PEARSON EDUCATION
SECONDARY GROUP

1 Lake Street
Upper Saddle River, NJ 07458
201-236-5401...781-455-1309
Fax: 201-236-5553...781-433-8425
E-Mail: marty.smith@phschool.com

Martha G. Smith
President
Pearson Education
Secondary Group

To the Teacher:

As a former social studies teacher, I cannot imagine a more important time to be a social studies educator.

Since the terrorist attacks on New York City and Washington, D.C., on September 11, 2001, you have served at the front line of efforts to understand the causes and effects of those momentous events. In the social studies classroom, you have helped your students understand our nation's heritage of unity and determination in times of crisis. You have had the opportunity to instill in your students the core values of democracy, free enterprise, and the rule of law. Your students have probably explored concepts of freedom and justice, through primary sources from the Declaration of Independence to the "I Have a Dream" speech, and the rights and responsibilities of citizenship, through the Constitution of the United States. They may be learning and applying critical thinking skills as well—debating, for example, the benefits and challenges of living in an open and tolerant society.

As a social studies educator, you can help your students master the fundamentals of history, geography, civics, and economics, providing a context within which to analyze current events. With your guidance, this knowledge can inform and encourage young people's participation in the democratic process.

Today more than ever, you play a crucial role in the maturing of responsible citizens. You help create tomorrow's leaders—the future defenders of America's freedoms, as defined by one President during another time of great crisis:

> *"In the future days which we seek to make secure, we look forward to a world founded upon four essential human freedoms. The first is freedom of speech and expression—everywhere in the world. The second is freedom of every person to worship God in his own way—everywhere in the world. The third is freedom from want . . . everywhere in the world. The fourth is freedom from fear . . . anywhere in the world."*
>
> —President Franklin Delano Roosevelt
> State of the Union Address, January 6, 1941

Sincerely,

Martha G. Smith

PRENTICE HALL

WORLD HISTORY

CONNECTIONS TO TODAY

TEACHER'S EDITION

Prentice
Hall

Upper Saddle River, New Jersey
Glenview, Illinois
Needham, Massachusetts

Especially for **NORTH CAROLINA!**
- North Carolina Standard Course of Study correlation inside
- North Carolina Assessment System

Block Scheduling Consultants

William J. McKee
Social Studies Department Chair
Brockport High School
Brockport, NY

Kathleen J. McKee
Social Studies Teacher
Brockport High School
Brockport, NY

ISBN 0-13-037020-7

1 2 3 4 5 6 7 8 9 10   06 05 04 03 02

CONTENTS

Teacher's Edition

Student Edition

Draw students into the drama of history.

Program Components
Student Edition
North Carolina Teacher's Edition

Teaching Resources
Program Overview
Pacing Chart With Block Scheduling Lessons
Creative Teaching Activities
Unit Books
  Guided Reading and Review
  Biographies
  Primary Sources
  Viewpoints
  Geography Quizzes
  Skill Applications
  Section Quizzes
  Chapter Tests
Chapter Extension Activities
Teaching With Themes
History Through Literature
Using the Internet
Simulations
Why Study History?
Why Study History? Poster
Guide to the Essentials of World History (English)
Guide to the Essentials of World History (Spanish)
Guide to the Essentials of World History, Teacher's Manual
Nystrom Desk Atlas

Reading
Section Reading Support Transparency System
Guided Reading and Review Workbook (English)
Guided Reading and Review Workbook Teacher's
  Edition (English)
Guide to the Essentials of World History (English)
Guide to the Essentials of World History,
  Teacher's Manual
Guided Reading Audiotapes (English)
Student Edition on Audio CD

Skills
World History Color Transparencies
Skills Transparencies
Treasures of the World Source Readings
World History Historical Outline Map Book
Humanities Pack, High School
Literature Library, World Studies High School
Social Studies Skills Tutor CD-ROM

Program Highlights:

- North Carolina Standard Course of Study Correlation in Teacher's Edition

- Makes key content accessible to all learners

- Builds skills for success

- Offers a variety of assessment options

Spanish

Guided Reading and Review Workbook (Spanish)
Guided Reading and Review Workbook Teacher's Edition (Spanish)
Guide to the Essentials of World History (Spanish)
Guided Reading Audiotapes (Spanish)

Assessment

Prentice Hall Assessment System
  Program Assessment
    Chapter Tests with ExamView® Test Bank CD-ROM
    Document-Based Assessment
    Alternative Assessment Handbook
  Test Prep
    Diagnose and Prescribe
      Diagnostic Tests for High School Social Studies Skills
    Review and Reteach
      Review Book for World History
    Practice and Assess
      Test Prep Book for World History
      Test-taking Strategies with Transparencies for High School
      Test-taking Strategies Posters
ExamView® Test Bank CD-ROM

Technology

Guided Reading Audiotapes (English)
Guided Reading Audiotapes (Spanish)
Student Edition on Audio CD
Passport to the World CD-ROM
Social Studies Skills Tutor CD-ROM
Resource Pro® CD-ROM
Prentice Hall Presentation Pro CD-ROM
World History Visions Voices Views
  Video Program
Companion Web Site
iText®

PH Success**Net**

But I'm Not a Reading Teacher!

Few people choose to be social studies teachers in order to focus on reading. Yet a significant number of today's students lack reading proficiency. Without it, they cannot access the wealth of social studies content they need to absorb from textbooks, primary sources, literature, and more. When students can't read well, they don't read and won't read.

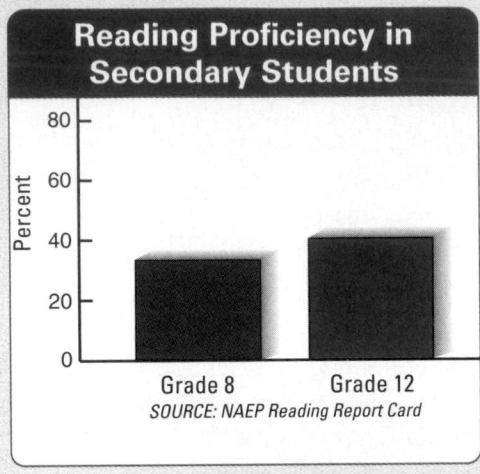

Reading Proficiency in Secondary Students

SOURCE: NAEP Reading Report Card

Best Practices in Reading

Instead of plunging in and plodding through a section, students need a plan of action, a strategy. Best practices for teaching reading in social studies focus on **comprehension strategies**—teaching students what to do *before reading, during reading,* and *after reading.*

Here are some ways to implement these strategies with struggling readers:

Before Reading Both teacher and student preparations precede reading.
- Use an anecdote, photo, artifact, or audio to set the scene.
- Display a map or other visual aid to encourage students to identify what they already know and to make predictions to apply this knowledge to a new situation.
- Model for students how to look at pictures, captions, and headings in order to predict what they will be learning.

During Reading Student-directed, individual activities take place during reading. Providing guided practice will help students develop these habits.
- Show students how to take notes, using graphic organizers that match the type of information they are reading. For example, use a Venn diagram for comparing and contrasting, a flowchart for sequencing, and a concept web for finding main ideas and supporting details.
- Teach students to ask themselves questions as they read.
- Demonstrate for students how to make connections between what they read and what they already know.

After Reading Both student-directed and teacher-directed activities can follow reading.
- Conduct a sample self-check for students—"What have I learned?"
- Teach students to ask themselves, "How does this relate to what I already know?"
- Demonstrate both formal and informal assessments that students will encounter.

Comprehension Strategies

Before Reading
- Activate prior knowledge
- Build needed prior knowledge
- Focus attention
- Set purpose for reading
- Make predictions

During Reading
- Confirm predictions
- Read and self-monitor
- Take notes and ask questions

After Reading
- Recall information
- Respond to new learning
- Extend and transfer new learning
- Assess reading success

 Reading success happens when students can construct meaning from information.

Prentice Hall Support Throughout the Program

The structure of each Prentice Hall program embeds the development of solid reading skills in the Student Edition. Each section of the text starts with suggestions to the student for *before reading* and *during reading*.

At the end of each section, students will find opportunities to recall and apply information and construct meaning from it.

Notice that the *Reading Focus* questions align with the subheadings in the section.

Notice how the section assessment questions relate back to the focus questions and section subheadings.

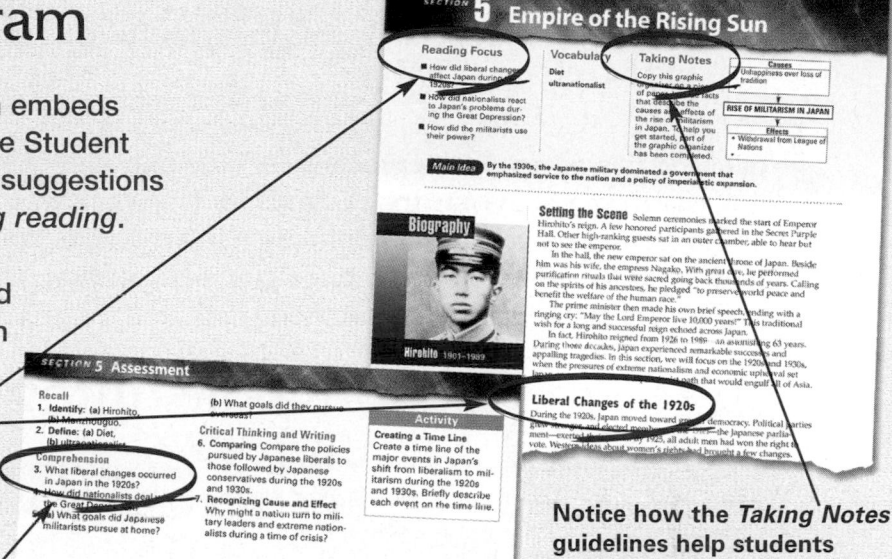

Notice how the *Taking Notes* guidelines help students understand the main idea.

Teacher's Edition

Additional reading strategies as well as ways of customizing instruction for less proficient readers and English language learners give you focused strategies to improve students' comprehension.

Section Reading Support Transparency System

Every section of the text has a companion reading support transparency that delivers the main points through a graphic organizer.

Guide to the Essentials

Look in the Teaching Resources box for the *Guide to the Essentials* in both English and Spanish. Students use this book to review and master new content through summaries written below grade level.

Student Edition on Audio

Auditory learners, less proficient readers, and English language learners can benefit from listening to the book on CD as they read the text.

Why Should I Teach Skills?

> "Give a man a fish, and he eats for a day. Teach a man to fish and he eats for a lifetime."
>
> —Author Unknown

*F*ollowing this advice, if we present our students with only content, we are, in essence, giving them the fish. If we are to prepare students for life, we need to teach the skills needed to make sense out of the increasing volume of information in the world. To help students become lifelong learners, we must develop their abilities to question, read, analyze, interpret, and evaluate information, as well as to communicate their ideas to others.

Best Practices in Skills Integration

These guidelines will help you embed skills development within content instruction.

1. **Plan each unit around an enduring understanding or big idea.** For example, if the unit you are about to teach is The Federal Government, the big idea might be "the powers of the three branches of the federal government are limited by a system of checks and balances."

Topic: How a Bill Becomes a Law		
	Example	**Skill**
Facts	Process in the House & Senate	Sequencing
Concepts	Checks and balances	Problem solving
Big Ideas	Process by which a bill becomes a law helps ensure democracy	Synthesizing information

2. **Develop each lesson around the facts, the concepts, the big idea, and the skills students need to be able to connect the content to the big idea.** For part of a lesson on the Supreme Court, you might want to focus on the Supremacy Clause and its impact.

3. **Teach skills that are new or that add another level of complexity to a previously mastered skill.** Follow the elements of good skill instruction:
   - Set a purpose for using the skill.
   - Present the steps to follow.
   - Model the process for using the skill.
   - Guide practice and provide feedback.
   - Apply to a prompt such as a picture, map, or reading passage.

4. **Reinforce skills whenever possible.** Ask critical thinking questions about maps, photos, graphs, charts, and primary sources.

5. **Assess both content and skills mastery regularly.** It is important to determine whether students are remembering important information, but equally important to determine whether they are internalizing skills as lifelong learners.

6. **Include skills in big projects.** Give students opportunities to combine their thinking and research abilities at least several times a year.

Elements of Skill Instruction

Teach the skill

Model applying the skill often

Guide practice of the skill

Give feedback and correction

Have students apply the skill independently

Prentice Hall Support for Skills

Skills mastery means developing habits of mind that enable us to turn information into meaning. Every Prentice Hall social studies program contains a wealth of resources to build skills for life.

Skills pages in the Student Edition provide three-step instruction strategy.

Social Studies Skills Tutor CD-ROM provides two levels of interactive instruction and practice in 20 core social studies skills.

Learn

Practice

Apply

Skills reinforcement appears in all caption questions.

Skills Assessment

Geography The region we call Southeast Asia consists of both a mainland area and thousands of islands. It was home to numerous ancient and diverse cultures.

1. **Location** On the map, locate (a) Pagan kingdom, (b) Angkor Wat, (c) the Moluccas, (d) Sunda Strait.
2. **Movement** From which direction did the Mongol invasion take place?
3. **Critical Thinking Understanding Sequence** During which centuries were these empires and kingdoms most likely to have come into contact with one another?

The Prentice Hall Vertical Alignment System

Mastery also requires that students learn skills at increasing levels of complexity as they progress through school. Prentice Hall takes the guesswork out of aligning skills instruction by developing 20 core social studies skills with increasing difficulty from grade to grade.

The 20 Core Social Studies Skills	
1. Using the Cartographer's Tools	**11.** Comparing and Contrasting
2. Using Special-Purpose Maps	**12.** Analyzing Primary Sources
3. Analyzing Graphic Data	**13.** Recognizing Bias and Propaganda
4. Analyzing Images	**14.** Identifying Frame of Reference and Point of View
5. Identifying Main Ideas/Summarizing	**15.** Decision Making
6. Sequencing	**16.** Problem Solving
7. Identifying Cause and Effect/Making Predictions	**17.** Using Reliable Information
8. Drawing Inferences and Conclusions	**18.** Transferring Information From One Medium to Another
9. Making Valid Generalizations	**19.** Synthesizing Information
10. Distinguishing Fact and Opinion	**20.** Supporting a Position

Should I Teach to the Test?

*T*he increasing importance of state standards and student accountability leads many teachers to wonder whether they must limit their classes to the content of high-stakes exams. While based on state standards and student needs, a truly effective social studies program requires **alignment of curriculum, instruction,** and **assessment.** When each of these elements dovetails with the others, *all* instruction prepares students for assessment based on curriculum objectives.

In an aligned system, both teacher and student know what is expected. There are no secrets or surprises. To ensure alignment:

- Teach the objectives in your standards to the specified level of understanding.
- Make sure that students know what they should learn before you teach.
- Test those same objectives as precisely as possible to the same depth of understanding that the standards require.

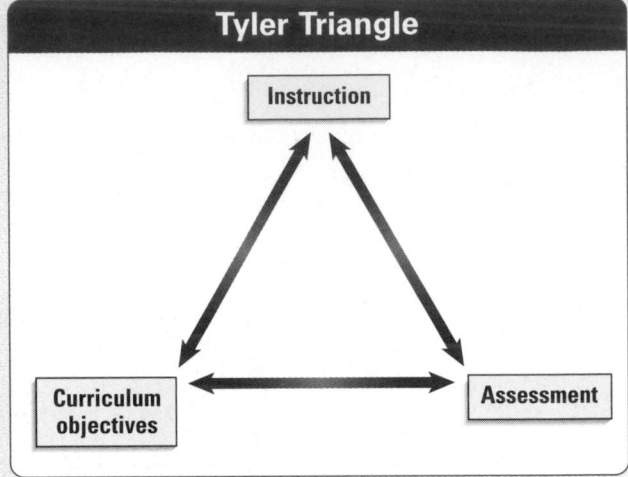

Tyler Triangle

Best Practices in Assessment

Here are some ways to integrate ongoing assessment into instruction:

Assessment Techniques	
Diagnose and Prescribe	• Evaluate student abilities at the beginning of the year.
Plan and Align Plan instruction to align with assessment.	• Examine objectives carefully and choose learning activities that require more than a knowledge level (or memorized level) from students. • Test students on all of the objectives, omitting none. • Test skill development at the same time you assess content.
Review and Reteach Weave ongoing review into aligned instruction and assessment.	• Connect instruction to prior learning and include review questions on each test.
Practice and Assess Apply assessment results to improve teaching and learning.	• Use individual student information for tutoring and devising individualized plans. • Use whole-class data to determine if your teaching was aligned to the assessment.

Prentice Hall Assessment System

The Prentice Hall Assessment System provides comprehensive support for program content assessment and preparation for high-stakes standardized tests.

Program Assessment

Use the *Chapter Tests* to assess core content for every chapter.

Develop your own customized tests and practice worksheets with the ExamView® Test Bank CD-ROM, selecting from hundreds of test questions and using the word-processing and editing capabilities. Create online tests and study guides and receive instant feedback on student progress.

Standardized Test Preparation

Prentice Hall Assessment System gives you the tools to help your students succeed on standardized tests, from the beginning of the year to the culminating high-stakes exam.

Diagnose and Prescribe

Profile student skills with Diagnostic Tests A & B.

Address student needs with program resources correlated to diagnostic test questions.

Review and Reteach

Provide cumulative content review with unit-level questions and study sheets.

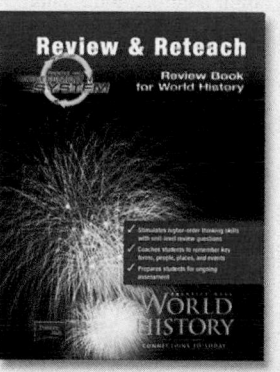

Practice and Assess

Build assessment skills using *Test-Taking Strategies With Transparencies*.

Reinforce assessment skills with *Test-Taking Posters*.

Develop students' test-taking skills and improve their scores on standardized tests with the *Test Prep Book*.

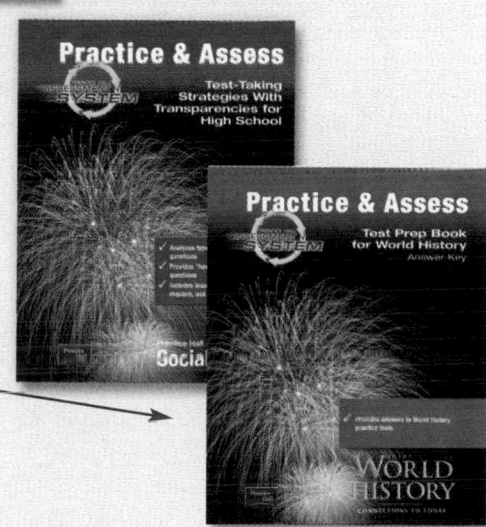

How Am I Doing?

*P*aired with the demand for high student achievement has come the drive for greater teacher accountability. More and more states and districts are establishing standards for teaching and new systems of teacher evaluation.

In the past, professional appraisals focused on teacher behaviors. Nationwide, the focus of teacher evaluation is now shifting to what students are able to do. Student success emerges as the most critical measure of teaching—the teacher has not taught if students have not learned. The goal is becoming the learner-centered class, alive with critical thinking, problem-solving activities, collaborative learning, projects, and investigations. Evaluation criteria now measure how well teachers promote this kind of learning.

Prentice Hall social studies programs provide a variety of ways to support learner-centered instruction. Below you will find a guide to program resources to help you address criteria commonly found in teacher evaluations.

Common Criteria	Where to Look for Support
Active, successful student participation in the learning process	• Structured reading support • Activities at section and chapter levels • Group and individual activities
Learner-centered instruction	• Critical thinking questions in every caption • Strategies for different learner needs • Technology for students: Social Studies Skills Tutor CD-ROM, World History Interactive Student Tutorial CD-ROM, **www.PHSchool.com** • Customize For… in Teacher's Edition
Evaluation and feedback on student progress	• Section and chapter assessments in Student Edition • ExamView® Test Bank CD-ROM
Classroom management of students, time, and materials	• Pacing chart in Teacher's Edition • Chapter interleafs in Teacher's Edition • Resource Pro® CD-ROM
Professional communications	• Letters to families • Resource Pro® CD-ROM lesson plans for supervisors
Improvement of student performance	• Prentice Hall Assessment System
Professional development	• eTeach • Skylight Professional Development services at www.skylightedu.com • PHSuccessNet.com

NORTH CAROLINA STANDARDS	STUDENT EDITION PAGES WHERE FOUND
COMPETENCY GOAL 1: Historical Tools and Practices—The learner will identify, evaluate, and use the methods and tools valued by historians, compare the views of historians, and trace the themes of history.	
1.01 Define history and the concepts of cause and effect, time, continuity, and perspective.	**defining history:** SE 6–10 **cause and effect:** SE xivi–xivii, 14, 19, 97, 114, 123, 124, 134, 150, 151, 190, 202, 219, 230, 260, 276, 288, 312, 345, 355, 360, 407, 408, 436, 487, 500, 533, 534, 554, 565, 577, 613, 614, 669, 697, 698, 705, 706, 733, 737, 741, 751, 774, 780, 795, 848, 854, 867, 878, 887, 893, 939, 943 **time:** SE 4–5, 22–23, 49–50, 71–72, 100–101, 126–127, 154–155, 174–175, 178–179, 204–205, 232–233, 362–363, 384–385, 410–411, 442–443, 466 467, 496–497, 516–517, 542–543, 568–569, 592–593, 616–617, 642–643, 674–675, 676–677, 700–701, 720–721, 744–745, 768–769, 804–805, 826–827, 856–857, 880–881, 906–907, 932–933 **continuity:** SE xxxi, 8, 47, 63, 96, 109, 116, 133, 168, 186, 199, 216, 247, 252, 297, 315, 320, 345, 378, 406, 424, 452, 477, 512, 531, 540, 546, 565, 580, 599, 630, 653, 682, 714, 727, 754, 776, 806, 840, 868, 888, 922, 946 **perspective:** SE 10, 39, 113, 119, 123, 219, 230, 239, 248, 270, 349, 448, 450, 464, 472, 477, 514, 547, 561, 565, 576, 602, 634, 662, 668, 679, 693, 718, 737, 747, 764, 776, 786, 796, 816, 838, 854, 887, 893
1.02 Analyze and interpret primary and secondary sources to compare views, trace themes, and detect bias.	SE xi–xii, xiii–xiiii, 6, 8, 12, 13, 21, 24, 26, 29, 33, 36, 38, 39, 40, 43, 46, 49, 55, 59, 65, 67, 76, 80, 83, 85, 91, 93, 95, 99, 104, 107, 111, 113, 114, 119, 125, 132, 137, 140, 143, 145, 149, 153, 156, 160, 162, 168, 171, 173, 191, 200, 201, 203, 206, 209, 211, 212, 213, 214, 216, 222, 226, 231, 240, 249, 252, 262, 263, 265, 266, 269, 270, 275, 277, 284, 287, 289, 290, 293, 299, 305, 307, 308, 312, 315, 316, 319, 320, 323, 327, 339, 340, 341, 347, 349, 350, 358, 361, 368, 369, 373, 379, 380, 383, 390, 393, 395, 400, 409, 417, 422, 428, 430, 433, 435, 437, 446, 448, 449, 460, 461, 465, 470, 479, 480, 481, 483, 490, 495, 505, 509, 512, 513, 515, 518, 520, 529, 535, 544, 547, 549, 555, 558, 562, 564, 567, 570, 572, 573, 575, 576, 577, 579, 584, 591, 594, 597, 602, 603, 605, 608, 615, 618, 619, 621, 625, 634, 636, 641, 644, 655, 656, 659, 663, 669, 679, 684, 689, 690, 691, 693, 695, 699, 704, 706, 710, 717, 719, 723, 726, 729, 737, 741, 743, 746, 748, 752, 764, 765, 767, 774, 776, 783, 784, 786, 793, 797, 806, 809, 816, 820, 825, 833, 836, 839, 844, 847, 855, 859, 863, 871, 873, 875, 879, 882, 894, 899, 905, 908, 910, 915, 920, 921, 931, 934, 949, 957 *Primary Sources and Literature:* SE 962, 963, 964, 965, 966, 967, 968, 969, 971, 974, 975, 976, 978, 979, 980, 981, 982, 987, 988, 989, 990, 993, 994, 995, 996, 997, 998, 999
1.03 Relate archaeology, geography, anthropology, political science, sociology, and economics to the study of history.	**archaeology:** SE 8–10, 12–14, 17, 18, 20–21, 29, 35, 53–54, 67, 133, 163, 283 **geography:** SE 6–7, 18, 44, 52, 88, 102, 156, 197, 244, 256, 284, 316, 336, 393, 433, 490, 504, 528, 560, 588, 613, 634, 662, 693, 702, 730, 750, 782, 807, 830, 867, 886, 916 **anthropology:** SE 8, 11, 20 **political science:** SE 16, 25–26, 35, 62, 90, 92, 106, 112, 114, 129, 160, 164–165, 236, 243, 294–245, 350, 401, 413, 417–418, 421, 422, 432, 447, 448, 451–452, 456–458, 461–463, 473, 475–476, 511–512, 521, 585, 594, 620, 693, 696–697, 713–717, 732, 758–759, 829–830, 838, 883, 898, 936 **sociology:** SE 16–17, 35, 55, 57, 62, 79, 86–87, 186–187, 188, 200, 267, 390–391, 508–509, 553–554, 555–556, 732, 885 **economics:** SE 42–43, 148, 199–200, 217, 226, 262, 390, 393, 395, 399, 404–406, 415, 450, 470, 501, 510–511, 513, 522, 528, 549–550, 597–598, 635, 659, 663–664, 708–709, 724–726, 746–748, 761–762, 814–815, 830, 832, 834, 841, 844, 846, 851, 859, 916, 937, 951, 955
1.04 Define the themes of society, technology, economics, politics, and culture and relate them to the study of history.	SE xxx–xxxi, 10, 11–14, 15–19, 20–21
1.05 Trace major themes in the development of the world from its origins to the rise of early civilizations.	SE 9, 10, 11–14, 15–19, 20–21, 24–27, 28–33, 34–37, 38, 40–44, 45–47, 48–49, 50–54, 55–58, 59–65, 66–67

(continued)

1.06 Examine the indicators of civilization, including writing, labor specialization, cities, technology, trade, and political and cultural institutions.	**writing:** SE 17, 32, 36–37, 44, 63, 65 **labor specialization:** SE 14, 16, 19 **cities:** SE 15, 35, 53 **technology:** SE 12, 13, 14, 26, 34–35, 41, 64 **trade:** SE 42–44, 54, 64 **political institutions:** SE 16, 18, 19, 25–27, 35, 38, 40–41, 62 **cultural institutions:** SE 12, 16, 17, 19, 28–33, 34–35, 43, 46–47, 54, 55–57, 58, 62–63

COMPETENCY GOAL 2: Emerging Civilizations—The learner will analyze the development of early civilizations in Africa, Asia, Europe, and the Americas.

2.01 Trace the development and assess the achievements of early river civilizations, including but not limited to those around the Huang-He, Nile, Indus, and Tigris-Euphrates rivers.	**Huang-He:** SE 15, 60–61, 303, 636 **Nile:** SE 15, 23–27, 36, 48–49 **Indus:** SE 15, 17, 22, 52–54, 66 **Tigris-Euphrates:** SE 15, 34–35 *Primary Sources and Literature:* SE 962, 963
2.02 Identify the roots of Greek civilization and recognize its achievements from the Minoan era through the Hellenistic period.	SE 100–101, 102–104, 105–109, 110–112, 114, 115–119, 120–123, 124–125 *Primary Sources and Literature:* SE 966, 967
2.03 Describe the developments and achievements of Roman civilization and analyze the significance of the fall of Rome.	SE 126–127, 128–131, 132–136, 137–138, 140, 141–142, 147–148, 152–153 **fall of Rome:** SE 149, 150, 151
2.04 Examine the importance of India as a hub of the world trade and as a cultural and religious center during its Golden Age.	SE 74–75, 76–80, 81–85, 86–88, 98–99 *Primary Sources and Literature:* SE 968, 969
2.05 Assess the distinctive achievements of Chinese and Japanese civilizations.	**Chinese civilizations:** SE 50–51, 60, 62–65, 66, 74–75, 89–90, 91, 92, 93–97, 98–99 *Primary Sources and Literature:* SE 965 **Japanese civilizations:** SE 300–301, 317–319, 320–325, 326–327 *Primary Sources and Literature:* SE 972
2.06 Describe the rise and achievements of the Byzantine and Islamic civilizations.	**Byzantine civilizations:** SE 232–233, 234, 235–239, 241, 248–249 **Islamic civilizations:** SE 250–251, 252–255, 256–260, 261–266, 267–268, 276–277 *Primary Sources and Literature:* SE 971
2.07 Describe the rise and achievements of African civilizations, including but not limited to Axum, Ghana, Kush, Mali, Namibia, and Songhai.	**Axum:** SE 127, 278, 282, 289–290, 292 **Ghana:** SE 284–285, 299 **Kush:** SE 27, 281 **Mali:** SE 285–287, 288 **Nubia:** SE 278, 281–282, 283 **Songhai:** SE 287, 288 **Zimbabwe:** SE 291–292
2.08 Evaluate the achievements of the major civilizations of the Americas during the pre-Columbian epoch, including but not limited to the Aztecs, Incas, and Mayas.	**Olmecs:** SE 154, 157–158, 162, 172 **Aztecs:** SE 155, 159–162, 172–173 **Incas:** SE 163–167, 172–173 **Mayas:** SE 154, 158–159, 162, 172

COMPETENCY GOAL 3: Monarchies and Empires—The learner will investigate significant events, people, and conditions in the growth of monarchical and imperial systems of government.

3.01 Trace the political and social development of monarchies and empires, including but not limited to the Ming and Manchu dynasties, the Mongol Empire, the Ottoman Empire, the Moghul Empire, and the British Empire.	**Ming dynasty:** SE 205, 310–312, 334, 377–378 **Manchu (Qing) dynasty:** SE 378–379, 380, 636, 638, 734 **Mongol Empire:** SE 241–242, 247, 251, 260, 301, 308–310, 315, 321–322 **Ottoman Empire:** SE 205, 251, 272–274, 275, 276, 412, 519, 520, 583 **Moghul (Mughal) Empire:** SE 269, 271, 276 **British Empire:** SE 616–617, 618–620, 622–624, 626, 630, 631–634, 635–636, 638, 640–641

(continued)

3.02 Describe events in Western Europe from the fall of Rome to the emergence of nation-states and analyze the impact of these events on economic, political, and social life in medieval Europe.	**economy of medieval Europe:** SE 186–190, 197–201, 203 **politics of medieval Europe:** SE 183–185, 193, 195, 196 **society of medieval Europe:** SE 186–190, 191–193, 196, 200–201, 202–203 *Primary Sources and Literature:* SE 973
3.03 Trace social, political, economic, and cultural changes associated with the Renaissance, Reformation, the rise of nation-states, and absolutism.	**Renaissance:** SE 334–335, 336–341, 342–345, 360–361 **Reformation:** SE 335, 346–348, 350, 351–355, 360–361 **rise of nation-states:** SE 204–205, 206–211, 212–214, 231 **absolutism:** SE 410–411, 412–415, 416–420, 421–426, 427–430, 431–435, 436–437 *Primary Sources and Literature:* SE 974
3.04 Examine European exploration and analyze the forces that caused and allowed the acquisition of colonial possessions and trading privileges in Africa, Asia, and the Americas	**Africa:** SE 398–402 **Asia:** SE 362–363, 364–368, 373–374, 376, 377 **the Americas:** SE 386–388, 394–397
3.05 Cite the effects of European expansion on Africans, pre-Columbian Americans, Asians, and Europeans.	**Africa:** SE 400, 402, 408–409 **the Americas:** SE 388, 391, 393, 397 **Asia:** SE 373–374, 376, 378, 380–381 **Europe:** SE 403–407, 409 *Primary Sources and Literature:* SE 975, 976
3.06 Compare the influence of religion, social structure, and colonial export economies on North and South American societies.	**North American societies:** SE 460–461, 463, 464 **South American societies:** SE 389–393
3.07 Evaluate the effects of colonialism on Africa, the Americas, Asia, and Europe.	**Africa:** SE 621–626, 663–665, 667, 669 **the Americas:** SE 389–393, 527–528, 658–662, 668–669 **Asia:** SE 631–634, 635–639, 640–641, 648–649, 650–652, 668–669 **Europe:** SE 618–620, 633, 641, 663–665, 666, 667, 668–669

COMPETENCY GOAL 4: Revolution and Nationalism—The learner will assess the causes and effects of movements seeking change, and will evaluate the sources and consequences of nationalism.

4.01 Analyze the causes and assess the influence of seventeenth to nineteenth century political revolutions in England, North America, and France on individuals, governing bodies, church–state relations, and diplomacy.	**England:** SE 421–426, 457–459, 464, 594–596, 597–600, 601, 614–615 **North America:** SE 460–463, 465, 609–613 **France:** SE 416–420, 436–437, 466–467, 468–472, 473–477, 478–483, 487, 494, 603–607, 614–615 *Primary Sources and Literature:* SE 978, 979

4.02 Describe the changes in economies and political control in nineteenth century Africa, Asia, Europe, and the Americas.	**Industrial Revolution:** SE 496–497, 498–500, 501–504, 505–509, 514–515, 544–550, 566–567, 611–613
	Africa: SE 621–626, 663–665, 667, 668–669
	Asia: SE 631–634, 635–639, 648–649, 650–652, 663–665, 667, 668–669
	Europe:
	    England: SE 594–596, 597–600, 601, 614–615
	    France: SE 603–607, 614–615
	    Germany: SE 570–573, 574–576, 590
	    the Balkans: SE 581–582, 590
	    Italy: SE 577–580, 590–591
	the Americas:
	    United States: SE 609–613, 652, 661–662
	    Latin America: SE 527–533, 534–535, 658, 662, 668–669
	Primary Sources and Literature: SE 982, 983

4.03 Evaluate the growth of nationalism as a contributor to nineteenth century European revolutions in areas such as the Balkans, France, Germany, and Italy.	**the Balkans:** SE 519–520, 581–583, 590 **France:** SE 484–487, 488–490, 492–493, 495, 521–522, 524 **Germany:** 525–526, 570–573, 574–576, 590 **Italy:** 525, 568, 577–580, 590–591

(continued)

4.04 Examine the causes and effects of the Russian Revolution and its effect on Russia and the world.	**causes:** SE 702–706, 718 **effects:** SE 707–712, 713–717, 718–719
4.05 Evaluate the causes and effectiveness of nineteenth and twentieth century nationalistic movements that challenged European domination in Africa, Asia, and Latin America.	**Africa:** SE 726–728, 908–913, 924–926, 928–929, 930 **Asia:** SE 731–732, 734–735, 739, 741, 882–883, 887 **Latin America:** SE 527–533, 534–535, 724–725

COMPETENCY GOAL 5: Global Wars—The learner will analyze the causes and results of twentieth century conflicts among nations

5.01 Analyze the causes and course of World War I and assess its consequences.	**causes of World War I:** SE 678, 680–681, 682–684, 698 **the war:** SE 685–689, 690–693, 699 **the effects:** SE 694–697, 698, 909 *Primary Sources and Literature:* SE 986
5.02 Assess the significance of the war experience on global foreign and domestic policies of the 1920s and 1930s.	SE 726–730, 731–733, 734–737, 738–741, 742–743, 746–751, 757–760, 761–765, 766–767
5.03 Analyze the causes and course of World War II and evaluate it as the end of one era and the beginning of another.	**causes of World War II:** SE 770–774, 796 **the war:** SE 775–780, 781–786, 787–790, 796 **the effects:** SE 791–795, 796–797 *Primary Sources and Literature:* SE 988
5.04 Trace the course of the Cold War and assess its impact on the global community including but not limited to the Korean War, the satellite nations of Eastern Europe, and the Vietnam War.	**Cold War:** SE 792–795, 796–797, 807–808, 828–829, 836–837, 846, 864, 878, 894–900, 912–913, 940–941 **Korean War:** SE 870–872 **Eastern Europe:** SE 793–794, 849–853, 878 **Vietnam War:** SE 873–875, 878–879 **Middle East:** 899–900 **Africa:** 912–913
5.05 Examine governmental policies, such as the Kellogg-Briand Pact, which were established and the role of organizations including the League of Nations, and the United Nations to maintain peace, and evaluate their continuing effectiveness.	**Kellogg-Briand Pact:** SE 747 **League of Nations:** SE 695, 697, 712, 739, 747, 750, 770 **United Nations:** SE 792, 809, 810–811, 819, 848, 853, 864, 870, 903, 922 **regional organizations:** SE 795, 809–810, 876, 932, 942, 946 *Primary Sources and Literature:* SE 989

COMPETENCY GOAL 6: Patterns of Social Order—The learner will investigate social and economic organization in various societies throughout time in order to understand the shifts in power and status that have occurred.

6.01 Compare the conditions, racial composition, and status of social classes, castes, and slaves in world societies and analyze changes in those elements.	**social classes:** SE 16–17, 35, 55, 57, 62, 79, 86–87, 186–187, 188, 267, 390–391, 508–509, 553–554, 555–556, 661, 732, 885 **castes:** SE 57, 79, 86–87, 267, 732, 885 **slaves:** SE 16, 17, 27, 35, 40, 45, 106–109, 136, 142, 242, 261, 273, 276, 288, 385, 390, 393, 398–399, 400–407, 527–529, 463, 483, 531, 533, 586, 589, 590, 592, 598, 611, 622, 810–811, 819, 823, 824
6.02 Analyze causes and results of ideas regarding superiority and inferiority in society and how those ideas have changed over time.	SE 57, 109, 560–561, 619, 658, 664–665, 764, 781–782, 810, 852 *Primary Source:* SE 989
6.03 Trace the changing definitions of citizenship and the expansion of suffrage.	**citizenship:** SE 106–109, 112–113, 129, 131, 135, 140, 208, 209, 426, 458, 462–463, 474, 475–477, 482, 522, 553–554, 558, 594–596, 599–600, 605–606, 609, 610, 611, 613, 724, 725, 727 *Primary Source:* SE 995 **suffrage:** SE 463, 509, 519, 553, 558, 573, 593, 595, 596, 597, 599–600, 604, 607, 610, 691, 738, 761, 771

6.04 Relate the dynamics of state economies to the well-being of their members and to changes in the role of government.	**capitalism:** SE 404–408, 450, 510, 511 **socialism:** SE 497, 510, 511–514 **communism:** SE 497, 512–513, 704–705, 707–708, 863–865 **welfare state:** SE 829–830
6.05 Analyze issues such as ecological/environmental concerns, political instability, and nationalism as challenges to which societies must respond.	**ecological/environmental concerns:** SE 54, 159, 816, 817, 891, 917, 942–943 **political instability:** SE 150, 151, 237–238, 376, 478–483, 484–485, 490, 519–520, 521–522, 524–526, 527–528, 530–533, 580–581, 586, 588–589, 602, 605–607, 636, 638–639, 645, 646, 659, 660–661, 696–697, 702–706, 722–724, 808–809, 815, 846–847, 849–853, 914–916, 921–922, 928, 936–938, 946, 948–949, 950–951, 953 **nationalism:** SE 483, 484–487, 488–490, 492–493, 495, 519–520, 521–522, 524, 525–526, 570–573, 568, 574–576, 581–583, 590–591, 600, 658, 678, 680–681, 721, 724–725, 727–728, 739–740, 757, 761–762, 806, 909, 911, 925
6.06 Trace the development of internal conflicts due to differences in religion, race, culture, and group loyalties in various areas of the world.	**religion:** SE 144, 196, 219, 245, 246, 346–348, 350, 351–352, 353–355, 606, 627, 733, 764, 765, 867, 898 **race:** SE 390, 598, 609, 611, 620 **culture:** SE 270, 457, 531, 600, 601, 633, 657, 764, 833, 847, 851, 852–853, 867, 885, 901–902 **group loyalties:** SE 257–258, 275, 310, 387, 421–426, 457–458, 461–462, 473–476, 478–482, 519–520, 521–522, 524–525, 527–528, 530–531, 553–554, 580, 599–600, 613, 628–629, 631–632, 636, 637, 644–646, 658, 661, 704–705, 736–737, 741, 757–760, 761–764, 865, 935–937, 949

COMPETENCY GOAL 7: Technology and Changing Global Connections—The learner will consider the short- and long-term consequences of the development of new technology

7.01 Assess the degree to which discoveries, innovations, and technologies have accelerated change.	**agricultural revolution:** SE iiv, 12, 14, 54, 157, 281 **discoveries:** SE 32, 83, 96, 122–123, 138, 337, 356–359, 496, 500, 504, 545, 546, 550, 551, 616, 752 **innovation:** SE 16–17, 26, 34–35, 36–37, 38, 39–40, 63, 94, 158–159 **technologies:** SE 14, 16, 19, 26–27, 35, 41, 65, 83, 96–97, 106, 122–123, 128, 138, 167, 197, 229, 265–266, 345, 500, 504, 540–541, 546–549, 776, 804–805, 820–822, 859
7.02 Examine the causes and effects of scientific revolutions and cite their major costs and benefits.	**16th century:** SE 356–359, 360 **18th century:** SE 446 **19th century:** SE 496, 497, 498–500, 501–504, 505–509, 510–513, 514–515, 542, 545–550, 551–554, 555–556, 558–561, 562–565, 566–567 **20th century:** SE 805, 820–822, 824, 942–943
7.03 Examine the causes and effects of industrialization and cite its major costs and benefits.	**causes of industrialization:** SE 498–500, 501–502 **impact of industrialization:** SE 498, 500, 503–504, 505–509, 510–513, 514–515, 542, 545–550, 551–554, 555–556, 558–561, 562–565, 566–567, 618–619 *Primary Sources and Literature:* SE 984
7.04 Describe significant characteristics of global connections created by technological change, and assess the degree to which cultures participate in that change.	**15th- and 16th-century technology that began European explorations:** SE 365, 367 **Columbian Exchange:** SE 403–404, 407, 409 **spread of the Industrial Revolution:** SE 544–545 **global economy created by technological change in the 19th century:** SE 663–667, 668–669 **the contemporary global economy created by technological change:** SE 812–815, 817, 818–823

COMPETENCY GOAL 8: Patterns of History—The learner will assess the influence of ideals, values, beliefs, and traditions on current global events and issues.

8.01 Trace developments in literary, artistic, and religious traditions over time as legacies of past societies or as cultural innovations.	**literary traditions:** SE 85, 116, 117–119, 137–138, 222–223, 296, 297, 307, 319, 323–325, 340–341, 343–345, 415, 418, 455, 562, 564, 754, 897 *Primary Sources and Literature:* SE 963, 967, 968, 972, 973, 977, 984, 986, 991 **artistic traditions:** SE 12, 30, 32–33, 85, 97, 116–117, 138, 223–224, 297, 311, 325, 339–340, 342, 414–415, 418, 453, 523, 563, 564–565, 753

(continued)

	religious traditions:
	    Buddhism: SE 74, 78–80, 81–82, 92, 323, 325, 370–371
	    Christianity: SE 141–146, 152, 183–184, 191–195, 241, 245, 254, 290, 346–355, 381, 389, 561, 622, 939; *Primary Source:* SE 970
	    Confucianism: SE 89, 90, 92, 372; *Primary Source:* SE 965
	    Hinduism: SE 76–78, 86–87, 267–269, 371; *Primary Source:* SE 968
	    Islam: SE 252–255, 257–258, 268–269, 272, 283, 285, 297, 372, 892–893
	    Primary Source: SE 971
	    Judaism: SE 45–47, 141–142, 196, 245–246, 290, 355, 588; *Primary Source:* SE 964
	    Shinto: SE 317

8.02 Compare major Eastern and Western beliefs and practices, including but not limited to Buddhism, Christianity, Confucianism, Hinduism, Islam, Judaism, and Shintoism, and locate their regions of predominance.	**Buddhism and Hinduism compared:** 79–80 **Eastern v. Western Christianity:** 236–237, 239 **Islam, Judaism, Christianity:** 254–255 **Hindu-Muslim differences:** 268, 271 **East/West views in India:** 633, 634 **Westernization:** 818, 892

8.03 Classify within the broad patterns of history those events that may be viewed as turning points.	**agricultural revolution:** SE liv, 12, 14, 54, 157, 281
	rise and spread of Christianity: SE 142–146
	rise and spread of Islam: SE 252–256
	Mongol invasions: SE 241–243, 247, 251, 301, 308–310, 312, 326
	development of cities: SE 15–19
	European exploration and colonization: SE 362–363, 364–368, 373–376, 377–381, 382–383, 384–385, 386–388, 389–393, 394–397, 398–402, 403–407, 408–409
	scientific and industrial revolutions:
	    16th century: SE 356–359, 360
	    18th century: SE 446
	    19th century: SE 496, 497, 498–500, 501–504, 505–509, 510–513, 514–515, 542, 545–550, 551–554, 555–556, 558–561, 562–565, 566–567
	    20th century: SE 805, 820–822, 824, 942–943
	    World War I: SE 676–677, 678, 680–681, 690–693, 694–698
	    World War II: SE 675, 775–780, 781–786, 787–790, 791–795, 804–805, 806–811

8.04 Characterize over time and place the interactions of world cultures.	**conflict:** SE 27, 41, 42, 45–47, 57, 63–64, 81–82, 110–112, 120–121, 131, 132–133, 136, 149, 159–160, 164, 183, 185, 216–217, 218–219, 236, 237–238, 241–242, 245, 247, 256–257, 267–269, 271, 272, 287, 302–303, 308–310, 373–374, 376, 386–387, 397, 401–402, 628–629, 639, 870–872, 873–875, 886–887 *Primary Sources and Literature:* SE 988, 993 **trade:** SE 42–44, 54, 95, 103, 158, 198, 218, 234, 262, 284–285, 289–290, 291, 376, 377–378, 380–381, 398–400, 635–636, 659, 663–664, 840, 860, 868–870 **colonization and imperialism:** SE 389–393, 527–528, 618–620, 621–626, 631–634, 635–639, 640–641, 648–649, 650–652, 658–662, 663–665, 667, 668–669 **global interdependence:** SE 225–226, 403–404, 407, 409, 688–689, 697, 781–786, 787–790, 791–795, 807–811, 812–815, 817, 818–823, 894–900, 912–913, 942–943 **cultural diffusion:** SE 19, 41–42, 57, 80, 82, 92, 143–145, 218, 221–222, 234–235, 239, 241, 257, 263–266, 283, 285, 290, 291, 311, 314, 317, 318, 323, 391–393, 397, 407, 409, 528, 628, 664–667, 728–729, 735, 821–823
8.05 Analyze how the changing and competing components of cultures have led to current global issues and conflicts, and hypothesize solutions to persistent problems.	SE i–ii, 806–811, 812–817, 818–820, 822–823, 828–833, 852–853, 854, 867, 870–871, 873–874, 886–887, 888–890, 892–893, 896, 898, 899–903, 908–909, 912–913, 917, 919, 934–939, 940–943; TE 852, 917, 942
8.06 Analyze the meanings of "civilization" in different times and places and demonstrate how such meanings reflect the societies of which they are a part.	**definition of civilization:** SE 16–19 **examples of civilizations:** SE 28–33, 35–37, 38, 40–43, 53–54, 55–58, 59–60, 62–65, 76–80, 81–85, 89–90, 93–97, 102–103, 105–109, 110–112, 115–119, 121–123, 129–131, 132–136, 137–138, 140, 157–162, 163–167, 183–185, 186–190, 191–196, 197–201, 206–211, 212–214, 215–219, 220–224, 225–229, 234–239, 240–243, 244–247, 252–255, 256–260, 261–266, 267–269, 271, 272–275, 280–283, 284–285, 287–288, 289–292, 293–297, 302–307, 308–312, 313–315, 316–319, 320–325

PRENTICE HALL
WORLD HISTORY
CONNECTIONS TO TODAY

Elisabeth Gaynor Ellis
Anthony Esler

With Senior Consultant
Burton F. Beers

Prentice
Hall

Upper Saddle River, New Jersey
Glenview, Illinois
Needham, Massachusetts

Authors

Elisabeth Gaynor Ellis

Elisabeth Gaynor Ellis is a historian and writer. She is a co-author of *World Cultures: A Global Mosaic*. Ms. Ellis, a former social studies teacher and school administrator, has taught world cultures, Russian studies, and European history. She holds a B.A. from Smith College and an M.A. and M.S. from Columbia University.

Anthony Esler

Anthony Esler is Professor of History at the College of William and Mary. He received his Ph.D. from Duke University and received Fulbright Fellowships to study at the University of London and to travel to Ivory Coast and Tanzania. Dr. Esler's books include *The Human Venture: A World History* and *The Western World: A History*, as well as several historical novels.

Senior Consultant

Burton F. Beers

Burton F. Beers is a retired Professor of History from North Carolina State University. He taught European history, Asian history, and American history. Dr. Beers has published numerous articles in historical journals and several books, including *The Far East: A History of Western Impacts and Eastern Responses*, with Paul H. Clyde, and *World History: Patterns of Civilization*.

PROGRAM REVIEWERS

ACADEMIC CONSULTANTS

Africa
Abraham Kuranga
Department of History
Cincinnati State, Technical
    and Community College
Cincinnati, Ohio

Ancient World
Maud Gleason
Department of Classics
Stanford University
Palo Alto, California

Chicano/a Studies
Shirlene Soto
California State University
Northridge, California

East Asia
Burton F. Beers
Department of History (retired)
North Carolina State University
Raleigh, North Carolina

Economics
Richard Roehl
Department of Economics
University of Michigan
Dearborn, Michigan

Richard Sylla
Department of Economics
Stern School of Business
New York University
New York, New York

Medieval Europe
Kathryn Reyerson
Department of History
University of Minnesota
Minneapolis, Minnesota

Modern Europe
Douglas Skopp
Distinguished University Teaching
    Professor of History
State University of New York
Plattsburgh, New York

Religion
William L. Pitts, Jr.
Department of Religion
Baylor University
Waco, Texas

Benjamin Ravid
Department of Near Eastern
    and Judaic Studies
Brandeis University
Waltham, Massachusetts

Michael Sells
Department of Religion
Haverford College
Haverford, Pennsylvania

Thomas Smith
Department of Religious Studies
Loyola University New Orleans
New Orleans, Louisiana

South Asia
David Gilmartin
Department of History
North Carolina State University
Raleigh, North Carolina

Susan Wadley
Department of Anthropology
Syracuse University
Syracuse, New York

Southwest Asia
Linda T. Darling
Department of History
University of Arizona
Tucson, Arizona

Women's History
Lyn Reese
Women in World History Curriculum
Berkeley, California

CONTENT REVIEWERS

David Beaulieu
Former State Human Rights Commissioner
St. Paul, Minnesota

Samuel Chu
Department of History
The Ohio State University
Columbus, Ohio

Susan Douglass
Educational Consultant
Falls Church, Virginia

Shabbir Mansuri
Founding Director, Council on Islamic
    Education
Fountain Valley, California

José Morales
Chair and Assistant Professor, Latin
    American, Caribbean, and Latino
    Studies Program
New Jersey City University
Jersey City, New Jersey

Mark Peterson
Coordinator of Asian Studies
Brigham Young University
Provo, Utah

Charlotte Stokes
Supervisor of Social Studies, K–12
Prince Georges County Public Schools
Prince Georges County, Maryland

Acknowledgments appear on page 1062, which constitutes an extension of this copyright page.

ISBN 0-13-062790-9

2 3 4 5 6 7 8 9 10   06 05 04 03 02

Stone Age cave painting

Coffin of an Egyptian king

Start Smart

Before you start your study of World History, check out these special pages.

▶ **Skills for Life** xxviii

▶ **Focus on Themes** xxx
Use themes to organize your understanding
of world history.

▶ **Skills Handbook** xxxiii
Build, practice, and apply key social studies skills.

Chinese soldier

Greek vase

Olmec stone head

Table of Contents

Viking ship carving

Byzantine Emperor Justinian

Table of Contents

Islamic law court

Benin bronze

Japanese shrine

Table of Contents

*Italian artist
Leonardo da Vinci*

Ocean-going ship

*Catherine the Great,
empress of Russia*

*American statesman
Benjamin Franklin*

Early steam engine

*South American liberator
Símon Bolívar*

Table of Contents

West African throne

Japanese textile workers

Mexican mural by Diego Rivera

Table of Contents

1920s "flapper"

Table of Contents

World War II battlefield

Namibian independence celebration

Honduran folk painting

Taos Pueblo, New Mexico

San Martín and O'Higgins cross the Andes, 1817

Why Study History?

See how history is relevant to your life today.

SPECIAL FEATURES

Biography

Meet fascinating history makers.

Indira Gandhi

Did You Know?

Find out something new or unusual about history.

Geography and History

Investigate the connection between history and geography.

SPECIAL FEATURES/PRIMARY SOURCES

Connections to Today

Explore links between historical events and your world today.

Global Connections

See connections between events in different parts of the world.

Primary Source

Relive history through eyewitness accounts, literature, and documents.

(continued)

PRIMARY SOURCES

> ### The Spirits Are Good
> *The poems in the* Book of Songs *offer
> a rare look into the everyday lives
> of average people in ancient China:*
>
> "The spirits are good,
>   They will give you many blessings.
>   The common people are contented,
>   For daily they have their drink and food.
>   The thronging herd, the many clans.
>   All side with you in deeds of power.
>
> To be like the moon advancing to its full,
>   Like the sun climbing the sky,
>   Like the everlastingness of the southern
>   hills,
>   Without failing or falling,
>   Like the pine-tree, the cypress in their
>   [foliage]
>   All these blessings may you receive!"
>
> —*Shih Ching (Book of Songs)*

Table of Contents

PRIMARY SOURCES: In Text

Middle Eastern market

(continued)

PRIMARY SOURCES

"Go, wondrous creature! mount where Science guides;
Go, measure earth, weigh air, and state the tides;
Instruct the planets in what orbs to run,
Correct old Time, and regulate the sun."
                                    —Alexander Pope, *Essay on Man*

Table of Contents

MAPS

African Kingdoms and Trading States, 1000 B.C.–A.D. 1600

(continued)

(continued)

REFERENCE SECTION MAPS

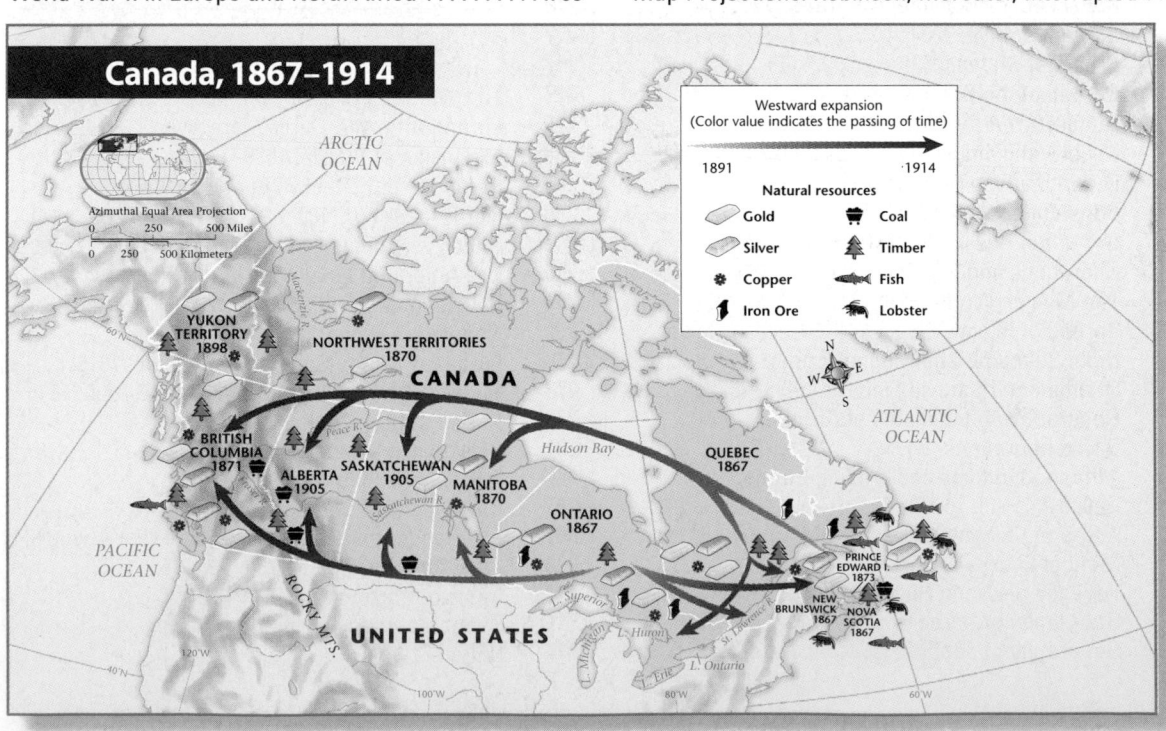

Canada, 1867–1914

CHARTS AND GRAPHS/SKILLS HANDBOOK

CHARTS AND GRAPHS

CAUSE AND EFFECT

FACT FINDER

UNIT TIME LINES

SKILLS HANDBOOK

Use This Book to Succeed in World History

You can use this book as a tool to master world history. Spend a few minutes to become familiar with the structure of the book and see how you can unlock the secrets of world history.

Find What Is Important

This book makes it easy to figure out what you really need to know about world history. Each section starts with Reading Focus questions that point out the most important ideas in that section. As you read, notice that the content is organized into several parts with red headings. As you read the paragraphs under the red headings, you can learn the answers to the Reading Focus questions. Later, you will find that the Section Assessment reviews each of these important ideas.

Reading Focus

- How did Napoleon rise to power?
- How were revolutionary reforms changed under Napoleon?
- How did Napoleon build an empire in Europe?

Vocabul

plebiscite
annex
blockade

Napoleon's Rise to Power

Napoleon Bonaparte was born in Corsica, a French-ruled island in the Mediterranean. His family were minor nobles, but had little money. At age nine, he was sent to France to be trained for a military career. When the revolution broke out, he was an ambitious 20-year-old lieutenant, eager to make a name for himself.

Napoleon favored the Jacobins and republican rule. However, he found the conflicting ideas and personalities of the revolution confusing. He wrote his brother in 1793: "Since one must take sides, one might as well choose the side that is victorious, the side which devastates, loots, and

Learn in Many Ways

Don't depend just on the main text. Discover world history through all parts of this book—from primary sources to pictures, from charts to activities. Preview each chapter by looking at photographs, a map, and a time line. See connections between main ideas and illustrations. Be transported back through time by reading primary sources. Read stories about real people who have changed the world. Witness grave disasters and relive great moments. Research exciting topics. Act out human dramas. Use all of your senses to explore world history.

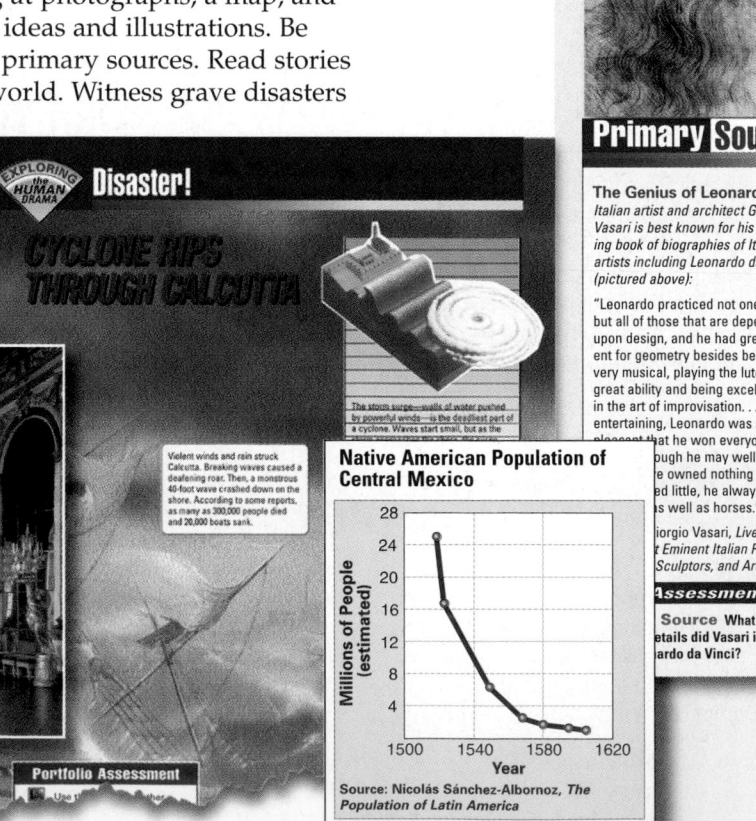

EXPLORING the HUMAN DRAMA **Disaster!**

CYCLONE RIPS THROUGH CALCUTTA

The storm surge—walls of water pushed by powerful winds—is the deadliest part of a cyclone. Waves start small, but as the

Violent winds and rain struck Calcutta. Breaking waves caused a deafening roar. Then, a monstrous 40-foot wave crashed down on the shore. According to some reports, as many as 300,000 people died and 20,000 boats sank.

Primary Source

The Genius of Leonardo
Italian artist and architect Giorgio Vasari is best known for his engaging book of biographies of Italian artists including Leonardo da Vinci (pictured above):

"Leonardo practiced not one art but all of those that are dependent upon design, and he had great talent for geometry besides being very musical, playing the lute with great ability and being excellent in the art of improvisation.... In entertaining, Leonardo was so pleasant that he won everyone's ... ugh he may well be ... e owned nothing and to ... ed little, he always kept ... s well as horses."

...iorgio Vasari, *Lives of the ... t Eminent Italian Painters, ... Sculptors, and Architects*

Assessment

Source What ...etails did Vasari include ...ardo da Vinci?

Native American Population of Central Mexico

Source: Nicolás Sánchez-Albornoz, *The Population of Latin America*

Palace of Versailles

Portfolio Assessment

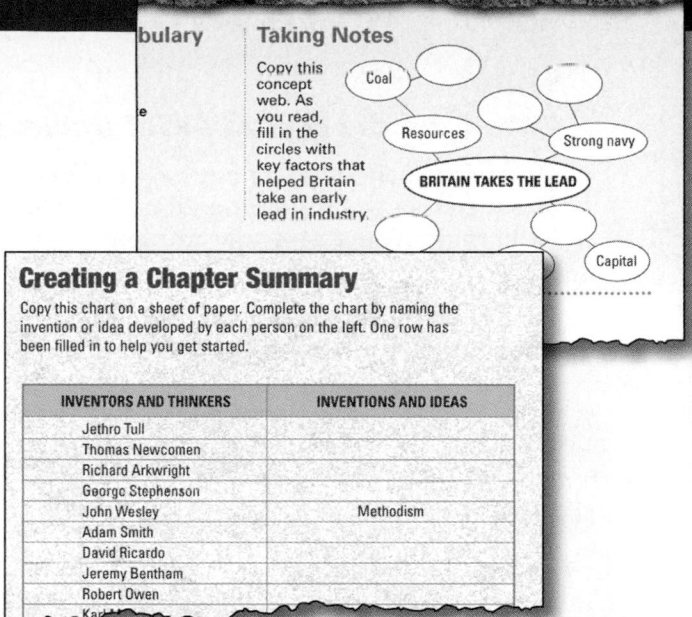

Organize Your Reading

Does so much world history content seem overwhelming? This book has ways to help you organize it. Use the Taking Notes exercise at the beginning of each section to help you take notes as you read. Then, at the end of the chapter, complete the Creating a Chapter Summary graphic organizer. This will help you capture the main ideas of the chapter in a visual way.

Creating a Chapter Summary

Copy this chart on a sheet of paper. Complete the chart by naming the invention or idea developed by each person on the left. One row has been filled in to help you get started.

INVENTORS AND THINKERS	INVENTIONS AND IDEAS
Jethro Tull	
Thomas Newcomen	
Richard Arkwright	
George Stephenson	
John Wesley	Methodism
Adam Smith	
David Ricardo	
Jeremy Bentham	
Robert Owen	
Karl	

Develop Your Skills

Success in world history requires you to master social studies skills. Learn these skills in the Skills Handbook. Practice them by answering questions on maps, pictures, primary sources, charts, and graphs. In each chapter, you can also find an Assessing Your Skills feature, which focuses on analyzing primary sources, synthesizing information, or comparing viewpoints. Then, review your skills by completing the Skills Assessment activities at the end of every chapter.

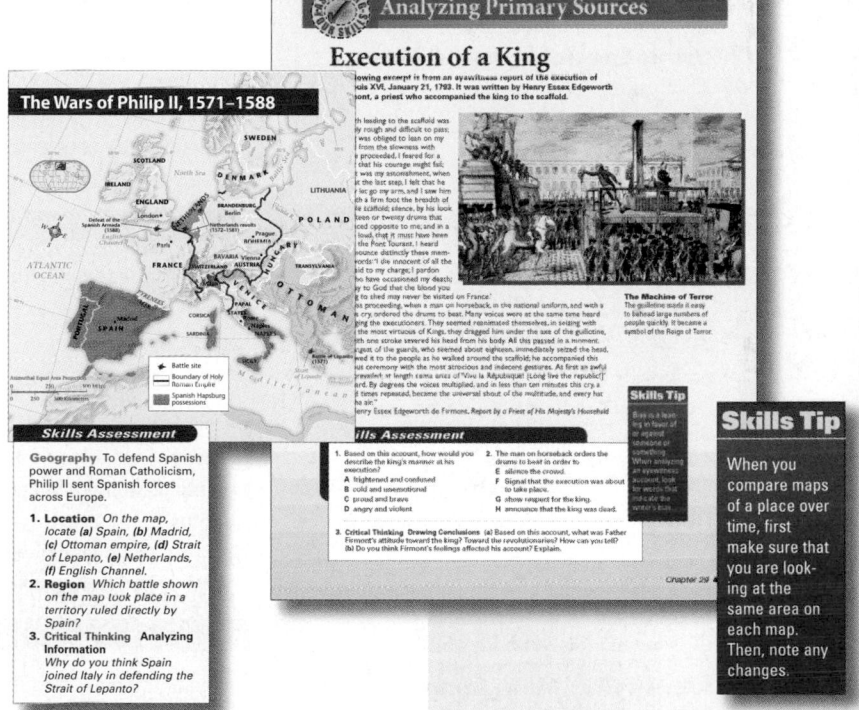

Prepare for Tests

This book will also help you prepare to take tests. To practice for standardized tests, answer the questions at the end of every section and chapter. Pay special attention to the critical-thinking questions. For portfolio assessment, complete activities in each Section Assessment and the portfolio assessment activities in Exploring the Human Drama features. Go to the **phschool.com** Web site to take a practice test for each chapter.

Web Site Self-Test
For practice test questions for Chapter 29, see
www.phschool.com

Skills for Life

What are the keys to social studies success?

In every social studies course you will ever take, you will need to know how to use the following 20 core skills. Building these skills year by year will make you a stronger student.

Read through this list of skills and their definitions. Which ones do you know well? Which ones do you need to strengthen? Beside each definition, a page where you can find help in developing that skill is listed.

Skill	Definition	Example
GEOGRAPHIC LITERACY		
1. Using the Cartographer's Tools	The ability to use the • compass rose to find directions and relative location. • scale to estimate distance. • latitude and longitude grid to determine exact location. • key, or legend, to understand map symbols and colors.	p. 49
2. Using Special-Purpose Maps	The ability to analyze and interpret maps of • natural features, such as elevation and climate. • features made by people, such as land use, roads, countries, population density, and battles.	p. 184
VISUAL ANALYZING		
3. Analyzing Graphic Data	The ability to read and interpret numeric information represented in • bar graphs. • line graphs. • circle graphs.	p. 515
4. Analyzing Images	The ability to identify and interpret symbols, tone, and message in • paintings and drawings. • photos. • posters and political cartoons.	p. 625
CRITICAL THINKING AND READING		
5. Identifying Main Ideas/ Summarizing	Identifying the main idea is the ability to distinguish the general idea of a passage from its supporting details. Summarizing is the ability to combine main ideas into an overview.	p. 614
6. Sequencing	The ability to organize items in order according to time, size, or priority.	p. 152
7. Identifying Cause and Effect/ Making Predictions	Identifying cause and effect is the ability to understand how an action or event leads to a result. Making predictions is the ability to use cause-and-effect understanding to determine the likely outcome of subsequent events or actions.	p. 534

Skill	Definition	Example
8. Drawing Inferences and Conclusions	Drawing inferences is the ability to determine the necessary consequences of an assumption: if this is true, that must be true. Drawing conclusions is the ability to analyze several inferences to make a reasoned judgment.	p. 838
9. Making Valid Generalizations	The ability to apply conclusions from specific circumstances to larger circumstances while maintaining accuracy.	p. 219
10. Distinguishing Fact and Opinion	The ability to separate those statements that can be proven to be true from those that reflect a personal viewpoint.	p. 824
11. Comparing and Contrasting	The ability to identify how different ideas, objects, historical figures, or situations are alike and/or different.	p. 98
12. Analyzing Primary Sources	The ability to evaluate a firsthand account for accuracy, tone, viewpoint, and frame of reference.	p. 296
13. Recognizing Bias and Propaganda	The ability to identify a stated or unstated viewpoint or slant that is designed to promote one set of beliefs over another.	p. 699
14. Identifying Frame of Reference and Point of View	The ability to identify an opinion expressed in writing or visual art and to understand the influences that shaped the writer's or artist's position.	p. 816
15. Decision making	The ability to state a question clearly, identify and evaluate possible choices, and select the option that seems to produce the best outcome.	p. 39
16. Problem solving	The ability to state a problem clearly, identify possible solutions, determine the likely outcome of each, select an option, and then evaluate its effectiveness.	p. 630

COMMUNICATIONS

Skill	Definition	Example
17. Using Reliable Information	The ability to locate and apply information for a variety of purposes that has been evaluated for its accuracy, age, authority, and bias.	p. 326
18. Transferring Information From One Medium to Another	The ability to translate numerical or visual information into text and to translate written information into graphs, tables, or diagrams.	p. 105
19. Synthesizing Information	The ability to analyze and combine information from several sources to draw conclusions and/or to create a new presentation of information.	p. 60
20. Supporting a Position	The ability to present evidence or reasoning that defends a given opinion or statement.	p. 838

Human History Is Fascinating and Complex

To make world history easier for you to grasp, this textbook emphasizes nine themes. They can help you focus on the key features of each society and event you read about.

Theme: Global Interaction

Different parts of the world may interact in many ways—through migration, trade, warfare, or the exchange of ideas. When people traveled by oxcart or sailing ship, interaction was a slow process. Today, communications networks can link all parts of the globe instantly.

Theme: Economics and Technology

Who controls vital resources? How are goods exchanged? What work do people do, and how are they paid for that work? Economic questions such as these are often closely linked to technology. From Stone Age farming tools to the printing press to the steam engine to the computer, technology has transformed the world again and again.

The first moon landing, 1969

Theme: Political and Social Systems

Monarchs, presidents, dictators, tribal councils—each society has a form of government to ensure order and guard against outside threats. Societies around the world have also developed other important institutions to ensure order, including legal systems, social classes, and the most basic unit of all—the family.

Theme: Impact of the Individual

Everyone who ever lived is part of the human story. Yet some people have such an impact on events that we remember them long after they die. For good or ill, individuals such as Confucius, Christopher Columbus, Marie Curie, Joseph Stalin, and Mohandas Gandhi have had a lasting influence on our world.

Theme: Diversity

The vast diversity of the world's cultures is reflected in many ways, including language, ethnic background, customs, beliefs, and clothing. Such diversity has enriched the human experience. Yet, at the same time, cultural or ethnic differences often lead to bitter conflict.

Ancient Indian Painting

A pipeline will carry water through the Arabian desert.

Theme: Geography and History

Geography influences where people settle, how they live, and how goods and ideas travel. Since ancient times, people have dug irrigation canals to water farmlands, and control of waterways or mountain passes has determined the outcome of wars. Today, environmental issues often stir heated debate.

Theme: Religions and Value Systems

Today, as in the past, religion exerts a powerful impact on the world. Belief in one God guided the histories of Jews, Christians, and Muslims. Buddhism and Hinduism shaped many Asian cultures. Nonreligious values, such as Greek ideals of beauty and individuality, have also had a wide influence.

Theme: Continuity and Change

History is the story of change. Some changes can be as quick as a revolution. Others, such as the spread of democratic ideas or the shifting roles of men and women in many nations, may take decades or even centuries. Although change is always taking place, enduring traditions and concerns link people across time and space.

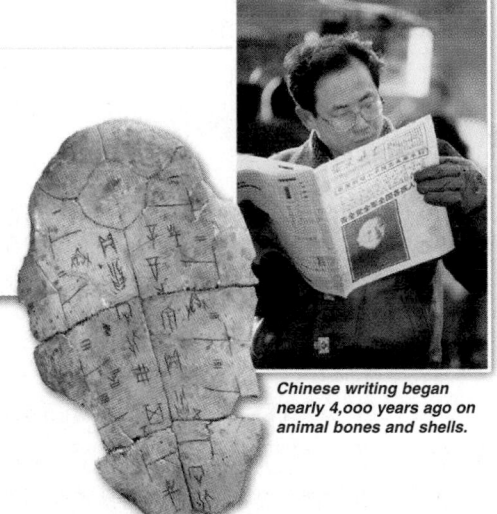

Chinese writing began nearly 4,000 years ago on animal bones and shells.

Pablo Picasso's African-inspired painting

Theme: Art and Literature

Since the days of Stone Age cave paintings, people have created art and literature to express their lives and values. In the Middle Ages, Europeans built soaring cathedrals to the glory of God. Today, novelists and filmmakers from Nigeria to Brazil vividly depict the challenges of modern life.

Explore World History Through the Internet

As you read this book, you will notice many opportunities to make world history come alive by using the Internet. By accessing a Web site designed specifically for Prentice Hall's *World History: Connections to Today* program, you can visit amazing places, develop exciting projects, and even review for tests.

Visit the Prentice Hall World History Web Site

Follow these easy steps to find the Web site that accompanies your book:
- Go to **www.phschool.com**.
- Click on the button that says **"Social Studies."**
- Under **"PH@School,"** open **"Program"** and click on **"World History: Connections to Today."**
    Find the edition of the book you use, and select the student version.
- Select a specific chapter.

Take Virtual Field Trips

Now you can take field trips around the world and across the ages through cyberspace. In every chapter, you will find a Virtual Field Trip feature that highlights a specially selected site on the Internet. Link there via the **www.phschool.com** Web site to begin your exploration.

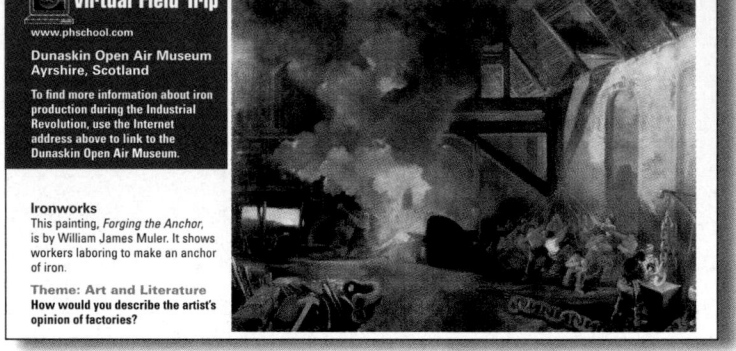

Virtual Field Trip

www.phschool.com

Dunaskin Open Air Museum Ayrshire, Scotland

To find more information about iron production during the Industrial Revolution, use the Internet address above to link to the Dunaskin Open Air Museum.

Ironworks
This painting, *Forging the Anchor*, is by William James Muler. It shows workers laboring to make an anchor of iron.

Theme: Art and Literature
How would you describe the artist's opinion of factories?

Learn Through Internet Activities

Throughout the entire program, you will find activities that are designed to use the strength of the Internet to supplement this textbook. Look for the Internet icon on Take It to the Net section and chapter review activities and Exploring the Human Drama portfolio activities.

Stay Up-to-Date With Current Events Online

For the latest developments in world history, go to the **www.phschool.com** Web site. Use the daily current events and content updates there to keep your learning up-to-date.

Take It to the NET
To learn about recent developments in Africa, visit the World History section of **www.phschool.com**.

Prepare for Tests With Web Site Self-Tests

For each chapter, you can take a practice test online at the **www.phschool.com** Web site. Completing this test will give you a quick review of the material and help you identify which areas you need to study further. You can also use the self-tests to prepare for unit tests, midterms, and finals.

CONTENTS

Learning the Skill Answers

1. "Civilizations of the Ancient Middle East" is the title of the map.
2. The distance between Ur and Kish is about 150 miles.
3. The locator map uses a black box and red land to indicate which area is shown on the main map.
4. A person would travel northeast to get from the Sinai Peninsula to the Caspian Sea.
5. The Arabian Desert is located around 30° N latitude.
6. Bodies of water include the Black Sea, Caspian Sea, Persian Gulf, Mediterranean Sea, Red Sea, Tigris River, Euphrates River, and Nile River. The Taurus Mountains are farther north.
7. A red border shows the Babylonian empire.
8. Possible answers: Mesopotamia is located in the Fertile Crescent, between the Tigris and Euphrates rivers. It is east of the Mediterranean Sea and northwest of the Persian Gulf. It lies between about 35–38° N latitude and 38–45° E longitude.

Learning From Maps

How Will I Use This Skill? Maps are not just for textbooks. They can help you find your way on a bus or in a car. They can help you understand about events in other parts of the world. You can even use them to learn about tomorrow's weather.

Learning the Skill

To learn from a map, you have to look closely at the map's features. Use the map and the information below to learn about the various parts of a map.

Civilizations of the Ancient Middle East

1. **Read the title** The title gives a clue to the main topic of the map. **What is the title of this map?**

2. **Use the scale** You can use the scale of miles and kilometers to calculate the distance between two points. A short distance on a map represents a larger distance on the Earth. For example, one inch may represent 100 miles. **How far is it from Ur to Kish?**

3. **Observe the locator map** The locator map shows which part of the whole Earth is shown on this map. **How does the locator indicate the area shown on the main map?**

4. **Check the compass** The compass shows which direction is north on the map. You can also find the other directions—south, east, and west. Some compasses also show intermediate directions, for example northeast, which is the direction between north and east. **In which direction would you travel to get from the Sinai Peninsula to the Caspian Sea?**

5. **Notice the latitude and longitude lines and numbers** Latitude lines indicate the distance north or south of the equator. Longitude lines show distance east or west from the Prime Meridian, an imaginary line that runs through Greenwich, England. Latitude and longitude are measured in degrees (°). **What desert is located around 30° N latitude?**

6. **Identify bodies of water and other physical features** Maps often show oceans, rivers, mountains, and other physical features. Sometimes, color or shading is used to identify different features. Water, for example, is usually blue. Mountains are indicated by gray shading called relief. **Name three bodies of water shown on this map. Which mountain range is farther north—the Taurus Mountains or the Zagros Mountains?**

7. **Use the key** The key explains colors or symbols used on the map. Here, purple shows Sumer. **How is the Babylonian empire shown?**

8. **Identify political areas** Political areas, such as countries, empires, or cities, can be shown with borders, colors, or other symbols. They may be labeled on the map or in the key. **Describe the location of Mesopotamia.**

xxxiv

Technology
Skills Transparencies Learning From Maps, p. 5

Practicing the Skill

Practice learning from maps by recalling the steps you just learned and by answering the following questions based on the map below.

1. What is the title of the map?
2. About how far would you travel to get from Beirut to Riyadh?
3. Study the locator map. What region of Africa is part of the Middle East? What region of Asia is part of the Middle East?
4. In what direction would you travel to get from Ankara to Tehran?
5. Use latitude and longitude to tell the location of the Strait of Hormuz.
6. (a) What are three important rivers in the Middle East? (b) What body of water separates Egypt from Saudi Arabia?
7. (a) A desalinization plant removes the salt from salt water to make it suitable for drinking and watering crops. How are desalinization plants shown on the map? (b) Where are most of them located?
8. (a) Through what countries does the Tigris River flow? (b) Through what countries does the Euphrates River flow? (c) Why do you think leaders from these countries meet to discuss water resources?

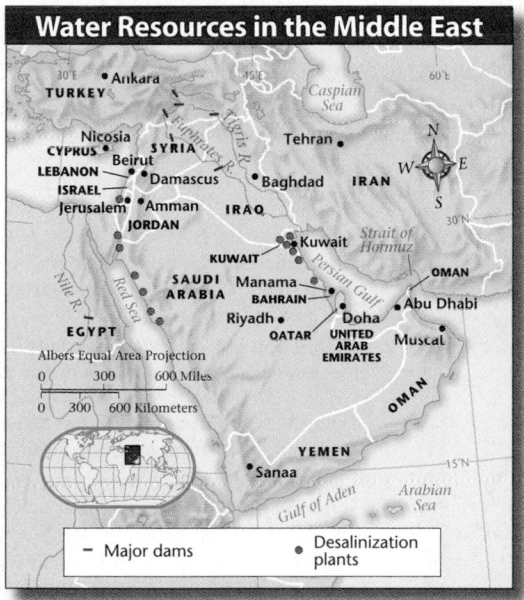

Applying the Skill

Choose a map in your textbook. Based on the skill lesson on these pages, write a series of questions that test understanding of how to read and use the map. Trade with a partner and answer each other's questions. Then, check your partner's answers.

xxxv

Practicing the Skill Answers

1. "Water Resources in the Middle East" is the title of the map.
2. The distance between Beirut and Riyadh is about 1,000 miles.
3. Northeast Africa and Southwest Asia are parts of the Middle East.
4. A person would travel southeast to get from Ankara to Tehran.
5. The Strait of Hormuz is located at about 27° N latitude and 56° E longitude.
6. (a) Three important rivers in the Middle East are the Nile, Tigris, and Euphrates rivers. (b) The Red Sea separates Egypt from Saudi Arabia.
7. (a) Desalinization plants are shown by purple dots. (b) There are six along the Persian Gulf coast and six along the Red Sea coast.
8. (a) The Tigris River flows through Turkey and Iraq. (b) The Euphrates River flows through Turkey, Syria, and Iraq. (c) These countries meet to discuss water resources because they all depend on and share the same sources of water.

Applying the Skill Rubrics

Share rubrics with students before they write their questions.

Attempted Student does not complete the assignment.

Minimal Student writes a few questions showing some understanding of how to read and use a map and is able to answer some of partner's questions.

Adequate Student writes a reasonable number of questions that show a clear understanding of how to read and use a map and is able to answer partner's questions.

Exemplary Student's questions are well written and reflect an in-depth comprehension of map information. Student is able to answer partner's questions and check answers.

UNDERSTANDING CHARTS AND GRAPHS

Learning the Skill Answers

1. "Travel Times to London" is the title of the bar graph.
2. The vertical axis of the bar graph refers to cities.
3. Travel times in 1830 are shown by a blue line.
4. Blue is used to show Catholic land ownership.
5. Protestants owned 78 percent of the land in 1685.
6. (a) The United States had the greatest rise in steel production from 1880 to 1910. **(b)** This rise probably benefited other segments of the economy because the steel producers needed to purchase more materials and services and because increased income for workers boosted consumer spending.

Understanding Charts and Graphs

How Will I Use This Skill? A graph shows numerical facts in picture form. Bar graphs and line graphs allow you to compare things at different times or in different places. You often see this type of graph in newspapers, where it might show a change such as the increase in student enrollment at your school or the average temperature over the last month. Circle graphs, or pie charts, show how a whole thing is divided into parts. The segments in a circle graph represent percentages of the whole, helping you better compare the parts.

Learning the Skill

To interpret a graph, you have to look closely at its features. Use the graphs and the information below to learn how to use various types of graphs.

Bar graph

Circle graph

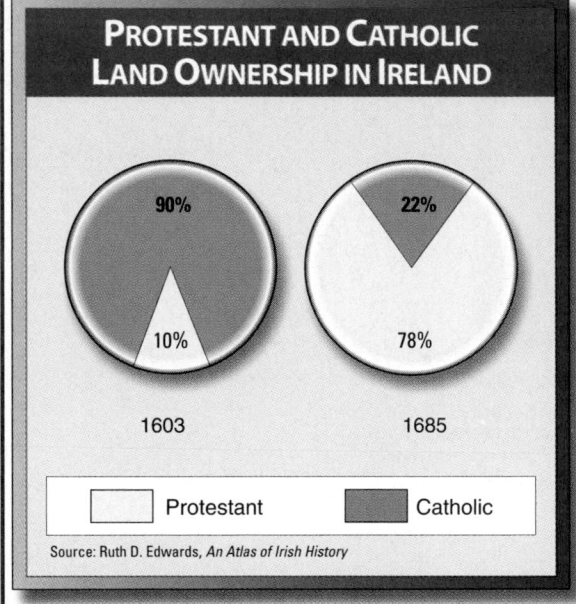

Source: Ruth D. Edwards, *An Atlas of Irish History*

1. **Read the title** The title of any kind of graph tells you the main topic of the graph. **What is the title of the bar graph?**

2. **On line and bar graphs, identify the labels** Notice the labels on the bottom and side of the graph. For example, on the bar graph, the bottom, or horizontal axis, refers to hours. **What does the side, or vertical axis, of the bar graph refer to?**

3. **Determine what the bars or lines represent** Graphs use labels or a key to make clearer what the graph is about. On the line graph, for example, the red line represents the amount of steel produced in Germany. **On the bar graph, how are travel times in 1830 shown?**

4. **On circle graphs, identify the parts into which the circle is divided** A circle graph may have labels on the parts to tell you how the circle is divided. Sometimes, however, the graph includes a key to explain the use of color on the graph. For example, on the circle graph, Protestant land ownership in Ireland is shown in beige. **What color is used to show Catholic land ownership?**

xxxvi

Resource Directory

Technology
Skills Transparencies Understanding Charts and Graphs, p. 7

Line graph

STEEL PRODUCTION, 1880–1910

Millions of Metric Tons (vertical axis: 5, 10, 15, 20, 25, 30)

Year (horizontal axis: 1880, 1890, 1900, 1910)

— United States — Germany — Great Britain

Sources: *European Historical Statistics, 1750–1970,* and *Historical Statistics of the United States*

5. **Read the graph** Use the title, labels, and colors to understand the meaning of the graph. You can learn from the circle graph that in 1603 Protestants owned 10 percent of the land in Ireland. **What percentage did Protestants own in 1685?**

6. **Interpret the graph** Often, graphs show trends, or tendencies in a given direction. The line graph shows steel production from 1880 to 1910 in three different countries. **(a) Which country had the greatest rise in steel production during this time? (b) Do you think this rise benefited other segments of the nation's economy? Why or why not?**

Practicing the Skill

Interpret the graph at right by recalling the steps you just learned and by answering the questions that follow.

1. What is the topic of the graph? How can you tell?
2. What percentage of enslaved Africans was shipped to Portuguese Brazil? To Europe and Asia?
3. To what other parts of the world were enslaved Africans shipped?
4. Can you learn from this graph how many slaves were shipped to North America in 1875? Why or why not?
5. Can you tell from this graph what percentage of enslaved Africans was shipped to the Caribbean? Why or why not?
6. Could this information be presented on a line graph instead of a circle graph? Explain.

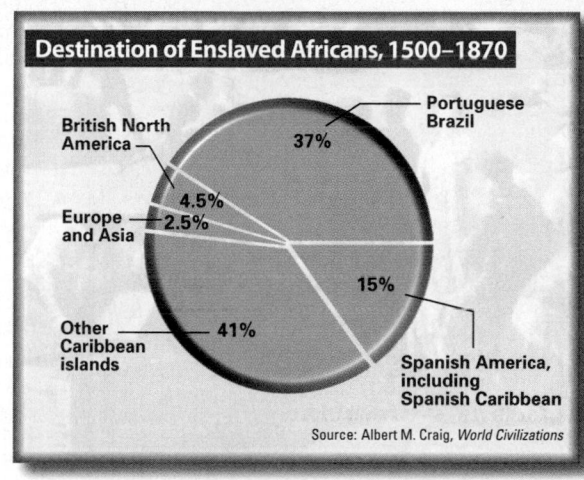

Destination of Enslaved Africans, 1500–1870

British North America

Portuguese Brazil 37%

Europe and Asia — 4.5% / 2.5%

Spanish America, including Spanish Caribbean — 15%

Other Caribbean islands — 41%

Source: Albert M. Craig, *World Civilizations*

Applying the Skill

Conduct a simple poll among your classmates about a topic related to school, such as the number of hours per day each student spends doing homework or the material used by each student to cover his or her textbooks. Then, create an appropriate graph to display the results of your poll. Be prepared to explain your graph to the class.

xxxvii

Interpreting Visuals

Learning the Skill Answers

1. The three main images in this photograph are the nuclear explosion, the "radiation-resistant" blanket, and the frightened boy cowering beneath the blanket.

2. The feelings of fear and insecurity are shown on the boy's face and through his crouched position hiding under the blanket.

3. This photograph was produced in 1954.

4. This visual was produced by the company that manufactured the "radiation-resistant" blanket. The purpose of this picture was to advertise a product that protected a person from the damage of a nuclear blast.

5. This information confirms the understanding that this picture is a result of widespread fear of nuclear war.

6. Possible answer: This picture was an effective advertisement because it capitalized on the fears that people felt in the 1950s.

How Will I Use This Skill? In today's fast-paced "information age," we are bombarded with visuals of all kinds. Television, film, the Internet, and print media all carry images that are designed to convey information or influence attitudes. People use drawings, art, photographs, and computer graphics to communicate facts and ideas. Today, literacy means not only the ability to read and write but also the ability to understand and interpret visuals.

Learning the Skill

Use this black-and-white photograph and the following steps to learn some of the methods involved in interpreting visuals.

In the 1950s, children in Europe and other parts of the world were taught they could survive a nuclear attack. This 1954 image was used to advertise a bogus "radiation-resistant" blanket.

1. **Identify the content of the visual** The content of a visual includes all the individual images that make up the larger visual. Be careful to look at both the foreground and background. Note which images seem to have the main importance in the visual. **What are the three main images in this photograph?**

2. **Note the emotional elements** An artist or photographer often tries to convey attitudes and emotions in a visual. **What feelings are conveyed by the boy's position and facial expression?**

3. **Read any text that accompanies the visual** A visual often has a title, caption, or other accompanying text that helps you to interpret it. **When was this photograph produced?**

4. **Determine the purpose of the visual** A visual may be intended to provide information, to persuade, or to entertain. A good starting point for determining the purpose of a visual is to consider the individual or group that produced it. **Who produced this visual? What do you think was its purpose?**

5. **Learn more about the visual or its creator** Sometimes, it is helpful to do some research to better understand the visual or its creator. If you did research on this photograph, you would learn that in the 1950s, the United States and the Soviet Union were engaged in a dangerous rivalry, including a race to build weapons. This rivalry was called the Cold War. Many people feared that a terrible nuclear conflict might erupt at any time. **Does this information refute or confirm your understanding of the picture? Explain.**

6. **React to the visual** React to the visual based on its apparent or intended purpose. If the visual was meant to inform, decide how well it conveys information to you. If it was meant to persuade, consider how effective it might be at influencing the attitudes of those who view it. If it was meant to be entertaining, react to it in those terms. **Do you think this photograph was an effective commercial advertisement that had an influence on people in the 1950s? Why or why not?**

xxxviii

Resource Directory

Technology
Skills Transparencies Interpreting Visuals, p. 9

Practicing the Skill

Interpret the visual below by recalling the steps you have just learned and by answering the questions that follow.

Honduran Street Scene
In this colorful folk art painting by Jorge Ferman, one can learn much about the culture of the Central American country of Honduras.

1. **(a)** What are some of the main images in the painting? **(b)** What images provide the background?
2. Do you think the painter portrays village life in Honduras in a favorable or unfavorable way? Explain.
3. How does the painting suggest that Honduras has a tropical climate?
4. What do you think is the purpose of this painting?
5. If you did some research about rural life in Honduras, you would learn that more than 50 percent of the population works in agriculture. Common crops among small farmers are corn, beans, and squash. On large plantations, people grow such cash crops as coffee and cotton. Based on this information, does the painting seem to convey an accurate or inaccurate vision of life in a Honduran village? Explain.
6. **(a)** What emotions does the painting cause you to feel? **(b)** Based on the painting, would you like to visit Honduras? Why or why not?

Applying the Skill

Select a visual in a current newspaper or magazine that appears in print or online. Print out, cut out, or reproduce a copy of the visual and any accompanying text. Use the steps that you have learned in this skill lesson to write an interpretation of the visual.

Practicing the Skill Answers

1. **(a)** The main images in the painting are the villagers walking the streets. **(b)** The brightly tiled houses and flowering trees and plants provide the background.
2. The painter shows village life in Honduras in an extremely favorable way. The colorful flowers, blue sky, and the happy looking villagers portray a feeling of happiness and contentment.
3. The bright colors and many flowers suggest a tropical climate.
4. Possible answer: The purpose of this painting is to demonstrate the richness and warmth of the culture of Honduras.
5. The painting seems accurate. The people carry bags of cotton or balance containers of produce on their heads.
6. **(a)** Emotions mentioned by students may include happiness, joy, or other positive feelings. **(b)** Students should support their preference with clear reasons.

Applying the Skill Rubrics

Share rubrics with students before they select the visual and write the interpretation.

Attempted Student does not complete the assignment.

Minimal Student's interpretation is missing some steps or shows incomplete understanding of the visual.

Adequate Student's interpretation shows understanding of all the steps and gives an appropriate response to each.

Exemplary Student's interpretation demonstrates deep understanding of steps and is clearly organized and well written.

xxxix

ANALYZING PRIMARY SOURCES

Analyzing Primary Sources

How Will I Use This Skill? Primary sources include official documents, as well as firsthand accounts of events. They may also include visual evidence, such as a news photograph, a painting by an eyewitness, or a political cartoon. They are a valuable source of information about the past. Historians often use primary sources to prepare their narratives, which are secondary sources. You use primary sources when you watch an interview on television or listen to a friend tell you about something that happened at school.

Learning the Skill

Use the excerpt, the cartoon, and the steps that follow to learn about analyzing primary sources.

> The following excerpt comes from *The Satires*, a series of poems written by Juvenal about life in Rome in the first century A.D. In this excerpt, Juvenal recounts a friend's reasons for moving away from Rome.
>
> 66 Since at Rome there is no place for honest pursuits, no profit to be got by honest toil—my fortune is less today than it was yesterday. . . .
>   What shall I do at Rome? I cannot lie; if a book is bad, I cannot praise it and beg a copy. I know not the motions of the stars . . . no one shall be a thief by my cooperation. . . .
>   Who, nowadays, is beloved except the confidant of crime? 99
>   —Juvenal, *The Satires* (tr. Lewis Evans)

Learning the Skill Answers

1. This primary source was written in the first century A.D. to speak about life and problems in Rome.

2. In this excerpt, the phrase *confidant of crime* literally means someone who is intimately familiar with crime—in other words, a criminal. The writer's main point is that no one can survive in Rome without turning to crime.

3. An opinion statement is ". . . at Rome there is . . . no profit to be got by honest toil . . . ."

4. The translator is Lewis Evans.

5. The fact that Juvenal was denied a government position would make his opinions suspect. He might be biased against the country that denied him his goal.

6. **(a)** The bulldozer in this cartoon represents overdevelopment and the excessive use of natural resources. **(b)** The cartoon portrays humanity using up the whole world and then having nothing left to stand on. **(c)** The artist is trying to show that people must be careful about what is taken from the world; otherwise, there may not be enough left to support life.

This cartoon by Arcadio Esquivel from Costa Rica shows the world being bulldozed. Costa Rica has been more successful than many other countries in balancing the need for development with the need to preserve the environment.

1. **Read the headnote or caption** Often, primary sources are presented with a short introduction about the writer or the document. The headnote with the excerpt above, for example, explains that the excerpt was written by Juvenal. **According to the headnote, when was this primary source written? Why was it written?**

2. **Read the primary source** As you read the primary source, identify unfamiliar words and try to gather the general meaning of the source. **In this excerpt, what is the writer's main point?**

3. **Identify facts and opinions in the written source** A fact can be proved true. An opinion, on the other hand, cannot be proved. Often, you can identify opinion statements by introductory words like "I think" or by strongly positive or negative words, like "gorgeous" or "despicable." Another clue is a statement that exaggerates. **Identify an opinion statement in the excerpt.**

4. **Read the source line** You can often get additional information about an excerpt by reading the source line. In this case, for example, you can learn that the excerpt is a translation. **Who translated Juvenal's words?**

Resource Directory

Technology
Skills Transparencies Analyzing Primary Sources, p. 11

5. **Identify bias and evaluate reliability** You have seen that primary sources include both facts and opinions. They may also reveal the bias of the author. These factors affect the reliability of the source. Other factors that affect reliability are the time that may have passed between an event and the author's writing about it and the author's own earlier experiences. Suppose you knew that Juvenal had served in the army, hoping to make his way into government service, but in the end, had not received the promotion he hoped for. **How might that fact affect Juvenal's reliability as a commentator on Roman society?**

6. **Learn from political cartoons** Political cartoons can also be primary sources. They reflect the observations of one artist about events of the time. They often use symbols to represent other things. **(a) In the cartoon on the opposite page, what does the bulldozer represent?** Cartoons also use exaggeration to make their point. **(b) What is exaggerated in this cartoon? (c) Explain the point of view expressed in the cartoon.**

Practicing the Skill

Analyze the primary source below by recalling the steps you have just learned and by answering the questions that follow.

In 1947, India gained independence after hundreds of years as a colony of Great Britain. India's new leader, Jawaharlal Nehru, had worked to bring about independence. He addressed the nation on its first independence day.

❝ We are a free and sovereign people today, and we have rid ourselves of the burden of the past. We look at the world with clear and friendly eyes, and at the future with faith and confidence. . . .

Our first and immediate objective must be to put an end to all internal strife and violence, which disfigure and degrade us and injure the cause of freedom. They come in the way of consideration of the great economic problems of the masses of the people which so urgently demand attention.

. . . Production today is the first priority, and every attempt to hamper or lessen production is injuring the nation, and more especially harmful to our laboring masses. . . . **❞**

—Jawaharlal Nehru, Independence Day speech, August 15, 1947

1. **(a)** Who wrote this document? **(b)** Under what circumstances?
2. **(a)** Identify one fact in Nehru's speech. **(b)** Identify one opinion statement.
3. **(a)** What was Nehru's purpose in giving this speech? **(b)** Do you think his purpose affected the words he spoke? **(c)** Do you think he achieved his purpose?
4. **(a)** Is the speech a reliable source for understanding Nehru's goal for his country? **(b)** Why or why not?

Applying the Skill

Use Internet or library sources to find a primary source that interests you. Remember that it can be either written or visual. Follow the steps outlined on these pages and then write a paragraph analzying the primary source.

xli

Comparing Viewpoints

How Will I Use This Skill? When people describe an idea or event, they usually provide some facts and their own personal viewpoints. A person's viewpoint is shaped by subjective influences such as feelings, prejudices, and past experiences. You often encounter divergent viewpoints, as when two of your friends describe the same event differently, when two politicians recommend different policies, or when two newspapers analyze a news event in different ways. By analyzing and comparing viewpoints, you will be able to better understand issues and form your own viewpoint.

Learning the Skill

Throughout history, people have tried to educate their children. But they have not always agreed on the goals of education. Read the excerpts below and compare the two viewpoints by using the steps that follow.

Henri Christophe, king of Haiti, set up schools for out-standing students of his nation. He believed these schools would help Haiti maintain the freedom it had won fewer than 15 years earlier. In 1817, he wrote:

❝ To form good citizens we must educate our children. From our national institutions will proceed a race of men capable of defending by their knowledge and talents those rights so long denied by tyrants. It is from these sources that light will be diffused among the whole mass of the population. ❞

—King Henri Christophe, 1817

Leo Tolstoy, a Russian aristocrat of the late 1800s, became a famous novelist as a young man. Later, he turned his attention to social issues. In 1902, he wrote:

❝ You can take a puppy and feed him, and teach him to carry something, and enjoy the sight of him; but it is not enough to rear and bring up a man, and teach him Greek; he has to be taught to live, that is, to take less from others, and give more. ❞

—Leo Tolstoy, 1902

---

1. **Identify the authors** It is important always to identify the writer or speaker. **Who are the authors of these two documents, and where and when did they live?**

2. **Make sure that you understand the arguments being made.** Try to identify the main idea and supporting arguments made by each author. **(a) According to Christophe, what is the goal of education? (b) Why does Tolstoy compare raising a puppy to teaching a person Greek?**

3. **Consider the authors' backgrounds** A person's attitudes, beliefs, and past experiences affect that person's viewpoint. By knowing the author's background, you can make judgments about the viewpoint. **How might the backgrounds of Christophe and Tolstoy affect their viewpoints?**

4. **Find common information** If two viewpoints are on the same topic, there should be some points that they agree on. Often, these will be basic facts. **According to both viewpoints, what is true about education?**

5. **Find opinions** Differentiate the opinions from the facts. The opinions represent the author's viewpoint. **Name two words used by Christophe that signal opinions.**

6. **Evaluate the validity of each viewpoint** Evaluate viewpoints by recalling the authors' background and determining if their opinions are based on facts or reasonable arguments. **Are the viewpoints of Christophe and Tolstoy based on reasonable arguments? Explain.**

xlii

Learning the Skill Answers

1. The authors of these passages are Henri Christophe, king of Haiti in the early 1800s, and Leo Tolstoy, a Russian aristocrat who lived during the late 1800s and early 1900s.

2. **(a)** According to Christophe, the goal of education is to make good citizens. **(b)** Tolstoy uses this comparison to demonstrate that it is not enough to educate someone; a person must also be taught moral values.

3. Both of these authors held higher positions than the common people of their countries. These lofty positions in society could certainly have affected their viewpoints.

4. Both viewpoints include the idea that education is necessary in society.

5. The words *must* and *will be* are often used to begin statements that are opinions. When absolute words such as these are used and the rest of the sentence is not a fact, then it is an opinion.

6. Both viewpoints seem to be opinions that are not based on facts. However, both seem to be reasonable arguments.

7. **(a)** It is likely that Tolstoy's view of the common man as an animal to be trained was a popular view among aristocrats. **(b)** The king of Haiti refers to rights that had long been denied by tyrants. He was concerned with maintaining freedom because he wanted to prevent a return to oppression.

Resource Directory

Technology
Skills Transparencies Comparing Viewpoints, p. 13

7. **Draw conclusions** After following the above steps, you are ready to draw conclusions about the viewpoints and the topic that they deal with. **(a) Do you think Tolstoy's view was typical of Russian aristocrats? (b) Why might the king of Haiti have been so concerned about maintaining the freedom of his nation?**

Practicing the Skill

The document and poster below reflect different viewpoints on industry and labor in the Soviet Union during the early 1900s. Compare the two viewpoints by answering the following questions:

1. Who are the authors of the letter?
2. Based on both documents, what was one goal of the Soviet Union?
3. **(a)** According to the poster, what was the general attitude of Soviet workers? **(b)** According to the letter, were most people in the camp treated justly? Explain.
4. Which viewpoint seems more trustworthy to you? Explain.
5. What methods did the Soviet Union use to increase economic production?

This letter protesting prison conditions was written to government leaders of the Soviet Union by former prisoners.

❝ We are prisoners who are returning from the Solovetsky concentration camp because of our poor health. We went there full of energy and good health, and now we are returning as invalids, broken and crippled emotionally and physically. . . . It is difficult for a human being even to imagine such terror, tyranny, violence, and lawlessness. . . . The Unified State Political Directorate [OGPU] without oversight and due process sends workers and peasants there who are by and large innocent. . . .

They die a slow and painful death . . . from hunger, cold, and backbreaking 14–16 hour days. . . . We . . . are asking you to improve the pathetic, tortured existence of those who are there who languish under the yoke of the OGPU's tyranny. . . . To this we subscribe: G. Zheleznov, Vinogradov, F. Belinskii. ❞

—Letter to the Presidium of the Central Executive
Committee of the Communist Party,
December 14, 1926

КОМСОМОЛ-УДАРНАЯ БРИГАДА ПЯТИЛЕТКИ.

Poster produced by the Soviet government, 1930s.

Applying the Skill

Use the Internet or library resources to find two documents expressing different viewpoints on a major turning point in world history. Some examples are the fall of the Roman empire, the Crusades, the Reformation, and World War I. Make copies of the documents. Then, use the steps that you have learned to write a paragraph comparing the viewpoints.

Practicing the Skill Answers

1. The authors of this letter are former prisoners in the Soviet Union.
2. One goal of the Soviet Union was to have all of its people constantly working for the good of the nation, regardless of whether the work was good for the individual.
3. **(a)** According to the poster, the workers were all industrious and liked their work. **(b)** According to the letter, those who worked in the prison camps were treated inhumanely and suffered, even though many were innocent.
4. The viewpoint of the prisoners seems more trustworthy because it is a personal account of hardship rather than an example of government propaganda.
5. The Soviet Union used prison labor to increase economic production.

Applying the Skill Rubrics

Share rubrics with students before they locate and compare two viewpoints.

Attempted Student does not complete the assignment.

Minimal Student locates two viewpoints but comparison is incomplete.

Adequate Student is able to compare the two viewpoints by including all steps in a clearly written paragraph.

Exemplary Student's comparison shows deep understanding of each viewpoint and its subjective influences and is well written.

xliii

SYNTHESIZING INFORMATION

Synthesizing Information

Learning the Skill Answers

1. All three items of information relate to sea transportation.

2. (a) The main idea of this passage is how important the improvements in technology were to Europeans' exploration of the oceans. **(b)** The caravel made it easier to sail across and into the wind. **(c)** Pigafetta's account tells how very difficult it was for Magellan's sailors to survive.

3. Both "Improved Technology" and the captioned illustration of a caravel show that European sailors became better equipped to sail the oceans.

4. The excerpt from Pigafetta's journal describes the extreme hardships faced by sailors.

5. Even with new and improved technology, sea travel was still extremely hazardous in the 1500s. It was difficult to store enough food and water for a long journey. It was also perilously easy to become lost when so much of the world was still uncharted.

How Will I Use This Skill? If you want to know whether a movie is worth seeing, you can read a review, watch a television commercial, view a film clip on the Internet, and talk to people who have seen the movie. You can combine the different pieces of evidence to develop a more complete impression of the movie. This process of combining pieces of evidence is called synthesizing. Today and in the future, synthesizing information will help you to become better informed and to make better decisions.

Learning the Skill

Study the three different pieces of information on this page about some developments in the 1400s and early 1500s. Then, follow the steps to learn how to synthesize information.

The caravel, shown above, helped Europeans sail across and into the wind.

Improved Technology Several improvements in technology helped Europeans conquer the vast oceans of the world. Cartographers, or mapmakers, created more accurate maps and sea charts. European sailors also learned to use the astrolabe, an instrument developed by the ancient Greeks and perfected by the Arabs, to determine their latitude at sea.

Along with more reliable navigational tools, Europeans designed larger and better ships. The Portuguese developed the caravel, which combined the square sails of European ships with Arab lateen, or triangular, sails. Caravels also adapted the sternpost rudder and numerous masts of Chinese ships. The new rigging made it easier to sail across or even into the wind. Finally, European ships added more weaponry, including sturdier cannons.

Hardships on the Uncharted Sea

In his journal, Italian sailor Antonio Pigafetta detailed the desperate conditions Magellan's sailors faced as they crossed the Pacific Ocean:

"We remained 3 months and 20 days without taking in provisions or other refreshments and ate only old biscuit reduced to powder, full of grubs and stinking from the dirt which rats had made on it. We drank water that was yellow and stinking. We also ate the ox hides from under the mainyard which we softened by soaking in seawater for several days."

—Journal of Antonio Pigafetta

1. **Focus on a topic** It is usually not very fruitful to synthesize bits of information that have little or nothing in common. The different pieces of information should be on some common topic. **To what common topic do all three bits of information relate?**

2. **Analyze each piece of information** The purpose of synthesizing is to gather evidence on a topic from more than one source. Before you can synthesize, you need to make sure that you understand the main idea and supporting details found in each source. **(a) What is the main idea of the Improved Technology paragraphs? (b) What was the benefit of the caravel? (c) What is the main idea of Pigafetta's firsthand account?**

3. **Look for similarities** Information is more complete and reliable if more than one source provides the same or similar information. Noting and analyzing the similarities will help you reach a more complete understanding of the topic. **Which two sources support the idea that European sailors became better equipped to sail the seas?**

4. **Look for differences** It is also important to look for inconsistent information or other perspectives. **Which sources convey the idea that European sailors still faced hardships at sea?**

5. **Draw conclusions** Our knowledge of a topic becomes more complete when we draw conclusions based on information synthesized from a variety of sources. **Was ocean travel easy or difficult for Europeans in the early 1500s? Explain.**

xliv

Resource Directory

Technology
Skills Transparencies Synthesizing Information, p. 15

Practicing the Skill

Study the different pieces of information on this page about developments that occurred between the 1500s and 1700s. Then, answer the following questions:

1. With what general topic do all three pieces of evidence deal?
2. **(a)** What does Las Casas complain about? **(b)** How does the painting show social change in the Americas? **(c)** What is the main idea of the graph?
3. Which two sources emphasize negative effects on Native Americans?
4. Do you think all Europeans were cruel to Native Americans? Explain.
5. Based on the evidence, were the early encounters between Native Americans and Europeans generally harmful or beneficial to the Native Americans? Explain.

Portrait of a Spanish man in the Americas, his wife of Native American ancestry, and their daughter.

A Brutal System
Bartolomé de las Casas, a conquistador turned priest, spoke out against the encomienda system and the treatment of Native Americans:

"It is impossible to recount the burdens with which their owners loaded them [75 to 100 pounds], making them walk [hundreds of miles]. . . . They had wounds on their shoulders and backs, like animals. . . . To tell likewise of the whip-lashings, the beatings, the cuffs, the blows, the curses, and a thousand other kinds of torments to which their masters treated them, while in truth they were working hard, would take much time and much paper; and would be something to amaze mankind."

—Bartolomé de las Casas,
Short Description of the Destruction of the Indies

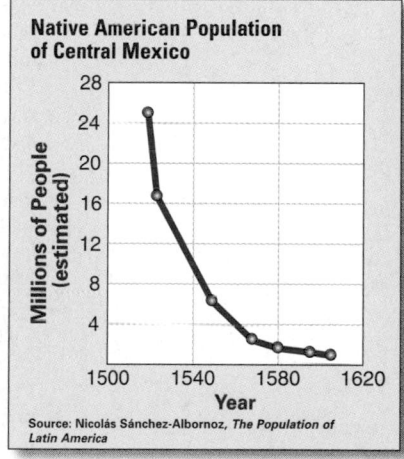

Native American Population of Central Mexico

Source: Nicolás Sánchez-Albornoz, *The Population of Latin America*

This graph shows the impact of diseases from Europe and of fighting against Europeans.

Applying the Skill

Select a current economics topic, such as e-commerce, international trade, or stock market trends. Find three different pieces of information on the topic, including at least one visual. Write questions to analyze and synthesize the information. Trade papers with a partner and answer each other's questions.

xlv

Practicing the Skill Answers

1. All three pieces of evidence deal with relations between the Spanish conquerors and Native Americans and their consequences.
2. **(a)** Las Casas complains about the inhumane treatment by the Spanish of the people of the Indies. **(b)** The painting shows that the two cultures were blending. **(c)** The main idea of the graph is to highlight the dramatic decrease in the Native American population in Central Mexico.
3. Both the graph and the description by Bartolomé de las Casas emphasize the negative effects on Native Americans.
4. Not all Europeans were cruel to Native Americans. In the portrait, the artist shows us a loving family with a Native American mother, a Spanish father, and their daughter.
5. Based on the presented evidence, it is logical to assume that the positive experience of Native Americans portrayed in the portrait was rare in this time period. For the most part, the Native Americans were enslaved, killed, or died from foreign diseases when they encountered Europeans.

Applying the Skill Rubrics

Share rubrics with students before they search for information and write the questions.

Attempted Fewer than three pieces of information were gathered.

Minimal Three pieces of information are included, but the questions do not fully analyze and synthesize the information.

Adequate Student's analysis and synthesis is comprehensive and well written.

Exemplary Student's analysis and synthesis is well researched, thoroughly understood, and presented in an organized and engaging style.

ANALYZING CAUSE AND EFFECT

Learning the Skill Answers

1. The central event is that a high school soccer team competed in the state tournament.

2. It is neither a cause nor an effect of the team's performance that the team's colors are blue and gold.

3. The causes of the central event in this story were: all the team members attended practice regularly, no team members were dropped due to poor academic performance, and the team won the division championship.

4. Effects of the central event were: the game was shown on cable television, college recruiters saw the game, and some of the team members were invited to apply for admission to various colleges.

5. A generalization based on this story is that good soccer players on a championship team will often be discovered and recruited by college coaches.

6. Possible answer: Any school sports team can improve its chances for success by having dedicated, talented players who work hard at practice and in classes, and also by having a good coach.

Analyzing Cause and Effect

How Will I Use This Skill? People often try to figure out the causes and effects of things. For example, government officials always conduct an investigation after an airplane accident. Their goals are to identify the causes of the mishap and to then use that knowledge to prevent future accidents. By analyzing causes and effects and by taking appropriate action based on what is learned, you can gain greater control over events and conditions that affect your life.

Learning the Skill

Read the passage below about a school soccer team. Then, follow the steps to learn how to analyze causes and effects.

> A high school soccer team has won the division championship. The team's coach was named coach of the year. The team's colors were blue and gold. All the team members attended practice regularly. Because they passed all their classes, no team members were dropped from the team. As a result of winning the division title, the soccer team competed in the state tournament. The championship game was seen by college coaches on cable television. Several weeks later, a few of those coaches invited some of the players to apply for admission to their colleges and play soccer for them.

1. **Identify the central event** Identify the central condition or event whose causes or effects you wish to study. In the introductory paragraph at the top of this page, for example, the central event was airplane accidents. **What is the central event in the soccer story?**

2. **Disregard irrelevant information** Disregard information that has little or nothing to do with the central event. **What information in the story is neither a cause nor an effect of the team's performance?**

3. **Identify possible causes** Causes precede the central event. They are the reasons that the central event or development occurred. In a reading passage, key words that can help you identify causes include *because* and *due to*. **What are the causes of the central event in the soccer story?**

4. **Identify possible effects** Effects come after the central event. They occur as a result of the central event. In a reading passage, key words that indicate effects include *therefore* and *as a result*. **What are the effects of the central event in the soccer story?**

5. **Make generalizations** After investigators find the causes of an accident, they do not think about one plane only. They generalize and consider how the same conditions might cause an accident for other planes. For example, faulty electrical wiring can cause a fire in all planes, not just the one under investigation. **Make a generalization based on the soccer story.**

6. **Make recommendations** By understanding causes and effects, you can recommend actions or make predictions based on what you have learned. **How can any school sports team improve its chances for success?**

Technology
Skills Transparencies Analyzing Cause and Effect, p. 17

Practicing the Skill

By A.D. 1000, East African port cities, such as Mogadishu, Kilwa, and Sofala, were thriving centers of trade. Study the facts below, which are listed in random order, and copy the blank cause-and-effect chart at right. Then, answer the questions below and fill in the chart. (As you work, you may want to consult the world map in the Atlas at the back of this book.)

- Muslim merchants from Arabia and other lands settled in East Africa.
- Africa had gold, ivory, and other valuable resources.
- East African trading cities thrived.
- Mansa Musa ruled an empire in West Africa.
- Favorable winds aided travel between Asia and Africa.
- There were natural harbors along the East African coast.
- Arabic words became part of the Swahili language in East Africa.
- Muslim merchants introduced their religion to East Africa.

1. Which of the facts above is the central event whose causes and effects can be determined? Write the central event in the appropriate place on the chart.
2. Which one fact is most probably neither a cause nor an effect of the central event?
3. What three facts were most probably causes of the central event? Write them in the appropriate place on the chart.
4. What three facts about Africa were most probably effects of the central event? Write the three facts in the appropriate place on the chart.
5. In general, what is often a common effect of thriving trade between different lands?
6. In general, if a government wanted to build a profitable center for overseas trade, what do you think would be a good geographic location for the trade center?

Applying the Skill

Suppose that your dentist tells you that you have two cavities. Create a chart identifying probable causes and effects of the cavities. Then, based on the chart, write two generalizations and two recommendations.

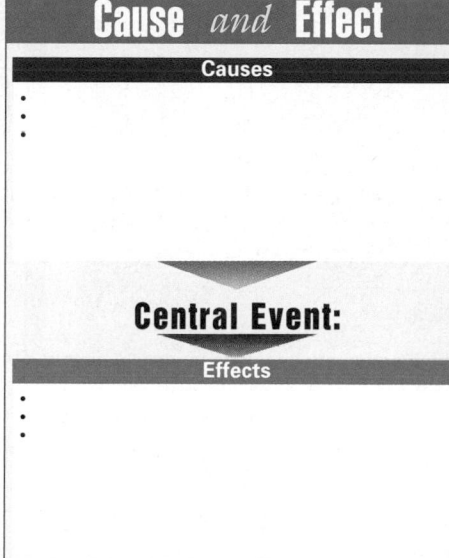

Cause *and* **Effect**

Causes

-
-
-

Central Event:

Effects

-
-
-

Practicing the Skill Answers

1. The central event is that East African trading cities thrived.
2. The fact that Mansa Musa ruled an empire in West Africa is neither a cause nor an effect.
3. Africa had gold, ivory, and other valuable resources. Favorable winds aided travel between Asia and Africa. There were natural harbors along the East African coast.
4. Muslim merchants settled in East Africa. Arabic words became part of the Swahili language. Muslim merchants introduced their religion to East Africa.
5. In general, a common effect of thriving trade between two lands is the integration of the two cultures.
6. In general, a profitable center for overseas trade should be built near a harbor.

Applying the Skill Rubrics

Share rubrics with students before they create the chart.

Attempted The chart has few causes or effects, or examples of causes and effects are incorrect.

Minimal The chart has a reasonable number of causes and effects, but the generalizations and recommendations are weak or unclear.

Adequate The chart includes appropriate causes and effects with logical generalizations and recommendations.

Exemplary The chart is creatively designed for effective communication, and generalizations and recommendations are well written and convincing.

xlvii

Asking Questions

Learning the Skill Answers

1. Two possible comprehension questions and their answers are: What did Queen Elizabeth I enjoy? She enjoyed dancing, music, and plays. Who was one of Elizabeth's favorite playwrights? She especially enjoyed the plays of William Shakespeare.
2. Another possible analytical question is: Why did Elizabeth I support and promote the arts?
3. Another possible evaluation question is: What is your opinion concerning Elizabeth's promotion of the arts?
4. A possible hypothetical question with its answer is: If Elizabeth I had never been queen, how might the arts be different today? We would probably not have as rich or varied a selection of music, books, and plays from that period, and the works of Shakespeare might not be well known.

How Will I Use This Skill? Asking questions is a key part of the critical-thinking process. By asking questions, you become an active thinker and learner rather than a passive observer. Using this skill will help you get the most out of any information that is presented to you.

Learning the Skill

Study the chart below and the biography on the left. Then, follow the steps to learn some of the techniques involved in asking useful questions.

Biography

Elizabeth I 1533–1603

"She takes great pleasure in dancing and music," noted an English observer of Queen Elizabeth I. The normally thrifty queen employed some 50 singers, 40 musicians, and several songwriters to stage concerts for her.

Elizabeth I also loved plays. She especially enjoyed the works of William Shakespeare, whom she helped to promote. The queen provided financial support and prestige for major acting groups, which led to a flowering of English theater.

Elizabeth's 45-year reign inspired other writers of the day. Poet Edmund Spenser dedicated *The Faerie Queene* to Elizabeth I.

Four Categories of Questions

Comprehension	Analysis	Evaluation	Prediction
Who?	How?	Is it beneficial or harmful?	If this occurs, then what might happen?
What?	Why?	Is it ethical or unethical?	If this does not occur, then what might happen?
Where?	What are the different points of view?	Is it logical or illogical?	If this had or had not happened, then what might be different?
When?	What are the causes and effects?	Is it relevant or irrelevant?	If this solution is implemented, how might the problem be affected?
How much?	What is the similarity or difference between this and that?	What are some advantages and disadvantages?	
What are the examples?	What is the problem?	What is the best solution?	
	What are some possible solutions?	What is my opinion?	
	What evidence supports the ideas?	What evidence supports my opinion?	

1. **Ask basic comprehension questions** Comprehension questions will help you to summarize or define the basic contents of what you are reading, seeing, or hearing. You might ask, "Who is discussed in the biography?" or "Where did she live?" **Ask and answer two more comprehension questions.**

2. **Ask analytical questions** Sample analytical questions are in the second column of the chart. Unlike comprehension questions, these questions involve some higher-level critical thinking. You might ask, "How do Elizabeth's accomplishments still have an impact on our lives today?" **What other analytical question could you ask?**

Resource Directory

Technology
Skills Transparencies Asking Questions, p. 19

3. **Ask questions that evaluate** Examples of these questions are in the third column of the chart. In this step, you make judgments and form opinions based on evidence. An evaluation question might be "Based on the biography, do you think Elizabeth's spending habits were beneficial or harmful to the English people?" **Ask another evaluation question.**

4. **Ask hypothetical questions** These questions usually involve the word *if*, as do the questions in the fourth column of the chart. At this stage of critical thinking, you ask yourself questions that lead to a hypothesis or theory about what *might happen* or what *might have happened.* **Ask and answer a hypothetical question.**

Practicing the Skill

Review the chart on the preceding page once again and study the three maps at right. Then, follow the steps below to practice the skill of asking questions.

1. Write a basic comprehension question about the main idea of the three maps.
2. Write an analytical question about what happened to Poland. (Clue: Note how the borders of the countries around Poland changed over the years.)
3. Write a question that evaluates some aspect of what happened to Poland.
4. Based on what the maps show about international relations in Europe in the 1700s, write a question that leads one to make a prediction about Europe in the 1800s.

Partitions of Poland, 1701–1795

Applying the Skill

Videotape a short segment from a national news report on television or cut out an article from the national news section of a newspaper. Write a series of questions on the news story. Include one or more questions for each of the following four categories: **(a)** comprehension, **(b)** analysis, **(c)** evaluation, **(d)** prediction. Write an answer to each of the questions.

Problem Solving and Decision Making

How Will I Use This Skill? Throughout your life, problems will arise. Today, a problem may be a dispute with a friend or a tough math test. Later, as a citizen and voter, you will be asked to make decisions about problems affecting the community, nation, or world. If you handle problems fearfully or haphazardly, they may overwhelm you. You will be more likely to find solutions if you make decisions in a logical, systematic way.

Learning the Skill

We will use a case study to learn the skills of problem solving and decision making. Study the situation described below and copy the incomplete chart. Then, follow the steps and answer the questions.

Learning the Skill Answers

1. Foreign powers were able to make demands on China and Japan because both countries had less industrial technology and weapons capability than those making the demands.
2. Possible answer: China and Japan could have chosen to ignore the demands but also to increase their industry and technology to the level of their competitors.
3. **Option 1 Advantages** Avoid conflict. Gain access to products of industrialized nations. **Option 1 Disadvantages** Native merchants lose profits to foreigners. Potential trade deficit. **Option 2 Advantages** Avoid conflict. Move toward a future position as an industrial power. **Option 2 Disadvantages** Difficulty of transition to modern industrial processes. Risk foreign discovery of weapons development. **Option 3 Advantages** Maintain the existing trade surplus. Satisfy the desire for isolationism. **Option 3 Disadvantages** Risk conflict. Fall behind in weapons and industrial development.
4. Possible answer: China decided on option 3 because it was a traditional country with a land-based economy whose leaders saw no need for increased trade or industrial development.
5. Possible answer: China should have chosen another option once it was realized that the decision left China vulnerable to the industrialized nations.

A Problem for Japan and China

In the 1800s, Japan and China faced a problem. Industrialized nations had developed machinery and weapons that were superior to what the Japanese and Chinese had. Some industrialized nations used their new power to demand special trading privileges in Asia.

Options for Japan and China		
Option	Advantages	Disadvantages
1. Give in to demands of the industrialized powers.	• Avoid conflict. •	• Native merchants lose profits to foreigners. •
2. Give in to demands, but also build modern machines and weapons.	• •	• •
3. Refuse the demands and reject much of the new technology.	• •	• •

The Decisions
- The Japanese government decided to follow option 2.
- The Chinese government decided to follow option 3.

Effects of the Decisions
- Japan quickly became a modern industrial and military power. After suffering defeat in World War II, Japan demilitarized. Today, it remains one of the world's leading industrial powers.
- China was defeated in several wars, first by Great Britain, and then by Japan. Foreign nations gained special privileges in China. Today, China is still struggling to become a leading industrial power.

1. **Identify the problem** It is almost impossible to solve a problem without examining it and having a clear understanding of its roots. **Why were foreign powers able to make demands on Japan and China?**

2. **Gather information and identify options** There is always more than one way to cope with a problem. Never follow the first option you think of. Instead, identify as many options as possible. **Describe an option, other than those in the chart, that Japan or China could have chosen.**

Resource Directory

Technology
Skills Transparencies Problem Solving and Decision Making, p. 21

3. **Consider advantages and disadvantages** Analyze each option by predicting the benefits and drawbacks of choosing that option. **On the chart that you copied, fill in advantages and disadvantages for each of the options that Japan and China had.**

4. **Make a decision and implement the solution** Choose the option that seems to offer the best advantages and the least significant disadvantages. **Why do you think China decided on option 3?**

5. **Evaluate the decision** After a while, study the effects of the option that was implemented. If the problem has been solved, then stay with the decision. If the problem persists, has worsened, or has given rise to new problems, then start the process again and choose another option. **Do you think China should have chosen another option after evaluating its decision? Explain.**

Practicing the Skill

Consider this situation. A friend of yours works at a restaurant. Each month, your friend spends more than he or she earns. The money is spent on food, clothing, movies, computer software, video games, and other items. To pay for all the expenses, your friend borrows money from other friends. The result is that your friend owes more and more money each month.

1. (a) What problem does your friend have? (b) What are the underlying causes of the problem?
2. What options does your friend have? List and describe as many options as you can think of. Do not weigh the advantages and disadvantages yet. Do not reject any options yet.
3. Make a chart similar to the one on the preceding page. In the chart, describe possible advantages and disadvantages for each option.
4. Study your finished chart. Which option seems to provide the most valuable advantages and the least harmful disadvantages? Write a paragraph identifying the decision that you think would be best for your friend. Include a brief explanation as to why you think that decision is best.
5. Ask a classmate to study the options, advantages, and disadvantages on your chart and to evaluate your decision. Does your classmate agree or disagree with your decision? Explain.

Applying the Skill

Think of a problem that is affecting your school or community today. Work with several of your classmates to try to solve the problem. Remember to follow each of the problem-solving and decision-making steps that you have learned in this lesson. When you have finished your work, consider submitting a proposal to a leader in your school or community.

li

Using the Internet

How Will I Use This Skill? By "surfing the Net," you can link to millions of computer sites sponsored by businesses, governments, schools, museums, and individuals all over the world. The Internet provides many services, including information, e-mail, and online shopping. As a student, you may often use the Internet as a valuable research tool.

Learning the Skill Answers

1. The search tool called HotBot provides both a directory and a search engine.
2. The help button is at the bottom of the left side of the home page.
3. On the home page, the box for typing keywords is in the dark blue strip to the right of the heading "Search Smarter." On the advanced search page, the box for keywords is directly beneath the "must contain" menu button.
4. The word *OR* should be used between "Crusades" and "Holy Wars" because there may be sites about the Crusades that do not contain the keyword "Holy Wars." However, sites about wars other than the Crusades may also be listed.
5. The search could be limited to the .com domain.
6. Colorado State University is the sponsor of the first site.
7. "Religious wars" and "Conquest in the Holy Land" are other possible keywords.

Learning the Skill

Use the steps below and the computer screen images to help you learn how to use the Internet. For this lesson, assume that you are searching for information on the Crusades, which were a series of holy wars between Christians and Muslims that began in the late 1000s.

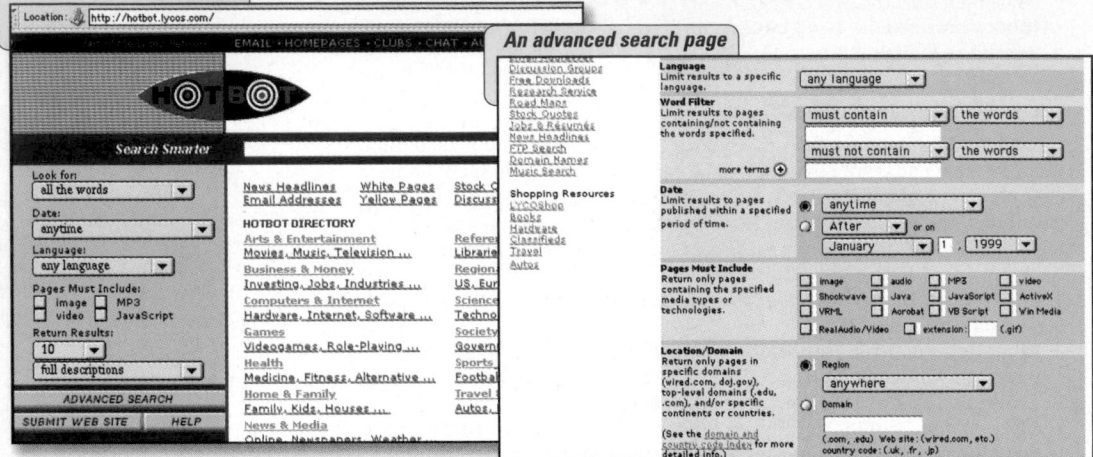

A search tool home page

An advanced search page

1. **Begin a search** Sometimes you know the Internet site you want and its URL, or Uniform Resource Locator. At other times, you must use search tools, such as AltaVista, HotBot, and NorthernLight, which are Internet sites that help you find other Internet sites. Some search tools are directories that list sites by category. For example, see the category called "Health" on the home page above. Other search tools are search engines that look for sites based on keywords that you choose and input yourself. Still others provide both a directory and an engine. **What does the search tool shown above provide?**

2. **Click on a help button** Search tools provide instructions on how to conduct a search. **Where is the help button on the above home page?**

3. **When you use a search engine, type in keywords** The keywords should briefly summarize your topic of choice. Usually, you should not input entire phrases or sentences like "When did the Crusades begin?" Instead, type in the word "Crusades" only. Then, click the search button. **Where is the box in the samples for typing keywords?**

4. **Use Boolean language** Two common Boolean terms are *AND* and *OR*. Use *AND* between two words when you want documents that contain both words. Use *OR* when you want documents that contain either of the words. **If you typed in "Crusades" and "Holy Wars," should you use *AND* or *OR* between them?**

lii

Resource Directory

Technology
Skills Transparencies Using the Internet, p. 23

5. **Try an advanced search** After clicking on the advanced search button, you can refine and limit your search. For example, you can specify documents produced only after a certain date or documents only from the .edu domain. Limiting the domain in this way will provide sites produced only by schools or other educational sites. The **.org** domain contains only sites produced by organizations. Another common domain is **.gov** which is used by government sites. **To what other domain could you limit your search?**

6. **Evaluate the quality of sites** When the search results page comes up, read the summaries and open those sites that seem to best match your topic. Note when each site was last updated. Note the sponsor or author, too. Universities, museums, libraries, and government agencies are usually the most useful and reliable for social studies research. **Who is the sponsor of the first site on the Crusades in the sample results page?**

7. **Explore, revise, and ask for help** Explore a variety of sites and compare them so you can select the one best suited to your needs. If the results are unsatisfactory, revise your search by typing in new keywords or by using another search tool. Seek guidance from teachers, librarians, and your parents. **What are two other keywords you could try in your search about the Crusades?**

Practicing the Skill

Use the Internet to do research on the Mongol empire, especially the Yuan dynasty that the Mongols established in China in 1279. Answer the following questions as you conduct your search:

1. What search tool do you choose? Why?
2. Describe one useful instruction that this search tool provides to users who click on the help button.
3. What keywords and/or Boolean language do you use in your search? Why?
4. How can an advanced search help you?
5. Which site provides the most useful and complete information about the Mongols and the Yuan dynasty? Explain.
6. Revise your search by inputting "Kublai Khan." How are your search results different from those of your earlier search?

Applying the Skill

Use the Internet to search for museum sites that have Native American art and artifacts. You may wish to limit your search to a particular Native American people. You could also limit your search to a particular type of art such as pottery or weaving. Print out your search result pages and circle the descriptions of those sites that you would recommend because they are the most appropriate. For each recommended site, identify the author or sponsor and explain why you recommend it.

A search results page

Practicing the Skill Answers

1. Students should give good reasons for their choice of search tools.
2. Students should describe one helpful instruction such as explaining the search screen.
3. Students will probably use "Mongol Empire" AND "Yuan Dynasty" as search keywords to locate specific sites where the dynasty is mentioned by name.
4. An advanced search enables the user to narrow the search topic or limit the types of material by various criteria.
5. Students should name the site and explain why it is the most useful and complete site of those they located.
6. In general, adding another keyword should limit the search further and reduce the number of sites listed in the search results.

Applying the Skill Rubrics

Share rubrics with students before they begin their Internet search.

Attempted Student does not complete the search.

Minimal Student locates some sites related to the topic but has difficulty using appropriate keywords or search tools.

Adequate Student uses keywords and search tools effectively to locate appropriate sites and evaluates descriptions of recommended sites.

Exemplary Student uses several search tools and advanced search techniques so that most sites listed are appropriate to the topic.

UNIT 1

UNIT OVERVIEW

Unit 1 examines human development and the rise of civilizations in Africa and Asia.

Chapter 1 focuses on human development during the Paleolithic age, the changes that came with the agricultural revolution, and the beginnings of civilization during the Neolithic age.

Chapter 2 focuses on the earliest civilizations of Egypt and the Middle East.

Chapter 3 deals with the rise of civilization along the Ganges and Indus rivers of India and the Huang He of China.

Early Civilizations

Prehistory–256 B.C.

OUTLINE

Chapter 1 **Toward Civilization** (Prehistory–3000 B.C.)

Chapter 2 **First Civilizations: Africa and Asia** (3200 B.C.–500 B.C.)

Chapter 3 **Early Civilizations in India and China** (2500 B.C.–256 B.C.)

THEMES

As you read about early human civilization, you will encounter the following unit themes.

Continuity and Change Using artifacts and written evidence, archaeologists and historians help us understand the ancient human past.

Economics and Technology During early human history, people gradually changed from the life of hunters and gatherers to the life of farmers. As civilizations developed, people began to specialize. They traded more, built large-scale public projects, and used mathematics and astronomy to better understand the world around them.

Geography and History Early people depended on their physical surroundings, using natural resources to provide food, shelter, and tools for survival. Gradually, people living in the river valleys of Egypt, the Middle East, India, and China developed complex civilizations.

Art and Literature The development of writing preserved some of the world's oldest literature, from the Egyptian *Tale of Sinuhe* and the Sumerian *Epic of Gilgamesh* to India's *Mahabharata* and ancient China's *Book of Songs*.

Unit Theme Activity

For Your Portfolio The chapters in this unit illustrate various connections between geography and history. As you read the chapters, prepare a portfolio project highlighting developments that show these connections. Your project might take one of the following forms:
- **PowerPoint presentation**
- **Museum exhibit**
- **Essay**

Resource Directory

Technology

World History Visions, Voices, Views Scenes of an Age, *Early Civilizations*, videodisc side 1 or videotape 1, running time 2:30 min.

Side 1: Fr. 5608-9095

Abu Simbel is a temple built along the Nile River in Egypt to honor the ruler Ramses II. Its huge size reflects the pharaoh's power and godlike status.

eTeach

🔔 **Bell Ringer** Ask students to think about events that have occurred during their lifetime that someday may be considered history by another group of students. Have volunteers tell the class those events they consider to be significant in history and explain why.

Activity

Cooperative Learning

Round Table Form students into groups, and assign one of the six pictures to each group. Have one student in each group write a paragraph about the picture, using information from the pages as well as prior knowledge, explaining what can be learned about a past society from the object shown. Then, have students pass their paragraphs to another group member, who adds any information or ideas that may be missing. Have the groups continue passing the paragraphs until all students in the group have had a chance to add to the paragraphs. Ask volunteers from each of the six groups to read the completed paragraphs to the class.

WHY STUDY HISTORY?
Because History Is a Fascinating Story!

Why would a man devote years to studying the letters of a long-dead king? Why would a woman spend thousands of hours digging in the mud and ruins of an ancient city? The answer is simple. These people are caught up in the fascinating time machine called human history. History is a story about people—how they lived, where they traveled, how they felt about their lives. Uncovering these stories is like unraveling a mystery. The more you search, the more you can discover about the world of the past.

Who was this man?

Today, he looks so fragile he might crumble at a touch. Once, though, this withered hand held incredible power. Pharaoh Ramses II ruled Egypt for 66 years, building scores of temples and monuments. Now, more than 3,000 years later, you can see the pharaoh's mummified remains at the Egyptian Museum in Cairo, Egypt. (Exactly how the Egyptians mummified their dead was itself a mystery for a long time.)

Why did someone write on this shell?

You may wonder why anyone would write on a tortoise shell or a deer bone. But to a priest in Shang China, oracle bones were an excellent way of predicting the future. The writing on this shell was actually a request for advice from a departed ancestor. Today, objects like oracle bones give us a window, not to the future, but to the past. They show us how past peoples differed from us—and how we are alike.

Where did the people go?

Suppose you walked into New York or Los Angeles today, only to find that everyone had vanished without a trace. That was how archaeologists felt when they uncovered the ruins of Mohenjo-Daro. About 3,500 years ago, these streets bustled with activity. Then, the people abandoned the city. What happened? A flood, an invasion—no one knows for certain. But you can be sure that historians will keep looking for clues.

2 *Unit 1*

Resource Directory

Teaching Resources

Why Study History? *Because History Is a Fascinating Story!,* Why Study History? booklet, pp. 5–6

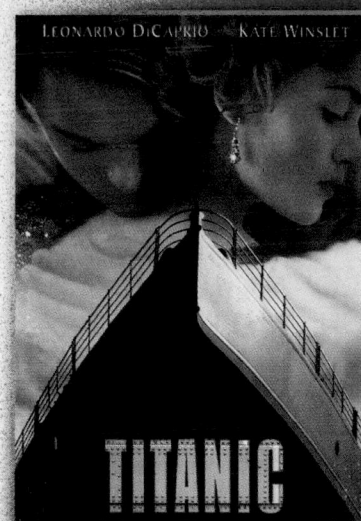

LEONARDO DiCAPRIO · KATE WINSLET

TITANIC

How was this pyramid built?

The Great Pyramid has stood in the Egyptian desert for nearly 5,000 years. Without machinery, workers fitted together huge hand-cut stones weighing an average of more than two tons each. The pyramid is so solidly built that it would survive a direct hit by an atomic bomb! Looking at this ancient monument, we come face to face with the awe and wonder of the human past.

Maybe you know someone who participates in Revolutionary War reenactments. Maybe you've joined in at a Renaissance Fair. Perhaps you've mused over dinosaur bones at a museum. Or maybe you've just watched a popular movie about a ship disaster of the past. The enormous popularity of such entertainments demonstrates the continuing fascination we have with history.

Portfolio Assessment

Connecting to Today Interview an older neighbor or family member. Ask the person to recount the most memorable or interesting event from his or her lifetime. Share the results of your interview with the class. What can you conclude from the collected memories of the class?

Resource Manager

	CORE INSTRUCTION	READING/SKILLS
Chapter Level Resources	📁 **Teaching Resources** 📄 **Pacing Charts,** Ch. 1 📄 **Teaching With Themes,** p. 4 🎞 **Color Transparencies,** p. F–3 💿 **Resource Pro®** Ch. 1 💻 **www.phschool.com** • eTeach	💿 **Book on CD,** Ch. 1 💿 **Interactive Student Tutorial CD-ROM,** Ch. 1 💿 **Social Studies Skills Tutor CD-ROM** 🎞 **Skills Transparencies**
1 Understanding Our Past 1. Explain how geography and history are linked. 2. Identify the methods that anthropologists and archaeologists use to find out about early people. 3. Describe the ways historians try to reconstruct the past.	📁 **Teaching Resources** 📄 **Creative Teaching Activities,** p. 8 💿 **Prentice Hall Presentation Pro,** Ch. 1, Section 1 🎞 **Section Reading Support Transparencies**	📁 **Teaching Resources** 📘 **Unit 1 booklet** • Guided Reading and Review, p. 2 📄 **Guide to the Essentials** 📼 **Guided Reading Audiotapes,** Ch. 1, Section 1

2 The Dawn of History
1. Identify the advances that people made during the Old Stone Age.
2. Describe the ways we can learn about the religious beliefs of early people.
3. Explain why the Neolithic agricultural revolution was a turning point in history.
	📁 **Teaching Resources**
	📘 **Unit 1 booklet**
	   • Biography Activity, p. 8
	   • Primary Source Activity, p. 9
	📄 **Creative Teaching Activities,** p. 9
	💿 **Prentice Hall Presentation Pro,** Ch. 1, Section 2
	🎞 **Section Reading Support Transparencies**
		📁 **Teaching Resources**
		📘 **Unit 1 booklet**
		   • Guided Reading and Review, p. 4
		   • Skill Application Activity, p. 11
		📄 **Guide to the Essentials**
		📼 **Guided Reading Audiotapes,** Ch. 1, Section 2

3 Beginnings of Civilization
1. Explain how the first cities emerged.
2. Identify the basic features of civilizations.
3. Describe the ways that cultures can spread and change.
	📁 **Teaching Resources**
	📘 **Unit 1 booklet**
	📄 **Creative Teaching Activities,** p. 10
	📘 **Teaching With Themes**
	   • Global View Activity, p. 41
	💿 **Prentice Hall Presentation Pro,** Ch. 1, Section 3
	🎞 **Section Reading Support Transparencies**
		📁 **Teaching Resources**
		📘 **Unit 1 booklet**
		   • Guided Reading and Review, p. 6
		📄 **Guide to the Essentials**
		📼 **Guided Reading Audiotapes,** Ch. 1, Section 3

ENRICHMENT/PRE-AP®

www.phschool.com
- Why Study History?

Teaching Resources
- Chapter Extension Activities, p. 7
- History Through Literature, pp. 3–4
- Simulations, pp. 2–3

www.phschool.com
- Take It to the Net: Internet Activities, Section 1

Teaching Resources
- Chapter Extension Activities, p. 8
- Color Transparencies, pp. C–23, E–21

www.phschool.com
- Take It to the Net: Internet Activities, Section 2

Teaching Resources
- Geography and History, p. 6

www.phschool.com
- Virtual Field Trip

ASSESSMENT

PRENTICE HALL ASSESSMENT SYSTEM

Core Assessment
- ExamView Test Bank booklet, Ch. 1
- ExamView Test Bank CD-ROM, Ch. 1

Standardized Test Preparation

Diagnose and Prescribe
- Diagnostic Tests for High School Social Studies Skills

Review and Reteach
- Review Book for World History

Practice and Assess
- Document-Based Assessment, pp. 3–7
- Test-Taking Strategies With Transparencies
- Alternative Assessment booklet
- Test Prep Book for World History

Teaching Resources
- Unit 1 booklet
  - Geography Quiz, p. 12
  - Section Quizzes, pp. 3, 5, 7
  - Chapter Tests A, B, and C, pp. 13–17

www.phschool.com
- Self-Test

CUSTOMIZE FOR INDIVIDUAL NEEDS

Gifted and Talented
- **Teacher's Edition**, Activities: Customize for Heterogeneous Groups, p. 16

Less Proficient Readers
- **Guide to the Essentials**, Ch. 1
- **Guided Reading Audiotapes, English**, Ch. 1
- **Book on CD**, Ch. 1
- **Teacher's Edition**, Reading Strategies: p. 8; p. 16
- **Teacher's Edition**, Activities: Customize for Kinesthetic Learners, p. 17; Customize for Heterogeneous Groups, p. 18

Less Proficient Writers
- **Teacher's Edition**, Activity: Cooperative Learning, p. 9

Students Acquiring English/ESL
- **Guide to the Essentials, English/Spanish**, Ch. 1
- **Guided Reading Audiotapes, English/Spanish**, Ch. 1
- **Book on CD**, Ch. 1
- **Teacher's Edition**, Activities marked with an *: Customize for Kinesthetic Learners, p. 17

Don't miss the exclusive interactive version of *World History: Connections to Today* on the Internet and CD-ROM.

INTRODUCTION

After discussing the work of geographers, historians, anthropologists, archaeologists, and others in uncovering the past, this chapter examines life in the Old Stone Age and the beginnings of civilization in the Middle East and elsewhere.

Focusing on Themes

Suggest that students focus on these theme questions as they read:

Continuity and Change
How have geographers, historians, anthropologists, and archaeologists helped us learn about the lives of people at different stages in history?

Economics and Technology
What breakthrough technologies did Stone Age people develop?

Religions and Value Systems
What religious beliefs and practices did early peoples develop?

Political and Social Systems
What basic features made the first civilizations differ from early farming societies?

◆ TIME LINE ACTIVITY

You may wish to share the About the Pictures note with your students before you ask questions about the time line such as the following:

1. Why do you think painting developed before writing? *(Answers should include the idea that writing is somewhat more abstract than painting.)*
2. When did people first begin to grow their own crops? *(in about 9000 B.C., or about 11,000 years ago)*
3. About how long ago did river valley civilizations emerge? *(in about 3000 B.C., or about 5,000 years ago)*

Don't Miss!

You Are There . . .
Unearthing the Past
(Section 1)

Analyzing Primary Sources
Clues to the Iceman Mystery (Section 2)

Toward Civilization
Prehistory–3000 B.C.

Chapter Preview

1 **Understanding Our Past**
2 **The Dawn of History**
3 **Beginnings of Civilization**

2 million B.C.
Early people first begin using stone tools, similar to this scraper and arrowhead.

30,000 B.C.
Stone Age people create cave paintings that show the animals they hunt. The Chauvet cave paintings in France, above, are the oldest ever found.

CHAPTER EVENTS

| 2 million B.C. | 35,000 B.C. | 27,000 B.C. |

Resource Directory

Teaching Resources
Teaching With Themes Chapter Theme Activities, p. 4
Pacing Chart With Block Scheduling Guide Ch. 1
Technology
World History Color Transparencies Ch. 1 Graphic Organizer, p. F–3

River Valley Civilizations

The earliest civilizations rose in fertile river valleys of Africa and Asia.

EUROPE

ASIA

Egypt
Mesopotamia
Indus Valley
Shang China

AFRICA

ATLANTIC
OCEAN

INDIAN
OCEAN

N
W E
S

Robinson Projection
0   1000   2000 Miles
0   1000   2000 Kilometers

40°N

20°N

Equator   0°

20°S

40°E   60°E   80°E   100°E   120°E   140°E

0°   20°E   40°E

18,000 B.C.
During the last ice age, huge glaciers spread across parts of Europe, Asia, and North America.

9000 B.C.
During the Neolithic agricultural revolution, people begin to grow their own crops and settle in farming villages. This ancient mortar was used to grind wheat into flour.

3000 B.C.
River valley civilizations emerge. As Egyptians (above) and others develop writing, they will preserve a written record of their history.

19,000 B.C.

11,000 B.C.

3000 B.C.

Bell Ringer Have students imagine that archaeologists of the twenty-fifth century discover the preserved and clothed body of an American student from the 1990s. Ask them to list information that archaeologists might learn about the student's way of life and to note the clues that would lead scientists to these conclusions.

Reading Focus

■ How are geography and history linked?

■ How do anthropologists and archaeologists find out about early peoples?

■ How do historians try to reconstruct the past?

Vocabulary

geography
latitude
longitude
prehistory
anthropology
culture
archaeology
artifact
technology
historian

Taking Notes

Make a concept web like the one at right. As you read the section, fill in each blank circle with important information about how experts learn about the past. Add as many circles as needed to complete the web.

Anthropology · History · LEARNING ABOUT THE PAST · Location · Geography

Main Idea Geographers, archaeologists, anthropologists, and historians work to unravel human history.

LESSON PLAN

1. Focus A key to understanding history is studying the five themes of geography—location, place, human-environment interaction, movement, and region. With the help of modern science, archaeologists analyze early human remains and reconstruct how early people lived. Historians learn about the past by examining and evaluating written evidence and other records.

2. Instruct Divide the class into five groups and have each group be responsible for one section of a chart on the five geographic themes. Each group should define its theme and list several examples to illustrate it. You may also wish to have students find magazine or newspaper photos to illustrate their themes. Compile the five themes into one class chart.

3. Assess Have representatives from each group explain the importance of their theme to the work of archaeologists and historians.

4. Reteach If students' Assess activity does not reflect adequate understanding of the lesson, you might assign the *Guide to the Essentials* or the *Interactive Student Tutorial CD-ROM* for this section.

Primary Source

A View of the Earth
An astronaut describes how world geography looks from space:

"As you eat breakfast you look out the window . . . and there's the Mediterranean area, Greece and Rome. . . . And you go down across North Africa, and out over the Indian Ocean and look up at that great subcontinent of India . . . out over the Philippines and up across that monstrous Pacific Ocean, that vast body of water—you've never realized how big that is before.

You finally come up across the coast of California, and you look for those friendly things, Los Angeles and Phoenix and on across to El Paso. . . . You look down there and you can't imagine how many borders and boundaries you cross, again and again and again, and you don't even see them."

—Russell L. Schweickart, quoted in *The Overview Effect* (White)

Skills Assessment

Primary Source Based on this reading, how is looking at the world from space different from looking at a world map?

Setting the Scene Austen Layard was sure that the large mounds held hidden secrets. In 1845, he hired workers to dig trenches in what is today Iraq. Day by day, they inched deeper into the hot desert sands.

One morning, Layard's foreman Awad ran toward him, yelling. Layard rushed to see what the diggers had found. He was amazed to see a huge stone head emerging from the sand. Excitement spread through the camp as the diggers unearthed a giant statue. Layard soon realized that they had begun to uncover remains of the Assyrians, known only from stories in the Bible. As Layard and others found additional evidence, they slowly pieced together a picture of these people who had lived some 3,000 years before.

Thanks to the work of scholars like Austen Layard, we know a lot about how people lived in different times and places. Among these scholars are people who study geography—the stage on which all human history takes place.

Geography and History

Geography is the study of people, their environments, and the resources available to them. By showing how people lived in different times and places, geographers have added to our knowledge of human history. Often, geographers must draw conclusions from limited evidence. For example, tons of river mud found in the ruins of an ancient city may indicate that the city was wiped out by a flood. Similarities in language and art in widely separated regions may suggest that there was once contact between the two places.

Five themes sum up the impact of geography on the human story. They are location, place, human-environment interaction, movement, and region.

Location Location tells where a place is on the surface of the Earth. You can locate any place on a map using latitude and longitude. Latitude measures distance north or south of the Equator. Longitude measures distance east or west of the Prime Meridian, an imaginary line that runs north to south through Greenwich, England. For example, you can locate the city of Seoul, South Korea, at 37° N latitude and 127° E longitude. These numbers give its exact location.

Relative location—where one place is located in relation to another—is sometimes more important than exact location. For example, ancient Athens was located on the eastern Mediterranean Sea, near much older

Skills Assessment

ANSWER From space you get a better idea of the size of things, and you cannot see political borders.

Resource Directory

Teaching Resources

Creative Teaching Activities Creative Teaching Activities booklet, p. 8
Guided Reading and Review Unit 1 booklet, p. 2
History Through Literature *The Source*, History Through Literature booklet, pp. 3–4

civilizations in Egypt and the Middle East. This relative location influenced the Athenians' way of life because they acquired valuable skills and ideas from their neighbors.

Place Geographers describe places in terms of their physical features and human characteristics. Physical features of a place include landforms, bodies of water, climate, soil quality, resources, and plant and animal life. Human characteristics include where most people live and their economic activities, religious beliefs, and languages.

Human-Environment Interaction Since the earliest times, people have interacted with their environment. That is, they have shaped and been shaped by the places in which they lived. Early farmers used water from rivers to irrigate their crops. Much later, European settlers in the Americas cut down trees to clear land for farms. As technology has advanced, we have changed the environment in more complex ways. Today, roads slice through deserts, and canals link distant bodies of water.

Movement The movement of people, goods, and ideas is another key link between geography and history. In early times, people followed herds of deer or buffalo on which they depended for food. In more recent times, people have migrated, or moved, from farms and villages to cities in search of jobs. Others have fled from war or religious persecution.

In ancient times, as today, traders have carried goods from one part of the Earth to another. Ideas also move, carried by people like missionaries or settlers. Today, communications satellites and television cables carry ideas faster and farther than ever before.

Region Geographers divide the world into many types of regions. Some regions are based on physical characteristics, such as location. The Gulf States, for example, are those countries bordering the Persian Gulf. They are part of a larger region of southwestern Asia, which we often call the Middle East. Regions may also be defined by political, economic, or cultural features. Culturally, the Gulf States are part of two larger regions, the Arabic-speaking world and the Muslim world.

Geography Makes a Difference Geographic features such as landforms, climate, and natural resources have helped to shape a wide variety of human cultures. This reindeer herder in Siberia (below) lives a far different life from that of these rice farmers in Vietnam (left).

Theme: Geography and History Identify two cultural differences shown in these photographs. How might geography contribute to these differences?

Chapter 1 **7**

Connections to Science

Dating the Past One method used by scientists to date the remains of living organisms is carbon-14 dating. Scientists know that, until they die, plants and animals absorb radioactive carbon 14 from the atmosphere. After they die, the carbon 14 decreases very slowly at a known rate. By measuring the amount of carbon 14 remaining in objects such as wood, seeds, and bones, scientists can estimate their ages.

Reinforcing Key Ideas

As preparation for reading, ask students to list each main heading and subheading in the section and then turn each subheading into a question. Have students skim the section to find answers to their questions. *(Less Advanced Readers)*

Connections to Today

History in a Garbage Dump

Can a 10,000-year-old garbage dump be a gold mine? It can—to an archaeologist. Prehistoric trash provides valuable clues as to how people lived long ago. For example, heaps of gnawed bones may show which animals people hunted or raised for food.

More recently, members of the University of Arizona Garbage Project gathered at the Fresh Kills landfill in New York—the world's largest garbage dump. Using a giant drill, the students dug deep into the rotting mounds. At 35 feet, they found newspapers, grass clippings, and hot dogs from 1984. At 60 feet, the drill had reached debris from the 1940s. From each layer, the team carefully collected and labeled samples. Despite the foul smell, the garbage hunters agreed that the landfill was full of "wonderful things."

Theme: Continuity and Change Name two things that you threw away in the last day. What clues might these items give to future anthropologists?

How Do We Know?

The search for the human past has led all over the globe and far back to prehistoric times. Prehistory refers to the long period of time before people invented systems of writing. Prehistoric people had no cities, countries, organized central governments, or complex inventions.

Anthropology About 200 years ago, scholars began studying the origins and development of people and their societies. Today we call this field of study anthropology. Modern anthropologists specialize. Some examine the origins of human life. Others focus on the variety of human cultures. In anthropology, culture refers to the way of life of a society that is handed down from one generation to the next by learning and experience.

Archaeology A specialized branch of anthropology is called archaeology (ahr kee AHL uh jee), the study of past people and cultures. Archaeologists find and analyze the material remains of human cultures to learn about prehistoric people and to add to the written records of historical times.

Archaeologists study artifacts, objects made by human beings. Artifacts include tools, weapons, pottery, clothing, and jewelry. By analyzing artifacts and other items, archaeologists draw conclusions about the beliefs, values, and activities of our ancestors. Writer Agatha Christie, who was married to an archaeologist, described how people of the past speak to us through artifacts:

> "'With these bone needles we sewed our clothes.' 'These were our houses, this our bathroom, here our system of sanitation!' . . . 'Here, in this little jar, is my make-up.' 'All these cook-pots are of a very common type. You'll find them by the hundred. We get them from the potter at the corner.'"
> —Agatha Christie, *Come, Tell Me How You Live*

Archaeologists at Work Analyzing ancient artifacts is difficult, but archaeologists have devised many useful techniques. In the 1800s and early 1900s, archaeologists picked a likely site, or place, and began digging. The farther down they dug, the older the artifacts they found. Some long-buried objects crumbled as soon as they were exposed to light and air. Today, scientists have ways to preserve such fragile artifacts.

By studying thousands of items, archaeologists have traced how early people developed new technologies. Technology refers to the skills and tools people use to meet their basic needs. The first stone tools, for example, were crudely made with jagged edges and rough surfaces. Stone tools from later times are smooth and polished, showing improved skills.

Archaeologists today also make detailed maps locating every artifact they find. By analyzing this evidence, they can tell what went on at different locations within a site. Flint chips, for example, might suggest the workplace of a toolmaker.

Technology and the Past Archaeologists use modern technology to study and interpret their findings. Computers can be used to store and sort data or to develop accurate site maps. Aerial photography can reveal patterns of how people used the land. Techniques for measuring radioactivity help chemists and physicists determine the age of objects.

Geologists, or experts on earth science, help archaeologists date artifacts by determining the age of nearby rocks. Botanists and zoologists, experts on plants and animals, examine seeds and animal bones to learn about the diet of early people. Experts on climate determine what conditions early people faced on the plains of Africa or in ice-covered parts of Europe. Biologists analyze human bones as well as bloodstains found on old stone tools and weapons.

Connections to Today

ANSWERS Answers depend on what students name as their discards.

Resource Directory

Teaching Resources

You Are There Chapter Extension Activities booklet, p. 7
Simulation *The Lost City of Vesuvia,* Simulations booklet, pp. 2–3

UNEARTHING THE PAST

Sweat runs down your forehead and into your eyes. It stings. Slowly, you stand up from where you've been kneeling in the dirt and wipe your face. You volunteered to spend your first summer after high school helping archaeologists at a dig in Mexico. Squinting against the bright sun, you wait for your eyes to adjust. . . .

You turn and you see a serene face on an urn that you helped excavate this morning. You feel a sense of pride as you realize that you have helped unearth a piece of the past.

You hear distant murmurs in English and Spanish, and you can pick out an occasional word. Louder are the clink of metal hammers on rock and the crunch of shovels in soft earth. These are the sounds of an archaeological dig.

Your eyes focus on a pit just in front of you. Archaeologists are examining a burial chamber. They are sketching and mapping the find. Precise records are needed for later analysis.

Paintbrush
Calipers
Toothbrush
Trowel

You gather your tools, lying scattered about you. You use the trowel to dig up an artifact, brushes to gently brush away dirt, and then calipers to measure it. You take great care, because you are unearthing ancient treasure.

Portfolio Assessment

The sun dips below the horizon, and you are through for the day. Alone in your tent, you pick up paper and pen and start a letter home. You explain how you have reached your decision about whether to volunteer at another dig next summer.

Bell Ringer Have students look at the photographs of the tools on this page and try to guess how each is used. Then have them read the caption to check their guesses.

Background
About the Scene

Archaeologists tailor their techniques to the site. Open sites—such as temples or forts—are visible on the surface. Closed sites are buried. *Sondages,* or provisional excavations, let archaeologists sample the layers of a closed site. Well-trained archaeologists are as careful as surgeons, working with pen knives, brushes, and trowels to carefully reveal and remove features of the dig. As they work, they make detailed notes and drawings and take photographs. Field notes from really good archaeologists are so carefully prepared that later archaeologists can re-create and reinterpret them as primary documents, once the reports are published.

Activity
Cooperative Learning

Organize the class into small groups to research one of the early civilizations of Mexico or Central America. Have students make a class chart that lists each civilization and the time that it flourished, some of its architectural and artistic achievements, its geographical location, and the names of its important centers. One student should make an outline map for the bulletin board, and a student from each group should label his or her group's civilization on the map.

Portfolio Assessment Rubrics

Share rubrics with students before they write their letters.

Attempted The letter is incomplete.

Minimal The letter is complete but shows minimal effort.

Adequate The letter is well written and shows knowledge of the work involved in an archaeological dig.

Exemplary The letter is well written, shows knowledge of the work, and shows an understanding of the grueling life at a dig.

Human Drama Note

The Murals of Bonampak The murals at Bonampak, Mexico, were begun as a celebration of the succession of the last Mayan dynasty, but they were never finished. Yale art history professor Mary Miller first visited the murals in the mid-1970s, before the Mexican government began restoring them. The following quotation describes Miller's reaction to the restored murals:

"Details . . . leaped from the walls. Pearls gleamed. Dancers paused for the next drumbeat. Ghostly bodies of defeated foes floated to the surface like drowned men rising from the depths."

✓ Test Preparation

Have students read the "Archaeology" section and the Agatha Christie quote on the opposite page, and then answer the question below.

To whom does the word *we* in the quotation refer?

A Christie and her husband

B workers at the site being investigated

C people in general

D people of the past who lived at the site being investigated

Recall

1. (a) geography, p. 6 (b) latitude, p. 6
(c) longitude, p. 6 (d) prehistory, p. 8
(e) anthropology, p. 8 (f) culture, p. 8
(g) archaeology, p. 8 (h) artifact, p. 8
(i) technology, p. 8 (j) historian, p. 10

Comprehension

2. (a) location, place, human-environment interaction, movement, region (b) Examples may include using water from rivers to irrigate crops, cutting trees to clear the land for farming, building roads and canals, mining metals from the earth. 3. by studying their physical remains and artifacts and by mapping the locations of these finds; scientists also help by dating and analyzing the objects 4. artifacts, written records, video and audio recordings

Critical Thinking and Writing

5. Answers should demonstrate an understanding that our past has helped shape the civilizations and cultures of today. By studying human behavior and decisions of the past, we can perhaps avoid the mistakes of the past and learn how to improve our lives today. 6. People have traditionally settled near bodies of water for transportation, irrigation, drinking water, and power.

Activity Rubrics

Share rubrics with students before they create their list of artifacts.

Attempted The list includes items that could not be considered artifacts, or descriptions are poor or missing.

Minimal The list is complete, but descriptions are sketchy.

Adequate The list is complete, and descriptions are thoughtful.

Exemplary The list is complete, and descriptions include several things that might be learned from each artifact.

Global Connections

What Year Is It?

Most nations today use a standard calendar that dates events from the birth of Christ. This calendar, sometimes called the Christian Era calendar, uses B.C. to stand for dates before the birth of Christ and A.D. for dates after the birth of Christ. Some modern books use C.E., or "common era," instead of A.D.

The Christian Era calendar, however, is not the only calendar used in the world. The year 2000 on the Christian Era calendar overlapped the Muslim year 1371, the Chinese year 4637, and the Jewish year 5761. In some cultures, people use the standard dates for everyday use and traditional dates for holidays and religious ceremonies.

Theme: Diversity What are the advantages of all nations using the same dating system?

Historians Reconstruct the Past

While archaeologists have uncovered useful information about the past, most of what goes into a textbook like this one comes from the work of historians. Historians study how people lived in the past. Like archaeologists, historians study artifacts, from clothing and coins to artwork and tombstones. However, they rely even more on written evidence.

About 5,000 years ago, some people in different parts of the world began to keep written records. That event marked the beginning of recorded history. Although these early records are often scanty, they do give us a narrative of events, as well as a number of names and dates. Historians carefully study written evidence, such as letters or tax records. Historians of the recent past also use such evidence as photographs or films.

Historical Detection Like a detective, the historian must evaluate the evidence to determine if it is reliable. Do records of a meeting between two officials tell us exactly what was said? Who was taking notes? Was a letter writer really giving an eyewitness report or just passing on rumors? Could the letter even be a forgery? The historian tries to find the answers.

Historians then must interpret the evidence, explaining what it means. Often, the historian's goal is to determine the causes of a certain development or event, such as a war or an economic collapse. By explaining why things happened in the past, the historian can help us understand what is going on today and what may happen tomorrow.

Generally, historians try to give a straightforward account of events. Sometimes, though, their personal experiences, cultural backgrounds, or political opinions may affect their interpretations. At times, historians disagree about what the evidence proves. Such differences can lead to lively debates.

The "Great" and the "Small" The first historians began writing thousands of years ago. These early historians wrote mostly about the deeds of well-known and powerful people such as monarchs, religious leaders, politicians, and generals.

Today, historians still write about famous people whose actions have had wide influence. Yet other historians are studying the lives of ordinary people. How did farmers or workers earn a living? What holidays did they celebrate? What was family life like? The answers to such questions have increased our understanding of the past.

SECTION 1 Assessment

Recall

1. **Define:** (a) geography, (b) latitude, (c) longitude, (d) prehistory, (e) anthropology, (f) culture (g) archaeology, (h) artifact, (i) technology, (j) historian.

Comprehension

2. (a) What are the five themes of geography? (b) Give two examples of how people interact with their environment.

3. How do anthropologists and archaeologists learn about the lives of prehistoric people?

4. What kinds of evidence do historians use to study the past?

Critical Thinking and Writing

5. **Linking Past and Present** Historians and archaeologists have worked to piece together the human story from prehistory up to today. Why do you think it is important for us to understand our past?

6. **Connecting to Geography** How can bodies of water play an important role in shaping human society and economy?

Activity

Learning From Artifacts Make a list of four or five artifacts that are in your classroom right now. Then, describe what these artifacts might tell archaeologists of the future about education in our time.

Global Connections

ANSWER It avoids confusion in planning and carrying out special events, in transportation, in communication, and so on.

Resource Directory

Teaching Resources

Section Quiz Unit 1 booklet, p. 3
Creative Teaching Activities Creative Teaching Activities booklet, p. 9
Guided Reading and Review Unit 1 booklet, p. 4
Biography Activity *Mary Leakey,* Unit 1 booklet, p. 8
Primary Source Activity *Ice Age Art in an Underwater Cave,* Unit 1 booklet, p. 9

Technology

Interactive Student Tutorial CD-ROM Ch. 1
Computer Test Bank Ch. 1
World History Color Transparencies *Pictographs, From Ancient Times to Today,* p. C–23; political cartoon about how technology changes the way people meet their basic need for food, p. E–21

Reading Focus

- What advances did people make during the Old Stone Age?

- How can we learn about the religious beliefs of early people?

- Why was the Neolithic agricultural revolution a turning point in history?

Vocabulary

nomad
glacier
animism
domesticate

Taking Notes

Copy the before-and-after chart shown below. As you read the section, add information about human history under each heading. Save the completed chart to help you recall what you learn in this section.

PEOPLE LEARN TO FARM	
Before	**After**
• Lived in small groups	• Populations grew
•	•

Main Idea The change from nomadic to farming life led to the emergence of civilizations.

Setting the Scene

A small band of hunters and food gatherers was camped on the shore of Lake Turkana in East Africa. One member of the group picked up a stone and chipped it with another stone to make a sharp, jagged edge. The toolmaker may have used this simple tool to cut meat from a dead animal or to sharpen a stick for digging up edible roots.

The toolmaker left the chipped stone near the lake. Some three million years later, anthropologist Richard Leakey picked it up. "It is a heart-quickening thought," Leakey later said, "that we share the same . . . heritage with the hand that shaped the tool that we can now hold in our own hands."

Very slowly, early people learned to make better tools and weapons from stone, bone, and wood. They also developed new skills. Technological advances like these helped more people to survive.

The Old Stone Age

Historians call the earliest period of human history the Old Stone Age, or Paleolithic age. This long period dates from about 2 million B.C., the time of the first stone toolmakers, to about 10,000 B.C.

African Beginnings Anthropologists have found startling evidence of early human life in East Africa. In 1959, Mary and Louis Leakey found pieces of bone embedded in ancient rock at Olduvai (OHL duh way) Gorge in Tanzania. After careful testing, they concluded that the bone belonged to early hominids, or humanlike primates. In 1974, Donald Johanson found part of a hominid skeleton in Ethiopia. Johanson named his find "Lucy" after a Beatles' song.

Because of such evidence, many scientists think that the earliest people lived in East Africa. Later, their descendants may have migrated north and east into Europe and Asia. In time, people reached the Americas, Australia, and the islands of the Pacific.

Hunters and Food Gatherers Paleolithic people lived in small hunting and food-gathering bands numbering about 20 or 30 people. Everyone contributed to feeding the group. In general, men hunted or fished. Women, with their small children, gathered berries, fruit, nuts, wild grain, roots, or even shellfish. This food kept the band alive when game was scarce. Paleolithic people were nomads, moving from place to place as they followed game animals and ripening fruit.

Biography

Louis Leakey 1903–1972

No one who heard Louis Leakey talk about Africa ever forgot it. "He cast a spell," recalled Donald Johanson, "making each listener believe he was speaking only to him or her." Leakey's enthusiasm inspired a whole generation of anthropologists.

Born in Kenya, Leakey began looking for early human remains in East Africa. He and his wife, Mary, found many tools, bones, and other artifacts. Even while working as a spy during World War II, Leakey continued digging in his free time. In later life, he traveled all over the world, lecturing and raising funds for new research projects.

Theme: Impact of the Individual Why might someone devote his or her life to studying human origins?

Primary Source

Art in a Cave
An artist describes seeing cave paintings near Lascaux, France:

"I left the wonderful cave of Lascaux feeling slightly dazed. In such a short time it was not possible to absorb fully the hundreds of painted animals that appeared to prance over the calcite-covered walls and ceilings. Heavy bulls—over sixteen feet long—jostled for space with tiny deer. Leaping cows straddled groups of small ponies, and ibex butted one another like animated bookends. Rounding a sharp corner, I was suddenly confronted by two large black bison, shown rushing away in opposite directions. In the stillness, one could almost hear the animals' stampeding hooves as they hurried to escape capture."
—Douglas Mazonowicz,
Voices From the Stone Age

Skills Assessment

Primary Source How does this artist's description of the Lascaux cave paintings convey a sense of excitement?

People depended wholly on their environment for survival. At the same time, they found ways to adapt to their surroundings. They made simple tools and weapons out of the materials at hand—stone, bone, or wood. At some point, Stone Age people developed spoken language, which let them cooperate during the hunt and perhaps discuss plans for the future.

Still, prehistoric people faced severe challenges from the environment. During several ice ages, the Earth cooled. Thick glaciers, or sheets of ice, spread across parts of Asia, Europe, and North America. To endure the cold, Paleolithic people invented clothing. Wrapped in animal skins, they took refuge in caves or under rocky overhangs during the long winters. They also learned to build fires for warmth and cooking. In this harsh life, only the hardy survived.

Early Religious Beliefs

About 30,000 years ago, people began to leave evidence of their belief in a spiritual world. To them, the world was full of spirits and forces that might reside in animals, objects, or dreams. Such beliefs are known as animism.

In France, Spain, and northern Africa, cave or rock paintings vividly portray animals such as deer, horses, and buffaloes. Some cave paintings show stick-figure people, too. The paintings often lie deep in the caves, far from a band's living quarters. Cave paintings may have been part of animist religious rituals in which hunters sought help from the spirit world for success in an upcoming hunt.

Archaeologists have also found small stone statues that probably had religious meaning. Statues of pregnant women, for example, may have been symbols meant to ensure survival of the band. They suggest that early people worshiped earth-mother goddesses, givers of food and life.

Toward the end of the Old Stone Age, some people began burying their dead with great care. This practice suggests a belief in life after death. They probably believed the afterlife would be similar to life in this world, so they provided the dead with tools, weapons, and other needed goods. Burial customs like these survived in many places into modern times.

The Neolithic Agricultural Revolution

About 11,000 years ago, nomadic bands made a breakthrough that had far-reaching effects. They learned to farm. By producing their own food, they could remain in one place. Farmers thus settled into permanent villages and developed a new range of skills and tools. This change from nomadic to settled farming life ushered in the New Stone Age, or Neolithic age.

The First Farmers No one knows when and how people began to plant seeds for food. Some scholars think that, in the Eastern Hemisphere, farming started in the Middle East and then spread. Others argue that farming developed independently in different regions. No matter which way it occurred, the change had such dramatic effects that historians call it the Neolithic agricultural revolution.

Food-gathering women may have been the first to notice that if seeds were scattered on the ground, new plants would grow the next year. They may also have seen that removing some plants enabled nearby ones to grow stronger. If game animals were scarce, a band might camp at a place where plants grew and begin cultivating them season after season.

The Neolithic revolution included a second feature. People learned to domesticate, or tame, some of the animals they had once hunted. Rather than wait for migrating animals to return each year, hunters rounded them up. Then they herded the animals to good grasslands or penned them in rough enclosures. The animals provided people with a source of protein.

Clues to the Iceman Mystery

In 1991, hikers in the Alps stumbled upon a gruesome sight: a man's head and shoulders sticking out of the ice. Investigators discovered that the man had not died recently. In fact, the Iceman, as newspapers called him, had been shot with an arrow more than 5,000 years earlier. Fascinated, scientists studied the Iceman and his belongings.

The Iceman and his possessions were preserved in a pocket of snow (right). The 4½-inch stone-and-wood dagger (below) was found near his body.

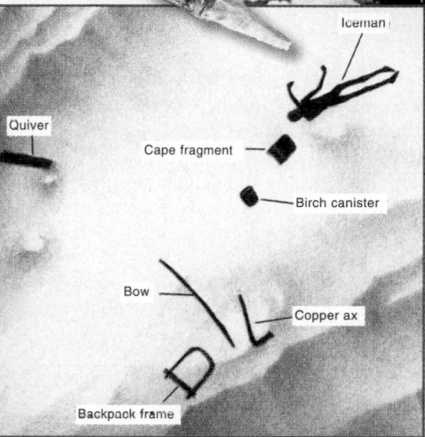

Quiver

Iceman

Cape fragment

Birch canister

Bow

Copper ax

Backpack frame

The Iceman's possessions, such as the bow and quiver shown on this diagram (left), give clues to his occupation. According to researcher Konrad Spindler, "In the high mountains, a shepherd would have to be armed with bow and arrow to defend himself from wild animals and human enemies, and also to secure food for himself."

Scientists were impressed by the complexity of the Iceman's ax. Its copper blade was bound onto a wooden handle with birch gum and leather.

Skills Assessment

1. Based on its size and shape, the dagger that was found with the Iceman might have been used to
   A chop wood for fires.
   B cut up meat or vegetables.
   C kill large animals.
   D carve through solid rock.

2. What conclusion can be made based on the discovery of the copper ax?
   E The Iceman used copper because stone was unavailable in the Alps.
   F People in the Alps knew how to mine and work with copper.
   G The early peoples of the Alps used copper for ornamental purposes.
   H Iron tools replaced copper tools.

3. **Critical Thinking Making Inferences** (a) Based on these artifacts, what can you infer about the Iceman's day-to-day life? (b) Consider the quality of workmanship of these artifacts. What does this tell you about the Iceman and the culture in which he lived?

Skills Tip

When using an artifact as a primary source, try to determine how that item might have been used at the time it was made.

Human Drama Note

Identifying the Iceman The hikers who found the Iceman notified police, who did not realize what he was. In removing his body, they destroyed artifacts and damaged his body. Then it was left to thaw during a press conference. Finally, after someone saw a fungus growing on the Iceman's skin, an expert—Konrad Spindler, of the Institute for Prehistory at Innsbruck—was called. He was astounded. "I thought this was perhaps what my colleague Howard Carter experienced when he opened the tomb of Tutankhamen. . . ."

Test Preparation

Have students read "The First Farmers" on the opposite page and then answer the question: Which is a fact from the passage?

A The Neolithic revolution took place first in the Middle East.

B Animals were first domesticated during the Neolithic revolution.

C The Neolithic revolution developed independently in different regions.

D Scientists know exactly when seeds were first planted for food.

Background
About the Primary Source

Clues to the Iceman's Culture The Iceman surprised scientists. His hair was short, proving that humans began cutting their hair much earlier than previously thought. He had several tattoos. Scientists had thought that tattooing began 2,500 years later.

The Iceman was wearing a fur robe that was a patchwork of the skins of different animals. His leather shoes were stuffed with grass for warmth, and he probably wore a fur cap. In a small leather pouch were mushrooms that could be consumed to fight infection, a sharpened piece of bone for making holes for sewing in leather, a stone drill, and a stone blade.

Activity
Interpreting the Primary Source

Use this additional question to generate class discussion.

Critical Thinking: Drawing Conclusions Weapons were found near the Iceman's body: a dagger, an ax, and a bow and arrow. Why do you suppose he was unable to defend himself against an attacker? *(Possible answers: He might have been surprised by his attacker or been unable to get a weapon out in time.)*

Skills Tip

Have students examine the ax to infer how the Iceman lived. The Skills Handbook in the front of the book has a lesson to help students with this feature.

Skills Assessment

ANSWERS 1. B 2. F 3. (a) He was prepared to live outdoors, hunting and gathering his foods. He could shoot game with his bow and arrows and skin and butcher it with tools. (b) He lived in a more technologically advanced culture than earlier Stone Age cultures.

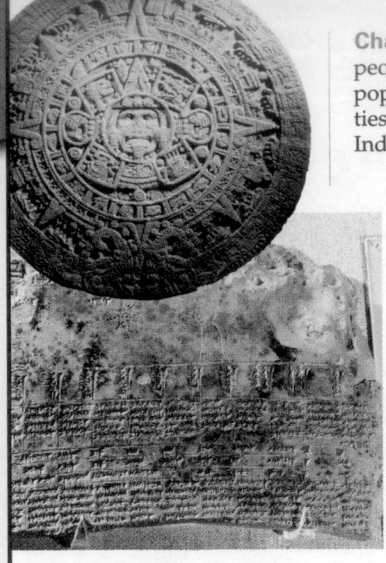

Early Calendars
From the Stone Age on, different cultures developed calendars based on the cycles of the sun and the moon. These calendars were created by the Aztecs of Mexico (top) and the Babylonians of the Middle East (bottom).

Theme: Economics and Technology Why was it important for farming societies to create calendars?

Changing Ways of Life The Neolithic agricultural revolution enabled people to become food producers for the first time. It led to a growth in population, which in turn led to more interaction among human communities. No greater change in the way people lived took place until the Industrial Revolution of the late 1700s.

Like their Paleolithic ancestors, early farmers still divided up the work by gender and age. Still, important differences began to emerge. In settled farming communities, the status of women declined as men came to dominate family, economic, and political life. Heads of families, probably older men, formed a council of elders and made decisions about when to plant and harvest.

When food was scarce, warfare increased, and some men gained prestige as warriors. These elite warriors asserted power over both women and other men. These changes did not mean that women lost all their influence or rights. Rather, they show that village life was reshaping the roles of both women and men.

Settled people had more personal property than their nomadic ancestors. Some people accumulated more possessions than their neighbors, so differences in wealth appeared. Yet big differences among social classes did not exist at this time.

New Technologies To farm successfully, people had to develop new technologies. Like farmers today, they had to find ways to protect their crops and measure out enough seed for the next year's harvest. They also needed to measure time accurately so that they would know when to plant and harvest. Gradually, they created the first calendars. In some places, farmers learned to use animals such as oxen or water buffalo to plow the fields.

Archaeological evidence shows that some villages had separate workshops where villagers made tools, including smooth, polished ax heads and chipped arrowheads. In some parts of the world, Neolithic people learned to weave cloth from animal hair or vegetable fibers.

Inventions did not appear everywhere at the same time. Technologies might travel slowly from one area to another, taking thousands of years to spread across continents. Other technologies may have been invented separately in different parts of the world.

By about 5,000 years ago, the advances made by early farming communities led to a new stage of development—the emergence of civilizations.

SECTION 2 Assessment

Recall

1. **Identify:** (a) Paleolithic age, (b) Mary and Louis Leakey, (c) Neolithic age.
2. **Define:** (a) nomad, (b) glacier, (c) animism, (d) domesticate.

Comprehension

3. How did Paleolithic people learn to adapt to their environment?
4. What do burial customs suggest about the beliefs of early peoples?
5. (a) What were the key features of the Neolithic agricultural revolution? (b) How did it change people's lives?

Critical Thinking and Writing

6. **Recognizing Causes and Effects** (a) Why would economic scarcity often lead to increased warfare between farming communities? (b) How do you think economic scarcity and warfare changed the status of women in Stone Age societies?
7. **Connecting to Geography** Why would geography probably have played a more important role in the lives of people during the Old Stone Age than it plays in your life today?

Activity
Take It to the NET

Use Internet sources to find out more about prehistoric cave paintings. Then, use the information to write a talk that a tour guide might give to visitors. Include the location of the caves, interesting features about the paintings, and information about the people who made them.

Resource Directory

Teaching Resources

Section Quiz Unit 1 booklet, p. 5
Creative Teaching Activities Creative Teaching Activities booklet, p. 10
Guided Reading and Review Unit 1 booklet, p. 6
Geography and History Activity *Choosing a Location for a Settlement*, Geography and History booklet, pp. 2–3

Technology

World History Color Transparencies *Pictographs, From Ancient Times to Today*, p. C–23
Interactive Student Tutorial CD-ROM Ch. 1
Computer Test Bank Ch. 1

SECTION **3** Beginnings of Civilization

Reading Focus

- How did the first cities emerge?

- What are the basic features of civilizations?

- How do cultures spread and change?

Vocabulary

civilization
surplus
polytheistic
artisan
pictogram
scribe
city-state
empire
steppe
cultural diffusion

Taking Notes

As you read, prepare an outline of this section. Use Roman numerals to indicate the major headings of the section, capital letters for the subheadings, and numbers for the supporting details. The sample at right will help you get started.

I. The rise of cities
  A. River valley civilizations
    1.
    2.
II. Features of civilization
  A.
    1.
    2.

Main Idea   The rise of cities was a central feature in the development and spread of civilizations.

Setting the Scene   Perhaps the best-known monuments of the ancient world are the great pyramids of Egypt. More than 100,000 workers labored for years under the hot North African sun to build these giant tombs. Without modern machinery, they fit into place more than two million stone blocks weighing an average of 2 ½ tons each!

Pyramid building required a society more highly organized and technologically advanced than Neolithic farming villages. In Egypt, as elsewhere, people were taking a giant step from prehistory into history.

The Rise of Cities

The rise of cities was the main feature of civilization. A civilization is a complex, highly organized social order. The first cities emerged after farmers began cultivating fertile lands along river valleys and producing surplus, or extra, food. These surpluses in turn helped populations to expand. As populations grew, some villages swelled into cities.

River Valley Civilizations   Cities rose independently in the valleys of the Tigris and Euphrates rivers in the Middle East, the Nile River in Egypt, the Indus River in India, and the Yellow River, or Huang He, in China. Conditions in these river valleys favored farming. Flood waters spread silt across the valleys, renewing the soil and keeping it fertile. The animals that flocked to the rivers to drink were another source of food. In addition, rivers provided a regular water supply and a means of transportation.

Rivers also posed challenges. Farmers had to control flooding and channel waters to the fields. To meet these challenges, cooperation was needed. Early farmers worked together to build dikes, dig canals, and carve out irrigation ditches. Such large-scale projects required leadership and a well-organized government.

Ancient cities were frequently surrounded by high walls. The walls of Babylon were so wide that a chariot could turn around on top of the wall without falling off. Early cities also boasted large temples and palaces and broad avenues used for public ceremonies. Still, most city streets were narrow and tangled, with houses as small as village huts.

Cities in the Americas   Unlike the civilizations in Asia, Africa, and Europe, civilizations in the Americas often did not rise in river valleys. Two major civilizations, the Aztecs and Incas, eventually emerged in the highlands of Mexico and Peru.

Did You Know?

The Walls of Jericho
The city of Jericho was tiny—just about the size of eight football fields—but it was home to several thousand people. Jericho, in present-day Jordan, is the oldest city yet found. Archaeologists believe it was first settled a stunning 10,000 years ago. Even more striking is the fact that archaeologists have uncovered a huge wall, 12 feet high and 6 feet thick, that once surrounded the city.

What can we conclude from this great wall? Jericho must have had a powerful government to oversee the building of the wall. We can also conclude that there must have been a very good reason to undertake such a difficult task. One historian put it this way: "The citizens of Jericho felt they had wealth worth defending, and they lived in a world where others would try to take it from them by force."

Theme: Economics and Technology   What might be the strategic advantages of a wall 12 feet high and 6 feet thick?

Bell Ringer Note that students will be reading about the eight features that constitute a civilization. Ask students to speculate on what those features may be.

LESSON PLAN

1. Focus Eight features of early civilizations were cities, centralized governments, complex religions, job specialization, social classes, arts and architecture, public works, and writing. Many of the first civilizations emerged along river valleys. Interaction among the various civilizations often brought about cultural change.

2. Instruct Inform students that several early civilizations constructed pyramids, often for religious and political purposes. If you wish, you could draw an example or two on the chalkboard or show some pictures. Have students analyze which features of civilization the pyramid reflects.

3. Assess Have a volunteer read aloud his or her responses. Ask the other students to add anything that the volunteer did not include.

4. Reteach If students' **Assess** activity does not reflect adequate understanding of the lesson, you might assign the *Guide to the Essentials* or the *Interactive Student Tutorial CD-ROM* for this section.

Block Scheduling Support

Pottery shards are probably the most common kinds of artifacts found at digs of ancient villages, towns, and cities. The art of pottery-making probably developed in response to the need to store grains and other foods, keeping them safe from rodents and protecting them from dampness. Have students research the history of pottery-making and create a bulletin board display with the results of their research. Illustrations, a time line, and a map should be included in the display. Possibly the art teacher could coordinate a lesson with this activity. In addition, a local craftperson might be invited to share his or her skills with the class.

Did You Know?

ANSWER too high to climb over, too thick to break through

In the Americas, the first cities may have begun as religious centers. There, powerful priests inspired people from nearby villages to build temples to their gods. Villagers would gather at the temples for regular worship. In time, many may have remained permanently, creating cities like those elsewhere.

Features of Civilization

How did civilizations differ from smaller farming societies? What did the early civilizations that rose in different parts of the globe have in common? Historians distinguish eight basic features found in most early civilizations. These eight features are (1) cities, (2) well-organized central governments, (3) complex religions, (4) job specialization, (5) social classes, (6) arts and architecture, (7) public works, and (8) writing.

Organized Governments As cities grew, they needed a steady food supply. To produce large amounts of food and oversee irrigation projects, new forms of government arose. City governments were far more powerful than the councils of elders and local chiefs of farming villages.

At first, priests probably had the greatest power. In time, warrior kings emerged as the chief political leaders. They took over the powers of the old councils of elders and set themselves up as hereditary rulers who passed power from father to son. Almost always, rulers claimed that their right to rule came from the gods. Early Chinese kings took the title "Son of Heaven," and Incan emperors declared that they were sons of the sun itself. Thus, political rulers gained religious power as well.

Government became more complex as rulers issued laws, collected taxes, and organized systems of defense. To enforce order, rulers relied on royal officials. Over time, separate government departments evolved that oversaw functions such as tax collection, irrigation projects, or the military.

Complex Religions Like their Stone Age ancestors, most ancient people were polytheistic, that is, they believed in many gods. People appealed to sun gods, river goddesses, and other spirits that they believed controlled natural forces. Other gods were thought to control human activities such as birth, trade, or war.

In ancient religions, priests and worshipers sought to gain the favor of the gods through complex rituals such as ceremonies, dances, prayers, and hymns. To ensure divine help, people built temples and sacrificed animals, crops, or sometimes other humans to the gods. Sacrifices and other ceremonies required the full-time attention of priests, who had special training and knowledge.

Job Specialization The lives of city dwellers differed from those of their Stone Age ancestors. Urban people developed so many new crafts that a single individual could no longer master all the skills needed to make tools, weapons, or other goods. For the first time, individuals began to specialize in certain jobs. Some became artisans, or skilled craftworkers, who made pottery or finely carved or woven goods. Among the crafts that developed in cities, metalworking was particularly important. People learned to make tools and weapons, first out of copper, then later out of bronze, a more durable mixture of copper and tin.

Cities had other specialists, too. Bricklayers built city walls. Soldiers defended them. Merchants sold goods in the marketplace. Singers, dancers, and storytellers entertained on public occasions. Such specialization made people dependent on others for their various needs.

Social Classes In cities, social organization became more complex. People were ranked according to their jobs. Such ranking led to the growth of social classes. Priests and nobles usually occupied the top level of an

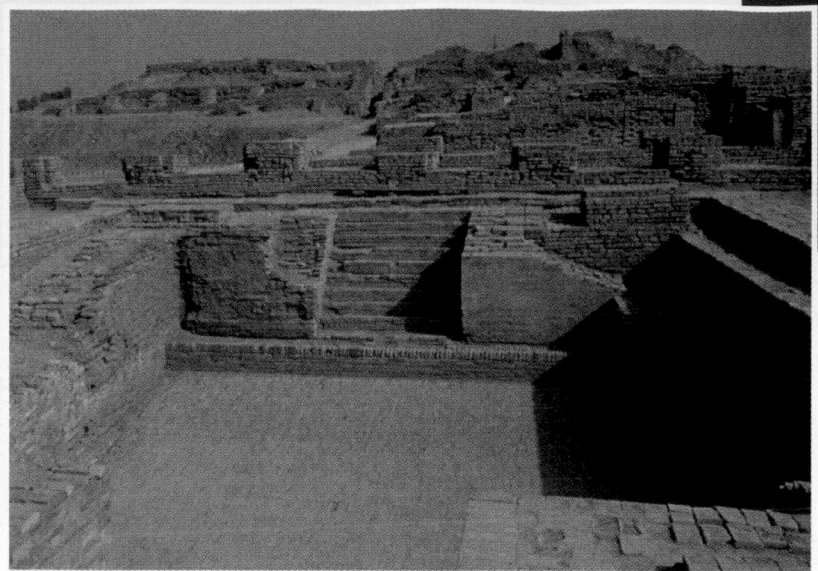

Virtual Field Trip

www.phschool.com
Harappa and Mohenjo-Daro Pakistan

To see other views and artifacts from these ancient cities, use the Internet address above to link to an ancient Indus Valley site.

Remains of an Ancient Civilization

One early civilization emerged in the Indus River valley. The Indus city of Mohenjo-Daro included a huge public water tank (left). Indus Valley artifacts (below) include stone seals with writing and a small statue of a priest-king.

Theme: Diversity **Describe how these pictures reflect some of the eight features of civilization.**

ancient society. Next came a small class of wealthy merchants, followed by humbler artisans. Below them stood the vast majority of people, peasant farmers who lived in the surrounding villages and produced food for the city.

Slaves occupied the lowest social level. Slaves sometimes came from poor families who sold themselves into slavery to pay their debts. Others were prisoners captured in war. Because male captives were often killed, women and children made up the largest number of these slaves.

Arts and Architecture The arts and architecture of ancient civilizations expressed the beliefs and values of the people who created them. Temples and palaces dominated the city scenery. Such buildings reassured people of the strength and power of their government and religion.

Skilled workers built and decorated massive buildings. In museums today, you can see statues of gods and goddesses, temple or palace wall paintings, and furniture and jewelry found in ancient tombs from around the world. They give ample evidence of the artistic genius of the first civilizations.

Public Works Closely linked to temples and palaces were vast public works that strong rulers ordered to be built. Such projects included irrigation systems, roads, bridges, and defensive walls. Although they were costly in human labor and even lives, such projects were meant to benefit the city, protecting it from attack and ensuring its food supply.

Writing A critical new skill developed by the earliest civilizations was the art of writing. It may have begun in temples, where priests needed to record amounts of grain collected, accurate information about the seasons, and precise rituals and prayers.

Archaeologists have found masses of ancient writings, ranging from treaties and tax rolls to business and marriage contracts. The earliest writing was made up of pictograms, or simple drawings that looked like the objects they represented. In time, symbols were added. They might stand for sounds of words or for ideas that could not be expressed easily in pictures.

Chapter 1 **17**

Chapter 1 **17**

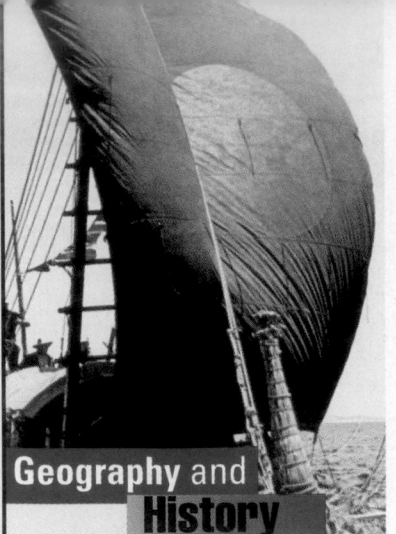

Geography and History

Ancient Travelers

Scientists long thought that ancient peoples tended to stay close to home. But startling new evidence from around the world has cast doubt on this idea.

In Europe, archaeologists found the remains of a sophisticated canoe that is 8,500 years old. In Oceania, we have learned that early people sailed small boats across hundreds, and perhaps thousands, of miles of open ocean. In Asia, scientists have mapped out ancient trade routes that crossed hundreds of miles of some of the most rugged terrain on the planet. These discoveries show that early peoples were much more mobile than anyone had ever imagined.

 Theme: Geography and History What might have motivated early peoples to travel?

As writing grew more complex, only specially trained people called scribes learned to read and write. Scribes were educated in temple schools and kept records for priests, rulers, and merchants. In only a few societies were women permitted to attend temple schools. As a result, women were generally excluded from becoming scribes, an occupation that could lead to political power.

Spread of Civilization

As ancient rulers gained more power, they conquered territories beyond the boundaries of their cities. This expansion led to the rise of the city-state, a political unit that included a city and its surrounding lands and villages. Rulers, nobles, and priests often controlled the land outside the city and forced peasants to grow crops on it. A large portion of each harvest went to support the government and temples.

The First Empires Rival leaders often battled for power. Sometimes, ambitious rulers conquered many cities and villages, creating the first empires. An empire is a group of states or territories controlled by one ruler. For the conquered people, defeat was painful and often cruel. At the same time, empire building also brought benefits. It helped end war between neighboring communities and created common bonds among people.

Interactions With Nomadic Peoples The first cities were scattered islands in a sea of older, simpler ways of life. Most peoples lived as their Stone Age ancestors had. They hunted, gathered food, or lived in simple farming villages. On some less-fertile lands or on sparse, dry grasslands, called steppes, nomadic herders tended cattle, sheep, goats, or other animals. Because the lands were poor in water and grass, these nomads had to keep moving to find new pasture.

Nomadic cultures were not "civilized," in the sense that they did not exhibit the characteristics of civilization. They built no cities and their governments were simpler than those of settled city-states or empires. However, many nomadic peoples developed sophisticated traditions in oral poetry, music, weaving, jewelry making, animal raising, and other areas of the arts and sciences.

Throughout history, relations between nomads and city dwellers have been complex. At times, the two groups cooperated in political, economic, or military matters. At other times, they have been in conflict, with cities subduing nomadic peoples or nomads overrunning cities. You will read about such encounters in later chapters.

Civilizations and Change

All societies and civilizations change. In fact, history itself might be defined as the story of these changes. Ancient civilizations changed in many ways over the centuries. Among the chief causes of change were shifts in the physical environment and interactions among people.

Environmental Changes Like their Stone Age ancestors, people of early civilizations depended heavily on the physical environment. They needed rain and fertile soil to produce crops. Resources such as stone, timber, or metals were also essential. Changes in the environment could have an immediate impact on people's lives.

At times, sudden, drastic events devastated a community. A tremendous volcano may have wiped out Minoan civilization on the island of Crete in the Mediterranean Sea. Overfarming could destroy soil fertility, or rivers might become too salty. Cities would then suffer famine, and survivors would be forced to move away.

Geography and History

ANSWER Answers may include curiosity about the world beyond, desire for adventure, desire for trade.

If people used up nearby timber or ran out of other building resources, they would have to adapt to this scarcity. They might, for example, trade with areas where such resources were available. Or they might use alternate building materials such as reeds.

Interactions Among People An even more important source of change was *cultural diffusion,* the spread of ideas, customs, and technologies from one people to another. Cultural diffusion occurred through migration, trade, and warfare.

As famine, drought, or other disasters led people to migrate, they interacted with others whose lives differed from their own. As a result, people often shared and adapted customs. Trade, too, introduced people to new goods or better methods of producing them. In ancient times, skills such as working bronze and writing, as well as religious beliefs, passed from one people to another.

Warfare also brought change. Often, victorious armies forced their way of life upon the people they defeated. On other occasions, the victors adopted the ways of a conquered people. Sometimes, nomadic rulers would become absorbed in city life.

Looking Ahead

In the next two chapters, you will read about the earliest civilizations that developed in the river valleys of Africa and Asia. They differed from one another in significant ways, each developing its own culture and traditions. At the same time, the civilizations of Egypt, Mesopotamia, India, and China all fit our definition of a civilization.

Cause *and* Effect

Long-Term Causes	Immediate Causes
• Silt deposits create fertile soil in river valleys • Neolithic people learn to farm • Hunters and gatherers settle into farming communities	• New technologies improve farming • Food surpluses support rising populations • First cities built in fertile valleys • Farmers cooperate to control flooding and channel water

Rise of River Valley Civilizations

Immediate Effects	Long-Term Effects
• Complex forms of government develop • Arts become more elaborate • Job specialization leads to social classes • Writing is invented	• Government bureaucracies emerge • Early civilizations conquer neighboring lands • Civilizations clash with nomadic peoples

Connections to Today

• Archaeologists mine rich stores of information in Egypt, Middle East, India, and China
• Large cities such as Cairo and Baghdad still flourish in river valley regions

Skills Assessment **Chart** Although river valley civilizations rose in different places, they shared many important features. **How did the rise of civilizations lead to the development of more complex governments?**

SECTION 3 Assessment

Recall

1. Define: (a) civilization, (b) surplus, (c) polytheistic, (d) artisan, (e) pictogram, (f) scribe, (g) city-state, (h) empire, (i) steppe, (j) cultural diffusion.

Comprehension

2. How did conditions in some river valleys favor the rise of early civilizations?
3. How were government and religion closely linked in early civilizations?

4. What are three causes of cultural change?

Critical Thinking and Writing

5. **Recognizing Causes and Effects** How did job specialization lead to the emergence of social classes in early civilizations?
6. **Linking Past and Present** (a) Give three examples that show cultural diffusion in today's world. (b) Why do you think that cultural changes occur more quickly today than in the past?

Activity
Take It to the NET

Use Internet sources to find out more about how early people learned to measure time. Then, use the information to create a time line about the evolution of time measurement.

SECTION 3 Assessment

Recall

1. (a) civilization, p. 15 (b) surplus, p. 15 (c) polytheistic, p. 16 (d) artisan, p. 16 (e) pictogram, p. 17 (f) scribe, p. 18 (g) city-state, p. 18 (h) empire, p. 18 (i) steppe, p. 18 (j) cultural diffusion, p. 19

Comprehension

2. Floods deposited silt that made river valleys fertile for farming. Rivers also provided constant water supplies and an easy means of transportation. Cities and civilization therefore prospered. 3. In early governments, priests often had the most power. Later, rulers claimed that their power came from the gods. 4. Answers may include any three of the following: environmental changes; cultural diffusion through migration, trade, or warfare.

Critical Thinking and Writing

5. Possible answer: People tended to live and work with those who had the same jobs as themselves, thus forming social classes. Social rank depended on the power and wealth connected to one's job. Priests and nobles usually enjoyed the highest status. 6. (a) Examples may include popular music of the United States being played in countries around the world; music from the Caribbean, Africa, and elsewhere being played in the United States; the popularity of American jeans worldwide; the demand for Japanese electronic equipment and games in the United States. (b) Cultural changes occur more quickly because of advances in communication and transportation.

Activity Rubrics

Share rubrics with students before they complete this time line activity.

Attempted The time line has few examples, or examples are out of order or mislabeled.

Minimal The time line includes a reasonable number of examples, but has little or no labeling.

Adequate The time line includes a reasonable number of examples with appropriate labels.

Exemplary The time line includes many examples and has thorough and interesting labels.

Skills Assessment

ANSWER As rulers issued laws, collected taxes, and organized systems of defense, separate departments developed to take care of these areas.

EXPLORING HUMAN DRAMA Human Drama Note

The Magic of Writing A scene from the 1991 movie *Black Robe,* based on the novel by Brian Moore, dramatically illustrates the magic of writing. In French Canada during the 1600s, a Jesuit missionary is trying unsuccessfully to demonstrate the value of writing to a Huron chief. The Huron knows nothing of writing and sees no benefit to this odd practice of making scratch marks. Then the Jesuit has an idea. "Tell me something I do not know," he says to the chief. The chief replies, "My woman's mother died in snow last winter." The Jesuit writes the message in the ground and then calls over another Frenchman from a distance away. The Frenchman, who could not have heard what was said, glances at the writing in the dirt and says to the chief, "Your mother-in-law died in a snowstorm?" The confused chief jumps back in fear of this stranger who finds knowledge in scratches on the ground. This was the Huron's first encounter with the powerful magic of writing.

Creating a Chapter Summary

As a reteaching opportunity, pair a more able student with a less able student to complete this chapter summary.

Additional entries that students might make on their Venn diagrams include the following: **Before First Civilizations** Learned to farm, Created first calendars; **Both** Relied on agriculture, Faced challenges from environment; **Early Civilizations** Differences among social classes, Job specialization, Arts, Public works, Trade.

Building Vocabulary

1–10. Sentences will vary but should show a clear understanding of the listed words.

Recalling Key Facts

11. chemists, physicists, geologists, botanists, zoologists, experts on climate, biologists
12. location, place, human-environment interaction, movement, region
13. **(a)** They survived as nomadic hunters and gatherers, taking shelter in caves or under rocky overhangs. **(b)** They learned to make tools of stone, wood, and bone, and they learned how to build fires and to make clothing.
14. the change from nomadic life to settled farming
15. They needed to be able to measure time so that they would know when to plant and harvest.
16. cities, well-organized central governments, complex religions, job specialization, social classes, arts and architecture, public works, writing
17. Tigris and Euphrates rivers, Nile River, Indus River, Yellow River (or Huang He)

Critical Thinking and Writing

18. Possible answer: Most countries use the Christian Era calendar, but some cultures—such as the Chinese, Jewish, and Muslim—also have different calendars.
19. **(a)** Possible answer: Khaldun stresses human interaction; Carlyle stresses the deeds of great people. **(b)** Possible answer: Khaldun probably wrote about groups of people and how they affected each other; Carlyle probably wrote about powerful men whose leadership affected others in the society.

Creating a Chapter Summary

Copy this Venn diagram on a sheet of paper. Use it to compare human life before and after the first civilizations began. Write information about life in both periods in the overlapping section of the circles. A few entries have been made to help you get started.

For additional review and enrichment activities, see the interactive version of *World History* available on the Web and on CD-ROM.

Before First Civilizations
• People lived in villages
• Not great difference among social classes
•

• Depended heavily on environment
•

Early Civilizations (from 5,000 years ago)
• Built cities
• Written language
•

Web Site Self-Test
For practice test questions for Chapter 1, see **www.phschool.com**.

Building Vocabulary

For each of the ten terms below, write a sentence using the term.

1. **geography**
2. **anthropology**
3. **prehistory**
4. **artifact**
5. **animism**
6. **domesticate**
7. **surplus**
8. **polytheistic**
9. **scribe**
10. **cultural diffusion**

Recalling Key Facts

11. Name five types of scientists who help archaeologists learn about the past.
12. What are the five themes of geography?
13. **(a)** How did Paleolithic people survive? **(b)** What technological advances did they make?
14. What change marked the beginning of the New Stone Age?
15. Why did early farmers need to create calendars?
16. List the eight features found in most early civilizations.
17. In which four river valleys did early civilizations emerge?

Critical Thinking and Writing

18. **Identifying Main Ideas** Reread the Global Connections feature in Section 1. Then, write a sentence stating the main idea of the feature.
19. **Recognizing Points of View** Thomas Carlyle, a Scottish writer, said that history was "the biography of great men." Ibn Khaldun, an Arab historian, defined history as "information about human social organizations." **(a)** What is the main difference between these two views of history? **(b)** How might each man's viewpoint have affected the way he wrote about history?
20. **Connecting to Geography (a)** Describe the community where you live in terms of each of the five themes of geography. **(b)** Explain two ways that geography affects your community and way of life.

21. **Recognizing Causes and Effects** Make a list of five major social or technological developments of the Old Stone Age and the New Stone Age. Then, for each development, identify one short-term and one long-term effect.

---

20. **(a)** Students should show an understanding of the five themes. **(b)** Students may discuss effects of geography on their diet, clothing, housing, transportation, etc.
21. List for the Old Stone Age may include simple tools, spoken language, fire building, cave paintings, and belief in an afterlife. List for the New Stone Age may include agriculture, domestication of animals, the wheel, declining status of women, and systems of measurement. Answers should show an understanding of the difference between long-term and short-term effects.

The excerpt below was written by an American historian. Read the passage, then answer the questions that follow.

How Historians Find Evidence

"Precisely because the historian must turn to all possible witnesses, he is the most bookish of men. For him, no printed statement is without its interest. For him, the destruction of old cookbooks, gazetteers, road maps, Sears Roebuck catalogues, children's books, railway timetables, or drafts of printed manuscripts, is the loss of potential evidence. Does one wish to know how the mail-order business was operated or how a Nebraska farmer might have dressed in 1930? Look to those catalogues. Does one wish to know whether a man from Washington just might have been in New York on a day in 1861 when it can be proved that he was in the capital on the day before and the day after? The timetables will help tell us of the opportunity."

—Robin Winks, *The Historian as Detective*

22. (a) Who is the author? (b) How does the author describe historians?
23. Why must the historian "turn to all possible witnesses"?
24. (a) According to the author, what could a historian learn from an old catalogue? (b) What might two other things be?
25. Based on this excerpt, do you think Winks considers the work of historians important?
26. Name three kinds of printed material a historian might consult that Winks does not name.

Use the Internet to research archaeological discoveries of early remains, such as "Lucy" or discoveries at Olduvai Gorge, in Africa. Then, imagine that you were present when a site was first discovered. Write an archaeological log describing what you found.

"Good effort, Sam, but it was a water jug!"

The cartoon above appeared in the British humor magazine *Punch* in May 1971. At that time, amateur archaeologists from many parts of the world were flocking to England to search for ancient artifacts and remains of early humans. Study the cartoon and then answer the following questions:

27. What kind of work are the three people in the cartoon doing?
28. (a) What has Sam pieced together? (b) Why do you think he is eager to show off his find?
29. How do the other archaeologists respond to what Sam has done?
30. What do you think is the cartoonist's view of amateur archaeologists?
31. (a) Based on the cartoon and on what you have read, what problems could a careless archaeologist cause? (b) How do professional archaeologists try to avoid such errors?

Skills Tip

Keep in mind that the cartoonist is presenting a point of view. Examine both the words and the pictures to understand what the subject matter is and how the cartoonist feels about it.

Chapter 1 **21**

22. (a) Robin Winks (b) as detectives and as the "most bookish of men"
23. to find the evidence needed to reconstruct the past
24. (a) how people dressed and how a mail-order business operated (b) possible answers: what tools people used, what appliances were available
25. yes
26. Possible answers include newspapers, magazines, posters, and airline schedules.

27. archaeological work reconstructing fragments that have been dug up
28. (a) a skull (b) because he had to put together tiny bits to make the skull
29. The woman doesn't seem to be paying any attention to it; the man tells Sam that he has tried hard, but that he has reconstructed the wrong thing.
30. possible answer: well meaning, industrious, but lacking in knowledge
31. (a) possible answer: destroying artifacts, obscuring site by careless digging, failing to keep adequate records of what was found and where it was found (b) possible answers: making detailed maps locating every article they find, using modern technology to carefully study and interpret their findings

Skills Tip

It will help students to answer question 29 if they note that the woman is looking down, not at the men. The Skills Handbook in the front of the book has a lesson that will help students with this feature.

Unit Theme Activity

Remind students about the Unit Theme Activity located on the unit opener page. Make sure students understand the assignment and have begun work.

Take It to the NET

Direct students to **www.phschool.com** for links to sites that will help them get started with this assignment. Share rubrics with students.
Attempted The log shows little research and lacks understanding of the discovery's importance.
Minimal The log shows that the research was done, but log entries are scanty.
Adequate The log shows an understanding of the discovery's importance and shows knowledge of the work involved in an archaeological dig.
Exemplary The log shows an understanding of the discovery's importance and of the work in an archaeological dig. Entries are imaginative and empathetic.

Resource Manager

Chapter Level Resources	CORE INSTRUCTION	READING/SKILLS
	Teaching Resources	**Book on CD**, Ch. 2
	Pacing Charts, Ch. 2	**Interactive Student Tutorial CD-ROM**, Ch. 2
	Teaching With Themes, p. 5	**Social Studies Skills Tutor CD-ROM**
	Color Transparencies, p. F–5	**Skills Transparencies**
	Resource Pro® Ch. 2	
	www.phschool.com • eTeach	
1 Ancient Egypt of the Nile 1. Explain how geography influenced ancient Egypt. 2. Identify and compare the main features and achievements of Egypt's kingdoms. 3. Describe how trade and warfare affected Egypt and Nubia.	**Teaching Resources** **Unit 1 booklet** • Primary Source Activity, p. 29 **Creative Teaching Activities**, p. 11 **Prentice Hall Presentation Pro**, Ch. 2, Section 1 **Section Reading Support Transparencies**	**Teaching Resources** **Unit 1 booklet** • Guided Reading and Review, p. 18 **Guide to the Essentials** **Guided Reading Audiotapes**, Ch. 2, Section 1
2 Egyptian Civilization 1. Summarize how religious beliefs shaped the lives of Egyptians. 2. Describe how Egyptian society was organized. 3. Identify the advances that Egyptians made in learning and the arts.	**Teaching Resources** **Creative Teaching Activities**, p. 12 **Prentice Hall Presentation Pro**, Ch. 2, Section 2 **Section Reading Support Transparencies**	**Teaching Resources** **Unit 1 booklet** • Guided Reading and Review, p. 20 • Skill Application Activity, p. 31 **Guide to the Essentials** **Guided Reading Audiotapes**, Ch. 2, Section 2
3 City-States of Ancient Sumer 1. Explain how geographic features influenced Fertile Crescent civilizations. 2. Describe the main features of Sumerian civilization. 3. Identify Sumerian advances in learning.	**Teaching Resources** **Creative Teaching Activities**, p. 13 **Prentice Hall Presentation Pro**, Ch. 2, Section 3 **Section Reading Support Transparencies**	**Teaching Resources** **Unit 1 booklet** • Guided Reading and Review, p. 22 **Guide to the Essentials** **Guided Reading Audiotapes**, Ch. 2, Section 3
4 Invaders, Traders, and Empire Builders 1. Describe how early empires arose in Mesopotamia. 2. Explain how ideas and technology spread. 3. Identify Phoenician contributions.	**Teaching Resources** **Unit 1 booklet** • Viewpoint Activity, p. 30 **Creative Teaching Activities**, p. 14 **Prentice Hall Presentation Pro**, Ch. 2, Section 4 **Section Reading Support Transparencies**	**Teaching Resources** **Unit 1 booklet** • Guided Reading and Review, p. 24 **Guide to the Essentials** **Guided Reading Audiotapes**, Ch. 2, Section 4
5 The Roots of Judaism 1. Summarize the main events in the early history of the Israelites. 2. Explain how the Jews viewed their relationship with God. 3. Describe the moral and ethical ideas that the prophets taught.	**Teaching Resources** **Unit 1 booklet** • Biography Activity, p. 28 **Creative Teaching Activities**, p. 15 **Prentice Hall Presentation Pro**, Ch. 2, Section 5 **Section Reading Support Transparencies**	**Teaching Resources** **Unit 1 booklet** • Guided Reading and Review, p. 26 **Guide to the Essentials** **Guided Reading Audiotapes**, Ch. 2, Section 5

ENRICHMENT/PRE-AP

- 🖥 **www.phschool.com**
  - Why Study History?

- 📖 **Color Transparencies,** p. B–71
- 📼 **Visions, Voices, Views,** Daily Life CloseUp, tape 1

- 📖 **Teaching Resources**
  - 📘 **Chapter Extension Activity,** p. 9
    - History Through Literature, pp. 5–6
  - 📖 **Color Transparencies,** pp. C–25, D–35
  - 📼 **Listening to Literature World Masterpieces,** Sumerian, Egyptian, and Hebrew Music, side 1
  - 🖥 **www.phschool.com**
    - Internet Activities, Egyptian Tomb Art
    - Internet Activities, Section 2

- 📖 **Color Transparencies,** p. B–71
- 📼 **Visions, Voices, Views,** Animated Map Story, tape 1
- 📼 **Listening to Literature World Masterpieces,** Sumerian, Egyptian, and Hebrew Music, side 1
- 🖥 **www.phschool.com**
  - Virtual Field Trip, Ch. 2

- 📖 **Teaching Resources**
  - 📘 **Chapter Extension Activity,** pp. 10–11
  - 📖 **Color Transparencies,** p. E–19
  - 📼 **Visions, Voices, Views,** Global Issues Forum, tape 1
  - 🖥 **www.phschool.com**
    - Internet Activities, Section 4

- 📖 **Color Transparencies,** p. C–27
- 📼 **Listening to Literature World Masterpieces,** Psalm 23, side 1

ASSESSMENT

PRENTICE HALL ASSESSMENT SYSTEM

Core Assessment
- 📘 ExamView Test Bank booklet, Ch. 2
- 💿 ExamView Test Bank CD-ROM, Ch. 2

Standardized Test Preparation

Diagnose and Prescribe
- 📘 Diagnostic Tests for High School Social Studies Skills

Review and Reteach
- 📘 Review Book for World History

Practice and Assess
- 📘 Test-Taking Strategies With Transparencies for High School
- 📘 Alternative Assessment booklet
- 📘 Test Prep Book for World History

📖 **Teaching Resources**
- 📘 **Unit 1 booklet**
  - Geography Quiz, p. 32
  - Section Quizzes, pp. 19, 21, 23, 25, 27
  - Chapter Tests A, B, and C, pp. 33–37
- 🖥 **www.phschool.com**
  - Self-Test

CUSTOMIZE FOR INDIVIDUAL NEEDS

Gifted and Talented
- **Teacher's Edition,** Activities: Connections to Science, p. 36

Less Proficient Readers
- **Guide to the Essentials,** Ch. 2
- **Guided Reading Audiotapes, English,** Ch. 2
- **Book on CD,** Ch. 2
- **Teacher's Edition,** Activities: Customize for Heterogeneous Groups, p. 26; Customize for Auditory Learners, p. 41; Reading Strategy, p. 43

Less Proficient Writers
- **Teacher's Edition,** Activities: Customize for Heterogeneous Groups, p. 26; Cooperative Learning Activity, p. 30

Students Acquiring English/ESL
- **Guide to the Essentials, English/Spanish,** Ch. 2
- **Guided Reading Audiotapes, English,** Ch. 2
- **Book on CD,** Ch. 2
- **Teacher's Edition,** Activities marked with an *: Customize for Heterogeneous Groups, p. 26; Connections to Science, p. 36

TEXT

Don't miss the exclusive interactive version of *World History: Connections to Today* on the Internet and CD-ROM.

INTRODUCTION

About 5,000 years ago, Egyptian pharaohs organized a strong central government and built pyramids as tombs. In Mesopotamia, Sumerians developed city-states, invented cuneiform writing, and studied mathematics and astronomy. Large empires of Babylonians, Assyrians, and Persians spread ideas and technology through warfare and trade. Hebrews and Phoenicians also contributed to civilization.

Focusing on Themes

Suggest that students focus on these theme questions as they read:

Geography and History
What role did rivers play in shaping Egypt and Mesopotamia?

Global Interaction
How did trade, warfare, and migration spread ideas and inventions?

Impact of the Individual
How did powerful rulers influence political, military, and religious developments in Egypt and the Fertile Crescent?

Diversity
What contributions to civilization were made by the Phoenicians and Hebrews?

TIME LINE ACTIVITY

You may wish to share the About the Pictures note with your students; then ask these questions about the time line:

1. Which came first: Sumerian city-states or Egypt's Old Kingdom? *(Sumerian city-states)*
2. How do you suppose Egyptians put enormous blocks of stone into place without machinery? *(Students may suggest use of levers, logs as rollers, or draft animals.)*
3. How much time passed between the beginnings of Egypt's Old Kingdom and the Olmec civilization in the Americas? *(1,300 years)*

Don't Miss!

Humanities Link
Egyptian Tomb Art
(Section 2)

Comparing Viewpoints
How Should Society Deal With Lawbreakers?
(Section 4)

First Civilizations: Africa and Asia

3200 B.C.–500 B.C.

Chapter Preview

1 Ancient Kingdoms of the Nile
2 Egyptian Civilization
3 City-States of Ancient Sumer
4 Invaders, Traders, and Empire Builders
5 The Roots of Judaism

3200 B.C.
City-states flourish in Sumer. Sumerians will develop an early form of writing and produce artworks like this statue.

2700 B.C.
Egypt's Old Kingdom begins. Rulers of the Old Kingdom build huge pyramids like these to serve as their tombs.

2300 B.C.
Sargon of Akkad conquers Sumer and builds the world's first known empire.

CHAPTER EVENTS

3500 B.C.   **2900 B.C.**   **2300 B.C.**

GLOBAL EVENTS

2500 B.C.
Cities are built in the Indus Valley of South Asia.

Resource Directory

Teaching Resources
Teaching With Themes Chapter Theme Activities, p. 5
Pacing Chart With Block Scheduling Guide Ch. 2

Technology
World History Color Transparencies Ch. 2 Graphic Organizer, p. F–5

Geography of Ancient Egypt and Mesopotamia

Legend:
- Arable land along the Nile
- Cataracts
- Fertile Crescent

The Nile in northeastern Africa and the Tigris and Euphrates rivers in southwestern Asia provided the fertile farmland needed to support early civilizations.

Map labels: Black Sea, CAUCASUS MTS., Caspian Sea, ASIA MINOR, ARMENIAN PLATEAU, Aegean Sea, TAURUS MTS., MESOPOTAMIA, Euphrates R., Tigris R., ASIA, ZAGROS MTS., Crete, Cyprus, Mediterranean Sea, SYRIA, SYRIAN DESERT, Nile Delta, LOWER EGYPT, Sinai Peninsula, UPPER EGYPT, ARABIAN DESERT, Persian Gulf, AFRICA, Nile R., Red Sea, NUBIA

Azimuthal Equal Area Projection
0   200   400 Miles
0   200   400 Kilometers

Timeline

1790s B.C.
Hammurabi, king of Babylon, issues the world's first written legal code.

1100 B.C.
The Assyrians expand across Mesopotamia. This huge winged bull guards the palace of an Assyrian emperor.

1000 B.C.
The kingdom of Israel is established. Israelite beliefs evolve into a major religion, Judaism. The carving above represents the Jewish menorah, a seven-branched candle holder.

| 2000 B.C. | 1700 B.C. | 1650 B.C. | 1400 B.C. | 1100 B.C. | 750 B.C. | 500 B.C. |

2000 B.C. The East African kingdom of Nubia develops.

1650 B.C. The Shang dynasty of China emerges.

1400 B.C. The Olmecs build the first civilization in the Americas.

750 B.C. Greek city-states such as Athens begin to develop.

Chapter 2 **23**

Geography of Ancient Egypt and Mesopotamia

Activating Prior Knowledge
You know that cultural diffusion was an important part of change among civilizations. How might art and ideas be exchanged between Egypt and Mesopotamia? *(by traders and others traveling overland through Syria and the Sinai or by boat across the Mediterranean)*

Previewing
Why might invaders have little trouble attacking Mesopotamian cities? *(Once the region had been entered, it would be easy to move across the flat plain.)*

Background
About the Pictures

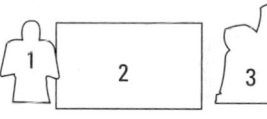

1. This Sumerian statue of a robed man with braided hair and braided beard was carved out of gypsum and covered with bitumen around 3000 B.C.

2. The pyramids of Giza were built between about 2575 B.C. and 2465 B.C.

3. Mythical creatures such as this were meant to keep evil spirits from the palace. It is carved with five legs so that seen from the front it appears to be standing; from the side it seems to be walking.

4. Located in the Museum of Israel in Jerusalem, this artifact depicting a menorah came originally from Ramat Ramel—Citadel of Kings. It dates from the seventh century, B.C.

Independent Assignments

Have students read one section as they prepare for class. After class, have them complete the assignment. Some students may benefit from using the Guided Reading and Review worksheets.

Section 1 Have students use the outline map *Ancient Egypt* in the Historical Outline Map Book, p. 2, to label important geographical features and political borders of ancient Egypt. Have them shade the Egyptian and Hittite empires.

Section 2 Have students complete the worksheet *Finding King Tut's Tomb* in the Unit 1 booklet, p. 29.

Section 3 Have students use the outline map *Ancient Middle East* in the Historical Outline Map Book, p. 3, to label major bodies of water around the ancient Middle East, to shade the Fertile Crescent, to outline Hammurabi's empire, and to label Akkad, Babylon, and Ur.

Section 4 Have students complete the worksheet *People of the Persian Empire View Their Rulers* in the Unit 1 booklet, p. 30.

Section 5 Have students complete the worksheet *Deborah* in the Unit 1 booklet, p. 28.

---

eTeach

Be sure to check out this month's online discussion with a World History Master Teacher.

Go to **www.phschool.com**.

Chapter 2 **23**

Bell Ringer Read aloud the quotation from Herodotus on this page. Then have students use the map in the Chapter Review and Assessment at the end of the chapter to trace the route of the Nile and to examine the surrounding terrain. What generalizations can they make about the importance of the Nile to the people of Egypt? Do they agree or disagree with Herodotus?

LESSON PLAN

1. Focus The benefits of the Nile supported the development of early Egyptian civilization. Interaction between the Egyptians and such peoples as the Hyksos, Hittites, and Nubians had lasting significance. Students will learn about three periods of ancient Egyptian history.

2. Instruct Organize the class into three groups and assign each group one of the kingdoms—Old, Middle, or New. Have the groups use the map in Section 1 and their textbook to create a list of the ways that the Nile influenced the history of each kingdom. Remind students to consider such things as government, agriculture, transportation, economics, and interaction with other peoples.

3. Assess Create a chart on the chalkboard as students discuss their findings about the Nile's influence on each kingdom.

4. Reteach If students' Assess activity does not reflect adequate understanding of the lesson, you might assign the *Guide to the Essentials* or the *Interactive Student Tutorial CD-ROM* for this section.

Reading Focus

- How did geography influence ancient Egypt?
- What were the main features and achievements of Egypt's three kingdoms?
- How did trade and warfare affect Egypt and Nubia?

Vocabulary

silt
cataract
delta
dynasty
pharaoh
vizier

Taking Notes

Copy the chart below. As you read, fill in the characteristics that distinguish each period in ancient Egyptian history.

	OLD KINGDOM	MIDDLE KINGDOM	NEW KINGDOM
GOVERNMENT	Pharaohs organize centralized state		
ACHIEVEMENTS		Land drained for farming	
DECLINE			

Main Idea The history of ancient Egypt is divided into three periods: Old Kingdom, Middle Kingdom, and New Kingdom.

Setting the Scene Every year, as the Nile River flooded its banks, the people of ancient Egypt sang a hymn of praise. They honored the river for nourishing the land and filling their storehouses with food:

"If the Nile smiles, the Earth is joyous
Every stomach is full of rejoicing
Every spine is happy,
Every jawbone crushes its food."
—"Hymn to the Nile," quoted in *The Literature of the Ancient Egyptians* (Erman)

The fertile lands of the Nile Valley attracted Stone Age farmers. People migrated from the Mediterranean area, from hills and deserts along the Nile, and from other parts of Africa. In time, a powerful civilization emerged that depended on the control of river waters.

Geography of the Nile Valley

"Egypt," said the ancient Greek historian Herodotus, "is wholly the gift of the Nile." Without the Nile, Egypt would be swallowed up by the barren deserts that surround it. While the desert protected Egypt from invasion, it also limited where people could settle.

In ancient times, as today, farming villages dotted the narrow band of land watered by the Nile. Beyond the rich, irrigated "Black Land," generally no more than 10 miles wide, lay the "Red Land," a sun-baked desert that stretches across North Africa. Farmers took advantage of the fertile soil of the Nile Valley to grow wheat and flax, a plant whose fibers were used for clothing.

Yearly Floods The Nile rises in the highlands of Ethiopia and the lakes of central Africa. Every spring, rains in this interior region send water racing down streams that feed the Nile River. In ancient times, Egyptians eagerly awaited the annual flood. It soaked the land with life-giving water and deposited a layer of rich silt, or soil.

People had to cooperate to control the Nile floods. They built dikes, reservoirs, and irrigation ditches to channel the rising river and store water for the dry season.

Uniting the Land Ancient Egypt had two distinct regions, Upper Egypt in the south and Lower Egypt in the north. Upper Egypt stretched from the

---

Resource Directory

Teaching Resources
Creative Teaching Activities Creative Teaching Activities booklet, p. 11
Guided Reading and Review Unit 1 booklet, p. 18
Technology
World History Color Transparencies *Ancient Egypt and Mesopotamia*, p. B–71

World History Visions, Voices, Views Daily Life CloseUp, *"Tomb Builders in Egypt,"* videodisc side 1 or videotape 1, running time 3:00 min.

Side 1: Fr. 9100-14590

first cataract, or waterfall, of the Nile northward to within 100 miles of the Mediterranean. Lower Egypt covered the delta region where the Nile empties into the Mediterranean. A delta is a triangular area of marshland formed by deposits of silt at the mouth of some rivers.

About 3100 B.C., Menes, the king of Upper Egypt, united the two regions. He and his successors used the Nile as a highway linking north and south. They could send officials or armies to towns along the river. The Nile thus helped make Egypt the world's first unified state.

The river also served as a trade route. Egyptian merchants traveled up and down the Nile in sailboats and barges, exchanging the products of Africa, the Middle East, and the Mediterranean world.

The Old Kingdom

The history of ancient Egypt is divided into three main periods: the Old Kingdom (about 2700 B.C.–2200 B.C.), the Middle Kingdom (about 2050 B.C.–1800 B.C.), and the New Kingdom (about 1550 B.C.–1100 B.C.). Although power passed from one dynasty, or ruling family, to another, the land generally remained united.

A Strong Government During the Old Kingdom, Egyptian rulers called pharaohs (FAIR ohz) organized a strong, centralized state. Pharaohs claimed divine support for their rule. Egyptians believed the pharaoh was a god. The pharaoh thus had absolute power, owning and ruling all the land in the kingdom.

Pharaohs of the Old Kingdom took pride in preserving justice and order. A pharaoh depended on a vizier, or chief minister, to supervise the business of government. Under the vizier, various departments looked after such matters as tax collection, farming, and the all-important irrigation system. Thousands of scribes carried out the vizier's instructions.

One wise vizier, Ptah-hotep (tah HOH tehp), took an interest in training young officials. Based on his vast experience of government, he wrote a

Farming the Nile Valley
This tomb painting shows the importance of agriculture to ancient Egyptian life. The man guides an ox-drawn plow. Then, the woman plants seeds in the newly turned soil.

Theme: Geography and History What does this painting show about the crops that were grown in the Nile Valley?

 Primary Sources and Literature

See "Instruction of Ptah-hotep" in the Reference Section at the back of this book.

Background
Connections to Today

Controlling the Nile Like their ancient ancestors, modern Egyptians have sought to control the Nile and secure more of its benefits. The Aswan High Dam, completed in 1970 at a cost of about $1 billion, prevents destructive floods and makes more land available for farming. Some lands now yield several crops a year because they can be irrigated year-round. The dam also provides about 25 percent of Egypt's electrical power needs.

Reading Strategy
Predicting Content

Write the section headings on the chalkboard. Ask students to think of at least two questions suggested by each heading and to look for answers to their questions as they read. *(More Advanced Readers)*

Block Scheduling Support

Have students reread the section about the pyramids on the following page. Remind students that the pyramids functioned as tombs for the deceased pharaohs and that these tombs took a great deal of planning and effort to build.

Divide the class into two groups. Have the first group plan the building of the tomb, considering such things as the size and location of the pyramid and the materials and labor needed to build it.

The second group should develop plans for the inside of the tomb, concentrating on issues such as how walls will be decorated and what items will be included in each chamber. Then have the two groups share their plans.

Caption Answer

The painting shows that Egyptians grew fields of grain, such as wheat, as well as fruit trees.

Writing a Letter Ask students to imagine that they are among the Hyksos who occupied Egypt in about 1700 B.C. Have them write a letter telling why they are impressed with Egyptian civilization. (Reteaching)

Customize for . . .
Heterogeneous Groups

Constructing a Time Line Have students construct a time line for important events in ancient Egypt. Tell them to first look in their textbook to identify the dates of key events. Then ask them to determine the span of years the time line should cover, divide the time line into equal parts, and label the beginning of each part with a year. Finally, have them place the events on the time line. Events might include
- Reign of Ramses II begins
- Nubia gains control of Egypt
- Period of pyramid-building begins
- Hyksos occupy the delta region
- Menes unites Upper and Lower Egypt
- Reign of Hatshepsut begins

(Reteaching) ✳

Background Biography

Ramses II Great building projects, as well as successful military campaigns, characterized the reign of Ramses II. His monuments and temples, raised throughout his reign, still exist in Egypt. Some major projects were the temple at Karnak, which was completed during his reign; the Rameseum, his funeral temple at Thebes; and the temple at Luxor. Perhaps the most notable structure was the great rock temple at Abu Simbel in Nubia, with its four seated figures of Ramses on the facade. Refer students to the picture of this temple in the Unit 1 opener of their textbook. All this construction required massive labor and resulted in an increase in slavery. Ramses II was probably the pharaoh in the Bible who dealt with Moses and released the Hebrew slaves.

Skills Assessment

ANSWERS 1. Review locations with students. 2. Crete, northern Syria, Assur 3. Possible answers: government records written on papyrus or monuments; maps or written accounts made by traders; archaeologists' discoveries of artifacts in Egypt or other lands

Egyptian Empire About 1450 B.C.

Egyptian empire
Hittite empire
Egyptian trade routes
Cataracts

Albers Equal Area Projection
0   200   400 Miles
0   200   400 Kilometers

Skills Assessment

Geography During the New Kingdom, Egyptian influence spread throughout the eastern Mediterranean region.

1. **Location** On the map, locate (a) Nile River, (b) Upper Egypt, (c) Lower Egypt, (d) Giza, (e) Hittite empire, (f) Nubia.
2. **Movement** What were the northernmost areas reached by Egyptian traders?
3. **Critical Thinking Applying Information** What sources of information might a mapmaker today use to draw Egyptian trade routes?

book, *Instruction of Ptah-hotep.* In it, he advised his son on how to avoid the errors he had seen in other officials:

> "If you are sitting at the table of one greater than you, take what he may give when it is set before you. Let your face be cast down until he addresses you, and you should speak only when he addresses you."
>
> —*Instruction of Ptah-hotep*

The Pyramids During the Old Kingdom, the Egyptians built the majestic pyramids that still stand at Giza. The pyramids were tombs for eternity. Because Egyptians believed in an afterlife, they preserved the bodies of their dead rulers and provided them with everything they would need in their new lives.

To complete the pyramids, workers hauled and lifted millions of limestone blocks, some weighing two tons or more. The builders had no iron tools or wheeled vehicles. Workers quarried the stones by hand, pulled them on sleds to the site, and hoisted them up earthen ramps. Building a pyramid took so long that often a pharaoh would begin to build his tomb as soon as he inherited the throne.

The pyramids suggest the strength of ancient Egyptian civilization. These costly projects required enormous planning and organization. Thousands of farmers, who had to be fed each day, worked on the pyramids when not planting or harvesting crops.

The Middle Kingdom

Power struggles, crop failures, and the cost of the pyramids contributed to the collapse of the Old Kingdom. After more than a century of disunity, new pharaohs reunited the land, ushering in the Middle Kingdom.

The Middle Kingdom was a turbulent period. The Nile did not rise as regularly as it had. Corruption and rebellions were common. Still, strong rulers did organize a large drainage project, creating vast new stretches of arable, or farmable, land. Egyptian armies occupied part of Nubia, the gold-rich land to the south. Traders also had greater contacts with the peoples of the Middle East and the Mediterranean island of Crete.

Catastrophe struck about 1700 B.C. when foreign invaders, the Hyksos (HIHK sohs), occupied the delta region. They awed the Egyptians with their horse-drawn war chariots. In time, the Egyptians mastered this new military technology. The Hyksos, in turn, were impressed by Egyptian civilization. They soon adopted Egyptian customs, beliefs, and even names. Finally, after more than 100 years, new Egyptian leaders arose. They drove out the Hyksos and set up the New Kingdom.

The New Kingdom

During the New Kingdom, powerful and ambitious pharaohs created a large empire. At its height, the Egyptian empire reached the Euphrates River. This age of conquest brought Egypt into greater contact with southwestern Asia as well as with other parts of Africa.

Resource Directory

Teaching Resources
Primary Source Activity *Finding King Tut's Tomb,* Unit 1 booklet, p. 29
Section Quiz Unit 1 booklet, p. 19

Technology
Interactive Student Tutorial CD-ROM Ch. 2
Chapter Test Bank Ch. 2

Powerful Rulers One monarch of the New Kingdom, Hatshepsut (hat SHEHP soot), was a woman who exercised all the rights of a pharaoh. From 1503 B.C. to 1482 B.C., she encouraged trade with eastern Mediterranean lands and along the Red Sea coast of Africa.

The most powerful pharaoh of the New Kingdom was Ramses II. Between 1290 B.C. and 1224 B.C., Ramses pushed Egyptian rule northward as far as Syria. On temples and monuments, he boasted of his conquests, though his greatest reported victory may not actually have taken place. In a battle against the Hittites of Asia Minor, only the desperate bravery of Ramses himself prevented a crushing defeat. Back home, however, Ramses had inscriptions carved on a monument that made the near defeat sound like a stunning victory.

After years of fighting, the Egyptians and Hittites signed a peace treaty, the first such document known to have survived in history. It declared that Egypt and the Hittites "shall be at peace and in brotherhood forever."

Decline After Ramses II, Egyptian power slowly declined. Invaders, such as the Assyrians and Persians, conquered the Nile region. Later, Greek and Roman armies came from the north. Each new conqueror was eager to add the fertile Nile Valley to a growing empire.

Egypt and Nubia

The Nile kingdom of Nubia (also known as Kush) developed to the south of Egypt. You will read more about Nubian civilization in a later chapter. Here, we will look at the relationship between the two kingdoms.

For centuries, Egyptians traded or fought with their southern neighbor. From Nubia, they acquired ivory, cattle, and slaves. During the New Kingdom, Egypt conquered Nubia. Ramses II used gold from Nubia to pay charioteers in his army. Nubians served in Egyptian armies and left their mark on Egyptian culture. Much Egyptian art of this period shows Nubian soldiers, musicians, or prisoners.

As Egypt declined, Nubia regained its independence. In 750 B.C., Nubian kings marched north, adding Egypt to their own lands. For 100 years, the Nubian empire stretched from what is today Sudan to the Mediterranean.

The Nubians saw themselves not as foreign conquerors but as restorers of Egyptian glory. They ruled Egypt like earlier pharaohs, respecting ancient Egyptian traditions. About 650 B.C., Assyrians, armed with iron weapons, descended on Egypt. They pushed the Nubians back into their original homeland, where Nubian monarchs ruled for 1,000 years more.

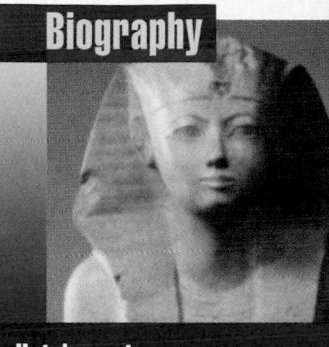

Biography

Hatshepsut
c. 1540 B.C.–1482 B.C.

Hatshepsut was the daughter of one pharaoh and the widow of another. Like some earlier Egyptian queens, she began ruling in the name of a male heir who was too young to take the throne. However, she then took the bold step of declaring herself pharaoh and won the support of key officials. Because Egyptians thought of their rulers as male, she wore a false beard as a sign of authority.

On the walls of her funeral temple, Hatshepsut left behind a record of her 20-year reign. Carvings depict an expedition she sent down the Red Sea coast of Africa, which brought back ivory, spices, and incense.

Theme: Impact of the Individual Why do you think Hatshepsut wanted to leave a record of her accomplishments?

SECTION 1 Assessment

Recall
1. **Identify: (a)** Menes, **(b)** Ptah-hotep, **(c)** Giza, **(d)** Hatshepsut, **(e)** Ramses II.
2. **Define: (a)** silt, **(b)** cataract, **(c)** delta, **(d)** dynasty, **(e)** pharaoh, **(f)** vizier.

Comprehension
3. Give two examples of how the Nile shaped ancient Egypt.
4. Describe one major achievement of each of Egypt's three ancient kingdoms.
5. Explain how Egypt was affected by its contacts with the Nubians.

Critical Thinking and Writing
6. **Drawing Conclusions** How are colossal monuments, such as the pyramids, a source of information about ancient Egypt?
7. **Making Inferences** Why do you think Ramses ordered misleading information about his battles to be inscribed on a public monument?

Activity

Writing Instructions
Write an instruction of your own that the Vizier Ptah-hotep might have written to advise a political leader of today. The topic might be how to work with other people or how to govern fairly.

Human Drama Activity

A Vizier's Autobiography Read students this excerpt from the autobiography of a vizier. Ask them to analyze what the excerpt reveals about Egyptian political values.

"I judged poor and rich alike. I rescued the weak from the strong. I opposed the rage of the angry. . . . I gave bread to the hungry, water to the thirsty, meat and oil and clothes to those who had nothing. . . . I caused both parties to leave my court in peace. . . . I never accepted anyone's bribe. I was . . . deliberate in counsel, ready to listen."

✓ Test Preparation

Have students reread the instructions of the vizier to his son at the top of the opposite page, and then answer the question below.

What does the vizier think is the key to success in government?

A eating with one's superiors

(D) being humble before one's superiors

C being quiet when with one's superiors

D looking sad when with one's superiors

Biography

ANSWER Possible answer: She wanted future generations to know about her accomplishments.

SECTION 2 Egyptian Civilization

Bell Ringer Ask students to describe ancient Egyptian mummies as they appear in fiction and horror films. Then, ask them to find and read information about mummies in the text. Have students discuss the differences between the fictional treatment and the historical treatment.

LESSON PLAN

1. Focus Religious beliefs about gods, values, and life after death affected ancient Egyptian life. The society was divided into a number of unequal classes. Scribes used a system of hieroglyphics to make written records. Other Egyptians made advances in science, mathematics, art, and literature.

2. Instruct Assign students a partner and ask each team to create a profile of someone from ancient Egypt. In addition to rulers such as Tutankhamen, Akhenaton, and Nefertiti, you might assign gods and goddesses such as Osiris, Isis, Amon-Re, and Aton. Other teams might profile a typical peasant, scribe, priest, artisan, doctor, astronomer, or engineer.

3. Assess Have each team share its finished profile with the class. Encourage students to suggest details that could be added to each profile.

4. Reteach If students' Assess activity does not reflect adequate understanding of the lesson, you might assign the *Guide to the Essentials* or the *Interactive Student Tutorial CD-ROM* for this section.

SECTION 2 Egyptian Civilization

Reading Focus

- How did religious beliefs shape the lives of Egyptians?
- How was Egyptian society organized?
- What advances did Egyptians make in learning and the arts?

Vocabulary

mummification
hieroglyphics
ideogram
demotic
papyrus
decipher

Taking Notes

Copy this concept web. As you read the section, fill in each blank circle with important facts to remember about Egyptian civilization. Part of the web has been filled in to help you get started.

Concept web: Society — EGYPTIAN CIVILIZATION — Learning — Hieroglyphics

Main Idea Religion and learning played an important role in ancient Egyptian civilization.

Honoring an Egyptian God
The ancient Egyptians were polytheistic, worshiping many gods and goddesses. In this painting, a musician plays for a falcon-headed god.

Theme: Religions and Value Systems What does this painting suggest about the relationship between the ancient Egyptian people and their gods?

Setting the Scene From an early age, Egyptian children heard stories about their gods and goddesses. A popular tale concerned the goddess Isis (Ī sihs) and the god Osiris (oh sī rihs). Osiris ruled Egypt until he was killed by his jealous brother, Set. The wicked Set then cut Osiris into pieces, which he tossed all over Egypt.

Osiris was saved by his faithful wife, Isis. She reassembled her husband's body and brought him back to life. Because Osiris could no longer rule over the living, he became god of the dead and judge of the souls seeking admission to the afterlife.

The symbol of the divine Isis was the ankh, a cross with a loop above the bar. To Egyptians, an ankh placed on a dead person assured the soul of eternal life. "The blood of Isis," they prayed, "the charms of Isis, the power of Isis are a protection unto me." The Egyptians' belief in eternal life had a profound effect on their civilization.

Egyptian Religion

Egyptians inherited from their earliest ancestors a variety of religious beliefs and practices. Inscriptions on monuments and wall paintings in tombs reveal how Egyptians appealed to the divine forces that they believed ruled this world and the afterlife.

Chief Gods and Goddesses In the sun-drenched land of Egypt, the chief god was the sun god, Amon-Re (AH muhn RAY). The pharaoh, whom Egyptians viewed as a god as well as a monarch, was closely linked to Amon-Re. Only the pharaoh could conduct certain ceremonies for the sun god.

Most Egyptians identified more easily with Osiris and Isis, whose story touched human emotions such as love, jealousy, and fear of death. According to the myth of Osiris and Isis, their son, Horus, later took revenge on the wicked god Set, killing his uncle.

To Egyptians, Osiris was especially important. Not only did he rule over the underworld, but he was also god of the Nile. In that role, he controlled the annual flood that made the land fertile. Isis had special appeal for women, who believed that she had first taught women to grind corn, spin flax, weave cloth, and care for children. Like Osiris, Isis promised the faithful that they would have life after death.

Caption Answer

Possible answers: The musician is kneeling, showing that Egyptians treated their gods with great respect or even fear. Also, the nonhuman head of the god may suggest that Egyptians viewed their gods as distant and mysterious.

Resource Directory

Teaching Resources
Creative Teaching Activities Creative Teaching Activities booklet, p. 12
Guided Reading and Review Unit 1 booklet, p. 20
History Through Literature *Poems of Ancient Egypt*, History Through Literature booklet, pp. 5–6

A Religious Rebel

About 1380 B.C., a young pharaoh challenged the powerful priests of Amon-Re. He devoted his life to the worship of Aton, a minor god whose symbol was the sun's disk. The pharaoh took the name Akhenaton (ah kuh NAH tuhn), meaning "he who serves Aton." With the support of his wife, Queen Nefertiti, Akhenaton tried to sweep away all other gods in favor of Aton. He ordered priests to stop worshiping other gods and to remove the names of these gods from their temples.

Scholars disagree about Akhenaton's goals. Some think the pharaoh was trying to introduce a new religion based on worship of a single god. Others argue that he just wanted to raise Aton to the highest place among the gods.

Akhenaton's radical ideas had little success. Priests of Amon-Re and of other gods resisted the revolutionary changes. The common people, too, were afraid to abandon their old gods in favor of Aton. Nobles also deserted the pharaoh because he neglected his duty of defending the empire. After Akhenaton's death, the priests of the old gods reasserted their power.

Belief in an Afterlife

As you read, Egyptians believed that Osiris and Isis had promised them eternal life after death. Belief in the afterlife affected all Egyptians, from the highest noble to the lowest peasant.

A Fateful Test The Egyptians believed that each soul had to pass a test in order to win eternal life. According to Egyptian belief, the dead soul would be ferried across a lake of fire to the hall of Osiris. There, Osiris would weigh the dead person's heart against the feather of truth. Those he judged to be sinners would be fed to the crocodile-shaped Eater of the Dead. Worthy souls would enter the Happy Field of Food, where they would live forever in bliss.

To survive the dangerous journey through the underworld, Egyptians relied on the Book of the Dead. It contained spells, charms, and formulas for the dead to use in the afterlife. The Book of the Dead includes a Negative Confession, which the dead soul could use to prove his or her worthiness to Osiris:

> "I have made no man to suffer hunger. I have made no one to weep. I have done no murder. . . . I have not encroached upon the fields of another. I have not added to the weights of the scales to cheat the seller. . . . I have not turned back water when it should flow. . . . I am pure. I am pure. I am pure."
> —Book of the Dead

The Book of the Dead was written on scrolls and placed in tombs. Today, these scrolls have given modern scholars a wealth of information about Egyptian beliefs and practices.

Mummification Egyptians believed that the afterlife would be much like life on Earth. As a result, they buried the dead with everything they would need for eternity.

To give a soul use of its body in the afterlife, Egyptians perfected skills in mummification (muhm mih fih KAY shuhn), the preservation of the dead. Skilled embalmers extracted the brain of the dead person through the nostrils and removed most of the internal organs. They filled the body cavity with spices, then later dried and wrapped the body in strips of linen. This costly process took months to complete. At first, mummification was a privilege reserved for rulers and nobles. Eventually, ordinary Egyptians also won the right to mummify their dead.

Did You Know?

Mummified Cats

When archaeologists unearthed a cemetery in Bubastis, Egypt, they found something unexpected—thousands of cat mummies! Why did the Egyptians mummify these animals? Archaeologists have discovered that Bubastis was a center for the worship of Bastet, a cat goddess. Some Egyptians prayed to Bastet for protection against diseases and demons. To honor her, worshipers made gifts of cat mummies to her shrines. Many of these mummies were topped with tiny death masks in the shape of a cat's face.

Theme: Continuity and Change Can you think of interesting beliefs that some people have about cats today?

Humanities Link

Bell Ringer Ask students to imagine they have spent ten years in search of an Egyptian tomb, and the patron will fund no further searches. Finally, they remove a large pile of rubble and find a tomb's unopened doors. Inside are thousands of golden objects. How do they feel? Explain that this is what happened to Howard Carter in 1922.

Background
Connections to Today

Hand-Crafted Coffins Though not so lavish as the coffins of King Tut, unique hand-crafted coffins are available today. A Tasmanian company offers coffins shaped like a mermaid on the sea and another replicating a luxury touring car.

In Ghana, Paa Joe's elaborate coffins include a 747 jet, a truck, a cow, a tiger, an eagle, a fish, and a chili pepper.

Activity
Cooperative Learning

Have small groups plan and design the objects they would place in the tomb of someone from the past whom they admire. The objects should have some significance to the life of the person. Some students may draw or make the objects. Others may write a brief description of the person and an explanation of the objects.

Portfolio Assessment Rubrics

Share rubrics with students before they create their exhibits.

Attempted Student's exhibit has fewer than five examples or descriptions.

Minimal Student's exhibit has the required number of examples and descriptions, but descriptions are poorly written, uninformative, or uninteresting.

Adequate Student's exhibit has the required number of examples, and the descriptions are well written, informative, and interesting.

Exemplary Student's exhibit has more than the five required examples, with well-written, informative, and interesting descriptions; or the required five examples are exceptional.

EGYPTIAN TOMB ART

Holding a candle, archaeologist Howard Carter allowed a ray of light to penetrate the blackness of Tutankhamen's tomb. When his eyes adjusted to the gloom, Carter was astonished by what he saw—exquisite artifacts, gold, and jewels. He knew he had found some of the finest examples of Egyptian art ever uncovered.

This coffin (left) held the dead man's vital organs. The realistic features of the face and the intricate inlays of precious stones show that the gold-smiths were masters of their craft.

In the wall painting below, Anubis—the jackal-headed god of the dead—prepares the body of the pharaoh for the afterlife.

Alabaster was delicately carved into a cup representing lotus flowers (below). To the Egyptians, the lotus symbolized immortality because the blossoms filled the Nile year after year.

Reflecting the artistic style developed in the New Kingdom, this small container (right) shows Tutankhamen looking more like a man than a god. He is shown in a natural sitting position.

Portfolio Assessment

Use the Internet or library resources to find other examples of Egyptian art. Create your own exhibit of five or more artifacts. Write a caption to describe each object, explaining why you included it in the exhibit.

Resource Directory

Teaching Resources

Skill Application Activity *Interpreting a Thematic Map,* Unit 1 booklet, p. 31
Humanities Link Chapter Extension Activities booklet, p. 9

Technology

World History Color Transparencies *Ipuy and His Wife Receiving Offerings From Their Children,* p. D–35

Evidence of the Tomb of Tutankhamen Many pharaohs were buried in the desolate Valley of the Kings. Their tombs, filled with fantastic riches, were a temptation to robbers in ancient times. As a result, most royal tombs were stripped of their treasures long ago. Then, in 1922, the British archaeologist Howard Carter unearthed the tomb of the pharaoh Tutankhamen (too tahng KAH muhn), the son-in-law of Akhenaton. It had remained almost untouched for more than 3,000 years. The tomb and its treasures have provided a wealth of evidence about Egyptian civilization.

The body of the 18-year-old "King Tut" had been placed in a solid-gold coffin, nested within richly decorated outer coffins. Today, the dazzling array of objects found in the tomb fills several rooms in the Egyptian Museum in Cairo. They include chariots, weapons, furniture, jewelry, toys, games, and food.

Tutankhamen was only a minor king. We can only imagine what treasures must have filled the tombs of great pharaohs like Ramses II.

Egyptian Society

Like other early civilizations, Egypt had its own class system. As both a god and an earthly leader, the pharaoh stood at the top of society, along with the royal family. Directly under the pharaoh were the high priests and priestesses, who served the gods and goddesses. Next came the nobles, who fought the pharaoh's wars. A tiny class of merchants, scribes, and artisans developed slowly. They provided for the needs of the rich and powerful.

The Life of the Farmer Most Egyptians were peasant farmers. Many were slaves. Men and women spent their days working the soil and repairing the dikes. One ancient record describes the life of a typical Egyptian peasant. "When the water is full he irrigates [the fields] and repairs his equipment. He spends the day cutting tools for cultivating barley, and the night twisting ropes."

In the off-season, peasant men were expected to serve the pharaoh, laboring to build palaces, temples, and tombs. Besides working in the fields, women also spent much time raising children, collecting water, and preparing food—tasks similar to those of peasant women today.

Social Change During the New Kingdom, society grew more fluid as trade and warfare increased. Trade offered new opportunities to the growing merchant class. Foreign conquests brought riches to Egypt, which in turn meant more business for artisans. These skilled craftworkers made fine jewelry, furniture, and fabrics for the palaces and tombs of pharaohs and nobles.

Women Egyptian women generally enjoyed a higher status and greater independence than women elsewhere in the ancient world. Ramses II declared, "The foot of an Egyptian woman may walk where it pleases her and no one may deny her." Under Egyptian law, women could inherit property, enter business deals, buy and sell goods, go to court, and obtain a divorce.

Although there were often clear distinctions between the occupations of women and men, women's work was not confined to the home. They manufactured perfume and textiles, managed farming estates, and served as doctors. Women could also enter the priesthood, especially in the service of goddesses. Despite their many rights and opportunities, few women learned to read and write. Even if they did, they were excluded from becoming scribes or holding other government jobs.

Egyptian Learning

Learned scribes played a central role in Egyptian society. Temple scribes kept records of ceremonies, taxes, and gifts. Other scribes served nobles or the pharaoh. With skill and luck, a scribe from a poor family might become rich

Background
Daily Life

Toys and Games Like people today, the ancient Egyptians enjoyed a variety of toys and games. Children liked to play with marbles, bouncing balls, and spinning tops. Adults favored board and dice games. Dice similar to those of today have been found in many Egyptian tombs, not just in Tutankhamen's. Egyptians also enjoyed games of chance. In a game called *atep*, players wagered on the number of fingers a person secretly held up.

 Human Drama Note

A Surprising Discovery When Carter first entered Tutankhamen's tomb, he was not exactly sure what he had uncovered. Carter later recorded those early moments:

"Our sensations were bewildering and full of strange emotion. . . . Was it a tomb or merely a cache? A sealed doorway between the two sentinel statues proved there was more beyond, and with the numerous cartouches bearing the name of Tutankhamen . . . there was little doubt that there behind was the grave of that Pharaoh."

✓ **Test Preparation**

Have students read the first paragraph under the heading "The Life of the Farmer" on this page, and then answer the question below.

The author of the passage gives you reason to believe that

A only men worked in the fields.

B Egyptian peasants were hardworking people.

C Egyptian peasants ate many different kinds of grains.

D when the floods came, peasants had nothing to do.

and powerful. Besides learning to read and write, scribes also acquired skills in mathematics, medicine, and engineering.

Written Records Like other early civilizations, the ancient Egyptians developed a form of picture writing. Hieroglyphics (hi er oh GLIHF ihks) were used to keep important records. Early on, priests and scribes carved hieroglyphics on stone. Inscriptions on temples and other monuments preserved records of Egyptian culture that have endured for thousands of years.

The earliest hieroglyphics were pictograms that depicted objects. Later, written language became more complex. The Egyptians added ideograms, pictures that symbolized an idea or action. For example, a picture of a reclining figure meant sleep.

Over time, scribes developed demotic, a simpler form of writing for everyday use. They also learned to make a paperlike writing material from papyrus (puh PĪ ruhs), a plant that grows along the banks of the Nile. (Paper would not be invented until about A.D. 100, in China.) Writing with reed pens and ink on the smooth surface of papyrus strips was much easier than chiseling words onto stone. When writing official histories, however, scribes continued to carve hieroglyphics.

The Rosetta Stone After the New Kingdom declined, Egyptians forgot the meanings of ancient hieroglyphics. Not until the early 1800s did a French scholar, Jean Champollion (ZHAHN shahm poh LYOHN), unravel the mysterious writings on Egypt's great monuments.

Champollion managed to decipher, or decode, the Rosetta Stone. This flat, black stone has the same message carved in three different forms of script—hieroglyphics, demotic, and Greek. By comparing the three versions, Champollion patiently worked out the meanings of many hieroglyphic symbols. As a result of that breakthrough, scholars could begin to read the thousands of surviving records from ancient Egypt.

Advances in Medicine and Science The ancient Egyptians accumulated a vast store of knowledge in fields such as medicine, astronomy, and mathematics. They were a practical people. When they had a problem, they used trial and error to find a solution.

Like most doctors until recent times, Egyptian physicians believed in various kinds of magic. Yet, through their knowledge of mummification, they learned a lot about the human body. They also became skilled at observing symptoms, diagnosing illnesses, and finding cures. Doctors performed complex surgical operations, which they described on papyrus scrolls. Many medicines that Egyptian doctors prescribed are still used, including anise, castor beans, and saffron.

Egyptian priest-astronomers studied the heavens, mapping constellations and charting the movements of the planets. With this knowledge, they developed a calendar that had 12 months of 30 days each and 5 days added at the end of each year. With a few changes, this ancient Egyptian calendar became the basis for our modern calendar.

Nile floods forced Egyptians to redraw the boundaries of fields each year. To do this, they developed practical geometry to survey the land. Egyptian engineers also used geometry to calculate the exact size and location of each block of stone to be placed in a pyramid or temple. Huge building projects such as pyramids and irrigation systems required considerable skills in design and engineering.

Arts and Literature

The Egyptians left a rich legacy of art and literature. Statues, paintings, poems, and tales have given us a wealth of information about ancient Egyptian attitudes and values.

Portrait of Queen Nefertiti
Most early Egyptian art focused on scenes of death and the afterlife. During the New Kingdom, many artists turned to likenesses of living people. This famous statue presents Nefertiti, wife of the pharaoh Akhenaton, as the image of perfect beauty.

Theme: Art and Literature
How did the artist use exaggeration to emphasize the beauty of Nefertiti?

Painting and Sculpture The arts of ancient Egypt included statues, wall paintings in tombs, and carvings on temples. Some show everyday scenes of trade, farming, family life, or religious ceremonies. Others boast of victories in battles.

Painting styles remained almost unchanged for thousands of years. The pharaohs and gods were always much larger than any other human figures. Artists usually drew people with their heads and limbs in profile but their eyes and shoulders facing the viewer.

Statues often depicted people in stiff, standard poses. Some human figures have animal heads that represent special qualities. The Great Sphinx that crouches near the pyramids at Giza portrays an early pharaoh as a powerful lion.

Besides the pyramids, Egyptians erected other great buildings. The magnificent temple of Ramses II at Karnak contains a vast hall with towering 80-foot columns. Much later, the Romans would adopt building techniques like those used at Karnak.

Egyptian Literature The oldest literature of ancient Egypt includes hymns and prayers to the gods, proverbs, and love poems. Other writings tell of royal victories in battle or, like *Instruction of Ptah-hotep*, give practical advice.

In Egypt, as in other early societies, folk tales were popular, especially *The Tale of Sinuhe*. It relates the wanderings of Sinuhe (sihn oo HAY), an Egyptian official forced to flee into what is now Syria. He fights his way to fame among the desert people, whom the Egyptians consider uncivilized. As he gets older, Sinuhe longs to return home. The story ends happily when the pharaoh welcomes him back to court. (See the Primary Source, right.) *The Tale of Sinuhe* helps us see how Egyptians viewed both themselves and the people of the surrounding desert.

Looking Ahead

Long after its power declined, Egypt remained a center of learning and culture in the African and Mediterranean worlds. It also retained economic importance as a source of grain and other riches.

In later ages, new Egyptian cities like Alexandria and Cairo would attract scholars, traders, and other visitors. Yet, from ancient times to today, foreigners have gazed in awe at the monuments of a culture that flourished for 3,000 years.

SECTION 2 Assessment

Recall
1. **Identify:** (a) Osiris, (b) Isis, (c) Amon-Re, (d) Akhenaton, (e) Tutankhamen, (f) Jean Champollion, (g) Rosetta Stone, (h) *The Tale of Sinuhe.*
2. **Define:** (a) mummification, (b) hieroglyphics, (c) ideogram, (d) demotic, (e) papyrus, (f) decipher.

Comprehension
3. (a) Which gods and goddesses were especially important to the ancient Egyptians? (b) What role did they play in Egyptian life?
4. (a) What social classes existed in ancient Egypt? (b) What rights did women have?
5. Describe three achievements of ancient Egyptians in the arts or learning.

Critical Thinking and Writing
6. **Synthesizing Information** How were religion, government, and the arts linked in ancient Egypt?
7. **Connecting to Geography** Describe two ways that Egyptian inventions or scientific advances were linked to geography.

Activity
Take It to the NET

Use the Internet to research the Rosetta Stone. Then, write a headline and a brief news account about the decoding of the Rosetta Stone. Include quotations from historians or archaeologists explaining why this discovery is so valuable.

Primary Source

An Egyptian Folk Tale
As Sinuhe concludes his story, he describes how he sheds the life of a nomad to live his remaining years in comfort in Egypt:

"His majesty said: 'Behold, thou art come. Thou hast trodden the foreign countries and made a flight. [But now] elderliness has attacked thee; thou hast reached old age. . . . Do not [live in exile] any longer.' . . . I answered it with the answer of one afraid: 'What is it that my lord says to me? . . . Behold, I am before thee. . . . May thy majesty do as he pleases. . . .'

I was put into the house of a royal son, in which were splendid things. . . . Years were made to pass away from my body. I was shaved, my hair was combed. . . . And I was dressed in the finest linen and anointed with the best oil. I slept on a bed, and gave up the sand to them who live [in the desert]."

—*The Tale of Sinuhe*

Skills Assessment

Primary Source What did the pharaoh propose to Sinuhe, and what was Sinuhe's response?

SECTION 2 Assessment

Recall
1. (a) Osiris, p. 28 (b) Isis, p. 28 (c) Amon-Re, p. 28 (d) Akhenaton, p. 29 (e) Tutankhamen, p. 31 (f) Jean Champollion, p. 32 (g) Rosetta Stone, p. 32 (h) *The Tale of Sinuhe,* p. 33 2. (a) mummification, p. 29 (b) hieroglyphics, p. 32 (c) ideogram, p. 32 (d) demotic, p. 32 (e) papyrus, p. 32 (f) decipher, p. 32

Comprehension
3. (a) Amon-Re, Osiris, Isis (b) Amon-Re was the sun god. Osiris was god of the Nile and the underworld. Isis taught women many important skills.
4. (a) Pharaohs, the highest class, were followed by priests and nobles; then merchants, scribes, and artisans; peasant farmers; and slaves. (b) Women could inherit property, engage in business, go to court, and obtain divorces. 5. Possible answer: They developed medical procedures, devised calendars, and built monuments.

Critical Thinking and Writing
6. Possible answer: The pharaoh was considered a god. Art works honored the pharaohs and the gods. 7. Possible answers: They used the papyrus from along the Nile to make a paperlike writing surface; they developed geometry to redraw boundaries after Nile floods.

Activity Rubrics

Share rubrics with students before they write their news story.

Attempted The account omits an element, such as a headline or quotation.

Minimal The account includes all elements, but is poorly organized or written.

Adequate The account includes all elements and is well organized and well written.

Exemplary The account includes all elements, is well organized and dramatically written, and the quotations chosen are especially apt or dramatic.

Primary Source

ANSWERS The pharaoh proposed that Sinuhe return from exile. Sinuhe humbly agreed.

Bell Ringer

Have students look at the map on the opposite page and tell them that the Fertile Crescent has been called the "crossroads of the world." Ask them to describe the geographic factors that might have given rise to this name.

LESSON PLAN

1. Focus The Tigris and Euphrates rivers supported the development of Sumerian civilization. In this section, students will focus on political, religious, and social life in Sumer. They will learn of many Sumerian accomplishments, especially those in writing and mathematics.

2. Instruct Draw on the chalkboard a chart with two columns and six rows. Label the columns Sumer and Egypt. Label the rows Geography, Religion, Economy, Government, Social Structure, and Achievements. Have students complete the charts by working individually or in groups. They should refer to Sections 1, 2, and 3 of this chapter.

3. Assess After students have finished their charts, lead the class in discussing the similarities and differences between Sumer and Egypt.

4. Reteach If students' **Assess** activity does not reflect adequate understanding of the lesson, you might assign the *Guide to the Essentials* or the *Interactive Student Tutorial CD-ROM* for this section.

Reading Focus

- How did geographic features influence the civilizations of the Fertile Crescent?
- What were the main features of Sumerian civilization?
- What advances in learning did Sumerians make?

Vocabulary

hierarchy

ziggurat

cuneiform

Taking Notes

As you read, prepare an outline of this section. Use Roman numerals to indicate the major headings of the section, capital letters for the subheadings, and numbers for the supporting details. The sample at right will help you get started.

I. Geography: The Fertile Crescent
A. The land between the rivers
  1.
  2.
B. Floods and irrigation
  1.
  2.
  3.

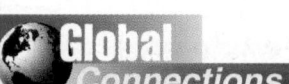 **Main Idea** The fertile land between the Tigris and Euphrates rivers supported the development of Sumerian civilization.

Setting the Scene "Why do you idle about? Go to school and recite your assignment. . . . After you have finished, come to me. Do not wander about in the street. Now, do you know what I said?" Almost 4,000 years ago, a father wrote those words to his son, who was studying to become a scribe. He then made his son copy the instructions so he would not forget them.

The father and son lived in Sumer, a region located between the Tigris and Euphrates rivers. The cities of Sumer lay to the northeast of the Nile in what we today call the Middle East. As builders of the earliest known civilization, the Sumerians made a lasting contribution to the world.

Geography of the Fertile Crescent

If you look at the map on the next page, you will notice an arc of land that curves from the Persian Gulf to the eastern Mediterranean coast. The dark, rich soils and golden wheat fields earned it the name Fertile Crescent.

Nomadic herders, ambitious invaders, and traders easily overcame the few natural barriers across the Fertile Crescent. As a result, the region became a crossroads where people and ideas met and mingled. Each new group that arrived made its own contributions to the turbulent history of the region.

The Land Between the Rivers The first known civilization in the Fertile Crescent was uncovered in the 1800s in Mesopotamia. The Tigris and Euphrates rivers define Mesopotamia, which means "between the rivers" in Greek. The two rivers flow from the highlands of modern-day Turkey through Iraq into the Persian Gulf.

In Sumer, as in Egypt, the fertile land of a river valley attracted Stone Age farmers from neighboring regions. In time, their descendants produced the surplus food needed to support growing populations.

Floods and Irrigation Just as control of the Nile was vital to Egypt, control of the Tigris and Euphrates was key to developments in Mesopotamia. The rivers frequently rose in terrifying floods that washed away topsoil and destroyed mud-brick villages. One story in the long Sumerian narrative poem *The Epic of Gilgamesh,* tells of a great flood that destroys the world. Archaeologists have indeed found evidence that a catastrophic flood devastated the Fertile Crescent some 4,900 years ago.

To survive and protect their farmland, villages along the riverbanks had to work together. Even during the dry season, the rivers had to be controlled

Global Connections

Flood Stories Around the World

The flood story in *The Epic of Gilgamesh* begins when the gods decide to destroy the world and its wickedness. They instruct Utnapishtim to build a boat to save his family and every species of animal. He sends out birds from his boat to search for dry land.

Stories involving floods that destroy the world can also be found in other cultures. In a tale from East Africa, a curious daughter-in-law ignores a warning not to touch a magical water pot. It breaks and a huge flood drowns everyone. In ancient China, Tse-gu-dzih sends a flood to destroy wicked humankind. Only the favored Du-mu, his family, and a few animals are saved in a hollowed-out log.

Theme: Religions and Value Systems What common theme exists in the flood stories of ancient China and Sumer?

Global Connections

ANSWER In both stories the gods send floods to destroy wicked humankind while preserving a good family and animals.

Resource Directory

Teaching Resources
Creative Teaching Activities Creative Teaching Activities booklet, p. 13
Guided Reading and Review Unit 1 booklet, p. 22

Technology
World History Color Transparencies *Ancient Egypt and Mesopotamia*, p. B–71
Listening to Literature World Masterpieces audiotapes Sumerian, Egyptian, and Hebrew Music, side 1, running time 3:08 min.

World History Visions, Voices, Views Animated Map Story, *Mesopotamia: The Land Between the Rivers (3000 B.C.–500 B.C.),* videodisc side 1 or videotape 1, running time 2:45 min.

Side 1: Fr. 14596-18425

to channel water to the fields. Temple priests or royal officials provided the leadership that was necessary to ensure cooperation. They organized villagers to build dikes to hold back flood waters and irrigation ditches to carry water to their fields.

The First Cities   Around 3200 B.C., the first Sumerian cities emerged in the southern part of Mesopotamia. The Sumerians had few natural resources, but they made the most of what they had. They lacked building materials, such as timber or stone, so they built with earth and water. They made bricks of clay, shaped in wooden molds and dried in the sun. These bricks were the building blocks for great cities like Ur and Erech.

Trade brought riches to Sumerian cities. Traders sailed along the rivers or risked the dangers of desert travel to carry goods to distant regions. (Although the wheel had been invented by some earlier unknown people, the Sumerians made the first wheeled vehicles.) Archaeologists have found goods from as far away as Egypt and India in the rubble of Sumerian cities.

Sumerian Civilization

Rival Sumerian city-states often battled for control of land and water. For protection, people turned to courageous and resourceful war leaders. Over time, these war leaders evolved into hereditary rulers.

Government and Society   In each city-state, the ruler was responsible for maintaining the city walls and the irrigation systems. He led its armies in war and enforced the laws. As government grew more complex, he employed scribes to carry out functions such as collecting taxes and keeping records. The ruler was seen as the chief servant of the gods and led ceremonies designed to please them.

Each Sumerian city-state had a distinct social hierarchy (HĪ uh rahr kee), or system of ranks. The highest class included the ruling family, leading officials, and high priests. A small middle class was made up of lesser priests and scribes. The middle class also included merchants and artisans. Artisans who practiced the same trade, such as weavers or carpenters, lived and worked in the same street.

At the base of society were the majority of people, peasant farmers. Some had their own land, but most worked land belonging to the king or temples. Sumerians also owned slaves. Most slaves had been captured in war. Some, though, had sold themselves into slavery to pay their debts.

The role of women in Sumerian society changed over time. In the earliest Sumerian myths, a mother-goddess reflected the honored role of mothers in farming communities. As large city-states emerged with warrior-leaders at their heads, male gods replaced the mother-goddess. Still, in the early city-states, wives of rulers enjoyed special powers and duties. Some supervised palace workshops and ruled for the king when he was absent. Over time, as men gained more power and wealth, women became more dependent on men. Yet women continued to have legal rights. Well-to-do women engaged in trade and owned property.

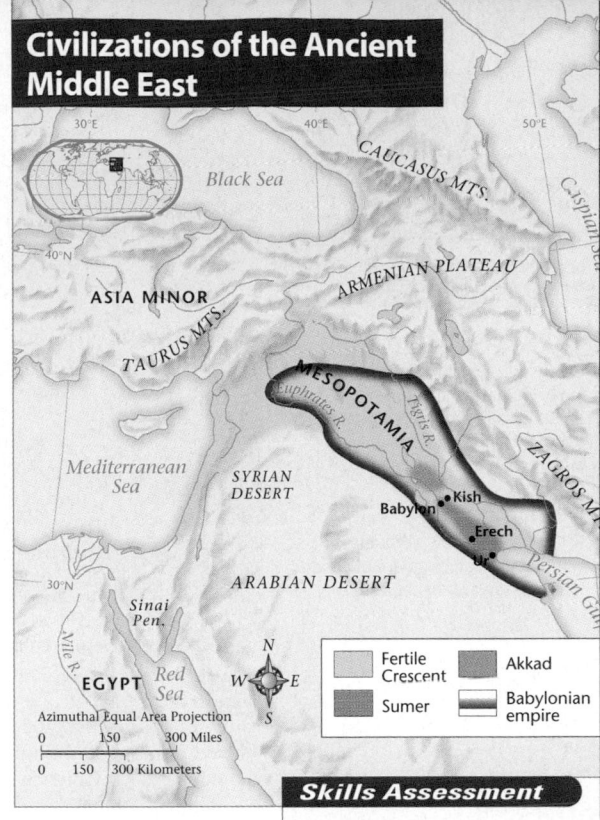

Civilizations of the Ancient Middle East

Fertile Crescent
Sumer
Akkad
Babylonian empire

Azimuthal Equal Area Projection

0   150   300 Miles
0   150   300 Kilometers

Skills Assessment

Geography   A series of early civilizations rose in the land between the Tigris and Euphrates rivers.

1. **Location**   On the map, locate **(a)** Tigris River, **(b)** Euphrates River, **(c)** Fertile Crescent, **(d)** Sumer, **(e)** Akkad, **(f)** Babylonian empire.
2. **Place**   What features may have limited the expansion of these early civilizations?
3. **Critical Thinking Comparing**   Review the map of the Egyptian empire in Section 1. Compare the location, physical features, and extent of the Egyptian and Babylonian empires.

Background
Connections to Today

Geographic Prize   The region of the Tigris and Euphrates rivers continues to play a critical role in contemporary life. During the 1980s, Iran and Iraq fought a war over control of the Shatt al Arab, the tidal river formed by the confluence of the two rivers. The Shatt al Arab extends some 120 miles along the Iran-Iraq border to the Persian Gulf. As a result of a 1975 agreement, Iran and Iraq shared navigation rights on the Shatt al Arab. However, when Iran's government fell into disarray in 1980, Iraq seized control of the valuable waterway. This action provoked a war that lasted until 1988 and cost the lives of an estimated one million people. The war ended with a cease-fire. Both countries withdrew their troops, and Iraq agreed to abide by the terms of the 1975 treaty it had signed with Iran.

Background
Historical Evidence

Destroying the Evidence   In addition to destroying lives, modern wars in the Middle East also destroy historical evidence. As a result of wars in Iraq, four bomb craters are now part of the Sumerian city of Ur, and trenches dug by soldiers have made it all but impossible to decipher an unexcavated site at Tell al-Lahm.

Block Scheduling Support

Have students read the excerpt from the *Epic of Gilgamesh* in the Reference Section in the back of this book. As they read, ask them to take notes on the kinds of information the story reveals about ancient civilizations. After they have read the selection and taken notes, discuss the story, reinforcing their ideas about how the story reveals useful insights on ancient peoples' lives and beliefs.

Skills Assessment

ANSWERS 1. Review locations with students. **2.** mountains and deserts **3.** The Egyptian empire was located west of the Red Sea and along the eastern Mediterranean coast. The Babylonian empire was east of the Red Sea; its only access to water was by way of the Persian Gulf. Both empires were centered on rivers. The Egyptian empire was bigger.

Virtual Field Trip
www.phschool.com

Ziggurat of Ur-Namma Haifa, Israel

To see other detailed views of this ziggurat, use the Internet address above to link to the University of Haifa.

A Sumerian Ziggurat
Using sun-baked bricks, workers in the Sumerian city-state of Ur built this ziggurat around 2100 B.C. Its wide steps were designed to allow the gods to descend from heaven to earth.

Theme: Religions and Value Systems What later religious structures were also built to reach toward the heavens?

▶ **Primary Sources and Literature**

See "The Epic of Gilgamesh" in the Reference Section at the back of this book.

Sumerian Religion Like most ancient peoples, the Sumerians were polytheistic, worshiping many gods. These gods were thought to control every aspect of life, especially the forces of nature. Sumerians believed that gods and goddesses behaved like ordinary people. They ate, drank, married, and raised families. Although the gods favored truth and justice, they were also responsible for violence and suffering.

To Sumerians, their highest duty was to keep these divine beings happy and thereby ensure the safety of their city-state. Each city built a ziggurat (ZIHG uh rat), a pyramid-temple that soared toward the heavens. At its top stood a shrine to the chief god or goddess of that city. To win the favor of the gods, the people prayed and offered sacrifices of animals, grain, and wine. They also celebrated holy days with ceremonies and processions. In one ritual, the king went through a symbolic wedding to Inanna, the life-giving goddess of love. This rite was meant to ensure a prosperous new year.

Like the Egyptians, the Sumerians believed in an afterlife. However, they saw the underworld as a grim place from which there was no release. One character in *The Epic of Gilgamesh* describes the underworld as

"the place where they live on dust, their food is mud,
. . . and they see no light, living in blackness
on the door and door-bolt, deeply settled dust."
—*The Epic of Gilgamesh*

This view of the afterlife contrasts with the Egyptian vision of the Happy Field of Food. Differences in geography may explain this contrast. The floods of the Tigris and Euphrates were less regular and more destructive than those of the Nile. As a result, Sumerians may have developed a pessimistic view of the world.

Advances in Learning

By 3200 B.C., the Sumerians had invented what may be the earliest known form of writing. This type of writing was later called cuneiform (kyoo NEE uh form), from the Latin word *cuneus* for "wedge," because it involved using a reed pen to make wedge-shaped marks on clay tablets.

Cuneiform grew out of a system of pictographs that priests used to record goods brought to temple storehouses. Later, priests developed symbols to represent more complicated thoughts. As their writing evolved, the Sumerians were able to use it to record not only grain harvests but also myths, prayers, laws, treaties, and business contracts.

Sumerian scribes had to go through years of difficult schooling to acquire their skills. Discipline was strict. Untidy copying or talking in class could be punished by "caning." Gifted students went on to gain a wide range of knowledge about religion, medicine, mathematics, geography, astronomy, and literature.

Over the centuries, Sumerian scholars made advances in mathematics. To measure and solve problems of calculation, they developed basic algebra and geometry. They based their number system on six, dividing the hour into 60 minutes and the circle into 360 degrees, as we still do today. Priests studied the skies, recording the movement of heavenly bodies. This knowledge enabled them to make accurate calendars, which are so essential to a farming society.

Looking Ahead

Armies of conquering peoples swept across Mesopotamia and overwhelmed the Sumerian city-states. Often the newcomers settled in the region and adopted ideas from the Sumerians. The myths and gods of these people became mingled with those of Sumer. Later peoples also elaborated on Sumerian literature, including *The Epic of Gilgamesh*.

The newcomers adapted cuneiform to their own languages and helped spread Sumerian learning across the Middle East. Building on Sumerian knowledge of the constellations and planets, later Mesopotamian astronomers developed ways to predict eclipses of the sun and moon.

By means of the various peoples who conquered the Middle East, Sumerian knowledge passed on to the Greeks and Romans. They, in turn, had a powerful impact on the development of the western world.

CUNEIFORM WRITING

Meaning	Outline character about 3000 B.C.	Sumerian about 2000 B.C.	Babylonian about 500 B.C.
Sun			
God or heaven			
Mountain			
Ox			
Fish			

Skills Assessment

Chart Cuneiform Writing Sumerian writing developed gradually from simple outline pictures to the wedged symbols of cuneiform. Later, Mesopotamian people adapted cuneiform. **Based on this chart, make a generalization about how cuneiform changed between 2000 B.C. and 500 B.C.**

SECTION 3 Assessment

Recall
1. **Identify: (a)** Fertile Crescent, **(b)** *The Epic of Gilgamesh*.
2. **Define: (a)** hierarchy, **(b)** ziggurat, **(c)** cuneiform.

Comprehension
3. How did geography influence the city-states of Sumer?
4. How was Sumerian society organized?
5. Describe how two Sumerian accomplishments influenced later peoples.

Critical Thinking and Writing
6. **Comparing** Compare the duties of Sumerian rulers to those of rulers of countries today. How are they similar? How are they different?
7. **Analyzing Information (a)** What are some of the benefits and drawbacks of keeping records in cuneiform on clay tablets? **(b)** What later inventions made it easier to preserve and pass on information?

Activity

Creating Symbols
Review the cuneiform chart in this section. Then, create cuneiform symbols for three objects or concepts that are important in your own life.

Chapter 2 **37**

SECTION 3 Assessment

Recall
1. **(a)** Fertile Crescent, p. 34 **(b)** *The Epic of Gilgamesh*, p. 34 **2. (a)** hierarchy, p. 35 **(b)** ziggurat, p. 36 **(c)** cuneiform, p. 36

Comprehension
3. Fertile land attracted farmers to the area. The need to cooperate for irrigation and flood control led people to form city-states with strong governments. **4.** Each city-state had a distinct hierarchy with the ruling family, leading officials, and high priests at the top; lesser priests, scribes, merchants, and artisans in the middle; and peasant farmers and slaves at the bottom. **5.** Possible answers: Their invention of cuneiform influenced the development of later writing systems. Their number system based on the number six influenced later methods of measuring time and circles.

Critical Thinking and Writing
6. Possible answers: Similar—Both are responsible for maintaining the public works, leading armies to war, and enforcing laws. Different—Today's leaders are unlikely to have religious functions.
7. Possible answers: **(a)** Benefits—Tablets last for a long time, and they are hard to alter for dishonest purposes. Drawbacks—They are time consuming to make and inscribe, and cumbersome to carry and store. **(b)** materials that are easier to carry and store such as paper

Activity Rubrics

Share rubrics with students before they create their pictographic and cuneiform symbols.

Attempted Fewer than three objects or concepts are depicted.

Minimal Three objects or concepts are depicted, but there is little difference between the pictographic version and the cuneiform version.

Adequate Three objects or concepts are depicted, and there is an appropriate difference between the pictographic version and the cuneiform version.

Exemplary Three or more objects or concepts are depicted, there is an appropriate difference between the pictographic and cuneiform versions, and the objects or concepts chosen are more difficult to convey.

Skills Assessment

ANSWER Possible answer: Early cuneiform was based on pictographs that resembled the objects or ideas that they represented, but later symbols were more stylized.

Human Drama Note

A Religious Reformer The political and economic power of Sumerian priests sometimes led to corruption. Priests took bribes, and their taxes and fees were so high that farmers and fishers barely survived. Disgusted, King Urukagina of Lagash introduced reforms that regulated temple taxes, reduced burial fees, and forbade priests' keeping the cattle given as offerings. Urukagina proclaimed that priests could no longer "come into the garden of a poor mother and take wood from there. . . ."

Test Preparation

Have students read the paragraph following the quotation from *The Epic of Gilgamesh* on the opposite page, and then complete the sentence below.

The word *pessimistic* in the paragraph means
A gloomy.
B hopeful.
C serious.
D fearful.

LESSON PLAN

1. Focus Strong rulers united the lands of the Fertile Crescent into empires that had well-organized systems of law and government. Middle Eastern civilizations of this period also developed ironworking, coins, and an alphabet. Through warfare and trade, these and other cultural achievements spread to new lands.

2. Instruct Divide the class into cooperative learning groups. Their task is to create matching quizzes based on the people and achievements described in this section. First, groups should collect the information and list individuals and civilizations and their major cultural achievements. In the first column each group should list the names of rulers and civilizations. In the second column they will list, in random order, descriptive phrases that identify each person or civilization listed in the first column.

3. Assess Ask each group to present its quiz for the class to complete.

4. Reteach If students' Assess activity does not reflect adequate understanding of the lesson, you might assign the *Guide to the Essentials* or the *Interactive Student Tutorial CD-ROM* for this section.

Skills Assessment

ANSWER by the authority of the gods

Reading Focus

- How did early empires arise in Mesopotamia?
- How did ideas and technology spread?
- How did the Persians unite a huge empire?
- What contributions did the Phoenicians make?

Vocabulary

codify
criminal law
civil law
tolerance
satrap
barter economy
money economy
colony
alphabet

Taking Notes

Copy the chart below. As you read, fill in the left-hand column with the names of ancient empires in the Middle East. Fill in the right-hand column with a major contribution of each empire.

EMPIRE	CONTRIBUTION
Babylon	Hammurabi's Code

Main Idea A series of strong rulers united the lands of the Fertile Crescent into well-organized empires.

Primary Source

The Code of Hammurabi
To establish respect for his laws, Hammurabi began his code with a statement of his authority and principles:

"Then [the gods] Anu and Bel called by name me, Hammurabi, the exalted prince, who feared God, to bring about the rule of righteousness in the land, to destroy the wicked and the evildoers; so that the strong should not harm the weak; so that I should rule over the [people] and enlighten the land, to further the well-being of mankind. Hammurabi, the prince, called of Bel am I, making riches and increase . . . who conquered the four corners of the world [and] made great the name of Babylon. . . . When [the god] Marduk sent me to rule over men, to give the protection of right to the land, I did right and righteousness. . . ."

Skills Assessment

Primary Source By what authority does Hammurabi claim to issue his legal code?

Setting the Scene

If you had visited the palace of the ancient Assyrian king Assurbanipal (ah soor BAH nuh pahl), you would have found the walls decorated with magnificent carvings. One scene shows Assurbanipal and his queen enjoying a picnic in their lush palace garden. Nearby, musicians entertain the royal couple.

The scene is relaxed and elegant. Look carefully, though, and you will see something startling. Hanging from a tree branch, just behind a harp player, is the head of a defeated king.

In the ancient Middle East, as elsewhere, bloody warfare and advanced culture often went hand in hand. In this section, we will look at the accomplishments of a series of Middle Eastern civilizations across 3,000 years of war and peace.

Ruling a Large Empire

Invasion and conquest were prominent features in the history of the ancient Middle East. Again and again, nomadic peoples or ambitious warriors descended on the rich cities of the Fertile Crescent. While many invaders simply looted and burned, some stayed to rule. Powerful leaders created large, well-organized empires, bringing peace and prosperity to the region.

The First Empire Builder About 2300 B.C., Sargon, the ruler of neighboring Akkad, invaded and conquered the city-states of Sumer. He built the first empire known to history. His astonishing achievement did not last long, however. Soon after his death, other invaders swept into the wide valley between the rivers, tumbling his empire into ruin.

In time, the Sumerian city-states revived, and their power struggles resumed. Eventually, however, new conquerors followed in the footsteps of Sargon and imposed unity over the Fertile Crescent.

Hammurabi the Lawgiver About 1790 B.C., Hammurabi (hah moo RAH bee), king of Babylon, brought much of Mesopotamia under his control. He took steps to unite the Babylonian empire. His most ambitious and lasting contribution was his publication of a remarkable set of laws known as the Code of Hammurabi.

Hammurabi was not the author of the code. Most of the laws had been around since Sumerian times. Hammurabi, however, wanted everyone in his empire to know the legal principles his government would follow. He had artisans carve nearly 300 laws on a stone pillar for all to see. On it, he

---

How Should Society Deal With Lawbreakers?

The question of how to deal fairly and effectively with lawbreakers is as old as society itself. To begin your own investigation, examine the following viewpoints.

Babylon 1790s B.C.

The Code of Hammurabi calls for strict justice:

❝ If a son strike his father, his hands shall be cut off. If a man put out the eye of another man, his eye shall be put out. If he break another man's bone, his bone shall be broken. . . . If a man knock out the teeth of his equal, his teeth shall be knocked out. ❞

Italy 1764

Cesare Beccaria was one of the first reformers to argue against torture, capital punishment, and harsh treatment of criminals:

❝ The purpose [of punishment] can only be to prevent the criminal from inflicting new injuries on its citizens and to deter others from similar acts. . . . Such punishments and such methods of inflicting them ought to be chosen, therefore, which will make the strongest and most lasting impression on the minds of men, and inflict the least torment on the body of the criminal. ❞

New England 1600

Puritans in colonial New England enforced their laws with stocks, which were both painful and humiliating.

Singapore 1994

In 1994, an American teenager living in Singapore was sentenced to a painful flogging for acts of vandalism. An official defended his country's harsh penalties:

❝ Unlike some other societies which tolerate acts of vandalism, Singapore has its own standards of social order as reflected in our laws. We are able to keep Singapore relatively crime-free. We do not have a situation where acts of vandalism are commonplace, as in cities like New York, where even police cars are not spared. ❞

Skills Assessment

1. Which of the following statements summarizes a Puritan view on punishment?
   - **A** Harsh penalties should be avoided.
   - **B** Punishments should not damage a criminal's body.
   - **C** Vandals should get the death penalty.
   - **D** Public humiliation is an effective way to prevent crime.

2. On what point would Beccaria agree with the official from Singapore?
   - **E** Criminals should be put in stocks.
   - **F** Punishments should stop people from committing future crimes.
   - **G** Capital punishment is an acceptable penalty for most crimes.
   - **H** Punishment should be as painful as possible.

3. **Critical Thinking Making Decisions** With which of the viewpoints above do you most strongly agree? Explain.

Skills Tip

When expressing a viewpoint, start with a statement of your opinion, and then give strong reasons to support your argument.

Background Other Viewpoints

Canaan, 700s B.C. The ancient Hebrews looked to the Torah as God's authority on the law. The Book of Leviticus contains a law similar to one of Hammurabi's laws:

"When a man causes disfigurement in his neighbor, as he has done it shall be done to him, fracture for fracture, eye for eye, tooth for tooth; as he has disfigured a man, he shall be disfigured."

China, 200s B.C. Hanfeizi, an influential scholar, believed that people were basically corrupt and that the only way to ensure an orderly society was to enforce strict laws:

"People become naturally spoiled by love, but are submissive to authority. . . . That being so, rewards should be rich and certain so that the people will be attracted to them; punishments should be severe and definite so that the people will fear them; and laws should be uniform and steadfast so that the people will be familiar with them."

Activity Interpreting Viewpoints

Critical Thinking: Comparing Use these additional questions to generate class discussion. **1.** What is the main difference between Beccaria's viewpoint and the other three viewpoints? *(The others call for some form of corporal punishment.)* **2.** Read aloud the Hanfeizi quote from the Background section above. With which part of Hanfeizi's philosophy do you think Beccaria would have been most likely to agree? *(Punishments should be uniform and steadfast.)*

Skills Tip

Inform students that to support an argument, it is better to have a few strong reasons than many weak ones. The Skills Handbook in the front of the book has a lesson that will help students with this feature.

Skills Assessment

ANSWERS **1.** D **2.** F **3.** Answers should be well supported.

Divide the class into groups. Ask each group to choose a different ancient civilization and work together to create a mural depicting that civilization's major achievements. Remind students to make sure that architecture, clothing, and artifacts portrayed in their murals are accurate for the time and place. Display the finished murals and ask each group to explain its work to the class. Use the murals to compare and contrast ancient civilizations.

Background
Daily Life

Hammurabi's Code Babylonian life was regulated by the Code of Hammurabi. A study of the code reveals much about Babylonian values and the problems that Babylonians faced in their daily lives. Some laws addressed economic activities. For example, the code established limits on prices and wages. Other laws dealt with family life. One such law shows that Babylonians believed it was important for children to honor and respect their parents. The law stated, "If a son has struck his father, his hand shall be cut off."

Most laws regulated criminal behavior and carried severe punishments. Crimes that were punishable by death included cowardice in battle, kidnapping, bigamy, adultery, giving false testimony in a legal proceeding, and wrongdoing by public officials.

Assyrian and Persian Empires

Assyrian empire about 625 B.C.

Persian empire about 500 B.C.

Great Royal Road

▲ Assyrian capitals ■ Persian capitals

Albers Equal Area Projection

Skills Assessment

Geography The Assyrians and Persians built huge empires in the ancient Middle East.

1. **Location** On the map, locate (a) Assyrian empire, (b) Nineveh, (c) Persian empire, (d) Asia Minor.
2. **Movement** What land and water routes might a trader have taken to travel from Memphis to Nineveh?
3. **Critical Thinking**
   Making Inferences (a) How many capital cities did the Persian empire have? (b) Why do you think the Persians set up so many capitals?

proclaimed that his goals were to "cause justice to prevail in the land / To destroy the wicked and evil / That the strong may not oppress the weak." Hammurabi's Code was the first important attempt by a ruler to codify, or arrange and set down in writing, all of the laws that would govern a state.

Crime and Punishment One section of Hammurabi's Code codified criminal law. This branch of law deals with offenses against others such as robbery, assault, or murder. Earlier traditions often permitted victims of crimes or their families to take the law into their own hands. By setting out specific punishments for specific offenses, Hammurabi's Code limited personal vengeance and encouraged social order.

By today's standards, the punishments in Hammurabi's Code often seem cruel, following the principle of "an eye for an eye and a life for a life." For example, if a house collapsed because of poor construction and the homeowner was killed, the builder of the house could be put to death. Still, such a legal code was more orderly than unrestricted personal vengeance.

Civil Law Another part of Hammurabi's Code involved civil law. This branch of law deals with private rights and matters, such as business contracts, property inheritance, taxes, marriage, and divorce.

Much of Hammurabi's civil code was designed to protect the powerless, such as slaves or women. Some laws, for example, allowed a woman to own property and pass it on to her children. Another law spelled out the rights of a married woman:

"If a woman so hated her husband that she has declared, `You may not have me,' her record shall be investigated at

40 Chapter 2

Skills Assessment

ANSWERS 1. Review locations with students. **2.** Possible answer: A traveler could have sailed down the Nile and across the Mediterranean to Asia Minor. Then the journey would have continued overland to Sardis and along the Great Royal Road to Nineveh. **3. (a)** four **(b)** Possible answer: They needed them because the empire was so large and contained so many different peoples.

her city council, and if she . . . was not at fault, that woman, without incurring any blame at all, may take her dowry and go off to her father's house."

—Code of Hammurabi

If the woman were not found blameless, however, the law instructed that she be thrown in the river.

In general, Babylonian civil law gave a husband both legal authority over his wife and a legal duty to support her. The code also gave a father nearly unlimited authority over his children. The Babylonians believed that an orderly household was necessary for a stable empire.

Other Accomplishments Although most famous for his law code, Hammurabi took other steps to unite his empire. He improved irrigation, organized a well-trained army, and had temples repaired. To encourage religious unity across his empire, he promoted the chief Babylonian god, Marduk, over older Sumerian gods.

Warfare and the Spread of Ideas

Later empires shaped the Middle East in different ways. Often, conquerors uprooted the peoples they defeated. By forcing people to move elsewhere, these invaders helped spread ideas. Other conquerors, like the Hittites, ought new skills to the region.

The Secret of Ironworking The Hittites pushed out of Asia Minor into Mesopotamia about 1400 B.C. Although they were less advanced than the peoples of Mesopotamia, they had learned to extract iron from ore. The Hittites heated iron ore and pounded out impurities before plunging it into cold water. The tools and weapons they made with iron were harder and had sharper edges than those made out of bronze or copper. Because iron was plentiful, the Hittites were able to arm more people at less expense.

The Hittites tried to keep this valuable technology secret. But as their empire collapsed about 1200 B.C., Hittite ironsmiths migrated to serve customers elsewhere. The new knowledge thus spread across Asia, Africa, and Europe, ushering in the Iron Age.

Assyrian Warriors The Assyrians, who lived on the upper Tigris, learned to forge iron weapons. By 1100 B.C., they began expanding across Mesopotamia. For 500 years, they earned a reputation for being among the most feared warriors in history.

Historians are unsure why warfare was so central to Assyrian culture. Was it to keep others from attacking or to please their god Assur by bringing peace and order to the region? Whatever the reason, Assyrian rulers boasted of their conquests. One told of capturing Babylon. He proclaimed, "The city and its houses, from top to bottom, I destroyed and burned with fire."

Despite their fierce reputation, Assyrian rulers encouraged a well-ordered society. They were the first rulers to develop extensive laws regulating life within

Contributions of the Fertile Crescent

Wheeled vehicles

Sumerians first used wheeled vehicles to transport goods in trade.

Alphabet

The Phoenician alphabet contained 22 symbols stand ing for consonant sounds, written in vertical columns from right to left. Later peoples adapted the Phoenician alphabet to produce our 26-letter alphabet.

Ironworking

Hittites learned to extract iron from ore and fashion tools and weapons that were harder than bronze or copper ones. They helped spread their knowledge of iron.

Connections to Today

Ancient civilizations of the Fertile Crescent made breakthroughs in writing, science, and technology. In some form or another, all three of the developments shown are still in use today.

Skills Assessment **Chart** Which technological advance shown on this chart do you think was the most important? Give reasons for your answer.

A Money Economy
Persia was the first large empire to create a uniform system of coinage. The Persian coin here depicts the emperor Darius. Today, every country in the world has its own system of coinage.
Theme: Economics and Technology What advantage does a money economy have over a barter economy?

PAST

PRESENT

42

the royal household. For example, women of the palace were confined in secluded quarters and had to be veiled when they appeared in public. Riches from trade and war loot paid for the splendid palaces in well-planned cities.

At Nineveh (NIHN uh vuh), King Assurbanipal founded one of the first libraries. He ordered his scribes to collect cuneiform tablets from all over the Fertile Crescent. Those tablets have given modern scholars a wealth of information about the ancient Middle East.

Babylon Revived In 612 B.C., shortly after Assurbanipal's death, neighboring people joined forces to crush the once-dreaded Assyrian armies. An aggressive and ruthless king, Nebuchadnezzar (neh buh kuhd NEHZ uhr), revived the power of Babylon. His new Babylonian empire stretched from the Persian Gulf to the Mediterranean Sea.

Nebuchadnezzar rebuilt the canals, temples, walls, and palaces of Babylon. Near his chief palace were the famous Hanging Gardens, known as one of the wonders of the ancient world. The gardens were probably made by planting trees and flowering plants on the steps of a huge ziggurat. According to legend, Nebuchadnezzar had the gardens built to please his wife, who was homesick for the hills where she had grown up.

Under Nebuchadnezzar, the Babylonians pushed the frontiers of learning into new areas. Priest-astrologers were especially eager to understand the stars and planets, which they believed had a great influence on all events on Earth. Their observations of the heavens contributed to the growing knowledge of astronomy.

The Persian Empire

The thick walls built by Nebuchadnezzar failed to hold back new conquerors. In 539 B.C., Babylon fell to the Persian armies of Cyrus the Great. Cyrus and his successors went on to conquer the largest empire yet seen. The Persians eventually controlled a wide sweep of territory from Asia Minor to India, including present-day Turkey, Iran, Egypt, Afghanistan, and Pakistan.

In general, Persian kings pursued a policy of tolerance, or acceptance, of the people they conquered. The Persians respected the customs and religious traditions of the diverse groups in their empire.

Uniting Many Peoples The real unification of the Persian empire was accomplished under the Persian emperor Darius, who ruled from 522 B.C. to 486 B.C. A skilled organizer, Darius set up a government that became a model for later rulers. He divided the Persian empire into provinces, each headed by a governor called a satrap. Each satrapy, or province, had to pay taxes based on its resources and wealth. Special officials, "the Eyes and Ears of the King," visited each province to check on the satraps.

Like Hammurabi, Darius adapted laws from the people he conquered and drew up a single code of laws for the empire. To encourage unity, he had hundreds of miles of roads built or repaired. Roads made it easier to communicate with different parts of the empire. Darius himself kept moving from one royal capital to another. In each, he celebrated important festivals and was seen by the people.

Economic Life To improve trade, Darius set up a common set of weights and measures. He also encouraged the use of coins, which the Lydians of Asia Minor had first introduced. Most

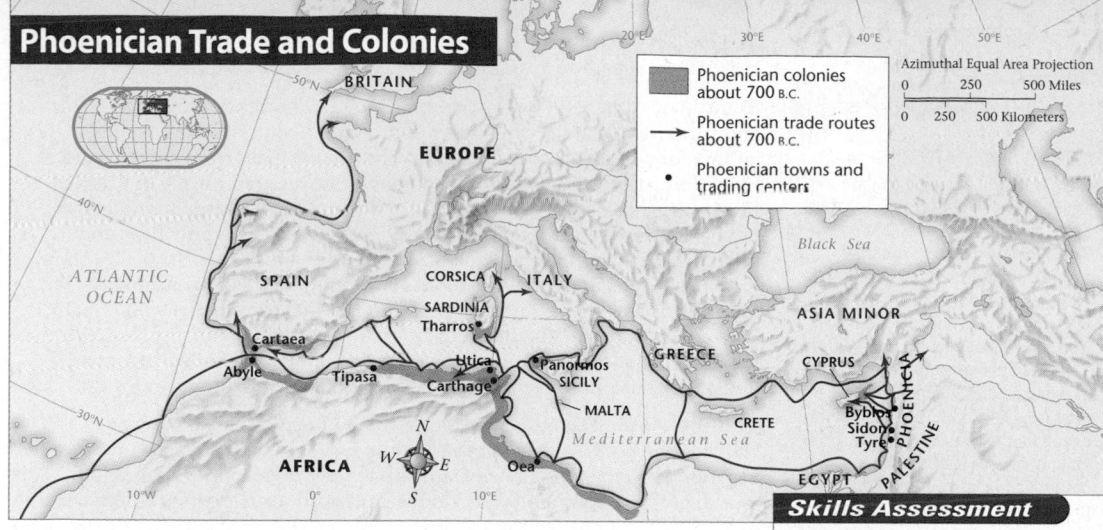

Phoenician Trade and Colonies

Legend:
- Phoenician colonies about 700 B.C.
- → Phoenician trade routes about 700 B.C.
- • Phoenician towns and trading centers

Azimuthal Equal Area Projection
0 250 500 Miles
0 250 500 Kilometers

Skills Assessment

Geography Although their homeland was small, the Phoenicians established trade and set up colonies throughout the Mediterranean world.

1. **Location** On the map, locate **(a)** Phoenicia, **(b)** Byblos, **(c)** Tyre, **(d)** Cyprus, **(e)** Greece, **(f)** Britain.
2. **Movement** What information on the map supports the claim that the Phoenicians were skilled sailors?
3. **Critical Thinking Drawing Conclusions** How did geography influence the type of economy that the Phoenicians developed?

---

people continued to be part of the barter economy, exchanging one set of goods or services for another. Coins, however, brought merchants and traders into an early form of a money economy. In this system, goods and services are paid for through the exchange of some token of an agreed value, such as a coin or a bill. By setting up a single Persian coinage, Darius created economic links among his far-flung subjects.

A New Religion Religious beliefs put forward by the Persian thinker Zoroaster (zoh roh AS tuhr) also helped to unite the empire. Zoroaster lived about 600 B.C. He rejected the old Persian gods. Instead, he taught that a single wise god, Ahura Mazda (ah HOO ruh MAHZ duh), ruled the world. Ahura Mazda, however, was in constant battle against Ahriman (AH rih muhn), the prince of lies and evil. Each individual, said Zoroaster, had to choose which side to support.

Zoroaster's teachings were collected in a sacred book, the *Zend-Avesta*. It taught that in the end Ahura Mazda would triumph over the forces of evil:

"There will come a day, the Judgment Day, when Ahura Mazda will conquer and banish Ahriman . . . when man allies himself with Ahura Mazda and helps him to banish all that is evil, all that is darkness, and all that is death."

—Zoroaster, *Zend-Avesta*

On the Judgment Day, taught Zoroaster, all individuals would be judged for their actions. Those who had done good would enter paradise. Evildoers would be condemned to eternal suffering. Two later religions that emerged in the Middle East, Christianity and Islam, stressed similar ideas about heaven, hell, and a final judgment day.*

Phoenician Sea Traders

While powerful rulers subdued large empires, many small states of the ancient Middle East made their own contributions to civilization. The Phoenicians (fuh NEE shuhns), for example, gained fame as sailors and

---

*Today, Zoroastrianism is still practiced by tens of thousands of people, mostly in India. They are known as Parsees, from the word for *Persian*.

Human Drama Note

Cyrus and the Taking of Babylon The Persian king Cyrus was noted for his generosity toward the peoples he conquered. He forbade his armies to loot and burn conquered cities, and he allowed people to worship as they pleased. Partly for that reason, he was able to take the city of Babylon peacefully. When he arrived, the people opened the city gates for him and welcomed him. In fact, if the Babylonian version of the story may be trusted, "Green twigs were spread in front of him. . . . To the inhabitants of Babylon a joyful heart is given now."

Reading Strategy
Check Comprehension

Write the following questions on the board: What did I read about in this section? What did I learn? What puzzled or confused me? What would help clarify things for me? What did I enjoy, dislike, or accomplish during my reading? Have students write for at least five minutes in response to these questions. *(Less Advanced Readers)*

Skills Assessment

ANSWERS 1. Review locations with students. **2.** Possible answer: It shows that they traveled as far away as Britain, a distance of more than 3,000 miles. **3.** Possible answers: They lived along the coast of the Mediterranean, so sailing was a natural development; they made glass from coastal sand and dye from sea snails.

SECTION 4 Assessment

Recall
1. (a) Sargon, p. 38 (b) Hammurabi, p. 38 (c) Assurbanipal, p. 38 (d) Nebuchadnezzar, p. 42 (e) Cyrus the Great, p. 42 (f) Darius, p. 42 (g) Zoroaster, p. 43 2. (a) codify, p. 40 (b) criminal law, p. 40 (c) civil law, p. 40 (d) tolerance, p. 42 (e) satrap, p. 42 (f) barter economy, p. 43 (g) money economy, p. 43 (h) colony, p. 44 (i) alphabet, p. 44

Comprehension
3. He brought much of Mesopotamia under his control and maintained control by having a uniform code of laws, by improving irrigation, maintaining a well-organized army, and promoting religious unity. 4. They learned how to make iron from iron ore. Their iron tools and weapons were superior to those made of softer metals. 5. Possible answers: He developed a well-organized government, had a single code of laws, and built a network of roads linking the various parts of the empire. 6. As traders and sailors, they spread Middle Eastern civilization around the Mediterranean.

Critical Thinking and Writing
7. There were few natural barriers to prevent a conqueror from reaching the cities of Mesopotamia. By the same token, it was relatively easy to get from one place to another, making it less of a problem to enforce laws, collect taxes, and so forth. 8. Possible answer: Darius hoped to strengthen the Persian empire by uniting it under a single religion.

Activity Rubrics

Share rubrics with students before they conduct their Internet research.

Attempted Student completed some research, but it does not cover both ancient and modern wonders adequately.

Minimal Both ancient and modern wonders are present, but the analysis is sketchy or lacking in depth.

Adequate Student has made comparisons and has drawn conclusions that are supported by good arguments.

Exemplary Research is complete and accurate. Comparisons and conclusions are insightful and well supported.

Geography and History

ANSWER The route would be from the Red Sea into the Gulf of Aden, into the Indian Ocean and south along the east coast of Africa, then north into the Atlantic Ocean and through the Strait of Gibraltar into the Mediterranean.

Geography and History

Phoenician Explorers

Did daring Phoenicians sail around Africa? No one knows for sure, but some historians believe that a Phoenician expedition rounded Africa's southern tip about 600 B.C. The only account of this expedition was written by the Greek historian Herodotus, close to 200 years later.

Herodotus gave no description of anything the Phoenicians saw in their travels—with one fascinating exception. The sailors reported that as they rounded Africa, the sun both rose and set on the right side of the ship. Because this unusual phenomenon would occur deep in the Southern Hemisphere, this statement suggests that the Phoenicians did indeed sail completely around Africa.

 Theme: Geography and History Plot a course the expedition could have taken, starting in the Red Sea and ending in the Mediterranean.

traders. They occupied a string of cities along the eastern Mediterranean coast, in the area that is today Lebanon and Syria.

Manufacturing and Trade The coastal land, though narrow, was fertile and supported farming. Still, the resourceful Phoenicians became best known for manufacturing and trade. They made glass from coastal sand. From a tiny sea snail, they produced a widely admired purple dye, called "Tyrian purple" after the city of Tyre. Phoenicians also used papyrus from Egypt to make scrolls, or rolls of paper, for books. The words *Bible* and *bibliography* come from the Phoenician city of Byblos.

Phoenicians traded with people all around the Mediterranean Sea. To promote trade, they set up colonies from North Africa to Sicily and Spain. A colony is a territory settled and ruled by people from another land. A few Phoenician traders braved the stormy Atlantic and sailed as far as England. There, they exchanged goods from the Mediterranean for tin.

The Alphabet Historians have called the Phoenicians "carriers of civilization" because they spread Middle Eastern civilization around the Mediterranean. Yet the Phoenicians made their own contribution to our world, giving us our alphabet. Unlike cuneiform or hieroglyphics, in which each symbol represents a word or concept, an alphabet contains letters that represent spoken sounds.

Phoenician traders needed a quick, flexible form of writing to record business deals. The wedges of cuneiform were too clumsy, so they developed a system of 22 symbols for consonant sounds. Later, the Greeks adapted the Phoenician alphabet and added symbols for the vowel sounds. From this Greek alphabet came the letters in which this book is written.

Looking Ahead

The Middle East continued to be a vital crossroads, where warriors and traders met, clashed, and mingled. Under Persian rule, scholars drew on 3,000 years of Mesopotamian learning and added their own advances to this rich heritage. In time, the achievements of this culture filtered eastward into India and westward into Europe.

Other conquerors would overwhelm the Persian empire, although different leaders revived Persian power at various times down to the present. The Middle East remained a region where diverse peoples came into close contact. Though these people lived thousands of years ago, some of their beliefs and ideas survived to shape our modern world.

SECTION 4 Assessment

Recall
1. **Identify:** (a) Sargon, (b) Hammurabi, (c) Assurbanipal, (d) Nebuchadnezzar, (e) Cyrus the Great, (f) Darius, (g) Zoroaster.
2. **Define:** (a) codify, (b) criminal law (c) civil law, (d) tolerance, (e) satrap, (f) barter economy, (g) money economy, (h) colony, (i) alphabet.

Comprehension
3. How did Hammurabi build and strengthen an empire?
4. How did the Hittites introduce a new age of technology?

5. Describe two steps Darius took to unite the Persian empire.
6. Why were the Phoenicians called "carriers of civilization"?

Critical Thinking and Writing
7. **Connecting to Geography** How did the geography of the Fertile Crescent help a series of leaders both to conquer and to unify Mesopotamia?
8. **Making Inferences** Why do you think Darius supported the spread of Zoroastrianism throughout the Persian empire?

44 Chapter 2

 ### Activity
Take It to the NET

Use the Internet to research the Seven Wonders of the Ancient World. Then, research a list of possible Wonders of the Modern World. How are these structures similar? How are they different? What do these structures tell you about the cultures that built them?

Resource Directory

Teaching Resources
Section Quiz Unit 1 booklet, p. 25
Creative Teaching Activities Creative Teaching Activities booklet, p. 15
Guided Reading and Review Unit 1 booklet, p. 26

Technology
Interactive Student Tutorial CD-ROM Ch. 2
Computer Test Bank Ch. 2
World History Color Transparencies *David and Goliath*, p. C–27

Reading Focus

- What were the main events in the early history of the Israelites?
- How did the Jews view their relationship with God?
- What moral and ethical ideas did the prophets teach?

Vocabulary

monotheistic
covenant
patriarchal
sabbath
prophet
ethics
diaspora

Taking Notes

Copy this concept web. As you read, fill in the circles with the major beliefs of Judaism. Two circles have been filled in to help you get started.

Torah

JUDAISM

Mono-theism

Main Idea The religion of the Israelites was unique in the ancient world because it was monotheistic.

Setting the Scene

"I am the Lord your God, who brought you out of the land of Egypt, out of the house of bondage. You shall have no other gods beside Me." These words—the first of the Ten Commandments—set the Israelites apart from all other people of the Fertile Crescent. Instead of worshiping many gods, the Israelites prayed to one God for guidance and protection. This promise of a unique relationship with God helped shape the history of the Israelites, later known as the Jews. Their early religion evolved into Judaism, one of the world's main faiths.

Early History of the Israelites

Early in their history, the Israelites, or Hebrews, came to believe that God was taking a hand in their lives. As a result, they recorded events and laws in the Torah, their most sacred text.

A Nomadic People According to the Torah, a man named Abraham lived near Ur in Mesopotamia. About 2000 B.C., he and his family migrated, herding their sheep and goats into a region called Canaan.* Abraham is considered the founder of the Israelite nation.

The Book of Genesis tells that a famine later forced many Israelites to migrate to Egypt. There, they were eventually enslaved. In time, Moses led the Israelites in their escape, or exodus, from Egypt. After Moses died, they entered Canaan, the land they believed God had promised them.

The Kingdom of Israel By 1000 B.C., the Israelites had set up a kingdom called Israel. David, a strong and shrewd king, united the feuding Israelite tribes into a single nation.

David's son Solomon turned Jerusalem into an impressive capital, with a splendid temple dedicated to God. Solomon won fame for his wisdom and understanding. He also tried to increase Israel's influence by negotiating with powerful empires in Egypt and Mesopotamia.

Division and Conquest Israel paid a heavy price for Solomon's ambitions. His building projects required such high taxes and so much forced labor that revolts erupted soon after his death about 922 B.C. The kingdom then split into Israel in the north and Judah in the south.

Weakened by this division, the Israelites could not fight off invading armies. In 722 B.C., Israel fell to the Assyrians. In 586 B.C., Babylonian

*Centuries later, under Roman rule, this land became known as Palestine.

Biography

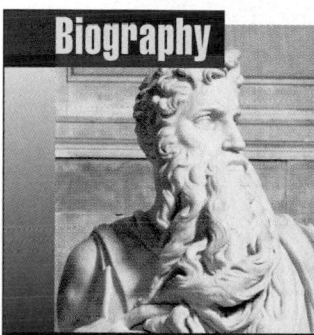

Moses
c. 1300s B.C.–1200s B.C.

According to the Bible, Moses was a reluctant hero. When God commanded him to free the Israelites from slavery in Egypt, Moses said fearfully, "Who am I that I should go to Pharaoh, and bring the sons of Israel out of Egypt?" When God insisted, Moses protested, "But I am slow of speech and of tongue." Because Moses' brother Aaron was a better public speaker, Moses asked for his help. When they saw the pharaoh, Moses told Aaron what to say, and Aaron did the talking.

Despite Moses' doubts about his abilities as a leader, he accomplished his goal. He finally freed his people from bondage in Egypt.

Theme: Impact of the Individual How did Moses conquer his fears?

Bell Ringer Select several passages from the early chapters of the Book of Exodus, which can be found in the Torah or in the Old Testament. Invite students to read these passages aloud to the class. Ask students to discuss what these passages reveal about how the Hebrews viewed themselves and their relationship with God.

LESSON PLAN

1. Focus The history of the Israelites is a story of enslavement and liberation, unity and division. The Israelites believed in one true God with whom they had a special covenant. They followed religious traditions and moral values that were contained in the Torah.

2. Instruct Work with the class to create on the chalkboard an annotated time line of Jewish history up to the Diaspora. References should include

- the covenant with Abraham
- the writing of the Torah
- the establishment of Israel
- the reigns of David and Solomon
- the division into Judah and Israel
- the exile in Babylon
- the rebuilding of the temple in Jerusalem

3. Assess Have students suggest the effects that each of these events had on the Jewish people.

4. Reteach If students' Assess activity does not reflect adequate understanding of the lesson, you might assign the *Guide to the Essentials* or the *Interactive Student Tutorial CD-ROM* for this section.

Block Scheduling Support

Share the information about King Solomon and the great temple of Jerusalem found in the Background section in the side column of the next page in the Teacher's Edition. Ask students to consider whether King Solomon or the northern Israelites were more justified in their actions. Then divide the class into several small groups. Assign half the groups to develop arguments defending Solomon's viewpoint and the other half to defend that of the northern Israelites. When students have finished, hold a class discussion in which the groups share and defend their views.

Biography

ANSWER He asked his brother Aaron to help him.

Jews Praying to God
After the Babylonian Captivity, the Jews rebuilt their temple in Jerusalem. Today, the Western Wall is all that remains of the great temple. Here, Jewish men gather at the wall to pray. Above is a morning prayer book.

Theme: Religions and Value Systems Why do you think the Western Wall is sacred to Jews around the world?

 Primary Sources and Literature

See "Psalm 23" in the Reference Section at the back of this book.

armies captured Judah. Nebuchadnezzar destroyed the great temple and forced many Israelites into exile in Babylon. During this period, called the Babylonian Captivity, the Israelites became known as the Jews.

Years later, when the Persian ruler Cyrus conquered Babylon, he freed the Jews from captivity. Many returned to their homeland, where they rebuilt a smaller version of Solomon's temple. Yet, like other small groups in the region, they continued to live under Persian rule.

A Covenant With God

What you have just read is an outline of Israelite history. To the Israelites, history and faith were interconnected. Each event reflected God's plan for them. In time, their beliefs evolved into the religion we know today as Judaism.

One True God The beliefs of the Israelites differed in basic ways from those of nearby peoples. The Israelites were monotheistic, believing in one true God. At the time, most other people worshiped many gods. A few religious leaders, such as the Egyptian pharaoh Akhenaton, spoke of a single powerful god. However, such ideas did not have the lasting impact that Israelite beliefs did.

The ancient Israelites prayed to God to save them from their enemies. Many other ancient people had also turned to particular gods as special protectors. But they thought of such gods as tied to certain places or people. The Israelites believed in an all-knowing, all-powerful God who was present everywhere.

The Chosen People The Israelites believed that God had made a covenant, or binding agreement, with Abraham:

> "I will make nations of you, and kings shall come forth from you. . . . And I will establish my covenant between me and you and your descendants after you throughout their generations for an everlasting covenant, to be God to you."
> —Book of Genesis

Moses later renewed this covenant. In return for faithful obedience, he said, God would lead the Israelites out of bondage and into the "promised land" of Canaan. Thus, the Israelites and, later, the Jews saw themselves as God's "chosen people."

Teachings on Law and Morality

From early times, the concept of law was central to the Israelites. The Torah set out many laws. Some dealt with everyday matters such as cleanliness and food preparation. Others were criminal laws.

Israelite society was patriarchal, that is, fathers and husbands held great legal and moral authority. The father or oldest male relative was head of the household and arranged marriages for his daughters. Women had few legal rights, although some laws protected them. In early times, a few outstanding women, such as the judge Deborah, won great honor.

The Ten Commandments At the heart of Judaism are the Ten Commandments, a set of laws that Jews believe God gave them through Moses. The first four Commandments stress religious duties toward God, such as keeping the sabbath, a holy day for rest and worship. The rest set out rules for conduct toward other people. They include "Honor your father and mother," "You shall not murder," and "You shall not steal."

An Ethical Worldview Often in Jewish history, spiritual leaders emerged to interpret God's will. These prophets, such as Isaiah and Jeremiah, warned that failure to obey God's law would lead their people to disaster.

The prophets also preached a strong code of ethics, or moral standards of behavior. They urged both personal morality and social justice, calling on the rich and powerful to protect the poor and weak. All people, they said, were equal before God. Unlike many ancient societies in which the ruler was seen as a god, Jews saw their leaders as fully human and bound to obey God's law.

Looking Ahead

More than 2,000 years ago, many Jews left their homeland. This diaspora (dī AS puhr uh), or scattering of people, sent Jews to different parts of the world. Wherever they settled, Jews maintained their identity as a people by living in close-knit communities and obeying their religious laws and traditions. These traditions helped them survive centuries of persecution.

Judaism is considered a major world religion for its unique contribution to religious thought. It also influenced Christianity and Islam, two other monotheistic faiths that rose in the Middle East. Today, Jews, Christians, and Muslims all honor Abraham, Moses, and the prophets, and they all teach the ethical worldview developed by the Israelites. In the west, this shared heritage of Jews and Christians is known as the Judeo-Christian tradition.

Connections to Today

Remembering the Exodus

Every year during the holiday of Passover, Jews retell the story of the Exodus from Egypt as part of an important family celebration called a seder. The storyteller, who is usually one of the adults in the family, explains the key events and symbols of the holiday to the children. The adult identifies with the Israelites who took part in the Exodus by beginning with the words "It is because of what the Lord did for me when I went free out of Egypt."

Special foods eaten during the seder also help Jews feel that they are taking part in the Exodus. A flat bread called matzo recalls how the Jews had to leave Egypt quickly and did not have time to wait for their bread to rise. Grated pieces of horseradish are eaten to symbolize the bitterness of slavery in Egypt.

Theme: Connections to Today Why is it important that the story of the Exodus be told to children as a first-person narrative?

SECTION 5 Assessment

Recall
1. **Identify:** (a) Torah, (b) Abraham, (c) Moses, (d) David, (e) Solomon, (f) Ten Commandments, (g) Judeo-Christian tradition.
2. **Define:** (a) monotheistic, (b) covenant, (c) patriarchal, (d) sabbath, (e) prophet, (f) ethics, (g) diaspora.

Comprehension
3. Why did Israel become divided?
4. How did the beliefs of the Israelites differ from those of other people of Mesopotamia?

5. Describe one Israelite teaching about each of the following: (a) family life, (b) ethics.

Critical Thinking and Writing
6. **Applying Information** Review what you have read about the Babylonian and Persian empires. Why do you think Nebuchadnezzar and Cyrus the Great treated the Jews differently?
7. **Linking Past and Present** How are the ethical beliefs of the Israelites similar to those commonly accepted in our society?

Activity

Playing a Role
With a partner, act out a conversation between an Israelite parent and child in Egypt or Babylon. The parent should try to explain why, even though they are in exile, the Israelites believe they are the "chosen people."

SECTION 5 Assessment

Recall
1. (a) Torah, p. 45 (b) Abraham, p. 45 (c) Moses, p. 45 (d) David, p. 45 (e) Solomon, p. 45 (f) Ten Commandments, p. 47 (g) Judeo-Christian tradition, p. 47
2. (a) monotheistic, p. 46 (b) covenant, p. 46 (c) patriarchal, p. 47 (d) sabbath, p. 47 (e) prophet, p. 47 (f) ethics, p. 47 (g) diaspora, p. 47

Comprehension
3. Israelites who opposed King Solomon's heavy taxes and forced labor policies revolted and split the kingdom in two.
4. Possible answers: They believed in one God, rather than many gods; they regarded their leaders as fully human, not as gods.
5. Possible answers: (a) Males were the heads of households and arranged marriages for the daughters of the family. Women had few legal rights. (b) All people are equal before God; the rich and powerful should protect the poor and weak; like the common people, leaders were bound to obey God's law.

Critical Thinking and Writing
6. Possible answer: Nebuchadnezzar was aggressive and ruthless, a conqueror who sought to subdue the people he defeated. Cyrus the Great and the Persians generally tolerated the customs and traditions of the people under their rule.
7. Students' answers should show an understanding of Hebrew ethics and recognize their enduring influence today.

Activity Rubrics

Share rubrics with students before they prepare this role-playing activity.

Attempted The conversation does not explain why the exiled Israelites believe they are the chosen people.

Minimal The conversation touches on the reasons for the exiled Israelites' belief but does not fully explain them.

Adequate The conversation fully explains why the exiled Israelites believe they are the chosen people.

Exemplary The conversation fully explains why the exiled Israelites believe they are the chosen people, and the role-playing is skillful.

Connections to Today

ANSWER Telling the story in the first person brings it alive for children by making the Exodus seem less like an event in the distant past and more like a current happening.

Human Drama Note

The Exodus The story of the Exodus contains many dramatic moments. For example, the Lord tries to impress the ruler of Egypt by sending hordes of locusts to devour the crops and by turning the water of the Nile to blood, thereby killing the fish and fouling the water for humans. When the Hebrews finally leave, the Lord parts the waters of the sea for them, and then allows the waters to rush back, drowning the army that the pharaoh had ordered to pursue the Hebrews.

Test Preparation

Have students reread the section under the heading "A Covenant With God" on the opposite page, and then answer the question below.

Which of these is *not* a characteristic of the Israelites' religion?

A a belief in one true God

B a belief in God's covenant with Abraham

C a belief that God wanted them to conquer other peoples

D a belief that God would lead them into the promised land of Canaan

Creating a Chapter Summary

As a reteaching opportunity, pair a more able student with a less able student to complete this chapter summary.

Possible answers: **Egyptian** viewed pharaoh as a god, believed in an afterlife, *Book of the Dead* contained spells and charms to guide souls through the underworld, mummified the dead **Sumerian** located in Mesopotamia, organized into city-states with hereditary rulers, polytheistic, believed gods controlled all aspects of life, each city-state had a god, ziggurats, cuneiform, number system based on six **Babylonian** located in Mesopotamia, Hammurabi ruled by a uniform set of laws, Hammurabi tried to unify empire under worship of Marduk, Hammurabi's code created civil and criminal law **Persian** from Asia Minor to India, divided into provinces, unified set of laws, Zoroastrianism, religious toleration, use of coins **Phoenician** located along Mediterranean coast, small cities which set up colonies along the Mediterranean, alphabet **Israelite** located at western tip of Fertile Crescent, ruled by kings, split into two kingdoms, belief in one God, Ten Commandments, Judaism, set of moral principles

Building Vocabulary

1–10. Quiz definitions should show a clear understanding of the meanings of the terms.

Recalling Key Facts

11. The Nile watered the land along its banks, making it good for farming.
12. to prepare the dead for the afterlife
13. in hieroglyphics
14. in the southern part of Mesopotamia
15. It was the first codification of all laws governing a state.
16. They thought that Abraham had made a binding agreement, or covenant, with God and that in return for faithful obedience, God would help them and lead them to the promised land of Canaan.

Critical Thinking and Writing

17. (a) The Sumerian view was gloomy; the Egyptian view was more hopeful. **(b)** Possible answer: The floods of the Tigris and Euphrates rivers were more destructive than those of the Nile, so Sumerians were more pessimistic.

Creating a Chapter Summary

Copy this graphic organizer on a sheet of paper. For each category on the chart, include from one to three facts that describe the characteristics of each civilization. To help you get started, the first row has been partly filled in.

CIVILIZATION	LOCATION	GOVERNMENT	RELIGION	CONTRIBUTIONS
EGYPTIAN	• Nile River valley in North Africa	• Strong centralized state • Pharaoh believed to be divine	• Polytheistic • •	• Knowledge of human body from mummification
SUMERIAN				
BABYLONIAN				
PERSIAN				
PHOENICIAN				
ISRAELITE				

For additional review and enrichment activities, see the interactive version of *World History* available on the Web and on CD-ROM.

Web Site Self-Test
For practice test questions for Chapter 2, see
www. phschool.com.

Building Vocabulary

Review the chapter vocabulary words listed below. Then, use the words and their definitions to create a matching quiz. Exchange quizzes with another student. Check each other's answers when you are finished.

1. dynasty
2. pharaoh
3. hieroglyphics
4. papyrus
5. hierarchy
6. cuneiform
7. civil law
8. barter economy
9. monotheistic
10. ethics

Recalling Key Facts

11. Why was the Nile River important to ancient Egyptian civilization?
12. Why did the people of ancient Egypt mummify their dead?
13. How did Egyptians record events?
14. Where did Sumerian civilization develop?
15. Explain the importance of Hammurabi's Code.
16. Why did the Israelites consider themselves to be God's "chosen people"?

Critical Thinking and Writing

17. Comparing Compare the view of the afterlife in the Sumerian and Egyptian religions. **(a)** What differences do you see between the two views? **(b)** Why do you think they might have been so different?
18. Drawing Conclusions One of Hammurabi's laws states, "If outlaws collect in the house of a wine-seller, and she does not arrest these outlaws and bring them to the palace, that wine-seller shall be put to death." **(a)** What was the purpose of this law? **(b)** Would you consider this a harsh law? **(c)** What similar laws do we have today?
19. Connecting to Geography Rivers played a major role in the development of ancient civilizations. Do rivers still play a major role in the world today? Why or why not?
20. Analyzing Information (a) What rights did women have in Egyptian, Sumerian, and Israelite civilizations? **(b)** How were these rights restricted? **(c)** What do these facts suggest about the status of women in ancient civilizations?

---

18. (a) to help officials capture outlaws and to make Babylonians responsible for enforcing laws **(b)** Answers may focus on the kind of crime and its punishment. **(c)** Possible answer: laws that prohibit the harboring of fugitives
19. Possible answer: Yes. Major cities still thrive along rivers; shipping bulky cargoes such as grain and coal, irrigation, and hydroelectric power still require rivers, but modern transportation such as railroads, trucks, and airplanes has made rivers less vital.
20. (a) Egyptian women could own property, engage in business, obtain divorces, and serve as doctors and priests. Some Sumerian women could engage in business and own property. Israelite women did not enjoy as many rights. **(b)** Possible answer: Most Egyptian women were kept illiterate, and even if they were literate, they could not become scribes or government officials. **(c)** Possible answer: The status of women varied, but, generally, they did not have as many rights as men.

In this essay, found on an ancient Sumerian tablet, a young student at a school for scribes describes his school day. Read the essay and answer the questions that follow.

A School for Scribes

"I recited my tablet, ate my lunch, prepared my new tablet, wrote it, finished it. Then they assigned me my oral work, and in the afternoon they assigned me my written work. When school was dismissed, I went home, entered the house, and found my father sitting there. I told my father of my written work, then recited my tablet to him, and my father was delighted. . . . When I awoke early in the morning, I faced my mother and said to her: 'Give me my lunch, I want to go to school.' My mother gave me two rolls and I set out. . . . In school, the monitor in charge of punctuality said to me, 'Why are you late?' Afraid and with pounding heart, I entered before my teacher and made a respectful curtsey."

—quoted in *History Begins at Sumer* (Kramer)

21. What invention of the Sumerians allowed this account to be preserved?
22. What type of schoolwork was assigned to Sumerian students?
23. What seems to be the attitude of the Sumerian student toward **(a)** his father, **(b)** his mother?
24. **(a)** How does the student approach his teacher? **(b)** Why do you think he behaves this way?
25. Would you consider this account a reliable source of information about Sumerian education and family life? Explain.
26. **(a)** Based on what you have read, what role did scribes play in Sumerian society? **(b)** How might this explain the strict discipline of the school described here?
27. Based on this account, compare life at a Sumerian school to life at a modern American high school.

Skills Tip

In evaluating a primary source, you should know whether the writer had firsthand knowledge of the events being described. This will help you determine whether the source is reliable.

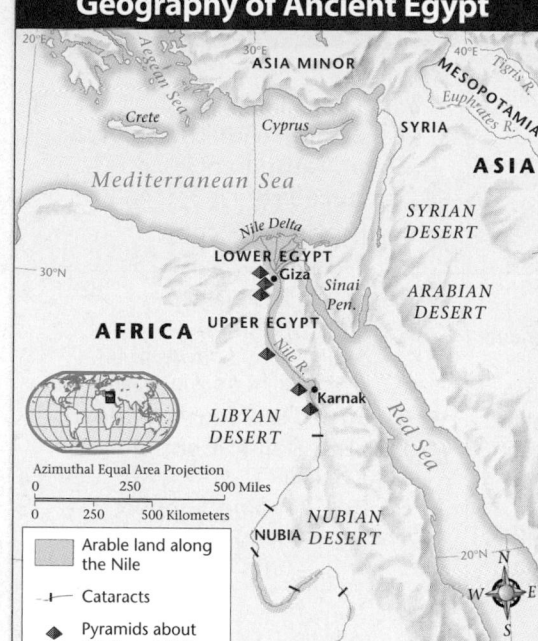

Geography of Ancient Egypt

Azimuthal Equal Area Projection

0 — 250 — 500 Miles
0 — 250 — 500 Kilometers

Arable land along the Nile
Cataracts
Pyramids about 2650 B.C.–2000 B.C.

Look at the map above and answer the following questions:

28. Describe the location of Lower Egypt.
29. About how far was it from Karnak to Giza?
30. Why did most people in ancient Egypt live near the Nile?
31. Why was travel toward the Nile Delta easier from the northernmost cataract?
32. Based on this map, do you think Egyptian traders would be more likely to travel by the Red Sea or the Mediterranean Sea? Explain.

Use the Internet to research hieroglyphics. Then, create a cartouche (kar TOOSH) of your name. A cartouche is a hieroglyphic spelling of a name, set within a formal, oval shape. What do the images used in hieroglyphics tell you about the society and environment of ancient Egypt?

21. writing or cuneiform
22. written and oral work
23. Possible answers: **(a)** respectful **(b)** disrespectful: he gives her orders
24. **(a)** fearfully and courteously **(b)** Possible answers: The teacher may have the power to reject him as a student; teachers are well respected in Sumerian society; the teacher may punish him by caning him.
25. Possible answer: yes, because it was written by someone with first-hand experience
26. **(a)** an important one; they were the ones who kept track of harvests and preserved the myths, prayers, laws, treaties, and business contracts **(b)** Possible answer: Students had to be well trained so that they would not make errors in important records.
27. Students may compare such things as daily routines, discipline, curriculum, educational differences for boys and girls, and student attitudes toward education.

28. in northeastern Africa on the Mediterranean Sea
29. about 300 miles (500 km)
30. The surrounding land was desert and too dry to farm.
31. because there were no more cataracts to go around
32. They would be more likely to travel by the Mediterranean Sea because they could reach the Mediterranean by way of the Nile. To reach the Red Sea, they would have to travel overland across the Nubian desert.

Skills Tip

Tell students that when they evaluate a firsthand account, they should first consider what sort of biases the writer might possess that would influence the account. The Skills Handbook in the front of the book has a lesson that will help students with this feature.

Direct students to **www.phschool.com** for links to sites that will help them get started on this assignment. Share rubrics with students.
Attempted The project is incomplete, missing either the cartouche or the answer to the question.
Minimal Project includes the cartouche and a very brief answer to the question.
Adequate Project includes the cartouche and a reasonable answer to the question.
Exemplary Project includes the cartouche and a thoughtful and thorough answer to the question.

Unit Theme Activity

Remind students to continue working on their Unit Theme Activity. See rubrics for the activity on the unit opener page in the Teacher's Edition.

Chapter 3 Planning Guide

Resource Manager

	CORE INSTRUCTION	READING/SKILLS
Chapter Level Resources	**Teaching Resources** 📖 Pacing Charts, Ch. 3 📖 Teaching With Themes, p. 6 🎞 Color Transparencies, p. F–7 💿 Resource Pro® Ch. 3 🖥 www.phschool.com • eTeach	🔊 Book on CD, Ch. 3 💿 Interactive Student Tutorial CD-ROM, Ch. 3 🔊 Social Studies Skills Tutor CD-ROM 🎞 Skills Transparencies

1 Cities of the Indus Valley
1. Describe how geography has influenced ancient India.
2. Explain how archaeology has provided clues about the Indus Valley civilization.
3. Identify the theories that scholars had about the decline of the Indus Valley civilization.
	Teaching Resources
	📖 Unit 1 booklet
	  • Biography Activity, p. 44
	  • Viewpoint Activity, p. 46
	📖 Creative Teaching Activities, p. 16
	💿 Prentice Hall Presentation Pro, Ch. 3, Section 1
	🎞 Section Reading Support Transparencies
		Teaching Resources
		📖 Unit 1 booklet
		  • Guided Reading and Review, p. 38
		  • Skill Application Activity, p. 47
		📖 Guide to the Essentials
		📼 Guided Reading Audiotapes, Ch. 3, Section 1

2 Kingdoms of the Ganges
1. Identify the main characteristics of Aryan civilization in India.
2. Describe how expansion led to changes in Aryan civilization.
3. Summarize what ancient Indian epics reveal about Aryan life.
	Teaching Resources
	📖 Unit 1 booklet
	  • Primary Source Activity, p. 45
	📖 Creative Teaching Activities, p. 17
	💿 Prentice Hall Presentation Pro, Ch. 3, Section 2
	🎞 Section Reading Support Transparencies
		Teaching Resources
		📖 Unit 1 booklet
		  • Guided Reading and Review, p. 40
		📖 Guide to the Essentials
		📼 Guided Reading Audiotapes, Ch. 3, Section 2

3 Early Civilization in China 1. Explain how geography influenced early Chinese civilization. 2. Describe how Chinese culture took shape under the Shang and the Zhou. 3. Identify the key cultural achievements in early China.	**Teaching Resources** 📖 Creative Teaching Activities, p. 18 💿 Prentice Hall Presentation Pro, Ch. 3, Section 3 🎞 Section Reading Support Transparencies	**Teaching Resources** 📖 Unit 1 booklet • Guided Reading and Review, p. 42 📖 Guide to the Essentials 📼 Guided Reading Audiotapes, Ch. 3, Section 3

ENRICHMENT/PRE-AP

Teaching Resources
- Teaching With Themes, Global View Activity, p. 41
- www.phschool.com
  - Why Study History?

Color Transparencies, p. B–73

Teaching Resources
- Chapter Extension Activities, p. 12
- Listening to Literature World Masterpieces, Indian Music; from the *Rig Veda*, side 1
- www.phschool.com
  - Internet Activities, Section 3

Teaching Resources
- Chapter Extension Activities, p. 13
  - History Through Literature, pp. 7–8
- Color Transparencies, p. D–37
- Listening to Literature World Masterpieces, Chinese Music; from *The Book of Songs*, side 2
- www.phschool.com
  - Internet Activities, The Huang He Floods
  - Internet Activities, Section 3
  - Virtual Field Trip

ASSESSMENT

PRENTICE HALL ASSESSMENT SYSTEM

Core Assessment
- ExamView Test Bank booklet, Ch. 3
- ExamView Test Bank CD-ROM, Ch. 3

Standardized Test Preparation

Diagnose and Prescribe
- Diagnostic Tests for High School Social Studies Skills

Review and Reteach
- Review Book for World History

Practice and Assess
- Document-Based Assessment, pp. 3-7
- Test-Taking Strategies With Transparencies
- Alternative Assessment booklet
- Test Prep Book for World History

Teaching Resources
- Unit 1 booklet
  - Geography Quiz, p. 48
  - Section Quizzes, pp. 39, 41, 43
  - Chapter Tests A, B, and C, pp. 49–53
- www.phschool.com
  - Self-Test

CUSTOMIZE FOR INDIVIDUAL NEEDS

Gifted and Talented
- **Teacher's Edition,** Activities: Customize for Heterogeneous Groups, p. 63

Less Proficient Readers
- **Guide to the Essentials,** Ch. 3
- **Guided Reading Audiotapes, English,** Ch. 3
- **Book on CD,** Ch. 3
- **Teacher's Edition,** Activities: Reading Strategy, p. 57; Reading Strategy, p. 60

Less Proficient Writers
- **Teacher's Edition,** Activities: Cooperative Learning Activity, p. 61

Students Acquiring English/ESL
- **Guide to the Essentials, English/Spanish,** Ch. 3
- **Guided Reading Audiotapes, English,** Ch. 3
- **Book on CD,** Ch. 3
- **Teacher's Edition,** Activities: Connections to Film, p. 63

Don't miss the exclusive inter-active version of *World History: Connections to Today* on the Internet and CD-ROM.

INTRODUCTION

Around 2500 B.C., the first civilization in India arose in the Indus River Valley where archaeologists have found the carefully planned cities of Harappa and Mohenjo-Daro. Although mountains protected the Indus River valley, eventually Aryans overran the civilization, mingled with the people, and formed a new Indian civilization.

Around 2000 B.C., Chinese civilization emerged along river valleys and the east coast of China. Desert and mountain barriers caused Chinese civilization to grow independently. Religion was important in both the Indian and Chinese civilizations. Both developed metalworking and a system of writing. The Chinese made strides in astronomy and learned to make books and silk.

Focusing on Themes

Suggest that students focus on these theme questions as they read:

Geography and History
How did geographic forces help shape early civilizations in India and China?

Art and Literature
How do the great epics of ancient India express basic social and religious values?

Continuity and Change
How did early Chinese traditions form the basis for a long-lasting civilization?

TIME LINE ACTIVITY

You may wish to share the About the Pictures note with your students before you ask these questions about the time line:

1. How can you tell that the Chinese developed writing after 2000 B.C.? *(Writing is a feature of civilization; it is not likely to have developed before Chinese civilization did.)*
2. When did Aryans invade India? *(1500 B.C.)*
3. How many years ago did the people of India begin to write the Vedas? *(2,500)*

Don't Miss!

Synthesizing Information
Tracing Migration Through Language
(Section 2)

Disaster!
The Huang He Floods
(Section 3)

CHAPTER 3

Early Civilizations in India and China

2500 B.C.–256 B.C.

Chapter Preview

1 Cities of the Indus Valley
2 Kingdoms of the Ganges
3 Early Civilization in China

1650 B.C.
The Shang dynasty, known for fine bronzeworks such as this cauldron, gains control of territory along the Huang He.

2500 B.C.
The first Indian civilization arises in the Indus River valley. Mohenjo-Daro, a principal city, is shown here.

2000 B.C.
Chinese civilization emerges along river valleys and the east coast of Asia.

CHAPTER EVENTS

3000 B.C.

2500 B.C.

2000 B.C.

GLOBAL EVENTS

3000 B.C. River valley civilizations begin to emerge.

2700 B.C. The pyramid age begins in Egypt.

50 Chapter 3

Resource Directory

Teaching Resources
Teaching With Themes Chapter Theme Activities, p. 6
Pacing Chart With Block Scheduling Guide Ch. 3
Global View Activity *How Did the First Civilizations Evolve?*
Teaching With Themes booklet, p.41

Technology
World History Color Transparencies Ch. 3 Graphic Organizer, p. F–7

Geography of India and China

Geographic barriers helped shape early civilizations in India and China.

1500 B.C.
The Aryans cross into India from the north and overrun existing cities and towns.

1027 B.C.
The Zhou overthrow the Shang. Richly adorned artworks reflect Zhou power and wealth.

500 B.C.
In India, people begin to write down Hindu sacred texts, called Vedas. The Vedas reflect Aryan belief in many deities, including Lakshmi, shown here.

1500 B.C.

1000 B.C.

500 B.C.

1400 B.C. The Olmecs develop the first civilization in the Americas.

750 B.C. Nubia conquers Egypt and gains control of the Nile Valley.

509 B.C. The Roman republic is established.

Geography of India and China

Activating Prior Knowledge
Given what you know about the location of North African and Middle Eastern civilizations, where would you expect civilizations to develop in India and China? *(along rivers such as the Indus, Ganges, Huang He, and Yangzi)*

Previewing
Mountains tended to isolate the Indus River civilization, but could not entirely prevent nomads from the west from invading it. How did the newcomers probably get over the mountains? *(through low spots such as the Bolan Pass and Khyber Pass)*

Background
About the Pictures

1. This view of Mohenjo-Daro shows the citadel with a dome-shaped shrine in the background. The shrine is Buddhist and dates from the second century A.D.—more than 2,000 years after the founding of Mohenjo-Daro.

2. The rich green patina on Chinese bronzes such as this one results from the piece's many centuries of entombment in the earth. Salts in the soil cause oxidation, which produces the color.

3. This dragon head is of bronze covered with gold. According to myth, dragons flew across the sky, gathering clouds and showering the earth with life-giving rain.

4. Lakshmi—goddess of fertility—was the gentle and submissive wife of Vishnu, the supreme Hindu god.

Independent Assignments

Have students read one section as they prepare for class. After class, have them complete the assignment. Some students may benefit from using the Guided Reading and Review worksheets.

Section 1 Have students use the outline map *Ancient India* in the Historical Outline Map Book, p. 5, to locate and label the area of the Indus Valley civilization and the major physical features of the Indian subcontinent

Section 2 Have students use the worksheet *Sita and Rama's First Meeting* in the Unit 1 booklet,

p. 45, to learn more about the beliefs of the people of ancient India.

Section 3 Have students use the worksheet *Two Chinese Parables* in the History Through Literature booklet, pp. 7–8, to learn more about the values of the ancient Chinese.

eTeach

Be sure to check out this month's online discussion with a World History Master Teacher.

Go to **www.phschool.com**.

SECTION 1 Cities of the Indus Valley

Bell Ringer Direct students' attention to the map of India and China on the chapter opener. Ask them to use the map to answer this question: How do you think geography benefited India's early civilizations?

LESSON PLAN

1. Focus The vast Indian subcontinent is a land of mountains, fertile plains, and arid regions. Rivers and monsoons have had much influence on Indian life. In the Indus River valley, archaeologists have uncovered the remains of India's first civilization.

2. Instruct Divide the class into cooperative learning groups. Explain that each group will create and submit plans for a museum exhibit on the cities that flourished in the Indus Valley about 2500 B.C. Each group's presentation should include maps, sketches of artifacts, diagrams of urban plans, and so on, all with brief descriptive captions. A written report might also accompany the project. The students in each group can divide the tasks so that some group members research, others illustrate, and others write.

3. Assess Have each group present its project to the class. Encourage questions and discussion. Ask students to describe the aspects of Indus Valley civilization that they were unable to illustrate.

4. Reteach If students' **Assess** activity does not reflect adequate understanding of the lesson, you might assign the *Guide to the Essentials* or the *Interactive Student Tutorial CD-ROM* for this section.

Reading Focus

- How has geography influenced India?
- How has archaeology provided clues about Indus Valley civilization?
- What theories do scholars hold about the decline of Indus Valley civilization?

Vocabulary

subcontinent
plateau
monsoon
veneration

Taking Notes

As you read this section, create an outline of the main ideas. Use Roman numerals to indicate the major headings of the section, capital letters for the subheadings, and numbers for the supporting details. The sample at right has been started for you.

I. Geography of the Indian subcontinent
  A. Three regions
    1.
    2.
    3.
  B.
    1.
    2.
II. Indus Valley civilization

Main Idea Archaeologists uncovered the remains of India's first civilization in the Indus River valley.

Setting the Scene In 1922, archaeologists made a startling discovery in northwestern India. While digging in the Indus River valley, they unearthed bricks, small statues, and other artifacts unlike any they had seen before. The archaeologists soon realized that they had uncovered a "lost civilization"—one that had been forgotten for some 3,500 years. Though later discoveries have added to our knowledge of the cities of the Indus Valley, many mysteries remain.

Geography of the Indian Subcontinent

The Indus Valley is located in the region known as South Asia or the subcontinent of India. A *subcontinent* is a large landmass that juts out from a continent. The Indian subcontinent is a huge, wedge-shaped peninsula extending into the Indian Ocean. Today, it includes 3 of the world's 10 most populous countries—India, Pakistan, and Bangladesh—as well as the island nation of Sri Lanka (sree LAHNG kah) and the mountain nations of Nepal and Bhutan.

Towering, snow-covered mountain ranges mark the northern border of the subcontinent, including the Hindu Kush and the Himalayas. These mountains limited contacts with other lands and helped India develop a distinct culture, yet the mountains were not a complete barrier. Steep passes through the Hindu Kush served as gateways to migrating and invading peoples for thousands of years.

Regions The Indian subcontinent is divided into three major zones: the well-watered northern plain, the dry triangular Deccan, and the coastal plains on either side of the Deccan.

The northern plain lies just south of the mountains. This fertile region is watered by mighty rivers: the Indus, which gives India its name, the Ganges (GAN jeez), and the Brahmaputra (brahm uh POO truh). These rivers and their tributaries carry melting snow from the mountains to the plains, making agriculture possible. To the people of the Indian subcontinent, rivers are sacred, especially the Ganges. This great importance is reflected in one Indian name for "river": *lok-mata,* or "mother of the people."

The most recognizable feature on any map of India is the Deccan. This triangular *plateau,* or raised area of level land, juts into the Indian Ocean. The Deccan lacks the melting snows that feed the rivers of the north and provide water for irrigation. As a result, much of the region is arid, unproductive, and sparsely populated.

Geography and History

River of Life

Beginning in an ice cave high in the Himalayas, the Ganges River flows through one of the most heavily cultivated and densely populated regions of the world. By the time it empties into the Bay of Bengal, it has touched the lives of 10 percent of the world's population.

For more than 3,500 years, Indians have drunk from the river, bathed in it, used it for irrigation, and honored it as a giver of life. Considered the most sacred of rivers, the Ganges is central to Hinduism, which teaches that the gods brought the river's water from heaven to purify the ashes of the dead.

Theme: Religions and Value Systems How does the Ganges satisfy the material and spiritual needs of Indians today?

Geography and History

ANSWER provides water for crops and people; is a sacred place for pilgrimages, purification rites, and funeral services

Resource Directory

Teaching Resources

Creative Teaching Activities Creative Teaching Activities booklet, p. 16
Guided Reading and Review Unit 1 booklet, p. 38
Viewpoint Activity *Did Democracy Begin in the Indus Valley?,* Unit 1 booklet, p. 46
Skill Application Activity *Using the Writing Process,* Unit 1 booklet, p. 47

Technology

World History Color Transparencies *Asia,* p. B–73

Block Scheduling Support

Archaeologists have recovered more than 2,000 seals from Harappa and Mohenjo-Daro. They believe each merchant family used its own seal to label its goods. The seals bear images of animals and other symbols, some with unknown meanings. Explain the uses and varied designs of the seals and have students design their own seals. Then, discuss how their seals and today's common trademarks and logos differ from the seals of ancient India. What do those differences communicate about the two societies?

The coastal plains, India's third region, are separated from the Deccan by low-lying mountain ranges, the Eastern and Western Ghats. Rivers and heavy seasonal rains provide water for farmers. From very early times, people used the seas for fishing and as highways for trade.

The Monsoons Today, as in the past, a defining feature of Indian life is the monsoon, a seasonal wind. In October, the winter monsoons blow from the northeast, bringing a flow of hot, dry air that withers crops. In late May or early June, the wet summer monsoons blow from the southwest. These winds pick up moisture over the Indian Ocean and then drench the land with daily downpours.

The monsoon has shaped Indian life. Each year, people welcome the rains that are desperately needed to water the crops. If the rains are late, famine and starvation may occur. Yet, if the rains are too heavy, rushing rivers unleash deadly floods.

Cultural Diversity India's great size and diverse languages made it hard to unite. Many groups of people, with differing languages and traditions, settled in different parts of India. At times, ambitious rulers conquered much of the subcontinent, creating great empires, yet the diversity of customs and traditions remained.

Indus Valley Civilization

The earliest Indian civilization is cloaked in mystery. It emerged in the Indus River valley, in present-day Pakistan, about 2500 B.C. This civilization flourished for about 1,000 years, then vanished without a trace. Only in this century have its once prosperous cities emerged beneath the archaeologists' picks and shovels.

Archaeologists have not fully uncovered many Indus Valley sites. We have no names of kings or queens, no tax records, no literature, no accounts of famous victories. Still, we do know that the Indus Valley civilization covered the largest area of any civilization until the rise of Persia more than 1,000 years later. We know, too, that its cities rivaled those of Sumer.

Well-Planned Cities The two main cities, Harappa and Mohenjo-Daro (moh HEHN joh DAH roh), may have been twin capitals. Both were large, some three miles in circumference. Each was dominated by a massive hilltop structure, probably a fortress or temple. Both cities had huge warehouses to store grain brought in from outlying villages.

The most striking feature of Harappa and Mohenjo-Daro is that they were so carefully planned. Each city was laid out in a grid pattern, with rectangular blocks larger than modern city blocks. All houses were built of uniform oven-fired clay bricks. Houses had surprisingly modern plumbing systems, with baths, drains, and water chutes that led into sewers beneath the streets. Merchants used a uniform system of weights and measures.

From such evidence, archaeologists have concluded that the Indus Valley cities had a well-organized government. Powerful leaders, perhaps priest-kings, made sure that the tens of thousands of city-dwellers had a steady supply of grain from the villages. The rigid pattern of building and

Indus Valley Civilization

Indus Valley civilization, 2500 B.C.–1500 B.C.

HINDU KUSH
Khyber Pass
Bolan Pass
ASIA
Indus R.
Harappa
30°N
Mohenjo-Daro
THAR DESERT
Brahmaputra R.
HIMALAYA MTS.
NORTHERN PLAIN
Ganges R.
VINDHYA MTS.
Narmada R.
INDIA
Arabian Sea
DECCAN PLATEAU
WESTERN GHATS
EASTERN GHATS
Bay of Bengal
15°N
75°E
90°E
INDIAN OCEAN

N W E S

Mercator Projection
0   250   500 Miles
0   250   500 Kilometers

Background
Historical Evidence

The Plunder of Indus Valley Cities In the 1800s, a British construction company built a railway through the Indus River valley. In the process, two engineers on the project nearly ruined some of India's most valuable historical treasures.

John Brunton was having difficulty laying track on sandy soil. He needed stones or bricks to use as a railway bed. Hearing that an ancient city was nearby, Brunton visited the site, where he found thousands of bricks used to build the city of Brahminabad. Brunton promptly commandeered the 4,000-year-old bricks and built his railway bed. Meanwhile, his brother William faced the same problem in the north, near the ancient city of Harappa. Like John, he plundered the city for its bricks. Between them, the Brunton brothers built 93 miles of railway bed with crushed bricks taken from these ancient Indus Valley cities.

Skills Assessment

Geography The earliest civilization in India developed in the Indus Valley.

1. **Location** On the map, locate (a) Himalaya Mountains, (b) Deccan Plateau, (c) Indus River, (d) Ganges River, (e) Harappa.
2. **Place** How has India's geography helped to protect the people living in the Deccan Plateau?
3. **Critical Thinking Making Inferences** Why do you think the Indus River valley was a more inviting location for the development of a civilization than was the Narmada River valley?

Human Drama Note

Indus Valley Empire The Indus Valley's two largest cities, Mohenjo-Daro and Harappa, were 3 miles in circumference, but the empire itself was larger. Archaeologists have found the remains of about 100 other early Indus cities. This empire, which started as Neolithic farming towns, may have spread to more than 403,000 square miles. Compare the Indus Valley civilizations to the Egyptian and the Mesopotamian civilizations, which flourished at the same time and had only about half as much land each.

Test Preparation

Have students read the section "The Monsoons" on this page, and then answer the question below.

What is a *monsoon*?

A an Indian holiday

B a type of crop

C an animal that eats snakes

D a seasonal wind

Skills Assessment

ANSWERS 1. Review locations with students. 2. Mountains provide a partial barrier to invasion and migration. 3. Possible answers: The Indus River valley is in a region with a more predictable supply of water for irrigation.

SECTION 1 Assessment

Recall
1. (a) subcontinent, p. 52 (b) plateau, p. 52 (c) monsoon, p. 53 (d) veneration, p. 54

Comprehension
2. Possible answers: Mountains partially protected India from invasion. India's vastness made it hard to unite. Monsoon rains benefited agriculture but also caused destructive floods. 3. well-planned cities of uniform design and a standardized system of weights and measures 4. Indus Valley records are lacking, and ancient sites have not yet been fully uncovered.

Critical Thinking and Writing
5. (a) Possible answers: A volcanic eruption might have blocked the Indus River and flooded cities. An earthquake might have devastated the region. (b) Possible answers: depletion of natural resources, global warming, pollution of the environment, reduction of the ozone layer, natural disasters such as floods and earthquakes, endangered species 6. Possible answers: Rivers are a source of life: they provide water for irrigation, drinking, and bathing; and they help create fertile soil.

Activity Rubrics

Share rubrics with students before they compile their lists.

Attempted The list is incomplete, or explanations are missing.

Minimal The list is complete, but explanations reveal little understanding of what one might learn from the items.

Adequate The list is complete, and explanations reveal an understanding of what one might learn from the items.

Exemplary The list contains items that would truly advance knowledge of the Indus civilization, and explanations reveal an understanding of what one might learn from the items.

Biography

Mortimer Wheeler
1890–1976

Much of what we know about Indus Valley civilization comes from the work of Sir Mortimer Wheeler, who began the excavation of Harappa and Mohenjo-Daro in the 1940s. Wheeler's great contribution to our knowledge was surpassed only by his skills as an organizer and promoter.

A noted scientist, Wheeler was also a colorful figure with a reputation as a scoundrel. His scandals, self-promotion, and success—combined with his brilliant manipulation of the press—drew thousands of visitors to his sites. Possibly more than any other person, Wheeler is responsible for the public's fascination with the work of archaeologists.

Theme: Impact of the Individual What did Wheeler contribute to archaeology?

the uniform brick sizes suggest government planners. These experts must also have developed skills in mathematics and surveying to lay out the cities so precisely.

Farming and Trade As in other early civilizations, most Indus Valley people were farmers. They grew a wide variety of crops, including wheat, barley, melons, and dates. They were also the first people to cultivate cotton and weave its fibers into cloth.

Some people were merchants and traders. Their ships carried cargoes of cotton cloth, grain, copper, pearls, and ivory combs to distant lands. By hugging the Arabian Sea coast and sailing up the Persian Gulf, Indian vessels reached the cities of Sumer. Contact with Sumer may have stimulated Indus Valley people to develop their own system of writing.

Religious Beliefs From clues such as statues, archaeologists have speculated about the religious beliefs of Indus Valley people. Like other ancient people, they were polytheistic. A mother goddess, the source of creation, seems to have been widely honored. Indus people also apparently worshiped sacred animals, including the bull. Some scholars think these early practices influenced later Indian beliefs, especially the veneration of, or special regard for, cattle.

Decline and Disappearance

By 1750 B.C., the quality of life in Indus Valley cities was declining. The once orderly cities no longer kept up the old standards. Crude pottery replaced the finer works of earlier days.

We do not know for sure what happened, but scholars have offered several explanations. Damage to the local environment may have contributed to the decline. Possibly too many trees were cut down to fuel the ovens of brick makers. Tons of river mud found in the streets of Mohenjo-Daro suggest that a volcanic eruption blocked the Indus, which flooded the city. Other evidence points to a devastating earthquake.

Scholars think that the deathblow fell about 1500 B.C., when nomadic people arrived in ever larger numbers from the north. The newcomers were the Aryans, whose ancestors had slowly migrated with their herds of cattle, sheep, and goats from what is now southern Russia. With their horse-drawn chariots and superior weapons, the Aryans overran the Indus region. The cities were soon abandoned and eventually forgotten.

SECTION 1 Assessment

Recall
1. **Define:** (a) subcontinent, (b) plateau, (c) monsoon, (d) veneration.

Comprehension
2. Describe two ways in which geography has influenced the people of South Asia.
3. What evidence shows that Indus Valley civilization had a well-organized government?
4. Why do we know so little about Indus Valley civilization?

Critical Thinking and Writing
5. **Linking Past and Present**
   (a) How could natural disasters have contributed to the decline of Indus Valley civilization?
   (b) What environmental problems does the world face today?
6. **Connecting to Geography** What characteristics of rivers might explain why many people in India still consider them sacred?

Activity

Thinking Like an Archaeologist
Imagine that you are an archaeologist digging in the Indus region. Write a "wish list" of three items you would like to uncover to learn more about Indus Valley civilization. Explain what you might learn from the items.

Biography

ANSWER He began the excavation of Harappa and Mohenjo-Daro, produced much of what is known about Indus Valley civilization, and raised public interest in archaeology.

Resource Directory

Teaching Resources
Biography Activity *Sir Mortimer Wheeler,* Unit 1 booklet, p. 44
Section Quiz Unit 1 booklet, p. 39
Creative Teaching Activities Creative Teaching Activities booklet, p. 17
Guided Reading and Review Unit 1 booklet, p. 40

Technology
Interactive Student Tutorial CD-ROM Ch. 3
Computer Test Bank Ch. 3

SECTION 2 Kingdoms of the Ganges

Reading Focus

■ What were the main characteristics of Aryan civilization in India?

■ How did expansion lead to changes in Aryan civilization?

■ What do ancient Indian epics reveal about Aryan life?

Vocabulary

caste

brahman

mystic

rajah

Taking Notes

Make a concept web like the one below. As you read this section, fill in each blank circle with important information about Aryan civilization. Use the completed web to help you focus on what you learned in this section.

Main Idea Aryan warriors invaded India and developed a new civilization.

Setting the Scene

The Aryans were warlike people. Their hymns praised their warriors as brave heroes and successful looters. In the *Satarudriya,* a poet lauded these warriors with the words:

"Hail to the lord of thieves . . . hail to the destructive ones armed with spears, hail to the lord of plunderers.
Hail to the archers, to those who stretch the bowstring, and to those who take aim."

—*Yajur Veda*

Over the centuries, the Aryans who destroyed and looted the cities of the Indus Valley became the builders of a new Indian civilization. It rose in the northeast along the Ganges River, rather than in the northwest along the Indus.

Aryan Civilization

The Aryans were among many groups of Indo-European people who migrated across Europe and Asia seeking water and pasture for their horses and cattle. The early Aryans built no cities and left no statues or stone seals. Most of what we know about them comes from the Vedas, a collection of prayers, hymns, and other religious teachings. Aryan priests memorized and recited the Vedas for a thousand years before they were written down. As a result, the period from 1500 B.C. to 500 B.C. is often called the Vedic age.*

In the Vedas, the Aryans appear as warriors who fought in chariots with bows and arrows. They loved eating, drinking, music, chariot races, and dice games. These nomadic herders valued cattle, which provided them with food and clothing. Later, when they became settled farmers, families continued to measure their wealth in cows and bulls.

Aryan Society From the Vedas, we learn that the Aryans divided people by occupation. The three basic groups were the Brahmins, or priests; the Kshatriyas (kuh SHAT ree yuhz), or warriors; and the Vaisyas (vīs yuhz), or herders, farmers, artisans, and merchants. At first, warriors enjoyed the highest prestige, but priests eventually gained the most respect. Their power grew because Brahmins claimed that they alone could conduct the ceremonies needed to win the favor of the gods.

*Our knowledge about the Aryans is very limited. Historians have re-created a picture of Aryan life from studying their language, but many conclusions are still open to debate.

Primary Source

Hymn to Indra
The Rig Veda *contains this hymn to the war god Indra:*

"The one who made firm the quaking earth; the one who made fast the shaken mountains; the one who measured out wide the atmosphere; the one who propped up heaven: he, O people, is Indra. . . .

The one in whose control are horses, cows, villages, all chariots; the one who has caused to be born the sun, the dawn; the one who is the waters' leader: he, O people, is Indra. . . .

The one without whom people do not conquer; the one to whom, when fighting, they call for help; the one who is a match for everyone; the one who shakes the unshakable: he, O people, is Indra."

—*Rig Veda*

Skills Assessment

Primary Source How can you tell from this source that the Aryans admired military prowess?

Block Scheduling Support

Vedic literature records the exploits of gods and goddesses who later evolved into the pantheon of Hindu gods. The deities include heroes, villains, demons, and animals. Among these many gods are the elephant-headed Ganesh, god of luck; the warrior goddess Durga, guardian against evil; Hanuman, the monkey-faced god; and Kali, the goddess of death, who is often surrounded by snakes.

Provide students with a brief profile of a Hindu god and discuss with them the god's unique characteristics, such as appearance, personality, and special powers. After the discussion, ask students to write a descriptive paragraph about the god. ✳

Bell Ringer Point out that for hundreds of years the Aryans preserved prayers, hymns, and long epic poems without the benefit of a written language. Ask students to speculate on how the Aryans accomplished this task. Then, have students discuss the special difficulties of maintaining an oral tradition.

LESSON PLAN

1. Focus The warlike Aryans invaded India and destroyed many Indus Valley cities. Over the centuries, they abandoned their nomadic life, mixed with the people they conquered, and developed a new Indian civilization. The sacred Vedas reveal much about the Aryans' religion and social structure.

2. Instruct Construct on the chalkboard a chart to show how Aryan culture changed over a period of 1,000 years. Set up two columns and label them Early Aryans and Later Aryans. Label the rows with such headings as Social System, Religious Beliefs, Literature, and Economics and Technology. Enlist students' assistance in completing the chart with specific details for each box. Students could also complete the charts individually or in groups.

3. Assess Ask students to review the information in their charts. Then have them write five sentences that summarize five main ideas they have learned.

4. Reteach If students' **Assess** activity does not reflect adequate understanding of the lesson, you might assign the *Guide to the Essentials* or the *Interactive Student Tutorial CD-ROM* for this section.

Primary Source

ANSWER Possible answer: The third paragraph refers to conquest and fighting.

Background
About the Evidence

Indo-European Origins The Indo-Iranian, Greek, Germanic, Romance, Slavic, Baltic, Celtic, Albanian, and Armenian languages are surviving branches of the Indo-European language. Some elements of the prehistoric language help scholars form theories about its origins. The ancient language had words for *snow, beech tree, bee,* and *wolf,* suggesting a northern European origin, but no word for *sea,* suggesting an inland central European location.

Activity
Interpreting the Evidence

Use these additional questions to generate class discussion.

1. Critical Thinking: Making Inferences Languages on the chart are different enough that speakers of one language cannot understand speakers of another. Why might this be so? *(Possible answers: geographical isolation; separate development over time)*

2. Critical Thinking: Analyzing Information The language of the Basques of the Pyrenees region of France and Spain is an enigma. Basque is unrelated to any other known language. Why might this be so? *(Accept any reasonable response.)*

Skills Tip

When answering multiple-choice questions, read all the choices before choosing an answer. Some choices may be distracters that are partially true, but do not answer the question as well as the correct answer. The Skills Handbook in the front of the book has a lesson to help students with this feature.

Skills Assessment

ANSWERS 1. C **2.** F **3.** Possible answers: The Indo-Europeans had ocean-going ships (routes on map); they were herders (pastureland on map); they could cross mountains (routes on map); they spoke similar languages (chart).

Tracing Migration Through Language

By studying the Indo-European language family, historians have learned about the migration of many peoples, including the Aryans. A *language family* is a group of related languages that developed from the same original, or parent, language. Use the map and chart below to draw conclusions about these Indo-European peoples.

Speakers of the parent Indo-European languages may have originated in north-central Europe. Over thousands of years, these people migrated across Europe and into Asia in search of good pastureland.

Comparing Languages

English	month	mother	new	night	nose	three
German	Monat	Mutter	neu	Nacht	Nase	drei
Persian	māh	mādar	nau	shab	bini	se
Sanskrit	mās	matar	nava	nakt	nās	trayas
Spanish	mes	madre	nuevo	noche	nariz	tres
Swedish	månad	moder	ny	natt	näsa	tre

The languages on the chart are all in the Indo-European language family. Similarities in words offer one clue that the languages share a common parent language. The similarities become even more apparent when the words are spoken out loud.

Skills Tip

Maps that show migrations use arrows to indicate movement. Trace routes by moving from the beginning of each arrow to its tip.

Skills Assessment

1. Which statement about Indo-European migrations can you base on the map?

  A Indo-European peoples migrated to the east coast of Asia.

  B Indo-European peoples migrated primarily along river and sea routes.

  C Indo-European peoples migrated across plains, mountains, and bodies of water.

  D Indo-European peoples migrated primarily to coastal areas.

2. Which statement best expresses the main idea of the chart?

  E There are six Indo-European languages.

  F There are similarities among words in Indo-European languages.

  G Indo-European languages are spoken in India and Europe.

  H Persian is unlike most other Indo-European languages.

3. Critical Thinking Drawing Conclusions What conclusions can you draw about Indo-European peoples, based solely on the information on this page? Explain how you arrived at each conclusion.

Resource Directory

Teaching Resources

Synthesizing Information Chapter Extension Activities booklet, p. 12

Technology

Listening to Literature World Masterpieces audiotapes Indian Music, side 1, running time 4:13 min.; from the *Rig Veda,* side 1, running time 3:48 min.

The Vedas also show that the Aryans felt vastly superior to the Dravidians, the people they conquered. Many scholars think that the Dravidians may have been descended from the original inhabitants of the Indus Valley. The Aryans separated Dravidians and non-Aryans into a fourth group, the Sudras (soo druhz). This group included farmworkers, servants, and other laborers who occupied the lowest level of society.

During the Vedic age, class divisions came to reflect social and economic roles more than ethnic differences between Aryans and non-Aryans. As these changes occurred, they gave rise to a more complex system of castes,* or social groups into which people are born and which they cannot change.

Aryan Religious Beliefs The Vedas show that the Aryans were polytheistic. They worshiped gods and goddesses that embodied natural forces such as sky and sun, storm and fire. Fierce Indra, the god of war, was the chief Aryan deity. Indra's weapon was the thunderbolt, which he used not only to destroy demons but also to announce the arrival of rain, so vital to Indian life. Other major gods included Varuna, the god of order and creation, and Agni, the god of fire. Agni also served as the messenger who communicated human wishes to the gods. The Aryans also honored animals, such as monkey gods and snake gods.

Brahmins offered sacrifices of food and drink to the gods. Through the correct rituals and prayers, the Aryans believed, they could call on the gods for health, wealth, and victory in war.

As the lives of the Aryans changed, so, too, did their beliefs. Some religious thinkers were moving toward the notion of a single spiritual power beyond the many gods of the Vedas, called brahman, that resided in all things. There was also a move toward mysticism. Mystics are people who devote their lives to seeking spiritual truth. Through meditation and yoga, or spiritual and bodily discipline, Aryan mystics sought direct communion with divine forces. The religions that emerged in India after the Vedic age reflected the impact of mysticism as well as the notion of brahman.

Expansion and Change

Over many centuries, waves of Aryans went through the mountain passes into northwestern India. Aryan tribes were led by chiefs called rajahs. A rajah was often the most skilled war leader, elected to his position by an assembly of warriors. He ruled with the advice of a council of elders made up of heads of families.

From Nomads to Farmers Aryans mingled with the people they conquered. Gradually, they gave up their nomadic ways and settled into villages to grow crops and breed cattle. From the local people, they learned farming and other skills and developed new crafts of their own.

In time, Aryans spread eastward to colonize the heavily forested Ganges basin. By about 800 B.C., they had learned to make tools out of iron. Equipped with iron axes and weapons, restless pioneers carved farms and villages out of the rain forests of the northeast. Tribal leaders fought to control trade and territory across the northern plain. Some rajahs became powerful hereditary rulers, extending their influence over many villages. Walled cities filled with multistory houses rose above the jungle.

By 500 B.C., a new Indian civilization had emerged. It consisted of many rival kingdoms. However, due to acculturation, or the blending of two or more cultures, the people shared a common culture rooted in both Aryan and Dravidian traditions. By this time, too, the Indian people had developed a written language, Sanskrit. Priests now began writing down the sacred texts.

---

*Indians use the word *jati* to describe their social system. The Portuguese, who reached India in the late 1400s, used the word *caste*, which other Europeans adopted.

Social Organization
Aryan society was divided into four distinct classes. One Vedic hymn explains how these classes corresponded to the human body: the Brahmins were the mouth, the Kshatriyas made up the arms, the legs were the Vaisyas, and the feet could be compared to the Sudras.

Theme: Political and Social Systems Which class does the hymn suggest was most important in Aryan society?

Chapter 3 **57**

Background
Perspectives

"A Desire for More Cows" In his book *Our Oriental Heritage*, historian Will Durant writes this of the Aryans:

"These Aryans were rather immigrants than conquerors. But they brought with them strong physiques, . . . a ready brutality, a skill and courage in war, which soon gave them the mastery of northern India. They fought with bows and arrows, led by armored warriors in chariots, who wielded battle-axes and hurled spears. They were too primitive to be hypocrites: they subjugated India without pretending to elevate it. They wanted land and pasture for their cattle; their word for war said nothing about national honor, but simply meant 'a desire for more cows.'"

You may wish to use this quotation as the basis for a class discussion on historical interpretation.

Reading Strategy
Check Comprehension

After students have finished reading about the Vedic age, ask them to make a rough sketch or drawing of what the text meant to them or what they learned from it. After students have completed their sketches, ask volunteers to share their illustrations. Discuss and compare what students chose to sketch and how their illustrations relate to the text. *(Less Advanced Readers)*

Human Drama Note

Jungle Warfare To transform the jungles of India into farmland and cities, people battled the lions, tigers, and elephants that occupied the land. Then, as today, the big cats would sometimes attack humans. But over the centuries, farmers, hunters, builders, and governments conquered the jungle, bringing several species close to extinction in India. Although the Indian government has established national parks and wildlife preserves, many animals remain on the endangered species list.

 Test Preparation

Have students read the paragraph headed "Aryan Religious Beliefs" on this page, and then answer the question below.

Which of the following best describes the main idea of the paragraph?

(A) Aryan gods and goddesses embodied natural forces and animals.

B The Aryans believed in only one god.

C The Aryans worshiped animals.

D The Aryans worshiped nature.

Caption Answer

Students may say that the Brahmins were the most important class because they could "speak" for the entire "body" of Indian society.

Recall
1. (a) Vedas, p. 55 (b) Brahmins, p. 55
(c) Kshatriyas, p. 55 (d) Vaisyas, p. 55
(e) Sudras, p. 57 (f) Indra, p. 57
2. (a) caste, p. 57 (b) brahman, p. 57
(c) mystic, p. 57 (d) rajah, p. 57

Comprehension
3. The Aryans categorized people by occupation: the Brahmins, or priests, were at the top; Kshatriyas, or warriors, followed; Vaisyas, or herders, farmers, artisans, and merchants were below warriors; and Sudras, or laborers, formed the lowest group in society. 4. A complex caste system developed. Mysticism and belief in brahman arose in religion. The Aryans began to farm and developed a written language. 5. They teach moral lessons embodying the values of the Aryans. Rama's actions show virtue, and Sita's actions are those of a loyal and obedient wife.

Critical Thinking and Writing
6. Possible answers: Epic poems mix moral lessons with dramatic action and exciting stories that appeal to a large audience. Good and evil are clear and distinct. Through moral action, the epic hero is victorious over evil. 7. Possible answer: Their relationship with their gods was all-important. Since the priests claimed that they were the only ones who could conduct ceremonies involving the gods, they assured themselves of greater power.

Activity Rubrics

Share rubrics with students before they prepare their lists.

Attempted Student's list shows no understanding of conflicting obligations or of dilemmas for characters in modern epics.

Minimal Student's list shows weak understanding of conflicting obligations and suggests weak and not well-thought-out dilemmas for modern epics.

Adequate Student's list shows good understanding of conflicting obligations and suggests several well-thought-out dilemmas for modern epics.

Exemplary Student's list shows an exceptional understanding of conflicting obligations and suggests several insightful and well-thought-out dilemmas for modern epics.

Epic Literature

Despite the new written language, the Aryans preserved a strong oral tradition. They continued to memorize and recite ancient hymns, as well as two long epic poems, the *Mahabharata* (muh HAH bah rah tuh) and the *Ramayana* (rah MAH yuh nuh). Like the Sumerian *Epic of Gilgamesh*, the *Mahabharata* and *Ramayana* mix history, mythology, adventure, and religion.

Mahabharata The *Mahabharata* is India's greatest epic. Through the tale's nearly 100,000 verses, we hear echoes of the battles that rival Aryan tribes fought to gain control of the Ganges region. Five royal brothers, the Pandavas, lose their kingdom to their cousins. After a great battle that lasts for 18 days, the Pandavas regain their kingdom and restore peace to India. One episode, known as the *Bhagavad-Gita* (BUHG uh vuhd GEE tuh), reflects important Indian religious beliefs about the immortality of the soul and the importance of duty.

Ramayana The *Ramayana* is much shorter but equally memorable. It recounts the fantastic deeds of the daring hero Rama and his beautiful bride Sita. Sita is kidnapped by the demon-king Ravana. The rest of the story tells how Rama finally rescues Sita with the aid of the monkey general Hanuman.

Like Aryan religion, these epics evolved over thousands of years. Priest-poets added new morals to the tales to teach different lessons. For example, they pointed to Rama as a model of virtue or as an ideal king. Likewise, Sita came to be honored as an ideal woman who remained loyal and obedient to her husband through many hardships.

> ▶ **Primary Sources and Literature**
>
> See "The Mahabharata" in the Reference Section at the back of this book.

Looking Ahead

The Aryans were the first of many people to filter into India through passes in the Hindu Kush. Even though scholars recognize that our knowledge of the Aryan migrations is very limited, most accept that Aryan traditions and beliefs formed a framework for later Indian civilization.

Aryan religious beliefs would evolve into major world religions. Just as the Middle East gave rise to three world religions—Judaism, Christianity, and Islam—South Asia was the birthplace of two influential faiths, Hinduism and Buddhism.

Recall
1. **Identify:** (a) Vedas, (b) Brahmins, (c) Kshatriyas, (d) Vaisyas, (e) Sudras, (f) Indra.
2. **Define:** (a) caste, (b) brahman, (c) mystic, (d) rajah.

Comprehension
3. What do the Vedas tell us about Aryan society and religion?
4. How did Aryan life change as a result of expansion in India?
5. What kinds of lessons do Rama and Sita teach in the epics of the *Ramayana*?

Critical Thinking and Writing
6. **Analyzing Information** Why might epic poems like the *Mahabharata* and *Ramayana* be good vehicles for teaching moral lessons?
7. **Making Generalizations** Based on what you have read about the shift in power from the Aryan warriors to the Brahmins, what generalization could you make about people and their relationship with their gods in Aryan civilization and society?

Activity
Take It to the NET

Use Internet sources to find out more about the moral dilemmas faced by characters in the *Ramayana*. Consider how these dilemmas stem from conflicting obligations. What types of dilemmas might be faced by characters in a modern-day epic?

Resource Directory

Teaching Resources
Section Quiz Unit 1 booklet, p. 41
Creative Teaching Activities Creative Teaching Activities booklet, p. 18
Guided Reading and Review Unit 1 booklet, p. 42
Primary Source Activity *Sita and Rama's First Meeting,* Unit 1 booklet, p. 45
History Through Literature *The Concealed Deer* and *The Man Who Forgot,* History Through Literature booklet, pp. 7–8

Technology
Interactive Student Tutorial CD-ROM Ch. 3
Computer Test Bank Ch. 3
World History Color Transparencies *Asia,* p. B–73; *Bronze Elephant,* p. D–37

SECTION 3 Early Civilization in China

Reading Focus

- How did geography influence early Chinese civilization?

- How did Chinese culture take shape under the Shang and the Zhou?

- What were key cultural achievements in early China?

Vocabulary

loess
clan
oracle bone
calligraphy
dynastic cycle
feudalism

Taking Notes

Make a chart like this one. As you read the section, add information about China under the Shang to the first column and information about the Zhou under the second column.

SHANG	ZHOU
• Clans controlled most of land	• Mandate of Heaven
•	•

Main Idea Early Chinese people developed a complex civilization and made many advances in learning and the arts.

Setting the Scene In very ancient times, relates a Chinese legend, flood waters rose to the top of the highest hills. Yu, a hard-working official, labored for 13 years to drain the waters:

> "I opened passages for the streams throughout the nine provinces, and conducted them to the sea. I deepened channels and canals, and conducted them to the streams."
> — *Shujing (Book of History)*

While taming the rivers, Yu did not once go home to see his wife and children. As a reward for his selfless efforts, he later became ruler of China.

The legend of Yu offers insights into early China. The ancient Chinese valued the ability to control flood waters and to develop irrigation systems for farming. The legend also shows how highly the Chinese prized devotion to duty. Both of these values played a key role in the development of Chinese civilization.

The Geography of China

The ancient Chinese called their land Zhongguo (JONG goo AW), the Middle Kingdom. China was the most isolated of the civilizations you have studied so far. Long distances and physical barriers separated it from Egypt, the Middle East, and India. This isolation contributed to the Chinese belief that China was the center of the Earth and the sole source of civilization.

Geographic Barriers To the west and southwest of China, high mountain ranges—the Tien Shan and the Himalayas—and brutal deserts blocked the easy movement of people. To the southeast, thick jungles divided China from Southeast Asia. To the north lay the forbidding desert, the Gobi. To the east, the vast Pacific Ocean rolled endlessly.

Despite formidable barriers, the Chinese did have contact with the outside world. They traded with neighboring people and, in time, Chinese goods reached the Middle East and beyond. More often, though, the outsiders whom the Chinese encountered were nomadic invaders. To the Chinese, these nomads were barbarians who did not speak Chinese and lacked the skills and achievements of a settled society. Nomads conquered China from time to time, but they were usually absorbed into the advanced Chinese civilization.

Mt. Everest
In the ancient world, the Himalayas served as one geographic barrier between China and the rest of the world. The range includes the world's highest peak, Mt. Everest, shown here.

Theme: Geography and History Why might a geographic barrier make it easier for a civilization to develop?

Chapter 3 **59**

SECTION 3

Bell Ringer Note that Chinese civilization grew up largely in isolation from other peoples and civilizations. Ask students to speculate on how that situation may have both fostered and hindered the growth of the civilization.

LESSON PLAN

1. Focus Geography isolated early Chinese civilization, yet the people developed a writing system, literature, silkmaking, and other arts. They honored nature and ancestor spirits. Politically, they believed in the Mandate of Heaven and the dynastic cycle.

2. Instruct Have small groups of students each outline one of the following topics concerning early Chinese civilization: effects of geography, politics, economics, society, religion, art and literature. Each outline should show the major developments and ideas pertaining to its assigned topic. Then regroup the students so that each new group has a student expert on each topic. Have students share their findings to learn more about early Chinese civilization.

3. Assess Ask the class to compare early Chinese civilization with the other early civilizations they have studied. How was Chinese civilization similar to the others? How did it differ?

4. Reteach If students' **Assess** activity does not reflect adequate understanding of the lesson, you might assign the *Guide to the Essentials* or the *Interactive Student Tutorial CD-ROM* for this section.

*B*ackground *Biography*

Yu the Great According to tradition, Yu the Great descended from one of the legendary Three Sovereigns of China. He invented the nets used for fishing and hunting. According to legend, all the people of north China helped Yu build a vast network of dikes and drainage ditches that kept the Huang He within its channel. A traditional saying shows their gratitude: "We should have been fish, but for Yu."

Caption Answer

Possible answer: Geographic barriers might allow a civilization to focus on development rather than on warding off attacks by other peoples.

Shang Civilization

Skills Assessment

Geography The huge landmass of China extends west from the Pacific Ocean deep into central Asia. More than two thirds of the land is made up of plateaus and mountains.

1. **Location** On the map, locate (a) Huang He, (b) Gobi, (c) Pacific Ocean.
2. **Region** What physical features acted as obstacles to contact with lands outside China?
3. **Critical Thinking Synthesizing Information** (a) Between which latitudes does most of China fall? (b) Use a map of the United States to find the latitude of your community. What part of China is at the same latitude?

Main Regions As the Chinese expanded over an enormous area, their empire came to include many regions with a variety of climates and land-forms. The Chinese heartland lay along the east coast and the valleys of the Huang He (HWAHNG HAY), or Yellow River, and the Yangzi (yahng DZEE). In ancient times, as today, these fertile farming regions supported the largest populations. Then, as now, the rivers provided water for irrigation and served as transportation routes.

Beyond the heartland are the outlying regions of Xinjiang (sheen jee AHNG), Mongolia, and Manchuria. The first two regions have harsh cli-mates and rugged terrain. Until recent times, they were mostly occupied by nomads and subsistence farmers. All three outlying regions played a key role in China's history. Nomads repeatedly attacked and plundered Chinese cities. At other times, powerful Chinese rulers conquered or made alliances with the people of these regions. China also extended its influence over the Himalayan region of Tibet, which the Chinese called Xizang (shee DZAHNG).

"River of Sorrows" Chinese history began in the Huang He valley, where Neolithic people learned to farm. As in other places, the need to control the flow of the river through large water projects probably led to the rise of a strong central government.

The Huang He got its name from the loess, or fine windblown yellow soil, that it carries eastward from Siberia and Mongolia. Long ago, the Huang He earned a bitter nickname, "River of Sorrows." As loess settles to the river bottom, it raises the water level. Chinese peasants labored constantly to build and repair dikes that kept the river from overflowing.

If the dikes broke, flood waters burst over the land. Such disasters destroyed crops and brought mass starvation. Fear of floods is reflected in Chinese writing. The character, or written symbol, for misfortune, 巛 represents a river with a blockage that causes flooding.

China Under the Shang

About 1650 B.C., a Chinese people called the Shang gained control of a cor-ner of northern China, along the Huang He. The Shang dynasty dominated this region until 1027 B.C. During the Shang period, Chinese civilization first took shape.

The Huang He Floods

For at least 4,000 years, farmers living along the Huang He in China have depended on the fertile yellow loess soil deposited along the river's banks. But they have also feared the devastating floods that the river brings every third or fourth year. In 2297 B.C., the Huang He burst its banks, destroying fields and drowning villagers.

After days of severe rains, the Huang He began to overflow its banks, spilling into the millet fields. Without the technology to dam the breach, the villagers could only flee or watch in horror as their crops and homes became completely submerged in the swirling, muddy, yellow water.

No one knows exactly how many people perished in this great flood. Worse yet, after the waters receded, many more people died as a result of a great famine that spread throughout the region. Despite this catastrophe, many villagers returned to the same spot to rebuild and plant, taking advantage of the fertile soil deposited by the flood waters.

The villagers' huts were quickly swept away in the flood. Unable to escape their pens, domestic animals reacted in fear as the waters surged toward them.

Portfolio Assessment

Use the Internet or other research sources to learn more about a recent flood. You can start your search at **www.phschool.com**. Use the information you find to write front-page newspaper articles about the flood. You may want to use pictures or diagrams to illustrate the articles.

Chapter 3 **61**

Bell Ringer Remind students of the damage done by a recent flood in the United States. Then have them imagine what it must have been like to be alive in 2297 B.C., when there was no technology to warn of the danger, prevent the flood, or minimize its effects.

Background
Connections to Today

Floods in China In 1998, and again in 1999, severe floods hit the Yangzi basin, where about 400 million people live. The flooding in 1998 killed more than 4,000 people and caused roughly $24 billion in property damage. The 1999 floods killed far fewer people and caused far less economic damage, even though the water rose higher in some places than in the previous year. The lessened damage was a result of the money the Chinese government—aided by World Bank and foreign loans—put into reinforcing embankments, removing silt, and relocating a million people to allow for the creation of lakes to help absorb excess water.

Activity
Cooperative Learning

Have student groups investigate recent disasters in the United States to find the cause of the disaster, the location and the number of people killed or injured, the amount of property damage, and the kinds of help the government gave victims. Have students suggest ways of preventing or reducing destruction in the future. Ask if government relief money encourages development of high-risk areas.

Portfolio Assessment Rubrics

Share rubrics with students before they create their articles.

Attempted Student's article fails to include all of the five *W*s (who, what, when, where, why).

Minimal Student's article has the five *W*s, but is poorly written.

Adequate Student's article has the five *W*s, and the article is clear.

Exemplary Student's article has the five *W*s, and is well written, informative, interesting, and accompanied by illustrations.

Background
Connections to Economics

Ancient Factories In early China, government officials supervised the production of bronze weapons, ritual vessels, and other objects in state-run factories. Production began in the countryside with the mining of metal ores. These raw materials were then transported to the capital and distributed among the factories. To enhance efficiency, labor in the workshops was divided according to specialized skills. Thus, instead of having to learn the entire process, workers would master one special skill, such as making clay molds or carving fine details. The ability of this system to produce large quantities of products contributed to the survival of many artifacts from early China. Factories today still use a division-of-labor system like that used in ancient China.

Background
Daily Life

Habits of Dress Chinese fashions did not vary greatly by social class or gender. Men and women of all classes wore pants and loose tunics, with no belts or corsets to constrict the figure or movements. All classes also used layering. In winter, men layered many tunics atop one another and shed them layer by layer as spring approached.

There were some exceptions to this generally egalitarian system, however. In the cities, women often wore a skirt over their pants. Upper-class people often wore silk instead of cotton. Also, age had its privileges. Men were not allowed to grow facial hair until the age of 45, and even then only a mustache was permitted. Not until the age of 60 was a full beard allowed.

Virtual Field Trip
www.phschool.com

The Tsui Museum of Art
Hong Kong, China

To see other artworks and artifacts relating to Shang bronzes, use the Internet address above to link to the Tsui Museum of Art.

Shang Bronzes
Bronzework was a high art during the Shang period. These bronze containers were crafted to resemble a snail (left) and a pair of owls (right).

Theme: Art and Literature
What features of the bronzes suggest that the Shang were skilled metalworkers?

Government Archaeologists have uncovered large palaces and rich tombs of Shang rulers. Shang kings led other noble warriors in battle. From their walled capital city at Anyang, they emerged to drive off nomads from the northern steppes and deserts.

In one Shang tomb, archaeologists discovered the burial place of Fu Hao (FOO HOW), wife of the Shang king Wu Ding. Artifacts show that she owned land and helped to lead a large army against invaders. This evidence suggests that noblewomen had considerable status during the Shang period.

Shang kings probably controlled only a small area. Loyal princes and nobles governed most of the land. They were likely the heads of important clans, or groups of families who claimed a common (often mythical) ancestor. Thus, Shang China probably more closely resembled the city-states of Sumer than the centralized government ruled by the Egyptian pharaohs.

Social Classes Shang society mirrored that in other early civilizations. Alongside the royal family was a class of noble warriors. Shang warriors used leather armor, bronze weapons, and horse-drawn chariots. The chariots may have come from other Asian peoples.

Early Chinese cities supported a class of artisans and merchants. Artisans produced goods for nobles, including bronze weapons, silk robes, and jade jewelry. Merchants exchanged food and crafts made by local artisans for salt, cowrie shells, and other goods not found in northeastern China.

Peasant Life Most people in Shang China were peasants. They clustered together in farming villages. Many lived in thatch-roofed pit houses whose earthen floors were dug several feet below the surrounding ground.

Peasants led grueling lives. All family members worked in the fields, using stone tools to prepare the ground for planting or to harvest grain. When they were not in the fields, peasants had to repair the dikes. If war broke out between noble families, men had to fight alongside their lords.

Religious Beliefs

By Shang times, the Chinese had developed complex religious beliefs, many of which continued to be practiced for thousands of years. They prayed to many gods and nature spirits. Chief among them were Shang Di

62 Chapter 3

Caption Answer

Possible answers: detailed designs, recognizable shape of snail's head, careful fit of lid to container

Block Scheduling Support

To help students understand the dynastic cycle and the Zhou's Mandate of Heaven, try the following activity. Have students form small groups. Instruct the groups that they are a new dynasty that is going to replace the "dynasty" that currently rules the United States. Have groups identify events that could be seen as signs of the end of the aging dynasty and also list improvements that they, as the new dynasty, would make. Each group should present its lists to the class. After each group has completed its presentation, lead a discussion comparing and contrasting the different lists. Finally, mention that this Mandate of Heaven still appears, to a lesser degree, in the rhetoric of politicians running against incumbents.

(SHAHNG DEE) and a mother goddess who brought plants and animals to Earth. The king was seen as the link between the people and Shang Di.

Gods as great as Shang Di, the Chinese believed, would not respond to the pleas of mere mortals. Only the spirits of the greatest mortals, such as the ancestors of the king, could get the ear of the gods. Thus, the prayers of rulers and nobles to their ancestors were thought to serve the community as a whole, ensuring good harvests or victory in war.

At first, only the royal family and other nobles had ancestors important enough to influence the gods. Gradually, other classes shared in these rituals. The Chinese called on the spirits of their ancestors to bring good fortune to the family. To honor their ancestors' spirits, they offered them sacrifices of food and other necessities. When westerners reached China, they mistakenly called this practice "ancestor worship."

The Chinese believed the universe reflected a delicate balance between two forces, yin and yang. Yin was linked to Earth, darkness, and female forces, while yang stood for Heaven, light, and male forces. To the Chinese, these forces were not in opposition. Rather, the well-being of the universe depended on maintaining balance between yin and yang. For example, the king had to make the proper sacrifices to Heaven while at the same time taking practical steps to rule well.

System of Writing

The ancient Chinese also developed a system of writing. Writing, like religious beliefs, was an early development that continued to influence cultures in China throughout history. This system used both pictographs and ideographs, signs that expressed thoughts or ideas.

Consulting the Ancestors Some of the oldest examples of Chinese writing are on oracle bones. On animal bones or turtle shells, Shang priests wrote questions addressed to the gods or the spirit of an ancestor. Priests then heated the bone or shell until it cracked. By interpreting the pattern of cracks, they provided answers or advice from the ancestors.

A Difficult Study Written Chinese took shape almost 4,000 years ago. Over time, it evolved to include tens of thousands of characters. Each character represented a word or idea and was made up of a number of different strokes. In recent years, the Chinese have simplified their characters, but Chinese remains one of the most difficult languages to learn. Students must still memorize up to 10,000 characters to read a newspaper. By contrast, languages based on an alphabet, such as English or Arabic, contain only two dozen or so symbols representing basic sounds.

Not surprisingly, in earlier times, only the well-to-do could afford the years of study needed to master the skills of reading and writing. Working with brush and ink, Chinese scholars turned calligraphy, or fine handwriting, into an elegant art form.

A Force for Unity Despite its complexity, the written language fostered unity. People in different parts of China often could not understand one another's spoken language, but they all used the same system of writing.

The Zhou Dynasty

In 1027 B.C., the battle-hardened Zhou (JOH) people marched out of their kingdom on the western frontier to overthrow the Shang. They set up the Zhou dynasty, which lasted until 256 B.C.

The Mandate of Heaven To justify their rebellion against the Shang, the Zhou promoted the idea of the Mandate of Heaven, or the divine right to rule. The cruelty of the last Shang king, they declared, had so outraged the

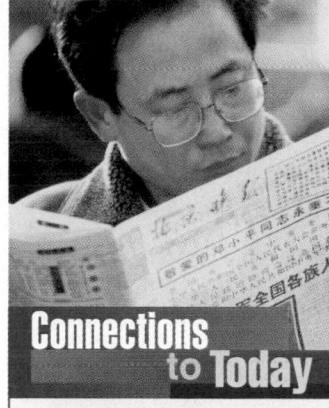

Connections to Today

Digital Chinese

The writing systems in China, Japan, Korea, Vietnam, and Taiwan are all based on a common set of thousands of characters developed in China centuries ago. Over time, each country has modified this system in a different way. These differences have made it difficult for writers in the various countries to communicate clearly with one another.

The computer age has added new communication problems. Since the 1970s, each East Asian country has developed its own code of Chinese characters to input and transmit computer data. The codes are not always compatible, and their differences can corrupt information sent from a computer in one country to that in another. To solve this problem, an international task force is attempting to develop a standard software set of digital Chinese characters.

Theme: Continuity and Change Why might there be so much interest in developing a common Chinese character code for computer communication?

Activity
Connections to Film

Drawing Conclusions *China: The Mandate of Heaven,* a program in the six-part 1991 public television series *Legacy,* describes an interesting investigation. For centuries, Chinese apothecaries had distributed ground bones as medicine. In the 1800s, Chinese scholars began to wonder where the bones came from. Their search for the answer took them to the site of the ancient Shang capital. To their dismay, the scholar-detectives discovered that, for centuries, Chinese druggists had been grinding ancient oracle bones!

Ask students to view the first few minutes of *China: The Mandate of Heaven.* Assign these questions: Why did Chinese druggists think ground bones were a valuable medicine? How did Chinese scholars probably feel about their discovery? Students should be able to draw conclusions based on the film and their knowledge of traditional Chinese religion. (*Legacy* is distributed by Ambrose Video Publishing, Inc.)

Customize for...
Heterogeneous Groups

Researching Because the modern dialects of China differ from one another as much as some languages do, Chinese who speak different dialects cannot understand one another's spoken language. They can, however, usually understand one another's written words. For example, although dialects may use different spoken words for *cat,* the symbol for *cat* is the same throughout China. Not all multilingual countries are this fortunate.

Have students research countries— such as Canada, Switzerland, and India— where more than one language is spoken. For each country, students should identify the languages used, the percentages of the population who use them, the areas where each language is prevalent, and examples of cooperation and conflict that result from this variety of languages. Students may use maps and graphs to present their findings. (*Enrichment*)

Connections to Today

ANSWER Possible answers: to avoid problems caused by incompatible codes; to permit computer users in the different Asian countries to communicate more easily with one another.

✓ Test Preparation

Have students read "A Difficult Study" on this page, and then complete the sentence:

In the passage the author provides evidence

A that the Chinese language is hard for English speakers to pronounce.

B that it is easier to learn to write in Chinese if you already know how to speak Chinese.

C that languages based on an alphabet contain up to 10,000 characters.

D that the Chinese writing system is complex and difficult to learn.

Background
Global Connections

International Espionage To protect its silkmaking monopoly and combat espionage, the Chinese government imposed strict measures on anyone who divulged to foreigners the secrets of silkmaking. Those found guilty would suffer torture and death. Despite such measures, the secret was eventually stolen. According to legend, the successful spies were a group of monks who stole some silkworm eggs, concealed them in hollow bamboo walking sticks, and smuggled the secret of silkmaking to Europe.

THE DYNASTIC CYCLE IN CHINA

The New Dynasty
Restores peace
Appoints loyal officials
Redistributes land to peasants
Builds canals, irrigation systems, and roads
Repairs defensive walls

After several generations, the new dynasty becomes an aging dynasty

The Aging Dynasty
Neglects government duties
Ignores corrupt officials
Loses control of the provinces
Imposes heavy taxes to pay for luxuries
Allows defensive walls to decay

Problems
Floods, famine, earthquakes
Invasions
Armed bandits in the provinces
Peasant revolts

New dynasty claims the Mandate of Heaven

Aging dynasty loses the Mandate of Heaven

Skills Assessment

Chart The Chinese believed that dynasties could gain or lose the Mandate of Heaven, depending on how wisely the emperor ruled. **According to this flowchart, how did a new dynasty try to repair the problems left by an aging dynasty?**

gods that they had sent ruin on him. The gods then passed the Mandate of Heaven to the Zhou, who "treated the multitudes of the people well." The Chinese later expanded the idea of the Mandate of Heaven to explain the dynastic cycle, or the rise and fall of dynasties. As long as a dynasty provided good government, it enjoyed the Mandate of Heaven. If the rulers became weak or corrupt, the Chinese believed that Heaven would withdraw its support.

Floods, famine, or other catastrophes were signs that a dynasty had lost the favor of Heaven. In the resulting chaos, an ambitious leader might seize power and set up a new dynasty. His success and strong government showed the people that the new dynasty had won the Mandate of Heaven. The dynastic cycle would then begin again.

A Feudal State The Zhou rewarded their supporters by granting them control over different regions. Thus, under the Zhou, China developed into a feudal state. Feudalism (FYOO duhl ihz uhm) was a system of government in which local lords governed their own lands but owed military service and other forms of support to the ruler. (In later centuries, feudal societies also developed in Europe and Japan.)

In theory, Zhou kings ruled China, and for about 250 years, they actually did enjoy great power and prestige. After about 771 B.C., though, feudal lords exercised the real power and profited from the lands worked by peasants within their domains.

Economic Growth During the Zhou period, China's economy grew. Knowledge of ironworking reached China about 500 B.C. As iron axes and ox-drawn iron plows replaced stone, wood, and bronze tools, farmers produced more food. Peasants also began to grow new crops, such as soybeans. Some feudal lords organized large-scale irrigation works, making farming even more productive.

Commerce expanded, too. The Chinese began to use money for the first time. Chinese copper coins had holes in the center so they could be strung on cords. This early form of a cash, or money, economy made trade easier. Merchants also benefited from new roads and canals constructed by feudal lords.

Economic expansion led to an increase in population. People from the Huang He heartland overflowed into central China and began to farm the immense Yangzi basin. Feudal nobles expanded their territories and encouraged peasants to settle in the conquered territories. Toward the end

Skills Assessment

ANSWER by restoring peace, appointing loyal officials, redistributing land, constructing public works, and repairing walls

Resource Directory

Teaching Resources
Section Quiz Unit 1 booklet, p. 43
Geography Quiz Unit 1 booklet, p. 48
Chapter Test A, B, and C Unit 1 booklet, pp. 49–53
Answer Key Unit 1 booklet, pp. 54–64

Technology
Listening to Literature World Masterpieces audio-tapes Chinese Music, side 2, running time 3:48 min.; from *The Book of Songs*, side 2, running time 1:14 min.
Interactive Student Tutorial CD-ROM Ch. 3
Computer Test Bank Ch. 3

of the Zhou era, China was increasing in area and population, as well as in prosperity.

Chinese Achievements

The Chinese made progress in many areas during the Shang and Zhou periods. For example, astronomers studied the movement of planets and recorded eclipses of the sun. Their findings helped them develop an accurate calendar with 365¼ days. The Chinese also made remarkable achievements in the art and technology of bronzemaking.

Silkmaking By 1000 B.C., the Chinese had discovered how to make silk thread from the cocoons of silkworms. Soon, the Chinese were cultivating both silkworms and the mulberry trees on which they fed. Women did the laborious work of tending the silkworms and processing the cocoons into thread. They then wove silk threads into a smooth cloth that was colored with brilliant dyes. Only royalty and nobles could afford robes made from this luxurious silk.

Silk became China's most valuable export. The trade route that eventually linked China and the Middle East became known as the Silk Road. To protect their control of this profitable trade, the Chinese kept the process of silkmaking a secret.

The First Books Under the Zhou, the Chinese made the first books. They bound thin strips of wood or bamboo together and then carefully drew characters on the flat surface with a brush and ink.

Among the greatest Zhou works is the lovely *Book of Songs.* Many of its poems describe such events in the lives of farming people as planting and harvesting. Others praise kings or describe court ceremonies. The book also includes tender or sad love songs.

Looking Ahead

By 256 B.C., China was a large, wealthy, and highly developed center of civilization. Chinese culture was already dominant in East Asia. Yet the Zhou dynasty was too weak to control feudal lords who ignored the emperor and battled one another in savage wars. Out of these wars rose a ruthless leader who was determined to impose political unity. His triumphs would leave a lasting imprint on Chinese civilization.

Primary Source

The Spirits Are Good
The poems in the Book of Songs *offer a rare look into the everyday lives of average people in ancient China:*

"The spirits are good,
 They will give you many blessings.
 The common people are contented,
 For daily they have their drink and food.
 The thronging herd, the many clans
 All side with you in deeds of power.

To be like the moon advancing to its full,
 Like the sun climbing the sky,
 Like the everlastingness of the southern hills,
 Without failing or falling,
 Like the pine-tree, the cypress in their [foliage]
 All these blessings may you receive!"

—*Shih Ching (Book of Songs)*

Skills Assessment

Primary Source Why might there be so many nature images in this poem?

Recall
1. (a) Zhongguo, p. 59 (b) Shang, p. 60 (c) yin and yang, p. 63 (d) Zhou, p. 63 (e) Mandate of Heaven, p. 63 (f) *Book of Songs,* p. 65 2. (a) loess, p. 60 (b) clan, p. 62 (c) oracle bone, p. 63 (d) calligraphy, p. 63 (e) dynastic cycle, p. 64 (f) feudalism, p. 64

Comprehension
3. People farmed in fertile river valleys, used rivers for transportation, or lived as nomads in areas of rugged terrain. In areas prone to flooding, Chinese peasants built dikes to hold back water.
4. Kings had rich palaces, but noble landowners wielded great power. Noblewomen may have had great status, and society was made up of noble warriors, artisans, merchants, and peasants.
5. bronzework, complex religion, system of writing, silkmaking, bookmaking

Critical Thinking and Writing
6. Possible answers: more time spent on learning to recognize characters; learning to read would take longer; homework would take more time because of greater need for care in writing 7. Environmental disasters such as floods, famines, and earthquakes were said to be signs that a dynasty had lost favor with Heaven. These disasters thus offered an opportunity for ambitious leaders to seize power and set up a new dynasty.

Recall
1. **Identify:** (a) Zhongguo, (b) Shang, (c) yin and yang, (d) Zhou, (e) Mandate of Heaven, (f) *Book of Songs.*
2. **Define:** (a) loess, (b) clan, (c) oracle bone, (d) calligraphy, (e) dynastic cycle, (f) feudalism.

Comprehension
3. How did people in China adapt to the environment?
4. What were the characteristics of Shang and Zhou government and social structure?

5. Identify major cultural achievements in early China.

Critical Thinking and Writing
6. **Predicting Consequences** Suppose that you had to learn a language written in unfamiliar characters, rather than in a language using an alphabet you know. Give three examples of how your life and schooling might be different.
7. **Connecting to Geography** How did environmental catastrophes affect Chinese government?

Activity
Take It to the NET

Use Internet sources to learn more about the silkworm. Then, use your information to create a fact sheet about this ancient source of silk. Post your fact sheet on a classroom bulletin board for others to read.

Activity Rubrics

Share rubrics with students before they create their fact sheets.

Attempted Student's fact sheet has little information.

Minimal Student's fact sheet has a reasonable number of facts but is poorly written.

Adequate Student's fact sheet has a reasonable number of facts and is well written.

Exemplary Student's choice of facts shows consideration of the relative importance of the information, and the fact sheet is well written and nicely designed.

Primary Source

ANSWER Possible answer: Part of Chinese religious beliefs included prayers to nature spirits.

Human Drama Note

Origin of Silkmaking Chinese legend says that silkmaking began because of the curiosity of a 14-year-old empress, Hsi Ling-shi. One day the young woman, who lived around 2500 B.C., noticed caterpillars eating the leaves of mulberry trees. A few days later, she saw cocoons attached to the leaves. Hsi Ling-shi took one of the cocoons and put it in a pot of water to see what would happen. As she watched, the cocoon softened and spread apart. When she took the mass out of the water, she was able to unravel it into a thread of silk.

Creating a Chapter Summary

As a reteaching opportunity, pair a more able student with a less able student to complete this chapter summary.

Possible entries that students might make on their tables include

Aryan Civilization Religion—moved toward monotheism; Class Structure—four fairly rigid castes formed by occupation; Government—elected rajahs; Cultural Achievements—Vedas, epic poems

Shang Civilization Religion—complex, many gods, honored ancestors (who communicated with gods), belief in yin and yang; Class Structure—royal family, landowning warriors, merchants and artisans, most people peasants; Government—kings and clan leaders; Cultural Achievements—system of writing, bronzemaking

Zhou Civilization Religion—similar to Shang; Class Structure—feudal; Government—feudal state, Mandate of Heaven; Cultural Achievements—silkmaking, books, calendar

Building Vocabulary

1–10. Students' sentences should show an understanding of each word.

Recalling Key Facts

11. People rely on the monsoon rains to water their crops. Also, monsoons often cause deadly floods.

12. warehouses to store grain, grid pattern in cities shows planning, advanced plumbing, uniform system of weights and measures, rigid building styles

13. The Aryans migrated to India from southeastern Europe looking for water and pastureland for their horses and cattle.

14. The caste system grew out of Aryan social classes.

15. The land in this area was good for farming, so the area could support many people.

16. developed a complex written language, studied planets and eclipses, designed an accurate calendar, made the first books

Critical Thinking and Writing

17. Possible answers: **(a)** Rivers provided water for agriculture and transportation routes. **(b)** Physical barriers limited contact with other lands and helped India and China develop distinct cultures.

Creating a Chapter Summary

Copy this table onto a sheet of paper. Use it to compare features of the Aryan, Shang, and Zhou civilizations. A few entries have been made to help you get started.

	ARYAN CIVILIZATION	SHANG CIVILIZATION	ZHOU CIVILIZATION
RELIGION	Polytheism		
CLASS STRUCTURE			
GOVERNMENT	Elected rajahs		Feudal state; Mandate of Heaven
CULTURAL ACHIEVEMENTS		System of writing; bronzemaking	Silk; books; calendar

For additional review and enrichment activities, see the interactive version of *World History* available on the Web and on CD-ROM.

Web Site Self-Test
For practice test questions for Chapter 3, see **www. phschool.com.**

Building Vocabulary

For each of the ten terms below, write a sentence using the term.

1. **subcontinent**
2. **monsoon**
3. **caste**
4. **brahman**
5. **rajah**
6. **loess**
7. **oracle bone**
8. **calligraphy**
9. **dynastic cycle**
10. **feudalism**

Recalling Key Facts

11. How has climate shaped life in the Indian subcontinent?
12. What signs of an advanced civilization can be seen in Harappa and Mohenjo-Daro?
13. Why did the Aryans migrate to India? From where did they come?
14. How did the caste system develop in early India?
15. Why was the area between the Huang He and the Yangzi the heartland of early China?
16. Describe Chinese accomplishments in writing, astronomy, and bookmaking.

Critical Thinking and Writing

17. **Connecting to Geography** In what ways might each of the following geographic features have influenced the development of civilization in ancient India and China: **(a)** rivers, **(b)** physical barriers?
18. **Linking Past and Present** Based on evidence uncovered by archaeologists, how were the cities of the ancient Indus Valley similar to and different from cities that exist around the world today?
19. **Applying Information** In the Vedas, "breaker of cities" is one of the titles of honor given to the god Indra. How might this title have linked Indra to actual events in the history of the Aryans?
20. **Making Generalizations** Based on what you have read about the ancient societies that existed in Egypt, Sumer, China, and the Indus Valley, make three generalizations about the role of religion and priests in early river valley civilizations.

---

18. Possible answer: They were similar to cities today because they were large and carefully planned and had well-organized governments. Unlike cities today, they were dominated by a fortress or temple, and they consisted of uniform clay-brick houses.
19. Possible answer: The Aryans looted and destroyed the cities of the Indus Valley civilization.
20. Students' answers should recognize the importance of religion and the power of priests in these early civilizations.

In the epic *Ramayana,* Rama is the oldest of four princes. His stepmother persuades the king to name her son heir instead of Rama, and to exile Rama from the kingdom for 14 years. Rama's wife, Sita, announces that she will join him in exile. In this excerpt, Sita persuades Rama to share his exile with her.

"Sita's beautiful face was streaked with tears which fell continuously from her large, dark eyes as drops of water from blue lotus flowers. Rama embraced her and gently wiped away her tears. He was still apprehensive about taking her, but he could not see her endure the pain of his separation. Making up his mind to take her with him, he spoke reassuringly.

'I would find no pleasure . . . if I obtained it at the cause of your suffering, O most pious lady! Not knowing your real feelings and being afraid that forest life would cause you pain, I discouraged you from following me. I see now that destiny has decreed you should dwell with me in the forest. Follow me then, O princess, and I will protect you in strict accord with the moral laws always followed by the virtuous.'

Rama made clear his firm intention to go into the deep forest and remain there for the full duration. . . . He was fixed in his determination to obey the command of his parents. . . . Earth, heaven, and the kingdom of God can all be achieved by one who serves his mother, father, and teacher. Explaining all of this to his devoted wife, Rama said, 'Not even truthfulness, charity, or sacrifice are comparable to serving one's mother and father. . . . Pious men, devoted to serving their parents, reach the regions of the gods and beyond.'"

— *Ramayana* (trans. Dharma)

21. Why does Rama decide to take Sita with him?
22. How does Rama say he will treat Sita during their exile?
23. What is Rama's attitude toward his parents?
24. What does this passage suggest about the importance of family in ancient India?

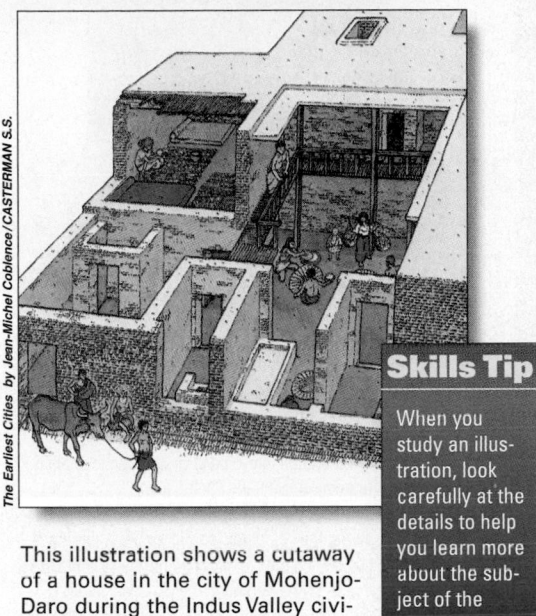

The Earliest Cities by Jean-Michel Coblence / CASTERMAN S.S.

This illustration shows a cutaway of a house in the city of Mohenjo-Daro during the Indus Valley civilization. Use the illustration to answer the following questions:

Skills Tip

When you study an illustration, look carefully at the details to help you learn more about the subject of the image.

25. How many stories are there in this house?
26. What area of the house seems to have been used for the greatest variety of activities?
27. What skills did people need to build a house like this?
28. What does the number of people in and around the house suggest?

Use the Internet to research population density in India and China today. Then, compare the information you find on the Internet with the information shown in the maps of the Indus Valley Civilization (in Section 1) and Shang Civilization (in Section 3). How do the settlement patterns of ancient India and China compare with the settlement patterns of these countries today?

Analyzing Primary Sources

21. She convinces him that she would be more unhappy without him.
22. He will protect her and maintain a high moral standard.
23. He is extremely respectful and places service to them above other values.
24. Possible answer: Family was a vital part of life in ancient India. Obedience to family members was almost a religious obligation.

Analyzing Illustrations

25. two
26. the large, two-story room on the right
27. Possible answer: brick making, architectural design, drafting, project planning
28. Possible answer: The homes were spacious enough to house large or extended families and possibly guests and servants.

Skills Tip

Tell students that a study of the details of this illustration will reveal how the roof was constructed. (See the cutaway of the roof at left.) The Skills Handbook in the front of the book has a lesson that will help students with this feature.

Unit Theme Activity

Evaluate students' Unit Theme Activities by referring to the rubrics on the unit opener page in the Teacher's Edition.

Take It to the NET

Direct students to **www.phschool.com** for links to sites that will help them get started on this assignment. Share rubrics with students.

Attempted The response is incomplete, missing information on one area or period or making no comparison.

Minimal The response includes some information on each area and period and makes some comparative comments.

Adequate The response includes clear information on each area and period and compares past to present.

Exemplary The response includes information on each area and period, insightful comparisons, and maps conveying the information visually.

Using These Pages

The Unit-in-Brief contains the main ideas of the unit chapters. You may use the Unit-in-Brief to preview, review, or condense the contents of each chapter.

The unit time line identifies key events in each world region that took place during the time span covered by the unit.

Activity
Unit Themes

Have students review the unit themes below. Then, ask them to find examples in the time line and summary to support each theme.

Continuity and Change Using artifacts and written evidence, archaeologists and historians help us understand the ancient human past.

Economics and Technology During early human history, people gradually changed from the life of hunters and gatherers to the life of farmers. As civilizations developed, people began to specialize. They traded more, built large-scale public projects, and used mathematics and astronomy to better understand the world around them.

Geography and History Early people depended on their physical surroundings, using natural resources to provide food, shelter, and tools for survival. Gradually, people living in the river valleys of Egypt, the Middle East, India, and China developed complex civilizations.

Art and Literature The development of writing preserved some of the world's oldest literature, from the Egyptian *Tale of Sinuhe* and the Sumerian *Epic of Gilgamesh* to India's *Mahabharata* and ancient China's *Book of Songs*.

Chapter 1

Toward Civilization
(Prehistory–3000 B.C.)

Archaeologists, historians, and other scholars are learning about our ancient human past through careful research. When the evidence they find is gathered, pieced together, and interpreted, a fascinating story of the emergence of civilization unfolds.

- Archaeologists analyze artifacts to trace how early people developed new technologies and ways of life.
- Historians also study how people lived in the past, but they rely more heavily on written evidence to interpret past events.
- Geographers use the themes of location, place, human-environment interaction, movement, and region to explain the impact of geography on the human story.
- People made tools, learned to build fires, and developed spoken languages during the Paleolithic period, or Old Stone Age.
- During the Neolithic period, or New Stone Age, people learned to farm, dramatically transforming the way they lived.
- By about 5,000 years ago, the advances made by early farming communities led to the rise of civilizations.
- Historians define eight basic features common to most early civilizations: (1) cities, (2) well-organized central governments, (3) complex religions, (4) job specialization, (5) social classes, (6) arts and architecture, (7) public works, and (8) writing.
- Cities first rose in river valleys where conditions favored farming and a surplus of food could be grown.

Chapter 2

First Civilizations: Africa and Asia
(3200 B.C.–500 B.C.)

The first civilizations to develop emerged in river valleys in Egypt and the Middle East more than 5,000 years ago. In these places, people developed a complex way of life and beliefs that continue to affect our world today.

- The three periods of ancient Egyptian history were the Old Kingdom, the Middle Kingdom, and the New Kingdom.
- Egyptian pharaohs organized a strong, centralized state and built majestic pyramids.
- Egyptians worshipped many deities and believed in an afterlife.
- Egyptian society was organized into a hierarchy of classes, with the pharaoh at the top and farmers and slaves at the bottom.
- Independent Sumerian city-states developed in Mesopotamia, an area of fertile land between the Tigris and Euphrates rivers.
- Sumerians invented the earliest form of writing, known as cuneiform, and made great strides in mathematics and astronomy.
- Many groups—including the Babylonians, the Assyrians, and the Persians—invaded Mesopotamia and built great empires.
- Warfare and trade in Mesopotamia helped to spread ideas and technology around the Mediterranean.
- The Hebrews developed Judaism, a monotheistic religion based on the worship of one God, whose laws are set out in the Torah and the Ten Commandments.

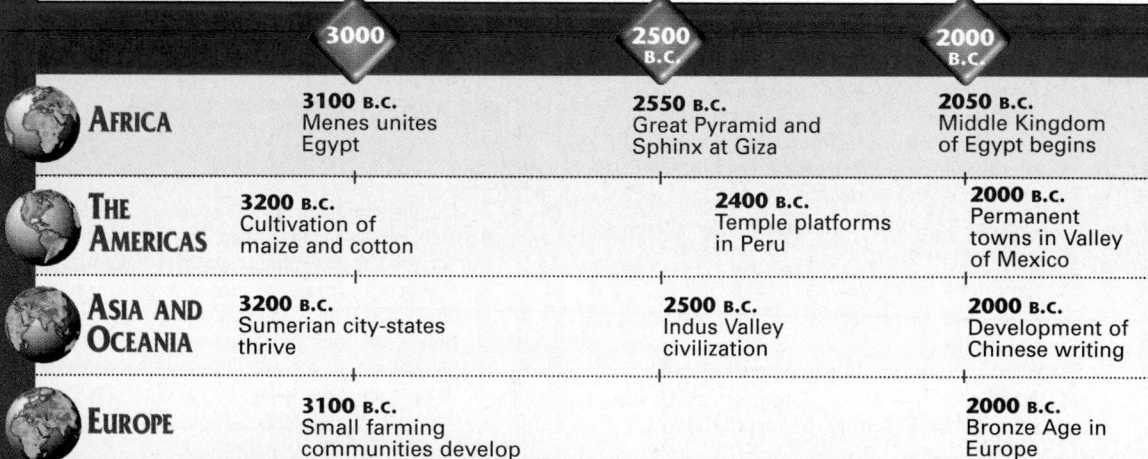

	3000	2500 B.C.	2000 B.C.
AFRICA	3100 B.C. Menes unites Egypt	2550 B.C. Great Pyramid and Sphinx at Giza	2050 B.C. Middle Kingdom of Egypt begins
THE AMERICAS	3200 B.C. Cultivation of maize and cotton	2400 B.C. Temple platforms in Peru	2000 B.C. Permanent towns in Valley of Mexico
ASIA AND OCEANIA	3200 B.C. Sumerian city-states thrive	2500 B.C. Indus Valley civilization	2000 B.C. Development of Chinese writing
EUROPE	3100 B.C. Small farming communities develop		2000 B.C. Bronze Age in Europe

Student Bibliography

Auel, Jean M. *The Clan of the Cave Bear*. Bantam, 1984. Fictional account of prehistoric life.

Gowlett, John. *Ascent to Civilization: The Archaeology of Early Humans*. McGraw-Hill, 1992. Beautifully illustrated account of the rise and development of human culture.

Grant, Michael. *The History of Ancient Israel*. Scribner's, 1984. Illustrated and readable account of the early Israelites.

Roaf, Michael. *Cultural Atlas of Mesopotamia and the Ancient Near East*. Facts On File, 1990. Richly illustrated synthesis of prehistory and early history of Southwest Asia.

Silverman, David P., ed. *Ancient Egypt*. Oxford University Press, 1997. Illustrated tour of the history and culture of ancient Egypt.

Chapter 3

Early Civilizations in India and China
(2500 B.C.–256 B.C.)

As civilizations took shape in the Nile Valley and the Fertile Crescent, people in India and China carved out their own civilizations. These two remarkable civilizations evolved distinct ways of life and thought that would exert a powerful influence on other civilizations.

- India's first civilization emerged in the Indus River valley.
- Excavations show that the Indus Valley covered the largest area of any ancient civilization and that its two main cities, Mohenjo-Daro and Harappa, were carefully planned.
- Aryan warriors invaded India and developed a new civilization.
- The Vedas and the great Aryan epic poems, the *Mahabharata* and the *Ramayana* reveal much about the lives and religious beliefs of the early Aryans.
- Long distances and physical barriers separated China from the other ancient civilizations and contributed to the Chinese belief that it was the sole source of civilization.
- The dynastic cycle explained the rise and fall of the many dynasties that came to rule China.
- Chinese religion centered around the veneration of ancestors and the balance of two opposing forces, yin and yang.
- During the Shang and Zhou periods, the Chinese made great strides in astronomy and bronzework, discovered how to make silk and books, and developed a complex system of writing.

1500 B.C.

1000 B.C.

500 B.C.

1503 B.C.
Reign of Hatshepsut begins

1290 B.C.–1224 B.C.
Reign of Ramses II

750 B.C.–650 B.C.
Nubian rule over Egypt

1400 B.C.
Rise of Olmec civilization

850 B.C.
Chavín culture in Peru

500 B.C.
Adena mounds in Ohio

1650 B.C.
Shang dynasty in China emerges

1100 B.C.
Assyrians expand power

539 B.C.
Persian empire created

1600 B.C.
Height of Minoan civilization

750 B.C.
Greeks colonize the Mediterranean

Teacher Bibliography

Chang, Kwang-chih. *The Archaeology of Ancient China.* Yale University Press, 1986. A comprehensive account of the origins of Chinese civilization and early Chinese dynasties.

Fagan, Brian D. *People of the Earth: An Introduction to World Prehistory.* HarperCollins, 1992. A comprehensive and clear survey of prehistoric peoples.

Gero, J.M., and M.W. Conkey, eds. *Engendering Archaeology: Women and Prehistory.* Blackwell, 1991. Brings together case studies addressing the role of women in the prehistoric past.

Grimal, Nicolas-Christophe. *A History of Ancient Egypt.* Blackwell, 1992. Well-written history from prehistory to Alexander the Great.

Kenoyer, Jonathan Mark. *Ancient Cities of the Indus Valley Civilization.* Oxford University Press, 1998. Introductory text on the Indus civilization.

Kramer, Samuel N. *History Begins at Sumer.* University of Pennsylvania Press, 1981. Authoritative overview emphasizing the achievements of Sumerian civilization.

UNIT OVERVIEW

Unit 2 examines the enduring and far-reaching significance of ancient empires in Asia, Europe, and the Americas.

Chapter 4 focuses on the powerful influence of ancient empires in India and China.

Chapter 5 examines the rise of ancient Greece and the development of Hellenistic civilization.

Chapter 6 studies the empire and civilization of ancient Rome and the rise of Christianity.

Chapter 7 focuses on the civilizations of the Mayas, the Aztecs, the Incas, and other peoples of the Americas.

Unit Theme Activity Rubrics

Share rubrics with students before they create their projects.

Attempted The project does not describe the development of several political and social systems.

Minimal The project is poorly executed or only vaguely describes the development of several political and social systems.

Adequate The project is well executed and clearly describes the development of several political and social systems.

Exemplary The project is extremely well executed, ably describes the development of several political and social systems, and is visually interesting or is extremely interesting and informative to read.

Empires of the Ancient World

1750 B.C.–A.D. 1570

OUTLINE

Chapter 4 **Empires of India and China** (600 B.C.–A.D. 550)

Chapter 5 **Ancient Greece** (1750 B.C.–133 B.C.)

Chapter 6 **Ancient Rome and the Rise of Christianity** (509 B.C.–A.D. 476)

Chapter 7 **Civilizations of the Americas** (1400 B.C.–A.D. 1570)

THEMES

As you read about the development of early empires in India, China, Europe, and the Americas, you will encounter the following unit themes.

Political and Social Systems Strong leaders centralized their power and created efficient government systems. These developments enabled the leaders to impose unity on diverse peoples and to strengthen their empires.

Global Interaction Civilizations in India, China, Greece, Rome, and the Americas spread ideas about government, technology, and religion through trade and conquest.

Religions and Value Systems Several major world religions and value systems, including Christianity, Buddhism, Confucianism, and Hinduism, developed among the peoples of the ancient world.

Continuity and Change From the Great Wall of China to the Incan royal road, ancient empires left behind impressive monuments. The civilizations of China, India, Greece, and Rome forged cultural legacies that still influence the world.

Unit Theme Activity

For Your Portfolio The chapters in this unit describe the development of several political and social systems. As you read the chapters, prepare a portfolio project highlighting examples of these developments. Your project might take one of the following forms:
- **Series of scenes or dialogues**
- **Chart or other detailed graphic organizer**
- **Essay or position paper**

Resource Directory

Teaching Resources

Teaching With Themes *What Characteristics Were Shared by Ancient Empires Around the World?,* p. 42

Technology

World History Visions, Voices, Views Scenes of an Age, *Empires of the Ancient World,* videodisc side 1 or videotape 2, running time 2:30 min.

Side 1: Fr. 26124–29555

The Colosseum was one of the great architectural achievements of the Roman empire. Completed about A.D. 82, the Colosseum was the site of spectacular competitions and other entertainments.

Bell Ringer Ask students to study the pictures on these two pages. Have them identify what areas of daily life are shown in the images *(play or entertainment, work, clothing, education, sports)*. Ask what other aspects of daily life they can think of. *(Possible answers include food, housing, health care, family life.)* Finally, have students suggest ways historians could learn about these areas of life in past societies.

Activity
Cooperative Learning

Changing Workforce Divide the class into two groups, males and females. Instruct the boys to list as many jobs or occupations as they can that were, until recently, traditionally held primarily by women. Ask the girls in the class to do the same for jobs that were, until recently, held primarily by men. Then, have the groups read their lists aloud. As students read items from the list, have the class discuss why those jobs would have been primarily male or female in the past. Then, have the class discuss how the roles of men and women have changed in today's society. What is different about modern life that has allowed for more variety in men's and women's jobs?

WHY STUDY HISTORY?
Because History Is the Story of Real People

Did you know that history is the story of *you*? True, history books often focus on kings and queens, presidents and generals, great writers and inventors. And, of course, these people are an important part of history. But the study of history is not complete unless it includes the lives of average people—their work, their play, their role in the events of their time. Historians must weave together the many strands of history to create a meaningful story of the world.

Children's toys and games tell us a lot about past cultures.

Aztec children enjoyed the board game *patolli* (left). A careful historian might note that they used beans for dice, a clue that food may have been plentiful in the Aztec empire. The ancient Greek toys (right) include a doll, a spinning top, and a baby's rattle in the shape of a pig. Toys like these are found in almost every culture. The materials used to make them or their shapes may provide important information about the past.

What jobs did people do?

In the past, women and men generally performed different jobs. In ancient Rome, young men, like these building a fort (above), were often required to serve in the army. Women, on the other hand, usually worked in jobs related to the home. Japanese women, like these shown at right, made an important contribution to the household economy.

72 Unit 2

Resource Directory

Teaching Resources

Why Study History? *Because History Is the Story of Real People,* Why Study History? booklet, pp. 7–8

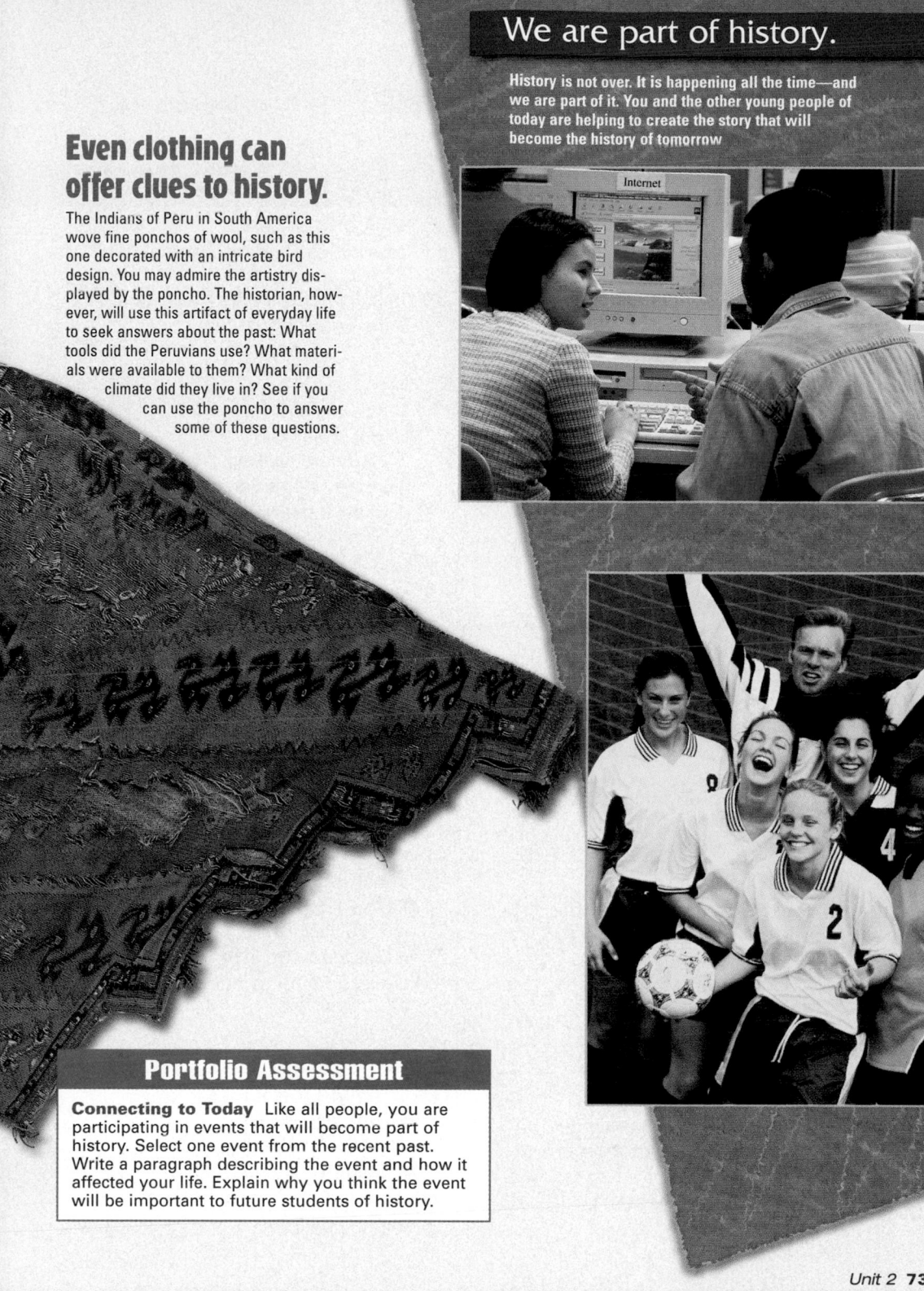

Even clothing can offer clues to history.

The Indians of Peru in South America wove fine ponchos of wool, such as this one decorated with an intricate bird design. You may admire the artistry displayed by the poncho. The historian, however, will use this artifact of everyday life to seek answers about the past: What tools did the Peruvians use? What materials were available to them? What kind of climate did they live in? See if you can use the poncho to answer some of these questions.

We are part of history.

History is not over. It is happening all the time—and we are part of it. You and the other young people of today are helping to create the story that will become the history of tomorrow

Portfolio Assessment

Connecting to Today Like all people, you are participating in events that will become part of history. Select one event from the recent past. Write a paragraph describing the event and how it affected your life. Explain why you think the event will be important to future students of history.

Unit 2 **73**

Resource Manager

	CORE INSTRUCTION	READING/SKILLS
Chapter Level Resources	**Teaching Resources** ■ **Pacing Charts**, Ch. 4 ■ **Teaching With Themes**, p. 7 ▥ **Color Transparencies**, p. F–9 ◉ **Resource Pro®** Ch. 4 ▣ **www.phschool.com** • eTeach	◉ **Book on CD**, Ch. 4 ◉ **Interactive Student Tutorial CD-ROM**, Ch. 4 ◉ **Social Studies Skills Tutor CD-ROM** ▥ **Skills Transparencies**
1 Hinduism and Buddhism 1. Explain how Hinduism is a complex religion. 2. Describe the major teachings of the Buddha. 3. Outline how Buddhism became a major world religion.	**Teaching Resources** ■ **Creative Teaching Activities**, p. 19 ◉ **Prentice Hall Presentation Pro**, Ch. 4, Section 1 ▥ **Section Reading Support Transparencies**	**Teaching Resources** ■ **Unit 2 booklet** • Guided Reading and Review, p. 2 ■ **Guide to the Essentials** ▦ **Guided Reading Audiotapes**, Ch. 4, Section 1
2 Powerful Empires of India 1. Explain how the Maurya rulers created a strong central government. 2. Describe some major achievements of the Deccan kingdoms. 3. Identify features of the Gupta period that led to an Indian golden age.	**Teaching Resources** ■ **Unit 2 booklet** • Biography Activity, p. 12 ■ **Creative Teaching Activities**, p. 20 ◉ **Prentice Hall Presentation Pro**, Ch. 4, Section 2 ▥ **Section Reading Support Transparencies**	**Teaching Resources** ■ **Unit 2 booklet** • Guided Reading and Review, p. 4 ■ **Guide to the Essentials** ▦ **Guided Reading Audiotapes**, Ch. 4, Section 2
3 Pillars of Indian life 1. Explain effects of the caste system. 2. Identify the values that influenced Indian family life. 3. Describe how the traditional Indian village functioned economically and politically.	**Teaching Resources** ■ **Creative Teaching Activities**, p. 21 ◉ **Prentice Hall Presentation Pro**, Ch. 4, Section 3 ▥ **Section Reading Support Transparencies**	**Teaching Resources** ■ **Unit 2 booklet** • Guided Reading and Review, p. 6 ■ **Guide to the Essentials** ▦ **Guided Reading Audiotapes**, Ch. 4, Section 3
4 Philosophy and Religion in China 1. Summarize the major teachings of Confucius. 2. Compare the views on government of Legalism and Daoism. 3. Explain why many Chinese people accepted Buddhist ideas.	**Teaching Resources** ■ **Creative Teaching Activities**, p. 22 ◉ **Prentice Hall Presentation Pro**, Ch. 4, Section 4 ▥ **Section Reading Support Transparencies**	**Teaching Resources** ■ **Unit 2 booklet** • Guided Reading and Review, p. 8 ■ **Guide to the Essentials** ▦ **Guided Reading Audiotapes**, Ch. 4, Section 4
5 Strong Rulers Unite China 1. Describe how Shi Huangdi united China. 2. Summarize how Han rulers strengthened the economy and government of China. 3. Identify features of the Han period that led to a Chinese golden age.	**Teaching Resources** ■ **Unit 2 booklet** • Primary Source Activity, p. 13 • Viewpoint Activity, p. 14 ■ **Creative Teaching Activities**, p. 23 ◉ **Prentice Hall Presentation Pro**, Ch. 4, Section 5 ▥ **Section Reading Support Transparencies**	**Teaching Resources** ■ **Unit 2 booklet** • Guided Reading and Review, p. 10 • Skill Application Activity, p. 15 ■ **Guide to the Essentials** ▦ **Guided Reading Audiotapes**, Ch. 4, Section 5

ENRICHMENT/PRE-AP

- **www.phschool.com**
  - Why Study History?

- **Color Transparencies**, pp. D–45, E–25
- **Visions, Voices, Views**, Animated Map Story, tape 2
- **www.phschool.com**
  - Virtual Field Trip
  - Internet Activities, Section 1

- **Teaching Resources**
  - **Chapter Extension Activities**, p. 14

- **Teaching Resources**
  - **History Through Literature**, pp. 9–10

- **Teaching Resources**
  - **Chapter Extension Activities**, p. 14
- **Listening to Literature World Masterpieces**, poems by T'ao Ch'ien, side 2

- **Color Transparencies**, p. D–47
- **www.phschool.com**
  - Internet Activities, Section 5

ASSESSMENT

PRENTICE HALL
ASSESSMENT *SYSTEM*

Core Assessment
- **ExamView Test Bank booklet**, Ch. 4
- **ExamView Test Bank CD-ROM**, Ch. 4

Standardized Test Preparation
Diagnose and Prescribe
- **Diagnostic Tests for High School Social Studies Skills**

Review and Reteach
- **Review Book for World History**

Practice and Assess
- **Test-Taking Strategies With Transparencies for High School**
- **Alternative Assessment booklet**
- **Test Prep Book for World History**

- **Teaching Resources**
  - **Unit 2 booklet**
    - Geography Quiz, p. 16
    - Section Quizzes, pp. 3, 5, 7, 9, 11
    - Chapter Tests A, B, and C, pp. 17–21
- **www.phschool.com**
  - Self-Test

CUSTOMIZE FOR INDIVIDUAL NEEDS

Gifted and Talented
- **Teacher's Edition**, Activities: Connections to Geography, p. 87

Less Proficient Readers
- **Guide to the Essentials**, Ch. 4
- **Guided Reading Audiotapes, English**, Ch. 4
- **Book on CD**, Ch. 4
- **Teacher's Edition**, Activities: Connections to Film, p. 77; Cooperative Learning, p. 78; Reinforcing Key Ideas, p. 78

Less Proficient Writers
- **Teacher's Edition**, Activities: Cooperative Learning, p. 78; Customize for Heterogeneous Groups, p. 79; Customize for Learning Styles, p. 90; Customize for Learning Styles, p. 96

Students Acquiring English/ESL
- **Guide to the Essentials, English/Spanish**, Ch. 4
- **Guided Reading Audiotapes, English/Spanish**, Ch. 4
- **Book on CD**, Ch. 4
- **Teacher's Edition**, Activities marked with an *: Connections to Film, p. 77; Cooperative Learning, p. 78

TEXT

Don't miss the exclusive interactive version of *World History: Connections to Today* on the Internet and CD-ROM.

CHAPTER 4

Empires of India and China 600 B.C.–A.D. 550

INTRODUCTION

Between 600 B.C. and A.D. 550, unified empires emerged in India and China. India became a trade center under the Maurya and Gupta dynasties. Religious and philosophical thought included the Hindu and Buddhist philosophies. Hindu beliefs spurred further development of the caste system. Shi Huangdi united China, built a strong government, and laid the groundwork for China's classical age. The teachings of Confucius influenced Chinese government and society, as did Legalism and Daoism.

Focusing on Themes

Suggest that students focus on these theme questions as they read:

Religions and Value Systems
What religious and moral ideas helped shape the civilizations of India and China?

Political and Social Systems
How did strong leaders centralize power and impose unity on diverse peoples in India and China?

Global Interaction
What factors encouraged or limited contacts between peoples across Asia?

Economics and Technology
What discoveries put Gupta India and Han China in the forefront of world technology?

Chapter Preview

1 Hinduism and Buddhism
2 Powerful Empires of India
3 Pillars of Indian Life
4 Philosophy and Religion in China
5 Strong Rulers Unite China

TIME LINE ACTIVITY

Share the About the Pictures note with students before asking these questions:

1. Did Asoka become emperor of the Maurya empire in India before or after Shi Huangdi united much of China? *(before)*
2. When did Buddhism spread from India to China? *(in the A.D. 100s)*
3. What empire from the west threatened Northern India before China's Great Wall was built? *(Greeks under Alexander the Great, 326 B.C.)*

221 B.C. Shi Huangdi unites much of China and has the Great Wall built to keep out invaders.

268 B.C. Asoka, whose authority was represented by regal sculptures such as this, becomes emperor of Maurya empire in India.

CHAPTER EVENTS

| 600 B.C. | | 350 B.C. | | 100 B.C. |

GLOBAL EVENTS

460 B.C. Age of Pericles begins in Greece.

326 B.C. Invading Greeks under Alexander the Great wage battle in northern India.

74 Chapter 4

Don't Miss!

Humanities Link
Indian Classical Dance
(Section 2)

Analyzing Primary Sources
Legalism (Section 4)

Resource Directory

Teaching Resources
Teaching With Themes Chapter Theme Activities, p. 7
Pacing Chart With Block Scheduling Guide Ch. 4
Technology
World History Color Transparencies Ch. 4 Graphic Organizer, p. F–9

Empires of India and China

Maurya empire about 250 B.C.
Gupta empire about A.D. 400
Qin empire, 221 B.C.–210 B.C.
Han empire, 206 B.C.–A.D. 220
Han protectorate

Strong rulers established empires in India and China and encouraged cultural achievements.

Map labels: CENTRAL ASIA, TAKLA MAKAN DESERT, MONGOLIA, GOBI DESERT, MANCHURIA, KUNLUN MTS., BACTRIA, HINDU KUSH, Kabul, GANDHARA, XIZANG (TIBET), CHINA, Handan, Huang He, Xianyang, KOREA, YELLOW SEA, HIMALAYA MTS., Chengdu, Yangzi R., EAST CHINA SEA, Ganges R., Pataliputra, Nalanda, MAGADHA, Ajanta, DECCAN PLATEAU, KALINGA, ARABIAN SEA, BAY OF BENGAL, VIETNAM, SOUTH CHINA SEA, Xi R., Tropic of Cancer, TAMIL KINGDOMS, SRI LANKA, INDIAN OCEAN, Mercator Projection, 0 250 500 Miles, 0 250 500 Kilometers

Timeline

A.D. 100s Buddhism spreads from India to China.

A.D. 320 Gupta golden age in India begins. The temple above is adorned with sculptures of Hindu gods and heroes.

A.D. 150 — A.D. 400 — A.D. 650

A.D. 300s Mayan city-states flourish in Central America and Mexico.

A.D. 476 The western Roman empire collapses.

Chapter 4 **75**

Independent Assignments

Have students read one section as they prepare for class. After class, have them complete the assignment. Some students may benefit from using the Guided Reading and Review worksheets.

Section 1 Have students read *A Buddhist Philosopher-King* in *Treasures of the World*, p. 26, to learn more about the content of Asoka's rock edicts.

Section 2 Have students use the worksheet *Kalidasa* in the Unit 2 booklet, p. 12, to learn more about this Indian writer.

Section 3 Have students read *Women Poets of Ancient India* in the History Through Literature booklet, pp. 9–10, to learn more about Sangram society.

Section 4 Have students read from *The Analects* of Confucius in the Reference Section at the back of the student textbook to explore some of the ideas of Confucius.

Section 5 Have students use the worksheet *Seven Feminine Virtues* in the Unit 2 booklet, p. 13, to learn more about using primary sources.

Empires of India and China

Activating Prior Knowledge

How was geography a key factor in the development of Indian and Chinese civilizations? *(Possible answer: Both are bordered by high mountains. Deserts and thick jungles separate China from neighboring regions. Isolated by geographic features, both civilizations developed a distinctive culture.)*

Previewing

Why do you think it would take strong rulers to maintain empires in India and China? *(Possible answer: India and China both cover large areas.)*

Background
About the Pictures

1. This lion capital adorned one of many stone pillars erected by Emperor Asoka throughout the Maurya empire. The pillars, carved with Asoka's edicts on humane conduct, guided the diverse peoples of the vast empire and fostered loyalty.

2. Emperor Shi Huangdi ordered the walls previously built by individual feudal states to be joined into one continuous wall to keep out invaders. The base of the largest part is 35 feet wide. The top is paved with brick and was used as a road by defending forces. Watchtowers up to forty feet high were spaced from 100 to 200 yards apart.

3. Siddhartha Gautama, the founder of Buddhism, is portrayed here characteristically meditating in lotus position.

4. In Ajanta, thirty Buddhist temples were elaborately carved in caves. Buddhist monks who lived in grottoes in the third century B.C. carved the first such temples. The practice developed over the next 500 years and reached its height during the Gupta empire.

eTeach

Be sure to check out this month's online discussion with a World History Master Teacher.

Go to **www.phschool.com**.

SECTION 1 Hinduism and Buddhism

Bell Ringer Write the words *Hinduism* and *Buddhism* on the chalkboard. Then, ask students to write three questions that they would like answered about each religion.

LESSON PLAN

1. Focus Students will learn about the basic beliefs and principles of Hinduism, a complex religion with many deities and many forms of worship. From these traditions, Gautama Buddha developed a new religion that spread through India and other Asian lands. Both religions emphasized spirituality and moral duties.

2. Instruct Assign partners and have each pair fill in the Venn diagrams from the Taking Notes section on this page. Remind students to consider the following information: origins, major beliefs, and sacred texts. Have students use their diagrams to compare and contrast Buddhism and Hinduism.

3. Assess Have students use their completed Venn diagrams to write two generalizations about Hinduism, two about Buddhism, and two that are true of both religions.

4. Reteach If students' **Assess** activity does not reflect adequate understanding of the lesson, you might assign the *Guide to the Essentials* or the *Interactive Student Tutorial CD-ROM* for this section.

Reading Focus

■ In what ways is Hinduism a complex religion?

■ What are the major teachings of the Buddha?

■ How did Buddhism spread beyond India to become a major world religion?

Vocabulary

atman
moksha
reincarnation
karma
dharma
ahimsa
nirvana
sect

Taking Notes

Copy the partially completed Venn diagram below. As you read about Hinduism and Buddhism, finish the diagram by writing key facts and ideas about the religions under the appropriate headings.

HINDUISM
• No single founder
• Caste system
•

• Belief in karma
•

BUDDHISM
• Four Noble Truths
•

Main Idea Hinduism and Buddhism, two major religions with a wide variety of beliefs, emerged in ancient India.

Setting the Scene Thousands of years ago, religious teachers in India tried to answer questions about the nature of the universe. Their ideas were later collected into the Upanishads (oo PAN ih shadz). These sacred texts use vivid images to examine complex ideas about the human soul and the connectedness of all life. In one story, a man tries to show his son that the essence of life cannot be seen. He orders the boy to break open the fruit of the banyan, or fig, tree:

"'What do you see?'
'Very tiny seeds, sir.'
'Break one.'
'I have broken it, sir.'
'Now, what do you see?'
'Nothing, sir.'
'My son,' the father said, 'what you do not perceive is the essence, and in that essence the mighty banyan tree exists. Believe me, my son, in that essence is the soul of all that is.'"

—Upanishads

Stories like this one helped people understand the teachings of Hinduism. Hinduism and Buddhism were two major religions that emerged in ancient India. The ethical and spiritual messages of both religions profoundly shaped the civilization of India.

The Beliefs of Hinduism

Unlike most major religions, Hinduism has no single founder and no single sacred text. Instead, it grew out of the overlapping beliefs of the diverse groups who settled India. The process probably began when the Aryans added the gods of the Indus Valley people to their own. Later people brought other gods, beliefs, and practices. As a result, Hinduism became one of the world's most complex religions, with countless gods and goddesses and many forms of worship existing side by side. Despite this diversity, all Hindus share certain basic beliefs.

Many Gods—or One? "God is one, but wise people know it by many names." This ancient proverb reflects a key feature of Hinduism—the belief that all the universe is part of the unchanging, all-powerful spiritual force called brahman. To Hindus, brahman is too complex a concept for most

Shiva
This bronze sculpture portrays the god Shiva crushing a demon into submission. The circle of fire represents the Hindu belief in a cycle of creation, death, and rebirth.
Theme: Diversity Why do you think various cultures use the circle to symbolize continuity?

Caption Answer

A circle has no end and no beginning.

Resource Directory

Teaching Resources
Creative Teaching Activities Creative Teaching Activities booklet, p. 19
Guided Reading and Review Unit 2 booklet, p. 2
Technology
World History Color Transparencies *Buddha and Shiva Nataraja, Lord of the Dance,* p. D–45; political cartoon of one tree in a grove, refusing to bend with the wind, p. E–25

Virtual Field Trip

www.phschool.com

Prince of Wales Museum of Western India Mumbai, India

To view other artworks relating to Hinduism and Indian history, use the Internet address above to link to the Prince of Wales Museum of Western India.

Bhagavad-Gita
This painting depicts a scene from the sacred Hindu text *Bhagavad-Gita*. The furious battle involves people, gods, goddesses, and demons.

Theme: Religions and Value Systems Why are sacred texts central to many religions?

Background
Daily Life

Forms of Worship In some religions, worshipers commonly gather in a central location, such as a church or synagogue. But for Hindus, daily worship may take place at a shrine, at a temple, or in the home. In each setting, Hindus worship different deities. For example, the deity worshiped at a temple may be the one associated with a person's particular caste. At home, Hindus have a shrine to their own family deity.

In all places of worship, Hindus offer flowers, food, and incense to their gods and goddesses. They also recite special hymns, prayers, or sacred words.

Activity
Connections to Film

Using Visual Evidence *India: The Empire of the Spirit*, a program in the six-part 1991 public television series *Legacy*, provides visual evidence of India's past and present. The early part of the hour-long program examines how Hindu traditions affect Indian life today. It includes scenes of castes and village life, the importance of the Ganges, the sacredness of the cow, and varied forms of worship. In one striking scene, village children gather outside around a television to view a production of the epic *Bhagavad-Gita*. As students view *India: The Empire of the Spirit*, ask them to identify and describe the ways in which Hindu traditions shape life in India today. (*Legacy* is distributed by Ambrose Video Publishing, Inc.) ✳

people to understand, so they worship a variety of gods that give a concrete form to brahman.

The most important Hindu gods are Brahma, the Creator; Vishnu, the Preserver; and Shiva, the Destroyer. Each represents aspects of brahman. Each of these gods can take many forms, human or animal, and each also has his own family. Some Hindus, for example, worship Shakti, the powerful wife of Shiva. She is both kind and cruel, a creator and destroyer.

Sacred Texts Over several thousand years, Hindu teachings were recorded in sacred texts such as the Vedas and Upanishads. The *Bhagavad-Gita*, for example, spells out many ethical ideas central to Hinduism. In that poem, the god Krishna instructs Prince Arjuna on the importance of duty over personal desires and ambitions.

The Goal of Life To Hindus, every person has an essential self, or atman (AHT muhn). But atman is really just another name for brahman. The ultimate goal of existence, Hindus believe, is achieving moksha (MAHK shuh), or union with brahman. To do that, individuals must free themselves from selfish desires that separate them from brahman. Most people cannot achieve moksha in one lifetime, but Hindus believe in reincarnation, or the rebirth of the soul in another bodily form. Reincarnation allows people to continue working toward moksha through several lifetimes.

Karma and Dharma In each existence, Hindus believe, a person can come closer to achieving moksha by obeying the law of karma. Karma refers to all the actions of a person's life that affect his or her fate in the next life. To Hindus, all existence is ranked. Humans are closest to brahman. Then come animals, plants, and objects like rocks or water. People who live virtuously earn good karma and are reborn at a higher level of existence. Those who do evil acquire bad karma and are reborn into suffering. In Indian art, this endless cycle of death and rebirth is symbolized by the image of the wheel.

To escape the wheel of fate, Hinduism stresses the importance of dharma (DAHR muh), the religious and moral duties of an individual. These duties vary according to class, occupation, gender, or age. By obeying one's dharma, a person acquires merit for the next life. The concepts of karma and dharma helped ensure the social order by supporting the caste system.

Block Scheduling Support

Invite a Hindu or Buddhist monk to speak to the class and to interact in a question-answer period. Guide students beforehand to develop questions based on information in the text or other sources. Assign one student to write an invitation to the speaker and another to act as guide and greeter. Have another student introduce the speaker to the class. Finally, assign a student to write a note of thanks for talking with the class and send it to the speaker.

Caption Answer

Sacred texts are important because they contain the central teachings and values of belief systems.

Another key moral principle of Hinduism is ahimsa (uh HIM sah), or nonviolence. To Hindus, all people and things are aspects of brahman and should therefore be respected. Many holy people have tried to follow the path of nonviolence.

Opposition to the Brahmins About 500 B.C., the teacher Mahavira (muh hah VEE ruh) founded Jainism (JĪN ihz um), a new religion that grew out of Hindu traditions. Mahavira rejected the idea that Brahmin priests alone could perform certain sacred rites. Jain teachings emphasized meditation, self-denial, and an extreme form of ahimsa. To avoid accidentally killing a living thing, even an insect, Jains carried brooms to sweep the ground in front of their feet.

Gautama Buddha: The Enlightened One

In the foothills of the Himalayas, another reformer, Siddhartha Gautama (sihd DAHR tuh go TUH muh), also founded a new religion, Buddhism. His teachings eventually spread across Asia to become the core beliefs of one of the world's most influential religions.

Early Life Gautama's early life is buried in legend. We know that he was born about 566 B.C. to a high-caste family. According to tradition, his mother dreamed that a radiant white elephant descended to her from heaven. Signs such as this led a prophet to predict that the boy would someday become a wandering holy man. To stop that from happening, Gautama's father kept him in the palace, surrounded by comfort and luxury. Prince Gautama married a beautiful woman, had a son, and enjoyed a happy life.

The Search One day, as Gautama rode beyond the palace gardens, he saw a sick person, an old person, and a dead body. For the first time, he became aware of human suffering. Deeply disturbed, he bade farewell to his wife and child and left the palace, never to return. He set out to discover "the realm of life where there is neither suffering nor death."

Gautama wandered for years, vainly seeking answers from Hindu scholars and holy men. He fasted and he meditated. One day, he sat under a giant tree, determined to stay there until he understood the mystery of life. For 48 days, evil spirits tempted him to give up his meditations. Then, he suddenly believed that he understood the cause and cure for suffering and sorrow. When he rose, he was Gautama no longer, but the Buddha, the "Enlightened One."

The Buddha
This image of the Buddha in Sri Lanka is carved out of granite. Traditionally, images of the Buddha lying down represent his achievement of nirvana.
Theme: Religions and Value Systems According to Buddhism, how does one achieve nirvana?

Side 1: Fr. 35570-40270

Spread of Buddhism and Hinduism to A.D. 500

Map Legend:
- Area where Buddhism originated
- Spread of Buddhism
- Area of Hindu influence

Labels on map: ASIA, JAPAN, KOREA, AFGHANISTAN, XIZANG (TIBET), CHINA, NEPAL, East China Sea, INDIA, BURMA, Arabian Sea, Bay of Bengal, SOUTHEAST ASIA, South China Sea, PACIFIC OCEAN, SRI LANKA, MALAY PEN., BORNEO, INDIAN OCEAN, SUMATRA, JAVA

Azimuthal Equal Area Projection
0   500   1000 Miles
0   500   1000 Kilometers

Four Noble Truths The Buddha spent the rest of his life teaching others what he had learned. In his first sermon after reaching enlightenment, he explained the Four Noble Truths that stand at the heart of Buddhism:

1. All life is full of suffering, pain, and sorrow.
2. The cause of suffering is the desire for things that are really illusions, such as riches, power, and long life.
3. The only cure for suffering is to overcome desire.
4. The way to overcome desire is to follow the Eightfold Path.

The Buddha described the Eightfold Path as "right views, right aspirations, right speech, right conduct, right livelihood, right effort, right mindfulness, and right contemplation." The first two steps involved understanding the Four Noble Truths and committing oneself to the Eightfold Path. Next, a person had to live a moral life, avoiding evil words and actions. Through meditation, a person might at last achieve enlightenment. For the Buddhist, the final goal is nirvana, union with the universe and release from the cycle of rebirth.

The Buddha saw the Eightfold Path as a middle way between a life devoted to pleasure and one based on harsh self-denial. He stressed moral principles such as honesty, charity, and kindness to all living creatures.

Buddhism and Hinduism Compared Buddhism grew from the same traditions as Hinduism. Both Hindus and Buddhists stressed nonviolence and believed in karma, dharma, moksha, and a cycle of rebirth.

Yet, the two religions differed in several ways. The Buddha rejected the priests, formal rituals, and many gods of Hinduism. Instead, he urged each person to seek enlightenment through meditation. Buddhists also rejected the caste system, offering the hope of nirvana to all regardless of birth.

Skills Assessment

Geography Missionaries and merchants spread Buddhism and Hinduism to many lands of Asia.

1. **Location** On the map, locate **(a)** India, **(b)** China, **(c)** Sri Lanka, **(d)** Japan.
2. **Movement** How did Buddhism spread to Japan?
3. **Critical Thinking Synthesizing Information** Based on the map and what you have read in this section, which arrows represent the spread of Theravada Buddhism?

Chapter 4 **79**

Recall

1. (a) Shiva, p. 77 (b) Jainism, p. 78 (c) Siddhartha Gautama, p. 78 (d) Four Noble Truths, p. 79 (e) Theravada, p. 80 (f) Mahayana, p. 80 2. (a) atman, p. 77 (b) moksha, p. 77 (c) reincarnation, p. 77 (d) karma, p. 77 (e) dharma, p. 77 (f) ahimsa, p. 78 (g) nirvana, p. 79 (h) sect, p. 80

Comprehension

3. Possible answer: Everything in the universe is part of the spiritual force called *brahman*. The goal of existence is achieving *moksha,* or union with brahman. To do so, one must be free of selfish desires and obey the laws of karma and dharma. 4. People escape worldly suffering by understanding the Four Noble Truths, following the Eightfold Path, living a moral life, and meditating. 5. (a) Missionaries and traders helped Buddhism spread across Asia. (b) Possible answer: Sri Lanka, Japan, and Tibet

Critical Thinking and Writing

6. Possible answer: In Mahayana teaching, Buddha and other holy beings offer compassionate help with problems and in achieving salvation and a heavenly afterlife. 7. (a) Both religions grew from the same traditions and stressed nonviolence and belief in karma, dharma, moksha, and a cycle of rebirth. (b) Hinduism has no single founder or sacred text, as Buddhism does. Buddhism rejects priests, formal rituals, the many Hindu gods, and the caste system. Buddhism stresses enlightenment through meditation.

Activity Rubrics

Share rubrics with students before they write their biographical sketches. Have students visit **www.phschool.com** to link to a site on the life of Buddha.

Attempted Project is attempted but not completed.

Minimal Biographical sketch has few details or is unclearly written.

Adequate Biographical sketch is well written with details to reflect the facts and the legendary aspects of Buddha's life.

Exemplary Sketch is original, well organized, well written, and well researched.

Primary Source

ANSWER A person who controls his anger is his own master and is approaching nirvana.

Primary Source

Buddha on Anger
This excerpt from the Tripitaka describes how a person should deal with anger:

"He who curbs his anger is like a charioteer controlling an unruly horse. Others merely hold the reins.

Overcome anger with kindness, evil with goodness, meanness with generosity and lying with truth.

Let a man be truthful and calm, and give to those who are in want. By these three means he will perfect himself.

The wise are free from hatred and are the controllers of their minds. They will approach Nirvana and go beyond sorrow. . . .

The wise man has control of body, tongue, and mind. He is the true master."

—*Tripitaka*

Skills Assessment

Primary Source According to this excerpt, what are the benefits of controlling one's anger?

Spread of Buddhism

The Buddha attracted many disciples, or followers, who accompanied him as he preached across northern India. Many men and women who accepted the Buddha's teachings set up monasteries and convents for meditation and study. Some Buddhist monasteries grew into major centers of learning.

The Buddha's death is clouded in legend. At age 80, he is said to have eaten spoiled food. As he lay dying, he told his disciples, "Decay is inherent in all things. Work out your own salvation with diligence."

Sacred Texts After the Buddha's death, some of his followers collected his teachings into a sacred text called the *Tripitaka,* or "Three Baskets of Wisdom." One of the "baskets" includes sayings like this one, which echoes the Hindu emphasis on duty: "Let a man, after he has discerned his own duty, be always attentive to his duty." Other sayings give the Buddha's version of the golden rule: "Overcome anger by not growing angry. Overcome evil with good. Overcome the liar by truth."

Two Sects Missionaries and traders spread Buddhism across India to many parts of Asia. Gradually, Buddhism split into two major sects, or smaller groups. These were Theravada (ther uh VAH duh) Buddhism and Mahayana (mah huh YAH nuh) Buddhism.

Theravada Buddhism closely followed the Buddha's original teachings. It required a life devoted to hard spiritual work. Only the most dedicated seekers, such as monks and nuns, could hope to reach nirvana. The Theravada sect spread to Sri Lanka and Southeast Asia.

The Mahayana sect made Buddhism easier for ordinary people to follow. Even though the Buddha had forbidden followers to worship him, Mahayana Buddhists pictured him and other holy beings as compassionate gods. People turned to these gods for help in solving daily problems as well as in achieving salvation. While the Buddha had said little about the nature of nirvana, Mahayana Buddhists described an afterlife filled with many heavens and hells. Mahayana Buddhism spread to China, Tibet, Korea, and Japan.

Decline in India Although Buddhism took firm root across Asia, it slowly declined in India. Hinduism eventually absorbed some Buddhist ideas and made room for Buddha as another Hindu god. A few Buddhist centers survived until the 1100s, when they fell to Muslim armies that invaded India.

SECTION 1 **Assessment**

Recall

1. **Identify:** (a) Shiva, (b) Jainism, (c) Siddhartha Gautama, (d) Four Noble Truths, (e) Theravada, (f) Mahayana.
2. **Define:** (a) atman, (b) moksha, (c) reincarnation, (d) karma, (e) dharma, (f) ahimsa, (g) nirvana, (h) sect.

Comprehension

3. What are three basic teachings of Hinduism?
4. According to Buddha, what actions would allow people to escape worldly suffering?

5. (a) How did Buddhism spread beyond India? (b) Name three of the lands in Asia to which Buddhism spread.

Critical Thinking and Writing

6. **Drawing Conclusions** How do you think Mahayana teachings increased the appeal of Buddhism?
7. **Comparing** (a) How were Hinduism and Buddhism similar? (b) How were the two religions different?

Activity
Take It to the NET

Use reliable Internet sources, such as university or museum sites, to find out more about the life story and legend of Buddha. Then, use the information that you find to write a biographical sketch of the founder of Buddhism.

Resource Directory

Teaching Resources

Section Quiz Unit 2 booklet, p. 3
Creative Teaching Activities Creative Teaching Activities booklet, p. 20
Guided Reading and Review Unit 2 booklet, p. 4

Technology

Interactive Student Tutorial CD-ROM Ch. 4
Computer Test Bank Ch. 4

Powerful Empires of India

Reading Focus

- How did Maurya rulers create a strong central government?

- What were some major achievements of the kingdoms of the Deccan?

- Why is the period of Gupta rule in India considered a golden age?

Vocabulary

dissent
missionary
golden age
decimal system
stupa
mural

Taking Notes

As you read, prepare an outline of this section. Use Roman numerals to indicate major headings of the section, capital letters for subheadings, and numbers for supporting details. The model at right will help you begin.

I. The Maurya empire
  A. Chandragupta
    1.
    2.
  B. Asoka
    1.
    2.
  C. Division and disunity
II. Kingdoms of the Deccan

Main Idea Two great empires, the Maurya and the Gupta, flourished in ancient India.

Setting the Scene

"The king's good is not that which pleases him, but that which pleases his subjects," insisted the author of an ancient Indian handbook for rulers. According to Hindu teachings, a ruler's duties included maintaining peace and order by enforcing laws, resisting invaders, and encouraging economic growth.

Achieving those goals was difficult. Northern India was often a battleground where rival rajahs fought for control of the rich Ganges Valley. Then, in 321 B.C., a young adventurer, Chandragupta Maurya (chun druh GUP tuh MOW uhr yuh), forged the first great Indian empire.

The Maurya Empire

We know about Chandragupta largely from reports written by Megasthenes (meh GAS thuh neez), a Greek ambassador to the Maurya court. He described the great Maurya capital at Pataliputra. It boasted schools and a library as well as splendid palaces and temples. An awed Megasthenes reported that the wall around the city "was crowned with 530 towers and had 64 gates."

Chandragupta Chandragupta first gained power in the Ganges Valley. He then conquered northern India. His son and grandson later pushed south, adding much of the Deccan to their empire. From 321 B.C. to 185 B.C., the Maurya dynasty ruled over a vast, united empire.

Chandragupta maintained order through a well-organized bureaucracy. Royal officials supervised the building of roads and harbors to benefit trade. Other officials collected taxes and managed state-owned factories and shipyards. People sought justice in royal courts.

Chandragupta's rule was effective but harsh. A brutal secret police reported on corruption, crime, and dissent, that is, any differing or opposing ideas. Fearful of his many enemies, Chandragupta had specially trained women warriors guard his palace.

Asoka The most honored Maurya emperor was Chandragupta's grandson, Asoka (uh SOH kuh). A few years after becoming emperor in 268 B.C., Asoka fought a long, bloody war to conquer the Deccan region of Kalinga. Then, horrified at the slaughter—over 100,000 dead—Asoka turned his

Pillar of Asoka
Asoka ordered that tall stone pillars be erected throughout India. Buddhist teachings were inscribed on each pillar.

Theme: Religions and Value Systems How did Asoka help Buddhism to spread?

SECTION 2

Bell Ringer Draw students' attention to the pillar of Asoka pictured on this page. Ask them to speculate on who Asoka was, why he had pillars inscribed with Buddhist virtues and ideals, and where he probably placed these pillars. Have students look for the answers as they study this section.

LESSON PLAN

1. Focus Maurya rulers created an empire in northern India, guided by an efficient bureaucracy and a strict system of justice. Indian merchants traded with people in Africa, elsewhere in Asia, and even in Rome. Under the rule of the Gupta dynasty, India enjoyed a golden age of peace, prosperity, and cultural advancements.

2. Instruct Ask students to imagine that they lived in India many hundreds of years ago. Have students write an eyewitness report of life in either the Maurya or Gupta empire. Instruct them to include references to government, city life, the economy, and religion. Their accounts should also refer to achievements in literature, art, and science and describe contacts with other peoples through warfare and trade. Have students share their eyewitness reports with the class.

3. Assess Suggest that students write three questions that they still have about life in these Indian empires. Challenge them to do research and find the answers.

4. Reteach If students' **Assess** activity does not reflect adequate understanding of the lesson, you might assign the *Guide to the Essentials* or the *Interactive Student Tutorial CD-ROM* for this section.

Block Scheduling Support

Have students read an example of Asoka's pillar edicts in the Reference Section of their texts and answer the questions. Then have small groups of students compose pillar edicts for a modern world based on their understanding of the principles Asoka championed. Have the groups share their edicts with the class. Then discuss the groups' edicts as a class. Were the groups' edicts similar? Did they reflect Asoka's principles?

Caption Answer

He sent missionaries to India and Sri Lanka, and his pillars helped spread Buddhist teachings.

Connections to Literature

Tamil Literature The Tamil kingdoms have left a rich literary tradition. Written in the Dravidian language, Tamil works are India's oldest non-Sanskrit literature. Unlike much of early Indian literature, which is religious, Tamil literature contains mostly secular writings. Tamil poets, for example, wrote mainly about two topics: the praise of kings with descriptions of their heroic deeds, and love. One noted Tamil poet, Avvaiyar (ahv vī yahr), praised the virtues of her king:

> "My king, when rich, freely gives food away,
> when poor he eats with his men.
> He is the head of the family of the poor,
> yet great is he...."

Primary Sources and Literature

See "Asoka: Edicts" in the Reference Section at the back of this book.

Biography

Asoka 304 B.C.(?)–232 B.C.(?)

Asoka's conversion to Buddhism was so complete that he even rejected violence against animals. He gave up hunting and banned the slaughter of animals in royal kitchens.

Asoka made his personal convictions the law of the land. On one pillar he proclaimed a list of protected species. It included several kinds of birds and fish and "all four-footed creatures that are neither useful nor edible." It also declared that "one animal is not to be fed to another."

On certain Buddhist holidays, horses could not be branded and the sale of fish was prohibited. To further emphasize Buddhist respect for life, Asoka also outlawed the burning of forests without good reason.

Theme: Impact of the Individual How did Asoka protect the animals of his kingdom?

---

back on further conquests. He converted to Buddhism, rejected violence, and resolved to rule by moral example.

True to the Buddhist principle of respect for all life, Asoka became a vegetarian and limited Hindu animal sacrifices. He sent missionaries, or people sent on a religious mission, to spread Buddhism across India and to Sri Lanka. He thus paved the way for the later spread of Buddhism throughout Asia. Although Asoka promoted Buddhism, he preached tolerance for other religions.

Asoka had stone pillars set up across India, announcing laws and promising righteous government. On one, he proclaimed: "All people are my children, and just as I desire for my children that they should obtain welfare and happiness, both in this world and the next, so do I desire the same for all people."

Asoka's rule brought peace and prosperity, and helped unite the diverse people within his empire. Asoka helped his "children" by building hospitals and Buddhist shrines. To aid transportation, he built roads and rest houses for travelers. "I have had banyan trees planted on the roads to give shade to people and animals," he noted. "I have planted mango groves, and I have had [wells] dug and shelters erected along the roads."

Division and Disunity After Asoka's death, Maurya power declined. By 185 B.C., the unity of the Maurya empire was shattered as rival princes again battled for power across the northern plain. In fact, during its long history, India has seldom been united. In ancient times, as today, the subcontinent was home to many peoples and cultures. Although the Aryan north shared a common civilization, fierce local rivalries kept it divided. Meanwhile, distance and cultural differences separated the peoples of the north and the peoples of the Deccan Plateau in the south.

Adding to the turmoil, foreign invaders frequently pushed through mountain passes into northern India. The divided northern kingdoms could not often resist such conquerors.

Kingdoms of the Deccan

Like the northern plain, the Deccan was divided into many kingdoms. Each had its own capital with magnificent temples and bustling workshops. Unlike the peoples of the Aryan north, the peoples of the Deccan were Dravidians with very different languages and traditions. Women, for example, enjoyed a high status and economic power. The Tamil kingdoms, which occupied much of the southernmost part of India, were sometimes ruled by queens.

Over the centuries, Hindu and Buddhist traditions and Sanskrit writings drifted south and blended with local cultures. Deccan rulers generally tolerated all religions as well as the many foreigners who settled in their busy ports.

Trade was important to the Tamil kingdoms. Tamil rulers improved harbors to support overseas trade. Indian merchants sent spices, fine textiles, and other luxuries westward to eager buyers in the Roman empire. As the Roman empire declined, Tamil trade with China increased.

The Tamil kingdoms have left a rich and diverse literature. Tamil poets described fierce wars, heroic deeds, and festive occasions, along with the ordinary routines of peasant and city life.

Golden Age of the Guptas

Although many kingdoms flourished in the Deccan, the most powerful Indian states rose in the north. About 500 years after the Mauryas, the Gupta dynasty again united much of India. Gupta emperors organized

Biography

ANSWER He outlawed the killing of certain species, banned the sale of fish and the branding of horses on certain days, and prohibited the indiscriminate burning of forests.

a strong central government that promoted peace and prosperity. Under the Guptas, who ruled from A.D. 320 to about 550, India enjoyed a golden age, or period of great cultural achievements.

Peace and Prosperity Gupta rule was probably looser than that of the Mauryas. Much power was left in the hands of individual villages and of city governments elected by merchants and artisans. Faxian (FAH shee EHN), a Chinese Buddhist monk who visited India in the 400s, reported on the mild nature of Gupta rule:

"The people are very well off, without poll tax or official restrictions. Only those who till the royal lands return a portion of the profit of the land as tax. . . . The kings govern without corporal punishment. Criminals are fined, according to circumstances, lightly or heavily."
—Faxian, *A Record of Buddhist Kingdoms*

Trade and farming flourished across the Gupta empire. Farmers harvested crops of wheat, rice, and sugar cane. In cities, artisans produced cotton cloth, pottery, and metalware for local markets and for export to East Africa, the Middle East, and Southeast Asia. The prosperity of Gupta India contributed to a flowering in the arts and learning.

Advances in Learning In India, as elsewhere during this period, students were educated in religious schools. However, in Hindu and Buddhist centers, learning was not limited to religion and philosophy. The large Buddhist monastery-university at Nalanda, which attracted students from other parts of Asia, taught mathematics, medicine, physics, languages, literature, and other subjects.

Indian advances in mathematics had a wide impact on the world. Gupta mathematicians devised the simple system of writing numbers that is used today. These numerals are now called "Arabic" numerals because it was Arabs who carried them from India to the Middle East and Europe. Indian mathematicians originated the concept of zero and developed the decimal system of numbers based on 10, which we still use today.

By Gupta times, Indian physicians were using herbs and other remedies to treat illness. Surgeons were skilled in setting bones and in simple surgery to repair facial injuries. Doctors also began vaccinating people against smallpox about 1,000 years before this practice was used in Europe.

Architecture Rajahs sponsored the building of magnificent stone temples. Sometimes, cities grew up around the temples to house the thousands of laborers working there. Hindu temples were designed to reflect cosmic patterns. The ideal shape was a square inscribed in a circle to symbolize eternity.

Buddhists built splendid stupas, large dome-shaped shrines that housed the sacred remains of the Buddha or other holy people. The stupas were ringed with enclosed walkways where Buddhist monks slowly walked, chanting their prayers.

Magnificent Carvings While stupas were quite plain, their gateways featured elaborate carvings that told stories of the life of the Buddha. He

Maurya and Gupta Empires

Maurya empire about 250 B.C.
Gupta empire about A.D. 400

BACTRIA
HINDU KUSH
Kabul
GANDHARA
XIZANG (TIBET)
Brahmaputra R.
Indus R.
HIMALAYA MTS.
30°N
Ganges R.
Pataliputra
Nalanda
MAGADHA
Narmada R.
Ajanta
Arabian Sea
DECCAN PLATEAU
KALINGA
Bay of Bengal
15°N
TAMIL KINGDOMS
INDIAN OCEAN
SRI LANKA
Mercator Projection
0   250   500 Miles
0   250   500 Kilometers
75°E   90°E

Skills Assessment

Geography Maurya and Gupta emperors were able to unite much of India under their rule.

1. **Location** On the map, locate (a) Ganges River, (b) Indus River, (c) Deccan Plateau.
2. **Region** What region of the Indian subcontinent remained separate from both the Maurya and the Gupta empires?
3. **Critical Thinking Connecting to Geography** How did geography limit the northward expansion of both empires?

✓ Test Preparation

Have students read the excerpt from Faxian's writings on this page, and then complete the sentence below.

Based on the passage, you can tell that the author probably felt that the Gupta emperors

A oppressed their subjects.
B were just and fair rulers.
C levied heavy taxes.
D did not govern strictly enough.

Skills Assessment

ANSWERS 1. Review locations with students. **2.** the southernmost region **3.** The Himalayas and other mountain ranges limited northward expansion.

🔔 **Bell Ringer** Draw students' attention to the photo of the woman dancing. Ask them to speculate about her costume. Do they think it is typical of costumes Indian dancers wear or simply a form of self-expression? Have students look for the answer as they read.

Background
Connections to Today

Bharata Natyam Although this dance form is ancient, it continues to be practiced today, especially in southern India, where it originated. Originally, only female temple dancers performed this dance. Not until 1930 was the dance performed on stage for the public.

For a discussion and demonstration of Bharata Natyam, see the video *Homage to Pandanallur Tradition of Bharata Natyam; Demonstration of Pandanallur Tradition of Bharata Natyam,* which is part of the Great Masters series (Indira Gandhi National Centre for Arts).

Activity
Cooperative Learning

Using Hand Gestures: Performance Have students form small groups and practice the three hand gestures illustrated on this page. Then have students compose a story to accompany the movements. One student can narrate as others perform. For additional hand gestures used in traditional Indian dance, see *History Alive!* ® "Ancient India," Section 4, "Connecting Past to Present: Legacies of Ancient India."

Portfolio Assessment Rubrics

Share rubrics with students before they create their own Humanities Link feature.

Attempted Assignment is attempted but fails to include information similar to that in the feature.

Minimal Student's feature shows some appropriate aspects of the dance.

Adequate Student's feature shows appropriate aspects of the dance and relates the dance to storytelling.

Exemplary Student's feature shows thorough research, reveals how the dance relates to storytelling, and presents insights into the chosen culture.

Indian Classical Dance

Centuries ago, the Hindus of India developed dances to express their religion. Classical Indian dance is elegant and complex. Dancers use elaborate body movements and facial expressions to tell religious stories. These unique dances captivate the interest of Indians today, as they have for hundreds of years.

Much of a dance's story is told through *mudras.* Mudras are complex hand gestures whose meanings the audience recognizes. Some mudras are designed to look like the items they represent. Others are purely symbolic.

Lion face

Fish

Opening in a bracelet

This woman is performing in the Bharata Natyam dance form. She is wearing radiant, flowing clothes and elaborate gold and silver jewelry typical of this form.

Bharata Natyam dancing is named for the sage Bharat, with whom an Indian god is said to have shared the secrets of dance. His name is a combination of the abbreviations for *Bhava* (expressions), *Raga* (melody), and *Tala* (rhythm) — the three basic parts of the dance.

It takes years to learn the 120 basic positions of Bharata Natyam. Thousands of variations on the basic moves can tell an infinite number of stories.

Most of the dance takes place in one spot, as the dancer constantly bends her knees and moves her feet to complicated rhythms. The bells on her ankles emphasize these movements and accompany the music to which she is dancing.

Portfolio Assessment

🖥️ **INTERNET** Use the Internet or library resources to research other cultures that use dance as a form of storytelling. Using this information, illustrate and write captions for your own Humanities Link.

Resource Directory

Teaching Resources
Biography Activity *Kalidasa,* Unit 2 booklet, p. 12
Humanities Link Chapter Extension Activities booklet, p. 14
Section Quiz Unit 2 booklet, p. 5

Technology
Interactive Student Tutorial CD-ROM Ch. 4
Computer Test Bank Ch. 4

was portrayed with a gentle smile, symbolizing the inner peace of someone who has reached nirvana. Hindu temples, too, were covered with carvings of gods and goddesses, elephants, monkeys, and ordinary people. A familiar figure is the four-armed god Shiva, who dances the world out of existence and then creates it again. (See the sculpture in Section 1.)

Paintings at Ajanta In the cave temples at Ajanta in western India, Buddhist artists painted rich murals, or wall paintings, recalling Buddhist stories and legends. The murals also reveal scenes of life in Gupta India, from beggars with bowls to sailors at sea to princes courting princesses in lovely flowered gardens. (See the mural on the following page.)

Literature During Gupta times, many fine writers added to the rich heritage of Indian literature. They collected and recorded fables and folk tales in the Sanskrit language. In time, Indian fables were carried west to Persia, Egypt, and Greece.

The greatest Gupta poet and playwright was Kalidasa. His most famous play, *Shakuntala,* tells the story of a king who marries the lovely orphan Shakuntala. Under an evil spell, the king forgets his bride. After many plot twists, he finally recovers his memory and is reunited with her. At the end of the play, the king's wise adviser blesses the royal couple:

> "For countless ages may the god of gods,
> Lord of the atmosphere, by plentiful showers
> Secure abundant harvest to your subjects;
> And you by frequent offerings preserve
> The Thunderer's friendship!"
> —Kalidasa, *Shakuntala*

Looking Ahead

The Gupta empire reached its height just as the Roman empire in the west collapsed. Before long, Gupta India declined under the pressure of weak rulers, civil war, and foreign invaders. From central Asia came the White Huns, a nomadic people who overran the weakened Gupta empire, destroying its cities and trade.

Once again, India split into many kingdoms. It would see no great empire like those of the Mauryas or Guptas for almost 1,000 years. Then, as you will read in a later chapter, another wave of invaders pushed into India and created a powerful new empire.

SECTION 2 Assessment

Recall

1. **Identify: (a)** Chandragupta Maurya, **(b)** Asoka, **(c)** Faxian, **(d)** Kalidasa.
2. **Define: (a)** dissent, **(b)** missionary, **(c)** golden age, **(d)** decimal system, **(e)** stupa, **(f)** mural.

Comprehension

3. How did Asoka bring peace and prosperity to India?
4. What were some achievements of the kingdoms of the Deccan?
5. Why is the Gupta period considered a golden age of India?

Give examples to support your answer.

Critical Thinking and Writing

6. **Defending a Position** "All faiths deserve to be honored for one reason or another," proclaimed Asoka. How do you think Asoka's policy of toleration helped him unite his empire?
7. **Drawing Conclusions** How did the promotion of peace and prosperity contribute to cultural advancements in the age of the Guptas?

Activity
Writing a Handbook on Government
Imagine that you are either Chandragupta, Asoka, or one of the Gupta emperors. Create a brief handbook listing ways in which an emperor can bring about peace, justice, and prosperity.

Chapter 4 **85**

SECTION 2 Assessment

Recall
1. **(a)** Chandragupta Maurya, p. 81 **(b)** Asoka, p. 81 **(c)** Faxian, p. 83 **(d)** Kalidasa, p. 85 2. **(a)** dissent, p. 81 **(b)** missionary, p. 82 **(c)** golden age, p. 83 **(d)** decimal system, p. 83 **(e)** stupa, p. 83 **(f)** mural, p. 85

Comprehension
3. He turned his back on further conquests. He rejected violence and resolved to rule by moral example. He set up stone pillars announcing laws and promising righteous government. He built hospitals, Buddhist shrines, roads, and rest houses. He planted trees for shade and dug wells.
4. They had a thriving overseas trade, improved harbors, and produced rich literature. 5. They made great advances in mathematics including the Arabic numeral system and the decimal system. They made medical advances; built great temples and shrines, called stupas; painted rich murals; and added to the rich literary heritage of India.

Critical Thinking and Writing
6. Possible answer: Indians of all faiths were willing to accept his rule because of his policy of toleration. 7. Possible answer: People could spend more time and energy on cultural interests when they didn't have to worry about war or economic issues.

Activity Rubrics

Share rubrics with students before they create their handbook.

Attempted Project is attempted but is not completed.

Minimal Student's rules show some understanding of the assignment.

Adequate Student's rules are consistent with the political philosophy of Maurya and Gupta rulers and show a good understanding of them.

Exemplary Student's rules demonstrate a keen application of the political philosophy of Maurya and Gupta rulers. The rules are clearly written and reflect the tone of the leaders who created them.

EXPLORING the HUMAN DRAMA   Human Drama Note

Kailasa Temple Indians considered caves holy and often built temples inside them. Inspired by this tradition, Indian stonemasons cut directly into rock cliffs to create Kailasa Temple (see the picture of the cave temple facade on the chapter opener), with its dark, cavernous rooms. The artists decorated the temple with numerous religious and cultural symbols. The creators of the temple dedicated it to the Hindu god Shiva and made it appear like the god's sacred mountain home. The temple was painted white to emulate the snow-capped peaks of the Himalayas. The elephant images throughout the temple are significant in several ways. Ganesha, the elephant-headed god, was the son of Shiva. Also, elephants were treasured throughout India for their power. Four pairs of elephants were believed to hold the dome of the Earth when time began. Elephants were the royal mounts of kings, and their size and strength made them formidable foes in war.

Bell Ringer

Bell Ringer Using a dictionary, write several definitions of *caste* on the board. Based on these definitions, ask students to describe what they think life would be like in a society based on a caste system.

LESSON PLAN

1. Focus The caste system, derived from Hindu beliefs, had much influence on village and family life in India. In this section, students will learn about the complex rules of caste and the values that guided Indian family life and the traditional organization of Indian villages.

2. Instruct Divide the class into three groups. Assign one group to explore the nature of the caste system, another to learn about family life, and the third to learn about village life. Explain that the members of each group will work together to become experts on their assigned topic. After students have completed this part of the lesson, regroup them so that each new group has experts on each of the three pillars of Indian life—caste, family, and village. Instruct each group to take part in a discussion that explores the influence and interdependence of these pillars.

3. Assess Have students write several questions and answers based on the contents of this section. Then, play a game in which students give an answer and call on other students to think of an appropriate question.

4. Reteach If students' **Assess** activity does not reflect adequate understanding of the lesson, you might assign the *Guide to the Essentials* or the *Interactive Student Tutorial CD-ROM* for this section.

Reading Focus

- How did the caste system affect Indian life?
- What values influenced family life?
- How did the traditional Indian village function economically and politically?

Vocabulary

joint family

dowry

Taking Notes

Copy the graphic organizer below. As you read the section, look for more characteristics and effects of the caste system. Add as many boxes to the organizer as you need.

COMPLEX CASTE SYSTEM

Stable social order

Main Idea The three important parts of Indian life were the caste system, the family, and the village.

Setting the Scene In the *Bhagavad-Gita,* the god Krishna proclaims: "It is better to do one's own duty badly than to do another's duty well." This advice from Krishna underlines an essential element of Indian life—devotion to one's duty.

Most Indians knew nothing of the dazzling courts of the Mauryas or Guptas. The vast majority were peasants who lived in the countless villages that dotted the Indian landscape. In Gupta times, as today, the caste system ensured stability and order. Two other pillars of Indian life were the family and the village. In Indian society, everyday life revolved around the rules and duties associated with caste, family, and village.

The Complex Caste System

In the previous chapter, you read how the Aryans had divided society into four occupational classes. Non-Aryans were considered outcastes and held the lowest jobs.

Many Castes By Gupta times, many additional castes and subcastes had evolved. As invaders were absorbed into Indian society, they formed new castes. Other castes grew out of new occupations and religions. By modern times, there were hundreds of major castes and thousands of subcastes.

Complex Rules Caste was closely linked to Hindu beliefs. To Hindus, people in different castes were different species of beings. A high-caste Brahmin, for example, was purer and therefore closer to moksha than someone from a lower caste.

To ensure spiritual purity, a web of complex caste rules governed every aspect of life—where people lived, what they ate, how they dressed, and how they earned a living. Rules forbade marrying outside one's caste or eating with members of another caste. High-caste people had the strictest rules to protect them from the spiritually polluted, or impure, lower castes.

For the lowest-ranked outcastes, or "Untouchables," life was harsh and restricted. To them fell "impure" jobs such as digging graves, cleaning streets, or turning animal hides into leather. Other castes feared that contact with an Untouchable could spread pollution. Untouchables had to live apart. They even had to sound a wooden clapper to warn of their approach.

Many Castes
Buddhist artists painted this mural in the Ajanta caves of western India. The painting depicts people of different castes and ethnic groups.

Theme: Diversity How does this mural reflect the Buddha's rejection of the caste system?

Caption Answer

Despite their differences, the people are grouped closely together.

Resource Directory

Teaching Resources
Creative Teaching Activities Creative Teaching Activities booklet, p. 21
Guided Reading and Review Unit 2 booklet, p. 6
History Through Literature *Women Poets of Ancient India,* History Through Literature booklet, pp. 9–10

Block Scheduling Support

Ask students to assume the role of a woman living in Gupta India and to write a diary entry that describes her thoughts, concerns, and activities. Before students begin, tell them to consider factors that will affect their diary entries. For instance, they need to determine the woman's caste, age, and marital status. When students are finished, ask for volunteers to read their entries to the class. Discuss how the entries reveal information about the status of women in India.

Effects Despite its inequalities, caste ensured a stable social order. People believed that the law of karma determined their caste. While they could not change their status in this life, they could reach a higher state in a future life by faithfully fulfilling the duties of their present caste.

The caste system gave people a sense of identity and interdependence. Each caste had its own occupation and its own leaders. Caste members cooperated to help one another. Further, each caste had its own special role in Indian society as a whole. Although strictly separated, different castes depended on one another for their basic needs. A lower-caste carpenter, for example, built the home of a higher-caste scholar.

The caste system also adapted to changing conditions, absorbing foreigners and new occupations into their own castes. This flexibility allowed people with diverse customs to live side by side in relative harmony.

Family Life

The family performed the essential function of training children in the traditions and duties of their castes. The family taught children their duties at home and in the village.

Structure The ideal family was the joint family, in which parents, children, grandchildren, uncles, and their offspring shared a common dwelling. The joint family was usually achieved only by the wealthy. In poor families, people often died young, so several generations seldom survived long enough to live together. Still, even when relatives did not share the same house, close ties linked brothers, uncles, cousins, and nephews.

The Indian family was patriarchal. The father or oldest male in the family headed the household. Because he was thought to have wisdom and experience, the head of the family enjoyed great authority. Still, his power was limited by sacred laws and tradition. Usually, he made decisions after consulting his wife and other family members. Property belonged to the whole family.

Children and Parents From an early age, children learned their family duties, which included obeying caste rules. Family interests came before individual wishes. Children worked with older relatives in the fields or at a family trade. While still young, a daughter learned that as a wife she would be expected to serve and obey her husband and his family. A son learned the rituals to honor the family's ancestors. Such rites linked the living and the dead, deepening family bonds across the generations.

For parents, an important duty was arranging good marriages for their children, based on caste and family interests. Marriage customs varied. In northern India, a bride's family commonly provided a dowry, or payment to the bridegroom, and financed the costly wedding festivities. After marriage, the daughter left her home and became part of her husband's family.

Women's Lives In early Aryan society, women seem to have enjoyed a higher status than in later times. Women even composed a few Vedic hymns. By early Gupta times, upper-caste Hindu women could still move freely in society and some were well educated.

Attitudes and customs affecting women varied across India and changed over time. By late Gupta times, upper-class women were increasingly restricted to the home. When they went outside the home, they were supposed to cover themselves from head to foot. Lower-class women, however, labored in the fields or worked at spinning and weaving.

Women were thought to have shakti, a creative energy, that men lacked. In marriage, a woman's shakti helped to make the husband complete. Still, shakti might also be a destructive force. A husband's duty was to channel his wife's energy in the proper direction.

Hindu Women
Hindu society valued the creative power of women. The women in this sculpture may be offering a ritual gift of wine to help increase the fruitfulness of their garden.

Theme: Continuity and Change How did the status of women in Hindu society change over time?

Background
Connections to Today

Caste System The caste system has undergone change since 1947. The Indian government abolished untouchability. It also set political and educational quotas to benefit the lowest castes. Nevertheless, caste still shapes much of Indian life. Hindus still adhere to the belief that caste reflects a person's level of spiritual purity, and most continue to marry within their caste in order to maintain that purity. Politicians frequently appeal to a particular caste when running for office, and caste members often unite to influence the government. Also, despite reform efforts, or perhaps because of them, violence between castes has remained a problem in recent years.

Activity
Connections to Geography

Researching Tell students that India's agricultural villages are still dependent on monsoon rains. Develop with students a list of library sources that may provide statistics on monsoon patterns and rainfall amounts. Assign students to gather and record such meteorological data for several regions of India. They may also wish to use the statistics to construct month-by-month rainfall charts or bar graphs. Ask students to draw conclusions, based on the weather statistics, about the effects of monsoons on Indian village life. Finally, ask them to discuss how modern methods of weather forecasting might benefit the people of Indian villages.

 Human Drama Note

Morality Tales Life in the courts of Maurya emperors was opulent. A ruler's heirs, however, were taught restraint and instructed to be disciplined, to value hard work, and to dutifully worship the gods. Paintings such as those on the Ajanta cave temple walls illustrated parables designed to instruct the royal heirs.

☑ **Test Preparation**

Have students read the subsection "Effects" on this page, and then complete the sentence below.

You can infer from reading this passage that the caste system

A promoted competition among classes

B encouraged movement to higher castes.

C was inflexible.

Ⓓ provided social stability despite its drawbacks.

Caption Answer

In early Aryan society, women seem to have enjoyed a higher status than in later times. By late Gupta times, upper-class women were increasingly restricted to the home. Over time, women had fewer and fewer rights.

Recall
1. **(a)** Untouchable, p. 86 **(b)** shakti, p. 87
(c) sati, p. 88 **2. (a)** joint family, p. 87
(b) dowry, p. 87

Comprehension
3. **(a)** The number of castes grew to accommodate new occupations, religions, and groups of people. **(b)** by developing rules that governed every aspect of life
4. **(a)** The structure of the traditional Indian family was patriarchal. **(b)** A woman's main responsibilities were devotion to her husband and raising children.
5. Village government was led by a headman and a council who made decisions.

Critical Thinking and Writing
6. Answers may vary, but students should recognize that both doctrines emphasized accepting one's status in life and fulfilling the duties of one's caste.
7. Possible answer: Caste rules governed each individual. Village life was based on the caste system. Family needs took precedence over individual desires.

Activity Rubrics

Share rubrics with students before they prepare their role-playing exercise.

Attempted The scene is incomplete.

Minimal The role-play demonstrates little understanding of Indian family life or the presentation is unconvincing and without energy.

Adequate The role-play accurately portrays Indian family life and traditions and is lively and involving.

Exemplary Students reflect a real comprehension of Indian family life and social traditions and give convincing performances.

Geography and History

Monsoons and Village Life

"With the monsoon, the tempo of life and death increases," writes one Indian author. "Almost overnight grass begins to grow and leafless trees turn green. . . . Showers start and stop without warning. . . . Lightning and thunder never cease."

Villagers count on monsoons to provide much of the water that they need to live. Since ancient times, the people of India have built dams and canals to capture and control the rainwater. But when they are not successful, the water comes down in driving torrents, flooding the land. Entire villages can be washed away, and thousands of people may die.

N W–E S **Theme: Economics and Technology** How do monsoons bring both life and death?

A woman's primary duties were to marry, show devotion to her husband, and raise children. Beyond these responsibilities, women had few rights within the family and society. For a woman, rebirth into a higher existence was gained through devotion to her husband.

As customs changed, a high-caste widow was forbidden to remarry. Often, a widow was expected to join her dead husband on his funeral fire. In this way, a widow became a sati, or "virtuous woman." Some widows accepted this painful death as a noble duty that wiped out their own and their husband's sins. However, other women bitterly resisted the custom.

Village Life

Throughout India's history, the village was at the heart of life. The size of villages varied, from a handful of people to hundreds of families. A typical village included a cluster of homes made of earth or stone. Beyond these dwellings stretched the fields, where farmers grew wheat, rice, cotton, sugar cane, or other crops according to region.

Each village included people of different castes who performed the tasks needed for daily life. Castes might include priests, landowners, herders, farmers, metalworkers, and carpenters, as well as such low castes as leather workers and sweepers.

In most of India, farming depended on the rains brought by the summer monsoons. Too much or too little rain meant famine. Landlords owned much of the land. Farmers who worked the land had to give the owner part of the harvest. Often, what remained was hardly enough to feed the farmers and their families.

Villages were usually self-sufficient. They produced most of the food and goods that they needed. Occasionally, however, people from different villages met and traded at regional markets.

Each village ran its own affairs based on caste rules and traditions. It faced little outside interference as long as it paid its share of taxes. A village headman and council made decisions. The council included the most respected people of the village. In early times, women served on the village council, but as Hindu law began to place greater restrictions on women, they were later excluded. The headman and council organized villagers to cooperate on vital local projects such as building or maintaining vital irrigation systems, as well as roads and temples.

SECTION 3 Assessment

Recall
1. **Identify: (a)** Untouchable, **(b)** shakti, **(c)** sati.
2. **Define: (a)** joint family, **(b)** dowry.

Comprehension
3. **(a)** Describe the development of the caste system after Aryan times. **(b)** How did the caste system provide a sense of order?
4. **(a)** Describe the structure of the traditional Indian family. **(b)** What were a woman's responsibilities in the family?

5. Describe the government of an Indian village.

Critical Thinking and Writing
6. **Analyzing Information** How did the traditional Hindu doctrines of karma and dharma support the caste system?
7. **Synthesizing Information** How did each of the three pillars of Indian life—caste, family, and village—place the needs of the community or group above the needs of the individual?

Activity

Role-Playing
With a partner, act out a conversation between a father and son or a mother and daughter about the duties of parents and children in the traditional Indian family. Your discussion should touch upon the influence of caste on family life.

Geography and History

Monsoons bring life-giving water to people and crops, but they also may cause devastating floods.

Resource Directory

Teaching Resources
Section Quiz Unit 2 booklet, p. 7
Creative Teaching Activities Creative Teaching Activities booklet, p. 22
Guided Reading and Review Unit 2 booklet, p. 8
Technology
Interactive Student Tutorial CD-ROM Ch. 4
Computer Test Bank Ch. 4

Philosophy and Religion in China

Reading Focus

- What were the major teachings of Confucius?
- How did Legalism and Daoism differ in their views on government?
- Why did many Chinese people accept Buddhist ideas?

Vocabulary

philosophy
filial piety

Taking Notes

Make a table like the one below to compare the philosophies and religions of China. Add information about each under the appropriate headings.

	CONFUCIANISM	LEGALISM	DAOISM	BUDDHISM
BELIEFS				
EFFECTS ON CHINESE LIFE				

Main Idea Confucianism, Legalism, Daoism, and Buddhism had a strong influence on China.

Setting the Scene

"Lead the people by laws and regulate them by punishments, and the people will simply try to keep out of jail, but will have no sense of shame. Lead the people by virtue . . . and they will have a sense of shame and moreover will become good."

The great philosopher Confucius* offered this advice to China's rulers. Confucius lived in late Zhou times, when war and social changes were disrupting old ways of life. In response to such chaos, thinkers like Confucius put forward ideas on how to restore social order.

The Wisdom of Confucius

Confucius was born in 551 B.C. to a noble but poor family. A brilliant scholar, Confucius hoped to become an adviser to a local ruler. For years, he wandered from court to court talking to rulers about how to govern. Unable to find a permanent government position, he turned to teaching. As his reputation for wisdom grew, he attracted many students.

Like two other influential thinkers who lived about the same time, Gautama Buddha in India and Socrates in Greece, Confucius never wrote down his ideas. After his death, students collected many of his sayings in the *Analects*.

Unlike the Buddha, Confucius took little interest in religious matters such as salvation. Instead, he developed a philosophy, or system of ideas, that was concerned with worldly goals, especially how to ensure social order and good government. Confucius studied ancient texts to learn the rules of conduct that had guided the ancestors.

Five Relationships Confucius taught that harmony resulted when people accepted their place in society. He stressed five key relationships: father to son, elder brother to younger brother, husband to wife, ruler to subject, friend to friend. Confucius believed that, except for friendship, none of these relationships was equal. For example, older people were superior to younger ones and men were superior to women.

According to Confucius, everyone had duties and responsibilities. Superiors should care for their inferiors and set a good example, while inferiors owed loyalty and obedience to their superiors. A woman's duty was to ensure the stability of the family and promote harmony in the home. Correct behavior, Confucius believed, would bring order and stability.

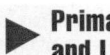

> **Primary Sources and Literature**
>
> See "Confucius: Analects" in the Reference Section at the back of this book.

*The name Confucius is the western version of the name Kong Fuzi, or Master Kong.

Bell Ringer Have students preview the text by reading and discussing the quotations from Confucius at the top of the next page.

LESSON PLAN

1. Focus The teachings of Confucius emphasized proper conduct, social order, and good government. Unlike Confucianism, Legalism said that human behavior had to be regulated by strict laws and harsh punishment. Daoism emphasized a life in harmony with nature. Students will learn how each of these schools of thought influenced the Chinese people.

2. Instruct On the board, draw a chart like the one on this page, with four columns and two rows. Label the columns Confucianism, Legalism, Daoism, and Buddhism. Label the rows Beliefs and Effects on Chinese Life. Divide the class into four groups, and assign each group one school of thought. Have students work together to compile information for their part of the chart. After they have finished, complete the chart on the board and use it to compare and contrast the four different schools of thought in China.

3. Assess Have students imagine that they are Chinese government officials. Ask them to discuss what they like and dislike about each philosophy.

4. Reteach If students' Assess activity does not reflect adequate understanding of the lesson, you might assign the *Guide to the Essentials* or the *Interactive Student Tutorial CD-ROM* for this section.

Block Scheduling Support

Tell students that Chinese people had a lasting respect for Confucius. Explain that Confucius sought to replace the conflicts of his time with harmony and order. He believed that education should train people in proper values and rules of conduct. Have students create a list of values and rules of conduct that they believe are important for today's students. Have volunteers share their lists. Which values and rules would be consistent with the teachings of Confucius? Which are purely modern?

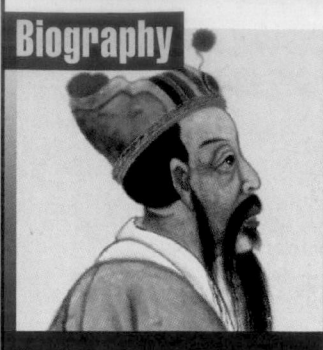

Biography

Confucius   551 B.C.–479 B.C.

Confucius decided at an early age to dedicate himself to education and public service. He felt that educated people had a responsibility to serve in government so they could translate their good ideas into action.

As a teacher, Confucius spread education to both rich and poor. He inspired thousands of followers with his guidelines about the proper way to live.

As a public servant, he did not fare so well, however. His high standards of conduct often brought him into conflict with corrupt officials. According to Confucius, "The superior man understands righteousness. The inferior man understands profit." Because some did not agree with his values, Confucius had to move from one part of China to another in search of a permanent government position.

Theme: Impact of the Individual How did Confucius try to improve government in China?

Confucius put filial piety, or respect for parents, above all other duties. Other Confucian values included honesty, hard work, and concern for others. "Do not do to others," he declared, "what you do not wish yourself."

Government According to Confucius, a ruler had the responsibility to provide good government. In return, the people would be respectful and loyal subjects. Confucius said the best ruler was a virtuous one who led people by good example.

Confucius believed that government leaders and officials should be well educated. "By nature, men are pretty much alike," he said. "It is learning and practice that set them apart." He urged rulers to take the advice of wise, educated men.

Spread of Confucianism In the centuries after Confucius died, his ideas influenced every area of Chinese life. Chinese rulers relied on Confucian ideas and chose Confucian scholars as officials. The Confucian emphasis on filial piety bolstered traditional customs such as reverence for ancestors.

As Chinese civilization spread, hundreds of millions of people in Korea, Japan, and Vietnam accepted Confucian beliefs. Close to a third of the world's population came under the influence of these ideas.

The Harsh Ideas of Legalism

A very different philosophy grew out of the teachings of Hanfeizi (HAHN fay DZEE), who died in 233 B.C. According to Hanfeizi, "the nature of man is evil. His goodness is acquired." Greed, he declared, was the motive for most actions and the cause of most conflicts.

Hanfeizi insisted that the only way to achieve order was to pass strict laws and impose harsh punishments. Because of this emphasis on law, Hanfeizi's teachings became known as Legalism. To Legalists, strength, not goodness, was a ruler's greatest virtue. "The ruler alone possesses power," declared Hanfeizi, "wielding it like lightning or like thunder."

Many feudal rulers chose Legalism as the most effective way to keep order. It was the official policy of the Qin (CHEENG) emperor who united China in 221 B.C. His laws were so cruel that later generations despised Legalism. Yet Legalist ideas survived in laws that forced people to work on government projects and punished those who shirked their duties.

Daoism: The Unspoken Way

The founder of Daoism was known as Laozi (LOW DZEE), or "Old Master." He is said to have lived at the time of Confucius. Although we know little about him, he is credited with writing *The Way of Virtue*, a book that had enormous influence on Chinese life. Unlike Confucianism and Legalism, Daoism was not concerned with bringing order to human affairs. Instead, Daoists sought to live in harmony with nature.

Seeking "the Way" Laozi looked beyond everyday cares to focus on the *Dao,* or "the way" of the universe. How does one find the Dao? "Those who know the Dao do not speak of it," replied Laozi. "Those who speak of it do not know it."

Daoists rejected conflict and strife. They wanted to end conflict between human desires and the simple ways of nature. They stressed the virtue of yielding. Water, they pointed out, does not resist, but yields to outside pressure. Yet it is an unstoppable force. Many Daoists turned from the "unnatural" ways of society. Some became hermits, artists, or poets.

Government Daoists viewed government as unnatural and, therefore, the cause of many problems. "If the people are difficult to govern," Laozi declared, "it is because those in authority are too fond of action." To

---

Analyzing Primary Sources

Legalism

Hanfeizi developed a philosophy, called Legalism because of its emphasis on strict laws. Legalism stood in stark contrast to Confucianism. In the following excerpt, Hanfeizi explains why he thinks his system is superior.

"When the [wise man] rules the state, he does not count on people doing good of themselves, but employs such measures as will keep them from doing any evil. If he counts on people doing good of themselves, there will not be enough such people to be numbered by the tens in the whole country. But if he employs such measures as will keep them from doing evil, then the entire state can be brought up to a uniform standard. [The ruler] does not busy himself with morals, but with laws. . . .

[The Confucianists] neither study affairs [of] law and government, nor observe the realities of vice and wickedness, but all exalt the supposed glories of remote antiquity and the achievements of the ancient kings. Sugar-coating their speech, the Confucianists say: 'If you listen to our words, you will be able to become the leader of all feudal lords.' . . . The intelligent ruler upholds solid facts and discards [such] useless frills. He does not speak about deeds of humanity and righteousness, and he does not listen to the words of [Confucianists].

Those who are ignorant about government insistently say: 'Win the hearts of the people.' . . . As if all that the ruler would need to do would be just to listen to the people. Actually, the intelligence of people is not to be relied upon any more than the mind of a baby. . . . The baby does not understand that suffering a small pain is the way to obtain a great benefit. . . .

The [ruler] regulates penalties and increases punishments for the purpose of repressing the wicked, but the people think the [ruler] is severe. . . . [This is a method] for attaining order and maintaining peace, but the people are too ignorant to appreciate [it]."

—*Hanfeizi*

Symbol of Rule
The dragon was the symbol of the Chinese emperor. Under the Legalistic emperors, the fierce appearance of the dragon may have seemed especially appropriate.

Skills Assessment

1. According to Hanfeizi, a good ruler must be sure to
   - A treat the people under his control with great respect.
   - B pass and enforce laws to make his people behave properly.
   - C obey the wishes of his people.
   - D teach his people about the achievements of ancient kings.

2. Which statement best summarizes Hanfeizi's view of Confucianism?
   - E Confucianism is unrealistic and therefore useless as a system of rule.
   - F Confucianism was effective in the past but is now obsolete.
   - G Confucianist rulers rely too much on the law and facts.
   - H Rulers who follow Confucianism are too strict.

3. **Critical Thinking Analyzing Information** (a) Identify the specific criticisms of the Confucianists that Hanfeizi makes. (b) Why do you think Legalist ideas were attractive to many rulers?

Skills Tip

Excerpts from documents often include brackets [ ]. The words within brackets are not direct quotations. They are added to clarify the quoted material.

Background
About the Primary Source

Hanfeizi's ideas impressed Zheng, the territorial leader who was to conquer and unify China under the Qin dynasty. With the ascendancy of the Qin (221–206 B.C.), Legalism became the first philosophy to be officially adopted in China's classical age. During the Qin, China censored books of history and burned books that glorified the past. Hundreds of scholars were executed. Legalism came to be despised for its harshness and the Qin dynasty did not last long. Hanfeizi's ideas profoundly influenced China's laws and are still characteristic of today's Communist rule.

Activity
Interpreting the Primary Source

Critical Thinking: Making Generalizations Use this additional question to generate class discussion: Why would a Legalist ruler not be likely to give a person the benefit of the doubt if the person were suspected of having broken a law? *(Possible answer: A Legalist ruler would not believe in the basic goodness of a person and so would assume that a person was guilty.)*

Skills Tip

Remind students that direct quotations are those in which a writer's words are copied verbatim and put in quotation marks. Any deletion must be indicated with an ellipsis (. . .). If words are added, they appear in brackets [ ]. The Skills Handbook in the front of the book has a lesson that will help students with this feature.

Skills Assessment

1. B **2.** E **3.** Possible answers: **(a)** Hanfeizi says the Confucianists are ignorant of law and government; they ignore the reality of wickedness; and they cite only dubious, ancient events to support their claims. **(b)** It encouraged them to impose their wills upon the people they ruled.

Human Drama Note

Chinese Philosophy Legalism, like Confucianism and Daoism, is a philosophy, not a religion. Fung Yu-lan, who has studied Confucianism, explains that the Chinese "have not had much concern with religion because they have had so much concern with philosophy." The moral principles of Chinese philosophy, however, are the result of a long tradition of reflection about man and his relation to Heaven. For the Chinese, virtue is rewarded by Heaven. Living morally elevates the mind and leads to transcendence of the material world.

Test Preparation

Have students read the subsection titled "Government" at the top of the opposite page, and then answer the question below.

Which phrase does *not* describe a good leader, according to Confucius?

 A is loyal and respectful of his subjects

B takes advice of well-educated men

C leads by setting a good example

D is virtuous and well educated himself

Recall

1. (a) *Analects*, p. 89 **(b)** Legalism, p. 90 **(c)** Daoism, p. 90 **2. (a)** philosophy, p. 89 **(b)** filial piety, p. 90

Comprehension

3. Confucius based his ethical code of conduct on duties and responsibilities. He placed special emphasis on the duties of filial piety, honesty, hard work, concern for others, and education. **4. (a)** The Legalists favored a government that passed strict laws and imposed harsh punishments. **(b)** Daoism was not concerned with bringing order to human affairs. Daoists believed the best government was one that governed the least. **5.** Many Chinese people liked the Buddhist idea of personal salvation. They welcomed the Buddhist promise that religious devotion could end suffering and lead to eternal happiness.

Critical Thinking and Writing

6. Hanfeizi. He believed that greed motivated most actions. He believed that harsh punishments were necessary to maintain social order. **7. (a)** Confucius taught that an orderly society was one in which people accepted their place in society and properly fulfilled their duties and responsibilities. **(b)** Hanfeizi believed that strict laws and harsh enforcement of those laws brought about an orderly society. **(c)** Laozi advised people to seek harmony with nature rather than an orderly society.

Activity Rubrics

Share rubrics with students before they write their dialogues.

Attempted Student attempts the assignment but does not complete it.

Minimal Dialogue shows some familiarity with historical figures and their views on government.

Adequate Student's dialogue shows careful preparation and understanding of historical content.

Exemplary Student's dialogue shows deep understanding of each figure's view of government and is well written.

Caption Answer

Merchants who traveled among the lands of Asia spread religious teachings and other elements of culture.

Buddhism in China
Buddhist missionaries built temples, monasteries, and rest houses along their routes between India and China. The golden images of the Buddha (above) are in the Temple of General Peace in China.

Theme: Global Interaction
How did trade aid the spread of Buddhism?

Daoists, the best government was one that governed the least.

A Blend of Ideas Although scholars kept to Laozi's teachings, Daoism evolved into a popular religion with gods, goddesses, and magical practices. Chinese peasants turned to Daoist priests for charms to protect them from unseen forces. Instead of accepting nature as it was, some Daoist priests searched for a substance to bring immortality. To achieve this goal, they conducted experiments. Sometimes, their work contributed to science and medicine.

Gradually, people blended Confucian and Daoist teachings. Although the two philosophies differed, people took beliefs and practices from each. Confucianism showed them how to behave. Daoism influenced their view of the natural world.

Buddhism in China

By A.D. 100, missionaries and merchants had spread Mahayana Buddhism from India into China. At first, the Chinese had trouble with the new faith. For example, Chinese tradition valued family loyalty, while Buddhism honored monks and nuns who gave up the benefits of family life for a life of solitary meditation.

Despite obstacles such as this, Buddhism became more popular, especially in times of crisis. Its great appeal was the promise of escape from suffering. Mahayana Buddhism offered the hope of eternal happiness and presented Buddha as a compassionate, merciful god. Through prayer, good works, and devotion, anyone could hope to gain salvation. Neither Daoism nor Confucianism emphasized this idea of personal salvation.

By A.D. 400, Buddhism had spread throughout China. Buddhist monasteries became important centers of learning and the arts. Buddhism absorbed many Confucian and Daoist traditions. Chinese Buddhist monks stressed filial piety and honored Confucius.

SECTION 4 Assessment

Recall

1. Identify: **(a)** *Analects*, **(b)** Legalism, **(c)** Daoism.
2. Define: **(a)** philosophy, **(b)** filial piety.

Comprehension

3. Describe the ethical code of conduct that Confucius promoted.
4. (a) What kind of government did Legalists favor? **(b)** Why did Daoists disagree with Legalist ideas on government?
5. Why did Buddhism appeal to many people in China?

Critical Thinking and Writing

6. Recognizing Points of View "Rewards should be rich and certain so that the people will be attracted by them. Punishments should be severe and definite so that the people will fear them." Which of the philosophers discussed in this section expressed these ideas? Explain.
7. Comparing Explain how each of these thinkers believed an orderly society could be achieved: **(a)** Confucius, **(b)** Hanfeizi, **(c)** Laozi.

Activity

Writing a Dialogue
Write a dialogue in which Confucius, Hanfeizi, and Laozi debate their ideas on the nature of the best kind of government and the role that government should play in Chinese society.

Resource Directory

Teaching Resources

Section Quiz Unit 2 booklet, p. 9
Creative Teaching Activities Creative Teaching Activities booklet, p. 23
Guided Reading and Review Unit 2 booklet, p. 10

Technology

World History Color Transparencies *Terra Cotta Soldiers*, p. D–47
Interactive Student Tutorial CD-ROM Ch. 4
Computer Test Bank Ch. 4

SECTION 5 Strong Rulers Unite China

Reading Focus

- How did Shi Huangdi unite China?
- How did Han rulers strengthen the economy and government of China?
- Why is the Han period considered a golden age of Chinese civilization?

Vocabulary

monopoly
expansionism
warlord
acupuncture

Taking Notes

Copy this partially completed concept web. As you read the section, add important events and developments to provide examples of how strong rulers united China. Add as many circles as you need to the web.

STRONG RULERS UNITED CHINA

Wudi improved roads

Main Idea Powerful emperors united much of China and encouraged cultural achievements.

Setting the Scene

From his base in western China, the powerful ruler of the state of Qin rose to unify all of China. An ancient Chinese poet and historian described how Zheng (JUHNG) crushed all his rivals: "Cracking his long whip, he drove the universe before him, swallowing up the eastern and the western Zhou and overthrowing the feudal lords."

In 221 B.C., Zheng proclaimed himself Shi Huangdi (SHEE hoo ahng DEE), or "First Emperor." Though his methods were brutal, he ushered in China's classical age. Historians call it a classical civilization because it set patterns in government, philosophy, religion, science, and the arts that served as the framework for later cultures.

Shi Huangdi

Shi Huangdi was determined to end the divisions that had splintered Zhou China. He spent 20 years conquering most of the warring states. Then, he centralized power with the help of Legalist advisers. Using rewards for merit and punishments for failure, he built the strong, authoritarian government of the Qin dynasty.

Sima Qian, who served later Chinese emperors as Grand Historian of the court, described a monument that Shi Huangdi had built atop a mountain, with an inscription praising the emperor's accomplishments:

"A new age is inaugurated by the Emperor;
Rules and measures are rectified,
The myriad things set in order, . . .
And there is harmony between fathers and sons.
The Emperor in his sagacity, benevolence and justice
Has made all laws and principles manifest."
—Sima Qian, quoted in *Records of the Historian*
(Yang Hsien-yi and Gladys Yang)

Unity Imposed Emperor Shi Huangdi abolished feudalism in China, whereby many local rulers had owed little allegiance to any central government. He replaced the feudal states with 36 military districts and appointed loyal officials to administer them. He then sent inspectors to spy on the local officials and report back to him. Shi Huangdi forced noble families to live in his capital at Xianyang, where he could monitor them. He distributed the lands of the displaced nobles to peasants. Still, peasants had to pay high taxes to support Shi Huangdi's armies and building projects.

Soldier of Shi Huangdi
This terra-cotta soldier is one of more than 8,000 that stand guard inside the tomb of Emperor Shi Huangdi. A farmer uncovered the tomb in 1974 while digging a well.
Theme: Impact of the Individual How does the figure symbolize the power and authority of Shi Huangdi?

Bell Ringer Have students read about the Great Wall and study the picture of the clay soldier. Ask students how these projects reflected the advancement of Chinese civilization during the time of Shi Huangdi.

LESSON PLAN

1. Focus China's classical age began with the unifying rule of Shi Huangdi in 221 B.C. Following his reign, emperors of the Han dynasty continued to strengthen government. Students will focus on these powerful emperors and the advances that were made in China under their rule.

2. Instruct Ask students to imagine that they are one of the following: a critic of Shi Huangdi, a laborer on the Great Wall, a silk trader, a Confucian scholar-official, a woman, or a scientist during the early classical age. In the role they have chosen, have students write a letter to a friend in which they describe their feelings and attitudes about life in China. In their letter, they should also describe some of their daily activities.

3. Assess Set aside time for students to share their letters with the class. Have students underline their feelings and attitudes and highlight the daily activities they describe before handing in their letters. Consider displaying the letters on a bulletin board.

4. Reteach If students' **Assess** activity does not reflect adequate understanding of the lesson, you might assign the *Guide to the Essentials* or the *Interactive Student Tutorial CD-ROM* for this section.

Block Scheduling Support

Have students complete the activity sheet *The Faults of the Qin Dynasty*, Unit 2 booklet, p. 14, containing two viewpoints of the Qin dynasty. When students have completed the activity, organize the class into debate teams, one affirmative and one negative, to debate the following proposition: Shi Huangdi should be revered as one of China's greatest leaders. Remind students to consider the elements of a classical civilization listed in the last paragraph of "Setting the Scene" on this page.

Caption Answer

The soldier is wearing armor and may once have held a weapon in his hands.

Historical Evidence

Translations Accurate historical knowledge depends on accurately translating the available records. Such work is not always easy, especially when dealing with ancient forms of languages or languages that are no longer used. Scholars sometimes develop different perspectives because they disagree on the correct translation of the written records. For example, there is disagreement about an incident during the reign of Shi Huangdi. Historians agree that as part of Shi Huangdi's crackdown on dissent, 460 scholars were arrested and executed for suspected plots against the government. Some historians say that the scholars were buried alive. However, other historians say that this misconception results from mistranslations of the Chinese records.

Qin and Han Empires, 221 B.C.–A.D. 220

Legend:
- Qin empire, 221 B.C.–210 B.C.
- Han empire, 206 B.C.–A.D. 220
- Han protectorate
- Silk Road
- Area of silk production during Han

Azimuthal Equal Area Projection

0   250   500 Miles
0   250   500 Kilometers

Skills Assessment

Geography Under the Qin and Han dynasties, Chinese rule expanded.

1. **Location** On the map, locate (a) Silk Road, (b) Great Wall, (c) Qin empire, (d) Han empire.
2. **Place** What natural barriers helped to protect China from invaders?
3. **Critical Thinking Drawing Conclusions** Based on the map, what Chinese town probably grew rich from the silk trade? Explain.

To promote unity, the First Emperor standardized weights and measures and replaced the diverse coins of the Zhou states with Qin coins. He also had scholars create uniformity in Chinese writing. Workers repaired and extended roads and canals to strengthen the transportation system. A new law even required cart axles to be the same width so that wheels could run in the same ruts on all Chinese roads.

Crackdown on Dissent Shi Huangdi moved harshly against critics. He jailed, tortured, and killed many who opposed his rule. Hardest hit were the feudal nobles and Confucian scholars who despised his laws. To end dissent, Shi Huangdi approved a ruthless campaign of book burning, ordering the destruction of all works of literature and philosophy. Only books on medicine and agriculture were spared.

The Great Wall Shi Huangdi's most remarkable and costly achievement was the Great Wall. In the past, individual feudal states had built walls to defend their lands against raiders. Shi Huangdi ordered the walls to be joined. Hundreds of thousands of laborers worked for years through bitter cold and burning heat. They pounded earth and stone into a mountainous wall almost 25 feet high topped with a wide brick road. Many workers died in the harsh conditions.

Over the centuries, the wall was extended and rebuilt many times. Eventually, it snaked for thousands of miles across northern China.

While the wall did not keep invaders out of China, it did demonstrate the emperor's ability to mobilize the vast resources of China. In the long run, the Great Wall became an important symbol to the Chinese people, dividing and protecting their civilized world from the nomadic, or wandering, bands north of the wall.

Skills Assessment

ANSWERS 1. Review locations with students. 2. the Gobi Desert, Takla Makan Desert, and mountains to the south and west of China 3. Xianyang may have benefited from the silk trade because it was located at the eastern end of the Silk Road.

Resource Directory

Teaching Resources

Viewpoint Activity *The Faults of the Qin Dynasty,* Unit 2 booklet, p. 14

Skill Application Activity *Classifying Sources of Information,* Unit 2 booklet, p. 15

Collapse Shi Huangdi thought his empire would last forever. But when he died in 210 B.C., anger over heavy taxes, forced labor, and cruel policies exploded into revolts. As Qin power collapsed, Liu Bang (LEE OO BAHNG), an illiterate peasant leader, defeated rival armies and founded the new Han dynasty. Like earlier Chinese rulers, Liu Bang claimed that his power was based on the Mandate of Heaven.

The Han Dynasty

As emperor, Liu Bang took the title Gao Zu (GOW DZOO) and set about restoring order and justice to his empire. Although he continued earlier efforts to unify China, he lowered taxes and eased the Qin emperor's harsh Legalist policies. In a key move, he appointed Confucian scholars as advisers. His policies created strong foundations for the Han dynasty, which lasted from 206 B.C. to A.D. 220.

Emperor Wudi The most famous Han emperor, Wudi, took China to new heights. During his long reign from 141 B.C. to 87 B.C., he strengthened the government and economy. Like Gao Zu, he chose officials from Confucian "men of wisdom and virtue." To train scholars, he set up an imperial university at Xian.

Wudi furthered economic growth by improving canals and roads. He had granaries set up across the empire so the government could buy grain when it was abundant and sell it at stable prices when it was scarce. He reorganized finances and imposed a government monopoly on iron and salt. A monopoly is the complete control of a product or business by one person or group. The sale of iron and salt gave the government a source of income other than taxes on peasants.

Wudi followed a policy of expansionism by increasing the amount of territory under Chinese rule. He fought many battles to expand China's borders and to drive nomadic peoples beyond the Great Wall. Chinese armies added outposts in Manchuria, Korea, northern Vietnam, Tibet, and Central Asia. Soldiers, traders, and settlers slowly spread Chinese influence across these areas.

Silk Road to the West The emperor Wudi opened up a trade route, later called the Silk Road, that would link China and the west for centuries. During the Han period, new foods such as grapes, figs, cucumbers, and walnuts flowed to China from western Asia. Lucky traders might return to China bearing furs from Central Asia, muslin from India, or glass from Rome. At the same time, the Chinese sent tons of silk westward to fill a growing demand for the prized fabric.

Eventually, the Silk Road stretched for 4,000 miles, linking China to the Fertile Crescent in southwestern Asia. Still, few traders covered the entire distance; instead, goods were relayed in stages from one set of traders to another. At the western end, trade was controlled by various people, including the Persians.

Scholar-Officials Han emperors made Confucianism the official belief system of the state. They relied on well-educated scholars to run the bureaucratic government. A scholar-official was expected to match the Confucian ideal of a gentleman. He would be courteous and dignified and possess a thorough knowledge of history, music, poetry, and Confucian teachings.

Civil Service Examination Han emperors adopted the idea that government officials should win positions by merit rather than through family background. To find the most qualified officials, they set up a system of exams. In time, these civil service exams were given at the local, provincial, and national levels. To pass, candidates studied the Confucian classics, a

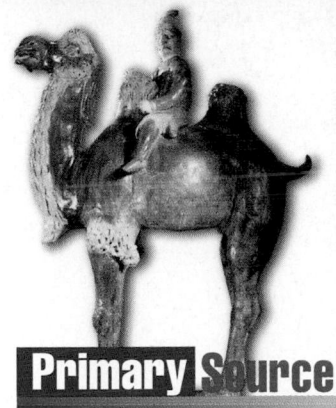

Primary Source

Travels on the Silk Road
Faxian, a Chinese Buddhist monk, described a journey crossing the Gobi on the Silk Road in A.D. 399:

"Le Hao, the [chief official] of T'un-hwang, had supplied them with the means of crossing the desert before them, in which there were many evil demons and hot winds. Travelers who encounter them perish all to a man. There is not a bird to be seen in the air above, nor an animal on the ground below. Though you look all round most earnestly to find where you can cross, you know not where to make your choice, the only mark and indication being the dry bones of the dead left upon the sand."

—Faxian, *A Record of Buddhist Kingdoms*

Skills Assessment

Primary Source According to Faxian, what landmarks did travelers use to follow the Silk Road across the Gobi?

Background
Connections to Economics

The Value of Silk There are several reasons for the great value associated with silk. First is its aesthetic beauty. Silk also offers practical benefits that no other natural fiber can match. It is one of the strongest natural fibers. As woven cloth, it is lightweight and retains warmth, which makes it an excellent insulating material in clothing. At the same time, silk has been prized by people of warmer climates because it is able to absorb moisture without feeling wet.

During the Han period, the price of silk was kept artificially high by the Chinese government. To maintain the Chinese monopoly on the silk industry, the government made it illegal to divulge any information about its production. The export of silkworm eggs was a crime punishable by death.

Background
Global Connections

An Unwelcome Exchange Commercial interaction between China and other areas of the world resulted in the beneficial exchange of goods and cultural items. However, such contact also resulted in the spread of deadly diseases. The caravans that traveled along the Silk Road and the ships that came to China from India transported all sorts of viruses and germs. Major epidemics of smallpox, measles, bubonic plague, and malaria frequently swept through China with appalling effects. When an epidemic struck in A.D. 317, the Chinese historian Ssuma Kuang noted, "One or two out of a hundred survived." The bubonic plague that decimated Europe in the 1300s was itself the result of international commerce. The plague began in Asia and traveled to Europe along the trade routes.

Human Drama Note

Chinese Folk Songs To provide cultural entertainment at his court, Emperor Wudi established a government organization called the Music Bureau. Its officials collected poems and folk songs from all parts of the country. The compositions' themes included, among others, love, loneliness, work, poverty, war, and the beauty of nature. They were sung to the music of flutes, bamboo mouth organs, drums, and other instruments. Some 100 of these Music Bureau ballads survive today to paint a vivid picture of the joys and hardships of the common people. Many may be found in anthologies of classical Chinese literature.

Skills Assessment

They followed the dry bones of the dead left upon the sand.

Customize for . . .
Learning Styles

Comparing Viewpoints The Chinese historian Sima Qian praised hard work, determination, and perseverance. Sima Qian seemed to place great value on success in the form of economic prosperity. Some people, however, saw disadvantages to a life of hard work in the pursuit of wealth and success. Robert Louis Stevenson, the Scottish novelist, essayist, and poet, once remarked, "Perpetual devotion to what a man calls his business is only to be sustained by perpetual neglect of many other things." On the same subject, the American poet Robert Frost commented, "By working faithfully eight hours a day, you may eventually get to be a boss and work twelve hours a day."

Read these quotations to the class and ask students to rephrase them in their own words. In a class discussion, ask students to compare the viewpoints of Stevenson and Frost with that of Sima Qian. Finally, ask students to discuss their own views on the nature of success and the means to achieving it. *(Auditory)* ✳

Background
Connections to Economics

The Paper Monopoly As with silk, the Chinese wanted to keep the art of making paper a secret in order to protect their industry from competition. They managed to keep the secret from other civilizations and maintain a paper monopoly for some 500 years. But sometime in the 600s the Japanese acquired the technology. Next, in the 700s, the Arab world learned the secret from Chinese prisoners of war, who were found to be knowledgeable about papermaking and were forced to construct and operate a paper mill.

collection of histories, poems, and handbooks on customs that Confucius was said to have compiled.

In theory, any man could take the exams. In practice, only those who could afford years of study, such as the sons of wealthy landowners or officials, could hope to succeed. Occasionally, a village or wealthy family might pay for the education of a brilliant peasant boy. If he passed the exams and obtained a government job, he, his family, and his clan all enjoyed immense prestige and moved up in society.

Confucian teachings about filial piety and the superiority of men kept women from taking the civil service exam. As a result, women were closed out of government jobs.

The civil service system had an enormous impact on China for almost 2,000 years. It put men trained in Confucian thought at every level of government and created an enduring system of values. Dynasties rose and fell, but Confucian influence survived.

Collapse of the Han Empire As the Han dynasty aged, signs of decay appeared. Court intrigues undermined emperors who could no longer control powerful warlords, or local military rulers. Weak emperors let canals and roads fall into disrepair. Burdened by heavy taxes and crushing debt, many peasants revolted. Thousands of rebellious peasants abandoned their villages and fled to the mountains. There they joined secret groups of bandits known by colorful names such as the "Red Eyebrows" and the "Green Woodsmen."

In A.D. 220, ambitious warlords overthrew the last Han emperor. After 400 years of unity, China broke up into several kingdoms. Adding to the disorder, invaders poured over the Great Wall and set up their own states. In time, many of these newcomers were absorbed into Chinese civilization.

Achievements of the Han Golden Age

The Han period was one of the golden ages of Chinese civilization. Han China made such tremendous advances in so many fields that the Chinese later called themselves "the people of Han."

Science Han scientists wrote texts on chemistry, zoology, botany, and other subjects. Han astronomers carefully observed and measured movements of the stars and planets, which enabled them to improve earlier calendars and invent better timekeeping devices. One scientist invented a simple seismograph to detect and measure earthquakes.

The scientist Wang Chong disagreed with the widely held belief that comets and eclipses showed Heaven's anger. "On the average, there is one moon eclipse about every 180 days," he wrote, "and a solar eclipse about every 41 or 42 months. Eclipses . . . are not caused by political action." Wang Chong argued that no scientific theories should be accepted unless they were supported by proof.

Medicine Chinese physicians diagnosed diseases, experimented with herbal remedies and other drugs, and developed anesthetics. Some doctors explored the uses of acupuncture. In this medical treatment, the doctor inserts needles under the skin at specific points to relieve pain or treat various illnesses.

Technology In its time, Han China was the most technologically advanced civilization in the world. Cai Lun, an official of the Han court, invented a method for making durable paper out of wood pulp. His basic method is still used to manufacture paper today. The Chinese also pioneered advanced methods of shipbuilding and invented the rudder to steer. Other practical inventions included bronze and iron stirrups, fishing reels, wheelbarrows, suspension bridges, and chain pumps. Some of these ideas

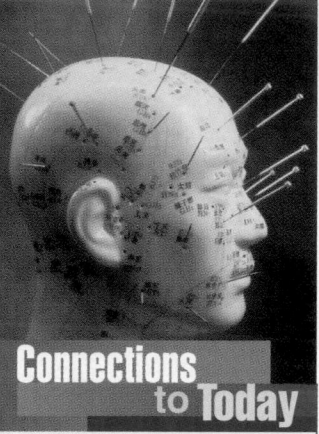

Connections to Today

How Acupuncture Works
For more than 2,500 years, Chinese physicians have used acupuncture to ease patients' suffering. There are several ways to explain how acupuncture works.

Traditional Chinese doctors believe that pain and illness are sometimes due to an imbalance of natural energy flow through the body. Equilibrium and good health can be restored by the insertion of needles at the proper points.

Other explanations involve the nervous system. Some doctors think that acupuncture works because the needles block nerves that carry pain. Another possibility is that the needles promote the release of endorphins in the brain. Endorphins are naturally produced substances that inhibit pain.

Theme: Connections to Today Why do you think some patients today are reluctant to undergo acupuncture?

ANSWER Possible answer: They are not familiar with the procedure.

Resource Directory

Teaching Resources
Primary Source Activity *Seven Feminine Virtues,* Unit 2 booklet, p. 13
Section Quiz Unit 2 booklet, p. 11
Geography Quiz Unit 2 booklet, p. 16
Chapter Test Forms A, B, and C Unit 2 booklet, pp. 17–21
Answer Key Unit 2 booklet, pp. 78–92

Technology
Interactive Student Tutorial CD-ROM Ch. 4
Computer Test Bank Ch. 4

moved west slowly, reaching Europe hundreds of years later.

The Arts The walled cities of Han China boasted splendid temples and palaces amid elegant parks. Although these wooden buildings have not survived, Han poets and historians have described their grandeur. Artisans produced delicate jade and ivory carvings and fine ceramic figures. Bronzeworkers and silkmakers improved on earlier techniques and set high standards for future generations.

In *Lessons for a Woman,* a handbook of behavior written by Ban Zhao (BAHN JOW) around A.D. 100, the proper behavior for women and men was carefully spelled out. Ban Zhao favored equal education for boys and girls. However, she stressed that women should be obedient, respectful, and submissive. "Let a woman modestly yield to others," she advised. "Let her respect others."

Looking Ahead

Shi Huangdi, Gao Zu, Wudi, and later Han rulers forged a vast and varied land into a united China. Han rulers created an empire roughly the size of the continental United States. During this period, Chinese officials established the pattern of government that would survive until 1912. China would undergo great changes. It would break up and be painfully reassembled over and over. On the whole, however, Chinese civilization flourished in a united land. After periods of disunity, a new dynasty would turn to Confucian scholars to revive the days of Han greatness.

Cause *and* Effect

Long-Term Causes	Immediate Causes
• Confucian ideas dominate education • China's isolation permits development without much outside interference • Common system of writing evolves	• Zheng conquers eastern and western Zhou and overthrows feudal lords • Zheng proclaims himself Shi Huangdi ("First Emperor")

Unification of China

Immediate Effects	Long-Term Effects
• Shi Huangdi standardizes weights and measures and money • Roads and canals unify distant provinces • Government cracks down on dissenters • Shi Huangdi supervises work on the Great Wall	• Han dynasty is founded by Liu Bang • China makes advances in government, trade, and transportation • Confucian-educated officials hold most government jobs • Common culture helps China survive upheavals

Connections to Today

• Mainland China remains a large, politically united country
• Chinese still share a common written language

Skills Assessment **Chart** Under Shi Huangdi, most of China united under a single ruler. **How did political unification benefit the Chinese economy?**

Recall
1. (a) Shi Huangdi, p. 93 (b) Great Wall, p. 94 (c) Gao Zu, p. 95 (d) Wudi, p. 95 (e) Silk Road, p. 95 (f) Wang Chong, p. 96 (g) Ban Zhao, p. 97 2. (a) monopoly, p. 95 (b) expansionism, p. 95 (c) warlord, p. 96 (d) acupuncture, p. 96

Comprehension
3. Possible answer: He centralized power in a strong authoritarian government, standardized weights and measures, and established a uniform currency. 4. They improved canals and roads, reorganized finances, and imposed a government monopoly on salt. 5. Possible answer: In science, they measured movements of stars and planets and invented a simple seismograph; in medicine, they developed anesthetics and explored acupuncture; in technology, they invented a way to make paper from wood pulp, pioneered methods of shipbuilding, and invented the rudder for steering; in the arts, they built temples and palaces, produced poems, and carved jade and ivory.

Critical Thinking and Writing
6. Possible answer: It created a system of values based on Confucian teachings that dominated Chinese government and society for years. 7. The Qin government suppressed Confucian scholars, but the Han government appointed Confucian scholars as advisers.

SECTION 5 Assessment

Recall
1. **Identify:** (a) Shi Huangdi, (b) Great Wall, (c) Gao Zu, (d) Wudi, (e) Silk Road, (f) Wang Chong, (g) Ban Zhao.
2. **Define:** (a) monopoly, (b) expansionism, (c) warlord, (d) acupuncture.

Comprehension
3. What were three steps Shi Huangdi took to unify China?
4. How did Han emperors further economic growth in China?
5. Describe several of the achievements that helped make the Han period a golden age in Chinese civilization.

Critical Thinking and Writing
6. **Drawing Conclusions** Based on what you know about Confucianism, how do you think the civil service examination system affected the nature of Chinese government?
7. **Comparing** Describe one major difference between Qin government and Han government.

Activity
Take It to the NET

Use Internet sources to find out more about Chinese art during the Qin and Han dynasties. In a scrapbook, collect photocopies of art objects that you find. Write a brief description of each image so that others can learn about Chinese art during these periods.

Activity Rubrics

Share rubrics with students before they complete their scrapbooks.

Attempted Project has few images and no labels.

Minimal Student's scrapbook has several images but sketchy annotations.

Adequate Student's scrapbook includes a variety of artifacts and art objects as well as informative descriptions of each.

Exemplary Student's scrapbook shows extensive research, is creatively and clearly organized, and has well written and informative annotations.

Skills Assessment

ANSWER Shi Huangdi standardized weights, measures, and money to make trade easier; roads and canals made it easier to trade over distances.

Test Preparation

Have students read the section "Collapse of the Han Empire" on the opposite page, and then answer the question below.

Which of the following did not contribute to the collapse of the Han dynasty?

A powerful warlords

B court intrigues

C civil service system

D peasant revolts

Creating a Chapter Summary

As a reteaching opportunity, pair a more able student with a less able student to complete this chapter summary.

India
Government
- Maurya emperors conquered northern India.
- The Deccan kingdom divided.

Society
- The caste system created inequalities and stability.
- Women's duties were marriage, devotion to husband and children.

Religions and Value Systems
- Hinduism and Buddhism became two major world religions.
- Both stressed nonviolence, karma, dharma, and reincarnation.

Arts and Sciences
- Concept of zero; medical advances
- Rajahs built stone temples; Buddhists built stupas.

China
Government
- Zheng unified all China in 221 B.C., proclaiming himself First Emperor.
- Emperor Wudi reigned from 141 B.C. to 87 B.C. and ushered in a golden age.
- Views of government came from Confucianism, Legalism, and Daoism.

Society
- Under the Han, education was limited to sons of officials and the wealthy.
- Confucian teachings kept women from civil service jobs.

Religions and Value Systems
- By A.D. 400 Confucianism became a central belief system.
- Buddhism offered personal salvation.

Arts and Sciences
- Doctors used acupuncture.
- Astronomers measured movements of stars.

Building Vocabulary

1–8. Students' crossword puzzle clues should show an understanding of each word.

Recalling Key Facts

9. to free oneself of selfish desires and become one with the all-powerful spiritual force, or brahman

10. All life is full of suffering; the cause of suffering is the desire for things that are really illusions; the only cure for

Creating a Chapter Summary

Copy this table on a sheet of paper. Fill in key facts about government, society, religions and value systems, and arts and sciences. To help you get started, some examples have been filled in already.

	GOVERNMENT	SOCIETY	RELIGIONS AND VALUE SYSTEMS	ARTS AND SCIENCES
INDIA	• Maurya emperors conquered northern India. •			
CHINA				• Doctors used acupuncture. •

iTEXT For additional review and enrichment activities, see the interactive version of *World History* available on the Web and on CD-ROM.

Web Site Self-Test For practice test questions for Chapter 4, see **www. phschool.com.**

Building Vocabulary

Use the words below to make a crossword puzzle. Then, exchange puzzles with a classmate and complete the puzzles.

1. reincarnation
2. dharma
3. nirvana
4. missionary
5. stupa
6. patriarchal
7. philosophy
8. expansionism

Recalling Key Facts

9. According to Hinduism, what is the ultimate goal of existence?

10. What are the Four Noble Truths of Buddhism?

11. Describe three cultural advances made by Indian scholars and artists in the Gupta empire.

12. How did caste rules affect the daily lives of Indians?

13. How did the primary goal of Daoism differ from the primary goal of Confucianism?

14. How did the Silk Road benefit the Chinese economy?

15. What was the purpose of the Great Wall?

16. Describe three advances of Han civilization in science and technology.

Critical Thinking and Writing

17. **Comparing** Both Indian and Chinese rulers faced difficult challenges in uniting their lands. **(a)** How were these challenges similar? **(b)** How were they different?

18. **Defending a Position** Confucius said that people are basically good and can be led by example. Hanfeizi felt that people are basically evil and have to be controlled by laws. Select one of these positions and write several arguments to defend it.

19. **Connecting to Geography** Review the map of India on the following page. **(a)** How did geography help protect India from invasion? **(b)** What land route might invaders have used to successfully enter India?

20. **Linking Past and Present** In Han China, government officials were required to be schooled in Confucian values. In the United States today, why is it important for government officials to be well educated?

21. **Drawing Conclusions** In China, Shi Huangdi used a policy of book burning to increase his power. Why is book burning so often a policy of authoritarian governments?

suffering is to overcome desire; the way to overcome desire is to follow the Eightfold Path.

11. Possible answers: Mathematicians invented "Arabic" numerals and the concept of zero; physicians began vaccinating people against smallpox; new forms of architecture and literature were created.

12. They gave Indians a sense of identity by telling them their roles in society.

13. Daoism aimed at harmony with nature; Confucianism aimed at order.

14. It established a trade route connecting China with the Fertile Crescent.

15. Possible answer: to keep out invaders and to

show Emperor Shi Huangdi's ability to mobilize vast resources

16. Possible answers: invention of a seismograph to detect and measure earthquakes; invention of a papermaking method; invention of the wheelbarrow

Critical Thinking and Writing

17. **(a)** Both rulers had to unite vast lands and diverse peoples, and deal with internal rivalries and foreign invaders. **(b)** China, unlike India, was influenced by the idea of the dynastic cycle.

18. Students' viewpoints should be clearly expressed and supported.

Read the excerpt below from *Lessons for a Woman,* written around A.D. 100 by Ban Zhao. Then, answer the questions that follow.

"Let a woman retire late to bed, but rise early to duties; let her not dread tasks by day or by night. Let her not refuse to perform domestic duties whether easy or difficult. That which must be done, let her finish completely, tidily, and systematically. When a woman follows such rules as these, then she may be said to be industrious.

Let a woman be correct in manner and upright in character in order to serve her husband. Let her live in purity and quietness of spirit, and attend to her own affairs. Let her love not gossip and silly laughter. Let her cleanse and purify and arrange in order the wine and the food for the offerings to ancestors. When a woman observes such principles as these, then she may be said to continue ancestor worship."

—Ban Zhao, *Lessons for a Woman*

22. According to Ban Zhao, what daily routines should an industrious woman follow?
23. **(a)** Whom should a woman serve? **(b)** How does a woman show proper worship of her ancestors?
24. How does a woman's role, as described by Ban Zhao, fulfill the Confucian ideas of order and harmony?
25. Do you think it was easy or difficult for Chinese women to follow the advice of Ban Zhao? Explain.
26. Do you agree or disagree with the teachings of Ban Zhao? Explain.

Use reliable Internet sources, such as university sites and online encyclopedias to learn more about one of the dynasties of ancient China. Then, use the information that you find to create a time line listing major events and achievements that occurred during that dynasty's reign.

Maurya and Gupta Empires

The map above shows the Maurya and Gupta empires in India. Use the map to answer the following questions:

27. The city of Kabul was part of which of the two empires shown?
28. What physical features marked the northern boundary of the Maurya empire?
29. Which lands included in the Maurya empire were not part of the Gupta empire?
30. How does the map help explain the differences in culture between the people of northern India and those in the south?
31. What part of India was not controlled by either the Gupta or the Maurya empire?

Skills Tip

To get the most information from a map, take careful note of the symbols in the map key.

19. **(a)** India is separated from other regions by high mountains in the north and water on the other three sides. **(b)** mountain passes in Hindu Kush
20. Possible answer: Well-educated officials can make decisions about complex issues.
21. Possible answer: Books contain ideas and facts that may not support the goals of an authoritarian government.

Analyzing Primary Sources

22. Go to bed late, get up early, never refuse to do duties, finish tasks completely and well.
23. **(a)** her husband **(b)** by cleansing, purifying, and arranging the wine and food for ancestral offerings
24. Possible answer: By accepting her duties and responsibilities, a woman would live in harmony.
25. Possible answer: It was easy to follow an expected routine.
26. Student answers should be supported by examples.

Analyzing Maps

Maurya and Gupta Empires
27. Maurya empire
28. Hindu Kush and Himalaya Mountains
29. lands south of the Narmada River; lands northwest of the Indus River
30. Distance and geography—plateau in the south, rivers in the north, surrounded by seas in the south, with mountainous land bordering the north—might account for differences in culture.
31. Tamil kingdoms and Sri Lanka

Skills Tip

Call students' attention to the inset Mercator Projection that highlights India in the map on this page. Explain that inset maps provide geographic information on the relation of countries to each other that is not possible in a close-up view. The Skills Handbook in the front of the book has a lesson that will help students with this feature.

Take It to the NET

Creating a Time Line
Visit the World Studies portion of the Prentice Hall home page **www.phschool.com** for information on ancient dynasties. Share rubrics with students before they complete their time lines.
Attempted Student has done some research, but the time line is incomplete.
Minimal Student creates a time line in chronological order, but with little understanding of coordinating how events are spaced relative to elapsed time.
Adequate Student creates a time line with significant dynastic events spaced appropriately on the continuum.
Exemplary Student's choice of several key events during the time of the chosen dynasty shows a sophisticated understanding of the events' importance and relationships.

Unit Theme Activity

Remind students about the Unit Theme Activity located on the unit opener page. Make sure students understand the assignment and have begun work.

Resource Manager

	CORE INSTRUCTION	**READING/SKILLS**
Chapter Level Resources	**Teaching Resources** 📘 Pacing Charts, Ch. 5 📘 Teaching With Themes, p. 8 🎬 Color Transparencies, p. F–11 💿 Resource Pro® Ch. 5	🎧 Book on CD, Ch. 5 💿 Interactive Student Tutorial CD-ROM, Ch. 5 💿 Social Studies Skills Tutor CD-ROM 🎬 Skills Transparencies
1 Early People of the Aegean 1. Identify the civilizations that influenced the Minoans. 2. Explain how the Mycenaean civilization affected the later Greeks. 3. Describe what the epics of Homer reveal.	**Teaching Resources** 📘 Creative Teaching Activities, p. 24 💿 Prentice Hall Presentation Pro, Ch. 5, Section 1 🎬 Section Reading Support Transparencies	**Teaching Resources** 📗 Unit 2 booklet • Guided Reading and Review, p. 22 📘 Guide to the Essentials 📼 Guided Reading Audiotapes, Ch. 5, Section 1
2 The Rise of Greek City-States 1. Describe the influence of geography. 2. Describe the kinds of governments the Greek city-states developed. 3. Compare Athens and Sparta. 4. Identify the unifying forces.	**Teaching Resources** 📗 Unit 2 booklet • Viewpoint Activity, p. 34 📘 Creative Teaching Activities, p. 25 💿 Prentice Hall Presentation Pro, Ch. 5, Section 2 🎬 Section Reading Support Transparencies	**Teaching Resources** 📗 Unit 2 booklet • Guided Reading and Review, p. 24 📘 Guide to the Essentials 📼 Guided Reading Audiotapes, Ch. 5, Section 2
3 Victory and Defeat in the Greek World 1. Describe the impact the Persian Wars had on Greece. 2. Explain how Athens enjoyed a golden age under Pericles. 3. Identify the causes and effects of the Peloponnesian War.	**Teaching Resources** 📘 Creative Teaching Activities, p. 26 💿 Prentice Hall Presentation Pro, Ch. 5, Section 3 🎬 Section Reading Support Transparencies	**Teaching Resources** 📗 Unit 2 booklet • Guided Reading and Review, p. 26 📘 Guide to the Essentials 📼 Guided Reading Audiotapes, Ch. 5, Section 3
4 The Glory That Was Greece 1. Outline the political and ethical ideas that Greek philosophers developed. 2. Describe architects' and artists' goals. 3. Identify the themes that Greek writers and historians explored.	**Teaching Resources** 📗 Unit 2 booklet • Biography Activity, p. 32 📘 Creative Teaching Activities, p. 27 💿 Prentice Hall Presentation Pro, Ch. 5, Section 4 🎬 Section Reading Support Transparencies	**Teaching Resources** 📗 Unit 2 booklet • Guided Reading and Review, p. 28 • Skill Application Activity, p. 35 📘 Guide to the Essentials 📼 Guided Reading Audiotapes, Ch. 5, Section 4
5 Alexander and the Hellenistic Age 1. Explain how Alexander built an empire. 2. Summarize the results of Alexander's conquests. 3. Describe how individuals contributed to Hellenistic civilization.	**Teaching Resources** 📗 Unit 2 booklet • Primary Source Activity, p. 33 📘 Creative Teaching Activities, p. 28 💿 Prentice Hall Presentation Pro, Ch. 5, Section 5 🎬 Section Reading Support Transparencies	**Teaching Resources** 📗 Unit 2 booklet • Guided Reading and Review, p. 30 📘 Guide to the Essentials 📼 Guided Reading Audiotapes, Ch. 5, Section 5

ENRICHMENT/PRE-AP

📖 **www.phschool.com**
  • Why Study History?

📖 Teaching Resources
  📖 **History Through Literature**, pp. 11–12
  📖 **Color Transparencies**, p. B–75
  📼 **Listening to Literature World Masterpieces**, excerpt from the *Iliad*, side 4
  📖 **www.phschool.com**
    • Internet Activities, Section 1

📼 **Listening to Literature World Masterpieces**, ancient Greek music, side 4
📼 **Visions, Voices, Views**, Daily Life CloseUp, tape 2

📖 Teaching Resources
  📖 **Chapter Extension Activities**, pp. 16–17
📼 **Visions, Voices, Views**, Global Issues Forum, tape 2

📖 Teaching Resources
  📖 **Chapter Extension Activities**, p. 18
  📖 **Color Transparencies**, pp. C–29, D–39
  📼 **Listening to Literature World Masterpieces**, poem by Sappho, side 4
  📖 **www.phschool.com**
    • Virtual Field Trip

📖 **Color Transparencies**, p. D–41
📖 **www.phschool.com**
  • Internet Activities, Section 5

ASSESSMENT

PRENTICE HALL
ASSESSMENT SYSTEM

Core Assessment
  📖 **ExamView Test Bank booklet**, Ch. 5
  💿 **ExamView Test Bank CD-ROM**, Ch. 5

Standardized Test Preparation
Diagnose and Prescribe
  📖 **Diagnostic Tests for High School Social Studies Skills**
Review and Reteach
  📖 **Review Book for World History**
Practice and Assess
  📖 **Test-Taking Strategies With Transparencies for High School**
  📖 **Alternative Assessment booklet**
  📖 **Test Prep Book for World History**

📖 Teaching Resources
  📖 **Unit 2 booklet**
    • Geography Quiz, p. 36
    • Section Quizzes, pp. 23, 25, 27, 29, 31
    • Chapter Tests A, B, and C, pp. 37–41
📖 **www.phschool.com**
  • Self-Test

CUSTOMIZE FOR INDIVIDUAL NEEDS

Gifted and Talented
  • **Teacher's Edition**, Activities: Customize for Auditory Learners, p. 116; Connections to Literature, p. 117
Less Proficient Readers
  • **Guide to the Essentials**, Ch. 5
  • **Guided Reading Audiotapes, English**, Ch. 5
  • **Book on CD**, Ch. 5
  • **Teacher's Edition**, Activities: Cooperative Learning, p. 107; Reading Strategy, p. 108; Reading Strategy, p. 121
Less Proficient Writers
  • **Teacher's Edition**, Activities: Cooperative Learning, p. 107; Cooperative Learning Activity, p. 118
Students Acquiring English/ESL
  • **Guide to the Essentials, English/Spanish**, Ch. 5
  • **Guided Reading Audiotapes, English/Spanish**, Ch. 5
  • **Book on CD**, Ch. 5
  • **Teacher's Edition**, Activities marked with an *: Cooperative Learning, p. 107

iTEXT

Don't miss the exclusive interactive version of *World History: Connections to Today* on the Internet and CD-ROM.

INTRODUCTION

Minoans built a brilliant civilization on Crete, but vanished by about 1400 B.C. Their Mycenaean successors conquered Greece, but were later destroyed by outsiders. Greece entered a dark age, but civilization gradually returned with the rise of city-states. Greece's golden age was followed by eventual decline and conquest at the hands of Alexander the Great, the Macedonian general who forged an extended empire.

Focusing on Themes

Suggest that students focus on these theme questions as they read:

Geography and History
How did geography influence the Greek way of life and their interaction with other people?

Impact of the Individual
How did political leaders, philosophers, and writers shape Greek civilization?

Political and Social Systems
What Greek ideas about government influenced later societies?

Global Interaction
How did Greek civilization affect peoples across many regions?

TIME LINE ACTIVITY

Share the About the Pictures note with your students before asking these questions about the time line:

1. Why is there a break in the time line between 1750 B.C. and 500 B.C.? *(to show a more extended time interval)*
2. What does the coin from 331 B.C. reveal about the Greek economy? *(They used money instead of barter.)*
3. What great empire was founded less than 100 years before the Age of Pericles in Athens? *(Persian)*
4. When did the Maurya Dynasty begin in India? *(321 B.C.)*

Don't Miss!

Comparing Viewpoints
How Should a Society's Leaders Be Chosen?
(Section 3)

Humanities Link
Greek Drama
(Section 4)

Ancient Greece
1750 B.C.–133 B.C.

Chapter Preview

1 Early People of the Aegean
2 The Rise of Greek City-States
3 Victory and Defeat in the Greek World
4 The Glory That Was Greece
5 Alexander and the Hellenistic Age

1600 B.C.
Minoan civilization on the island of Crete is at its height. The palace at Knossos (above) was the center of Minoan civilization.

460 B.C.
The Age of Pericles marks the height of democracy in Athens.

431 B.C.
The Peloponnesian War begins, pitting Athens against its rival city-state, Sparta. This painting shows soldiers in the Peloponnesian War.

CHAPTER EVENTS

1750 B.C.   500 B.C.   400 B.C.

GLOBAL EVENTS

539 B.C. Cyrus the Great founds the Persian empire.

450 B.C. The Roman Republic publishes its legal code.

Resource Directory

Teaching Resources
Teaching With Themes Chapter Theme Activities, p. 8
Pacing Chart With Block Scheduling Guide Ch. 5
Technology
World History Color Transparencies Ch. 5 Graphic Organizer, p. F–11

Centers of Greek Civilization About 500 B.C.

A common language and civilization linked the many Greek city-states. Although Greek civilization arose in a small corner of southeastern Europe, it had a worldwide impact.

PINDUS MTS.

Mt. Olympus ▲

Peneus R.

Aegean Sea

ASIA MINOR

Delphi

GREECE

Corinth • Athens

Olympia • Mycenae

PELOPONNESUS

Sparta

Milos

Mediterranean Sea

Crete

Albers Equal Area Projection
0   50   100 Miles
0   50   100 Kilometers

331 B.C.
Alexander the Great conquers the Persian empire. The young Macedonian general already rules all of Greece.

323 B.C.
The Hellenistic Age begins, spreading Greek culture through the lands conquered by Alexander. This statue, called *Nike* or Winged Victory, is a masterpiece of Hellenistic art.

133 B.C.
Greek dominance of the Mediterranean world ends.

300 B.C.   **200 B.C.**   **100 B.C.**

321 B.C.
The Maurya dynasty begins in India.

221 B.C.
Shi Huangdi unites China.

Chapter 5 **101**

Independent Assignments

Have students read one section as they prepare for class. After class, have them complete the assignment. Some students may benefit from using the Guided Reading and Review worksheets.

Section 1 Have students use the worksheet *The Odyssey* in the History Through Literature booklet, pp. 11–12, to learn more about Greek literature.
Section 2 Have students use the worksheet *The Values of Sparta and Athens* in the Unit 2 booklet, p. 34, to learn more about each of these city-states.
Section 3 Have students use the Chapter Extension Activities worksheet *Comparing Viewpoints*, pp. 16–17, to learn how viewpoints can differ.

Section 4 Have students use the worksheet *Herodotus Visits the Pyramids of Egypt* in the Unit 2 booklet, p. 33, to learn what impressed this ancient Greek historian.
Section 5 Have students label major physical features and important cities on the outline map *Empire of Alexander the Great* in the Historical Outline Map Book, p. 8.

Centers of Greek Civilization About 500 B.C.

Activating Prior Knowledge
Given Greece's location in the Mediterranean, which ancient civilization would you expect to have the greater influence on Greece: that of Egypt or that of India? Why? *(Egypt; it is much closer than India and easily accessible via the Mediterranean Sea.)*

Previewing
What clue does the map give you that, for the Greeks, farming was a less important economic activity than trade? *(Greece's mountainous land limited farming.)*

Background
About the Pictures

1. Architects designed Minoan palaces to take advantage of the region's sunny climate. Openings in the roof let in the sunlight.

2. Greek foot soldiers were called *hoplites*. As the painting shows, they carried a spear in one hand and a shield in the other. They marched into battle in formidable phalanxes of 8 or 16 men.

3. This Greek *tetradrachm* silver coin was made with the image of Alexander the Great in about 320 B.C. The Lydians of Asia Minor had started the practice of coinmaking about 300 years earlier. Lumps of gold and silver were stamped with official symbols before then, but each had to be weighed and tested before use.

4. The *Nike of Samothrace*, named after the island on which it was found, was sculpted about 190 B.C. Made of marble, it originally stood on the prow of a sculpture of a warship. Today, the 8-foot-high *Nike* is in the Louvre. (Nike was the goddess of victory, hence the name *Winged Victory*.)

eTeach

Be sure to check out this month's online discussion with a World History Master Teacher.

Go to **www.phschool.com**.

SECTION 1

Bell Ringer Ask students to recall the Greek myths and legends that they have encountered in films and literature. Then, invite volunteers to list some Greek gods and heroes on the chalkboard. Have students describe what they know about each. Suggest that students keep these stories in mind as they study this section.

LESSON PLAN

1. Focus Influenced by the civilizations of Egypt and Mesopotamia, Minoan civilization developed on the island of Crete. Later, Mycenaean civilization developed in numerous city-states on the Greek mainland. The epics of Homer tell us much about the values of the ancient Greeks.

2. Instruct Have students work in groups to dramatize information and events in the section. The groups might base their presentations on one of the following: the story of Europa, Minoan life on Crete, the *Iliad*, or the *Odyssey*. Suggest that students prepare scripts, assign roles, and rehearse their dramatizations. They might also do additional research. Advise students that they should be prepared to answer questions or further explain their presentations.

3. Assess Ask students to write three main ideas that they learned about Minoan life, Mycenaean epics, or other aspects of early Greek cultures covered in this section. In a class discussion, have students identify their ideas and support them with details from the section.

4. Reteach If students' *Assess* activity does not reflect adequate understanding of the lesson, you might assign the *Guide to the Essentials* or the *Interactive Student Tutorial CD-ROM* for this section.

SECTION 1 Early People of the Aegean

Reading Focus

- What civilizations influenced the Minoans?
- How did Mycenaean civilization affect the later Greeks?
- What do the epics of Homer reveal about the Greeks?

Vocabulary

shrine
fresco
strait

Taking Notes

Copy this time line. As you read, fill in the major civilizations and events that occurred.

Trojan War
1250 B.C.

| 1800 B.C. | 1600 B.C. | 1400 B.C. | 1200 B.C. | 1000 B.C. | 800 B.C. |

1750 B.C.–1500 B.C.
Minoan civilization at its height

Main Idea The Minoans and Mycenaeans shaped the first Greek civilizations.

Geography and History

From Egypt to Crete

When Minoan traders sailed the Mediterranean, they often headed for Egypt. Some Egyptian tomb paintings even show Minoan traders offering gifts to the pharaoh. In return, the traders brought valuable items such as linen home to Crete.

Trading goods led to cultural borrowing. Early Greek painting, with its stiff, formal poses, resembles Egyptian art styles. In addition, Egyptian notions of life after death—including a ferry ride across a river to the underworld—may have influenced Greek religious ideas.

 Theme: Geography and History How does Egyptian influence on Minoan culture reflect the geographic themes of location and movement?

Setting the Scene Europa, the beautiful daughter of the king of Phoenicia, was gathering flowers when she saw a bull quietly grazing with her father's herds. The bull was actually Zeus, king of the gods, who had fallen in love with her. When Europa reached to place flowers on his horns, he suddenly bounded into the air and carried the weeping princess far across the Mediterranean Sea to the island of Crete. Eventually, Europa married the king of Crete and gave her name to a new continent—Europe.

This Greek legend carries seeds of truth. Crete was the cradle of an early civilization that later influenced Greeks on the European mainland. The people of Crete, however, had absorbed many ideas from the older civilizations of Egypt and Mesopotamia. Europa's journey from Phoenicia to Crete thus suggests the movement of ideas from east to west.

Minoan Civilization

Washed by the warm waters of the Aegean (uh JEE uhn) Sea, Crete was home to a brilliant early civilization. We do not know what the people who built this civilization called themselves. However, the British archaeologist who unearthed its ruins called them Minoans after Minos, a legendary king of Crete. Minoan civilization reached its height, or greatest success, between 1750 B.C. and 1500 B.C.

The success of the Minoans was based on trade, not conquest. Minoan traders set up outposts throughout the Aegean world. From their island home in the eastern Mediterranean, they crossed the seas to the Nile Valley and the Middle East. Through contact with Egypt and Mesopotamia, they acquired ideas and technology that they adapted to their own culture.

The Palace at Knossos The rulers of this trading empire lived in a vast palace at Knossos (NAHS uhs). It housed rooms for the royal family, banquet halls, and working areas for artisans. It also included religious shrines, areas dedicated to the honor of gods and goddesses.

The walls of the palace at Knossos are covered with colorful frescoes, watercolor paintings done on wet plaster. These frescoes tell us much about Minoan society. Leaping dolphins reflect the importance of the sea to the Minoan people. Religious images indicate that the Minoans worshiped the bull and a mother goddess. Other paintings show young men and women strolling through gardens or jumping through the horns of a charging bull. They suggest that women appeared freely in public and may have enjoyed more rights than women in most other ancient civilizations.

Geography and History

ANSWERS Location: Crete is located only a few hundred miles from the mouth of the Nile River. **Movement:** Egyptian cultural influences were carried by traders who traveled by sea.

Resource Directory

Teaching Resources
Creative Teaching Activities Creative Teaching Activities booklet, p. 24
Guided Reading and Review Unit 2 booklet, p. 22

Technology
World History Color Transparencies *Lands of the Mediterranean*, p. B–75

Block Scheduling Support

Play for students the excerpt from the *Iliad* on Listening to Literature World Masterpieces Audiotapes. As they listen, have them note what the excerpt reveals about Greek values. Then, have them write a paragraph explaining their observations. Remind students to organize their observations before they write and to begin their paragraphs with a clear topic sentence.

A Civilization Disappears By about 1400 B.C., Minoan civilization had vanished. Archaeologists are not sure of the reasons for its disappearance. A sudden volcanic eruption on a nearby island may have rained flaming death on Knossos. An earthquake may have destroyed the palace, followed by a tidal wave that drowned the inhabitants of the island.

However, invaders certainly played a role in the destruction of Minoan civilization. These intruders were the Mycenaeans (mī suh NEE uhnz), the first Greek-speaking people of whom we have a written record.

Rulers of Mycenae

Like the Aryans who swept into India, the Mycenaeans were an Indo-European people. They conquered the Greek mainland before overrunning Crete.

Successful Sea Traders Mycenaean civilization dominated the Aegean world from about 1400 B.C. to 1200 B.C. Like the Minoans, the Mycenaeans were sea traders. They reached out beyond the Aegean to Sicily, Italy, Egypt, and Mesopotamia. The newcomers learned many skills from the Minoans, including the art of writing. They, too, absorbed Egyptian and Mesopotamian influences, which they passed on to later Greeks.

The Mycenaeans lived in separate city-states on the mainland. In each, a warrior-king built a thick-walled fortress from which he ruled the surrounding villages. Wealthy rulers amassed hoards of treasure, including fine gold ornaments that archaeologists have unearthed from their tombs.

The Trojan War The Mycenaeans are best remembered for their part in the Trojan War, which took place around 1250 B.C. The conflict may have had its origins in economic rivalry between Mycenae and Troy, a rich trading city in present-day Turkey. Troy controlled the vital straits, or narrow water passages, that connect the Mediterranean and Black seas. However, Greek legend attributes the war to a more romantic cause. After the Trojan prince Paris kidnapped Helen, the beautiful wife of a Greek king, the Mycenaeans sailed to Troy to rescue her. For the next 10 years, the two sides battled until the Greeks finally seized Troy and burned the city to the ground.

For centuries, most people regarded the Trojan War as purely a legend. Then, in the 1870s, a wealthy German businessman, Heinrich Schliemann (HĪN rihk SHLEE mahn), set out to prove that the legend was rooted in fact. As he excavated the site of ancient Troy, Schliemann found evidence of fire and war dating to about 1250 B.C. Though most of the details remain lost in legend, modern scholars agree that the Trojan War was an actual event.

The Age of Homer

Not long after the fall of Troy, Mycenaean civilization crumbled under the attack of sea raiders. About the same time, another wave of Greek-speaking people, the Dorians, invaded from the north. As Mycenaean power faded, people abandoned the cities, and trade declined. From 1100 B.C. to 800 B.C., Greek civilization seemed to step backward. People forgot many skills, including the art of writing.

We get hints about life during this period from two great epic poems, the *Iliad* and the *Odyssey*. These epics may have been the work of many

A Minoan Fresco
These dolphins from the palace at Knossos show the lightness and sense of movement of Minoan frescoes.
Theme: Geography and History Why do you think Minoan artists chose dolphins as a subject?

Recall
1. **(a)** Trojan War, p. 103 **(b)** Heinrich Schliemann, p. 103 **(c)** Homer, p. 104
2. **(a)** shrine, p. 102 **(b)** fresco, p. 102 **(c)** strait, p. 103

Comprehension
3. Through trade, Minoans and Mycenaeans learned ideas and technology from Egypt and Mesopotamia. 4. Mycenaeans passed on writing, legends, and other cultural features to later Greeks.
5. Homer's poems tell of honor, courage, and eloquence.

Critical Thinking and Writing
6. Students may mention resources needed to build boats, such as wood, as well as rock-free harbors that can be reached safely. 7. Possible answers: Yes and no. Homer's epics are based partly on fact. For example, the remains of Troy have been found. However, his epics are filled with myths and legends.

Activity Rubrics

Share rubrics with students before they create their lists.

Attempted The list contains fewer than five words or is missing some or all explanations.

Minimal The list contains five words, but explanations are unclear.

Adequate The list contains five words, and explanations are clear.

Exemplary The list contains five or more words, and explanations are clear and interesting.

Hero of the *Odyssey*
Odysseus was admired for cleverness. Here, he outwits the siren, whose song lures sailors to their doom. He fills his crew's ears with beeswax. Then, he has himself tied to the ship's mast so he can hear the siren's song without endangering the ship.

Theme: Art and Literature Name some fictional heroes of the past and present. What admirable qualities do they possess?

people, but they are credited to the poet Homer, who probably lived about 750 B.C. According to tradition, Homer was a blind poet who wandered from village to village, singing of heroic deeds. Like the great Indian epics, Homer's tales were passed on orally for generations before they were finally written down.

The *Iliad* is our chief source of information about the Trojan War, although the story involves gods, goddesses, and even a talking horse. At the start of the poem, Achilles (uh KIHL eez), the mightiest Greek warrior, is sulking in his tent because of a dispute with his commander. Although the war soon turns against the Greeks, Achilles stubbornly refuses to listen to pleas that he rejoin the fighting. Only after his best friend is killed does Achilles return to battle.

The *Odyssey* tells of the struggles of the Greek hero Odysseus (oh DIHS ee uhs) to return home to his faithful wife, Penelope, after the fall of Troy. On his long voyage, Odysseus encounters a sea monster, a race of one-eyed giants, and a beautiful sorceress who turns men into swine.

The *Iliad* and *Odyssey* reveal much about the values of the ancient Greeks. The heroes display honor, courage, and eloquence, as when Achilles rallies his troops:

> "Every man make up his mind to fight
> And move on his enemy! Strong as I am,
> It's hard for me to face so many men
> And fight with all at once. . . .
> And yet I will!"
>
> —Homer, *Iliad*

For almost 3,000 years, the epics of Homer have inspired European writers and artists.

Looking Ahead

For centuries after the Dorian invasions, the Greeks lived in small, isolated villages. They had no writing and few contacts with the outside world. From this unpromising start, they would develop a civilization that influenced many parts of the world. As they emerged from obscurity, they benefited from the legacy of earlier civilizations. Over time, the stories they heard about Crete and Mycenae underwent changes and became part of the Greek heritage.

SECTION 1 Assessment

Recall
1. **Identify:** **(a)** Trojan War, **(b)** Heinrich Schliemann, **(c)** Homer.
2. **Define:** **(a)** shrine, **(b)** fresco, **(c)** strait.

Comprehension
3. How did trade contribute to the development of Minoan and Mycenaean civilizations?
4. What impact did Mycenaean civilization have on later Greeks?
5. What values of the ancient Greeks are found in the poems of Homer?

Critical Thinking and Writing
6. **Connecting to Geography** In addition to location near water, what other geographic features or natural resources would have been important to an early people who made their living as sea traders?
7. **Drawing Conclusions** Do you think the epics of Homer are probably a reliable source of information about the history of the ancient Greeks? Why or why not?

Activity
Take It to the NET

Use the Internet to research ancient Greek myths such as the story of Europa. Then, make a list of five words, like *Europe*, that are derived from these myths. For each word, include an explanation of the connection between the English word and its Greek origin.

Caption Answer

Possible answers: Hercules, King Arthur, Rama, John Henry, Superman, Indiana Jones, Luke Skywalker. Their heroic qualities may include courage, intelligence, determination, and a sense of justice.

Resource Directory

Teaching Resources
History Through Literature *The Odyssey*, History Through Literature booklet, pp. 11–12
Section Quiz Unit 2 booklet, p. 23
Creative Teaching Activities Creative Teaching Activities booklet, p. 25
Guided Reading and Review Unit 2 booklet, p. 24

Technology
Listening to Literature World Masterpieces audiotapes ancient Greek music, side 4, running time 3:14 min.; excerpt from the *Iliad* (in English), sample of lines in Greek, side 4, running time 9:25 min.
Interactive Student Tutorial CD-Rom Ch. 5
Computer Test Bank Ch. 5

The Rise of Greek City-States

Reading Focus

- How did geography influence the Greek city-states?
- What kinds of government did the Greek city-states develop?
- How did Athens and Sparta differ?
- What forces unified the Greek city-states?

Vocabulary

polis
acropolis
monarchy
aristocracy
oligarchy
phalanx
helot
democracy
tyrant
legislature

Taking Notes

Copy this diagram. As you read, fill in both similarities and differences between Athens and Sparta. Parts of these circles have been completed to help you get started.

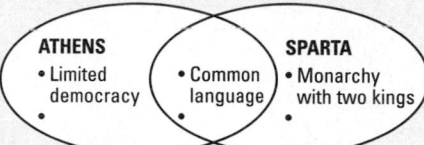

ATHENS
- Limited democracy

- Common language

SPARTA
- Monarchy with two kings

Main Idea As Greek city-states grew, they developed different types of government, including an early form of democracy.

Setting the Scene "We live around the sea like frogs around a pond," noted the Greek thinker Plato. Indeed, the Mediterranean and Aegean seas were as central to the development of Greek civilization as the Nile was to the Egyptians. The ancient Greeks absorbed many ideas and beliefs from the older civilizations of Mesopotamia and Egypt. At the same time, they evolved their own unique ways. In particular, the Greeks developed new ideas about how best to govern a society.

Geography of the Greek Homeland

As you have read, the earliest civilizations rose in fertile river valleys. There, strong rulers organized irrigation works that helped farmers produce food surpluses needed to support large cities. A very different set of geographic conditions influenced the rise of Greek civilization.

Mountains and Valleys Greece is part of the Balkan peninsula, which extends southward into the eastern Mediterranean Sea. Mountains divide the peninsula into isolated valleys. Beyond the rugged coast, hundreds of rocky islands spread toward the horizon.

The Greeks who farmed the valleys or settled on the scattered islands did not create a large empire such as that of the Egyptians or Persians. Instead, they built many small city-states, cut off from one another by mountains or water. Each included a city and its surrounding countryside. Greeks fiercely defended the independence of their tiny city-states. Endless rivalry led to frequent wars.

The Seas While mountains divided Greeks, the seas were a vital link to the world outside. With its hundreds of bays, the Greek coastline provided safe harbors for ships. The Greeks became skilled sailors, carrying cargoes of olive oil, wine, and marble around the eastern Mediterranean. They returned not only with grains and metals but also with ideas, which they adapted to their own needs. For example, the Greeks expanded the Phoenician alphabet. The resulting Greek alphabet became the basis for all western alphabets.

By 750 B.C., rapid population growth was forcing many Greeks to leave their own overcrowded valleys. With fertile land limited, the Greeks expanded overseas. Gradually, a scattering of Greek colonies took root all around the Mediterranean from Spain to Egypt. Wherever they traveled, Greek settlers and traders carried their ideas and culture.

DEVELOPMENT OF THE ALPHABET

Phoenician	Greek	Roman
∤	A	A
⊿	B	B
⊿	△	D
Ψ	K	K
⎿	∧	L
⌐	N	N

Skills Assessment

Chart Our alphabet comes to us from the Phoenicians by way of the Greeks. The word *alphabet* itself comes from the first two Greek letters, *alpha* and *beta*. **Describe how the modern letter A changed over time.**

Bell Ringer Draw students' attention to the vocabulary word *polis* and ask them to identify places in the United States whose names end with *-polis* as a suffix. What do students think the term means? What does this suggest about Greek civilization?

LESSON PLAN

1. Focus Although mountains separated Greek communities from one another, this land of islands and jagged coastlines had a common focus—the sea. One result of geographic divisions was the growth of separate city-states, two of which were Sparta, with its rigorous, warrior society, and Athens, with its limited democracy.

2. Instruct Have pairs of students write dialogues between an Athenian and a Spartan citizen that reveal some of the key differences they cited in the Taking Notes activity for this section.

3. Assess Ask students to read their dialogues before the class. Then have the class discuss the differences brought out in the dialogues.

4. Reteach If students' **Assess** activity does not reflect adequate understanding of the lesson, you might assign the *Guide to the Essentials* or the *Interactive Student Tutorial CD-ROM* for this section.

Skills Assessment

ANSWER The Phoenican letter was on its side. The Greeks rotated it clockwise and dropped the bottom of the left leg. The Romans kept that orientation, but replaced the bottom left leg.

Background
Historical Evidence

Helot Rewards The Spartans used helots in their army, but they feared that helots who showed exceptional ability might one day lead rebellions against them. To avert this danger, the *ephors*, or magistrates, gave a secret police force the power to kill helots at any time. The Greek historian Thucydides reports a major incident that occurred sometime before the Peloponnesian War:

"The Helots were invited by a proclamation to pick out those of their number who claimed to have distinguished themselves against the enemy, in order that they might receive their freedom. . . . As many as 2,000 were selected accordingly, who crowned themselves and went round the temples, rejoicing in their new freedom. The Spartans, however, soon did away with them, and no one ever knew how each of them perished."

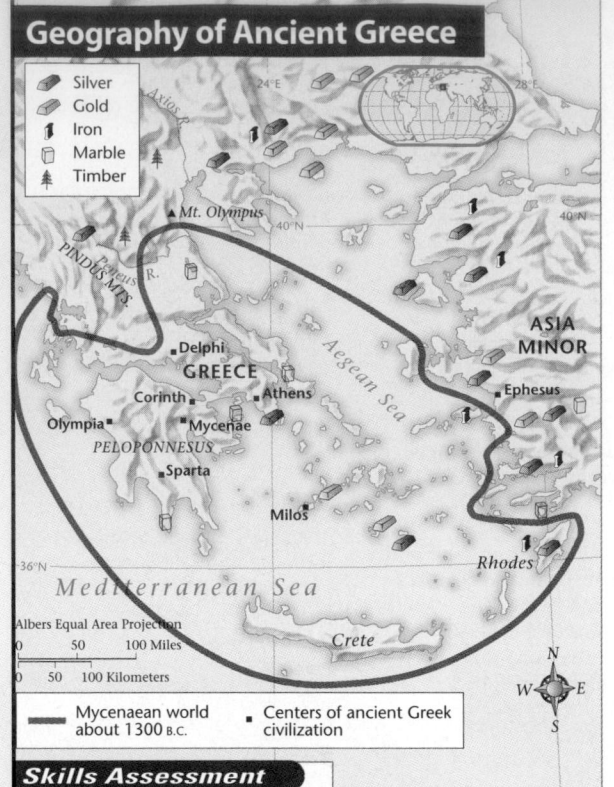

Geography of Ancient Greece

Silver
Gold
Iron
Marble
Timber

Mycenaean world about 1300 B.C.

Centers of ancient Greek civilization

Skills Assessment

Geography Greek civilization was shaped by both rugged mountains and the surrounding seas.

1. **Location** On the map, locate (a) Aegean Sea, (b) Mediterranean Sea, (c) Greece, (d) Crete, (e) Mycenae, (f) Athens, (g) Sparta, (h) Mt. Olympus.
2. **Region** How did the geography of Greece present obstacles to unity?
3. **Critical Thinking** **Comparing** How did the geography of Greece differ from that of other ancient civilizations?

Governing the City-States

As their world expanded after 750 B.C., the Greeks evolved a unique version of the city-state, which they called the **polis**. Typically, the city itself was built on two levels. On a hilltop stood the **acropolis** (uh KRAHP uh lihs), or high city, with its great marble temples dedicated to different gods and goddesses. On flatter ground below lay the walled main city with its market-place, theater, public buildings, and homes.

The population of each city-state was fairly small, which helped citizens share a sense of responsibility for its triumphs and defeats. In the warm climate of Greece, free men spent much time outdoors in the marketplace, debating issues that affected their lives. The whole community joined in festivals honoring the city's special god or goddess.

Early Governments Between 750 B.C. and 500 B.C., Greeks evolved different forms of government. At first, the ruler of the polis, like those in the river valley empires, was a king. A government in which a king or queen exercises central power is a **monarchy**. Slowly, though, power shifted to a class of noble landowners. They were also the military defenders of the city-states, because only they could afford bronze weapons and chariots. At first these nobles defended the king. In time, they won power for themselves. The result was an **aristocracy**, or rule by a landholding elite.

As trade expanded, a new middle class of wealthy merchants, farmers, and artisans emerged in some cities. They challenged the landowning nobles for power and came to dominate some city-states. The result was a form of government called an **oligarchy**. In an oligarchy, power is in the hands of a small, powerful elite, usually from the business class.

Changes in Warfare Changes in military technology increased the power of the middle class. By about 650 B.C., iron weapons replaced bronze ones. Since iron was cheaper, ordinary citizens could afford iron helmets, shields, and swords. Meanwhile, a new method of fighting emerged. The **phalanx** was a massive formation of heavily armed foot soldiers. It required long hours of drill. Shared training created a strong sense of unity among citizen-soldiers.

By putting the defense of the city-state in the hands of ordinary citizens, the phalanx reduced class differences. The new type of warfare, however, led the two most influential city-states to develop very different ways of life. While Sparta stressed military virtues and stern discipline, Athens glorified the individual and extended political rights to more citizens.

Sparta: A Nation of Soldiers

The Spartans were Dorians who conquered Laconia. This region lies in the Peloponnesus (pehl uh puh NEE suhs), the southern part of Greece. The invaders turned the conquered people into state-owned slaves, called **helots**, and made them work the land. Because the helots greatly outnumbered their rulers, the Spartans set up a brutal system of strict control.

The Spartan government included two kings and a council of elders who advised the monarchs. An assembly made up of all citizens approved

Skills Assessment

ANSWERS 1. Review locations with students. 2. The many Greek city-states were divided by mountains and seas, making united action difficult. 3. Early civilizations in Africa and Asia developed along river valleys, allowing for widespread agriculture. Greek civilization developed on a mountainous peninsula jutting into the sea, where farming was more limited.

Resource Directory

Teaching Resources
Viewpoint Activity *The Values of Sparta and Athens,* Unit 2 booklet, p. 34

Technology
World History Visions, Voices, Views Daily Life CloseUp, *A Young Woman in Sparta,* videodisc side 1 or videotape 2, running time 3:00 min.

Side 1: Fr. 29590-35565

major decisions. Citizens were male, native-born Spartans over the age of 30. The assembly also elected five ephors, officials who held the real power and ran day-to-day affairs.

The Rigors of Citizenship From childhood, a Spartan prepared to be part of a military state. Officials examined every newborn, and sickly children were abandoned to die. Spartans wanted future soldiers or mothers of soldiers to be healthy.

At the age of seven, boys began training for a lifetime in the military. They moved into barracks, where they endured a brutal existence. Toughened by a coarse diet, hard exercise, and rigid discipline, Spartan youths became excellent soldiers. To develop cunning and supplement their diet, boys were even encouraged to steal food. If caught, though, they were beaten severely.

At the age of 20, a man could marry, but he continued to live in the barracks for another 10 years and to eat there for another 40 years. At the age of 30, after further specialized training, he took his place in the assembly.

Women Girls, too, had a rigorous upbringing. As part of a warrior society, they were expected to produce healthy sons for the army. They therefore were told to exercise and strengthen their bodies—something no other Greek women did.

Like other Greek women, Spartan women had to obey their fathers or husbands. Under Spartan law, though, they had the right to inherit property. Because men were occupied with war, some women took on responsibilities such as running the family's estates.

Sparta and Its Neighbors The Spartans isolated themselves from other Greeks. They looked down on trade and wealth, forbade their own citizens to travel, and had little use for new ideas or the arts. While other Greeks admired the Spartans' military skills, no other city-state imitated their rigorous way of life. "Spartans are willing to die for their city," some suggested, "because they have no reason to live."

Athens: A Limited Democracy

Athens was located in Attica, just north of the Peloponnesus. As in many Greek city-states, Athenian government evolved from a monarchy into an aristocracy. Around 700 B.C., noble landowners held power and chose the chief officials. Nobles judged major cases in court and dominated the assembly.

Demands for Change Under the aristocracy, Athenian wealth and power grew. Yet discontent spread among ordinary people. Merchants and soldiers resented the power of the nobles. They argued that their service to Athens entitled them to more rights. Foreign artisans, who produced many goods that Athens traded abroad, were resentful that foreigners were barred from becoming citizens. Farmers, too, demanded change. During hard times, many farmers were forced to sell their land to nobles. A growing number even sold themselves and their families into slavery to pay their debts.

As discontent spread, Athens moved slowly toward democracy, or government by the people. As you will see, the term had a different meaning for the ancient Greeks than it has for us today.

Solon's Reforms Solon, a wise and trusted leader, was appointed archon (AHR kahn), or chief official, in 594 B.C. Athenians gave Solon a free hand to make needed reforms. He outlawed debt slavery and freed those who had already been sold into slavery for debt. He opened high offices to more citizens, granted citizenship to some foreigners, and gave the Athenian assembly more say in important decisions.

Primary Source

A Spartan Education
An Athenian historian explains the system of education set up by Lycurgus, the Spartan lawgiver:

"Instead of softening the boys' feet with sandals he required them to harden their feet by going without shoes. He believed that if this habit were cultivated it would enable them to climb hills more easily and descend steep inclines with less danger, and that a youth who had accustomed himself to go barefoot would leap and jump and run more nimbly than a boy in sandals. And instead of letting them be pampered in the matter of clothing, he introduced the custom of wearing one garment throughout the year, believing that they would thus be better prepared to face changes of heat and cold."

—Xenophon, *Constitution of the Lacedaemonians*

Skills Assessment

Primary Source Describe the Spartan student dress code. What was its purpose?

Slavery and Democracy Ironically, the existence of slavery probably had a great deal to do with the success of democracy in ancient Athens. Athenians who owned slaves were freed from the necessity of daily chores and the routine work of commerce and manufacturing. Thus, they could devote their time to discussing public affairs in the marketplace, taking part in the assembly, and holding public office.

Background
Connections to Today

Valuable Oil Olive oil had indispensable value for the ancient Greeks. They used it as a cooking oil and as a fuel oil in lamps. They anointed people with it in religious rituals, and they also used it as a valuable export commodity that could be traded for grain and other foods.

In recent years, people have found olive oil valuable for another reason. Scientists noted that people of Mediterranean countries had a relatively low incidence of heart disease despite a relatively high intake of fats and oils. Studies indicate that the high level of monounsaturates found in olive oil may be the reason.

Reading Strategy
Check Comprehension

After students read Section 2, ask them to recall as many facts as they can without looking back. List their points on the board without correcting errors or supplying additional information. Have students reread or skim the material, checking to see if the ideas listed were correct and adding ideas that were not listed the first time. Have students organize the facts and ideas into a summary of the reading. *(Less Advanced Readers)*

Athenian Education
Athenians believed that education should teach all arts for the development of well-rounded citizens. This vase painting shows young men learning music and grammar at an Athenian school.

Theme: Continuity and Change How is the ideal of education shown in this painting reflected in American schools today?

Solon introduced economic reforms as well. He encouraged the export of wine and olive oil. This policy helped merchants and farmers by increasing demand for their products.

Although Solon's reforms ensured greater fairness and justice to some groups, citizenship remained limited, and many positions were open only to wealthy landowners. Widespread and continued unrest led to the rise of tyrants, or people who gained power by force. Tyrants often won support of the merchant class and the poor by imposing reforms to help these groups. (Although Greek tyrants often governed well, the word *tyrant* has come to mean a vicious and brutal ruler.)

Later Reforms The Athenian tyrant Pisistratus (pi SIHS truh tuhs) seized power in 546 B.C. He helped farmers by giving them loans and land taken from nobles. New building projects gave jobs to the poor. By giving poor citizens a greater voice, he further weakened the aristocracy.

In 507 B.C., another reformer, Cleisthenes (KLIS thuh neez), broadened the role of ordinary citizens in government. He set up the Council of 500, whose members were chosen by lot from among all citizens. The council prepared laws for the assembly and supervised the day-to-day work of government. Cleisthenes made the assembly a genuine legislature, or lawmaking body, that debated laws before deciding to approve or reject them. All male citizens over the age of 30 were members of the assembly.

Limited Rights By modern standards, Athenian democracy was quite limited. Only male citizens could participate in government, and citizenship was severely restricted. Also, tens of thousands of Athenians were slaves without political rights or personal freedom. In fact, it was the labor of slaves that gave citizens the time to participate in government. Still, Athens gave more people a say in decision making than did the other ancient civilizations we have studied.

Women In Athens, as in other Greek city-states, women had no share in public life. The respected thinker Aristotle saw women as imperfect beings who lacked the ability to reason as well as men. "The man is by nature fitter for command than the female," he wrote, "just as an older person is superior to a younger, more immature person."

In well-to-do Athenian homes, women lived a secluded existence. There, they managed the entire household. They spun and wove, cared for their children, and prepared food. Their slaves or children were sent to buy

Possible answer: American schools try to give students a well-rounded education. They offer courses in many areas, including music and literature.

Teaching Resources
Section Quiz Unit 2 booklet, p. 25
Technology
Interactive Student Tutorial CD-ROM Ch. 5
Computer Test Bank Ch. 5

food and to fetch water from the public well. Poorer women worked outside the home, tending sheep or working as spinners, weavers, or potters.

Education for Democracy   Unlike girls, who received little or no formal education, boys attended school if their families could afford it. Besides learning to read and write, they studied music and memorized poetry. They studied to become skilled public speakers because, as citizens in a democracy, they would have to voice their views. Young men received military training and, to keep their bodies healthy, participated in athletic contests. Unlike Sparta, which put military training above all else, Athens encouraged young men to explore many areas of knowledge.

Forces for Unity

Strong local ties, an independent spirit, and economic rivalry led to fighting among the Greek city-states. Despite these divisions, Greeks shared a common culture. They spoke the same language, honored the same ancient heroes, participated in common festivals, and prayed to the same gods.

Religious Beliefs   Like most other ancient people, the Greeks were polytheistic. They believed that the gods lived on Mount Olympus in northern Greece. The most powerful Olympian was Zeus, who presided over the affairs of gods and humans. His children included Aphrodite (af ruh DĪ tee), goddess of love, and Ares, god of war. His daughter Athena, goddess of wisdom, gave her name to Athens.

Greeks honored their gods with temples and festivals. To discover the will of the gods, Greeks consulted the oracles, priests or priestesses through whom the gods were thought to speak. Although religion was important, some Greek thinkers came to believe that the universe was regulated, not by the will of gods, but by natural laws.

View of Non-Greeks   As trade and colonies expanded, the Greeks came in contact with people with different languages and customs. Greeks felt superior to non-Greeks and called them *barbaroi,* people who did not speak Greek. The English word *barbarian* comes from this Greek root. These "barbarians" included such people as the Phoenicians and Egyptians, from whom the Greeks borrowed important ideas and inventions. Still, this sense of uniqueness would help the Greeks face a threat from the mightiest power in the Mediterranean world—the Persian empire.

Connections to Today

The Olympic Games

Every four years, in the city-state of Olympia, the Greeks held athletic contests to honor Zeus. Winning athletes, such as wrestlers or discus throwers, would be crowned with a wreath. The Olympic games helped unify the Greek world. Warring city-states would even call a truce so that people could attend the games.

Today, thousands of athletes from around the world compete in the summer and winter Olympics. To honor the Greek origins of the games, relay runners carry a torch from Greece to the host city.

Theme: Global Interaction
Do you think the Olympic games are a force for unity in the world? Why or why not?

SECTION 2 Assessment

Recall

1. **Identify:** (a) Peloponnesus, (b) Solon, (c) Cleisthenes, (d) Zeus.
2. **Define:** (a) polis, (b) acropolis, (c) monarchy, (d) aristocracy, (e) oligarchy, (f) phalanx, (g) helot, (h) democracy, (i) tyrant, (j) legislature.

Comprehension

3. Identify two ways that geography influenced Greece.
4. (a) How did noble landowners gain power in Greek city-states? (b) How did the phalanx affect Greek society and government?
5. Describe the system of education in (a) Sparta and (b) Athens.
6. What cultural ties united the Greek world?

Critical Thinking and Writing

7. **Drawing Conclusions** (a) In what ways was Athenian democracy limited? (b) Despite such limits, Athens is still admired as an early model of democracy. Why do you think this is so?
8. **Analyzing Ideas** Like the early Chinese, the Greeks felt superior to people outside their own land. How might such an attitude be both a strength and a weakness?

Activity

Creating a Dialogue
Create a dialogue between an Athenian and a Spartan in which they discuss the best form of government and the responsibilities of citizenship.

 Human Drama Activity

Artistic Pride Vase painters captured the myths, legends, wars, and domestic affairs of ancient Greece. People throughout the Greek world cherished and desired their beautiful creations, especially those vases decorated with the Athenian red-figure style of painting. Driven by this popularity, Athenian artisans surpassed their rivals in other city-states, becoming the leading vase exporters. They also began to sign their names to their creations. This artistic pride has allowed historians to trace the influence and style of individual artists.

SECTION 2 Assessment

Recall
1. (a) Peloponnesus, p. 106 (b) Solon, p. 107 (c) Cleisthenes, p. 108 (d) Zeus, p. 109 2. (a) polis, p. 106 (b) acropolis, p. 106 (c) monarchy, p. 106 (d) aristocracy, p. 106 (e) oligarchy, p. 106 (f) phalanx, p. 106 (g) helot, p. 106 (h) democracy, p. 107 (i) tyrant, p. 108 (j) legislature, p. 108

Comprehension
3. Possible answers: Because mountains and water divided the land, the Greeks formed separate city-states. The need for fertile land pushed the Greeks to expand overseas. 4. (a) They were able to afford costly weapons, which were used to gain power. (b) Since ordinary citizens formed the phalanx, class differences were reduced. The citizens who worked in a phalanx developed a sense of unity. 5. (a) Spartan boys received strict military training. (b) Athenian boys learned reading, writing, music, poetry, public speaking, and military and athletic skills. 6. The Greeks shared the same myths, language, and religious beliefs.

Critical Thinking and Writing
7. (a) Only male citizens could participate in government, and citizenship was severely limited. Tens of thousands of Athenians were slaves with no political rights or personal freedom. (b) Athens gave more people a say in government than did any other civilization of its time. 8. Possible answers: Such an attitude can lead to a sense of confidence and can bring people together in a crisis. However, feelings of superiority may stop people from learning new ways.

Activity Rubrics

Share rubrics with students before they write their dialogues.

Attempted The dialogue is attempted but not completed.

Minimal The dialogue is poorly written or presents only one point of view.

Adequate The dialogue is clear and explains both points of view but clearly favors one position.

Exemplary The dialogue is thoughtful, well written, and shows empathy with each person's ideas.

Connections to Today

ANSWERS Possible answers: Although the games encourage competition among countries, they also bring athletes from many nations together in a friendly atmosphere. Different nations must cooperate in planning the games.

Bell Ringer Ask this question: What are the causes of war in the world today? After students have responded, direct their attention to the map of the Persian Wars on the opposite page. Ask students to offer opinions—based on their consideration of modern wars and on the map—on what they think caused the Persian Wars.

Reading Focus

- What impact did the Persian Wars have on Greece?
- How did Athens enjoy a golden age under Pericles?
- What were the causes and effects of the Peloponnesian War?

Vocabulary

alliance
direct democracy
stipend
jury
ostracism

Taking Notes

Copy this flowchart. As you read, fill in the boxes with the major events of the many wars in the Greek world. The first box has been completed to help you get started.

THE WARS OF THE GREEK WORLD

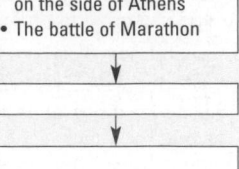

- Athens fights Persia
- Other city-states fight on the side of Athens
- The battle of Marathon

Main Idea   Competition among the Greek city-states led to conflict.

LESSON PLAN

1. Focus After the Persian Wars, democracy thrived in Athens as it became the most powerful and prosperous Greek city-state. However, rivalry among the Greek city-states led to conflict. The resulting Peloponnesian War ended Athenian greatness.

2. Instruct Lead students in creating a cause-and-effect diagram that shows the rise and fall of Athens between 500 B.C. and 359 B.C. Events for students to consider include key battles of the Persian Wars, Athenian achievements under Pericles, Athenian domination of the Delian League, and the Peloponnesian War and its aftermath. Encourage students to analyze and discuss how these various factors contributed to Athenian greatness and to Athenian decline.

3. Assess Based on their cause-and-effect diagrams, ask students to write a brief paragraph answering this question: How can political power and economic prosperity sometimes lead to a nation's downfall?

4. Reteach If students' Assess activity does not reflect adequate understanding of the lesson, you might assign the *Guide to the Essentials* or the *Interactive Student Tutorial CD-ROM* for this section.

Did You Know?

The First Marathon
After the battle of Marathon, the Greeks sent Pheidippides, their fastest runner, to carry home news of the stunning victory. Though exhausted, he sprinted 26.2 miles to Athens. "Rejoice, we conquer," he gasped—then dropped dead. Today, in honor of Pheidippides, marathon runners still cover the same distance that he ran 2,500 years ago.

Theme: Continuity and Change Today, many American communities hold annual marathons. Why do you think such races are popular?

Setting the Scene In 492 B.C., King Darius I of Persia cast an angry eye across the Aegean to the proud Greek city-states. Seeking revenge for a Greek insult, he sent messengers throughout Greece. The messengers demanded gifts of "earth and water"—symbols of submission to Darius I.

Many of the city-states obeyed Darius' demand. After all, the Persian empire was the most powerful in the Mediterranean world. But Athens and Sparta were not so quick to submit. Instead, the Athenians threw Darius' messengers into a well, while the Spartans tossed them into a pit. The Persians, they said, could collect their own earth and water.

The Greek historian Herodotus (hih RAHD uh tuhs) told this story of Greek defiance and pride. Despite their cultural ties, the Greek city-states were often bitterly divided. Yet, when the Persians threatened, the Greeks briefly put aside their differences to defend their freedom.

The Persian Wars

By 500 B.C., Athens had emerged as the wealthiest Greek city-state. But Athens and the entire Greek world soon faced a fearsome threat from outside. The Persians, you will recall, conquered a huge empire stretching from Asia Minor to the border of India. Their subjects included the Greek city-states of Ionia in Asia Minor.

Though under Persian rule, these Ionian city-states were largely self-governing. Still, they resented their situation. In 499 B.C., Ionian Greeks rebelled against Persian rule. Athens sent ships to help them. As Herodotus wrote some years later, "These ships were the beginning of mischief both to the Greeks and to the barbarians."

Victory at Marathon The Persians soon crushed the rebel cities. However, Darius I was furious at Athens' role in the uprising. To keep his anger hot, reported Herodotus, he had a servant whisper to him at every meal, "Master, remember the Athenians."

In time, Darius I sent a huge force across the Aegean to punish Athens for its interference. The mighty Persian army landed near Marathon, a plain north of Athens, in 490 B.C. The Athenians asked for help from neighboring city-states, but received little support.

The Persians greatly outnumbered Athenian forces. Yet the invaders were amazed to see "a mere handful of men coming on at a run without either horsemen or archers." The Persians responded with a rain of arrows, but the Greeks rushed onward. They broke through the Persian line and

Did You Know?

ANSWER Possible answer: Marathons offer a great challenge to participants. Athletes can compete for the glory of winning. Others just enjoy the satisfaction of finishing. Activities such as walk-a-thons and bike-a-thons are popular fundraising events.

Resource Directory

Teaching Resources
Creative Teaching Activities Creative Teaching Activities booklet, p. 26
Guided Reading and Review Unit 2 booklet, p. 26

engaged the enemy in fierce hand-to-hand combat. Overwhelmed by the fury of the Athenian assault, the Persians hastily retreated to their ships.

The Athenians celebrated their triumph. Still, the Athenian leader, Themistocles (thuh MIHS tuh kleez), knew the victory at Marathon had bought only a temporary lull in the fighting. He urged Athenians to build a fleet of warships and prepare other defenses.

Renewed Attacks Darius died before he could mass his troops for another attack. But in 480 B.C., his son Xerxes (ZERK seez) sent a much larger force to conquer Greece. By this time, Athens had persuaded Sparta and other city-states to join in the fight against Persia.

Once again, the Persians landed an army in northern Greece. A small Spartan force guarded the narrow mountain pass at Thermopylae (thuhr MAHP uh lee). Led by the great warrior-king Leonidas, the Spartans held out heroically against the enormous Persian force. Herodotus described the heroic stand of the Spartans:

"Here they defended themselves to the last, such as still had swords using them, and the others resisting with their hands and teeth; till the barbarians who . . . now encircled them upon every side, overwhelmed and buried the remnant that was left beneath showers of missile weapons."

—Herodotus, *The Persian Wars*

After defeating the Spartans, the Persians marched south and burned Athens. The city was empty, however. The Athenians had withdrawn to safety.

The Greeks now put their faith in the fleet of ships that Themistocles had urged them to build. The Athenians lured the Persian navy into the narrow strait of Salamis. Athenian warships, powered by rowers, drove into the Persian boats with underwater battering rams. On the shore, Xerxes watched helplessly as his mighty fleet sank.

The following year, the Greeks defeated the Persians on land in Asia Minor. This victory marked the end of the Persian invasions. Although fighting continued for years, Greek raiders were on the offensive from this time on. In a brief moment of unity, the Greek city-states had saved themselves from the Persian threat.

Results Victory in the Persian Wars increased the Greeks' sense of their own uniqueness. The gods, they felt, had protected their superior form of government—the city-state—against invaders from Asia.

Athens emerged from the war as the most powerful city-state in Greece. To continue the struggle against Persia, it organized the Delian League, an alliance with other Greek city-states. An **alliance** is a formal agreement between two or more nations or powers to cooperate and come to one another's defense.

From the start, Athens dominated the Delian League. It slowly used its position of leadership to create an Athenian empire. It moved the league treasury from the island of Delos to Athens, using money contributed by other city-states to rebuild its own city. When its allies protested and tried

Persian Wars, 490 B.C.–479 B.C.

Areas settled by Greeks
Route of Xerxes' fleet
Route of Persian army
Battle sites
Athenian empire about 450 B.C.

Alber's Equal Area Projection
0   50   100 Miles
0   50   100 Kilometers

Skills Assessment

Geography When the Persian empire attacked Greece, the Greek city-states briefly joined forces to defend their independence.

1. **Location** On the map, locate **(a)** Athens, **(b)** Sparta, **(c)** Marathon, **(d)** Thermopylae, **(e)** Salamis.
2. **Movement** Describe the route of the Persian army toward Athens.
3. **Critical Thinking Making Inferences** Why do you think Xerxes' fleet hugged the coastline instead of sailing directly across the Aegean?

Background
Historical Evidence

Competing Values Most of what we know about the Persian Wars comes to us from the Greek historian Herodotus. During the wars, according to Herodotus, some Greek deserters informed King Xerxes that the Greeks were holding their Olympic games. Xerxes asked about the prize for which the athletes were contending. Hearing that the prize was not money, but a wreath of olives, Xerxes exclaimed aloud, "Good heavens, what manner of men are these against whom you have brought us to fight—men who contend with one another, not for money, but for honor!"

You may wish to use this story as the basis for a class activity or discussion. Ask students why Herodotus might have included this story in his history. Also ask them how Herodotus' history might be a biased account.

Background
Global Connections

Disinformation A warring nation sometimes misleads its enemies by deliberately allowing false information to fall into their hands. According to Herodotus, the Greeks played this game well. He writes that Themistocles wished to draw the Persian fleet into the narrow strait of Salamis, where the enemy ships could be trapped and outmaneuvered. To lure the fleet into the strait, Themistocles sent a trusted slave, in the guise of a traitor, to the Persian commanders. The Greek agent gave the Persians this false message: "Fear has seized the Greeks and they are meditating a hasty flight." The Persians went for the bait and rushed into the trap that the Greeks had set. The clever bit of disinformation led to the Athenian victory at the strait of Salamis.

Block Scheduling Support

The Athenians used clever war tactics to win the Battle of Marathon. These included the use of hoplites manning phalanxes. Have students find out details about the battle, including leaders, numbers of troops, and how the battle was fought. Then have them write a newspaper article describing the battle, including a diagram or map of it. Remind students that newspaper articles begin with a lead paragraph that contains answers to the questions—sometimes called the five *W*s—of who, what, when, where, and why.

Skills Assessment

ANSWERS 1. Review locations with students. **2.** The army traveled northwest from Sardis, crossed into Europe, then marched west and south to attack Athens from the north. **3.** Possible answer: The fleet sailed along the coast to protect the route of their army. Also, the Persians may have been unwilling to face the fine Athenian fleet in the middle of the Aegean Sea.

to withdraw from the league, Athens used force to make them remain. Yet, while Athens was enforcing its will abroad, Athenian leaders were championing political freedom at home.

Athens in the Age of Pericles

The years after the Persian Wars were a golden age for Athens. Under the able statesman Pericles (PEHR uh kleez), the economy thrived and the government became more democratic. Because of his wise and skillful leadership, the period from 460 B.C. to 429 B.C. is often called the Age of Pericles.

Political Life Periclean Athens was a direct democracy. Under this system, a large number of citizens take direct part in the day-to-day affairs of government. By contrast, in most democratic countries today, citizens participate in government indirectly through elected representatives.

By the time of Pericles, the Athenian assembly met several times a month. At least 6,000 members had to be present in order to decide important issues. Pericles believed that all male citizens, regardless of wealth or social class, should take part in government. Athens therefore began to pay a stipend, or fixed salary, to men who held public office. This reform enabled poor men to serve in government.

In addition to serving in the assembly, Athenians served on juries. A jury is a panel of citizens who have the authority to make the final judgment in a trial. Unlike a modern American trial jury, which is usually made up of 12 members, an Athenian jury might include hundreds or even thousands of jurors. Male citizens over 30 years of age were chosen by lot to serve on the jury for a year. Like members of the assembly, jurors received a stipend.

Athenian citizens could also vote to banish, or send away, a public figure whom they saw as a threat to their democracy. This process was called ostracism (AHS trah sihzm). To ostracize someone, a citizen wrote that person's name on a piece of pottery. Depending on the number of votes cast, an ostracized individual would have to live outside the city, usually for a period of 10 years.

▶ **Primary Sources and Literature**

See "Thucydides: A History of the Peloponnesian War" in the Reference Section at the back of this book.

The Funeral Oration Thucydides (thoo SIHD uh deez), a historian who lived in the Age of Pericles, recorded a speech given by Pericles at the funeral of Athenians slain in battle. In this famous Funeral Oration, Pericles praised the Athenian form of government. He pointed out that, in Athens, power rested in the hands "not of a minority but of the whole people."

In the Funeral Oration, Pericles stressed not only the rights but also the duties of citizenship. As citizens of a democracy, he said, Athenians bore a special responsibility. "We alone," he stated, "regard a man who takes no interest in public affairs, not as a harmless but as a useless character." Today, Pericles' Funeral Oration is considered one of the earliest and greatest expressions of democratic ideals.

Economic and Cultural Life Athens prospered during the Age of Pericles. With the riches of the Athenian empire, Pericles hired the best architects and sculptors to rebuild the Acropolis, which the Persians had destroyed. Magnificent new temples and colossal statues rose from the ruins of the Acropolis. Such building projects increased Athenians' prosperity by creating jobs for artisans and workers. They also served as a further reminder to both citizens and visitors that the gods had favored the Athenians.

With the help of an educated foreign-born woman named Aspasia, Pericles turned Athens into the cultural center of Greece. Pericles and Aspasia surrounded themselves with thinkers, writers, and artists. Through building programs and public festivals, they supported the arts. In the next section, you will read about Greek contributions to architecture, art, literature, history, and philosophy.

How Should a Society's Leaders Be Chosen?

In his Gettysburg Address, Abraham Lincoln expressed his abiding belief in democracy, which he described as "government of the people, by the people, and for the people." But through the years, not everyone has agreed that democracy is the best form of government. Consider the following viewpoints.

Greece 400s B.C.

In a famous Funeral Oration, Pericles praised the Athenian form of government:

❝ Our constitution is called a democracy because power is in the hands not of a minority but of the whole people.... When it is a question of putting one person before another in positions of public responsibility, what counts is not membership of a particular class, but the ability the man possesses. ❞

United States 1787

Alexander Hamilton, a Caribbean-born statesman who helped shape the Constitution, distrusted ordinary citizens:

❝ All communities divide themselves into the few and the many. The first are rich and well-born, the other the mass of the people.... The people are turbulent and changing; they seldom judge or determine right. Give therefore to the first class a distinct, permanent share in the government. ❞

Algeria 1990s

The Arabic writing on this poster says "Your election equals the restoration of the country's glory."

Chile 1986

Santiago Sinclair, an aide to Chilean military dictator Augusto Pinochet, defended the right of strong leaders to take power into their own hands:

❝ Command is voice, conscience, justice.... Command guides spirits and unites wills, carrying them to success.... ❞

Background
Other Viewpoints

India, c. 200 B.C.: In the *Mahabharata*, a wise man explains that kings became necessary when people grew too greedy to rule themselves: "To institute order, the gods approached Vishnu, the lord of the creatures, and said: 'Indicate to us that one person among mortals who alone is worthy of the highest rank.' Then the blessed lord god Vishnu reflected, and brought forth a glorious son, called Virajas, who became the first king."

Tanzania, 1961: Julius Nyerere, first president of Tanzania, described the practice of government by consensus: "The traditional African society, whether it had a chief or not... was a society of equals, and it conducted its business through discussion.... 'They talk till they agree.' That gives you the essence of traditional African democracy."

Activity
Interpreting Viewpoints

Critical Thinking: Comparing

Use these additional questions to generate class discussion.

1. What is the difference between Hamilton's view and Sinclair's view? *(Possible answers: Hamilton thinks leaders should be chosen from the rich; Sinclair thinks strong leaders should seize power.)* **2.** Among the people quoted on this page, which two share similar views? *(Possible answer: Both Lincoln and Pericles advocate government by the people.)*

Skills Assessment

1. Which writer seems most opposed to choosing leaders in a democratic way?
   A Pericles
   B Hamilton
   C Sinclair
   D the creator of the voting poster

2. With which statement would Pericles agree?
   E Class is more important than ability.
   F The minority should rule.
   G Leaders know best.
   H Power should be shared by all.

3. **Critical Thinking Making Decisions** For more than 200 years, people in the United States have been concerned with the way elections are run. If you could change one thing about the American elections, what would it be? Why?

Skills Tip

Someone may express an opinion that is not necessarily what you would expect. A person's background, as well as the time and place in which he or she lived, may have influenced his or her way of thinking.

Human Drama Activity

Governing Groups Share with students the Nyerere viewpoint on this page. Then discuss how students make decisions when they are with groups of friends. Is it pretty much the same as the procedure described by Nyerere? If not, how does it differ? Perhaps they use more than one way: sometimes one person will take the lead and the others follow, and at other times it is a group decision. Ask students what they think happens in group discussions when members end up agreeing. *(compromise)*

Test Preparation

Have students read the Alexander Hamilton quotation on this page, and then answer the question below.

What does the word *turbulent* in this quotation mean?

A just
B irresponsible
C restless
D unchanging

Skills Tip

Sometimes verbal context can be a clue to someone's bias. Ask students what detail in the headnote for Santiago Sinclair's quote may provide a clue to his bias. The Skills Handbook in the front of the book has a lesson to help students with this feature.

Skills Assessment

ANSWERS 1. C **2.** H **3.** Students may want to change the length of time candidates have to campaign or the amount of money they spend on television ads.

Recall

1. **(a)** Marathon, p. 110 **(b)** Themistocles, p. 111 **(c)** Delian League, p. 111 **(d)** Pericles, p. 112 **(e)** Aspasia, p. 112 **2. (a)** alliance, p. 111 **(b)** direct democracy, p. 112 **(c)** stipend, p.112 **(d)** jury, p. 112 **(e)** ostracism, p. 112

Comprehension

3. Possible answers: Athens became the most powerful city-state. Greek city-states formed the Delian League under Athenian leadership. **4.** He extended democracy to common people, encouraged extensive public building of temples and statues, increased general prosperity, and fostered the arts and philosophy. **5.** Many Greeks came to resent Athenian domination.

Critical Thinking and Writing

6. **(a)** Citizens participate in government by helping make the laws. Education and civic responsibilities are valued. **(b)** Athens had a direct democracy in which many citizens took part, while in American democracy people participate indirectly by electing representatives. In Athens, only male citizens could participate in government, while in the United States both men and women participate. Athens had slavery, unlike the United States today. **7. (a)** Athens formed the Delian League with other Greek city-states to defend against attacks by Persia. Sparta formed the Peloponnesian League to counter domination by Athens. **(b)** Students should recognize various types of alliances today—political, military, economic.

Activity Rubrics

Share rubrics with students before they draw their political cartoons.

Attempted The cartoon does not show an understanding of the chosen viewpoint or is incomplete.

Minimal The cartoon reveals little understanding of the chosen viewpoint or is messily prepared.

Adequate The cartoon reveals an understanding of the chosen viewpoint and is clearly drawn.

Exemplary The cartoon reveals in-depth understanding of the chosen viewpoint, is clearly drawn, and is clever.

Skills Assessment

Answer: It would cause a breakdown in law, religion, and customs.

The Peloponnesian War

The power of Athens contained the seeds of disaster. Many Greeks outside of Athens resented Athenian domination. Before long, the Greek world split into rival camps. To counter the Delian League, Sparta and other enemies of Athens formed the Peloponnesian League. Sparta encouraged oligarchy in the cities of the Peloponnesian League, while Athens supported democracy among its allies.

In 431 B.C., warfare broke out in earnest between Athens and Sparta. The Peloponnesian War soon engulfed all of Greece. The fighting would drag on for 27 years.

Greek Against Greek Despite its riches and powerful navy, Athens faced a serious geographic disadvantage. Sparta was located inland, so it could not be attacked from the sea. Yet Sparta had only to march north to attack Athens by land.

When Sparta invaded Athens, Pericles allowed people from the surrounding countryside to move inside the city walls. The overcrowded conditions soon led to disaster. A terrible plague broke out, killing at least a third of the population, including Pericles himself. His successors were much less able leaders. Their power struggles quickly undermined the city's democratic government.

As the war dragged on, each side committed savage acts against the other. Sparta even allied itself with Persia, the longtime enemy of the Greeks. Finally, in 404 B.C., with the help of the Persian navy, the Spartans captured Athens. The victors stripped Athenians of their fleet and empire. However, Sparta rejected calls from its allies to destroy Athens, possibly out of respect for the city's role in the Persian Wars.

The Aftermath of War The Peloponnesian War ended Athenian domination of the Greek world. The Athenian economy eventually revived and Athens remained the cultural center of Greece. However, its spirit and vitality declined. In Athens, as elsewhere in the Greek world, democratic government suffered. Corruption and selfish interests replaced older ideals such as service to the city-state.

For the next century, fighting continued to disrupt the Greek world. Sparta itself soon suffered defeat at the hands of Thebes, another Greek city-state. As Greeks battled among themselves, a new power rose in Macedonia (mas uh DOHN ee yuh), a kingdom to the north. By 359 B.C., its ambitious ruler stood poised to conquer the quarrelsome Greek city-states.

Primary Source

The Plague in Athens
The Greek historian Thucydides describes the unknown plague that struck Athens in 430 B.C.:

"Bodies of dying men lay one upon another, and half-dead people rolled about in the streets and, in their longing for water, near all the fountains. The temples, too, in which they had quartered themselves were full of the corpses of them who had died in them; for the calamity which weighed upon them was so overpowering that men, not knowing what was to become of them, became careless of all law, sacred as well as profane [worldly]. And the customs which they had hitherto observed regarding burial were all thrown into confusion, and they buried their dead each one as he could."

—Thucydides, *A History of the Peloponnesian War*

Skills Assessment

Primary Source What strains would a plague such as this put on a society?

Recall

1. **Identify: (a)** Marathon, **(b)** Themistocles, **(c)** Delian League, **(d)** Pericles, **(e)** Aspasia.
2. **Define: (a)** alliance, **(b)** direct democracy, **(c)** stipend, **(d)** jury, **(e)** ostracism.

Comprehension

3. Describe two effects of the Persian Wars.
4. How did Pericles contribute to Athenian greatness?
5. How did the growth of Athenian power lead to war?

Critical Thinking and Writing

6. **Linking Past and Present** Compare Athenian democracy during the Age of Pericles to American democracy today. **(a)** How are they similar? **(b)** How are they different?
7. **Recognizing Causes and Effects (a)** What were the reasons that the Athenians and the Spartans formed their rival alliances? **(b)** Do nations today form alliances with one another for the same reasons? Explain.

Activity

Drawing a Political Cartoon Draw a political cartoon commenting on the causes or effects of the Peloponnesian War. Take the viewpoint of either an Athenian or a Spartan.

Resource Directory

Teaching Resources

Section Quiz Unit 2 booklet, p. 27
Creative Teaching Activities Creative Teaching Activities booklet, p. 27
Guided Reading and Review Unit 2 booklet, p. 28

Technology

Interactive Student Tutorial CD-ROM Ch. 5
Computer Test Bank Ch. 5

The Glory That Was Greece

Reading Focus

- What political and ethical ideas did Greek philosophers develop?

- What were the goals of Greek architects and artists?

- What themes did Greek writers and historians explore?

Vocabulary

logic
rhetoric
tragedy
comedy

Taking Notes

Copy the concept web at right. Include three or four blank circles. As you read, fill in each blank circle with important facts to remember about Greek civilization. Two circles have been completed to help you get started.

Philosophy

GREEK CIVILIZATION

Plato describes ideal government

Main Idea Greek thinkers, artists, and writers explored the nature of the universe and the place of people in it.

Setting the Scene

Despite wars and political turmoil, Greeks had confidence in the power of the human mind. "We cultivate the mind," boasted Pericles. "We are lovers of the beautiful, yet simple in our tastes." Driven by curiosity and a belief in reason, Greek thinkers, artists, and writers explored the nature of the universe and the place of people in it.

To later admirers, Greek achievements in the arts represented the height of human development in the western world. They looked back with deep respect on what one poet called "the glory that was Greece."

Greek Philosophers

As you read, some Greek thinkers challenged the belief that events were caused by the whims of gods. Instead, they used observation and reason to find causes for what happened. The Greeks called these thinkers philosophers, meaning "lovers of wisdom."

Greek philosophers explored many subjects, from mathematics and music to logic, or rational thinking. Through reason and observation, they believed, they could discover laws that governed the universe. Much modern science traces its roots to the Greek search for such principles.

Ethical Issues Other Greek philosophers were more interested in ethics and morality. They debated such questions as what was the best kind of government and what standards should rule human behavior.

In Athens, the Sophists questioned accepted ideas. To them, success was more important than moral truth. They developed skills in rhetoric, the art of skillful speaking. Ambitious men could use clever rhetoric to advance their careers. The turmoil of the Peloponnesian War led many young Athenians to follow the Sophists. Older citizens, however, accused the Sophists of undermining traditional values.

Socrates One outspoken critic of the Sophists was Socrates, an Athenian stonemason and philosopher. Most of what we know about Socrates comes from his student Plato. Socrates himself wrote no books. Instead, he lounged around the marketplace, asking his fellow citizens about their beliefs. Using a process we now call the Socratic method, he would pose a series of questions to his students and challenge them to examine the implications of their answers. To Socrates, this patient examination was a way to help others seek truth and self-knowledge. To many Athenians, however, such questioning was a threat to accepted traditions.

Biography

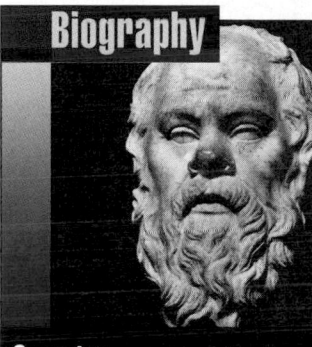

Socrates 469 B.C.–399 B.C.

To most Athenians, Socrates was not an impressive figure. Tradition tells us that his clothes were untidy and he made a poor living. But young men loved to watch him as he questioned citizens, leading them to contradict themselves.

Many Athenians found Socrates annoying—and he knew it. When he was put on trial, he told the jury, "All day long and in all places I am always fastening upon you, stirring you and persuading you and reproaching you. You will not easily find another like me." But Plato had a different view of his teacher. He called Socrates "the wisest, justest, and best of all I have ever known."

Theme: Impact of the Individual Socrates said, "The unexamined life is not worth living." How did his actions support this idea?

Chapter 5 **115**

Block Scheduling Support

Have students read the excerpt from *The Clouds* in *Treasures of the World,* p. 16. Then have them draw conclusions about Greek culture based on what they read. Have students present their findings creatively—for example, in a poster, in a bulletin board, or as a magazine article. Remind students that good presentations will have both verbal and visual elements that will support their analyses of Greek culture as revealed in *The Clouds.*

SECTION **4**

Bell Ringer Have students read the statement by Socrates in the Biography feature on this page, and then ask what they think the philosopher means.

LESSON PLAN

1. Focus Armed with their faith in human reason, Greek philosophers developed ideas about government, morality, and the purpose of life. In literature and the arts, the Greeks sought beauty, harmony, and order. Their achievements set standards for future generations.

2. Instruct Divide the class into several groups, each responsible for one of the following topics: philosophy of Socrates, philosophy of Plato, philosophy of Aristotle, art and architecture, drama, history. Ask each group to list the major characteristics of Greek achievements in its assigned area. Then, have students share their findings in a class discussion.

3. Assess Ask students to identify the common beliefs and ideals that guided the Greeks in all these areas of achievement. Lead the class in a discussion of how classical Greek culture continues to influence western culture today.

4. Reteach If students' **Assess** activity does not reflect adequate understanding of the lesson, you might assign the *Guide to the Essentials* or the *Interactive Student Tutorial CD-ROM* for this section.

Biography

ANSWER Possible answer: By questioning people, he forced them to think about their beliefs and actions.

Auditory Learners

Debating Because he favored a system of government based on reasoning and knowledge, Socrates found democracy to be seriously deficient. Choosing officials by lot did not produce qualified leaders. Allowing everyone to vote on issues, whether or not they used proper reasoning, did not produce good laws. According to the Greek historian Xenophon, Socrates summed up the weakness of democracy this way:

> "It is absurd to choose magistrates by lot where no one would dream of drawing lots for a pilot, a mason, a flute-player, or any craftsman at all, though the shortcomings of such men are far less harmful than those that disorder our government."

Read the quote to the class and discuss its meaning. Then, ask students to debate this question: "Is democracy the best form of government?" Ask for volunteers to argue in favor of democracy and others to argue against it. Before they debate the issue, have students work in groups to gather and organize their thoughts.

▶ Primary Sources and Literature

See "Aristotle: The Politics" in the Reference Section at the back of this book.

Connections to Today

The Parthenon in Danger
The Parthenon has survived nearly 2,500 years. It even withstood being blown up. In 1687, the temple was used to store gunpowder. An explosion damaged the roof and many of the columns.

Today, the Parthenon faces an even greater danger. Air pollution is slowly eating away the ancient marble. Scientists say the temple could be destroyed in a century. International teams are now working to shore up the building. Restorers are using a different-colored stone, so visitors can tell which parts are original.

Theme: Global Interaction
Why do you think people from many different countries are interested in saving the Parthenon?

When he was about 70 years old, Socrates was put on trial. His enemies accused him of corrupting the city's youth and failing to respect the gods. Standing before a jury of 501 citizens, Socrates offered a calm defense. But the jurors condemned him to death. Loyal to the laws of Athens, Socrates accepted the death penalty. He drank a cup of hemlock, a deadly poison.

Plato The execution of Socrates left Plato with a lifelong distrust of democracy. He fled Athens for 10 years. When he returned, he set up a school called the Academy. There, he taught and wrote about his own ideas. Like Socrates, Plato emphasized the importance of reason. Through rational thought, he argued, people could discover unchanging ethical values, recognize perfect beauty, and learn how best to organize society.

In *The Republic*, Plato described his vision of an ideal state. He rejected Athenian democracy because it had condemned Socrates. Instead, Plato argued that the state should regulate every aspect of its citizens' lives in order to provide for their best interests. He divided his ideal society into three classes: workers to produce the necessities of life, soldiers to defend the state, and philosophers to rule. This elite class of leaders would be specially trained to ensure order and justice. The wisest of them, a philosopher-king, would have the ultimate authority.

Plato thought that, in general, men surpassed women in mental and physical tasks, but that some women were superior to some men. Talented women, he said, should be educated to serve the state. The ruling elite, both men and women, would take military training together and raise their children in communal centers for the good of the republic.

Aristotle Plato's most famous student, Aristotle, developed his own ideas about government. He analyzed all forms of government, from monarchy to democracy, and found good and bad examples of each. Like Plato, he was suspicious of democracy, which he thought could lead to mob rule. In the end, he favored rule by a single strong and virtuous leader.

Aristotle also addressed the question of how people ought to live. In his view, good conduct meant pursuing the "golden mean," a moderate course between extremes. He promoted reason as the guiding force for learning.

Aristotle set up a school, the Lyceum, for the study of all branches of knowledge. He left writings on politics, ethics, logic, biology, literature, and many other subjects. When the first European universities evolved some 1,500 years later, their courses were largely based on the works of Aristotle.

Architecture and Art

Plato argued that every object on Earth had an ideal form. The work of Greek artists and architects reflected a similar concern with balance, order, and beauty.

Architecture Greek architects sought to convey a sense of perfect balance to reflect the harmony and order of the universe. The most famous example of Greek architecture is the Parthenon, a temple dedicated to the goddess Athena. The basic plan of the Parthenon is a simple rectangle, with tall columns supporting a gently sloping roof. The delicate curves add dignity and grace.

Greek architecture has been widely admired for centuries. Today, you can see many public buildings that have adopted various kinds of Greek columns.

Sculpture and Painting Early Greek sculptors carved figures in rigid poses, perhaps imitating Egyptian styles. By 450 B.C., Greek sculptors had developed a new style that emphasized natural poses. While their work was lifelike, it was also idealistic. That is, sculptors carved gods, goddesses,

Connections to Today

ANSWER Many people in western countries view Greek culture as an important part of their own heritage.

Resource Directory

Teaching Resources
Biography Activity *Aeschylus*, Unit 2 booklet, p. 32
Skill Application Activity *Working in a Group*, Unit 2 booklet, p. 35

Technology
World History Color Transparencies *The Parthenon and the Lincoln Memorial*, p. C–29; *Discobolos, the Discus Thrower*, p. D–39
Humanities Pack Transparencies *The Charioteer of Delphi*, Transparency 1
Listening to Literature World Masterpieces audiotapes poem by Sappho, side 4, running time 1:45 min.

Virtual Field Trip

www.phschool.com

The Acropolis
Athens, Greece

To see other images of the ancient buildings on the Acropolis, use the Internet address above to link to the Ancient City of Athens.

The Acropolis
The buildings on the Acropolis stand as proud monuments of classical Greek architecture. The most revered temple on the Acropolis is the Parthenon, with its balanced rows of majestic columns.

Theme: Art and Literature
Based on this picture, what kinds of modern buildings were influenced by the style of the Parthenon?

Activity
Connections to Literature

Analyzing a Speech In his play *Medea*, Euripides exposes the low status of women and foreigners in Greek society. Medea, a woman and a foreigner, is abandoned by Jason, who feels marriage to a Greek woman offers more advantages. In her first speech, Medea asks the women of Greece to help her gain revenge against Jason. She describes the prejudices and injustices that women and non-Greeks have endured.

Choose a student to read Medea's speech to the class. Ask students to take notes on Medea's complaints about her position in society. Then, have students discuss what Medea's speech reveals about the nature of Greek society.

athletes, and famous men in a way that showed individuals in their most perfect, graceful form.

The only Greek paintings to survive are on vases and other pottery. They offer intriguing views of Greek life. Women carry water from wells, warriors race into battle, and athletes compete in javelin contests. Each scene is designed to fit the shape of the pottery.

Poetry and Drama

In literature, as in art, the ancient Greeks developed their own style. To later Europeans, Greek styles were a model of perfection. They admired what they called the "classical style," referring to the elegant, balanced forms of traditional Greek works.

Greek literature began with the epics of Homer, whose stirring tales inspired later writers. In later times, Sappho sang of love and of the beauty of her island home, and Pindar celebrated the victors in athletic contests.

Beginnings of Greek Drama Perhaps the most important Greek contribution to literature was in the field of drama. The first Greek plays evolved out of religious festivals, especially those held in Athens to honor Dionysus (di uh NI suhs), god of fertility and wine. Plays were performed in large outdoor theaters with little or no scenery. Actors wore elaborate costumes and stylized masks. A chorus sang or chanted comments on the action.

Greek dramas were often based on popular myths and legends. Through these familiar stories, playwrights discussed moral and social issues or explored the relationship between people and the gods.

Tragedy The greatest Athenian playwrights were Aeschylus (EHS kuh luhs), Sophocles (SAHF uh kleez), and Euripides (yu RIHP uh deez). All three wrote tragedies, plays that told stories of human suffering that usually ended in disaster. The purpose of tragedy, the Greeks felt, was to stir emotions of pity and fear. In *The Oresteia* (ohr eh STEE uh), for example, Aeschylus showed a powerful family torn apart by betrayal, murder, and revenge. Audiences saw how pride could cause horrifying misfortune and how the gods could bring down even the greatest heroes.

In *Antigone* (an TIHG uh nee), Sophocles explored what happens when an individual's moral duty conflicts with the laws of the state. Antigone

Caption Answer

Students may mention courthouses, older libraries and post offices, and government buildings such as the White House.

GREEK DRAMA

Ancient Greek drama reached the height of its popularity in the 400s B.C. In every Greek city, enthusiastic audiences attended festivals in which playwrights competed to win prizes for their work. Though changed in form, today's theater arts still use many techniques perfected over 2,000 years ago.

This modern production of Sophocles' *Antigone* (above) differs from the original. Because only men could be actors in ancient Greece, a man wearing both a mask and a woman's costume would have played Antigone.

Aristotle Describes a Tragedy

A philosopher of wide-ranging interests, Aristotle turned his attention to Greek drama in his book *Poetics*, written in the 300s B.C. He defined characteristics of a tragedy:

66 In the finest kind of tragedy . . . it is evident that good men ought not to be shown passing from prosperity to misfortune, for this does not inspire either pity or fear, but only disgust; nor evil men rising from ill fortune to prosperity, for this is the most untragic plot of all—it lacks every requirement, in that it neither appeals to human sympathy nor stirs pity or fear. And again, neither should an extremely wicked man be seen falling from prosperity into misfortune, for a plot so constructed might indeed call forth human sympathy, but would not excite pity or fear. . . . We are left with the man who on the one hand does not excel in virtue or justice, and yet on the other hand does not fall into misfortune through vice or corruption, but falls because of some mistake. 99

Fast Facts

- At the government's request, wealthy Athenian citizens paid part of the production costs.

- Actors held high social status because of their speaking skills, and some served as diplomats.

- Greek judges awarded garlands of ivy leaves to recognize superior Greek playwrights and actors.

This carved marble relief (left) shows the playwright Menander, who wrote some of the most popular comedies in ancient Greece. He holds a mask that would be worn by an actor in a comedy. In both tragedies and comedies, actors wore leather masks with exaggerated features to help define the different characters.

Portfolio Assessment

Find a character in a play, novel, or movie who matches Aristotle's definition of a tragic character. Identify the character's strengths and weaknesses and describe the mistake that leads to his or her downfall.

118 *Chapter 5*

Bell Ringer Ask students whether they have ever seen a live play. Ask them to explain the differences between that experience and seeing a movie.

Background
Connections to Today

Special FX Like their modern counterparts, Greek theaters used special effects to make productions more exciting and dramatic. As the text notes, one technique was the use of masks. They were two-faced, with a peaceful expression on one side and an angry or grotesque one on the other. Thus, with a sharp turn of the head, actors could grab the attention of the audience with a sudden, and often terrifying, mood change. To create a larger-than-life look, performers wore boots with 10-inch soles and robes with huge, flowing sleeves. Trapdoors were used for dramatic exits, and various sound devices were used to re-create booms of thunder and cracks of lightning. With the aid of special cranes, actors in the role of gods were able to soar above the stage.

Activity
Cooperative Learning

Have students work together to perform a scene or two from one of the tragedies. (The comedies are too sexually explicit for use in public schools.) Some students should be the actors, and some should be the chorus. Others should make the masks and costumes, gather or make props, and prepare the scenery.

Portfolio Assessment Rubrics

Share rubrics with students before they complete their projects.

Attempted The character is inappropriate, and analysis is weak or incomplete.

Minimal The character is appropriate, but analysis is sketchy.

Adequate The character is appropriate, and strengths, weaknesses and mistakes are catalogued.

Exemplary The character choice is insightful and the analysis is complete, well written, and very informative.

Resource Directory

Teaching Resources
Humanities Link Chapter Extension Activities booklet, p. 18
Section Quiz Unit 2 booklet, p. 29

Technology
Interactive Student Tutorial CD-ROM Ch. 5
Computer Test Bank Ch. 5

is a young woman whose brother has been killed leading a rebellion. King Creon forbids anyone to bury the traitor's body. When Antigone buries her brother anyway, she is sentenced to death. She defiantly tells Creon that duty to the gods is greater than human law:

> "For me, it was not Zeus who made that order. Nor did I think your orders were so strong that you, a mortal man, could overrule the gods' unwritten and unfailing laws."
> —Sophocles, *Antigone*

Like Sophocles, Euripides survived the horrors of the Peloponnesian War. That experience probably led him to question accepted ideas. His plays suggested that people, not the gods, were the cause of human misfortune. In *The Trojan Women*, he stripped war of its glamour by showing the suffering of women who were victims of the war.

Comedy Some Greek playwrights wrote comedies, humorous plays that mocked people or customs. Almost all surviving Greek comedies were written by Aristophanes (ar ihs TAHF uh neez). In *Lysistrata*, he shows the women of Athens banding together to force their husbands to end a war against Sparta. Through ridicule, comic playwrights sharply criticized society, much as political cartoonists do today.

The Writing of History

The Greeks applied observation, reason, and logic to the study of history. Herodotus is often called the "Father of History" in the western world because he went beyond listing names of rulers or retelling ancient legends. Before writing *The Persian Wars*, Herodotus visited many lands, collecting information from people who remembered the events he chronicled.

Herodotus cast a critical eye on his sources, noting bias and conflicting accounts. Yet, his writings reflected his own view that the war was a clear moral victory of Greek love of freedom over Persian tyranny. He also invented conversations and speeches for historical figures.

Thucydides wrote about the Peloponnesian War, a much less happy subject for the Greeks. He had lived through the war and vividly described its savagery and its corrupting influence on all those involved. Although he was an Athenian, he tried to be fair to both sides.

Both writers set standards for future historians. Herodotus stressed the importance of research. Thucydides showed the need to avoid bias.

SECTION 4 Assessment

Recall
1. **Identify: (a)** Socrates, **(b)** Aristotle, **(c)** Parthenon, **(d)** Sophocles, **(e)** Euripides, **(f)** Herodotus, **(g)** Thucydides.
2. **Define: (a)** logic, **(b)** rhetoric, **(c)** tragedy, **(d)** comedy.

Comprehension
3. **(a)** Why did Plato reject democracy as a form of government? **(b)** Describe the ideal form of government as set forth in Plato's *Republic*.
4. What standards of beauty did Greek artists follow?
5. **(a)** How were Greek plays performed? **(b)** What were the topics of Greek poetry and plays?

Critical Thinking and Writing
6. **Making Inferences** Why do you think many Greeks condemned the ideas of the Sophists?
7. **Recognizing Bias** Do you think it is ever possible for a historian to be completely free of bias? Why or why not?

Activity

Writing a Paragraph
Thucydides wrote about an event he had lived through because he believed it would have a lasting impact. Choose a recent event that you think historians will write about 100 years from now. Write a paragraph explaining the importance of this event.

SECTION 4 Assessment

Recall
1. **(a)** Socrates, p. 115 **(b)** Aristotle, p. 116 **(c)** Parthenon, p. 116 **(d)** Sophocles, p. 117 **(e)** Euripides, p. 117 **(f)** Herodotus, p. 119 **(g)** Thucydides, p. 119 **2. (a)** logic, p. 115 **(b)** rhetoric, p. 115 **(c)** tragedy, p. 117 **(d)** comedy, p. 119

Comprehension
3. **(a)** He rejected Athenian democracy because it had condemned Socrates. **(b)** In Plato's ideal state the government would regulate the lives of citizens, who would be divided into workers, soldiers, and philosophers. The ruling class would be the philosophers, and the king would be chosen from that class. **4.** balance, order, beauty **5. (a)** Plays were performed in large outdoor theaters. Little scenery was used, but actors wore elaborate costumes and masks. A chorus accompanied the action on stage. **(b)** They explored moral and social issues and the relationship between people and the gods.

Critical Thinking and Writing
6. Possible answer: The Sophists placed success above morality. Many Greeks thought they were undermining traditional values. **7.** Students should recognize that all historians have a point of view, which influences how they interpret and analyze events and sources.

Activity Rubrics

Share rubrics with students before they write their paragraphs.

Attempted The paragraph fails either to describe the event or explain its importance.

Minimal The paragraph describes the event and explains its importance but only in a cursory way.

Adequate The paragraph describes the event and its importance and is thoughtful and well written.

Exemplary The paragraph thoroughly describes the event and its importance and is thoughtful, well written, and convincing.

☑ Test Preparation

Have students read about the plays of Euripides in the paragraph after the quotation on this page, and then complete the sentence below.

Euripides was concerned with

A complaining about the gods.

(B) showing how humans caused their own problems.

C telling people to be more respectful of gods.

D ridiculing the gods' laws.

Reading Focus

■ How did Alexander the Great build a huge empire?

■ What were the results of Alexander's conquests?

■ How did individuals contribute to Hellenistic civilization?

Vocabulary

assassination
assimilate
heliocentric

Taking Notes

Copy this chart. As you read, fill in the chart with examples of contributions made during the Hellenistic period. Parts of the chart have been filled in to help you get started.

ACHIEVEMENTS OF THE HELLENISTIC AGE

| • Art and architecture | • Philosophy | • Mathematics and science | • Medicine |
| • | • | • | • |

Main Idea Alexander the Great created a large empire and spread Greek culture throughout the region.

Bell Ringer

Bell Ringer Inform students that historians have referred to Alexander as "Alexander the Great." Invite students to suggest the qualities of a "great" ruler.

LESSON PLAN

1. Focus Alexander created a vast empire that included Greece, Persia, Egypt, and other lands. A blending of eastern and western cultures took place, especially in cities such as Alexandria in Egypt. In the many lands that Alexander conquered, Hellenistic civilization flourished.

2. Instruct Have students work in groups to prepare a multimedia presentation on Alexander and Hellenistic civilization. Each group should cover topics such as Philip of Macedonia, Alexander's conquests, the significance of new urban centers, and Hellenistic civilization. Suggest that students use wall maps and illustrations of Greek and Hellenistic cultural achievements to show routes of conquest, the birth of towns, and the blending of cultures. Group members should be prepared to answer questions from the class.

3. Assess Ask students to define Hellenistic civilization and to give examples drawn from the material they collected for their presentations that show the influence of Hellenistic civilization on the world today.

4. Reteach If students' *Assess* activity does not reflect adequate understanding of the lesson, you might assign the *Guide to the Essentials* or the *Interactive Student Tutorial CD-ROM* for this section.

Biography

Alexander the Great
356 B.C.–323 B.C.

As a boy, Alexander had heard tales of Achilles, hero of the *Iliad*. The legendary Greek warrior was all a soldier should be—brave, daring, strong, and almost unbeatable. Alexander saw himself as a second Achilles.

From his tutor, Aristotle, young Alexander acquired a love of learning and the arts, but he was first and foremost a warrior. When Thebes rebelled, he ordered the city to be burned and its inhabitants to be killed or sold into slavery. But he told his soldiers to spare one house—the house where the Greek poet Pindar had once lived.

Theme: Impact of the Individual Why do you think Alexander refused to burn Pindar's house?

Setting the Scene

"He is always taking in more, everywhere casting his net around us, while we sit idle and do nothing!" Demosthenes (dih MAHS thuh neez) was warning his fellow Athenians about Philip II, the king of Macedonia. Bit by bit, Philip was bringing Greece under his rule. "When," asked Demosthenes, "will you Athenians take the necessary action?"

When Athenians finally did take action against Philip, it was too late. Athens and the other Greek city-states lost their independence. Yet the disaster ushered in a new age in which Greek influence spread from the Mediterranean to the borders of India. The architect of this new era was Philip's son, known to history as Alexander the Great.

Alexander the Great

To the Greeks, the rugged, mountainous kingdom of Macedonia was a backward, half-civilized land. The rulers of this frontier land, in fact, were of Greek origin and kept ties to their Greek neighbors. As a youth, Philip had lived in Thebes and had come to admire Greek culture. Later, he hired Aristotle as a tutor to his young son Alexander.

Philip's Dream When Philip gained the throne in 359 B.C., he dreamed of conquering the prosperous city-states to the south. He built a superb army. Through threats, bribery, and diplomacy, he formed alliances with many Greek city-states. Others he conquered. In 338 B.C., when Athens and Thebes joined forces against him, he defeated them at the battle of Chaeronea (kehr uh NEE uh). Philip then brought all of Greece under his control.

Philip had a still grander dream—to conquer the Persian empire. Before he could achieve that plan, though, he was assassinated at his daughter's wedding. Assassination is the murder of a public figure, usually for political reasons. Philip's determined wife, Olympias, then outmaneuvered his other wives and children to put her own son, Alexander, on the throne.

Conquest of Persia Alexander was only 20 years old. Yet he was already an experienced soldier who shared his father's ambitions. With Greece subdued, he began organizing the forces needed to conquer Persia. By 334 B.C., he had enough ships to cross the Dardanelles, the strait separating Europe from Asia Minor.

Persia was no longer the great power it had once been. The emperor Darius III was weak, and the provinces were often in rebellion against him. Still, the Persian empire stretched more than 2,000 miles from Egypt to India.

120 Chapter 5

Biography

ANSWER Possible answer: Despite his anger at the Thebans, Alexander admired Greek culture and wanted to show his respect for a great poet.

Resource Directory

Teaching Resources

Creative Teaching Activities Creative Teaching Activities booklet, p. 28

Guided Reading and Review Unit 2 booklet, p. 30

Primary Source Activity *Herodotus Visits the Pyramids of Egypt,* Unit 2 booklet, p. 33

Empire of Alexander the Great

☐ Macedonia, 336 B.C.	☐ Alexander's empire at its height, 323 B.C.	→ Route of Alexander, 334 B.C.–323 B.C.	○ Towns founded by Alexander and his followers

Albers Equal Area Projection

0   250   500 Miles

0   250   500 Kilometers

Activity
Connections to Film

Constructing an Outline *Alexander the Great*, program 7 of the public television series *The Western Tradition,* focuses on Alexander and the birth of the Hellenistic age. Students view artifacts from the Metropolitan Museum of Art and visit various sites of Alexander's empire. Of particular interest is a tour through the well-preserved ruins of a Hellenistic city in present-day Afghanistan.

After students watch the film, have them list its major ideas. Then, have them view the film a second time to note the details and examples that support each major idea. Finally, ask students to use their notes to construct a well-organized outline of the features of Hellenistic culture. Before assigning this activity, you may wish to review some standard outline format with the students. (*The Western Tradition,* released in 1989 as part of the Annenberg/CPB Collection, is distributed by Intellimation.)

Alexander won his first victory against the Persians at the Granicus River. He then moved from victory to victory, marching through Asia Minor into Palestine and south to Egypt. In 331 B.C., he took Babylon, then seized the other Persian capitals. But before Alexander could capture Darius, the Persian emperor was murdered.

Onward to India With much of the Persian empire under his control, the restless Alexander headed farther east. He crossed the Hindu Kush into northern India. There, in 326 B.C., his troops for the first time faced soldiers mounted on war elephants. Although Alexander never lost a battle, his soldiers were tired of the long campaign and refused to go farther east. Reluctantly, Alexander agreed to turn back. After a long, hard march, they reached Babylon, where Alexander began planning a new campaign.

Sudden Death Before he could set out again, Alexander fell victim to a sudden fever. As he lay dying, his commanders asked to whom he left his immense empire. "To the strongest," he is said to have whispered.

In fact, no one leader proved strong enough to succeed Alexander. Instead, after years of disorder, three generals divided up the empire. Macedonia and Greece went to one general, Egypt to another, and most of Persia to a third. For 300 years, their descendants competed for power over the lands Alexander had conquered.

The Legacy of Alexander

Although Alexander's empire soon crumbled, he had unleashed changes that would ripple across the Mediterranean world and the Middle East for centuries. His most lasting achievement was the spread of Greek culture.

Skills Assessment

Geography Alexander's ambitions led him to conquer lands across a wide area.

1. **Location** On the map, locate **(a)** Aegean Sea, **(b)** Arabian Sea, **(c)** Euphrates River, **(d)** Indus River, **(e)** Macedonia, **(f)** Persia.
2. **Region** Locate the map Assyrian and Persian Empires, *which appears in an earlier chapter. Which parts of Alexander's empire had not been part of the Persian empire?*
3. **Critical Thinking Predicting Consequences** *Judging from this map, do you think Alexander's empire would be difficult to keep united? Explain.*

Reading Strategy
Structured Overview

Ask students to write the main section headings on a sheet of paper. Then have students scan the section and note the subheadings under each of the headings. Ask them to fill in details from the text as they read. *(Less Advanced Readers)*

▣ Block Scheduling Support

Have students complete World History Activity 2, p. 14, of the Using the Internet booklet. The activity requires students to read and take notes on the information they find at the given Web site, create a time line, and produce an exhibit. Discuss possible components of students' exhibits, such as posters, drawings or paintings, artifacts, or brochures. You may wish to allow students to work in pairs or small groups for this activity.

Skills Assessment

ANSWERS 1. Review locations with students. **2.** Greece, the Indus Valley of India, and lands west of Egypt **3.** Students should recognize that the great extent of Alexander's empire and the many different peoples it contained would make it hard to unite.

Global Connections

The Seven Wonders of the Ancient World

Around 100 B.C., a Hellenistic traveler named the lighthouse at Alexandria as one of the Seven Wonders of the World. This famous list of awesome structures also included the Hanging Gardens of Babylon and the Colossus, a 100-foot bronze statue on the Aegean island of Rhodes.

Since then, six of the Seven Wonders of the Ancient World have been destroyed, including the Pharos. Only the pyramids of ancient Egypt—the oldest structures on the list—are still standing.

Theme: Arts and Literature
What structures would you include on a list of Seven Wonders of the Modern World?

A Blending of Cultures Across his far-flung empire, Alexander founded many new cities, most of them named after him. The generals who succeeded him founded still more. Greek soldiers, traders, and artisans settled these new cities. From Egypt to the borders of India, they built Greek temples, filled them with Greek statues, and held athletic contests as they had in Greece. Local people assimilated, or absorbed, Greek ideas. In turn, Greek settlers adopted local customs.

Gradually, a blending of eastern and western cultures occurred. Alexander had encouraged this blending when he married a Persian woman and urged his soldiers to follow his example. He had also adopted many Persian customs, including Persian dress. After his death, a vital new culture emerged which blended Greek, Persian, Egyptian, and Indian influences. This Hellenistic civilization would flourish for centuries.

Alexandria At the very heart of the Hellenistic world stood the city of Alexandria, Egypt. Located on the sea lanes between Europe and Asia, its markets boasted a wide range of goods, from Greek marble to Arabian spices to East African ivory. A Greek architect had drawn up plans for the city, which would become home to almost a million people. Greeks, Egyptians, Persians, Hebrews, and many others crowded its busy streets. Among the city's marvelous sights was the Pharos, an enormous lighthouse that soared 440 feet into the air.

Alexander and his successors encouraged the work of scholars. The rulers of Alexandria built the great Museum as a center of learning.* The Museum boasted laboratories, lecture halls, and a zoo. Its well-stocked library had thousands of scrolls representing the accumulated knowledge of the ancient world. Unfortunately, the library was later destroyed in a fire.

Opportunities for Women Paintings, statues, and legal codes show that women were no longer restricted to their homes during the Hellenistic period. More women learned to read and write. Some became philosophers or poets. Royal women held considerable power, working alongside husbands and sons who were the actual rulers. In Egypt, the able and clever queen Cleopatra came to rule in her own right.

Hellenistic Civilization

The cities of the Hellenistic world employed armies of architects and artists. Temples, palaces, and other public buildings were much larger and grander than the buildings of classical Greece. The elaborate new style reflected the desire of Hellenistic rulers to glorify themselves as godlike monarchs.

New Schools of Thought Political turmoil during the Hellenistic age contributed to the rise of new schools of philosophy. The most influential was Stoicism. Its founder, Zeno, urged people to avoid desires and disappointments by accepting calmly whatever life brought. Stoics preached high moral standards, such as the idea of protecting the rights of fellow humans. They taught that all people, including women and slaves, though unequal in society, were morally equal because all had the power of reason. Stoicism later influenced many Roman and Christian thinkers.

Advances in Learning During the Hellenistic age, thinkers built on earlier Greek, Babylonian, and Egyptian knowledge. In mathematics, Pythagoras (pih THAG uhr uhs) derived a formula ($a^2 + b^2 = c^2$) to calculate the relationship between the sides of a right triangle. Euclid wrote *The Elements*, a textbook that became the basis for modern geometry.

Using mathematics and careful observation, the astronomer Aristarchus (ar ihs TAHR kuhs) argued that the Earth rotated on its axis and orbited

---

* *Museum* means "house of the Muses." The Muses were nine Greek goddesses who presided over the arts and sciences.

around the sun. This theory of a **heliocentric**, or sun-centered, solar system was not accepted by most scientists until almost 2,000 years later. Another Hellenistic astronomer, Eratosthenes, (air uh TAHS thu neez), showed that the Earth was round and accurately calculated its circumference.

The most famous Hellenistic scientist, Archimedes (ahr kuh MEE deez), applied principles of physics to make practical inventions. He mastered the use of the lever and pulley. He boasted, "Give me a lever long enough and a place to stand on, and I will move the world." An awed audience watched as he used his invention to draw a ship onto shore.

Medicine About 400 B.C., the Greek physician Hippocrates (hih PAHK ruh teez) studied the causes of illnesses and looked for cures. His Hippocratic oath set ethical standards for doctors. Physicians swore to "help the sick according to my ability and judgment but never with a view to injury and wrong" and to protect the privacy of patients. Doctors today take a similar oath.

Looking Ahead

During the Hellenistic period, Rome emerged as a powerful new state. After its conquest of Asia Minor in 133 B.C., it replaced Greece as the dominant power in the Mediterranean world. Still, by then, the Greeks had already made their greatest contributions.

Greek ideas about law, freedom, justice, and government have influenced political thinking to the present day. In the arts and sciences, Greek works set a standard for later people of Europe. These achievements were especially remarkable because they were produced by a scattering of tiny city-states whose rivalries cost them their freedom. In later chapters, you will see how the Greek legacy influenced the civilizations of Rome and of Western Europe.

Cause and Effect

Causes

- Rise of civilizations in Persia, Egypt, and Greece
- Macedonian conquest of Greece
- Growth of Alexander's empire from Greece to northern India
- Growing contacts among kingdoms of eastern Mediterranean and Middle East

Rise of Hellenistic Civilization

Effects

- Learning and arts encouraged by Alexander and his successors
- Alexandria, Egypt, becomes center of trade and learning
- Spread of Greek, Middle Eastern, and Persian religions
- Spread of Christianity

Connections to Today

- Continued practice of Christianity and Judaism in the region
- Alexandria, Egypt, still a center of learning
- Greek architecture still visible in ruins across Middle East

Skills Assessment **Chart** Although Alexander's empire split apart soon after his death, his conquests had an impact that endured for centuries. **How did the conquests of Alexander the Great encourage contact among different Mediterranean civilizations?**

SECTION 5 Assessment

Recall
1. **Identify: (a)** Philip of Macedonia, **(b)** Stoicism, **(c)** Pythagoras, **(d)** Euclid, **(e)** Archimedes, **(f)** Hippocrates.
2. **Define: (a)** assassination, **(b)** assimilate, **(c)** heliocentric.

Comprehension
3. What was the extent of Alexander's vast empire?
4. How did Alexander's conquests lead to a new civilization?
5. What new ideas did the Stoics introduce?

Critical Thinking and Writing
6. **Defending a Position** Would you agree that Alexander deserved to be called "the Great"? Why or why not?
7. **Ranking** What do you think were the three most important contributions made by Hellenistic scientists and mathematicians? Explain.

Activity
Take It to the NET

Use the Internet to research the lasting effects of Alexander and his ideas on the areas he conquered. Then, create a poster entitled "The Lasting Legacy of Alexander the Great."

Human Drama Activity

Constructing a Time Line By the time Alexander died in 323 B.C., he had won an empire of more than 1.5 million square miles. It is said that when he reached the Indus River, he wept "because there were no more worlds to conquer." Have students create a time line of the events of Alexander's life, consulting both the chapter material and outside sources. Have students illustrate their time lines with artwork of their own or with photocopies of outside resources. Display finished time lines. ✳

Test Preparation

Have students read the subsection titled "New Schools of Thought" on the opposite page, and then answer the question below.

Which of the following would be most likely to be a Stoic's reaction to receiving a prize of $100,000?

A jumping up and down in excitement

B burning the money

C quietly thanking the giver of the prize

D giving the money away

SECTION 5 Assessment

Recall
1. **(a)** Philip of Macedonia, p. 120 **(b)** Stoicism, p. 122 **(c)** Pythagoras, p. 122 **(d)** Euclid, p. 122 **(e)** Archimedes, p. 123 **(f)** Hippocrates, p. 123 2. **(a)** assassination, p. 120 **(b)** assimilate, p. 122 **(c)** heliocentric, p. 123

Comprehension
3. Alexander's empire stretched from Greece to northern India and included Persia, Palestine, Asia Minor, and Egypt. 4. Greeks left their country to settle in newly conquered lands. Eastern and western cultures blended, resulting in the new Hellenistic civilization. 5. high moral standards; calm acceptance of life; moral equality of all people, including women and slaves

Critical Thinking and Writing
6. Students should recognize Alexander's military victories, the size of his empire, the creation of a new culture, and the advancements in learning during his era. They may also point to the short duration of his empire. 7. Students' answers should accurately describe three contributions made by Hellenistic scientists and mathematicians.

Activity Rubrics

Share rubrics with students before they create their posters.

Attempted The poster was attempted but is sketchy or incomplete.

Minimal The poster combines words and pictures, but the design is weak.

Adequate The poster is effective, using both words and images.

Exemplary The poster has an eye-catching design, demonstrates careful research, and reflects insights into Alexander's legacy.

Skills Assessment

ANSWERS Alexander's conquests encouraged trade among the lands of the Hellenistic world. Hellenistic culture united the eastern Mediterranean.

CHAPTER **5** **Review and Assessment**

Creating a Chapter Summary

As a reteaching opportunity, pair a more able student with a less able student to complete this chapter summary.

Possible answers: **Minoan** 1750 B.C.–1500 B.C.: located on Crete; sea traders; built vast palace at Knossos with beautiful frescoes; worshiped a bull and a mother goddess; disappeared for unknown reasons; **Mycenaean** 1400 B.C.–1200 B.C.: based on Greek mainland but dominated the Mediterranean; sea traders; Trojan War; epics of Homer; **Greek City-States** 750 B.C.–323 B.C.: stages of government included monarchy, aristocracy, oligarchy, limited democracy; Athenian Golden Age, with achievements in philosophy, art, drama, and history; **Hellenistic** 323 B.C.–133 B.C.: empire of Alexander the Great from Greece to India; blending of Greek and other cultures; advances in philosophy, mathematics, and science

Building Vocabulary

1–10. Sentences should show a clear understanding of the meanings of the terms.

Recalling Key Facts

11. epics written by Homer about 750 B.C.
12. Because mountains divided Greece into many separate areas, Greeks developed separate, independent city-states. Mountains also limited farming.
13. **(a)** In Athens, women were treated as second-class citizens and were not educated. Spartan females were trained to strengthen their bodies and were expected to produce healthy sons for the military. They had to obey males but were allowed to inherit property. **(b)** They enjoyed many more freedoms—including education and greater power.
14. Persia's invasion of Greece was defeated; Greek morale rose; Athens emerged as the dominant city-state.
15. method used by Socrates to teach by asking a series of questions
16. Greek, Persian, Egyptian, Indian

Critical Thinking and Writing

17. The mountainous terrain contributed to the development of independent city-states and pushed Greeks away from farming; the mild climate allowed outdoor life; proximity to

---

Creating a Chapter Summary

Copy this graphic organizer on a sheet of paper. For each period of ancient Greek history, identify the time period and list three or four characteristics and achievements.

MINOAN CIVILIZATION 1750 B.C.–1500 B.C.
1. Traded with other Mediterranean people.
2.

MYCENAEAN CIVILIZATION
1.
2.

GREEK CITY-STATES
1.
2.

HELLENISTIC CIVILIZATION
1.
2.

iTEXT

For additional review and enrichment activities, see the interactive version of *World History* available on the Web and on CD-ROM.

Web Site Self-Test
For practice test questions for Chapter 5, see **www.phschool.com**.

Building Vocabulary

Write sentences using the chapter vocabulary words listed below; leave blanks where the vocabulary words should go. Exchange your sentences with another student and fill in the blanks in each other's sentences.

1. fresco
2. strait
3. aristocracy
4. tyrant
5. alliance
6. direct democracy
7. jury
8. logic
9. tragedy
10. assimilate

Recalling Key Facts

11. What were the *Iliad* and the *Odyssey*?
12. How did mountains help shape the development of Greek civilization?
13. **(a)** What was the social status of women in Sparta and in Athens? **(b)** How did the status of women change during the Hellenistic period?
14. What were the results of the Persian Wars?
15. What is the Socratic method?
16. What cultures blended to form Hellenistic civilization?

Critical Thinking and Writing

17. **Connecting to Geography** How did the geography and climate of Greece and the Aegean influence the development of Greek civilization?
18. **Analyzing Information** **(a)** How did Athenian culture stress the importance of the individual? Give two examples. **(b)** Do you think there is a relationship between the importance placed on the individual and the development of democracy? Explain.
19. **Recognizing Causes and Effects** **(a)** Identify two immediate and two long-range causes of the Peloponnesian War. **(b)** Why might it be said that all Greeks were losers in this war?
20. **Synthesizing Information** **(a)** How was the form of government outlined in Plato's *Republic* similar to the government of Sparta? **(b)** How was it different?
21. **Linking Past and Present** Reread the description of the Hippocratic oath. **(a)** How did Hippocrates address the question of medical ethics? **(b)** What ethical issues do doctors face today?

---

the sea made it possible for the Greeks to become sea traders.
18. Possible answers: **(a)** Greek democracy stressed individual political power. Greek philosophy stressed individual reasoning. **(b)** As individuals gained importance, they acquired more political rights.
19. **(a)** Immediate causes include Athenian domination, formation of the Peloponnesian League; long-range causes include creation of the Delian League, rivalry between Athens and Sparta. **(b)** The war weakened the Greeks and led to their conquest by Philip of Macedonia.
20. **(a)** Both systems had kings who regulated the

lives of their citizens. **(b)** Plato's rulers were philosophers; Sparta's were soldiers.
21. **(a)** He swore to use medicine to help patients, and never to injure or betray them. **(b)** Answers may include euthanasia, experimental treatments, and accusations of malpractice.

Analyzing Primary Sources

22. They criticize it.
23. Common people man the boats of the navy and are responsible for the city's strength.
24. **(a)** the poor and the common people **(b)** the high-born and wealthy

The excerpt below is from a pamphlet written by an anonymous Greek calling himself the Old Oligarch. Read the excerpt and answer the questions that follow.

"[The Athenians] have chosen to let the worst people be better off than the good. Therefore, on this account I do not think well of their constitution. But since they have decided to have it so, I intend to point out how well they preserve their constitution and accomplish those other things for which the rest of the Greeks criticize them.

First I want to say this: There the poor and the people generally are right to have more than the highborn and wealthy for the reason that it is the people who man the ships and impart strength to the city. . . .

Everywhere on earth the best element is opposed to democracy. For among the best people there is minimal wantonness [undisciplined behavior] and injustice but a maximum of care for what is good, whereas among the people there is a maximum of ignorance, disorder, and wickedness."

—Old Oligarch, *The Constitution of the Athenians*

22. According to the Old Oligarch, what do the other Greek city-states think about the Athenian political system?

23. According to the Old Oligarch, why is it proper that Athens have a democracy?

24. **(a)** According to the Old Oligarch, who would support democracy in Athens? **(b)** Who would oppose it?

25. This anonymous author chose to call himself the Old Oligarch. **(a)** What was an oligarchy? **(b)** What does the writer's choice of a name indicate about his own social and economic status?

26. What do you think the Old Oligarch means when he refers to the "best" and the "worst" people?

27. Would you consider the Old Oligarch's view of Athenian democracy to be biased? Explain.

Skills Tip

When you analyze a primary source, keep in mind the author's own background. Factors such as age, education, social class, or economic status often influence a person's point of view.

The scene below is from a Greek painting that was created in the 400s B.C. It shows a group of Athenian women preparing a young bride for her wedding. Look at the painting, and then answer the questions that follow.

28. **(a)** What is the subject of this picture? **(b)** Who are the central figures?

29. To what social class would you say these women belonged?

30. What kinds of information about the lives of these women can you get from this painting? Identify at least three details.

31. Based on what you have read about surviving Greek artworks, where would you find this painting?

32. Compare the representations of the human form in Greek painting and Egyptian painting. **(a)** How are the two styles similar? **(b)** How are they different? **(c)** Why might there be some similarities between these two styles of painting?

Use the Internet to research information about the city-states in ancient Greece other than Athens and Sparta. Locate five of these city-states on a blank map of Greece. Then, make a fact sheet that includes two or three facts about each of these five city-states.

25. **(a)** An oligarchy is rule by a small, powerful elite. **(b)** He was probably wealthy and of the higher class, as all oligarchs were.

26. He identifies the wealthy elite as the "best people." The "worst people" are the poor.

27. Yes. As an "old oligarch," he is a member of a class that has less power in Athens. His own aristocratic values affect his judgment.

Analyzing Pictures

28. **(a)** women preparing for a wedding **(b)** the bride and the woman who is about to put jewelry on her

29. They are probably wealthy.

30. Possible answers: The women attending the bride are wearing tiaras. The central woman is holding a necklace. The bride is seated on a finely carved chair. The woman holding the necklace has well-coiffed hair. The bride is about to receive a gift of some sort.

31. probably on a vase

32. **(a)** Both depict scenes of people in everyday life. **(b)** Egyptian art portrayed people in stiff, unnatural poses with heads and limbs in profile and eyes and shoulders facing the viewers. Greek art portrayed people in more realistic and graceful poses. **(c)** because there was much interaction between the two societies

Skills Tip

Tell students that when they read a primary source, they should watch for sweeping generalizations, which are a clue that what follows is probably not entirely true. In this excerpt, for example, the Old Oligarch says, *"Everywhere on earth* the best element is opposed to democracy" (emphasis added). The Skills Handbook in the front of the book has a lesson that will help students with this feature.

Take It to the NET

Direct students to **www.phschool.com** for links to sites that will help them get started on this assignment. Share rubrics with students.

Attempted The project is incomplete.

Minimal The project includes the map and a fact sheet with just two facts for each of the five city-states.

Adequate The project includes the map and a fact sheet with three facts for each of the five city-states.

Exemplary The project includes the map and a fact sheet with at least three interesting facts for each of the five city-states.

Unit Theme Activity

Remind students to continue working on their Unit Theme Activity. See rubrics for the activity on the unit opener page in the Teacher's Edition.

Chapter 6 Planning Guide

Resource Manager

Chapter Level Resources	CORE INSTRUCTION	READING/SKILLS
Chapter Level Resources	📘 Teaching Resources 📄 Pacing Charts, Ch. 6 📄 Teaching With Themes, p. 9 📺 Color Transparencies, p. F–13 💿 Resource Pro® Ch. 6 💻 www.phschool.com 　• eTeach	💿 Book on CD, Ch. 6 💿 Interactive Student Tutorial CD-ROM, Ch. 6 💿 Social Studies Skills Tutor CD-ROM 📺 Skills Transparencies
1 The Roman World Takes Shape 1. Identify ways that geography shaped the early development of Rome. 2. Describe the major characteristics of government and society in the Roman republic. 3. Explain how Rome succeeded in expanding in Italy.	📘 Teaching Resources 📄 Creative Teaching Activities, p. 29 💿 Prentice Hall Presentation Pro, Ch. 6, Section 1 📺 Section Reading Support Transparencies	📘 Teaching Resources 📓 Unit 2 booklet 　• Guided Reading and Review, p. 42 📙 Guide to the Essentials 📼 Guided Reading Audiotapes, Ch. 6, Section 1
2 From Republic to Empire 1. Describe how Rome won an empire. 2. Explain why the republic declined. 3. Outline how Roman emperors promoted peace and stability in the empire.	📘 Teaching Resources 📓 Unit 2 booklet 　• Biography Activity, p. 52 　• Primary Source Activity, p. 53 📄 Creative Teaching Activities, p. 30 💿 Prentice Hall Presentation Pro, Ch. 6, Section 2	📘 Teaching Resources 📓 Unit 2 booklet 　• Guided Reading and Review, p. 44 📙 Guide to the Essentials 📼 Guided Reading Audiotapes, Ch. 6, Section 2
3 The Roman Achievement 1. Analyze how Greco-Roman civilization was formed. 2. Outline Roman contributions to literature, the arts, and technology. 3. Identify principles of Roman law.	📘 Teaching Resources 📄 Creative Teaching Activities, p. 31 💿 Prentice Hall Presentation Pro, Ch. 6, Section 3 📺 Section Reading Support Transparencies	📘 Teaching Resources 📓 Unit 2 booklet 　• Guided Reading and Review, p. 46 📙 Guide to the Essentials 📼 Guided Reading Audiotapes, Ch. 6, Section 3
4 The Rise of Christianity 1. Describe Rome's policy toward different religions in the early empire. 2. Summarize the major teachings of Jesus and how they spread. 3. Explain how the early Christian Church developed.	📘 Teaching Resources 📓 Unit 2 booklet 　• Viewpoint Activity, p. 54 📄 Creative Teaching Activities, p. 32 💿 Prentice Hall Presentation Pro, Ch. 6, Section 4 📺 Section Reading Support Transparencies	📘 Teaching Resources 📓 Unit 2 booklet 　• Guided Reading and Review, p. 48 📙 Guide to the Essentials 📼 Guided Reading Audiotapes, Ch. 6, Section 4
5 The Long Decline 1. Outline how Roman emperors tried to end the crisis in the empire. 2. Explain how the Hun invasions contributed to the decline of Rome. 3. Describe how economic and social problems led to the fall of Rome.	📘 Teaching Resources 📄 Creative Teaching Activities, p. 32 💿 Prentice Hall Presentation Pro, Ch. 6, Section 5 📺 Section Reading Support Transparencies	📘 Teaching Resources 📓 Unit 2 booklet 　• Guided Reading and Review, p. 50 　• Skill Application Activity, p. 55 📙 Guide to the Essentials 📼 Guided Reading Audiotapes, Ch. 6, Section 5

ENRICHMENT/PRE-AP

📖 **www.phschool.com**
  • Why Study History?

🏛 **Color Transparencies**, p. B–75
📖 **www.phschool.com**
  • Virtual Field Trip

🏛 **Color Transparencies,** pp. B–19, B–21, B–23, B–25

📚 Teaching Resources
  📄 **Chapter Extension Activities,** p. 19
  📄 **History Through Literature,** pp. 13–15
  🏛 **Color Transparencies,** p. C–31
  📼 **Listening to Literature World Masterpieces,** Roman Music, side 5; from *The Aeneid,* side 5
  📖 **www.phschool.com**
    • Internet Activities, Vesuvius Erupts!
    • Internet Activities, Section 3

🏛 **Color Transparencies,** pp. B–27, B–29, B–31, B–33
📖 **www.phschool.com**
  • Internet Activities, Section 4

📚 Teaching Resources
  📄 **Chapter Extension Activities,** p. 20
  📄 **Geography and History,** pp. 4–5

ASSESSMENT

PRENTICE HALL
ASSESSMENT SYSTEM

Core Assessment
  📄 ExamView Test Bank booklet, Ch. 6
  💿 ExamView Test Bank CD-ROM, Ch. 6

Standardized Test Preparation
Diagnose and Prescribe
  📄 Diagnostic Tests for High School Social Studies Skills
Review and Reteach
  📄 Review Book for World History
Practice and Assess
  📄 Test-Taking Strategies With Transparencies for High School
  📄 Alternative Assessment booklet
  📄 Test Prep Book for World History

📚 Teaching Resources
  📄 Unit 2 booklet
    • Geography Quiz, p. 56
    • Section Quizzes, pp. 43, 45, 47, 49, 51
    • Chapter Tests A, B, and C, pp. 57–61
  📖 www.phschool.com
    • Self-Test

CUSTOMIZE FOR INDIVIDUAL NEEDS

Gifted and Talented
  • **Teacher's Edition,** Activities: Customize for Heterogeneous Groups, p. 135; Customize for Heterogeneous Groups, p. 142
Less Proficient Readers
  • **Guide to the Essentials,** Ch. 6
  • **Guided Reading Audiotapes, English,** Ch. 6
  • **Book on CD,** Ch. 6
  • **Teacher's Edition,** Activities: Connections to Geography, p. 138; Reading Strategy, p. 143
Less Proficient Writers
  • **Teacher's Edition,** Activities: Cooperative Learning Activity, p. 135
Students Acquiring English/ESL
  • **Guide to the Essentials, English/Spanish,** Ch. 6
  • **Guided Reading Audiotapes, English/Spanish,** Ch. 6
  • **Book on CD,** Ch. 6
  • **Teacher's Edition,** Activities marked with an *: Connections to Geography, p. 138

𝒊 TEXT

Don't miss the exclusive interactive version of *World History: Connections to Today* on the Internet and CD-ROM.

INTRODUCTION

Conquest and diplomacy helped Rome build a diverse empire, extending its rule throughout the Mediterranean, including the regions of Greece, Egypt, and the Fertile Crescent. During the Pax Romana, emperors brought peace, order, unity, and prosperity to the lands under their control. Christianity spread quickly throughout the empire, reshaping Roman beliefs. Foreign invasions, the division of the empire, corruption, poverty, and the breakdown of moral values contributed to the decline and downfall of the Roman empire.

Focusing on Themes

Suggest that students focus on these theme questions as they read:

Political and Social Systems
How did Rome conquer and rule a diverse empire?

Global Interaction
How was Rome a bridge between the civilizations of east and west?

Religions and Value Systems
How did Christianity become a central institution of western civilization?

Continuity and Change
Why did Roman power fade?

TIME LINE ACTIVITY

You may wish to share the About the Pictures note with your students before you ask questions such as these about the time line:

1. The Carthaginian general Hannibal invaded Italy during which wars? *(Punic Wars)*
2. How much time elapsed between the beginning of the Maurya dynasty in India and the unification of much of China under Shi Huangdi? *(100 years)*
3. When was Christianity made the official religion of the Roman empire? *(A.D. 392)*

Don't Miss!

Disaster!
Vesuvius Erupts!
(Section 3)

Synthesizing Information
Why Did Rome Fall?
(Section 5)

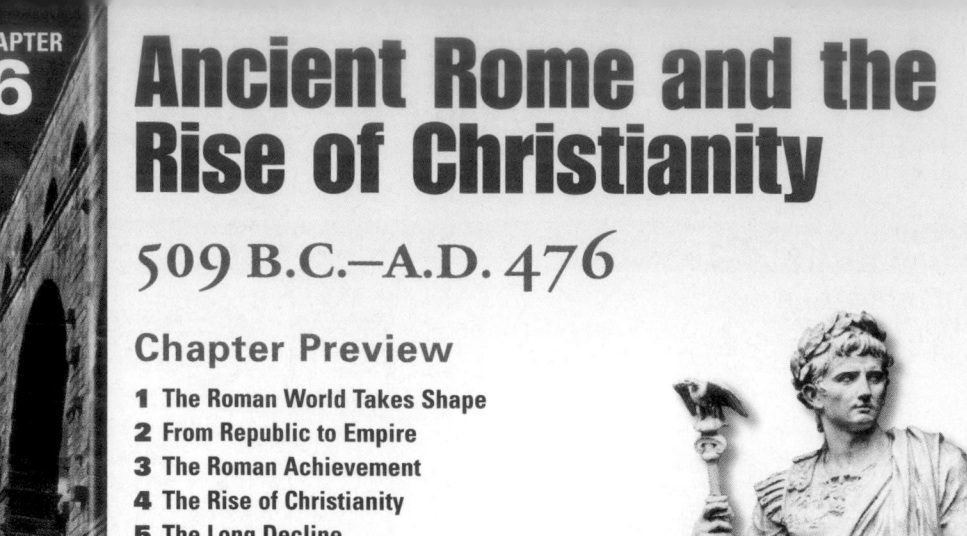

Ancient Rome and the Rise of Christianity

509 B.C.–A.D. 476

Chapter Preview

1 The Roman World Takes Shape
2 From Republic to Empire
3 The Roman Achievement
4 The Rise of Christianity
5 The Long Decline

218 B.C.
The Carthaginian general Hannibal invades Italy during the Punic Wars between Rome and Carthage.

509 B.C.
Romans set up a republic.

27 B.C.
The Roman republic ends, and the Roman empire begins under Emperor Augustus.

CHAPTER EVENTS

500 B.C.

300 B.C.

100 B.C.

GLOBAL EVENTS

321 B.C. Chandragupta begins the Maurya dynasty in India.

221 B.C. Shi Huangdi unites much of China.

Resource Directory

Teaching Resources
Teaching With Themes Chapter Theme Activities, p. 9
Pacing Chart With Block Scheduling Guide Ch. 6
Technology
World History Color Transparencies Ch. 6 Graphic Organizer, p. F–13

The Roman Empire at Its Height

BRITAIN
GERMANY
GAUL
ALPS
PYRENEES MTS.
Rhine R.
Danube R.
Black Sea
SPAIN
CORSICA
Rome
MACEDONIA
Byzantium
New Carthage
SARDINIA
ASIA MINOR
Antioch
Carthage
Zama
SICILY
Athens
SYRIA
NUMIDIA
Mediterranean Sea
CRETE
CYPRUS
Damascus
ARABIA
Cyrene
Alexandria
EGYPT
AFRICA
Thebes
Euphrates R.
Tigris R.
Nile R.

At its height, the Roman empire included lands in Europe, Africa, and Asia.

Roman empire, A.D. 117

Azimuthal Equal Area Projection
0   250   500 Miles
0   250   500 Kilometers

A.D. 392
Emperor Theodosius makes Christianity the official religion of the Roman empire. The cross and fish were Christian symbols.

A.D. 400s
Roman armies battle Hun and Germanic invaders. In A.D. 476, a Germanic leader seizes Rome.

A.D. 100

A.D. 300

A.D. 500

A.D. 220 In China, warlords overthrow the last Han emperor.

A.D. 350s About this time in Africa, armies from the kingdom of Axum conquer Nubia.

Chapter 6 **127**

Independent Assignments

Have students read one section as they prepare for class. After class, have them complete the assignment. Some students may benefit from using the Guided Reading and Review worksheets.

Section 1 Have students use the outline map *Roman Empire to 117 A.D.* in the Historical Outline Map Book, p. 9, to learn how the Roman empire expanded.
Section 2 Have students use the worksheet *Cleopatra VII* in the Unit 2 booklet, p. 52, to learn more about political rivalries at the beginning of the empire.
Section 3 Have students use the worksheet *The*

Aeneid in the History Through Literature booklet, pp. 13–15, to learn more about different standards of courage.
Section 4 Have students use the worksheet *What To Do About the Christians?* in the Unit 2 booklet, p. 54, to learn more about official Roman policy.
Section 5 Have students use the worksheet in the Chapter Extension Activities booklet, p. 20, to learn more about the decline and fall of Rome.

The Roman Empire at Its Height

Activating Prior Knowledge
Have students think about the other empires they have studied, and then look at a map of the Roman empire. Ask students how the Roman empire differs from others they have read about. *(It is built around a sea, not adjacent lands in the interior of a continent.)*

Previewing
Ask students to speculate about how geography helped Christianity spread relatively quickly throughout the Roman empire. *(The position on the Mediterranean Sea made it easier to travel the empire and spread the Christian faith.)*

Background
About the Pictures

1. *The Punic War: Hannibal in Italy.* This depiction of Hannibal is a fresco, a painting on a wet plaster wall. Painted by Jacopo Ripanda c. 1508, this fresco is in the Museo Capitolino in Rome, Italy.

2. *Statue of Augustus.* Rome's first emperor, Octavian, brought an end to ninety years of civil war in the Roman republic. In gratitude and respect, the Senate gave him the title *Augustus.*

3. *Secret symbols of Christianity.* The cross and the fish are ancient Christian symbols that date from the time of the Christian persecution. The Greek word for fish is *ichthys.* These letters are also the initials for the expression "Jesus Christ Son of God Saviour" in Greek (*Iesous Christos theou hyios soter*).

4. *Arch of Constantine, A.D. 315.* This frieze is from the Arch of Constantine, erected by the Senate as a tribute to Emperor Constantine, who defeated the pagan Maxentius (A.D. 306), a rival for power. After having a vision on the battlefield, Constantine converted to Christianity and officially ended persecution of Christians in the empire.

eTeach

Be sure to check out this month's online discussion with a World History Master Teacher.
Go to **www.phschool.com.**

SECTION 1

SECTION 1 — The Roman World Takes Shape

Bell Ringer Direct students' attention to the map on the opposite page titled "Ancient Italy About 600 B.C." Ask students to describe the location of Italy and to explain how this location might have benefited the growth of Roman power.

LESSON PLAN

1. Focus The central location of Rome helped the Romans unite Italy and all of the Mediterranean world under their rule. Through skillful diplomacy and military victories, they created a vast empire. Through gradual reforms, they made their republican form of government more democratic.

2. Instruct Ask students to assume one of the following roles: a Roman patrician, a Roman plebeian, a Roman soldier, a Roman woman, or a citizen of a land conquered by Rome. Then ask them to write a letter to a friend which describes their lives and the important developments taking place around them. Their letters should comment on the conditions with which they are happy and those with which they are unhappy. They should also describe their hopes and goals for the future. Invite volunteers to read their letters to the class.

3. Assess Have students look at the heads, subheads, illustrations, captions, and boldface and italicized words and then prepare a summary of the key points in this section.

4. Reteach If students' **Assess** activity does not reflect adequate understanding of the lesson, you might assign the *Guide to the Essentials* or the *Interactive Student Tutorial CD-ROM* for this section.

Reading Focus

- How did geography shape the early development of Rome?
- What were the major characteristics of government and society in the Roman republic?
- Why was Rome's expansion in Italy successful?

Vocabulary

republic
patrician
consul
dictator
plebeian
tribune
veto
legion

Taking Notes

At right is a partially completed outline of this section. As you read, finish the outline. Use Roman numerals for major headings, capital letters for subheadings, and numbers for supporting details.

I. Geography and peoples of Italy
   A. Geography
      1. Peninsula
      2.
   B.
II. The Roman republic
   A. The government takes shape
      1.
      2.
   B.

Main Idea Rome developed a republican form of government based on strong civic virtues and gained control over much of the Italian peninsula.

Setting the Scene Romans loved stories about great heroes of the past. One of their favorite heroes was Horatius, who was said to have single-handedly saved Rome from an invading Etruscan army.

As the enemy approached, Horatius rushed to the far end of the bridge that led into the city. Standing alone, he held off the attackers while his fellow Romans tore down the bridge behind him. As the last timber fell, Horatius flung himself into the river below. Dodging the spears raining down all around him, he swam safely to the other side.

The story of Horatius is more legend than it is history. Still, it helps us to understand the virtues that the Romans admired. Courage, loyalty, and devotion to duty were the pillars on which Romans would build an empire.

Geography and Peoples of Italy

Rome began as a small city-state in Italy but ended up ruling the entire Mediterranean world. The story of the Romans and how they built a world empire starts with the land where they lived.

Geography The Italian peninsula looks like a boot, jutting into the Mediterranean Sea. The peninsula is centrally located in the Mediterranean, and the city of Rome is in the center of Italy. That location helped the Romans as they expanded, first in Italy, and then into lands around the Mediterranean.

Because of its geography, Italy was much easier to unify than Greece. Unlike Greece, Italy is not broken up into small, isolated valleys. In addition, the Apennine Mountains, which run like a backbone down the length of the Italian peninsula, are less rugged than the mountains of Greece. Finally, Italy has the advantage of broad, fertile plains, both in the north under the shadow of the Alps, and in the west, where the Romans settled. These plains supported a growing population.

Peoples The ancestors of the Romans, the Latins, migrated into Italy by about 800 B.C. The Latins settled along the Tiber River in small villages scattered over seven low-lying hills where they herded and farmed. Those villages would in time grow into Rome, the city on seven hills.

The Romans shared the Italian peninsula with other peoples. Among them were Greek colonists whose city-states dotted southern Italy and the Etruscans who lived north of Rome. For a time, the Etruscans ruled much of central Italy, including Rome itself.

Etruscan Helmet
The Etruscans were skilled in metalworking, as is shown by the bronze helmet above. Romans learned much from the other peoples in Italy.

Theme: Diversity What other peoples lived in the Italian peninsula?

Caption Answer

the Latins and Greek colonists, among others

Resource Directory

Teaching Resources
Creative Teaching Activities Creative Teaching Activities booklet, p. 29
Guided Reading and Review Unit 2 booklet, p. 42

Technology
World History Color Transparencies *Lands of the Mediterranean*, p. B–75

The Romans learned much from Etruscan civilization. They adapted the alphabet that the Etruscans had earlier acquired from the Greeks. They also learned to use the arch in building and adapted Etruscan engineering techniques to drain the marshy lands along the Tiber. Etruscan gods and goddesses merged with Roman deities.

The Roman Republic

The Romans drove out their Etruscan ruler in 509 B.C. This date is traditionally considered to mark the founding of the Roman state.

The Romans set up a new government in which some officials were chosen by the people. They called it a republic, or "thing of the people." A republic, Romans thought, would keep any individual from gaining too much power.

The Government Takes Shape In the early republic, the most powerful governing body was the senate. Its 300 members were all patricians, members of the landholding upper class. Senators, who served for life, made the laws.

Each year, the senators elected from the patrician class two consuls. Their job was to supervise the business of government and command the armies. Consuls, however, could serve only one term. They were also expected to consult with the senate. By limiting their time in office and making them responsible to the senate, Rome had a system of checks on the power of government.

In the event of war, the senate might choose a dictator, or ruler who has complete control over a government. Each Roman dictator was granted power to rule for six months. Then, he had to give up power. Romans admired Cincinnatus as a model dictator. Cincinnatus organized an army, led the Romans to victory over the attacking enemy, attended victory celebrations, and returned to his farmlands—all within 16 days.

Plebeians Demand Equality At first, all government officials were patricians. Plebeians (plih BEE uhnz), the farmers, merchants, artisans, and traders who made up the bulk of the population, had little influence. The efforts of the plebeians to gain power shaped politics in the early republic.

The plebeians' first breakthrough came in 450 B.C., when the government had the laws of Rome inscribed on 12 tablets and set up in the Forum, or marketplace. Plebeians had protested that citizens could not know what the laws were, because they were not written down. The Laws of the Twelve Tables made it possible for the first time for plebeians to appeal a judgment handed down by a patrician judge.

In time, the plebeians gained the right to elect their own officials, called tribunes, to protect their interests. The tribunes could veto, or block, those laws that they felt were harmful to plebeians. Little by little, plebeians forced the senate to choose plebeians as consuls, appoint plebeians to other high offices, and finally to open the senate itself to plebeians.

A Lasting Legacy Although the senate still dominated the government, the common people had gained access to power and won safeguards for their rights without having to resort to war or revolution. More than 2,000 years later, the framers of the United States Constitution would adapt such Roman ideas as the senate, the veto, and checks on political power.

Ancient Italy About 600 B.C.

Mercator Projection

0   100   200 Miles
0   100   200 Kilometers

ALPS

Po R.
Genoa
Rubicon R.
Arno R.
APENNINE MTS.
Adriatic Sea
CORSICA • Alalia
Rome
Tiber R.
SARDINIA
Tyrrhenian Sea
Ionian Sea
Mediterranean Sea
SICILY
Carthage • Syracuse
AFRICA

Greeks
Etruscans
Carthaginians

Skills Assessment

Geography The Romans shared the Italian peninsula with other peoples, many of whose ideas they adapted for their own use.

1. **Location** On the map, locate (a) Rome, (b) Alps, (c) Mediterranean Sea, (d) Carthage, (e) Sicily.
2. **Region** Based on this map, which group do you think had the most influence on the Romans? Explain.
3. **Critical Thinking Comparing** Why was Italy easier to unite than Greece?

Virtual Field Trip

Roman Women
In this wall painting, a woman of the patrician class is shown playing a lyre. The girl standing behind her is probably a servant or slave.

Theme: Political and Social Systems Describe how a portrait of a plebeian scene might appear different from the scene shown here.

Roman Society

The family was the basic unit of Roman society. Under Roman law, the male head of the household, usually the father, had absolute power in the family. He enforced strict discipline and demanded total respect for his authority. His wife was subject to his authority and was not allowed to administer her own affairs. The ideal Roman woman was loving, dutiful, dignified, and strong.

Changing Role of Women Roman women played a larger role in society than did Greek women. In later Roman times, women from all classes ran a variety of businesses, from small shops to major shipyards. Those who made their fortunes earned respect by supporting the arts or paying for public festivals. Most women, though, worked at home, raising their families, spinning, and weaving.

Over the centuries, Roman women gained greater freedom and influence. Patrician women went to the public baths, dined out, and attended the theater or other public entertainments with their husbands. Some women, such as Livia and Agrippina the Younger, had highly visible public roles and exercised significant political influence.

Education Girls and boys alike learned to read and write. Even lower-class Romans were taught to write, as can be seen from the jokes and other graffiti that archaeologists found scrawled on walls around the city.

By the late republic, many wealthy Romans were hiring private tutors, often Greeks, to supervise the education of their children. Under their guidance, children memorized major events and developments in Roman history. Rhetoric was an important subject for boys who wanted to pursue political careers.

Religion Roman gods and goddesses resembled those of the Etruscans and Greeks. Like the Greek god Zeus, the Roman god Jupiter ruled over the sky and the other gods. Juno, his wife, like the Greek goddess Hera, protected marriage. Romans also prayed to Neptune, god of the sea, whose powers were the same as those of the Greek god Poseidon. On the battlefield, they turned to Mars, the god of war.

The Roman calendar was full of feasts and other celebrations to honor the gods and to ensure divine favor for the city. As loyal citizens, Romans joined in these festivals, which inspired a sense of community. Throughout Rome were dozens of temples where statues of the gods were housed. Inside these temples, Romans worshiped and asked for divine assistance.

Expansion in Italy

As Rome's political and social systems evolved at home, its armies expanded Roman power across Italy. Roman armies conquered first the Etruscans and then the Greek city-states in the south. By about 270 B.C., Rome controlled most of the Italian peninsula.

Citizen-Soldiers Rome's success was due to skillful diplomacy and to its loyal, well-trained army. The basic military unit was the legion, made up of about 5,000 men. As in Greece, Roman armies consisted of citizen-soldiers who fought without pay and supplied their own weapons. Roman citizens often made good soldiers because they were brought up to value loyalty, courage, and respect for authority.

To ensure success, Roman commanders mixed rewards with harsh punishment. Young soldiers who showed courage in action won praise and gifts. If a unit fled from battle, however, 1 out of every 10 men from the disgraced unit was put to death.

Conquered Lands Rome generally treated its defeated enemies with justice. Conquered peoples had to acknowledge Roman leadership, pay taxes, and supply soldiers for the Roman army. In return, Rome let them keep their own customs, money, and local government.

To a few privileged groups among the conquered people, Rome gave the highly prized right of full citizenship. Others became partial citizens, who were allowed to marry Romans and carry on trade in Rome. As a result of such generous policies, most conquered lands remained loyal to Rome even in troubled times.

Protection and Unification To protect its conquests, Rome posted soldiers throughout the land. It also built a network of all-weather military roads to link distant territories to Rome. As trade and travel increased, local peoples incorporated Latin into their languages and adopted many Roman customs and beliefs. Slowly, Italy began to unite under Roman rule.

SECTION 1 Assessment

Recall
1. **Identify:** (a) Latins, (b) Etruscans, (c) Laws of the Twelve Tables, (d) Jupiter.
2. **Define:** (a) republic, (b) patrician, (c) consul, (d) dictator, (e) plebeian, (f) tribune, (g) veto, (h) legion.

Comprehension
3. Describe two ways that the geography of Italy influenced the rise of Rome.
4. (a) What reforms did plebeians win during the early republic?

(b) How did male and female roles differ in the Roman family?
5. What were two reasons for Rome's success in expanding its power across Italy?

Critical Thinking and Writing
6. **Linking Past and Present** Roman heroes were admired for their courage, loyalty, and devotion to duty. What qualities do American heroes display?
7. **Analyzing Information** Did the Roman republic have a democratic government? Why or why not?

SECTION 1 Assessment

Recall
1. **(a)** Latins, p. 128 **(b)** Etruscans, p. 128 **(c)** Laws of the Twelve Tables, p. 129 **(d)** Jupiter, p. 130 **2. (a)** republic, p. 129 **(b)** patrician, p. 129 **(c)** consul, p. 129 **(d)** dictator, p. 129 **(e)** plebeian, p. 129 **(f)** tribune, p. 129 **(g)** veto, p. 129 **(h)** legion, p. 131

Comprehension
3. A central location helped the Romans expand their power. The lack of major geographic barriers helped Rome unify Italy. **4. (a)** the Twelve Tables, the right to elect tribunes who could veto laws, the right to serve as government officials **(b)** The male head of the household had absolute power in the family. His wife was subject to his authority and was not allowed to administer her own affairs. However, women, especially patricians, gained more freedom and influence over the centuries. **5.** Possible answer: a loyal, well-trained army and skilled diplomacy

Critical Thinking and Writing
6. Students' answers should reflect qualities they consider admirable. **7.** Students should present a definition of democracy and demonstrate an understanding of Roman republican government.

Activity Rubrics

Share rubrics with students before they write their newspaper headlines.

Attempted The project is attempted, but headlines do not identify significant events.

Minimal Headlines show some awareness of events leading to the rise of Rome.

Adequate Headlines are well written and demonstrate a good understanding of events leading to the rise of Rome.

Exemplary Headlines are well written, original, accurate, and show a keen perception of events.

Human Drama Note

Dangerous Family Liaisons Agrippina enjoyed power and privilege as the sister of Emperor Caligula, but she lost power when the emperor learned she was plotting against him. When he died, he was succeeded by their uncle Claudius, who took Agrippina as his wife. She convinced Claudius to favor his stepson Nero over his own son. Agrippina is thought to have poisoned Claudius, to enable Nero to become emperor. Nero eventually had his mother murdered in A.D. 59. The modern city of Cologne, Germany, was originally called Colonia Agrippinensis after her.

Test Preparation

Have students read the text on this page under the heading "Conquered Lands," and then answer the question below.

According to the passage, which word best describes Rome's defeated enemies?

A privileged

B just

C generous

D loyal

SECTION 2

From Republic to Empire

LESSON PLAN

1. Focus Roman expansion brought about new economic classes, corruption, and attempted reforms. After a period of civil wars, the republic ended and the reign of Augustus ushered in the Pax Romana. In this section, students will learn about the strengths and weaknesses of imperial Rome.

2. Instruct Have students work in groups to construct annotated time lines for the years between 264 B.C. and A.D. 180. Remind students to include references to the Punic wars; the rise of a new class of wealthy people; the Gracchus reforms; civil wars; the rise and fall of Julius Caesar; and the reigns of Augustus, Nero, Marcus Aurelius, and other emperors. Follow up with a discussion of the strengths and weaknesses of the Roman empire.

3. Assess Have pairs of students create quizzes based on the materials in this section, and then exchange their quizzes with those of another team. The teams should take each other's quizzes and discuss any questions about which they disagree on the answers.

4. Reteach If students' Assess activity does not reflect adequate understanding of the lesson, you might assign the *Guide to the Essentials* or the *Interactive Student Tutorial CD-ROM* for this section.

Reading Focus

- How did Rome win an empire?
- Why did the Roman republic decline?
- How did Roman emperors promote peace and stability in the empire?

Vocabulary

imperialism
province
latifundia
census

Taking Notes

Copy this concept web. As you read the section, fill in the blank circles with important facts about the decline of the Roman republic. Add more circles if you need them.

THE REPUBLIC DECLINES

Gracchus brothers are killed

Main Idea As Roman power spread around the Mediterranean, the republic ended and the age of the Roman empire began.

Setting the Scene

After gaining control of the Italian peninsula, Rome began to build an empire around the Mediterranean Sea. Expansion created strains and conflicts in Roman society. Addressing plebeians, the Roman tribune Tiberius Gracchus described one of the injustices that he saw in Roman society:

> "The beasts of the field and the birds of the air have their holes and their hiding places, but the men who fight and die for Italy enjoy only the light and the air. . . . You fight and die to give wealth and luxury to others. You are called the masters of the world, but there is not a foot of ground that you can call your own."
>
> —Plutarch, *Parallel Lives*

The effects of territorial expansion gradually weakened and finally crushed the republic. Out of the rubble, though, rose the Roman empire and a new chapter in Rome's long history.

Winning an Empire

Rome's conquest of the Italian peninsula brought it into contact with Carthage, a city-state on the northern coast of Africa. Settled by North Africans and Phoenician traders, Carthage ruled over an empire that stretched across North Africa and the western Mediterranean. As Rome expanded westward, conflict between these two powers became inevitable.

Wars With Carthage Between 264 B.C. and 146 B.C., Rome fought three wars against Carthage. They are called the Punic Wars, from *Punicus*, the Latin word for Phoenician. In the First Punic War, Rome defeated Carthage and won Sicily, Corsica, and Sardinia.

The Carthaginians sought revenge in the Second Punic War. In 218 B.C., the Carthaginian general Hannibal led his army, including dozens of war elephants, on an epic march across the Pyrenees, through France, and over the Alps into Italy. The trek cost Hannibal nearly half his army. However, the Carthaginian general had surprised the Romans who had expected an invasion from the south. For 15 years, Hannibal and his army moved across Italy, winning battle after battle.

The Carthaginians, however, failed to capture Rome itself. In the end, the Romans outflanked Hannibal by sending an army to attack Carthage.

Wars With Carthage
Hannibal crossed the Alps into Italy with an invasion force that included thousands of troops and more than three dozen elephants. From towers on the elephants' backs, soldiers rained arrows and spears on their Roman enemies.

Theme: Impact of the Individual How did Hannibal's invasion route surprise the Romans?

Caption Answer

The Romans had expected an invasion from the south, but Hannibal attacked from the north.

Resource Directory

Teaching Resources
Creative Teaching Activities Creative Teaching Activities booklet, p. 30
Guided Reading and Review Unit 2 booklet, p. 44

Hannibal returned to defend his homeland, where the Romans defeated him at last. Carthage gave up all its lands except those in Africa.

Nevertheless, many Romans still saw Carthage as a rival and wanted revenge for the terrible destruction that Hannibal's army had brought to Italy. For years, Cato, a wealthy senator, ended every speech he made with the words "Carthage must be destroyed."

Finally, in the Third Punic War, Rome completely destroyed Carthage. Survivors were killed or sold into slavery. The Romans poured salt over the earth so that nothing would grow there again. The Romans were now masters of the western Mediterranean.

Other Conquests "The Carthaginians fought for their own preservation and the sovereignty of Africa," observed a Greek witness to the fall of Carthage; "the Romans, for supremacy and world domination." The Romans were committed to a policy of imperialism, or establishing control over foreign lands and peoples. While Rome fought Carthage in the west, it was also expanding into the eastern Mediterranean. There, Romans confronted the Hellenistic rulers who had divided up the empire of Alexander the Great.

Sometimes to defend Roman interests, sometimes simply for plunder, Rome launched a series of wars in the area. One by one, Macedonia, Greece, and parts of Asia Minor surrendered and became Roman provinces, that is, lands under Roman rule. Other regions, like Egypt, allied with Rome. By 133 B.C., Roman power extended from Spain to Egypt. Truly, the Romans were justified in calling the Mediterranean *Mare Nostrum*, or "Our Sea."

Social and Economic Effects Conquests and control of busy trade routes brought incredible riches into Rome. Generals, officials, and traders amassed fortunes from loot, taxes, and commerce. A new class of wealthy Romans emerged. They built lavish mansions and filled them with luxuries imported from the east. Wealthy families bought up huge estates, called latifundia. As the Romans conquered more and more lands, they forced people captured in war to work as slaves on the latifundia.

The widespread use of slave labor hurt small farmers, who were unable to produce food as cheaply as the latifundia could. The farmers' problems were compounded when huge quantities of grain pouring in from the conquered lands drove down grain prices. Many farmers fell into debt and had to sell their land.

In despair, landless farmers flocked to Rome and other cities looking for jobs. There, they joined a restless class of unemployed people. As the gap between rich and poor widened, angry mobs began to riot.

The new wealth also increased corruption. Greed and self-interest replaced virtues such as simplicity, hard work, and devotion to duty so prized in the early republic.

Attempts at Reform Two young patricians, brothers named Tiberius and Gaius Gracchus (GAY uhs GRAK uhs), were among the first to attempt reform. Tiberius, who was elected a tribune in 133 B.C., called on the state to distribute land to poor farmers. Gaius, elected tribune 10 years later, sought a wider range of reforms, including the use of public funds to buy grain to feed the poor.

The reforms of the Gracchus brothers angered the senate, which saw them as a threat to its power. The brothers, along with thousands of their followers, were killed in waves of street violence set off by senators and their hired thugs.

Connections to Today

Ancient Ruins Under the Sea
Swimming among brightly colored fish, archaeologists are exploring an underwater treasure off the coast of Egypt. In a rare find, they have uncovered remains of the ancient city of Alexandria beneath the waters of the Mediterranean. Divers can swim among sphinxes, columns, and temples—a rich mix of Egyptian, Greek, and Roman artifacts.

Mingled among the ruins created long ago by earthquakes are the wrecks of Roman ships that failed to navigate the dangerous harbor. Cargoes of olive oil and wine are still intact after resting on the sea floor for some 2,000 years.

Theme: Geography and History How did geography contribute to the creation of this archaeological site?

134 Chapter 6

Background
Biography

Spartacus Between 73 and 71 B.C., Spartacus, a former slave and gladiator, led a rebellion that humbled mighty Rome. With an army of some 90,000 escaped slaves, he conquered much of southern Italy and for two years fought off every Roman army sent against him. The rebellion came to an end when Spartacus was killed in a battle at Lucania. After the battle, 3,000 Roman captives were found unharmed in Spartacus' camp. To deter any future rebellions, the Romans crucified 6,000 of the rebel slaves along the road to Rome.

Background
Global Connections

East Meets West Julius Caesar's pursuit of Pompey took him to Egypt, where he learned that Pompey was dead. Now, however, Caesar found himself in the midst of another civil war. The Egyptian queen Cleopatra VII, of the Ptolemaic line that had been established by a Macedonian general in the army of Alexander, was at war with her brother, Ptolemy XIII. Caesar allied himself with the youthful queen and turned the royal palace into a fortress. With his army, he fought off Egyptian and Roman forces for nine months until reinforcements could arrive.

According to the biographer Suetonius, Caesar "often feasted with Cleopatra till daybreak," and "would have gone through Egypt with her in her royal barge almost to Ethiopia," had not his soldiers threatened mutiny. In 47 B.C., Cleopatra bore Caesar a son, named Caesarion. After achieving victory in Egypt, Caesar returned to Rome and to his wife, Calpurnia. Cleopatra and Caesarion followed Caesar to Rome, where they remained until his assassination in 44 B.C.

Growth of Roman Power to 44 B.C.

	500 B.C.
	to 264 B.C.
	to 146 B.C.
	to 44 B.C.
▨	Territory gained from Carthage
→	Hannibal's invasion route

Azimuthal Equal Area Projection
0 — 250 — 500 Miles
0 — 250 — 500 Kilometers

Geography Through wars and diplomacy, the Roman republic gradually gained control of lands around the Mediterranean Sea.

1. **Location** On the map, locate (a) Spain, (b) Gaul, (c) Carthage, (d) Egypt, (e) Macedonia.
2. **Place** During what period did Asia Minor come under Roman control?
3. **Critical Thinking Recognizing Causes and Effects** How did Rome gain so much territory between 264 B.C. and 146 B.C?

Decline of the Republic

Unable to resolve its problems peacefully, Rome was plunged into a series of civil wars. At issue was who should hold power—the senate, which wanted to govern as it had in the past, or popular political leaders, who wanted to weaken the senate and enact reforms.

The turmoil sparked slave uprisings and revolts among Rome's allies. Meanwhile, the old legions of Roman citizen-soldiers became professional armies whose first loyalty was to their commanders. Rival generals marched their armies into Rome to advance their ambitions.

Julius Caesar's Rise to Power Out of this chaos emerged Julius Caesar, an ambitious military commander. For a time, Caesar dominated Roman politics with Pompey, another brilliant general. Then, in 59 B.C., Caesar set out with his army to make new conquests. After nine years of fighting, he completed the conquest of Gaul—the area that is now France.

Fearful of Caesar's rising fame, Pompey persuaded the senate to order Caesar to disband his army and return to Rome. Caesar defied the order. Swiftly and secretly, he led his army across the Rubicon River into northern Italy and then headed toward Rome. Once again, civil war erupted across the Roman world.

Caesar crushed Pompey and his supporters. He then swept around the Mediterranean, suppressing rebellions. *"Veni, vidi, vici"*—"I came, I saw, I conquered"—he announced after one victory. Later, returning to Rome, he forced the senate to make him dictator. Although he kept the senate and other features of the republic, he was in fact the absolute ruler of Rome.

Caesar's Reforms Between 48 B.C. and 44 B.C., Caesar pushed through a number of reforms intended to deal with Rome's many problems. He

ANSWER 1. Review locations with students. 2. between 146 B.C. and 44 B.C. 3. Winning the Punic Wars against Carthage gave Rome a foothold in Spain.

Resource Directory

Teaching Resources

Biography Activity *Cleopatra VII,* Unit 2 booklet, p. 52
Primary Source Activity *Nero Sings While Rome Burns,* Unit 2 booklet, p. 53

Technology

World History Color Transparencies *Roman Expansion* base map and overlay transparencies, set 1, pp. B–19, B–21, B–23, B–25

launched a program of public works to employ the jobless and gave public land to the poor. He also reorganized the government of the provinces and granted Roman citizenship to more people. Caesar's most lasting reform was the introduction of a new calendar based on Egyptian knowledge. The Julian calendar, as it was later called, was used in western Europe for over 1,600 years. With minor changes, it is still our calendar today.

Assassination and Civil Wars Caesar's enemies worried that he planned to make himself king of Rome. In order to save the republic, they plotted against him. In March 44 B.C., as Caesar arrived in the senate, his enemies stabbed him to death.

The death of Julius Caesar plunged Rome into a new round of civil wars. Mark Antony, Caesar's chief general, and Octavian, Caesar's grand-nephew, joined forces to hunt down the murderers. The two men soon quarreled, however, setting off a bitter struggle for power. In 31 B.C., Octavian finally defeated Antony and his powerful ally Queen Cleopatra of Egypt.

Roman Empire and Roman Peace

The senate gave the triumphant Octavian the title of *Augustus,* or Exalted One, and declared him *princeps,* or first citizen. Although he was careful not to call himself king, a title that Romans had hated since Etruscan times, Augustus exercised absolute power and named his successor, just as a king would do.

Under Augustus, who ruled from 31 B.C. to A.D. 14, the 500-year-old republic came to an end. Romans did not know it at the time, but a new age had dawned—the age of the Roman empire.

A Stable Government Through firm but moderate policies, Augustus laid the foundation for a stable government. Although he left the senate in place, Augustus created an efficient, well-trained civil service to enforce the laws. High-level jobs were open to men of talent, regardless of their class. In addition, he cemented the allegiance of cities and provinces to Rome by allowing them a large measure of self-government.

Augustus undertook economic reforms, too. To make the tax system more fair, he ordered a census, or population count, to be taken in the empire. He set up a postal service and issued new coins to make trade easier. He put the jobless to work building roads and temples and sent others to farm the land.

The government that Augustus organized functioned well for 200 years. Still, a serious problem kept arising: Who would rule after an emperor died? Romans did not accept the idea of power passing automatically from father to son. As a result, the death of an emperor often led to intrigue and violence.

Bad Emperors and Good Emperors Not all of Augustus' successors were great rulers. Indeed, some were weak and incompetent. Two early emperors, Caligula and Nero, were downright evil and perhaps insane. Caligula, for example, appointed his favorite horse as consul. Nero viciously persecuted Christians and was even blamed for setting a great fire that destroyed much of Rome.

Between A.D. 96 and A.D. 180, the empire benefited from the rule of a series of "good emperors." The emperor Hadrian, for example, codified Roman law, making it the same for all provinces. He also had soldiers build a wall across Britain to hold back attackers from the non-Roman north.

The emperor Marcus Aurelius, who read philosophy while on military campaigns, was close to Plato's ideal of a philosopher-king. His *Meditations* show his Stoic philosophy and commitment to duty: "Hour by hour resolve firmly . . . to do what comes to hand with correct and natural dignity."

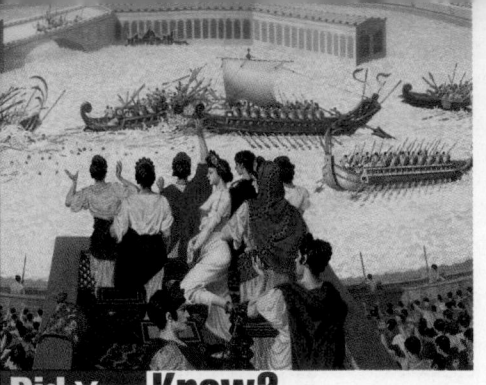

Did You Know?

The Colosseum

Romans marveled at the shows put on at the Colosseum, ancient Rome's largest stadium. Spectators watched the slaughter of exotic animals, gladiators battling to the death, and mock naval battles, like the one shown above.

The Colosseum was an architectural marvel. Its floor was about the size of a modern football field. As many as 50,000 spectators could crowd onto the Colosseum's marble and wooden benches. There, they were protected from the hot Roman sun by a giant canvas roof.

Theme: Political and Social Systems How does the architectural accomplishment of the Colosseum contrast with what took place there?

The Pax Romana The 200-year span that began with Augustus and ended with Marcus Aurelius is known as the period of the *Pax Romana,* or "Roman Peace." During that time, Roman rule brought peace, order, unity, and prosperity to lands stretching from the Euphrates River in the east to Britain in the west, an area approximately equal in size to the continental United States.

During the Pax Romana, Roman legions maintained and protected the roads, and Roman fleets chased pirates from the seas. Trade flowed freely to and from distant lands in Africa and Asia. Egyptian farmers in the Nile Valley supplied Romans with grain. From other parts of Africa came ivory and gold, as well as lions and other wild animals that were used in public entertainments. From India came spices, cotton, and precious stones. Trade caravans traveled along the great Silk Road, bringing silk and other goods from China.

People too, moved easily within the Roman empire, spreading ideas and knowledge, especially the advances of the Hellenistic east. As you will read, ideas from Greece and Judea would have tremendous impact on Rome and the western world.

Bread and Circuses Throughout the empire, rich and poor alike loved spectacular entertainments. At the Circus Maximus, Rome's largest racecourse, chariots thundered around an oval course, making dangerously tight turns at either end. Fans bet feverishly on their favorite teams—the Reds, Greens, Blues, or Whites—and successful charioteers were hailed as heroes.

Gladiator contests were even more popular. Many gladiators were slaves who had been trained to fight. In the arena, they battled one another, either singly or in groups. Crowds cheered a skilled gladiator, and a good fighter might even win his freedom. But if a gladiator made a poor showing, the crowd turned thumbs down, a signal that he should be killed.

To the emperors who paid for them with the taxes they collected from the empire, these amusements were a way to pacify the city's restless mobs. In much the same spirit, the government provided free grain to feed the poor. Critics warned against this policy of "bread and circuses," but few listened.

During the Pax Romana, the general prosperity hid underlying social and economic problems. Later Roman emperors, however, would face problems that could not be solved with "bread and circuses."

SECTION 2 Assessment

Recall

1. Identify: (a) Punic Wars, **(b)** Hannibal, **(c)** Tiberius and Gaius Gracchus, **(d)** Julius Caesar, **(e)** Augustus, **(f)** Hadrian, **(g)** Pax Romana, **(h)** Circus Maximus.

2. Define: (a) imperialism, **(b)** province, **(c)** latifundia, **(d)** census.

Comprehension

3. How did Rome build an empire around the Mediterranean Sea?

4. What problems contributed to the decline of the Roman republic?

5. How did Augustus lay the foundation for stable government in the Roman empire?

Critical Thinking and Writing

6. Analyzing Information How do you think the founders of the Roman republic would have viewed the government of the Roman empire? Explain.

7. Predicting Consequences What were some possible negative consequences of following the policy of "bread and circuses"?

136 Chapter 6

Reading Focus

- How was Greco–Roman civilization formed?
- What were some Roman contributions to literature, the arts, and technology?
- What principles of law did Romans develop?

Vocabulary

satirize
mosaic
engineering
aqueduct

Taking Notes

Make a table like the one below to focus on the cultural achievements of the Romans. Add more information and more rows as you read the section.

LAW	Civil law, law of nations
LITERATURE	Virgil's *Aeneid*
HISTORY	

Main Idea Romans absorbed ideas from other cultures and made great advances in law, literature, engineering, and other areas.

Setting the Scene

Marcus Tullius Cicero was a philosopher, politician, and passionate defender of law. As the republic declined, he attacked ambitious men such as Julius Caesar. When Caesar came to power, however, he forgave Cicero, noting that it was "more glorious to have enlarged the limits of the Roman mind than the boundaries of Roman rule."

Romans such as Cicero and Caesar both had a lasting impact. Through war and conquest, Roman generals carried the achievements of Roman civilization to distant lands. Yet the civilization that developed was not simply Roman. Rather, it blended Greek, Hellenistic, and Roman achievements.

Greco-Roman Civilization

In its early days, Rome absorbed ideas from Greek colonists in southern Italy, and it continued to borrow heavily from Greek culture after it conquered Greece. To the Romans emerging from their villages, Greek art, literature, philosophy, and scientific genius represented the height of cultural achievement. Their admiration never wavered, leading the Roman poet Horace to note, "Greece has conquered her rude conqueror."

The Romans adapted Greek and Hellenistic achievements, just as the Greeks had once absorbed ideas from Egypt and the Fertile Crescent. The blending of Greek, Hellenistic, and Roman traditions produced what is known as Greco-Roman civilization. Trade and travel during the Pax Romana helped spread this vital new civilization.

Literature, Philosophy, and History

In the field of literature, the Romans owed a great debt to the Greeks. Many Romans spoke Greek and imitated Greek styles in prose and poetry. Still, the greatest Roman writers used Latin to create their own literature.

Poetry In his epic poem, the *Aeneid*, Virgil tried to show that Rome's past was as heroic as that of Greece. He linked his epic to Homer's work by telling how Aeneas escaped from Troy to found Rome. Virgil wrote the *Aeneid* soon after Augustus came to power. He hoped it would arouse patriotism and help unite Rome after years of civil wars.

Other poets used verse to satirize, or make fun of, Roman society. Horace's satires were gentle, using playful wit to attack human folly. Juvenal and Martial were more biting. Martial's poems were so harsh that he had to use fictitious names to protect himself from retribution.

Primary Source

A Roman Epic
In the opening lines of the Aeneid, *Virgil introduces "the hero" Aeneas and hints at his daring and destiny:*

"I tell about war and the hero who first from Troy's frontier,
Displaced by destiny, came . . .
To Italy—a man much travailed on sea and land
By the powers above, because of the brooding anger of [the goddess] Juno,
Suffering much in war until he could found a city
And march his gods into Latium, whence rose the Latin race,
. . . and the high walls of Rome."

—Virgil, *Aeneid*

Skills Assessment

Primary Source What forces caused Aeneas' suffering and led to his founding of Rome?

Bell Ringer On the chalkboard, list students' responses to this question: What legal principles guide judges and lawyers in American courtrooms today? Have the students compare their list to the list of Roman legal principles at the end of Section 3, under the subsection "Roman Law."

LESSON PLAN

1. Focus Because Rome absorbed ideas from the lands it conquered, Roman civilization became a blend of Greek, Hellenistic, and Roman traditions. The Romans made important advances in architecture, engineering, and practical science. Students will also learn about Roman contributions in literature, history, philosophy, and, most importantly, law.

2. Instruct Work with the class to create a Venn diagram showing the achievements of Greco-Roman civilization. Draw two large overlapping circles on the chalkboard. Have students list Greek achievements in one circle and Roman achievements in the other. Greco-Roman traditions should be listed in the part of the diagram where the two circles overlap.

3. Assess Ask groups of students to design and create bulletin boards that highlight Rome's accomplishments. Invite volunteers from each group to describe their presentations to the class.

4. Reteach If students' **Assess** activity does not reflect adequate understanding of the lesson, you might assign the *Guide to the Essentials* or the *Interactive Student Tutorial CD-ROM* for this section.

Block Scheduling Support

Have students create an enlarged design for a Roman coin celebrating an important achievement of Roman civilization. Have them explain their creation to the class. Remind students that some parts of a coin's design may be literal, such as a portrait or a building; other parts may be symbolic. Have students use leader lines to label the design elements on the coin and explain their significance.

Test Preparation

Have students read the section titled "Poetry," and then answer the question below.

Who wrote the *Aeneid*?

A Martial

B Juvenal

C Augustus

D Virgil

Primary Source

ANSWER Both his suffering and his founding of Rome were caused by the involvement of the gods, especially Juno.

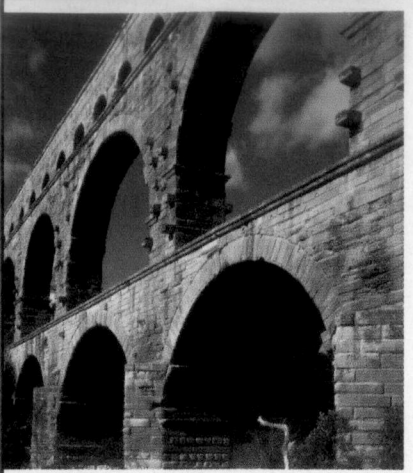

A Roman Aqueduct
Roman engineers built this aqueduct across the Gardon River in present-day France.
Theme: Economics and Technology Why were aqueducts important to Roman towns?

History Roman historians pursued their own theme—the rise and fall of Roman power. Like the poet Virgil, the historian Livy sought to rouse patriotic feeling and restore traditional Roman virtues by recalling images of Rome's heroic past. In his history of Rome, Livy recounted tales of great heroes such as Horatius and Cincinnatus.

Another historian, Tacitus, wrote bitterly about Augustus and his successors, who, he felt, had destroyed Roman liberty. He admired the simple culture of the Germans who lived on Rome's northern frontier and would later invade the empire.

Philosophy Romans borrowed much of their philosophy from the Greeks. The Hellenistic philosophy of Stoicism impressed Roman thinkers like the emperor Marcus Aurelius. Stoics stressed the importance of duty and acceptance of one's fate. They also showed concern for the well-being of all people, an idea that would be reflected in Christian teachings. (See Section 4 of this chapter.)

Art and Architecture

To a large degree, Roman art and architecture were based on Greek and Etruscan models. However, as with literature, the Romans made adaptations to develop their own style.

Art Like the Greeks before them, Roman sculptors stressed realism, portraying their subjects with every wart and vein in place. The Romans also broke new ground, however, by revealing an individual's character. A statue of a soldier, a writer, or an emperor might capture an expression of smugness, discontent, or haughty pride.

Some Roman sculpture was more idealistic. For example, sculptors transformed Augustus, who was neither handsome nor imposing, into a symbol of power and leadership.

Romans beautified their homes with works of art. Examples of these works were preserved in Pompeii, a city buried by the volcanic eruption of Mount Vesuvius in A.D. 79. Artists depicted scenes from Roman literature and daily life in splendid frescoes and mosaics. A mosaic is a picture made from chips of colored stone or glass.

Architecture While the Greeks aimed for simple elegance in architecture, the Romans emphasized grandeur. Immense palaces, temples, and stadiums stood as mighty monuments to Roman power and dignity. The Romans improved on devices such as the column and the arch. Using concrete as a building material, they developed the rounded dome to roof large spaces. The most famous domed structure is the Pantheon, a temple to all the Roman gods, which still stands in Rome.

Technology and Science

The Romans excelled in engineering, which is the application of science and mathematics to develop useful structures and machines. Roman engineers built roads, bridges, and harbors throughout the empire. Roman roads were so solidly built that many of them were still used long after the fall of the empire.

Roman engineers also built many immense aqueducts, or bridgelike stone structures that brought water from the hills into Roman cities. The wealthy had water piped in, and almost every city boasted public baths. Here, people gathered not only to wash themselves but to hear the latest news and exchange gossip.

The Romans generally left scientific research to the Greeks who were by that time citizens of the empire. In Alexandria, Egypt, Hellenistic scientists

Vesuvius Erupts!

One summer day in A.D. 79, the townspeople of Pompeii, a wealthy Roman resort town, felt tremors and heard a low rumble but were not alarmed. Though they lived in the shadow of a huge volcano, no one could remember the last time it had erupted. Within hours, a giant explosion had ripped off the mountaintop. Within two days, the town of Pompeii had disappeared.

Before the eruption, Pompeii was a busy town. Its fanciest homes boasted beautiful mosaic floors and colorful murals.

As ash started to fall, many people tried to flee while others sought safety in their cellars. Still, most people suffocated and were buried in the ash. Rain hardened the ash, forming perfect molds of people and preserving articles of everyday living.

With little warning, Mt. Vesuvius exploded. Gas and hot, liquid rock burst through the cone, shooting ash and whole rocks into the air. Spectacular lightning bolts and clouds of ash filled the sky.

This is a cast of the body of a child who was entombed in the hardened ash.

Portfolio Assessment

 Use the Internet or other research sources to learn about a recent volcanic eruption. Use the information you find to write articles about the event for the front page of a newspaper. You may want to use pictures or diagrams to illustrate the articles.

EXPLORING the HUMAN DRAMA Human Drama Activity

Persuasive Letter The debate continues about how to preserve Pompeii from further deterioration wrought by people and the environment. A law recently passed in Italy allows industrialists to adopt a block of Pompeii to protect and restore. In return, they get tax breaks and commercial rights to use any images in their adopted area. Some have suggested going further, letting business people take over the blocks they restore and turn them into entertainment areas with concession stands and activities such as Pompeian parties. Others want a more traditional approach to preservation, such as building a visitors' center where tourists can get an orientation about the ruins from an archaeologist. Have students write letters to the Italian Minister of Culture expressing their views on the best way to preserve the ruins. If students are also doing the Cooperative Learning activity suggested on the page, these letters can be an extension of the research and discussion they do for the group activity.

Bell Ringer Ask students to speculate why people might choose to live near an active volcano if they had a choice of places to live.

Background Connections to Today

Assault on Pompeii This archaeological site is deteriorating so quickly that Pompeii may one day be off-limits to the public. Weather, tourists, thieves, pollution, neglect, and mismanagement all have damaged this site that shows the life of this time so clearly. Sun and rain have faded some frescoes. After thieves stole jewelry and coins from the museum, it closed in 1975.

Activity Cooperative Learning

Pompeii Today Have students form small groups to write a problem-solving essay about preserving Pompeii. Suggest that students focus on problems the site faces, proposed solutions and their drawbacks, and the solution the students recommend. Each group member should be assigned one of the following tasks: researching, making an outline, writing a rough draft, revising, writing the final draft, or proofreading. The group should discuss possible solutions and their drawbacks, and then reach a consensus about the best solution. Initiate a class discussion using the groups' ideas.

Portfolio Assessment Rubrics

Share rubrics with students before they write their newspaper articles.

Attempted The article is poorly researched, omits important information, and is poorly written.

Minimal The article has adequate research but is poorly written.

Adequate The research and writing are carefully done and some graphic elements are included.

Exemplary The article shows careful research and is clearly and dramatically written; graphic elements are well done and informative.

SECTION 3 Assessment

Recall
1. (a) Greco-Roman civilization, p. 137 (b) Virgil, p. 137 (c) Livy, p. 138 (d) Pantheon, p. 138 (e) Galen, p. 140 (f) civil law, p. 140 (g) law of nations, p. 140 2. (a) satirize, p. 137 (b) mosaic, p. 138 (c) engineering, p. 138 (d) aqueduct, p. 138

Comprehension
3. Possible answer: Romans admired and adapted Greek culture, which influenced literature, philosophy, and art. 4. Possible answer: Engineers built huge aqueducts into Roman cities to carry water from the outlying hills directly to public baths or homes. 5. People of the same status were equal before the law; an accused person was innocent until proven guilty; accused people could defend themselves; and judges had broad authority.

Critical Thinking and Writing
6. Students' answers will vary but should reflect an understanding of Roman and American legal principles. 7. (a) He meant that Roman civilization was built on Greek accomplishments. (b) Possible answer: The Romans copied Greek sculpture, architecture, and literature.

Activity Rubrics

Share rubrics with students before they create their portfolios on Roman life.

Attempted The project is attempted but bears little relation to the assignment.

Minimal The project shows some research, but the examples collected are few or the presentation is messy.

Adequate The project shows careful research, and the printouts of various aspects of Roman daily life are compiled neatly in a portfolio.

Exemplary The project is interesting, reflects excellent research and comprehension, and is clearly presented.

Law and Government
Knowledge of the laws and legal procedures of Rome was helpful in pursuing a career in government. Many Roman officials, such as the senator depicted in this sculpture, had argued cases in court and served as judges.

Theme: Continuity and Change Today, many American government officials are lawyers. How do you think this affects the quality of government?

exchanged ideas freely. It was there that astronomer-mathematician Ptolemy (TAHL uh mee) proposed his theory that the Earth was the center of the universe, a mistaken idea that was accepted in the western world for nearly 1,500 years.

The Greek doctor Galen advanced the frontiers of medical science by insisting on experiments to prove a conclusion. Galen compiled a medical encyclopedia summarizing what was known at the time. It remained a standard text for more than 1,000 years.

Although the Romans did little original research, they did put science to practical use. They applied geography to make maps, and medical knowledge to help doctors improve public health. Like Galen, they collected knowledge into encyclopedias. Pliny the Elder, a Roman scientist, compiled volumes on geography, zoology, botany, and other topics, all based on other people's works.

Roman Law

"Let justice be done," proclaimed a Roman saying, "though the heavens fall!" Probably the greatest legacy of Rome was its commitment to the rule of law and to justice. During the Roman empire, the rule of law fostered unity and stability. Many centuries later, the principles of Roman law would become the basis for legal systems in Europe and Latin America.

Two Systems During the republic, Rome developed a system of law, known as the civil law, that applied to its citizens. As Rome expanded, however, it ruled many foreigners who were not covered under the civil law. Gradually, a second system of law, known as the law of nations, emerged. It applied to all people under Roman rule, citizens and noncitizens. Later, when Rome extended citizenship across the empire, the two systems merged.

Common Principles As Roman law developed, certain basic principles evolved. Many of these principles are familiar to Americans today. An accused person was presumed innocent until proven guilty. The accused was allowed to face the accuser and offer a defense against the charge. Guilt had to be established "clearer than daylight" through evidence. Judges were allowed to interpret the laws and were expected to make fair decisions.

SECTION 3 Assessment

Recall
1. **Identify:** (a) Greco-Roman civilization, (b) Virgil, (c) Livy, (d) Pantheon, (e) Galen, (f) civil law, (g) law of nations.
2. **Define:** (a) satirize, (b) mosaic, (c) engineering, (d) aqueduct.

Comprehension
3. How did Greek culture influence the development of Roman civilization?
4. How did Romans use technology to improve life in the empire?
5. What principles of law did Romans develop?

Critical Thinking and Writing
6. **Linking Past and Present** Give two examples of how the principles of law developed by Rome affect life in the United States today.
7. **Analyzing Primary Sources** The Roman poet Horace said of Roman civilization: "Greece has conquered her rude conqueror." (a) What did he mean by this? (b) Give three examples that support his statement.

140 Chapter 6

Activity
Take It to the NET

Roman art often depicted scenes of daily life. Find Internet sites with information about Roman clothing, foods, entertainment, and other aspects of daily life. Use printouts of the sites you visit to create a portfolio on Roman life.

Caption Answer

Possible answer: It improves the quality of government because it is helpful for officials to know the laws and how they are made and applied.

Resource Directory

Teaching Resources
Section Quiz Unit 2 booklet, p. 47
Creative Teaching Activities Creative Teaching Activities booklet, p. 32
Guided Reading and Review Unit 2 booklet, p. 48

Technology
Interactive Student Tutorial CD-ROM Ch. 6
Computer Test Bank Ch. 6

The Rise of Christianity

Reading Focus

- What was Rome's policy toward different religions in the early empire?
- What were the major teachings of Jesus, and how were they spread?
- How did the early Christian Church develop?

Vocabulary

messiah
apostle
martyr
bishop
diocese
patriarch
pope
heresy

Taking Notes

Copy the partially completed flowchart at right. As you read, finish the flowchart by writing in the main events in the rise of Christianity. Add more boxes as needed.

Romans tolerate various religions
↓
Jesus preaches his ideas
↓
Followers of Jesus spread Christianity
↓
↓

Main Idea A new religion, Christianity, emerged in the Roman empire. It gradually spread and became the official religion of the empire.

Setting the Scene

Early in the Pax Romana, a new religion, Christianity, sprang up in a distant corner of the Roman empire. At first, Christianity was just one of many religions practiced in the empire. But despite many obstacles, the new faith grew rapidly, and by A.D. 395, it had been declared the official religion of the Roman empire.

As it gained strength and spread through the empire, Christianity reshaped Roman beliefs. And when the Roman empire fell, the Christian Church took over much of its role, becoming the central institution of western civilization for nearly 1,000 years.

Religious Diversity in the Early Empire

Within the culturally diverse Roman empire, a variety of religious beliefs and practices coexisted. Jupiter, Mars, Juno, and other traditional Roman gods remained important to some people. However, a growing number of people were looking elsewhere for spiritual fulfillment.

Mystery Religions Some turned to mystery religions that emphasized secret rituals and promised special rewards. One of the most popular of these was the cult of Isis, which originated in Egypt and offered women equal status with men. Others worshiped the Persian god Mithras, who championed good over evil and offered life after death. Mithraism was especially favored by Roman soldiers.

Religious Toleration Generally, Rome tolerated the varied religious traditions. As long as citizens showed loyalty by honoring Roman gods and acknowledging the divine spirit of the emperor, they were allowed to worship other gods as they pleased. Because most people at the time were polytheistic, they were content to worship the Roman gods along with their own.

Divisions in Judea By 63 B.C., the Romans had conquered Judea, where most Jews of the time lived. As you have learned, the Jews were devoted to their monotheistic traditions. To avoid violating the Jewish belief in one god, the Romans excused Jews from worshiping Roman gods.

Among the Jews themselves, however, religious ferment was creating deep divisions. During the Hellenistic age, many Jews absorbed Greek customs and ideas. Concerned about the weakening of their religion, Jewish conservatives rejected these influences and called for strict obedience to Jewish laws and traditions.

Global Connections

A Jewish-Greek Connection

During Roman times and before, many Jews left their homeland in Judea. They settled in lands around the Mediterranean and elsewhere.

Many of those who migrated began to speak Greek instead of Hebrew, and two Greek words became an important part of Jewish history. The Greek word *diaspora*, which means "scattering," refers to the fact that some Jews migrated and settled in various parts of the world. The Greek word *synagogue*, "a bringing together," was used for the places where Jews gathered to read the sacred Torah. Meeting in synagogues helped Jews share ideas, hold their community together, and preserve traditions. Today, synagogues can be found in most major cities throughout the world.

Theme: Global Interaction
How did synagogues help Jewish culture survive the diaspora?

Block Scheduling Support

Have pairs of students imagine that they are members of a group similar to a modern think tank. Roman rulers have asked them to prepare a paper in which they analyze the factors within the empire and within the teachings of Jesus that have caused the rapid spread of this new religion. Have volunteers read their papers to the class, and then have them discuss whether Christianity represents a threat to the Roman Empire.

Bell Ringer Write "The Rise of Christianity" on the chalkboard. Ask students to write down three questions that they would like to explore about this subject. Suggest that they look for this information as they study this section.

LESSON PLAN

1. Focus The Romans tolerated the different religions of the peoples they conquered but also required loyalty to their gods and emperor. In Palestine, Jesus promised spiritual salvation to all who followed his teachings of love, kindness, mercy, and forgiveness. Despite persecution, the new religion of Christianity spread throughout the Roman empire.

2. Instruct Ask students to imagine that they are living in the Roman empire during the early years of Christianity. Have them write diary entries from the point of view of one of the following: a Roman soldier in Palestine, a Jewish Zealot, a disciple of Jesus, a Christian missionary, a Roman emperor, a persecuted Christian, or a Christian bishop. Remind students that their diary entries should refer to historical events and the beliefs of the time. Ask for volunteers to read their entries aloud. Ask students to discuss how accurately these entries reflect the people and events of this historical period.

3. Assess Play a game in which students read their diary entries to the class without identifying their assumed role. Have the class try to identify the historical character who would have written that diary entry.

4. Reteach If students' Assess activity does not reflect adequate understanding of the lesson, you might assign the *Guide to the Essentials* or the *Interactive Student Tutorial CD-ROM* for this section.

Global Connections

ANSWER They helped Jews come together to share ideas, develop communities, and preserve traditions.

Jesus Healing a Woman
Jesus promised everlasting life to all who followed his teachings. This Roman mural depicts Jesus miraculously healing an afflicted woman.
Theme: Religions and Value Systems Which social classes were most attracted to Christianity? Why?

While most Jews were reluctantly willing to live under Roman rule, others, called Zealots, were not. They called on Jews to revolt against Rome and reestablish an independent state. Some Jews believed that a messiah, or anointed king sent by God, would soon appear to lead the Jewish people to freedom.

Jewish Revolt In A.D. 66, discontent flared into rebellion. Roman forces crushed the rebels, captured Jerusalem, and destroyed the Jewish temple. When revolts broke out again in the next century, Roman armies leveled Jerusalem. Thousands of Jews were killed in the fighting, and many others were enslaved and transported to various parts of the empire. Faced with the destruction that resulted from the rebellions, growing numbers of Jews decided to leave Judea.

Although they were defeated in their efforts to regain political independence, Jews survived in scattered communities around the Mediterranean. Over the centuries, Jewish rabbis, or scholars, extended and preserved the religious law, as set forth in the Talmud. Commitment to learning Jewish law and traditions enabled the Jews to survive over the centuries.

Jesus and His Message

As turmoil engulfed the Jews in Palestine, a new religion, Christianity, rose among them. Its founder was a Jew named Jesus.

Almost all that we know about the life of Jesus comes from the Gospels, the first four books of the New Testament of the Bible. These accounts were attributed by early Christians to Matthew, Mark, Luke, and John, four followers of Jesus. *Gospel* comes from the Old English word for "good news."

Life of Jesus Jesus was born about 4 B.C. in Bethlehem, near Jerusalem. According to the Gospels, he was a descendant of King David of Israel. An angel, the Gospels say, told Jesus' mother, Mary, that she would give birth to the messiah. "He will be great," said the angel, "and will be called the Son of the Most High God."

Growing up in the small town of Nazareth, Jesus worshiped God and followed Jewish law. As a young man, he may have worked as a carpenter, the occupation of Mary's husband Joseph. At the age of 30, the Gospels relate, he began preaching to villagers near the Sea of Galilee. To help him in his mission, he recruited twelve close followers, known as the apostles, from the Greek word meaning "a person sent forth." Chief among these was one called Peter.

Large crowds gathered to hear Jesus' teachings, especially when word spread that he had performed miracles of healing. Jesus often used parables, or short stories with simple moral lessons, to communicate his ideas. After three years, he and his disciples, or loyal followers, went to Jerusalem to spread his message there.

The Message Jesus' teachings were firmly rooted in Jewish tradition. Jesus believed in one God and accepted the Ten Commandments. He preached obedience to the laws of Moses and defended the teachings of the Jewish prophets.

At the same time, Jesus preached new beliefs. According to his followers, he called himself the Son of God. Many people believed he was the messiah whose appearance Jews had long predicted. Jesus proclaimed that his mission was to bring spiritual salvation and eternal life to anyone who would believe in him.

In the Sermon on the Mount, Jesus summed up his ethical message, which echoed Jewish ideas of mercy and sympathy for the poor and helpless:

> "Blessed are the meek, for they shall inherit the earth.
> Blessed are those who hunger and thirst for righteousness,
>   for they shall be satisfied.
> Blessed are the merciful, for they shall obtain mercy.
> Blessed are the pure in heart, for they shall see God.
> Blessed are the peacemakers, for they will be called sons of God."
> —Gospel According to Matthew

Jesus emphasized God's love and taught the need for justice, morality, and service to others. According to Jesus, a person's major responsibilities were to "love the Lord your God with all your heart" and to "love your neighbor as yourself." Jesus emphasized the importance of forgiveness. "Love your enemies," he told his followers. "If anyone hits you on one cheek, let him hit the other one, too."

Death on the Cross Some Jews welcomed Jesus to Jerusalem. Others, however, regarded him as a dangerous troublemaker. Jewish priests, in particular, felt that he was challenging their leadership. To the Roman authorities, Jesus was a revolutionary who might lead the Jews in a rebellion against Roman rule.

Jesus was betrayed by one of his disciples, the Gospels state. Arrested by the Romans, he was tried and condemned to be crucified. In crucifixion, a Roman method of execution, a person was nailed to or hung on a cross and left to die.

Jesus' disciples were thrown into confusion. But then rumors spread through Jerusalem that Jesus was not dead at all. His disciples, the Gospels say, saw and talked with Jesus, who had risen from the dead. They say Jesus commanded them to spread his teachings, and that he then ascended into heaven.

Spread of Christianity

Following Jesus' death, the apostles and other disciples spread Jesus' message and helped establish Christian communities. First, they preached only among the Jews of Judea. Slowly, some Jews accepted the teaching that Jesus was the messiah, or the Christ, from the Greek for "the anointed one." These people became the first Christians. For a time, Christianity remained a sect within Judaism.

Gradually, disciples of Jesus began to preach in Jewish communities throughout the Roman world. According to tradition, Peter established Christianity in the city of Rome itself. However, it was Paul, a Jew from Asia Minor, who played the most influential role in the spread of Christianity.

Work of Paul Paul had never seen Jesus. In fact, he had been among those who persecuted Jesus' followers. Then one day, Paul had a vision in which Jesus spoke to him. Immediately converting to the new faith, Paul made an important decision. He would spread the teachings of Jesus beyond Jewish communities to gentiles, or non-Jews.

Paul's missionary work set Christianity on the road to becoming a world religion. A tireless traveler, Paul journeyed around the Mediterranean and set up churches from Mesopotamia to Rome. In long letters to the Christian communities, he explained difficult doctrines, judged disputes, and expanded Christian teachings. These letters are part of the New Testament. In his writings, Paul emphasized the idea that Jesus had sacrificed his life out of love for humankind. Paul promised that those

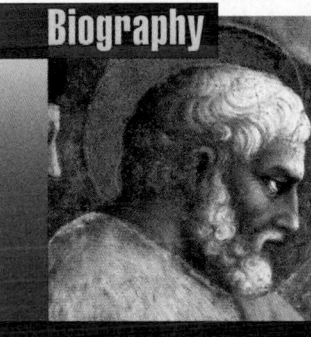
Peter means "rock" in Greek. The name was given to Simon by Jesus, who is quoted in the New Testament as saying, "Thou art Peter, and upon this rock I will build my church."

Peter, the chief apostle, devoted his life to spreading the teachings of Jesus. Peter became a missionary. He is said to have become the first bishop of both Antioch and Rome.

Peter's devotion cost him his life. Tradition tells of Peter's persecution under the Roman Emperor Nero. In one account, when Peter learns he is to be crucified, he insists on being turned upside down. He says he is not worthy of dying in the same way that Jesus had died.

Theme: Impact of the Individual Why do you think that much of what we know of Peter comes from legend rather than historical evidence?

 Primary Sources and Literature

See "St. Paul: First Letter to the Corinthians" in the Reference Section at the back of this book.

Have students read the subsection titled "Work of Paul" on this page, and then answer the question below.

According to the passage, which of the following did Paul *not* do?

A persecute followers of Jesus

B write letters to Christian communities

C meet Jesus and speak to him

D help make Christianity a world religion

ANSWER Possible answer: Historical evidence from that time period is not available, especially since Peter was a little-known religious leader during his own time.

Reading Strategy
Reinforcing Key Ideas

As they read, ask students to look for issues, events, ideas, and beliefs that led to the rise of Christianity during the Pax Romana. Have them list specific ways in which Christianity spread across the Roman empire. *(Less Advanced Readers)*

Background
Connections to Today

Religious Persecution Religious persecution has occurred throughout history. It has happened in many lands, and it has victimized people of many religions. Unfortunately, it still continues today.

In the 1990s, religious differences and intolerance ignited conflicts around the world. In the Balkan states of southeastern Europe, Roman Catholics, Eastern Orthodox Christians, and Muslims participated in civil wars and international struggles based on centuries-old animosities. In Israel, Jews and Palestinian Arabs still found lasting peace elusive. After the Persian Gulf War of 1991, thousands of Shiite Muslims fled Iraq to escape the army of Iraq's Sunnite government. In Tibet, Buddhists still found the Chinese government intolerant of their religious beliefs as military crackdowns took place yet again.

As an enrichment exercise, you may wish to assign some students to do a research activity on these or other examples of modern religious conflict.

Spread of Christianity to A.D. 476

- Christian areas, A.D. 325
- Christian areas added by A.D. 476
- Boundary of Roman empire, A.D. 476
- → Paul's first journey
- --→ Paul's second journey
- ---→ Paul's third journey
- ····→ Paul's journey to Rome

Skills Assessment

Geography Aided by the work of Paul and other missionaries, Christianity gradually spread across the Roman empire.

1. **Location** On the map, locate (a) Jerusalem, (b) Asia Minor, (c) Antioch, (d) Constantinople, (e) Alexandria.
2. **Movement** In what areas did Paul travel on his first journey?
3. **Critical Thinking** **Connecting to Geography** How was the Mediterranean Sea important in the spread of Christianity?

who believed Jesus was the son of God and followed his teachings would achieve salvation, or eternal life.

Persecution Rome's tolerant attitude toward religion did not extend to Christianity. Roman officials suspected Christians of disloyalty to Rome because they refused to make sacrifices to the emperor or to honor the Roman gods. When Christians met in secret to avoid persecution, rumors spread that they were engaged in evil practices.

In times of trouble, persecution increased. Roman rulers like Nero used Christians as scapegoats, blaming them for social or economic ills. Over the centuries, thousands of Christians became martyrs, people who suffer or die for their beliefs. According to tradition, both Peter and Paul were killed in Rome during the reign of Nero.

Reasons for Christianity's Appeal Despite the attacks, Christianity continued to spread. The reasons were many. Jesus had welcomed all people, especially the humble, poor, and oppressed. They found comfort in his message of love. Equality, human dignity, and the promise of a better life beyond the grave were very attractive teachings.

As they did their work, Christian missionaries like Paul added ideas from Plato, the Stoics, and other Greek thinkers to Jesus' message. Educated Romans, in particular, were attracted to a religion that incorporated the discipline and moderation of Greek philosophy.

The work of missionaries such as Paul was made easier by the unity of the Roman empire. Christians traveled along Roman roads and across the Mediterranean Sea, which was protected by Roman fleets. Early Christian documents were usually written in Greek or Latin, languages that many people in the empire understood.

144 Chapter 6

Skills Assessment

ANSWERS 1. Review locations with students. **2.** From Antioch, he traveled through Asia Minor to Ephesus, Philippi, and Athens. Then he traveled to Corinth, north to Thessalonica, back to Philippi, down the eastern coast of Asia Minor, and by land to Jerusalem. **3.** Paul and other missionaries crossed the sea to carry the teachings of Jesus to various parts of the Roman empire.

Even persecution brought new converts. Observing the willingness of Christians to die for their religion, people were impressed by the strength of Christians' belief. "The blood of the martyr is the seed of the [Christian] Church," noted one Roman.

Triumph The persecution of Christians finally ended in A.D. 313, when the emperor Constantine issued the Edict of Milan. It granted freedom of worship to all citizens of the Roman empire. In making his decision, Constantine was influenced by his mother, who was a devout Christian. Some 80 years later, the emperor Theodosius (thee uh DOH shuhs) made Christianity the official religion of the Roman empire.

The Early Christian Church

Early Christian communities shared a common faith in the teachings of Jesus and a common way of worship. Only gradually did the scattered communities organize a structured Church.

Patterns of Life and Worship A person fully joined the Christian community by renouncing evil in the rite of baptism. Christians believed that through baptism their sins were forgiven by the grace of God. Members of the community were considered equals, and they addressed each other as "brother" or "sister." Each Sunday, Christians gathered for a ceremony of thanksgiving to God. The baptized ate bread and drank wine in a sacred meal called the Eucharist. They did this in memory of Jesus, whose last supper was described in the Gospels. Justin, an early Christian philosopher and martyr, tried to explain the Eucharist in a letter to the Roman emperor and senate:

> "And this food is called among us the Eucharist. . . . For not as common bread and common drink do we receive these; but in like manner as Jesus Christ our Savior, having been made flesh by the Word of God . . . so likewise we have been taught that the food which is blessed by the prayer of his word, and from which our blood and flesh by transformation are nourished, is the flesh and blood of that Jesus who was made flesh."
>
> —*First Apology of Justin*

Role of Women Women often led the way to Christianity. Many welcomed its promise that in the Church "there is neither Jew nor Greek . . . neither slave nor free . . . neither male nor female." In early Christian communities, women served as teachers and administrators. Even when they were later barred from any official role in the Church, they still worked to win converts across the Roman world.

Structure of the Church Each Christian community had its own priest. Only men were allowed to become members of the Christian clergy. Priests came under the authority of a **bishop**, a Church official who was responsible for all Christians in an area called a **diocese** (dī uh sihs). Bishops traced their spiritual authority to the apostles, and through the apostles, to Jesus himself. In the early Christian Church, all bishops were considered equal successors of the apostles.

Gradually, the bishops of the most important cities in the Roman empire gained greater authority. The bishops of Rome, Antioch, Alexandria, Jerusalem, and Constantinople gained the honorary title of **patriarch**, and exercised authority over other bishops in their area. Except for Rome, the cities in which patriarchs resided were all in the eastern empire. The Christian Church thus developed into a hierarchy, or organization in which officials are arranged according to rank.

A Sacred Meal
Christians gathered frequently to celebrate the sacred meal of the Eucharist. The gilded plate and chalice shown here held the bread and wine of the Eucharist.

Theme: Religions and Value Systems Why did Christians consider the Eucharist so important?

Simeon Stylites The early years of Christianity included ascetics who chose to inflict physical punishment on themselves. Some ate only unlikely things such as grass or wore heavy iron chain belts. A man called Simeon Stylites (A.D. 388–459) lived as a hermit after being dismissed from a monastery for excessive attempts to do penance. In an effort to escape the crowds who came to see him, Simeon sat on top of a stone column for the rest of his life—37 years. Throughout Syria, other believers erected their own pillars. The practice of sitting on pillars remained in use among a small number of followers in the Near East for six centuries.

The practice has not completely died out. In the 1990s, a man on the Indonesian island of Sulawesi lived in a cashew-nut tree for several years. His reason, however, was not religious. He climbed 60 feet to the top of the tree after an argument with his wife.

Caption Answer

They believed that through the Eucharist they were receiving the body and blood of Jesus.

Recall

1. (a) Jesus, p. 142 (b) Gospels, p. 142
(c) Paul, p. 143 (d) Edict of Milan, p. 145
2. (a) messiah, p. 142 (b) apostle, p. 142
(c) martyr, p. 144 (d) bishop, p. 145
(e) diocese, p. 145 (f) patriarch, p. 145
(g) pope, p. 146 (h) heresy, p. 146

Comprehension

3. Generally, Rome tolerated different religious traditions, as long as citizens showed loyalty by honoring Roman gods and acknowledging the divine spirit of the emperor. Rome even excused Jews from worshiping Roman gods. 4. (a) Possible answer: A person's main duties were to love God "with all your heart," "love your neighbor as yourself," and to forgive others. (b) Possible answer: Jesus welcomed all people, especially the humble, poor, and oppressed. People found comfort in his message of love. 5. Early Christians joined the church by renouncing evil through baptism; they considered all community members equal; they gathered on Sundays for ceremonies of thanksgiving; the baptized partook of a sacred meal called the Eucharist; women served as teachers and administrators; each community had a priest.

Critical Thinking and Writing

6. Answers may vary, but most students will agree that Roman geography and Roman roads made it easy for Christian missionaries to safely reach all parts of the empire. 7. Possible answer: If the Christians did not honor Roman gods, maybe they would also not honor the emperor.

Activity Rubrics

Share rubrics with students before they write their biographical sketches.

Attempted Students attempt the project but fail to conduct sufficient research or prepare an incomplete biographical sketch.

Minimal Biographical sketches show some research and are in the correct format.

Adequate Biographical sketches show good research, include sufficient information, and are in the correct format.

Exemplary Biographical sketches are well organized and well written, show thorough research, and include interesting facts.

Divisions in the Church As the rituals and structure of the Church became more defined, divisions began to arise. A major divisive force was rivalry among the patriarchs. In the Latin-speaking west, bishops of Rome, who came to be called popes, began to claim greater authority over all other bishops. In the Greek-speaking east, the patriarchs felt that the five patriarchs should share spiritual authority as equals.

Another source of disunity was the emergence of heresies, or beliefs said to be contrary to official Church teachings. To end disputes over questions of faith, councils of Church leaders met to decide official Christian teachings. The Church also sent out missionaries both within the Roman empire and beyond to convert people to Christianity.

Theology and Scholarship Early Christians produced an abundance of works on Judeo-Christian theology. The word *theology* was borrowed from Greek philosophy and literally means "talk or discourse about God."

Two leading scholars of the early Christian Church were Clement and Origen. Both lived and worked as teachers in the Egyptian city of Alexandria, a major center of learning in the Roman world. And, like most Christian scholars of their time, they both wrote in Greek.

Origen was most respected for his intellectual achievements. Though he fully accepted the traditions of the Gospels, he also believed that he and other Christians could reach a deeper understanding of Jesus' teachings through reflection. Several of his works, such as *On Prayer* and *On First Principles,* exerted a lasting influence on Christianity.

Perhaps the greatest of the early Church scholars was Augustine, who was bishop of Hippo in North Africa. He combined Greco-Roman learning, especially the philosophy of Plato, with Christian doctrine. Shocked by the sack of Rome in 410, Augustine wrote *The City of God.* In this work, Augustine said the City of God was the community of those who loved God and would one day live with him in heaven. Those whose minds and hearts were set only on worldly things lived outside the City of God.

Looking Ahead

While the Christian Church was growing in strength and influence, Roman power was fading. When the western Roman empire finally collapsed, the Church inherited many of its functions. The Church preserved and spread not only Christian teachings but also the achievements of Greco-Roman civilization. In this way, the foundation was laid for the future development of western civilization.

SECTION 4 Assessment

Recall

1. **Identify:** (a) Jesus, (b) Gospels, (c) Paul, (d) Edict of Milan.
2. **Define:** (a) messiah, (b) apostle, (c) martyr, (d) bishop, (e) diocese, (f) patriarch, (g) pope, (h) heresy.

Comprehension

3. What was Rome's policy toward most of the religions in the empire?
4. (a) Describe three basic teachings of Jesus. (b) Why did many people find Jesus' ideas attractive?
5. What beliefs and practices did early Christians have in common?

Critical Thinking and Writing

6. **Synthesizing Information** How do you think the geography of the Roman empire and Rome's extensive road system helped Christianity to spread?
7. **Making Inferences** Some emperors persecuted Christians for their refusal to make sacrifices to the emperor or to honor Roman gods. Why do you think emperors considered this refusal a threat to the empire?

Activity
Take It to the NET

Use Internet sources to find information about the life and career of Origen or Augustine. Use the information to write a brief biographical sketch of the person you have chosen.

Resource Directory

Teaching Resources

Section Quiz Unit 2 booklet, p. 49
Creative Teaching Activities Creative Teaching Activities booklet, p. 33
Guided Reading and Review Unit 2 booklet, p. 50
Geography and History Activity *Examining Empires Geographically,* Geography and History booklet, pp. 4–5

Technology

Interactive Student Tutorial CD-ROM Ch. 6
Computer Test Bank Ch. 6

The Long Decline

Reading Focus

- How did Roman emperors try to end the crisis in the empire?
- How did Hun invasions contribute to the decline of Rome?
- How did economic and social problems lead to the fall of Rome?

Vocabulary

inflation
mercenary

Taking Notes

Copy the partially completed cause-and-effect chart below. As you read, fill in two more categories of causes. Then, add individual causes under the appropriate categories.

Military	Political		
• German invasions			
•			

DECLINE OF ROME

Main Idea Foreign invasions, along with political, social, and economic problems, led to the fall of the Roman empire.

Setting the Scene More than 1,500 years ago, the western half of the Roman empire stumbled into ruin. At the time, the spectacle of decline and defeat left Romans stunned. Some looked for reasons for the decay. The Roman historian Ammianus Marcellinus pointed to declining values. "Centers of learning," he wrote, "are now filled with ridiculous amusements . . . and the libraries are closed forever like so many graves." Marcellinus witnessed moral decay among Romans of all classes. Of the powerful, he complained that they "fall away into error and vice." Of the lower classes, he reported that "some spend the whole night in the wine shops . . . or else they play at dice." He was also alarmed about external threats to the empire, such as the invading Huns, who he feared could "force their way through all obstacles."

The end of Roman greatness did not occur overnight. Decay had set in centuries before the final fall. In the late 200s, for example, the empire was divided into two parts, each ruled by a co-emperor. A complex combination of problems led to the decline and fall of the western Roman empire.

Crisis and Reforms

After the death of the emperor Marcus Aurelius in 180, the golden age of the Pax Romana ended. For the next 100 years, political and economic turmoil rocked the Roman empire.

Struggles for Power During this period, a disruptive political pattern emerged. Again and again, emperors were overthrown by political intriguers or ambitious generals who seized power with the support of their troops. Those who rose to the imperial throne in this way ruled for just a few months or years until they, too, were overthrown or assassinated. In one 50-year period, at least 26 emperors reigned. Only one died of natural causes. Political violence and instability, rather than order and efficiency, thus became the rule.

Economic and Social Problems At the same time, the empire was shaken by disturbing social and economic trends. High taxes to support the army and the bureaucracy placed heavy burdens on business people and small farmers. Farmland that had been overcultivated for too many years lost its productivity.

Many poor farmers left their land and sought protection from wealthy landowners. Living on large estates, they worked for the landowners and

Sharing Power
Co-emperors Diocletian and Maximian shared the responsibility of ruling and defending the empire. Both established mobile imperial courts so that they could move swiftly to wherever a crisis broke out.

Theme: Political and Social Systems How do you think the division of the empire might have hastened Rome's decline?

Bell Ringer On the chalkboard, write "The Decline and Fall of the Roman Empire." Ask students to speculate about the kinds of problems that could have caused this fall. Have students write down three possible explanations. Tell the class that, after they have finished studying this section, they will refer to their theories to see how accurate they were.

LESSON PLAN

1. Focus Political turmoil marked the end of the Pax Romana. Emperors Diocletian and Constantine attempted to solve the empire's problems through reforms, but the results were mixed and the gradual decline of the empire continued. Students will learn that complex political, social, and economic problems, along with foreign invasions, ended the western Roman empire.

2. Instruct Have students consult the Taking Notes diagram on this page and construct a cause-and-effect chart of factors that caused the decline of the Roman empire. Their charts may include: political, military, economic, and social causes. Remind students that Rome faced serious problems both before and after the reigns of Diocletian and Constantine. Also, advise students to make good use of the map on the following page.

3. Assess Lead students in a discussion of the causes they have outlined. Then, have students select the two problems that they think had the most negative impact on the empire. Encourage students to explain the reasons for their choices.

4. Reteach If students' Assess activity does not reflect adequate understanding of the lesson, you might assign the *Guide to the Essentials* or the *Interactive Student Tutorial CD-ROM* for this section.

Block Scheduling Support

To help students form a deeper appreciation of the power struggles that plagued the Roman empire after A.D. 180, organize the class into four groups and assign each group a 25-year period between A.D. 180 and A.D. 280. Have each group create a time line of Roman rulers. Students should identify the date of each ruler's ascent to power, the date he left power, and the cause of his loss of the imperial throne. Then, assemble the time lines from each group and discuss them with the class.

Caption Answer

Possible answer: At times, the two co-emperors might not have cooperated.

Digging Up the Past Have students look at the map "Invasions of the Roman Empire to A.D. 500" on this page. Note that the northernmost area of the western Roman empire in Britain was invaded several times.

Today, archaeologists continue to unearth evidence of earlier Roman battles at Dorset in England, as well as foundations and mosaics from Roman buildings of the fourth century A.D. The Dorset County Museum today exhibits 12 mosaics, many of which are from Durnovaria, or Roman Dorchester.

One of the unique displays at the museum is of two skeletons, each with battle wounds linked to the campaigns of Vespasian and the Second Legion Augusta in the first century A.D. One skeleton has an iron weapon tip in its spine. The other has a head wound from a Roman pilum.

Artifacts from the Roman period still lie beneath present-day Dorchester.

Invasions of the Roman Empire to A.D. 500

Western Roman empire
Eastern Roman empire
★ Major battle sites

Skills Assessment

Geography Under Roman emperors like Diocletian and Constantine, the eastern empire prospered, but invasions and other problems led to the decline of the west.

1. **Location** On the map, locate **(a)** Rhine River, **(b)** Danube River, **(c)** Adrianople, **(d)** Troyes.
2. **Movement** Which Germanic peoples moved into Britain?
3. **Critical Thinking Analyzing Information** How does the map suggest that the eastern empire was stronger than the western empire?

farmed small plots for themselves. Although technically free, they were not allowed to leave the land.

Emperor Diocletian In 284, the emperor Diocletian (DĪ uh KLEE shuhn) set out to restore order. To make the empire easier to govern, he divided it into two parts. He kept control of the wealthier eastern part himself but appointed a co-emperor to rule the western provinces. The co-emperor was responsible to Diocletian, who retained absolute power.

Diocletian tried to increase the prestige of the emperor by surrounding himself with elaborate ceremonies. He wore purple robes embroidered with gold and a crown encrusted with jewels. Anyone who approached the throne had to kneel and kiss the hem of the emperor's robe.

Diocletian also took steps to end the empire's economic decay. To slow inflation, or the rapid rise of prices, he fixed prices for goods and services. Other laws forced farmers to remain on the land. In cities, sons were required to follow their fathers' occupations. These rules were meant to ensure steady production of food and other goods.

Emperor Constantine In 312, the talented general Constantine gained the throne. As emperor, Constantine continued Diocletian's reforms. More important, he took two steps that changed the course of European history.

First, as you have read, Constantine granted toleration to Christians. By doing so, he encouraged the rapid growth of Christianity within the empire and guaranteed its future success.

Second, he built a new capital, Constantinople, on the Bosporus, the strait that connects the Black and Mediterranean seas. By making his capital there, Constantine made the eastern portion of the empire the center of power. The western Roman empire was in decline, but the eastern Roman

Skills Assessment

ANSWERS 1. Review locations with students. **2.** Angles, Saxons, and Jutes **3.** Possible answer: Unlike the western empire, the eastern empire did not suffer from numerous invasions.

empire, which had more people and greater resources, would prosper for centuries to come.

Mixed Results The reforms of Diocletian and Constantine had mixed results. They revived the economy. And by increasing the power of government, they helped hold the empire together for another century. Still, the reforms failed to stop the long-term decline. In the end, internal problems combined with attacks from outside to bring the empire down.

Foreign Invasions

For centuries, Rome had faced attacks from the Germanic peoples who lived east of the Rhine and north of the Danube rivers. When Rome was powerful, the legions on the frontiers were successful in holding back the invaders. Some of the Germanic peoples who lived along the borders learned Roman ways and became allies of the Romans.

Impact of the Huns As early as A.D. 200, wars in East Asia set off a chain of events that would eventually overwhelm Rome, thousands of miles to the west. Those wars sent the Huns, a nomadic people, migrating across Central Asia. By 350, the Huns reached eastern Europe. These skilled riders fought fierce battles to dislodge the Germanic peoples in their path. The Visigoths, Ostrogoths, and other Germanic peoples crossed into Roman territory seeking safety.

Men armed with spears moved in bands along with women and children, carts and herds, hoping to settle on Roman land. With the empire in decline, Roman legions were hard pressed to halt the invading peoples. Under pressure from attacks, the Roman empire surrendered first Britain, then France and Spain. It was only a matter of time before foreign invaders marched into Italy and took over Rome itself.

Rome Defeated In 378, when a Roman army tried to turn back the Visigoths at Adrianople, it suffered a stunning defeat. Roman power was fading. New waves of invaders were soon hammering at Rome's borders, especially in the west. In 410, the Visigoth general Alaric overran Italy and plundered Rome. Meanwhile, the Vandals moved through Gaul and Spain into North Africa. Gradually, other Germanic peoples occupied more and more of the western Roman empire.

For Rome, the worst was yet to come. Starting in 434, the Hun leader Attila embarked on a savage campaign of conquest across much of Europe. Christians called Attila the "scourge of God" because they believed his attacks were a punishment for the sins of humankind. Attila died in 453. Although his empire collapsed soon after, the Hun invasion sent still more Germanic peoples fleeing into the Roman empire.

Finally, in 476, Odoacer (oh doh AY suhr), a Germanic leader, ousted the emperor in Rome. Later, historians referred to that event as the "fall" of Rome. By then, however, Rome had already lost many of its territories, and Roman power in the west had ended.

Causes of the Fall of Rome

The passing of Rome's power and greatness was a major turning point in the history of western civilization. Why did Rome "fall"? Modern historians identify a number of interrelated causes.

Military Causes Perhaps the most obvious cause of Rome's fall was the Germanic invasions. Still, these attacks were successful in part because Roman legions of the late empire lacked the discipline and training of past Roman armies. To meet its need for soldiers, Rome hired mercenaries, or foreign soldiers serving for pay, to defend its borders. Many were German warriors who, according to some historians, felt little loyalty to Rome.

Background
About the Evidence

Rome's Last Major Historian In all, Ammianus Marcellinus wrote 31 books for his history *Rerum gestarum libri (The Chronicles of Events),* which covered the period from Nerva to the death of Valens in Roman history. Of these, only the last 18 survive, covering the years from A.D. 353 to 378.

Marcellinus wrote vivid accounts of the period's economic and social problems and made insightful judgments of the period's politics. His straightforward accounts often use elaborate literary allusions, metaphors, and other rhetorical devices to give drama to events and characters who made history during this time.

Activity
Interpreting the Evidence

Use these additional questions to generate class discussion.

1. Critical Thinking: Analyzing Information How does the information on this page convey the complex nature of this historical event? *(Possible answer: graphic organizer gives an overview of causes, quotation and illustration give details of information in the graphic organizer)*

2. Critical Thinking: Recognizing Causes and Effects What cause shown in the graphic organizer does the quotation illustrate? *(social cause)*

Skills Tip

Arrows in graphic organizers show how its parts are related. Here, they show that military, political, social, and economic causes all caused Rome's decline and fall. The Skills Handbook at the front of this book has a lesson that will help students with this feature.

Skills Assessment

ANSWERS 1. D **2.** E **3.** Possible answers: Agree: we can imitate their successes; disagree: knowing why the empire failed can help us avoid similar mistakes.

Why Did Rome Fall?

Although historians often cite 476 as the official date of the fall of Rome, the Roman empire had been in trouble for centuries. The illustration, the quotation, and the graphic organizer on this page all give clues to why Rome declined.

Hun Warrior

Hun warriors struck fear in the hearts of their enemies. Swooping down on horseback, they shot arrows great distances with deadly accuracy. The Huns were among the many groups of invaders who defeated weakened Roman legions.

Corruption in Rome

"Rome is still looked upon as the queen of the earth, and the name of the Roman people is respected and venerated. But the magnificence of Rome is defaced by the [stupidity] of a few, who never recollect where they are born, but fall away into error and [corruption]. . . . The Romans have even sunk so far, that not long ago, when [there was a famine] and the foreigners were driven from the city, [scholars] were expelled instantly, yet the followers of actresses and all their ilk were [allowed] to stay. . . . "

—Ammianus Marcellinus,
The Luxury of the Rich in Rome

The Decline and Fall of Rome

Military Causes
• Germanic invasions
• Weakened Roman legions

Political Causes
• Oppressive government
• Corrupt officials
• Divided empire

The Decline and Fall of Rome

Social Causes
• Erosion of traditional values
• Self-serving upper class
• "Bread and circuses"

Economic Causes
• Heavy taxes
• Population decline

Skills Tip

Graphic organizers show information in an easy-to-read format. Read the information in the boxes and trace the arrows to determine the main idea of the graphic organizer.

Skills Assessment

1. What type of cause shown in the graphic organizer does the Hun warrior illustrate?
A social cause
B political cause
C economic cause
D military cause

2. According to Ammianus Marcellinus, Rome's greatness was threatened by
E Romans who wanted only amusements.
F an increase in interest in liberal studies.
G invasion by the Huns.
H a shrinking population of foreigners.

3. Critical Thinking Synthesizing Information According to one historian, Rome's decline and fall were a result of its prosperity and power. He said that we should not concern ourselves with why the Roman empire fell, but with why it lasted as long as it did. Using the information above, explain why you agree or disagree with this idea.

Resource Directory

Teaching Resources
Skill Application Activity *Analyzing a Primary Source,* Unit 2 booklet, p. 55
Synthesizing Information Chapter Extension Activities booklet, p. 20
Section Quiz Unit 2 booklet, p. 51
Geography Quiz Unit 2 booklet, p. 56
Chapter Test Forms A, B, and C Unit 2 booklet, pp. 57–61
Answer Key Unit 2 booklet, pp. 78–89

Technology
Interactive Student Tutorial CD-ROM Ch. 6
Computer Test Bank Ch. 6

Political Causes Political problems also contributed to Rome's decline. First, as the government became more oppressive and authoritarian, it lost the support of the people. Growing numbers of corrupt officials undermined loyalty, too. So did frequent civil wars over succession to the imperial throne. Again and again, rival armies battled to have their commanders chosen as emperor. Perhaps most important, dividing the empire at a time when it was under attack may have weakened it beyond repair. The richer eastern Roman empire did little to help the west.

Economic Causes Economic problems were widespread in the empire. Heavier and heavier taxes were required to support the vast government bureaucracy and huge military establishment. At the same time, reliance on slave labor discouraged Romans from exploring new technology. The wealth of the empire dwindled as farmers abandoned their land and the middle classes sank into poverty. Some scholars have suggested that climatic change was yet another reason for reduced agricultural productivity. In addition, the population itself declined as war and epidemic diseases swept the empire.

Social Causes For centuries, worried Romans pointed to the decline in values such as patriotism, discipline, and devotion to duty on which the empire was built. The need to replace citizen soldiers with mercenaries testified to the decline of patriotism. The upper class, which had once provided leaders, devoted itself to luxury and self-interest. Besides being costly, providing "bread and circuses" may also have undermined the self-reliance of the masses.

Did Rome Fall? Although we talk of the "fall" of Rome, the Roman empire did not disappear from the map in 476. An emperor still ruled the eastern Roman empire, which later became known as the Byzantine empire and lasted for another 1,000 years.

The phrase "the fall of Rome" is, in fact, shorthand for a long, slow change from one way of life to another. Roman civilization survived the events of 476. In Italy, people continued to live much as they had before, though under new rulers. Many still spoke Latin and obeyed Roman laws.

Over the next centuries, however, German customs and languages replaced much of Roman culture. Old Roman cities crumbled, and Roman roads disappeared. Still, the Christian Church preserved elements of Roman civilization. In later chapters, you will read how Roman and Christian traditions gave rise to medieval civilization in western Europe.

SECTION 5 Assessment

Recall
1. **Identify:** (a) Diocletian, (b) Constantine, (c) Huns, (d) Visigoths, (e) Alaric, (f) Attila, (g) Odoacer.
2. **Define:** (a) inflation, (b) mercenary.

Comprehension
3. (a) Describe the crisis that afflicted the Roman empire after the Pax Romana ended. (b) List two ways in which Diocletian tried to ease the crisis.
4. How did the invasion of the Huns weaken the Roman empire?

5. What social problems contributed to the decline of the Roman empire?

Critical Thinking and Writing
6. **Linking Past and Present** Imagine that the United States government in Washington no longer existed. What would be the effects on (a) your life, (b) your state, (c) the United States?
7. **Recognizing Causes and Effects** What were the causes and effects of the division of the Roman empire into two parts?

Activity

Creating a Booklet
Create an illustrated booklet explaining why the Roman empire fell. You may wish to use pictures, maps, cartoons, and graphic organizers to illustrate your booklet.

SECTION 5 Assessment

Recall
1. (a) Diocletian, p. 148 (b) Constantine, p. 148 (c) Huns, p. 149 (d) Visigoths, p. 149 (e) Alaric, p. 149 (f) Attila, p. 149 (g) Odoacer, p. 149 2. (a) inflation, p. 148 (b) mercenary, p. 149

Comprehension
3. (a) Political turbulence and economic instability rocked the Roman empire. (b) Diocletian divided the empire into two parts, appointed a co-emperor, and fixed prices for goods and services to help slow inflation. 4. As the Huns migrated across Central Asia and into Eastern Europe, they dislodged Germanic peoples who lay in their path. The Germanic tribes in turn invaded Roman territory seeking safety. Roman armies could not halt the invaders. 5. a decline in values such as patriotism, discipline, devotion to duty, and self-reliance

Critical Thinking and Writing
6. Answers will vary. Possible answer: Without a national government, local governments' powers would increase. Without government restrictions, personal freedoms might increase, but many problems would result from increased lawlessness. 7. A cause of the division of the Roman empire into two parts was to make it easier to govern the empire and to help restore order. An effect of the division was that it may have weakened the empire beyond repair.

Activity Rubrics

Share rubrics with students before they begin making their booklets.

Attempted Students attempt the project, but booklets are incomplete.

Minimal Projects show understanding of the assignment and include one or two visual elements.

Adequate Projects explain the fall of the Roman empire clearly and include helpful illustrations and charts.

Exemplary Projects explain the fall of the Roman empire clearly, include excellent illustrations, and are well executed.

Human Drama Note

What's in a Name? Attila the Hun was so feared that his name, in several cultures, became the stuff of epic poems. In Latin, Attila was called *Flagellum Dei,* Scourge of God. He appears as Etzel in the *Nibelungenlied,* a middle German epic written about 1200, and as Atli in a Norse heroic poem, *The Lay of Atli.* In the *Nibelungenlied,* Etzel and his wife Kriemhild invite her brothers to their court and then proceed to kill nearly everyone. In *The Lay of Atli,* Atli has the heart of one of the brothers cut out and the other brother thrown into a snakepit and then put to death. Did Attila deserve his bloodthirsty reputation? Consider some actual historic events. Attila captured—and then destroyed—a number of important cities. Unable to breach the great walls of Constantinople, Attila destroyed what remained of the eastern Roman troops after they withdrew into Gallipoli. In about 445, he murdered his brother and then ruled the Huns as an autocrat. He was defeated only once in battle; two years later, he invaded Italy and sacked several cities including Azuleia, Patavium, Verona, Brixia, Bergonum, and Mediolanum (Milan). Even today, the name of Attila the Hun is synonymous with ruthless violence.

Creating a Chapter Summary

As a reteaching opportunity, pair more able students with less able students to complete this chapter summary.

Additional entries students might make on their time lines include: 450 B.C.—Laws of the Twelve Tables published; 146 B.C.—Punic Wars end; 133–123 B.C.—reform of the Gracchus brothers; 59 B.C.—Julius Caesar rises to power; 31 B.C.—Octavian Augustus/End of republic and beginning of empire; 4 B.C.—Jesus born; early A.D.—Jesus preaches Christianity; A.D. 66—Romans capture Jerusalem; A.D. 180—Pax Romana ends; A.D. 284—Diocletian's reforms; A.D. 312–313—Constantine becomes Christian/Edict of Milan; A.D. 378—defeat by Visigoths; A.D. 434—beginning of Attila's attacks

Building Vocabulary

1–10. Students' quizzes should show an understanding of each word.

Recalling Key Facts

11. Tribunes could veto laws they felt were harmful to plebeians.
12. Carthage was entirely destroyed; Rome made the surrounding area the new province of Africa; Rome no longer had a rival in the western Mediterranean.
13. It marked the end of the Roman republic and the start of the Roman empire.
14. Peace, order, unity, and prosperity characterized the Pax Romana. Roman legions maintained and protected the roads, Roman fleets protected the seas from piracy, trade flowed freely, and people moved freely throughout the empire, spreading ideas and knowledge.
15. People of the same status are equal before the law; an accused person is presumed innocent until proven guilty; the accused is allowed to face his or her accuser; guilt must be established clearly through evidence; decisions should be based on fairness, allowing judges to interpret the law.
16. Christian missionaries like Paul traveled to Asia Minor and Europe, gaining converts; people adopted the religion because it offered hope.
17. Possible answers: decline in army discipline; government inefficiency and corruption; heavier taxes; lack of patriotism

---

Creating a Chapter Summary

On a sheet of paper create a time line like the one started here. Add other important dates and events. Use the time line to review the events and developments that you have learned about in this chapter.

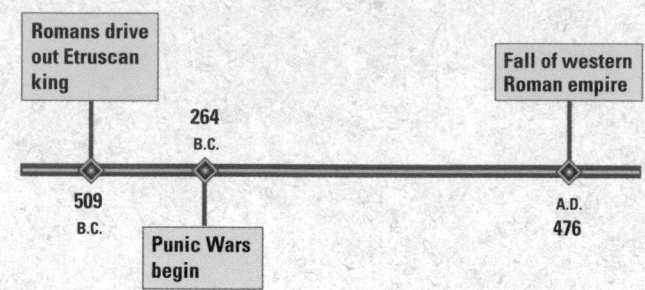

Romans drive out Etruscan king

264 B.C.

509 B.C.

Punic Wars begin

Fall of western Roman empire

A.D. 476

For additional review and enrichment activities, see the interactive version of *World History* available on the Web and on CD-ROM.

Web Site Self-Test
For practice test questions for Chapter 6, see **www.phschool.com**.

Building Vocabulary

Review the chapter vocabulary words listed below. Then, use the words and their definitions to create a matching quiz. Exchange quizzes with another student. Check each other's answers when you are finished.

1. republic
2. dictator
3. plebeian
4. imperialism
5. census
6. satirize
7. aqueduct
8. messiah
9. heresy
10. mercenary

Recalling Key Facts

11. How did tribunes protect plebeian interests in the Roman republic?
12. What were the results of the wars between Rome and Carthage?
13. How did Augustus' rise to power mark a significant change in Rome's form of government?
14. What were the major characteristics of the Pax Romana?
15. What were the important principles of Roman law?
16. How did Christianity spread through the Roman empire?

17. Describe three reasons for the fall of the Roman empire.

Critical Thinking and Writing

18. **Connecting to Geography** **(a)** How did geographic conditions make it easier to unite Italy than to unite Greece? **(b)** How did both Greece and Rome benefit from their location on the Mediterranean Sea?
19. **Making Decisions** Imagine that you were a Roman senator living at the time of Cato. Would you have supported his call to destroy Carthage? Why or why not?
20. **Linking Past and Present** "History," said Cicero, "illuminates reality, vitalizes memory, provides guidance in daily life, and brings us tidings of antiquity." **(a)** How did the work of Roman historians like Livy and Tacitus illustrate Cicero's idea? **(b)** Do you think Cicero's views on the value of history are still valid today? Why or why not?
21. **Solving Problems** **(a)** Describe two policies that Rome might have followed to restore its strength in the later years of the empire. **(b)** Do you think it would have been possible for the Romans to follow such policies? Why or why not?

Critical Thinking and Writing

18. **(a)** The mountains of Italy are not as rugged and widespread as those of Greece. Italy has more fertile land than Greece. **(b)** They prospered from trade and imperialism.
19. Answers will vary. Students who support Cato might refer to the many hardships of the earlier Punic Wars. Students who oppose Cato might express concern for the innocent people of Carthage, especially women and children.
20. **(a)** Possible answer: They analyzed and interpreted the events of Rome's past. They both hoped their histories would influence the people of their own time. **(b)** Answers will vary.
21. **(a)** Possible answer: Rome could have made peace treaties with the invading peoples. The Roman government could have reduced corruption among its officials. **(b)** Students should use critical reasoning to evaluate the feasibility of their suggested solutions.

The excerpt below is from a letter sent by Emperor Trajan to Pliny the Younger, one of his governors. After reading the excerpt, answer the questions that follow.

"The method you have pursued, my dear Pliny, in sifting the cases of those denounced to you as Christians is extremely proper. . . . No search should be made for these people; when they are denounced and found guilty they must be punished, with the restriction, however, that when the party denies himself to be a Christian and shall give proof that he is not (that is, by adoring our gods), he shall be pardoned on the ground of repentance, even though he may have formerly incurred suspicion. Information without the accuser's name subscribed [affixed] must not be admitted in evidence against anyone, as it is introducing a very dangerous precedent and by no means agreeable to the spirit of the age."

—quoted in Pliny the Younger, *Letters*

22. Based on this letter, why do you think Trajan supported the persecution of Christians?
23. Why do you think Trajan felt the need to write this letter to Pliny?
24. **(a)** How could a person accused of being a Christian be pardoned? **(b)** Do you think many Christians avoided punishment in this way? Explain.
25. What kind of evidence does Trajan declare to be inadmissible evidence?
26. Based on this letter, do you think Trajan was strongly committed to the policy of persecution? Why or why not?

Take It to the NET

Use the Internet to research the territorial expansion of the Roman empire. Then, create a map of the empire at its height. Draw present-day national boundaries on the map to show which nations were once part of the Roman empire.

INFLUENTIAL ROMAN EMPERORS

Leader Years in Office	Major Policies
Augustus 31 B.C.–A.D. 14	Ended civil war; reformed government; established empire
Nero A.D. 54–A.D. 68	Persecuted Christians after fire destroyed much of Rome
Vespasian A.D. 69–A.D. 79	Authorized building projects in Rome; reorganized government finance
Hadrian A.D. 117–A.D. 138	Built Hadrian's Wall in Britain; codified Roman law
Marcus Aurelius A.D. 161–A.D. 180	Helped unify empire economically; made legal reforms
Constantine A.D. 306–A.D. 337	Ended persecution of Christians; called Nicaea council to settle Church disputes; built new capital of Constantinople

Study the table above and then answer the following questions:

27. Which emperor's reign was the longest? Which was the shortest?
28. How did the religious policies of Nero and Constantine differ?
29. Which emperor built a structure to help keep invaders out of Britain?
30. How did Constantine reduce the importance and power of the city of Rome?
31. Which emperor had the longest reign?

Skills Tip

When you use a table, be sure to read the title and the headings first.

22. because they do not adore Roman gods
23. Possible answer: He wanted to ensure that proper procedures were used in keeping with the tolerant spirit of Roman law regarding different religions.
24. **(a)** adore Roman gods **(b)** Possible answer: possibly, although the martyrs are the ones history remembers
25. information without the name of the accuser
26. Possible answer: no, because he advises Pliny not to search out Christians but merely to punish those who are denounced

27. Augustus had the longest reign; Vespasian the shortest
28. Nero persecuted Christians, whereas Constantine ended the persecution.
29. Hadrian
30. Constantine constructed the capital of Constantinople.
31. Augustus

Skills Tip

In addition to reading the headings, remind students to look at the structure of a chart. The Skills Handbook at the front of the book has a lesson that will help students with this feature.

Unit Theme Activity

Remind students to continue working on their Unit Theme Activity. See rubrics for the activity on the unit opener page in the Teacher's Edition.

Take It to the NET

Direct students to **www.phschool.com** for links to sites that will help them get started with this assignment. Share rubrics with students.

Attempted Map is incomplete.
Minimal Map is complete but is unclear, poorly labeled, or inaccurate.
Adequate Map clearly depicts the Roman empire and present-day national boundaries and is neat and accurate.
Exemplary Map depicts the Roman empire and present-day boundaries and is neat, accurate, and visually interesting.

Resource Manager

Chapter Level Resources	CORE INSTRUCTION	READING/SKILLS
	Teaching Resources	**Book on CD**, Ch. 7
	Pacing Charts, Ch. 7	**Interactive Student Tutorial CD-ROM**, Ch. 7
	Teaching With Themes, p. 10	**Social Studies Skills Tutor CD-ROM**
	Color Transparencies, p. F–15	**Skills Transparencies**
	Resource Pro® Ch. 7	
	www.phschool.com • eTeach	
1 Civilizations of Middle America 1. Explain how geography affected the development of cultures in the Americas. 2. Compare the main features of Olmec and Mayan civilizations. 3. Describe the development of Aztec culture.	**Teaching Resources** **Unit 2 booklet** • Biography Activity, p. 68 **Creative Teaching Activities**, p. 34 **Prentice Hall Presentation Pro**, Ch. 7, Section 1 **Section Reading Support Transparencies**	**Teaching Resources** **Unit 2 booklet** • Guided Reading and Review, p. 62 **Guide to the Essentials** **Guided Reading Audiotapes**, Ch. 7, Section 1
2 The World of the Incas 1. Outline the main achievements of the early peoples of Peru. 2. Summarize how Incan emperors extended and maintained their empire. 3. Describe how the Incas lived.	**Teaching Resources** **Unit 2 booklet** • Viewpoint Activity, p. 70 **Creative Teaching Activities**, p. 35 **Prentice Hall Presentation Pro**, Ch. 7, Section 2 **Section Reading Support Transparencies**	**Teaching Resources** **Unit 2 booklet** • Guided Reading and Review, p. 64 • Skill Application Activity, p. 71 **Guide to the Essentials** **Guided Reading Audiotapes**, Ch. 7, Section 2
3 Peoples of North America 1. Describe how people in the desert southwest adapted to their environment. 2. Explain how the culture of the Mound Builders reflected their contact with other regions. 3. Identify how the diverse regional cultures in the Americas differed from one another.	**Teaching Resources** **Unit 2 booklet** • Primary Source Activity, p. 69 **Creative Teaching Activities**, p. 36 **Prentice Hall Presentation Pro**, Ch. 7, Section 3 **Section Reading Support Transparencies**	**Teaching Resources** **Unit 2 booklet** • Guided Reading and Review, p. 66 **Guide to the Essentials** **Guided Reading Audiotapes**, Ch. 7, Section 3

ENRICHMENT/PRE-AP

Teaching Resources
Teaching With Themes, Global View Activity, p. 42
www.phschool.com
• Why Study History?

Teaching Resources
Chapter Extension Activities, p. 21
www.phschool.com
• Internet Activities, Section 1

Teaching Resources
Chapter Extension Activities, p. 22
Color Transparencies, p. C–39
www.phschool.com
• Internet Activities, Section 2

ASSESSMENT

PRENTICE HALL
ASSESSMENT *SYSTEM*

Core Assessment
ExamView Test Bank booklet, Ch. 7
ExamView Test Bank CD-ROM, Ch. 7

Standardized Test Preparation
Diagnose and Prescribe
Diagnostic Tests for High School Social Studies Skills
Review and Reteach
Review Book for World History
Practice and Assess
Document-Based Assessment, pp. 8–12
Test-Taking Strategies With Transparencies
Alternative Assessment booklet
Test Prep Book for World History

Teaching Resources
Unit 2 booklet
• Geography Quiz, p. 72
• Section Quizzes, pp. 63, 65, 67
• Chapter Tests A, B, and C, pp. 73–77
www.phschool.com
• Self-Test

CUSTOMIZE FOR INDIVIDUAL NEEDS

Gifted and Talented
• **Teacher's Edition,** Activities: Customize for Heterogeneous Groups, p. 159
Less Proficient Readers
• **Guide to the Essentials,** Ch. 7
• **Guided Reading Audiotapes, English,** Ch. 7
• **Book on CD,** Ch. 7
• **Teacher's Edition,** Activities: Connections to Art, p. 166; Reading Strategy, p. 169
Less Proficient Writers
• **Teacher's Edition,** Activities: Customize for Heterogeneous Groups, p. 159; Cooperative Learning, p. 161
Students Acquiring English/ESL
• **Guide to the Essentials, English/Spanish,** Ch. 7
• **Guided Reading Audiotapes, English/Spanish,** Ch. 7
• **Book on CD,** Ch. 7
• **Teacher's Edition,** Activities marked with an *: Customize for Heterogeneous Groups, p. 156; Connections to Art, p. 166

TEXT

Don't miss the exclusive interactive version of *World History: Connections to Today* on the Internet and CD-ROM.

INTRODUCTION

America's first people, nomadic hunter-gatherers, crossed a land bridge from Siberia to Alaska. Their descendants spread from North America into South America, forming distinctive cultures, each with its own language and way of life. In time they became the advanced civilizations of the Mayas, Aztecs, and Incas. Each had features of a complex civilization—job specialization, a well-organized central government, and a complex religion. The Mayas and Aztecs had systems of writing.

Focusing on Themes

Suggest that students focus on these theme questions as they read:

Diversity
How did people in different parts of the Americas create distinct civilizations?

Continuity and Change
How did the Mayas, Aztecs, and Incas build on earlier achievements?

Political and Social Systems
What methods did Aztec and Incan rulers use to organize their large empires?

Religions and Value Systems
How did religion play a central role in early American societies?

TIME LINE ACTIVITY

Share the About the Pictures note before asking these questions:

1. This Olmec head is 9 feet 4 inches high and is carved from stone quarried a great distance away. What does that suggest about its makers? *(advanced civilization; skilled engineering)*
2. How many years passed between the building of the temple at Chavín de Huantar and the start of Mayan city construction? *(550)*
3. Which came first: the expansion of the Aztec empire or the beginning of Akbar's rule? *(Aztec expansion)*

Don't Miss!

You Are There . . .
Buying Treasures in an Aztec Market
(Section 1)

Synthesizing Information
Incan Government
(Section 2)

Civilizations of the Americas 1400 B.C.–A.D. 1570

Chapter Preview

1 Civilizations of Middle America
2 The World of the Incas
3 Peoples of North America

1400 B.C.

The Olmecs establish the first American civilization. Remains of their culture include giant heads carved in stone.

850 B.C.

Construction takes place on a huge temple in Chavín de Huantar.

A.D. 300

The Mayas begin to build elaborate cities, which include enormous pyramids such as the Temple of the Magician, shown here.

CHAPTER EVENTS

1400 B.C.

1000 B.C.

A.D. 400

GLOBAL EVENTS

1027 B.C. The Zhou dynasty is founded in China.

A.D. 392 Christianity becomes the official religion of the Roman empire.

Resource Directory

Teaching Resources
Teaching With Themes, Chapter Theme Activities, p. 10
Pacing Chart With Block Scheduling Guide Ch. 7
Global View Activity *What Characteristics Were Shared by Ancient Empires Around the World?*
Teaching With Themes booklet, p. 42

Technology
World History Color Transparencies Ch. 7 Graphic Organizer, p. F–15

Trade Routes in the Americas

NORTH AMERICA

ROCKY MTS.

GREAT PLAINS

MISSISSIPPI R.

APPALACHIAN MTS.

ATLANTIC OCEAN

160°E 180° 160°W

140°W 120°W 100°W 80°W 60°W 40°W

60°N

40°N

20°N

SIBERIA

Bering Strait

— Trade routes

Early civilizations throughout the Americas traded a wide variety of goods.

SIERRA MADRE

W. SIERRA MADRE

Gulf of Mexico

Yucatán Peninsula

CENTRAL AMERICA

Caribbean Sea

Robinson Projection

0   1000   2000 Miles

0   1000   2000 Kilometers

PACIFIC OCEAN

N W E S

0° Equator

Amazon R.

ANDES MTS.

SOUTH AMERICA

Atacama Desert

Brazilian Highlands

20°S

40°S

A.D. 900s

The Anasazis build pueblo towns and create elaborately decorated pottery, such as these clay mugs.

A.D. 1200

The Mississippian center of Cahokia thrives.

A.D. 1400s

The Aztec empire expands across Mexico, from the Gulf of Mexico to the Pacific Ocean.

A.D. 800

A.D. 1200

A.D. 1600

A.D. **800** Pope Leo III crowns Charlemagne emperor of the Romans.

A.D. **1556** Akbar begins his rule of Mughal India.

Chapter 7 **155**

Independent Assignments

Have students read one section as they prepare for class. After class, have them complete the assignment. Some students may benefit from using the Guided Reading and Review worksheets.

Section 1 Have students use the worksheet *Nezahualcoyotl* in the Unit 2 booklet, p. 68, to learn more about this much admired Aztec ruler.

Section 2 Have students use the worksheet *Two Views of Life Under the Incas* in the Unit 2 booklet, p. 70, to learn about Incan life.

Section 3 Have students use the worksheet *The Greenlanders' Saga* in the Unit 2 booklet, p. 69, to learn more about early contact between Native Americans and Europeans.

Trade Routes in the Americas

Activating Prior Knowledge

Based on what you have read about trade in other regions, what other function did these trade routes probably serve? *(conduits for the spread of ideas and technology)*

Previewing

Ask students what clue the map gives that civilization in South America probably developed independently of that in Central America. *(No trade route connects the two areas.)*

Background
About the Pictures

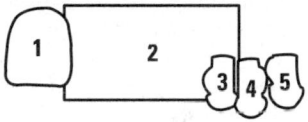

1. The Olmecs transported the stones for the heads more than 50 miles. Also found at Olmec sites were large earthen mounds, ruins of what are probably religious centers, mirrors of polished iron ore, and smaller carvings in stone and in jade.

2. The Temple of the Magician is at Uxmal on the Yucatán Peninsula. Legend has it that this temple was built in one night by the magician-god Itzamna. Actually, it was built in five phases.

3. These mugs were found at the Anasazi Pueblo Bonito site in New Mexico. Extending out from this site are several mysterious lines that run ten to twenty miles long and are perfectly straight, regardless of the terrain. These lines can be found throughout the Anasazi realm. Their exact purpose is still being debated.

---

eTeach

Be sure to check out this month's online discussion with a World History Master Teacher.

Go to **www.phschool.com**.

LESSON PLAN

1. Focus In this section, students will learn about the achievements of the Mayas, the Aztecs, and other peoples of Middle America.

2. Instruct Have three groups of students compile data for a three-part chart that compares the Olmec, Mayan, and Aztec civilizations, using the note-taking activity at the head of this section as needed. One group will gather information about the Olmecs, another will study the Mayas, and the third will learn about the Aztecs. Each group should organize their information under headings such as Location, Time Period, Religious Beliefs, Social Structure, Advances, and Achievements. Finally, have students use the chart to compare the three civilizations in a class discussion.

3. Assess Have students play an answer-and-question game that measures knowledge of Middle American civilizations by giving an answer and calling on others to respond with a question that matches that answer.

4. Reteach If students' Assess activity does not reflect adequate understanding of the lesson, you might assign the *Guide to the Essentials* or the *Interactive Student Tutorial CD-ROM* for this section.

SECTION 1 Civilizations of Middle America

Reading Focus
- How did geography affect the development of cultures in the Americas?
- What were the main features of Olmec and Mayan civilizations?
- How did the Aztec culture develop?

Vocabulary
global warming
plains
chinampas
tribute

Taking Notes
As you read this section, prepare an outline of the contents. Use Roman numerals to indicate major headings. Use capital letters for the subheadings and numbers for the supporting details. The sample at right will help you get started.

I. Civilizations of Middle America
A. Geography of the Americas
1. Earth grows warmer
2. Agricultural revolution
B. Olmecs develop first American civilization

Main Idea Climate and geography contributed to the rise of several powerful civilizations in Middle America.

Setting the Scene The Aztecs of Middle America evolved a complex system of religious beliefs. Their religions, like those of many other people, included a belief that the world and all of its inhabitants would someday come to a fiery end.

According to the Aztec Legend of the Suns, the universe had been created and destroyed four times in the past. People living under the First Sun had been destroyed by jaguars. Next, people living under the Second Sun were swept away by wind. People living under the Third Sun perished in the fire and ash of volcanoes, while those people who lived under the Fourth Sun had been swallowed by water. The Fifth Sun represented the time of the Aztec empire:

"This is our Sun, the one in which we now live. And here is its sign, how the Sun fell into the fire, into the divine hearth . . . . And as the elders continue to say, under the Sun there will be earthquakes and hunger, and then our end shall come."
—quoted in *Seeds of Change* (Viola)

The Legend of the Suns reflects the important role of the sun in Aztec religion. It also suggests a feeling of helplessness in the face of the harsh forces of nature. Despite this sense of impending doom, the Aztecs were able to create a remarkable civilization. In order to do so, they built on the achievements of earlier peoples. To understand more about these early American civilizations, we must go far back in time to the arrival of the first people in the Americas.

Geography of the Americas
Perhaps as early as 30,000 years ago,* according to some scholars, small family groups of Paleolithic hunters and food gatherers reached North America from Asia. This great migration took place during the last ice age. At that time, so much water froze into thick ice sheets that the sea level dropped, exposing a land bridge between Siberia and Alaska, in the area now known as the Bering Strait. Many historians believe that hunters followed herds of bison and mammoths across this land bridge. Other migrating people may have paddled small boats and fished along the coasts.

*Scholars disagree about exactly when the first people reached the Americas. They have proposed dates ranging from 70,000 to 10,000 years ago.

Geography and History

When Were the Americas First Settled?
For many years, scientists believed that human migration to the Americas from Siberia began about 11,500 years ago. But recent finds challenge that view.

In New Mexico, fingerprints were found preserved in clay at least 13,000 years old. In Virginia, stone tools more than 15,000 years old were found.

Based on such finds, archaeologists are beginning to question when the first people migrated to the Americas from Asia, and even if they may have come from other places as well.

Theme: Geography and History A skeleton found in Brazil is believed to be 11,500 years old. How would this information contradict the theory that people first migrated from Siberia to Alaska 11,500 years ago?

Geography and History
ANSWER Possible answer: It took thousands of years for the newcomers to spread out across the Americas, and Brazil is very far from Alaska.

Resource Directory
Teaching Resources
Creative Teaching Activities Creative Teaching Activities booklet, p. 34
Guided Reading and Review Unit 2 booklet, p. 62
Biography Activity *Nezahualcoyotl*, Unit 2 booklet, p. 68

Global Warming About 10,000 B.C., the Earth's climate grew warmer. As the ice melted, water levels rose, covering the land bridge under the Bering Strait. The global warming—or world-wide temperature increase—along with the hunting skills of the first Americans, may have killed off large game animals like the mammoth. People adapted by hunting smaller animals, fishing, and gathering fruit, roots, and shellfish. These nomadic hunter-gatherers slowly migrated eastward and southward across the Americas.

Regions What lands did the first Americans explore and settle? The Americas are made up of the two continents of North America and South America. Within these two geographic regions is a cultural region that historians call Middle America. Middle America includes Mexico and Central America and was home to several early civilizations.

Great mountain chains form a spiny backbone down the western Americas. In North America, the Rocky Mountains split into the East and West Sierra Madre of Mexico. The towering Andes run down the length of South America. The continents are drained by two of the world's three longest rivers, the Amazon of South America and the Mississippi of North America.

The first Americans adapted to a variety of climates and resources. Far to the north and the south, people learned to survive in icy, treeless lands. Closer to the Equator, people settled in the hot, wet climate and thick vegetation of the Amazon rain forests. Elsewhere, hunters adapted to deserts like the Atacama of Chile, woodlands like those in eastern North America, and the fertile plains, or rolling flatlands, of both continents.

The Agricultural Revolution In the Americas, as elsewhere, the greatest adaptation occurred when some people learned to cultivate plants and domesticate animals. Archaeologists think that farming was partly a response to the disappearance of the large mammals. With fewer animals to hunt, people came to depend more on other food sources. In Mexico, or perhaps farther south, Neolithic people began cultivating a range of crops, from corn and beans to sweet potatoes, peppers, tomatoes, and squash. These changes took place slowly between about 8500 B.C. and 2000 B.C.

Early American farmers learned to domesticate animals. In South America, domesticated animals include the llama and other creatures valued for their wool. However, the Americas had no large animals such as oxen or horses that were capable of bearing heavy loads or pulling wagons. This lack of draft animals would limit development in some areas.

In the Americas, as in Africa and Eurasia, the agricultural revolution helped to cause other changes. Farming people settled into villages. Populations expanded. Some villages grew into large religious centers and then into the great cities of the first American civilizations.

Legacy of the Olmecs

The earliest American civilization emerged in the tropical forests along the Mexican Gulf Coast. The Olmec civilization lasted from about 1400 B.C. to 500 B.C.

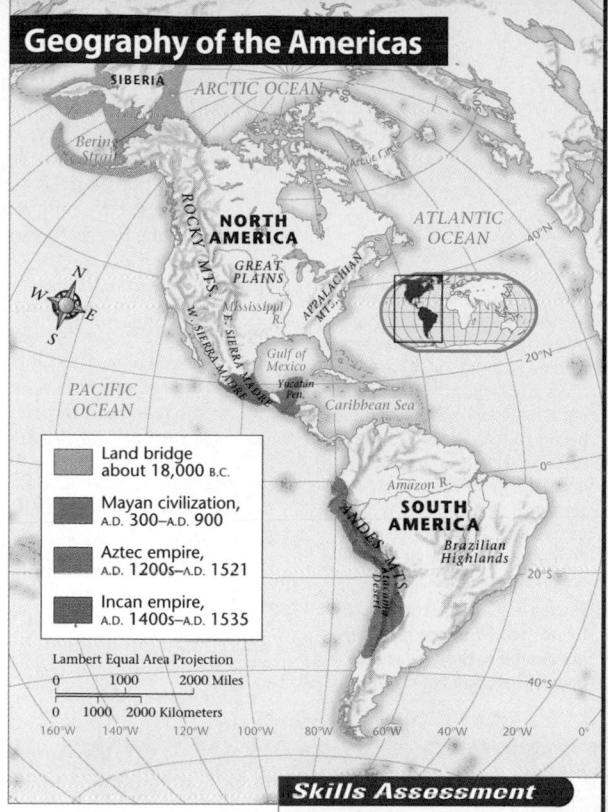

Geography of the Americas

Land bridge about 18,000 B.C.

Mayan civilization, A.D. 300–A.D. 900

Aztec empire, A.D. 1200s–A.D. 1521

Incan empire, A.D. 1400s–A.D. 1535

Lambert Equal Area Projection

0   1000   2000 Miles

0   1000   2000 Kilometers

Legendary Ball Games In the *Popol Vuh*, or *Book of Counsel,* of the Quiché Maya, there is a great legend that begins in a ball court. Two brothers are so skilled at the game that they arouse the jealousy of two death gods who challenge them to a game in the underworld. The brothers lose and die in sacrifice. But one of the dead brothers had twin sons, the Hero Twins, who themselves become masters of the ritual ball game. Again, the death gods send a fateful challenge. The Hero Twins descend on an epic journey through the realm of the dead, where they must pass many tests and overcome many obstacles. Finally, they meet the evil gods on the ball court, defeat and dismember them, and ascend to the heavens to become the sun and the moon.

Mayan Ball Games

Ball courts (PAST) were a key feature of Mayan cities. Spectators watched as two teams competed to drive a solid rubber ball through a stone ring that hung from a wall. Opposing players moved the ball across the court by using their bodies, but not their hands and feet. Players wore protective helmets and padding, but injuries were still common. Today, ball games such as soccer (PRESENT) continue to be popular with players and spectators alike.

Theme: Continuity and Change What modern games are similar to the Mayan ball game? Describe the similarities.

PAST

PRESENT

158 Chapter 7

Archaeologists know very little about the Olmecs. However, rich tombs and temples suggest that a powerful class of priests and aristocrats stood at the top of Olmec society. The Olmecs did not build true cities. Rather, they built ceremonial centers made up of pyramid-shaped temples and other buildings. People came from nearby farming villages to work on the temples or attend religious ceremonies.

The most dramatic remains of the Olmec civilization are the giant carved stone heads found in the ruins of a religious center at La Venta. No one knows how the Olmecs moved these colossal 40-ton stones from distant quarries without wheeled vehicles or draft animals.

Through trade, Olmec influence spread over a wide area. The grinning jaguars and serpents that decorate many Olmec carvings appear in the arts of later peoples. The Olmecs also invented a calendar and used carved inscriptions as a form of writing. But their most important legacy may have been the tradition of priestly leadership and religious devotion that became a basic part of later Middle American civilizations.

The World of the Mayas

Among the peoples influenced by the Olmecs were the Mayas. Between A.D. 300 and 900, Mayan city-states flourished from the Yucatán in southern Mexico through much of Central America.

Scientists have recently determined how Mayan farming methods allowed them to thrive in the tropical environment. Mayan farmers cleared the dense rain forests and then built raised fields that caught and held rainwater. They also built channels that could be opened to drain excess water. This complex system produced enough native corn, called maize, and other crops to support rapidly growing cities.

Temples and Palaces Towering pyramid temples dominated the largest Mayan city of Tikal (tee KAHL), in present-day Guatemala. Priests climbed steep temple stairs to perform sacrifices on high platforms, while ordinary people watched from the plazas far below. Some temples also served as burial places for nobles and priests. The Mayan pyramids remained the tallest structures in the Americas until 1903, when the Flatiron Building, a skyscraper, was built in New York City.

Tikal also boasted large palaces and huge stone pillars covered with elaborate carvings. The carvings, which usually record events in Mayan history, preserve striking images of haughty aristocrats, warriors in plumed headdresses, and captives about to be sacrificed to the gods.

Much of the wealth of Tikal and the other Mayan cities came from trade. Along roads made of packed earth, traders carried valuable cargoes of honey, cocoa, cotton cloth, and feathers to exchange with other people across Middle America.

Social Classes Each Mayan city had its own ruling chief. He was surrounded by nobles who served as military leaders and officials who managed public works, collected taxes, and enforced laws. Rulers were usually men, but Mayan records and carvings show that women occasionally governed on their own or in the name of young sons. Priests held great power because only they could conduct the elaborate ceremonies needed to ensure good harvests and success in war.

Caption Answer

basketball—putting ball through hoop; soccer—moving ball without using hands; volleyball—moving ball without using feet; football—protective helmets and padding

Most Mayas were farmers. They grew corn, beans, and squash—the basic food crops of Middle America—as well as fruit trees, cotton, and brilliant tropical flowers. Men usually cultivated the crops, while women turned them into food. To support the cities, farmers paid taxes in food and helped build the temples.

Advances in Learning Along with their magnificent buildings and carvings, the Mayas made impressive advances in learning. They developed a hieroglyphic writing system, which has only recently been deciphered. Mayan scribes kept their sacred knowledge in books made of bark. Though Spanish conquerors later burned most of these books, a handful were taken to Europe and survive in European museums.

Mayan priests needed to measure time accurately in order to hold ceremonies at the correct moment. As a result, many priests became expert mathematicians and astronomers. They developed an accurate 365-day solar calendar, as well as a 260-day calendar based on the orbit of the planet Venus. Mayan priests also invented a numbering system and understood the concept of zero.

Decline About A.D. 900, the Mayas abandoned their cities, leaving their great stone palaces and temples to be swallowed up by the jungle. Not until modern times were these "lost cities" rediscovered.

No one knows for sure why Mayan civilization declined. Possibly, frequent warfare forced the Mayas to abandon their traditional agricultural methods. Or overpopulation may have led to overfarming, which in turn exhausted the soil. Heavy taxes to finance wars and temple building may have sparked peasant revolts. Still, remnants of Mayan culture have survived. Today, millions of people in Guatemala and southern Mexico speak Mayan languages and are descended from the builders of this early American civilization.

Roots of Aztec Culture

Long before Mayan cities rose to the south, the city of Teotihuacán (tay oh tee wah KAHN) had emerged in the Valley of Mexico. The Valley of Mexico is a huge oval basin ringed by snowcapped volcanoes, located in the high plateau of central Mexico. From A.D. 100 to A.D. 750, Teotihuacán dominated a large area.

Teotihuacán The city of Teotihuacán was well planned, with wide roads, massive temples, and large apartment buildings. Along the main avenue, the Pyramid of the Sun and the Pyramid of the Moon rose majestically toward the sky. Citizens of Teotihuacán worshiped a powerful nature goddess and rain god, whose images often appear on public buildings and on everyday objects. Teotihuacán eventually fell to invaders, but its culture influenced later peoples, especially the Aztecs.

Arrival of the Aztecs In the late 1200s, bands of nomadic people, the ancestors of the Aztecs, migrated into the Valley of Mexico from the north. According to Aztec legend, the gods had told them to search for an eagle perched atop a cactus holding a snake in its beak. They finally saw the sign on a swampy island in Lake Texcoco. Once settled, the Aztecs shifted from hunting to farming. Slowly, they built the city of Tenochtitlán (tay nawch tee TLAHN), on the site of present-day Mexico City.

As their population grew, the Aztecs found ingenious ways to create more farmland. They built chinampas, artificial islands made of earth piled on reed mats that were anchored to the shallow lake bed. On these "floating gardens," they raised corn, squash, and beans. They gradually filled in parts of the lake and created canals for transportation. Wide stone causeways linked Tenochtitlán to the mainland.

Mayan Society in Art
Mayan potters fashioned clay figurines depicting people at all levels of society. Here, an aristocrat (top) poses in his robes, while a peasant woman (bottom) holds tortillas.

Theme: Art and Literature
How do these figurines suggest that these two people were from different social classes?

Customize for . . .
Heterogeneous Groups

Constructing a Poster Have students conduct outside research in order to construct posters on early Mayan civilization. Each poster should include a special-purpose map that shows the extent of Mayan civilization and the location of Mayan cities. It should also include diagrams to illustrate the designs of temples and palaces. Students could also illustrate their posters with drawings or photocopies of Mayan writing and works of art. Have students display their finished posters and explain their contents in a class presentation. *(Enrichment)* ✳

Background
Connections to Music

Aztec Musicians Aztec musicians played a variety of musical instruments, including trumpets, rasps, drums, tambourines, rattles, and whistles. Music played an important role in religious rituals, and Aztec musicians therefore enjoyed many rewards and privileges. They were exempt from paying certain taxes and tribute. In addition, musicians had the sacred task of calling the people to prayers at specific hours each day.

Background
Global Connections

Sacred Plant Corn was so important in the lives of early Americans that many cultures considered it a sacred plant. In the desert southwest of North America, people performed special corn dances to induce rain, to promote fertility, and to thank the gods for the harvest. In the southeastern region of North America, people performed the green corn dance to celebrate an early harvest. They gave thanks for the corn, prayed for continued fertility, and sought prevention of disease.

Human Drama Note

Mayan Warfare To prepare for war, the Mayas fasted for days, went through purification rituals, and made sacrifices. Wearing battle jackets and helmets, the warriors carried knives, long lances, and shields. Around their necks hung the shrunken heads of captives from previous battles. Advancing toward the enemy, the warriors shouted insults and challenges at the opposing army, and then backed off, repeating these actions until the tension became too great, and a fierce battle erupted.

Caption Answer

The top figure is in a very formal, erect posture and appears to be wearing ornate clothing. The bottom figure is smiling and looks more informal; it is carrying items that may be food.

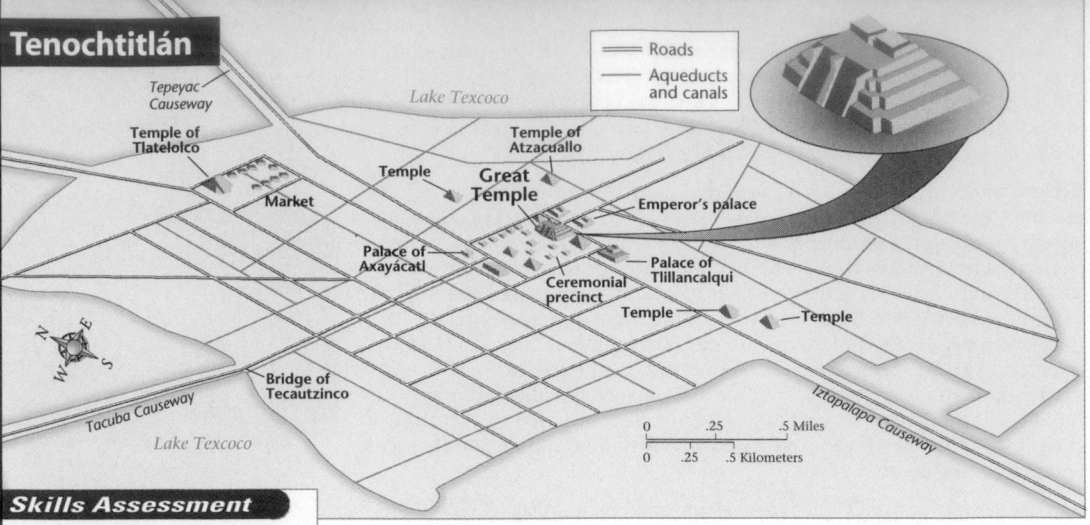

Roads
Aqueducts and canals

Tepeyac Causeway
Lake Texcoco
Temple of Tlatelolco
Market
Temple
Temple of Atzacuallo
Great Temple
Emperor's palace
Palace of Axayácatl
Ceremonial precinct
Palace of Tlillancalqui
Temple
Temple
Bridge of Tecautzinco
Tacuba Causeway
Lake Texcoco
Iztapalapa Causeway

0 .25 .5 Miles
0 .25 .5 Kilometers

Background
Daily Life

Agricultural Bounty Aztec farmers grew a variety of crops for a variety of purposes. In addition to corn, squash, and beans, important food crops included the sweet potato, manioc, avocado, tomato, pineapple, and papaya. Cotton provided fibers for weaving. A fermented sugar was used to make an intoxicating beverage. Cacao provided chocolate, a luxury drink that was cherished by the upper classes. Tapped trees yielded rubber, which was used to make the balls for the important ritual games.

Background
Daily Life

The Original Taco The Aztecs prepared corn by mixing ground kernels with water impregnated with unslaked lime (an alkaline, inorganic compound, calcium oxide) to form a thick paste. They then formed the paste into a thin round *tlaxcali*, which the Spaniards would later call *tortilla*, and toasted it on a griddle. The *tlaxcali* often served as a utensil for scooping up food. Aztec diners also used it as a wrapper folded around a mixture of meats and vegetables. Today, we know this item of Aztec cuisine as the taco.

Skills Assessment

Geography The Aztec capital, Tenochtitlán, was located in Lake Texcoco and connected to the mainland by causeways. In the center of the city, people gathered at the Great Temple, the emperor's palace, the market, or other public centers.

1. **Location** On the map, locate **(a)** Great Temple, **(b)** market, **(c)** emperor's palace, **(d)** Lake Texcoco.
2. **Interaction** Give two examples of ways the Aztecs adapted their environment to meet their needs in Tenochtitlán.
3. **Critical Thinking Analyzing Information** How does the map suggest that religion played an important role in Aztec life?

Conquering an Empire In the 1400s, the Aztecs greatly expanded their territory. Through a combination of fierce conquests and shrewd alliances, they spread their rule across most of Mexico, from the Gulf of Mexico on the east to the Pacific Ocean on the west. By 1500, the Aztec empire numbered an estimated 30 million people.

War brought immense wealth as well as power. Tribute, or payment from conquered peoples, helped the Aztecs turn their capital into a magnificent city.

The World of the Aztecs

When the Spanish reached Tenochtitlán in 1519, they were awestruck at its magnificence. The Spanish conqueror Hernán Cortés described the city as it looked then:

"The city has many squares where markets are held and trading is carried on. There is one square . . . where there are daily more than 60,000 souls, buying and selling, and where are found all the kinds of merchandise produced in these countries, including food products, jewels of gold and silver, lead, brass, copper, zinc, bones, shells, and feathers."
—Hernán Cortés, quoted in
Latin American Civilization (Keen)

From its temples and royal palaces to its zoos and floating gardens, Tenochtitlán was a city of wonders. It was also the center of a complex, well-ordered empire.

Government and Society Unlike the Mayan city-states, each of which had its own king, the Aztecs had a single ruler. The emperor was chosen by a council of nobles and priests to lead in war. Below him, nobles served as officials, judges, and governors of conquered provinces. They enjoyed special privileges such as wearing luxurious feathered cloaks and gold jewelry. Next came the warriors, who could rise to noble status by killing or capturing enemy soldiers. The majority of people were commoners who farmed the land.

At the bottom of society were the slaves, mostly criminals or prisoners of war. Despite their low status, slaves' rights were clearly spelled out by law. For example, slaves could own land and buy their freedom.

Skills Assessment

ANSWERS 1. Review locations with students. 2. Possible answers: built aqueducts and canals, built causeways 3. The Great Temple is at the center of the city and is larger than any other building.

Resource Directory

Teaching Resources
You Are There Chapter Extension Activities booklet, p. 21

Buying Treasures in an Aztec Market

Thoughts of shopping fill you with excitement. Although Tenochtitlán's market is packed with eager buyers and sellers today, the crowd doesn't bother you. You are a wealthy Aztec noble, and your servants carry you above it all. Carefully, you clutch your bag of cocoa beans; they are very valuable and you will use them to buy what you want.

Thousands of different goods spill out over the vendors' tables. Some are ordinary—food products like tomatoes, chili peppers, or turkeys. Others dazzle you—turquoise masks and fine gold and silver jewelry.

First, you buy a fan made of brilliantly colored feathers. You will give it to your brother, an important government official. It will show his high rank in society.

After shopping for hours, you are ready to go home. Then, a cup carved like a rabbit catches your eye. You could use it to drink chocolate. Only the wealthy can drink this brew made from cocoa beans, so chocolate deserves a special cup. You decide to buy it.

Portfolio Assessment

Write a shopping list for your next trip to the market. Briefly explain why you need each item on the list. Refer to the mural above for ideas.

Chapter 7 **161**

☑ Test Preparation

Have students read the section titled "Government and Society" on the opposite page, and then answer the question below.

Which term below best describes the Aztec government system?

A aristocracy

B patriarchy

Ⓒ monarchy

D democracy

Bell Ringer Ask students to study the picture of Tenochtitlán and identify as many items as they can.

Background About the Scene

This is a section of a Diego Rivera fresco painted in 1945 at the National Palace in Mexico City. In the background is the city of Tenochtitlán, with the Sierra Madres rising in the far distance. The Great Temple is visible, as are causeways and canals. In the foreground is a bustling market, probably the large one, although the city had several local markets. At the upper left are slaves with huge rolls of cloth. The seated figure in the center is the magistrate who presided at the market. At the bottom right, people are selling various kinds of maize.

Activity Cooperative Learning

Have students work together in small groups to prepare an exhibit on some other aspect of Aztec life, such as crafts or housing. Artifacts in the exhibit may be student drawings or models or photographs taken from magazines or the Internet. Each artifact should have a brief descriptive label, and the exhibit as a whole should have a written introduction. Students should divide the tasks among the group members, so that each person is responsible for some aspect, such as research or drawing.

Portfolio Assessment Rubrics

Share rubrics with students before they create their shopping lists.

Attempted The list is attempted, but explanations are missing.

Minimal The list names very few market goods, or explanations for each are sketchy.

Adequate The list names several market items and explains why each item is needed.

Exemplary The list shows exceptional understanding of the markets of Tenochtitlán and offers detailed explanations of the items.

Recall
1. (a) Olmecs, p. 157 (b) Tikal, p. 158
(c) Teotihuacán, p. 159 (d) Tenochtitlán,
p. 159 2. (a) global warming, p. 157
(b) plains, p. 157 (c) chinampas, p. 159
(d) tribute, p. 160

Comprehension
3. Global warming and migration required
people to adapt to new environments.
While some remained hunters, many
others began cultivating crops and
domesticating pack animals. Villages
grew into religious centers and cities.
4. (a) Religion was the center of life.
(b) Mayan priests became expert mathematicians and astronomers, and the
Mayas also built huge temples. 5. by a
combination of fierce conquests and
shrewd alliances

Critical Thinking and Writing
6. Possible answer: A lack of draft animals would require smaller-scale farming
because there would be no way to pull
heavy equipment. 7. Possible answer:
They might look for similarities in subject
matter or artistic styles in artwork and
architecture. Similarities could indicate
that the later civilizations were
influenced by the Olmecs.

Activity Rubrics

Share rubrics with students before they
write their diary entries.

Attempted The diary entries show no
evidence of research or do not include
the required descriptions.

Minimal The diary entries show some
evidence of research but are very brief,
poorly written, or lacking in interest.

Adequate The diary entries show evidence of research and are thoughtful
and well written.

Exemplary The diary entries show
evidence of extensive research, are
thoughtful and well written, and show
empathy with the migratory people.

Primary Source

ANSWER Like all things of the Earth,
they will die out and their glory will vanish
from the Earth.

Primary Source

A Vision of a Grim Future
*In the 1400s, poet-king
Nezahualcoyotl (neh tsah wahl
cuh YOH tuhl) warned of impending
doom:*

"All the Earth is a grave and
    nothing escapes it;
Nothing is so perfect that it does
    not descend to its tomb . . .
Filled are the depths of the Earth
    with dust
Once flesh and bone, once living
    bodies of men
Who sat upon thrones, decided
    cases, presided in council,
Commanded armies, conquered
    provinces, possessed treasures,
    destroyed temples,
Exulted in their pride, majesty,
    fortune, praise and power.
Vanished are these glories."

    —Nezahualcoyotl, quoted in *The
    Flute of the Smoking Mirror*
    (Gilmor)

Skills Assessment

Primary Source **What does
Nezahualcoyotl predict will
happen to the civilizations of
the Valley of Mexico?**

Protected by Aztec power, a class of long-distance traders ferried goods
across the empire and beyond. From the highlands, they took goods such
as weapons, tools, and rope to barter for tropical products such as jaguar
skins and cocoa beans. They also served as spies, finding new areas for
trade and conquest.

Religious Beliefs The priests were a class apart. They performed rituals
they believed pleased the Aztec gods and prevented droughts or other disasters. The chief Aztec god was Huitzilopochtli (wee tsee loh POHKT lee),
the sun god. His pyramid-temple towered above central Tenochtitlán.

Huitzilopochtli, the Aztecs believed, battled the forces of darkness each
night and was reborn each morning. As the Legend of the Suns shows,
there was no guarantee that the sun would always win. To give the sun
strength to rise each day, the Aztecs offered human sacrifices. Priests
offered the hearts of tens of thousands of victims to Huitzilopochtli and
other Aztec gods. Most of the victims were prisoners of war, but sometimes
a noble family gave up one of its own members to appease the gods.

Other cultures, such as the Olmecs and the Mayas, had practiced human
sacrifice, but not on the massive scale of the Aztecs. The Aztecs carried on
almost continuous warfare, using the captured enemy soldiers for a regular
source of sacrificial victims. Among the conquered peoples, discontent festered and rebellion often flared up. When the armies from Spain later arrived,
they found ready allies among peoples who were ruled by the Aztec empire.

Education and Learning Priests were the keepers of Aztec knowledge.
They recorded laws and historical events. Some ran schools for the sons of
nobles. Others used their knowledge of astronomy and mathematics to
foretell the future. The Aztecs, like the Mayas, had an accurate calendar.

Like many other ancient peoples, the Aztecs believed that illness was a
punishment from the gods. Still, Aztec priests used herbs and other medicines to treat fevers and wounds. Aztec physicians could set broken bones
and treat dental cavities. They also prescribed steam baths as cures for various ills, a therapy still in use today.

Looking Ahead

The Aztecs developed a sophisticated and complex culture, but their world
would not last forever. At the height of Aztec power, word reached
Tenochtitlán that pale-skinned, bearded men had landed on the east coast.
Later, you will read about the results of the encounter between the Aztecs
and the newcomers from far-off Spain.

SECTION 1 Assessment

Recall
1. **Identify:** (a) Olmecs, (b) Tikal,
    (c) Teotihuacán, (d) Tenochtitlán.
2. **Define:** (a) global warming,
    (b) plains, (c) chinampas,
    (d) tribute.

Comprehension
3. How did early people adapt to
    different environments in the
    Americas?
4. (a) What role did religion play
    in Olmec and Mayan culture?
    (b) How did religion influence
    Mayan ideas and technology?

5. How did the Aztecs build and con-
    trol a powerful empire in Mexico?

Critical Thinking and Writing
6. **Connecting to Geography**
    Explain why a lack of large draft
    animals might limit agricultural
    development in some regions.
7. **Analyzing Information** How
    would archaeologists use
    evidence such as artwork and
    public buildings to trace the
    influence of the Olmecs or similar
    civilizations on later Middle
    American people?

Activity
Take It to the NET

Use the Internet to
research the migration of
people across the land
bridge. Then, write a series
of diary entries describing
the crossing from Siberia
into the Americas. Include
descriptions of the animal
and plant life encountered
along the way.

162 *Chapter 7*

Resource Directory

Teaching Resources
Section Quiz Unit 2 booklet, p. 63
Creative Teaching Activities Creative Teaching
Activities booklet, p. 35
Guided Reading and Review Unit 2 booklet, p. 64

Technology
Interactive Student Tutorial CD-ROM Ch. 7
Computer Test Bank Ch. 7
World History Color Transparencies *Textiles From
the Incas*, p. C–39

The World of the Incas

Reading Focus

- What were the main achievements of the early peoples of Peru?
- How did Incan emperors extend and maintain their empire?
- How did the Incas live?

Vocabulary

glyph
quipu
alloy

Taking Notes

Copy this flowchart, adding information about each of the successive cultures that inhabited Peru. When possible, indicate how cultures influenced later peoples. Add more boxes as necessary.

```
┌─────────────────────┐
│       CHAVÍN         │
│      850 B.C.        │
│ Influenced art and  │
│   religion          │
│  of later cultures  │
└─────────────────────┘
          ↓
┌─────────────────────┐
│                     │
└─────────────────────┘
          ↓
┌─────────────────────┐
│                     │
└─────────────────────┘
```

Main Idea) The Incas built a complex civilization that relied on order and absolute authority.

Setting the Scene
The Sapa Inca lifted a golden cup to the rising sun, a gesture to honor his divine ancestor. He then entered the temple, where sunlight glinted off the golden statues along the walls. A priest placed a bundle of fibers on the altar. With a copper mirror, he directed the magical power of the sun's rays to explode the fibers into flame.

Other rituals followed. Priests sacrificed a llama and prayed for success in the coming year. When the ceremonies ended, horns blared the news to the crowds outside the temple. A shout rose: *"Hailli!"*—"Victory!" Reed pipes and flutes echoed the joy as people prepared for a day of feasting and dancing.

This ceremony honoring the sun god took place each year in Cuzco, capital of the Incan empire of Peru. By the early 1500s, the Incas, like the Aztecs, ruled a mighty empire.

Early Peoples of Peru
Western South America includes a wide variety of climates and terrains. The narrow coastal plain is a dry, lifeless desert crossed by occasional river valleys. Further inland, the snow-capped Andes Mountains rise steeply, leveling off into high plateaus that bake by day and freeze at night. East of the Andes lie dense jungles that stretch from Peru into Brazil.

Native American peoples developed many different styles of life across South America. Hunters and gatherers thrived in some regions, while farmers grew root crops in the Amazon rain forests. Thousands of years ago, people settled in fishing villages along the desert coast of Peru. Gradually they expanded inland, farming the river valleys that run up into the highland plateaus. Using careful irrigation, they grew corn, cotton, squash, and beans. On mountain slopes, they cultivated potatoes, eventually producing 700 varieties. In high plateaus, they domesticated the llama and the alpaca. Like the Mayas, they built large ceremonial centers and developed skills in pottery and weaving.

Chavín Through painstaking work at many sites, archaeologists have pieced together a chronology of various cultures that left their mark on the region. The earliest of these was the Chavín (chah VEEN) culture, named for ruins at Chavín de Huantar in the Andes. There, about 850 B.C., people built a huge temple complex. Stone carvings and pottery show that the Chavín people worshiped a ferocious-looking god, part jaguar and part human with grinning catlike features. The arts and religion of the Chavín culture influenced later peoples of Peru.

Peruvian Textile
Artisans among the Paracas, an early people of Peru, produced this cloak around the 500s B.C. Spinners, weavers, and skillful dyers worked together to create this fabric adorned with complex and imaginative designs.

Theme: Art and Literature
What does this fabric suggest about cultural development among the Paracas?

Chapter 7 **163**

Bell Ringer Have students look at the map at the beginning of Section 1 and the picture of Machu Picchu in this section. Discuss how geography might have affected Incan civilization.

LESSON PLAN

1. Focus The diverse lands of the Incan empire were united by a strong government, a common language, and an impressive communication system. Religious practices influenced much of daily life.

2. Instruct Divide the class into groups to create catalogs for a museum exhibit on the Incas. The exhibit will have galleries for geography, government, communication, economy, religion, and the Chosen Women. Each catalog should include a written guide. With the help of outside research, catalogs might also include maps, sketches, or photocopies of artifacts, diagrams of urban plans, and the like. Invite the groups to display and discuss their catalogs.

3. Assess Ask students to compare the Incan empire with other empires that they have studied. What characteristics do the empires share?

4. Reteach If students' **Assess** activity does not reflect adequate understanding of the lesson, you might assign the *Guide to the Essentials* or the *Interactive Student Tutorial CD-ROM* for this section.

Background
Connections to Economics

A Complex Process It took years to produce a Peruvian textile. First, farmers grew cotton and raised alpacas for their wool. Skilled workers then spun yarn. Dyers used minerals, vegetables, and tree barks to add brilliant color to the natural fibers. Then, weavers attached the colored yarn to looms and wove large pieces of cloth. Finally, artists decorated each cloth with a unique design.

Caption Answer

It shows that the Paracas were creative, good at planning, and highly skilled.

Block Scheduling Support

Have students complete the History Through Literature activity *The Children of the Sun* in the History Through Literature booklet, pp. 16–17. The reading is an Incan myth that explains how the Incas came to be civilized and to spread their civilization among the peoples of the region. You may wish to have volunteers read their answers to the Drawing Conclusions question and then discuss the answers with the class.

The Swift Runners The messengers of the Incan empire were called *chasquis*. In times of crisis, chasquis carried urgent messages about uprisings or disasters throughout the mountainous realm. At other times, they relayed information about the day-to-day operation of the Incan empire.

Chasquis served 15-day shifts, during which they lived in small roadside huts. Each runner was expected to know a particular stretch of roadway well enough to run the distance barefoot on a starless night. The blasts of a conch shell trumpet and the sounds of pounding feet signaled the approach of another chasqui. A message was relayed from one runner to the other, and it continued on its rapid way. In this way, the swift runners of the Incas moved messages across their empire at the amazing rate of about 200 miles a day.

Biography

Pachacuti 1391(?)–1473(?)

Growing up, Pachacuti did not seem destined to rule the Incan people. True, his father, Viracocha, was their king. But Pachacuti was neither the eldest son—that was Urcon—nor his father's favorite.

Then one day, the army of a powerful neighboring people, the Chancas, swept down on Cuzco. Soon, the battle was going against the Incan army. Viracocha and Urcon fled the field for the safety of a mountain stronghold. But Pachacuti fought on, commanding the army and inspiring his warriors to turn almost certain defeat into a stunning victory. Within days, Pachacuti deposed the shamed Viracocha, denied the throne to Urcon, and seized it for himself.

Theme: Impact of the Individual From what you have read about Pachacuti, what traits and skills must he have had?

Mochica Between about A.D. 100 and 700, the Mochica people forged an empire along the arid north coast of Peru. The Mochicas were skilled farmers, developing methods of terracing, irrigation, and fertilization of the soil. Their leaders built roads and organized networks of relay runners to carry messages, ideas that the Incas would later adopt.

Remains of Mochica cities and temples dot the land. To build one temple, workers had to produce 130 million sun-dried adobe bricks. The people perfected skills in textile production, goldwork, and woodcarving. They produced remarkable pots decorated with realistic scenes of daily life. On these painted vases, helmeted warriors go into battle, musicians play pipes and drums, and women weave textiles on small portable looms.

Nazca Many other cultures left tantalizing clues to their lives and beliefs. In southern Peru, the Nazca people etched glyphs in the desert. A glyph is a pictograph or other symbol carved into a surface. Nazca glyphs include straight lines that run for miles, as well as giant figures of birds, whales, and other creatures. These figures may have been family symbols or part of an ancient calendar.

For more than 2,000 years, diverse civilizations rose and fell in Peru. Then, in the mid-1400s, the Incas emerged from high in the Andes. Incan armies rapidly conquered an empire that stretched 2,500 miles down the Andes and along the Pacific coast. Like the Romans, who also ruled a diverse empire, the Incas drew heavily on the ideas and skills of the peoples they conquered.

The Incan Empire

Pachacuti, a skilled warrior and leader, was the founder of the Incan empire. In 1438, he proclaimed himself Sapa Inca, or emperor, and set out on a policy of conquest. From a small kingdom in the high mountain valley of Cuzco, he came to dominate an immense empire. Once he had subdued neighboring peoples, he enlisted them in his armies for future campaigns. In this way, he and his son extended Incan rule from Ecuador in the north to Chile in the south.

Government The Sapa Inca exercised absolute power over the empire. Claiming that he was divine, the son of the sun itself, he was also the chief religious leader. Like the pharaohs of ancient Egypt, the Incan god-king owned all the land, herds, mines, and people. Gold, the "sweat of the sun," was his symbol. He lived in splendor, eating from golden plates and dressing in richly embroidered clothes. In fact, the Sapa Inca never wore the same royal garments twice. His queen, the Coya, carried out important religious duties and sometimes governed when the Sapa Inca was absent.

From Cuzco, the Incas ran an efficient government with a chain of command reaching into every village. Nobles ruled the provinces along with local chieftains whom the Incas had conquered. Below them, officials carried out the day-to-day business of collecting taxes and enforcing laws. Specially trained officials kept records on a quipu, a collection of knotted, colored strings. Modern scholars think that quipus noted dates and events as well as statistics on population and crops.

Roads and Runners To unite their empire, the Incas imposed their own language, Quechua (KEHCH wuh), and religion on the people. They also created one of the great road systems of history. It wound more than 12,000 miles through mountains and deserts. Hundreds of bridges spanned rivers and deep gorges. Steps were cut into steep slopes and tunnels dug through hillsides. Even more impressive than the roads that united the Roman empire, the Incan road system was unmatched until modern times.

The roads allowed armies and news to move rapidly throughout the empire. At regular stations, runners waited to carry messages. Relays of

Biography

ANSWER He must have had courage, military skills, self-confidence, and ambition.

Resource Directory

Teaching Resources
Synthesizing Information Chapter Extension Activities booklet, p. 22

Incan Government

People of the Incan empire lived in one of the most highly ordered societies in history. Use the quotation, chart, and diagram below to draw conclusions about the government that created this order.

Incan System of Rule

Leader	Responsibility
The Inca	• Ruled the entire Incan empire
Suyuyuq Apu	• Controlled one of four regions of the empire
Hunu Kamayoq	• Governed a province containing 10,000 families
Waranq Kamayoq	• Acted as head of 1,000 families
Pichqa Pachaq Kamayoq	• Acted as head of 500 families
Pachaq Kamayoq	• Acted as head of 100 families
Pichqa Chunka Kamayoq	• Acted as head of 50 families
Chunka Kamayoq	• Acted as head of 10 families
Pichqa Kamayoq	• Acted as head of 5 families
Pureq	• Acted as head of 1 family

The Incan bureaucracy controlled life, even at the individual family level.

A Sapa Inca's Purpose

In the following quotation, the Inca explains what he believes the sun has ordered Incan rulers to do.

"'Each day that passes,' said our father, the sun, 'I go around the world in order to have a better knowledge of men's needs and to satisfy those needs. Follow my example: Do unto all of them as a merciful father would do to his well-beloved children; for I have sent you on earth for the good of men, that they might cease to live like wild animals. You shall be the kings and lords of all the peoples who accept our law and our rule.'"

—Garcilaso de la Vega, *The Royal Commentaries of the Inca*

Incan Farming System

Field of the sun god, used for priests

Field of the sick, orphans, widows, and those away on government service

Field of the Inca, used for the state and the community

Field assigned for the needs of the individual families

All land belonged to the community. Farmers grew crops in different fields.

Skills Tip

Start by reading the title of the activity to identify its general topic. Then, when you examine each source, ask yourself how the specific information presented relates to the general topic.

Skills Assessment

1. Like the sun god, the Inca was supposed to
   A satisfy his people's needs.
   B act like a favorite child.
   C prevent the division of land by the community.
   D accept the rule of the high priests.

2. How were orphans provided for by Incan society?
   E They became priests of the sun god.
   F They went to live with the Hunu Kamayoq.
   G They received crops from land assigned to them.
   H They were adopted by Incan nobles.

3. **Critical Thinking Drawing Conclusions** How might an Incan ruler explain the need to have such an extensive bureaucracy?

Test Preparation

Have students read the Biography feature in this section, and then answer the question below.

Which of the following is a fact supported by the information in the feature?

A Viracocha was ashamed of himself.

B Urcon was unpopular.

C Pachacuti was destined to rule.

(D) Pachacuti deposed his father.

Background
About the Evidence

In addition to the division of land shown on the diagram, one area of land was left fallow so that crops could be rotated. The amount of land provided to each family was based on the size of the family.

Most men between the ages of 25 and 50 were farmers but were also called upon each year for road construction, army service, bridge building, mining, erecting public buildings, or other service to the empire. Such service, called *mita,* was considered a kind of tax.

Activity
Interpreting the Evidence

Use these additional questions to generate class discussion.
1. **Critical Thinking: Drawing Conclusions** Into what four purposes was farmland divided? *(fields for priests; fields for the sick, orphans, widows, and those away in the military; fields for the Inca, used for state and community; fields for individual families)*
2. **Critical Thinking: Making Inferences** What does this arrangement reveal about Incan government? *(Possible answers: concern for the people, highly structured)*

Skills Tip

When you look at the chart on this page, don't get bogged down with trying to pronounce or remember the titles of the officials. What is important is the great degree of structure that the chart reveals. The Skills Handbook in the front of the book has a lesson that will help students with this feature.

Skills Assessment

ANSWERS 1. A **2.** G **3.** Possible answer: He might say that in order to satisfy his people's needs, the government had to have information about, and an official responsible for, every person in his empire.

Activity
Connections to Art

Creating an Illustration *The Incas,* a presentation of the PBS Odyssey series, takes viewers on a fascinating journey to the Incan past. The cameras focus on the remains of Incan cities, temples, warehouses, postal stations, bridges, roads, and terraced fields. To demonstrate Incan artistry, the program examines textiles and pottery. Throughout the documentary, actual Incan drawings of such items as clothing, jewelry, quipus, musical instruments, and more appear.

Ask for volunteers to view *The Incas* and to look for several images that they can illustrate for the class. As they watch the video, students may want to freeze-frame or stop and replay certain images. Their illustrations should be large enough for display and include brief descriptive notes. Students should present their work to the class and be prepared to answer questions. (*The Incas,* released in 1980, is distributed by Pacific Arts.) ✳

Virtual Field Trip

www.phschool.com

Machu Picchu, Peru

To learn more about Machu Picchu, use the Internet address above to link to the Web site of Machu Picchu, Peru.

Machu Picchu

Machu Picchu lies some 7,000 feet above sea level. The sturdy walls have withstood centuries of earthquakes. Incan workers cut and fitted the stones together without the aid of mortar. Abandoned for some 300 years, the ruins of Machu Picchu were rediscovered in 1911.

Theme: Economics and Technology How do the ruins of Machu Picchu show that the Incan empire was well organized and technologically advanced?

Global Connections

Finding a Way Across

Like the Romans, the Incas were inventive road builders. But the deep gorges of the Andes presented a formidable obstacle: How can a road cross from one steep canyon wall to another, often high above a rushing river? The Incans built massive stone piers on either side and slung five cables of twisted fiber between them. They attached wooden crosspieces to three cables and made the other two handrails.

When Europeans first saw these flimsy-looking suspension bridges swaying in the wind, they were terrified of them. But they marveled too, knowing no way to improve upon their design.

Theme: Economics and Technology How did the environment affect Incan construction methods?

runners could carry news of a revolt swiftly from a distant province to the capital. The Incas kept soldiers at outposts throughout the empire. Within days of an uprising, they would be on the move to crush the rebels. Ordinary people, though, were restricted from using the roads at all.

Cuzco All roads led through Cuzco. The population was made up of representatives of all the peoples of the empire, each living in a particular part of the city. They wore regional costumes and practiced traditional crafts. In the heart of the city stood the great Temple of the Sun, its interior walls lined with gold. Like Incan palaces and forts, the temple was made of enormous stone blocks, each polished and carved to fit exactly in place. The engineering was so precise that, although no mortar was used to hold the stones together, Incan buildings have survived severe earthquakes.

Daily Life

The Incas strictly regulated the lives of millions of people within their empire. People lived in close-knit communities, called ayllus (ī LOOZ). Leaders of each ayllu carried out government orders, assigning jobs to each family and organizing the community to work the land. Government officials arranged marriages to ensure that men and women were settled at a certain age.

Farming Farmers expanded the step terraces built by earlier peoples. On steep hillsides, they carved out strips of land to be held in place by stone walls. These terraces kept rains from washing away the soil and made farming possible in places where flat land was scarce.

Farmers had to spend part of each year working land for the emperor and the temples as well as for their own communities. All land belonged to the Inca, but cultivation and crops were allotted to specific groups of

---

Caption Answer

Possible answers: expertly cut and fitted stones, solid construction, orderly layout of city

Global Connections

ANSWERS Possible answer: The rugged terrain made it necessary for the Incas to develop new bridge-building technology.

Resource Directory

Teaching Resources

Section Quiz Unit 2 booklet, p. 65
Viewpoint Activity *Two Views of Life Under the Incas,* Unit 2 booklet, p. 70
Skill Application Activity *Answering Essay Questions,* Unit 2 booklet, p. 71

Technology

Interactive Student Tutorial CD-ROM Ch. 7
Computer Test Bank Ch. 7

people or for particular purposes. The government took possession of each harvest, dividing it among the people and storing part of it in case of famine.

Metalworking The Incas were the best metalworkers in the Americas. They learned to work and alloy, or blend, copper, tin, bronze, silver, and gold. While they employed copper and bronze for useful objects, they used precious metals for statues of gods and goddesses, eating utensils for the aristocracy, and decorations.

Medical Advances The Incas developed some important medical practices, including surgery on the human skull. In such operations, they first cleaned the operating area and then made the patient unconscious with a drug—procedures much closer to the use of modern antiseptics and anesthesia than anything practiced in Europe at that time.

Religion Like other early peoples, the Incas were polytheistic, worshiping many gods linked to the forces of nature. People offered food, clothing, and drink to the guardian spirits of the home and the village. Religion was tied to the routines of life. Each month had its own festival, from the great ripening and the dance of the young maize to the festival of the water. Festivals were celebrated with ceremonies, sports, and games. A powerful class of priests served the gods, celebrating their special festivals and tending to their needs.

Chief among the gods was Inti, the sun god. His special attendants, the "Chosen Women," were selected from each region of the empire. During years of training, they studied the mysteries of the religion, learned to prepare ritual food and drink, and made the elaborate wool garments worn by the Sapa Inca and the Coya. At the end of their training, most of the Chosen Women continued to serve the sun god. Others, however, joined the Inca's court or married nobles.

Looking Ahead

At its height, the Incan civilization, like those of Middle America, was a center of learning and political power. Then, in 1525, the emperor Huayna Capac (wī nah KAH pahk) died suddenly of an unknown plague that swept across the land. As he had not named a successor, civil war broke out between two of his sons. The fighting weakened the empire at a crucial moment. Like the Aztecs to the north, the Incas soon faced an even greater threat from Spanish invaders.

SECTION 2 Assessment

Recall
1. **Identify: (a)** Pachacuti, **(b)** Quechua.
2. **Define: (a)** glyph, **(b)** quipu, **(c)** alloy.

Comprehension
3. Describe one achievement of each of the following early peoples of Peru: **(a)** Chavín, **(b)** Mochica.
4. Describe two ways in which the Incas united their empire.
5. What were some elements of daily life for the Incas?

Critical Thinking and Writing
6. **Connecting to Geography**
   (a) How did geography pose a challenge to the Incas as they built their empire? **(b)** How did they meet this challenge? **(c)** What does this suggest about the level of government and learning among the Incas?
7. **Recognizing Points of View** For the average Inca, what might be the benefits of the absolute rule of the Sapa Inca? What might be the disadvantages?

Activity
Take It to the NET

Use the Internet to research the ancient Incan city of Machu Picchu. Then, create a museum exhibit describing the discovery of this "lost city" in 1911, as well as the buildings and artifacts found there.

Recall
1. **(a)** Pachacuti, p. 164 **(b)** Quechua, p. 164 2. **(a)** glyph, p. 164 **(b)** quipu, p. 164 **(c)** alloy, p. 167

Comprehension
3. Possible answers: **(a)** developed arts and religion that may have influenced later cultures; **(b)** skilled farmers with techniques that included terracing, irrigation, and fertilization 4. Possible answers: The Incas imposed their own language and religion on the people. They created one of the great road systems in history, which allowed armies and runners to move swiftly throughout the empire. Soldiers stationed throughout the empire could move to put down uprisings within days. 5. Incas lived in close-knit communities where government leaders assigned jobs to each family and organized the community to work the land. Government officials arranged marriages to ensure that men and women were settled by a certain age.

Critical Thinking and Writing
6. **(a)** The Incas lived on steep mountain slopes. **(b)** They built terraces for farming to keep rains from washing away the soil. This made farming possible in places where land was scarce. They built bridges across deep gorges, steps up steep slopes, and tunnels through hillsides. **(c)** These achievements suggest advanced learning and a well-organized central government. 7. Possible answer: The Sapa Inca provided order, safety, and stability, but the average Incan had little personal freedom and no say in decision making.

Activity Rubrics

Share rubrics with students before they create their exhibits.

Attempted The exhibit is attempted but contains few items and scanty or no descriptions.

Minimal The exhibit contains several items with brief descriptions.

Adequate The exhibit contains an account of the discovery of Machu Picchu by Hiram Bingham in 1911 and includes many items with informative descriptions.

Exemplary The exhibit contains an account of the discovery of Machu Picchu by Hiram Bingham in 1911 and includes many items with excellent descriptions.

Human Drama Activity

Writing a Diary Entry The Chosen Women were selected at the age of eight, on the basis of looks, weaving skills, or rank. Near the main temple in each provincial capital was a house of the chosen where the girls lived and studied in strict seclusion. The house at Cuzco, which admitted only those of royal blood, had a long narrow corridor with rooms along each side. Doorkeepers guarded each door. Porters fetched and carried whatever was needed, but were allowed to go only as far as the second door, even if they were called in. The penalty for breaking that rule was death, both for the porter and for anyone who called him in. The girls' training ended at the age of 16. In old age, a Chosen Woman might be allowed to return home, where she would live in comfort, venerated by all for her lifetime of service.

Have students imagine that they have been selected as Chosen Women and write several diary entries describing their emotions and the reasons for their feelings. Entries should be based on the above information and that in the text. ✳

🔔 **Bell Ringer** Have students use the map and chart in this section to identify and describe the Native American culture group that inhabited the area where the students now live. Call on volunteers to describe what they know about Native American cultures in the time before Europeans arrived.

Reading Focus

- How did people in the desert southwest adapt to their environment?

- How did the culture of the Mound Builders reflect their contact with other regions?

- How did the diverse regional cultures in the Americas differ from one another?

Vocabulary

pueblo
kiva
potlatch

Taking Notes

Create a table that compares three culture areas in North America. This sample will help you get started.

CULTURE AREA	GEOGRAPHY	WAY OF LIFE	OTHER
ARCTIC	Harsh climate		
NORTHWEST COAST			Shared wealth
EASTERN WOODLANDS		Built villages in forests	

Main Idea Geographic diversity contributed to the growth of a great variety of cultures in North America.

LESSON PLAN

1. Focus As farming spread northward from Middle America, the people of North America began to build permanent settlements. Objects found in mounds in the Mississippi and Ohio valleys provide evidence of technology and trade. In this section, students will learn about the wide variety of cultural traditions in North America.

2. Instruct Divide the class into several teams, each assigned to explore one of the North American culture groups covered in this section. Ask students to describe the geographic setting, the culture, and the advances made by the people assigned to them. Challenge students to find some additional details by conducting research. After students have completed this part of the lesson, regroup them so that each new team consists of students who have learned about different cultural groups. Instruct team members to use their expertise to instruct the other students in the group about the culture group that they have studied.

3. Assess In a class discussion, ask students to explain how, in North America, geographic diversity led to cultural diversity. Encourage students to support their ideas with examples.

4. Reteach If students' **Assess** activity does not reflect adequate understanding of the lesson, you might assign the *Guide to the Essentials* or the *Interactive Student Tutorial CD-ROM* for this section.

Connections to Today

Apartment Living

"Cliff dwellers"—today that term could describe people who live in tall apartment buildings. But it was first used to describe the Anasazi.

Named because it backed up against a sheer cliff, the Cliff Palace was one of the Anasazi's major "apartment buildings." With 217 rooms and 250 residents, it was larger than many modern apartment buildings. In place of brick, its walls were made of carefully cut slabs of stone, fitted tightly together. Rather than flat boards, great logs formed its floors and roofs. There were no elevators, though—its residents reached their rooms by either climbing ladders or mounting steps carved in the stone.

Theme: Continuity and Change Why do you think that the Anasazi and modern city dwellers developed similar types of housing?

Setting the Scene

Climate and natural resources had profound effects on daily life for the first people in North America. A traditional southwest song reflects how the natural world provided beauty as well as the necessities of life:

"The whole Southwest was a House Made of Dawn. It was made of pollen and of rain. The land was old and everlasting. There were many colors on the hills and on the plain, and there was a dark wilderness on the mountains beyond. The land was tilled and strong and it was beautiful all around."
—quoted in *The Native Americans: An Illustrated History*
(Ballantine)

The impact of the environment stretched far beyond the southwest. Hundreds of cultural groups emerged in the present-day United States and Canada. For centuries, they lived by hunting, fishing, and gathering wild plants. As farming spread north from Middle America, many people raised corn and other food crops. Some people farmed so successfully that they built large permanent settlements. Here, we will look at the earliest of these farming cultures, in the desert southwest and in the Mississippi Valley.

The Desert Southwest

More than 1,000 years ago, fields of corn, beans, and squash bloomed in the desert southwest. The farmers who planted these fields were called the Hohokams, or "Vanished Ones," by their later descendants, the Pimas and Papagos. To farm the desert, they built a complex irrigation system.

The Hohokams lived near the Gila River in present-day Arizona. They may have acquired skills such as irrigation from the civilizations of Middle America. They built temple mounds and ball courts, as the Mayas did. The Hohokams survived until about A.D. 1500, when drought seems to have forced them to leave their settlements.

Anasazi The best-known society of the southwest was that of the Anasazi. They lived in what is today the Four Corners region of Arizona, New Mexico, Colorado, and Utah. Between about A.D. 900 and 1300, the Anasazi built large villages, later called pueblos by the Spanish.

Remains of Pueblo Bonito still stand in New Mexico. The village consisted of a huge complex with 800 rooms that housed about 6,000 people.

Connections to Today

ANSWERS Apartment buildings are efficient in allowing a large number of people to live on a fairly limited area of land.

Resource Directory

Teaching Resources
Creative Teaching Activities Creative Teaching Activities booklet, p. 36
Guided Reading and Review Unit 2 booklet, p. 66

Builders used stone and adobe bricks to erect a crescent-shaped compound rising five stories high.

At the center of the great complex was a plaza. There, the Anasazi dug their kiva, a large underground chamber used for religious ceremonies. Paintings on the walls show their concern with weather, including storms that might damage crops.

Cliff Dwellings In the late 1100s, the Anasazi began building housing complexes in the shadow of canyon walls, where the cliffs offered protection from raiders. The largest of these cliff dwellings at Mesa Verde, in present-day Colorado, had over 200 rooms. People had to climb ladders to reach their fields on the flatlands above or the canyon floor below.

In the late 1200s, a long drought forced the Anasazi to abandon their cliff dwellings. Without rain, they could no longer live in large settlements. Attacks by Navajos and Apaches may have contributed further to their decline. Anasazi traditions survived, however, among the Hopis and other Pueblo Indians of the present-day southwestern United States.

The Mound Builders

Far to the east of the Anasazi, in the Mississippi and Ohio valleys, other farming cultures emerged as early as 700 B.C. The Adena and Hopewell people left behind giant earthen mounds. Some mounds were cone-shaped, while others were made in the shape of animals. The Great Serpent Mound in Ohio wriggles and twists for almost a quarter of a mile.

Objects found in Hopewell mounds show that traders extended their influence over a wide area. They brought back shells and shark teeth from the Gulf of Mexico and copper from the Great Lakes region. Skilled artisans hammered and shaped the copper into fine ornaments.

Cahokia By A.D. 800, these early cultures had disappeared, but a new people, the Mississippians, gained influence. As their culture spread, the Mississippians built clusters of earthen mounds and ever larger towns and ceremonial centers.

Their greatest center, Cahokia in present-day Illinois, housed as many as 40,000 people by about A.D. 1200. Cahokia boasted at least 60 mounds. On top of some mounds stood the homes of rulers and nobles. The largest mound probably had a temple on its summit, where priests and rulers offered prayers and sacrifices to the sun. Archaeologists think that this temple mound shows the influence of Middle American civilizations.

Heirs of the Mound Builders The Mississippians left no written records, and their cities had disappeared by the time Europeans reached the area. Still, their traditions survived among the Natchez people, whose ruler, the Great Sun, had absolute power. He and his family lived on the top of pyramid mounds.

Diverse Regional Cultures

Many other groups of Native Americans emerged in North America prior to 1500. Modern scholars have identified 10 culture areas based on the environments in which people lived: the Arctic, Subarctic, Northwest Coast, California, Great Basin, Plateau, Southwest, Great Plains, Eastern Woodlands, and Southeast. In each area, people adapted to geographic conditions that influenced their ways of life.

Legacy of the Mound Builders
The Great Serpent Mound (center) in Ohio shows careful planning in its even curves. Archaeologists have discovered artifacts such as this mica bird's claw (top) and carved frog (bottom) in mounds built by the Adena, Hopewell, and Mississippian peoples.

Theme: Global Interaction
Why do scholars think that Mississippian mounds may show the influence of Middle American civilizations?

Background
Daily Life

The Bow The Mississippian people benefited from a relatively new technology—the bow. For thousands of years, Native American hunters had relied on spears thrown by hand or with the aid of a throwing stick. To capture small game, they had also used snares and nets. But by the time Cahokia reached its height, Native American inventors had discovered how to cut a pliable length of tree branch and string it with tough plant fiber to create a bow. The bow revolutionized both hunting and warfare. A hunter or warrior armed with a bow could shoot an arrow three times the distance that he could throw a spear. The bow also provided greater accuracy. This new technology, along with advances in agriculture, enabled the Mississippians to feed the populations of their growing towns.

Reading Strategy
Graphic Organizer

Ask students to write three column headings at the top of a sheet of paper: The Desert Southwest, The Mound Builders, Diverse Regional Cultures. Have them list the Native American societies appropriate to each heading. Also, ask students to fill in details from the text that describe these societies. *(Less Advanced Readers)*

Block Scheduling Support

Divide the class into seven groups. Have each group create a presentation that illustrates the culture of one of the Native American groups included on the chart on the next page. Help students search the Internet to complete this activity. Each group's presentation should include one or more maps, drawings or photocopies of cultural artifacts, and short descriptive captions. Each group might also produce a brief essay that gives more detailed information on the culture group assigned to it. Suggest to students that they divide the tasks so that some group members do research, others create illustrations, and others write. Students should be prepared to present their findings to the class. ✳

Caption Answer

The largest mound in Cahokia probably had a temple on its summit for prayers and sacrifices, which archaeologists think may show Middle American influence.

Oral Tradition Native Americans had a rich oral tradition that was passed from generation to generation. While various culture groups produced their own unique traditions, their stories often displayed certain common themes, such as reverence for nature and devotion to ancestral spirits. Many traditional myths reinforced cultural values and justified the natural order of the world. Other stories explained how people, animals, plants, geographic formations, or natural phenomena came into the world. For example, one common myth explained the beginning of the world by telling of an animal that dove into the waters of the universe and emerged with a speck of dirt that grew into the world. Much of the Native American oral tradition has been preserved and recorded. You may wish to have students visit the library to find anthologies of Native American literature.

North American Culture Areas About 1450

Skills Assessment

Geography As Native Americans spread out to populate North America, they developed a wide variety of cultures. The map shows culture areas in which tribes shared similar environments and ways of life.

1. **Location** On the map, locate **(a)** Northwest Coast culture area, **(b)** Eastern Woodlands culture area, **(c)** Great Basin culture area.
2. **Place (a)** Name two tribes in the Great Plains culture area. **(b)** With which culture area are the Cherokees associated?
3. **Critical Thinking Making Inferences** The Navajos lived in the Southwest culture area but spoke a Subarctic language. **(a)** How might this be explained? **(b)** What were some other characteristics of peoples in the Southwest culture area?

Map legend:
- Arctic/Subarctic
- Northwest Coast
- California/Great Basin/Plateau
- Southwest
- Great Plains
- Eastern Woodlands
- Southeast

Azimuthal Equal Area Projection

0   500   1000 Miles

0   500   1000 Kilometers

Native American Culture Groups of North America

Arctic/Subarctic
Beavers, Crees, Inuits, Kutchins

Lived as nomadic hunters and food gatherers in cold climate; honored ocean, weather, and animal spirits

California/Great Basin/Plateau
Nez Percés, Pomos, Shoshones

Lived as hunters and gatherers in small family groups; ate mainly fish, berries, acorns

Southwest
Apaches, Hohokams, Hopis, Navajos, Pueblos

Lived in villages in homes made of adobe; built irrigation systems to grow corn and other crops; honored earth, sky, and water spirits

Southeast
Cherokees, Natchez

Grew corn, squash, beans, and other crops; held yearly Green Corn Ceremony to mark end of year and celebrate harvest

Northwest Coast
Bella Coolas, Coos, Kwakiutls, Tlingits

Lived in villages; benefited from rich natural resources in forests, rivers, and ocean; held potlatches, or ceremonial dinners, where host families gave gifts to guests to show wealth and gain status

Great Plains
Apaches, Arapahos, Blackfeet, Cheyennes, Comanches, Crows, Lakotas, Mandans, Osages

Lived in tepees; animals hunted by men; crops grown by women; relied on buffalo to meet basic needs of food, shelter, and clothing

Eastern Woodlands
Algonquins, Chippewas, Hurons, Iroquois, Leni-Lenapes, Miamis, Pequots, Shawnees

Lived in farming villages, but also hunted for food; long houses shared by several families; women held social and political power

170 Chapter 7

Skills Assessment

ANSWERS 1. Review locations with students. **2. (a)** Any two of the following: Blackfeet, Mandans, Crows, Lakotas, Cheyennes, Arapahos, Osages, Apaches, Comanches **(b)** Southeast **3. (a)** migration between regions **(b)** homes made of adobe, built irrigation systems, honored nature spirits

Resource Directory

Teaching Resources
Primary Source Activity *The Greenlanders' Saga,* Unit 2 booklet, p. 69
Section Quiz Unit 2 booklet, p. 67
Geography Quiz Unit 2 booklet, p. 72
Chapter Test Forms A, B, and C Unit 2 booklet, pp. 73–77
Answer Key Unit 2 booklet, pp. 78–89

Technology
Interactive Student Tutorial CD-ROM Ch. 7
Computer Test Bank Ch. 7

Here, we will look in greater detail at the distinct ways of life that developed in three regions—the Arctic, the Northwest Coast, and the Eastern Woodlands.

A Frozen World In the far north, the Inuits* adapted to a harsh climate, using the resources of the frozen land to survive. Small bands lived by hunting and fishing. Seals and other sea mammals provided them with food, skins for clothing, bones for needles and tools, and oil for cooking. They paddled kayaks in open waters or used dog sleds to transport goods across the ice. In some areas, Inuits constructed igloos, or dome-shaped homes made from snow and ice. In others, they built sod dwellings that were partly underground.

A Land of Plenty The people of the Northwest Coast lived in a far richer environment than the Inuits. Rivers teemed with salmon, and the Pacific Ocean offered other fish and sea mammals. Hunters tracked deer, wolves, and bears in the forests. In this land of plenty, people built large permanent villages with homes made of wood. They traded their surplus goods, gaining wealth that was shared in ceremonies like the potlatch. At this ceremony, which continues in Canada today, a person of rank and wealth distributes lavish gifts to large numbers of guests. By accepting the gifts, the guests acknowledge the host's high status.

The Iroquois League The Eastern Woodlands, stretching from the Atlantic Coast to the Great Lakes, was home to a number of groups, including the Iroquois. They cleared land and built villages in the forests. While women farmed, men hunted and frequently warred against rival nations.

According to Iroquois tradition, the prophet Dekanawidah (deh kan ah WEE dah) urged rival Iroquois nations to stop their constant wars. In the late 1500s, he became one of the founders of the unique political system known as the Iroquois League. This was an alliance of five nations who spoke the same language and shared similar traditions.

The Iroquois League did not always succeed in keeping the peace. Still, it was the best-organized political group north of Mexico. Member nations governed their own villages but met jointly in a council when they needed to address larger issues. Only men sat on the council, but each clan had a "clan mother" who could name or depose members of the council.

The Iroquois League emerged just at the time when Europeans arrived in the Americas. Encounters with Europeans would take a fearful toll on the peoples of North America and topple the Aztec and Incan empires.

* The Inuits were late immigrants from Siberia. Other Native Americans called them Eskimos, "eaters of raw flesh," but they called themselves the Inuits, the "people."

Primary Source

A Plea for Peace
In about 1570, the prophet Dekanawidah persuaded warring Iroquois nations to form a confederacy:

"I, Dekanawidah, and the confederate lords now uproot the tallest tree and into the cavity thereby made we cast all weapons of war. Into the depths of the earth we cast all weapons of strife. We bury them from sight forever and plant again the tree. Thus shall all Great Peace be established and hostilities shall no longer be known between the Five Nations but only peace to a united people."

—Iroquois Constitution

Skills Assessment

Primary Source What does Dekanawidah believe the Iroquois must do to achieve the Great Peace?

SECTION 3 Assessment

Recall
1. **Identify: (a)** Hohokams,
   (b) Anasazi, **(c)** Mound Builders,
   (d) Inuits, **(e)** Iroquois League.
2. **Define: (a)** pueblo, **(b)** kiva,
   (c) potlatch.

Comprehension
3. How did the Hohokams farm the desert southwest?
4. How do we know about the lives of the Mound Builders and their contacts with other peoples?

5. Give examples of how the environment influenced three early cultures of North America.

Critical Thinking and Writing
6. **Asking Questions** If you were an archaeologist studying the Adena and Hopewell people, what three questions might you ask about the giant mounds they built?
7. **Linking Past and Present** How does environment affect your community?

Activity

Creating a Poster
With a partner, create a poster that expresses the ideas behind the formation of the Iroquois League. Use symbols to represent the five Iroquois nations.

Chapter 7 **171**

SECTION 3 Assessment

Recall
1. **(a)** Hohokams, p. 168 **(b)** Anasazi, p. 168 **(c)** Mound Builders, p. 169 **(d)** Inuits, p. 171 **(e)** Iroquois League, p. 171 2. **(a)** pueblo, p. 168 **(b)** kiva, p. 169 **(c)** potlatch, p. 171

Comprehension
3. They built a complex irrigation system.
4. Archaeologists have learned about their lives by studying the remains of their mounds, towns, and ceremonial centers. They also study the artifacts that the people left inside the mounds. 5. Possible answers: Drought forced the Anasazi to abandon their cliff dwellings. The Inuits survived in the frozen north by building homes from sod or snow and ice. In the forest lands of the Northwest Coast, people enjoyed plentiful natural resources and could therefore live in large permanent villages.

Critical Thinking and Writing
6. Possible answers: What was the purpose of the mounds? Why are some mounds cone-shaped and others in the shape of animals? Do the mounds or the objects in them resemble artifacts of other nearby people? 7. Answers depend on where students live, but students should recognize that climate, geographic features, and the presence or absence of natural resources affect the life of their community.

Activity Rubrics

Share rubrics with students before they make their posters.

Attempted The poster is attempted but is incomplete.

Minimal The poster reflects limited understanding of the ideas behind the formation of the Iroquois League or is messy.

Adequate The poster reflects an understanding of the ideas behind the formation of the Iroquois League and is visually appealing.

Exemplary The poster reflects an understanding of the ideas behind the formation of the Iroquois League and is dramatic and eye-catching.

Primary Source

ANSWERS They must get rid of all the weapons that encourage them to make war among themselves, and they must join together in unity and brotherhood.

Human Drama Note

Bury the Hatchet Dekanawidah's call for burying the weapons of war came from an actual practice which stated that, when smoking the peace pipe, all such weapons must be buried, putting all reminders of aggression out of sight. Longfellow refers to the peacemaking in "The Song of Hiawatha."

Buried was the bloody hatchet.
Buried was the dreadful war club;
Buried were all warlike weapons,
And the war-cry was forgotten.
There was peace among the nations.

Test Preparation

Have students read the Primary Source on this page, and then answer the question below.

Which is the best summary of the passage?

A We will bury our weapons under a tree and resume hostilities among the Five Nations.

B We will establish peace among the Five Nations by burying our weapons under a tree.

C Peace among the Five Nations will begin when we bury our weapons inside a tree.

D We will unite the Five Nations by uprooting a tree.

Creating a Chapter Summary

As a reteaching opportunity, pair a more able student with a less able student to complete this chapter summary.

Completed time lines should include the following dates and events (items to be filled in by students are shown in italics):

- A.D. 100 *Rise of Teotihuacán*
- A.D. 300 *Mayan civilization develops*
- A.D. *900* Mayas abandon their cities
- A.D. 1200 Aztecs arrive in Valley of Mexico, build Tenochtitlán
- A.D. 1400 Aztecs expand their territory
- A.D. *1438 Incan empire founded*
- A.D. 1500 *Drought may have forced the Hohokams to leave Arizona settlements.*

Building Vocabulary

1–10. Quiz definitions should show a clear understanding of the meanings of the terms.

Recalling Key Facts

11. They may have traveled over a land bridge that formed between Siberia and North America during the last ice age.
12. They developed a hieroglyphic writing system and an accurate 365-day solar calendar, invented a numbering system, and understood the concept of zero.
13. At the top of society was a single ruler. Below him, nobles served as officials, judges, and governors of conquered provinces. Next came the warriors, who could rise to noble status by killing or capturing enemy soldiers. The majority of people were commoners who farmed the land. At the bottom of society were the slaves, mostly criminals or prisoners of war.
14. to unite their great empire
15. There was a long drought.
16. to put an end to constant wars

Critical Thinking and Writing

17. **(a)** The Mayas built raised fields with channels to drain excessive water. The Aztecs built artificial islands to create more farmland. By carving terraces into hillsides, Incan farmers prevented soil erosion. **(b)** By developing farming methods that were suited to their geographic environment, all three civilizations were able to produce enough crops to support their growing populations.

CHAPTER **7** **Review and Assessment**

Creating a Chapter Summary

Fill in the missing events and dates on the following time line. Add more events and dates to create a time line that includes the major cultures discussed in this chapter.

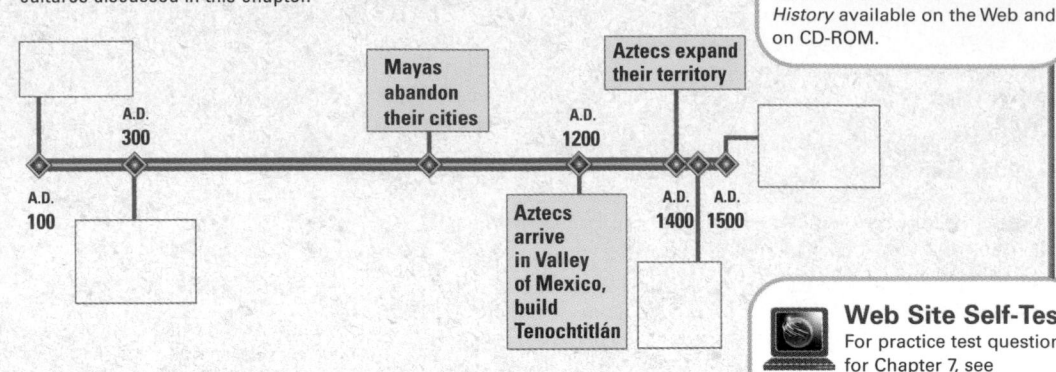

A.D. 300

Mayas abandon their cities

Aztecs expand their territory

A.D. 1200

A.D. 100

Aztecs arrive in Valley of Mexico, build Tenochtitlán

A.D. 1400 A.D. 1500

iTEXT

For additional review and enrichment activities, see the interactive version of *World History* available on the Web and on CD-ROM.

Web Site Self-Test

For practice test questions for Chapter 7, see **www.phschool.com**.

Building Vocabulary

Review the vocabulary words listed below. Then, use the words and their definitions to create a matching quiz. Exchange quizzes with another student. Check each other's answers when you are finished.

1. global warming
2. plains
3. chinampas
4. tribute
5. glyph
6. quipu
7. alloy
8. pueblo
9. kiva
10. potlatch

Recalling Key Facts

11. How and when do historians think that people first migrated to the Americas?
12. Name three advances in learning made by the Mayas.
13. Describe the social structure of the Aztec empire.
14. Why did the Incas build an extensive road system?
15. Why did the Anasazis abandon their cliff dwellings?
16. What was the main goal of the Iroquois League?

Critical Thinking and Writing

17. **Analyzing Information (a)** What advances in agriculture did the Mayas, Aztecs, and Incas make? **(b)** Why were these farming methods critical to the development of each of these civilizations?
18. **Predicting Consequences** How do you think the people conquered by the Aztecs might respond to an invasion by a foreign power? Explain.
19. **Synthesizing Information (a)** How were religion and government linked in the Incan empire? **(b)** Identify two other ancient civilizations you have read about in which rulers claimed divine powers.
20. **Comparing** Review the information on the Roman empire in the previous chapter. Then, compare the methods used by the Incas and the Romans to unite and control their diverse, far-flung empires.
21. **Connecting to Geography (a)** Describe the environment of the Northwest Coast. **(b)** How did people adapt to this environment?

---

18. Possible answers: They might help the invaders to overthrow the Aztecs. The conquered people might hope that foreign invaders would free them or not see them as a source of sacrificial victims.
19. **(a)** The Sapa Inca claimed divinity as the son of the sun and was the religious as well as the political leader. **(b)** China and Egypt
20. Possible answers: Both empires had powerful emperors, a large bureaucracy, an extensive system of roads, and a strong army. The Romans were more tolerant of local customs and allowed more self-government than the Incas did.
21. **(a)** The Northwest Coast people lived in a hospitable environment that enabled them to develop a

comfortable way of life. **(b)** They had plentiful food; lived in permanent villages; traded surplus goods.

Father Bernabe Cobo was a seventeenth-century Spanish missionary who worked with the Indians of Peru. Over the years, Cobo closely observed the Incas. In the excerpt below, Cobo describes the great majesty and splendor of the Sapa Inca. Read the excerpt and answer the questions that follow.

"The multitude of servants that they had in their palace was incredible. They were served all the exquisite, precious, and rare things that the land produced. . . . Serving women brought him all of his food. . . . When he pointed out the dish that he wanted, . . . one of these serving women would take it to him and hold it in her hand while he ate. . . . All leftovers from the meal and whatever the Inca touched with his hands were kept by the Indians in chests; thus, in one chest they placed the little [mats] that they placed before him when he ate; in another, the bones of the poultry and meat left over from his meals; in another, the clothes that he discarded. Finally, everything that the Inca had touched was kept in a hut, . . . and on a certain day each year it was all burned. They said that since the Incas were children of the Sun, whatever they touched had to be burned, . . . and no one was to touch it."

—Bernabe Cobo, *History of the Inca Empire*

22. What is the source of the excerpt?
23. According to Cobo, how was the Inca treated by his subjects?
24. **(a)** What happened to things that the Inca touched? **(b)** Why?
25. Do you think this is a reliable source of information about the Incas? Explain.

Skills Assessment
Take It to the NET

Use the Internet to research Aztec, Incan, or Mayan art. Then, create a sketch, sculpture, or textile in the artistic style of the civilization you have researched. If you prefer, write a description of a piece of art you have researched, focusing on special features of that civilization's style.

This picture is from an Aztec codex, or book. It is a symbolic representation of the rise of Tenochtitlán, the Aztec capital. Study the picture and review what you have learned about the Aztec empire to answer the following questions:

26. **(a)** Identify two symbols in the top portion of the picture. **(b)** What might they represent?
27. **(a)** What is the bird in the center of the picture? **(b)** What is the bird perched on? **(c)** Why do you think the Aztec artist placed it there?
28. Canals divided Tenochtitlán into four quarters. How did the artist represent the canals?
29. **(a)** What might the symbols at the bottom of the panel represent? **(b)** What do the symbols suggest about Aztec culture?

Skills Tip

Artists often use symbols to represent ideas. Study the symbols and compare them with your own knowledge to identify their meaning.

Analyzing Primary Sources

22. *History of the Inca Empire* by a Spanish priest, Father Bernabe Cobo
23. He was treated with great respect and worship.
24. **(a)** They were placed in a box until they were burned. **(b)** The Incas believed that the Sapa Inca was the child of the sun and whatever he touched had to be burned and made into ashes.
25. Students should recognize that since the Incas left no written record, carefully researched reports like this one by Cobo are important historical documents. They might note, however, that Cobo's views are those of a conqueror.

Analyzing Art

26. **(a)** Possible answers: crops, house **(b)** the importance of people (families) and agriculture in the building of the city of Tenochtitlán
27. **(a)** an eagle **(b)** a cactus **(c)** The eagle is an important symbol of the Aztec empire. According to legend, the gods told the Aztecs to search for an eagle perched on a cactus holding a snake in its beak. That is where they were to build Tenochtitlán.
28. The crossed blue bands represent the canals.
29. **(a)** Aztec warriors in battle **(b)** that warfare played an important role in Aztec culture

Skills Tip

Background knowledge about a subject makes it easier to decipher the symbols used in art. Therefore, sometimes additional research may be required to understand a work of art. The Skills Handbook in the front of the book has a lesson that will help students with this feature.

Unit Theme Activity

Evaluate students' Unit Theme Activities by referring to the rubrics on the unit opener page in the Teacher's Edition.

Take It to the NET

Direct students to **www.phschool.com** for links to sites that will help them get started on this assignment. Share rubrics with students.
Attempted The project is attempted but is incomplete.
Minimal The project shows little research and is poorly executed.
Adequate The project shows appropriate research, and the artwork is well executed, or the description is well written.
Exemplary The project shows extensive research, and the artwork is very well executed, or the description is very well written.

USING THESE PAGES

The Unit-in-Brief contains the main ideas of the unit chapters. You may use the Unit-in-Brief to preview, review, or condense the contents of each chapter.

The unit time line identifies key events in each world region that took place during the time span covered by the unit.

Activity
Unit Themes

Have students review the unit themes below. Then, ask them to find examples in the time line and summary to support each theme.

Political and Social Systems Strong leaders centralized their power and created efficient government systems. These developments enabled the leaders to impose unity on diverse peoples and to strengthen their empires.

Global Interaction Civilizations in India, China, Greece, Rome, and the Americas spread ideas about government, technology, and religion through trade and conquest.

Religions and Value Systems Several major world religions and value systems, including Christianity, Buddhism, Confucianism, and Hinduism, developed among the peoples of the ancient world.

Continuity and Change From the Great Wall of China to the Incan royal road, ancient empires left behind impressive monuments. The civilizations of China, India, Greece, and Rome forged cultural legacies that still influence the world.

Chapter 4

Empires of India and China
(600 B.C.–A.D. 550)

Between 600 B.C. and A.D. 550, strong, unified empires with complex belief systems emerged in India and China. These civilizations set patterns in government, religion, and philosophy that influenced later cultures.

- Hindu beliefs, including the concepts of reincarnation, karma, and dharma, profoundly influenced Indian civilization.
- The Buddha, an Indian religious reformer, sought spiritual enlightenment. His teachings gave rise to a new religion, Buddhism, that spread through Southeast and East Asia.
- Under the Maurya and Gupta dynasties, India developed into a center of trade and had contacts with civilizations in Africa, the Middle East, and Central and Southeast Asia.
- The caste system, the village, and the family influenced many aspects of Indian life.
- The teachings of Confucius, based on ideals of duty and social good, influenced Chinese government and society.
- Legalism and Daoism were two other important philosophies that arose in China.
- Shi Huangdi united China and built a strong authoritarian government, which laid the groundwork for China's classical age.
- Under Han rulers, the Chinese made huge advances in trade, government, technology, and the arts.

Chapter 5

Ancient Greece
(1750 B.C.–133 B.C.)

Despite bitter rivalry, Greek city-states gave rise to a civilization that set a standard of excellence for later civilizations. Greek ideas about the universe, the individual, and government still live on in the world today.

- Through trading contacts, Minoan and Mycenaean culture acquired many ideas from older civilizations of Egypt and Mesopotamia.
- Separated by mountains, the Greek city-states often warred with one another but united to defeat the Persians.
- After the Persian Wars, democracy flourished and culture thrived in Athens under the leadership of Pericles.
- Guided by a belief in reason, Greek artists, writers, and philosophers used their genius to seek order in the universe.
- The conquests of Alexander the Great spread Greek civilization throughout the Mediterranean world and across the Middle East to the outskirts of India.
- Greek culture blended with Persian, Egyptian, and Indian cultures to create the Hellenistic civilization, in which art, science, mathematics, and philosophy flourished.

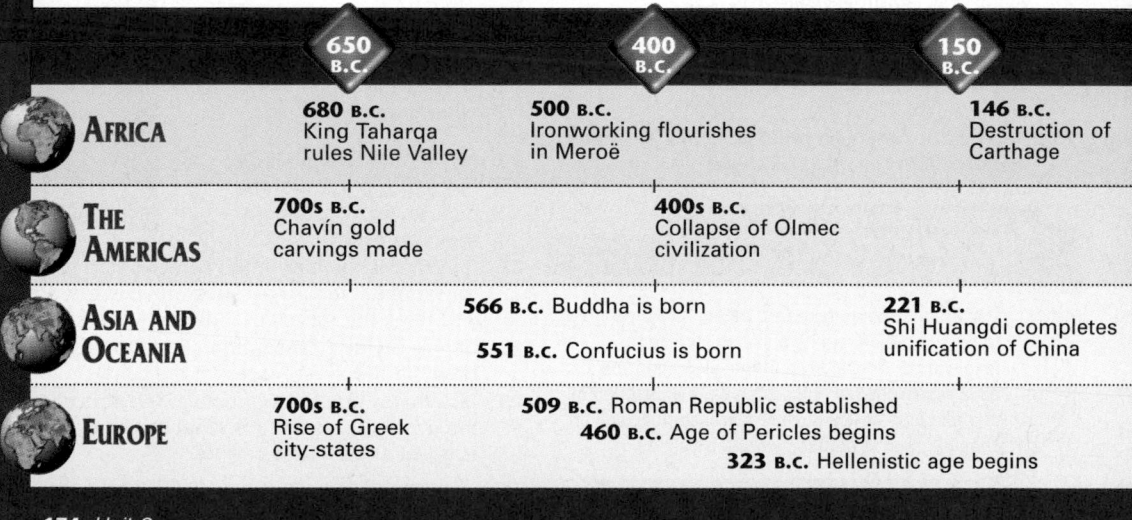

	650 B.C.	400 B.C.	150 B.C.
AFRICA	**680 B.C.** King Taharqa rules Nile Valley	**500 B.C.** Ironworking flourishes in Meroë	**146 B.C.** Destruction of Carthage
THE AMERICAS	**700s B.C.** Chavín gold carvings made	**400s B.C.** Collapse of Olmec civilization	
ASIA AND OCEANIA	**566 B.C.** Buddha is born **551 B.C.** Confucius is born		**221 B.C.** Shi Huangdi completes unification of China
EUROPE	**700s B.C.** Rise of Greek city-states	**509 B.C.** Roman Republic established **460 B.C.** Age of Pericles begins **323 B.C.** Hellenistic age begins	

Student Bibliography

Andrewes, A. *Greek Society.* D.C. Heath, 1992. A clear and accessible survey of Greek history from archaic to classical periods.

Coe, Michael D. *The Maya (Ancient Peoples and Places).* Thames & Hudson, 1999. Detailed account of the ancient Mayan civilization.

Fairbank, John K., and Edwin O. Reischauer. *China: Tradition and Transformation.* Houghton Mifflin, 1989. Rich textbook with many illustrations by two eminent scholars.

Feuerstein, Georg, and Subhash Kak. *In Search of the Cradle of Civilization: New Light on Ancient India.* Quest Books, 1995. A scholarly study arguing that India, not Sumer, was the cradle of civilized humanity.

Grant, Michael. *History of Rome.* Macmillan, 1978. Comprehensive and highly readable history of Rome from its beginnings to its fall.

Thomas, David Hurst. *Exploring Ancient Native America: An Archaeological Guide.* Routledge, 1994. Illustrated reference to ancient Indian cultures in North America.

Chapter 6

Ancient Rome and the Rise of Christianity
(509 B.C.–A.D. 476)

Rome expanded across the Mediterranean to build a huge, diverse empire. In the process, it spread the civilizations of Greece, Egypt, and the Fertile Crescent westward into Europe.

- After the Romans threw out their Etruscan king, they set up a republic. Eventually, commoners were allowed to be elected to the Roman senate.
- Conquest and diplomacy helped the Romans to extend their rule from Spain to Egypt. However, expansion created social and economic problems that led to the decline of the republic and the rule of an emperor.
- During the Pax Romana, Roman emperors brought peace, order, unity, and prosperity to the lands under their control.
- Rome acted as a bridge between the east and the west by borrowing and transforming Greek and Hellenistic achievements to produce Greco-Roman civilization.
- Christianity, which emerged in Roman-held lands in the Middle East, spread quickly throughout the Roman empire. The new faith reshaped Roman beliefs.
- Foreign invasions, the division of the empire, a corrupt government, poverty and unemployment, and declining moral values finally contributed to the downfall of the Roman empire.

Chapter 7

Civilizations of the Americas
(1400 B.C.–A.D. 1570)

Four advanced civilizations—those of the Olmecs, the Mayas, the Aztecs, and the Incas—developed in Middle and South America. In North America, diverse culture groups emerged.

- The first settlers in the Americas were nomadic hunters who migrated across a land bridge between Siberia and Alaska and gradually populated two vast continents.
- From about 1400 B.C to 500 B.C., the Olmec civilization flourished along the Mexican Gulf Coast. Their religious, scientific, and architectural contributions influenced later civilizations in Mexico.
- Mayan civilization flourished from southern Mexico through Central America between A.D. 300 and A.D. 900. Its system of city-states supported a complex religious structure.
- In the 1400s, the Aztecs conquered most of Mexico and built a highly developed civilization led by a single ruler.
- By the 1500s, the Incas established a centralized government in Peru, ruled by a god-king and a powerful class of priests.
- Ten culture groups developed in the Arctic, Subarctic, Northwest Coast, California, Great Basin, Plateau, Southwest, Great Plains, Southeast, and Eastern Woodlands. Their diverse ways of life were strongly influenced by geography.

Activity
Summarizing the Main Idea

Have students use both the Unit-in-Brief and Chapters 4–7 to answer the following questions in order to summarize Unit 2: (1) What religions and philosophies spread as ancient empires of Asia and Europe expanded their influences? (2) How did conquest and trade increase the lasting significance of ancient empires? (3) How did cultural blending enrich Greco-Roman civilization? (4) Describe the type of government that was most common among ancient empires.

PRENTICE HALL
ASSESSMENT SYSTEM

Diagnose and Prescribe
- **Profile student skills with Diagnostic Tests A & B.**
- **Address student needs with program materials identified in the test.**

Review and Reteach
- **Provide cumulative content review with the Review Book.**

Practice and Assess
- **Build test-taking skills with Test-Taking Strategies With Transparencies.**

A.D. 100

A.D. 350

A.D. 600

LATE A.D. 100s
Camel caravans create new trade patterns

A.D. 350
Axum converts to Christianity

A.D. 100s
Mochica civilization rises

A.D. 200s
Hopewell culture flourishes

A.D. 500s
Height of Mayan civilization

A.D. 100
Paper invented in Han China

A.D. 320
Gupta Golden Age begins

27 B.C.
Pax Romana begins

A.D. 135
Jewish diaspora begins

A.D. 476
Western Roman empire falls

Teacher Bibliography

Boardman, J., J. Griffin, and O. Murray, eds. *Oxford History of Greece and the Hellenistic World.* Oxford University Press, 1991. Sixteen essays by prominent scholars serve as an excellent introduction to many topics.

Liu, Xinru. *Ancient India and Ancient China: Trade and Religious Exchanges, A.D. 1–600.* Oxford University Press, 1988. Examination of commercial and religious interchange between India and China.

Longhena, Maria. *Ancient Mexico: The History and Culture of the Maya, Aztec, and Other Precolumbian Peoples.* Stewart Tabori & Chang, 1998. Nicely illustrated cultural history that discusses many topics, including art and religion.

Schele, Linda, Peter Mathews, et al. *The Code of Kings: The Language of Seven Sacred Maya Temples and Tombs.* Scribner, 1998. Unique guide to seven major sites of Mayan civilization.

Scullard, H.H. *A History of the Roman World: 753–146 B.C.* Methuen, 1980. History of Rome from earliest times, including daily life and culture.

UNIT 3

UNIT OVERVIEW

Unit 3 examines how regional civilizations, from about 500 to 1500, linked people of diverse lands.

Chapter 8 focuses on feudalism, Christianity, and economic change in medieval Europe.

Chapter 9 examines Western Europe during the High Middle Ages.

Chapter 10 describes the history of the Byzantine empire, Russia, and other lands of Eastern Europe.

Chapter 11 examines the birth, development, and far-reaching influence of Muslim civilization.

Chapter 12 studies early African civilizations and the economic patterns that linked Africa to other regions.

Chapter 13 focuses on the cultural interaction that linked East Asian lands.

Unit Theme Activity Rubrics

Share rubrics with students before they create their projects.

Attempted The project does not include examples of artistic expression from all the regional civilizations.

Minimal The project is poorly executed or only vaguely highlights examples of artistic expression from all the regional civilizations.

Adequate The project is well executed, with well-chosen examples of artistic expression from all the regional civilizations.

Exemplary The project is extremely well executed, with many examples of artistic expression from all the regional civilizations, and is visually interesting or is extremely interesting and informative to read.

UNIT 3

Regional Civilizations

750 B.C.–A.D. 1650

OUTLINE

THEMES

As you read about the rise of regional civilizations around the world, you will encounter the following themes.

Religions and Value Systems Religions and value systems such as Christianity, Islam, and Confucianism united people across wide areas.

Art and Literature Rich regional cultures found expression in such art forms as the Gothic cathedrals of Europe, bronze sculptures of West Africa, and kabuki theater of Japan.

Geography and History Geographic features such as the Sahara, the Mediterranean Sea, and the steppes of Russia influenced the development of regional civilizations.

Diversity As regional civilizations learned more about one another through trade and war, they became lands of diverse peoples and ideas. Sometimes this diversity led to tolerance and a flowering of ideas; sometimes it led to conflict.

Unit Theme Activity

For Your Portfolio The chapters in this unit discuss various ways in which societies expressed themselves through the arts. As you read the chapters, prepare a portfolio project highlighting examples of this artistic expression. Your project might take one of the following forms:
- **Museum exhibit and catalog**
- **Annotated map**
- **Collage**

Resource Directory

Technology
World History Visions, Voices, Views Scenes of an Age, *Regional Civilizations,* videodisc side 2 or videotape 3, running time 2:30 min.

Side 2: Fr. 228-2769

Built during the Ming dynasty, the Forbidden City was home to the emperors of China for nearly five centuries. All but a chosen few were forbidden to enter the imperial palace.

Background
About the Picture

The Forbidden City Representing the seat of Chinese power for 500 years, the imperial palace was called the "Forbidden City" because not even members of the imperial family had full access to all of its buildings—only the emperor could go wherever he wished. Built on a north-south line, the buildings all faced south, paying homage to the sun. In addition, the buildings and open spaces were all constructed so as to glorify the emperor's power while continually diminishing the individual's. It is for this reason that the Hall of Supreme Harmony, which housed the emperor's throne, is the largest single building in the compound.

After the 1911–1912 Chinese Revolution, the Forbidden City lost its status as the center of power. However, once Pu Yi, China's last emperor, abdicated, he was allowed to inhabit the palace. He remained there until 1924, when he secretly left. The Forbidden City was used in the filming of the 1987 movie *The Last Emperor,* which detailed the life of Pu Yi.

TEXT

Don't miss the exclusive interactive version of *World History: Connections to Today* on the Internet and CD-ROM.

Block Scheduling Support

Using the Unit-in-Brief The Unit-in-Brief, found at the end of the unit, contains the main ideas of the unit chapters. You may use the Unit-in-Brief to preview, review, or condense the contents of each chapter.

Using the Unit Time Line The Unit Time Line, at the end of the unit, provides a chronology of world events during the period covered by this unit. By studying the time line in conjunction with the Unit-in-Brief, students may compare developments in various regions. You may use the time line to help condense the contents of the chapters.

Using the *Guide to the Essentials* The *Guide to the Essentials of World History* contains summaries and graphic organizers for each section of every chapter in this unit. You may use the *Guide to the Essentials* to help poor readers or students acquiring English to access the main ideas of the chapters. You may also use it with all students to review or to condense topics in your world history course.

eTeach

Be sure to check out this month's online discussion with a World History Master Teacher.

Go to **www.phschool.com**.

Bell Ringer Before students read the feature, ask them to think of examples of the various kinds of heroes throughout history and how and why they have changed. For example, monarchs may once have been considered heroes, but with most countries having democratic governments, they are less likely to be seen as heroes now. Have students suggest their ideas, and discuss how heroism has changed.

Activity
Cooperative Learning

Writing and Presenting a Skit As an enrichment activity, have students work in small groups to write a skit portraying an act of heroism. Suggest that each group make a list of the tasks needed to complete the assignment. For example, some students may do research, others can write the script, and others can prepare props. Students should decide what roles will be played and who will play them. When the groups are prepared, have them perform their skits for the class.

WHY STUDY HISTORY?
Because Past Heroes Can Be Today's Role Models

We are all capable of heroism. And we can learn from the heroes of the past. Throughout history, exceptional men and women have acted boldly to change the world. Some were great leaders. Others revolutionized the way we think. Many were simply people who refused to accept injustice and unfairness as a condition of everyday life. Whoever they were, these past heroes can serve as role models for us today. By studying their lives, we may discover new ways to make our own world a better place.

Heroes strive to reach their potential.

In the Middle Ages, Europeans looked on educated women as oddities. Women, they believed, belonged in the home, managing the household and raising children. Christine de Pizan refused to accept this role. After her husband's death, she dared to support herself as a writer, an occupation usually reserved for men. In her many works, she celebrated the achievements of women and defended them against unfair attacks.

Heroes promote new ideas.

내 히 이 러 발 래 가 나 니
ㄱ 무 래 아 니 ㄱ 츨 ㅆ
ㅅ ㅣ 미 기 쁜 ㅁ 를
곳 됴 코 열 ㅁ 하 ㄴ 니
ᄆ ᄅ ᄆ 아 니 뮐 ㅆ
ᄇ 휘 기 쁜 남 ᄆ 인

It takes great courage for a leader to promote unpopular ideas. In Korea, in the 1400s, King Sejong instituted a bold reform. Ignoring the objections of scholars, Sejong introduced a new alphabet to simplify the system of writing that Koreans had used for centuries. Sejong's policy paid off. With the help of the new alphabet, Korea became one of the most literate nations in the world.

Resource Directory

Teaching Resources
Why Study History? *Because Past Heroes Can Be Today's Role Models,* Why Study History? booklet, pp. 9–10

Heroes expand our knowledge of the universe.

Scientists have always challenged accepted ideas about the nature of the world. In the early 1900s, physicist Albert Einstein advanced a series of theories that suggested entirely new ways of thinking about space, time, and gravitation. Einstein's theories of relativity and gravitation revolutionized the fields of science and philosophy.

Heroes lead the fight for freedom.

Mohandas Gandhi (above left) was a new kind of leader. Although he organized India's struggle for independence from British rule, he renounced the use of force. Instead, he called on his followers to adopt the weapon of nonviolent resistance. His campaigns of civil disobedience eroded British power and won wide support for India's cause. Gandhi's teachings continue to inspire people throughout the world today.

Who are today's heroes?

Study the daily newspaper or watch TV—you are certain to find people who qualify as heroes. For example, Colin Powell (right) was the first African American to serve as chairman of the Joint Chiefs of Staff, the highest military post in the United States. General Powell has chosen to use his celebrity to run America's Promise—The Alliance for Youth, an organization devoted to helping children at risk.

Portfolio Assessment

Connecting to Today Select either a person you know or a public figure whom you would consider a role model. Write a paragraph explaining why you think this person is a hero.

Unit 3 **179**

Background
Connections to Today

Unsung Heroes Point out to students that a person does not necessarily have to be famous to qualify as a hero. Every day, throughout the world, ordinary people help others to keep out of danger, or to learn about the world, or to recognize right from wrong. Parents, coaches, police officers, and even friends can all be unsung heroes.

Background
About the Pictures

1. Christine de Pizan (c. 1363–1431) *(opposite page, top left)* wrote poetry and prose, including a life of Charles V, an educational and social compendium for women, and celebrations of Joan of Arc's early successes.

2. King Sejong of Korea *(opposite page, bottom right)* ordered Korean scholars to invent a simple writing system based on the way their language was pronounced.

3. German-born Albert Einstein *(top left)* was a Jew who fled his homeland during the rise of the Nazis. Here he is shown writing an equation for the density of the Milky Way galaxy.

4. In addition to Mohandas Gandhi *(top right)*, Martin Luther King, Jr., and Caesar Chavez also believed nonviolence would effect greater change than violence.

5. America's Promise—The Alliance for Youth, founded by General Colin Powell *(bottom right)*, is dedicated to building and strengthening the character and competence of America's youth.

Portfolio Assessment Rubrics

Share rubrics with students before they write their paragraphs.

Attempted The paragraph is incomplete.

Minimal The paragraph was written but does not explain why the person is a hero, or it is poorly organized or written.

Adequate The paragraph is complete and well written with few errors and ably explains why the chosen person is a hero.

Exemplary The paragraph is complete and very well written with no errors and shows insight into the person chosen and the reasons given.

Resource Manager

	CORE INSTRUCTION	READING/SKILLS
Chapter Level Resources	📁 Teaching Resources 📓 Pacing Charts, Ch. 8 📓 Teaching With Themes, p. 11 📺 Color Transparencies, p. F–17 💿 Resource Pro® Ch. 8 🖥 www.phschool.com • eTeach	💿 Book on CD, Ch. 8 💿 Interactive Student Tutorial CD-ROM, Ch. 8 💿 Social Studies Skills Tutor CD-ROM 📺 Skills Transparencies

1 The Early Middle Ages
1. Explain why Western Europe was a frontier land in the early Middle Ages.
2. Identify how Germanic kingdoms gained power in the early Middle Ages.
3. Summarize how Charlemagne briefly reunited much of Western Europe.
	📁 Teaching Resources
	📓 Unit 3 booklet
	  • Primary Source Activity, p. 11
	📓 Creative Teaching Activities, p. 37
	💿 Prentice Hall Presentation Pro, Ch. 8, Section 1
	📺 Section Reading Support Transparencies
		📁 Teaching Resources
		📓 Unit 3 booklet
		  • Guided Reading and Review, p. 2
		📓 Guide to the Essentials
		📼 Guided Reading Audiotapes, Ch. 8, Section 1

2 Feudalism and the Manor Economy
1. Explain how feudalism shaped medieval society.
2. Describe what feudal life was like for nobles and peasants.
3. Identify the basis of the manor economy.
	📁 Teaching Resources
	📓 Unit 3 booklet
	  • Biography Activity, p. 10
	  • Viewpoint Activity, p. 12
	📓 Creative Teaching Activities, p. 38
	💿 Prentice Hall Presentation Pro, Ch. 8, Section 2
	📺 Section Reading Support Transparencies
		📁 Teaching Resources
		📓 Unit 3 booklet
		  • Guided Reading and Review, p. 4
		  • Skill Application Activity, p. 13
		📓 Guide to the Essentials
		📼 Guided Reading Audiotapes, Ch. 8, Section 2

3 The Medieval Church 1. Relate how the Church and its monks and nuns shaped medieval life. 2. Describe how the power of the Church grew. 3. Explain how reformers worked for change in the Church. 4. Outline the problems that Jewish communities faced.	📁 Teaching Resources 📓 Creative Teaching Activities, p. 39 💿 Prentice Hall Presentation Pro, Ch. 8, Section 3 📺 Section Reading Support Transparencies	📁 Teaching Resources 📓 Unit 3 booklet • Guided Reading and Review, p. 6 📓 Guide to the Essentials 📼 Guided Reading Audiotapes, Ch. 8, Section 3
4 Economic Expansion and Change 1. Explain how new technologies sparked an agricultural revolution. 2. Identify how the revival of trade revolutionized commerce. 3. Describe how guilds were linked to the rise of towns and cities.	📁 Teaching Resources 📓 Creative Teaching Activities, p. 40 💿 Prentice Hall Presentation Pro, Ch. 8, Section 4 📺 Section Reading Support Transparencies	📁 Teaching Resources 📓 Unit 3 booklet • Guided Reading and Review, p. 8 📓 Guide to the Essentials 📼 Guided Reading Audiotapes, Ch. 8, Section 4

ENRICHMENT/PRE-AP

📟 **www.phschool.com**
- Why Study History?

🎞 **Color Transparencies**, p. B–77
📼 **Visions, Voices, Views**, Animated Map Story, tape 3
💻 **www.phschool.com**
- Internet Activities, Section 1

📖 **Teaching Resources**
📘 **Chapter Extension Activities**, p. 23
📘 **History Through Literature**, pp. 18–19
💻 **www.phschool.com**
- Internet Activities, Section 2

📖 **Teaching Resources**
📘 **Chapter Extension Activities**, p. 24
🎞 **Color Transparencies**, pp. D–51, D–53
📼 **Listening to Literature World Masterpieces**, *Veni Creator Spiritus*, side 5
💻 **www.phschool.com**
- Virtual Field Trip

📖 **Teaching Resources**
📘 **Geography and History**, pp. 6–7
🎞 **Color Transparencies**, pp. B–41, B–43, B–45, C–37

ASSESSMENT

PRENTICE HALL
ASSESSMENT SYSTEM

Core Assessment
📘 **ExamView Test Bank booklet**, Ch. 8
💿 **ExamView Test Bank CD-ROM**, Ch. 8

Standardized Test Preparation
Diagnose and Prescribe
📘 **Diagnostic Tests for High School Social Studies Skills**

Review and Reteach
📘 **Review Book for World History**

Practice and Assess
📘 **Test-Taking Strategies With Transparencies for High School**
📘 **Alternative Assessment booklet**
📘 **Test Prep Book for World History**

📖 **Teaching Resources**
📗 **Unit 3 booklet**
- Geography Quiz, p. 14
- Section Quizzes, pp. 3, 5, 7, 9
- Chapter Tests A, B, and C, pp. 15–19
💻 **www.phschool.com**
- Self-Test

CUSTOMIZE FOR INDIVIDUAL NEEDS

Gifted and Talented
- **Teacher's Edition**, Activities: Customize for Heterogeneous Groups, p. 184; Connections to Music, p. 187; Customize for Heterogeneous Groups, p. 199

Less Proficient Readers
- **Guide to the Essentials**, Ch. 8
- **Book on CD**, Ch. 8
- **Teacher's Edition**, Activities: Reading Strategy, p. 189; Reading Strategy, p. 193; Customize for Heterogeneous Groups, p. 195

Less Proficient Writers
- **Teacher's Edition**, Activities: Cooperative Learning Activity, p. 194

Students Acquiring English/ESL
- **Guide to the Essentials**, English/Spanish, Ch. 8
- **Book on CD**, Ch. 8
- **Teacher's Edition**, Activities marked with an *

ⓘTEXT

Don't miss the exclusive interactive version of *World History: Connections to Today* on the Internet and CD-ROM.

INTRODUCTION

From 500 to 1000, Germanic invaders carved Europe into small kingdoms. Charlemagne temporarily reunited much of Western Europe in the 800s, reviving learning and blending German, Roman, and Christian traditions. The dominant forces during the early Middle Ages were feudalism, the manor economy, and the Roman Catholic Church. By the 1000s, advances in agriculture and commerce had spurred economic revival in Western Europe.

Focusing on Themes

Suggest that students focus on these theme questions as they read:

Political and Social Systems
How did feudalism and the manor economy provide a measure of political, economic, and social order?

Religions and Value Systems
How did the Roman Catholic Church spread Christian civilization throughout Western Europe?

Economics and Technology
What new technologies sparked a revolution in agriculture and commerce?

Continuity and Change
How did Western Europeans blend Greco-Roman, Christian, and Germanic traditions to build a new civilization?

◆ TIME LINE ACTIVITY

Share the About the Pictures note with your students before you ask these questions about the time line:

1. Who briefly united much of Western Europe in the 800s? *(Charlemagne)*
2. Name a contributing factor to the emergence of European feudalism. *(Viking invasions of Europe)*
3. How much time passed between the origins of feudalism in Europe and in Japan? *(about 200 years)*

Don't Miss!

Synthesizing Information
Feudalism
(Section 2)

You Are There . . .
Seeking Shelter in a Medieval Monastery
(Section 3)

The Rise of Europe
500–1300

Chapter Preview

1 The Early Middle Ages
2 Feudalism and the Manor Economy
3 The Medieval Church
4 Economic Expansion and Change

500s
Germanic tribes such as the Franks dominate Western Europe. This bronze brooch depicts a Frankish warrior.

732
Frankish forces defeat Muslim armies at the battle of Tours.

800
Frankish King Charlemagne is crowned emperor by the pope. Under Charlemagne, much of Western Europe is briefly united.

CHAPTER EVENTS

400 · 600 · 800

GLOBAL EVENTS

527 Justinian rules Byzantine empire.

622 The Muslim prophet Muhammad leaves Mecca.

Resource Directory

Teaching Resources
Teaching With Themes Chapter Theme Activities, p. 11
Pacing Chart With Block Scheduling Guide Ch. 8
Technology
World History Color Transparencies Ch. 8 Graphic Organizer, p. F–17

Geography and Resources of Europe

Europe is rich in natural resources. But in the early Middle Ages, many of these resources remained largely untapped.

Legend:
- Coal
- Fish
- Furs
- Iron
- Other metals
- Timber

Azimuthal Equal Area Projection
0   250   500 Miles
0   250   500 Kilometers

900s

Sailing out of Scandinavia in long ships, Viking raiders plunge much of Europe into disorder. Such invasions contribute to the emergence of European feudalism.

1000s

The European economy begins to recover. The growth of bustling new towns is one sign of revival.

1200s

The Dominican and Franciscan orders of Christian friars are founded.

1000   1200   1400

1100s Feudalism develops in Japan.

1230s Sundiata founds the empire of Mali in West Africa.

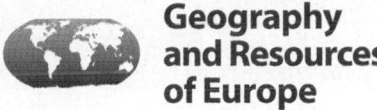

Geography and Resources of Europe

Activating Prior Knowledge

What external forces compelled the Roman empire to give up its territories? *(Rome buckled under attacks by Germanic peoples who lived along its northern borders.)*

Previewing

Ask students to speculate how a natural resource such as iron could have contributed to the growth in agriculture. *(Possible answer: Iron could be used to make farming implements such as plows.)*

Background
About the Pictures

1. This bronze brooch shows an armed Frankish warrior. Several regiments of Franks are listed in the *Notitia Dignitatum,* an early fifth century Roman document. Some commanders in the Roman army of the fourth century were also Franks.

2. Pope Leo crowned Charlemagne as Holy Roman Emperor on Christmas Day in 800 A.D. Charlemagne, however, was said to be reluctant to receive the crown and would not have entered the church that day had he known the pope's intention.

3. The Oseberg ship, discovered in Norway in 1903, was probably built in about 800 A.D. The ship measured 19 feet 2 inches in length and had 15 pairs of oars.

4. Trade flourished throughout Paris's history. In 1220 the right to collect duties on incoming goods was granted to Paris merchants. They, in turn, were required to maintain fair weights and measures.

Independent Assignments

Have students read one section as they prepare for class. After class, have them complete the assignment. Some students may benefit from using the Guided Reading and Review worksheets.

Section 1 Have students use the map *Charlemagne's Empire* in the Historical Outline Map Book, p. 16, to locate and label the homelands and surrounding geographic features of the various ethnic groups that Charlemagne battled. Then have students add the boundaries of the modern-day countries where Charlemagne's empire once stood.

Section 2 Have students use the worksheet *Two Views of Medieval Life* in the Unit 3 booklet, p. 12, to learn more about the lives of members of the different classes in feudal society.

Section 3 Have students use the worksheet in the Chapter Extension Activities booklet, p. 24, to explore life in a medieval monastery.

Section 4 Have students use the map *Europe in the Middle Ages* in the Historical Outline Map Book, p. 17, to locate and label the major medieval European commercial centers. Then have them draw lines to indicate the major trade routes of medieval Europe.

---

eTeach

Be sure to check out this month's online discussion with a World History Master Teacher.

Go to **www.phschool.com**.

LESSON PLAN

1. Focus As Roman civilization declined, Europe became an isolated land of disunity, conflict, and poverty. Charlemagne, allied with the Roman Catholic Church, created a new empire with a blend of German, Roman, and Christian traditions. After his death, however, internal divisions and invasions once again disrupted European life.

2. Instruct Group students into pairs to write a dialogue. Have one partner assume the role of Charlemagne and the other the role of a poor Frankish farmer. In the dialogue, the farmer will complain to Charlemagne about the terrible conditions under which he is living. To each complaint, Charlemagne will explain an action that he will take to remedy the problem. Have students use the text to research their roles and write a script for their dialogue. When each dialogue is prepared, have students present them to the class.

3. Assess Charlemagne achieved limited and temporary success. Ask students to think about other measures that Charlemagne could have taken. Then, ask them to complete the following sentence: "If I had been Charlemagne, I would have . . ." Have students explain the reason for their proposed actions.

4. Reteach If students' **Assess** activity does not reflect adequate understanding of the lesson, you might assign the *Guide to the Essentials* or the *Interactive Student Tutorial CD-ROM* for this section.

The Early Middle Ages

Reading Focus

- Why was Western Europe a frontier land during the early Middle Ages?
- How did Germanic kingdoms gain power in the early Middle Ages?
- How did Charlemagne briefly reunite much of Western Europe?

Vocabulary

medieval
frontier
missi dominici
curriculum

Taking Notes

As you read, prepare an outline of this section. Use Roman numerals to indicate the major headings of the section, letters for the subheadings, and numbers for the supporting details. The sample at right will help you get started.

I. Geography of Western Europe
  A. Location
    1.
    2.
  B.
II. The Germanic kingdoms
  A. The Franks
    1.
    2.
  B.

Main Idea After the fall of Rome, Germanic tribes divided Western Europe into many small kingdoms.

Setting the Scene Pope Gregory the Great sat at his desk, thinking about the perils facing Italy. The Lombards were attacking from the north. Once again, Rome might fall to plundering invaders. "Where is the senate?" Gregory wrote. "Where are the people? The bones are all dissolved, the flesh is consumed. . . . The whole mass is boiled away."

Gregory was writing around A.D. 600, as waves of invaders swept across Europe. Trade slowed to a trickle, towns emptied, and learning virtually ceased. During the early Middle Ages,* from about 500 to 1000, Europe was a relatively backward region largely cut off from advanced civilizations in the Middle East, China, and India. Slowly, though, a new European civilization would emerge that blended Greco-Roman, Germanic, and Christian traditions. Much later, it would be called medieval civilization, from the Latin for "middle age."

Geography of Western Europe

Rome had linked its distant European territories with miles of roads and had spread classical ideas, the Latin language, and Christianity to the tribal peoples of Western Europe. But Rome was a Mediterranean power. The Germanic peoples who ended Roman rule in the West shifted the focus of European history to the north.

Location Europe is relatively small—the second smallest in land area of the seven continents. It lies on the western end of Eurasia, the giant landmass that stretches from present-day Portugal in the west all the way to China in the east. Despite Europe's size, its impact on the modern world has been enormous.

Resources From about 500 to 1000, this region was a frontier land—a sparsely populated, undeveloped area on the outskirts of a civilization. Still, it had great untapped potential. Dense forests flourished in the north. The region's rich earth was better suited to raising crops than were the dry soils of the Mediterranean. Underground lay mineral resources. Nearby seas provided fish for food and served as transportation routes. Europe's large rivers were ideal for trade, and its mountain streams could turn water wheels.

---

* The period from about 500 to 1450 is known today as the Middle Ages because it came between the fall of Rome and the start of the modern era.

Resource Directory

Teaching Resources
Creative Teaching Activities Creative Teaching Activities booklet, p. 37
Guided Reading and Review Unit 3 booklet, p. 2
Technology
World History Color Transparencies *Europe*, p. B–77

The Germanic Kingdoms

The Germanic tribes who migrated across Europe were farmers and herders. Their culture differed greatly from that of the Romans. They had no cities or written laws. Instead, they lived in small communities governed by unwritten customs. They elected kings to lead them in war. Warrior nobles swore loyalty to the king in exchange for weapons and loot.

The Franks Between 400 and 700, Germanic tribes carved Western Europe into small kingdoms. The strongest kingdom to emerge was that of the Franks. In 486, Clovis, king of the Franks, conquered the former Roman province of Gaul. He ruled his new lands according to Frankish custom but did preserve much of the Roman legacy in Gaul.

Clovis took an important step when he converted to Christianity, the religion of the people in Gaul. Not only did he earn their support, but he also gained a powerful ally in the Christian Church of Rome.

Europe and the Muslim World As the Franks and other Germanic peoples carved up Europe, a new power was emerging across the Mediterranean. The religion of Islam appeared in Arabia in 622. From there, Muslims, or believers in Islam, built a huge empire and created a new civilization, as you will read in Chapter 11.

European Christians were stunned when Muslim armies overran Christian lands from Palestine to North Africa to Spain. When a Muslim army crossed into France, Charles Martel rallied Frankish warriors. At the battle of Tours in 732, Christian warriors triumphed. To them, the victory was a sign that God was on their side. Muslims advanced no farther into Western Europe, although they continued to rule most of Spain.

To European Christians, the Muslim presence was a source of anxiety. Even when Islam was no longer a threat, Christians viewed the Muslim world with hostility. In time, though, medieval Europeans would learn much from Muslims, whose learning in many areas exceeded their own.

The Age of Charlemagne

Around 800, Western Europe had a moment of unity when the grandson of Charles Martel built an empire reaching across France, Germany, and part of Italy. This emperor is known to history as Charlemagne (SHAHR luh mayn), or Charles the Great. Charlemagne towered over most people of his time. He loved battle and spent much of his 46-year reign fighting Muslims in Spain, Saxons in the north, Avars and Slavs in the east, and Lombards in Italy. His conquests reunited much of the old Roman empire.

A Christian Emperor In 800, Pope Leo III called on Charlemagne for help against rebellious nobles in Rome. Frankish armies marched south and crushed the rebellion. On Christmas Day, the pope showed his gratitude by placing a crown on Charlemagne's head and proclaiming him Emperor of the Romans.

The ceremony would have enormous significance. A Christian pope had crowned a German king successor to the Roman emperors. In doing so,

Empire of Charlemagne, 768–843

Legend:
- Kingdom of the Franks, 768
- Area conquered by Charlemagne, 768–814
- ★ Battle sites
- — Division of Charlemagne's empire (Treaty of Verdun, 843)

Azimuthal Equal Area Projection

0   150   300 Miles
0   150   300 Kilometers

North Sea · ENGLAND · ATLANTIC OCEAN · Seine R. · Paris · Tours · Loire R. · Aachen · Rhine R. · Verdun · Danube R. · SAXONS · Süntel · SLAVS · AVARS · Roncesvalles · Po R. · LOMBARDS · CORSICA · Rome · SPAIN · Mediterranean Sea

Skills Assessment

Geography Charlemagne built an empire in Europe, but his descendants were unable to hold it together.

1. **Location** On the map, locate **(a)** the Frankish kingdom in 768, **(b)** Charlemagne's empire in 814, **(c)** Tours, **(d)** Aachen.
2. **Region** Look at a map of the Roman empire in Chapter 6. Compare the location and extent of Charlemagne's empire with that of Rome.
3. **Critical Thinking Predicting Consequences** What might be one result of the division of Charlemagne's empire?

Background
Global Connections

Muslim Influence Muslim influence in Europe went well beyond the introduction of new fruits and vegetables. Muslim scholars preserved works of Greek philosophy and helped reintroduce them to Europe. Muslim influence in mathematics and science was significant and enduring, which can be seen in such terms of Arabic origin as *algebra, zero, azimuth, zenith,* and *almanac.* Muslim culture in Spain influenced the music and poetry of French troubadours. From India, Muslims brought the game of chess, with the Persian term *shah mat,* meaning the "king is dead," becoming *checkmate.* Also from India came Hindu fables and the numerals that would become known as Arabic numerals. New technology that came to Europe by way of the Muslims included papermaking, new irrigation techniques, and the distillation of liquids.

Block Scheduling Support

The Life of Charlemagne, written by the Frankish historian Einhard, is a valuable and highly readable primary source on Charlemagne and his time. Einhard, educated in Charlemagne's palace school at Aachen, was a favorite of the emperor. His account, therefore, is somewhat colored by his gratitude for the emperor's patronage.

Have the students read the selections from Einhard's *Life of Charlemagne* in *Treasures of the World.* Ask students to outline the admirable achievements and qualities of Charlemagne as described by Einhard, and write their responses on the chalkboard. Then, have students analyze Einhard's appraisal of Charlemagne by answering the following questions as a class: (1) How is Einhard a reliable source for information about Charlemagne? (2) How and why might Einhard's account be biased? Students should support their ideas with examples from Einhard's *Life of Charlemagne.*

Skills Assessment

ANSWERS 1. Review locations with students. **2.** Both empires included northern Italy and present-day France. While Charlemagne's empire extended farther north, the Roman empire included all the lands around the Mediterranean. **3.** Possible answers: The divided empire could be more open to invasion; disunity might make it harder to carry on trade.

Interpreting History As a class, have students brainstorm about the problems Charlemagne may have faced in uniting such a large area as medieval Europe. Ask students why they think Charlemagne may have welcomed the support of the Church. Then, ask students to explain how local nobles and peasants might have reacted to being part of Charlemagne's united empire. How would being part of this empire benefit these groups? How would it hinder them? Finally, ask students to suggest reasons that Charlemagne's heirs were unable to continue his legacy. *(Enrichment)*

Invasions of Europe, 700–1000

→ Viking invasions
→ Magyar invasions
→ Muslim invasions
Vikings
Magyars
Muslims
Areas of Viking settlement outside Scandinavia

Azimuthal Equal Area Projection
0   250   500 Miles
0   250   500 Kilometers

Skills Assessment

Geography Between 700 and 1000, Western Europe was battered by invaders.

1. **Location** On the map, locate **(a)** Byzantine empire, **(b)** Scandinavia, **(c)** Ireland, **(d)** England, **(e)** Cordoba.
2. **Place** **(a)** From where did the Magyars set out? **(b)** Where did the Vikings and Muslims build settlements?
3. **Critical Thinking Comparing** How did the Viking invasions differ from those of the Magyars and the Muslims?

he revived the ideal of a united Christian community. He also laid the ground for desperate power struggles between future Roman Catholic popes and German emperors.

The pope's action outraged the emperor of the eastern Roman empire in Constantinople. The eastern emperor saw himself, and not some backward Frankish king, as the sole Roman ruler. In the long run, the crowning of Charlemagne helped widen the split between the eastern and western Christian worlds.

Government Charlemagne tried to exercise control over his many lands and create a united Christian Europe. Working closely with the Church, he helped spread Christianity to the conquered peoples on the fringes of his empire. Missionaries converted many Saxons and Slavs.

Like other Germanic kings, Charlemagne appointed powerful nobles to rule local regions. He gave them land so that they could offer support and supply soldiers for his armies. To keep control of these provincial rulers, he sent out officials called *missi dominici* (MIH see dohm in NEE kee) to check on roads, listen to grievances, and see that justice was done. Charlemagne instructed the *missi* to "administer the law fully and justly in the case of the holy churches of God and of the poor, of wards and of widows, and of the whole people."

Revival of Learning Charlemagne wanted to make his court at Aachen (AH kuhn) a "second Rome." To do so, he set out to revive Latin learning in his empire. Education had declined so much that even supposedly educated clergy were often sadly ignorant. Charlemagne himself could read but not write. Still, as a ruler, he saw the need for officials to keep accurate records and write clear reports.

Skills Assessment

ANSWERS 1. Review locations with students. **2. (a)** from Hungary **(b)** Vikings: mainly in the British Isles and the coast of France; Muslims: mainly Spain, Sardinia, Corsica, and Sicily **3.** Possible answer: The Vikings mostly traveled by water, while the Magyars and Muslims primarily traveled by land.

Resource Directory

Teaching Resources
Section Quiz Unit 3 booklet, p. 3
Primary Source Activity *A Personal Portrait of Charlemagne,* Unit 3 booklet, p. 11
Technology
Interactive Student Tutorial CD-ROM Ch. 8
Computer Test Bank Ch. 8

World History Visions, Voices, Views Animated Map Story, *Viking Invasions of Europe (790s–1000s),* videodisc side 2 or videotape 3, running time 3:00 min.

Side 2: Fr. 14556-20110

Charlemagne founded a school at Aachen under the direction of a respected scholar, Alcuin (AL kwihn) of York. Alcuin created a curriculum, or formal course of study, based on Latin learning. It included grammar, rhetoric, logic, arithmetic, geometry, music, and astronomy. Alcuin also hired scholars to copy ancient manuscripts, including the Bible and Latin works of history and science. Alcuin's system would become the educational model for medieval Europe.

After Charlemagne

After Charlemagne died in 814, his empire soon fell apart. His heirs battled for power for nearly 30 years. Finally, in 843, Charlemagne's grandsons drew up the Treaty of Verdun, which split the empire into three regions.

Legacy of Charlemagne Still, Charlemagne left a lasting legacy. He extended Christian civilization into northern Europe and furthered the blending of German, Roman, and Christian traditions. He also set up strong, efficient governments. Later medieval rulers looked to his example when they tried to strengthen their own kingdoms.

A New Wave of Invasions Charlemagne's heirs faced new waves of invasions. Despite the Christian victory at Tours, Muslim forces still posed a threat to Europe. In the late 800s, they conquered Sicily, which became a thriving center of Islamic culture. Not until the 900s, when power struggles erupted in the Middle East, did Muslim attacks finally subside.

About 896, a new wave of nomadic people, the Magyars, settled in what is today Hungary. From there, they overran eastern Europe and moved on to plunder Germany, parts of France, and Italy. Finally, after about 50 years, they were pushed back into Hungary.

The Vikings snapped the last threads of unity in Charlemagne's empire. These expert sailors burst out of Scandinavia, a northern region that now includes Norway, Sweden, and Denmark. Starting in the 900s, they looted and burned communities along the coasts and rivers of Europe.

The Vikings were not just destructive raiders. They were also traders and explorers who sailed around the Mediterranean Sea and across the Atlantic Ocean. Vikings opened trade routes that linked northern Europe to Mediterranean lands. Vikings also settled in England, Ireland, northern France, and parts of Russia. Around the year 1000, Leif Erikson set up a short-lived Viking colony on North America.

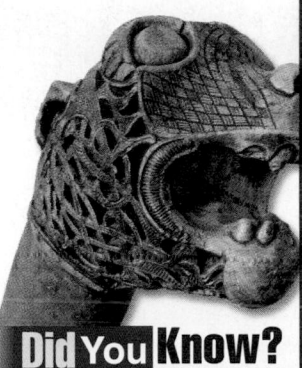

Did You Know?

The Voyage to Valhalla

According to Viking mythology, Valhalla was a great hall in the grandest palace of Odin, king of the gods. The walls of Valhalla were gold, and its roof was made of battle shields. Vikings believed that if they died heroically in battle, they would spend eternity fighting and then feasting in Valhalla with Odin.

To make the voyage to Valhalla, a Viking hero needed a proper funeral. This included being buried with his weapons, his clothing, and a ship. The servants of Viking warriors were buried with them to serve their masters on the journey and beyond. Sometimes, instead of being buried, the fully stocked ship was cast adrift and burned.

Theme: Religions and Value Systems How might a Viking's beliefs have affected his behavior in battle?

SECTION 1 Assessment

Recall
1. (a) Clovis, p. 183 (b) Islam, p. 183
(c) Charlemagne, p. 183 (d) Alcuin, p. 185
(e) Treaty of Verdun, p. 185 (f) Vikings, p. 185 2. (a) medieval, p. 182 (b) frontier, p. 182 (c) *missi dominici*, p. 184
(d) curriculum, p. 185

Comprehension
3. dense forests, rich earth, rich minerals, seas, large rivers, and mountain streams
4. He became a Christian and gained the alliance of the Roman Catholic Church.
5. (a) He spread Christianity to the conquered peoples of his empire, appointed powerful nobles to rule local regions, and sent out *missi dominici* to check on roads, listen to grievances, and see that justice was done. (b) It fell apart.

Critical Thinking and Writing
6. Students' answers should reflect the knowledge that other civilizations did not span the same period of years as the European civilization. Thus, the years 500 to 1450 would not necessarily be their Middle Ages. 7. His accomplishments included creating a large empire, centralizing government, helping Christianity spread, and promoting education. Students' appraisals should be supported by valid reasons.

SECTION 1 Assessment

Recall
1. **Identify:** (a) Clovis, (b) Islam, (c) Charlemagne, (d) Alcuin, (e) Treaty of Verdun, (f) Vikings.
2. **Define:** (a) medieval, (b) frontier, (c) *missi dominici*, (d) curriculum.

Comprehension
3. What untapped resources did Western Europe possess in the early Middle Ages?
4. How did Clovis increase the power of the Frankish kingdoms?
5. (a) What steps did Charlemagne take to improve government and unify his empire? (b) What happened to his empire after he died?

Critical Thinking and Writing
6. **Recognizing Points of View** The term *Middle Ages* was coined by Europeans to describe the period from 500 to 1450. Do you think that other civilizations use the same term for that period? Why or why not?
7. **Ranking** List the accomplishments of Charlemagne. Which do you think had the most lasting importance? Why?

Activity
Take It to the NET

The Vikings did not produce much art, but they did decorate many of their possessions with elaborate designs. Use the Internet to find out about Viking ornamentation. Then, draw an example to share with the class. Explain how or where the Vikings might have used the design.

Chapter 8 **185**

Activity Rubrics

Share rubrics with students before they draw their examples.

Attempted The drawing shows little or no research and does not reflect Viking ornamentation.

Minimal The drawing shows some research and resembles a Viking design.

Adequate The drawing shows research, effort, understanding, and careful work.

Exemplary The drawing is extremely well executed and shows excellent research and planning.

Human Drama Note

Writing and Storytelling Vikings carved stories in wood, metal, and stone using letters called *runes*. Rune stones often tell about Viking history. Oral storytelling was also important in Viking culture. Viking poets, called *skalds*, recited tales of Viking heroes and told legends about their gods, such as Thor and Odin. Many of these stories, known as *sagas*, were written down centuries later in Iceland.

Test Preparation

Have students read the paragraphs under the heading "Government" on the opposite page, and then answer the question below.

Which of the following was the main reason that Charlemagne sent out the *missi dominici*?

A to listen to grievances

B to administer the law

C to control provincial rulers

D to check on roads

Caption Answer

It may have made him more determined to fight heroically.

Bell Ringer

Ask students to recall how popular games, films, and literary works portray life during the Middle Ages. Then, ask them to write down five or more major characteristics of medieval life as suggested by these modern sources. As they study this section, have students compare the popular image of medieval life with the actual historical conditions.

LESSON PLAN

1. Focus Through interdependence and mutual responsibilities, feudalism provided people with protection and other benefits. Everyone in medieval society had a clearly defined role. Women's rights were generally restricted, but noblewomen played significant roles. Agriculture was the major economic activity on the medieval manor.

2. Instruct Ask students to imagine that they live in a future society where a team of time travelers is planning a trip to the Middle Ages. In order to blend undetected into medieval life, the time travelers plan to assume the roles of lord, vassal, noblewoman, serf, and other members of medieval society.

Assign students to write down careful instructions for the role of each time traveler. The instructions should include advice on how to behave, how to treat other people, what responsibilities to fulfill, what services to expect, and the like. Ask for volunteers to read their instructions aloud to the class. Ask the listeners to determine whether any important information has been omitted.

3. Assess Form the class into groups, and have students make believe that they are the time travelers who are visiting the Middle Ages. In a series of skits, have them play the roles of various medieval characters.

4. Reteach If students' Assess activity does not reflect adequate understanding of the lesson, you might assign the *Guide to the Essentials* or the *Interactive Student Tutorial CD-ROM* for this section.

Connections to Today

ANSWER Yes, the people who participate in the festivals create a sense of what it was like to live during the Middle Ages. No, festivals are not always accurate and may be romanticized.

Reading Focus

- How did feudalism shape medieval society?
- What was feudal life like for nobles and peasants?
- What was the basis of the manor economy?

Vocabulary

feudalism
vassal
feudal contract
fief
knight
tournament
chivalry
troubadour
manor
serf

Taking Notes

Copy the table below. Then, fill it in as you read. Part of the table has been filled in to help you get started.

	NOBLES	PEASANTS
OBLIGATIONS	• Military service to lord •	
RIGHTS AND BENEFITS		• Protection from lord •
LIVES		

Main Idea A new political and social system, called feudalism, shaped medieval life.

Connections to Today

The Middle Ages Are Alive and Well!

The town is abuzz: Soon the king and queen will be passing by! Peasants crowd the muddy street. Shopkeepers loudly peddle food and drink. Minstrels wander through the crowd, singing and playing instruments. On the outskirts of town, knights in armor prepare to joust.

Scenes like this are common today all over this country at medieval festivals. Professional actors and others dress up in period costumes, pretend to have European accents, and play people from all levels of medieval society. The results are very romanticized and not always accurate. Still, the fairs give thousands of visitors a small taste of medieval life.

Theme: Continuity and Change Do you think a medieval festival would be a good place to learn about the Middle Ages? Why or why not?

Setting the Scene Count William had just inherited the rich lands of Flanders. The local nobles gathered to pledge loyalty to their new lord. One by one, they knelt before him and took a solemn oath. "I promise on my faith," pledged each lord, "that I will in future be faithful to Count William and will observe my [loyalty] to him completely against all persons in good faith and without deceit."

The count then touched the noble with a small rod. With that gesture, he granted the noble a parcel of land, which included any towns, castles, or people on it.

Although the words might vary, ceremonies like this one took place across Europe during the Middle Ages. In public, before witnesses, great nobles and lesser lords exchanged vows of loyalty and service. Those vows were part of a new political and social system that governed medieval life.

The Emergence of Feudalism

In the face of invasions by Vikings, Muslims, and Magyars, kings and emperors were too weak to maintain law and order. People needed protection for themselves, their homes, and their lands. In response to this basic need for protection, a new system evolved, known as feudalism. Feudalism was a loosely organized system of rule in which powerful local lords divided their landholdings among lesser lords. In exchange, these lesser lords, or vassals, pledged service and loyalty to the greater lord.

Mutual Obligations The relationship between lords and vassals was established by custom and tradition and by an exchange of pledges known as the feudal contract. A lord granted his vassal a fief (FEEF), or estate. Fiefs ranged from a few acres to hundreds of square miles. In addition to the land itself, the fief included peasants to work the land, as well as any towns or buildings on the land.

As part of the feudal contract, the lord promised to protect his vassal. In return, the vassal pledged loyalty to his lord. He also agreed to provide the lord with 40 days of military service each year, certain money payments, and advice.

A Structured Society Everyone had a place in feudal society. Below the monarch were powerful lords, such as dukes and counts, who held the largest fiefs. Each of these lords had vassals, and these vassals in turn had their own vassals. In many cases, the same man was both vassal and

Resource Directory

Teaching Resources

Creative Teaching Activities Creative Teaching Activities booklet, p. 38
Guided Reading and Review Unit 3 booklet, p. 4
Biography Activity *Eleanor of Aquitaine,* Unit 3 booklet, p. 10
Skill Application Activity *Interpreting Diagrams,* Unit 3 booklet, p. 13
History Through Literature *Song of Roland,* History Through Literature booklet, pp. 18–19

lord—vassal to a more powerful lord above him and lord to a less powerful vassal below him.

Because vassals often held fiefs from more than one lord, feudal relationships grew very complex. A vassal who had pledged loyalty to several lords could have serious problems if his overlords quarreled with each other. What was he to do if both demanded his aid? To solve this problem, a vassal usually had a liege lord to whom he owed his first loyalty.

The World of Nobles

For feudal nobles, warfare was a way of life. Rival lords battled constantly for power. Many nobles trained from boyhood for a future occupation as a knight, or mounted warrior.

Achieving Knighthood At the age of seven, a boy slated to become a knight was sent away to the castle of his father's lord. There, he learned to ride and fight. He also learned to keep his armor and weapons in good condition. Training was difficult and discipline was strict. Any laziness was punished with an angry blow or even a severe beating.

With his training finished, the youth was ready to become a knight. Kneeling before an older knight, he bowed his head. The knight struck the young man with his hand or the flat side of his sword and declared something like the following: "In the name of God, Saint Michael, and Saint George, I dub thee knight. Be valiant." After this "dubbing," the young knight took his place beside other warriors.

As feudal warfare decreased in the 1100s, tournaments, or mock battles, came into fashion. A lord would invite knights from the surrounding area to enter contests of fighting skill. Early tournaments were as dangerous as real battles, and captured knights were held for ransom. In time, tournaments acquired more ceremony and ritual.

Castles During the early Middle Ages, powerful lords fortified their homes to withstand attack. Their strongholds included a keep, or wooden tower, ringed by a fence. The keep was separated from the surrounding area by a moat, or water-filled ditch.

The strongholds gradually became larger and grander. By the 1100s, monarchs and nobles owned sprawling stone castles with high walls, towers, and drawbridges over wide moats. Wars often centered on seizing

A Medieval Castle
By the late Middle Ages, some feudal castles had become vast fortresses. This castle at Carcassonne in France, which people still visit today, had a double outer wall to protect it from attack.

Theme: Economics and Technology What do you think was the function of the high turrets, or towers, that surround this castle?

Chapter 8 **187**

Background
About the Evidence

The Church supported the feudal relationship. The hierarchy from serf to monarch was seen as a divine relationship, much as the hierarchy of clergy with the pope as head. In addition, the Church was directly involved through the participation of Church officials in feudal relationships. Bishops and abbots were granted lands by secular rulers in return for their homage.

Activity
Interpreting the Evidence

Use these additional questions to generate class discussion.

1. Critical Thinking: Analyzing Primary Sources How did John of Toul plan to balance his feudal commitments should any of his overlords go to war with his liege? *(He planned to aid the count of Grandpré personally and send his knights to fight for the count and countess of Champagne.)*

2. Critical Thinking: Drawing Conclusions What does the John of Toul quotation illustrate about the weakness of the feudal system? *(Possible answer: It was tenuous. Conflict of interest was inherent in a system where a vassal had many overlords.)*

Skills Tip

Explain to students that the chart on this page is simplified and that the relationships were really much more complex. Remind students that charts are often generalized. The reader must often read more to fully understand the structure of the subject. The Skills Handbook in the front of the book has a lesson that will help students with this feature.

Skills Assessment

ANSWERS 1. A **2.** F **3.** Possible answers: **(a)** people to work and maintain the land, soldiers to protect his lands, people to stand behind him in a conflict **(b)** Those in a position of power could provide protection to the lesser lords and peasants who needed it.

Feudalism

For centuries, feudalism was the way of life in Western Europe. Everyone, from the poorest peasant to the richest king, was touched in some way by feudal relationships. The painting, the chart, and the quotation on this page all provide information about these relationships.

Feudal Society

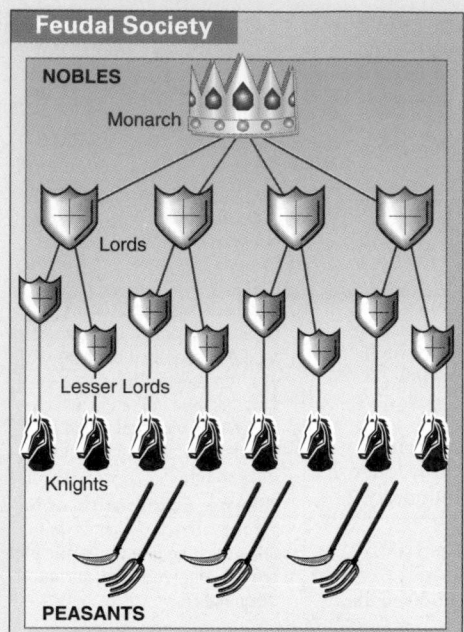

Under the feudal system, everyone had a well-defined place in society. At the head of society was the monarch. Peasants, who made up the bulk of the population, were at the bottom.

A King Grants Land

In exchange for a pledge of loyalty, a king grants a fief of land.

A Vassal Pledges Loyalty

"I John of Toul, make it known that I am the faithful man of the lady Beatrice, Countess of Troyes, and of my most dear lord, Theobald, Count of Champagne, her son, against all persons living or dead, except for my allegiance to lord Enjorand of Coucy, lord John of Arcis and the count of Grandpré. If it should happen that the count of Grandpré should be at war with the countess and count of Champagne on his own quarrel, I will aid the count of Grandpré in my own person and will send to the count and countess of Champagne the knights whose service I owe them for the fief which I hold of them."

—quoted in *Institutions in European History* (Esler)

Skills Tip

In a chart showing hierarchy, the lines show relationships between those of lesser and greater positions.

Skills Assessment

1. According to the chart of feudal society, the person kneeling in the picture is a
   A lord.
   B lesser lord.
   C knight.
   D peasant.

2. In a battle between the Count of Champagne and the Count of Grandpré, John of Toul would
   E remain neutral.
   F fight for Grandpré.
   G fight for Champagne.
   H send knights to each.

3. Critical Thinking Drawing Conclusions (a) Lords provided for their vassals. In return, what did a lord gain from his vassals? **(b)** Feudalism was based partly on the assumption that only the powerful could maintain peace and provide protection. What conclusions about life in medieval Europe can you draw from this?

Resource Directory

Teaching Resources

Synthesizing Information Chapter Extension Activities booklet, p. 23

castles that commanded strategic river crossings, harbors, or mountain passes. Castle dwellers stored up food and water so that they could withstand a long siege. If attackers failed to starve the defender into submission, they might try to tunnel under the castle walls.

Noblewomen Noblewomen played active roles in this warrior society. While her husband or father was off fighting, the "lady of the manor" took over his duties. She supervised vassals, managed the household, and performed necessary agricultural and medical tasks. Sometimes she might even have to go to war to defend her estate.

A few medieval noblewomen took a hand in politics. For example, Eleanor of Aquitaine inherited lands in southwestern France. Through two marriages, she became, first, queen of France and, later, queen of England. Eleanor was a leading force in European politics for more than 50 years.

Women's rights to inheritance were severely restricted under the feudal system. Land usually passed to the eldest son in a family. A woman did, however, receive land as part of her dowry, and fierce negotiations swirled around an unmarried or widowed heiress. If her husband died before her, a woman regained rights to her land.

Like their brothers, the daughters of nobles were sent to friends or relatives for training. Before her parents arranged her marriage, a young woman was expected to know how to spin and weave and how to supervise servants. A few learned to read and write. As a wife, she was expected to bear many children and be dutiful to her husband.

Chivalry In the later Middle Ages, knights adopted a code of conduct called chivalry. Chivalry required knights to be brave, loyal, and true to their word. In warfare, they had to fight fairly. A knight, for example, agreed not to attack another knight before the opponent had a chance to put on his armor. Chivalry also dictated that warriors treat a captured knight well or even release him if he promised to pay his ransom. Chivalry had limits, though. It applied to nobles only, not to commoners.

In theory, if not always in practice, chivalry placed women on a pedestal. The code of chivalry called for women to be protected and cherished. Troubadours, or wandering poets, adopted this view. Their love songs praised the perfection, beauty, and wit of women. Much later, ideas of chivalry would shape western ideas of romantic love.

Peasants and Manor Life

The heart of the medieval economy was the manor, or lord's estate. Most manors included one or more villages and the surrounding lands. Peasants, who made up the majority of the population in medieval society, lived and worked on the manor.

Most peasants on a manor were serfs, bound to the land. Serfs were not slaves who could be bought and sold. Still, they were not free. They could not leave the manor without the lord's permission. If the manor was granted to a new lord, the serfs went along with it.

Mutual Obligations Peasants and their lords were tied together by mutual rights and obligations. Peasants had to work several days a week farming the lord's lands. They also repaired his roads, bridges, and fences. Peasants paid the lord a fee when they married, when they inherited their father's acres, or when they used the local mill to grind grain. Other payments fell due at Christmas and Easter. Because money had largely disappeared from medieval Europe, they paid with products such as grain, honey, eggs, or chickens.

In return for a lifetime of labor, peasants had the right to farm several acres for themselves. They were also entitled to their lord's protection from Viking raids or feudal warfare. Although they could not leave the manor

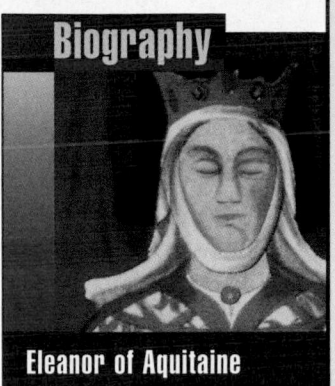

Biography

Eleanor of Aquitaine
1122–1204

Eleanor of Aquitaine married King Louis VII of France when she was 15. Not content just to enjoy her wealth and status, Eleanor joined in the Second Crusade, wearing armor and riding on horseback alongside male crusaders.

Soon afterward, she ended her marriage to Louis. She then wed another king, Henry II of England, with whom she had eight children. Later, Eleanor spurred several of her sons in an attempt to overthrow Henry. The revolt failed, and Eleanor landed in prison, where she spent 15 years. After Henry died, her son Richard (known as "the Lion-Hearted") became king of England. Richard freed his mother, and she later ruled in his place while he went on a crusade to the Holy Land.

Theme: Impact of the Individual Eleanor has been called the "Grandmother of Europe." Why do you think she was given this title?

Reading Strategy
Reinforcing Key Ideas

Ask students to write the headings Noblemen, Noblewomen, and Serfs on a sheet of paper and to take notes about each group as they read. When students have finished reading the section, ask them to write a paragraph comparing and contrasting nobles and serfs in the Middle Ages. *(Less Advanced Readers)*

Human Drama Note

Knights of Christ During the 1000s and 1100s, groups of knights founded military orders that embraced the ideals of chivalry combined with Christian values such as charity, fidelity, piety, and service to God. The knights protected Christians who went on pilgrimages to the Holy Land. The first chivalric order, the Knights of St. John of Jerusalem, was founded in 1070 to protect a pilgrim's hospital in Jerusalem. The order of Knights Templars was founded in 1119 to defend Christ's tomb in Jerusalem.

Test Preparation

Have students read the section titled "Noblewomen" on this page, and then complete the sentence below.

In general, noblewomen were expected to do all of the following except

A be dutiful to their husbands.

B oversee their servants.

C learn to read and write.

D bear many children.

Caption Answer

Her children's children became rulers in many different parts of Europe.

SECTION 2 Assessment

Recall

1. (a) feudalism, p. 186 (b) vassal, p. 186 (c) feudal contract, p. 186 (d) fief, p. 186 (e) knight, p. 187 (f) tournament, p. 187 (g) chivalry, p. 189 (h) troubadour, p. 189 (i) manor, p. 189 (j) serf, p. 189

Comprehension

2. Possible answer: Everyone had duties to others. Nobles had responsibilities as both lords and vassals. Serfs were tied to the land. 3. (a) The lord promised protection for his vassals. The vassals pledged loyalty and 40 days a year of military service, money payments, and advice. (b) It raised women to a new status because it called for women to be protected and cherished. 4. (a) The peasants' responsibilities included working several days a week farming the lord's lands; repairing the lord's roads, bridges, and fences; and paying the lord occasional fees. (b) The lord had to provide peasants with protection and with land for them to farm.

Critical Thinking and Writing

5. Possible answer: With no central authority to provide protection, people developed feudalism as a way to protect their lives and property. 6. Possible answer: Students might compare the concepts of being brave, loyal, true, and fighting fairly with fair play in today's sports.

Caption Answer

They might have idealized peasant life so the nobles would not have to see the harsher aspects of peasant life, such as hunger or hard work.

A View of Peasant Life
This French painting from the late Middle Ages presents an idealized picture of farm life in winter. While a peasant takes cattle to market, his family members warm themselves by the fire in their hut.

Theme: Art and Literature Illustrations like these were created for nobles. Why do you think they might have idealized peasant life?

freely, they also could not be forced off it. In theory, at least, they were guaranteed food, housing, and land.

A Self-Sufficient World The manor was generally self-sufficient. That is, peasants produced almost everything they needed, from food and clothing to simple furniture and tools. Most peasants never ventured more than a few miles from their village. They had no schooling and no knowledge of a larger world outside.

A typical manor included a few dozen one-room huts clustered close together in a village. Nearby stood a water mill to grind grain, a tiny church, and the manor house. The fields surrounding the village were divided into narrow strips. Each family had strips of land in different fields so that good land and bad land were shared evenly.

Peasant Life For most peasants, life was harsh. Men, women, and children worked long hours, from sunup to sundown. During planting season, a man might guide an ox-drawn plow through the fields while his wife walked alongside, goading the ox into motion with a pointed stick. Children helped plant seeds, weeded, and took care of pigs or sheep.

The peasant family ate a simple diet of black bread with vegetables such as peas, cabbage, turnips, or onions. They seldom had meat unless they poached wild game on their lord's manor, at the risk of harsh punishment. If they lived near a river, a meal might include fish. At night, the family and any cows, chickens, pigs, or sheep slept together in their one-room hut.

Like farmers everywhere, European peasants worked according to the season. In spring and autumn, they plowed and harvested. In summer, they hayed. At other times, they weeded, repaired fences, and performed chores. In late winter, when the harvest was exhausted and new crops had not yet ripened, hunger was common. Disease took a heavy toll, and few peasants lived beyond the age of 35.

Still, peasants found occasions to celebrate, such as marriages and births. Welcome breaks came at Christmas and Easter, when peasants had a week off from work. Dozens of other festivals in the Christian calendar brought days off. At these times, people might butcher an animal so that they could feast on meat. There would also be dancing and rough sports, from wrestling to ball games.

SECTION 2 Assessment

Recall

1. **Define:** (a) feudalism, (b) vassal, (c) feudal contract, (d) fief, (e) knight, (f) tournament, (g) chivalry, (h) troubadour, (i) manor, (j) serf.

Comprehension

2. Describe three features of feudal society.
3. (a) What obligations did lords and vassals have under the feudal system? (b) How did the code of chivalry affect medieval ideas about women?

4. (a) What responsibilities did the peasant have toward the lord of a manor? (b) What responsibilities did the lord of the manor have toward the peasants?

Critical Thinking and Writing

5. **Recognizing Causes and Effects** How did the breakdown of central authority in Europe lead to the development of feudalism?
6. **Linking Past and Present** Compare the code of chivalry to ideas about "good sportsmanship" today.

 Activity
Take It to the NET

Use the Internet to learn more about the way knights in the early Middle Ages dressed. Make a diagram showing the various items in a knight's armor and add labels to identify them. Display your diagram on a bulletin board.

Resource Directory

Teaching Resources

Viewpoint Activity *Two Views of Medieval Life,* Unit 3 booklet, p. 12
Section Quiz Unit 3 booklet, p. 5
Creative Teaching Activities Creative Teaching Activities booklet, p. 39
Guided Reading and Review Unit 3 booklet, p. 6

Technology

Interactive Student Tutorial CD-ROM Ch. 8
Computer Test Bank Ch. 8

The Medieval Church

Reading Focus

- How did the Church and its monks and nuns shape medieval life?
- How did the power of the Church grow?
- How did reformers work for change in the Church?
- What problems did Jewish communities face?

Vocabulary

sacrament
tithe
secular
papal supremacy
canon law
excommunication
interdict
simony
friar
antisemitism

Taking Notes

Copy this concept web. As you read, add information about the role of the Church in medieval times. Add as many circles as you need to complete the web.

THE MEDIEVAL CHURCH
Daily life
Worldly power

Main Idea The Church played a vital role in medieval life and in time grew into a secular power as well.

Setting the Scene

Charlemagne waged battle in the name of Christianity. "It is our task," he said, "with the aid of divine goodness, to defend the holy church of Christ everywhere . . . and to strengthen it within through the knowledge of the Catholic faith."

It took centuries for Christian missionaries to spread their faith across Europe. But in time, the medieval Church emerged as the most powerful force in Europe. The Church's teachings and practices shaped the lives of Christian Europeans.

The Church and Medieval Life

During the early Middle Ages, the Church's most important achievement was to Christianize the diverse peoples of Western Europe. In 597, Pope Gregory I sent Augustine to convert the Anglo-Saxons in England. From Britain, later missionaries went back to the continent to spread their faith among Germanic tribes.

Women also spread the faith even at the risk of their own lives. Some women married pagan kings and brought their husbands into the Church. Clothilde, for example, persuaded her husband Clovis, who was king of the Franks, to accept Christianity.

The Parish Priest In manor villages, the priest of the parish, or local region, was usually the only contact people had with the Church. The priest cared for the souls of his parishioners by celebrating the mass and by administering the sacraments, the sacred rites of the Church. Christians believed that faith in Christ and participation in the sacraments would lead them to salvation, or everlasting life with God.

In addition to administering the sacraments, priests preached the Gospels and the teachings of the Church. They guided people on issues regarding values and morality. They offered assistance to the sick and needy.

Christian rituals and faith were part of the fabric of everyday life. Priests married peasants and nobles, baptized their children, and buried the dead in sacred ground.

The Village Church The church was a social center as well as a place of worship. After services, peasants gossiped or danced, although the priest might condemn their rowdy songs or behavior. In the later Middle Ages, some parish priests ran schools.

Primary Source

The Role of the Parish Priest

The English poet Geoffrey Chaucer describes an ideal parish priest:

"Wide was his parish, with houses far asunder,
But he would not be kept by rain or thunder,
If any had suffered a sickness or a blow
From visiting the farthest, high or low,
Plodding his way on foot, his staff in hand,
He was a model his flock could understand,
For first he did and afterward he taught."

—Geoffrey Chaucer,
The Canterbury Tales

Skills Assessment

Primary Source What were some of the duties of this fictional parish priest?

Spread of Christianity in Europe

Mostly Christian, 476

Mostly Christian, added by 1050

Muslim, 1050

⊕ Monastery

Azimuthal Equal Area Projection

0   250   500 Miles

0   250   500 Kilometers

NORWAY
SWEDEN
SCOTLAND
North Sea
IRELAND
DENMARK
Baltic Sea
ENGLAND
RUSSIA
Canterbury
GERMANY
Bingen
ATLANTIC OCEAN
FRANCE
Cluny
Black Sea
ITALY
PAPAL STATES
SPAIN
CORSICA Assisi
Rome Monte Cassino
Constantinople
Nicaea
SARDINIA
BYZANTINE EMPIRE
SICILY
CRETE
Mediterranean Sea

Villages took pride in their church buildings and decorated them with care. In later medieval times, prosperous communities built stone churches rather than wooden ones. Some churches housed relics, or remains of martyrs or other holy figures. Local people, as well as visitors, might make pilgrimages, or journeys, to pray before the relics.

To support itself and its parishes, the Church required Christians to pay a tithe, or tax equal to a tenth of their income. The tithe had its origins in the Bible. Tithing is still common in many Christian churches today.

Daily life revolved around the Christian calendar, which marked "holy days" such as Easter in addition to changes in the seasons. In medieval times, many holidays were added to the calendar to honor saints.

Views of Women The Church taught that men and women were equal before God. But on Earth, women were viewed as "daughters of Eve," weak and easily led into sin. Thus, they needed the guidance of men. At the same time, the Church offered a view of the ideal woman, as modest and pure as Mary, the mother of Jesus. Many churches were dedicated to the "mother of God" and "queen of heaven." Men and women asked Mary to pray to God on their behalf.

The Church tried to protect women. It set a minimum age for marriage. Church courts could fine men who seriously injured their wives. Yet they often punished women more harshly than men for the same offense.

Monks and Nuns

During the early Middle Ages, both women and men withdrew from worldly life to become nuns and monks. Behind the walls of monasteries and convents, they devoted their lives to spiritual goals.

The Benedictine Rule About 530, a monk named Benedict organized the monastery of Monte Cassino in southern Italy. He drew up a set of rules to regulate monastic life. In time, the Benedictine Rule was used by monasteries and convents across Europe.

Under the Benedictine Rule, monks and nuns took three vows. The first was obedience to the abbot or abbess, who headed the monastery or convent. The second was poverty, and the third was chastity, or purity. Each day was divided into periods for worship, work, and study. Benedict believed in the spiritual value of manual labor, so he required monks to work in the fields or at other physical tasks. As part of their labor, monks and nuns cleared and drained land and experimented with crops.

A Life of Service In a world without hospitals or schools, monasteries and convents often provided basic services. Monks and nuns looked after the poor and sick and sometimes set up schools for children. They gave food and lodging to travelers, especially to Christian pilgrims traveling to holy shrines. Some monks and nuns became missionaries. St. Patrick, for example, was a monk who set up the Irish Church. Later, the Church honored many missionaries by declaring them saints.

Virtual Field Trip

www.phschool.com

**Trinity College Library
Dublin, Ireland**

To see other pages from this illuminated manuscript, use the Internet address above to link to the *Book of Kells,* Trinity College, Dublin.

The Book of Kells

As monks and nuns copied books, they illuminated, or illustrated, each page. They decorated the letters and framed the text with intricate designs or scenes. This page is from the *Book of Kells,* illuminated by Irish monks on the island of Iona in the 800s.

Theme: Religions and Value Systems Why do you think copiers wanted to make this book so beautiful?

Background
Connections to Art

Illuminated Manuscripts Monks and nuns reproduced the Bible in order to help spread the teachings of Christ. They considered their copies to be forms of worship whose beauty had to match the importance of their contents. At first, there was some hesitation to render images of Christ and other holy persons, but in the sixth century, Pope Gregory the Great proclaimed that "painting can do for the illiterate what writing does for those who can read."

Inspired by the pope's commission, copyists labored day after day in special workshops called *scriptoria.* They became specialists at their work, with *antiquarii* creating the flowing calligraphy, *rubricatores* illuminating the initial letters, and *miniatores* illustrating the margins. They endured the pains of bent backs, aching muscles, and fingers numbed by winter cold. But religious devotion drove them on. In their own words, the work of writing and illuminating manuscripts was a way of "fighting the Devil by pen and ink."

Centers of Learning Monasteries and convents also performed a vital role in preserving the writings of the ancient world. Often, monks and nuns copied ancient works as a form of labor. Once copied, the work might remain unread for centuries. Still, it would be there when later scholars took an interest in ancient learning.

Educated monks and nuns kept learning alive. In Italy, Abbot Cassiodorus wrote useful summaries of Greek and Latin works and taught the classics to other monks. In Britain, the Venerable Bede wrote the earliest known history of England. Bede introduced the use of B.C. and A.D. to date historical events.

Convents Although women could not become priests, many did enter convents. There, capable, strong-minded women could escape the limits of society. In the 1100s, Abbess Hildegard of Bingen composed religious music and wrote books on many subjects. Because of her mystical visions, popes and rulers sought her advice. She spoke her mind freely. "Take care that the Highest King does not strike you down because of the blindness that prevents you from governing justly," she warned one ruler.

In the later Middle Ages, the Church put more restrictions on nuns. It withdrew rights that nuns had once enjoyed, such as preaching the Gospel, and placed most independent convents under the control of Church officials. It frowned on too much learning for women, preferring them to accept Church authority. Although women's role within the Church was limited, they made valuable contributions to their faith.

The Power of the Church Grows

In the centuries after the fall of Rome, the Church carved out a unique position in Western Europe. It not only controlled the spiritual life of Christians but gradually became the most powerful secular, or worldly, force in medieval Europe.

The Church and Feudal Society During the Middle Ages, the pope was the spiritual leader of the Roman Catholic Church. As representatives of Christ on Earth, medieval popes eventually claimed papal supremacy, or authority over all secular rulers.

*R*eading Strategy
Structured Overview

Point out the heading "The Power of the Church Grows" on this page. Have students scan Section 3 for ideas that relate to the growing spiritual and secular power of the Roman Catholic Church. List these ideas on the board. *(Less Advanced Readers)*

✓ Test Preparation

Have students read the paragraph titled "The Benedictine Rule" under "Monks and Nuns" on the opposite page, and then answer the question below.

Why did Benedict require monks and nuns to do manual labor?

A He believed it had a spiritual value.

B Manual labor conformed to their vow of poverty.

C The monastery needed more farmland to grow food.

D It made them physically as well as spiritually strong.

Caption Answer

Possible answer: They wanted to glorify and please God. Also, monks believed that hard work was a virtue in itself.

EXPLORING the HUMAN DRAMA
You Are There . . .

Bell Ringer Ask students to imagine what it would be like to stay in a monastery for a few days. Have students list what they might expect to encounter.

Background
About the Scene

With roots in a Christian monastic tradition that started in Egypt, the Benedictine order, founded by Benedict of Nursia, became the most influential order in Western Europe. The order observed the *Regula sancti Benedicti* (Rule of St. Benedict), which explains Benedict's philosophy of monasticism and gives rules for living a monastic life. In time, the Benedictine order spread across Europe. Today the order maintains retreat houses for quiet prayer and meditation.

Activity
Cooperative Learning

As an alternative to the individual portfolio assessment activity on this page, small groups of students may complete the assignment together. Students should brainstorm ideas for their manuscripts, and determine each group member's responsibility. One student could research a monastery's daily schedule, and another student could create the calligraphy for the manuscript. A third student could illuminate the initial letters, and a fourth student could illustrate the margins. All group members should be responsible for revising and proofreading.

Portfolio Assessment Rubrics

Share rubrics with students before they create their illuminated manuscripts.

Attempted Manuscript shows little research and is poorly executed.

Minimal Manuscript shows some research, but the pictures and text do not go beyond the student text.

Adequate Manuscript shows sufficient research, and the pictures and text illustrate aspects of the lives and accomplishments of the monks not shown in the student text.

Exemplary Manuscript is well researched, and the pictures and text go beyond what is in the student text. The project is exceptionally well executed.

Seeking Shelter in a Medieval Monastery

You've been walking since dawn, and the sun is now setting. You and another knight are on a long journey. After many days of travel, you look forward to a day of rest at a Benedictine monastery along the way. A monk welcomes you at the gate. You are curious about what life is like in the monastery.

After a simple meal of oatmeal, you spend the night on a straw mattress. A bell wakes you before dawn. The monks begin the day with prayers and household chores. They pray together seven times a day, including once in the middle of the night.

The bell rings again—it is time for study. Many of the monks are copying books. You see one monk spend hours illuminating, or illustrating, just one page.

Another bell sounds, and the monks head for the fields. You watch them hard at work farming. According to St. Benedict, "Idleness is the enemy of the soul!"

In the evening, you share a light supper with the monks. The day ends with the monks praying and singing hymns. The next day's routine will be the same.

Portfolio Assessment

When you get home, you decide to create an illuminated manuscript similar to the ones you saw at the monastery. In it, you include pictures and text detailing the lives and accomplishments of the monks you met.

Resource Directory

Teaching Resources
You Are There Chapter Extension Activities booklet, p. 24

The pope headed an army of churchmen who supervised Church activities. High clergy, such as bishops and archbishops, were usually nobles. Like other feudal lords, some had their own territories. The pope himself held vast lands in central Italy, later called the Papal States.

Church officials were closely linked to secular rulers. Because churchmen were often the only educated people, feudal rulers appointed them to high government positions.

Religious Authority The medieval Christian Church was dedicated to the worship of God. At the same time, Christians believed that all people were sinners and that many were doomed to eternal suffering. The only way to avoid the tortures of hell was to believe in Christ and participate in the sacraments. Because the medieval Church administered the sacraments, it had absolute power in religious matters.

The medieval Church developed its own body of laws, known as canon law, as well as its own courts. Canon law applied to religious teachings, the clergy, marriages, and morals. Anyone who disobeyed Church law faced a range of penalties. The most severe and terrifying was excommunication. If excommunicated, people could not receive the sacraments or a Christian burial. A powerful noble who opposed the Church could face the interdict, an order excluding an entire town, region, or kingdom from receiving most sacraments and Christian burial. Even the strongest ruler gave in rather than face the interdict.

A Force for Peace The Church tried to use its great authority to end feudal warfare. It declared periods of truce, or temporary peace, known as the Peace of God. It demanded that fighting stop between Friday and Sunday each week and on religious holidays. Such efforts may have contributed to the decline of feudal warfare in the 1100s.

Reform Movements

The very success of the medieval Church brought problems. As its wealth and power grew, discipline weakened. Pious Christians left their wealth and lands to monasteries and convents, leading some monks and nuns to ignore their vows of poverty. Some clergy lived in luxury. Priests could marry, but some spent more time on family matters than on Church duties, and some even treated the priesthood as a family inheritance. Throughout the Middle Ages, voices called for reform in the Church.

Cluniac Reforms One reform movement swept across Western Europe in the early 900s. Abbot Berno of Cluny, a monastery in eastern France, set out to end abuses. First, he revived the Benedictine Rule, which had been allowed to lapse. Then, he declared that he would no longer allow nobles to interfere in monastery affairs. Finally, he filled the monastery at Cluny with men devoted to religious pursuits. In time, many monasteries and convents copied the Cluniac reforms.

In 1073, Pope Gregory VII, a former monk, extended the Cluniac reforms to the entire Church. He outlawed marriage for priests and prohibited simony, the selling of Church offices. He then called on Christians to renew their faith. To end secular influence, Gregory insisted that the Church, not kings or nobles, choose Church officials. That policy, as you will read, would spark a bitter battle of wills with the German emperor.

Preaching Orders Over the centuries, other reform movements battled corruption and worldliness. In the early 1200s, Francis of Assisi and Dominic took a new approach. They set up orders of friars, monks who did not live in isolated monasteries but traveled around Europe's growing towns preaching to the poor.

Francis left a comfortable home in the Italian town of Assisi to preach the Gospel and teach by example. The Franciscan order he set up preached

Biography

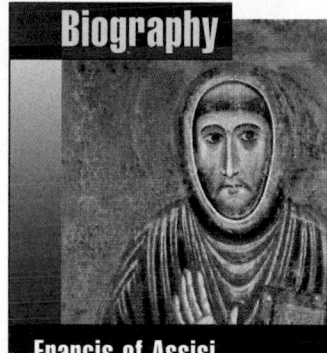

Francis of Assisi
c. 1181–1226

Today, Francis of Assisi is often portrayed talking with birds and animals. But as a young man, he loved going to parties, wearing fine clothes, and writing lively poems and songs. Then, in his mid-20s, he heard a voice speak to him while he was praying. He decided to give up all of his wealth and accept a life of poverty and charity. He was soon joined by a small group of followers—the first Franciscan friars—and together they served the poor and the sick.

Francis continued to write poetry. In his new poems, he expressed love for nature and the joy he felt in being part of God's family. One of his famous poems begins, "Praise to thee, my Lord, for all thy creatures/Above all Brother Sun/Who brings us the day and lends us his light."

Theme: Impact of the Individual How did Francis set an example for his followers?

Chapter 8 **195**

Recall

1. (a) Benedictine Rule, p. 192 (b) Cluny, p. 195 (c) Francis of Assisi, p. 195 (d) Dominicans, p. 196 (e) Beguines, p. 196 2. (a) sacrament, p. 191 (b) tithe, p. 192 (c) secular, p. 193 (d) papal supremacy, p. 193 (e) canon law, p. 195 (f) excommunication, p. 195 (g) interdict, p. 195 (h) simony, p. 195 (i) friar, p. 195 (j) antisemitism, p. 196

Comprehension

3. (a) Possible answer: The Church administered sacraments, offered spiritual guidance, and provided care for the needy. Daily life revolved around the Christian calendar. (b) They emphasized the value in hard work; preserved knowledge by copying and storing important texts; provided basic social services by tending the sick, helping the poor, setting up schools for children, and caring for travelers. 4. Feudal rulers often appointed Church officials to high government positions. The Church tried to end feudal warfare by declaring periods of truce. 5. Francis preached poverty, humility, and love of God. Dominic tried to combat heresy by preaching official Catholic beliefs. 6. The Muslims who controlled Spain tolerated both Jews and Christians.

Critical Thinking and Writing

7. (a) The Church taught that men and women were equal before God. However, it also considered women to be weak and needful of guidance and protection. (b) Possible answer: They believed that she had visions from God. They respected her as a wise counselor. 8. Students should recognize main ideas and convey information concisely.

Activity Rubrics

Share rubrics with students before they write their letters.

Attempted The letter is incomplete, missing either the reasons for the rules or the argument to follow them.

Minimal The letter has both parts but is very brief.

Adequate The letter has both parts, and both are well written.

Exemplary The letter has both parts, and both are very detailed and very well written.

Caption Answer

Both are beautiful, intricately designed, and used in religious observances.

---

poverty, humility, and love of God. Soon after, Dominic, a Spanish priest, set up the Dominican order. Its chief goal was to combat heresy by teaching official Roman Catholic beliefs.

Women joined this reform movement by creating new religious groups. One such group was the Beguines (BEHG eenz). Most convents accepted only well-born women whose families gave a dowry, or gift, to the Church. The Beguines welcomed women without the wealth to enter a regular convent. Using funds from selling their weavings and embroidery, they helped the poor and set up hospitals and shelters.

Jews in Europe

Jewish communities existed across Europe. In their homes, Jews preserved the oral and written laws that were central to their faith.

Jews flourished in Spain, where they became known as Sephardim, from the Hebrew word for Spain. The Muslims who conquered Spain in 711 were tolerant of both Jews and Christians. Muslim Spain became a center of Jewish culture and scholarship. There, Sephardic Jews served as officials in Muslim royal courts.

During the Middle Ages, Jewish farmers migrated to other parts of Western Europe. Later, they became known as Ashkenazim, or "German" Jews. For centuries, Christians and Jews lived side by side in relative peace. Early German kings gave educated Jews positions at court. Many rulers in northern Europe valued and protected Jewish communities, although they taxed them heavily.

In the late 1000s, Christian persecution of Jews increased. Many Church leaders charged that Jews were responsible for the death of Jesus. As the Church grew in power, it issued orders forbidding Jews to own land or practice most occupations. Yet popes and rulers still turned to educated Jews as financial advisers and physicians.

In bad times, antisemitism, or prejudice against Jews, worsened. Faced with disasters they could not understand, such as illness or famine, many Christians blamed Jews. People also blamed their economic woes on Jews, as many Jews barred from other professions had become moneylenders. In response to growing persecution, thousands of Jews migrated to Eastern Europe. There, rulers welcomed the newcomers' skills and knowledge. Jewish communities thrived in Eastern Europe until modern times.

Preserving a Jewish Tradition
Jewish communities in medieval Europe observed their unique customs. This plate belonged to a Jewish family in Spain. On Passover, it was filled with the traditional foods of the Seder, or Passover meal.

Theme: Diversity In what way is this Seder plate similar to the illuminated manuscript on page 193?

SECTION 3 Assessment

Recall

1. **Identify:** (a) Benedictine Rule, (b) Cluny, (c) Francis of Assisi, (d) Dominicans, (e) Beguines.
2. **Define:** (a) sacrament, (b) tithe, (c) secular, (d) papal supremacy, (e) canon law, (f) excommunication, (g) interdict, (h) simony, (i) friar, (j) antisemitism.

Comprehension

3. (a) Describe three ways in which the Church shaped medieval life. (b) How did monks and nuns help build Christian civilization in Europe?
4. How did the Church increase its secular power?
5. What reforms did Francis and Dominic promote?
6. Why were Jewish communities able to flourish in Spain?

Critical Thinking and Writing

7. **Analyzing Information** (a) What views did the Church put forth about women? (b) Why do you think important leaders were willing to accept the advice of Hildegard of Bingen?
8. **Identifying Main Ideas** Choose one of the main headings from this section. Write a sentence describing the main idea of the material in that subsection.

Activity

Writing a Letter
Write a letter that Benedict might have sent to a neighboring monastery in the 500s. Explain why you have drawn up a set of rules for the monks at Monte Cassino and why you think it would be worthwhile for other monasteries to follow the Benedictine Rule.

Resource Directory

Teaching Resources
Section Quiz Unit 3 booklet, p. 7
Creative Teaching Activities Creative Teaching Activities booklet, p. 40
Guided Reading and Review Unit 3 booklet, p. 8

Technology
Interactive Student Tutorial CD-ROM Ch. 8
Computer Test Bank Ch. 8

Economic Expansion and Change

Reading Focus

■ How did new technologies spark an agricultural revolution?

■ How did the revival of trade revolutionize commerce?

■ How were guilds linked to the rise of towns and cities?

Vocabulary

charter
capital
partnership
bill of exchange
tenant farmer
middle class
usury
guild
apprentice
journeyman

Taking Notes

Create a diagram like the one shown below. As you read the section, fill in the main causes for the economic recovery in Europe. The first one has been partially filled in for you.

New Technology
• Iron plows
• Windmills

ECONOMIC RECOVERY IN EUROPE

Main Idea During the High Middle Ages, Europe's economy grew, cities and towns expanded, and a middle class arose.

Setting the Scene

The castle of Count William of Flanders was a bustling place. Hundreds of people lived and worked there, from nobles to servants. Such a large castle had many needs, and people came from near and far to supply them. "There began to throng before the gate near the castle bridge, traders and merchants selling costly goods," wrote one medieval chronicler. After that, other merchants came and built inns where visitors could eat and sleep, "and the houses so increased that there grew up a town."

The appearance of new towns was a symbol of Europe's economic recovery. This revival, which lasted from about 1000 to 1300, is called the High Middle Ages.

An Agricultural Revolution

By 1000, Europe's economic recovery was well underway. It had begun in the countryside, where peasants adapted new farming technologies that made their fields more productive. The result was an agricultural revolution that transformed Europe.

New Technologies By the 800s, peasants were using new iron plows that carved deep into the heavy soil of northern Europe. These plows were a big improvement over the old wooden plows, which had been designed for the light soils of the Mediterranean region. Also, a new kind of harness allowed peasants to use horses rather than oxen to pull the plows. Because faster-moving horses could plow more land in a day than could oxen, peasants were able to enlarge their fields and plant more crops.

A peasant might look up and see another new device, a windmill, turning slowly against the sky. Where there were no fast-moving streams to turn a water mill, the power of the wind had been harnessed to grind the peasants' grain into flour.

Expanding Production Other changes brought still more land into use. Feudal lords who wanted to boost their incomes pushed peasants to clear forests, drain swamps, and reclaim wasteland for farming and grazing.

Peasants also adopted the three-field system. They planted one field with grain, a second with legumes, such as peas and beans, and they left the third fallow, or unplanted. The legumes restored soil fertility while adding variety to the peasant diet. Unlike the old two-field system, the new method left only a third of the land unplanted.

Geography and History

Roadblock

The roads to places like Count William's castle in Flanders bustled with travelers. Among them were peasants, carrying farm products to the marketplace.

In those days, wealthy travelers might ride horses, but the farmers walked. Neither riders nor walkers were comfortable on the road, however, because of the ruts, cracks, and potholes. The roads built by the Romans were still in use but had been poorly maintained. Other minor roads had been added since Roman times, but these were little more than narrow tracks. Worse, peasants would dig up the roads for clay to repair their houses. The story goes that one miller dug a deep hole in the middle of a nearby road. When it rained, the hole filled with water and a traveling glovemaker fell in, drowning both himself and his horse!

Theme: Economics and Technology What conditions or developments might lead to the improvement of medieval roads?

🔔 **Bell Ringer** Ask students to describe what comes to mind when they think of a trade fair or an arts and crafts show. Discuss the purpose of such fairs and shows. Then, point out that trade fairs date back to the Middle Ages, when they served similar purposes.

LESSON PLAN

1. Focus Iron plows, new types of harnesses, windmills, and other new technologies led to an agricultural revolution in Europe. As population grew, so did the demand for goods. In response, trade revived and towns prospered. In this section, students will learn about an economic revival, the birth of a new middle class, and the advantages and disadvantages of town life.

2. Instruct Divide the class into groups. Tell students that each group will become experts on one of the economic changes that occurred in Europe between 1000 and 1300. Assign each group one of the following topics: Agricultural Revolution, Revival of Trade, Commercial Revolution, Role of Guilds, Life in a Medieval City. Have each group work together to learn about its assigned topic. You may wish to suggest that students do some additional research in the library. When they have finished their research, have each group present its findings to the class in a panel discussion. Encourage students to ask questions of the panel members. Continue rotating panels until each topic has been covered.

3. Assess Ask students to write five newspaper headlines that cover the important economic events or trends of the High Middle Ages.

4. Reteach If students' Assess activity does not reflect adequate understanding of the lesson, you might assign the *Guide to the Essentials* or the *Interactive Student Tutorial CD-ROM* for this section.

Block Scheduling Support

Tell students that some aspects of city or town life have survived from medieval to modern times. In addition to medieval festivals that are still popular today, have students think of other similarities between city or town life then and now. Ask students to create Venn diagrams. They should list activities and features found in medieval cities in one circle and activities and features of modern city or town life in the other. In the space where the circles overlap, students should list activities and features that have not changed since the Middle Ages. Encourage students to illustrate their diagrams and share their observations with the class.

Geography and History

ANSWER technological advances for paving roads; increased demand for good roads because more people want or need to travel; stronger governments that can organize the improvement of roads

Connections to Economics

Banking Trade fairs brought together merchants from all over Europe and beyond. As a result, there was a profusion of different currencies that included English marks, Westphalian groats, Venetian ducats, Florentine florins, Muslim dinar, and other varieties of coins. However, this apparent confusion did not pose a serious problem due to the development of banking services. Merchants and their customers relied on Italian moneychangers who weighed and tested the various coins to determine their values. They provided their services at a *banc,* or bench. Thus began the institutions that we know today as banks.

Trade in Medieval Europe, 1000–1300

- ● Towns holding fairs
- ○ Major commercial centers
- — Major trade routes

Skills Assessment

Geography As trade revived in medieval Europe, trade routes multiplied and many towns hosted trade fairs.

1. **Location** On the map, locate *(a) Constantinople, (b) Adriatic Sea, (c) Venice, (d) Flanders, (e) London, (f) Baltic Sea.*
2. **Region** In which two areas were most of the principal commercial centers located?
3. **Critical Thinking Linking Past and Present** *(a) Identify two medieval towns that held trade fairs. (b) What might be today's equivalent of a medieval trade fair? Explain.*

All these improvements let farmers produce more food. With more food available, the population grew. Between about 1000 and 1300, the population of Europe doubled.

Trade Revives

Europe's growing population needed goods that were not available on the manor. Peasants needed iron for farm tools. Wealthy nobles wanted fine wool, furs, and spices from Asia. As foreign invasions and feudal warfare declined, traders crisscrossed Europe to meet the growing demand for goods.

New Trade Routes Enterprising traders formed merchant companies that traveled in armed caravans for safety. They followed regular trade routes. Along these routes, merchants exchanged local goods for those from remote markets in the Middle East and further east into Asia.

In Constantinople, merchants bought Chinese silks, Byzantine gold jewelry, and Asian spices. They shipped these goods to Venice on the Adriatic Sea. In Venice, traders loaded their wares onto pack mules and headed north over the Alps and up the Rhine River to Flanders. In Flanders, other traders bought the goods to send on to England and the lands along the Baltic Sea. Northern Europeans paid for the goods with products such as honey, furs, cloth, tin, and lead.

Trade Fairs At first, traders and their customers did business at local trade fairs. These fairs took place each year near navigable rivers or where busy trade routes met.

People from the surrounding villages, towns, and castles flocked to the fairs. Peasants traded farm goods and animals. As they ate and drank, they

Skills Assessment

ANSWERS **1.** Review locations with students. **2.** Flanders and northern Italy **3. (a)** Answers include Winchester, Ghent, Ypres, and Milan. **(b)** Possible answer: a shopping mall. Like a trade fair, a mall is located in a high-traffic area and attracts many merchants and customers.

Resource Directory

Technology

World History Color Transparencies *European Knowledge of the World* base map and overlay transparencies, set 4, pp. B–41, B–43, B–45; *Medieval Guilds, Protecting Group Interests*, p. C–37

enjoyed the antics of jugglers, acrobats, or even dancing bears. Still, peasants had no money to buy fine swords, sugar, and silks. The customers for these luxuries were the feudal rulers, nobles, and wealthy churchmen.

New Towns Trade fairs closed in the autumn when the weather made roads impassable. Merchants might wait out the winter months near a castle or in a town with a bishop's palace. These settlements attracted artisans who made goods that the merchants could sell.

Slowly, these small centers of trade and handicraft developed into the first real medieval cities. Some boasted populations of 10,000, and a few topped 100,000. Europe had not seen towns of this size since Roman times. The richest cities grew up in northern Italy and Flanders—the two ends of the profitable north-south trade route. Both areas were centers of the wool trade and had prosperous textile industries.

To protect their interests, the merchants who set up a new town would ask the local lord, or if possible the king himself, for a charter. This written document set out the rights and privileges of the town. In return, merchants paid the lord or the king a large sum of money, a yearly fee, or both.

Although charters varied from place to place, they almost always granted townspeople the right to choose their own leaders and control their own affairs. Most charters also had a clause, popular with runaway serfs, that declared that anyone who lived in the town for a year and a day was free. "Town air makes free," was a common medieval saying.

A Commercial Revolution

As trade revived, money reappeared, which in turn led to more changes. Merchants, for example, needed money to buy goods so they borrowed from moneylenders. In time, their need for capital, or money for investment, spurred the growth of banking houses.

New Business Practices To meet the needs of the changing economy, Europeans developed new ways of doing business. For example, many merchants joined together in an organization known as a partnership. Under this setup, a group of merchants pooled their funds to finance a large-scale venture that would have been too costly for any individual trader. This practice made capital available more easily. It also reduced the risk for any one partner in the venture because no one had to invest all his or her capital in the company.

Merchants also developed a system of insurance to help reduce business risks. For a small fee, an underwriter would insure the merchant's shipment. If the shipment was lost or destroyed, the underwriter paid the merchant most of its value. If the goods arrived safely, the merchant lost only the insurance payment.

Europeans adopted other practices from Middle Eastern merchants. Among the most important was the bill of exchange. A merchant deposited money with a banker in his home city. The banker issued a bill of exchange, which the merchant exchanged for cash in a distant city. A merchant could thus travel without carrying gold coins, which were easily stolen.

Social Changes These new ways of doing business were part of a commercial revolution that transformed the medieval economy. Slowly, they also reshaped medieval society.

For example, the use of money undermined serfdom. Feudal lords needed money to buy fine goods. As a result, many peasants began selling farm products to townspeople and fulfilling their obligations to their lords by paying their rent in cash rather than in labor. By 1300, most peasants in Western Europe were either tenant farmers, who paid rent for their land, or hired farm laborers.

Connections to Today

Taking Care of Business

A medieval merchant visiting the United States today might understand many modern business practices. Like medieval merchants, today's mutual fund investors pool their money to make possible much larger-scale investments than they could make as individuals. The medieval idea of insurance is also alive and well. Today's insurance possibilities are endless—life, business, car, home, jewelry. A famous dancer was even able to insure her legs!

The bill of exchange has echoes in today's automated teller machines, or ATMs. With hundreds of thousands of them in operation internationally, anyone with a bank account can access the money in it instantly, around the corner or halfway across the world.

Theme: Continuity and Change How is an ATM like a bill of exchange?

Customize for . . .
Auditory Learners

Linking Past and Present Tell students that the annual state and county fairs that are held across the United States have their roots in medieval trade fairs. Even the World's Fair is a form of trade fair where nations display their wares. Ask students to name and describe fairs put on by their town, county, or state. Have students discuss the purposes that these fairs serve. Also, have students describe the forms of entertainment offered at these fairs.

Customize for . . .
Heterogeneous Groups

Writing a Report Assign students to research and write a report on the history of a major European city in the Middle Ages. Students could choose London, Paris, Bruges, Antwerp, Venice, or others. In their reports, students should discuss the city's population, economic activities, government, social problems, cultural activities, and architecture. *(Enrichment)*

Human Drama Note

Medieval Tapestries Explain to students that medieval tapestries were more than merely decorative—they were symbols of wealth and a means of telling a story. Often their scenes depicted snapshots from daily life, the conquests and adventures of heroes, or stories from the lives of saints. Have students imagine that this practice suddenly became fashionable in modern times. Have students sketch designs for contemporary tapestries that meet the same criteria as their medieval counterparts. Ask students to explain why they chose their subjects and what colors and shapes they would use to depict their designs.

Connections to Today

ANSWER It makes it possible for a person to access money at a distance from where it is deposited.

Background
Daily Life

City Life Medieval cities retained many of the features of rural life. Many houses had vegetable gardens, and many city dwellers kept pigs and cows in sties or stables. As people walked along the unpaved city streets, they would frequently pass herds of sheep or flocks of geese.

In other ways, medieval cities were quite different. Because most city buildings were crowded together and made of wood, fire posed a serious threat. The Swiss city of Bern, for example, was consumed by fire in less than 30 minutes, despite the efforts of a bucket brigade to extinguish the flames. Another serious problem was that crowding and unsanitary conditions created a perfect environment for the rapid spread of contagious diseases.

Guild Members at Work
All over Europe, artisans in many fields organized craft guilds. These Italian pictures show medieval artisans weaving tapestries (top) and building cabinets (bottom).

Theme: Economics and Technology How do modern factories differ from these medieval workshops?

In towns, the old social order of nobles, clergy, and peasants gradually changed. By 1000, a new class appeared that included merchants, traders, and artisans. They formed a middle class, standing between nobles and peasants.

Nobles and the clergy despised the new middle class. To nobles, towns were a disruptive influence beyond their control. To the clergy, the profits that merchants and bankers made from usury (YOO zhuh ree), or lending money at interest, were immoral.*

During the Middle Ages, the Church forbade Christians to lend money at interest. As a result, many Jews who were barred from other professions became moneylenders. Although moneylenders played an essential role in the growing medieval economy, the need to pay them back led to much resentment and a rise in antisemitism, as you have read.

Role of Guilds

In medieval towns, merchants and artisans formed associations known as guilds. Merchant guilds appeared first. They dominated town life, passing laws and levying taxes. They also decided whether to spend funds to pave the streets with cobblestones, build protective walls, or raise a new town hall.

In time, artisans came to resent the powerful merchants. They organized craft guilds. Each guild represented workers in one occupation, such as weavers, bakers, brewers, or goldsmiths. In some towns, struggles between craft guilds and the wealthier merchant guilds led to riots.

Guild members cooperated to protect their own economic interests. To prevent competition, they limited membership in the guild. No one except guild members could work in any trade. Guilds made rules to protect the quality of their goods, regulate hours of labor, and set prices. Guilds also provided social services. Besides operating schools and hospitals, they looked after the needs of their members. For example, the regulations of a craft guild in the leather-making trade stated:

> "If by chance any of the said trade shall fall into poverty, whether through old age or because he cannot labor or work, and have nothing with which to keep himself, he shall have every week from the said box 7d for his support, if he be a man of good repute."
> —*Ordinances of the White-Tawyers*

Guilds also pledged to provide support for the widows and orphans of their members.

Becoming a Guild Member To become a guild member meant many years of hard work. At the age of seven or eight, a child might become an apprentice, or trainee, to a guild master. The apprentice usually spent seven years learning the trade. The guild master paid no wages, but was required to give the apprentice bed and board.

Few apprentices ever became guild masters unless they were related to one. Most worked for guild members as journeymen, or salaried workers. Journeymen often accused masters of keeping their wages low so that they could not save enough to open a competing shop.

Women and the Guilds Women worked in dozens of crafts. A woman often engaged in the same trade as her father or husband and might inherit his workshop if he died. Because she knew the craft well, she kept the shop

---

*Today, the term *usury* refers to charging excessive interest.

---

going and sometimes might become a guild master herself. Young girls became apprentices in trades ranging from ribbonmaking to papermaking to surgery.

Women dominated some trades and even had their own guilds. In Paris, they far outnumbered men in the profitable silk and woolen guilds. A third of the guilds in Frankfurt were composed entirely of women.

Town and City Life

Medieval towns and cities were surrounded by high, protective walls. As the city grew, space within the walls filled to overflowing, and newcomers had to settle in the fields outside the walls. To keep up with this constant growth, every few years the city might rebuild its walls farther and farther out.

A typical medieval city was a jumble of narrow streets lined with tall houses. Upper floors hung out over the streets, making those below dim even in daytime. In the largest cities, a great cathedral, where a bishop presided, or a splendid guild hall might tower above humbler residences.

During the day, streets echoed with the cries of hawkers selling their wares and porters grumbling under heavy loads. A wealthy merchant might pass, followed by a procession of servants. At night, the unlit streets were deserted.

Even a rich town had no garbage collection or sewer system. Residents simply flung their wastes into the street. Larger cities might pass laws, such as one requiring butchers to dump their garbage on the edge of town. But towns remained filthy, smelly, noisy, and crowded.

Looking Ahead

By 1300, Western Europe was a different place from what it had been in the early Middle Ages. Although most people had no way of knowing it, slow but momentous changes were sending shock waves through medieval life. Trade, for example, put ideas as well as money into circulation. New riches revised the social structure. In politics, too, new forces were at work.

In the global sphere, the economic revival of the High Middle Ages was bringing Europeans into contact with civilizations much more advanced than their own. From these lands to the east came products, ideas, and technologies that would spark an even greater transformation in how Europeans thought and lived.

SECTION 4 Assessment

Recall
1. **Identify**: High Middle Ages.
2. **Define**: (a) charter, (b) capital, (c) partnership, (d) bill of exchange, (e) tenant farmer, (f) middle class, (g) usury, (h) guild, (i) apprentice, (j) journeyman.

Comprehension
3. What were two effects of the agricultural revolution that took place during the Middle Ages?
4. What new ways of doing business evolved in the Middle Ages?

5. **(a)** How did a merchant guild differ from a craft guild? **(b)** How did guilds improve life for townspeople?

Critical Thinking and Writing
6. **Synthesizing Information** Give three pieces of evidence to support the idea that the High Middle Ages were a time of economic growth.
7. **Comparing** Compare economic life in the early Middle Ages to economic life in the High Middle Ages.

Activity

Creating an Advertisement Imagine that a growing medieval city has hired you to attract people to move there. Create an ad that describes opportunities the city provides for merchants, artisans, and peasants.

Test Preparation

Have students read the section titled "Becoming a Guild Member" on the opposite page, and then answer the question below.

What were the steps involved in becoming a guild member?

A apprentice, trainee, guild master

(B) apprentice, journeyman, guild master

C apprentice, guild master, journeyman

D apprentice, journeyman, salaried worker

SECTION 4 Assessment

Recall
1. High Middle Ages, p. 197 2. **(a)** charter, p. 199 **(b)** capital, p. 199 **(c)** partnership, p. 199 **(d)** bill of exchange, p. 199 **(e)** tenant farmer, p. 199 **(f)** middle class, p. 200 **(g)** usury, p. 200 **(h)** guild, p. 200 **(i)** apprentice, p. 200 **(j)** journeyman, p. 200

Comprehension
3. Possible answer: Farmers produced more food, and the population grew.
4. the use of money, banking, partnerships, insurance, bills of exchange
5. **(a)** Merchant guilds passed laws, levied taxes, and made decisions about how to spend funds. Each craft guild represented workers in one occupation. Members protected their economic interests by limiting membership, establishing quality control, regulating hours of labor, and setting prices. **(b)** They provided schools, hospitals, and support for members and widows and orphans.

Critical Thinking and Writing
6. Possible answer: Trade increased throughout Europe. Cities and towns grew as centers of trade. New business practices evolved. 7. During the early Middle Ages, trade was limited. The center of the economy was the manor, an economic unit that relied on farming. The High Middle Ages brought increased trade, the growth of towns, and a commercial revolution.

Activity Rubrics

Share rubrics with students before they create their advertisements.

Attempted Advertisement does not describe opportunities for all three groups and shows little awareness of medieval city life.

Minimal Advertisement describes some of what a medieval city offered for each group.

Adequate Advertisement is well written, creative, and shows a good grasp of the opportunities for each group.

Exemplary Advertisement is original, creative, catchy, and highlights appealing opportunities for each group.

Primary Source

ANSWER The sports are similar to present-day activities, although the equipment, such as ice skates, has changed.

Creating a Chapter Summary

As a reteaching opportunity, pair a more able student with a less able student to complete this chapter summary.

Students should list additional relevant points under each heading. For example: **Early Middle Ages** limited trade, farm economy, strong influence of Church. **High Middle Ages** agricultural revolution, increased trade, commercial revolution, less Church influence, increased population.

Building Vocabulary

1–10. Students' sentences should show an understanding of each word.

Recalling Key Facts

11. Unlike the Romans, the Germanic tribes had no cities or written laws and they were ruled by elected kings.
12. It fell apart.
13. The pope was the leader of the Roman Catholic Church and ruler of the Papal States, and he claimed authority over all secular rulers.
14. Monks and nuns copied ancient books, helping to preserve them. They also wrote summaries of classical works.
15. The use of money undermined serfdom, and a new middle class emerged.
16. Students' answers should demonstrate a clear understanding of what a medieval city may have been like.

Critical Thinking and Writing

17. Possible answer: A medieval manor was more self-sufficient because it was expected to produce all the needs of people who lived on it. Modern farmers tend to specialize in one or a few crops and depend on others for their equipment and even food.
18. Possible answer: As feudalism weakened, monarchs gained power. The Church and the monarchs competed for power and influence.
19. Possible answer: In times of trouble, people often look for a scapegoat on whom to blame their problems. Jews may have been considered safe targets because they were not protected by the Church or by feudal lords.
20. Order of occurrence: new technologies, agricultural revolution, population growth, revival of trade, growth of towns. Technology made

---

Creating a Chapter Summary

On a sheet of paper start a table like the one shown here. Add important facts under each heading to help you review the events you have learned about in this chapter. Part of the table has been filled in to help you get started.

EARLY MIDDLE AGES	HIGH MIDDLE AGES
Feudal society	Rise of middle class
Life centered on manors	Cities develop

TEXT For additional review and enrichment activities, see the interactive version of *World History* available on the Web and on CD-ROM.

Web Site Self-Test
For practice test questions for Chapter 8, see **www.phschool.com**.

Building Vocabulary

Write sentences using the chapter vocabulary words listed below, leaving blanks where the vocabulary words would go. Exchange your sentences with another student and fill in the blanks in each other's sentences.

1. medieval
2. feudalism
3. vassal
4. fief
5. tithe
6. secular
7. interdict
8. charter
9. guild
10. journeyman

Recalling Key Facts

11. How did the culture of the Germanic tribes differ from that of the Romans?
12. What happened to Charlemagne's empire after his death?
13. Why was the pope a powerful figure in medieval Europe?
14. What role did monasteries and convents play in the preservation of ancient culture?
15. What social changes were caused by the commercial revolution of the Middle Ages?
16. Describe the typical medieval city.

Critical Thinking and Writing

17. **Connecting to Geography** Compare life on a medieval manor with life on an American farm today. Which do you think would be more self-sufficient? Why?

18. **Predicting Consequences** How do you think the weakening of the feudal system affected the Church? Explain your answer.
19. **Recognizing Causes and Effects** As you have read, antisemitism increased during economic bad times. Why do you think this was so?
20. **Understanding Sequences** Arrange the following developments in the order in which they occurred: new technologies, growth of towns, agricultural revolution, population growth, revival of trade. Then, explain why they occurred in that order.
21. **Making Decisions** If you had been a European peasant during the High Middle Ages, do you think you would have chosen to stay in the countryside or move to a town? Give reasons to support your decision.

---

farming more productive. Greater food production supported more people, which led to increased demand for goods. Trade increased and towns grew.
21. In describing the reasons for their choice, students should show an understanding of manor life and town life during the Middle Ages.

Einhard, a medieval monk at the court of Charlemagne, wrote a life of the king. In this letter, quoted by Einhard, Charlemagne instructs one of his lords, Abbot Fulrad, about what to bring to a meeting of nobles. Read the passage and answer the questions that follow.

"[Arrive] so prepared with your men that you may be able to go thence well equipped in any direction which our command shall order, that is with arms and accoutrements [equipment] and other provisions for war in the way of food and clothing. Each horseman is expected to have a shield, lance, sword, dagger, bow, quiver with arrows, and in your cart shall be . . . axes, planes, augers, boards, spades, iron shovels and other utensils which are necessary in any army. In the wagons shall be supplies for three months, together with arms and clothing for six months."

—Einhard, *Life of Charlemagne*

22. What is each horseman expected to bring to the meeting?
23. Why do you think Charlemagne wants the men prepared in the way that he describes?
24. How long might these men be engaged in the king's service?
25. **(a)** Based on what you have learned about feudalism, what does the lord abbot owe Charlemagne? **(b)** What do the lord's men owe the lord?
26. Fulrad was both an abbot and a lord. What does this fact suggest about the role of the Church at this time?

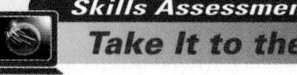

Skills Assessment
Take It to the NET

Use the Internet to research daily life in early medieval Europe. Then, write a diary entry from the point of view of a medieval European. You might choose to take the role of a lord, noblewoman, knight, monk, nun, serf, or town merchant. Include information about how your status in medieval society affects your tasks, beliefs, and expectations of life.

A FEUDAL MANOR OF MEDIEVAL EUROPE

Manor house
Blacksmith's shop
Lord's oven
Fallow field
Well
Serfs' houses
Kitchen garden
Church
Priest's house
Mill
Wheat field
Peas, oats, barley, and beans

The diagram above represents a medieval manor. Study the diagram and answer the following questions:

27. **(a)** What kinds of buildings does the diagram show? **(b)** How many fields are shown?
28. Describe the purpose of: **(a)** the kitchen garden, **(b)** the blacksmith's shop, **(c)** the lord's oven, **(d)** the mill.
29. How does the diagram show that religion played an important role in manor life?
30. Does this diagram represent a manor before or after the agricultural revolution of the High Middle Ages? How can you tell?
31. How does the diagram support the statement that the medieval manor was self-sufficient?
32. Do you think this diagram represents an actual manor? Give reasons for your answer.

Skills Tip

Some diagrams represent an actual place or object, such as the blueprint of a house. Others give a more general picture of a typical place or object.

Chapter 8 **203**

22. shield, lance, sword, dagger, bow, quiver with arrows
23. He is most likely preparing for war.
24. from three to six months
25. **(a)** loyalty, allegiance, military service **(b)** the same
26. Possible answer: The roles of secular and spiritual leadership were blended. The Church was a powerful presence among the landowning nobility.

Analyzing Diagrams

27. **(a)** residences, work areas, and a place of worship **(b)** three
28. **(a)** food for the nobles or the serfs **(b)** to shoe horses and make tools **(c)** to bake food for the nobles or the serfs **(d)** to grind the grain into flour
29. There was a church on the manor grounds.
30. after; the crops are planted according to the three-field system rather than the older two-field system
31. The manor included facilities to meet all the people's needs.
32. Students should be able to support their answers with specific reasons.

Skills Tip

Explain to students that diagrams that represent a more general picture of an object or a place often do so to emphasize the most important features of that object or place. More specific diagrams are more concerned with emphasizing very detailed parts of a particular object. The Skills Handbook in the front of this book has a lesson to help students with this feature.

Unit Theme Activity

Remind students about the Unit Theme Activity located on the unit opener page. Make sure the students understand the assignment and have begun work.

Take It to the NET

Direct students to **www.phschool.com** for links to sites that will help them get started on this assignment. Share rubrics with students.
Attempted The diary entry shows little or no research and a lack of understanding about how status would affect point of view.
Minimal The diary entry indicates some research was done and that the student has some understanding of how status determines the type of life a person may lead.
Adequate The diary entry shows sufficient research was done and illustrates fairly well how status influenced a person's work, beliefs, and expectations in life.
Exemplary The diary entry is well researched and well written. The supporting details illustrate clearly how a medieval person's work, beliefs, and expectations were determined by his or her status in society.

Chapter 9 Planning Guide

Resource Manager

	CORE INSTRUCTION	READING/SKILLS
Chapter Level Resources	**Teaching Resources** ▪ Pacing Charts, Ch. 9 ▪ Teaching With Themes, p. 12 ▫ Color Transparencies, p. F–19 ◉ Resource Pro® Ch. 9 ▣ www.phschool.com • eTeach	◉ Book on CD, Ch. 9 ◉ Interactive Student Tutorial CD-ROM, Ch. 9 ◉ Social Studies Skills Tutor CD-ROM ▫ Skills Transparencies
1 Growth of Royal Power in England and France 1. Explain how monarchs gained power over the nobles and the Church. 2. Summarize the traditions of government developed under King John and others. 3. Describe how strong monarchs succeeded in unifying France.	**Teaching Resources** ▪ Creative Teaching Activities, p. 41 ◉ Prentice Hall Presentation Pro, Ch. 9, Section 1 ▫ Section Reading Support Transparencies	**Teaching Resources** ▪ Unit 3 booklet • Guided Reading and Review, p. 20 ▪ Guide to the Essentials ▣ Guided Reading Audiotapes, Ch. 9, Section 1
2 The Holy Roman Empire and the Church 1. Explain why Holy Roman emperors failed to unify Germany. 2. Describe how power struggles affected Italy's rulers. 3. Identify Church powers at its height.	**Teaching Resources** ▪ Creative Teaching Activities, p. 42 ◉ Prentice Hall Presentation Pro, Ch. 9, Section 2 ▫ Section Reading Support Transparencies	**Teaching Resources** ▪ Unit 3 booklet • Guided Reading and Review, p. 22 ▪ Guide to the Essentials ▣ Guided Reading Audiotapes, Ch. 9, Section 2
3 Europeans Look Outward 1. Identify the advanced civilizations of 1050. 2. Analyze Crusades' causes and effects. 3. Summarize the Christian Reconquista in Spain.	**Teaching Resources** ▪ Creative Teaching Activities, p. 43 ◉ Prentice Hall Presentation Pro, Ch. 9, Section 3 ▫ Section Reading Support Transparencies	**Teaching Resources** ▪ Unit 3 booklet • Guided Reading and Review, p. 24 ▪ Guide to the Essentials ▣ Guided Reading Audiotapes, Ch. 9, Section 3

4 Learning, Literature, and the Arts
1. Describe how medieval universities advanced learning.
2. Explain how "new" learning affected medieval thought.
3. Identify the styles of literature, architecture, and art that developed.
	Teaching Resources
	▪ Unit 3 booklet
	  • Biography Activity, p. 30
	  • Primary Source Activity, p. 31
	▪ Creative Teaching Activities, p. 44
	◉ Prentice Hall Presentation Pro, Ch. 9, Section 4
	▫ Section Reading Support Transparencies
		Teaching Resources
		▪ Unit 3 booklet
		  • Guided Reading and Review, p. 26
		  • Skill Application Activity, p. 33
		▪ Guide to the Essentials
		▣ Guided Reading Audiotapes, Ch. 9, Section 4

5 A Time of Crisis
1. Explain how the Black Death caused social and economic decline.
2. Identify problems of the Church.
3. Analyze the causes, turning points, and effects of the Hundred Years' War.
	Teaching Resources
	▪ Unit 3 booklet
	  • Viewpoint Activity, p. 32
	◉ Prentice Hall Presentation Pro, Ch. 9, Section 5
	▫ Section Reading Support Transparencies
		Teaching Resources
		▪ Unit 3 booklet
		  • Guided Reading and Review, p. 28
		▪ Guide to the Essentlals
		▣ Guided Reading Audiotapes, Ch. 9, Section 5

ENRICHMENT/PRE-AP

- **www.phschool.com**
  - Why Study History?

Teaching Resources
- **Chapter Extension Activities**, p. 25

Color Transparencies, p. C–41
www.phschool.com
- Virtual Field Trip

Teaching Resources
- **History Through Literature**, pp. 20–22
- **Color Transparencies**, pp. D–51, D–53
- **Listening to Literature World Masterpieces**, excerpt from *Dante's Inferno*, side 5
- **www.phschool.com**
  - Internet Activities, Section 4

Teaching Resources
- **Chapter Extension Activities**, p. 26
- **www.phschool.com**
  - Internet Activities, The Black Death Strikes
  - Internet Activities, Section 5

ASSESSMENT

PRENTICE HALL
ASSESSMENT SYSTEM

Core Assessment
- ExamView Test Bank booklet, Ch. 9
- ExamView Test Bank CD-ROM, Ch. 9

Standardized Test Preparation
Diagnose and Prescribe
- Diagnostic Tests for High School Social Studies Skills

Review and Reteach
- Review Book for World History

Practice and Assess
- Test-Taking Strategies With Transparencies for High School
- Alternative Assessment booklet
- Test Prep Book for World History

Teaching Resources
- **Unit 3 booklet**
  - Geography Quiz, p. 34
  - Section Quizzes, pp. 21, 23, 25, 27, 29
  - Chapter Tests A, B, and C, pp. 35–39
- **www.phschool.com**
  - Self-Test

CUSTOMIZE FOR INDIVIDUAL NEEDS

Gifted and Talented
- **Teacher's Edition,** Activities: Customize for Heterogeneous Groups, p. 210

Less Proficient Readers
- **Guide to the Essentials,** Ch. 9
- **Guided Reading Audiotapes, English,** Ch. 9
- **Book on CD,** Ch. 9
- **Teacher's Edition,** Activities: Customize for Visual Learners, p. 216; Reading Strategy, p. 222; Customize for Heterogeneous Groups, p. 226

Less Proficient Writers
- **Teacher's Edition,** Activities: Cooperative Learning, p. 227; Cooperative Learning, p. 228

Students Acquiring English/ESL
- **Guide to the Essentials, English/Spanish,** Ch. 9
- **Guided Reading Audiotapes, English/Spanish,** Ch. 9
- **Book on CD,** Ch. 9
- **Teacher's Edition,** Activities marked with an *

TEXT

Don't miss the exclusive interactive version of *World History: Connections to Today* on the Internet and CD-ROM.

CHAPTER 9

INTRODUCTION

During the High Middle Ages, the economy, learning, and the arts flourished. In England and France, royal government evolved. In the Holy Roman Empire, conflicts erupted between popes and monarchs. The Crusades revived interest in trade with other cultures. By the 1300s, famine, plague, and war marked the decline of medieval Europe.

Focusing on Themes

Suggest that students focus on these theme questions as they read:

Political and Social Systems
How did feudal monarchs build the foundations for strong national governments?

Global Interaction
How did Western Europeans come in contact with more advanced civilizations?

Art and Literature
How did the revival of trade and the growth of towns influence medieval culture?

Religions and Value Systems
How did Christian scholars try to fit the learning of ancient Greece and the Arab world into their culture?

Continuity and Change
How did disasters of the late Middle Ages help set the stage for the modern age?

◆ TIME LINE ACTIVITY

Share the About the Pictures note with your students before asking these questions about the time line:

1. How can you tell that there was more than one crusade? *(The 1096 event would not be labeled First Crusade if there had been only one.)*
2. In which century did the Black Death break out, 13th or 14th? *(14th)*
3. *Reconquista* is a Spanish word. From the English meaning of the prefix *re-* and words similar to *conquista,* you can infer the meaning of *reconquista.* What is it? *(reconquest or reconquering)*

Don't Miss!

Analyzing Primary Sources
Magna Carta
(Section 1)

Disaster!
The Black Death
Strikes (Section 5)

The High Middle Ages
1050–1450

Chapter Preview

1 Growth of Royal Power in England and France
2 The Holy Roman Empire and the Church
3 Europeans Look Outward
4 Learning, Literature, and the Arts
5 A Time of Crisis

1215

King John, shown above, signs the Magna Carta limiting royal power in England.

1096

Christians launch the First Crusade. The siege of Antioch is shown above.

CHAPTER EVENTS

| 1000 | 1100 | 1200 |

GLOBAL EVENTS

1000s Kilwa, Sofala, and other East African port cities thrive on trade.

1192 Minamoto Yoritomo establishes the Kamakura shogunate in Japan.

Resource Directory

Teaching Resources
Teaching With Themes Chapter Theme Activities, p. 12
Pacing Chart With Block Scheduling Guide Ch. 9
Technology
World History Color Transparencies Ch. 9 Graphic Organizer, p. F–19

Europe About 1300

By the 1300s, monarchs in Western Europe were increasing their power and building strong united kingdoms.

Boundary of the Holy Roman Empire

Azimuthal Equal Area Projection

0   250   500 Miles

0   250   500 Kilometers

1347
Black Death breaks out in Italy.

1429
After leading French troops to victory over the English, Joan of Arc marches triumphantly into Orléans.

1492
Spanish complete the Reconquista.

1300

1400

1500

1368 Ming dynasty is established in China.

1453 Ottoman Turks capture Constantinople.

Independent Assignments

Have students read one section as they prepare for class. After class, have them complete the assignment. Some students may benefit from using the Guided Reading and Review worksheets.

Section 1 Have students complete the Guided Reading and Review sheet on p. 20 of the Unit 3 booklet to learn about key figures of England and France.

Section 2 Have students use the map *Europe at the Time of the Crusades* in the Historical Outline Map Book, p. 18, to identify the lands covered by the Papal States and the Holy Roman Empire.

Section 3 Have students read the excerpt *The Crusaders Capture Jerusalem* in Treasures of the World, pp. 42–43, to learn more about the only successful crusade.

Section 4 Have students use the worksheet *Lady Margaret Beaufort* in the Unit 3 booklet, p. 30, to learn about this influential woman.

Section 5 Have students use the worksheet *Historians Look at the Middle Ages* in the Unit 3 booklet, p. 32, to compare two historians' views on the Middle Ages.

Europe About 1300

Activating Prior Knowledge

Compare this map with the one at the beginning of Chapter 8. What similarities and differences do you see? *(Europe is divided politically into many regions resembling modern states.)*

Previewing

What clue does the map give you of the great power of the popes? *(They have their own territory—the Papal States.)*

Background
About the Pictures

1.
2.
3.

1. This elaborate drawing is from an illuminated manuscript. Monks and, later, craftworkers decorated their book pages with small drawings like this and with fanciful designs and elaborate initial letters.

2. This is a detail from the effigy of King John in Worcester Cathedral. Although John, youngest son to King Henry II, was his father's favorite and named the original heir to Henry's throne, for little-known reasons Richard I, Henry's oldest son, became king. Only after many years and much political maneuvering did John become king.

3. This oil-on-canvas painting of Joan of Arc's entrance into Orléans (8 May 1429) is by Jean Jacques Sherrer (1855–1916). Lead students to see that the flag and the figure of Joan are well lit while the rest of the painting is somewhat dark. The effect emphasizes Joan's heroism.

---

eTeach

Be sure to check out this month's online discussion with a World History Master Teacher.

Go to **www.phschool.com**.

Growth of Royal Power in England and France

Bell Ringer Have a volunteer read aloud the quote that begins this section. Then, lead a discussion on the meaning of the quote. Ask students to describe what these words reveal about the relationship between churchmen and monarchs.

LESSON PLAN

1. Focus During the Middle Ages, strong monarchs in England and France worked to increase their landholdings and the numbers of their subjects. In England, people established political traditions such as common law, the jury system, protection of rights, and representative assemblies. In France, strong leaders built an efficient bureaucracy, set up the Estates General, and expanded their territory.

2. Instruct Have students work with a partner to create an illustrated biographical profile for a key figure from this section. Tell students that their biographies will consist of three to five illustrations highlighting important moments in the person's life with captions explaining each illustration. Have each team share its profile with the class. You may wish to display the profiles on a bulletin board or in a scrapbook.

3. Assess Ask students to think of an award for each of the historical figures profiled. Explain that the awards do not necessarily have to be flattering, but should reflect an important legacy left by that person.

4. Reteach If students' **Assess** activity does not reflect adequate understanding of the lesson, you might assign the *Guide to the Essentials* or the *Interactive Student Tutorial CD-ROM* for this section.

Reading Focus

- How did monarchs gain power over nobles and the Church?
- What traditions of government developed under John and later English monarchs?
- How did strong monarchs succeed in unifying France?

Vocabulary

exchequer
common law
jury

Taking Notes

Copy this incomplete Venn diagram. As you read, write key facts about royal power in England and France in the appropriate sections. Write common characteristics in the overlapping section.

ENGLAND
- Royal power limited by Magna Carta
-

Bureaucracy

FRANCE
- Crusade against Albigensians
-

Main Idea In England and France, monarchs expanded royal authority and laid the foundations for united nation-states.

Biography

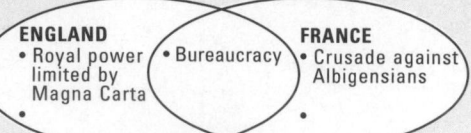

William of Normandy
1028–1087

From the time he became Duke of Normandy at age seven, William's life and position were in constant danger, mostly from jealous relatives. Four of his guardians were murdered—one in the very room in which William lay sleeping.

As an adult, William did all that he could to get and keep power. At age 20, he led an army to defeat a rebellious cousin. When an abbot condemned his marriage to Matilda of Flanders because they were too closely related, an enraged William burned down a monastery. But when the pope validated the marriage, William had a new abbey built.

Theme: Impact of the Individual How did William's experience as duke prepare him to be king of England?

Setting the Scene

A monarch could not always count on the loyalty of powerful nobles and Church officials. A medieval chronicle tells of the difficulties faced by one English king in the 1100s:

> "King Stephen . . . seized . . . Alexander, bishop of Lincoln, and Roger, the chancellor, his nephew, and he kept them all in prison. . . . They had done homage to him, and sworn oaths, but they . . . broke their allegiance, for every rich man built his castles, and defended them against him."
> —*Anglo-Saxon Chronicle*

During the Middle Ages, monarchs struggled to exert royal authority over nobles and churchmen. Bit by bit over many centuries, they built the framework for what would become the European nation-states of today.

Monarchs, Nobles, and the Church

Feudal monarchs in Europe stood at the head of society, but had limited power. While they ruled their own domains, they relied on vassals for military support. Nobles and the Church had as much—or more—power as the monarch. Both nobles and the Church had their own courts, collected their own taxes, and fielded their own armies. They jealously guarded their rights and privileges against any effort by rulers to increase royal authority.

Monarchs used various means to centralize power. They expanded the royal domain and set up a system of royal justice that undermined feudal or Church courts. They organized a government bureaucracy, developed a system of taxes, and built a standing army. Monarchs strengthened ties with the middle class. Townspeople, in turn, supported royal rulers, who could impose the peace and unity that were needed for trade.

Strong Monarchs in England

During the early Middle Ages, Angles, Saxons, and Vikings invaded and settled in England. Although feudalism developed, English rulers generally kept their kingdoms united.

In 1066, the Anglo-Saxon king Edward died without an heir. A council of nobles chose Edward's brother-in-law Harold to rule. But Duke William of Normandy, a tough, ruthless descendant of the Vikings, also claimed the English throne. The answer to the rival claims lay on the battlefield.

Biography

ANSWER The threats against him as the young ruler of Normandy led William to be both strong and ruthless in establishing control over others.

Resource Directory

Teaching Resources

Creative Teaching Activities Creative Teaching Activities booklet, p. 41
Guided Reading and Review Unit 3 booklet, p. 20

Norman Conquest Duke William raised an army and won the backing of the pope. He then sailed across the English Channel. At the Battle of Hastings, William and his Norman knights triumphed over Harold. On Christmas Day 1066, William the Conqueror, as he was now called, assumed the crown of England.

Although William's French speaking nobles dominated England, the country's Anglo-Saxon population survived. Over the next 300 years, a gradual blending occurred of Norman French and Anglo-Saxon customs, languages, and traditions.

Growth of Royal Power William exerted firm control over his new lands. Like other feudal monarchs, he granted fiefs to the Church and his Norman lords, or barons, but he kept a large amount of land for himself. He monitored who built castles and where. He required every vassal to swear first allegiance to him rather than to any other feudal lord.

To learn about his kingdom, William had a complete census taken in 1086. The result was the *Domesday Book* (pronounced "doomsday"), which listed every castle, field, and pigpen in England. As the title suggests, the survey was as thorough and inevitable as doomsday, believed to be God's final day of judgment that no one could escape. Information in the *Domesday Book* helped William and later English monarchs build an efficient system of tax collecting.

William's successors continued to increase royal authority. In the area of finance, they created the royal exchequer, or treasury, to collect taxes. Into the exchequer flowed fees, fines, and other dues.

A Unified Legal System In 1154, an energetic, well-educated king, Henry II, inherited the throne. He broadened the system of royal justice. As a ruler, he could not simply write new laws but had to follow accepted customs. Henry found ways to expand customs into law. He then sent out traveling justices to enforce royal laws. The decisions of the royal courts became the foundation of English common law, a legal system based on custom and court rulings. Unlike local feudal laws, common law applied to all of England. In time, people chose royal courts over those of nobles or the Church. Because royal courts charged fees, the exchequer benefited from the growth of royal justice.

Under Henry II, England also developed an early jury system. When traveling justices visited an area, local officials collected a jury, or group of men sworn to speak the truth. (The word *jury* is derived from the French *juré,* meaning "sworn on oath.") These early juries determined which cases should be brought to trial and were the ancestors of today's grand jury. Later, another jury evolved that was composed of 12 neighbors of an accused. It was the ancestor of today's trial jury.

Conflict With the Church Henry's efforts to extend royal power led to a bitter dispute with the Church. Henry claimed the right to try clergy in royal courts. Thomas Becket, the archbishop of Canterbury and once a close friend of Henry's, fiercely opposed the king's move. The conflict simmered for years.

At last, Henry's fury exploded. "What a pack of fools and cowards I have nourished," he cried, "that not one of them will avenge me of this turbulent priest." Four hot-headed knights took Henry at his word. In 1170, they murdered the archbishop in his own cathedral. Henry denied any part in the attack. Still, to make peace with the Church,

FACT FINDER

Evolution of English Government

1066	**Norman Conquest** William of Normandy defeats Anglo-Saxons at Hastings.
1086	***Domesday Book*** William I uses this survey as a basis for taxation.
1160s–1180s	**Common Law** Henry II lays foundation for English legal system.
1215	**Magna Carta** John signs this document limiting royal power and extending rights.
1295	**Model Parliament** Edward I summons Parliament, which includes representatives of common people.

Skills Assessment

Chart Traditions of English government and law evolved during the Middle Ages. **How did the *Domesday Book* benefit William I? How did the Magna Carta affect English government?**

Background
Daily Life

Medieval Justice Although Henry II used juries to dispense justice, many Western European monarchs and nobles doled out harsh punishments without the benefit of juries. A thief might have his hand cut off. A woman who verbally abused family or friends could be punished by being forced to wear a bridle whose bit held her tongue. Hanging was a common punishment. It was used not only for serious offenses such as murder, but also for rioting and robbery. Public punishments were common. For fighting, a person might be whipped or confined in a stock. A man accused of assault might be ordered to stand for a day in a pillory and then be branded on the forehead with a red-hot iron so that he was marked forever.

Background
Connections to Film

Becket The political struggle between church and state and the personal struggle between Henry II and Thomas Becket are brought to life in the 1964 film *Becket.* The award-winning film, starring Richard Burton and Peter O'Toole, was based on a play by Jean Anouilh. It was filmed on location in England with the aid of elaborate sets and costuming.

The film traces the relationship between Henry II and Becket from its early days of friendship to its tragic and fatal conclusion. It accurately portrays the causes of their conflict. Henry desired to tax the clergy, to appoint bishops, and to extend the power of royal courts. Becket, meanwhile, desired to maintain the traditional powers and privileges of the Church. (*Becket* is available on both videocassette and laserdisc.)

Block Scheduling Support

Show students Transparency 4 of the Humanities Pack Transparencies, which shows a section of the Bayeux Tapestry, a valuable piece of historical evidence that chronicles the Norman conquest. Then have students use library resources or the Internet to find out more about the tapestry. Students may download or photocopy sections and explain what is going on in that particular section.

Remind students that history is often written—or in this case, embroidered—by the victors. After students have explained various sections of the tapestry, conduct a class discussion about the events in 1066. How might the presentation have been different if Harold had won?

Skills Assessment

ANSWERS The *Domesday Book* helped William form the basis for tax collection. The Magna Carta limited the power of the monarch and established a foundation for the rights of citizens.

Visual Learners

Constructing a Diagram Some students may gain a better understanding of King John's troubles if they diagram them. Tell students to draw a circle in the center of a sheet of paper. In the center of the circle, write "John." Then draw three lines branching out from the circle. On each line, write the name of one of John's three enemies: King Philip II, Pope Innocent III, and the English nobles. Then draw a circle at the end of each line. In these surrounding circles, have students write the problems that John faced in dealing with each of his opponents. Have students continue the web by drawing more circles in which they write the outcomes of each of John's conflicts.

Background
Connections to Today

Traditions of Parliament Since Parliament's first days, it has been a tradition to begin each session with a prayer. In his book *The Great Palace*, BBC correspondent Christopher Jones points out that during the prayer, members of Parliament turn their backs to one another and face the walls. According to Jones, the reason for this curious practice dates back to medieval days when members of Parliament wore swords. If members had faced one another when they kneeled for prayer, their weapons would have gotten tangled. Therefore, members turned and kneeled toward the wall—a tradition that has endured to this day.

Edward I and Parliament
In this scene, King Edward I presides over what was later called the Model Parliament. On both sides of him are his vassals, the rulers of Scotland and Wales. Clergy sit on the left, and lords sit on the right.

Theme: Political and Social Systems What other social class was represented in the Model Parliament?

he eased his attempts to regulate the clergy. Becket, meantime, was honored as a martyr and declared a saint. Pilgrims flocked to his tomb at Canterbury, where miracles were said to happen.

Evolving Traditions of English Government

Later English rulers repeatedly clashed with nobles and the Church. Most battles developed as a result of efforts by the monarch to raise taxes or to impose royal authority over traditional feudal rights. Out of those struggles evolved traditions of government that would influence the modern world.

John's Troubles Henry's son John was a clever, greedy, cruel, and untrustworthy ruler. During his reign, he faced three powerful enemies: King Philip II of France, Pope Innocent III, and his own English nobles. He lost his struggles with each.

Ever since William the Conqueror, Norman rulers of England had held vast lands in France. In 1205, John suffered a major setback when he lost a war with Philip II and had to give up English-held lands in Anjou and Normandy.

Next, John battled with Innocent III over selecting a new archbishop of Canterbury. When John rejected the pope's nominee, the pope responded by excommunicating him. He also placed England under the interdict—as you recall, a papal order that forbade Church services in an entire kingdom. Even the strongest ruler was likely to give in to that pressure. To save himself and his crown, John had to accept England as a fief of the papacy and pay a yearly fee to Rome.

The Magna Carta Finally, John angered his own nobles with oppressive taxes and other abuses of power. In 1215, a group of rebellious barons cornered John and forced him to sign the Magna Carta, or great charter. In this document, the king affirmed a long list of feudal rights.

Besides protecting their own privileges, the barons included a few clauses recognizing the legal rights of townspeople and the Church. Among the most significant of these was a clause protecting every freeman from arbitrary arrest, imprisonment, and other legal actions, except "by legal judgment of his peers or by the law of the land." This famous clause formed the basis of the right now known as "due process of law."

The king also agreed not to raise new taxes without first consulting his Great Council of lords and clergy. Many centuries later, American colonists would claim that those words meant that any taxation without representation was unjust. In 1215, though, neither the king nor his lords could have imagined such an idea.

The Magna Carta contained two very important ideas that in the long run would shape government traditions in England. First, it asserted that the nobles had certain rights. Over time, the rights that had been granted to nobles were extended to all English citizens. Second, the Magna Carta made it clear that the monarch must obey the law.

Development of Parliament In keeping with the Magna Carta, English rulers often called on the Great Council for advice. During the 1200s, this body evolved into Parliament. Its name comes from the French word *parler*, meaning "to talk." As Parliament acquired a larger role in government, it helped unify England.

In 1295, Edward I summoned Parliament to approve money for his wars in France. "What touches all," he declared, "should be approved by all." He had representatives of the "common people" join with the lords and clergy. The

Knights and townspeople represented the common people at the Model Parliament.

Teaching Resources
Analyzing Primary Sources Chapter Extension Activities booklet, p. 25

Magna Carta

King John of England was forced to sign the Magna Carta, which means "Great Charter," in 1215. Ideas from the Magna Carta still influence the systems of government in many countries around the world. Below are excerpts from 5 of the 63 articles of this important document.

1. We also have granted to all the freemen of our kingdom, for us and for our heirs forever, all the underwritten liberties, to be had and holden by them and their heirs, of us and our heirs forever. . . .

12. No scutage [tax] or aid shall be imposed in our kingdom, unless by the general council of our kingdom; except for ransoming our person, making our eldest son a knight and once for marrying our eldest daughter; and for these there shall be paid no more than a reasonable aid.

14. And for holding the general council of the kingdom concerning the assessment of aids, except in the three cases aforesaid, and for assessing of scutage, we shall cause to be summoned the archbishops, bishops, abbots, earls, and greater barons of the realm, singly by our letters. And furthermore, we shall cause to be summoned generally, by our sheriffs and bailiffs all others who hold of us in chief, for a certain day, that is to say, forty days before the meeting at least, and to a certain place. And in all letters of such summons we will declare the cause of such summons. And summons being thus made, the business shall proceed on the day appointed, according to the advice of such as shall be present, although all that were summoned come not.

39. No freeman shall be taken or imprisoned, or diseised [deprived], or outlawed, or banished, or in any way destroyed . . . unless by the lawful judgment of his peers, or by the law of the land.

40. We will sell to no man, we will not deny to any man, either justice or right.

—Magna Carta

A group of nobles forced King John to sign the Magna Carta at Runnymede.

Skills Tip

Very old documents often contain unfamiliar words. Sometimes they are explained in brackets. Others, however, require the reader to consult a dictionary. This helps the reader both to understand the words themselves and to understand the full meaning of the document.

Skills Assessment

1. In Article 1, who is granted the rights described elsewhere in the Magna Carta?
   A only the king and his heirs
   B only the general council
   C all freemen and their heirs
   D only nobles assembled at the signing

2. Approval by the general council was not required for any tax that would
   E fund the building of roadways.
   F pay for schools.
   G support the general council.
   H ransom the king.

3. **Critical Thinking Making Inferences (a)** What do Articles 14 and 40 suggest about royal abuse of power during this period of English history? **(b)** Think about the membership of the general council, as described in Article 14. Who is *not* included? What can you infer from this?

Background
About the Primary Source

The Magna Carta was written in Latin on parchment. Copies of the document were sent to churches throughout England. Four times a year, the sheriffs had to read it aloud in the county courts. After John's death in 1216, it was modified and reissued.

Activity
Interpreting the Primary Source

Use these questions to generate class discussion.

Critical Thinking: Comparing Article 20 of the Magna Carta stated that a freeman could be fined "only according to the measure of his offenses." Which amendment to the U.S. Constitution reflects this same idea? *(Amendment VIII)* Article 28 of the Magna Carta protected people from government seizure of their goods. Which amendment to the U.S. Constitution reflects this same idea? *(Amendment V)*

Skills Tip

Dictionaries often list several definitions for a word. Choose the most appropriate meaning for the context of the material in the reading. The right definition may not be the first meaning that is listed. The Skills Handbook at the front of this book also has a lesson that will help students with this feature.

Test Preparation

Have students read Article 14 on this page, and then answer the question below.

Using what you have read on the opposite page, into what did the "general council" in Article 14 evolve?

(A) the Parliament
B the Knights of the Round Table
C the King's Council
D the House of Commons

Skills Assessment

ANSWERS 1. C **2.** H **3.** Possible answers: **(a)** Requiring that meetings be announced far in advance suggests that the king used short-notice meetings to circumvent the council. Article 40 suggests that wrong-doers could buy their way out of trouble. **(b)** Common people, such as peasants, are not present or represented in the general council, which implies low status with no representation.

Royal Lands in France, 987–1328

Legend:
- French royal lands, 987
- Added to French royal lands by 1180
- Added to French royal lands by 1328
- Held by French nobles, 1328
- English holdings in France, 1328
- → Route of royal attack on Albigensians

Azimuthal Equal Area Projection
0   100   200 Miles
0   100   200 Kilometers

Skills Assessment

Geography From a small area around the city of Paris, Capetian monarchs gradually extended royal control over almost all of France.

1. **Location** On the map, locate **(a)** Paris, **(b)** Normandy, **(c)** Avignon.
2. **Place** What territories were held by the English in 1328?
3. **Critical Thinking** **Identifying Main Ideas** What main idea does the map show about royal lands in France between 987 and 1328?

"commons" included two knights from each county and representatives of the towns.

Much later, this assembly became known as the Model Parliament because it set up the framework for England's legislature. In time, Parliament developed into a two-house body: the House of Lords with nobles and high clergy and the House of Commons with knights and middle-class citizens.

Looking Ahead Like King Edward I, later English monarchs summoned Parliament for their own purposes. Over the centuries, though, Parliament gained the crucial "power of the purse." That is, it won the right to approve any new taxes. With that power, Parliament could insist that the monarch meet its demands before voting for taxes. In this way, it could check, or limit, the power of the monarch.

Successful Monarchs in France

Unlike William the Conqueror in England, monarchs in France did not rule over a unified kingdom. The successors to Charlemagne had little power over a patchwork of French territories ruled by great feudal nobles.

The Capetians In 987, these feudal nobles elected Hugh Capet, the count of Paris, to fill the vacant throne. They probably chose him because he was too weak to pose a threat to them. Hugh's own lands around Paris were smaller than those of many of his vassals.

Hugh and his heirs slowly increased royal power. First, they made the throne hereditary, passing it from father to son. Fortunately, the Capetians enjoyed an unbroken succession for 300 years. Next, they added to their lands by playing rival nobles against each other. They also won the support of the Church.

Perhaps most important, the Capetians built an effective bureaucracy. Government officials collected taxes and imposed royal law over the king's domain. By establishing order, they added to their prestige and gained the backing of the new middle class of townspeople.

Philip Augustus An outstanding French king of this period was Philip II, often called Philip Augustus. A bald, red-faced man who ate and drank too much, Philip was a shrewd and able ruler. He strengthened royal government in many ways. Instead of appointing nobles to fill government positions, he used paid middle-class officials who would owe their loyalty to him. He granted charters to many new towns, organized a standing army, and introduced a new national tax.

Philip also quadrupled royal land holdings. Through trickery, diplomacy, and war, he brought English-ruled lands in Normandy, Anjou, and elsewhere under his control. He then began to take over southern France. Informed by the pope that the Albigensian (al buh JEHN see uhn) heresy had sprung up in the south, he sent his knights to suppress it and add this vast area to his domain. Before his death in 1223, Philip had become the most powerful ruler in Europe.

Louis IX, King and Saint Perhaps the most admired French ruler of this time was Louis IX. Louis, who ascended to the throne in 1226, embodied the ideal of the perfect medieval monarch—generous, noble, and devoted to justice and chivalry. Within 30 years of his death, he was declared a saint. A knight at Louis's court praised the king's charity:

> "The king daily gave countless generous alms, to poor religious, to poor hospitals, to poor sick people, to other poor convents, to poor gentlemen and gentlewomen and girls . . . and to poor minstrels who from old age or sickness were unable to work."
>
> —John of Joinville, *The Life of St. Louis*

Saint Louis was a deeply religious man, and he pursued religious goals that were acceptable to Christians in his day. He persecuted heretics and Jews and led thousands of French knights in two wars against Muslims.

Louis did much to improve royal government. Like Charlemagne, he sent out roving officials to check on local officials. He expanded the royal courts, outlawed private wars, and ended serfdom in his lands. To ensure justice, he even heard cases himself under a tree in the royal park of Vincennes. His enormous personal prestige helped create a strong national feeling among his subjects. By the time of his death in 1270, France was an efficient centralized monarchy.

Philip IV Clashes With the Pope Louis's grandson, Philip IV, ruthlessly extended royal power. To raise cash, he tried to collect new taxes from the clergy. These efforts led to a clash with Pope Boniface VIII.

Declaring that "God has set popes over kings and kingdoms," Pope Boniface VIII forbade Philip to tax the clergy without papal consent. Philip countered by threatening to arrest any clergy who did not pay up. As their quarrel escalated, Philip sent troops to seize Boniface. The pope escaped, but he was badly beaten and died soon afterward.

Shortly after, a Frenchman was elected pope. He moved the papal court to Avignon (ah veen YOHN) on the border of southern France, ensuring that future French rulers would control religion within their own kingdoms.

The Estates General During this struggle with the pope, Philip rallied French support by setting up the Estates General in 1302. This body had representatives from all three estates, or classes: clergy, nobles, and townspeople. Although later French kings consulted the Estates General, it did not develop the same role that the English Parliament did. It never gained the power of the purse or otherwise served as a balance to royal power.

SECTION 1 Assessment

Recall
1. **Identify:** (a) *Domesday Book*, (b) Henry II, (c) Thomas Becket, (d) Parliament, (e) Louis IX, (f) Philip IV, (g) Estates General.
2. **Define:** (a) exchequer, (b) common law, (c) jury.

Comprehension
3. (a) How were nobles and the Church obstacles for monarchs who wanted more power? (b) How did William increase royal power in England?
4. What principles were established by the Magna Carta?
5. How did the Capetians increase royal power in France?

Critical Thinking and Writing
6. **Analyzing Information** (a) Based on the map in this section, identify three groups of people who stood in the way of expanding royal power in France. (b) Which of the three do you think was the most difficult challenge for French kings? Explain.
7. **Linking Past and Present** How is the jury system important to us today?

Activity
Writing an Editorial Write a newspaper editorial supporting or opposing the actions of one of the following kings: Henry II of England, John of England, Louis IX of France, or Philip IV of France. Be sure to identify clearly which royal action you are discussing.

Recall
1. (a) *Domesday Book*, p. 207 (b) Henry II, p. 207 (c) Thomas Becket, p. 207 (d) Parliament, p. 208 (e) Louis IX, p. 210 (f) Philip IV, p. 211 (g) Estates General, p. 211 2. (a) exchequer, p. 207 (b) common law, p. 207 (c) jury, p. 207

Comprehension
3. (a) The nobles held the real power over the lands claimed by the monarchs. The Church had the power to appoint Church officials. (b) William kept large amounts of land for himself, monitored the building of castles, and required every vassal to swear first allegiance to him. He used census information recorded in the *Domesday Book* to create an efficient tax collection system. 4. Principles included that nobles and freemen had certain rights and that the monarch must obey the law. The king also agreed not to raise new taxes without consulting a representative body. 5. The Capetians made the throne hereditary, added to their lands, and won the support of the Church. They also built an efficient bureaucracy and imposed order, thus gaining the support of the middle class. Philip II granted charters to new towns, set up a standing army, and introduced a new national tax.

Critical Thinking and Writing
6. (a) French nobles, the English, and the Albigensians (b) Students will probably choose the French nobles because they were spread throughout France, and they held the most territory. The English holdings were mostly concentrated in one area, which would make control easier. The Albigensians were a minority. 7. Possible answer: Trial by jury is a crucial element of our justice system today. All people accused of a crime are tried by an impartial group of people. This increases their chance of receiving a fair trial.

Activity Rubrics

Share rubrics with students before they write their editorials.

Attempted The editorial does not accurately represent the king's actions or clearly describe the position being taken.

Minimal The editorial makes a weak case, although it accurately represents the king's actions.

Adequate The editorial makes a strong case and accurately represents the king's actions.

Exemplary The editorial makes a strong case, accurately represents the king's actions, and is well organized and well written.

Human Drama Activity

Writing Advice The values of Louis IX are clearly revealed in a letter of advice he wrote to his oldest son, who was to become King Philip III. Much of the advice dealt with religious concerns, but it also included advice on the administration of the kingdom. This letter is available on the Internet. Ask students to access the site and choose one item that deals with administering the realm, one that concerns religious values, and one that deals with justice. (Each piece of advice is numbered, which makes choosing easier.) Have students explain the items in their own words.

Bell Ringer Draw students' attention to the quote from Pope Innocent III at the beginning of this section. Ask students to discuss what the quote suggests about the power of the Church during this period.

Reading Focus

- Why did Holy Roman emperors fail to build a unified state in Germany?
- How did power struggles and rivalry in Italy affect popes and emperors?
- What powers did the Church have at its height?

Vocabulary

lay investiture
annul
crusade

Taking Notes

As you read, complete this table listing the actions of Holy Roman emperors and popes. Add as many rows as needed to finish the table.

POPE OR EMPEROR	ACTIONS	EFFECTS
OTTO I	• Cooperated with Church • Helped pope defeat Roman nobles	• Pope crowned Otto emperor •
GREGORY VII		
HENRY IV		

Main Idea With secular and religious rulers advancing rival claims to power, explosive conflicts erupted between monarchs and popes.

LESSON PLAN

1. Focus Conflicts with the Church and with independent nobles prevented Holy Roman emperors from unifying Germany. The Church and German emperors finally resolved the issue of investiture with the signing of the Concordat of Worms. However, new struggles arose as Pope Innocent III claimed supremacy over all rulers.

2. Instruct Have students work with a partner. Tell each pair to imagine that one of them is Pope Gregory VII and the other is Emperor Henry IV. Ask the partners, in their assumed roles, to write letters to each other expressing their viewpoints on lay investiture. Remind students that their letters should reflect the viewpoint of the historical figure they are pretending to be. Then have partners exchange letters. After students read their partners' letters, have them write a response. Invite pairs of students to read their letters aloud.

3. Assess Ask students to draw a political cartoon based on the struggle between the Roman Catholic Church and the monarchs of Europe. Have them write titles and captions for their cartoons.

4. Reteach If students' Assess activity does not reflect adequate understanding of the lesson, you might assign the *Guide to the Essentials* or the *Interactive Student Tutorial CD-ROM* for this section.

Imperial Crown
Holy Roman emperors first wore this crown around the 900s. Some, however, claimed that Charlemagne had worn it almost two centuries earlier.

Theme: Continuity and Change Why do you think emperors wanted people to believe that Charlemagne had worn the crown?

Setting the Scene The Church, you will recall, spread its influence across Europe during the early Middle Ages. By the High Middle Ages, both popes and monarchs were extending their authority. In the early 1200s, Pope Innocent III claimed broad powers:

"Just as the moon gets her light from the sun, and is inferior to the sun in quality, quantity, position, and effect, so the royal power gets the splendor of its dignity from the papal authority."

—Letter of Innocent III to Nobles of Tuscany, 1198

With secular rulers advancing their own claims to power, explosive conflicts erupted between monarchs and Church officials. The longest and most destructive struggle pitted popes against Holy Roman emperors who ruled vast lands from Germany to Italy.

The Holy Roman Empire

In the early Middle Ages, as you have learned, the emperor Charlemagne had brought much of present-day France and Germany under his rule. After Charlemagne's death, his empire dissolved into a number of separate states. In time, the dukes of Saxony extended their power over neighboring German lands. In 936, Duke Otto I of Saxony took the title King of Germany.

Like Charlemagne, Otto I worked closely with the Church. He appointed bishops to top government jobs. He also took an army into Italy to help the pope defeat rebellious Roman nobles. In 962, a grateful pope crowned Otto emperor. Later, Otto's successors took the title Holy Roman emperor—"holy" because they were crowned by the pope, "Roman" because they saw themselves as heirs to the emperors of ancient Rome.

German emperors claimed authority over much of central and eastern Europe as well as parts of France and Italy. In fact, the real rulers of these lands were the emperor's vassals—hundreds of nobles and Church officials. For German emperors, the challenge was to control their vassals. In the end, as you will see, it was a challenge they never met.

Another problem for the emperors was conflict with the popes over the appointment of Church officials. Like other monarchs, the Holy Roman emperors often decided who would become bishops and abbots within their realm. As the Cluny reforms strengthened the Church, popes tried to end such outside interference from secular rulers.

212 Chapter 9

Caption Answer

Possible answer: Since Charlemagne was revered for his many accomplishments, Holy Roman emperors might have thought that they would receive greater respect if people viewed them as Charlemagne's successors.

Resource Directory

Teaching Resources
Creative Teaching Activities Creative Teaching Activities booklet, p. 42
Guided Reading and Review Unit 3 booklet, p. 22

Block Scheduling Support

Have students do additional research on the conflicts between the pope and the rulers. Students may choose to study papal conflicts with King John of England, Philip II of France, the German emperor Frederick II, or another ruler of the period. Have students focus especially on the causes and effects of the various conflicts. Ask students to share their findings with the class by means of oral presentations or dramatizations.

Conflict Between Popes and Emperors

Under the reforming pope Gregory VII, the conflict between emperors and the Church burst into flames. Gregory was one of the greatest medieval popes. He was also among the most controversial.

Pope Gregory VII Few Europeans of the time had a neutral view of Pope Gregory VII. Many admired and revered him. Among his enemies, however, he probably aroused more hatred and contempt than did any other pope of this time period.

Gregory was determined to make the Church independent of secular rulers. To do so, he banned the practice of lay investiture. Under this practice, the emperor or another lay person (a person who is not a member of the clergy) "invested," or presented, bishops with the ring and staff that symbolized their office. Only the pope, said Gregory, had the right to appoint and install bishops in office.

Emperor Henry IV Pope Gregory's ban brought an angry response from the Holy Roman emperor Henry IV. He argued that bishops held their lands as royal fiefs. Since he was their overlord, Henry felt entitled to give them the symbols of office. The feud heated up as the two men exchanged insulting notes. Meanwhile, rebellious German princes saw a chance to undermine Henry by supporting the pope.

The Struggle Intensifies In 1076, Gregory excommunicated Henry, freeing his subjects from their allegiance to the emperor. The pope then headed north to crown a new emperor. Faced with revolts at home, Henry was forced to make peace with the pope. In January 1077, Henry crossed the icy Alps to Canossa. There, "with bare feet and clad only in a wretched woolen garment," he presented himself to the pope as a repentant sinner.

Gregory knew that Henry was just trying to save his throne. Still, as a priest, Gregory had no choice but to forgive a confessed sinner. He lifted the order of excommunication, and Henry quickly returned to Germany to subdue his rebellious nobles. In later years, he took revenge on Gregory when he led an army to Rome and forced the pope into exile.

Concordat of Worms The struggle over investiture dragged on for almost 50 years. Finally, in 1122, both sides accepted a treaty known as the Concordat of Worms (VOHRMS). In it, they agreed that the Church had the sole power to elect and invest bishops with spiritual authority. The emperor, however, had the right to invest them with fiefs.

The Struggle for Italy

Although the investiture struggle was over, new battles were soon raging between popes and emperors. During the 1100s and 1200s, ambitious German emperors sought to master Italy. As they did so, they came into conflict with popes and with the wealthy towns of northern Italy.

Frederick Barbarossa The emperor Frederick I, called Barbarossa, or "Red Beard," dreamed of building an empire from the Baltic to the Adriatic. For years, he fought to bring the wealthy cities of northern Italy under his control. With equal energy, they resisted. By joining forces with the pope in the Lombard League, they managed to defeat Barbarossa's armies.

Barbarossa did succeed, however, in arranging a marriage between his son Henry and Constance, heiress to Sicily and southern Italy. That move entangled German emperors even more deeply in Italian affairs.

Frederick II The child of Henry and Constance, Frederick II, was raised in southern Italy. He was an able, arrogant leader, willing to use any means to achieve his ends.

Primary Source

A Pope Deposes a King
On February 22, 1076, Pope Gregory VII issued this decree against Henry IV:

"O St. Peter, chief of the apostles . . . I withdraw, through thy power and authority, from Henry the king, . . . who has risen against thy church with unheard of insolence, the rule over the whole kingdom of the Germans and over Italy. And I absolve all Christians from the bonds of the oath which they have made . . . to him; and I forbid anyone to serve him as king. For it is fitting that he who strives to lessen the honour of thy church should himself lose the honour which belongs to him. And since he has scorned to obey . . . my commands which . . . I issued to him for his own salvation . . . I bind him in thy stead with the chain of [excommunication]."

—Gregory VII, First Deposition and Banning of Henry IV

Skills Assessment

Primary Source What reasons does Gregory give for excommunicating Henry?

Recall

1. **(a)** Holy Roman Empire, p. 212 **(b)** Gregory VII, p. 213 **(c)** Henry IV, p. 213 **(d)** Concordat of Worms, p. 213 **(e)** Frederick II, p. 213 **(f)** Innocent III, p. 214 **(g)** Albigensian Crusade, p. 214 **2. (a)** lay investiture, p. 213 **(b)** annul, p. 214 **(c)** crusade, p. 214

Comprehension

3. The emperors never succeeded in controlling the nobles who ruled German lands. They also spent much energy trying to control Italy and the Church.
4. **(a)** They kept the empire in turmoil for many years and prevented German unity. **(b)** Italy endured centuries of destruction and upheaval. 5. As head of the Church, he claimed supremacy over all other rulers, and in clashes with secular rulers, he usually came out ahead. He excommunicated King John of England and placed his kingdom under interdict when the king defied him. He ordered the same punishment for Philip II of France.

Critical Thinking and Writing

6. **(a)** English and French monarchs increased their power and united their kingdoms. Meanwhile, the Holy Roman Empire remained disunited and relatively weak. **(b)** Possible answer: German emperors were too involved in conflicts with the Church and in efforts to gain control of northern Italy. 7. **(a)** the moon **(b)** that monarchs received their authority from the pope

Activity Rubrics

Share rubrics with students before they label their maps.

Attempted The map is attempted but does not show all the places mentioned in the text, or illustrations are missing.

Minimal The map shows all the places mentioned in the text, but some or all illustrations are missing.

Adequate The map shows all the places mentioned in the text and includes illustrations.

Exemplary The map shows all the places mentioned in the text and includes illustrations and explanatory notes.

Biography

ANSWER He came from an influential family with strong religious ties and became an expert on theology and canon law.

Biography

Innocent III 1160(?)–1216

Lotario de' Conti grew up in an influential Roman family. Several of his uncles were leading Church figures, including one pope. Lotario attended the finest schools of Europe, studying theology in Paris and law in Bologna. He became a leading expert on canon law and rose quickly through Church ranks. In 1198, he was elected pope, just one month before he was ordained a priest.

One of Innocent's most lasting achievements was to convene an important Church council in Rome. There, more than 1,000 Church officials established several practices that are still followed by Catholics today, such as regular confession of sins.

Theme: Impact of the Individual How did Innocent's background prepare him to assume the role of pope?

As Holy Roman emperor, Frederick spent little time in Germany. Instead, he pursued his ambitions in Italy. There, he clashed repeatedly and unsuccessfully with several popes. Like his grandfather, Frederick also tried but failed to subdue the cities of northern Italy.

Effects on Germany and Italy While Frederick was embroiled in Italy, German nobles grew more independent. The Holy Roman Empire survived, but it remained fragmented into many feudal states. The German people paid a high price for their emperors' ambitions. Unlike France and England, Germany would not achieve unity for another 600 years.

Southern Italy and Sicily also faced centuries of upheaval. There, popes turned to the French to overthrow Frederick's heirs. A local uprising against French rule in Sicily led to 200 years of chaos as French and Spanish rivals battled for power. The region that had once been a thriving center of culture was left in ruins.

The Height of Church Power

Pope Innocent III, who took office in 1198, embodied the triumph of the Church. As head of the Church, he claimed supremacy over all other rulers. The pope, he said, stands "between God and man, lower than God but higher than men, who judges all and is judged by no one."

Innocent clashed with all the powerful rulers of his day. More often than not, the pope came out ahead. As you have read, when King John of England dared to appoint an archbishop of Canterbury without the pope's approval, Innocent excommunicated the king and placed his kingdom under interdict. Innocent ordered the same punishment for France when Philip II tried unlawfully to annul, or invalidate, his marriage. The Holy Roman emperor Frederick II also felt the wrath of the powerful pope.

In 1209, Innocent, aided by Philip II, launched a brutal crusade, or holy war, against the Albigensians in southern France. The Albigensians wanted to purify the Church and return to the simple ways of early Christianity. Tens of thousands of people were slaughtered in the Albigensian Crusade.

After Innocent's death, popes continued to press their claim to supremacy. During this period, though, the French and English monarchies were growing stronger. In 1296, Philip IV of France successfully challenged Pope Boniface VIII on the issue of taxing the clergy. After Philip engineered the election of a French pope, the papacy entered a period of decline.

SECTION 2 Assessment

Recall

1. **Identify:** **(a)** Holy Roman Empire, **(b)** Gregory VII, **(c)** Henry IV, **(d)** Concordat of Worms, **(e)** Frederick II, **(f)** Innocent III, **(g)** Albigensian Crusade.
2. **Define:** **(a)** lay investiture, **(b)** annul, **(c)** crusade.

Comprehension

3. Why was the power of German emperors limited?
4. How did conflicts between popes and emperors affect **(a)** the Holy Roman Empire, and **(b)** Italy?

5. How did Pope Innocent III assert the power of the Church?

Critical Thinking and Writing

6. **Comparing (a)** How did the political development of the Holy Roman Empire differ from that of England and France? **(b)** What were the causes of these differences?
7. **Analyzing Primary Sources** Review the words of Innocent III at the beginning of this section. **(a)** To what does Innocent compare a monarch? **(b)** What point was he trying to make?

Activity

Making a Map
On an outline map of Europe, label the places that you have read about in this section. Illustrate your map to show what happened in each location.

Resource Directory

Teaching Resources

Section Quiz Unit 3 booklet, p. 23
Creative Teaching Activities Creative Teaching Activities booklet, p. 43
Guided Reading and Review Unit 3 booklet, p. 24

Technology

Interactive Student Tutorial CD-ROM Ch. 9
Computer Test Bank Ch. 9

SECTION 3 Europeans Look Outward

Reading Focus

- What advanced civilizations flourished around the world in 1050?
- What were the causes and effects of the Crusades?
- How did Christians in Spain carry out the Reconquista?

Vocabulary

schism
levy
religious toleration

Taking Notes

As you read, complete the following chart showing the effects that the Crusades had on life in Europe.

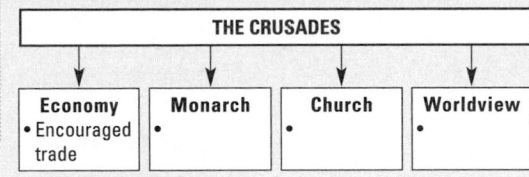

THE CRUSADES

Economy	Monarch	Church	Worldview
• Encouraged trade	•	•	•

Main Idea The Crusades stimulated economic and political change in Europe and broadened Europeans' view of the world.

Setting the Scene

Nearly 23 weeks after departing France, Count Stephen of Blois reached the city of Antioch in Syria. There, in March 1098, he composed a letter to his wife, Adele. He described the battles he had fought and the riches he had won. Stephen proudly told Adele that he and his fellow knights were "full of fury" and "prepared to die for Christ."

Stephen of Blois was one of thousands of Europeans who took part in a series of wars known as the Crusades. In these wars, which began in 1096, Christians battled Muslims for control of lands in the Middle East. As they streamed eastward over the next 200 years, Western Europeans learned that the world was much larger than they had ever dreamed. Their encounters outside Europe would serve to stimulate the pace of change.

The World in 1050

In 1050, as Western Europe was just emerging from a period of isolation, civilizations were thriving elsewhere. These civilizations are described in detail in other chapters. What follows here is an overview of the world at the time that medieval Europe was first beginning to test its strength.

During Europe's Middle Ages, Islam had given rise to a brilliant new civilization that stretched from Spain to India. Muslim traders and scholars spread goods and ideas even further. Trading caravans regularly crossed the Sahara to West Africa. Arab ships visited East African ports and sailed to India and East Asia.

Although India was politically divided, it was a land of thriving cities. Hindu and Buddhist traditions flourished, and wealthy princes built stunning temples and palaces. Indian mathematicians invented a number system, which Arabs adapted and eventually passed to Europeans.

China had a strong central government. Under the Tang and Song dynasties, China's culture flourished and influenced neighboring peoples. The Chinese made amazing advances in technology, inventing paper, printing, and gunpowder. In dozens of cities, traders used coins and paper money, unknown to medieval Europeans.

In West Africa, the Soninke people were building the great trading empire of Ghana. Its merchants traded goods, especially gold, across the Sahara to North Africa, the Middle East, and even Europe.

Across the Atlantic, in the Americas, the Mayas had cleared rain forests and built cities dominated by towering temples. In Peru, Native Americans were building empires and creating great works of art, including elegant

Global Connections

A Mongol Alliance?

Later during the Crusades, Pope Innocent IV sent a diplomatic mission to the Mongols in Central Asia. The pope hoped that the Mongol khan would halt his invasions of Christian lands, convert to Christianity, and join European Christians in their struggle against the Muslims. In a letter written in Mongol, Arabic, and Latin, the khan rejected the pope's proposal.

The pope's mission failed to win an alliance, but it did bring the Europeans new knowledge about the world. Giovanni da Pian del Carpini, the monk who had led the mission, wrote a text based on his extensive travels. His book on the Mongol empire consisted of chapters on climate, customs, religion, character, history, policy, and tactics.

Theme: Global Interaction
How can increased knowledge of other cultures improve international relations?

Chapter 9 **215**

Customize for . . .
Visual Learners

Creating an Advertisement Inform students that the Church offered powerful incentives to those who joined the Crusades. The pope promised forgiveness of sins and entrance into the kingdom of heaven for anyone who died in the Crusades. Serfs could obtain freedom from their lords. Citizens who enlisted were freed from paying taxes. Those who owed debts were allowed to pay them back without additional fees. Prisoners were released from jails, and sentences of death were commuted to life service in Palestine.

Ask students to imagine that the Church has asked them to create an advertisement to convince people to join the Crusades. Their advertisements should mention one or more of the incentives described above as well as those discussed in the text. To complete the assignment, students may wish to use any combination of persuasive words, drawings, maps, or other illustrations. You may wish to display students' finished projects in the classroom. ✳

Connections to Today

A Holy City
Today, Jews, Christians, and Muslims still consider Jerusalem sacred. Each year, the city's population is swelled by thousands of pilgrims who arrive to visit places that are holy to their faiths. Christian pilgrims make certain to visit the Church of the Holy Sepulcher, believed to be the site of Jesus' resurrection. Equally sacred to Muslims is the Dome of the Rock, from which the Prophet Muhammad is believed to have ascended to heaven. Jewish pilgrims join in prayer at the Old City's western wall, all that remains of the city's ancient temple.

Theme: Religions and Value Systems Why do Muslims consider Jerusalem a holy city?

pottery, textiles, and jewelry. The civilizations of the Americas, however, remained outside the contacts that were taking place among Africans, Europeans, and Asians.

Closer to Western Europe, the Byzantine empire was generally prosperous and united. Byzantine scholars still studied ancient Greek and Roman writings. In Constantinople, Byzantine and Muslim merchants mingled with traders from Venice and other Italian cities.

In the 1050s, the Seljuk Turks invaded the Byzantine empire. The Turks had migrated from Central Asia into the Middle East, where they converted to Islam. By 1071, the Seljuks had overrun most Byzantine lands in Asia Minor (present-day Turkey). The Seljuks also extended their power over Palestine to the Holy Land* and attacked Christian pilgrims.

The Crusades

The Byzantine emperor Alexius I urgently asked Pope Urban II for Christian knights to help him fight the Turks. Although Roman popes and Byzantine emperors were longtime rivals, Urban agreed.

At the Council of Clermont in 1095, Urban incited bishops and nobles to action. "From Jerusalem and the city of Constantinople comes a grievous report," he began. "An accursed race . . . has violently invaded the lands of those Christians and has depopulated them by pillage and fire." Urban then called for a crusade to free the Holy Land:

> "Both knights and footmen, both rich and poor . . . strive to help expel [the Seljuks] from our Christian lands before it is too late. . . . Christ commands it. Remission of sins will be granted for those going thither."
> —Fulcher of Chartres, *Chronicle of the First Crusade*

Motives "God wills it!" roared the assembly. By 1096, thousands of knights were on their way to the Holy Land. As the crusading spirit swept through Western Europe, armies of ordinary men and women inspired by fiery preachers left for the Holy Land, too. Few returned.

Religious zeal and other factors motivated the crusaders. Many knights hoped to win wealth and land. Some crusaders sought to escape troubles at home. Others yearned for adventure.

The pope, too, had mixed motives. Urban hoped to increase his power in Europe and perhaps heal the schism, or split, between the Roman and Byzantine churches. (See the next chapter.) He also hoped that the Crusades would set Christian knights to fighting Muslims instead of one another.

Victories and Defeats Only the First Crusade came close to achieving its goals. After a long, bloody campaign, Christian knights captured Jerusalem in 1099. They capped their victory with a massacre of Muslim and Jewish residents of the city.

The Crusades continued, off and on, for over 200 years. The crusaders divided their captured lands into four small states. The Muslims repeatedly sought to destroy these Christian kingdoms, prompting Europeans to launch new crusades. By 1187, Jerusalem had fallen to the able Muslim leader Salah al-Din, known to Europeans as Saladin. On the Third Crusade, Europeans tried but failed to retake Jerusalem. After negotiations, though, Saladin did reopen the holy city to Christian pilgrims.

Europeans also mounted crusades against other Muslim lands, especially in North Africa. All ended in defeat. During the Fourth Crusade, the crusaders were diverted from fighting Muslims to fighting Christians. After

---

*Christians called Jerusalem and other places in Palestine where Jesus had lived and taught the Holy Land. Jerusalem was also a holy place for Jews and Muslims.

Connections to Today

ANSWER Because it contains the Dome of the Rock, from which Muhammad is believed to have ascended to heaven.

Crusades, 1096–1204

North Sea

Baltic Sea

ENGLAND

ATLANTIC OCEAN

POLAND

RUSSIA

HOLY

Metz • Regensburg

Vézeley • ROMAN

FRANCE

EMPIRE

Clermont •

Venice

Genoa

HUNGARY

CROATIA

Black Sea

PORTUGAL

CASTILE

Marseille •

SERBIA

Rome •

Córdoba •

KINGDOM OF SICILY

BYZANTINE

EMPIRE

Constantinople

SELJUK TURKS

Tangier •

CYPRUS

Mediterranean Sea

CRETE

Tripoli •

Azimuthal Equal Area Projection

Cairo •

Edessa

Antioch

Baghdad •

Damascus

Acre

Jerusalem

Area of inset map

Legend:
- Predominantly Muslim lands, 1095
- First Crusade, 1096–1099
- Second Crusade, 1147–1149
- Third Crusade, 1189–1192
- Fourth Crusade, 1202–1204

0   250   500 Miles
0   250   500 Kilometers

Crusader States, 1099

Edessa •

Antioch •

COUNTY OF EDESSA

PRINCIPALITY OF ANTIOCH

Tripoli •

COUNTY OF TRIPOLI

Acre •

Damascus •

KINGDOM OF JERUSALEM

Jerusalem •

0   50   100 Miles
0   100 Kilometers

---

helping Venetian merchants defeat their Byzantine trade rivals in 1204, crusaders captured and looted Constantinople, the Byzantine capital.

Muslim armies, meanwhile, overran the crusader states. By 1291, they captured the last Christian outpost, the port city of Acre. As in Jerusalem 200 years earlier, the victors massacred their defeated enemies. This time, the victims were Christians.

Effects of the Crusades on Europe

The Crusades left a bitter legacy of religious hatred behind them. In the Middle East, both Christians and Muslims committed appalling atrocities in the name of religion. In Europe, crusaders sometimes turned their religious fury against Jews, massacring entire communities.

Though the Crusades failed to conquer the Holy Land, they did have significant effects on life in Europe. The wars helped to quicken the pace of changes already underway.

Economic Expansion Even before the Crusades, Europeans had a taste for luxuries from the Byzantine empire. The Crusades increased trade. Crusaders introduced fabrics, spices, and perfumes from the Middle East to Europe.

Merchants in Venice and other northern Italian cities built large fleets to carry crusaders to the Holy Land. They later used those fleets to carry on trade with the Middle East. Our words *sugar, cotton,* and *rice,* borrowed from Arabic, show the range of trade goods involved.

The Crusades further encouraged the growth of a money economy. To finance a journey to the Holy Land, nobles needed money. They allowed peasants to pay rents in money rather than in grain or labor, which helped undermine serfdom.

Chapter 9 **217**

Background
Biography

Incredible Tales When Marco Polo and his father returned to Venice, they looked so foreign that their relatives refused to let them in. The Polos finally beat their way in and proved their identity. Shortly thereafter, the Polos held a grand feast. In front of astonished family and friends, the two men slit the seams of their tattered clothes, and out poured piles of rubies, diamonds, and other jewels. Still, many refused to believe Marco Polo's stories. A book about his travels was denounced as full of lies. On his deathbed, Polo's friends pleaded with him to retract the outlandish statements in his book. His reply was, "I have not told half of what I saw."

Virtual Field Trip

www.phschool.com

University of Calgary
Calgary, Canada

For more images and information about the Reconquista and the history of Spain, use the Internet address above to link to the department of history at the University of Calgary.

The Reconquista
In 1492, the fall of the Muslim city of Granada completed the Christian reconquest of Spain. This Spanish woodcarving shows Granada surrendering to Queen Isabella and King Ferdinand.

Theme: Economics and Technology How were Granada and other medieval towns designed to provide defense?

Increased Power for Monarchs The Crusades helped to increase the power of feudal monarchs. Rulers won new rights to levy, or collect, taxes in order to support the Crusades. Some rulers, including the French king Louis IX, led crusades, which added greatly to their prestige.

The Church Enthusiasm for the Crusades brought papal power to its greatest height. This period of enhanced prestige was short-lived, however. As we have seen, popes were soon involved in bitter clashes with feudal monarchs. Also, the Crusades did not end the split between the Roman and Byzantine churches. In fact, Byzantine resentment against the West hardened as a result of the Fourth Crusade.

A Wider Worldview Contacts with the Muslim world led Christians to realize that millions of people lived in regions they had never known existed. Soon, a few curious Europeans visited far-off places like India and China.

In 1271, a young Venetian, Marco Polo, set out for China with his merchant father and uncle. After many years in China, he returned to Venice full of stories about the wonders of Chinese civilization. Doubting Europeans called Marco Polo the "prince of liars." To them, his tales of a government-run mail service and black stones (coal) that were burned to heat homes were totally untrue.

The experiences of crusaders and of travelers like Marco Polo expanded European horizons. They brought Europe into a wider world from which it had been cut off since the fall of Rome. By the 1400s, a desire to trade directly with India and China led Europeans to a new age of exploration.

The Reconquista in Spain

The crusading spirit continued long after the European defeat at Acre. It flourished especially in Spain, where Christian warriors had been battling Muslims for centuries. Muslims had conquered most of Spain in the 700s. Several tiny Christian kingdoms survived in the north, however. As they slowly expanded their borders, they sought to take over Muslim lands. Their campaign to drive the Muslims from Spain became known as the Reconquista, or "reconquest."

Resource Directory

Teaching Resources
Section Quiz Unit 3 booklet, p. 25
Technology
World History Color Transparencies *Protective Armor in Europe and Japan*, p. C–41
Interactive Student Tutorial CD-ROM Ch. 9
Computer Test Bank Ch. 9

Christian Advances Efforts by Christian warriors to expel the Muslims began in the 700s. Their first real success did not come, however, until 1085, when they recaptured the city of Toledo. During the next 200 years, Christian forces pushed slowly and steadily southward. By 1300, Christians controlled the entire Iberian Peninsula except for Granada. Muslim influences remained strong, though, and helped shape the arts and literature of Christian Spain.

Ferdinand and Isabella In 1469, Isabella of Castile married Ferdinand of Aragon. This marriage between the rulers of two powerful kingdoms opened the way for a unified state. Using their combined forces, the two monarchs made a final push against the Muslim stronghold of Granada. In 1492, Granada fell. The Reconquista was complete.

Isabella and Ferdinand tried to impose unity on their diverse peoples. They joined forces with townspeople against powerful nobles. Isabella was determined to bring religious as well as political unity to Spain.

Under Muslim rule, Spain had enjoyed a tradition of religious toleration, that is, a policy of allowing people to worship as they choose. Christians, Jews, and Muslims lived there in relative peace. Isabella ended that policy of toleration. With the support of the Inquisition, a Church court set up to try people accused of heresy, Isabella launched a brutal crusade against Jews and Muslims. Often, those who refused to convert to Christianity were burned at the stake.

The queen achieved religious unity but at a high price. More than 150,000 people fled Spain. Many of these exiles were skilled, educated people who had contributed much to Spain's economy and culture.

Cause and Effect

Western European Emergence From Isolation

Long-Term Causes	Immediate Causes
• Growth of strong monarchs • Growth of towns and cities • Growth of representative bodies • Crusades • Increased trade • Population decline	• Economic revival • New technology and agricultural productivity • Development of universities • Wider worldview

Immediate Effects	Long-Term Effects
• Population growth • End of feudalism • Centralized monarchies • Growth of Italian trading centers • Increased productivity	• Renaissance • Age of Exploration • Scientific Revolution • Western European colonies in Asia, Africa, and the Americas

Connections to Today

• Growth of strong central governments
• Spread of representative government
• Capitalism and powerful business classes
• Influence of Western European culture around the world
• Influence of technology on everyday life

Skills Assessment **Chart** During the late Middle Ages, Europe was emerging from a period of isolation. **How did the Crusades contribute to economic revival?**

SECTION 3 Assessment

Recall

1. **Identify:** (a) Crusades, (b) Council of Clermont, (c) Saladin, (d) Reconquista, (e) Ferdinand and Isabella.
2. **Define:** (a) schism, (b) levy, (c) religious toleration.

Comprehension

3. What advanced civilizations existed around the world at the time of the First Crusade?
4. (a) Why did Europeans join the Crusades? (b) What were three results of the Crusades?
5. How did Spain achieve political and religious unity?

Critical Thinking and Writing

6. **Analyzing Information** How did the Crusades reflect the growing strength of medieval Europe?
7. **Making Generalizations** (a) How was the Reconquista part of the crusading spirit that appealed to many Europeans? (b) How were the goals of Ferdinand and Isabella similar to the goals of other monarchs in Europe?

Activity

Expressing Different Points of View
Write two articles reporting on the First Crusade: one from the point of view of a Christian knight, and another from the point of view of a Muslim living in Jerusalem.

SECTION 3 Assessment

Recall
1. (a) Crusades, p. 215 (b) Council of Clermont, p. 216 (c) Saladin, p. 216 (d) Reconquista, p. 218 (e) Ferdinand and Isabella, p. 219 2. (a) schism, p. 216 (b) levy, p. 218 (c) religious toleration, p. 219

Comprehension
3. Islamic civilization stretching across lands from Spain to India; Hindu and Buddhist civilizations in India and China; the African civilization of the Soninke; Native American civilizations in the Americas; Byzantine civilization in Eastern Europe
4. (a) Europeans joined the Crusades out of religious zeal, to win wealth and land, to escape troubles at home, and to experience adventure. (b) Answers should include three of the following: increased trade with the Middle East, increased tensions between popes and monarchs, increased power for monarchs, growth of a money economy, weakening of serfdom, increased knowledge of the world outside Europe. 5. Spain achieved political and religious unity through the Reconquista, the Inquisition, and powerful monarchs.

Critical Thinking and Writing
6. Possible answer: The Crusades reflected the growing power and influence of the Church. European monarchs displayed their growing power by being able to wage wars in a region far away from their homeland. 7. (a) The Reconquista, like the Crusades, was an attempt to expel Muslims. (b) They wanted to unify their nation and achieve religious unity by expelling or killing non-Christians.

Activity Rubrics

Share rubrics with students before they write their articles.

Attempted The articles are attempted but are incomplete.

Minimal The articles are poorly written or reveal little understanding of the different points of view.

Adequate The articles are well written and reflect different points of view.

Exemplary The articles are thoughtful, well written, and show empathy with each point of view.

Skills Assessment

ANSWER The Crusades led to increased trade between Europe and the Middle East.

Human Drama Note

Quinsay Marco Polo stayed in China for many years, serving as an official for the Mongol emperor Kublai Khan, a grandson of Genghiz Khan and founder of the Mongol dynasty. Polo was impressed with the city of Hangzhou, also call Quinsay, the Khan's southern capital. Quinsay was surrounded by water. Its numerous canals were spanned by stone bridges, each of which was posted with sentries who regularly struck the hour and patrolled the streets. Polo's description below reveals the city's character. "Each guard is provided with a hollow instrument of wood, a metal basin, and a time-keeper to enable them to know the hour of the day or night. . . . Part of the watch patrols the quarter to see if any light or fire is burning after the lawful hours; if they find any they mark the door, and in the morning the owner is summoned before the magistrates, and unless he can plead a good excuse, he is punished. Also, anyone going about the streets at unlawful hours is arrested. . . . Likewise, any poor cripple unable to work for his livelihood [is taken] to one of the [many] hospitals . . . endowed with great revenue."

Bell Ringer Ask students to write down five characteristics of a typical day at their school. Then, ask students to read about student life on this and the next page in the text. Ask students to discuss how their daily routine compares to the typical day of students during the Middle Ages.

Reading Focus

- How did medieval universities advance learning?
- How did "new" learning affect medieval thought?
- What styles of literature, architecture, and art developed in the High Middle Ages?

Vocabulary

scholasticism
vernacular
epic
flying buttress
illumination

Taking Notes

Copy this concept web. As you read, complete the web. Add circles as needed.

Universities — CULTURAL ACHIEVEMENTS — Literature — Epics praise virtues — The arts

Main Idea As economic and political conditions improved, Europeans made notable achievements in learning, literature, and the arts.

LESSON PLAN

1. Focus Sparked by improving economic and political conditions, a revival of learning took place in the High Middle Ages. Writers across Western Europe began publishing works in the vernacular. Gothic cathedrals served as symbols of wealth and religious devotion.

2. Instruct Ask students to imagine that they are living during the High Middle Ages. Have students write at least three diary entries that give their impressions of the new universities, new works of literature, and the new forms of architecture. Tell students that they should write their diary entries from the point of view of one of the following: a Catholic priest, a woman friend of Christine de Pizan, or a man whose son is attending a university.

3. Assess Have volunteers read their diary entries aloud. Then, discuss how the learning, literature, and architecture of the High Middle Ages affect us today.

4. Reteach If students' Assess activity does not reflect adequate understanding of the lesson, you might assign the *Guide to the Essentials* or the *Interactive Student Tutorial CD-ROM* for this section.

Setting the Scene By the 1100s, Europe was experiencing dynamic changes. No longer was everyone preoccupied with the daily struggle to survive. Improvements in agriculture were creating a steadier food supply. The revival of trade and the growth of towns were signs of increased prosperity. Within the towns and cities of medieval Europe, a few people were acquiring wealth. In time, towns contributed a vital spark that ignited the cultural flowering of the High Middle Ages.

Medieval Universities

As economic and political conditions improved in the High Middle Ages, the need for education expanded. The Church wanted better-educated clergy. Royal rulers also needed literate men for their growing bureaucracies. By getting an education, the sons of wealthy townspeople might hope to qualify for high jobs in the Church or royal governments.

Academic Guilds By the 1100s, schools had sprung up around the great cathedrals to train the clergy. Some of these cathedral schools evolved into the first universities. They were organized like guilds with charters to protect the rights of members and set standards for training.

University of Paris
Students listened as teachers read aloud five logic books and two grammar books, as part of the course of study for a bachelor of arts.

Theme: Economics and Technology Why do you think there was not a book for each student?

Salerno and Bologna in Italy boasted the first universities. Paris and Oxford soon had theirs. In the 1200s, other cities rushed to organize universities. Students often traveled from one university to another. They might study law in Bologna, medicine in Montpellier, and theology, or religion, in Paris.

Student Life University life offered few comforts. A bell wakened students at about 5 A.M. for prayers. Students then attended classes until 10 A.M., when they had their first meal of the day—perhaps a bit of beef and soup mixed with oatmeal. Afternoon classes continued until 5 P.M. Students usually ate a light supper and then studied until it was time for bed.

Because medieval universities did not have permanent buildings, classes were held in rented rooms or in the choir loft of a church. Students sat for hours on hard benches as the teacher dictated and then explained Latin texts. Students were expected to memorize what they heard.

Caption Answer

There were relatively few books because they were written by hand and often took many years to produce. Books were expensive and students could not afford them.

Resource Directory

Teaching Resources

Creative Teaching Activities Creative Teaching Activities booklet, p. 44

Guided Reading and Review Unit 3 booklet, p. 26

Biography Activity *Lady Margaret Beaufort*, Unit 3 booklet, p. 30

A program of study covered the seven liberal arts: arithmetic, geometry, astronomy, music, grammar, rhetoric, and logic. To show that they had mastered a subject, students took an oral exam. Earning a degree as a bachelor of arts took between three and six years. Only after several more years of study could a man qualify to become a master of arts and a teacher.

Women and Education Women were not allowed to attend the universities. This exclusion seriously affected their lives. Without a university education, they could not become doctors, lawyers, administrators, church officials, or professors. They were also deprived of the mental stimulation that was an important part of university life.

An exception was Christine de Pizan (duh pee ZAHN), an Italian-born woman who came to live in the French court. De Pizan was married at 15, but her husband died before she was 25. Left with three children to raise, De Pizan earned her living as a writer, an unusual occupation for a woman of that time.

De Pizan used her pen to examine the achievements of women. In *The City of Ladies,* she questions several imaginary characters about men's negative views of women. She asks Lady Reason, for example, whether women are less capable of learning and understanding, as men insist. Lady Reason replies: "If it were customary to send daughters to school like sons, and if they were then taught the same subjects, they would learn as thoroughly and understand the subtleties of all arts and sciences as well as sons."

Still, men continued to look on educated women as oddities. Women, they felt, should pursue their "natural" gifts at home, raising children, managing the household, and doing needlework, and leave books and writing to men.

Europeans Acquire "New" Learning

Universities received a further boost from an explosion of knowledge that reached Europe in the High Middle Ages. Many of the "new" ideas had originated in ancient Greece but had been lost to Western Europeans after the fall of Rome.

Spread of Learning In the Middle East, Muslim scholars had translated the works of Aristotle and other Greek thinkers into Arabic, and their texts had spread across the Muslim world. In Muslim Spain, Jewish scholars translated these works into Latin, the language of Christian European scholars. By the 1100s, these new translations were seeping into Western Europe. There they set off a revolution in the world of learning.

Philosophy The writings of the ancient Greeks posed a challenge to Christian scholars. Aristotle taught that people should use reason to discover basic truths. Christians, however, accepted many ideas on faith. They believed that the Church was the final authority on all questions. How could they use the logic of Aristotle without undermining their Christian faith?

Christian scholars, known as scholastics, tried to resolve the conflict between faith and reason. Their method, known as scholasticism, used reason to support Christian beliefs. Scholastics studied the works of the Muslim philosopher Averroës (ah VEHR oh eez) and the Jewish rabbi Maimonides (mī MAHN uh deez). These thinkers, too, used logic to resolve the conflict between faith and reason.

The writings of these thinkers influenced the scholastic Thomas Aquinas (uh KWĪ nuhs). In a monumental work, *Summa Theologica,* Aquinas examined Christian teachings in the light of reason. Faith and reason, he concluded, existed in harmony. Both led to the same truth, that God ruled over an orderly universe. He thus brought together Christian faith and classical Greek philosophy.

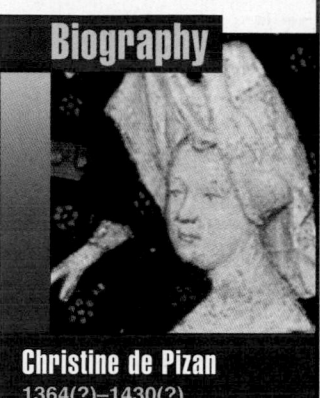

Biography

Christine de Pizan
1364(?)–1430(?)

Christine de Pizan was more educated than most men of her time. Her father, a physician and astronomer in the French court of Charles V, had seen that she received an excellent education. She spoke French, Italian, and possibly Latin as well.

To support her family, De Pizan wrote poems, songs, and ballads. Her work was supported by lords and ladies, by King Charles VI of France, and by his wife, Queen Isabella. Because of her desire to comment on social issues, De Pizan gradually switched her focus to prose. In much of her work, she promoted women's rights and accomplishments. Shortly before her death, she wrote the poem "Hymn to Joan of Arc" to honor a young Frenchwoman who was leading French soldiers to victory over the English.

Theme: Impact of the Individual What was a major theme of De Pizan's writing?

Background
Historical Evidence

Profile of a Bad Student Alvarus Palagius, a Franciscan friar of the Middle Ages, noted some of the habits of bad students. Students in your class might be surprised to learn that some of the items on Palagius's list would describe students' bad habits today. His list included attending classes but making no effort to learn anything; learning what should be ignored, such as "forbidden sciences" and superstitions; depriving their masters of their salaries by not paying tuition; missing church on feast days; and spending allowances received from their parents in taverns and on games.

Background
Daily Life

Medieval Fashion Advice Although few women received a formal university education, they were thoroughly instructed in the proper way to dress. Medieval etiquette books and clerical writers provided noblewomen with advice such as this:

"Shun foreign fashions at festivals and tourneys, lest one become foolishly conspicuous; and above all beware of lofty headgear, lest you resemble stags who must lower their heads on entering a wood, and in order that you may not by your loud fashions make everyone stare at you as if you were a wild beast."

Block Scheduling Support

Have students complete the Skill Application Activity, *Analyzing Literature as Historical Evidence,* Unit 3 booklet, p. 33, which is an excerpt from the *Morte d'Arthur.* Ask students to explain how literature can aid our understanding of history. Ask students what they can infer about medieval society based on this reading. Then, ask students to list on the board other epics that have contributed to our knowledge of the past, such as the works of Homer. Use this list to lead a discussion on the importance of literature in studying history.

Biography

ANSWER women's rights and accomplishments

Primary Source

The Adventures of Roland
This passage, located near the end of the epic the Song of Roland, *describes Roland's final moments:*

"The Count Roland, beneath a pine he sits . . .
Remembering so many [different] things:
So many lands where he went conquering,
And France the [sweet], the heroes of his kin,
And Charlemagne, his lord who nourished him.
Nor can we help but weep and sigh at this. . . .
His right-hand glove, to God he offers it
Saint Gabriel from's hand hath taken it . . .
He joins his hand: and so is life finish'd
God sent him down His angel cherubim . . .
So the count's soul they bear to Paradis[e]."

—*Song of Roland*

Skills Assessment

Primary Source Why would the *Song of Roland* be considered an epic poem?

Science and Mathematics Works of science, translated from Arabic and Greek, also reached Europe from Spain and the Byzantine empire. Christian scholars studied Hippocrates on medicine and Euclid on geometry, along with works by Arab scientists. They saw, too, how Aristotle had used observation and experimentation to study the physical world.

Yet science made little real progress in the Middle Ages because most scholars still believed that all true knowledge must fit with Church teachings. It would take many centuries before Christian thinkers changed the way they viewed the physical world.

In mathematics, as we have seen, Europeans adopted Hindu-Arabic numerals. This system was much easier to use than the cumbersome system of Roman numerals that had been traditional throughout Europe for centuries. In time, Arabic numerals allowed both scientists and mathematicians to make extraordinary advances in their fields.

Medieval Literature

While Latin was the language of scholars and churchmen, new writings began to appear in the vernacular, or the everyday languages of ordinary people, such as French, German, and Italian. These writings captured the spirit of the High Middle Ages. Medieval literature included epics, or long narrative poems, about feudal warriors and tales of the common people.

Heroic Epics Across Europe, people began writing down oral traditions in the vernacular. French pilgrims traveling to holy sites loved to hear the *chansons de geste,* or "songs of heroic deeds." The most popular was the *Song of Roland,* which praises the courage of one of Charlemagne's knights who died while on a military campaign in Muslim Spain. A true feudal hero, Roland loyally sacrifices his life out of a sense of honor.

Spain's great epic, *Poem of the Cid,* also involves battle against Muslim forces. The Cid was Rodrigo Díaz, a bold and fiery Christian lord who battled Muslims in Spain. Calling to his warriors, he surges into battle full of zeal:

"There are three hundred lances that each a pennant bears.
At one blow every man of them his Moor has slaughtered there,
And when they wheeled to charge anew as many more were slain,
You might see great clumps of lances lowered and raised again. . . .
Cried the Moor "Muhammed!" The Christians shouted on St. James of Grace,
On the field Moors thirteen hundred were slain in little space."

—*Poem of the Cid*

Dante's *Divine Comedy* "In the middle of the journey of life, I found myself in a dark wood, where the straight way was lost." So begins the *Divine Comedy* by the famed Italian poet Dante Alighieri (DAHN tay al lee GYEH ree). The poem takes the reader on an imaginary journey into hell and purgatory, where souls await forgiveness. Finally, Dante describes a vision of heaven.

"Abandon all hope, ye that enter here" is the warning Dante receives as he approaches hell. There, he talks with people from history who tell how they earned a place in hell. Humor, tragedy, and the endless medieval quest for religious understanding are all ingredients in Dante's poem. His journey summarizes Christian ethics. It also highlights in vivid detail a key idea of Christianity—that people's actions in life will determine their fate in the afterlife.

Chaucer's *Canterbury Tales* In *The Canterbury Tales*, Geoffrey Chaucer follows a band of English pilgrims traveling to Thomas Becket's tomb. In brilliant word portraits, he sketches a range of characters, including a knight, a plowman, a merchant, a miller, a monk, a nun, and the five-times-widowed "wife of Bath." Each character tells a story. Whether funny, romantic, or bawdy, each tale adds to our picture of medieval life.

Architecture and Art

"In the Middle Ages," wrote French author Victor Hugo, "men had no great thought that they did not write down in stone." With riches from trade and commerce, townspeople, nobles, and monarchs indulged in a flurry of building. Their greatest achievements were the towering stone cathedrals that served as symbols of their wealth and religious devotion.

Romanesque Strength About 1000, monasteries and towns built solid stone churches that reflected Roman influences. These Romanesque churches looked like fortresses with thick walls and towers. Typically, the roof of a Romanesque church was a barrel vault, a long tunnel of stone that covered the main part of the structure. It was so heavy that it had to be supported by massive thick walls. Builders provided no windows or only tiny slits of windows for fear of weakening the walls that supported the roof. As a result, the interior of a Romanesque church was dark and gloomy.

Gothic Grace About 1140, Abbot Suger wanted to build a new abbey church at St. Denis near Paris. He hoped that it "would shine with wonderful and uninterrupted light." Urged on by the abbot, builders developed what became known as the Gothic style of architecture. A key feature of this style was the flying buttresses, or stone supports that stood outside the church. These supports allowed builders to construct higher walls and leave space for huge stained-glass windows.

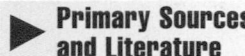
▶ **Primary Sources and Literature**

See "Geoffrey Chaucer: The Canterbury Tales" in the Reference Section at the back of this book.

Gothic Style
The Cathedral of Notre Dame in Paris is a fine example of the Gothic style. Medieval artists adorned Gothic cathedrals with brilliant stained-glass windows and a variety of sculptures, such as the mythical beast shown here.

Theme: Art and Literature
How did Gothic style differ from Romanesque style?

Background
Connections to Art

Reaching for the Heights Architects and artists of the Middle Ages designed Gothic cathedrals as places of worship and inspiration. The community came to worship in a building whose towers and spires reached to the heavens. The light that filtered down through the stained glass symbolized God's divine presence. The spirits of the people could rise into the immensity of the vaulted ceilings. Sculptures and stained glass art inspired the congregation with Bible stories and examples of saints and apostles.

Background
Connections to Today

Stained by Pollution The huge stained glass windows that adorn Gothic cathedrals are works of art in themselves. The glass for the windows was made from sand, salt, and ashes that were heated to a thick liquid and colored with copper (red), iron (yellow), or cobalt (blue). Stained glass was once believed to be immune to aging. However, today their brilliance is fading. Experts have recently learned that the pollution of our modern industrial age does indeed do damage to these medieval works of art.

Human Drama Note

The Spread of the Lute We know that the lute dates to ancient times because a Babylonian relief, dating from about 1700 B.C., shows the instrument. The oldest known actual lute was found in an Egyptian tomb and dates to about 1500 B.C. Medieval poets often accompanied their recitations on the lute, which came to Europe via Spaniards, who copied it from the Moors in the 1200s. In France, the instrument became so popular that the word *luthier*, meaning "lute manufacturer," is still used to refer to any maker of stringed instruments.

☑ **Test Preparation**

Have students read the excerpt from *Poem of the Cid* on the opposite page, and then answer the question below.

Which lines probably are exaggerations?

A Lines 1 and 2
B Lines 2 and 3
C Lines 1 and 5
D Lines 4 and 5

Caption Answer

Gothic churches had higher walls and more space for windows than Romanesque churches. The Gothic churches had graceful spires and lofty ceilings.

Recall
1. (a) Christine de Pizan, p. 221
(b) Thomas Aquinas, p. 221 (c) *Song of Roland*, p. 222 (d) *Poem of the Cid*, p. 222
(e) Dante Alighieri, p. 222 (f) Geoffrey Chaucer, p. 223 2. (a) scholasticism, p. 221 (b) vernacular, p. 222 (c) epic, p. 222 (d) flying buttress, p. 223
(e) illumination, p. 224

Comprehension
3. A program of study covered the seven liberal arts: arithmetic, geometry, astronomy, music, grammar, rhetoric, and logic.
4. Much of the new learning was based on reason, while Christianity was based largely on faith. Christian scholars had to resolve the conflict between faith and reason. 5. Gothic architecture featured flying buttresses, graceful spires, enormous stained glass windows, and lofty ceilings.

Critical Thinking and Writing
6. Sculptures, stained glass windows, and carvings portrayed people and stories from the Bible. These portrayals helped teach Christian principles to the illiterate masses. 7. MMMMCCCXL; 1,980 + 2,360 = 4,340. Students should recognize that the use of Arabic numerals made it much easier to perform mathematical calculations and therefore encouraged more advanced mathematical inquiry in Western Europe.

Activity Rubrics

Share rubrics with students before they conduct their interview.

Attempted The interview is attempted but does not reveal much research or understanding of the chosen writer.

Minimal The interview reveals some research and understanding of the chosen writer.

Adequate The interview reveals appropriate research and understanding of the chosen writer.

Exemplary The interview reveals appropriate research and understanding of the chosen writer, and the program is well acted.

Caption Answer

Sculptures, stained glass windows, and ⸺ ⸺ and stories

Art and Religion
Stained-glass windows depicted biblical or other religious scenes. In the 1100s, a monk wrote that his church was filled with "the most radiant windows" to "illuminate men's minds so that they may travel through it [light] to an apprehension of God's light."
Theme: Art and Literature
How did medieval art help illiterate Christians learn about the Bible?

The new Gothic churches soared to incredible heights. Their graceful spires, lofty ceilings, and enormous windows carried the eye upward to the heavens. "Since their brilliance lets the splendor of the True Light pass into the church," declared a medieval visitor, "they enlighten those inside."

Cities all over Europe competed to build grander, taller cathedrals. The faithful contributed money, labor, and skills to help build these monuments "to the greater glory of God."

Art in Stone and Glass As churches rose, stonemasons carved sculptures to decorate them inside and out. The sculptors portrayed scenes from the Bible and other religious themes. They also carved images of everyday life that included lifelike forms of plants and animals. Among the most interesting of their creations were whimsical or frightening images of mythical creatures such as dragons, griffins, and unicorns.

At the same time, other skilled craftworkers created stained-glass windows that added to the brilliant splendor of Gothic churches. The artisans stained small pieces of glass in glowing colors. They then set the pieces in thin lead frames to create pictures depicting the life of Jesus, a biblical event, or other religious themes. Stained glass and carvings served as a religious education for the people, most of whom were illiterate.

Illuminated Manuscripts In the 1300s and 1400s, the Gothic style was applied to paintings and illumination, that is, the artistic decoration of books. Since the early Middle Ages, monks, nuns, and other skilled artisans had illuminated books with intricate designs and miniature paintings of biblical scenes and daily life. Characteristics of the new Gothic style included bold, brilliant colors and decorative detail. Some fine examples of Gothic painting appeared in prayer books known as Books of Hours. Artists decorated these prayer books with depictions of towns and castles, knights and ladies in gardens or at banquet, and peasants working in the fields.

SECTION 4 Assessment

Recall
1. **Identify:** (a) Christine de Pizan, (b) Thomas Aquinas, (c) *Song of Roland*, (d) *Poem of the Cid*, (e) Dante Alighieri, (f) Geoffrey Chaucer.
2. **Define:** (a) scholasticism, (b) vernacular, (c) epic, (d) flying buttress, (e) illumination.

Comprehension
3. What subjects were included in the course of study in medieval universities?
4. How did new knowledge pose a challenge to Christian scholars?

5. What were the characteristics of Gothic architecture?

Critical Thinking and Writing
6. **Making Inferences** Why do you think Gothic churches are sometimes referred to as "Bibles in stone"?
7. **Solving Problems** Solve this problem using Roman numerals: MCMLXXX + MMCCCLX. Then, translate and solve the problem using Arabic numerals. How do you think the introduction of Arabic numerals might have affected mathematics in Western Europe?

Activity
Take It to the NET

Use the Internet to learn more about the literature and views of Dante or Chaucer. Then, with a small group of classmates, stage a TV program in which you interview one of the writers. Develop your questions and answers by referring to what you learned in your research.

Resource Directory

Teaching Resources
Section Quiz Unit 3 booklet, p. 27
Creative Teaching Activities Creative Teaching Activities booklet, p. 45
Guided Reading and Review Unit 3 booklet, p. 28
Viewpoint Activity *Historians Look at the Middle Ages,* Unit 3 booklet, p. 32
History Through Literature *The Decameron,* History Through Literature booklet, pp. 20–22

Technology
Interactive Student Tutorial CD-ROM Ch. 9
Computer Test Bank Ch. 9

SECTION 5 A Time of Crisis

Reading Focus

■ How did the Black Death cause social and economic decline?

■ What problems afflicted the Church in the late Middle Ages?

■ What were the causes, turning points, and effects of the Hundred Years' War?

Vocabulary

epidemic
inflation
longbow

Taking Notes

Copy the chart at right on conditions before and after the Hundred Years' War. As you read, fill in each column with appropriate information.

HUNDRED YEARS' WAR	
Before	After
• Castles offered adequate protection	• English hold only Calais in France
•	•

Main Idea Plague, upheaval in the Church, and war made the 1300s and early 1400s a time of crisis for Europeans.

Setting the Scene

In the autumn of 1347, a fleet of Genoese trading ships, loaded with grain, left the Black Sea port of Caffa and set sail for Messina, Sicily. By midvoyage, sailors were falling sick and dying. Soon after the ships tied up at Messina, townspeople, too, fell sick and died. A medieval chronicler described how the people of Messina "drove (the Genoese) in all haste from their city and port." Nevertheless, "the sickness remained and a terrible mortality ensued." Within months, the disease that Europeans called the Black Death was raging through Italy.

To Europeans in the mid-1300s, the end of the world seemed to have come. First, widespread crop failures brought famine and starvation. Then, plague and war deepened the crisis. Europe eventually recovered from these disasters. Still, the upheavals of the 1300s and 1400s marked the end of the Middle Ages and the beginning of the early modern age.

The Black Death

By 1348, the Black Death had reached beyond Italy to Spain and France. From there, it ravaged the rest of Europe. One in three people died—worse than in any war in history.

A Global Epidemic The sickness was bubonic plague, a disease spread by fleas on rats. Bubonic plague had broken out before in Europe, Asia, and North Africa but had subsided. One strain, though, had survived in Mongolia. In the 1200s, Mongol armies conquered much of Asia, probably setting off the new epidemic, or outbreak of rapid-spreading disease.

In the premodern world, rats infested ships, towns, and even the homes of the rich and powerful, so no one took any notice of them. In the early 1300s, rats scurrying through crowded Chinese cities spread the plague, which killed about 35 million people there.

Fleas jumped from those rats to infest the clothes and packs of traders traveling west. As a result, the disease spread from Asia to the Middle East. Terrible reports reached Europe: "India was depopulated," wrote a chronicler. "Mesopotamia, Syria, and Armenia were covered with dead bodies." In Cairo, one of the world's largest cities, the plague at its peak killed about 7,000 people a day.

Social Upheaval In Europe, the plague brought terror and bewilderment, as people had no way to stop the disease. Some people turned to magic and witchcraft for cures. Others plunged into wild pleasures, believing they

Chapter 9 **225**

Bell Ringer Ask students to read the first paragraph under "Joan of Arc and French Victory" in this section. Then ask students to speculate on what might happen if a young woman came before a world leader today with such a message.

LESSON PLAN

1. Focus The late Middle Ages was a period of decline. The Black Death wreaked havoc throughout Europe. The Church suffered from poor leadership and accusations of corruption. England and France fought the Hundred Years' War, in which Joan of Arc emerged as a French national hero.

2. Instruct Ask students to imagine that they are living in Europe during the late Middle Ages. Have each student write an eyewitness report on one of the following: the Black Death, problems faced by the Church, the Hundred Years' War, or the trial of Joan of Arc. Collect students' reports and bind them into a scrapbook.

3. Assess Have students write four generalizations about life during the late Middle Ages.

4. Reteach If students' **Assess** activity does not reflect adequate understanding of the lesson, you might assign the *Guide to the Essentials* or the *Interactive Student Tutorial CD-ROM* for this section.

Block Scheduling Support

To review Chapter 9, have students play the following game. In large letters, label four bags with the four themes of the chapter (Political and Social Systems, Global Interaction, Art and Literature, Religions and Value Systems). Have each student write four questions—one for each of the four themes. Have students drop their questions in the appropriate bags. Then, label four pieces of cardboard with the chapter themes and place them in a separate bag labeled Categories.

Now, divide the class into two teams. Allow a student from Team 1 to pick a theme from the category bag. A student from Team 2 then picks a question from the bag marked with that theme and asks the question. A correct answer is worth five points. An incorrect answer results in a penalty of two points. Have teams take turns asking and answering questions. The first team to get 50 points wins. ✳

A First-Hand Account The following description of the effects of the Black Death was given by a resident of Siena, Italy:

"And so they died. And nobody could be found to bury the dead for money or for friendship. . . . And in many places in Siena huge pits were dug and piled deep with great heaps of the dead. . . . And I buried my five children with my own hands and many others did likewise. And there were many corpses about the city who were so sparsely covered with earth that dogs dragged them out and devoured their bodies."

Customize for . . .
Heterogeneous Groups

Writing a Headline Ask students to imagine that they are newspaper editors during the late Middle Ages. Have them write at least five headlines about the effects of the Black Death on Europe. You may wish to offer extra credit for articles based on the headlines. *(Reteaching)* ✳

would soon die anyway. Still others saw the plague as God's punishment. They beat themselves with whips to show that they repented their sins. Christians blamed Jews for the plague, charging that they had poisoned the wells. "The whole world," a French friar noted, "rose up against [the Jews] cruelly on this account." In the resulting hysteria, thousands of Jews were slaughtered.

Normal life broke down. The Italian poet Boccaccio described the social decay that he witnessed in Florence as people tried to avoid contracting the plague from neighbors and relatives:

> "In the horror thereof brother was forsaken by brother . . . and oftentimes husband by wife; nay, what is more, and scarcely to be believed, fathers and mothers were found to abandon their own children, untended, unvisited, to their fate, as if they had been strangers."
> —Boccaccio, *The Decameron*

Economic Effects As the plague kept recurring in the late 1300s, the European economy plunged to a low ebb. As workers and employers died, production declined. Survivors demanded higher wages. As the cost of labor soared, inflation, or rising prices, broke out too.

Landowners and merchants pushed for laws to limit wages. To stop rising costs, landowners converted croplands to sheep raising, which required less labor. Villagers forced off the land sought work in towns. There, guilds limited apprenticeships, refused to accept new members, and denied journeymen the chance to become masters.

Coupled with the fear of the plague, these restrictions sparked explosive revolts. Bitter, angry peasants rampaged in England, France, Germany, and elsewhere. In cities, too, artisans fought, usually without success, for more power. The plague had spread both death and social unrest. Western Europe would not fully recover from its effects for more than 100 years.

Upheaval in the Church

The late Middle Ages brought spiritual crisis, scandal, and division to the Roman Catholic Church. Many priests and monks died during the plague. Their replacements faced challenging questions. "Why did God spare some and kill others?" asked survivors.

Divisions Within the Catholic Church The Church was unable to provide the strong leadership needed in this desperate time. In 1309, Pope Clement V had moved the papal court to Avignon on the border of southern France. There it remained for about 70 years under French domination. This period is often called the Babylonian Captivity of the Church, referring to the time when the ancient Israelites were held captive in Babylon.

In Avignon, popes reigned over a lavish court. Critics lashed out against the worldly, pleasure-loving papacy, and anticlergy sentiment grew. Within the Church itself, reformers tried to end the "captivity."

In 1378, reformers elected their own pope to rule from Rome. French cardinals responded by choosing a rival pope. For decades, there was a schism, or split, in the Church as two and sometimes even three popes claimed to be the true "vicar of Christ." Not until 1417 did a Church council at Constance finally end the crisis.

New Heresies With its moral authority weakened, the Church faced still more problems. Popular preachers challenged its power. In England, John Wycliffe, an Oxford professor, attacked Church corruption.

Wycliffe insisted that the Bible, not the Church, was the source of all Christian truth. His followers began translating the Bible into English so

Resource Directory

Teaching Resources
Disaster! Chapter Extension Activities booklet, p. 26

Disaster!

The Black Death Strikes

Between 1347 and 1353, the Black Death, or bubonic plague, killed one person out of every three in Europe. In this short time, over 25 million people died.

The Black Death struck with stunning speed. Within hours, victims developed egg-sized lumps under their arms. Then, horrible black spots appeared on their skin. Once they started spitting blood, death was certain. The sickness seemed all the more terrifying because it could strike anyone. The image above shows Death dancing (left to right) with a woman, a noble, a priest, a peasant, and a monk.

Unsanitary conditions spread disease. During the Middle Ages, people threw garbage and human waste into the streets.

"Bring out your dead!" This gruesome call sounded through deserted streets. The death toll was so high that gravediggers used carts to collect corpses. Piles of bodies were buried in vast pits.

Flea-covered rats thrived in the filthy streets. One bite from an infected flea could bring an agonizing death.

Spread of the Black Death

ATLANTIC OCEAN

DENMARK
ENGLAND
HOLY ROMAN EMPIRE
POLAND
LITHUANIA
RUSSIA
FRANCE
HUNGARY
PORTUGAL
SPAIN
ITALY
Black Sea
OTTOMAN EMPIRE
Mediterranean Sea

0   500 Miles
0   500 Kilometers

Extent of plague in:
☐ 1347   ☐ 1353

By 1347, the bubonic plague had arrived in Europe. Spreading outward in waves of terror, it soon ravaged most of the continent.

Portfolio Assessment

 Use the Internet or other research sources to learn about a recent epidemic. Create a chart tracing the spread of the disease. Describe how people are trying to prevent or cure this modern plague.

Test Preparation

Have students read the paragraph headed "Divisions Within the Catholic Church" on the opposite page, and then answer the question below.

To what does the term *Babylonian Captivity* refer?

A the time when the popes were held at Babylon

B the time when the popes were held in prison

C the time when the Hebrews were held in southern France

Ⓓ the time when the popes were under French control in southern France

---

Bell Ringer Ask students to study the map and pictures on this page and then describe the probable effects of the Black Death on medieval society. Ask students if they think huge epidemics are still possible.

Background
Connections to Today

Modern Epidemics Although relatively rare in the developed world, epidemics are still common in Third World countries. A recent outbreak of cholera occurred in Peru in 1991. Another killer is Ebola hemorrhagic fever, which has caused epidemics in various African countries. AIDS, probably the best known modern epidemic disease, is found in both developed and developing countries. It is devastating populations in Africa.

Activity
Cooperative Learning

Presenting an Informational Poster Divide the class into groups of five students. Have groups prepare and present an informational poster about the spread of the bubonic plague that includes a graphic representation such as a chart or map, illustrations, and some text. Two students should conduct the research, and two more should create the graphic and textual material using this research. A fifth student should be responsible for assembling the pieces and laying out the poster and presenting it to the class.

Portfolio Assessment Rubrics

Share rubrics with students before they create their charts.

Attempted The project is attempted, but either the chart or the description is missing.

Minimal The chart and description reveal little understanding of the topic.

Adequate The chart and description reveal an understanding of the topic.

Exemplary The chart and description reveal a thorough understanding of the topic.

Cooperative Learning

Writing a Skit As an enrichment activity, have students work in small groups to write a skit reenacting the trial of Jan Hus. Suggest that groups make a list of the tasks needed to complete the assignment. For example, some students may do research, others can write the script, and others can prepare props. Students should decide what roles will be played and who will play them. When groups are prepared, have them perform their skits for the class.

Turning Points of the Hundred Years' War

Longbow

During the early years of the war, English armies equipped with the longbow overpowered their French counterparts equipped with the crossbow. An English archer could shoot three arrows in the time it took a French archer to shoot one.

Joan of Arc

From 1429 to 1431, Joan's successes in battle rallied the French forces to victory. French armies continued to win even after she was executed by the English.

Cannon

The cannon helped the French to capture English-held castles and defeat England's armies. French cannons were instrumental in defeating English forces in Normandy.

Connections to Today

England, which is now part of the United Kingdom, and France have friendly relations today. Their economies are closely linked in that both nations are members of the European Union. The two cooperate militarily as members of the North Atlantic Treaty Organization.

Skills Assessment **Chart** Changes in leadership and new technology marked some of the major turning points in the Hundred Years' War. **How did technology benefit the English in the early years of the war?**

---

that people could read it themselves rather than rely on the clergy to read it. Czech students at Oxford carried Wycliffe's ideas to Bohemia—what is today the Czech Republic. There, Jan Hus led the call for reforms.

The Church responded by persecuting Wycliffe and his followers and suppressing the Hussites. Hus was tried for preaching heresy—ideas contrary to Church teachings. Found guilty, he was burned at the stake in 1415. The ideas of Wycliffe and Hus survived, however. A century later, other reformers took up the same demands.

The Hundred Years' War

On top of the disasters of famine, plague, and economic decline came a long, destructive war. Between 1337 and 1453, England and France fought a series of conflicts, known as the Hundred Years' War.

Causes As you have read, English rulers had battled for centuries to hold onto the French lands of their Norman ancestors. French kings, for their part, were intent on extending their own power in France. When Edward III of England claimed the French crown in 1337, war erupted anew between these rival powers. Once fighting started, economic rivalry and a growing sense of national pride made it hard for either side to give up the struggle.

English Victories At first, the English won a string of victories—at Crécy in 1346, Poitiers 10 years later, and Agincourt in 1415. They owed much of their success to the longbow wielded by English archers. This powerful new weapon was six feet long and took years to master. But it could discharge three arrows in the time a French archer with his crossbow fired just one, and its arrows pierced all but the heaviest armor.

The English victories took a heavy toll on French morale. England, it seemed, was likely to bring all of France under its control. Then, in what seemed to the French a miracle, their fortunes were reversed.

Joan of Arc and French Victory In 1429, a 17-year-old peasant woman, Joan of Arc, appeared at the court of Charles VII, the uncrowned king of France. She told Charles that God had sent her to save France. She persuaded the desperate French king to let her lead his army against the English.

To Charles's amazement, Joan inspired the battered and despairing French troops to fight anew. In an astonishing year of campaigning, she led the French to several victories and planted the seeds for future triumphs.

Joan paid for success with her life. She was taken captive by allies of the English and turned over to her enemies for trial. The English wanted to discredit her, and they had her tried for witchcraft. She was convicted and burned at the stake. Much later, however, the Church declared her a saint.

The execution of Joan rallied the French, who saw her as a martyr. After Joan's death, the French took the offensive. With a powerful new weapon, the cannon, they

---

Skills Assessment

ANSWER The English longbow was superior to the crossbows used by the French. This advantage helped the English win battles.

Resource Directory

Teaching Resources
Section Quiz Unit 3 booklet, p. 29
Geography Quiz Unit 3 booklet, p. 34
Chapter Test Forms A, B, and C Unit 3 booklet, pp. 35–39
Answer Key Unit 3 booklet, pp. 114–128

Technology
Interactive Student Tutorial CD-ROM Ch. 9
Computer Test Bank Ch. 9

attacked English-held castles. By 1453, the English held only the port of Calais in northwestern France.

Effects The Hundred Years' War set France and England on different paths. The war created a growing sense of national feeling in France and allowed French kings to expand their power. During the war, English rulers turned repeatedly to Parliament for funds, which helped that body win the "power of the purse." The loss of French lands shattered English dreams of a continental empire, but English rulers soon began looking at new trading ventures overseas.

The Hundred Years' War brought many changes to the late medieval world. The longbow and cannon gave common soldiers a new importance on the battlefield and undermined the value of armored knights. Castles and knights were doomed to disappear because their defenses could not stand up to the more deadly firepower. Feudal society was changing. Monarchs needed large armies, not feudal vassals, to fight their wars.

Looking Ahead

In the 1400s, as Europe recovered from the Black Death, other changes occurred. The population expanded and manufacturing grew. These changes, in turn, led to increased trade. Italian cities flourished as centers of shipping. They sent European cloth to the Middle East in exchange for spices, sugar, and cotton. Europeans developed new technologies. German miners, for example, used water power to crush ore and built blast furnaces to make cast iron.

The recovery of the late Middle Ages set the stage for further changes during the Renaissance, Reformation, and Age of Exploration. As Europe grew stronger over the next few centuries, it would take a more prominent role on the global stage.

Hundred Years' War, 1337–1453

Map shows England, France, and surrounding regions with battle sites including London, Calais, Agincourt, Crécy, Flanders, Normandy, Rouen, Reims, Paris, Brittany, Patay, Orléans, Chinon, Poitiers, Bordeaux, Avignon, Burgundy, Holy Roman Empire, Atlantic Ocean, English Channel, North Sea, Bay of Biscay, Mediterranean Sea. Joan of Arc's death, 1431.

Azimuthal Equal Area Projection
0   200   400 Miles
0   200   400 Kilometers

- France, 1337
- Held by England, 1337
- Held by England, 1429
- ★ Battle sites
- → Route of Joan of Arc
- Boundary of France, 1453

Skills Assessment

Geography The English and French fought for control of France in the Hundred Years' War.

1. **Location** On the map, locate (a) Normandy, (b) Poitiers, (c) Calais.
2. **Place** What city in northern France was still under English control in 1453?
3. **Critical Thinking Analyzing Information** What regions of France did England gain between 1337 and 1429?

SECTION 5 Assessment

Recall
1. **Identify:** (a) Black Death, (b) Babylonian Captivity, (c) John Wycliffe, (d) Jan Hus, (e) Hundred Years' War, (f) Joan of Arc.
2. **Define:** (a) epidemic, (b) inflation, (c) longbow.

Comprehension
3. What were three effects of the bubonic plague on late medieval Europe?
4. (a) Why did reformers criticize the Church? (b) How did the Church respond to this criticism?
5. (a) How did new technologies affect fighting during the Hundred Years' War? (b) What were the results of the war?

Critical Thinking and Writing
6. **Understanding Sequence** Make a step-by-step list showing how the bubonic plague spread from Asia to Europe and resulted in the deaths of millions of Europeans.
7. **Comparing** Compare the effects of the Hundred Years' War on France and on England.

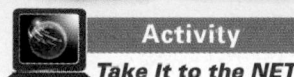

Activity
Take It to the NET

Use the Internet to research the Black Death in Europe, especially its effects on population and the economy. Then, use the information you have found to create graphs showing the decline of Europe's population and economy during the plague years. You might download pictures from the Net to illustrate your graphs.

Human Drama Activity

Analyzing Historical Films A number of movies on Joan of Arc have been made, including one released in 1999. If time permits, have students view a videotape of one of these movies. Then, discuss how true to life they think the movie potrayal is. Is the movie too sensational? Too sentimental? Does the movie depict the time period accurately? Is the war shown accurately, or is it glamorized?

SECTION 5 Assessment

Recall
1. (a) Black Death, p. 225 (b) Babylonian Captivity, p. 226 (c) John Wycliffe, p. 226 (d) Jan Hus, p. 228 (e) Hundred Years' War, p. 228 (f) Joan of Arc, p. 228
2. (a) epidemic, p. 225 (b) inflation, p. 226 (c) longbow, p. 228

Comprehension
3. Answers should include three of the following: a decrease in population, severe economic decline, inflation, social upheaval, explosive revolts, violence against Jews. 4. (a) Reformers believed the Church had become too powerful and corrupt. They lashed out against the worldly, pleasure-loving papacy. (b) The Church persecuted its critics. 5. (a) The longbow helped the English win many victories. The French used cannons to attack castles held by the English. (b) French kings expanded their power, and England sought new ventures overseas. Feudal society began changing as monarchs sought large armies, not feudal vassals.

Critical Thinking and Writing
6. The plague, which was spread by fleas carried by rats, killed millions in Chinese cities. The fleas jumped from the rats to the clothing and packs of traders traveling west, spreading the plague through India, Mesopotamia, Syria, Egypt, and Europe. Flea-infested rats on ships helped spread the disease as well. 7. In France, nationalism and royal power increased. In England, the power of Parliament increased and there was new interest in overseas trade.

Activity Rubrics

Share rubrics with students before they make their graphs.

Attempted The graphs are attempted but are incorrectly plotted or labeled, or only one graph was completed.

Minimal The graphs are correctly plotted and labeled, but no pictures are included.

Adequate The graphs are correctly plotted and labeled, and pictures are included.

Exemplary The graphs are correctly plotted and labeled, pictures are included, and the graphs are visually very well done.

Skills Assessment

ANSWERS 1. Review locations with students. 2. Calais 3. Brittany, Normandy, Flanders, and Burgundy

Creating a Chapter Summary

As a reteaching opportunity, pair a more able student with a less able student to complete this chapter summary.

The High Middle Ages

Students' charts should include the following developments: **Political** Monarchs expanded royal power; English common law, jury system developed; King John signed Magna Carta; representative bodies in France acquired a larger role; German emperors failed to control nobles; Holy Roman emperors and popes clashed; Ferdinand and Isabella expelled Muslims, unified Spain; England and France fought the Hundred Years' War. **Economic** Crusades increased trade; plague caused economic collapse and inflation. **Cultural** New learning in Europe; new writings in the vernacular; architects built Gothic cathedrals. **Religious** Holy Roman emperors battled the Church for power; Christians went on the Crusades; Inquisition targeted Jews and Muslims; Babylonian Captivity; reformers challenged the Church.

Building Vocabulary

1–10. Students' sentences should show an understanding of the words.

Recalling Key Facts

11. Possible answers: They began efficient tax collection and issued royal laws.
12. They wanted the power to appoint Church officials and to control Italy.
13. **(a)** to expel the Muslims from the Holy Land **(b)** The Crusades failed to permanently conquer the Holy Land. They did, however, cause economic expansion and a wider world view for Europeans.
14. **(a)** Isabella ended Spain's policy of religious toleration. The Inquisition launched a brutal crusade against Muslims and Jews. Those who refused to convert to Christianity were burned at the stake. **(b)** Isabella achieved religious unity for Spain. However, more than 15,000 people— many who were skilled—fled Spain.
15. Much of the new knowledge was contained in the works of Aristotle and other ancient Greek philosophers, and in scientific works such as those of Hippocrates, Euclid, and Arab scientists. The Hindu-Arabic numerical system also reached Europe.

Creating a Chapter Summary

On a separate sheet of paper, copy and complete the following chart showing the major political, economic, cultural, and religious developments of the High Middle Ages.

POLITICAL	ECONOMIC	CULTURAL	RELIGIOUS
Monarchs expanded royal power.	Crusades spurred growth of a money economy.	Universities were established.	Church reached height of its power.

Web Site Self-Test
For practice test questions for Chapter 9, see **www.phschool.com**.

iTEXT
For additional review and enrichment activities, see the interactive version of *World History* available on the Web and on CD-ROM.

Building Vocabulary

Review the meaning of the chapter vocabulary words listed below. Then, write a sentence for each word, describing its significance in medieval Europe.

1. common law
2. jury
3. lay investiture
4. crusade
5. schism
6. scholasticism
7. vernacular
8. epidemic
9. inflation
10. longbow

Recalling Key Facts

11. List two ways English and French monarchs increased royal power.
12. Why did Holy Roman emperors come into conflict with the Church?
13. **(a)** What was the goal of the Crusades? **(b)** Did they achieve their goal? Explain.
14. **(a)** What steps did Isabella take to bring religious unity to Spain? **(b)** What were the results of her policy?
15. What new knowledge reached Europe in the High Middle Ages?
16. **(a)** What steps did reformers take to end the Babylonian Captivity of the Church? **(b)** What were the results?

Critical Thinking and Writing

17. **Analyzing Information (a)** List four goals of medieval monarchs. **(b)** Explain how one ruler furthered these goals.
18. **Defending a Position** Review the conflict between Gregory VII and Henry IV. Cite two arguments each man might have given to defend his position.
19. **Ranking** List four effects of the Crusades. Then, rank them in order of their importance. Give reasons for your ranking.
20. **Connecting to Geography** Review the map titled "Trade in Medieval Europe" in the last chapter and the map titled "Spread of the Black Death" in this chapter. How might trade routes and the spread of the disease be linked?
21. **Making Inferences** How might the rise of medieval literature written in the vernacular reflect a change in education and literacy rates?
22. **Recognizing Causes and Effects (a)** How did the creation of the Magna Carta affect government in England? **(b)** How do you think the lack of a similar document in France affected the development of government there?

---

16. **(a)** In 1378, reformers elected their own pope to rule from Rome. French cardinals responded by choosing a rival pope. **(b)** For decades there was a schism in the Church, with rival popes claiming to be the true head of the Church.

Critical Thinking and Writing

17. **(a)** centralized power, expanded lands, a system of royal justice, an efficient royal bureaucracy, an efficient taxation system, and a strong army **(b)** Possible answer: William the Conqueror used

the *Domesday Book* to create efficient taxation.
18. Possible answer: The conflict was over lay investiture. Pope Gregory VII might have argued that papal authority came from God; the Church was not subject to secular rulers; and only the pope could invest bishops. Henry IV might have argued that bishops held lands as royal fiefs; that the emperor was the overlord of bishops; and that therefore he could invest them.
19. Students' answers should include four of the following: increased level of trade, growth of a money economy, increased power and prestige

Roger of Wendover, an English monk, describes how King John came to sign the Magna Carta. Read the excerpt and answer the questions that follow.

> "In Easter week of [1215], the . . . nobles assembled . . . with horses and arms; for they had now induced almost all the nobility of the whole kingdom to join them . . . and when the king learned this, he sent . . . to them to inquire [what] they demanded. The barons then delivered to the messengers a paper, containing in great measure the laws and ancient customs of the kingdom, and declared that, unless the king immediately granted them . . . they would, by taking possession of his fortresses, force him to give them sufficient satisfaction. . . .
>
> King John, when he saw that he was deserted by almost all, . . . deceitfully pretended to make peace with the aforesaid barons, and . . . told them that . . . he would willingly grant them the laws and liberties they required."

—Roger of Wendover, quoted in *Source Book of English History* (Kendall)

23. **(a)** What demands did the nobles make? **(b)** What did they threaten to do if King John did not agree?
24. Do you think Roger of Wendover expected King John to keep his word and honor the Magna Carta? Explain.
25. What was contained in the Magna Carta?
26. What does this excerpt suggest about English royal power in 1215? Explain.

Use the Internet to research medieval Gothic cathedrals. Based on information that you find on the Internet, draw a simple diagram of part of a cathedral. With your diagram, include a description of the technology used to build that section of the cathedral, or an explanation of that section's significance to medieval architects, clergy, and citizens.

Royal Lands in France, 987–1328

Legend:
- French royal lands, 987
- Added to French royal lands by 1180
- Added to French royal lands by 1328
- Held by French nobles, 1328
- English holdings in France, 1328
- → Route of royal attack on Albigensians

Azimuthal Equal Area Projection
0   125   250 Miles
0   125   250 Kilometers

The map above shows the growth of royal lands over a period of several hundred years. Use the map to answer the following questions:

27. Describe the extent of French royal lands in 987.
28. **(a)** Between what years did Anjou become part of French royal lands? **(b)** Between what years did royal lands increase the most?
29. **(a)** Describe the route used by Philip Augustus's army to attack the Albigensians. **(b)** About how many miles did the army travel?
30. In 1328, who controlled **(a)** Normandy? **(b)** Brittany? **(c)** Bordeaux?

Skills Tip

To understand a map, compare the information on the map with what you have read in your textbook.

for feudal monarchs, increased papal power, increased Byzantine resentment against the West, an expanded world view for Europeans. Students' rankings should reflect an understanding of the events' long-range effects.

20. The spread of the plague closely paralleled the major trade routes of the time.
21. Previously, all writing was in Latin, which was understood by very few people, primarily those connected with the Church. With works in the vernacular, literature was accessible to ordinary people.
22. **(a)** It led to the development of Parliament. **(b)** The Estates General never really had the power to act as a balance to royal power.

Analyzing Primary Sources

23. **(a)** that he grant them the rights covered by the laws and ancient customs of the kingdom **(b)** They threatened to take his lands.
24. No, he says that the king "deceitfully pretended to make peace."
25. most of the laws and ancient customs of the kingdom
26. Possible answer: It suggests that the king's power was not absolute and that he needed the support of the nobles in order to govern.

Analyzing Maps

27. a small area around the city of Paris
28. **(a)** between 1180 and 1328 **(b)** between 1180 and 1328
29. **(a)** From Dijon near the eastern border, the knights traveled south and then west to Beziers. **(b)** about 325 miles
30. **(a)** the French monarch **(b)** French nobles **(c)** England

Skills Tip

Tell students to note that on the map, regions and cities are labeled in different styles of type. Knowing this common convention of mapmaking helps you decipher a map. The Skills Handbook in the front of the book has a lesson that will help students with this feature.

Direct students to **www.phschool.com** for links to sites that will help them get started on this assignment. Share rubrics with students.

Attempted The project is attempted but incomplete, missing either the diagram or the description or explanation.

Minimal The project includes the diagram and a very brief or unclear description or explanation.

Adequate The project includes the diagram and a description or explanation that is clear and informative.

Exemplary The project includes the diagram and a thoughtful and thorough description or explanation.

Unit Theme Activity

Remind students to continue working on their Unit Theme Activity. See rubrics for the activity on the unit opener page in the Teacher's Edition.

Chapter 10 Planning Guide

Resource Manager

	CORE INSTRUCTION	READING/SKILLS
Chapter Level Resources	📓 **Teaching Resources** 📘 **Pacing Charts**, Ch. 10 📘 **Teaching With Themes**, p. 13 🎞 **Color Transparencies**, p. F–21 💿 **Resource Pro®** Ch. 10 💻 **www.phschool.com** • eTeach	💿 **Book on CD**, Ch. 10 💿 **Interactive Student Tutorial CD-ROM**, Ch. 10 💿 **Social Studies Skills Tutor CD-ROM** 🎞 **Skills Transparencies**
1 The Byzantine Empire 1. Summarize how Justinian extended Byzantine power. 2. Outline the key elements of Byzantine Christianity. 3. Explain why the Byzantine empire collapsed. 4. Describe the Byzantine heritage.	📓 **Teaching Resources** 📁 **Unit 3 booklet** • Biography Activity, p. 46 📘 **Creative Teaching Activities**, p. 46 💿 **Prentice Hall Presentation Pro**, Ch. 10, Section 1 🎞 **Section Reading Support Transparencies**	📓 **Teaching Resources** 📁 **Unit 3 booklet** • Guided Reading and Review, p. 40 📘 **Guide to the Essentials** 📼 **Guided Reading Audiotapes**, Ch. 10, Section 1
2 The Rise of Russia 1. Identify how geography helped shape early Russia and the growth of Kiev. 2. Describe how the Mongol conquest affected Russia. 3. Explain why Moscow emerged as the chief power in Russia.	📓 **Teaching Resources** 📁 **Unit 3 booklet** • Primary Source Activity, p. 47 • Viewpoint Activity, p. 48 📘 **Creative Teaching Activities**, p. 47 💿 **Prentice Hall Presentation Pro**, Ch. 10, Section 2 🎞 **Section Reading Support Transparencies**	📓 **Teaching Resources** 📁 **Unit 3 booklet** • Guided Reading and Review, p. 42 • Skill Application Activity, p. 49 📘 **Guide to the Essentials** 📼 **Guided Reading Audiotapes**, Ch. 10, Section 2
3 Shaping Eastern Europe 1. Identify how geography influenced developments in Eastern Europe. 2. Explain why Eastern Europe became a cultural crossroads with a diverse mix of people. 3. Describe the threats that the early kingdoms of Eastern Europe faced.	📓 **Teaching Resources** 📘 **Creative Teaching Activities**, p. 48 💿 **Prentice Hall Presentation Pro**, Ch. 10, Section 3 🎞 **Section Reading Support Transparencies**	📓 **Teaching Resources** 📁 **Unit 3 booklet** • Guided Reading and Review, p. 44 📘 **Guide to the Essentials** 📼 **Guided Reading Audiotapes**, Ch. 10, Section 3

ENRICHMENT/PRE-AP

www.phschool.com
- Why Study History?

Teaching Resources
Chapter Extension Activities, p. 27
History Through Literature, pp. 23–24
www.phschool.com
- Internet Activities, *The Church of Hagia Sophia*
- Virtual Field Trip
- Internet Activities, Section 1

Color Transparencies, p. E–29

Teaching Resources
Chapter Extension Activities, p. 28
www.phschool.com
- Internet Activities, Section 3

ASSESSMENT

PRENTICE HALL ASSESSMENT SYSTEM

Core Assessment
ExamView Test Bank booklet, Ch. 10
ExamView Test Bank CD-ROM, Ch. 10

Standardized Test Preparation
Diagnose and Prescribe
Diagnostic Tests for High School Social Studies Skills
Review and Reteach
Review Book for World History
Practice and Assess
Test-Taking Strategies With Transparencies for High School
Alternative Assessment booklet
Test Prep Book for World History

Teaching Resources
Unit 3 booklet
- Geography Quiz, p. 50
- Section Quizzes, pp. 41, 43, 45
- Chapter Tests A, B, and C, pp. 51–55
www.phschool.com
- Self-Test

CUSTOMIZE FOR INDIVIDUAL NEEDS

Gifted and Talented
- **Teacher's Edition,** Activities: Connections to Literature, p. 236

Less Proficient Readers
- **Guide to the Essentials,** Ch. 10
- **Guided Reading Audiotapes, English,** Ch. 10
- **Book on CD,** Ch. 10
- **Teacher's Edition,** Activities: Connections to Film, p. 237

Less Proficient Writers
- **Teacher's Edition,** Activities: Cooperative Learning Activity, p. 235

Students Acquiring English/ESL
- **Guide to the Essentials, English/Spanish,** Ch. 10
- **Guided Reading Audiotapes, English/Spanish,** Ch. 10
- **Book on CD,** Ch. 10
- **Teacher's Edition,** Activities marked with an *: Connections to Film, p. 237

TEXT

Don't miss the exclusive interactive version of *World History: Connections to Today* on the Internet and CD-ROM.

INTRODUCTION

After Rome fell, the Byzantine empire preserved the Greco-Roman heritage and spread Byzantine culture and Orthodox Christianity to Russia and Eastern Europe. In Russia, Czars Ivan III and Ivan IV expanded the Russian empire and established a tradition of autocratic rule. The geography of Eastern Europe made it a cultural crossroads. Many invasions and migrations contributed to the diversity and political turmoil of the region.

Focusing on Themes

Suggest that students focus on these theme questions as they read:

Continuity and Change
How did the Byzantine empire preserve the political and cultural heritage of Rome?

Religions and Value Systems
Why did a new form of Christianity emerge in the Byzantine empire and Russia?

Political and Social Systems
How did the rulers of Moscow build a powerful centralized Russian state?

Diversity
What peoples and cultural traditions shaped the Slavic kingdoms of Eastern Europe?

◆ TIME LINE ACTIVITY

Share the About the Pictures note with your students before you ask these questions about the time line:

1. When did Constantinople become the capital of the eastern Roman empire? *(330)*
2. Which pope crowned Charlemagne Emperor of the Romans? *(Pope Leo III)*
3. What structure was built to show Kiev's ties to the Byzantine empire? *(Kiev's Cathedral of St. Sophia)*
4. What symbol did Ivan the Great use to show his connections to the Byzantine empire? *(the double-headed eagle)*

Don't Miss!

Humanities Link
The Church of Hagia Sophia (Section 1)

Synthesizing Information
Jewish Migrations in Europe (Section 3)

The Byzantine Empire and Russia 330–1613

Chapter Preview

1 The Byzantine Empire
2 The Rise of Russia
3 Shaping Eastern Europe

527
Justinian (above) begins his rule of the Byzantine empire.

330
Constantinople becomes capital of the eastern Roman empire.

1019
The reign of Yaroslav the Wise begins in Kiev. Soon, the golden-domed Cathedral of St. Sophia (above) is built to show Kiev's ties to the Byzantine empire.

CHAPTER EVENTS

300

600

900

GLOBAL EVENTS

622 Muhammad makes a journey, known as the hijra, from Mecca to Yathrib.

800 Pope Leo III crowns Charlemagne emperor of the Romans.

232 *Chapter 10*

◖ Resource Directory ◗

Teaching Resources
Teaching With Themes Chapter Theme Activities, p. 13
Pacing Chart With Block Scheduling Guide Ch. 10
Technology
World History Color Transparencies Ch. 10 Graphic Organizer, p. F–21

Major Religions About 1300

Several religious traditions—including Roman Catholic Christianity, Orthodox Christianity, and Islam—reflect the diversity of Eastern Europe and interaction with its neighbors.

ATLANTIC OCEAN

North Sea

Moscow

Warsaw

Kiev

Rome

Black Sea
Constantinople

Caspian Sea

Mediterranean Sea

Azimuthal Equal Area Projection

0   500   1000 Miles

0   500   1000 Kilometers

1386

Duke Wladyslav Jagiello of Lithuania marries Queen Jadwiga of Poland, making Poland-Lithuania the largest state in Europe.

1462

Ivan the Great begins his reign in Russia. He uses the double-headed eagle, shown above, to show his connections to the Byzantine empire.

1613

The Romanov dynasty begins its 304-year reign in Russia.

1200   **1500**   **1800**

1076 Pope Gregory VII excommunicates Henry IV, the Holy Roman emperor.

1324 Mansa Musa, ruler of Mali, makes a pilgrimage to Mecca.

1556 Akbar becomes ruler of the Mughal empire in India.

Chapter 10 **233**

Independent Assignments

Have students read one section as they prepare for class. After class, have them complete the assignment. Some students may benefit from using the Guided Reading and Review worksheets.

Section 1 Have students use the worksheet *Anna Comnena* in the Unit 3 booklet, p. 46, to learn more about one of the first woman historians in western civilization. Then have students use the worksheet *The Alexiad* in the History Through Literature booklet, pp. 23–24, to read an excerpt from Anna Comnena's writing.

Section 2 Have students use the worksheet *Prince Vladimir's Testament to His Sons* in the Unit 3 booklet, p. 47, to read an excerpt of the early Russian work *The Primary Chronicle.* In this excerpt, Prince Vladimir gives advice to his sons.

Section 3 Have students use the Synthesizing Information worksheet in the Chapter Extension Activities booklet, p. 28.

Major Religions About 1300

Activating Prior Knowledge

What happened to the western Roman empire during this period? *(Rome declined, and power shifted to Germanic rulers under feudalism. The Christian Church became the core of European culture, incorporating many Roman traditions.)*

Previewing

Ask students to speculate how geography could have helped Constantinople develop into a crossroads for world trade. *(Possible answer: The city is on a narrow waterway that controls access to the Black Sea and the Mediterranean Sea; hence, the city was a geographically favorable meeting place for trade routes to converge from all directions.)*

Background
About the Pictures

1.   2.   3. 4.   5.

1. Justinian, Emperor of the Byzantine Empire (527–565), is best known for codifying Roman laws, which greatly influenced Western laws in use today.

2. Cathedral of St. Sophia, Kiev, was built in 1036 to complement the grandeur of Hagia Sophia in Constantinople.

3. Wladyslav II Jagiello, Grand Duke of Lithuania from 1377. At the time of the Duke's marriage to Jadwiga of Poland in 1386, the combined state was one of the largest kingdoms in medieval Europe.

4. Jadwiga, Queen of Poland from 1384. Her union with Wladyslav II Jagiello combined Poland and Lithuania into a large and powerful kingdom ruled by the same dynasty for more than 200 years.

5. Ivan III (the Great), Grand Duke of Moscow, reigned from 1462–1505 and unified most of Russia. To establish a connection to the Byzantine Empire he married its heir, Sophia-Zöe Paleologus.

eTeach

Be sure to check out this month's online discussion with a World History Master Teacher.

Go to **www.phschool.com**.

Bell Ringer Have students scan the boldface headings in this section, and ask them to speculate on possible reasons for the rise and fall of the Byzantine empire. Encourage students to share their speculations with the class.

LESSON PLAN

1. Focus The emperor Justinian expanded the Byzantine empire, built magnificent buildings, and established a code of laws. A strong central government and a prosperous economy enabled the empire to survive for more than 1,000 years. Byzantine civilization, based on Roman and Hellenistic achievements, influenced and enriched later civilizations.

2. Instruct As they read this section, have students find evidence to support these generalizations: (1) Justinian was an autocrat. (2) Women could attain positions of power in the Byzantine empire. (3) Religious differences divided Byzantine Christians from Roman Catholics. (4) The Byzantine empire preserved the achievements of earlier civilizations and influenced later civilizations. Have students share their findings in a class discussion on each of the four generalizations.

3. Assess Ask students to imagine that they are writing a 10-chapter history book about the Byzantine empire. Ask them to write 10 chapter titles that would cover the history of the empire.

4. Reteach If students' *Assess* activity does not reflect adequate understanding of the lesson, you might assign the *Guide to the Essentials* or the *Interactive Student Tutorial CD-ROM* for this section.

Reading Focus

- How did Justinian extend Byzantine power?
- What were the key elements of Byzantine Christianity?
- Why did the Byzantine empire collapse?
- What was the heritage of the Byzantine empire?

Vocabulary

autocrat
patriarch
icon

Taking Notes

As you read this section, create an outline of the main ideas. Use Roman numerals to indicate the major headings of the section, capital letters for the subheadings, and numbers for the supporting details. The sample at right will help you get started.

I. The growth of Byzantine power
  A. Constantinople
    1.
    2.
    3.
  B. A blending of cultures
II. The age of Justinian

Main Idea The emperor Justinian expanded the Byzantine empire, erected grand buildings, and established a code of laws.

Setting the Scene The bazaars of Constantinople awed visitors. Benjamin of Tudela, a Jewish traveler from Spain, saw merchants there from the Middle East, Egypt, and Eastern Europe. "The city's daily income," he noted, "what with rent from shops and markets and taxes levied on merchants coming by sea and by land, reaches 20,000 gold pieces." As the cities of the western Roman empire crumbled, Constantinople prospered. With its high walls and golden domes, it stood as the proud capital of the Byzantine empire.

The Growth of Byzantine Power

You will recall that, as German invaders pounded the Roman empire in the west, emperors shifted their base to the eastern Mediterranean. The emperor Constantine rebuilt the Greek city of Byzantium and gave it the name Constantinople. In 330, he made Constantinople the new capital of the empire. From this "New Rome," roads fanned out to the Balkans, to the Middle East, and to North Africa. In time, the eastern Roman empire became known as the Byzantine empire.

Constantinople The vital center of the empire was Constantinople. The city was located on the shores of the Bosporus, a strait that linked the Mediterranean and Black seas. Constantinople had an excellent harbor and was guarded on three sides by water. Later emperors built an elaborate system of land and sea walls to bolster its defenses. Equally important, Constantinople commanded key trade routes linking Europe and Asia. For centuries, the city's favorable location made it Europe's busiest marketplace. There, merchants sold silks from China, wheat from Egypt, gems from India, spices from Southeast Asia, and furs from Viking lands in the north.

At the center of the city, Byzantine emperors and empresses lived in glittering splendor. Dressed in luxurious silk, they attended chariot races at the Hippodrome, an arena built in the 200s. Crowds cheered wildly as rival charioteers careened their vehicles around and around. The spectacle was another reminder of the city's glorious Roman heritage.

A Blending of Cultures After rising to spectacular heights, the Byzantine empire eventually declined to a small area around Constantinople itself. Yet it was still in existence nearly 1,000 years after the fall of the western Roman empire. As the heir to Rome, it promoted a brilliant civilization that blended ancient Greek, Roman, and Christian influences with other traditions of the Mediterranean world.

Global Connections

The Quest for Silk

It is nearly impossible for us today to imagine how rare and costly silk was in the Byzantine empire. Wars made the supply unreliable. Persia, which controlled the silk trade with China, levied high taxes that made silk outrageously expensive.

The Byzantine emperor Justinian wanted a reliable supply of silk at a reasonable price. He tried to set up other trade routes, but with little success. In the end, smugglers changed the picture. According to one legend, monks sneaked silkworm eggs out of China in their walking sticks. Although the details are unclear, the results are not. By the 700s, state-owned silk factories in the Byzantine empire fed a growing and profitable silk industry.

Theme: Economics and Technology Why did the Persians want to keep control over the silk trade with China?

Global Connections

ANSWER If Persia kept control of the trade route, they could levy high taxes on all silk passing through, thus benefiting from the silk trade.

Resource Directory

Teaching Resources
Creative Teaching Activities Creative Teaching Activities booklet, p. 46
Guided Reading and Review Unit 3 booklet, p. 40
Humanities Link Chapter Extension Activities booklet, p. 27

The Church of Hagia Sophia

The Church of Hagia Sophia survives as an important legacy of the Byzantine empire. During a revolt in 532, the original Hagia Sophia was destroyed. Emperor Justinian quickly began the task of rebuilding the church as Constantinople's brightest jewel. He divided 10,000 workers into two crews and had them compete to finish opposite sides of the church.

Sunlight filters through the windows and highlights the interior of the Hagia Sophia. In its early days, gold glittered from the ceiling, and marble gleamed from the walls.

Inside the church, dazzling mosaics adorn the walls. This mosaic shows Christ Pantocrator, center, flanked by Emperor Constantine IX Monamachus and the Empress Zoë.

Completed in less than six years, Justinian's Church of Hagia Sophia stood as the largest religious building of its day. A huge dome dominated the church. Four minarets, or narrow towers, were added later. After the empire's fall in 1453, the Hagia Sophia served as a mosque and, in recent years, as a museum.

Portfolio Assessment

INTERNET Use the Internet or library resources to find out more about Byzantine art or architecture. Then, choose one example of Byzantine art or architecture. Create a model, diagram, or drawing that points out important features of the work. Prepare a presentation to summarize your research.

Chapter 10 **235**

Block Scheduling Support

Divide the class into two groups to debate whether it is appropriate for the spouse of a government leader to take an active role in political affairs, as Theodora did. Assign one group to defend the idea and the other to oppose it. Direct each group to develop two lists. One list should contain arguments that support the group's position. The other should have points the group can use to refute arguments it believes the other side will make. During the debate, give both sides the same amount of time to present their arguments and to rebut the arguments of the other side. After the debate is concluded, have the class vote to determine which position they accept.

EXPLORING the HUMAN DRAMA

Humanities Link

Bell Ringer Have students note the blending of architectural styles in the church of Hagia Sophia. Which elements of the structure are Roman, and which are not characteristic of Roman architecture?

Background Connections to Today

Preserving the Past Restoration of the church of Hagia Sophia began in the late twentieth century with funding from the Turkish government. In addition to restoring some of the mosaics and repairing the lead roofing, the building is being monitored for its resistance to earthquakes. Weakened by an earthquake in the previous year, the dome of the church collapsed in 558, but was rebuilt. During a deadly quake in 1998, the church of Hagia Sophia remained intact. A computer model of the church was recently constructed so archaeologists and engineers can learn more about this historic treasure.

Activity Cooperative Learning

Creating a Mosaic Have small groups create a mosaic using construction paper. Suggest that students choose as a model one of the pictures in this chapter, or allow them to tie this activity into the Portfolio Assessment activity described on this page. One student should design the picture, and others should create the tiles from colored paper. All students can help assemble the mosaic.

Activity Rubrics

Share rubrics with students before they create their models, diagrams, or drawings.

Attempted The project reflects little or no research, lacks important features of the art or architecture, and fails to summarize features about the topic.

Minimal The project demonstrates some research and preparation and illustrates and summarizes a few important features of the chosen topic.

Adequate The project is neatly done, shows many important features of the chosen topic, and is well organized.

Exemplary The project is detailed, well executed, interesting, informative, and reflects extensive research.

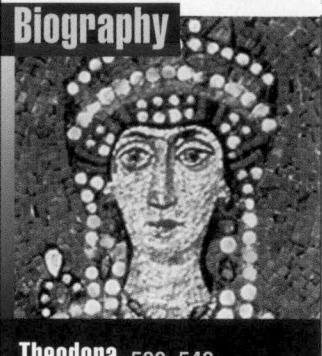

Activity
Connections to Literature

Reading Historical Fiction *The Belt of Gold,* by best-selling novelist Cecilia Holland, weaves a tale of intrigue and murder in ninth-century Constantinople. Have students read Chapter Three of the novel, which establishes the historical setting. The chapter begins with Constantine's founding of the "New Rome" and Justinian's wave of expansion. It then describes Arab and Bulgar attacks and the shrinking of the empire. In this chapter, students will also meet Empress Irene, who rises to power by deposing and blinding the previous emperor, her son Constantine VI.

Invite interested students to learn more about one of the events described in the chapter by doing additional research. Then, have students share their findings in an oral presentation.

Reading Strategy
Predicting Content

Ask students to skim Section 1, listing the main headings and subheadings on a piece of paper. Have them write a sentence or phrase under each heading that predicts the content of that section. When they have finished reading, ask students to test their predictions against the actual text. *(More Advanced Readers)*

Biography

Theodora 500–548

From humble beginnings as the daughter of a bearkeeper, Theodora rose to become Justinian's adviser and co-ruler. A shrewd, tough, and sometimes ruthless politician, Theodora did not hesitate to challenge the emperor and pursue her own policies.

Her most dramatic act came during a revolt in 532. "Emperor, if you wish to flee, well and good, you have the money, the ships are ready, the sea is clear," calmly spoke Theodora. "But I shall stay," she concluded. "I accept the ancient proverb: Royal purple is the best burial sheet." Theodora's courageous words inspired Justinian to remain in Constantinople and crush the revolt that threatened his power.

Theme: Impact of the Individual How did Theodora affect the outcome of the revolt?

Biography

ANSWER She convinced Justinian to stand his ground and crush the rebellion.

The Age of Justinian

The Byzantine empire reached its greatest size under the emperor Justinian, who ruled from 527 to 565. Justinian was determined to revive ancient Rome by recovering the provinces that had been overrun by invaders. Led by the brilliant general Belisarius, Byzantine armies reconquered North Africa, Italy, and southern Spain. The fighting exhausted Justinian's treasury and weakened his defenses in the east. In the end, the victories were temporary. Justinian's successors lost the bitterly contested lands.

Hagia Sophia Justinian left a more lasting monument in his buildings. To restore Roman glory, he launched a program to beautify Constantinople. His great triumph was the church of Hagia Sophia ("Holy Wisdom"). Its immense, arching dome improved on earlier Roman buildings. The interior glowed with colored marble and embroidered silk curtains. Seeing this church, the emperor recalled King Solomon's temple in Jerusalem. "Glory to God who has judged me worthy of accomplishing such a work as this!" Justinian exclaimed. "O Solomon, I have surpassed you!"

Code of Laws Justinian is best remembered for his reform of the law. Early in his reign, he set up a commission to collect, revise, and organize all the laws of ancient Rome. The result was the *Corpus Juris Civilis,* or "Body of Civil Law," popularly known as Justinian's Code. This massive collection included laws passed by Roman assemblies or decreed by Roman emperors, as well as the legal writings of Roman judges and a handbook for students.

Justinian's Code had an impact far beyond the Byzantine empire. By the 1100s, it had reached Western Europe. There, both the Roman Catholic Church and medieval monarchs modeled their laws on its principles. Centuries later, the code also guided legal thinkers who began to put together the international law in use today.

Absolute Power Justinian used the law to unite the empire under his control. He ruled as an autocrat, or sole ruler with complete authority. The emperor also had power over the Church. He was deemed Christ's co-ruler on Earth. As a Byzantine official wrote, "The emperor is equal to all men in the nature of his body, but in the authority of his rank he is similar to God, who rules all." Unlike feudal monarchs in Western Europe, he combined both political power and spiritual authority. His control was aided by his wife, Theodora. A shrewd politician, she served as adviser and co-ruler to Justinian and even pursued her own policies.

Changing Fortunes In the centuries after Justinian, the fortunes of the empire rose and fell. Attacks by Persians, Slavs, Vikings, Mongols, and Turks were largely unsuccessful. The empire thus served as a buffer for Western Europe. Beginning in the 600s and 700s, however, Arab armies gained control of much of the Mediterranean world. Constantinople itself withstood their attack, and the Byzantines held onto their heartland in the Balkans and Asia Minor. The empire's greatest strengths came from a strong central government and a prosperous economy.

Peasants formed the backbone of the empire, working the land, paying taxes, and providing soldiers for the military. In the cities of the empire, trade and industry flourished. While Western Europe was reduced to a barter economy, the Byzantine empire preserved a healthy money economy. The bezant, the Byzantine gold coin stamped with the emperor's image, circulated from England to China.

Byzantine Christianity

Christianity was as influential in the Byzantine empire as it was in Western Europe. But religious divisions grew between the two regions.

Virtual Field Trip

www.phschool.com

**Byzantine Museum
Athens, Greece**

To see other examples of Orthodox Christian icons, use the Internet address above to link to the Byzantine Museum.

Icons

In this early Byzantine icon, the figures of Christ (right) and a saint stare directly outward, inviting the viewer into a personal relationship. The figures and their golden halos seem to glow because the artist painted on a background of reflecting gold paint. Over the centuries, Byzantine artists tended to use similar styles and techniques.

Theme: Art and Literature
What do you think the artist was trying to accomplish with this icon?

Differences East and West   Since early Christian times, differences had emerged over Church leadership. Although the Byzantine emperor was not a priest, he controlled Church affairs and appointed the patriarch, or highest Church official, in Constantinople. Byzantine Christians rejected the pope's claim to authority over all Christians.

Further differences developed. Unlike priests in Western Europe, the Byzantine clergy kept their right to marry. Greek, not Latin, was the language of the Byzantine Church. The chief Byzantine holy day was Easter, celebrated as the day Jesus rose from the dead. In contrast, western Christians placed greater emphasis on Christmas, the birthday of Jesus.

Schism   During the Middle Ages, the two branches of Christianity drew farther apart. A dispute over the use of icons, or holy images, contributed to the split. Many Byzantine Christians prayed to images of Christ, the Virgin Mary, and the saints. In the 700s, however, a Byzantine emperor outlawed the veneration of icons, saying it violated God's commandment against worshiping "graven images."

The ban set off violent battles within the empire. From the west, the pope took a hand in the dispute, excommunicating the emperor. Although a later empress eventually restored the use of icons, the conflict left great resentment against the pope.

In 1054, other controversies provoked a schism, or permanent split, between the Byzantine, or Eastern (Greek) Orthodox, and the Roman Catholic churches. The pope and the patriarch excommunicated each other. Thereafter, contacts between the two churches were guarded and distant. They treated each other as rivals rather than as branches of the same faith.

Crisis and Collapse

By the time of the schism, the Byzantine empire was declining. Struggles over succession, court intrigues, and constant wars undermined its strength. As in Western Europe, powerful local lords gained control of large areas. As the empire faltered, its enemies advanced. The Normans conquered southern Italy. Even more serious, the Seljuk Turks advanced across Asia Minor.

Chapter 10 **237**

A nomadic people out of central Asia, the Seljuks had converted to Islam in their migrations westward.

The Crusades In the 1090s, the Byzantine emperor called for western help to fight the Seljuks, who had closed the pilgrimage routes to Jerusalem. The result was the First Crusade. During later crusades, however, trade rivalry sparked violence between the Byzantine empire and Venice. Venetian merchants persuaded knights on the Fourth Crusade to attack Constantinople in 1204. For three days, crusaders burned and plundered the city, sending much treasure westward. Western Christians ruled Constantinople for 50 years. Although a Byzantine emperor reclaimed the capital in the 1260s, the empire never recovered. Venetian merchants gained control of Byzantine trade, draining the wealth of the empire. More threatening, the Ottoman Turks overran most of Asia Minor and the Balkans.

Constantinople Falls In 1453, Ottoman forces surrounded the city of Constantinople. After a siege lasting two months, they stormed the broken walls. When the last Byzantine emperor was offered safe passage, he replied, "God forbid that I should live an emperor without an empire." He chose instead to die fighting.

Forces led by Ottoman ruler Muhammad II entered the city in triumph. The ancient Christian city was renamed Istanbul and became the capital of the Ottoman

Constantinople About 550

Byzantine Empire to 1000

- Byzantine empire, 565
- Byzantine empire about 1000
- Ancient Byzantium
- City under Constantine and later rulers

Azimuthal Equal Area Projection
0   250   500 Miles
0   250   500 Kilometers

empire. Hagia Sophia was turned into an Islamic house of worship, and Istanbul soon emerged as a great center of Muslim culture.

The Byzantine Heritage

Although Byzantine power had faded long before, the fall of Constantinople marked the end of an era. To Europeans, the empire had stood for centuries as the enduring symbol of Roman civilization. Throughout the Middle Ages, Byzantine influence radiated across Europe. Even the Ottoman conquerors adapted features of Byzantine government, social life, and architecture.

What was the Byzantine heritage? For 1,000 years, the Byzantines built on the culture of the Hellenistic world. Byzantine civilization blended Christian religious beliefs with Greek science, philosophy, arts, and literature. The Byzantines also extended Roman achievements in engineering and law.

The Arts Byzantine artists made unique contributions, especially in religious art and architecture, that influenced western styles from the Middle Ages to the present. Icons, designed to evoke the presence of God, gave viewers a sense of personal contact with the sacred. Mosaics brought scenes from the Bible to glowing life. In architecture, Byzantine palaces and churches blended Greek, Roman, Persian, and other Middle Eastern styles.

The World of Learning Byzantine scholars preserved the classic works of ancient Greece. In addition, they produced their own great books, especially in the field of history.

Like the Greek historians Herodotus and Thucydides, Byzantine historians were mostly concerned with writing about their own times. Procopius, an adviser to the general Belisarius, chronicled the Byzantine campaign against Persia. In his *Secret History*, Procopius savagely criticized Justinian and Theodora. He called the emperor "both an evil-doer and easily led into evil . . . never of his own accord speaking the truth." Anna Comnena is considered by many scholars to be the western world's first important female historian. In the *Alexiad*, she analyzed the reign of her father, Emperor Alexius I. Comnena's book portrayed Latin crusaders as greedy barbarians.

As the empire tottered in the 1400s, many Greek scholars left Constantinople to teach at Italian universities. They took valuable Greek manuscripts to the West, along with their knowledge of Greek and Byzantine culture. The work of these scholars contributed to the European cultural flowering that became known as the Renaissance.

Recall
1. (a) Hagia Sophia, p. 236 (b) *Corpus Juris Civilis*, p. 236 (c) Theodora, p. 236 (d) Procopius, p. 239 (e) Anna Comnena, p. 239 2. (a) autocrat, p. 236 (b) patriarch, p. 237 (c) icon, p. 237

Comprehension
3. Possible answer: He oversaw the building of the Hagia Sophia, set up a commission to collect, revise, and organize all the laws of ancient Rome, and united the empire under his control.
4. selection process for pope and patriarch, ability of clergy to marry, church language, chief holy day 5. (a) led to Western Christian control of Constantinople, loss of control of trade routes (b) The Ottoman Turks captured the city and renamed it Istanbul. 6. Possible answer: made unique contributions to religious art and architecture and preserved classic works of ancient Greece

Critical Thinking and Writing
7. Possible answer: preservation of ancient Greek works, because it allowed later peoples to learn from them 8. Possible answer: Justinian's Code, because laws today are based on it

SECTION 1 Assessment

Recall
1. **Identify:** (a) Hagia Sophia, (b) *Corpus Juris Civilis,* (c) Theodora, (d) Procopius, (e) Anna Comnena.
2. **Define:** (a) autocrat, (b) patriarch, (c) icon.

Comprehension
3. Describe three of Justinian's major accomplishments.
4. What were some differences between Byzantine Christianity and Roman Catholic Christianity?
5. (a) How did the Crusades affect the Byzantine empire? (b) Why did the empire finally fall?
6. Describe the legacy of Byzantine civilization.

Critical Thinking and Writing
7. **Defending a Position** The Byzantine empire preserved part of the heritage of the Roman empire. What, in your opinion, was the most important result of this legacy? Why do you think so?
8. **Drawing Conclusions** As emperor, Justinian made many contributions to the strength and prosperity of the Byzantine empire. Which contribution do you think had the most lasting impact? Explain your answer.

Activity
Take It to the NET
Use the Internet to research the history of Hagia Sophia in Istanbul. Then, use your information to create a time line showing important events in the building's history. If possible, include illustrations of the interior and exterior.

Activity Rubrics

Share rubrics with students before they create their time lines.

Attempted The time line is missing some important historical events, reflecting little or no research.

Minimal The time line includes some of the important historical events and demonstrates sufficient research, but it is poorly drawn and labeled.

Adequate The time line lists all the important historical events and is neatly done.

Exemplary The time line lists all the important historical events and is well executed and visually pleasing. It may include illustrations of the interior and exterior of the building.

✓ Test Preparation

Have students read the section titled "The Crusades" on the opposite page, and then answer the question below.

What was the cause of the First Crusade?

A Venetian merchants supported an attack on Constantinople.

B Venice and the Byzantine empire were rivals for trade.

C The Seljuks closed pilgrimage routes to Jerusalem.

D Ottoman Turks overran the Balkans.

Bell Ringer

Bell Ringer Draw students' attention to the picture of Ivan the Terrible on the last page in this section. Ask students to describe the emotions that they feel as they look at this portrait. How do they think the Russian people felt under such a ruler?

LESSON PLAN

1. Focus Early Russia was influenced by the Slavs, Vikings, Byzantines, and Mongols. The princes of Moscow rose to power by leading Russian resistance against Mongol rule. As the first czars, they began a long tradition of autocratic rule in Russia.

2. Instruct As students complete their time lines for the Taking Notes activity, advise them to include references to various migrations and invasions, the influence of diverse cultures on Russian civilization, and the significant actions of powerful leaders. Encourage students to use maps and other illustrations to support their time lines. Use the time lines as the basis for a class discussion on the rise of Russia.

3. Assess Have students point out events on their time lines that were shaped by geography. Lead a discussion on the role of geography in Russian history.

4. Reteach If students' Assess activity does not reflect adequate understanding of the lesson, you might assign the *Guide to the Essentials* or the *Interactive Student Tutorial CD-ROM* for this section.

Reading Focus

- How did geography help shape early Russia and the growth of Kiev?
- How did the Mongol conquest affect Russia?
- Why did Moscow emerge as the chief power in Russia?

Vocabulary

steppe
boyar
czar

Taking Notes

Create a time line that shows events in the rise of Russia between the 700s and 1613. The sample on this page will help you get started.

700s	900	1100	1300	1500	1613

Varangians
appear

Main Idea In its early years, Russia was influenced by the Slavs, Vikings, Byzantines, and Mongols.

Setting the Scene In Russia, a patriotic monk saw a special meaning in the fall of Constantinople. Moscow, he declared, was a "third Rome," the successor to the Roman and Byzantine empires:

> "The third Rome . . . shines like the sun . . . throughout the whole universe. . . . Two Romes have fallen, and the third one stands, and a fourth one there shall not be."
> —Philotheos, quoted in *Tsar and People* (Cherniavsky)

Moscow had reason to claim itself heir to the Byzantine empire. Over many centuries, Byzantine culture greatly influenced the development of Russian society.

The Geography of Russia

Russia lies on the vast Eurasian plain that reaches from Europe to the borders of China. Although mapmakers use the Ural Mountains to mark the boundary between Europe and Asia, these ancient mountains were long ago worn away to wooded hills. They posed no obstacle to migration.

Three broad zones with different climates and resources helped shape early Russian life. The northern forests supplied lumber for building and fuel. Fur-bearing animals attracted hunters, but poor soil and a cold, snowy climate hindered farming. Farther south, a band of fertile land attracted early farmers. This region—today the country of Ukraine—was home to Russia's first civilization.

A third region, the southern steppe, is an open, treeless grassland. It offered splendid pasture for the herds and horses of nomadic peoples. With no natural barriers, the steppe was a great highway, along which streams of nomads migrated from Asia into Europe.

Russia's network of rivers provided transportation for both people and goods. The Dnieper (NEE puhr) and Volga rivers became productive trade routes. Major rivers ran from north to south, linking the Russians early on to the advanced Byzantine world in the south.

Growth of Kiev

During Roman times, the Slavs expanded into southern Russia. Like the Germanic peoples who pushed into Western Europe, the Slavs had a simple political organization and were organized into clans. They lived in small

Primary Source

The Russians Become Christians

Prince Vladimir of Kiev sent representatives to visit the churches of many lands:

"The envoys reported, 'When we journeyed among the Bulgars, we beheld how they worship in their temple. . . . Their religion is not good. Then we went among the Germans, . . . but we beheld no glory there. Then we went on to Greece, and the Greeks led us to the edifices [buildings] where they worship their God, and we knew not whether we were in heaven or on earth. For on earth there is no such splendor or such beauty, and we are at a loss how to describe it. We know only that God dwells there among men, and their service is fairer than the ceremonies of other nations. For we cannot forget that beauty.'"

—*The Primary Chronicle*

Skills Assessment

Primary Source What impressed the Russians about the Greek Orthodox Church?

Primary Source

ANSWER its splendor and beauty and the feeling of God's presence

Resource Directory

Teaching Resources
Creative Teaching Activities Creative Teaching Activities booklet, p. 47
Guided Reading and Review Unit 3 booklet, p. 42
Primary Source Activity *Prince Vladimir's Advice to His Sons,* Unit 3 booklet, p. 47

villages, farmed, and traded along the rivers that ran between the Baltic and the Black seas.

The Varangians   In the 700s and 800s, the Vikings steered their long ships out of Scandinavia. These expert sailors were as much at home on Russian rivers as on the stormy Atlantic. The Vikings, called Varangians by later Russians, worked their way south along the rivers, trading with and collecting tribute from the Slavs. They also conducted a thriving trade with Constantinople.

Located at the heart of this vital trade network was the city of Kiev. In time, it would become the center of the first Russian state. Within a few generations, the Varangians who had settled among the Slavs were absorbed into the local culture. Viking names like *Helga* and *Waldemar* became the Slavic names *Olga* and *Vladimir*.

Byzantine Influences   Early on, trade had brought Kiev into the Byzantine orbit. Constantinople later sent Christian missionaries to convert the Slavs. About 863, two Greek monks, Cyril and Methodius, adapted the Greek alphabet so they could translate the Bible into Slavic languages. This Cyrillic (suh RIHL ihk) alphabet became the written script used in Russia and Ukraine to the present.

In 957, Princess Olga of Kiev converted to Byzantine Christianity. But it was not until the reign of her grandson Vladimir that the new religion spread widely. After his own conversion, Vladimir married the sister of a Byzantine emperor. Soon, Greek priests arrived in Kiev to preside over the mass baptisms organized by the prince.

As Byzantine Christianity gained strength in Russia, princes began to see themselves as heirs to many cultural and political aspects of the Byzantine empire. The Russians acquired a written language, and a class of educated Russian priests emerged. Russians adapted Byzantine religious art, music, and architecture. Byzantine domes capped with colorful, carved "helmets" became the onion domes of Russian churches.

Byzantine Christianity set the pattern for close ties between Church and state. Russian rulers, like the Byzantine emperor, eventually controlled the Church, making it dependent on them for support. The Russian Orthodox Church would long remain a pillar of state power.

Yaroslav   Kiev enjoyed a golden age under Yaroslav the Wise, who ruled from 1019 to 1054. Like Justinian, he issued a written law code to improve justice. A scholar, he translated Greek works into his language. Yaroslav arranged marriages between his children and some of the royal families of Western Europe.

Kiev declined in the 1100s as rival families battled for the throne. Also, Russian trading cities were hurt because Byzantine prosperity faded. As Russian princes squabbled among themselves, Mongol invaders from central Asia struck the final blow.

Mongol Conquest

In the early 1200s, a young leader united the nomadic Mongols of central Asia. As his mounted bowmen overran lands from China to Eastern Europe, he took the title Genghiz Khan (GEHNG gihz KAHN), "World Emperor."

The Golden Horde   Between 1236 and 1241, Batu, the grandson of Genghiz, led Mongol armies into Russia. Known as the Golden Horde, from

Constantinople and Russia
Cyril and Methodius became saints in both the Orthodox and Roman Catholic churches. Modern Russian script is based on the Cyrillic alphabet developed by the two Greek monks.

Theme: Impact of the Individual   How does this image, from a church fresco, reflect the contributions of Cyril and Methodius?

Background
Global Connections

The Livonian War Like later Russian czars, Ivan IV hoped to open his land-locked country to foreign trade by gaining access to the seas. In 1558, therefore, Ivan the Terrible invaded the Baltic Sea region of Livonia. In the war that followed, Russia found itself opposed by Swedish, Lithuanian, and Polish forces. The Livonian War lasted more than 20 years until finally, in 1582, Russia agreed to a peace settlement. Exhausted by the years of fighting, Russia surrendered the territory it had gained and remained a landlocked state. The mission of opening Russia to the West was left for future czars.

Growth of Russia, 1330–1584

Extent of Mongol conquest, 1300
Moscow, 1300
★ Battle site
Land added, 1330–1462
Land added, 1462–1533
Land added, 1533–1584

Azimuthal Equal Area Projection

Skills Assessment

Geography Between 1300 and 1584, Russian lands grew from a small area around Moscow to a large territory.

1. **Location** On the map, locate (a) Black Sea, (b) Volga River, (c) Danube River, (d) Caspian Sea, (e) Kulikovo.
2. **Place** During what years did Novgorod come under Russian rule?
3. **Critical Thinking Synthesizing Information** Locate the natural feature many mapmakers consider the boundary between Europe and Asia. In 1584, were Russian lands mostly in Europe or in Asia?

the color of their tents, they looted and burned Kiev and other Russian towns. So many inhabitants were killed, declared a Russian historian, that "no eye remained to weep for the dead." From their capital on the Volga, the Golden Horde ruled Russia for the next 240 years.

The Mongols, although fierce conquerors, were generally tolerant rulers. They demanded regular payments of heavy tribute, and Russian princes had to acknowledge the Mongols as their overlords. But as long as the tribute was paid, the Mongols left Russian princes to rule without much interference.

Mongol Influences Historians have long debated how Mongol rule affected Russia. Peasants felt the burden of heavy taxes. Some fled to remote regions, and others sought protection from Mongol raids by becoming serfs of Russian nobles. Even though the Golden Horde converted to Islam, the Mongols tolerated the Russian Orthodox Church, which grew more powerful during this period. The Mongol conquest brought peace to the huge swath of land between China and Eastern Europe, and Russian merchants benefited from new trade routes across this region.

During the period of Mongol rule, Russians adopted the practice of isolating upper-class women in separate quarters. Beginning in the 1200s, women became totally subject to male authority in the household. Husbands could even sell their wives into slavery to pay family debts.

The absolute power of the Mongols served as a model for later Russian rulers. Russian princes developed a strong desire to centralize their own power without interference from nobles, the clergy, or wealthy merchants. Perhaps most important, Mongol rule cut Russia off from contacts with Western Europe at a time when Europeans were making rapid advances in the arts and sciences.

Moscow Takes the Lead

During the Mongol period, the princes of Moscow steadily increased their power. Their success was due in part to the city's location near important river trade routes. They also used their positions as tribute collectors for the Mongols to subdue neighboring towns. When the head of the Russian Orthodox Church made Moscow his capital, the city became not just Russia's political center, but its spiritual center as well.

As Mongol power declined, the princes of Moscow took on a new role as patriotic defenders of Russia against foreign rule. In 1380, they rallied other Russians and defeated the Golden Horde at the battle of Kulikovo. Although the Mongols continued their terrifying raids, their strength was much reduced.

Ivan the Great A driving force behind Moscow's successes was Ivan III, known as Ivan the Great. Between 1462 and 1505, he brought much of northern Russia under his rule. He also recovered Russian territories that had fallen into the hands of neighboring Slavic states.

Ivan built the framework for absolute rule. He tried to limit the power of the boyars, or great landowning nobles. After he married Sophia-Zoë

242 Chapter 10

Skills Assessment

ANSWERS 1. Review locations with students. **2.** 1462–1533 **3.** Europe

Resource Directory

Teaching Resources
Viewpoint Activity *Two Views of the Czarina Sophia,* Unit 3 booklet, p. 48
Skill Application Activity *Organizing Your Writing,* Unit 3 booklet, p. 49
Section Quiz Unit 3 booklet, p. 43

Technology
World History Color Transparencies political cartoon on the advantages and disadvantages of a government being dominated by a single powerful individual, p. E–29
Interactive Student Tutorial CD-ROM Ch. 10
Computer Test Bank Ch. 10

Paleologus, niece of the last Byzantine emperor, he adopted Byzantine court rituals to emphasize Russia's role as the heir to Byzantine power. Like the Byzantine emperors, he used a double-headed eagle as his symbol. Ivan and his successors took the title czar, the Russian word for Caesar. "The czar," claimed Ivan, "is in nature like all men, but in authority he is like the highest God."

Ivan the Terrible Ivan IV, grandson of Ivan the Great, further centralized royal power. He limited the privileges of the old boyar families and granted land to nobles in exchange for military or other service. At a time when the manor system was fading in Western Europe, Ivan IV introduced new laws that tied Russian serfs to the land.

About 1560, Ivan IV became increasingly unstable. He trusted no one and became subject to violent fits of rage. In a moment of madness, he even killed his own son. He organized the *oprichniki* (aw PREECH nee kee), agents of terror who enforced the czar's will. Dressed in black robes and mounted on black horses, they slaughtered rebellious boyars and sacked towns where people were suspected of disloyalty. Their saddles were decorated with a dog's head and a broom, symbols of their constant watchfulness to sweep away their master's enemies.

The czar's awesome power, and the ways he used it, earned him the title "Ivan the Terrible." When he died in 1584, he left a land seething with rebellion. But he had introduced Russia to a tradition of extreme absolute power.

Looking Ahead

Disputes over succession, peasant uprisings, and foreign invasions soon plunged Russia into a period of disorder. This "Time of Troubles" lasted from 1604 to 1613. Finally, the zemsky sobor (ZEHM skee suh BAWR), an assembly of clergy, nobles, and townsmen, chose a new czar, 17-year-old Michael Romanov. His reign established the Romanov dynasty, which would rule Russia until 1917.

In the 1600s, Russia was an emerging power. Like monarchs in France or Spain, the czars expanded national borders and centralized royal control. But Russia developed along far different lines. Byzantine influences had helped establish a strong tradition of autocratic rule. Later Russian rulers were generally more autocratic than western kings and queens. Authoritarian leaders, from Peter the Great and Catherine the Great to Joseph Stalin, would shape Russian history down to this century.

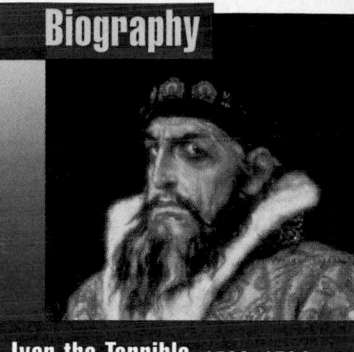

Biography

Ivan the Terrible 1530–1584

"I grew up on the throne," explained Ivan of his unhappy childhood. His father, Vasily, died when Ivan was only three years old. Intelligent, well read, and religious, young Ivan was crowned czar at age 17.

Though Ivan had long been a harsh ruler, his behavior became increasingly unstable after his wife died. Prone to violence, he crushed any opposition, real or imagined. He had thousands of people killed in the city of Novgorod because he feared a plot. Almost every noble family was affected by his murders. "From Adam to this day I have surpassed all sinners," he confessed in his will.

Theme: Impact of the Individual How did Ivan's reign affect Russia?

SECTION 2 Assessment

Recall
1. **Identify:** (a) Cyril and Methodius, (b) Vladimir, (c) Yaroslav, (d) Genghiz Khan, (e) Golden Horde, (f) "Time of Troubles," (g) Michael Romanov.
2. **Define:** (a) steppe, (b) boyar, (c) czar.

Comprehension
3. Describe how Russia's geography affected the rise of Kiev.
4. How did Mongol rule influence the economy and political structure of Russia?

5. How did Ivan III and Ivan IV establish royal power in Russia?

Critical Thinking and Writing
6. **Recognizing Points of View** Supporters of Ivan III called Moscow "the third Rome." (a) Why do you think they wanted to compare Moscow to Rome? (b) Do you agree that Moscow was truly the heir to Rome? Why or why not?
7. **Connecting to Geography** How did geography aid the princes of Moscow in gaining power?

Activity
Creating a Chart
Create a chart that summarizes the various cultural, religious, and political influences of the following groups on Russia: Varangians, Byzantines, Mongols.

Chapter 10 **243**

Recall
1. (a) Cyril and Methodius, p. 241
(b) Vladimir, p. 241 (c) Yaroslav, p. 241
(d) Genghiz Khan, p. 241 (e) Golden Horde, p. 241 (f) Time of Troubles, p. 243
(g) Michael Romanov, p. 243 2. (a) steppe, p. 240 (b) boyar, p. 242 (c) czar, p. 243

Comprehension
3. Fertile land attracted farmers, and proximity to the steppe aided migration. Additionally, the river network encouraged migration and trade. 4. economy—high taxation rates contributed to growth of serfdom as people sought protection of Russian lords; political structure—encouraged autocratic rule and absolute power 5. Ivan III—recovered lost territories, limited power of boyars, adopted Byzantine court rituals; Ivan IV—further limited power of boyars, reinforced serfdom, organized *oprichniki*

Critical Thinking and Writing
6. (a) Possible answer: They regarded Rome as the height of civilization and power and wanted others to regard Moscow in the same way. (b) Possible answer: Moscow had little in common with Rome. For example, Russia at this time made relatively few contributions to the arts and sciences. 7. Possible answer: The proximity of important river trade routes enabled princes to gain wealth because Moscow was a trading center.

Activity Rubrics

Share rubrics with students before they create their charts.

Attempted The chart contains erroneous information, is messy and is incomplete.

Minimal The chart does not include important cultural, religious, and political influences of the groups on Russia and is messy.

Adequate The chart accurately summarizes the cultural, religious, and political influences of the groups on Russia and is neatly done.

Exemplary The chart summaries provide an accurate and complete overview of the various influences on Russia and are very well done and imaginative.

Biography

ANSWER His rule enlarged the nation, but left the people terrorized and weakened. He created a tradition of the ruler's absolute power.

Human Drama Note

Italian Influence Sophia-Zoë Paleologus was known for her great intelligence. After she married Ivan III, she was instrumental in encouraging her husband to rebuild Moscow. One of her projects, the Cathedral of the Assumption of Our Lady, still exists, and is an example of the work of one of the Italian craftsmen she brought with her, the architect Fioraventi.

Test Preparation

Have students read the section titled "Looking Ahead" on this page, and then answer the question below.

Which of the following did not contribute to the "Time of Troubles"?

A peasant uprisings

B zemsky sobor

C foreign invasions

D succession disputes

Bell Ringer
Have students study the political map of Europe today in the Reference Section at the back of the book. Ask them to compare the number of countries in Eastern Europe with those in Western Europe. Why do they think there are many more countries in Eastern Europe? How do they think this situation has affected the development of the region?

Reading Focus
- How did geography influence developments in Eastern Europe?
- Why did Eastern Europe become a cultural crossroads with a diverse mix of peoples?
- What threats did the early kingdoms of Europe face?

Vocabulary
ethnic group
diet

Taking Notes
On a sheet of paper begin a concept web like this one. As you read the section, fill in the blank circles with relevant information about Eastern Europe. Add more circles if needed.

EASTERN EUROPE — Diverse geography — Early kingdoms

Main Idea Ethnic diversity contributed to the varied cultural traditions of Eastern Europe.

LESSON PLAN

1. Focus Geography and ethnic diversity contributed to the varied cultural traditions of Eastern Europe. During the Middle Ages, small kingdoms were frequently at war with one another. Without strong central governments, these kingdoms were often threatened by their larger neighbors.

2. Instruct Have students work with partners to complete the concept webs described in the Taking Notes section on this page. Suggest that they use the heads and subheads as guidelines. Also, advise them to use the map in this section. Encourage students to add specific details for each subsection of their concept web. Have students compare their webs with those of other students to see how similar they are.

3. Assess Have students write summaries based on their concept webs. Have them develop topic sentences for each main circle note and add sentences using other facts as supporting detail.

4. Reteach If students' Assess activity does not reflect adequate understanding of the lesson, you might assign the *Guide to the Essentials* or the *Interactive Student Tutorial CD-ROM* for this section.

Geography and History

The Blue Danube
"The Danube is Eastern Europe's great throbbing artery," wrote one journalist. "No other river in Europe . . . flows through as many nations . . . or echoes to as many languages." For more than 2,500 years, the Danube River has been a pathway for armies, goods, and ideas. Greek traders sailed along the lower part of the river as early as 600 B.C. Roman and, later, Ottoman armies built forts along its banks. Some of those fortresses grew into major cities, including Budapest and Belgrade. Today, dams on the 1,800 mile-long "Blue Danube" are a vital source of electric power.

Theme: Geography and History What resources has the Danube provided over the centuries?

Setting the Scene Many times in the past hundred years, people have opened their newspapers to find news about turbulent events in Eastern Europe. In 1914, a political assassination by Serbian nationalists triggered World War I. In 1938 and 1939, German aggression in Czechoslovakia and Poland sparked World War II. In 1989, revolts in Eastern European nations helped topple the Soviet empire. In the 1990s, war again erupted in the Balkans as rival national groups clashed in Bosnia and Kosovo.

The roots of such conflicts lie deep in the history of Eastern Europe. As you will see, it has been a history often marked by war, revolution, and foreign conquest. At the same time, its diverse mix of peoples has enriched the culture of the region.

The Geography of Eastern Europe
The region known as Eastern Europe is a wide swath of territory lying between German-speaking Central Europe to the west and the largest Slavic nation, Russia, to the east. Many peoples and many nations have flourished in the area over the centuries.

Eastern Europe reaches from the chilly waters of the Baltic Sea, down across the plains of Poland, then through the mountainous Balkans. The Balkan Peninsula, a roughly triangular arm of land, juts southward into the warm Mediterranean. Several geographic features contributed to developments in Eastern Europe. Much of the region lies on the great European plain that links up with the steppes of southern Russia.

The main rivers of Eastern Europe, like the Danube and the Vistula, flow either south into the Black Sea or north into the Baltic Sea. Goods and cultural influences traveled along these river routes. As a result, the Balkans in the south felt the impact of the Byzantine empire and, later, the Muslim Ottoman empire. In contrast, the northern regions bordering Germany and the Baltic Sea forged closer links to Western Europe.

A Diverse Mix of Peoples
Eastern Europe's geography has made it a cultural crossroads. The ease of migration encouraged many different peoples to seek new homes, as well as increased power, in the region. As a result, Eastern Europe now includes a wealth of languages and cultures.

Geography and History

ANSWER The Danube has been a pathway for travel, goods, and ideas for 2,500 years, and in modern times, a source of hydroelectric power.

Resource Directory

Teaching Resources
Creative Teaching Activities Creative Teaching Activities booklet, p. 48
Guided Reading and Review Unit 3 booklet, p. 44

The Balkans In the early Middle Ages, the Slavs spread out from a central heartland in Russia. The West Slavs filtered into present-day Poland and the Czech and Slovak republics. The South Slavs descended into the Balkans and became the ancestors of the Serbs, Croats, and Slovenes.

The Balkans were peopled by other ethnic groups as well. An **ethnic group** is a large group of people who share the same language and cultural heritage. Waves of Asian peoples migrated into Eastern Europe, among them the Huns, Avars, Bulgars, Khazars, and Magyars. Vikings and other Germanic peoples added to the mix.

Powerful neighboring states exercised strong cultural influences on Eastern Europe. Byzantine missionaries carried Eastern Orthodox Christianity and Byzantine culture throughout the Balkans. German knights and missionaries from the West spread Roman Catholic Christianity to Poland, Hungary, the Czech area, and the western Balkans. In the 1300s, the Ottomans invaded the Balkans, spreading Islam into pockets of that area.

Jewish Settlements In the late Middle Ages, Eastern Europe was a refuge for many Jewish settlers. Western European Christians launched brutal attacks on Jewish communities, particularly during the Crusades and the Black Death. To escape persecution, many Jews fled east. Monarchs in England, France, and Spain also expelled Jews from their lands. (See "Synthesizing Information" on the next page.)

In the 1300s, Polish kings followed a policy of toleration toward Jews. As a result, Jewish villages sprang up in Poland and other sparsely populated areas of Eastern Europe. Jewish merchants and scholars contributed to the economic and cultural development of Poland during this period.

Early Kingdoms

During the Middle Ages, Eastern Europe included many kingdoms and small states. Sometimes, empires absorbed national groups. Alliances or royal marriages might bind others together for a time. To get a sense of these shifting fortunes, we will look at the kingdoms of Poland, Hungary, and Serbia.

Poland Missionaries brought Roman Catholicism to the West Slavs of Poland in the 900s. A century later, the first Polish king was crowned. To survive, Poland often had to battle Germans, Russians, and Mongols.

Poland's greatest age came after Queen Jadwiga (yahd VEE gah) married Duke Wladyslav Jagiello (vwah DIHS wahv yahg YEH loh) of Lithuania in 1386. Poland-Lithuania controlled the largest state in Europe, stretching from the Baltic to the Black Sea. Jadwiga supported a university in Cracow, which became a major center of science and the arts.

Byzantine Cavalry
Although Byzantine civilization influenced many people in Eastern Europe, conflict often erupted. In this illustration from the 1300s, Byzantine knights defeat Bulgar soldiers.

Theme: Political and Social Systems What reasons might the Bulgars have had for fighting the Byzantine empire?

Customize for . . .
Visual Learners

Refer students to the map on the Chapter 9 opener. As students read the section titled "Early Kingdoms," have them find Poland, Hungary, and Serbia on the map. Then refer students to the modern map in the Atlas in the textbook's Reference Section to compare the changes undergone by the three countries. (Reteaching)

Block Scheduling Support

Tell students they are going to play a version of a television game show. Have them form groups. Assign each group a number before giving them part of Section 3 to read. Give note cards to each group, and tell students to skim their section and write a question on one side and the answer on the other. Have them write their group number at the bottom of each card. Set a time limit for this part of the activity, and, at the end of it, collect the cards. Write the number of each group on the board, and then quiz the class by reading the answers. Assign a point to the group that can supply the correct question for that answer. The group that wrote the question does not participate. The group with the most points wins.

Caption Answer

Possible answer: They might have wanted to maintain their independence or even conquer the Byzantine empire themselves.

Synthesizing Information

Jewish Migrations in Europe

The late Middle Ages were a time of troubles for the Jews of Europe. Though masters of trade, finance, and learning, Jews were expelled from several of the Christian nations of Western Europe. The map and the time line below show events related to their migrations.

Migrations and Expulsions, 1100–1650

→ Migrations
→ Expulsions

Azimuthal Equal Area Projection
0   250   500 Miles
0   250   500 Kilometers

During the early Middle Ages, Jews created economically and intellectually vital communities in Western Europe. Beginning in the 1200s, however, the rulers of several nations formally expelled the Jews from their lands. Many migrated to Poland and other parts of Eastern Europe, where they were allowed to build their own communities.

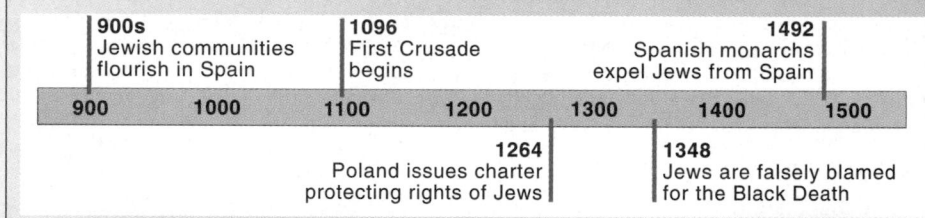

900s Jewish communities flourish in Spain	1096 First Crusade begins		1492 Spanish monarchs expel Jews from Spain
900 1000	1100 1200	1300	1400 1500
	1264 Poland issues charter protecting rights of Jews	1348 Jews are falsely blamed for the Black Death	

Skills Assessment

1. When expelled from France in 1394, Jews migrated to
   A England.
   B Italy and Germany.
   C Spain and Portugal.
   D Poland and Eastern Europe.

2. Which event resulted in a widespread scattering of the Jewish population outside Europe?
   E expulsion from Spain
   F Polish charter
   G Black Death
   H First Crusade

3. **Critical Thinking Drawing Conclusions** Based on the evidence provided, where were Jews more likely to settle after 1350? Why?

Skills Tip

Time lines show a sequence of events over time. Follow the dates from left to right to find the chronological order of events.

Synthesizing Information

Background
About the Evidence

Diaspora Jews were relatively secure in Europe until the Middle Ages. Then, during the Crusades, entire Jewish communities in Germany and France were massacred. Violence against Jews escalated again during the Black Death. Throughout the Middle Ages, Western European monarchs expelled Jews.

The Jews who migrated to Poland and Lithuania led segregated lives— living in close-knit communities and speaking Yiddish, a German dialect mixed with Hebrew and Slavic words. For a time they were granted limited self-government through the Council of the Four Lands.

Activity
Interpreting the Evidence

Use these additional questions to generate class discussion.

1. Critical Thinking: Connecting to Geography Where did many Jews who left Spain settle? *(in areas bordering the Mediterranean)*

2. Critical Thinking: Analyzing Information How did the movement of Jews in the early Middle Ages differ from that in the late Middle Ages? *(In the early Middle Ages, Jews migrated northward from southern Italy into France and Germany. Later, they migrated to Poland, Russia, and non-European lands around the Mediterranean.)*

Skills Tip

Time lines can be helpful in seeing relationships between events. The Skills Handbook in the front of the book has a lesson that will help students with this feature.

Skills Assessment

ANSWERS 1. B **2.** E **3.** Eastern Europe. They were blamed for the Black Death, but in Eastern Europe they were allowed to build their own communities.

Resource Directory

Teaching Resources
Synthesizing Information Chapter Extension Activities booklet, p. 28
Section Quiz Unit 3 booklet, p. 45
Geography Quiz Unit 3 booklet, p. 50
Chapter Test Forms A, B, and C Unit 3 booklet, pp. 51–55
Answer Key Unit 3 booklet, pp. 114–128

Technology
Interactive Student Tutorial CD-ROM Ch. 10
Computer Test Bank Ch. 10

Unlike Russia or Western Europe, Poland gradually increased the power of its nobles at the expense of the monarch. They met in a **diet,** or assembly, where the vote of a single noble was enough to block the passage of a law. This liberum veto, or "free veto," made it hard for the government to take decisive action.

Without a strong central government, Poland declined. It enjoyed a final moment of glory in 1683 when the Polish king Jan Sobieski (YAHN SAW BYEH skee) broke the Ottoman siege of Vienna. In the next century, however, Poland was gobbled up by ambitious neighbors and disappeared from the map entirely.

Hungary The Magyars raided Europe from the Asian steppes and settled in Hungary. Like the West Slavs of Poland, they adopted Roman Catholic Christianity. During the Middle Ages, the country was much larger than it is today. Hungarian rulers controlled present-day Slovakia, Croatia, and parts of Romania.

Like King John of England, the Hungarian king was forced to sign a charter recognizing the rights of his nobles. Known as the Golden Bull of 1222, it strictly limited royal power.

The Mongols overran Hungary in 1241, killing perhaps as much as half its population. They soon withdrew, so their invasion did not have the same impact it had on Russia. The expansion of the Ottoman Turks, though, ended Hungarian independence in 1526.

Serbia During the 600s, South Slavs settled the mountainous Balkans. Serbs, Croats, Slovenes, and other Slavic peoples in the Balkans had different histories during the Middle Ages. The Serbs accepted Orthodox Christianity. By the late 1100s, they had set up their own state, which reached its height under Stefan Dušan (STEH fahn DOO shahn). Stefan also encouraged Byzantine culture, even modeling his law code on that of Justinian.

Dušan's successors lacked his political gifts, however, and Serbia could not withstand the advance of Ottoman Turks. At the battle of Kosovo in 1389, Serbs fought to the death, a memory still honored by their descendants more than 600 years later.

Looking Ahead

Migration, conquest, dynastic marriages, and missionary activity helped produce a tangle of overlapping claims to territories in Eastern Europe. During the 1600s and 1700s, large empires to the east and west swallowed up much of the region. Yet whenever they had a chance, the peoples of Eastern Europe tried to recover their independence. In later chapters, we will see how the desire to rebuild separate states repeatedly ignited new turmoils.

Connections to Today

Balkan Boiling Pot

Throughout the 1990s, violence exploded in the Balkans. In 1992, Eastern Orthodox Serbs, Bosnian Muslims, and Catholic Croats fought a bloody civil war in Bosnia. In 1998, Christian Serbs and Muslims of Albanian heritage clashed in Kosovo.

The modern-day wars echo ethnic struggles that have gone on for more than 600 years in the Balkans. In 1389, Turkish soldiers from the Ottoman empire defeated Serbs at the Battle of Kosovo and took over the region. Different ethnic groups practicing different religions dispersed throughout the area. Even though they were forced to live together, the different groups have remained fiercely independent. Instead of being a melting pot of cultures, the Balkan region has continued to simmer and occasionally boil over.

Theme: Religions and Value Systems How have religions and ethnic groups affected life in the Balkans?

SECTION 3 Assessment

Recall

1. **Identify: (a)** Jadwiga and Wladyslav Jagiello, **(b)** Jan Sobieski, **(c)** Golden Bull of 1222, **(d)** Stefan Dušan.
2. **Define: (a)** ethnic group, **(b)** diet.

Comprehension

3. What role did rivers play in Eastern Europe?
4. How did Eastern Europe become home to many ethnic groups?

5. What relationship did the Ottoman Turks have with the early kingdoms of Eastern Europe?

Critical Thinking and Writing

6. **Comparing (a)** How were the histories of Poland, Hungary, and Serbia similar? **(b)** How were their histories different?
7. **Linking Past and Present** Why is Kosovo so important to modern-day Serbs?

Activity
Take It to the NET

Use the Internet to research old Cracow in Poland. Use your information to create a guide to the old part of the city. Then, take your classmates on a virtual tour.

SECTION 3 Assessment

Recall

1. **(a)** Jadwiga and Wladyslav Jagiello, p. 245 **(b)** Jan Sobieski, p. 247 **(c)** Golden Bull of 1222, p. 247 **(d)** Stefan Dušan, p. 247 2. **(a)** ethnic group, p. 245 **(b)** diet, p. 247

Comprehension

3. provided a link for culture and trade; as a result, Balkans forged ties with Byzantine and Muslim Ottoman empires, while northern regions forged ties with Western Europe 4. its location made it a cultural crossroads; its geography eased migration 5. They invaded the Balkans, spreading Islam there. They expanded into Hungary, ending Hungarian independence.

Critical Thinking and Writing

6. **(a)** For a time, they were powerful kingdoms, but eventually they were overrun by ambitious neighbors. **(b)** Poland and Hungary became mostly Roman Catholic lands, while Serbia became mostly Eastern Orthodox. They were conquered and absorbed by different empires. 7. They fought to the death there against the Ottoman Turks in 1389.

Activity Rubrics

Share rubrics with students before they create their guides to old Cracow.

Attempted The guide and the tour are missing important historical sites in the old part of the city, reflecting inadequate research.

Minimal The guide and the tour include few important historical sites, reflecting some research, but the guide is not complete or well organized.

Adequate The guide and the tour include important historical sites, and the guide is well organized and well written.

Exemplary The guide and the tour include important historical sites, and are well organized; details convey a sense of what old Cracow must have been like.

Human Drama Note

The Crown of St. Stephen To celebrate Hungary's first Christian king, Pope Sylvester II sent Stephen I a crown. When Stephen was canonized in 1083, this crown became known as the "Crown of St. Stephen." Worn by Hungarian kings for centuries, the crown was an important national symbol for Hungarians. This historical artifact is now on display in Budapest's National Museum.

Test Preparation

Read the section titled "Hungary" on this page, and then answer the question below.

Which group was responsible for ending Hungarian independence?

A Mongols

B West Slavs

C Ottoman Turks

D Magyars

Connections to Today

ANSWER The different groups have lived uneasily together in a state of conflict, violence, and tension.

Creating a Chapter Summary

As a reteaching opportunity, pair a more able student with a less able student to complete this chapter summary.

Students should complete the table. Possible entries: **Byzantine Empire** Justinian and Theodora; Eastern Orthodox; *Corpus Juris Civilis*, Hagia Sophia, preservation of Greek culture **Russia** Ivan the Great, Ivan the Terrible; Russian Orthodox; influence of Mongols, absolute power **Eastern Europe** Jadwiga and Jagiello in Poland, Stefan Dušan in Serbia; Roman Catholic in Poland and Hungary, Orthodox in Serbia

Building Vocabulary

1–8. Students' puzzle clues should show an understanding of each word.

Recalling Key Facts

9. The Byzantine empire was once the eastern part of the Roman empire.
10. The Eastern Orthodox and Roman Catholic churches split.
11. a Mongol army that invaded Russia
12. He expanded Moscow's control over neighboring parts of Russia, strengthened the power of the czar, and adopted Byzantine court rituals.
13. Peoples include Slavs, Asians, Vikings, and other Germanic groups; religions include Roman Catholic Christianity, Eastern Orthodox Christianity, Islam, and Judaism.
14. to escape persecution in Western Europe
15. Poland lacked a strong central government. The vote of a single noble could block passage of a law.

Critical Thinking and Writing

16. Possible answer: Without the Byzantine empire to act as a buffer, invaders might have reached Western Europe. Also, Byzantine civilization might not have influenced Eastern Europe.
17. Answers will probably involve the question of whether the end ever justifies the means. Students' answers should reflect an understanding of autocracy.
18. **(a)** To support their answers, students should refer to recent articles in newspapers and periodicals. **(b)** Possible answer: The institution of slavery, although abolished more than a century ago, was based on ethnicity and continues to affect the lives of many people.

Creating a Chapter Summary

Copy the table shown below. Fill in the spaces under each heading to help you review key facts about the chapter.

	BYZANTINE EMPIRE	RUSSIA	EASTERN EUROPE
IMPORTANT CITIES	Constantinople	Kiev, Moscow	Cracow (Poland), Kosovo (Serbia)
RULERS			
RELIGION			
OTHER CONTRIBUTIONS			

For additional review and enrichment activities, see the interactive version of *World History* available on the Web and on CD-ROM.

Web Site Self-Test
For practice test questions for Chapter 10, see
www.phschool.com.

Building Vocabulary

Use the chapter vocabulary words listed below to create a crossword puzzle. Exchange puzzles with a classmate. Complete the puzzles and then check each other's answers.

1. **autocrat**
2. **patriarch**
3. **icon**
4. **steppe**
5. **boyar**
6. **czar**
7. **ethnic group**
8. **diet**

Recalling Key Facts

9. How was the Byzantine empire an outgrowth of the Roman empire?
10. What important split in Christianity occurred in 1054?
11. What was the Golden Horde?
12. What were the accomplishments of Ivan the Great?
13. What peoples and religions are represented in Eastern Europe?
14. Why did many Jews migrate to Eastern Europe?
15. Why did the kingdom of Poland decline?

Critical Thinking and Writing

16. **Drawing Conclusions** How might European history have been different if the Byzantine empire had fallen after the death of Justinian?
17. **Defending a Position** Autocratic rule helped leaders of Moscow and Russia create a strong central state. Do you think that there is any justification for autocratic rule? Explain.
18. **Linking Past and Present (a)** How have long-standing ethnic differences in Eastern Europe influenced events in modern times? **(b)** Do you think that ethnic differences have played a similar role in the growth of American society? Explain.
19. **Synthesizing Information (a)** Construct a time line showing events in the Byzantine empire, Russia, and Eastern Europe. **(b)** Identify influences that had a significant impact on the history of all three regions.
20. **Connecting to Geography** Describe the role that bodies of water played in linking the Byzantine empire with Russia and Eastern Europe.

---

19. **(a)** Time lines should accurately represent significant events in all three regions. Refer students to their Note Taking activities and the chart on the opposite page to help construct their time lines. **(b)** Possible answer: the spread of Christianity, migrations, the blending of cultures
20. Rivers created trade routes; Constantinople is on the Black Sea with access to the Mediterranean Sea.

Skills Assessment
Analyzing Primary Sources

During the reign of Czar Ivan IV, a book called the *Domostroi* was published. The title means "house order." The *Domostroi* contains instructions on all aspects of a noble's home life, including the preparation and serving of food; the treatment of children, guests, merchants, and servants; and the celebration of religious holidays. The author may have been a priest who served at the Kremlin Cathedral of the Annunciation in Moscow. Read the excerpt below and answer the questions that follow.

"If God send any disease or ailment down upon a person let him cure himself through the grace of God, through tears, prayer, fasting, charity to the poor, and true repentance. Let him thank the Lord and beg His forgiveness, and show mercy and undisguised charity to everybody. . . .

When a sick person is in the house, let the homeowner invite seven or more priests and as many deacons as he can find. They will pray over commemorative beer for health and over frumenty [a kind of pudding] to bring peace of mind.

After someone departs this life, the priest or deacon will cense [perfume with incense] every room, sprinkling it with holy water and making the sign of the cross. Then those in the house, praising God according to the divine liturgy, should at once set up a table so that the priests and monks, along with the rest of the guests and the neighborhood poor, may eat and drink. Then all, contented and replete [full], will go to their homes praising God."

—Domostroi

21. **(a)** According to the writer, what should a person do if he or she becomes ill? **(b)** What does this suggest about the author's view of sickness?
22. What does the author say a homeowner should do when someone in the home is ill?
23. What actions should follow the death of a sick person?
24. What does this passage suggest about the role of religious figures in everyday Russian life?
25. Based on this passage, would you say that rituals were important in the Russian Orthodox religion? Explain.

Skills Assessment
Analyzing Charts

DECLINE OF THE BYZANTINE EMPIRE

EXTERNAL FACTORS	OUTCOMES
Invasions	Normans conquer southern Italy.
	Seljuk Turks advance through Asia Minor.
Crusades	Trade rivalries lead to conflict with Venice.
	Knights capture Constantinople during Fourth Crusade.
Ottoman Attack	Constantinople is captured by Turks.
	Constantinople is transformed into Muslim Istanbul.

This chart summarizes information about the decline of the Byzantine empire. Study the chart and answer the following questions:

26. What was the result of the invasion in southern Italy?
27. Name two results of the Crusades that contributed to the decline of the Byzantine empire.
28. Why did Constantinople become Istanbul?
29. What do the three events listed on the chart have in common?

Skills Tip

When conducting research on the Internet, try to determine if the information seems inaccurate or presents only one point of view. Check facts against sites provided by governments or universities.

Skills Assessment
Take It to the NET

Use the Internet to research a period of Byzantine history—for example, the age of Justinian, the schism, the Crusades, or the fall of Constantinople. Then, write a brief explanation of how the events of that period affected life in the Byzantine empire.

Analyzing Primary Sources

21. **(a)** cure himself through prayer, fasting, and acts of charity **(b)** Possible answer: Good health depends on God.
22. bring in seven or more priests and as many deacons as can be found
23. room should be blessed, and a feast should be held for priests, monks, poor neighbors, and guests
24. Possible answer: It shows their close involvement and influence.
25. Possible answer: Yes, because the rituals are explained very specifically in the book.

Analyzing Charts

26. The Normans took over.
27. Trade rivalries led to a conflict with Venice, and knights captured Constantinople during the Fourth Crusade.
28. It was captured by the Turks, renamed, and transformed into a Muslim city.
29. They all involved fighting; they all contributed to the decline of the Byzantine empire.

Skills Tip

Tell students to take a look at the domain of a Web site. Students need to know that .com at the end of a Web address indicates a commercial site, which may present inaccurate or biased information. Have students begin their search with a university (.edu) or government (.gov) domain. Also, many public libraries subscribe to a time-saving service that filters unreliable sites from their Internet databases. The Skills Handbook in the front of the book has a lesson that will help students with this feature.

Unit Theme Activity

Remind students to continue working on their Unit Theme Activity. See rubrics for the activity on the unit opener page in the Teacher's Edition.

Take It to the NET

Direct students to **www.phschool.com** for links to sites that will help them get started on this assignment. Share rubrics with students.

Attempted The report is missing some events or fails to explain how the events affected Byzantine life.

Minimal The report includes some pertinent events, but is disorganized and not clearly written.

Adequate The report is well organized and clear, includes several pertinent events, and explains how events affected Byzantine life.

Exemplary The report is well written, informative, and interesting. It includes all pertinent events and explains how they affected Byzantine life.

Resource Manager

	CORE INSTRUCTION	READING/SKILLS
Chapter Level Resources	**Teaching Resources** 📖 Pacing Charts, Ch. 11 📖 Teaching With Themes, p. 14 📺 Color Transparencies, p. F–23 💿 Resource Pro® Ch. 11 💻 www.phschool.com 　• eTeach	💿 Book on CD, Ch. 11 💿 Interactive Student Tutorial CD-ROM, Ch. 11 💿 Social Studies Skills Tutor CD-ROM 📺 Skills Transparencies
1 Rise of Islam 1. Explain how Muhammad became the prophet of Islam. 2. Summarize the teachings of Islam. 3. Describe how Islam helped shape the lives of believers.	**Teaching Resources** 📖 Creative Teaching Activities, p. 49 💿 Prentice Hall Presentation Pro, Ch. 11, Section 1 📺 Section Reading Support Transparencies	**Teaching Resources** 📁 Unit 3 booklet 　• Guided Reading and Review, p. 56 📖 Guide to the Essentials 📼 Guided Reading Audiotapes, Ch. 11, Section 1
2 Islam Spreads 1. Summarize how Muslims conquered many lands. 2. Describe the movements that emerged within Islam. 3. Explain why the empire of the caliphs declined.	**Teaching Resources** 📁 Unit 3 booklet 　• Viewpoint Activity, p. 68 📖 Creative Teaching Activities, p. 50 💿 Prentice Hall Presentation Pro, Ch. 11, Section 2 📺 Section Reading Support Transparencies	**Teaching Resources** 📁 Unit 3 booklet 　• Guided Reading and Review, p. 58 📖 Guide to the Essentials 📼 Guided Reading Audiotapes, Ch. 11, Section 2
3 Golden Age of Muslim Civilization 1. Describe how the Muslim society and economy were organized. 2. Explain what traditions influenced Muslim arts and literature. 3. Identify the advances Muslims made in centers of learning.	**Teaching Resources** 📁 Unit 3 booklet 　• Biography Activity, p. 66 📖 Creative Teaching Activities, p. 51 💿 Prentice Hall Presentation Pro, Ch. 11, Section 3 📺 Section Reading Support Transparencies	**Teaching Resources** 📁 Unit 3 booklet 　• Guided Reading and Review, p. 60 📖 Guide to the Essentials 📼 Guided Reading Audiotapes, Ch. 11, Section 3
4 Muslims in India 1. Describe the impact of the Delhi sultanate on India. 2. Outline how Muslim and Hindu traditions clashed and blended. 3. Explain how Akbar strengthened Mughal rule.	**Teaching Resources** 📁 Unit 3 booklet 　• Primary Source Activity, p. 67 📖 Creative Teaching Activities, p. 52 💿 Prentice Hall Presentation Pro, Ch. 11, Section 4 📺 Section Reading Support Transparencies	**Teaching Resources** 📁 Unit 3 booklet 　• Guided Reading and Review, p. 62 　• Skill Application Activity, p. 69 📖 Guide to the Essentials 📼 Guided Reading Audiotapes, Ch. 11, Section 4
5 The Ottoman and Safavid Empires 1. Explain how the Ottoman empire expanded. 2. Identify the characteristics of Ottoman culture. 3. Describe how Abbas the Great strengthened the Safavid empire.	**Teaching Resources** 📖 Creative Teaching Activities, p. 53 💿 Prentice Hall Presentation Pro, Ch. 11, Section 5 📺 Section Reading Support Transparencies	**Teaching Resources** 📁 Unit 3 booklet 　• Guided Reading and Review, p. 28 📖 Guide to the Essentials 📼 Guided Reading Audiotapes, Ch. 11, Section 5

ENRICHMENT/PRE-AP

💻 **www.phschool.com**
  • Why Study History?

💻 **www.phschool.com**
  • Internet Activities, Section 1

🏛 **Color Transparencies,** pp. B–35, B–37, B–39, C–33
📼 **Visions, Voices, Views,** Daily Life CloseUp, tape 3

📗 Teaching Resources
  📘 **Creative Teaching Activities,** p. 31
  📘 **History Through Literature,** pp. 25–26
  🏛 **Color Transparencies,** pp. C–33, D–55
  📼 **Listening to Literature World Masterpieces,** *Persian and Arabic Music,* side 1; from *The Rubáiyát,* side 1
  💻 **www.phschool.com**
    • Virtual Field Trip
    • Internet Activities, *Art of the Muslim World*
    • Internet Activities, Section 3

📗 Teaching Resources
  📘 **Chapter Extension Activities,** pp. 29–30
  🏛 **Color Transparencies,** p. E–27
  📼 **Visions, Voices, Views,** Global Issues Forum, tape 3

💻 **www.phschool.com**
  • Internet Activities, Section 5

ASSESSMENT

PRENTICE HALL
ASSESSMENT SYSTEM

Core Assessment
  📘 ExamView Test Bank booklet, Ch. 11
  💿 ExamView Test Bank CD-ROM, Ch. 11

Standardized Test Preparation
Diagnose and Prescribe
  📘 Diagnostic Tests for High School Social Studies Skills
Review and Reteach
  📘 Review Book for World History
Practice and Assess
  📘 Test-Taking Strategies With Transparencies for High School
  📘 Alternative Assessment booklet
  📘 Test Prep Book for World History

📗 Teaching Resources
  📁 **Unit 3 booklet**
    • Geography Quiz, p. 34
    • Section Quizzes, pp. 21, 23, 25, 27, 29
    • Chapter Tests A, B, and C, pp. 35–39
💻 **www.phschool.com**
  • Self-Test

CUSTOMIZE FOR INDIVIDUAL NEEDS

Gifted and Talented
  • **Teacher's Edition,** Activities: Cooperative Learning Activity, p. 264; Customize for Heterogeneous Groups, p. 268

Less Proficient Readers
  • **Guide to the Essentials,** Ch. 11
  • **Book on CD,** Ch. 11
  • **Guided Reading Audiotapes, English,** Ch. 11
  • **Teacher's Edition,** Activities: Reading Strategy, p. 253; Connections to Film, p. 257; Customize for Kinesthetic Learners, p. 258; Reading Strategy, p. 263; Reading Strategy, p. 274

Less Proficient Writers
  • **Teacher's Edition,** Activities: Customize for Heterogeneous Groups, p. 258

Students Acquiring English/ESL
  • **Guide to the Essentials, English/Spanish,** Ch. 11
  • **Guided Reading Audiotapes, English/Spanish,** Ch. 11
  • **Book on CD,** Ch. 11
  • **Teacher's Edition,** Activities marked with an *

TEXT

Don't miss the exclusive interactive version of *World History: Connections to Today* on the Internet and CD-ROM.

INTRODUCTION

Islam emerged on the Arabian peninsula in the 600s. Founded by Muhammad, the religion spread east to India and west across North Africa and southern Europe. The Arab empire was ruled at first by powerful caliphs; later independent dynasties ruled separate states. During the Muslim golden age, learning, literature, science, medicine, and trade flourished. By the 1500s, the Mughals, Ottomans, and Safavids dominated the Muslim world.

Focusing on Themes

Have students focus on these questions:

Religions and Value Systems
What are the central religious and moral teachings of Islam?

Diversity
How did Muslim rulers deal with the diversity among their subjects?

Global Interaction
How did Muslim civilization create links among three continents?

Art and Literature
What artistic and literary traditions flourished in the Muslim world?

◆ TIME LINE ACTIVITY

Share the About the Pictures note with your students before you ask these questions about the time line:

1. The Muslim calendar and the Christian Era calendar differ. What year in the Christian Era calendar do you suppose is the Muslim year 1? *(622)*
2. How many years passed between the rise of Islam and the battle of Tours? *(110)*
3. How can you tell from this time line that the Muslims of India had skilled architects? *(Advanced architectural knowledge is needed to build a tall, tapering tower which is still standing centuries later.)*

Don't Miss!

Humanities Link
Art of the Muslim World (Section 3)

Comparing Viewpoints
Does Diversity Strengthen or Weaken a Society? (Section 4)

The Muslim World
622–1629

Chapter Preview

1 Rise of Islam
2 Islam Spreads
3 Golden Age of Muslim Civilization
4 Muslims in India
5 The Ottoman and Safavid Empires

750
Abu al-Abbas establishes the Abbassid dynasty. Over the next several centuries, Muslim merchant ships travel around the Abbassid empire and beyond.

622
Muhammad journeys from Mecca to Yathrib, an event that marks the rise of Islam. The Quran, shown above, is the sacred book of Islam.

1099
Christian crusaders from Europe capture Jerusalem from the Muslims.

CHAPTER EVENTS

600 • 800 • 1000

GLOBAL EVENTS

732 At the battle of Tours, the Muslim advance into Europe is stopped.

843 In Europe, the Frankish empire is split in three by the Treaty of Verdun.

1000s East African port cities flourish.

250 Chapter 11

Resource Directory

Teaching Resources
Teaching With Themes Chapter Theme Activity, p. 14
Pacing Chart With Block Scheduling Guide Ch. 11
Technology
World History Color Transparencies Ch. 11 Graphic Organizer, p. F–23

The Muslim World, 1150

During its early centuries, Islam spread from Arabia across the Middle East and North Africa and into Spain.

Robinson Projection

0   500   1000 Miles

0   500   1000 Kilometers

Muslim world, 1150

1206

Muslims set up Delhi sultanate in northern India. From atop the tower shown here, Indian Muslims are called to prayer.

1520

Suleiman becomes ruler of the Ottoman empire. During his reign, the empire grows and enjoys a golden age.

1620s

Under Shah Abbas the Great, Persian culture thrives.

1200

1400

1600

1279 Mongols complete the conquest of China.

1389 Serbs defeat Ottoman forces at the battle of Kosovo.

Chapter 11 **251**

The Muslim World, 1150

Activating Prior Knowledge

What would you expect, based on your knowledge of earlier empires, to be some of the effects of the spread of Islam through such diverse regions? *(Possible answers: blending of cultures, adaptation of art and literature and music, loss of some aspects of the previous cultures)*

Previewing

Why do you suppose the spread of Islam around the Mediterranean was mostly to lands along the coasts? *(Overland travel into the interior was more difficult than sea travel.)*

*B*ackground
About the Pictures

1	2
3	4

1. As Islam spread, Muslim artists learned new artistic styles. By the 1100s, Muslim artists used techniques from India and the Christian West. For the first time, Islamic artists began to illuminate both secular and religious texts.

2. Arabs developed the astrolabe, compass, and the lateen sail that allowed traders to travel great distances.

3. Criers called *muezzins* give the stirring *adhan,* or call to prayer, five times a day. According to legend, the first muezzin was one of Muhammad's first converts, an Ethiopian with a beautiful voice.

4. Suleiman (or Suleyman) was proud of his position as ruler: "Slave of God, master of the world, I am Suleyman and my name is read in all the prayers in all the cities of Islam. I am the Shah of Baghdad and Iraq, Caesar of all the lands of Rome, and the Sultan of Egypt."

eTeach

Be sure to check out this month's online discussion with a World History Master Teacher.

Go to **www.phschool.com**.

Independent Assignments

Have students read one section as they prepare for class. After class, have them complete the assignment. Some students may benefit from using the Guided Reading and Review worksheets.

Section 1 Have students read *In the Name of Allah* in *Treasures of the World,* pp. 53–55, to learn about the moral principles of the Quran.

Section 2 Have students use the worksheet *Views of the Muslim World* in the Unit 3 booklet, p. 68, to learn about Muslim culture in Spain.

Section 3 Have students use the worksheet *Firdawsi* in the Unit 3 booklet, p. 66, to learn about the life of this Persian poet.

Section 4 Have students use the worksheet *Babur's Army Crosses the Mountains* in the Unit 3 booklet, p. 67, to learn about this military leader's invasion of India.

Section 5 Have students use the map *Ottoman Empire, 1566* in the Historical Outline Map Book, p. 29, to study the extent of the Ottoman Empire.

Bell Ringer Ask students to read the words of Muhammad quoted on this page. Have them use the quote to describe some basic beliefs of Islam. Ask them if they note any similarities between these beliefs and those of other religions.

LESSON PLAN

1. Focus According to Muslim tradition, Muhammad was chosen to be the last and greatest prophet of Allah, the one true God. Muhammad devoted his life to spreading Islam. All Muslims embrace five pillars of faith. For Muslims, the Quran is the final authority on all matters of religion and daily life.

2. Instruct Ask students to outline this section. First, have them list the subheads. Then, tell them to list under each subhead the boldfaced run-in heads. Remind students to leave some space to write under each heading. Finally, have them summarize the content of each subhead in a sentence or two. Have students use their outlines as the basis for a class discussion on the rise of Islam.

3. Assess Point out that Islam is one of the world's major religions today. Ask students to discuss why, based on information in this section, they think Islam won many converts.

4. Reteach If students' **Assess** activity does not reflect adequate understanding of the lesson, you might assign the *Guide to the Essentials* or the *Interactive Student Tutorial CD-ROM* for this section.

Connections to Today

ANSWER They believe that Abraham built the first house of worship for God there—the Kaaba.

Reading Focus

■ How did Muhammad become the prophet of Islam?

■ What are the teachings of Islam?

■ How did Islam help shape the way of life of its believers?

Vocabulary

oasis
hijra
monotheistic
mosque
hajj
jihad

Taking Notes

Copy this chart. As you read, fill in the first column with key events concerning the emergence of Islam. In the second column, write down some of the basic teachings of Islam.

KEY EVENTS	TEACHINGS

Main Idea Islam arose in the Arabian Peninsula and became one of the world's major religions.

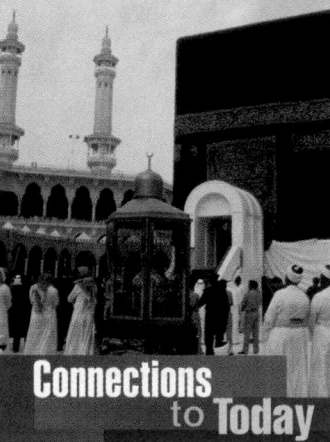

Connections to Today

A Sacred Duty

Today, more than two million Muslims gather each year in Mecca. Every Muslim who is physically and financially able must make a journey there at least once. Muslims believe that Abraham built the Kaaba in Mecca as the first house of worship for God. Today, it is adorned with a black cloth containing religious verses embroidered in gold. Pilgrims wear special clothes: simple garments that erase cultural and class differences so that all stand equal before God. The simple attire also symbolizes the abandonment of the material world for the sake of God.

Theme: Religions and Value Systems Why do Muslims consider Mecca sacred?

Setting the Scene In the Arabian town of Mecca, the marketplace echoed with the bustle of bargaining. One corner, though, was hushed. There, a husky, black-bearded man spoke to a handful of followers:

"In the name of God, the Compassionate, the Merciful,
Praise be to God, Lord of the Universe,
The Compassionate, the Merciful,
Sovereign of the Day of Judgment!
You alone we worship, and to You alone we turn for help."
—Quran

Some bowed their heads, moved by Muhammad's words. But many merchants scoffed. Muhammad had once been a good merchant himself. Surely, they thought, he had gone mad.

In years to come, Muhammad would be recognized by millions of Muslims as the Prophet. His followers would carry the message of Islam to people on three continents and set off one of the most powerful forces in world history.

The Prophet Muhammad

Islam emerged in the Arabian Peninsula, part of southwestern Asia. (See the map in Section 2 of this chapter.) Its deserts and trade centers helped shape the early life of Muhammad.

Geographic Setting The Arabian Peninsula is mostly desert, but farming is possible through irrigation or in scattered oases. An oasis is a fertile area in a desert, watered by a natural well or spring.

Many Arab clans occupied Arabia at the time of Muhammad. Nomadic herders, called Bedouins (BEHD oo ihnz), used camels to cross the scorching desert in search of seasonal pasturelands. Raids for scarce grazing land led to frequent warfare. The Bedouins would form the backbone of the armies that conquered a huge empire in the 600s and 700s. Bedouins traded with other Arabs who had settled in oasis towns. One of these was Mecca.

Mecca was a bustling market town at the crossroads of two main caravan routes. One route linked southern Arabia to Syria and Palestine on the Mediterranean coast. The other route crossed from Mesopotamia to eastern Africa. Mecca was also a thriving pilgrimage center. Arabs came to pray at the Kaaba, an ancient shrine that Muslims today believe was built by the prophet Abraham. In Muhammad's time, though, the Kaaba housed statues

---

Resource Directory

Teaching Resources
Creative Teaching Activities Creative Teaching Activities booklet, p. 49
Guided Reading and Review Unit 3 booklet, p. 56

of many local gods and goddesses. The pilgrim traffic brought good profits to the local merchants.

Muhammad's Vision Muhammad was born in Mecca about 570. In his youth, he worked as a shepherd among the Bedouins. Later, he led caravans across the desert and became a successful merchant. When he was about 25, Muhammad married Khadija (kah DEE jah), a wealthy widow who ran a prosperous caravan business. By all accounts, he was a devoted husband and a loving father to his daughters.

Muhammad was troubled by the idol worship and moral ills of society. When he was about 40, he went to a desert cave to meditate. According to Muslim belief, he heard a voice saying, "Recite!" Muhammad replied, "What shall I recite?" The voice explained: "Recite in the name of your God, the Creator, who created man from clots of blood."

Muhammad understood that it was the voice of the angel Gabriel calling him to be the messenger of God. But Muhammad was terrified and puzzled. How could he, an illiterate merchant, become the messenger of God? But Khadija encouraged him to accept the call. She became the first convert to the faith called Islam, from the Arabic word for "submission." Muhammad devoted the rest of his life to spreading Islam. He urged Arabs to give up their false gods and submit to the one true God. In Arabic, the word for god is *Allah*.

The Hijra: A Turning Point At first, few people listened to the teachings of Muhammad. His rejection of the traditional Arab gods angered Meccan merchants who feared neglecting their idols and disrupting the pilgrim trade. In 622, faced with the threat of murder, Muhammad and his followers left Mecca for Yathrib, a journey known as the hijra. Later, Yathrib was renamed Medina, or "city of the Prophet," and 622 became the first year of the Muslim calendar.*

The hijra was a turning point for Islam. In Medina, Muhammad was welcomed by Muslim converts, not only as God's prophet, but also as ruler and lawgiver. As his reputation grew, thousands of Arabs adopted Islam. From Medina, Muslims launched attacks on Meccan caravans and defeated the Meccans in battle.

Finally, in 630, Muhammad returned in triumph to Mecca, where he destroyed the idols in the Kaaba. In the next two years, Muhammad worked to unite the Arabs under Islam. Muhammad died in 632, but the faith that he proclaimed continued to spread. Today, Islam is one of the world's major religions.

Teachings of Islam

Like Judaism and Christianity, Islam is monotheistic, based on belief in one God. The Quran (ku RAHN), the sacred text of Islam, teaches that God is all-powerful and compassionate. It also states that people are responsible for their own actions: "Whoever strays bears the full responsibility for straying." According to the Quran, each individual will stand before God on the final judgment day to face either eternal punishment in hell or eternal bliss in paradise. Muslims recognize no official priests who mediate between the people and God.

---

* The Muslim calendar uses A.H. for dates after the hijra. However, this chapter, like the rest of the book, will continue to use dates based on the Christian Era calendar.

Messenger of God
On several occasions Muhammad heard the angel Gabriel calling him to be the messenger of God. In this miniature painting, an angel's announcement is symbolized by the blowing of a horn.

Theme Religions and Value Systems How did Muhammad respond to God's calling?

Background
Historical Evidence

Muhammad's Second Vision After his vision of the angel Gabriel, two years passed as Muhammad watched and waited for further signs from God. Finally, while walking near Mecca, an awestruck Muhammad saw an angel seated on a throne in the sky. Terrified, Muhammad ran to Khadija, his wife, and said, "Cover me." Khadija covered him with a cloak, whereupon the following words, contained in the Quran, came down to Muhammad: "O thou who wrappest thyself up, Arise and warn, And thy Lord do magnify, And thy garments do purify, And uncleanness do shun, And do no favourseeking gain, And for the sake of thy Lord be patient." It was the command "Arise and warn" that prompted Muhammad to begin to spread the teachings of Islam.

Reading Strategy
Check Comprehension

Have students read Section 1. Ask them to work in small groups to recall as many facts as they can without looking back at the section. Have them list their points on a sheet of paper. Then ask students to reread or skim the material, checking to see if the ideas listed were correct. Ask them to add ideas that were not listed the first time and to correct any inaccurate points from their first lists. *(Less Advanced Readers)*

Block Scheduling Support

Many films are available to provide students with more in-depth information on Islam. One that is recommended is *Islam* (19 min., color/bw), from the "Great Religions" series of the National Film Board of Canada. This film gives a good general introduction to Islam. As students view the film, ask them to make notes of interesting facts, ideas, or questions. Use students' notes as a basis for a class discussion of Islam. (*Islam* is distributed by McGraw-Hill Films.)

Caption Answer

He devoted his life to spreading Islam, urging Arabs to give up false gods and submit to the one true God.

A Revered Islamic Site
One of the holiest sites in the Muslim world is the Dome of the Rock in Jerusalem. It was built in the 690s above a rock from which Muslims believed Muhammad had risen into heaven.
Theme: Religions and Value Systems Why is the city of Jerusalem also sacred to Christians and Jews?

▶ **Primary Sources and Literature**

See "The Quran" in the Reference Section at the back of this book.

Five Pillars All Muslims accept five basic duties, known as the Five Pillars of Islam. The first is a declaration of faith. "There is no god but God, Muhammad is the messenger of God." Muslims believe that God had sent other prophets, including Abraham, Moses, and Jesus, but that Muhammad was the last and greatest prophet. The second pillar is daily prayer. After a ritual washing, Muslims face the holy city of Mecca to pray. Although Muslims may pray anywhere, they often gather in houses of worship called *masjids* or mosques. The third pillar is giving charity to the poor. The fourth is fasting from sunrise to sunset during the holy month of Ramadan. The fifth pillar is the hajj, or pilgrimage to Mecca. All Muslims who are able are expected to visit the Kaaba at least once in their lives.

Some Muslims look on jihad (jee HAHD), or effort in God's service, as another duty. Jihad has often been mistakenly translated simply as "holy war." In fact, it may include acts of charity or an inner struggle to achieve spiritual peace, as well as any battle in defense of Islam.

The Quran To Muslims, the Quran contains the sacred word of God as revealed to Muhammad. It is the final authority on all matters. The Quran not only teaches about God but also provides a complete guide to life. Its ethical standards emphasize honesty, generosity, and social justice. It sets harsh penalties for crimes such as stealing or murder.

Muslims believe that, in its original Arabic form, the Quran is the direct, unchangeable word of God. Because the meaning and beauty of the Quran reside in its original language, converts to Islam learn Arabic. This shared language has helped unite Muslims from many regions.

"People of the Book" Muslims profess faith in the same God as that worshiped by Jews and Christians. The Quran teaches that Islam is God's final and complete revelation, and that the Torah and Bible contain partial revelation from God. To Muslims, Jews and Christians are "People of the Book," spiritually superior to polytheistic idol worshipers. Although some later Muslims overlooked Muhammad's principle of tolerance, in general, the People of the Book enjoyed religious freedom in early Muslim societies.

A Way of Life

Islam is both a religion and a way of life. Its teachings help shape the lives of Muslims around the world. Islamic law governs many aspects of daily life, and Islamic traditions determine ethical behavior and influence family relations.

Sharia Over time, Muslim scholars developed an immense body of law interpreting the Quran and applying its teachings to daily life. This Islamic system of law, called the Sharia, regulates moral conduct, family life, business practices, government, and other aspects of a Muslim community. Like the Quran, the Sharia helped unite the many peoples who converted to Islam.

Unlike the law codes that evolved in the west, the Sharia does not separate religious matters from criminal or civil law. The Sharia applies the Quran to all legal situations.

Impact of Islam on Women Before Islam, the position of women in Arab society varied. In some communities, women took a hand in religion, trade, or warfare. Most women, however, were under the control of a male guardian and could not inherit property. Furthermore, among a few tribes, unwanted daughters were sometimes killed at birth.

Islam affirmed the spiritual equality of women and men. "Whoever does right, whether male or female," states the Quran, "and is a believer, all such will enter the Garden." Women therefore won greater protection under the law. The Quran prohibited the killing of daughters. Inheritance laws guaranteed a woman a share of her parents' or husband's property. Muslim women had to consent freely to marriage and had the right to an education. In the early days of Islam, some Arab women participated actively in public life.

Though spiritually equal, men and women had different roles and rights. For example, the amount of an inheritance given to a daughter was less than that given to a son. A woman could seek a divorce, but it was harder for her to get one than for a man.

As Islam spread, Arabs sometimes absorbed attitudes from the peoples they conquered. In Persian and Byzantine lands, Arabs adopted the practice of veiling upper-class women and secluding them in a separate part of the home. There, they managed the affairs of the household but seldom ventured out. Still, as in other cultures, women's lives varied according to region and class. Veiling and seclusion were not so strictly followed among lower-class city women. In rural areas, peasant women continued to contribute to the economy in many ways.

Islamic Law Court
The Sharia applies Islamic teachings to legal issues. In this Persian painting, a man and woman seek a decision before a judge.

Theme: Political and Social Systems What does this picture suggest about the rights of Muslim women?

SECTION 1 Assessment

Recall
1. **Identify:** **(a)** Mecca, **(b)** Bedouins, **(c)** Kaaba, **(d)** Khadija, **(e)** Quran, **(f)** People of the Book, **(g)** Sharia.
2. **Define:** **(a)** oasis, **(b)** hijra, **(c)** monotheistic, **(d)** mosque, **(e)** hajj, **(f)** jihad.

Comprehension
3. How did Muhammad become the prophet of Islam?
4. **(a)** What are the Five Pillars of Islam? **(b)** How do they help unite Muslims?

5. How do the Quran and Sharia guide the lives of Muslims?

Critical Thinking and Writing
6. **Comparing** In what ways are the religious teachings of Islam similar to those of Judaism and Christianity?
7. **Identifying Main Ideas** Review the three paragraphs that appear in this section under the heading "The Hijra: A Turning Point." For each paragraph, identify the main idea and two details that support the main idea.

Activity
Take It to the NET

Use the Internet to learn more about the hajj, or pilgrimage to Mecca, today. Then, assume the role of a news reporter in Mecca. Write a news article describing the special customs and rites associated with the hajj.

Human Drama Activity

The Hajj The following is part of a description of a young American woman's first experience of the hajj. "Before me was the Kaaba, a great black cube partly submerged in a torrent of white-robed pilgrims circling round and round. . . . High above, the muezzin began the evening call to prayer: *'Allahu Akbar!* . . . God is Most Great!' Up on the hills the thin reedy voices of the muezzins in the smaller mosques joined in, each voice picking up the call in a fugue of prayer soaring into the golden crest of the afternoon."

Test Preparation

Have students read the paragraph on the opposite page under the heading "People of the Book," and then complete the sentence below.

The word *polytheistic* in the passage means

A having many heads.

B having many gods.

C having many ideas.

D having many books.

SECTION 1 Assessment

Recall
1. (a) Mecca, p. 252 (b) Bedouins, p. 252 (c) Kaaba, p. 252 (d) Khadija, p. 253 (e) Quran, p. 253 (f) "People of the Book," p. 254 (g) Sharia, p. 255 2. (a) oasis, p. 252 (b) hijra, p. 253 (c) monotheistic, p. 253 (d) mosque, p. 254 (e) hajj, p. 254 (f) jihad, p. 254

Comprehension
3. He received visions from God telling him to preach against false gods and to urge people to worship Allah. 4. (a) faith that there is one God and Muhammad is his messenger; daily prayer; charity to the poor; observance of the fast during Ramadan; pilgrimage to Mecca (b) The Five Pillars bind Muslims together through common beliefs and practices. 5. The Quran is the final word on all matters. It addresses many ethical matters and explains proper behavior for Muslims. The Sharia is a body of law that applies the teachings of the Quran to the daily life of Muslims and regulates many aspects of Muslim society.

Critical Thinking and Writing
6. Islam, like Judaism and Christianity, is monotheistic and teaches rules for moral behavior. Islam also teaches that the Torah and Bible are revelations from God. Islam accepts Moses and Jesus as prophets sent from God. Islam and Christianity also believe in Judgment Day, heaven, and hell. 7. Answers should show that students understand the difference between main ideas and details.

Activity Rubrics

Share rubrics with students before they write their articles.

Attempted The article reveals little knowledge of the customs and rites of the hajj and is poorly written.

Minimal The article reveals some knowledge of the customs and rites of the hajj, but is poorly written.

Adequate The article reveals knowledge of the customs and rites of the hajj and is well written.

Exemplary The article reveals a great deal of knowledge of the customs and rites of the hajj and is very well written.

Caption Answer

It suggests that women as well as men had the right to bring a case before a court of law.

SECTION 2 — Islam Spreads

SECTION 2

Bell Ringer Draw students' attention to the "Spread of Islam" map in this section. Ask students to speculate on possible causes for this rapid and far-reaching growth.

LESSON PLAN

1. Focus Arab armies, inspired by Muhammad's teachings, spread Islam through parts of three continents. In many areas, people welcomed Islamic teachings and the benefits of Muslim rule. After Muhammad's death, a split over leadership arose between the Sunnis and the Shiites. By the 1200s, the Arab empire began to decline due to civil wars and foreign invasions.

2. Instruct Divide the class into several groups. Instruct each group to make up three discussion questions covering the main points in this section. Have the groups take turns presenting their questions and leading class discussions based on them. Conclude by asking students to analyze which questions made them consider the content most thoughtfully.

3. Assess Tell students to imagine that they are newspaper editors. Have them write three or four headlines that summarize the main points in the section.

4. Reteach If students' **Assess** activity does not reflect adequate understanding of the lesson, you might assign the *Guide to the Essentials* or the *Interactive Student Tutorial CD-ROM* for this section.

Reading Focus

- How did Muslims conquer many lands?
- What movements emerged within Islam?
- Why did the empire of the caliphs decline?

Vocabulary

caliph
minaret
muezzin
sultan

Taking Notes

On a piece of paper, make a time line like the model below. As you read, fill in the time line with major events concerning the spread of Islam and the rise and fall of Muslim empires.

Muslims
enter Spain
711

600	800	1000	1200	1400

Main Idea Inspired by Muhammad's teachings, Arab armies spread Islam through parts of three continents.

Setting the Scene The death of Muhammad plunged his followers into grief. The Prophet had been a pious man and a powerful leader. No one else had ever been able to unify the Bedouin tribes. Could his legacy survive without him?

Abu Bakr, an early convert to Islam, was determined to continue the Prophet's work. He sternly told the faithful, "If you worship Muhammad, Muhammad is dead. If you worship God, God is alive."

Despite some bitter struggles, Arab unity did not collapse. Inspired by the teachings of the Prophet, Arab armies surged across the Byzantine and Persian empires. In a stunningly short time, an Arabic empire reached from the Atlantic to the borders of India.

An Age of Conquests

As the first caliph, or successor to Muhammad, Abu Bakr faced an immediate crisis. The loyalty of some Arab tribal leaders had been dependent on Muhammad's personal command. They now refused to follow Abu Bakr and withdrew their loyalty to Islam. Abu Bakr succeeded in reuniting the Arabs, based first and foremost on their allegiance to Islam. Once reunited, the Arabs set out on a remarkable series of military conquests.

From Victory to Victory Under the first four caliphs, Arab armies marched from victory to victory. They conquered great chunks of the Byzantine empire, including the provinces of Syria and Palestine, with the cities of Damascus and Jerusalem. Next, they rapidly demolished the Persian empire. The Arabs then swept into Egypt.

Later Muslim armies conquered even more lands. From Egypt, Muslims dashed west, defeating Byzantine forces across North Africa. In 711, they crossed the Strait of Gibraltar into Spain and pushed north into France. There, in 732, they were defeated at the battle of Tours. The Muslim advance into Western Europe was halted. Even so, Muslims would rule parts of Spain for centuries. Elsewhere, Muslims besieged the Byzantine capital of Constantinople, but failed to take the well-defended city. Later waves of conquests would expand Muslim rule farther into the continents of Asia and Africa.

Reasons for Success Why did the Arabs have such an astonishing series of victories? One reason was the weakness of the Byzantine and Persian empires. These longtime rivals had fought each other to exhaustion. Many people in the Fertile Crescent welcomed the Arabs as liberators from harsh

Geography and History

Desert Warfare

"Fight the enemy in the desert," said one wounded Muslim leader. "There you will be victorious . . . you will have the friendly and familiar desert at your backs. The enemy cannot follow you there."

In response to the geographic conditions of the Arabian Peninsula, Arab soldiers became skilled in the special tactics of desert warfare. They knew how to use horses and camels to cross broad areas quickly and then sweep down to catch their enemies by surprise. The sudden charge of an Arab cavalry overwhelmed unprepared defenders. The elements of surprise and speed, as well as maneuverability, helped the Arabs conquer much of the Byzantine and Persian empires.

Theme: Geography and History Why were Arab soldiers skilled in the tactics of desert warfare?

Geography and History

ANSWER They lived and trained in the desert.

Resource Directory

Teaching Resources

Creative Teaching Activities Creative Teaching Activities booklet, p. 50
Guided Reading and Review Unit 3 booklet, p. 58
Viewpoint Activity *Views of the Medieval Muslim World*, Unit 3 booklet, p. 68

Technology

World History Color Transparencies *Spread of Islam* base map and overlay transparencies, set 3, pp. B–35, B–37, B–39

Byzantine or Persian rule. Bold, efficient fighting methods also contributed to the Arab success. The Bedouin camel and horse cavalry mounted aggressive and mobile offensives that overwhelmed more traditional armies.

Perhaps the key reason for Arab success, however, was the common faith Muhammad had given his people. Islam knitted a patchwork of tribes into a determined, unified state. Belief in Islam and the certainty of paradise for those who fell in battle spurred the Arab armies to victory.

Treatment of Conquered People The advancing Arabs brought many people under their rule. Muslim leaders imposed a special tax on non-Muslims, but allowed Christians, Jews, and Zoroastrians to practice their own faiths and follow their own laws. As Muslim civilization developed, many Jews and Christians played key roles as officials, doctors, and translators. In time, many non-Muslims converted to Islam.

Many nomadic peoples in North Africa and Central Asia chose Islam immediately. Its message was simple and direct, and they saw its triumph as a sign of God's favor. Moreover, Islam had no religious hierarchy or class of priests. In principle, it emphasized the equality of all believers, regardless of race, sex, class, or wealth. In later centuries, Turkish and Mongol converts helped spread Islam far across Asia.

Muslims in Europe For centuries after the battle of Tours, Christian forces fought to reconquer Spain. Only in 1492 did they seize the last Muslim stronghold. In the meantime, Spain flourished as a center of Muslim civilization.

Muslim rulers in Spain presided over brilliant courts, where the arts and learning thrived. In general, they were more tolerant of other religions than Christian rulers of the time. At centers of learning such as the city of Córdoba, rulers employed Jewish officials and welcomed Christian scholars to study science and philosophy. Architects built grand buildings, such as the Alhambra, a fortified palace in Granada. Its lovely gardens, reflecting pools, and finely decorated marble columns mark a high point of Muslim civilization in Spain.

Great Mosque of Córdoba
Córdoba was the cultural center of Muslim Spain. The columns and arches of this mosque in Córdoba show the elaborate nature of Muslim architecture.

Theme: Continuity and Change What earlier civilizations pioneered the use of columns and arches?

Muslim civilization also thrived in Sicily and other Mediterranean islands seized by Arab forces in the late 800s. Muslim rule lasted briefly. But even after knights from Normandy gained control of Sicily, it remained strongly Arabic in culture. Muslim officials governed the island well, and merchants and farmers helped the economy prosper. Muslim poets, philosophers, and scientists enriched the courts of Norman kings.

Movements Within Islam

Not long after Muhammad's death, divisions arose within Islam over his successor. The split between Sunni (SOO nee) and Shiite (SHEE ite) Muslims had a profound impact on later Islamic history.

Sunni and Shiites The Sunni felt that the caliph should be chosen by leaders of the Muslim community. Although the Sunni agreed that the caliph should be a pious Muslim, they viewed him simply as a leader, not as a religious authority.

Background Biography

Skillful Leadership The Arabs' military success began with Muhammad himself, who proved to be not only an inspiring religious leader, but a capable war strategist as well. In the Battle of the Ditch, Muhammad prevailed over an army of 10,000 Meccans with only 3,000 of his own forces. He did so by digging deep trenches around Medina. Any attempts the Meccan cavalry made to breach the trench were thwarted by Muslim foot soldiers. This success vastly increased Muhammad's prestige.

Activity Connections to Film

Constructing a Diagram *The Byzantine Empire,* Program 15 of the public television series *The Western Tradition,* provides a well-organized outline of the various developments and circumstances that caused one empire to fall and another to rise. Ask students who view *The Byzantine Empire* to construct a web that outlines the many causes of the rise and spread of Islam. Students' diagrams should include branches for religious, economic, cultural, political, and military reasons. (*The Western Tradition,* released in 1989 as part of the Annenberg/CPB Collection, is distributed by Intellimation.) ✻

Block Scheduling Support

Have students compare the spread of Islam with the spread of Christianity, Judaism, Buddhism, and Hinduism. Divide the class into five groups and assign each group one of the religions mentioned above. Each group should use what they have read in their textbooks to create a chart that shows the spread of their assigned religion. Have a representative from each group present their chart to the class. After each group has presented, use the charts to generate a class discussion.

Caption Answer

Greek, Roman, and Byzantine civilizations

Customize for...
Heterogeneous Groups

Writing a Dialogue Have small groups of students create dialogues in which a Sunni, Shiite, and Sufi discuss their thoughts and beliefs about Islam. The dialogue should reflect both similarities and differences in their beliefs. Suggest that students first review the text and summarize the ideas of each group. When students have finished writing their dialogues, ask volunteers to perform them for the class. *(Reteaching)*

Customize for...
Kinesthetic Learners

Making a Map Have students make a map, similar to the one on this page, showing the spread of Islam from the time of Muhammad to 750. You may distribute copies of the outline map *Islamic Empire* from the Historical Outline Map Book, p. 20, or assign students to draw maps of their own. Remind students that their maps should be accurately labeled and should include an appropriate key. Display the maps around the classroom.
✳

Spread of Islam

Key:
- Boundary of Byzantine empire, 565
- Muslim lands at death of Muhammad, 632
- Lands conquered by Muslims under first four caliphs, 632–661
- Lands conquered by Muslims under Umayyad caliphs, 661–750

Robinson Projection

Skills Assessment

Geography In less than 150 years, Islam spread from Arabia across southwest Asia and North Africa and into Europe.

1. **Location** On the map, locate **(a)** Arabian Desert, **(b)** Mecca, **(c)** Medina, **(d)** Persia, **(e)** Cairo, **(f)** Constantinople, **(g)** Córdoba.
2. **Region** During what period did Spain come under Muslim rule?
3. **Critical Thinking**
   Applying Information How might the spread of Islam have contributed to Muslim success in trade?

The Shiites, on the other hand, argued that the only true successors to the Prophet were descendants of Muhammad's daughter and son-in-law, Fatima and Ali. The Shiites believed that the descendants of the Prophet were divinely inspired. The Sunni believed that inspiration came from the example of Muhammad as recorded by his early followers.

Ali became the fourth caliph, but he was assassinated in 661 in a struggle for leadership. Later, his son, too, was killed. Many other Shiites died in battle against Sunni, trying to install their candidates for caliph. Shiites grew to admire martyrdom as a demonstration of their faith.

Like the schism between Roman Catholic and Eastern Orthodox Christians, the division between Sunni and Shiite Muslims has survived to the present day. Members of both branches of Islam believe in the same one God, look to the Quran for guidance, and make the hajj. But numerous differences have emerged in such areas as religious practice, law, and daily life. Today, about 90 percent of Muslims are Sunni. Most Shiites live in Iran, Lebanon, Iraq, and Yemen. The Shiite movement itself has split into several different factions.

Sufi A third tradition in Islam emerged with the Sufis, Muslim mystics who sought communion with God through meditation, fasting, and other rituals. Sufis were respected for their piety and miraculous powers.

Like Christian monks and nuns, some Sufis helped spread Islam through missionary work. They carried the faith to remote villages, where they blended local traditions and beliefs into Muslim culture.

Empire of the Caliphs

After the death of Ali, the Umayyad (oh MĪ ad) family set up a dynasty that ruled the Islamic world until 750. From their capital at Damascus in Syria, they directed the spectacular conquests that carried Islam from the Atlantic to the Indus Valley.

Umayyads Even as victories expanded the Arab empire, the Umayyads faced numerous problems. First, they had to adapt from desert life to ruling large cities and huge territories. To govern their empire, the Umayyads often relied on local officials, including educated Jews, Greeks, and Persians. As a result, Byzantine and Persian traditions of government influenced Arab rulers.

While conquests continued, vast wealth flowed into Umayyad hands. When conquests slowed in the 700s, economic tensions increased between

Skills Assessment

ANSWERS 1. Review locations with students. 2. between 661 and 750 3. Possible answer: Muslims controlled much of the land around the Mediterranean. Muslim control allowed merchants to travel safely through many parts of the region.

Resource Directory

Technology
World History Color Transparencies *Chess, A Traveling Game,* p. C–33

World History Visions, Voices, Views Daily Life CloseUp, *A Court Singer and a Merchant in Baghdad,* videodisc side 2 or videotape 3, running time 3:00 min.

Side 2: Fr. 8582-14540

wealthy Arabs and those who had less. Many Muslims criticized the court at Damascus for abandoning the simple ways of the early caliphs. Shiites hated the Umayyads because they had defeated Ali and killed his son, dishonoring the Prophet's family. Unrest also festered among non-Arab converts to Islam, who under the Umayyads had fewer rights than Arabs.

Abbassids Discontented Muslims found a leader in Abu al-Abbas, who captured Damascus in 750. Soon after, one of his generals invited members of the defeated Umayyad family to a banquet—and killed them all. Abu al-Abbas then founded the Abbassid dynasty, which lasted until 1258.

The Abbassid dynasty ended Arab dominance and helped make Islam a truly universal religion. Under the early Abbassids, the empire of the caliphs reached its greatest wealth and power, and Muslim civilization enjoyed a golden age.

Splendors of Baghdad The Abbassid caliph al-Mansur chose as the site of his new capital Baghdad, a small market town in present-day Iraq. "It is an excellent military camp," he wrote. "Besides here is the Tigris to put us in touch with lands as far as China and bring us all that the seas yield." Under the Abbassids, Baghdad exceeded Constantinople in size and wealth.

In Baghdad, Persian traditions strongly influenced Arab life, but Islam remained the religion and Arabic the language of the empire. Poets, scholars, philosophers, and entertainers from all over the Muslim world flocked to the Abbassid court. Visitors no doubt felt that Baghdad deserved its title "City of Peace, Gift of God, Paradise on Earth."

Many gardens, dotted with fabulous fountains, gleamed in the sunlight. Above the streets loomed domes and minarets, the slender towers of mosques. Each day, a mosque official called a muezzin climbed to the top of the minaret and called the faithful to prayer. In busy market courtyards, merchants sold goods from Africa, Asia, and Europe. The palace of the caliph echoed with the music of flutes, cymbals, and tambourines, along with the voices of female singers.

The city of Baghdad reached its peak under the reign of caliph Harun al-Rashid, who ruled from 786 to 809. For centuries, in both Europe and the Muslim world, Harun was admired as a model ruler. He was viewed as a symbol of wealth and splendor.

Decline of the Caliphate

Starting about 850, Abbassid control over the Arab empire fragmented. In Spain, Egypt, and elsewhere, independent dynasties ruled separate Muslim states. As the caliph's power faded, civil wars erupted, and Shiite rulers took over parts of the empire. Between 900 and 1400, a series of invasions added to the chaos.

Seljuks In the 900s, the Seljuk Turks migrated into the Middle East from Central Asia. They adopted Islam and built a large empire across the Fertile Crescent. By 1055, a Seljuk sultan, or authority, controlled Baghdad, but he left the Abbassid caliph as a figurehead. As the Seljuks pushed into Asia Minor, they threatened the Byzantine empire. Reports of Seljuk interference with Christian pilgrims traveling to Jerusalem led Pope Urban II, in 1095, to call for the First Crusade.

Crusaders In 1099, after a long and bloody siege, Christian crusaders captured Jerusalem. For 150 years, the city passed back and forth between Muslims and Christians. The Muslim general Salah al-Din, or Saladin, ousted Christians from Jerusalem in 1187. They regained it after his death, holding it until 1244.

Christians also ruled a few tiny states in Palestine, but they were eventually expelled. In the long term, as you read, the Crusades had a much greater impact on Europe than on the Muslim world.

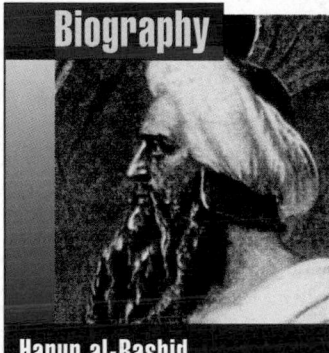

Biography

Harun al-Rashid
763(?)–809

Many stories and legends recall Caliph Harun al-Rashid's wealth, generosity, and support of learning. Poets, physicians, philosophers, and artists all gathered at his court in Baghdad. One story tells how Harun rewarded a favorite poet with a robe of honor, a splendid horse, and 5,000 dirhams—a vast sum of money.

Harun used his generosity to create closer ties with other rulers. He sent the Frankish king Charlemagne several gifts, including a mechanical clock and an elephant. Harun hoped that the Franks would join him in an alliance against the rival Umayyad caliphate in Spain.

Despite his lavishness and generosity, Harun amassed a great fortune. At his death, he had millions of dirhams, plus huge stores of jewels and gold.

Theme: Impact of the Individual How did Harun help make Baghdad a major center of Muslim culture?

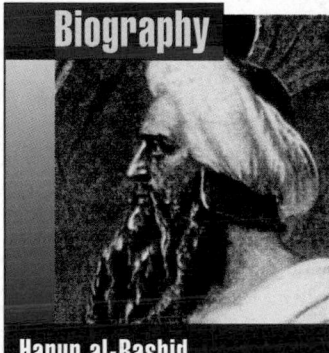

Background
Global Connections

A Traveling Game Chess originated in India, with game pieces that represented a king, an elephant, a horse, a chariot, and four footmen. The original Indian game had four players who threw dice to determine their moves. By the 500s, the game had spread to Persia. After Persia was conquered by the Arabs, chess spread throughout the Muslim world. During this time, its use of dice was abandoned, and it became a game of two players. During the Crusades, Europeans learned chess from Muslims.

Background
Biography

An Iron Hand Harun al-Rashid was known for swift and determined action. On one occasion, the Byzantine emperor Nicephorus sent a letter to the caliph informing him that he would not be able to deliver his tribute payments. Harun's response was swift:

"In the name of Allah the Merciful, the Compassionate. From Harun, Commander of the Faithful, to Nicephorus, dog of a Roman: I have your letter, O son of an infidel mother. The answer shall be for your eyes to see, not for your ears to hear. Salaam."

When Harun marched a huge army against Asia Minor, the Byzantine emperor quickly agreed to resume payments.

Human Drama Note

Language English contains many words of Arabic derivation. Have students trace the history of the following words:

admiral	baroque	elixir	mattress
adobe	borax	gauze	racquet
alchemy	caliber	gypsum	retina
alcove	cataract	hazard	sash
almanac	cipher	jasmine	sugar
arsenal	crimson	macabre	traffic
azure	damask	magnet	zero

✓ Test Preparation

Have students read the paragraphs on this page under the heading "Crusaders," and then answer the question below.

When did Salah al-Din drive the Christians out of Jerusalem?

A in the 900s

B in the 1000s

C in the 1100s

D in the 1200s

Biography

ANSWER His generosity to artists like the poet must have encouraged them to produce great art, believing that their efforts would be rewarded.

Recall

1. **(a)** Abu Bakr, p. 256 **(b)** battle of Tours, p. 256 **(c)** Fatima and Ali, p. 258 **(d)** Sufi, p. 258 **(e)** Umayyads, p. 258 **(f)** Abbassids, p. 259 **(g)** Harun al-Rashid, p. 259 **(h)** Seljuks, p. 259 **(i)** Tamerlane, p. 260
2. **(a)** caliph, p. 256 **(b)** minaret, p. 259 **(c)** muezzin, p. 259 **(d)** sultan, p. 259

Comprehension

3. **(a)** Syria, Palestine, the Persian empire, Egypt, North Africa, Spain, Sicily **(b)** Possible answers: the weakness of nearby empires; bold, efficient fighting methods; unity under one faith 4. Sunnis and Shiites had fundamental differences about the nature of Islamic leadership. 5. The Abbassid empire was divided by independent dynasties that ruled separate Muslim states. There were civil wars and foreign invasions.

Critical Thinking and Writing

6. The Turks threatened the Byzantine empire. Reports that they had interfered with Christian pilgrims led Pope Urban II to call for a crusade. 7. Possible answer: They might have liked the ideas of unity and equality that brotherhood implied.

Activity Rubrics

Share rubrics with students before they write their diary entries.

Attempted The diary entry is unimaginative and has few details.

Minimal The diary entry is poorly written, but does discuss country and city life.

Adequate The diary entry is detailed, thoughtful, and well written.

Exemplary The diary entry is detailed, thoughtful, and well written. It includes humor or anecdotes to help involve the reader.

Skills Assessment

ANSWER Muslims learn Arabic because it is the language of the Quran. Wherever Islam spread, so did knowledge of Arabic.

Cause and Effect

Long-Term Causes	Immediate Causes
• Weakness of Byzantine and Persian empires • Economic and social changes in Arabia	• Tribes of Arabia unified by Islam around a central message • Wide acceptance of religious message of Islam • Easy acceptance of social ideas of Islam, such as equality among believers

Spread of Islam

Immediate Effects	Long-Term Effects
• Islam spreads from the Atlantic coast to the Indus Valley • Centers of learning flourish in Cairo, Córdoba, and elsewhere	• Muslim civilization emerges • Linking of Europe, Asia, and Africa through Muslim trade network • Arabic becomes shared language of Muslims • Split between Sunni and Shiites

Connections to Today

• Islam is religion of nearly one fifth of world population
• Millions of Muslims make pilgrimages to Mecca
• Arabic is among the most widely spoken languages in the world

Skills Assessment **Chart** Religion, politics, and culture all played a significant role in the rapid spread of Islam. **How does the spread of Islam help explain the wide knowledge of Arabic in today's world?**

Mongols In 1216, Genghiz Khan led the Mongols out of Central Asia across Persia and Mesopotamia. Mongol armies returned again and again. In 1258, Hulagu, grandson of Genghiz, burned and looted Baghdad, killing the last Abbassid caliph. Later, the Mongols adopted Islam.

In the late 1300s, another Mongol leader, Timur the Lame, or Tamerlane, led his armies into the Middle East. Though he himself was a Muslim, Tamerlane's ambitions led him to conquer Muslim as well as non-Muslim lands. His victorious armies overran Persia and Mesopotamia before invading Russia and India.

Looking Ahead

As the 1200s drew to a close, the Arab empire had fragmented and fallen. Independent Muslim caliphates and states were scattered across North Africa and Spain, while a Mongol khan ruled the Middle East. After five centuries of relative unity, the Muslim world was as politically divided as Christian Europe.

Even though the empire crumbled, Islam continued to link diverse people across an enormous area that Muslims called the *Dar al-Islam,* or "Abode of Islam." In the future, other great Muslim empires would arise in the Middle East and India. Muslims also benefited from an advanced civilization that had taken root under the Abbassids. In the next section, you will read about the achievements of their Muslim civilization in art, literature, and other fields of endeavor.

SECTION 2 Assessment

Recall

1. **Identify:** **(a)** Abu Bakr, **(b)** battle of Tours, **(c)** Fatima and Ali, **(d)** Sufi, **(e)** Umayyads, **(f)** Abbassids, **(g)** Harun al-Rashid, **(h)** Seljuks, **(i)** Tamerlane.
2. **Define:** **(a)** caliph, **(b)** minaret, **(c)** muezzin, **(d)** sultan.

Comprehension

3. **(a)** What areas did Arab armies conquer? **(b)** Give three reasons for the rapid success of the Arab conquests.
4. What issues divided Sunni Muslims and Shiite Muslims?

5. Why did the empire of the Abbassid caliphs decline and eventually break up?

Critical Thinking and Writing

6. **Connecting to Geography** How did the migration of the Turks lead to conflict in the Middle East?
7. **Drawing Conclusions** Muhammad said, "Know ye that every Muslim is a brother to every other Muslim and that ye are now one brotherhood." How might this idea have increased the appeal of Islam to conquered peoples?

Activity

Writing a Diary
Imagine that you are a Bedouin who is visiting Baghdad for the first time during the reign of Harun al-Rashid. Record in your diary how city life differs from nomadic life in the desert.

260 *Chapter 11*

Resource Directory

Teaching Resources

Section Quiz Unit 3 booklet, p. 59
Creative Teaching Activities Creative Teaching Activities booklet, p. 51
Guided Reading and Review Unit 3 booklet, p. 60

Technology

World History Color Transparencies *Chess, A Traveling Game,* p. C–33; *An Arms Workshop,* p. D–55
Interactive Student Tutorial CD-ROM Ch. 11
Computer Test Bank Ch. 11

SECTION 3 Golden Age of Muslim Civilization

Reading Focus

■ How were the Muslim society and economy organized?

■ What traditions influenced Muslim art and literature?

■ What advances did Muslims make in centers of learning?

Vocabulary

social mobility
arabesque
calligraphy

Taking Notes

Copy this partially completed concept web. As you read, finish the diagram by adding advances made during the golden age of Muslim civilization. Draw as many circles as you need to complete the web.

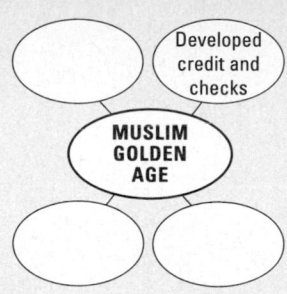

Main Idea During the Abbassid golden age, Muslims made advances in economics, art, literature, and science.

Setting the Scene

One night, Caliph al-Mamun had a vivid dream. There in his chambers he came upon a balding, blue-eyed stranger sitting on the low couch.

"Who are you?" the caliph demanded.

"Aristotle," the man replied. The caliph was delighted. He plied the great Greek philosopher with questions about ethics, reason, and religion.

Although al-Mamun soon awoke, his dream inspired him to action. He had scholars collect the great works of the classical world and translate them into Arabic. By 830, the caliph had set up the "House of Wisdom," a library and university in Baghdad.

Under the Abbassids, Islam absorbed traditions from many cultures. In the process, a vital new civilization rose that flourished in cities from Damascus to Cairo to Córdoba and later to Delhi in India. The great works produced by scholars of the Abbassid golden age shaped the Muslim world just as Greek and Roman classics shaped western culture.

Society and the Economy

Muslim rulers united people from diverse cultures, including Arabs, Persians, Egyptians and other Africans, and Europeans. Later, Mongols, Turks, Indians, and people in Southeast Asia declared their faith in Islam. In time, Muslim civilization absorbed and blended many traditions.

Social Classes Muslim society was more open than that of medieval Christian Europe. Although Arabs had held themselves apart from non-Arab Muslims at first, that distinction faded under the Abbassids. People enjoyed a certain degree of social mobility, the ability to move up in social class. People could improve their social rank through religious, scholarly, or military achievements.

As in Greece and Rome, slavery was a common institution in the cities of the Muslim world. Slaves were brought from conquered lands in Spain, Greece, Africa, India, and Central Asia. Muslims could not be enslaved. If non-Muslim slaves converted to Islam, they did not automatically gain their freedom, but their children did. A female slave who married her owner also gained freedom.

Most slaves worked as household servants. Some were skilled artisans. The Abbassids used slave-soldiers who fought loyally for the caliph. Slaves of rulers sometimes rose to high positions in government, and a number of caliphs were the sons of slave mothers. Islamic law encouraged the freeing

Muslim Scholars
During the golden age of Muslim civilization, scholars made advances in a variety of fields. Here, some learned men gather in an observatory for studying the heavens.

Theme: Global Interaction
How did Muslim conquests contribute to advances in the arts and sciences?

Bell Ringer Ask students to describe what they know about the stories of Aladdin, Ali Baba, or Sindbad. Inform them that these tales are just a small sample of Muslim achievements in literature. Muslims also made significant achievements in art and science.

LESSON PLAN

1. Focus A vast international trade network helped to support manufacturing and agriculture. During the golden age of Muslim civilization, Muslims of many lands made advances in art, literature, and science.

2. Instruct Have students work in groups to research and report on a particular aspect of Muslim civilization during its golden age. Assign each group a different topic. Possible topics include: Social Classes, Economy, Art, Literature, and Science. Encourage students to use library resources as well as information in the text. For their reports to the class, advise students to use illustrations, maps, charts, videos, or other visual aids.

3. Assess Ask students to write down three achievements of Muslim civilization that they consider to have the greatest importance. Invite students to read their choices to the class and to explain the reasons for their choices.

4. Reteach If students' **Assess** activity does not reflect adequate understanding of the lesson, you might assign the *Guide to the Essentials* or the *Interactive Student Tutorial CD-ROM* for this section.

Block Scheduling Support

World History Color Transparencies contain two transparencies that can help students visualize aspects of this section. One is *Chess, A Traveling Game*, p. C–33. Background information and lesson suggestions are found on p. C–8. The other appropriate transparency is *An Arms Workshop*, p. D–57, which shows a Persian manuscript illumination. Background information and lesson suggestions are on p. D–15. Also of interest is Transparency 7, *Polo Game*, in the Humanities Pack Transparencies. This Persian miniature will help students learn about the mixing of artistic traditions in the Middle East. Use these transparencies to generate a class discussion on the legacy of Muslim arts and crafts.

Caption Answer

Muslims absorbed traditions and knowledge of conquered people, then brought these traditions to newly conquered lands.

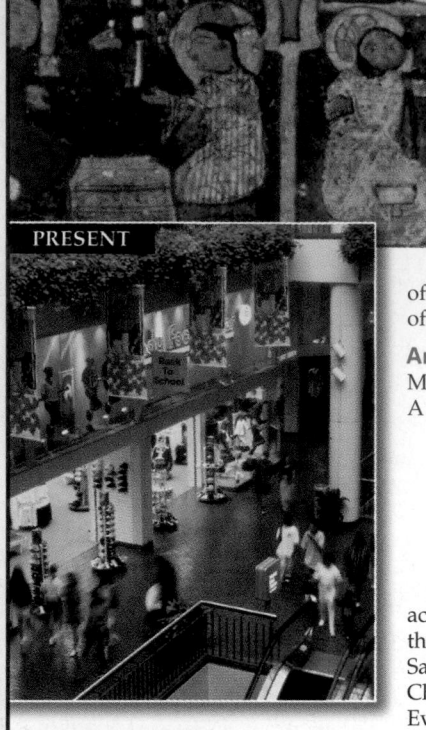

PAST

PRESENT

In the Marketplace
In the painting (top), Muslim merchants sell their wares. In cities like Baghdad, merchants sold goods in roofed bazaars containing miles of streets. Today's multilevel shopping mall (bottom) is a modern version of the bazaar.

Theme: Economics and Technology In what businesses are the four bazaar merchants engaged?

of slaves. Many slaves bought their freedom, often with the help of charitable donations or even state funds.

An International Trade Network Merchants were honored in the Muslim world, in part because Muhammad had been a merchant. A traditional collection of deeds and sayings stated:

> "The honest, truthful Muslim merchant will stand with the martyrs on the Day of Judgment. I commend the merchants to you, for they are the couriers of the horizon and God's trusted servants on Earth."
> —Sayings of the Prophet

Between 750 and 1350, merchants built a vast trading network across the Muslim world and beyond, spreading Islam peacefully in their wake. Camel caravans—the "ships of the desert"—crossed the Sahara into West Africa. Muslim traders traveled the Silk Road from China. Monsoon winds carried Arab ships from East Africa to India. Everywhere Muslim traders bought and exchanged goods, creating great fortunes for the most successful.

Trade spread both products and technologies. As you have read, Muslim merchants brought Arabic numerals from India to the western world. Arabs also carried sugar from India and papermaking from China. A common language and a common religion helped this global exchange to grow and thrive.

Extensive trade and a prosperous money economy led Muslims to pioneer new business practices. They set up partnerships, bought and sold on credit, and formed banks to change currency. To transfer money more easily, Muslims invented the ancestors of today's bank checks. We get our word *check* from the Arabic word *sakk*. Bankers developed a sophisticated system of accounting. They opened branch banks in all major cities, so that a check written in Baghdad might be cashed in Cairo.

Manufacturing As in medieval Europe, handicraft manufacturing in Muslim cities was typically organized by guilds. The heads of the guilds, chosen by their members, often had the authority to regulate prices, weights and measures, methods of production, and the quality of the product. Most labor was done by wage workers.

Across the Muslim world, artisans produced a wealth of fine goods. Steel swords from Damascus, leather goods from Córdoba, cotton textiles from Egypt, and carpets from Persia were highly valued. Workshops also turned out fine glassware, furniture, and tapestries.

Agriculture Outside the cities, agriculture flourished across a wide variety of climates and landforms. Muslim farmers cultivated sugar cane, cotton, dyes, medicinal herbs, fruits, vegetables, and flowers that were bought and sold in world markets.

The more arid regions of the Muslim world were basically divided into two kinds of land, "the desert and the sown." Small farming communities faced a constant scarcity of water. To improve farm output, the Abbassids organized massive irrigation projects and drained swamplands between the Tigris and Euphrates. Farmers in Mesopotamia, Egypt, and the Mediterranean coast produced grain, olives, dates, and other crops.

The deserts continued to support independent nomads who lived by herding. Still, nomads and farmers shared economic ties. Nomads bought dates and grain from settled peoples, while farming populations acquired meat, wool, and hides from the nomads.

Art and Literature

As in Christian Europe and Hindu India, religion shaped the arts and literature of the Islamic world. The great work of Islamic literature was the poetic Quran itself. Scholars studied the sacred words of the Quran in Arabic and then produced their own works interpreting its meaning.

Muslim art and literature reflected the diverse traditions of the various peoples who lived under Muslim rule. Muslim artists and writers were also influenced by the skills and styles of the many peoples with whom they came in contact, including Greeks, Romans, Persians, and Indians.

Design and Decoration Because the Quran strictly banned the worship of idols, Muslim religious leaders forbade artists to portray God or human figures in religious art. The walls and ceilings of mosques were decorated with elaborate abstract and geometric patterns. The arabesque, an intricate design composed of curved lines that suggest floral shapes, appeared in rugs, textiles, and glassware. Muslim artists also perfected skills in calligraphy, the art of beautiful handwriting. They worked the flowing Arabic script, especially verses from the Quran, into decorations on buildings and objects of art.

In nonreligious art, some Muslim artists did paint human and animal figures. Arabic scientific works were often lavishly illustrated. Literary works and luxury objects sometimes showed stylized figures. In later periods, Persian, Turkish, and Indian artists excelled at painting miniatures to illustrate books of poems and fables.

Architecture Muslim architects adapted the domes and arches of Byzantine buildings to new uses. In Jerusalem, they built the Dome of the Rock, a great shrine capped with a magnificent dome. Domed mosques and high minarets dominated Muslim cities in the same way that cathedral spires dominated medieval Christian cities.

Poetry Long before Muhammad, Arabs had a rich tradition of oral poetry. In musical verses, Bedouin poets chanted the dangers of desert journeys, the joys of battle, or the glories of their clans. Their most important themes, chivalry and the romance of nomadic life, recurred in Arab poetry throughout the centuries. Through Muslim Spain, these traditions came to influence medieval European literature and music.

Later Arab poets developed elaborate formal rules for writing poetry and explored both religious and worldly themes. The poems of Rabiah al-Adawiyya expressed Sufi mysticism and encouraged the faithful to worship God selflessly without hope of reward. "If I worship Thee in hope of Paradise / Exclude me from Paradise," she wrote in one prayer poem. Other poets praised important leaders, described the lavish lives of the wealthy, sang of the joys and sorrows of love, or conveyed nuggets of wisdom.

Persian Muslims also had a fine poetic tradition. Firdawsi (fihr DOW see) wrote in Persian using Arabic script. His masterpiece, the *Shah Namah*, or *Book of Kings*, tells the history of Persia. Omar Khayyám (kī YAHM),

Primary Source

A Hero's Super Powers

Firdawsi's Shah Namah *tells the story of many Persian heroes— among them, Rustam:*

"The tale is told that Rustam had at first
Such strength bestowed by Him who giveth all
That if he walked upon a rock his feet
Would sink therein. Such [power] as that
Proved an abiding trouble, and he prayed
To God in bitterness of soul to [diminish]
His strength that he might walk like other men."

—Firdawsi, *Shah Namah*

Skills Assessment

Primary Source Why was Rustam's strength both an advantage and a disadvantage?

 Human Drama Activity

Constructing a Model Have students bring a bar of soap to class. If possible, ask the art teacher to provide you with some small sculpting tools. You will also need art history books that describe and illustrate elements of Muslim architecture. Inform students that they will be creating soap sculptures replicating details of Muslim architecture.

First, have students browse through the text and art books to find an architectural detail they wish to sculpt. Next, instruct them to sketch the detail on a sheet of paper the same size as their bar of soap. Finally, have students begin to sculpt. After they have completed their sculptures, tell them to write a brief description of their work. Display students' finished work in class. ✳

Primary Source

ANSWER Rustam's strength would perhaps make him a great hero in battle, but it presented him with many everyday inconveniences.

Reading Strategy
Graphic Organizer

Ask students to write four column headings at the top of a sheet of paper: Society and the Economy, Art, Literature, and Learning. Have students fill in details from the text that illustrate Muslim accomplishments in these areas. *(Less Advanced Readers)*

Bell Ringer Have students try to guess which two animals are combined in the mythological griffin. *(Usually an eagle and a lion, but it is hard to tell which four-legged creature is represented in this griffin.)*

Background
Connections to Today

Muslim Art Because Muhammad declared that God loves beauty and preached that whatever people do they should do it excellently, Muslim art extends into most aspects of daily life. For example, in the past and in some areas today, many Muslim women learned embroidery and fine crocheting. A young girl and her mother would make beautiful towels, prayer rugs, table-cloths, and other linens that the girl would take with her when she married.

Activity
Cooperative Learning

Comparing Arts and Crafts Have students work together in small groups to research and present the arts or crafts of other groups, such as the Shakers, whose religion affected their artistic styles or their crafts. Have students compare the work of their chosen group with that of Islamic artists.

Portfolio Assessment Rubrics

Share rubrics with students before they make their presentations.

Attempted Student's presentation is cursory or incomplete.

Minimal Student's presentation shows some understanding of the topic, but comparisons are unclear.

Adequate Student's presentation is informative and interesting.

Exemplary Student's presentation has more than the required number of examples and is informative and interesting.

Art of the Muslim World

Throughout the Middle Ages, Muslim artists from Spain to India created paintings, sculptures, and mosaics in many different forms and styles, often borrowing ideas from the local cultures. Some of the artwork reflected religious themes, while other pieces focused on more worldly concerns, such as war, nature, and wealth.

This sixteenth-century painting was created by a Muslim artist from India. As a rule, representations of humans and animals were prohibited in Muslim art. But some people considered images of living creatures harmless if they were small, appeared on everyday objects, or did not cast a shadow.

Muslim artists showed their praise for Allah by decorating mosques with intricate mosaics. This sixteenth-century niche is created from ceramic tiles fitted together in geometric designs and decorated with floral patterns and calligraphy.

Fast Facts

- Calligraphy became a major Muslim art form because it reflected the holiness of the written Quran.

- As a sign of respect, Muhammad's face is never depicted in Muslim art.

- In the Middle Ages, Europeans prized Persian carpets so highly that they used them to cover tables instead of floors.

Portfolio Assessment

INTERNET Use the Internet or library resources to discover other examples of Muslim art. Choose two pieces from different time periods and geographic regions. Using what you have learned here, prepare a presentation comparing the two pieces.

This large sculpture, created by Muslim metalworkers around the year 1000, portrays an ancient mythological figure called a griffin. Arabic inscriptions on the figure wish its owner health and good fortune.

264 *Chapter 11*

Resource Directory

Teaching Resources
Humanities Link Chapter Extension Activities booklet, p. 31
Technology
Listening to Literature World Masterpieces audiotapes
Persian and Arabic Music, side 1, running time 2:10; from *The Rubáiyát,* side 1, running time 1:46

famous in the Muslim world as a scholar and astronomer, is best known to westerners for *The Rubáiyát* (ROO bī yaht). In this collection of four-line poems, Khayyám meditates on fate and the fleeting nature of life:

> "The Moving Finger writes; and having writ,
> Moves on; nor all your Piety nor Wit
> Shall lure it back to cancel half a line,
> Nor all your Tears wash out a word of it."
>
> —Omar Khayyám, *The Rubáiyát*

Tales Arab writers prized the art of storytelling. Across their empire, they gathered and adapted stories from Indian, Persian, Greek, Jewish, Egyptian, and Turkish sources. The best-known collection is *The Thousand and One Nights,* a group of tales narrated by the fictional princess Scheherezade (shu hehr uh ZAH duh). They include romances, fables, adventures, and humorous anecdotes, many set in the Baghdad of Harun al-Rashid. Later versions filtered into Europe, where millions of children thrilled to "Aladdin and His Magic Lamp" or "Ali Baba and the Forty Thieves."

The World of Learning

"Seek knowledge even as far as China," said Muhammad. Although he could not read or write, his respect for learning inspired Muslims to make great advances in learning.

Centers of Learning Both boys and girls were provided with elementary education. This training emphasized reading and writing, especially study of the Quran. Institutions of higher learning included schools for religious instruction and for the study of Islamic law.

Al-Mamun and later caliphs made Baghdad into the greatest Muslim center of learning. Its vast libraries attracted a galaxy of scholars, who were well paid and highly respected. Other cities, like Cairo, Bukhara, Timbuktu, and Córdoba, had their own centers of learning. In all these places, Muslim scholars made advances in philosophy, mathematics, medicine, and other fields. They preserved the learning of earlier civilizations by translating ancient Persian, Sanskrit, and Greek texts into Arabic.

Philosophy Muslim scholars translated the works of the Greek philosophers, as well as many Hindu and Buddhist texts. Like later Christian thinkers in Europe, Muslim scholars tried to harmonize Greek ideas about reason with religious beliefs based on divine revelation. In Córdoba, the philosopher Ibn Rushd—known in Europe as Averroës—put all knowledge except the Quran to the test of reason. His writings on Aristotle were translated into Latin and influenced Christian scholastics in medieval Europe.

Another Arab thinker, Ibn Khaldun, set standards for the scientific study of history. He stressed the importance of economics and social structure as causes of historical events. He also warned about common sources of error in historical writing. These included bias, exaggeration, and overconfidence in the accuracy of one's sources. Khaldun urged historians to trust sources only after a thorough investigation.

Mathematics Muslim scholars studied both Indian and Greek mathematics before making their original contributions. The greatest Muslim mathematician was al-Khwarizmi (ahl kwah REEZ mee). His work pioneered the study of algebra (from the Arabic word *al-jabr*). In the 800s, he wrote a book that was later translated into Latin and became a standard mathematics textbook in Europe.

Astronomy Like many scholars of the time, al-Khwarizmi made contributions in other fields. He developed a set of astronomical tables based on Greek and Indian discoveries. At observatories from Baghdad to Central

Biography

Ibn Rushd (Averroës)
1126–1198

While growing up in Spain, Muslim scholar Ibn Rushd (known to Europeans as Averroës) was interested in almost every subject and profession. He first focused on medicine and became chief physician to the Muslim ruler in Spain. Later, he studied astronomy and wrote several important books on the subject. Ibn Rushd also studied law, became a famous judge, and wrote a digest of Islamic law.

Ibn Rushd is best known as a philosopher—both Muslims and Christians have studied his commentaries on Aristotle for centuries. For part of his life, however, Ibn Rushd was forced to live in exile outside Spain because some Muslim religious leaders felt that his writings contradicted the teachings of Islam.

Theme: Impact of the Individual What role did Ibn Rushd play in increasing the knowledge of people during the Middle Ages?

Recall

1. **(a)** Omar Khayyám, p. 263 **(b)** Averroës, p. 265 **(c)** Muhammad al-Razi, p. 266 **(d)** Avicenna, p. 266 **2. (a)** social mobility, p. 261 **(b)** arabesque, p. 263 **(c)** calligraphy, p. 263

Comprehension

3. Partnerships made it easier to start businesses. Credit and banks made it easier to conduct business. **4.** Because of religious teachings, Muslim artists did not portray God or human figures in religious art. They instead used abstract and geometric patterns, such as the arabesque, and calligraphy. **5.** Possible answers: **(a)** Algebra was developed. **(b)** The circumference of the earth was calculated. **(c)** Surgeons developed a method for treating cataracts.

Critical Thinking and Writing

6. Possible answers: **(a)** Knowledge was more important than sacrificing one's life in battle. **(b)** Muslim scholars pursued learning and made many advances in literature, art, and science. **7.** Students may cite similarities such as the dominance of religious architecture in cities, the scholarly attempt to combine reason and divine revelation, and the use of guilds for conducting business. Students may cite as differences the amount of trade, social mobility, and advanced learning that existed in Muslim society.

An Arabic Medical Text
At hospitals in Baghdad, Cairo, and Damascus, libraries were well stocked with medical textbooks. This page is from an Arabic textbook on anatomy.

Theme: Economics and Technology Identify three details that suggest that this drawing was based on the study of actual human skeletons.

Asia, Muslim astronomers studied eclipses, observed the Earth's rotation, and calculated the circumference of the Earth to within a few thousand feet. The work of Muslim astronomers and navigators helped pave the way for later explorers like Christopher Columbus.

Medicine Building on the knowledge of the ancient Greeks, Muslims made remarkable advances in medicine and public health. Under the caliphs, physicians and pharmacists had to pass a test before they could practice their profession. The government set up hospitals, with separate wards for women. Injured people could get quick treatment at a facility similar to today's emergency room. Physicians traveled to rural areas to provide health care to those who could not get to a city, while others regularly visited jails.

One of the most original medical thinkers was Muhammad al-Razi, head physician at Baghdad's chief hospital. He wrote many books on medicine, including a pioneering study of measles and smallpox. He also challenged accepted medical practices. Treat the mind as well as the body, he advised young doctors. If a doctor made hopeful comments, he taught, patients would recover faster.

Equally famous was the Persian physician Ibn Sina, known in Europe as Avicenna. By the age of 16, he was already a doctor to the Persian nobility. His great work was the *Canon on Medicine,* a huge encyclopedia of what the Greeks, the Arabs, and he himself had learned about the diagnosis and treatment of disease. The book includes a list of more than 4,000 prescriptions, made with such ingredients as mercury from Spain, myrrh from East Africa, and camphor from India.

Behind these two great names stood dozens of others. Muslim surgeons developed a way to treat cataracts, drawing fluid out of the lenses with a hollow needle. For centuries, surgeons around the world used this method to save patients' eyesight. Arab pharmacists were the first to mix bitter medicines into sweet-tasting syrups and gums.

Knowledge Moves West Over time, Muslim scholars helped knowledge move into Christian Europe. The two main routes of entry were through Spain and through Sicily. Christian European scholars were reintroduced to achievements of Greco-Roman civilization. They studied Muslim philosophy, art, and science. Eventually, European physicians began to attend Muslim universities in Spain and to translate Arabic medical texts. For 500 years, the works of Avicenna and al-Razi were the standard medical textbooks at European schools.

SECTION 3 Assessment

Recall

1. **Identify: (a)** Omar Khayyám, **(b)** Averroës, **(c)** Muhammad al-Razi, **(d)** Avicenna.
2. **Define: (a)** social mobility, **(b)** arabesque, **(c)** calligraphy.

Comprehension

3. How did new business methods encourage trade and industry?
4. How did the teachings of Islam influence the arts?
5. Describe one advance made by Muslim civilization in each of the following areas: **(a)** mathematics, **(b)** astronomy, **(c)** medicine.

Critical Thinking and Writing

6. **Analyzing Primary Sources** Muhammad taught that "the ink of the scholar is holier than the blood of the martyr." **(a)** What do you think he meant? **(b)** How might this attitude have contributed to the development of Muslim civilization?
7. **Comparing** What were the similarities and differences between Muslim society under the Abbassids and European society in the early Middle Ages?

Activity
Take It to the NET

Visit some Internet museum sites that contain descriptions and examples of Muslim art and architecture. Then, make a poster that shows the major characteristics of Muslim art during the Abbassid golden age.

Activity Rubrics

Share rubrics with students before they create their posters.

Attempted The poster has very few examples and is sloppily executed.

Minimal The poster has several examples, but is poorly executed.

Adequate The poster has numerous examples and is well executed.

Exemplary The poster has many examples and is imaginative and strikingly well executed.

Caption Answer

Possible answer: The drawing shows that the spinal column is made up of discs, that ribs branch off from the spinal column, and that the hands and feet are made up of many bones separated by joints.

Resource Directory

Teaching Resources
Section Quiz Unit 3 booklet, p. 61
Creative Teaching Activities Creative Teaching Activities booklet, p. 52
Guided Reading and Review Unit 3 booklet, p. 62

Technology
Interactive Student Tutorial CD-ROM Ch. 11
Computer Test Bank Ch. 11

SECTION 4 Muslims in India

Reading Focus

- What impact did the Delhi sultanate have on India?
- How did Muslim and Hindu traditions clash and blend?
- How did Akbar strengthen Mughal India?

Vocabulary

sultanate

caste

rajah

Taking Notes

Copy the partially completed outline at right. As you read this section, finish the outline. Use Roman numerals to indicate the major headings of the section, capital letters for the subheadings, and numbers for the supporting details.

I. The Delhi sultanate
  A. Origins of the sultanate
    1.
    2.
  B. Effects of Muslim rule
    1.
    2.
II. Muslims and Hindus

Main Idea Muslim invasions and rule over India led to cultural diffusion as well as bloody clashes between Muslims and Hindus.

Setting the Scene "The whole of India is full of gold and jewels," advisers told Sultan Mahmud of Ghazni. "And since the inhabitants are chiefly infidels and idolaters, by the order of God and his Prophet, it is right for us to conquer them." In 1001, Mahmud led his armies into northern India. Smashing and looting Hindu temples, Mahmud used the fabulous riches of India to turn his capital into a great Muslim center. Later Muslim invaders did more than loot and destroy. They built a dazzling new Muslim empire in India.

The arrival of Islam brought changes to India as great as those caused by the Aryan migrations 2,000 years earlier. As Muslims mingled with Indians, each civilization absorbed elements from the other.

The Delhi Sultanate

After the Gupta empire fell in about 550, India again fragmented into many local kingdoms. Rival princes battled for control of the northern plain. Despite power struggles, Indian culture flourished. Hindu and Buddhist rulers spent huge sums to build and decorate magnificent temples. Trade networks linked India to the Middle East, Southeast Asia, and China.

Origins of the Sultanate Although Arabs conquered the Indus Valley in 711, they advanced no farther into the subcontinent. Then about 1000, Muslim Turks and Afghans pushed into India. At first, they were adventurers like Mahmud, who pillaged much of the north. However, in the late 1100s, the sultan of Ghur defeated Hindu armies across the northern plain. He made Delhi his capital. From there, his successors organized a sultanate, or land ruled by a sultan. The Delhi sultanate, which lasted from 1206 to 1526, marked the start of Muslim rule in northern India.

Why did the Muslim invaders triumph? They won on the battlefield in part because Muslim mounted archers had far greater mobility than Hindu forces, who rode slow-moving war elephants. Also, Hindu princes wasted resources battling one another instead of uniting against a common enemy. In some places, large numbers of Hindus, especially from low castes, converted to Islam. In the Hindu social system, you will recall, people were born into castes, or social groups from which they could not change.

Effects of Muslim Rule Muslim rule brought changes to Indian government and society. Sultans introduced Muslim traditions of government. Many Turks, Persians, and Arabs migrated to India to serve as soldiers

Global Connections

Ibn Battuta: World Traveler

In 1333, the sultan of Delhi was seeking the services of educated foreigners. To fill the position of judge, he hired a scholarly traveler from Morocco. The name of the traveler was Ibn Battuta.

Ibn Battuta was no ordinary traveler. By the time he reached India, he had already visited Egypt, the eastern coast of Africa, Asia Minor, and Central Asia. After eight years in India, he sailed on to Southeast Asia and China. Still later, he trekked across the Sahara to tour West Africa. In all, he logged an estimated 75,000 miles. After finally returning to Morocco, Ibn Battutta dictated an account of his extraordinary travels that has survived to this day.

Theme: Global Interaction
Why was it so rare for people of the time to travel as widely as Ibn Battuta had?

Bell Ringer Have students read the questions in the Section 4 Assessment. Then ask students to write three general statements predicting what they will learn in this section.

LESSON PLAN

1. Focus Muslim invasions resulted in the establishment of the Delhi sultanate and Muslim rule over northern India. Some Muslim and Hindu traditions blended, but there were also bloody clashes between the two peoples. Akbar the Great strengthened Muslim rule by instituting a policy of religious toleration.

2. Instruct As a class project, create a cause-and-effect web showing the developments that occurred in India as a result of Muslim invasions. Encourage students to name as many changes as they can and then to list the causes and effects of each change.

3. Assess Use the completed web as the focus of a class discussion on the interaction between Muslim and Hindu culture in India.

4. Reteach If students' Assess activity does not reflect adequate understanding of the lesson, you might assign the *Guide to the Essentials* or the *Interactive Student Tutorial CD-ROM* for this section.

Block Scheduling Support

Divide the class into two groups. Have one group imagine that they are Muslim commoners living in India during the Delhi sultanate and the Mughal empire. Have the other group imagine that they are Hindu commoners living in India during the same period.

Have each group reread this section and then describe how their lives would be affected under the Delhi sultanate rule, and later, under Mughal rule. A representative from each group should present that group's findings to the class. Use the findings to generate a class discussion about what it means to be part of the ruling group and what it means to be part of the subjugated group.

Global Connections

ANSWER Travel was difficult and often dangerous.

Heterogeneous Groups

Researching Point out to students that both Muslims and Hindus still reside in India. Ask them to find news articles about Muslims and Hindus in India. What conclusions can students draw from the articles that they find?

Delhi Sultanate and Mughal Empire

HINDU KUSH
Lahore
Delhi
Agra
HIMALAYA MTS.
Brahmaputra R.
Ganges R.
Arabian Sea
Tropic of Cancer
Narmada R.
DECCAN PLATEAU
Bay of Bengal
Goa (Portuguese)
INDIAN OCEAN

Mercator Projection
0   300   600 Miles
0   300   600 Kilometers

▭ Delhi sultanate about 1300
→ Route of Tamerlane's invasion, 1398
■ Mughal empire, 1526
■ Lands added to the empire by 1605
▨ Lands added to the empire by 1707
◇ Taj Mahal

Skills Assessment

Geography Two Muslim dynasties ruled much of the Indian subcontinent. The Delhi sultanate lasted more than 300 years before the Mughal dynasty replaced it.

1. **Location** On the map, locate **(a)** Delhi, **(b)** Hindu Kush, **(c)** Ganges River, **(d)** Taj Mahal.
2. **Movement** Describe Tamerlane's invasion route into India.
3. **Critical Thinking**
   Linking Past and Present Use the map of Asia in the Reference Section to identify the present-day countries that now occupy the lands of the Mughal empire.

or officials. Trade between India and the Muslim world increased. During the Mongol raids of the 1200s, many scholars and adventurers fled from Baghdad to India, bringing Persian and Greek learning. The newcomers helped create a brilliant civilization at Delhi, where Persian art and architecture flourished.

Decline In 1398, Tamerlane invaded India. He plundered the northern plain and smashed into Delhi. "Not a bird on the wing moved," reported stunned survivors. Thousands of artisans were enslaved to build Tamerlane's capital at Samarkand. Delhi, an empty shell, slowly recovered. But the sultans no longer controlled a large empire, and northern India again fragmented, this time into rival Hindu and Muslim states.

Muslims and Hindus

At its worst, the Muslim conquest of northern India inflicted disaster on Hindus and Buddhists. The widespread destruction of Buddhist monasteries contributed to the drastic decline of Buddhism as a major religion in India. During the most violent onslaughts, many Hindus were killed. Others may have converted to escape death. In time, though, relations became more peaceful.

Hindu-Muslim Differences The Muslim advance brought two utterly different religions and cultures face to face. Hinduism was an ancient religion that had evolved over thousands of years. Hindus recognized many sacred texts and prayed before statues representing many gods and goddesses. Islam, by contrast, was a newer faith with a single sacred text. Muslims were devout monotheists who saw the statues and carvings in Hindu temples as an offense to the one true god.

Hindus accepted differences in caste status and honored Brahmans as a priestly caste. Muslims taught the equality of all believers before God and had no religious hierarchy. Hindus celebrated religious occasions with music and dance, a practice that many strict Muslims condemned.

Interactions Eventually, the Delhi sultans grew more tolerant of their subject population. Some Muslim scholars argued that behind the many Hindu gods and goddesses was a single god. Hinduism was thus accepted as a monotheistic religion. Although Hindus remained second-class citizens, as long as they paid the non-Muslim tax, they could practice their religion. Some sultans even left rajahs, or local Hindu rulers, in place.

During the Delhi sultanate, a growing number of Hindus converted to Islam. Some lower-caste Hindus preferred Islam because it rejected the caste system. Other converts came from higher castes. They chose to adopt Islam either because they accepted its beliefs or because they served in the Muslim government. Indian merchants were attracted to Islam in part because of the strong trade network across Muslim lands.

Cultural Blending During this period, too, Indian Muslims absorbed elements of Hindu culture, such as marriage customs and caste ideas. A new language, Urdu, evolved as a marriage of Persian, Arabic, and Hindi. Local artisans applied Persian art styles to Indian subjects. Indian music and dance reappeared at the courts of the sultan.

Skills Assessment

ANSWERS 1. Review locations with students. **2.** Tamerlane's force came from the northwest through the Hindu Kush, then crossed the northern plain. **3.** parts of India, Pakistan, Bangladesh, and Nepal

Resource Directory

Teaching Resources
Primary Source Activity *Babur's Army Crosses the Mountains,* Unit 3 booklet, p. 67

Virtual Field Trip

www.phschool.com

Prince of Wales Museum
of Western India
Mumbai, India

To see more artworks from the
Mughal period, as well as other
periods in Indian history, use the
Internet address above to link to
the Prince of Wales Museum of
Western India.

Akbar the Great
As ruler of the Mughal empire,
Akbar tried to promote harmony
among the diverse peoples of India.
Here, Akbar enjoys a performance
of traditional Hindu dance.
Theme: Diversity How does
this picture reflect Akbar's policy
of toleration?

Background
Historical Evidence

Regulations of Akbar Akbar commissioned Abul Fazl to write his biography.
Abul Fazl's task, according to Akbar,
was to "write with the pen of sincerity
the account of the glorious events and
of our dominion-increasing victories."

Abul Fazl produced two works: *History of Akbar* and *Regulations of Akbar.* In
the latter, Fazl relates that before Akbar
ate his sole daily meal, his food was
tasted for poison three times after it left
the pot and before it reached his plate.
After each taste, the dish was marked
with the seal of the master of the kitchen.
Abul Fazl also says that Akbar never
drank anything but water from the
Ganges River, no matter where in his
empire he might be.

An Indian holy man, Nanak, sought to blend Islamic and Hindu beliefs.
He preached "the unity of God, the brotherhood of man, the rejection of
caste, and the futility of idol worship." His teachings led to the rise of a
new religion, Sikhism, in northern India. (See the chart in the Chapter
Review and Assessment.) The Sikhs later organized into military forces
that clashed with the powerful Mughal rulers of India.

Mughal India

In 1526, Turkish and Mongol invaders again poured through the mountain
passes in India. At their head rode Babur (BAH buhr), who claimed descent
from Genghiz Khan and Tamerlane. Babur was a military genius, poet, and
author of a fascinating book of memoirs.

Babur Founds a Dynasty Just north of Delhi, Babur met a huge army led
by the sultan Ibrahim. "I placed my foot in the stirrup of resolution and my
hands on the reins of confidence in God," recalled Babur. His force was
small but had cannons, which he put to good use:

> "The sun had mounted spear-high when the onset began,
> and the battle lasted till midday, when the enemy was com-
> pletely broken and routed. By the grace and mercy of
> Almighty God, this difficult affair was made easy to me, and
> that mighty army . . . was crushed in the dust."
> —Babur, *Memoirs*

In no time, Babur swept away the remnants of the Delhi sultanate and
set up the Mughal dynasty, which ruled from 1526 to 1857. (*Mughal* is the
Persian word for "Mongol.") Babur and his heirs conquered an empire that
stretched from the Himalayas to the Deccan Plateau.

Akbar the Great The chief builder of the Mughal empire was Babur's
grandson Akbar. During his long reign, from 1556 to 1605, he created a strong
central government, earning the title Akbar the Great.

Akbar was a leader of unusual abilities. Although a Muslim, he won
the support of Hindu subjects through his policy of toleration. He opened

Human Drama Note

Babur's Death Babur seems to have been a charming man, who commanded great loyalty among his
people and who was willing to forgo his own comfort for the sake of his goals. The legend of his death
illustrates this view of the ruler.
"Babur's son and heir, Humayun, lay dying when a sage told Babur that the boy could be saved if the
most precious thing in the world were sacrificed. Babur walked around his son's bed three times, praying, 'Oh God, I sacrifice my life, the most precious thing to me, for the sake of my son.' Humayun began
to get well; immediately Babur himself became ill. The king died in a short time. . . ."
A weak ruler, Humayun died in 1556, leaving his remaining Indian lands to his son, Akbar the Great,
who was then 13 years old.

Caption Answer

Although he was a Muslim, Akbar
allowed traditional Hindu dancers
to perform at his court.

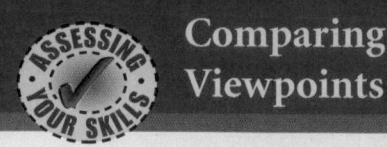

Comparing Viewpoints

Background
Other Viewpoints

Mexico, 1853 Lucas Alamán, a conservative leader, believed that religious unity was vital to his recently independent nation:

"First and foremost is the need to preserve the Catholic religion, because we believe in it and because . . . we consider it to be the only common bond that links all Mexicans when all the others have been broken."

United States, 1935 Anthropologist Margaret Mead based her views on observations of both American and Pacific island societies:

"If we are to achieve a richer culture, rich in contrasting values, we must recognize the whole gamut of human potentialities, and so weave a less arbitrary social fabric, one in which each diverse human gift will find a fitting place."

Activity
Interpreting Viewpoints

Critical Thinking: Comparing Share with students the information in the Background above. Then, use these additional questions to generate class discussion. **1.** Which person would be most likely to agree with Margaret Mead: Mazzini or Husayn? *(Husayn)* **2.** Which person would be most likely to agree with Lucas Alamán: Mazzini or Akbar? *(Mazzini)*

Skills Tip

When you look at a political cartoon, you need to compare the words with the picture. Note that the two trains in the picture in this cartoon have left their parallel course and seem to be headed for a collision. (Notice the expressions of dismay on the faces in the smoke from the trains.) The Skills Handbook in the front of the book has a lesson that will help students with this feature.

Skills Assessment

ANSWERS 1. D **2.** G **3.** Possible answers: Advantages—richer and more interesting; disadvantages—possibility of strife between groups, possibility of discrimination

_270_ Chapter 11

Comparing Viewpoints

Does Diversity Strengthen or Weaken a Society?

"India has not ever been an easy country to understand," commented Indian prime minister Indira Gandhi in the 1970s. "Perhaps it is too deep, contradictory, and diverse." Should a nation encourage diversity? Or can lack of unity weaken the fabric of a society? Keep these questions in mind as you examine the following viewpoints.

India Late 1500s

Akbar the Great spoke eloquently about the diversity he found in his land:

❝ O God, in every temple I see people that seek You. In every language I hear spoken, people praise You. If it be a mosque, people murmur the holy prayer. If it be a Christian church, they ring the bell for love of You. . . . It is You whom I seek from temple to temple. ❞

Italy 1835

Giuseppe Mazzini, who led a movement to unite Italy into a single state, defined the ties that bind a nation:

❝ A nation is an association of those who are brought together by language, by given geographical locations, or by the role assigned them by history, who acknowledge the same principles and who march together to the conquest of a single definite goal under the rule of a common body of law. . . . It is necessary that [a nation's] ideas be shown to other lands in their beauty and purity, free from any alien mixture. ❞

Egypt 1933

Taha Husayn, a respected scholar, pointed out that his nation's culture was a blend of three distinct traditions. The first came from ancient Egypt, the second from Arabian Muslims:

❝ As for the third element, it is the foreign element which has always influenced Egyptian life, and will always do so. It is what has come to Egypt from its contacts with the civilized peoples in the east and west. . . . I should like Egyptian education to be firmly based on a certain harmony between these three elements. ❞

Canada 1980s

This cartoon comments on long-standing tensions between French-speaking Canadians and those who speak English. René Levesque was a leader who called for French Quebec to break away from the rest of Canada.

"CANADA IS MADE UP OF TWO DISTINCT NATIONS. JUST LIKE TWO TRAINS ON PARALLEL TRACKS THAT WILL NEVER MEET" *PREMIER RENE LEVESQUE*

Skills Assessment

1. Whose points of view least favor diversity?
   A Akbar and Mazzini
   B Mazzini and Husayn
   C Husayn and Levesque
   D Mazzini and Levesque

2. Akbar and Husayn would probably agree that
   E diversity weakens a society.
   F members of a society must share the same religion.
   G diversity can enhance a society.
   H a society should try to repel diversity.

3. **Critical Thinking Recognizing Points of View** As an American, you live in a highly diverse society. Write a statement in which you identify and explain two advantages and two disadvantages this diversity brings to American society.

Skills Tip

To help you understand the context in which a point of view developed, try to identify the place and time in which it arose.

_270_ Chapter 11

Resource Directory

Teaching Resources

Comparing Viewpoints Chapter Extension Activities booklet, pp. 29–30
Skill Application Activity *Recognizing Points of View,* Unit 3 booklet, p. 69
Section Quiz Unit 3 booklet, p. 63

Technology

World History Color Transparencies political cartoon dealing with issue of diversity, p. E–27
Interactive Student Tutorial CD-ROM Ch. 11
Computer Test Bank Ch. 11

World History Visions, Voices, Views Global Issues Forum, *Should the United States' Immigration Policy Encourage or Discourage Diversity?,* videodisc side 2 or videotape 3, running time 4:00 min.

Side 2: Fr. 20142-27425

government jobs to Hindus of all castes and treated Hindu princes as his partners in ruling the vast empire. He ended the tax on non-Muslims and himself married a Hindu princess.

Akbar could not read or write, but he consulted leaders of many faiths, including Muslims, Hindus, Buddhists, and Christians. Like the early Indian leader Asoka, he hoped to promote religious harmony through toleration. By recognizing India's diversity, Akbar placed Mughal power on a firm footing.

Akbar strengthened his empire in other ways as well. To improve government, he used paid officials in place of hereditary officeholders. He modernized the army, encouraged international trade, standardized weights and measures, and introduced land reforms.

Akbar's Successors Akbar's son Jahangir (juh hahn GIR) was a weaker ruler than his father. He left most details of government in the hands of his wife, Nur Jahan. Fortunately, she was an able leader whose shrewd political judgment was matched only by her love of poetry and royal sports. She was the most powerful woman in Indian history up until the twentieth century.

The high point of Mughal literature, art, and architecture came with the reign of Shah Jahan, Akbar's grandson. When his wife, Mumtaz Mahal, died at age 39, Shah Jahan was distraught. "Empire has no sweetness," he cried, "life itself has no relish left for me now." He then had a stunning tomb built for her, the Taj Mahal (TAHZH muh HAHL). It was designed in Persian style, with spectacular white domes and graceful minarets mirrored in clear blue reflecting pools. Verses from the Quran adorn its walls. The Taj Mahal stands as perhaps the greatest monument of the Mughal empire.

Shah Jahan planned to build a twin structure to the Taj Mahal as a tomb for himself. However, before he could do so, his son Aurangzeb usurped the throne in 1658. Shah Jahan was kept imprisoned until he died several years later.

Looking Ahead

In the late 1600s, the emperor Aurangzeb rejected Akbar's tolerant policies and resumed persecution of Hindus. Economic hardships increased under heavy taxes, and discontent sparked revolts against Mughal rule. As you will read, this climate of discontent helped European traders gain a foothold in the once powerful Mughal empire.

SECTION 4 Assessment

Recall
1. **Identify:** (a) Sikhism, (b) Babur, (c) Mughal, (d) Nur Jahan, (e) Taj Mahal.
2. **Define:** (a) sultanate, (b) caste, (c) rajah.

Comprehension
3. **(a)** Why were the founders of the Delhi sultanate able to conquer India? **(b)** How did Delhi sultans affect life in northern India?
4. How did relations between Hindus and Muslims evolve over time?
5. What policies did Akbar follow to strengthen his empire?

Critical Thinking and Writing
6. **Applying Information** How does the history of Muslims in India illustrate the process of cultural diffusion?
7. **Predicting Consequences** Rulers after Akbar rejected the policy of toleration of other religious beliefs. How do you think this rejection of toleration affected relations between Hindus and Muslims? Explain.

Activity
Creating a Chart
Using information from this chapter and other chapters in this book, create a chart showing differences between Islam and Hinduism. Include information such as when each emerged, where they spread, and their major beliefs. Consult the table of contents and index to find the information you need.

Chapter 11 **271**

Recall
1. **(a)** Sikhism, p. 269 **(b)** Babur, p. 269 **(c)** Mughal, p. 269 **(d)** Nur Jahan, p. 271 **(e)** Taj Mahal, p. 271 2. **(a)** sultanate, p. 267 **(b)** caste, p. 267 **(c)** rajah, p. 268

Comprehension
3. **(a)** Muslim mounted archers had greater mobility than Hindus who rode elephants. Also, Hindu princes wasted time and resources battling each other, while Muslims were united. **(b)** They introduced Muslim traditions of government. Trade between India and the Muslim world increased. Persian and Greek scholars emigrated to India, where Persian art and architecture flourished. 4. At first, Muslims killed many Hindus. In time, however, Muslims became more tolerant of Hindus. Many Hindus converted to Islam, and Muslims adopted elements of Hindu culture. 5. Akbar won popular support by following a policy of toleration. His rule benefited people of various castes and religions. He also reformed the civil service and tax policies, modernized the army, encouraged trade, and introduced land reform.

Critical Thinking and Writing
6. Possible answers: As Hindus and Muslims lived together, they gradually adopted elements of each other's culture. The Urdu language and Sikh religion were products of cultural diffusion. 7. Students should realize that such a rejection would be likely to lead to increased tensions and possibly to violence between Hindus and Muslims.

Activity Rubrics

Share rubrics with students before they create their charts.

Attempted The chart has very few entries, contains factual errors, and is messy or difficult to read.

Minimal The chart has several entries, contains few factual errors, and is legible.

Adequate The chart has numerous entries, contains no factual errors, and is easily readable.

Exemplary The chart has many entries, contains no factual errors, and is easy to read and visually attractive.

Test Preparation

Have students read the paragraph headed "Akbar's Successors" on this page, and then answer the question below.

Which of the following best describes Nur Jahan?

A She was a clever politician but she was not a fan of poetry or sports.

B She liked poetry and sports more than politics.

C She liked politics more than poetry and sports.

D She was a clever politician who was also a lover of poetry and sports.

Bell Ringer

Bell Ringer Direct students to study the map in this section showing the extent of the Ottoman and Safavid empires. Then, have them compare this map with the "Spread of Islam" map in Section 2. Invite students to comment on the size of the empires. Ask what they might conclude about the influence of these empires on the Muslim world.

LESSON PLAN

1. Focus New military technology helped both the Ottomans and the Safavids to create large and powerful empires. Although both empires were united by the beliefs and laws of Islam, at times other religions were tolerated. Strong leaders like Suleiman and Abbas the Great encouraged the arts.

2. Instruct On the chalkboard, create a chart that compares the Ottoman and Safavid empires. Include headings such as Important Leaders, Religions, Military Strength, Government and Laws, Territory, Social Organization, Arts and Literature, Decline. Have students contribute facts for each heading. Then, use the chart as the basis for a class discussion comparing and contrasting the two empires.

3. Assess Ask students to write three generalizations about how the Ottoman and Safavid empires were similar. Then, have them write three generalizations about how they differed.

4. Reteach If students' Assess activity does not reflect adequate understanding of the lesson, you might assign the *Guide to the Essentials* or the *Interactive Student Tutorial CD-ROM* for this section.

Reading Focus

- How did the Ottoman empire expand?
- What were the characteristics of Ottoman culture?
- How did Abbas the Great strengthen the Safavid empire?

Vocabulary

millet

janizary

shah

Taking Notes

Copy this Venn diagram. As you read, fill in key characteristics of the Ottoman and Safavid empires in the appropriate sections of the diagram. The diagram has been partially completed to help you get started.

OTTOMAN EMPIRE
-
-

• Centralized government

SAFAVID EMPIRE
• Capital was Isfahan
-

Main Idea Ottoman and Safavid rulers governed large empires and encouraged cultural achievements.

Setting the Scene While the Mughals ruled India, two other dynasties, the Ottomans and Safavids, dominated the Middle East and parts of Eastern Europe. All three empires owed much of their success to new weapons. In 1453, Ottoman cannons blasted gaps in the great defensive walls of Constantinople. Later, muskets gave greater firepower to ordinary foot soldiers, thus reducing the importance of mounted warriors.

The new military technology helped the Ottomans and Safavids create strong central governments. As a result, this period from about 1450 to 1650 is sometimes called "the age of gunpowder empires."

Expanding the Ottoman Empire

The Ottomans were yet another Turkish-speaking nomadic people who had migrated from Central Asia into northwestern Asia Minor. In the 1300s, they expanded across Asia Minor and into southeastern Europe. They established a capital in the Balkan Peninsula.

Fall of Constantinople Ottoman expansion threatened the crumbling Byzantine empire. After several failed attempts to capture Constantinople, Muhammad II finally succeeded in 1453. In the next 200 years, the Ottoman empire continued to expand.

Suleiman The Ottoman empire enjoyed its golden age under the sultan Suleiman (soo lay mahn), who ruled from 1520 to 1566. Called Suleiman the Magnificent by westerners, he was known to his own people as the "Lawgiver." A brilliant general, Suleiman modernized the army and conquered many new lands. He extended Ottoman rule eastward into Mesopotamia, and also into Kurdistan and Georgia in the Caucasus Mountain region. In the west, Suleiman advanced deeper into Europe. He was able to gain control of nearly all of Hungary through diplomacy and warfare. In 1529, his armies besieged the Austrian city of Vienna, sending waves of fear through Western Europe.

Although they failed to take Vienna, the Ottomans ruled the largest, most powerful empire in both Europe and the Middle East for centuries. At its height, the empire stretched from Hungary to Arabia and Mesopotamia and across North Africa.

Suleiman felt justified in claiming to be the rightful heir of the Abbassids and caliph of all Muslims. To the title of "Emperor," he added the symbolic name of "Protector of the Sacred Places" (Mecca and Medina).

Resource Directory

Teaching Resources

Creative Teaching Activities Creative Teaching Activities booklet, p. 53

Guided Reading and Review Unit 3 booklet, p. 64

Ottoman Culture

Suleiman was a wise and capable ruler. He strengthened the government of the rapidly growing empire and improved its system of justice. As sultan, Suleiman had absolute power, but he ruled with the help of a grand vizier and a council. A huge bureaucracy supervised the business of government, and the powerful military kept the peace. As in other Muslim states, Ottoman law was based on the Sharia, supplemented by royal edicts. Government officials worked closely with religious scholars who interpreted the law.

Social Organization The Ottomans divided their subjects into four classes, each with its appointed role. At the top were "men of the pen"—such as scientists, lawyers, judges, and poets—and "men of the sword," soldiers who guarded the sultan and defended the state. Below them were "men of negotiation"—such as merchants, tax collectors, and artisans, who carried out trade and production—and "men of husbandry," farmers and herders who produced food for the community.

The Ottomans ruled diverse peoples who had many religions. The men of the sword and men of the pen were almost all Muslims, while the other classes included non-Muslims as well. Non-Muslims were organized into millets, or religious communities. These included Greek Christians, Armenian Christians, and Jews. Each millet had its own religious leaders who were responsible for education and some legal matters.

Janizaries Like earlier Muslim empires, the Ottomans recruited officers for the army and government from among the huge populations of conquered peoples in their empire. The Ottomans levied a "tax" on Christian families in the Balkans, requiring them to turn over young sons to the government.

The boys were converted to Islam and put into rigorous military training at the palace school. The best soldiers won a prized place in the janizaries, the elite force of the Ottoman army. The brightest students received special education to become government officials. They might serve as judges, poets, or even grand vizier.

Like the boys, non-Muslim girls from Eastern Europe were brought to serve as slaves in wealthy Muslim households. There, they might be accepted as members of the household. Some of the enslaved girls were freed after the death of their masters.

Literature and the Arts The arts blossomed under Suleiman. Ottoman poets adapted Persian and Arab models to produce works in their own Turkish language. Influenced by Persian artistic styles, Ottoman painters produced magnificently detailed miniatures and illuminated manuscripts.

The royal architect Sinan, a janizary military engineer, designed hundreds of mosques and palaces. He compared his most famous building, the Selimiye Mosque at Edirne, to the greatest church of the Byzantine empire. "With God's help and the Sultan's mercy," Sinan wrote, "I have succeeded in building a dome for the mosque which is greater in diameter and higher than that of Hagia Sophia."

The Ottomans Take Constantinople
In this French painting, Turkish land and sea forces lay siege to the fortified city of Constantinople in 1453. In a surprise move, the Ottomans hauled ships overland and launched them into the harbor outside the city.

Theme: Geography Compare this picture to the map of Constantinople in the previous chapter. In what ways does the picture accurately reflect the geography of the city?

Reading Strategy
Graphic Organizer

Have students work in pairs to create a diagram or graphic organizer that incorporates the main ideas and some of the supporting details discussed in this section. *(Less Advanced Readers)*

Ottoman and Safavid Empires, 1453–1629

Map legend:
- Ottoman empire, 1453
- Lands added, 1453–1520
- Lands added under Suleiman, 1520–1566
- Safavid empire at death of Shah Abbas the Great, 1629

Mercator Projection

0   250   500 Miles
0   250   500 Kilometers

Skills Assessment

Geography At its greatest extent, the Ottoman empire stretched across three continents. During the same period, the Safavid empire controlled most of present-day Iran.

1. **Location** On the map, locate **(a)** Constantinople, **(b)** Black Sea, **(c)** Isfahan, **(d)** Hungary.
2. **Region** Into what regions did the Ottoman empire expand under Suleiman?
3. **Critical Thinking**
   Recognizing Points of View How do you think Russians probably felt about the expansion of the Ottoman and Safavid empires? Explain.

Decline By the 1700s, European advances in both commerce and military technology were leaving the Ottomans behind. While European industry and trade pressed ahead, the aging Ottoman empire remained dependent on agriculture. Russia and other European powers chipped away at Ottoman lands, while local rulers in North Africa and elsewhere broke away from Ottoman control. From time to time, able sultans tried to revive Ottoman power, but with limited success.

The Safavid Empire

By the early 1500s, the Safavid (sah FAH weed) dynasty had united a strong empire in Persia, present-day Iran. Sandwiched between two other expansionist powers, Mughal India and the Ottoman empire, the Safavids engaged in frequent warfare. Religion played a major role in the conflict. The Safavids were Shiite Muslims who enforced their beliefs throughout their empire. The Ottomans were Sunni Muslims who despised the Shiites as heretics.

Abbas the Great The outstanding Safavid shah, or king, was Abbas the Great. Shah Abbas revived the glory of ancient Persia. From 1588 to 1629, he centralized the government and created a powerful military force modeled on the Ottoman janizaries. Abbas used a mixture of force and diplomacy against the Ottomans. He also sought alliances with European states that had reason to fear Ottoman power.

To strengthen the economy, Abbas reduced taxes on farmers and herders and encouraged the growth of industry. While earlier Safavids had imposed their faith on the empire, Abbas tolerated non-Muslims and valued their economic contributions. He built a magnificent new capital

274 Chapter 11

Skills Assessment

ANSWERS 1. Review locations with students. **2.** Tripoli, Algeria, Hungary, and lands bordering Persia **3.** Possible answer: The Russians may have feared Ottoman or Safavid expansion northward into Russian territory. Also, they may have resented Ottoman control of the Black Sea, which kept Russia landlocked.

Resource Directory

Teaching Resources

Section Quiz Unit 3 booklet, p. 65
Geography Quiz Unit 3 booklet, p. 70
Chapter Test Forms A, B, and C Unit 3 booklet, pp. 71–75
Answer Key Unit 3 booklet, pp. 114–128

Technology

Interactive Student Tutorial CD-ROM Ch. 11
Computer Test Bank Ch. 11

at Isfahan (is fuh HAHN), a center of the international silk trade. Because the trade was controlled by Armenians, Abbas had thousands of Armenians brought to Isfahan. Even though they were Christians, he had a settlement built for them just outside the capital, where they could govern themselves.

Under Abbas, Isfahan flourished as a center of Persian culture. The shah welcomed artists, poets, and scholars to the court. Palace workshops produced magnificent porcelains, clothes, and rugs. Women and men wove intricately designed flowers and animals into marvelous garden scenes.

Abbas liked to walk the streets of Isfahan in disguise, mingling with the crowds in bazaars. Amid the cries of street vendors and swarms of traders and customers, he asked people about their problems. If he heard stories of corruption, he punished the guilty.

Decline Safavid glory slowly faded after the death of Shah Abbas. One cause of the decline was continuing pressure from Ottoman armies. Another factor was that conservative Shiite scholars challenged the authority of the shah by stressing their own authority to interpret law. They also encouraged persecution of religious minorities. In the end, Sunni Afghans rebelled. They defeated imperial armies, captured Isfahan, and forced the last Safavid ruler to abdicate in 1722.

In the late 1700s, a new dynasty, the Qajars (kah JAHRZ), won control of Iran. They made Tehran their capital and ruled until 1925. Still, the Safavids had left a lasting legacy. They planted Shiite traditions firmly in Iran and gave Persians a strong sense of their own identity.

Looking Ahead

By 1500, Islam had become the dominant faith across a large part of the world from West Africa to Southeast Asia. An extraordinary diversity of peoples—Arabs, Berbers, Turks, Persians, Slavs, Mongols, Indians, and many others—answered the muezzin's call to prayer each day. This vast world was not politically united, but the Quran, the Sharia, and a network of cultural and economic ties linked Muslims across the *Dar al-Islam*.

Three large states dominated the Muslim world in the 1500s. The Ottomans, the Safavids, and the Mughals were reaching their peak of power. At the same time, however, the nations of Europe were undergoing a period of dynamic growth. Several of these nations would soon challenge Muslim power.

Primary Source

Shah Abbas the Great
In 1604, a Carmelite missionary visited the Persian court. The monk recorded his observations of Shah Abbas the Great:

"He is sagacious in mind, likes fame and to be esteemed: he is courteous in dealing with everyone and at the same time very serious. For he will go through the public streets, eat from what they are selling there and . . . speak at ease freely with the lower classes . . . or will sit down beside this man or that. He says that is how to be a king, and that the king of Spain and other Christians do not get any pleasure out of ruling, because they are obliged to comport themselves with so much pomp and majesty as they do."
—*A Chronicle of the Carmelites in Persia*

Skills Assessment

Primary Source According to Abbas, how does his style of leadership differ from that of Christian rulers?

SECTION 5 Assessment

Recall
1. **Identify:** (a) Sinan, (b) Isfahan.
2. **Define:** (a) millet, (b) janizary, (c) shah.

Comprehension
3. Describe the geographic extent of the Ottoman empire at its height.
4. (a) How was the Ottoman empire governed under Suleiman? (b) How did the arts flourish under Suleiman?
5. What policies did Abbas the Great use to strengthen the Safavid empire?

Critical Thinking and Writing
6. **Drawing Conclusions** Why do you think Ottoman and Safavid rulers allowed some religious toleration in their empires?
7. **Linking Past and Present** (a) How did new military technology benefit the Ottoman and Safavid empires? (b) Explain how new military technology affects international relations today.

Activity
Take It to the NET
Use the Internet to research the Ottoman sultan Suleiman the Magnificent. Then, write a brief essay explaining why Suleiman earned the title "magnificent." Discuss military, political, and cultural achievements.

SECTION 5 Assessment

Recall
1. (a) Sinan, p. 273 (b) Isfahan, p. 275
2. (a) millet, p. 273 (b) janizary, p. 273
(c) shah, p. 274

Comprehension
3. It stretched from Hungary to Arabia and Mesopotamia and across North Africa. 4. (a) A huge bureaucracy ran the government, while a powerful military kept the peace. In addition, society was organized into four classes to aid in the rule of a diverse people. (b) Ottoman poets adapted Persian and Arab models to produce works in the Turkish language. Influenced by Persian artistic styles, Ottoman painters produced detailed miniatures and illuminated manuscripts. Hundreds of mosques and palaces designed by Sinan were built. 5. He centralized the government, strengthened the military, formed alliances with European countries, reduced taxes, encouraged industry, built a new capital, and supported culture.

Critical Thinking and Writing
6. Religious toleration allowed the Muslim rulers to raise money through taxes and provided officers for the military. 7. (a) The Ottomans and Safavids both used these new weapons to expand their power. Cannons were used to blast defensive walls. Muskets increased the effectiveness of their infantry. (b) Possible answer: Countries whose military forces have long-range missiles or powerful air forces are able to strike targets at very great distances.

Activity Rubrics

Share rubrics with students before they write their essays.

Attempted The essay fails to include all the required elements.

Minimal The essay has all the required elements but is poorly written and organized and has mechanical errors.

Adequate The essay has all the required elements, is well written and organized, and has few mechanical errors.

Exemplary The essay has all the required elements, is very well written and organized, and is free of mechanical errors.

Primary Source

ANSWER Possible answer: He is much more casual, and he is more concerned about the lives and concerns of his subjects.

Test Preparation

Have students read the section "Abbas the Great," beginning on the opposite page, and then complete the sentence below.

One reason Abbas was called Great is that

A he remained distant from his subjects.

B he was harsh.

C he revived the glory of ancient Persia.

D he converted to Christianity.

Creating a Chapter Summary

As a reteaching opportunity, pair a more able student with a less able student to complete this chapter summary.

Possible answers: **Rise of Islam** Muhammad introduces Islam in Arabia, Quran and Sharia become the way of life for Muslims **Teaching of Islam** one God, all powerful and compassionate, people responsible for own actions, final judgment determines whether a person ends in heaven or hell **Umayyads** capital in Damascus, extended Islam to the Atlantic **Abbassids** capital at Baghdad, golden age of Muslim culture **Mughals** located in India, toleration of Hindus, building of Taj Mahal **Ottomans** capital at Istanbul, Turkey, division into four social classes, millets and janizaries, Suleiman is greatest sultan **Safavids** capital in Isfahan, Persia, flowering of Persian culture

Building Vocabulary

1–6. Sentences should show a clear understanding of the meanings of the terms.

Recalling Key Facts

7. faith that there is one God and Muhammad is his messenger; daily prayer; charity to the poor; observance of the fast during Ramadan; pilgrimage to Mecca
8. They were generally tolerant, especially toward other monotheistic religions.
9. Muslim scholars translated the works of Greek, Hindu, and Buddhist thinkers, and studied Indian and Greek mathematics. Muslim scholars also made advances in both philosophy and mathematics.
10. (a) created a strong central government; opened government jobs to Hindus of all castes, and treated Hindu princes as partners in ruling the empire; ended tax on non-Muslims; promoted religious harmony; used paid officials in place of hereditary officeholders; modernized the army; encouraged international trade; introduced land reforms **(b)** Later rulers rejected religious tolerance and resumed persecution of Hindus; economic hardship increased under heavy taxes, sparking revolts.
11. (1) men of the pen (scientists, lawyers, judges, poets, and others) **(2)** men of the sword (soldiers) **(3)** men of negotiation (merchants, tax collectors,

---

CHAPTER **11** Review and Assessment

Creating a Chapter Summary

Copy this partially completed graphic organizer on a piece of paper. For each item in the left column, provide two or more main ideas in the right column.

Rise of Islam	•
Teaching of Islam	•
Umayyads	•
Abbassids	•
Mughals	•
Ottomans	•
Safavids	•

 TEXT For additional review and enrichment activities, see the interactive version of *World History* available on the Web and on CD-ROM.

 Web Site Self-Test For practice test questions for Chapter 11, see **www.phschool.com**.

Building Vocabulary

Using the chapter vocabulary words listed below, write sentences, leaving blanks where the words would go. Exchange your sentences with another student and fill in the blanks in each other's sentences.

1. **mosque**
2. **caliph**
3. **social mobility**
4. **arabesque**
5. **janizary**
6. **shah**

Recalling Key Facts

7. What are the Five Pillars of Islam?
8. How did Muslims treat conquered peoples?
9. Describe some of the cultural achievements made by Muslim scholars.
10. **(a)** How did Akbar's rule affect life in India? **(b)** Why did the Mughal empire decline after the reign of Akbar?
11. From the highest to the lowest, what were the four social classes in the Ottoman empire?

Critical Thinking and Writing

12. **Comparing** How does the Christian belief about Jesus differ from the Muslim belief about Muhammad?
13. **Analyzing Information** In what ways was traditional Bedouin society different from the society that was formed under Islam?
14. **Recognizing Causes and Effects** Do you think there would have been a split between Sunni and Shiites if Muhammad had designated a successor before he died? Explain.
15. **Connecting to Geography** How do you think the geography of the Middle East might have helped Muslims spread the teachings of Islam throughout the region?
16. **Making Inferences** Do you think Ottoman policies encouraged Christians in the empire to be loyal or disloyal to their Muslim rulers? Explain the reasons for your answer.
17. **Solving Problems** How do you think Safavid shahs might have been able to halt or slow the decline of their empire after the reign of Abbas the Great?

---

artisans, others) **(4)** men of husbandry (farmers and herders)

Critical Thinking and Writing

12. Christians believe that Jesus is the Son of God and should be worshiped. Muslims believe that Muhammad is a fully human prophet of God and should not be worshiped.
13. Bedouin society was based on clan or tribal loyalty. It was nomadic and frequently at war. Islamic society was based on common religious beliefs and loyalty to God. It stressed education and, because of many conquests, was multicultural.

14. Students should recognize that the initial disagreement was over who was the rightful successor to Muhammad.
15. few natural barriers to overcome and the desire to control the many trade routes crossing the area
16. Students should realize that by allowing various religious groups some autonomy within their millets, the Ottomans encouraged their loyalty.
17. Students' answers should reveal understanding of the causes of decline (pressure from Ottoman armies; competition for power from conservative Shiites; religious persecution).

The excerpt below describes the capture of the Turkish city of Antioch by the crusaders during the First Crusade. Read the description and answer the questions that follow.

"After the siege had been going on for a long time, the Franks made a deal with one of the men who were responsible for the towers. He was an armor-maker called Ruzbih whom they bribed. . . . The Franks sealed their pact with the armor-maker, God curse him! And made their way to the water gate. They opened it and entered the city. Another gang of them climbed the tower with ropes. At dawn, when more than 500 of them were in the city, and the defenders were worn out after the night watch, they sounded their trumpets. . . . This happened in 491."

—Ibn al-Athir, *Account of the First Crusade*

18. **(a)** Were the Franks Christian or Muslim?
(b) Was the armor-maker Christian or Muslim?
19. According to this account, how were the crusaders able to capture Antioch?
20. Why does the author curse Ruzbih?
21. According to Christian historians, the Franks captured Antioch in 1098. Why did al-Athir give the date of the event as 491?
22. Do you consider this account a reliable source of information about the Crusades? Why or why not?

Use the Internet to learn more about one of the Muslim scholars described in the text. Based on your research, write a brief biography. Try to explain how the person's early life helped lead to a life of significant achievement. Focus especially on the contributions that the scholar made. Describe in some detail a few of the scholar's most influential works.

SIKHISM: A BLEND OF RELIGIOUS BELIEFS

Hinduism
- Belief in many gods, all part of brahman
- Religious and moral duties, or dharma, stressed
- Belief in cycle of birth, death, and rebirth
- Priests are part of the social caste system

Islam
- Belief in one God
- Religious and moral duties defined in Five Pillars
- Belief in Heaven and Hell, and a Day of Judgment
- No priests; all believers are religious equals

Sikhism
- Belief in the "unity of God"
- Belief in reincarnation
- Rejection of caste

The chart above shows some teachings of Hinduism, Islam, and Sikhism. Use the chart to answer the following questions:

23. **(a)** Which teachings of Sikhism are similar to those of Hinduism? **(b)** Which are different?
24. Which teachings of Sikhism are similar to those of Islam?
25. According to the chart, what is the relationship of Sikhism to both Hinduism and Islam?
26. Based on what you have read, do you think Sikhism would attract followers in India? Explain.

Skills Tip

As you analyze a chart with arrows, note the directions of the arrows. They indicate relationships between items on the chart.

Analyzing Primary

18. **(a)** Christian **(b)** Muslim
19. They had help from someone inside the city and they struck at dawn when the defenders were tired from their night watch.
20. He was a traitor.
21. Muslims used a different calendar.
22. Students should recognize that the author was not present and that the siege had been futile until this point. He appears to be making excuses for the Muslim defeat.

Analyzing Charts

23. **(a)** belief in reincarnation **(b)** belief in one God, rejection of caste
24. belief in one God; all believers are equal
25. It is a blend of Hinduism and Islam.
26. Students should demonstrate knowledge of the appeal of eliminating castes to poor people.

Skills Tip

Look at the title for a clue about how to read a chart. The Skills Handbook in the front of the book has a lesson that will help students with this feature.

Unit Theme Activity

Remind students to continue working on their Unit Theme Activity. See rubrics for the activity on the unit opener page in the Teacher's Edition.

Take It to the NET

Direct students to **www.phschool.com** for links to sites that will help them get started on this assignment. Share rubrics with students.

Attempted The biography fails to include the required elements, is poorly written and organized, and contains many mechanical errors.

Minimal The biography includes the required elements, but is poorly written and organized, and contains many mechanical errors.

Adequate The biography includes the required elements, is well written and organized, and contains few mechanical errors.

Exemplary The biography includes the required elements, is very well written and organized, and contains no mechanical errors.

Chapter 12 Planning Guide

Resource Manager

	CORE INSTRUCTION	READING/SKILLS
Chapter Level Resources	📦 **Teaching Resources** 📄 Pacing Charts, Ch. 12 📄 Teaching With Themes, p. 15 📖 Color Transparencies, p. F–25 💿 Resource Pro® Ch. 12 🖥 **www.phschool.com** • eTeach	💿 Book on CD, Ch. 12 💿 Interactive Student Tutorial CD-ROM, Ch. 12 💿 Social Studies Skills Tutor CD-ROM 📖 Skills Transparencies
1 Early Civilizations in Africa 1. Explain how geography affected cultural development. 2. Identify the achievements of the kingdom of Nubia. 3. Relate how outside influences led to change in North Africa.	📦 **Teaching Resources** 📄 Creative Teaching Activities, p. 54 💿 Prentice Hall Presentation Pro, Ch. 12, Section 1 📖 Section Reading Support Transparencies	📦 **Teaching Resources** 📁 Unit 3 booklet • Guided Reading and Review, p. 76 📄 Guide to the Essentials 📼 Guided Reading Audiotapes, Ch. 12, Section 1

2 Kingdoms of West Africa
1. Analyze why gold and salt were important to early Africa.
2. Describe how rulers of Ghana, Mali, and Songhai built strong kingdoms.
3. Summarize the development of other West African kingdoms.
	📦 **Teaching Resources**
	📁 Unit 3 booklet
	    • Biography Activity, p. 84
	📄 Creative Teaching Activities, p. 55
	💿 Prentice Hall Presentation Pro, Ch. 12, Section 2
	📖 Section Reading Support Transparencies
		📦 **Teaching Resources**
		📁 Unit 3 booklet
		    • Guided Reading and Review, p. 78
		    • Skill Application Activity, p. 87
		📄 Guide to the Essentials
		📼 Guided Reading Audiotapes, Ch. 12, Section 2

3 Trade Routes of East Africa
1. Explain how religion influenced the development of Axum and Ethiopia.
2. Enumerate the effects of trade on city-states in East Africa.
3. Outline what archaeologists discovered about Great Zimbabwe.
	📦 **Teaching Resources**
	📁 Unit 3 booklet
	    • Primary Source Activity, p. 85
	    • Viewpoint Activity, p. 86
	📄 Creative Teaching Activities, p. 56
	💿 Prentice Hall Presentation Pro, Ch. 12, Section 3
	📖 Section Reading Support Transparencies
		📦 **Teaching Resources**
		📁 Unit 3 booklet
		    • Guided Reading and Review, p. 80
		📄 Guide to the Essentials
		📼 Guided Reading Audiotapes, Ch. 12, Section 3

4 Many Peoples, Many Traditions 1. Identify how the interaction of people and the environment led to diverse societies. 2. Describe how government, family, and religion held African societies together. 3. Illustrate how artistic and literary traditions reflected the values of African society.	📦 **Teaching Resources** 📄 Creative Teaching Activities, p. 57 💿 Prentice Hall Presentation Pro, Ch. 12, Section 4 📖 Section Reading Support Transparencies	📦 **Teaching Resources** 📁 Unit 3 booklet • Guided Reading and Review, p. 82 📄 Guide to the Essentials 📼 Guided Reading Audiotapes, Ch. 12, Section 4

ENRICHMENT/PRE-AP

- 📖 **www.phschool.com**
  - Why Study History?

- 🎨 **Color Transparencies**, p. B–81
- 📖 **www.phschool.com**
  - Internet Activities, Section 1

- 📚 **Teaching Resources**
  - 📘 **Creative Teaching Activities**, p. 32
  - 📘 **History Through Literature**, pp. 27–29
- 🎨 **Color Transparencies**, p. D–55
- 📖 **www.phschool.com**
  - Virtual Field Trip

- 📖 **www.phschool.com**
  - Internet Activities, Section 3

- 📚 **Teaching Resources**
  - 📘 **Chapter Extension Activities**, p. 33

ASSESSMENT

PRENTICE HALL ASSESSMENT *SYSTEM*

Core Assessment
- 📘 ExamView Test Bank booklet, Ch. 12
- 💿 ExamView Test Bank CD-ROM, Ch. 12

Standardized Test Preparation

Diagnose and Prescribe
- 📘 Diagnostic Tests for High School Social Studies Skills

Review and Reteach
- 📘 Review Book for World History

Practice and Assess
- 📘 Test-Taking Strategies With Transparencies for High School
- 📘 Alternative Assessment booklet
- 📘 Test Prep Book for World History

- 📚 **Teaching Resources**
  - 📕 **Unit 3 booklet**
    - Geography Quiz, p. 88
    - Section Quizzes, pp. 77, 79, 81, 83
    - Chapter Tests A, B, and C, pp. 89–93
- 📖 **www.phschool.com**
  - Self-Test

CUSTOMIZE FOR INDIVIDUAL NEEDS

Gifted and Talented
- Teacher's Edition, Activities: Interpreting Viewpoints, p. 291

Less Proficient Readers
- Guide to the Essentials, Ch. 12
- Guided Reading Audiotapes, English, Ch. 12
- Book on CD, Ch. 12
- Teacher's Edition, Activities: Connections to Film, p. 282; Reading Strategy, p. 295

Less Proficient Writers
- Teacher's Edition, Activities: Cooperative Learning Activity, p. 286

Students Acquiring English/ESL
- Guide to the Essentials, English/Spanish, Ch. 12
- Guided Reading Audiotapes, English/Spanish, Ch. 12
- Book on CD, Ch. 12
- Teacher's Edition, Activities marked with an *: Connections to Film, p. 282; Interpreting Viewpoints, p. 291

iTEXT

Don't miss the exclusive inter-active version of *World History: Connections to Today* on the Internet and CD-ROM.

INTRODUCTION

Many civilizations rose and flourished in Africa, despite geographical barriers. Bantu migrations and contacts with Egypt, Rome, Christianity, and Islam contributed to diversity. A succession of powerful West African kingdoms controlled the Saharan trade routes between 800 and 1600. Along the coast of East Africa, Indian Ocean trade routes led to the growth of prosperous city-states. Art and oral literature fostered common values.

Focusing on Themes

Suggest that students focus on these theme questions as they read:

Geography and History
How did geography both help and hinder the peoples of Africa?

Diversity
What conditions contributed to the development of varied cultures in Africa?

Global Interaction
How were parts of Africa tied into major trading networks?

Art and Literature
What literary and artistic traditions developed in Africa?

TIME LINE ACTIVITY

Share the About the Pictures note with your students before you ask these questions about the time line:

1. After Nubia conquers Egypt, how do the Nubians blend their culture with Egyptian culture? *(They adopt many aspects of Egyptian culture but worship their own gods.)*
2. When and why did Hannibal cross the Alps? *(218 B.C., to attack Rome during the Second Punic War)*
3. What major religion spread to North Africa in the A.D. 600s? *(Islam)*
4. What impact do you think the spread of Islam will have on African cultures? *(It will contribute to their diversity.)*

Don't Miss!

You Are There . . .
Traveling With Mansa Musa (Section 2)

Analyzing Primary Sources
The Griots of Africa (Section 4)

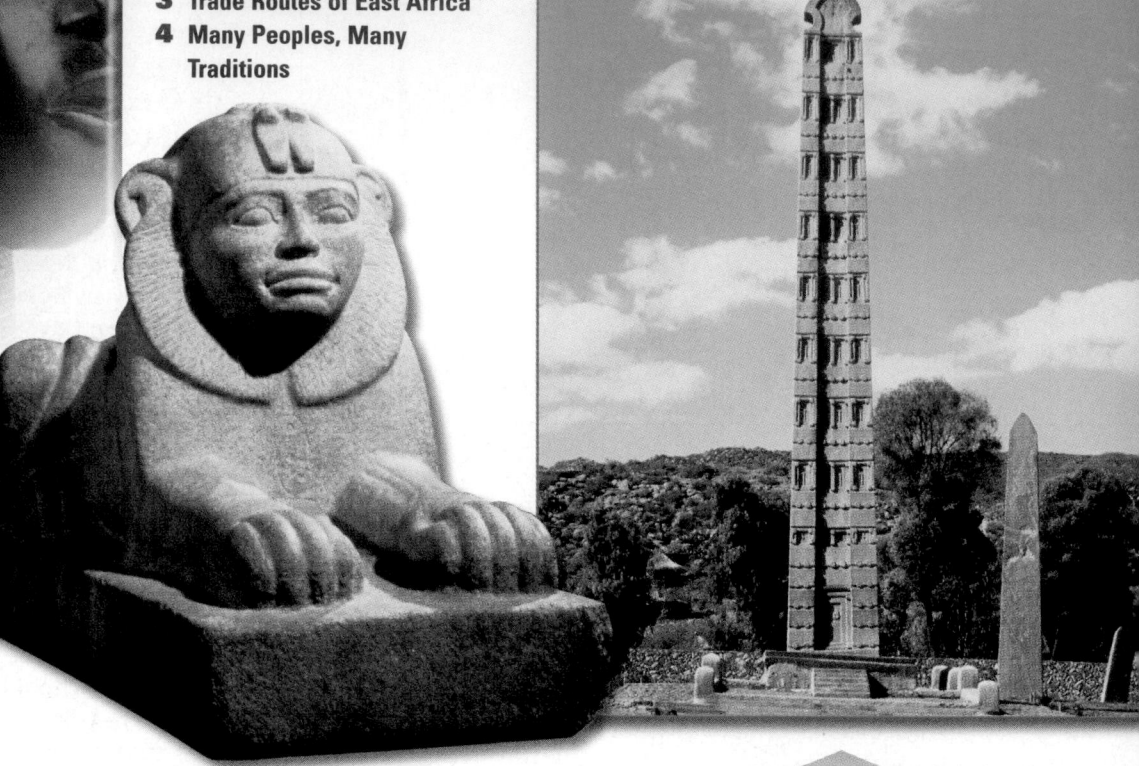

Kingdoms and Trading States of Africa 750 B.C.–A.D. 1586

Chapter Preview

1 Early Civilizations of Africa
2 Kingdoms of West Africa
3 Trade Routes of East Africa
4 Many Peoples, Many Traditions

750 B.C.
Nubia conquers Egypt. Nubians adopt many aspects of Egyptian culture but worship their own gods. Here, King Taharqa is shown as the lion-headed warrior god, Apedemak.

200 B.C.
Axum gains control of an extensive trade network. The Axumites carve granite pillars such as the Great Stela, pictured above, to show their power.

CHAPTER EVENTS

800 B.C.   400 B.C.   B.C. A.D.

GLOBAL EVENTS

500 B.C. In India, the sacred Hindu texts are recorded.

460 B.C. The Age of Pericles begins in Athens.

218 B.C. Hannibal crosses the Alps to attack Rome during the Second Punic War.

278 Chapter 12

Resource Directory

Teaching Resources
Teaching With Themes Chapter Theme Activities, p. 15
Pacing Chart With Block Scheduling Guide Ch. 12

Technology
World History Color Transparencies Ch. 12 Graphic Organizer, p. F–25

Geography and Climates of Africa

Climates

- Rain forest
- Savanna
- Desert
- Mediterranean
- Dry woodland

Africa's many climate zones and landforms have encouraged the development of a wide variety of cultures.

A.D. 600s
Islam spreads to North Africa.

A.D. 1200s
King Lalibela has churches built into the mountains of Ethiopia.

A.D. 1500
The kingdom of Kongo flourishes in central Africa.

A.D. 400

A.D. 1200

A.D. 1600

A.D. 668 The Shilla dynasty unites Korea.

A.D. 1492 Christopher Columbus reaches Hispaniola.

Independent Assignments

Have students read one section as they prepare for class. After class, have them complete the assignment. Some students may benefit from using the Guided Reading and Review worksheets.

Section 1 Have students use the outline map *Early Kingdoms in Africa* in the Historical Outline Map Book, p. 14, to label the major physical features and important cities of ancient Africa.

Section 2 Have students use the worksheet *Ibn Battuta* in the Unit 3 booklet, p. 84, to learn about the famous Muslim who traveled through fourteenth-century Africa.

Section 3 Have students use the worksheet *Who Built Great Zimbabwe?* in the Unit 3 booklet, p. 86, to learn about differing viewpoints regarding the construction of Great Zimbabwe.

Section 4 Have students use the worksheet *Sundiata: An Epic of Old Mali* in the History Through Literature booklet, pp. 27–29, to read an oral legend about the empire of ancient Mali.

Geography and Climates of Africa

Activating Prior Knowledge
What kinds of geographic barriers may have prevented people from migrating easily from one area to another in Africa? *(deserts, rain forests, and mountains)*

Previewing
Inform students that the Sahara became an area for migration and trade. Ask them to speculate why. *(Possible answer: Lands bordering the Sahara to the west, north, and east have access by sea to goods from the other lands. With no rivers going from the interior to these coasts, traders had to cross the Sahara.)*

Background
About the Pictures

1. This sphinx represents King Taharqa, one of the Nubian kings who became pharaoh in 690 B.C. Taharqa was overthrown by Assyrian King Esarhaddon, who ruled from 680 to 669 B.C.

2. This stela from Axum, Ethiopia, is the tallest of the stelae that still stand. In all, 126 stelae, or obelisks, once stood in one central area of the city; many are still standing. The tallest one, which has fallen, was 110 feet tall. By comparison, the Washington Monument stands 555 feet, 5 inches tall.

3. Churches like this Ethiopian rock church were built during the thirteenth century. Workers dug a deep pit around a solid rock. Then they carved the rock into the shape of a cross, hollowed out the interior, and cut doors and windows.

eTeach

Be sure to check out this month's online discussion with a World History Master Teacher.

Go to **www.phschool.com**.

Bell Ringer

Bell Ringer Ask students to study the *Geography and Climates of Africa* map on the chapter opener page. Then, have them describe how geographic factors might have both hindered and promoted the development of African civilizations.

Reading Focus

- How did geography affect cultural development and the migration of peoples?
- What were the achievements of the kingdom of Nubia?
- How did outside influences lead to change in North Africa?

Vocabulary

savanna
desertification
outpost

Taking Notes

Copy this concept web. As you read the section, complete the circles with important facts to remember about desertification. Add as many circles as you need.

Main Idea Africa's geographic features had a major impact on the development of societies.

LESSON PLAN

1. Focus The varied climate zones, physical features, and natural resources of Africa have helped create diverse ways of life. Nubian civilization adopted much from ancient Egyptian culture and, at the same time, developed advances of its own. Over the centuries, North Africa was influenced by Carthaginian, Roman, and Muslim civilizations.

2. Instruct Ask students to imagine that they are responsible for planning a museum exhibit on the development of civilization in early Africa. The exhibit will occupy three separate galleries, one for African prehistory, another for the kingdom of Nubia, and a third for the civilizations of North Africa. Have students write descriptions of the artifacts, maps, illustrations, and photographs that they will place in each gallery of their exhibit. Invite volunteers to present their exhibit plans to the class in an oral presentation.

3. Assess As a concluding activity, have students create colorful posters that advertise their museum exhibits. Display the finished posters for the class to share.

4. Reteach If students' **Assess** activity does not reflect adequate understanding of the lesson, you might assign the *Guide to the Essentials* or the *Interactive Student Tutorial CD-ROM* for this section.

Shown twice actual size

Did You Know?

The Tsetse Fly

The tsetse fly carries one of Africa's most troublesome diseases—sleeping sickness. Flies pass on the deadly disease by biting humans and large animals. Some people have abandoned their villages in heavily infested areas. In other regions, people have stopped raising horses and cattle because of the pests. Many tourists arrange their trips to avoid the tsetse fly.

How can Africans overcome this menace? Tsetse flies are attracted to moving vehicles, dark colors, and perfume and after-shave. Using this knowledge, scientists have built traps. A dark blue cloth, treated to smell like ox breath—irresistible to the tsetse fly—acts as a lure. The cloth is also treated with insecticide, to kill the flies.

Theme: Economics and Technology How might African economies be affected by eliminating the tsetse fly?

Setting the Scene

Setting the Scene As the sun rose above the east bank of the Nile, workers hurried to the construction site. They had only a few hours to work in comfort before the sun turned the desert into a furnace. Still, as long as King Taharqa (tuh HAHR kuh) was determined to turn the old mud-brick temple into a magnificent monument, their work would continue. An ancient inscription explains how the monument was "built of good white sandstone, excellent, hard, . . . the house being of gold, the columns of gold, the inlays thereof being of silver."

About 680 B.C., Taharqa commanded the Nile Valley from Nubia to the Mediterranean. By that time, Nubia was already 3,000 years old. Along with Egypt, it stood as one of the world's early civilizations.

The Geography of Africa

After Asia, Africa is the second largest continent, covering one fifth of all the Earth's land surface. Its geography is immensely varied. However, certain geographic features, such as distinct climate zones, have had a major impact on its development.

Climate Zones Many outsiders, misled by movies, imagine Africa as a continent covered with thick jungles. In fact, tropical rain forests cover less than five percent of the land, mostly along the Equator. Thick trees and roots make this region unsuitable for farming.

Africa's largest and most populated climate zone is the savanna, or grassy plain, which stretches north and south of the forest zone. Although the savanna has good soil, irregular patterns of rainfall sometimes cause long, deadly droughts. In parts of the savanna, the tsetse fly infects people and cattle with sleeping sickness. But in other parts, cattle herding is a common occupation.

The savanna belts trail off into increasingly dry steppe zones and then into two major deserts. The blistering Sahara in the north is the world's largest desert. Although the Sahara did become a highway for migration and trade, its size and harsh terrain limited movement. The Kalahari and Namib in the south are smaller but equally forbidding. Finally, along the Mediterranean coast of North Africa and at the tip of southern Africa lie areas of fertile farmland. These varied regions also offer a variety of mineral resources, such as salt, gold, iron, copper, diamonds, and oil, all of which have spurred trade.

Did You Know?

ANSWER Possible answer: Agriculture and tourism might increase if people did not have to worry about contracting sleeping sickness.

Resource Directory

Teaching Resources

Creative Teaching Activities Creative Teaching Activities booklet, p. 54

Guided Reading and Review Unit 3 booklet, p. 76

Technology

World History Color Transparencies *Africa*, p. B–81

Movement In addition to deserts and rain forests, other geographic features have acted as barriers to easy movement of people and goods. Africa has an enormous coastline, but few good natural harbors. In addition, much of the interior is a high plateau. As rivers approach the coast, they cascade through a series of rapids and cataracts that hinder travel between the coast and the interior.

Despite geographic barriers, people did migrate within Africa and to neighboring lands. The Great Rift Valley of East Africa served as one interior corridor. Many rivers were navigable in the interior of the continent. The Red Sea and Indian Ocean linked East Africa to the Middle East and other Asian lands, while North Africa was a part of the Mediterranean world.

Resources Mineral resources spurred trade among various African regions. Salt, gold, iron, and copper were particularly valuable to early trade. In later centuries, diamonds and oil would also gain importance.

Migration of Peoples

Archaeologists have uncovered evidence that the Great Rift Valley of East Africa was the home of the earliest people. Gradually, their descendants spread to almost every corner of the Earth.

The Changing Sahara In Africa, as elsewhere, Paleolithic people developed skills as hunters and food gatherers. By 5500 B.C., Neolithic farmers had learned to cultivate the Nile Valley and to domesticate animals. As farming spread across North Africa, Neolithic villages even appeared in the Sahara, which was then a well-watered zone. Ancient rock paintings show a Sahara full of forests and rivers.

About 2500 B.C., a climate change slowly dried out the Sahara. As the land became parched, the desert spread. This process of *desertification* has continued to the present, devouring thousands of acres of cropland and pastureland each year. Desertification has also encouraged migration, as people are forced to seek new areas to maintain their ways of life.

The Bantu Migrations Over thousands of years, migrations contributed to the rich diversity of peoples and cultures. Scholars have traced these migrations by studying language patterns. They have learned that West African farmers and herders migrated to the south and east between about 1000 B.C. and A.D. 1000. Like the Indo-European peoples of Europe and Asia, these West African peoples spoke a variety of languages that derived from a common root language. We call this root language Bantu.

As people migrated across Africa, they adapted to its many climates and developed a diversity of cultures. While some were nomadic cattle herders, others cultivated grain or root crops. In several regions, farming people built great empires.

The Nile Kingdom of Nubia

While Egyptian civilization was developing, another African civilization took shape on a wide band of fertile land among the cataracts of the upper Nile. The ancient kingdom of Nubia, also called Kush, was located in present-day Sudan.

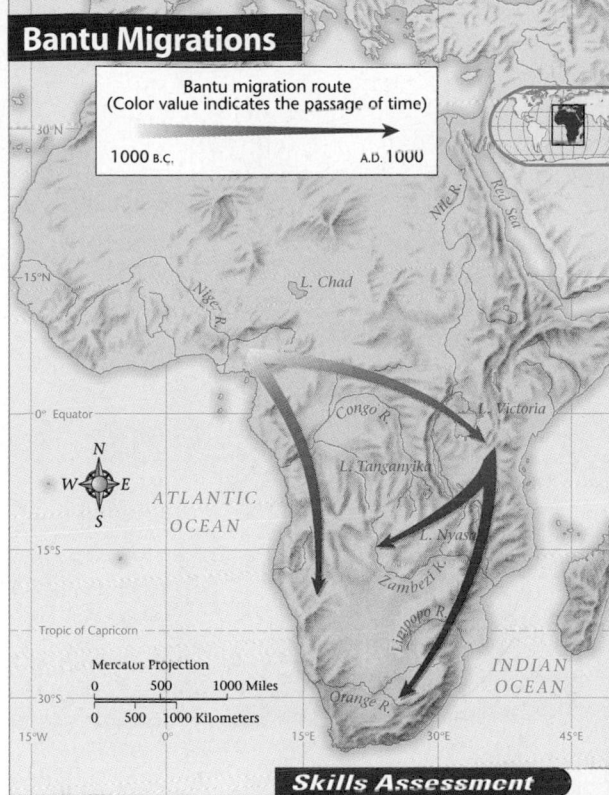

Bantu Migrations

Bantu migration route
(Color value indicates the passage of time)

1000 B.C.   A.D. 1000

Mercator Projection

| 0 | 500 | 1000 Miles |
| 0 | 500 | 1000 Kilometers |

Skills Assessment

Geography Over a period of 2,000 years, Bantu peoples migrated to southern Africa. Today, as many as one third of Africans speak a Bantu language.

1. **Location** On the map, locate **(a)** Lake Victoria, **(b)** Orange River, **(c)** Lake Nyasa.
2. **Movement** **(a)** Where did Bantu peoples originate? **(b)** About when did Bantu-speaking peoples reach the Orange River?
3. **Critical Thinking Solving Problems** How have scientists learned about the Bantu migrations?

Background
Global Connections

West African Droughts Due to changing weather patterns, West Africa is particularly prone to unpredictable periods of protracted drought. Drought occurs in the region when the pattern of westerlies, or winds from the west, changes. Between 1968 and 1974, and again in the mid-1980s, West African westerlies shifted in a southward direction. As a result, the summer monsoon rains that normally soak the area bypassed it completely. These periods of prolonged drought result in massive crop failures and loss of livestock. Hundreds of thousands, and sometimes millions, of people die of starvation and disease.

Reading Strategy
Predicting Content

Before they read, have students predict how the migration of peoples contributed to Africa's diversity. Ask students to look for data to support their predictions as they read. *(More Advanced Readers)*

☐ Block Scheduling Support

Pair up students to create separate concept webs for "The Nile Kingdom of Nubia" and "North Africa" sections. Their webs should be similar to the Taking Notes feature at the beginning of this section. While one student orally summarizes information about the Nubian kingdom, the other student can draw the web. After the pair agrees on the design of and information in their web, they should switch roles to create their North African concept web. Once all pairs agree on the design of and information in that second concept web, ask students to share their concept webs with the rest of the class. Invite volunteers to draw their webs on the chalkboard. Ask other students if these webs differ from their own. If so, have them explain how their webs differ.

Skills Assessment

ANSWERS 1. Review locations with students. **2. (a)** near Atlantic coast, in the southern portion of West Africa **(b)** about A.D. 1000 **3.** by studying language patterns

Nubian Carvings
Conquest and trade provided Nubia with opportunities to learn about Egyptian culture. Many traditions and beliefs were adapted to become part of Nubian civilization.

Theme: Art and Literature
How do these Nubian carvings reflect the influence of Egyptian art?

From time to time, ambitious Egyptian pharaohs subdued Nubia, but the Nubians always regained their independence. As a result of conquest and trade, Nubian rulers adapted many Egyptian traditions. They modeled palaces and pyramids on Egyptian styles. About 750 B.C., the Nubian king Piankhi (pee AHNG kee) conquered Egypt. For a century, Nubian kings ruled Egypt. But their armies could not match the iron weapons of the invading Assyrians. The Nubians retreated south from Egypt.

The Furnaces of Meroë By 500 B.C., Nubian rulers moved their capital to Meroë (MEHR uh wee). Meroë commanded both the north-south Nile route and the east-west route from the Red Sea into the savanna and North Africa. Along this wide trade network, Nubia sent gold, ivory, animal skins, perfumes, and slaves to the Mediterranean world and the Middle East.

Equally important, Meroë was rich in iron ore. Its furnaces, fueled by large quantities of timber, produced iron. Today, giant heaps of iron waste remain as evidence of ancient Meroë's industry.

Splendor and Decline Although Nubia absorbed much from Egypt, it later followed an independent course. Nubians worshiped their own gods including Apedemak, a lion-headed warrior god. At Meroë, artistic styles reflected a greater sense of freedom than did Egyptian styles. Nubians also created their own system of writing, using an alphabet instead of hieroglyphics. Unfortunately, the Nubian alphabet has yet to be deciphered.

After the joint reign of King Natakamani and Queen Amanitere in the first century A.D., Nubia's golden age dimmed. Finally, about A.D. 350, armies from the kingdom of Axum on the Red Sea overwhelmed Nubia. King Ezana of Axum boasted, "I burnt their towns, both those built of brick and those built of reeds, and my army carried off their food and copper and iron . . . and destroyed the statues in their temples." As you will read later, Axum would make its own mark on this region beyond the Nile.

North Africa

Early African civilizations had strong ties to the Mediterranean world. At the opposite end of the Mediterranean from Nubia and Axum, Carthage rose as a great North African power. Like Nubia, its wealth came from trade. Founded by Phoenician traders, Carthage came to dominate trade in the western Mediterranean and North Africa. Between 800 B.C. and 146 B.C., it forged an empire that stretched from the Maghreb (present-day Tunisia, Algeria, and Morocco) to southern Spain and Sicily. Carthage also established outposts, or distant military stations, in England and France.

As Rome expanded, territorial and trade rivalries erupted between the two powers, resulting in the Punic Wars. Despite the efforts of Hannibal, Rome eventually crushed Carthage. Trade, however, continued.

Roman Rule The Romans built roads, dams, aqueducts, and cities across North Africa. They developed its farmlands and imported lions and other fierce animals to do battle with gladiators. North Africa also provided soldiers for the Roman army. One of them, Septimius Severus, later became emperor of Rome.

Under Roman rule, Christianity spread to the cities of North Africa. St. Augustine, the most influential Christian thinker of the late Roman empire, was born in present-day Algeria. From A.D. 395 to A.D. 430, Augustine was bishop of Hippo, a city near the ruins of ancient Carthage.

Camels and Trade By A.D. 200, camels had been brought to North Africa from Asia. These hardy "ships of the desert" revolutionized trade across the Sahara. Camels could carry loads of up to 500 pounds and could plod 20 or 30 miles a day, often without water. Although daring traders had earlier made the difficult desert crossing in horse-drawn chariots, camel caravans created new trade networks.

Spread of Islam Further changes came in the 600s, when Arab armies carried Islam into North Africa. At first, the Arabs occupied the cities and battled the Berbers in the desert. Later, Berbers and Arabs joined forces to conquer Spain. Islam replaced Christianity as the dominant religion of North Africa, and Arabic replaced Latin as its language.

North Africa benefited from the blossoming of Muslim civilization. Cities like Cairo, Fez, and Marrakesh were famed for their mosques and libraries. Linked into a global trade network, North African ports did a busy trade in grain, wine, fruit, ivory, and gold. Along with their goods, Muslim traders from North Africa carried Islam into West Africa.

SECTION 1 Assessment

Recall
1. **Identify:** (a) Taharqa, (b) Bantu, (c) Piankhi, (d) Meroë, (e) St. Augustine.
2. **Define:** (a) savanna, (b) desertification, (c) outpost.

Comprehension
3. (a) What geographic barriers hindered movement in Africa? (b) Describe two examples of migration in Africa.
4. How did Nubia prosper?
5. Describe one way each of the following influenced North Africa: (a) the growth of the Roman empire, (b) the spread of Islam.

Critical Thinking and Writing
6. **Linking Past and Present** (a) What effects did desertification have on African peoples? (b) How might life in the United States today be affected if well-watered areas began to turn into desert?
7. **Connecting to Geography** Explain the link between geography and the introduction of camel caravans.

Activity
Take It to the NET

Search on the Internet for Lepcis Magna, an archaeological site on the Mediterranean coast of North Africa. Write a paragraph about the city's history and its link to Septimius Severus.

SECTION 1 Assessment

Recall
1. (a) Taharqa, p. 280 (b) Bantu, p. 281 (c) Piankhi, p. 282 (d) Meroë, p. 282 (e) St. Augustine, p. 283 2. (a) savanna, p. 280 (b) desertification, p. 281 (c) outpost, p. 283

Comprehension
3. (a) Deserts and tropical rain forests hindered land travel. River rapids and the small number of natural harbors limited travel by water. (b) Possible answer: As the Sahara dried out, the people who had lived there retreated to the north and south. Later, between A.D. 500 and 1500, West African farmers and herders migrated south and east. 4. Nubia conquered Egypt and commanded trade. Additionally, its capital was rich in iron ore. 5. Possible answers: (a) The growth of the Roman empire led to the construction of roads, dams, aqueducts, and cities. (b) Islam replaced Christianity as the dominant religion of North Africa.

Critical Thinking and Writing
6. (a) It forced them to migrate to other parts of the continent. (b) Possible answer: People would migrate to other areas of the country. This would lead to changes in population density. The nation might have to start importing food on a large scale. Food prices would rise. In the worst-case scenario, malnutrition and starvation could occur. 7. The Sahara's size and harsh terrain limited movement. Camels could carry loads of up to 500 pounds and could plod 20 or 30 miles a day, often without water. This made them better-suited than horses to desert travel. Camel caravans created new trade networks after camels were brought to North Africa from Asia.

Activity Rubrics

Share rubrics with students before they begin their research and write their paragraphs.

Attempted The paragraph fails to explain adequately the city's link to Septimius Severus; the paragraph is disorganized.

Minimal The paragraph explains the link between the city and Septimius Severus but is poorly developed.

Adequate The paragraph clearly explains the link between Lepcis Magna and Septimius Severus and is well written.

Exemplary The paragraph clearly explains the link between Lepcis Magna and Septimius Severus, is well written, and provides interesting supporting details and elaboration.

Human Drama Activity

Destruction of Nubia Ask students to imagine that they are citizens of Nubia living during the time when Nubia was invaded by armies from Axum. Have students write a journal entry describing their feelings as they witness the destruction of this once-powerful kingdom. Ask students to be imaginative and use very descriptive language.

Test Preparation

Have students read the subsection titled "Spread of Islam" on this page, and then answer the question below.

Which of the following is not an effect of Muslim civilization coming into North Africa?

A North African ports had more global connections.

B Muslim traders spread Islam into West Africa.

C Christianity continued to spread in North Africa.

D Muslim civilization benefited several cities.

Bell Ringer

Ask students to observe the illustrations in this section and to study the map of Africa in Section 3. Then, ask students to identify and describe two economic activities that brought wealth to West Africa.

LESSON PLAN

1. Focus Trade played an important role in linking and strengthening the kingdoms of West Africa. Rulers built powerful kingdoms by gaining control of key trade routes and defeating their enemies. Muslim civilization spread through much of West Africa.

2. Instruct Ask students to imagine that they are living in a West African kingdom during the 1500s. Have them write a diary entry describing their life. Suggest that students choose one of the following and write the entry from that person's point of view: a caravan leader, someone in the entourage of Mansa Musa on his pilgrimage to Mecca, a marketplace trader, a student in Timbuktu, a Benin sculptor. Have students read their diary entries to the class and be prepared to answer questions.

3. Assess In closing, ask students to answer this question: If you could have visited one of these West African kingdoms, which one would it be? Why?

4. Reteach If students' **Assess** activity does not reflect adequate understanding of the lesson, you might assign the *Guide to the Essentials* or the *Interactive Student Tutorial CD-ROM* for this section.

Reading Focus

- Why were gold and salt important in early Africa?
- How did the rulers of Ghana, Mali, and Songhai build strong kingdoms?
- How did other West African kingdoms develop?

Vocabulary

surplus

commodity

mansa

oba

Taking Notes

Copy and complete the time line below. As you read, add entries for the establishment of kingdoms mentioned in this section. One has been included as an example.

550	800	1050	1300	1550
	Ghana			

Main Idea Between about A.D. 800 and A.D. 1600, several powerful kingdoms won control of the Sahara trade and built prosperous cities in West Africa.

Setting the Scene In the early 1500s, the scholar Hassan ibn Muhammad—known in the West as Leo Africanus—described the commercial wealth and bustling markets of the West African city of Timbuktu:

> "Here are many shops of . . . merchants, and especially such as weave linen and cotton cloth. And here do the Barbary (North African) merchants bring the cloth of Europe. All the women of this region, except maidservants, go with their faces covered and sell all the necessary foods."
>
> —Hassan ibn Muhammad, quoted in *Ancient African Kingdoms* (Shinnie)

Timbuktu stood at one end of a trade network that reached north to Cairo and then across the Mediterranean Sea to Italy. Between about 800 and 1600, several powerful kingdoms in turn won control of the prosperous Sahara trade. Among the richest of these West African states were Ghana, Mali, and Songhai.

Trading Gold and Salt

As the Sahara dried out, you will recall, some Neolithic people migrated southward into the savanna. There, farmers grew beans, melons, and cereal grains. By A.D. 100, settled farming villages were expanding, especially along the Senegal and Niger rivers and around Lake Chad.

Villagers traded any **surplus**, or excess, food they produced. Gradually, a trade network linked the savanna to forest lands in the south and then funneled goods across the Sahara to civilizations along the Mediterranean and in the Middle East.

Two products, gold and salt, dominated the Sahara trade. Gold was plentiful in present-day Ghana, Nigeria, and Senegal. Men dug the gold-bearing soil from pits. Women then washed the soil to extract the gold dust. The precious metal was stuffed into hollow feather quills for safe travel to the markets of North Africa and Europe.

In return, West Africans received an equally important **commodity**, or valuable product, salt. People need salt in their diet to prevent dehydration, especially in hot, tropical areas. The Sahara had an abundance of salt. At Taghaza, in the central Sahara, people even built homes of salt blocks. But in the savanna, several hundred miles south, salt was scarce. A block of salt was easily worth its weight in gold.

Geography and History

The Salt Trade

The camel changed the Saharan salt trade. For centuries, trade was limited because the horses that transported the salt were not suited to desert travel. However, about A.D. 300, the Berbers, an Arabic people of North Africa, began using camels to carry their goods. When the caravans reached Ghana, merchants would pay one pound of gold dust for one pound of salt. The salt trade began to thrive.

Now, more than 1,000 years later, the salt trade still exists. As late as 1975, workers in Taghaza (now called Taoudenni) were living in salt huts and mining several thousand tons of salt per year. Small caravans of camels carrying salt still arrive in Timbuktu today.

Theme: Continuity and Change Why are camels still used in the salt trade in today's technological age?

Geography and History

ANSWER Students may speculate about tradition and the camel's suitability for the desert environment.

Resource Directory

Teaching Resources

Creative Teaching Activities Creative Teaching Activities booklet, p. 55

Guided Reading and Review Unit 3 booklet, p. 78

Skill Application Activity *Making Presentations*, Unit 3 booklet, p. 87

History Through Literature *Sundiata: An Epic of Old Mali*, History Through Literature booklet, pp. 27–29

As farming and trade prospered, cities developed on the northern edges of the savanna. Strong monarchs gained control of the most profitable trade routes and built powerful kingdoms.

Gold Wealth of Ghana

By A.D. 800, the rulers of the Soninke people had united many farming villages to create the kingdom of Ghana.* Ghana was located in the broad "V" made by the Niger and Senegal rivers. From there, the king controlled gold-salt trade routes across West Africa. The two streams of trade met in the marketplaces of Ghana, where the king collected tolls on all goods entering or leaving his land. So great was the flow of gold that Arab writers called Ghana "land of gold."

Capital and King The capital of Ghana was Kumbi Saleh, made up of two separate, walled towns, some six miles apart. The first town was dominated by the royal palace, surrounded by a complex of domed buildings. Here, in a court noted for its wealth and splendor, the king of Ghana presided over elaborate ceremonies. To the people, he was a semidivine figure who dispensed justice and kept order.

In the second town of Kumbi Saleh, prosperous Muslim merchants from north of the Sahara lived in luxurious stone buildings. Lured by the gold wealth of Ghana, these merchants helped make Kumbi Saleh a bustling center of trade.

Influence of Islam Muslim merchants, settled in their own communities throughout the kingdom, brought their Islamic faith to Ghana. Islam spread slowly at first. The king employed Muslims as counselors and officials, gradually absorbing Muslim military technology and ideas about government. Muslims also introduced their written language, coinage, business methods, and styles of architecture. In time, a few city dwellers adopted Islam, but most of the Soninke people continued to follow their own traditional beliefs.

About 1050, the Almoravids (al MOR uh veedz), pious Muslims of North Africa, launched a campaign to spread their form of Islam. They eventually overwhelmed Ghana, but were unable to maintain control over such a distant land. In time, Ghana was swallowed up by a rising new power, the West African kingdom of Mali.

The Kingdom of Mali

Amid the turmoil of Ghana's collapse, the Mandinka people on the upper Niger suffered a bitter defeat by a rival leader. Their king and all but one of his sons were executed. According to tradition, the survivor was Sundiata. By 1235, he had crushed his enemies, won control of the gold trade routes, and founded the empire of Mali.

Mali is an Arab version of the Mandinka word meaning "where the king dwells." The mansas, or kings, expanded their influence over both the gold-mining regions to the south and the salt supplies of Taghaza. Where caravan routes crossed, towns like Timbuktu mushroomed into great trading cities.

The greatest emperor of Mali was Mansa Musa (MAHN sah MOO sah), who came to the throne in about 1312. He expanded Mali's borders westward to the Atlantic Ocean and pushed northward to conquer many cities. During Mansa Musa's 25-year reign, he worked to ensure peace and order in his empire. "There is complete and general safety throughout the land,"

---

*Ghana, meaning ruler, was the name used for the kingdom by Arab traders. The modern nation of Ghana is not located on the site of the ancient kingdom, but lies several hundred miles to the south.

The Gold Trade
This gold scorpion was probably used as a weight by West African merchants. Along with salt, gold dominated the Sahara trade and was a mainstay of the West African economy.

Theme: Economics and Technology Why might someone choose to make a weight from so valuable a material as gold?

Bell Ringer Ask students to imagine that they are setting out on a pilgrimage that will take over a year. Have them think about what things they will need to take and what kinds of adventures they might encounter.

Background
About the Scene

The hajj had its origins in the hijra, the journey made by Mohammad in 622. Muslims undertook the pilgrimage to show their religious devotion, yet personal reasons often came into play as well. Mansa Musa was said to have killed his mother accidentally. He traveled to Mecca to fast and pray and to become at peace with himself.

Details of Mansa Musa's journey were gathered by Al-Umari of Cairo. During the hajj, so much gold was put into circulation that it took twelve years for the gold market to recover.

Activity
Cooperative Learning

Creating a Booklet Divide the class into small groups to create an illustrated booklet detailing Mansa Musa's pilgrimage. Students could focus on who participated in the hajj, preparations for the journey, stopovers in Timbuktu and Cairo, and the return home. Each student could be responsible for taking notes and writing a rough draft on one part of the hajj. Other parts of the activity could be divided among members of the group: collecting illustrations or drawing pictures, creating the page design, revising the rough drafts, and proofreading.

Portfolio Assessment Rubrics

Share rubrics with students before they compose their song.

Attempted The song lacks sufficient details.

Minimal The song has details, but they are not very vivid.

Adequate The song has interesting details and allows readers to visualize the journey.

Exemplary The song draws the listener into the journey. Details are striking.

Traveling With Mansa Musa

Despite the blistering heat of the Sahara, your heart is light. As a minor official, you feel honored to be a part of the *hajj*—or pilgrimage—of your emperor, Mansa Musa. Although there are still many miles between you and the holy city of Mecca, you know that the people of Mali will sing songs about this trip for generations to come.

You began the 4,800-mile trip in Niani, the capital of Mali. Musa's caravan followed the Niger River to Timbuktu, then headed toward the salt mines of Taghaza. Now, you are near the Egyptian city of Cairo. After visiting Mecca, your party must return to Mali. The hajj will take over a year.

Musa's enormous caravan snakes along as far as the eye can see. You travel with thousands of people and camels, as well as enough food and supplies for months.

It seems as if you have been riding a camel forever. Although it can be a mean-tempered beast, your camel is the best form of transportation through this vast desert.

Musa dazzles everyone with Mali's wealth. At each city and oasis, Musa showers gifts of gold on local leaders and gives alms to the poor. He can afford to be generous, because the caravan boasts 100 camels heavily laden with gold. Five hundred slaves each carry a golden staff.

Portfolio Assessment

Write a song to commemorate the great pilgrimage of Mansa Musa. Be sure to add details about your journey and the impression Musa made on the people he met.

286 Chapter 12

Resource Directory

Teaching Resources
Biography Activity *Ibn Battuta,* Unit 3 booklet, p. 84
You Are There Chapter Extension Activities booklet, p. 32

commented Ibn Battuta when he visited Mali. "The traveler here has no more reason to fear thieves than the man who stays at home."

Mansa Musa converted to Islam and based his system of justice on the Quran. At the same time, he did not adopt all customs associated with some nearby Muslim societies. For example, women in Mali wore no veils and were not secluded within the home.

In 1324, Mansa Musa fulfilled one of the Five Pillars of Islam by making the hajj, or pilgrimage to Mecca. Through his pilgrimage, Mansa Musa showed his devotion to Islam. He also forged new diplomatic and economic ties with other Muslim states. The movement of wealth, people, and ideas increased Mali's renown. By the 1400s, Timbuktu had become a leading center of learning. The city drew some of the best scholars from all over the Muslim world.

A New Empire in Songhai

In the 1400s, disputes over succession weakened Mali. Subject peoples broke away, and the empire shriveled. By 1450, the wealthy trading city of Gao (GOW) had emerged as the capital of a new West African kingdom, Songhai (SAWNG hī).

Two Great Leaders Songhai grew up on the bend of the Niger River in present-day Niger and Burkina Faso. Between 1464 and 1492, the soldier-king Sonni Ali used his powerful army to forge the largest state that had ever existed in West Africa. Sonni Ali brought trade routes and wealthy cities like Timbuktu under his control. Unlike the rulers of Mali, he did not adopt the practices of Islam. Instead, he followed traditional religious beliefs.

Soon after Sonni Ali's death, though, the emperor Askia Muhammad set up a Muslim dynasty. He further expanded the territory of Songhai and improved the government. Askia Muhammad set up a bureaucracy with separate departments for farming, the army, and the treasury.

Like Mansa Musa, Askia Muhammad made a pilgrimage to Mecca that led to increased ties with the Muslim world. Scholars and poets from Muslim lands flocked to his court at Gao. In towns and cities across Songhai, Askia Muhammad built mosques and opened schools for the study of the Quran.

Invaders From the North Songhai prospered until about 1586, when disputes over succession led to civil war. Soon after, the ruler of Morocco sent his armies south to seize the West African gold mines. The invaders used gunpowder weapons to defeat the disunited forces of Songhai.

Like the Almoravids in Ghana, however, the Moroccans were not able to rule an empire across the Sahara. With the downfall of Songhai, this part of West Africa splintered into many small kingdoms.

Other Kingdoms of West Africa

In the period from 500 to 1500, other kingdoms flourished in various parts of West Africa. The fertile northern lands of modern-day Nigeria were home to the Hausa people, who had probably migrated there when the Sahara dried out. They were successful at both farming and trading.

Walled City-States of the Hausa By the 1300s, the Hausa had built a number of clay-walled cities. While these city-states remained independent of one another, in time they expanded into thriving commercial centers. In the cities, cotton weavers and dyers, leatherworkers, and other artisans produced goods for sale. Merchants traded with Arab and Berber caravans from north of the Sahara. Hausa goods were sold as far away as North Africa and southern Europe.

Kano was the most prosperous Hausa city-state. Its walls, 14 miles in circumference, protected a population of more than 30,000. Kano's greatest

Primary Source

A Description of Timbuktu
In 1526, Hassan ibn Muhammad, also known as Leo Africanus, published an account of his travels. For the next 300 years, his book was Europe's main source of information about Africa:

"The houses of Timbuktu are huts made of clay-covered wattles [poles interwoven with reeds and branches] and thatched roofs. In the center of the city is a temple built of stone and mortar, . . . and in addition there is a large palace, . . . where the king lives. The shops . . . are very numerous. Fabrics are also imported from Europe to Timbuktu. . . .

The people of Timbuktu are of a peaceful nature. They have a custom of almost continuously walking about the city in the evening (except for those that sell gold), between 10 P.M. and 1 A.M., playing musical instruments and dancing."

—Hassan ibn Muhammad, *The Description of Africa*

Skills Assessment

Primary Source What information does this account give about the economy of Timbuktu?

***B*ackground**
Global Connections

Timbuktu There was an African proverb that said, "Salt comes from the north, gold from the south, and silver from the country of the white men, but the word of God and the treasures of wisdom are to be found only in Timbuktu." Timbuktu was an important learning center for Muslims of Africa and beyond. The city's scholars, many of whom had studied in Mecca or Egypt, attracted students from diverse areas. In Timbuktu students could pursue the study of Arabic grammar, the Quran, theology, law, and other subjects.

But as a result of the Moroccan conquest of Songhai, Timbuktu suffered a rapid decline. The new Moroccan rulers doubted the loyalty of the city's scholars and ordered that they be arrested. Some were killed and many others were exiled. In the years ahead, Timbuktu continued to experience invasions and political instability, and its importance as an educational center declined.

Human Drama Note

Abu Ishaq as-Sahili When Mansa Musa returned to Mali from the Middle East, he invited the architect as-Sahili to join him and commissioned him to design Sankore mosque, which is still standing. As-Sahili's designs influenced the architecture of the region. He introduced two changes to houses: flat-topped roofs and the addition of wooden posts to the outside walls, which needed annual repairs after the rainy season. The wooden framework helped hold the mud walls in place and made repairs easier.

 Test Preparation

Have students read the first paragraph under the heading "Two Great Leaders," and then complete the sentence below.

Sonni Ali was an important leader because

A he adopted the practices of Islam.

B he gave up traditional religion.

C he forged the largest West African state that ever existed.

D he isolated Songhai from other countries.

Primary Source

ANSWER It was a prosperous and busy trade and manufacturing center, and textiles were especially important.

SECTION 2 Assessment

Recall

1. (a) Almoravids, p. 285 (b) Sundiata, p. 285 (c) Sonni Ali, p. 287 (d) Askia Muhammad, p. 287 (e) Amina, p. 288
2. (a) surplus, p. 284 (b) commodity, p. 284 (c) mansa, p. 285 (d) oba, p. 288

Comprehension

3. North Africans wanted gold for trade with Europeans, while West Africans needed salt in their diet to prevent dehydration. Each possessed an item of trade that was coveted by the other. 4. Each emphasized trade to increase his nation's wealth and renown. Mansa Musa and Askia Muhammad also were Muslims who made pilgrimages to Mecca and forged new economic and political ties.
5. (a) The Hausa city-states were successful at farming and trading, and they developed a written language. (b) Benin sculptors developed a unique style for representing the human face and form.

Critical Thinking and Writing

6. Possible answers: (a) Musa showed his devotion to Islam and forged new trading and diplomatic ties with Muslim states. (b) Word of Mali's wealth spread to Europe and caused European traders to become interested in Africa. 7. Possible answer: Benin bronzeworks depict warriors, indicating Benin's military readiness, and the queen mother, indicating that Benin's oba shared leadership with women. Benin bronzeworks of Portuguese merchants indicate when trade with Portugal began, and imply that new trade benefited Benin prior to the opening of the slave trade.

Activity Rubrics

Share rubrics with students before they create their maps.

Attempted Maps are incomplete, reflecting insufficient research.

Minimal Maps include the required information, but the labeling is messy and difficult to read.

Adequate Maps are complete, accurate, and legible.

Exemplary Maps are accurately and neatly labeled and color is used to depict the different regions in a visually pleasing way.

Caption Answer

ornate headdress, carefully designed features, highly polished surface

---

Virtual Field Trip

www.phschool.com

**The British Museum
London, England**

To see other examples of Benin bronzework, use the Internet address above to link to the British Museum.

Benin Bronzes
The forest kingdom of Benin was famous for its sculptures, such as this depiction of a queen mother. Benin artisans used a lost-wax process to create sculptures of bronze and brass. In this process, the sculptor formed a wax model inside a clay shell and then poured molten metal into the shell. The melting wax ran out, leaving behind a finished metal sculpture.

Theme: Political and Social Systems How does this casting suggest that the subject was an important person in Benin?

---

king, Muhammad Rumfa, was a Muslim, as were many merchants and officials. The Hausa developed a written language based on Arabic.

Many Hausa rulers were women, such as Amina of the city-state of Zaria. In the 1500s, she conquered Kano and expanded the boundary of Zaria as far as the Niger River. Under Amina, the Hausa came to dominate many Saharan trade routes.

The Forest Kingdom of Benin South of the savanna, Benin (beh NIN) rose in the rain forests of the Guinea coast. The forest peoples carved out farming villages and traded pepper, ivory, and, later, slaves to their neighbors in the savanna.

The rulers of Benin organized their kingdom in the 1300s, probably building on the achievements of earlier forest cultures. An oba, or king, was both a political and a religious leader. Still, much power was spread among other figures, including the queen mother and a council of hereditary chiefs. A three-mile-long wall surrounded the capital, Benin City. Its broad avenues were dotted with tidy homes and a great palace.

The palace, in particular, was decorated with elaborate brass plaques and sculptures. According to tradition, artisans from Ife (EE fay), an earlier forest society, had taught the people of Benin how to cast bronze and brass. Benin sculptors developed their own unique style for representing the human face and form. Their works depicted warriors armed for battle, queen mothers with upswept hairstyles, and the oba himself.

Looking Ahead

Later Benin bronzeworks showed helmeted and bearded Portuguese merchants. These newcomers began to arrive in growing numbers in the 1500s. At first, Benin benefited from the new trade with European countries. However, increasing contacts with Europe opened the door to a booming slave trade that would have far-reaching consequences for all of West Africa.

SECTION 2 Assessment

Recall

1. **Identify:** (a) Almoravids, (b) Sundiata, (c) Sonni Ali, (d) Askia Muhammad, (e) Amina.
2. **Define:** (a) surplus, (b) commodity, (c) mansa, (d) oba.

Comprehension

3. How did the gold-salt trade develop between West Africa and North Africa?
4. How did Mansa Musa, Sonni Ali, and Askia Muhammad change their kingdoms?

5. What were the achievements of the (a) Hausa city-states, (b) kingdom of Benin?

Critical Thinking and Writing

6. **Recognizing Causes and Effects** (a) Describe two short-term effects of Mansa Musa's hajj. (b) What do you think was the most important long-term effect?
7. **Drawing Conclusions** What might historians learn about the kingdom of Benin by studying its sculpture?

Activity

Creating a Map
Research the pilgrimages of Mansa Musa and Askia Muhammad. On a map, trace the routes of the pilgrimages. What regions and kingdoms did each ruler visit during his pilgrimage? Label each of these regions.

Resource Directory

Teaching Resources
Section Quiz Unit 3 booklet, p. 79
Creative Teaching Activities Creative Teaching Activities booklet, p. 56
Guided Reading and Review Unit 3 booklet, p. 80

Technology
World History Color Transparencies *Nigerian Relief Plaque, Spear Carrier*, p. D–55
Interactive Student Tutorial CD-ROM Ch. 12
Computer Test Bank Ch. 12

Reading Focus

- How did religion influence the development of Axum and Ethiopia?

- What effects did trade have on city-states in East Africa?

- What have archaeologists discovered about Great Zimbabwe?

Taking Notes

Copy this table. As you read, fill in the columns with trade goods from Africa, Asia, and Europe and the Mediterranean that passed through the markets of Axum and the East African coast.

AFRICA	ASIA	EUROPE AND THE MEDITERRANEAN
		Linen cloth
Hides, skins, and animal products		
		Copper
	Cotton cloth and silk	
	Porcelain, china, and glassware	

Main Idea ▶ **Religion and trade played an important role in Ethiopia and East African city-states.**

Setting the Scene

According to Ethiopian tradition, the first emperor of Ethiopia was the son of the Israelite king Solomon and Makeda, the queen of Sheba. An ancient chronicle described how Makeda decided to journey to Jerusalem after hearing of Solomon's wisdom. "Learning is better than treasures of silver and gold," she said. The queen spent six months at Solomon's court, gathering knowledge to bring back to her people.

According to the chronicle, when Makeda was about to return to Sheba, Solomon gave her a ring and a blessing:

> "May the peace of God be with thee. While I was sleeping . . .
> I had a vision. The sun which before my eyes was shining
> upon Israel, moved away. It went and soared above Ethiopia.
> It remained there. Who knows but that thy country may be
> blessed because of thee? Above all keep the truth which I
> have brought thee. Worship God."
> —*The Glory of Kings*

The kingdom of Ethiopia was proud of its ancient Jewish roots and Christian traditions of Byzantine origin. In later centuries, other areas in Africa were joining the Islamic world. Ethiopia, however, remained mainly Christian and established the Coptic church.

Axum and Its Successors

About A.D. 350, as you will recall, King Ezana of Axum conquered and absorbed the ancient Nile kingdom of Nubia. Located to the southeast of Nubia, Axum extended from the mountains of present-day Ethiopia to the sun-bleached shores of the Red Sea. The peoples of Axum were descended from African farmers and from traders who brought Jewish religious traditions through Arabia. This merging of cultures introduced another religion to Axum. It also gave rise to a unique written and spoken language, Geez.

A Trade Network The kingdom of Axum profited from the strategic location of its two main cities, the port of Adulis on the Red Sea and the upland capital city of Axum. From about 200 B.C. to A.D. 400, Axum commanded a triangular trade network that connected Africa to India by way of the Arabian Sea and to the Mediterranean world.

From the interior of Africa, traders brought ivory, animal hides, rhinoceros horns, and gold to the markets of Axum. Goods from farther south along the African coast came to the harbor of Adulis. There, too, markets

Chapter 12 **289**

Bell Ringer Write this quotation from Makeda, the Queen of Sheba, on the chalkboard: "Learning is better than treasures of silver and gold." Ask students to discuss the meaning of this quote. How do they think this value might have affected the development of Ethiopian culture?

LESSON PLAN

1. Focus The kingdom of Axum prospered by controlling a triangular trade network that linked Africa, India, and the Mediterranean world. Judaism, Christianity, and Islam all influenced East Africa. Trade routes across the Indian Ocean linked East Africa with other regions.

2. Instruct As they study this section, ask students to find evidence to support each of the following generalizations: (1) Ethiopia was influenced by several religious traditions. (2) Trade routes played a key role in the rise of Axum. (3) The blending of cultures occurred in East African city-states. (4) The prosperity of Great Zimbabwe was based on a variety of economic activities.

3. Assess Ask students to write three questions that they still have about the early civilizations of East Africa. Encourage them to do independent research to find the answers.

4. Reteach If students' Assess activity does not reflect adequate understanding of the lesson, you might assign the *Guide to the Essentials* or the *Interactive Student Tutorial CD-ROM* for this section.

Block Scheduling Support

Have students imagine that they are Muslim visitors to Ethiopia during the high point of Ethiopian civilization and are writing a newspaper article about that country as a Christian outpost in the predominantly Muslim area. Have them use the information in their text to re-create the Ethiopian Christians' lives. Inform students that the article should describe the character of the country itself, explain the differences between Ethiopia and its neighbors, and include information about the experiences of individual Ethiopian Christians.

King Lalibela During the early 1200s, the ruler of Ethiopia was King Lalibela, a devout Christian monarch. Under his leadership, Ethiopian workers constructed a number of churches like the one pictured at the beginning of this chapter. Each of the remarkable structures was hewn out of solid rock. The memory of King Lalibela remains strong in Ethiopia today—he is considered a saint by the Ethiopian Coptic Church. The region where the church buildings hewn from rock are located is called Lalibela.

offered iron, spices, precious stones, and cotton cloth from India and other lands beyond the Indian Ocean. Ships bore these goods up the Red Sea, where they collected linen cloth, brass, copper, iron tools, wine, and olive oil from Europe and countries along the Mediterranean.

The Spread of Christianity In these great centers of international trade, Greek, Egyptian, Arab, and Jewish merchants mingled with traders from Africa, India, and other regions. As elsewhere, ideas spread along with goods. In the 300s, Axum's great king, Ezana, converted to Christianity. As the new religion took hold among the people, Christian churches replaced older temples.

At first, Christianity strengthened the ties between Axum, North Africa, and the Mediterranean world. Axum's other African neighbors, however, were not Christian. In the 600s, Islam began spreading across Africa. Many African rulers embraced this new faith, creating strong cultural ties across much of the continent. Axum was now isolated from its own trade network—by distance from Europe and by religion from many former trading partners. Civil war and economic decline combined to weaken Axum, and the kingdom slowly declined.

Ethiopia, a Christian Outpost Though Axum's political and economic power faded, its cultural and religious influence did not vanish. This legacy survived among the peoples of the interior uplands, in what today is Ethiopia. Protected by rugged mountains, descendants of the Axumites were able to maintain their independence for centuries. Their success was due in part to the unifying power of their Coptic Christian faith, which gave them a unique sense of identity and helped establish a culture distinct from that of neighboring peoples.

During the reign of King Lalibela in the early 1200s, Christian monks built a number of remarkable churches. They were carved into the solid rock of the mountains. According to Ethiopian chronicles, the builders had divine help:

> "Angels joined the workers, the quarry men, the stone cutters, and the laborers. The angels worked with them by day and by themselves at night. The men . . . doubted whether the angels were doing this work because they could not see them, but Lalibela knew, because the angels, who understood his virtue, did not hide from him."
> —*The Ethiopian Royal Chronicles*

Despite their isolation, Ethiopian Christians kept ties with the Holy Land. Some made pilgrimages to Jerusalem. Ethiopians also were in touch with Christian communities in Egypt. Still, Ethiopians saw their country as a Christian outpost. Over time, Ethiopian Christians absorbed many local customs. They adapted traditional East African drum music and dances that are still used in church services today.

The kings of Ethiopia claimed descent from the Israelite king Solomon and the queen of Sheba. This belief was recorded in an ancient Ethiopian book called *The Glory of Kings* and reinforced by observing Jewish holidays and dietary laws. One group of Ethiopians practiced Judaism rather than Christianity. These Ethiopian Jews, known as the Falasha, survived in the mountains of Ethiopia until recent years, when they were evacuated to Israel during a famine.

East African City-States

While Axum declined, a string of commercial cities—including Kilwa, Mogadishu, Mombasa, and Sofala—gradually rose along the East African coast. Since ancient times, Phoenician, Greek, Roman, and Indian traders had visited this coast. Under the protection of local African rulers, Arab and

Trade in Mogadishu
In 1331, the North African scholar Ibn Battuta visited East Africa. His account of his travels provides the only eyewitness description of Mogadishu during this period:

"Among the customs of the people of this town is the following: when a ship comes into port, it is boarded from . . . little boats. Each [boat] carries a crowd of young men, each carrying a covered dish, containing food. Each one of them presents his dish to a merchant on board, and calls out, 'This man is my guest.' . . . Not one of the merchants disembarks except to go to the house of his host. . . .

When a merchant has settled in his host's house, the latter sells for him what he has brought and makes his purchases for him. Buying anything from a merchant below its market price or selling him anything except in his host's presence is disapproved of by the people of Mogadishu."

—*Les Voyages d'Ibn Batoutah*

Skills Assessment

Primary Source How did the people of Mogadishu control trade?

ANSWER They controlled the activities of foreign traders when they were in port, the times traders could sell, and the prices of goods bought and sold.

Resource Directory

Teaching Resources

Primary Source Activity *Swahili Cities of East Africa,* Unit 3 booklet, p. 85
Viewpoint Activity *Who Built Great Zimbabwe?,* Unit 3 booklet, p. 86

Persian merchants set up Muslim communities beginning in the A.D. 600s. Later, Bantu-speaking peoples migrated into the region and adopted Islam. Port cities, as well as offshore islands like Lamu and Zanzibar, were ideally located for trade with Asia. As a result, Asian traders and immigrants from as far away as Indonesia soon added to the rich cultural mix.

Growing Trade Early mariners learned that the annual monsoon winds could carry sailing ships northeast to India in summer and back to Africa in winter. On the East African coast, rulers saw the advantages of trade. They welcomed ships from Arabia, Persia, and China. Traders acquired ivory, leopard skins, iron, copper, and gold from the interior of Africa, as well as from coastal regions. From India, Southeast Asia, and China came cotton cloth, silk, spices, porcelain, glassware, and swords. A thriving slave trade also developed, sending captured people from the African interior to the Middle East and beyond.

Trade helped local rulers build strong city-states. A Muslim visitor described Kilwa as "one of the most beautiful and well-constructed towns in the world." Its royal palace stands on cliffs that today overlook the modern city. The complex of courtyards and large rooms runs for two acres. Built of coral and cut stone, the structure is evidence of the city's splendor.

A Blend of Cultures International trade created a rich and varied mix of cultures in the East African city-states. Bantu-speaking Africans, Arabs, and other Middle Easterners mingled in the streets with people from Southeast Asia, India, and China. With the spread of Islam, Middle Eastern influences grew stronger. Marriages between African women and non-African Muslim men furthered the spread of Muslim culture. An African wife's traditional property rights allowed her husband to settle and own land, creating opportunities for these non-African men. Their children often gained positions of leadership.

Both private houses and palaces show strong Arab and Middle Eastern influences in the East African cities. Additionally, the blend of cultures gave rise to a new language. Known as Swahili, it fused many Arabic words onto a Bantu base and was written in Arabic script.

Great Zimbabwe

To the south and inland from the coastal city-states, massive stone ruins sprawl across rocky hilltops near the great bend in the Limpopo River. The looming walls, great palace, and cone-shaped towers testify that these structures were part of the powerful and prosperous capital of a great inland empire. Today, these impressive ruins are known as Great Zimbabwe, which means "great stone buildings."

Europeans who came upon these ruins in the 1800s thought they were the work of the ancient Phoenicians. In fact, the builders were a succession of Bantu-speaking peoples who settled in the region between 900 and 1500. The newcomers brought improved farming skills, iron, and mining methods. On the relatively fertile land, they produced enough food to support a growing population.

African Kingdoms and Trading States, 1000 B.C. – A.D. 1600

Mercator Projection

	Egypt, 712 B.C.–525 B.C.
	Nubia, 1000 B.C.–A.D.150
	Axum, 900 B.C.–A.D. 600
	Ghana, A.D. 800–A.D.1000
	Mali, A.D.1200–A.D.1450
	Ethiopia, A.D.1270–A.D.1550
	Songhai, A.D.1450–A.D.1600
—	Major trade routes

Skills Assessment

Geography From 1000 B.C. in Nubia to the A.D. 1400s and 1500s in Songhai, Africans built strong trading kingdoms in East Africa and West Africa. Many of the kingdoms developed because of profitable trade with other lands.

1. **Location** On the map, locate **(a)** Indian Ocean, **(b)** Nile River, **(c)** Axum, **(d)** Ghana, **(e)** Malindi.
2. **Region** **(a)** What was the major hub of West Africa? **(b)** Which cities were most likely to trade directly with India?
3. **Critical Thinking Drawing Conclusions** Explain why West and East Africa saw a series of kingdoms develop within the same general areas, rather than in different places.

Activity Interpreting Viewpoints

Researching Divide the class into four groups for doing research on the East African countries of Somalia, Kenya, Tanzania, and Mozambique. Assign one group to find out which religions are currently practiced in each country and the percentages of the population that belong to each of these faiths. Assign another group to find out which languages are spoken in each country and the percentages of the population that speak each language. Have a third group locate similar information about each nation's ethnic groups. Assign the fourth group to find cultural traditions in each nation that reflect a mixing of cultures. When groups have finished their research, have them report their information to the class. ✻

Human Drama Activity

Architectural Structures Divide the class into small groups and have students brainstorm a list of remarkable architectural structures, such as the rock churches of Ethiopia and Great Zimbabwe, that they have encountered so far in their study of world history. Have students develop criteria for ranking the structures in terms of engineering skill and explain their choices. Criteria might include difficulty of obtaining materials, choice of materials, amount of time and labor required for construction, and so forth.

Test Preparation

Have students read the section titled "Ethiopia, a Christian Outpost" on the opposite page, and then answer the question below.

Which is a fact from the passage?

A Axumites were a conquered people who worshiped in secret.

B King Lalibela ruled until the 1400s.

C Stonecutters carved churches.

D Over the centuries, Lalibela had churches carved.

Skills Assessment

ANSWERS 1. Review locations with students. 2. **(a)** Timbuktu **(b)** Mogadishu, Malindi, Mombasa, Kilwa, Sofala 3. They probably grew up around the same set of resources, such as gold.

SECTION 3 Assessment

Recall
1. **(a)** Queen of Sheba, p. 289 **(b)** Ezana, p. 289 **(c)** Geez, p. 289 **(d)** Lalibela, p. 290 **(e)** Falasha, p. 290 **(f)** Swahili, 291 **(g)** Great Zimbabwe, 291

Comprehension
2. Christianity, Judaism, and traditional East African religions 3. **(a)** Interior and coastal cities provided trade centers for merchants from Africa, Asia, and Europe. **(b)** Traders exposed those with whom they came in contact to different languages and religions. 4. **(a)** Archaeologists have found Indian beads and Chinese porcelain among the ruins of Great Zimbabwe. **(b)** overfarming, civil war, and dwindling trade

Critical Thinking and Writing
5. Possible answer: It adhered to Christianity while much of North Africa became Muslim, and its mountainous terrain offered protection from invaders.
6. Possible answer: International trade in the East African city-states brought together Bantu-speaking Africans, Arabs, and other Middle Easterners. The fusion of these influences created the need for a common language.

Great Zimbabwe
The ruins of Great Zimbabwe suggest a rich and varied society. This aerial view of the stone structures shows the extent of the empire's capital.

Theme: Economics and Technology Which of the structures appears to have been most significant in the capital? Explain your answer.

Economy and Government
We know little about how this civilization developed. Early settlers raised cattle. They built stone enclosures to protect their livestock. In time, they improved their building methods and erected large walls and palaces. The capital probably reached its height about 1300. By then, it had tapped nearby gold resources and created profitable commercial links with coastal cities like Sofala. Archaeologists have found beads from India and porcelain from China, showing that Great Zimbabwe was part of a trade network that reached across the Indian Ocean.

Besides controlling trade, Zimbabwe was a center for manufacturing. Artisans turned gold and copper into beautiful jewelry and made iron tools for everyday use. Weaving cotton into cloth seems to have been an important craft.

Very little is known about the government in Great Zimbabwe. Some scholars have suggested, however, that the ruler was a god-king who presided over a large court. He may have shared authority with a powerful queen mother as well as nine queens, each of whom had her own court. Below the king, a central bureaucracy may have ruled an inner ring of provinces, while appointed governors had authority in more distant villages.

Decline By 1500, Zimbabwe was in decline. Some scholars suggest that overfarming had exhausted the soil. In addition, civil war and dwindling trade probably contributed to the breakup of Zimbabwe. By then, Portuguese traders were pushing inland to find the source of gold that they were able to buy in cities along the coast. They failed to discover the gold mines, and their intrusion helped undermine later small states that formed in the region.

SECTION 3 Assessment

Recall
1. **Identify: (a)** queen of Sheba, **(b)** Ezana, **(c)** Geez, **(d)** Lalibela, **(e)** Falasha, **(f)** Swahili, **(g)** Great Zimbabwe.

Comprehension
2. What religious traditions came together in Ethiopia?
3. **(a)** Why did Axum become a key trading center for three continents? **(b)** How did trade encourage a blending of cultures in East African city-states such as Kilwa, Mombasa, and Mogadishu?

4. **(a)** What evidence suggests that Great Zimbabwe was a center of trade? **(b)** What do historians think were the reasons that Great Zimbabwe declined?

Critical Thinking and Writing
5. **Analyzing Information** Why did Ethiopia become increasingly isolated from its neighbors over the centuries?
6. **Making Inferences** Why might the language of Swahili have emerged in the East African city-states?

Activity
Take It to the NET

Research African beadmaking between 10,000 B.C. and A.D. 1200. Write a paragraph about the impact of shell, stone, clay, metal, and glass beads on Africa's trade networks and cultures.

Many Peoples, Many Traditions

Reading Focus

- How did the interaction of people and the environment lead to diverse societies?
- How did government, family, and religion hold African societies together?
- How did artistic and literary traditions reflect the values of African societies?

Vocabulary

slash-and-burn agriculture
nuclear family
patrilineal
matrilineal
lineage
griot

Taking Notes

As you read, prepare an outline of this section. Use Roman numerals to indicate the major headings of the section, capital letters for the subheadings, and numbers for the supporting details. The sample at right has been started for you.

I. People and the environment
  A. Hunting and food gathering
    1. Lived in Africa's fringe areas
    2.
  B. Herding and fishing

Main Idea   The process of adapting to the land contributed to the development of many different cultures in Africa.

Setting the Scene   At harvest time, the Kikuyu (kee koo yoo) people of East Africa offered prayers of thanksgiving to their traditional gods. A modern writer recorded one ancient prayer:

> "Mwene-Nyaga, you who have brought us rain and have given us good harvest, let people eat grain of this harvest calmly and peacefully. . . . Guard us against illness of people or our herds and flocks so that we may enjoy this season's harvest in tranquility."
> —Jomo Kenyatta, *Facing Mount Kenya*

In West African mosques, Muslims recited a different prayer: "Praise be to God, Lord of the Universe, the Compassionate, the Merciful."

Differing religious traditions contributed to the diversity of the vast continent of Africa. At the same time, religious beliefs formed deep bonds that united individual societies.

People and the Environment

Over thousands of years, Bantu-speaking peoples migrated across Africa. With them, they carried farming skills and knowledge of ironworking to its many regions. Wherever these people settled, they adapted to local environments and absorbed ideas from the peoples they encountered. Trade or other contacts brought additional changes. As a result, the ways of life of African societies varied greatly from place to place.

Hunting and Food Gathering   Bantu migrations pushed many hunting and food-gathering peoples of Africa to fringe areas. The Khoisan people, for example, adapted to the harsh conditions of the Kalahari Desert by gathering roots and herbs and hunting small game.

Because food was scarce, hunting-gathering people lived in small bands numbering only about 20 or 30. Their knowledge of the natural world, however, was unmatched by city dwellers or farming villagers. They could track animals across long distances and identify the food and healing properties of many different plants.

Herding and Fishing   In parts of the savanna free from the tsetse fly, some peoples raised herds of cattle. Because grazing areas were limited, these societies were often nomadic. To protect their herds against raiders, these peoples perfected skills in warfare.

Chapter 12 **293**

Block Scheduling Support

Remind students that people in American society preserve their cultural heritage in many ways. For example, they may dress in a certain way, listen to certain kinds of music, decorate their homes in a particular fashion, or prepare distinctive foods.

Divide the class into groups and ask them to consider the diverse cultural traditions of people in American society. Ask them to work together to make a list of traditional styles, fashions, designs, and the like that are associated with particular cultural heritages. When the groups have finished, ask for volunteers to read their lists to the class. Then have the class discuss why people maintain these various cultural traditions across generations. ✳

SECTION 4

Bell Ringer Begin by asking students to discuss the following question: What are the bonds that hold a society together? Have students look for more answers as they read this section.

LESSON PLAN

1. Focus African peoples developed ways of life that were best suited to the conditions of their environment. Village governments, family bonds, and religious beliefs gave people a sense of community. Art and literature reinforced the beliefs and history of each society.

2. Instruct Have students work together in cooperative groups. Assign each group one of the following topics: Obtaining Food, Village Government, Family Patterns, Religious Beliefs, Arts, Literature. Explain that all students should become experts on their group's topic. After the groups have finished this part of the lesson, regroup the class so that each new group has an expert for each topic. Have the new groups conduct round-table discussions on the various topics. Suggest that each expert lead that particular part of the discussion.

3. Assess Ask students to discuss examples of literature, art, and music that strengthen the bonds of American society.

4. Reteach If students' **Assess** activity does not reflect adequate understanding of the lesson, you might assign the *Guide to the Essentials* or the *Interactive Student Tutorial CD-ROM* for this section.

African Farming Practices In the past, slash-and-burn agriculture worked well for African farming societies. Farmers provided adequate food by working one area of land while allowing another to lay fallow. Today, however, because of rapidly growing populations, the system does not work as it once did. Many African farmers no longer let fields lie fallow to renew their fertility. As a result, the soil is exhausted, farmlands are lost, and erosion and desertification expand. An article in the June 1, 1992, issue of *Time* magazine vividly describes the devastating results:

"Since 1900, Ethiopia's burgeoning population has stripped 90 percent of the country's forests for firewood and farmland, allowing 1 billion tons of topsoil to wash away every year. Some 8,000 acres [3,200 hectares] of the once fertile highlands can no longer bear crops, and an area the size of Switzerland may be bare rock by 2010."

African Masks
Many societies in Africa used masks in political, religious, and social rituals. Carved masks might be elaborately decorated with paint or items such as shells to show the authority of the wearer or to represent a particular spiritual force.

Theme: Art and Literature
What kinds of artistic skills would be needed to create these masks?

Along the coasts and rivers, fish was the basic food for some people. Most fishing peoples used nets. They traded any surplus fish for grain, animal skins, and other products made by people who lived inland. Some fishing areas had enough food resources to support large populations.

Settled Farming Societies Farming communities raised a variety of crops from grains to root crops like yams or tree crops like bananas. Most farming peoples practiced a method that is today called slash-and-burn agriculture. They cleared forest and brush land with iron axes and hoes, then burned the remains, using the ash for fertilizer. Because the land lost its fertility within a few years, villagers would move on to clear other land. Eventually, after giving the soil time to renew its fertility, they might return to the abandoned fields.

Forms of Village Government

Farming peoples generally lived in tightknit communities and helped one another in tasks such as clearing the land, planting, and harvesting. Both men and women planted, but they usually were responsible for different crops. Political patterns varied, depending in part on the size of the communities. However, village governments often had similar features.

Sharing Power In these pre-urban societies, power was usually shared among a number of people rather than centralized in the hands of a single leader. In some villages, a chief had a good deal of authority, but in many others, elders made the major decisions. In some places, especially in parts of West Africa, women took the dominant role in the marketplace or acted as official peacemakers in the village.

Villages often made decisions by a process known as consensus. In open discussions, people whose opinions were valued voiced their views before

Caption Answer

carving, painting, beading

a general agreement was reached. The opinions of older women and men usually held the greatest weight.

Villages within a large kingdom like that of Songhai had to obey decisions made at a distant court. These villagers had to pay taxes and provide soldiers to the central government.

The Kingdom of Kongo The kingdom of Kongo, which flourished about 1500 in central Africa, illustrates one of the many forms of government organization in Africa. It consisted of many villages grouped into districts and provinces and governed by officials appointed by the king. Each village had its own chief, a man chosen on the basis of the descent of his mother's family.

The king of Kongo might seem to have absolute power, but actually that power was limited. The king was chosen by a board of electors and had to govern according to traditional laws. Unlike rulers of West African states, who maintained strong standing armies, kings of Kongo could only call upon men to fight in times of need. Through local governors, the king collected taxes either in goods or in cowrie shells, a common African currency.

Family Patterns

In Africa, as elsewhere, the family was the basic unit of society. Patterns of family life varied greatly. In hunting-and-gathering societies, for example, the nuclear family was typical, with parents and children living and working together as a unit. In other African communities, people lived in joint families. Several generations shared the same complex of houses.

Lines of Descent Family organization varied in other ways. Some families were patrilineal. In these families, important kinship ties and inheritance were passed through the father's side. Other families were matrilineal, with inheritance traced through the mother's side. In a patrilineal culture, a bride would move to her husband's village to become part of his family. In a matrilineal culture, the husband joined his wife's family.

Matrilineal cultures also forged strong ties between brothers and sisters. Brothers were expected to protect their sisters, and sisters made their sons available to help their brothers whenever needed.

Wider Ties Each family belonged to a lineage, or group of households who claimed a common ancestor. Several lineages formed a clan that traced its descent to an even more remote and often legendary ancestor. Belonging to a particular family, lineage, or clan gave people a sense of community.

An individual's place in society was also determined by a system of age grades. An age grade included all girls or boys born in the same year. Each age grade had particular responsibilities and privileges. In the older age grades, children began to take part in village activities, which created social ties beyond the family.

Religious Beliefs

Across Africa, religious beliefs were varied and complex. Like Hindus or ancient Greeks and Romans, village Africans worshiped many gods and goddesses. They identified the forces of nature with divine spirits and tried to influence those forces through rituals and ceremonies.

Many African peoples believed that a single, unknowable supreme being stood above all the other gods and goddesses. This supreme being was the creator and ruler of the universe and was helped by the lesser spirits, who were closer to the people. Like the Chinese, many African peoples believed that the spirits of their ancestors could help, warn, or punish their descendants on Earth. Just as Christians in medieval Europe called on the saints, people in Africa turned to the spirits of their departed ancestors.

After students read Section 4, have them reread and answer the questions listed under Reading Focus at the beginning of this section. Then ask them to rewrite the questions as statements that illustrate the main ideas of the section. *(Less Advanced Readers)*

✔ Test Preparation

Have students read the first four paragraphs beginning on the opposite page under the heading "Forms of Village Government," and then complete the sentence below.

Based on the passage, you can tell that village governments in Africa were

A rigidly structured under a single model.

(B) often systems in which power was shared by a group of people.

C always the lowest level of hierarchy in a centralized government.

D never under the power of a chief or king.

Analyzing Primary Sources

Background
About the Primary Sources

The influence of griots extended beyond the African continent. African slaves brought their folk tales to America. The Uncle Remus stories about Brer Rabbit and Brer Fox were brought to the United States by the Mandinkas. Modern day American writer Alex Haley, author of the enormously popular *Roots,* was also influenced by Africa's oral tradition. Listening to a griot, Haley pieced together the story of his family's origins in West Africa.

Activity
Interpreting the Primary Source

Use this additional question to generate class discussion.

Critical Thinking: Making Inferences Since modern societies do not have to rely upon oral history alone to impart history, literature, and values, how do you account for the continued existence of griots? *(Possible answer: Storytelling is a more immediate, sometimes more interactive way to impart the knowledge, entertainment, and values of a culture. Griots provide a cultural link to their people in a more personal way than book knowledge.)*

Skills Tip

Tell students that *ellipsis* is the grammatical term for these dots, and that they can be used to reduce the length of a direct quotation. Students most likely will use them when they incorporate direct quotations into their own essays or research papers. The Skills Handbook in the front of the book has a lesson that will help students with this feature.

Skills Assessment

ANSWERS 1. C 2. G 3. Possible answers: **(a)** They remind kings of ancient rulers and settle disputes between tribes for the people's well being. They know tradition and put problems into historical context. **(b)** No. Kouyate keeps secrets. Some information could damage a ruler's prestige.

The Griots of Africa

As historians, poets, and musicians, the griots of West Africa have captivated their audiences for centuries. They are greatly respected for their knowledge, wisdom, and honesty. Becoming a griot takes years of training. Here is part of a speech by a modern griot from Guinea.

"I am a griot. It is I, Djeli Mamoudou Kouyate, son of Bintou Kouyate and Djeli Kedian Kouyate, master in the art of eloquence. Since time immemorial the Kouyates have been in the service of the Keita princes of Mali; we are vessels of speech, we are the repositories which harbor secrets many centuries old. The art of eloquence has no secrets for us; without us the names of kings vanish into oblivion, we are the memory of mankind; by the spoken word we bring to life the deeds and exploits of kings for younger generations.

I derive my knowledge from my father, Djeli Kedian, who also got it from his father; history holds no mystery for us. . . .

I know the list of all the sovereigns who succeeded to the throne of Mali. I know how the black people divided into tribes, for my father bequeathed to me all his learning; I know why such and such is called Kamara, another Keita, and yet another Sibibe or Traore; every name has a meaning, a secret import.

From Generation to Generation History—and the lessons to be learned from it—becomes lively stories in the mouth of the griot. Here, children listen to the stories of their people.

I teach kings the history of their ancestors so that the lives of the ancients might serve them as an example, for the world is old, but the future springs from the past.

My word is pure and free of all untruth; it is the word of my father; it is the word of my father's father. I will give you my father's words just as I received them; royal griots do not know what lying is. When a quarrel breaks out between tribes it is we who settle the difference, for we are the depositories of oaths which the ancestors swore.

Listen to my word, you who want to know . . . . To acquire my knowledge I have journeyed all round Mali. . . . Everywhere I was able to see and understand what my masters were teaching me, but between their hands I took an oath to teach only what is to be taught and to conceal what is to be kept concealed."

—Djeli Mamoudou Kouyate, *Through African Eyes* (Clark)

Skills Assessment

1. From whom did Kouyate learn to be a griot?
   A the ruler of Mali
   B his mother
   C his father
   D his grandfather

2. Kamara, Keita, Sibibe, and Traore are
   E griots.
   F Kouyate's ancestors.
   G tribes of Mali.
   H rulers of Mali.

3. **Critical Thinking Analyzing Information (a)** According to Kouyate, for what two special tasks besides relating history are griots responsible? What purposes do these tasks serve? Why might griots be especially well equipped to handle these tasks? **(b)** Does Kouyate relate everything he knows to everyone who hears him? How do you know? What might be the reason for this?

Skills Tip

In an excerpt, dots indicate where something has been left out. Three spaced dots (. . .) usually indicate that part of a sentence has been omitted. A period followed by three spaced dots (. . . .) usually indicates the omission of the last part of a sentence.

Resource Directory

Teaching Resources
Analyzing Primary Sources Chapter Extension Activities booklet, p. 33
Section Quiz Unit 3 booklet, p. 83
Geography Quiz Unit 3 booklet, p. 88
Chapter Test Forms A, B, and C Unit 3 booklet, pp. 89–93
Answer Key Unit 3 booklet, pp. 114–128

Technology
Interactive Student Tutorial CD-ROM Ch. 12
Computer Test Bank Ch. 12

Christianity and Islam, as you have seen, influenced peoples in some parts of Africa. Converts often associated the God of Christians and Muslims with their traditional supreme being. In this way, Christianity and Islam absorbed many local practices and beliefs.

Artistic and Literary Traditions

In art and architecture, African traditions extend far back in time to the ancient rock paintings of the Sahara. The pyramids of Egypt and Nubia, the rock churches of Ethiopia, and the palace of Great Zimbabwe bear lasting witness to the creative power of these early civilizations. Sadly, many wooden buildings and works of art have not survived.

Arts African artists created works in ivory, wood, and bronze. Sometimes, their work was decorative. Artisans wove and dyed cloth, inscribed jugs and bowls, and shaped bracelets and neck ornaments simply for beauty. Much art, though, served social and religious purposes.

Art strengthened bonds within the community and linked both the makers and the users of the work. Patterns used to decorate textiles, baskets, swords, and other objects had important meanings. Often, they identified an object as the work of a particular clan or the possession of royalty.

In Africa, as elsewhere, much art was closely tied to religion. Statues and other objects were used in religious ceremonies. In many rituals, leaders wore impressively carved wooden masks decorated with cowrie shells or grass. Once the mask was in place, both the wearer and the viewers could feel the presence of the spiritual force it represented.

Literature African societies preserved their histories and values through both oral and written literature. Ancient Egypt, Nubia, and Axum left written records of their past. Later, Arabic provided a common written language in parts of Africa influenced by Islam. African Muslim scholars gathered in cities like Timbuktu and Kilwa as well as in North African cities. Documents in Arabic offer invaluable evidence about law, religion, and history.

Oral traditions date back many centuries. In West Africa, griots (GREE ohs), or professional poets, recited ancient stories. They preserved both histories and traditional folk tales in the same way that the epics of Homer or Aryan India were passed orally from generation to generation.

Histories praised the heroic deeds of famous ancestors or kings. Folk tales, which blended fanciful stories with humor and sophisticated word play, taught important moral lessons. Oral literature, like religion and art, thus encouraged a sense of community and common values.

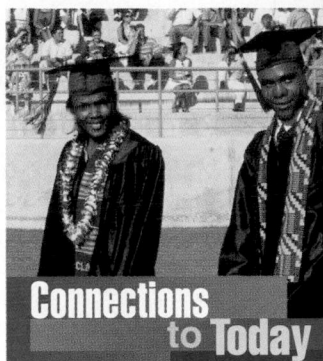

Connections to Today

Kente Cloth

Centuries ago, the Asante people of Ghana developed a colorful, intricately designed cloth called kente. Once the apparel of Asante royalty, today kente designs represent the philosophy, moral values, and code of conduct in Ghanaian culture. Some designs symbolize good omens and spiritual rebirth, while others may represent family unity, cooperation, or sharing.

In recent years, many Americans have begun wearing kente cloth as a celebration of their African heritage. Traditionally the garb of joyous occasions, imported kente is used in a wide variety of items, from shirts to neckties to backpacks.

Theme: Religions and Value Systems Why might the people in this picture have chosen to wear kente cloth?

SECTION 4 Assessment

Recall
1. **Identify:** (a) Khoisan people, (b) Kongo.
2. **Define:** (a) slash-and-burn agriculture, (b) nuclear family, (c) patrilineal, (d) matrilineal, (e) lineage, (f) griot.

Comprehension
3. List three examples of how the environment influenced African societies.
4. What types of institutions and traditions held African societies together?

5. How was art connected to religion in African cultures?

Critical Thinking and Writing
6. **Analyzing Information** How might a matrilineal line of descent allow women to exercise greater authority in village affairs?
7. **Predicting Consequences** (a) Describe the process of slash-and-burn agriculture. (b) What might be some dangers of the extensive use of slash-and-burn agriculture?

Activity

Retelling a Tale
Find an African folk tale and read it. Then, retell it without using the book. Based on this experience, write two or three sentences describing the challenges that a griot faces.

SECTION 4 Assessment

Recall
1. (a) Khoisan people, p. 293 (b) Kongo, p. 295 2. (a) slash-and-burn agriculture, p. 294 (b) nuclear family, p. 295 (c) patrilineal, p. 295 (d) matrilineal, p. 295 (e) lineage, p. 295 (f) griot, p. 297

Comprehension
3. Possible answer: Khoisan people became hunter-gatherers; people in parts of savanna became cattle herders; people along coasts relied on fishing 4. family structures, lineages, clans, age grades, religious beliefs, artistic and literary traditions 5. Art objects were used in religious ceremonies. In many rituals, leaders wore impressively carved wooden masks.

Critical Thinking and Writing
6. Possible answer: Women were given greater respect in a matrilineal society, and their opinions and ideas regarding village affairs were accorded greater weight. 7. (a) Forest and bush were cleared and burned, with the ash used for fertilizer. (b) Possible answer: The land can become infertile. There is destruction of natural habitats.

Activity Rubrics

Share rubrics with students before they perform their retellings and write their descriptions.

Attempted Retelling lacks important details from the story, or sentences do not specifically address the challenges a griot faces.

Minimal Retelling includes the main details from the story, and sentences describe the challenges a griot faces but are poorly written.

Adequate Retelling includes all the important details from the story and the description is clearly written.

Exemplary Retelling captures the spirit of the folk tale and holds the listener's interest. The description is well written and clearly states the challenges that a griot may face.

Human Drama Note

African Origins Many African words can be found in the English language. In some cases, the words entered the English language indirectly through such languages as Spanish and Portuguese. In other cases, words were brought directly into the English language by enslaved Africans. For example, the word *banana* was derived from a word in the Wolof language. *Goober* is from the Bantu word *nguba*, meaning peanut. *Coffee* is derived from Kaffa, a region in Ethiopia.

Connections to Today

ANSWER to show the importance of education and their respect for their heritage and traditions

Creating a Chapter Summary

As a reteaching opportunity, pair a more able student with a less able student to complete this chapter summary.

Possible answers: **Nubia** 750 B.C.–A.D. 350, Piankhi, local religion, trade and iron ore **Axum** A.D. 350–A.D. 600s, Ezana, Christianity, trade **Ghana** A.D. 800–A.D. 1050, king, Islam, gold **Mali** A.D. 1250–A.D. 1400s, Mansa Musa, Islam, trade **Hausa** A.D. 1300s–A.D. 1500s, Amina, Islam, trade **Great Zimbabwe** A.D. 900s–A.D. 1500s, possible god-king with queen mother and central bureaucracy, unknown, trade **Songhai** A.D. 1450–A.D. 1586, Sonni Ali, local traditions and Islam, trade and gold

Building Vocabulary

1–10. Students' answers should reflect clear understanding of vocabulary terms.

Recalling Key Facts

11. Ancient rock paintings show a Sahara full of forests and rivers.

12. present-day Tunisia, Algeria, and Morocco to southern Spain and Sicily, as well as outposts in England, France, and possibly West Africa

13. Amina, of the city-state of Zaria, conquered Kano and expanded the boundary of Zaria as far as the Niger River.

14. People in the interior uplands maintained Christianity after the fall of Axum. Kings of Ethiopia claimed descent from Hebrew king Solomon through the Queen of Sheba.

15. They gathered edible roots and herbs and hunted small game, and lived in small bands numbering only about 20 or 30.

Critical Thinking and Writing

16. The traditional African belief in a superior being corresponded to the God of Christianity or Islam.

17. **(a)** Possible answer: A lineage was a group of households claiming a common ancestor. A clan included several lineages and traced its descent to a legendary ancestor. An age grade referred to all children born in a given year. **(b)** Answers may compare and contrast African traditions with modern-day social clubs, activity groups, and families.

18. **(a)** She went to gather knowledge to bring back to Ethiopia. **(b)** that she

---

Creating a Chapter Summary

Copy this chart on a sheet of paper. For each kingdom listed, fill in the row by naming the kingdom's characteristics. To help you get started, one row has been filled in.

KINGDOM	ERA	RULER	RELIGION	ECONOMIC BASE
NUBIA				
AXUM				
GHANA				
MALI				
HAUSA				
BENIN	1300s	Oba, queen mother, and council	Unknown	Farming, pepper, ivory
GREAT ZIMBABWE				
SONGHAI				

For additional review and enrichment activities, see the interactive version of *World History* available on the Web and on CD-ROM.

Web Site Self-Test
For practice test questions for Chapter 12, see **www.phschool.com.**

Building Vocabulary

Write sentences using the vocabulary words listed below, leaving blanks for the vocabulary words. Exchange your sentences with another student, and complete each other's sentences.

1. savanna
2. desertification
3. outpost
4. commodity
5. oba
6. nuclear family
7. patrilineal
8. matrilineal
9. lineage
10. griot

Recalling Key Facts

11. How do ancient rock paintings help scholars determine that the Sahara was a well-watered zone during the Neolithic age?

12. Into what present-day countries did the empire of Carthage extend?

13. How did the Hausa come to dominate Saharan trade routes under Amina's rule?

14. Why did Ethiopia's roots embrace both Jewish and Christian traditions?

15. How did the Khoisan people adapt to their environment?

Critical Thinking and Writing

16. **Drawing Conclusions** From what you have learned about African religions, why do you think many Africans found it easy to accept the monotheism of Christianity or Islam?

17. **Linking Past and Present (a)** Describe three traditions that created social bonds in African communities. **(b)** How are these traditions similar to the traditions that create bonds in your community? How are they different?

18. **Analyzing Information** Reread Setting the Scene, including the selection from *The Glory of Kings* in Section 3. **(a)** What reason does Makeda give for going to Jerusalem? **(b)** According to Solomon, what is the great lesson he has taught Makeda? **(c)** Would you consider *The Glory of Kings* a reliable source of historical information? Explain.

19. **Connecting to Geography** Look at the maps in this chapter. **(a)** Into which areas did Bantu-speaking peoples migrate? **(b)** Why might certain climate zones act as barriers?

---

should worship God, as he had taught her **(c)** Answers will vary, but should recognize that the selection is more folklore than history.

19. **(a)** Possible answers: Mali, Ghana, Benin, Ethiopia, Zimbabwe **(b)** Deserts and tropical rain forests hindered travel. River rapids and few natural harbors also hindered travel.

In the 1000s, the Spanish Arab geographer al-Bakri wrote an encyclopedia of the entire world he knew about. Here, he describes the ceremonies when the king of ancient Ghana held court. Read the passage and answer the questions that follow.

"The king adorns himself . . . with neck-laces and bracelets, and when he sits before the people he puts on a high cap decorated with gold and wrapped in tur-bans of fine cotton. The court of appeal is held in a domed pavilion around which stand ten horses with gold embroidered trappings. Behind the king stand ten pages holding shields and swords decorated with gold, and on his right are the sons of the secondary kings of his country, all wearing splendid garments and with their hair mixed with gold. On the ground around him are seated his ministers, whilst the governor of the city sits before him. . . . The royal audience is announced by the beating of a drum which they call 'deba' made out of a long piece of hollowed-out wood. When the people have gathered, those who profess the same religion as the king draw near upon their knees, sprinkling dust upon their heads as a sign of respect, whilst the Muslims clap hands as their form of greeting."

—al-Bakri, *Book of Roads and Kingdoms*

20. How does this passage reflect the image of Ghana as a "land of gold"?

21. What details show the importance of the king's audience?

22. How does al-Bakri's description illustrate the people's view of their king as a semidivine figure?

23. How do the Muslims at court differ from the followers of the king's own religion?

24. Would you consider this a reliable source of information about the ancient kingdom of Ghana? Why or why not?

Skills Tip

Secondary sources are accounts by people who did not directly witness the events they are describing. In reading a secondary source, be aware of what sources of information the writer used.

The sculpted panel above depicts a family at work in an African agricultural village. Look at the panel and answer the following questions:

25. What economic and social activities are depicted in this sculpture?

26. How does the sculpture depict a nuclear family?

27. How does the picture reflect the importance of family in African societies?

28. What seems to be the principal source of food for this family?

29. What does this picture suggest about the family's living conditions?

Skills Assessment
Take It to the NET

Use the Internet to research the history of Swahili and the countries in which it is commonly spoken today. Then, create a simple map that indicates concentrations of Swahili-speaking peoples. Compare your map to the Bantu Migrations map in this chapter. Using both maps, prepare a brief oral report that explains the development of the Swahili language.

Chapter 12 **299**

Chapter 13 Planning Guide

Resource Manager

	CORE INSTRUCTION	READING/SKILLS
Chapter Level Resources	📁 **Teaching Resources** 📄 **Pacing Charts**, Ch. 13 📄 **Teaching With Themes**, p. 16 📰 **Color Transparencies**, p. F–27 💿 **Resource Pro®** Ch. 13 🖥 **www.phschool.com** 　• eTeach	🔊 **Book on CD**, Ch. 13 🔊 **Interactive Student Tutorial CD-ROM,** Ch. 13 🔊 **Social Studies Skills Tutor CD-ROM** 📰 **Skills Transparencies**
1 Two Golden Ages of China 1. Explain how Tang and Song rulers ensured Chinese unity and prosperity. 2. Describe how Chinese society reflected Confucian traditions. 3. Identify literary and artistic movements.	📁 **Teaching Resources** 📄 **Creative Teaching Activities**, p. 58 💿 **Prentice Hall Presentation Pro,** Ch. 13, Section 1 📰 **Section Reading Support Transparencies**	📁 **Teaching Resources** 📁 **Unit 3 booklet** 　• Guided Reading and Review, p. 94 　• Skill Application Activity, p. 107 📄 **Guide to the Essentials** 📼 **Guided Reading Audiotapes,** Ch. 13, Section 1
2 The Mongol and Ming Empires 1. Summarize how the Mongols conquered and ruled a huge empire. 2. Describe effects of Mongol rule on China. 3. Explain how Ming restored Chinese rule. 4. Outline the policies the Ming pursued regarding the outside world.	📁 **Teaching Resources** 📁 **Unit 3 booklet** 　• Primary Source Activity, p. 105 📄 **Creative Teaching Activities**, p. 59 💿 **Prentice Hall Presentation Pro,** Ch. 13, Section 2 📰 **Section Reading Support Transparencies**	📁 **Teaching Resources** 📁 **Unit 3 booklet** 　• Guided Reading and Review, p. 20 📄 **Guide to the Essentials** 📼 **Guided Reading Audiotapes,** Ch. 13, Section 2
3 Korea and Its Traditions 1. Describe how geography affected life in the Korean peninsula. 2. Explain how Korea maintained unity and independence despite Chinese influence. 3. Identify achievements of Choson dynasty.	📁 **Teaching Resources** 📁 **Unit 3 booklet** 　• Biography Activity, p. 104 📄 **Creative Teaching Activities**, p. 60 💿 **Prentice Hall Presentation Pro,** Ch. 13, Section 3 📰 **Section Reading Support Transparencies**	📁 **Teaching Resources** 📁 **Unit 3 booklet** 　• Guided Reading and Review, p. 98 📄 **Guide to the Essentials** 📼 **Guided Reading Audiotapes,** Ch. 13, Section 3
4 The Emergence of Japan 1. Identify geographic features that influenced Japan's early development. 2. Explain how Chinese civilization influenced early Japanese traditions. 3. Describe the traditions that emerged at the Heian court.	📁 **Teaching Resources** 📄 **Creative Teaching Activities**, p. 61 💿 **Prentice Hall Presentation Pro,** Ch. 13, Section 4 📰 **Section Reading Support Transparencies**	📁 **Teaching Resources** 📁 **Unit 3 booklet** 　• Guided Reading and Review, p. 100 📄 **Guide to the Essentials** 📼 **Guided Reading Audiotapes,** Ch. 13, Section 4
5 Japan's Feudal Age 1. Explain how feudalism developed in Japan. 2. Summarize the changes that took place under the Tokugawa shoguns. 3. Describe the cultural and artistic traditions that emerged in feudal Japan.	📁 **Teaching Resources** 📁 **Unit 3 booklet** 　• Viewpoint Activity, p. 106 📄 **Creative Teaching Activities**, p. 62 💿 **Prentice Hall Presentation Pro,** Ch. 13, Section 5 📰 **Section Reading Support Transparencies**	📁 **Teaching Resources** 📁 **Unit 3 booklet** 　• Guided Reading and Review, p. 102 📄 **Guide to the Essentials** 📼 **Guided Reading Audiotapes,** Ch. 13, Section 5

ENRICHMENT/PRE-AP

Teaching Resources
Teaching With Themes, Global View Activity, p. 43
www.phschool.com
- Why Study History?

Teaching Resources
- **Chapter Extension Activities,** p. 34
- **Color Transparencies,** pp. C–35, C–59
- **Listening to Literature World Masterpieces,** works by Li Po and Tu Fu, side 2
- **www.phschool.com**
  - Virtual Field Trip

Teaching Resources
- **Chapter Extension Activities,** p. 60

Teaching Resources
- **History Through Literature,** pp. 30–31
- **Visions, Voices, Views,** Daily Life CloseUp
- **www.phschool.com**
  - Internet Activities, Section 4

Teaching Resources
- **Chapter Extension Activities,** p. 35
- **Color Transparencies,** pp. C–41, C–45
- **Listening to Literature World Masterpieces,** *Sakura,* side 3; Japanese poems, side 3
- **www.phschool.com**
  - Internet Activities, Kabuki Theater
  - Internet Activities, Section 5
  - Global View Essay

ASSESSMENT

PRENTICE HALL ASSESSMENT SYSTEM

Core Assessment
- ExamView Test Bank booklet, Ch. 13
- ExamView Test Bank CD-ROM, Ch. 13

Standardized Test Preparation
Diagnose and Prescribe
- Diagnostic Tests for High School Social Studies Skills

Review and Reteach
- Review Book for World History

Practice and Assess
- Document-Based Assessment, pp. 13–17
- Test-Taking Strategies With Transparencies
- Alternative Assessment booklet
- Test Prep Book for World History

Teaching Resources
- Unit 3 booklet
  - Geography Quiz, p. 108
  - Section Quizzes, pp. 95, 97, 99, 101, 103
  - Chapter Tests A, B, and C, pp. 109–113
- **www.phschool.com**
  - Self-Test

CUSTOMIZE FOR INDIVIDUAL NEEDS

Gifted and Talented
- **Teacher's Edition,** Activities: Customize for Heterogeneous Groups, p. 303; Customize for Heterogeneous Groups, p. 309; Customize for Heterogeneous Groups, p. 321

Less Proficient Readers
- **Guide to the Essentials,** Ch. 13
- **Guided Reading Audiotapes, English,** Ch. 13
- **Book on CD,** Ch. 13
- **Teacher's Edition,** Activities: Reading Strategy, p. 309

Less Proficient Writers
- **Teacher's Edition,** Activities: Customize for Kinesthetic Learners, p. 311; Cooperative Learning, p. 324

Students Acquiring English/ESL
- **Guide to the Essentials, English/Spanish,** Ch. 13
- **Guided Reading Audiotapes, English/Spanish,** Ch. 13
- **Book on CD,** Ch. 13
- **Teacher's Edition,** Activities marked with an *

iTEXT

Don't miss the exclusive interactive version of *World History: Connections to Today* on the Internet and CD-ROM.

INTRODUCTION

After 400 years of fragmentation, a united China expanded and prospered under the Tang and Song dynasties. During the 1200s and 1300s, the Mongols ruled much of Asia. After the fall of the Mongols, the Ming dynasty restored Chinese culture. While Korea and Japan were heavily influenced by Chinese civilization, each maintained its own identity.

Focusing on Themes

Suggest that students focus on these theme questions as they read:

Continuity and Change
What traditions helped preserve Chinese civilization despite the rise and fall of dynasties?

Global Interaction
How did Chinese civilization come to influence people in Korea and Japan?

Political and Social Systems
How did Japan develop into a feudal society?

Art and Literature
What distinct literary and artistic traditions emerged in China and Japan?

◆ TIME LINE ACTIVITY

You may wish to share the About the Pictures note with students before you ask these questions about the time line:

1. Which empire was larger, the Mongol or the Byzantine? *(the Mongol)*
2. Which of the dynasties named on the time line lasted to the twentieth century? *(Choson dynasty of Korea)*
3. Was the Tokugawa shogunate still in power in 1853? How do you know? *(Yes; caption says it lasted more than 250 years, and 1603 + 250 = 1853.)*

Spread of Civilizations in East Asia 500–1650

Chapter Preview

1 Two Golden Ages of China
2 The Mongol and Ming Empires
3 Korea and Its Traditions
4 The Emergence of Japan
5 Japan's Feudal Age

618
The Tang dynasty begins in China. The achievements of the Tang included fine porcelain figures, such as this soldier.

668
Shilla rulers unite Korea.

794
The Japanese royal court moves to Heian. The shrine above is a duplicate of one in the Heian imperial palace.

CHAPTER EVENTS

450 · · 700 · · 950

GLOBAL EVENTS

527 Justinian becomes ruler of the Byzantine empire.

800 Charlemagne is crowned emperor by the pope.

Don't Miss!

Analyzing Primary Sources
Advice for Families in China (Section 1)

Humanities Link
Kabuki Theater (Section 5)

▶ Resource Directory

Teaching Resources
Teaching With Themes Chapter Theme Activity, p. 16
Pacing Chart With Block Scheduling Guide Ch. 13
Global View Activity *How Did Regional Civilizations Expand the Scope of World History?*, Teaching With Themes booklet, p. 43

Technology
World History Color Transparencies Ch. 13 Graphic Organizer, p. F–27

Areas of Chinese Influence, 900

For centuries, Chinese culture dominated much of Asia. Confucian ideals spread from China to many neighboring lands.

China, 900

Area of Chinese influence, 900

TIEN SHAN

TAKLA MAKAN DESERT

KUNLUN SHAN

GOBI DESERT

Sea of Japan

JAPAN

KOREA

Yellow Sea

XIZANG (TIBET)

Indus R.

HIMALAYA MTS.

Brahmaputra R.

Ganges R.

Huang He

CHINA

Yangzi R.

East China Sea

PACIFIC OCEAN

Bay of Bengal

South China Sea

INDOCHINA PENINSULA

VIETNAM

Azimuthal Equal Area Projection

0 500 1000 Miles

0 500 1000 Kilometers

1279
The Mongol conquest of China is completed. Skilled Mongol warriors on horseback helped forge the largest empire in the world up to that time.

1392
The Choson dynasty begins its 518-year reign in Korea. This Choson vase shows the lasting influence of Chinese culture on Korea.

1603
Tokugawa Ieyasu becomes shogun of Japan. The Tokugawa shogunate will rule Japan for more than 250 years.

1200

1450

1700

1300s Kingdom of Benin established in West Africa.

1492 Christopher Columbus voyages from Spain to the Americas.

Chapter 13 **301**

Areas of Chinese Influence, 900

Activating Prior Knowledge
Compare this map to the map of the Qin and Han empires in Chapter 4. How do the borders of China in 900 compare with the borders of the Han empire? (*They are about the same, but in 900, China included the area in the east that was not part of China in Han times.*)

Previewing
Japan was influenced but never conquered by China. Why do you suppose that is true? (*Japan is an island nation, that could be approached only by sea. It was difficult to carry enough forces by ship for conquest.*)

Background
About the Pictures

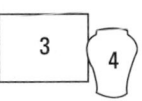

1. Most ceramics from the Tang period, like this soldier, have been found in tombs. Chinese artisans made porcelains by mixing a pure white clay called kaolin with a special mineral called china stone.

2. The Heian Jingu shrine in Kyoto was built in the mid-1800s in honor of the 1,100th anniversary of the transfer of the capital to Heian. Enshrined are emperors Kammu, who moved the capital, and Komei, the last ruler to live in Kyoto. (His shrine was added in 1940.)

3. Mongol warriors carried two bows: one for short-range fighting, and the other for long-range. Other weapons included small swords, javelins, and hooked lances for dragging enemy soldiers off their saddles. Leather stirrups helped warriors stay mounted while in combat.

4. Korean pottery is similar to Chinese, but distinct. For example, it is simpler in form and decoration, which includes more white space.

Independent Assignments

Have students read one section as they prepare for class. After class, have them complete the assignment. Some students may benefit from using the Guided Reading and Review worksheets.

Section 1 Have students use the worksheet *Interpreting a Chart* in the Unit 3 booklet, p. 107, to learn about the hierarchy of Chinese society.

Section 2 Have students use the map *Mongol Empire About 1294* in the Historical Outline Map Book, p. 22, and label the various political and geographical features of the Mongol empire.

Section 3 Have students use the worksheet *King Sejong* in the Unit 3 booklet, p. 104, to learn about this important Korean ruler.

Section 4 Consult lesson ideas at the front of the Historical Outline Map Book and have students use the map *Ancient Japan*, p. 23, to show various places and boundaries in Japan.

Section 5 Have students use the worksheet *The Samurai in Fact and Fiction* in the Unit 3 booklet, p. 106, to learn about samurai ideals.

---

eTeach

Be sure to check out this month's online discussion with a World History Master Teacher.

Go to **www.phschool.com**.

LESSON PLAN

1. Focus The Tang and Song dynasties restored culture and prosperity to China. Social and political order was maintained by using Confucian ideas of duty, rank, and behavior. During this period, the Chinese made important contributions in porcelain, landscape painting, calligraphy, prose, and poetry.

2. Instruct Work with students to create a chart on the chalkboard comparing the Tang and Song dynasties. Headings for the chart might include: Government, Size of Empire, Economy, Society, and Arts. Encourage students to contribute as many details as they can. Then, use the chart to discuss how the two dynasties were both similar and different.

3. Assess Direct students' attention to the entries they made on the chart under Society, and ask them to draw a diagram showing the organization of Chinese society.

4. Reteach If students' **Assess** activity does not reflect adequate understanding of the lesson, you might assign the *Guide to the Essentials* or the *Interactive Student Tutorial CD-ROM* for this section.

Reading Focus

- How did Tang and Song rulers ensure Chinese unity and prosperity?
- How did Chinese society reflect Confucian traditions?
- What were the literary and artistic achievements of Tang and Song China?

Vocabulary

usurp
tributary state
land reform
gentry
pagoda

Taking Notes

On a sheet of paper, copy this Venn diagram. As you read, add information about the Tang and Song. Include information that applies to both dynasties in the intersecting parts of the circles. Part of the diagram has been filled out to help you get started.

TANG
- Conquered Vietnam, Tibet, Korea

- Well-ordered society

SONG
- Ruled less territory

Main Idea The Tang and Song dynasties restored culture and prosperity to China.

Setting the Scene Many people in China had reason to distrust Empress Wu Zhao (woo jow). From humble beginnings, she had risen to a position of influence with the emperor. After his death, she had ruthlessly taken power into her own hands, unseating her own sons from the throne. She had even declared herself "Son of Heaven," the age-old title of China's emperors. No other woman had ever dared do such a thing!

Now, rival princes and Confucian scholars were raising the banner of revolt against her. The poet Lo Binwang wrote a declaration condemning the empress as a "vile character" who had usurped, or illegally taken over, the throne. "Rise, rise, all men!" Lo Binwang wrote. "Consider, the orphans of our emperor are left helpless and defenseless while their father's grave is hardly dry!"

When the empress saw the declaration, she demanded to know who wrote it. But, surprisingly, she did not direct her anger at Lo Binwang. Rather, she berated her own ministers for failing to bring such a talented writer into her service! Like other educated Chinese, Wu prized a skilled and brilliant writer, no matter what side he was on.

In the late 600s, Wu Zhao became the only woman to rule China in her own name. Her strong rule helped guide China through one of its most brilliant periods. At a time when Europe was fragmented into many small feudal kingdoms, China remained unified under two powerful dynasties—the Tang and the Song.

The Brilliant Tang

After the Han dynasty collapsed in 220, China remained divided for nearly 400 years. Yet China escaped the decay that disrupted Western Europe after the fall of Rome. Farm production expanded and technology slowly improved. Buddhism spread, while learning and the arts continued. Even Chinese cities survived. Although invaders stormed northern China, they often adopted Chinese civilization rather than demolishing it.

Meanwhile, various dynasties rose and fell in the south. During the brief Sui dynasty (589–618), the emperor Sui Wendi reunited the north and south. But China was not restored to its earlier glory until the emergence of the Tang dynasty in 618.

Building an Empire The first Tang emperor, Li Yuan, was a general under the Sui dynasty. When the Sui began to crumble, his ambitious 16-year-old son, Li Shimin, urged him to lead a revolt. Father and son crushed all rivals and established the Tang dynasty. Eight years later, Li Shimin compelled his aging father to step down and mounted the throne himself, taking the name Tang Taizong. Brilliant general, government reformer, historian, and master of the calligraphy brush, Tang Taizong would become China's most admired emperor.

Later Tang rulers carried empire building to new heights, conquering territories deep into Central Asia. Chinese armies forced the neighboring lands of Vietnam, Tibet, and Korea to become tributary states. That is, while these states remained independent, their rulers had to acknowledge Chinese supremacy and send regular tribute to the Tang emperor. At the same time, students from Korea and Japan traveled to the Tang capital to learn about Chinese government, law, and arts.

Government and the Economy Tang rulers, such as Empress Wu Zhao, helped restore the Han system of uniform government throughout China. They rebuilt the bureaucracy and enlarged the civil service system to recruit talented officials trained in Confucian philosophy. They also set up schools to prepare male students for the exams and developed a flexible new law code.

Tang emperors instituted a system of land reform. That is, they broke up large agricultural holdings and redistributed the land to peasants. This policy strengthened the central government by weakening the power of large landowners. It also increased government revenues, since the peasants who farmed their own land would be able to pay taxes.

Under the Tang, a system of canals encouraged internal trade and transportation. The Grand Canal linked the Huang He to the Yangzi River. As a result, food grown in the south could be shipped to the capital in the north. At the time, the Grand Canal was the longest waterway ever dug by human labor.

Decline Like earlier dynasties, the Tang eventually weakened. Later Tang emperors lost territories in Central Asia to the Arabs. Corruption, high taxes, drought, famine, and rebellions all contributed to the downward swing of the dynastic cycle. In 907, a rebel general overthrew the last Tang emperor. This time, however, the chaos following the collapse of a dynasty did not last long.

Prosperity Under the Song

In 960, a scholarly general reunited much of China and founded the Song dynasty. The Song ruled 319 years, slightly longer than the Tang; however, the Song controlled less territory than the Tang. In addition, the Song faced the constant threat of invaders in the north. In the early 1100s, the battered Song retreated south of the Huang He. There, the Southern Song continued to rule for another 150 years.

Despite military setbacks, the Song period was a golden age. Chinese wealth and culture dominated East Asia even when its armies did not. Under the Song, the

Technology of Tang and Song China

Mechanical clock, 700s

The Chinese learned of water-powered clocks from Middle Easterners. Mechanical clocks used a complex series of wheels, shafts, and pins, turning at a steady rate, to tell exact time.

Gunpowder, 850

The earliest form of gunpowder was made from a mixture of saltpeter, sulfur, and charcoal, all found in abundance in China. It was first used in fireworks and later in weapons.

Block printing, 700s
Movable type, 1040s

Both printing processes were based on earlier techniques, such as seals (first used in the Middle East). In block printing, a full page of characters was carved onto a wooden block. Movable type was made up of pre-cut characters that were combined to form a page.

Connections to Today

In addition to the advances shown here, the Chinese developed a smallpox vaccine, invented a spinning wheel, and pioneered the use of arches in bridge building. In time, many of these developments traveled westward. Modernized versions of most of these inventions are still widely used today.

Skills Assessment **Chart** Explain how one of the inventions shown here could have aided the spread of Chinese civilization to other lands.

Background
Daily Life

Government Under the Song The Song dynasty developed a centralized government with a Council of State, which was responsible for general policy. The council was composed of five to nine members and was chaired by the emperor. The council decided policy based on discussions in which different opinions were voiced on the issues. Most of the time, the emperor simply ratified decisions made by the council. Only in the case of a deadlock did the emperor impose his will by casting the deciding vote.

Did You Know?

The Real Reason Sunglasses Were Invented

Add "sunglasses" to the long list of Chinese inventions. But unlike modern sunglasses, they were not invented to shade people's eyes from the sun. Instead, they had a role to play in the efficient Chinese bureaucracy.

The Chinese made the lenses for their glasses from clear quartz. The lenses were tinted, or darkened, by exposing them to smoke. The lenses were so dark that they kept others from seeing the wearer's eyes. And that is exactly what the Chinese wanted.

The darkened glasses were worn only by judges in Chinese courts to prevent people from reading their eye expressions. If people arguing a case could read the judge's reaction in his eyes, they might alter their statements to sway him.

Theme: Religion and Value Systems Based on this information, what can you conclude about the role of Chinese judges?

Chinese economy expanded. The center of farming shifted from the wheat fields of the north to the rice paddies of the Yangzi in the south. New strains of rice and improved irrigation methods helped peasants produce two rice crops a year. The rise in productivity created surpluses, allowing more people to pursue commerce, learning, or the arts.

Under both the Tang and Song, foreign trade flourished. Merchants arrived from India, Persia, and Arabia. Chinese merchants carried goods to Southeast Asia in exchange for spices and special woods. Song porcelain has been found as far away as East Africa. To improve trade, the government issued paper money. China's cities, which had been mainly centers of government, now prospered as centers of trade.

Chinese Society

Under the Tang and Song, China was a well-ordered society. At its head was the emperor, whose court was filled with aristocratic families. The court supervised a huge bureaucracy, from which officials fanned out to every part of China. Aside from the court, China's two main social classes were the gentry and the peasantry.

Gentry Most scholar-officials at court came from the gentry, or wealthy landowning class. They alone could afford to spend years studying the Confucian classics in order to pass the grueling civil service exam. When not in government service, the gentry often served in the provinces as allies of the emperor's officials.

The Song scholar-gentry valued learning more than physical labor. They supported a revival of Confucian thought. New schools of Confucian philosophers emphasized social order based on duty, rank, and proper behavior. Although corruption and greed existed among civil servants, the ideal Confucian official was a wise, virtuous scholar who knew how to ensure harmony in society.

Peasants Most Chinese were peasants who worked the land, living on what they produced. Drought and famine were a constant threat, but new tools and crops did improve the lives of many peasants. To add to their income, some families produced handicrafts such as baskets or embroidery. They carried these products to nearby market towns to sell or trade for salt, tea, or iron tools.

Peasants lived in small, largely self-sufficient villages that managed their own affairs. "Heaven is high," noted one Chinese saying, "and the emperor far away." Peasants relied on one another rather than the government. When disputes arose, a village leader and council of elders put pressure on the parties to resolve the problem. Only if such efforts failed did villagers take their disputes to the emperor's county representative.

In China, even peasants could move up in society through education and government service. If a bright peasant boy received an education and passed the civil service examinations, both he and his family rose in status.

Merchants In market towns and cities, some merchants acquired vast wealth. Still, according to Confucian tradition, merchants had an even lower social status than peasants because their riches came from the labor of others. An ambitious merchant therefore might buy land and educate at least one son to enter the ranks of the scholar-gentry.

The Confucian attitude toward merchants affected economic policy. Some rulers favored commerce but sought to control it. They often restricted where foreign merchants could live and even limited the activities of private traders. Still, Chinese trade flourished during Song times.

Status of Women Women had higher status in Tang and early Song times than they did later. Within the home, women were called upon to

Did You Know?

ANSWERS Possible answer: Chinese judges were expected to be neutral or impartial when hearing a case.

Resource Directory

Teaching Resources

Skill Application Activity *Interpreting a Chart*, Unit 3 booklet, p. 107

Analyzing Primary Sources Chapter Extension Activities booklet, p. 34

Advice for Families in China

During the Tang and Song dynasties, women sometimes enjoyed higher status than they did later. The following excerpt is from a collection of essays offering practical advice to families. A scholar, Yüan Tsai, wrote it in the 1100s, during the Song dynasty. Here, he discusses how to treat daughters and how women want to help family members.

A Tang Woman
This ceramic figurine of a woman kneeling at the imperial court, holding a bamboo flute, dates from the Tang dynasty.

"Without going overboard, people should marry their daughters with dowries appropriate to their family's wealth. Rich families should not consider their daughters outsiders but should give them a share of the property. Sometimes people have incapable sons and so have to entrust their affairs to their daughters' families; even after their deaths, their burials and sacrifices are performed by their daughters. So how can people say that daughters are not as good as sons?

Generally speaking, a woman's heart is very sympathetic. If her parents' family is wealthy and her husband's family is poor, she wants to take her parents' wealth to help her husband's family prosper. If her husband's family is wealthy but her parents' family is poor, then she wants to take from her husband's family to enable her parents to prosper. Her parents and husband should be sympathetic toward her feelings and indulge some of her wishes. When her own sons and daughters are grown and married, if either her son's family or her daughter's family is wealthy while the other is poor, she wishes to take from the wealthy one to give to the poor one. Her sons and daughters should understand her feelings and be somewhat indulgent. But taking from the poor to make the rich richer is unacceptable, and no one should ever go along with it."

—Yüan Tsai, quoted in *Chinese Civilization and Society* (Ebery)

Skills Assessment

1. Yüan would agree that
   A daughters should be allowed to choose their own husbands.
   B sons take better care of their families than daughters.
   C daughters are as good as sons.
   D dowries are not necessary.

2. Yüan suggests that
   E a married daughter should be allowed to help her poor relatives.
   F poor relatives should go to work for rich ones.
   G daughters should have nothing to do with their parents after they are married.
   H sons and daughters should make their own way in the world.

3. **Critical Thinking Making Inferences** What responsibility does Yüan imply that family members have toward one another? Explain.

Skills Tip

As you read a historical document, look for statements that the author assumes everyone in the audience will accept without question. Such assumptions can help you understand the accepted beliefs and values of the author's culture.

Background
About the Primary Source

Yüan Tsai's book also included advice on raising children, living in large families, arranging marriages, managing family businesses, dividing family property, showing sympathy for elderly women, and providing shelter and support for female relatives whose families do not support them.

Activity
Interpreting the Primary Source

Use these additional questions to generate class discussion.

Critical Thinking: Making Inferences
According to Yüan, how should a woman's parents and husband treat her? *(They should be sympathetic to her feelings and indulge some of her wishes.)* Based on this passage, how would you characterize Yüan's view of women? *(Yüan seems to respect women and thinks they can be the equal of men.)*

Skills Tip

To help students remember what they have read, they can try summarizing each paragraph in their own words. The Skills Handbook in the front of the book has a lesson that will help students with this feature.

Test Preparation

Have students read the section "Peasants" on the opposite page, and then answer the question below.

Which sentence *best* explains the meaning of the saying "Heaven is high and the emperor is far away"?

A Peasants lived far away on farms.

B The emperor died and went to heaven.

C The emperor ignores the peasants when there are disputes.

(D) Peasants were left to handle their own affairs.

Skills Assessment

ANSWERS **1.** C **2.** E **3.** Wealthier families are responsible for sharing their wealth with poorer family members. A married daughter is responsible for ensuring that a poorer new family member, either on her side or her husband's, receives assistance from the wealthier family. She also is similarly responsible for ensuring the prosperity of her children.

Virtual Field Trip

www.phschool.com

Council of Cultural Affairs Taipei, Republic of China

To see other Chinese paintings, use the Internet address above to link to the Council of Cultural Affairs.

Song Landscape Painting Landscapes painted during the Song dynasty stressed the harmony of nature. In *Travelers Among Mountains and Streams*, painter Fan Kuan balances a towering mountain against the rushing stream below. In the lower right, a tiny line of travelers on horseback emerges from the woods.

Theme: Arts and Literature Why do you think the painter made the human figures so small?

run family affairs. Wives and mothers-in-law had great authority, managing servants and family finances. Still, families valued boys more highly than girls. When a young woman married, she completely became a part of her husband's family. She could not keep her dowry and could never remarry.

Women's subordinate position was reinforced in late Song times when the custom of footbinding emerged. The custom probably began at the imperial court but later spread to the lower classes. The feet of young girls were bound with long strips of cloth, producing a lily-shaped foot about half the size of a foot that was allowed to grow normally. Tiny feet and a stilted walk became a symbol of nobility and beauty.

Footbinding was extremely painful. Yet the custom survived and in time spread to lower classes. Even peasant parents feared that they could not find a husband for a daughter with large feet.

Not all girls in China had their feet bound. Peasants who needed their daughters to work in the fields did not accept the practice. Yet most women did have to submit to footbinding. Women with bound feet often could not walk without help. Thus, footbinding reinforced the Confucian tradition that women should remain inside the home.

Arts and Literature of the Tang and Song

A prosperous economy supported the rich culture of Tang and Song China. The splendid palaces of the emperors were long ago destroyed, but many paintings, statues, temples, and ceramics have survived.

Landscape Painting Along with poetry, painting and calligraphy were essential skills for the scholar-gentry. In both of these crafts, artists sought balance and harmony through the mastery of simple strokes and lines. The Song period saw the triumph of Chinese landscape painting. Steeped in the Daoist tradition, painters sought to capture the spiritual essence of the natural world. "When you are planning to paint," instructed a Song artist, "you must always create a harmonious relationship between heaven and earth."

Misty mountains and delicate bamboo forests dominated Chinese landscapes. Yet Chinese painters also produced realistic, vivid portraits of emperors or lively scenes of city life.

Other Arts Buddhist themes dominated sculpture and influenced Chinese architecture. The Indian stupa evolved into the graceful Chinese pagoda, a multistoried temple with eaves that curve up at the corners. Chinese sculptors created striking statues of the Buddha. These statues created such a strong impression that, today, many people picture the Buddha as a Chinese god rather than an Indian holy man.

The Chinese perfected skills in making porcelain, a shiny, hard pottery that was prized as the finest in the world. They developed beautiful glazes to decorate vases, tea services, and other objects that westerners would later call "chinaware." Artists also produced porcelain figures of neighing camels, elegant court ladies playing polo, and bearded foreigners fresh from their travels on the Silk Road.

A Flood of Literature Prose and poetry flowed from the brushes of Tang and Song writers. Scholars produced works on philosophy, religion, and history. Short stories that often blended fantasy, romance, and adventure made their first appearance in Chinese literature.

Still, among the gentry, poetry was the most respected form of Chinese literature. Confucian scholars were expected to master the skills of poetry. We know the names of some 200 major and 400 minor Tang and Song poets. Their works touched on Buddhist and Daoist themes as well as on social issues. Many poems reflected on the shortness of life and the immensity of the universe.

Probably the greatest Tang poet was Li Bo (LEE BOW). A zestful lover of life and freedom, he spent most of his life moving from place to place. He wrote some 2,000 poems celebrating harmony with nature or lamenting the passage of time. A popular legend says that Li Bo drowned when he tried to embrace the reflection of the moon in a lake.

More realistic and less romantic were the poems of Li Bo's friend Du Fu. His verses described the horrors of war or condemned the lavishness of the court. A later poet, Li Qingzhao (LEE CHING jow), described the experience of women left behind when a loved one goes off to war. Her poems reflect a time when invasion threatened to bring the brilliant Song dynasty to an end.

Primary Source

Li Bo: Devoted Father
Separated from his children, Li Bo wrote a poem to them:

"This is the tree I myself put in
  When I left you, nearly three
    years past;
A peach tree, level with the eaves,
And I sailing cannot yet turn
    home!

Pretty daughter, P'ing-yang is
    your name,
Breaking blossom, there beside
    my tree,
Breaking blossom, you cannot
    see me
And your tears flow like the
    running stream;

And little son, Po-ch'in you are
    called,
Your big sister's shoulder you
    must reach
When you come there underneath
    my peach,
Oh, to pat and pet you too, my
    child!"

—Li Bo, "Letter to His
Two Small Children"

Skills Assessment

Primary Source How do Li Bo's feelings still relate to our lives?

SECTION 1 Assessment

Recall
1. (a) Sui Wendi, p. 302 **(b)** Tang Taizong, p. 303 **(c)** Wu Zhao, p. 303 **(d)** Grand Canal, p. 303 **(e)** Li Bo, p. 307 **2. (a)** usurp, p. 302 **(b)** tributary state, p. 303 **(c)** land reform, p. 303 **(d)** gentry, p. 304 **(e)** pagoda, p. 307

Comprehension
3. Under the two dynasties, China enjoyed political stability, efficient government, thriving agriculture, and expanding trade. There were also many achievements in the arts and sciences.
4. (a) At the top of Chinese society were the emperor and the royal family. Below them were the gentry, followed by peasants, and finally merchants. **(b)** It was a stable social order based on rank and duty. Reflecting Confucian tradition, women were encouraged to remain inside the home. **5. (a)** balance, harmony, and the Daoist tradition of seeking the spiritual essence of the natural world **(b)** Chinese poets focused on Buddhist and Daoist themes, as well as social issues, the shortness of life, and the immensity of nature. They also wrote about harmony with nature, the passage of time, and the lives of the people.

Critical Thinking and Writing
6. Possible answer: The later map would show more areas under Chinese control. It would also show the Grand Canal, built during the Tang. **7.** The saying reflects the fact that peasants turned to their village leaders and council of elders for leadership instead of the distant emperor and his representatives.

SECTION 1 Assessment

Recall
1. Identify: (a) Sui Wendi, **(b)** Tang Taizong, **(c)** Wu Zhao, **(d)** Grand Canal, **(e)** Li Bo.
2. Define: (a) usurp, **(b)** tributary state, **(c)** land reform, **(d)** gentry, **(e)** pagoda.

Comprehension
3. In what ways did the rise of the Tang and Song dynasties benefit China?
4. (a) Describe the social structure of China under the Tang and Song dynasties. **(b)** How did the social structure reflect Confucian traditions?

5. (a) What ideas and traditions shaped Chinese painting? **(b)** What themes did Chinese poets address?

Critical Thinking and Writing
6. Connecting to Geography How might a map of China before the Tang dynasty look different from a map of China afterward? Give two examples.
7. Applying Information "Distant water cannot put out a nearby fire." How does this saying reflect the nature of village government under the Tang and Song dynasties?

Activity

Preparing a Museum Guide
Find two illustrations of Chinese porcelain or painting from the Tang or Song periods. (If possible, make copies of them.) Then, for each selection, write an entry that might appear in a guide to a museum exhibit. List the date and artist (if known), and briefly describe what the work shows.

Activity Rubrics

Share rubrics with students before they create their museum guide entries.

Attempted Only one example or description has been written.

Minimal Entries are poorly written, uninformative, or uninteresting.

Adequate Entries are well written, informative, and interesting.

Exemplary The student's guide has more than two examples, with well-written, informative, and exceptionally interesting descriptions.

Human Drama Note

A Painful Tradition Footbinding continued in China even after it was officially banned at the start of the twentieth century. One modern woman who experienced binding had this to say:

"My feet hurt so much that for two years I had to walk on my hands and knees. Sometimes at night they hurt so much I could not sleep. I stuck my feet under my mother and she lay on them so they hurt less."

Footbinding broke the instep of the foot and, in the most severe cases, resulted in feet only three inches long. Women whose feet had been bound stayed close to home, as they found walking to be extremely painful.

Primary Source

ANSWERS Possible answer: The poem tells how a father misses his children and how a child can miss a parent. These are universal feelings people certainly have today.

Bell Ringer Ask students to answer this question: What was the largest empire ever to exist? Tally their responses on the chalkboard. Then, ask them to look at the map on the opposite page.

LESSON PLAN

1. Focus In the 1200s, powerful Mongol armies conquered China, much of Asia, and portions of Europe. The lands under Mongol control enjoyed a long-lasting period of peace, order, and economic prosperity. However, most Chinese welcomed the Ming dynasty, which ended foreign rule and restored Chinese traditions.

2. Instruct Arrange students into partnerships, and have each choose one of the following people as the subject for an interview: Genghiz Khan, Kublai Khan, Marco Polo, Zhu Yuanzhang, or Zheng He. Ask students to prepare a list of questions that address their selected figure's goals, methods, achievements, and the like. Each partnership should work together to provide answers to these questions. When students are finished, ask each team to present its interview. One student should assume the role of the historical figure and the other should be the interviewer.

3. Assess Remind students that, after the voyages of Zheng He, China adopted a policy of turning inward. Ask students to predict how this policy might have affected the development of Chinese civilization.

4. Reteach If students' Assess activity does not reflect adequate understanding of the lesson, you might assign the *Guide to the Essentials* or the *Interactive Student Tutorial CD-ROM* for this section.

Reading Focus

■ How did the Mongols conquer and rule a huge empire?

■ What were the effects of Mongol rule on China?

■ How did the Ming restore Chinese rule?

■ What policies did the Ming pursue with regard to the outside world?

Taking Notes

On a sheet of paper create a flowchart like this one. Add important events as you read this section. Use the chart to help you focus on key events in the section.

```
Mongols advance into
China; cannons used
        ↓
Kublai Khan topples
Song emperor
        ↓
┌──────────────┐
│              │
└──────────────┘
        ↓
┌──────────────┐
│              │
└──────────────┘
```

Main Idea Mongol armies conquered China, much of Asia, and part of Europe, but in time, the Ming dynasty regained control in China.

Biography

Genghiz Khan 1162–1227

When Temujin—later known as Genghiz Khan—was a boy, his father was poisoned by a rival Mongol clan. Then, at the age of 15, Temujin was taken prisoner. For the rest of his life, he never forgot the humiliation of being locked in a wooden collar and paraded before his enemies.

Though he regained his freedom, Temujin wandered among drifting clans. He grew up with a reputation for courage and leadership. He took revenge on the clan that had imprisoned him and, in time, became supreme ruler of all the Mongols. Once despised, Genghiz Khan would be admired and feared across two continents.

Theme: Impact of the Individual How might Temujin's experiences have motivated him to unite the Mongol clans?

Setting the Scene The Mongols were tough, skilled warriors who lived in the saddle. They could travel for days at a time on their shaggy ponies, drinking mare's milk and eating only a few handfuls of grain. They were also considered the most skilled horse riders in the world. An observer described Mongol battle tactics:

"They keep hovering about the enemy, discharging their arrows first from one side and then from the other. . . . Their horses are so well broken-in to quick changes of movement, that upon the signal given, they instantly turn in any direction, and by these rapid maneuvers many victories have been obtained."

—Marco Polo, *A Description of the World*

About 1200, the Mongols burst out of Central Asia to conquer an empire stretching across Asia and Europe. In the process, they overran Song China and imposed Mongol rule on its people.

Building the Mongol Empire

The Mongols were a nomadic people who grazed their horses and sheep on the steppes of Central Asia. Rival Mongol clans spent much of their time warring with one another. In the early 1200s, however, a brilliant Mongol chieftain united these warring tribes. This chieftain took the name Genghiz Khan, meaning "World Emperor." Under his leadership, Mongol forces triumphantly conquered a vast empire that stretched from the Pacific Ocean to Eastern Europe.

Conquests Genghiz Khan imposed strict military discipline and demanded absolute loyalty. His highly trained, mobile armies had some of the most skilled horsemen in the world. Genghiz Khan had a reputation for fierceness. He could order the massacre of an entire city. Yet he also could be generous, rewarding the bravery of a single fighter.

Mongol armies conquered the Asian steppe lands with some ease, but as they turned on China, they faced the problem of attacking walled cities. Chinese and Turkish military experts taught them to use cannons and other new weapons. The Mongols and Chinese launched missiles against each other from metal tubes filled with gunpowder. This use of cannons in warfare would soon spread westward to Europe.

Biography

ANSWER Possible answer: The tragedies of Temujin's early life were a result of clan rivalries among the Mongols. By uniting them he would eliminate the cause of much suffering.

Resource Directory

Teaching Resources

Creative Teaching Activities Creative Teaching Activities booklet, p. 59

Guided Reading and Review Unit 3 booklet, p. 96

Genghiz Khan did not live to complete the conquest of China. His heirs, however, continued to expand the Mongol empire. For the next 150 years, they dominated much of Asia. Their furious assaults toppled empires and spread destruction from southern Russia through Muslim lands in the Middle East to China. In China, the Mongols devastated the flourishing province of Sichuan (see CHWAHN) and annihilated its great capital city of Chengdu.

Mongol Rule Once conquest was completed, the Mongols were not oppressive rulers. Often, they allowed conquered people to live much as they had before—as long as they regularly paid tribute to the Mongols.

Genghiz Khan had set an example for his successors by ruling conquered lands with toleration and justice. Although the Mongol warrior had no use for city life, he respected scholars, artists, and artisans. He listened to the ideas of Confucians, Buddhists, Christians, Muslims, Jews, and Zoroastrians.

The Mongol Peace In the 1200s and 1300s, the sons and grandsons of Genghiz Khan established peace and order within their domains. Today, many historians refer to this period of order as the *Pax Mongolica*, or Mongol Peace.

Political stability set the stage for economic growth. Under the protection of the Mongols, who now controlled the great Silk Road, trade flourished across Eurasia. According to a contemporary, Mongol rule meant that people "enjoyed such a peace that a man might have journeyed from the land of sunrise to the land of sunset with a golden platter upon his head without suffering the least violence from anyone."

Cultural exchanges increased as foods, tools, inventions, and ideas spread along the protected trade routes. From China, the use of windmills and gunpowder moved westward into Europe. Techniques of papermaking reached the Middle East, and crops and trees from the Middle East were carried into East Asia.

Mongol Empire

Mongol empire at Genghiz Khan's death, 1227
Mongol empire at its greatest extent, 1294
Boundary of Yuan dynasty of Kublai Khan
Route of Marco Polo, 1271–1295

Robinson Projection
0   500   1000 Miles
0   500   1000 Kilometers

China Under Mongol Rule

Although Genghiz Khan had subdued northern China, the Mongols needed nearly 70 more years to conquer the south. Genghiz Khan's grandson, Kublai (KOO blī), finally toppled the last Song emperor in 1279. From his capital at Cambulac, present-day Beijing, Kublai Khan ruled all of China as well as Korea, Tibet, and Vietnam.

Government Kublai Khan tried to prevent the Mongols from being absorbed into Chinese civilization as other conquerors of China had been. He decreed that only Mongols could serve in the military. He also reserved the highest government jobs for Mongols or for other non-Chinese officials whom he employed. Still, because there were too few Mongols to control so vast an empire, Kublai allowed Chinese officials to continue to rule in the provinces.

Under Mongol rule, an uneasy mix of Chinese and foreign ways developed. Kublai adopted a Chinese name for his dynasty, the Yuan (yoo AHN), and turned Cambulac into a Chinese walled city. At the same time, he had Arab architects design his palace, and many rooms reflected Mongol steppe dwellings.

Kublai Khan was a capable but demanding emperor. He rebuilt and extended the Grand Canal to his new capital, though at a terrible cost in human lives. He also welcomed many foreigners to his court, including the African Muslim world traveler Ibn Battuta.

A Western Visitor The Italian merchant Marco Polo was one of many visitors to China during the Yuan dynasty. In 1271, Polo left Venice with his father and uncle. He crossed Persia and Central Asia to reach China. During his stay in China, he spent 17 years in Kublai's service. He returned to Venice by sea after visiting Southeast Asia and India.

In his writings, Marco Polo left a vivid account of the wealth and splendor of China. He described the royal palace of Kublai Khan, with its walls "covered with gold and silver and decorated with pictures of dragons and birds and horsemen and various breeds of beasts and scenes of battle." Polo also described China's efficient royal mail system, with couriers riding swift ponies along the empire's well-kept roads. Furthermore, he reported that the city of Hangzhou was 10 or 12 times the size of Venice, one of Italy's richest city-states.

As you have read, Marco Polo's book astonished readers in medieval Europe. In the next centuries, Polo's reports sparked European interest in the riches of Asia.

Other Contacts As long as the Mongol empire prospered, contacts between Europe and Asia continued. The Mongols tolerated a variety of beliefs. The pope sent Christian priests to Beijing, while Muslims set up their own communities in China. Meanwhile, some Chinese products moved toward Europe. They included gunpowder, porcelain, and playing cards.

The Ming Restore Chinese Rule

The Yuan dynasty declined after the death of Kublai Khan. Most Chinese despised the foreign Mongol rulers. Confucian scholars retreated into their own world, seeing little to gain from the barbarians. Heavy taxes, corruption, and natural disasters led to frequent uprisings. Finally, Zhu Yuanzhang (DZOO yoo ahn DZUHNG), a peasant leader, forged a rebel army that toppled the Mongols and pushed them back beyond the Great Wall. In 1368, he founded a new Chinese dynasty, which he called the Ming, meaning brilliant.

Ming Porcelain
Ming dynasty artisans created a unique form of blue and white porcelain. Today, collectors have paid over a million dollars for genuine Ming vases like this one.

Theme: Continuity and Change How does this vase build on earlier Chinese achievements?

Voyages of Zheng He

PERSIAN EMPIRE
Persian Gulf
Ormuz
ARABIA
ASIA
MUGHAL EMPIRE
MING EMPIRE
Canton
30°N
Jiddah
Mecca
Red Sea
Aden
Arabian Sea
1413–1415
Chittagong
20°N
PACIFIC OCEAN
AFRICA
Calicut
Bay of Bengal
Vijaya
1413–1415
10°N
Exploration routes
Mogadishu
1417–1419
1405–1407
1413–1415
Malacca
South China Sea
Robinson Projection
0   500   1000 Miles
0   500 1000 Kilometers
INDIAN OCEAN
EAST INDIES
1421–1422
20°E   30°E   40°E   50°E   60°E   70°E   80°E   90°E   100°E   110°E   120°E   130°E
1417–1419

Early Ming rulers sought to reassert Chinese greatness after years of foreign rule. The Ming restored the civil service system, and Confucian learning again became the road to success. The civil service exams became more rigorous than ever. A board of censors watched over the bureaucracy, rooting out corruption and disloyalty.

Economic Revival Economically, Ming China was immensely productive. The fertile, well-irrigated plains of eastern China supported a population of more than 100 million. In the Yangzi Valley, peasants produced huge rice crops. Better methods of fertilizing helped to improve farming. In the 1500s, new crops reached China from the Americas, especially corn and sweet potatoes.

Chinese cities were home to many industries, including porcelain, paper, and tools. The Ming repaired the extensive canal system that linked various regions and made trade easier. New technologies increased output in manufacturing. Better methods of printing, for example, led to the production of a flood of books.

Cultural Flowering Ming China also saw a revival of arts and literature. Ming artists developed their own styles of landscape painting and created brilliant blue and white porcelain. Ming vases were among the most valuable and popular Chinese products exported to the West.

Confucian scholars continued to produce classical poetry. At the same time, new forms of popular literature, meant to be enjoyed by the common people, began to emerge. Ming writers composed novels, including *The Water Margin,* about an outlaw gang that tries to end injustice by corrupt officials. Ming writers also produced the world's first detective stories. Performing artists developed a popular tradition of Chinese opera that combined music, dance, and drama.

China and the World

Early Ming rulers proudly sent Chinese fleets into distant waters. The most extraordinary of these overseas ventures were the voyages of the Chinese admiral Zheng He (DZUHNG HEH).

The Voyages of Zheng He In 1405, Zheng He commanded the first of seven expeditions. He departed at the head of a fleet of 62 huge ships and hundreds of smaller ones, carrying a crew of more than 25,000 sailors. The largest ships measured 400 feet long. The goal of each expedition was to promote trade and collect tribute from lesser powers across the "western seas."

SECTION 2 Assessment

Recall
1. (a) Kublai Khan, p. 310 (b) Marco Polo, p. 310 (c) Zheng He, p. 311

Comprehension
2. Trade and cultural exchange flourished because Mongol rule ensured safe passage along the Silk Road and other trade routes. The goods of many lands and the ideas of many cultures traveled with merchants along these routes.
3. He tried to keep Mongols from being absorbed into Chinese society; allowed only Mongols in the military; reserved the highest government positions for Mongols or other non-Chinese people; and allowed Chinese rule of provinces.
4. Ming rulers restored Confucian values and the civil service system. 5. to promote trade, collect tribute from lesser powers, show strength of Chinese empire

Critical Thinking and Writing
6. Possible answer: Polo's reaction suggests that Europe was not as prosperous and politically organized as China.
7. Possible answers: (a) Overseas explorations were halted. (b) Cultural and technological exchanges took place as trade expanded. (c) The Ming dynasty restored Chinese traditions.

Activity Rubrics

Share rubrics with students before they present their debates.

Attempted The student is poorly prepared, offering weak and disorganized arguments that contain factual errors.

Minimal The student offers arguments that are weak and poorly organized.

Adequate The student is well prepared and offers strong, well-organized arguments and convincing support.

Exemplary The student's arguments are thoroughly researched, carefully prepared, well presented, and insightful.

Global Connections

Beasts From Across the Sea

Zheng He's voyages from China left a lasting impression on the peoples he visited. But his return to China left an equally powerful —and totally unexpected— impression on the Chinese.

Wherever Zheng He went, he collected animals to bring back to China. Back in China, they were kept in the imperial zoo.

One of these animals was known to the Chinese as a *qilin,* a legendary beast whose appearance was a sign of heaven's favor. People flocked to marvel at this bizarre creature. It stood 15 feet tall, had the body of a deer and the tail of an ox, and was covered with red spots.

Today, we call it the giraffe.

Theme: Global Interaction
Why might Zheng He have collected animals from foreign lands?

Between 1405 and 1433, Zheng He explored the coasts of Southeast Asia and India and the entrances to the Red Sea and the Persian Gulf. He also dropped anchor and visited many ports in East Africa. In the wake of the expeditions, Chinese merchants settled in Southeast Asian and Indian trading centers. The voyages also showed local rulers the power and strength of the Middle Kingdom. Many acknowledged the supremacy of the Chinese empire.

Zheng He set up an engraved stone tablet listing the dates, places, and achievements of his voyages. The tablet proudly proclaimed that the Ming had unified the "seas and continents" even more than the Han and Tang had done:

> "The countries beyond the horizon and from the ends of the earth have all become subjects. . . . We have crossed immense water spaces and have seen huge waves like mountains rising sky-high, and we have set eyes on barbarian regions far away . . . while our sails loftily unfurled like clouds day and night continued their course, crossing those savage waves as if we were walking on a public highway. . . ."
> —Zheng He, quoted in *The True Dates of the Chinese Maritime Expeditions in the Early Fifteenth Century* (Duyvendak)

Turning Inward In 1433, the year Zheng He died, the Ming emperor suddenly banned the building of seagoing ships. Later, ships with more than two masts were forbidden. Zheng He's huge ships were retired and rotted away.

Why did China, with its advanced naval technology, turn its back on overseas exploration? Historians are not sure. However, some speculate that the fleets were costly and did not produce any profits. Also, Confucian scholars at court had little interest in overseas ventures. To them, Chinese civilization was the most successful in the world. They wanted to preserve its ancient traditions, which they saw as the source of stability. In fact, such rigid loyalty to tradition would eventually weaken China and once again leave it prey to foreign domination.

Fewer than 60 years after China halted overseas expeditions, the explorer Christopher Columbus would sail west from Spain in search of a sea route to Asia. As you will see, this voyage made Spain a major power and had a dramatic impact on the entire world. We can only wonder how the course of history might have changed if the Chinese had continued the explorations they had begun under the Ming.

SECTION 2 Assessment

Recall
1. **Identify:** (a) Kublai Khan, (b) Marco Polo, (c) Zheng He.

Comprehension
2. How did the Mongol conquests promote trade and cultural exchanges?
3. How did Kublai Khan organize Mongol rule in China?
4. How did the Ming emperors try to restore Chinese culture?
5. What was the purpose of Zheng He's overseas expeditions?

Critical Thinking and Writing
6. **Making Inferences** What does Marco Polo's awe at the glories of China suggest about the differences between China and Europe at that time?
7. **Recognizing Causes and Effects** Describe one effect of each of the following on China: (a) the rise of the Ming dynasty, (b) the Mongol invasion, (c) the expulsion of the Mongols.

Activity

Organizing a Debate Organize a debate that might have taken place at the Ming court between Confucian scholars, who want to end overseas voyages, and court officials, who want to finance more expeditions by Zheng He.

312 Chapter 13

Global Connections

ANSWERS Possible answer: The animals were new to Zheng He and the Chinese. Like other explorers, Zheng He was intrigued by the new and different.

Resource Directory

Teaching Resources
Section Quiz Unit 3 booklet, p. 97
Creative Teaching Activities Creative Teaching Activities booklet, p. 60
Guided Reading and Review Unit 3 booklet, p. 98

Technology
Interactive Student Tutorial CD-ROM Ch. 13
Computer Test Bank Ch. 13

312 Chapter 13

Korea and Its Traditions

Reading Focus

- How did geography affect life in the Korean peninsula?
- How did Korea maintain its unity and independence despite Chinese Influence?
- What were the major achievements of the Choson dynasty?

Vocabulary

celadon
hangul
literacy rate

Taking Notes

Begin a concept web like this one. As you read this section, fill in the blank circles with relevant information about Korea. Add more circles as needed.

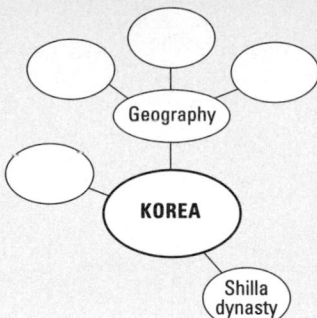

Geography

KOREA

Shilla dynasty

Main Idea Korea's history and culture were linked closely to those of China and Japan.

Setting the Scene

For centuries, Korea survived in the shadow of powerful neighbors, China and Japan. Koreans thus came to see their land as a "shrimp among whales." Yet Korea had another name, "Land of the Morning Calm." Whether tossed in turbulent seas or at rest in a calm land, Koreans had their own identity.

As early as Han times, China extended its influence to Korea. Although Koreans absorbed many Chinese traditions, they maintained a separate and distinct culture.

Geography of the Korean Peninsula

Korea is located on a peninsula that juts south from the Asian mainland with its tip pointing toward Japan. At the northern end of the peninsula, mountains and the Yalu River separate Korea from China.

Mountains and Seas An early visitor once compared Korea's landscape to "a sea in a heavy gale." Low but steep mountains cover nearly 70 percent of the Korean peninsula. The most important range is the T'aebaek (TEH BEHK). It runs from the north to the south along the eastern coast, with smaller chains branching off to form hilly areas. Because farming is difficult on the mountains, most people live along the western coastal plains, Korea's major farming region.

Korea has a 5,400-mile coastline with hundreds of good harbors. In addition, the offshore waters feature thousands of islands. Since earliest times, Koreans have depended upon seafood for most of the protein in their diet. Today, South Korea has the third largest fishing industry in the world.

The Impact of Location Korea's location on China's doorstep has played a key role in its development. From its powerful mainland neighbor, Korea received many cultural and technological influences. At various times in history, China extended political control over the Korean peninsula. Throughout its history, Korea has also served as a cultural bridge linking China and Japan. From early times, Koreans adapted and transformed Chinese traditions before passing them on to the Japanese.

Despite these strong ties, the Korean language is not related to Chinese. The earliest Koreans probably migrated eastward from Siberia and northern Manchuria during the Stone Age. They evolved

Mountains of Korea
"Over the mountains, mountains!" says one Korean proverb. This photograph shows a steep ridge in the T'aebaek Range.

Theme: Geography and History How would mountains affect settlement patterns?

Bell Ringer Draw students' attention to the map of Korea on the next page. Have them use the map to answer this question: How do you think geography affected life in Korea? Ask students to confirm or revise their answers as they read this section.

LESSON PLAN

1. Focus Korea's history and culture are closely linked to those of China and Japan. Chinese social values, political ideas, farming methods, and writing spread to Korea. The Korean people adapted Chinese influences to fit their own needs and passed those influences on to Japan.

2. Instruct Draw a Venn diagram on the board as the basis for a discussion of China's influence on Korean civilization. In one circle, have students list Chinese inventions, cultural contributions, political characteristics, and the like. In the second circle, have them list historical and cultural characteristics that were unique to Korea. In the portion of the circles that overlap, have students list things that the Koreans borrowed from China. Encourage students to use the diagram as they discuss the historical relationship between China and Korea.

3. Assess Ask students to write a generalization about Chinese traditions and another about Korean traditions. Then, have them write a third generalization that is true of both traditions.

4. Reteach If students' **Assess** activity does not reflect adequate understanding of the lesson, you might assign the *Guide to the Essentials* or the *Interactive Student Tutorial CD-ROM* for this section.

Block Scheduling Support

Have available books showing various Korean art forms. Ask students to research one of them and write a brief paragraph about it. Ask students to draw or photocopy an image to illustrate the paragraph or to download images from the Internet. One interesting art form is pyrography, the art of drawing on wood, bamboo, or paper with heated irons. It took great skill to execute pyrographic drawings on paper without setting it on fire. Invite an art teacher to demonstrate modern wood burning techniques.

Test Preparation

Have students read the second paragraph under "Mountains and Seas" on this page, and then answer the question below.

Which of the following would be a good title for this paragraph?

A Koreans and Seafood
B The Importance of the Sea
C Harbors and Islands
D The Korean Fishing Industry

Caption Answer

Possible answer: People would probably tend to settle along the coasts and in river valleys.

Background
Global Connections

Poor Relations In the 700s, the Chinese emperor received an urgent message from Korea, written in a dialect that his ministers could not translate. The emperor summoned the poet Li Bo, who was capable of many things. Li Bo, however, refused to appear, saying that he had failed the civil service examinations and must, therefore, be incompetent to perform such a delicate service. Finally, the ministers persuaded Li Bo to come.

When he arrived, Li Bo found his examiners among the ministers and, in retribution, he forced them to remove his boots. He then coolly translated the message, in which the Koreans threatened to wage war to regain their freedom. The Chinese government sent a terrifying letter in response. The Koreans sent apologies and tribute, and the conflict was avoided.

Geography of Korea

Map showing the Three Kingdoms of Korea:

Kingdoms, A.D. 300–A.D. 600
- Koguryo
- Paekche
- Shilla

Labels on map: CHINA, Paektu Mt., Korea Bay, Kaesong, Yellow Sea, Yalu R., Taedong R., Imjin R., Nangnim Range, Taebaek Range, Sobaek Range, Han R., Sea of Japan, Korea Strait, JAPAN, East China Sea

Skills Assessment

Geography Korea occupies a peninsula that juts south from China toward the islands of Japan.

1. **Location** On the map, locate **(a)** T'aebaek Range, **(b)** Yalu River, **(c)** Korea Strait, **(d)** Koguryo, **(e)** Paekche, **(f)** Shilla.
2. **Region** Why do most Koreans live along the western coastal plain?
3. **Critical Thinking** **Predicting Consequences** In the 1590s, Japan made plans to invade China. What effect might this have had on Korea?

their own ways of life before the first wave of Chinese influence reached the peninsula during the Han dynasty. In 108 B.C., the Han emperor Wudi invaded Korea and set up a military colony there. From this outpost, Confucian traditions and Chinese ideas about government, as well as Chinese writing and farming methods, spread to Korea.

Korea United

Between about A.D. 300 and 600, powerful local rulers forged three separate kingdoms: Koguryo (KOH GUH REE OH) in the north, Paekche (PEHK CHEH) in the southwest, and Shilla (SHIL LAH) in the southeast. Although they shared the same language and cultural background, the three kingdoms often warred with one another or with China. Still, Chinese influences continued to arrive. Missionaries spread Mahayana Buddhism, which took root among the rulers and nobles. Korean monks then traveled to China and India to learn more about Buddhism. They brought home the arts and learning of China.

In 668, with the support of the Tang empress Wu Zhao, the Shilla kingdom united the Korean peninsula. Unlike China, Korea had only three dynasties in its history. The Shilla ruled from 668 to 918, the Koryo (KOR EE OH) ruled from 918 to 1392, and the Choson (CHOH SUHN), or Yi, ruled from 1392 to 1910.

Chinese Influence Under the Shilla dynasty, Korea became a tributary state, acknowledging Chinese overlordship but preserving its independence. Over the centuries, Korea came to see its relationship to China in Confucian terms, as that of a younger brother who owed respect and loyalty to an older brother. Koreans also adopted the Confucian emphasis on the family as the foundation of the state.

Confucian ideas affected the rights of women. Early on, Korean women had the right to inherit property. Some upper-class women held public roles. Over time, as Confucian views took root, women's rights became restricted. Women could no longer inherit property, and a woman's position within the family became more subordinate.

At the same time, Koreans adapted and modified Chinese ideas. For example, they adapted the Chinese civil service examination to reflect their own system of inherited ranks. In China, even a peasant could win political influence by passing the exam. In Korea, only aristocrats were permitted to take the test.

Buddhist Influence During the Koryo age, Buddhism reached its greatest influence in Korea. Korean scholars wrote histories and poems based on Chinese models, and artists created landscape paintings following Chinese principles. The Koryo dynasty built their capital at Kaesong (KEH SUNG) following the plan of the Tang capital at Chang'an.

Koreans used woodblock printing from China to produce a flood of Buddhist texts. Later, Korean inventors made movable metal type to print large numbers of books. Koreans improved on other Chinese inventions. They learned to make porcelain from China, but then perfected techniques of making celadon, a porcelain with an unusual blue-green glaze. Korean

ANSWERS **1.** Review locations with students. **2.** because the interior is mountainous and difficult to farm. **3.** Possible answer: Korea is between Japan and China, so it might have been invaded as well.

Resource Directory

Teaching Resources
Section Quiz Unit 3 booklet, p. 99
Biography Activity *King Sejong,* Unit 3 booklet, p. 104
Technology
Interactive Student Tutorial CD-ROM Ch. 13
Computer Test Bank Ch. 13

celadon vases and jars were prized throughout Asia. In the 1200s, when the Mongols overran Korea and destroyed many industries, the secret of making celadon was lost forever.

Choson: The Longest Dynasty

The Mongols occupied Korea until the 1350s. In 1392, the brilliant Korean general Yi Song-gye (EE SUNG KEH) set up the Choson dynasty. In *Songs of the Flying Dragons,* Korea's leading poets held Yi up as a model of virtue and wisdom for future rulers:

> "When you have men at your beck and call,
> When you punish men and sentence them,
> Remember, my Lord, His mercy and temperance.
> If you are unaware of people's sorrow,
> Heaven will abandon you.
> Remember, my Lord, His labor and love."
> —*Songs of the Flying Dragons*

Yi reduced Buddhist influence and set up a government based upon Confucian principles. Within a few generations, Confucianism had made a deep impact on Korean life.

A Korean Alphabet Despite Chinese influence, Korea preserved its distinct identity. In 1443, Korea's most celebrated ruler, King Sejong (SEH JONG) decided to replace the complex Chinese system of writing. "The language of this land," he noted, "is different from China's." Sejong had experts develop hangul, an alphabet using symbols to represent the sounds of spoken Korean.

Although Confucian scholars rejected hangul at the outset, its use quickly spread. Hangul was easier for Koreans to use than the thousands of characters of written Chinese. Its use led to an extremely high literacy rate, or percentage of people who can read and write.

Japanese Invasions In the 1590s, an ambitious Japanese ruler decided to invade China by way of Korea. Japanese armies landed and for years looted and burned across the peninsula. To stop the invaders at sea, the Korean admiral Yi Sun-shin used metal-plated "turtle boats." After six years, the Japanese armies withdrew from Korea. As they left, however, they carried off many Korean artisans to introduce their skills to Japan.

Connections to Today

A Peninsula Divided

Korean unity lasted almost 1,300 years. But today, the Korean peninsula is again divided into hostile camps.

North Korea is a communist country. South Korea is a democracy. Each nation wants to rule the entire peninsula. Both sides have massed soldiers and equipment along the border in preparation for war.

The United States is South Korea's most powerful ally. North Korea maintains close ties to Communist China. As a result, Korea is one of the world's hot spots. The Korean War (1950–1953) was fought there, and there is a constant fear that the troubled Korean Peninsula may be the site of more bloodshed.

Theme: Continuity and Change How is today's division of Korea different from that created by early kingdoms?

SECTION 3 Assessment

Recall
1. **Identify:** (a) Shilla, (b) Koryo, (c) Choson, (d) Yi Song-gye, (e) Sejong.
2. **Define:** (a) celadon, (b) hangul, (c) literacy rate.

Comprehension
3. How did the relative location of the Korean peninsula influence the development of Korean civilization?
4. Give two examples of how Koreans adapted or modified Chinese ideas under the Shilla or Koryo dynasty.

5. (a) How did Confucianism influence Korea during the Choson dynasty? (b) How did Korea preserve its own identity?

Critical Thinking and Writing
6. **Analyzing Literature** Reread the excerpt from *Songs of the Flying Dragons* in this section. How does this poem reflect Confucian influences?
7. **Analyzing Information** Today, Hangul Day is a holiday in South Korea. Why do you think Koreans celebrate the creation of their alphabet?

Activity

Making a Poster
Draw a poster that expresses the relationship between Korea and China during either the Shilla, Koryo, or Choson dynasty. Use symbols to show the exchange of ideas.

Human Drama Activity

Korean Proverbs Like people the world over, Koreans have many traditional proverbs, some of which express the same ideas that American proverbs do. Give students the following and have them interpret their meaning and, if appropriate, give an equivalent American proverb. **1.** To begin is to be half done. **2.** Even a sweet song, sung overmuch, becomes disagreeable. **3.** Cousin buys a farm, and I get a stomachache. **4.** Does smoke rise from a chimney where no fire burns? **5.** A great vessel takes time to be made. **6.** Hearing 100 times is not like seeing once. *(1. Getting started is half the battle. 2. It is possible to have too much of a good thing. 3. The grass is always greener on the other side of the fence. 4. Where there's smoke there's fire. 5. Rome wasn't built in a day. 6. One picture is worth a thousand words.)*

Recall
1. (a) Shilla, p. 314 (b) Koryo, p. 314 (c) Choson, p. 315 (d) Yi Song-gye, p. 315 (e) Sejong, p. 315 2. (a) celadon, p. 314 (b) hangul, p. 315 (c) literacy rate, p. 315

Comprehension
3. Located on the border of China, Korea was influenced by Chinese culture and technology. At various times, both China and Japan have exerted political control over Korea. 4. Possible answer: Koreans adapted the Chinese civil service examination so that only aristocrats were permitted to take the exam. Koreans made books using movable metal type instead of the Chinese woodblock method; they altered the Chinese way of making porcelain by creating celadon ware with its distinctive blue-green glaze. 5. (a) Korea saw its relationship to China in Confucian terms, as a younger sibling who owed respect and loyalty. Koreans also placed emphasis on the family as the foundation of the state. (b) It developed a new alphabet, hangul, better fitted to the Korean language than the Chinese system; hangul helped spread literacy.

Critical Thinking and Writing
6. Possible answer: The poem reflects the Confucian notion that a leader has a duty to care for those under him and to rule by virtuous example. 7. Possible answer: It is a symbol of their unique identity.

Activity Rubrics

Share rubrics with students before they begin their posters.

Attempted The poster is not complete or reveals little understanding of the relationship between Korea and China.

Minimal The poster shows some awareness of the relationship between Korea and China, but is poorly executed.

Adequate The poster is well conceived, clear, and demonstrates a good grasp of the relationship between Korea and China.

Exemplary The poster is original, creative, well researched, well presented, and shows a thorough understanding of the topic.

Connections to Today

ANSWERS Possible answers: Earlier kingdoms divided the peninsula into three nations; today it is divided into two. The division today is ideological, whereas the past division was power-based.

Bell Ringer Have students use the map of Japan on the opposite page to list possible ways geography has affected this island nation. Invite students to make generalizations based on the map. Ask them to verify or revise their ideas as they read the section.

Reading Focus

- What geographic features influenced the early development of Japan?
- How did Chinese civilization influence early Japanese traditions?
- What traditions emerged at the Heian court?

Vocabulary

archipelago
tsunami
selective borrowing
kana

Taking Notes

On a sheet of paper copy this concept web. As you read the section, add circles to the left with more information about the influence of China and circles to the right with more information about Japan's own traditions.

Ideas of government

China's influence — **EMERGENCE OF JAPAN** — Japanese traditions

Shinto

Main Idea Japan borrowed elements of Chinese civilization but remained free of Chinese control.

LESSON PLAN

1. Focus Mountainous lands, surrounding seas, and violent forces of nature affected the development of Japan. Japan adopted elements of Chinese civilization but remained free of Chinese control. During the Heian period, Japanese culture flourished.

2. Instruct Divide the class into four or more groups, and assign each group one of the following topics: Geography, Early Traditions, The Influence of China, The Heian Period. Ask members of each group to work together to compile information on their assigned topic for a data bank on Japan. Collect each group's document and place it in a binder or booklet accessible to the entire class. You may also wish to make copies and distribute them to the students.

3. Assess Have students use the class data bank on Japan to answer the Section 4 Assessment questions.

4. Reteach If students' **Assess** activity does not reflect adequate understanding of the lesson, you might assign the *Guide to the Essentials* or the *Interactive Student Tutorial CD-ROM* for this section.

Geography and History

Tsunami: The Killer Wave

Picture an ocean wave seven stories tall—heading right at you. That's what the people on the Japanese island of Honshu faced on June 15, 1896. The huge wave—a tsunami—slammed into 200 miles of Japanese coastline. Whole villages were swept away. Nearly 30,000 people were killed.

Tsunamis begin far out at sea, when an undersea earthquake, landslide, or volcano sets the water in motion. The wave can travel at up to 600 miles per hour. In deep water, the wave is barely noticeable on the surface. But in shallow water, it reaches horrific height, sometimes as much as 100 feet.

Theme: Geography and History How might Japan's geography have increased death tolls from tsunamis?

Setting the Scene Prince Shotoku of Japan's ruling Yamato clan wanted to create an orderly society. In 604, he outlined ideals of behavior for both the royal court and ordinary people. "Harmony should be valued," he wrote, "and quarrels avoided." Shotoku's words reflected a strong Confucian influence about social order. As he stated:

"Everyone has his biases, and few men are far-sighted. Therefore some disobey their lords and fathers and keep up feuds with their neighbors. But when the superiors are in harmony with each other and inferiors are friendly, then affairs are discussed quietly and the right view of matters prevails."

—Prince Shotoku, *Laws*

Like Korea, Japan felt the powerful influence of Chinese civilization early in its history. At the same time, the Japanese continued to maintain their own distinct culture.

Geography: Japan, a Land Apart

Japan is located on an **archipelago** (ahr kuh PEHL uh goh), or chain of islands, about 100 miles off the Asian mainland and east of the Korean peninsula. Its four main islands are Hokkaido (hoh KĪ doh), Honshu (hahn SHOO), Kyushu (kee oo SHOO), and Shikoku (shee KOH koo).

Land and Sea Japan is about the size of Montana, but four fifths of its land is too mountainous to farm. As a result, most people settled in narrow river valleys and along the coastal plains. A mild climate and sufficient rainfall, however, helped Japanese farmers make the most of the limited arable land. As in ancient Greece, the mountainous terrain at first was an obstacle to unity.

The surrounding seas have both protected and isolated Japan. It was close enough to the mainland to learn from Korea and China, but too far away for the Chinese to conquer. Japan thus had greater freedom to accept or reject Chinese influences than did other East Asian lands. At times, the Japanese sealed themselves off from foreign influences, choosing to go their own way.

The seas that helped Japan preserve its identity also served as trade routes. The Inland Sea was an especially important link among various

Geography and History

ANSWER Possible answer: The mountains of Japan have forced most people to live along the coasts, putting them at greater risk from tsunamis.

Resource Directory

Teaching Resources
Creative Teaching Activities Creative Teaching Activities booklet, p. 61
Guided Reading and Review Unit 3 booklet, p. 100

Japanese islands. The seas also offered plentiful food resources. The Japanese, like the Koreans, developed a thriving fishing industry.

Ring of Fire Japan lies in a Pacific region known as the Ring of Fire, which also includes the Philippines, Indonesia, and parts of Australia and South America. This region is subject to frequent earthquakes and volcanoes. Underwater earthquakes can launch killer tidal waves, called tsunami (tsoo NAH mee), that sweep over the land without warning, wiping out everything in their path.

The Japanese came to fear and respect the dramatic forces of nature. Today, as in the past, soaring Mount Fuji, with its snowcapped volcanic crater, is a sacred symbol of the beauty and majesty of nature.

Early Traditions

The people we know today as the Japanese probably migrated from the Asian mainland more than 2,000 years ago. They slowly pushed the earlier inhabitants, the Ainu, onto the northernmost island of Hokkaido.

Yamato Clan Early Japanese society was divided into uji, or clans. Each uji had its own chief and a special god or goddess who was seen as the clan's original ancestor. Some clan leaders were women, suggesting that women enjoyed a respected position in society.

By about A.D. 500, the Yamato clan came to dominate a corner of Honshu, the largest Japanese island. For the next 1,000 years, the Yamato Plain was the heartland of Japanese government. The Yamato set up Japan's first and only dynasty. They claimed direct descent from the sun goddess, Amaterasu, and chose the rising sun as their symbol. Later Japanese emperors were revered as living gods. While this is no longer the case, the current Japanese emperor still traces his roots to the Yamato clan.

Shinto Early Japanese clans honored kami, or nature spirits. This worship of the forces of nature became known as Shinto, meaning "the way of the gods." Shinto never evolved into an international religion like Christianity, Buddhism, or Islam. Still, its traditions have survived to the present day. Hundreds of Shinto shrines dot the Japanese countryside. Though simple in design, they are generally located in beautiful, natural surroundings. Shinto shrines are dedicated to special sites or objects such as mountains or waterfalls, ancient gnarled trees, or even oddly shaped rocks.

The Korean Bridge The Japanese language is distantly related to Korean but completely different from Chinese. From early on, Japan and Korea were in continuous contact with each other. Korean artisans and metalworkers settled in Japan, bringing sophisticated skills and technology. Japanese and Korean warriors crossed the sea in both directions to attack each other's strongholds. Some of the leading families at the Yamato court claimed Korean ancestors.

By about A.D. 500, missionaries from Korea had introduced Buddhism to Japan. With it came knowledge of Chinese writing and culture. This opening sparked a sudden surge of Japanese interest in Chinese civilization.

Geography of Japan

▲ Volcano
● Yamato influence

Skills Assessment

Geography Japan is located on an archipelago. In addition to its four main islands, Japan includes over 3,000 smaller islands.

1. **Location** On the map, locate (a) Hokkaido, (b) Honshu, (c) Kyushu, (d) Shikoku, (e) Mount Fuji.
2. **Interaction** Explain how two geographic features might have influenced Japanese life.
3. **Critical Thinking Drawing Conclusions** Which city was more likely to feel the influence of the Yamato clan—Osaka or Edo? Why?

Chapter 13 **317**

Protector of a Buddhist Monastery
In the 700s, a Japanese emperor ordered that pagodas and Buddhist monasteries be built throughout Japan. The warrior god shown here was meant to protect a Buddhist temple from evil spirits.

Theme: Global Interaction
How does this statue show the influence of China on Japan?

▶ **Primary Sources and Literature**

See "Murasaki Shikibu: The Tale of Genji" in the Reference Section at the back of this book.

Japan Looks to China

In the early 600s, Prince Shotoku of the Yamato clan decided to learn about China directly instead of through Korean sources. He sent young nobles to study in China. Over the next 200 years, many Japanese students, monks, traders, and officials visited the Tang court.

Imported From China Each mission spent a year or more in China—negotiating, trading, but above all studying. They returned to Japan eager to spread Chinese thought, technology, and arts. They also imported Chinese ideas about government. Japanese rulers adopted the title "Heavenly Emperor" and claimed absolute power. They strengthened the central government, set up a bureaucracy, and adopted a law code similar to that of China. Still, the new bureaucracy had little real authority beyond the royal court. Out in the countryside, the old clans remained strong.

In 710, the Japanese emperor built a new capital at Nara, modeled on the Tang capital at Chang'an. There, Japanese nobles spoke Chinese and dressed in Chinese fashion. Their cooks prepared Chinese dishes and served food on Chinese-style pottery. Tea drinking, along with an elaborate tea ceremony, was imported from China. Japanese officials and scholars used Chinese characters to write official histories. Tang music and dances became very popular, as did gardens designed along Chinese lines.

As Buddhism spread, the Japanese adopted pagoda architecture. Buddhist monasteries grew rich and powerful. Confucian ideas and ethics also took root. They included the emphasis on filial piety, the relationships between superior and inferior, and respect for learning.

Selective Borrowing In time, the initial enthusiasm for everything Chinese died down. The Japanese kept some Chinese ways but discarded or modified others. This process is known as selective borrowing. Japan, for example, never accepted the Chinese civil service examination to choose officials based on merit. Instead, they maintained their tradition of inherited status through family position. Officials were the educated sons of nobles.

By the 800s, as Tang China began to decline, the Japanese court turned away from its model. After absorbing all they could from China, the Japanese spent the next 400 years digesting and modifying these cultural acquisitions to produce their own unique civilization. The Japanese asserted their identity by revising the Chinese system of writing and adding kana, or phonetic symbols representing syllables. Japanese artists developed their own styles.

The Heian Period

This blending of cultures took place from 794 to 1185. During this time, the imperial capital was in Heian (hay AHN), present-day Kyoto. There, emperors performed traditional religious ceremonies, while wealthy court families like the Fujiwara wielded real power. The Fujiwara married their daughters to the heirs to the throne, thus ensuring their authority.

An Elegant Court At the Heian court an elegant and sophisticated culture blossomed. Noblewomen and noblemen lived in a fairy-tale atmosphere of beautiful pavilions, gardens, and lotus pools. Elaborate rules of etiquette governed court ceremony. Courtiers dressed with extraordinary care in delicate, multicolored silk. Draping one's sleeve out a carriage window was a fine art.

Although men at court still studied Chinese, women were forbidden to learn the language. Despite these restrictions, it was Heian women who produced the most important works of Japanese literature of the period. Using the new kana, women of the court produced fine diaries, essays, and collections of poetry.

In the 900s, Sei Shonagon, a lady-in-waiting to the empress, wrote *The Pillow Book*. In a witty series of anecdotes and personal observations, she provides vivid details of court manners, amusements, decor, and dress. In one section, Shonagon discusses the importance of keeping up a good appearance at court:

> "Nothing can be worse than allowing the driver of one's ox-carriage to be poorly dressed. It does not matter too much if the other attendants are shabby, since they can remain at the rear of the carriage; but the drivers are bound to be noticed and, if they are badly turned out, it makes a painful impression."
>
> —Sei Shonagon, *The Pillow Book*

Lady Murasaki The best-known Heian writer was Sei Shonagon's rival, Murasaki Shikibu. Her monumental work, *The Tale of Genji*, was the world's first full-length novel.

The Tale of Genji recounts the adventures and loves of the fictional Prince Genji and his son. In one scene, Genji moves with ease through the festivities at an elaborate "Chinese banquet." After dinner, "under the great cherry tree of the Southern court," the entertainment begins. There is music—Genji performs skillfully on the 13-stringed zither and does the Wave Dance. But the main event of the evening is a Chinese poetry contest. Genji and other guests are given a "rhyme word," which they must use to compose a poem in Chinese. Genji's word is "Spring" and his poem is the hit of the banquet.

Elegant though they are, the Heian poems and romances are haunted by a sense of sadness. The writers lament that love does not last and the beauty of the world is soon gone. Perhaps this feeling of melancholy was prophetic. While noble men and women strolled through manicured gardens, outside the walls of the court, clouds of rebellion and civil war were gathering.

Biography

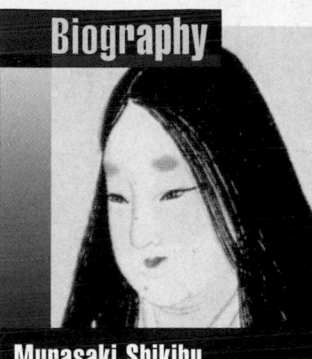

Murasaki Shikibu
978 (?) –1031(?)

"If only you were a boy, how happy I would be!" said Murasaki Shikibu's father. Although he was praising her intelligence, he was also revealing how Japan valued men over women. Growing up, Murasaki studied with her brother. This fact was probably kept secret, because learning by girls was considered improper.

After the death of her husband and child, she went to the imperial court as a lady-in-waiting. There, as Lady Murasaki, she penned the world's first novel, *The Tale of Genji*, which has been celebrated for over a thousand years.

Theme: Impact of the Individual What personal qualities can you infer that Lady Murasaki possessed?

SECTION 4 Assessment

Recall
1. **Identify:** (a) Ring of Fire,
(b) Yamato clan, (c) Amaterasu,
(d) Shinto, (e) Shotoku, (f) Sei Shonagon, (g) Murasaki Shikibu.
2. **Define:** (a) archipelago,
(b) tsunami, (c) selective borrowing, (d) kana.

Comprehension
3. Describe two ways in which geography affected Japanese life and culture.
4. (a) What early Japanese traditions were influenced by China?
(b) How did the Japanese preserve their own identity and culture?

5. How did women influence culture at the Heian court?

Critical Thinking and Writing
6. **Comparing** How was the Japanese development of kana similar to the Korean development of hangul?
7. **Understanding Sequence** (a) Arrange the following events in the order in which they occurred: Emperor builds a new capital at Nara; Shotoku sends nobles to China; the Japanese court turns away from its Chinese model; missionaries introduce Buddhism to Japan. (b) Explain why the events occurred in that order.

Activity
Take It to the NET

Use the Internet to view photographs or paintings of Mount Fuji on the Japanese island of Honshu. (If possible, print out two or three of these images.) Then, write a short poem or essay describing your impression of the mountain and its surroundings.

SECTION 4 Assessment

Recall
1. (a) Ring of Fire, p. 317 (b) Yamato clan, p. 317 (c) Amaterasu, p. 317 (d) Shinto, p. 317 (e) Shotoku, p. 318 (f) Sei Shonagon, p. 319 (g) Murasaki Shikibu, p. 319
2. (a) archipelago, p. 316 (b) tsunami, p. 317 (c) selective borrowing, p. 318 (d) kana, p. 318

Comprehension
3. Possible answers: Mountainous lands caused people to settle in river valleys and along coastal plains. The surrounding seas provided protection, trade routes, and a source of food. 4. (a) Possible answers: government, law, food, music, dance, and architecture (b) The Japanese discarded some Chinese ways and adapted others. For example, they revised the Chinese system of writing and added kana to it. 5. Women wrote important works of literature using kana.

Critical Thinking and Writing
6. Both systems of writing reflected more accurately the spoken language.
7. (a) Missionaries introduce Buddhism to Japan; Shotoku sends nobles to China; emperor builds new capital at Nara; the Japanese court turns away from its Chinese model. (b) Korea was in early contact with Japan and brought an interest in Chinese civilization including Buddhism. Prince Shotoku then decided to learn about China directly by sending nobles there to study. The Japanese capital at Nara was modeled after the Tang capital at Changan. When the Tang dynasty began to decline, Japan turned away from its model.

Activity Rubrics

Share rubrics with students before they write their poems or essays.

Attempted The poem or essay is attempted, but is poorly written and organized and contains many mechanical errors.

Minimal The poem or essay is poorly written and organized and contains some mechanical errors.

Adequate The poem or essay is well written and organized and contains few mechanical errors.

Exemplary The poem or essay is very well written and organized and contains no mechanical errors.

Biography

ANSWER Possible answer: Lady Murasaki was probably intelligent, talented, devoted, and perhaps strong willed.

SECTION 5

Bell Ringer
Have students look at the picture of armorers on the opposite page and the picture of a Buddhist temple and garden on the page following that. Ask what the two pictures suggest about life in Japan during its feudal age.

LESSON PLAN

1. Focus A warrior aristocracy controlled by a shogun dominated Japanese society during feudal times. The Tokugawa shoguns developed a system of centralized feudalism. Zen Buddhism, kabuki theater, haiku, and woodblock prints blossomed.

2. Instruct Have students work in groups to create an elementary-school book about Japan's feudal age. Assign each group one of the following chapters to develop: Age of the Samurai, The Tokugawa Shogunate, Zen Buddhism, Artistic Traditions. Each group should write about its topic in a way that elementary students would understand and enjoy. Encourage students to do additional research and to illustrate their reports with maps, drawings, or photocopies of pertinent subjects. Have each group end its chapter with a series of review questions. Compile the finished chapters into a class book.

3. Assess Use the review questions that the students have written as the basis for a class discussion on each of the four topics.

4. Reteach If students' Assess activity does not reflect adequate understanding of the lesson, you might assign the *Guide to the Essentials* or the *Interactive Student Tutorial CD-ROM* for this section.

Reading Focus
- How did feudalism develop in Japan?
- What changes took place under the Tokugawa shoguns?
- What cultural and artistic traditions emerged in feudal Japan?

Vocabulary
shogun
daimyo
samurai
bushido
kabuki
bunraku
haiku

Taking Notes
As you read this section, prepare an outline of Japan's feudal age. Use Roman numerals to indicate major headings, capital letters for the subheadings, and numbers for the supporting details. The sample at right has been started for you.

I. Japanese feudalism emerges
  A. The world of warriors
    1. Daimyo
    2. Samurai
  B. Status of noble-women
    1.
    2.

Main Idea During feudal times, military rulers called shoguns dominated Japanese society and eventually created a strong central government.

Connections to Today

The Martial Arts

Nearly 1,500 years ago, warriors in China, Japan, and Korea learned ways to fight without weapons. These techniques, developed originally by Buddhist monks from India and Tibet, were called the martial, or military, arts.

Today, millions of people around the world learn and practice different forms of martial arts. Discipline—both physical and mental—is a key to success. Those who practice the Korean art of tae kwon do agree to be committed to 11 "tenets," or principles. These include showing respect for teachers, parents, and other elders and always finishing what you begin.

Theme: Continuity and Change Why do you think the martial arts are still popular?

Setting the Scene
The poet Sogi was one of the leading writers of Japan in the 1400s. In verses like this one, he expresses a sense of uncertainty and despair:

> "To live in the world
> Is sad enough without this rain
> Pounding on my shelter."
> —Sogi, *Haiku*

The 1400s, when Sogi lived, were a time of political intrigue, rebellions, and feudal warfare in Japan. Disorder continued through the following century. Yet, despite the turmoil, a new Japanese culture blossomed.

Japanese Feudalism Emerges

While the emperor presided over the splendid court at Heian, rival clans battled for control of the countryside. Local warlords and even Buddhist temples formed armed bands loyal to them rather than to the central government. As these armies struggled for power, Japan evolved a feudal system. As in the feudal world of medieval Europe, a warrior aristocracy dominated Japanese society.

In theory, the emperor stood at the head of Japanese feudal society. In fact, he was a powerless, though revered, figurehead. Real power lay in the hands of the shogun, or supreme military commander. Minamoto Yoritomo was appointed shogun in 1192. He set up the Kamakura shogunate, the first of three military dynasties that would rule Japan for almost 700 years.

The World of Warriors Often the shogun controlled only a small part of Japan. He distributed lands to vassal lords who agreed to support him with their armies in time of need. These great warrior lords were later called daimyo (DĪ myoh). They, in turn, granted land to lesser warriors called samurai, meaning "those who serve." Samurai were the fighting aristocracy of a war-torn land.

Like medieval Christian knights in Europe, samurai were heavily armed and trained in the skills of fighting. They also developed their own code of values. Known as bushido (BOO shee doh), or the "way of the warrior," the code emphasized honor, bravery, and absolute loyalty to one's lord.

Connections to Today

ANSWERS Possible answers: Some people may be intrigued with the grace and discipline involved in martial arts; others may have had their interest sparked by movies or television shows.

Resource Directory

Teaching Resources
Creative Teaching Activities Creative Teaching Activities booklet, p. 62
Guided Reading and Review Unit 3 booklet, p. 102
Viewpoint Activity *The Samurai in Fact and Fiction,* Unit 3 booklet, p. 106

Technology
World History Color Transparencies *Protective Armor in Europe and Japan,* p. C–41

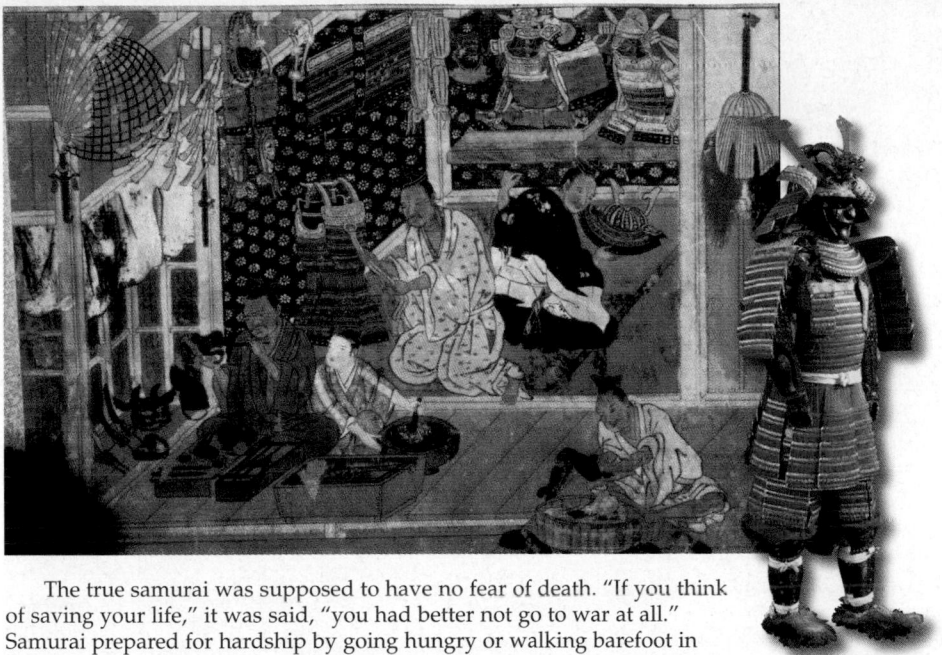

The true samurai was supposed to have no fear of death. "If you think of saving your life," it was said, "you had better not go to war at all." Samurai prepared for hardship by going hungry or walking barefoot in the snow. For a samurai, it was said, "when his stomach is empty, it is a disgrace to feel hungry." A samurai who betrayed the code of bushido was expected to commit *seppuku* (seh POO koo), or ritual suicide, rather than live without honor.

Status of Noblewomen At first, some noblewomen in Japanese feudal society trained in the military arts. A few even became legendary warriors. At times, some noblewomen supervised their family's estates.

As the age of the samurai progressed, however, the position of women declined steadily. When feudal warfare increased, inheritance was limited to sons. Unlike the European ideal of chivalry, the samurai code did not set women on a pedestal. Instead, the wife of a warrior had to accept the same hardships as her husband and owed the same loyalty to his overlord.

Peasants, Artisans, and Merchants Far below the samurai in the social hierarchy were the peasants, artisans, and merchants. Peasants, who made up 75 percent of the population, formed the backbone of feudal society in Japan. Peasant families cultivated rice and other crops on the estates of samurai. Some peasants also served as foot soldiers in feudal wars. On rare occasions, an able peasant soldier might rise through the ranks to become a samurai himself.

Artisans, such as armorers and swordmakers, provided necessary goods for the samurai class. Merchants had the lowest rank in Japanese feudal society. However, as you will see, their status gradually improved.

Mongol Invasions During the feudal age, most fighting took place between rival warlords, but the Mongol conquest of China and Korea also threatened Japan. When the Japanese refused to accept Mongol rule, Kublai Khan launched an invasion from Korea in 1274. After a fleet carrying 30,000 troops arrived, a typhoon wrecked many Mongol ships.

In 1281, the Mongols landed an even larger invasion force, but again a typhoon destroyed much of the Mongol fleet. The Japanese credited their miraculous delivery to the *kamikaze* (kah mih KAH zee), or divine winds. The Mongol failure reinforced the Japanese sense that they were a people set apart who enjoyed the special protection of the gods.

Armor for a Warrior
This painting shows Japanese artisans constructing armor and weapons for a samurai warrior. Unlike the solid steel plates worn by European feudal knights, the samurai's armor was made up of thin strips of steel held together by brightly colored silk cords.
Theme: Economics and Technology What might be the advantages and disadvantages of the type of armor used by a samurai?

A Zen Buddhist Temple Zen monks were the leading scholars and artists of feudal Japan. This temple was a Zen monastery and a peaceful retreat for visiting shoguns seeking advice.

Theme: Religions and Value Systems How does the setting of this temple reflect Zen values?

Order and Unity Under the Tokugawas

The Kamakura shogunate crumbled in the aftermath of the Mongol invasions. A new dynasty took power in 1338, but the level of warfare increased after 1450. To defend their castles, daimyo armed peasants as well as samurai, which led to even more ruthless fighting. A popular saying of the time declared, "The warrior does not care if he's called a dog or beast. The main thing is winning."

Gradually, several powerful warriors united large parts of Japan. By 1590, the brilliant general Toyotomi Hideyoshi (hee day YOH shee), a commoner by birth, had brought most of Japan under his control. He then tried, but failed, to conquer Korea and China. In 1600, the daimyo Tokugawa Ieyasu (toh kuh GAH wah ee YAY yah soo) defeated his rivals to become master of Japan. Three years later, he was named shogun. The Tokugawa shogunate ruled Japan until 1868.

Centralized Feudalism The Tokugawa shoguns were determined to end feudal warfare. They kept the outward forms of feudal society but imposed central government control on all Japan. For this reason, their system of government is called centralized feudalism.

The Tokugawas created a unified, orderly society. To control the daimyo, they required these great lords to live in the shogun's capital at Edo (present-day Tokyo) every other year. A daimyo's wife and children had to remain in Edo full time, giving the shogun a powerful check on the entire family. The shogun also forbade daimyo to repair their castles or marry without permission.

New laws fixed the old social order rigidly in place and upheld a strict moral code. Only samurai were allowed to serve in the military or hold government jobs. They were expected to follow the traditions of bushido. Peasants had to remain on the land. Lower classes were forbidden to wear luxuries such as silk clothing.

Women, too, faced greater restrictions under the Tokugawas. One government decree, sent to all villages, stated, "However good-looking a wife

322 *Chapter 13*

may be, if she neglects her household duties by drinking tea or sightseeing or rambling on the hillsides, she must be divorced." Women's freedom to move about, or even travel with their husbands, was strictly regulated.

Economic Growth While the shoguns tried to hold back social change, the Japanese economy grew by leaps and bounds. With peace restored to the countryside, agriculture improved and expanded. New seeds, tools, and the use of fertilizer led to greater output of crops.

Food surpluses supported rapid population growth. Towns sprang up on the lands around the castles of daimyo. Edo grew into a booming city, where artisans and merchants flocked to supply the needs of the daimyo and their families.

Trade flourished within Japan. New roads linked castle towns and Edo. Each year, daimyo and their servants traveled to and from the capital, creating a demand for food and services along the route. In the cities, a wealthy merchant class emerged. In accordance with Confucian tradition, merchants had low social status. Still, Japanese merchants gained influence by lending money to daimyo and samurai. Sometimes, merchants further improved their social position by arranging to marry their daughters into the samurai class.

Zen Buddhism and Japanese Culture

During Japan's feudal age, a Buddhist sect from China won widespread acceptance among samurai. Known in Japan as Zen, it emphasized meditation and devotion to duty.

Zen had seemingly contradictory traditions. Zen monks were great scholars, yet they valued the uncluttered mind and stressed the importance of reaching a moment of "non-knowing." Zen stressed compassion for all, yet samurai fought to kill. In Zen monasteries, monks sought to experience absolute freedom, yet rigid rules gave the master complete authority over his students.

Zen beliefs shaped Japanese culture in many ways. At Zen monasteries, upper-class men learned to express devotion to nature in such activities as landscape gardening. Zen Buddhists believed that people could seek enlightenment, not only through meditation, but through the precise performance of everyday tasks. For example, the elaborate rituals of the tea ceremony reflected Zen values of peace, simplicity, and love of beauty. Zen reverence for nature also influenced the development of fine landscape paintings.

Changing Artistic Traditions

Cities such as Edo and Osaka were home to an explosion in the arts and theater. At stylish entertainment quarters, sophisticated nobles mixed with the urban middle class. Urban culture emphasized luxuries and pleasures and differed greatly from the feudal culture that had dominated Japan for centuries.

Theater In the 1300s, feudal culture had produced Nō plays performed on a square, wooden stage without scenery. Men wore elegant carved masks while a chorus chanted important lines to musical accompaniment. The action was slow. Each movement had a special meaning. Many Nō plays presented Zen Buddhist themes, emphasizing the need to renounce selfish desires. Others recounted fairy tales or the struggles between powerful feudal lords.

In the 1600s, towns gave rise to a popular new form of drama, kabuki (kuh BOO kee). Kabuki was influenced by Nō plays, but it was less refined and included comedy or melodrama. Kabuki plays often portrayed family or historical events. Dressed in colorful costumes, actors used lively and

Zen Gardens Zen ideals of self-discipline, avoiding over-intellectualization, simplicity, and freeing the mind of clutter affected the style of Japanese gardens. While still portraying in miniature a natural scene, they became sparer and less concerned with decoration. A few artfully placed shrubs, some rocks, and sand or pebbles swept into a pattern aimed to impart a sense of rest and peacefulness. A comment about Zen art by modern-day Zen teacher Issan Dorsey applies equally well to Zen gardens: When asked, "What is the essence of Zen art?" Dorsey replied, "Nothing extra."

Primary Source

Perfect Serenity
Kenko, a Zen Buddhist priest of feudal Japan, wrote of the fleeting nature of worldly things:

"If we were never to fade away . . . but linger on forever in the world, how things would lose their power to move us! The most precious thing in life is its uncertainty. The May fly waits not for the evening, the summer cicada knows neither spring nor autumn. What a wonderfully unhurried feeling it is to live even a single year in perfect serenity! If that is not enough for you, you might live a thousand years, and still feel it was but a single night's dream. We cannot live forever in this world."

—Kenko, *Essays in Idleness*

Skills Assessment

Primary Source How do Kenko's words reflect what you know about Buddhist beliefs?

Test Preparation

Have students read the section "Economic Growth" on this page, and then answer the question below.

How did economic prosperity affect Japan's merchant class?

A It lost influence.

(B) It gained influence.

C It was sent into exile.

D It gave up trade for agriculture.

Primary Source

ANSWER Possible answer: Buddhists celebrate the eternal and the achievement of inner peace.

EXPLORING the HUMAN DRAMA   **Humanities Link**

Kabuki Theater

For nearly 400 years, audiences in Japan have enjoyed kabuki theater. Kabuki plays combine drama, dance, and music. Dressed in colorful costumes, actors use lively and exaggerated movements. The stories range from thrilling adventures to comedies of family life.

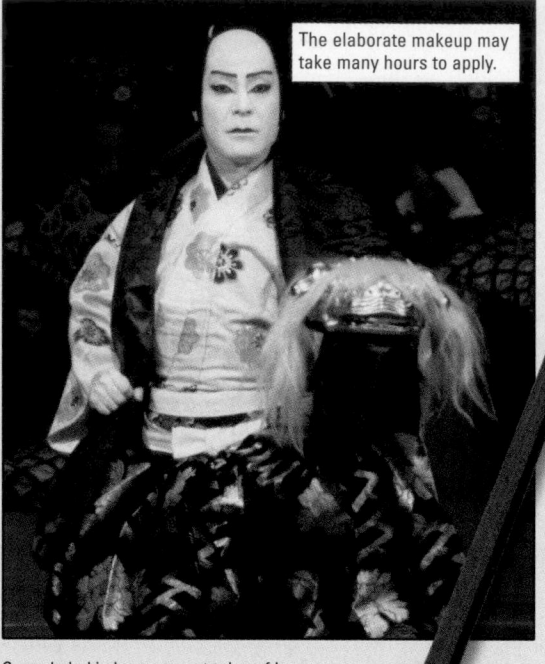

The elaborate makeup may take many hours to apply.

Some kabuki plays recount tales of honor and betrayal in feudal Japan. In this modern performance, a samurai must identify the head of his brother, a traitor.

Musicians accompany the drama on traditional instruments such as this samisen.

Kabuki was founded by a woman named Okuni. However, women were soon banned from performing. Here, men play the women's roles, as they still do today.

Fast Facts

- In the 1700s, a single kabuki performance might last an entire day.

- Scenery is changed in full view of the audience by stage hands in black costumes.

- Kabuki fans shout the names of their favorite actors during pauses in the action.

Portfolio Assessment

INTERNET   Use the Internet or library resources to find out more about Japanese theater. Then, prepare a class presentation. If possible, include visual aids.

Bell Ringer Point out that in kabuki drama, lines are spoken in stylized, formal patterns, and actors often wear masks. The plays are of two basic types: those dealing with feudal nobles or warriors and those dealing with the lives of commoners in the past.

Background
Connections to Today

Kabuki In the late 1600s, kabuki plays became more sophisticated and stylized, reaching the height of their popularity around 1700. After a period of decline, the plays enjoyed a revival in the late 1800s. New works were created and performed.

Kabuki remains a very popular form of entertainment, both with Japanese people and tourists. Kyoto and Osaka each have important kabuki theaters, and Tokyo boasts several.

Activity
Cooperative Learning

Performing a Play Divide the class into groups and assign the following roles: researchers, writers, costume designers, actors. Researchers should gather more information about kabuki plays and about the plots of specific plays. Using this information, writers should collaborate to create a script for a short kabuki play. Costume designers should use old clothing to simulate the kabuki costumes worn in the 1600s. Finally, performers should put on the play for the rest of the class.

Portfolio Assessment Rubrics

Share rubrics with students.

Attempted The student's presentation shows little understanding of the topic.

Minimal The student's presentation shows some understanding of the topic but is poorly written and uninteresting.

Adequate The student's presentation is well written, informative, and interesting.

Exemplary The student's presentation is exceptionally well written, informative, and interesting.

Resource Directory

Teaching Resources

Humanities Link Chapter Extension Activities booklet, p. 35
Section Quiz Unit 3 booklet, p. 103
Geography Quiz Unit 3 booklet, p. 108
Chapter Test Forms A, B, and C Unit 3 booklet, pp. 109–113
Answer Key Unit 3 booklet, pp. 114–128

Technology

World History Color Transparencies *Theater in Ancient Japan,* p. C–45
Listening to Literature World Masterpieces audiotapes *Sakura,* side 3, running time 2:51 min.; Japanese poems, side 3, running time 7:34 min.
Interactive Student Tutorial CD-ROM Ch. 13
Computer Test Bank Ch. 13

exaggerated movements to convey action. Kabuki was originated by an actress and temple dancer named Okuni, who became famous for her performance of warrior roles. However, women were soon banned from performing on stage.

Puppet plays, known as bunraku, were also enormously popular in towns. A narrator told a story while handlers silently manipulated near-life-sized puppets. Bunraku plays catered to popular middle-class tastes.

Literature The feudal age produced stories like the *Tale of the Heike* about a violent conflict between two families. Another important prose work was *Essays in Idleness*, a collection of short essays by Kenko, a Zen Buddhist priest. Many of the essays express Zen values, but others contain witty observations about human nature. "How boring it is," Kenko wrote, "when you meet a man after a long separation and he insists on relating at interminable length everything that has happened to him in the meantime."

Japanese poets adapted Chinese models, creating miniature poems called haiku. In only three lines—totaling 17 syllables in the Japanese language—these tiny word pictures express a feeling, thought, or idea. The poem by Sogi at the beginning of this section is an example of haiku.

Painting and Printmaking Japanese paintings often reflected the influence of Chinese landscape paintings, yet Japanese artists developed their own styles. On magnificent scrolls, painters boldly recreated historical events, such as the Mongol invasions.

In the 1600s, the vigorous urban culture produced a flood of colorful woodblock prints to satisfy middle-class tastes. Some woodblock artists produced humorous prints. Their fresh colors and simple lines give us a strong sense of the pleasures of town life in Japan.

Looking Ahead

The Tokugawa shogunate brought peace and stability to Japan. Trade flourished, merchants prospered, and prosperity contributed to a flowering of culture. Still, the shoguns were extremely conservative. They tried to preserve samurai virtues and ancient beliefs.

In the 1500s, Japan faced a new wave of foreign influence. The shogun at first welcomed the outsiders, then moved to sever foreign ties. In the next unit, you will read about Japan's uneasy relationship with an expanding Europe.

SECTION 5 Assessment

Recall
1. **Identify:** (a) Minamoto Yoritomo, (b) Toyotomi Hideyoshi, (c) Tokugawa Ieyasu, (d) Zen.
2. **Define:** (a) shogun, (b) daimyo, (c) samurai, (d) bushido, (e) kabuki, (f) bunraku, (g) haiku.

Comprehension
3. (a) What groups or individuals held the most power in feudal Japan? (b) What values did bushido emphasize?
4. Describe three results of the centralized feudalism imposed by the Tokugawas.
5. How did the growth of towns influence Japanese arts and literature?

Critical Thinking and Writing
6. **Analyzing Information** Why do you think the Tokugawas wanted to restrict the role of women?
7. **Linking Past and Present** Elaborate rituals such as the tea ceremony reflected Zen values. Are there any activities in our society today that follow a clearly defined ritual? If so, what values do these rituals reflect?

Activity
Take It to the NET
Use the Internet to learn more about the life of the Tokugawa shoguns. Then, write a descriptive essay to share what you learn. Include visuals if you wish.

Human Drama Activity

Haiku This poetic form consists of one line of five syllables, followed by a seven-syllable line and another five-syllable line. Traditional haiku includes a reference to an animal, a plant, or an event associated with a particular season. In this haiku by Bashō, for example, the reference is to the cicada, an insect that appears in summer and emits a pulsating, reedy sound.

"The cicada's cry
Gives no sign
It is about to die."

Have students find and read more examples of haiku, and then try their hand at writing their own verses. Invite the language arts teacher to devote a class period to this project.

SECTION 5 Assessment

Recall
1. (a) Minamoto Yoritomo, p. 320 (b) Toyotomi Hideyoshi, p. 322 (c) Tokugawa Ieyasu, p. 322 (d) Zen, p. 323 2. (a) shogun, p. 320 (b) daimyo, p. 320 (c) samurai, p. 320 (d) bushido, p. 320 (e) kabuki, p. 323 (f) bunraku, p. 325 (g) haiku, p. 325

Comprehension
3. (a) the shogun, or supreme military commander, and the daimyo (b) honor, bravery, and absolute loyalty to one's lord
4. Possible answer: The social system became more rigid. Agriculture improved, which caused population growth. Trade thrived, and a merchant class emerged in the cities. 5. The urban culture emphasized luxury and pleasure. In response, a new form of drama known as kabuki arose. Literature and painting also served to satisfy urban tastes.

Critical Thinking and Writing
6. Possible answer: The Tokugawa shoguns set up a rigid social system in which everyone's role was defined. They believed that women should support and obey their husbands. 7. Possible answer: The ritual of standing and singing the national anthem at the start of sports events reflects patriotism.

Activity Rubrics

Share rubrics with students before they write their essays.

Attempted The essay is attempted but reveals little research, is poorly written and organized, and contains many mechanical errors.

Minimal The essay includes basic information but is poorly written and organized and contains some mechanical errors.

Adequate The essay reflects good research, is well written and organized, contains few mechanical errors, and includes interesting descriptions.

Exemplary The essay is highly interesting, very well written, and carefully researched; it includes visual material and contains no mechanical errors.

Creating a Chapter Summary

As a reteaching opportunity, pair a more able student with a less able student to complete this chapter summary.

Possible entries: **China** Periods—Tang, Song, Yuan, Ming; Outside Influences—Mongol rule, voyages of Zheng He, conquering of neighboring lands; Type of Society—powerful rulers, civil service, gentry, peasants, merchants; Main Achievements—built Grand Canal, painting, poetry, prose, inventions, advanced technology **Korea** Periods—three kingdoms, Shilla dynasty, Koryo dynasty, Choson dynasty; Outside Influences—contact with China, Mongols; Type of Society—powerful rulers, civil service for aristocrats only; Main Achievements—movable metal type, celadon, hangul, iron-clad "turtle boats" **Japan** Periods—Yamato clan, Heian Period, Kamakura shogunate, Tokugawa shogunate; Outside Influences—Korea, China; Type of Society—clans, court society, feudalism; Main Achievements—Zen; literature, trade, agriculture

Building Vocabulary

1–10. (a) Art and Literature celadon, hangul, bunraku **Political and Social Systems** tributary state, land reform, gentry, shogun, bushido **Geography and History** archipelago, tsunami **(b)** Students' sentences should show an understanding of the chosen words.

Recalling Key Facts

11. the Tang and Song dynasties
12. The Mongols, while demanding tribute, generally let conquered people live as they had before.
13. Southeast and South Asia, the Middle East, and East Africa
14. Korea is located between China and Japan.
15. As an island, Japan was protected against invasion by China and had greater freedom to accept or reject foreign influences. Japan also used the seas that surrounded it for fishing and trade.
16. The central government was strengthened; new laws specified behavior for each class; the economy grew and trade flourished.

Critical Thinking and Writing

17. Possible answers: **(a)** Mongol warriors killed many and destroyed cities

Creating a Chapter Summary

On a sheet of paper copy the table shown here. Fill in the spaces under each heading to help you review key information about China, Korea, and Japan.

	CHINA	KOREA	JAPAN
PERIODS OR DYNASTIES	Tang, Song, Yuan, Ming		
OUTSIDE INFLUENCES			
TYPE OF SOCIETY			
MAIN ACHIEVEMENTS			

For additional review and enrichment activities, see the interactive version of *World History* available on the Web and on CD-ROM.

Web Site Self-Test
For practice test questions for Chapter 13, see **www.phschool.com**.

Building Vocabulary

(a) Classify each of the chapter vocabulary words listed below under *one* of the following themes: Art and Literature, Political and Social Systems, Geography and History. **(b)** Choose *one* word in each category and write a sentence explaining how that word relates to the theme.

1. tributary state
2. land reform
3. gentry
4. celadon
5. hangul
6. archipelago
7. tsunami
8. shogun
9. bushido
10. bunraku

Recalling Key Facts

11. Which two dynasties united and ruled China between the 600s and 1200s?
12. What impact did Mongol rule have on Asia?
13. What lands did Zheng He visit?
14. Describe the location of Korea in relation to China and Japan.
15. How has Japan's island status affected its history?
16. How did life in Japan change under the Tokugawas?

Critical Thinking and Writing

17. **Synthesizing Information** Review what you have read about the Mongol empire in this chapter and in earlier chapters. **(a)** How was the Mongol period both destructive and constructive? **(b)** What do you think were the three greatest effects of the Mongol conquests?
18. **Applying Information** Using the information in this chapter and in earlier chapters, construct a time chart of major Chinese dynasties. **(a)** When did each dynasty rise and fall? **(b)** What periods fall between major dynasties? **(c)** Make one generalization about the history of dynasties in China.
19. **Drawing Conclusions (a)** Describe the Japanese practice of selective borrowing. **(b)** How have Americans borrowed from other cultures? Give two examples. **(c)** What are some of the benefits and disadvantages of borrowing from other cultures?
20. **Connecting to Geography (a)** In what ways are the geographies of Japan and Korea similar? **(b)** What similar effects has geography had on these nations?

to conquer new lands. Afterward, however, the Mongols promoted religious and cultural tolerance, trade, and the arts. **(b)** the expansion of trade, cultural exchanges, the isolation of Russia from close contacts with the West
18. **(a)** Shang (1650–1027 B.C.); Zhou (1027–256 B.C.); Qin (221–207 B.C.); Han (206 B.C.–A.D. 220); Sui (589–618); Tang (618–907); Song (960–1279); Yuan (1279–1368); Ming (1368–1644) **(b)** 256–221 B.C.; 220–589; 907–960 **(c)** Possible answer: Dynasties may rule for short or long periods.
19. **(a)** The Japanese kept some Chinese ways but discarded or modified others. **(b)** Possible answer: They have borrowed from immigrants

and Native Americans. **(c)** Possible answer: Technology from other cultures can make work more efficient and productive. However, people sometimes resent the influence of foreign ideas.
20. **(a)** Both have mountains and long coastlines. **(b)** Because the mountains are hard to farm, people settled along the coasts. The surrounding seas provided seafood for large fishing industries.

21. Concentrate on the book and keep a dignified appearance.
22. Read the piece the assigned number of times, and reread until the student has memorized the text.
23. **(a)** books that expound virtues **(b)** those that are useless **(c)** it should improve character
24. It emphasizes duty, proper behavior, and virtue.
25. Students may note that they are not usually assigned to read a text a specific number of times. Today, students do not memorize books, and have considerable freedom of choice in what they read.

Analyzing Charts

26. **(a)** the emperor **(b)** He is at the top of the chart.
27. merchants
28. peasants
29. Possible answer: The chart shows hierarchy, and peasants, merchants, and artisans were all roughly in the same category.

Skills Tip

In addition to observing the lines on a chart, it is important to read the verbal descriptions. The Skills Handbook in the front of the book has a lesson that will help students with this feature.

Unit Theme Activity

Evaluate students' Unit Theme Activity by referring to the rubrics for the activity on the unit opener page in the Teacher's Edition.

Skills Assessment
Analyzing Primary Sources

The following passage is from a 1315 book of regulations for Chinese students. Read the passage, then answer the questions that follow.

"You should concentrate on your book and keep a dignified appearance. You should count the number of times you read an assigned piece. If, upon completion of the assigned number, you still have not memorized the piece, you should continue until you are able to recite it. On the other hand, if you have memorized the piece quickly, you should still go on to complete the assigned number of readings.

Only after a book has been thoroughly learned should you go on to another. Do not read too many things on a superficial level. Do not attempt to memorize a piece without understanding it. Read only those books which expound virtues. Do not look into useless writings."

—Chieng Tuan-li, *A Schedule for Learning*

21. According to the author, how should a student behave while reading a book?
22. What are two key procedures to follow when reading?
23. **(a)** What kinds of books does the author think a student should read? **(b)** What kinds of books does he advise students to avoid? **(c)** What does this suggest about his view of the goal of education?
24. How does this instruction reflect the new school of Confucian thought that emerged during the Song dynasty?
25. Compare the way a Chinese student of the fourteenth century read a book to the way you read a book.

Skills Assessment
Take It to the NET

Use the Internet to research an invention or technological discovery from early China during the time period discussed in this chapter. Then, create and deliver a brief presentation about it. You should tell when the item or technique was invented, how it was discovered or created, and whether it is still used today.

Skills Assessment
Analyzing Charts

FEUDAL SOCIETY IN JAPAN

Emperor
Held highest rank in society but had no political power

Shogun
Actual ruler

Daimyo
Large landowners

Samurai
Warriors loyal to daimyo

Peasants
Three fourths of population

Artisans
Made swords and armor

Merchants
Low status but gradually gained influence

The organization chart above illustrates the social levels of feudal society in Japan. Study the chart and then answer the following questions:

26. **(a)** Who occupied the highest position in Japanese feudal society? **(b)** How does the chart show this?
27. Who occupied the lowest position in Japanese feudal society?
28. What group made up the largest part of the population?
29. Why does the chart show no lines connecting the peasants, artisans, and merchants?

Skills Tip

Organization charts are usually arranged from highest (top) to lowest (bottom). Connecting lines show relationships between groups.

Take It to the NET

Direct students to **www.phschool.com** for links to sites that will help them get started on this assignment. Share rubrics with students.
Attempted The student's presentation is attempted but is missing one or more of the required elements.
Minimal The student's presentation has the required elements, but organization and delivery are poor.
Adequate The student's presentation has the required elements, organization is good, and delivery is informative and interesting.
Exemplary The student's presentation has the required elements, organization is excellent, and delivery is informative and exceptionally interesting.

Unit-in-Brief
3 Regional Civilizations

USING THESE PAGES

The Unit-in-Brief contains the main ideas of the unit chapters. You may use the Unit-in-Brief to preview, review, or condense the contents of each chapter.

The unit time line identifies key events in each world region that took place during the time span covered by the unit.

Activity
Unit Themes

Have students review the unit themes below. Then, ask them to find examples in the time line and summary to support each theme.

Religions and Value Systems Religions and value systems such as Christianity, Islam, and Confucianism united people across wide areas.

Art and Literature Rich regional cultures found expression in such art forms as the Gothic cathedrals of Europe, bronze sculptures of West Africa, and kabuki theater of Japan.

Geography and History Geographic features such as the Sahara, the Mediterranean Sea, and the steppes of Russia influenced the development of regional civilizations.

Diversity As regional civilizations learned more about one another through trade and war, they became lands of diverse peoples and ideas. Sometimes this diversity led to tolerance and a flowering of ideas; sometimes it led to conflict.

Chapter 8

The Rise of Europe
(A.D. 500–A.D. 1300)

From 500 to 1000, Europe was a fragmented, largely isolated region. Feudalism, the manor economy, and the Roman Catholic Church were dominant forces during the early Middle Ages.

* Between 400 and 700, Germanic invaders carved Europe up into small kingdoms.
* In the 800s, Charlemagne temporarily reunited much of Europe. He revived learning and furthered the blending of German, Roman, and Christian traditions.
* Feudalism, based on mutual obligations among lords and vassals, gave a strict order to medieval society.
* The Church guided the spiritual lives of Christians and was the most powerful political force in medieval Europe.
* By the 1000s, advances in agriculture and commerce spurred economic revival.

Chapter 9

The High Middle Ages
(A.D. 1050–A.D. 1450)

During the High Middle Ages, economic conditions improved, and learning and the arts flourished. At the same time, feudal monarchs moved to centralize their power, building a framework for the modern nation-state.

* In England and France, long-lasting traditions of royal government evolved.
* In the Holy Roman Empire, conflicts erupted between popes and secular rulers.
* European contacts with the Middle East during the Crusades revived interest in trade and exploration.
* Beginning in the 1300s, famine, plague, and war marked the decline of medieval Europe.

Chapter 10
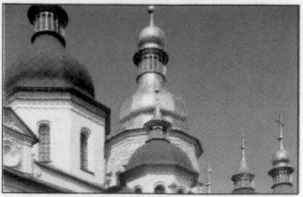

The Byzantine Empire and Russia (A.D. 330–A.D. 1613)

After the fall of Rome, the Greco-Roman heritage survived in the Byzantine empire. Byzantine civilization shaped the developing cultures of Russia and Eastern Europe.

* The Byzantine empire served as a center of world trade and a buffer between Western Europe, and the Arab empire.
* Traders and missionaries carried Byzantine culture and Eastern Orthodox Christianity to Russia, Eastern Europe, and Ethiopia.
* Czars Ivan III and Ivan IV expanded the Russian empire and laid the foundation for extreme absolute power.
* Invasions and migrations created a mix of ethnic and religious groups in Eastern Europe.
* Jews fleeing the Crusades and the Inquisition migrated further into Eastern Europe and the Middle East.

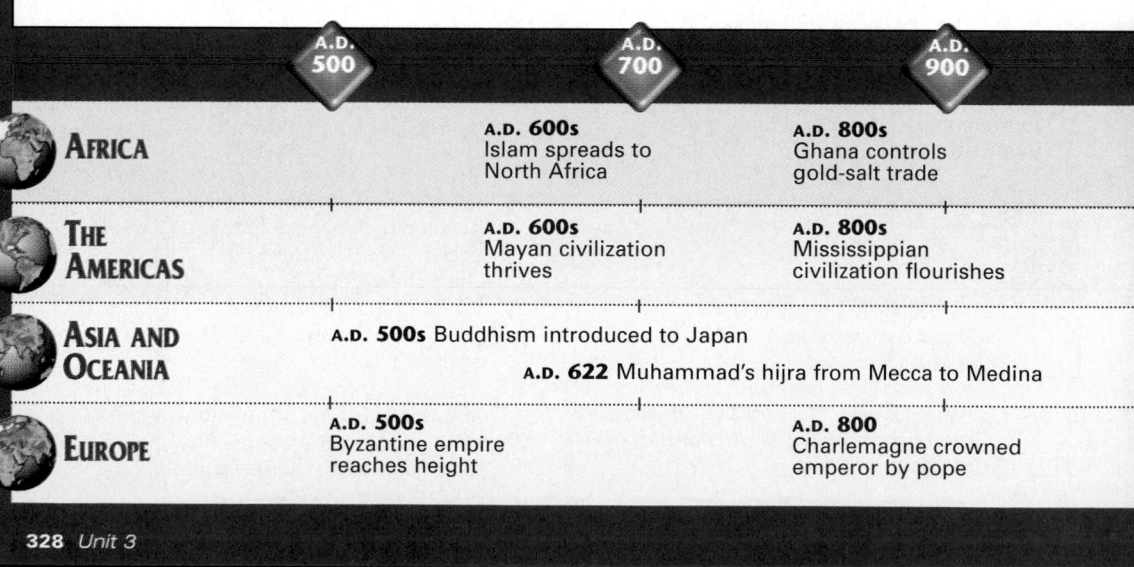

	A.D. 500	A.D. 700	A.D. 900
AFRICA		A.D. 600s Islam spreads to North Africa	A.D. 800s Ghana controls gold-salt trade
THE AMERICAS		A.D. 600s Mayan civilization thrives	A.D. 800s Mississippian civilization flourishes
ASIA AND OCEANIA	A.D. 500s Buddhism introduced to Japan	A.D. 622 Muhammad's hijra from Mecca to Medina	
EUROPE	A.D. 500s Byzantine empire reaches height		A.D. 800 Charlemagne crowned emperor by pope

Student Bibliography

Billings, Malcolm. *The Cross and the Crescent: A History of the Crusades.* Sterling, 1988. Well-illustrated history of the Crusades.

Browning, Robert. *The Byzantine Empire.* Catholic University of America Press, 1992. A short survey of Byzantine history from 500 to 1453.

Farris, W.W. *Heavenly Warriors: The Evolution of Japan's Military, 500–1300.* Harvard University Press, 1992. Excellent study of the emergence of the samurai.

Garlake, Peter S. *The Kingdoms of Africa.* Bedrick, 1990. Illustrated archaeological approach to social history of African kingdoms from the 300s to the 1500s.

Levathes, Louise. *When China Ruled the Seas: The Treasure of the Dragon Throne, 1405–1433.* Simon and Schuster, 1994. Detailed account of the sea voyages of Zheng He during the Ming dynasty.

Southern, R.W. *The Making of the Middle Ages.* Yale University Press, 1992. An introduction to the medieval period.

Chapter 11	Chapter 12	Chapter 13

The Muslim World
(A.D. 622–A.D. 1629)

The religion of Islam emerged on the Arabian Peninsula in the 600s. Muslim civilization eventually created cultural ties among diverse peoples across three continents.

- Muhammad was the prophet of Islam, a monotheistic religion. Through the Quran, the Five Pillars, and the Sharia, Islam was both a religion and a way of life.
- The Arab empire was ruled by several powerful caliphates. After 850, they were replaced by independent dynasties ruling separate Muslim states.
- Learning, literature, science, medicine, and trade flourished during the golden age of Muslim civilization.
- By the 1500s, the Mughals, Ottomans, and Safavids dominated the Muslim world with powerful empires in India, Eastern Europe, the Middle East, and North Africa.

Kingdoms and Trading States
of Africa (750 B.C.–A.D. 1586)

Despite geographic barriers, many civilizations rose and flourished in Africa. Kingdoms in the west and city-states in the east became important commercial and political centers.

- The Bantu migrations, contacts with Greece and Rome, the spread of Islam, and trade with Asia contributed to Africa's diversity.
- Between 800 and 1600, a succession of powerful West African kingdoms controlled the rich Sahara trade route.
- Indian Ocean trade routes led to the growth of prosperous city-states along the East African coast.
- Art and oral literature fostered common values and a sense of community among the peoples of Africa.

Spread of Civilizations in
East Asia (A.D. 500–A.D. 1650)

After 400 years of fragmentation, China reemerged as a united empire and the most powerful force in East Asia. Although Korea and Japan were heavily influenced by Chinese civilization, each maintained its own identity.

- China expanded and prospered under the powerful Tang and Song dynasties.
- During the 1200s and 1300s, the Mongols ruled much of Asia. After the fall of the Mongols, the Ming restored Chinese culture and later imposed a policy of isolation.
- While maintaining its own identity, Korea served as a cultural bridge linking China and Japan.
- The seas allowed Japan to preserve its unique culture while selectively borrowing religious, political, and artistic traditions from China.
- During the 1100s, Japan created a feudal society that was ruled by powerful military lords.

A.D. 1100   **A.D. 1300**   **A.D. 1500**

A.D. 1000
East African trading cities prosper

A.D. 1250
Empire of Mali reaches height

A.D. 1500
Kongo kingdom flourishes

A.D. 1000s
Anasazis build pueblo towns

A.D. 1438 Incan empire founded

A.D. 1500 Aztec empire reaches height

A.D. 960
Song dynasty in China founded

A.D. 1206
Delhi sultanate founded

A.D. 1368
Ming dynasty ends Mongol rule

A.D. 1520
Reign of Suleiman begins

A.D. 1066
Normans conquer Britain

A.D. 1215
English Magna Carta signed

A.D. 1389 Ottomans defeat Serbs at Kosovo

A.D. 1462 Reign of Ivan the Great begins

Activity
Summarizing the
Main Idea

Have students use both the Unit-in-Brief and Chapters 8–13 to answer the following questions in order to summarize Unit 3: (1) What religion, political system, and economic system were dominant features of medieval European civilization? (2) How did the Byzantine empire influence neighboring lands? (3) What cultural ties united people of the Muslim world? (4) How did trade affect the development of African civilizations? (5) Describe the cultural relationship that existed between China, Korea, and Japan.

PRENTICE HALL
ASSESSMENT SYSTEM

Diagnose and Prescribe
- **Profile student skills with Diagnostic Tests A & B.**
- **Address student needs with program materials identified in the test.**

Review and Reteach
- **Provide cumulative content review with the Review Book.**

Practice and Assess
- **Build test-taking skills with Test-Taking Strategies With Transparencies.**

Teacher Bibliography

Cantor, Norman F. *The Civilization of the Middle Ages: A Completely Revised and Expanded Edition of Medieval History, the Life and Death of a Civilization.* HarperPerennial Library, 1994. Considered the standard history.

Davidson, Basil. *Africa in History: Themes and Outlines.* Macmillan/Collier, 1991. Readable survey by noted journalist-historian.

Norwich, John Julius. *A Short History of Byzantium.* Knopf, 1998. An overview of the author's three-volume history of Byzantium.

Riley-Smith, Jonathan, ed. *The Atlas of the Crusades.* Facts On File, 1990. An account of the Crusades, including 150 high-quality color maps.

Rossabi, M., ed. *China Among Equals: The Middle Kingdom and Its Neighbors, 10th to 14th Centuries.* University of California Press, 1983. Foreign relations during Song and Mongol times described by experts.

Saunders, J.J. *History of Medieval Islam.* Routledge, 1990. A brief introduction to medieval Muslim history from Muhammad to the Mongol invasions.

UNIT 4

Unit 4 studies the major developments that led to the emergence of modern Europe and an age of global conquest, interdependence, and exchange.

Chapter 14 examines the Renaissance, Reformation, and Scientific Revolution.

Chapter 15 describes the growth of European trading empires in Asia.

Chapter 16 studies the impact of Europe's age of exploration on the Americas, Africa, and Europe itself.

Chapter 17 focuses on the role of absolute monarchs in Europe from the 1500s through the 1700s.

Unit Theme Activity Rubrics

Share rubrics with students before they create their projects.

Attempted The project does not include examples of the changes that led to the first era of global interaction.

Minimal The project is poorly executed or only vaguely highlights examples of the changes that led to the first era of global interaction.

Adequate The project is well executed, with well-chosen examples of the changes that led to the first era of global interaction.

Exemplary The project is extremely well executed, with many examples of the changes that led to the first era of global interaction, and is visually interesting or is extremely interesting and informative to read.

UNIT 4

Early Modern Times

1300–1800

OUTLINE

Chapter 14 **The Renaissance and Reformation**
(1300–1650)

Chapter 15 **The First Global Age: Europe and Asia**
(1415–1796)

Chapter 16 **The First Global Age: Europe, the Americas, and Africa** (1492–1750)

Chapter 17 **The Age of Absolutism**
(1550–1800)

Themes

As you read about developments that led to the emergence of modern Europe and the first age of global interaction, you will encounter the following unit themes.

Economics and Technology A scientific revolution enabled explorers to travel the world in search of trade and riches. Dramatic economic developments, such as the rise of capitalism, affected all social classes.

Global Interaction Exploration by powerful nations led to increased competition for trade. The spread of cultural beliefs and the exchange of material goods often were accomplished by conquest and by destruction of native cultures.

Political and Social Systems Absolute monarchs forged modern nation-states with strong central governments. The struggle between monarchs and Parliament in England was an important step in the development of modern democracy.

Religions and Value Systems Classical and Christian humanist ideals shaped the Renaissance. While the Protestant Reformation shattered the religious unity of Europe, Christianity continued to spread to new lands.

330 *Unit 4*

Unit Theme Activity

For Your Portfolio The chapters in this unit illustrate changes that led to the first era of global interaction. As you read the chapters, prepare a portfolio project highlighting these developments. Your project might take one of the following forms:
• **Chart or other detailed graphic organizer**
• **Debate**
• **Diary**

Resource Directory

Technology

World History Visions, Voices, Views Scenes of an Age, *Early Modern Times,* videodisc side 2 or videotape 4, running time 2:30 min.

Side 2: Fr. 27440-31883

The Palace of Versailles was designed to glorify the power of France and its monarch, Louis XIV. It served as the capital of France and as the royal residence from 1682 until the French Revolution.

Background
About the Picture

Palace of Versailles Originally built as a hunting lodge by King Louis XIII, the Palace of Versailles did not gain its famed extravagance until the time of Louis XIV. One of its most famous features is the Hall of Mirrors, which is flanked by the Salon of Peace and the Salon of War. This hall, shown at left, includes 17 wide, arched mirrors with 17 large windows opposite them. It was here that the famous Treaty of Versailles was signed between the Allies and Germany at the end of World War I.

In the Hall of Mirrors, Louis XIV requested that Charles Le Brun, the painter in charge of the interior of the palace, use the ceiling to depict the achievements of the king's government. Le Brun used the 31 ceiling panels to depict Louis XIV as a Roman emperor and a victor over foreign powers and in various other scenes suggestive of the king's power.

Don't miss the exclusive interactive version of *World History: Connections to Today* on the Internet and CD-ROM.

eTeach

Be sure to check out this month's online discussion with a World History Master Teacher.

Go to **www.phschool.com**.

Block Scheduling Support

Using the Unit-in-Brief The Unit-in-Brief, found at the end of the unit, contains the main ideas of the unit chapters. You may use the Unit-in-Brief to preview, review, or condense the contents of each chapter.

Using the Unit Time Line The Unit Time Line, at the end of the unit, provides a chronology of world events during the period covered by this unit. By studying the time line in conjunction with the Unit-in-Brief, students may compare developments in various regions. You may use the time line to help condense the contents of the chapters.

Using the *Guide to the Essentials* The *Guide to the Essentials of World History* contains summaries and graphic organizers for each section of every chapter in this unit. You may use the *Guide to the Essentials* to help poor readers or students acquiring English access the main ideas of the chapters. You may also use it with all students to review or to condense topics in your world history course.

Bell Ringer After students have looked at the pictures and read the paragraphs on these two pages, ask them to give examples of a problem that has been successfully corrected or solved within the recent past. Examples may be the invention of nicotine patches to help people quit smoking or of airbags in cars to protect people during crashes.

Activity
Cooperative Learning

Constructing a Chart Arrange students into groups of four. Instruct each group to make a chart with the columns Modern Problems and Modern Solutions, and the following categories: Food, Travel, Communications, and Health. Each group member should be responsible for one of the categories. They should list all problems or difficulties they can think of that belong to their category. Then, they should list the solutions that have been devised for each problem. Tell students that there may be more entries of problems or difficulties than of solutions. Urge them to use their imaginations to invent solutions or improvements. Groups should then share their lists with the entire class. Have the class discuss solutions to other groups' problems where possible.

WHY STUDY HISTORY?
Because Problem Solving of the Past Can Provide Insight for Today

How do you lift a million two-ton limestone blocks to build a pyramid? How do you unite a vast empire stretching some 2,000 miles? These were real problems faced by real people—the ancient Egyptians and the Incas of Peru. These pages show how Europeans of the fifteenth century solved a problem in their time. By studying how people solved problems in the past, we can gain new insights about how to solve today's problems.

Fifteenth-century problem: Gaining control of the pepper trade

Pepper plant

The Problem Long ago, in the jungles of India, a woody climbing vine was discovered whose small berries imparted a wonderful flavor to food. Soon, pepper had emerged as the world's most precious spice. During the Middle Ages in Europe, pepper was worth its weight in gold, and taxes and rents were often paid in peppercorns.

Europeans knew they could make much money by trading pepper and other spices. But Arab traders controlled the route across the Mediterranean Sea. And marauding bandits and forbidding geography made it very dangerous to travel overland to Asia.

Possible Solutions There seemed to be two ways to solve the problem. Traders could travel overland to Asia. To do so, though, they would have to seize the trade route from the Arabs, defeat dangerous bandits, and survive the hostile terrain. Or they could try to find a new, ocean route to the East. But this solution would require them to learn new navigation techniques, while overcoming their fear of ocean travel. Many Europeans at the time believed that the oceans were full of sea monsters—terrifying creatures with "horns, flames, and huge eyes 16 or 20 feet across."

Solution: Education

The nation of Portugal led the way in Europe's exploration of the seas. Prince Henry, known as the Navigator (left), spearheaded the drive. At Sagres in southern Portugal, Henry gathered astronomers, cartographers, and other experts. Under his direction, they prepared maps, redesigned ships, and trained captains and crews for long voyages on the open sea. Henry sent out expedition after expedition. At last, in 1434, Captain Gil Eanes rounded Cape Bojador off the coast of West Africa and then returned to Portugal. This journey brought a swift end to the terrifying myths about the "Sea of Darkness" and set the stage for the European Age of Discovery.

332

Resource Directory

Teaching Resources

Why Study History? *Because Problem-Solving of the Past Can Provide Insight for Today,* Why Study History? booklet, pp. 11–12

Solution: New navigational tools

Early European sailors had no way to determine their location in the open sea. Fearful of getting lost, they hugged the coastline, keeping well in sight of land. Then, in the 1400s, Portuguese mariners learned to trust astronomy and mathematics to guide them safely to and from their destinations. Cartographers produced more accurate maps. Sailors learned to use the astrolabe and the sextant, instruments that helped them to calculate latitude at sea. The magnetic compass enabled them to determine direction. Armed with these new tools, Europeans could now set out across the ocean, traveling for weeks without sighting land.

Astrolabe

Magnetic compass

Sextant

Solution: Improved ships

To meet the challenge of prolonged ocean voyages, Europeans had to design larger and better ships. The Portuguese again led the way with the caravel, a long, shallow ship whose steering rudder and triangular sails allowed it to sail against the wind. The highly maneuverable caravel was the ideal ship for exploring unknown seas.

Caravel

Twenty-first-century problem and solution

The problems we face today may be different from those faced by people in the past. But problem-solving techniques remain the same. First, we must identify the problem. Then, we look for solutions. For example, environmental pollution is a serious problem. One way people are working to solve this problem is by learning more about it and by seeking new laws to regulate the sources of pollution.

Earth Day has become an annual opportunity to draw attention to environmental problems. Here, teenagers in Los Angeles are preparing an antipollution petition to present to their city government.

Portfolio Assessment

Connecting to Today Identify a problem in your school or community. Then, list three steps you might take to solve the problem.

Background
Connections to Today

Information Revolution When the printing press was invented in the fifteenth century, it created an information revolution by allowing more copies of books to be produced more easily. Common people—not just religious scholars—could read and study. Today, the Internet has caused a similar information revolution by allowing instantaneous access to millions of books and other resources.

Background
About the Pictures

1. **Pepper plant** *(opposite page, top right)*. Pepper is the fruit of a vine originally found in the East Indies. It is not related to peppers, which are the fruits of the *Capsicum* bush and include both sweet bell peppers and spicy chili peppers.

2. **Sea monsters** *(opposite page, middle right)* were sometimes portrayed as mythical unicorns and dragons.

3. **Prince Henry the Navigator** *(opposite page, bottom left)*. In 1441, one of Henry's explorers returned to Portugal from Africa with some Africans he had captured. These people were the first slaves brought from West Africa to Europe.

4. **Astrolabe, magnetic compass, and sextant** *(top)*. These instruments revolutionized sailing much the same as radar helped to revolutionize flying.

5. **The Portuguese caravel** *(middle)* was innovative for its time, borrowing the design for its sails from early Arab ships.

6. **Students working on poster** *(bottom)*. Earth Day observations began in 1970. An estimated 20 million people participated in demonstrations across the country.

Portfolio Assessment Rubrics

Share rubrics with students before they identify a problem faced by the school community and list the possible solutions.

Attempted The assignment is incomplete.

Minimal The assignment was completed but is poorly organized and presented.

Adequate The assignment is complete, well written, and well organized.

Exemplary The assignment is complete, very well written, and very well organized.

Chapter 14 Planning Guide

Resource Manager

Chapter Level Resources	CORE INSTRUCTION	READING/SKILLS
Chapter Level Resources	📗 Teaching Resources 📖 Pacing Charts, Ch. 14 📖 Teaching With Themes, p. 17 📜 Color Transparencies, p. F–29 💿 Resource Pro® Ch. 14 💻 **www.phschool.com** • eTeach	💿 Book on CD, Ch. 14 💿 Interactive Student Tutorial CD-ROM, Ch. 14 💿 Social Studies Skills Tutor CD-ROM 📜 Skills Transparencies

1 The Renaissance in Italy
1. Explain why the Italian city-states were a favorable setting for a cultural rebirth.
2. Define the Renaissance.
3. Identify the themes and techniques Renaissance artists and writers explored.
	📗 Teaching Resources
	📕 **Unit 4 booklet**
	   • Biography Activity, p. 12
	   • Primary Source Activity, p. 13
	📖 **Creative Teaching Activities**, p. 63
	💿 **Prentice Hall Presentation Pro**, Ch. 14, Section 1
	📜 **Section Reading Support Transparencies**
		📗 Teaching Resources
		📕 **Unit 4 booklet**
		   • Guided Reading and Review, p. 2
		   • Skill Application Activity, p. 15
		📘 **Guide to the Essentials**
		📼 **Guided Reading Audiotapes**, Ch. 14, Section 1

2 The Renaissance Moves North 1. Cite the artists who brought the Renaissance to Northern Europe. 2. Paraphrase the themes that humanist thinkers and other writers explored. 3. Relate the impact that the printing revolution had on Europe.	📗 Teaching Resources 📖 **Creative Teaching Activities**, p. 64 💿 **Prentice Hall Presentation Pro**, Ch. 14, Section 2 📜 **Section Reading Support Transparencies**	📗 Teaching Resources 📕 **Unit 4 booklet** • Guided Reading and Review, p. 4 📘 **Guide to the Essentials** 📼 **Guided Reading Audiotapes**, Ch. 14, Section 2
3 The Protestant Reformation 1. State how abuses in the Church sparked widespread criticism. 2. Relate how Martin Luther challenged Catholic authority. 3. Identify the role John Calvin played in the Reformation.	📗 Teaching Resources 📖 **Creative Teaching Activities**, p. 65 💿 **Prentice Hall Presentation Pro**, Ch. 14, Section 3 📜 **Section Reading Support Transparencies**	📗 Teaching Resources 📕 **Unit 4 booklet** • Guided Reading and Review, p. 6 📘 **Guide to the Essentials** 📼 **Guided Reading Audiotapes**, Ch. 14, Section 3
4 Reformation Ideas Spread 1. Outline what ideas radical reformers supported. 2. Explain why England formed a new church. 3. Describe how the Catholic Church reformed itself. 4. Enumerate why some groups faced persecution.	📗 Teaching Resources 📕 **Creative Teaching Activities**, p. 66 💿 **Prentice Hall Presentation Pro**, Ch. 14, Section 4 📜 **Section Reading Support Transparencies**	📗 Teaching Resources 📕 **Unit 4 booklet** • Guided Reading and Review, p. 8 📘 **Guide to the Essentials** 📼 **Guided Reading Audiotapes**, Ch. 14, Section 4

5 The Scientific Revolution
1. Assess how astronomers changed the way people viewed the universe.
2. Describe the new scientific method.
3. Summarize the advances made by Newton and other scientists.
	📗 Teaching Resources
	📕 **Unit 4 booklet**
	   • Viewpoint Activity, p. 14
	📖 **Creative Teaching Activities**, p. 67
	💿 **Prentice Hall Presentation Pro**, Ch. 14, Section 5
	📜 **Section Reading Support Transparencies**
		📗 Teaching Resources
		📕 **Unit 4 booklet**
		   • Guided Reading and Review, p. 10
		📘 **Guide to the Essentials**
		📼 **Guided Reading Audiotapes**, Ch. 14, Section 5

ENRICHMENT/PRE-AP

🖥 **www.phschool.com**
- Why Study History?

📕 **Teaching Resources**
📘 **History Through Literature**, pp. 32–33
🎞 **Color Transparencies**, p. D–61
📼 **Listening to Literature World Masterpieces**, *Fa una canzione*, side 6; two poems by Francesco Petrarch, side 6
🖥 **www.phschool.com**
- Virtual Field Trip
- Internet Activities, Section 1

🎞 **Color Transparencies**, pp. C–43, D–63, D–65
📼 **Listening to Literature World Masterpieces**, poems by Pierre Ronsard, side 6
🖥 **www.phschool.com**
- Internet Activities, Shakespeare's World of Drama

📕 **Teaching Resources**
📘 **Chapter Extension Activities**, pp. 37–38
📼 **Visions, Voices, Views**, Daily Life CloseUp, tape 4

🎞 **Color Transparencies**, p. D–49

🖥 **www.phschool.com**
- Internet Activities, Section 5

ASSESSMENT

PRENTICE HALL
ASSESSMENT SYSTEM

Core Assessment
📘 **ExamView Test Bank booklet**, Ch. 14
💿 **ExamView Test Bank CD-ROM**, Ch. 14

Standardized Test Preparation
Diagnose and Prescribe
📘 **Diagnostic Tests for High School Social Studies Skills**
Review and Reteach
📘 **Review Book for World History**
Practice and Assess
📘 **Test-Taking Strategies With Transparencies for High School**
📘 **Alternative Assessment booklet**
📘 **Test Prep Book for World History**

📕 **Teaching Resources**
📗 **Unit 4 booklet**
- Geography Quiz, p. 16
- Section Quizzes, pp. 3, 5, 7, 9, 11
- Chapter Tests A, B, and C, pp. 17–21
🖥 **www.phschool.com**
- Self-Test

CUSTOMIZE FOR INDIVIDUAL NEEDS

Gifted and Talented
- **Teacher's Edition**, Activities: Customize for Heterogeneous Groups, p. 352

Less Proficient Readers
- **Guide to the Essentials**, Ch. 14
- **Guided Reading Audiotapes, English**, Ch. 14
- **Book on CD**, Ch. 14
- **Teacher's Edition**, Activities: Reading Strategy, p. 357

Less Proficient Writers
- **Teacher's Edition**, Activities: Cooperative Learning Activity, p. 344

Students Acquiring English/ESL
- **Guide to the Essentials, English/Spanish**, Ch. 14
- **Guided Reading Audiotapes, English/Spanish**, Ch. 14
- **Book on CD**, Ch. 14
- **Teacher's Edition**, Activities marked with an *: Connections to Film, p. 339

TEXT

Don't miss the exclusive interactive version of *World History: Connections to Today* on the Internet and CD-ROM.

CHAPTER
14

The Renaissance and Reformation

1300–1650

INTRODUCTION

Europe's cultural rebirth, known as the Renaissance, began in Italy around 1300, and then spread to northern Europe. This period emphasized artistic expression, the study of Greek and Roman cultures, secular concerns, and the development of the individual. In the 1500s the Protestant Reformation grew in response to the widespread corruption in the Catholic Church. In the 1600s, scientific discoveries changed the way Europeans viewed the physical world.

Focusing on Themes

Suggest that students focus on these theme questions as they read:

Art and Literature
How did the rediscovery of classical models influence Renaissance arts and literature?

Impact of the Individual
How did the Renaissance create a new emphasis on individual achievement?

Religions and Value Systems
How did discontent with the Church lead to the Protestant Reformation?

Economics and Technology
What influence did the new technology of printing have on European life and culture?

Continuity and Change
How did the Scientific Revolution transform the way people viewed the physical world?

Chapter Preview

1 The Renaissance in Italy
2 The Renaissance Moves North
3 The Protestant Reformation
4 Reformation Ideas Spread
5 The Scientific Revolution

TIME LINE ACTIVITY

Share the About the Pictures note before asking these questions:

1. While Mansa Musa began his pilgrimage in Africa, what was happening in Italy? *(The Renaissance began.)*
2. Identify the act that started the Protestant Reformation. *(Martin Luther posted his 95 Theses in Wittenberg, Germany.)*
3. Why was Galileo tried by the Inquisition? *(He said the Earth moves around the sun.)*

1300s

The Renaissance begins in Italian city-states. The cathedral in Florence, topped by this magnificent dome, reflects the wealth and artistic brilliance of Renaissance Italy.

1434

The Medici family gains control of the government of Florence.

1456

The first Gutenberg Bible is printed. The introduction of the printing press with movable type ushers in a printing revolution in Europe.

CHAPTER EVENTS

1300 — 1375 — 1450

GLOBAL EVENTS

1324 Mansa Musa makes hajj.

1368 The Ming dynasty is founded in China.

1453 Constantinople falls to the Ottoman Turks.

Don't Miss!

Humanities Link
Shakespeare's World of Drama (Section 2)

Comparing Viewpoints
What Is the Goal of Education? (Section 3)

Resource Directory

Teaching Resources
Teaching With Themes Chapter Theme Activities, p. 17
Pacing Chart With Block Scheduling Guide Ch. 14

Technology
World History Color Transparencies Ch. 14 Graphic Organizer, p. F–29

Artists of the Renaissance

During the Renaissance, the arts flowered in Italy and northern Europe. Renaissance artists built on Greek and Roman traditions and pioneered new techniques.

Pieter Bruegel
1525–1569

Peter Paul Rubens
1577–1640

Jan van Eyck
1395–1441

Albrecht Dürer
1471–1528

FLANDERS (SMALL STATES)

Leonardo da Vinci
1452–1519

Michelangelo
1475–1564

Donatello
1386–1466

Raphael
1483–1520

Boundary of Holy Roman Empire

Azimuthal Equal Area Projection

0   200   400 Miles

0   200   400 Kilometers

1506
Leonardo da Vinci completes the *Mona Lisa*, one of the greatest paintings of the Italian Renaissance.

1517
Martin Luther posts his 95 Theses in Wittenberg, Germany. This protest against Church policy launches the Protestant Reformation.

1633
Galileo is tried before the Inquisition for claiming that the Earth moves around the sun.

1525 1600 1675

1532 Spanish forces defeat the Incan empire of South America.

1620 Pilgrims found the Plymouth Colony in Massachusetts.

Chapter 14 **335**

Artists of the Renaissance

Activating Prior Knowledge

Ask students to speculate why the northern Renaissance centered on Flanders. *(Students might recall that during the Middle Ages Flanders was a prosperous trading center which attracted many artisans. Hence, it was a natural place for artists to congregate.)*

Previewing

The Renaissance was a time when artists rediscovered the art of classical Rome. Given that, what region or country do you suppose led the way in Renaissance art? Why? *(Italy had once been the center of Roman culture, and many architectural ruins and artifacts still remained.)*

Background
About the Pictures

1. Cathedral of Florence. Architectural historians consider this dome to mark the beginning of Renaissance architecture. The dome was built between 1420 and 1436.

2. Early printing press. The invention of the printing press with movable type helped the spread of literacy. Early printed books were mostly religious or classical in nature.

3. The Gutenberg Bible is named after Johann Gutenberg of Germany, who is credited with printing the first book in Europe using a movable type press.

4. The *Mona Lisa* hangs in the Louvre Museum in Paris. This portrait, noted for the woman's enigmatic smile, is among the world's most famous paintings.

5. This late sixteenth-century Bible depicts Martin Luther on its leather cover.

eTeach

Be sure to check out this month's online discussion with a World History Master Teacher.

Go to **www.phschool.com**.

Chapter 14 **335**

Bell Ringer
Tell students that the city of Florence was known for its wealth, its beauty, and the creative geniuses who worked there. Then, ask these questions: What cities today are known as centers of art and literature? Why do many artists and writers move to cities?

LESSON PLAN

1. Focus The Renaissance was characterized by creativity, interest in learning, and a desire to explore the human experience. Spurred by renewed interest in the culture of ancient Rome, the Renaissance began in the independent and prosperous cities of Italy. At the heart of the Renaissance was a set of ideas known as humanism.

2. Instruct Ask students to enumerate the general characteristics of Renaissance art and literature in Italy. Then, ask them to list all the artists and writers who are named in this section. Have them write a sentence or two describing one specific example of how each person displayed a characteristic of Renaissance art or literature in his or her work. Next, ask volunteers to read aloud one item in their list of Renaissance characteristics. Each time a characteristic is read, have other students respond aloud with a specific example of how a Renaissance figure displayed that characteristic.

3. Assess Ask students to put away their textbooks, outlines, and notes. Then, assign them to write a paragraph describing any one characteristic of the Renaissance style. Instruct them to explain how one or two Renaissance figures displayed this general characteristic in their work.

4. Reteach If students' Assess activity does not reflect adequate understanding of the lesson, you might assign the *Guide to the Essentials* or the *Interactive Student Tutorial CD-ROM* for this section.

Geography and History

ANSWER They made good use of canals as an efficient way to transport trade goods.

Reading Focus

- Why were the Italian city-states a favorable setting for a cultural rebirth?
- What was the Renaissance?
- What themes and techniques did Renaissance artists and writers explore?

Vocabulary

patron
humanism
humanities
perspective

Taking Notes

As you read, prepare an outline of this section. Use Roman numerals to indicate major headings, capital letters for the sub-headings, and numbers for the supporting details. The sample at right will help you get started.

I. The Italian city-states
  A. Why Italy?
    1. Remains of Roman heritage
    2. Prosperous city-states
    3.
  B. Florence and the Medicis
    1.
    2.
II.

Main Idea The Renaissance that began in Italy was characterized by an interest in learning and the arts and a desire to explore the human experience.

Geography and History

The Islands of Venice

One of the world's most remarkable cities was born after the fall of the western Roman empire. As invaders began conquering Italy, refugees fled to the islands in the Adriatic Sea. They drove wooden pilings into the marshy area to make a flat surface so that they could build houses. By Renaissance times, Venetian sailors were bringing back a wealth of trade goods from East and West.

The Grand Canal, an S-shaped waterway, became the main "street." Venetians row from island to island in flat-bottomed boats, called gondolas. Over 150 canals and 400 bridges link the islands into a single, unique city.

Theme: Geography and History How did Venetians adapt to geography?

Setting the Scene The philosopher Marsilio Ficino smiled with pleasure as he watched the sun cast a golden glow over his native city of Florence. To Ficino, this glow symbolized the revival of art and thought taking place in Italy. Dipping his pen in ink, he began to write. "This century," he wrote, "like a golden age has restored to light the liberal arts, which were almost extinct: grammar, poetry, rhetoric, painting, sculpture, architecture, music." What a glorious time to be alive, he thought.

As Ficino recognized, a new age had dawned in Western Europe. Europeans called it the Renaissance, meaning "rebirth." It began in the 1300s and reached its peak around 1500.

The Italian City-States

The Renaissance began in Italy, then spread north to the rest of Europe. Italy was the birthplace of the Renaissance for several reasons.

Why Italy? The Renaissance was marked by a new interest in the culture of ancient Rome. Because Italy had been the center of the Roman empire, it was a logical place for this reawakening to begin. Architectural remains, statues, coins, and inscriptions—all were visible reminders of Roman grandeur.

Italy differed from the rest of Europe in other ways. Its cities survived the Middle Ages. In the north, city-states like Florence, Milan, Venice, and Genoa grew into prosperous centers of trade and manufacturing. Rome, in central Italy, and Naples, in the south, along with a number of smaller city-states, also contributed to the Renaissance cultural revival.

A wealthy and powerful merchant class in these city-states further promoted the cultural rebirth. These merchants exerted both political and economic leadership, and their attitudes and interests helped to shape the Italian Renaissance. They stressed education and individual achievement. They also spent lavishly to support the arts.

Florence and the Medicis Florence, perhaps more than any other city, came to symbolize the energy and brilliance of the Italian Renaissance. Like the ancient city of Athens, it produced a dazzling number of gifted poets, artists, architects, scholars, and scientists in a short span of time.

Resource Directory

Teaching Resources

Creative Teaching Activities Creative Teaching Activities booklet, p. 63
Guided Reading and Review Unit 4 booklet, p. 2

In the 1400s, the Medici (MEH dee chee) family of Florence organized a successful banking business. Before long, the family expanded into wool manufacturing, mining, and other ventures. The Medicis ranked among the richest merchants and bankers in Europe. Money translated into cultural and political power. Cosimo de' Medici gained control of the Florentine government in 1434, and the family continued as uncrowned rulers of the city for many years.

Cosimo's grandson Lorenzo, known as "the Magnificent," represented the Renaissance ideal. A clever politician, he held Florence together in the late 1400s during difficult times. He was also a generous patron, or financial supporter, of the arts. Under Lorenzo, poets and philosophers frequently visited the Medici palace. Artists learned their craft by sketching ancient Roman statues displayed in the Medici gardens.

What Was the Renaissance?

The Renaissance was a time of creativity and change in many areas—political, social, economic, and cultural. Perhaps most important, however, were the changes that took place in the way people viewed themselves and their world.

A New Worldview Spurred by a reawakened interest in the classical learning of Greece and Rome, creative Renaissance minds set out to transform their own age. Their era, they felt, was a time of rebirth after what they saw as the disorder and disunity of the medieval world.

In reality, Renaissance Europe did not break completely with its medieval past. After all, monks and scholars of the Middle Ages had preserved much of the classical heritage. Latin had survived as the language of the Church and of educated people. And the mathematics of Euclid, the astronomy of Ptolemy, and the works of Aristotle were well known to late medieval scholars.

Yet the Renaissance did produce new attitudes toward culture and learning. Unlike medieval scholars, who were more likely to focus on life after death, Renaissance thinkers explored the richness and variety of human experience in the here and now. At the same time, there was a new emphasis on individual achievement. Indeed, the Renaissance ideal was the person with talent in many fields.

A Spirit of Adventure The Renaissance supported a spirit of adventure and a wide-ranging curiosity that led people to explore new worlds. The Italian navigator Christopher Columbus, who sailed to the Americas in 1492, represented that spirit. So did Nicolaus Copernicus, a Polish scientist who revolutionized the way people viewed the universe. Renaissance writers and artists, eager to experiment with new forms, were also products of that adventurous spirit.

Humanism At the heart of the Italian Renaissance was an intellectual movement known as humanism. Based on the study of classical culture, humanism focused on worldly subjects rather than on the religious issues that had occupied medieval thinkers. Most humanist scholars were pious

Renaissance Italy, 1505

Duchy of Milan
Republic of Genoa
Republic of Florence
Papal States
Republic of Venice
Kingdoms under Spanish sovereignty
Other city-states

Mercator Projection
0   100   200 Miles
0   100   200 Kilometers

Skills Assessment

Geography At the time of the Renaissance, Italy was made up of numerous republics, kingdoms, and city-states.

1. **Location** On the map, locate (a) Florence, (b) Venice, (c) Rome, (d) Papal States, (e) Duchy of Milan.
2. **Place** (a) In which state was Pisa an important city? (b) Who controlled Corsica and Sicily?
3. **Critical Thinking Making Inferences** Based on this map, why was Venice in a good position to trade with the Muslim world?

Background Biography

Patron of the Arts Lorenzo de' Medici gave a helping hand to dozens of famous painters and sculptors. Michelangelo was a boy of 15 when he arrived at the school that Lorenzo had established in Florence for sculptors. One day, the boy scrounged a scrap of marble and carved it into the mask of a mythical figure. Lorenzo passed by as Michelangelo was polishing the mask. He talked to the boy, recognized his genius, and invited him to become part of the Medici household. For the next four years, the young Michelangelo lived in the Medici palace while sharpening the skills that would make him one of the premier artists of the Renaissance.

Block Scheduling Support

Have students read the selection from *The Prince* in the History Through Literature booklet, pp. 32–33. After students complete the questions at the end of the selection, hold a class discussion that brings out the nature of practical politics for Machiavelli. Discuss how Machiavelli's approach to the world contrasts with attitudes during the Middle Ages. Ask what makes Machiavelli a man of his time. The discussion can be extended to examine the general question of morality and ethics in politics and whether leaders in present times are justified in using Machiavellian principles. Ask students to support their opinions with evidence, which may include examples, facts, or statistics.

Skills Assessment

ANSWERS 1. Review locations with students. **2. (a)** Republic of Florence **(b)** Corsica: Republic of Genoa; Sicily: Kingdom under Spanish sovereignty **3.** The Republic of Venice bordered the Muslim Ottoman empire, and the city of Venice was a major port on the Adriatic Sea.

Christians who hoped to use the wisdom of the ancients to increase their understanding of their own times.

Humanists believed that education should stimulate the individual's creative powers. They returned to the humanities, the subjects taught in ancient Greek and Roman schools. The main areas of study were grammar, rhetoric, poetry, and history, based on Greek and Roman texts. Humanists did not accept the classical texts without question, however. Rather, they studied the ancient authorities in light of their own experiences.

Francesco Petrarch (PEE trahrk), a Florentine who lived in the 1300s, was an early Renaissance humanist. In monasteries and churches, he found and assembled a library of Greek and Roman manuscripts. Through his efforts and those of others encouraged by his example, the works of Cicero, Homer, and Virgil again became known to Western Europeans. Petrarch also wrote literature of his own. His *Sonnets to Laura*, love poems inspired by a woman he knew only from a distance, greatly influenced later writers.

A Golden Age in the Arts

The Renaissance attained its most glorious expression in its paintings, sculpture, and architecture. Wealthy patrons played a major role in this artistic flowering. Popes and princes supported the work of hundreds of artists. Wealthy and powerful women such as Isabella d'Este of Mantua were important patrons of the arts as well.

Humanist Concerns Renaissance art reflected humanist concerns. Like artists of the Middle Ages, Renaissance artists portrayed religious figures such as Jesus and Mary. However, they often set these figures against Greek or Roman backgrounds. Painters also produced portraits of well-known figures of the day, reflecting the humanist interest in individual achievement.

Perspective
Renaissance artists used perspective to create an illusion of depth. The diagram below shows how the lines in this painting by Antonello da Messina recede from the viewer toward a single vanishing point.

Theme: Arts and Literature How does the size of objects in this painting add to the sense of depth?

Renaissance artists studied ancient Greek and Roman works and revived many classical forms. The sculptor Donatello, for example, created a life-size statue of a soldier on horseback. It was the first such figure done since ancient times.

New Techniques Roman art had been very realistic, and Renaissance painters developed new techniques for representing both humans and landscapes in a realistic way. Renaissance artists learned the rules of perspective. By making distant objects smaller than those close to the viewer, artists could paint scenes that appeared three-dimensional.

Renaissance painters used shading to make objects look round and real. Painters and sculptors also studied human anatomy and drew from live models. As a result, they were able to portray the human body more accurately than medieval artists had done.

Women Artists Some women overcame the limits on education and training to become professional artists. Sometimes, these women kept their work secret, allowing their husbands to pass it off as their own. Still, a few women artists did gain acceptance. In the 1500s, Sofonisba Anguissola (soh foh NIHZ bah ahn gwee SOH lah), an Italian noblewoman, became court painter to King Philip II of Spain.

Architecture Renaissance architects rejected the Gothic style of the late Middle Ages as cluttered and disorderly. Instead, they adopted the columns, arches, and domes that had been favored by the Greeks and Romans. For the cathedral in Florence, Filippo Brunelleschi (broo nehl LEHS kee) created a majestic dome, which he modeled on the dome of the Pantheon in Rome.

Three Geniuses of Renaissance Art

Renaissance Florence was home to many outstanding painters and sculptors. The three most celebrated Florentine masters were Leonardo da Vinci, Michelangelo, and Raphael.

Leonardo Leonardo da Vinci (dah VIHN chee) was born in 1452. His exploring mind and endless curiosity fed a genius for invention. He made sketches of nature and of models in his studio. He even dissected corpses to learn how bones and muscles work. "Indicate which are the muscles and which the tendons, which become prominent or retreat in the different movements of each limb," he wrote in his notebook.

Today, people admire Leonardo's paintings for their freshness and realism. Most popular is the *Mona Lisa*, a portrait of a woman whose mysterious smile has baffled viewers for centuries. *The Last Supper*, showing Christ and his apostles on the night before the crucifixion, is both a moving religious painting and a masterpiece of perspective. Because Leonardo was experimenting with a new type of paint, much of *The Last Supper* decayed over the years, but it has recently been restored.

Leonardo thought of himself as an artist, but his talents and accomplishments ranged over many areas. His interests extended to botany, anatomy, optics, music, architecture, and engineering. He made sketches for flying machines and undersea boats centuries before the first airplane or submarine was actually built.

Michelangelo Like Leonardo, Michelangelo was a many-sided genius—sculptor, engineer, painter, architect, and poet. As a young man, he shaped marble into masterpieces like the *Pietà*, which captures the sorrow of Mary as she cradles the dead Christ on her knees. Michelangelo's statue of David, the biblical shepherd who killed the giant Goliath, recalls the harmony and grace of ancient Greek tradition.

Primary Source

The Genius of Leonardo
Italian artist and architect Giorgio Vasari is best known for his engaging book of biographies of Italian artists, including Leonardo da Vinci (pictured above):

"Leonardo practiced not one art but all of those that are dependent upon design, and he had great talent for geometry besides being very musical, playing the lute with great ability and being excellent in the art of improvisation. . . . In entertaining, Leonardo was so pleasant that he won everyone's heart. Although he may well be said to have owned nothing and to have worked little, he always kept a servant as well as horses."

—Giorgio Vasari, *Lives of the Most Eminent Italian Painters, Sculptors, and Architects*

Skills Assessment

Primary Source What personal details did Vasari include about Leonardo da Vinci?

A Masterpiece by Michelangelo

Michelangelo spent four years painting biblical scenes on the ceiling of the Sistine Chapel. One of the most dramatic images, the *Creation of Adam*, shows God bringing the first man to life with a touch.

Theme: Religions and Value Systems How does Michelangelo suggest the power of God?

One of Michelangelo's greatest projects was painting a huge mural to decorate the ceiling of the Sistine Chapel in Rome. It was an enormous task, depicting the biblical history of the world, from the Creation to the Flood. For four years, the artist lay on his back on a wooden platform suspended just a few inches below the chapel ceiling. In a poem, Michelangelo later described his ordeal:

"My stomach is thrust toward my chin
 My beard curls up toward the sky
 My head leans right over onto my back . . .
 The brush endlessly dripping onto my face."
 —Michelangelo, *Poems*

Michelangelo was also a talented architect. His most famous design was for the dome of St. Peter's Cathedral in Rome. It served as a model for many later structures, including the United States Capitol building in Washington, D.C.

Raphael A few years younger than Leonardo and Michelangelo, Raphael (RAF ee uhl) studied the works of those great masters. His paintings blend Christian and classical styles. He is probably best known for his tender portrayals of the madonna, the mother of Jesus.

In *The School of Athens,* Raphael pictures an imaginary gathering of great thinkers and scientists, such as Plato, Aristotle, Socrates, and the Arab philosopher Averroës. With typical Renaissance self-confidence, Raphael included the faces of Michelangelo, Leonardo—and himself.

Italian Renaissance Writers

Poets, artists, and scholars mingled with politicians at the courts of Renaissance rulers. A literature of "how-to" books sprang up to help ambitious men and women who wanted to rise in the Renaissance world.

Castiglione's Ideal Courtier The most widely read of these handbooks was *The Book of the Courtier.* Its author, Baldassare Castiglione (bahl dahs

SAHR ray kahs steel YOHN ay), describes the manners, skills, learning, and virtues that a member of the court should have. Castiglione's ideal courtier was a well-educated, well-mannered aristocrat who mastered many fields, from poetry to music to sports.

Castiglione's ideal differed for men and women. The ideal man, he wrote, is athletic but not overactive. He is good at games, but not a gambler. He plays a musical instrument and knows literature and history but is not arrogant. The ideal woman offers a balance to men. She is graceful and kind, lively but reserved. She is beautiful, "for outer beauty," wrote Castiglione, "is the true sign of inner goodness."

Machiavelli's Successful Prince Niccolò Machiavelli (mahk ee uh VEHL ee) wrote a different kind of handbook. Machiavelli had served Florence as a diplomat and had observed kings and princes in foreign courts. He also had studied ancient Roman history. In *The Prince,* published in 1513, Machiavelli combined his personal experience of politics with his knowledge of the past to offer a guide to rulers on how to gain and maintain power.

Unlike earlier political writers, such as Plato, Machiavelli did not discuss leadership in terms of high ideals. Instead, *The Prince* looked at real rulers, such as the Medicis, in an age of ruthless power politics. Machiavelli stressed that the end justifies the means. He urged rulers to use whatever methods were necessary to achieve their goals. On the issue of honesty in government, for example, he taught that getting results was more important than keeping promises. He wrote:

> "How praiseworthy it is for a prince to keep his word and live with integrity rather than craftiness, everyone understands; yet . . . those princes have accomplished most who paid little heed to keeping their promises, but who knew how craftily to manipulate the minds of men."
> —Niccolò Machiavelli, *The Prince*

Machiavelli saw himself as an enemy of oppression and corruption. But critics attacked his cynical advice. Some even claimed that he was inspired by the devil. (In fact, the term "Machiavellian" came to refer to the use of deceit in politics.) Later students of government, however, argued that Machiavelli provided a realistic look at politics. His work continues to spark debate because it raises important ethical questions about the nature of government and the use of power.

▶ **Primary Sources and Literature**

See "Niccolò Machiavelli: Discourses," in the Reference Section at the back of this book.

SECTION 1 Assessment

Recall
1. (a) Lorenzo de' Medici, p. 337 (b) Francesco Petrarch, p. 338 (c) Leonardo da Vinci, p. 339 (d) Michelangelo, p. 339 (e) Raphael, p. 340 (f) Baldassare Castiglione, p. 340 (g) Niccolò Machiavelli, p. 341 2. (a) patron, p. 337 (b) humanism, p. 337 (c) humanities, p. 338 (d) perspective, p. 339

Comprehension
3. Italy had been the center of ancient Roman culture. The wealthy merchant class of Italian cities supported learning and the arts. 4. In the Renaissance, people explored the richness and variety of human experience in the here and now rather than focusing on life after death. There was a new emphasis on human achievement. 5. Renaissance artists used Greek and Roman settings, depicted worldly subjects, portrayed well-known individuals, and emphasized realism.

Critical Thinking and Writing
6. Possible answer: to increase their own prestige and the prestige of their city-state
7. Possible answers: (a) He meant that rulers can best maintain their power by instilling fear in their subjects. (b) No. When people are used to democratic ideas, harsh rule may lead people to rebel.

SECTION 1 Assessment

Recall
1. **Identify:** (a) Lorenzo de' Medici, (b) Francesco Petrarch, (c) Leonardo da Vinci, (d) Michelangelo, (e) Raphael, (f) Baldassare Castiglione, (g) Niccolò Machiavelli.
2. **Define:** (a) patron, (b) humanism, (c) humanities, (d) perspective.

Comprehension
3. What conditions in Italy contributed to the emergence of the Renaissance?
4. Identify the concerns and attitudes emphasized during the Renaissance.
5. How did Renaissance art reflect humanist concerns?

Critical Thinking and Writing
6. **Making Inferences** Why might powerful rulers and wealthy business people choose to become patrons of the arts during the Renaissance?
7. **Linking Past and Present** In *The Prince,* Machiavelli advised rulers that it "is much safer to be feared than loved." (a) What did he mean by that? (b) Do you think a political leader today would be wise to follow that advice? Why or why not?

Activity
Take It to the NET

Use the Internet to learn more about a major artist of the Italian Renaissance. You may choose one of the artists mentioned in this section or another artist such as Fra Angelico, Benvenuto Cellini, Sandro Botticelli, or Titian. Prepare a report on one artwork. Include a copy of the work.

Activity Rubrics

Share rubrics with students before they complete their reports.

Attempted The report fails to follow specifications or is not complete.

Minimal The report is complete but lacks evidence of understanding the artist.

Adequate The report reflects the necessary research and is well written.

Exemplary The report is well researched, well written, and interesting and shows extra effort.

Chapter 14 **341**

☑ Test Preparation

Have students read the quotation in the subsection titled "Machiavelli's Successful Prince" on this page, and then answer the question below.

According to Machiavelli, which of the following character traits is not absolutely essential for a prince to have?

A craftiness
(B) trustworthiness
C shrewdness
D effectiveness

Bell Ringer
Before reading the section, have students turn to the picture of the printing press on the opening page of this chapter. Invite them to comment on the impact of this invention. Follow up by asking students to list the different print materials they have used today.

LESSON PLAN

1. Focus After a slow recovery from the devastating Black Death, northern Europe joined in the Renaissance that had earlier swept Italy. Northern artists and writers imitated Italian styles while adding new methods and ideas of their own. As a result of printing, books became more available, and people became more literate.

2. Instruct Have students work with a partner to prepare and present a profile of a northern Renaissance writer or artist. As their subject, each partnership may select a figure mentioned in the text or another of their own choosing. Their profiles, which will require some outside research, should include information about the person's background and training, a description of the person's artistic or literary style, and examples of his or her work. Students may use slides, videos, or art books to illustrate the work of artists. For writers, students should be prepared to read aloud one or more excerpts from the author's works. They might also want to distribute copies of the excerpts to the class. Have each partnership present its profiles to the class, and encourage students to ask questions of one another.

3. Assess Have students create a bulletin board display that features the works of northern Renaissance artists and writers.

4. Reteach If students' **Assess** activity does not reflect adequate understanding of the lesson, you might assign the *Guide to the Essentials* or the *Interactive Student Tutorial CD-ROM* for this section.

Reading Focus

- Which artists brought the Renaissance to northern Europe?
- What themes did humanist thinkers and other writers explore?
- What impact did the printing revolution have on Europe?

Vocabulary

engraving
vernacular
utopian

Taking Notes

On a sheet of paper begin a table like the one shown here. Add information about the Renaissance under each heading as you read the section.

DUTCH	GERMAN	FLEMISH	ENGLISH	FRENCH	SPANISH
Erasmus	Dürer				

Main Idea The Renaissance slowly spread to northern Europe, where artists and writers experimented with new methods and ideas.

Setting the Scene "Had I not torn myself from Rome, I could never have resolved to leave," wrote Dutch priest Desiderius Erasmus. "There one enjoys sweet liberty, rich libraries, the charming friendship of writers and scholars, and the sight of antique monuments." Inspired by his visit to Italy, Erasmus helped spread the Renaissance to northern Europe.

Unlike Italy, northern Europe recovered slowly from the ravages of the Black Death. Only after 1450 did the north enjoy the economic growth that had earlier supported the Renaissance in Italy.

Artists of the Northern Renaissance

The northern Renaissance began in the prosperous cities of Flanders, a region that included parts of present-day northern France, Belgium, and the Netherlands. Spain, France, Germany, and England enjoyed their great cultural rebirth 100 years later, in the 1500s.

A "German Leonardo" Albrecht Dürer traveled to Italy in 1494 to study the techniques of the Italian masters. Returning home, he employed these methods in paintings and, especially, in engravings. In this form of art, an artist etches a design on a metal plate with acid. The artist then uses the plate to make prints. Many of Dürer's engravings portray the religious upheaval of his age.

Through his art as well as through essays, Dürer helped to spread Italian Renaissance ideas in his homeland. Because of his wide-ranging interests, which extended far beyond art, he is sometimes called the "German Leonardo."

Flemish Painters Among the many artists of Flanders in the 1400s, Jan and Hubert van Eyck (van ĪK) stand out. Their portrayals of townspeople as well as religious scenes abound in rich, realistic details. The van Eycks also developed oil paint. Northern artists used this new medium to produce strong colors and a hard surface that could survive the centuries.

In the 1500s, Pieter Bruegel (PEE tuhr BROY guhl) used vibrant colors to portray lively scenes of peasant life. Bruegel's work influenced later Flemish artists, who painted scenes of daily life rather than religious or classical themes.

In the 1600s, Peter Paul Rubens blended the realistic tradition of Flemish painters like Bruegel with the classical themes and artistic freedom of the Italian Renaissance. Many of his enormous paintings portray pagan figures from the classical past.

Resource Directory

Teaching Resources

Creative Teaching Activities Creative Teaching Activities booklet, p. 64
Guided Reading and Review Unit 4 booklet, p. 4

Technology

World History Color Transparencies *Music and Dance in the Renaissance,* p. C–43; *Peasant Wedding,* p. D–63; *The Moneylender and His Wife,* p. D–65
Listening to Literature World Masterpieces audiotapes Poems by Pierre Ronsard, side 6, running time 2:25 min.

Northern Humanists

Like Italian humanists, northern European humanist scholars stressed education and classical learning. At the same time, they emphasized religious themes. They believed that the revival of ancient learning should be used to bring about religious and moral reform.

Erasmus The great Dutch priest and humanist Desiderius Erasmus used his knowledge of classical languages to produce a new Greek edition of the New Testament. He also called for a translation of the Bible into the vernacular, or everyday language of ordinary people. He scorned "those who are unwilling that Holy Scripture, translated into the vernacular, be read by the uneducated . . . as if the strength of the Christian religion consisted in the ignorance of it."

To Erasmus, an individual's chief duties were to be open-minded and of good will toward others. As a priest, he was disturbed by corruption in the Church and called for reform. In *The Praise of Folly*, Erasmus uses humor to expose the ignorant and immoral behavior of many people of his day, including the clergy.

More Erasmus's friend, the English humanist Thomas More, also pressed for social reform. In *Utopia*, More describes an ideal society in which men and women live in peace and harmony. No one is idle, all are educated, and justice is used to end crime rather than to eliminate the criminal. Today, the word *utopian* has come to describe any ideal society.

Writers for a New Audience

Scholars like More and Erasmus wrote mostly in Latin. In northern towns and cities, the growing middle class demanded new works in the vernacular. This audience particularly enjoyed dramatic tales and earthy comedies.

Rabelais The French humanist François Rabelais had a varied career as a monk, physician, Greek scholar, and author. In *Gargantua and Pantagruel*, he chronicles the adventures of two gentle giants. On the surface, the novel is

Dürer, the "German Leonardo"
Albrecht Dürer, shown in a self-portrait (below right), helped bring the genius of the Italian Renaissance to northern Europe. Many of his finest works were engravings, such as the portrait of a peasant couple (below left).
Theme: Arts and Literature How do these works reflect the Renaissance interest in the individual?

Background
Connections to Art

Oil Paint Before artists used oil paint, their chief medium was tempera, consisting of ground pigments and egg yolk. According to the art historian H. W. Janson, "It [tempera] produced a thin, tough, quick-drying coat . . . suited to the medieval taste for high-keyed, flat color surfaces. However, in tempera the different tones . . . cannot be smoothly blended, and the continuous progression of values necessary for three-dimensional effects was difficult to achieve; also, the darks tended to look muddy."

Oil paint has a sticky, adhesive quality and dries much more slowly than tempera. It can be applied thinly or thickly and can produce a continuous scale of tones that blend together to create a more three-dimensional effect. Janson believes that from a technical viewpoint, the Flemish Renaissance painters "deserve to be called the 'fathers of modern painting,' for oil has been the painter's basic medium ever since."

Background
Historical Evidence

Religion in Utopia The following excerpt is taken from More's *Utopia*. You may wish to use it as the basis for a discussion on freedom of religion.
"At the first constitution of their government, Utopus . . . made a law that every man might be of what religion he pleased, and might endeavor to draw others to it by the force of argument, and by amicable and modest ways, but without bitterness against those of other opinions."

Block Scheduling Support

Have students form small groups to write a brief essay about this section. They should use the Main Idea listed at the beginning of the section for their thesis statement and turn the three questions under Reading Focus into statements that can serve as topic sentences for body paragraphs. Each student can be responsible for writing the first draft of one of the body paragraphs. All students in the group should contribute to the revision process.

Caption Answer

Both works are realistic portraits of actual people, rather than ideal types. In particular, the peasants are drawn with great attention to individual details.

Humanities Link

Bell Ringer

Bell Ringer Read the following quote aloud to students and ask them to identify it: "O Romeo, Romeo! wherefore art thou Romeo?" *(Romeo and Juliet, II, ii, I. 33)* Most students will recognize the line immediately; many will identify the line as part of the balcony scene. Shakespeare's words are among the best known in the world.

Background
Connections to Art

The Globe Theater The South Bank of the Thames River in London is home again to the Globe Theater. First built in 1598–1599, the theater presented many of Shakespeare's plays. The Globe burned in 1613 and was rebuilt, but it was closed in 1642 by the Puritans and torn down in 1644. Nearly 400 years later, the theater was again rebuilt, near its original site. The new Globe reproduces the original, including building materials used in Elizabethan times.

Activity
Cooperative Learning

In preparation for the portfolio activity, have students form small groups and read Act I, scene 7 of *Macbeth,* where Macbeth and Lady Macbeth hatch their plan to kill the king. Have students choose readers. As the remaining students listen to the performance, have them list and describe the emotions portrayed by the actors. Then, have students discuss how these emotions still influence human behavior today.

Portfolio Assessment Rubrics

Share rubrics with students before they perform their passages.

Attempted Students' performances show insufficient preparation and understanding of the passage.

Minimal Students' performances show some preparation and understanding of the passage.

Adequate Students' performances show preparation and a good understanding of the passage.

Exemplary Students' performances show a good understanding of the passage and are especially entertaining or moving.

Shakespeare's World of Drama

"He was not of an age, but for all time," said one of Shakespeare's contemporaries of him. A later poet said, "He was the man who of all modern, and perhaps ancient poets, had the largest and most comprehensive soul." Today, no plays are performed more frequently around the world than those of William Shakespeare.

In *A Midsummer Night's Dream,* a love potion causes confusion among two young couples and makes Titania, the queen of the fairies, fall in love with a man who has the head of a donkey. One character comments:

"Alas, poor Yorick! I knew him, Horatio, a fellow of infinite jest."

Prince Hamlet mourns his father's deceased court jester.

"What fools these mortals be"

"All the world's a stage, / And all the men and women merely players:/ They have their exits and their entrances;/ And one man in his time plays many parts."

—William Shakespeare, *As You Like It*

Portfolio Assessment

INTERNET Use the Internet or library resources to find out more about the dramas of William Shakespeare. Form small groups, and have each group choose a different play. Then, pick out a passage from the play, cast and rehearse it, and perform it for the rest of the class.

Resource Directory

Teaching Resources

Humanities Link Chapter Extension Activities booklet, p. 36
Prentice Hall World History Literature Library *A Midsummer Night's Dream*
Section Quiz Unit 4 booklet, p. 5

Technology

Interactive Student Tutorial CD-ROM Ch. 14
Computer Test Bank Ch. 14

a comic tale of travel and war. But Rabelais uses his characters to offer opinions on religion, education, and other serious subjects.

Shakespeare The towering figure of Renaissance literature was the English poet and playwright William Shakespeare. Between 1590 and 1613, he wrote 37 plays that are still performed around the world.

Shakespeare's comedies, such as *Twelfth Night,* laugh at the follies of young people in love. His history plays, such as *Richard III,* depict the power struggles of English kings. His tragedies show people crushed by powerful forces or their own weaknesses. In *Romeo and Juliet,* two teenagers fall victim to an old family feud.

Shakespeare's love of words vastly enriched the English language. More than 1,700 words appeared for the first time in his works, including *bedroom, lonely, generous, gloomy, heartsick, hurry,* and *sneak.*

Cervantes The Renaissance in Spain in the early 1600s also led to the production of great works. Best known is *Don Quixote* (DAHN kee HOH tay), by Miguel de Cervantes (suhr VAN teez), an entertaining tale that mocks romantic notions of medieval chivalry. The novel follows the adventures of Don Quixote, a foolish but idealistic knight, and Sancho Panza, his faithful servant. (You will read more about *Don Quixote* in a later chapter.)

The Printing Revolution

In 1456, Johann Gutenberg of Mainz, Germany, printed the first complete edition of the Bible using the first printing press and printing inks in the West. Within twenty years, the development of movable type made book production even easier. A printing revolution had begun that would transform Europe. By 1500, more than 20 million volumes had been printed.

Gutenberg and his successors built on earlier advances. Methods of making paper had reached Europe from China about 1300. The Chinese and Koreans had been using movable metal type for centuries, although Europeans may have developed their technology independently.

The printing revolution brought immense changes. Printed books were cheaper and easier to produce than hand-copied works. With books more readily available, more people learned to read. Readers gained access to a broad range of knowledge, from medicine and law to astrology and mining. Printed books exposed educated Europeans to new ideas, greatly expanding their horizons. As you will read, the new presses would contribute to the religious turmoil that engulfed Europe in the 1500s.

SECTION 2 Assessment

Recall
1. (a) Albrecht Dürer, p. 342 (b) Jan van Eyck, p. 342 (c) François Rabelais, p. 343 (d) William Shakespeare, p. 345 (e) Miguel de Cervantes, p. 345 (f) Johann Gutenberg, p. 345 2. (a) engraving, p. 342 (b) vernacular, p. 343 (c) utopian, p. 343

Comprehension
3. He traveled to Italy in 1494, studied the Italian masters, and used their methods in his work. 4. Erasmus called for reforms in the Church. He opposed ignorance and immorality while calling for open-mindedness and good will. More described an ideal society based on peace, harmony, communal living, hard work, education, and justice. 5. Possible answer: Books became more available, more people became literate, and more people were exposed to new ideas.

Critical Thinking and Writing
6. Possible answer: Before this time, people lacked wealth and leisure time for learning and the arts. 7. Possible answers: Shakespeare's plays are still read and performed; lines from his works are still quoted; many of his plays have been made into movies.

SECTION 2 Assessment

Recall
1. **Identify:** (a) Albrecht Dürer, (b) Jan van Eyck, (c) François Rabelais, (d) William Shakespeare, (e) Miguel de Cervantes, (f) Johann Gutenberg.
2. **Define:** (a) engraving, (b) vernacular, (c) utopian.

Comprehension
3. How did Dürer help bring the Renaissance to northern Europe?
4. What themes did Erasmus and More raise in their writings?

5. What were three effects of the printing revolution?

Critical Thinking and Writing
6. **Recognizing Causes and Effects** Why do you think the cultural flowering of the northern Renaissance did not begin until after economic growth had taken place?
7. **Linking Past and Present** What are some ways in which Shakespeare's plays and sonnets still "live" today?

Activity

Creating Compound Words Shakespeare invented new words by combining two existing words. Examples of these compound words are *eyesore, heartsick, hot-blooded, leapfrog,* and *tongue-tied.* Look up definitions of these words. Then, create five compound words of your own.

Human Drama Activity

Analyzing Literature Explain that in Miguel de Cervantes's comic novel *Don Quixote* Sancho Panza, Quixote's servant, provides a foil or contrast to his master. Panza is grounded in reality and common sense; Quixote imagines himself to be a brave, chivalrous knight in a world of romance. Have students read the opening paragraph of Book I, Chapter 8, in which Quixote mistakes windmills for giants and decides he must fight them. Then, discuss how the passage shows Quixote's romanticism.

 Test Preparation

Have students read the section titled "The Printing Revolution" on this page, and then answer the question below.

Which of the following is a cause of the printing revolution?

A More people gained access to knowledge.

B The invention contributed to religious turmoil.

C Books were cheaper and easier to produce.

D Gutenberg built upon earlier advances.

Bell Ringer Write the words *Protestant Reformation* on the chalkboard, and ask students to identify their root words. After students recognize the words *protest* and *reform,* ask them to predict how these words might have applied to the Catholic Church in the 1500s.

LESSON PLAN

1. Focus In the late Middle Ages, reformers criticized Church abuses and desired greater simplicity and piety. Martin Luther opposed Church authority by attacking the Church practice of selling indulgences. The ideas of Martin Luther and John Calvin led people to separate from the Roman Catholic Church and form new Protestant churches.

2. Instruct On the chalkboard, create a chart to compare the teachings of the Roman Catholic Church with those of the new Protestant churches. Set up three columns labeled Roman Catholic, Lutheran, and Calvinist. Set up the rows with such labels as Sources of Doctrine, Beliefs About Salvation, Church Hierarchy, Religious Practices, and the like. Assign students to work together in groups to complete the chart. After they have finished, use the students' charts as the basis for a class discussion.

3. Assess Have students put away their charts. Then, describe a religious idea or practice that the students charted and discussed. Ask for volunteers to identify the religion or religions to which the belief or practice applies.

4. Reteach If students' **Assess** activity does not reflect adequate understanding of the lesson, you might assign the *Guide to the Essentials* or the *Interactive Student Tutorial CD-ROM* for this section.

The Protestant Reformation

Reading Focus

■ How did abuses in the Church spark widespread criticism?

■ How did Martin Luther challenge Catholic authority and teachings?

■ What role did John Calvin play in the Reformation?

Vocabulary

indulgence

recant

predestination

theocracy

Taking Notes

On a sheet of paper draw a flowchart like the one shown here. As you read this section, add important events and ideas that contributed to the Protestant Reformation.

Church involved in worldly affairs
↓
Tetzel sells indulgences to raise money for new cathedral
↓
↓

Main Idea The ideas of Martin Luther and John Calvin led people to separate from the Roman Catholic Church and form new Protestant churches.

Setting the Scene During the Renaissance, the Church increasingly came under fire. Christians at all levels of society accused the clergy of corruption and worldliness. One peasant even compared the clergy to "wicked wolves." He protested, "Instead of saving the souls of the dead and sending them to Heaven, they gorge themselves at banquets after funerals."

During the Middle Ages, the Church had renewed itself from within. In the 1500s, though, new calls for reform unleashed forces that would shatter Christian unity. This movement is known as the Protestant Reformation.

Abuses in the Church

Beginning in the late Middle Ages, the Church had become increasingly caught up in worldly affairs. Popes competed with Italian princes for political power. They fought long wars to protect the Papal States against invasions by secular rulers. They intrigued against powerful monarchs who tried to seize control of the Church within their lands.

Like other Renaissance rulers, popes maintained a lavish lifestyle. Popes were also patrons of the arts. They hired painters and sculptors to beautify churches.

To finance such projects, the Church increased fees for services such as marriages and baptisms. Some clergy also promoted the sale of indulgences. According to Church teaching, an indulgence was a lessening of the time a soul would have to spend in purgatory, a place where souls too impure to enter heaven atoned for sins committed during their lifetimes. In the Middle Ages, the Church had granted indulgences only for good deeds, such as going on a crusade. By the late 1400s, however, indulgences could also be obtained in exchange for money gifts to the Church.

Many Christians protested such practices, especially in northern Europe. Christian humanists such as Erasmus urged a return to the simple ways of the early Christian Church. They stressed Bible study and rejected what they saw as the worldliness of the Church.

Luther's Protest

In 1517, protests against Church abuses erupted into a full-scale revolt. The man who triggered the revolt was a German monk and professor of theology named Martin Luther.

Resource Directory

Teaching Resources

Creative Teaching Activities Creative Teaching Activities booklet, p. 65

Guided Reading and Review Unit 4 booklet, p. 6

Technology

World History Visions, Voices, Views Daily Life CloseUp, *A Student in Renaissance Europe,* videodisc side 2 or videotape 4, running time 3:00 min.

Side 2: Fr. 31888-37600

As a young man, Luther prayed and fasted and tried to lead a holy life. Still, he believed he was doomed to eternal damnation. He also grew disillusioned with what he saw as Church corruption and worldliness. At last, an incident in the town of Wittenberg prompted him to take action.

The 95 Theses In 1517, a priest named Johann Tetzel set up a pulpit on the outskirts of Wittenberg. He offered indulgences to any Christian who contributed money for the rebuilding of the Cathedral of St. Peter in Rome. Tetzel claimed that purchase of these indulgences would assure entry into heaven not only for the purchasers but for their dead relatives as well. "Don't you hear the voices of your dead parents and other relatives crying out?" he demanded.

To Luther, Tetzel's actions were the final outrage. He drew up 95 theses, or arguments, against indulgences. Among other things, he argued that indulgences had no basis in the Bible, that the pope had no authority to release souls from purgatory, and that Christians could be saved only through faith. In accordance with the custom of the time, he posted his list on the door of Wittenberg's All Saints Church.

Luther Versus the Church Almost overnight, copies of Luther's 95 Theses were printed and distributed across Europe, where they stirred furious debate. The Church called on Luther to recant, or give up his views. Luther refused. Instead, he developed even more radical new doctrines. Before long, he was urging Christians to reject the authority of Rome. Because the Church would not reform itself, he wrote, it must be reformed by secular authorities.

In 1521, the pope excommunicated Luther. Later that year, the new Holy Roman emperor, Charles V, summoned Luther to the diet, or assembly of German princes, at Worms. Luther went, expecting to defend his writings. Instead, the emperor simply ordered him to give them up. Luther again refused to recant:

"Unless I am convicted by Scripture and plain reason—I do not accept the authority of popes and councils, for they have contradicted each other—I am captive to the Word of God. I cannot and will not recant anything, for to go against conscience is neither right nor safe."
—Martin Luther, Speech Before the Diet of Worms

Charles declared Luther an outlaw, making it a crime for anyone in the empire to give him food or shelter. Still, Luther had many powerful supporters. One prince hid him at a castle in Wartburg. Luther remained in hiding for nearly a year. Throughout Germany, in the meantime, thousands hailed him as a hero. They accepted his teachings and, following his lead, renounced the authority of the pope.

Selling Indulgences
This 1517 cartoon shows Johann Tetzel selling indulgences to the people of Wittenberg. A jingle in the upper left corner said, "As soon as the coin in the coffer rings, a soul from purgatory springs."

Theme: Religions and Value Systems Do you think the artist who drew this picture approved of Tetzel's actions? Why or why not?

Background
Daily Life

The Relics Trade In addition to purchasing indulgences, many Christians also acquired relics of Christ and the saints. In some regions, the relics trade became a booming business. One avid collector was Frederick the Wise of Saxony, who reportedly accumulated thousands of relics. By his own account, his prized possessions included fragments of Moses' burning bush, pieces of the holy cradle, splinters from the holy cross, and a swatch of fabric from Christ's swaddling clothes.

Reading Strategy
Finding Evidence

Read aloud to students the following statement from the second paragraph of Section 3. "In the 1500s, . . . new calls for reform unleashed forces that would shatter Christian unity." Have students look for and note on a piece of paper the specific disagreements among Christians that led to the Protestant Reformation. *(More Advanced Readers)*

Block Scheduling Support

Divide the class into groups and have each group prepare a newspaper that reports on events of 1517. Tell students that the focus of the newspaper should be Luther's attack on the Church. Newspapers should include news stories, interviews, and profiles of the personalities involved. There might also be editorials, letters to the editor, and cartoons about the controversy. Encourage students to divide the work so that some do research, others write, and others provide artwork.

Test Preparation

Have students read the section titled "The 95 Theses" on this page, and then answer the question below.

Which of the following was *not* a reason that Luther objected to indulgences?

A Indulgences had no biblical basis.

B Only a few people could afford them.

C The pope lacked authority to release souls from purgatory.

D Christians are saved through faith.

Caption Answer

Possible answer: No. The figure of Tetzel is a monk, but is drawn without any indications of holiness or spirituality. The emphasis is on money and greed.

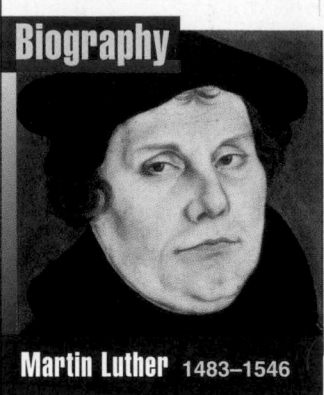
Luther's Teachings At the heart of Luther's teachings were several beliefs. First, he rejected the Church doctrine that good deeds were necessary for salvation. Instead, Luther argued that salvation was achieved through faith alone.

Second, Luther upheld the Bible as the sole source of religious truth. He denied other authorities, such as Church councils or the pope.

Third, Luther rejected the idea that priests and the Church hierarchy had special powers. Instead, he talked of a "priesthood of all believers." All Christians, he said, had equal access to God through faith and the Bible. Luther translated the Bible into the German vernacular so that ordinary people could study it by themselves. Every town, he said, should have a school so that girls and boys could learn to read the Bible.

Luther wanted to change other church practices. He rejected five of the seven sacraments because the Bible did not mention them. He banned indulgences, confession, pilgrimages, and prayers to saints. He simplified the elaborate ritual of the mass and instead emphasized the sermon. And he permitted the clergy to marry. These and other changes were adopted by the Lutheran churches that were set up by Luther's followers.

Spread of Lutheran Ideas

Luther's ideas found a fertile field in northern Germany and Scandinavia. While the new printing presses spread Luther's writings, fiery preachers denounced Church abuses. By 1530, the Lutherans were using a new name, Protestant, for those who "protested" papal authority.

Widespread Support Why did Lutheranism win widespread support? Many clergy saw Luther's reforms as the answer to Church corruption. A number of German princes, however, embraced Lutheran beliefs for more selfish reasons. Some saw Lutheranism as a way to throw off the rule of both the Church and the Holy Roman emperor. Others welcomed a chance to seize Church property in their territory. Still other Germans supported Luther because of feelings of national loyalty. They were tired of German money going to support churches and clergy in Italy.

The Peasants' Revolt Many peasants also took up Luther's banner. They hoped to gain his support for social and economic change.

In 1524, a Peasants' Revolt erupted across Germany. The rebels called for an end to serfdom and demanded other changes in their harsh lives. Luther, however, strongly favored social order and respect for political authority. As the Peasants' Revolt grew more violent, Luther denounced it. With his support, nobles suppressed the rebellion, killing tens of thousands of people and leaving thousands more homeless.

The Peace of Augsburg During the 1530s and 1540s, Holy Roman emperor Charles V tried to force Lutheran princes back into the Catholic Church, but with little success. Finally, after a number of brief wars, Charles and the princes reached a settlement. The Peace of Augsburg, signed in 1555, allowed each prince to decide which religion—Catholic or Lutheran—would be followed in his lands. Most northern German states chose Lutheranism. The south remained largely Catholic.

John Calvin

Two other reformers, Ulrich Zwingli and John Calvin, presented further challenges to the Catholic Church. Zwingli, a priest and an admirer of Erasmus, lived in the Swiss city of Zurich. Like Luther, he rejected elaborate church rituals and stressed the importance of the Bible. John Calvin had a logical, razor-sharp mind. His ideas had a profound effect on the direction of the Reformation.

Comparing Viewpoints

What Is the Goal of Education?

Both the Renaissance and the Reformation stressed the importance of education. What is your goal in pursuing an education? Think about the goals of modern-day schools as you compare the following viewpoints.

China 500 B.C.

Chinese philosopher Confucius explained how learning was essential for both the individual and the community:

66 Extension of knowledge comes from the investigation of things. When things are investigated, knowledge is extended. When knowledge is extended, the will becomes sincere. When the will is sincere, the heart can be set right. When the heart is right, the personal life can be cultivated. When the personal life is cultivated, the community can be regulated. When the community is regulated, the government can be made orderly. And when the government is orderly, there will be peace in the world. 99

Germany 1524

Protestant reformer Martin Luther called for German communities to set up and pay for Christian schools:

66 The world has need of educated men and women to the end that men may govern the country properly and women may properly bring up their children, care for their domestics, and direct the affairs of the household.... The welfare of the state depends on the intelligence and virtue of its citizens. 99

United States 1990s

This poster was designed for school guidance counselors.

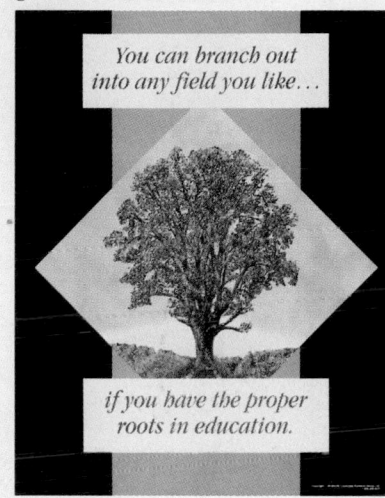

You can branch out into any field you like...

if you have the proper roots in education.

Cuba 1883

José Martí, a poet and political leader, turned away from classical ideas about what should be taught:

66 The schools teach classes in ancient geography, rules of rhetoric, and similar things of long ago, but in their place there should be courses in health; advice on hygiene; practical counseling; clear and simple studies of the human body, its parts, functions, ways of adjusting one to the other, economizing one's strength, and directing it well so that there will be no reason to restore it later. 99

Skills Assessment

1. What goal of education is stressed by both Confucius and Luther?
   A gaining knowledge for its own sake
   B making a good living
   C cultivating the personal life
   D contributing to the community

2. Who would be most likely to favor classes in physical education?
   E Confucius
   F Luther
   G Martí
   H the designer of the poster

3. **Critical Thinking Making Decisions** Identify a future career for yourself. Which educational theory would be most useful in helping you achieve this goal? Why? Explain why more than one type of education would be helpful.

Skills Tip

It is important to recognize that a writer may express his or her point of view as an absolute truth to convince others of its validity.

Recall

1. (a) Protestant Reformation, p. 346
(b) Martin Luther, p. 346 (c) Peace of Augsburg, p. 348 (d) John Calvin, p. 348 (e) Huguenot, p. 350 (f) John Knox, p. 350
2. (a) indulgence, p. 346 (b) recant, p. 347 (c) predestination, p. 350 (d) theocracy, p. 350

Comprehension

3. Many felt that the Church had become too worldly. They opposed corruption and desired a return to the simpler ways of the early Church. 4. Possible answers: (a) In opposition to Catholic Church teachings, Luther taught that salvation came through faith alone, the Bible was the sole source of religious truth, and priests and Church leaders had no special powers. (b) Many saw Lutheranism as the answer to Church corruption. Also, many German princes supported Luther as a way to throw off domination by the Catholic Church and the Holy Roman emperor. 5. Possible answer: Salvation is gained through faith alone. The Bible is the only source of religious truth. Humans are by nature sinful. God predetermines who will gain salvation. A theocracy is the best type of government.

Critical Thinking and Writing

6. Possible answer: It reflected the individualism and critical spirit that characterized humanism. 7. Possible answer: Abuses in the Church had worsened. The printing press allowed Luther's teachings to spread.

Activity Rubrics

Share rubrics with students before they write their obituaries.

Attempted The obituary lacks key events in Luther's life and fails to explain why he will be remembered.

Minimal The obituary has all the key events but lacks a clear explanation as to why he will be remembered.

Adequate The obituary has all the key events and a clear explanation as to why he will be remembered.

Exemplary The obituary has all the key events, a clear explanation as to why he will be remembered, and is extremely well written.

Primary Source

ANSWER Calvin warned against the pursuit of wealth, honor, and power.

Primary Source

Calvin on Greed
John Calvin warns his followers in Geneva and elsewhere against worldly values:

"We have a frenzied desire, an infinite eagerness, to pursue wealth and honor, intrigue for power, accumulate riches, and collect all those frivolities [extras] which seem conducive to luxury and splendor. On the other hand, we have a remarkable dread, a remarkable hatred of poverty, mean birth, and a humble condition, and feel the strongest desire to guard against them. . . . The course which Christian men must follow is this: first, they must not long for, or hope for, or think of any kind of prosperity apart from the blessing of God; on it they must cast themselves, and there safely and confidently recline."

—John Calvin, *On the Christian Life*

Skills Assessment

Primary Source What activities did John Calvin warn against?

Teachings Calvin was born in France and trained as a priest and lawyer. In 1536, Calvin published the *Institutes of the Christian Religion*. In this book, which was read by Protestants everywhere, he set forth his religious beliefs. He also provided advice on how to organize and run a Protestant church.

Like Luther, Calvin believed that salvation was gained through faith alone. He, too, regarded the Bible as the only source of religious truth. But Calvin put forth a number of ideas of his own. He preached predestination, the idea that God had long ago determined who would gain salvation. To Calvinists, the world was divided into two kinds of people—saints and sinners. Calvinists tried to live like saints, believing that only those who were saved could live truly Christian lives.

Calvin's Geneva In 1541, Protestants in the city-state of Geneva in Switzerland asked Calvin to lead their community. In keeping with his teachings, Calvin set up a theocracy, or government run by church leaders.

Calvin's followers in Geneva came to see themselves as a new "chosen people" entrusted by God to build a truly Christian society. Calvinists stressed hard work, discipline, thrift, honesty, and morality. Citizens faced fines or other harsher punishments for offenses such as fighting, swearing, laughing in church, or dancing. Calvin closed theaters and frowned on elaborate dress. To many Protestants, this emphasis on strict morality made Calvinist Geneva seem a model community.

Like Luther, Calvin believed in religious education for girls as well as for boys. Women, he felt, should read the Bible—in private. Calvin also allowed women to sing in church, a practice that many church leaders criticized.

Spread of Calvinism Reformers from all over Europe visited Geneva and then returned home to spread Calvin's ideas. By the late 1500s, Calvinism had taken root in Germany, France, the Netherlands, England, and Scotland. This new challenge to the Roman Catholic Church set off bloody wars of religion across Europe.

In Germany, Calvinists faced opposition not only from Catholics, but from Lutherans as well. In France, wars raged between French Calvinists, called Huguenots, and Catholics. Calvinists in the Netherlands organized the Dutch Reformed Church. To avoid persecution, "field preachers" gave sermons in the countryside, away from the eyes of town authorities.

In Scotland, a Calvinist preacher named John Knox led a religious rebellion. Under Knox, Scottish Protestants overthrew their Catholic queen. They then set up the Scottish Presbyterian Church.

SECTION 3 Assessment

Recall

1. **Identify:** (a) Protestant Reformation, (b) Martin Luther, (c) Peace of Augsburg, (d) John Calvin, (e) Huguenot, (f) John Knox.
2. **Define:** (a) indulgence, (b) recant, (c) predestination, (d) theocracy.

Comprehension

3. Why did many Christians call for Church reform?
4. (a) How did Martin Luther's ideas differ from those expressed by the Catholic Church?

(b) Why did Luther gain wide-spread support?
5. Identify five ideas taught by John Calvin.

Critical Thinking and Writing

6. **Synthesizing Information** How did the Reformation reflect humanist ideas?
7. **Analyzing Information** Why do you think Luther's teachings caused a split in the Catholic Church when earlier reform movements did not?

Activity

Writing an Obituary
Read some obituaries, or death notices, in a current newspaper. Then, using the same style of writing, prepare a brief obituary of Martin Luther. The obituary should list key events in Luther's life and explain why he will be remembered. Try to avoid bias.

350 Chapter 14

Resource Directory

Teaching Resources
Section Quiz Unit 4 booklet, p. 7
Creative Teaching Activities Creative Teaching Activities booklet, p. 66
Guided Reading and Review Unit 4 booklet, p. 8

Technology
Interactive Student Tutorial CD-ROM Ch. 14
Computer Test Bank Ch. 14
World History Color Transparencies *The Tower of London With London Bridge Behind,* p. D–49

Reformation Ideas Spread

Reading Focus

- What ideas did radical reformers support?
- Why did England form a new church?
- How did the Catholic Church reform itself?
- Why did some groups face persecution?

Vocabulary

annul
canonize
compromise
scapegoat
ghetto

Taking Notes

On a sheet of paper draw a Venn diagram like the one shown here. As you read the section, add information from the text.

ENGLISH REFORMATION
- King Henry VIII establishes Church of England

• Widespread persecution

CATHOLIC REFORMATION
- Council of Trent

Main Idea Both the Protestant and Catholic reformations brought sweeping changes to Europe.

Setting the Scene

Henry III, the Catholic king of France, was deeply disturbed by Calvinist reformers in Geneva. "It would have been a good thing," he wrote, "if the city of Geneva were long ago reduced to ashes, because of the evil doctrine which has been sown from that city."

Throughout Europe, Catholic monarchs and the Catholic Church fought back against the Protestant challenge. They also took steps to reform the Church and to restore its spiritual leadership of the Christian world. At the same time, Protestant ideas continued to spread.

Radical Reformers

As the Reformation continued, hundreds of new Protestant sects sprang up. These sects often had ideas that were even more radical than those of Luther and Calvin. A number of groups, for example, rejected infant baptism. Infants, they argued, are too young to understand what it means to accept the Christian faith. Only adults, they felt, should receive the sacrament of baptism. They became known as Anabaptists.

A few Anabaptist sects sought radical social change as well. Some wanted to abolish private property. Others sought to speed up the coming of God's day of judgment by violent means. When radical Anabaptists took over the city of Munster in Germany, even Luther advised his supporters to join Catholics in suppressing the threat to the traditional order.

Most Anabaptists were peaceful. They called for religious toleration and separation of church and state. Despite harsh persecution, these groups influenced Protestant thinking in many countries. Today, the Baptists, Quakers, Mennonites, and Amish all trace their ancestry to the Anabaptists.

The English Reformation

In England, religious leaders such as John Wycliffe had called for Church reform as early as the 1300s. By the 1520s, some English clergy were toying with Protestant ideas. The break with the Catholic Church, however, was the work not of religious leaders but of King Henry VIII. For political reasons, Henry wanted to end papal control over the English church.

Seeking an Annulment At first, Henry VIII stood firmly against the Protestant revolt. The pope even awarded him the title "Defender of the Faith" for a pamphlet that he wrote denouncing Luther.

Henry VIII
Henry VIII wrote love songs, played tennis, and married six times. He was also ruthless to his enemies. He had dozens of people beheaded, including his second and fifth wives.

Theme: Impact of the Individual What impression of Henry do you get from this picture?

Chapter 14 **351**

Block Scheduling Support

Have students complete the Guided Reading and Review worksheet for this section in the Unit 4 booklet, p. 8. Then, assign the map activities *Europe About 1600* in the Historical Outline Map Book, p. 25, in which students identify the European countries where Protestant sects dominated and where the Catholic Church prevailed. Based on the activities, have students evaluate the success of the Protestant Reformation and of the Catholic Reformation.

SECTION 4

Bell Ringer Ask students to find a news article about religious conflict in the world today. Have students share and display their stories, and then point out that conflicting ideas and practices played an important part in the Reformation.

LESSON PLAN

1. Focus By breaking with Rome and forming the Church of England, King Henry VIII gained both political and personal benefits. As part of the Catholic Reformation, Church leaders instituted a program of reforms at the Council of Trent. Both the Protestant and Catholic Reformations brought sweeping changes to Europe.

2. Instruct Have students work in groups to dramatize one of the events or developments described in this section. Each group might choose one of the following topics: Henry VIII's Break With the Catholic Church, the Conflict Between Mary and Elizabeth Tudor, the Council of Trent, the Inquisition, the Life of Ignatius Loyola, or an appropriate topic of their choice. Advise students that they will need to do research, prepare scripts, assign roles, and rehearse their dramas. Remind them to be prepared to answer questions about their presentations.

3. Assess Ask students to draw a political cartoon that illustrates one aspect of the religious conflict that marked the Reformation.

4. Reteach If students' **Assess** activity does not reflect adequate understanding of the lesson, you might assign the *Guide to the Essentials* or the *Interactive Student Tutorial CD-ROM* for this section.

Caption Answer

that he is arrogant, self-confident, and self-willed

Biography

Elizabeth I 1533–1603

"She takes great pleasure in dancing and music," noted an English observer of Queen Elizabeth I. "In her youth she danced very well and composed measures and music and had played them herself." The normally thrifty queen employed some 50 singers, 40 musicians, and several songwriters to stage concerts for her.

Elizabeth also loved to see plays. She especially enjoyed the works of William Shakespeare, whom she helped to promote. The queen provided financial support and prestige for major acting groups, which led to a flowering of English theater.

Elizabeth's popular 45-year reign inspired other writers of the day. Poet Edmund Spenser dedicated *The Faerie Queene* to Elizabeth.

Theme: Impact of the Individual How did Queen Elizabeth help promote English arts?

In 1527, an issue arose that set Henry at odds with the Church. After 18 years of marriage, Henry and his Spanish wife, Catherine of Aragon, had one surviving child, Mary Tudor. Henry felt that England's stability depended on his having a male heir. He wanted to marry Anne Boleyn, hoping that she would bear him a son. Because Catholic law does not permit divorce, he asked the pope to annul, or cancel, his marriage. Popes had annulled royal marriages before. But the current pope refused. He did not want to offend the Holy Roman emperor Charles V, Catherine's nephew.

Break With Rome Henry was furious. Spurred on by his advisers, many of whom leaned toward Protestant teachings, he decided to take over the English church. Acting through Parliament, he had a series of laws passed. They took the English church from the pope's control and placed it under Henry's rule. In 1534, the Act of Supremacy made Henry "the only supreme head on Earth of the Church of England." Many loyal Catholics refused to accept the Act of Supremacy and were executed for treason. Among them was Sir Thomas More, the great English humanist. More was later canonized, or recognized as a saint, by the Catholic Church.

At the same time, Henry appointed Thomas Cranmer archbishop. Cranmer annulled the king's marriage. Henry then wed Anne Boleyn, who bore him a second daughter, Elizabeth. In the years ahead, Henry married four more times but had only one son, Edward.

The Church of England Between 1536 and 1540, royal officials investigated English convents and monasteries. Claiming that they were centers of immorality, Henry ordered them closed. He then confiscated, or seized, their lands and wealth. Henry shrewdly granted some of these lands to nobles and other high-ranking citizens. He thus secured their support for the Anglican Church, as the new Church of England was called.

Despite these actions, Henry was not a religious radical. He rejected most Protestant doctrines. Aside from breaking away from Rome and allowing use of the English Bible, he kept most Catholic forms of worship.

Religious Turmoil When Henry died in 1547, his 10-year-old son, Edward VI, inherited the throne. The young king's advisers were devout Protestants. Under Edward, Parliament passed new laws that brought the Protestant reforms to England. Thomas Cranmer drew up the *Book of Common Prayer.* It imposed a moderate form of Protestant service, while keeping many Catholic doctrines. Even so, the changes sparked uprisings that were harshly suppressed.

When Edward died in his teens, his half-sister, Mary Tudor, became queen. She was determined to return England to the Catholic faith. Under Queen Mary, hundreds of English Protestants were burned at the stake.

The Elizabethan Settlement On Mary's death in 1558, the throne passed to Elizabeth. For years, Elizabeth had survived court intrigues, including the religious swings under Edward and Mary. As queen, Elizabeth had to determine the future of the Church of England. Moving cautiously at first, she slowly enforced a series of reforms that later were called the Elizabethan settlement.

The queen's policies were a compromise, or acceptable middle ground, between Protestant and Catholic practices. The Church of England preserved much Catholic ceremony and ritual. It kept the hierarchy of bishops and archbishops, but the queen reaffirmed that the monarch was the head of the Anglican Church. At the same time, Elizabeth restored a version of the *Book of Common Prayer,* accepted moderate Protestant doctrine, and allowed English to replace Latin in church services.

During a long reign, Elizabeth used all her skills to restore unity to England. Even while keeping many Catholic traditions, she made England a firmly Protestant nation. After her death, England faced new religious

Major European Religions About 1600

- Mainly Roman Catholic
- Mainly Anglican
- Mainly Lutheran
- Areas of Calvinist minorities
- Areas of Muslim minorities
- Mainly Orthodox Christian
- Boundary of Holy Roman Empire

Note: Not all minority religious groups are shown. Jews were dispersed throughout Europe.

Azimuthal Equal Area Projection
0   250   500 Miles
0   250   500 Kilometers

storms. But it escaped the endless religious wars that tore apart France and many other European states during the 1500s.

The Catholic Reformation

As the Protestant Reformation swept across northern Europe, a vigorous reform movement took hold within the Catholic Church. The leader of this movement, known as the Catholic Reformation, was Pope Paul III. During the 1530s and 1540s, he set out to revive the moral authority of the Church and roll back the Protestant tide. To end corruption within the papacy itself, he appointed reformers to key posts. They and their successors guided the Catholic Reformation for the rest of the century.

Council of Trent To establish the direction that reform should take, the pope called the Council of Trent in 1545. It met off and on for almost 20 years. The council reaffirmed traditional Catholic views, which Protestants had challenged. Salvation comes through faith and good works, it declared. The Bible, while a major source of religious truth, is not the only source.

The council also took steps to end abuses in the Church. It provided stiff penalties for worldliness and corruption among the clergy. It also established schools to create a better-educated clergy who could challenge Protestant teachings.

The Inquisition To deal with the Protestant threat more directly, Pope Paul strengthened the Inquisition. As you have read, the Inquisition was a Church court set up during the Middle Ages. The Inquisition used secret testimony, torture, and execution to root out heresy. It also prepared the Index of Forbidden Books, a list of works considered too immoral or irreligious for Catholics to read. It included books by Luther and Calvin.

Ignatius of Loyola In 1540, the pope recognized a new religious order, the Society of Jesus, or Jesuits. Founded by Ignatius of Loyola, the Jesuit order was determined to combat heresy and spread the Catholic faith.

Skills Assessment

Geography As a result of the Reformation, Europe was largely divided into Catholic and Protestant lands.

1. **Location** On the map, locate (a) England, (b) Scotland, (c) Wittenberg, (d) Worms, (e) Geneva.
2. **Region** (a) What was the majority religion in France? (b) Name one country that was mainly Lutheran.
3. **Critical Thinking Predicting Consequences** Based on this map, identify two areas where you think religious conflicts would be least likely to break out. Explain.

Background Connections to Today

The Index Books that the Church placed on its Index of Forbidden Books were of two sorts—those considered harmful to morals and those believed to undermine Church doctrine. The first sort included books by Rabelais, who used coarse language about sexual conduct and bodily functions.

Even prominent Catholic thinkers might have their books banned if they strayed from accepted Church teachings. Thus, books by Erasmus were placed on the Index because his reformist tendencies sometimes challenged official Church doctrine. The Church stopped keeping an Index in 1966, but it still declares certain books unsuitable for Catholics to read.

Background Biography

Two Catholic Leaders Two major figures of the Catholic Reformation were the Italian cardinal Carlo Borromeo and the French bishop Francis de Sales. Borromeo helped organize the Council of Trent and was in charge of carrying out its decrees. He issued the Roman Catechism, a handbook on Church teachings that was used by parish priests for hundreds of years. De Sales taught that busy people could lead holy lives without withdrawing from the world. He founded the Visitation of Holy Mary, an order of nuns devoted largely to teaching. Today, the Visitation Nuns run schools in many nations, including the United States.

Background
Historical Evidence

Evidence of Witchcraft As the witchcraft mania spread, popular superstitions came to be treated as legal truths. For example, until the late 1600s, most magistrates accepted that there were physical tests for witchcraft. If the body of the accused exhibited unusual marks, the person was considered to be a witch. If the accused had body parts that were insensitive to the prick of a needle, the person was judged to be a witch. Storms, diseases, and sexual impotence were other indications of sorcery at work.

The 1664 trial of an accused witch in England is most revealing. The accused had cursed and threatened one of his neighbors. After this, the neighbor testified that his pig, having just birthed piglets, jumped, ran about, and fell down dead. Furthermore, the neighbor was "vexed with a number of lice of extraordinary bigness." Sir Matthew Hale, the Lord Chief Justice, declared the accused guilty and condemned him to hang.

Background
Historical Evidence

Responding to Persecution In 1648, the members of one Jewish community in Ukraine accepted torture and death rather than renounce their faith. A Jewish chronicler wrote:

> "The head of the yeshiva [religious school] was the first to offer up his body as a burnt-offering. Young and old, boys and girls saw the tortures, sufferings, and wounds of our teacher, who did not cease exhorting them to accept martyrdom in the name of [God]. As one man they all exclaimed, '. . . Let us offer up our souls to God and our bodies to the wild waves, to our enemies. . . .' When our enemies heard these words, they started a horrible butchery . . . . Husbands and wives and children fell in heaps."

Global Connections

Witch Hunt in Salem
Witch hunts were not just a European phenomenon. They also took place across the Atlantic in the English colonies. In 1692, a witch hunt broke out in the town of Salem Village, Massachusetts. The panic began when two girls suffered strange fits. When coaxed to explain their behavior, the girls accused neighbors of casting spells on them. Soon, accusations spread like wildfire throughout the town. Before the witch hunt ended the following year, at least 200 people had been named, and 20 people had been executed as witches.

Theme: Political and Social Systems How did witch hunts disrupt communities during the Renaissance?

Ignatius was a Spanish knight raised in the crusading tradition. After his leg was shattered in battle, he found comfort reading about saints who had overcome mental and physical torture. Vowing to become a "soldier of God," Ignatius drew up a strict program for the Jesuits. It included spiritual and moral discipline, rigorous religious training, and absolute obedience to the Church. Led by Ignatius, the Jesuits embarked on a crusade to defend and spread the Catholic faith throughout the world.

To further the Catholic cause, Jesuits became advisers to Catholic rulers, helping them combat heresy in their lands. They set up schools that taught humanist and Catholic beliefs and enforced discipline and obedience. Daring Jesuits slipped into Protestant lands in disguise to minister to the spiritual needs of Catholics. Jesuit missionaries spread their Catholic faith to distant lands, including Asia, Africa, and the Americas.

Teresa of Avila As the Catholic Reformation spread, many Catholics experienced renewed feelings of intense faith. Teresa of Avila symbolized this renewal. Born into a wealthy Spanish family, Teresa entered a convent in her youth. Finding convent routine not strict enough, she set up her own order of nuns. They lived in isolation, eating and sleeping very little and dedicating themselves to prayer and meditation.

Impressed by her spiritual life, her superiors in the Church asked Teresa to reorganize and reform convents and monasteries throughout Spain. Teresa was widely honored for her work, and after her death the Church canonized her. Her mystical writings rank among the most important Christian texts of her time.

Results Did the Catholic Reformation succeed? By 1600, Rome was a far more devout city than it had been 100 years earlier. Across Catholic Europe, piety and charity flourished. The reforms did slow the Protestant tide and even returned some areas to the Catholic Church. Still, Europe remained divided into a Catholic south and a Protestant north.

Widespread Persecution

During this period of heightened religious passion, persecution was widespread. Both Catholics and Protestants fostered intolerance. Catholic mobs attacked and killed Protestants. Protestants killed Catholic priests and wrecked Catholic churches. Both Catholics and Protestants persecuted radical sects like the Anabaptists.

Witch Hunts Almost certainly, the religious fervor of the times contributed to a wave of witch hunting. Those accused of being witches, or agents of the devil, were usually women, although some men faced similar attacks. Between 1450 and 1750, tens of thousands of women and men died as victims of witch hunts.

Scholars have offered various reasons for this persecution. At the time, most people believed in magic and spirits. They saw a close link between magic and heresy. In addition, during times of trouble, people often look for scapegoats on whom they can blame their problems. People accused of witchcraft were often social outcasts—beggars, poor widows, midwives blamed for infant deaths, or herbalists whose potions were seen as gifts from the devil.

Most victims of the witch hunts died in the German states, Switzerland, and France, all centers of religious conflict. When the wars of religion came to an end, the persecution of witches also declined.

Jews and the Reformation The Reformation brought hard times to Europe's Jews. For many Jews in Italy, the early Renaissance had been a time of relative prosperity. Unlike Spain, which had expelled its Jews in 1492, Italy allowed Jews to remain. Some Jews followed the traditional trades they had

Global Connections

ANSWER Witch hunts fostered suspicion among neighbors and led to persecution and deaths of innocent people.

Resource Directory

Teaching Resources
Section Quiz Unit 4 booklet, p. 9
Technology
Interactive Student Tutorial CD-ROM Ch. 14
Computer Test Bank Ch. 14

been restricted to in medieval times. They were goldsmiths, artists, traders, and moneylenders. Others expanded into medicine, law, government, and business. Still, pressure remained strong on Jews to convert. By 1516, Venice ordered Jews to live in a separate quarter of the city, which became known as a **ghetto**. Other Italian cities also forced Jews into walled ghettos.

During the Reformation, restrictions on Jews increased. At first, Luther hoped that Jews would be converted to his teachings. However, when they did not convert, he called for them to be expelled from Christian lands and for their synagogues and books to be burned. In time, some German princes did expel Jews. Others confined Jews to ghettos, requiring them to wear a yellow badge if they traveled outside.

In the 1550s, Pope Paul IV placed added restrictions on Jews. Even Emperor Charles V, who supported toleration of Jews in the Holy Roman Empire, banned them from Spanish colonies in the Americas. After 1550, many Jews migrated to Poland-Lithuania and to parts of the Ottoman empire, where they were permitted to prosper. Dutch Calvinists allowed Jewish families who were driven out of Portugal and Spain to settle in the Netherlands.

Looking Ahead

The upheavals of the Catholic and Protestant reformations sparked wars of religion in Europe until the mid-1600s. At that time, issues of religion began to give way to issues of national power. As you will read, Catholic and Protestant rulers often made decisions based on political interests rather than for purely religious reasons.

Cause *and* Effect

Long-Term Causes	Immediate Causes
• Roman Catholic Church becomes more worldly • Humanists urge a return to simple religion • Strong national monarchs emerge	• Johann Tetzel sells indulgences in Wittenberg • Martin Luther posts 95 Theses • Luther translates the Bible into German • Printing press allows spread of reform ideas • Calvin and other reformers preach against Roman Catholic traditions

Protestant Reformation

Immediate Effects	Long-Term Effects
• Peasants' Revolt • Founding of Lutheran, Calvinist, Anglican, Presbyterian, and other Protestant churches • Weakening of Holy Roman Empire • Luther calls for Jews to be expelled from Christian lands	• Religious wars in Europe • Catholic Reformation • Strengthening of the Inquisition • Jewish migration to Eastern Europe • Increased antisemitism

Connections to Today

• About one fourth of Christians are Protestant
• Religious conflict in Northern Ireland

Skills Assessment **Chart** The Protestant Reformation brought sweeping changes to Western Europe. **Identify one religious and one political effect of the Reformation.**

SECTION 4 Assessment

Recall
1. (a) Henry VIII, p. 351 (b) Elizabeth I, p. 352 (c) Council of Trent, p. 353 (d) Inquisition, p. 353 (e) Jesuits, p. 353 (f) Teresa of Avila, p. 354 2. (a) annul, p. 352 (b) canonize, p. 352 (c) compromise, p. 352 (d) scapegoat, p. 354 (e) ghetto, p. 355

Comprehension
3. They rejected infant baptism. Some Anabaptists also favored social reform and turned to violence. 4. Henry VIII wanted to end his marriage so he could marry another woman who might bear him a male heir. When the pope refused him an annulment, Henry had laws passed to place the English Church under his own control. Chief of these was the Act of Supremacy. 5. to end corrupt Church practices, to revive morality, and to stop and reverse the spread of Protestantism 6. Both Catholics and Protestants fostered intolerance.

Critical Thinking and Writing
7. Possible answer: No; if the Catholic Church had reformed itself earlier, there would have been no need for the Protestant Reformation. 8. Possible answer: Protestants may have seen the reform movement primarily as an effort to reverse Protestant gains. To Catholics, it was a movement to revive the moral authority of the Church.

SECTION 4 Assessment

Recall
1. **Identify: (a)** Henry VIII, **(b)** Elizabeth I, **(c)** Council of Trent, **(d)** Inquisition, **(e)** Jesuits, **(f)** Teresa of Avila.
2. **Define: (a)** annul, **(b)** canonize, **(c)** compromise, **(d)** scapegoat, **(e)** ghetto.

Comprehension
3. Why were the Anabaptists considered radical?
4. Describe the steps by which England became a Protestant country.
5. What were the goals of the Catholic Reformation?
6. Why did persecution increase after the Reformation?

Critical Thinking and Writing
7. **Recognizing Causes and Effects** If the Catholic Church had undertaken reform earlier, do you think that the Protestant Reformation would have occurred? Explain.
8. **Recognizing Point of View** The Protestant term for the Catholic Reformation was the Counter-Reformation. (The prefix *counter* means "against.") How do these two terms reflect different points of view?

Activity

Writing a News Report Prepare a script for a TV news program reporting on King Henry VIII and his break with the Catholic Church. You might wish to include visuals and interviews as well.

Activity Rubrics

Share rubrics with students before they complete their scripts.

Attempted The script is incomplete, not providing enough details on the king's break with the Church.

Minimal The script is complete and shows a general understanding of the event but does not provide sufficient detail.

Adequate The script shows good understanding of the event, provides sufficient detail, and is well written.

Exemplary The script shows a keen understanding of Henry's break with the Church, is presented in an interesting way with many details, and includes visuals or interviews.

Skills Assessment

Religious effects include the founding of Protestant churches and the launching of the Catholic Reformation. Political effects include the weakening of the Holy Roman emperor and the Peasants' Revolt.

Human Drama Note

McCarthyism: A Modern Day Witch Hunt In the 1950s, a congressional investigation of the State Department was led by Senator Joseph McCarthy, who charged that the department had been infiltrated by communists. Although he was unable to prove this allegation, McCarthy capitalized upon the fears of a country concerned by recent communist political and military advances in Asia and Europe. Launching a crusade to investigate several government departments, he questioned numerous people about their suspected communist affiliation, and many innocent people lost their jobs. This persecution and the conformity that it forced upon America became known as *McCarthyism*.

In his 1953 play *The Crucible,* American playwright Arthur Miller used the Salem witchcraft trials of 1692 as a metaphor for McCarthyism. Miller was called before the House Un-American Activities Committee for being present at a writer's meeting that was said to have taken place a decade earlier. Refusing to name people he had seen at that meeting, Miller was convicted of contempt of Congress. Later he appealed the conviction and won.

SECTION 5

Bell Ringer On the chalkboard, draw a diagram of Ptolemy's view of the universe with Earth as its center. Ask students to comment on it and then correct it. Tell them to read the section to learn how the Scientific Revolution changed this and other ancient views.

LESSON PLAN

1. Focus Astronomers advanced their knowledge of the universe by rejecting ancient ideas. They and other scientists developed a new method based on experimentation, observations, and mathematical calculations. In his theories on gravity, Newton linked physics and astronomy. Other scientists made advances in medicine and chemistry.

2. Instruct Divide the class into cooperative learning groups. Tell the groups to create a quiz based on information in this section. First, students should collect and organize major ideas and key facts about the Scientific Revolution. Then, they should decide on a form for their quiz, such as matching, multiple choice, or fill-in. They may decide to use a combination of question types. Have students use their data to construct their quizzes. Then, ask each group to present its quiz to the class to complete.

3. Assess Ask students to imagine that they are the hosts of a science awards show. Have them select three figures of the Scientific Revolution who they think should receive a special award. For each of their honorees, ask them to write a speech summarizing his or her major achievements. Invite volunteers to deliver their speeches.

4. Reteach If students' **Assess** activity does not reflect adequate understanding of the lesson, you might assign the *Guide to the Essentials* or the *Interactive Student Tutorial CD-ROM* for this section.

SECTION 5 The Scientific Revolution

Reading Focus

- How did astronomers change the way people viewed the universe?
- What was the new scientific method?
- What advances did Newton and other scientists make?

Vocabulary

heliocentric
hypothesis
scientific method
gravity

Taking Notes

On a sheet of paper, begin a concept web like this one. As you read this section, fill in the blank circles with information about the Scientific Revolution. Add as many other circles as you need.

Main Idea A new way of thinking, based on experimentation and observation, changed the way Europeans looked at the world.

Galileo
In addition to his work in astronomy, Galileo made important discoveries about the motion of pendulums and falling objects. This statue honors Galileo.

Theme: Impact of the Individual In this statue, what might be the meaning of the object Galileo holds in his hand?

Setting the Scene In 1609, Galileo Galilei trained his new telescope on the night sky. Its specially ground lens allowed him to view amazing sights. He saw mountains on the moon, fiery spots on the sun, and four moons circling the planet Jupiter. "I did discover many particulars in Heaven that had been unseen and unheard of until this our age," he later wrote. Galileo's observations supported a new view of the universe.

Leaders of the Renaissance and the Reformation looked to the past for models. Humanists turned to ancient classical ideas. Religious reformers were inspired by the Bible and early Christian times. By contrast, the profound change that took place in science in the mid-1500s pointed ahead, toward a future shaped by a new way of thinking about the physical universe. We call that historical change the Scientific Revolution.

Changing Views of the Universe

Until the mid-1500s, European scholars accepted the theory of the ancient Greek astronomer Ptolemy. Ptolemy taught that the Earth was the center of the universe. Not only did this view seem to agree with common sense, it also matched the teachings of the Church. In the 1500s and 1600s, some startling discoveries radically changed the way Europeans viewed the physical world.

A Revolutionary Theory In 1543, Polish scholar Nicolaus Copernicus (koh PER nuh kuhs) published *On the Revolutions of the Heavenly Spheres.* In it, he proposed a heliocentric, or sun-centered, model of the universe. The sun, he said, stood at the center of the universe. The Earth was just one of several planets that revolved around the sun.

Most experts rejected this revolutionary theory. In Europe at the time, all scientific knowledge and many religious teachings were based on the arguments developed by classical thinkers. If Ptolemy's reasoning about the planets was wrong, they believed, then the whole system of human knowledge might be called into question. But in the late 1500s, the Danish astronomer Tycho Brahe (TEE koh BRAH uh) provided evidence that supported Copernicus's theory. Brahe set up an astronomical observatory. Every night for years, he carefully observed the sky, accumulating data about the movement of the heavenly bodies.

After Brahe's death, his assistant, the brilliant German astronomer and mathematician Johannes Kepler, used Brahe's data to calculate the

Caption Answer

The item might be a pendulum, representing Galileo's work in the study of motion. It might also be the sun or one of the planets, representing his work in astronomy.

Resource Directory

Teaching Resources
Creative Teaching Activities Creative Teaching Activities booklet, p. 67
Guided Reading and Review Unit 4 booklet, p. 10
Viewpoint Activity *Does the Earth Move?*, Unit 4 booklet, p. 14

orbits of the planets revolving around the sun. His calculations supported Copernicus's heliocentric view. At the same time, however, they showed that each planet did not move in a perfect circle, as both Ptolemy and Copernicus believed, but in an oval-shaped orbit called an ellipse.

Galileo Scientists of many lands built on the foundations laid by Copernicus and Kepler. In Italy, Galileo Galilei assembled an astronomical telescope. As you have read, he observed the four moons of Jupiter moving slowly around that planet—exactly, he realized, the way Copernicus said that the Earth moved around the sun.

Galileo's discoveries caused an uproar. Other scholars attacked him because his observations contradicted ancient views about the world. The Church condemned him because his ideas challenged the Christian teaching that the heavens were fixed, unmoving, and perfect.

In 1633, Galileo was tried before the Inquisition. Threatened with death unless he withdrew his "heresies," Galileo agreed to state publicly that the Earth stood motionless at the center of the universe. "Nevertheless," he is said to have muttered as he left the court, "it does move."

A New Scientific Method

Despite the opposition of religious authorities, by the early 1600s a new approach to science had emerged. Unlike most earlier approaches, it did not rely on authorities like Aristotle or Ptolemy or even the Bible. It depended instead upon observation and experimentation.

A Step-by-Step Process The new approach to science required scientists to collect and accurately measure data. To explain the data, scientists used reasoning to propose a logical hypothesis, or possible explanation. They then tested the hypothesis with further observation or experimentation. Complex mathematical calculations were used to convert the observations and experiments into scientific laws. After reaching a conclusion, scientists repeated their work at least once—and usually many times—to confirm their findings. This step-by-step process of discovery became known as the scientific method.

Bacon and Descartes The new scientific method was really a revolution in thought. Two giants of this revolution were the Englishman Francis Bacon and the Frenchman René Descartes (ruh NAY day KAHRT). Each devoted himself to the problem of knowledge.

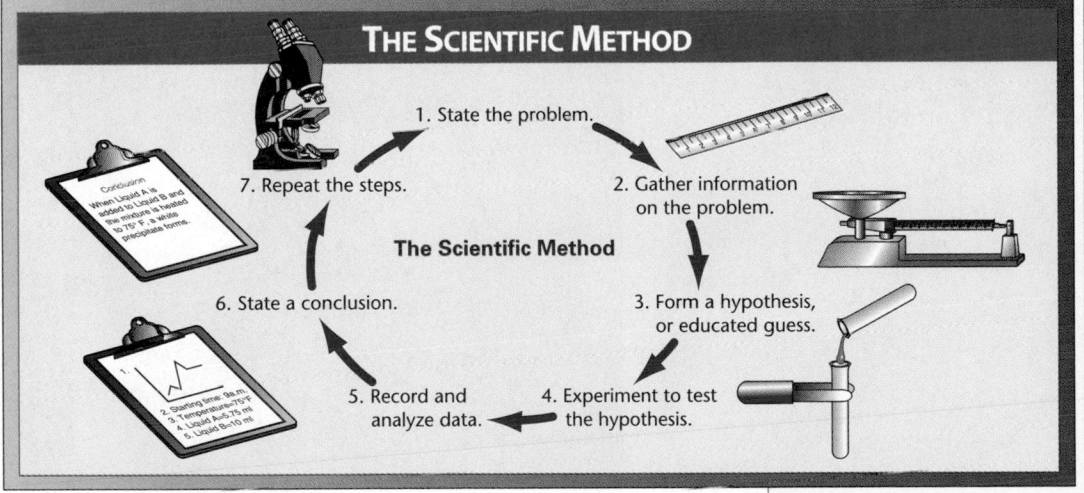

THE SCIENTIFIC METHOD

1. State the problem.
2. Gather information on the problem.
3. Form a hypothesis, or educated guess.
4. Experiment to test the hypothesis.
5. Record and analyze data.
6. State a conclusion.
7. Repeat the steps.

The Scientific Method

Exploring Human Anatomy
Leonardo da Vinci dissected more than 30 corpses in order to create precise sketches of the human body (PAST). Today, doctors study anatomy with the aid of advanced computer technology (PRESENT).

Theme: Economics and Technology How were anatomical drawings useful to Leonardo? How is computer imaging useful to doctors today?

Both Bacon and Descartes rejected Aristotle's scientific assumptions. They also challenged the scholarly traditions of the medieval universities that sought to make the physical world fit in with the teachings of the Church. Both argued that truth is not known at the beginning of inquiry but at the end, after a long process of investigation.

Bacon and Descartes differed in their methods, however. Bacon stressed experimentation and observation. He wanted science to make life better for people by leading to practical technologies. Descartes emphasized human reasoning as the best road to understanding. In his *Discourse on Method*, he explains how he decided to discard all traditional authorities and search for provable knowledge. Left only with doubt, he concluded that the doubter had to exist and made his famous statement, "I think, therefore I am."

Newton Ties It All Together

As a student in England, Isaac Newton devoured the works of the leading scientists of his day. By age 24, he had formed a brilliant theory to explain why the planets moved as they did. According to one story, Newton saw an apple fall from a tree. He wondered whether the force that pulled that apple to the Earth might not also control the movements of the planets.

In the next 20 years, Newton perfected his theory. Using mathematics, he showed that a single force keeps the planets in their orbits around the sun. He called this force gravity.

In 1687, Newton published *Mathematical Principles of Natural Philosophy*, explaining the law of gravity and other workings of the universe. Nature, argued Newton, follows uniform laws. All motion in the universe can be measured and described mathematically.

To many, Newton's work seemed to link physics and astronomy, to bind the new science as gravity itself held the universe together. An English poet caught the spirit of what would later be called the Newtonian revolution:

> "Nature and Nature's Laws lay hid in night,
>   God said, Let Newton be! and all was light."
> —Alexander Pope, *Epitaphs*

For over 200 years, Newton's laws held fast. In the early 1900s, startling new theories of the universe called some of Newton's ideas into question.

PAST

PRESENT

Yet Newton's laws of motion and mechanics continue to have many practical uses. Newton also helped develop an important new branch of mathematics—calculus.

Other Scientific Advances

The 1500s and 1600s saw breakthroughs in many branches of science. Some of the most significant advances occurred in chemistry and medicine.

Chemistry Chemistry slowly freed itself from the magical notions of medieval alchemists, who had believed it was possible to transform ordinary metals into gold. In the 1600s, Robert Boyle distinguished between individual elements and chemical compounds. He also explained the effect of temperature and pressure on gases. Boyle's work opened the way to modern chemical analysis of the composition of matter.

Medicine Medieval physicians relied on the ancient works of Galen. Galen, however, had made many errors, in part because he had limited knowledge of human anatomy. During the Renaissance, artists and physicians made new efforts to study the human body. In 1543, Andreas Vesalius published *On the Structure of the Human Body*, the first accurate and detailed study of human anatomy. A French physician, Ambroise Paré, developed a new and more effective ointment for preventing infection. He also developed a technique for closing wounds with stitches.

In the early 1600s, William Harvey, an English scholar, described the circulation of the blood for the first time. He showed how the heart serves as a pump to force blood through veins and arteries. Later in the century, the Dutch inventor Anthony van Leeuwenhoek perfected the microscope and became the first human to see cells and microorganisms. These pioneering scientists opened the way for further advances.

Looking Ahead

The rapid advance in science and technology that began in the 1500s has continued to this day. Thinkers like Bacon, Descartes, and Newton applied the scientific method to the pursuit of knowledge. Their work encouraged others to search for scientific laws governing the universe. Such ideas opened the way to the Enlightenment of the 1700s and a growing belief in human progress.

SECTION 5 Assessment

Recall
1. **Identify:** (a) Nicolaus Copernicus, (b) Johannes Kepler, (c) Galileo Galilei, (d) Francis Bacon, (e) René Descartes, (f) Isaac Newton, (g) Robert Boyle.
2. **Define:** (a) heliocentric, (b) hypothesis, (c) scientific method, (d) gravity.

Comprehension
3. Why did some people oppose the heliocentric theory of the universe?
4. How did the scientific method differ from earlier approaches?
5. How did Newton try to explain the workings of the universe?

Critical Thinking and Writing
6. **Making Inferences** Newton wrote, "If I have seen further [than others] it is by standing on the shoulders of giants." (a) What do you think he meant? (b) Who might be some of the "giants" to whom Newton was referring?
7. **Applying Information** Identify three ways in which your life today might have been different if the Scientific Revolution had never occurred.

Activity
Take It to the NET

Use the Internet to learn more about the life and work of William Harvey. Then, prepare a brief biographical sketch of Harvey. Include a diagram of the circulatory system that he described.

Chapter 14 **359**

SECTION 5 Assessment

Recall
1. (a) Nicolaus Copernicus, p. 356 (b) Johannes Kepler, p. 356 (c) Galileo Galilei, p. 357 (d) Francis Bacon, p. 357 (e) René Descartes, p. 357 (f) Isaac Newton, p. 358 (g) Robert Boyle, p. 359
2. (a) heliocentric, p. 356 (b) hypothesis, p. 357 (c) scientific method, p. 357 (d) gravity, p. 358

Comprehension
3. Scholars feared that by contradicting the teachings of Ptolemy, Copernicus called all classical knowledge into question. Church officials thought Copernicus's theory contradicted Christian teachings.
4. It started not with Aristotle, Ptolemy, or the Bible, but with observation and experimentation. Complex mathematical calculations were used to convert observations and experiments into scientific laws.
5. Newton used mathematics to develop his theory of gravity. He asserted that nature followed uniform laws that can be measured through mathematics.

Critical Thinking and Writing
6. (a) His discoveries were based on the work of the great scientists who came before him. (b) Answers include Copernicus, Brahe, Kepler, and Galileo.
7. Answers should reflect recent advances in astronomy, mathematics, medicine, or chemistry.

Creating a Chapter Summary

As a reteaching opportunity, pair a more able student with a less able student to complete this chapter summary.

Answers may include these and others.
Renaissance—Causes: Humanism; Important Events: Gutenberg's printing press; Key People: Petrarch, Leonardo, Lorenzo de' Medici, Michelangelo, Raphael, Machiavelli, Erasmus, Dürer, Shakespeare
Protestant Reformation—What It Was: Protest against the Catholic Church; Causes: Abuses of clergy; Important Events: Peace of Augsburg, establishment of Church of England; Key People: Luther, Calvin, Henry VIII
Catholic Reformation—What It Was: Revival of Church's authority; Causes: Reaction to Protestant Reformation; Important Events: Council of Trent, Inquisition; Key People: Pope Paul III
Scientific Revolution—What It Was: Change of view about physical world; Causes: Copernicus proposes heliocentric theory; Important Events: discovery of telescope; Key People: Copernicus, Kepler, Galileo, Newton, Bacon, Descartes, Harvey

Building Vocabulary

1–10. Students' sentences should show a clear understanding of the meaning of each word.

Recalling Key Facts

11. **(a)** The Renaissance was the rebirth of culture and learning in Europe. **(b)** in Italy in the 1300s
12. comedies, histories, and tragedies
13. to protest selling of indulgences
14. When the pope refused Henry's request to annul his marriage, Henry took over the English church.
15. a way to draw conclusions by testing hypotheses
16. He meant that his ability to reason proved the basic truth of his own existence.

Critical Thinking and Writing

17. They used perspective to show objects in a realistic way; distant objects were painted smaller than those close to the viewer. They also used shading to make objects look round and real.
18. Possible answers: **(a)** Both stressed education and classical learning. Northern Europeans emphasized

---

Creating a Chapter Summary

On a sheet of paper make a table like the one shown here. Use it to summarize major events that you have learned about in this chapter. Some cells have been partly filled in to help you get started.

	RENAISSANCE	PROTESTANT REFORMATION	CATHOLIC REFORMATION	SCIENTIFIC REVOLUTION
WHAT IT WAS	• Time of creativity and change			
CAUSES				
IMPORTANT EVENTS		• Luther posts 95 Theses •		
KEY PEOPLE			• Ignatius of Loyola •	

For additional review and enrichment activities, see the interactive version of *World History* available on the Web and on CD-ROM.

Web Site Self-Test
For practice test questions for Chapter 14, see **www.phschool.com**.

Building Vocabulary

Write sentences using the chapter vocabulary words listed below, leaving blanks where the vocabulary words would go. Then, exchange your sentences with another student, and fill in the blanks in each other's sentences.

1. **patron**
2. **humanism**
3. **vernacular**
4. **utopian**
5. **indulgence**
6. **predestination**
7. **annul**
8. **ghetto**
9. **heliocentric**
10. **hypothesis**

Recalling Key Facts

11. **(a)** What was the Renaissance? **(b)** When and where did it begin?
12. What three different kinds of plays did William Shakespeare write?
13. Why did Martin Luther post his 95 Theses?
14. How did the English Reformation occur?
15. What is the scientific method?
16. What did Descartes mean by the statement "I think, therefore I am"?

Critical Thinking and Writing

17. **Connecting to Geography** How did artists translate new techniques of the Renaissance to their landscape paintings?
18. **Comparing (a)** Compare and contrast the Renaissance in Italy with the Renaissance in northern Europe. **(b)** How would you account for the differences?
19. **Understanding Sequence** An English author wrote, "The preaching of sermons is speaking to a few of mankind, but printing books is talking to the whole world." How does this statement suggest a relationship between two of the key events discussed in this chapter?
20. **Recognizing Causes and Effects** Why did England escape the kinds of religious wars that tore apart other European nations?
21. **Linking Past and Present** Modern scientists refer to the discoveries of Copernicus as the Copernican Revolution. Why do you think they use that term?

---

religious themes and believed education should lead to moral and religious reform. Italians focused on worldly subjects and believed education should stimulate individual creativity. **(b)** Wealthy merchants exerted leadership in Italy. In Northern Europe, the Renaissance was influenced by religious thinkers and reformers.
19. Possible answer: The statement suggests that Gutenberg's invention of the printing press in the 1400s helped to advance the Protestant Reformation in the 1500s. Printing allowed ideas like those of Luther and Calvin to spread rapidly across Europe.

20. Possible answer: Queen Elizabeth I adopted a policy of religious compromise.
21. Possible answer: Copernicus's discoveries revolutionized the way people viewed the universe. After Copernicus, other scientists challenged traditional views and developed new knowledge.

The passage below is from the Council of Trent called by Pope Paul III in 1545 to establish the direction of Catholic reform. Read the passage, then answer the questions that follow.

"This holy Council cautions all bishops so to live . . . that they can bring together truth and behavior as a kind of constant example of thrift, modesty, and decency, and especially of that holy humility that so strongly commends men to God. Therefore, following the example set by our fathers at the Council of Carthage, it is ordered that bishops shall content themselves not only with modest household furniture and simple food, but with regard to the rest of their manner of living and to their whole house, so that nothing appears that is alien to this holy institution of the Church and that does not show simplicity, zeal for God, and contempt for worldly things."

—Canons and Decrees of the
Holy Council of Trent

22. To what group of people is this passage mainly addressed?
23. **(a)** What orders are given in the passage? **(b)** On what authority are these orders given?
24. What does this document imply about the situation in the Church before the Council?
25. How can you tell that the reformers at the Council of Trent looked to the example of the early Christian Church?
26. **(a)** Do you think the reformers at Trent would agree with Protestant reformers about worldliness in the Church? **(b)** Do you think they would agree about the subject of papal authority?

Use the Internet to research the invention of the printing press and its effects on Renaissance Europe. Then, write an essay in which you try to persuade the reader that the invention of the Internet either will or will not have a similar effect on world civilization in the future.

Michelangelo sculpted this huge statue of the Israelite prophet Moses for the tomb of Pope Julius II. It stands almost eight feet tall and took years to complete. Study the statue, then answer the following questions:

27. How was this choice of subject typical of the Renaissance?
28. How does the sculpture show Renaissance humanism?
29. How does the sculpture show Michelangelo's attention to anatomical detail?
30. Why would an artist like Michelangelo need the support of a powerful patron like the pope?

Skills Tip

When you study a work of art, use what you know about the period in which it was created. In particular, it is important to understand what themes and topics were of concern to artists of that period.

---

22. bishops of the Roman Catholic Church
23. **(a)** Bishops were told to live modestly, to show zeal for God and contempt for worldly things, and not to enrich their relations from Church revenues. **(b)** on the authority of the Council of Trent called by the Pope
24. It implies that many bishops lived in wealth and misused Church revenues.
25. The passage refers to "our fathers at the Council of Carthage."
26. **(a)** Yes. Like Protestant reformers, the reformers at Trent believed that the clergy should live simply. **(b)** No. Protestant reformers rejected the pope's authority. The pope called the Council at Trent and used papal authority to forbid abuses.

27. Much Renaissance art emphasized religious themes, especially when the patron was a religious leader.
28. Although Moses is larger than life, the statue also emphasizes his human characteristics—a natural, human pose and a strong facial expression.
29. The statue emphasizes physical details, such as veins and muscles.
30. Such works took years to complete. Without a patron, an artist had a hard time earning a living.

Skills Tip

Comparing the ways similar subjects are treated by different artists can help students understand art better. The Skills Handbook in the front of the book has a lesson that will help students with this feature.

Unit Theme Activity

Remind students about the Unit Theme Activity located on the unit opener page. Make sure students understand the assignment and have begun work.

 Take It to the NET

Direct students to **www.phschool.com** for links to sites that will help them get started on this assignment. Share rubrics with students before they write their persuasive essays.
Attempted The essay fails to make connections between the effects on society of the two inventions, reflecting insufficient research.
Minimal The essay makes connections between the two inventions and reflects sufficient research but lacks adequate development of persuasive details to support the thesis.
Adequate The essay is well organized, and supporting details are developed sufficiently to be convincing.
Exemplary The essay is well developed, and the supporting details are very interesting as well as convincing.

Chapter 15 Planning Guide

Resource Manager

	CORE INSTRUCTION	READING/SKILLS
Chapter Level Resources	📖 **Teaching Resources** 📄 **Pacing Charts**, Ch. 15 📄 **Teaching With Themes**, p. 18 ▦ **Color Transparencies**, p. F–31 💿 **Resource Pro®** Ch 15 🖥 **www.phschool.com** • eTeach	💿 **Book on CD**, Ch. 15 💿 **Interactive Student Tutorial CD-ROM**, Ch. 15 💿 **Social Studies Skills Tutor CD-ROM** ▦ **Skills Transparencies**
1 The Search for Spices 1. Explain why Europeans crossed the seas. 2. Identify how Portugal's eastward explorations led to the development of a trading empire. 3. Trace how Columbus's voyages affected the search for a passage to the Indies.	📖 **Teaching Resources** 📄 **Creative Teaching Activities**, p. 68 💿 **Prentice Hall Presentation Pro**, Ch. 15, Section 1 ▦ **Section Reading Support Transparencies**	📖 **Teaching Resources** 📕 **Unit 4 booklet** • Guided Reading and Review, p. 22 📄 **Guide to the Essentials** 📼 **Guided Reading Audiotapes**, Ch. 15, Section 1
2 Diverse Traditions of Southeast Asia 1. Determine the key geographic features of Southeast Asia. 2. Summarize the impact Indian civilization had on new kingdoms and empires. 3. Identify the factors that contributed to the growth of Vietnamese culture.	📖 **Teaching Resources** 📄 **Creative Teaching Activities**, p. 69 💿 **Prentice Hall Presentation Pro**, Ch. 15, Section 2 ▦ **Section Reading Support Transparencies**	📖 **Teaching Resources** 📕 **Unit 4 booklet** • Guided Reading and Review, p. 24 📄 **Guide to the Essentials** 📼 **Guided Reading Audiotapes**, Ch. 15, Section 2

3 European Footholds in Southeast Asia and India
1. Explain how the Portuguese and the Dutch built empires in the East.
2. Describe how Spain controlled the Philippines.
3. Analyze how the decline of Mughal India affected European traders.
	📖 **Teaching Resources**
	📕 **Unit 4 booklet**
	   • Primary Source Activity, p. 31
	📄 **Creative Teaching Activities**, p. 70
	💿 **Prentice Hall Presentation Pro**, Ch. 15, Section 3
	▦ **Section Reading Support Transparencies**
		📖 **Teaching Resources**
		📕 **Unit 4 booklet**
		   • Guided Reading and Review, p. 26
		   • Skill Application Activity, p. 33
		📄 **Guide to the Essentials**
		📼 **Guided Reading Audiotapes**, Ch. 15, Section 3

4 Encounters in East Asia
1. Illustrate how European trade with China was affected by the Manchu conquest.
2. Explain why Korea isolated itself from other nations.
3. Describe the attitude Tokugawa shoguns took toward foreign traders.
	📖 **Teaching Resources**
	📕 **Unit 4 booklet**
	   • Biography Activity, p. 30
	   • Viewpoint Activity, p. 32
	📄 **Creative Teaching Activities**, p. 66
	💿 **Prentice Hall Presentation Pro**, Ch. 15, Section 4
	▦ **Section Reading Support Transparencies**
		📖 **Teaching Resources**
		📕 **Unit 4 booklet**
		   • Guided Reading and Review, p. 8
		📄 **Guide to the Essentials**
		📼 **Guided Reading Audiotapes**, Ch. 15, Section 4

ENRICHMENT/PRE-AP

www.phschool.com
- Why Study History?

Teaching Resources
- Geography and History, pp. 8–9
- Color Transparencies, pp. B–41, B–43, B–45
- www.phschool.com
  - Internet Activities, Section 1

Teaching Resources
- History Through Literature, p. 34
- www.phschool.com
  - Virtual Field Trip

Teaching Resources
- Chapter Extension Activities, p. 39
- Visions, Voices, Views, Animated Map Story, side 2
- www.phschool.com
  - Internet Activities, Cyclone Rips Through Calcutta
  - Internet Activities, Section 3

Teaching Resources
- Chapter Extension Activities, p. 40
- Simulations, p. 7

ASSESSMENT

PRENTICE HALL ASSESSMENT SYSTEM

Core Assessment
- ExamView Test Bank booklet, Ch. 15
- ExamView Test Bank CD-ROM, Ch. 15

Standardized Test Preparation

Diagnose and Prescribe
- Diagnostic Tests for High School Social Studies Skills

Review and Reteach
- Review Book for World History

Practice and Assess
- Test-Taking Strategies With Transparencies for High School
- Alternative Assessment booklet
- Test Prep Book for World History

Teaching Resources
- Unit 4 booklet
  - Geography Quiz, p. 34
  - Section Quizzes, pp. 23, 25, 27, 29
  - Chapter Tests A, B, and C, pp. 35–39
- www.phschool.com
  - Self-Test

CUSTOMIZE FOR INDIVIDUAL NEEDS

Gifted and Talented
- Teacher's Edition, Activities: Connections to Literature, p. 380

Less Proficient Readers
- Guide to the Essentials, Ch. 15
- Guided Reading Audiotapes, English, Ch. 15
- Book on CD, Ch. 15
- Teacher's Edition, Activities: Reading Strategy, p. 378

Less Proficient Writers
- Teacher's Edition, Activities: Cooperative Learning Activity, p. 375

Students Acquiring English/ESL
- Guide to the Essentials, English/Spanish, Ch. 15
- Guided Reading Audiotapes, English/Spanish, Ch. 15
- Book on CD, Ch. 15
- Teacher's Edition, Activities marked with an *: Cooperative Learning Activity, p. 375

TEXT

Don't miss the exclusive interactive version of *World History: Connections to Today* on the Internet and CD-ROM.

The First Global Age: Europe and Asia
1415–1796

INTRODUCTION

The desire for a share in the valuable spice trade spurred Portugal and Spain to search for new routes to Asia. Aided by better ships and other technological advances, Europeans explored the world, coming upon the Americas in their travels. Europeans established trading posts in Asia. India, too, established a presence in Southeast Asia, where geography contributed to the development of a number of diverse Southeast Asian cultures.

Focusing on Themes

Suggest that students focus on these theme questions as they read:

Economics and Technology
How did technology help Europeans explore the seas and build trading empires in Asia?

Diversity
What patterns of civilization emerged in Southeast Asia?

Global Interaction
What new global patterns resulted from the European age of exploration?

Continuity and Change
How did the first global age affect the civilizations of Asia?

Chapter Preview

1 The Search for Spices
2 Diverse Traditions of Southeast Asia
3 European Footholds in Southeast Asia and India
4 Encounters in East Asia

TIME LINE ACTIVITY

You may wish to share the About the Pictures note with your students before you ask questions about the time line such as these:

1. Vasco da Gama was the first European to reach India by sailing around Africa. Why do you suppose no one had been able to do that earlier? *(Da Gama had better ships or navigational tools.)*
2. When did Japan bar western merchants? *(1630s)*
3. How many years had the Portuguese held Malacca before the Dutch seized it from them? *(130)*

CHAPTER EVENTS

1498
Portuguese explorer Vasco da Gama reaches India after rounding Africa. His voyage sets the stage for the rise of a Portuguese trading empire.

1511
Portugal seizes Malacca.

1522
The *Vittoria* completes the first circumnavigation of the globe. The expedition's original leader, Ferdinand Magellan, and four other ships do not survive the voyage.

1400   1480   1560

GLOBAL EVENTS

1456 The Gutenberg Bible is printed.

1500 The kingdom of Kongo thrives.

1519 Hernan Cortés lands in Mexico.

362 *Chapter 15*

Don't Miss!

Disaster!
Cyclone Rips Through Calcutta (Section 3)

Analyzing Primary Sources
Letter From the Celestial Emperor to the "Barbarian" King (Section 4)

Resource Directory

Teaching Resources
Teaching With Themes Chapter Theme Activities, p. 18
Pacing Chart With Block Scheduling Guide Ch. 15
Technology
World History Color Transparencies Ch. 15 Graphic Organizer, p. F–31

Trade Between Europe, Africa, and Asia About 1700

Ocean trade routes permitted the development of cultural and economic ties between Europe, Africa, and Asia.

Ports controlled by
- England
- Portugal
- France
- Netherlands
- Spain
- Trade routes

20°W · 0° · ENGLAND · NETHERLANDS · EUROPE · FRANCE · PORTUGAL · SPAIN · Canary Islands · Cape Verde Islands · Bissau · AFRICA · Accra · São Tomé · ATLANTIC OCEAN · From Europe · PERSIA · ARABIA · Arabian Sea · ASIA · INDIA · Bombay · Goa · Madras · Cochin · Calcutta · Bay of Bengal · CHINA · Macao · East China Sea · JAPAN · Deshima · PACIFIC OCEAN · From Mexico · Manila · PHILIPPINES · South China Sea · Malacca · INDIAN OCEAN · Batavia · EAST INDIES · Mombasa · Zanzibar · Mozambique · Sofala · MADAGASCAR · Ft. Dauphin · Cape Town · AUSTRALIA

Robinson Projection
0 500 1000 Miles
0 500 1000 Kilometers

1641
The Dutch seize Malacca from the Portuguese.

1736
China's Emperor Qianlong, shown here, begins a long reign. Qianlong expands China's territory but rejects western efforts to increase trade with China.

1640 — 1720 — 1800

1630s Japan bars western merchants.

1642 The English Civil War begins.

1789 The French Revolution begins.

Independent Assignments

Have students read one section as they prepare for class. After class, have them complete the assignment. Some students may benefit from using the Guided Reading and Review worksheets.

Section 1 Have students use the map *The World During the Age of Discovery* in the Historical Outline Map Book, p. 26, to locate and label the various continents, bodies of water, and major political boundaries during this time period.

Section 2 Have students use the worksheet *Poetry from 15th-Century Vietnam* in the History Through Literature booklet, p. 34, to learn about Vietnamese poetry.

Section 3 Have students use the worksheet *An Unusual Dinner Party* in the Unit 4 booklet, p. 31, to learn how a Hindu merchant felt about a dinner party put on by an Indian who had converted to Christianity.

Section 4 Have students use the worksheet *Japan's Shoguns Reject the West* in the Unit 4 booklet, p. 32, to learn how two historians view Japan's decision to be isolated from the West.

Trade Between Europe, Africa, and Asia About 1700

Activating Prior Knowledge
Before the Portuguese established the sea route around Africa, how had Europeans obtained goods from India, China, and other Asian countries? *(mainly from Muslim traders who traveled overland)*

Previewing
How do you suppose Europeans were able to gain control of the African and Asian ports shown on the map? *(Students will probably guess that most of the ports were taken by force.)*

Background About the Pictures

1   2   3

1. Painted in the sixteenth century, this portrait is of Vasco da Gama. On his second voyage to India, da Gama established the colonies of Mozambique and Sofala in East Africa.

2. One of Magellan's five ships was lost when it was beached while exploring the coast of what is now Argentina. The crew of a second ship mutinied in the Strait of Magellan and turned back for Spain. A third ship was abandoned because so many crewmen had died that there weren't enough sailors to man all three remaining ships. The fourth ship was captured by the Portuguese.

3. Although Qianlong (1711–1799) ruled China from 1736 until 1796, when he abdicated the throne in favor of his son, Qianlong held political power even after leaving the throne, making him the longest ruling monarch in Chinese history.

eTeach

Be sure to check out this month's online discussion with a World History Master Teacher.

Go to **www.phschool.com**.

Bell Ringer Before introducing this section, have students brainstorm a list of qualities that they think an explorer would need. Ask students to be prepared to explain and defend their suggestions. Tell the class to look for these qualities in the explorers they will read about.

Reading Focus

- Why did Europeans cross the seas?
- How did Portugal's eastward explorations lead to the development of a trading empire?
- How did Columbus's voyages affect the search for a passage to the Indies?

Vocabulary

cartographer
astrolabe
caravel
scurvy
circumnavigate

Taking Notes

Copy the table below. As you read the section, add information about the explorations of Portugal and Spain in the 1400s and 1500s.

PORTUGAL	SPAIN
• Henry the Navigator sponsors voyages	• Columbus sails for India; reaches Caribbean
•	•

Main Idea A desire to share in the rich spice trade of the East spurred Europeans to explore the oceans.

LESSON PLAN

1. Focus Muslim and Italian control of the valuable spice trade spurred the Atlantic nations of Europe to seek new routes to Asia. The Portuguese and Spanish, aided by reliable navigational tools, better ships, and other technological advances, led the overseas exploration.

2. Instruct Divide the class into cooperative learning groups and assign each group one of the following figures: Prince Henry of Portugal, Bartholomeu Dias, Vasco da Gama, Christopher Columbus, Pedro Alvarez Cabral, Amerigo Vespucci, Vasco Núñez de Balboa, Ferdinand Magellan. Tell students that their assignment is to create a portrait in words of their figure. In addition to information in the text, students should consult library resources and other reference works. Have each group share its finished portrait; then, bind your "portrait gallery" into a file folder for future use.

3. Assess Ask students to write a brief dialogue between the explorer assigned to their group and someone he met in his travels.

4. Reteach If students' **Assess** activity does not reflect adequate understanding of the lesson, you might assign the *Guide to the Essentials* or the *Interactive Student Tutorial CD-ROM* for this section.

The Spice Trade
Voyages of exploration were driven by the desire for access to spices. Nutmeg, cinnamon, cloves, and pepper were among the most prized trade items.

Theme: Economics and Technology Why were spices so costly?

Setting the Scene

Today, we take pepper for granted. To Europeans of past ages, though, this spice was as valuable as gold. Ancient Romans paid as much as $125 for 12 ounces of pepper. During the Middle Ages, the pepper in your local supermarket could have paid a year's rent. By the late 1400s, the desire to share in the rich spice trade of the East spurred Europeans to explore the oceans.

Europeans Explore the Seas

Europeans had traded with Asia long before the Renaissance. The Crusades introduced Europeans to many luxury goods from Asia. Later, when the Mongol empire united much of Asia in the 1200s and 1300s, Asian goods flowed to Europe along complex overland trade routes.

The Black Death and the breakup of the Mongol empire disrupted trade. By the 1400s, though, Europe was recovering from the plague. As its population grew, so did the demand for trade goods. The most valued items were spices, such as cinnamon, cloves, nutmeg, and pepper. People used spices in many ways—to preserve food, add flavor to dried and salted meat, and make medicines and perfumes. The chief source of spices was the Moluccas, an island chain in present-day Indonesia, which Europeans then called the Spice Islands.

Motives In the 1400s, Muslim and Italian merchants controlled most trade between Asia and Europe. Muslim traders brought prized goods to eastern Mediterranean ports. Traders from Venice and other Italian cities then carried the precious cargoes to European markets. Europeans, however, wanted to gain direct access to the riches of Asia. To do so, the Atlantic powers—first Portugal, then Spain—sought a route to Asia that bypassed the Mediterranean.

The desire for wealth was not the only motive that lured people to sea. Some voyagers were still fired by the

Caption Answer

They had to be transported a long way and were handled by many middlemen, driving the prices up.

Resource Directory

Teaching Resources
Creative Teaching Activities Creative Teaching Activities booklet, p. 68
Guided Reading and Review Unit 4 booklet, p. 22
Technology
World History Color Transparencies *European Knowledge of the World* base map and overlay transparencies, set 4, pp. B–41, B–43, B–45

centuries-old desire to crusade against the Muslims. The Renaissance spirit of inquiry further fired people's desire to learn more about the lands beyond Europe.

Improved Technology Several improvements in technology helped Europeans conquer the vast oceans of the world. Cartographers, or mapmakers, created more accurate maps and sea charts. European sailors also learned to use the astrolabe, an instrument developed by the ancient Greeks and perfected by the Arabs, to determine their latitude at sea.

Along with more reliable navigational tools, Europeans designed larger and better ships. The Portuguese developed the caravel, which combined the square sails of European ships with Arab lateen, or triangular, sails. Caravels also adapted the sternpost rudder and numerous masts of Chinese ships. The new rigging made it easier to sail across or even into the wind. Finally, European ships added more weaponry, including sturdier cannons.

Portugal Sails Eastward

Portugal, a small nation on the western edge of Spain, led the way in exploration. By the 1400s, Portugal was strong enough to expand into Muslim North Africa. In 1415, the Portuguese seized Ceuta (say oo tah) on the North African coast. The victory sparked the imagination of Prince Henry, known to history as Henry the Navigator.

Mapping the African Coast Prince Henry embodied the crusading drive and the new spirit of exploration. He hoped to expand Christianity and find the source of African gold.

At Sagres, in southern Portugal, Henry gathered scientists, cartographers, and other experts. They redesigned ships, prepared maps, and trained captains and crews for long voyages. Henry then sent out ships that slowly worked their way south to explore the western coast of Africa.

Henry died in 1460, but the Portuguese continued their quest. In 1488, Bartholomeu Dias rounded the southern tip of Africa. Despite the turbulent seas, the tip became known as the Cape of Good Hope because it opened the way for a sea route to Asia.

On to India In 1497, Vasco da Gama led four ships around the Cape of Good Hope. After a 10-month voyage, da Gama finally reached the great spice port of Calicut on the west coast of India. The long voyage home took a heavy toll. The Portuguese lost half their ships. Many sailors died of hunger, thirst, and scurvy, a disease caused by a lack of vitamin C in their diets during months at sea. Still, the venture proved highly profitable to the survivors. In India, da Gama had acquired a cargo of spices that he sold at a profit of 3,000 percent.

Da Gama quickly outfitted a new fleet. In 1502, he forced a treaty of friendship on the ruler of Calicut. Da Gama then left Portuguese merchants there to buy spices when prices were low and to store them near the dock until the next fleet could return. Soon, the Portuguese seized key ports around the Indian Ocean to create a vast trading empire.

Columbus Sails to the West

News of Portugal's successes spurred other nations to look for a sea route to Asia. An Italian navigator from the port of Genoa, Christopher Columbus, sought Portuguese backing for his own plan. He wanted to reach the Indies* by sailing west across the Atlantic. Like most educated Europeans, Columbus knew that the Earth was a sphere. A few weeks

*The Indies, or East Indies, was the European name for a group of islands in Southeast Asia. Today, they are a part of Indonesia.

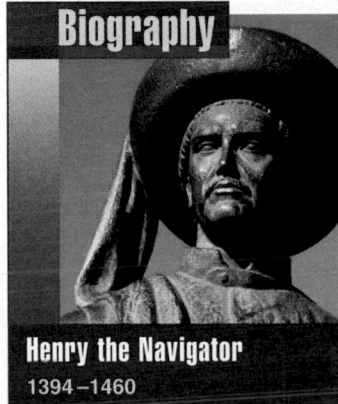

Biography

Henry the Navigator
1394–1460

As a younger son of Portugal's King John I and Queen Philippa, Henry was not destined to rule his nation. This did not stop him, however, from carving out a place in history. During the campaign to conquer Ceuta, in northern Africa, he found his true calling. Inspired by stories of gold beyond the Sahara, he recognized Portugal's need for a sea route to distant lands.

Henry's interest in gaining wealth for Portugal was equaled by his desire to spread Christianity. In 1420, he was made a knight in a religious order. Already the governor of a province in southern Portugal, Henry paid for voyages of exploration with funds provided by the order. Each ship that set out from his court in Sagres bore a red cross on its sails, indicating the dual quest to find new lands and new converts to Christianity.

Theme: Impact of the Individual How might Portugal's history have been different if Henry had been the oldest son?

Chapter 15 **365**

Connections to Science

A Science Show On his final voyage to the Americas, Columbus and his crew were shipwrecked on the island of Jamaica. Stranded for over a year, they came perilously close to starvation—until Columbus used science to win the support of the island's natives.

In an astronomy book, Columbus had noted that a lunar eclipse was predicted for February 29 of that year. Columbus called together the native leaders and told them that God was angry with them for letting his men starve. He was so angry, in fact, that he was going to blot out the moon. The chiefs laughed at such folly—until the eclipse began. The astonishing event convinced them that God was on the side of the Europeans, and they provided them with food until help arrived.

Early Voyages of European Exploration, 1487–1609

Explorers for Portugal

- - → Dias, 1487–1488

——→ Da Gama, 1497–1499

Explorers for Spain

- - → Columbus, 1492–1493

——→ Balboa, 1510–1513

- - → Magellan and Elcano, 1519–1522

Explorers for England

——→ Cabot, 1497

Explorers for France

——→ Cartier, 1534–1535

Explorers for the Netherlands

——→ Hudson, 1609

Skills Assessment

Geography Beginning in the later 1400s, European nations sent explorers across the oceans in search of riches. New technology, such as the astrolabe and the caravel, made these voyages possible.

1. **Location** On the map, locate (a) Ottoman empire, (b) West Indies, (c) Strait of Magellan.
2. **Movement** (a) What region seems to have been of the most interest to explorers for England and the Netherlands? (b) What tool would they have used to determine location during their voyage?
3. **Critical Thinking** **Making Inferences** Why do you think explorers tended to take similar routes?

sailing west, he reasoned, would bring a ship to eastern Asia. His plan made sense, but Columbus made two errors. First, he greatly underestimated the size of the Earth. Second, he had no idea that two continents lay in his path.

Voyages of Columbus After Portugal refused to help him, Columbus persuaded Ferdinand and Isabella of Spain to finance his "enterprise of the Indies." In 1492, the Catholic rulers had driven the Muslims from their last stronghold in Spain. To strengthen their power, they sought new sources of wealth. Queen Isabella was also anxious to spread Christianity in Asia.

On August 3, 1492, Columbus sailed west with three small ships, the *Pinta*, the *Niña*, and the *Santa María*. Although the expedition encountered good weather and a favorable wind, no land came into sight. Provisions ran low, and the crew became anxious. Finally, on October 12, a lookout yelled, "Land! Land!"

Columbus then spent several months cruising the islands of the Caribbean. Because he thought he had reached the Indies, he called the people of the region Indians. In 1493, he returned to Spain to a hero's welcome. In three later voyages, Columbus remained convinced he had reached the coast of East Asia. Before long, though, other Europeans realized that Columbus had found a route to continents previously unknown to them.

Line of Demarcation Spain and Portugal pressed rival claims to the lands Columbus explored. In 1493, Pope Alexander VI stepped in to keep the peace. He set a Line of Demarcation dividing the non-European world

Skills Assessment

ANSWERS 1. Review locations with students. **2. (a)** North America **(b)** astrolabe **3.** Possible answer: They followed the same currents and winds.

Tools of Ocean Navigation

Astrolabe This device was used to measure the angles of the sun and stars above the horizon. It was difficult to use accurately in rough seas.

Caravel This ship combined the square sails of European vessels with the lateen (triangular) sails of their Arab counterparts. The new rigging made it easier to sail across and into the wind.

Scurvy This vitamin C deficiency disease was a frequent problem for sailors on long voyages. One sufferer described the horrors of scurvy in graphic terms: "It rotted all my gums, which gave out a black and putrid blood. My thighs and lower legs were black and gangrenous, and I was forced to use my knife each day to cut into the flesh in order to release this black and foul blood. I also used my knife on my gums, which were livid and growing over my teeth. . . . Many of our people died of it every day, and . . . for the most part they died with no aid given them, expiring behind some case or chest."

Native Americans of Canada, who were familiar with the disease, offered afflicted Europeans a cure made from brewed hemlock boughs. It wasn't until 1753 that Scottish naval surgeon James Lind prescribed the consumption of orange, lemon, or lime juice as a preventive and curative measure.

Trickery at Sea According to Antonio Pigafetta, a most deceitful incident occurred as Magellan's fleet took refuge in a Patagonian bay to await the passing of winter. Magellan decided that he would capture two Native Americans of the region. However, the two that he selected were very large men, and Magellan feared that his own men might be injured. He therefore devised a scheme.

When the unsuspecting victims visited, Magellan offered them gifts of knives, mirrors, bells, and glass, which the Patagonians gladly accepted. Then the captain offered leg irons, which the unknowing Patagonians took to be another generous gift. However, because their hands were full of the other treasures, they could not take hold of the irons. Magellan solved their problem by obligingly placing the shackles on their legs. Too late, the hapless Patagonians realized their mistake as they sailed out of the bay in chains.

---

into two zones. Spain had trading and exploration rights in any lands west of the line. Portugal had the same rights east of the line.

In 1500, the Portuguese captain Pedro Alvarez Cabral was blown off course as he sailed around Africa. Landing in Brazil, which lay east of the Line of Demarcation, he claimed it for Portugal.

Naming the "New World" In 1507, a German cartographer read reports about the "New World" written by an Italian sailor, Amerigo Vespucci. The mapmaker labeled the region America. The islands Columbus had explored in the Caribbean became known as the West Indies.

The Search Continues

Europeans continued to seek new routes around or through the Americas. In 1513, the Spanish adventurer Vasco Núñez de Balboa, with the help of Native Americans, hacked a passage through the tropical forests of Panama. From a ridge on the west coast, he gazed at a huge body of water that he called the South Sea. On September 20, 1519, a minor Portuguese noble named Ferdinand Magellan set out from Spain with five ships. His crew included men from Europe, Africa, and Southeast Asia.

Perils at Sea As the ships sailed south and west, through storms and calms and tropical heat, Magellan had to put down more than one mutiny. At last, the fleet reached the coast of South America. Carefully, they explored each bay, hoping for one that would lead to the Pacific.

Chapter 15 **367**

SECTION 1 Assessment

Recall
1. (a) Henry the Navigator, p. 365 (b) Vasco da Gama, p. 365 (c) Christopher Columbus, 365 (d) Vasco Núñez de Balboa, p. 367 (e) Ferdinand Magellan, p. 367 2. (a) cartographer, p. 365 (b) astrolabe, p. 365 (c) caravel, p. 365 (d) scurvy, p. 365 (e) circumnavigate, p. 368

Comprehension
3. They wanted to bypass the existing trading routes that were controlled by foreign powers and gain direct access to the spices and other goods of Asia.
4. (a) south along the coast of Africa, around the Cape of Good Hope, and on to Calicut on the west coast of India (b) Portugal seized key ports around the Indian Ocean to create a vast trading empire.
5. (a) He wanted to reach the Indies by sailing west across the Atlantic. (b) Columbus found previously unknown continents and expanded Spain's trading and exploration rights.

Critical Thinking and Writing
6. Students' answers should show an understanding of the dangers of ocean sailing at the time, as well as the potential for huge financial reward. 7. (a) They both underestimated the circumference of Earth. (b) Magellan thought he could find a sea route through the Americas, while Columbus didn't know they were there.

Activity Rubrics

Share rubrics with students before they begin researching Columbus's coat of arms.

Attempted The presentation is missing either the description or the drawing.

Minimal The presentation includes both a description and a drawing but is poorly organized and delivered.

Adequate The presentation includes both a description and a drawing and is well organized and delivered.

Exemplary The presentation includes both a description and a drawing, is very well organized, and is exceptionally well delivered.

Primary Source

ANSWER The voyage took longer than Magellan had calculated, and he failed to provide enough provisions for his crew. Also, they found no islands at which to stop and get fresh supplies as they crossed the Pacific.

Primary Source

Hardships on the Uncharted Sea
In his journal, Italian sailor Antonio Pigafetta detailed the desperate conditions Magellan's sailors faced as they crossed the Pacific Ocean:

"We remained 3 months and 20 days without taking in provisions or other refreshments and ate only old biscuit reduced to powder, full of grubs and stinking from the dirt which rats had made on it. We drank water that was yellow and stinking. We also ate the ox hides from under the mainyard which we softened by soaking in seawater for several days."

—Journal of Antonio Pigafetta

Skills Assessment

Primary Source Why was Magellan's crew forced to consume spoiled food and water?

In November 1520, Magellan's ships entered a bay at the southern tip of South America. Amid brutal storms, rushing tides, and unpredictable winds, Magellan charted a passage that became known as the Strait of Magellan. The ships emerged from this lashing into Balboa's South Sea, which Magellan renamed the Pacific—peaceful—Ocean.

Circumnavigating the Globe Their mission accomplished, most of the crew wanted to return to Spain the way they had come. Magellan, however, insisted they push on across the Pacific to the East Indies. Three more weeks, he thought, would bring them to the Spice Islands.

Magellan soon found that the Pacific was much wider than he imagined. For nearly four months, the ship plowed across the uncharted ocean. Finally in March 1521, the fleet reached the Philippines. There, Magellan was killed when he got involved in a local conflict. In the end, only one ship and 18 sailors completed the voyage. On September 8, 1522, nearly three years after setting out, the survivors reached Seville. The Spanish hailed them as the first people to circumnavigate, or sail around, the world.

Search for a Northwest Passage "I believe that never more will any man undertake to make such a voyage," predicted Antonio Pigafetta, a survivor of the Magellan voyage. But he was wrong. While Spain and Portugal claimed their zones, English, Dutch, and French explorers searched the coast of North America for a northwest passage to Asia.

In 1497, King Henry VII of England sent a Venetian navigator known as John Cabot to seek a more northerly route than the one Columbus had charted. Cabot found rich fishing grounds off Newfoundland, which he claimed for England. Later the French captain Jacques Cartier explored the St. Lawrence River, while Henry Hudson, sailing for the Dutch, explored the Hudson River. None of them found the hoped-for route to Asia, but the search for a Northwest Passage continued for centuries.

Looking Ahead

The European age of exploration set off a period of growing global interdependence that continues today. Yet the activities of European explorers brought both tragedy and triumph. As trade increased, conflicts between Europe and other civilizations would become more pronounced. These conflicts emerged first in Asia.

SECTION 1 Assessment

Recall
1. **Identify:** (a) Henry the Navigator, (b) Vasco da Gama, (c) Christopher Columbus, (d) Vasco Núñez de Balboa, (e) Ferdinand Magellan.
2. **Define:** (a) cartographer, (b) astrolabe, (c) caravel, (d) scurvy, (e) circumnavigate.

Comprehension
3. Why did European nations seek a sea route to Asia?
4. (a) Describe the routes taken by explorers for Portugal during the 1400s and early 1500s. (b) How did this affect Portugal's trade?
5. (a) Why did Columbus decide to sail westward? (b) What influence did his voyages have on other explorers?

Critical Thinking and Writing
6. **Making Decisions** What pros and cons would you weigh if you were a sailor trying to decide whether to sign on with da Gama, Columbus, or Magellan?
7. **Comparing** (a) In what way were the mistakes that Columbus and Magellan made similar? (b) How did their mistakes differ?

Activity
Take It to the NET

Use the Internet to find out about the coat of arms that Christopher Columbus used after his voyages. How did Columbus modify the original plan for his coat of arms? Present your findings and a drawing of the coat of arms to the class.

Resource Directory

Teaching Resources
Geography and History Activity *Mapmaking and Relative Location,* Geography and History booklet, pp. 8–9
Section Quiz Unit 4 booklet, p. 23
Creative Teaching Activities Creative Teaching Activities booklet, p. 69
Guided Reading and Review Unit 4 booklet, p. 24

Technology
Interactive Student Tutorial CD-ROM Ch. 15
Computer Test Bank Ch. 15

Reading Focus

- What are the key geographic features of Southeast Asia?

- What impact did Indian civilization have on new kingdoms and empires?

- What factors contributed to the growth of Vietnamese culture?

Vocabulary

matrilineal
stupa
padi

Taking Notes

As you read this section, prepare an outline of the contents. Use Roman numerals to indicate major headings. Use capital letters for the subheadings and numbers for the supporting details. The sample at right will help you get started.

I. Geography of
   Southeast Asia
  A. Location
    1. Mainland set apart
      by mountains and
      plateaus
    2.
  B. Trade routes in the
    southern seas

Main Idea   Because of its location, Southeast Asia was affected by the cultures of both China and India.

Setting the Scene

According to the chronicles of early Burma (modern Myanmar), King Anawrata spoke to a Buddhist monk named Thera Arahanta.

> "'Preach to me somewhat—yea, but a little—of the Law preached by the Lord, the Master.'
> And Arahanta preached the Law, beginning with the things not to be neglected. . . . Then the king's heart was full of faith, steadfast, and immovable. Faith sank into him as oil filtered a hundred times soaks into cotton."
> —*The Glass Palace Chronicle of the Kings of Burma*

Buddhism was one of many exports from India that had a profound effect on the peoples of Southeast Asia. Sandwiched between China and India, the region known today as Southeast Asia was strongly influenced by both of these powerful neighbors. Yet the distinct cultures of Southeast Asia retained their own unique identities.

Geography of Southeast Asia

Southeast Asia is made up of two major regions. The first region, mainland Southeast Asia, includes several peninsulas that jut south between India and China. Today, the mainland is home to Myanmar (MEE uhn mahr), Thailand, Cambodia, Laos, Vietnam, and part of Malaysia. The second region, island Southeast Asia, consists of more than 20,000 islands scattered between the Indian Ocean and the South China Sea. It includes the present-day nations of Indonesia, Singapore, Brunei (bru NĪ), and the Philippines.

Location The mainland is separated from the rest of Asia by mountains and high plateaus. Still, traders and invaders did push overland into the region. Mountains also separate the four main river valleys of Southeast Asia—the Irrawaddy (ihr uh WAHD ee), Chao Phraya, Mekong, and Red. These river valleys were home to early civilizations.

Island Southeast Asia has long been of strategic importance. All seaborne trade between China and India had to pass through either the Malacca or Sunda straits. Whoever commanded the straits controlled rich trade routes.

Trade Routes in the Southern Seas The monsoons, or seasonal winds, shaped trading patterns in the "southern seas." Ships traveled northeast in

Southeast Asia
As the Irrawaddy River reaches the sea, its valley flattens out into a broad delta. The Irrawaddy River valley, like other Southeast Asian river valleys, served as a home to the region's early civilizations.

Theme: Geography and History What are the other major rivers of Southeast Asia?

Bell Ringer Draw students' attention to the photograph of Angkor Wat on the next page. Invite the class to make generalizations about the civilization that produced elaborate temples such as this.

LESSON PLAN

1. Focus Due to favorable location and seasonal winds, Southeast Asia was linked by trade with East Africa, the Middle East, India, and China. Indian and Chinese civilizations had the greatest impact on the development of Southeast Asian cultures. The leading states of the region included Pagan, the Khmer empire, and Vietnam.

2. Instruct Have students imagine that they are aboard a merchant ship that is visiting ports of various Southeast Asian lands. Inform students that their merchant ship will stop at Pagan, the Khmer empire, the Srivijaya empire, and Vietnam. As they arrive at each port, they will record observations in their ship's journal. They should note the effects of geography on the culture, evidence of cultural diffusion, political relations with other countries, monuments that they see, and stories of great leaders. After their journey, invite volunteers to read their journal entries to the class. Encourage other students to ask pertinent questions about the journey.

3. Assess Ask students to refer to their journals and write four generalizations that describe Southeast Asian history, geography, or culture.

4. Reteach If students' **Assess** activity does not reflect adequate understanding of the lesson, you might assign the *Guide to the Essentials* or the *Interactive Student Tutorial CD-ROM* for this section.

Block Scheduling Support

Divide the class into small groups and have them imagine that they are part of a team writing a cultural history of India. The history will include information on both Indian culture and Indian influences on neighboring cultures. The students' team is responsible for writing the section on Indian influences. Using what they have read, have each group create an outline for their section. Then have a representative from each group present the group's findings to the class, while another group member records the group's response on the chalkboard. When each group has presented, use the notes on the board to compile a master outline. Use this master outline for further class discussion.

Caption Answer

the Chao Phraya, Mekong, and Red rivers

Virtual Field Trip

www.phschool.com

Angkor Wat
Cambodia

To learn more about Angkor Wat, use the Internet address above to link to the Web site for Angkor Wat.

Khmer Temple
Although Angkor Wat lies in ruins today, its intricate carvings suggest the magnificence of the original complex. The central towers represent the peaks of mythical Mount Meru, which was believed to be the home of the gods.

Theme: Religions and Value Systems Why might the builders of Angkor Wat have chosen to represent Mount Meru in their design?

summer and southwest in winter. Between seasons, while waiting for the winds to shift, merchants harbored their vessels in Southeast Asian ports, which became important centers of trade and culture. Soon, an international trade network linked India, Southeast Asia, and China to East Africa and the Middle East.

The key products of Southeast Asia were spices. Only a fraction of the spices traded in the region was destined for markets in Europe. Most cargoes went to East Asia, the Middle East, and East Africa.

Early Traditions The peoples of Southeast Asia developed their own cultures before Indian or Chinese influences shaped the region. At Bang Chiang in Thailand, archaeologists have found jars and bronze bracelets at least 5,000 years old. This evidence is challenging old theories about when civilization began in the region.

Over the centuries, diverse ethnic groups speaking many languages settled in Southeast Asia. Living in isolated villages, they followed their own religious and cultural patterns. Many societies were built around the nuclear family rather than the extended families of India and China.

Women had greater equality in Southeast Asia than elsewhere in Asia. Female merchants took part in the spice trade, gaining fame for their skill in bargaining, finance, and languages. In some port cities, they gained enough wealth and influence to become rulers. Matrilineal descent, or inheritance through the mother, was an accepted custom in Southeast Asia. Women also had some freedom in choosing or divorcing marriage partners. Even after Indian and Chinese influences arrived, women retained their traditional rights.

Impact of India

Indian merchants and Hindu priests filtered into Southeast Asia, slowly spreading their culture. Later, Buddhist monks and scholars introduced Theravada beliefs. Following the path of trade and religion came the influence of writing, law, government, art, architecture, and farming.

Increasing Contacts In the early centuries A.D., Indian traders settled in port cities in growing numbers. They gave presents to local rulers and married into influential families. Trade brought prosperity as merchants exchanged products such as cottons, jewels, and perfume for raw materials such as timber, spices, and gold.

In time, local Indian families exercised considerable power. Also, people from Southeast Asia visited India as pilgrims or students. As these contacts increased, Indian beliefs and ideas won widespread acceptance. Indian influence reached its peak between 500 and 1000.

Islam Long after Hinduism and Buddhism took root in Southeast Asia, Indians carried a third religion, Islam, into the region. By the 1200s, Muslims ruled northern India. From there, traders spread Islamic beliefs and Muslim civilization throughout the islands of Indonesia and as far east as the Philippines.* Arab merchants, too, spread the new faith. The prevalence of Islam in lands surrounding the Indian Ocean contributed to the growth of a stable, thriving trade network.

New Kingdoms and Empires

The blend of Indian influences with local cultures produced a series of kingdoms and empires in Southeast Asia. Some of these states rivaled those of India.

Pagan The kingdom of Pagan (pah GAHN) arose in the fertile rice-growing Irrawaddy Valley in present-day Myanmar. In 1044, King Anawrata (ah nuh RAH tuh) united the region. He is credited with bringing Buddhism to the Burman people. Buddhism had reached nearby cultures long before, but Anawrata made Pagan a major Buddhist center. He filled his capital city with magnificent stupas, or dome-shaped shrines, at about the same time that people in medieval Europe were beginning to build Gothic cathedrals.

Pagan flourished for some 200 years after Anawrata's death, but fell in 1287 to conquering Mongols. When the Burmans finally threw off foreign rule, they looked back with pride to the great days of Pagan.

The Khmer Empire Indian influences also helped shape the Khmer (kuh MEHR) empire, which reached its peak between 800 and 1350. Its greatest rulers controlled much of present-day Cambodia, Thailand, and Malaysia. The Khmer people adapted Indian writing, mathematics, architecture, and art. Khmer rulers became pious Hindus. Like the princes and emperors of India, they saw themselves as god-kings. Most ordinary people, however, preferred Buddhism.

In the 1100s, King Suryavarman II built the great temple complex at Angkor Wat. The ruins that survive today, though overgrown with jungle and pocked by the bullets of recent wars, are among the most impressive in the world. Hundreds of carved figures tell Hindu myths and glorify the king. Although the images of Vishnu, Shiva, and the Buddha reflect strong Indian influence, the style is uniquely Khmer.

Srivijaya The trading empire of Srivijaya (shree vah JĪ yah), in Indonesia, flourished from the 600s to the 1200s. Srivijaya controlled the Strait of

_____

*Today, Indonesia has the largest Muslim population of any nation in the world.

Empires and Kingdoms of Southeast Asia

Pagan kingdom, A.D. 1044–A.D. 1287
Khmer empire, A.D. 800–A.D. 1350
Srivijaya empire, A.D. 600s–A.D. 1200s
Vietnam kingdom, A.D. 939–A.D. 1883
→ Mongol invasion, A.D. 1287

INDIA
CHINA
Red R.
Pagan •
Bay of Bengal
Chao Phraya R.
Mekong R.
Angkor Wat •
Gulf of Thailand
Strait of Malacca
Sumatra
Malacca •
Palembang •
Sunda Strait
Java
PACIFIC OCEAN
Philippine Islands
Manila •
South China Sea
Borneo
The Moluccas (Spice Islands)
INDIAN OCEAN
90°E
110°E
120°E
100°E
30°N
20°N
0°
10°S

Azimuthal Equal Area Projection
0   400   800 Miles
0   400   800 Kilometers

Skills Assessment

Geography The region we call Southeast Asia consists of both a mainland area and thousands of islands. It was home to numerous ancient and diverse cultures.

1. **Location** On the map, locate (a) Pagan kingdom, (b) Angkor Wat, (c) the Moluccas, (d) Sunda Strait.
2. **Movement** From which direction did the Mongol invasion take place?
3. **Critical Thinking**
   Understanding Sequence During which centuries were these empires and kingdoms most likely to have come into contact with one another?

Human Drama Note

Angkor Wat The temple complex at Angkor Wat is a monumental work. A wide causeway leads to the enormous entrance gate. Along the causeway are sculptures that symbolize fertility. Beyond the entrance gate are terraces arranged in a series of three diminishing stories and crowned by five towers. The central tower, shaped like a mountain, represented the Khmer god-kings. The interior walls of each room are adorned with reliefs illustrating elements of Hindu mythology. Many of the scenes relate to the god Vishnu, to whom the temple was dedicated.

Test Preparation

Have students read the section titled "Increasing Contacts," which begins on the opposite page and ends on this page, and then complete the sentence below.

Southeast Asians visited India as students or

A to visit relatives.

B to start new trading outposts.

C to spread Christianity.

D for religious reasons.

Recall

1. **(a)** Pagan, p. 371 **(b)** Anawrata, p. 371 **(c)** Khmer, p. 371 **(d)** Suryavarman II, p. 371 **(e)** Trung sisters, p. 372 **2. (a)** matri-lineal, p. 370 **(b)** stupa, p. 371 **(c)** padi, p. 372

Comprehension

3. Sea trade had to pass through either the Malacca or Sunda strait; command of these straits meant control of a rich trade.
4. Indian influences included religion, writing, mathematics, architecture, and art. **5. (a)** Han armies controlled Vietnam for 1,000 years, introducing their civil service system, government bureaucracy, language, and Mahayana and Daoist beliefs. **(b)** A Vietnamese uprising in A.D. 39 briefly drove out the Chinese. Vietnam broke free of Chinese rule again in 939.

Critical Thinking and Writing

6. Possible answer: The traditional rights and freedoms of women were deeply rooted in Southeast Asian culture. As a result, Indian and Chinese influence had relatively little impact. **7.** Possible answer: Indian influence was spread through trade and intermarriage, while Chinese influence depended on conquest.

Activity Rubrics

Share rubrics with students before they make their maps.

Attempted The map is missing most standard elements; labels are difficult to read, missing, or inaccurately placed.

Minimal The map is missing some standard elements; most labels are included, but they are somewhat difficult to read, and several are inaccurately placed.

Adequate The map includes most standard elements; all labels are included, and most are easy to read and accurately placed.

Exemplary The map includes all appropriate standard elements; all labels are included, easy to read, and accurately placed.

Biography

ANSWER They rose up, fought, and overthrew the conquering Chinese, which appeals to the Vietnamese people's sense of nationalism.

Biography

Trung Sisters
d. A.D. 42(?)

Although the Chinese conquest of Annam introduced Confucian values, many local traditions continued for centuries. Women remained involved in politics, law, and trade. Still, officials were surprised when sisters Trung Trac and Trung Nhi forged a legacy for themselves as freedom fighters.

The sisters managed to do what no one else could. They forced the conquering Chinese out and established home rule. They did this by recruiting and training over 80,000 men and women to fight. Thirty-six of their generals were women.

After three years, however, the Chinese emperor sent an army against the sisters. According to legend, after a terrible defeat, the Trung sisters drowned themselves to avoid capture.

Theme: Impact of the Individual Why are the Trung sisters still revered in Vietnam today?

Malacca, which, as you have learned, was vital to shipping. Both Hinduism and Buddhism reached this island empire. As elsewhere in Southeast Asia, however, the local people often blended Indian beliefs into their own forms of worship, based on nature spirits.

Later, Islam spread to Sumatra, Java, and other islands. Local rulers adopted the new religion, which cemented commercial links with other Muslim trading centers around the Indian Ocean.

Vietnam Emerges

In most of Southeast Asia, Indian influence outweighed Chinese influence. Indian traditions spread mostly through trade rather than conquest. China, however, sent military forces to conquer the neighboring state of Annam (now northern Vietnam).

The heart of northern Vietnam was the Red River delta, around present-day Hanoi. There, the river irrigated fertile rice **padis,** or fields, which provided food for a growing population. The Vietnamese had their own distinct culture. As in other parts of Southeast Asia, women often held positions of authority.

Chinese Domination In 111 B.C., Han armies conquered the region. China remained in control for 1,000 years. During that time, the Vietnamese absorbed Confucian ideas. They adopted the Chinese civil service system and built a government bureaucracy similar to that found in China. Vietnamese nobles learned to speak the Chinese language and read Chinese characters. Unlike the rest of Southeast Asia, where Theravada Buddhism had the strongest impact, Vietnam adopted Mahayana beliefs from China. Daoism also helped shape Vietnamese society.

Resistance Despite these powerful Chinese influences, the Vietnamese preserved a strong sense of their separate identity. In A.D. 39, two noble sisters, Trung Trac and Trung Nhi, led an uprising that briefly drove the Chinese occupiers from the land. They tried to restore a simpler form of government based on ancient Vietnamese traditions. To this day, the Trung sisters are remembered as great martyrs and heroes. Finally in 939, as the Tang dynasty collapsed in China, Vietnam was able to break free from China. The Vietnamese turned back repeated Chinese efforts to reconquer their land, but did remain a tributary state of China.

SECTION 2 **Assessment**

Recall

1. **Identify:** **(a)** Pagan, **(b)** Anawrata, **(c)** Khmer, **(d)** Suryavarman II, **(e)** Trung sisters.
2. **Define:** **(a)** matrilineal, **(b)** stupa, **(c)** padi.

Comprehension

3. How did geography make Southeast Asia of strategic importance?
4. How did India influence Pagan, the Khmer empire, and Srivijaya?
5. **(a)** How did China influence Vietnam? **(b)** How did Vietnam preserve its identity?

Critical Thinking and Writing

6. **Analyzing Information** Women's social status was limited in both India and China. Why do you think Southeast Asian women were able to retain their equality despite strong Indian and Chinese cultural influence?
7. **Comparing** How did the spread of Indian influence through Southeast Asia differ from the spread of Chinese influence through the same region?

Activity

Making a Map
Create a map showing foreign influences in Southeast Asia. First, draw or trace an outline map of the region. Use arrows to show the origins and directions of influences—for example, blue arrows for trade routes, red arrows for invasion routes. Then, show what products or ideas traveled along these routes.

Resource Directory

Teaching Resources

History Through Literature *Poetry from 15th-Century Vietnam,* History Through Literature booklet, p. 34
Section Quiz Unit 4 booklet, p. 25
Creative Teaching Activities Creative Teaching Activities booklet, p. 70
Guided Reading and Review Unit 4 booklet, p. 26

Technology

Interactive Student Tutorial CD-ROM Ch. 15
Computer Test Bank Ch. 15

World History Visions, Voices, Views Animated Map Story, *The Global Trade in Pepper (1100s–1700s),* videodisc side 2 or videotape 4, running time 3:00 min.

Side 2: Fr. 37618-42985

SECTION **3** European Footholds in Southeast Asia and India

Reading Focus

- How did the Portuguese and the Dutch build empires in the East?
- How did Spain control the Philippines?
- How did the decline of Mughal India affect European traders?

Vocabulary

outpost
sepoy

Taking Notes

Begin a concept web like this one. As you read this section, fill in the blank circles with information about European influence in Southeast Asia and India. Add more circles as necessary.

Main Idea Europeans used military power to build trading empires in Southeast Asia.

Setting the Scene

In 1511, a Portuguese fleet commanded by Afonso de Albuquerque (ahl boo KEHR keh) dropped anchor off Malacca, a rich Muslim trading port that controlled the sea route linking India, Southeast Asia, and China. "Have you come in peace or in war?" asked the sultan. "Peace," replied Albuquerque. The true goal of the Portuguese, however, was not peace, but conquest.

The fleet remained at anchor for several weeks. Then they opened fire. The Portuguese quickly took the city, killing its inhabitants and seizing its wealth. On the ruins of a mosque, Albuquerque built a fort. The sultan had fled, thinking the invaders would loot and leave. But when he heard about the fort, he realized that the Portuguese had come to stay.

Portugal was the first European power to gain a foothold in Asia. The Portuguese ships were small in size and number, but the firepower of their shipboard cannons was unmatched. In time, this superior firepower helped them win control of the rich Indian Ocean spice trade and build a Portuguese trading empire in Asia. Before long, however, other European nations would challenge Portugal.

Portugal's Empire in the East

After Vasco da Gama's voyage, the Portuguese, under Albuquerque's command, burst into the Indian Ocean. In 1510, they seized the island of Goa off the coast of India, making it their major military and commercial base. Albuquerque then moved to end Muslim power and turn the Indian Ocean into a "Portuguese lake."

Trading Outposts Albuquerque burned coastal towns and crushed Arab fleets at sea. The Portuguese attacked Aden, at the entrance to the Red Sea, and took Ormuz, gateway to the Persian Gulf. In 1511, Albuquerque took Malacca, massacring the city's Muslims and making the Europeans hated and feared.

In less than 50 years, the Portuguese had built a trading empire with military and merchant outposts, or distant areas under their control, rimming the southern seas. They seized cities on the east coast of Africa so they could resupply and repair their ships. For most of the 1500s, Portugal controlled the spice trade between Europe and Asia.

Impact Despite their sea power, the Portuguese remained on the fringe of Asian trade. They had neither the strength nor the resources to conquer

Primary Source

The Portuguese in India
Afonso de Albuquerque explained to his soldiers why the Portuguese wanted to capture Malacca:

"The king of Portugal has often commanded me to go to the Straits, because . . . this was the best place to intercept the trade which the Moslems . . . carry on in these parts. So it was to do Our Lord's service that we were brought here; by taking Malacca, we would close the Straits so that never again would the Moslems be able to bring their spices by this route. . . . I am very sure that, if this Malacca trade is taken out of their hands, Cairo and Mecca will be completely lost."

—*The Commentaries of the Great Afonso de Albuquerque*

Skills Assessment

Primary Source Why did Portugal want to control Malacca?

Block Scheduling Support

Divide the class into two randomly selected groups. Instruct students in Group A to consider Albuquerque's actions from the viewpoint of Albuquerque himself or another Portuguese invader. Students in Group B should take the viewpoint of native Malaccans or other Muslims faced with Albuquerque and his men. Ask students in both groups to write brief position papers and have one or two volunteers from each group share theirs with the class. Then, have the groups switch sides to consider the opposite point of view. Again, have students write brief position papers and ask volunteers from each group to read theirs to the class.

Bell Ringer Write the word *monopoly* on the board, and ask students to explain how one wins the board game that bears that name. Then, have students skim the section and read the words of Afonso de Albuquerque quoted in the Primary Source feature on this page. Ask students to describe Portugal's goal. Ask them to name the other players in this real-life and very deadly game of "monopoly."

LESSON PLAN

1. Focus The Portuguese used military power to build an empire in Southeast Asia. By the same means, the Dutch replaced the Portuguese as the region's leading commercial power. As Mughal rule collapsed during the 1700s, European nations were also able to extend their influence into India.

2. Instruct Have students work in groups to construct annotated time lines. Their time lines will chart European policies and actions in Southeast Asia and India between the 1500s and 1700s. Have each group focus on the influence of one of these European nations: Portugal, the Netherlands, Spain, Britain, France. Encourage students to supplement information in the text by consulting additional resources.

3. Assess Have each group display its finished time line and explain its contents in an oral presentation.

4. Reteach If students' Assess activity does not reflect adequate understanding of the lesson, you might assign the *Guide to the Essentials* or the *Interactive Student Tutorial CD-ROM* for this section.

Primary Source

ANSWER so it could control the spice trade dominated by Muslim traders and thus weaken Islam

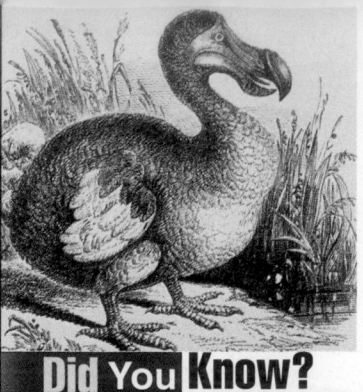

much territory on land. In India and China, where they faced far stronger empires, they merely sought permission to trade.

The intolerance of Portuguese missionaries caused resentment. In Goa, they attacked Muslims, destroyed Hindu temples, and introduced the Inquisition. Portuguese ships even sank Muslim pilgrim ships on their way to Mecca. Some Asian merchants chose to trade with the Portuguese. Others, however, chose to bypass Portuguese-controlled towns and continue their older trade patterns.

Rise of the Dutch

The Dutch were the first Europeans to challenge Portuguese domination in Asia. The land we know today as the Netherlands included a group of provinces and prosperous cities on the North Sea. The region had long been a center of handicrafts and trade. Through royal marriages, it fell under Spanish rule in the early 1500s. Later, the Protestant northern provinces won independence.

Sea Power In 1599, a Dutch fleet returned to Amsterdam from Asia after more than a year's absence. It carried a cargo of pepper, cloves, and other spices. Church bells rang to celebrate this "Happy Return." Those who had invested in the venture received 100 percent profit. The success of this voyage led to a frenzy of overseas activity.

By the late 1500s, Dutch warships and trading vessels put the Netherlands in the forefront of European commerce. They used their sea power to set up colonies and trading posts around the world. At the southwestern tip of Africa, the Dutch built the Cape Town settlement, where they could repair and resupply their ships.

Dutch Dominance In 1602, a group of wealthy Dutch merchants formed the Dutch East India Company. In the next decades, the Dutch strove to make themselves the major European power in the east. In 1641, they captured Malacca from the Portuguese and opened trade with China. Before long, they were able to enforce a monopoly in the Spice Islands, controlling shipments to Europe as well as much of the trade within Southeast Asia.

Like the Portuguese, the Dutch used military force to further their trading goals. At the same time, they forged closer ties with local rulers than the Portuguese had. Many Dutch merchants married Asian women.

Trade brought the Dutch enormous wealth. At home, Dutch merchants built tall mansions along the canals of Amsterdam and hired artists like Rembrandt to paint their portraits. In the 1700s, however, the growing power of England and France contributed to the decline of the Dutch trading empire in the East.

Spain Seizes the Philippines

While the Portuguese and Dutch set up bases on the fringes of Asia, Spain took over the Philippines. Magellan had claimed the archipelago for Spain in 1521. Within about 50 years, Spain had conquered and colonized the islands, renaming them for the Spanish king Philip II. Unlike most other peoples of Southeast Asia, the Filipinos were not united. As a result, they could be conquered more easily.

In the spirit of the Catholic Reformation, Spanish priests set out to convert the Filipino people to Christianity. Later, missionaries from the Philippines tried to spread Catholic teachings in China and Japan.

The Philippines became a key link in Spain's overseas trading empire. The Spanish shipped silver mined in Mexico and Peru across the Pacific to the Philippines. From there, they used the silver to buy goods in China. In this way, large quantities of American silver flowed into the economies of East Asian nations.

Disaster!

CYCLONE RIPS THROUGH CALCUTTA

When the English East India Company chose the location for the port city of Calcutta (Kolkata) in 1696, they did not realize its danger. Calcutta was built on the Hooghly River, part of the Ganges River delta system that flows into the Bay of Bengal. The bay is hit several times a year with devastating tropical storms. On October 11, 1737, the region was hit by one of the most destructive cyclones in history.

The storm surge—walls of water pushed by powerful winds—is the deadliest part of a cyclone. Waves start small, but as the storm approaches the shore, the surge grows. Finally, huge waves crash onto the shore, flooding the land.

Violent winds and rain struck Calcutta. Breaking waves caused a deafening roar. Then, a monstrous 40-foot wave crashed down on the shore. According to some reports, as many as 300,000 people died and 20,000 boats sank.

Desperate sailors were tossed from their ships and drowned. Of the nine British ships anchored in the Ganges before the storm hit, only one remained afloat. After the storm, bits of the shattered ships were found hanging in trees six miles upriver.

Portfolio Assessment

Use the Internet or other research sources to learn about other tropical storms such as a hurricane in the United States. Make a chart listing precautions that people in coastal areas can take to minimize damage and loss of life.

Chapter 15 **375**

Disaster!

Bell Ringer Point out that the Calcutta area, like neighboring Bangladesh, is on a low-lying plain with many river channels forming one huge delta. This terrain makes the area prone to flooding from the frequent storms.

Background
Connections to Today

Cyclones Today Eastern and northeastern India and Bangladesh suffer from frequent storm damage and flooding. On October 29, 1999, for example, a cyclone struck the state of Orissa on India's east coast with wind gusts up to 190 miles an hour. More than 9,500 people died, some by drowning and many others from disease brought on by contaminated water or lack of adequate food.

Activity
Cooperative Learning

Making a Map Have students work together in five groups to find the most devastating storms of the twentieth century in each of the following five types: typhoons, cyclones, hurricanes, tornadoes, and blizzards. Another group should make a large world map for the bulletin board. Each of the five groups should write a brief definition of its storm type and details of the worst storm and place it on the outside of the map. Then group members should show on the map where their storm occurred.

Portfolio Assessment Rubrics

Share rubrics with students before they make their charts.

Attempted The chart lists few precautions and is poorly written, with many mechanical errors.

Minimal The chart lists some precautions but contains numerous errors.

Adequate The chart lists numerous precautions; contains few mechanical errors; and is well written, informative, and interesting.

Exemplary The chart lists many precautions; contains no mechanical errors; and is informative, interesting, and presented effectively.

Human Drama Note

Tipu Sultan The British made great gains in India by making alliances with local rulers. But one ruler, Tipu Sultan of Mysore, refused to make such an alliance with the European invaders. For a while, he won many battles against the British and their Indian allies. But in 1799, he died in an unsuccessful defense of his capital. Tipu's hatred of the British was reflected in one of his favorite objects—a model of a clockwork tiger eating an Englishman. His famous model ended up in the Victoria and Albert Museum in London.

Test Preparation

Have students read the last paragraph on the opposite page, and then answer the question below.

Which of the following would be a good title for this paragraph?

A Global Trade

B The Philippines

C Mexican Silver

D East Asian Economics

SECTION 3 Assessment

Recall

1. (a) Afonso de Albuquerque, p. 373
(b) Robert Clive, p. 376 2. (a) outpost, p. 373 (b) sepoy, p. 376

Comprehension

3. (a) Armed with guns and cannons, the Portuguese waged war on the inhabitants of coastal towns, burned their towns, and overwhelmed their fleets. (b) The Dutch were successful in trading by sea and were at the forefront of European commerce. They eventually captured Malacca from the Portuguese and opened trade with China. 4. (a) The people were not united. (b) Its location between the Americas and Asia helped expand Spain's trading empire. Queen Isabella also wished to spread Christianity. 5. (a) Civil wars and political corruption weakened the Mughal government. (b) The decline led to competition between Britain and France for control of India. By the late 1700s, the British were victorious.

Critical Thinking and Writing

6. Possible answer: Through negotiation and military force, they gained control of trade networks that had been established by Asians. They then extended these networks to include Europe. 7. Possible answer: Trade was controlled by whichever nation was able to use force most effectively.

Caption Answer

The wall hanging incorporates Indian design motifs, but also depicts Europeans.

Prized Imports
Indian artisans created products like this hand-painted cotton wall hanging for European markets. Indian cottons became so popular in England that, to protect the English textile industry, Parliament tried to ban them.

Theme: Global Interaction
How does this wall hanging reflect both Indian and European culture?

Mughal India and European Traders

Before the 1700s, European traders made very little impression on India, which was enjoying one of its greatest periods of strength and prosperity. In 1526, Babur had founded the Mughal dynasty. European merchants were dazzled by India's splendid court and its many luxury goods. There seemed little of value that Europeans could offer to the sophisticated civilization of Mughal India.

Industry and Commerce Besides producing spices, India was the world leader in textile manufacturing. It exported large quantities of silk and cotton cloth, from sheer muslins to elaborate chintzes. Handicrafts and shipbuilding added to the country's wealth.

The Mughal empire was larger, richer, and more powerful than any kingdom in Europe. When Europeans sought trading rights, Mughal emperors saw no threat in granting such concessions. The Portuguese and later the Dutch, English, and French thus were permitted to build forts and warehouses in coastal towns.

Turmoil and Decline When Akbar's successors ended his policy of religious toleration, conflicts rekindled between Hindu and Muslim princes. Years of civil war drained Mughal resources. Rulers then increased taxes, sparking peasant rebellions. Several weak rulers held the throne in the early 1700s. Corruption became widespread, and the central government eventually collapsed.

British-French Rivalry As Mughal power faltered, French and English traders played off rival Indian princes against one another. Both the English and French East India companies made alliances with local officials and independent rajahs. Each company organized its own army of sepoys, or Indian troops.

By the mid-1700s, the British and the French had become locked in a bitter struggle for global power. In 1756, war between Britain and France erupted in Europe. The fighting soon spread, involving both nations' lands in Asia and the Americas.

In India, Robert Clive, an agent of the British East India Company, used an army of British troops and sepoys to drive the French from their trading posts. The Company then forced the Mughal emperor to recognize its right to collect taxes in Bengal in the northeast. By the late 1700s, the Company had become the real ruler of Bengal, able to use its great wealth to spread its influence into other parts of India.

SECTION 3 Assessment

Recall

1. **Identify:** (a) Afonso de Albuquerque, (b) Robert Clive.
2. **Define:** (a) outpost, (b) sepoy.

Comprehension

3. (a) How did the Portuguese gain control of the spice trade? (b) How were they challenged by the Dutch?
4. (a) Why was Spain easily able to conquer the Philippines? (b) Why did Spain want to control the islands?

5. (a) Why did Mughal power decline? (b) What effect did the decline have on France and Britain?

Critical Thinking and Writing

6. **Analyzing Information** How did Europeans build on existing trade networks in the Indian Ocean?
7. **Drawing Conclusions** Some people have argued "to the victors belong the spoils [riches] of the enemy." How do events in this section support this statement?

Resource Directory

Reading Focus

- How was European trade with China affected by the Manchu conquest?

- What factors led Korea to isolate itself from other nations?

- What attitude did the Tokugawa shoguns have toward foreign traders?

Taking Notes

As you read this section, make a table to show how westerners acted and were received in East Asia. Use this table as a model.

	CHINA	KOREA	JAPAN
WESTERN BEHAVIOR AND ATTITUDES	• Matteo Ricci speaks Chinese • Macartney offends emperor		
RESPONSE TO WESTERNERS	• Restrict trade		

Main Idea China, Korea, and Japan limited contact with western nations.

Setting the Scene

The Europeans who reached Asia in the 1500s often made a poor impression on their hosts. The Italian traveler Niccoló Manucci told how Asians thought that Europeans "have no polite manners, that they are ignorant, wanting in ordered life, and very dirty."

Europeans, by contrast, wrote enthusiastically about China. In 1590, a visitor described Chinese artisans "cleverly making devices out of gold, silver and other metals." He was also impressed with their abilities in handicrafts and gunsmithing, and wrote: "They daily publish huge multitudes of books."

Portuguese ships first reached China by way of the South China Sea during the Ming dynasty. To the Chinese, the Portuguese were "southern barbarians." Like other foreigners, they lacked the civilized ways of the Middle Kingdom.

European Trade With China

The Ming dynasty, you will recall, ended its overseas explorations in the mid-1400s. Confucian officials had little use for foreigners. "Since our empire owns the world," said a Ming document, "there is no country on this or other sides of the seas which does not submit to us."

Strict Limits on Trade Portuguese traders reached China by sea in 1514. To the Chinese, the newcomers had little to offer in exchange for silks and porcelains. European textiles and metalwork were inferior to Chinese products. The Chinese therefore demanded payment in gold or silver.

The Ming eventually allowed the Portuguese a trading post at Macao, near Canton, present-day Guangzhou (gwahng JOH). Later, they let Dutch, English, and other Europeans trade with Chinese merchants, but only under strict limits. Foreigners could trade only at Canton under the supervision of imperial officials. When each year's trading season ended, they had to sail away.

Scholars and Missionaries A few European scholars, like the brilliant Jesuit priest Matteo Ricci, did make a positive impression on Ming China.

China and Foreign Trade
This fan shows the harbor in Canton, with European flags flying over warehouses in the background. Strict limits on foreign trade kept Europeans from gaining a foothold in China.

Theme: Economics and Technology How does the scene on this fan suggest the limitations placed on European merchants?

In the 1580s, Ricci learned to speak Chinese and adopted Chinese dress. Ricci and other priests had little success spreading their religious beliefs, although Chinese rulers welcomed the chance to learn the arts and sciences of Renaissance Europe.

The Manchu Conquest

By the early 1600s, the aging Ming dynasty was decaying. Revolts erupted, and Manchu invaders from the north pushed through the Great Wall. The Manchus ruled a region in the northeast that had long been influenced by Chinese civilization. In 1644, victorious Manchu armies seized Beijing and made it their capital.

Qing Rule The Manchus set up a new dynasty called the Qing (CHIHNG), meaning "pure." To preserve their distinct identity, the Manchus barred intermarriage between Manchus and Chinese. Manchu women were forbidden to follow the traditional Chinese practice of footbinding. Still, the Manchus won the support of the Chinese scholar-officials because they adopted the Confucian system of government. For each top government position, the Qing chose two people, one Manchu and one Chinese. Local government remained in the hands of the Chinese, but Manchu troops stationed across the empire ensured loyalty.

Two rulers oversaw the most brilliant age of the Qing. Kangxi (kahng SHEE), who ruled from 1661 to 1722, was an able administrator and military leader. He extended Chinese power into Central Asia and promoted Chinese culture. Kangxi's grandson Qianlong (chyehn LOHNG) had an equally successful reign from 1736 to 1796. He expanded China's borders to rule the largest area in the nation's history. Qianlong retired after 60 years because he did not want to rule longer than his grandfather had.

Prosperity The Chinese economy expanded under both emperors. New crops from the Americas, such as potatoes and corn, boosted farm output, which in turn contributed to a population boom. China's population rose from 140 million in 1740 to over 300 million by 1800. Peace and prosperity encouraged further growth in handicraft industries, including silk, cotton, and porcelain. Internal trade grew, as did the demand for Chinese goods from all over the world.

Response to Westerners The Qing maintained the Ming policy of restricting foreign traders. Still, Europeans kept pressing to expand trade to cities other than Guangzhou. In 1793, Lord Macartney arrived in China at the head of a British diplomatic mission. He brought samples of British-made goods to show the Chinese the advantages of trade with westerners. The Chinese thought the goods were gifts offered as tribute to the emperor and looked on them as rather crude products.

Further misunderstandings followed. Macartney insisted on an audience with the emperor. The Chinese told Macartney he would have to perform the traditional kowtow, touching his head to the ground to show respect to the emperor. Macartney refused. He also offended the Chinese by speaking of the natural superiority of the English. The negotiations faltered. In the end, Qianlong did receive Macartney, but the meeting accomplished nothing. Later, in a letter to King George III of Britain, Qianlong rejected the request for trading rights.

At the time, Qianlong's attitude seemed justified by China's successes. After all, he already ruled the world's greatest empire. Why should he negotiate with a nation as distant as Britain? In the long run, however, his policy proved disastrous. Even then, there was much the Chinese could have learned from the West. In the 1800s, China would learn about western advances—especially in military technology—the hard way.

Connections to Today

Guangzhou's International Trade

For centuries, the thriving port of Guangzhou has welcomed merchants from many lands. Today, thousands of business people from all over the world attend the twice-yearly Guangzhou Fair. There they buy Chinese products to sell overseas and market their own goods to sell in China.

Many foreign companies have opened branches in Guangzhou. They have done so because of its status as one of 14 "coastal open cities." This special designation allows Guangzhou to extend privileges, including lower taxes, to foreign companies that want to do business there.

Theme: Economics and Technology How has Guangzhou continued to thrive from international trade?

Connections to Today

ANSWER Trade fairs help sell Chinese products; its status as "coastal open city" encourages foreign investment.

Resource Directory

Teaching Resources
Analyzing Primary Sources Chapter Extension Activities booklet, p. 40

Letter From the Celestial Emperor to the "Barbarian" King

In the following excerpt, Emperor Qianlong denies the request of King George III for greater trading rights in China.

"We have perused [read] the text of your state message and the wording expresses your earnestness. From it your sincere humility and obedience can clearly be seen. It is admirable and we fully approve. . . .

As to what you have requested in your message, O King, namely to be allowed to send one of your subjects to reside in the Celestial Empire to look after your country's trade, this does not conform to the Celestial Empire's ceremonial system, and definitely cannot be done. . . .

Moreover, the territories ruled by the Celestial Empire are vast, and for all the envoys of vassal [inferior] states coming to the capital there are definite regulations. . . . There has never been any precedent for allowing them to suit their own convenience. . . . Furthermore, there are a great many Western Ocean countries altogether, and not merely your one country. If, like you, O King, they all beg to send someone to reside at the capital, how could we grant their request in every case? It would be absolutely impossible for us to do so. How can we go so far as to change the regulations of the Celestial Empire . . . because of the request of one man—of you, O King? . . .

We have never valued ingenious articles, nor do we have the slightest need of your country's manufacturers. . . . You, O King, should simply act in conformity with our wishes by strengthening your loyalty and swearing perpetual obedience so as to ensure that your country may share the blessings of peace."

—Qianlong, letter to George III

Lord Macartney's Mission
Artist William Alexander traveled to China with Lord Macartney. He did not attend the British meeting with the emperor, however, and had to rely on a British officer's firsthand drawings to produce this picture.

Skills Assessment

1. Emperor Qianlong seems to treat King George as
   - A an equal.
   - B an inferior.
   - C a superior.
   - D a threat.

2. What reason does the emperor not give for denying the king's request?
   - E historical precedent
   - F current regulations
   - G lack of interest in British goods
   - H fear of foreign influence

3. **Critical Thinking Recognizing Points of View** (a) What words or phrases convey Emperor Qianlong's view of the British king? (b) How does the emperor characterize his own nation?

✓ Test Preparation

Have students read the last paragraph on this page, and then answer the question below.

What does the word *perpetual* mean in this passage?

- A loyal
- B heartfelt
- Ⓒ everlasting
- D slavish

Background
About the Primary Source

Versions of Qianlong's Letter Qianlong wrote his letter to King George weeks before Lord Macartney's audience with the emperor. After Macartney refused to kowtow, the letter's language was strengthened, but there was really little hope for the mission's success. Missionaries who translated the letter into Latin had softened the language. Then, Macartney and a colleague summarized the letter in English and carefully removed anything that might offend King George. Long after everyone involved was dead, the original version, excerpted here, was made public.

Activity
Interpreting the Primary Source

Use this additional question to generate class discussion.
Critical Thinking: Predicting Consequences Given the technological superiority of the British, what would you expect to be the results of China's refusal to accept increased trade? *(Students should recognize that China would be at a disadvantage if hostilities should break out.)*

Skills Tip

The language used in the letter, starting with the name Celestial (heavenly) tells you how the emperor views himself and his country. The Skills Handbook in the front of the book has a lesson that will help students with this feature.

Skills Assessment

ANSWERS 1. B 2. H 3. (a) He praises King George's "sincere humility and obedience," mentions that England is only one of "a great many Western Ocean countries," calls the king "one man," and advises the king to ensure peace by "strengthening your loyalty and swearing perpetual obedience." (b) He characterizes China as the "Celestial Empire" that controls vast territories and rules many vassal states.

Japanese Screens
Shoguns and daimyo filled their castles with brilliant, multipaneled screen paintings. Many screens depicted the beauties of nature or scenes of everyday life. This screen shows the activities of Japanese and Portuguese seafarers aboard a large ship.

Theme: Art and Literature
How did the artist create a sense of motion?

Korea and Isolation

Like China, Korea restricted outside contacts in the 1500s and 1600s. Earlier, Korean traders had far-ranging contacts across East Asia. A Korean map from the 1300s accurately outlines lands from Japan to the Mediterranean. Koreans probably acquired this knowledge from Arab traders who had visited Korea.

The Choson dynasty, you will recall, firmly embraced Confucian ideas. Like the Chinese, Koreans felt that Confucian learning was the most advanced in the world. The low status of merchants in Confucianism also led Koreans to look down on foreign traders.

Two other events led the Koreans to turn inward. A Japanese invasion in the 1590s devastated the land of Korea. Then in 1636, the Manchus conquered Korea before overrunning Ming China. When the Manchus set up the Qing dynasty in China, Korea became a tributary state, run by its own government but forced to acknowledge China's supremacy. The two invasions left Korea feeling like "a shrimp among whales."

In response, the Koreans chose isolation, excluding all foreigners except the Chinese and a few Japanese. When European sailors were shipwrecked on Korean shores, they were imprisoned or killed. As a result, Korea became known in the West as the "Hermit Kingdom."

Even though Korea had few contacts with the world for about 250 years, this period was a great age for Korean arts and literature. In one satirical tale, author Pak Chi-won describes a poor scholar who breaks with tradition to become a merchant. Here, Master Ho describes doing business in an isolated country:

> "Our country has no trade with other countries, and . . . everything we use is produced and consumed in the same province. . . . With ten thousand yang, you can buy just about all of one particular item produced in the country. You can buy the whole lot, whether you load it on a cart or on a boat."
>
> —Pak Chi-won, "The Story of Ho"

Japan and Foreign Traders

Unlike the Chinese or Koreans, the Japanese at first welcomed western traders. In 1543, the Portuguese reached Japan. Later came the Spanish, Dutch, and English. They arrived at the turbulent time when strong daimyo were struggling for power. The Japanese quickly acquired western firearms and built castles modeled on European designs. In fact, the new weapons may have helped the Tokugawa shoguns centralize power and impose order.

Japan was much more open to European missionaries than China. Jesuits, like the Spanish priest Francis Xavier, found the Japanese curious and eager to learn about Christianity. A growing number of Japanese adopted the new faith.

The Tokugawa shoguns, however, grew increasingly hostile toward foreigners. After learning how Spain had seized the Philippines, they may have seen the newcomers as agents of an invading force. In addition, Japanese officials disliked the intrigues and competition among Christian missionaries. They also suspected that Japanese Christians—who may have numbered as many as 300,000—owed their allegiance to the pope, rather than to Japanese leaders. In response, the Tokugawas expelled foreign missionaries. They brutally persecuted Japanese Christians, killing many thousands of people.

By 1638, the Tokugawas had barred all western merchants and forbidden Japanese to travel abroad. To further their isolation, they outlawed the building of large ships, thereby ending foreign trade. In order to keep informed about world events, they permitted just one or two Dutch ships each year to trade at a small island in Nagasaki harbor. Through this tiny gateway, a few Japanese did learn about some foreign ideas. They studied Dutch medical texts, for example, which they found to be more accurate than Chinese ones.

Looking Ahead

Japan maintained its policy of strict isolation for more than 200 years. Isolation had a profound effect on Japan. Without outside influence, Japanese culture turned inward. Still, art and literature spread beyond the upper classes. Artists found new ways to interpret traditions.

During this time, internal trade boomed. Cities grew in size and importance, and some merchant families gained wealth and status. By the early 1700s, Edo (present-day Tokyo) had a million inhabitants, more than either London or Paris.

In 1853, Japan was forced to reopen contacts with the western world. Renewed relations unleashed an extraordinary period of change that helped Japan emerge as a major world power.

Global Connections

The Jesuits in Asia

Although Jesuit missionaries in Asia failed to win many converts to Christianity, they succeeded in spreading western ideas and technology. In China, Jesuit priest Matteo Ricci introduced an accurate world map and helped manufacture European-style cannons. Later Jesuits served as heads of the bureau that planned China's official calendar. The Jesuits also translated more than 100 books on science, math, and technology into Chinese. In Japan, Jesuits introduced the printing press.

Cultural influences also flowed in the other direction. The Jesuits introduced Europeans to the works of Confucius.

Theme: Religions and Value Systems What western ideas did the Jesuits introduce in Asia?

SECTION 4 Assessment

Recall
1. Identify: (a) Matteo Ricci, **(b)** Manchus, **(c)** Kangxi, **(d)** Qianlong, **(e)** Hermit Kingdom, **(f)** Francis Xavier.

Comprehension
2. (a) How was economic prosperity reflected in Qing China? **(b)** How did the Qing restrict trade with other nations?
3. Why did Korea pursue a policy of isolation?
4. Why did the Japanese policy toward trade and foreigners change over time?

Critical Thinking and Writing
5. Linking Past and Present Why do some people in the United States today support limited overseas ties?
6. Making Generalizations **(a)** Based on your reading, what generalization might you make about the attitude of European traders to the countries of East Asia? **(b)** What generalization might you make about how East Asians felt toward Europeans? **(c)** What evidence might you give to support each generalization?

Activity

Writing a Dialogue
Write a dialogue between two officials in China, Korea, or Japan. One official should express a willingness to establish relations with European powers. The other should argue in favor of a policy of isolation.

Chapter 15 **381**

Human Drama Activity

Recreating History Have students participate in the Simulation activity *Will the Shogun Close Japan to Foreigners?*, Simulations booklet, p. 7. Have students prepare for the simulation by reading the Biography Activity, *Francis Xavier*, Unit 4 booklet, p. 70, and the Viewpoint Activity, *Japan's Shoguns Reject the West*, Unit 4 booklet, p. 72, and by gathering a few props. The simulation requires eight actors and recreates the Japanese decision to become an isolationist country. This activity may be repeated with different students in each role.

SECTION 4 Assessment

Recall
1. **(a)** Matteo Ricci, p. 377 **(b)** Manchus, p. 378 **(c)** Kangxi, p. 378 **(d)** Qianlong, p. 378 **(e)** Hermit Kingdom, p. 380 **(f)** Francis Xavier, p. 381

Comprehension
2. **(a)** There was a rise in population due to increased farm output, growth in handicraft industries, and increased trade. **(b)** Like Ming rulers before them, Qing emperors restricted where and when foreign merchants could conduct trade.
3. The Japanese invasion in the 1590s and the Manchu invasion in 1636 led to Korea's policy of isolation. The low status assigned to merchants also made Koreans reluctant to welcome foreign traders. 4. At first, Japanese leaders were divided in their own power struggles and European weapons were useful. Later, the Japanese were concerned about invasion following Spain's conquest of the Philippines. Also, they felt that Christianity was divisive and encouraged loyalties outside Japan.

Critical Thinking and Writing
5. Possible answer: Some people fear that the United States will get involved in other countries' wars. 6. Possible answers: **(a)** Europeans thought that East Asia was a region to be exploited, a source of wealth. Europeans thought they were superior to East Asians. **(b)** East Asians thought their goods and cultures were superior; they feared the intent of Europeans. **(c)** Europeans continued sending ships and pressing to open new cities to trade. Asians rejected European overtures to trade.

Activity Rubrics

Share rubrics with students before they write their dialogues.

Attempted The dialogue is incomplete.

Minimal The dialogue is complete but does not adequately present each viewpoint.

Adequate The dialogue presents each viewpoint clearly.

Exemplary The dialogue skillfully presents each viewpoint, cites numerous examples, and is well written.

Global Connections

ANSWER Western scientific ideas, such as geographic and astronomical knowledge

Creating a Chapter Summary

As a reteaching opportunity, pair a more able student with a less able student to complete this chapter summary.

Possible entries: **Causes** desire for wealth, crusade against Muslims, desire to learn about other lands, improved technology **Effects** Spain gains foothold in Americas, seizes the Philippines; French ousted from India, British East India Company founded, British rule Bengal; Dutch monopolize Spice Islands; China, Korea, Japan turn inward

Building Vocabulary

1–10. Students' sentences should show an understanding of each word.

Recalling Key Facts

11. to gain wealth, to lead crusades against Muslims, to learn more about distant lands, to spread Christianity
12. line that divided the non-European world between Spain and Portugal
13. It resulted in a westward path to Asia.
14. After the Spanish conquest of the Philippines, Catholic priests set out to convert the Filipinos.
15. Britain and France
16. strict isolation from other nations

Critical Thinking and Writing

17. **(a)** Spices, desired by Europeans for preserving and flavoring food, offered merchants huge profits. **(b)** Possible answer: petroleum, Internet companies
18. Possible answer: Europeans tried to gain profits, spread their religious beliefs, and win control of lands in India and East Asia. Students might mention missionary activity and the seizure of ports as examples.
19. Possible answer: The Tokugawa shoguns might have chosen to sponsor their own voyages of exploration and forge stronger trading ties with other nations.
20. Possible answers: **(a)** Europeans might consider them heroic. Native Americans and people of India might condemn them. **(b)** Defenders of the explorers might cite their successful ocean voyages. Those who condemn them might cite their use of force to exert control over other people.

CHAPTER **15 Review and Assessment**

Creating a Chapter Summary

On a sheet of paper make a cause-and-effect diagram like the one shown here. Fill in the causes and effects of European exploration to help you review this chapter. Add more boxes as needed.

Demand for Asian goods

EUROPEAN EXPLORATION AND FOOTHOLDS IN ASIA

Portuguese gain Goa, Macao

Dutch East India Company formed

For additional review and enrichment activities, see the interactive version of *World History* available on the Web and on CD-ROM.

Web Site Self-Test
For practice test questions for Chapter 15, see www.phschool.com.

Building Vocabulary

Review the meaning of the chapter vocabulary words listed below. Then, write a sentence for each word in which you define the word and describe its relation to the first global age.

1. cartographer
2. astrolabe
3. caravel
4. scurvy
5. circumnavigate
6. matrilineal
7. stupa
8. padi
9. outpost
10. sepoy

Recalling Key Facts

11. What different motives led Europeans to explore the oceans?
12. What was the Line of Demarcation?
13. Why was Magellan's voyage of 1519–1522 important?
14. How did Christianity spread to the Philippines?
15. Which two European nations competed for influence in India?
16. What important policy did Japanese leaders follow between 1638 and 1853?

Critical Thinking and Writing

17. **Linking Past and Present** **(a)** Why were spices such valued trading goods in the 1400s? **(b)** What goods and resources play a similar role in the world economy today?
18. **Analyzing Information** How did European encounters with India, China, and Japan link economic, religious, and political activity?
19. **Identifying Alternatives** How might Tokugawa policy have been changed to encourage greater contact with other civilizations?
20. **Recognizing Points of View** Many people admire explorers such as Columbus and da Gama as bold adventurers. Others condemn them as vicious conquerors. **(a)** Who do you think might hold each of these viewpoints? **(b)** What evidence can be given to support each opinion?
21. **Connecting to Geography** How did weather conditions in the "southern seas" contribute to travel in the region and cultural exchange in Southeast Asian ports?

21. Ships had to take into account the monsoons or winds by sailing northeast in the summer and southwest in the winter and waiting in ports in between. These ports became centers of trade and places for cultural exchange.

Analyzing Primary Sources

22. near Japan
23. China (Asia)
24. (a) They were dissatisfied at his orders and complained. (b) He continued with his plans.
25. Possible answer: He might become too independent and opinionated and cause trouble with the crew, or he might rebel.

Analyzing Maps

26. Khmer empire
27. to the southeast
28. It sits on the Strait of Malacca, which was an important east-west trade route.
29. (a) north (b) south (c) Sumatra, Borneo, the Moluccas
30. Eastern Hemisphere

Skills Assessment
Analyzing Primary Sources

The following diary entry is from the log that Christopher Columbus kept on his first voyage. To dispel the crew's fears of how long the voyage was, Columbus always reckoned "fewer leagues than we actually made" and kept confidential records of the actual distance traveled. Martín Alonso Pinzón was the captain of the *Pinta*. Read the entry, then answer the questions that follow.

"*Saturday, 6 October 1492 I maintained my course to the west and made 120 miles between day and night, but told the people 99. This evening Martín Alonso Pinzón told me that he thought it would be wise to steer to the SW by west in order to reach the island of Japan, which is marked on the chart that I had shown him. In my opinion it is better to continue directly west until we reach the mainland. Later we can go to the islands on the return voyage to Spain. My decision has not pleased the men, for they continue to murmur and complain. Despite their grumblings I held fast to the west.*"

—*The Log of Christopher Columbus* (Fuson, tr.)

22. Where did Martín Alonso Pinzón think they were?
23. What mainland did Columbus think they were near?
24. (a) What problem did Columbus face with the crew? (b) How did Columbus respond?
25. How might a captain like Martín Alonso Pinzón be a problem for Columbus?

Skills Assessment
Take It to the NET

Use the Internet to research one of the European voyages that began the first global age. If possible, find a primary source from the voyage, such as the letters of Christopher Columbus. Then, write a series of news reports that the voyager might have written if he had been able to send news flashes about his travels back to his home country.

Skills Assessment
Analyzing Maps

Empires and Kingdoms of Southeast Asia

Pagan kingdom, A.D. 1044–A.D. 1287	Srivijaya empire, A.D. 600s–A.D. 1200s
Khmer empire, A.D. 800–A.D. 1350	Vietnam kingdom, A.D. 939–A.D. 1883

→ Mongol invasion, A.D. 1287

INDIA · CHINA · PACIFIC OCEAN
Pagan · 20°N
Bay of Bengal · South China Sea · Philippine Islands · Manila
Chao Phraya R. · Angkor Wat
INDIAN OCEAN · Gulf of Thailand · 10°N
Strait of Malacca
Malacca · Borneo · The Moluccas (Spice Islands)
Sumatra
Palembang · Sunda Strait
Java · 10°S
90°E · 100°E · 110°E · 120°E

Azimuthal Equal Area Projection
0   400   800 Miles
0 400 800 Kilometers

Use the map to answer the following questions:

26. In which empire was Angkor Wat located?
27. What is the location of the Philippine Islands in relation to China?
28. Why did the location of the city of Malacca make the city important to Southeast Asian trade?
29. (a) Is China north or south of the Equator? (b) Is Java north or south of the Equator? (c) Identify the islands through which the Equator runs.
30. Does the region shown in this map lie in the Eastern Hemisphere or the Western Hemisphere?

Skills Tip

Lines of latitude run horizontally and identify whether an area is north or south of the Equator. Lines of longitude show if an area is in the Eastern or Western Hemisphere.

Skills Tip

The Prime Meridian and the 180° line of longitude divide the earth into Eastern and Western Hemispheres. The Skills Handbook in the front of the book has a lesson that will help students with this feature.

Unit Theme Activity

Remind students to continue working on their Unit Theme Activity. See rubrics for the activity on the unit opener page in the Teacher's Edition.

Take It to the NET

Direct students to **www.phschool.com** for links to sites that will help them get started on this assignment. Share rubrics with students.

Attempted There are fewer than three news reports; they are poorly written and organized and contain many mechanical errors.

Minimal There are at least three news reports, but they are poorly written or organized and contain a number of mechanical errors.

Adequate There are at least three news reports, and they are well written and organized and contain few mechanical errors.

Exemplary There are more than three news reports, and they are very well written and organized, contain no mechanical errors, and include interesting or amusing anecdotes.

Chapter 16 Planning Guide

Resource Manager

	CORE INSTRUCTION	READING/SKILLS

Chapter Level Resources	📒 **Teaching Resources**
	  📄 **Pacing Charts**, Ch. 16
	  📄 **Teaching With Themes**, p. 19
	  🎞 **Color Transparencies**, p. F–33
	  💿 **Resource Pro®** Ch. 16
	  💻 **www.phschool.com**
	    • eTeach
		💿 **Book on CD**, Ch. 16
		💿 **Interactive Student Tutorial CD-ROM**, Ch. 16
		💿 **Social Studies Skills Tutor CD-ROM**
		🎞 **Skills Transparencies**

1 Conquest in the Americas
1. Summarize the first encounters between the Spanish and Native Americans.
2. Describe how Spanish conquistadors conquered the Aztec and Incan empires.
3. Explain why the Spanish were victorious.
	📒 **Teaching Resources**
	  📄 **Unit 4 booklet**
	    • Primary Source Activity, p. 51
	💿 **Prentice Hall Presentation Pro**, Ch. 16, Section 1
	🎞 **Section Reading Support Transparencies**
		📒 **Teaching Resources**
		  📄 **Unit 4 booklet**
		    • Guided Reading and Review, p. 40
		📕 **Guide to the Essentials**
		📼 **Guided Reading Audiotapes**, Ch. 16, Section 1

2 Spanish and Portuguese Colonies in the Americas
1. Outline Spain's rule in the Americas.
2. Describe colonial society and culture.
3. Explain challenges to Spanish power.
	📒 **Teaching Resources**
	  📄 **Unit 4 booklet**
	    • Viewpoint Activity, p. 52
	💿 **Prentice Hall Presentation Pro**, Ch. 16, Section 2
	🎞 **Section Reading Support Transparencies**
		📒 **Teaching Resources**
		  📄 **Unit 4 booklet**
		    • Guided Reading and Review, p. 42
		📕 **Guide to the Essentials**
		📼 **Guided Reading Audiotapes**, Ch. 16, Section 2

3 Struggle for North America
1. Identify problems in New France.
2. Describe colonies' new traditions of government.
3. Assess how power struggles affected Europeans and Native Americans.
	📒 **Teaching Resources**
	  📕 **Creative Teaching Activities**, p. 74
	💿 **Prentice Hall Presentation Pro**, Ch. 16, Section 3
	🎞 **Section Reading Support Transparencies**
		📒 **Teaching Resources**
		  📄 **Unit 4 booklet**
		    • Guided Reading and Review, p. 44
		    • Skill Application Activity, p. 53
		📕 **Guide to the Essentials**

4 Turbulent Centuries in America
1. Explain how Europeans in Africa led to slave trade.
2. Describe how slave trade gave rise to new African states.
3. Identify battling groups in southern Africa.
	📒 **Teaching Resources**
	  📄 **Unit 4 booklet**
	    Biography Activity, p. 50
	💿 **Prentice Hall Presentation Pro**, Ch. 16, Section 4
	🎞 **Section Reading Support Transparencies**
		📒 **Teaching Resources**
		  📄 **Unit 4 booklet**
		    • Guided Reading and Review, p. 46
		📕 **Guide to the Essentials**
		📼 **Guided Reading Audiotapes**, Ch. 16, Section 4

5 Changes in Europe
1. Summarize how European explorations led to a global exchange.
2. Identify the impact that the commercial revolution and mercantilism had on European economies.
3. Describe how changes affected ordinary people.
	📒 **Teaching Resources**
	  📕 **Creative Teaching Activities**, p. 76
	💿 **Prentice Hall Presentation Pro**, Ch. 16, Section 5
	🎞 **Section Reading Support Transparencies**
		📒 **Teaching Resources**
		  📄 **Unit 4 booklet**
		    • Guided Reading and Review, p. 48
		📕 **Guide to the Essentials**

ENRICHMENT/PRE-AP

- **www.phschool.com**
  - Why Study History?

Teaching Resources
- **History Through Literature,** pp. 35–36
- **Simulations,** p. 8
- **www.phschool.com**
  - Virtual Field Trip
  - Internet Activities, Section 1

Teaching Resources
- **Chapter Extension Activities,** p. 41

Color Transparencies, p. E–33

Teaching Resources
- **Geography and History,** pp. 8–9
- **www.phschool.com**
  - Internet Activities, Section 4

Teaching Resources
- **Chapter Extension Activities,** p. 42

ASSESSMENT

PRENTICE HALL
ASSESSMENT SYSTEM

Core Assessment
- ExamView Test Bank booklet, Ch. 16
- ExamView Test Bank CD-ROM, Ch. 16

Standardized Test Preparation

Diagnose and Prescribe
- **Diagnostic Tests for High School Social Studies Skills**

Review and Reteach
- **Review Book for World History**

Practice and Assess
- **Test-Taking Strategies With Transparencies for High School**
- **Alternative Assessment booklet**
- **Test Prep Book for World History**

Teaching Resources
- **Unit 4 booklet**
  - Geography Quiz, p. 54
  - Section Quizzes, pp. 41, 43, 45, 47, 49
  - Chapter Tests A, B, and C, pp. 55–59
- **www.phschool.com**
  - Self-Test

CUSTOMIZE FOR INDIVIDUAL NEEDS

Gifted and Talented
- **Teacher's Edition,** Activities: Connections to Literature, p. 396

Less Proficient Readers
- **Guide to the Essentials,** Ch. 16
- **Guided Reading Audiotapes, English,** Ch. 16
- **Book on CD,** Ch. 16

Less Proficient Writers
- **Teacher's Edition,** Activities: Cooperative Learning Activity, p. 392

Students Acquiring English/ESL
- **Guide to the Essentials, English/Spanish,** Ch. 16
- **Guided Reading Audiotapes, English/Spanish,** Ch. 16
- **Book on CD,** Ch. 16
- **Teacher's Edition,** Activities marked with an *

TEXT

Don't miss the exclusive interactive version of *World History: Connections to Today* on the Internet and CD-ROM.

INTRODUCTION

During the age of exploration, Europeans enslaved Native Americans and European diseases decimated the Native American populations. The importation of African slaves to American colonies led to the rise and fall of African states. In the 1500s, a commercial revolution in Europe gave rise to capitalism and a global exchange of ideas and goods. By the 1600s, European countries were competing for New World trade and colonies.

Focusing on Themes

Suggest that students focus on these theme questions as they read:

Economics and Technology
How did the winning of overseas empires affect the economy of Europe?

Political and Social Systems
How were the governments of the Spanish, French, and English colonies similar? How were they different?

Diversity
How were different cultures around the world brought into contact during the 1500s and 1600s?

Religions and Value Systems
What role did Christian values play in the European colonization of the Americas?

TIME LINE ACTIVITY

Share the About the Pictures note with students before asking these questions:

1. What do you think was stored in the trading post in Ghana? *(people)*
2. Who conquered the Aztecs, and what were the implications? *(Cortés; Spain acquired vast stores of gold.)*
3. When was the British colony of Jamestown founded? *(1607)*

CHAPTER
16

The First Global Age: Europe, the Americas, and Africa 1492–1750

Chapter Preview

1 Conquest in the Americas
2 Spanish and Portuguese Colonies in the Americas
3 Struggle for North America
4 Turbulent Centuries in Africa
5 Changes in Europe

1492
Columbus lands in the Americas. A global exchange of goods and ideas begins.

1521
Cortés completes conquest of the Aztecs, acquiring for Spain vast stores of gold, including ornaments such as this one.

1607
Jamestown is founded by British colonists.

CHAPTER EVENTS

1500   1550   1600

GLOBAL EVENTS
1498 Portuguese explorer da Gama rounds Africa and reaches India.

Don't Miss!

Humanities Link
Southwestern Architecture: A Blending of Cultures (Section 2)

Synthesizing Information
The Commercial Revolution (Section 5)

Resource Directory

Teaching Resources
Teaching With Themes Chapter Theme Activities, p. 19
Pacing Chart With Block Scheduling Guide Ch. 16

Technology
World History Color Transparencies Ch. 16 Graphic Organizer, p. F–33

Land Claims in the Americas and Africa, 1675

Legend:
- Dutch territory
- English territory
- French territory
- Portuguese territory
- Spanish territory
- Independent African states

By 1675, Spain, France, Britain, and Portugal possessed sizable overseas empires. Oceangoing trade ships carried tons of goods between Europe and the Americas and Africa.

Map labels: NETHERLANDS, ENGLAND, FRANCE, PORTUGAL, SPAIN, New France, Newfoundland, Nova Scotia, English Colonies, Florida, Mexico, Gulf of Mexico, Caribbean Sea, ATLANTIC OCEAN, Mediterranean Sea, Danube R., Nile R., MOROCCO, Futa Toro, SENEGAMBIA, ASANTE, HAUSA STATES, DAHOMEY, Gold Coast, Niger R., Congo R., KONGO, Angola, Zambezi R., Amazon R., Brazil, Peru, Panama R., Parana R., Chile, PACIFIC OCEAN

Robinson Projection
0   1000   2000 Miles
0   1000   2000 Kilometers

140°W 120°W 100°W 80°W 60°W 40°W 20°W 0° 20°E 40°E

Timeline

1600s — Enslaved Africans continue to be shipped to the Americas. Europeans use forts on the west coast of Africa as trading posts. The one shown here, in Ghana, is held at various times by the Portuguese, Dutch, and British.

1700s — Islamic revival spreads across West Africa.

1759 — British defeat French at Quebec.

1650 — **1630s** Japan bars western merchants.

1700

1750 — **1736** Reign of Emperor Qianlong of China begins.

Activating Prior Knowledge
Ask students to explain why most of the land claims border the sea. (*Students should note the limited means of inland transportation available to explorers; hence, most explorations took place on or near a body of water.*)

Previewing
Which two countries do you think would go to war over North America? Why? (*France and Britain because their colonies were near each other*)

Background
About the Pictures

1. *Landing of Columbus at San Salvador (Guanahani) in Bahamas, 12 October 1492.* Before his arrival in Cuba, Columbus landed on five islands. More than 500 years later, the identities of all but the fifth island are still being disputed.

2. This fifteenth-century gold breastplate found in a Mixtec tomb is remarkable for its detailed symbols. Round dots on both sides of the ornament are signs for calendar units. The deity Quetzalcoatl, whom the Aztecs believed invented the calendar, appears on the left side. The symbol for house is on the right.

3. Sao Jorge da Mina, also known as Elmina Castle, was built by the Portuguese in 1482 in what is now Ghana. The first major European building erected in West Africa, this fortress allowed the Portuguese to dominate the African gold trade for more than 100 years.

eTeach
Be sure to check out this month's online discussion with a World History Master Teacher.

Go to **www.phschool.com**.

Independent Assignments

Have students read one section as they prepare for class. After class, have them complete the assignment. Some students may benefit from using the Guided Reading and Review worksheets.

Section 1 Have students use the worksheet *The Massacre in the Temple of Tenochtitlán* in the Unit 4 booklet, p. 51, to read an account of the Spanish conquest of Mexico as told by Aztec authors.

Section 2 Have students use the worksheet in the Chapter Extension Activities booklet, p. 41, to learn more about Southwestern architecture.

Section 3 Have students use the outline map *Claims in the Americas, 1700* in the Historical Outline

Map Book, p. 27, to label and shade in with different colors the lands claimed by European countries.

Section 4 Have students use the worksheet *Olau-dah Equiano* in the Unit 4 booklet, p. 50, to learn more about an African slave's experience in the New World.

Section 5 Have students use the worksheet in the Chapter Extension Activities booklet, p. 42, to learn more about the Commercial Revolution.

LESSON PLAN

1. Focus Desire for wealth, as well as religious zeal, encouraged Spanish explorers to travel to the Americas. The Aztecs and Incas, weakened by disunity and disease, fell victim to superior Spanish military technology. The Spanish empire in the Americas brought power and wealth to Spain. Meanwhile, Native American peoples struggled to survive.

2. Instruct Ask students to imagine that they are living during the time of Spanish conquests in the Americas. Have students work in pairs. Assign one partner to assume the role of a Native American and the other to be a Spanish explorer. Then, from their assigned point of view, have students write an eyewitness account of one of the following events: (1) the arrival of Christopher Columbus in the West Indies in 1492, (2) the arrival of Hernan Cortés in Mexico in 1519, (3) the fall of Tenochtitlán, (4) Francisco Pizarro's capture of Atahualpa. Have partners read their reports to each other and compare viewpoints.

3. Assess Based on their eyewitness reports, have students write down who, what, where, when, and why questions for their partners. Then, have students exchange papers and answer the questions they were given.

4. Reteach If students' Assess activity does not reflect adequate understanding of the lesson, you might assign the *Guide to the Essentials* or the *Interactive Student Tutorial CD-ROM* for this section.

Reading Focus

■ What were the results of the first encounters between the Spanish and Native Americans?

■ How did Spanish conquistadors conquer the Aztec and Incan empires?

■ Why were the Spanish victorious?

Vocabulary

conquistador
immunity
alliance
civil war

Taking Notes

Copy this diagram. As you read, add other factors that help to explain why the Spanish were able to conquer Native American empires. Add as many boxes as you need.

> Disease weakens Native Americans ▷ ▷ ▷
>
> **EUROPEANS CONQUER NATIVE AMERICANS**

Main Idea Various factors enabled the Spanish to conquer the Aztec and Incan empires.

Setting the Scene Spanish soldiers who reached the Aztec capital of Tenochtitlán in 1519 were amazed by its size and splendor. From the emperor's palace, reported one soldier, "We had a clear view of the . . . [majestic temples] of the nearby cities, built in the form of towers and fortresses, . . . and others . . . all whitewashed, and wonderfully brilliant."

Within a few years, the Spanish had captured and destroyed the Aztec capital. In its place, they built a new capital, Mexico City, that became the heart of the Spanish empire in the Americas.

First Encounters

In 1492, Christopher Columbus landed in the islands that are now called the West Indies, in the Caribbean. There, he encountered the Taíno people. The Taínos lived in villages and grew corn, yams, and cotton, which they wove into cloth. They were friendly and generous toward the Spanish.

Friendly relations soon evaporated, however. Spanish conquistadors (kahn KEES tuh dohrz), or conquerors, followed in the wake of Columbus. They settled on the islands of Hispaniola (now the Dominican Republic and Haiti), Cuba, and Puerto Rico. They seized the gold ornaments worn by the Taínos, then made them pan for more gold. At the same time, the newcomers forced the Taínos to convert to Christianity.

Meanwhile, a deadly but invisible invader was at work—disease. Europeans unknowingly carried diseases such as smallpox, measles, and influenza to which Native Americans had no immunity, or resistance. These diseases spread rapidly and wiped out village after village. As a result, the Native American population of the Caribbean islands declined by as much as 90 percent in the 1500s. This cycle of disease and death was repeated in many other places across the Western Hemisphere.

The Conquistadors

From Cuba, Spanish explorers probed the coasts of the Americas. They spread stories of empires rich in gold. Attracted by the promise of riches as well as by religious zeal, a flood of adventurers soon followed.

Cortés in Mexico Among the earliest conquistadors was Hernan Cortés. Cortés landed on the coast of Mexico in 1519 with about 600 men, 16 horses, and a few cannons. As he headed inland toward Tenochtitlán, he was helped

Resource Directory

Teaching Resources
Creative Teaching Activities Creative Teaching Activities booklet, p. 72
Guided Reading and Review Unit 4 booklet, p. 40
Primary Source Activity *The Massacre in the Temple of Tenochtitlán,* Unit 4 booklet, p. 51
History Through Literature *The Broken Spears,* History Through Literature booklet, pp. 35–36

Virtual Field Trip

www.phschool.com

University of Minnesota
Duluth, Minnesota

For more images and information about the Aztecs and the Spanish conquest, use the Internet address above to link to the department of history at the University of Minnesota.

Conquistadors in Mexico
Pedro de Alvarado was one of the Spanish conquistadors who conquered Mexico. This illustration shows Alvarado and his men facing off against a troop of Aztec soldiers.

Theme: Economics and Technology Based on this picture, identify two technological advantages the Spanish had over the Aztecs.

by Malinche (mah LIHN chay), a young Indian woman who served as his translator and adviser. The Spanish called her Doña Marina. Malinche knew both the Mayan and Aztec languages, and she learned Spanish quickly.

From Malinche, Cortés learned that many conquered peoples hated their Aztec overlords. The Aztecs, you will recall, sacrificed thousands of captives to their gods each year. Malinche helped Cortés arrange alliances with these discontented groups. They would help one another fight the Aztecs.

Moctezuma's Dilemma Meanwhile, messengers brought word about the newcomers to the Aztec emperor Moctezuma. He wondered if the leader of the pale-skinned, bearded strangers might be Quetzalcoatl, the god-king who had long ago vowed to return from the east. Moctezuma sent gifts of gold and silver, but urged the strangers not to continue to Tenochtitlán.

Cortés had no intention of turning back. Fighting and negotiating by turns, he led his forces inland toward the capital. At last, they arrived in Tenochtitlán, where they were dazzled by the grandeur of the city.

Fall of Tenochtitlán Moctezuma welcomed Cortés to his capital. However, relations between the Aztecs and Spaniards soon grew strained, and the Aztecs drove the Spanish from the city. Moctezuma was killed in the fighting.

Cortés retreated to plan an assault. In 1521, in a brutal struggle, Cortés and his Indian allies captured and demolished Tenochtitlán. An unknown Aztec lamented, "Broken spears lie in the road; / We have torn our hair with grief. / The houses are roofless now, and their walls are red with blood." On the ruins of Tenochtitlán, the Spanish later built Mexico City.

Pizarro in Peru Cortés's success inspired other adventurers. Among them was Francisco Pizarro. He arrived in Peru in 1532, just after the Incan ruler Atahualpa (ah tah WAHL pah) won the throne from his brother in a bloody civil war. A civil war is fought between groups of people in the same nation.

Helped by Indian allies, Pizarro captured Atahualpa after slaughtering thousands of his followers. The Spanish demanded a huge ransom for the ruler. The Incas paid it, but the Spanish killed Atahualpa anyway.

Despite continuing resistance, the invaders overran the Incan heartland. From Peru, Spanish forces surged across Ecuador and Chile. Before long, Spain added much of South America to its growing empire.

▶ **Primary Sources and Literature**

See "Bernal Díaz: The True History of the Conquest of New Spain" in the Reference Section at the back of this book.

Recall

1. **(a)** Taínos, p. 386 **(b)** Hernan Cortés, p. 386 **(c)** Malinche, p. 387 **(d)** Moctezuma, p. 387 **(e)** Francisco Pizarro, p. 387 **(f)** Atahualpa, p. 387 **2. (a)** conquistador, p. 386 **(b)** immunity, p. 386 **(c)** alliance, p. 387 **(d)** civil war, p. 387

Comprehension

3. The Spanish seized the Native Americans' gold and forced them to convert to Christianity. Their population was decimated by diseases from Europe. 4. He used diplomacy, force, and deceit; enlisted the aid of some Indians; captured and killed Atahualpa; and slaughtered thousands of Incas. 5. **(a)** Peoples conquered by Incas and Aztecs helped the conquistadors. **(b)** superior military technology, diseases, a belief by some Native Americans that the gods had abandoned them

Critical Thinking and Writing

6. Possible answers: **(a)** In all three cases, religious motives played a role. **(b)** The Spanish conquered much of the Americas and drove the Muslims from Spain; the Crusaders were not as successful. 7. Possible answer: The friendly Taínos welcomed Christopher Columbus in 1492. The conquistadors then stole from the Taínos and forced them to convert to Christianity. Deadly diseases carried by Europeans devastated Native American populations.

Activity Rubrics

Share rubrics with students before they write their paragraphs.

Attempted The paragraph shows insufficient research and is poorly written.

Minimal The paragraph shows sufficient research but is poorly written.

Adequate The paragraph is well written, and explanations are clear.

Exemplary A well-written paragraph clearly explains the writer's position and uses interesting supporting details.

Skills Assessment

ANSWER The population decreased from about 25 million in 1519 to about 1 million in 1605.

FACT FINDER

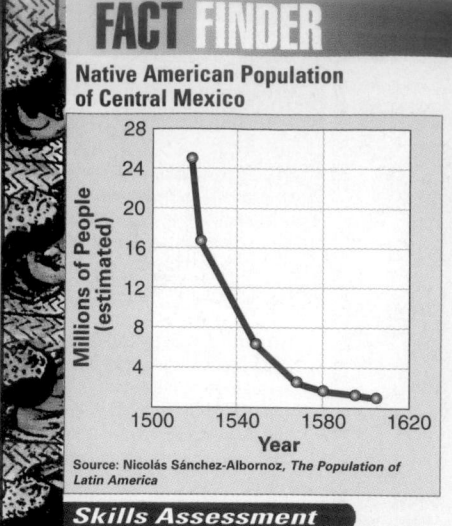

Native American Population of Central Mexico

Source: Nicolás Sánchez-Albornoz, *The Population of Latin America*

Skills Assessment

Graph Disease and conquest combined to reduce drastically the Native American population. This graph shows what happened to central Mexico's Native Americans after the arrival of the Spanish in 1519. **How did the Native American population change during the period shown on the graph?**

Reasons for Victory

How could a few hundred European soldiers conquer huge Native American empires with populations in the millions? Several reasons explain the amazing Spanish success.

1. Superior military technology was a key factor. The Spaniards' horses frightened some Indians, who had never seen such animals. Spanish muskets and cannons killed Indian soldiers, while metal helmets and armor protected the Spanish from the Indians' arrows and spears.
2. Division and discontent among the Indians aided the Spanish. The Spanish won allies by playing on old hatreds among rival Indian groups. In fact, Indians provided Cortés and Pizarro with much of their fighting power.
3. Disease brought by the Europeans weakened the Aztecs and Incas. As tens of thousands of Indians died, some of the bewildered and demoralized survivors felt that their gods were less powerful than the god of their conquerors.
4. Many Indians believed that the disasters they suffered marked the world's end. To Aztecs, the destruction of Tenochtitlán signaled the end of the reign of the sun god.

Ongoing Resistance Native Americans continued to resist the invaders, however. For years, Mayas fought Spanish rule. Long after the death of Atahualpa, revolts erupted among the Incas. Throughout the Americas, Indians resisted Europeans by preserving aspects of their own culture, such as language, religious traditions, and clothing.

Looking Ahead

The Spanish seized gold and silver statues and ornaments from the Aztecs and Incas. After depleting these sources, they forced Native Americans to mine silver in Peru and Mexico. In the 1500s and early 1600s, treasure fleets sailed each year to Spain or the Spanish Philippines loaded with gold and silver. As you will read, this flood of wealth created both benefits and problems for the economy of Europe.

SECTION 1 Assessment

Recall

1. **Identify:** **(a)** Taínos, **(b)** Hernan Cortés, **(c)** Malinche, **(d)** Moctezuma, **(e)** Francisco Pizarro, **(f)** Atahualpa.
2. **Define:** **(a)** conquistador, **(b)** immunity, **(c)** alliance, **(d)** civil war.

Comprehension

3. How were Native Americans of the Caribbean region affected by their early encounters with Europeans?
4. What methods did Pizarro use to conquer the Incan empire?
5. **(a)** How did divisions within the Aztec and Incan empires help the Spanish? **(b)** What other reasons explain the rapid success of the Spanish conquistadors over Native Americans?

Critical Thinking and Writing

6. **Comparing** Compare the Spanish conquest of the Americas with the Reconquista or the Crusades. **(a)** How were they similar? **(b)** How were they different?
7. **Identifying Main Ideas** Review the three paragraphs under the heading First Encounters. For each paragraph, write a single sentence identifying the main idea of the paragraph.

Activity

Take It to the NET

Use the Internet to research the life of Malinche, whose name means "traitor." Then, write a paragraph explaining why you believe she does or does not deserve this name.

Resource Directory

Teaching Resources

Section Quiz Unit 4 booklet, p. 41
Creative Teaching Activities Creative Teaching Activities booklet, p. 73
Guided Reading and Review Unit 4 booklet, p. 42

Technology

Interactive Student Tutorial CD-ROM Ch. 16
Computer Test Bank Ch. 16

Spanish and Portuguese Colonies in the Americas

Reading Focus

- How did Spain rule its empire in the Americas?
- What were the chief features of colonial society and culture?
- How did Portugal and other European nations challenge Spanish power?

Vocabulary

viceroy
plantation
encomienda
peon
peninsular
creole
mestizo
mulatto
privateer

Taking Notes

Copy this partially completed concept web. As you read, write key facts and ideas about the Spanish empire in the Americas in the appropriate circles. Add as many circles as you need.

Economy — **SPANISH EMPIRE** — **Government** — **Society** — **Culture**

Main Idea Native American, African, and European traditions blended to form new cultures in the Americas.

Bell Ringer Have students use the glossary to define the vocabulary words listed at the start of this section. Ask them what these terms suggest about the nature of government, society, and culture in Spanish America.

LESSON PLAN

1. Focus Spanish monarchs appointed viceroys and set up the Council of the Indies to keep strict control over their American empire. When new laws forbade the enslavement of Native Americans, the Spanish brought enslaved Africans to the Americas. Native American, African, and European traditions blended to form the distinct cultures of the Americas.

2. Instruct Divide the class into four groups. Assign each group one of the following topics concerning life in Spanish America: Government, Economy, Society, Culture. Have students in each group work together to outline the major ideas and details that pertain to their assigned topic. When students have finished this part of the assignment, regroup them so that each new group has at least one "expert" for each of the four topics. Instruct students to take turns teaching the other members of their group about their area of expertise.

3. Assess Ask students to make a list of the injustices that existed in the American empires of Spain and Portugal. Invite volunteers to read their lists to the class.

4. Reteach If students' **Assess** activity does not reflect adequate understanding of the lesson, you might assign the *Guide to the Essentials* or the *Interactive Student Tutorial CD-ROM* for this section.

Setting the Scene

Spain was immensely proud of its rich silver mines in the Potosí region of Peru. By the 1540s, tons of Potosí silver filled Spanish treasure ships. Year after year, thousands of Native Americans were forced to extract the rich ore from dangerous shafts deep inside the Andes Mountains. Many Indians died in the terrible conditions, only to be replaced by thousands more.

Scenes such as this were repeated in Mexico, the Caribbean, and other parts of Spain's empire. A flood of Spanish settlers and missionaries followed the conquistadors. Wherever they went, they claimed the land and its people for their king and Church. When there was resistance, the newcomers imposed their will by force. As devout Christians, they thought it was their duty to bring their religion and civilization to the Indians.

From the first, though, Christian Europeans had much to learn from the peoples that they conquered. In the end, a new culture emerged that reflected European, Native American, and African traditions.

Ruling the Spanish Empire

In the 1500s, Spain claimed a vast empire stretching from California to South America. In time, it divided these lands into five provinces. The most important were New Spain (Mexico) and Peru.

Spain was determined to maintain strict control over its empire. To achieve this goal, the king set up the Council of the Indies to pass laws for the colonies. He also appointed viceroys, or representatives who ruled in his name, in each province. Lesser officials and *audiencias*, or advisory councils of Spanish settlers, helped the viceroy rule. The Council of the Indies in Spain closely monitored these colonial officials to make sure they did not assume too much authority.

The Catholic Church To Spain, winning souls for Christianity was as important as gaining land. The Catholic Church played a key role in the colonies, working with the government to convert Native Americans to Christianity. Church leaders often served as royal officials and helped to regulate the activities of Spanish settlers. As Spain's American empire expanded, Church authority expanded along with it.

Franciscan, Jesuit, and other missionaries baptized thousands of Native Americans. In frontier regions, they built mission churches and worked to turn new converts into loyal subjects of the Catholic king of Spain. They forcibly imposed European culture over Native American culture.

Block Scheduling Support

Have students read *Two Views of the Treatment of Indians* in the Unit 4 booklet, p. 52, which provides differing opinions on official Spanish policy toward the original inhabitants of the Americas. Then have students form small groups and imagine they are Native Americans who have witnessed the actions of conquistadors. Tell each group to focus on the last paragraph of Solorzano y Pereyra's opinion. Have each group draft a letter to Spanish officials explaining why the Spanish policy is unfair and inhumane. Encourage each group to share its letter with the rest of the class.

Connections to Film

Preparing a Speech In 1680, the Pueblo Indians of present-day New Mexico rose up against Spanish rule. They drove the invaders from their land and remained free of foreign control for the next 12 years. This event and the conditions that precipitated it are recalled in a 1992 public television production entitled *Surviving Columbus: The Story of the Pueblo People*. The two-hour presentation, divided into six parts, tells its dramatic and often painful story through extensive use of primary sources and oral history.

Have students view parts 2 and 3 of the program to learn about the hardships and injustices that the Pueblos endured under Spanish rule. Then, ask them to assume the role of a Pueblo leader living near Santa Fe in 1680. Their assignment is to write a speech that will convince the people that they must rise up and fight against the Spanish. Ask volunteers to deliver their speeches to the class, and have students comment on whether or not they would have participated in the rebellion. (*Surviving Columbus: The Story of the Pueblo People* was produced by KNME of Albuquerque and is distributed by Pacific Arts.)

Primary Source

A Brutal System
Bartolomé de las Casas, a conquistador turned priest, spoke out against the encomienda system and the treatment of Native Americans:

"It is impossible to recount the burdens with which their owners loaded them, more than [75 to 100 pounds], making them walk [hundreds of miles]. . . . They had wounds on their shoulders and backs, like animals. . . . To tell likewise of the whip-lashings, the beatings, the cuffs, the blows, the curses, and a thousand other kinds of torments to which their masters treated them, while in truth they were working hard, would take much time and much paper; and would be something to amaze mankind."

—Bartolomé de las Casas,
Short Description of the Destruction of the Indies

Skills Assessment

Primary Source How were the conditions Las Casas describes linked to the encomienda system?

They also introduced European clothing, the Spanish language, and new crafts such as carpentry and locksmithing.

The Economy To make the empire profitable, Spain closely controlled its economic activities, especially trade. Colonists could export raw materials only to Spain and could buy only Spanish manufactured goods. Laws forbade colonists from trading with other European nations or even with other Spanish colonies. The most valuable resources shipped from Spanish America to Spain were silver and gold.

Sugar cane was introduced into the West Indies and elsewhere and quickly became a profitable resource. The cane was refined into sugar, molasses, and rum. Sugar cane, however, had to be grown on plantations, large estates run by an owner or the owner's overseer. Finding the large numbers of workers needed to make the plantations profitable was a major problem.

At first, Spanish monarchs granted the conquistadors encomiendas, the right to demand labor or tribute from Native Americans in a particular area. The conquistadors used this system to force Native Americans to work under the most brutal conditions. Those who resisted were hunted down and killed. Disease, starvation, and cruel treatment caused catastrophic declines in the population.

Bartolomé de las Casas A few bold priests, like Bartolomé de las Casas, condemned the evils of the encomienda system. In vivid reports to Spain, Las Casas detailed the horrors that Spanish rule had brought to Native Americans and pleaded with the king to end the abuse.

Prodded by Las Casas, Spain passed the New Laws of the Indies in 1542, forbidding enslavement of Native Americans. The laws were meant to end abuses against Native Americans, but Spain was too far away to enforce them. Many Native Americans were forced to become peons, workers forced to labor for a landlord in order to pay off a debt. Landlords advanced them food, tools, or seeds, creating debts that workers could never pay off in their lifetime.

Bringing Workers From Africa To fill the labor shortage, Las Casas urged colonists to import workers from Africa. Africans were immune to tropical diseases, he said, and had skills in farming, mining, and metalworking. Las Casas later regretted that advice because it furthered the brutal African slave trade. Colonists had begun bringing Africans to the Americas as early as 1502.

As demand for sugar products skyrocketed, the settlers imported millions of Africans as slaves. They were forced to work as field hands, miners, or servants in the houses of wealthy landowners. Others became peddlers, skilled artisans, artists, and mechanics.

In time, Africans and their American-born descendants greatly outnumbered European settlers in the West Indies and parts of South America. Often, they resisted slavery by rebelling or running away. In the cities, some enslaved Africans earned enough money to buy their freedom.

Colonial Society and Culture

In Spanish America, the mix of diverse peoples gave rise to a new social structure. The blending of Native American, African, and European peoples and traditions resulted in a new American culture.

Social Structure At the top of colonial society were peninsulares, people born in Spain. (The term *peninsular* referred to the Iberian Peninsula, on which Spain is located.) Peninsulares filled the highest positions in both colonial governments and the Catholic Church. Next came creoles,

---

Primary Source

ANSWER The encomienda system allowed Spaniards to demand labor from Native Americans. The treatment Las Casas describes is this forced labor carried to its most horrific extreme.

Resource Directory

Teaching Resources
Viewpoint Activity *Two Views of the Treatment of Indians,*
Unit 4 booklet, p. 52

American-born descendants of Spanish settlers. Creoles owned most of the plantations, ranches, and mines.

Other social groups reflected the mixing of populations. They included mestizos, people of Native American and European descent, and mulattoes, people of African and European descent. Native Americans and people of African descent formed the lowest social classes.

Cities   Spanish settlers preferred to live in towns and cities. The population of Mexico City grew so quickly that by 1550 it was the largest Spanish-speaking city in the world.

Colonial cities were centers of government, commerce, and European culture. Around the central plaza, or square, stood government buildings and a Spanish-style church. Broad avenues and public monuments symbolized European power and wealth. Cities were also centers of intellectual and cultural life. Architecture and painting, as well as poetry and the exchange of ideas, flourished.

Education   To meet the Church's need for educated priests, the colonies built universities. The University of Mexico was established as early as 1551. A dozen Spanish American universities were busy educating young men long before Harvard, the first university in the 13 English colonies, was founded in 1636.

Women wishing an education might enter a convent. One such woman was Sor Juana Inés de la Cruz. Refused admission to the University of Mexico because she was a girl, Juana entered a convent at the age of 16. There, she devoted herself to study and the writing of poetry. She earned a reputation as one of the greatest poets ever to write in the Spanish language.

Cultural Blending   Although Spanish culture was dominant in the cities, the blending of diverse traditions changed people's lives throughout the Americas. Settlers learned Native American styles of building, ate foods native to the Americas, and traveled in Indian-style canoes. Indian artistic styles influenced the newcomers. At the same time, settlers taught their religion to Native Americans. They also introduced animals, especially the horse, that transformed the lives of many Native Americans.

Africans added to this cultural mix with their farming methods, cooking styles, and crops, including okra and palm oil. African drama, dance, and song heightened Christian services. In Cuba, Haiti, and elsewhere, Africans forged new religions that blended African and Christian beliefs.

The Portuguese Colony in Brazil

A large area of South America remained outside the Spanish empire. By the Treaty of Tordesillas in 1494, Portugal claimed Brazil. (See the map in Section 3.) Portugal issued grants of land to Portuguese nobles, who agreed to develop the land and share profits with the crown. Landowners sent settlers to build towns, plantations, and churches.

The Economy   Unlike Spain's American lands, Brazil offered no instant wealth from silver or gold. Early settlers clung to the coast, where they cut and exported brazilwood, used to produce a precious dye. Before long,

A New Society and Culture
The social structure and culture of Spain's American empire reflected its unique blend of people. This portrait depicts a Spanish man, his Mexican wife, and their mestizo daughter.

Theme: Diversity What were the social classes in Spain's American empire?

Background
Connections to Today

Lasting Divisions   In 1545, after securing adoption of the New Laws of the Indies forbidding enslavement of Native Americans, Bartolomé de las Casas became the bishop of Chiapas in Mexico. The Spanish slaveowners in Chiapas greeted him with open hostility. Children sang loud and insulting songs as they passed the bishop's house. Spanish settlers even rioted. After many stormy months, Las Casas gave up and returned to Spain.

In 1994, almost 450 years later, rebels known as Zapatistas took up arms in the Mexican state of Chiapas to dramatize Native American grievances against the government. In the Chiapas city of San Cristóbal de las Casas, Bishop Samuel Ruiz García tried to mediate between the rebels and the government. Like Las Casas before him, Ruiz García became a hero to many Native Americans—and the enemy to local landowners, who saw him as a troublemaker.

Background
Perspectives

Women's Rights   Sor Juana Inés de la Cruz, in addition to being a poet and a dramatist, was an ardent defender of a woman's right to an education. Most men of her time, however, believed that educating women was excessive and even harmful. In fact, a bishop wrote her a letter calling her scholarly work inappropriate and ordering her to stop.

Sor Juana responded to such prejudices in a poem called "Hombres Necios," or "Foolish Men." In the poem, she pointed out that men often dismissed women as being ignorant. Yet it was the men themselves who, by their social restrictions, perpetuated the ignorance of women.

Human Drama Note

Distinguished Scholar   Carlos de Sigüenza y Góngora possessed an intellectual curiosity that was reflected in his study of such diverse subjects as mathematics, astronomy, geography, and poetry. He served as professor of mathematics at the Royal University of Mexico and as the royal cosmographer for King Charles II. His interest in writing led to the publication of many fictional works, the last of which was *The Misadventures of Alonso Ramírez*. In organizing the adventure narrative, Sigüenza y Góngora set the standard for colonial fiction and later Mexican novels. Moreover, his fictional device of a narrator relating someone else's firsthand account has been used in modern literature, most notably by the prize-winning Latin American writer Gabriel García Márquez.

Caption Answer

peninsulares, creoles, mestizos, mulattoes, Native Americans, and Africans

Background
Connections to Today

Taos Pueblo From the outside the Taos
Pueblo appears to be a single large
dwelling, but it is actually a collective
of individual houses that share exterior
walls but do not have connecting
interior doorways.

A sovereign nation within the United
States, the Taos Pueblo is considered by
some to be the longest continually inhabited community in the United States.
Today, there are approximately 150 full-
time dwellers in the pueblo, and more
than 1900 Taos Indians living on Taos
Pueblo property. Because Taos traditions mandate that the pueblo must not
have electricity or running water, most
members live in more modern homes
nearby, returning to the pueblo only
for ceremonial occasions.

Activity
Cooperative Learning

Creating a Display Have students form
small groups to make a display about
one of the Native American groups that
populated the Southwest during Spanish
colonial times: the Hopi, Pueblo, Navajo,
or Apache. Each student should be
responsible for a part of this activity:
research, collecting photographs and
drawings, creating maps, making models
of the buildings or artifacts, or designing
the display.

Portfolio Assessment Rubrics

Share rubrics with students before they
make their presentations.

Attempted Presentation fails to meet
outlined requirements.

Minimal Presentation demonstrates
adequate research and some preparation.

Adequate Presentation identifies key
features of the selected building and is
well organized.

Exemplary Presentation is well done
and includes photographs, drawings, or
a model of the building.

Southwestern Architecture: A Blending of Cultures

When the Spanish explorers entered what is today the American Southwest,
they found Native American buildings that had existed for centuries. The
Spanish settlers and the Native Americans influenced each other's building
styles and created a unique architecture that survives to this day.

The Pueblo Indians used a mixture of mud and
sand, called adobe, to construct the Taos Pueblo
in New Mexico (below). Built around 1350, this
collection of apartment-style houses has flat
roofs formed by long poles, closely grouped
rooms, and small windows. For protection,
the main entrances were in the rooftops.
The front doorways are a modern addition.

Known as "The White Dove
of the Desert," San Xavier del
Bac (right) was completed in
the late 1700s. Spanish priests
directed the work of Tohono
O'odham Indian laborers to
create this outpost of Spanish
culture in the desert near
Tucson, Arizona.

Built in the 1920s in Santa Fe,
New Mexico, the Institute of
American Indian Arts Museum,
(right) blends Native American
and Spanish architecture. The
twin towers resemble the bell
towers of a Spanish church.
The main contours of the
building follow the shape
of an Indian pueblo.

Creativity Is Our Tradition

Portfolio Assessment

INTERNET Use the Internet or library resources to
find out more about the architecture of
the American Southwest. Then, prepare a class
presentation that identifies Native American
and Spanish features of a particular building.
If possible, include photographs, drawings,
or a model of the building you have selected.

Fast Facts

- Pueblo Indians used "puddled," or
  poured, adobe before the Spanish
  arrived. Spanish settlers introduced
  the use of adobe bricks.

- Both the Pueblos and the Spanish
  built their communities around a
  central plaza, or square.

- Taos Pueblo is still inhabited today.

Resource Directory

Teaching Resources
Humanities Link Chapter Extension Activities booklet, p. 41
Section Quiz Unit 4 booklet, p. 43
Technology
Interactive Student Tutorial CD-ROM Ch. 16
Computer Test Bank Ch. 16

they turned to plantation agriculture and cattle raising. They forced Indians and Africans to clear land for sugar plantations. As many as five million Africans were sent to Brazil.

The thickly forested Amazon basin remained largely unexplored by settlers. However, ruthless adventurers slowly pushed inland. They attacked and enslaved Native American peoples and claimed for themselves land for immense cattle ranches. Some even discovered gold.

A New Culture As in Spanish America, a new culture emerged in Brazil that blended European, Native American, and African patterns. European culture dominated the upper and middle classes, but Native American and African influences left their mark. Portuguese settlers, for example, eagerly adopted Indian hammocks. A settler expressed his enthusiasm:

> "Would you believe that a man could sleep suspended in a net in the air like a bunch of hanging grapes? Here this is the common thing. . . . I tried it, and will never again be able to sleep in a bed, so comfortable is the rest one gets in the net."
> —quoted in *Latin America: A Concise Interpretive History* (Burns)

Challenging Spanish Power

In the 1500s, the wealth of the Americas helped make Spain the most powerful country in Europe. Its lofty position fueled envy among its European rivals. Many English and Dutch shared the resentment that French king Francis I felt when he declared, "I should like to see Adam's will, wherein he divided the Earth between Spain and Portugal."

European nations challenged Spain's power in various ways. To get around Spain's strict control over colonial trade, smugglers traded illegally with Spanish colonists. In the Caribbean and elsewhere, Dutch, English, and French pirates preyed on Spanish treasure ships. Some pirates, called privateers, even operated with the approval of European governments. England's Queen Elizabeth, for example, knighted Francis Drake for his daring raids on Spanish ships and towns.

Like the Spanish, the Dutch, English, and French hunted for gold empires and for a northwest passage to Asia. As you will read, these nations explored the coasts and planted settlements in North America.

Piracy on the Seas

Of all the privateers who plundered Spanish colonies, none was bolder than the Englishman whom the Spanish called *El Draque* (the Dragon). But Sir Francis Drake was more than just a pirate. He was also a skilled and daring explorer.

Drake led the second expedition ever to sail around the world. After a violent storm, he rounded the tip of South America in 1578 with only his flagship, the *Golden Hind*. But that one ship was enough. Spain's settlements along the Pacific coast were unguarded. After all, no hostile ship had ever made it into these waters before! Drake plundered one Spanish town and captured two treasure ships before continuing on his mission. Thanks to these raids and others, *El Draque* enriched his queen—and won the lasting hatred of the Spanish.

Theme: Geography and History Why was Drake able to surprise the Spanish?

SECTION 2 Assessment

Recall
1. **(a)** Council of the Indies, p. 389 **(b)** Bartolomé de las Casas, p. 390 **(c)** New Laws of the Indies, p. 390 **(d)** Sor Juana Inés de la Cruz, p. 391 **2. (a)** viceroy, p. 389 **(b)** plantation, p. 390 **(c)** encomienda, p. 390 **(d)** peon, p. 390 **(e)** peninsular, p. 390 **(f)** creole, p. 390 **(g)** mestizo, p. 391 **(h)** mulatto, p. 391 **(i)** privateer, p. 393

Comprehension
3. Spain ruled its empire through the Council of the Indies and viceroys. Church leaders also helped the government. Spain controlled the economy by regulating imports and exports and by granting encomiendas. 4. **(a)** One's place in society was based primarily on ethnicity. Spaniards and people of Spanish descent were at the top of the social structure. People of mixed ancestry ranked next. The lowest classes consisted of Africans and Native Americans. **(b)** Possible answer: Spanish settlers built their homes in the style of Native Americans. The majority of people adopted Christianity. African farming methods, cooking styles, and arts enriched the cultures of Spanish America. 5. They established their own colonies and seized Spanish treasure ships.

Critical Thinking and Writing
6. Possible answers: **(a)** Both Spanish and Portuguese colonies used plantation agriculture and African slaves. **(b)** The Spanish settled the interior of the Americas while Portuguese settled along the coast. Also, Portuguese colonies did not provide the rich sources of gold and silver that the Spanish colonies did. 7. Possible answer: offer incentives to poor Spaniards living in Spain to come settle in the colonies

---

SECTION 2 **Assessment**

Recall
1. **Identify: (a)** Council of the Indies, **(b)** Bartolomé de las Casas, **(c)** New Laws of the Indies, **(d)** Sor Juana Inés de la Cruz.
2. **Define: (a)** viceroy, **(b)** plantation, **(c)** encomienda, **(d)** peon, **(e)** peninsular, **(f)** creole, **(g)** mestizo, **(h)** mulatto, **(i)** privateer.

Comprehension
3. Describe how Spain controlled its American empire.
4. **(a)** How did the mix of peoples in Spanish America result in a new social structure? **(b)** Give three examples of cultural blending in Spain's American empire.
5. How did other European nations challenge Spanish power in the Americas?

Critical Thinking and Writing
6. **Comparing (a)** In what ways were the Spanish and Portuguese empires in the Americas similar? **(b)** In what ways were they different?
7. **Solving Problems** How might the Spanish have solved the problem of finding a dependable labor supply without resorting to the use of slavery?

Activity

Making a Poster
Review what you have read about Spanish treatment of Native Americans. Then, design a poster Bartolomé de las Casas could have used to rouse public opinion in Spain to protect the Indians.

Activity Rubrics

Share rubrics with students before they design their posters.

Attempted Poster lacks sufficient detail to persuade people to protect the Indians.

Minimal Poster has sufficient detail to persuade people to protect the Indians.

Adequate Poster persuades people to protect the Indians and is attractively done.

Exemplary Poster demonstrates a good understanding of the issue, is persuasive, and is visually appealing.

Geography and **History**

ANSWER by rounding the southern tip of South America and reaching the west coast, which no enemy ship had ever done before

---

✓ Test Preparation

Have students read the section titled "Challenging Spanish Power" on this page, and then answer the question below.

Which of the actions listed below was *not* a response from other European countries to Spain's position of power in Europe?

A Privateers raided Spanish treasure ships.

B Spanish colonists traded illegally with European smugglers.

C Other European countries sided with Portugal and declared war on Spain.

D Pirates were rewarded for raids on Spanish ships.

Reading Focus

■ What problems did settlers in New France face?

■ What traditions of government evolved in the 13 English colonies?

■ How did competition for power affect Europeans and Native Americans?

Vocabulary

missionary
revenue
compact

Taking Notes

Copy this partially completed table. As you read, fill in key information on the French and English colonies in North America.

	FRENCH COLONIES	ENGLISH COLONIES
LOCATION		East coast of North America
ECONOMY	Based mostly on fishing and fur trading	
GOVERNMENT		
GROWTH		

Main Idea France and England set up colonies and competed for dominance in North America.

Bell Ringer Ask students to preview this section by scanning its pages and observing maps, illustrations, and boldface heads. Ask them to name three peoples who competed for control of North America. Based on their knowledge of the United States and Canada today, who do they suppose won the struggle? Have them explain their reasoning.

LESSON PLAN

1. Focus Due to its harsh climate and vast wilderness, the population of New France grew slowly. People in the English colonies enjoyed traditions of representative self-government and political rights and freedoms. After defeating France, Britain became the dominant power in North America. European settlers in North America learned new ways from the Native American peoples.

2. Instruct Remind students that many of them first learned about early American history when they were in elementary school. Have students work in groups to summarize the contents of this section for elementary school students. Assign each group to work on one of the following topics: New France, The English Colonies, Competition for Colonies, and The Native Americans. Suggest that each group summarize its material by identifying the main idea of each pertinent paragraph and expressing it in one or two simple sentences. Ask for volunteers to read their group's summary to the class.

3. Assess Have each group make a list of at least six illustrations that would make the summary more interesting and understandable for elementary school students.

4. Reteach If students' Assess activity does not reflect adequate understanding of the lesson, you might assign the *Guide to the Essentials* or the *Interactive Student Tutorial CD-ROM* for this section.

Biography

Samuel de Champlain
1567(?)–1635

Samuel de Champlain was an explorer, geographer, and mapmaker. As founder and first governor of the French colony of Quebec, he is known as the Father of New France, the French colonial empire in North America.

Champlain explored many of the waterways of New France. He especially loved the St. Lawrence River, which he said was "beautiful as the Seine, rapid as the Rhône, and deep as the sea." He helped to make it the main highway for trade through New France and to make himself the force behind the colony's settlement.

Theme: Impact of the Individual Why is Champlain considered the Father of New France?

Biography

ANSWER He was the founder and first governor of the French colony of Quebec; he became the force behind the colony's settlement.

Setting the Scene

In the 1600s, other European powers moved into the Americas and began building settlements. France, the Netherlands, England, and Sweden joined Spain in claiming parts of North America.

At first, the Europeans were disappointed. North America did not yield vast treasure or offer a water passage to Asia, as they had hoped. Before long, though, the English and French were turning large profits by growing tobacco in Virginia, fishing off the North Atlantic coast, and trading fur from New England to Canada.

By 1700, France and England controlled large parts of North America. As their colonies grew, they developed their own governments, different from each other and from that of Spanish America.

Building New France

By the early 1500s, French fishing ships were crossing the Atlantic each year to harvest rich catches of cod off Newfoundland, Canada. Distracted by wars at home, however, French rulers at first paid little attention to Canada—New France, as they called it. Not until 1608 did Samuel de Champlain build the first permanent French settlement in Quebec. Jesuits and other missionaries, hoping to spread Christianity to Native Americans, soon followed. They advanced into the wilderness, trying to convert Native Americans they met.

Slow Growth Helped by Native American allies, French explorers and fur traders traveled inland, claiming vast territory. Soon, France's American empire reached from Quebec to the Great Lakes and down the Mississippi to Louisiana and the Gulf of Mexico.

The population of New France grew slowly. Wealthy landlords owned huge tracts, or areas of land, along the St. Lawrence River. They sought settlers to farm the land, but the harsh Canadian climate attracted few French peasants.

Many who went to New France soon abandoned farming in favor of fur trapping and trading. They faced a hard life in the wilderness, but the soaring European demand for fur ensured good prices. Fishing, too, supported settlers who lived in coastal villages and exported cod and other fish to Europe.

Government Policy In the late 1600s, the French king Louis XIV set out to strengthen royal power and boost revenues, or income from taxes, from

Resource Directory

Teaching Resources

Creative Teaching Activities Creative Teaching Activities booklet, p. 74

Guided Reading and Review Unit 4 booklet, p. 44

Skill Application Activity *Using a Computerized Card Catalog,* Unit 4 booklet, p. 53

his overseas empire. He appointed officials to oversee justice and economic activities in New France. He also sent more settlers and soldiers to North America. The Catholic Louis, however, prohibited Protestants from settling in New France.

By the early 1700s, French forts, missions, and trading posts stretched from Quebec to Louisiana. Yet the population of New France remained small compared to that of the 13 English colonies expanding along the Atlantic coast.

The 13 English Colonies

The English built their first permanent colony at Jamestown, Virginia, in 1607. Its early years were filled with disaster. Many settlers died of starvation and disease. The rest survived with the help of friendly Native Americans. The colony finally made headway when the settlers started to grow and export tobacco, a crop they learned about from the Indians.

In 1620, other English settlers, the Pilgrims,* landed at Plymouth, Massachusetts. They were seeking religious freedom, rather than commercial profit. Before coming ashore, they signed the Mayflower Compact, in which they set out guidelines for governing their North American colony. A compact is an agreement among people. Today, we see this document as an important early step toward self-government. It read:

> "We, whose names are underwritten . . . having undertaken for the Glory of God, and Advancement of the Christian Faith . . . a voyage to plant [a] colony in the [Americas] . . . do enact, constitute, and frame, such just and equal Laws . . . as shall be thought most [fitting] and convenient for the general Good of the Colony."
>
> —Mayflower Compact

Many Pilgrims died in the early years of the Plymouth colony. Local Indians, however, taught them to grow corn and helped them survive in the new land. Soon, a new wave of Puritan immigrants arrived to establish the Massachusetts Bay Colony.

Growth In the 1600s and 1700s, the English established 13 colonies. Some, like Virginia and New York, were commercial ventures, organized for profit. Others, like Massachusetts, Pennsylvania, and Maryland, were set up as havens for persecuted religious groups.

Geographic conditions helped shape different ways of life in the New England, middle, and southern colonies. In New England, many settlers were farmers who transferred to North America the village life they had enjoyed in England. In parts of the South, there emerged a plantation economy based on tobacco, rice, and other crops.

Like New Spain, the English colonies needed workers to clear land and raise crops. A growing number of Africans were brought to the colonies and sold as slaves. In several mainland colonies, enslaved Africans and their descendants outnumbered people of European descent.

Government Like the rulers of Spain and France, English monarchs asserted control over their American colonies. They appointed royal governors to oversee colonial affairs and had Parliament pass laws to regulate colonial trade. Yet, compared with settlers in the Spanish and French colonies, English colonists enjoyed a large degree of self-government. Each

---

*Pilgrims were a band of English Puritans, a Protestant group, who rejected the practices of the official Church of England.

Pilgrim Courage

Governor William Bradford of Plymouth Colony wrote a first-hand account of its early days, describing what happened after half the Pilgrims had died:

"[Of the 50 left . . . only six or seven were sound. These six or seven] . . . spared no pains night nor day, but with abundance of toil and hazard of their own health, fetched them wood, made them fires, dressed them meat, made their beds, washed their [filthy] clothes, clothed and unclothed them. . . . All this [was done] willingly and cheerfully, without any grudging in the least, showing herein their true love unto their friends and brethren."

—William Bradford, *Of Plymouth Plantation: 1620–1647*

Skills Assessment

Primary Source Why were the "sound" Pilgrims' actions necessary to the survival of Plymouth Colony?

Background
Global Connections

French Influences As the French explored and settled North American lands, they gave French names to forts, towns, and natural features. Many of these names remain familiar to us today and remind us of the extent of France's North American empire. Here are some French place names and their original meaning:

Detroit (narrow water passage)
Des Moines (belonging to the monks)
Baton Rouge (red stick)
Vermont (green mountain)
Terre Haute (high land)
Boise (wooded)

Global Connections

War of Jenkins' Ear This very descriptive name refers to one of the conflicts fought by European powers in the Americas during the 1700s. This war between Britain and Spain lasted from 1739 to 1748. Competition for trade was the underlying cause of the war, but the colorful testimony of Captain Robert Jenkins before Parliament actually precipitated the fighting. Jenkins alleged that his ear had been cut off eight years earlier when Spanish coast guards had boarded and looted his ship. British leaders used the incident to justify war with Spain. During the war's course, Spanish forces invaded Georgia and British forces invaded Florida, but the war ended with neither side making any significant gains.

Activity
Connections to Literature

Drawing Conclusions The novel *Northwest Passage*, by Kenneth Roberts, is an exciting tale of nations and cultures in conflict. It focuses on Rogers' Rangers, an American militia unit fighting in the British army during the French and Indian War. As the Americans and British fight alongside one another, they become increasingly aware of the growing differences and distrust that threaten to divide them.

Have students read the first few pages of Chapters 10 and 14. Then, ask them to answer the following questions based on their reading: (1) How were the tactics used by Rogers' Rangers different from those used by the British regular army? (2) What was the American attitude toward British military leadership and tactics? (3) How might the French and Indian War have helped lead to the American Revolution?

Land Claims in the Americas About 1750

Land claims about 1750
- Dutch
- English
- French
- Portuguese
- Spanish

Skills Assessment

Geography In the 1700s, European nations competed for colonies and trade in the Americas.

1. **Location** On the map, locate (a) New France, (b) Florida, (c) West Indies.
2. **Region** In what regions of North America did England have colonies?
3. **Critical Thinking Synthesizing Information** Based on the map and what you have read, why did England and France clash several times during the 1700s?

colony had its own representative assembly elected by propertied men. The assemblies advised the royal governor and made decisions on local issues.

The tradition of consulting representative assemblies grew out of the English experience. Beginning in the 1200s, Parliament had played an increasingly important role in English affairs. Slowly, too, English citizens had gained certain legal and political rights. England's American colonists expected to enjoy the same rights. When colonists later protested British policies in North America, they viewed themselves as "freeborn Englishmen" who were defending their traditional rights.

Competing for Power

By the 1600s, Spain, France, England, and the Netherlands were competing for colonies and trade around the world. All four of these nations had colonies in North America, where they often fought over territory. After several naval wars with the Netherlands, the English seized the Dutch colony of New Netherland in 1664 and renamed it New York. English settlers in Georgia clashed with the Spanish in nearby Florida.

Competition was also fierce in the Caribbean region. Dutch planters developed sugar production in the Caribbean into a big business. The French acquired Haiti, the richest of the sugar colonies, as well as Guadeloupe and Martinique. The English took Barbados and Jamaica. By the 1700s, the French and English Caribbean islands, worked by enslaved Africans, had surpassed the whole of North America in exports to Europe.

British-French Rivalry During the 1700s, Britain and France emerged as bitter rivals for power around the globe. They clashed in Europe, North America, Africa, and Asia. In North America, the French and Indian War raged from 1754 to 1763. A worldwide struggle, known as the Seven Years' War, erupted in Europe in 1756 and spread to India and Africa.

Although France held more territory in North America, the British colonies had more people. Trappers, traders, and farmers from the English colonies were pushing west into the Ohio Valley, a region claimed by France. The French, who had forged alliances with local Indians, fought to oust the intruders.

During the war, British soldiers and colonial troops launched a series of campaigns against the French in Canada and on the Ohio frontier. At first, France won several victories. Then, in 1759, the tide turned in Britain's favor. From ships anchored in the St. Lawrence River, British troops launched an attack on Quebec, the capital of New France. The British scaled steep cliffs along the river and captured the city. Though the war dragged on until 1763, the British had won control of Canada.

The Peace Treaty The 1763 Treaty of Paris officially ended the worldwide war. The treaty ensured British dominance in North America. France ceded Canada and its lands east of the Mississippi River to Britain. As you have read, the British also forced the French out of India. France, however,

Skills Assessment

ANSWERS 1. Review locations with students. **2.** north of New France and along the eastern coast of North America **3.** England and France were competing for territory in the same general area of North America.

Resource Directory

Teaching Resources
Section Quiz Unit 4 booklet, p. 45
Technology
World History Color Transparencies political cartoon on how the form of government influences people's lives, p. E–33
Interactive Student Tutorial CD-ROM Ch. 16
Computer Test Bank Ch. 16

regained the rich sugar-producing islands in the Caribbean and the slave-trading outposts in Africa that the British had seized during the war.

Impact on Native Americans

As in Spanish America, the arrival of European settlers in North America had a profound impact on Native Americans. Some Native Americans traded or formed alliances with the newcomers. On the Great Plains, as we will see, the arrival of the horse transformed the lifestyle of buffalo-hunting Indians.

War and Disease Frequently, however, clashes erupted. As settlers claimed more land, Native Americans resisted their advance. Bitter fighting resulted. In the end, superior weapons helped the English to victory. Year by year, the flood of new settlers pushed the frontier—and the Indians—slowly westward.

As elsewhere, the Native American population of North America plummeted. Disease weakened or killed large numbers. For example, in 1608, an estimated 30,000 Algonquins lived in Virginia. By 1670, there were only about 2,000 Algonquins remaining.

Native American Legacy While encounters with Europeans often brought disaster to Native American societies, the Indian way of life helped shape the emerging new culture of North America. Settlers adopted Native American technologies. From Indians, they learned to grow corn, beans, squash, and tomatoes and to hunt and trap forest animals. Today's Thanksgiving menu of turkey and pumpkin pie reflects Indian foods.

Trails blazed by Indians became highways for settlers moving west. Across the continent, rivers like the Mississippi, lakes like Okeechobee, and mountains like the Appalachians bear Indian names. Some Europeans came to respect Native American medical knowledge. Today, many people are taking a new look at Indian religious traditions that stress respect for the natural environment.

Impact on Native Americans
In their contest for North America, European nations enlisted Indian allies. This leader of the Iroquois sided with the English.

Theme: Global Interaction How did the flood of European settlers affect the Indians of North America?

SECTION 3 Assessment

Recall
1. (a) Samuel de Champlain, p. 394 (b) Louis XIV, p. 394 (c) Jamestown, p. 395 (d) Pilgrims, p. 395 (e) Mayflower Compact, p. 395 (f) French and Indian War, p. 396 (g) Treaty of Paris, p. 396
2. (a) missionary, p. 394 (b) revenue, p. 394 (c) compact, p. 395

Comprehension
3. The harsh Canadian climate attracted few French peasants. 4. Each colony had its own representative assembly elected by propertied men. The assemblies advised the governor who was appointed by the king and made decisions about local issues. 5. (a) by winning the French and Indian War (b) It had a profound, mostly negative impact on Native Americans who lost their land to settlers and succumbed to disease.

Critical Thinking and Writing
6. (a) the Atlantic Ocean, St. Lawrence River, Gulf of Mexico, Mississippi River (b) By controlling these waterways, France's rivals could disrupt trade between France and its colonies.
7. (a) The population of the 13 colonies was much larger than that of New France. (b) English colonies had more self-government than French colonies. (c) New France relied on fishing and fur trading. The English colonies relied more on farming. In the South, a plantation economy based on slavery emerged.

SECTION 3 Assessment

Recall
1. **Identify:** (a) Samuel de Champlain, (b) Louis XIV, (c) Jamestown, (d) Pilgrims, (e) Mayflower Compact, (f) French and Indian War, (g) Treaty of Paris.
2. **Define:** (a) missionary, (b) revenue, (c) compact.

Comprehension
3. Why did New France grow slowly?
4. What form of government did the 13 English colonies set up?
5. (a) How did Britain come to dominate North America? (b) What impact did European competition for colonies have on Native Americans?

Critical Thinking and Writing
6. **Connecting to Geography** Study the map in this section and the physical map of North America in the Reference Section of this book. (a) Which waterways were vitally important to French colonies in North America? (b) How might France's rivals take advantage of this geographic dependence?
7. **Comparing** Compare New France and the 13 English colonies in terms of (a) population, (b) government, (c) economy.

Activity

Making a Travel Brochure
Suppose you are a minister to Louis XIV of France. To attract people to New France, he has asked you to advertise the benefits of life in the Americas. Make a colorful brochure with maps, illustrations, and persuasive messages.

Activity Rubrics

Share rubrics with students before they create their brochures.

Attempted Brochure is not historically accurate or persuasive.

Minimal Brochure is historically accurate and persuasive and has some illustrations and maps.

Adequate Brochure is historically accurate and persuasive, and the illustrations and maps are colorful and neat.

Exemplary Brochure is historically accurate, persuasive, and well designed. The illustrations and maps are colorful and neat.

Human Drama Note

Herbal Medicine European settlers brought their own medicinal plants to North America, but they also learned herbal remedies from Native Americans. In the 1700s, steeped witch hazel bark was used by the Mohawks to treat bruised eyes. The Menominees of Wisconsin used the boiled leaves of the plant as a liniment for aching legs. Around 1850, the American Medical Association recognized witch hazel as being useful for treating eye inflammations and internal hemorrhages.

✓ Test Preparation

Have students read the first paragraph in the subsection titled "British-French Rivalry" on the opposite page, and then complete the sentence below.

Clashes between Britain and France sparked conflicts everywhere except

(A) China.

B North America.

C India.

D Africa.

Caption Answer

Native Americans clashed with settlers and gradually lost lands. Diseases from Europe spread among the Indians.

LESSON PLAN

1. Focus Contact between Europeans and Africans led to commerce and conflict. The Atlantic slave trade caused some African nations to decline and others to rise. The Asante kingdom was one of several powerful states to emerge in West Africa. In southern Africa, the Zulus battled the Dutch for control of the land.

2. Instruct Assign students to write an essay on the causes of turbulence in Africa between the 1400s and early 1800s. Have them begin by reading the section and listing the major causes of turbulence. Then, have them read the section a second time to find supporting details that help explain and develop their major ideas. Students should now organize their data into an outline and use it to write a first draft. At this point, you may wish to review the proper structure of an essay.

Now, allow students to work with a partner so that they can critically review each other's work. Based on these reviews, students should revise their first drafts. Remind students to proofread their work carefully before submitting their finished essays. Invite volunteers to read their essays to the class. Also, display essays around the classroom for others to read.

3. Assess Ask students to bring in periodical articles that address the causes of turbulence in Africa today. Use these articles as the basis for discussion.

4. Reteach If students' **Assess** activity does not reflect adequate understanding of the lesson, you might assign the *Guide to the Essentials* or the *Interactive Student Tutorial CD-ROM* for this section.

Reading Focus

- How did the arrival of Europeans in Africa lead to the Atlantic slave trade?
- How did the slave trade contribute to the rise of new African states?
- What groups battled for power in southern Africa?

Vocabulary

triangular trade
repeal
monopoly

Taking Notes

Copy this partially completed flowchart. As you read, fill in key events in the development of the Atlantic slave trade. Add as many boxes to the chart as you need.

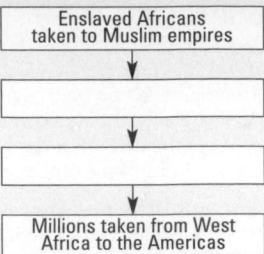

Enslaved Africans taken to Muslim empires

↓

↓

Millions taken from West Africa to the Americas

Main Idea The Atlantic slave trade, the rise of new states, and power struggles created turbulence in Africa.

Setting the Scene "The first object which saluted my eyes when I arrived on the coast was the sea, and a slave ship which was then riding at anchor and waiting for its cargo. These filled me with astonishment, which was soon converted into terror when I was carried on board." So wrote Olaudah Equiano. In the 1750s, when he was 11 years old, Equiano was seized from his Nigerian village by slave traders. He was then transported as human cargo from West Africa to the Americas.

Enslaved Africans like Equiano formed part of an international trade network that arose during the first global age. Encounters between Europeans and Africans had been taking place since the 1400s. By then, as you have read, Africa was home to diverse societies, and Islam had become an important force in some parts of the continent. As Europeans arrived, they would bring their own influences to Africa.

European Outposts in Africa

In the 1400s, Portuguese ships explored the coast of West Africa, looking for a sea route to India. They built small forts along the West African coast to trade for gold, collect food and water, and repair their ships.

The Portuguese lacked the power to push into the African interior. They did, however, attack the coastal cities of East Africa, such as Mombasa and Malindi, which were hubs of international trade. With cannons blazing, they expelled the Arabs who controlled the East African trade network and took over this thriving commerce for themselves.

The Portuguese, however, gained little profit from their victories. Trade between the interior and the coast soon dwindled. By 1600, the once-prosperous East African coastal cities had sunk into poverty.

Other Europeans soon followed the Portuguese into Africa. The Dutch, the English, and the French established forts along the western coast of Africa. Like the Portuguese, they exchanged muskets, tools, and cloth for gold, ivory, hides, and slaves.

The Atlantic Slave Trade

In the 1500s, Europeans began to view slaves as the most important item of African trade. Slavery had existed in Africa, as elsewhere around the world, since ancient times. Egyptians, Greeks, Romans, Persians, Indians, and Aztecs often enslaved defeated foes. Our word *slave* comes from the large number of Slavs taken from southern Russia to work as unpaid laborers in Roman times.

The Arab empire also used slave labor, often captives taken from Africa. In the Middle East, many enslaved Africans worked on farming estates or large-scale irrigation projects. Others became artisans, soldiers, or merchants. Some rose to prominence in the Muslim world even though they were officially slaves.

European and African Slave Traders   The Atlantic slave trade began in the 1500s, to fill the need for labor in Spain's American empire. In the next 300 years, it grew into a huge and profitable business. Each year, traders shipped tens of thousands of enslaved Africans across the Atlantic to work on tobacco and sugar plantations in the Americas.

Europeans seldom went into the interior to take part in slave raids. Instead, they relied on African rulers and traders to seize captives in the interior and bring them to coastal trading posts and fortresses. There, the captives were exchanged for textiles, metalwork, rum, tobacco, weapons, and gunpowder. The slave trade intensified as the demand for slaves increased in the Americas and as the demand for luxury goods increased in Africa.

Triangular Trade   The Atlantic slave trade formed one part of a three-legged trade network known as the triangular trade. On the first leg, merchant ships brought goods to Africa to be traded for slaves. On the second leg, known as the Middle Passage, the slaves were transported to the West Indies. There, the enslaved Africans were exchanged for sugar, molasses, and other products. On the final leg, these products were shipped to Europe or European colonies in the Americas. The prosperity of port cities such as Nantes in France, Bristol in England, and Salem in Massachusetts thus depended in large part on the slave trade.

Horrors of the Middle Passage   For enslaved Africans, the Middle Passage was a horror. Once purchased, Africans were packed below the decks of slave ships. Hundreds of men, women, and children were crammed into a single vessel. Slave ships became "floating coffins" on which up to half the Africans on board died from disease or brutal mistreatment.

The Slave Trade
Merchants from many lands engaged in the slave trade. Arabs, such as those on the ship below, brought human cargoes out of East Africa. Portuguese traders carried slaves to the Americas from West Africa. A Portuguese soldier is depicted in the delicate ivory carving.

Theme: Global Interaction
Why was there a growing demand for slaves in the Americas?

Check Comprehension

After they read Section 4, have students write for at least five minutes in response to the following questions: What did I read about in this section? What did I already know? What did I learn? What did I think about or feel as I read about the slave trade? *(Less Advanced Readers)*

Background

Connections to Economics

The Economics of Slavery Many cultures have practiced slavery or other forced labor. People were enslaved for debt, as punishment for crimes, or as prisoners of war. From the 1400s to the 1800s, millions of serfs in Eastern Europe and Russia were bound to the land. In the Middle East, some slaves rose to positions in government.

During this same time period, the slave trade in Africa expanded. Some African societies used war captives as slaves. However, Arab slave traders carried millions of Africans to southwestern Asia, where Europeans took millions more to the Americas.

English colonists had tried to use Native Americans and indentured servants to fill their labor needs, but many of them died as a result of poor treatment. They turned to imported Africans to clear land and work on plantations.

Enslaved Africans who worked as household servants were sometimes treated better than field hands. In the Caribbean, some had skilled trades, lived in cities, and earned money. In South America, some met with less severe racial prejudice. In the American South, the Caribbean Islands, and Brazil, slaves produced tobacco, sugar, and cotton for export.

Slaves in the Americas could not integrate into society or achieve power or wealth. They were a commodity in a new world of capitalism.

Biography

King Affonso 1456–1543

"Most powerful and excellent King of the Kongo, We convey you greetings in that We much love and esteem you." So wrote the king of Portugal to King Affonso in 1512. Affonso (born Nzinga Mbemba) had a long and warm relationship with the Portuguese. However, some years later, in 1526, Affonso wrote in dismay to the king of Portugal: "Merchants are taking every day our natives, sons of the land and sons of our nobles and vassals and our relatives, because the thieves and men of bad conscience . . . grab them and get them to be sold. . . . Our country is being completely depopulated."

In the end, Affonso's ties to Portugal were not strong enough. He sought help to build modern ships, but no Portuguese shipbuilders ever arrived. And his attempts to end the slave trade had no effect.

Theme: Impact of the Individual Why do you think Affonso is admired today, even though his efforts failed?

 Primary Sources and Literature

See "King Affonso I: Letter to King John of Portugal" in the Reference Section at the back of this book.

Some enslaved Africans resisted. A few tried to seize control of the ship and return to Africa. Others committed suicide by leaping overboard. One African recalled such an incident during the Middle Passage:

"One day . . . two of my wearied countrymen who were chained together . . . jumped into the sea; immediately another . . . followed their example. . . . two of the wretches were drowned, but [the ship's crew] got the other, and afterwards flogged him unmercifully for thus attempting to prefer death to slavery."

—Olaudah Equiano, *The Life of Gustavus Vassa*

African Leaders Resist Some African leaders tried to slow down the transatlantic slave trade or even to stop it altogether. They used different forms of resistance. But in the end, the system that supported the trade was simply too strong for them.

An early voice raised against the slave trade was that of Affonso I, ruler of Kongo in west-central Africa. As a young man, Affonso was tutored by Portuguese missionaries. After becoming king in 1505, he called on the Portuguese to help him develop Kongo as a modern Christian state.

Before long, however, Affonso grew alarmed. Each year, more and more Portuguese came to Kongo to buy slaves. They offered high prices, and government officials and local chiefs eagerly entered the trade. Even Christian missionaries began to buy and sell Africans.

Affonso insisted that "it is our will that in these Kingdoms there should not be any trade of slaves nor outlet for them." Kongo, he stated, could benefit from contacts with Europe, but the trade in human lives was evil. His appeal failed, and the slave trade continued.

In the late 1700s, another African ruler, the almamy of Futa Toro in northern Senegal, tried to halt the slave trade in his lands. Since the 1500s, French sea captains had bought slaves from African traders in Futa Toro. The almamy decided to put a stop to this practice. In 1788, he forbade anyone to transport slaves through Futa Toro for sale abroad. The sea captains and local chiefs protested, and called on the almamy to repeal, or cancel, the law. The almamy refused. He returned the presents the captains had sent him in hopes of winning him over to their cause. "All the riches in the world would not make me change my mind," he said.

The almamy's victory was short-lived, however. The inland slave traders simply worked out a new route to the coast. Sailing to this new market, the French captains easily purchased the slaves that the almamy had prevented them from buying in Senegal. There was nothing the almamy could do to stop them.

Impact of the Atlantic Slave Trade Historians are still debating the number of Africans who were affected by the Atlantic slave trade. In the 1500s, they estimate, about 2,000 enslaved Africans were sent to the Americas each year. In the 1780s, when the slave trade was at its peak, that number topped 80,000 a year. By the 1800s, when the overseas slave trade was finally stopped, an estimated 11 million enslaved Africans had reached the Americas. Another 2 million probably died under the brutal conditions of the voyage between Africa and the Americas.

The slave trade caused the decline of some African states and the rise of others. In West Africa, the loss of countless numbers of young women and men resulted in some small states disappearing forever. At the same time, there arose new African states whose way of life depended on the slave trade. The rulers of these powerful new states waged war against other Africans so they could gain control of the slave trade in their region and reap the profits.

Biography

ANSWER because he attempted to end the slave trade

Resource Directory

Teaching Resources
Biography Activity *Olaudah Equiano,* Unit 4 booklet, p. 50

Triangular Trade

Destinations of Enslaved Africans, 1500–1870

British North America — 4.5%
Europe and Asia — 2.5%
Portuguese Brazil — 37%
Spanish America, including Spanish Caribbean — 15%
Other Caribbean islands — 41%

Source: Albert M. Craig, *World Civilizations*

Rise of New African States

Among the large states that rose in West Africa in the 1600s and 1700s were Oyo, Bornu, and Dahomey. Another state, the Asante kingdom, emerged in the area occupied by modern Ghana.

The Asante Kingdom In the late 1600s, an able military leader, Osei Tutu, won control of the trading city of Kumasi. From there, he conquered neighboring peoples and organized the Asante kingdom. Osei Tutu claimed that his right to rule came from heaven. Leading chiefs served as a council of advisers but were subject to the royal will.

Officials chosen by merit rather than by birth supervised an efficient bureaucracy. They managed the royal monopolies over gold mining and the slave trade. A monopoly is the exclusive control of a business or industry. The Asante traded with Europeans on the coast, exchanging gold and slaves for firearms. But they shrewdly played off rival Europeans against one another to protect their own interests.

Islamic Crusades In the 1700s and early 1800s, an Islamic revival spread across West Africa. It began among the Fulani people in northern Nigeria. The scholar and preacher Usman dan Fodio denounced the corruption of the local Hausa rulers. He called for social and religious reforms based on the Sharia, or Islamic law. In the early 1800s, Usman inspired Fulani herders and Hausa townspeople to rise up against their rulers.

Usman and his successors set up a powerful Islamic state. Under their rule, literacy increased, local wars quieted, and trade improved. Their success inspired other Muslim reform movements in West Africa. Between

Failure to Understand In 1900, when the British sought to take control of what is now Ghana, they claimed the Asantes' famed Golden Stool for their own Queen Victoria. A British representative told the Asante leaders: "[You have] failed to give to the Queen, who is the paramount power in this country, the stool to which she is entitled. Where is the Golden Stool? Why am I [as the queen's representative] not sitting on the Golden Stool at this moment?"

The British did not understand that the Asante ruler would never have thought of sitting on the Golden Stool. It was a sacred religious symbol, not a mere throne. To the Asante people, it symbolized royal power and contained the spirits of their ancestors. Insulted by the British demand, the Asante, in the name of their own Queen Mother, Yaa Asantewaa, went to war against the British. However, they lost the war, and Britain became their colonial master.

Skills Assessment

Geography The Atlantic slave trade was part of the triangular trade network that linked merchants in Africa, Europe, and the Americas.

1. **Location** On the map, locate **(a)** Africa, **(b)** West Indies, **(c)** New York, **(d)** Charleston.
2. **Movement** What goods were sent to Africa?
3. **Critical Thinking Analyzing Information** Between 1500 and 1870, most enslaved Africans were taken to what two regions of the Americas?

Human Drama Activity

Writing a Journal Entry Have students review the section "Africa Leaders Resist" on the opposite page. Then ask students to imagine they are either King Affonso I or the almamy of Futa Toro and that they are trying to stop the slave trade in Kongo or northern Senegal. Have students write a journal entry detailing the hopes and frustrations they feel about this issue. The journal should also record the reactions to the proposed reforms by those who favored or relied upon the slave trade.

Test Preparation

Have students read the subsection titled "Impact of the Atlantic Slave Trade" on the opposite page, and then answer the question below.

About how many slaves reached the Americas by the 1800s?

A 80,000

B 11 million

C 2,000

D 2 million

Skills Assessment

ANSWERS 1. Review locations with students. 2. tobacco, rum, and manufactured goods 3. Brazil and the West Indies

SECTION 4 Assessment

Recall
1. (a) Middle Passage, p. 399 **(b)** Asante, p. 401 **(c)** Usman dan Fodio, p. 401 **(d)** Boer, p. 402 **(e)** Shaka, p. 402 **(f)** Great Trek, p. 402 **2. (a)** triangular trade, p. 399 **(b)** repeal, p. 400 **(c)** monopoly, p. 401

Comprehension
3. (a) King Affonso wrote to the king of Portugal, asking him to end the slave trade. The almamy of Futa Toro passed a law forbidding anyone to transport slaves through his area. **(b)** The population of some regions of Africa decreased dramatically. Some societies and states were ruined. The African states that profited from the slave trade grew more powerful. **4.** Asante rulers claimed to rule by divine right, created an efficient bureaucracy, conquered neighboring peoples, engaged in the slave trade, and avoided conflict with European powers. **5.** Various groups, including the Zulu, Dutch, and British, migrated there and competed with one another for control of the land.

Critical Thinking and Writing
6. Possible answers: **(a)** Modern historians could study population figures for each African society whose people were enslaved. They could also study the cargo records of slave ships. **(b)** Such records may not have been kept, may be incomplete, or may have been lost or destroyed. **7.** Possible answers: **(a)** There were enough African traders who would perform the raids. **(b)** It had a devastating effect on many West African states whose populations were decimated.

Activity Rubrics

Share rubrics with students before they write their newspaper articles.

Attempted Article is incomplete or reflects insufficient research.

Minimal Article describes Shaka's role in Zulu history, reflecting sufficient research.

Adequate Article describes Shaka's role in Zulu history and is written in an objective newspaper style.

Exemplary Article is well written and describes Shaka's role in Zulu history in an informative, yet entertaining manner.

Caption Answer

The guns that Europeans had were superior to the weapons used by the Zulus.

about 1780 and 1880, more than a dozen Islamic leaders rose to power, replacing old rulers or founding new states in the western Sudan.

Battles for Power in Southern Africa

Over many centuries, Bantu-speaking peoples had migrated into southern Africa. In 1652, Dutch immigrants also arrived in the region. They built Cape Town to supply ships sailing to or from the East Indies. Dutch farmers, called Boers, settled around Cape Town. Over time, they ousted or enslaved the Khoisan herders who lived there. The Boers held to a Calvinist belief that they were the elect, or chosen, of God. They looked on Africans as inferiors.

In the 1700s, Boer herders and ivory hunters began to push north from the Cape Colony. As they did, they had to battle several powerful African groups.

Shaka and the Zulus The Zulus had migrated into southern Africa in the 1500s. In the early 1800s, they emerged as a major force under a ruthless and brilliant leader, Shaka. He built on the successes of earlier leaders who had begun to organize young fighters into permanent regiments.

Between 1818 and 1828, Shaka waged relentless war and conquered many nearby peoples. He absorbed their young men and women into Zulu regiments. By encouraging rival groups to forget their differences, he cemented a growing pride in the Zulu kingdom.

Shaka's wars disrupted life across southern Africa. Groups driven from their homelands by the Zulus adopted Shaka's tactics. They then migrated north, conquering still other peoples and creating their own powerful states.

Later Shaka's half brother took over the Zulu kingdom. About this time, the Zulus faced a new threat, the arrival of well-armed, mounted Boers migrating north from the Cape Colony.

Boers Versus Zulus In 1815, the Cape Colony passed from the Dutch to the British. Many Boers resented British laws that abolished slavery and otherwise interfered in their way of life. To escape British rule, they loaded their goods into covered wagons and started north. In the late 1830s, several thousand Boer families joined this "Great Trek."

As the migrating Boers came into contact with Zulus, fighting quickly broke out. At first, Zulu regiments held their own. But in the end, Zulu spears could not defeat Boer guns. The struggle for control of the land would rage until the end of the century, as you will read later.

Zulu Weapons
The Zulus developed a new type of stabbing spear with a short shaft and a broad blade. For protection, they used ox-hide shields that were four feet high. Zulu armies won battles against the Boers, the English, and neighboring African peoples.

Theme: Economics and Technology Why were Europeans eventually able to defeat the Zulus?

SECTION 4 Assessment

Recall
1. Identify: (a) Middle Passage, **(b)** Asante, **(c)** Usman dan Fodio, **(d)** Boer, **(e)** Shaka, **(f)** Great Trek.
2. Define: (a) triangular trade, **(b)** repeal, **(c)** monopoly.

Comprehension
3. (a) Describe attempts by Africans to stop the slave trade. **(b)** What was the impact of the slave trade on life in Africa?
4. What steps did the Asante ruler take to ensure his power?
5. How did southern Africa become a battleground for rival groups?

Critical Thinking and Writing
6. Solving Problems (a) What kinds of information would a modern historian need to determine the number of Africans involved in the slave trade? **(b)** Why might a historian have trouble finding this information?
7. Analyzing Information (a) Why do you think European traders rarely took part directly in slave raids? **(b)** What effect did participation in the slave trade have on West African states?

Activity
Take It to the NET

Use the Internet to research the Zulu leader, Shaka. Then, write a newspaper article that describes his life, his character, and his role in the history of southern Africa.

Resource Directory

Teaching Resources

Section Quiz Unit 4 booklet, p. 47
Creative Teaching Activities Creative Teaching Activities booklet, p. 76
Guided Reading and Review Unit 4 booklet, p. 48
Geography and History Activity *Mapmaking and Relative Location,* Geography and History booklet, pp. 8–9

Technology

Interactive Student Tutorial CD-ROM Ch. 16
Computer Test Bank Ch. 16

SECTION 5 Changes in Europe

Reading Focus

■ How did European explorations lead to a global exchange?

■ What impact did the commercial revolution and mercantilism have on European economies?

■ How did these changes affect ordinary people?

Vocabulary

inflation
capitalism
entrepreneur
joint stock company
mercantilism
tariff

Taking Notes

Copy this diagram. As you read, fill in ways in which exploration and increased trade affected life in Europe. To help you get started, part of the diagram has been filled in.

EUROPEAN EXPLORATION AND TRADE

New foods from the Americas

Main Idea European exploration and increased trade stimulated a global exchange, a commercial revolution, and other changes in Europe.

Setting the Scene

In 1570, Joseph de Acosta visited the Americas. He wrote in amazement about the many strange forms of life that he saw there. "[There are] a thousand different kinds of birds and beasts of the forest, which have never been known, neither in shape nor name. . . ." To Europeans like Acosta, the Americas seemed like a "new world."

As you have read, European explorations between 1500 and 1700 brought major changes to Asia, Africa, and the Americas. Here, we will look at the impact that these explorations had on Europe itself.

A Global Exchange

When Columbus returned to Spain in March 1493, he brought with him "new" plants and animals that he had found in the Americas. Later that year, Columbus returned to the Americas. With him were some 1,200 settlers and a collection of European animals and plants. In this way, Columbus began a vast global exchange that would have a profound effect on the world. In addition to people, plants, and animals, it included technology and even disease. Because this global exchange began with Columbus, we call it the Columbian Exchange.

New Foods From the Americas, Europeans brought home a variety of foods, including tomatoes, pumpkins, and peppers. Perhaps the most important foods from the Americas, however, were corn and the potato. Easy to grow, the potato helped feed Europe's rapidly growing population. Corn spread all across Europe and to Africa and Asia, as well.

At the same time, Europeans carried a wide variety of plants and animals to the Americas. Foods included wheat and grapes from Europe itself, and bananas and sugar cane from Africa and Asia. Cattle, pigs, goats, and chickens, unknown before the European encounter, added protein to the Native American diet. Horses and donkeys also changed the lives of Native Americans. The horse, for example, gave the nomadic peoples of western North America a new, more effective way to hunt buffalo.

Impact on Population The transfer of food crops from continent to continent took time. By the 1700s, however, corn, potatoes, manioc, beans, and tomatoes were contributing to population growth around the world. While other factors help account for the population explosion that began at this time, new food crops from the Americas were probably a key cause.

Global Connections

Europe's Sweet Tooth

Today, we take sugar for granted. But at one time, it was strictly a luxury item that few European households could afford. Then, in 1493, Columbus brought sugar cane plants to the Caribbean. The new crop thrived. As sugar supplies increased, sugar prices fell, and the former luxury item appeared on more and more European tables. It was also used to sweeten a popular new treat from the Americas—chocolate.

Still, Europe's new "sweet tooth" had a tragic side effect. In just 150 years, close to 4 million Africans were shipped as slaves to the Caribbean and Brazil to work the sugar plantations there.

Theme: Global Interaction
Who was originally responsible for bringing sugar cane to the Americas?

Chapter 16 **403**

Making a Profit In a capitalist market system, almost anything can be traded. If demand is great, prices rise and traders earn profits. When demand falls, however, traders lose money. The trick is knowing when to buy and when to sell.

For Europeans of the 1600s, the tulip was a luxury item. In the Netherlands, the enormous demand for tulips attracted numerous profit-seeking investors and led to a buying frenzy that became known as *tulipomania*. At first, tulip prices skyrocketed. But a bust soon followed. Prices—and the dreams of many investors—crashed.

Today, many young people collect trading cards. For those who are lucky, an initial purchase price of a few dollars may result in a handsome profit in the future.

The Columbian Exchange sparked the migration of millions of people. Each year, shiploads of European settlers sailed to the Americas. Europeans also settled on the fringes of Africa and Asia. As you have read, the Atlantic slave trade forcibly brought millions of Africans to the Americas. The Native American population declined drastically.

The vast movement of peoples led to the transfer of ideas and technologies. Language also traveled. Words such as *pajama* (from India) or *hammock* and *canoe* (from the Americas) entered European languages.

A Commercial Revolution

The opening of direct links with Asia, Africa, and the Americas had far-reaching economic consequences for Europeans. Among these consequences were an upsurge in prices, known as the price revolution, and the rise of modern capitalism.

The Price Revolution In the early modern age, prices began to rise in parts of Europe. The economic cycle that involves a rise in prices linked to a sharp increase in the amount of money available is today called inflation.

European inflation had several causes. As the population grew, the demand for goods and services rose. Because goods were scarce, sellers could raise their prices. Inflation was also fueled by an increased flow of silver and gold. By the mid-1500s, tons of these precious metals were flowing into Europe from the Americas. Rulers used much of the silver and gold to make coins. The increased money in circulation, combined with the scarcity of goods, caused prices to rise.

Growth of Capitalism Expanded trade and the push for overseas empires spurred the growth of European capitalism, the investment of money to make a profit. Entrepreneurs, or enterprising merchants, organized, managed, and assumed the risks of doing business. They hired workers and paid for raw materials, transport, and other costs of production.

As trade increased, entrepreneurs sought to expand into overseas ventures. Such ventures were risky. Capitalist investors were more willing to take the risks when demand and prices were high. Thus, the price revolution of the early modern age gave a boost to capitalism.

Entrepreneurs and capitalists made up a new business class devoted to the goal of making profits. Together, they helped change the local European economy into an international trading system.

New Business Methods Early capitalists discovered new ways to create wealth. From the Arabs, they adapted methods of bookkeeping to show profits and losses from their ventures. During the late Middle Ages, as you have read, banks sprang up, allowing wealthy merchants to lend money at interest. The joint stock company, also developed in late medieval times, grew in importance. It allowed people to pool large amounts of capital needed for overseas ventures.

Bypassing the Guilds The growing demand for goods led merchants to find ways to increase production. Traditionally, guilds controlled the manufacture of goods. But guild masters often ran small-scale businesses without the capital to produce for large markets. They also had strict rules regulating quality, prices, and working conditions.

Enterprising capitalists devised a way to bypass the guilds. The putting out system, as it was called, was first used to produce textiles but later spread to other industries. Under the putting out system, a merchant capitalist distributed raw wool to peasant cottages. Cottagers spun the wool into thread and then wove the thread into cloth. Merchants bought the wool cloth from the peasants and sent it to the city for finishing and dyeing. Finally, the merchants sold the finished product for a profit.

Resource Directory

Teaching Resources
Synthesizing Information Chapter Extension Activities booklet, p. 42

The Commercial Revolution

The Commercial Revolution spurred trade, promoted new business methods, and increased competition for profits among European nations. Use the quotation, picture, and graph to learn about this revolution.

The Clove Market

In his book published in 1998, journalist Charles Corn described one way the Dutch East India Company maintained its profits in cloves:

"The Dutch East India Company by now had gained the power to restrict production to meet Europe's demand for cloves, thereby maintaining high prices and preventing a glutted market. To achieve this end, the company engaged in a ploy . . . : balancing off the island's supply of spices against what it perceived to be the world's demand for them. Such a scheme introduced the practice of [required] cultivation of spice trees in groves officially authorized and the careful [destruction] of those the company did not approve."
—Charles Corn, *The Scents of Eden*

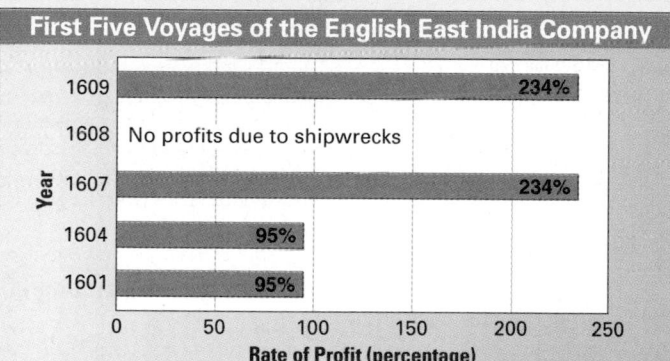

The Port of Marseille, France, 1700s

First Five Voyages of the English East India Company

Year	Rate of Profit (percentage)
1609	234%
1608	No profits due to shipwrecks
1607	234%
1604	95%
1601	95%

Source: Sir William Wilson Hunter, *A History of British India*

Skills Assessment

1. The range of profits on the English East India Company's first five voyages was from
   A 95 percent to 234 percent.
   B total loss to 234 percent.
   C 1601 to 1609.
   D $0 to $234.

2. The Dutch East India Company tried to improve its profits on cloves by
   E planting more clove trees.
   F using extra ships to bring cloves to market.
   G keeping production low in relation to demand.
   H increasing the supply of cloves on the market.

3. **Critical Thinking Drawing Conclusions** (a) What evidence here might lead you to conclude that shipping was important to the Commercial Revolution? (b) What role did the profit motive play in the Commercial Revolution? Use evidence to support your answer.

Skills Tip

Bar graphs have both a vertical axis and a horizontal axis, with each measuring a different element. Distinguish between the two before turning to the rest of the graph.

Chapter 16 **405**

✓ Test Preparation

Have students read the section titled "Growth of Capitalism" on the opposite page, and then complete the sentence below.

The investment of money to make a profit is called

A circulation.

B inflation.

C capitalism.

D joint stock.

Background
About the Evidence

Dutch Trading The Netherlands, although a small country, had a major role in the commercial revolution of the seventeenth century. Half its population lived in cities, making it the most urbanized country in Europe. The country's roads and waterways were filled with people and goods. By the 1560s, Holland—one of the country's seven provinces—had 1800 ships, six times the number found in Venice a century earlier, when that Italian city-state was at its height of prosperity.

Activity
Interpreting the Evidence

Interpreting the Evidence Use these additional questions to generate class discussion.

1. Critical Thinking: Making Inferences If the 1608 voyage of the English East India Company had not shipwrecked, what rate of profit might have been expected? Why? *(probably around 234 percent, because that was the rate of profit for the years before and after 1608)*

2. Critical Thinking: Analyzing Information How might the English East India Company have used the methods employed by the Dutch East India Company to achieve higher profits? *(They might have decreased the supply to increase the demand.)*

Skills Tip

Ask students to distinguish verbally between the vertical and horizontal lines on the bar graph by stating what each one measures. The Skills Handbook in the front of the book has a lesson that will help students with this feature.

Skills Assessment

ANSWERS 1. D **2.** G **3. (a)** the many trading ships shown in the Marseille harbor and the total loss incurred due to shipwrecks **(b)** The Dutch company kept supply intentionally low to increase demand, and therefore, profit. The English company also strove to increase their rate of profit.

Pick Your Poison Both the potato and the tomato are members of the night-shade plant family. Because Europeans were familiar with poisonous night-shades, they initially refused to accept these American plants as food. Many, however, believed the plants to have special powers. The tomato was known as the love apple and was used as a special ornament.

Background
Daily Life

Later Marriages During the Middle Ages, Church law set the minimum age for marriage at 12 for women and 14 for men. By the 1500s, however, men and women were marrying at much later ages—typically in the mid-twenties and late-twenties rather than the teens. Due to inflation and other economic pressures, it took the average couple a longer time to gather the material resources needed for married life. An increasing number never married at all. It is estimated that, during the 1500s, 20 percent of all women remained single.

"TAKE US TO YOUR LEADER . . . WE'VE COME TO NEGOTIATE A FREE TRADE AGREEMENT WITH EARTH."

Connections to Today

The Banana Wars
Governments have been using tariffs to protect their own indus-tries for years. This practice con-tinues today, as the "Banana Wars" between the United States and Europe demonstrate. American multinational compa-nies produce bananas in coun-tries like Honduras and Ecuador. Former European colonies in the Caribbean also produce bananas. European governments decided to let Caribbean bananas come into their countries more cheaply than the bananas produced by American firms, thus taking mar-ket share from the American firms. To retaliate, the United States government placed a 100 percent tariff on certain goods from Europe, making them much more expensive. Some 500 years after they began, tariff wars go on.

Theme: Continuity and Change Why do tariff wars develop?

The putting out system separated capital and labor for the first time. From this system controlled by merchants, the next step would be the capitalist-owned factories of the Industrial Revolution of the 1700s, as you will read.

Mercantilism

European monarchs enjoyed the benefits of the commercial revolution. In the fierce competition for trade and empire, they adopted a new economic policy, known as mercantilism, aimed at strengthening their national economies.

Mercantilists supported several basic ideas. They believed that a nation's real wealth was measured in its gold and silver treasure. To build its supply of gold and silver, they said, a nation must export more goods than it imported.

The Role of Colonies Overseas empires were central to the mercantile system. Colonies, said mercantilists, existed for the benefit of the parent country. They provided resources and raw materials not available in Europe. In turn, they enriched a par-ent country by serving as a market for its manufactured goods. To achieve these goals, European powers passed strict laws regulating trade with their colonies. Colonists could not set up their own industries to manufacture goods. They were also forbidden to buy goods from a foreign country. In addition, only ships from the parent country or the colonies themselves could be used to send goods in or out of the colonies.

Increasing National Wealth Mercantilists urged rulers to adopt policies to increase national wealth and government revenues. To boost production, governments exploited mineral and timber resources, built roads, and backed new industries. They imposed a single national currency and estab-lished standard weights and measures.

Governments also sold monopolies to large producers in certain indus-tries as well as to big overseas trading companies. Finally, governments imposed tariffs, or taxes on imported goods. Tariffs were designed to pro-tect local industries from foreign competition by increasing the price of imported goods.

The Lives of Ordinary People

How did these economic changes affect Europeans? In general, their impact depended on a person's social class. Merchants who invested in overseas ventures acquired wealth. But the price revolution hurt nobles. Their wealth was in land, and they had trouble raising money to pay higher costs for stylish clothing and other luxuries. Some sold off land, which in turn reduced their income. In towns and cities, the wages of hired workers did not keep up with inflation, creating poverty and discontent.

Most Europeans were still peasants. Europe's growing involvement in the world had little immediate effect on their lives. Changes took genera-tions, even centuries, to be felt. For example, tradition-bound peasants were often reluctant to grow foods brought from the Americas. Only in the later 1700s did German peasants begin to raise potatoes. Even then, many com-plained that these strange-looking tubers tasted terrible.

Within Europe's growing cities, there were great differences in wealth and power. Successful merchants dominated city life. Guilds, too, remained powerful. And as trade grew, another group—lawyers—gained importance for their skills in writing contracts. Middle-class families enjoyed a comfort-able life. Servants cooked, cleaned, and waited on them. Other city residents, such as journeymen and other laborers, were not so lucky. They often lived in crowded quarters on the edge of poverty.

Connections to Today

ANSWER Governments use tariffs to try to gain an advantage over other coun-tries, and the other countries retaliate with their own tariffs.

Resource Directory

Teaching Resources
Section Quiz Unit 4 booklet, p. 49
Geography Quiz Unit 4 booklet, p. 54
Chapter Test Forms A, B, and C Unit 4 booklet, pp. 55–59
Answer Key Unit 4 booklet, pp. 80–90

Technology
Interactive Student Tutorial CD-ROM Ch. 16
Computer Test Bank Ch. 16

Regardless of social class, European families were patriarchal. As husband and father, a man was responsible for the behavior of his wife and children. Women had almost no property or legal rights. A woman's chief roles were as wife and mother. Society stressed such womanly virtues as modesty, household economy, obedience, and caring for the family. Middle-class women might help their husbands in a family business. Peasant women worked alongside their husbands in the fields.

Looking Ahead

In the 1500s and 1600s, Europe emerged as a powerful new force on the world scene. The voyages of exploration marked the beginning of what would become European domination of the globe. In the centuries ahead, competition for empire would spark wars in Europe and on other continents.

European expansion would spread goods and other changes throughout the world. It would also revolutionize the European economy and transform its society. The concept of "the West" itself emerged as European settlers transplanted their culture to the Americas and, later, to Australia and New Zealand.

For centuries, most Europeans knew little or nothing about other lands. Exposure to different cultures was both unsettling and stimulating. As their horizons broadened, they had to reexamine old beliefs and customs.

Cause and Effect

Long-Term Causes	Immediate Causes
• Scientific Revolution • Europeans search for a sea route to Asia	• Columbus and other Europeans arrive in the Americas • Europeans encounter new plants and animals in the Americas

Columbian Exchange

Immediate Effects	Long-Term Effects
• Millions of Native Americans die from diseases • Enslaved Africans sent to the Americas • American foods introduced into Europe	• Exchange of ideas, foods, art, and language between Europe and the Americas • Population migration from Europe to the Americas • Growth of capitalism

Connections to Today

• Multicultural societies in the Americas
• Worldwide reliance on staples such as corn and potatoes

Skills Assessment Chart The arrival of Columbus in the Americas set off a global exchange of people, goods, and ideas. **Based on the chart, name one immediate and one long-term effect of the Columbian Exchange.**

SECTION 5 Assessment

Recall

1. **Identify: (a)** Columbian Exchange, **(b)** commercial revolution, **(c)** putting out system.
2. **Define: (a)** inflation, **(b)** capitalism, **(c)** entrepreneur, **(d)** joint stock company, **(e)** mercantilism, **(f)** tariff.

Comprehension

3. How did the voyages of Columbus lead to global exchanges of goods and ideas?
4. Explain how each of the following contributed to economic changes in Europe: **(a)** the price revolution, **(b)** capitalism, **(c)** mercantilism.

5. How did the economic changes of the 1500s and 1600s affect the lives of ordinary people?

Critical Thinking and Writing

6. **Linking Past and Present** Global exchanges of goods, ideas, and even diseases continue today. How has modern technology quickened the speed with which global exchanges occur? Provide examples to support your answer.
7. **Inferring** Do you think the European policy of mercantilism was beneficial or harmful for the people of Africa and the Americas? Explain.

Activity

Creating a Map
Create an illustrated map of the world showing the movement of items in the Columbian Exchange. Label Europe, Asia, Africa, and North and South America. Create symbols to stand for products and use arrows to indicate the direction in which they traveled.

EXPLORING the HUMAN DRAMA ## Human Drama Note

The Columbian Exchange In Ireland, the potato had a profound effect on the way people lived. The potato was introduced into Ireland from the Americas in the 1580s. The new crop was easy to grow and highly nutritious. Before long, Irish peasants depended on it as their main source of food. Then, in 1845, disaster struck. In a single month, a blight wiped out the entire potato crop. More than a million Irish died of starvation and disease in the famine that followed. In a strange twist of history, hundreds of thousands of starving Irish left their homeland to seek a new life in the Americas—from where the potato had first come.

SECTION 5 Assessment

Recall
1. **(a)** Columbian Exchange, p. 403 **(b)** commercial revolution, p. 404 **(c)** putting out system, p. 404
2. **(a)** inflation, p. 404 **(b)** capitalism, p. 404 **(c)** entrepreneur, p. 404 **(d)** joint stock company, p. 404 **(e)** mercantilism, p. 406 **(f)** tariff, p. 406

Comprehension
3. Columbus brought people, plants, and animals from the Americas to Europe. Returning to the Americas, he brought European settlers and European plants and animals, thus beginning a vast global exchange. 4. **(a)** The rise in prices made merchants wealthy but hurt nobles, whose wealth was tied up in land, and workers, whose wages did not keep up with inflation. **(b)** Investors provided the capital that financed international trade. **(c)** It encouraged the growth of overseas empires and the regulation of trade. 5. Students' answers should reflect how changes to the economy affected different social groups.

Critical Thinking and Writing
6. Possible answer: Modern transportation has sped up global exchanges. Ideas can spread rapidly over the Internet. Jets speed people and goods across the world. As people travel, they can carry disease with them. 7. Possible answer: Mercantilism was harmful to many people in Africa and the Americas. Europeans took gold and silver from them, exploited and enslaved their peoples, and established colonies.

Activity Rubrics

Share rubrics with students before they design their maps.

Attempted Map is incomplete.

Minimal Map labels some continents, uses some symbols and arrows to show the movement of items in the Columbian Exchange, but is not thorough.

Adequate Map labels continents, uses symbols and arrows to show the movement of items in the Columbian Exchange, and is neatly done.

Exemplary Map labels continents; uses symbols and arrows to show the movement of items in the Columbian Exchange; and is neatly labeled, colored, and visually appealing.

Skills Assessment

ANSWER Possible answer: immediate effect—millions of Native Americans died from diseases; long-term effect—the growth of capitalism

Creating a Chapter Summary

As a reteaching opportunity, pair a more able student with a less able student to complete this chapter summary.

Possible answers: **The Americas** Aztec and Incan civilizations destroyed by Spanish; the Americas were divided into Spanish, Portuguese, British, French, and Dutch colonial empires; the slave trade brought Africans to the Americas; the introduction of new products and ideas; the creation of new culture blending European, African, and Native American traditions **Africa** decrease in population due to slave trade; development of new states dependent on the slave trade; conflicts between Zulus, Dutch, and English in southern Africa **Europe** Spain's wealth due to gold and silver from America; wars among European powers to control empires; introduction of new products; development of new business practices; changes in social structure

Building Vocabulary

1–10. Student's crossword puzzles should demonstrate a clear understanding of the vocabulary words.

Recalling Key Facts

11. Some Native Americans were forced to convert to Christianity; some were enslaved; some died of diseases acquired from Europeans.
12. Possible answer: Spanish settlers adapted Native American building styles; Native Americans converted to Christianity; African dance and song heightened Christian worship.
13. by defeating the French in the Seven Years' War
14. to work as slaves on plantations and in mines
15. Zulus, Boers, and British competed for control of the region.
16. exchange of people, plants, and other items between the Americas and Europe

Critical Thinking and Writing

17. Possible answer: The location of Spain and Portugal on the western-most peninsula of Europe, bordered by the Atlantic Ocean, might have encouraged overseas exploration.
18. Possible answer: French, rather than English, might be the primary language of most Americans.

Creating a Chapter Summary

Copy this graphic organizer. Complete the organizer by writing in major changes that occurred in Europe, the Americas, and Africa as a result of the first global age from 1492 through the 1700s.

For additional review and enrichment activities, see the interactive version of *World History* available on the Web and on CD-ROM.

Web Site Self-Test
For practice test questions for Chapter 16, see www.phschool.com.

Building Vocabulary

Use the chapter vocabulary words listed to create a crossword puzzle. Exchange your puzzle with a classmate. Complete the puzzle and then check each other's answers.

1. conquistador
2. civil war
3. encomienda
4. creole
5. mestizo
6. missionary
7. compact
8. capitalism
9. mercantilism
10. tariff

Recalling Key Facts

11. How did the Spanish conquistadors treat the Native Americans they encountered?
12. Describe three examples of cultural blending in Spain's empire in the Americas.
13. How did Britain gain control of North America from the French?
14. Why were Africans brought to Spanish colonies in the Americas?
15. Why was there conflict in southern Africa in the 1700s and 1800s?
16. What was the Columbian Exchange?

Critical Thinking and Writing

17. **Connecting to Geography** Look at the map of the world in the Reference Section at the back of the book. How might geography have contributed to Spain and Portugal becoming the first European nations to explore the Americas?
18. **Linking Past and Present** How might your life be different if France had defeated England in the Seven Years' War?
19. **Recognizing Points of View** How might each of the following people have viewed European conquests in the 1500s and 1600s: **(a)** a Spaniard, **(b)** a Native American, and **(c)** an African?
20. **Recognizing Causes and Effects** **(a)** What were three causes of the growth of the Atlantic slave trade? **(b)** What were three immediate effects of the slave trade on Africa? **(c)** What do you think might have been some long-term effects of the slave trade on Africa's later development? Explain.

---

19. Possible answers: **(a)** A Spaniard might be proud of the power and wealth that Spain acquired. **(b)** A Native American might feel that Europeans stole Native American lands and destroyed their way of life. **(c)** An African might think of the millions of Africans who were forced to serve as slaves.
20. Possible answers: **(a)** Spain's American empire needed labor. Ships' captains could profit by transporting slaves. African traders could profit by supplying them. **(b)** Slavers removed millions of Africans. Some African states declined. Others

rose in power. **(c)** Some Africans might have been reluctant to do business with Europeans and Americans. There might have been conflicts between African nations whose people were enslaved and other African nations who helped supply the slaves.

Read the excerpt below about the Middle Passage. Then, answer the questions that follow.

"I now saw myself deprived of all chances of returning to my native country. . . [and] my present situation. . .was filled with horrors of every kind. . . .The stench of the hold, while we were on the coast was so intolerably loathsome that it was dangerous to remain there for any time. . . .The closeness of the place, and the heat of the climate, added to the number in the ship, which was so crowded that each had scarcely room to turn himself, almost suffocated us. . . .The shrieks of the women, and the groans of the dying, rendered the whole a scene of horror almost inconceivable."

—Olaudah Equiano, *The Life of Gustavus Vassa*

21. **(a)** Who was the author of the excerpt? **(b)** Do you consider him a reliable source of information about the Middle Passage? Why or why not?
22. **(a)** What are some of the descriptive words used by the author about conditions aboard a slave ship? **(b)** What emotions are these words likely to arouse in the reader?
23. How did climate conditions affect the Middle Passage?
24. **(a)** Did the author think that he might one day return to Africa? **(b)** Why do you think he felt this way?
25. Many enslaved Africans died during the Middle Passage. Based on the above account, what were some of the reasons for the high death toll?

Skills Assessment
Take It to the NET

Use the Internet to research the exports of Brazil or another European colony in the Americas during the first global age. Then, write a business report describing how that colony helped increase the wealth of the colonizing nation. If possible, compare the colonial exports with the exports that the area produces as an independent nation today.

THE COLUMBIAN EXCHANGE

From the Americas to Europe, Africa, and Asia	From Europe, Africa, and Asia to the Americas
maize	wheat
potato	sugar
sweet potato	banana
beans	rice
peanut	grape (wine)
squash	olive oil
pumpkin	dandelion
peppers	horse
pineapple	pig
tomato	cow
cocoa	goat
	chicken
	smallpox
	typhus

Use the chart above and information that you have learned in this chapter to answer the following questions:

26. When and with what event did this global exchange begin?
27. **(a)** Name three food crops that spread from the Americas to Europe, Africa, and Asia. **(b)** Name three domesticated animals that were introduced to the Americas.
28. How did the exchange cause a decline in the Native American population?
29. What effects did the Columbian Exchange have on the European economy?
30. How would life improve for people in both Europe and the Americas as a result of the global exchange?

Skills Tip

A flowchart represents a process in a simplified form. Some show a step-by-step process. Others show a cycle. Look at the arrows to understand the direction of the process.

Analyzing Primary Sources

21. **(a)** The author was an African slave. **(b)** Possible answer: He is a reliable source because he was an eyewitness to the event.
22. Possible answers: **(a)** intolerable, horror, loathsome, inconceivable **(b)** Such words may arouse sadness, shock, or anger.
23. The hot climate made the cramped conditions feel even worse.
24. **(a)** He felt he had no chance of returning to his native land. **(b)** Possible answer: He might have known how far across the ocean he was going to travel.
25. Heat, overcrowding, and lack of fresh air contributed to the death toll.

Analyzing Charts

26. 1492; Columbus arrived in the West Indies
27. Possible answers: **(a)** maize, potato, pumpkin **(b)** horse, pig, goat
28. Diseases that destroyed Native American populations were spread to the Americas.
29. Increased trade helped the economy prosper.
30. Students should demonstrate knowledge that the lives of Europeans generally benefited more from the introduction of new products than the lives of Native Americans.

Skills Tip

Reading the headings is also essential to understanding the graphic representations in a flow chart. The Skills Handbook in the front of the book has a lesson that will help students with this feature.

Unit Theme Activity

Remind students to continue working on their Unit Theme Activity. See rubrics for the activity on the unit opener page in the Teacher's Edition.

Take It to the NET

Direct students to **www.phschool.com** for links to sites that will help them get started on this assignment. Share rubrics with students.
Attempted Report is incomplete.
Minimal Report demonstrates some research and preparation but does not show a clear understanding of how that colony helped increase the wealth of the colonizing nation.
Adequate Report demonstrates extensive research and a clear understanding of how that colony helped increase the wealth of the colonizing nation.
Exemplary Report demonstrates extensive research and a clear understanding of how that colony helped increase the wealth of the colonizing nation, resulting in an interesting, informative, and well-written report.

Chapter 17 Planning Guide

Resource Manager

	CORE INSTRUCTION	READING/SKILLS
Chapter Level Resources	**Teaching Resources** 📖 **Pacing Charts**, Ch. 17 📖 **Teaching With Themes**, p. 20 📽 **Color Transparencies**, p. F–35 💿 **Resource Pro®** Ch. 17 💻 **www.phschool.com** 　• eTeach	🎧 **Book on CD**, Ch. 17 💿 **Interactive Student Tutorial CD-ROM**, Ch. 17 💿 **Social Studies Skills Tutor CD-ROM** 📽 **Skills Transparencies**
1 Extending Spanish Power 1. Summarize how Spanish power increased. 2. Describe how arts flourished during the Golden Age. 3. State why the Spanish economy declined in the late 1600s.	**Teaching Resources** 📖 **Creative Teaching Activities**, p. 77 💿 **Prentice Hall Presentation Pro**, Ch. 17, Section 1 📽 **Section Reading Support Transparencies**	**Teaching Resources** 📕 **Unit 4 booklet** 　• Guided Reading and Review, p. 60 📖 **Guide to the Essentials** 📼 **Guided Reading Audiotapes**, Ch. 17, Section 1
2 France Under Louis XIV 1. Summarize how France rebuilt after the religious wars. 2. Explain how Louis XIV strengthened royal power. 3. Contrast the successes and failures of Louis XIV.	**Teaching Resources** 📕 **Unit 4 booklet** 　• Primary Source Activity, p. 71 💿 **Prentice Hall Presentation Pro**, Ch. 17, Section 2 📽 **Section Reading Support Transparencies**	**Teaching Resources** 📕 **Unit 4 booklet** 　• Guided Reading and Review, p. 62 📖 **Guide to the Essentials** 📼 **Guided Reading Audiotapes**, Ch. 17, Section 2
3 Triumph of Parliament in England 1. Outline how the Tudors and Stuarts differed in their relations with Parliament. 2. Analyze how the English Civil War led to the rise of the Commonwealth. 3. Identify the causes and results of the Glorious Revolution.	**Teaching Resources** 📕 **Unit 4 booklet** 　• Biography Activity, p. 70 💿 **Prentice Hall Presentation Pro**, Ch. 17, Section 3 📽 **Section Reading Support Transparencies**	**Teaching Resources** 📕 **Unit 4 booklet** 　• Guided Reading and Review, p. 64 📖 **Guide to the Essentials** 📼 **Guided Reading Audiotapes**, Ch. 17, Section 3
4 Rise of Austria and Prussia 1. Identify the causes and results of the Thirty Years' War. 2. Relate how Austria and Prussia emerged as great powers. 3. Describe how European diplomats tried to maintain the balance of power.	**Teaching Resources** 📕 **Unit 4 booklet** 　• Viewpoint Activity, p. 72 📖 **Creative Teaching Activities**, p. 80 📽 **Section Reading Support Transparencies**	**Teaching Resources** 📕 **Unit 4 booklet** 　• Guided Reading and Review, p. 66 📖 **Guide to the Essentials** 📼 **Guided Reading Audiotapes**, Ch. 17, Section 4
5 Absolute Monarchy in Russia 1. Describe how Peter the Great tried to make Russia into a modern state. 2. Identify the steps Peter the Great took to expand Russia's borders. 3. Explain how Catherine the Great strengthened Russia.	**Teaching Resources** 📖 **Creative Teaching Activities**, p. 81 💿 **Prentice Hall Presentation Pro**, Ch. 17, Section 5 📽 **Section Reading Support Transparencies**	**Teaching Resources** 📕 **Unit 4 booklet** 　• Guided Reading and Review, p. 68 　• Skill Application Activity, p. 73 📖 **Guide to the Essentials**

ENRICHMENT/PRE-AP

Teaching Resources
Teaching With Themes, Global View Activity, p. 44
www.phschool.com
   • Why Study History?

www.phschool.com
   • Internet Activities, Section 1

Teaching Resources
Chapter Extension Activities, p. 43
History Through Literature, pp. 37–38
Color Transparencies, pp. C–49, C–51, E–29, E–33
www.phschool.com
   • Virtual Field Trip

Teaching Resources
Chapter Extension Activities, p. 44
Visions, Voices, Views, Global Issues Forum, tape 4

www.phschool.com
   • Global View Essay

www.phschool.com
   • Internet Activities, Section 5

ASSESSMENT

PRENTICE HALL
ASSESSMENT SYSTEM

Core Assessment
   ExamView Test Bank booklet, Ch. 17
   ExamView Test Bank CD-ROM, Ch. 17

Standardized Test Preparation
Diagnose and Prescribe
   Diagnostic Tests for High School Social Studies Skills
Review and Reteach
   Review Book for World History
Practice and Assess
   Document-Based Assessment, pp. 18–22
   Test-Taking Strategies With Transparencies for High School
   Alternative Assessment booklet
   Test Prep Book for World History

Teaching Resources
   Unit 4 booklet
      • Geography Quiz, p. 74
      • Section Quizzes, pp. 61, 63, 65, 67, 69
      • Chapter Tests A, B, and C, pp. 75–79
   www.phschool.com
      • Self-Test

CUSTOMIZE FOR INDIVIDUAL NEEDS

Gifted and Talented
   • **Teacher's Edition,** Activities: Customize for Visual Learners, p. 414
Less Proficient Readers
   • **Guide to the Essentials,** Ch. 17
   • **Guided Reading Audiotapes, English,** Ch. 17
   • **Book on CD,** Ch. 17
   • **Teacher's Edition,** Activities: Reading Strategy, p. 414
Less Proficient Writers
   • **Teacher's Edition,** Activities: Cooperative Learning Activity, p. 419; Customize for Heterogeneous Groups, p. 422
Students Acquiring English/ESL
   • **Guide to the Essentials, English/Spanish,** Ch. 17
   • **Guided Reading Audiotapes, English/Spanish,** Ch. 17
   • **Book on CD,** Ch. 17
   • **Teacher's Edition,** Activities marked with an *

TEXT

Don't miss the exclusive interactive version of *World History: Connections to Today* on the Internet and CD-ROM.

INTRODUCTION

During the 1500s and 1600s, several European monarchs became absolute rulers. In England, Parliament gained control. After the Thirty Years' War, Prussia emerged as a strong Protestant state. In Austria, the Hapsburgs expanded their territory. Peter the Great gained land and brought reforms to Russia but worsened the condition of the serfs.

Focusing on Themes

Suggest that students focus on these theme questions as they read:

Political and Social Systems
How did absolute monarchs centralize power?

Impact of the Individual
What role did individual rulers such as Louis XIV of France and Peter the Great of Russia play in shaping their nations?

Continuity and Change
How did struggles between monarchs and Parliament affect the development of Britain?

Art and Literature
How did European monarchs contribute to cultural flowering?

◆ TIME LINE ACTIVITY

You may wish to share the About the Pictures note with your students before you ask these questions about the time line:

1. What might be the effect on the German people of a war that lasted 30 years? *(fewer male citizens, destruction of property, depopulation, hunger, poverty)*
2. If the Hall of Mirrors at Versailles symbolizes the reign of Louis XIV, what would you expect to be characteristic of that reign? *(luxury, wealth)*
3. What happened in North America in 1754? *(The French and Indian War started.)*

Don't Miss!

You Are There . . .
Living at Versailles
(Section 2)

Synthesizing Information
The Struggle Between King and Parliament
(Section 3)

The Age of Absolutism
1550–1800

Chapter Preview

1. **Extending Spanish Power**
2. **France Under Louis XIV**
3. **Triumph of Parliament in England**
4. **Rise of Austria and Prussia**
5. **Absolute Monarchy in Russia**

THE
Exerciſe of the English, in the
Militia of the Kingdome of
ENGLAND.

Time Line

1556
Philip II (second from right) becomes king of Spain. Under Philip, Spain is the wealthiest and most powerful state in Europe.

1618
Religious conflict between German Protestants and Catholics sparks the Thirty Years' War.

1642
The English Civil War begins, pitting the king's troops (left) against the armies of Parliament (right).

CHAPTER EVENTS

1550 — 1600 — 1650

GLOBAL EVENTS

1556 Akbar the Great becomes emperor of India.

1607 British colonists found Jamestown.

▶ Resource Directory

Teaching Resources
Teaching With Themes Chapter Theme Activities, p. 20
Pacing Chart With Block Scheduling Guide Ch. 17
Global View Activity *How Did Changes in Western Europe Help Bring About the First Global Age?* Teaching With Themes booklet, p. 44

Technology
World History Color Transparencies Ch. 17
Graphic Organizer, p. F–35

European Nation-States, 1700

By 1700, powerful European monarchs had set aside the feudal past and built strong, centralized nation-states. Most of these rulers held absolute power.

Major European monarchies

North Sea

SWEDEN

Moscow

RUSSIA

ENGLAND
London

Berlin · PRUSSIA
Baltic Sea
POLAND

Rhine R.

Paris ·
FRANCE

· Prague

· Vienna
AUSTRIA

Vistula R.

Dnieper R.

Danube R.

Black Sea

Rhône R.

ALPS

PYRENEES MTS

· Madrid
SPAIN

· Rome

Mediterranean Sea

OTTOMAN EMPIRE

ATLANTIC OCEAN

Azimuthal Equidistant Projection
0   250   500 Miles
0   250   500 Kilometers

1697
Czar Peter the Great of Russia tours Europe to study western technology and ideas.

1715
King Louis XIV of France dies. The palace of Versailles, shown here, is a symbol of his 72-year reign.

1795
Russia, Prussia, and Austria complete the partition of Poland.

1700 — 1750 — 1800

1680s Asante kingdom is organized in West Africa.

1754 The French and Indian War erupts in North America.

1793 The emperor of China rejects British trade.

Chapter 17 **411**

Activating Prior Knowledge
You learned earlier that Spain and other nations built trading empires in Asia, Africa, and the Americas. How do you suppose that helped monarchs unite their lands into the nation-states shown on this map? *(brought in vast wealth, some of which could be used to build armies and buy loyalty)*

Previewing
Why do you suppose Germany is not shown on this map? *(It was not yet united into one nation.)*

Background
About the Pictures

1 2   3 4

1. The women in this bronze statue are three of Philip's four wives. His first wife was his cousin Princess Maria of Portugal, who died four days after the birth of their son Don Carlos. Philip's next wife was Mary I of England, daughter of Henry VIII and Catherine of Aragon. After Mary's death, Philip married Princess Elizabeth of France, who died in childbirth in 1568. In that year, Don Carlos also died. Since Philip had no male heir, he married Anna of Austria in 1570. That union produced the future Philip III.

2. The title page from this tract shows militiamen representing the two sides of the conflict between the English monarch and Parliament. The Cavalier on the left supported Charles I. The Roundhead on the right supported Parliament.

3. As an adult, Peter the Great was a huge bear of a man who could, with his bare hands, roll a heavy silver plate into a scroll.

4. The palace of Versailles was built in several stages. The dazzling Hall of Mirrors shown here was added in 1684.

eTeach

Be sure to check out this month's online discussion with a World History Master Teacher.

Go to **www.phschool.com**.

Independent Assignments

Have students read one section as they prepare for class. After class, have them complete the assignment. Some students may benefit from using the Guided Reading and Review worksheets.

Section 1 Have students read Chapter 13, pp. 98–104, of *I, Juan de Pareja* to learn more about life in Spain's Golden Age.

Section 2 Have students use the worksheet *A Busy Day at the Sun King's Court* in the Unit 4 booklet, p. 71, to learn about life at Louis XIV's court.

Section 3 Have students use the worksheet *George Fox* in the Unit 4 booklet, p. 70, to learn about this English Quaker.

Section 4 Have students use the worksheet *Empress Maria Theresa: Two Views* in the Unit 4 booklet, p. 72, to learn what two historians thought about this Hapsburg ruler.

Section 5 Have students use the worksheet *Interviewing* in the Unit 4 booklet, p. 73, to learn about the skill of interviewing through an imaginary interview with Peter I.

Reading Focus

- How did Spanish power increase under Charles V and Philip II?

- How did the arts flourish during Spain's golden age?

- Why did the Spanish economy decline in the 1600s?

Vocabulary

absolute monarch

divine right

armada

Taking Notes

As you read this section, prepare an outline of the contents. Use Roman numerals to indicate major headings. Use capital letters for the sub-headings and numbers for the supporting details. The example will help you get started.

I. Charles V and the Hapsburg Empire
  A. Wearing two crowns
    1. Spain
    2. Holy Roman Empire and Netherlands
  B. An empire divided
    1.
    2.
II.

Main Idea Philip II extended Spain's power and helped establish a golden age.

Global Connections

Cartloads of Silver and Gold

Old Spanish shipping records tell a tale about amazing wealth: "On 22 March 1595, ships from the Indies . . . began to discharge and deposit with the Chamber of Commerce 332 cartloads of silver, gold, and pearls of great value." This was the haul for *just one day*—and the flow of riches continued for *years!*

A major part of this wealth enriched the royal family. Most of the rest went into the hands of private traders. For Spain, American silver and gold financed a golden age of art, literature—and power.

Theme: Economics and Technology What impact could wealth from the Americas have on the arts in Renaissance Spain?

Setting the Scene

"It is best to keep an eye on everything," Philip II of Spain often said—and he meant it. As king of the most powerful nation in Europe, he gave little time to pleasure. Instead, he plowed through a mountain of paperwork each day, making notes on even the most trivial matters. Once the Spanish ambassador to England wrote about an unfamiliar kind of insect he had seen in London. "Probably fleas," Philip scribbled on the letter.

Philip's determination to "keep an eye on everything" extended far beyond trivia. It helped him build Spain into a strong centralized state. By the late 1500s, he had concentrated all power into his own hands. Over the next 200 years, other European monarchs would pursue similar goals.

Charles V and the Hapsburg Empire

By the 1500s, Spain had shaken off the feudal past and emerged as the first modern European power. Under Queen Isabella and King Ferdinand, Spain had expelled the last Muslim rulers and enforced religious unity. In 1492, Isabella financed Columbus's voyage across the Atlantic, leading to the Spanish conquest of the Americas.

Wearing Two Crowns In 1519, Charles V,* grandson of Ferdinand and Isabella, inherited a huge empire. The new king faced a nearly impossible challenge. He not only inherited the crown of Spain but was also the heir of the Austrian Hapsburgs. The sprawling Hapsburg empire included the Holy Roman Empire and the Netherlands.

Ruling two empires involved Charles in constant warfare. As a devout Catholic, he fought to suppress the Protestant movement in the German states. After years of religious warfare, however, Charles was forced to allow the German princes to choose their own religions.

His greatest foe was the Ottoman empire. Under Suleiman, Ottoman forces advanced across central Europe to the walls of Vienna, Austria. Although Austria held firm, the Ottomans occupied much of Hungary. Ottoman naval forces also challenged Spanish power in the Mediterranean.

An Empire Divided Perhaps the Hapsburg empire was too scattered and diverse for any one person to rule. Exhausted and disillusioned, Charles V gave up his titles and entered a monastery in 1556. He divided his empire,

* Within Spain, the king was known as Charles I. However, historians usually refer to him as Charles V, his title as ruler of the Austrian Hapsburg empire.

Bell Ringer Ask students to look at the map "The Wars of Philip II" in this section. What does this map tell them about the rule of Philip II?

LESSON PLAN

1. Focus As an absolute monarch claiming to rule by divine right, Philip II extended the power of Spain. He increased his personal power, defended the Catholic Church, and engaged in numerous wars. By supporting literature and the arts, he helped establish Spain's "golden century." However, inflation, costly wars, and other problems led to economic decline in the 1600s.

2. Instruct Inform students that they will produce a newspaper about Spain during the reigns of Charles V and Philip II. Divide the class into groups, and designate each group as a particular department of a newspaper. Students might be assigned to any of the following departments: national news, international news, the arts, literature, the economy, or editorial. Members of each group will work together to make a list of articles that the department will develop. Then, each member of the department should assume responsibility for writing one of the articles. Encourage students to use library resources as well as the text. Compile the finished articles into a class newspaper on Spain's golden century.

3. Assess Have each student create a ten-question quiz based on the newspaper articles. Collect the quizzes, and have each student take a quiz that he or she did not create.

4. Reteach If students' Assess activity does not reflect adequate understanding of the lesson, you might assign the *Guide to the Essentials* or the *Interactive Student Tutorial CD-ROM* for this section.

Global Connections

ANSWER It could lead to a flourishing of the arts.

Resource Directory

Teaching Resources
Creative Teaching Activities Creative Teaching Activities booklet, p. 77
Guided Reading and Review Unit 4 booklet, p. 60

leaving the Hapsburg lands in central Europe to his brother Ferdinand, who became Holy Roman emperor. He gave Spain, the Netherlands, southern Italy, and Spain's overseas empire to his 29 year old son Philip.

Philip II and Divine Right

Like his father, King Philip II was hard-working, devout, and ambitious. During his 42-year reign, he sought to expand Spanish influence, strengthen the Catholic Church, and make his own power absolute. Thanks in part to silver from the Americas, he made Spain the foremost power in Europe.

Unlike many other monarchs, Philip devoted much time to government work. He seldom hunted, never jousted, and lived as sparsely as a monk. His isolated, somber palace outside Madrid reflected the King's character. Known as the Escorial (ehs KOHR ee uhl), it served as a church, a residence, and a tomb for members of the royal family.

As did Ferdinand and Isabella, Philip further centralized royal power, making every part of the government responsible to him. He reigned as an absolute monarch, a ruler with complete authority over the government and the lives of the people. Like other European rulers, Philip asserted that he ruled by divine right. That is, he believed that his authority to rule came directly from God.

Partly as a result of the concept of divine right, Philip saw himself as the guardian of the Roman Catholic Church. The great undertaking of his life was to defend the Catholic Reformation and turn back the rising Protestant tide in Europe. Within his own lands, Philip enforced religious unity. He turned the Inquisition against Protestants and other people thought to be heretics.

The Wars of Philip II

Philip fought many wars as he attempted to advance Spanish Catholic power. At the battle of Lepanto in 1571, Spain and its Italian allies soundly defeated an Ottoman fleet in the Mediterranean. Although Christians hailed this as a great victory, the Ottoman empire remained a major power in the Mediterranean region.

Revolt in the Netherlands During the last half of his reign, Philip battled Protestant rebels in the Netherlands. At the time, the region included 17 provinces that are today Belgium, the Netherlands, and Luxembourg. It was the richest part of Philip's empire. Protestants in the Netherlands resisted Philip's efforts to crush their faith. Protestants and Catholics alike opposed high taxes and autocratic Spanish rule, which threatened local traditions of self-government.

In the 1560s, riots against the Inquisition sparked a general uprising in the Netherlands. Savage fighting raged for decades. In 1581, the northern, largely Protestant provinces declared their independence from Spain and became known as the Dutch Netherlands. They did not gain official recognition, however, until 1648. The southern, mostly Catholic provinces of the Netherlands remained part of the Spanish empire.

Invading England By the 1580s, Philip saw England's Queen Elizabeth I as his chief Protestant enemy. First secretly, then openly, Elizabeth had supported the Dutch against Spain. She even encouraged English captains,

Philip II of Spain
From 1556 to 1598, Philip II ruled the wealthiest, most powerful nation in Europe. Devoted to his family and to the Catholic Church, Philip could also be ruthless toward his enemies.

Theme: Impact of the Individual What impression of Philip II does this painting give you? Explain.

Chapter 17 **413**

The Wars of Philip II, 1571–1588

known as Sea Dogs, to plunder Spanish treasure ships. Francis Drake, the most daring Sea Dog, looted Spanish cities in the Americas. To Philip's dismay, instead of punishing the pirate, Elizabeth made him a knight.

To end English attacks and subdue the Dutch, Philip prepared a huge *armada*, or fleet, to carry a Spanish invasion force to England. In 1588, the Armada sailed with more than 130 ships, 20,000 men, and 2,400 pieces of artillery. The Spanish were confident of victory. "When we meet the English," predicted one Spanish commander, "God will surely arrange matters so that we can grapple and board them, either by sending some strange freak of weather or, more likely, just by depriving the English of their wits."

The "strange freak of weather," however, favored the other side. In the English Channel, lumbering Spanish ships took losses from the lighter, faster English ships. Suddenly, a savage storm blew up, scattering the Armada. After further disasters at sea, the tattered remnants limped home in defeat.

While the defeat of the Spanish Armada ended Philip's plan to invade England, it had little short-term effect on his power. In the long term, however, Spain's naval superiority did dwindle. In the 1600s and 1700s, Dutch, English, and French fleets challenged—and surpassed—Spanish power both in Europe and around the world.

Spain's Golden Age

The century from 1550 to 1650 is often called Spain's *siglo de oro,* or "golden century," for the brilliance of its arts and literature. Philip II was a patron of the arts and also founded academies of science and mathematics.

Painters Among the famous painters of this period was El Greco, meaning "the Greek." Born on the Greek island of Crete, El Greco had studied in

Renaissance Italy before settling in Spain. He produced haunting religious pictures, dramatic views of the city of Toledo, and striking portraits of Spanish nobles, done in a dramatically elongated style.

El Greco's use of vibrant colors influenced the work of Diego Velázquez (vuhl LAHS kehs), court painter to King Philip IV. Velázquez is perhaps best known for his vivid portraits of Spanish royalty.

Writers Spain's golden century produced outstanding writers like Lope de Vega. A peasant by birth, he wrote more than 1,500 plays, including witty comedies and action-packed romances. In *The Sheep Well*, Lope de Vega shows King Ferdinand and Queen Isabella saving a village from the hands of a villainous feudal lord.

Miguel de Cervantes wrote *Don Quixote*, the first modern novel in Europe. It pokes fun at medieval tales of chivalry. Dressed in rusty armor, the madman Don Quixote rides out on his broken-down plowhorse in search of adventure. He battles a windmill, which he thinks is a giant, and mistakes two flocks of sheep for opposing armies. He is accompanied by Sancho Panza, a practical-minded peasant.

Don Quixote mocked the traditions of Spain's feudal past. Yet Cervantes admired both the unromantic, earthy realism of Sancho Panza and the foolish but heroic idealism of Don Quixote.

Economic Decline

In the 1600s, Spanish power and prosperity slowly declined. Lack of strong leadership was one reason. The successors of Philip II were far less able rulers than he.

Economic problems were also greatly to blame. Costly overseas wars drained wealth out of Spain almost as fast as it came in. Then, too, treasure from the Americas led Spain to neglect farming and commerce. The government heavily taxed the small middle class, weakening a group that in other European nations supported royal power. The expulsion of Muslims and Jews from Spain deprived the economy of many skilled artisans and merchants. Finally, American gold and silver led to soaring inflation, with prices rising much higher in Spain than elsewhere in Europe.

Even though Spain continued to rule a huge colonial empire, its strength slipped away. By the late 1600s, France had replaced Spain as the most powerful European nation.

▶ **Primary Sources and Literature**

See "Miguel de Cervantes: Don Quixote" in the Reference Section at the back of this book.

SECTION 1 Assessment

Recall
1. **Identify:** (a) Hapsburgs, (b) *siglo de oro*, (c) El Greco, (d) Diego Velázquez, (e) Miguel de Cervantes.
2. **Define:** (a) absolute monarch, (b) divine right, (c) armada.

Comprehension
3. (a) How did Philip II ensure absolute power? (b) How did he try to further Catholicism?
4. Why is the period from 1550 to 1650 considered Spain's golden age?
5. Why did Spanish power and prosperity decline?

Critical Thinking and Writing
6. **Recognizing Points of View** The English referred to the fierce storm that battered the Spanish Armada in 1588 as "the Protestant wind." (a) What does this nickname mean? (b) What nickname might the Spanish have given to the storm?
7. **Understanding Sequence** Create a time line showing key events in Spain's history between the rise of King Ferdinand and Queen Isabella and the end of its "golden century." Include events from this chapter and earlier chapters.

 Activity

Take It to the NET

Use the Internet to learn more about the life and times of Miguel de Cervantes and his famous novel *Don Quixote*. Then, prepare a presentation giving examples of how the author used the characters of Don Quixote and Sancho Panza to satirize society.

Chapter 17 **415**

SECTION 1 Assessment

Recall
1. (a) Hapsburgs, p. 412 (b) *siglo de oro*, p. 414 (c) El Greco, p. 414 (d) Diego Velázquez, p. 415 (e) Miguel de Cervantes, p. 415 2. (a) absolute monarch, p. 413 (b) divine right, p. 413 (c) armada, p. 414

Comprehension
3. (a) He made all parts of the government responsible to him. He claimed to rule by divine right. He devoted much time to government, paying attention to even the most trivial matters. (b) He defended the Catholic Reformation and turned the Inquisition against Protestants and others he thought heretics. He fought wars against Protestant countries. 4. During this time, Spain achieved much in the arts, literature, and science. 5. The successors of Philip II were less able than he. Costly wars drained the Spanish economy. Treasure from the Americas caused Spain to neglect farming and commerce and led to inflation.

Critical Thinking and Writing
6. (a) The nickname meant that the storm helped Protestant England defeat Catholic Spain. (b) Students' answers should reflect the shock and disappointment that the Spaniards must have felt. 7. Students' time lines should reflect careful research, thoughtful judgment, and accurate chronology.

Activity Rubrics

Share rubrics with students before they make their presentations.

Attempted The presentation suggests limited research and little understanding of the satirical element of the examples cited.

Minimal The presentation offers only one or two examples of Cervantes's satire, or the examples are unclear.

Adequate The presentation offers several strong examples of Cervantes's satire.

Exemplary The presentation reflects a thorough understanding of the satirical element of the examples or is very creative.

 Human Drama Activity

Art Appreciation Have available books showing the works of El Greco and Velázquez. Ask students to choose their favorite painting and explain why it attracts them. Students may consider color, arrangement, subject matter, or other elements of the painting. Ask students to identify elements of Spanish life that are reflected in the paintings.

 Test Preparation

Have students read the second full paragraph on the opposite page, and then answer the question below.

What are the "tattered remnants" that "limped home"?

A wounded sailors walking back to Spain

B shredded scraps of sails that couldn't hold the wind

C broken masts

D damaged ships returning to Spain

Bell Ringer
Draw students' attention to the quotation from Louis XIV on the opposite page. Invite student comments. What kind of government do they think France had at this time? How do they think the French people felt about such a government?

LESSON PLAN

1. Focus Violent warfare between Catholics and Protestants divided France for a time. Cardinals Richelieu and Mazarin increased royal power at the expense of nobles and Huguenots, or French Protestants. Under the absolutist rule of Louis XIV, France became the leading state of Europe. But costly wars and religious persecution undermined French power.

2. Instruct Ask students to write letters to Louis XIV commenting on his policies. In their letters, students should touch upon Louis's political philosophy, his economic policies, his personal living arrangements, his cultural achievements, his wars, and his treatment of the Huguenots. If students disagree with any of the king's beliefs and policies, they should express their reasons for doing so. Have students conclude their letters by predicting what will happen to France in the years after Louis XIV's reign.

3. Assess Invite volunteers to read their letters aloud to the class. Encourage discussion of the ideas students present.

4. Reteach If students' Assess activity does not reflect adequate understanding of the lesson, you might assign the *Guide to the Essentials* or the *Interactive Student Tutorial CD-ROM* for this section.

Reading Focus

- How did France rebuild after its wars of religion?
- How did Louis XIV strengthen royal power?
- What successes and failures did Louis XIV experience?

Vocabulary

intendant
levée
balance of power

Taking Notes

Begin a concept web like this one. As you read this section, fill in the blank circles with relevant information about Louis XIV. Add as many circles as you need.

LOUIS XIV
- Sun as symbol
- No meetings of Estates General

Main Idea Under the absolute rule of Louis XIV, France became the leading power of Europe.

Setting the Scene "I have had an idea that will . . . give much pleasure to the people here," wrote Louis XIV, the young king of France. His plan was to throw a grand party. Each guest would receive a lottery ticket for a prize of jewelry—and every ticket would be a winner. At Louis's bidding, some 600 noble guests flocked to the royal palace for a week of sumptuous feasts, pageants, sports, dances, plays, and music. This extravaganza was the first of many spectacles organized by Louis XIV.

By the late 1600s, Louis was absolute monarch of France and the most powerful ruler in Europe. Yet, just 100 years earlier, France had been torn apart by turbulent wars of religion.

Rebuilding France

From the 1560s to the 1590s, religious wars between Huguenots (French Protestants) and the Catholic majority tore France apart. Leaders on both sides used the strife to further their own ambitions.

The worst incident began on St. Bartholomew's Day, August 24, 1572. As Huguenot and Catholic nobles gathered to celebrate a royal wedding, violence erupted that led to the massacre of 3,000 Huguenots. In the next few days, thousands more were slaughtered. For many, the St. Bartholomew's Day Massacre symbolized the complete breakdown of order in France.

Catholics vs. Huguenots In the war between French Catholics and Protestants, both sides committed acts of violence. Here, Huguenot rioters destroy and loot a Catholic church.
Theme: Political and Social Systems Why did some French nobles encourage actions like these?

Caption Answer

Noble families, both Catholic and Protestant, were competing for power and used the religious conflict to further their own ambitions.

Resource Directory

Teaching Resources
Creative Teaching Activities Creative Teaching Activities booklet, p. 78
Guided Reading and Review Unit 4 booklet, p. 62

Henry IV In 1589, a Huguenot prince inherited the French throne as Henry IV. Knowing that a Protestant would face severe problems ruling a largely Catholic land, he became Catholic. "Paris is well worth a Mass," he is supposed to have said. To protect Protestants, however, he issued the Edict of Nantes in 1598. It granted the Huguenots religious toleration and let them fortify their own towns and cities.

Henry IV then set out to heal his shattered land. His goal, he said, was not the victory of one sect over another, but "a chicken in every pot"—a good Sunday dinner for every peasant. Under Henry, the government reached into every area of French life. Royal officials administered justice, improved roads, built bridges, and revived agriculture. By building the royal bureaucracy and reducing the influence of nobles, Henry IV laid the foundations for royal absolutism.

Richelieu When Henry IV was killed by an assassin in 1610, his nine-year-old son, Louis XIII, inherited the throne. For a time, nobles reasserted their power. Then, in 1624, Louis appointed Cardinal Armand Richelieu (RIHSH uh loo) as his chief minister. This cunning, capable leader spent the next 18 years strengthening the central government.

Richelieu sought to destroy the power of the Huguenots and nobles, two groups that did not bow to royal authority. He smashed the walled cities of the Huguenots and outlawed their armies, while still allowing them to practice their religion. At the same time, he defeated the private armies of the nobles and destroyed their fortified castles. While reducing their independence, Richelieu tied nobles to the king by giving them high posts at court or in the royal army.

Richelieu handpicked his able successor, Cardinal Jules Mazarin. When five-year-old Louis XIV inherited the throne in 1643, the year after Richelieu's death, Mazarin was in place to serve as chief minister. Like Richelieu, Mazarin worked tirelessly to extend royal power.

Louis XIV, the Sun King

Soon after Louis XIV became king, disorder again swept France. In an uprising called the *Fronde,* nobles, merchants, peasants, and the urban poor rebelled—each group for its own reasons. On one occasion, rioters drove the boy king from his palace. It was an experience Louis would never forget.

When Mazarin died in 1661, Louis resolved to take over the government himself. "I have been pleased to entrust the government of my affairs to the late Cardinal," he declared. "It is now time that I govern them myself."

"I Am the State" Like his great-grandfather Philip II of Spain, Louis IV firmly believed in divine right. He wrote:

> "God's power is felt in an instant from one end of the world to the other; royal power takes the same time to act throughout the kingdom. It preserves the order of the whole kingdom, as does God with the whole world."
> —Louis XIV, quoted in *From Absolutism to Revolution* (Rowen)

Louis took the sun as the symbol of his absolute power. Just as the sun stands at the center of the solar system, he argued, so the Sun King stands at the center of the nation. Louis is often quoted as saying, *"L'etat, c'est moi"*—"I am the state."

During his reign, Louis did not once call a meeting of the Estates General, the medieval council made up of representatives of all French social classes. In fact, the Estates General did not meet between 1614 and 1789. Thus, unlike the English Parliament, the Estates General played no role in checking royal power.

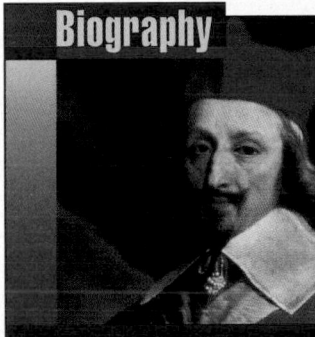

Background
Connections to Art

Louis XIV Immortalized The stucco relief *Louis XIV on Horseback,* by Antoine Coysevox, which dominates the Salon de la Guerre at Versailles, is considered by many art historians to be the most successful decorative work in the palace. Extending from floor to ceiling, the piece glorifies the king and his accomplishments.

In the center of the relief, Louis XIV, depicted as a conquering Roman, masters his enemies, who are strewn beneath his horse. A figure meant to represent Eternity bestows the French crown on the king's head. Leaning into the relief from above, two winged Victories blow a trumpet and extend a laurel crown. As if supporting the king on their backs, two chained prisoners writhe in the pain of defeat. The lowest part of the relief shows the seated figure of Fame, inscribing the immortal feats of Louis XIV.

The oil painting in this section has a similar theme, with Louis as a warrior in Roman garb receiving a crown of laurel. The artist was Pierre Mignard, who rendered it around 1658.

Background
Daily Life

Court Etiquette The strictness of etiquette at Versailles made it almost impossible to relax. A noble would never consider walking out of his appointed place in a royal procession. Knocking on a door was forbidden. Instead, one was to scratch on the door with the fingernail of the little finger. Any digression from court etiquette subjected one to open derision and ridicule for days and might even result in banishment from court. One duchess who sat down at a gaming table when she was not playing was never invited to the Palace of Versailles again.

Did You Know?

A High-Maintenance King

"No expense is too great." Applying this rule certainly helped Louis XIV make sure his every wish was fulfilled. For example:

• As much as $1.5 billion may have been taken from France's treasury to build his lavish palace at Versailles. Tens of thousands of workers spent several decades building the palace.

• One minor item for the Versailles palace was his bathtub, which was carved out of a single piece of priceless Languedoc marble.

• Guards were stationed at every fountain in Versailles's gardens. The guards' job was to whistle whenever the king approached so that the water would be turned on fully.

Theme: Impact of the Individual What does the extravagance of Louis XIV say about the power of the French monarch?

Strengthening Royal Power Louis spent many hours each day attending to government affairs. To strengthen the state, he followed the policies of Richelieu. He expanded the bureaucracy and appointed intendants, royal officials who collected taxes, recruited soldiers, and carried out his policies in the provinces. The office of intendant and other government jobs often went to wealthy middle-class men. In this way, Louis cemented ties between the middle class and the monarchy.

Under Louis XIV, the French army became the strongest in Europe. The state paid, fed, trained, and supplied up to 300,000 soldiers. Louis used this highly disciplined army to enforce his policies at home and abroad.

Colbert and the Economy Louis's brilliant finance minister, Jean Baptiste Colbert (kohl BEHR), followed mercantilist policies to bolster the economy. Colbert had new lands cleared for farming, encouraged mining and other basic industries, and built up luxury trades such as lacemaking. To protect French manufacturers, he put high tariffs on imported goods. He also encouraged overseas colonies, such as New France in North America, and regulated trade with the colonies to enrich the royal treasury.

Colbert's policies helped make France the wealthiest state in Europe. Yet Louis XIV was often short of cash. Not even the financial genius of Colbert could produce enough income to support the huge costs of Louis's court or pay for his many foreign wars.

Versailles, Symbol of Royal Power

In the countryside near Paris, Louis XIV turned a royal hunting lodge into the immense palace of Versailles (ver sī). He spared no expense to make it the most magnificent building in Europe. Its halls and salons displayed the finest paintings and statues, and glittering chandeliers and mirrors. In the royal gardens, millions of flowers, trees, and fountains were set out in precise geometric patterns.

Versailles became the perfect symbol of the Sun King's wealth and power. As both the king's home and the seat of government, it housed at least 10,000 people, from nobles and officials to servants.

Court Ceremonies Louis XIV perfected elaborate ceremonies that emphasized his own importance. Each day began in the king's bedroom with a major ritual known as the levée, or rising. High-ranking nobles competed for the honor of holding the royal wash basin or handing the king his diamond-buckled shoes. At night, the ceremony was repeated in reverse. Wives of nobles vied to attend upon women of the royal family.

Rituals such as the levée served a serious purpose. French nobles were descendants of the feudal lords who held power in medieval times. Left at their estates, these nobles were a threat to the power of the monarchy. By luring nobles to Versailles, Louis turned them into courtiers angling for privileges rather than warriors battling for power. Louis carefully protected their prestige and left them free from paying taxes.

Cultural Flowering The king and his court supported a "splendid century" of the arts. Louis sponsored musical entertainments and commissioned plays by the best writers. The age of Louis XIV was the classical age of French drama. Jean Racine (rah SEEN) wrote tragedies based on ancient Greek myths. The actor-playwright Molière (mohl YAIR) turned out comedies, such as *The Miser*, that poked fun at French society.

In painting, music, architecture, and decorative arts, French styles became the model for all Europe. A new form of dance drama, ballet, gained its first great popularity at the French court. As a leading patron of culture, Louis sponsored the French Academies, which set high standards for both the arts and the sciences.

Did You Know?

ANSWER It reinforces how absolute this power was. Not only could the monarch govern as he wished, but he could use his country's money and human resources according to his whim.

Resource Directory

Teaching Resources

Primary Source Activity *A Busy Day at the Sun King's Court,* Unit 4 booklet, p. 71
History Through Literature *The Would-Be Gentleman,* History Through Literature booklet, pp. 37–38
You Are There Chapter Extension Activities booklet, p. 44

Technology

Listening to Literature World Masterpieces audiotapes poems by Pierre de Ronsard, side 6, running time 2:25 min.
World History Color Transparencies *A Craze for Porcelain Figures,* p. C–49; *High Fashion in France,* p. C–51

You Are There . . .

Living at Versailles

King Louis XIV has summoned you to live at Versailles. As a French noble, you are both honored and intimidated. After all, life at court can be demanding. Dress, conduct, and events are strictly prescribed. One mistake and you may be ridiculed—or even banished. But the chance is too good to miss!

As you ride through the front gate, under the golden seal, you are stunned by the size of the main palace. It stretches for more than a quarter of a mile and contains 1,300 rooms.

An explosion of color commands your attention as you stroll through the formal gardens of Versailles with other nobles. Flower beds are divided into geometric patterns, and you are amazed at the endless variety of plants, bubbling fountains, and impressive statues.

You find it easy to believe that the king has said, "My dominant passion is certainly love of glory." Everything you have seen at Versailles is extravagant. All this magnificence does not come without a price, however. The kitchen is so far away from your apartments that your food often arrives cold.

Portfolio Assessment

To gain favor with the king, you decide to create a tour brochure of Versailles. You are so taken by the beauty of a particular site within the palace or on the grounds that you focus the guide on that area.

Chapter 17 **419**

Human Drama Activity

Molière Have students do the History Through Literature activity, *The Would-Be Gentleman*, History Through Literature booklet, pp. 37–38. It contains an excerpt from the play of that name, which is a comedy about a newly rich merchant trying to mimic the manners of a gentleman. You may wish to discuss the answers to questions 4 and 5 as a class.

Test Preparation

Have students read the paragraph headed "Court Ceremonies" on the opposite page, and then answer the question below.

Which words in the paragraph are synonyms?

A *competed* and *vied*

B *elaborate* and *ritual*

C *perfected* and *emphasized*

D *ritual* and *rising*

You Are There . . .

Bell Ringer So students can grasp the immensity and grandeur of the Palace of Versailles, ask them to look at the photos on this page as well as photos from other sources.

Background
About the Scene

The palace, which is now a national museum, includes the living quarters of the king and queen, the Room of Hercules, the Hall of Mirrors, a magnificent royal chapel, and a private theater. The ceiling of the Hall of Mirrors is decorated with paintings glorifying Louis XIV's achievements.

Activity
Cooperative Learning

Ask students to work together in small groups to research and compare the Palace of Versailles during the time of Louis XIV with the present-day White House. Groups should prepare a floor plan or map of both buildings, noting similarities and differences. For example, each building contains residences, important works of art, formal gardens, and so on, but the White House is not the center of U.S. government. Invite volunteers from each group to present their findings to the class.

Activity Rubrics

Share rubrics with students before they create their brochures.

Attempted The brochure is incomplete.

Minimal The brochure is sketchy, unclear, or full of errors.

Adequate The brochure is full of details and is clearly written, free of errors, and contains visuals.

Exemplary The brochure demonstrates extensive research and results in an interesting and informative travelogue that includes lively writing and appealing visual aids.

SECTION 2 Assessment

Recall
1. (a) St. Bartholomew's Day Massacre, p. 416 (b) Edict of Nantes, p. 417 (c) *Fronde*, p. 417 (d) Versailles, p. 418 (e) War of the Spanish Succession, p. 420 2. (a) intendant, p. 418 (b) levée, p. 418 (c) balance of power, p. 420

Comprehension
3. (a) The wars divided the country. Both sides committed terrible atrocities. Rival leaders used the wars to further their own ambitions. (b) Henry IV converted to Catholicism but issued the Edict of Nantes, which granted the Huguenots religious toleration. He extended government influence into every area of life, including the courts, agriculture, and public works. 4. He expanded the bureaucracy and appointed intendants to collect taxes and carry out his policies. He cemented the ties between the middle class and the monarchy and strengthened the army. He made France the wealthiest state in Europe. 5. By expelling many of France's most prosperous and hard-working citizens, Louis harmed the French economy.

Critical Thinking and Writing
6. Both kings believed in divine right, that their authority to rule came directly from God. 7. Possible answer: Louis XIV's many wars and personal extravagances had drained the French treasury and weakened France.

Activity Rubrics

Share rubrics with students before they make their lists.

Attempted The list contains very few items or includes items that are anachronistic.

Minimal The list contains a few items, most of which are appropriate.

Adequate The list contains many items, all of which are appropriate.

Exemplary The list contains many items and reveals that the student has done research on Versailles.

Caption Answer

Possible answer: Louis is riding a horse and dressed in Roman military attire, which symbolizes the glory of ancient Rome. The representation of Eternity hovers over the king and places a laurel wreath upon his head, symbolizing that the king's power comes from heaven. The flag has the image of the sun, which was Louis's symbol of power. He carries a scepter, also a symbol of royal power.

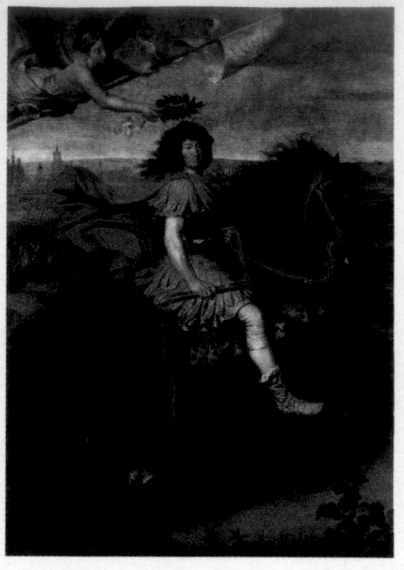

The King as Warrior
Although Louis XIV is best remembered for his extravagant court, he also expanded France's military might. This painting depicts Louis as a gallant warrior.

Theme: Impact of the Individual What symbols does this artist use to glorify Louis XIV?

Successes and Failures

Louis XIV ruled France for 72 years, far longer than any other monarch. During his reign, French culture, manners, and customs replaced those of Renaissance Italy as the standard for European taste. In both foreign and domestic affairs, however, many of Louis's policies were costly failures.

Wars of Louis XIV Louis XIV poured vast resources into wars to expand French borders. At first, he did gain some territory. His later wars were disastrous, though, because rival rulers joined forces to check French ambitions. Led by the Dutch or the English, these alliances fought to maintain the balance of power, a distribution of military and economic power that would prevent any one nation from dominating Europe.

In 1700, Louis's grandson Philip V inherited the throne of Spain. Louis declared that France and Spain "must regard themselves as one." But neighboring powers led by England were determined to prevent this union. The War of the Spanish Succession dragged on until 1713, when an exhausted France signed the Treaty of Utrecht. Philip remained on the Spanish throne, but France agreed never to unite the two crowns.

Persecution of the Huguenots Louis saw France's Protestant minority as a threat to religious and political unity. In 1685, he revoked the Edict of Nantes. More than 100,000 Huguenots fled France.

The persecution of the Huguenots was perhaps the king's most costly blunder. The Huguenots had been among the most hard-working and prosperous of Louis's subjects. Their loss was thus a serious blow to the French economy, just as the expulsion of Muslims and Jews had hurt Spain.

Looking Ahead

Louis XIV outlived his sons and grandsons. When he died in 1715, his five-year-old great-grandson inherited the throne as Louis XV. Although France was then the strongest state in Europe, years of warfare had drained the treasury. The prosperity nurtured by Colbert evaporated under the burden of bad harvests, heavy taxes, and other problems.

Louis XV was too weak a king to deal with such problems. He devoted his days to pleasure, ignoring the growing need for reform. He often quoted an old proverb, "After us, the deluge." As you will read, the deluge came during the reign of the next king.

SECTION 2 Assessment

Recall
1. **Identify:** (a) St. Bartholomew's Day Massacre, (b) Edict of Nantes, (c) *Fronde*, (d) Versailles, (e) War of the Spanish Succession.
2. **Define:** (a) intendant, (b) levée, (c) balance of power.

Comprehension
3. (a) What were the effects of the French wars of religion? (b) How did Henry IV rebuild French unity?
4. Describe how Louis XIV strengthened the power of the monarchy.

5. How did Louis's persecution of the Huguenots harm France?

Critical Thinking and Writing
6. **Comparing** How were the ideas of Louis XIV about monarchy similar to those of Philip II of Spain?
7. **Applying Information** On his deathbed, Louis XIV told his heir, "I have loved war too well; do not copy me in this, nor in the lavish expenditures I have made." Why do you think Louis gave this advice?

Activity

Designing a Set
Imagine that your school is putting on a play about Louis XIV at Versailles. You have been asked to design the set. Make a list of furniture, paintings, and other items you would want to include in the set.

Resource Directory

Teaching Resources
Section Quiz Unit 4 booklet, p. 63
Creative Teaching Activities Creative Teaching Activities booklet, p. 79
Guided Reading and Review Unit 4 booklet, p. 64

Technology
World History Color Transparencies political cartoon suggesting the result when government is dominated by a single powerful individual, p. E–29; political cartoon suggesting how people's lives are affected by the form of government under which they live, p. E–33
Interactive Student Tutorial CD-ROM Ch. 17
Computer Test Bank Ch. 17

Reading Focus

- How did the Tudors and Stuarts differ in their relations with Parliament?
- How did the English Civil War lead to the rise of the Commonwealth?
- What were the causes and results of the Glorious Revolution?

Vocabulary

dissenter
habeas corpus
limited monarchy

Taking Notes

Create a flowchart that shows the events in England that ultimately led to the strengthening of Parliament. Use this chart as a model, and add boxes as needed.

```
┌─────────────────────────────────┐
│ Tudors consult with and control │
│ Parliament                      │
└─────────────────────────────────┘
              ↓
┌─────────────────────────────────┐
│ James asserts claim to absolute │
│ power and clashes with Parliament│
└─────────────────────────────────┘
              ↓
┌─────────────────────────────────┐
│                                 │
└─────────────────────────────────┘
              ↓
┌─────────────────────────────────┐
│                                 │
└─────────────────────────────────┘
```

Main Idea During the 1600s, the British Parliament asserted its rights against royal claims to absolute power.

Setting the Scene "The most high and absolute power in the realm consists in the Parliament," wrote an English statesman in the 1560s. He was voicing a tradition that had roots in the Middle Ages. But in 1603, a monarch with far different ideas took the throne of England. "Kings are called gods," declared James I, "because they sit upon God's throne on Earth." Before long, James was on a collision course with Parliament.

In the 1600s, while Louis XIV perfected royal absolutism in France, England developed in a different direction. In this section, we will look at why and how Parliament asserted itself against royal power.

The Tudors and Parliament

From 1485 to 1603, England was ruled by the Tudor dynasty. Although the Tudors believed in divine right, they shrewdly recognized the value of good relations with Parliament. As you have read, when Henry VIII broke with the Roman Catholic Church, he turned to Parliament to legalize his actions. Parliament approved the Act of Supremacy, making the monarch head of the Church of England.

A constant need for money also led Henry to consult Parliament frequently. Although he had inherited a bulging treasury, he quickly used up his funds fighting overseas wars. To levy new taxes, the king had to seek the approval of Parliament. Members of Parliament tended to vote as Henry's agents instructed. Still, they became accustomed to being consulted on important matters.

Like her father, Elizabeth I both consulted and controlled Parliament. Her advisers conveyed the queen's wishes to Parliament and forbade discussion of certain subjects, such as foreign policy or the queen's marriage. Her skill in handling Parliament helped make "Good Queen Bess" a popular and successful ruler.

The Early Stuarts

Elizabeth died in 1603 without a direct heir. The throne passed to her relatives the Stuarts, the ruling family of Scotland. The Stuarts were neither as popular as the Tudors nor as skillful in dealing with Parliament. They also inherited problems that Henry and Elizabeth had long suppressed. The result was a "century of revolution" that pitted the Stuart monarchs against Parliament.

Chapter 17 **421**

SECTION 3

Bell Ringer Have students preview this section by reading the Reading Focus questions on this page and the Section 3 Assessment questions. Ask them to write five generalizations predicting what they will learn in the section. After they have finished studying the section, ask students to review and revise their generalizations.

LESSON PLAN

1. Focus The Stuart kings clashed with Parliament over money, foreign policy, and religion. A civil war erupted when Charles I tried to arrest the radical leaders in the House of Commons. Parliament's triumph led to the execution of the king, the abolition of the monarchy, and the creation of a republic headed by Oliver Cromwell. After the monarchy was restored, the Glorious Revolution limited royal power and protected the rights of English citizens.

2. Instruct Have students work with a partner to create an annotated chart or diagram portraying English rulers from 1603 to 1689. Remind students that the ruler may be an individual or a group. For each ruler, students should provide the name of the ruler, the dates of the ruler's reign, a description of the ruler's significant policies and actions, and a description of any checks or limits on the ruler's power. After students have finished, create new student partnerships so that students can compare and, if necessary, revise their charts. Then, use the charts as the basis for a class discussion.

3. Assess Have students select one ruler from their chart and ask them to identify two mistakes that they think the ruler made. If they had been that ruler, what would they have done differently?

4. Reteach If students' Assess activity does not reflect adequate understanding of the lesson, you might assign the *Guide to the Essentials* or the *Interactive Student Tutorial CD-ROM* for this section.

🖥 Block Scheduling Support

Use the political cartoon in World History Color Transparencies, p. E–33, to discuss how people's lives are affected by their form of government. The Lesson Suggestions on p. E–9 include background information about the issue and about the cartoon, as well as a writing and a mapmaking activity. You may want also to discuss the political cartoon in World History Color Transparencies, p. E–29, which suggests the result when government is dominated by a single powerful individual. Background information on p. F–7 and student activities compare history's tyrants. This page includes an interdisciplinary activity and a writing activity to help students evaluate the qualities of a strong leader.

Customize for . . .
Heterogeneous Groups

Writing a News Article Ask students to imagine that they are newspaper reporters covering the following events: (1) James I addressing Parliament on the divine right of kings, (2) the execution of Charles I, and (3) Cromwell declaring himself Lord Protector. You may wish to assign other significant events as well. Ask students to write a brief article on each event, reporting what happened and the reactions of the people involved. *(Reteaching)* ✳

Primary Source

A Voice for Absolutism

In 1651, two years after the English Civil War ended, English political philosopher Thomas Hobbes published Leviathan. *In the book, he explained why he favored an absolute monarch:*

"During the time men live without a common power to keep them all in awe, they are in that condition which is called war. . . . In such condition, there is no place for industry . . . no arts; no letters; no society; and, which is worst of all, continual fear and danger of violent death. And the life of man [is] solitary, poor, nasty, brutish, and short."

—Thomas Hobbes, *Leviathan*

Skills Assessment

Primary Source How might people who supported Parliament over the monarch have argued against Hobbes's view?

Primary Source

ANSWER Opponents of an absolute monarch might say that a democratic government, rather than an absolute monarch, can keep people in enough "awe" to get them to obey laws and thus to let society function productively.

The Royal Challenge The first Stuart monarch, James I, had agreed to rule according to English laws and customs. Soon, however, he was lecturing Parliament about divine right. "I will not be content that my power be disputed upon," he declared. Leaders in the House of Commons fiercely resisted the king's claim to absolute power.

James repeatedly clashed with Parliament over money and foreign policy. He needed funds to finance his lavish court and wage wars. When members wanted to discuss foreign policy before voting funds, James dissolved Parliament and collected taxes on his own.

James also found himself embroiled in disputes with dissenters, Protestants who differed with the Church of England. One group, called Puritans, sought to "purify" the church of Catholic practices. Puritans called for simpler services and a more democratic church without bishops. James rejected their demands, vowing to "harry them out of this land or else do worse."

A positive result of the king's dispute with the Puritans was his call for a new translation of the Bible. The King James version that appeared in 1611 has had a lasting influence on English language and literature.

Parliament Responds In 1625, Charles I inherited the throne. Like his father, Charles behaved like an absolute monarch. He imprisoned his foes without trial and squeezed the nation for money. By 1628, though, his need to raise taxes forced Charles to summon Parliament. Before voting any funds, Parliament insisted that Charles sign the Petition of Right. It prohibited the king from raising taxes without the consent of Parliament or from imprisoning anyone without just cause.

Charles did sign the petition, but he then dissolved Parliament in 1629. For 11 years, he ignored the petition and ruled the nation without Parliament. During that time, he created bitter enemies, especially among Puritans. His Archbishop of Canterbury, William Laud, tried to force all clergy to follow strict Anglican rules, dismissing or imprisoning dissenters. Many people felt that the archbishop was trying to revive Catholic practices.

In 1637, Charles and Laud tried to impose the Anglican prayer book on Scotland. The Calvinist Scots revolted. To get funds to suppress the Scottish rebellion, Charles finally had to summon Parliament in 1640. When it met, however, Parliament launched its own revolt.

The Long Parliament The 1640 Parliament became known as the Long Parliament because it lasted on and off until 1653. Its actions triggered the greatest political revolution in English history. In a mounting struggle with the king, Parliament tried and executed his chief ministers, including Archbishop Laud. It further declared that the Parliament could not be dissolved without its own consent and called for the abolition of bishops.

Charles lashed back. In 1642, he led troops into the House of Commons to arrest its most radical leaders. They escaped through a back door and soon raised their own army. The clash now moved to the battlefield.

The English Civil War

The civil war that followed lasted from 1642 to 1649. Like the *Fronde* that occurred about the same time in France, the English Civil War posed a major challenge to absolutism. But while the forces of royal power won in France, in England the forces of revolution triumphed.

Cavaliers and Roundheads At first, the odds seemed to favor the Cavaliers, or supporters of Charles I. Many Cavaliers were wealthy nobles, proud of their plumed hats and fashionably long hair. Well trained in dueling and warfare, the Cavaliers expected a quick victory. But their foes proved to be tough fighters with the courage of their convictions. The

Virtual Field Trip

www.phschool.com

Cromwell Museum Huntington, England

To see other images relating to the career of Oliver Cromwell, use the Internet address above to link to the Cromwell Museum.

A Victory for Parliament The Battle of Marston Moor was a turning point in the English Civil War. Though wounded in the neck, Oliver Cromwell (center, on horse) rallied his troops to defeat the forces of King Charles I.

Theme: Continuity and Change How would a modern battle scene differ from this one?

Background
Historical Evidence

British Redcoats During the English Civil War, Oliver Cromwell proved himself to be an excellent military strategist. He was responsible for the well-known brilliant red color of the English soldier's uniform. In the heat of battle, the bright red coats helped soldiers distinguish between friendly forces and enemy forces. The red color also camouflaged any blood stains from wounds, thus helping to keep morale high.

forces of Parliament were composed of country gentry, town-dwelling manufacturers, and Puritan clergy. They were called Roundheads because their hair was cut close around their heads.

The Roundheads found a leader of genius in Oliver Cromwell. A Puritan member of the lesser gentry, Cromwell was a skilled general. He organized the "New Model Army" for Parliament into a disciplined fighting force. Inspired by Puritan chaplains, Cromwell's army defeated the Cavaliers in a series of decisive battles. By 1647, the king was in the hands of parliamentary forces.

Execution of a King Eventually, Parliament set up a court to put the king on trial. It condemned him to death as "a tyrant, traitor, murderer, and public enemy." On a cold January day in 1649, Charles I stood on a scaffold surrounded by his foes. "I am a martyr of the people," he declared.

Showing no fear, the king told the executioner that he himself would give the sign for him to strike. After a brief prayer, Charles knelt and placed his neck on the block. On the agreed signal, the executioner severed the king's head with a single stroke.

The execution sent shock waves throughout Europe. In the past, kings had occasionally been assassinated or died in battle. But for the first time, a ruling monarch had been tried and executed by his own people. The parliamentary forces had sent a clear signal that, in England, no ruler could claim absolute power and ignore the rule of law.

The Commonwealth

After the execution of Charles I, the House of Commons abolished the monarchy, the House of Lords, and the official Church of England. It declared England a republic, known as the Commonwealth, under the leadership of Oliver Cromwell.

Challenges to the Commonwealth The new government faced many threats. Supporters of Charles II, the uncrowned heir to the throne, attacked England by way of Ireland and Scotland. Cromwell led forces into Ireland to crush the uprising. He then took harsh measures against the Irish Catholic majority. In 1652, Parliament passed a law exiling most Catholics to barren

Test Preparation

Have students read the section titled "Execution of a King" on this page, and then answer the question below.

What was the significance of King Charles's execution?

A It showed he had courage.

B It showed trial by jury works for kings, too.

C It showed the law was above the ruler.

D It showed the king was a tyrant.

Caption Answer

Possible answer: In a modern battle, there might be tanks instead of horses and automatic rifles instead of swords. The soldiers would not be wearing armor. The commander probably would not be in the midst of the battle.

land in the west of Ireland. Any Catholic found disobeying this order could be killed on sight.

Squabbles also splintered forces within the Commonwealth. One group, called Levellers, thought that poor men should have as much say in government as the gentry, lawyers, and other leading citizens. "The poorest he that is in England hath a life to live as the greatest he," wrote one Leveller. In addition, female Levellers asserted their right to petition Parliament.

These Leveller ideas horrified the gentry who dominated Parliament. Cromwell and his generals suppressed the Levellers, as well as more radical groups who threatened property ownership. As the challenges to order grew, Cromwell took the title Lord Protector in 1653. From then on, he ruled through the army.

Puritan Society Under the Commonwealth, Puritan preachers tried to root out godlessness and impose a "rule of saints." The English Civil War thus ushered in a social revolution as well as a political one.

Parliament enacted a series of laws designed to make sure that Sunday was set aside for religious observance. Anyone over the age of 14 who was caught "profaning the Lord's Day" could be fined. To the Puritans, theaters were "spectacles of pleasure too commonly expressing mirth and levity." So, like John Calvin in Geneva, Cromwell closed all theaters. Puritans also frowned on lewd dancing, taverns, and gambling.

Puritans felt that every Christian, rich and poor, must be able to read the Bible. To spread religious knowledge, they encouraged education for all people. By mid-century, families from all classes were sending their children to school, girls as well as boys.

Puritans pushed for changes in marriage to ensure greater fidelity. In addition to marriages based on business interests, they encouraged marriages based on love. As in the past, women were seen mainly as caretakers of the family, subordinate to men. When some radical Protestant groups allowed women to preach sermons, most Puritans were shocked.

Although Cromwell could not accept open worship by Roman Catholics, he believed in religious freedom for other Protestant groups. He even welcomed Jews back to England, after more than 350 years of exile.

End of the Commonwealth Oliver Cromwell died in 1658. Soon after, the Puritans lost their grip on England. Many people were tired of military rule and strict Puritan ways. In 1660, a newly elected Parliament invited Charles II to return to England from exile.

England's "kingless decade" ended with the restoration of the monarchy. Yet Puritan ideas about morality, equality, government, and education endured. In the following century, these ideas would play an important role in shaping the United States of America.

From Restoration to Glorious Revolution

In late May 1660, cheering crowds welcomed Charles II back to London. One supporter wrote:

> "This day came his Majesty, Charles the Second to London, after a sad and long exile . . . with a triumph of above 20,000 horse and [soldiers], brandishing their swords, and shouting with inexpressible joy; the ways strewd with flowers, the bells ringing, the streets hung with tapestry."
>
> —John Evelyn, *Diary*

With his charm and flashing wit, young Charles II was a popular ruler. He reopened theaters and taverns and presided over a lively court in the manner of Louis XIV. Charles restored the official Church of England but tolerated other Protestants such as Presbyterians, Quakers, and Baptists.

Synthesizing Information

The Struggle Between King and Parliament

In England, a battle for power raged between king and Parliament during the 1600s. The monarchy was abolished and then restored. The picture, the source, and the time line depict a few highlights of that struggle.

King Versus Parliament

James I and Divine Right (1603)

"Kings are called gods because they sit upon God's throne on earth."

English Bill of Rights (1689)

"1. That . . . suspending of laws . . . by regal authority, without consent of Parliament is illegal.
4. That levying money for or to the use of the crown . . . without grant of Parliament . . . is illegal. "

Restoration: Charles II in Triumph

1603 Stuart rule begins	1629 Charles I dissolves Parliament	1649 Parliament orders execution of Charles I; Cromwell rules	1688 Glorious Revolution	1689 Parliament passes Bill of Rights

1600	1620	1640	1660	1680	1700

1640 Long Parliament meets	1642 English Civil War	1660 Parliament restores Stuart rule; Charles II is crowned

Skills Tip

On a time line, equal intervals of time should be represented by an equal amount of space.

Skills Assessment

1. In which of the following years did Parliament seem to have the most power?
   A 1629
   B 1640
   C 1660
   D 1689

2. The person who painted the picture of Charles II probably
   E favored the monarchy.
   F fought for Cromwell.
   G supported Parliament.
   H disliked the new king.

3. **Critical Thinking Applying Information** (a) What advice would you give to an English monarch in the 1600s who wanted to keep his or her throne? (b) What advice would you give to a member of Parliament in the 1600s who wanted the monarchy to continue?

Human Drama Note

James II When James II became king in 1685, he favored Catholics in his appointments and published the Declaration of Indulgence in 1687, providing "liberty of conscience" for all denominations. The birth of James's son in 1688 aroused public fear of continued Catholic rule and caused English nobles to offer the throne to James's Protestant daughter, Mary, and her husband, William of Orange, thus establishing Parliament's right to control succession to the throne and to limit the monarch's power.

---

*B*ackground
About the Evidence

English Bill of Rights In addition to the provisions listed here and on the next page, the English Bill of Rights forbade the monarch to keep a standing army in peace time without Parliament's consent, to deny the right of the people to petition the monarch, and to interfere in the elections to Parliament.

*A*ctivity
Interpreting the Evidence

Use these additional questions to generate class discussion.

Critical Thinking: Summarizing 1. How would you state the articles from the English Bill of Rights in your own words? *(Possible answers: It is illegal for the monarch to set aside laws without Parliament's agreement. Parliament must approve all taxes.)*

Critical Thinking: Comparing 2. How is this document similar to the Magna Carta? *(Possible answers: Both were drawn up in response to abuses by the crown. Both deal with levying taxes, trial by jury, and obedience to the law by the monarch.)*

Skills Tip

On the time line, note the close sequence of events leading to the passage of the English Bill of Rights. The Skills Handbook in the front of the book has a lesson that will help students with this feature.

Skills Assessment

ANSWERS **1.** D **2.** E **3.** Possible answers: **(a)** A monarch must obey the laws of the land, even if they limit his or her power. **(b)** A member of Parliament must allow the monarch some power.

Recall

1. (a) James I, p. 421 **(b)** Charles I, p. 422 **(c)** Petition of Right, p. 422 **(d)** Cavalier, p. 422 **(e)** Roundhead, p. 423 **(f)** Oliver Cromwell, p. 423 **(g)** Leveller, p. 424 **(h)** English Bill of Rights, p. 426 **2. (a)** dissenter, p. 422 **(b)** habeas corpus, p. 426 **(c)** limited monarchy, p. 426

Comprehension

3. (a) Although they believed in divine right, the Tudors fostered good relations with Parliament in order to raise money and gain political support. **(b)** The Stuarts behaved as absolute monarchs. They dismissed Parliament, jailed people without trial, collected excessive taxes, and engaged in religious conflicts. **4.** Possible answers: **(a)** After signing the Petition of Right, Charles I dissolved Parliament. When Parliament reconvened, it executed the king's ministers. Charles responded by trying to arrest the radical leaders of Parliament. **(b)** Many people opposed the Commonwealth government because of its military rule and strict Puritan ways. **5.** Possible answer: The power of Parliament was superior to that of the monarchy. The Bill of Rights protected the traditional rights of English citizens.

Critical Thinking and Writing

6. Possible answers: **(a)** The Puritan emphasis on education might have encouraged women to pursue knowledge and learning. **(b)** Men were accustomed to women confining themselves to the home. By speaking out publicly, women threatened the traditional order of society. **7.** part of American society—public education for boys and girls, marriages based on love, female preachers, religious freedom for Protestants and Jews; not part of American society—laws requiring religious observance on Sunday, closing of theaters, forbidding of Catholic worship

Activity Rubrics

Share rubrics with students before they draw their cartoons.

Attempted The cartoon fails to reflect a point of view.

Minimal The cartoon presents a point of view but shows limited understanding of the subject and is poorly rendered.

Adequate The cartoon shows understanding of the subject, clearly presents a point of view, and is well rendered.

Exemplary The cartoon shows a clear understanding of the subject, presents a point of view, and is particularly well rendered.

Although Charles accepted the Petition of Right, he shared his father's faith in absolute monarchy and secretly had Catholic sympathies. Still, he shrewdly avoided his father's mistakes in dealing with Parliament.

A New Clash With Parliament Charles's brother, James II, inherited the throne in 1685. Unlike Charles, James flaunted his Catholic faith. He further angered his subjects by suspending laws at whim and appointing Catholics to high office. Many English Protestants feared that James would restore the Roman Catholic Church.

In 1688, alarmed parliamentary leaders invited James's Protestant daughter, Mary, and her Dutch Protestant husband, William III of Orange, to become rulers of England. When William and Mary landed with their army late in 1688, James II fled to France. This bloodless overthrow of a king became known as the Glorious Revolution.

English Bill of Rights Before they could be crowned, William and Mary had to accept several acts passed by Parliament in 1689 that became known as the English Bill of Rights. The Bill of Rights ensured the superiority of Parliament over the monarchy. It required the monarch to summon Parliament regularly and gave the House of Commons the "power of the purse." A king or queen could no longer interfere in Parliamentary debates or suspend laws. The Bill of Rights also barred any Roman Catholic from sitting on the throne.

The Bill of Rights also restated the traditional rights of English citizens, such as trial by jury. It abolished excessive fines and cruel or unjust punishment. It affirmed the principle of habeas corpus. That is, no person could be held in prison without first being charged with a specific crime.

Later, the Toleration Act of 1689 granted limited religious freedom to Puritans, Quakers, and other dissenters, though not yet to Catholics. Still, only members of the Church of England could hold public office.

Looking Ahead

The Glorious Revolution did not create democracy, but a type of government called limited monarchy, in which a constitution or legislative body limits the monarch's powers. English rulers still had much power, but they had to obey the law and govern in partnership with Parliament. In the age of absolute monarchy elsewhere in Europe, the limited monarchy in England was radical enough.

> ► **Primary Sources and Literature**
>
> See "The English Bill of Rights" in the Reference Section at the back of this book.

SECTION 3 Assessment

Recall

1. Identify: (a) James I, **(b)** Charles I, **(c)** Petition of Right, **(d)** Cavalier, **(e)** Roundhead, **(f)** Oliver Cromwell, **(g)** Leveller, **(h)** English Bill of Rights.
2. Define: (a) dissenter, **(b)** habeas corpus, **(c)** limited monarchy.

Comprehension

3. (a) How did Tudor monarchs handle Parliament? **(b)** Why did the early Stuarts clash with Parliament?
4. (a) Explain two causes of the English Civil War. **(b)** Why did many people welcome the return of the monarchy?
5. Describe two results of the Glorious Revolution.

Critical Thinking and Writing

6. Analyzing Information (a) How might Puritan teachings have led some women to seek greater liberties? **(b)** Why do you think many men were upset by the idea of women speaking in public?
7. Linking Past and Present Which aspects of Commonwealth society are part of American society today? Which are not?

Activity

Drawing a Political Cartoon
Draw a political cartoon that might have appeared in England in 1649 about the execution of Charles I. Take the point of view of either a Roundhead or a Cavalier.

426 Chapter 17

> ## Resource Directory
>
> ### Teaching Resources
>
> **Section Quiz** Unit 4 booklet, p. 65
> **Creative Teaching Activities** Creative Teaching Activities booklet, p. 80
> **Guided Reading and Review** Unit 4 booklet, p. 66
>
> ### Technology
>
> **Interactive Student Tutorial CD-ROM** Ch. 17
> **Computer Test Bank** Ch. 17

Rise of Austria and Prussia

Reading Focus

- What were the causes and results of the Thirty Years' War?

- How did Austria and Prussia emerge as great powers?

- How did European diplomats try to maintain a balance of power?

Vocabulary

elector
mercenary
depopulation

Taking Notes

On a sheet of paper, copy the chart shown at right. As you read this section, add events that occurred before and after the Peace of Westphalia.

PEACE OF WESTPHALIA

Before	After
• Thirty Years' War	• Germany divided into many states
• Frederick becomes Holy Roman emperor	•

Main Idea Two great empires, Austria and Prussia, rose out of the ashes of the Thirty Years' War.

Setting the Scene

Year after year, war ravaged the German states of central Europe. Bodies of victims littered fields and roads. As the Thirty Years' War dragged on, almost every European power was sucked into the conflict. "We have had blue coats and red coats and now come the yellow coats," cried the citizens of one German town. "God have pity on us!"

Finally, two great German-speaking powers, Austria and Prussia, rose out of the ashes. Like Louis XIV in France, their rulers perfected skills as absolute monarchs.

The Thirty Years' War

The French philosopher Voltaire noted that, by early modern times, the Holy Roman Empire was neither holy, nor Roman, nor an empire. Instead, it was a patchwork of several hundred small, separate states. In theory, these states were under the authority of the Holy Roman emperor, who was chosen by seven leading German princes called electors. In practice, the emperor had little power over the many rival princes. Religion further divided the German states. The north was largely Protestant, and the south was Catholic. This power vacuum sparked the Thirty Years' War.

The War Begins The war had both religious and political causes. It began in Bohemia, the present-day Czech Republic. Ferdinand, the Hapsburg king of Bohemia, sought to suppress Protestants and to assert royal power over local nobles. In May 1618, a few rebellious Protestant noblemen tossed two royal officials out of a castle window in Prague. This act sparked a general revolt, which Ferdinand moved to suppress. As both sides sought allies, what began as a local conflict widened into a general European war.

The following year, Ferdinand was elected Holy Roman emperor. With the support of Spain, Poland, and other Catholic states, he tried to roll back the Reformation. In the early stages of the war, he defeated the Bohemians and their Protestant allies. Alarmed, Protestant powers like the Netherlands and Sweden sent troops into Germany.

Before long, political motives outweighed religious issues. Catholic and Protestant rulers shifted alliances to suit their own interests. At one point, Catholic France joined Lutheran Sweden against the Catholic Hapsburgs.

The Thirty Years' War Begins

In an act known as the Defenestration of Prague, rebellious nobles in Bohemia tossed two royal officials out of a castle window. Both men survived, but the defiant act sparked the terrible Thirty Years' War.

Theme: Diversity What opposing groups do the men shown in this picture represent?

Chapter 17 **427**

SECTION 4

Bell Ringer Read aloud to the class the quote on the next page, which describes the sack of a peasant village during the Thirty Years' War. Then, ask students to imagine living under such conditions for 30 years.

LESSON PLAN

1. **Focus** The Thirty Years' War severely reduced local populations and left Germany divided. France gained territory, while Hapsburg control of the Holy Roman Empire waned. Gradually, the Hapsburgs of Austria added new European lands to their empire. In north Germany, meanwhile, Prussia emerged as a powerful militaristic state.

2. **Instruct** Divide the class into groups and assign each group to cover one of the following topics: (1) The Thirty Years' War, (2) The War of the Austrian Succession, (3) The Rise of Prussia. Assign each group to work together to outline the causes and effects of its assigned topic. After students have completed this part of the lesson, regroup the students so that each new group has at least one "expert" on each of the three topics. Then, have students take turns teaching one another about their area of expertise.

3. **Assess** Ask students to use the information they learned to answer the Reading Focus questions on this page.

4. **Reteach** If students' **Assess** activity does not reflect adequate understanding of the lesson, you might assign the *Guide to the Essentials* or the *Interactive Student Tutorial CD-ROM* for this section.

Block Scheduling Support

Have students work with the outline map *Europe After the Peace of Westphalia, 1648* on p. 28 of the Historical Outline Map Book. Suggestions for map activities and questions for discussion appear on p. T–7. The activity stimulates interpretive and thinking skills in students.

Test Preparation

Have students read the picture caption on this page, and then answer the question below.

What would you guess to be the meaning of the word *defenestration*?

A the act of cutting down trees, completely clearing the land

B the act of throwing something or someone out of a window

C an act of rebellion against the state

D the act of protesting a war

Caption Answer

The men being thrown out the window represent the Roman Catholics who ruled the Holy Roman Empire. The other men represent rebellious Protestant nobles.

Write the headings and subheadings for Section 4 on the board. Ask students to predict what each section will be about. List their predictions on the board. After students read Section 4, ask them to compare their predictions to what they learned from the text. *(More Advanced Readers)*

Background
Daily Life

Repopulating Germany It is estimated that the Thirty Years' War reduced the German population from 20 million to 13.5 million. This massive depopulation presented a crisis for German rulers, and they responded with drastic measures. At the Congress of Franconia, in 1650, German princes adopted the following resolution:

"[M]en under sixty years of age shall not be admitted to monasteries. . . . Priests and curates (if not ordained), and the canons of religious establishments, shall marry. . . . [E]very male shall be allowed to marry two wives; and each and every male is earnestly reminded, and shall often be warned from the pulpit, to so comport himself in this matter."

Europe After the Thirty Years' War

Legend:
- Controlled by Spanish Hapsburgs
- Controlled by Austrian Hapsburgs
- Italian city-states
- Prussia
- Boundary of Holy Roman Empire

Azimuthal Equal Area Projection
0 250 500 Miles
0 250 500 Kilometers

Skills Assessment

Geography After the Thirty Years' War, the Peace of Westphalia redrew the map of Europe.

1. **Location** On the map, locate (a) Poland, (b) Sweden, (c) Spanish Netherlands, (d) Westphalia.
2. **Region** (a) In 1648, who controlled Bohemia? (b) What lands did the Spanish Hapsburgs control?
3. **Critical Thinking Drawing Conclusions** How can you tell from the map that the Holy Roman Empire was not a strong, unified state?

A Brutal Conflict The fighting took a terrible toll. Roving armies of mercenaries, or soldiers for hire, burned villages, destroyed crops, and killed without mercy. A novel of the time describes episodes of nightmare violence, such as the plundering of a village by marauding soldiers:

"For one of [the peasants] they had taken they thrust into the baking oven and there lit a fire under him, . . . as for another, they put a cord around his head and twisted it so tight with a piece of wood that the blood gushed from his mouth and nose and ears. In a word each had his own device to torture the peasants."

—Jacob von Grimmelshausen, *Simplicissimus*

Murder and torture were followed by famine and disease. Wolves, not seen in settled areas since the Middle Ages, stalked the deserted streets of once-bustling villages. The war led to severe depopulation, or reduction in population. Although exact population statistics do not exist, historians estimate that as many as one third of the people in the German states may have died as a result of the war.

Peace at Last Finally, in 1648, the exhausted combatants accepted a series of treaties, known as the Peace of Westphalia. Because so many powers had been involved in the conflict, the war ended with a general European peace and an attempt to settle other international problems as well.

France emerged a clear winner, gaining territory on both its Spanish and German frontiers. The Hapsburgs were big losers because they had to accept the almost total independence of all the princes of the Holy Roman Empire. The Netherlands and the Swiss Federation (present-day Switzerland) won recognition as independent states.

Skills Assessment

ANSWERS 1. Review locations with students. **2. (a)** Austrian Hapsburgs **(b)** Spain, Balearic Islands, Sardinia, Sicily, the area that is today southern Italy, Spanish Netherlands, and some lands in the Holy Roman Empire **3.** The map shows that areas within the Holy Roman Empire were actually ruled by a number of different powers, including Prussia.

Resource Directory

Teaching Resources

Viewpoint Activity *Empress Maria Theresa: Two Views,* Unit 4 booklet, p. 72

The Thirty Years' War left Germany divided into more than 360 separate states, "one for every day of the year." These states still formally acknowledged the leadership of the Holy Roman emperor. Yet each state had its own government, coinage, state church, armed forces, and foreign policy. Germany, potentially the most powerful nation in Europe, thus remained fragmented for another 200 years.

Hapsburg Austria

Though weakened by war, the Hapsburgs still wanted to create a strong united state. They kept the title of Holy Roman emperors, but focused their attention on expanding their own lands. To Austria, they added Bohemia, Hungary, and, later, parts of Poland and Italy.

Unity and Diversity Uniting these lands proved difficult. Divided by geography, they also included diverse peoples and cultures. By the 1700s, the Hapsburg empire included Germans, Magyars, Slavs, and others. In many parts of the empire, people had their own languages, laws, assemblies, and customs.

The Hapsburgs did exert some control over these diverse peoples. They sent German-speaking officials to Bohemia and Hungary and settled Austrians on confiscated lands in these provinces. The Hapsburgs also put down revolts in Bohemia and Hungary. Still, the Hapsburg empire never developed a centralized system like that of France.

Maria Theresa In the early 1700s, the emperor Charles VI faced a new crisis. He had no son. His daughter, Maria Theresa, was intelligent and capable, but no woman had yet ruled Hapsburg lands in her own name. Charles persuaded other European rulers to recognize his daughter's right to succeed him. When he died, however, many ignored their pledge.

The greatest threat came in 1740, when Frederick II of Prussia seized the rich Hapsburg province of Silesia. Maria Theresa set off for Hungary to appeal for military help from her Hungarian subjects. The Hungarians were ordinarily unfriendly to the Hapsburgs. But she made a dramatic plea before an assembly of Hungarian nobles. According to one account, the nobles rose to their feet and shouted, "Our lives and blood for your Majesty!" She eventually got further help from Britain and Russia.

During the eight-year War of the Austrian Succession, Maria Theresa was not able to force Frederick out of Silesia. Still, she did preserve her empire and win the support of most of her people. Equally important, she strengthened Hapsburg power by reorganizing the bureaucracy and improving tax collection. She even forced nobles and clergy to pay taxes and tried to ease the burden of taxes and labor services on peasants. As you will read, many of her reforms were later extended by her son and successor, Joseph II.

The Rise of Prussia

While Austria was molding a strong Catholic state, Prussia emerged as a new Protestant power. In the 1600s, the Hohenzollern (HOH uhn tsahl ern) family ruled scattered lands across north Germany. After the Peace of Westphalia, ambitious Hohenzollern rulers united their lands by taking over the states between them. Like absolute rulers elsewhere, they set up an efficient central bureaucracy and reduced the independence of their nobles, called Junkers (YOON kerz).

To achieve their goals, Prussian rulers like Frederick William I forged one of the best-trained armies in Europe. Great emphasis was placed on military values. One Prussian military leader boasted, "Prussia is not a state which possesses an army, but an army which possesses a state."

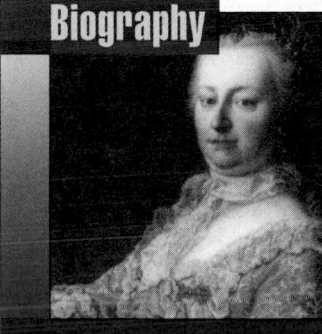

Biography

Maria Theresa 1717–1780

When Maria Theresa became Hapsburg empress at the age of 23, her chances of remaining in power seemed very slim. She later said, "I found myself . . . without money, without credit, without army, without experience and knowledge of my own, and finally without counsel, because each one of them first wanted to wait and see what would happen."

But the determined empress survived. She appointed superb advisers and was able to maintain control of her empire. During her 40-year reign, Vienna became a center for music and the arts.

Maria Theresa had one thing in common with most women of her day—her duties included motherhood. She gave birth to a total of 16 children—11 girls and 5 boys. Among them were future emperors Joseph II and Leopold II and Queen Marie Antoinette of France.

Theme: Impact of the Individual What traits did Maria Theresa need to stay in power?

Recall

1. (a) Peace of Westphalia, p. 428 (b) Maria Theresa, p. 429 (c) War of the Austrian Succession, p. 429 (d) Frederick the Great, p. 430 (e) Seven Years' War, p. 430 2. (a) elector, p. 427 (b) mercenary, p. 428 (c) depopulation, p. 428

Comprehension

3. Germany was left divided into more than 360 states, each with its own government, coinage, state church, armed forces, and foreign policy. These states were almost totally independent of the Holy Roman Empire. 4. (a) Austria and Prussia (b) Both countries wished to create a strong, unified state as well as expand their lands. 5. (a) They did not want any one state to dominate Europe. (b) They formed alliances and went to war.

Critical Thinking and Writing

6. (a) Possible answers: Because so many countries were involved in the war, a conference was necessary to propose, discuss, and agree on peace terms. (b) They hold peace conferences or submit to arbitration by a third party. The third party may be one or more other countries or an international organization, such as the United Nations. They also go to war. 7. Possible answer: bravery, physical strength and agility, discipline, loyalty, determination, quick thinking

Activity Rubrics

Share rubrics with students before they create their lists of rules.

Attempted The list fails to include the required number of rules.

Minimal The list includes the required number of items but shows limited understanding of the times or has many errors.

Adequate The list shows understanding of the age of absolutism and is clearly written.

Exemplary The list includes more than the required ten items or shows very deep understanding of the requirements of being an absolute monarch.

Frederick William won the loyalty of the Junkers by giving them positions in the army and government. By 1740, Prussia was strong enough to challenge its rival Austria.

Frederick II Frederick William made sure that, from an early age, his son Frederick was trained in the art of war:

> "His tutor must take the greatest pains to imbue my son with a sincere love for the soldier's profession and to impress upon him that nothing else in the world can confer upon a prince such fame and honor as the sword."
> —Frederick William, quoted in *The Heritage of World Civilizations* (Craig)

In fact, young Frederick preferred playing the flute and writing poetry. Frederick William despised these pursuits and treated the young prince so badly that he tried to flee the country. Discovering these plans, Frederick William put his son in solitary confinement. A friend who had helped Frederick was beheaded while the 18-year-old prince was forced to watch.

Military Successes Frederick's harsh military training did have an effect. After becoming king in 1740, Frederick II lost no time in using his army. As you read, he boldly seized Silesia from Austria, sparking the War of the Austrian Succession. In several later wars, Frederick made brilliant use of his disciplined army, forcing all to accept Prussia as a great power. His exploits earned him the name Frederick the Great.

Keeping the Balance of Power

By 1750, the great powers of Europe included Austria, Prussia, France, England, and Russia. They formed various alliances to maintain the balance of power. Though nations sometimes switched partners, two rivalries persisted. Prussia battled Austria for control of the German states, while Britain and France competed for overseas empire.

On occasion, European rivalries ignited a worldwide conflict. The Seven Years' War, which lasted from 1756 until 1763, was fought on four continents. Prussia, Austria, Russia, France, and Britain battled in Europe. Britain and France also fought in India and Africa. In North America, the French and Indian War also involved Native American nations. The Treaty of Paris ending the wars gave Britain a huge empire.

SECTION 4 Assessment

Recall

1. **Identify:** (a) Peace of Westphalia, (b) Maria Theresa, (c) War of the Austrian Succession, (d) Frederick the Great, (e) Seven Years' War.
2. **Define:** (a) elector, (b) mercenary, (c) depopulation.

Comprehension

3. What impact did the Thirty Years' War have on the German states?
4. (a) What two major powers emerged in Europe at the end of the Thirty Years' War? (b) How were the goals of these two nations similar?

5. (a) Why did European nations seek a balance of power? (b) What methods did they use?

Critical Thinking and Writing

6. **Linking Past and Present** Westphalia was the first modern peace conference. (a) Why was such a conference needed? (b) How do nations try to settle disputes today?
7. **Making Inferences** "Prussia is not a state which possesses an army, but an army which possesses a state." What values do you think would be emphasized in such a state?

Activity

Mentoring a Monarch
Both Louis XIV and Frederick William wrote instructions for training their sons to rule. With a partner, create a list of eight to ten rules for a successful absolute monarch in the 1600s and 1700s.

Resource Directory

Teaching Resources

Section Quiz Unit 4 booklet, p. 67
Creative Teaching Activities Creative Teaching Activities booklet, p. 81
Guided Reading and Review Unit 4 booklet, p. 68
Skill Application Activity *Interviewing*, Unit 4 booklet, p. 73

Technology

Interactive Student Tutorial CD-ROM Ch. 17
Computer Test Bank Ch. 17

Reading Focus

- How did Peter the Great try to make Russia into a modern state?
- What steps did Peter take to expand Russia's borders?
- How did Catherine the Great strengthen Russia?

Vocabulary

westernization
boyar
warm-water port
partition

Taking Notes

As you read this section, make a Venn diagram to compare events in the reigns of Peter the Great and Catherine the Great. Use this diagram as a model, and add more information.

```
     PETER          CATHERINE
  • Visited    • Adopted   • Established
    western      western     port on the
    countries    ideas       Black Sea
```

Main Idea Czar Peter the Great and his successor, Catherine the Great, strengthened Russia and expanded Russian territory.

Setting the Scene

Along the Dutch waterfront, curious observers noticed that Peter Mikhailov was no ordinary man. For one thing, he stood almost seven feet tall. He had a booming laugh but also a furious temper. By day, he dressed in shabby clothes and worked as a shipyard carpenter. At night, he was entertained by royalty. For Peter Mikhailov was none other than Peter the Great, czar of Russia. His mission was to learn all he could about the more advanced nations of Western Europe.

In the early 1600s, Russia was still a medieval state, untouched by the Renaissance and Reformation and largely isolated from Western Europe. As you have read, the "Time of Troubles" had plunged the state into a period of disorder and foreign invasions. The reign of the first Romanov czar in 1613 restored a measure of order. Not until 1682, however, did a czar emerge who was strong enough to regain the absolute power of earlier czars. Peter the Great pushed Russia on the road to becoming a great modern power.

Peter the Great

Peter, just 10 years old when he came to the throne, did not take control of the government until 1689. Though he was not well educated, the young czar was immensely curious. He spent hours in the "German quarter," the Moscow suburb where many Dutch, Scottish, English, and other foreign artisans and soldiers lived. There, he heard of the advanced technology that was helping Western European monarchs forge powerful empires.

Journey to the West In 1697, Peter set out to study western technology for himself. He spent hours walking the streets of European cities, noting the manners and homes of the people. He visited factories and art galleries, learned anatomy from a doctor, and even had a dentist teach him how to pull teeth. In England, Peter was impressed by Parliament. "It is good," he said, "to hear subjects speaking truthfully and openly to their king."

Returning to Russia, Peter brought along a group of technical experts, teachers, and soldiers he had recruited in the West. He then embarked on a policy of westernization, that is, the adoption of western ideas, technology, and culture. But persuading fellow Russians to change their way of life proved difficult. To impose his will, Peter became the most autocratic of Europe's absolute monarchs.

Peter Westernizes Russia

As part of his program of westernization, Peter the Great ordered Russian nobles to shave their beards and dress in western style. Those who refused had to pay a special "beard tax."

Theme: Continuity and Change How is the noble in this cartoon reacting to Peter's beard policy?

Expansion of Russia, 1689–1796

▢ Russia, 1689	▢ Austria, 1796
▢ Land added by Peter the Great by 1725	▢ Prussia, 1796
▢ Land added by Catherine the Great by 1795	— Trade routes
▢ Land added by 1796	→ Bering's exploration route, 1725–1729

Azimuthal Equal Area Projection
0   500   1000 Miles
0   500   1000 Kilometers

Activity
Connections to Literature

Using Biographical Information Robert K. Massie traces the personal life and political career of Peter the Great in his biography *Peter the Great: His Life and World.* Ask students to read Chapter 59, "Commerce by Decree," in which Massie examines Peter's program to westernize and modernize the Russian economy. Students will learn how the czar's complex plan encountered resistance from Russian nobles and peasants reluctant to accept change. Furthermore, according to Massie, the monarch, although enthusiastic about building canals, factories, and efficient farms, lacked the consistent leadership needed to see the ideas through.

After students have read the chapter, ask them to answer the following questions: (1) What were the specific goals of Peter the Great's commerce plan? (2) What specific methods did he use to achieve his goals? (3) To what degree did he succeed or fail? (4) What were the reasons for his failures and successes? Have students present their findings in a written or an oral presentation.

Skills Assessment

Geography During the 1600s and 1700s, Russia expanded both eastward and westward to become the largest nation in the world.

1. **Location** On the map, locate (a) Sweden, (b) Baltic Sea, (c) St. Petersburg, (d) Black Sea, (e) Siberia, (f) Bering Sea.
2. **Place** Why were ports on the Black Sea more appealing to Russia than those on the Baltic?
3. **Critical Thinking Predicting Consequences** How might this map look different if Peter the Great had not modernized Russia?

Autocrat and Reformer At home, Peter pursued several related goals. He wanted to strengthen the military, expand Russian borders, and centralize royal power. To achieve his ends, he brought all Russian institutions under his control, including the Russian Orthodox Church. He forced the haughty boyars, or landowning nobles, to serve the state in civilian or military jobs.

Under Peter, serfdom spread in Russia, long after it had died out in Western Europe. By tying peasants to land given to nobles, he ensured that nobles could serve the state. Further, he forced some serfs to become soldiers or labor on roads, canals, and other government projects.

Using autocratic methods, Peter pushed through social and economic reforms. He imported western technology, improved education, simplified the Russian alphabet, and set up academies for the study of mathematics, science, and engineering. To pay for his sweeping reforms, Peter adopted mercantilist policies, such as encouraging exports. He improved the waterways and canals, developed mining and textile manufacturing, and backed new trading companies.

Some changes had a symbolic meaning. As you read, after returning from the West, Peter insisted that boyars shave their beards. He also forced them to replace their old-fashioned robes with Western European clothes. To end the practice of secluding upper-class women in separate quarters, he held grand parties at which women and men were expected to dance together. Russian nobles resisted this radical mixing of the sexes in public.

Peter had no mercy for any who resisted the new order. When elite palace guards revolted, he had over 1,000 of the rebels tortured and executed. As an example of his power, he left their rotting corpses outside the palace walls for months.

432 Chapter 17

Skills Assessment

ANSWERS 1. Review locations with students. 2. The warmer climate of the Black Sea would allow ships to come and go all year round. 3. Possible answer: Russia might not have conquered territories along the Baltic and Black seas if Peter had not modernized the army.

Expansion Under Peter

From his earliest days as czar, Peter worked to build Russian's military power. He created the largest standing army in Europe and set out to extend Russian borders to the west and south.

Search for a Warm-Water Port Russian seaports, located along the Arctic Ocean, were frozen over in the winter. To increase Russia's ability to trade with the West, Peter desperately wanted a warm-water port—one that would be free of ice all year round.

The nearest warm-water coast was located along the Black Sea. To gain control of this territory, Peter had to push through the powerful Ottoman empire. In the end, Peter was unable to defeat the Ottomans and gain his warm-water port. However, the later Russian monarch Catherine the Great would achieve that goal before the century ended.

War With Sweden In 1700, Peter began a long war against the kingdom of Sweden. At the time, Sweden dominated the Baltic region. Early on, Russia suffered humiliating defeats. A Swedish force of only 8,000 men defeated a Russian army five times its size. Undaunted, Peter rebuilt his army along western lines. In 1709, he defeated the Swedes and won land along the Baltic Sea.

Peter's City On land won from Sweden, Peter built a magnificent new capital city, St. Petersburg. Seeking to open a "window on the West," he located the city on the swampy shores of the Neva River near the Baltic coast. He forced tens of thousands of serfs to drain the swamps. Many thousands died, but Peter got his city. He then invited Italian architects and artisans to design great palaces in western style. Peter even planned the city's parks and boulevards himself.

Just as Versailles became a monument to French absolutism, St. Petersburg became the great symbol of Peter's desire to forge a modern Russia. A hundred years later, Russia's best-known poet, Alexander Pushkin, portrayed Peter as a larger-than-life ruler, determined to tame nature no matter what the cost:

> "Here we at Nature's own behest
> Shall break a window to the West,
> Stand planted on the ocean level;
> Here flags of foreign nations all
> By waters new to them will call
> And unencumbered we shall revel."
> —Alexander Pushkin, *The Bronze Horseman*

Toward the Pacific Russian traders and raiders also crossed the plains and rivers of Siberia, blazing trails to the Pacific. Under Peter, Russia signed a treaty with Qing China, defining their common border in the east. The treaty recognized Russia's right to lands north of Manchuria.

In the early 1700s, Peter hired the Danish navigator Vitus Bering to explore what became known as the Bering Strait between Siberia and Alaska. Russian pioneers crossed into Alaska and migrated as far south as California. Few Russians moved east of the Ural Mountains at this time, but on a map, Russia was already the largest country in the world, as it still is today.

Legacy of Peter the Great

When Peter died in 1725, he left behind a mixed legacy. He had expanded Russian territory, gained ports on the Baltic Sea, and created a mighty army. He had also ended Russia's long period of isolation. From the 1700s on, Russia would be increasingly involved in the affairs of Western Europe. Yet

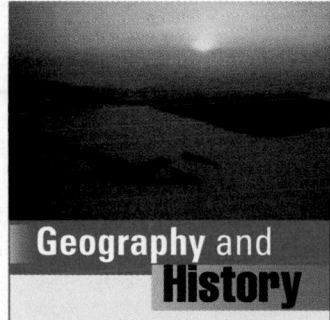

Geography and History

Being "Sent to Siberia"

Russia's absolute monarchs needed a place to exile both criminals and political opponents for long periods of time. What place was better than the arctic region of Siberia to the north? Siberia had an extremely inhospitable climate—temperatures could average −59°F in winter—and it was far away from everything Russian. There was little chance for escape, as it was almost impossible to survive the vast, frozen, sparsely populated region. In fact, approximately 10 to 15 percent of the exiles never made it to Siberia. They died along the way.

Exiles started with a trickle in the early 1600s, but by the early 1800s, the number grew to 2,000 a year. After a revolt in 1825, the czar sent 150,000 people off to their freezing fate. Today, the expression "sent to Siberia" still implies that a person is being punished or has become an outcast.

Theme: Geography and History Why was Siberia chosen as a place for exile?

Geography and History

ANSWER The inhospitable climate of Siberia and its distance from family and friends made banishment there a horrible punishment. Also, banishment to Siberia got criminals and political opponents safely away from the rest of Russian society.

Just and Necessary? The treaties that partitioned Poland always included a statement to show the justice and necessity of seizing Polish territory. Here is part of the introductory statement for the Partition Treaty of 1772:

"The spirit of faction, turmoils, and civil war that has been agitating the Kingdom of Poland for so many years, and the anarchy which every day gathers there new forces to the point of annihilating all the authority of a regular government. . . . [A]t the same time, the neighboring powers of the Republic have ancient and legitimate claims and rights which they have never been able to maintain and which they risk to lose forever, unless they take measures to assert them and reinstall tranquillity and order in the interior of this Republic."

You may wish to use this excerpt as the basis for a class discussion on the foreign policies of absolute monarchs.

The Wealth of Catherine the Great

Catherine the Great (pictured above) enjoyed the splendor of being an absolute monarch. The ornate horse-drawn carriage was a gift from one of the Russian nobles who had conspired in the murder of her husband.

Theme: Political and Social Systems Compare this picture to pictures of the French court at Versailles in this chapter. Why do you think great displays of wealth were important to absolute monarchs?

many of Peter's ambitious reforms died with him. Nobles, for example, soon ignored his policy of service to the state.

Like earlier czars, Peter the Great had brandished terror to enforce his absolute power. His policies contributed to the growth of serfdom, which served only to widen the gap between Russia and the West that Peter had sought to narrow.

Catherine the Great

Peter died without naming a successor, setting off power struggles among various Romanovs. Under a series of ineffective rulers, Russian nobles reasserted their independence. Then, a new monarch took the reins of power firmly in hand. She became known to history as Catherine the Great.

A German princess by birth, Catherine had come to Russia at the age of 15 to wed the heir to the Russian throne. She learned Russian, embraced the Russian Orthodox faith, and won the loyalty of the people. In 1762, her mentally unstable husband, Czar Peter III, was murdered by a group of Russian army officers. Whether or not Catherine was involved in the assassination plot, she certainly benefited from it. With the support of the military, she ascended the Russian throne herself.

An Efficient Ruler Catherine proved to be an efficient, energetic empress. She reorganized the provincial government, codified laws, and began state-sponsored education for boys and girls.

Like Peter the Great, she embraced western ideas. At court, she encouraged French language and customs, wrote histories and plays, and organized court performances. As you will read in the next chapter, she was also a serious student of the French thinkers who led the intellectual movement known as the Enlightenment.

A Ruthless Absolute Monarch Like other absolute monarchs, Catherine could be ruthless. She granted a charter to the boyars outlining important rights, such as exemption from taxes. At the same time, she allowed them to increase their stranglehold on the peasants. When peasants rebelled against the harsh burdens of serfdom, Catherine took firm action to repress them. As a result, conditions grew worse for Russian peasants. Under Catherine, even more peasants were forced into serfdom.

Like Peter the Great, Catherine was determined to expand Russia's borders. After a war against the Ottoman empire, she finally achieved Peter's dream of a warm-water port on the Black Sea. She also took steps to seize territory from neighboring Poland.

Partition of Poland As you have read, Poland had once been a great European power. However, Polish rulers were unable to centralize their power or diminish the influence of the Polish nobility. The divided Polish government was ill prepared to stand up to the increasing might of its neighbors Russia, Prussia, and Austria.

In the 1770s, Catherine the Great, Frederick the Great, and Emperor Joseph II of Austria hungrily eyed Poland. To avoid fighting one another, the three monarchs agreed to partition, or divide up, Poland. At the first partition, in 1772, Catherine took part of eastern Poland, where many Russians and Ukrainians lived. Frederick and Joseph nibbled at Polish territory from the west.

Poland was partitioned again in 1793 and a third time in 1795. By the time Austria, Prussia, and Russia had taken their final slices, the independent kingdom of Poland had vanished from the map. Not until 1919 would a free Polish state reappear.

Looking Ahead

By the mid-1700s, absolute monarchs ruled four of the five leading powers in Europe. Britain, with its strong Parliament, was the only exception. As these five nations competed with one another, they often ended up fighting to maintain the balance of power.

At the same time, new ideas were in the air. Radical changes would soon shatter the French monarchy, upset the balance of power, and revolutionize European societies. In the next unit, you will read about how the Enlightenment, the French Revolution, the rise of Napoleon Bonaparte, and the Industrial Revolution would transform Europe.

SECTION 5 Assessment

Recall
1. **Identify:** (a) Peter the Great, (b) St. Petersburg, (c) Vitus Bering, (d) Catherine the Great.
2. **Define:** (a) westernization, (b) boyar, (c) warm-water port, (d) partition.

Comprehension
3. (a) List three goals of Peter the Great. (b) Explain one reform that Peter undertook to achieve each goal.
4. Why did Peter seek to expand Russian territory?
5. Describe how two policies of Catherine the Great strengthened Russia.

Critical Thinking and Writing
6. **Comparing** Compare the goals and policies of Peter the Great to those of *one* of the following monarchs: (a) Louis XIV of France, (b) Frederick II of Prussia, (c) Maria Theresa of Austria.
7. **Drawing Conclusions** Peter the Great said of the English Parliament, "It is good to hear subjects speaking truthfully and openly to their king." Based on what you have read, do you think Peter followed this idea in his own kingdom? Give a reason to support your answer.

Activity
Take It to the NET

Use the Internet to learn about the city of St. Petersburg today. Then, write a commentary that Peter the Great might make on the city if he were to see it today. Tell how he would react to a statue such as *The Bronze Horseman* or to the Hermitage Museum.

Primary Source

An Empress Writes Her Epitaph
Catherine the Great wrote her own epitaph, or gravestone inscription. Her words show how she wished to be remembered:

"When she had ascended the throne of Russia, she wished to do good and tried to bring happiness, freedom, and prosperity to her subjects.
She forgave easily and hated no one.
She was good-natured and easygoing; she had a cheerful temperament, republican sentiments, and a kind heart.
She had friends.
Work was easy for her; she loved sociability and the arts."
—Catherine the Great, *Memoirs*

Skills Assessment

Primary Source What image of herself was Catherine trying to create? Do you think this image was accurate?

Human Drama Note

Taxes and Census Peter the Great faced the same problem many other autocrats faced, namely, how to raise money to support his projects and his wars. With his usual ingenuity, he found several ways to do that. One was by levying taxes on everything from coffins to beehives. Another was to replace the old household tax with a so-called soul tax. In the past, peasants and serfs had gotten around the household tax by gathering large numbers of people in one home. To find all the males in the land— each of whom would be eligible for the soul tax— Peter sent out soldiers to scour the land, beginning in 1718. After six years of brutal searching, more than five million persons were registered.

SECTION 5 Assessment

Recall
1. (a) Peter the Great, p. 431 (b) St. Petersburg, p. 433 (c) Vitus Bering, p. 433 (d) Catherine the Great, p. 434 2. (a) westernization, p. 431 (b) boyar, p. 432 (c) warm-water port, p. 433 (d) partition, p. 435

Comprehension
3. (a) modernize Russia, centralize royal power, build Russian military power (b) imported western technology, brought the Russian Orthodox Church under his control, created the largest standing army in Europe 4. He wanted to increase Russia's power and wealth. He especially wanted to increase trade by acquiring warm-water ports. 5. She expanded Russian territory to include a warm-water port on the Black Sea and, through a partition agreement with Prussia and Austria, gained control of part of Poland.

Critical Thinking and Writing
6. Students should recognize that absolute monarchs often pursued similar policies and goals, but differed because of various personal qualities, national needs, and changing circumstances.
7. Students most likely will say that Peter did not follow this concept because he showed no mercy for those who resisted his orders.

Activity Rubrics

Share rubrics with students before they complete their commentary.

Attempted The commentary is sketchy, shows limited research, or has many errors.

Minimal The commentary reflects St. Petersburg today but not from Peter's perspective or has some errors.

Adequate The commentary has plentiful information on St. Petersburg today and reflects Peter's ideas.

Exemplary The commentary shows a deep understanding of Peter's ideas and how he might view the city today.

Primary Source

ANSWER She tried to create an image of a benevolent ruler who was well-liked by her subjects. It was not totally accurate, since she allowed the boyars to increase their stranglehold on the peasants.

Creating a Chapter Summary

As a reteaching opportunity, pair a more able student with a less able student to complete this chapter summary.

Spain Philip II; absolute ruler; defeats Ottomans in 1571; Catholic; wealthy nation; inflation, costly wars, and other problems led to economic decline in the 1600s

France Louis XIV, absolute ruler, "Sun King"; violent warfare between Catholics and Huguenots; Protestant, Catholic; wealthy nation; religious persecution undermined French power

England Tudor and Stuart monarchies, Cromwell and the Commonwealth; Civil War, Glorious Revolution; Protestant, Puritan, Catholic; good economy; execution of King Charles I

Austria/Prussia Ferdinand, Charles VI, Maria Theresa, Frederick William, Frederick the Great; Thirty Years' War, Seven Years' War; Protestant, Catholic; war-torn countries; Germany is divided, Prussia grows strong

Russia Absolute monarchies of Peter the Great and Catherine the Great; war with Sweden, war against Ottoman empire; Russian Orthodox; serfdom, mercantilist policies, westernization of Russia; St. Petersburg built

Building Vocabulary

1–10. Students' crossword puzzle clues should show an understanding of each word.

Recalling Key Facts

11. The Spanish Armada was a fleet sent by Spain in 1588 to invade England. It was defeated by the English and by weather.
12. It meant that under Louis XIV, the French monarchy had complete control over the government.
13. King Charles I was overthrown and executed; the monarchy was abolished; Oliver Cromwell took power.
14. Parliament forced William and Mary, before they were crowned, to accept the English Bill of Rights, which ensured Parliament's supremacy over the monarchy.
15. imported technology, improved education, simplified the alphabet, set up academies, improved waterways and canals, developed mining and textiles, backed new trading companies
16. Poland was divided in the late 1700s among Austria, Prussia, and Russia.

CHAPTER **17** Review and Assessment

Creating a Chapter Summary

On a sheet of paper make a table to compare the nations of Europe during the Age of Absolutism. Use the table shown here as a guide to get started.

	SPAIN	FRANCE	ENGLAND	AUSTRIA/ PRUSSIA	RUSSIA
GOVERNMENT	Philip II; absolute ruler				
WARS	Defeats Ottomans in 1571				
RELIGION	Catholic				
ECONOMY					
OTHER					

For additional review and enrichment activities, see the interactive version of *World History* available on the Web and on CD-ROM.

Web Site Self-Test
For practice test questions for Chapter 17, see **www.phschool.com.**

Building Vocabulary

Use the chapter vocabulary words listed below to create a crossword puzzle. Exchange puzzles with a classmate. Complete the puzzles and then check each other's answers.

1. **absolute monarch**
2. **divine right**
3. **balance of power**
4. **habeas corpus**
5. **limited monarchy**
6. **mercenary**
7. **depopulation**
8. **westernization**
9. **boyar**
10. **partition**

Recalling Key Facts

11. What was the Spanish Armada?
12. Explain what the statement "I am the state" meant.
13. Describe the results of the English Civil War.
14. How did the Glorious Revolution limit royal power in England?
15. What reforms did Peter the Great carry out?
16. How and when did the kingdom of Poland lose its independence?

Critical Thinking and Writing

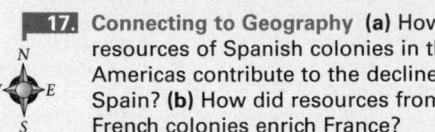

17. **Connecting to Geography** **(a)** How did resources of Spanish colonies in the Americas contribute to the decline of Spain? **(b)** How did resources from French colonies enrich France?

18. **Analyzing Primary Sources** Bishop Bossuet, a court preacher under Louis XIV, wrote, "Let God take away his hand and the world will fall back into nothingness; let authority fail in the kingdom, and total confusion will result." **(a)** According to Bossuet, what is the benefit of absolute monarchy? **(b)** What assumption does he make about the source of royal power? **(c)** How might the history of France in the late 1500s have influenced Bossuet's viewpoint?

19. **Recognizing Causes and Effects** **(a)** What were the immediate causes of the English Civil War? **(b)** What were some of the long-term causes?

20. **Recognizing Points of View** How might each of the following have viewed Peter the Great: **(a)** a boyar, **(b)** a serf, **(c)** Catherine the Great?

Critical Thinking and Writing

17. **(a)** Treasure from the Americas led the Spanish to neglect farming and commerce; it also led to soaring inflation. **(b)** The French regulated trade with the colonies and put high tariffs on imported goods.
18. **(a)** Absolute monarchy ensured order and security. **(b)** He assumes that royal power comes from God. **(c)** Possible answer: France's wars of religion might have made Bossuet fearful of political and social disorder.
19. Possible answers: **(a)** Parliament declared that it could not be dissolved, and it executed the king's chief ministers. Charles I led troops into the House of Commons to arrest its most radical leaders. **(b)** Long-term causes include England's long tradition of limiting the power of monarchs, the Protestant Reformation, and the Stuarts' desire to impose absolute power.

Skills Assessment
Analyzing Primary Sources

This passage is from a letter written to Louis XIV by a tutor to the king's children. Read the excerpt, then answer the questions that follow.

"For nearly thirty years, your principal Ministers have destroyed and reversed all the ancient customs of the state in order to raise your authority to its highest pitch. They no longer speak of the state and its constitution; they only speak of the King and his royal pleasure. They have pushed your revenues and your expenses to unprecedented heights. They have raised you up to the sky in order, they say, to out-shine the grandeur of all your predecessors; that is to say, in order to impoverish the whole of France for the introduction of monstrous luxuries of court. . . .

Meanwhile, your people die of hunger. The cultivation of the soil is almost stag-nant, and no longer offers employment to working men. All commerce is destroyed."

—Archbishop François de Fénelon, *Letters*

21. **(a)** What did Fénelon criticize about the rule of Louis XIV? **(b)** Whom did he blame besides the king?
22. Fénelon wrote the letter anonymously, that is, unsigned. Why do you think he sent it this way?
23. What reforms do you think Fénelon would have welcomed?
24. Do you think the letter is a reliable source of information about the reign of Louis XIV? Why or why not?
25. How do you think the king might have respond-ed to the charges made in the letter? Explain.

Skills Assessment
Take It to the NET

Use the Internet to research one of the absolute monarchs described in the text. Then, write a brief biography of the monarch. Focus on the charac-teristics that made this person an example of absolutism, and on how this ruler affected the country he or she ruled. Be sure to list the sources you used in writing your biography.

Skills Assessment
Analyzing Maps

The maps below, which show Poland in three different years, make it possible to see how the area changed over time. Study the maps, then answer the questions that follow.

Partitions of Poland 1701–1795

26. What country was divided into two separate territories by Poland in 1701?
27. **(a)** How did the size of Poland's territory change from 1701 to 1772? **(b)** What was the status of Warsaw in 1795?
28. **(a)** What had happened to Poland by 1795? **(b)** What three countries divided the Polish territory?
29. In addition to the partition of Poland, what other territorial change can you see on these maps?
30. What do you think happened to the Polish people after the final partition?

Skills Tip

When you compare maps of a place over time, first make sure that you are looking at the same area on each map. Then, note any changes.

20. Possible answers: **(a)** A boyar might have resented forced service to the state. **(b)** A serf might have regretted that serfdom had spread under Peter's reign. **(c)** Catherine might have viewed Peter's reign as a model.

Analyzing Primary Sources

21. **(a)** He criticized the royal expendi-tures on grandeur and the lack of food and employment for the people. **(b)** the ministers
22. Possible answer: He did not wish to incur the king's wrath and to lose his position as tutor.
23. Possible answer: less expenditures on royal pleasure and more money spent to help the French people
24. Most students will probably say *yes* because Fénelon was close to the court and in a good position to observe what went on.
25. Students might say that Louis would be angry at being criticized because he was an absolute monarch; he did not seek this advice from Fénelon.

Analyzing Maps

26. Prussia
27. **(a)** It became smaller. **(b)** It was in Prussia.
28. **(a)** It ceased to exist. **(b)** Prussia, Austria, and Russia
29. Between 1701 and 1772, Prussia gained some land from Austria.
30. Possible answer: They probably became second-class citizens, and may have been persecuted.

Skills Tip

To help you locate political areas at various times, you can use natural features such as rivers or mountains. The Skills Handbook in the front of the book has a lesson that will help students with this feature.

Unit Theme Activity

Evaluate students' Unit Theme Activity by referring to the rubrics for the activity on the unit opener page in the Teacher's Edition.

Take It to the NET

Direct students to **www.phschool.com** for links to sites that will help them get started on this assignment. Share rubrics with students.
Attempted The biography fails to include the required elements, is poorly written and organ-ized, contains many mechanical errors, and fails to list sources.
Minimal The biography includes the required elements and lists sources but is poorly written and organized and contains some mechanical errors.
Adequate The biography includes the required elements, lists sources, is well written and organized, and contains few mechanical errors.
Exemplary The biography includes the required elements, lists sources, is very well written and organized, and contains no mechanical errors.

USING THESE PAGES

The Unit-in-Brief contains the main ideas of the unit chapters. You may use the Unit-in-Brief to preview, review, or condense the contents of each chapter.

The unit time line identifies key events in each world region that took place during the time span covered by the unit.

Activity
Unit Themes

Have students review the unit themes below. Then, ask them to find examples in the time line and summary to support each theme.

Economics and Technology A scientific revolution enabled explorers to travel the world in search of trade and riches. Dramatic economic developments, such as the rise of capitalism, affected all social classes.

Global Interaction Exploration by powerful nations led to increased competition for trade. The spread of cultural beliefs and the exchange of material goods often were accomplished by conquest and by destruction of native cultures.

Political and Social Systems Absolute monarchs forged modern nation-states with strong central governments. The struggle between monarchs and Parliament in England was an important step in the development of modern democracy.

Religions and Value Systems Classical and Christian humanist ideals shaped the Renaissance. While the Protestant Reformation shattered the religious unity of Europe, Christianity continued to spread to new lands.

Chapter 14

The Renaissance and Reformation (1300–1650)

Between the 1300s and 1500s, Europe experienced a period of cultural rebirth known as the Renaissance. During the same period, the Protestant Reformation and the Scientific Revolution reshaped European civilization.

- Beginning in Italy and later spreading to northern Europe, the Renaissance reached its most glorious expression in painting, sculpture, and architecture.
- The intellectual movement known as humanism stressed the study of classical Greek and Roman cultures and the development of the individual.
- Reformers like Martin Luther and John Calvin challenged church corruption and eventually broke away from the Roman Catholic Church entirely.
- In response to the Protestant Reformation, the Catholic Church undertook its own vigorous reform movement.
- Religious fervor led to widespread intolerance and persecution by both Protestants and Catholics.
- During the Scientific Revolution, startling discoveries by individuals such as Copernicus, Newton, and Galileo changed the way Europeans viewed the physical world.

Chapter 15

The First Global Age: Europe and Asia (1415–1796)

Beginning in the 1500s, European powers gradually built trading empires in Asia. Thus began a period of increasing global interdependence that has continued to the present day.

- Improvements in technology helped European explorers navigate the vast oceans of the world.
- In his search for a sea route to Asia, Christopher Columbus came upon the Americas, two continents previously unknown to Europeans.
- Although they were strongly influenced by China and India, the nations of Southeast Asia retained their own unique cultural identities.
- The desire for spices led Europeans to seek control of the Indian Ocean trade network.
- By the late 1500s, the Dutch replaced the Portuguese as the major European power in Asia. In the 1700s, England and France vied for dominance.
- During the 1500s and 1600s, China and Korea restricted contact with the outside world.
- The Japanese initially welcomed western traders, but they later adopted a similar policy of isolation.

	1300	1400	1500
AFRICA	**1300s** Kingdom of Benin flourishes		**1460s** Sonni Ali founds Songhai
THE AMERICAS		**1400s** Aztec and Incan empires expand	**1492** Columbus reaches the Caribbean
ASIA AND OCEANIA		**1405–1433** Voyages of Zheng He	**1510** Portuguese seize Goa
EUROPE	**Mid–1300s** Renaissance begins in Italy	**1456** Gutenberg Bible printed	**1517** 95 Theses

Student Bibliography

Miller, John. *Bourbon and Stuart: Kings and Kingship in France and England in the 17th Century.* Watts, 1987. Examination of monarchies and governments of England and France in the 1600s.

Morison, Samuel Eliot. *Admiral of the Ocean Sea: A Life of Christopher Columbus.* Fine Communications, 1997. New paperback edition of the Pulitzer Prize-winning biography.

Nash, Gary B. *Red, White, and Black: The Peoples of Early North America.* Prentice Hall, 1992. General overview of colonial history, including interactions of Native Americans, Africans, and Europeans.

Parry, J.H. *The Age of Reconnaissance.* University of California Press, 1981. Detailed study of European exploration, trade, and settlement outside Europe from the 1400s through the 1600s.

Thomas, Hugh. *Conquest: Montezuma, Cortés, and the Fall of Old Mexico.* Touchstone Books, 1995. Richly detailed history.

Chapter 16

The First Global Age: Europe, the Americas, and Africa (1492–1750)

During the age of exploration, European powers built colonial empires in the Americas. New patterns of conquest and global exchange had an enormous impact on the civilization of Africa as well.

- Spanish conquistadors vanquished the Aztec and Incan civilizations and set up a vast empire in the Americas.
- By the 1600s, Spain, France, England, and the Netherlands were competing for trade and colonies.
- The arrival of European settlers in the Americas brought disaster to Native Americans.
- Beginning in the 1400s, Europeans began establishing trading outposts in Africa.
- Millions of slaves were imported from Africa to meet labor needs in American colonies. The slave trade led to the fall of some African states and the rise of others.
- The Columbian Exchange was a vast global interchange of people, animals, culture, ideas, and technology.
- Beginning in the 1500s, Europe experienced a commercial revolution that brought about dramatic economic changes, including the rise of capitalism.

Chapter 17

The Age of Absolutism (1550–1800)

During the 1500s and 1600s, European monarchs struggled to centralize their power. As they vied for the lead in overseas empires, the center of world civilization shifted to Europe.

- During the 1500s, wealth from the Americas helped make Spain the most powerful nation in Europe.
- Following a period of religious and social turmoil, Louis XIV achieved royal absolutism and helped France become the most powerful nation in Europe during the 1600s.
- Despite efforts at absolutism by several English monarchs, Parliament successfully asserted itself against royal power.
- The Thirty Years' War involved most of Europe. After the Peace of Westphalia, Prussia emerged as a new Protestant power.
- The Hapsburgs expanded Austrian territory but were unable to develop a strong centralized system.
- Peter the Great of Russia centralized royal power, embarked on a program of modernization, and sought to expand Russian territory from Europe to the Pacific.

Activity
Summarizing the Main Idea

Have students use both the Unit-in-Brief and Chapters 14–17 to answer the following questions in order to summarize Unit 4: (1) Define each of the following terms: Renaissance, Reformation, Scientific Revolution. (2) Why did Europeans desire closer contacts with the lands of East and Southeast Asia? (3) What effects did European power and imperialism have on civilizations in Africa and the Americas? (4) Describe examples of the cultural diffusion that took place during the first global age. (5) What were some of the policies typically favored by Europe's absolute monarchs?

PRENTICE HALL
ASSESSMENT *SYSTEM*

Diagnose and Prescribe
- Profile student skills with Diagnostic Tests A & B.
- Address student needs with program materials identified in the test.

Review and Reteach
- Provide cumulative content review with the Review Book.

Practice and Assess
- Build test-taking skills with Test-Taking Strategies With Transparencies.

Timeline

1500s Zulus migrate into southern Africa

1500s Atlantic slave trade grows

1556 Akbar begins reign in India

1558 Elizabeth begins reign

1600 (marker)

1607 British found Jamestown

1608 French build Quebec

1600 Tokugawas gain power in Japan

1643 Age of Louis XIV begins

1644 Manchus found Qing dynasty

1652 Dutch build Cape Town

Late 1600s Asante kingdom established

1687 Newton explains theory of gravity

1700 (marker)

1736 Qianlong becomes emperor of China

1754 French and Indian War begins

1700s Peter the Great modernizes Russia

1800 (marker)

Teacher Bibliography

Black, Jeremy. *The Rise of the European Powers, 1679–1793.* Arnold, 1990. A survey focusing on the forces that shaped diplomacy and international relations during the era.

Caponetto, Salvatore, with Anne C. and John Tedeschi, translators. *The Protestant Reformation in Sixteenth-Century Italy.* Truman State University Press, 1998. A study of the overall movement of reform in Italy.

Curtin, Philip D., ed. *Africa Remembered: Narratives by West Africans from the Era of the Slave Trade.* Waveland Press, 1997. A non-European viewpoint of the African slave trade.

Kinsbruner, Jay. *Independence in Spanish America: Civil Wars, Revolutions, and Underdevelopment.* University of New Mexico Press, 1994. Insightful interpretation of this pivotal era in world history.

Miller, John, ed. *Absolutism in Seventeenth Century Europe.* St. Martin's, 1990. A survey of absolute monarchies in principal states by various historians.

Reid, Anthony. *Southeast Asia in the Age of Commerce, 1460–1680.* Yale University Press, 1988–1993. An overview of the region based mainly on European travelers' accounts and records.

UNIT OVERVIEW

Unit 5 studies the revolutionary ideas of the Enlightenment, the violent revolutions that brought political and social change to Europe and the Americas, and the start of the Industrial Revolution.

Chapter 18 focuses on Enlightenment philosophy, constitutional government in Britain, and the American Revolution.

Chapter 19 examines the French Revolution and the rise and fall of Napoleon Bonaparte.

Chapter 20 profiles the many changes brought by the early Industrial Revolution.

Chapter 21 highlights the many revolutions that swept Europe and the Americas from the 1790s through the 1840s.

Unit Theme Activity Rubrics

Share rubrics with students before they create their projects.

Attempted The project does not show the impact of the development of factories.

Minimal The project is poorly executed or only vaguely shows the impact of the development of factories.

Adequate The project is well executed and clearly shows the impact of the development of factories.

Exemplary The project is extremely well executed, ably shows the impact of the development of factories, and is visually interesting or is extremely interesting and informative to read.

UNIT 5

Enlightenment and Revolution

1707–1850

OUTLINE

Chapter 18 **The Enlightenment and the American Revolution** (1707–1800)

Chapter 19 **The French Revolution and Napoleon** (1789–1815)

Chapter 20 **The Industrial Revolution Begins** (1750–1850)

Chapter 21 **Revolutions in Europe and Latin America** (1790–1848)

Themes

As you read about the revolutionary ideas that brought dramatic changes to western society and government, you will encounter the following themes.

Continuity and Change Enlightenment ideas about society and government stood in sharp contrast to the prevailing standards. Since the 1700s, Enlightenment ideas have spread around the world.

Economics and Technology During the 1700s, advances in farming, transportation, and manufacturing contributed to the Industrial Revolution. Production of goods shifted from the home to the factory. Laissez-faire economists, utilitarians, and socialists offered plans to deal with the consequences of this change.

Impact of the Individual Thinkers such as John Locke, Voltaire, and Jean-Jacques Rousseau and political leaders such as Napoleon Bonaparte and Simón Bolívar encouraged national pride and human rights.

Political and Social Systems Revolutionaries, inspired by the Enlightenment, urged radical changes in government. Early industrialization created a new working class, while merchants and skilled artisans formed a growing new middle class.

Unit Theme Activity

For Your Portfolio The chapters in this unit describe the revolutionary changes in governments and economies that occurred in the 1700s. As you read the chapters, prepare a portfolio project showing the impact of development of factories. Your project might take one of the following forms:
• **Diary**
• **Report**
• **Illustration**

Resource Directory

Technology
World History Visions, Voices, Views Scenes of an Age, *Enlightenment and Revolution,* videodisc side 3 or videotape 5, running time 2:30 min.

Side 3: Fr. 228-4225

These monuments at the Plaza General San Martín in Buenos Aires, Argentina, display pride in national revolutionary heroes. Most nations in Latin America had won their independence by 1825.

Background
About the Picture

José de San Martín Buenos Aires's Plaza General San Martín is named after the South American liberator José de San Martín. Although San Martín was born in Argentina, his parents were Spanish. When San Martín was young, his family returned to Spain, where he soon joined the military. Early in his career, he advanced fairly easily although—as a Creole—he was never fully accepted. Then, in 1811, he resigned his post and left for Buenos Aires, where he would soon fight for the liberation of his native land.

Under his command, Argentina gained its independence. But San Martín did not cease at the liberation of his homeland. After victory in Argentina, he led a daring maneuver through the Andes Mountains, a move that has invoked comparisons to Hannibal and Napoleon. This successful maneuver led to the liberation of Chile. Rejecting the governorship of Chile, he pushed on toward his ultimate goal, the liberation of Lima, Peru, which he accomplished on July 28, 1821.

About a year later, San Martín met with the other great liberator of South America, Simón Bolívar. Due to political differences with Bolívar, San Martín left the continent. He had clearly had an impact on South America's history, however.

TEXT

Don't miss the exclusive interactive version of *World History: Connections to Today* on the Internet and CD-ROM.

Be sure to check out this month's online discussion with a World History Master Teacher.

Go to **www.phschool.com**.

Block Scheduling Support

Using the Unit-in-Brief The Unit-in-Brief, found at the end of the unit, contains the main ideas of the unit chapters. You may use the Unit-in-Brief to preview, review, or condense the contents of each chapter.

Using the Unit Time Line The Unit Time Line, at the end of the unit, provides a chronology of world events during the period covered by this unit. By studying the time line in conjunction with the Unit-in-Brief, students may compare developments in various regions. You may use the time line to help condense the contents of the chapters.

Using the *Guide to the Essentials* The *Guide to the Essentials of World History* contains summaries and graphic organizers for each section of every chapter in this unit. You may use the *Guide to the Essentials* to help poor readers or students acquiring English access the main ideas of the chapters. You may also use it with all students to review or to condense topics in your world history course.

Bell Ringer After students have read the text and studied the pictures on these two pages, ask them to give examples of the freedoms they enjoy today. If students have difficulty giving examples, prompt them with such ideas as choosing which radio program to listen to or what television show to watch.

Activity
Cooperative Learning

A Living Bill of Rights Organize the students into small groups and assign each group one of the Constitution's first eight amendments. (The First Amendment could be subdivided into the four freedoms of religion, speech, the press, and assembly. You may wish to skip the Third Amendment, which prohibits the quartering of troops in homes.) Ask the groups to prepare presentations, either written or oral, giving examples of how their assigned amendment applies to life today.

Democracy is hard work. Sure, you enjoy many rights and freedoms. You can speak out against the government if you think it's doing something wrong. You can own property, call a public meeting, practice your religion, travel wherever you wish. The list goes on. But you also have responsibilities. Being a good citizen requires you to obey the laws of the nation, to vote, to practice tolerance. For centuries, people struggled and died to achieve democracy. It is up to you to maintain and protect the unique system they won.

Americans Proclaim the Principles of Democracy

In July 1776, American colonists issued the Declaration of Independence. Besides proclaiming American independence from Great Britain, this document set out the basic principles of democracy—that "all men are created equal," with the right to "life, liberty, and the pursuit of happiness." Governments, it went on, can exist only if they have the "consent of the governed." If the government is unjust, then people have the right to "alter or abolish it." These twin ideals of democratic self-government and individual liberty remain the foundation of our nation today.

Signing of the Declaration of Independence

Democratic Stirrings in France

Stirrings of democracy helped inspire the French Revolution of 1789. People from all levels of French society, such as the Parisian women shown here, fought to overthrow the absolute monarchy that had ruled the nation for centuries. Inspired by the American Declaration of Independence, a new French national assembly adopted the Declaration of the Rights of Man and the Citizen. In it, they asserted the equality of all men, the sovereignty of the people, and the inalienable rights of the individual to liberty, property, and security.

442 Unit 5

Resource Directory

Teaching Resources

Why Study History? *Because the Spread of Democracy Requires Informed Citizens,* Why Study History? booklet, pp. 13–14

Fighting for Freedom in Latin America

The new democratic ideas soon reached Spain's colonies in Latin America. Most colonists had no say in government, and discontent was widespread. Spurred by the revolutions in France and North America, colonists embarked on a series of wars of independence that continued until they had thrown off European rule. Simón Bolívar, the principal leader in the battle for freedom, is shown here.

Spread of Democracy in the Twentieth Century

The quest for democratic self-government continued in the twentieth century. Here, Indonesians in 1999 vote in their first free elections in over 40 years.

What You Can Do: Stay Informed

Our democratic way of life is not guaranteed. We must work to maintain it. And the first step is to keep informed. Two hundred years ago, when our nation was founded, news spread slowly. Today, however, we have a continuous stream of information—radio, TV, newspapers, the Internet. Here, a man reads a newspaper to find out about the events of the day.

Portfolio Assessment

Connecting to Today List three specific ways in which you keep informed about current affairs. Create a poster encouraging others to keep informed in the same or similar ways.

Unit 5 **443**

Background
Connections to Today

Being Informed Point out to students that it is easier to stay informed in modern times than ever before. Internet sites give voters the opportunity to access news reports from across the country—and around the world. At other sites, voters can read the speeches of candidates to hear their views on different issues. They can also visit the sites of different citizens groups to see outsiders' views of candidates' stands.

Background
About the Pictures

1. The Signing of the Declaration of Independence *(opposite page, top)*. This 1786 oil painting by John Trumbull shows John Hancock, sitting at the right; before him stand, left to right, John Adams, Roger Sherman, Robert R. Livingston, Thomas Jefferson, and Benjamin Franklin, the five members of the committee charged with drafting the Declaration of Independence.
2. The French Revolution *(opposite page, bottom)*, which lasted from 1789 to 1799, introduced democratic ideals to France but did not make the nation a democracy.
3. Simón Bolívar *(top left)*, often called the "George Washington of South America," won independence from Spain for Bolivia, Colombia, Ecuador, Peru, and Venezuela.
4. Man with newspaper *(middle right)*. From the invention of the printing press in the fifteenth century to today, newspapers have been important sources of information.
5. Voters chose from 48 political parties in Indonesia's 1999 election *(bottom left)*.

Portfolio Assessment Rubrics

Share rubrics with students before they create their posters.

Attempted The poster is incomplete.

Minimal The poster is complete but is poorly organized and presented and has little visual appeal.

Adequate The poster is complete, well organized, and well presented with considerable visual appeal.

Exemplary The poster is complete and very well done, with great visual impact.

Chapter 18 Planning Guide

Resource Manager

	CORE INSTRUCTION	READING/SKILLS
Chapter Level Resources	**Teaching Resources** ■ Pacing Charts, Ch. 18 ■ Teaching With Themes, p. 21 ▥ Color Transparencies, p. F–37 ◉ Resource Pro® Ch. 18 ▣ www.phschool.com 　• eTeach	◉ Book on CD, Ch. 18 ◉ Interactive Student Tutorial CD-ROM, Ch. 18 ◉ Social Studies Skills Tutor CD-ROM ▥ Skills Transparencies
1 Philosophy in the Age of Reason 　1. Describe how scientific progress promoted trust in human reason. 　2. Explain how the social contract and separation of powers affected views on government. 　3. Outline how new ideas affected society and the economy.	**Teaching Resources** ▨ Unit 5 booklet 　• Biography Activity, p. 10 　• Viewpoint Activity, p. 12 ◉ Prentice Hall Presentation Pro, Ch. 18, Section 1 ▥ Section Reading Support Transparencies	**Teaching Resources** ▨ Unit 5 booklet 　• Guided Reading and Review, p. 2 ▧ Guide to the Essentials ▦ Guided Reading Audiotapes, Ch. 18, Section 1
2 Enlightenment Ideas Spread 　1. Point out the roles censorship and salons played in the spread of new ideas. 　2. Identify how *philosophes* influenced Enlightenment despots. 　3. Summarize how the Enlightenment affected the arts and literature. 　4. Explain why the lives of the majority were unaffected by the Enlightenment.	**Teaching Resources** ▨ Unit 5 booklet 　• Primary Source Activity, p. 11 ▧ Creative Teaching Activities, p. 52 ◉ Prentice Hall Presentation Pro, Ch. 18, Section 2 ▥ Section Reading Support Transparencies	**Teaching Resources** ▨ Unit 5 booklet 　• Guided Reading and Review, p. 4 ▧ Guide to the Essentials ▦ Guided Reading Audiotapes, Ch. 18, Section 2
3 Britain at Mid-Century 　1. Identify the influences that spurred Britain's rise to global power. 　2. Relate how the growth of constitutional government reflected conditions in politics and society. 　3. Explain how George III reasserted royal power.	**Teaching Resources** ▧ Creative Teaching Activities, p. 84 ◉ Prentice Hall Presentation Pro, Ch. 18, Section 3 ▥ Section Reading Support Transparencies	**Teaching Resources** ▨ Unit 5 booklet 　• Guided Reading and Review, p. 6 ▧ Guide to the Essentials ▦ Guided Reading Audiotapes, Ch. 18, Section 3
4 Birth of the American Republic 　1. Identify the chief characteristics of the 13 colonies. 　2. Describe how growing discontent led to the American Revolution. 　3. Summarize how the new Constitution reflected the ideas of the Enlightenment.	**Teaching Resources** ▧ Creative Teaching Activities, p. 85 ◉ Prentice Hall Presentation Pro, Ch. 18, Section 4 ▥ Section Reading Support Transparencies	**Teaching Resources** ▨ Unit 5 booklet 　• Guided Reading and Review, p. 8 　• Skill Application Activity, p. 13 ▧ Guide to the Essentials

ENRICHMENT/PRE-AP

🖥 **www.phschool.com**
- Why Study History?

📖 Teaching Resources
📕 **Chapter Extension Activities,** pp. 39–40
📕 **History Through Literature,** pp. 39–40
📼 **Visions, Voices, Views,** Global Issues Forum, tape 5

📖 Teaching Resources
📕 **Chapter Extension Activities,** p. 47
📕 **History Through Literature,** pp. 39–40
📼 **Listening to Literature World Masterpieces,** *Fugue in G Minor,* side 6
🖥 **www.phschool.com**
- Virtual Field Trip
- Internet Activities, Section 2

🖥 **www.phschool.com**
- Internet Activities, Section 4

ASSESSMENT

PRENTICE HALL
ASSESSMENT *SYSTEM*

Core Assessment
📘 **ExamView Test Bank booklet,** Ch. 18
💿 **ExamView Test Bank CD-ROM,** Ch. 18

Standardized Test Preparation
Diagnose and Prescribe
📗 **Diagnostic Tests for High School Social Studies Skills**
Review and Reteach
📗 **Review Book for World History**
Practice and Assess
📗 **Test-Taking Strategies With Transparencies for High School**
📗 **Alternative Assessment booklet**
📗 **Test Prep Book for World History**

📖 Teaching Resources
📁 **Unit 5 booklet**
- Geography Quiz, p. 14
- Section Quizzes, pp. 3, 5, 7, 9
- Chapter Tests A, B, and C, pp. 15–19
🖥 **www.phschool.com**
- Self-Test

CUSTOMIZE FOR INDIVIDUAL NEEDS

Gifted and Talented
- **Teacher's Edition,** Activities: Customize for Heterogeneous Groups, p. 449; Connections to Literature, p. 457

Less Proficient Readers
- **Guide to the Essentials,** Ch. 18
- **Guided Reading Audiotapes, English,** Ch. 18
- **Book on CD,** Ch. 18
- **Teacher's Edition,** Activities: Reading Strategy, p. 452

Less Proficient Writers
- **Teacher's Edition,** Activities: Cooperative Learning Activity, p. 449

Students Acquiring English/ESL
- **Guide to the Essentials, English/Spanish,** Ch. 18
- **Guided Reading Audiotapes, English/Spanish,** Ch. 18
- **Book on CD,** Ch. 18
- **Teacher's Edition,** Activities marked with an *

i TEXT

Don't miss the exclusive interactive version of *World History: Connections to Today* on the Internet and CD-ROM.

INTRODUCTION

New advances in science led to the application of reason as a means of governing human nature. Enlightenment ideas spread, challenging the old order and creating new forms of art and literature. Britain wrestled with changes, meanwhile becoming a dominant global power. On the American continent, Enlightenment ideas gave birth to a new nation.

Focusing on Themes

Suggest that students focus on these theme questions as they read:

Religions and Value Systems
How did the Enlightenment challenge the traditional order in Europe?

Economics and Technology
How did the ideas of the physiocrats clash with mercantilist policy?

Continuity and Change
Why did Enlightenment ideas at first affect only the upper levels of European society?

Political and Social Systems
How did constitutional government evolve in Britain and the United States?

◆ TIME LINE ACTIVITY

You may wish to share the About the Pictures note with your students before you ask questions about the time line such as the following:

1. When did the Act of Union take place, and what two countries did it unite? *(The Act of Union took place in 1707, uniting England and Scotland.)*
2. Why do you think revolutionary ideas in Europe could affect changes in North America? *(Answers should include the idea of global interaction.)*
3. When did the Parisians storm the Bastille? *(in 1789)*

Don't Miss!

Comparing Viewpoints
What Limits Should There Be on Freedom of Speech? (Section 1)

Humanities Link
The Great Mozart (Section 2)

The Enlightenment and the American Revolution
1707–1800

Chapter Preview

1 **Philosophy in the Age of Reason**
2 **Enlightenment Ideas Spread**
3 **Britain at Mid-Century**
4 **Birth of the American Republic**

1707
The Act of Union unites England and Scotland. This British flag uses symbols from each country's flag to show unity.

1721
Johann Sebastian Bach publishes his Brandenburg Concertos. Bach composes music for the harpsichord, shown here, and for many other instruments.

1740
Frederick II begins his reign in Prussia.

CHAPTER EVENTS

1700   1720   1740

GLOBAL EVENTS

1736 Qianlong begins a 60-year reign as emperor of China.

444 Chapter 18

Resource Directory

Teaching Resources
Teaching With Themes Chapter Theme Activities, p. 21
Pacing Chart With Block Scheduling Guide Ch. 18

Technology
World History Color Transparencies Ch. 18 Graphic Organizer, p. F–37

North America, 1783

The American Revolution transformed maps of North America as the United States became an independent nation.

United States territory	Russian territory	Claimed by U.S. and Spain
British territory	Spanish territory	Claimed by Russia, Spain, and Great Britain
French territory	Claimed by U.S. and Great Britain	

ALASKA
Yukon R.
Mackenzie R.
Arctic Circle
Hudson Bay
CANADA
St. Lawrence R. • Quebec
Saskatchewan R.
• Halifax
• Boston
Missouri R. • New York
Snake R. Columbia R. Ohio R. • Philadelphia
CALIFORNIA
LOUISIANA UNITED STATES
ATLANTIC OCEAN
• Charleston
New Orleans •
Rio Grande
NEW SPAIN FLORIDA
Gulf of Mexico
BAHAMAS (Br.)
HISPANIOLA
Tropic of Cancer
CUBA PUERTO RICO
MARTINIQUE (Fr.)
Mexico City • BELIZE
JAMAICA GUADELOUPE (Fr.)
Caribbean Sea
PACIFIC OCEAN
MOSQUITO COAST
SOUTH AMERICA

Azimuthal Equal Area Projection
0 500 1000 Miles
0 500 1000 Kilometers

1759
The *philosophe* Voltaire, shown here, publishes *Candide*. The novel mocks French society.

1762
Jean-Jacques Rousseau publishes *The Social Contract*.

1781
The British army surrenders to the Americans after the Battle of Yorktown. This painting shows American and French officers planning the siege.

1760 — 1780 — 1800

1763 The Treaty of Paris is signed by France and Great Britain.

1789 Parisians storm the Bastille.

Activating Prior Knowledge
Ask students how this map would be different if it reflected the situation in 1750. *(The territory of the United States would be divided between Britain and France.)*

Previewing
Point out to students that this map represents the first appearance of the United States on the world scene. Ask them if they know the opening words of the Declaration of Independence. (If they do not, write the words on the chalkboard.) Tell them that in this chapter they will learn about the intellectual movement that led to those words.

Background
About the Pictures

1 2 3 4

1. Developed in 1606, the Union Jack included the red cross of St. George, symbolizing England, and the white cross of St. Andrew, representing Scotland. In 1801, the diagonal cross of St. Patrick was added to represent Ireland.

2. The harpsichord, a keyboard instrument with strings, was used by composers like Johann Sebastian Bach. The harpsichord pictured here belonged to Franz Joseph Haydn (1732–1809).

3. Voltaire, one of the most famous French writers of the Enlightenment, used biting wit in his writing to expose inequality, injustice, and superstition.

4. With the help of the French, George Washington was able to defeat the British in 1781 at Yorktown. With this defeat, the British war against the Americans crumbled. Two years later, American, British, and French diplomats signed the Treaty of Paris, ending the American Revolution.

eTeach

Be sure to check out this month's online discussion with a World History Master Teacher.

Go to **www.phschool.com**.

Independent Assignments

Have students read one section as they prepare for class. After class, have them complete the assignment. Some students may benefit from using the Guided Reading and Review worksheets.

Section 1 Have students use the worksheet *Enlightenment Views on Education* in the Unit 5 booklet, p. 12, to compare and contrast Rousseau's and Wollstonecraft's opinions on education.

Section 2 Have students read the excerpt from Voltaire's *Candide* in the History Through Literature booklet, pp. 39–40, to learn how literature can be used to critique society.

Section 3 Have students use the transparency worksheet *The British Government* in the Treasures of the World Transparency set, p. 51, to learn more about the structure of British government.

Section 4 Have students use the map *North America, 1783* in the Historical Outline Map Book, p. 31, to locate and label the different territories and countries of North America after the Revolutionary War.

Reading Focus

- How did scientific progress promote trust in human reason?

- How did the social contract and separation of powers affect views on government?

- How did new ideas affect society and the economy?

Main Idea Enlightenment thinkers tried to apply reason and the laws of nature to human society.

Vocabulary

natural law
social contract
natural right
philosophe
physiocrat
laissez faire

Taking Notes

Make a table like the one here. Add information about each thinker as you read this section.

THINKER	WORKS AND IDEAS
Hobbes	• Wrote *Leviathan* •
Locke	
Montesquieu	
Voltaire	
Diderot	
Rousseau	
Wollstonecraft	
Smith	

Smallpox Vaccinations In this painting, Edward Jenner vaccinates a child against smallpox. The smallpox vaccine was one of many scientific developments of the 1700s.

Theme: Art and Literature What elements of the painting suggest that smallpox was a major problem before Jenner developed his vaccine?

Setting the Scene By the early 1700s, European thinkers felt that nothing was beyond the reach of the human mind. The following lines by the English poet Alexander Pope celebrated the successes of humans—the "wondrous creature"—in the Scientific Revolution:

"Go, wondrous creature! mount where Science guides;
Go, measure earth, weigh air, and state the tides;
Instruct the planets in what orbs to run,
Correct old Time, and regulate the sun."
—Alexander Pope, *Essay on Man*

Progress and Reason

The Scientific Revolution of the 1500s and 1600s had transformed the way people in Europe looked at the world. In the 1700s, other scientists expanded European knowledge. Joseph Priestley and Antoine Lavoisier (ahn TWAHN lah vwah ZYAY), for example, built the framework for modern chemistry. Edward Jenner developed a vaccine against smallpox, a disease whose path of death spanned the centuries.

Scientific successes convinced educated Europeans of the power of human reason. If people used reason to find laws that governed the physical world, why not use reason to discover natural laws, or laws that govern human nature? Using the methods of the new science, reformers set out to study human behavior and solve the problems of society. Thus, the Scientific Revolution led to another revolution in thinking, known as the Enlightenment. Through the use of reason, insisted Enlightenment thinkers, people and governments could solve every social, political, and economic problem. Heaven could be achieved here on Earth.

Two Views of the Social Contract

In the 1600s, two English thinkers, Thomas Hobbes and John Locke, set forth ideas that were to become key to the Enlightenment. Both men lived through the upheavals of the English Civil War. Yet they came to very different conclusions about human nature and the role of government.

Hobbes Thomas Hobbes set out his ideas in a work titled *Leviathan*. In it, he argued that people were naturally cruel, greedy, and selfish. If not strictly controlled, they would fight, rob, and oppress one another. Life in the "state of nature"—without laws or other control—would be "solitary, poor, nasty, brutish, and short."

To escape that "brutish" life, said Hobbes, people entered into a social contract, an agreement by which they gave up the state of nature for an organized society. Hobbes believed that only a powerful government could ensure an orderly society. For him, such a government was an absolute monarchy, which could impose order and compel obedience.

Locke John Locke had a more optimistic view of human nature. People were basically reasonable and moral, he said. Further, they had certain natural rights, or rights that belonged to all humans from birth. These included the right to life, liberty, and property.

In *Two Treatises of Government*, Locke argued that people formed governments to protect their natural rights. The best kind of government, he said, had limited power and was accepted by all citizens. Thus, unlike Hobbes, Locke rejected absolute monarchy.

Locke then set out a radical idea. A government, he said, has an obligation to the people it governs. If a government fails its obligations or violates people's natural rights, the people have the right to overthrow that government. This right to revolution would echo across Europe and around the world in the centuries that followed.

Separation of Powers

In the 1700s, France saw a flowering of Enlightenment thought. An early and influential thinker was the Baron de Montesquieu (MON tehs kyoo). Montesquieu studied the governments of Europe, from Italy to England. He read all he could about ancient and medieval Europe and learned about Chinese and Native American cultures. His sharp criticism of absolute monarchy opened the doors for later debate.

In 1748, Montesquieu published *The Spirit of the Laws*. In it, he discussed governments throughout history and wrote admiringly about Britain's limited monarchy. Montesquieu felt that the British had protected themselves against tyranny by dividing the various functions and powers of government among three separate branches: the legislative, executive, and judicial. (In fact, he had misunderstood the British system, which did not separate powers in this way.) Still, he felt that the separation of powers was the best way to protect liberty. Montesquieu also felt that each branch of government should be able to serve as a check on the other two, an idea that we call checks and balances.

The *Philosophes* and Society

In France, a group of Enlightenment thinkers applied the methods of science to better understand and improve society. They believed that the use of reason could lead to reforms of government, law, and society. These thinkers were called *philosophes,* which means "lovers of wisdom." Their ideas soon spread beyond France and even beyond Europe.

Voltaire Defends Freedom of Thought Probably the most famous of the *philosophes* was François-Marie Arouet, who took the name Voltaire. "My trade," said Voltaire, "is to say what I think," and he did so throughout his long, controversial life. Voltaire used biting wit as a weapon to expose the abuses of his day. He targeted corrupt officials and idle aristocrats. With his pen, he battled inequality, injustice, and superstition. He detested the slave trade and deplored religious prejudice.

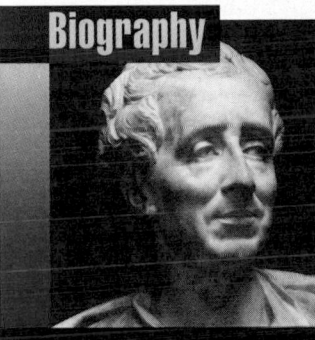

Biography

Montesquieu 1689–1755

Born to wealth, Charles Louis de Secondat inherited the title Baron de Montesquieu. Like many other reformers, his privileged status did not keep him from becoming a voice for democracy. His *Persian Letters* ridiculed the French elite. In *The Spirit of the Laws,* he advanced the idea of separation of powers—a foundation of modern democracy.

Montesquieu's belief in democracy did not mean that he considered all people equal. For example, he held a common view of his time that men were superior to women. However, he thought that women would make good government officials. According to Montesquieu, women's "weakness" would make them "gentle" rulers, thus benefiting the people.

Theme: Impact of the Individual What reforms did Montesquieu promote?

Background Connections to Science

Science and Philosophy Sociology, the study of human behavior and the development of human societies, came out of the science practiced by the eighteenth-century *philosophes,* in particular Baron de Montesquieu. He can legitimately be called the father of sociology. In his great treatise, *The Spirit of the Laws,* Montesquieu wrote that the extent of freedom in a society is determined by its institutions, climate controls behavior, and religion shapes politics. His method of study was to compare the features of past and present societies. This is similar to the methods of comparative sociology today.

Background Global Connections

Archaeological Discoveries Enlightenment thinkers found inspiration not only in the cultures of other lands, but also in the cultures of other times. The relatively new science of archaeology gave thinkers more access to the knowledge of past civilizations. For example, archaeological discoveries in Italy during the early 1700s unearthed the ruins of the ancient Roman cities of Herculaneum and Pompeii, buried under volcanic debris for many centuries.

Block Scheduling Support

Divide the class into small groups. Have each group think of areas in modern society that are based on or represent Enlightenment ideas. Have each group make a list that charts this correlation. Possible areas include government, human rights, education, gender roles, and the economy. Have students evaluate some of the more salient influences and outline the similarities and differences between the original Enlightenment ideas and the present-day manifestation of these ideas.

Human Drama Activity

Writing a Letter Have students read the selections from *Two Treatises on Government* by John Locke and *The Social Contract* by Jean-Jacques Rousseau found in the Reference Section in the back of the book. Then ask students to choose one of the documents and write a letter to the author. Letters should state the student's opinion about the ideas expressed in the document and why the student thinks this way.

Biography

ANSWER Montesquieu advocated the separation of powers and believed that women would be good government officials.

Comparing Viewpoints

Background
Other Viewpoints

France, 1700s Writing in response to the efforts of government and Church authorities to censor books, Voltaire commented:

"I know many books which have bored their readers, but I know of none which has done real evil. . . . Does a book displease you? Refute it. Does it bore you? Don't read it."

Activity
Interpreting Viewpoints

Critical Thinking: Comparing Share with students the information in the background note above. Then use these additional questions to generate class discussion. **1.** Which of the quotes on the Student Edition page would be most likely to directly oppose the writings of Voltaire? *(Mao Zedong)* **2.** Would modern audiences in the United States today be more likely to agree or disagree with Voltaire? *(Some may agree that books do no real evil, others may disagree. Have students support their ideas with examples and logical reasons.)*

Skills Tip

To compare differing points of view, look at the evidence each writer or speaker uses to support the argument and any biases that might color the argument. The Skills Handbook in the front of the book has a lesson that will help students with this feature.

What Limits Should There Be on Freedom of Speech?

"I do not agree with a word that you say, but I will defend to the death your right to say it." Whether or not Voltaire said these exact words, he passionately believed in this idea. But his idea has not been universally accepted. To consider whether there should be limits on freedom of speech, examine these viewpoints.

England 1643

John Milton, Puritan writer, expressed views about freedom of expression that later influenced Enlightenment thinkers:

❝ Give me liberty to know, to utter, and to argue freely according to conscience, above all liberties. ❞

China 1957

Mao Zedong led a government in China based on the ideals of the communist philosopher Karl Marx:

❝ What should our policy be toward non-Marxist ideas? As far as unmistakable counterrevolutionaries and saboteurs of the socialist cause are concerned, the matter is easy. We simply deprive them of their freedom of speech. ❞

Canada 1985

The criminal code of Canada outlaws public remarks against religious, racial, or ethnic groups:

❝ Everyone who, by communicating statements other than in private conversation, willfully promotes hatred against any identifiable group is guilty of . . . an indictable offense and is liable to imprisonment for a term not exceeding two years. ❞

United States 1942

Uncle Sam silences an American who is careless in his speech during World War II. "Loose talk" could reveal important secrets to the enemy, costing American lives.

QUIET!

LOOSE TALK CAN COST LIVES

Skills Assessment

1. Who seems to support complete freedom of speech, free from all restrictions?
   A John Milton
   B Uncle Sam
   C Mao Zedong
   D Karl Marx

2. According to Canadian law, freedom of speech
   E does not apply to immigrants.
   F is everyone's right.
   G should be limited under certain circumstances.
   H exists only in public situations.

3. **Critical Thinking Analyzing Information** **(a)** Study the poster. What does it seem to say about freedom of speech? **(b)** Should freedom of speech ever be limited? If so, under what conditions?

Skills Tip

Before comparing points of view, you must identify the main idea of each separate point of view. Then, look for ways in which the views are the same or different.

Skills Assessment

ANSWERS 1. A **2.** G **3.** Possible answers: **(a)** The poster implies that freedom of speech should not be exercised to its fullest extent in wartime, when doing so could endanger American lives. **(b)** Students might say that freedom of speech should be limited when it is exercised in a way that endangers others.

Resource Directory

Teaching Resources
Comparing Viewpoints Chapter Extension Activities booklet, pp. 39–40
Viewpoint Activity *Enlightenment Views on Education,* Unit 5 booklet, p. 12

Technology
World History Visions, Voices, Views Global Issues Forum, *Should Colleges and Universities Regulate Hateful Speech?,* videodisc side 3 or videotape 5, running time 4:00 min.

Side 3: Fr. 16600-23815

Voltaire's outspoken attacks offended both the French government and the Catholic Church. He was imprisoned and forced into exile. Even as he saw his books outlawed and even burned, he continued to defend the principle of freedom of speech.

The *Encyclopedia* Another *philosophe*, Denis Diderot (dee DROH), labored for some 25 years to produce a 28-volume *Encyclopedia*. As the editor of this huge work, Diderot did more than just gather articles on human knowledge. His purpose was "to change the general way of thinking" by explaining the new ideas on topics such as government, philosophy, and religion. Diderot's *Encyclopedia* included articles by leading thinkers of the day, including Montesquieu and Voltaire.

In their *Encyclopedia* articles, the *philosophes* denounced slavery, praised freedom of expression, and urged education for all. They attacked divine-right theory and traditional religions. Critics raised an outcry. The French government argued that the *Encyclopedia* was an attack on public morals, and the pope threatened to excommunicate Roman Catholics who bought or read the volumes.

Despite these and other efforts to ban the *Encyclopedia*, as many as 20,000 copies were printed between 1751 and 1789. When translated into other languages, it helped spread Enlightenment ideas throughout Europe and across the Atlantic to the Americas.

Rousseau The most controversial *philosophe*, Jean-Jacques Rousseau (ZHAHN ZHAHK roo SOH), was a strange, difficult man. Coming from a poor family, he never felt comfortable in the glittering social world of Enlightenment thinkers.

Rousseau believed that people in their natural state were basically good. This natural innocence, he felt, was corrupted by the evils of society, especially the unequal distribution of property. This view was later adopted by many reformers and revolutionaries.

In 1762, Rousseau set forth his ideas about government and society in *The Social Contract*. Rousseau felt that society placed too many limitations on people's behavior. He believed that some controls were necessary, but that they should be minimal. Additionally, these controls should be imposed only by governments that had been freely elected.

Rousseau put his faith in the "general will," or the best conscience of the people. The good of the community as a whole, he said, should be placed above individual interests. Thus, unlike many Enlightenment thinkers who put the individual first, Rousseau felt that the individual should be subordinate to the community.

Rousseau has influenced political and social thinkers for more than 200 years. Woven through his work is a profound hatred of all forms of political and economic oppression. His bold ideas would help fan the flames of revolt in years to come.

Women and the Enlightenment The Enlightenment slogan "free and equal" did not apply to women. Women did have "natural rights," said the *philosophes*. But unlike the natural rights of men, these rights were limited to the areas of home and family.

By the mid-1700s, a small but growing number of women protested this view. They questioned the notion that women were by nature inferior to men and that men's domination of women was therefore part of "nature's plan." Germaine de Staël in France and Catharine Macaulay and Mary Wollstonecraft in Britain argued that women were being excluded from the social contract itself. Their arguments, however, were ridiculed and often sharply condemned.

Wollstonecraft was a well-known British social critic. She accepted that a woman's first duty was to be a good mother. At the same time, however,

Primary Source

The *Encyclopedia*
Diderot's Encyclopedia *contains this passage on the concept of liberty:*

"The first state that man acquires by nature and that is esteemed the most precious of all his possible possessions is the state of liberty. He can neither exchange himself for another, nor sell himself, nor be enslaved, for all men are naturally born free. . . .

By virtue of this state, all men hold from nature itself the power to do what seems right to them and to regulate their actions and their property at will, provided they do not act against the laws of the government. . . ."

—Diderot, Encyclopedia, or Classified Dictionary of the Sciences, Arts, and Occupations

Skills Assessment

Primary Source What arguments does Diderot offer against slavery?

Activity
Cooperative Learning

Interviewing Organize students into small groups. Assign one of the following four thinkers to each group: Thomas Hobbes, John Locke, Baron de Montesquieu, and Jean-Jacques Rousseau. Instruct students to imagine that they are living in Enlightenment Europe and have the opportunity to interview the philosopher who has been assigned to them. First, students should formulate questions for their interview. Next, they should write possible answers that the thinker might have given. Students should also prepare follow-up questions and answers to these questions. Finally, ask volunteers to conduct their interviews for the class. ✷

Customize for . . .
Heterogeneous Groups

Analyzing a Quotation Desiring equal rights for women, Mary Wollstonecraft argued that the environment, not nature, made women seem shallow and intellectually limited. She explained her belief in these words:

"Taught from infancy that beauty is woman's sceptre, the mind shapes itself to the body, and roaming round its gilt cage, only seeks to adorn its prison."

Ask students to explain the meaning of the quotation. Invite comments on whether or not it has any significance for women today. *(Enrichment)*

☑ **Test Preparation**

Have students read the section titled "Rousseau" on this page, and then complete the sentence below.

Rousseau believed that people are

(A) basically good, but corrupted by society.

B basically neutral, and their behavior depends solely on their environment.

C basically corrupt, but reformed by society.

D unchangeable by nature.

Primary Source

ANSWER The passage says that a person cannot sell himself or herself because "all men are naturally born free." Diderot either wrote this passage himself or agreed to include it, so one can assume it represents his views.

Recall

1. (a) Thomas Hobbes, p. 447 (b) John Locke, p. 447 (c) Baron de Montesquieu, p. 447 (d) Voltaire, p. 447 (e) Denis Diderot, p. 449 (f) Jean-Jacques Rousseau, p. 449 (g) Mary Wollstonecraft, p. 449 (h) *The Wealth of Nations*, p. 450 2. (a) natural law, p. 446 (b) social contract, p. 447 (c) natural right, p. 447 (d) *philosophe*, p. 447 (e) physiocrat, p. 450 (f) laissez faire, p. 450

Comprehension

3. They led to greater faith in the power of reason. People began to apply reason to human nature and government as well as to the physical world. 4. Hobbes: He has a negative view of human nature; people need to be controlled by a powerful government. Locke: People are basically reasonable and moral; they need a limited government to protect their rights. Montesquieu: People need to create governments that protect against tyranny through separation of powers. 5. Their belief in reason led them to support freedom of thought, oppose slavery, and encourage education. These attitudes were extended to limit government involvement in the economy as well as in people's lives.

Critical Thinking and Writing

6. Possible answer: Rousseau was wrong; the general good may be actively harmful to individuals, and they should not be forced to act against their own interests. 7. Possible answer: Wollstonecraft might want to know why the *philosophes* did not focus more on the plight of women. The *philosophe* might say women's rights are different from men's and that therefore the subjects are too different to discuss.

Activity Rubrics

Share rubrics with students before they draw their cartoons.

Attempted The cartoon does not illustrate an idea and does not contain a caption.

Minimal The cartoon illustrates an idea but is poorly or messily drawn or unclear.

Adequate The cartoon illustrates an idea, is well drawn, and contains a clear caption.

Exemplary The cartoon illustrates an idea, is very well drawn, and has a well-written caption.

Caption Answer

Women's rights were limited to the home and family.

Germaine de Staël
Madame de Staël argued that women had been excluded from the ideals of the Enlightenment. She wrote a number of books, including an analysis of Rousseau.

Theme: Diversity According to the *philosophes*, how were natural rights different for men and for women?

---

she felt that a woman should be able to decide what is in her own interest and should not be completely dependent on her husband. In 1792, Wollstonecraft published *A Vindication of the Rights of Woman*. In it, she called for equal education for girls and boys. Only education, she argued, could give women the tools they needed to participate equally with men in public life.

New Economic Thinking

Other thinkers known as physiocrats focused on economic reforms. Like the *philosophes*, physiocrats looked for natural laws to define a rational economic system.

Laissez Faire Physiocrats rejected mercantilism, which required government regulation of the economy to achieve a favorable balance of trade. Instead, they urged a policy of laissez faire (LEHS ay FAIR), allowing business to operate with little or no government interference. Unlike mercantilists, who called for acquiring gold and silver wealth through trade, the physiocrats claimed that real wealth came from making the land more productive. Extractive industries, they said, such as agriculture, mining, and logging, produced new wealth. Physiocrats also supported free trade and opposed tariffs, or taxes on trade.

Adam Smith British economist Adam Smith greatly admired the physiocrats. In his influential work, *The Wealth of Nations*, he argued that the free market should be allowed to regulate business activity. Smith tried to show how manufacturing, trade, wages, profits, and economic growth were all linked to the market forces of supply and demand. Wherever there is a demand for goods or services, he said, suppliers will seek to meet it. They do so because of the profits and other economic rewards they can get from fulfilling the demand.

Smith was a strong supporter of laissez faire. He believed that the marketplace was better off without any government regulation. At the same time, however, he argued that government had a duty to protect society, administer justice, and provide public works.

Adam Smith's ideas would gain increasing influence as the Industrial Revolution spread across Europe and beyond. His emphasis on the free market and the law of supply and demand would help to shape immensely productive economies in the 1800s and 1900s.

SECTION 1 Assessment

Recall

1. **Identify:** (a) Thomas Hobbes, (b) John Locke, (c) Baron de Montesquieu, (d) Voltaire, (e) Denis Diderot, (f) Jean-Jacques Rousseau, (g) Mary Wollstonecraft, (h) *The Wealth of Nations*.
2. **Define:** (a) natural law, (b) social contract, (c) natural right, (d) *philosophe*, (e) physiocrat, (f) laissez faire.

Comprehension

3. How did the achievements of the Scientific Revolution contribute to the Enlightenment?

4. Explain the views of Thomas Hobbes, John Locke, and the Baron de Montesquieu.
5. How did the *philosophes* influence ideas on society and the economy?

Critical Thinking and Writing

6. **Defending a Position** Rousseau put the common good over the interest of the individual. Do you agree with that position? Explain.
7. **Predicting Consequences** Suppose that Mary Wollstonecraft encountered another important *philosophe*. What course might their conversation follow?

Activity

Creating a Cartoon
Draw a cartoon to illustrate the ideas of one or more of the *philosophes* you read about in this section. Write a brief caption to accompany your cartoon.

Resource Directory

Teaching Resources

Section Quiz Unit 5 booklet, p. 3
Creative Teaching Activities Creative Teaching Activities booklet, p. 83
Guided Reading and Review Unit 5 booklet, p. 4
History Through Literature *Candide*, History Through Literature booklet, pp. 39–40

Technology

Interactive Student Tutorial CD-ROM Ch. 18
Computer Test Bank Ch. 18

SECTION 2 Enlightenment Ideas Spread

Reading Focus

- What roles did censorship and salons play in the spread of new ideas?
- How did *philosophes* influence enlightened despots?
- How did the Enlightenment affect arts and literature?
- Why were the lives of the majority unaffected?

Vocabulary

censorship
salon
enlightened despot
baroque
rococo

Taking Notes

On a sheet of paper draw a concept web to help you record information from this section. The web at right has been started for you. Add more circles as needed.

SPREAD OF ENLIGHTEN-MENT IDEAS

Salons

Courts of monarchs

Main Idea Enlightenment ideas spread across Europe and prompted some rulers to make reforms.

Setting the Scene

Paris, the heart of the Enlightenment, drew many intellectuals and others eager to debate the new ideas. Reforms proposed one evening became the talk of the town the next day. Even an enemy of the Enlightenment admitted that "an opinion launched in Paris was like a battering ram launched by 30 million men."

From France, Enlightenment ideas flowed across Europe and beyond. Everywhere, thinkers examined traditional beliefs and customs in the light of reason and found them flawed. Even absolute monarchs experimented with Enlightenment ideas, although they drew back when changes threatened the established way of doing things.

The Challenge of New Ideas

The ideas of the Enlightenment spread quickly through many levels of society. Educated people all over Europe eagerly read not only Diderot's *Encyclopedia* but also the small, cheap pamphlets that printers churned out on a broad range of issues. More and more, they saw the need for reform to achieve a just society.

During the Middle Ages, most Europeans had accepted without question a society based on divine-right rule, a strict class system, and a belief in heavenly reward for earthly suffering. In the Age of Reason, such ideas seemed unscientific and irrational. A just society, Enlightenment thinkers taught, should ensure social justice and happiness in this world.

Censorship Government and church authorities felt they had a sacred duty to defend the old order. They believed that the old order had been set up by God. To protect against the attacks of the Enlightenment, they waged a war of censorship, or restricting access to ideas and information. They banned and burned books and imprisoned writers.

Philosophes and writers like Montesquieu and Voltaire sometimes disguised their ideas in works of fiction. In the *Persian Letters*, Montesquieu uses two fictional Persian travelers, named Usbek and Rica, to mock French society. The hero of Voltaire's humorous novel *Candide*, published in 1759, travels across Europe and even to the Americas and the Middle East in search of "the best of all possible worlds." Voltaire slyly uses the tale to expose the corruption and hypocrisy of European society.

Salons The new literature, the arts, science, and philosophy were regular topics of discussion in salons, informal social gatherings at which writers,

Global Connections

An American *Philosophe*

Benjamin Franklin first traveled to Europe when he was just 18. There, he wrote in his *Autobiography*, "... I spent little upon myself except ... in books. I had improved my knowledge, ... though I had by no means improved my fortune. But I had made some very ingenious acquaintance, whose conversation was of great advantage to me, and I had read considerably."

Franklin's activities in Europe gave him firsthand exposure to Enlightenment ideas. He carried this new knowledge back to the American colonies, where he helped to create a country based on those ideas—the United States.

Theme: Global Interaction How was the transmission of ideas across the Atlantic different in Franklin's time than it is today?

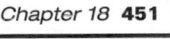

Salons Another famous *salonière* of this period was Germaine de Staël, who, in the 1780s, established a Paris salon that became a center of progressive discussion. Unlike Madame Geoffrin, de Staël was no stranger to intellectual thought, since she had grown up in the salon environment created by her mother, Suzanne Necker.

Politicians, writers, and musicians frequented Madame de Staël's salon. It remained a popular salon until 1803, when her opposition to Napoleon forced her into exile in Switzerland. De Staël, however, was more than a spirited conversationalist. She was also a talented writer. Her novels *Delphine* (1802) and *Corinne* (1807) noted the dilemma of gifted women who found themselves caught in a time and place that left them lonely and unfulfilled.

Reading Strategy
Predicting Content

Before reading, have students read the boldfaced headings in Section 2. Ask students to predict the content of the section in one sentence. *(Less Advanced Readers)*

Connections to Today

Virtual Salons

Salons provided a way for people to gather and share ideas. Today, many people do this without ever meeting—through the Internet.

Every day, millions of people use the Internet to exchange ideas easily. In "chat rooms," people send messages instantly, even if the recipient is on the other side of the world. In "newsgroups," people submit thoughts on a given topic and respond to the comments of others.

Many discussions on the Internet lack the serious-minded tone of a salon conversation. And because participants meet only through computers, there is no way to be sure who is on the other end of the line. But the popularity of the Internet shows that people will find a way to gather and discuss their ideas, even in a "virtual" living room.

Theme: Continuity and Change How does a "virtual" salon compare to the salons of the 1700s?

artists, *philosophes*, and others exchanged ideas. The salon originated in the 1600s, when a group of noblewomen in Paris began inviting a few friends to their homes for poetry readings. By the 1700s, some middle-class women began holding salons. In the drawing rooms of these *salonières* (sah lohn YAIR), middle-class citizens could meet with the nobility on an equal footing to discuss and spread Enlightenment ideas.

One of the most respected salons was run by Madame Geoffrin. In her home on the Rue St. Honoré, she brought together the brightest and most talented people of her day. The young musical genius Wolfgang Amadeus Mozart played for her guests, and Diderot was a regular at her weekly dinners for philosophers and poets.

Enlightened Despots

Discussions of Enlightenment ideas also enlivened the courts of Europe. *Philosophes* tried to persuade European rulers to adopt their ideas. If they could "enlighten" the ruling classes, they thought, they could bring about reform. Some monarchs did accept Enlightenment ideas. They became enlightened despots, or absolute rulers who used their power to bring about political and social change.

Frederick the Great As king of Prussia from 1740 to 1786, Frederick II exerted extremely tight control over his subjects. Still, he saw himself as the "first servant of the state," with a duty to work for the common good.

Frederick admired Voltaire's work and lured the *philosophe* to Berlin to develop a Prussian academy of science. When Frederick was not busy fighting wars, he had swamps drained and forced peasants to grow new crops such as the potato. He had seed and tools distributed to peasants who had suffered in Prussia's wars. Frederick also tolerated religious differences, welcoming victims of religious persecution. "In my kingdom," he said, "everyone can go to heaven in his own fashion."

Frederick's reforms were directed mainly at making the Prussian government more efficient. He reorganized the civil service and simplified laws. But a "rationalized" bureaucracy also meant a stronger monarchy— and more power for Frederick himself.

Catherine the Great Catherine II of Russia read the works of the *philosophes* and exchanged letters with Voltaire and Diderot. She praised Voltaire as someone who had "fought the united enemies of humankind: superstition, fanaticism, ignorance, trickery."

Catherine, who became empress in 1762, toyed with Enlightenment ideas. Early in her reign, she made some limited reforms in law and government. She granted nobles a charter of rights and criticized the institution of serfdom. Still, like Frederick in Prussia, Catherine intended to give up no power. In the end, her political contribution to Russia was not reform but an expanded empire.

Joseph II The most radical of the enlightened despots was the Hapsburg emperor Joseph II, son and successor of Maria Theresa. An eager student of the Enlightenment, Joseph traveled in disguise among his subjects to learn of their problems. His efforts to improve their lives won him the nickname the "peasant emperor."

Maria Theresa had begun to modernize Austria's government. Joseph continued her reforms. Despite opposition, he granted toleration to Protestants and Jews in his Catholic empire. He ended censorship and attempted to bring the Catholic Church under royal control. He sold the property of many monasteries and convents and used the proceeds to build hospitals. Joseph even abolished serfdom. Like many of his other reforms, however, this measure was canceled after his death.

Connections to Today

ANSWER Internet discussion offers the advantage of interacting with a great many people, on a worldwide basis, but the meetings are not face-to-face.

Resource Directory

Teaching Resources
Primary Source Activity *A Court Musician's Problems,* Unit 5 booklet, p. 11
Technology
Listening to Literature World Masterpieces audiotapes
Fugue in G Major, side 6, running time 3:16 min.

Virtual Field Trip

www.phschool.com

Utah Museum of Fine Arts Salt Lake City, Utah

For more information about the works of Elisabeth Vigée LeBrun, use the Internet address above to link to the Web site of the Utah Museum of Fine Arts.

Enlightenment Painters
During the 1700s, many artists began painting very personal, detailed scenes. In *The Marquise de Peze and the Marquise de Rouget with Her Two Children,* French artist Elisabeth Vigée LeBrun shows the relationships between mothers and young children.

Theme: Art and Literature
What elements of this painting identify its style as rococo rather than baroque?

The Arts and Literature

In the 1600s and 1700s, the arts evolved to meet changing tastes. As in earlier periods, artists and composers had to please their patrons, the men and women who commissioned works from them or gave them jobs.

Courtly Art   In the age of Louis XIV, courtly art and architecture were either in the Greek and Roman tradition or in a grand, complex style known as baroque. Baroque paintings were huge, colorful, and full of excitement. They glorified historic battles or the lives of saints. Such works matched the grandeur of European courts.

By the mid-1700s, architects and designers developed the rococo style. Unlike the heavy splendor of the baroque, rococo art was personal, elegant, and charming. Furniture and tapestries featured delicate shells and flowers. Portrait painters showed noble subjects in charming rural settings, surrounded by happy servants and pets.

Middle-Class Audiences   A new audience, the growing middle class, emerged with its own requirements. Successful merchants and prosperous town officials wanted their portraits painted, but without frills. They liked pictures of family life or realistic town or country scenes. Dutch painters such as Rembrandt van Rijn (REHM brant van RĪN) conferred great dignity on merchants and other ordinary, middle-class subjects.

Trends in Music   New kinds of musical entertainment evolved during this era. Ballets and operas—plays set to music—were performed at royal courts. Before long, opera houses sprang up from Italy to England to amuse the paying public. The music of the period followed ordered, structured forms well suited to the Age of Reason.

Among the towering musical figures of the era was Johann Sebastian Bach. A devout German Lutheran, Bach wrote complex and beautiful religious works for organ and choirs. Another German-born composer, George Frederick Handel, spent much of his life in England. There, he wrote *Water Music* and other pieces for King George I, as well as many operas. His most celebrated work, the *Messiah,* combines instruments and voices. Today, it is a standard at Christmas and Easter concerts.

Activity
Connections to Film

Outlining   In *The Enlightened Despots,* Program 33 of the public television series *The Western Tradition,* UCLA professor Eugene Weber describes how some absolute monarchs exploited Enlightenment ideals for their own advantage. Rulers used rational thinking to make warfare, government, and the economy more efficient. While freedoms were introduced to gain the support of the powerful middle class, a well-ordered state under royal authority remained the primary goal.

After students have viewed *The Enlightened Despots,* ask them to answer this question: According to Professor Weber, why did European monarchs embrace the ideas of the Enlightenment? Then, ask students to outline the policies that enlightened monarchs followed in such areas as international affairs, government, and the economy. (*The Western Tradition,* released in 1989 as part of the Annenberg/CPB Collection, is distributed by Intellimation.)

✓ Test Preparation

Have students read the first paragraph under the heading "Enlightened Despots" on the opposite page, and then answer the question below.

A *despot* is what?

A   a poor person

B   an absolute monarch

C   a philosopher

D   a performer

Caption Answer

It shows a personal, happy scene of a noblewoman and her children.

Humanities Link

Bell Ringer Have students look at the photographs on this page and try to guess what each has to do with Mozart. Then have students read the page and check their guesses.

Background
About the Evidence

Classical Music By the 1700s, baroque music began to give way to a new musical style called "classical," named for the classical Greek principles of order, clarity, and symmetry.

Classical composers focused on secular themes. For some composers, such as Mozart, this made earning a living difficult. Unless composers secured a job with a family wealthy enough to maintain its own private orchestra, employment and income were uneven.

Activity
Cooperative Learning

Compare and Contrast Organize the class into four groups and have each group research one of the following: J.S. Bach, G.F. Handel, F.J. Haydn, or W.A. Mozart. Each group should identify the following: biographical information, number of works written, and different types of works. Ask volunteers from each group to list this information on a large class chart to graphically display and organize the information. A representative work by each composer can then be played for the class.

Portfolio Assessment Rubrics

Share rubrics with students before they write their journal entries.

Attempted The journal entry is not complete or fails to answer all of the questions.

Minimal The journal entry answers all of the questions but only briefly.

Adequate The journal entry answers all the questions and reveals some thought about the Mozart piece.

Exemplary The journal entry demonstrates extensive thought and results in an interesting and informative response to Mozart's work.

The Great Mozart

Wolfgang Amadeus Mozart died when he was just 35 years old. His musical genius, however, has lived for centuries. Today, his work is celebrated around the world.

Mozart was a prolific composer. He wrote operas, symphonies, piano concertos, string quartets, and scores of other works, including church music. In all, he composed more than 600 pieces of music.

Mozart wrote the opera *The Magic Flute* during the last year of his life. Here, the high priest is passing judgment on a kidnapper. Mozart's operas are famous for their outstanding arias (solos), recitatives (sung dialogues), and ensembles (group singing).

Mozart's music is admired throughout the world today. It can be playful, serious, uplifting, or somber. Many of his melodies are instantly recognized. People use his music in everything from car commercials to Internet greeting cards.

Portfolio Assessment

Listen to a recording of one of Mozart's compositions. Then, write a journal entry in which you tell how the music affected you. What feelings did it evoke? What images did it bring to mind? Explain why you think Mozart's music is held in such high regard.

Fast Facts

- Mozart was a child prodigy. He played the harpsichord at age 4 and began to compose music at age 5. A year later, he performed for the empress of Austria.

- Mozart's father, Leopold, was an accomplished musician. He took his young son on performing tours throughout Europe. Wolfgang never attended school.

Resource Directory

Teaching Resources
Section Quiz Unit 5 booklet, p. 5
Humanities Link Chapter Extension Activities booklet, p. 47
Technology
Independent Student Tutorial CD-ROM Ch. 18
Computer Test Bank Ch. 18

In 1762, a six-year-old prodigy, Wolfgang Amadeus Mozart, burst onto the European scene to gain instant celebrity as a composer and performer. Over the next three decades, his brilliant operas, graceful symphonies, and moving religious music helped define the new style of composition. Although he died in poverty at age 35, his musical legacy thrives today.

The Novel By the 1700s, literature developed new forms and a wide new audience. Middle-class readers, for example, liked stories about their own times told in straightforward prose. One result was an outpouring of novels, or long works of prose fiction. English novelists created many popular works. Daniel Defoe wrote *Robinson Crusoe*, an exciting tale about a sailor shipwrecked on a tropical island. In *Pamela*, Samuel Richardson used a series of letters to tell a story about a servant girl. This technique was adopted by other authors of the period.

Lives of the Majority

Most Europeans were untouched by either courtly or middle-class culture. They remained what they had always been—peasants living in small rural villages. Their culture, based on centuries-old traditions, changed slowly.

Peasant life varied across Europe. Villages in Western Europe were relatively more prosperous than those in Eastern Europe. In the West, serfdom had largely disappeared. Instead, some peasants worked their own patches of land. Others were tenants of large landowners, paying a yearly rent for the land they farmed. Still others were day laborers who hired themselves out to work on other people's farms.

In central and Eastern Europe, however, serfdom was firmly rooted. In Russia, it spread and deepened in the 1700s. Peasants owed labor services to their lords and could be bought and sold with the land.

Despite advances, some echoes of serfdom survived in Western Europe. In France, peasants still had to provide free labor, repairing roads and bridges after the spring floods just as their ancestors had done. In England, country squires had the right to hunt foxes across their tenants' lands, tearing up plowed and planted fields.

By the late 1700s, radical ideas about equality and social justice seeped into peasant villages. While some peasants eagerly sought to topple the old order, others resisted efforts to bring about change. In the 1800s, war and political upheaval, as well as changing economic conditions, would transform peasant life in Europe.

SECTION 2 Assessment

Recall
5. How did the Enlightenment affect **(a)** arts and literature, **(b)** the lives of the majority?

Recall
1. **Identify: (a)** *Candide*, **(b)** Joseph II, **(c)** Johann Sebastian Bach, **(d)** George Frederick Handel, **(e)** Wolfgang Amadeus Mozart, **(f)** Daniel Defoe.
2. **Define: (a)** censorship, **(b)** salon, **(c)** enlightened despot, **(d)** baroque, **(e)** rococo.

Comprehension
3. Explain how each of the following affected the spread of new ideas: **(a)** censorship, **(b)** salons.
4. What were the goals of enlightened despots?

Critical Thinking and Writing
6. **Analyzing Information (a)** What did Frederick II mean when he said, "In my kingdom, everyone can go to heaven in his own fashion"? **(b)** How did his actions reflect that idea?
7. **Making Inferences** How did the Enlightenment bring together ideas of both the Renaissance and the Reformation?

Activity
Take It to the NET

Search the Internet for information about salons in the 1700s. Identify types of people who attended salons in the 1700s, and create a list of people you would invite to a modern salon. Explain your choices.

SECTION 2 Assessment

Recall
1. **(a)** *Candide*, p. 451 **(b)** Joseph II, p. 452 **(c)** Johann Sebastian Bach, p. 453 **(d)** George Frederick Handel, p. 453 **(e)** Wolfgang Amadeus Mozart, p. 455 **(f)** Daniel Defoe, p. 455 **2. (a)** censorship, p. 451 **(b)** salon, p. 451 **(c)** enlightened despot, p. 452 **(d)** baroque, p. 453 **(e)** rococo, p. 453

Comprehension
3. **(a)** Censorship was an effort to limit the spread of ideas, but *philosophes* found ways to spread their thoughts in spite of censorship. **(b)** Salons provided a setting for people to share ideas in a social situation. **4.** Their goals were to bring about political and social change. However, most monarchs still maintained their personal power. **5. (a)** New forms and styles of art and literature developed. **(b)** Most people's lives were unchanged.

Critical Thinking and Writing
6. **(a)** He was referring to freedom of religion. **(b)** He tolerated religious differences and welcomed victims of religious persecution. **7.** Possible answer: People questioned traditional beliefs and believed in the human ability to bring about change and to explore new creative outlets.

Activity Rubrics

Share rubrics with students before they make their lists.

Attempted The list is exceedingly short or does not explain why people would be invited.

Minimal The list is brief, and the explanations are sketchy or contain many mechanical errors.

Adequate The list has a reasonable number of persons, and the explanations are clear and thoughtful.

Exemplary The list is extensive and well thought out, with clear, concise, and well-written explanations.

Did You Know?

ANSWER Possible answer: Defoe thought Selkirk's story was interesting.

LESSON PLAN

1. Focus Britain's island location, colonial possessions, favorable business climate, and powerful navy contributed to its rise to world power. Britain's constitutional government, with political parties, a prime minister, and a cabinet, was more democratic than other European governments. Still, most political and economic power was held by a ruling class of landowning aristocrats.

2. Instruct After students have finished the outlining described in the Taking Notes feature, ask each group to make up five essay questions that cover the content of the section. When students have completed this task, invite volunteers to read their questions to the class. Encourage students to answer each question after it is read.

3. Assess Choose several of the essay questions that students formulated. Present the questions to students and ask them to write a brief essay in response to the question of their choice.

4. Reteach If students' **Assess** activity does not reflect adequate understanding of the lesson, you might assign the *Guide to the Essentials* or the *Interactive Student Tutorial CD-ROM* for this section.

Reading Focus
■ What influences spurred Britain's rise to global power?

■ How did the growth of constitutional government reflect conditions in politics and society?

■ How did George III reassert royal power?

Vocabulary
constitutional government

cabinet

prime minister

oligarchy

Taking Notes
As you read this section, make an outline of the information. Use Roman numerals for the main headings. Use capital letters for the subheadings, and use numbers for the supporting details. The outline at right has been started for you.

I. Rise to global power
  A. Geography
    1. Location good for trade
    2. From outposts to empire
  B. Success in war
    1. Won Nova Scotia and Newfoundland
    2.

Main Idea Britain's island location, colonial possessions, and powerful navy contributed to its rise to world power.

A Powerful Navy
By the mid-1700s, Britain controlled territories in North America, South America, Asia, and the Pacific. These scattered holdings required a strong navy, including men-of-war like the one shown here.

Theme: Political and Social Systems How might a strong navy benefit trade?

Setting the Scene Supporters of mercantilism found success in England. In the mid-1600s, a mercantilist wrote, "Foreign trade is . . . the honor of the kingdom, the noble profession of the merchant, . . . the means of our treasure, the sinews of our wars, the terror of our enemies."

Over the next century, Britain embraced mercantilism and built a colonial and commercial empire that reached around the world. At the same time, Britain developed a constitutional monarchy, a political system somewhere between the absolute monarchies of Europe and later democracies.

Rise to Global Power

Why did Britain, a small island kingdom on the edge of Europe, rise to global prominence in the 1700s? Here, we can look at a few reasons for the nation's success.

Geography Location placed England in a position to control trade during the Renaissance. In the 1500s and 1600s, English merchants sent ships across the world's oceans and planted outposts in the West Indies, North America, and India. From these tiny settlements, England would build a global empire.

Success in War In the 1700s, Britain was generally on the winning side in European conflicts. Each victory brought valuable rewards. With the Treaty of Utrecht, France gave Britain Nova Scotia and Newfoundland in North America. Britain also monopolized the slave trade in Spanish America. The slave trade brought enormous wealth to British merchants, who invested their profits in other ventures. In 1763, the Treaty of Paris ending the French and Indian War and the Seven Years' War brought Britain all of French Canada. The British East India Company also pushed the French out of India.

Unlike its European rivals, Britain had no large standing army. Instead, it built up its fleet. By 1763, Britain had developed a more powerful navy than its greatest rival, France. With superior naval power, it could protect its growing empire and trade.

A Favorable Business Climate England offered a more favorable climate to business and commerce than did its European rivals. Although England followed mercantilist policies, it put fewer restrictions on trade than France. Also, while British nobles, like most other nobles in Europe, looked down on trade, some did engage in business activities.

Caption Answer

A strong navy provides safety for merchant ships and secures port areas.

Resource Directory

Teaching Resources

Creative Teaching Activities Creative Teaching Activities booklet, p. 84

Guided Reading and Review Unit 5 booklet, p. 6

Union With Scotland At home, England expanded by merging with its neighbor, Scotland. In 1707, the Act of Union joined the two countries in the United Kingdom of Great Britain. The United Kingdom also included Wales. The union brought economic advantages to both lands. Free trade between the two created a larger market for farmers and manufacturers. Many Scots, however, resented the union. On two occasions, they supported the claims of Stuart princes who sought to regain the British throne. Eventually, though, growing prosperity made the union more acceptable.

Ireland England had controlled Ireland since the 1100s. In the 1600s, English rulers tried to subdue Catholic Ireland by sending Protestants from England and Scotland to settle there. They gave Protestant settlers title to Irish Catholics' lands. The Irish fiercely resisted Protestant rule. Uprisings led to increased repression. Catholics were forbidden to own weapons, marry non-Catholics, or teach.

Growth of Constitutional Government

In the century following the Glorious Revolution, three new political institutions arose in Britain: political parties, the cabinet, and the office of prime minister. The appearance of these institutions was part of the evolution of Britain's constitutional government—that is, a government whose power is defined and limited by law. The British constitution is not a single document. Instead, it consists of all acts of Parliament over the centuries. It also includes documents such as the Magna Carta and Bill of Rights, as well as unwritten traditions that protect citizens' rights.

Political Parties Two political parties emerged in England in the late 1600s—Tories and Whigs. Tories were generally landed aristocrats who

United Kingdom of Great Britain

Land Ownership in Ireland

90% Protestant / 10% Catholic — 1603

22% Protestant / 78% Catholic — 1685

Protestant / Catholic

Source: Ruth D. Edwards, *An Atlas of Irish History*

United Kingdom
Controlled by Britain
Battle sites

Azimuthal Equal Area Projection
0 100 200 Miles
0 100 200 Kilometers

Political Campaigns
William Hogarth's painting *The Election II—Canvassing for Votes* shows campaigners trying to win votes for their candidates. In England during the 1700s, only men who owned land could vote.
Theme: Political and Social Systems Why might leaders have thought that voting should be limited to landowning men?

sought to preserve older traditions. They supported broad royal powers and a dominant Anglican Church. Whigs backed the policies of the Glorious Revolution. They were more likely to reflect urban business interests, support religious toleration, and favor Parliament over the crown.

These early political parties were unlike the party organizations that we know today. They represented exclusive social circles among rich, powerful men in Parliament. The modern political party, which represents groups of voters and has a distinct platform, did not appear until the 1800s.

The Cabinet System The cabinet, another new feature of government, evolved in the 1700s after the British throne was inherited by a German Protestant prince. George I spoke no English and relied on the leaders in Parliament to help him rule. Under George I and his German-born son George II, a handful of parliamentary advisers set policy. They were called the cabinet because they met in a small room, or "cabinet."

In time, the cabinet gained official status. It was made up of leaders of the majority party in the House of Commons. The cabinet remained in power so long as it enjoyed the support of the Commons. If the Commons voted against a cabinet decision, the cabinet resigned. This cabinet system (also called a parliamentary system) was later adopted by other countries.

The Prime Minister Heading the cabinet was the prime minister. The prime minister was the leader of the majority party in Parliament and in time the chief official of the British government. From 1721 to 1742, the able Whig leader Robert Walpole molded the cabinet into a unified body, requiring all members to agree on major issues. Although the title was not yet used, Walpole is often called Britain's first prime minister.

Politics and Society

The age of Walpole was a time of peace and prosperity. But even as Parliament and the cabinet assumed new powers, British government was far from democratic. Rather, it was an oligarchy—a government in which the ruling power belongs to a few people.

In Britain as on the continent, landowning aristocrats were seen as the "natural" ruling class. The highest nobles held seats in the House of Lords. Other wealthy landowners and rich business leaders in the cities controlled elections to the House of Commons. The right to vote was limited to a relatively few male property owners, and their votes were bought openly.

The lives of most people contrasted sharply with those of the ruling elite. The majority made a meager living from the land. In the 1700s, even that poor existence was threatened. Wealthy landowners bought up farms and took over common lands, evicting tenant farmers and small landowners. Many landless families drifted into towns, where they faced a harsh existence.

A small but growing middle class included successful merchants and manufacturers. They controlled affairs in the towns and cities. Some improved their social standing by marrying into the landed gentry. The middle class also produced talented inventors and entrepreneurs who helped usher in the Industrial Revolution.

George III Reasserts Royal Power

In 1760, George III began a 60-year reign. Unlike his father and grandfather, the new king was born in England. He spoke English and loved Britain. But George was eager to recover the powers the crown had lost. Following his mother's advice, "George, be a king!" he set out to reassert royal power. He wanted to end Whig domination, choose his own ministers, dissolve the cabinet system, and make Parliament follow his will.

Personal Rule Gradually, George found seats in Parliament for "the king's friends." Then, with their help, he began to assert his leadership. Many of his policies, however, would prove disastrous.

After the Seven Years' War, George and his advisers decided that English colonists in North America must pay the costs of their own defense. When colonists protested, Parliament passed harsh measures to force them to obey. In 1775, these and other conflicts triggered the American Revolution, which ended in a loss for Britain.

Cabinet Rule Restored Britain's loss of its American colonies discredited the king. Increasingly, too, he suffered from bouts of mental illness. In the crisis of leadership that followed, cabinet rule was restored in 1788.

In the decades ahead, revolution engulfed France, and Napoleon Bonaparte's armies stormed across Europe, dragging Britain into long wars. During that time, the cabinet controlled the government. The British came to see the prime minister as their real political leader.

George III
This portrait shows the king just a few years after the start of his reign. One of his priorities was to regain power for the throne.

Theme: Art and Literature
What elements of the painting reflect the king's authority?

SECTION 3 Assessment

Recall
1. **Identify:** (a) Act of Union, (b) Tories, (c) Whigs, (d) Robert Walpole, (e) George III.
2. **Define:** (a) constitutional government, (b) cabinet, (c) prime minister, (d) oligarchy.

Comprehension
3. Explain how each of the following contributed to Britain's rise to global power: (a) geography, (b) success in war, (c) attitudes toward business and commerce.

4. How did the British cabinet and office of prime minister develop?
5. What goals did George III have when he became king?

Critical Thinking and Writing
6. **Analyzing Information** How did the British political party system affect most people in Britain?
7. **Predicting Consequences** How might people in Ireland and the American colonies react to British attempts to increase control over those regions?

SECTION 3 Assessment

Recall
1. (a) Act of Union, p. 457 (b) Tories, p. 457 (c) Whigs, p. 457 (d) Robert Walpole, p. 458 (e) George III, p. 459 2. (a) constitutional government, p. 457 (b) cabinet, p. 458 (c) prime minister, p. 458 (d) oligarchy, p. 458

Comprehension
3. (a) Britain's island location helped it to control trade and build a global empire. (b) Military successes won Britain more overseas territories and a monopoly on the slave trade in Spanish America. (c) The British government promoted business by imposing fewer trade restrictions than other nations. 4. George I and II needed advisory help in Parliament because they were from a German state and did not speak English. This body became known as the cabinet and eventually gained official status. The head of the cabinet was the prime minister, leader of the majority party. 5. to reassert royal power by ending Whig domination, to choose his own ministers, to dissolve the cabinet system and gain control of Parliament

Critical Thinking and Writing
6. The lives of most people were not affected. The majority of people were busy making a meager living from the land. 7. Possible answer: Catholics in Ireland would remain poor and politically weak but would protest and rebel against the British government. In the American colonies, people might also rebel.

Activity

Creating a Diagram
Make a diagram showing the relationship among the English crown, prime minister, cabinet, and Parliament during the reigns of George I and George II.

Activity Rubrics

Share rubrics with students before they create their diagrams.

Attempted The diagram is incomplete or does not show the interrelationships of the institutions.

Minimal The diagram depicts all the institutions and shows their relationship to each other but is messy or unclear.

Adequate The diagram depicts all the institutions and clearly shows their relationship to each other.

Exemplary The diagram depicts the different institutions, shows their relationship to each other, and draws conclusions from these relationships.

Caption Answer

elaborate, fur-trimmed cloak; regal expression; and stance

Bell Ringer
Read aloud the quotation from Thomas Paine on this page. Ask students what they believe Paine was saying in this quotation. How did Paine's statements affect the colonies and Britain? Also ask students how Paine's idea reflects those of the Enlightenment.

LESSON PLAN

1. Focus Colonists in the 13 English colonies opposed British taxes and trade restrictions, especially since they had no representation in Parliament. Enlightenment ideas influenced the American Declaration of Independence and the framing of the United States Constitution. The successful American Revolution helped inspire future revolutions in Europe and Latin America.

2. Instruct Divide the class into cooperative learning groups and explain that students will work together to plan a television documentary on the birth of the American republic. The hour-long program will consist of four segments addressing the following topics: American Discontent, The American Revolution Begins, The Long Struggle to Victory, A New Constitution. Assign one of these topics to each group. Instruct students to use the text and outside resources to plan their documentary segment. They should produce a script outline, a list of visuals, and a list of interview subjects. Ask students to present their plans to the class.

3. Assess Tell students that their documentary is being sold as a videotape. Have them describe the documentary in a five-sentence summary that could appear on the videotape box.

4. Reteach If students' Assess activity does not reflect adequate understanding of the lesson, you might assign the *Guide to the Essentials* or the *Interactive Student Tutorial CD-ROM* for this section.

Caption Answer

It suggests that Franklin thought unity was essential to success.

Reading Focus

- What were the chief characteristics of the 13 English colonies?
- How did growing discontent lead to the American Revolution?
- How did the new constitution reflect the ideas of the Enlightenment?

Vocabulary

popular sovereignty
Loyalist
federal republic

Taking Notes

On a sheet of paper draw a time line to show important dates leading up to the emergence of the United States government. Use the time line shown here to help you get started.

French and Indian War ends	Boston Massacre		
1763	1770	1776	1789

Main Idea Colonial opposition to British trade and tax policies led to independence and the founding of the United States of America.

Setting the Scene Early in 1776, English colonists in North America eagerly read the newly published *Common Sense*. The pamphlet called on them to declare their independence from Britain. Its author, Thomas Paine, a recent immigrant from England, wrote with passion tempered by reason. "In the following pages," he declared, "I offer nothing more than simple facts, plain arguments, and common sense."

In *Common Sense*, Paine echoed the themes of the Enlightenment. He rejected ancient prejudice and tyranny, while appealing to reason, natural laws, and the promise of freedom. He wrote:

> "'Tis repugnant to reason, to the universal order of things, to all examples from former ages, to suppose that this Continent can long remain subject to any external power."
> —Thomas Paine, *Common Sense*

Colonists hotly debated Paine's arguments. As resentment of British policies grew, however, many came to agree with his radical ideas.

The 13 English Colonies

By 1750, a string of 13 prosperous colonies stretched along the eastern coast of North America. They were part of Britain's growing empire. Colonial cities such as Boston, New York, and Philadelphia were busy commercial centers that linked North America to the West Indies, Africa, and Europe. Colonial shipyards produced many vessels used in that global trade.

Britain applied mercantilist policies to its colonies. In the 1600s, Parliament had passed the Navigation Acts to regulate colonial trade and manufacturing. For the most part, these acts were not rigorously enforced. Smuggling was common and was not considered a crime by the colonists. Even prominent colonists might gain part of their wealth from smuggled goods.

By the mid-1700s, too, the colonies were home to diverse religious and ethnic groups. Social distinctions were more blurred than in Europe, although government and society were dominated

Colonial Unity
Benjamin Franklin created this political cartoon at the beginning of the French and Indian War. The segmented snake represents Britain's colonies in North America.

Theme: Political and Social Systems How does this cartoon suggest Franklin's attitude toward colonial involvement in the war?

JOIN, or DIE.

Resource Directory

Teaching Resources
Creative Teaching Activities Creative Teaching Activities booklet, p. 85
Guided Reading and Review Unit 5 booklet, p. 8
Skill Application Activity *Distinguishing Facts From Opinions*, Unit 5 booklet, p. 13

by wealthy landowners and merchants. In politics as in much else, there was a good deal of free discussion. Colonists felt entitled to the rights of English citizens, and their colonial assemblies exercised much control over local affairs.

Although the ways of life between the colonists of New England and those in the south differed, they all shared common values, respect for individual enterprise, and a growing self-confidence. Many also had an increasing sense of their own destiny separate from Britain.

Growing Discontent

After 1763, relations between Britain and the 13 colonies grew strained. The Seven Years' War and the French and Indian War in North America had drained the British treasury. King George III and his advisers thought that the colonists should help pay for the war and for troops still stationed along the frontier. Britain began to enforce the long-neglected laws regulating colonial trade, and Parliament passed new laws to increase the taxes paid by the colonies.

The British measures were not burdensome, but colonists bitterly resented what they saw as an attack on their rights. "No taxation without representation," they protested. Because they had no representatives in Parliament, they believed, Parliament had no right to tax them. Parliament did repeal some of the hated measures, such as a tax on all paper, but in general, it asserted its right to impose taxes on the colonies.

Early Clashes A series of violent clashes intensified the crisis. In March 1770, British soldiers in Boston opened fire on a crowd that was pelting them with stones and snowballs. Colonists called the death of five protesters the "Boston Massacre." In December 1773, a handful of colonists hurled a cargo of recently arrived British tea into the harbor to protest a tax on tea. The incident became known as the Boston Tea Party. When Parliament passed harsh laws to punish Massachusetts for the destruction of the tea, other colonies rallied to oppose the British response.

As tensions increased, fighting spread, representatives from each colony gathered in Philadelphia. There, they met in a Continental Congress to decide what action to take. Members included some extraordinary men. Among the participants were the radical yet fair-minded Massachusetts lawyer John Adams, who had defended at trial the British soldiers involved in the Boston Massacre; Virginia planter and soldier George Washington; and political and social leaders from all 13 colonies.

Declaring Independence The Congress set up a Continental Army, with George Washington in command. In April 1775, the crisis exploded into war. Although many battles ended in British victories, they showed that the Patriots were determined to fight at any cost. In 1776, the Second Continental Congress took a momentous step, voting to declare independence from Britain. Thomas Jefferson of Virginia was the principal author of the Declaration of Independence, a document that clearly reflects the ideas of John Locke.

The Declaration claimed that people had the right "to alter or to abolish" unjust governments—a right to revolt. It also emphasized the principle of popular sovereignty, which states that all government power comes from the people. Jefferson carefully detailed the colonists' grievances against Britain. Because the king had trampled colonists' natural rights, he argued, the colonists had the right to rebel and set up a new government that would protect them. Aware of the risks involved, on July 4, 1776, American leaders adopted the Declaration, pledging "our lives, our fortunes, and our sacred honor" to creating and protecting the new United States of America.

Inspiring Words

The Declaration of Independence stands as one of the most important documents in all of history. It still serves as inspiration for people around the world. Here is one of its most moving passages:

"We hold these truths to be self-evident, that all men are created equal, that they are endowed by their Creator with certain unalienable Rights, that among these are Life, Liberty and the pursuit of Happiness. That to secure these rights, Governments are instituted among Men, deriving their just powers from the consent of the governed; That whenever any Form of Government becomes destructive of these ends it is the Right of the People to alter or to abolish it, and to institute new Government, laying its foundation on such principles and organizing its powers in such form, as to them shall seem most likely to effect their Safety and Happiness."

—Declaration of Independence

Skills Assessment

Primary Source How does this excerpt reflect the ideas of John Locke?

Activity
Connections to Geography

Discussing a Topic The philosophical writings of the Enlightenment certainly influenced leading Americans such as Thomas Jefferson and Benjamin Franklin. However, simpler thoughts motivated many of the soldiers in the Continental Army. When Captain Levi Preston was asked if he joined the fight for independence because of having read the writings of Locke and others on liberty, he replied:

"Never heard of 'em. We read only the Bible, the Catechism, Watt's Psalms and Hymns, and the Almanack. Young man, what we meant in going for those red-coats was this: we always had governed ourselves, and we always meant to. They didn't mean we should."

Use the quotation to stimulate discussion on how geography helped bring about this attitude. Also, discuss the democratic traditions that the 13 colonies inherited from England.

Reading Strategy
Finding Evidence

Read aloud to students the following sentence at the top of this page: "Colonists felt entitled to the rights of English citizens. . . ." Ask students to look for evidence to support this statement as they read. *(More Advanced Readers)*

Block Scheduling Support

Organize the class into small groups. Assign each group a member of the Continental Congress, including John Adams, Benjamin Franklin, John Dickinson, John Hancock, John Jay, or Thomas Jefferson. Have each group research what their representative thought about British rule and American independence. Then have a volunteer from each group present to the class that representative's argument for or against independence.

Test Preparation

Have students read the selection from the Declaration of Independence in the Primary Source feature on this page, and then complete the sentence below.

The word *unalienable* in the passage means

A only true in this country.

B only true on this planet.

C unable to be taken away.

D unable to be confirmed.

Primary Source

ANSWER The first sentence identifies natural rights, and the second and third allude to a social contract.

Global Connections

The Spanish Alliance The Spanish government in the territory of Louisiana aided the American cause even before the Battle of Saratoga. In 1776, George Gibson of Virginia sailed to New Orleans to request military supplies from the governor of Spanish Louisiana. After temporarily jailing the American agent to allay British suspicions, the governor began secret shipments of desperately needed supplies. The Spanish supplied medicine, cloth, muskets, and gunpowder to American troops.

In 1779, Spain openly joined in the war against Britain. Spanish forces seized British forts along the Mississippi River and Gulf of Mexico. They also wrested Florida from British control.

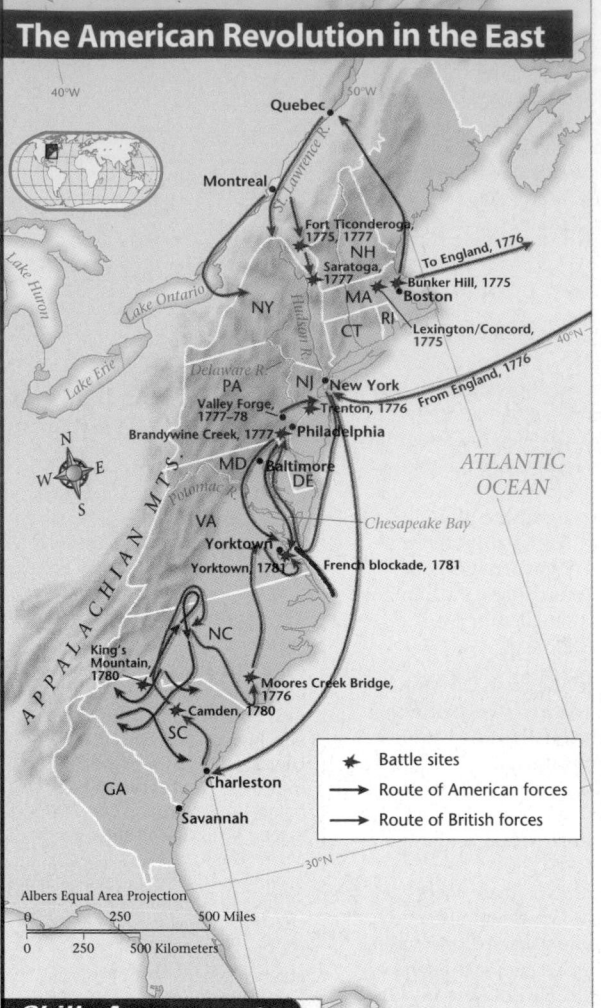

The American Revolution in the East

Skills Assessment

Geography Battles were fought across the colonies, but toward the end of the war, most took place in the southern colonies.

1. **Location** On the map, locate (a) Saratoga, (b) Valley Forge, (c) Yorktown.
2. **Movement** What route did British troops take after landing at Charleston?
3. **Critical Thinking Making Inferences** How was the arrival of the French fleet important during the Battle of Yorktown?

The American Revolution

At first, the American cause looked bleak. The British had professional soldiers, a huge fleet, and plentiful money. They occupied most major American cities. Also, about one third of the colonists were Loyalists, who supported Britain. Many others refused to fight for either side.

The Continental Congress had few military resources and little money to pay its soldiers. Still, colonists battling for independence had some advantages. They were fighting on their own soil for their farms and towns. Although the British held New York and Philadelphia, rebels controlled the countryside.

To counteract these advantages, the British worked to create alliances within the colonies. A number of Native American groups sided with the British, while others saw potential advantages in supporting the Patriot cause. Additionally, the British offered freedom to any enslaved people who were willing to fight the colonists.

The French Alliance A turning point in the war came in 1777, when the Americans triumphed over the British at the Battle of Saratoga. This victory persuaded France to join the Americans against its old rival, Britain. The alliance brought the Americans desperately needed supplies, trained soldiers, and French warships. Spurred by the French example, the Netherlands and Spain added their support.

Hard times continued, however. In the brutal winter of 1777–1778, Continental troops at Valley Forge suffered from cold, hunger, and disease. Throughout this crisis and others, Washington proved a patient, courageous, and determined leader able to hold the ragged army together.

Treaty of Paris Finally in 1781, with the help of the French fleet, which blockaded the Chesapeake Bay, Washington forced the surrender of a British army at Yorktown, Virginia. With that defeat, the British war effort crumbled. Two years later, American, British, and French diplomats signed the Treaty of Paris ending the war. In that treaty, Britain recognized the independence of the United States of America. It also accepted the new nation's western frontier as the Mississippi River.

A New Constitution

The national government set up by a document that Americans called the Articles of Confederation was too weak to rule the new United States effectively. To address this problem, the nation's leaders gathered once more in Philadelphia. During the hot summer of 1787, they met in secret to hammer out the Constitution of the United States. This framework for a strong yet flexible government has adapted to changing conditions for more than 200 years.

The Impact of Enlightenment Ideas The framers of the Constitution had absorbed the ideas of Locke, Montesquieu, and Rousseau and had

---

Skills Assessment

***ANSWERS* 1.** Review locations with students. **2.** They headed northwest through South Carolina then north through North Carolina, turned southeast toward the coast, and turned north again into Virginia before swinging east. **3.** It blockaded the British navy, preventing aid from reaching British troops.

Resource Directory

Teaching Resources

Section Quiz Unit 5 booklet, p. 9
Geography Quiz Unit 5 booklet, p. 14
Chapter Test Forms A, B, and C Unit 5 booklet, pp. 15–19
Answer Key Unit 5 booklet, pp. 74–83

Technology

Interactive Student Tutorial CD-ROM Ch. 18
Computer Test Bank Ch. 18

studied history. They saw government in terms of a social contract into which "We the People of the United States" entered. They provided not only for an elective legislature but also for an elected president rather than a hereditary monarch. For the first president, voters would choose George Washington, who had led the army during the war.

The Constitution created a **federal republic**, with power divided between the federal, or national, government and the states. A central feature of the new federal government was the separation of powers among the legislative, executive, and judicial branches, an idea borrowed directly from Montesquieu. Within that structure, each branch of government was provided with checks and balances on the other branches.

The Bill of Rights, the first 10 amendments to the Constitution, recognized the idea that people had basic rights that the government must protect. These rights included freedom of religion, speech, and the press, as well as the rights to trial by jury and to private property.

Limited Freedom In 1789, the Constitution became the supreme law of the land. It set up a representative government with an elected legislature to reflect the wishes of the governed.

Yet most Americans at the time did not have the right to vote. Only white men who were able to meet certain property requirements could vote. Women could not cast a ballot, nor could African Americans—enslaved *or* free—or Native Americans. It would take more than a century of struggle before the right to vote and equal protection under the law were extended to all adult Americans.

Looking Ahead

Despite these limitations, the Constitution of the United States created the most progressive government of its day. From the start, the new republic shone as a symbol of freedom to European countries and to reformers in Latin America. Its constitution would be copied or adapted by many lands throughout the world.

The Enlightenment ideals that had inspired American colonists brought changes in Europe, too. In 1789, a revolution in France toppled the monarchy in the name of liberty and equality. Before long, other Europeans took up the cry for freedom. By the mid-1800s, most absolute monarchs across Europe would see their powers greatly reduced.

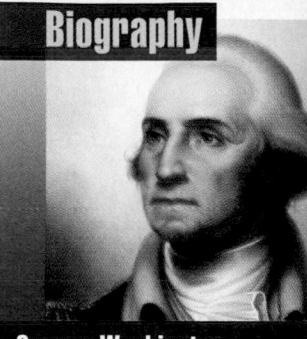

George Washington
1732–1799

As president, George Washington acted on the Enlightenment ideals given form in the Constitution. Some leaders felt that the president should have a grand title. Instead, Washington chose to be addressed as "Mr. President." He believed that a simple form of address was more appropriate for the leader of a republic.

Toward the end of his second term in office, some hoped that he would run again, becoming a president for life. Again, Washington disagreed. Later presidents followed this example. No president would run for a third term until 1940—nearly 150 years after Washington left office.

Theme: Impact of the Individual How did Washington's presidency reflect the ideas of the Enlightenment?

SECTION 4 Assessment

Recall
1. **Identify:** **(a)** Navigation Acts, **(b)** Continental Congress, **(c)** George Washington, **(d)** Battle of Saratoga, **(e)** Treaty of Paris of 1783, **(f)** Bill of Rights.
2. **Define:** **(a)** popular sovereignty, **(b)** Loyalist, **(c)** federal republic.

Comprehension
3. Describe colonial law, society, and politics in the mid-1700s.
4. Explain why conflict between the colonists and Britain increased after 1763.
5. Give an example of how Enlightenment ideas were reflected in each of the following: **(a)** the Declaration of Independence, **(b)** the United States Constitution.

Critical Thinking and Writing
6. **Analyzing Information** Describe the idea of separation of powers. Then, give two examples of how your life would be different if the Constitution did not guarantee separation of powers.
7. **Recognizing Point of View** What reasons might a Loyalist have for opposing the American Revolution?

Activity
Take It to the NET

Use the Internet to research the Battle of Saratoga during the American Revolution. Then, write a letter that an American officer might have written home describing the battle and its significance.

Chapter 18 **463**

Human Drama Activity

Writing a Letter Ask students to put themselves in the position of one of the following:
• a southern slave owner
• a northern merchant
• a New England farmer
• a mother of three sons
• a slave

Have students write a letter to Thomas Jefferson about the Declaration of Independence from the viewpoint of one of these people.

SECTION 4 Assessment

Recall
1. **(a)** Navigation Acts, p. 460 **(b)** Continental Congress, p. 461 **(c)** George Washington, p. 461 **(d)** Battle of Saratoga, p. 462 **(e)** Treaty of Paris of 1783, p. 462 **(f)** Bill of Rights, p. 463 2. **(a)** popular sovereignty, p. 461 **(b)** Loyalists, p. 462 **(c)** federal republic, p. 463

Comprehension
3. Trade was controlled by Britain, while politics and society were generally controlled by wealthy landowners. Religious and social diversity, however, helped reduce the types of social distinctions that would be found in Europe. 4. The colonists resented the new taxes that Britain imposed to help pay for the French and Indian War. They opposed the taxes because they had no representation in Parliament. 5. Possible answers: **(a)** The Declaration of Independence claimed that all men are born with rights that governments must protect. **(b)** The Constitution was based on the social contract theory of government. It created a government with power divided among three branches, just as Montesquieu had recommended.

Critical Thinking and Writing
6. Students' answers should reflect an understanding of how the separation of powers prevents any one branch from exercising too much power. 7. Possible answer: The colonies belonged to Britain and owed allegiance to it; Britain supported and protected the colonies; revolution was dangerous.

Activity Rubrics

Share rubrics with students before they write their letters.

Attempted The letter is incomplete.

Minimal The letter is complete but lacks significant details or has many mechanical errors.

Adequate The letter accurately and clearly describes the battle as well as its significance.

Exemplary The letter accurately and clearly describes the battle, shows thorough understanding of the significance of the battle, and is imaginatively written.

Biography

ANSWER It represented democratic ideas of equality (taking a common title) and elective government (in not running for a third term).

Creating a Chapter Summary

As a reteaching opportunity, pair a more able student with a less able student to complete this chapter summary.

Students might supply the following additional answers: **Ideas of Enlightenment**—Authority lies with people; government is responsible to people it serves **American Constitution**—equality before law; separation of three branches of government; government responsible to people; guaranteed rights

Building Vocabulary

1–10. Students' classifications should show a clear understanding of each word.

Recalling Key Facts

11. The people have the right to overthrow the government.
12. by the natural forces of supply and demand
13. Serfdom largely disappeared in Western Europe but remained common in Eastern Europe.
14. England, Wales, and Scotland
15. Britain sought to tax the colonies to pay for their defense, while colonists thought Britain had no right to tax them.

Critical Thinking and Writing

16. **(a)** Answers should describe a current event in which the human rights of an individual or group are being challenged or asserted. **(b)** The suggested response should be plausible for the *philosophe* chosen.
17. Possible answers: **(a)** ideas connected with the Enlightenment, the Magna Carta, the Petition of Right, the Glorious Revolution, and the English Bill of Rights **(b)** Colonists believed that the British government was violating their traditional, legal, and natural rights. They believed that they were entitled to rebel.
18. **(a)** People place the greatest value on the things that are the most difficult to attain. **(b)** Encourage students to express their opinions clearly and to support them with pertinent examples.
19. **(a)** Americans were fighting on their own ground for their farms and towns, which gave them a strong incentive. **(b)** The British soldiers were unfamiliar with the unsettled land and had no strong motive for winning.

Creating a Chapter Summary

On a sheet of paper, draw a web like the one shown here. Add information to the empty circles to help you recall important ideas of the Enlightenment and important ideas from the Enlightenment that were used in the American Constitution.

For additional review and enrichment activities, see the interactive version of *World History* available on the Web and on CD-ROM.

Web Site Self-Test
For practice test questions for Chapter 18, see **www.phschool.com**.

Building Vocabulary

Classify each of the chapter vocabulary words listed below under *one* of the following themes: art and literature; political and social systems; religions and value systems.

1. **natural law**
2. *philosophe*
3. **enlightened despot**
4. **baroque**
5. **rococo**
6. **constitutional government**
7. **cabinet**
8. **prime minister**
9. **Loyalist**
10. **federal republic**

Recalling Key Facts

11. According to John Locke, what should happen if a government violates people's natural rights?
12. According to Adam Smith, how should wages and prices be regulated?
13. How did serfdom differ in Eastern and Western Europe?
14. What areas combined to form the United Kingdom of Great Britain?
15. How did taxation create tensions between the American colonies and the British government?

Critical Thinking and Writing

16. **Linking Past and Present** Today, we talk about human rights rather than natural rights. **(a)** Describe a human rights issue that has been in the news recently. **(b)** Choose one *philosophe* from this chapter and describe how he or she might respond to the issue.
17. **Analyzing Information** **(a)** What ideas about government do you think English settlers brought with them to the Americas? **(b)** How might those ideas have contributed to the outbreak of the American Revolution?
18. **Defending a Position** During the American Revolution, Thomas Paine used the following words to encourage the colonists during a particularly grim time: "What we obtain too cheaply, we esteem too light; it is [costliness] only that gives everything its value." **(a)** What did he mean by this? **(b)** Do you agree or disagree? Give an example to defend your position.
19. **Connecting to Geography** **(a)** During the American Revolution, how did the location of the war help the Americans? **(b)** Why was it a problem for the British?

Skills Assessment
Analyzing Primary Sources

This passage is from a selection by Voltaire titled "Tolerance." In it, Voltaire describes people who abuse their power. In the first part of the excerpt, he uses the first person, "I," to show how these people think. In the remainder, he uses the third person, "they," to describe the effects of their actions on others. Read the passage, then answer the questions that follow.

> "I possess a dignity and power founded on ignorance; I walk on the heads of the men who lie at my feet; if they should rise and look me in the face, I am lost; I must bind them to the ground, therefore, with iron chains. Thus have reasoned the men whom centuries of bigotry have made powerful. They have other powerful men beneath them, and these have still others, who all grow rich with the spoils of the poor, grow fat on their blood, and laugh at their stupidity. They all hate tolerance, as . . . tyrants dread the word liberty."

—Voltaire, *Philosophical Dictionary*

20. Why would people who abuse their power be "lost" if others were to "rise and look me in the face"?

21. What do you think Voltaire meant by the phrase "grow fat on their blood"?

22. What is Voltaire's tone in this passage? How does it suggest Voltaire's own beliefs?

23. Who are some of the intolerant people Voltaire might have had in mind when he wrote this?

24. **(a)** Identify a simile used in this excerpt. **(b)** Identify a metaphor in the excerpt.

Skills Tip

To illustrate a point, authors may use similes and metaphors. A simile is a description that uses "like" or "as" to draw comparisons. A metaphor uses the comparison as the description itself.

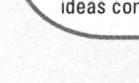

Skills Assessment
Take It to the NET

Use the Internet to research one of the political thinkers described in the text. Then, write a letter to that person explaining whether you think his or her ideas continue to be relevant in the present day.

Skills Assessment
Analyzing Charts

SEPARATION OF POWERS

Executive Branch
(President)
Carries out laws
Proposes laws
Can veto laws
Negotiates foreign treaties
Serves as commander in chief of the armed forces
Appoints federal judges, ambassadors, and other high officials
Can grant pardons to federal offenders

Legislative Branch
(Congress)
Passes laws
Can override President's veto
Approves treaties and presidential appointments
Can impeach and remove President and other high officials
Creates lower federal courts
Appropriates money
Prints and coins money
Raises and supports the armed forces
Can declare war
Regulates foreign and interstate trade

Judicial Branch
(Supreme Court and Other Federal Courts)
Interprets laws
Can declare laws unconstitutional
Can declare executive actions unconstitutional

This table shows the powers held by each branch of the United States government. Study the table and answer the following questions:

25. Who heads the executive branch?
26. What is the main role of the legislative branch?
27. In 1748, Montesquieu wrote, "There is no liberty, if the power of judging is not separated from the legislative and executive powers. Were it joined with the legislative, the life and liberty of the subject would be exposed to arbitrary control, for the judge would then be the legislator. Were it joined to the executive power, the judge might behave with all the violence of an oppressor." How does this table relate to Montesquieu's statement?

Analyzing Primary Sources

20. because the position of power depends on the perception of power; if the others saw that the powerful are human too, the powerful could no longer maintain their status
21. Possible answer: People who are intolerant and powerful rely on the work of others for their own riches.
22. He is angry—even scathing—in his denunciation. He obviously thinks tolerance is important.
23. Possible answer: clergy, monarchs, nobles
24. **(a)** "They hate all tolerance, as . . . tyrants dread the word liberty." **(b)** "I walk on the heads of the men who lie at my feet."

Analyzing Charts

25. the President
26. to pass laws
27. The chart shows how the United States government incorporates Montesquieu's ideas by creating a separate judicial branch.

Skills Tip

Once a simile or metaphor has been identified, analyze it to try to find what emotional impact the words have. The Skills Handbook in the front of the book has a lesson that will help students with this feature.

Unit Theme Activity

Remind students to continue working on their Unit Theme Portfolio Activity. Make sure students understand the assignment and have begun work.

Take It to the NET

Direct students to **www.phschool.com** for links to sites that will help them get started on their assignments. Share rubrics with students.
Attempted The letter is incomplete and does not address the ideas of the political thinker.
Minimal The letter is complete but does not adequately address ideas of the political thinker.
Adequate The letter addresses ideas of the political thinker and evaluates their relevance to the present day.
Exemplary The letter addresses ideas of the political thinker, evaluates their relevance to the present day by citing numerous examples, and is creative and well written.

Chapter 19 Planning Guide

Resource Manager

	CORE INSTRUCTION	READING/SKILLS
Chapter Level Resources	📚 Teaching Resources 　📖 Pacing Charts, Ch. 19 　📖 Teaching With Themes, p. 22 🏛 Color Transparencies, p. F–39 💿 Resource Pro® Ch. 19 💻 **www.phschool.com** 　• eTeach	💿 Book on CD, Ch. 19 💿 Interactive Student Tutorial CD-ROM, Ch. 19 💿 Social Studies Skills Tutor CD-ROM 🏛 Skills Transparencies
1 On the Eve of Revolution 1. Describe the social structure of the old regime. 2. Outline why France faced economic troubles in 1789. 3. Explain why Louis XVI called the Estates General. 4. Summarize why a Paris crowd stormed the Bastille.	📚 Teaching Resources 　📖 Creative Teaching Activities, p. 86 💿 Prentice Hall Presentation Pro, Ch. 19, Section 1 🏛 Section Reading Support Transparencies	📚 Teaching Resources 　📒 Unit 5 booklet 　• Guided Reading and Review, p. 20 　📖 Guide to the Essentials 📼 Guided Reading Audiotapes, Ch. 19, Section 1
2 Creating a New France 1. Describe how popular revolts contributed to the French Revolution. 2. Enumerate the moderate reforms enacted by the National Assembly. 3. Explain how foreign reaction to the revolution helped lead to war.	📚 Teaching Resources 　📒 Unit 5 booklet 　• Primary Source Activity, p. 31 　📖 Creative Teaching Activities, p. 87 💿 Prentice Hall Presentation Pro, Ch. 19, Section 2	📚 Teaching Resources 　📒 Unit 5 booklet 　• Guided Reading and Review, p. 22 　📖 Guide to the Essentials 📼 Guided Reading Audiotapes, Ch. 19, Section 2
3 Radical Days 1. Explain why radicals abolished the monarchy. 2. Describe how the excesses of the Convention led to the Directory. 3. Specify what impact the revolution had on women and daily life.	📚 Teaching Resources 　📒 Unit 5 booklet 　• Biography Activity, p. 30 　📖 Creative Teaching Activities, p. 88 💿 Prentice Hall Presentation Pro, Ch. 19, Section 3	📚 Teaching Resources 　📒 Unit 5 booklet 　• Guided Reading and Review, p. 24 　📖 Guide to the Essentials 📼 Guided Reading Audiotapes, Ch. 19, Section 3
4 The Age of Napoleon Begins 1. Explain how Napoleon rose to power. 2. Specify how revolutionary reforms changed under Napoleon. 3. Describe how Napoleon built an empire in Europe.	📚 Teaching Resources 　📒 Unit 5 booklet 　• Viewpoint Activity, p. 32 　📖 Creative Teaching Activities, p. 89 💿 Prentice Hall Presentation Pro, Ch. 19, Section 4	📚 Teaching Resources 　📒 Unit 5 booklet 　• Guided Reading and Review, p. 26 　📖 Guide to the Essentials 📼 Guided Reading Audiotapes, Ch. 19, Section 4
5 The End of an Era 1. Identify the challenges that threatened Napoleon's empire. 2. Describe the events that led to Napoleon's defeat. 3. Enumerate the goals of the Congress of Vienna.	📚 Teaching Resources 　📖 Creative Teaching Activities, p. 90 💿 Prentice Hall Presentation Pro, Ch. 19, Section 5 🏛 Section Reading Support Transparencies	📚 Teaching Resources 　📒 Unit 5 booklet 　• Guided Reading and Review, p. 28 　• Skill Application Activity, p. 33 　📖 Guide to the Essentials

ENRICHMENT/PRE-AP

- www.phschool.com
  - Why Study History?

Teaching Resources
- History Through Literature, pp. 41–42
- Color Transparencies, p. C–51
- www.phschool.com
  - Virtual Field Trip

- www.phschool.com
  - Internet Activities, Section 2

Teaching Resources
- Chapter Extension Activities, p. 48
  - Simulations, pp. 9–11

- Color Transparencies, p. D–69
- www.phschool.com
  - Internet Activities, Section 4

Teaching Resources
- Chapter Extension Activities, p. 49
- Visions, Voices, Views, Animated Map Story, tape 5
- www.phschool.com
  - Internet Activities, *Napoleon's Retreat From Moscow*

ASSESSMENT

PRENTICE HALL ASSESSMENT SYSTEM

Core Assessment
- ExamView Test Bank booklet, Ch. 19
- ExamView Test Bank CD-ROM, Ch. 19

Standardized Test Preparation

Diagnose and Prescribe
- Diagnostic Tests for High School Social Studies Skills

Review and Reteach
- Review Book for World History

Practice and Assess
- Test-Taking Strategies With Transparencies for High School
- Alternative Assessment booklet
- Test Prep Book for World History

Teaching Resources
- Unit 5 booklet
  - Geography Quiz, p. 34
  - Section Quizzes, pp. 21, 23, 25, 27, 29
  - Chapter Tests A, B, and C, pp. 35–39
- www.phschool.com
  - Self-Test

CUSTOMIZE FOR INDIVIDUAL NEEDS

Gifted and Talented
- Teacher's Edition, Activities: Customize for Heterogeneous Groups, p. 482

Less Proficient Readers
- Guide to the Essentials, Ch. 19
- Book on CD, Ch. 19
- Teacher's Edition, Activities: Reading Strategy, p. 474; Reading Strategy, p. 489

Less Proficient Writers
- Teacher's Edition, Activities: Customize for Auditory Learners, p. 492

Students Acquiring English/ESL
- Guide to the Essentials, English/Spanish, Ch. 19
- Guided Reading Audiotapes, English/Spanish, Ch. 19
- Book on CD, Ch. 19
- Teacher's Edition, Activities marked with an *

iTEXT

Don't miss the exclusive interactive version of *World History: Connections to Today* on the Internet and CD-ROM.

INTRODUCTION

In 1789, a financial crisis, an outmoded social system, and an indecisive king burdened France. Reformers called for a constitution, limitations on the monarch's power, and equality among citizens. Peasants and the urban poor rioted. The crisis deepened, moderates lost control, and the execution of the king and queen in 1793 ushered in the Reign of Terror. Between 1799 and 1815, Napoleon Bonaparte controlled the government, conquered the forces of Europe's major powers, and spread the ideas of the revolution across Europe. After his defeat, the Congress of Vienna tried to undo the effects of the French Revolution.

Focusing on Themes

Suggest that students focus on these theme questions as they read:

Religions and Value Systems
What beliefs and attitudes inspired the leaders of the French Revolution?

Political and Social Systems
How did the French Revolution reshape social and political institutions?

Impact of the Individual
How did Napoleon Bonaparte create upheaval across Europe?

Continuity and Change
What were the effects of the French Revolution?

TIME LINE ACTIVITY

You may wish to share the About the Pictures note with your students before you ask these questions about the time line:

1. In what year would you guess the French Revolution began? *(1789)*
2. What does Reign of Terror mean? *(rule by fear)*
3. What event in the New World took place about the time Napoleon became emperor? *(Haiti declares independence from France, 1804)*

Don't Miss!

Analyzing Primary Sources
Execution of a King
(Section 3)

Disaster!
Napoleon's Retreat
From Moscow
(Section 5)

The French Revolution and Napoleon
1789–1815

Chapter Preview

1 On the Eve of Revolution
2 Creating a New France
3 Radical Days
4 The Age of Napoleon Begins
5 The End of an Era

1793

During the Reign of Terror, which begins in 1793, the guillotine is used to execute thousands of French citizens.

1789

After a battle with royal troops, Parisians capture the Bastille on July 14, 1789.

CHAPTER EVENTS

1799

Napoleon overthrows the Directory.

| 1790 | 1795 | 1800 |

GLOBAL EVENTS

1789 The United States Constitution is ratified.

1793 China rejects British trade offer.

Resource Directory

Teaching Resources

Teaching With Themes Chapter Theme Activities, p. 22
Pacing Chart With Block Scheduling Guide Ch. 19

Technology

World History Color Transparencies Ch. 19 Graphic Organizer, p. F–39

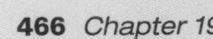

Revolutionary France at War, 1793

France, 1793

Allied countries against France

Boundary of Holy Roman Empire

By 1793, the French Revolution had plunged France into a general European war that would last on and off for more than 20 years and transform Europe.

(Map labels: IRELAND, GREAT BRITAIN, North Sea, KINGDOM OF DENMARK AND NORWAY, SWEDEN, Baltic Sea, PRUSSIA, NETHERLANDS, HANOVER, PRUSSIA, SAXONY, POLAND, RUSSIAN EMPIRE, AUSTRIAN NETHERLANDS, ATLANTIC OCEAN, PRUSSIA, BAVARIA, AUSTRIA, HUNGARY, FRANCE, SWISS CONFED., ALPS, VENETIAN REPUBLIC, OTTOMAN EMPIRE, Danube R., PORTUGAL, SPAIN, PYRENEES MTS., KINGDOM OF SARDINIA, PAPAL STATES, Adriatic Sea, Mediterranean Sea, KINGDOM OF NAPLES, Azimuthal Equal Area Projection, 0 150 300 Miles, 0 150 300 Kilometers)

1804
In a magnificent ceremony, Napoleon crowns himself emperor of the French.

1805

1804 Haiti declares independence from France.

1812
Napoleon invades Russia.

1810

1812 The United States declares war on Britain.

1815
Napoleon abdicates after British and Prussian forces defeat him at Waterloo. The Duke of Wellington is the victorious British general.

1815

Chapter 19 **467**

Independent Assignments

Have students read one section as they prepare for class. After class, have them complete the assignment. Some students may benefit from using the Guided Reading and Review worksheets.

Section 1 Have students use the worksheet *A Tale of Two Cities* in the History Through Literature booklet, pp. 41–42, to explore the passions that drove the French people.
Section 2 Have students use the worksheet *The Royal Family in Prison* in the Unit 5 booklet, p. 31, to learn how Louis XVI and his family were treated in prison.
Section 3 Have students use the worksheet *Maximilien Robespierre* in the Unit 5 booklet, p. 30,

to learn about this leader of the Reign of Terror.
Section 4 Have students use the worksheet *Two Views of Napoleon* in the Unit 5 booklet, p. 32, to learn what two of Napoleon's contemporaries thought of him.
Section 5 Have students use the maps *Europe in 1812* and *Europe After the Congress of Vienna, 1815* in the Historical Outline Map Book, pp. 32–33, to compare the boundaries of Europe under Napoleon and after his fall.

Revolutionary France at War, 1793

Activating Prior Knowledge
What kind of government was found in most of Europe at this time—including in France before the revolution? *(Most European governments were monarchies.)*

Previewing
Given that many nations were at war against France, under what circumstances might France be able to hold its own against its enemies? *(Possible answers: disorganization of or lack of cooperation by the allies, poor allied military leaders, excellent French military leaders)*

Background
About the Pictures

1 2 3 4

1. The Bastille was a symbol of royal power because it was used mainly for political prisoners, especially in the 1600s and 1700s. Anyone the monarch didn't like could be arrested on a secret warrant, called a *lettre de cachet*, and kept there without a trial.

2. Use of the guillotine survived in France as a method of execution until 1981, when the death penalty was abolished.

3. In Ingres's idealization of Napoleon, power and authority are symbolized by the scepter of Charles V on one side and Charlemagne's hand of justice and sword on the other.

4. This British medal commemorates the battle of Waterloo. People still refer to a disastrous defeat as "meeting one's Waterloo." Napoleon's nemesis, Wellington, was known as the Iron Duke for his resolute will.

eTeach

Be sure to check out this month's online discussion with a World History Master Teacher.

Go to **www.phschool.com**.

Bell Ringer Ask students to study the first paragraph on this page and the graphs and picture on the opposite page. Then, have them write five generalizations about the social structure of France at the start of the French Revolution.

LESSON PLAN

1. Focus In 1789, French society consisted of three social classes: the clergy, or First Estate; the nobility, or Second Estate; and the rest of the population, who comprised the Third Estate. The nation faced social unrest, enormous debt, and food shortages. When the king summoned the Estates General to carry out reforms, members of the Third Estate broke away and formed the National Assembly. On July 14, 1789, angry Parisians stormed the Bastille.

2. Instruct Have students work with a partner. Have each pair of students write brief profiles for three of the following: a nun, priest, nobleman, banker, manufacturer, lawyer, peasant, member of the royal family, journeyman, and servant. In their profiles, students should identify the estate to which the person belonged, privileges that the person might have had, complaints that the person might have had, and changes that the person might have desired. After students have finished their profiles, invite volunteers to read them to the class.

3. Assess Have students draw a political cartoon that represents the views of one or more of the persons whom they profiled.

4. Reteach If students' *Assess* activity does not reflect adequate understanding of the lesson, you might assign the *Guide to the Essentials* or the *Interactive Student Tutorial CD-ROM* for this section.

Reading Focus

- What was the social structure of the old regime?
- Why did France face economic troubles in 1789?
- Why did Louis XVI call the Estates General?
- Why did a Paris crowd storm the Bastille?

Vocabulary

bourgeoisie
deficit spending

Taking Notes

As you read this section, create a chart to identify causes of the French Revolution. Use the incomplete chart below as a model. Add more arrows for causes if you need them.

Burden of debt

THE FRENCH REVOLUTION

Main Idea Social unrest, economic troubles, and the desire for political reforms led to the French Revolution.

Setting the Scene On April 28, 1789, unrest exploded at a Paris wallpaper factory. A rumor had spread that the factory owner was planning to cut wages even though bread prices were soaring. Enraged workers vandalized the owner's home. Later, they stopped some nobles returning from an afternoon at the racetrack. They forced the nobles to shout: "Long live the Third Estate [the common people]!"

Riots like these did not worry most nobles. They knew that France faced a severe economic crisis but thought that financial reforms would ease the problem. Then, rioters would be hanged, as they deserved.

The nobles were wrong. The crisis went deeper than government finances. Reform would not be enough. By July, the hungry, unemployed, and poorly paid people of Paris had taken up arms. Their actions would push events further and faster than anyone could have foreseen.

The Old Regime

In 1789, France, like the rest of Europe, still clung to an outdated social system that had emerged in the Middle Ages. Under this *ancien regime,* or old order, everyone in France belonged to one of three classes: the First Estate, made up of the clergy; the Second Estate, made up of the nobility; or the Third Estate, the vast majority of the population.

The Clergy In the Middle Ages, the Church had exerted great influence throughout Christian Europe. In 1789, the French clergy still enjoyed enormous wealth and privilege. The Church owned about 10 percent of the land, collected tithes, and paid no direct taxes to the state. High Church leaders such as bishops and abbots were usually nobles who lived very well. Parish priests, however, often came from humble origins and might be as poor as their peasant congregations.

The First Estate did provide some social services. Nuns, monks, and priests ran schools, hospitals, and orphanages. But during the Enlightenment, *philosophes* targeted the Church for reform. They criticized the idleness of some clergy, Church interference in politics, and its intolerance of dissent. In response, many clergy condemned the Enlightenment for undermining religion and moral order.

The Nobles The Second Estate was the titled nobility of French society. In the Middle Ages, noble knights had defended the land. In the 1600s, Richelieu and Louis XIV had crushed the nobles' military power but given

Resource Directory

Teaching Resources
Creative Teaching Activities Creative Teaching Activities booklet, p. 86
Guided Reading and Review Unit 5 booklet, p. 20

Technology
World History Color Transparencies *High Fashion in France,* p. C–51

them other rights—under strict royal control. Those rights included top jobs in government, the army, the courts, and the Church.

At Versailles, ambitious nobles competed for royal appointments while idle courtiers enjoyed endless entertainments. Many nobles, however, lived far from the center of power. Though they owned land, they had little money income. As a result, they felt the pinch of trying to maintain their status in a period of rising prices.

Many nobles hated absolutism and resented the royal bureaucracy that employed middle-class men in positions that once had been reserved for the aristocracy. They feared losing their traditional privileges, especially their freedom from paying taxes.

The Third Estate In 1789, the Third Estate numbered about 27 million people, or 98 percent of the population. It was a diverse group. At the top sat the bourgeoisie (boor zhwah ZEE), or middle class. The bourgeoisie included prosperous bankers, merchants, and manufacturers. It also included the officials who staffed the royal bureaucracy, as well as lawyers, doctors, journalists, professors, and skilled artisans.

The bulk of the Third Estate—9 out of 10 people in France—were rural peasants. Some were prosperous landowners who hired laborers to work for them. Others were tenant farmers or day laborers.

The poorest members of the Third Estate were urban workers. They included apprentices, journeymen, and others who worked in industries such as printing or clothmaking. Many women and men earned a meager living as servants, stable hands, porters, construction workers, or street sellers of everything from food to pots and pans. A large number of the urban poor were unemployed. To survive, some turned to begging or crime.

Discontent From rich to poor, members of the Third Estate resented the privileges enjoyed by their social "betters." Wealthy bourgeois families could buy political office and even titles, but the best jobs were still reserved for nobles. Urban workers earned miserable wages. Even the smallest rise in the price of bread, their main food, brought the threat of greater hunger or even starvation.

The Old Regime
In this cartoon, a priest and a noble stand on a stone crushing a peasant. The stone represents burdensome taxes and feudal dues. Taken together, the pie graphs below show inequalities among France's three estates.

Theme: Political and Social Systems Why did the Third Estate consider the distribution of land unfair?

Population and Land Ownership in France, 1789

Population by Estate

1.5%
98%
0.5%

First Estate
Second Estate
Third Estate

Land Owned by Estate

20%
70%
10%

Chapter 19 **469**

Customize for . . .
Visual Learners

Constructing Graphs and Charts After students have studied the graphs on this page, ask them to create other visual means of looking at land ownership and the social structure of France in 1789. Students might draw line graphs or bar graphs. They also might create a pyramid chart displaying the relative size and status of each of the three estates.

Customize for . . .
Auditory Learners

Analyzing a Primary Source Read aloud the following excerpt from Abbé Sieyès's pamphlet *What Is the Third Estate?* Then, ask students to respond to the questions that follow. For students who need extra help, distribute copies of the excerpt and preteach difficult vocabulary words.

"Thus, what is the third estate? Everything; but an everything shackled and oppressed. What would it be without the privileged order? Everything, but an everything free and flourishing. Nothing can progress without it; everything would proceed infinitely better without the others. . . . [The] nobility does not belong to the social organization at all . . . indeed, it may be a burden upon the nation."

(1) How would you feel and respond to these words if you were a member of the Third Estate? (2) What might your reaction be if you were a member of the nobility? ✳

Block Scheduling Support

Have students write one or two paragraphs showing how the two quotations below are related to the events and conditions described in Section 1.
(1) "Man is born free and everywhere is in chains." (Rousseau)
(2) "People have a natural right to life, liberty, and property. Rulers have a responsibility to protect these rights. People have the right to change a government that fails to do so." (Locke)

Test Preparation

Have students read "The Clergy" on the opposite page, and then answer the question below.

Which of the following is supported by the passage?

A All members of the clergy were wealthy.

B All members of the clergy lived in luxury.

C High ranking clergymen were usually nobles.

D Most nuns, monks, and priests were idle.

Caption Answer

The First and Second Estates owned 30 percent of the land even though they comprised only 2 percent of the population.

Petitioning the King The following excerpt is from a petition to King Louis XVI from the village of Lion-en-Sullias, dated March 1, 1789. It reflects the popular feeling that government policies were responsible for the famine that afflicted the countryside.

"Relying on His Majesty's paternal goodness, they dare to hope that he will . . . exempt their sons and domestics from militia service in order to let them attend to the cultivation of the land and provide the kingdom with more grain, as useful to the State as military service and they ask this with all more reason because hands are lacking in the countryside. What causes the countryside to be deserted is the too great misery that reigns over it, . . . a result of the extreme misery caused by the excessive burden of numerous taxes."

You may wish to use this primary source to stimulate a class discussion about French peasant life and the policies of the French government.

Primary Source

Bread Riots in France
The British embassy in Paris sent regular reports to London. The excerpts below describe the effects of rising bread prices:

"November 27, 1788
The price of bread has again been raised . . . the consequences of which has already been felt in the instance of more than 40 bakers having been obliged to shut up shop. In the provinces these discontents have still risen higher. . . . The public magazines of wheat have been broken open and pillaged.

December 11, 1788
Bread has again been raised. . . . The distress of the poor is already very great as may be conceived, and the unusual severity of the weather is at this moment peculiarly unfortunate for them; nor on this account, is it very surprising that robberies should be frequent, which at present is the case in an alarming degree. It is by no means safe to walk the streets late in the evening."

—O. Browning, *Dispatches from Paris*

Skills Assessment

Primary Source What were the effects of the rising prices?

Peasants were burdened by taxes on everything from land to soap to salt. Though they were technically free, many owed fees and services that dated back to medieval times, such as the corvée (kohr VAY), which was unpaid labor to repair roads and bridges. Peasants were also incensed when nobles, hurt by rising prices, tried to reimpose old manor dues. Also, only nobles had the right to hunt wild game. Peasants were even forbidden to kill rabbits that ate their crops.

In towns and cities, Enlightenment ideas led people to question the inequalities of the old regime. Why, people demanded, should the first two estates have such great privileges at the expense of the majority? It did not meet the test of reason! Throughout France, the Third Estate called for the privileged classes to pay their share.

Economic Troubles

Economic woes added to the social unrest and heightened tensions. One of the causes of the decline was a mushrooming financial crisis that was due in part to years of deficit spending, that is, a government's spending more money than it takes in.

The Burden of Debt Louis XIV had left France deeply in debt. Wars like the Seven Years' War and the American Revolution strained the treasury even further. Costs generally had risen in the 1700s, and the lavish court soaked up millions. To bridge the gap between income and expenses, the government borrowed more and more money. By 1789, half its tax income went just to pay interest on this enormous debt.

To solve the financial crisis, the government would have to increase taxes, reduce expenses, or both. However, the nobles and clergy fiercely resisted any attempt to end their exemption from taxes.

Poor Harvests Other economic troubles added to the financial crisis. A general economic decline had begun in the 1770s. Then, in the late 1780s, bad harvests sent food prices soaring and brought hunger to poorer peasants and city dwellers.

Hard times and lack of food inflamed these people. In towns, people rioted, demanding bread. In the countryside, peasants began to attack the manor houses of the nobles. Arthur Young, an English visitor to France, witnessed the violence:

"Everything conspires to render the present period in France critical: the [lack] of bread is terrible; accounts arrive every moment from the provinces of riots and disturbances, and calling in the military, to preserve the peace of the markets."
—Arthur Young, *Travels in France During the Years 1787–1789*

Failure of Reform The heirs of Louis XIV were not the right men to solve the economic crisis that afflicted France. Louis XV, who ruled from 1715 to 1774, pursued pleasure before serious business and ran up more debts. His grandson, Louis XVI, was well-meaning but weak and indecisive. He wisely chose Jacques Necker, a financial wizard, as an adviser. Necker urged the king to reduce extravagant court spending, reform government, and abolish burdensome tariffs on internal trade. When Necker proposed taxing the First and Second estates, however, the nobles and high clergy forced the king to dismiss the would-be reformer.

As the crisis deepened, the pressure for reform mounted. Finally, the wealthy and powerful classes demanded that the king summon the Estates General before making any changes. French kings had not called the Estates General for 175 years, fearing that nobles would use it to recover the feudal powers that they had lost under absolute rule. To reform-minded nobles, the Estates General seemed to offer a chance to carry out changes

Primary Source

ANSWER Many bakers went out of business; stores of wheat were broken into and wheat stolen; the poor endured great hardship and discontent; robberies increased to the point where it was no longer safe to walk the streets in late evening.

Virtual Field Trip

www.phschool.com

WebMuseum
Paris, France

To see other David paintings of the French Revolution and Napoleonic era, use the Internet address above to link to the WebMuseum.

The Tennis Court Oath
In this painting, Jacques Louis David captures the moment when delegates at the National Assembly took the Tennis Court Oath.

Theme: Continuity and Change Why did the Third Estate want to change the voting system used in the Estates General?

Background
Daily Life

Life at the Bastille The seven prisoners who were freed from the Bastille on July 14 may not have been as jubilant as their rescuers expected. Ironically, inmates at the Bastille were treated more as guests of the king than as criminals. If they desired, they were provided with furniture. Or, if they had the means, as many did, they were permitted to bring their own furnishings, including works of art and musical instruments. Meals at the Bastille consisted of several courses, and often catered to personal tastes. Prisoners could hire personal servants and could have parties attended by fellow prisoners as well as outside guests.

like those that had come with the Glorious Revolution in England. They hoped that they could bring the absolute monarch under the control of the nobles and guarantee their own privileges.

Louis XVI Calls the Estates General

As 1788 came to a close, France tottered on the verge of bankruptcy. Bread riots were spreading, and nobles, fearful of taxes, were denouncing royal tyranny. A baffled Louis XVI finally summoned the Estates General to meet at Versailles the following year.

The Cahiers In preparation, Louis had all three estates prepare *cahiers* (kah YAY), or notebooks, listing their grievances. Many cahiers called for reforms such as fairer taxes, freedom of the press, or regular meetings of the Estates General. In one town, shoemakers denounced regulations that made leather so expensive they could not afford to make shoes. Some peasants demanded the right to kill animals that were destroying their crops. Servant girls in the city of Toulouse demanded the right to leave service when they wanted and that "after a girl has served her master for many years, she receive some reward for her service."

The cahiers testified to boiling class resentments. One called tax collectors "bloodsuckers of the nation who drink the tears of the unfortunate from goblets of gold." Another one of the cahiers condemned the courts of nobles as "vampires pumping the last drop of blood" from the people. Another complained that "20 million must live on half the wealth of France while the clergy . . . devour the other half."

The Tennis Court Oath Delegates to the Estates General from the Third Estate were elected, though only propertied men could vote. Thus, they were mostly lawyers, middle-class officials, and writers. They were familiar with the writings of Voltaire, Rousseau, and other *philosophes*. They went to Versailles not only to solve the financial crisis but also to insist on reform.

The Estates General convened in May 1789. From the start, the delegates were deadlocked over the issue of voting. Traditionally, each estate had met and voted separately. Each group had one vote. Under this system, the First and Second estates always outvoted the Third Estate two to one.

Human Drama Note

Storming the Bastille The storming of the Bastille is described in the textbook on the following page. When the crowd attempted to enter the Bastille, its commander, the Marquis de Launay, ordered his troops to open fire. In the ensuing four-hour battle, revolutionary fervor seized Paris. Some soldiers joined the besiegers and turned their cannons against the fortress. Finally, after killing 98 of the attackers, de Launay surrendered. An angry mob beheaded him, stuck his head on a pike, and paraded it through the streets, foreshadowing the violent days that lay ahead.

Caption Answer

One vote per estate meant that the First and Second Estates usually outvoted the Third Estate two to one.

Recall

1. **(a)** *ancien regime,* p. 468 **(b)** Jacques Necker, p. 470 **(c)** cahiers, p. 471 **(d)** Tennis Court Oath, p. 471 **(e)** National Assembly, p. 472 **(f)** Bastille, p. 472
2. **(a)** bourgeoisie, p. 469 **(b)** deficit spending, p. 470

Comprehension

3. The Third Estate resented the privileges enjoyed by the other estates. Peasants suffered from poor wages, heavy taxes, poor harvests, and lack of rights. 4. Deficit spending, made necessary by a large debt and expensive wars, weakened the economy. Other problems included an economic recession and poor harvests. 5. France was on the verge of bankruptcy, bread riots were spreading, and nobles were denouncing royal tyranny. 6. It was the symbolic beginning of the French Revolution.

Critical Thinking and Writing

7. 1788—France on brink of bankruptcy; bread riots spreading; nobles denounce tyranny, bad harvests increase discontent 1789—workers from wallpaper factory sack owner's home; Louis asks three estates to prepare cahiers of grievances; Estates General convenes; Third Estate delegates declare themselves National Assembly; Tennis Court Oath; July 14: storming of Bastille 8. Paragraphs should reflect an understanding of Necker's policies.

Activity Rubrics

Share rubrics with students before they write their cahiers.

Attempted The cahier fails to include all of the required information.

Minimal The cahier includes the required information and shows some understanding of France's problems but is poorly written and organized and contains many mechanical errors.

Adequate The cahier includes the required information, shows understanding of France's problems, is well written and organized, and contains few mechanical errors.

Exemplary The cahier includes the required information, shows deep understanding of France's problems, is very well written and organized, and contains no mechanical errors.

This time, the Third Estate wanted all three estates to meet in a single body, with votes counted "by head."

After weeks of stalemate, delegates of the Third Estate took a daring step. Claiming to represent the people of France, they declared themselves to be the National Assembly. They then invited delegates from the other estates to help them write a constitution, a document that describes the basic rules and laws of government.

A few days later, the National Assembly found its meeting hall locked and guarded. Fearing that the king planned to dismiss them, the delegates moved to a nearby indoor tennis court. As curious spectators looked on, the delegates took their famous Tennis Court Oath. They swore "never to separate and to meet wherever the circumstances might require until we have established a sound and just constitution."

When reform-minded clergy and nobles joined the Assembly, Louis XVI grudgingly accepted it. But royal troops gathered around Paris, and rumors spread that the king planned to dissolve the Assembly.

Suspicion and rumor continued to poison the atmosphere as the crisis deepened in early July. The king, who had brought back Necker to deal with the financial crisis, again dismissed the popular minister. Food shortages were also getting worse because of the disastrous harvest of 1788.

Storming the Bastille

On July 14, 1789, Paris seized the spotlight from the National Assembly meeting in Versailles. The streets buzzed with rumors that royal troops were going to occupy the capital. More than 800 Parisians assembled outside the Bastille, a grim medieval fortress used as a prison for political and other prisoners. The crowd was demanding weapons and gunpowder believed to be stored there.

The commander of the Bastille refused to open the gates and opened fire on the crowd. In the battle that followed, many people were killed. Finally, the enraged mob broke through the defenses. They killed the commander and five guards and released a handful of prisoners, but found no weapons.

When told of the attack, Louis XVI asked, "Is it a revolt?" "No, sire," replied a noble. "It is a revolution." The storming of the Bastille quickly became a symbol of the French Revolution. Supporters saw it as a blow to tyranny, a step toward freedom. Today, the French still celebrate July 14 as Bastille Day, the French national holiday.

SECTION 1 **Assessment**

Recall

1. **Identify:** **(a)** *ancien regime,* **(b)** Jacques Necker, **(c)** cahiers, **(d)** Tennis Court Oath, **(e)** National Assembly, **(f)** Bastille.
2. **Define:** **(a)** bourgeoisie, **(b)** deficit spending.

Comprehension

3. Why were members of the Third Estate discontented with conditions under the old regime?
4. What economic troubles did France have in 1789?
5. What issues arose when Louis XVI called the Estates General in 1789?

6. What was the significance of the storming of the Bastille?

Critical Thinking and Writing

7. **Understanding Sequence** List key decisions and events of 1788 and 1789 in the order in which they occurred. Briefly explain the significance or effects of each decision and event in your list.
8. **Defending a Position** Suppose that you are Jacques Necker. Write a paragraph or two explaining how your economic reform program will benefit France.

Activity

Writing a Cahier
Imagine that you belong to one of the following groups in 1789 France: nobles, high clergy, parish priests, bourgeoisie, peasants, urban workers. Write a cahier describing who you are and what you think is the chief problem facing the nation.

472 Chapter 19

Resource Directory

Teaching Resources
History Through Literature *A Tale of Two Cities,* History Through Literature booklet, pp. 41–42
Section Quiz Unit 5 booklet, p. 21
Creative Teaching Activities Creative Teaching Activities booklet, p. 87
Guided Reading and Review Unit 5 booklet, p. 22

Technology
Interactive Student Tutorial CD-ROM Ch. 19
Computer Test Bank Ch. 19

SECTION 2 Creating a New France

Reading Focus

- How did popular revolts contribute to the French Revolution?
- What moderate reforms did the National Assembly enact?
- How did foreign reaction to the revolution help lead to war?

Vocabulary

faction
émigré
republic

Taking Notes

As you read this section, prepare an outline following this model. Use Roman numerals for major headings, capital letters for subheadings, and numbers for supporting details.

I. Revolts in Paris and the provinces
  A. The Great Fear
    1. Inflamed by famine and rumors
    2.
  B. Paris in arms
II. Moderate reforms

Main Idea The National Assembly instituted political and social reforms in the moderate first stage of the revolution.

Setting the Scene

Excitement, wonder, and fear engulfed France as the revolution unfolded at home and spread abroad. Today, historians divide this revolutionary era into four phases. The moderate phase of the National Assembly (1789–1791) turned France into a constitutional monarchy. Then, a phase (1792–1793) of escalating violence led to a Reign of Terror (1793-1794). There followed a period of reaction against extremism, known as the Directory (1795–1799). Finally, the Age of Napoleon (1799–1815) consolidated many revolutionary changes. In this section, you will read about the moderate start of the French Revolution.

Revolts in Paris and the Provinces

The political crisis of 1789 coincided with the worst famine in memory. Starving peasants roamed the countryside or flocked to the towns, where they swelled the ranks of the unemployed. As grain prices soared, even people with jobs had to spend up to 80 percent of their income on bread.

The Great Fear In such desperate times, rumors ran wild and set off what was later called the "Great Fear." Tales of attacks on villages and towns spread panic. Other rumors asserted that government troops were seizing peasant crops.

    Inflamed by famine and fear, peasants unleashed their fury on nobles who were trying to reimpose medieval dues. Defiant peasants attacked the homes of nobles, set fire to old manor records, and stole grain from storehouses. The violent attacks died down after a period of time, but they clearly demonstrated peasant anger with an unjust regime.

Paris in Arms Paris, too, was in turmoil. As the capital and chief city of France, it was the revolutionary center. A variety of factions, or small groups, competed to gain power. Moderates looked to the Marquis de Lafayette, the aristocratic "hero of two worlds" who had fought alongside George Washington in the American Revolution. Lafayette headed the National Guard, a largely middle-class militia organized in response to the arrival of royal troops in Paris. The Guard was the first group to don the tricolor—a red, white, and blue badge which was eventually adopted as the national flag of France.

Paris in Arms

In this engraving, an angry mob of men and women march through the streets of Paris.

Theme: Geography and History Why do you think Paris was the center of the French Revolution?

Chapter 19 473

Bell Ringer Ask students to preview this section by scanning its pictures and boldface heads. Then, have them write down four changes that took place in France between 1789 and 1791.

LESSON PLAN

1. Focus Popular uprisings encouraged the National Assembly to take swift action. It ended feudal privileges, issued a declaration of rights, reorganized the Church, and established a limited monarchy. Throughout Europe, the supporters of the Enlightenment applauded the reforms, while rulers and nobles denounced them. By 1792, revolutionary France was at war with much of Europe.

2. Instruct Ask students to write an eyewitness account of one of the following events: peasants attacking the home of a nobleman; the August 4 meeting of the National Assembly; the women of Paris marching on Versailles; the procession of the royal family from Versailles to Paris; the writing of the Constitution of 1791; the unsuccessful flight of the royal family; an émigré describing events in France to the Austrian emperor. Students' accounts should include a vivid description of the event and the emotions of the people involved. Suggest that students do additional library research to make their reports more authentic. Invite volunteers to read their accounts to the class.

3. Assess After students have listened to the eyewitness accounts, ask them to predict what will happen next. After students read Section 2, have them review their predictions to see how accurate they were.

4. Reteach If students' **Assess** activity does not reflect adequate understanding of the lesson, you might assign the *Guide to the Essentials* or the *Interactive Student Tutorial CD-ROM* for this section.

Caption Answer

Possible answer: The capital city was a center of intellectual activity where Enlightenment ideas spread. Discontent spread quickly among the urban unemployed.

A more radical group, the Paris Commune, replaced the royalist government of the city. It could mobilize whole neighborhoods for protests or violent action to further the revolution. Newspapers and political clubs—many even more radical than the Commune—blossomed everywhere. Some demanded an end to the monarchy and spread scandalous stories about the royal family and members of the court.

Moderate Reforms

Peasant uprisings and the storming of the Bastille stampeded the National Assembly into action. On August 4, in a combative all-night meeting, nobles in the National Assembly voted to end their privileges. They agreed to give up their old manorial dues, exclusive hunting rights, special legal status, and exemption from taxes.

An End to Special Privilege "Feudalism is abolished," announced the proud and weary delegates at 2 A.M. As the president of the Assembly later observed, "We may view this moment as the dawn of a new revolution, when all the burdens weighing on the people were abolished, and France was truly reborn."

Were the votes on the night of August 4 voluntary? Both contemporary observers and modern historians note that the nobles gave up nothing that they had not already lost. In the months ahead, the National Assembly turned the reforms of August 4 into law, meeting a key Enlightenment goal—the equality of all citizens before the law.

Declaration of the Rights of Man In late August, as a first step toward writing a constitution, the Assembly issued the Declaration of the Rights of Man and the Citizen. The document was modeled in part on the American Declaration of Independence, written 13 years earlier. All men, the French declaration announced, were "born and remain free and equal in rights." They enjoyed natural rights to "liberty, property, security, and resistance to oppression." Like the writings of Locke and the *philosophes*, the constitution insisted that governments exist to protect the natural rights of citizens.

The Declaration further proclaimed that all male citizens were equal before the law. Every Frenchman had an equal right to hold public office "with no distinction other than that of their virtues and talents." In addition, the Declaration asserted freedom of religion and called for taxes to be levied according to ability to pay. Its principles were captured in the enduring slogan of the French Revolution, "Liberty, Equality, Fraternity."

Uncertain and hesitant, Louis XVI was slow to accept the reforms of the National Assembly. Parisians grew suspicious as more royal troops arrived. Nobles continued to enjoy gala banquets while people were starving. By autumn, anger again turned to action.

Women March on Versailles On October 5, thousands of women streamed down the road that led from Paris to Versailles. "Bread!" they shouted. They demanded to see the king.

Much of the crowd's anger was directed at the queen, Marie Antoinette. Ever since she had married Louis in 1770, she had come under attack for being frivolous and extravagant. She eventually grew more serious and even advised the king to compromise with moderate reformers. Still, she remained a source of scandal. Early in the revolution, the radical press spread the story that she had answered the cries of hungry people for bread by saying, "Let them eat cake." Though the story was untrue, it helped inflame feelings against the queen.

The women refused to leave Versailles until the king met their most important demand—to return to Paris. Not too happily, the king agreed. The next morning, the crowd, with the king in tow, set out for the city. At the head of the procession rode women perched on the barrels of seized cannons. They told bewildered spectators that they were bringing Louis XVI, Marie Antoinette, and their son back to Paris. "Now we won't have to go so far when we want to see our king," they sang. Crowds along the way cheered the king, who now wore the tricolor.

In Paris, the royal family moved into the Tuileries (TWEE luh reez) palace. For the next three years, Louis was a virtual prisoner.

The National Assembly Presses Onward

The National Assembly soon followed the king to Paris. Its largely bourgeois members worked to draft a constitution and to solve the continuing financial crisis. To pay off the huge government debt—much of it owed to the bourgeoisie—the Assembly voted to take over and sell Church lands.

Reorganizing the Church In an even more radical move, the National Assembly put the French Catholic Church under state control. Under the Civil Constitution of the Clergy, issued in 1790, bishops and priests became elected, salaried officials. The Civil Constitution ended papal authority over the French Church and dissolved convents and monasteries.

Reaction was swift and angry. Many bishops and priests refused to accept the Civil Constitution. The pope condemned it. Large numbers of French peasants, who were conservative concerning religion, also rejected the changes. When the government punished clergy who refused to support the Civil Constitution, a huge gulf opened between revolutionaries in Paris and the peasantry in the provinces.

Constitution of 1791 The National Assembly completed its main task by producing a constitution. The Constitution of 1791 set up a limited monarchy in place of the absolute monarchy that had ruled France for centuries. A new Legislative Assembly had the power to make laws, collect taxes, and decide on issues of war and peace. Lawmakers would be elected by tax-paying male citizens. Still, only about 50,000 men in a population of more than 27 million could qualify as candidates to run for the Assembly.

To make government more efficient, the constitution replaced the old provinces with 83 departments of roughly equal size. It abolished the old provincial courts, and it reformed laws. The middle-class framers of the constitution protected private property and supported free trade. They compensated nobles for land seized by the peasants, abolished guilds, and forbade urban workers to organize labor unions.

Women March on Versailles

As famine gripped Paris, poor mothers did not have enough food for their children. On October 5, 1789, thousands of women decided to bring Louis XVI to Paris, where he could no longer ignore their suffering.

Theme: Continuity and Change Based on this painting, in what ways do you think the march challenged traditional roles of women?

Political	Social and Economic	Religious
• Proclaimed all male citizens equal before the law	• Abolished special privileges of the nobility	• Declared freedom of religion
• Limited the power of the monarchy	• Announced an end to feudalism	• Took over and sold Church lands
• Established the Legislative Assembly to make laws	• Called for taxes to be levied according to ability to pay	• Placed the French Catholic Church under control of the state
• Granted all tax-paying male citizens the right to elect members of the Legislative Assembly	• Abolished guilds and forbade labor unions	• Provided that bishops and priests be elected and receive government salaries
	• Compensated nobles for lands seized by peasants	

Background
Daily Life

Revolutionary Language As part of the French Revolution, everyday language was altered to demonstrate the abolition of social ranks and privileges. For example, people stopped using the formal *vous* for "you," which peasants had customarily used to address nobility or merchants, and instead used the informal *tu,* which in the past had been used only to address good friends. The titles *Monsieur* and *Madame* were also considered too formal. The proponents of social equality changed the titles—by law—to "Citizen" and "Citizeness." In these ways, the leaders of the revolution attempted to erase the differences among social classes and create bonds of equality among all French citizens.

Customize for . . .
Heterogeneous Groups

Recognizing Viewpoints As a reinforcement activity, assign students to write a paragraph about one of the events discussed in this section from the viewpoint of a person who supports the French Revolution. Then, have them write another paragraph that describes the same event from the viewpoint of a person who opposes the French Revolution. *(Reteaching)*

Skills Assessment

Chart The National Assembly produced the Declaration of the Rights of Man and the Citizen, the Civil Constitution of the Clergy, and the Constitution of 1791. These documents brought far-reaching change to France. **Which reforms in the chart were due to the Civil Constitution of the Clergy?**

To moderate reformers, the Constitution of 1791 seemed to complete the revolution. Reflecting Enlightenment goals, it ended Church interference in government and ensured equality before the law for all male citizens. At the same time, it put power in the hands of men with the means and leisure to serve in government.

Louis's Failed Flight Meanwhile, Marie Antoinette and others had been urging the king to escape their humiliating situation. Louis finally gave in. One night in June 1791, a coach rolled north from Paris toward the border. Inside sat the king disguised as a servant, the queen dressed as a governess, and the royal children.

The attempted escape failed. In a town along the way, Louis's disguise was uncovered by someone who held up a piece of currency with the king's face on it. A company of soldiers escorted the royal family back to Paris, as onlooking crowds hurled insults at the king. To many, Louis's dash to the border showed that he was a traitor to the revolution.

Reaction Outside France

Events in France stirred debate all over Europe. Supporters of the Enlightenment applauded the reforms of the National Assembly. They saw the French experiment as the dawn of a new age for justice and equality. European rulers and nobles, however, denounced the French Revolution.

Widespread Fears European rulers increased border patrols to stop the spread of the "French plague." Fueling those fears were the horror stories that were told by émigrés (EHM ih grayz)—nobles, clergy, and others who had fled France and its revolutionary forces. Émigrés reported attacks on their privileges, their property, their religion, and even their lives. "Enlightened" rulers turned against French ideas. Catherine the Great of Russia burned Voltaire's letters and locked up her critics.

In Britain, Edmund Burke, who earlier had defended the American Revolution, bitterly condemned revolutionaries in Paris. He predicted all too accurately that the revolution would become more violent. "Plots and assassinations," he wrote, "will be anticipated by preventive murder and preventive confiscation." Burke warned: "When ancient opinions and rules of life are taken away . . . we have no compass to govern us."

Threats From Abroad The failed escape of Louis XVI brought further hostile rumblings from abroad. In August 1791, the king of Prussia and the

Skills Assessment

ANSWER taking over and selling Church lands, placing of the Church under state control, providing for bishops and priests to be elected and to receive government salaries

Resource Directory

Teaching Resources
Section Quiz Unit 5 booklet, p. 23
Primary Source Activity *The Royal Family in Prison*, Unit 5 booklet, p. 31
Technology
Interactive Student Tutorial CD-ROM Ch. 19
Computer Test Bank Ch. 19

emperor of Austria—who was Marie Antoinette's brother—issued the Declaration of Pilnitz. In this document, the two monarchs threatened to intervene to protect the French monarchy. The declaration may have been mostly bluff, but revolutionaries in France took the threat seriously and prepared for war. The revolution was about to enter a new, more radical phase of change and conflict.

War at Home and Abroad

In October 1791, the newly elected Legislative Assembly took office. Faced with crises at home and abroad, it would survive for less than a year. Economic problems fed renewed turmoil. Assignats, the revolutionary currency, dropped in value, which caused prices to rise rapidly. Uncertainty about prices led to hoarding and additional food shortages.

Internal Divisions In Paris and other cities, working-class men and women, called sans-culottes* (sanz kyoo LAHTZ), pushed the revolution into more radical action. By 1791, many sans-culottes demanded a republic, or government ruled not by a monarch, but by elected representatives.

Within the Legislative Assembly, several hostile factions competed for power. The sans-culottes found support among radicals in the Legislative Assembly, especially the Jacobins. A revolutionary political club, the Jacobins were mostly middle-class lawyers or intellectuals. They used pamphleteers and sympathetic newspaper editors to advance the republican cause. Opposing the radicals were moderate reformers and political officials who wanted no more reforms at all.

War on Tyranny The radicals soon held the upper hand in the Legislative Assembly. In April 1792, the war of words between French revolutionaries and European monarchs moved onto the battlefield. Eager to spread the revolution and destroy tyranny abroad, the Legislative Assembly declared war first on Austria, then on Prussia, Britain, and other states. The great powers expected to win an easy victory against France, a land divided by revolution. In fact, however, the fighting that began in 1792 lasted on and off until 1815.

---

*Sans-culottes means "without culottes," the fancy knee breeches worn by upper-class men. Shopkeepers, artisans, and other working-class men wore trousers, not culottes.

SECTION 2 Assessment

Recall
1. **Identify:** (a) Great Fear, (b) tricolor, (c) Legislative Assembly, (d) Declaration of Pilnitz, (e) Jacobins.
2. **Define:** (a) faction, (b) émigré, (c) republic.

Comprehension
3. What role did the people of Paris play in the French Revolution?
4. Describe one reform that the National Assembly enacted through each of the following documents: (a) the Declaration of the Rights of Man and the Citizen, (b) the Civil Constitution of the Clergy, (c) the Constitution of 1791.
5. (a) Why did some people outside France react negatively to the French Revolution? (b) How did these feelings lead to war?

Critical Thinking and Writing
6. **Comparing** Compare the women's march on Versailles to the storming of the Bastille in terms of goals and results.
7. **Defending a Position** The Declaration of the Rights of Man has been called the "death certificate" of the old regime. Do you agree? Why or why not?

Activity
Take It to the NET

Use the Internet to research the life of Marie Antoinette. Then, write a feature article about her as it might appear in a popular magazine of today. Include interesting details about her family, friends, and habits that would appeal to your readers.

Connections to Today

Knowing Left From Right

Have you ever wondered how political positions came to be described as *right* or *left*?

It began in France's Legislative Assembly in 1791. Members with similar views always sat together in the meeting hall in Paris. On the right sat those who felt that reform had gone far enough; some even wanted to turn the clock back to 1788. In the center of the hall sat supporters of moderate reform. On the left were the Jacobins and other republicans who wanted to abolish the monarchy and promote radical changes.

Today, the terms *right, center,* and *left* continue to reflect those long-ago seating arrangements.

Theme: Political and Social Systems To what kind of political position might *far right* refer? *Far left?*

SECTION 2 Assessment

Recall
1. (a) Great Fear, p. 473 (b) tricolor, p. 473 (c) Legislative Assembly, p. 475 (d) Declaration of Pilnitz, p. 477 (e) Jacobins, p. 477
2. (a) faction, p. 473 (b) émigré, p. 476 (c) republic, p. 477

Comprehension
3. Paris was the capital and revolutionary center of France. Parisians marched on Versailles for bread and insisted that the royal family accompany them back to the city. 4. Possible answers: (a) declared that all men were equal and had natural rights (b) made bishops and priests elected and salaried officials (c) set up a limited monarchy and a new Legislative Assembly 5. (a) Rulers and nobles feared similar attacks on their privileges. (b) The rulers of Prussia and Austria threatened to protect the French monarchy.

Critical Thinking and Writing
6. Students should recognize that both events were impelled by a simple objective but resulted in a profound consequence. 7. Students should address the sweeping changes brought about by the declaration.

Activity Rubrics

Share rubrics with students before they write their articles.

Attempted The article fails to include all the required information.

Minimal The article includes all the required information and reflects some research but is poorly written and has many mechanical errors.

Adequate The article includes all the required information, is well researched and written, and has few mechanical errors.

Exemplary The article includes all the required information, shows thorough research, is very interesting and informative, and has no mechanical errors.

Test Preparation

Have students read the Edmund Burke quote in the last paragraph on the opposite page, and then answer the question below.

Which of the following does Burke expect?

A People will be killed to keep them from killing others.

B People will be living in chaos because the old laws have been abandoned.

C People's property will be taken away from them.

(D) All of the above

Connections to Today

ANSWER A far right position might be one that is considered highly conservative, while a far left position might be one that is considered highly liberal.

Bell Ringer

Bell Ringer Note that the French Revolution, like other revolutions, had a radical stage of excessive violence. Have students look at the pictures and read the captions in this section. Then, ask students to write down some possible reasons for the atrocities and excessive violence that often take place in revolutions.

LESSON PLAN

1. Focus The French Revolution, driven by leaders determined to preserve and extend the revolution, entered a new and radical phase. During the Reign of Terror, thousands of French citizens were sent to their deaths by Maximilien Robespierre and the Committee of Public Safety. Meanwhile, the revolution brought dramatic changes to many aspects of daily life.

2. Instruct Tell students that they will publish a newspaper chronicling the events of the French Revolution. Assign various students to write news articles about the invasion of the Tuileries; the National Convention; the executions of the king and queen; the Committee of Public Safety; the Reign of Terror; changes in daily life; and other significant developments. Other assignments might include an editorial on rights for women, a review of paintings by Jacques Louis David, and a feature on the popularity of "La Marseillaise." Some students might also produce political cartoons and word puzzles. Encourage students to do additional research, if necessary. Display the pages of the finished newspaper or place them where students can read them.

3. Assess Note that many actions during the Terror were very undemocratic. Discuss with students the question of whether a democratic government is ever justified in using nondemocratic means to protect itself and ensure its survival.

4. Reteach If students' Assess activity does not reflect adequate understanding of the lesson, you might assign the *Guide to the Essentials* or the *Interactive Student Tutorial CD-ROM* for this section.

Did You Know?

ANSWER Tussaud escaped the guillotine by agreeing to make wax models of the revolutionaries and their victims.

Reading Focus

- Why did radicals abolish the monarchy?
- How did the excesses of the Convention lead to the Directory?
- What impact did the revolution have on women and daily life?

Vocabulary

suffrage
nationalism
secular

Taking Notes

On a sheet of paper, make a time line like the one begun here. The time line should extend from August 1792 to July 1794. Add dates and important events as you read this section.

August 1792	September 1792	January 1793	July 1794
Mob invades royal palace	September massacres		

Main Idea A radical phase of the revolution led to the monarchy's downfall and a time of violence known as the Reign of Terror.

Did You Know?

The Origin of Madame Tussaud's Wax Museum

In the 1780s, Marie Tussaud ran two wax museums in Paris and was art tutor to the sister of Louis XVI. During the revolution, she was imprisoned as a royalist. Even so, the leaders of the revolution admired her art skills. Tussaud escaped the guillotine by agreeing to make wax models of the revolutionaries and their victims, such as Louis XVI and Marie Antoinette, shown above.

After the revolution, Tussaud took her collection to London. There she established the wax museum that still bears her name. Today, tourists from around the world marvel at the realistic sculptures of the famous and infamous in Madame Tussaud's Wax Museum.

Theme: Art and Literature
How did Tussaud's art skills save her life?

Setting the Scene Someone who had left Paris in 1791 and returned in 1793 could have gotten lost. Almost 4,000 streets had new names. Louis XV Square was renamed the Square of the Revolution. King-of-Sicily Street, named for the brother of Louis XVI, had become the Rights of Man Street.

Renaming streets was one way that Jacobins tried to wipe out all traces of the old order. In 1793, the revolution entered a radical phase. For a year, France experienced one of the bloodiest regimes in its long history as determined leaders sought to extend and preserve the revolution.

The Monarchy Abolished

Dismal news about the war heightened tensions. Well-trained Prussian forces were cutting down raw French recruits. Royalist officers deserted the French army, joining émigrés and others hoping to restore the king's power.

Outbreaks of Violence Battle disasters quickly inflamed revolutionaries who thought the king was in league with the invaders. On August 10, 1792, a crowd of Parisians stormed the Tuileries and slaughtered the king's guards. The royal family fled to the Legislative Assembly.

A month later, citizens attacked prisons that held nobles and priests accused of political offenses. These prisoners were killed, along with many ordinary criminals. Historians disagree about the people who carried out the "September massacres." Some call them bloodthirsty mobs. Others describe them as patriots defending France from its enemies. In fact, most were ordinary citizens fired to fury by real and imagined grievances.

The French Republic Backed by Paris crowds, radicals took control of the Assembly. Radicals called for the election of a new legislative body called the National Convention. Suffrage, the right to vote, was to be extended to all male citizens, not just to property owners.

The Convention that met in September 1792 was a more radical body than earlier assemblies. It voted to abolish the monarchy and declare France a republic. Deputies then drew up a new constitution for France. The Jacobins, who controlled the Convention, set out to erase all traces of the old order. They seized lands of nobles and abolished titles of nobility.

Death of the King and Queen During the early months of the Republic, the Convention also put Louis XVI on trial as a traitor to France. The king was convicted by a single vote and sentenced to death. On a foggy morning

Resource Directory

Teaching Resources

Creative Teaching Activities Creative Teaching Activities booklet, p. 88
Guided Reading and Review Unit 5 booklet, p. 24
Analyzing Primary Sources Chapter Extension Activities booklet, p. 48

Execution of a King

The following excerpt is from an eyewitness report of the execution of King Louis XVI, January 21, 1793. It was written by Henry Essex Edgeworth de Firmont, a priest who accompanied the king to the scaffold.

"The path leading to the scaffold was extremely rough and difficult to pass; the King was obliged to lean on my arm, and from the slowness with which he proceeded, I feared for a moment that his courage might fail; but what was my astonishment, when arrived at the last step, I felt that he suddenly let go my arm, and I saw him cross with a firm foot the breadth of the whole scaffold; silence, by his look alone, fifteen or twenty drums that were placed opposite to me; and in a voice so loud, that it must have been heard at the Pont Tourant, I heard him pronounce distinctly these memorable words: 'I die innocent of all the crimes laid to my charge; I pardon those who have occasioned my death; and I pray to God that the blood you are going to shed may never be visited on France.'

He was proceeding, when a man on horseback, in the national uniform, and with a ferocious cry, ordered the drums to beat. Many voices were at the same time heard encouraging the executioners. They seemed reanimated themselves, in seizing with violence the most virtuous of Kings, they dragged him under the axe of the guillotine, which with one stroke severed his head from his body. All this passed in a moment. The youngest of the guards, who seemed about eighteen, immediately seized the head, and showed it to the people as he walked around the scaffold; he accompanied this monstrous ceremony with the most atrocious and indecent gestures. At first an awful silence prevailed; at length some cries of 'Vive la République! [Long live the republic!]' were heard. By degrees the voices multiplied, and in less than ten minutes this cry, a thousand times repeated, became the universal shout of the multitude, and every hat was in the air."

—Henry Essex Edgeworth de Firmont, *Report by a Priest of His Majesty's Household*

The Machine of Terror
The guillotine made it easy to behead large numbers of people quickly. It became a symbol of the Reign of Terror.

Skills Assessment

1. Based on this account, how would you describe the king's manner at his execution?
   A frightened and confused
   B cold and unemotional
   C proud and brave
   D angry and violent

2. The man on horseback orders the drums to beat in order to
   E silence the crowd.
   F signal that the execution is about to take place.
   G show respect for the king.
   H announce that the king is dead.

3. **Critical Thinking Drawing Conclusions** (a) Based on this account, what was Father Firmont's attitude toward the king? Toward the revolutionaries? How can you tell? (b) Do you think Firmont's feelings affected his account? Explain.

Skills Tip
Bias is a leaning in favor of or against someone or something. When analyzing an eyewitness account, look for words that indicate the writer's bias.

Block Scheduling Support

Have students read Olympe de Gouges's Declaration of the Rights of Woman and the Female Citizen in the Reference Section at the back of the book. Have students compare and contrast this document with the Declaration of the Rights of Man and of the Citizen, also in the Reference Section. Ask students to identify passages in de Gouges's work that directly echo the French National Assembly's document. Have students speculate on why de Gouges may have done this. Finally, have students reread the section on Mary Wollstonecraft in Chapter 18 and compare her ideas to the ideas expressed in de Gouges's document.

---

*B*ackground
About the Primary Source

A King's Request According to Henry de Firmont, the king did not command his attendance, but merely requested it.

"A King, though in chains, had a right to command, but he commanded not. My attendance was requested merely *as a pledge of my attachment for him, and as a favour, which he hoped I would not refuse. But as [there] was likely to be . . . some danger for me, he dared not to insist. . . .* I made answer to the most unfortunate of Kings, that whether he lived or died, I would be his friend to the last. . . ."

*A*ctivity
Interpreting the Primary Source

Use this additional question to generate class discussion.
Critical Thinking: Making Inferences Why do you suppose the king was able to maintain his dignity and composure? *(Students may surmise that he had been trained from boyhood to maintain his dignity.)*

Skills Tip

Look also for any relationship between the writer and the person or persons in the account. In this case, the priest was a member of the king's household. The Skills Handbook in the front of the book has a lesson that will help students with this feature.

Skills Assessment

ANSWERS 1. C 2. F 3. (a) Students should see that he is proud of the king's dignity and courage, but dislikes the revolutionaries. They can cite word choice as evidence. (b) Yes, The priest clearly loved the king.

Connections to Film

Drawing Conclusions Assign students to watch any film version of Charles Dickens's *A Tale of Two Cities*. Have them describe three scenes that portray injustices in France before the French Revolution. Then, have them describe three scenes that depict injustices that were carried out by the revolutionaries themselves. Finally, ask students to answer this question: Why do you think revolutions commonly go through a radical stage characterized by excessive cruelty, extreme violence, and denial of rights and freedoms?

Biography

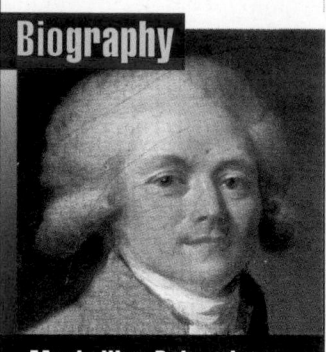

Maximilien Robespierre
1758–1794

Robespierre was the son and grandson of lawyers, but his early life was difficult. His mother died when he was only 6 years old. Just two years later, his father abandoned him and his three siblings. The children were raised by their grandfather and their aunts.

As a result, Robespierre had to assume responsibilities at an early age. He also experienced poverty. However, with the help of a scholarship, he was able to study law at the University of Paris. His performance was so noteworthy that he was chosen to deliver a speech to Louis XVI on the occasion of the king's coronation. But young Robespierre was snubbed. After listening to the address in a pouring rainstorm, the king and queen quickly left without acknowledging Robespierre in any way. Years later, in 1789, Robespierre was elected to the Estates General where his career as a revolutionary began.

Theme: Impact of the Individual How do you think Robespierre's early life might have influenced his political ideas?

---

in January 1793, Louis mounted a scaffold in a public square in Paris. He tried to speak, but his words were drowned out by a roll of drums. Moments later, the king was beheaded.

In October, Marie Antoinette was also executed. The popular press celebrated her death. The queen, however, showed great dignity as she went to her death. Their son, the uncrowned Louis XVII, died of unknown causes in the dungeons of the revolution.

The Convention Defends the Republic

By early 1793, danger threatened France on all sides. The country was at war with much of Europe, including Britain, the Netherlands, Spain, and Prussia. In the Vendée (vahn DAY) region of France, royalists and priests led peasants in rebellion against the government. In Paris, the sans-culottes demanded relief from food shortages and inflation. The Convention itself was bitterly divided between Jacobins and a rival group, the Girondins.

Committee of Public Safety To deal with the threats to France, the Convention created the Committee of Public Safety. The 12-member committee had almost absolute power as it battled to save the revolution. The Committee prepared France for all-out war, issuing a *levée en masse*, or mass levy that required all citizens to contribute to the war effort:

> "All Frenchmen are in permanent requisition for the service of the armies. The young men shall go to battle; the married men shall forge arms and transport provisions; the women shall make tents and clothing and shall serve in the hospitals; the children shall turn old lint into linen; the aged shall take themselves to the public places in order to arouse the courage of the warriors and preach the hatred of kings and the unity of the Republic."
> —*Proclamation of the National Convention*, August 23, 1793

Spurred by revolutionary fervor, French recruits marched off to defend the republic. Young officers developed effective new tactics to win battles with masses of ill-trained but patriotic forces. Soon, French armies overran the Netherlands. They later invaded Italy. At home, they crushed peasant revolts. European monarchs shuddered as the revolutionaries carried "freedom fever" into conquered lands.

Robespierre At home, the government battled counterrevolutionaries under the guiding hand of Maximilien Robespierre (ROHBZ pyair). Robespierre, a shrewd lawyer and politician, quickly rose to the leadership of the Committee of Public Safety. Among Jacobins, his selfless dedication to the revolution earned him the nickname "the incorruptible." The enemies of Robespierre called him a tyrant.

Robespierre had embraced Rousseau's idea of the general will as the source of all legitimate law. He promoted religious toleration and wanted to abolish slavery. Though cold and humorless, he was popular with the sans-culottes, who hated the old regime as much as he did. He believed that France could achieve a "republic of virtue" only through the use of terror, which he coolly defined as nothing more than "prompt, severe, inflexible justice." "Liberty cannot be secured," Robespierre cried, "unless criminals lose their heads."

The Reign of Terror Robespierre was one of the chief architects of the Reign of Terror, which lasted from about July 1793 to July 1794. Revolutionary courts conducted hasty trials. Spectators greeted death sentences with cries of "Hail the Republic!" or "Death to the traitors!"

Biography

ANSWER Possible answer: The early death of his mother and abandonment by his father probably made it hard for him to give and receive love and to feel empathy for others. That plus the snubbing by the king and queen probably influenced his decision to join the revolution and his ruthless dealings with criminals and political enemies.

Resource Directory

Teaching Resources
Biography Activity *Maximilien Robespierre*, Unit 5 booklet, p. 30
Simulation *Monarchy on Trial in France*, Simulations booklet, pp. 9–11

Perhaps 40,000 people died during the Terror. About 15 percent were nobles and clergy. Another 15 percent were middle-class citizens, often moderates who had supported the revolution in 1789. The rest were peasants and sans-culottes involved in riots or revolts against the Republic. Many were executed, including victims of mistaken identity or false accusations by their neighbors. Many more were packed into hideous prisons, where deaths were common.

The engine of the Terror was the guillotine. Its fast-falling blade extinguished life instantly. A member of the legislature, Dr. Joseph Guillotin (GEE oh tan), had introduced it as a more humane method of beheading than the uncertain ax. But the guillotine quickly became a symbol of horror. In a speech given on February 5, 1794, Robespierre explained why the horror was necessary to achieve the goals of the revolution:

"It is necessary to stifle the domestic and foreign enemies of the Republic or perish with them. . . . The first maxim of our politics ought to be to lead the people by means of reason and the enemies of the people by terror. . . . If the basis of popular government in time of peace is virtue, the basis of popular government in time of revolution is both virtue and terror."

—Maximilien Robespierre, quoted in
Pageant of Europe (Stearns)

Within a year, however, the Reign of Terror consumed its own. Weary of bloodshed and fearing for their own lives, members of the Convention turned on the Committee of Public Safety. On the night of July 27, 1794, Robespierre was arrested. The next day he was executed. After the heads of Robespierre and other radicals fell, executions slowed down dramatically.

Reaction and the Directory

In reaction to the Terror, the revolution entered a third stage. Moving away from the excesses of the Convention, moderates produced another constitution, the third since 1789. The Constitution of 1795 set up a five-man Directory and a two-house legislature elected by male citizens of property.

The Reign of Terror
During the Reign of Terror, lists of those to be executed, such as the one below, were posted for all to see. In Paris and other cities, cartloads of the condemned rolled to the guillotine.

Theme: Impact of the Individual Why did Robespierre think the Terror was justified?

LISTE
DES
GUILLOTINÉS

SUR la place de la Révolution, et au ci-devant Carouzel

Background
Connections to Literature

William Wordsworth At first a supporter of the French Revolution, Wordsworth later regarded it with revulsion. In his long poem "The Prelude," he described the Terror.

"The Mother from the Cradle
of her Babe,
The Warrior from the Field, all
perished, all,
Friends, enemies, of all parties,
ages, ranks,
Head after head, and never
heads enough
For those that bade them fall."

Chapter 19 **481**

Human Drama Activity

Interpreting History So that students may understand the reasons behind the French king and queen's execution, have them complete the Simulation activity *Monarchy on Trial in France* in the Simulations booklet, pp. 9–11. The class can prepare for the simulation by reviewing this section and by reading *A Tale of Two Cities* in the History Through Literature booklet, pp. 41–42, and the worksheet *The Royal Family in Prison* in the Unit 5 booklet, p. 31. The simulation requires 15 actors and challenges students to role-play the different personalities involved in a fictitious trial of Louis XVI and Marie Antoinette that leads to their executions.

Caption Answer

He considered the use of terror to be a just way to defend the revolution against its enemies.

Customize for . . .
Heterogeneous Groups

Creating Illustrations As an enrichment activity, assign students to research the fashion changes that took place in France during the French Revolution. To illustrate these changes, have students draw sketches that show styles before and after the revolution. Their illustrations should be accompanied by brief captions that explain the changes and any symbolic meaning that they might have had. *(Enrichment)* ✳

The middle-class and professional people of the bourgeoisie were the dominant force during this stage of the French Revolution. The Directory held power from 1795 to 1799.

Weak but dictatorial, the Directory faced growing discontent. Peace was made with Prussia and Spain, but war with Austria and Great Britain continued. Corrupt leaders lined their own pockets but failed to solve pressing problems. When rising bread prices stirred hungry sans-culottes to riot, the Directory quickly suppressed them. Another threat to the Directory was the revival of royalist feeling. Many émigrés were returning to France, and they were being welcomed by devout Catholics, who resented measures that had been taken against the Church. In the election of 1797, supporters of a constitutional monarchy won the majority of seats in the legislature.

As chaos threatened, politicians turned to Napoleon Bonaparte, a popular military hero who had won a series of brilliant victories against the Austrians in Italy. The politicians planned to use him to advance their own goals—a bad miscalculation! Before long, Napoleon would outwit them all to become ruler of France.

Women in the Revolution

As you have seen, women of all classes participated in the revolution from the very beginning. Working-class women protested and fought in street battles. In Paris and elsewhere, women formed their own political clubs. A few women, like Jeanne Roland, were noted leaders. Roland supported the revolution through her writings, her salon, and her influence on her husband, a government minister.

Rights for Women Many women were very disappointed when the Declaration of the Rights of Man did not grant equal citizenship to women. Olympe de Gouges (oh LAMP duh GOOZH), a journalist, demanded equal rights in her *Declaration of the Rights of Woman.* "Woman is born free," she proclaimed, "and her rights are the same as those of man." Therefore, Gouges reasoned, "all citizens, be they men or women, being equal in the state's eyes, must be equally eligible for all public offices, positions, and jobs." After opposing the Terror and accusing certain Jacobins of corruption, Gouges was sent to the guillotine.

Women did gain some rights for a time. The government made divorce easier, a move that was aimed at weakening Church authority. Government officials also allowed women to inherit property, hoping to undermine the tradition of nobles leaving large estates to their oldest sons. These reforms and others did not last long after Napoleon gained power.

Setbacks As the revolution progressed, women's right to express their views in public came under attack. In 1793, a committee of the National Convention declared that women lacked "the moral and physical strength necessary to practice political rights." Women's revolutionary clubs were banned and violators were arrested.

Women were imprisoned and sent to the guillotine. Among the many women who became victims of the Terror were republicans like Gouges and moderates like Roland. As she mounted the steps to the guillotine, Roland cried, "O liberty, what crimes are committed in your name!"

Changes in Daily Life

By 1799, the 10-year-old French Revolution had dramatically changed France. It had dislodged the old social order, overthrown the monarchy, and brought the Church under state control.

New symbols such as the red "liberty caps" and the tricolor confirmed the liberty and equality of all male citizens. The new title "citizen" applied

Resource Directory

Teaching Resources
Section Quiz Unit 5 booklet, p. 25
Technology
Interactive Student Tutorial CD-ROM Ch. 19
Computer Test Bank Ch. 19

to people of all social classes. Titles were eliminated. Before he was executed, Louis XVI was called Citizen Capet, from the name of the dynasty that had ruled France in the Middle Ages. Elaborate fashions and powdered wigs gave way to the practical clothes and simple haircuts of the sans-culottes. To show their revolutionary spirit, enthusiastic parents gave their children names like Constitution, Republic, or August Tenth.

Nationalism Revolution and war gave the French people a strong sense of national identity. In earlier times, people had felt loyalty to local authorities. As monarchs centralized power, loyalty shifted to the king or queen. Now, the government rallied sons and daughters of the revolution to defend the nation itself.

Nationalism, a strong feeling of pride in and devotion to one's country, spread throughout France. The French people attended civic festivals that celebrated the nation and the revolution. A variety of dances and songs on themes of the revolution became immensely popular.

By 1793, France was a nation in arms. From the port city of Marseilles (mahr SAY), troops marched to a rousing new song. It urged the "children of the fatherland" to march against the "bloody banner of tyranny." This song, "La Marseillaise" (mahr say EHZ), would later become the French national anthem. The second verse and chorus appear at right.

Social Reform Revolutionaries pushed for social reform and religious toleration. They set up state schools to replace religious ones and organized systems to help the poor, old soldiers, and war widows. With a major slave revolt raging in the colony of St. Domingue (Haiti), the government also abolished slavery in their Caribbean colonies.

The Convention tried to de-Christianize France. It created a secular, or nonreligious, calendar with 1793 as the Year I of the new era of freedom. It banned many religious festivals, replacing them with secular celebrations. Huge public ceremonies boosted support for republican and nationalist ideals.

The Arts In the arts, France adopted a grand classical style that echoed the grandeur of ancient Rome. A leading artist of this period was Jacques Louis David (dah VEED). He immortalized on canvas such stirring events as the Tennis Court Oath and, later, Napoleon's coronation. David helped shape the way future generations pictured the French Revolution.

SECTION 3 Assessment

Recall
1. (a) Committee of Public Safety, p. 480
(b) Maximilien Robespierre, p. 480
(c) Directory, p. 481 (d) Olympe de Gouges, p. 482 (e) "La Marseillaise," p. 483 (f) Jacques Louis David, p. 483
2. (a) suffrage, p. 478 (b) nationalism, p. 483 (c) secular, p. 483

Comprehension
3. They thought the king was in league with the Prussian invaders. 4. Weary of bloodshed and fearing for their own lives, members of the Convention executed Robespierre and other radicals and wrote a new constitution, which created the Directory. 5. Possible answers: (a) Women were allowed to inherit property. (b) Practical clothes replaced elaborate costumes.

Critical Thinking and Writing
6. Students' opinions should reflect an understanding of the quote and the conditions that existed in France in 1793.
7. Possible answer: It boosted morale and encouraged the French to keep fighting.

Activity Rubrics

Share rubrics with students before they create their posters.

Attempted The student fails to complete the poster, or the poster does not clearly reflect a point of view or address an issue.

Minimal The poster shows some awareness of the issue and reflects a point of view but is messy or poorly executed.

Adequate The poster is well conceived and clear, reflects a point of view, and addresses a relevant issue.

Exemplary The poster is original, creative, well researched, and well presented; shows a thorough understanding of the issue; and clearly reflects a point of view.

SECTION 3 Assessment

Recall
1. **Identify:** (a) Committee of Public Safety, (b) Maximilien Robespierre, (c) Directory, (d) Olympe de Gouges, (e) "La Marseillaise," (f) Jacques Louis David.
2. **Define:** (a) suffrage, (b) nationalism, (c) secular.

Comprehension
3. Why did radical revolutionaries oppose the monarchy?
4. How did the Reign of Terror cause the National Convention to be replaced by the Directory?

5. Describe one effect of the French Revolution on each of the following: (a) women, (b) daily life.

Critical Thinking and Writing
6. **Analyzing Primary Sources** Robespierre wrote, "Terror is nothing but prompt, severe, inflexible justice." Explain why you agree or disagree with Robespierre.
7. **Predicting Consequences** How do you think French nationalism affected the war between France and the powers of Europe?

Activity

Presenting a Poster
Create a poster that might have been used to support or oppose *one* of the following: the goals of the Jacobins; the abolition of the monarchy; the policies of the Committee of Public Safety; French nationalism; equal rights for women.

Test Preparation

Have students read the first paragraph of "Social Reform" on this page, and then answer the question below.

What does "compulsory elementary education" mean?

A By law, elementary-age students must be provided with schools and must attend school.

B By law, teachers must teach only elementary-age students.

C Elementary-age students may choose not to attend school.

D Elementary-age students are the only ones who need schools.

SECTION 4

The Age of Napoleon Begins

Bell Ringer
Write this quotation from Napoleon on the chalkboard, and ask students to comment on its meaning: "It is better to eat than be eaten." Ask students to look for evidence of this philosophy as they read about Napoleon.

LESSON PLAN

1. Focus Napoleon's early fame was based on military victories. After overthrowing the Directory, he used clever political maneuvering to become emperor. While his new law code reflected Enlightenment principles, it also undid some revolutionary reforms. Defeating the European powers in battle, Napoleon built a vast empire by annexing lands, making alliances, and placing members of his family on the thrones of Europe.

2. Instruct Have students work together in pairs to construct an outline of the contents of this section. Begin by reviewing with the class a standard outline format. Advise students to base the structure of their outlines on the Reading Focus questions on this page. Students should also pay attention to the boldface heads found throughout the section.

3. Assess When students have finished, ask them to use their outlines to answer the Section 4 Assessment questions. Students should revise their outlines to include any significant ideas or details that may be lacking.

4. Reteach If students' Assess activity does not reflect adequate understanding of the lesson, you might assign the *Guide to the Essentials* or the *Interactive Student Tutorial CD-ROM* for this section.

Reading Focus
- How did Napoleon rise to power?
- How were revolutionary reforms changed under Napoleon?
- How did Napoleon build an empire in Europe?

Vocabulary
plebiscite
annex
blockade

Taking Notes
Begin a concept web like this one. As you read, fill in the blank circles with relevant information about Napoleon. Add as many circles as you need.

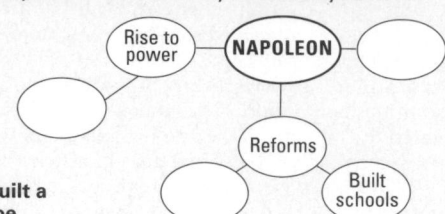

Main Idea Napoleon rose to power in France and built a vast empire that included much of Europe.

Setting the Scene "He was like an expert chess player, with the human race for an opponent, which he proposed to checkmate." Thus did Madame Germaine de Staël (STAHL), a celebrated writer and intellectual, describe Napoleon Bonaparte. Napoleon himself expressed a more humble view of his rise to power. "Nothing has been simpler than my elevation," he once observed. "It is owing to the peculiarities of the time."

From 1799 to 1815, Napoleon would dominate France and Europe. A hero to some, an evil force to others, he gave his name to the final phase of the revolution—the Age of Napoleon.

Napoleon's Rise to Power

Napoleon Bonaparte was born in Corsica, a French-ruled island in the Mediterranean. His family were minor nobles, but had little money. At age nine, he was sent to France to be trained for a military career. When the revolution broke out, he was an ambitious 20-year-old lieutenant, eager to make a name for himself.

Napoleon favored the Jacobins and republican rule. However, he found the conflicting ideas and personalities of the French Revolution confusing. He wrote to his brother in 1793: "Since one must take sides, one might as well choose the side that is victorious, the side which devastates, loots, and burns."

Early Successes During the turmoil of the revolution, Napoleon rose quickly in the army. In December 1793, he drove British forces out of the French port of Toulon (too LOHN). He then went on to win several dazzling victories against the Austrians, capturing most of northern Italy and forcing the Hapsburg emperor to make peace. Hoping to disrupt British trade with India, he led a colorful expedition to Egypt in 1798. The Egyptian campaign proved to be a disaster, but Napoleon managed to hide stories of the worst losses from his admirers in France.

Success fueled his ambition. By 1799, he moved from victorious general to political leader. That year, he helped overthrow the weak Directory and set up a three-man

FACT FINDER

The Rise of Napoleon

1769	Born on island of Corsica
1785	Becomes officer in French army
1793	Helps capture Toulon from British; promoted to brigadier general
1795	Crushes rebels opposed to the National Convention
1796–1797	Becomes commander in chief of the army of Italy; wins victories against Austria
1798–1799	Loses to the British in Egypt and Syria
1799	Overthrows Directory and becomes First Consul of France
1804	Crowns himself emperor of France

Skills Assessment

Chart Napoleon's successes on the battlefield helped him become emperor. **Where and when did Napoleon experience a military setback? Did that setback affect his rise to power? Explain.**

Skills Assessment

ANSWER He was defeated in Egypt and Syria in 1798 and 1799. Despite these defeats, he overthrew the Directory in 1799.

Resource Directory

Teaching Resources

Creative Teaching Activities Creative Teaching Activities booklet, p. 89
Guided Reading and Review Unit 5 booklet, p. 26
Viewpoint Activity *Two Views of Napoleon,* Unit 5 booklet, p. 32

Technology

World History Color Transparencies *Bonaparte Crossing the Alps,* p. D–69

governing board known as the Consulate. Another constitution was drawn up, but Napoleon soon took the title First Consul. In 1802, he had himself named consul for life.

A Self-made Emperor Two years later, Napoleon had acquired enough power to assume the title Emperor of the French. He invited the pope to preside over his coronation in Paris. During the ceremony, however, Napoleon took the crown from the pope's hands and placed it on his own head. By this action, Napoleon meant to show that he owed his throne to no one but himself.

At each step on his rise to power, Napoleon had held a *plebiscite* (PLEHB ih sīt), or ballot in which voters say yes or no. Each time, the French strongly supported him. To understand why, we must look at his policies.

France Under Napoleon

During the consulate and empire, Napoleon consolidated his power by strengthening the central government. Order, security, and efficiency replaced liberty, equality, and fraternity as the slogans of the new regime.

Reforms To restore economic prosperity, Napoleon controlled prices, encouraged new industry, and built roads and canals. To ensure well-trained officials and military officers, he set up a system of public schools under strict government control.

At the same time, Napoleon backed off from some of the revolution's social reforms. He made peace with the Catholic Church in the Concordat of 1801. The Concordat kept the Church under state control but recognized religious freedom for Catholics. Revolutionaries who opposed the Church denounced the agreement, but Catholics welcomed it.

Napoleon won support across class lines. He encouraged émigrés to return, provided that they took an oath of loyalty. Peasants were relieved when he recognized their right to lands they had bought from the Church and nobles during the revolution. The middle class, who had benefited most from the revolution, approved Napoleon's economic reforms and the restoration of order after years of chaos. Napoleon also made jobs "open to

The Coronation
David depicted the splendor and power of the new French emperor in the painting *Napoleon Crowning the Empress Josephine*. Years later, Napoleon would divorce Josephine and marry an Austrian princess.

Theme: Impact of the Individual How did Napoleon emphasize his personal power at the coronation ceremony?

Activity
Connections to Today

Drawing Conclusions Although Napoleon did away with some of the reforms that came out of the French Revolution, he did keep the metric system. The metric system was enacted by the French National Assembly between 1790 and 1795. Most nations around the world today use the system for mathematics, science, and daily life. Nevertheless, the people of the United States are reluctant to abandon their traditional systems and "go metric."

Ask students the following questions: (1) What advantages does the metric system offer? (2) What problems does the United States face by not fully adopting the system? (3) Why do you think many Americans are reluctant to learn and use the metric system? ☀

Chapter 19 **485**

Block Scheduling Support

Have students create a flowchart spanning the time from before the storming of the Bastille until Napoleon's self-coronation as emperor. Flowcharts should accurately depict the causes and effects of the French Revolution. Once the flowcharts are complete, instruct students to review them to answer this question: Why do you think that the French, who overthrew and executed their monarch, would return enthusiastically to a monarchy under Napoleon Bonaparte?

EXPLORING HUMAN DRAMA Human Drama Note

The Egyptian Connection The Egyptian campaign mentioned on the opposite page was a military failure but a cultural success. Napoleon sent a commission of scientists, artists, and scholars to collect extensive information on Egypt. Their work introduced Egyptian culture to Europe and launched a craze for Egyptian styles. More important, French troops discovered the Rosetta Stone, which French scholar Jean Champollion was eventually able to use to decipher ancient Egyptian hieroglyphics.

Caption Answer

Possible answer: He seized the crown from the pope and placed it on his own head.

Napoleon's Power in Europe, 1812

Legend:
- French territory
- States ruled by Napoleon's family
- States under French influence
- French allies, 1812
- ★ Battle sites, 1800–1815
- → Route of Napoleon's invasion of Russia

Azimuthal Equal Area Projection
0   250   500 Miles
0   250   500 Kilometers

Activity
Connections to Literature

Writing a Letter *Master and Commander* is the first in Patrick O'Brian's series of novels that capture the excitement and drama of naval warfare during the Napoleonic Era. Have some students read the latter half of Chapter 10. They will meet Jack Aubrey, captain of the British armed brig *Sophie,* as he is engaged in a deadly duel with a Spanish frigate. The chapter recreates the fury of battle with the blasts of broadsides, the crashes of falling masts and rigging, and the cries of the wounded and dying.

After students have read Chapter 10, ask them to assume the role of a sailor aboard the *Sophie.* Have them write a letter to a family member back in England describing how Captain Aubrey was able to lead his ship to victory. In their letters, they should describe the terrible sights and sounds of the battle. They should also share their feelings, hopes, fears, and the like. Ask students to read their letters aloud to the class.

Background
Historical Evidence

A Double Victory At the Battle of Austerlitz, which took place in 1805, Napoleon won not only on the field of battle but also in the hearts of the French people. After the battle, Napoleon made a grand gesture that won him the loyalty and adoration of the masses. He announced in a public speech that he would adopt the children of all the French soldiers killed in the battle—a number that was in the thousands. To fulfill his promise, he ordered the state to pay for the children's support and education, arrange marriages for the girls, and find jobs for the boys. One final provision was perhaps the most cherished—he permitted "his children" to add the name Napoleon to theirs.

Skills Assessment

Geography Napoleon won a vast empire in Europe. But resistance in Spain and a disastrous invasion of Russia would turn the tide against him.

1. **Location** On the map, locate **(a)** Spain, **(b)** Moscow, **(c)** Waterloo.
2. **Place** What part of the Italian peninsula was French territory?
3. **Critical Thinking Drawing Conclusions** Do you think the spread of nationalism would weaken or strengthen Napoleon's power? Explain.

all talent," a popular policy among those who remembered the old aristocratic monopoly of power.

Napoleonic Code Among Napoleon's most lasting reforms was a new law code, popularly called the Napoleonic Code. It embodied Enlightenment principles such as the equality of all citizens before the law, religious toleration, and advancement based on merit.

But the Napoleonic Code undid some reforms of the French Revolution. Women, for example, lost most of their newly gained rights and could not exercise the rights of citizenship. Male heads of households regained complete authority over their wives and children. Again, Napoleon valued order and authority over individual rights.

Building an Empire

From 1804 to 1814, Napoleon furthered his reputation on the battlefield. He successfully faced down the combined forces of the greatest European powers. He took great risks and even suffered huge losses. "I grew up on the field of battle," he once said, "and a man such as I am cares little for the life of a million men." By 1810, his Grand Empire reached its greatest extent.

As a military leader, Napoleon valued rapid movements and made effective use of his large armies. He developed a new plan for each battle, so opposing generals could never anticipate what he would do next. His enemies paid tribute to his leadership. Napoleon's presence on the battlefield, said one, was "worth 40,000 troops."

The Grand Empire As Napoleon created a vast French empire, he redrew the map of Europe. He annexed, or added outright, some areas to France, including the Netherlands, Belgium, and parts of Italy and Germany. He also abolished the tottering Holy Roman Empire and created a 38-member Confederation of the Rhine under French protection. He cut Prussian territory in half, turning part of old Poland into the Grand Duchy of Warsaw.

Napoleon controlled much of Europe through forceful diplomacy. One tactic was to put friends and relatives on the thrones of Europe. For example, after unseating the king of Spain, he placed his own brother, Joseph

Skills Assessment

ANSWERS: 1. Review locations with students. **2.** Rome and much of the west-central part of the peninsula **3.** It would weaken his empire because nationalism would spur conquered peoples to rebel against French rule.

Resource Directory

Teaching Resources
Section Quiz Unit 5 booklet, p. 27
Technology
Interactive Student Tutorial CD-ROM Ch. 19
Computer Test Bank Ch. 19

Bonaparte, on the throne. He also forced alliances on European powers from Madrid to Moscow. At various times, the rulers of Austria, Prussia, and Russia reluctantly signed treaties with the "Corsican upstart," as his enemies called him

In France, Napoleon's successes boosted the spirit of nationalism. Great victory parades filled the streets of Paris with cheering crowds. The people celebrated the glory and grandeur that Napoleon had won for France.

France Versus Britain Britain alone remained outside Napoleon's European empire. With only a small army, Britain relied on its sea power to stop Napoleon's drive to rule the continent. In 1805, Napoleon prepared to invade England. But at the Battle of Trafalgar, fought off the southwest coast of Spain, British admiral Horatio Nelson smashed a French fleet.

With an invasion ruled out, Napoleon struck at Britain's lifeblood, its commerce. He waged economic warfare through the Continental System, which closed European ports to British goods. Britain responded with its own blockade of European ports. A blockade involves shutting off ports to keep people or supplies from moving in or out. During their long struggle, both Britain and France seized neutral ships suspected of trading with the other side. British attacks on American ships sparked anger in the United States and eventually triggered the War of 1812.

In the end, Napoleon's Continental System failed to bring Britain to its knees. Although British exports declined, its powerful navy kept open vital trade routes to the Americas and India. Meanwhile, trade restrictions created a scarcity of goods in Europe, sent prices soaring, and intensified resentment against French power.

Cause and Effect

Long-Term Causes	Immediate Causes
• Corrupt, inconsistent, and insensitive leadership • Prosperous members of Third Estate resent privileges of First and Second estates • Spread of Enlightenment ideas	• Huge government debt • Poor harvests and rising price of bread • Failure of Louis XVI to accept financial reforms • Formation of National Assembly • Storming of Bastille

The French Revolution

Immediate Effects	Long-Term Effects
• Declaration of the Rights of Man and the Citizen adopted • France adopts its first written constitution • Monarchy abolished • Revolutionary France fights coalition of European powers • Reign of Terror	• Napoleon gains power • Napoleonic Code established • French public schools set up • French conquests spread nationalism • Revolutions occur in Europe and Latin America

Connections to Today

• French law reflects Napoleonic Code
• France is a democratic republic

Skills Assessment **Chart** The French Revolution was a major turning point. Its impact spread far beyond France. **How did Napoleon spread the ideas of the French Revolution?**

SECTION 4 Assessment

Recall
1. **Identify: (a)** Consulate, **(b)** Concordat of 1801, **(c)** Napoleonic Code, **(d)** Confederation of the Rhine, **(e)** Battle of Trafalgar, **(f)** Continental System.
2. **Define: (a)** plebiscite, **(b)** annex, **(c)** blockade.

Comprehension
3. Describe Napoleon Bonaparte's rise to power.
4. **(a)** What revolutionary reforms were undone by Napoleon? **(b)** How did Napoleon preserve some of the principles of the Enlightenment?

5. **(a)** How did Napoleon come to dominate most of Europe? **(b)** Why did his efforts to subdue Britain fail?

Critical Thinking and Writing
6. **Analyzing Information** What opinions do you think each of the following had of Napoleon? **(a)** royalists, **(b)** Catholic priests, **(c)** soldiers, **(d)** republicans.
7. **Making Decisions** Suppose you were a French voter in 1803. How would you have voted on the plebiscite to make Napoleon emperor? Explain your reasons.

Activity
Take It to the NET

Use the Internet to research one of the battles identified on the map in this section. Make a map that shows the terrain of the battle site, and the positions, strengths, and movements of the opposing forces. Write a paragraph or two explaining the outcome.

SECTION 4 Assessment

Recall
1. **(a)** Consulate, p. 485 **(b)** Concordat of 1801, p. 485 **(c)** Napoleonic Code, p. 486 **(d)** Confederation of the Rhine, p. 486 **(e)** Battle of Trafalgar, p. 487 **(f)** Continental System, p. 487 2. **(a)** plebiscite, p. 485 **(b)** annex, p. 486 **(c)** blockade, p. 487

Comprehension
3. After a successful military career, in 1799 he helped overthrow the Directory and set up the Consulate. In 1802, he had himself named consul for life. In 1804, he had himself crowned emperor. 4. **(a)** He kept the Church under state control but recognized religious freedom for Catholics. Women lost most of their newly gained rights. **(b)** His laws supported equality before the law, religious toleration, and merit-based advancement.
5. **(a)** He conquered European powers by moving large armies rapidly, taking risks, and being willing to suffer great losses. He annexed some lands and forced alliances on others. He put friends and family members on the thrones of Europe. **(b)** The British navy was superior. The Continental System, which Napoleon was unable to enforce, hurt European trade and caused resentment.

Critical Thinking and Writing
6. Possible answers: royalists—angry that he kept some reforms of the French Revolution; Catholic priests—upset that he kept state control of the Church but happy that he allowed religious freedom for Catholics; soldiers—admired him for leadership and skills; republicans—annoyed with him for centralizing power
7. Students' responses should demonstrate understanding of the issues.

Activity Rubrics

Share rubrics with students before they make their maps.

Attempted Either the map or paragraph is missing or incomplete.

Minimal The map is unclear or inaccurate, and the explanation is poorly written with many mechanical errors.

Adequate The map is clear and correct, and the explanation is well written, with few mechanical errors.

Exemplary The map is clear, correct, and attractively prepared, and the explanation is very well written with no mechanical errors.

Skills Assessment

ANSWER He spread revolutionary ideas to the lands he conquered.

Bell Ringer

Ask students to compare the map "Napoleon's Power in Europe, 1812" in Section 4 with the map "Europe After the Congress of Vienna, 1815" in this section. Have students list five changes that resulted from Napoleon's fall from power.

LESSON PLAN

1. Focus The Continental System and the spread of nationalism led to rebellions against French rule. After defeats in Russia and at Leipzig and Waterloo, Napoleon lost power. European leaders at the Congress of Vienna sought to restore stability and order based on the status quo of 1792. They redrew national boundaries, restored monarchs, established a balance of power, and created the Quadruple Alliance.

2. Instruct On the chalkboard, write these five generalizations: (1) Other nations in Europe benefited from the reforms of the French Revolution. (2) Nationalism was a major reason for Napoleon's downfall. (3) Geography played an important role in Napoleon's defeat in Russia. (4) The French people supported Napoleon. (5) The Congress of Vienna achieved its goals. As students read the section, have them find evidence that supports or disputes each generalization.

3. Assess Have students use their evidence to write a paragraph in response to each generalization. Their paragraphs should agree or disagree with each statement and provide pertinent facts to support their opinions.

4. Reteach If students' Assess activity does not reflect adequate understanding of the lesson, you might assign the *Guide to the Essentials* or the *Interactive Student Tutorial CD-ROM* for this section.

Reading Focus

- What challenges threatened Napoleon's empire?
- What events led to Napoleon's downfall?
- What were the goals of the Congress of Vienna?

Vocabulary

guerrilla warfare
abdicate
legitimacy

Taking Notes

On a sheet of paper, make a flowchart like the partially completed one at right. As you read this section, add events that led to the downfall of Napoleon. Add as many boxes as you need.

DOWNFALL OF NAPOLEON

Nationalism spurs opposition to French rule
↓
↓
↓
Waterloo

Main Idea Napoleon was finally defeated, but revolutionary ideals and the postwar peace settlement affected Europe for many years.

Biography

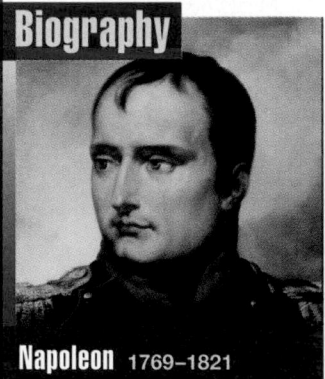

Napoleon 1769–1821

Perhaps history has seen no greater believer in nepotism than Napoleon. Nepotism is favoritism shown to relatives by a person in high office.

"I am building a family of kings," Napoleon proudly said. In addition to making his brother Joseph king of Spain, he made Louis king of Holland and Jerome king of Westphalia. His sister Caroline became queen of Naples, and Elisa was named Grand Duchess of Tuscany. Then, his mother wanted a title, too! He named her Imperial Highness, Lady, Mother of the Emperor. His final family appointment went to his son, whom he named king of Rome.

Theme: Impact of the Individual How do you think nepotism benefited Napoleon?

Setting the Scene

Napoleon watched the battle for the Russian city of Smolensk from a chair outside his tent. As fires lit up the walled city, he exclaimed:

"It's like Vesuvius erupting. Don't you think this is a beautiful sight?"

"Horrible, Sire," replied an aide.

"Bah!" snorted Napoleon. "Remember, gentlemen, what a Roman emperor said: 'The corpse of an enemy always smells sweet.'"

In 1812, Napoleon pursued his dream of empire by invading Russia. The campaign began a chain of events that eventually led to his downfall. Napoleon's final defeat brought an end to the era of the French Revolution.

Challenges to Napoleon's Empire

Under Napoleon, French armies spread the ideas of the revolution across Europe. They backed liberal reforms in the lands they conquered. In some places, they helped install revolutionary governments that abolished titles of nobility, ended Church privileges, opened careers to men of talent, and ended serfdom and manorial dues. The Napoleonic Code, too, was carried across Europe. French occupation sometimes brought economic benefits as well, by reducing trade barriers and stimulating industry.

Impact of Nationalism Napoleon's successes, however, contained the seeds of defeat. Although nationalism spurred French armies to success, it worked against them, too. Many Europeans who had welcomed the ideas of the French Revolution nevertheless saw Napoleon and his armies as foreign oppressors. They resented the Continental System and Napoleon's effort to impose French culture.

From Rome to Madrid to the Netherlands, nationalism unleashed revolts against France. In the German states, leaders encouraged national loyalty among German-speaking people to counter French influence.

Resistance in Spain Resistance to foreign rule bled French occupying forces in Spain. In 1808, Napoleon replaced the king of Spain with his own brother, Joseph Bonaparte. He also introduced reforms that sought to undermine the Spanish Catholic Church. But many Spaniards remained loyal to their former king and devoted to the Church. When the Spanish resisted the invaders, well-armed French forces responded with brutal repression. Far from crushing resistance, however, the French reaction further inflamed Spanish nationalism. Efforts to drive out the French intensified.

Biography

ANSWER It increased his control over other nations.

Resource Directory

Teaching Resources

Creative Teaching Activities Creative Teaching Activities booklet, p. 90

Guided Reading and Review Unit 5 booklet, p. 28

Spanish patriots conducted a campaign of guerrilla warfare, or hit-and-run raids, against the French. (In Spanish, *guerrilla* means "little war.") Small bands of guerrillas ambushed French supply trains or troops before melting into the countryside. These attacks kept large numbers of French soldiers tied down in Spain, when Napoleon needed them elsewhere. Eventually, the British sent an army under Arthur Wellesley, later the Duke of Wellington, to help the Spanish fight France.

War With Austria Spanish resistance encouraged Austria to resume hostilities against the French. In 1805, at the Battle of Austerlitz, Napoleon had won a crushing victory against an Austro-Russian army of superior numbers. Now, in 1809, the Austrians sought revenge. But once again, Napoleon triumphed—this time at the battle of Wagram. By the peace agreement that followed, Austria surrendered lands populated by more than three million subjects.

The next year, after divorcing his wife Josephine, Napoleon married the Austrian princess Marie Louise. By marrying the daughter of the Hapsburg emperor, he and his heirs could claim kinship with the royalty of Europe.

Defeat in Russia Napoleon's alliance with the Austrian royal family was especially disturbing to Czar Alexander I of Russia. The Russians were also unhappy with the economic effects of Napoleon's Continental System. Yet another cause for concern was that Napoleon had enlarged the Grand Duchy of Warsaw that bordered Russia on the west. These and other issues led the czar to withdraw Russia from the Continental System. Napoleon responded to the czar's action by assembling his Grand Army.

In 1812, more than 400,000 soldiers from France and other countries invaded Russia. To avoid battles with Napoleon, the Russians retreated eastward, burning crops and villages as they went. This "scorched earth" policy left the French hungry and cold as winter came. Napoleon entered Moscow in September. He realized, though, that he

Resistance in Spain
Spanish artist Francisco Goya stressed raw human emotions. Goya's *The Third of May, 1808* shows French soldiers executing Spanish prisoners. His drawing *And They Are Like Wild Beasts* depicts a furious battle between Spanish women and the French.
Theme: Art and Literature How did Goya emphasize nationalism in these artworks?

Chapter 19 **489**

Background Perspectives

Napoleon on Napoleon While on St. Helena, Napoleon reviewed his career in conversations with the Marquis Las Cases, who recorded them in *Mémorial*. Napoleon believed that he had conquered Europe in self-defense. His conquests benefited those under his rule by bringing them his code of laws and other revolutionary reforms. If not for the jealousy of Britain and the hatred of the monarchs that he had overthrown, Europe under his guidance would have become a federation of free peoples, allied with enlightened France in eternal peace. Napoleon characterized Britain as a mischief-maker and pirate whose petty ambitions had destroyed a noble future for France and Europe.

You may wish to have students compare Napoleon's views with the views of the *London Times*, quoted in the note that follows.

Background Perspectives

Wretch and Villain As Napoleon was departing for exile on St. Helena, the *London Times* reviewed his career in these words:

"This wretch has lived in the commission of every crime so long, that he has lost all sight of and knowledge of the difference that exists between good and evil, and hardly knows when he is doing wrong, except to be taught by proper chastisement. A creature who ought to be greeted by a gallows as soon as he lands. . . . It has been the constant trick of this villain, whenever he had got his companions into a scrape, to leave them in it, and seek his own safety by flight. In Egypt, in the Moscow expedition, and at Waterloo, such was his conduct."

Geography and History

The Battle of Waterloo

Waterloo—to this day it symbolizes utter defeat. But on the morning of the battle, Napoleon felt certain of victory. "This whole affair will not be more serious than swallowing one's breakfast," he said.

But both weather and terrain conspired against him. First, he held off his attack until the rain-soaked ground could dry. (Cannonballs just stick in mud; they can do more damage bouncing along dry ground.) These lost hours gave the enemy time to move in more troops. Second, Napoleon ordered a frontal attack against an enemy positioned on an upward slope. The crest of its ridge helped shield the opposition from French artillery barrages. At Waterloo, more than 20,000 French soldiers died, and Napoleon suffered his final defeat.

Theme: Geography and History How did geography help defeat Napoleon at Waterloo?

---

was not able to feed and supply his army through the long Russian winter. In October, he turned homeward.

The 1,000-mile retreat from Moscow turned into a desperate battle for survival. Russian attacks and the brutal Russian winter took a terrible toll. Philippe Paul de Ségur, an aide to Napoleon, described the grim scene as the remnants of the Grand Army returned:

> "In Napoleon's wake [was] a mob of tattered ghosts draped in . . . odd pieces of carpet, or greatcoats burned full of holes, their feet wrapped in all sorts of rags. . . . [We] stared in horror as those skeletons of soldiers went by, their gaunt, gray faces covered with disfiguring beards, without weapons . . . with lowered heads, eyes on the ground, in absolute silence."
> —*Memoirs of Philippe Paul de Ségur*

Only about 10,000 soldiers of the once-proud Grand Army survived. Many died. Others deserted. French general Michel Ney sadly concluded: "General Famine and General Winter, rather than Russian bullets, have conquered the Grand Army." Napoleon rushed to Paris to raise a new force to defend France. His reputation for success had been shattered.

Downfall of Napoleon

The disaster in Russia brought a new alliance of Russia, Britain, Austria, and Prussia against a weakened France. In 1813, they defeated Napoleon in the Battle of the Nations at Leipzig.

Exile and Return The next year, Napoleon abdicated, or stepped down from power. The victors exiled him to Elba, an island in the Mediterranean. They then recognized Louis XVIII, brother of Louis XVI, as king of France.

The restoration of Louis XVIII did not go smoothly. The Bourbon king agreed to accept the Napoleonic Code and honor the land settlements made during the revolution. However, many émigrés rushed back to France bent on revenge. An economic depression and the fear of a return to the old regime helped rekindle loyalty to Napoleon.

As the victorious allies gathered in Vienna for a general peace conference, Napoleon escaped his island exile and returned to France. Soldiers flocked to his banner. As citizens cheered Napoleon's advance, Louis XVIII fled. In March 1815, the emperor of the French entered Paris in triumph.

Battle of Waterloo Napoleon's triumph was short-lived. His star soared for only 100 days, while the allies reassembled their forces. On June 18, 1815, the opposing armies met near the town of Waterloo in Belgium. British forces under the Duke of Wellington and a Prussian army commanded by General Blücher crushed the French in an agonizing day-long battle. Once again, Napoleon was forced to abdicate and to go into exile on St. Helena, a lonely island in the South Atlantic. This time, he would not return.

Legacy of Napoleon Napoleon died in 1821, but his legend lived on in France and around the world. His contemporaries as well as historians have long debated his legacy. Was he "the revolution on horseback," as he claimed? Or was he a traitor to the revolution?

No one, however, questions Napoleon's impact on France and on Europe. The Napoleonic Code consolidated many changes of the revolution. The France of Napoleon was a centralized state with a constitution. Elections were held with expanded, though limited, suffrage. Many more citizens had rights to property and access to education than under the old regime. Still, French citizens lost many rights promised so fervently by republicans during the Convention.

On the world stage, Napoleon's conquests spread the ideas of the revolution. He failed to make Europe into a French empire. Instead, he sparked

---

Geography and History

ANSWER Weather delayed him, letting the enemy grow stronger, and the enemy's position on a hill doomed his frontal attack.

Teaching Resources
Disaster! Chapter Extension Activities booklet, p. 49

Technology
World History Visions, Voices, Views Animated Map Story, *Napoleon's Russian Campaign* (1812), videodisc side 3 or videotape 5, running time 3:00 min.

Side 3: Fr. 9366-16594

Napoleon's Retreat From Moscow

"My greatest and most difficult enterprise," said Napoleon in June 1812 as he eagerly took on the challenge of conquering Russia. A few months later, he would see things differently, and so would his troops. After a disheartening defeat, Napoleon had to hurry back to Paris to squelch rumors that he had been killed, leaving his shrinking army to face the long, brutal winter in Russia.

Fast Facts

- Russian soldiers set Moscow ablaze to avoid handing it over intact to Napoleon's army.
- When the Grand Army retreated from Moscow in October, the line of French troops stretched for more than 50 miles.
- French troops experienced temperatures as low as −40° F.

As French troops stumbled their way through blinding snow, they grew desperate for shelter. Soldiers resorted to building huts using the frozen corpses of their fallen comrades, stacking them like logs to create walls.

Russian forces harassed the retreating French army throughout November.

The Grand Army of France was forced to follow the same path retreating from Moscow that it used to get there. As the army passed over an old battlefield, one observer commented, "It was covered with the debris of helmets . . . wheels, weapons, rags of uniforms—and 30,000 corpses half-eaten by wolves."

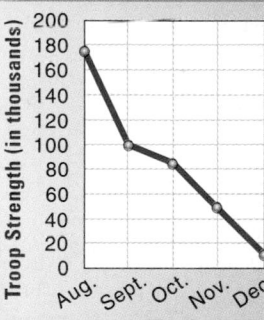

Napoleon's Troops in Russia

Troop Strength (in thousands) vs. Month (Aug., Sept., Oct., Nov., Dec.)

Source: Charles Joseph Minard, 1861

Starting with 422,000 troops in June, Napoleon lost almost half of his forces to fighting, desertion, and famine by August. Grand Army troop strength continued to fall drastically from August through December.

Portfolio Assessment

INTERNET Use the Internet or library resources to learn about another disastrous march in history. Some such marches were the Trail of Tears in North America in 1838–1839, the Long March in China in 1934–1935, or the Bataan Death March in the Philippines in 1942. Write a news story in which you include a map of the route and statistics on loss of life.

✓ Test Preparation

Have students read the quote from Philippe Paul de Ségur on the opposite page, and then answer the question below.

Which is a fact from the passage?

- **A** Napoleon was bothered by ghosts.
- **B** The retreating French soldiers were starving and poorly clothed.
- **C** Many French soldiers deserted.
- **D** The retreating French soldiers were carrying skeletons.

Bell Ringer Have students study the graph and read its caption. Then have them study the illustration of Napoleon and his army, concentrating on the expressions of the faces. Ask students to express what three men looking at Napoleon might want to say to him. Then, have students express what Napoleon might be thinking.

*B*ackground Connections to Today

Persian Gulf War Although Napoleon's invasion of Russia and his retreat are different in many ways from the 1991 Persian Gulf War, there are some similarities. One is that Napoleon's army burned crops and villages as they retreated from Russia; the Iraqi army burned Kuwait's oil wells when they retreated from the allied forces.

*A*ctivity Cooperative Learning

Fleshing Out the Story Have small groups of students find out more about the invasion and retreat, to answer these questions: Why were the French forced to retreat along the same route they had used to enter, and why was the retreat a disaster? Why couldn't the French army simply stay in Moscow until the winter ended? Was the severe weather unusual for that time of year in Russia? Then, reform the groups so that an "expert" from the original groups can share information.

Portfolio Assessment Rubrics

Share rubrics with students before they write their news story.

Attempted The news story is incomplete, and the graphics are missing or poorly done.

Minimal The news story is poorly written and organized, and the graphics are included but are messy or unclear.

Adequate The news story is well written and organized, and the graphics are well executed.

Exemplary The news story is very well written and organized, and the graphics are striking.

Analyzing a Quotation One of the most successful diplomats at the Congress of Vienna was Prince Charles Maurice de Talleyrand. His skillful maneuvering saved defeated France from harsh retribution and won it recognition as an equal among the powers of Europe. He was at Vienna, he said, "not to collect trophies, but to bring the world back to peaceful habits." Concerning the balance of power and the proper treatment of France, he said, "No arrangement could be wise that carried ruin to one of the countries between which it was concluded."

Read the above quotations to the class and ask students to respond to the following questions: (1) Why do you think Talleyrand was against the collecting of "trophies"? (2) How was a balance of power in the best interest of France? (3) How might Talleyrand have felt and spoken differently if France had been one of the victorious countries?

Europe After the Congress of Vienna, 1815

Boundary of the German Confederation

Quadruple Alliance, 1815
- Great Britain
- Prussia
- Austrian Empire
- Russian Empire

Azimuthal Equal Area Projection
0   250   500 Miles
0   250   500 Kilometers

Skills Assessment

Geography At the Congress of Vienna, European leaders redrew the map of Europe in order to contain France and keep a balance of power.

1. **Location** On the map, locate **(a)** German Confederation, **(b)** Netherlands, **(c)** Vienna.
2. **Region** Name three states that were in the German Confederation.
3. **Critical Thinking Recognizing Causes and Effects** Why did the Congress enlarge some of the countries around France?

nationalist feeling across Europe. The abolition of the Holy Roman Empire would eventually help in creating a new Germany. Napoleon also had a dramatic impact across the Atlantic. In 1803, his decision to sell France's vast Louisiana Territory to the American government doubled the size of the United States and ushered in an age of American expansion.

The Congress of Vienna

After Waterloo, diplomats and heads of state again sat down at the Congress of Vienna. They faced the monumental task of restoring stability and order in Europe after years of revolution and war.

Gathering of Leaders The Congress met for 10 months, from September 1814 to June 1815. It was a brilliant gathering of European leaders. Diplomats and royalty dined and danced, attended concerts and ballets, and enjoyed parties arranged by their host, Emperor Francis I of Austria.

While the entertainment kept thousands of minor players busy, the real work fell to Prince Clemens von Metternich of Austria, Czar Alexander I of Russia, and Lord Robert Castlereagh (KAS uhl ray) of Britain. Defeated France was represented by Prince Charles Maurice de Talleyrand.

Goals of the Congress The chief goal of the Vienna decision makers was to create a lasting peace by establishing a balance of power and protecting the system of monarchy. Each of the leaders also pursued his own goals. Metternich, the dominant figure at the Congress, wanted to restore the *status quo* (Latin for "the way things are") of 1792. Alexander I urged a "holy alliance" of Christian monarchs to suppress future revolutions. Lord Castlereagh was determined to prevent a revival of French military power.

ANSWERS 1. Review locations with students. 2. any three: Hanover, Prussia, Saxony, Bohemia, Bavaria, Austria 3. to prevent France from expanding and upsetting the balance of power

Resource Directory

Teaching Resources

Skill Application Activity *Identifying Relevant Facts*, Unit 5 booklet, p. 33
Section Quiz Unit 5 booklet, p. 29
Geography Quiz Unit 5 booklet, p. 34
Chapter Test, Forms A, B, and C Unit 5 booklet, pp. 35–39
Answer Key Unit 5 booklet, pp. 74–83

Technology

Interactive Student Tutorial CD-ROM Ch. 19
Computer Test Bank Ch. 19

The aged diplomat Talleyrand shrewdly played the other leaders against one another to get defeated France accepted as an equal partner.

Balance of Power The peacemakers also redrew the map of Europe. To contain French ambitions, they ringed France with strong countries. In the north, they added Belgium and Luxembourg to Holland to create the kingdom of the Netherlands. To prevent French expansion eastward, they gave Prussia lands along the Rhine River. They also allowed Austria to reassert control over northern Italy. This policy of containment proved fairly successful in maintaining the peace.

Restoration of Monarchs To turn back the clock to 1792, the architects of the peace promoted the principle of legitimacy, restoring hereditary monarchies that the French Revolution or Napoleon had unseated. Even before the Congress began, they had put Louis XVIII on the French throne. Later, they restored "legitimate" monarchs in Portugal, Spain, and the Italian states.

Problems of the Peace To protect the new order, Austria, Russia, Prussia, and Great Britain extended their wartime alliance into the postwar era. In the Quadruple Alliance, the four nations pledged to act together to maintain the balance of power and to suppress revolutionary uprisings.

The Vienna statesmen achieved their immediate goals, but they failed to foresee how powerful new forces such as nationalism would shake the foundations of Europe. They redrew national boundaries without any concern for national cultures. In Germany, they created a loosely organized German Confederation with Austria as its official head. But many Germans who had battled Napoleon were already dreaming of a strong, united German nation. Their dream would not come true for more than 50 years, but the story of German unification began in this period.

Looking Ahead

Despite clashes and controversies, the Congress created a framework for peace. Its decisions influenced European politics for the next 100 years. Europe would not see war on a Napoleonic scale until 1914.

The ideals of the French Revolution were not destroyed at Vienna. In the next decades, the French Revolution would inspire people in Europe and Latin America to seek equality and liberty. The spirit of nationalism ignited by Napoleon also remained a powerful force.

SECTION 5 Assessment

Recall
1. **Identify:** (a) Joseph Bonaparte, (b) Duke of Wellington, (c) Marie Louise, (d) scorched earth policy, (e) Waterloo, (f) Clemens von Metternich, (g) Quadruple Alliance.
2. **Define:** (a) guerrilla warfare, (b) abdicate, (c) legitimacy.

Comprehension
3. What challenges did Napoleon face in: (a) Spain, (b) Austria?
4. How did the defeat in Russia lead to Napoleon's downfall?
5. What were the chief goals of the Congress of Vienna?

Critical Thinking and Writing
6. **Linking Past and Present** The powers of Europe used the Quadruple Alliance to protect the postwar order. How do international alliances and organizations help provide order in the world today?
7. **Connecting to Geography** Review the map on the preceding page. (a) What two states were the leading powers in the German Confederation? (b) How do you think this affected future attempts to unify Germany?

Creating a Chapter Summary

As a reteaching opportunity, pair a more able student with a less able student to complete this chapter summary.

Possible additions: 1789 French Revolution begins; 1791 National Assembly adopts Constitution; 1793 Louis XVI and Marie Antoinette executed; Reign of Terror begins; 1795 Directory set up; 1799 Napoleon overthrows Directory; 1804 Napoleon becomes emperor; 1805 Napoleon defeats Austro-Russian army at the Battle of Austerlitz; 1810 Grand Empire at its height; 1813 Napoleon defeated and imprisoned; 1815 Battle of Waterloo/Congress of Vienna

Building Vocabulary

1–10. Quizzes should show a clear understanding of the terms.

Recalling Key Facts

11. Nobles got best government jobs; urban workers earned poor wages; peasants' taxes were high; nobles did not pay their fair share.

12. Rumors that royal troops were going to occupy Paris sent a crowd to the Bastille for arms. The commander denied access and fired upon the crowd, which started a battle in which the peasants broke into the prison.

13. "Liberty, Equality, Fraternity"

14. a ruthless campaign against people suspected of being enemies of the revolution

15. modernized finance, controlled prices, promoted public schools and public works, instituted new law code

16. (a) annexed areas to France, made alliances with nations, put family members on the thrones of nations, used forceful diplomacy (b) defeat in Russia, a unified Europe opposed him

17. redrew national boundaries, surrounded France with strong countries, created Quadruple Alliance

Critical Thinking and Writing

18. Possible answers: (a) France was in debt because of deficit spending, the extravagances of the monarchy, and the costs of many wars. (b) by raising taxes paid by the Third Estate (c) The taxes raised the price of goods, making it difficult for the poor to get food.

19. Possible answers: (a) Distance and climate took a huge toll on Napoleon's forces. (b) Students should recognize that terrain and distance to supplies

---

CHAPTER **19** Review and Assessment

Creating a Chapter Summary

On a sheet of paper, make a time line to recall the chief events of the French Revolution and Napoleonic era. Use the model shown here as a guide for getting started.

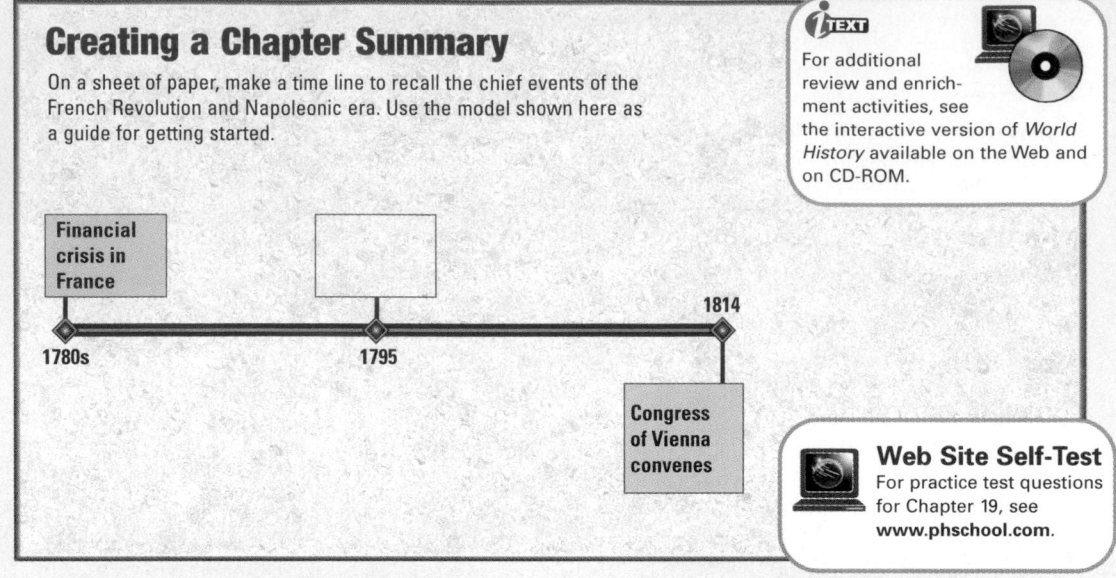

Financial crisis in France

1780s

1795

1814

Congress of Vienna convenes

iTEXT
For additional review and enrichment activities, see the interactive version of *World History* available on the Web and on CD-ROM.

Web Site Self-Test
For practice test questions for Chapter 19, see **www.phschool.com**.

Building Vocabulary

Use these vocabulary words and their definitions to create a matching quiz. Exchange quizzes with another student. Check each other's answers when you are finished.

1. **bourgeoisie**
2. **deficit spending**
3. **émigré**
4. **republic**
5. **suffrage**
6. **nationalism**
7. **plebiscite**
8. **annex**
9. **abdicate**
10. **legitimacy**

Recalling Key Facts

11. Why was there discontent with the old regime in France?

12. Why did a crowd storm the Bastille?

13. What was the slogan of the French Revolution?

14. What was the Reign of Terror?

15. List the reforms that Napoleon made as leader of France.

16. (a) How did Napoleon build an empire in Europe? (b) What were two reasons for his downfall?

17. How did the Congress of Vienna try to restore the balance of power in Europe?

Critical Thinking and Writing

18. **Synthesizing Information** A French noble wrote this on the causes of the revolution: "The most striking of the country's troubles was the chaos in its finances, the result of years of extravagance. . . . No one could think of any remedy, except to search for fresh funds." (a) What did the noble mean by "chaos in its finances"? (b) How were fresh funds raised? (c) How did this lead to revolution?

19. **Connecting to Geography** (a) How did the geography of the Russian empire work against Napoleon's Grand Army? (b) Do you think geography can affect the outcome of modern warfare? Explain.

20. **Analyzing Primary Sources** Review the words of "La Marseillaise," which appears in Section 3. How does the song express some of the ideals of the French Revolution?

21. **Comparing** Review the English Civil War. (a) How were the English Civil War and the French Revolution similar? (b) How were they different?

---

always have an impact on war although the effects will be different in present times because the technology of war has changed.

20. Possible answers: It mentions love of the fatherland and fighting for liberty.

21. Possible answers: (a) both caused in part by royal abuses; both involved tax conflicts; both were conflicts between supporters of the monarchy and supporters of the common people; both included the execution of a monarch; both ended with restoration of a monarchy (b) The English Civil War was fought to restore

traditional rights of citizens and to force the monarch to obey the law and allow Parliament to exercise its duties. French society was still based on the feudal system and had few such rights, thus revolutionaries wanted to reform the entire political and social system.

Read the excerpt below from an eyewitness account of the battle at Waterloo. Then answer the questions that follow.

"Our division, which had stood upwards of 5000 men at the commencement of the battle, had gradually dwindled down into a solitary line of skirmishers. . . . Presently a cheer which we knew to be British commenced far to the right, and made everyone prick up his ears; it was Lord Wellington's long-wished-for orders to advance. . . . [To] people who had been so many hours enveloped in darkness, in the midst of destruction, and naturally anxious about the result of the day, the scene which now met the eye conveyed a feeling of more exquisite gratification than can be conceived. . . . The French were flying in one confused mass. British lines were seen in close pursuit, and in admirable order, as far as the eye could reach to the right, while the plain to the left was filled with Prussians."

—Captain J. Kincaid,
Adventures in the Rifle Brigade

22. What nationality is the writer?
23. What evidence is given that the French fought fiercely?
24. Why do the soldiers cheer?
25. How does the writer feel about victory?
26. How does this battle differ from the guerrilla warfare fought against the French in Spain?

Skills Assessment
Take It to the NET

Use the Internet to research one of the symbols of the French Revolution or the French republic, such as the Bastille, the tricolor, or "La Marseillaise." Then, write a brief historical analysis of the symbol. Explain how it originated, what it represented to French citizens during the revolution, and how it continues to be an important symbol to the French people today.

The Plumb-pudding in danger, or State Epicures taking un Petit Soup
the great Globe itself and all which it went is too small to satisfy such insatiable appetites

In the political cartoon (above), the figure at left represents the British and the figure at right represents Napoleon. Use the cartoon to answer the following questions:

27. What is represented by the meal on the table?
28. Why are the two figures carving the meal?
29. Does the cartoonist portray Napoleon favorably? Explain.
30. How would people of the time have known which nations were represented by the two men in the cartoon?
31. Which of the two sides, if any, does the cartoon favor? Explain.
32. (a) Compose a title for the cartoon. (b) Explain the meaning of the title you created.

Skills Tip

To understand a political cartoon's point of view, first try to figure out the meaning of the cartoon's various figures and symbols.

22. British
23. Kincaid's division had lost most of its men.
24. They received orders to advance and can see what had been happening.
25. happy and gratified
26. The British are fighting in orderly lines, not the hit-and-run raids of guerrilla warfare.

Analyzing Political Cartoons

27. the world
28. France and Britain want to divide up the world into their empires.
29. No, he is portrayed as greedy and insatiable.
30. by the physical characteristics of the two men and by their clothing
31. It is equally critical of each side.
32. Possible answers: (a) "Insatiable Greed" (b) greed that cannot be satisfied

Skills Tip

To find the meaning of the figures and symbols, look at clothing and labels and read the caption. The Skills Handbook in the front of the book has a lesson that will help students with this feature.

Unit Theme Activity

Remind students to continue working on their Unit Theme Activity. See rubrics for the activity on the unit opener page in the Teacher's Edition.

Take It to the NET

Direct students to **www.phschool.com** for links to sites that will help them get started on this assignment. Share rubrics with students.
Attempted The analysis fails to include all the required information.
Minimal The analysis includes all the required information but is poorly written and organized and contains many mechanical errors.
Adequate The analysis includes all the required information, is well written and organized, and contains few mechanical errors.
Exemplary The analysis includes more than the required information; is exceptionally well written, organized and insightful; and contains no mechanical errors.

Chapter 20 Planning Guide

Resource Manager

	CORE INSTRUCTION	READING/SKILLS
Chapter Level Resources	**Teaching Resources** ⬛ Pacing Charts, Ch. 20 ⬛ Teaching With Themes, p. 23 ▥ Color Transparencies, p. F–41 ⬤ Resource Pro® Ch. 20 ⬛ www.phschool.com 　• eTeach	⬤ Book on CD, Ch. 20 ⬤ Interactive Student Tutorial CD-ROM, Ch. 20 ⬤ Social Studies Skills Tutor CD-ROM ▥ Skills Transparencies
1 Dawn of the Industrial Age 1. Specify the reasons that the Industrial Revolution was a turning point. 2. State the ways that an agricultural revolution contributed to population growth. 3. Describe new technologies that triggered the Industrial Revolution.	**Teaching Resources** ⬛ Creative Teaching Activities, p. 91 ⬤ Prentice Hall Presentation Pro, Ch. 20, Section 1 ▥ Section Reading Support Transparencies	**Teaching Resources** ⬛ Unit 5 booklet ⬛ • Guided Reading and Review, p. 40 　• Skill Application Activity, p. 51 ⬛ Guide to the Essentials ▦ Guided Reading Audiotapes, Ch. 20, Section 1
2 Britain Leads the Way 1. Cite the reasons that Britain was the starting point for the Industrial Revolution. 2. Describe changes that transformed the textile industry. 3. Outline the new technologies that were part of the revolution in transportation.	**Teaching Resources** ⬛ Unit 5 booklet 　• Biography Activity, p. 48 　• Primary Source Activity, p. 49 ⬛ Creative Teaching Activities, p. 92 ⬤ Prentice Hall Presentation Pro, Ch. 20, Section 2	**Teaching Resources** ⬛ Unit 5 booklet 　• Guided Reading and Review, p. 42 ⬛ Guide to the Essentials ▦ Guided Reading Audiotapes, Ch. 20, Section 2
3 Hardships of Early Industrial Life 1. Describe life in the new industrial city. 2. Explain how the factory system changed the way people worked. 3. Enumerate the benefits and problems industrialization brought to the working class and the new middle class.	**Teaching Resources** ⬛ Unit 5 booklet 　• Viewpoint Activity, p. 50 ⬛ Creative Teaching Activities, p. 88 ⬤ Prentice Hall Presentation Pro, Ch. 20, Section 3 ▥ Section Reading Support Transparencies	**Teaching Resources** ⬛ Unit 5 booklet 　• Guided Reading and Review, p. 24 ⬛ Guide to the Essentials ▦ Guided Reading Audiotapes, Ch. 20, Section 3
4 New Ways of Thinking 1. Explain laissez-faire economics. 2. Compare how the views of utilitarians differed from those of socialists. 3. Summarize the ideas of "scientific socialism" introduced by Karl Marx.	**Teaching Resources** ⬛ Creative Teaching Activities, p. 89 ⬤ Prentice Hall Presentation Pro, Ch. 20, Section 4 ▥ Section Reading Support Transparencies	**Teaching Resources** ⬛ Unit 5 booklet 　• Guided Reading and Review, p. 26 ⬛ Guide to the Essentials ▦ Guided Reading Audiotapes, Ch. 20, Section 4

ENRICHMENT/PRE-AP

- **www.phschool.com**
  - Why Study History?

- **Color Transparencies**, p. E–35

- **Teaching Resources**
  - **Chapter Extension Activities**, p. 50
- **www.phschool.com**
  - Internet Activities, Section 2

- **Teaching Resources**
  - **Chapter Extension Activities**, p. 51
    - Geography and History, pp. 10–11
  - **History Through Literature**, pp. 43–44
- **www.phschool.com**
  - Virtual Field Trip
  - Internet Activities, Section 3

ASSESSMENT

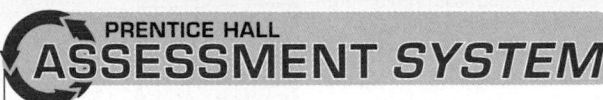
**PRENTICE HALL
ASSESSMENT SYSTEM**

Core Assessment
- ExamView Test Bank booklet, Ch. 20
- ExamView Test Bank CD-ROM, Ch. 20

Standardized Test Preparation

Diagnose and Prescribe
- Diagnostic Tests for High School Social Studies Skills

Review and Reteach
- Review Book for World History

Practice and Assess
- Test-Taking Strategies With Transparencies for High School
- Alternative Assessment booklet
- Test Prep Book for World History

- **Teaching Resources**
  - **Unit 5 booklet**
    - Geography Quiz, p. 52
    - Section Quizzes, pp. 41, 43, 45, 47
    - Chapter Tests A, B, and C, pp. 53–57
- **www.phschool.com**
  - Self-Test

CUSTOMIZE FOR INDIVIDUAL NEEDS

Gifted and Talented
- **Teacher's Edition**, Activities: Cooperative Learning Activity, p. 512

Less Proficient Readers
- **Guide to the Essentials**, Ch. 20
- **Book on CD**, Ch. 20
- **Teacher's Edition**, Activities: Reading Strategy, p. 502

Less Proficient Writers
- **Teacher's Edition**, Activities: Cooperative Learning Activity, p. 507

Students Acquiring English/ESL
- **Guide to the Essentials**, English/Spanish, Ch. 20
- **Guided Reading Audiotapes**, English/Spanish, Ch. 20
- **Book on CD**, Ch. 20
- **Teacher's Edition**, Activities marked with an *

*i*TEXT

Don't miss the exclusive interactive version of *World History: Connections to Today* on the Internet and CD-ROM.

INTRODUCTION

During the 1700s, the Industrial Revolution transformed the world. An agricultural revolution contributed to a population explosion that, in turn, supplied the labor force. Production shifted to complex machines, fueled by new sources of energy. Urbanization and the factory system created dismal conditions for the poor. Laissez-faire economists, utilitarians, socialists, and communists put forth ideas for solving industrial society's problems.

Focusing on Themes

Suggest that students focus on these theme questions as they read:

Continuity and Change
How did the Industrial Revolution transform traditional ways of life?

Economics and Technology
What roles did capital and technology play in the Industrial Revolution?

Impact of the Individual
How did individual contributions shape the industrial age?

Political and Social Systems
Why did new social and political philosophies develop during the industrial age?

◆ TIME LINE ACTIVITY

You may wish to share the About the Pictures note with your students before you ask questions about the time line such as these:

1. How many years passed between Watt's improvement to the steam engine and Fulton's first successful steamboat? *(between 38 and 47 years)*
2. Who published *The Communist Manifesto* and when? *(Karl Marx and Friedrich Engels in 1848)*
3. Why was 1847 an important year for freed African Americans? *(The country they settled, Liberia, became an independent nation.)*

Don't Miss!

Synthesizing Information
Impact of the Railroad
(Section 2)

You Are There . . .
Spinning Thread in a Textile Mill
(Section 3)

The Industrial Revolution Begins

1750–1850

Chapter Preview

1 Dawn of the Industrial Age
2 Britain Leads the Way
3 Hardships of Early Industrial Life
4 New Ways of Thinking

1760s
James Watt improves on the steam engine. Watt's engine, shown here, provides a vital source of power.

1800
Robert Owen begins social reforms at New Lanark.

1807
Robert Fulton develops the first successful steamboat, the *Clermont*. Steam power allows the vessel, shown here, to travel against the current without difficulty.

CHAPTER EVENTS

1750   1775   1800

GLOBAL EVENTS

1762 Catherine the Great comes to power in Russia.

1804 Napoleon becomes emperor of France.

◆ Resource Directory

Teaching Resources
Teaching With Themes Chapter Theme Activities, p. 23
Pacing Chart With Block Scheduling Guide Ch. 20

Technology
World History Color Transparencies Ch. 20 Graphic Organizer, p. F–41

Major Centers of Industry in Great Britain, 1825

Lambert Azimuthal Equal Area Projection

The Industrial Revolution first took hold in Britain, encouraging the growth of cities and factory towns.

Population of urban centers
- • 30,000 or more
- • 80,000 or more
- • 1,000,000 or more

SCOTLAND
Glasgow
Edinburgh
ATLANTIC OCEAN
Newcastle
Belfast
Tyne R.
North Sea
Irish Sea
Mersey R.
Humber R.
Liverpool
Manchester
IRELAND
ENGLAND
Birmingham
WALES
Severn R.
Thames R.
Bristol
London

Activating Prior Knowledge
Why do you suppose London became a major urban center? *(It was located on the Thames River not far from the sea.)*

Previewing
How did geography contribute to Britain's economic prosperity? *(There are many rivers and being an island nation made it easy to trade with overseas colonies and other countries.)*

Background
About the Pictures

1 | 2 | 3

1. James Watt's first improvement to the Newcomen engine was to harness the energy lost by the engine's wasted steam. His famous patent was titled "A New Invented Method of Lessening the Consumption of Steam and Fuel in Fire Engines."

2. Robert Fulton actually named his first working steamboat *North River Steamboat* and made several trips with it between New York and Albany in 1807. However, in the winter of 1807–1808, he made such massive improvements to it that it was essentially a different ship. For that reason, he renamed it *North River Steamboat of Clermont,* which was soon shortened to *Clermont.*

3. The Crystal Palace was built in Hyde Park, London, for the Great Exhibition of 1851. After the exhibition, it was moved to Sydenham Hill, where it burned in 1936. The move was possible because the building was made entirely of prefabricated parts that could be taken down and reassembled.

1830
The Liverpool-Manchester Railroad opens.

1848
Karl Marx and Friedrich Engels publish *The Communist Manifesto.*

1851
The Great Exhibition is held in London. A display of industrial developments, housed in the Crystal Palace, is shown here.

1825   1850   1875

1847 Liberia, settled by freed African Americans, becomes an independent nation.

Chapter 20 **497**

Independent Assignments

Have students read one section as they prepare for class. After class, have them complete the assignment. Some students may benefit from using the Guided Reading and Review worksheets.

Section 1 Have students use the worksheet *Recognizing Faulty Reasoning* in the Unit 5 booklet, p. 51, to learn more about the arguments for and against the enclosure system.

Section 2 Have students use the worksheet *Riding the Liverpool-Manchester Line* in the Unit 5 booklet, p. 49, to learn about the reaction of a passenger on a trial run of an early railroad.

Section 3 Have students use the worksheet *Rules for Workers* in the Unit 5 booklet, p. 50, to learn more about the harsh working conditions of factory workers.

Section 4 Have students read *How I Became a Socialist* in Treasures of the World, pp. 113–115, for an Austrian woman's explanation of why she embraced socialism.

🔔 **Bell Ringer** Write the word *revolution* on the chalkboard and ask students to recall what they have learned about the French Revolution. Have students think of other kinds of revolutions that affect government, the economy, society, and culture. Ask them to write descriptions of three revolutions that they are familiar with.

Reading Focus

- Why was the Industrial Revolution a turning point in world history?
- How did an agricultural revolution contribute to population growth?
- What new technologies helped trigger the Industrial Revolution?

Vocabulary

anesthetic
enclosure
smelt

Taking Notes

As you read, create a chart of causes of the Industrial Revolution. This sample will help you get started. Add categories as needed.

Agricultural Revolution	Population Explosion	New Technology	
• Dikes	• Declining	•	
• Fertilizer	death rates	•	

INDUSTRIAL REVOLUTION

Main Idea The Industrial Revolution had an impact on every aspect of life in Western Europe and the United States.

LESSON PLAN

1. Focus Several factors triggered the Industrial Revolution. Improved farming methods and the enclosure movement created a revolution in agriculture. Due to increased food production and better living conditions, the population of Europe soared. The Industrial Revolution was driven by a growing labor force and by new sources of fuel and power.

2. Instruct Divide the class into three or more groups and assign each group one of the following topics: A New Agricultural Revolution, The Population Explosion, New Technologies. Each group should work together on their topic to learn about changes that took place and the effects that those changes had on European life. After students have finished this part of the assignment, organize them into new groups so that each new group has at least one "expert" on each of the three topics. Have students take turns teaching one another about their particular topic.

3. Assess Have students consider the many changes that are occurring in the world today. Do they think the world is experiencing an agricultural revolution, a population explosion, or a technological revolution today? Encourage students to support their opinions with relevant examples.

4. Reteach If students' Assess activity does not reflect adequate understanding of the lesson, you might assign the *Guide to the Essentials* or the *Interactive Student Tutorial CD-ROM* for this section.

Setting the Scene For thousands of years following the rise of civilization, most people lived and worked in small farming villages. However, a chain of events set in motion in the mid-1700s changed that way of life for all time. Today, we call this period of change the Industrial Revolution.

The Industrial Revolution started in Britain. In contrast with most political revolutions, it was neither sudden nor swift. Instead, it was a long, slow, uneven process in which production shifted from simple hand tools to complex machines. New sources of power replaced human and animal power. In the 250 years since it began, the Industrial Revolution has spread from Britain to the rest of Europe, to North America, and around the globe.

A Turning Point in History

In 1750, most people worked the land, using handmade tools. They lived in simple cottages lit by firelight and candles. They made their own clothes and grew their own food. In nearby towns, they might exchange goods at a weekly outdoor market.

Like their ancestors, these people knew little of the world that existed beyond their village. The few who left home traveled only as far as their feet or a horse-drawn cart could take them. Those bold adventurers who dared to cross the seas were at the mercy of the winds and tides.

With the beginning of the Industrial Revolution, the rural way of life began to disappear. By the 1850s, many country villages had grown into industrial towns and cities. Their inhabitants bought food and clothing in stores that offered a large variety of machine-made goods. Their homes were crowded, multistory apartment buildings.

Industrial-age travelers moved rapidly between countries and continents by train or steamship. Urgent messages flew along telegraph wires. New inventions and scientific "firsts" poured out each year. Between 1830 and 1855, for example, an American dentist first used an anesthetic, or drug that prevents pain during surgery; an American inventor patented the first sewing machine; a French physicist measured the speed of light; and a Hungarian doctor introduced antiseptic methods to reduce the risk of women dying in childbirth.

Still more stunning changes occurred in the next century, creating our familiar world of skyscraper cities and carefully tended suburbs. How and why did these great changes occur? Historians point to a series of interrelated causes that helped trigger the industrialization of the West.

Resource Directory

Teaching Resources

Creative Teaching Activities Creative Teaching Activities booklet, p. 91
Guided Reading and Review Unit 5 booklet, p. 40
Skill Application Activity *Recognizing Faulty Reasoning,* Unit 5 booklet, p. 51

Technology

World History Color Transparencies political cartoon about the effect of technology on people's lives, p. E–35

Block Scheduling Support

Tell students to imagine they are tenant farmers for a rich landowner who is considering enclosing his land. Such an action means they will be forced off the land. Have them write a letter to their landlord explaining their situation and asking him to reconsider. You may wish to assign the Skill Application Activity *Recognizing Faulty Reasoning* in the Unit 5 booklet, p. 51, before having students write their letters.

A New Agricultural Revolution

Oddly enough, the Industrial Revolution was made possible in part by a change in the farming fields of Western Europe. The first agricultural revolution took place some 11,000 years ago, when people learned to farm and domesticate animals. About 300 years ago, a second agricultural revolution took place. It greatly improved the quality and quantity of farm products.

Improved Methods of Farming The Dutch led the way in this new agricultural revolution. They built earthen walls known as dikes to reclaim land from the sea. They combined smaller fields into larger ones to make better use of the land and used fertilizer from livestock to renew the soil.

In the 1700s, British farmers expanded on Dutch experiments. Some farmers mixed different kinds of soils to get higher crop yields. Others tried out new methods of crop rotation. Lord Charles Townshend urged farmers to grow turnips, which restored exhausted soil. Jethro Tull invented a new mechanical device, the seed drill, to aid farmers. It deposited seeds in rows rather than scattering them wastefully over the land.

Educated farmers exchanged news of experiments through farm journals. King George III himself, nicknamed "Farmer George," wrote articles about his model farm near Windsor Castle.

Enclosure Movement Meanwhile, rich landowners pushed ahead with enclosure, the process of taking over and fencing off land formerly shared by peasant farmers. In the 1500s, they had enclosed land to gain pastures for sheep and increased wool output. By the 1700s, they wanted to create larger fields that could be cultivated more efficiently.

As millions of acres were enclosed, farm output rose. Profits also rose because large fields needed fewer workers. But such progress had a human cost. Many farm laborers were thrown out of work, and small farmers were forced off their land because they could not compete with large landholders. Villages shrank as cottagers left in search of work.

In time, jobless farmworkers migrated to towns and cities. There, they formed a growing labor force that would tend the machines of the Industrial Revolution.

Changes in Agriculture

New inventions contributed to an agricultural revolution during the 1600s and 1700s. Today, the development of new sources of fuel encourages even more use of machine power in farming.

Theme: Economics and Technology How might agricultural developments increase farm productivity and efficiency?

 PAST

This four Wheel Drill Plow, with a Seed and a Manure Hopper, was first Invented in the Year 1... and is now in Use with W. Ellis at Little Gaddesden, near Hempstead in Hertfordshire, where anype... may View the same. It is so light that a Man may Draw it, but Generally drawn by a pony or little Hor...

 PRESENT

Recall
1. (a) Charles Townshend, p. 499 (b) Jethro Tull, p. 499 (c) Thomas Newcomen, p. 500 (d) James Watt, p. 500 (e) Abraham Darby, p. 500 2. (a) anesthetic, p. 498 (b) enclosure, p. 499 (c) smelt, p. 500

Comprehension
3. Possible answer: The Industrial Revolution changed the way people worked, traveled, acquired food, and organized their living space. 4. Possible answers: the agricultural revolution, better hygiene and sanitation, improved medical care 5. (a) It was a key power source of the early Industrial Revolution. (b) cheaper, better-quality iron was used in construction, especially in building railroads

Critical Thinking and Writing
6. Immediate effects included increased crop yields, more efficient farming, and a decreased demand for farm laborers. Long-term effects included population growth and migration. 7. Possible answer: It provided new sources of human labor and increased demand for manufactured goods.

Activity Rubrics

Share rubrics with students before they draw their sketches.

Attempted Student's sketch is incomplete.

Minimal Student's sketch is complete, but solution is far-fetched or impossible to build.

Adequate Student's sketch is complete and well thought-out.

Exemplary Student's sketch is well rendered, feasible to build, and creative and innovative.

Biography

James Watt 1736–1819

How did a clever Scottish engineer become the "Father of the Industrial Revolution"? After repairing a Newcomen steam engine, James Watt had become fascinated with the idea of improving the device. Within a few months, he knew he had a product that would sell.

Still, Watt lacked the money needed to produce and market it. Fortunately, he found a series of partners, including the shrewd Matthew Boulton. Soon, Boulton could boast, "I have at my disposal what the whole world demands, something which will uplift civilization more than ever by relieving man of all undignified drudgery. I have *steam power*."

Theme: Impact of the Individual How might the Industrial Revolution have been different if Watt had not found a business partner?

The Population Explosion

The agricultural revolution contributed to a rapid growth of population that continues today. Precise population statistics for the 1700s are rare, but those that do exist are striking. Britain's population, for example, soared from about 5 million in 1700 to almost 9 million in 1800. The population of Europe as a whole shot up from roughly 120 million to about 190 million during the same period. Such growth had never before been seen.

The population boom of the 1700s was due more to declining death rates than to rising birthrates. The agricultural revolution reduced the risk of famine. Because they ate better, women were healthier and had stronger babies. In the 1800s, better hygiene and sanitation, along with improved medical care, further slowed deaths from disease.

New Technology

A third factor that helped trigger the Industrial Revolution was the development of new technology. New sources of energy, along with new materials, enabled business owners to change the ways work was done.

An Energy Revolution From the beginning of human history, the energy for work was provided mostly by the muscles of humans and animals. In time, water mills and windmills were added to muscle power.

During the 1700s, people began to harness new sources of energy. One vital power source was coal, used to develop the steam engine. In 1712, inventor Thomas Newcomen had developed a steam engine powered by coal to pump water out of mines. About 1769, Scottish engineer James Watt improved on Newcomen's engine. Watt's engines would become a key power source of the Industrial Revolution.

Improved Iron Coal was also a vital source of fuel in the production of iron, a material needed for construction of machines and steam engines. The Darby family of Coalbrookdale pioneered new methods of producing iron. In 1709, Abraham Darby used coal to smelt iron, or separate iron from its ore. When he discovered that coal gave off impurities that damaged the iron, Darby found a way to remove the impurities from coal.

Darby's experiments led him to produce better-quality and less expensive iron, and his son and grandson continued to improve on his methods. In the decades that followed, high-quality iron was used more and more widely, especially after the world turned to building railroads.

SECTION 1 Assessment

Recall
1. **Identify:** (a) Charles Townshend, (b) Jethro Tull, (c) Thomas Newcomen, (d) James Watt, (e) Abraham Darby.
2. **Define:** (a) anesthetic, (b) enclosure, (c) smelt.

Comprehension
3. Describe how the Industrial Revolution changed daily life, becoming a turning point in history.
4. Identify three causes of the population explosion in Europe.

5. Explain the impact of each of the following technologies: (a) steam power, (b) improved iron.

Critical Thinking and Writing
6. **Recognizing Causes and Effects** What were the immediate and long-term effects of the agricultural revolution?
7. **Predicting Consequences** How do you think increased population contributed to the Industrial Revolution?

Activity

Creating a Mechanical Drawing Suppose that you are trying to develop a way to draw water from a well that is faster than pulling up one bucket of water at a time. Draw a sketch of a machine that would speed up the process and require less human labor.

Biography

ANSWER Possible answer: Watt's improved steam engine might not have been marketed right away, which could have meant a delay in the spread of the Industrial Revolution.

Resource Directory

Teaching Resources
Section Quiz Unit 5 booklet, p. 41
Creative Teaching Activities Creative Teaching Activities booklet, p. 92
Guided Reading and Review Unit 5 booklet, p. 42
Biography Activity *Josiah Wedgwood,* Unit 5 booklet, p. 48

Technology
Interactive Student Tutorial CD-ROM Ch. 20
Computer Test Bank Ch. 20

SECTION **2** Britain Leads the Way

Reading Focus

- Why was Britain the starting point for the Industrial Revolution?
- What changes transformed the textile industry?
- What new technologies were part of the revolution in transportation?

Vocabulary

capital

factory

turnpike

Taking Notes

Copy this concept web. As you read, fill in the circles with key factors that helped Britain take an early lead in industry.

Coal

Resources

Strong navy

BRITAIN TAKES THE LEAD

Capital

Main Idea The Industrial Revolution originated in Britain.

Setting the Scene Visitors crowded into London's Crystal Palace in 1851. The immense structure housed the Great Exhibition, a display of the "Works of Industry of all Nations." The palace itself was specially built for the occasion. A vast cavern of glass and iron, it symbolized the triumph of the industrial age.

In the century before the exhibition, Britain had been the first nation to industrialize. Its success became the model for other countries, in Europe and around the world.

Why Britain?

Why did the Industrial Revolution begin in Britain? Historians have identified a number of key factors that helped Britain lead the way.

Resources Britain was a small nation in area. However, it had large supplies of coal to power steam engines. It also had plentiful iron to build the new machines. In addition to natural resources, a labor supply was necessary. Large numbers of workers were needed to mine the coal and iron, build the factories, and run the machines. The agricultural revolution of the 1600s and 1700s freed many people in Britain from farm labor and led to a population boom.

New Technology In the 1700s, Britain had plenty of skilled mechanics who were eager to meet the growing demand for new, practical inventions. Technology was an important part of the Industrial Revolution, but it did not cause it. After all, other societies, such as the ancient Greeks or Chinese, had advanced technology for their time but did not move on to industrialization. Only when other necessary conditions existed, including demand and capital, did technology pave the way for industrialization.

Economic Conditions From the mid-1600s to 1700s, trade from a growing overseas empire helped the British economy prosper. Beginning with the slave trade, the business class accumulated capital, or wealth to invest in enterprises such as shipping, mines, railroads, and factories. Many were ready to risk their capital in new ventures.

At home, the population explosion boosted demand for goods. However, a growing population alone would not have resulted in increased production. General economic prosperity also helped make the new consumer goods affordable to members of every social class.

Chapter 20 **501**

Britain's Overseas Markets The vast British empire provided world-wide markets for British industrial goods. In fact, during the 1700s, the overseas export market grew at a much faster rate than the domestic market. Between 1750 and 1770, for example, production for the export market increased by 80 percent, while production for the domestic market grew by only 7 percent. Although investing in new industries carried risks, the lucrative overseas trade made the gamble seem well worth taking.

After they read the section, ask students to make a list of key British resources, conditions, and inventions that brought about industrialization. Remind them to use their completed concept webs from the Taking Notes activity to help them make their lists. Then ask them to write a sentence about Britain and industrialization. *(Less Advanced Readers)*

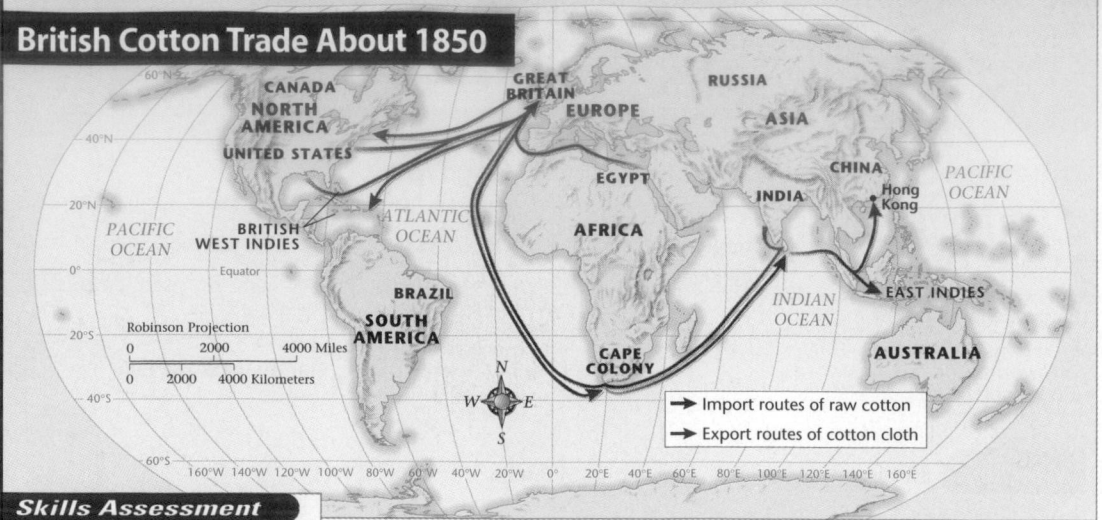

British Cotton Trade About 1850

→ Import routes of raw cotton
→ Export routes of cotton cloth

Skills Assessment

Geography As its textile industry grew, Great Britain needed more raw cotton. It also sought out new markets for finished cotton cloth.

1. **Location** *On the map, locate* **(a)** *Great Britain,* **(b)** *United States,* **(c)** *British West Indies.*
2. **Movement** **(a)** *Name two overseas sources that supplied raw cotton to Britain.* **(b)** *Name two overseas markets to which Britain exported its cotton cloth.*
3. **Critical Thinking Predicting Consequences** *What might have happened to the British cotton industry if Britain had lost control of India?*

Political and Social Conditions Britain had a stable government that supported economic growth. It built a strong navy to protect its empire and overseas trade. Although the upper class tended to look down on business people, it did not reject the wealth produced by the new entrepreneurs.

Religious attitudes also played a role. Many entrepreneurs came from religious groups that encouraged thrift and hard work. At the same time, many people focused more on worldly concerns than on the afterlife. Thus, risk takers such as inventors and bankers felt free to devote their energies to material achievements.

Changes in the Textile Industry

The Industrial Revolution first took hold in Britain's largest industry, textiles. In the 1600s, cotton cloth imported from India had become popular. British merchants tried to organize a cotton cloth industry at home. They developed the putting out system, in which raw cotton was distributed to peasant families who spun it into thread and then wove the thread into cloth. Skilled artisans in the towns then finished and dyed the cloth.

Major Inventions Under the putting out system, production was slow. As the demand for cloth grew, inventors came up with a string of remarkable devices that revolutionized the British textile industry. For example, using John Kay's flying shuttle, weavers worked so fast that they soon outpaced spinners. James Hargreaves solved that problem by producing the spinning jenny in 1764, which spun many threads at the same time. A few years later, Richard Arkwright invented the waterframe, which used water power to speed up spinning still further.

The First Factories The new machines doomed the putting out system. They were too large and expensive to be operated at home. Instead, manufacturers built long sheds to house the machines. At first, they located the sheds near rapidly moving streams, which provided water power to run the machines. Later, machines were powered by steam engines.

Spinners and weavers came each day to work in these first factories— places that brought together workers and machines to produce large quantities of goods. Early observers were awed at the size and output of these establishments. One onlooker noted: "The same [amount] of labor is now performed in one of these structures which formerly occupied the industry of an entire district."

Skills Assessment

ANSWERS 1. Review locations with students. **2.** Possible answers: **(a)** India, Egypt, the United States **(b)** Africa, India, China, East Indies, North America, Caribbean **3.** It could have harmed the cotton industry, because Britain would have lost an important source of raw materials as well as a major market.

Resource Directory

Teaching Resources
Primary Source Activity *Riding the Liverpool-Manchester Line,* Unit 5 booklet, p. 49
Synthesizing Information Chapter Extension Activities booklet, p. 50

Synthesizing Information

Impact of the Railroad

The steam locomotive was one of the key inventions of the Industrial Revolution. The maps, the cartoon, and the graph below all relate to the growth of railroads in Great Britain.

English Cartoon, Early 1800s

Railways in Great Britain

1840

SCOTLAND
Edinburgh
IRELAND
Dublin
Manchester ENGLAND
Birmingham
WALES
London
Brighton

1850

SCOTLAND
Edinburgh
ENGLAND
IRELAND Manchester
Dublin
Birmingham
WALES London
Brighton

——— Railway lines

Travel Times to London

Birmingham

Brighton

Manchester

| 0 | 10 | 20 | 30 | 40 | 50 | 60 | 70 | 80 |

Hours

- 1750
- 1830
- 1850

Source: E. J. Hobsbaum, *Industry and Empire*

Skills Assessment

1. Between 1750 and 1830, travel time from Birmingham to London decreased by about
   A 12 hours.
   B 24 hours.
   C 36 hours.
   D 48 hours.

2. Which of the three pieces of evidence above supports the conclusion that railroads reached more places in 1850 than in 1830?
   E the maps only
   F the graph only
   G the maps and the graph
   H the maps and the cartoon

3. **Critical Thinking Drawing Conclusions** (a) Based on the evidence provided here, what were some of the benefits and drawbacks of railroads? (b) What other positive or negative effects do you think railroads might have had? Give two examples.

Skills Tip

Bar graphs often show change over time. To determine the amount of change, subtract the smaller measure from the larger one.

Background
About the Evidence

Trains of the Future Steam locomotives revolutionized rail travel during the Industrial Revolution, but today's high-speed trains are even more revolutionary. As late as the early 1970s, developers thought the top speed possible for flanged-wheel trains was from 150 to 200 miles per hour. By the 1990s Japanese and German engineers had achieved speeds of more than 300 miles per hour by using magnetic levitation (called *maglev*).

Maglev trains travel not *on* a track, but above it, lifted a few inches above the guideway surface by magnetic fields. Maglev enthusiasts believe that the invention will eventually provide comfortable, economic, and almost maintenance-free transportation.

Activity
Interpreting the Evidence

Use these additional questions to generate class discussion.

1. **Critical Thinking: Applying Information** Between which years was there a decrease of about 2 hours travel time between Brighton and London? *(between 1830 and 1850)*

2. **Critical Thinking: Making Inferences** Why do you suppose there were no railroads in northern Scotland and western Ireland in 1850? *(possible answer: isolated locations and fewer population centers)*

Skills Tip

Point out that graphs use color coding to facilitate comparisons between entries. The Skills Handbook in the front of the book has a lesson that will help students with this feature.

Skills Assessment

***ANSWERS* 1.** C **2.** E **3.** Possible answers: **(a)** benefits—faster travel times between cities; drawbacks—accidents between trains and horse-drawn carriages **(b)** Positive effects included increased communication between cities and easier transport of goods. Negative effects were noise pollution and the carving up of the countryside.

 EXPLORING HUMAN DRAMA

Human Drama Note

The Cotton Cycle The Industrial Revolution in Britain had an unforeseen effect in the United States. American planters supplied raw cotton for the British textile industry but could not keep up with demand. The invention of the cotton gin speeded up cotton processing. With enormous profits to be made, American planters wanted to sell more cotton. They used their profits to buy more land and more slaves, who worked in the cotton fields. In this way, slavery became entrenched in the American economy.

✓ Test Preparation

Have students review the chart "Travel Times to London" on this page, and then answer the question below.

Between 1750 and 1830, which route saw the biggest decrease in travel time?

A Birmingham to London

B Brighton to London

C Manchester to London

D All travel times decreased equally.

SECTION 2 Assessment

Recall
1. (a) John Kay, p. 502 (b) James Hargreaves, p. 502 (c) Richard Arkwright,
p. 502 (d) George Stephenson, p. 504
2. (a) capital, p. 501 (b) factory, p. 502
(c) turnpike, p. 504

Comprehension
3. plentiful natural and human resources,
Britain's technological lead, capital and
demand, a stable government, and a society that valued hard work and worldly
achievements 4. New inventions required
more space than was available in homes.
To increase efficiency, business owners
built factories in which many people completed tasks under one roof, rather than
in their own homes on a smaller scale.
5. Capitalists invested in turnpikes and
canals, Stephenson invented the railroad,
and Fulton invented the steamboat.

Critical Thinking and Writing
6. (a) As population grew, demand
increased because there were more people who needed more goods. (b) As people became more prosperous, they had
more money to buy goods. 7. (a) North
America, Africa, Asia (b) Transportation
improved shipping and opened up new
resources and markets.

Geography and History

Europe's Canal Boom

People have dug canals since
ancient times, but it took the
Industrial Revolution to set off a
canal-building frenzy in Europe.
During the late 1700s and early
1800s, European factories needed
an efficient, inexpensive way to
receive coal and raw materials
and then to ship finished goods to
market. The many navigable rivers
in Europe did not reach every town
and sometimes followed indirect—
and lengthy—courses. Canals
solved the problem. They connected towns to more distant
rivers and provided direct routes
from factories to markets.

The canals soon lost some of
their importance to railroads, but
today Europe is still crisscrossed
by a 13,000-mile network of canals
and rivers.

 **Theme: Geography
and History** How did
canals help to advance the
Industrial Revolution?

Revolution in Transportation

As production increased, entrepreneurs needed faster and cheaper methods
of moving goods from place to place. Some capitalists invested in turnpikes,
which were privately built roads that charged a fee to travelers who used
them. Others had canals dug to link rivers or connect inland towns with
coastal ports. Engineers also built stronger bridges and upgraded harbors
to help the expanding overseas trade.

On Land The great revolution in transportation, however, was the invention of the steam locomotive. It was this invention that made possible the
growth of railroads. In the early 1800s, pioneers like George Stephenson
developed steam-powered locomotives to pull carriages along iron rails.
The railroad did not have to follow the course of a river. This meant
that tracks could go places rivers did not, allowing factory owners and
merchants to ship goods over land.

The world's first major rail line, from Liverpool to Manchester, opened
in England in 1830. In the following decades, railroad travel became faster
and railroad building boomed. By 1870, rail lines crisscrossed Britain,
Europe, and North America.

On Sea Other inventors applied steam power to improve shipping. In
1807, an American, Robert Fulton, used Watt's steam engine to power the
Clermont up the Hudson River in New York. Fulton's steamboat traveled
at a record-breaking speed of more than five miles an hour!

Designing steamships for ocean voyages was more difficult. The coal
needed for the voyage took up much of the cargo space. But by the late
1800s, steam-powered freighters with iron hulls were carrying 10 to 20
times the cargo of older wooden ships.

Looking Ahead

As the Industrial Revolution got under way, it triggered a chain reaction.
In response to growing demand, inventors developed machines that could
produce large quantities of goods more efficiently. As the supply of goods
increased, prices fell. Lower prices made goods more affordable and thus
created more consumers who further fed the demand for goods. The Industrial Revolution affected not only how goods were made but also how people lived. It brought a tidal wave of economic and social changes that
swept the industrializing nations of the world.

SECTION 2 Assessment

Recall
1. **Identify:** (a) John Kay, (b) James
   Hargreaves, (c) Richard Arkwright,
   (d) George Stephenson.
2. **Define:** (a) capital, (b) factory,
   (c) turnpike.

Comprehension
3. Describe four factors that helped
   bring about the Industrial
   Revolution in Britain.
4. How did the Industrial Revolution
   transform the textile industry?
5. How did transportation improve
   in the early 1800s? Give three
   examples.

Critical Thinking and Writing
6. **Analyzing Information** Explain
   how each of the following helped
   contribute to demand for consumer goods in Britain: (a) population explosion, (b) general
   economic prosperity.
7. **Connecting to Geography** Look
   at the map of the British cotton
   trade in this section. (a) To what
   continents did Britain export its
   cotton cloth? (b) Explain how
   advances in transportation, such
   as the steamboat, contributed to
   Britain's global cotton trade.

Activity
Take It to the NET
Research connections
between mining and
transportation. Write
a brief explanation of
how canals affected the
coal industry.

504 Chapter 20

Geography and History

ANSWER They provided interconnec-
tions between different rivers to link ports
and manufacturing centers throughout
Europe.

Reading Focus

- What was life like in the new industrial city?
- How did the factory system change the way people worked?
- What benefits and problems did industrialization bring to the working class and the new middle class?

Vocabulary

urbanization
tenement
labor union

Taking Notes

Copy this table. As you read, list the characteristics of the working class and the middle class. Add more entries as needed.

THE WORKING CLASS	THE MIDDLE CLASS
Factory and mine workers	Merchants, inventors, skilled artisans
Tenement housing	

Main Idea The Industrial Revolution created material benefits as well as social problems.

Setting the Scene The Industrial Revolution brought great riches to most of the entrepreneurs who helped set it in motion. For the millions of workers who crowded into the new factories, however, the industrial age brought poverty and harsh living conditions. One observer commented on the disease-ridden neighborhoods and polluted air:

> "The population . . . is crowded into one dense mass of cottages separated by unpaved and almost pestilential streets. This is an atmosphere loaded with the exhalation of a large manufacturing city."
> —J. P. Kay, quoted in *Mill Life at Styal*

In time, reforms would curb many of the worst abuses of the early industrial age in Europe and the Americas, and people at all levels of society would benefit from industrialization. Until then, working people could look forward only to lives marked by dangerous working conditions; unsafe, unsanitary, and overcrowded housing; and unrelenting poverty.

The New Industrial City

The Industrial Revolution brought rapid urbanization, or the movement of people to cities. Changes in farming, soaring population growth, and an ever-increasing demand for workers led masses of people to migrate from farms to cities. Almost overnight, small towns around coal or iron mines mushroomed into cities. Other cities grew up around the factories that entrepreneurs built in once-quiet market towns.

The British market town of Manchester numbered 17,000 people in the 1750s. Within a few years, it exploded into a center of the textile industry. Its population soared to 40,000 by 1780 and 70,000 by 1801. Visitors described the "cloud of coal vapor" that polluted the air, the pounding noise of steam engines, and the filthy stench of its river.

In Manchester, as elsewhere, a gulf divided the urban population. The wealthy and the middle class lived in pleasant neighborhoods. Vast numbers of poor, however, struggled to survive in foul-smelling slums. They packed into tiny rooms in tenements, multistory buildings divided into crowded apartments. These buildings had no running water, only community pumps. There was no sewage or sanitation system, and wastes and garbage rotted in the streets. Cholera and other diseases spread rapidly. In time, reformers pushed for laws to improve conditions in city slums.

▶ **Primary Sources and Literature**

See "Charles Dickens: Hard Times" in the Reference Section at the back of this book.

Bell Ringer Ask students to read the excerpt from Charles Dickens's novel, *Hard Times,* in the Reference Section at the back of this book. Then, have them list three hardships of industrial life that Dickens describes. Ask students to offer a possible remedy for each problem.

LESSON PLAN

1. Focus Factory work meant long hours, backbreaking jobs, unsafe conditions, and low pay. Many women worked both at home and in the factories. Child labor was a common practice. In the cities, working-class families endured filthy and overcrowded living conditions. At the same time, however, the Industrial Revolution gradually brought more jobs, higher pay, and other material benefits.

2. Instruct Ask students to imagine that they are living during the early years of the Industrial Revolution. Assign each student one of the following roles: a miner, a factory worker, a child laborer, a working-class mother, a factory owner, a government inspector, a Luddite, a middle-class woman. Have students write a diary entry in the role of their assumed character. Instruct students to record the events of a complete day and to include specific details of the person's life. In their diaries, students should include not only their activities and observations but also their feelings and emotions. Have students take turns sharing their diary entries with the class.

3. Assess Ask students to list three or four ways that life today would be different for the person whose role they assumed.

4. Reteach If students' Assess activity does not reflect adequate understanding of the lesson, you might assign the *Guide to the Essentials* or the *Interactive Student Tutorial CD-ROM* for this section.

Block Scheduling Support

In 1816, a teenager named Mary Shelley had a nightmare vision that inspired her to write *Frankenstein,* a novel about a scientist who tries to make a human being but creates a monster instead. The story reflected the fear of many Europeans during the Industrial Revolution that humans were using technology to tamper with nature. Have students form small groups to discuss the following questions. Why did people during the Industrial Revolution worry that technology had gone too far? Are those concerns still valid today? Then have each group draft a scenario for a modern-day *Frankenstein* in which they address today's concerns about technology. Encourage each group to share their scenarios with the rest of the class.

Background
Daily Life

Child Labor Thousands of children worked in Britain's coal mines during the Industrial Revolution. In the cramped, narrow mine shafts, children crawled on all fours, pushing coal carts or dragging them behind. "Some places are scarcely fit for a dog to go in, not being more than from two feet and a half to a yard in height," one young miner said.

The horrors of child labor were slowly exposed in the 1830s and 1840s, when British lawmakers looked into abuses in factories and mines. Government commissions heard about children as young as five years old working in factories. Some died. Others were stunted in growth or had twisted limbs. Most remained uneducated.

Members of the Ashley Mines Commission heard about life in the coal mines from 17-year-old Patience Kershaw, whose sisters had started in the mines but switched to mill work. One changed jobs when her legs swelled from standing in the cold water that covered the mine floor. Kershaw's job was "hurrying"—pushing carts of coal to the surface of the mine:

"I go to [the mine] at 5 o'clock in the morning and come out at 5 in the evening. . . . The bald place upon my head is made by [pushing] the corves [carts full of coal]. . . . I hurry the corves a mile and more underground and back. . . . I wear a belt and chain . . . to get the corves out."

Virtual Field Trip

www.phschool.com

**Dunaskin Open Air Museum
Ayrshire, Scotland**

To find more information about iron production during the Industrial Revolution, use the Internet address above to link to the Dunaskin Open Air Museum.

Forging the Anchor
This painting by William James Muler shows workers laboring to make an anchor of iron. The image provides a glimpse of the factory system.

Theme: Art and Literature
How would you describe the artist's opinion of factories?

The Factory System

The heart of the new industrial city was the factory. There, the technology of the machine age imposed a harsh new way of life on workers.

Rigid Discipline The factory system differed greatly from farmwork. In rural villages, people worked hard, but their work varied according to the season. In factories, workers faced a rigid schedule set by the factory whistle. "While the engine runs," said an observer, "people must work—men, women, and children are yoked together with iron and steam."

Working hours were long. Shifts lasted from 12 to 16 hours. Exhausted workers suffered accidents from machines that had no safety devices. They might lose a finger, a limb, or even their lives. Workers were exposed to other dangers, as well. Coal dust destroyed the lungs of miners, and textile workers constantly breathed air filled with lint. If workers were sick or injured, they lost their jobs.

Women Workers Employers often preferred to hire women workers rather than men. They thought women could adapt more easily to machines and were easier to manage than men. More important, they were able to pay women less than men, even for the same work.

Factory work created special problems for women. Their new jobs took them out of their homes for 12 hours or more a day. They then returned to crowded slum tenements to feed and clothe their families, clean, and cope with sickness and other problems. Family life had been hard for poor rural cottagers. In industrial towns, it was even grimmer.

Child Labor Factories and mines also hired many boys and girls. Often, nimble-fingered and quick-moving children changed spools in textile mills. Others clambered through narrow mine shafts, pushing coal carts. Because children had helped with farmwork, parents accepted the idea of child labor. And the wages the children earned were needed to keep their families from starving.

Employers often hired orphans, making deals with local officials who were glad to have the children taken off their hands. Overseers beat children accused of idling. A few enlightened factory owners did provide basic education and a decent life for child workers. More often, though, children, like their parents, were slaves to the machines.

506 *Chapter 20*

The artist seems to glorify factories and factory workers, although the work does look difficult and hot.

Teaching Resources

Geography and History Activity *The Widening Spiral of Resource Extraction and Environmental Damage,* Geography and History booklet, pp. 10–11
History Through Literature *Mary Barton,* History Through Literature booklet, pp. 43–44
Viewpoint Activity *Rules for Workers,* Unit 5 booklet, p. 50
You Are There Chapter Extensions Activities booklet, p. 51

Spinning Thread in a Textile Mill

It is your first day at work and you're already exhausted. You wanted to help your family by earning extra money, so you came to Manchester to work with your uncle in a textile mill. You must work on several machines at once, keeping the thread from tangling and breaking. The factory still seems so strange.

The thunder of the spinning mule vibrates through the floor. This machine allows you to make thread faster by yourself than hundreds of people spinning by hand.

It is hard to breathe. Cotton dust flies out of the machines. You hear other workers coughing, their lungs filled with the thick dust.

Children dart in and out, untying knots in the thread. You wince as you see a little boy almost get his hand caught in a machine. The boss gives you a disapproving look, so you try to focus on your own work.

Portfolio Assessment

After a 12-hour day at the mill, you decide to write a letter to your family. In your letter, describe your new job and say whether you want to keep working here in Manchester or go back home to the farm.

Chapter 20 **507**

Bell Ringer After students study the illustration, ask them what they find striking about the working conditions and the workers. How do they differ from modern working conditions and workers?

Background
About the Scene

"The Chimney Sweeper" William Blake, an English poet of the 1800s, wrote two volumes of poems reflecting the social effects of the Industrial Revolution. These volumes, titled *Songs of Innocence* and *Songs of Experience,* describe similar experiences, but from different perspectives.

Two poems, both titled "The Chimney Sweeper," explore child labor. In *Songs of Innocence,* a child chimney sweep describes the hardships of his life, but repeats, ironically, what he has been told: he is doing his duty and will be rewarded in heaven. The chimney sweep in *Songs of Experience,* however, finds not even that poor consolation for his pain.

Activity
Cooperative Learning

Planning a Presentation Have small groups of students imagine that they are members of an organization during this period that opposes child labor. They are seeking to get new laws passed banning the practice. Have each group plan a campaign in which they will make a presentation to lawmakers against child labor. The group should brainstorm ways to get their message across most effectively and then assign individuals to specific functions: research, creating visuals, writing speeches, and so on.

Activity Rubrics

Share rubrics with students before they complete their letters.

Attempted Letter fails to address the issues.

Minimal Letter addresses the issues, but description is superficial.

Adequate Letter describes job in sufficient detail and addresses the issues.

Exemplary Letter gives detailed descriptions, striking examples, and compelling reasons for the writer's choice.

EXPLORING the HUMAN DRAMA

Human Drama Activity

Analyzing a Film Assign students to watch a film version of Dickens' *Oliver Twist.* Many film critics consider the 1948 British production, directed by David Lean and starring Alec Guinness, to be the classic rendition. The film alternates scenes that depict middle-class life with those that portray the terrible conditions endured by the working class. As students view the film, ask them to list the problems that characterized life for England's lower classes during the early Industrial Revolution. Also, have them list the advantages enjoyed by the wealthier upper classes. Finally, have them write an essay that compares the living conditions of England's lower and upper classes during the early Industrial Revolution. ✳

Worker Protests
On a hot August day in 1819, workers gathered in St. Peter's Fields in Manchester to hear reformers speak. Suddenly, soldiers attacked the crowd. The incident became known as the Peterloo Massacre.

Theme: Art and Literature Did the artist who created this cartoon favor the workers or the soldiers? Explain.

In the 1830s and 1840s, British lawmakers looked into abuses in factories and mines. Government commissions heard about children as young as five years old working in factories. Some died; others were stunted in growth or had twisted limbs. Most were uneducated. Slowly, Parliament passed laws to regulate child labor in mines and factories.

The Working Class

In rural villages, farm families had strong ties to a community in which they had lived for generations. When they moved to the new industrial cities, many felt lost and bewildered. In time, though, factory and mine workers developed their own sense of community.

Protests As the Industrial Revolution began, weavers and other skilled artisans resisted the new "labor-saving" machines that were costing them their jobs. Some smashed machines and burned factories. In England, such rioters were called Luddites after a mythical figure, Ned Ludd, who supposedly destroyed machines in the 1780s.

Protests met harsh repression. When workers held a rally in Manchester in 1819, soldiers charged the crowd, killing a dozen and injuring hundreds more. Workers were forbidden to organize in groups to bargain for better pay and working conditions. Strikes were outlawed.

Spread of Methodism Many working-class people found comfort in a new religious movement. In the mid-1700s, John Wesley had founded the Methodist Church. Wesley stressed the need for a personal sense of faith. He urged Christians to improve their lot by adopting sober, moral ways.

Methodist meetings featured hymns and sermons promising forgiveness of sin and a better life to come. Methodist preachers took this message of salvation into the slums. There, they tried to rekindle hope among the working poor. They set up Sunday schools where followers not only studied the Bible but also learned to read and write. Methodists helped channel workers' anger away from revolution and toward social reform.

The New Middle Class

Those who benefited most from the Industrial Revolution were the entrepreneurs who set it in motion. This new middle class came from several sources. Some members were merchants who invested their growing profits in factories. Others were inventors or skilled artisans who developed new technologies. Some rose from "rags to riches," a pattern that the age greatly admired.

Middle-class families lived in solid, well-furnished homes. They dressed and ate well. Middle-class men gained influence in Parliament, where they opposed any effort to improve conditions for workers.

As a sign of their new standard of living, middle-class women were encouraged to become "ladies." They took up "ladylike" activities, such as drawing, embroidery, or playing the piano. A "lady" did not work outside the home or do housework. Instead, the family hired a maid-servant. The family then set about educating its daughters to provide the same type of happy, well-furnished home for their future husbands. Sons gained an education that allowed them to become businessmen.

The new middle class valued hard work and the determination to "get ahead." They had confidence in themselves and often little sympathy for the poor. If they thought of the faceless millions in the factories and mines, they generally supposed the poor to be responsible for their own misery. Some believed the poor were so lazy or ignorant that they could not "work their way up" out of poverty.

Benefits and Problems

Since the 1800s, people have debated whether the Industrial Revolution was a blessing or a curse. The early industrial age brought terrible hardships. Said English writer Thomas Carlyle, "Something [ought] to be done."

In time, "something" would be done. Reformers pressed for laws to improve working conditions. Workers' organizations called **labor unions** won the right to bargain with employers for better wages, hours, and working conditions. Eventually, working-class men gained the right to vote, which gave them political power.

Despite the social problems created by the Industrial Revolution—low pay, unemployment, dismal living conditions—the industrial age did bring material benefits. As demand for mass-produced goods grew, new factories opened, creating more jobs. Wages rose so that workers had enough left after paying rent and buying food to buy a newspaper or visit a music hall. As the cost of railroad travel fell, people could visit family in other towns. Horizons widened; opportunities increased.

Industrialization has spread around the world today. Often, it begins with great suffering. In the end, however, it produces more material benefits for more people.

Primary Source

"Badly Cooked Dinners and Untidy Ways"
Women who reached middle-class status in the Industrial Revolution eagerly sought advice on how to be proper "ladies":

"What moved me . . . to attempt a work like this was the discomfort and suffering I had seen brought upon men and women by household management. I have always thought there is no more fruitful source for family discontent than a housewife's badly cooked dinners and untidy ways. [These lead husbands to "flee" from home to] clubs, well-ordered taverns and dining houses."

—Isabella Beeton, *Beeton's Book of Household Management*

Skills Assessment

Primary Source What does the excerpt suggest about the role and status of middle-class women during the Industrial Revolution?

SECTION 3 Assessment

Recall
1. **Identify:** (a) Luddite, (b) John Wesley, (c) Methodism.
2. **Define:** (a) urbanization, (b) tenement, (c) labor union.

Comprehension
3. Describe life in the new industrial city.
4. (a) What were the main characteristics of factory work? (b) What special problems did factory work create for women?

5. How did the conditions of the early industrial age improve?

Critical Thinking and Writing
6. **Comparing** Compare the life of a farmworker with that of an early factory worker.
7. **Connecting to Geography** Look at the chapter opener map. What geographic feature do many of the industrial centers share? Why do you think this is so?

Activity
Take It to the NET

Search the Internet for information about working conditions during the Industrial Revolution. Draw a political cartoon that illustrates the life of factory workers. Write a caption for your cartoon.

Chapter 20 **509**

Test Preparation

Read the section "Benefits and Problems" on this page, and then complete the sentence below.

The main idea of this section is that the Industrial Revolution

A was either a blessing or a curse for people.

B had both positive and negative effects on workers.

C brought terrible hardships to the working class.

D broadened horizons and increased opportunities.

Bell Ringer

Bell Ringer Direct students' attention to the vocabulary words that appear at the start of this section. Ask them to define any of the words with which they are familiar. Have them use the glossary to verify their definitions and to define the words that are unfamiliar to them.

Reading Focus

■ What was laissez-faire economics?

■ How did the views of utilitarians differ from those of socialists?

■ What were the ideas of "scientific socialism," introduced by Karl Marx?

Vocabulary

utilitarianism

socialism

means of production

communism

proletariat

Taking Notes

As you read this section, prepare an outline of its contents. Use Roman numerals to indicate major headings. Use capital letters for subheadings, and use numbers for the supporting details. The example here will help you get started.

I. Laissez-faire economics
  A. Legacy of Adam Smith
    1. Benefits of free market
    2.
  B. Malthus on population
    1. Population outpaces food supply
    2.

LESSON PLAN

1. Focus The industrial age gave rise to economic philosophies such as utilitarianism, socialism, and communism. Individual thinkers offered a variety of opinions on what government should do to improve social and economic conditions. Socialists condemned the evils of industrial capitalism and urged radical changes in the way the economy operated.

2. Instruct Ask students to choose one of the following people and write a position paper in which they explain that thinker's point of view: Adam Smith, Thomas Malthus, David Ricardo, Jeremy Bentham, John Stuart Mill, Robert Owen, Karl Marx. Students should use the text and library resources to set forth the philosophy of the person they choose. Tell students to be prepared to read their papers to the class and to answer any questions that you or the students might have.

3. Assess Have students construct a table that compares the views of all the philosophers discussed in this section.

4. Reteach If students' Assess activity does not reflect adequate understanding of the lesson, you might assign the *Guide to the Essentials* or the *Interactive Student Tutorial CD-ROM* for this section.

Main Idea

The Industrial Revolution fostered new ideas about business and economics.

Biography

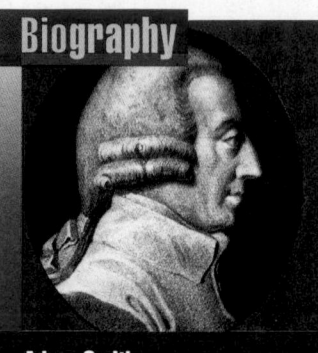

Adam Smith 1723–1790

If anyone fit the image of the "absent-minded professor," it was Adam Smith. He forgot things, spoke awkwardly, and rambled as he walked. "I am a beau in nothing but my books," Smith once said. Still, he had one of history's keenest minds.

At the age of 14, Smith was a student at a university in his native Scotland. There, and later in Paris, he met many influential thinkers of the Enlightenment. He also met local merchants, gaining practical knowledge about business.

Smith spent 10 years writing *The Wealth of Nations*. Published in 1776, it became an instant bestseller. Readers embraced Smith's ideas about laissez-faire and the benefits of capitalism.

Theme: Impact of the Individual How did Smith's education shape his work?

Setting the Scene Everywhere in Britain, Thomas Malthus saw the effects of the population explosion—crowded slums, hungry families, unemployment, and widespread misery. After careful study, in 1798 he published his "Essay on the Principle of Population." Poverty and misery, he concluded, were unavoidable because the population was increasing faster than the food supply. Malthus wrote: "The power of population is [far] greater than the power of the Earth to produce subsistence for man."

Malthus was one of many thinkers who tried to understand the staggering changes taking place in the early industrial age. As heirs to the Enlightenment, these thinkers looked for natural laws that governed the world of business and economics.

Laissez-Faire Economics

During the Enlightenment, physiocrats argued that natural laws should be allowed to operate without interference. As part of this philosophy, they believed that government should not interfere in the free operation of the economy. In the early 1800s, middle-class business leaders embraced this laissez-faire, or "hands-off," approach.

Legacy of Adam Smith The main prophet of laissez-faire economics was Adam Smith, author of *The Wealth of Nations*. Smith asserted that a free market—the unregulated exchange of goods and services—would come to help everyone, not just the rich.

The free market, Smith said, would produce more goods at lower prices, making them affordable by everyone. A growing economy would also encourage capitalists to reinvest profits in new ventures. Supporters of this free-enterprise capitalism pointed to the successes of the industrial age, in which government had played no part.

Malthus on Population Like Smith's book, Thomas Malthus's writings on population shaped economic thinking for generations. Malthus grimly predicted that population would outpace the food supply. The only checks on population growth, he said, were war, disease, and famine. As long as population kept increasing, he went on, the poor would suffer. He thus urged families to have fewer children.

During the early 1800s, many people accepted Malthus's bleak view. It proved to be too pessimistic, however. Although the population boom did continue, the food supply grew even faster. As the century progressed,

Biography

ANSWER His early encounters with Enlightenment thought influenced his later work.

Resource Directory

Teaching Resources

Creative Teaching Activities Creative Teaching Activities booklet, p. 94

Guided Reading and Review Unit 5 booklet, p. 46

living conditions for the western world also slowly improved—and then people began having fewer children. By the 1900s, population growth was no longer a problem in the West, but it did continue to afflict many nations elsewhere.

Ricardo on Wages Another influential British economist, David Ricardo, agreed with Malthus that the poor had too many children. In his "iron law of wages," Ricardo pointed out that when wages were high, families had more children. But more children meant a greater supply of labor, which led to lower wages and higher unemployment. Like Malthus, Ricardo did not hold out hope for the working class to escape poverty. Because of such gloomy predictions, economics became known as the "dismal science."

Neither Malthus nor Ricardo was a cruel man. Yet both opposed any government help for the poor. To these supporters of laissez-faire economics, the best cure for poverty was not government relief but the unrestricted "laws of the free market." They felt that individuals should be left to improve their lot through thrift, hard work, and limiting the size of their families.

The Utilitarians

Others adapted laissez-faire doctrines to justify some government intervention. By 1800, Jeremy Bentham was preaching utilitarianism, the idea that the goal of society should be "the greatest happiness for the greatest number" of its citizens. To Bentham, all laws or actions should be judged by their "utility." Did they provide more pleasure (happiness) than pain? He strongly supported individual freedom, which he believed guaranteed happiness. Still, he saw the need for government to become involved under certain circumstances.

Bentham's chief follower, John Stuart Mill, also argued that actions are right if they promote happiness and wrong if they cause pain. He reexamined the idea that unrestricted competition in the free market was always good. Often, he said, it favored the strong over the weak.

Although he believed strongly in individual freedom, Mill wanted the government to step in to improve the hard lives of the working class. "The only purpose for which power can be rightfully exercised over any member of a civilized community, against his will," Mill wrote, "is to prevent harm to others. His own good, either physical or moral, is not a sufficient warrant [cause]." While middle-class business and factory owners were entitled to increase their own happiness, therefore, government should prevent them from doing so in a manner that harmed workers.

Mill further called for giving the vote to workers and women. These groups could then use their political power to win reforms. Utilitarians also worked for reforms in many other areas affecting workers and the poor, from child labor to public health.

Most middle-class people rejected Mill's ideas. Only in the later 1800s were his views slowly accepted. Today's democratic governments, however, have absorbed many ideas from Mill and the other utilitarians.

Emergence of Socialism

While the champions of laissez-faire economics praised individual rights, other thinkers focused on the good of society in general. They condemned the evils of industrial capitalism, which they believed had created a gulf between rich and poor. To end poverty and injustice, they offered a radical solution—socialism. Under socialism, the people as a whole rather than private individuals would own and operate the means of production—the

Overcrowded Conditions
Thomas Malthus warned that population growth could exhaust the food supply, bringing misery to the poor. In *Bishopsgate Street*, artist Gustave Doré captures the squalor and overcrowded conditions of a London slum.

Theme: Political and Social Systems What did Malthus recommend as a solution to the problems of the early industrial age?

Connections to Today

Day Care

Robert Owen founded a model village, shown above, for his workers. Owen was not the last employer to provide for the children of his employees. Today, many businesses provide child-care services, either on site or at a separate day care center.

Companies find that child care is an important issue for many people seeking jobs. One center in Denmark has tried to go a step further. Staff at the day care center will also do laundry, shop for groceries, and cook take-out dinners. Additionally, the center has a video camera hooked up to the Internet so parents can log on and see how their child is doing.

Theme: Economics and Technology Why might some companies choose to provide day care for employees' children?

---

farms, factories, railways, and other large businesses that produced and distributed goods.

Socialism grew out of the Enlightenment faith in progress, its belief in the basic goodness of human nature, and its concern for social justice. Socialists wanted to develop a world in which society would operate for the benefit of all members, rather than just for the wealthy. In a socialist society, one reformer predicted:

> "There will be no war, no crime, no administration of justice, as it is called, no government. Besides there will be neither disease, anguish, melancholy, nor resentment. Every man will seek . . . the good of all."
> —William Godwin, "Political Justice"

The Utopians Early socialists tried to build self-sufficient communities in which all work was shared and all property was owned in common. When there was no difference between rich and poor, they felt, fighting between people would disappear. These early socialists were called Utopians, after Thomas More's ideal community. The name implied that they were impractical dreamers. However, the Utopian Robert Owen did set up a model community to put his ideas into practice.

Robert Owen A poor Welsh boy, Owen became a successful mill owner. Unlike most industrialists at the time, he refused to use child labor. He campaigned vigorously for laws that limited child labor and encouraged the organization of labor unions.

Owen insisted that the conditions in which people lived shaped their character. To prove his point, he set up his factory in New Lanark, Scotland, as a model village. He built homes for workers, opened a school for children, and generally treated employees well. He showed that an employer could offer decent living and working conditions and still run a profitable business. By the 1820s, many people were visiting New Lanark to study Owen's reforms.

The "Scientific Socialism" of Karl Marx

In the 1840s, Karl Marx, a German philosopher, condemned the ideas of the Utopians as unrealistic idealism. He put forward a new theory, "scientific socialism," which he claimed was based on a scientific study of history.

As a young man in Germany, Marx agitated for reform. Forced to leave his homeland because of his radical ideas, he lived first in Paris and then settled in London. He teamed up with another German socialist, Friedrich Engels, whose father owned a textile factory in England.

Marx and Engels wrote a pamphlet, *The Communist Manifesto*, which they published in 1848. "A spectre is haunting Europe," it began, "the spectre of communism." Communism is a form of socialism that sees class struggle between employers and employees as unavoidable.

Marxism In *The Communist Manifesto*, Marx theorized that economics was the driving force in history. The entire course of history, he argued, was "the history of class struggles" between the "haves" and the "have-nots." The "haves" have always owned the means of production and thus controlled society and all its wealth. In industrialized Europe, Marx said, the "haves" were the bourgeoisie. The "have-nots" were the proletariat, or working class.

According to Marx, the modern class struggle pitted the bourgeoisie against the proletariat. In the end, he predicted, the proletariat would be triumphant. It would then take control of the means of production and set up a classless, communist society. Such a society would mark the end of the struggles people had endured throughout history, because wealth and power would be equally shared.

Marx despised capitalism. He believed it created prosperity for only a few and poverty for many. He called for an international struggle to bring about its downfall. "Working men of all countries," he urged, "unite!"

Looking Ahead

At first, Marxism gained popularity with many people around the world. Leaders of a number of reform movements adopted the idea that power should be held by workers rather than by business owners. Marx's ideas would never be practiced exactly as he imagined them, however.

Failures As time passed, the failures of Marxist governments would illustrate the flaws in his arguments. Marx claimed that his ideas were based on scientific laws. However, many of the assumptions on which he based his theories were wrong. He predicted that the misery of the proletariat would touch off a world revolution. Instead, by 1900, the efforts of reformers and governments led to improved conditions for the working class. As a result, Marxism lost some of its appeal in the industrially developed countries of Europe and North America.

Marx also predicted that workers would unite across national borders to wage class warfare. Instead, nationalism won out over working-class loyalty. In general, people felt stronger ties to their own countries than to the international communist movement.

Revolutions These failures did not doom the movement instantly. In the late 1800s, Russian socialists embraced Marxism, and the Russian Revolution of 1917 set up a communist-inspired government. For much of the 1900s, revolutionaries around the world would adapt Marxist ideas to their own needs. Independence leaders in Asia, Latin America, and Africa would turn to Marxism. By the 1990s, however, nearly every nation would incorporate elements of free-market capitalism. To many people, Adam Smith's ideas seemed to be of more lasting value than those of Karl Marx.

SECTION 4 Assessment

Recall
1. **Identify:** (a) Thomas Malthus, (b) iron law of wages, (c) John Stuart Mill, (d) Utopians, (e) Karl Marx.
2. **Define:** (a) utilitarianism, (b) socialism, (c) means of production, (d) communism, (e) proletariat.

Comprehension
3. Describe the views of laissez-faire economists (a) Adam Smith, (b) Thomas Malthus, and (c) David Ricardo.
4. Contrast the approaches of utilitarians and socialists to solving economic problems.

5. (a) Describe Karl Marx's view of history. (b) How have events challenged that view?

Critical Thinking and Writing
6. **Linking Past and Present** Choose one economic or political theory discussed in this section. Does that theory seem to apply to the American economy today? Explain.
7. **Applying Information** How might the rise of Methodism and workplace reforms alter Marxist predictions of world revolution?

Creating a Chapter Summary

As a reteaching opportunity, pair a more able student with a less student to complete this chapter summary.

Answers: **Tull** seed drill **Newcomen** steam engine **Arkwright** waterframe **Stephenson** steam-powered locomotive **Smith** laissez-faire economics **Ricardo** "iron law of wages" **Bentham** utilitarianism **Owen** Utopian communities **Marx** communism, Marxism

Building Vocabulary

1–9. **(a) Continuity and Change** urbanization, labor union **Political and Social Systems** utilitarianism, means of production, proletariat **Economics and Technology** anesthetic, smelt, capital, factory **(b)** Sentences should reflect an understanding of how the word relates to the theme.

Recalling Key Facts

10. Many farm workers lost their jobs; small farmers were forced off their land; villages shrank; many people moved to cities in search of work.
11. coal-powered steam engine
12. Answers should include three of the following: resources such as coal and iron, plenty of workers, new technology, capital, stable government, religious attitudes
13. Farm jobs were declining, and the supply of jobs in the cities was rising.
14. government efforts to improve workers' lives, giving the vote to workers and women, child labor and public health reforms

Critical Thinking and Writing

15. Britain had plentiful coal and iron, rapidly moving streams that powered the waterframe, coastal ports, and rivers that could be linked by canals to inland towns.
16. **(a)** worker protests **(b)** British soldiers **(c)** workers holding a rally in Manchester in 1819 **(d)** Possible answer: The cartoonist wanted to gain public attention and sympathy for the workers.
17. **(a)** Better food supplies, sanitary conditions, and medical care caused a population explosion. **(b)** City populations grew. Within the city a gulf existed that divided the wealthy and middle class from the working poor. **(c)** Factory workers endured unvarying

---

CHAPTER **20 Review and Assessment**

Creating a Chapter Summary

Copy this chart on a sheet of paper. Complete the chart by naming the invention or idea developed by each person on the left. One row has been filled in to help you get started.

INVENTORS AND THINKERS	INVENTIONS AND IDEAS
Jethro Tull	
Thomas Newcomen	
Richard Arkwright	
George Stephenson	
John Wesley	Methodism
Adam Smith	
David Ricardo	
Jeremy Bentham	
Robert Owen	
Karl Marx	

For additional review and enrichment activities, see the interactive version of *World History* available on the Web and on CD-ROM.

Web Site Self-Test
For practice test questions for Chapter 20, see
www.phschool.com.

Building Vocabulary

(a) Classify each of the chapter vocabulary words listed below under *one* of the following themes: Continuity and Change; Political and Social Systems; Economics and Technology. **(b)** Choose one word in each category and write a sentence explaining how that word relates to the theme.

1. anesthetic
2. smelt
3. capital
4. factory
5. urbanization
6. labor union
7. utilitarianism
8. means of production
9. proletariat

Recalling Key Facts

10. How did the enclosure movement affect people?
11. What new source of energy helped trigger the Industrial Revolution?
12. List three reasons why the Industrial Revolution began in Britain.
13. Why did large numbers of people migrate to cities?
14. List the government reforms sought by John Stuart Mill.

Critical Thinking and Writing

15. **Connecting to Geography** Explain the link between Britain's natural resources and its rise as an industrial nation.
16. **Analyzing Political Cartoons** Study the political cartoon in Section 3. **(a)** What is the subject of the cartoon? **(b)** Who are the men on horseback? **(c)** Who are the people under attack? **(d)** What do you think was the artist's purpose in creating the cartoon?
17. **Analyzing Information** Describe how the Industrial Revolution affected each of the following: **(a)** size of population, **(b)** cities, **(c)** working and living conditions, **(d)** women and children.
18. **Linking Past and Present (a)** How did thinkers in the 1800s disagree about the role of government in helping the poor? **(b)** Give three examples to show that this debate continues today.
19. **Defending a Position** Do you think that the negative social consequences of the Industrial Revolution could have been avoided? Use material from this chapter to defend your position.

---

routines, long hours, and unsafe conditions. Workers lived in overcrowded and filthy city slums. **(d)** Women and children made up a large part of the new work force.

18. **(a)** Some thinkers, such as Adam Smith and Thomas Malthus, believed that government had no place helping the poor, while others, such as the socialists and Karl Marx, believed that it was the government's duty to aid the poor. **(b)** Students might cite such issues as social security, federal budget reductions, the welfare-to-work program, affirmative action laws, subsidized housing, and school lunch programs.

19. Students may argue that greater government regulation at an earlier stage could have reduced human suffering. Other students may argue that short-term costs were inevitable.

In the excerpt below, a British newspaper correspondent details the daily life of cotton-mill workers in the northern industrial town of Manchester. Read the excerpt, then answer the questions that follow.

"The streets in the neighborhood of the mills are thronged with men and women and children flocking to their labour. . . . The factory bell rings from five minutes before six until the hour strikes. Then—to the moment—the engine starts and the day's work begins. Those who are [late], be it but a moment, are fined twopence, and in many mills, after the expiration of a very short time of grace, the doors are locked, and the laggard, besides the fine, loses his morning work.

. . . I fear that I cannot say much for the cleanliness of the workpeople. They have an essentially greasy look, which makes me sometimes think that water would run off their skins, as it does off a duck's back. In this respect the women are just as bad as the men. . . . The spinners and piecers . . . fling shoes and stockings aside, but I fear it is very seldom that their feet see the interior of a tub, with plenty of hot water and soap."

—from "A Working Day" in *Labour and the Poor in England and Wales, 1849–1851*

20. Who made up the work force at the mill?

21. How were workers punished for being late?

22. How did the correspondent view the workers' personal hygiene habits?

23. Why might the spinners and piecers work barefoot?

24. Based on what you have read, would the correspondent view himself as a member of the proletariat? Explain your answer.

When you read a primary source, try to determine whether the writer identifies with the people or events being described. Is the writer's viewpoint sympathetic or unsympathetic?

BRITISH OUTPUT OF COAL, 1820–1850

Coal Output (in thousands of metric tons) — Year

Source: B. R. Mitchell, *European Historical Statistics 1750–1970*

BRITISH EXPORTS OF COAL, 1820–1850

Coal Export (in thousands of metric tons) — Year

Source: B. R. Mitchell, *European Historical Statistics 1750–1970*

Use the graphs to answer the following questions:

25. By what year had the coal output of 1820 doubled?

26. **(a)** By about how many metric tons did coal output increase between 1820 and 1840? **(b)** Between 1840 and 1850?

27. Write a sentence that summarizes the information about coal output and exports presented in these graphs.

Use the Internet to research primary or secondary sources on the daily life of factory workers during the Industrial Revolution. Then, write a paper explaining why you do or do not think that the benefits of living in an industrialized nation today outweigh some of the social consequences of the Industrial Revolution.

20. men, women, and children

21. They were fined, locked out, or both.

22. The writer noted that the hygiene habits did not stress cleanliness.

23. Possible answer: It may have been more comfortable for the workers to be barefoot.

24. Possible answer: No, the writer seems to distance himself from the workers, or proletariat, criticizing their lack of hygiene.

25. 1840

26. **(a)** about 17,000 **(b)** about 16,000

27. Possible answer: Coal output and export both rose dramatically, although the increase in exports was more extreme than that in production.

Remind students that the third-person point of view, which uses the pronouns *he* or *she*, puts more distance between writer and reader than the first-person point of view, which uses the pronouns *I* or *we*. The Skills Handbook in the front of the book has a lesson that will help students with this feature.

Remind students to continue working on their Unit Theme Activity. See rubrics for the activity on the unit opener page in the Teacher's Edition.

Direct students to **www.phschool.com** for links to sites that will help them get started on this assignment. Share rubrics with students.

Attempted Paper fails to support writer's opinion.

Minimal Paper supports writer's opinion but lacks specific examples and is poorly written.

Adequate Paper supports writer's opinion, has specific examples, and is well written.

Exemplary Paper supports writer's opinion, uses convincing examples, and is very well written.

Chapter 21 Planning Guide

Resource Manager

	CORE INSTRUCTION	READING/SKILLS
Chapter Level Resources	📘 Teaching Resources 📖 Pacing Charts, Ch. 21 📖 Teaching With Themes, p. 24 📺 Color Transparencies, p. F–43 💿 Resource Pro® Ch. 21 💻 www.phschool.com • eTeach	💿 Book on CD, Ch. 21 💿 Interactive Student Tutorial CD-ROM, Ch. 21 💿 Social Studies Skills Tutor CD-ROM 📺 Skills Transparencies
1 An Age of Ideologies 1. Identify the goals of conservatives. 2. Describe how liberalism and nationalism challenged the old order. 3. Outline why Europe was plagued by revolts after 1815.	📘 Teaching Resources 📖 Creative Teaching Activities, p. 95 💿 Prentice Hall Presentation Pro, Ch. 21, Section 1 📺 Section Reading Support Transparencies	📘 Teaching Resources 📂 Unit 5 booklet • Guided Reading and Review, p. 58 📖 Guide to the Essentials 📼 Guided Reading Audiotapes, Ch. 21, Section 1

2 Revolutions of 1830 and 1848
1. Explain why revolutions occurred in France in 1830 and 1848.
2. Discuss how revolution spread in 1830.
3. Summarize the results of the 1848 revolutions.
	📘 Teaching Resources
	📂 Unit 5 booklet
	  • Primary Source Activity, p. 65
	📖 Creative Teaching Activities, p. 96
	💿 Prentice Hall Presentation Pro, Ch. 21, Section 2
	📺 Section Reading Support Transparencies
		📘 Teaching Resources
		📂 Unit 5 booklet
		  • Guided Reading and Review, p. 60
		📖 Guide to the Essentials
		📼 Guided Reading Audiotapes, Ch. 21, Section 2

3 Latin American Wars of Independence
1. Analyze the causes of discontent in Latin America.
2. Explain how Haitians, Mexicans, and people in Central America won independence.
3. Describe how the nations of South America won independence.
	📘 Teaching Resources
	📂 Unit 5 booklet
	  • Biography Activity, p. 64
	  • Viewpoint Activity, p. 66
	📖 Creative Teaching Activities, p. 97
	💿 Prentice Hall Presentation Pro, Ch. 21, Section 3
	📺 Section Reading Support Transparencies
		📘 Teaching Resources
		📂 Unit 5 booklet
		  • Guided Reading and Review, p. 62
		  • Skill Application Activity, p. 67
		📖 Guide to the Essentials
		📼 Guided Reading Audiotapes, Ch. 21, Section 3

ENRICHMENT/PRE-AP

📖 Teaching Resources
📖 Teaching With Themes
- Global View Activity, p. 45

💻 www.phschool.com
- Why Study History?

💻 www.phschool.com
- Internet Activities, Section 1
- Global View Essay

📖 Teaching Resources
📖 Chapter Extension Activities, p. 52
📼 History Through Literature, pp. 45–46
💻 www.phschool.com
- Internet Activities, Art and Revolution
- Internet Activities, Section 2

📖 Teaching Resources
📖 Chapter Extension Activities, p. 53
📼 Visions, Voices, Views, Daily Life CloseUp, tape 5
💻 www.phschool.com
- Virtual Field Trip

ASSESSMENT

PRENTICE HALL
ASSESSMENT SYSTEM

Core Assessment
- 📖 ExamView Test Bank booklet, Ch. 21
- 💿 ExamView Test Bank CD-ROM, Ch. 21

Standardized Test Preparation

Diagnose and Prescribe
- 📖 Diagnostic Tests for High School Social Studies Skills

Review and Reteach
- 📖 Review Book for World History

Practice and Assess
- 📖 Document-Based Assessment, pp. 23–27
- 📖 Test-Taking Strategies With Transparencies
- 📖 Alternative Assessment booklet
- 📖 Test Prep Book for World History

📖 Teaching Resources
📁 Unit 5 booklet
- Geography Quiz, p. 68
- Section Quizzes, pp. 59, 61, 63
- Chapter Tests A, B, and C, pp. 69–73

💻 www.phschool.com
- Self-Test

CUSTOMIZE FOR INDIVIDUAL NEEDS

Gifted and Talented
- **Teacher's Edition,** Activities: Customize for Heterogeneous Groups, p. 531

Less Proficient Readers
- **Guide to the Essentials,** Ch. 21
- **Guided Reading Audiotapes, English,** Ch. 21
- **Book on CD,** Ch. 21
- **Teacher's Edition,** Activities: Reading Strategy, p. 519

Less Proficient Writers
- **Teacher's Edition,** Activities: Customize for Kinesthetic Learners, p. 528

Students Acquiring English/ESL
- **Guide to the Essentials, English/Spanish,** Ch. 21
- **Guided Reading Audiotapes, English/Spanish,** Ch. 21
- **Book on CD,** Ch. 21
- **Teacher's Edition,** Activities marked with an *

i TEXT

Don't miss the exclusive interactive version of *World History: Connections to Today* on the Internet and CD-ROM.

CHAPTER 21

Revolutions in Europe and Latin America
1790–1848

Chapter Preview

1 An Age of Ideologies
2 Revolutions of 1830 and 1848
3 Latin American Wars of Independence

TIME LINE ACTIVITY

1810
Father Miguel Hidalgo urges Mexicans to fight for independence from Spain.

1804
Haiti declares independence from France.

1819
Simón Bolívar, later known as "The Liberator," seizes Bogota from the Spanish.

CHAPTER EVENTS

GLOBAL EVENTS

1800

1810

1820

1803 United States buys Louisiana from France.

1820 Several thousand British colonists settle in South Africa

Don't Miss!

Humanities Link
Art and Revolution
(Section 2)

Analyzing Primary Sources
Toussaint L'Ouverture on Slavery (Section 3)

Resource Directory

Teaching Resources
Teaching With Themes Chapter Theme Activities, p. 24
Pacing Chart With Block Scheduling Guide Ch. 21
Global View Activity *How Did the New Ideas of the Enlightenment Lead to a Wave of Democratic Revolutions?*
Teaching With Themes booklet, p. 45

Technology
World History Color Transparencies Ch. 21
Graphic Organizer, p. F–43

Revolutions in Europe, 1815–1829

Despite the order imposed by the Congress of Vienna, several revolutions erupted in Europe between 1815 and 1829. The spread of revolutionary ideals would ignite new uprisings in 1830 and 1848.

Map labels: DENMARK, NETHERLANDS, HANOVER, PRUSSIA, RUSSIA, BAVARIA, SAXONY, AUSTRIAN EMPIRE, FRANCE, SWITZ., ALPS, LOMBARDY-VENETIA, PAPAL STATES, TUSCANY, PIEDMONT-SARDINIA, SERBIA, OTTOMAN EMPIRE, GREECE, KINGDOM OF THE TWO SICILIES, PORTUGAL, SPAIN, PYRENEES MTS., ATLANTIC OCEAN, Mediterranean Sea, Adriatic Sea, Black Sea, Seine R., Loire R., Rhône R., Rhine R., Elbe R., Oder R., Vistula R., Danube R., Tiber R.

Azimuthal Equal Area Projection

0   150   300 Miles
0   150   300 Kilometers

Areas where revolutions occurred

Repression of revolutions
→ French forces
→ Austrian forces
→ Ottoman forces

1830
French revolutionaries battle the king's troops in the streets of Paris.

1848
Revolutions break out across much of Europe.

1830   1840   1850

1839 China and Britain clash in the Opium War.

1850 Taiping Rebellion begins in China.

Chapter 21 **517**

Revolutions in Europe, 1815–1829

Activating Prior Knowledge
Did the French Revolution achieve its goals? *(No, the monarchy was restored, and social class differences reinstated.)* What impact might that have? *(leave simmering discontent)*

Previewing
How do you think revolution spread to Latin America? *(Revolutionary ideas were picked up by Latin American colonists from European countries.)*

Background
About the Pictures

1. Unlike most Mexican clergymen, Father Miguel Hidalgo sympathized with Native Americans, teaching them how to grow olives, mulberries, and grapevines and to make pottery and leather. These actions, illegal at the time, enraged the Spanish viceroy, who had the crops destroyed.

2. Simón Bolívar's most successful campaign was possibly his most daring. With a force of only 800, Bolívar invaded Venezuela in 1813, facing up to 15,000 Spanish troops. Amazingly, he succeeded, and his forces briefly occupied Caracas.

3. *Fighting at the Hotel de Ville, 28th July, 1830* by Jean Victor Schnetz uses symbolism to depict the passion and glory—not the violence—of the 1830 Paris revolution. The youth at the center of the painting symbolizes a bright and hopeful future, and the body at the forefront, which shows no blood, symbolizes the sacrifices that led to victory. This painting hangs at the Musée du Petit Palais in Paris.

eTeach

Be sure to check out this month's online discussion with a World History Master Teacher.

Go to **www.phschool.com**.

Independent Assignments

Have students read one section as they prepare for class. After class, have them complete the assignment. Some students may benefit from using the Guided Reading and Review worksheets.

Section 1 Have students use the Section 1 Guided Reading and Review worksheet in the Unit 5 booklet, p. 58, to gain a better understanding of the issues raised in this section.

Section 2 Have students use the worksheet *A Movement for Democracy* in the Unit 5 booklet, p. 65, to learn about the student movement in Bonn, Germany, in 1848.

Section 3 Have students use the worksheet *Miguel Hidalgo y Costilla* in the Unit 5 booklet, p. 64, to learn about the life of this famous Mexican revolutionary.

Bell Ringer

Bell Ringer Write the words *conservative* and *liberal* on the chalkboard. Ask students to try to define the words by examining their roots. (*Conservative* is from the Latin *com,* an intensifier, and *servare,* to preserve. *Liberal* comes from the Latin *liberalis,* which means free.) Have students list three goals that they think conservative politicians might have had and three goals that liberal politicians might have had in this period.

LESSON PLAN

1. Focus After 1815, conservatives called for a return to the political and social structure that existed before 1789. Liberals embraced the ideas of the Enlightenment and wanted to limit the power of monarchs. Nationalists, by urging national independence, threatened the powerful empires of Europe. Conflicts emerged as conservative leaders opposed liberal and nationalist demands.

2. Instruct Divide the class into three groups—one for conservatism, another for liberalism, and a third for nationalism. Assign each group to outline its political movement by listing its attitudes, goals, policies, and actions. When students have finished this part of the assignment, regroup them so that each new group has at least one "expert" on each of the three political movements. Have students take turns teaching the group about their area of expertise.

3. Assess Call on students to describe any characteristic of liberalism, conservatism, or nationalism. Then, ask for volunteers to name the political philosophy that included that characteristic. You may wish to use this activity as the basis for a game or a quiz.

4. Reteach If students' Assess activity does not reflect adequate understanding of the lesson, you might assign the *Guide to the Essentials* or the *Interactive Student Tutorial CD-ROM* for this section.

Reading Focus

- What were the goals of conservatives?
- How did liberalism and nationalism challenge the old order?
- Why was Europe plagued by revolts after 1815?

Vocabulary

ideology

universal manhood suffrage

autonomy

Taking Notes

Copy this chart. As you read this section, list the ideas of conservatism, liberalism, and nationalism.

CONSERVATISM	LIBERALISM	NATIONALISM

Main Idea After 1815, the clash of people with opposing ideologies plunged Europe into an era of turmoil that lasted more than 30 years.

The Conservative Order Conservatives were determined to preserve the old order. At the heart of that order was the monarchy, symbolized in the Austrian empire by the Hapsburg coat of arms shown here.

Theme: Political and Social Systems What other institutions besides the monarchy were part of the old order?

Setting the Scene A "revolutionary seed" had been planted in Europe, warned Prince Clemens von Metternich. The ideas spread by the French Revolution and Napoleon Bonaparte, he believed, not only threatened Europe's monarchs but also undermined its basic social values:

"Passions are let loose . . . to overthrow everything that society respects as the basis of its existence: religion, public morality, laws, customs, rights, and duties, all are attacked, confounded, overthrown, or called in question."
—*Memoirs of Prince Metternich*

At the Congress of Vienna, the powers of Europe tried to uproot that "revolutionary seed." Other voices, however, kept challenging the order imposed in 1815. The clash of people with opposing ideologies, or systems of thought and belief, plunged Europe into more than 30 years of turmoil.

Conservatives and the Old Order

The Congress of Vienna was a victory for the conservative forces, which included monarchs and their officials, noble landowners, and church leaders. Conservatives supported the political and social order that had existed before the French Revolution. Conservative ideas also appealed to peasants, who wanted to preserve traditional ways.

Conservatives of the early 1800s wanted to turn the clock back to the way things had been before 1789. After all, they had benefited under the old order. They wanted to restore royal families to the thrones they had lost when Napoleon swept across Europe. They supported a social hierarchy in which lower classes were expected to respect and obey their social superiors. Conservatives also backed an established church—Catholic in Austria and southern Europe, Protestant in northern Europe, and Orthodox in eastern Europe.

Conservatives believed that talk about natural rights and constitutional government could lead only to chaos, as it had in France in 1789. If change had to come, they argued, it must come slowly. Conservatives felt that they benefited all people by defending peace and stability. Conservative leaders like Metternich sought to suppress revolutionary ideas. Metternich urged monarchs to oppose freedom of the press, crush protests in their own countries, and send troops to douse the flames of rebellion in neighboring lands.

Caption Answer

Possible answers: an established church, the nobility, a rigid class system

Resource Directory

Teaching Resources
Creative Teaching Activities Creative Teaching Activities booklet, p. 95
Guided Reading and Review Unit 5 booklet, p. 58

Block Scheduling Support

Explain to students that some areas where revolutionary tensions existed in the 1800s continue to be volatile today. One such example can be found in the Balkans. Ethnic identity and nationalism have continued to contribute to unrest in Serbia over the years. Have students research and create a time line of major events in Serbian history from 1800 to the present.

The Liberal and Nationalist Challenge

Challenging the conservatives at every turn were liberals and nationalists who were inspired by the Enlightenment and the French Revolution. Liberalism and nationalism ignited a number of revolts against established rule.

Liberal Goals Because liberals spoke mostly for the bourgeoisie, or middle class, their ideas are sometimes called "bourgeois liberalism." Liberals included business owners, bankers, and lawyers, as well as politicians, newspaper editors, writers, and others who helped to shape public opinion.

Liberals wanted governments to be based on written constitutions and separation of powers. Liberals spoke out against divine-right monarchy, the old aristocracy, and established churches. They defended the natural rights of individuals to liberty, equality, and property. They called for rulers elected by the people and responsible to them. Thus, most liberals favored a republican form of government over a monarchy, or at least wanted the monarch to be limited by a constitution.

The liberals of the early 1800s saw the role of government as limited to protecting basic rights such as freedom of thought, speech, and religion. They believed that only male property owners or others with a financial stake in society should have the right to vote. Only later in the century did liberals support the principle of universal manhood suffrage, giving all adult men the right to vote.

Liberals strongly supported the laissez-faire economics of Adam Smith and David Ricardo. They saw the free market as an opportunity for capitalist entrepreneurs to succeed. As capitalists and often employers, liberals had different goals from those of workers laboring in factories, mines, and other enterprises of the early Industrial Revolution.

Nationalist Goals For centuries, European rulers had gained or lost lands through wars, marriages, and treaties. They exchanged territories and the people in them like pieces in a game. As a result, by 1815 Europe had several empires that included many nationalities. The Austrian, Russian, and Ottoman empires, for example, each included diverse peoples.

In the 1800s, national groups who shared a common heritage set out to win their own states. Within the diverse Austrian empire, for example, various nationalist leaders tried to unite and win independence for each particular group. Nationalism gave people with a common heritage a sense of identity and the goal of creating their own homeland. At the same time, however, nationalism often bred intolerance and led to persecution of other ethnic or national groups.

Revolts Against the Old Order

Spurred by the ideas of liberalism and nationalism, revolutionaries fought against the old order. During the early 1800s, rebellions erupted in the Balkan Peninsula and elsewhere along the southern fringe of Europe. The Balkans, in southeastern Europe, were inhabited by people of various religions and ethnic groups. These peoples had lived under Ottoman rule for more than 300 years.

The Serb Revolt
In 1804, the Serb leader Karageorge, shown below, led a revolt against Ottoman rule. Ottoman troops crushed this rebellion by 1813, but renewed resistance would eventually lead to Serbian independence.

Theme: Political and Social Systems Why did the Ottoman empire face frequent rebellions in the 1800s?

SECTION 1 Assessment

Recall
1. **(a)** conservatives, p. 518 **(b)** liberals, p. 519 **(c)** nationalists, p. 519 **(d)** Karageorge, p. 520 **(e)** Milos Obrenovic, p. 520
2. **(a)** ideology, p. 518 **(b)** universal manhood suffrage, p. 519 **(c)** autonomy, p. 520

Comprehension
3. returning to the pre-French Revolution way of life; restoring monarchies, traditional social hierarchies, and established churches; imposing peace and stability by suppressing revolutionaries 4. **(a)** Liberals favored republican governments based on written constitutions, separation of powers, and protection of natural rights, while conservatives supported the power of monarchs and opposed natural rights and written constitutions. **(b)** Nationalists wanted each national group to be unified in its own independent state. 5. **(a)** They wanted to be free from Ottoman domination and form their own state. **(b)** Rebels in those countries wanted to set up constitutional governments.

Critical Thinking and Writing
6. They urged people to free themselves of foreign rule and monarchical power.
7. Possible answer: Liberals were generally middle-class capitalists who probably felt that only property owners or others with a financial stake in society would have the knowledge and background to vote wisely.

Activity Rubrics

Share rubrics with students before they write their explanations.

Attempted The explanation is poorly written, contains many mechanical errors, and reveals little understanding of Metternich's ideas.

Minimal The explanation reveals some understanding of Metternich's ideas but is poorly written and has some mechanical errors.

Adequate The explanation reveals an understanding of Metternich's ideas, is well written, and contains few mechanical errors.

Exemplary The explanation reveals excellent understanding of Metternich's ideas, is very well written and organized, and contains no mechanical errors.

Primary Source

ANSWER Possible answer: He, like many other Europeans, had a deep admiration for ancient Greek civilization—for its history, its arts, and its culture.

Primary Source

Byron, Glory, and Greece
The English poet Lord Byron went to Greece to aid the fight for independence. He wrote these lines:

"The sword, the banner, and the field,
  Glory and Greece, around me see!
The Spartan, borne upon his shield,
  Was not more free.

Awake! (not Greece—she is awake!)
  Awake, my spirit! Think through whom
Thy lifeblood tracks its parent lake,
  And then strike home! . . ."

—George Gordon, Lord Byron, "On This Day I Complete My Thirty-Sixth Year"

Skills Assessment

Primary Source Why did Lord Byron admire Greece?

Independence for Serbia The first Balkan people to revolt were the Serbs. From 1804 to 1813, the Serb leader Karageorge led a guerrilla war against the Ottomans. The bitter struggle was unsuccessful, but it fostered a sense of Serbian identity. A revival of Serbian literature and culture added to the sense of nationhood.

In 1815, Milos Obrenovic led the Serbs in a second, more successful rebellion. One reason for the success was that Obrenovic turned to Russia for assistance. Like the Serbs, the Russian people were Slavic in language and Christian Orthodox in religion. By 1830, Russian support helped the Serbs win autonomy, or self-rule, within the Ottoman empire. The Ottoman sultan later agreed to formal independence. In the future, Russia would continue to defend Serbian interests and affect events in the Balkans.

Independence for Greece In 1821, the Greeks, too, revolted, seeking to end centuries of Ottoman rule. At first, the Greeks were badly divided. But years of suffering in long, bloody wars of independence helped shape a national identity. Leaders of the rebellion justified their struggle as "a national war, a holy war, a war the object of which is to reconquer the rights of individual liberty." They sought help from Western Europeans, who admired ancient Greek civilization.

The Greeks won sympathy in the West. In the late 1820s, Britain, France, and even conservative Russia forced the Ottomans to grant independence to some Greek provinces. By 1830, Greece was independent. The European powers, however, pressured the Greeks to accept a German king, a move meant to show that they did not support revolution. Still, liberals were enthusiastic, and nationalists everywhere saw reasons to hope for a country of their own.

Other Challenges Several other challenges to the Vienna peace settlement erupted in the 1820s. Revolts occurred along the southern fringe of Europe. In Spain, Portugal, and various states in the Italian peninsula, rebels struggled to gain constitutional governments.

Metternich urged conservative rulers to act decisively and crush the dangerous uprisings. In response, a French army marched over the Pyrenees to suppress a revolt in Spain. Austrian forces crossed the Alps to smash rebellious outbreaks in Italy.

Troops dampened the fires of liberalism and nationalism, but could not smother them. In the next decades, sparks would flare anew. Added to liberal and nationalist demands were the goals of the new industrial working class. By the mid-1800s, social reformers and agitators were urging workers to support socialism or other ways of reorganizing property ownership.

SECTION 1 Assessment

Recall
1. **Identify:** **(a)** conservatives, **(b)** liberals, **(c)** nationalists, **(d)** Karageorge, **(e)** Milos Obrenovic.
2. **Define:** **(a)** ideology, **(b)** universal manhood suffrage, **(c)** autonomy.

Comprehension
3. What were the goals of conservative leaders?
4. **(a)** How did the political goals of liberals differ from those of conservatives? **(b)** How did nationalists threaten the system set up by Metternich?
5. **(a)** Why did the Serbs and Greeks revolt? **(b)** Why were there uprisings in Spain, Portugal, and the Italian states?

Critical Thinking and Writing
6. **Applying Information** How did ideologies like liberalism and nationalism contribute to unrest?
7. **Analyzing Information** Why do you think liberals of the early 1800s supported limited voting rights?

Activity
Take It to the NET

On the Internet, find a site that contains some of the writings of Metternich. Print an excerpt that describes one of the key ideas of conservatism. Explain the main idea of the excerpt and explain why Metternich supported this idea.

Resource Directory

Teaching Resources

Section Quiz Unit 5 booklet, p. 59
Creative Teaching Activities Creative Teaching Activities booklet, p. 96
Guided Reading and Review Unit 5 booklet, p. 60

Technology

Interactive Student Tutorial CD-ROM Ch. 21
Computer Test Bank Ch. 21

Reading Focus

- Why did revolutions occur in France in 1830 and 1848?
- How did revolution spread in 1830?
- What were the results of the 1848 revolutions?

Vocabulary

ultraroyalist
recession

Taking Notes

Copy this graphic organizer. As you read, fill in information about conditions before and after the revolutions of 1848.

REVOLUTIONS OF 1848	
Before	**After**
• France is a monarchy	• France is a republic
•	•

Main Idea Revolutions broke out across Europe in 1830 and 1848, but most failed to achieve their goals.

Setting the Scene The quick suppression of liberal and nationalist uprisings in the 1820s did not end Europe's age of revolutions. "We are sleeping on a volcano," warned Alexis de Tocqueville, a liberal French leader who saw widespread discontent. "Do you not see that the Earth trembles anew? A wind of revolution blows, the storm is on the horizon."

In 1830 and 1848, Europeans saw street protests explode into full-scale revolts. As in 1789, the upheavals began in Paris and radiated out across the continent.

The French Revolution of 1830

When the Congress of Vienna restored Louis XVIII to the French throne, he wisely issued a constitution, the Charter of French Liberties. It created a two-house legislature and allowed limited freedom of the press. Still, although Louis was careful to avoid absolutism, the king retained much power.

Sources of Unrest Louis's efforts at compromise satisfied few people. Ultraroyalists, the king's supporters on the far right, despised constitutional government and wanted to restore the old regime. The "ultras" included many high clergy and émigré nobles who had returned to France in the years after the revolution.

The ultras faced bitter opposition from other factions. Liberals wanted to extend suffrage and win a share of power for middle-class citizens like themselves. On the left, radicals yearned for a republic like that of the 1790s. And in working-class slums, men and women wanted what they had wanted in 1789—a decent day's pay and bread they could afford.

The July Revolution When Louis XVIII died in 1824, his younger brother, Charles X, inherited the throne. Charles, a strong believer in absolutism, rejected the very idea of the charter. In July 1830, he suspended the legislature, limited the right to vote, and restricted the press.

Liberals and radicals responded forcefully to the king's challenge. In Paris, angry citizens threw up barricades across the narrow streets. From behind them, they fired on the soldiers and pelted them with stones and roof tiles. Within days, rebels controlled Paris. The revolutionary tricolor flew from the towers of Notre Dame cathedral. A frightened Charles X abdicated and fled to England.

With the king gone, radicals wanted to set up a republic. Moderate liberals, however, insisted on a constitutional monarchy. The Chamber of

 Bell Ringer Draw students' attention to the map "Revolutions in Europe, 1830 and 1848" in this section. Ask them to explain how the map illustrates Alexis de Tocqueville's comment, "We are sleeping on a volcano."

LESSON PLAN

1. Focus Charles X's attempt to restore absolutism in France resulted in the July revolution of 1830. An economic slump, coupled with discontent over social and political issues, sparked revolution again in 1848. These French uprisings inspired revolts in other parts of Europe. Many of the revolutions failed because they were put down by military force and because they did not have mass support.

2. Instruct Work with the class to construct a chart that profiles the revolutions that occurred in Europe between 1800 and 1848. Draw a chart with six columns on the chalkboard. Label the columns with the following heads: Country, Date, Goals, Opponent, Outcome, Reasons for Success or Failure. Instruct students to use information from Sections 1 and 2 of this chapter to fill in the chart. Have students take turns coming up to the board and filling in the chart. If you prefer, have students complete the charts in cooperative learning groups.

3. Assess Ask students to use the charts that they have developed to write three generalizations about this period in Europe.

4. Reteach If students' **Assess** activity does not reflect adequate understanding of the lesson, you might assign the *Guide to the Essentials* or the *Interactive Student Tutorial CD-ROM* for this section.

☐ Block Scheduling Support

As a reinforcement activity, assign students to review one of the revolutions of 1848 in two different editorials. Have them write one editorial from the viewpoint of a liberal and the other from the viewpoint of a conservative. Editorials should cite specific examples that each side might use to argue for or against the revolution. Explain to students that their editorials will be evaluated based upon the strength of their arguments. Have volunteers read their editorials aloud and ask the class to identify the viewpoint that each editorial represents.

Activity
Connections to Literature

Analyzing Literature In *Les Misérables*, Victor Hugo provides this vivid description of one of the many barricades built by the revolutionaries of 1848 in Paris:

"The barricade Saint Antoine was monstrous; it was three stories high and seven hundred feet long. . . . It was the collaboration of the pavement, the pebble, the timber, the iron bar, the chip, the broken square, the stripped chair, the cabbage stump, the scrap, the rag. . . . Its crest was thorny with muskets, with swords, with clubs, with axes, with pikes, and with bayonets; a huge red flag fluttered in the wind; there were heard cries of command, songs of attack, the roll of the drum, the sobs of women, and the dark wild laughter of the starving. . . . The spirit of revolution covered . . . that summit whereon growled this voice of the people which is like the voice of God; a strange majesty emanated from that titanic hodful of refuse. It was a garbage heap and it was Sinai."

Distribute copies of the passage to students or read it aloud. Before reading the passage, explain to students that *titanic,* which means "huge," comes from *Titan.* The Titans were Greek gods, who were gigantic in size. Also, a *hod* is a trough used for carrying bricks or mortar. Finally, *Sinai* is a reference to the mountain on which Moses received the Ten Commandments. Then use the following questions as the basis of a class discussion: (1) How does Hugo describe the structure and size of the barricade? (2) What weapons did the revolutionaries use? (3) Describe the various emotions of the revolutionaries. (4) Why do you think Hugo compares the people's voices to the voice of God? (5) Basing your answer on this excerpt, how would you describe Hugo's political views?

The "Citizen King" The French called Louis Philippe the "citizen king" because he owed his throne to the people. Louis got along well with the liberal bourgeoisie. Like them, he dressed in a frock coat and top hat. Sometimes, he strolled the streets, shaking hands with well-wishers. Liberal politicians and professionals filled his government.

Under Louis Philippe, the upper bourgeoisie prospered. Louis extended suffrage, but only to France's wealthier citizens. The vast majority of the people still could not vote. The king's other policies also favored the middle class at the expense of the workers.

The French Revolution of 1848

In the 1840s, discontent grew. Radicals formed secret societies to work for a French republic. Utopian socialists called for an end to private ownership of property. (See the previous chapter.) Even liberals denounced Louis Philippe's government for corruption and called for expanded suffrage.

Near the end of the decade, discontent was heightened by a recession, or period of reduced economic activity. Factories shut down and people lost their jobs. Poor harvests caused bread prices to rise. Newspapers blamed government officials for some of the problems. As in 1789, Paris was ripe for revolution.

"February Days" In February 1848, when the government took steps to silence critics and prevent public meetings, angry crowds took to the streets. During the "February Days," iron railings, overturned carts, paving stones, and toppled trees again blocked the streets of Paris. Church bells rang alarms, while women and men on the barricades sang the revolutionary "La Marseillaise." A number of demonstrators clashed with royal troops and were killed.

As the turmoil spread, Louis Philippe abdicated. A group of liberal, radical, and socialist leaders proclaimed the Second Republic. (The First Republic had lasted from 1792 until 1804, when Napoleon became emperor.)

From the start, deep differences divided the new government. Middle-class liberals wanted moderate political reforms. Socialists wanted far-reaching social and economic change that would help hungry workers. In the early days of the new republic, the socialists forced the government to set up national workshops to provide jobs for the unemployed.

"June Days" By June, however, upper- and middle-class interests had won control of the government. They saw the national workshops as a waste of money, and they shut them down.

Furious, workers took to the streets of Paris, rallying to the cry "Bread or Lead!" This time, however, bourgeois liberals turned violently against the protesters. Peasants, who feared that socialists might take their land, also attacked the rioting workers. At least 1,500 people were killed before the government crushed the rebellion.

The fighting of the "June Days" left a bitter legacy. The middle class both feared and distrusted the left, while the working class nursed a deep hatred for the bourgeoisie.

Louis Napoleon By the end of 1848, the National Assembly, dominated by members who wanted to restore order, issued a constitution for the Second Republic. It created a strong president and a one-house legislature. But it also gave the vote to all adult men, the widest suffrage in the world at the time. Nine million Frenchmen now could vote, compared with only 200,000 who had that right before.

Did You Know?

How Banquets Helped Spark a Revolution

Paris in 1847 was the scene of a series of public banquets. Food was served, but the real purpose of the gatherings was to call for changes in the French government. Organized by reform groups, these "reform banquets," as they were called, were marked by antigovernment speeches and resolutions, voted on by the banqueters.

The government's response was to ban the dinners. But this action only stirred the passions of the reformers. They called for the biggest banquet yet. It was planned for February 22, 1848. When the government sought to keep the banquet from taking place, a mob of students and workers formed. The next night, another large group of protesters clashed with soldiers— and the revolution was under way.

Theme: Political and Social Systems Why did the government ban the public banquets?

Did You Know?

ANSWER Possible answer: The government was trying to prevent critics from speaking out.

Resource Directory

Teaching Resources
History Through Literature *Les Misérables,* History Through Literature booklet, pp. 45–46
Humanities Link Chapter Extension Activities booklet, p. 52

Humanities Link

Art and Revolution

Art became more than an expression of beauty and truth in Europe during the mid-1800s. Many European painters, writers, and composers took an active role in the politics of the time. They used their artistic works to fuel the revolutionary spirit.

This painting (above), called *The Uprising,* captures the passion of the French revolutionaries. The painter Honoré Daumier (1808–1879), who was a revolutionary in his own right, used a paintbrush as others might have used a gun or a sword. As a young man, Daumier was imprisoned for drawing caricatures of Emperor Louis Philippe. Daumier's satirical works helped inspire further protests, and much of his work captured the spirit of the revolution he helped to create.

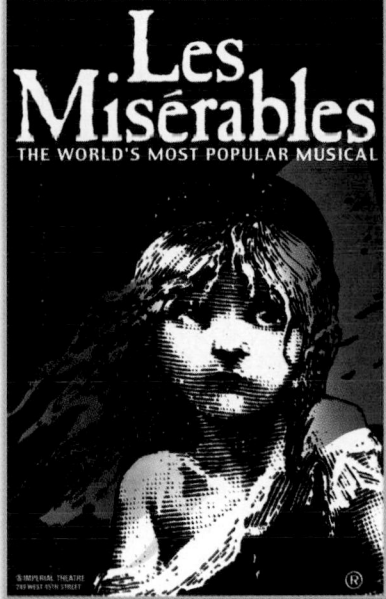

Les Misérables
THE WORLD'S MOST POPULAR MUSICAL

French writer Victor Hugo is still revered as a champion of French democracy. His novel *Les Misérables* offers a bleak view of French society in the years leading up to the revolution of 1848. The above poster was created to promote the modern theatrical version of *Les Misérables.*

European composers, such as Richard Wagner of Germany (right), also felt the revolutionary spirit and expressed it through their music. The popular music of the day was marked by a new passion and freedom of expression. It seemed to carry the revolutionary and republican spirit through the air.

Portfolio Assessment

INTERNET

Using the Internet or library resources, create a display of revolutionary art. You may use works of art, including paintings or drawings. You may choose to illustrate the display with excerpts of revolutionary writings, including poetry, song lyrics, or prose.

Chapter 21 **523**

Test Preparation

Have students read the section under the heading "June Days" on the opposite page, and then answer the question below.

Who shut down France's national workshops?

A workers who protested in the streets of Paris

B members of the liberal bourgeoisie and the upper class

C peasants who attacked protesting workers

D socialists who took control of the government

EXPLORING the HUMAN DRAMA
Humanities Link

Bell Ringer Ask students to look at the Daumier painting and explain how they could tell its subject without reading the caption. If necessary, point out the mass of people; their forward movement; the dark, oppressive colors; and the upraised, clenched fist.

Background
Connections to Today

Revolutionary Ideas In the early 1960s, color television programs first crossed the ocean via satellite, but programming was limited to 15 minutes—the length of time satellites stayed in sight of relay stations. Soon, however, "stationary" satellites that hovered above the same place on the Earth's surface allowed unlimited international transmissions. By 1964 the Tokyo Olympic Games appeared on North American TV. Less than a decade later, almost every place on Earth had access to satellite transmissions, and ideas had a worldwide audience.

Activity
Cooperative Learning

Analyzing a Song Have small groups find some of the protest songs of the 1960s. Group members should find information about the singer or group, what the song is protesting, and the songwriter (if different from the performer). Have students share their songs and background information with the class. Then, discuss how music continues to be a force for social change.

Portfolio Assessment Rubrics

Share rubrics with students.

Attempted Display has only one or two pieces of art, unlabeled, and it has few or no excerpts.

Minimal Display has three or four pieces of art, labeled, and includes an excerpt or two.

Adequate Display has five or more pieces of art, clearly labeled with title and artist's name and dates, and includes excerpts.

Exemplary Display has many pieces of art, clearly labeled with title and the artist's name and dates, and it includes many excerpts.

Nationalist Expansion While nationalism was causing revolutions and repression in Europe, it was also causing conflict in North America. Nationalism was partly responsible for the United States' belief in its "Manifest Destiny" to expand across the continent. This doctrine led to war with Mexico in 1846. Defeated in the war, Mexico agreed to the Treaty of Guadalupe Hidalgo in 1848. By this treaty, Mexico gave up claims to Texas, recognized the Rio Grande as its northern boundary, and ceded to the United States most of the lands in New Mexico, Utah, Nevada, Arizona, California, and western Colorado. In effect, Mexico had granted more than two-fifths of its territory to the United States. Driven by the spirit of nationalism, American settlers continued to move westward in ever-increasing numbers.

Revolutions in Europe, 1830 and 1848

Legend:
- Gained independence, 1830–1831
- Revolutions of 1830
- Revolutions of 1848
- Repression of revolutions in 1830
- Repression of revolutions in 1848

Azimuthal Equal Area Projection

Skills Assessment

Geography In 1830 and again in 1848, revolutions in France sparked uprisings throughout Europe. Although most rebellions were quickly crushed, their ideals survived.

1. **Location** On the map, locate (a) Paris, (b) Warsaw, (c) Budapest.
2. **Place** Which countries gained independence in 1830 and 1831?
3. **Critical Thinking Making Inferences** How can you tell from the map that the revolution in Budapest was unsuccessful?

When elections for president were held, the overwhelming winner was Louis Napoleon, nephew of Napoleon Bonaparte. The "new" Napoleon attracted the working classes by presenting himself as a man who cared about social issues such as poverty. At the same time, his famous name, linked with order and past French glory, helped him with conservatives.

Once in office, Louis Napoleon used his position as a steppingstone to greater power. By 1852, he had proclaimed himself emperor, taking the title Napoleon III. (He was the third Napoleon because the son of Napoleon I had died in his youth without ever ruling France.) Thus ended the short-lived Second Republic.

Like his celebrated uncle, Louis Napoleon used a plebiscite to win public approval for his seizure of power. A stunning 90 percent of voters supported his move to set up the Second Empire. Many thought that a monarchy was more stable than a republic. Millions of French hoped that Napoleon III would restore the glory days of Napoleon Bonaparte.

Napoleon III, like Louis Philippe, ruled at a time of rapid economic growth. For the bourgeoisie, the early days of the Second Empire brought prosperity and contentment. In time, however, Napoleon III would embark on foreign adventures that would bring down his empire and end French leadership in Europe.

The Spread of Revolution

In both 1830 and 1848, the revolts in Paris inspired uprisings to break out elsewhere in Europe. As Metternich said, "When France sneezes, Europe catches cold." Most of the uprisings were suppressed by military force. But here and there, rebels did win changes from conservative governments. Even when they failed, revolutions frightened rulers badly enough to encourage reform later in the century.

Belgium The one notable success for Europe's revolutionaries in 1830 took place in Belgium. In 1815, the Congress of Vienna had united the Austrian Netherlands (present-day Belgium) and the Kingdom of Holland under the Dutch king. The Congress had wanted to create a strong barrier to help prevent French expansion in the future.

The Belgians resented the new arrangement. The Belgians and Dutch had different languages, religions, and economic interests. The Belgians were Catholic, while the Dutch were Protestant. The Belgian economy was based on manufacturing; the Dutch, on trade.

In 1830, news of the Paris uprising that toppled Charles X ignited a revolutionary spark in Belgium. Students and workers threw up barricades in Brussels, the capital. The Dutch king turned to the other European powers for help. Britain and France knew that the Belgians were threatening to disrupt the boundaries set up by the Congress of Vienna, but they believed that they would benefit from the separation of Belgium and Holland. They therefore supported Belgian demands for independence. The conservative powers—Austria, Prussia, and Russia—were too busy putting down revolts of their own to help the Dutch king. As a result, in 1831, Belgium became an independent state with a liberal constitution.

Skills Assessment

ANSWERS 1. Review locations with students. 2. Belgium and Greece 3. Arrow symbol shows that Russian forces suppressed the revolution.

Resource Directory

Teaching Resources

Primary Source Activity *A Movement for Democracy,* Unit 5 booklet, p. 65

Poland Nationalists in Poland also staged an uprising in 1830. But, unlike the Belgians, the Poles failed to win independence for their country.

In the late 1700s, Russia, Austria, and Prussia had divided up Poland. Poles had hoped that the Congress of Vienna would restore their homeland in 1815. Instead, the great powers handed most of Poland to Russia.

In 1830, Polish students, army officers, and landowners rose in revolt. The rebels failed to gain widespread support, however, and were brutally crushed by Russian forces. Some survivors fled to Western Europe and the United States, where they kept alive the dream of freedom.

1848: Another Wave of Rebellion

In 1848, revolts in Paris again unleashed a tidal wave of revolution across Europe. For opponents of the old order, it was a time of such hope that they called it the "springtime of the peoples."

Sources of Discontent Although events in France touched off the revolts, grievances had been piling up for years. Unrest came from many sources. Middle-class liberals wanted a greater share of political power for themselves, as well as protections for the basic rights of all citizens. Workers demanded relief from the miseries of the Industrial Revolution. And nationalists of all classes ached to throw off foreign rule. By 1848, discontent was so widespread that it was only a matter of time before it exploded into full-scale revolution.

Metternich Falls In the Austrian empire, a revolt broke out in Vienna, taking the government by surprise. Metternich, who had dominated Austrian politics for more than 30 years, tried to silence the students who took to the streets. But when workers supported the students, Metternich resigned and fled in disguise. The Austrian emperor then promised reform.

Revolution quickly spread to other parts of the empire. In Budapest, Hungarian nationalists led by Louis Kossuth demanded an independent government. They also called for an end to serfdom and a written constitution to protect basic rights. In Prague, the Czechs made similar demands. Overwhelmed by events, the Austrian government agreed to the reforms.

The gains were temporary. Austrian troops soon regained control of Vienna and Prague. With Russian help, Austrian forces also smashed the rebels in Budapest. Many were imprisoned, executed, or forced into exile.

Revolution in Italy Uprisings also erupted in the Italian states. Nationalists wanted to end domination of Italy by the Austrian Hapsburgs. As elsewhere, nationalist goals were linked to demands for liberal reforms such as constitutional government. Workers suffering economic hardships demanded even more radical changes. From Venice in the north to Naples in the south, Italians set up independent republics. Revolutionaries even expelled the pope from Rome and installed a nationalist government.

Before long, however, the forces of reaction surged back here, too. Austrian troops ousted the new governments in northern Italy. A French army restored the pope to power in Rome. In Naples, local rulers canceled the reforms they had reluctantly accepted.

Turmoil in the German States In the German states, university students passionately demanded national unity and liberal reforms. Economic hard times and a potato famine brought peasants and workers into the struggle. Workers destroyed the machines that threatened their livelihood, while peasants burned the homes of wealthy landowners.

In Prussia, liberals forced King Frederick William IV to agree to a constitution written by an elected assembly. Within a year, though, he dissolved the assembly. Later, he issued his own constitution keeping power in his own hands or those of the upper classes.

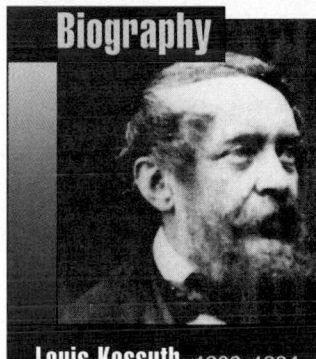

Biography

Louis Kossuth 1802–1894

For two decades, Louis Kossuth had been an activist, writing pamphlets designed to inflame patriotic feelings in the Hungarians. As a result, he was imprisoned by Austrian officials for three years. When he was released, he immediately renewed his activities. He became editor of a nationalistic newspaper and was recognized as the leading voice for Hungarian independence.

Kossuth went on to organize Hungarian revolutionary forces and to declare Hungary's independence in 1848. When Russia intervened, however, Kossuth was forced to flee.

He traveled to the United States, where he spoke before both houses of Congress. His subsequent tour of the country was so well received that a county in Iowa and towns in five states were named in his honor. Tragically, Kossuth would never return to his Hungarian homeland.

Theme: Impact of the Individual Why was Kossuth unable to win Hungarian independence?

Human Drama Activity

Discussing a Poem British poet Arthur H. Clough wrote "Say Not the Struggle Nought Availeth," reprinted below, in 1849 after witnessing the 1848 revolutions in France and Italy. Ask students how the poem relates to the revolutionary spirit.

Say not the struggle nought availeth,
   The labor and the wounds are vain,
The enemy faints not, nor faileth,
   And as things have been they remain.

If hopes were dupes, fears may be liars;
   It may be, in yon smoke concealed,
Your comrades chase e'en now the fliers,
   And, but for you, possess the field.

For while the tired waves, vainly breaking,
   Seem here no painful inch to gain,
Far back, through creeks and inlets making,
   Comes silent, flooding in, the main.

And not by eastern windows only,
   When daylight comes, comes in the light,
In front, the sun climbs slow, how slowly,
   But westward, look, the land is bright.

Biography

ANSWER Possible answer: The Russians aided Austria, and their combined forces were too much for the rebels to overcome.

Recall

1. **(a)** Charter of French Liberties, p. 521 **(b)** Charles X, p. 521 **(c)** Louis Philippe, p. 522 **(d)** Louis Napoleon, p. 522 **(e)** Louis Kossuth, p. 525 **(f)** Frankfurt Assembly, p. 526 **(g)** Frederick William IV, p. 526 **2. (a)** ultraroyalist, p. 521 **(b)** recession, p. 522

Comprehension

3. Possible answers: **(a)** Causes: Charles X rejected the Charter of French Liberties, suspended the legislature, limited the right to vote, and restricted the press. Effects: Charles X abdicated the throne; a constitutional monarchy was established with Louis Philippe as king. The middle class dominated this new government.
(b) Causes: discontent with limited extent of reforms, corruption in government, limited suffrage, economic hardships caused by recession, repression of reformers, closing of the national workshops. Effects: fear and distrust between the middle class and the left; hatred of the bourgeoisie by the working class; creation of the Second Republic with a new constitution, a strong president, and a legislature; expanded male suffrage; election of Louis Napoleon as president, who once in office declared himself emperor with popular support
4. **(a)** Belgium and Poland **(b)** In Belgium, the revolution succeeded, and Belgium gained independence. In Poland, Russian troops crushed the revolution. **5.** Conservative governments helped one another and used military force to suppress the revolutions. The revolutionaries did not agree on their goals and did not have mass support.

Critical Thinking and Writing

6. Arguments should be clear and logical.
7. Accept all reasonable responses.

Activity Rubrics

Share rubrics with students.

Attempted The essay is sketchy, with very little information, or is full of errors.

Minimal The essay has some information but is unclear or has many errors.

Adequate The essay is clear and well written, with few errors.

Exemplary The essay reveals in-depth research, is very clear and interesting, and has no errors.

Caption Answer

(a) liberty **(b)** They seem frightened by the threat of liberty.

THE GREAT SEA SERPENT OF 1848

An Eventful Year
This English cartoon comments on the revolutions of 1848 and the reaction of European rulers.

Theme: Political and Social Systems Based on the cartoon, **(a)** What ideal caused the revolutions of 1848? **(b)** How did the revolutions affect Europe's monarchs?

Frankfurt Assembly Throughout 1848, delegates from German states met in the Frankfurt Assembly. "We are to create a constitution for Germany, for the whole land," declared one leader with great optimism.

Divisions soon emerged. Delegates debated endlessly on such topics as whether the new Germany should be a republic or a monarchy, and whether or not to include Austria in a united German state. Finally, the assembly offered Prussia's Frederick William IV the crown of a united Germany. To their dismay, the conservative king rejected the offer because it came not from the German princes but from the people—"from the gutter," as he described it. By early 1849, the assembly was dissolved, under threat from the Prussian military. Outside the assembly, middle-class reformers and workers with radical demands clashed. Conservative forces rallied, dousing the last flames of revolt. Hundreds of people were killed. Many more went to prison. Thousands of Germans left their homeland. Most traveled to the United States, attracted by the young nation's promise of democratic government and economic opportunity.

Looking Ahead

By 1850, rebellion faded, ending the age of liberal revolution that had begun in 1789. Why did the uprisings fail? The rulers' use of military force was just one reason. In general, revolutionaries did not have mass support. In Poland in 1830, for example, peasants did not take part in the uprising. In 1848, a growing gulf divided workers seeking radical economic change and liberals pursuing moderate political reform.

By mid-century, Metternich was gone from the European scene. Still, his conservative system remained in force. In the decades ahead, liberalism, nationalism, and socialism would win successes not through revolution but through political activity. Ambitious political leaders would unify Germany and Italy. Workers would campaign for reforms through unions and the ballot box, as they increasingly won the right to vote.

SECTION 2 Assessment

Recall

1. **Identify: (a)** Charter of French Liberties, **(b)** Charles X, **(c)** Louis Philippe, **(d)** Louis Napoleon, **(e)** Louis Kossuth, **(f)** Frankfurt Assembly, **(g)** Frederick William IV.
2. **Define: (a)** ultraroyalist, **(b)** recession.

Comprehension

3. Describe one cause and one effect of **(a)** the French revolution of 1830, **(b)** the French revolution of 1848.
4. **(a)** To what lands did revolution spread in 1830? **(b)** Were these revolutions successful? Explain.
5. Why did most of the revolutions of 1848 fail to achieve their goals?

Critical Thinking and Writing

6. **Identifying Alternatives** Do you think that European rulers could have prevented nationalist revolts by granting autonomy to some groups of people? Why or why not?
7. **Making Decisions** Suppose you had been a conservative adviser to King Frederick William IV of Prussia. Would you have advised the king to accept the crown offered by the Frankfurt Assembly? Explain the reasons for your decision.

Activity
Take It to the NET

In recent years, various ethnic groups have sought independence, just as national groups did in 1830 and 1848. Use the Internet to find news articles about the people of East Timor, Chechnya, Bosnia, or another land where people have struggled to win an independent nation. Write a brief essay describing their struggle.

Resource Directory

Teaching Resources

Section Quiz Unit 5 booklet, p. 61
Creative Teaching Activities Creative Teaching Activities booklet, p. 97
Guided Reading and Review Unit 5 booklet, p. 62
Viewpoint Activity *Why Latin Americans Wanted Independence,* Unit 5 booklet, p. 66

Technology

Interactive Student Tutorial CD-ROM Ch. 21
Computer Test Bank Ch. 21

SECTION 3 Latin American Wars of Independence

Reading Focus

- What caused discontent in Latin America?
- How did Haitians, Mexicans, and people in Central America win independence?
- How did the nations of South America win independence?

Vocabulary

peninsular

creole

mestizo

mulatto

truce

Taking Notes

Copy the partially completed table below. As you read, fill in the left column with the names of leaders who led independence movements in Latin America. Fill in the right column with the name of the country or countries that each leader helped liberate.

LEADERS	COUNTRIES
Iturbide	Mexico
San Martín	Argentina, Chile, Peru

Main Idea In the early 1800s, many new nations emerged In Latin America as independence movements freed people from European rule.

Setting the Scene

Like many wealthy Latin Americans,* young Simón Bolívar (boh LEE vahr) was sent to Europe to complete his education. There, he became a strong admirer of the ideals of the Enlightenment and the French Revolution.

One afternoon, Bolívar and his Italian tutor sat talking about freedom and the rights that ordinary people should have. Bolívar's thoughts turned to his homeland, held as a colony by Spain. He fell on his knees and swore a solemn oath: "I swear before God and by my honor never to allow my hands to be idle nor my soul to rest until I have broken the chains that bind us to Spain."

In later years, Bolívar would fulfill his oath, leading the struggle to liberate northern South America from Spain. Elsewhere in Latin America, other leaders organized independence movements. By 1825, most of Latin America had been freed from colonial rule.

Sources of Discontent

By the late 1700s, the revolutionary fever that gripped Western Europe had spread to Latin America. There, discontent was rooted in the social, racial, and political system that had emerged during 300 years of Spanish rule.

Ethnic and Social Hierarchy Spanish-born peninsulares dominated Latin American political and social life. Only they could hold top jobs in government and the Church. Many creoles—the European-descended Latin Americans who owned the haciendas, ranches, and mines—bitterly resented their second-class status. Merchants fretted under mercantilist policies that tied the colonies to Spain.

Meanwhile, a growing population of mestizos, people of Native American and European descent, and mulattoes, people of African and European descent, were angry at being denied the status, wealth, and power that were available to whites. Native Americans suffered economic misery under the Spanish, who had conquered the lands of their ancestors. In the Caribbean region and parts of South America, masses of enslaved Africans who worked on plantations longed for freedom.

*Latin America refers to the regions in Middle and South America colonized by Europeans, especially the Spanish, French, and Portuguese, whose languages are rooted in Latin. It includes Spanish-speaking countries from Mexico to Argentina, Portuguese-speaking Brazil, and French-speaking Haiti.

The Ruling Class
This is a portrait of Don Tomas Mateo Cervantes, an aristocrat and government official of Cuba in the late 1700s. The portrait was painted by Vincente Escobar, a Cuban of African descent.

Theme: Political and Social Systems How was ethnic background linked to class in Latin America?

Geography and History

A Deadly, Microscopic Enemy

French forces in Haiti were up against much more than Toussaint L'Ouverture's brilliant leadership and brave soldiers. They also had to fight an enemy they couldn't see or begin to understand. It was yellow fever.

Soldiers who caught the virus became dizzy and developed high fevers and muscle aches. Their gums would bleed. Many became comatose and eventually died. Historians estimate that of the 33,000 French troops sent to the Caribbean, 29,000 contracted yellow fever within a year.

The source of the disease was the mosquito, so prevalent in tropical Haiti. Mosquitoes can carry the yellow fever virus and transmit it by biting humans.

Might history be different if Haiti were not a tropical island where mosquitoes thrived? Some historians think so. One said simply, "Mosquitoes liberated Haiti."

 Theme: Geography and History Why didn't the French take steps to protect themselves from mosquitoes and yellow fever?

Beyond dissatisfaction with Spanish rule, the different classes had little in common. In fact, they distrusted and feared one another. At times, they worked together against the Spanish. But once independence was achieved, the creoles, who had led the revolts, dominated the governments.

Enlightenment Ideas In the 1700s, educated creoles read the works of Enlightenment thinkers. They watched colonists in North America throw off British rule. Translations of the Declaration of Independence and the Constitution of the United States even circulated among the creole elite.

Women actively participated in the exchange of ideas. In some cities, women hosted and attended salons, called tertulias, where independence and revolution were discussed.

During the French Revolution, young creoles like Simón Bolívar traveled in Europe and were inspired by the ideals of "liberty, equality, and fraternity." Despite their admiration for Enlightenment ideas and revolutions in other lands, most creoles were reluctant to act.

Napoleon Bonaparte The spark that finally ignited widespread rebellion in Latin America was Napoleon's invasion of Spain in 1808. Napoleon ousted the Spanish king and placed his brother Joseph on the Spanish throne. In Latin America, leaders saw Spain's weakness as an opportunity to reject foreign domination and demand independence from colonial rule.

Haiti's Struggle for Independence

Even before Spanish colonists hoisted the flag of freedom, revolution had erupted elsewhere in Latin America, in a French-ruled colony on the island of Hispaniola. Haiti, as it is now called, was France's most valued possession in the 1700s.

In Haiti, French planters owned very profitable sugar plantations worked by nearly a half million enslaved Africans. Sugar plantations were labor intensive. The slaves were overworked and underfed. Haiti also had about 25,000 free mulattoes. Many were wealthy, and some also owned slaves. However, they did not have full equality with the French creoles.

A Slave Revolt In the 1790s, revolutionaries in France were debating ways to abolish slavery in the West Indies. However, debating the issue in Paris did not help enslaved Haitians gain their freedom. Embittered by suffering and inspired by the talk of liberty and equality, Haiti's slaves exploded in revolt in 1791.

The rebels were fortunate to find an intelligent and skillful leader in Toussaint L'Ouverture (too SAN loo vuhr TYOOR), a self-educated former slave. Although untrained, Toussaint was a brilliant general. He was also an inspiring commander. On the eve of one crucial battle, he rallied his troops with these stirring words: "We are fighting so that liberty—the most precious of all earthly possessions—may not perish."

The struggle was long and complex. Toussaint's army of former slaves faced many enemies. Some mulattoes joined French planters against the rebels. France, Spain, and Britain each sent armies to Haiti. The fighting took more lives than any other revolution in the Americas.

By 1798, the rebels had achieved their goal; enslaved Haitians had been freed. And even though Haiti was still a French colony, Toussaint's forces controlled most of the island.

Independence In France, meantime, Napoleon Bonaparte rose to power. In 1802, he sent a large army to reconquer Haiti. Toussaint urged Haitians once again to take up arms, this time to fight for full independence from France. The guerrilla forces were aided by a deadly ally, yellow fever, a disease which took a growing toll on the invaders. In April 1802, the French agreed to a truce, or temporary peace.

Geography and History

ANSWER The cause and method of transmission of the disease were not yet known.

Toussaint L'Ouverture on Slavery

In the late 1700s, Toussaint L'Ouverture led a successful revolt in Haiti to eliminate slavery. But Toussaint was haunted by the fear that the French, who still held Haiti as a colony, would try to reestablish slavery. Many French officials, as well as colonists, had already expressed such a desire. Toussaint wrote to the French Directory to oppose any plans to reimpose slavery.

Above, Toussaint L'Ouverture and his army of former slaves battle for independence from France.

"The attempts on . . . liberty which the colonists propose are all the more to be feared because it is with the veil of patriotism that they cover their detestable plans. We know that they seek to impose some of them on [the French government] by illusory and [deceptive] promises, in order to see renewed in this colony its former scenes of horror. . . . My attachment to France, my knowledge of the blacks, make it my duty not to leave you ignorant either of the crimes which they meditate or the oath that we renew, to bury ourselves under the ruins of a country revived by liberty rather than suffer the return of slavery. . . .

Blind as they are! They cannot see how [their] odious conduct . . . can become the signal of new disasters and irreparable misfortunes, and far from making them regain what in their eyes liberty for all has made them lose, they expose themselves to a total ruin and the colony to its inevitable destruction. Do they think that men who have been unable to enjoy the blessing of liberty will calmly see it snatched away? They supported their chains only so long as they did not know any condition of life more happy than that of slavery. But today when they have left it, if they had a thousand lives they would sacrifice them all rather than be forced into slavery again. . . .

But if, to re-establish slavery in [Haiti], this was to be done, then I declare to you it would be to attempt the impossible: we have known how to face dangers to obtain our liberty, we shall know how to brave death to maintain it."

—Toussaint L'Ouverture, quoted in *The Black Jacobins* (James)

Skills Tip

Italics in excerpts from old documents may represent underlining or some other form of emphasis in the original document.

Skills Assessment

1. What is the tone of Toussaint's letter?
   A diplomatic
   B peaceful
   C warning
   D friendly

2. What does Toussaint say will happen if the French try to reestablish slavery?
   E The British will take over.
   F The colony will be ruined by war.
   G The blacks will feel resentful.
   H The French will be condemned.

3. **Critical Thinking Making Inferences** (a) Why do you think Toussaint emphasized that one paragraph in his letter? (b) What might you infer about Toussaint himself from this letter?

✓ Test Preparation

Have students read the introductory paragraph and the first paragraph of the Primary Source on this page, and then answer the question below.

What are the "former scenes of horror" to which Toussaint refers?

A the mistreatment of enslaved Haitians
B the battles Haitians fought to free the colony from French rule
C the battles Haitians fought to free the colony from Spanish rule
D the battles Haitians fought to eliminate slavery

Background
About the Primary Source

Haitian Slavery The officials to whom Toussaint refers were not only in favor of a return to slavery, they were trying to suppress revolutionary clubs and reverse other achievements of the French Revolution. At first, the weak and corrupt Directory was unable to do anything to stop these reactionaries. Then it discovered proof that they were plotting to restore the monarchy. With that proof, the Directory was able to arrest and banish 65 of the conspirators to the Guianas. When Toussaint wrote to the Directory, he did not know of their banishment. Soon, the Directory itself would be overthrown by the next threat to Haitian liberty—Napoleon Bonaparte.

Activity
Interpreting the Primary Source

Use this additional question to generate class discussion.

Critical Thinking: Predicting Consequences Share with students the information in the background note above, and then ask: If the Directory had not been able to banish the reactionaries, what do you think would have been the consequences for Haiti? *(Slavery might have been reintroduced into Haiti.)*

Skills Tip

When you see italics used for emphasis, ask yourself why the writer might have wanted to emphasize that particular passage. The Skills Handbook in the front of the book has a lesson that will help students with this feature.

Skills Assessment

ANSWERS 1. C 2. G 3. Possible answers: **(a)** Toussaint emphasized it because it reiterates the essence of his message: the consequences of an attempt to reestablish slavery (revolt), the reasons for the consequences (the fight for liberty), and the inevitable outcome (failure to reinstate slavery). **(b)** Toussaint was a literate, passionate man, dedicated to freedom.

Toussaint's Fate Historians hold different views on the treatment that Toussaint L'Ouverture received while a prisoner in France. In his work *Black Liberator: The Life of Toussaint L'Ouverture,* Stephen Alexis maintains that Napoleon virtually murdered Toussaint through cruel treatment and slow starvation. He writes that Toussaint was placed in a cold, damp cell, denied writing materials, and woken up three or four times each night. His food rations were gradually decreased, until he finally died.

An opposing view is held by Ralph Korngold, author of *Citizen Toussaint,* who writes that "the charge that Toussaint was systematically starved is unfounded. Four francs a day, which the Government paid to a tavernkeeper in the town for Toussaint's food, washing, and mending, did not condemn a man to starvation. Many a student [in Paris] lived on less than half that amount."

Independent Nations of Latin America About 1844

Independent nations with date of independence

*United Provinces of Central America had dissolved by 1841

**Gran Colombia had dissolved by 1830

Skills Assessment

Geography In the early 1800s, many Latin American nations won independence from European rule.

1. **Location** *On the main map, locate (a) Mexico, (b) Gran Colombia, (c) Haiti.*

2. **Place** *Which nation of South America was once a Portuguese colony?*

3. **Critical Thinking** **Synthesizing Information** *Why did so many nations of Latin America gain independence by 1830?*

Shortly after, the French captured Toussaint and carried him in chains to France. Ten months later, he died there in a cold mountain prison. But Haiti's struggle for freedom continued. In 1804, Haitian leaders declared independence. With yellow fever destroying his army, Napoleon abandoned Haiti. In the following years, rival Haitian leaders fought for power. Finally, in 1820, Haiti became a republic.

Independence for Mexico and Central America

The slave revolt in Haiti frightened creoles in Spanish America. Although they wanted power themselves, most had no desire for economic or social changes that might threaten their way of life. In 1810, however, a creole priest in Mexico, Father Miguel Hidalgo (hih DAHL goh), raised a cry for freedom that would echo across the land.

El Grito de Dolores Father Hidalgo presided over the poor rural parish of Dolores. On September 15, 1810, he rang the church bells summoning the people to prayer. When they gathered, he startled them with an urgent

ANSWERS 1. Review locations with students. **2.** Brazil **3.** The French Revolution and American Revolution caused Enlightenment ideas to spread to Latin America. Napoleon's conquest of Spain weakened Spanish rule in the Americas.

Resource Directory

Teaching Resources
Biography Activity *Miguel Hidalgo y Costilla,* Unit 5 booklet, p. 64

Technology
World History Visions, Voices, Views Daily Life CloseUp, *A Latin American Revolutionary,* videodisc side 3 or videotape 5, running time 3:00 min.

Side 3: Fr. 4254-9362

appeal. We do not know his exact words, but his message is remembered: "My children, will you be free? Will you make the effort to recover the lands stolen from your forefathers by the hated Spaniards 300 years ago?" Father Hidalgo's speech became known as "el Grito de Dolores"—the cry of Dolores. It called Mexicans to fight for "Independence and Liberty."

A ragged army of poor mestizos and Native Americans rallied to Father Hidalgo and marched to the outskirts of Mexico City. At first, some creoles supported the revolt. However, they soon rejected Hidalgo's call for an end to slavery and his plea for reforms to improve conditions for Native Americans. They felt that these policies would cost them power.

After some early successes, the rebels faced growing opposition. Less than a year after he issued the "Grito," Hidalgo was captured and executed, and his followers scattered.

José Morelos   Another priest picked up the banner of revolution. Father José Morelos was a mestizo who called for wide-ranging social and political reform. He wanted to improve conditions for the majority of Mexicans, abolish slavery, and give the vote to all men. For four years, Morelos led rebel forces before he, too, was captured and shot in 1815.

Spanish forces, backed by conservative creoles, hunted down the surviving guerrillas. They had almost succeeded in ending the rebel movement when events in Spain had unexpected effects on Mexico.

Independence Achieved   In Spain in 1820, liberals forced the king to issue a constitution. This move alarmed Agustín de Iturbide (ee toor BEE day), a conservative creole in Mexico. He feared that the new Spanish government might impose liberal reforms on the colonies as well.

Iturbide had spent years fighting Mexican revolutionaries. Suddenly in 1821, he reached out to them. Backed by creoles, mestizos, and Native Americans, he overthrew the Spanish viceroy. Mexico was independent at last. Iturbide took the title Emperor Agustín I. Soon, however, liberal Mexicans toppled the would-be monarch and set up the Republic of Mexico.

Although Mexico was free of Spanish rule, the lives of most people changed little. Military leaders dominated the government and ruled by force of arms. The next 100 years would see new struggles to improve conditions for Mexicans.

New Republics in Central America   Spanish-ruled lands in Central America declared independence in the early 1820s. Iturbide tried to add these areas to his Mexican empire. After his overthrow, local leaders set up a republic called the United Provinces of Central America. The union was short-lived. It soon fragmented into the separate republics of Guatemala, Nicaragua, Honduras, El Salvador, and Costa Rica. Like Mexico, the new nations faced many social and economic problems.

Independence in South America

In South America, Native Americans had rebelled against Spanish rule as early as the 1700s. These rebellions had limited results, however. It was not until the 1800s that discontent among the creoles sparked a widespread drive for independence.

A Native American Revolt   The strongest challenge to Spanish rule by Native Americans was led by Tupac Amaru, who claimed descent from Incan kings. He demanded that the government end the brutal system of forced Indian labor. Spanish officials rejected the demand for reform. In 1780, Tupac Amaru organized a Native American revolt. A large army crushed the rebels and captured and killed their leader. Still, the revolt did have some positive effects. The Spanish king ordered officials to look into the system of forced labor and eventually abolished it.

▶ **Primary Sources and Literature**

See "Miguel Hidalgo: Decree of Hidalgo" in the Reference Section at the back of this book.

Connections to Today

Mexican Independence Day

Today, the people of Mexico remember Father Hidalgo's speech as "el Grito de Dolores," which means "the cry of Dolores." Every September 15, the anniversary of the speech, the president of Mexico rings a bell—suggestive of the church bell in Dolores. The president then honors the Grito de Dolores by repeating it.

The next day, September 16, marks the anniversary of the beginning of the fight against the Spanish. It is celebrated as Mexican Independence Day, a national holiday. Schools and businesses shut down, and people throw huge parties. Fireworks light the night sky.

The massive celebration is very different from the event at Dolores that it celebrates, but the spirit of independence is the same.

Theme: Continuity and Change Why is the ringing of bells an important custom of Mexican Independence Day?

Customize for . . .
Heterogeneous Groups

Constructing a Chart As an enrichment activity, have students make a chart with three columns titled Countries of Latin America, Government in the mid-1800s, and Government Today. Have students do research to fill in the chart with information for at least three Latin American countries. When students have completed their charts, conduct a class discussion comparing Latin American governments of the past with those of today. Ask students to make predictions about future political developments in Latin America. *(Enrichment)*

Connections to Today

ANSWER Possible answer: It commemorates Father Hidalgo's ringing of the church bell to summon the people to hear his appeal.

Activity
Interpreting Viewpoints

Writing an Editorial *The Price of Freedom*, Program IV in the 1991 five-part video series titled *The Buried Mirror: Reflections on Spain and the New World,* combines paintings, drawings, and reenactments to immerse viewers in the revolutions that swept Latin America during the early 1800s. The first part of the program provides in-depth and provocative profiles of Simón Bolívar and José de San Martín. Students will learn about these leaders' formative years in Europe during the Napoleonic Era and their victorious campaigns against the Spanish in the Americas. They will learn that in their final years, both men experienced failure, rejection, and exile.

Ask students who view *The Price of Freedom* to assume the role of a Latin American newspaper editor at the time of Bolívar's and San Martín's deaths. Their assignment is to write an editorial reviewing the life of either of the two figures. Their composition should summarize key events in the leader's life and outline his successes and failures. The editorial should offer an opinion as to whether the leader should be considered a successful hero or a tragic hero. (*The Buried Mirror: Reflections on Spain and the New World,* produced by Sogetel in association with the Smithsonian Institution, is a Films Incorporated Video.)
✳

Virtual Field Trip

www.phschool.com

The Library of Congress
Washington, D.C.

To learn more about the Latin American wars of independence and the history of Chile, use the Internet address above to link to the Library of Congress.

San Martín Crossing the Andes
In this painting, José de San Martín and Bernardo O'Higgins lead their army in a dramatic march over the Andes into Chile. San Martín won independence for Chile when he defeated the Spanish at the battle of Maipú in 1818.

Theme: Geography and History How do you think the successful march across the Andes affected San Martín's army?

 Primary Sources and Literature

See "Simón Bolívar: Address to the Congress of Venezuela" in the Reference Section at the back of this book.

Bolívar In the early 1800s, discontent spread across South America. Educated creoles like Simón Bolívar admired the French and American revolutions. They dreamed of winning their own independence from Spain.

In 1808, when Napoleon Bonaparte occupied Spain, Bolívar and his friends saw it as a signal to act. In 1810, Bolívar led an uprising that established a republic in his native Venezuela. Bolívar's new republic was quickly toppled by conservative forces. For years, civil war raged in Venezuela. The revolutionaries suffered many setbacks. Twice Bolívar was forced into exile on the island of Haiti.

Then, Bolívar conceived a daring plan. He would march his army across the Andes and attack the Spanish at Bogotá, the capital of the viceroyalty of New Granada (present-day Colombia). First, he cemented an alliance with the hard-riding *llaneros,* or Venezuelan cowboys. Then, in a grueling campaign, he led an army through swampy lowlands and over the snowcapped Andes. Finally, in August 1819, he swooped down to take Bogotá from the surprised Spanish.

Other victories followed. By 1821, Bolívar had succeeded in freeing Caracas, Venezuela. "The Liberator," as he was now called, then moved south into Ecuador, Peru, and Bolivia. There, he joined forces with another great South American leader, José de San Martín.

San Martín Like Bolívar, San Martín was a creole. He was born in Argentina but went to Europe for military training. In 1816, this gifted general helped Argentina win freedom from Spain. He then joined the independence struggle in other areas. He, too, led an army across the Andes, from Argentina into Chile. He defeated the Spanish in Chile before moving into Peru to strike further blows against colonial rule.

Bolívar and San Martín tried to work together, but their views were too different. In 1822, San Martín stepped aside, letting Bolívar's forces win the final victories against Spain.

Dreams and Disappointments The wars of independence had ended by 1824. Bolívar now worked tirelessly to unite the lands he had liberated into a single nation, called Gran Colombia. Bitter rivalries, however, made that dream impossible. Before long, Gran Colombia split into three independent countries: Venezuela, Colombia, and Ecuador.

Caption Answer

It was probably a very difficult journey and many horses and men probably were lost to the cold and to disease, but for those who survived, it was probably a big morale booster.

Resource Directory

Teaching Resources

Skill Application Activity *Identifying Ideologies,* Unit 5 booklet, p. 67
Section Quiz Unit 5 booklet, p. 63
Geography Quiz Unit 5 booklet, p. 68
Chapter Test Forms A, B, and C Unit 5 booklet, pp. 69–73
Answer Key Unit 5 booklet, pp. 74–83

Technology

Interactive Student Tutorial CD-ROM Ch. 21
Computer Test Bank Ch. 21

Bolívar faced another disappointment as power struggles among rival leaders triggered destructive civil wars. Spain's former South American colonies faced a long struggle to achieve stable governments—and an even longer one for democracy. Before his death in 1830, a discouraged Bolívar wrote, "We have achieved our independence at the expense of everything else." Contrary to his dreams, no social revolution took place. South America's common people had simply changed one set of masters for another.

Independence for Brazil When Napoleon's armies conquered Portugal, the Portuguese royal family fled to Brazil. During his stay in Brazil, the Portuguese king introduced many reforms, including free trade. He encouraged the development of local industries and allowed Brazilian merchants to trade with nations other than Portugal.

When the king returned to Portugal, he left his son Dom Pedro to rule Brazil. "If Brazil demands independence," the king advised Pedro, "proclaim it yourself and put the crown on your own head."

In 1822, Pedro followed his father's advice. A revolution had brought new leaders to Portugal. They planned to abolish the reforms that had benefited Brazil and they demanded that Dom Pedro return to Portugal. Dom Pedro refused to leave and submit to the Portuguese officials. Instead, he became emperor of an independent Brazil. He accepted a constitution that provided for freedom of the press, freedom of religion, and an elected legislature. Brazil remained a monarchy until 1889, when social and political turmoil led it to become a republic.

Cause and Effect

Long-Term Causes	Immediate Causes
• European domination of Latin America • Spread of Enlightenment ideas • American and French revolutions • Growth of nationalism in Latin America	• People of Latin America resent colonial rule and social injustices • Revolutionary leaders emerge • Napoleon invades Spain and ousts Spanish king

Independence Movements in Latin America

Immediate Effects	Long-Term Effects
• Toussaint L'Ouverture leads slave revolt in Haiti • Bolívar, San Martín, and others lead successful revolts in Latin America • Colonial rule ends in much of Latin America • Attempts made to rebuild economies	• 18 separate republics set up • Continuing efforts to achieve stable democratic governments and to gain economic independence

Connections to Today

• Numerous independent nations in Latin America
• Ongoing efforts to expand prosperity and democracy in Latin America

Skills Assessment **Chart** The French Revolution and the Napoleonic wars had a lasting impact on Latin America. **What difficulties did Latin Americans face after independence?**

SECTION 3 Assessment

Recall
1. Identify: **(a)** Toussaint L'Ouverture, **(b)** Miguel Hidalgo, **(c)** el Grito de Dolores, **(d)** José Morelos, **(e)** Tupac Amaru, **(f)** Simón Bolívar, **(g)** Dom Pedro.
2. Define: **(a)** peninsular, **(b)** creole, **(c)** mestizo, **(d)** mulatto, **(e)** truce.

Comprehension
3. How did social structure contribute to discontent in Latin America?
4. (a) What was the first step on Haiti's road to independence?

(b) Why did creoles refuse to support Hidalgo or Morelos?
5. How did successful military campaigns lead to the creation of independent nations in South America?

Critical Thinking and Writing
6. Comparing Compare the ways in which Mexico and Brazil achieved independence.
7. Connecting to Geography Review the subsection Independence in South America and the map in this section. How does the map show that Bolívar failed to achieve one of his dreams?

Chapter 21 **533**

Activity

Creating a Poster
Imagine that you are an artist in the service of Bolívar or San Martín. You have been hired to create a poster urging people to join the armies fighting against Spain. Your poster should highlight the goals of the revolutionary armies. It should also be eye-catching and convincing.

SECTION 3 Assessment

Recall
1. **(a)** Toussaint L'Ouverture, p. 528 **(b)** Miguel Hidalgo, p. 530 **(c)** el Grito de Delores, p. 531 **(d)** José Morelos, p. 531 **(e)** Tupac Amaru, p. 531 **(f)** Simón Bolívar, p. 532 **(g)** Dom Pedro, p. 533 2. **(a)** peninsular, p. 527 **(b)** creole, p. 527 **(c)** mestizo, p. 527 **(d)** mulatto, p. 527 **(e)** truce, p. 528

Comprehension
3. Creoles were unhappy with their second-class status, merchants disliked mercantilist policies that tied them to Spain, and mestizos and mulattoes resented the discrimination that they faced. Also, the classes distrusted and feared one another. 4. **(a)** a slave revolt in 1791, led by Toussaint L'Ouverture **(b)** They feared that the liberal ideas of Hidalgo and Morelos would cost them power. 5. Bolívar led armies to free Colombia, Venezuela, and Ecuador and—with San Martín—Peru and Bolivia. San Martín's armies freed Argentina and Chile.

Critical Thinking and Writing
6. Mexico's revolutionaries fought many battles before independence was won. Brazil's revolutionaries were granted independence by their king, Dom Pedro, without bloodshed. 7. Bolívar's goal of independence from Spain was achieved for Venezuela, Ecuador, Peru, and Bolivia, but his goal for unity as a single nation failed.

Activity Rubrics

Share rubrics with students before they begin their posters.

Attempted The poster is incomplete or reveals little understanding of the goals of the revolutionaries.

Minimal The poster shows some understanding of the goals of the revolutionaries but is poorly executed.

Adequate The poster is well conceived and clear and demonstrates a good grasp of the goals of the revolutionaries.

Exemplary The poster shows a thorough understanding of the goals of the revolutionaries and is original, creative, and eye-catching.

Skills Assessment

ANSWER Their economies needed to be rebuilt. They had to work to achieve stable democratic government.

Human Drama Activity

Discussing a Quotation Not everyone considered Simón Bolívar to be "The Liberator." His own chief of staff was greatly dismayed by Bolívar's behavior after freeing the Venezuelan city of Caracas. He included the following report in his memoirs.

"Meanwhile he organized his government, in which he united in himself the three powers—legislative, executive, and judicial; in virtue of which, he became absolute master of the liberty, prosperity, and lives of his countrymen. He named to offices those who could flatter him most. This dictatorship was . . . an absolute, despotic, military government."

You may wish to use this excerpt to stimulate class discussion on the leadership of Simón Bolívar. You may also wish to assign students to research other perspectives on Simón Bolívar.

Creating a Chapter Summary

As a reteaching opportunity, pair a more able student with a less able student to complete this chapter summary.

Possible additional responses: Conservatives resisted change; liberals promoted ideas of freedom; nationalists called for national liberation; Ottoman empire weakened; Spanish power was reduced by Napoleon's invasions; class and ethnic differences divided society in Latin America

Building Vocabulary

1–8. Sentences should show a clear understanding of the relationship of the terms to the revolutionary period.

Recalling Key Facts

9. **(a)** to restore royal families to power, to preserve the hierarchy of social classes, to oppose change **(b)** written constitutions, separation of powers, elections, laissez-faire economic policies **(c)** to unify and gain independence for people with a common national heritage
10. Charles X rejected the Charter of French Liberties, suspended the legislature, limited the right to vote, and restricted the press.
11. Revolutions occurred in France, Austria, Hungary, Italy, and the German states. Except for those in France, they were unsuccessful because the revolutionaries did not agree on their goals, and they lacked widespread support and outside help.
12. He invaded Spain and replaced the king with his brother. Latin American leaders saw Spain's weakness as an opportunity to gain independence.
13. **(a)** In 1821, the combined efforts of Mexican conservatives and reformers overthrew Spanish power in Mexico. **(b)** Most people's lives changed little after independence.
14. because his armies freed several South American countries from Spanish control

Critical Thinking and Writing

15. Possible answers: Conservatives tried to squash rebellions and maintain the old order but were opposed at every turn by liberals. Nationalists opposed the old order also because it had thrown together people of various nationalities in arbitrary ways.

Creating a Chapter Summary

Below is a partially completed graphic organizer on the causes of revolution in Europe and Latin America between 1800 and 1848. Copy the organizer and fill in the causes that led to revolutions.

> Enlightenment ideas spread

REVOLUTIONS IN EUROPE AND LATIN AMERICA

 iTEXT

For additional review and enrichment activities, see the interactive version of *World History* available on the Web and on CD-ROM.

Web Site Self-Test
For practice test questions for Chapter 21, see **www.phschool.com**.

Building Vocabulary

For each term below, write a sentence in which you show some connection between the term and the revolutions that occurred between 1800 and 1848.

1. **ideology**
2. **autonomy**
3. **ultraroyalist**
4. **recession**
5. **peninsular**
6. **creole**
7. **mestizo**
8. **mulatto**

Recalling Key Facts

9. In the early 1800s, what were the main goals of **(a)** conservatives, **(b)** liberals, **(c)** nationalists?
10. What were the causes of the French revolution of 1830?
11. Describe the outcomes of the 1848 rebellions in Europe.
12. How did Napoleon spark the revolutions that erupted in Latin America?
13. **(a)** How did Mexico gain independence from Spain? **(b)** How did Mexico's independence change the lives of its people?
14. Why is Simón Bolívar known as "The Liberator"?

Critical Thinking and Writing

15. **Recognizing Causes and Effects** How did the clash of conservatism, liberalism, and nationalism contribute to unrest in Europe in the 1800s?
16. **Recognizing Points of View** In the 1820s, Britain, France, and Russia supported the Greek struggle for independence. **(a)** Why did these European powers support the Greeks? **(b)** Did the European powers usually respond to revolution in this way? Explain.
17. **Analyzing Information** You have read Metternich's comment: "When France sneezes, Europe catches cold." **(a)** What did he mean by those words? **(b)** Was Metternich correct? Explain.
18. **Predicting Consequences** Do you think that the suppression of nationalist revolutions in the mid-1800s put an end to nationalism? Why or why not?
19. **Connecting to Geography** **(a)** How did climatic conditions help Haitians defeat the French? **(b)** Do you think the distance between Europe and Latin America affected the Latin American wars for independence? Explain.

---

16. **(a)** They had a great admiration for ancient Greek civilization. **(b)** No. They usually saw revolution as a threat to their power and to national stability.
17. **(a)** He meant that revolutions in France caused revolutions elsewhere. **(b)** Possible answer: yes, because the revolutions in France inspired others to revolt
18. Students' answers should recognize the continued influence of nationalism in the world today.
19. **(a)** Thousands of French soldiers contracted yellow fever from the mosquitoes that lived in tropical Haiti; many died. **(b)** Possible answer: yes, because the great distance led to slow communications and prevented European governments from sending more soldiers

Skills Assessment
Analyzing Primary Sources

In 1814, after a defeat in Caracas, Venezuela, Simón Bolívar fled to the British colony of Jamaica. There, he wrote a letter stating his principles. Read the excerpt below and answer the questions that follow.

"There is nothing we have not suffered at the hands of that unnatural stepmother— Spain. . . . Americans, under the existing Spanish system, occupy a position in society no better than that of serfs suitable for labor. . . . And even this status is surrounded with galling restrictions, such as the prohibition against the cultivation of European crops, the existence of royal monopolies, or the ban on factories. . . . To this add the exclusive trading privileges. . . . In short, do you wish to know what our future was?— simply the cultivation of the fields of indigo, grain, coffee, sugar cane, cacao, and cotton; raising cattle on the empty plains, hunting wild game in the wilderness; digging in the earth to mine gold for the insatiable greed of Spain."

—Simón Bolívar, "Letter From Jamaica"

20. Why do you think Bolívar calls Spain an "unnatural stepmother"?
21. According to Bolivar, what position in society did Latin Americans occupy?
22. What restriction was placed on Latin American farmers?
23. Who had monopolies on some industries?
24. Why do you think there was a ban on factories?
25. What does Bolívar say was the ultimate purpose of all Latin American labor?
26. What do you think were the effects of the publication of this letter?

Skills Assessment
Take It to the NET

Use the Internet to do an in-depth study of one of the revolutions that you have studied in this chapter. Create an outline that identifies the causes, key events, and results of the revolution. Note the Internet sites that you used by listing their titles, authors, and addresses.

Skills Assessment
Analyzing Political Cartoons

"You have the floor; explain yourself!"

In his satirical cartoons, French artist Honoré Daumier (1808–1879) protested unfair social conditions, legal injustices, and middle-class corruption. He was once imprisoned for drawing an unflattering caricature of the king. Study his cartoon titled "You have the floor; explain yourself!" Then, answer the following questions:

27. In this court scene, **(a)** who is the speaker? **(b)** What do his words mean?
28. How well do you think the accused will be able to defend himself?
29. In this cartoon, what do the unbalanced scales of justice symbolize?
30. Based on the cartoon, what was Daumier's view of the French justice system?
31. Do you think Daumier's cartoons helped bring about change? Explain.

Skills Tip

A political cartoon expresses one person's point of view. The cartoon may be factually accurate or inaccurate. To amuse the reader, a cartoon's message is often exaggerated.

Analyzing Primary Sources

20. Possible answer: because Spain treated its colonies and the colonists so poorly
21. a position no better than that of serfs
22. couldn't grow European crops
23. the crown (Spain)
24. Possible answer: to maintain Spain's monopoly on manufactured goods
25. Possible answer: to serve Spain
26. Possible answer: It would have angered Spanish officials and inspired revolutionaries.

Analyzing Political Cartoons

27. **(a)** the judge **(b)** Possible answer: By granting the gagged defendant the right to speak, the judge creates only the illusion of justice.
28. He won't be able to defend himself at all.
29. bias and injustice
30. Daumier viewed the French justice system of his day as corrupt and unjust.
31. yes, because they increased people's awareness of injustice

Skills Tip

Look for details in the background of the cartoon (such as the executioner with ax in hand ready to kill the man whose head is on the block) that may help explain its message. The Skills Handbook in the front of the book has a lesson that will help students with this feature.

Unit Theme Activity

Evaluate students' Unit Theme Activities by referring to the rubrics on the unit opener page in the Teacher's Edition.

Take It to the NET

Direct students to **www.phschool.com** for links to sites that will help them get started on this assignment. Share rubrics with students.

Attempted The outline reveals little research and fails to include all the required elements or doesn't follow standard outline form.

Minimal The outline reveals some research and includes all the required elements but doesn't follow standard outline form or is messy.

Adequate The outline reveals appropriate research, includes all the required elements, and follows standard outline form.

Exemplary The outline reveals extensive research, includes all the required elements, and follows standard outline form.

USING THESE PAGES

The Unit-in-Brief contains the main ideas of the unit chapters. You may use the Unit-in-Brief to preview, review, or condense the contents of each chapter.

The unit time line identifies key events in each world region that took place during the time span covered by the unit.

Activity
Unit Themes

Have students review the unit themes below. Then, ask them to find examples in the time line and summary to support each theme.

Continuity and Change Enlightenment ideas about society and government stood in sharp contrast to the prevailing standards. Since the 1700s, Enlightenment ideas have spread around the world.

Economics and Technology During the 1700s, advances in farming, transportation, and manufacturing contributed to the Industrial Revolution. Production of goods shifted from the home to the factory. Laissez-faire economists, utilitarians, and socialists offered plans to deal with the consequences of this change.

Impact of the Individual Thinkers such as John Locke, Voltaire, and Jean-Jacques Rousseau and political leaders such as Napoleon Bonaparte and Simón Bolívar encouraged national pride and human rights.

Political and Social Systems Revolutionaries, inspired by the Enlightenment, urged radical changes in government. Early industrialization created a new working class, while merchants and skilled artisans formed a growing new middle class.

---

5 Enlightenment and Revolution

Chapter 18

The Enlightenment and the American Revolution (1707–1800)

The Enlightenment was a movement in Western Europe and North America that sought to discover natural laws and apply them to social, political, and economic problems. Since the 1700s, Enlightenment ideas have spread around the world, creating upheaval and change as they have challenged established traditions.

- The ideas of thinkers such as Locke, Montesquieu, and Rousseau would justify revolutions and inspire principles of representative government.
- Enlightenment thinkers called *philosophes* applied the methods of science to their efforts to understand and improve society.
- Physiocrats rejected mercantilism in favor of laissez-faire economics.
- Despite a growing middle class, most Europeans remained peasants who lived in small rural villages, untouched by Enlightenment ideas.
- England established a constitutional monarchy and built the most powerful commercial empire in the world.
- After years of growing dissent, Britain's North American colonies won independence in the American Revolution.
- Inspired by Enlightenment ideas, the United States adopted a constitution that would serve as a model for other democratic nations.

Chapter 19

The French Revolution and Napoleon (1789–1815)

Between 1789 and 1815, the French Revolution destroyed an absolute monarchy and disrupted a social system that had existed for over a thousand years. These events ushered in the modern era in European politics.

- France was burdened by an outdated class system, a severe financial crisis, and a monarchy too indecisive to enact reforms.
- In 1789, dissatisfied members of the middle class called for a constitution and other reforms. Meanwhile, hunger and social resentment sparked rioting among peasants and poor city dwellers.
- In the first phase of the French Revolution, moderates attempted to limit the power of the monarchy and guarantee basic rights of the people.
- In 1793, as enemies outside France denounced the revolution, radicals executed the king and queen and began a Reign of Terror.
- From 1799 to 1815, Napoleon Bonaparte consolidated his power within France and subdued the combined forces of the greatest powers of Europe.
- Under Napoleon, French armies spread the ideas of revolution across Europe.
- In 1815, the Congress of Vienna sought to undo the effects of the French Revolution and the Napoleonic era.

	1725	**1750**	**1775**
AFRICA	**1700s** Islamic revival in Africa		
THE AMERICAS		**1763** Britain wins control of Canada	**1775** American Revolution begins
ASIA AND OCEANIA		**1756** Seven Years' War affects India / **1770** Cook claims Australia for Britain	
EUROPE		**1751** Diderot publishes *Encyclopedia* / **1764** Spinning jenny invented	

Student Bibliography

Ashton, Thomas S. *The Industrial Revolution, 1760 to 1830.* Greenwood, 1986. Comprehensive history of Great Britain's Industrial Revolution.

Bell, Madison Smartt. *All Souls' Rising.* Penguin USA, 1996. Powerful historical novel of the slave rebellion that brought an end to white rule in Haiti.

Clare, John D., ed. *Industrial Revolution.* Harcourt Trade Publishers, 1994. Describes the Industrial Revolution's origins in Great Britain and its spread to America and the rest of Europe.

Doyle, William. *The Oxford History of the French Revolution.* Oxford University Press, 1990. Comprehensive account of the revolution.

Fast, Howard. *The Call of the Fife and Drum: Three Novels of the American Revolution.* Lyle Stuart, 1987. The well-known novelist wrote these entertaining tales in the early years of his career.

Ford, Franklin L. *Europe 1780–1830.* Longman, 1989. Introductory summary of social, political, economic, and cultural transformations.

Chapter 20

The Industrial Revolution Begins
(1750–1850)

During the 1700s, production began to shift from simple hand tools to complex machines, and new sources of energy replaced human and animal power. Known as the Industrial Revolution, this transformation marked a crucial turning point in history and changed the lives of people all over the world.

- An agricultural revolution contributed to a population explosion that, in turn, fed the growing industrial labor force.
- Abundant resources and a favorable business climate allowed Britain to take an early lead in industrialization.
- New sources of energy, such as coal and steam, fueled factories and paved the way for faster means of transporting people and goods.
- A series of remarkable inventions revolutionized the British textile industry and led to the creation of the first factories.
- Rapid urbanization and the rise of the factory system at first created dismal living and working conditions.
- Laissez-faire economists, utilitarians, and socialists put forth their own ideas for solving the problems of industrial society.
- Karl Marx promoted communism, a radical form of socialism that would have a worldwide influence.

Chapter 21

Revolutions in Europe and Latin America
(1790–1848)

With the Congress of Vienna, the great powers sought to return to the political and social order that had existed prior to 1789. However, in the early 1800s, a wave of violent uprisings swept across Western Europe and Latin America, fueled by the political ideas of the French Revolution and the economic problems of the Industrial Revolution.

- Two opposing ideologies emerged in Europe. Liberals embraced Enlightenment ideas of democracy and individual rights, while conservatives sought to preserve the old political and social order.
- Nationalism inspired independence movements among peoples with a shared heritage but also bred intolerance and persecution of minorities.
- In 1830 and 1848, ideological tensions and social inequalities sparked uprisings in France and elsewhere in Europe. Although most of these democratic revolutions were suppressed, they served to hasten reform later in the century.
- In Latin America, discontent with foreign domination led to a series of independence movements that freed most of the region from colonial rule by 1825.

1800   **1825**   **1850**

1788 Futa Toro outlaws slave trade

1830s Boers begin Great Trek

1818 Shaka begins Zulu conquests

1847 Liberia becomes independent

1789 United States Constitution takes effect

1819 Bolívar captures Bogotá

1810 "El Grito de Dolores" in Mexico

1793 Emperor Qianlong rejects British trade

1839 Opium War begins in China

1789 French Revolution begins

1804 Napoleon becomes emperor

1815 Congress of Vienna

1830 First railway opens in Britain

1848 Revolutions sweep Europe; *The Communist Manifesto* published

Activity
Summarizing the Main Idea

Have students use both the Unit-in-Brief and Chapters 18–21 to answer the following questions in order to summarize Unit 5: (1) How did the ideas of the Enlightenment encourage revolution? (2) How did political, social, and economic conditions contribute to the start of the French Revolution? (3) Describe the major characteristics of the Industrial Revolution in Britain. (4) Describe how each of the following contributed to the revolutions that took place in Europe and Latin America during the early 1800s: liberalism, nationalism, conservatism.

PRENTICE HALL
ASSESSMENT SYSTEM

Diagnose and Prescribe
- Profile student skills with Diagnostic Tests A & B.
- Address student needs with program materials identified in the test.

Review and Reteach
- Provide cumulative content review with the Review Book.

Practice and Assess
- Build test-taking skills with Test-Taking Strategies With Transparencies.

Teacher Bibliography

Best, Geoffrey. *War and Society in Revolutionary Europe, 1770–1870.* St. Martin's, 1982. Broad survey covering the Old Regime, the French Revolution, post-Napoleonic Europe, and revolutions to the 1860s.

Collier, Christopher, and James Lincoln Collier. *The American Revolution.* Benchmark Books, 1998. Examines the people and events involved in the revolution.

Dallas, Gregor, and George Dallas. *The Final Act: The Roads to Waterloo.* Henry Holt, 1997. Engaging account of the Congress of Vienna.

Lefebvre, Georges. *The Coming of the French Revolution.* Princeton University Press, 1989. Classic account of the causes and early development of the revolution.

Stearns, Peter N., and John H. Hinshaw, eds. *ABC-Clio World History Companion to the Industrial Revolution.* ABC-Clio, 1996. Encyclopedia focusing on manufacturing changes from the eighteenth century to the present.

UNIT 6

UNIT OVERVIEW

Unit 6 examines the Industrial Revolution of the 1800s and the expansion of nationalism, western democracy, and imperialism.

Chapter 22 studies the effects of the Industrial Revolution on western society and culture.

Chapter 23 studies the rising tide of nationalism in Europe, the formation of new nation-states, and the weakening of multinational empires.

Chapter 24 examines developments in the western democracies of Britain, France, and the United States.

Chapter 25 describes how western industrial powers dominated much of the world by building global empires.

Chapter 26 studies various responses to western imperialism and the effects of imperialism around the world.

UNIT 6

Industrialism and a New Global Age

1800–1914

OUTLINE

Themes

As you read about imperialism and the new global age, you will encounter the following themes.

Diversity Rulers strengthened their nations by incorporating surrounding states and colonies. Conflicts arose as new subjects, often of different ethnic backgrounds, demanded independence. Women struggled to end restrictions on their lives and gain recognition of their rights.

Economics and Technology Developing factory systems, improved transportation and communication, and scientific advances contributed to overseas expansion by European powers. Industrialized nations grew wealthy, often at the expense of colonies.

Impact of the Individual Nationalist leaders in Italy and Germany used warfare and political alliances to forge new nations out of fragmented provinces.

Political and Social Systems In the 1800s, as the middle class grew, democratic rights were extended in Britain, France, and the United States. Urbanization and the impact of industrialization led to major changes in social values.

Unit Theme Activity

For Your Portfolio The chapters in this unit describe the effects of developing technology on national growth. As you read the chapters, prepare a portfolio project showing the significance of industrialization to imperialism. Your project might take one of the following forms:
• Editorial
• Debate
• Time line

The Gateway of India was built in 1911 to honor the visit of King George V and Queen Mary to India. Located on the harbor of Mumbai (Bombay), it combines Indian, Islamic, and Persian styles of art and architecture.

Background
About the Picture

The Gateway of India One of the most famous landmarks of Mumbai, the city that was once called Bombay but was renamed to reflect its native roots, is the Gateway of India. This structure is located at Apollo Bunder, on the water's edge. Built of yellow basalt, the Gateway's design is a variation of the conventional Arch of Triumph. At its highest point, the structure stands 83 feet above the ground, and the diameter of the central dome is 48 feet. On the ground, there are eight open doorways. Just beyond the main doorway is a staircase leading to the top, where one finds four spires between two large balconies that overlook the harbor.

In 1948, the last of the British troops to leave India, the First Battalion of the Somerset Light Infantry, passed through the Gateway. This ended 194 years of British military presence in India.

TEXT

Don't miss the exclusive interactive version of *World History: Connections to Today* on the Internet and CD-ROM.

eTeach

Be sure to check out this month's online discussion with a World History Master Teacher.

Go to **www.phschool.com**.

Block Scheduling Support

Using the Unit-in-Brief The Unit-in-Brief, found at the end of the unit, contains the main ideas of the unit chapters. You may use the Unit-in-Brief to preview, review, or condense the contents of each chapter.

Using the Unit Time Line The Unit Time Line, at the end of the unit, provides a chronology of world events during the period covered by this unit. By studying the time line in conjunction with the Unit-in-Brief, students may compare developments in various regions. You may use the time line to help condense the contents of the chapters.

Using the *Guide to the Essentials* The *Guide to the Essentials of World History* contains summaries and graphic organizers for each section of every chapter in this unit. You may use the *Guide to the Essentials* to help poor readers or students acquiring English access the main ideas of the chapters. You may also use it with all students to review or to condense topics in your world history course.

Bell Ringer After students have read the text accompanying the pictures, ask them to name modern conveniences they have used today. Then, have them name a predecessor or earlier stage of this convenience.

Activity
Cooperative Learning

Presenting Research Divide the class into groups of five or six students each. Assign each group one of the following organizations to research: the United Nations, the Olympic games, the Boy Scouts or Girl Scouts, major league baseball, or the motion picture industry. Groups should trace the history, growth, and development of their assigned organization, and present their research to the class in a format of their choosing—skit, oral report, written report, or poster.

WHY STUDY HISTORY?
Because the Past Has an Impact on Us Today

Most of us take the marvels of our modern world for granted. Without a second thought, we microwave a frozen pizza, watch TV, fly in airplanes, surf the Net. But these "new" inventions did not come about overnight, in a single inspired flash. Instead, over decades, or even centuries, innovators have built on the discoveries and ideas of the past. The process continues today. Our twenty-first-century achievements will serve as building blocks for even more amazing technology in the future.

Architects Defy Gravity

In the 1890s, in Chicago, architects built the 16-story Reliance Building—one of the world's first "skyscrapers" (left). Elevators made it practical for the first time to erect a building of more than 6 stories, and the use of steel made it possible for the frame to carry the weight of the building. Chicagoans of the time marveled at the structure's light and airy facade, composed almost entirely of windows. The Reliance Building is considered the direct ancestor of today's glass-and-steel skyscrapers, such as the Petronas Towers in Kuala Lumpur (right), which rise 88 stories, or 1,453 feet, in the air.

540

Resource Directory

Teaching Resources
Why Study History? *Because the Past Has an Impact on Us Today,* Why Study History? booklet, pp. 15–16

Easing Human Suffering

In 1859, Jean Henri Dunant, a Swiss banker, witnessed a battle during the Italian war for independence. Horrified at the suffering, Dunant helped to organize the International Red Cross to care for battle victims. One of the first groups of Red Cross volunteers, during the Franco-Prussian War in 1870, is shown above at left. Later, the Red Cross expanded its mission to include prevention and relief of human suffering generally. Today, the Red Cross operates in more than 100 countries. In the picture above at right, Red Cross workers join the relief effort in Puebla, Mexico, after a devastating earthquake in 1999.

Trains— Fast and Faster!

The invention of the steam-powered locomotive (above) in the early 1800s revolutionized transportation. Pulled by these massive engines, early railroad trains moved at what seemed startling speed—nearly 40 miles an hour! For more than a century, railroads enjoyed enormous success, carrying tons of freight and millions of passengers each year. Then, in the late 1900s, automobiles and airplanes eroded the popularity of rail travel. Today, thanks to new technology, people are turning once again to the railroad. The reason? High-speed trains, such as the streamlined French "bullet train"(right), now achieve speeds of nearly 200 miles per hour!

Portfolio Assessment

Connecting to Today List three features of modern life that you might research to discover their roots in the past. Describe your plan for conducting the research on one of them.

Unit 6 **541**

Chapter 22 Planning Guide

Resource Manager

	CORE INSTRUCTION	READING/SKILLS
Chapter Level Resources	**Teaching Resources** ◼ Pacing Charts, Ch. 22 ◼ Teaching With Themes, p. 25 ▦ Color Transparencies, p. F–45 ◉ Resource Pro® Ch. 22 ▣ **www.phschool.com** • eTeach	◉ Book on CD, Ch. 22 ◉ Interactive Student Tutorial CD-ROM, Ch. 22 ◉ Social Studies Skills Tutor CD-ROM ▦ Skills Transparencies
1 The Industrial Revolution Spreads 1. Identify the industrial powers that emerged in the 1800s. 2. Outline the impact new technology had on industry. 3. Relate how big business emerged in the late 1800s.	**Teaching Resources** ◼ Creative Teaching Activities, p. 98 ◉ Prentice Hall Presentation Pro, Ch. 22, Section 1 ▦ Section Reading Support Transparencies	**Teaching Resources** ◻ Unit 6 booklet • Guided Reading and Review, p. 2 ◼ Guide to the Essentials ▣ Guided Reading Audiotapes, Ch. 22, Section 1
2 The World of Cities 1. Summarize the impact of medical advances in the late 1800s. 2. Describe how cities had changed by 1900. 3. Outline how working-class struggles led to improved conditions for workers.	**Teaching Resources** ◻ Unit 6 booklet • Primary Source Activity, p. 11 • Viewpoint Activity, p. 12 ◼ Creative Teaching Activities, p. 99 ◉ Prentice Hall Presentation Pro, Ch. 22, Section 2	**Teaching Resources** ◻ Unit 6 booklet • Guided Reading and Review, p. 4 • Skill Application Activity, p. 13 ◼ Guide to the Essentials ▣ Guided Reading Audiotapes, Ch. 22, Section 2
3 Changing Attitudes and Values 1. Point out the values that shaped the new social order. 2. State how women and educators sought change. 3. Summarize how science challenged existing beliefs. 4. Explain the role religion played in urban society.	**Teaching Resources** ◼ Creative Teaching Activities, p. 100 ◉ Prentice Hall Presentation Pro, Ch. 22, Section 3 ▦ Section Reading Support Transparencies	**Teaching Resources** ◻ Unit 6 booklet • Guided Reading and Review, p. 6 ◼ Guide to the Essentials ▣ Guided Reading Audiotapes, Ch. 22, Section 3
4 A New Culture 1. Enumerate the themes that shaped romantic art, literature, and music. 2. Describe how realists responded to the industrialized, urban world. 3. Explain how the visual arts changed.	**Teaching Resources** ◻ Unit 6 booklet • Biography Activity, p. 10 ◼ Creative Teaching Activities, p. 101 ◉ Prentice Hall Presentation Pro, Ch. 22, Section 4 ▦ Section Reading Support Transparencies	**Teaching Resources** ◻ Unit 6 booklet • Guided Reading and Review, p. 8 ◼ Guide to the Essentials ▣ Guided Reading Audiotapes, Ch. 22, Section 4

ENRICHMENT/PRE-AP

- **www.phschool.com**
  - Why Study History?

Teaching Resources
- **Chapter Extension Activities,** pp. 54–55
- **Visions, Voices, Views,** Global Issues Forum, tape 5

Color Transparencies, p. D–79

Teaching Resources
- **Chapter Extension Activities,** p. 56
- **History Through Literature,** pp. 47–48
- **www.phschool.com**
  - Internet Activities, Section 3

Color Transparencies, p. D–73
Listening to Literature World Masterpieces, Beethoven's *Sonata no. 14,* works by Heinrich Holmes, Victor Hugo, and Charles Baudelaire, sides 7 and 8
www.phschool.com
  - Virtual Field Trip
  - Internet Activities, Section 4

ASSESSMENT

PRENTICE HALL ASSESSMENT SYSTEM

Core Assessment
- **ExamView Test Bank booklet,** Ch. 22
- **ExamView Test Bank CD-ROM,** Ch. 22

Standardized Test Preparation

Diagnose and Prescribe
- **Diagnostic Tests for High School Social Studies Skills**

Review and Reteach
- **Review Book for World History**

Practice and Assess
- **Test-Taking Strategies With Transparencies for High School**
- **Alternative Assessment booklet**
- **Test Prep Book for World History**

Teaching Resources
- **Unit 6 booklet**
  - Geography Quiz, p. 14
  - Section Quizzes, pp. 3, 5, 7, 9
  - Chapter Tests A, B, and C, pp. 15–19
- **www.phschool.com**
  - Self-Test

CUSTOMIZE FOR INDIVIDUAL NEEDS

Gifted and Talented
- **Teacher's Edition,** Activities: Customize for Heterogeneous Groups, p. 545

Less Proficient Readers
- **Guide to the Essentials,** Ch. 22
- **Guided Reading Audiotapes, English,** Ch. 22
- **Book on CD,** Ch. 22
- **Teacher's Edition,** Activities: Reading Strategy, p. 558; Customize for Visual Learners, p. 564

Less Proficient Writers
- **Teacher's Edition,** Activities: Connections to Film, p. 552

Students Acquiring English/ESL
- **Guide to the Essentials, English/Spanish,** Ch. 22
- **Guided Reading Audiotapes, English/Spanish,** Ch. 22
- **Book on CD,** Ch. 22
- **Teacher's Edition,** Activities marked with an *

TEXT

Don't miss the exclusive interactive version of *World History: Connections to Today* on the Internet and CD-ROM.

INTRODUCTION

A second Industrial Revolution spread across Europe, North America, and beyond in the mid-1800s. By late century, "big business" ruled the industrial world. A complex social structure evolved, dominated by middle-class values. The women's suffrage movement began. The overall standard of living improved, but the poor still suffered. Through art, romanticism, realism, and impressionism responded to social and technological changes.

Focusing on Themes

Suggest that students focus on these theme questions as they read:

Economics and Technology
How did science and new ways of doing business promote industrial growth?

Religions and Value Systems
What social, economic, and intellectual developments reshaped western social values?

Art and Literature
How did literature, music, and visual arts reflect changing attitudes and values?

Impact of the Individual
What contributions did individuals make in science, business, and the arts?

◆ TIME LINE ACTIVITY

Share the About the Pictures note before asking these questions:

1. When and where did the Industrial Revolution begin on the European continent? *(Belgium in 1807)*
2. What publication, denounced by several religious leaders, appeared in 1859? *(On the Origin of Species)*
3. Why was 1869 an important year for labor unions? *(Germany legalized them.)*
4. What 1914 event was linked to growing world trade? *(Panama Canal opened)*

Don't Miss!

Comparing Viewpoints
Is Technology a Blessing or a Curse? (Section 1)

You Are There . . .
Sipping Tea in a Victorian Parlor (Section 3)

Life in the Industrial Age 1800–1914

Chapter Preview

1 The Industrial Revolution Spreads
2 The World of Cities
3 Changing Attitudes and Values
4 A New Culture

TIME LINE

Early 1800s
Romanticism shapes western art and literature. Painters such as J.M.W. Turner seek to glorify nature and stir powerful emotions.

1807
First factories open in Belgium, setting off the Industrial Revolution on the European continent.

1839
French inventor Louis Daguerre perfects an effective method of photography.

CHAPTER EVENTS

1790 — 1815 — 1840

GLOBAL EVENTS

1819 Simón Bolívar establishes Gran Colombia.

1842 The Treaty of Nanjing gives Britain trading rights in China.

542 *Chapter 22*

Resource Directory

Teaching Resources
Chapter Theme Activities Teaching With Themes booklet, p. 25
Pacing Chart With Block Scheduling Guide Ch. 22
Technology
World History Color Transparencies Ch. 22 Graphic Organizer, p. F–45

Industrial Growth, 1800–1900

From its beginnings in eighteenth-century Britain, the Industrial Revolution spread through Europe and beyond.

Map legend:
- Industrializing by 1800
- Industrializing by 1850
- Industrializing by 1900

Robinson Projection

0   1500   3000 Miles
0   1500   3000 Kilometers

1859
Charles Darwin publishes *On the Origin of Species*. His theory of evolution is denounced by many religious leaders.

1869
Germany legalizes labor unions.

1903
Wilbur and Orville Wright demonstrate the first airplane at Kitty Hawk, North Carolina.

1861 Czar Alexander II emancipates Russian serfs.

1884 European nations carve up Africa at the Berlin Conference.

1914 The Panama Canal opens.

1865   1890   1915

Chapter 22 **543**

Independent Assignments

Have students read one section as they prepare for class. After class, have them complete the assignment. Some students may benefit from using the Guided Reading and Review worksheets.

Section 1 Have students use the outline map *Europe About 1870* in the Historical Outline Map Book, p. 34, to identify countries and cities and to indicate locations of iron ore deposits and coal fields.

Section 2 Have students use the worksheet *The People of Paris Earn a Living* in the Unit 6 booklet, p. 11, to learn more about the differences between business owners and workers.

Section 3 Have students read an excerpt from *Pride and Prejudice* in the History Through Literature booklet, pp. 47–48, to learn more about the manners and social distinctions of the British middle and upper classes.

Section 4 Have students use the worksheet *Julia Margaret Cameron* in the Unit 6 booklet, p. 10, to learn more about how this English woman helped develop photography as a new art.

Industrial Growth, 1800–1900

Activating Prior Knowledge
Why was Britain the first place to industrialize? *(It had a large supply of coal and iron, a large number of displaced agricultural workers, new technology, and the right economic conditions.)*

Previewing
What factors might explain why western nations came to dominate the world more than ever before during this time? *(Those countries industrialized before eastern nations did.)*

Background
About the Pictures

1. This painting, *Fisherman Upon a Lee Shore,* by English artist J. M. W. Turner (1775–1851), reflects light and color to reveal the new romantic interpretation of nature. It also foreshadows impressionism.

2. This early daguerreotype of a family, c. 1850, represents hi-tech photography in the mid-nineteenth century. Developed by Louis-Jacques-Mandé Daguerre and Joseph-Nicéphore Niepce, daguerreotypes were the first successful photography.

3. This Rosewood-veneered daguerreotype camera, 1845, represented a great advance in photography. Earlier photographs required up to eight hours exposure time; daguerreotypes needed only 20 to 30 minutes.

4. Charles Darwin, the subject of this John Collier (1850–1934) painting, is best known as author of *On the Origin of Species* and *The Descent of Man,* which detailed the role of natural selection in human evolution.

5. This first successful heavier-than-air aircraft, built by the Wright brothers, is on display at the Smithsonian Institution.

Be sure to check out this month's online discussion with a World History Master Teacher.

Go to **www.phschool.com**.

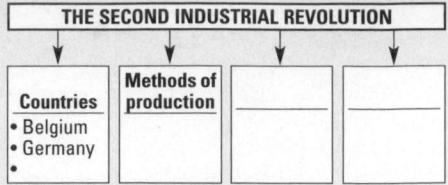

Bell Ringer

Ask students to preview this section by scanning its pictures, maps, and boldface heads. Have them write at least five questions that they believe they will be able to answer by studying this section.

LESSON PLAN

1. Focus During the 1800s, the United States, Japan, and several European countries joined Britain in the Industrial Revolution. New machines and scientific advances helped business grow. Large companies developed new ways to get the capital they needed. The leaders of big business created monopolies and trusts that controlled entire industries.

2. Instruct Divide the class into small groups. Tell students to imagine that they are living in the 1800s and are members of a commission that will decide the contents of a time capsule. The time capsule, scheduled to be opened by people of the twenty-first century, should reveal the changes that the industrialized world experienced in the 1800s. The time capsule should contain 10 to 15 items. It may include artifacts, maps, graphs, photographs, artworks, and documents. Each commission should list the contents of its time capsule. They should also write a clear description of the nature and significance of each item. Have the groups take turns presenting their lists to the class.

3. Assess Ask students to read aloud the questions that they prepared as part of their Bell Ringer activity. Invite volunteers to answer the questions based on what they have learned in this section.

4. Reteach If students' Assess activity does not reflect adequate understanding of the lesson, you might assign the *Guide to the Essentials* or the *Interactive Student Tutorial CD-ROM* for this section.

Reading Focus

- What industrial powers emerged in the 1800s?
- What impact did new technology have on industry, transportation, and communication?
- How did big business emerge in the late 1800s?

Vocabulary

dynamo
interchangeable parts
assembly line
stock
corporation
cartel

Taking Notes

Copy the diagram below. As you read, fill in the major developments of the Industrial Revolution.

THE SECOND INDUSTRIAL REVOLUTION

Countries	Methods of production		
• Belgium • Germany •			

Main Idea The second Industrial Revolution was marked by the spread of industry, the development of new technologies, and the rise of big business.

Setting the Scene By the 1880s, steel had replaced steam as the great symbol of the Industrial Revolution. Steel girders could support stronger bridges and taller buildings. Steel rails could carry faster steel railway cars. In huge steel mills, visitors watched with awe as tons of molten metal were poured into giant mixers:

> "At night the scene is indescribably wild and beautiful. The flashing fireworks, the terrific gusts of heat, the gaping, glowing mouth of the giant chest, the quivering light from the liquid iron, the roar of a near-by converter . . . combine to produce an effect on the mind that no words can translate."
> —J. H. Bridge, *History of the Carnegie Steel Company*

The first phase of industrialization had largely been forged from iron, powered by steam engines, and driven by the British textile industry. By the mid-1800s, the Industrial Revolution entered a new phase. New industrial powers emerged. New factories powered by new sources of energy used new processes to turn out new products. And new forms of business organization contributed to the rise of giant new companies. As the twentieth century dawned, this second Industrial Revolution transformed the economies of the western world.

New Industrial Powers

During the early Industrial Revolution, Britain stood alone as the world's industrial giant. To protect its head start, Britain tried to enforce strict rules against exporting inventions.

For a while, the rules worked. Then, in 1807, British mechanic William Cockerill opened factories in Belgium to manufacture spinning and weaving machines. Belgium became the first European nation outside Britain to industrialize. By the mid-1800s, other nations had joined the race, and several newcomers were challenging Britain's industrial supremacy.

The New Pacesetters How were other nations able to catch up to Britain so quickly? First, nations such as Germany, France, and the United States had more abundant supplies of coal, iron, and other resources than did Britain. Also, they had the advantage of being able to follow Britain's lead. Like Belgium, latecomers often borrowed British experts or technology. The first American textile factory was built in Pawtucket, Rhode Island, with

Resource Directory

Teaching Resources

Creative Teaching Activities Creative Teaching Activities booklet, p. 98
Guided Reading and Review Unit 6 booklet, p. 2

plans smuggled out of Britain. American inventor Robert Fulton powered his steamboat with one of James Watt's steam engines.

Two countries in particular thrust their way to industrial leadership. Germany united into a powerful nation in 1871. (See the next chapter.) Within a few decades, it became Europe's leading industrial power. Across the Atlantic, the United States advanced even more rapidly, especially after the Civil War. By 1900, American industry led the world in production.

Uneven Development Other nations industrialized more slowly, particularly those in eastern and southern Europe. These nations often lacked natural resources or the capital to invest in industry. Although Russia did have resources, social and political conditions slowed its economic development. Only in the late 1800s, more than 100 years after Britain, did Russia lumber toward industrialization.

In East Asia, however, Japan offered a remarkable success story. Although it lacked many basic resources, it industrialized rapidly after 1868. Canada, Australia, and New Zealand also built thriving industries.

Impact Like Britain, the new industrial nations underwent social changes, such as rapid urbanization. Men, women, and children worked long hours in difficult and dangerous conditions. As you will read, by 1900, these conditions had begun to improve in many industrialized nations.

The factory system produced huge quantities of new goods at lower prices than ever before. In time, workers were buying goods that in earlier times only the wealthy could afford. The demand for goods created jobs, as did the building of cities, railroads, and factories. Politics changed, too, as leaders had to meet the demands of an industrial society.

Globally, industrial nations competed fiercely, altering patterns of world trade. Thanks to their technological and economic advantage, western powers came to dominate the world more than ever before, as you will read.

Skills Assessment

Geography Deposits of raw material such as iron and coal could be the key to a nation's industrial success.

1. **Location** On the map, locate (a) Belgium, (b) Germany, (c) Saar, (d) Ruhr.
2. **Interaction** Which American city probably grew because of its location near coal fields?
3. **Critical Thinking Applying Information** Why would you expect Lyon, France, to become a major industrial city?

Centers of Industry, 1871

United States

CANADA
Boston
Pittsburgh • New York
ATLANTIC OCEAN
Gulf of Mexico
0   500   1000 Miles
0   500   1000 Kilometers
MEXICO

Glasgow
Newcastle
North Sea
SWEDEN
IRELAND
GREAT
Liverpool • Manchester
BRITAIN
Birmingham
London
DENMARK
Hamburg
NETH.
Berlin
Brussels
RUHR
GERMANY
RUSSIA
BELG.
Frankfurt
Dresden
LUX.
SAAR
Paris
Loire R.
FRANCE
Munich
Vienna
Limoges
Lyon
SWITZ.
AUSTRIA-HUNGARY
ATLANTIC OCEAN
Marseille
PORTUGAL
SPAIN
Madrid
Barcelona
ITALY
Rome
Mediterranean Sea

Azimuthal Equal Area Projection
0   200   400 Miles
0   200   400 Kilometers

• Major industrial cities
■ Iron ore deposits
▨ Coal fields

Skills Assessment

ANSWERS 1. Review locations with students. **2.** Pittsburgh **3.** It was located near both coal fields and iron ore deposits.

Technology and Industry

During the early Industrial Revolution, inventions such as the steam engine were generally the work of gifted tinkerers. They experimented with simple machines to make them better. By the 1880s, the pace of change quickened as companies hired professional chemists and engineers to create new products and machinery. The marriage of science, technology, and industry spurred economic growth.

Steel In 1856, British engineer Henry Bessemer developed a process to purify iron ore and produce a new substance, steel. Steel was lighter, harder, and more durable than iron. Others improved on the Bessemer process, so steel could be produced very cheaply. It rapidly became the major material used in tools, bridges, and railroads.

As steel production soared, industrialized countries measured their success in steel output. In 1880, for example, the average German steel mill produced less than five million metric tons of steel a year. By 1910, that figure had reached nearly fifteen million metric tons.

Chemicals Chemists created hundreds of new products, from medicines such as aspirin to perfumes and soaps. Newly developed chemical fertilizers played a key role in increasing food production.

In 1866, the Swedish chemist Alfred Nobel invented dynamite, an explosive much safer than others used at the time. It was widely used in construction and, to Nobel's dismay, in warfare. Dynamite earned Nobel a huge fortune, which he willed to fund the famous Nobel prizes that are still awarded today.

Electricity In the late 1800s, a new power source—electricity—replaced steam as the dominant source of industrial power. Scientists like Benjamin Franklin had tinkered with electricity a century earlier. The Italian scientist Alessandro Volta developed the first battery about 1800. Later, the English chemist Michael Faraday created the first simple electric motor and the first dynamo, a machine that generates electricity. Today, all electrical generators and transformers work on the principle of Faraday's dynamo.

In the 1870s, the American inventor Thomas Edison made the first electric light bulb. Soon, Edison's "incandescent lamps" illuminated whole cities. The pace of city life quickened, and factories could continue to operate after dark. By the 1890s, cables carried electrical power from dynamos to factories.

New Methods of Production The basic features of the factory system remained the same during the 1800s. Factories still used large numbers of workers and power-driven machines to mass-produce goods. To improve efficiency, however, manufacturers designed products with interchangeable parts, identical components that could be used in place of one another. Interchangeable parts simplified both assembly and repair.

By the early 1900s, manufacturers introduced another new method of production, the assembly line. Workers on an assembly line add parts to a product that moves along a belt from one work station to the next. Like interchangeable parts, the assembly line made production faster and cheaper, lowering the price of goods.

Technology Speeds Transportation and Communication

During the second Industrial Revolution, transportation and communications were transformed by technology. Steamships replaced sailing ships, and railroad building took off. In Europe and North America, rail lines connected inland cities and seaports, mining regions and industrial centers. In

Is Technology a Blessing or a Curse?

After the second Industrial Revolution, technology began to have an increasing influence on people's lives. Does technology always benefit us, or can it have some harmful effects? Think about the influence of technology as you compare the following viewpoints.

United States 1876

Writer William Dean Howells attended the Centennial Exposition in Philadelphia. He marveled at Machinery Hall, filled with examples of recent American technology:

❝ The superior elegance, aptness, and ingenuity of our machinery is observable at a glance. Yes, it is still in these things of iron and steel that the national genius speaks most freely; by and by the inspired marbles, the breathing canvases, the great literature [will be recognized]; for the present America is [expressed] in the strong metals and their infinite uses. ❞

India 1955

After India's independence, Prime Minister Jawaharlal Nehru commented on its need for industrial development:

❝ There can be no real well-being or advance in material standards in India without the big factory. I shall venture to say that we cannot even maintain our freedom and independence as a nation without the big factory and all it represents. ❞

South Africa 1988

This cartoon uses imagery borrowed from the pyramid builders of ancient Egypt to comment on modern technology.

BERRY *THE STAR* Johannesburg SOUTH AFRICA

Japan 1984

Ikeda Daisaku spoke of the effects of technology from the viewpoint of a Buddhist philosopher:

❝ The man who rides in a car all of the time loses the ability to walk long distances vigorously. Even when we employ mechanical devices, we must realize that it is we humans who are at the controls and that whether the machine is a blessing or a curse depends on what is inside us. ❞

Background
Other Viewpoints

Ireland 1895 Writer and wit Oscar Wilde wrote:

"The fact is, that civilization requires slaves.... Unless there are slaves to do the ugly, horrible, uninteresting work, culture and contemplation become almost impossible. Human slavery is wrong, insecure, and demoralizing. On mechanical slavery, on the slavery of the machine, the future of the world depends."

Iran 1964 Ruhollah Khomeini, a Muslim reformer, belittled the West's technological progress:

"Let them go all the way to Mars or beyond the Milky Way; they will still be deprived of true happiness.... For the solution of social problems and the relief of human misery require foundations in faith and morals; merely acquiring material power and wealth, conquering nature and space, have no effect in this regard."

Activity
Interpreting Viewpoints

Critical Thinking: Comparing Use these additional questions to generate class discussion.

1. Which views represented here seem least critical of modern technology? *(those of Howells and Nehru)*

2. How does Ikeda Daisaku's view of western technology differ from William Dean Howells's? *(Daisaku recognizes the potential of machines to control us; Howells sees technology as an expression of American genius.)*

Skills Assessment

1. The viewpoints most favorable toward technology are expressed by
   A Howells and Daisaku.
   B Nehru and Daisaku.
   C Howells and Nehru.
   D Nehru and the cartoon.

2. Ikeda Daisaku would probably agree with the cartoonist that technology
   E can rule people.
   F expresses the ideals of a nation.
   G is key to economic development.
   H is always destructive.

3. **Critical Thinking Making Decisions** Decide whether you think technology is a blessing or a curse in today's society. Write a short essay explaining your point of view. Be sure to provide several clear examples to support your decision.

Skills Tip

A person's point of view may be influenced by such factors as time and place of birth, historical period, occupation, economic status, religious values, and political opinions.

✔ Test Preparation

Have students read the viewpoint titled "Japan" on this page, and then complete the sentence below.

The word *vigorously* means
Ⓐ energetically.
B quietly.
C directly.
D slowly.

Skills Tip

Tell students to look at the country, date, and biographical information about the speaker for clues to the factors that can influence point of view. The Skills Handbook in the front of the book has a lesson that will help students with this feature.

Skills Assessment

ANSWERS 1. C **2.** E **3.** Students' answers should have a clearly expressed opinion supported by several examples.

Radio Broadcasting The first known radio program in the United States was aired in 1906 on Christmas Eve. Originating from Brant Rock, Massachusetts, the program consisted of two musical selections, a poem, and a short talk for the benefit of wireless operators at sea. During World War I, growth of the radio industry was limited by a government ban on nonmilitary broadcasting. After the war, however, the industry developed rapidly. The first commercial radio station was KDKA, which began operating in Pittsburgh in 1920. Within two years, more than 550 stations were on the air.

Ford's Automobile Assembly Line
The use of the assembly line allowed cars to be produced more quickly and cheaply. These pictures show three stages in the creation of the Ford Model T.

Theme: Economics and Technology Based on these pictures, what words would you use to describe working on an assembly line?

the United States, a transcontinental railroad provided rail service from the Atlantic to the Pacific. In the same way, Russians built the Trans-Siberian Railroad, linking Moscow in European Russia to Vladivostok on the Pacific. Railroad tunnels and bridges crossed the Alps in Europe and the Andes in South America. Passengers and goods rode on rails in India, China, Egypt, and South Africa.

The Automobile Age Begins The transportation revolution took a new turn when a German engineer, Nikolaus Otto, invented a gasoline-powered internal combustion engine. In 1886, Karl Benz received a patent for the first automobile, which had three wheels. A year later, Gottlieb Daimler (DĪM luhr) introduced the first four-wheeled automobile. People laughed at the "horseless carriages," which quickly transformed transportation.

The French nosed out the Germans as early automakers. Then the American Henry Ford started making models that reached the breathtaking speed of 25 miles an hour. In the early 1900s, Ford began using the assembly line to mass-produce cars, making the United States a leader in the automobile industry.

Conquest of the Air The internal combustion engine powered more than cars. Motorized threshers and reapers boosted farm production. Even more dramatically, the internal combustion engine made possible the dream of human flight. In 1903, two American bicycle makers, Orville and Wilbur Wright, designed and flew a flimsy airplane at Kitty Hawk, North Carolina. Although their flying machine stayed aloft for only a few seconds, it ushered in the air age.

Soon, daredevil pilots were flying airplanes across the English Channel and over the Alps. Commercial passenger travel, however, would not begin until the 1920s.

Rapid Communication A revolution in communications also made the world smaller. An American inventor, Samuel F. B. Morse, developed the telegraph, which could send coded messages over wires by means of electricity. His first telegraph line went into service between Baltimore and Washington, D.C., in 1844. By the 1860s, an undersea cable was relaying messages between Europe and North America.

Communication soon became even faster. In 1876, the Scottish-born American inventor Alexander Graham Bell patented the telephone. By the

Unfinished car frames move along a belt.

At this station, workers attach the engine.

Possible answers: efficient, fast, boring

1890s, the Italian pioneer Guglielmo Marconi had invented the radio. In 1901, Marconi transmitted a radio message from Britain to Canada, using Morse's dot-and-dash code. Radio would become a cornerstone of today's global communications network that links every corner of the world.

New Directions for Business

New technologies required the investment of large amounts of money. To get the needed capital, entrepreneurs developed new ways of organizing businesses. Owners sold stock, or shares in their companies, to investors. Each stockholder thus became owner of a tiny part of a company.

Rise of Big Business By the late 1800s, what we call "big business" came to dominate industry. Large-scale companies such as steel foundries needed so much capital that they sold hundreds of thousands of shares. These businesses formed giant corporations, businesses that are owned by many investors who buy shares of stock. Stockholders risk only the amount they invest in the company and cannot be held personally responsible for any debts of the corporation.

With large amounts of capital, corporations could expand into many areas. In the novel *Germinal* by the French writer Émile Zola, two investors discuss the growth of a large coal mining company. "And is your company rich?" one asks. "Ah! yes. Ah! yes," the other replies:

> "Ten thousand workers, concessions reaching over sixty-seven towns, an output of five thousand tons a day, a railway joining all the pits, and workshops, and factories! Ah! yes! Ah, yes! There's money there!"
>
> —Émile Zola, *Germinal*

Move Toward Monopolies Powerful business leaders created monopolies and trusts, huge corporate structures that controlled entire industries or areas of the economy. In Germany, Alfred Krupp inherited a steelmaking business from his father. He bought up coal and iron mines as well as ore-shipping lines that fed the steel business. Later, he and his son acquired plants that made tools, railroad cars, and weapons. In the United States, John D. Rockefeller built Standard Oil Company of Ohio into an empire. By

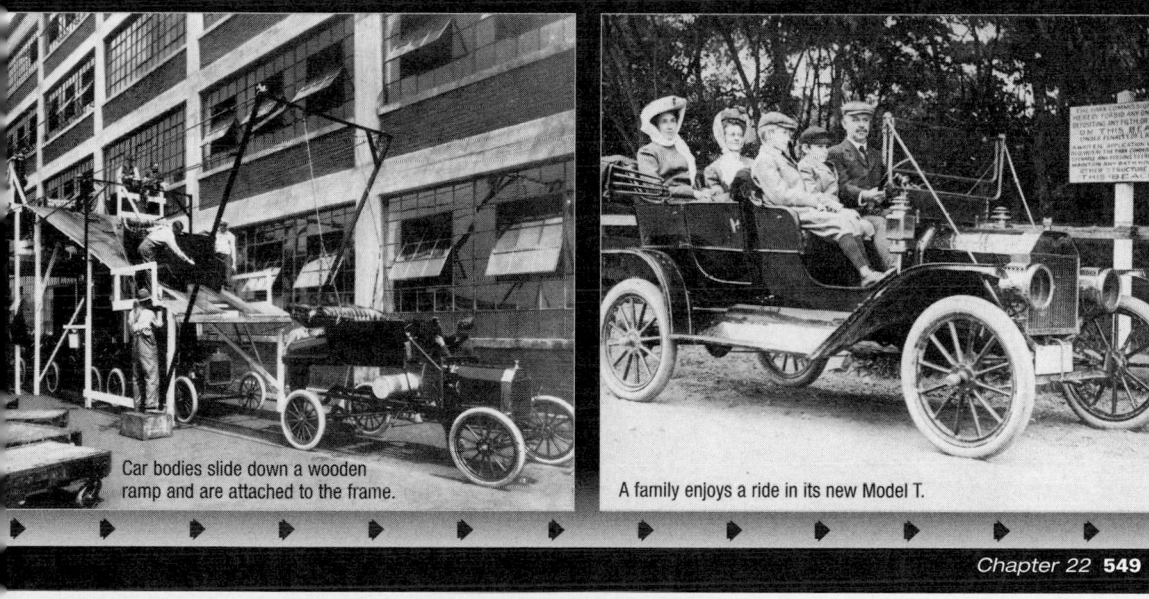

Car bodies slide down a wooden ramp and are attached to the frame.

A family enjoys a ride in its new Model T.

One View of Big Business
To some critics, the growth of monopolies had a dangerous effect on society. This American cartoon of 1899 shows a monopoly as an octopus-like monster.

Theme: Economics and Technology Do you think this cartoonist favored or opposed government regulation of business? Explain.

gaining control of oil wells, oil refineries, and oil pipelines, he dominated the American petroleum industry.

In their pursuit of profit, ruthless business leaders destroyed competing companies. Then, with the competition gone, they were free to raise prices to any level. Sometimes, a group of large corporations would join forces and form a cartel, an association to fix prices, set production quotas, or control markets. In Germany, a single cartel fixed prices for 170 coal mines. An international shipping cartel of British, German, French, Dutch, and Japanese shippers came close to setting freight rates on the sea lines of the world.

Move Toward Regulation The rise of big business and the creation of such great wealth sparked a stormy debate. Some people saw the Krupps and Rockefellers as "captains of industry" and praised their vision and skills. They pointed out that capitalists invested their wealth in worldwide ventures, such as railroad building, that employed thousands of workers and added to the general prosperity.

To others, the aggressive magnates were "robber barons." Any effort to destroy competition, critics argued, damaged the free-enterprise system. Reformers called for laws to prevent monopolies and regulate large corporations. By the early 1900s, some governments did move against monopolies. However, the political and economic power of business leaders often hindered efforts at regulation.

Looking Ahead

By the late 1800s, European and American corporations were setting up factories, refineries, and other production facilities around the world. Banks, too, were involved in this global economy. They invested vast sums—the money coming from rich and small depositors—in undertakings such as building ports, railroads, and canals. As western capital flowed into Africa, Asia, and Latin America, western governments became increasingly involved in these areas.

SECTION 1 Assessment

Recall
1. **Identify:** (a) Bessemer process, (b) Alfred Nobel, (c) Michael Faraday, (d) Thomas Edison, (e) Henry Ford, (f) Orville and Wilbur Wright, (g) Guglielmo Marconi, (h) Alfred Krupp.
2. **Define:** (a) dynamo, (b) interchangeable parts, (c) assembly line, (d) stock, (e) corporation, (f) cartel.

Comprehension
3. How did the Industrial Revolution spread in the 1800s?

4. How did technology help industry expand?
5. How did the need for capital lead to new business methods?

Critical Thinking and Writing
6. **Connecting to Geography** "The availability of natural resources is the most important condition for industrialization." Do you agree or disagree? Explain.
7. **Ranking** Which three technological advances in this section do you think were the most important? Explain.

Activity
Drawing a Political Cartoon Draw a political cartoon that might have appeared in a newspaper in the late 1800s. In your cartoon, take a stand for or against the passage of laws to prevent monopolies or regulate big business.

Resource Directory

Teaching Resources
Section Quiz Unit 6 booklet, p. 3
Creative Teaching Activities Creative Teaching Activities booklet, p. 99
Guided Reading and Review Unit 6 booklet, p. 4

Technology
Interactive Student Tutorial CD-ROM Ch. 22
Computer Test Bank Ch. 22

Reading Focus

- What was the impact of medical advances in the late 1800s?

- How had cities changed by 1900?

- How did working-class struggles lead to improved conditions for workers?

Vocabulary

germ theory

urban renewal

mutual-aid society

standard of living

Taking Notes

As you read, prepare an outline of this section. Use Roman numerals to indicate the major headings, capital letters for the subheadings, and numbers for the supporting details. The sample at right will help you get started.

I. Medicine and population
  A. The fight against disease
    1.
    2.
  B. In the hospital
    1.
    2.
II. The life of the cities

Main Idea   The population of cities grew as people moved to urban centers for jobs.

Setting the Scene   In the 1870s, a citizen of Berlin, Germany, boasted of his city's rapid growth. "We have already 800,000 inhabitants, next year we shall have 900,000, and the year after that a million." He predicted that Berlin's population would soon rival those of Paris and even London.

The population explosion that had begun during the 1700s continued through the 1800s. Cities grew as rural people streamed into urban areas. By the end of the century, European and American cities had begun to take on many of the features of cities today.

Medicine and Population

Between 1800 and 1900, the population of Europe more than doubled. This rapid growth was not due to larger families. In fact, families in most industrializing countries had fewer children. Instead, populations soared because the death rate fell. People ate better, thanks in part to improved methods of farming, food storage, and distribution. Medical advances and improvements in public sanitation also slowed death rates.

The Fight Against Disease   Since the 1600s, scientists had known of microscopic organisms, or microbes. Some scientists speculated that certain microbes might cause specific infectious diseases. Yet most doctors scoffed at this germ theory. Not until 1870 did French chemist Louis Pasteur clearly show the link between microbes and disease. Pasteur went on to make other major contributions, including the development of vaccines against rabies and anthrax and the discovery of a process called pasteurization, named after him, for killing disease-carrying microbes in milk.

In the 1880s, the German doctor Robert Koch identified the bacteria that caused tuberculosis, a respiratory disease that claimed about 30 million human lives in the 1800s. The search for a tuberculosis cure, however, took half a century. By 1914, yellow fever and malaria had been traced to microbes carried by mosquitoes.

As people understood how germs caused disease, they bathed and changed their clothes more often. In western cities, better hygiene caused a marked drop in the rate of disease and death.

FACT FINDER

Average Life Expectancy in Selected Industrial Areas, 1850–1910

Year	Male	Female
1850	40.3 years	42.8 years
1870	42.3 years	44.7 years
1890	45.8 years	48.5 years
1910	52.7 years	56.0 years

Source: E. A. Wrigley, *Population and History* (based on data for parts of Western Europe and the United States)

Skills Assessment

Chart Improved medicine and sanitation played a major role in increasing life expectancy in the industrialized world. **Between 1850 and 1910, how much did life expectancy increase for men? For women?**

Bell Ringer Ask students to consider the nature of city life today. Have them list advantages and disadvantages of living in a big city.

LESSON PLAN

1. Focus Advances in medicine extended life expectancy in the 1800s. The population of cities soared as people flocked to urban centers for jobs. New wealth enabled cities to provide improved living conditions and cultural opportunities. For the poor, however, life in urban slums remained harsh. Conditions for workers gradually improved as the efforts of labor unions and government leaders brought reforms.

2. Instruct Divide the class into groups. Ask them to imagine that they are living during the 1800s and working as tour guides in a major city. Their assignment is to plan a tour of a typical city of the late 1800s. To make their tour more realistic and interesting, they may wish to do research on a specific city such as London, Paris, Berlin, or Vienna. They should note the places that their tour will visit, and they should draft a script telling what they will say about each place. Remind students that their tour should go through parts of the city inhabited by both the rich and the poor. When students have finished, invite them to take the class on their tours.

3. Assess Ask students to write two paragraphs describing life in a European city of the late 1800s. Have them write one paragraph from the perspective of a middle-class or upper-class person and the other paragraph from the perspective of a working-class person.

4. Reteach If students' **Assess** activity does not reflect adequate understanding of the lesson, you might assign the *Guide to the Essentials* or the *Interactive Student Tutorial CD-ROM* for this section.

Skills Assessment

ANSWERS men: a little over 12 years; women: a little over 13 years

---

Block Scheduling Support

During the Industrial Revolution, life changed drastically. Have students complete the Viewpoint Activity *Looking at London in the 1820s* in the Unit 6 booklet, p. 12, in which Thomas Carlyle and Felix Mendelssohn record their views of London in the early nineteenth century. Initiate a class discussion that examines life in a contemporary large city with which students are familiar. Ask students to give their impressions of the city, comparing point for point Carlyle's and Mendelssohn's observations. Have students evaluate whether they think things have changed much in large industrial centers between the 1820s and the 2000s. Some points to compare include noise, animals, crowds, excitement, agitation, chaos, order, nature, cleanliness, visual clutter, and traffic. Then ask students to write a descriptive paragraph modeled on one of the readings in which they describe in vivid words a city they have experienced. Have volunteers read their paragraphs to the class.

Biography

Florence Nightingale
1820–1910

When Florence Nightingale arrived at a British military hospital in the Crimea in 1854, she was horrified by what she saw. The sick and wounded lay on bare ground. With no sanitation and a shortage of food, some 60 percent of all patients died. But Nightingale was a fighter. Bullying the military and medical staff, she soon had every available person cleaning barracks, digging latrines, doing laundry, and caring for the wounded. Six months later, the death rate had dropped to 2 percent.

Back in England, Nightingale was hailed as a saint. Ballads were even written about her. She took advantage of her popularity and connections to pressure the government for reforms.

Nightingale lived most of the last 50 years of her life as an invalid. Yet from her couch, she continued to write letters and reports and to command her vast network of supporters.

Theme: Impact of the Individual How did Nightingale achieve reforms in British army hospitals?

In the Hospital In the early 1840s, anesthesia was first used to relieve pain during surgery. The use of anesthetics allowed doctors to experiment with operations that had never before been possible.

Yet, throughout the century, hospitals could be dangerous places. Surgery was performed with dirty instruments in dank operating rooms. Often, a patient would survive an operation, only to die days later of infection. For the poor, being admitted to a hospital was often a death sentence. Wealthy or middle-class patients insisted on treatment in their own homes.

"The very first requirement in a hospital," said British nurse Florence Nightingale, "is that it should do the sick no harm." As an army nurse during the Crimean War, Nightingale insisted on better hygiene in field hospitals. After the war, she worked to introduce sanitary measures in British hospitals. She also founded the world's first school of nursing.

The English surgeon Joseph Lister discovered how antiseptics prevented infection. He insisted that surgeons wash their hands before operating and sterilize their instruments. Eventually, the use of antiseptics drastically reduced deaths from infection.

The Life of the Cities

As industrialization progressed, cities came to dominate the West. City life, as old as civilization itself, underwent dramatic changes.

The Changing City Landscape Growing wealth and industrialization altered the basic layout of western cities. City planners gouged out spacious new squares and boulevards. They lined these avenues with government buildings, offices, department stores, and theaters.

The most extensive urban renewal, or rebuilding of the poor areas of a city, took place in Paris in the 1850s. Georges Haussmann, chief planner for Napoleon III, destroyed many tangled medieval streets full of tenement housing. In their place, he built wide boulevards and splendid public buildings. The project put many people to work, decreasing the threat of social unrest. The wide boulevards also made it harder for rebels to put up barricades and easier for troops to reach any part of the city.

Gradually, settlement patterns shifted. In most American cities, the rich lived in pleasant neighborhoods on the outskirts of the city. The poor crowded into slums near the city center, within reach of factories. Trolley lines made it possible to live in one part of the city and work in another.

Sidewalks, Sewers, and Skyscrapers Paved streets made urban areas much more livable. First gas lamps, then electric street lights, increased safety at night. Cities organized police forces and expanded fire protection.

Beneath the streets, sewage systems made cities healthier places to live. City planners knew that clean water supplies were needed to combat epidemics of cholera and tuberculosis. The massive new sewer systems of London and Paris were costly, but they cut death rates dramatically.

By 1900, architects were using steel to construct soaring buildings. The steel Eiffel Tower became a symbol of Paris. American architects like Louis Sullivan pioneered a new structure, the skyscraper. In large cities, single-family middle-class homes gave way to multistory apartment buildings.

Slums Despite efforts to improve cities, urban life remained harsh for the poor. Some working-class families could afford better clothing, newspapers, or tickets to a music hall. But they went home to small, cramped row houses or tenements in overcrowded neighborhoods.

In the worst tenements, whole families were often crammed into a single room. Unemployment or illness meant lost wages that could ruin a family. High rates of crime and alcoholism were a constant curse. Conditions had improved somewhat from the early Industrial Revolution, but slums remained a fact of city life.

The Lure of the City Despite their drawbacks, cities attracted millions. New residents were drawn as much by the excitement as by the promise of work. For tourists, too, cities were magnetic centers of action. One reporter described the hustle and bustle of holiday crowds in London:

> "Cyclists of both sexes covered the roads. River steamers and pleasure boats carried their thousands to Kew and the upper reaches of the Thames. The London parks were crowded. The Botanic Gardens and Zoological Gardens formed great attractions, and the flowers of Battersea Park drew large crowds all day."
>
> —*Times* (London), quoted in *Crises in English History, 1066–1945* (Henning)

Music halls, opera houses, and theaters provided entertainment for every taste. Museums and libraries offered educational opportunities. Sports, from tennis to bare-knuckle boxing, drew citizens of all classes. Few of these enjoyments were available in country villages.

Working-Class Struggles

Workers tried to improve the harsh conditions of industrial life. They protested low wages, long hours, unsafe conditions, and the constant threat of unemployment. At first, business owners and governments tried to silence protesters. Strikes and unions were illegal. Demonstrations were crushed.

By mid-century, workers slowly began to make progress. They formed mutual-aid societies, self-help groups to aid sick or injured workers. Men and women joined socialist parties or organized unions. The revolutions of 1830 and 1848 left vivid images of worker discontent.

By the late 1800s, most western countries had granted all men the vote. Workers also won the right to organize unions to bargain on their behalf.

The Lure of a City
The photograph of Paris in 1900 (bottom) shows two of its most famous attractions—the Eiffel Tower and a giant Ferris wheel. The city also won worldwide fame for its theaters, music halls, museums, and circuses.

Theme: Continuity and Change How might this photograph of Paris look different if it were taken today?

553

Background
Connections to Art

Psychological Horror Some artists saw the darker side of the new industrial city. Edvard Munch believed that impressionism's interest in colorful landscapes failed to address the "inner landscape" of man. Munch felt that artists should express the complexity of the human psyche and its depth of emotions. A forerunner of modern expressionists, he replaced the realistic portrayal of people and nature with distorted figures and scenery based on emotional perceptions. By distorting the human form, Munch hoped to convey the alienation he believed permeated life—especially life in an industrial city. In the painting *Spring Evening on Karl Johan Street, Oslo,* Munch conveys emptiness by portraying the people as skeletal figures with wide eyes and expressionless faces. Munch's paintings were so dismal and haunting that in 1892, authorities in Berlin shut down a show displaying his works.

Human Drama Activity

Writing a Letter Ask students to imagine that they have moved from a rural village to London or Paris in the late 1800s. As working-class people, they have paid attention to the reform laws that were passed in this time. Have students write a letter home describing their feelings about city life and the reforms enacted to protect workers. Have students rank the reforms in the order of their importance and explain why they ranked the reforms in this particular order.

Test Preparation

Have students read the subsection titled "The Changing City Landscape" on the opposite page, and then answer the question below.

Which of the following was *not* a result of urban renewal?

A Settlement patterns shifted.

B Poor areas of cities were rebuilt.

C The rich lived near city centers.

D Many new jobs were created.

Caption Answer

Possible answer: Today, you might see cars and trucks on the road, taller buildings, fewer trees, and perhaps some signs of air pollution over the city.

Recall

1. (a) Louis Pasteur, p. 551 (b) Robert Koch, p. 551 (c) Florence Nightingale, p. 552 (d) Joseph Lister, p. 552 2. (a) germ theory, p. 551 (b) urban renewal, p. 552 (c) mutual-aid society p. 553 (d) standard of living, p. 554

Comprehension

3. People were eating better and practicing better hygiene. Medical discoveries were eliminating some diseases. 4. Possible answers: Paved streets, wide boulevards, and trolley lines made transportation easier. Gas and electric street lights increased safety at night. New sewer systems reduced the impact of waterborne diseases. 5. New laws allowed workers to unionize, expanded the right to vote, regulated working conditions, limited child labor, and set up old age pensions and disability insurance.

Critical Thinking and Writing

6. Advantages might include jobs, entertainment, museums and libraries, sports and medical facilities. Disadvantages might include crowded housing, poverty, crime, and disease. 7. Students should recognize that laws continue to set limits on child labor, working hours and safety, wages, retirement pensions and disability insurance. They should also recognize that laws today go even farther in protecting the worker.

Activity Rubrics

Share rubrics with students before they write their letters.

Attempted The letter is incomplete or fails to describe the writer's feelings or express a viewpoint; it is messy.

Minimal The letter describes the writer's feelings and expresses a viewpoint but is poorly written and organized.

Adequate The letter describes the writer's feelings, expresses a viewpoint, and is well written and organized.

Exemplary The letter describes the writer's feelings, expresses a viewpoint, uses persuasive and historically accurate details, and is well written.

Skills Assessment

ANSWERS Social effects include urbanization and the expansion of the middle class. Economic effects include the growth of labor unions and the rise of big business.

Cause and Effect

Causes

- Increased agricultural productivity
- Growing population
- New sources of energy, such as steam and coal
- Growing demand for textiles and other mass-produced goods
- Improved technology
- Available natural resources, labor, and money
- Strong, stable governments that promoted economic growth

Industrial Revolution

Immediate Effects

- Rise of factories
- Changes in transportation and communication
- Urbanization
- New methods of production
- Rise of urban working class
- Growth of reform movements

Long-Term Effects

- Growth of labor unions
- Inexpensive new products
- Spread of industrialization
- Rise of big business
- Expansion of public education
- Expansion of middle class
- Competition for world trade among industrialized nations
- Progress in medical care

Connections to Today

- Improvements in world health
- Growth in population
- Industrialization in developing nations
- New energy sources, such as oil and nuclear power
- Mass media and mass entertainment
- Efforts to regulate world trade

Skills Assessment **Chart** The long-term effects of the Industrial Revolution touched nearly every aspect of life. **Identify two social and two economic effects of the Industrial Revolution.**

Germany legalized labor unions in 1869. Britain, Austria, and France followed. Unions grew rapidly. In France, membership grew from 140,000 in 1890 to over a million in 1912.

Pressured by unions, reformers, and working-class voters, governments passed laws to regulate working conditions. Over time, laws were passed outlawing child labor and banning the employment of women in mines. Other laws limited work hours and improved safety. By 1909, British coal miners had won an eight-hour day, setting a standard for workers in other countries.

First in Germany, and then elsewhere, western governments established old-age pensions, as well as disability insurance for workers who were hurt or became ill. These programs protected workers from poverty once they were no longer able to work.

Rising Standards of Living Wages varied throughout the industrialized world, with unskilled laborers earning much less than skilled workers. Women received less than half the pay of men doing the same work. Farm laborers barely scraped by during the economic slump of the late 1800s. Periods of unemployment brought desperate hardships to industrial workers and helped boost union membership.

Overall, though, standards of living for workers did rise. The standard of living measures the quality and availability of necessities and comforts in a society. Families ate more varied diets, lived in better homes, and dressed in inexpensive, mass-produced clothing. Advances in medicine improved health. Some workers moved to suburbs, traveling to work on subways and trams. Still, the gap between workers and the middle class widened.

SECTION 2 Assessment

Recall

1. **Identify:** (a) Louis Pasteur, (b) Robert Koch, (c) Florence Nightingale, (d) Joseph Lister.
2. **Define:** (a) germ theory, (b) urban renewal, (c) mutual-aid society, (d) standard of living.

Comprehension

3. Why did the rate of population growth increase in the late 1800s?
4. Describe three ways that city life changed in the 1800s.

5. What laws helped workers in the late 1800s?

Critical Thinking and Writing

6. **Analyzing Information** What were the advantages and disadvantages of city life in the late 1800s?
7. **Linking Past and Present** By the early 1900s, governments had passed many laws that improved conditions for the working class. What are some laws that regulate working conditions today?

Activity

Writing a Letter
You have moved from a rural village to London or Paris in the late 1800s. Write a letter home describing your feelings about city life. Suggest both positive and negative aspects.

Resource Directory

Teaching Resources

Section Quiz Unit 6 booklet, p. 5
Creative Teaching Activities Creative Teaching Activities booklet, p. 100
Guided Reading and Review Unit 6 booklet, p. 6

Technology

Interactive Student Tutorial CD-ROM Ch. 22
Computer Test Bank Ch. 22

Changing Attitudes and Values

Reading Focus

- What values shaped the new social order?
- How did women and educators seek change?
- How did science challenge existing beliefs?
- What role did religion play in urban society?

Vocabulary

cult of domesticity

temperance movement

women's suffrage

racism

social gospel

Taking Notes

Copy this chart. As you read, list new attitudes and values in the left-hand column. List supporting details in the right-hand column.

CHANGES IN ATTITUDES AND VALUES

1. A new social order	• Upper class—old nobility, new industrialists, and business families
2. Middle-class values	•
3.	•

Main Idea — The Industrial Revolution changed the social order in the western world, and new ideas challenged long-held traditions.

Setting the Scene

"Once a woman has accepted an offer of marriage, all she has . . . becomes virtually the property of the man she has accepted as husband." This advice appeared in an 1859 British publication called *The What-Not or Ladies' Handbook*. But not all women accepted such restrictions. One Italian crusader for women's rights denounced the inferior legal status of women:

"For her, taxes but not an education; for her, sacrifices but not employment; . . . strong enough to be laden with an array of painful duties, but sufficiently weak not to be allowed to govern herself."

—Anna Mazzoni, *La Liberazione della Donna*

Demand for women's rights was one of many issues that challenged the traditional social order in the late 1800s. By then, the social order itself was changing. In many countries, the middle class increasingly came to dominate society.

A New Social Order

The Industrial Revolution slowly changed the old social order in the western world. For centuries, the two main classes were nobles and peasants. Their roles were defined by their relationship to the land. While middle-class merchants, artisans, lawyers, and officials played important roles, they still occupied a secondary position in society. With the spread of industry, a more complex social structure emerged.

By the late 1800s, Western Europe's new upper class included superrich industrial and business families as well as the old nobility. Wealthy entrepreneurs married into aristocratic families, gaining the status of noble titles. Nobles needed the money brought by the industrial rich to support their lands and lifestyle. By tradition, the upper class held the top jobs in government and the military.

Below this tiny elite, a growing middle class was pushing its way up the social ladder. Its highest rungs were filled with midlevel business people and professionals such as doctors, scientists, and lawyers. With comfortable incomes, they enjoyed a wide range of material goods. Next came the lower middle class, which included teachers, office workers, shopkeepers, and clerks. Even though they earned much smaller incomes, they struggled to keep up with their "betters."

Chapter 22 **555**

SECTION 3

Bell Ringer Ask students to paraphrase the two quotations that appear at the beginning of this section. When they have finished, discuss with students the meaning of the two quotations. Ask students to describe how conditions for women have changed since the 1800s.

LESSON PLAN

1. Focus During the 1800s, wealthy industrialists and the old nobility comprised the upper class. The influential middle class consisted of professionals, shop owners, and office workers. Peasants and industrial workers made up the lower class. A strict code of behavior guided middle-class life. Women, meanwhile, struggled to gain political and economic rights. During this era, scientific advances challenged traditional beliefs.

2. Instruct Ask students to imagine that they are reporters for a newspaper or magazine of the 1800s that is devoting a special issue to the changing attitudes and values in society. Divide the class into four groups. Have students in one group write advice columns telling readers how to act, dress, and speak in middle-class society. Assign students in the second group to write editorials defending or opposing women's efforts at social reform. Have students in the third group write articles about the many changes taking place in education. Have the fourth group cover the debate between science and religion. Invite some students to read their articles aloud to the class. Display other articles around the class.

3. Assess Ask students to discuss how the attitudes and values of the late 1800s have survived or changed in western society today.

4. Reteach If students' Assess activity does not reflect adequate understanding of the lesson, you might assign the *Guide to the Essentials* or the *Interactive Student Tutorial CD-ROM* for this section.

Block Scheduling Support

Have students review the subsections "Middle-Class Values" and "Rights for Women" in this section. Divide the class into small discussion groups, and have them describe middle-class society's way of life and women's rebellion against the rigidity of social expectations. Encourage students to share their observations with the class. Then, ask students to imagine that they are living in the late 1800s. Have them write an editorial for the newspaper explaining why they agree or disagree with the conventional marriage arrangements and clearly defined roles of men and women in the 1800s. Encourage students to share their ideas with the class.

Using Fiction as Historical Evidence
Read aloud the following excerpt from *Buddenbrooks,* a novel published in 1901 by the German author Thomas Mann. Ask students to describe the middle-class customs and values that are revealed in the passage.

"The maid-servant passed the cabbage soup and toast, assisted by the maid from upstairs. The guests began to use their soup-spoons. . . . An enormous brick-red boiled ham appeared, strewn with crumbs and served with a sour brown onion sauce, and so many vegetables that the company could have satisfied their appetites from that one vegetable dish. . . . There they all sat, on heavy, high-backed chairs, consuming good heavy food from good heavy silver plates, drinking full-bodied wines and expressing their views freely on all subjects."

Did You Know?

The Proper Victorians

In England, the period from 1837 to 1901 is known as the Victorian Era because Queen Victoria's long reign spanned those years. Middle-class Victorians had a strict code of manners:

• In respectable Victorian homes, fabric drapes concealed piano legs, which, like people's legs, were considered immodest if shown.
• A widow was expected to dress in black from head to toe and never to remarry. In contrast, a widower wore a black crepe band around his hat or sleeve and was expected to find a new wife quickly.
• Wealthy businessmen wore knee-length frock coats and silk top hats to the office.
• Women wore suffocating corsets pulled tightly enough to achieve the ideal waist measurement of 18 to 20 inches.

Theme: Religions and Value Systems How did Victorian rules for men and women differ?

At the base of the social ladder were workers and peasants. In highly industrialized Britain, workers made up more than 30 percent of the population in 1900. In Western Europe and the United States, the number of farmworkers dropped, but many families still worked the land. The rural population was even higher in eastern and southern Europe, where industrialization was limited.

Middle-Class Values

By mid-century, the modern middle class had developed its own way of life. The nuclear family lived in a large house, or perhaps in one of the new apartment houses. Rooms were crammed with large overstuffed furniture, and paintings and photographs lined the walls. Clothing reflected middle-class tastes for luxury and respectability. A strict code of etiquette governed social behavior. Rules dictated how to dress for every occasion, how to give a dinner party, how to pay a social call, when to write letters, and how long to mourn for relatives who died.

Parents strictly supervised their children, who were expected to be "seen but not heard." A child who misbehaved was considered to reflect badly on the entire family. Servants, too, were seen as a reflection of their employers. Even a small middle-class household was expected to have at least a cook and a housemaid.

Courtship and Marriage As in the past, middle-class families had a large say in choosing whom their children married. At the same time, young people had more freedom to choose a marriage partner. The notion of "falling in love" was more accepted than ever before.

Yet most women and men carefully considered the practical side of marriage. Mothers and daughters discussed the "likely prospects" of a possible husband. A young man was expected to court his bride-to-be with tender sentiments, but he also had to convince her father that he could support her in style. Until the late 1800s in most western countries, a husband controlled his wife's property, so marriage contracts were drawn up to protect a daughter's property rights.

The Ideal Home Within the family circle, the division of labor between wife and husband changed. In earlier times, middle-class women had often helped run family businesses out of the home. By the later 1800s, most middle-class husbands went to work in an office or shop. A successful husband was one whose income was enough to keep his wife at home. Women spent their working hours raising children, directing the servants, and perhaps doing religious or charitable service.

Books, magazines, and popular songs supported a cult of domesticity that idealized women and the home. Sayings like "home, sweet home" were stitched into needlework and hung on parlor walls. The ideal woman was seen as a tender, self-sacrificing caregiver who provided a nest for her children and a peaceful refuge for her husband.

This ideal rarely applied to the lower classes. Working-class women labored for low pay in garment factories or worked as domestic servants. Young women might leave domestic service after they married but often had to seek other employment. Despite long days working for wages, they were still expected to take full responsibility for child care and homemaking.

Rights for Women

Some individual women and women's groups protested restrictions on women. Like earlier pioneers Olympe de Gouges and Mary Wollstonecraft, they sought a broad range of rights. Across Europe and the United States, politically active women campaigned for fairness in marriage, divorce, and

Did You Know?

ANSWER Widowed women were expected to dress in black from head to toe and never remarry, but men wore a black crepe band around their hat or sleeve and were expected to remarry quickly.

Resource Directory

Teaching Resources
You Are There Chapter Extension Activities booklet, p. 56
History Through Literature *Pride and Prejudice,* History Through Literature booklet, pp. 47–48

You Are There . . .

Sipping Tea in a Victorian Parlor

You are visiting friends in London. As part of Victorian England's middle class, they think of their home as an island of peace away from the hustle and bustle of the new factories. As you gaze at their lavishly decorated parlor, you are impressed with their good taste.

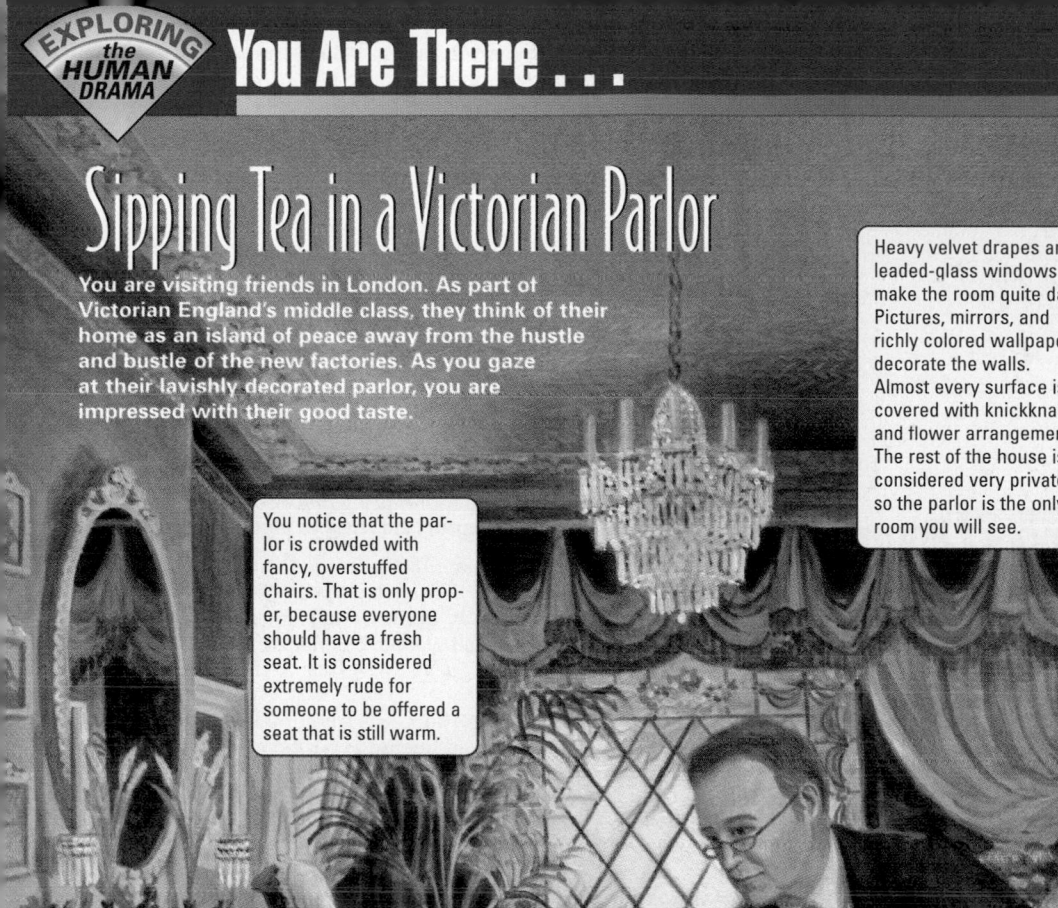

Heavy velvet drapes and leaded-glass windows make the room quite dark. Pictures, mirrors, and richly colored wallpaper decorate the walls. Almost every surface is covered with knickknacks and flower arrangements. The rest of the house is considered very private, so the parlor is the only room you will see.

You notice that the parlor is crowded with fancy, overstuffed chairs. That is only proper, because everyone should have a fresh seat. It is considered extremely rude for someone to be offered a seat that is still warm.

The butler has just come in to announce another caller. He presents your friend with the visitor's calling card—a small, decorative card that contains the visitor's name. Good manners demand that the lady of the house return the visit, or at least a card, to every caller within three days.

Portfolio Assessment

When you get home from your visit, you decide to redecorate your parlor in the Victorian style. Draw up a floor plan with doorways, windows, and furniture. Write an explanation of how the room will impress your visitors.

Chapter 22 **557**

 Human Drama Note

The Water Closet Early Victorian homes did not have indoor bathrooms as we know them today. Instead, every bedroom had a washstand consisting of a waist-high table with a basin and pitcher that rested on a hole in the top shelf. A lower shelf held the commode set—toothbrush, soap dish, cup, and shaving mug—often hidden behind a door. A chamber pot was used at night and often disguised as a rocking chair. A servant emptied the pot each morning.

Only the wealthy could afford indoor plumbing because it was very expensive. Early indoor bathrooms, or water closets, were usually converted bedrooms. Sinks and toilets were disguised as furniture or hidden behind curtains or screens, and tubs were boxed-in wooden structures that looked like cabinets. As people became less shy about their indoor bathrooms, the rooms eventually came to resemble their modern-day counterparts.

Bell Ringer Have students study the drawing of a Victorian parlor on this page. Ask how it reflects the middle-class values of mid-century England. What might they expect to see today in a middle-class home?

Background
About the Evidence

Victorian Homes Homes during the Victorian era were not necessarily large. However, close attention was paid to interior decoration. During the early part of the Victorian era, the dining room was in the basement because people believed it was better to digest food in the dark. Eventually, the dining room moved to the ground floor. To ensure that food carried upstairs from the kitchen stayed warm, owners installed a dumb waiter, a shelf inside the wall that could move up and down a chute with ropes and pulleys.

Activity
Interpreting Viewpoints

Cooperative Learning Have students form small groups to research the Victorian home. Each student should find information about one room other than the parlor—the kitchen, the scullery, servants' quarters, bed chambers, or the nursery. All group members should write a paragraph about their findings and share it with the group.

Activity Rubrics

Share the following rubrics with students before they draw up their floor plans and write their explanations.

Attempted The activity does not reflect an understanding of Victorian home decorating.

Minimal The activity reflects some understanding of Victorian home decorating.

Adequate The activity reflects a good understanding of Victorian home decorating. The floor plan is neatly drawn, and the explanation has sufficient detail.

Exemplary The activity reflects an excellent understanding of Victorian home decorating. The floor plan is well drawn, and the explanation detailed.

Primary Source

ANSWER Education would teach women the skills needed to be personally responsible and self-sufficient.

Reading Strategy
Reinforcing Key Ideas

Ask students to write the phrase "Women and the Industrial Revolution" in the center of a piece of paper. As they read, students should write six phrases around the central concept which indicate important concepts or events affecting women during the Second Industrial Revolution. *(Less Advanced Readers)*

Background
Perspectives

English Feminism In England, the feminist movement of the mid-and late-1800s favored gradual and moderate means. Women had to counter men's fears that suffrage would somehow make women less womanly. In 1884, Frances Power Cobbe, a leading proponent of women's rights in the late 1800s, responded to the charge in a letter to an English feminist magazine.

"It is not so much that our opponents ... despise women, as that they really prize what women now are in the home and in society so highly that they cannot bear to risk losing it by any serious change in their condition. These fears are futile and faithless .... To remove them, we must not use violent words, for every such violent word confirms their fears; but, on the contrary, show the world that while the revolutions brought by men have been full of bitterness and rancor and stormy passions, if not of bloodshed, we women will at least strive to accomplish our great emancipation calmly and by persuasion and reason."

Primary Source

An Equal Right to Learn

In an 1892 address, American women's rights leader Elizabeth Cady Stanton argued that women should have an equal right to education:

"The strongest reason for giving woman all the opportunities for higher education ... is the solitude and personal responsibility of her own individual life. ... As an individual, she must rely on herself. ... To throw obstacles in the way of a complete education is like putting out the eyes. ... In talking of education, how shallow the argument that [men and women] must be educated for the special work [they propose] to do, and that all of the faculties not needed in this special work must lie dormant and utterly wither for lack of use, when, perhaps, these will be the very faculties needed in life's greatest emergencies!"

—Elizabeth Cady Stanton, "The Solitude of Self"

Skills Assessment

Primary Source How does Stanton believe that an education would help women better control their own lives?

property laws. Women's groups also supported the temperance movement, a campaign to limit or ban the use of alcoholic beverages. Temperance leaders argued that drinking threatened family life.

These reformers faced many obstacles. In Europe and the United States, women could not vote. They were barred from most schools and had little, if any, protection under the law. A woman's husband or father controlled her property.

Early Voices Before 1850, some women had become leaders in the union movement. Others, mostly from the middle class, had campaigned for the abolition of slavery. In the process, they realized the severe restrictions on their own lives. In the United States, Elizabeth Cady Stanton and Susan B. Anthony crusaded against slavery before organizing a movement for women's rights.

Many women broke the barriers that kept them out of universities and professions. By the late 1800s, a few brave women overcame opposition to train as doctors or lawyers. Others became explorers, researchers, or inventors, often without recognition. For example, Julia Brainerd Hall worked with her brother to develop an aluminum-producing process. Their company became hugely successful, but Charles Hall received almost all of the credit.

The Suffrage Struggle By the late 1800s, married women in some countries had won the right to control their own property. The struggle for political rights proved far more difficult. In the United States, the Seneca Falls Convention of 1848 demanded that women be granted the right to vote. In Europe, groups dedicated to women's suffrage, or women's right to vote, emerged in the later 1800s.

Among men, some liberals and socialists supported women's suffrage. In general, though, suffragists faced intense opposition. Some critics claimed that women were too emotional to be allowed to vote. Others argued that women needed to be "protected" from grubby politics or that a woman's place was in the home, not in government. To such claims, Sojourner Truth, an African American suffragist, is believed to have replied, "Nobody ever helps me into carriages, or over mudpuddles, or gives me any best place! And ain't I a woman?"

On the edges of the western world, women made faster strides. In New Zealand, Australia, and some western territories of the United States, women won the vote before 1900. There, women who had "tamed the frontier" alongside men were not dismissed as weak and helpless. In Europe and most of the United States, however, the suffrage struggle succeeded only after World War I. (You will read more about the suffrage movement in later chapters.)

Growth of Public Education

By the late 1800s, reformers persuaded many governments to set up public schools and require basic education for all children. Teaching "the three Rs"—reading, writing, and 'rithmetic—was thought to produce better citizens. In addition, industrialized societies recognized the need for a literate work force. Schools taught punctuality, obedience to authority, disciplined work habits, and patriotism. In European schools, children also received basic religious education.

Public Education At first, elementary schools were primitive. Many teachers had little schooling themselves. In rural areas, students attended class only during the times when they were not needed on the farm or in their parents' shops.

By the late 1800s, more and more children were in school, and the quality of elementary education improved. Also, governments began to expand secondary schools, known as high schools in the United States.

In secondary schools, students learned the "classical languages," Latin and Greek, along with history and mathematics.

In general, only middle-class families could afford to have their sons attend these schools, which trained students for more serious study or for government jobs. Middle-class girls were sent to school primarily in the hope that they might marry well and become better wives and mothers.

Higher Education Colleges and universities expanded in this period, too. Most university students were the sons of middle- or upper-class families. The university curriculum emphasized ancient history and languages, philosophy, religion, and law. By the late 1800s, universities added courses in the sciences, especially in chemistry and physics. At the same time, engineering schools trained students who would have the knowledge and skills to build the new industrial society.

Some women sought greater educational opportunities. By the 1840s, a few small colleges for women opened, including Bedford College in England and Mount Holyoke in the United States. In 1863, the British reformer Emily Davies campaigned for female students to be allowed to take the entrance examinations for Cambridge University. She succeeded, but as late as 1897, male Cambridge students rioted against granting degrees to women.

New Directions in Science

As you have seen, science in the service of industry brought great changes in the later 1800s. At the same time, researchers advanced startling theories about the natural world. Their new ideas challenged long-held beliefs.

Atomic Theory A crucial breakthrough in chemistry came in the early 1800s when the English Quaker schoolteacher John Dalton developed modern atomic theory. The ancient Greeks had speculated that all matter was made of tiny particles called atoms. Dalton showed how different kinds of atoms combine to make all chemical substances. In 1869, the Russian chemist Dmitri Mendeleyev (mehn duh LAY ehv) drew up a table that grouped

Public Education
By the late 1800s, poor children often attended elementary school, although many would drop out before high school. Above left, students in a cramped New York City classroom copy their lessons.

Theme: Continuity and Change Why are poor children today more likely to attend high school than the children shown here?

Background
Perspectives

A Diploma at Last! By the late 1800s, women in Germany were permitted to attend university lectures—but only if they stood in the back of the lecture hall or listened from outside an open window or door. Despite such obstacles, determined women struggled to complete their educations.

Background
Global Connections

Soccer Western schools encouraged physical fitness as well as learning. In the early 1800s, English schoolboys began playing a game that developed into soccer. School representatives drew up the first set of soccer rules in 1848. The game spread to the rest of Europe, then to Chile, Canada, and the United States. The first international soccer association formed in 1904, and the first World Cup match took place in 1930. Today, soccer is probably the most widely played sport in the world.

Basketball In the United States, James Naismith, a physical education teacher at the Young Men's Christian Association (YMCA) Training School of Springfield, Massachusetts, used a soccer ball in an entirely new game. In December 1891, he developed the game of basketball. Naismith devised the sport as an indoor athletic activity for the winter months. He hung up two peach basket goals, one at each end of the gym, and his YMCA athletes played the first game of basketball—with a soccer ball.

The new game spread swiftly. The metal hoop was introduced in 1893 and backboards were added in 1895. The first men's intercollegiate game was played in 1897, and the first professional league was established in 1898. By 1900, college women were also playing the game. The first collegiate association—the Eastern Intercollegiate League—was created in 1901. As basketball grew more popular, it assumed its now familiar characteristics.

Writing a Dialogue The phrase "survival of the fittest" was coined by the English philosopher Herbert Spencer. Spencer was a Social Darwinist who completely opposed government assistance programs. He believed that competition made people stronger, and that, conversely, government handouts made people weaker. In 1891, he wrote, "The ultimate result of shielding men from the effects of folly is to fill the world with fools."

Discuss the philosophy of Herbert Spencer and other Social Darwinists with the class. Then, have them read about the social gospel movement discussed in the subsection "Religion in an Urban Age" in this section. Have students work in pairs to write a dialogue between a Social Darwinist and a member of the social gospel movement in which they debate the value to the working class of government-sponsored social services. Invite volunteers to present their dialogues to the class.

Christian Reformers Like many devout Christians, John Wood of Yorkshire, England, was horrified by the cruel treatment of child workers. A mill owner himself, Wood shortened the workday and built a school and a church near his factory.

Christian activists like Wood focused attention on many social ills of the early 1800s and campaigned for reform. They believed that people living in misery could not respond to the message of Christianity. They also felt that the nation had a moral obligation to care for its weaker members. During the 1800s, they slowly achieved their goals for social reform.

Geography and History

A "Living Laboratory"

In 1835, the British ship *Beagle* reached the volcanic Galapagos Islands in the Pacific Ocean, some 600 miles west of South America. The islands were well known for their giant tortoises, which sailors prized as a delicacy. But one crew member, Charles Darwin, was far more interested in how the tortoises, marine and land iguanas, and numerous species of finches survived on the isolated islands.

The specimens he collected and studied helped Darwin develop his theory of evolution. Even today, scientists consider the Galapagos Islands a "living laboratory" for the study of animal life.

Theme: Geography and History Why would the isolation of the Galapagos Islands attract scientists?

elements according to their atomic weights. Mendeleyev's table became the basis for the periodic table of elements used today.

The Age of the Earth The new science of geology opened disturbing avenues of debate. In *Principles of Geology* (1830–1833), Charles Lyell offered evidence to show that the Earth had formed over millions of years. His successors concluded that the Earth was at least two billion years old and that life had not appeared until long after Earth was formed. These ideas did not seem to agree with biblical accounts of creation.

Archaeology added other pieces to an emerging debate about the origins of life on Earth. In 1856, workers in the Neander valley of Germany accidentally uncovered the fossilized bones of prehistoric people, whom scientists called Neanderthal. Later scholars found fossils of other prehistoric humans and animals. These pioneering archaeologists had limited evidence and often drew mistaken conclusions. But as more discoveries were made around the world, scholars developed new ideas about early human life.

The Darwin Challenge

The most disturbing new idea came from the British naturalist Charles Darwin. In 1859, after years of research, he published *On the Origin of Species*. Darwin argued that all forms of life had evolved into their present state over millions of years. To explain the long, slow process of evolution, he put forward his theory of natural selection.

Theory of Natural Selection Darwin adopted Thomas Malthus's idea that all plants and animals produced more offspring than the food supply could support. As a result, he said, members of each species constantly competed to survive. Natural forces "selected" those with physical traits best adapted to their environment. For example, short-necked giraffes, unable to reach the leaves at the tops of trees, would starve. Longer-necked giraffes, however, would survive and pass the trait on to their offspring. This process of natural selection came to be known as "survival of the fittest."

Over time, said Darwin, natural selection would give rise to entirely new species. He applied this theory to humans. "Man," he declared, "is descended from some less highly organized form." He claimed that humans, like all life forms, were still evolving.

The Darwin Furor Like the ideas of Nicolaus Copernicus and Galileo Galilei in earlier times, Darwin's theory ignited a furious debate between scientists and theologians. To many Christians, the Bible contained the only true account of creation. It told how God created the

---

Geography and History

ANSWER The isolation could help prove Darwin's theory of evolution.

Resource Directory

Teaching Resources
Section Quiz Unit 6 booklet, p. 7
Technology
Interactive Student Tutorial CD-ROM Ch. 22
Computer Test Bank Ch. 22

world and all forms of life in six days. Darwin's theory, they argued, reduced people to the level of animals and undermined belief in God and the soul.

While some Christians eventually came to accept the idea of evolution, others did not. Controversy over Darwin's theory has continued to the present day, especially in the United States.

Social Darwinism Darwin himself never promoted any social ideas. However, some thinkers used Darwin's theories to support their own beliefs about society. Their ideas became known as Social Darwinism, applying the idea of survival of the fittest to war and economic competition. Industrial tycoons, argued Social Darwinists, were more "fit" than those they put out of business. War brought progress by weeding out weak nations. Victory was seen as proof of superiority.

Social Darwinism encouraged racism, the belief that one racial group is superior to another. By the late 1800s, many Europeans and Americans claimed that the success of western civilization was due to the supremacy of the white race. Karl Pearson, a British mathematician, wrote, "History shows me one way, and one way only, in which a high state of civilization has been produced, namely the struggle of race with race, and the survival of the physically and mentally fitter race." By the end of the century, as you will read, such ideas would be used to justify the global expansion of imperialism, as well as racial discrimination and segregation.

Religion in an Urban Age

Despite the challenge of new ideas, religion continued to be a major force in western society. Christian churches and Jewish synagogues remained at the center of communities. Religious leaders influenced political, social, and educational developments.

The grim realities of industrial life stimulated feelings of compassion and charity. In Europe, Christian labor unions and political parties pushed for reforms. Individuals and church groups tried to help the working poor. Catholic priests and nuns set up schools and hospitals in urban slums. In the United States, Jewish organizations such as B'nai B'rith provided similar social services.

In Europe and the United States, many Protestant churches backed the social gospel, a movement that urged Christians to social service. They campaigned for reforms in housing, health care, and education. By 1878, William and Catherine Booth had set up the Salvation Army in London. It both spread Christian teachings and provided social services.

Comfort for the Poor
Evangeline Booth, daughter of William and Catherine, helped bring the Salvation Army from Britain to the United States and Canada. This picture shows Booth with two slum children.

Theme: Religions and Value Systems How does this picture express the values of groups like the Salvation Army?

SECTION 3 Assessment

Recall
1. **Identify:** (a) atomic theory, (b) Charles Lyell, (c) natural selection, (d) Social Darwinism, (e) Salvation Army.
2. **Define:** (a) cult of domesticity, (b) temperance movement, (c) women's suffrage, (d) racism, (e) social gospel.

Comprehension
3. (a) How did the social order change in industrial nations? (b) Describe three values associated with the middle class.

4. (a) What were the main goals of the women's movement? (b) Why did it face strong opposition?
5. Why did the ideas of Charles Darwin cause controversy?
6. What services did religious organizations provide?

Critical Thinking and Writing
7. **Defending a Position** Why do you think reformers pushed for free public education?
8. **Linking Past and Present** What charitable services do religious organizations perform today?

Activity
Take It to the NET

Use Internet resources to find out about entertaining in a middle-class English home in the 1800s. Then, with two other students, plan a party. Write an invitation, plan a menu, and demonstrate a game that you might play.

SECTION 3 Assessment

Recall
1. (a) atomic theory, p. 559 (b) Charles Lyell, p. 560 (c) natural selection, p. 560 (d) Social Darwinism, p. 561 (e) Salvation Army, p. 561 2. (a) cult of domesticity, p. 556 (b) temperance movement, p. 558 (c) women's suffrage, p. 558 (d) racism, p. 561 (e) social gospel, p. 561

Comprehension
3. (a) A more complex social structure emerged. The upper class expanded to include rich industrial and business families, a growing middle class enjoyed prosperity, while the lower middle class struggled to keep up. The number of farm-workers fell, but workers and peasants were still at the base of the social ladder. (b) luxury, respectability, and a strict etiquette 4. (a) to secure suffrage and gain access to education and jobs (b) Men believed that women belonged in the home and that they were too emotional to vote. 5. Darwin's ideas contradicted the accepted biblical account of creation. 6. They worked for reforms in the workplace, housing, health care, and education. They also set up schools and hospitals in urban slums.

Critical Thinking and Writing
7. Possible answer: It would improve opportunities for working-class children.
8. provide food and housing for the poor, care of the sick, and counseling

Activity Rubrics

Share rubrics with students before they plan a party.

Attempted The party plan is historically inaccurate or incomplete, reflecting insufficient research.

Minimal The party plan is historically accurate but lacks some details.

Adequate The party plan is historically accurate and complete, showing careful research.

Exemplary The details of the invitation and menu accurately reflect Victorian tastes and rules of etiquette; it is complete, organized, and accurate.

Caption Answer

It expresses the ideal of the social gospel that Christians had a duty to help the poor.

Bell Ringer Ask students to read the subsection titled "Music" on the next page. Then, play a portion of a Beethoven symphony for the class. Ask students to describe how the symphony fits the description of romantic music.

Reading Focus

- What themes shaped romantic art, literature, and music?
- How did realists respond to the industrialized, urban world?
- How did the visual arts change?

Vocabulary

romanticism
realism
impressionism

Taking Notes

Copy the diagram below. As you read, fill in the major features of the artistic movements in the 1800s. To help you get started, some answers have been provided.

	GOALS	CHARACTERISTICS	MAJOR FIGURES
ROMANTICISM	• Rebellion against the Enlightenment emphasis on reason •	• Romantic hero in literature •	• Lord Byron • Wordsworth •
REALISM			
IMPRESSIONISM			

Main Idea New artistic styles emerged as a reaction to the Industrial Revolution.

LESSON PLAN

1. Focus In the 1800s, the arts were dominated by two very different movements. Reacting against the rationalism of the Enlightenment, the romantic movement embraced vibrant emotions, heroism, and glorification of the past. Realism, meanwhile, emerged as an attempt to show the harsh realities of the real world. In the visual arts, impressionists and post-impressionists presented their own views of the world.

2. Instruct Organize the students into groups for the purpose of creating a festival that celebrates the arts of the 1800s. Assign each group responsibility for one art genre. Students may choose romantic literature, art, or music; realistic literature or art; women's literature; impressionism; or postimpressionism. Tell students to use their school and local libraries to find examples of their chosen art form. Each group should write a general introduction for the genre that they will present. Also, each item in their collection should be preceded by a brief oral presentation. Have groups take turns making their presentations to the class. If you wish, you may also invite other classes to the festival.

3. Assess Have students write responses to the following questions: Which of the artists, writers, and musicians presented in the festival affected me the most? Why?

4. Reteach If students' Assess activity does not reflect adequate understanding of the lesson, you might assign the *Guide to the Essentials* or the *Interactive Student Tutorial CD-ROM* for this section.

Biography

Ludwig van Beethoven
1770–1827

Composer Ludwig van Beethoven wrote from the heart. An accomplished musician by age 12, he agonized over every note of every composition. The result was stunning music that expresses intense emotion. The famous opening of his Fifth Symphony conveys the sense of fate knocking at the door. His Sixth Symphony captures a joyful day in the countryside, interrupted by a violent thunderstorm.

Beethoven's career was haunted by perhaps the greatest tragedy a musician can face. In 1798, he began to lose his hearing. Still, he continued to compose music he could hear only in his mind.

Theme: Impact of the Individual How did Beethoven's music reflect romanticism?

Setting the Scene In the 1800s, many writers turned away from the harsh realities of industrial life to celebrate the natural world. The English poet William Wordsworth described the peace and beauty of sunset:

> "It is a beauteous evening, calm and free,
> The holy time is quiet as a Nun
> Breathless with adoration; the broad sun
> Is sinking down in its tranquillity."
> —William Wordsworth,
> *Complete Poetical Works*

Other writers, however, made the new industrialized, urban society the subject of their work.

The Romantic Revolt Against Reason

Wordsworth was part of a cultural movement called romanticism. From about 1750 to 1850, romanticism shaped western literature and arts. Romantic writers, artists, and composers rebelled against the Enlightenment emphasis on reason and progress. They glorified nature and sought to excite strong emotions in their audiences.

The Romantic Hero Romantic writers created a new kind of hero—a mysterious, melancholy figure who felt out of step with society. "My joys, my grief, my passions, and my powers, / Made me a stranger," wrote Britain's Lord Byron. He himself was a larger-than-life figure equal to those he created. Public interest in his poetry and adventures was so great that moody, isolated romantic heroes came to be described as "Byronic."

The romantic hero often hid a guilty secret and faced a grim destiny. Germany's greatest writer, Johann Wolfgang von Goethe (GEH tuh), wrote the dramatic poem *Faust*. The aging scholar Faust makes a pact with the devil, exchanging his soul for youth. After much agony, Faust wins salvation by accepting his duty to help others. In *Jane Eyre*, British novelist Charlotte Brontë weaves a tale about a quiet governess and her brooding, Byronic employer, whose large mansion conceals a terrifying secret.

Romance of the Past Romantic writers combed history, legend, and folklore. Sir Walter Scott's novels and ballads evoked the turbulent history of Scottish clans or medieval knights. Alexandre Dumas (doo MAH) re-created France's past in novels like *The Three Musketeers*.

Biography

ANSWER His music aroused strong emotions.

Resource Directory

Teaching Resources
Creative Teaching Activities Creative Teaching Activities booklet, p. 101
Guided Reading and Review Unit 6 booklet, p. 8

Technology
World History Color Transparencies *Ballet Rehearsal*, p. D–73
Prentice Hall Listening to Literature World Masterpieces audiotapes Ludwig van Beethoven's *Piano Sonata no. 14*, side 7, running time 5:20 min.; works by Heinrich Heine, Victor Hugo, and Charles Baudelaire, sides 7 and 8, running time 17:25 min.

Music Romantic composers also tried to stir deep emotions. The passionate music of German composer Ludwig van Beethoven combined classical forms with a stirring range of sound. He was the first composer to take full advantage of the broad range of instruments in the modern orchestra. In all, Beethoven produced nine symphonies, five piano concertos, a violin concerto, an opera, two masses, and dozens of shorter pieces. To many, he is considered the greatest composer of his day.

Other romantic composers wove traditional folk melodies into their works to glorify their nations' pasts. In his piano works, Frederic Chopin (shoh PAN) used Polish peasant dances to convey the sorrows and joys of people living under foreign occupation.

Romanticism in Art Painters, too, broke free from the discipline and strict rules of the Enlightenment. Landscape painters like J.M.W. Turner sought to capture the beauty and power of nature. Using bold brush strokes and colors, Turner showed tiny human figures struggling against sea and storm.

Romantics painted many subjects, from simple peasant life to medieval knights to current events. Bright colors conveyed violent energy and emotion. The French painter Eugène Delacroix (deh luh KRWAH) filled his canvases with dramatic action. In *Liberty Leading the People*, the Goddess of Liberty carries the revolutionary tricolor as French citizens rally to the cause.

The Call to Realism

By the mid-1800s, a new artistic movement, realism, took hold in the West. Realism was an attempt to represent the world as it was. Realists often focused their work on the harsh side of life in cities or villages. Many writers and artists were committed to improving the lot of the unfortunates whose lives they depicted.

Realism in Art
After seeing two men working on a road, Gustave Courbet invited them to pose for him in his studio. In 1849, *The Stone Breakers* became his first important work of realist art.

Theme: Arts and Literature Many critics denounced Courbet's work for being vulgar and unspiritual. Why do you think his work caused such a reaction?

Chapter 22 **563**

Background
Biography

Background
Biography

"Immoral and Subversive" Henrik Ibsen originally planned to study medicine at the University of Norway. However, after failing entrance examinations in Greek and arithmetic, he decided to work as a playwright and stage manager of the newly founded Norwegian Theater. He began writing historical and romantic plays for the small company before venturing into his "problem plays." These plays, one of which is *A Doll's House,* openly criticize social conventions of the 1800s, such as subjugation of women, political hypocrisy, bourgeois mediocrity, and corrupt journalism. These forthright attacks on social structures caused his critics to label him "immoral and subversive." Yet, Ibsen's willingness to probe the foundations of society eventually earned him the title of "father of modern drama."

Customize for...
Visual Learners

Using a Photograph as a Primary Source Ask volunteers to bring to class family photographs dating from the late 1800s or early 1900s. Have students examine the photographs for evidence of the artistic movement that may have influenced them. For example, ask students to examine the backdrop of the photograph. Have them decide if the photograph is perhaps romantic or realistic in style. Have students also study the photographs to gather information about the time period in which they were taken. They should take note of such things as the poses, the styles of clothing, and the occasion that was photographed. Ask students to share their observations with the rest of the class.

WebMuseum
Paris, France

To see more paintings by Claude Monet and other impressionists, use the Internet address above to link to WebMuseum, Paris.

Impressionism
In his many paintings of Rouen Cathedral, Claude Monet showed how light and atmosphere can affect perception. These three paintings show the cathedral at different times of day and in different weather conditions.

Theme: Arts and Literature Why do you think Monet always painted the cathedral from a similar angle?

The Novel The English novelist Charles Dickens vividly portrayed the lives of slum dwellers and factory workers, including children. In *Oliver Twist,* he tells the story of a nine-year-old orphan raised in a grim poorhouse. One day, young Oliver gets up the nerve to ask for extra food:

> "Child as he was, he was desperate with hunger, and reckless with misery. He rose from the table, and advancing on the master, basin and spoon in hand, said somewhat alarmed at his own [boldness]:
> 'Please, sir, I want some more.'"
> —Charles Dickens, *Oliver Twist*

In response to that simple request, Oliver is smacked on the head and sent away to work. Later, he runs away to London. There he is taken in by Fagin, a villain who trains homeless children to become pickpockets. *Oliver Twist* shocked many middle-class readers with its picture of poverty, mistreatment of children, and urban crime. Yet, Dickens's humor and colorful characters made him one of the most popular novelists in the world.

French novelists also portrayed the ills of their time. In *Les Misérables* (LAY mih zehr AHB bluh), Victor Hugo revealed how hunger drove a good man to crime and how the law hounded him ever after. The novels of Émile Zola painted an even grimmer picture. In *Germinal,* Zola exposed class warfare in the French mining industry. To Zola's characters, neither the Enlightenment's faith in reason nor romantic feelings mattered at all.

Drama Norwegian dramatist Henrik Ibsen brought realism to the stage. His plays attacked the hypocrisy he observed around him. *A Doll's House* showed a woman caught in a straitjacket of social rules. In *An Enemy of the People,* a doctor discovers that the water in a local spa is polluted. Because the town's economy depends on its spa, the citizens denounce the doctor and suppress the truth. Ibsen's realistic dramas had a wide influence in Europe and the United States.

Realism in Art Painters also represented the realities of their time. Rejecting the romantic emphasis on imagination, they focused on ordinary subjects, especially working-class men and women. "I cannot paint an angel," said the French realist Gustave Courbet (koor BAY), "because I have never seen one." Instead, he painted works such as *The Stone Breakers,*

Caption Answer

Other painters might have shown the church as it looked from different angles. By keeping to the same basic viewpoint, Monet could concentrate on the differences created by light and atmosphere.

Resource Directory

Teaching Resources

Biography Activity *Julia Margaret Cameron,* Unit 6 booklet, p. 10
Section Quiz Unit 6 booklet, p. 9
Geography Quiz Unit 6 booklet, p. 14
Chapter Test Forms A, B, and C Unit 6 booklet, pp. 15–19
Answer Key Unit 6 booklet, pp. 98–112

Technology

Interactive Student Tutorial CD-ROM Ch. 22
Computer Test Bank Ch. 22

which shows two rough laborers on a country road. Later in the century, *The Gross Clinic*, by American painter Thomas Eakins, shocked viewers with its realistic depiction of a medical class conducting a dissection.

New Directions in the Visual Arts

By the 1840s, a new art form, photography, was emerging. Louis Daguerre (dah GAYR) in France and William Fox Talbot in England had improved on earlier technologies to produce successful photographs. At first, many photos were stiff, posed portraits of middle-class families or prominent people. Other photographs reflected the romantics' fascination with faraway places.

In time, photographers used the camera to present the grim realities of life. During the American Civil War, Mathew B. Brady preserved a vivid, realistic record of the corpse-strewn battlefields. Other photographers provided vivid evidence of harsh conditions in industrial factories or slums.

The Impressionists Photography posed a challenge to painters. Why try for realism, some artists asked, when a camera could do the same thing better? By the 1870s, a group of painters took art in a new direction, seeking to capture the first fleeting impression made by a scene or object on the viewer's eye. The new movement, known as impressionism, took root in Paris, capital of the western art world.

Since the Renaissance, painters had carefully finished their paintings so that not a brush stroke showed. But impressionists like Claude Monet (moh NAY) and Edgar Degas (day GAH) brushed strokes of color side by side without any blending. According to new scientific studies of optics, the human eye would mix these patches of color.

By concentrating on visual impressions rather than realism, artists achieved a fresh view of familiar subjects. Monet, for example, painted the cathedral at Rouen (roo AHN), France, dozens of times from the same angle, capturing how it looked in different lights at different times of day.

The Postimpressionists Later painters, called postimpressionists, developed a variety of styles. Georges Seurat (suh RAH) arranged small dots of color to define the shapes of objects. The Dutch painter Vincent van Gogh experimented with sharp brush lines and bright colors.

Paul Gauguin (goh GAN) developed a bold, personal style. He rejected the materialism of western life and went to live on the island of Tahiti. In his paintings, people look flat, as in "primitive" folk art. But his brooding colors and black outlining of shapes convey intense feelings and images.

Connections to Today

A Van Gogh at Auction

Vincent van Gogh sold few paintings during his short, unhappy life. In 1890, after several attacks of epilepsy and depression, he began to see the noted doctor Paul-Ferdinand Gachet. Soon after, his doctor became his model. Van Gogh wrote that he had painted Gachet "with the heart-broken expression of our time."

Van Gogh died nearly penniless a year later, but his *Portrait of Dr. Gachet* became one of the most valuable paintings of all time. In 1990, exactly 100 years after it was painted, the portrait sold at an auction in New York for more than $82 million—then an all-time record for any work of art sold at auction.

Theme: Art and Literature
How has the value of Van Gogh's paintings changed?

SECTION **4** **Assessment**

Recall

1. **Identify:** (a) Lord Byron, (b) Johann Wolfgang von Goethe, (c) Ludwig van Beethoven, (d) Charlotte Brontë, (e) Charles Dickens, (f) Gustave Courbet, (g) Claude Monet, (h) postimpressionists.
2. **Define:** (a) romanticism, (b) realism, (c) impressionism.

Comprehension

3. (a) How did romantics respond to the Enlightenment? (b) Describe three subjects romantics favored.

4. How did Dickens and Ibsen explore realistic themes?
5. How did photography influence the development of painting?

Critical Thinking and Writing

6. **Recognizing Causes and Effects** In what ways were the new artistic styles of the 1800s a reaction to changes in society?
7. **Defending a Position** (a) What did Courbet mean when he said, "I cannot paint an angel because I have never seen one"? (b) Do you agree with his attitude? Explain.

Activity
Take It to the NET

Use the Internet to research one of the artists mentioned in this section. Then, write a review of one of his paintings. Consider such questions as the following: What style is used? What is the artist trying to do? What is your opinion of the work?

SECTION **4** **Assessment**

Recall
1. (a) Lord Byron, p. 562 (b) Johann Wolfgang von Goethe, p. 562 (c) Ludwig van Beethoven, p. 562 (d) Charlotte Brontë, p. 562 (e) Charles Dickens, p. 564 (f) Gustave Courbet, p. 564 (g) Claude Monet, p. 565 (h) postimpressionists, p. 565
2. (a) romanticism, p. 562 (b) realism, p. 563 (c) impressionism, p. 565

Comprehension
3. (a) They rebelled against the Enlightenment's emphasis on reason and progress and responded to industrialism by largely ignoring it. Instead, they emphasized rural landscapes and historical subjects. (b) Possible answers: They were interested in history, legends, and folklore. They celebrated dramatic action and heroism. They sought to portray and arouse strong emotions. 4. Dickens vividly portrayed the lives of slum dwellers and factory workers in his novels. Ibsen used his plays to attack the hypocrisy that he saw around him. 5. The realism of photography made some artists turn away from realistic painting. Instead, they sought to capture the first fleeting impression that a scene or object made on the viewer's eye.

Critical Thinking and Writing
6. Possible answers: Romantics sought to escape or ignore the industrial society around them. Realists sought to expose the evils of the industrial world. Impressionists responded to the development of photography. 7. (a) He meant that he painted only what he saw and not what he imagined. (b) Student answers should explain why they agree or disagree with his attitude.

Activity Rubrics

Share rubrics with students before they write their reviews.

Attempted The review does not address the suggested questions and reflects insufficient research.

Minimal The review addresses some of the suggested questions correctly and reflects sufficient research.

Adequate The review addresses many of the suggested questions correctly and is well written.

Exemplary The review goes beyond the suggested questions, is well written, the supporting details well developed, and the opinion is thoughtful.

Connections to Today

ANSWER They have greatly increased in value.

Human Drama Note

The Brontë Sisters By the mid-1800s, a growing number of women were getting their works into print. In northern England, the sisters Charlotte, Emily, and Anne Brontë lived quietly at home, the dutiful daughters of a country clergyman, but every day they wrote. Using the names Currer, Ellis, and Acton Bell, they found a publisher for their poems and novels. Later, the publisher was shocked to discover his authors were women.

Test Preparation

Have students read the last paragraph in "The Novel," on the opposite page, and then answer the question below.

Which is the main idea in the paragraph?

A Poverty drove people to crime.

B French novelists of the time wrote about social ills.

C The Enlightenment's faith in reason did not matter.

D Hugo and Zola were great novelists.

CHAPTER **22** Review and Assessment

Creating a Chapter Summary

As a reteaching opportunity, pair a more able student with a less able student to complete this chapter summary.

Possible answers: **New technology**—assembly line, electricity, steel, chemicals **City life**—population explosion, germ theory, city planning, slums, and an improved standard of living **New communication**—telegraph, telephone, radio **New transportation**—steamships, railroads, airplane **New attitudes and values**—middle-class dominance, cult of domesticity, women's suffrage, public education, Social Darwinism, and social gospel **New culture**—romanticism, realism, and impressionism

Building Vocabulary

1–10. Students' sentences should reflect an understanding of each word.

Recalling Key Facts

11. Germany and the United States
12. Some people praised the economic benefits created by big business, while others argued that big business was greedy and aimed to hurt competition.
13. jobs, music halls, opera houses, theaters, museums, libraries, sports, and parks
14. child labor outlawed, women refused employment in mines, eight-hour workday, old age pensions, disability insurance
15. emphasis on emotion, glorification of nature, the romantic hero, history and folklore, nationalism
16. Photography was used to expose the harsh conditions of industrial life. Impressionism replaced realism as a style of painting.

Critical Thinking and Writing

17. Possible answer: The development of steamships, railroads, airplanes, automobiles, and subways made it possible for people to move from one country to another and from rural to urban areas more easily.
18. (a) The first phase was centered in Britain and based on coal and steam. The second phase involved a number of countries and was based more on steel, electricity, and new methods of production. **(b)** Students should support their opinions with pertinent evidence.

Creating a Chapter Summary

Copy this graphic organizer on a piece of paper. Include information about the developments that occurred in each category during the 1800s. Add more circles as needed.

LIFE IN THE INDUSTRIAL AGE — New technology — Assembly line — Electricity — City life

For additional review and enrichment activities, see the interactive version of *World History* available on the Web and on CD-ROM.

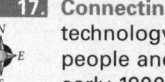

Web Site Self-Test
For practice test questions for Chapter 22, see **www.phschool.com**.

Building Vocabulary

Review the meaning of the chapter vocabulary words listed below. Then, write a sentence for each word in which you define the word and describe its relationship to life in the Industrial Revolution.

1. **assembly line**
2. **corporation**
3. **cartel**
4. **urban renewal**
5. **standard of living**
6. **cult of domesticity**
7. **temperance movement**
8. **social gospel**
9. **romanticism**
10. **realism**

Recalling Key Facts

11. Which two nations became industrial leaders in the late 1800s?
12. What arguments were made for and against the rise of big business?
13. What kinds of attractions did cities offer their residents?
14. What improvements in working conditions occurred in the late 1800s?
15. Name three characteristics or concerns of romanticism.
16. How did the visual arts change in response to new technology?

Critical Thinking and Writing

17. Connecting to Geography How did technology affect the movement of people and goods in the 1800s and early 1900s?
18. Linking Past and Present (a) How did the second Industrial Revolution differ from the first? **(b)** Some historians believe that we are now in the midst of a "third" Industrial Revolution. Do you agree or disagree? Explain.
19. Recognizing Points of View How might each of the following have viewed the Industrial Revolution: **(a)** an inventor, **(b)** an entrepreneur, **(c)** a worker?
20. Applying Information Did the lives of women improve as a result of the Industrial Revolution? Why or why not?
21. Making Inferences Referring to *Oliver Twist*, Dickens wrote that "to show [criminals] as they really are, for ever skulking uneasily through the dirtiest paths of life . . . would be a service to society." **(a)** What do you think he meant? **(b)** How does his claim reflect the goals of realism?

---

19. Possible answers: **(a)** approved of the opportunity to use his education and talents to create new inventions **(b)** enthusiastic about the ability to make huge profits by investing in industry **(c)** welcomed the stable job market, higher wages, and the improved standard of living his skills provided
20. Yes. Women in some countries won the right to vote and to get an education.
21. (a) He meant that upper and middle-class people should be exposed to the details of the terrible lives lived by criminals. **(b)** Possible answer: By painting a realistic picture of the criminal world, he may hope to inspire society to solve the problem.

Skills Assessment
Analyzing Primary Sources

John Hollingshead was an English journalist who had himself been raised in poverty in London. He wrote this description of city life in 1862. Read the passage and answer the questions that follow.

"We are a little too apt to pride ourselves on our national growth and to overlook the quality in the quantity of our population. Thirty millions of people in the United Kingdom, one-tenth of whom belong to London proper . . . show an undoubted advance in capital and prosperity. Taken in detail [however] they show that the spreading limbs of a great city may be healthy and vigorous, while its heart may gradually become more choked and decayed. A vast deal of life that skulks or struggles in London is only familiar to the hard-working clergy, certain medical practitioners, and a few [parish] officers. It burrows in holes and corners at the back of busy thoroughfares. . . . Its records, if truthfully given, have little romance, little beauty, and less variety. Poverty, ignorance, dirt, immorality, and crime are the five great divisions of its history."

—John Hollingshead, "London Poor"

22. According to the author, what percentage of people in London had experienced an improvement in their standard of living as a result of the Industrial Revolution?

23. What does Hollingshead say are the main problems facing the poor?

24. What does the author mean when he says that "the spreading limbs of a great city may be healthy and vigorous, while its heart may gradually become more choked and decayed"?

25. How does this passage reflect what you have learned about the role of religion in urban society?

26. **(a)** Who do you think was the intended audience for this article? **(b)** Why does Hollingshead say, "We are a little too apt to pride ourselves on our national growth"? **(c)** What effect do you think the author hoped to have on his audience?

27. Do you think Hollingshead's description of London in the 1860s could also apply to cities today? Explain.

Skills Assessment
Analyzing Graphs

STEEL PRODUCTION, 1880–1910

Millions of Metric Tons / Year

Legend: —— United States —— Germany —— Great Britain

Sources: *European Historical Statistics, 1750–1970*, and *Historical Statistics of the United States*

The graph above shows the amount of steel produced by three major industrialized nations. Look at the graph and answer the following questions:

28. About how much steel did Britain produce in 1880? In 1910?

29. List the three countries shown in the graph in order from highest to lowest steel production in **(a)** 1890, **(b)** 1900.

30. Between 1890 and 1910, which nation had the greatest increase in steel production? The smallest?

31. Based on what you have read, how can you explain Germany's rise in steel production?

Skills Tip

When you analyze a graph, look for increases and decreases, as well as similarities and differences over time.

Skills Assessment
Take It to the NET

Use the Internet to research an invention or breakthrough from the second Industrial Revolution. Then, create and deliver a presentation about it. Include when and how it was discovered or created, its importance at the time it was discovered or created, and whether it is still in use today.

Analyzing Primary Sources

22. 10 percent
23. poverty, ignorance, dirt, immorality, and crime
24. Possible answer: In many cities, the rich moved to the outskirts and built beautiful homes, while the poor remained in the center of the city in slums.
25. Hollingshead says that the condition of the poor is familiar to "the hard-working clergy." This reflects the role of church groups in administering to the poor and the philosophy of the social gospel.
26. Possible answers: **(a)** middle-class readers **(b)** He means that the well-to-do are proud of the economic benefits of industrialization but ignore many of the hardships. **(c)** He hoped that they would take action to improve the lives of the poor.
27. Students should cite examples of city life today and compare them to the conditions described in the excerpt.

Analyzing Graphs

28. about a million tons; about 6 million tons
29. **(a)** United States, Great Britain, Germany **(b)** United States, Germany, Great Britain
30. greatest: United States; smallest: Great Britain
31. Germany became a united nation in 1871, which aided its industrial development.

Skills Tip

Tell students that increasing or decreasing the intervals of values can significantly alter the graph's appearance. The Skills Handbook in the front of this book has a lesson that will help students with this feature.

Unit Theme Activity

Remind students about the Unit Theme Activity located on the unit opener page. Make sure students understand the assignment and have begun work.

Take It to the NET

Direct students to **www.phschool.com** for links to sites that will help them get started on this assignment. Share rubrics with students.
Attempted The presentation does not meet requirements.
Minimal The presentation demonstrates some research and addresses a few of the requirements.
Adequate The presentation addresses many of the requirements and is well organized.
Exemplary The presentation addresses all of the requirements, is very informative and well organized, and conveys the significance of the inventions, and the delivery is smooth.

Chapter 23 Planning Guide

Resource Manager

Chapter Level Resources	CORE INSTRUCTION	READING/SKILLS
Chapter Level Resources	📀 Teaching Resources 📄 Pacing Charts, Ch. 23 📄 Teaching With Themes, p. 26 🎞 Color Transparencies, p. F–47 💿 Resource Pro® Ch. 23 💻 **www.phschool.com** • eTeach	🔊 Book on CD, Ch. 23 🔊 Interactive Student Tutorial CD-ROM, Ch. 23 🔊 Social Studies Skills Tutor CD-ROM 🎞 Skills Transparencies
1 Building a German Nation 1. Relate the early changes that promoted German unity. 2. Explain how Bismarck unified Germany. 3. Describe the new German empire's political organization.	📀 Teaching Resources 📄 Creative Teaching Activities, p. 102 💿 Prentice Hall Presentation Pro, Ch. 23, Section 1 🎞 Section Reading Support Transparencies	📀 Teaching Resources 📘 Unit 6 booklet • Guided Reading and Review, p. 20 📄 Guide to the Essentials 📼 Guided Reading Audiotapes, Ch. 23, Section 1
2 Strengthening Germany 1. Identify factors marking Germany as an industrial giant. 2. Explain why Bismarck was called the Iron Chancellor. 3. Describe the policies Kaiser William II followed.	📀 Teaching Resources 📘 Unit 6 booklet • Viewpoint Activity, p. 32 📄 Creative Teaching Activities, p. 103 💿 Prentice Hall Presentation Pro, Ch. 23, Section 2	📀 Teaching Resources 📘 Unit 6 booklet • Guided Reading and Review, p. 22 📄 Guide to the Essentials 📼 Guided Reading Audiotapes, Ch. 23, Section 2
3 Unifying Italy 1. Identify the obstacles to Italian unity. 2. Describe the roles that Cavour and Garibaldi played in the struggle for Italy. 3. Outline the challenges that faced the new nation of Italy.	📀 Teaching Resources 📘 Unit 6 booklet • Biography Activity, p. 30 📄 Creative Teaching Activities, p. 104 💿 Prentice Hall Presentation Pro, Ch. 23, Section 3	📀 Teaching Resources 📘 Unit 6 booklet • Guided Reading and Review, p. 24 📄 Guide to the Essentials 📼 Guided Reading Audiotapes, Ch. 23, Section 3
4 Nationalism Threatens Old Empires 1. Analyze how nationalism contributed to the decline of the Austrian empire. 2. Relate the main characteristics of the Dual Monarchy. 3. Describe how the growth of nationalism affected the Balkans.	📀 Teaching Resources 📄 Creative Teaching Activities, p. 105 💿 Prentice Hall Presentation Pro, Ch. 23, Section 4 🎞 Section Reading Support Transparencies	📀 Teaching Resources 📘 Unit 6 booklet • Guided Reading and Review, p. 26 • Skill Application Activity, p. 33 📄 Guide to the Essentials
5 Russia: Reform and Reaction 1. Analyze how conditions in Russia affected progress. 2. Explain why the czars followed a cycle of absolutism, reform, and reaction. 3. Describe how the problems of industrialization contributed to the growing crisis and outbreak of revolution in Russia.	📀 Teaching Resources 📘 Unit 6 booklet • Primary Source Activity, p. 31 📄 Creative Teaching Activities, p. 106 💿 Prentice Hall Presentation Pro, Ch. 23, Section 5	📀 Teaching Resources 📘 Unit 6 booklet • Guided Reading and Review, p. 28 📄 Guide to the Essentials 📼 Guided Reading Audiotapes, Ch. 23, Section 5

ENRICHMENT/PRE-AP

www.phschool.com
- Why Study History?

Teaching Resources
- Chapter Extension Activities, p. 57
- Color Transparencies, p. C–53

www.phschool.com
- Internet Activities, Section 2

www.phschool.com
- Virtual Field Trip

Teaching Resources
- Chapter Extension Activities, p. 58
- History Through Literature, pp. 49–50

www.phschool.com
- Internet Activities, Russian Ballet
- Internet Activities, Section 5

ASSESSMENT

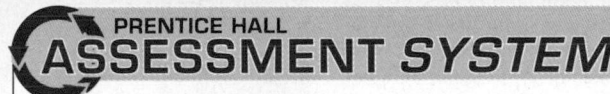

PRENTICE HALL ASSESSMENT SYSTEM

Core Assessment
- ExamView Test Bank booklet, Ch. 23
- ExamView Test Bank CD-ROM, Ch. 23

Standardized Test Preparation

Diagnose and Prescribe
- Diagnostic Tests for High School Social Studies Skills

Review and Reteach
- Review Book for World History

Practice and Assess
- Test-Taking Strategies With Transparencies for High School
- Alternative Assessment booklet
- Test Prep Book for World History

Teaching Resources
- Unit 6 booklet
  - Geography Quiz, p. 34
  - Section Quizzes, pp. 21, 23, 25, 27, 29
  - Chapter Tests A, B, and C, pp. 35–39
- **www.phschool.com**
  - Self-Test

CUSTOMIZE FOR INDIVIDUAL NEEDS

Gifted and Talented
- Teacher's Edition, Activities: Customize for Heterogeneous Groups, p. 588

Less Proficient Readers
- Guide to the Essentials, Ch. 23
- Guided Reading Audiotapes, English, Ch. 23
- Book on CD, Ch. 23
- Teacher's Edition, Activities: Customize for Visual Learners, p. 582

Less Proficient Writers
- Teacher's Edition, Activities: Cooperative Learning Activity, p. 587

Students Acquiring English/ESL
- Guide to the Essentials, English/Spanish, Ch. 23
- Guided Reading Audiotapes, English/Spanish, Ch. 23
- Book on CD, Ch. 23
- Teacher's Edition, Activities marked with an *

*i*TEXT

Don't miss the exclusive interactive version of *World History: Connections to Today* on the Internet and CD-ROM.

CHAPTER 23

Nationalism Triumphs in Europe

1800–1914

INTRODUCTION

In the last half of the nineteenth century, much of Europe was in turmoil. Germany and Italy achieved unification, but in other areas, nationalist groups fought for independence. The old Ottoman and Hapsburg empires began to break up. In Russia, some czars experimented with reforms, but they soon reverted to repressive ways.

Focusing on Themes

Suggest that students focus on these theme questions as they read:

Political and Social Systems
What effect did nationalism and demands for reform have on European governments?

Impact of the Individual
How did tough-minded political leaders help unify both Germany and Italy?

Diversity
How did nationalism affect diverse empires in central and eastern Europe?

Religions and Value Systems
How were religion and nationalism linked in the Russian empire?

Chapter Preview

1 Building a German Nation
2 Strengthening Germany
3 Unifying Italy
4 Nationalism Threatens Old Empires
5 Russia: Reform and Reaction

◆ TIME LINE ACTIVITY

Share the About the Pictures note with your students before you ask these questions about the time line:

1. What elements, in addition to folk tales, form part of a people's heritage? *(possible answers: language, common history, tradition, religion)*
2. Why was Mazzini's society a secret one? *(Possible answer: The government was probably trying to suppress such organizations.)*
3. What events on the time line show that there was unrest in other regions too? *(the Global Events in 1804, 1848, and 1898)*

1812
Jacob and William Grimm publish the first in a series of folk tales such as "Hansel and Gretel," shown here. The tales reflect the common heritage of people throughout the German states.

1814
The Congress of Vienna begins.

1831
Giuseppe Mazzini, shown here, founds a secret society called Young Italy. The society encourages Italian unification.

CHAPTER EVENTS

1800 — 1825 — 1850

GLOBAL EVENTS

1804 Haiti declares independence from France.

1848 Revolutions take place throughout Europe.

Don't Miss!

Analyzing Primary Sources
Crowning the German Emperor (Section 1)

Humanities Link
Russian Ballet (Section 5)

Resource Directory

Teaching Resources
Teaching With Themes Chapter Theme Activities, p. 26
Pacing Chart With Block Scheduling Guide Ch. 23
Technology
World History Color Transparencies Ch. 23 Graphic Organizer, p. F–47

Unification in Europe, 1873

Nationalist movements led to the creation of several new nations across Europe.

ATLANTIC OCEAN

UNITED KINGDOM
NETHERLANDS
BELGIUM
GERMANY
LUXEMBOURG
SWITZERLAND
FRANCE
PORTUGAL
SPAIN

KINGDOM OF SWEDEN AND NORWAY
DENMARK
St. Petersburg
Berlin
RUSSIA
Don R.

AUSTRIA-HUNGARY
Vienna
Budapest

ALPS
Rome
ITALY
Adriatic Sea
Danube R.
Black Sea

OTTOMAN EMPIRE

Mediterranean Sea

Azimuthal Equal Area Projection
0   200   400 Miles
0   200   400 Kilometers

1885
Construction begins on the parliament building in Budapest. Although Austria and Hungary have been united under the Dual Monarchy since 1867, each state has its own parliament.

1905
In Russia, the czar's troops, standing in front of the arch, fire on peaceful protesters. The massacre becomes known as Bloody Sunday.

1914
World War I begins.

1875 — 1900 — 1925

1898 The Philippines declares independence from Spain.

1903 In North Carolina, the Wright brothers complete the first flight in an airplane.

Unification in Europe, 1873

Activating Prior Knowledge
Prior to unification, how was the area labeled Germany on the map divided? *(Prussia and a number of small German states)*

Previewing
Why do you suppose Austria-Hungary has two capitals? *(Possible answer: Each state has retained some political power of its own, while forming one nation.)*

Background
About the Pictures

1 | 2 | 3 | 4

1. The Grimm brothers (Jacob and William) were scholars and university teachers. Each wrote several books, including works on the grammar and history of the German language and collections of legends.

2. Mazzini (1805–1872) spent his life working for the cause of Italian unification. He was disappointed with the 1861 unification because the government was a monarchy, not a republic. Italy did not become a republic until 1946.

3. The city of Budapest consists of two sections—Buda and Pest—divided by the Danube, which flows past the Parliament building. The building, which was completed in 1902, is on the east bank of the river, in the Pest section.

4. The protesters were workers and their wives and children. Estimates of the dead and wounded run from hundreds to thousands. The arch in the picture is a monument to the defeat of Napoleon. At its top is a statue of Victory on her horse-drawn chariot.

Independent Assignments

Have students read one section as they prepare for class. After class, have them complete the assignment. Some students may benefit from using the Guided Reading and Review worksheets.

Section 1 Consult lesson ideas at the front of the Historical Outline Map Book and have students use the map *Unification of Germany*, p. 37, to see how the German state was formed.

Section 2 Have students use the worksheet *Bismarck and His Strategies* in the Unit 6 booklet, p. 32, to learn how two historians view this historical figure.

Section 3 Have students use the worksheet *Giuseppe Verdi* in the Unit 6 booklet, p. 30, to learn

about this famous Italian composer and his role in Italian unification.

Section 4 Have students use the worksheet *Drawing Inferences From Maps* in the Unit 6 booklet, p. 33, to learn about continuing strife in the Balkans.

Section 5 Have students use the worksheet *The Execution in Semyonovsky Square* in the Unit 6 booklet, p. 31, to learn about the effects of the desperate efforts of Czar Nicholas I to control dissent.

eTeach

Be sure to check out this month's online discussion with a World History Master Teacher.

Go to **www.phschool.com**.

LESSON PLAN

1. Focus During the early 1800s, the rise of German nationalism fueled desires for a strong, united German state. As chancellor of Prussia, Otto von Bismarck led the drive for German unity. Following his ideas of *Realpolitik* and "blood and iron," Bismarck used a minor dispute to create war between France and the German states. As a result of the Franco-Prussian War, France was defeated and a powerful German state, the Second Reich, was born.

2. Instruct Have students work with a partner to outline Section 1. Remind students to use the boldface heads to help them organize the structure of their outlines. Also remind students that they should determine the main ideas of the paragraphs that develop each subsection. Encourage students to also make use of the map *Unification of Germany, 1865–1871*. After students have completed their outlines, have each team write two or three questions for each portion of its outline.

3. Assess Review the material by making use of the questions that the students have written. You may wish to use their questions for a class discussion, a written quiz, or a quiz game.

4. Reteach If students' **Assess** activity does not reflect adequate understanding of the lesson, you might assign the *Guide to the Essentials* or the *Interactive Student Tutorial CD-ROM* for this section.

SECTION 1 Building a German Nation

Reading Focus

- What early changes promoted German unity?
- How did Bismarck unify Germany?
- What was the basic political organization of the new German empire?

Vocabulary

chancellor
Realpolitik
annex
kaiser
Reich

Taking Notes

On a sheet of paper, make a flowchart showing the key events that led to a united Germany. Use this flowchart to help you get started. Add more boxes as needed

Bismarck becomes chancellor
↓
Bismarck enters alliance with Austria to "liberate" Holstein and Schleswig
↓

Main Idea Otto von Bismarck, the chancellor of Prussia, led the drive for German unity.

Setting the Scene The Prussian legislators waited restlessly for Otto von Bismarck to speak. They knew he wanted them to vote more money to build up the Prussian army. Liberal members of the parliament, however, opposed the move. At last, Bismarck rose and dismissed their concerns:

> "Germany does not look to Prussia's liberalism, but to her power. . . . The great questions of the day are not to be decided by speeches and majority resolutions—that was the mistake of 1848 and 1849—but by blood and iron!"
> —Otto von Bismarck, quoted in *Modern and Contemporary European History, 1815–1940* (Schapiro)

Bismarck delivered his "blood and iron" speech in 1862. It set the tone for his policies in the years ahead. Bismarck was determined to build a strong, unified German state, with Prussia at its head.

Steps Toward Unity

In the early 1800s, German-speaking people lived in a number of small and medium-sized states as well as in Prussia and the Austrian Hapsburg empire. Napoleon's invasions unleashed new forces in these territories.

Impact of Napoleon Between 1807 and 1812, Napoleon made important territorial changes in German-speaking lands. He annexed lands along the Rhine River for France. He dissolved the Holy Roman Empire and organized a number of German states into the Rhine Confederation.

At first, some Germans welcomed the French emperor as a hero with enlightened, modern policies. He encouraged freeing the serfs, made trade easier, and abolished laws against Jews. However, not all Germans appreciated Napoleon and his changes. As people fought to free their lands from French rule, they began to demand a unified German state.

Napoleon's defeat did not resolve the issue. At the Congress of Vienna, Metternich pointed out that a united Germany would require dismantling the government of each German state. Instead, the peacemakers created the German Confederation, a weak alliance headed by Austria.

Prussian Leadership In the 1830s, Prussia created an economic union called the *Zollverein* (TSAWL fuh rīn). It dismantled tariff barriers between many German states. Still, Germany remained politically fragmented.

Resource Directory

Teaching Resources

Creative Teaching Activities Creative Teaching Activities booklet, p. 102
Guided Reading and Review Unit 6 booklet, p. 20

Technology

World History Color Transparencies *A Dream Castle in Bavaria*, p. C–53

In 1848, liberals meeting in the Frankfurt Assembly again demanded German political unity. They offered the throne of a united German state to Frederick William IV of Prussia. The Prussian ruler, however, rejected the notion of a throne offered by "the people."

Bismarck and German Unity

Otto von Bismarck succeeded where others had failed. Bismarck came from Prussia's Junker (YUNG ker) class, made up of conservative landowning nobles. Bismarck first served Prussia as a diplomat. In 1862, King William I made him chancellor, or prime minister. Within a decade, the new chancellor had united the German states under Prussian rule.

Master of *Realpolitik* Bismarck's success was due in part to his strong will. He was a master of *Realpolitik,* or realistic politics based on the needs of the state. Power was more important than principles.

Although Bismarck was the architect of German unity, he was not really a German nationalist. His primary loyalty was to the Hohenzollerns, the ruling dynasty of Prussia. Through unification, he hoped to bring more power to the Hohenzollerns.

Strengthening the Army As chancellor, Bismarck moved first to build up the Prussian army. Despite his "blood and iron" speech, the liberal legislature refused to vote funds for the military. In response, Bismarck strengthened the army with money that had been collected for other purposes. He then was ready to pursue an aggressive foreign policy.

In the next decade, Bismarck led Prussia into three wars. Each war increased Prussian power and paved the way for German unity.

Skills Assessment

Geography In the early 1800s, people living in German-speaking states had local loyalties. By the mid-1800s, however, they were developing a national identity.

1. **Location** On the map, locate **(a)** Prussia, **(b)** Silesia, **(c)** Bavaria, **(d)** Schleswig.
2. **Region** What area did Prussia add to its territory in 1866?
3. **Critical Thinking**
   Analyzing Information Why do you think Austrian influence was greater among the southern German states than among the northern ones?

Reading Strategy
Problem Solving

Read aloud to students the following sentence from the opposite page: "In the early 1800s, German-speaking people lived in a number of small and medium-sized states as well as in Prussia and the Austrian Hapsburg empire." Tell students that a rise in nationalism helped bring about a united German state. As they read, ask students to think up and list practical alternatives to Bismarck's ruthless policy of "blood and iron"—that is, alternative ways that German-speaking people might have achieved unification. Ask volunteers to share their ideas with the class. *(More Advanced Readers)*

Unification of Germany, 1865–1871

Map legend:
- Prussia, 1865
- Added to Prussia, 1866
- Added to form North German Confederation, 1867
- Added to form German empire, 1871
- Boundary of German empire, 1871
- ✳ Battle sites
- → Route of Prussian armies in Austro-Prussian War
- → Route of German armies in Franco-Prussian War

Azimuthal Equal Area Projection

Chapter 23 **571**

Block Scheduling Support

Some of the short stories by French writer Alphonse Daudet (1840–1897) deal with life during the Franco-Prussian War. One is "The Siege of Berlin," in which a young Parisian woman tries to keep her ailing grandfather, a retired cavalry officer, from learning how badly the war is going for the French. The title of the story comes from the false report that she gives him about how the French are laying siege to Berlin. In actuality, it is Paris that is under siege. Another story, "The Last Lesson," is set in a rural Alsatian school. The story describes the last day of class before the new Prussian teacher arrives to replace M. Hamel, who has taught in the village school for 40 years. These stories should be available in anthologies in the library. After students read one, have a class discussion about their reaction to it. Ask what these stories reveal about the times and character of the people.

Skills Assessment

ANSWERS 1. Review locations with students. 2. 1866—Schleswig, Holstein, Hanover 3. Austria was physically closer to the southern German states.

Analyzing Primary Sources

Crowning the German Emperor

This painting by Anton von Werner shows the coronation of William I (center on the steps) as emperor of the united Germany. The ceremony took place at Versailles in 1871.

*B*ackground
About the Primary Source

A Successful Scheme Bismarck had trouble convincing William I to accept the crown of a united Germany. Bismarck bribed Ludwig II of Bavaria, who was in financial difficulty, to help. Bismarck instructed Ludwig, William's old and trusted friend, to write a letter paying homage to William and urging him to accept the imperial throne. Soon after receiving the letter, William accepted Bismarck's offer and became Kaiser William I of the Second German Reich.

*A*ctivity
Interpreting the Primary Source

Use this additional question to generate class discussion.
Critical Thinking: Making Generalizations What is one generalization that could be made about the predominance of military uniforms in this scene? *(Possible answer: Military strength was important to the leaders of Germany.)*

Skills Tip

When analyzing a painting, note where your eye goes first. That is likely to be what the artist thought was most important. The Skills Handbook in the front of the book has a lesson that will help students with this feature.

Skills Tip

Keep in mind that a painting is an artist's vision of an event. Unlike a photograph of an actual scene, a painting may embellish or exaggerate certain aspects of an event.

Skills Assessment

1. In the painting, William I is saluted by
   A common citizens.
   B the royal court.
   C uniformed men.
   D foreign dignitaries.

2. How is Otto von Bismarck (at center, in white jacket) portrayed?
   E as equal to the emperor
   F as superior to the emperor
   G as unimportant to the coronation
   H as a central part of the coronation

3. **Critical Thinking Analyzing Primary Sources** **(a)** What feelings does the painting evoke about the coronation and the union of Germany? Which details support your view? **(b)** Write three questions that the painting raises about the event, then find the answers through further research.

Skills Assessment

ANSWERS **1.** C **2.** H **3. (a)** pride in the new German nation's military strength; proud men in uniform saluting the emperor **(b)** Questions might include: Who made up the audience? *(German princes)* Why were they in uniform? *(Military victories unified Germany.)* Why was the coronation held in France? *(The Palace of Versailles was German military headquarters in the Franco-Prussian War.)*

Resource Directory

Teaching Resources
Analyzing Primary Sources Chapter Extension Activities booklet, p. 57
Section Quiz Unit 6 booklet, p. 21

Technology
Interactive Student Tutorial CD-ROM Ch. 23
Computer Test Bank Ch. 23

Wars With Denmark and Austria Bismarck's first maneuver was to form an alliance in 1864 with Austria. They seized the provinces of Schleswig and Holstein from Denmark. Prussia and Austria "liberated" the two provinces, which were largely inhabited by Germans, and divided up the spoils.

In 1866, Bismarck invented an excuse to attack Austria. The Austro-Prussian War lasted just seven weeks and ended in a decisive Prussian victory. Prussia then annexed, or took control of, several other north German states.

Bismarck dissolved the Austrian-led German Confederation and created a new confederation dominated by Prussia. He allowed Austria and four other southern German states to remain independent. Bismarck's motives, as always, were strictly practical. "We had to avoid leaving behind any desire for revenge," he later wrote.

The Franco-Prussian War In France, the Prussian victory over Austria worried Napoleon III. A growing rivalry between the two nations led to the Franco-Prussian War of 1870.

Germans recalled only too well the invasions of Napoleon I some 60 years earlier. Bismarck played up the image of the French menace to spur German nationalism. For his part, Napoleon III did little to avoid war, hoping to mask problems at home with military glory.

Bismarck furthered the crisis by rewriting and then releasing to the press a telegram that reported on a meeting between King William I and the French ambassador. Bismarck's editing of the "Ems dispatch" made it seem that William I had insulted the Frenchman. Furious, Napoleon III declared war on Prussia, as Bismarck had hoped.

A superior Prussian force, supported by troops from other German states, smashed the badly organized and poorly supplied French soldiers. Napoleon III, old and ill, surrendered within a few weeks. France had to accept a humiliating peace.

The German Empire

Delighted by the victory over France, princes from the southern German states and the North German Confederation persuaded William I of Prussia to take the title kaiser (KĪ zer), or emperor. In January 1871, German nationalists celebrated the birth of the Second Reich, or empire. They called it that because they considered it heir to the Holy Roman Empire.

A constitution drafted by Bismarck set up a two-house legislature. The Bundesrat, or upper house, was appointed by the rulers of the German states. The Reichstag, or lower house, was elected by universal male suffrage. Because the Bundesrat could veto any decisions of the Reichstag, real power remained in the hands of the emperor and his chancellor.

SECTION 1 Assessment

Recall
1. **Identify:** (a) *Zollverein*, (b) Otto von Bismarck, (c) William I.
2. **Define:** (a) chancellor, (b) *Realpolitik*, (c) annex, (d) kaiser, (e) Reich.

Comprehension
3. What territorial and economic changes promoted German unity?
4. Describe the techniques Bismarck used to unify the German states.

5. How did the emperor and his chancellor retain power in the new German government?

Critical Thinking and Writing
6. **Applying Information** Identify three examples of Bismarck's use of *Realpolitik*.
7. **Comparing** How did the nationalism represented by Bismarck differ from that embraced by liberals in the early 1800s?

Primary Source

War and Power
In 1866, Field Marshal Helmuth von Moltke analyzed the importance of Prussia's war against Austria.

"The war of 1866 was entered on not because the existence of Prussia was threatened, nor was it caused by public opinion and the voice of the people; it was a struggle, long foreseen and calmly prepared for, recognized as a necessity by the Cabinet, not for territorial expansion, for an extension of our domain, or for material advantage, but for an ideal end—the establishment of power. Not a foot of land was exacted from Austria. . . . Its center of gravity lay out of Germany; Prussia's lay within it. Prussia felt itself called upon and strong enough to assume the leadership of the German races."

—Helmuth von Moltke, quoted in *Readings in European History* (Robinson)

Skills Assessment

Primary Source Why, according to von Moltke, did Prussia go to war against Austria?

Activity

Making a Map
Create an illustrated map and time line showing the unification of Germany. Include a legend that explains symbols on your map, such as those used for battle sites.

SECTION 1 Assessment

Recall
1. (a) *Zollverein*, p. 570 (b) Otto von Bismarck, p. 571 (c) William I, p. 571
2. (a) chancellor, p. 571 (b) *Realpolitik*, p. 571 (c) annex, p. 573 (d) kaiser, p. 573 (e) Reich, p. 573

Comprehension
3. annexation of Rhine lands by Napoleon, creation of *Zollverein* 4. based actions on *Realpolitik*, strengthened army, directed military in three successful wars 5. The upper house, which could veto decisions of the lower house, was appointed by the rulers of the German states.

Critical Thinking and Writing
6. Possible answers: Bismarck funded the Prussian army with money appropriated for other purposes. He treated Austria as an ally or enemy depending on his changing needs. He edited a telegram in order to start a war with France.
7. Possible answer: European liberals who embraced nationalism also favored democracy. Bismarck's nationalism was combined with military expansionism and increased royal power.

Activity Rubrics

Share rubrics with students before they make their maps and time lines.

Attempted The map and time line are incomplete, missing important places or events.

Minimal Map and time line labels are included but are difficult to read or are inaccurately placed.

Adequate Map and time line labels are included, easy to read, and accurately placed.

Exemplary Map and time line labels are included, easy to read, and accurately placed, and both are exceptionally well presented.

Human Drama Note

Carrier Pigeons Because the roads were blocked during the German siege of Paris, the French used carrier pigeons to send and receive messages. Hundreds of notes were set in tiny type and then reduced by photography to a small strip of film. The film was placed in a tiny tube and strapped to the leg of a pigeon. When the pigeon reached its destination, the film was projected onto a screen. The messages were copied down by transcribers and passed on to their intended recipients.

Test Preparation

Have students read the third paragraph after the heading "The Franco-Prussian War" on this page, and then answer the question below.

What was the "Ems dispatch"?

A a telegram that insulted the German king

B a telegram that insulted the French king

C a telegram that insulted the French ambassador

D a telegram that insulted the German ambassador

Primary Source

ANSWER to establish Prussia's power and to assert its leadership of the German states

SECTION 2 Strengthening Germany

Bell Ringer Draw students' attention to the boldface heads and the picture that appear on this page. Ask students to write a paragraph explaining why the countries of Europe might have been alarmed by developments in the new Germany.

LESSON PLAN

1. Focus The growth of German industry was based on ample resources and a highly skilled work force. To increase unity and devotion to the state, Bismarck applied the principles of *Realpolitik* toward socialists and Catholics. After asking Bismarck to resign, Kaiser William II limited democratic reform and increased the military power of Germany.

2. Instruct Divide the class into two groups. Ask students to imagine that they are newspaper editors who have been assigned to write an editorial on events in Germany between 1871 and 1890. One group will write editorials that generally support and praise German policies. The second group will write editorials that criticize those policies and express fears about the future. Advise students to also include an appraisal of Bismarck's style of leadership. Allow each group time to discuss the ideas that they might develop. Then, have students work individually to write their editorials. Invite some students to read their finished editorials to the class.

3. Assess Ask students to write a "letter to the editor" disagreeing with the ideas that they developed in their own editorial.

4. Reteach If students' *Assess* activity does not reflect adequate understanding of the lesson, you might assign the *Guide to the Essentials* or the *Interactive Student Tutorial CD-ROM* for this section.

Reading Focus

- What marked Germany as an industrial giant?
- Why was Bismarck called the Iron Chancellor?
- What policies did Kaiser William II follow?

Vocabulary

Kulturkampf
social welfare

Taking Notes

On a sheet of paper, make a diagram like the one started here. As you read the section, add other causes that led to a strong German nation.

- Plentiful resources for industry
- Educated work force

STRONG GERMAN NATION

Main Idea Germany increased its power by building up its industry and armed forces.

Setting the Scene In January 1871, German princes gathered in the glittering Hall of Mirrors at the French palace of Versailles. They had just defeated Napoleon III in the Franco-Prussian War. The palace of Louis XIV seemed the perfect place to proclaim the new German empire. To the winners as well as to the losers, the symbolism was clear. French domination of Europe, dating from the age of Louis XIV, had ended. Germany, headed by William I and his chancellor, Otto von Bismarck, was now the dominant power in Europe.

The German Industrial Giant

In the aftermath of unification, the German empire emerged as the industrial giant of the European continent. By the late 1800s, German chemical and electrical industries were setting the standard worldwide. German shipping was second only to Britain's among the European powers.

Economic Progress Germany, like Great Britain, possessed several of the factors that made industrialization possible. Germany's spectacular growth was due in part to ample iron and coal resources, the basic ingredients for industrial development. A disciplined and educated work force also helped the economy, and a rapidly growing population—from 41 million in 1871 to 67 million by 1914—provided a huge home market along with a larger supply of industrial workers.

The new nation also benefited from earlier progress. During the 1850s and 1860s, Germans had founded large companies and built many railroads. The house of Krupp boomed after 1871. It became an enormous industrial complex that produced steel and weapons for a world market. Between 1871 and 1914, the business tycoon August Thyssen built a small steel factory of 70 workers into a giant empire with 50,000 employees.

Science, Government, and Industry German industrialists were the first to see the value of applied science in developing new products such as synthetic chemicals and dyes. They supported research and development in the universities and hired trained scientists to solve technological problems in their factories.

German Industry
The Krupp works was a major German industrial company. This huge cannon was displayed at an international industrial exhibition to demonstrate the might of the house of Krupp and of Germany.

Theme: Economics and Technology What advantages would a cannon like this one offer to an army?

Caption Answer

It would be able to shoot larger ammunition, resulting in more destruction. Also, it has a very intimidating appearance, so people would be impressed with Germany's military power.

Resource Directory

Teaching Resources

Creative Teaching Activities Creative Teaching Activities booklet, p. 103
Guided Reading and Review Unit 6 booklet, p. 22
Viewpoint Activity *Bismarck and His Strategies,* Unit 6 booklet, p. 32

Block Scheduling Support

Have students explain the meaning of the following of Bismarck's aphorisms. Then, ask students to write a paragraph in which they connect the aphorisms with Bismarck's actions.
- "When you want to fool the world, tell the truth."
- "Universal suffrage is the government of a house by its nursery."
- "People never lie so much as after a hunt, during a war, or before an election."

The German government promoted economic development. After 1871, it issued a single currency for Germany, reorganized the banking system, and coordinated railroads built by the various German states. When a worldwide depression hit in the late 1800s, Germany raised tariffs to protect home industries from foreign competition. The leaders of the new German empire were determined to maintain economic strength as well as military power.

The Iron Chancellor

As chancellor of the new German empire, Bismarck pursued several foreign-policy goals. He wanted to keep France weak and isolated while building strong links with Austria and Russia. He respected British naval power but did not seek to compete in that arena. "Water rats," he said, "do not fight with land rats." Later, however, he would take a more aggressive stand against Britain as the two nations competed for colonies to expand their overseas empires.

On the domestic front, Bismarck applied the same ruthless methods he had used to achieve unification. The Iron Chancellor, as he was called, sought to erase local loyalties and crush all opposition to the imperial state. He targeted two groups—the Catholic Church and the socialists. In his view, both posed a threat to the new German state.

Campaign Against the Church After unification, Catholics made up about a third of the German population. The Lutheran Bismarck distrusted Catholics—especially the clergy—whose first loyalty, he believed, was to the pope instead of to Germany.

In response to what he saw as the Catholic threat, Bismarck launched the *Kulturkampf,* or "battle for civilization." His goal was to make Catholics put loyalty to the state above allegiance to the Church. The chancellor had laws passed that gave the state the right to supervise Catholic education and approve the appointment of priests. Other laws closed some religious orders, expelled the Jesuits from Prussia, and made it compulsory for couples to be married by civil authority.

Bismarck's moves against the Catholic Church backfired. The faithful rallied behind the Church, and the Catholic Center party gained strength in the Reichstag. A realist, Bismarck saw his mistake and worked to make peace with the Church.

Campaign Against the Socialists Bismarck also saw a threat to the new German empire in the growing power of socialism. By the late 1870s, German Marxists had organized the Social Democratic party, which called for parliamentary democracy and laws to improve conditions for the working class. Bismarck feared that socialists would undermine the loyalty of German workers and turn them toward revolution. He had laws passed that dissolved socialist groups, shut down their newspapers, and banned their meetings. Once again, repression backfired. Workers were unified in support of the socialist cause.

Bismarck then changed course. He set out to woo workers away from socialism by sponsoring laws to protect them. Bismarck made it clear that *Realpolitik* influenced social reform as well as foreign policy:

"Give the workingman the right to work as long as he is healthy, assure him care when he is sick, and maintenance when he is old . . . then the socialists will sing their siren songs in vain, and the workingmen will cease to throng to their banner."
—Otto von Bismarck, quoted in *Economic Development of Europe* (Ogg and Sharp)

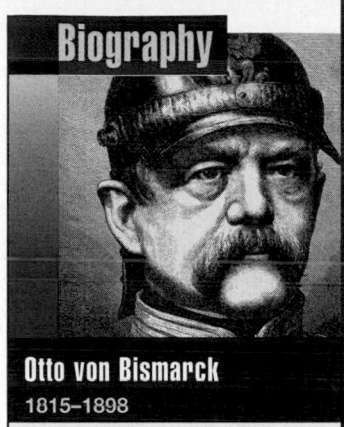

Biography

Otto von Bismarck
1815–1898

Bismarck spent his early years on his father's country estate. He worked briefly as a civil servant, but found the work boring. At 24, Bismarck resigned his post as a bureaucrat. "My ambition strives more to command than to obey," the independent-minded young man explained.

The resignation did not end his career in government. While he was a delegate to the Prussian assembly in 1847, his conservative views and passionate speeches in defense of government policies won him the support of the Prussian king. He was rewarded with appointment to the post of prime minister, a position he held for 28 years.

Theme: Impact of the Individual What path did Bismarck take to win political power?

Human Drama Note

Bismarck's Other Side Bismarck seems to have been as sentimental about his family and pets as he was ruthless in politics. He very much enjoyed being at home with his wife and children and, later, grandchildren. He kept a kennel full of dogs, of whom he was very fond. After watching over the death of one of his dogs, Bismarck is said to have told his son that he wished that upon his death he could be reunited with his faithful canines in the heavenly hunting ground of German folklore.

Test Preparation

Have students read the Bismarck quotation at the bottom of this page, and then answer the question below.

Why does Bismarck advocate giving government benefits to workingmen?

A to prevent workingmen from supporting the socialists

B to give workingmen a fair deal

C to keep workingmen from putting up banners

D to keep socialists from singing siren songs

Skills Assessment

ANSWER Bismarck rejected the traditional road of rising through the bureaucracy. As a delegate to the assembly, he won the support of the king by defending the government's policies.

SECTION 2 Assessment

Recall

1. **(a)** house of Krupp, p. 574 **(b)** August Thyssen, p. 574 **(c)** Iron Chancellor, p. 575 **2. (a)** *Kulturkampf*, p. 575 **(b)** social welfare, p. 576

Comprehension

3. Germany had ample coal and iron resources, a disciplined and educated work force, a growing population, and previous progress in building industries and railroads. 4. They both commanded loyalties to something other than the state. He saw them as threats to German power. 5. While he limited democratic reform, William II did provide social welfare benefits, more efficient transportation, and improved education. He also strengthened German military power around the world.

Critical Thinking and Writing

6. Possible answer: Because Bismarck and William I had gathered so much power that democratic reformers were easily sidestepped. 7. Possible answer: No, because an able politician should have been able to achieve these results without Bismarck's level of ruthlessness.

Photography and Daily Life
The invention of photography in the mid-1800s provided artists with a new way to reflect and comment on real life. This photograph is from a series depicting workers at the beginning of the 1900s.

Theme: Art and Literature
What do you think the photographer is trying to say about German workers?

By the 1890s, Germans had health and accident insurance as well as old-age insurance to provide retirement benefits. Thus, under Bismarck, Germany was a pioneer in social reform. Its system of economic safeguards became the model for other European nations.

Bismarck's plan was only partly successful. Although workers benefited from his measures, they did not abandon socialism. In fact, the Social Democratic party continued to grow in strength. By 1912, it had more seats in the Reichstag than were held by any other party. Yet Bismarck's program showed that conditions for workers could be improved without the upheaval of a revolution. Later, Germany and other European nations would build on Bismarck's social policies, greatly increasing government's role in providing for the needs of its citizens.

Kaiser William II

In 1888, William II succeeded his grandfather as kaiser. The new emperor was supremely confident of his abilities and wished to put his own stamp on Germany. In 1890, he shocked Europe by asking the dominating Bismarck to resign. "There is only one master in the Reich," he said, "and that is I."

William II seriously believed that his right to rule came from God. He expressed this view when he said:

> "My grandfather considered that the office of king was a task that God had assigned to him. . . . That which he thought I also think. . . . Those who wish to aid me in that task . . . I welcome with all my heart; those who oppose me in this work I shall crush."
> —William II, quoted in *Europe Since 1815* (Hazen)

Not surprisingly, William resisted efforts to introduce democratic reforms. At the same time, his government provided services, from programs for social welfare, or programs to help certain groups of people, to cheap transportation and electricity. An excellent system of public schools, begun under Bismarck, taught students obedience to the emperor along with reading, writing, and mathematics.

Like his grandfather, William II lavished funds on the German military machine, already the most powerful in Europe. He also launched an ambitious campaign to expand the German navy and win an overseas empire to rival those of Britain and France. You will read in later chapters how William's nationalism and aggressive militarism helped increase tensions on the eve of World War I.

SECTION 2 Assessment

Recall

1. **Identify:** (a) house of Krupp, (b) August Thyssen, (c) Iron Chancellor.
2. **Define:** (a) *Kulturkampf*, (b) social welfare.

Comprehension

3. How did Germany become an industrial giant in the late 1800s?
4. Why did Bismarck try to crush the Catholic Church and socialists?
5. What policies did William II introduce?

Critical Thinking and Writing

6. **Recognizing Causes and Effects** Why do you think supporters of democratic government had little hope of success in Germany in the late 1800s?
7. **Defending a Position** Were Bismarck's methods justified by his social reforms? Explain.

Activity
Take It to the NET

Use the Internet to research the Krupp family of Germany. Then, write a report explaining their role in the military and industrial history of Germany.

Unifying Italy

Reading Focus

- What were the key obstacles to Italian unity?
- What roles did Count Camillo Cavour and Giuseppe Garibaldi play in the struggle for Italy?
- What challenges faced the new nation of Italy?

Vocabulary

anarchist
emigration

Taking Notes

As you read, make a time line to show events from 1831 to 1871 in Italy. Use the time line shown here to help you get started.

1831	1849	1852	1871
Mazzini founds Young Italy	Mazzini's revolutionary republic in Rome toppled	Cavour becomes prime minister in Sardinia	

Main Idea During the 1800s, influential leaders helped to create a unified Italy.

Setting the Scene At the Congress of Vienna, Italian nationalists hoped to end centuries of foreign rule and achieve unity. To Metternich, the idea of a unified Italy was laughable. Italy, he was convinced, was a mere "geographic expression."

Although the people of the Italian peninsula spoke the same language, they had not experienced political unity since Roman times. By the early 1800s, though, Italian patriots were determined to build a new, united Italy. As in Germany, unification was brought about by the efforts of a strong state and a shrewd, ruthless politician—Count Camillo Cavour.

Obstacles to Italian Unity

For centuries, Italy had been a battleground for ambitious foreign and local princes. Frequent warfare and foreign rule had led people to identify with local regions. The people of Florence considered themselves Tuscans, those of Venice Venetians, the people of Naples Neapolitans, and so on. But as in Germany, the invasions of Napoleon had sparked dreams of national unity.

The Congress of Vienna, however, ignored the nationalists. At Vienna, Austria took control of much of northern Italy, while Hapsburg monarchs ruled various other Italian states. In the south, a French Bourbon ruler was put in charge of Naples and Sicily.

In response, nationalists organized secret patriotic societies and focused their efforts on expelling Austrian forces from northern Italy. Between 1820 and 1848, nationalist revolts exploded across the region. Each time, Austria sent in troops to crush the rebels.

Mazzini's Young Italy In the 1830s, the nationalist leader Giuseppe Mazzini founded Young Italy. The goal of this secret society was "to constitute Italy, one, free, independent, republican nation." In 1849, Mazzini helped set up a revolutionary republic in Rome, but French forces soon toppled it. Like many other nationalists, Mazzini spent much of his life in exile, plotting and dreaming of a united Italy.

The Tide of Nationalism "Ideas grow quickly," Mazzini once said, "when watered by the blood of martyrs." Although revolution had failed, nationalist agitation had planted seeds for future harvests.

To nationalists like Mazzini, a united Italy made sense not only because of geography, but also because of a common language and history. Nationalists reminded Italians of the glories of ancient Rome and the medieval

Primary Source

First Stirrings of Nationalism
After the failed revolution in northern Italy, many rebels came through Genoa, begging for funds to pay for safe passage to Spain. An impressionable Giuseppe Mazzini described his reaction to the situation:

"He held out a white handkerchief, merely saying, 'For the refugees of Italy.' My mother . . . dropped some money into the handkerchief. . . . That day was the first in which a confused idea presented itself to my mind—I will not say of country or of liberty—but an idea that we Italians could and ought to struggle for the liberty of our country. . . . The idea of an existing wrong on my own country, against which it was a duty to struggle, flashed before my mind on that day for the first time, never again to leave me."

—Giuseppe Mazzini,
Life and Writings

Skills Assessment

Primary Source How did the man's request influence Mazzini's thinking?

Bell Ringer Have students use the map *Unification of Italy, 1858–1870* in this section to answer the following questions: (1) What was the political condition of Italy in 1858? (2) How might this situation have slowed the development of Italy's economy?

LESSON PLAN

1. Focus For centuries, Italy had been a collection of separate states ruled by foreign and local princes who competed with each other for power. In the 1800s, influential leaders such as Giuseppe Mazzini, Giuseppe Garibaldi, and Count Camillo Cavour helped to create a united Italy. However, Italy still faced regional differences, disputes between the Church and state, and opposition to a conservative government.

2. Instruct Divide the class into small groups. Assign each group to create a biographical profile of one of the following people: Giuseppe Mazzini, Victor Emmanuel II, Count Camillo Cavour, Giuseppe Garibaldi. Explain that the profiles should focus on how these leaders contributed to Italy's unification. Students should consider how the person rose to leadership, what his ideals and goals were, what methods he used, and the reasons for his success or failure. Suggest that students in each group assume responsibility for a different part of the profile. Advise students to use library resources to supplement the information in the text. When they have finished, have the groups take turns sharing their profiles with the class.

3. Assess Play a game in which you describe some aspect of one or more of the Italian leaders whom the students have profiled. Ask students to identify the person or persons being described.

4. Reteach If students' Assess activity does not reflect adequate understanding of the lesson, you might assign the *Guide to the Essentials* or the *Interactive Student Tutorial CD-ROM* for this section.

Skills Assessment

ANSWER It gave Mazzini his first inkling that Italians should fight to free their country from foreign rule.

Block Scheduling Support

Political and social movements are shaped by leaders who inspire people and orchestrate events. Artists, too, have a significant impact on the life of a people, reinforcing specific visions and attitudes, including nationalistic sentiments. Renowned Italian composer Giuseppe Verdi inspired nationalistic feelings. His operas helped drive the patriotic movement for unification.

Have students read the Biography Activity *Giuseppe Verdi* in the Unit 6 booklet, p. 30; answer the questions; and discuss them in class. Then, invite a music teacher or music students to speak to the class on Verdi's nationalistic music and play some examples from recordings.

Background
Biography

Giuseppe Garibaldi After being sentenced to death for his revolutionary activities in the 1830s, Giuseppe Garibaldi fled to South America, where he lived from 1836 to 1848. He took part in a local rebellion against Emperor Pedro II of Brazil. He then helped Uruguay gain independence from Argentina by serving as the commander of the tiny Uruguayan navy and by leading a battalion of Italian volunteers. When news of the revolutions of 1848 reached him in Montevideo, he quickly returned to Italy. In 1848, he fought against the Austrians in Milan and against the French in the Papal States. Exiled once again, Garibaldi, known now as the "hero of two worlds," lived for a time in North Africa, the United States, and Peru. He finally returned to Italy in 1854 to assume a new role of leadership in the drive for Italian unification.

papacy. To others, unity made practical economic sense. It would end trade barriers among the Italian states and stimulate industry.

The Struggle for Italy

After 1848, leadership of the Risorgimento (ree sor jee MEHN toh), or Italian nationalist movement, passed to the kingdom of Sardinia. Its constitutional monarch, Victor Emmanuel II, hoped to join other states to his own, thereby increasing his power.*

Cavour In 1852, Victor Emmanuel made Count Camillo Cavour his prime minister. Cavour came from a noble family but favored liberal goals. He was a flexible, practical, crafty politician, willing to use almost any means to achieve his goals. Like Bismarck in Prussia, Cavour was a monarchist who believed in *Realpolitik*.

Once in office, Cavour moved first to reform Sardinia's economy. He improved agriculture, had railroads built, and encouraged commerce by supporting free trade. Cavour's long-term goal, however, was to end Austrian power in Italy and annex its provinces of Lombardy and Venetia.

Intrigue With France In 1855, led by Cavour, Sardinia joined Britain and France in the Crimean War against Russia. Sardinia did not win territory, but it did have a voice at the peace conference. Sardinia also gained the attention of Napoleon III.

In 1858, Cavour negotiated a secret deal with Napoleon, who promised to aid Sardinia in case it faced a war with Austria. A year later, the shrewd

---

*The kingdom of Sardinia included Piedmont, Nice, and Savoy, as well as the island of Sardinia.

Giuseppe Garibaldi
As leader of a volunteer army (below, right) that fought to unify Italy, Garibaldi told his troops, "I offer hunger, thirst, . . . battles, and death. Let him who loves his country in his heart, and not with his lips only, follow me."
Theme: Impact of the Individual What leadership qualities might someone like Garibaldi have?

Caption Answer

Possible answers: personal involvement and conviction, bravery, commitment to people who fight with him

Cavour provoked that war. With help from France, Sardinia defeated Austria and annexed Lombardy. Meanwhile, nationalist groups overthrew Austrian-backed rulers in several other northern Italian states. These states then joined with Sardinia.

Garibaldi's Red Shirts Next, attention shifted to the kingdom of the Two Sicilies in southern Italy. There, Giuseppe Garibaldi, a longtime nationalist and an ally of Mazzini, was ready for action. Like Mazzini, Garibaldi wanted to create an Italian republic. He did not, however, hesitate to accept aid from the monarchist Cavour. By 1860, Garibaldi had recruited a force of 1,000 red-shirted volunteers. Cavour provided weapons and allowed two ships to take Garibaldi and his "Red Shirts" south to Sicily.

With surprising speed, Garibaldi's forces won control of Sicily, crossed to the mainland, and marched triumphantly north to Naples. An English volunteer recalled his impression of Garibaldi during one battle:

"I saw Garibaldi, with his red shirt wringing wet with perspiration, his eye sternly gleaming, his face flushed with the heat of conflict. . . . I heard his voice commanding—but it was no longer now the calm, clear voice of quieter times. It was hoarse and guttural, and choked with emotion. For the good general saw his gallant band unfalteringly pouring out their life-blood."
—W. B. Brooke, quoted in *Garibaldi: Great Lives Observed* (Smith)

Unity at Last Garibaldi's success alarmed Cavour, who feared that the nationalist hero would set up his own republic in the south. To prevent this, Cavour urged Victor Emmanuel to send Sardinian troops to deal with Garibaldi. Instead, the Sardinians overran the Papal States and linked up with Garibaldi and his forces in Naples.

In a patriotic move, Garibaldi turned over Naples and Sicily to Victor Emmanuel. Shortly afterward, southern Italy voted to approve the move, and in 1861, Victor Emmanuel II was crowned king of Italy.

Two areas remained outside the new Italian nation: Rome and Venetia. Cavour died in 1861, but his successors completed his dream. In a deal negotiated with Bismarck, Italy acquired Venetia after the Austro-Prussian War. Then, during the Franco-Prussian War in 1870, France was forced to withdraw its troops from Rome. For the first time since the fall of the Roman empire, Italy was a united land.

Challenges Facing the New Nation

Italy faced a host of problems. Like the many states Bismarck cemented into the German empire, Italy had no tradition of unity. Few Italians felt ties to the new nation. Strong regional rivalries left Italy unable to solve critical national issues.

Unification of Italy, 1858–1870

Kingdom of Sardinia, 1858

Added to Sardinia, 1859 and 1860

Route of Garibaldi's expedition, 1860

Added to Italy, 1866

Added to Italy, 1870

Mercator Projection

Recall

1. (a) Giuseppe Mazzini, p. 577 (b) Risorgimento, p. 578 (c) Victor Emmanuel II, p. 578 (d) Camillo Cavour, p. 578 (e) Giuseppe Garibaldi, p. 579 2. (a) anarchist, p. 580 (b) emigration, p. 580

Comprehension

3. (a) Italy was divided into many states, and Italians were more loyal to their local regions than to Italy. (b) common language, shared traditions, nationalist opposition to Napoleonic invasions 4. Cavour used *Realpolitik* policies to strengthen Sardinia's economy and form alliances. Garibaldi recruited volunteers to fight for unification. 5. Italy still faced regional differences, disputes between the Church and state, and opposition to a conservative government.

Critical Thinking and Writing

6. (a) Both leaders wanted to increase royal power. Both sought national unity, prosperity, and power. They were willing to use any means to attain their goals. (b) Bismarck could always rely on Prussian military force to attain his goals through war. Because Sardinia was weaker than Prussia, Cavour had to rely more on careful diplomacy and alliances. 7. (a) Cavour feared that Garibaldi would set up a rival nation in the south. (b) Garibaldi turned over his conquered territories to Victor Emmanuel II.

Activity Rubrics

Share rubrics with students before they create their comic strip.

Attempted The comic strip is attempted but is missing important historical events, is poorly drawn, and has no continuity.

Minimal The comic strip includes the important historical events and has some continuity but is not clear or well presented.

Adequate The comic strip includes key historical events, has continuity, and is clear and well presented.

Exemplary The comic strip includes key historical events and is imaginative, sophisticated, and well drawn.

Caption Answer

Italy gave the pope control of Vatican City so that the Catholic Church would have political independence and not be subject to any nation.

Connections to Today

Vatican City

As Italian nationalists unified Italy, the Papal States lost their independence. Today, only one Papal State exists: Vatican City. Located in Rome, Vatican City is the world's smallest and least populated nation. At just over 108 acres, it is "just big enough to keep body and soul together," noted Pope Pius XI. In 1929, the Italian government granted the pope control of Vatican City. This gave him political independence as head of the Catholic Church. Named a United Nations world heritage site, Vatican City houses St. Peter's Basilica, the Sistine Chapel, and other churches and museums.

Theme: Political and Social Systems Why do you think the government granted the pope control of Vatican City?

Divisions The greatest regional differences were between the north and the south. The north was richer and had more cities than the south. For centuries, northern Italian cities had flourished as centers of business and culture. The south, on the other hand, was rural and poor. Its population was booming, but illiterate peasants could wring only a meager existence from the exhausted farmland.

Hostility between Italy and the Roman Catholic Church further divided the nation. Popes bitterly resented the seizure of the Papal States and of Rome. The government granted the papacy the small territory of the Vatican. Popes, however, saw themselves as "prisoners" and urged Italian Catholics—almost all Italians—not to cooperate with their new government.

Turmoil Under Victor Emmanuel, Italy was a constitutional monarchy with a two-house legislature. The king appointed members to the upper house, which could veto bills passed by the lower house. Although the lower house consisted of elected representatives, only a small number of men had the right to vote.

In the late 1800s, unrest increased as radicals on the left struggled against a conservative government. Socialists organized strikes while anarchists, people who want to abolish all government, turned to sabotage and violence. Slowly, the government extended suffrage to more men and passed laws to improve social conditions. Still, the turmoil continued. To distract attention from troubles at home, the government set out to win an overseas empire.

Progress Despite its problems, Italy did develop economically, especially after 1900. Although the nation lacked important natural resources such as coal, industries did sprout up in northern regions. Industrialization, of course, brought urbanization as peasants flocked to the cities to find jobs in factories. As in other countries, reformers campaigned to improve education and working conditions.

The population explosion of this period created tensions. One important safety valve for many people was emigration, or movement away from their homeland. Many Italians left for the United States, Canada, and Latin American nations.

Looking Ahead

Although unification brought great challenges, it also brought increased strength. By 1914, Italy was significantly better off than it had been in 1861. But it was hardly prepared for the great war that broke out in that year and into which it was soon drawn.

SECTION 3 Assessment

Recall

1. **Identify:** (a) Giuseppe Mazzini, (b) Risorgimento, (c) Victor Emmanuel II, (d) Camillo Cavour, (e) Giuseppe Garibaldi.
2. **Define:** (a) anarchist, (b) emigration.

Comprehension

3. (a) What obstacles to unity did Italian nationalists face? (b) What conditions favored unity?
4. How did Cavour and Garibaldi work for Italian unity?

5. Describe the problems Italians faced after unification.

Critical Thinking and Writing

6. **Comparing** Compare the goals and methods of Cavour in Italy and Bismarck in Germany. (a) How were they similar? (b) How were they different?
7. **Analyzing Information** (a) What was the source of conflict between Garibaldi and Cavour? (b) How was the conflict resolved?

Activity

Creating a Comic Strip Create a historical comic strip that illustrates the events leading to Italian unification. Include important historical figures and locations.

Resource Directory

Teaching Resources

Section Quiz Unit 6 booklet, p. 25
Creative Teaching Activities Creative Teaching Activities booklet, p. 105
Guided Reading and Review Unit 6 booklet, p. 26

Technology

Interactive Student Tutorial CD-ROM Ch. 23
Computer Test Bank Ch. 23

SECTION 4 · Nationalism Threatens Old Empires

Reading Focus

- How did nationalism contribute to the decline of the Austrian empire?
- What were the main characteristics of the Dual Monarchy?
- How did the growth of nationalism affect the Balkans?

Taking Notes

Start a table like the one shown here. As you read this section, add information about the threats and changes that led to the decline of the Hapsburg and Ottoman empires.

HAPSBURGS	OTTOMAN TURKS
• Oldest ruling house in Europe	•
•	•

Main Idea Desires for national independence threatened to break up the Austrian and Ottoman empires.

Setting the Scene

The Hapsburgs had controlled the Holy Roman Empire for nearly 400 years when Napoleon invaded the German-speaking states. Austria's center of power now lay in Eastern Europe. Further wars resulted in continued loss of territory to Germany and Italy. Why did nationalism bring new strength to some countries and weaken others?

In Eastern Europe, the Austrian Hapsburgs and the Ottoman Turks ruled lands that included diverse ethnic groups. Nationalist feelings among these subject people contributed to tensions building across Europe.

A Declining Empire

In 1800, the Hapsburgs were the oldest ruling house in Europe. In addition to their homeland of Austria, over the centuries they had acquired the territories of Bohemia and Hungary, as well as parts of Romania, Poland, Ukraine, and northern Italy.

Challenge of Change Since the Congress of Vienna, the Austrian emperor Francis I and Metternich, his foreign minister, had upheld conservative goals against liberal forces. "Rule and change nothing," the emperor told his son. Under Francis and Metternich, newspapers could not even use the word *constitution*, much less discuss this key demand of liberals. The government also tried to limit industrial development, which would threaten traditional ways of life.

Austria, however, could not hold back the changes that were engulfing the rest of Europe. By the 1840s, factories were springing up. Soon, the Hapsburgs found themselves facing the problems of industrial life that had long been familiar in Britain—the growth of cities, worker discontent, and the stirrings of socialism.

A Patchwork of People Equally disturbing to the old order were the urgent demands of nationalists. The Hapsburgs presided over a multinational empire. Of its 50 million people at mid-century, fewer than a quarter were German-speaking Austrians. Almost half belonged to different

The Imperial Hub
Vienna was a glittering, glamorous city that attracted many of the best minds and talents of Europe. Here, Vienna's leading citizens enjoy an evening of gaiety at an imperial ball.

Theme: Political and Social Systems Based on this painting, what generalization might you make about the Hapsburg ruling class?

Virtual Field Trip
www.phschool.com

Schönbrunn Palace
Vienna, Austria

To find more information about the Austrian empire, use the Internet address above to link to Schönbrunn Palace.

The Hapsburg Empire
Schönbrunn Palace was the summer home of Hapsburg rulers. The imposing structure and extensive gardens were designed during the 1700s and 1800s to show the power of the Hapsburgs.

Theme: Political and Social Systems Why might the Hapsburgs have wanted a showplace palace?

Slavic groups, including Czechs, Slovaks, Poles, Ukrainians, Romanians, Serbs, Croats, and Slovenes. Often, rival groups shared the same region. The empire also included large numbers of Hungarians and Italians.

The Hapsburgs ignored nationalist demands as long as they could. "Peoples?" Francis I once exclaimed. "What does that mean? I know only subjects." As you have read, when nationalist revolts broke out across the Hapsburg empire in 1848, the government crushed them.

Early Reforms Amid the turmoil, 18-year-old Francis Joseph inherited the Hapsburg throne. He would rule until 1916, presiding over the empire during its fading days into World War I.

An early challenge came when Austria suffered its humiliating defeat at the hands of France and Sardinia in 1859. Francis Joseph realized he needed to strengthen the empire at home. Accordingly, he made some limited reforms. He granted a new constitution that set up a legislature. This body, however, was dominated by German-speaking Austrians. The reforms thus satisfied none of the other national groups that populated the empire. The Hungarians, especially, were determined to settle for nothing less than total self-government.

The Dual Monarchy

Austria's disastrous defeat in the 1866 war with Prussia brought renewed pressure for change from Hungarians within the empire. One year later, Francis Deák (deh AHK), a moderate Hungarian leader, helped work out a compromise that created a new political power known as the Dual Monarchy of Austria-Hungary.

Under the agreement, Austria and Hungary were separate states. Each had its own constitution and parliament. Francis Joseph ruled both, as emperor of Austria and king of Hungary. The two states also shared ministries of finance, defense, and foreign affairs, but were independent of each other in all other areas.

Although Hungarians welcomed the compromise, other subject peoples resented it. Restlessness increased among various Slavic groups, especially the Czechs in Bohemia. Some nationalist leaders called on Slavs to unite, insisting that "only through liberty, equality, and fraternal solidarity" could Slavic peoples fulfill their "great mission in the history of mankind." By the early 1900s, nationalist unrest often left the government paralyzed in the face of pressing political and social problems.

Balkan Nationalism

Like the Hapsburgs, the Ottomans ruled a multinational empire. It stretched from Eastern Europe and the Balkans to North Africa and the Middle East. There, as in Austria, nationalist demands tore at the fabric of the empire.

In the Balkans, Serbia had won autonomy in 1817, and southern Greece won independence in the 1830s. But many Serbs and Greeks still lived in the Balkans under Ottoman rule. The Ottoman empire was home to other national groups, such as Bulgarians and Romanians. During the 1800s, various subject peoples staged revolts against the Ottomans, hoping to set up their own independent states.

Such nationalist stirrings became mixed up with the ambitions of the great European powers. In the mid-1800s, Europeans came to see the Ottoman empire as "the sick man of Europe." Eagerly, they scrambled to divide up Ottoman lands. Russia pushed south toward the Black Sea and Istanbul, which Russians still called Constantinople. Austria-Hungary took control of the provinces of Bosnia and Herzegovina. This action angered the Serbs, who also had hoped to expand into that area. Meanwhile, Britain and France set their sights on other Ottoman lands in the Middle East and North Africa.

In the end, a complex web of competing interests contributed to a series of crises and wars in the Balkans. Russia fought several wars against the Ottomans. France and Britain sometimes joined the Russians and sometimes the Ottomans. Germany supported Austrian authority over the discontented national groups. But Germany also encouraged the Ottomans because of their strategic location in the eastern Mediterranean. In between, the subject peoples revolted and then fought among themselves. By the early 1900s, observers were referring to the region as the "Balkan powder keg." The explosion that came in 1914 helped set off World War I.

The Balkans, 1878

▨ Independent Balkan states
▢ Ottoman empire

RUSSIA
AUSTRIA–HUNGARY
BOSNIA–HERZEGOVINA (occupied by Austria)
ROMANIA
SERBIA
MONTENEGRO
BULGARIA (autonomous)
EASTERN RUMELIA (administered by Turkey)
Constantinople
ITALY
GREECE
Crete
Adriatic Sea
Aegean Sea
Black Sea
Mediterranean Sea
Danube R.

Azimuthal Equal Area Projection
0   200   400 Miles
0   200   400 Kilometers

40°N   20°E   30°E

Skills Assessment

Geography In the late 1800s, the Balkans had become a center of conflict, as various peoples and empires competed for power.

1. **Location** On the map, locate (a) Black Sea, (b) Ottoman empire, (c) Serbia, (d) Greece, (e) Austria-Hungary.
2. **Place** Which three large seas border the Balkan Peninsula?
3. **Critical Thinking Predicting Consequences** Why do you think competing interests in the Balkans led the region to be called a powder keg?

SECTION 4 Assessment

Recall
1. (a) Francis Joseph, p. 582 (b) Dual Monarchy, p. 582

Comprehension
2. In 1867, Austria formed the Dual Monarchy with Hungary. Other ethnic groups felt left out and continued to press the government for national freedom. 3. (a) Austria and Hungary were united by a common king and various ministries, but each had its own constitution and parliament. (b) Other nationalities in the empire gained little from this settlement and continued to demand national independence.
4. Possible answer: Various ethnic groups were demanding independence from the Ottoman empire. European powers competed for influence in the region.

Critical Thinking and Writing
5. Students' answers should indicate an understanding of the many difficulties faced by a multinational state. 6. (a) introduced limited reforms, kept legislature filled with German-speaking Austrians (b) Possible answer: He might have encouraged inclusion of more ethnic groups in the legislature, giving them a voice in government.

Activity Rubrics

Share rubrics with students before they write their reports.

Attempted The report reveals little research, misses important recent developments, is poorly written and organized, and contains many mechanical errors.

Minimal The report reveals some research and includes important recent developments but is poorly written and organized and contains many mechanical errors.

Adequate The report reveals ample research, includes important recent developments, is well written and organized, and contains few mechanical errors.

Exemplary The report reveals extensive research, includes important recent developments, is very well written and organized, and contains no mechanical errors.

Skills Assessment

ANSWERS 1. Review locations with students. **2.** Adriatic, Mediterranean, Aegean, and Black seas **3.** Possible answer: As outside nations competed for power over the Balkans, the region gained potential as a location for an outbreak of violence.

SECTION 4 Assessment

Recall
1. **Identify:** (a) Francis Joseph, (b) Dual Monarchy.

Comprehension
2. Explain how nationalism affected the Austrian empire.
3. (a) How was the Dual Monarchy organized? (b) Why did it fail to end nationalist demands?
4. How did Balkan nationalism contribute to the decline of the Ottoman empire?

Critical Thinking and Writing
5. **Solving Problems** Do you think that either the Hapsburgs or the Ottoman Turks could have built a modern, unified nation from their multinational empires? Explain.
6. **Identifying Alternatives** (a) What actions did Francis Joseph take to maintain power in Austria-Hungary? (b) How else might he have responded to nationalist demands?

Activity

Studying Current Events Research recent developments in the Balkans. Organize your findings into a report that can be presented orally or in writing.

Human Drama Activity

Balkan Culture Have students use library or Internet resources to find a folk song, a national anthem, or a folk tale from one of the Balkan countries. Call on a few volunteers to read aloud (or sing) their song, anthem, or story. Post the remaining songs, anthems, and stories on the bulletin board for students to read later.

✓ Test Preparation

Have students read the paragraph that begins at the bottom of the opposite page, and then answer the question below.

What does *fraternal solidarity* mean in this paragraph?

A   a pact between brothers

B   unity between brothers

C   unity among all peoples

Ⓓ   unity among Slavic peoples

Bell Ringer

Ask students to read the first paragraph and the quotation in "Setting the Scene" on this page and look at the picture of peasant women on the next page. How would students describe the life of the serfs? To what group in American history could serfs be compared?

LESSON PLAN

1. Focus Russian czars recognized the need to reform Russia. However, they were reluctant to undermine absolutist rule, social stability, the Orthodox Church, and the dominant role of the Russian ethnic group. The emancipation of the serfs in 1861 and the development of industry in the 1890s failed to stem popular unrest. War with Japan, the events of Bloody Sunday, and long-term disaffection ignited a revolution in 1905. Promised reforms were abandoned soon after the revolution.

2. Instruct Have students create an annotated time line of Russian history from 1800 to 1914. Students may work individually or in groups. Advise students that their time lines should include significant events having to do with each of the following czars: Alexander I, Nicholas I, Alexander II, Alexander III, Nicholas II. Ask students to write on a separate sheet of paper a descriptive or explanatory note for each event on their time lines. Display the finished time lines around the classroom. Have students use their notes to discuss the significance of each of the events on their time lines.

3. Assess Ask students to review their notes and time lines, and then write four generalizations about this period of Russian history.

4. Reteach If students' Assess activity does not reflect adequate understanding of the lesson, you might assign the *Guide to the Essentials* or the *Interactive Student Tutorial CD-ROM* for this section.

Reading Focus

■ How did conditions in Russia affect progress?

■ Why did czars follow a cycle of absolutism, reform, and reaction?

■ How did the problems of industrialization contribute to the growing crisis and outbreak of revolution?

Vocabulary

colossus
emancipation
zemstvo
pogrom
Duma

Taking Notes

As you read this section, make an outline of the information. Use Roman numerals for the main headings. Use capital letters for the subheadings, and use numbers for the supporting details. The outline has been started for you.

I. Conditions in Russia
  A. Obstacles to progress
    1. Economically undeveloped
    2. Rigid social structure
  B. Serfdom
II. Russian absolutism
  A. Alexander I
    1. Initially open to liberal ideas
    2.

Main Idea Industrialization and reform came more slowly to Russia than to Western Europe.

Setting the Scene Although serfdom had almost disappeared in Western Europe by the 1700s, it survived and spread in Russia. Masters exercised almost total power over their serfs. In the 1800s, a noble who became a revolutionary described the brutal treatment of serfs:

> "I heard . . . stories of men and women torn from their families and their villages, and sold, or lost in gambling, or exchanged for a couple of hunting dogs, and then transported to some remote part of Russia to create a [master's] new estate; . . . of children taken from their parents and sold to cruel masters."
> —Peter Kropotkin, *Memoirs of a Revolutionist*

Reformers hoped to free Russia from autocratic rule, economic backwardness, and social injustice. But efforts to modernize Russia had little success, as czars imprisoned critics or sent them into icy exile in Siberia.

Conditions in Russia

By 1815, Russia was not only the largest, most populous nation in Europe but also a great world power. Since the 1600s, explorers had pushed the Russian frontier eastward across Siberia to the Pacific. Peter the Great and Catherine the Great had added lands on the Baltic and Black seas, and czars in the 1800s had expanded into Central Asia. Russia had thus acquired a huge multinational empire, part European and part Asian.

Other European nations looked on the Russian colossus, or giant, with a mixture of wonder and misgiving. It had immense natural resources. Russia's vast size gave it global interests and influence. But Western Europeans disliked its autocratic government and feared its expansionist aims.

Obstacles to Progress Despite efforts by Peter and Catherine to westernize Russia, it remained economically undeveloped. By the 1800s, czars saw the need to modernize but resisted reforms that would undermine their absolute rule. While the czars wavered, Russia fell further behind Western Europe in economic and social developments.

A great obstacle to progress was the rigid social structure. Landowning nobles dominated society and rejected any change that would threaten their privileges. The middle class was too small to have much influence. The majority of Russians were serfs, laborers bound to the land and to masters who controlled their fates.

Resource Directory

Teaching Resources

Creative Teaching Activities Creative Teaching Activities booklet, p. 106
Guided Reading and Review Unit 6 booklet, p. 28
Primary Source Activity *The Execution in Semyonovsky Square,* Unit 6 booklet, p. 31

Technology

Prentice Hall Listening to Literature World Masterpieces audiotapes *The Bridegroom,* side 7, running time 6:25 min.

Serfdom Most serfs were peasants. Others might be servants, artisans, or soldiers forced into the czar's army. As industry expanded, some masters sent serfs to work in factories but took much of their pay.

Many enlightened Russians knew that serfdom was inefficient. As long as most people had to serve the whim of their masters, Russia's economy would remain backward. Landowning nobles had no reason to improve agriculture and took little interest in industry.

Russian Absolutism

For centuries, czars had ruled with absolute power, imposing their will on their subjects. The changes brought about by the Enlightenment and the French Revolution had almost no effect on Russian autocracy.

Alexander I When Alexander I inherited the throne in 1801, however, he seemed open to liberal ideas. The new czar eased censorship and promoted education. He even talked about freeing the serfs.

By the time Napoleon invaded Russia in 1812, Alexander had drawn back from reform. Like earlier czars, he feared losing the support of nobles. At the Congress of Vienna, he joined the conservative powers in opposing liberal and nationalist impulses in Europe.

Revolt and Repression When Alexander I died in 1825, a group of army officers led an uprising known as the Decembrist Revolt. They had picked up liberal ideas while fighting Napoleon in Western Europe and now demanded a constitution and other reforms. The new czar, Nicholas I, suppressed the Decembrists and cracked down on all dissent.

Nicholas used police spies to hunt out critics. He banned books from Western Europe that might spread liberal ideas. Only approved textbooks were allowed in schools and universities. Many Russians with liberal or revolutionary ideas were judged to be insane and shut up in mental hospitals. Up to 150,000 others were exiled to Siberia.

Nicholas I and Absolutism To bolster his regime, Nicholas I embraced the three pillars of Russian absolutism symbolized in the motto "Orthodoxy, Autocracy, and Nationalism." *Orthodoxy* referred to the strong ties between the Russian Orthodox Church and the government. *Autocracy* was the absolute power of the state. *Nationalism* involved respect for Russian traditions and suppression of non-Russian groups within the empire.

Still, Nicholas realized that Russia needed to modernize. He issued a new law code and made some economic reforms. He even tried to limit the power of landowners over serfs. But he could see no way to change the system completely without angering Russian nobles and weakening the power of the czar. Before he died, he told his son, "I am handing you command of the country in a poor state."

Reforms of Alexander II

Alexander II came to the throne in 1855 during the Crimean War. The war had broken out after Russia tried to seize Ottoman lands along the Danube. Britain and France stepped in to help the Turks, invading the Crimean peninsula that juts into the Black Sea. The war, which ended in a Russian defeat, revealed the country's backwardness. It had only a few miles of

Russian Serfs
Masters held great power over serfs in Russia, and a large labor supply meant that few landowners invested in machines that could speed up agricultural labor. Here, women clear large stones from a field.

Theme: Economics and Technology How did the continuation of serfdom keep the Russian economy from advancing as quickly as that of Western Europe?

Background
Daily Life

A Miserable Existence The daily life of Russian serfs was scarcely better than that of workhorses or other animals. They lived in dirt-floored huts. Windows were covered with pigs' bladders, which allowed no light to enter. Pigs and calves slept with the serfs in their huts. Fires that burned for warmth and cooking filled the homes with thick smoke.

The labor requirements imposed on serfs had changed little over the centuries. They still had to work several days a week on their masters' estates. Some worked as domestic servants; most worked the land. They also spent part of the year building roads, canals, and railways for the state. When Russia began to industrialize, serfs were compelled to live and work in factory towns under quasi-military discipline.

Global Connections

Freedom for Enslaved Americans

Emancipation was a troublesome issue around the world. For many years, the United States had been divided over slavery. In 1861, civil war erupted, in part over slavery. President Abraham Lincoln issued the Emancipation Proclamation in 1863, declaring the slaves in rebel areas to be free.

Neither Lincoln's action nor four years of bloody fighting settled the question. Finally, in 1865, the Thirteenth Amendment to the United States Constitution abolished slavery throughout the United States.

Even after emancipation, African Americans continued to face great challenges. Former slaves, like former serfs in Russia, had trouble acquiring farm land. Many worked for wages on the farms of former slaveholders, and others left to work in factories.

Theme: Political and Social Systems What settled the issue of slavery in the United States?

railroads, and the military bureaucracy was hopelessly inefficient. Many felt that dramatic changes were needed.

Emancipation A widespread popular reaction followed. Liberals demanded changes, and students demonstrated for reform. Pressed from all sides, Alexander II finally agreed to reforms. In 1861, he issued a royal decree that required emancipation, or freeing the serfs.

Freedom brought problems. Former serfs had to buy the land they had worked for so long. Many were too poor to do so. Also, the lands allotted to peasants were often too small to farm efficiently or to support a family. As a result, peasants remained poor, and discontent festered.

Still, emancipation was a turning point. Many peasants moved to the cities, taking jobs in factories and building Russian industries. Equally important, freeing the serfs boosted the drive for further reform.

Other Reforms Along with emancipation, Alexander set up a system of local government. Elected assemblies, called zemstvos, were made responsible for matters such as road repair, schools, and agriculture. At the local level, at least, Russians gained some experience of self-government.

The czar also introduced legal reforms based on ideas such as trial by jury. He eased censorship and tried to reform the military. A soldier's term of service was reduced from 25 years to 15, and brutal discipline was limited. Alexander also encouraged the growth of industry in Russia, which still relied almost entirely on agriculture.

A movement to liberate women also swept the urban centers of Russia. Since they were denied education in Russia, hundreds of privileged young women left their homes and families to study abroad in the few universities that would accept them. Many came to support revolutionary goals.

Reaction to Change

Alexander's reforms failed to satisfy many Russians. Peasants had freedom but not land. Liberals wanted a constitution and an elected legislature. Radicals, who had adopted socialist ideas from the West, demanded even more revolutionary changes. The czar, meantime, moved away from reform and toward repression.

Revolutionary Currents In the 1870s, some socialists carried the message of reform to the peasants. They went to live and work among the peasants, sometimes preaching rebellion. These educated young men and women had little success. The peasants scarcely understood them and sometimes turned them over to the police.

The failure of this "Go to the People" movement, combined with renewed government repression, sparked anger among radicals. Some turned to terrorism. A revolutionary group calling itself the People's Will assassinated officials and plotted to kill the czar. Their first attempts failed. Then, on a cold March day in 1881, terrorists hurled two bombs at Alexander's carriage. One struck down several guards. The second killed the leader known to some as the "czar emancipator."

Crackdown Alexander III responded to his father's assassination by reviving the harsh methods of Nicholas I. To wipe out liberals and revolutionaries, he increased the power of the secret police, restored strict censorship, and exiled critics to Siberia. He relied on his adviser and former tutor, Constantine Pobedonostsev (puh beh duh NAWS tsehv), who rejected all talk of democracy and constitutional government as "the lies of hollow and flabby people."

The czar also launched a program of Russification aimed at suppressing the cultures of non-Russian peoples within the empire. Alexander insisted on one language, Russian, and one church, the Russian Orthodox Church.

Global Connections

ANSWER the Thirteenth Amendment

Resource Directory

Teaching Resources
Humanities Link Chapter Extension Activities booklet, p. 58

Russian Ballet

Although French and Italian in origin, ballet took on a bold, unique form in Russia. Beginning in the eighteenth century, European ballet teachers introduced the classical style to Russia. By the late 1800s, Russian choreographers and dancers had developed an expressive, muscular style that was to rejuvenate and dominate ballet in the twentieth century.

Russian dancer and choreographer Vaslav Nijinsky won worldwide fame while touring with the Ballet Russe in the early 1900s. Many consider him the greatest male ballet dancer of the twentieth century.

The ballet *Firebird*, shown here in a modern production, debuted in Paris in 1910. It was one of the first ballets to be created by a Russian choreographer and inspired by a Russian folk tale.

Twice destroyed by fires, Moscow's ornate Bolshoi ("Big") Theater took on its present form in 1856. Tiers of seats line the opulent interior of the theater, which can seat more than 2,000. Today, the grand theater is considered "the main theater of the country."

Fast Facts

- Until the early 1900s, common people in Russia were thought to be too ignorant to understand and appreciate ballet. Only nobles and people from the wealthy classes attended performances.

- In 1911, Sergey Diaghilev's Ballet Russe began to spread the influence of Russian dance worldwide.

- During World War II, dancers from the Bolshoi traveled from place to place, entertaining Russian troops in the field.

Portfolio Assessment

 INTERNET Use the Internet or library resources to find out more about Russian ballet. Then, prepare a presentation on the significance of a particular Russian choreographer or dancer. If possible, include photographs or drawings of the individual you have selected.

Bell Ringer Ask students whether they have ever seen a ballet performed. How would they describe the experience? What did they like best about it?

Background Connections to Today

Russian Ballet Today As a search of the Internet under the words *Russian ballet* reveals, ballet is alive and well in Russia today. In one recent month, more than ten different ballets were performed by various companies in Moscow alone. In addition to performing classical ballet, Russian companies, some of which are quite new, perform modern and experimental dance. Several companies go on tour to the United States, Japan, and other countries around the world.

Activity Cooperative Learning

Divide the class into small groups and have each group choose some aspect of ballet for a presentation. Students may choose to investigate techniques and steps, training, music, costuming, history, or an individual ballet. Students may also choose to play clips from a ballet video and provide commentary on them.

Portfolio Assessment Rubrics

Share rubrics with students before they complete this presentation.

Attempted The presentation shows little understanding of the subject or his or her significance.

Minimal The presentation shows some understanding of the subject, but organization and delivery are poor.

Adequate The presentation shows understanding of the subject, organization is good, and delivery is informative and interesting.

Exemplary The presentation is exceptionally full of detail and well organized, and delivery is informative and especially interesting.

EXPLORING the HUMAN DRAMA | **Human Drama Note**

Using Fiction as Historical Evidence Feodor Dostoyevsky's novel *The House of the Dead* reveals—through the eyes of one of the "dead," a prisoner—life in one of the Siberian prison camps to which critics were exiled (mentioned on the opposite page). Based on the Russian writer's own exile, the novel describes a daily life of confinement, compulsory work, rotten food, and power struggles among the convicts.

Ask students to read Chapters 1 and 2 of *The House of the Dead*. Have students refer to Chapter 1 and draw and label a diagram of the prison camp. After they have read Chapter 2, ask students to write and present a monologue representing the viewpoint of a prisoner in the camp or the major who is in charge of the camp. In their monologue, students should speak in the "voice" of the assumed character. They should identify themselves, tell why they are in the camp, describe a typical day, and explain how they endure their experience. ❋

Customize for . . .
Heterogeneous Groups

Relating Cause and Effect As an enrichment activity, ask students to explore the causes and effects of the Russo-Japanese War, fought in 1904 and 1905. Advise students that they will need to do outside research. They should recognize both immediate and long-term causes and effects. They should focus their attention on Russia more than Japan. Students may present their findings in any of various formats, including a cause-and-effect chart, an essay, or an oral presentation. *(Enrichment)*

Geography and History

Russia's Long Iron Road

Beginning in the 1890s, Russian workers laid more than 5,000 miles of track to build the Trans-Siberian Railroad, the longest railroad in the world at that time. Siberia's harsh landscape and climate challenged workers. Iron, stone, hardwoods, and food had to be shipped thousands of miles to the crews.

In the chilling winters, many workers died from hypothermia. With no safety devices, some fell to their deaths onto frozen rivers. To lay tracks in some areas, workers had to dynamite permanently frozen soil. These explosions often proved fatal, as did epidemics of bubonic plague, anthrax, and cholera.

Theme: Geography and History What geographic and climatic challenges did the railroad builders face in Siberia?

Poles, Ukrainians, Finns, Armenians, and many others suffered persecution. The Russification campaign also targeted Jews and Muslims in the empire.

Persecution and Pogroms Russia had acquired a large Jewish population when it carved up Poland and expanded into Ukraine. Under Alexander III, persecution of Russian Jews increased. The czar limited the number of Jews who were allowed to study in universities and practice professions such as law and medicine. He revived old laws that forced Jews to live in certain restricted areas.

Official persecution encouraged pogroms, or violent mob attacks on Jews. Gangs beat and killed Jews and looted and burned their homes and stores. The police did nothing to stop the violence. Faced with savage persecution, many Jews escaped from Russia. They became refugees, or people who flee their homeland to seek safety elsewhere. Large numbers of Russian Jews went to the United States. Though they often faced prejudice and great hardship there, they were safe from pogroms and official persecution. Jewish immigrants sent joyful news back to Russia: "There is no czar in America!"

Building Russian Industry

Under Alexander III and his son, Nicholas II, Russia finally entered the industrial age. In the 1890s, Count Serge Witte, finance minister to Nicholas, focused on economic development. Witte encouraged railroad building to connect iron and coal mines with factories and to transport goods across Russia. He secured foreign capital to invest in transportation systems and industry. Loans from France helped build the Trans-Siberian Railroad. Begun in the 1890s, it linked European Russia to the Pacific Ocean.

The drive to industrialize increased political and social problems. Government officials and business leaders applauded and encouraged economic growth. Nobles and peasants opposed it, fearing the changes brought by the new ways.

Industrialization also created new social ills as peasants flocked to cities to work in factories. Instead of a better life, they found long hours and low pay in dangerous conditions. In the slums around the factories, poverty, disease, and discontent multiplied.

Radicals sought supporters among the new industrial workers. At factory gates, socialists handed out pamphlets that preached the revolutionary ideas of Karl Marx. Among the revolutionaries of the 1890s was young Vladimir Ulyanov, whose older brother had been executed for plotting to kill Alexander III. Like many revolutionaries, Ulyanov used an alias, or false name—Lenin. In 1917, Lenin would take power in a revolution that transformed Russia.

Turning Point: Crisis and Revolution

War broke out between Russia and Japan in 1904. Nicholas II called on his people to fight for "the Faith, the Czar, and the Fatherland." But despite their efforts, the Russians suffered one humiliating defeat after another.

A Peaceful March News of the military disasters unleashed pent-up discontent created by years of oppression. Protesters poured into the streets. Workers went on strike with demands for shorter hours and better wages. Liberals called for a constitution and reforms to overhaul the inefficient, corrupt government.

As the crisis deepened, a young Orthodox priest, Father George Gapon, organized a march for Sunday, January 22, 1905. Father Gapon felt certain that the "Little Father," as many Russians called the czar, would help his people if only he understood their sufferings. The parade flowed through

588 Chapter 23

Skills Assessment

ANSWER Many resources had to be shipped long distances; extreme cold caused many accidents and deaths; permafrost had to be blasted.

Resource Directory

Teaching Resources
Treasures of the World *The Cause of Bloody Sunday,* pp. 127–129
History Through Literature *How I Found America,* History Through Literature booklet, pp. 49–50
Section Quiz Unit 6 booklet, p. 29
Geography Quiz Unit 6 booklet, p. 34
Chapter Test Forms A, B, and C Unit 6 booklet, pp. 35–39
Answer Key Unit 6 booklet, pp. 98–112

Technology
Interactive Student Tutorial CD-ROM Ch. 23
Computer Test Bank Ch. 23

588 Chapter 23

the icy streets of St. Petersburg toward the czar's lavish Winter Palace. Chanting prayers and singing hymns, workers carried holy icons and pictures of the czar. They also brought a petition for justice and freedom, which was addressed to Nicholas.

Bloody Sunday Fearing the marchers, the czar had fled the palace and called in soldiers. As the people approached, they saw troops lined up across the square. Suddenly, gunfire rang out. Men and women ran and fell. More shots left hundreds dead or wounded in the snow.

A woman stumbling away from the scene of the massacre moaned: "The czar has deserted us! They shot away the orthodox faith." Indeed, the slaughter marked a turning point for Russians. "Bloody Sunday" killed the people's faith and trust in the czar.

The Revolution of 1905 In the months that followed Bloody Sunday, discontent exploded across Russia. Strikes multiplied. In some cities, workers took over local government. In the countryside, peasants revolted and demanded land. Minority nationalities called for autonomy from Russia. Terrorists targeted officials, and some assassins were cheered as heroes by discontented Russians.

At last, the clamor grew so great that Nicholas was forced to announce sweeping reforms. In the October Manifesto, he promised "freedom of person, conscience, speech, assembly, and union." He agreed to summon a Duma, or elected national legislature. No law, he declared, would go into effect without approval by the Duma.

Results of the Revolution The manifesto won over moderates, leaving socialists isolated. These divisions helped the czar, who had no intention of letting strikers, revolutionaries, and rebellious peasants challenge him.

In 1906, the first Duma met, but the czar quickly dissolved it when leaders criticized the government. Nicholas then appointed a new prime minister, Peter Stolypin (stuh LEE pihn). Arrests, pogroms, and executions followed as the conservative Stolypin sought to restore order.

Stolypin soon realized that Russia needed reform, not just repression. To regain peasant support, he introduced moderate land reforms. He strengthened the zemstvos and improved education. These reforms were too limited to meet the broad needs of most Russians, and dissatisfaction still simmered. Stolypin was assassinated in 1911. Several more Dumas met during this period, but new voting laws made sure they were conservative. By 1914, Russia was still an autocracy, simmering with unrest.

Biography

Peter Stolypin 1862–1911

Violence surrounded Peter Stolypin, who was once described as "a tall stiff man with a dead white face and a dead white beard." As governor and later prime minister, he used harsh measures to silence opposition. On his orders, trials of terrorists were held within 24 hours of arrest; executions were held immediately upon conviction. More than 1,000 suspected terrorists were executed in less than a year. The noose used to hang them came to be known as "Stolypin's necktie."

Stolypin and his family were also the targets of violence. In 1907, his opponents bombed his house, killing many servants and severely injuring his children. Four years later, Stolypin himself was assassinated while attending the theater.

Theme: Impact of the Individual How did Stolypin deal with terrorism?

SECTION 5 Assessment

Recall
1. (a) Decembrist Revolt, p. 585 (b) Alexander II, p. 585 (c) Russification, p. 586 (d) Bloody Sunday, p. 589 (e) October Manifesto, p. 589 (f) Peter Stolypin, p. 589 2. (a) colossus, p. 584 (b) emancipation, p. 586 (c) zemstvo, p. 586 (d) pogrom, p. 588 (e) Duma, p. 589

Comprehension
3. economic underdevelopment, rigid social structure, continuation of serfdom
4. by increasing repression 5. (a) worker discontent, desire for a liberal constitution, Russo-Japanese War, Bloody Sunday (b) Nicholas issued the October Manifesto, in which he promised personal freedoms and the summoning of the Duma. Soon after the revolution, however, the czar dismissed the Duma and continued to limit rights and freedoms.

Critical Thinking and Writing
6. Possible answer: He felt that if he did not end serfdom himself, revolutionaries would eventually do so. By freeing the serfs, he hoped to avoid revolution.
7. Possible answer: Bloody Sunday revealed that the czar feared the Russian people and was willing to use force to suppress them. Many Russians, realizing that peaceful reform was unlikely, were willing to use violence against the czar.

SECTION 5 Assessment

Recall
1. **Identify:** (a) Decembrist Revolt, (b) Alexander II, (c) Russification, (d) Bloody Sunday, (e) October Manifesto, (f) Peter Stolypin.
2. **Define:** (a) colossus, (b) emancipation, (c) zemstvo, (d) pogrom, (e) Duma.

Comprehension
3. What conditions in Russia posed challenges during the early 1800s?
4. How did Russian czars often react to change?

5. (a) What were the causes of the revolution of 1905? (b) How did Nicholas II respond?

Critical Thinking and Writing
6. **Analyzing Information** Alexander II declared that it is "better to abolish serfdom from above than to wait until it will be abolished by a movement from below." Explain his statement.
7. **Making Inferences** What does Bloody Sunday suggest about the relationship between the czar and the Russian people?

Activity
Take It to the NET

Use the Internet to find the decree of Alexander II to free the serfs. Write a paragraph that summarizes Alexander's reasons for emancipation.

✔ Test Preparation

Have students read "Bloody Sunday" on this page, and then answer the question below.

Why was Bloody Sunday a turning point for Russians?

A People were massacred.

Ⓑ It destroyed people's belief in the czar as a protector.

C It destroyed people's faith in God.

D Blood was shed in the snow.

Activity Rubrics

Share rubrics with students before they write their paragraphs.

Attempted The paragraph shows limited understanding of the decree, is poorly written and organized, and contains many mechanical errors.

Minimal The paragraph shows reasonable understanding of the decree but is poorly written and organized and contains many mechanical errors.

Adequate The paragraph shows good understanding of the decree, is well written and organized, and contains few mechanical errors.

Exemplary The paragraph shows excellent understanding of the decree, is very well written and organized, and contains no mechanical errors.

Biography

ANSWER Trials were held within 24 hours after arrest, and execution came immediately after conviction.

Creating a Chapter Summary

As a reteaching opportunity, pair a more able student with a less able student to complete this chapter summary.

Possible answers: **Germany** German states unite under William I; Empire takes leading role in Europe; Bismarck/Iron Chancellor **Italy** Mazzini founds Young Italy; Garibaldi leads Red Shirts; Victor Emmanuel II makes Cavour prime minister of Sardinia; Italian states become unified by 1871 **Austria** Francis I and Metternich uphold conservative goals; Dual Monarchy with Hungary set up; National groups restless; Empire weakened **Balkans** Serbian independence in 1817; Greek independence in 1830s; European nations move in; Balkan powder keg **Russia** Serfs freed in 1861; Persecutions of Alexander III; Enters industrial age late; Bloody Sunday leads to revolution in 1905; Duma with limited power

Building Vocabulary

1–10. Sentences should show a clear understanding of the meanings of the terms.

Recalling Key Facts

11. ample iron and coal resources, a disciplined and educated work force, large companies and many railroads
12. He sponsored social reform laws, such as health and accident insurance, that benefited workers.
13. to create a unified, independent, republican Italy
14. They ignored nationalist demands and crushed nationalist revolts.
15. They sought to divide up Ottoman lands in the Balkans for themselves.
16. Military defeats increased popular discontent with the government, and a demonstration for better government was met by gunfire, which encouraged the spread of revolutionary violence.

Critical Thinking and Writing

17. (a) coronation of William I as emperor of Germany **(b)** in the Hall of Mirrors at Versailles **(c)** Bismarck **(d)** that the chancellor was at least as powerful as the emperor
18. Possible answers: **(a)** The French will seek revenge against Germany. **(b)** Germany will become involved in more wars. **(c)** Austria-Hungary will continue to face national unrest and violence. **(d)** More nationalist groups

---

CHAPTER 23 Review and Assessment

Creating a Chapter Summary

On a sheet of paper, make a table like the one shown here to list events that led to nationalism in Germany, Italy, Austria, the Balkans, and Russia in the 1800s.

GERMANY	ITALY	AUSTRIA	BALKANS	RUSSIA
• German states unite under William I • Empire takes leading role in Europe • Bismarck/Iron Chancellor		• Francis I and Metternich uphold conservative goals •		

Web Site Self-Test For practice test questions for Chapter 23, see **www.phschool.com.**

For additional review and enrichment activities, see the interactive version of *World History* available on the Web and on CD-ROM.

Reviewing Vocabulary

Review the meaning of the chapter vocabulary words listed below. Then, write a sentence for each word in which you define the word and describe its relation to nationalism in Europe.

1. *Realpolitik*
2. annex
3. Reich
4. *Kulturkampf*
5. anarchist
6. colossus
7. emancipation
8. zemstvo
9. pogrom
10. Duma

Recalling Key Facts

11. What factors aided German economic growth in the late 1800s?
12. How did Bismarck try to persuade workers not to support the socialists?
13. What was the goal of Mazzini's Young Italy society?
14. How did the Hapsburg leaders deal with the ethnic diversity of their empire?
15. How did European powers react to Ottoman weakness?
16. How did war with Japan contribute to the Revolution of 1905 in Russia?

Critical Thinking and Writing

17. **Analyzing Information** Study the painting that appears in the feature in Section 1. **(a)** What is the subject of the painting? **(b)** Where does the scene take place? **(c)** Who seems to be the central figure of the painting? **(d)** What conclusions can you draw from this about the power structure in Germany at the time?
18. **Predicting Consequences** Based on your reading of the chapter, predict the consequences of the following: **(a)** defeat of France in the Franco-Prussian War, **(b)** growth of German nationalism and militarism in the late 1800s, **(c)** failure to satisfy nationalist ambitions in Austria-Hungary, **(d)** weakening of the Ottoman empire.
19. **Connecting to Geography** How did regional differences contribute to continued divisions in Italy after unification?
20. **Linking Past and Present** Is nationalism a force in the world today? Give examples from current events to support your answer.

---

in Ottoman lands will gain independence.
19. People had loyalty to local regions rather than to the nation. In the southern part of Italy people struggled to farm in poor rural areas with exhausted soil. Northern Italy had more cities that were cultural and business centers.
20. Most students probably will agree that nationalism still plays an important role around the world today. Examples may include nationalist strife in the former Yugoslavia and the former Soviet Union.

On January 22, 1905, Father George Gapon led Russian workers to the Winter Palace to deliver a petition to the czar. Unfortunately, Nicholas II had called in soldiers and fled. The result was the massacre known as Bloody Sunday. Read the workers' petition, then answer the questions that follow.

"We, the workers of the town of St. Petersburg, with our wives, our children and our aged and feeble parents, have come to you, Sire, in search of justice and protection. We have fallen into poverty, we are oppressed, we are loaded with a crushing burden of toil, we are insulted, we are not recognized as men, we are treated as slaves who should bear their sad and bitter lot in patience and silence. . . . Do not refuse to protect your people; raise [Russia] from the grave of arbitrary power, poverty and ignorance; permit it to dispose of its own fate; free it from the intolerable oppression of officials; destroy the wall between yourself and your people—and let it govern the country with you."

—quoted in *Revolution From 1789 to 1906*
(Postgate)

21. **(a)** On whose behalf is the petition presented? **(b)** Whom does the petition blame?
22. What hardships does the petition describe?
23. What are the demonstrators' goals?
24. What is the tone of this petition?
25. If Nicholas had stayed to receive this petition, do you think he would have acted differently? Why or why not?

Skills Assessment
Take It to the NET

Use the Internet to research the history of the Hapsburgs and their roles in European history. Create a time line that shows major political events relating to the Hapsburgs. Illustrate your time line with copies of photographs or paintings of significant locations, battles, and rulers.

Unification of Italy, 1858–1870

Use the map to answer the following questions:

26. **(a)** When was the largest part of Italy added to the Kingdom of Sardinia? **(b)** When was the last part added?
27. To what country did Corsica belong?
28. In degrees of longitude, approximately how much farther east is Naples than Rome?
29. What body of water lies between Italy and the Ottoman empire?
30. **(a)** Describe the route of Garibaldi's expedition in 1860. **(b)** About how many miles did the expedition travel?
31. Why, in your opinion, was Rome the last area to become part of unified Italy?

Skills Tip

Degrees of longitude tell you how far east or west a point lies from the Prime Meridian.

Analyzing Primary Sources

21. **(a)** workers and their families **(b)** oppressive government officials
22. extreme poverty, oppression, extremely hard work, insults, treatment as slaves, ignorance
23. to be free from oppression and poverty, to be educated, to govern the country with the czar, to have a say in their own fate
24. possible answers: beseeching, pleading, respectful
25. Possible answer: No. Nicholas believed in the total power of the czar and that the people had no rights but to obey.

Analyzing Maps

26. **(a)** in 1859 and 1860 **(b)** 1870
27. France
28. about one and a half degrees
29. Adriatic Sea
30. **(a)** The expedition sailed from Genoa to Tuscany to Sicily, where it split up. Some forces marched across Sicily, and some sailed along the coast of Sicily. It then crossed to the Italian mainland, and marched north to Naples. **(b)** between about 900 and 1,000 miles
31. Possible answer: It was last because it was so close to the Papal States, and Vatican City lay within its borders.

Skills Tip

Degrees of latitude tell you how far north or south of the Equator a place is. The Skills Handbook in the front of the book has a lesson that will help students with this feature.

Unit Theme Activity

Remind students to continue working on their Unit Theme Activity. See rubrics for the activity on the unit opener page in the Teacher's Edition.

Take It to the NET

Direct students to **www.phschool.com** for links to sites that will help them get started on their time lines. Share rubrics with students.

Attempted The time line's divisions are not proportionally spaced, and labels are difficult to read, missing, or inaccurately placed. Few or no illustrations are included.

Minimal The time line's divisions are proportionally spaced, and most labels are included but are somewhat difficult to read. Several are inaccurately placed. Several illustrations are included.

Adequate The time line's divisions are proportionally spaced, and all labels are included. Most are easy to read and accurately placed. Many illustrations are included.

Exemplary The time line's divisions are proportionally spaced, and all labels are included. All are easy to read and accurately placed. Many illustrations are included.

Chapter 24 Planning Guide

Resource Manager

	CORE INSTRUCTION	READING/SKILLS
Chapter Level Resources	**Teaching Resources** 📖 Pacing Charts, Ch. 24 📖 Teaching With Themes, p. 27 🎬 Color Transparencies, p. F–49 💿 Resource Pro® Ch. 24 💻 www.phschool.com • eTeach	🎧 Book on CD, Ch. 24 🎧 Interactive Student Tutorial CD-ROM, Ch. 24 🎧 Social Studies Skills Tutor CD-ROM 🎬 Skills Transparencies

1 Britain Becomes More Democratic
1. Summarize why reformers sought to change Parliament in the 1800s.
2. Describe the values Queen Victoria represented.
3. Identify how the Liberal and Conservative parties helped bring a new era to British politics.
	Teaching Resources
	📘 Unit 6 booklet
	    • Primary Source Activity, p. 49
	📖 Creative Teaching Activities, p. 107
	💿 Prentice Hall Presentation Pro, Ch. 24, Section 1
	🎬 Section Reading Support Transparencies
		Teaching Resources
		📘 Unit 6 booklet
		    • Guided Reading and Review, p. 40
		📖 Guide to the Essentials
		📼 Guided Reading Audiotapes, Ch. 24, Section 1

2 A Century of Reform
1. Identify the social and economic reforms that benefited British workers and others.
2. Explain how British women worked to win the vote.
3. Specify the goals of Irish nationalists.
	Teaching Resources
	📘 Unit 6 booklet
	    • Biography Activity, p. 48
	📖 Creative Teaching Activities, p. 108
	💿 Prentice Hall Presentation Pro, Ch. 24, Section 2
		Teaching Resources
		📘 Unit 6 booklet
		    • Guided Reading and Review, p. 42
		    • Skill Application Activity, p. 51
		📖 Guide to the Essentials

3 Division and Democracy in France 1. Outline the domestic and foreign policies of Napoleon III. 2. Describe the impact of the Dreyfus affair and other challenges on the Third Republic. 3. Specify the steps the French government took toward reform in the early 1900s.	**Teaching Resources** 📖 Creative Teaching Activities, p. 109 💿 Prentice Hall Presentation Pro, Ch. 24, Section 3 🎬 Section Reading Support Transparencies	**Teaching Resources** 📘 Unit 6 booklet • Guided Reading and Review, p. 44 📖 Guide to the Essentials 📼 Guided Reading Audiotapes, Ch. 24, Section 3

4 Expansion of the United States
1. Explain how the United States extended its territory.
2. Outline the ways American democracy grew before and after the Civil War.
3. Summarize the impact that economic growth and social reform had on the United States.
	Teaching Resources
	📘 Unit 6 booklet
	    • Viewpoint Activity, p. 50
	📖 Creative Teaching Activities, p. 110
	💿 Prentice Hall Presentation Pro, Ch. 24, Section 4
		Teaching Resources
		📘 Unit 6 booklet
		    • Guided Reading and Review, p. 46
		📖 Guide to the Essentials
		📼 Guided Reading Audiotapes, Ch. 24, Section 4

ENRICHMENT/PRE-AP

- 🖳 www.phschool.com
  - Why Study History?

🎞 Teaching Resources
- 📕 History Through Literature, pp. 51–52
- 🖳 www.phschool.com
  - Internet Activities, Section 1

🎞 Teaching Resources
- 📕 Chapter Extension Activities, p. 59
- 🖳 www.phschool.com
  - Internet Activities, Famine Devastates Ireland

🎞 Teaching Resources
- 📕 Chapter Extension Activities, p. 60
- 🖳 www.phschool.com
  - Virtual Field Trip
  - Internet Activities, Section 4

ASSESSMENT

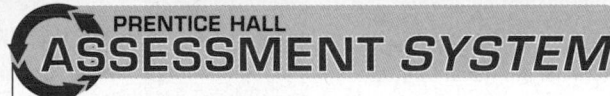

Core Assessment
- 📕 ExamView Test Bank booklet, Ch. 24
- 💿 ExamView Test Bank CD-ROM, Ch. 24

Standardized Test Preparation
Diagnose and Prescribe
- 📕 Diagnostic Tests for High School Social Studies Skills

Review and Reteach
- 📕 Review Book for World History

Practice and Assess
- 📕 Test-Taking Strategies With Transparencies for High School
- 📕 Alternative Assessment booklet
- 📕 Test Prep Book for World History

🎞 Teaching Resources
- 📂 Unit 6 booklet
  - Geography Quiz, p. 52
  - Section Quizzes, pp. 41, 43, 45, 47
  - Chapter Tests A, B, and C, pp. 53–57
- 🖳 www.phschool.com
  - Self-Test

CUSTOMIZE FOR INDIVIDUAL NEEDS

Gifted and Talented
- Teacher's Edition, Activities: Heterogeneous Groups, p. 606

Less Proficient Readers
- Guide to the Essentials, Ch. 24
- Guided Reading Audiotapes, English, Ch. 24
- Book on CD, Ch. 24
- Teacher's Edition, Activities: Reading Strategy, p. 598; Reading Strategy, p. 604

Less Proficient Writers
- Teacher's Edition, Activities: Cooperative Learning Activities, p. 601; Cooperative Learning Activity, p. 609

Students Acquiring English/ESL
- Guide to the Essentials, English/Spanish, Ch. 24
- Guided Reading Audiotapes, English/Spanish, Ch. 24
- Book on CD, Ch. 24
- Teacher's Edition, Activities marked with an *

𝒾 TEXT

Don't miss the exclusive inter-active version of *World History: Connections to Today* on the Internet and CD-ROM.

INTRODUCTION

During the Victorian era, reformers worked for changes in Britain. Reforms helped the working class, but women's suffrage remained a controversy. Irish nationalists campaigned for home rule. In France, Napoleon III set up the Second Empire before the Franco-Prussian War forced him out and created the Third Republic. Meanwhile, the United States followed an expansionist policy. The states fought a Civil War over slavery and economic differences. After the war, the United States focused on economic growth and social reform.

Focusing on Themes

Suggest that students focus on these theme questions as they read:

Religions and Value Systems
What role did nationalism play in the western democracies?

Continuity and Change
How did western democracies adapt to the new demands of industrial society?

Political and Social Systems
How did Britain, France, and the United States become more democratic?

Diversity
How did women and members of religious and ethnic groups seek greater rights?

TIME LINE ACTIVITY

You may wish to share the About the Pictures note with your students before you ask questions about the time line such as the following:

1. When did the American Civil War begin? *(1861)*
2. Why do you think Theodor Herzl might want to found a Jewish state? *(Jews were often persecuted.)*
3. What was the first country to give women the right to vote and in what year? *(New Zealand in 1893)*

Don't Miss!

Disaster!
Famine Devastates Ireland (Section 2)

Synthesizing Information
The Growth of American Suffrage (Section 4)

Growth of Western Democracies 1815–1914

Chapter Preview

1. **Britain Becomes More Democratic**
2. **A Century of Reform**
3. **Division and Democracy in France**
4. **Expansion of the United States**

1832
The Great Reform Act gives more British men the right to vote. The houses of Parliament, shown here, will be the center of a century of political reform.

1845
Ireland's Great Hunger begins, leading to widespread death and disease and mass emigration.

1861
The American Civil War begins. The four-year battle between North and South will lead to the end of slavery in the United States.

CHAPTER EVENTS

1815   1835   1855

GLOBAL EVENTS

1821 Mexico wins independence from Spain.

1858 Britain begins direct rule of India.

592 Chapter 24

Resource Directory

Teaching Resources
Teaching With Themes Chapter Theme Activities, p. 27
Pacing Chart With Block Scheduling Guide Ch. 24
Technology
World History Color Transparencies Ch. 24 Graphic Organizer, p. F–49

Western Democracies, 1900

Mr. John Bull - No it does not John I must have one of MY own

THE VOTE — John Bull My umbrella protects us all!

PACIFIC OCEAN

UNITED STATES ★ Washington, D.C.

ATLANTIC OCEAN

GREAT BRITAIN   GERMANY   RUSSIA
London ★   ★ Paris   ★ Berlin   ★ St. Petersburg
FRANCE   ★ Vienna   ★ Budapest
Mediterranean Sea   *Black Sea*

| | Democratic governments |
| | Autocratic governments |

The Industrial Revolution uprooted old ways of life. While Germany and Russia tried to stem the tide of change, Britain, France, and the United States slowly extended democratic rights.

Robinson Projection
0   1000   2000 Miles
0   1000   2000 Kilometers

1897
Theodor Herzl organizes the First Zionist Congress for the purpose of founding a Jewish state.

1870
The Franco-Prussian War leads to the fall of Napoleon III and the founding of a new French republic.

1900s
The women's suffrage movement grows in Britain. This 1911 cartoon expresses the determination of British women to win the vote.

1875   **1895**   **1915**

1869 The French-built Suez Canal opens in Eygpt.

1889 Brazil becomes a republic.

1893 New Zealand is the first nation to give women the vote.

1910 The Union of South Africa is formed.

Chapter 24 **593**

Independent Assignments

Have students read one section as they prepare for class. After class, have them complete the assignment. Some students may benefit from using the Guided Reading and Review worksheets.

Section 1 Have students use the worksheet *The London Street Markets* in the Unit 6 booklet, p. 49, to learn about the division between the rich and poor in Britain.
Section 2 Have students use the worksheet *Emmeline Pankhurst* in the Unit 6 booklet, p. 40, to learn about the sacrifices people make for causes they believe in.

Section 3 Have students use the Section 3 Guided Reading and Review worksheet in the Unit 6 booklet, p. 44, to gain a better understanding of how democracy took shape in France.
Section 4 Have students use the map *Growth of the United States, 1783–1853* in the Historical Outline Map book, p. 35, to trace the expansion of the United States' territory.

Western Democracies, 1900

Activating Prior Knowledge
Ask students what the difference is between an autocracy and a democracy. *(An autocratic government is rule by one person with unlimited power; a democratic government is rule by the people through elected representatives.)*

Previewing
Ask students why the English might believe Ireland should be a part of Great Britain. *(Ireland is located very near Great Britain.)*

Background About the Pictures

1   2   3   4

1. Designated as a UNESCO World Heritage site in 1987, the British Houses of Parliament are a group of buildings designed by Sir Charles Barry in the Gothic Revival style. During World War II, the Commons chamber was burned. The restored House of Commons reopened in 1950.

2. In the American Civil War, Southern states demanded the right to secede from the Union. They named themselves the Confederate States of America and elected Jefferson Davis as their president.

3. Theodor Herzl believed the only solution to antisemitism was for Jews to form their own state. He died more than 40 years before Israel was a reality.

4. Although the women's suffrage movement was strong in Britain in the 1800s, Britain was not the first country to grant women the vote. New Zealand was first in 1893, followed by Australia in 1902, Finland in 1906, and Norway in 1913. It wasn't until 1918 that women could vote in Great Britain and 1920 in the United States.

eTeach

Be sure to check out this month's online discussion with a World History Master Teacher.

Go to **www.phschool.com**.

Bell Ringer Inform students that even though Britain had elections in the early 1800s, the government was not truly democratic. Ask students to list specific ways in which a country that has elections might still be undemocratic.

Reading Focus

■ Why did reformers seek to change Parliament in the 1800s?

■ What values did Queen Victoria represent?

■ How did the Liberal and Conservative parties help bring a new era to British politics?

Vocabulary

rotten borough
electorate
secret ballot

Taking Notes

As you read this section, prepare an outline of the contents. Use Roman numerals to indicate major headings. Use capital letters for subheadings, and use numbers for the supporting details. The example at right will help you get started.

I. Reforming Parliament
  A. Pressure for change
    1. Religious restrictions on voting
    2.
    3.
  B. Reform Act of 1832
    1.
    2.

Main Idea Throughout the 1800s, political reform gradually expanded suffrage and made Parliament more democratic.

LESSON PLAN

1. Focus As the 1800s began in Britain, wealthy landowners dominated government and most people still could not vote. Then, political parties began to compete for the support of the British working class by backing democratic reforms. By the end of the century, universal male suffrage and many other democratic measures had been achieved. In Britain, political change came through gradual reform rather than violent revolution.

2. Instruct Divide the class into several groups. Assign some groups to identify the undemocratic conditions that existed in Britain in the 1800s. Assign other groups to list and describe the reforms that made British government more democratic. Have a last set of groups work to explain how the Chartists, the Victorian age, and British political parties all contributed to peaceful, gradual change in Britain. When students have finished this part of the assignment, regroup them so that each new group has at least one "expert" on each of the previous topics. Have students take turns teaching the group about their area of expertise.

3. Assess Ask students to identify areas in which reforms were still needed in Britain at the close of the 1800s.

4. Reteach If students' Assess activity does not reflect adequate understanding of the lesson, you might assign the *Guide to the Essentials* or the *Interactive Student Tutorial CD-ROM* for this section.

Primary Source

The Need to Reform Parliament

English-born Thomas Paine significantly influenced political thought in Europe and North America:

"What is government more than the management of the affairs of a Nation? It is not, and from its nature cannot be, the property of any particular man or family, but the whole community. . . .

The county of York, which contains near a million souls, sends two county members; and so does the county of Rutland which contains not a hundredth part of that number. The old town of Sarum, which contains not three houses, sends two members; and the town of Manchester, which contains upwards of sixty thousand souls, is not admitted to send any. Is there any principle in these things?"

—Thomas Paine,
Rights of Man, 1791

Skills Assessment

Primary Source Why was representation in Parliament unfair, according to Paine?

Setting the Scene Charles Egremont, a wealthy young man, is proud to be British. One day, he boasts to strangers that Victoria, the queen of England, "reigns over the greatest nation that ever existed." "Which nation?" asks one of the strangers, "for she reigns over two":

"Two nations: between whom there is no [communication] and no sympathy; who are as ignorant of each other's habits, thoughts, and feelings, as if they were . . . inhabitants of different planets; who are formed by a different breeding, are fed by a different food, are ordered by different manners, and are not governed by the same laws."

—Benjamin Disraeli, *Sybil*

What are these "two nations," Egremont wonders. "THE RICH AND THE POOR," the stranger replies.

Egremont is the hero of Benjamin Disraeli's novel *Sybil*. Disraeli, a leading political figure at the time of the Industrial Revolution, had seen both the world of aristocratic luxury and the appalling poverty of factory towns and rural villages. In the 1800s, Disraeli and other political leaders slowly worked to bridge Britain's "two nations" and extend democratic rights. Unlike some of its neighbors in Europe, Britain generally achieved change through reform rather than revolution.

Reforming Parliament

In 1815, Britain was a constitutional monarchy with a parliament and two political parties. Still, it was far from democratic. Although members of the House of Commons were elected, less than five percent of the people had the right to vote. Wealthy nobles and squires, or country landowners, dominated politics and heavily influenced voters. In addition, the House of Lords—made up of hereditary nobles and high-ranking clergy—could veto any bill passed by the House of Commons.

Pressure for Change Long-standing laws kept many people from voting. Catholics and non-Anglican Protestants, for example, could not vote or serve in Parliament. In the 1820s, reformers pushed to end religious restrictions. After fierce debate, Parliament finally granted Catholics and non-Anglican Protestants equal political rights.

An even greater battle soon erupted over making Parliament more representative. During the Industrial Revolution, centers of population shifted.

Primary Source

ANSWER Population size was not considered when the number of parliamentary representatives per district was determined. In some cases, the new industrial cities had no representation at all.

Resource Directory

Teaching Resources
Creative Teaching Activities Creative Teaching Activities booklet, p. 107
Guided Reading and Review Unit 6 booklet, p. 40
Primary Source Activity *London Street Markets*, Unit 6 booklet, p. 49
History Through Literature *Pickwick Papers*, History Through Literature booklet, pp. 51–52

Block Scheduling Support

Hold a class discussion on human rights. Begin by asking students to define freedom, in terms of what it means both to them personally and to the people of a nation. Then, ask what basic rights all human beings are entitled to expect. Discuss whether any nation has a right to interfere in another country's affairs if human rights are violated and what individuals can do to further human rights.

Some rural towns lost so many people that they had few or no voters. Yet local landowners in these rotten boroughs still sent members to Parliament. At the same time, populous new industrial cities like Manchester and Birmingham had no seats in Parliament at all because they had not existed as important population centers in earlier times.

Reform Act of 1832 By 1830, Whigs and Tories* were battling over a bill to reform Parliament. In the streets, supporters of reform chanted, "The Bill, the whole Bill, and nothing but the Bill!" Their shouts seemed to echo the cries of revolutionaries on the continent.

Parliament finally passed the Great Reform Act in 1832. It redistributed seats in the House of Commons, giving representation to large towns and cities and eliminating rotten boroughs. It also enlarged the electorate, the body of people allowed to vote, by granting suffrage to more men. The Act did, however, keep a property requirement for voting.

The Reform Act of 1832 did not bring full democracy, but it did give a greater political voice to middle-class men. Landowning nobles, however, remained a powerful force in the government and in the economy.

The Chartist Movement The reform bill did not help rural or urban workers. Some of them demanded more radical change. In the 1830s, protesters known as Chartists drew up the People's Charter. This petition demanded universal male suffrage, annual parliamentary elections, and salaries for members of Parliament. Another key demand was for a secret ballot, which would allow people to cast their votes without announcing them publicly.

Twice the Chartists presented petitions with over a million signatures to Parliament. Both petitions were ignored. In 1848, as revolutions swept Europe, the Chartists prepared a third petition and organized a march on Parliament. Fearing violence, the government moved to suppress the march. Soon after, the unsuccessful Chartist movement declined. In time, however, Parliament would pass most of the major reforms proposed by the Chartists.

The Victorian Age

From 1837 to 1901, the great symbol in British life was Queen Victoria. Her reign was the longest in British history. Although she exercised little real political power, she set the tone for what is now called the Victorian age.

Symbol of a Nation's Values As queen, Victoria came to embody the values of her age. These Victorian ideals included duty, thrift, honesty, hard work, and—above all—respectability. Today, we associate most of these qualities with the Victorian middle class. However, people at all levels of society shared these ideals, even if they could not always live up to them.

Victoria herself embraced a strict code of morals and manners. As a young woman, she married a German prince, Albert, and they raised a large family. Albert held a lower rank than Victoria. Still, she treated him with the devotion a dutiful wife was expected to have for her husband. When he died in 1861, Victoria went into deep mourning and dressed in black for the rest of her reign.

*The Whig party largely represented middle-class and business interests. The Tory party spoke for nobles, landowners, and others whose interests and income were rooted in agriculture.

Victoria, Queen of England
Although she held little political power, Queen Victoria came to stand for the values of her age. This plate was presented to Victoria on the occasion of her fiftieth year on the throne.

Theme: Political and Social Systems How do the words and images on this plate reflect Britain's sense of optimism and self-confidence?

Recall

1. (a) Benjamin Disraeli, p. 594 (b) Chartism, p. 595 (c) Victoria, p. 595 (d) William Gladstone, p. 596 2. (a) rotten borough, p. 595 (b) electorate, p. 595 (c) secret ballot, p. 595

Comprehension

3. It redistributed seats in the House of Commons, giving representation to large towns and eliminating rotten boroughs. It also extended suffrage to men with a certain amount of property, and it gave a greater political voice to middle-class men. 4. duty, thrift, honesty, hard work, and respectability 5. Reforms gave the vote to working-class men, farm workers, and most other men; the power of the Lords was restricted, including their power to veto tax bills.

Critical Thinking and Writing

6. (a) so politicians could not use bribes and threats to influence the way people voted (b) so Englishmen without wealth or an independent source of income could afford to serve in the government 7. (a) The poor and the rich in England occupy entirely unequal worlds. (b) The wealthy Egremont is unaware of the conditions of the poor. (c) reliable, because it reflects the disparity that existed between the rich and poor in Britain at the time

---

Activity Rubrics

Share rubrics with students before they begin their presentation.

Attempted Presentation is very brief and provides few details about Victoria outside those in the textbook.

Minimal Presentation includes basic information about Victoria's life but does not hold audience's interest.

Adequate Presentation has ample information about Victoria's life given in an interesting way.

Exemplary Presentation is full of information about Victoria's life and is lively and entertaining.

Caption Answer

Political caricatures and cartoons show that people have the freedom to laugh at and criticize their leaders.

Two Political Giants
As the leading political figures of Victorian England, Benjamin Disraeli (left) and William Gladstone (right) were often the subjects of caricatures.

Theme: Political and Social Systems Why are political caricatures like these often seen as a sign of a healthy democracy?

A Confident Age Under Victoria, the British middle class—and growing numbers of the working class—felt great confidence in the future. That confidence grew as Britain expanded its already huge empire. Victoria, the empress of India and ruler of some 300 million subjects around the world, became a revered symbol of British might.

As she aged from teenaged monarch to grieving widow to revered national symbol, Victoria witnessed growing agitation for social reform. The queen herself commented that the lower classes "earn their bread and riches so deservedly that they cannot and ought not to be kept back." As the Victorian era went on, reformers continued the push toward greater social and economic justice.

A New Era in British Politics

In the 1860s, a new era dawned in British politics. The old political parties regrouped under new leadership. Benjamin Disraeli forged the Tories into the modern Conservative party. The Whigs, led by William Gladstone, evolved into the Liberal party. Between 1868 and 1880, as the majority in Parliament swung between the two parties, Gladstone and Disraeli alternated as prime minister. Both fought for important reforms.

Expanding Suffrage Disraeli and the Conservative party pushed through the Reform Bill of 1867. By giving the vote to many working-class men, the new law almost doubled the size of the electorate.

In the 1880s, it was the turn of Gladstone and the Liberal party to extend suffrage. Their reforms gave the vote to farmworkers and most other men. By century's end, almost-universal male suffrage, the secret ballot, and other Chartist ambitions had been achieved.

Limiting the Lords In the early 1900s, Liberals in the House of Commons pressed ahead with social reforms. But many bills passed by the Commons met defeat in the House of Lords. In particular, the Lords used their veto power to block any attempt to increase taxes on the wealthy.

In 1911, a Liberal government passed measures to restrict the power of the Lords, including their power to veto tax bills. The Lords resisted. Finally, the government threatened to create enough new lords to approve the law, and the Lords backed down. People hailed the change as a victory for democracy. In time, the House of Lords would become largely a ceremonial body with little power. The elected House of Commons would reign supreme.

SECTION 1 Assessment

Recall

1. **Identify:** (a) Benjamin Disraeli, (b) Chartism, (c) Victoria, (d) William Gladstone.
2. **Define:** (a) rotten borough, (b) electorate, (c) secret ballot.

Comprehension

3. How did the Reform Act of 1832 change Parliament?
4. What middle-class values are associated with the Victorian age?
5. What reforms did the Liberal and Conservative parties achieve?

Critical Thinking and Writing

6. **Drawing Conclusions** Why do you think the Chartists demanded (a) a secret ballot, (b) salaries for members of Parliament?
7. **Analyzing Literature** Reread the excerpt from *Sybil* at the beginning of this section. (a) Restate the stranger's main idea in your own words. (b) Why is Egremont surprised by this view of Britain? (c) Would you consider this novel a reliable source of information about Britain in the early 1800s? Why or why not?

Activity
Take It to the NET

Use the Internet to research the life of Queen Victoria. Then, with a group of classmates, present your findings in a "This Is Your Life" format. Have one student play Victoria and another the host. Other students will play surprise guests who can tell about highlights of Victoria's life.

Resource Directory

Teaching Resources

Section Quiz Unit 6 booklet, p. 41
Creative Teaching Activities Creative Teaching Activities booklet, p. 108
Guided Reading and Review Unit 6 booklet, p. 42

Technology

Interactive Student Tutorial CD-ROM Ch. 24
Computer Test Bank Ch. 24

Reading Focus

- What social and economic reforms benefited British workers and others?
- How did British women work to win the vote?
- What were the goals of Irish nationalists?

Vocabulary

free trade
repeal
capital offense
penal colony
absentee landlord
home rule

Taking Notes

On a sheet of paper, create a concept web like this one. As you read the section, add information to the web. Add as many circles as you need.

Main Idea Parliament passed a wide variety of reform measures, but women's suffrage and the status of Ireland remained difficult issues.

Setting the Scene

Her aristocratic family would have been shocked. Here was Lady Constance Lytton, disguised as a seamstress—and lying in a prison hospital! Lytton had been arrested for taking part in a women's suffrage protest. Now, she refused to eat. Her hunger strike, she vowed, would go on until the British government granted the vote to women. Lytton later recalled:

> "I was visited again by the Senior Medical Officer, who asked me how long I had been without food. I said I had eaten a buttered scone and a banana sent in by friends to the police station on Friday at about midnight. He said, 'Oh, then, this is the fourth day; that is too long, I shall feed you, I must feed you at once.'"
>
> —Constance Lytton, *Prisons and Prisoners*

In the end, the doctor—with the help of five prison matrons—force-fed Lytton through a tube. Yet the painful ordeal failed to weaken her resolve. "No surrender," she whispered. "No surrender."

Lytton's 1910 hunger strike was part of the long struggle for women's suffrage in Britain. Suffragists were not the only people to fight for change. Between 1815 and 1914, Parliament responded to widespread discontent with a series of social and economic reforms. At the same time, the question of British control over Ireland was becoming a dominant and divisive political issue.

Social and Economic Reforms

During the early and mid-1800s, Parliament passed a wide variety of important new laws. One of the most controversial measures involved the issue of free trade, or trade between countries without quotas, tariffs, or other restrictions.

Free Trade and the Corn Laws In the early 1800s, Britain, like other European nations, taxed foreign imports in order to protect local economies. But supporters of free trade demanded an end to such protective tariffs. Free traders, usually middle-class business leaders, agreed with Adam Smith that a policy of laissez faire would increase prosperity for all. If tariffs were abolished, merchants everywhere would have larger markets in which to sell their goods, and consumers would benefit from open competition.

Bell Ringer Ask students to read the Reading Focus questions that appear at the start of this section and the Section Assessment questions that appear at the end. Have them use the questions to write three generalizations about the reforms that occurred in Britain between 1815 and 1914.

LESSON PLAN

1. Focus During the 1800s, Britain passed laws to bolster free trade, abolish slavery, reduce capital offenses, and improve working conditions. The government improved health care and education and enacted social welfare laws. Women used both peaceful and violent protest to gain the right to vote. Meanwhile, Irish nationalists struggled for self-rule.

2. Instruct Ask students to select an issue that is discussed in this section. Have them write two editorials addressing the issue—one that advocates the status quo and another that calls for reform. Remind students that the purpose of an editorial is to express an opinion and to persuade others to share that opinion. Encourage students to include persuasive and emotional arguments in their editorials. Suggest that they do additional research if needed. Have students read their editorials to the class. Then, call on volunteers to summarize the main ideas of each editorial.

3. Assess Ask students to discuss the current status of women in various parts of the world. To what degree have women achieved political, social, and economic equality? In what ways is the role of women still limited?

4. Reteach If students' **Assess** activity does not reflect adequate understanding of the lesson, you might assign the *Guide to the Essentials* or the *Interactive Student Tutorial CD-ROM* for this section.

Block Scheduling Support

Organize students into two groups. Assign one group the viewpoint of Queen Victoria on women's suffrage and the other group the viewpoint of women working for suffrage. Groups are to write and present a 10-minute presentation, either live or videotaped, about their subject. Presentations should include interesting and accurate portrayals of both viewpoints and may include mock interviews, historical reenactments, and commentary from "experts." Have each group assign the roles of producer, scriptwriter, narrator, actors, and if needed, camera person, and director.

Punishing Crime

These pictures are from an 1862 study of Britain's new system of reformed prisons. The cell at left reflects the new idea that prisoners should be confined to individual cells instead of milling around a common prison yard. At right, female convicts take care of their children in a prison nursery.

Theme: Political and Social Systems What does the picture on the left show you about how many prisoners spent their day?

Some British tariffs were repealed in the 1820s. However, fierce debate erupted over the Corn Laws, which imposed high tariffs on imported grain. (In Britain, "corn" refers to all cereal grains, such as wheat, barley, and oats.) Farmers and wealthy landowners supported the Corn Laws because they kept the price of British grain high. Free traders, however, wanted Parliament to repeal, or cancel, the Corn Laws. They argued that repeal of these laws would lower the price of grain, make bread cheaper for city workers, and open up trade in general.

Parliament finally repealed the Corn Laws in 1846, after widespread crop failures swept many parts of Europe. Liberals hailed the repeal as a victory for free trade and laissez-faire capitalism. However, in the late 1800s, economic hard times led Britain and other European countries to impose protective tariffs on many goods again.

Campaign Against Slavery During the 1700s, Enlightenment thinkers had turned the spotlight on the evils of the slave trade. At the time, British ships were carrying more Africans to the Americas than was any other European country. Under pressure from middle-class reformers, the campaign against the slave trade and slavery slowly took off. In 1807, Britain became the first leading European power to abolish the slave trade.

Banning the slave trade did not end slavery. Although the Congress of Vienna had condemned slavery, it had taken no action. In Britain, liberals preached the immorality of slavery. Finally, in 1833, Parliament passed a law banning slavery in all British colonies. Yet British textile manufacturers still imported cheap cotton produced by enslaved African Americans in the United States.

Crime and Punishment Other reforms were aimed at the criminal justice system. In the early 1800s, more than 200 crimes were punishable by death. Such capital offenses included not only murder but also shoplifting, sheep stealing, and impersonating an army veteran. In practice, some juries refused to convict criminals, because the punishments were so harsh. Executions were public occasions, and the hanging of a well-known murderer might attract thousands of curious spectators. Afterward, instead of receiving a proper burial, the criminal's body might be given to a medical college for dissection.

Victorian reformers began to reduce the number of capital offenses. By 1850, the death penalty was reserved for murder, piracy, treason, and arson. Many petty criminals were instead transported to penal colonies, or special settlements for convicts, in the new British territories of Australia and New

Zealand. In 1868, Parliament ended public hangings. Additional reforms improved prison conditions and outlawed imprisonment for debt.

Victories for the Working Class

"Four [ghosts] haunt the Poor: Old Age, Accident, Sickness and Unemployment," declared Liberal politician David Lloyd George in 1905. "We are going to [expel] them." By the early 1900s, Parliament gradually passed a series of reforms designed to help the men, women, and children whose labor supported the new industrial society.

Working Conditions As you have read, working conditions in the early industrial age were grim and often dangerous. Gradually, Parliament passed laws to regulate conditions in factories and mines. In 1842, for example, mineowners were forbidden to employ women or children under age 10. An 1847 law limited women and children to a 10-hour day. Later in the 1800s, the government regulated many safety conditions in factories and mines—and sent inspectors to see that the laws were enforced. Other laws set minimum wages and maximum hours of work.

Labor Unions Early in the Industrial Revolution, labor unions were outlawed. Under pressure, government and business leaders slowly accepted worker organizations. Trade unions were made legal in 1825. At the same time, though, strikes remained illegal.

Despite restrictions, unions spread, and gradually they won additional rights. Between 1890 and 1914, union membership soared. Besides winning higher wages and shorter hours for workers, unions pressed for other laws to improve the lives of the working class.

Later Reforms During the late 1800s and early 1900s, both political parties enacted social reforms to benefit the working class. Disraeli sponsored laws to improve public health and housing for workers in cities. Under Gladstone, an Education Act called for free elementary education for all children. Gladstone also pushed to open up government jobs based on merit rather than on birth or wealth.

Another force for reform was the Fabian Society, a socialist organization founded in 1883. The Fabians promoted gradual change through legal means rather than by violence. Though small in number, the Fabians had a strong influence on British politics.

In 1900, socialists and union members backed the formation of a new political party, which became the Labour party. ("Labour" is the British spelling of "labor.") The Labour party would grow in power and membership until, by the 1920s, it surpassed the Liberal party as one of Britain's two major parties.

In the early 1900s, Britain began to pass social welfare laws to protect the well-being of the poor and disadvantaged. These laws were modeled on those Bismarck had introduced in Germany. They protected workers with accident, health, and unemployment insurance as well as old-age pensions. One result of such reforms was that Marxism gained only limited support among the British working classes. The middle class hailed reforms as proof that democracy was working.

Votes for Women

In Britain, as elsewhere, women struggled for the right to vote against strong opposition. Just as Parliament had rejected the Chartist demand for universal male suffrage in 1848, so it resisted the demands of the women's suffrage movement 50 years later.

Women themselves were divided on the issue. Some women opposed suffrage altogether. Queen Victoria, for example, called the suffrage struggle

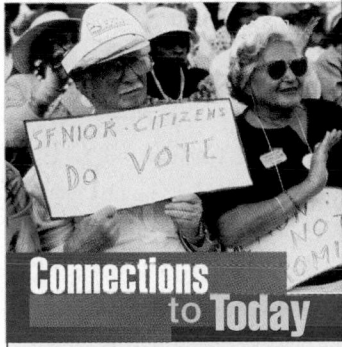

Connections to Today

Your Senior Years: Is Your Future Secure?

The United States created its Social Security system in 1935. It is similar to some of the social reforms Britain introduced years earlier. But Social Security was designed to supplement other pension plans and personal savings. Today, it has become a primary source of retirement income for many older Americans.

Social Security is now facing increasing challenges. The rising cost of living forces retirees to stretch their Social Security benefits more than ever. Also, life expectancies have increased dramatically. In 1900, only 4 percent of the American population was age 65 or over. By the year 2000, that figure was almost 13 percent—and growing. In the future, there will be many more retirees who live longer and healthier lives. These changes will put strains on the Social Security system, and some experts predict that funds will be exhausted by 2032.

Theme: Continuity and Change What might happen if the Social Security system were to run completely out of funding?

Background Historical Evidence

Health Care Reform In 1842, Edwin Chadwick, a government commissioner serving the poor, released a detailed report on "sanitary conditions of the laboring population." The evidence clearly indicated that disease was directly related to filthy environmental conditions caused by lack of drainage, sewers, and garbage collection. The report concluded that putrefying excrement was not only smelly and disgusting, but also a threat to the health of the community.

To alleviate the danger, Chadwick recommended clean piped water for personal hygiene, public bathhouses, and street cleaning. He also stated that communal outhouse wastes should be carried off through sewers, not removed by hand. Parliament took action, but only after a devastating cholera epidemic in 1846. Britain's first public health law, enacted in 1848, created a national health board and encouraged cities to build modern sanitary systems.

Activity Heterogeneous Groups

Constructing a Chart As a reinforcement activity, have students construct a chart that lists nineteenth-century reforms in Great Britain. Students might use colors to categorize the reforms. For example, red could indicate political reforms, blue could indicate labor reforms, and brown could indicate social reforms. *(Reteaching)*

Human Drama Note

Mauve Decade Eighteen-year-old William Henry Perkin launched the synthetic dye industry while attempting to make a synthetic drug to cure malaria. Earlier failed experiments had consistently resulted in a black powder. Curious, Perkins dissolved the substance in alcohol, which resulted in a colorfast mauve dye. The color became so popular in Britain that the 1850s became known as the "Mauve Decade." Synthetic dyes were created as a direct outgrowth of the drug industry.

Connections to Today

ANSWER People would have to rely on other sources of funding for retirement and some people may have to wait longer to retire.

Fighting Hunger Strikes The last thing the British government wanted was to see a suffragist die in prison and become a martyr to women throughout the nation. To prevent this from happening, the government passed the "Cat and Mouse" Act. This act allowed prison officials to release a prisoner to stop her hunger strike. The law also permitted police to rearrest the woman after she had regained her strength.

Background
Perspectives

Women Against Pankhurst The women's suffrage movement in Britain was not a unified force. Many women opposed Emmeline Pankhurst and her followers for advocating such tactics as arson, window breaking, and sabotage of postal boxes. Millicent Fawcett, a rival of Pankhurst, led the moderate National Union of Women's Suffrage Societies. Her view was that women could convince Parliament to take action only through respectable and responsible political activity. Fawcett, the wife of a former Liberal party politician, favored the peaceful reform efforts used by English liberals. In 1908, her National Union organized a rally that was attended by a half million women in London.

Biography

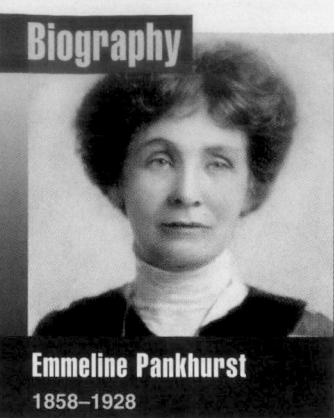

Emmeline Pankhurst
1858–1928

From the time she attended her first women's suffrage meeting at the age of 14, Emmeline Pankhurst was a "conscious and confirmed suffragist." Years of peaceful protest and demonstrations did little to win women the vote, however. After newspapers stopped reporting on suffrage rallies, Pankhurst turned to more aggressive tactics.

Tireless and fiercely determined, Pankhurst fought for her cause on many fronts—on the streets, from a prison cell, and in the courtroom. She even went on 10 hunger strikes within 18 months. With England's entrance into World War I in 1914, Pankhurst suspended her militant activities to support the war effort. Continuing to fight from the podium, however, Pankhurst spoke at home and abroad, refusing to let women's suffrage be forgotten.

Theme: Impact of the Individual Why did Emmeline Pankhurst believe that strong measures were necessary?

"mad, wicked folly." Even women in favor of suffrage disagreed about how best to achieve it.

Suffragists Revolt By the early 1900s, Emmeline Pankhurst, a leading suffragist, had become convinced that only aggressive tactics would bring victory. Pankhurst and other radical suffragists interrupted speakers in Parliament, shouting, "Votes for women!" until they were carried away. They collected petitions and organized huge public demonstrations. During one suffragist rally in London's Hyde Park, organizers brought demonstrators from all over Britain. An astonished newspaper reporter wrote, "It is probable that so many people have never before stood in one square mass anywhere in England."

When mass meetings and other peaceful efforts brought no results, some women turned to violent protest. They smashed windows or even burned buildings. Pankhurst justified such tactics as necessary to achieve victory. "There is something that governments care far more for than human life," she declared, "and that is the security of property, so it is through property that we shall strike the enemy."

Pankhurst and other women, including her daughters Christabel and Sylvia, were arrested and jailed. As you have read, some went on hunger strikes, risking their lives to achieve their goals. One radical suffragist died when she threw herself in front of the king's horse.

A Belated Victory Many middle-class women disapproved of such radical and violent actions. Yet they, too, spoke up in increasing numbers, demanding votes for women and equality under the law. Still, Parliament refused to grant women's suffrage. Not until 1918 did Parliament finally grant suffrage to women over age 30. Younger women did not win the right to vote for another decade.

The Irish Question

Throughout the 1800s, Britain faced the ever-present "Irish question." The English had begun conquering Ireland in the 1100s. In the 1600s, English and Scottish settlers colonized Ireland, taking possession of much of the best farmland.

The Irish never accepted English rule. They bitterly resented settlers, especially absentee landlords who owned large estates but did not live on them. Many Irish peasants lived in desperate poverty, while paying high rents to landlords living in England. In addition, the Irish, most of whom were Catholic, had to pay tithes to support the Church of England. Under these conditions, resistance and rebellion were common.

Irish Nationalism Like the national minorities in the Austrian empire, Irish nationalists campaigned vigorously for freedom and justice in the 1800s. Nationalist leader Daniel O'Connell, nicknamed "the Liberator," organized an Irish Catholic League and held mass meetings to demand repeal of unfair laws. "My first object," declared O'Connell, "is to get Ireland for the Irish."

Under pressure from O'Connell and other Irish nationalists, Britain slowly moved to improve conditions in Ireland. In 1829, Parliament passed the Catholic Emancipation Act, which allowed Irish Catholics to vote and hold political office. Yet many injustices remained. Absentee landlords could evict tenants almost at will. Other British laws forbade the teaching and speaking of the Irish language.

The Great Hunger Under British rule, three quarters of Irish farmland was used to grow crops that were imported to England. The potato, introduced from the Americas, became the main source of food for most of the Irish people themselves. Still, potatoes were abundant and nutritious enough to support a growing population.

Biography

ANSWER Peaceful means had not produced results, and she believed that the government cared more for property than human rights.

Resource Directory

Teaching Resources
Biography Activity *Emmeline Pankhurst,* Unit 6 booklet, p. 48
Skill Application Activity *Holding a Debate,* Unit 6 booklet, p. 51
Disaster! Chapter Extension Activities booklet, p. 59

Famine Devastates Ireland

The first potatoes harvested in the Irish countryside in October 1845 looked fine. But within days the potatoes had turned black and rotten. Soon, half the potato crop was ruined, the result of a deadly plant disease. For seven years the potato blight lingered, leading to a disastrous famine.

Like this family bound for Detroit, many Irish during the famine chose to emigrate rather than face certain starvation. The number of Irish who left between 1845 and 1851 totaled more than one million—greater than the number who had emigrated in the previous 30 years. The majority went to the United States.

During the "Great Hunger," many Irish homes such as this one were stripped of food and belongings. Many farmers sold furniture and clothing to buy food. Few families could even afford to buy fuel for heat.

In 1846, Mary Rush of Ardnaglass, Ireland, wrote to her parents in Quebec, Canada:
"Pen cannot dictate the poverty of this country at present. . . . For God's sake take us out of the poverty, and don't let us die with the hunger."
— Mary Rush, letter to her parents

Portfolio Assessment

INTERNET Use the Internet or library resources to find out more about a recent famine. Then, prepare a class presentation on the causes and results of the famine. If possible, include first-person accounts or photographs of the topic you have selected.

Fast Facts

- Irish peasants could not afford to buy the wheat, meat, and dairy products that continued to be shipped from Ireland to England.

- When the Irish protested against taxes, rents, and evictions, thousands of British troops arrived in Ireland to restore order.

- Due to rampant malnutrition, more people died from diseases such as typhus and cholera than from starvation during the famine.

Chapter 24 **601**

✓ Test Preparation

Have students read the Disaster! feature on this page, and then answer the question below.

What was the greatest cause of death during the Great Hunger?

A starvation

B malnutrition

C hypothermia

D homelessness

 Disaster!

Bell Ringer Have students look at the picture on this page and then write their thoughts about hunger in Ireland during the Great Hunger and about hunger in the world today.

Background
Connections to Today

World Hunger In today's world, nearly 800 million people in the developing world and 34 million in developed countries are undernourished. Around 200 million children in the developing world are underweight and face other health problems because of malnutrition.

Activity
Cooperative Learning

Making a Chart Organize the class into two groups: a global hunger research team and a local hunger research team. Have the global research team use the Internet or contact organizations to learn more about world hunger. Have the local research team contact local food banks, homeless shelters, and other community organizations.

Assign each student a task related to the group's topic, such as writing a contact letter or thank-you note, researching to find names and phone numbers of organizations, calling the organization, creating a chart, or preparing a presentation. Have presenters explain their group's chart and information to the class. Suggest the class take some action to help alleviate hunger in their community.

Portfolio Assessment Rubrics

Share rubrics with students before they write their presentation.

Attempted Student's work is incomplete or fails to meet outlined requirements.

Minimal Student's work presents basic information but in little depth.

Adequate Student's work shows extensive research and identifies the causes and results of a recent famine.

Exemplary Student's work shows extensive research and preparation; identifies causes and results of a recent famine; and includes first-person accounts or photographs.

Recall
1. (a) Corn Laws, p. 597 (b) Fabian Society, p. 599 (c) Emmeline Pankhurst, p. 600 (d) Catholic Emancipation Act, p. 600 (e) Great Hunger, p. 600 (f) Charles Stewart Parnell, p. 602 2. (a) free trade, p. 597 (b) repeal, p. 598 (c) capital offense, p. 598 (d) penal colony, p. 598 (e) absentee landlord, p. 600 (f) home rule, p. 602

Comprehension
3. The British government improved public health and housing for urban workers. The Education Act set up free elementary education. Social welfare laws provided accident, health, and unemployment insurance and old-age pensions. 4. Women suffragists collected petitions and held rallies. Some smashed windows and burned buildings. 5. (a) Irish nationalists wanted home rule. They resented English landlords who imposed high rents and evictions. They opposed paying a tithe to the Anglican church. They also opposed British laws that limited the use of the Irish language. Many blamed the British for the Great Hunger. (b) Gladstone ended the use of Irish tithe money to support the Anglican church. Other laws protected the rights of Irish tenants.

Critical Thinking and Writing
6. Free trade is an extension of laissez-faire economics, based on the idea that removing trade regulations would increase prosperity for all. 7. Encourage students to give reasons for their opinions.

Activity Rubrics

Share rubrics with students before they design their posters.

Attempted The poster is incomplete.

Minimal The poster is complete but is ineffective or messily presented.

Adequate The poster is well researched, well designed, and effective.

Exemplary Poster is well researched and well designed and offers a very persuasive argument for home rule.

 Global Connections

ANSWER People today respond much the same way the groups responded to Ireland's Great Hunger. Once they learn about the plight of the hungry, groups work to aid them. Many organizations work together today to help alleviate hunger. Still more effort is needed.

Global Connections

Aid for Ireland

Americans from all walks of life rushed to the aid of the starving Irish. Quakers were the first to organize relief efforts. Catholic churches, Jewish synagogues, and women's groups worked to raise funds. The American government encouraged food shipments by announcing that no road or canal tolls would be charged on any supplies headed for Ireland.

The Choctaw people, whose own forced relocation in the 1830s resulted in great hardship and many deaths, identified with the plight of the Irish people. Still recovering from food shortages of their own, the Choctaws contributed over $700—a large sum in the 1840s.

Theme: Global Interaction How do groups and individuals today respond to disasters around the world?

Then, in 1845, disaster struck. A blight, or disease, destroyed the potato crop. Other crops, such as wheat and oats, were not affected. Yet British landowners continued to ship these crops outside Ireland, leaving little for the Irish except the blighted potatoes. The result was a terrible famine that the Irish called the "Great Hunger."

Witnesses described many "scenes of frightful hunger." One official told of entering what he thought was a deserted village. In one home, he saw "six famished and ghastly skeletons, to all appearances dead . . . huddled in a corner on some filthy straw."

"I approached with horror, and found by a low moaning they were alive—they were in a fever, four children, a woman and what had once been a man. . . . In a few minutes I was surrounded by at least 200 such phantoms, such frightful spectres as no words can describe, either from famine or from fever."

—letter to the *Times* (London), December 24, 1846

In four years, at least one million Irish men, women, and children died of starvation or disease. More than one million emigrated to the United States and Canada. The Great Hunger left a legacy of Irish bitterness toward the English that still exists today.

Struggle for Home Rule Throughout the century, Irish demands for self-rule intensified. In the 1850s, some Irish militants organized the Fenian Brotherhood. Its goal was to liberate Ireland from British rule by force. In the 1870s, moderate Irish nationalists found a rousing leader in Charles Stewart Parnell. He rallied Irish members of Parliament to press for home rule, or local self-government. The debate dragged on for decades.

The "Irish question" disrupted English politics. At times, political parties were so deeply split over the Irish question that they could not take care of other business. As prime minister, Gladstone pushed for reforms in Ireland. He ended the use of Irish tithe money to support the Anglican church and tried to ease the hardships of Irish tenant farmers. New laws prevented landlords from charging unfair rents and protected the rights of tenants to the land they worked.

Finally, in 1914, Parliament passed a home rule bill. But it delayed putting the new law into effect when World War I broke out that year. As you will read, the southern counties of Ireland finally became independent in 1921.

SECTION 2 Assessment

Recall
1. **Identify:** (a) Corn Laws, (b) Fabian Society, (c) Emmeline Pankhurst, (d) Catholic Emancipation Act, (e) Great Hunger, (f) Charles Stewart Parnell.
2. **Define:** (a) free trade, (b) repeal, (c) capital offense, (d) penal colony, (e) absentee landlord, (f) home rule.

Comprehension
3. Describe three social reforms that helped the British working class.
4. What actions did women suffragists take to achieve their goals?

5. (a) Why did Irish nationalists oppose British rule? (b) Describe two reforms that improved conditions in Ireland.

Critical Thinking and Writing
6. **Analyzing Ideas** How is the idea of free trade linked to the principles of laissez faire and competition?
7. **Defending a Position** Do you agree that the tactics used by suffragists like Emmeline Pankhurst were necessary at the time? Why or why not?

Activity

Designing a Poster
Design a poster that an Irish nationalist of the late 1800s or early 1900s might have used in the struggle for home rule. First, decide whether your main goal is to win support from the Irish or to persuade members of the British Parliament.

Resource Directory

Teaching Resources
Section Quiz Unit 6 booklet, p. 43
Creative Teaching Activities Creative Teaching Activities booklet, p. 109
Guided Reading and Review Unit 6 booklet, p. 44

Technology
Interactive Student Tutorial CD-ROM Ch. 24
Computer Test Bank Ch. 24

SECTION **3** Division and Democracy in France

Reading Focus

- What domestic and foreign policies did Napoleon III pursue?

- What impact did the Dreyfus affair and other challenges have on the Third Republic?

- How did the French government take steps toward reform in the early 1900s?

Vocabulary

provisional
premier
coalition
libel

Taking Notes

On a sheet of paper, draw a time line to show the main events of this section. Use the time line shown here to help you get started.

```
1848        1860s        1863           1914
 |            |            |              |
Second    Napoleon III  Napoleon III
Empire    eases controls tries to put
                        Maximilian on
                        throne of
                        Mexico
```

Main Idea Democratic reforms in France took place under the Second Empire of Napoleon III and its successor, the Third Republic.

Bell Ringer Have students skim through the first three pages of this section to identify any three reasons for conflict and division in France during the mid-1800s.

LESSON PLAN

1. Focus Ruling France much like a dictator, Napoleon III limited liberties, encouraged economic growth, and pursued imperialistic ventures. After his fall from power, the Third Republic arose. Its coalition governments regulated working conditions, limited the power of the Church, and gradually extended suffrage. The Dreyfus affair split France and reflected antisemitism in Europe. It also helped give birth to the Zionist movement.

2. Instruct Divide the class into groups and assign each group one of the following topics: Napoleon III; The Events of 1870–1871; Coalition Governments and Scandals; The Dreyfus Affair; Reforms in France. Ask students to work together to describe three or more ways in which their topic affected the people of France or other areas of the world. Have representatives of each group take turns presenting their findings to the class. Encourage students to ask questions about each topic.

3. Assess Ask students to write five or more statements in answer to this question: How was France in the early 1900s different from France in the 1860s?

4. Reteach If students' **Assess** activity does not reflect adequate understanding of the lesson, you might assign the *Guide to the Essentials* or the *Interactive Student Tutorial CD-ROM* for this section.

Setting the Scene

The news sent shock waves throughout Paris. An entire French army under the emperor Napoleon III had surrendered to the Prussians at the city of Sedan. Still worse, Prussian forces were now about to advance on Paris. Could the city survive?

Georges Clemenceau (KLEHM uhn soh), a young French doctor who had entered politics, rallied the people of Paris to defend their city and their homeland. "Citizens," he cried, "must France destroy herself and disappear, or shall she resume her old place in the vanguard of nations?" Clemenceau concluded:

"Each of us knows his duty. We are children of the Revolution. Let us seek inspiration in the example of our forefathers in 1792, and like them we shall conquer. V*ive la France!* [Long Live France!]"
—Georges Clemenceau, quoted in *Clemenceau and the Third Republic* (Jackson)

For four months, Paris did resist the German onslaught. But finally, in January 1871, the French government at Versailles was forced to accept Prussian surrender terms.

The Franco-Prussian War ended a long period of French domination of Europe that had begun under Louis XIV. Yet the Third Republic rose from the ashes of the Second Empire of Napoleon III. Economic growth, democratic reforms, and the fierce nationalism expressed by Clemenceau all played a part in shaping modern France.

France Under Napoleon III

After the revolution of 1848, Napoleon III set up the Second Empire. His appeal cut across lines of class and ideology. The bourgeoisie saw him as a strong leader who would restore order. His promise to end poverty gave hope to the lower classes. People of all classes were attracted by his name, a reminder of the days when France had towered over Europe. Unlike his famous uncle, however, Napoleon III would bring France neither glory nor an empire.

Limits on Liberty On the surface, the Second Empire looked like a constitutional monarchy. In fact, Napoleon III ruled almost as a dictator, with the power to appoint his cabinet, the upper house of the legislature, and

Napoleon III
This portrait of Emperor Napoleon III suggests his pride and love of pomp. Like many monarchs of his day, Napoleon often had himself painted or photographed in military garb.

Theme: Political and Social Systems Why do you think many monarchs favored military dress?

Block Scheduling Support

Ask students to imagine that they are living in Paris during the second half of the 1800s, and that, as journalists for an underground newspaper, they are able to write editorials expressing their opinions of issues or events affecting France during this period. Have each student pick an issue or event and write an editorial, pro or con, about that event or issue. Have volunteers read their editorials to the class. Then, use them as a basis for class discussion on the divisions within the country.

Caption Answer

They believe it makes them look like strong leaders.

Background
Historical Evidence

Traitor? As Paris lay under siege, so did a huge French army at the fortress of Metz. Under the command of Marshal Achille François Bazaine, an army of more than 150,000 troops lay immobile following a battle that had cost it 23,000 casualties. During the two-month siege that followed, the army was further decimated by famine and outbreaks of smallpox, dysentery, and typhus. Marshal Bazaine finally surrendered the entire army. After the war, a court-martial found Bazaine responsible not only for the loss of Metz, but also for the defeat of France. He was sentenced to death but escaped to Spain, where he lived until his death in 1888.

One reason for Marshal Bazaine's surrender at Metz was perhaps the memory of his experience in Algeria some 30 years earlier. Bazaine, then a captain with the Foreign Legion, had commanded an outpost with a garrison of 1,200 men. For four months, Algerian forces laid siege to the fort. Bazaine's garrison was ravaged by disease and almost daily enemy raids. When help arrived, only 60 of the original 1,200 remained, and 20 of that number died the next day.

Reading Strategy
Check Comprehension

Write the following questions on the board: What did I read about in this section? What did I already know? What did I learn? What puzzled me? What did I enjoy or dislike about my reading? What conclusions can I draw from my reading? Have students write for at least five minutes in response to these questions. *(Less Advanced Readers)*

Map legend:

— Prussian siege line
— French defensive line
→ French attacks
⚓ Prussian batteries
⬛ French forts
▨ City walls
→ Prussian attacks

Skills Assessment

Geography For four months, Prussian troops surrounded Paris. In the painting at right, a hot air balloon leaves the city.

1. **Location** On the map, locate (a) Paris, (b) Seine River, (c) Marne River, (d) Versailles.
2. **Movement** In what area did the Prussians launch attacks?
3. **Critical Thinking Synthesizing Information** Based on the map, why do you think Parisians made use of hot air balloons during the Prussian siege?

many officials. Although the assembly was elected by universal male suffrage, appointed officials "managed" elections so that supporters of the emperor would win. Debate was limited, and newspapers faced strict censorship.

In the 1860s, the emperor began to ease controls. He lifted some censorship and gave the legislature more power. On the eve of his disastrous war with Prussia, Napoleon III even issued a new constitution that extended democratic rights.

Economic Growth Like much of Europe, France prospered at mid-century. Napoleon III promoted investment in industry and large-scale ventures such as railroad building and the urban renewal of Paris. During this period, a French entrepreneur, Ferdinand de Lesseps (duh LEHS uhps), organized the building of the Suez Canal to link the Mediterranean with the Red Sea and thus the Indian Ocean.

Workers enjoyed some benefits from economic growth. Napoleon legalized labor unions, extended public education to girls, and created a small public health program. Still, in France, as in other industrial nations, many people lived in great poverty.

Foreign Adventures Napoleon's worst failures were in foreign affairs. In the 1860s, he tried to place Maximilian, an Austrian Hapsburg prince, on the throne of Mexico. Through Maximilian, Napoleon hoped to turn Mexico into a French satellite. But after a large commitment of troops and money, the adventure failed. Mexican patriots resisted fiercely, and the United States protested. After four years, France withdrew its troops. Maximilian was overthrown and shot by Mexican patriots.

Napoleon's successes were almost as costly as his failures. He helped Italian nationalists defeat Austria, gaining Nice (NEES) and Savoy. But this

Skills Assessment

1. Review locations with students. **2.** from the east **3.** German troops surrounded Paris, cutting off roads, railway lines, and access to the Seine River. Hot air balloons may have been the only way Parisians could communicate with the outside world.

victory backfired when a united Italy emerged as a rival on France's border. And, though France and Britain won the Crimean War, France had little to show for its terrible losses except a small foothold in the Middle East.

War With Prussia At this time, France grew increasingly concerned about the rise of a great rival, Prussia. The Prussian leader Otto von Bismarck shrewdly manipulated French worries to lure Napoleon into war in 1870.

As you have read, the Franco-Prussian War was a disaster for France. After Napoleon III was captured at Sedan, German forces began the four-month siege of Paris. Encircled by Prussian troops, starving Parisians were reduced to catching rats and killing circus animals for food.

Challenges of the Third Republic

After Napoleon's capture, republicans in Paris had declared an end to the Second Empire. They set up a **provisional,** or temporary, government that evolved into France's Third Republic.

In 1871, the newly elected National Assembly accepted a harsh peace with Germany. France had to surrender the provinces of Alsace and Lorraine and pay a huge sum to Germany. The French burned to avenge their loss.

The Paris Commune In 1871, an uprising broke out in Paris. Rebels set up the Paris Commune. Like the radical government during the French Revolution, its goal was to save the Republic from royalists. Communards, as the rebels were called, included workers and socialists as well as bourgeois republicans. As patriots, they rejected the harsh peace that the National Assembly had signed with Germany. Radicals dreamed of creating a new socialist order.

The National Assembly ordered the Commune to disband. When the Communards refused, the government sent troops to besiege Paris. For weeks, civil war raged. As government troops advanced, the rebels toppled great Paris monuments and slaughtered hostages. Finally, government forces butchered some 20,000 Communards. The suppression of the Paris Commune left bitter memories that deepened social divisions within France.

Government Structure Despite its shaky beginnings, the Third Republic remained in place for 70 years. The new republic had a two-house legislature. The powerful lower house, or Chamber of Deputies, was elected by universal male suffrage. Together with the Senate, it elected the president of the republic. However, he had little power and served mostly as a figurehead. Real power was in the hands of the **premier** (prih MIR), or prime minister.

Unlike Britain, with its two-party system, France had many parties, reflecting the wide splits within the country. Among them were divine-right royalists, constitutional monarchists, moderate republicans, and radicals. With so many parties, no single party could win a majority in the legislature. In order to govern, politicians had to form **coalitions,** or alliances of various parties. Once a coalition controlled enough votes, it could then name a premier and form a cabinet.

Multiparty systems and coalition governments are common in Europe. Such alliances allow citizens to vote for a party that most nearly matches their own beliefs. Coalition governments, however, are often unstable. If one party deserts a coalition, the government might lose its majority in the legislature. The government then falls, and new elections must be held. In the first 10 years of the Third Republic, 50 different coalition governments were formed and fell.

Scandals Despite frequent changes of governments, France made economic progress. It paid Germany the huge sum required by the peace treaty and expanded its overseas empire. But in the 1880s and 1890s, a series of political scandals shook public trust in the government.

Dreyfus in Disgrace
The cover of this 1895 French magazine shows Alfred Dreyfus being drummed out of the army. By tradition, a disgraced officer stood at attention while his shoulder pads were ripped off and his sword was broken.

Theme: Diversity How do you think people in France reacted to this magazine cover?

One crisis erupted when a popular minister of war, General Georges Boulanger (boo lahn ZHAY), rallied royalists and ultranationalists eager for revenge on Germany. Accused of plotting to overthrow the republic, Boulanger fled to Belgium and later committed suicide. In another scandal, a nephew of the president was caught selling nominations for the Legion of Honor, France's highest award. The president was forced to resign.

The Dreyfus Affair

The most divisive scandal began in 1894, when a high-ranking army officer, Alfred Dreyfus, was accused of spying for Germany. At his military trial, neither Dreyfus nor his lawyer was allowed to see the evidence against him. The injustice was rooted in antisemitism. The military elite detested Dreyfus, the first Jew to reach such a high position in the army. Although Dreyfus proclaimed his innocence, he was convicted and condemned to life imprisonment on Devil's Island, a desolate penal colony off the coast of South America.

By 1896, new evidence pointed to another officer, Ferdinand Esterhazy, as the spy. Still, the army refused to grant Dreyfus a new trial.

Deep Divisions The Dreyfus affair, as it was called, scarred French politics and society for decades. Royalists, ultranationalists, and Church officials charged Dreyfus supporters, or "Dreyfusards," with undermining France. Paris echoed with cries of "Long live the army!" and "Death to traitors!" Dreyfusards, mostly liberals and republicans, upheld ideals of justice and equality in the face of massive public anger. In 1898, French novelist Émile Zola joined the battle. In an article headlined *J'Accuse!* (I Accuse!), he charged the army and government with suppressing the truth. As a result, Zola was convicted of libel, or the knowing publication of false and damaging statements. He fled into exile.

Slowly, though, the Dreyfusards made progress. They revealed that the evidence against Dreyfus was forged. In 1906, a French court finally cleared Dreyfus of all charges and restored his honors. That move was a victory for justice, but the political scars of the Dreyfus affair took longer to heal.

Calls for a Jewish State The Dreyfus case reflected the rise of antisemitism in Europe. The Enlightenment and the French Revolution had spread ideas about religious toleration. In Western Europe, some Jews had gained jobs in government, universities, and other areas of life. A few were successful in banking and business, though most struggled to survive in the ghettos of Eastern Europe or slums of Western Europe.

By the late 1800s, however, antisemitism was again on the rise. Antisemites were often members of the lower middle class who felt insecure in their social and economic position. Steeped in the new nationalist fervor, they adopted an aggressive intolerance for outsiders and a violent hatred of Jews.

The Dreyfus case and the pogroms in Russia stirred Theodor Herzl (HEHRT suhl), a Hungarian Jewish journalist living in France. He called for Jews to form their own separate state, where they would have the rights denied to them in European countries. Herzl helped launch modern Zionism, a movement devoted to rebuilding a Jewish state in Palestine. Many Jews had kept alive this dream since the Roman destruction of Jerusalem. In 1897, Herzl organized the First Zionist Congress in Basel, Switzerland.

Reforms in France

Though shaken by the Dreyfus affair, France achieved serious reforms in the early 1900s. Like Britain, France passed laws regulating wages, hours, and safety conditions for workers. It set up a system of free public elementary schools. Creating public schools was also part of a campaign to reduce the power of the Roman Catholic Church, which controlled education.

Separating Church and State Like Germany, France tried to end Church involvement in government. Republicans viewed the Church as a conservative force that opposed progressive policies. In the Dreyfus affair, it had backed the army and ultranationalists.

The government closed Church schools, along with many convents and monasteries. In 1905, it passed a law to separate church and state and stopped paying the salaries of the clergy. Catholics, Protestants, and Jews enjoyed freedom of worship, but none had any special treatment from the government.

Women's Rights Under the Napoleonic Code, French women had few rights. Women could not even control their own property. By the 1890s, a growing women's rights movement sought legal reforms. It made some gains, such as an 1896 law giving married women the right to their own earnings.

In 1909, Jeanne-Elizabeth Schmahl founded the French Union for Women's Suffrage. Rejecting the radical tactics used in Britain, Schmahl favored legal protests. Yet even liberal men were reluctant to grant women suffrage. They feared that women would vote for Church and conservative causes. In the end, French women did not win the vote until after World War II.

Looking Ahead

By 1914, France was the largest democratic country in Europe, with a constitution that protected basic rights. France's economy was generally prosperous, and its overseas empire was second only to that of Britain.

Yet the outlook was not all smooth. Coalition governments rose and fell at the slightest pressure. To the east loomed the industrial might of Germany. Many French citizens were itching for a chance to avenge the defeat in the Franco-Prussian War and liberate the "lost provinces" of Alsace and Lorraine. That chance came in 1914, when all of Europe exploded into World War I.

SECTION 3 Assessment

Recall
1. **Identify:** (a) Paris Commune, (b) Georges Boulanger, (c) Alfred Dreyfus, (d) Theodor Herzl, (e) Jeanne-Elizabeth Schmahl.
2. **Define:** (a) provisional, (b) premier, (c) coalition, (d) libel.

Comprehension
3. Describe the government of France during the Second Empire.
4. Explain how each of the following heightened divisions in France: (a) the Paris Commune, (b) the Dreyfus affair.

5. Describe two reforms enacted in France in the early 1900s.

Critical Thinking and Writing
6. **Comparing** (a) How does the French system of political parties differ from the American system? (b) How do these differences affect the stability of governments under each system?
7. **Solving Problems** (a) What solution did Zionists propose for the problem of widespread antisemitism? (b) Why do you think they felt it was the best solution?

Activity

Drawing a Political Cartoon
Draw a political cartoon about one event or development during the reign of Napoleon III. You may focus either on domestic affairs, such as limitations on liberty, or on foreign affairs, such as the Franco-Prussian War.

SECTION 3 Assessment

Recall
1. **(a)** Paris Commune, p. 605 **(b)** Georges Boulanger, p. 606 **(c)** Alfred Dreyfus, p. 606 **(d)** Theodor Herzl, p. 606 **(e)** Jeanne-Elizabeth Schmahl, p. 607
2. **(a)** provisional, p. 605 **(b)** premier, p. 605 **(c)** coalition, p. 605 **(d)** libel, p. 606

Comprehension
3. During the Second Empire, the government of France was like a dictatorship. Napoleon III held the power to appoint his cabinet, the upper house of the legislature, and many officials. Elections were managed and there was strict censorship. 4. **(a)** The violent suppression of the Paris Commune left bitter memories for those who fought on opposing sides. **(b)** The Dreyfus affair heightened tensions between ultranationalists, royalists, and the Church on one side and liberals and republicans on the other. 5. France passed laws regulating wages, hours, and safety conditions for workers. It set up a system of free public elementary schools. It passed a law to separate Church and state. It gave married women the right to their own earnings.

Critical Thinking and Writing
6. **(a)** Under the French system, there are many parties that must form coalitions in order to govern. Under the American system, there are two major parties. **(b)** The American system is more stable. When a coalition fails, the government falls and new elections must be held. In the American system, the government stays in place until the next regularly scheduled election. 7. **(a)** Zionists proposed forming a separate Jewish state in Palestine. **(b)** Antisemitism appeared to be on the rise again. The Dreyfus affair and the pogroms in Russia provided evidence of this.

Activity Rubrics

Share rubrics with students before they create their cartoons.

Attempted The cartoon is incomplete.

Minimal The point of the cartoon is not clear, or the presentation is messy or illegible.

Adequate The cartoon takes a clear position on an issue.

Exemplary The cartoon is well executed, reflecting thought, research, and a good understanding of issues during the reign of Napoleon III.

Bell Ringer

Read aloud the poem inscribed on the base of the Statue of Liberty, reproduced on this page. Ask students what they believe Emma Lazarus was saying in this poem. Why was the United States a beacon of hope for many people?

Reading Focus

- How did the United States extend its territory?
- How did American democracy grow before and after the Civil War?
- What impact did economic growth and social reform have on the United States?

Vocabulary

expansionism
abolitionist
secede
segregation
isolationism

Taking Notes

On a sheet of paper, start a before-and-after chart like the one shown here. As you read this section, list events under the appropriate columns.

CIVIL WAR	
Before	After
• Expansion and western settlement	
• Manifest Destiny	
• Calls for abolition of slavery	

Main Idea In the United States, the 1800s were a time of changing borders, growing industry, and expanding democracy.

LESSON PLAN

1. Focus During the 1800s, the United States expanded across the continent to the Pacific Ocean. The slavery issue, economic differences between the North and South, and the election of Abraham Lincoln in 1860 brought about the Civil War. Though slavery ended after the war, African Americans faced difficult times ahead. Starting in the late 1800s, reformers campaigned to extend suffrage to women and to protect the rights of workers.

2. Instruct Divide the class into groups and ask each group to imagine that it is an archaeological team in the twenty-third century. They are uncovering items that can be traced to the United States of the 1800s. List the following headings on the chalkboard: Territorial Expansion; Expanding Democracy; The Civil War and Its Aftermath; Economic Growth and Social Reform. Have each group list at least two items that it might find for each of the topics on the board. After students have finished this part of the lesson, have them work individually to write a brief descriptive paragraph for each item on their list. Their paragraphs should explain how each item is important for understanding life in the United States during the 1800s.

3. Assess Have students write four generalizations describing how the United States of 1900 was different from the United States of 1800.

4. Reteach If students' Assess activity does not reflect adequate understanding of the lesson, you might assign the *Guide to the Essentials* or the *Interactive Student Tutorial CD-ROM* for this section.

Setting the Scene

For many Irish families fleeing hunger, Russian Jews escaping pogroms, or poor Italian farmers seeking economic opportunity, the answer was the same—America! A poem inscribed on the base of the Statue of Liberty expressed the hopes of millions of immigrants:

"Give me your tired, your poor,
  Your huddled masses yearning to breathe free,
  The wretched refuse of your teeming shore.
  Send these, the homeless, tempest-tossed to me.
  I lift my lamp beside the golden door."
      —Emma Lazarus, "The New Colossus"

In the 1800s, the United States was a beacon of hope for many people. The American economy was growing rapidly, offering jobs to newcomers. The Constitution and Bill of Rights held out the hope of political and religious freedom. Not everyone shared in the prosperity or the ideals of democracy. Still, by the turn of the century, Americans were increasingly proud of their status as an emerging world power.

Territorial Expansion

From the earliest years of its history, the United States followed a policy of expansionism, or extending a nation's boundaries. At first, the United States stretched only from the Atlantic coast to the Mississippi River. In 1803, President Thomas Jefferson bought the Louisiana territory from France. In one stroke, the Louisiana Purchase virtually doubled the size of the nation.

Manifest Destiny By 1846, the United States had expanded to include Florida, Oregon, and the Republic of Texas. The Mexican War (1846–1848) added California and the Southwest. With growing pride and confidence, Americans claimed that their nation was destined to spread across the entire continent, from sea to sea. This idea became known as Manifest Destiny. Some expansionists even hoped to absorb Canada and Mexico. In fact, the United States did go far afield. In 1867, it bought Alaska from Russia and in 1898 annexed the Hawaiian Islands.

Settling the West During the 1800s, settlers flocked to newly acquired western lands. The discovery of gold in California drew floods of easterners.

Resource Directory

Teaching Resources

Creative Teaching Activities Creative Teaching Activities booklet, p. 110
Guided Reading and Review Unit 6 booklet, p. 46
Viewpoint Activity *Democracy in America,* Unit 6 booklet, p. 50

Other people, like the Mormons, sought a place to practice their religion freely. Still others headed west in the spirit of adventure.

The waves of settlers brought tragedy to Native Americans. Following a pattern that began in colonial days, newcomers pushed the Indians off their lands, sometimes by treaty, but more often by force. Some Native American nations resisted the invaders, but they were outgunned and outnumbered. As settlers moved westward, they destroyed the buffalo herds on which the Plains Indians depended. By the 1890s, most surviving Native Americans had been driven onto reservations, usually the least desirable parts of a territory.

Expanding Democracy

In 1800, the United States had the most liberal suffrage in the world, but still only white men who owned property could vote. States slowly chipped away at requirements. By the 1830s, most white men had the right to vote. Democracy was far from complete, however. Women, Native Americans, and free blacks had no vote. Enslaved African Americans had no rights at all.

By mid-century, reformers were campaigning for many changes. Some demanded a ban on the sale of alcoholic beverages. Others called for better treatment of the mentally ill or pushed for free elementary schools. Two crusades, especially, highlighted the limits of American democracy—the abolition movement and the women's rights movement.

Calls for Abolition In the early 1800s, a few Americans demanded an immediate and complete end to slavery. These abolitionists included William Lloyd Garrison, who pressed the antislavery cause through his newspaper, the *Liberator*. Frederick Douglass, who had himself escaped slavery, spoke eloquently in the North about the evils of slavery.

Skills Assessment

Geography Through wars and treaties, the United States expanded its borders to its present size.

1. **Location** On the map, locate (a) Louisiana Purchase, (b) Florida, (c) Texas, (d) Alaska, (e) Hawaii.
2. **Region** Identify three countries that sold territories to the United States.
3. **Critical Thinking Linking Past and Present** Compare this map to a map of the present-day United States. How did the area where you live become part of the United States?

Activity
Cooperative Learning

Writing a Dialogue Assign students to work in pairs. Ask one member of each partnership to assume the role of a displaced Native American. Ask the other member of each partnership to assume the role of a settler moving westward. The students' assignment is to write a dialogue in which they discuss, in their assumed roles, their feelings about Manifest Destiny, the future development of the United States, and their place in American society. Invite teams to present their dialogues to the class. ✳

Activity
Connections to Literature

Writing a Speech Have students read Chapter 11 of Frederick Douglass's autobiography, *The Narrative of the Life of Frederick Douglass, an American Slave*. In this chapter, students will learn about Douglass's final days as a slave, his frustration with his powerlessness, his first experiences at work when he traveled North, and his forging of a new identity as a free man.

After students have read the chapter, ask them to pretend that they are abolitionists who must write a speech calling for an end to slavery. In their speeches, students should use Frederick Douglass's experiences to highlight the terrible hardships of a slave's life, the effects that slaveholding has on a society, and the benefits that would come with a society of free and equal people. Call on students to deliver their speeches to the class. Encourage students to comment on the impact and effectiveness of each speech.

Expansion of the United States, 1783–1898

CEDED BY GREAT BRITAIN (Convention of 1818)

DISPUTED WITH GREAT BRITAIN UNTIL 1842

CANADA

OREGON COUNTRY (Agreement with Great Britain, 1846)

ROCKY MTS.

MEXICAN CESSION (Treaty of Guadalupe Hidalgo, 1848)

LOUISIANA PURCHASE (Purchased from France, 1803)

THE UNITED STATES IN 1783

APPALACHIAN MTS.

PACIFIC OCEAN

ATLANTIC OCEAN

GADSDEN PURCHASE (Purchased from Mexico, 1853)

TEXAS ANNEXATION (Annexed by Congress, 1845)

FLORIDA CESSION (Treaty with Spain, 1819)

ALASKA (Purchased from Russia, 1867)

0 400 Miles
0 400 Kilometers

MEXICO

Gulf of Mexico

HAWAII (Annexed, 1898)

0 100 Miles
0 100 Kilometers

Albers Conic Equal Area Projection

0 250 500 Miles
0 250 500 Kilometers

Chapter 24 **609**

Block Scheduling Support

Organize students into four groups. Assign each group one of the following categories: Native Americans, African Americans, your community's history, your state's history. Have students contact organizations such as the local and state historical societies, Native American councils, or the National Association for the Advancement of Colored People to ask for a representative to speak to the class about how the people in your community or the region were affected by either Manifest Destiny or the Civil War. Have students prepare a list of guidelines for the speakers they invite, telling them when and where to appear and suggesting topics that will interest the class. Have other students prepare a list of questions that they would like to ask each speaker. Remind student groups to prepare an introduction for each speaker and to write a thank-you note to the speakers once they have finished.

Skills Assessment

ANSWERS 1. Review locations with students. **2.** Russia, France, and Mexico **3.** Check students' answers for accuracy.

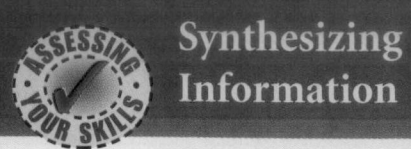

Synthesizing Information

Background
About the Evidence

Susan B. Anthony Susan B. Anthony fearlessly led a group of women to the voting polls to push for women's right to vote. After being arrested, she attended a highly publicized lecture while awaiting trial. She even tried to vote again and was arrested again. She continued to campaign for a federal suffrage amendment to give women the civil and political rights granted to African American men under the Fourteenth and Fifteenth Amendments.

Activity
Interpreting the Evidence

Use these additional questions to generate class discussion.

1. Critical Thinking: Drawing Conclusions Should women have had the right to vote under the Fifteenth Amendment? Why or why not? *(The Fifteenth Amendment specifically mentions "race, color, or previous conditions of servitude." Students may say that even though the amendment does not mention women, women should have had the right to vote.)*

2. Critical Thinking: Recognizing Causes and Effects How do you think publicity helps a cause such as women's suffrage? *(Publicity brings public attention to an issue.)*

Skills Tip

Political cartoons reflect a certain era. To understand the cartoon, it helps to read about the culture and the time. The Skills Handbook at the front of the book has a lesson that will help students with this feature.

Skills Assessment

ANSWERS 1. D **2.** E **3. (a)** by state laws and constitutional amendments **(b)** Gradually, the United States extended suffrage to all its citizens, regardless of economic class, race, or gender.

The Growth of American Suffrage

The right to vote in the United States has gradually expanded over time. When the Constitution was approved, only white men over age 21 who owned property could vote. The chart, cartoon, and primary source below all relate to the growth of American suffrage.

Expansion of Suffrage in the United States

Year	People Granted the Vote
Late 1700s	Most white men aged 21 or older who meet property requirements (state laws)
Early 1800s–1850s	Most white men aged 21 or older (state laws)
1870	Black men (Amendment 15)
1920	Women (Amendment 19)
1961	People in the District of Columbia in presidential elections (Amendment 23)
1971	People aged 18 or older (Amendment 26)

Fifteenth Amendment

"Section 1. The right of citizens of the United States to vote shall not be denied or abridged by the United States or by any state on account of race, color, or previous condition of servitude.
Section 2. The Congress shall have power to enforce this article by appropriate legislation."
—Fifteenth Amendment to the United States Constitution, adopted 1870

"The Latest Suffrage Recruit"

Secretary of State William Jennings Bryan unfurls the suffragist flag in 1915.

Skills Tip

Be careful not to draw conclusions from political cartoons when you do not have enough information. Political cartoons can be misleading, particularly when they depict events that happened a long time ago.

Skills Assessment

1. According to the chart, which amendment to the Constitution gave all citizens aged 18 or older the right to vote in the United States?
A Fifteenth
B Nineteenth
C Twenty-third
D Twenty-sixth

2. What can you conclude about William Jennings Bryan from this cartoon?
E He supported votes for women.
F Defending women's suffrage helped his political career.
G His endorsement alone earned women the right to vote.
H He sponsored the Fifteenth Amendment.

3. Critical Thinking Making Inferences (a) By what means was suffrage extended to an increasingly broader group of people? **(b)** Based on these sources, how would you describe the expansion of suffrage in the United States?

Resource Directory

Teaching Resources
Synthesizing Information Chapter Extension Activities booklet, p. 60

By the 1850s, the battle over slavery intensified. As new states entered the union, proslavery and antislavery forces met in violent confrontations to decide whether slavery would be legal in the new state. Harriet Beecher Stowe's novel *Uncle Tom's Cabin* helped convince many northerners that slavery was a great social evil.

Women's Rights Movement   Women worked hard in the antislavery movement. Lucretia Mott and Elizabeth Cady Stanton traveled to London for the World Antislavery Convention—only to find they were forbidden to speak because they were women. Gradually, American women began to protest the laws and customs that limited their lives.

In 1848, in Seneca Falls, New York, Mott and Stanton organized the first women's rights convention. The convention passed a resolution, based on the Declaration of Independence. It began, "We hold these truths to be self evident: that all men and women are created equal." The women's rights movement set as its goal equality before the law, in the workplace, and in education. Some women also demanded the vote.

The Civil War and Its Aftermath

Economic differences, as well as the slavery issue, drove the North and South apart. The division reached a crisis in 1860 when Abraham Lincoln was elected president. Lincoln opposed extending slavery into new territories. Southerners feared that he would eventually abolish slavery altogether and that the federal government would infringe on their states' rights.

North Versus South   Soon after Lincoln's election, most southern states seceded, or withdrew, from the Union and formed the Confederate States of America. This action sparked the Civil War. From 1861 to 1865, the agonizing ordeal divided families as well as a nation.

The South had fewer resources, people, and industry than the North. Still, southerners fought fiercely to defend their cause. They won many early victories. At one point, Confederate armies under General Robert E. Lee drove northward as far as Gettysburg, Pennsylvania. In a bloody three-day battle, the Union army turned back the southern advance for good.

In the last years of the war, General Ulysses S. Grant used the massive resources of the North to launch a full-scale offensive against the South. The Confederacy finally surrendered in 1865. The struggle cost more than 600,000 lives—the largest casualty figures of any American war. Although the war left a bitter legacy, it did guarantee that the nation would remain united.

Challenges for African Americans   During the war, Lincoln declared that enslaved African Americans in the South were free. After the war, three amendments to the Constitution banned slavery throughout the country and granted political rights to African Americans. Under the Fifteenth Amendment, African American men won the right to vote.

Still, African Americans faced many restrictions. In the South, laws imposed segregation, or legal separation of the races, in hospitals, schools, and other public places. Other laws bypassed the Fifteenth Amendment to prevent African Americans from voting. Thus, in the United States, as in Europe, democracy remained a goal rather than a reality for many citizens.

African Americans also faced economic hardships. Freed from slavery but without land, many ended up working as tenant farmers. To escape the bleak poverty of the postwar South, some headed west. Others migrated to the northern cities, seeking jobs in the factories that were springing to life.

Economic Growth and Social Reform

After the Civil War, the United States grew to lead the world in industrial and agricultural production. With seemingly unlimited natural resources

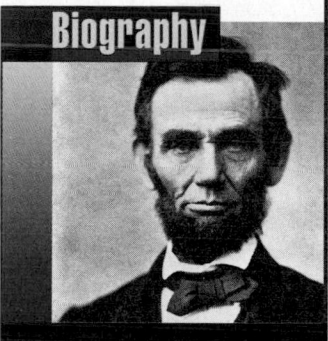

Biography

Abraham Lincoln 1809–1865

When he arrived in Washington in 1861, Abraham Lincoln was an unpolished Illinois lawyer with little political experience and no formal education. Yet for four years, he skillfully led the Union through the Civil War, the bloodiest conflict in American history. Throughout the long ordeal, Lincoln's dedication to preserving the Union never faltered.

He has been called "the Grand Harmonizer of the North" for his ability to solidify public opinion behind him as the war raged on. Yet Lincoln looked beyond the war to the future of the whole nation. In his second inaugural address, he expressed his dream for a reunited country: "With malice toward none; with charity for all; let us strive . . . to bind up the nation's wounds . . . to do all which may achieve and cherish a just, and a lasting peace, among ourselves, and with all nations."

Theme: Impact of the Individual How would you describe the popular image of Abraham Lincoln today?

Background
Historical Evidence

Another Victim of the Civil War When Mathew Brady set out to make a complete photographic record of the Civil War in the United States, he was sure that the War Department would buy his photographs once the war ended. Working with Alexander Gardner and Timothy H. O'Sullivan, Brady and his staff documented the war through photographs—and Brady spent $100,000 to do it. Today, Brady's photographs are collector's items and a valuable historical record of Civil War battles, but at the time, the War Department and others showed little interest in them.

When the financial panic in 1873 forced Brady into bankruptcy, the War Department purchased his negatives at auction for $2,840. Although Congress later granted Brady $25,000, the grant was too little, too late. Mathew Brady died in 1896 in a hospital charity ward in New York City.

Customize for . . .
Visual Learners

Several Internet sites and many books contain examples of Civil War photographs from the Brady studio. Have students locate examples of some of Brady's photographs and create a classroom display. Then, use the photographs to spark a discussion of this question: How might photographs of the war create a different kind of historical record than written accounts?

Human Drama Note

Fighting for Freedom About 178,000 African Americans volunteered to serve in the Union Army during the Civil War. Of these, 21 were awarded the Congressional Medal of Honor for heroism. The secretary of war noted that the African American regiments "have proved themselves among the bravest of the brave, performing deeds of daring and shedding their blood with . . . heroism."

After the Civil War, African Americans continued to serve in the military, in all–African American regiments in the West, where they were called "Buffalo Soldiers." Members of the Ninth and Tenth Cavalry regiments of Buffalo Soldiers collected 18 additional medals of honor for heroism between 1868 and 1890.

Biography

ANSWER Many think of him as Honest Abe. Historians have recorded many of Lincoln's qualities to support the image: his personal integrity and sense of fairness; his direct, straightforward, concise manner of speaking; his trustworthiness; his sharp wit.

New Immigrants to the United States
In this 1902 photograph, European immigrants crowd onto the deck of a ship as they sail into New York Harbor. For many, their first stop in the United States was the immigration center at Ellis Island.

Theme: Global Interaction Why do you think these immigrants might have decided to come to the United States?

and the help of European capital, the economy boomed. Farm output soared as settlers flooded into the fertile farmlands of the Midwest. Mechanical reapers, plows, and threshers led to huge increases in farm production.

Industry and Transportation Industry grew even more rapidly. As in Europe, early progress came in the textile industry. Cotton mills used machines and cheap labor to turn out great quantities of mass-produced goods. Rich coal and iron resources fed other industries. A huge work force, swelled by waves of immigrants, labored in mines and factories.

A growing network of transportation and communication aided economic growth. The first transcontinental railroad was completed in 1869, opening up new opportunities for settlement and growth. In the early 1900s, Americans took to the automobile faster than Europeans. Henry Ford's "Model T" became the symbol of a new automobile era.

Immigration and the Growth of Cities The Industrial Revolution brought rapid urbanization. Millions of Americans left farms for jobs in the growing industrial cities. The nation's population soared as millions of immigrants arrived in the 1800s and early 1900s. They represented nearly every nationality and ethnic group, including Irish, German, Chinese, Italian, Scandinavian, Japanese, Eastern European Jews, and many others.

Most European immigrants settled first in cities on the Atlantic coast, while Asian immigrants filled cities on the Pacific coast. In time, newcomers spread out across the country. They worked in mines and factories, built railroads, and opened up farmlands in the West. Immigration made the United States "a nation of nations," with roots around the world.

Immigrants faced harsh conditions in crowded slum tenements. Often, newcomers suffered from prejudice and even violence from native-born Americans. In the West, whites hostile to Chinese workers pushed for laws to end immigration from China. For the first time, the United States began to close its "golden door."

612 Chapter 24

Business and Labor By 1900, giant monopolies controlled whole industries. Scottish-born Andrew Carnegie built the nation's largest steel company, while John D. Rockefeller's Standard Oil Company dominated the world's petroleum industry. Big business enjoyed tremendous profits.

But the growing prosperity was not shared by all. In factories, wages were low and conditions were often brutal. To defend their interests, American workers organized labor unions such as the American Federation of Labor. Unions sought better wages, hours, and working conditions. Struggles with management sometimes erupted into violent confrontations. Slowly, however, workers made gains.

Populists and Progressives In the economic hard times of the late 1800s, farmers, too, organized to defend their interests. In the 1890s, they joined city workers to support the new Populist party. The Populists never became a major party, but their platform of reforms, such as an eight-hour workday, eventually became law.

By 1900, reformers known as Progressives again pressed for change. They sought laws to ban child labor, limit working hours, regulate monopolies, and give voters more power. Another major goal of the Progressives was votes for women. After a long struggle, American suffragists finally won the vote in 1920, when the Nineteenth Amendment went into effect.

Looking Ahead

By 1900, the United States was the world's largest democracy and its leading industrial giant. It was also acquiring a new role—that of a global power. In the Spanish American War of 1898, the United States acquired overseas territories, including the Philippines, Guam, and Puerto Rico.

Many Americans wanted to maintain their tradition of isolationism, or limited involvement in world affairs. This tradition dated back to George Washington, who had advised Americans to "steer clear of permanent alliances" with other nations. Expansionists, however, urged the nation to pursue global economic and military interests. "Whether they will or no, Americans must now begin to look outward," wrote influential expansionist Alfred T. Mahan. "The growing production of the country demands it."

In 1914, rivalries among European nations exploded into war. Although Americans sought to stay out of the conflict, World War I would eventually force the United States to take an even greater role on the world stage.

Geography and History

Conserving the Wilderness

Progressives wanted to do more than protect workers and voters. Under President Theodore Roosevelt, they made it their goal to protect the environment, too.

Roosevelt was a keen outdoorsman who loved camping in the woods. He grew alarmed that the American wilderness was being destroyed and its resources rapidly exhausted. "The rights of the public to natural resources outweigh private rights," he said. For example, he wanted lumber companies to replant trees in the forests they were clearing. Under Roosevelt, the government also created some 170,000 acres of national parkland.

 Theme: Geography and History Identify two ways that Americans today try to protect the environment and conserve natural resources.

SECTION 4 Assessment

Recall
1. **(a)** Louisiana Purchase, p. 608
(b) Manifest Destiny, p. 608 **(c)** Frederick Douglass, p. 609 **(d)** Abraham Lincoln, p. 611 **(e)** Fifteenth Amendment, p. 611 **(f)** Progressives, p. 613 2. **(a)** expansionism, p. 608 **(b)** abolitionist, p. 609 **(c)** secede, p. 611 **(d)** segregation, p. 611 **(e)** isolationism, p. 613

Comprehension
3. **(a)** Mexican War, Louisiana Purchase, purchase of Alaska, and annexation of Hawaiian islands **(b)** Millions of immigrants came from Europe and Asia. **(c)** By 1900, the United States led the world in industrial and agricultural production.
4. Reformers worked to abolish slavery and to secure voting rights for women.
5. **(a)** Because of the growth of industry after the war, there were plenty of jobs and opportunities to get ahead. **(b)** Workers faced harsh living and working conditions in slums and factories.

Critical Thinking and Writing
6. Economic growth enabled the United States to increase its international trade and military power. 7. People continue to come in search of freedom and a new chance.

SECTION 4 Assessment

Recall
1. **Identify:** (a) Louisiana Purchase, **(b)** Manifest Destiny, **(c)** Frederick Douglass, **(d)** Abraham Lincoln, **(e)** Fifteenth Amendment, **(f)** Progressives.
2. **Define:** (a) expansionism, **(b)** abolitionist, **(c)** secede, **(d)** segregation, **(e)** isolationism.

Comprehension
3. Describe how the United States grew in each of these areas in the 1800s: **(a)** territory, **(b)** population, **(c)** economy.
4. Describe two ways that democracy expanded.

5. **(a)** How did immigrants benefit from economic growth in the United States after the Civil War? **(b)** What problems did workers face?

Critical Thinking and Writing
6. **Recognizing Causes and Effects** How do you think economic growth helped make the United States a world power?
7. **Linking Past and Present** Reread the poem by Emma Lazarus at the beginning of this section. How do these words still apply to the United States today?

 Activity
Take It to the NET

Use the Internet to research the legacy of Andrew Carnegie's philanthropic efforts. Then, prepare a map of the United States showing places that benefited from his libraries and other gifts.

Activity Rubrics

Share rubrics with students before they prepare their maps.

Attempted Maps are incomplete.

Minimal Maps are complete but unclear or inaccurate.

Adequate Maps are accurate and clear.

Exemplary Maps are comprehensive, clear, and attractive.

Chapter 24 **613**

Test Preparation

Have students read the section under the heading "Immigration and the Growth of Cities" on the opposite page, and then complete the sentence below.

The Industrial Revolution

A pushed people back to the farms.

B brought rapid urbanization.

C caused a decline in the nation's population.

D benefited farmers.

Geography and History

ANSWER recycling, laws to regulate pollution or ban illegal dumping of hazardous materials

Creating a Chapter Summary

As a reteaching opportunity, pair a more able student with a less able student to complete this chapter summary.

Possible additions to web: **Britain** 1830s—suffrage for male property owners; fair division of seats in Parliament; end of slavery in Britain and colonies; suffrage for working-class men in 1867; elections by secret ballot in 1880s; limits on power of House of Lords in 1911; more rights for workers; free education for all children **France** rights for workers; system of education for all; separation of church and state; increased rights for women **United States** slavery abolished; all men gain the vote; growth of labor unions

Creating a Chapter Summary

On a sheet of paper, create a concept web to identify the main democratic reforms in Britain, France, and the United States during the 1800s. Use the web shown here to help you get started. Add as many circles as you need.

For additional review and enrichment activities, see the interactive version of *World History* available on the Web and on CD-ROM.

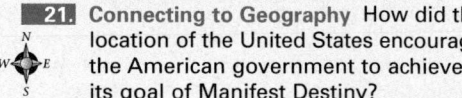

Web Site Self-Test
For practice test questions for Chapter 24, see **www.phschool.com**.

Building Vocabulary

1–10. Students' crossword puzzles should show a clear understanding of each word.

Recalling Key Facts

11. It did not bring full democracy but did increase the political power of middle-class males.

12. In that year, slavery was outlawed.

13. They collected petitions and organized rallies. Some turned to violence and went on hunger strikes.

14. Unlike in Britain, where there were two major parties, French governments were made up of coalitions of several smaller parties.

15. to build a Jewish state in Palestine

16. laws banning child labor, limiting working hours, regulating monopolies, giving voters more power, and giving women the vote

Critical Thinking and Writing

17. In the late 1800s, both major political parties worked to expand suffrage and limit the power of the lords.

18. Britain was more experienced with democratic methods than France was. Also, the legacy of the French Revolution remained strong.

19. (a) Long-term causes: The British controlled Irish farmlands. The potato was the main source of food for the Irish. Immediate causes: A blight destroyed the potato crop. The British continued to ship other crops out of Ireland. **(b)** One million Irish people died of starvation or disease. Millions emigrated to the United States. **(c)** The Irish blamed Britain for continuing to

Building Vocabulary

Use the chapter vocabulary words listed below to create a crossword puzzle. Exchange puzzles with a classmate. Complete the puzzles, and then check each other's answers.

1. **rotten borough**
2. **secret ballot**
3. **free trade**
4. **penal colony**
5. **home rule**
6. **provisional**
7. **coalition**
8. **abolitionist**
9. **segregation**
10. **isolationism**

Recalling Key Facts

11. What were the effects of the Reform Bill of 1832?

12. How did British policy toward slavery change in 1833?

13. How did British women's suffragists try to win the vote?

14. How did the party system in France's Third Republic differ from the British party system?

15. What was the main goal of the Zionist movement?

16. List two goals of progressive reformers in the United States.

Critical Thinking and Writing

17. Identifying Main Ideas Reread the subsection "A New Era in British Politics" in Section 1. Then, write a sentence summarizing the main idea of this subsection.

18. Drawing Conclusions Britain and France faced many similar political and social problems in the 1800s. Why do you think Britain was able to avoid the upheavals that plagued France?

19. Recognizing Causes and Effects (a) List two long-term and two immediate causes of the Great Hunger. **(b)** List two immediate effects. **(c)** Why do you think the famine sparked lasting feelings of bitterness against Britain?

20. Applying Information Describe how each of the following was related to nationalism: **(a)** the prestige of Queen Victoria, **(b)** the revolt of the Paris Commune, **(c)** the rise of Zionism.

21. Connecting to Geography How did the location of the United States encourage the American government to achieve its goal of Manifest Destiny?

ship food out of Ireland even when famine was devastating the country.

20. (a) The British were proud of her long and successful reign. **(b)** The rebels considered themselves patriots who rejected the peace with Germany. **(c)** Zionists sought to create a Jewish nation-state.

21. The United States was on the eastern part of a large continent; the vast expanses of land to the west seemed available for the taking. Although Native Americans resisted, the settlers overwhelmed them and took their land for farming, ranching, and building railroads.

Skills Assessment
Analyzing Primary Sources

The passage below is from *"J'Accuse!"* the letter that Émile Zola published in 1898. Read the passage, then answer the questions that follow.

"It is a crime to misdirect public opinion and to pervert it until it becomes delirious. It is a crime to poison small and simple minds, to rouse the passions of intolerance and reaction through the medium of that miserable antisemitism of which great and liberal France, with her Rights of Man, will expire if she is not soon cured. It is a crime to exploit patriotism for motives of hatred and it is a crime, finally, to make of the sword the modern god when all human science is at work to bring about a future of truth and justice. . . .

I have but one passion—that of light. . . . Let them dare to bring me before the court of appeals and let an inquiry be made in broad daylight. I wait."

—Émile Zola, *Aurore,* January 13, 1898

22. What historical event is Zola describing?
23. **(a)** Whom is Zola accusing of crimes? **(b)** What are the crimes that Zola lists?
24. What does Zola say will happen to France if intolerance and antisemitism continue?
25. How does Zola appeal to the French people's pride in their history?
26. What does Zola mean when he says, "I have but one passion—that of light"?
27. What is the tone of this passage?
28. **(a)** What does Zola dare his opponents to do? **(b)** Why does he want them to do this? **(c)** Based on what you have read, did Zola succeed in his aim?

Skills Assessment
Take It to the NET

Use the Internet to research leading figures in the women's suffrage movement in Britain, such as Emily Davidson, Constance Lytton, Christabel Pankhurst, or Annie Kenney. Then, with a partner, conduct a mock interview with one of these women. Include questions about her goals and what actions she took to achieve them. If possible, include actual quotations.

Skills Assessment
Analyzing Political Cartoons

This cartoon appeared in Britain in 1831. The man on the stilts is saying, "REFORM is become absolutely necessary—the Representation is corrupt—we have now representatives of Green Mounds, of Stone Walls, even of a Pig-sty, while many of our most populous manufacturing towns remain unrepresented." Study the cartoon, then answer the following questions:

29. What are "Green Mounds," "Stone Walls," and "Pig-sty"?
30. Why does the man on stilts say reform is necessary?
31. **(a)** What political position do the people on the ground represent? **(b)** Why are they in danger?
32. **(a)** Why would a British newspaper publish a cartoon about this issue in 1831? **(b)** How do you think the cartoonist felt about the issue? **(c)** Could the same cartoon have appeared in 1833? Why or why not?

Skills Tip

A political cartoon comments on events of its time. Knowing the date of a cartoon and the issues that were important at that time can help you understand the meaning of the cartoon.

Analyzing Primary Sources

22. the Dreyfus affair
23. **(a)** members of the French military and government who unjustly accused and convicted Dreyfus of treason **(b)** misdirecting and perverting public opinion, poisoning minds, rousing passions of intolerance, exploiting patriotism for motives of hatred, making a god of the sword or military
24. It will expire as a nation respecting the Rights of Man.
25. He refers to the principles of the French Revolution in the Declaration of the Rights of Man.
26. All he cares about is the truth.
27. angry, outraged, indignant, excited
28. **(a)** to take him to court **(b)** He hopes that a court case would lead to an honest, open inquiry into the Dreyfus case. **(c)** Yes and no. His opponents did bring him to court, but Zola was convicted of libel.

Analyzing Political Cartoons

29. rotten boroughs
30. The representation in Parliament is corrupt because it doesn't represent real people.
31. **(a)** the aristocrats and country squires who are against reform **(b)** Reform will cost them their seats in parliament.
32. **(a)** In 1831, Whigs and Tories were debating passage of a Reform Bill. **(b)** He favored the Bill because it would eliminate rotten boroughs and give representation to manufacturing towns. **(c)** No. In 1832, the Reform Act of 1832 was passed. The issue was no longer active.

Skills Tip

Look for exaggerated characteristics to see which side of an issue a cartoonist is taking. The Skills Handbook in the front of the book has a lesson that will help students with this feature.

Take It to the NET

Direct students to **www.phschool.com** for links to sites that will help them get started on their assignments. Share rubrics with students.
Attempted The interview is incomplete and does not address the ideas of the woman.
Minimal The interview is complete but does not adequately present the ideas of the woman.
Adequate The interview presents ideas of the woman and evaluates their relevance to the present day.
Exemplary The interview presents ideas of the woman, evaluates their relevance to the present day, and is creative and well written.

Unit Theme Activity

Remind students to continue working on their Unit Theme Portfolio Activity. See rubrics for the activity on the unit opener page in the Teacher's Edition.

Chapter 25 Planning Guide

Resource Manager

Chapter Level Resources	CORE INSTRUCTION	READING/SKILLS
Chapter Level Resources	📚 Teaching Resources 📖 Pacing Charts, Ch. 25 📖 Teaching With Themes, p. 28 🎞 Color Transparencies, p. F–51 💿 Resource Pro® Ch. 25 🖥 **www.phschool.com** • eTeach	🔊 Book on CD, Ch. 25 🔊 Interactive Student Tutorial CD-ROM, Ch. 25 🔊 Social Studies Skills Tutor CD-ROM 🎞 Skills Transparencies

1 A Western-Dominated World
1. Outline causes of the "new imperialism."
2. Explain why western imperialism was so successful.
3. Describe how governments ruled their empires.
	📚 Teaching Resources
	📖 Creative Teaching Activities, p. 111
	💿 Prentice Hall Presentation Pro, Ch. 25, Section 1
	🎞 Section Reading Support Transparencies
		📚 Teaching Resources
		📁 Unit 6 booklet
		  • Guided Reading and Review, p. 58
		  • Skill Application Activity, p. 71
		📖 Guide to the Essentials

2 The Partition of Africa
1. Identify forces shaping Africa in the early 1800s.
2. Describe how European contact with Africa increased.
3. Summarize how Leopold II started a scramble for colonies.
4. Explain how Africans resisted imperialism.
	📚 Teaching Resources
	📁 Unit 6 booklet
	  • Viewpoint Activity, p. 624
	📖 Creative Teaching Activities, p. 112
	💿 Prentice Hall Presentation Pro, Ch. 25, Section 2
	🎞 Section Reading Support Transparencies
		📚 Teaching Resources
		📁 Unit 6 booklet
		  • Guided Reading and Review, p. 60
		📖 Guide to the Essentials
		📼 Guided Reading Audiotapes, Ch. 25, Section 2

3 European Challenges to the Muslim World 1. Identify stresses in the Muslim world. 2. Define problems faced by the Ottoman empire. 3. Outline how Egypt sought to modernize. 4. Explain the European powers' interest in Iran.	📚 Teaching Resources 📖 Creative Teaching Activities, p. 113 💿 Prentice Hall Presentation Pro, Ch. 25, Section 3 🎞 Section Reading Support Transparencies	📚 Teaching Resources 📁 Unit 6 booklet • Guided Reading and Review, p. 62 📖 Guide to the Essentials 📼 Guided Reading Audiotapes, Ch. 25, Section 3

4 The British Take Over India
1. Summarize the causes and effects of the Sepoy Rebellion.
2. Assess how British rule affected India.
3. Explain how Indians viewed western culture.
4. Trace the origins of Indian nationalism.
	📚 Teaching Resources
	📁 Unit 6 booklet
	  • Biography Activity, p. 68
	📖 Creative Teaching Activities, p. 114
	💿 Prentice Hall Presentation Pro, Ch. 25, Section 4
		📚 Teaching Resources
		📁 Unit 6 booklet
		  • Guided Reading and Review, p. 64
		📖 Guide to the Essentials
		📼 Guided Reading Audiotapes, Ch. 25, Section 4

5 China and the New Imperialism
1. Enumerate trade rights westerners sought in China.
2. Summarize the internal problems that Chinese reformers tried to solve.
3. Describe how the Qing dynasty came to an end.
	📚 Teaching Resources
	📁 Unit 6 booklet
	  • Primary Source Activity, p. 69
	📖 Creative Teaching Activities, p. 115
	💿 Prentice Hall Presentation Pro, Ch. 25, Section 5
		📚 Teaching Resources
		📁 Unit 6 booklet
		  • Guided Reading and Review, p. 66
		📖 Guide to the Essentials
		📼 Guided Reading Audiotapes, Ch. 25, Section 5

ENRICHMENT/PRE-AP

www.phschool.com
- Why Study History?

Teaching Resources
- Geography and History, pp. 12–13
- Color Transparencies, pp. D–71, E–41

Teaching Resources
- Chapter Extension Activities, p. 61
- History Through Literature, pp. 53–54
- Color Transparencies, pp. B–47, B–49, B–51
- www.phschool.com
  - Virtual Field Trip
  - Internet Activity, Section 2

- Color Transparencies, p. C–55
- Visions, Voices, Views, Daily Life CloseUp, tape 6

Teaching Resources
- Chapter Extension Activities, p. 62
- www.phschool.com
  - Internet Activity, Section 5

ASSESSMENT

PRENTICE HALL ASSESSMENT SYSTEM

Core Assessment
- ExamView Test Bank booklet, Ch. 25
- ExamView Test Bank CD-ROM, Ch. 25

Standardized Test Preparation

Diagnose and Prescribe
- Diagnostic Tests for High School Social Studies Skills

Review and Reteach
- Review Book for World History

Practice and Assess
- Test-Taking Strategies With Transparencies for High School
- Alternative Assessment booklet
- Test Prep Book for World History

Teaching Resources
- Unit 6 booklet
  - Geography Quiz, p. 72
  - Section Quizzes, pp. 59, 61, 63, 65, 67
  - Chapter Tests A, B, and C, pp. 73–77
- www.phschool.com
  - Self-Test

CUSTOMIZE FOR INDIVIDUAL NEEDS

Gifted and Talented
- Teacher's Edition, Activities: Customize for Heterogeneous Groups, p. 629; Customize for Heterogeneous Groups, p. 638

Less Proficient Readers
- Guide to the Essentials, Ch. 25
- Guided Reading Audiotapes, English, Ch. 25
- Book on CD, Ch. 25
- Teacher's Edition, Activities: Customize for Visual Learners, p. 628

Less Proficient Writers
- Teacher's Edition, Activities: Cooperative Learning Activity, p. 637

Students Acquiring English/ESL
- Guide to the Essentials, English/Spanish, Ch. 25
- Guided Reading Audiotapes, English/Spanish, Ch. 25
- Book on CD, Ch. 25
- Teacher's Edition, Activities marked with an *

TEXT

Don't miss the exclusive interactive version of *World History: Connections to Today* on the Internet and CD-ROM.

INTRODUCTION

The Industrial Revolution gave Europeans the means and the motives to seek global domination during the Age of Imperialism. The Europeans divided most of Africa among themselves and extended their influence over Ottoman lands. The British took over much of India, and even China was forced to accept western trade. Although local populations resisted these encroachments, they were overcome by the superior military technology of the Europeans.

Focusing on Themes

Suggest that students focus on these theme questions as they read:

Economics and Technology
How was the Industrial Revolution linked to imperialism?

Global Interaction
How did western powers gain global empires?

Political and Social Systems
What conditions in Africa and Asia helped western powers make inroads there?

Continuity and Change
How did people in Africa and Asia respond to western imperialism?

◆ TIME LINE ACTIVITY

You may wish to share the About the Pictures note with your students before you ask questions about the time line such as these:

1. Which entries on the time line deal with events in Africa? *(Muhammad Ali named governor of Egypt, France tries to conquer Algeria, Berlin Conference, Boer War)*
2. Which entries on the time line deal with events in Asia? *(Sepoy Rebellion, Sun Yixian becomes Chinese president)*
3. What is the most significant global event in this period? *(World War I)*

Don't Miss!

Analyzing Primary Sources
A Schoolroom in East Africa (Section 2)

You Are There . . .
Meeting the Emperor (Section 5)

The New Imperialism
1800–1914

Chapter Preview

1 A Western-Dominated World
2 The Partition of Africa
3 European Challenges to the Muslim World
4 The British Take Over India
5 China and the New Imperialism

1857
The Sepoy Rebellion breaks out in India. At the battle of Cawnpore, shown here, Indian cavalry charges a British line.

1805
Muhammad Ali is named governor of Egypt. This mosque in Cairo is named in his honor.

1830
France begins efforts to conquer Algeria in North Africa.

CHAPTER EVENTS

1800   1825   1850

GLOBAL EVENTS

1807 In the United States, Robert Fulton uses a steam engine to power a ship.

1848 Revolutions break out through much of Europe.

Resource Directory

Teaching Resources
Teaching With Themes Chapter Theme Activities, p. 28
Pacing Chart With Block Scheduling Guide Ch. 25
Technology
World History Color Transparencies Ch. 25 Graphic Organizer, p. F–51

Imports From Africa and Asia About 1870

40°W 20°W 0° 20°E 40°E 60°E 80°E 100°E 120°E 140°E 160°E 60°N 40°N 20°N 0° 20°S 40°S

EUROPE

ASIA

AFRICA

INDIAN OCEAN

PACIFIC OCEAN

ATLANTIC OCEAN

AUSTRALIA

Legend
- Industrialized nations
- Coal
- Coffee
- Copper
- Cotton
- Jute
- Silk
- Sugar
- Timber
- Wheat
- → Trade routes

N W E S

Robinson Projection
0   1000   2000 Miles
0   1000   2000 Kilometers

In the late 1800s, during the Age of Imperialism, the industrial powers of Europe sought raw materials from Africa and Asia.

1884
European officials meet at the Berlin Conference to settle rival land claims in Africa. No Africans are invited.

1899
Boer War erupts in South Africa.

1911
Sun Yixian becomes president of Chinese republic.

1875   1900   1925

Mid 1880s German engineers develop the first automobile.

1914 World War I begins in Europe.

Imports From Africa and Asia About 1870

Activating Prior Knowledge
What technological change that began in the 1700s do you think spurred the trade shown on this map? *(Industrial Revolution)*

Previewing
Why do you suppose Europeans went such great distances to get these raw materials? *(Possible answers: couldn't produce enough at home or not available at home)*

Background About the Pictures

1. Also known as the Alabaster Mosque because its walls are faced with that stone, this mosque was built between 1830 and 1857. Noted for its twin minarets, it is the largest of the four mosques in the Citadel, a complex of structures in eastern Cairo. Because the Citadel is on high ground, the mosque's domes and minarets are visible throughout the city.

2. Sepoys captured Cawnpore in early summer in 1857, but the British regained it in July. The side column in Section 4 has details on atrocities committed by both sides at Cawnpore.

3. Sun Yixian abandoned his medical profession and devoted himself to leading China's reform and modernization program, which included forming a democratic government.

Independent Assignments

Have students read one section as they prepare for class. After class, have them complete the assignment. Some students may benefit from using the Guided Reading and Review worksheets.

Section 1 Have students use the worksheet *Identifying Alternatives* in the Unit 6 booklet, p. 71, to learn about two views of imperialism and economic health.

Section 2 Have students use the worksheet *Two Views of Imperialism in Africa* in the Unit 6 booklet, p. 70, to compare two views of imperialism.

Section 3 Have students use the map on p. 38 of the Historical Outline Map Book to identify the sites or regions mentioned in this section.

Section 4 Have students use the worksheet *Rabindranath Tagore* in the Unit 6 booklet, p. 68, to learn about the first non-European to win the Nobel Prize for literature.

Section 5 Have students use the worksheet *The Great Powers Divide China* in the Unit 6 booklet, p. 69, to study a political cartoon about relations between the West and China.

eTeach

Be sure to check out this month's online discussion with a World History Master Teacher.

Go to **www.phschool.com**.

SECTION 1

A Western-Dominated World

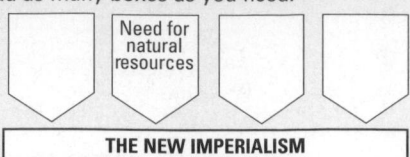

🔔 **Bell Ringer** Write on the board "The sun never sets on the British empire." Then, ask students what they think the statement means.

LESSON PLAN

1. Focus Economic, political, and military interests spurred European imperialism in the 1800s. Other motivating factors included humanitarianism, religious fervor, and racism. Europeans of all classes supported imperialism. The imperialist powers of Europe established colonies, protectorates, and spheres of influence all around the world.

2. Instruct Ask students to outline the contents of this section. Advise them to construct their outlines with three parts, titled Reasons for Imperialism, Reasons for European Success, and Forms of Imperial Control. Encourage students to use the boldfaced heads for guidance in finding the major ideas for each part of the outline. Remind them that each major idea should be supported by specific facts or examples. Students may work on this assignment in groups or as individuals. When students have finished their outlines, review the material in a class discussion.

3. Assess Have students put away their outlines and, for each part, list as many major ideas as they can.

4. Reteach If students' Assess activity does not reflect adequate understanding of the lesson, you might assign the *Guide to the Essentials* or the *Interactive Student Tutorial CD-ROM* for this section.

Reading Focus

■ What were the causes of the "new imperialism"?

■ Why was western imperialism so successful?

■ How did governments rule their empires?

Vocabulary

imperialism
protectorate
sphere of influence

Taking Notes

As you read, make an organizer like the model below showing the causes of imperialism in the 1800s. Add as many boxes as you need.

| Need for natural resources | | | |

THE NEW IMPERIALISM

Main Idea In the late 1800s, industrial nations of the West engaged in imperialism and dominated much of the world.

Setting the Scene When Edward VII inherited the British throne in 1901, his empire extended far beyond Britain. One writer boasted, "The sun never sets" on the British empire. In other words, because the empire circled the globe, the sun always shone on some part of it.

Like Britain, other western powers built overseas empires in the late 1800s. The Industrial Revolution and the growth of science and technology had transformed the West. Armed with new economic and political power, western nations set out to dominate the world.

The New Imperialism and Its Causes

European imperialism did not begin in the 1800s. Imperialism is the domination by one country of the political, economic, or cultural life of another country or region. As you have learned, European states won empires in the Americas after 1492, established colonies in South Asia, and gained toeholds on the coasts of Africa and China. Despite these gains, between 1500 and 1800, Europe had little influence on the lives of the peoples of China, India, or Africa.

By the 1800s, however, Europe had gained considerable power. Strong, centrally governed nation-states had emerged, and the Industrial Revolution had greatly enriched European economies. Encouraged by their new economic and military strength, Europeans embarked on a path of aggressive expansion that today's historians call the "new imperialism." Like other key developments in world history, the new imperialism exploded out of a combination of causes.

Economic Interests The Industrial Revolution created needs and desires that spurred overseas expansion. Manufacturers wanted access to natural resources such as rubber, petroleum, manganese for steel, and palm oil for machinery. They also hoped for new markets where they could sell their factory goods. In addition, colonies offered a valuable outlet for Europe's growing population. Lord Frederick Lugard, a British empire builder, tried to justify imperialism in Africa with these words:

> "The necessity that is upon us [is] to provide for our ever-growing population—either by opening new fields for emigration, or by providing work and employment . . . and to stimulate trade by finding new markets."
> —Lord Lugard, *The Rise of Our East African Empire*

Resource Directory

Teaching Resources

Creative Teaching Activities Creative Teaching Activities booklet, p. 111
Guided Reading and Review Unit 6 booklet, p. 58
Geography and History Activity *The Geography of Gateway Cities,* Geography and History booklet, pp. 12–13

Technology

World History Color Transparencies political cartoon on the responsibilities of powerful nations toward the less powerful, p. E–41

🔲 Block Scheduling Support

Ask students whether they agree or disagree with the following statement: "Western nations continue to exert some imperialistic control over other parts of the world today." Encourage students to explain the reasons for their opinion, either in class discussion or as a written assignment.

Have students work in pairs to examine copies of the week's newspapers for examples of imperialism in today's world. Ask students to report to the class on their findings.

Political and Military Interests Closely linked to economic motives were political and military issues. Steam-powered merchant ships and naval vessels needed bases around the world to take on coal and supplies. Industrial powers seized islands or harbors to satisfy these needs.

Nationalism played an important role, too. When France, for example, moved into West Africa, rival nations like Britain and Germany seized lands nearby to halt further French expansion. Western leaders claimed that colonies were needed for national security. They also felt that ruling a global empire increased a nation's prestige around the world.

Humanitarian Goals Many westerners felt a genuine concern for their "little brothers" beyond the seas. Missionaries, doctors, and colonial officials believed they had a duty to spread what they saw as the blessings of western civilization, including its medicine, law, and Christian religion.

Social Darwinism Behind the idea of a civilizing mission was a growing sense in the West of racial superiority. Many westerners had embraced the ideas of Social Darwinism. They applied Darwin's ideas about natural selection and survival of the fittest to human societies. European races, they argued, were superior to all others, and imperial conquest and destruction of weaker races were simply nature's way of improving the human species!

The Success of Western Imperialism

In just a few decades, from about 1870 to 1914, imperialist nations gained control over much of the world. Leading the way were soldiers, merchants, settlers, missionaries, and explorers. In Europe, imperial expansion found favor with all classes, from bankers and manufacturers to workers. Western imperialism succeeded for a number of reasons.

Weakness of Nonwestern States While European nations had grown stronger in the 1800s, several older civilizations were in decline, especially the Ottoman Middle East, Mughal India, and Qing China. In West Africa, wars among African peoples and the draining effect of the slave trade had undermined established empires, kingdoms, and city-states. Newer African states were not strong enough to resist the western onslaught.

Western Advantages Europeans had the advantages of strong economies, well-organized governments, and powerful armies and navies. Superior technology and improved medical knowledge also played a role. Quinine and other new medicines helped Europeans survive deadly tropical diseases. And, of course, advances such as Maxim machine guns, repeating rifles, and steam-driven warships were very strong arguments in persuading Africans and Asians to accept western control. As an English writer sarcastically noted: "Whatever happens, we have got the Maxim gun, and they have not."

Resistance Africans and Asians strongly resisted western expansion into their lands. Some people fought the invaders, even though they had no weapons to equal the Maxim gun. As you will read, ruling groups in certain areas tried to strengthen their societies against outsiders by reforming their own Muslim, Hindu, or Confucian traditions. Finally, many western-educated Africans and Asians organized nationalist movements to expel the imperialists from their lands.

Primary Source

"The White Man's Burden"
In the photo above, British writer Rudyard Kipling (front right) is one of several journalists in South Africa. Kipling promoted imperialism in his controversial poem, "The White Man's Burden":

"Take up the White Man's burden—
  Send forth the best ye breed—
Go bind your sons to exile
  To serve your captives' need. . . .
Take up the White Man's burden—
  The savage wars of peace—
Fill full the mouth of Famine,
  And bid the sickness cease;
And when your goal is nearest
  (The end for others sought)
Watch sloth and heathen folly
  Bring all your hope to nought.
              —Rudyard Kipling,
              "The White Man's Burden"

Skills Assessment

Primary Source Why did Kipling consider imperialism to be beneficial?

Background
Historical Evidence

National Greatness National rivalry played a major role in the scramble for colonies. In a work published in 1897, German historian Heinrich von Treitschke used nationalism to justify German imperialism.

"All over the globe today we see the peoples of Europe creating a mighty aristocracy of the white races. Those who take no share in this great rivalry will play a pitiable part in time to come. The colonizing impulse has become a vital question for a great nation. . . . We . . . [in Germany] realize today what opportunities we have missed. The consequences of the last half-century have been appalling, for in them England has conquered the world. . . . We must, and will, take our share in the domination of the world by white races."

You may wish to use this excerpt as the basis for a class discussion on how nationalism and racism helped cause imperialism.

Human Drama Note

Might Makes Right To gain control in Africa, Europeans cajoled, manipulated, and threatened African leaders. Pierre Brazza, a French naval officer, related how he offered his hand to an African chief in the Congo. Holding rifle cartridges in his right hand and a piece of cloth in his left, he said, "White men have two hands. The stronger hand is the hand of war. The other hand is the hand of trade. Which hand do the Abanhos want?" The tribe cried out in unison, "Trade."

✓ **Test Preparation**

Have students read "Humanitarian Goals" on this page, and then complete the sentence below.

Europeans referred to Africans and Asians as "little brothers" because they thought that

A most Africans and Asians were short.

B most Africans and Asians were young males.

C Africans and Asians, like children, needed help and guidance.

D Africans and Asians were sickly.

Primary Source

ANSWER He thought the "captive" peoples would benefit from the imperialists' efforts to end famine and disease.

SECTION 1 Assessment

Recall

1. (a) new imperialism, p. 618 (b) direct rule, p. 620 (c) indirect rule, p. 620
2. (a) imperialism, p. 618 (b) protectorate, p. 620 (c) sphere of influence, p. 620

Comprehension

3. Possible answer: Industrial powers desired sources of raw materials and markets for manufactured goods. They also desired naval bases to support trade and military operations. Nationalism and racism also motivated countries. 4. Possible answers: (a) Many older civilizations were in decline and therefore not strong enough to resist. African nations were weakened by wars and the slave trade. Europeans had strong economies, well-organized governments, and powerful military forces. (b) Some lands resisted imperialism. In others, rulers tried to reform society to strengthen it. 5. colonies, with either direct or indirect rule; protectorates, in which local rulers were expected to follow European advice; spheres of influence, which were areas claimed by various European powers for their exclusive investment or trading privileges

Critical Thinking and Writing

6. Possible answer: because Britain needed to provide for its growing population, either by starting new colonies or by providing work for the people, and to stimulate trade 7. Possible answers: biased, because it assumes that Asian and African cultures were inferior to western culture

Caption Answer

European armies had more modern weapons than had African or Asian armies.

The Maxim Gun
Britain's future King Edward VII tries his hand at the Maxim machine gun. Standing next to him is Sir Hiram Maxim, the gun's inventor.

Theme: Economics and Technology Why were European armies often able to defeat African or Asian forces?

Criticism at Home In the West itself, a small group of anti-imperialists emerged. Some argued that colonialism was a tool of the rich. Others said it was immoral. Westerners, they pointed out, were moving toward greater democracy at home but were imposing undemocratic rule on other people. "The new imperialism stood," one English critic protested, "not for a widened and ennobled sense of national responsibility, but for a hard assertion of racial supremacy and material force."

Forms of Imperial Rule

The new imperialism took several forms. In some areas, imperial powers established colonies. Elsewhere, they set up protectorates and spheres of influence.

Colonies France and Britain, the leading imperial powers, developed different kinds of colonial rule. The French practiced direct rule, sending officials and soldiers from France to administer their colonies. Their goal was to impose French culture on their colonies and turn them into French provinces.

The British, by contrast, relied on a system of indirect rule. To govern their colonies, they used sultans, chiefs, or other local rulers. They then encouraged the children of the local ruling class to get an education in Britain. In that way, they groomed a new "westernized" generation of leaders to continue indirect imperial rule and to spread British civilization. Like France and other imperialist nations, however, Britain could still resort to military force if its control over a colony was threatened in any way.

Protectorates In a protectorate, local rulers were left in place but were expected to follow the advice of European advisers on issues such as trade or missionary activity. A protectorate cost less to run than a colony did, and usually did not require a large commitment of military forces.

Spheres of Influence A third form of western control was the sphere of influence, an area in which an outside power claimed exclusive investment or trading privileges. Europeans carved out these spheres in China and elsewhere to prevent conflicts among themselves. The United States claimed Latin America as its sphere of influence.

SECTION 1 Assessment

Recall

1. **Identify:** (a) new imperialism, (b) direct rule, (c) indirect rule.
2. **Define:** (a) imperialism, (b) protectorate, (c) sphere of influence.

Comprehension

3. Describe three causes of the new imperialism.
4. (a) What were three reasons for the success of western imperialism? (b) How did people oppose western imperialism?
5. Describe three different forms of imperial rule.

Critical Thinking and Writing

6. **Analyzing Primary Sources** Review the words of Lord Lugard quoted at the start of this section. Explain why Lugard thought that it was necessary for Britain to pursue a policy of imperialism in Africa.
7. **Recognizing Bias** Western colonial officials and missionaries thought that they had a duty to spread the "blessings of western civilization" to their "little brothers" in Africa and Asia. How was this a biased viewpoint?

Activity

Making a Graphic Organizer
Make a graphic organizer that shows the various reasons for the success of western imperialism. Use the graphic organizers at the start of each section and at the end of each chapter for ideas on how to design your chart.

SECTION 2 The Partition of Africa

Reading Focus

- What forces were shaping Africa in the early 1800s?

- How did European contact with Africa increase?

- How did Leopold II start a scramble for colonies?

- How did Africans resist imperialism?

Vocabulary

jihad
missionary
elite

Taking Notes

As you read, create a concept web like the model below that lists examples of African resistance against imperialism. Add as many circles as needed to complete the web.

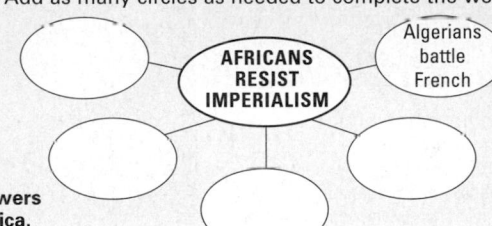

AFRICANS RESIST IMPERIALISM

Algerians battle French

Main Idea By the end of the 1800s, the imperialist powers of Europe claimed control over most of Africa.

Setting the Scene

In the late 1800s, Britain, France, Germany, and other European powers swept into Africa. Chief Machemba of the Yao people in East Africa wrote in Swahili to a German officer:

> "If it be friendship that you desire, then I am ready for it . . . but to be your subject, that I cannot be. . . . I do not fall at your feet, for you are God's creature just as I am."
> —Chief Machemba, Letter to Herman von Wissman

Though the Yao and others resisted, they could not prevent European conquest. Within about 20 years, the Europeans had carved up the continent and dominated millions of Africans.

Africa in the Early 1800s

To understand the impact of European domination, we must look at Africa in the early 1800s, before the scramble for colonies began. Africa is a huge continent, four times the size of Europe. Across its many regions, people spoke hundreds of languages and had developed varied governments. Some people lived in large centralized states, others in village communities.

North Africa North Africa includes the enormous Sahara and the fertile land along the Mediterranean. Since long before 1800, the region had close ties to the Muslim world. In the early 1800s, much of North Africa remained under the rule of the declining Ottoman empire.

West Africa On the grasslands of West Africa, an Islamic reform movement had brought change. Leaders like Usman dan Fodio preached jihad, a holy struggle, to revive and purify Islam. Under these leaders, several new Muslim states arose, built on trade, farming, and herding.

In the forest regions, strong states like the Asante kingdom had arisen. The Asante traded with Europeans and Muslims and controlled several smaller states. However, these tributary states were ready to turn to Europeans or others who might help them defeat their Asante rulers.

East Africa Islam had long influenced the east coast of Africa, where port cities like Mombasa and Kilwa carried on profitable trade. The cargoes were often slaves. Captives were marched from the interior to the coast to be shipped as slaves to the Middle East. Ivory and copper from Central Africa were also exchanged for goods such as cloth and firearms from India.

The Ivory Trade
East African merchants profited from the ivory trade. For centuries, artists around the world made beautiful ivory carvings. Today, international law severely limits the trade in order to protect declining elephant populations.

Theme: Economics and Technology Besides ivory, what was another source of profits for merchants in East Africa?

Chapter 25 **621**

Block Scheduling Support

Fables are stories with animal characters that illuminate a truth about human nature or life. They allow members of the audience to step out of themselves and view a situation from a dramatically different perspective. In this way, fables are often able to expose bias in an effective way. They may also express the yearnings of certain segments of society.

Have students read *The Gentlemen of the Jungle* in the History Through Literature booklet, pp. 53–54, and then answer the questions about this fable that deals with the injustice of imperialist treatment of native populations and its possible consequences.

SECTION 2

Bell Ringer Have students read the words of Chief Machemba quoted at the start of this section. Ask them to imagine that they are the German officer to whom the chief wrote. Have them write a letter in response to Machemba.

LESSON PLAN

1. Focus In the early 1800s, most of Africa was free of European control. Each African group enjoyed individual religious, economic, political, and social traditions. In the late 1800s, however, Britain, France, and other European powers began carving up the continent. Many Africans fought against European domination, but in the end only Ethiopia and Liberia remained independent.

2. Instruct Divide the class into four groups, and assign each group one of the following regions: North Africa, West Africa, East Africa, South Africa. Explain that each group will make two posters using words and images to portray conditions in their assigned region. Both posters should be designed from an African point of view. One poster will portray conditions as they existed before the arrival of European imperialists. The second poster will depict some of the changes that European imperialism brought to the region. Suggest to students that their posters might include maps, illustrations, concept charts, and the like. Encourage students to supplement information in the text by doing additional research. Have each group present and explain their posters to the class. Then display the posters around the classroom.

3. Assess Ask students to comment on how their posters would have been different if they had been designed to express a European point of view.

4. Reteach If students' **Assess** activity does not reflect adequate understanding of the lesson, you might assign the *Guide to the Essentials* or the *Interactive Student Tutorial CD-ROM* for this section.

Caption Answer

Possible answers: copper, slaves

Virtual Field Trip

www.phschool.com

David Livingstone National Memorial Blantyre, Scotland

To learn more about the life and work of Dr. David Livingstone, use the Internet address above to link to the David Livingstone National Memorial.

Livingstone and Victoria Falls

After recovering from bouts of malaria and rheumatic fever, Dr. David Livingstone set out in 1853 to explore the Zambesi River valley. On November 17, 1855, he viewed the magnificent site that we know today as Victoria Falls.

Theme: Geography and History Why was exploration of Africa difficult?

Southern Africa In the early 1800s, southern Africa was in turmoil. Shaka, you will recall, united the Zulu nation. His conquests, however, set off mass migrations and wars, creating chaos across much of the region. By the 1830s, the Zulus were also battling the Boers, who were migrating north from the Cape Colony.

The Slave Trade In the early 1800s, European nations began to outlaw the transatlantic slave trade, though it took years to end it. Meanwhile, the East African slave trade, continued to the Middle East and Asia.

Some people in Britain and the United States helped freed slaves resettle in Africa. In 1787, the British organized Sierra Leone in West Africa as a colony for former slaves. Later, some free blacks from the United States settled in nearby Liberia. By 1847, Liberia became an independent republic.

European Contacts Increase

From the 1500s through the 1700s, Europeans traded along the African coast. Difficult geography and diseases kept them from reaching the interior. Medical advances and river steamships changed all that in the 1800s.

Explorers In the early 1800s, European explorers began pushing into the interior of Africa. Daring adventurers like Mungo Park and Richard Burton set out to map the course and sources of the great African rivers such as the Niger, the Nile, and the Congo. These explorers were fascinated by African geography, but they had little understanding of the peoples they met. All, however, endured great hardships in pursuit of their dreams.

Missionaries Catholic and Protestant missionaries followed the explorers. All across Africa, they sought to win people to Christianity. The missionaries were sincere in their desire to help Africans. They built schools and medical clinics alongside churches. They also focused attention on the evils of the slave trade.

Still, missionaries, like most westerners, took a paternalistic view of Africans. They saw them as children in need of guidance. To them, African cultures and religions were "degraded." They urged Africans to reject their own traditions in favor of western civilization.

Livingstone The best known explorer-missionary was Dr. David Livingstone. For 30 years, he crisscrossed Africa. He wrote about the many peoples he met with more sympathy and less bias than did most Europeans. He relentlessly opposed the slave trade, which remained a profitable business for some African rulers and foreign traders. The only way to end this cruel traffic, he believed, was to open up the interior of Africa to Christianity and trade.

Livingstone blazed a trail that others soon followed. In 1869, the journalist Henry Stanley trekked into Central Africa to find Livingstone, who had not been heard from for years. He finally tracked him down in 1871 in what is today Tanzania, greeting him with the now-legendary phrase "Dr. Livingstone, I presume?"

A Scramble for Colonies

Shortly afterward, King Leopold II of Belgium hired Stanley to explore the Congo River basin and arrange trade treaties with African leaders. Publicly, Leopold spoke of a civilizing mission to carry the light "that for millions of men still plunged in barbarism will be the dawn of a better era." Privately, he dreamed of conquest and profit.

Skills Assessment

Geography During the late 1800s, European countries took part in a scramble for Africa. They claimed control of nearly the whole continent by 1914.

1. **Location** On the map, locate **(a)** Algeria, **(b)** Belgian Congo, **(c)** Ethiopia.
2. **Region** In which part of Africa were most of France's colonies located?
3. **Critical Thinking Making Inferences** How can you tell from the map that Africans did not willingly accept European domination?

Activity
Connections to Film

Writing a News Story On January 23, 1879, a Zulu army of 20,000 soldiers struck back at the British empire. When the Battle of Isandlwana was over, 858 British soldiers and 471 native troops lay dead. This British defeat is the subject of *Zulu Dawn*, a 1979 film starring Burt Lancaster, Peter O'Toole, and John Mills. The film shows how Sir Bartle Frere, the British governor, forced the war by issuing the Zulus a humiliating and unacceptable ultimatum. It also shows how Lord Chelmsford, the British military commander, underestimated the Zulu army.

Ask students who view *Zulu Dawn* to imagine that they are newspaper reporters covering the Zulu war. Their assignment is to write a news article on the Battle of Isandlwana, describing the key events that led to the battle and the circumstances that led to the British defeat. (*Zulu Dawn* is available on both videocassette and videodisc.)

Imperialism in Africa to 1914

European Colonies in Africa About 1850

Chapter 25 623

Test Preparation

Have students read the second paragraph after the heading "Livingstone" on this page, and then answer the question below.

Why are Stanley's words remembered?

A They were the first words he spoke to Dr. Livingstone.

(B) They were a supreme understatement from a man who had spent so long searching for Livingstone.

C They were very stilted.

D Stanley was a very famous man.

Skills Assessment

ANSWERS 1. Review locations with students. **2.** northwestern Africa **3.** The map shows many sites where anticolonial resistance took place.

624 Chapter 25

A Royal Gift
In 1908, German colonizers met with Njoya, ruler of the West African kingdom of Bamum. King Njoya presented this ornate throne as a gift for Kaiser William II.

Theme: Global Interaction
Why do you think Njoya wanted to give a gift to the German ruler?

King Leopold's activities in the Congo set off a scramble by other European nations. Before long, Britain, France, and Germany were pressing rival claims to the region.

Berlin Conference To avoid bloodshed, European powers met at an international conference in 1884. It took place not in Africa but in Berlin, Germany. No Africans were invited to the conference.

At the Berlin Conference, European powers recognized Leopold's private claims to the Congo Free State but called for free trade on the Congo and Niger rivers. They further agreed that a European power could not claim any part of Africa unless it had set up a government office there. This principle led Europeans to send officials who would exert their power over local rulers and peoples.

The rush to colonize Africa was on. In the 20 years after the Berlin Conference, the European powers partitioned almost the entire continent. As Europeans carved out their claims, they established new borders and frontiers. They redrew the map of Africa with little regard for traditional patterns of settlement or ethnic boundaries.

Horrors in the Congo Leopold and other wealthy Belgians, meantime, exploited the riches of the Congo, including its copper, rubber, and ivory. Soon, there were horrifying reports of Belgian overseers brutalizing villagers. Forced to work for almost nothing, laborers were savagely beaten or mutilated. The population of some areas declined drastically.

Eventually, international outrage forced Leopold to turn over his colony to the Belgian government. It became the Belgian Congo in 1908. Under Belgian rule, the worst abuses were ended. Still, the Belgians regarded the Congo as a possession to be exploited. Africans were given little or no role in either the government or the economy of the colony.

French Expansion France took a giant share of Africa. In the 1830s, it had invaded and conquered Algeria in North Africa. The victory cost tens of thousands of French lives and killed many times more Algerians. In the late 1800s, France extended its influence along the Mediterranean into Tunisia. It also won colonies in West and Central Africa. At its height, the French empire in Africa was as large as the continental United States.

Britain Takes Its Share Britain's share of Africa was smaller and more scattered than that of France. However, it included more heavily populated regions with many rich resources. Britain took chunks of West and East Africa. It gained control of Egypt, and pushed south into the Sudan.

In southern Africa, Britain clashed with the Boers, who were descendants of Dutch settlers. Britain had acquired the Cape Colony from the Dutch in 1815. At that time, many Boers fled British rule. They migrated north and set up their own republics. In the late 1800s, however, the discovery of gold and diamonds in the Boer lands led to conflict with Britain. The Boer War, which lasted from 1899 to 1902, involved bitter guerrilla fighting. The British won, but at great cost.

In 1910, the British united the Cape Colony and the former Boer republics into the Union of South Africa. The new constitution set up a government run by whites and laid the foundation for a system of complete racial segregation that would remain in force until 1993.

Others Join the Scramble Other European powers joined the scramble for colonies, in part to bolster their national image, in part to further their economic growth and influence. The Portuguese carved out large colonies in Angola and Mozambique. Italy reached across the Mediterranean to occupy Libya and then pushed into the "horn" of Africa, at the southern end of the Red Sea. The newly united German empire took lands in eastern and southwestern Africa. A German politician, trying to ease the worries of

A Schoolroom in East Africa

This photograph, dated 1903, was taken in a German missionary school in East Africa. The pictures on the wall are of Kaiser William II and his wife, Augusta.

Background
About the Primary Source

Colonial Schools Children in the colonial schools were taught in the language of the colonial power. They were also taught from a European perspective: they might learn about the Alps or the great rivers of Europe, but nothing of the geography of Africa. Textbooks, of course, also were written from a European perspective, so that African students might read about "our ancestors, the Picts and the Scots" and similar incongruities.

Activity
Interpreting the Primary Source

Use the additional question to generate class discussion.
Critical Thinking: Making Inferences In what language are the students probably being taught? *(German)*

Skills Tip

Although photographs show real scenes, be careful not to draw conclusions that are too broad. A single photograph may not show important details. A different picture might suggest a different story.

Skills Tip

Even the same scene shot from a different angle may present new or different information. Encourage students to pay close attention to the photographer's vantage point. The Skills Handbook in the front of the book has a lesson that will help students with this feature.

Skills Assessment

1. When this picture was taken, the students were taking a lesson in
   A arithmetic.
   B reading.
   C art.
   D music.

2. Which is the most valid conclusion that you can draw from this photograph?
   E Africans resented German colonial rule.
   F Germany educated young Africans to help rule their colonies.
   G Colonial classrooms did not allow girls.
   H In some lands, colonial powers provided basic education.

3. **Critical Thinking Drawing Conclusions** Select three details that you see in this photograph. **(a)** What does each detail suggest about this classroom and the people in it? **(b)** What additional information might help you check if your conclusions are valid?

Human Drama Activity

Using Fiction as Historical Evidence The novel *Heart of Darkness* by Joseph Conrad is set in Africa during the age of imperialism. Marlowe, the narrator of the story, leaves England to seek adventure in Africa. Like others of his time, he is confident that European civilization benefits the people of Africa. But when he arrives at his company's station near the mouth of the Congo, he is shocked by what he finds. Through their mining, industrialists have ravaged the countryside. Africans are chained together, working and dying so that Europeans can reap financial profits. All that matters to the imperialists is satisfaction of their personal greed.

Ask students to read Part One of *Heart of Darkness*. In an oral presentation or written essay, have them describe the atrocities that Marlowe witnesses when he arrives at the company station in the Congo.

Skills Assessment

ANSWERS **1.** B **2.** H **3.** Possible answers: **(a)** Students may that the teacher is a man, which suggests that most teachers might have been men; and that students seem to be using slates, which suggests that paper is scarce or expensive. **(b)** Additional photographs, contemporary diaries, mission records, and secondary sources would help to confirm or refute those theories.

Recall
1. **(a)** Asante, p. 621 **(b)** Liberia, p. 622 **(c)** David Livingstone, p. 623 **(d)** Berlin Conference, p. 624 **(e)** Boer War, p. 624 **(f)** Nehanda, p. 626 **(g)** Menelik II, p. 626
2. **(a)** jihad, p. 621 **(b)** missionary, p. 622 **(c)** elite, p. 626

Comprehension
3. Possible answer: *North*—Ottoman control was weakening. *West*—An Islamic reform movement encouraged the rise of new Muslim states. *East*—Slave trade with the Middle East continued. *South*—The Zulu nation conquered neighboring peoples. 4. through explorers, missionaries, and traders 5. France, Britain 6. Possible answer: The Zulus battled against the Boers and British in southern Africa. The Ethiopians defeated an Italian army at the battle of Adowa in 1896. The Yao people rebelled against German rule but were defeated by a scorched-earth policy.

Critical Thinking and Writing
7. Possible answers: **(a)** European leaders believed that they knew what was best for Africa and had the right to decide its fate. **(b)** Later African leaders might disregard any decisions made at the meeting. 8. Possible answer: Somaliland was near the important water route that connected the Arabian Sea and the Indian Ocean with the Mediterranean by way of the Suez Canal and the Red Sea.

Activity Rubrics

Share rubrics with students before they write their biographies.

Attempted The biography is sketchy, or the map and chart are missing or incomplete.

Minimal The biography is poorly written and organized and has some mechanical errors. The map and chart are messy and unclear.

Adequate The biography is well written and organized and has few mechanical errors. The map and chart are well executed.

Exemplary The biography is very well written and organized and has no mechanical errors. The map and chart are strikingly well executed.

Biography

ANSWER by uniting the peoples of Ethiopia and by adopting western technology

---

Biography

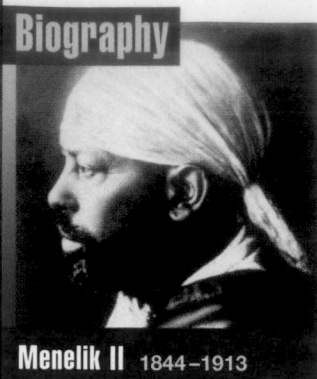

Menelik II 1844–1913

Before becoming emperor of Ethiopia, Menelik II ruled the Shoa region in central Ethiopia. He ensured that he would succeed John IV as emperor by marrying John's daughter. After John died in 1889, Menelik took the throne.

Menelik used profits from ivory sales to buy modern weapons. He then hired European advisers to teach his soldiers how to use the new guns. Menelik's army conquered neighboring lands and won a stunning victory over the Italians at Adowa. European nations rushed to establish diplomatic ties with Ethiopia. Around the world, people of African descent hailed Menelik's victory over European imperialism.

Theme: Impact of the Individual How did Menelik preserve Ethiopian independence?

European rivals, explained, "We do not want to put anyone in the shade, but we also demand our place in the sun."

Africans Resist Imperialism

Europeans met armed resistance across the continent. The Algerians battled the French for years. Samori Touré fought French forces in West Africa, where he was building his own empire. The British battled the Zulus in southern Africa and the Asante in West Africa. When their king was exiled, the Asante put themselves under the command of their queen, Yaa Asantewaa. She led the fight against the British in the last Asante war. Another woman who became a military leader was Nehanda, of the Shona in Zimbabwe. Although a clever tactician, Nehanda was captured and executed. However, the memory of her achievements inspired later generations to fight for freedom.

In East Africa, the Germans fought wars against people like the Yao and Herero. Fighting was especially fierce in the Maji-Maji Rebellion of 1905. The Germans triumphed only after using a scorched-earth policy. To crush resistance, they burned acres and acres of farmland, leaving thousands of local people to die of starvation.

Ethiopia Survives Successful resistance was mounted by Ethiopia. This ancient Christian kingdom had survived in the highlands of East Africa. But, like feudal Europe, it had been divided up among a number of rival princes who ruled their own domains.

In the late 1800s, a reforming ruler, Menelik II, began to modernize his country. He hired European experts to plan modern roads and bridges and set up a western school system. He imported the latest weapons and European officers to help train his army. Thus, when Italy invaded Ethiopia in 1896, Menelik was prepared. At the battle of Adowa (ah DUH wah), the Ethiopians smashed the Italian invaders. Ethiopia was the only African nation, aside from Liberia, to preserve its independence.

New African Elite During the Age of Imperialism, a western-educated African elite, or upper class, emerged. Some middle-class Africans admired western ways and rejected their own culture. Others valued their African traditions and condemned western societies that upheld liberty and equality for whites only. By the early 1900s, African leaders were forging nationalist movements to pursue self-determination and independence.

SECTION 2 Assessment

Recall
1. **Identify:** **(a)** Asante, **(b)** Liberia, **(c)** David Livingstone, **(d)** Berlin Conference, **(e)** Boer War, **(f)** Nehanda, **(g)** Menelik II.
2. **Define:** **(a)** jihad, **(b)** missionary, **(c)** elite.

Comprehension
3. Describe one development in each region of Africa in the early 1800s.
4. How did European contact with Africa increase?
5. Which European nations were most successful in the scramble for African colonies?

6. Describe two examples of African resistance to European imperialism.

Critical Thinking and Writing
7. **Making Inferences (a)** Why do you think the Europeans did not invite Africans to the Berlin Conference? **(b)** What might be the effect of this exclusion upon later African leaders?
8. **Connecting to Geography** Review the maps of Africa in this section. Why do you think Britain, France, and Italy were all interested in controlling part of Somaliland?

Activity
Take It to the NET

Use the Internet to find out more about explorer-missionary David Livingstone. Then, prepare a brief biography of him. You may wish to illustrate the biography with a map showing Livingstone's explorations and a chart describing his missionary activities.

Resource Directory

Teaching Resources
Section Quiz Unit 6 booklet, p. 61
Creative Teaching Activities Creative Teaching Activities booklet, p. 113
Guided Reading and Review Unit 6 booklet, p. 62

Technology
Interactive Student Tutorial CD-ROM Ch. 25
Computer Test Bank Ch. 25

SECTION 3 European Challenges to the Muslim World

Reading Focus

- What were sources of stress in the Muslim world?
- What problems did the Ottoman empire face?
- How did Egypt seek to modernize?
- Why were European powers interested in Iran?

Vocabulary

pasha
genocide
concession

Taking Notes

As you read, prepare an outline. Use Roman numerals for major headings, capital letters for subheadings, and numbers for supporting details. The incomplete model below will help you get started.

> I. Stresses in the Muslim world
> A. Empires in decline
> 1.
> 2.
> B.
> C.
> II. Problems for the Ottoman empire
> A.

Main Idea During the 1800s, European nations extended their power into parts of the Muslim world.

Setting the Scene "Europe is a molehill," said Napoleon Bonaparte in 1797. He felt it offered too few chances for glory. "We must go to the East," he declared. "All great glory has been acquired there." In 1798, he put his thoughts into action by invading Egypt, a province of the Ottoman empire.

Napoleon's Egyptian campaign highlighted Ottoman decline and opened a new era of European contact with the Muslim world. In the early 1800s, European countries were just nibbling at the edges of the Muslim world. Before long, they would strike at its heartlands.

Stresses in the Muslim World

The Muslim world extended from western Africa to Southeast Asia. In the 1500s, three giant Muslim empires ruled much of this world—the Mughals in India, the Ottomans in the Middle East, and the Safavids in Iran.

Empires in Decline By the 1700s, all three Muslim empires were in decline. The decay had many causes. Central governments had lost control over powerful groups such as landowning nobles, military elites, and urban craft guilds. Corruption was widespread. In some places, Muslim scholars and religious leaders were allied with the state. In other areas, they helped to stir discontent against the government.

Islamic Reform Movement In the 1700s and early 1800s, reform movements sprang up across the Muslim world. Most stressed religious piety and strict rules of behavior. The Wahhabi movement in Arabia, for example, rejected the schools of theology and law that had emerged in the Ottoman empire. In their place, they wanted to recapture the purity and simplicity of Muhammad's original teachings. An Arab prince led the Wahhabis against Ottoman rule. Although the revolt was crushed, the Wahhabi movement survived. Its teachings are influential in the kingdom of Saudi Arabia today.

Islamic revivals rose in Africa, too. As you have read, Usman dan Fodio led the struggle to reform Muslim practices. In the Sudan, south of Egypt, Muhammad Ahmad announced that he was the Mahdi, the long-awaited savior of the faith. In the 1880s, the Mahdi and his followers fiercely resisted British expansion into the region.

European Imperialism In addition to internal decay and stress, the old Muslim empires faced western imperialism. Through diplomacy and military threats, European powers won treaties giving them favorable

Bell Ringer Draw students' attention to the map "The Suez Canal, 1869" in this section. Ask students to discuss how the canal might have brought both benefits and problems to the people of Egypt.

LESSON PLAN

1. Focus During the 1800s, the Ottoman empire was threatened by economic decline, political corruption, nationalism, and the ambitions of European powers. In Egypt, Muhammad Ali hoped to modernize his country through political and economic reforms. Russia and Britain battled for influence in Iran, especially after the discovery of oil there.

2. Instruct Ask each student to imagine that he or she is a government official of Egypt, Iran, or the Ottoman empire during the 1800s. Government leaders, aware of the declining power of the state, have given the "official" a special assignment: Outline the problems that are causing our state to decline and describe some actions that we can take to slow or reverse this trend. Students may work individually or in groups to complete this assignment. When students have finished this part of the lesson, invite volunteers to read their reports to the class. Encourage other students to critique the remedial policies that students propose in their reports.

3. Assess Ask students to summarize how the Ottoman empire, Egypt, and Iran faced similar problems and sought similar solutions.

4. Reteach If students' Assess activity does not reflect adequate understanding of the lesson, you might assign the *Guide to the Essentials* or the *Interactive Student Tutorial CD-ROM* for this section.

Block Scheduling Support

Help students find resources on the Internet about the Suez Canal. Divide the class into small groups and have each group be responsible for finding information on different aspects of the canal, including history, technical descriptions, current use, images, and interesting facts. Have groups share their findings.

Constantinople
People from all over the world met and traded at Constantinople. The capital of the Ottoman empire was located on the Bosporus.

Theme: Geography and History Why did Russia hope to gain control of the Bosporus?

trading terms. They then demanded special rights for Europeans residing in Muslim lands. At times, European powers protected those rights by intervening in local affairs. Sometimes, they took over an entire region.

Problems for the Ottoman Empire

At its height, the Ottoman empire had extended across the Middle East, North Africa, and Southeastern Europe. By the early 1800s, however, it faced serious challenges. Ambitious pashas, or provincial rulers, had increased their power. Economic problems and corruption added to Ottoman decay.

Nationalist Revolts As ideas of nationalism spread from Western Europe, internal revolts weakened the multiethnic Ottoman empire. Subject peoples in Eastern Europe, the Middle East, and North Africa threatened to break away. In the Balkans, Greeks, Serbs, Bulgarians, and Romanians gained their independence. Revolts against Ottoman rule also erupted in Arabia, Lebanon, and Armenia. The Ottomans suppressed these uprisings, but another valuable territory, Egypt, slipped out of their control.

European Pressure European states sought to benefit from the slow crumbling of the Ottoman empire. After seizing Algeria in the 1830s, France hoped to gain more Ottoman territory. Russia schemed to gain control of the Bosporus and the Dardanelles. Control of these straits would give the Russians access to the Mediterranean Sea. Britain tried to thwart Russia's ambitions, which it saw as a threat to its own power in the Mediterranean and beyond it to India. And in 1898, the new German empire jumped onto the bandwagon, hoping to increase its influence in the region by building a Berlin-to-Baghdad railway.

Efforts to Westernize Since the late 1700s, several Ottoman rulers had seen the need for reform and looked to the West for ideas. They reorganized the bureaucracy and system of tax collection. They built railroads, improved education, and hired European officers to train a modern military. Young men were sent to the West to study the new sciences and technology. Many returned home with western ideas about democracy and equality.

The reforms also brought better medical care and revitalized farming. These improvements, however, were a mixed blessing. Better living conditions resulted in a population explosion. The growing population increased competition for the best land, which led to unrest.

The adoption of western ideas about government also increased tension. Many officials objected to changes that were inspired by a foreign culture. For their part, repressive sultans rejected reform and tried to rebuild the autocratic power enjoyed by earlier rulers.

Young Turks In the 1890s, a group of liberals formed a movement called the Young Turks. They insisted that reform was the only way to save the empire. In 1908, the Young Turks overthrew the sultan. Before they could achieve their planned reforms, however, the Ottoman empire was plunged into the world war that erupted in 1914.

Massacre of Armenians Traditionally, the Ottomans had let minority nationalities live in their own communities and practice their own religions. By the 1890s, however, nationalism was igniting new tensions, especially between

Turkish nationalists and minority peoples who sought their own states. These tensions triggered a brutal genocide of the Armenians, a Christian people concentrated in the eastern mountains of the empire. **Genocide** is a deliberate attempt to destroy an entire religious or ethnic group.

The Muslim Turks distrusted the Christian Armenians and accused them of supporting Russian plans against the Ottoman empire. When Armenians protested repressive Ottoman policies, the sultan had tens of thousands of them slaughtered. Over the next 25 years, a million or more Armenians in the Ottoman empire were killed.

Egypt Seeks to Modernize

Egypt in 1800 was a semi-independent province of the Ottoman empire. In the early 1800s, it made great strides toward reform. Its success was due to Muhammad Ali, who was appointed governor of Egypt in 1805.

Muhammad Ali Muhammad Ali is sometimes called the "father of modern Egypt." To strengthen Egypt, he introduced a number of political and economic reforms. He improved tax collection, reorganized the landholding system, and backed large irrigation projects to increase farm output. By expanding cotton production and encouraging the development of local industry, he increased Egyptian participation in world trade.

Muhammad Ali also brought western military experts to Egypt to help him build a well-trained, modern army. He conquered the neighboring lands of Arabia, Syria, and Sudan. Before he died in 1849, he had set Egypt on the road to becoming a major Middle Eastern power.

The Suez Canal Muhammad Ali's successors lacked his skills, and Egypt came increasingly under foreign control. In 1859, a French entrepreneur, Ferdinand de Lesseps, organized a company to build the Suez Canal. This

Skills Assessment

Chart By linking the Mediterranean and Red seas, the Suez Canal shortened the travel distance from Western Europe to ports in East Africa and Asia. European ships no longer had to go around the southern tip of Africa. **On a journey from London to Bombay, how many miles could a ship save by going through the Suez Canal?**

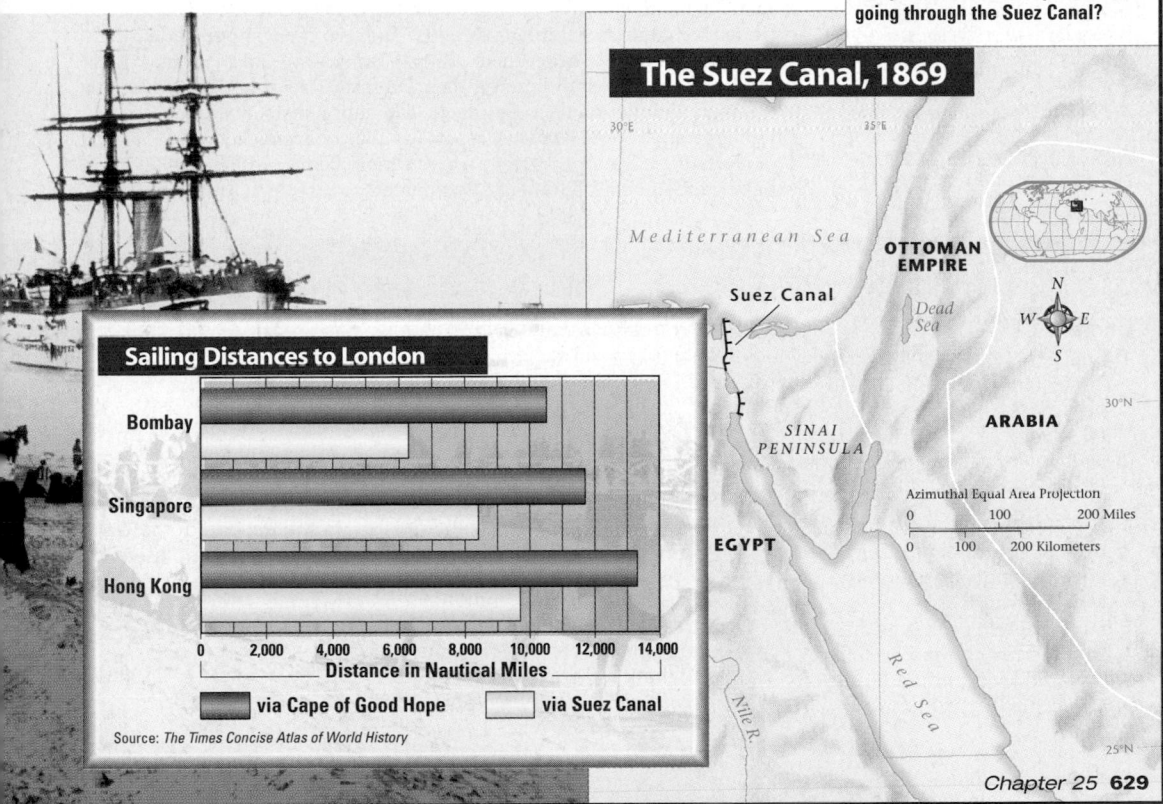

The Suez Canal, 1869

Mediterranean Sea

OTTOMAN EMPIRE

Suez Canal

Dead Sea

SINAI PENINSULA

ARABIA

30°N

EGYPT

Azimuthal Equal Area Projection
0   100   200 Miles
0   100   200 Kilometers

Red Sea

Nile R.

25°N

30°E   35°E

N W E S

Sailing Distances to London

Bombay

Singapore

Hong Kong

0   2,000   4,000   6,000   8,000   10,000   12,000   14,000
Distance in Nautical Miles

■ via Cape of Good Hope   □ via Suez Canal

Source: *The Times Concise Atlas of World History*

Customize for...
Heterogeneous Groups

Writing a Dialogue As an enrichment activity, have students work in pairs to write a dialogue about the conflict between Muslim Turks and Christian Armenians in the late 1800s. Have one student assume the role of a Turkish government official and the other assume the role of an Armenian protester. In their dialogues, students should describe some of the reasons for the conflict and some of the actions carried out by both Turks and Armenians. Remind students that the historical characters in their dialogue will view motivations and events from two very different perspectives. Students will need to do additional research to complete this assignment. When students have finished writing their dialogues, have them present the results to the class. Encourage other students to ask questions about the dialogues. *(Enrichment)*

Background
Daily Life

A Profitable Friendship When Ferdinand de Lesseps was French consul at Cairo, he enjoyed a certain amount of influence at the court of Muhammad Ali. During those days, Ali's son, Prince Said, would often slip away from his guards and tutors and sneak into the French consulate. The boy would enter de Lesseps' office, whereupon the consul would lead him to the kitchen. There, the overweight boy would eat large amounts of spaghetti, French pastries, or whatever food was available. Had his father known, he would have been outraged. Muhammad Ali had ordered strict exercise and a limited diet for his son. Years later, after Said had succeeded to the throne, he permitted his French friend to build the Suez Canal. Perhaps one of the reasons for his decision was fond memories of the kindness that the French consul had shown a hungry boy.

Skills Assessment

ANSWER about 4,000

Human Drama Note

De Lesseps' Downfall De Lesseps was much honored for his engineering and management of the Suez Canal project. For that reason he was made president of the company that tried to build a canal across Panama in the 1880s. Unfortunately, design problems arose and were compounded by the geography and climate of the region and by mosquito-borne disease. Also, de Lesseps and his son were accused of, and tried for, mismanagement and illegal use of company funds. They were convicted but never served their prison terms.

Test Preparation

Have students look at the chart on this page, and then answer the question below.

Of the three trips shown, which one saved the greatest percentage of miles?

(A) London to Bombay

B London to Singapore

C London to Hong Kong

D They all saved about the same percentage.

Recall

1. **(a)** Mahdi, p. 627 **(b)** Young Turks, p. 628 **(c)** Armenians, p. 629 **(d)** Muhammad Ali, p. 629 **(e)** Suez Canal, p. 629 **(f)** Qajars, p. 630 **2. (a)** pasha, p. 628 **(b)** genocide, p. 629 **(c)** concession, p. 630

Comprehension

3. Through diplomacy or the threat of force, European nations sometimes gained control of an entire region. 4. Provincial rulers had increased their powers, challenging the central government. Economic problems and corruption also contributed to the decline. 5. He improved tax collection, reorganized the landholding system, backed irrigation projects, expanded the cotton industry, encouraged trade, and brought in western military experts to build a modern army. 6. Russia wanted to protect its southern frontier and expand into Central Asia. Britain wanted to protect its interests in India. Both nations wanted control of oil fields.

Critical Thinking and Writing

7. Possible answers: **(a)** Tensions arose between Turkish nationalists and minorities who sought their own states. These tensions led to the persecution and attempted genocide of the Armenians. **(b)** Students might mention present-day examples from Africa or southeastern Europe. 8. Students may propose giving various national groups more independence.

Activity Rubrics

Share rubrics with students before they make their time lines.

Attempted The time line has no apparent scale and few items, some of which are inaccurate or misspelled.

Minimal The time line has a rough scale and an adequate number of items; some are inaccurate or illegible.

Adequate The time line has an appropriate number of entries and an accurate scale and contains few mechanical errors.

Exemplary The time line has carefully chosen items, an accurate scale, no mechanical errors, and a striking appearance.

Connections to Today

ANSWER If OPEC cuts production, prices rise because there is less oil to meet the demand.

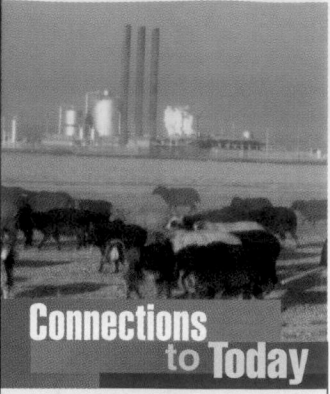

Connections to Today

The Power of Oil
In the early 1900s, Russia and Britain competed for oil in the Middle East. Today, the vast petroleum deposits in the region are controlled by Middle Eastern countries themselves.

Oil produces enormous wealth for countries in the Middle East. Industrialized nations rely on imported oil to produce electricity, run factories, and fuel vehicles. In the Organization of Petroleum Exporting Countries (OPEC), oil-producing countries of the Middle East and other world regions try to maximize their profits through cooperation. They influence oil prices by controlling how much oil is produced.

Theme: Global Interaction
What do you think happens to oil prices if OPEC cuts production? Explain.

100-mile waterway links the Mediterranean and Red seas. (See the map on the previous page.) Europeans hailed its opening in 1869 because it greatly shortened the sea route from Europe to South and East Asia. To Britain, especially, the canal was a "lifeline" to India.

In 1875, the ruler of Egypt was unable to repay loans he had contracted for the canal and other modernization projects. To pay his debts, he was forced to sell his shares in the canal. British prime minister Disraeli quickly bought the shares, giving Britain a controlling interest in the canal.

A British Protectorate When Egyptian nationalists revolted against foreign influence in 1882, Britain made Egypt a protectorate. In theory, the governor of Egypt was still an official of the Ottoman government. In fact, he followed policies dictated by Britain. Under British influence, Egypt continued to modernize. At the same time, however, nationalist discontent simmered and flared into protests and riots well into the next century.

Iran and the European Powers

Like the Ottoman empire, Iran faced major challenges in the 1800s. The Qajar (kah JAHR) shahs, who ruled Iran from 1794 to 1925, exercised absolute power like the Safavids before them. Still, they did take steps to introduce reforms. The government improved finances, sponsored the building of telegraph lines and railroads, and even experimented with a liberal constitution.

Reform, however, did not save Iran from western imperialism. Both Russia and Britain battled for influence in the area. Russia wanted to protect its southern frontier and expand into Central Asia. Britain was concerned about protecting its interests in India.

For a time, each nation set up its own sphere of influence in Iran. Russia operated in the north and Britain in the south. The discovery of oil in the early 1900s heightened foreign interest in the region. Both Russia and Britain intrigued for control of Iranian oil fields. The two powers persuaded the Iranian government to grant them concessions, or special economic rights given to foreign powers. To protect their interests, they sent troops into Iran.

Iranian nationalists were outraged. The nationalists included two very different groups. Some Iranians, especially the urban middle class, wanted to move swiftly to adopt western ways. Others, led by Muslim religious leaders, condemned the Iranian government and western influences.

SECTION 3 Assessment

Recall

1. **Identify: (a)** Mahdi, **(b)** Young Turks, **(c)** Armenians, **(d)** Muhammad Ali, **(e)** Suez Canal, **(f)** Qajars.
2. **Define: (a)** pasha, **(b)** genocide, **(c)** concession.

Comprehension

3. How did European nations take advantage of stresses in the Muslim world?
4. Describe two problems that contributed to Ottoman decline.
5. How did Muhammad Ali seek to modernize Egypt?

6. Why did Russia and Britain compete for power in Iran?

Critical Thinking and Writing

7. **Linking Past and Present (a)** How did Turkish nationalism lead to intolerance of minorities in the Ottoman empire? **(b)** Describe a present-day example of nationalism's causing intolerance of others.
8. **Solving Problems** Suppose you are an Ottoman government official in the 1800s. Recommend and explain a series of actions that you think will solve the problems afflicting the Ottoman empire.

Activity

Making a Time Line Conduct research to learn more about Iran in the late 1800s and early 1900s. Then, make a time line that identifies key events in the decline of the Qajar government and the rise of Russian and British influence in the region.

Resource Directory

Teaching Resources
Section Quiz Unit 6 booklet, p. 63
Creative Teaching Activities Creative Teaching Activities booklet, p. 114
Guided Reading and Review Unit 6 booklet, p. 64
Technology
Interactive Student Tutorial CD-ROM Ch. 25
Computer Test Bank Ch. 25

SECTION 4 The British Take Over India

Reading Focus

- What were the causes and effects of the Sepoy Rebellion?

- How did British rule affect India?

- How did Indians view western culture?

- What were the origins of Indian nationalism?

Main Idea Despite Indian opposition, Britain gradually extended its control over most of India.

Vocabulary

sati
sepoy
viceroy
deforestation
purdah

Taking Notes

As you read this section, make a flowchart to show the events that led to increased British control of India. Use the incomplete chart below as a model.

> British East India Company gets trading rights
>
> ↓
>
> British officials introduce western education and law
>
> ↓
>
> ☐
>
> ↓
>
> ☐

SECTION 4

Bell Ringer Have students scan the boldfaced heads and subheads of this section. Ask them to write three questions that they believe they will be able to answer after reading the section.

Setting the Scene

Ranjit Singh ruled the large Sikh empire in northwestern India during the early 1800s. He had cordial dealings with the British but saw only too well where their ambitions were headed. One day, he was looking at a map of India on which British-held lands were shaded red. "All will one day become red!" he predicted.

Not long after Ranjit Singh's death in 1839, the British conquered the Sikh empire. They added its 100,000 square miles to their steadily growing lands. As Singh had forecast, India was falling under British control.

East India Company and Sepoy Rebellion

In the early 1600s, the British East India Company won trading rights on the fringe of the Mughal empire. As Mughal power declined, the company's influence grew. By the mid-1800s, it controlled three fifths of India.

Exploiting Indian Diversity The British were able to conquer such a vast territory by exploiting the diversity of India. Even when Mughal power was at its height, India was home to many people and cultures. As Mughal power crumbled, India fragmented. Indians with different traditions and dozens of different languages were not able to unite against the newcomers. The British took advantage of Indian divisions by encouraging competition and disunity among rival princes. Where British diplomacy or intrigue did not work, their superior weapons overpowered local rulers.

British Policies The East India Company's main goal in India was to make money, and leading officials often got very rich. At the same time, the company did work to improve roads, preserve peace, and reduce banditry.

By the early 1800s, British officials introduced western education and legal procedures. Missionaries tried to convert Indians to Christianity, which they felt was far superior to Indian religions. The British also pressed for social change. They worked to end slavery and the caste system and to improve the position of women within the family. One law outlawed *sati*, a Hindu custom practiced mainly by the upper classes. It called for a widow to join her husband in death by throwing herself on his funeral fire.

Causes of Discontent In the 1850s, the East India Company made several unpopular moves. First, it required *sepoys*, or Indian soldiers in its service, to serve anywhere, either in India or overseas. For high-caste Hindus, however, overseas travel was an offense against their religion. Second, it

Global Connections

"Thank God for Tea!"

The British East India Company made a fortune by importing tea—a drink with a long history. According to legend, a Chinese emperor discovered tea thousands of years ago when windblown leaves fell into a pot of boiling water. Buddhist monks brought the drink to Japan and made it part of their meditation rites. Europeans did not become acquainted with the pleasure of tea until the 1600s—but they caught on quickly.

In England, tea was first used as a medicinal drink only. However, it soon became common to have tea every afternoon. The custom became a regular social event. People invited friends for afternoon tea served with cake, bread, and butter. By the 1800s, tea was considered an essential part of English culture, moving one writer to offer special thanks: "Thank God for tea! What would the world do without tea?—how did it exist? I am glad I was not born before tea."

Theme: Global Interaction
Why did the British East India Company earn huge profits?

LESSON PLAN

1. Focus British rule and policies that were insensitive to Indian culture led to the Sepoy Rebellion in 1857. After the failed rebellion, the British government increased its control, bringing both benefits and injustice to the people of India. Indians resisted by forming the Indian National Congress and the Muslim League.

2. Instruct Divide the class into three groups. Assign students in one group to assume the role of a British entrepreneur with a variety of investments in India. Have students in another group take the role of an upper-class Indian who supports British rule. Ask students in the third group to assume the role of an Indian who resents British domination. Ask each student to write a letter to a member of the British Parliament commenting on British policies in India during the 1800s. Advise students that their letter should reflect the probable interests and attitudes of their assigned character. When students finish, invite volunteers to read their work to the class. Encourage students to ask questions about each letter.

3. Assess Ask students to write three policies that Britain could have followed to reduce Indian resentment and opposition. Use these ideas as the basis for a class discussion on Britain's India policies during the 1800s.

4. Reteach If students' Assess activity does not reflect adequate understanding of the lesson, you might assign the *Guide to the Essentials* or the *Interactive Student Tutorial CD-ROM* for this section.

Block Scheduling Support

Distribute copies of the following excerpt from a speech made by a member of the Indian National Congress in 1885.

"It is under the civilizing rule of the Queen and the people of England that we meet here together . . . and are freely allowed to speak our minds without the least fear [or] hesitation. Such a thing is possible . . . under British rule only. Then I put the question plainly: Is this Congress a nursery for sedition and rebellion against the British Government; or is it another stone in the foundation of the stability of that government? There could be but one answer . . . because we are thoroughly sensible to the numberless blessings conferred upon us, of which the very existence of this Congress is proof. . . ."

(1) According to the speaker, how do British colonial policies compare to those of other countries? (2) What is the speaker's answer to the rhetorical question? (3) What was the immediate goal of the Indian National Congress in 1885? (4) Do you think the author of this speech was a clever politician? Explain.

Global Connections

ANSWER because it imported tea

Rumors When the British realized their mistake in greasing rifle cartridges with animal fat, they quickly recalled the tainted ammunition and reissued cartridges coated with pure vegetable fat. But no official announcements, tours of fat-producing factories, or scientific tests could stop rumors from spreading. Many sepoys were convinced that the problem was a devious British plot. Christian officers, it was said, were deliberately polluting the sepoys so that they would have to abandon their own religion and convert to Christianity. Other rumors claimed that British generals were under orders from Christian church leaders and that British soldiers were pouring pig and cow fat into wells.

Background
Historical Evidence

Massacres Both sides committed atrocities during the Sepoy Rebellion (also known as the Sepoy Mutiny). One incident occurred at Cawnpore, where a British garrison of some 400, along with several hundred civilians, surrendered in return for a promise of safe conduct. But as the British entered the boats that would take them to safety, they found themselves caught in a murderous crossfire. All but a few of the soldiers were killed. The women and children who survived were later cut down with knives and swords.

The British responded to incidents such as this with atrocities of their own. When the British retook Cawnpore, they forced their captives to lick the dried blood of the murdered women and children off the floor and then executed them. In Delhi, one Englishman boasted that "all the people found within the walls when our troops entered were bayoneted on the spot." Rebels were hanged or shot without trial. Some were tied to the muzzles of cannons and blown to bits.

Imperialism in India to 1858

■	British colonies in 1765
■	Territory under British rule in 1805
■	Territory under British rule in 1858
▨	Main area affected by Sepoy Rebellion

Skills Assessment

Geography Britain controlled all of India by 1858. British officials ruled some areas directly and other areas through local Indian rulers.

1. **Location** On the map, locate **(a)** Punjab, **(b)** Delhi, **(c)** Hyderabad, **(d)** Madras.
2. **Region** Which regions were most greatly affected by the Sepoy Rebellion?
3. **Critical Thinking Asking Questions** Write three questions based on information on the map.

passed a law that allowed Hindu widows to remarry. Hindus viewed both moves as a Christian conspiracy to undermine their beliefs.

Then, in 1857, the British issued new rifles to the sepoys. Troops were told to bite off the tips of cartridges before loading them into the rifles. The cartridges, however, were greased with animal fat—either from cows, which Hindus considered sacred, or from pigs, which were forbidden to Muslims. When the troops refused the order to "load rifles," they were sent home without pay.

Rebellion and Aftermath Angry sepoys rose up against their British officers. The Sepoy Rebellion swept across northern and central India. Several sepoy regiments marched off to Delhi, the old Mughal capital. There, they hailed the last Mughal ruler as their leader.

The sepoys brutally massacred British men, women, and children in some places. But the British soon rallied and crushed the revolt. They then took terrible revenge for their earlier losses, torching villages and slaughtering thousands of unarmed Indians.

The Sepoy Rebellion left a bitter legacy of fear, hatred, and mistrust on both sides. It also brought major changes in British policy. In 1858, Parliament ended the rule of the East India Company and put India directly under the British crown. It sent more troops to India, taxing Indians to pay the cost of these occupying forces. While it slowed the "reforms" that had angered Hindus and Muslims, it continued to develop India for Britain's own economic benefit.

British Colonial Rule

After 1858, Parliament set up a system of colonial rule in India. A British **viceroy** in India governed in the name of the queen, and British officials held the top positions in the civil service and army. Indians filled most other jobs. With their cooperation, the British made India the "brightest jewel" in the crown of their empire.

British policies were designed to fit India into the overall British economy. At the same time, British officials felt they were helping India to modernize. In their terms, modernizing meant adopting not only western technology but also western culture.

An Unequal Partnership Britain saw India as a market and as a source of raw materials. To this end, the British built roads and an impressive railroad network. Improved transportation let the British sell their factory-made goods across the subcontinent and carry Indian cotton, jute, and coal to coastal ports for transport to factories in England. New methods of communication, such as the telegraph, also gave Britain better control of India.

After the Suez Canal opened in 1869, British trade with India soared. But it remained an unequal partnership, favoring the British. The British flooded India with inexpensive, machine-made textiles, ruining India's once-prosperous hand-weaving industry.

Britain also transformed Indian agriculture. It encouraged nomadic herders to settle into farming and pushed farmers to grow cash crops, such

Skills Assessment

ANSWERS 1. Review locations with students. **2.** north central India and northern India along the Ganges **3.** Students may write questions about territories under British rule at different times and about the names of the different regions.

Resource Directory

Teaching Resources
Biography Activity *Rabindranath Tagore*, Unit 6 booklet, p. 68
Prentice Hall Literature Library *Literature From Around the World*, pp. 97–102

Technology
World History Color Transparencies *The Sounds of India*, p. C–55

World History Visions, Voices, Views Daily Life CloseUp, *A Railway Laborer in Colonial India*, videodisc side 3 or videotape 6, running time 3:00 min.

Side 3: Fr. 27370-33110

as cotton and jute, that could be sold on the world market. Clearing new farmlands led to massive deforestation, or cutting of trees.

Population Growth and Famine The British introduced medical improvements and new farming methods. Better health care and increased food production led to rapid population growth. The rising numbers, however, put a strain on the food supply, especially as farmland was turned over to growing cash crops instead of food. In the late 1800s, terrible famines swept India.

Benefits of British Rule On the positive side, British rule brought peace and order to the countryside. The British revised the legal system to promote justice for Indians regardless of class or caste. Railroads helped Indians move around the country, while the telegraph and postal system improved communication. Greater contact helped bridge regional differences and opened the way for Indians to develop a sense of national unity.

The upper classes, especially, benefited from some British policies. They sent their sons to British schools, where they were trained for posts in the civil service and military. Indian landowners and princes, who still ruled their own territories, grew rich from exporting cash crops.

Different Views on Culture

During the Age of Imperialism, Indians and British developed different views of each other's culture. Both the British and the Indians were divided in their opinions.

Indian Attitudes Some educated Indians were impressed by British power and technology and urged India to follow a western model of progress. These mostly upper-class Indians learned English and adopted western ways. Other Indians felt that the answer to change lay with their own Hindu or Muslim cultures.

In the early 1800s, Ram Mohun Roy combined both views. A great scholar, he knew Sanskrit, Persian, and Arabic classics, as well as English, Greek, and Latin works. Roy felt that India could learn from the West. At the same time, he wanted to revitalize and reform traditional Indian culture.

Roy condemned some traditions, such as rigid caste distinctions, child marriage, sati, and purdah, the isolation of women in separate quarters. But he also set up educational societies that helped revive pride in Indian culture. Because of his influence on later leaders, he is often hailed today as the founder of Indian nationalism.

Western Attitudes The British disagreed among themselves about India. A few admired Indian theology and philosophy. As western scholars translated Indian classics, they acquired respect for India's ancient heritage. Western writers and philosophers borrowed ideas from Hinduism and Buddhism.

However, most British people knew little about Indian achievements and dismissed Indian culture with contempt. In an essay on whether Indians should be taught in English or their own languages, the English historian Thomas Macaulay wrote that "a single shelf of a good European library is worth the whole native literature of India and Arabia."

Cotton: A Valuable Cash Crop
In the 1800s, British officials encouraged Indian farmers to grow cash crops rather than food crops. Today, India is one of the world's largest producers of cotton.

Theme: Global Interaction
How did British policy contribute to famine in India?

Geography and History

British Railroads and Indian Nationalism

The British railway system in India
was massive in size and importance. By 1900, 25,000 miles of track
crisscrossed the Asian subcontinent, providing easy transportation for tea, cotton, jute, and
other goods destined to enrich the
British economy.

The vast rail network aided India
as well. India had long been divided
by geography, cultural differences,
and rival rulers. British railroads
helped to bridge some of these
divisions and promote a sense of
nationalism. They enabled Indians
to travel across the country. The
trains also helped ideas spread by
transporting books, newspapers,
and letters.

One British official compared
the railroad system in India to "the
aqueducts of Rome, the pyramids
of Egypt, the great wall of China . . .
monuments not merely of intelligence and power, but of utility and
beneficence."

 **Theme: Geography
and History** How did
railroads encourage Indian
nationalism?

Indian Nationalism

During the years of British rule, a class of western-educated Indians
emerged. In the view of Macaulay and others, this elite class would
bolster British power:

> "We must at present do our best to form a class who may be
> interpreters between us and the millions whom we govern; a
> class of persons, Indian in blood and color, but English in
> taste, in opinions, in morals, and in intellect."
>
> —Thomas Macaulay, quoted in
> *Sources of Indian Tradition* (deBary)

As it turned out, exposure to European ideas had the opposite effect.
By the late 1800s, western-educated Indians were spearheading a nationalist
movement. Schooled in western ideals such as democracy and equality,
they dreamed of ending imperial rule.

Indian National Congress In 1885, nationalist leaders organized the
Indian National Congress, which became known as the Congress party. Its
members were mostly professionals and business leaders who believed in
peaceful protest to gain their ends. They called for greater democracy,
which they felt would bring more power to Indians like themselves.
The Indian National Congress looked forward to eventual self-rule but
supported western-style modernization.

Muslim League At first, Muslims and Hindus worked together for
self-rule. In time, however, Muslims grew to resent Hindu domination of
the Congress party. They also worried that a Hindu-run government would
oppress Muslims. In 1906, Muslims formed the Muslim League to pursue
their own goals. Soon, they were talking of a separate Muslim state.

Looking Ahead

By the early 1900s, protests and resistance to British rule increased. Some
Indian nationalists urged that Indian languages and cultures be restored.
More and more Indians demanded not simply self-rule but complete independence. Their goal finally would be achieved in 1947, but only after a
long struggle against the British and a nightmare of bloody conflict
between Hindus and Muslims.

SECTION 4 Assessment

Recall
1. **Identify:** (a) East India Company,
(b) Sepoy Rebellion, (c) Ram
Mohun Roy, (d) Indian National
Congress, (e) Muslim League.
2. **Define:** (a) sati, (b) sepoy,
(c) viceroy, (d) deforestation,
(e) purdah.

Comprehension
3. What were the causes and effects of
the Sepoy Rebellion?
4. Describe three effects of British
colonial rule on India.
5. How did Indians differ in their views
on Indian and British culture?

6. How did British rule lead to
growing Indian nationalism?

Critical Thinking and Writing
7. **Analyzing Primary Sources**
Review the words of Thomas
Macaulay, quoted above. What
kind of education did Macaulay
favor for Indians? Why?
8. **Defending a Position** Do you
think that the British were right to
pass laws that tried to reform the
caste system and end sati? Explain and defend your position.

Activity

**Drawing a Political
Cartoon**
Draw a cartoon that either
praises or criticizes a
British colonial policy in
India. Give your cartoon a
title and a caption. Consider
using symbolism such as
a lion, which is a traditional
symbol of Britain.

Reading Focus

- What trade rights did westerners seek in China?
- What internal problems did Chinese reformers try to solve?
- How did the Qing dynasty come to an end?

Vocabulary

trade surplus
trade deficit
indemnity
extraterritoriality

Taking Notes

As you read, create a concept web, like this partially completed model, to show key events and developments in the decline of Qing China. Add as many circles as you need to finish the web.

- Opium War
- Boxer Uprising
- DECLINE OF QING CHINA

Main Idea During the 1800s, Qing China declined as western powers used diplomacy and war to gain power in East Asia.

Setting the Scene

By the 1830s, British merchant ships were arriving in China loaded with opium to sell to the Chinese. One Chinese official complained bitterly to Britain's Queen Victoria. "I have heard that smoking opium is strictly forbidden in your country," he wrote. "Why do you let this evil drug be sent to harm people in other countries?"

For centuries, Chinese regulations had ensured that China had a favorable balance of trade with other nations. The phrase *balance of trade* refers to the difference between how much a country imports and how much it exports. By the 1800s, however, western nations were using their growing power to gain more influence over East Asia.

The Trade Issue

Prior to the 1800s, Chinese rulers placed strict limits on foreign traders. European merchants were restricted to a small area in southern China. China sold them silk, porcelain, and tea in exchange for gold and silver. Under this arrangement, China enjoyed a trade surplus, exporting more than it imported. Westerners, on the other hand, had a trade deficit with China, buying more from the Chinese than they sold to them.

By the late 1700s, two developments were underway that would transform China's relations with the western world. First, China entered a period of decline. Second, the Industrial Revolution created a need for expanded markets for European goods. At the same time, it gave the West superior military power.

The Opium War During the late 1700s, British merchants began making huge profits by trading opium grown in India for Chinese tea, which was popular in Britain. Soon, many Chinese had become addicted to the drug. Silver flowed out of China in payment for the drug, disrupting the economy.

The Chinese government outlawed opium and executed Chinese drug dealers. They called on Britain to stop the trade. The British refused, insisting on the right of free trade.

The Opium War

The Opium War began when Chinese officials tried to keep British ships from bringing the addictive drug into China. Here, a British warship sinks Chinese junks during the war.

Theme: Economics and Technology How does the picture suggest Britain's superior military technology?

LESSON PLAN

1. Focus During the 1800s, western powers used diplomacy and war to win favorable trade agreements in China. The Qing dynasty suffered from a poor economy, a corrupt bureaucracy, and the devastating Taiping Rebellion. Reformers sought to modernize China by importing technology and ideas from the West. In 1911, China was declared a republic with Sun Yixian as its president.

2. Instruct Assign students to assume the role of one of the following historical characters: a British diplomat in China; a peasant in the Taiping Rebellion; a sympathizer with the "self-strengthening movement"; emperor Guang Xu; a participant in the Boxer Rebellion; a member of the imperial court of Ci Xi; a member of the Righteous Harmonious Fists; Sun Yixian. Instruct students to write a speech, in the role of their assigned character, addressing the following question: What is the best course of action for China? Advise students that their speech should be written as a persuasive speech. Ask volunteers to read their speeches to the class. Encourage the other students to agree or disagree with the facts and messages contained in each speech.

3. Assess Ask students to draw a propaganda poster or cartoon that reflects the contents of their speech.

4. Reteach If students' **Assess** activity does not reflect adequate understanding of the lesson, you might assign the *Guide to the Essentials* or the *Interactive Student Tutorial CD-ROM* for this section.

Chapter 25 **635**

The Opium Trade The amount of opium imported into China increased from around 1,000 chests in 1767 to about 40,000 chests by 1838. Levels of addiction grew despite Chinese legislation banning the importation, sale, and use of the drug. Opium addiction became so rampant that it began to compromise the ability of Chinese troops and government officials.

But in the 1850s, during another dispute over the opium trade, Sir Henry Pottinger, a British envoy to China, was able to appraise the situation in this way:

"I take this opportunity unhesitatingly to declare that after the most unbiased and careful observations, I have become convinced that during my stay in China the alleged demoralizing and debasing evils of opium have been and are vastly exaggerated. I have neither myself seen such vicious consequences . . . nor have I been able to obtain authentic proofs or information of their existence."

In 1839, Chinese warships clashed with British merchants, triggering the Opium War. British gunboats, equipped with the latest in firepower, bombarded Chinese coastal and river ports. With outdated weapons and fighting methods, the Chinese were easily defeated.

Unequal Treaties In 1842, Britain made China accept the Treaty of Nanjing. Britain received a huge indemnity, or payment for losses in the war. The British also gained the island of Hong Kong. (See the map later in this section.) China had to open five ports to foreign trade and grant British citizens in China extraterritoriality, the right to live under their own laws and be tried in their own courts.

The treaty was the first of a series of "unequal treaties" that forced China to make concessions to western powers. During the mid-1800s, under pressure from the West, China agreed to open more ports to foreign trade and to let Christian missionaries preach in China.

Internal Problems

By the 1800s, the Qing dynasty was in decline. Irrigation systems and canals were poorly maintained, leading to massive flooding of the Huang He valley. The population explosion that had begun a century earlier created a terrible hardship for China's peasants. An extravagant court, tax evasion by the rich, and widespread official corruption added to the peasants' burden. Even the honored civil service system was rocked by bribery scandals.

The Taiping Rebellion As poverty and misery increased, peasants rebelled. The Taiping Rebellion, which lasted from 1850 to 1864, was probably the most devastating peasant revolt in history. The leader, Hong Xiuquan (howng shyoo CHWAHN), was a village schoolteacher. Inspired by religious visions, he set himself up as a revolutionary prophet. He wanted to establish a "Heavenly Kingdom of Great Peace"—the Taiping (ti PIHNG).

Influenced by the teachings of Christian missionaries, Hong endorsed social ideas that Chinese leaders considered radical. These included land reform, community ownership of property, and equality of women and men. Above all, he called for an end to the hated Qing dynasty.

The Taiping rebels won control of large parts of China. They held out for 14 years. However, with the help of loyal regional governors and generals, the government crushed the rebellion in the end.

Effects The Taiping Rebellion almost toppled the Qing dynasty. It is estimated to have caused the deaths of between 20 million and 30 million Chinese. The Qing government survived, but it had to share power with regional commanders. During the rebellion, Europeans kept up pressure on China. Russia seized lands in northern China.

Reform Efforts

By the mid-1800s, educated Chinese were divided over the need to adopt western ways. Most scholar-officials saw no reason for new industries because China's wealth and taxes came from land. Although Chinese merchants were allowed to do business, they were not seen as a source of prosperity.

Scholar-officials also disapproved of the ideas of western missionaries, whose emphasis on individual choice challenged the Confucian order. They saw western technology as dangerous, too, because it threatened Confucian ways that had served China successfully for so long.

The imperial court was a center of conservative opposition. By the late 1800s, the empress Ci Xi (tsee SHYEE) had gained power. A strong-willed ruler, she surrounded herself with advisers who were deeply committed to Confucian traditions.

Primary Source

The Taiping Rebellion
The rebels of the Taiping Rebellion were peasants. Here, some of the captured rebels explain why they joined the rebellion:

"We men from Kwangtung . . . were born in a time of prosperity and were good people. We lived in towns and were taught to distinguish right from wrong. But because of continuous flooding in our area, we could not get a grain of rice to eat even if we worked hard in the fields, and we could not engage in business because we lacked the funds. As a result we all joined the bandits.

Not long ago we came to Kwangsi to try to make a living. We met others who had come from our hometowns. We pitied each other because of our sad situation, and together we began to imitate outlaws in order to relieve our hungry stomachs . . . no one forced us to join the outlaws. We were driven to join them because we were desperate. Given the chance, we would have returned gladly to our normal way of life."

—Kwangsi Bandit Group, quoted in *Chinese Civilization and Society* (Ebrey)

Skills Assessment

Primary Source Why did these men join the rebellion?

Primary Source

ANSWER They were desperate because they were hungry and had no way to earn a living.

Resource Directory

Teaching Resources
You Are There Chapter Extension Activities booklet, p. 62

You Are There...

Meeting the Emperor

After years of education, you have finally made it. You are about to be installed as a government official in the service of the emperor. You stand in the throne room known as the Hall of Supreme Harmony. Yet today, there is little harmony. Wars and rebellion have weakened China, and the foreigners are gaining power. Here in Beijing, meanwhile, leaders quarrel over what to do.

The room fell silent when Emperor Guang Xu entered. Now, as he begins the ceremony, you reflect on his recent actions as emperor. You know that he is trying to modernize China. However, conservatives in the government are fighting his reforms.

The Dowager Empress Ci Xi is not present. You have heard that she does not approve of the emperor's reforms. When the ceremony ends, you feel confused. You want to be loyal to your emperor, but you have spent years studying traditional Confucian ways of governing. Should you support reform?

Portfolio Assessment

In your new government post, you can either support or oppose the emperor's reforms. Write a poem explaining your decision. Be sure to include both reasons for and possible consequences of your decision.

Chapter 25 **637**

You Are There...

Bell Ringer Point out that the central figure is Emperor Guang Xu, seated on the throne. Have students speculate on the identities of the other men shown.

Background
About the Scene

The Forbidden City The hall depicted here is part of the Forbidden City, a complex of buildings that takes up about 860,000 square yards inside Beijing. Surrounding the complex is a nearly 33-foot-high wall. Outside the wall is a moat about 170 feet in width. The city was begun during the Ming dynasty and was used by Ming and Qing emperors from 1421 until the monarchy fell in 1911. The ministers wear the traditional queues, or long strands of hair gathered in the back. These were outlawed after the revolution in 1911.

Activity
Cooperative Learning

The Forbidden City Have students work in small groups and choose one aspect of the Forbidden City for further study. Students may use library resources or the Internet for information. Alternately, students may choose to learn the fate of Guang Xu, the reforming emperor.

Portfolio Assessment Rubrics

Share rubrics with students before they write their poems.

Attempted The poem does not explain reasons for the decision or give possible effects.

Minimal The poem explains reasons for the decision and gives possible effects, but it is unclear or full of mechanical errors.

Adequate The poem explains reasons for the decision, gives possible effects, and has few errors.

Exemplary The poem ably explains reasons for the decision, decribes possible effects, is well written with no errors, and reveals an understanding of issues in China at the time.

☑ Test Preparation

Have students read the first three paragraphs under the heading "Reform Efforts" on the opposite page, and then answer the question below.

Which is a fact from the passage?

A New industries would not have improved China's economy.

B New industries were springing up in western Europe.

C China's wealth did not come from merchants.

D Western missionaries had a bad influence on the Chinese people.

Background
Historical Evidence

Rebellions The Taiping Rebellion was only one of numerous rebellions that swept China in the second half of the 1800s. From 1853 to 1868, the Nien Rebellion took place in northern China. In the southwest and northwest, there were bloody uprisings by Chinese Muslims during the 1860s and 1870s. The Chinese government was able to put down these rebellions with the aid of western military technology.

Customize for . . .
Heterogeneous Groups

Interviewing Organize students into pairs. Have each pair choose one of the following people mentioned in this section: Hong Xiuquan; Empress Ci Xi; Guang Xu; Sun Yixian. After researching the person that they choose, have students write and then conduct an interview in front of the class. Tell students to prepare questions that will reveal as much as possible about the character and ideals of the personality being interviewed. Instruct pairs to formulate answers to the questions from the perspective of the person they choose. Ask volunteers to conduct their interviews for the class. *(Enrichment)*

Imperialism in China to 1914

Spheres of Influence
- Occupied by Russia, 1897–1905
- Occupied by Japan by 1905
- Main area of Boxer Uprising
- British
- French
- German
- Japanese
- Russian

Skills Assessment

Geography The European powers and Japan carved China into spheres of influence.

1. **Location** On the map, locate (a) Vladivostok, (b) Korea, (c) Hong Kong, (d) Taiwan.
2. **Place** What river was the center of Britain's sphere of influence?
3. **Critical Thinking Recognizing Causes and Effects** Use information on the map to identify causes of the growth of Chinese nationalism.

Self-Strengthening Movement In the 1860s, reformers launched what became known as the "self-strengthening movement." They imported western technology, setting up factories to make modern weapons. They developed shipyards, railroads, mining, and light industry. The Chinese translated western works on science, government, and the economy. However, the movement made limited progress because the government did not rally behind it.

War With Japan Meanwhile, the western powers and nearby Japan moved rapidly ahead. Japan began to modernize after 1868. It then joined the western imperialists in the competition for a global empire.

In 1894, Japanese pressure on China led to the Sino-Japanese War. It ended in disaster for China, with Japan gaining the island of Taiwan off the coast of China. When the two powers met at the peace table, there was a telling difference. Japanese officials were dressed in western clothes, the Chinese in traditional robes.

Spheres of Influence The crushing defeat revealed China's weakness. Western powers moved swiftly to carve out spheres of influence along the Chinese coast. The British took the Yangzi River valley. The French acquired the territory near their colony of Indochina. Germany and Russia gained territory in northern China.

The United States, a longtime trader with the Chinese, did not take part in the carving up of China. It feared that European powers might shut out American merchants. A few years later, in 1899, it called for a policy to keep Chinese trade open to everyone on an equal basis. The imperial powers more or less accepted the idea of an Open Door Policy, as it came to be called. No one, however, consulted the Chinese about the policy.

Hundred Days of Reform Defeated by Japan and humiliated by westerners, the Chinese looked for a scapegoat. Reformers blamed conservative officials for not modernizing China. They urged conservative leaders to stop looking back at China's past golden ages and instead to modernize as Japan had.

In 1898, a young emperor, Guang Xu (gwawng SHYOO), launched the Hundred Days of Reform. New laws set out to modernize the civil service exams, streamline government, and encourage new industries. Reforms affected schools, the military, and the bureaucracy. Conservatives soon rallied against the reform effort. The emperor was imprisoned, and the aging empress Ci Xi reasserted control. Reformers fled for their lives.

The Qing Dynasty Falls

As the century ended, China was in turmoil. Anger grew against Christian missionaries who belittled Chinese thinkers like Confucius. The presence of foreign troops was another source of discontent. Protected by extraterritoriality, foreigners ignored Chinese laws and lived in their own communities.

Boxer Uprising Antiforeign feeling finally exploded in the Boxer Uprising. In 1899, a group of Chinese had formed a secret society, the Righteous

638 Chapter 25

Skills Assessment

ANSWERS 1. Review locations with students. **2.** Yangzi River **3.** Possible answer: Many Chinese people united in their opposition to foreign influence and control. Westerners spread their ideas about nationalism to the Chinese.

Resource Directory

Teaching Resources
Primary Source Activity *The Great Powers Divide China,* Unit 6 booklet, p. 69
Section Quiz Unit 6 booklet, p. 67
Geography Quiz Unit 6 booklet, p. 72
Chapter Test Forms A, B, and C Unit 6 booklet, pp. 73–77
Answer Key Unit 6 booklet, pp. 98–112

Technology
Interactive Student Tutorial CD-ROM Ch. 25
Computer Test Bank Ch. 25

Harmonious Fists. Westerners watching them train in the martial arts dubbed them Boxers. Their goal was to drive out the "foreign devils" who were polluting the land with their un-Chinese ways, strange buildings, machines, and telegraph lines.

In 1900, the Boxers attacked foreigners across China. In response, the western powers and Japan organized a multinational force. It crushed the Boxers and rescued foreigners besieged in Beijing. The empress Ci Xi had at first supported the Boxers but reversed her policy as they retreated.

Aftermath of the Uprising   China once again had to make concessions to foreigners. The defeat, however, forced even Chinese conservatives to support westernization. In a rush of reforms, China admitted women to schools and stressed science and mathematics in place of Confucian thought. More students were sent abroad to study.

China expanded economically, as well. Mining, shipping, railroads, banking, and exports of cash crops grew. With foreign capital, small-scale Chinese industry developed. A Chinese business class emerged, and a new urban working class began to press for rights as western workers had done.

Three Principles of the People   Although the Boxer Uprising failed, the flames of Chinese nationalism spread. Reformers wanted to strengthen China's government. By the early 1900s, they had introduced a constitutional monarchy. Some reformers called for a republic.

A passionate spokesman for a Chinese republic was Sun Yixian* (soon yee SHYAHN). Sun had studied in the West. In the early 1900s, he organized the Revolutionary Alliance. His goal was to rebuild China on "Three Principles of the People." The first principle was nationalism, freeing China from foreign domination. The second was democracy, or representative government. The third was "livelihood," or economic security for all Chinese.

Birth of a Republic   When Ci Xi died in 1908 and a two-year-old boy inherited the throne, China slipped into chaos. In 1911, uprisings in the provinces swiftly spread. Peasants, students, local warlords, and even court politicians helped topple the Qing dynasty.

Sun Yixian hurried home from a trip to the United States. In December 1911, he was named president of the new Chinese republic. From the outset, the republic faced overwhelming problems. For the next 37 years, China was almost constantly at war with itself or fighting off foreign invasion.

*In earlier history books, this name appears as Sun Yat-sen.

Biography

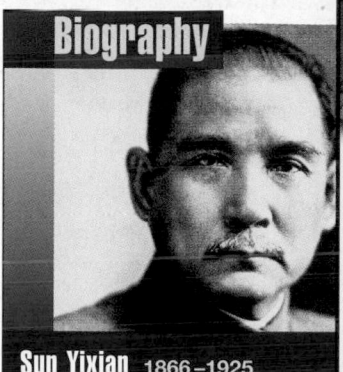

Sun Yixian 1866–1925

Sun Yixian was not born to power. His parents were poor farmers. Sun's preparation for leadership came from his travels, education, and personal ambitions. In his teen years, he lived with his brother in Hawaii and attended British and American schools. Later on, he earned a medical degree.

Sun left his career in medicine to struggle against the Qing government. After a failed uprising in 1895, he went into exile. Sun visited many nations, seeking support against the Qing dynasty. When revolution erupted in China, Sun was in Denver, Colorado. He returned to China to begin his leading role in the new republic.

Theme: Impact of the Individual   How did Sun's background prepare him to lead?

SECTION 5 Assessment

Recall
1. **(a)** Opium War, p. 635 **(b)** Treaty of Nanjing, p. 636 **(c)** Taiping Rebellion, p. 636 **(d)** Ci Xi, p. 636 **(e)** Open Door Policy, p. 638 **(f)** Boxer Uprising, p. 638 **(g)** Sun Yixian, p. 639 2. **(a)** trade surplus, p. 635 **(b)** trade deficit, p. 635 **(c)** indemnity, p. 636 **(d)** extraterritoriality, p. 636

Comprehension
3. through wars and unfair treaties
4. **(a)** Irrigation systems and canals were poorly maintained. A population explosion caused great hardship for Chinese peasants. Corruption afflicted the upper class and government officials. The Taiping Rebellion devastated the Yangzi basin region of China. **(b)** to adapt western ideas for use in China; to bring new technology and learning to China 5. Peasants, students, warlords, and politicians joined in uprisings that toppled the Qing dynasty, which was replaced by a republic with Sun Yixian as president.

Critical Thinking and Writing
6. Possible answer: European nations gained trading rights and sometimes control of entire regions through diplomacy, the threat of military force, or the actual use of force. 7. Students will probably choose to support reform efforts, either because change was inevitable or for other reasons.

SECTION 5 Assessment

Recall
1. **Identify:** **(a)** Opium War, **(b)** Treaty of Nanjing, **(c)** Taiping Rebellion, **(d)** Ci Xi, **(e)** Open Door Policy, **(f)** Boxer Uprising, **(g)** Sun Yixian.
2. **Define:** **(a)** trade surplus, **(b)** trade deficit, **(c)** indemnity, **(d)** extraterritoriality.

Comprehension
3. How did western powers gain greater trading rights in China?
4. **(a)** What internal problems threatened the Qing dynasty? **(b)** What were the goals of Chinese reformers?
5. How was the Qing dynasty replaced by a republic?

Critical Thinking and Writing
6. **Making Generalizations** Based on what you have learned about western imperialism in Africa and Asia, what methods did European states use to gain power around the world?
7. **Making Decisions** If you had been a Chinese government official in the 1800s, would you have decided to support or oppose reform efforts designed to westernize China? Explain the reasons for your decision.

Activity

Planning a Debate
Work with a partner to plan a debate between a British merchant and a Chinese government official. The topic is extraterritoriality in China. Each of you should be prepared to present and defend your own position and to criticize the opposing position. Conduct your debate before the class.

Chapter 25 **639**

Activity Rubrics

Share rubrics with students before they present their debates.

Attempted The student does not work with a partner to complete the assignment or offers only sketchy, poorly prepared arguments.

Minimal The debate shows limited research; arguments are weak and poorly organized.

Adequate The debate reflects good research with strong, well-organized arguments and convincing support.

Exemplary The student's arguments are thoroughly researched, carefully prepared, well presented, and insightful.

Biography

ANSWER Sun's travels and education abroad prepared him for leadership.

Human Drama Activity

The Good Earth This novel by Pearl Buck (1892–1973) won the 1932 Pulitzer Prize for fiction. Pearl Buck also won the 1938 Nobel Prize for literature for her novels about life in China. A good source of information about everyday life in China, *The Good Earth* tells the story of a peasant named Wang Lung. Have students choose a chapter to read, and then write a paragraph or two describing what they learned about peasant life in China.

Creating a Chapter Summary

As a reteaching opportunity, pair a more able student with a less able student to complete this chapter summary.

Possible answers: **Political** Belgian Congo, Union of South Africa, Indian National Congress **Military** conflicts with native peoples, Boer War, Opium Wars, Sepoy Rebellion **Economic** Suez Canal, spheres of influence in China, Indians forced to raise cash crops **Social** western-educated African elite, Indian famines

Building Vocabulary

1–10. Quiz definitions should show a clear understanding of the meanings of the terms.

Recalling Key Facts

11. economic interests, such as trade; political and military interests, such as colonies and prestige; humanitarian and religious interests, such as spreading western religion; and Social Darwinism
12. Menelik II, the Ethiopian emperor, imported modern weapons and European officers to train his army. This army then defeated an invading Italian army.
13. reorganized the bureaucracy and tax-collection system, built railroads, improved education, hired European officers to train modern military, sent young men to the West to study new sciences and technology, improved medical care, revitalized farming
14. (a) resentment over the requirement that sepoys serve overseas; anger caused by a new law allowing widows to remarry, which went against Hindu traditions; fear that the British were trying to force them to give up their religion by causing them to ingest animal fat that coated rifle cartridges; opposition to British domination and interference in traditional life (b) atrocities on both sides; a legacy of hatred, fear, and distrust on both sides
15. China entered a period of decline, and the Industrial Revolution gave western nations greater need for commerce with China and greater military power.
16. (a) to drive foreigners out of China (b) nationalism, democracy, and economic security

---

CHAPTER 25 Review and Assessment

Creating a Chapter Summary

On a sheet of paper, create a chart showing the effects of imperialism in the late 1800s and early 1900s. Use the partially completed model below to help you get started. Add as many boxes as you need.

WESTERN IMPERIALISM

Political
- Europeans set up spheres of influence

Military

Economic

Social
- Britain tries to change Indian caste system

For additional review and enrichment activities, see the interactive version of *World History* available on the Web and on CD-ROM.

Web Site Self-Test
For practice test questions for Chapter 25, see www.phschool.com.

Building Vocabulary

Use these words and their definitions to create a matching quiz. When you are finished, exchange quizzes with another student and check each other's answers.

1. imperialism
2. protectorate
3. jihad
4. missionary
5. pasha
6. genocide
7. sepoy
8. viceroy
9. indemnity
10. extraterritoriality

Recalling Key Facts

11. List the four main motives of the new imperialists.
12. How did Ethiopia successfully resist European imperialism?
13. How did the Ottoman empire try to westernize?
14. (a) What were the causes of the Sepoy Rebellion? (b) What were its effects?
15. Give two main reasons that China's policy of limiting trade with foreigners ended after the 1700s.
16. (a) What was the goal of the Boxer Uprising? (b) Describe the three principles that guided Sun Yixian.

Critical Thinking and Writing

17. **Linking Past and Present (a)** How did the opening of the Suez Canal in 1869 transform world trade? **(b)** Do you think the canal might be less important today? Why or why not?
18. **Analyzing Information** Western industrial nations set up colonies in Africa and India. In China, however, they established spheres of influence rather than colonies. Why do you think they did not colonize China?
19. **Comparing** In the late 1800s, several nonwestern nations instituted programs of western reforms and modernization. **(a)** Describe the reform efforts of two of the following: Egypt, the Ottoman empire, China. **(b)** Compare the results of these efforts.
20. **Connecting to Geography** Why were the natural resources of African and Asian lands so important to Europeans in the 1800s?
21. **Predicting Consequences** How do you think rivalries between religious groups affected anti-imperialism efforts in India? Explain your answer.

Critical Thinking and Writing

17. (a) It greatly reduced travel time between Europe and Asia. (b) Possible answer: Modern communications technology and air travel have reduced the importance of the canal for communications and passenger travel, though it would still be valuable for shipping heavy goods.
18. Possible answer: China would have been more difficult to colonize because its government was more powerful than governments in Africa and India.
19. Students' answers should reflect an understanding that reformers in each of these areas sought to apply western ideas about government, economy, and technology to solve their problems.
20. The Industrial Revolution created a need for African and Asian resources (such as rubber, coal, petroleum, palm oil, manganese, copper, gold, and diamonds) to manufacture goods.
21. prevented Indians from putting up a united front against British imperialism

In 1896, Liang Ch'i-ch'ao, an influential Chinese thinker, was unhappy with conditions in China. Read the excerpt below and answer the questions that follow.

"The age of China as a country is equal to that of India and the fertility of her land is superior to that of Turkey, but her conformity to the defective ways which have accumulated and her incapacity to stand up and reform make her also like a brother of these two countries. . . . Whenever there is a flood or drought, communications are severed, there is no way to transport famine relief, the dead are abandoned to fill the ditches or are disregarded, and nine out of ten houses are emptied. . . . The members of secret societies are scattered over the whole country, waiting for the chance to move. Industry is not developed, commerce is not discussed, the native goods daily become less salable. . . ."

—Liang Ch'i-ch'ao,
On the Harm of Not Reforming

22. According to Liang Ch'i-ch'ao, how is China similar to India and Turkey?
23. What does he say are some of China's most serious problems?
24. What kind of "move" do you think "secret societies" were waiting to make? Explain.
25. What do you think Liang Ch'i-ch'ao wanted Chinese leaders to do?
26. **(a)** What important event occurred in China four years after this was written? **(b)** Based on what you have read, how do you think Liang Ch'i-ch'ao may have felt about this event?

Use the Internet to find primary sources having to do with imperialism in the late 1800s and early 1900s. Select two documents or excerpts of documents and print them out. Explain the meaning of each primary source in your own words.

The cartoon above was published in France in 1904, at the height of the Age of Imperialism. The figure at left is a French soldier. The figure at right is a British soldier. Study the cartoon and answer the following questions:

27. What continent appears on the map?
28. Why are the soldiers in the cartoon ripping the map apart?
29. **(a)** Which part of the continent are the British getting? **(b)** Which part of the continent are the French getting?
30. Why do you think part of the continent was not colored red?
31. How do you think the situation depicted in the cartoon affected relations between Britain and France?
32. How do you think people of the time knew which nations the two figures represented?
33. What prediction about future international relations can you make based on information in the cartoon? Explain.
34. Create an interesting title for the political cartoon. Explain the reason for your choice of title.

Skills Tip

Use information that you already have about a historical topic to help you understand a political cartoon.

Analyzing Primary Sources

22. in age and in the incapacity to reform
23. poor infrastructure to respond to floods and famines, poor communication, undeveloped industry and commerce, scattered secret societies
24. possible answer: drive out the foreigners
25. to break the habit of resignation and adopt western methods to solve problems of reform and development
26. **(a)** Boxer Uprising **(b)** Students might say he would disapprove because the Boxers wanted to get rid of foreigners and their industry, trade, and technology.

Analyzing Political Cartoons

27. Africa
28. They are symbolic of the roles of France and Britain in the partition of Africa.
29. **(a)** eastern **(b)** northwestern
30. It was already claimed by another country.
31. possible answer: probably improved them, because they didn't have to go to war
32. They would have recognized the soldiers' uniforms.
33. Other countries may resent Britain and France gobbling up most of Africa. They will want a share and may go to war for it.
34. Answer should express a point of view about the action pictured.

Skills Tip

Reading all labels and the caption, if any, will also help you interpret a cartoon. The Skills Handbook in the front of the book has a lesson that will help students with this feature.

Unit Theme Activity

Remind students to continue working on their Unit Theme Activity. See rubrics for the activity on the unit opener page in the Teacher's Edition.

Direct students to **www.phschool.com** for links to sites that will help them get started on this assignment. Share rubrics with students.
Attempted The student provides only one document, or the explanations reveal little understanding of the document.
Minimal The explanations reveal some understanding of the documents, but they are poorly written and organized and contain many mechanical errors.
Adequate The explanations reveal some understanding of the documents, are well written and organized, and contain few mechanical errors.
Exemplary The explanations reveal deep understanding of the documents, are very well written and organized, and contain no mechanical errors.

Resource Manager

	CORE INSTRUCTION	READING/SKILLS
Chapter Level Resources	📓 **Teaching Resources** 📄 **Pacing Charts**, Ch. 26 📄 **Teaching With Themes**, p. 29 📖 **Color Transparencies**, p. F–53 💿 **Resource Pro®** Ch. 26 🖥 **www.phschool.com** 　• eTeach	🔵 **Book on CD**, Ch. 26 🔵 **Interactive Student Tutorial CD-ROM**, Ch. 26 🔵 **Social Studies Skills Tutor CD-ROM** 📖 **Skills Transparencies**
1 Japan Modernizes 1. Outline how discontent in society and the opening of Japan led to the Meiji restoration. 2. Summarize the main reforms under the Meiji. 3. State how Japanese military strength promoted imperialism.	📓 **Teaching Resources** 📘 **Unit 6 booklet** 　• Biography Activity, p. 88 📕 **Creative Teaching Activities**, p. 116 💿 **Prentice Hall Presentation Pro**, Ch. 26, Section 1 📖 **Section Reading Support Transparencies**	📓 **Teaching Resources** 📘 **Unit 6 booklet** 　• Guided Reading and Review, p. 78 　• Skill Application Activity, p. 91 📘 **Guide to the Essentials** 📼 **Guided Reading Audiotapes**, Ch. 26, Section 1
2 Southeast Asia and the Pacific 1. Discuss the impact of European colonization on Southeast Asia. 2. Explain how Siam remained independent. 3. Outline the ways imperialism spread to the Philippines and other Pacific islands.	📓 **Teaching Resources** 📕 **Creative Teaching Activities**, p. 117 💿 **Prentice Hall Presentation Pro**, Ch. 26, Section 2 📖 **Section Reading Support Transparencies**	📓 **Teaching Resources** 📘 **Unit 6 booklet** 　• Guided Reading and Review, p. 80 📘 **Guide to the Essentials** 📼 **Guided Reading Audiotapes**, Ch. 26, Section 2
3 Self-Rule for Canada, Australia, and New Zealand 1. Summarize how Canada achieved self-rule. 2. Give examples that show how European settlement changed the course of Australian history. 3. Identify how New Zealand emerged as an independent nation.	📓 **Teaching Resources** 📘 **Unit 6 booklet** 　• Viewpoint Activity, p. 90 📕 **Creative Teaching Activities**, p. 118 💿 **Prentice Hall Presentation Pro**, Ch. 26, Section 3	📓 **Teaching Resources** 📘 **Unit 6 booklet** 　• Guided Reading and Review, p. 82 📘 **Guide to the Essentials** 📼 **Guided Reading Audiotapes**, Ch. 26, Section 3
4 Economic Imperialism in Latin America 1. Describe the political and economic problems that faced new Latin American nations. 2. Relate how Mexico struggled for stability. 3. Analyze United States influence in Latin America.	📓 **Teaching Resources** 📘 **Unit 6 booklet** 　• Primary Source Activity, p. 89 📕 **Creative Teaching Activities**, p. 119 💿 **Prentice Hall Presentation Pro**, Ch. 26, Section 4	📓 **Teaching Resources** 📘 **Unit 6 booklet** 　• Guided Reading and Review, p. 84 📘 **Guide to the Essentials** 📼 **Guided Reading Audiotapes**, Ch. 26, Section 4
5 Impact of Imperialism 1. Explain how imperialism led to new economic patterns. 2. Describe cultural impact of imperialism. 3. Summarize how new political tensions developed as a result of imperialism.	📓 **Teaching Resources** 📕 **Creative Teaching Activities**, p. 120 💿 **Prentice Hall Presentation Pro**, Ch. 26, Section 5 📖 **Section Reading Support Transparencies**	📓 **Teaching Resources** 📘 **Unit 6 booklet** 　• Guided Reading and Review, p. 86 📘 **Guide to the Essentials** 📼 **Guided Reading Audiotapes**, Ch. 26, Section 5

ENRICHMENT/PRE-AP

Teaching Resources
Teaching With Themes
- Global View Activity, p. 46

www.phschool.com
- Global View Activity
- Why Study History?

Teaching Resources
Chapter Extension Activities, p. 63
History Through Literature, pp. 55–56

www.phschool.com
- Virtual Field Trip
- Internet Activities, Section 1

www.phschool.com
- Internet Activities, Section 3

Listening to Literature World Masterpieces, *Sonatina,* side 9

www.phschool.com
- Internet Activities, Section 4

Teaching Resources
Chapter Extension Activities, p. 64

www.phschool.com
- Internet Activities, The Influence of African Art on Picasso

ASSESSMENT

PRENTICE HALL
ASSESSMENT SYSTEM

Core Assessment
- ExamView Test Bank booklet, Ch. 26
- ExamView Test Bank CD-ROM, Ch. 26

Standardized Test Preparation
Diagnose and Prescribe
- Diagnostic Tests for High School Social Studies Skills

Review and Reteach
- Review Book for World History

Practice and Assess
- Document-Based Assessment, pp. 28–32
- Test-Taking Strategies With Transparencies
- Alternative Assessment booklet
- Test Prep Book for World History

Teaching Resources
Unit 6 booklet
- Geography Quiz, p. 92
- Section Quizzes, pp. 79, 81, 83, 85, 87
- Chapter Tests A, B, and C, pp. 93–97

www.phschool.com
- Self-Test

CUSTOMIZE FOR INDIVIDUAL NEEDS

Gifted and Talented
- **Teacher's Edition,** Activities: Customize for Heterogeneous Groups, p. 660

Less Proficient Readers
- **Guide to the Essentials,** Ch. 26
- **Guided Reading Audiotapes, English,** Ch. 26
- **Book on CD,** Ch. 26
- **Teacher's Edition,** Activities: Customize for Visual Learners, p. 660

Less Proficient Writers
- **Teacher's Edition,** Activities: Customize for Auditory Learners, p. 645

Students Acquiring English/ESL
- **Guide to the Essentials, English/Spanish,** Ch. 26
- **Guided Reading Audiotapes, English/Spanish,** Ch. 26
- **Book on CD,** Ch. 26
- **Teacher's Edition,** Activities marked with an *

iTEXT

Don't miss the exclusive interactive version of *World History: Connections to Today* on the Internet and CD-ROM.

INTRODUCTION

Imperialism profited industrial nations but disrupted economies elsewhere, forcing nonwestern peoples to accept western ways. Japan became a modern industrialist power with its own imperialist goals. By 1900, western powers claimed most of the Pacific islands and Southeast Asia. The British colonies of Canada, Australia, and New Zealand won independence. In Latin America, a pattern of military rule and economic dependency emerged. The United States created its own sphere of influence in the Western Hemisphere.

Focusing on Themes
Suggest that students focus on these theme questions as they read:

Continuity and Change
How did western domination threaten traditional cultures around the world?

Economics and Technology
How did imperialism create a new western-dominated world economy?

Political and Social Systems
Why was it difficult for Latin American nations to achieve political stability?

Diversity
How did responses to imperialism differ in various parts of the world?

TIME LINE ACTIVITY

Share the About the Pictures note with students before asking these questions about the time line:

1. What was one result of Britain's annexation of New Zealand? *(The Maori population was devastated.)*
2. What happened in Ireland shortly after Britain's annexation of New Zealand? *(In 1845, potato blight led to the Great Hunger.)*
3. What event would lead to greater United States involvement in Latin America? *(construction of the Panama Canal)*

Don't Miss!

Synthesizing Information
Industrialization in Japan (Section 1)

Humanities Link
The Influence of African Art on Picasso (Section 5)

New Global Patterns
1800–1914

Chapter Preview

1 Japan Modernizes
2 Southeast Asia and the Pacific
3 Self-Rule for Canada, Australia, and New Zealand
4 Economic Imperialism in Latin America
5 Impact of Imperialism

1840
Britain annexes New Zealand, leading to devastation for the Maori population. This carved figure is an example of Maori art.

1823
The United States issues the Monroe Doctrine.

1853
American ships commanded by Commodore Matthew Perry arrive in Japan. This woodblock print shows the American "black ships" and Japanese onlookers.

CHAPTER EVENTS

1800 • • 1825 • • 1850

GLOBAL EVENTS

1804 Haiti declares independence from France.

1818 Shaka begins Zulu conquests.

1845 Potato blight leads to the Great Hunger in Ireland.

642 Chapter 26

Resource Directory

Teaching Resources
Teaching With Themes Chapter Theme Activities, p. 29
Pacing Chart With Block Scheduling Guide Ch. 26
Global View Activity *How Did Industrialization, Nationalism, and the Growth of Democracy Reshape the World?* Teaching With Themes booklet, p. 46

Technology
World History Color Transparencies Ch. 26 Graphic Organizer, p. F–53

Imperialism in Asia, the Pacific, and the Americas, 1900

Industrialized nations competed for control of territories around the world.

PACIFIC OCEAN

INDIAN OCEAN

Colonial possessions:
- British
- Dutch
- French
- German
- Japanese
- United States
- Russian
- Portuguese

Spheres of influence:
- British
- French
- German
- Japanese
- Russian
- United States
- British and French

Robinson Projection

0   1500   3000 Miles
0   1500   3000 Kilometers

1885
The Canadian Pacific Railway opens, linking eastern and western Canada.

1898
The Philippines declares independence from Spain.

1914
The Panama Canal opens, linking the Pacific Ocean and the Caribbean Sea. Construction of the canal, shown here, will lead to greater United States involvement in Latin America.

1875 — 1900 — 1925

1871 Germany is unified under Prussian leadership in the Second Reich.

1914 World War I begins.

Imperialism in Asia, the Pacific, and the Americas, 1900

Activating Prior Knowledge
How did geography enable Japan's shoguns to forbid its people to travel overseas and close the country to foreigners? *(Japan is an island nation, making it relatively easy to prevent people from leaving or coming in.)*

Previewing
What dilemma might the countries of Southeast Asia face as a result of resisting imperialism? *(Possible answer: By resisting imperialism, countries might be invaded.)*

Background
About the Pictures

1. In this Maori wood carving, the head was given special prominence because Maoris believed that the soul resided there. Intricate curving surface designs imitate tattoos worn by Maori people.

2. *Commodore Perry arrives in Japan August 7, 1853* is a Japanese wood-block print by Yoshitoshi. Called *ukiyo-e,* or "scenes of transitory importance," these prints depicted scenes of everyday life and, like a poster or postcard, were not considered formal art.

3. One of the world's most strategic human-made waterways, the Panama Canal is 51 miles (82 km) long. Duplicate locks allow ships to pass in opposite directions during the 15- to 20-hour trip through the locks. The canal saves 8,000 nautical miles for ships traveling between the east and west coasts of the United States.

eTeach

Be sure to check out this month's online discussion with a World History Master Teacher.

Go to **www.phschool.com**.

Independent Assignments

Have students read one section as they prepare for class. After class, have them complete the assignment. Some students may benefit from using the Guided Reading and Review worksheets.

Section 1 Have students use the worksheet *Hiroshige* in the Unit 6 booklet, p. 88, to learn about the life and art of a Japanese printmaker.

Section 2 Have students use the worksheet *East Asia to 1914* in the Historical Outline Map Book, p. 43, to locate and label the countries and outline imperialist expansion in East Asia.

Section 3 Have students use the worksheet *Australia's Convict Colonists* in the Unit 6 booklet, p. 90,

to learn about the country's colonial beginnings as a penal colony.

Section 4 Have students use the worksheet *Jose Martí's "Our America"* in the Unit 6 booklet, p. 89, to learn about a Cuban hero and patriot and what he believed the people of Spanish America must do.

Section 5 Have students read *A Defense of Imperialism,* pp. 119–120, and *First Doubts in My Imperialist Soul,* pp. 121–122, in Treasures of the World to compare differing viewpoints on imperialism.

Bell Ringer Ask students to skim the Reading Focus questions at the start of this section and the Section Assessment questions at the end. Have them use these questions to write three generalizations about the Japanese experience in the latter half of the 1800s.

LESSON PLAN

1. Focus To avoid domination by the West, Japan opened its doors to foreign influences and transformed itself into a modern industrial power. The change occurred rapidly because of Japan's homogeneous society, great determination, and experience in cultural adaptation. As a small island nation with few resources, Japan began building an empire to feed its industrial growth.

2. Instruct Assign students to construct a cause-and-effect chart on the Meiji restoration. Working individually or in groups, students should indicate the factors that led to the overthrow of the shogun and restoration of the emperor in 1868. They should then identify the major changes that occurred as a result of the restoration. Encourage students to identify long-term effects by referring to their knowledge of twentieth-century history and conditions in Japan today.

3. Assess Ask students to compare the different ways in which Japan and China responded to the growing power of the West. Which policy do they think was the wiser? Encourage students to explain their answers.

4. Reteach If students' Assess activity does not reflect adequate understanding of the lesson, you might assign the *Guide to the Essentials* or the *Interactive Student Tutorial CD-ROM* for this section.

Reading Focus

- How did discontent in Japanese society and the opening of Japan lead to the Meiji restoration?
- What were the main reforms under the Meiji?
- How did Japanese military strength promote imperialism?

Vocabulary

Diet
zaibatsu
homogeneous society

Taking Notes

Copy this chart. As you read, fill in the major reforms of the Meiji restoration. The sample has been started for you.

REFORMS DURING MEIJI RESTORATION

Political	Economic	Social
• Adopted German model of government	•	•
•		

Main Idea During the late 1800s, Japan opened its doors to foreign influence and became a modern industrial power.

Setting the Scene In 1853, the United States displayed its new military might, sending a naval force to make Japan open its ports to trade. Japanese leaders debated how to respond. While some resisted giving up their 215-year-old policy of seclusion, others felt that it would be wiser to learn from the foreigners. One Japanese lord pointed out:

> "There is a saying that when one is besieged in a castle, to raise the drawbridge is to imprison oneself. . . . Even though the Shogun's ancestors set up seclusion laws, they left the Dutch and Chinese to act as a bridge. . . . Might this bridge not now be of advantage to us, . . . providing us with the means whereby we may for a time avert the outbreak of hostilities and then, after some time has elapsed, gain a complete victory?"
> —Ii Naosuke, quoted in *Selected Documents on Japanese Foreign Policy* (Beasley)

In the end, Japan chose to abandon its centuries of isolation and to learn from the West. The country swiftly transformed itself into a modern industrial power and then set out on its own imperialist path.

Discontent in Tokugawa Japan

After the Tokugawa shoguns gained power in 1600, they reimposed centralized feudalism, closed Japan to foreigners, and forbade Japanese to travel overseas. The nation's only window on the world was through Nagasaki, where the Dutch were allowed very limited trade.

For more than 200 years, Japan developed in isolation. Although internal commerce expanded, economic changes introduced severe strains in Japanese society. By the 1800s, shoguns were no longer strong leaders, and corruption was common. Discontent simmered throughout Japan.

Many daimyo suffered financial hardship. Money was needed in a commercial economy, but a daimyo's wealth was in land rather than cash. Daimyo also had the heavy expense of maintaining households in both Edo and their own domains. Lesser samurai were unhappy, too, because they were no longer fighters. Many were bureaucrats. Even though they were noble, they lacked the money to live as well as urban merchants.

Merchants in turn resented their place at the bottom of the social ladder. No matter how rich they were, they had no political power. Peasants, meanwhile, suffered under heavy taxes.

Resource Directory

Teaching Resources
Creative Teaching Activities Creative Teaching Activities booklet, p. 116
Guided Reading and Review Unit 6 booklet, p. 78

The government responded by trying to revive old ways, emphasizing farming over commerce and praising traditional values. These efforts at reform, however, had scant success. Many groups felt little loyalty to the old system.

Opening Up Japan

While the shogun faced troubles at home, disturbing news reached him from abroad during the 1830s and 1840s. He was alarmed by news of the British victory over China in the Opium War. Even more disturbing was the way in which imperialists had forced China to sign the unequal treaties. Surely, the shogun reasoned, it would not be long before western powers began seeking trading rights in Japan.

External Pressure and Internal Revolt Then, in July 1853, a fleet of well-armed American ships commanded by Commodore Matthew Perry sailed into Tokyo Bay. Perry had a letter from the President of the United States. The letter demanded that Japan open its ports to diplomatic and commercial exchange.

The shogun's advisers debated what to do. As Lord Ii noted, Japan did not have the ability to defend itself against the powerful United States Navy. In the Treaty of Kanagawa in 1854, the shogun agreed to open two Japanese ports to American ships, though not for trade.

The United States soon won trading and other rights, including the right of extraterritoriality and a "most favored nation" clause. European nations demanded and won similar rights. Like the Chinese, the Japanese deeply resented the terms of these unequal treaties, which they found humiliating. Some bitterly criticized the shogun for not taking a strong stand against the foreigners.

Foreign pressure deepened the social and economic unrest. In 1867, discontented daimyo and samurai led a revolt that unseated the shogun and "restored" the 15-year-old emperor to power. He moved from the old imperial capital in Kyoto to the shogun's palace in Edo, which was renamed Tokyo, or "eastern capital."

Tea Ceremony
In Japan, the tea ceremony was developed to provide a peaceful setting for social activity (PAST). Today, the rituals provide a reminder of the nation's cultural heritage, as well as an oasis of calm in an otherwise busy world (PRESENT).

Theme: Continuity and Change Why might people choose to maintain traditions along with modernization?

PRESENT

PAST

Synthesizing Information

Industrialization in Japan

The emperor Meiji wrote a poem to provide inspiration for Japan's efforts to become a modern country: "May our country, / Taking what is good, / and rejecting what is bad, / Be not inferior / To any other." The picture, the song, and the chart on this page relate to Japan's efforts to modernize in the late 1800s.

Clothing Manufacturing in Japan

Japanese manufacturing grew rapidly in the late 1800s. As in Europe and the United States, women played a key role in Japan's industrial revolution. In this 1897 print, women make clothing in a Japanese workshop.

Children's Game

In 1878, a song composed for Japanese children impressed on them the 10 objects that their country should adopt from the West to be truly modern. As they named each object, the children bounced a ball:

"Gas Lamps
Steam Engines
Horse Carriages
Cameras
Telegrams
Lightning Conductors
Newspapers
Schools
[Postal System]
Steamboats"

Investments by Industry in Meiji Japan

Activity	1877	1883	1893
Agriculture	–	1,053,000	2,542,000
Trading	454,000	35,904,000	57,616,000
Manufacturing	–	14,725,000	68,259,000
Railways	–	12,080,000	57,945,000
Banking	24,981,000	75,375,000	111,635,000

All figures are in yen.
Source: S. Uyehara, *The Industry and Trade of Japan*

Skills Assessment

1. According to the picture, Japanese women
   A adopted western ways.
   B worked long hours.
   C opposed organized labor unions.
   D earned less than men.

2. In which economic activity did the investments increase by about 46 million yen between 1883 and 1893?
   E agriculture
   F trading
   G manufacturing
   H railways

3. **Critical Thinking Evaluating Information**   Name two things about modernization in Japan that you cannot learn from the sources on this page. Explain why it would be useful to have that information.

Background
About the Evidence

Changing Styles During the 1870s and 1880s, Japanese officials thought they could rid themselves of unequal treaties only if the West viewed Japan as modern and civilized. They set out to change their image. Kimonos, swords, and top-knots were abandoned for frock coats, top hats, and short haircuts. The Meiji emperor appeared publicly in western-style military uniforms. Leading Japanese officials gathered in the new Rokumeikan, or Deer Cry Pavilion, to play billiards or attend fancy-dress balls complete with western drinks and music. They shocked traditionalists by often attending these balls with their wives.

Activity
Interpreting the Evidence

Use these additional questions to generate class discussion.

1. **Critical Thinking: Analyzing Information** Which industry dropped in rank from second to fourth in terms of amount of money invested between 1883 and 1893? *(trading)*

2. **Critical Thinking: Making Inferences** Why was manufacturing invested in more heavily than agriculture in the last two decades of the century? *(The government had made it a major priority for the nation to develop western-style industry.)*

Skills Tip

In charts such as this one, read across to compare spending in the same category for different years and read down to compare spending in the same year for different categories. The Skills Handbook in the front of the book has a lesson that will help students with this feature.

Skills Assessment

ANSWERS **1.** A **2.** H **3.** Possible answers: what goods were manufactured, what resources Japan had. Answers should be well supported.

Skills Tip

In tables containing numbers, a dash is often used to indicate a value of zero or to indicate that no value is given.

Resource Directory

Teaching Resources

Synthesizing Information Chapter Extension Activities booklet, p. 63
History Through Literature *Under Reconstruction,* History Through Literature booklet, pp. 55–56

Meiji Restoration

The young emperor began a long reign known as the Meiji (MAY jee) restoration. This period, which lasted from 1868 to 1912, was a major turning point in Japanese history. *Meiji* means "enlightened rule." The Meiji reformers, who ruled in the emperor's name, were determined to strengthen Japan. Their goal was summarized in their motto, "A rich country, a strong military."

The new leaders set out to study western ways, adapt them to Japanese needs, and eventually beat westerners at their own game. In 1871, members of the government traveled overseas to learn about western governments, economies, technology, and customs. The government brought experts from western countries to Japan and sent young samurai to study abroad.

Reforms Under the Meiji

The Meiji reformers faced an enormous task. They were committed to replacing the rigid feudal order with a completely new political and social system and to building a modern industrial economy. Change did not come easily. In the end, however, Japan adapted foreign ideas with amazing speed and success.

Government The reformers wanted to create a strong central government, equal to those of western powers. After studying various European governments, they adapted the German model. In 1889, the emperor issued the Meiji constitution. It set forth the principle that all citizens were equal before the law. Like the German system, however, it gave the emperor autocratic power. A legislature, or Diet, was formed, made up of one elected house and one house appointed by the emperor. Additionally, voting rights were sharply limited.

Japan then established a western-style bureaucracy with separate departments to supervise finance, the army, the navy, and education. To strengthen the military, it turned to western technology and ended the special privilege of samurai. In the past, samurai alone were warriors. In modern Japan, as in the West, all men were subject to military service.

Economic Reforms Meiji leaders made the economy a major priority. They encouraged Japan's business class to adopt western methods. The government set up a banking system, built railroads, improved ports, and organized a telegraph and postal system.

To get industries started, the government typically built factories and then sold them to wealthy business families who developed them further. With such support, business dynasties like the Kawasaki family soon ruled over industrial empires that rivaled those of the Rockefellers in the United States or the Krupps in Germany. These powerful banking and industrial families were known as zaibatsu (zī baht soo).

By the 1890s, industry was booming. With modern machines, silk manufacturing soared. Shipyards, copper and coal mining, and steel making also helped make Japan an industrial powerhouse. As in other industrial countries, the population grew rapidly, and many peasants flocked to the growing cities for work.

Social Change The constitution ended legal distinctions between classes, thus providing the opportunity for more people to become involved in nation-building. The government set up schools and a university. It hired westerners to teach the new generation modern technology.

Despite the reforms, class distinctions survived in Japan as they did in the West. Also, although literacy increased and some women gained an education, women in general were still assigned a secondary role in society.

The reform of the Japanese family system, and women's position in it, became the topic of major debates in the 1870s. Reformers wanted women to become full partners in the process of nation-building and to learn skills

► **Primary Sources and Literature**

See "Fukuzawa Yukichi: Autobiography" in the Reference Section at the back of this book.

Background
Connections to Today

Zaibatsu The zaibatsu continued to grow and expand until World War II. At the end of the war, the victorious Allies forced them to disband. After a treaty was signed in 1951, however, new industrial combines known as *keiretsu* emerged and became important forces in Japan's economy. The *keiretsu* are often considered direct successors to the old zaibatsu. Today, *keiretsu* such as Mitsubishi enjoy worldwide success.

Human Drama Note

Fukuzawa Yukichi English-speaking Japanese student Fukuzawa Yukichi was an early visitor to the West. In 1860, even before the Meiji restoration, he sailed on the first Japanese steamship to cross the Pacific to California. Later, he traveled in Europe.

In his *Autobiography,* Fukuzawa set out to explain western culture to the Japanese and Japanese culture to the West. Upon visiting a hotel in San Francisco, he and the other Japanese visitors were stunned to find the hotel floor covered with "valuable carpets that in Japan only the more wealthy could buy." Even more shocking, "Upon this costly fabric walked our hosts wearing shoes with which they had come in from the streets!" (At home, the Japanese, who highly value cleanliness, remove their shoes before entering a house.)

Among many bewildering American customs was a dancing party. "To our dismay, we could not make out what they were doing. The ladies and gentlemen seemed to be hopping about the room together. As funny as it was, we knew it would be rude to laugh, and we controlled our expressions with difficulty. . . ."

that would allow them to live on their own. Although the government agreed to some increases in education for women, it dealt harshly with other attempts at change. After 1898, Japanese women were forbidden any political participation and legally were lumped together with minors.

Amazing Success During the Meiji period, Japan modernized with amazing speed. Its success was due to a number of causes. It was a homogeneous society—that is, it had a common culture and language that gave it a strong sense of identity. Economic growth during Tokugawa times had set Japan on the road to development. Also, the Japanese had experience in learning from foreign nations, such as China.

Like other people faced with western imperialism, the Japanese were determined to resist foreign rule. In fact, in the 1890s, Japan was strong enough to force western powers to revise the unequal treaties. By then, it was already acquiring its own overseas empire.

Growing Military Strength

As with western industrial powers, Japan's economic needs fed its imperialist desires. A small island nation, Japan lacked many basic resources that were essential for industrial growth. Yet, spurred by nationalism and a strong ambition to equal the West, Japan built an empire. With its modern army and navy, it maneuvered for power in East Asia.

Japan Gains Power In 1894, competition between Japan and China led to the Sino-Japanese War. Although China had greater resources, Japan had benefited from modernization. To the surprise of China and the West, Japan won easily. It used its victory to gain treaty ports in China and control over the island of Taiwan, thus joining the West in the race for empire.

Ten years later, Japan successfully challenged Russia, its rival for power in Korea and Manchuria. During the Russo-Japanese War, Japan's armies defeated Russian troops in Manchuria, and its navy destroyed almost an entire Russian fleet. For the first time in modern history, an Asian power humbled a European nation. In the 1905 Treaty of Portsmouth, Japan gained control of Korea as well as rights in parts of Manchuria. This foothold on the East Asian mainland would fuel its ambitions.

Competition for Korea Imperialist rivalries put the spotlight on Korea. Located at a crossroads of East Asia, the Korean peninsula was a focus of competition among Russia, China, and Japan.

Although Korea had long been influenced by its powerful neighbor, it had its own traditions and government. Like China and Japan, Korea had shut its doors to foreigners. It did, however, maintain relations with China and sometimes with Japan.

By the 1800s, Korea faced pressure from outsiders. As Chinese power declined, Russia expanded into East Asia. Then, as Japan industrialized, it too eyed Korea. In 1876, Japan used its superior power to force Korea to open its ports to Japanese trade. Faced with similar demands from western powers, the "Hermit Kingdom" had to accept unequal treaties.

As Japan extended its influence in Korea, it came into conflict with China, which still saw Korea as a tributary state. After defeating China and then Russia, Japan made Korea a protectorate. In 1910, it annexed Korea outright, absorbing the kingdom into the Japanese empire.

Japan Rules Korea Japan ruled Korea for 35 years. Like western imperialists, the Japanese set out to modernize their newly acquired territory. They built factories, railroads, and communications systems. Development, however, generally benefited Japan. Under Japanese rule, Koreans produced more rice than ever before, but most of it went to Japan.

The Japanese were as unpopular in Korea as western imperialists were elsewhere. They imposed harsh rule on their colony and deliberately set out to erase the Korean language and identity. Repression bred resentment. And resentment, in turn, nourished a Korean nationalist movement.

Nine years after annexation, a nonviolent protest against the Japanese began on March 1, 1919, and soon spread throughout Korea. The Japanese crushed the uprising and massacred many Koreans. The violence did not discourage people who worked to end Japanese rule. Instead, the March First Movement became a rallying symbol for Korean nationalists.

Looking Ahead

The Koreans would have to wait many years for freedom. By the early 1900s, Japan was the strongest power in Asia. It continued to expand in East Asia during the years that followed, seeking natural resources and territory. In time, Japanese ambitions to control a sphere of influence in the Pacific would put it on a collision course with several western powers, especially Britain and the United States.

Global Connections

The Russo-Japanese War

The Russo-Japanese War began and ended on the sea. On February 19, 1904, Japanese torpedo boats made a surprise attack on part of the Russian fleet, near Manchuria. Most of those ships were wiped out.

The rest of the Russian navy was based in the Baltic Sea, more than 10,000 miles away. The Russian ships began a slow 15-month journey around Africa. When they chugged into the waters of East Asia on May 27, 1905, the Japanese navy attacked again. Japan's faster ships and more accurate gunnery forced the Russians to surrender within a single day.

Theme: Economics and Technology Why were the Japanese forces able to defeat their opponents so easily?

SECTION 1 Assessment

Recall
1. **Identify:** (a) Matthew Perry, (b) Treaty of Kanagawa, (c) Meiji restoration, (d) Russo-Japanese War, (e) Treaty of Portsmouth.
2. **Define:** (a) Diet, (b) zaibatsu, (c) homogeneous society.

Comprehension
3. (a) What problems did Tokugawa Japan face in the early 1800s? (b) Why did Japan end 200 years of seclusion?
4. (a) List three ways in which Japan modernized. (b) Explain how each of these actions helped strengthen Japan so it could resist western pressure.
5. How did Japan demonstrate its growing military strength?

Critical Thinking and Writing
6. **Connecting to Geography** How did the geographic location of Korea make it desirable to both China and Japan?
7. **Predicting Consequences** What might have happened to Japan if the Meiji reformers had not decided to modernize in the late 1800s? Explain.

Activity
Take It to the NET

Use the Internet to research the opening of Japan by Matthew Perry. Then, write a news article for either an American or a Japanese newspaper describing the event.

Chapter 26 **649**

Test Preparation

Have students read the section titled "Japan Rules Korea" on this page, and then answer the question below.

Which of the following events does *not* show how the Japanese modernized Korea?

(A) They repressed Korean culture.

B They built communications systems.

C They built factories and railroads.

D They increased agricultural output.

SECTION 1 Assessment

Recall
1. (a) Matthew Perry, p. 645 (b) Treaty of Kanagawa, p. 645 (c) Meiji restoration, p. 647 (d) Russo-Japanese War, p. 648 (e) Treaty of Portsmouth, p. 648 2. (a) Diet, p. 647 (b) zaibatsu, p. 647 (c) homogeneous society, p. 648

Comprehension
3. (a) corrupt leadership, financial hardship among daimyo and samurai, and peasant unrest because of heavy taxes (b) The Japanese had been humbled by the unequal treaties with western powers. They believed that adopting western technology would help them resist western domination. 4. Possible answers: (a) Japan established a western-style bureaucracy; built modern factories; and developed railroads, ports, and telegraph systems. (b) A western-style bureaucracy enabled the government to direct industry, the military, and education. Modern industries supplied needed military equipment. Improved communication and transportation allowed a quick response to any military threat. 5. It forced ports in China to open, gained control of Taiwan, and defeated the Russians in the Russo-Japanese War.

Critical Thinking and Writing
6. Possible answer: Korea was located at a major crossroads of East Asia. For China, Korea provided a buffer from Japan. For Japan, Korea provided a stepping stone onto the Asian mainland. 7. Possible answer: Japan might have been divided into western spheres of influence. To support this response, students could refer to China's experience.

Activity Rubrics

Share rubrics with students before they write their news articles.

Attempted Article is incomplete.

Minimal Article reflects sufficient research but is poorly written.

Adequate Article has sufficient research, is well written with few mechanical errors, and contains a convincing point of view.

Exemplary Article is well researched, is well written with no mechanical errors, and contains interesting details and a convincing point of view.

Global Connections

ANSWER by combining a surprise attack and using fast, accurate, modern weapons

SECTION 2

Bell Ringer Ask students to read about Phan Thanh Gian, a Vietnamese official who is discussed in the first few paragraphs of Section 2. Have students describe the dilemma that he faced. Then, ask them to describe the course of action that they would take in his situation and to explain the reasons for their decisions.

Reading Focus

■ What impact did European colonization have on Southeast Asia?

■ How did Siam maintain its independence?

■ How did imperialism spread to the Philippines and other Pacific islands?

Taking Notes

Copy this table. As you read, fill in information on imperialism in Asia and the Pacific. To help you get started, portions of the table have been completed.

REGION	IMPERIALIST POWER	REASONS FOR COLONIZATION
INDONESIA	The Netherlands	
MALAYA		Rubber and tin
INDOCHINA		
SIAM		
HAWAII		
PHILIPPINES		

Main Idea Western industrialized powers divided up Southeast Asia in pursuit of raw materials, new markets, and converts to Christianity.

LESSON PLAN

1. Focus Imperialist rivalries in Southeast Asia resulted in the colonization of many countries. Siam, however, remained independent by avoiding conflicts and serving as a neutral zone between British and French colonies. In 1898, the United States annexed Hawaii. It also acquired the Philippines as a result of the Spanish-American War.

2. Instruct Have students work in groups to produce radio broadcasts reporting from different parts of Southeast Asia and the Pacific during the 1800s. Each team should focus on the impact of western imperialism and include newscasts from Burma, Indonesia, Vietnam, Siam, Samoa, Hawaii, and the Philippines. Tell students to include facts about the advance of imperialism as well as interviews with national leaders and people on the street. Have the groups present some of their broadcasts to the class.

3. Assess Encourage each broadcast team to field comments and questions from classmates in the audience.

4. Reteach If students' Assess activity does not reflect adequate understanding of the lesson, you might assign the *Guide to the Essentials* or the *Interactive Student Tutorial CD-ROM* for this section.

Setting the Scene A Vietnamese official, Phan Thanh Gian, faced a dilemma in 1867. The French were threatening to invade. As a patriot, Phan Thanh Gian wanted to resist. But as a devoted follower of Confucius, he was obliged "to live in obedience to reason." And based on the power of the French military, he concluded that the only reasonable course was to surrender. Phan Thanh Gian made his choice with a heavy heart. By avoiding a useless war that would hurt his people, he became a traitor to his king. For that decision, he wrote, "I deserve death."

Leaders throughout Southeast Asia faced the same dilemma during the Age of Imperialism. As they had in Africa, western industrial powers gobbled up the region in their relentless race for raw materials, new markets, and Christian converts.

Europeans Colonize Southeast Asia

Southeast Asia commanded the sea lanes between India and China and had been influenced by both civilizations. From the 1500s through the 1700s, European merchants gained footholds in the region, but most of the area remained independent. This changed in the 1800s. Westerners— notably the Dutch, British, and French—played off local rivalries and used modern armies and technology to colonize much of Southeast Asia.

During the 1600s, the Dutch East India Company gained control of the fabled riches of the Moluccas, or Spice Islands. They then reached out to dominate the rest of Indonesia. The Dutch expected their Southeast Asian colonies to produce profitable crops of coffee and indigo as well as spices.

In the early 1800s, rulers of Burma (present-day Myanmar) clashed with the British, who were expanding eastward from India. In several wars, the Burmese suffered disastrous defeats. They continued to resist British rule, however, even after Britain annexed Burma in 1886.

The British also pushed south through Malaya. The bustling port of Singapore, on the sea route between the Indian Ocean and the China Sea, grew up at the southern tip of the peninsula. Soon, natural resources and profits from Asian trade flowed through Singapore to enrich Britain.

The French, meanwhile, were building an empire on the Southeast Asian mainland. In the early 1800s, French missionaries began winning converts in what is today Vietnam. The region had long been influenced by Confucian traditions. Vietnamese officials tried to suppress Christianity by killing converts and missionary priests.

Resource Directory

Teaching Resources

Creative Teaching Activities Creative Teaching Activities booklet, p. 117

Guided Reading and Review Unit 6 booklet, p. 80

Block Scheduling Support

Have students explore the effects of imperialism on both the ruler and the ruled by reading "Shooting an Elephant," George Orwell's famous essay about his experiences as a police officer in Burma. He writes about a working elephant that goes on a rampage and kills a laborer. Orwell is expected to kill the animal, but he has mixed feelings about it.

After they read the essay, have small groups debate the proposition: Imperialism has done more good than harm. Tell students to use evidence to support their arguments.

As with Burma and the British, the Vietnamese misjudged European power. In the 1860s, the French invaded and seized a chunk of Vietnam. Over the next decades, they added more lands, eventually seizing all of Vietnam, Laos, and Cambodia. The French and other westerners referred to these holdings as French Indochina.

By the 1890s, Europeans controlled most of Southeast Asia. They introduced modern technology and expanded commerce and industry. They set up new enterprises to mine tin and harvest rubber, brought in new crops of corn and cassava, and built harbors and railroads. But these changes benefited Europeans far more than the people of Southeast Asia.

Many Chinese migrated to Southeast Asia to escape hardship and turmoil at home and to benefit from growing economic opportunities. Despite persistent local resentment, these communities of "overseas" Chinese formed vital networks in trade, banking, and other economic activities.

Siam Survives

Sandwiched between British-ruled Burma and French Indochina lay the kingdom of Siam—present-day Thailand. King Mongkut, who ruled from 1851 to 1868, did not underestimate western power. Before inheriting the throne, he had studied foreign languages and read widely on modern science and mathematics. He thus had a greater understanding of the West than many other Asian rulers.

Although Mongkut had to accept some unequal treaties, Siam escaped becoming a European colony. He and his son, Chulalongkorn, set Siam on the road to modernization. They reformed government, modernized the army, and hired western experts to train Thais in the new technology. They abolished slavery and gave women some choice in marriage. As Siam modernized, Chulalongkorn bargained to remove the unequal treaties.

In the end, both Britain and France saw the advantage of making Siam a buffer, or neutral zone, between them. In the early 1900s, they guaranteed its independence.

Imperial Powers in the Pacific

In the 1800s, the industrial powers began to take an interest in the islands of the Pacific.* At first, American, French, and British whaling and sealing ships looked for bases to take on supplies. Missionaries, too, moved into the Pacific region and opened the way for political involvement.

In 1878, the United States secured an unequal treaty from Samoa, gaining rights such as extraterritoriality and a naval station. Other nations gained similar agreements. As their rivalry increased, the United States, Germany, and Britain agreed to a triple protectorate over Samoa.

From the mid-1800s, American sugar growers pressed for power in Hawaii. When the Hawaiian queen Liliuokalani (lee lee oo oh kah LAH nee)

*The thousands of islands splashed across the Pacific are known as Oceania. Besides Australia and New Zealand, Oceania includes three regions: Melanesia, Micronesia, and Polynesia. (See the map in the Reference Section at the back of this book.)

SECTION 2 Assessment

Recall
1. (a) French Indochina, p. 651
(b) Mongkut, p. 651 (c) Liliuokalani, p. 651
(d) Spanish-American War, p. 652
(e) Emilio Aguinaldo, p. 652

Comprehension
2. Dutch—used trade to expand from island strongholds; British—used force and trade; French—missionaries spread religion while merchants spread trade
3. Siam avoided incidents that might provoke invasion. Its leaders reformed the government, modernized the army, and hired western experts to teach them about new technology. They also abolished slavery and expanded rights for women. 4. (a) secured an unequal treaty with the Samoans (b) annexed Hawaii after American planters in Hawaii overthrew the queen (c) defeated Spain in the Spanish-American War and crushed a Filipino rebellion

Critical Thinking and Writing
5. Possible answers: (a) As in Africa, the western powers used military force and treaties to gain control of Southeast Asia. (b) One difference is that the United States acquired the Philippines in Southeast Asia, but had no colonies in Africa.
6. Possible answer: All three areas are along strategic trade and naval routes between Asia and Europe.

Activity Rubrics

Share rubrics with students before they create their time lines.

Attempted Time line does not show the main events in Southeast Asia and the Pacific during the Age of Imperialism.

Minimal Time line shows fewer than five of the main events in Southeast Asia and the Pacific during the Age of Imperialism.

Adequate Time line shows five to ten of the main events in Southeast Asia and the Pacific during the Age of Imperialism and is neatly done.

Exemplary Time line shows ten or more of the main events of Southeast Asia and the Pacific during the Age of Imperialism, is accurate and is visually pleasing.

Biography

ANSWER He gave his life to help win independence for the people of his country.

---

tried to reduce foreign influence, American planters overthrew her in 1893. They then asked the United States to annex Hawaii, which it did in 1898. Supporters of annexation argued that if the United States did not take Hawaii, Britain or Japan might do so.

Biography

José Rizal 1861–1896

José Rizal was a pacifist and never fought in any battle himself. Still, he inspired other Filipinos to fight for independence from Spain.

Rizal was a talented man. He was a doctor, sculptor, novelist, and philosopher who spoke many languages fluently. He also wrote two novels that criticized Spanish leaders in the Philippines. The books were banned and even burned. The rulers later arrested Rizal as a revolutionary and had him executed by a firing squad. He is still recognized as a martyr of the cause for independence and a national hero.

Theme: Impact of the Individual Why does Rizal's life make him a national hero?

The United States and the Philippines

In the 1500s, Spain had seized the Philippines. Catholic missionaries spread Christianity among the Filipinos, and the Catholic Church gained enormous power and wealth. Many Filipinos accused the Church of abusing its position. By the late 1800s, their anger had fueled strong resistance to Spanish rule. Inspired by leaders such as José Rizal, many Filipinos worked to end Spanish control of the islands.

The United States became involved in the fate of the Philippines almost by accident. In 1898, war broke out between Spain and the United States over Cuba's independence from Spain. During the Spanish-American War, American battleships destroyed the Spanish fleet, which was stationed in the Philippines. Seizing the moment, Filipino leaders declared their independence from Spain. Rebel soldiers threw their support into the fight against Spanish troops.

In return for their help, the Filipino rebels had expected the Americans to recognize their independence. The peace settlement with Spain, however, placed the Philippines under American control.

Bitterly disappointed, Filipino nationalists renewed their struggle. From 1899 to 1901, Filipinos led by Emilio Aguinaldo (ah gee NAHL doh) battled American forces. Thousands of Americans and hundreds of thousands of Filipinos died. In the end, the Americans crushed the rebellion. The United States set out to modernize the Philippines through education, improved health care, economic reform, and construction of dams, roads, railways, and ports. Additionally, the United States promised Filipinos self-rule some time in the future.

Looking Ahead

By 1900, the United States, Britain, France, and Germany had claimed nearly every island in the Pacific. Japan, too, wanted a share of the region. Eventually, it would gain control of German possessions in the Pacific. Japanese territorial expansion would set the stage for a growing rivalry with the United States.

SECTION 2 Assessment

Recall
1. **Identify:** (a) French Indochina, (b) Mongkut, (c) Liliuokalani, (d) Spanish-American War, (e) Emilio Aguinaldo.

Comprehension
2. Compare imperialist policies of the Dutch, British, and French.
3. What steps did Siam take to preserve its independence?
4. Describe how the United States acquired each of the following territories in the Pacific: (a) Samoa, (b) Hawaii, (c) Philippines.

Critical Thinking and Writing
5. **Comparing** Compare the partition of Southeast Asia to the partition of Africa during the Age of Imperialism. (a) How was it similar? (b) How was it different?
6. **Connecting to Geography** Why were the Philippines, Singapore, and Indonesia of strategic value?

Activity

Creating a Time Line Create a time line showing the colonialization of Southeast Asia and the Pacific during the Age of Imperialism.

Resource Directory

Teaching Resources
Section Quiz Unit 6 booklet, p. 81
Creative Teaching Activities Creative Teaching Activities booklet, p. 118
Guided Reading and Review Unit 6 booklet, p. 82

Technology
Interactive Student Tutorial CD-ROM Ch. 26
Computer Test Bank Ch. 26

Reading Focus

- How did Canada achieve self-rule?
- How did European settlement change the course of Australian history?
- How did New Zealand emerge as an independent nation?

Vocabulary

indigenous
confederation
dominion

Taking Notes

Copy this Venn diagram. As you read, fill in the information on the similarities and differences between the colonial experiences of Canada and those of Australia. To help you get started, some entries have been made.

CANADA
- Two distinct populations, British and French

- Set up government based on British model

AUSTRALIA
- Established as penal colony for Britain

Main Idea The British colonies of Canada, Australia, and New Zealand won independence faster and with greater ease than territories in other regions.

Setting the Scene The pattern of imperialism in the British colonies of Australia and New Zealand differed from that in other parts of the world. The indigenous (ihn DIHJ uh nuhs), or original, inhabitants of these regions were relatively few in number, and white settlers quickly subdued and replaced them. Still, the process of "replacement" was as deadly as it had been in the Americas some 200 years earlier.

These two English-speaking colonies, as well as Canada, won independence faster and with greater ease than England's territories in Africa or Asia. One reason was that they, unlike nonwestern peoples, had cultural roots in western-style government. However, western racial attitudes also played a part. Imperialist nations like Britain felt that whites could govern themselves. Nonwhites in places like India were thought to be incapable of shouldering such responsibility.

Canada Achieves Self-Rule

Canada's first European rulers were the French. When France lost Canada to Britain in 1763, thousands of French-speaking settlers remained. After the American Revolution, an estimated 30,000 or more colonists who had remained loyal to Britain fled to Canada. Unlike the French-speaking Catholics, the newcomers were English-speaking and Protestant.

Native Americans formed another strand of the Canadian heritage. In the 1790s, various Native American people still lived in eastern Canada. Others, in the west and the north, remained largely undisturbed by the movement of white settlers.

The Two Canadas To ease ethnic tensions, Britain passed the Canada Act in 1791. It created two provinces: English-speaking Upper Canada (now Ontario) and French-speaking Lower Canada (now Quebec). Each had its own laws, legislature, and royal governor. French traditions and the Catholic Church were protected in Lower Canada, while English traditions and laws guided Upper Canada.

During the early 1800s, unrest grew in both colonies. The people of Upper Canada resented the power held by a small British elite. In Lower Canada, too, people felt that British officials ignored their needs. In 1837, discontent flared into rebellion in both Upper and Lower Canada. "Put down the villains who oppress and enslave our country," cried William Lyon Mackenzie, a leader of the Upper Canada revolt.

Connections to Today

A Quandary for Quebec

Today, travelers to Canada who visit Quebec often feel that they have entered a different country. The French language and culture are evident everywhere, from traffic signs to radio shows.

Many Quebecers want Quebec to become independent. They believe that the cultural differences between French and English speakers are too deep for them to share the same country. They feel allegiance to Quebec rather than to Canada as a whole.

In 1995, a referendum on secession was held in Quebec. The final vote was almost a tie, with 50.5 percent voting against separation and 49.5 percent supporting the idea. Thus, the stage is set for continuing tension.

Theme: Diversity In what ways are Quebecers different from citizens of other Canadian provinces?

Chapter 26 **653**

Background
Global Connections

The Aroostook "War" The borderlands between Canada and the United States, which had been a battleground of the French and Indian War, the American Revolution, and the War of 1812, remained an area of contention into the mid-1800s. In one incident, a border dispute almost caused war between the United States and Canada. The conflict centered on the Aroostook Valley claimed by both Maine and New Brunswick. In 1827, the United States and Britain submitted the dispute for arbitration to the king of the Netherlands. He offered a compromise, which was accepted by Britain but rejected by the United States.

A crisis emerged in 1838 when Canadian lumberjacks entered the disputed region and began lumbering operations. The arrest of an American official and the refusal of the Canadians to leave caused the United States Congress to authorize a force of 50,000 men to respond to the potential emergency. The Canadian governments of New Brunswick and Nova Scotia took similar measures. But war was averted through the mediation of General Winfield Scott, sent by President Martin Van Buren to arrange a truce. The Aroostook War ended without any significant bloodshed, and the issue was finally settled by a treaty in 1842.

Canada, 1867–1914

Skills Assessment

Geography By the end of the 1800s, railroads were moving people from one coast of Canada to the other.

1. **Location** *On the map, locate (a) Quebec, (b) Ontario, (c) Alberta, (d) British Columbia.*
2. **Region** *Which of the provinces on this map was organized last?*
3. **Critical Thinking Drawing Conclusions** *What major geographic feature might have provided an obstacle to large-scale migration before the construction of railroads?*

The Durham Report The British had learned a lesson from the American Revolution. While they hurried to put down the disorder, they sent an able politician, Lord Durham, to study the causes of the unrest. In 1839, the Durham Report called for the two Canadas to be reunited and given control over their own affairs.

In 1840, Parliament passed the Act of Union, a major step toward self-government. It gave Canada an elected legislature to determine domestic policies. Britain kept control of foreign policy and trade.

Dominion of Canada Like the United States, Canada expanded westward in the 1800s. As the country grew, two Canadians, John Macdonald and George Étienne Cartier, urged confederation, or unification, of all Canada's provinces. Like many Canadians, Macdonald and Cartier feared that the United States might try to dominate Canada. A strong union, they felt, would strengthen the nation against United States ambitions and help Canada develop economically.

Britain finally agreed. In 1867, it passed the British North America Act of 1867, creating the Dominion of Canada. It united four provinces into a dominion, or self-governing nation. Six additional provinces later joined the union.

As a dominion, Canada had its own parliament, modeled on that of Britain. By 1900, Canada had also been granted some control over its own foreign policy. Still, although self-governing, Canada maintained close ties with the British monarchy.

Expansion John Macdonald, Canada's first prime minister, encouraged expansion across the continent. To unite the far-flung regions of Canada, he called for a transcontinental railroad. In 1885, the Canadian Pacific Railway opened, linking eastern and western Canada. Wherever the railroad went,

Skills Assessment

ANSWERS **1.** Review locations with students. **2.** Alberta and Saskatchewan were both organized in 1905. **3.** Rocky Mountains settlers followed. It moved people and products, such as timber and manu-factured goods, across the country.

As in the United States, westward expansion destroyed the way of life of Native Americans in Canada. Most were forced to sign treaties giving up their lands. Some resisted. Louis Riel led a revolt of the métis, people of mixed Native American and European descent. Many were French-speaking Catholics who accused the government of stealing their land and trying to destroy their language and religion. Government troops put down the uprising and executed Riel.

Immigration In the late 1800s and early 1900s, immigration increased as people flooded into Canada from across Europe and Asia. Newcomers from Germany, Italy, Poland, Russia, Ukraine, China, and Japan enriched Canada economically and culturally.

By 1914, Canada was a flourishing nation. Two issues continued to plague it, however. First, French-speaking Canadians were determined to preserve their separate heritage, making it hard for Canadians to create a single national identity. Second, the United States exerted a powerful eco-nomic and cultural influence that threatened to dominate its neighbor to the north. Both issues have continued to affect Canada to the present day.

Europeans in Australia

The Dutch in the 1600s were the first Europeans to reach Australia—the world's smallest continent. In 1770, Captain James Cook claimed Australia for Britain. For a time, however, it remained too distant to attract European settlers.

The First Settlers Like most regions claimed by imperialist powers, Australia had long been inhabited by other people. The first settlers had reached Australia perhaps 50,000 years earlier, probably from Southeast Asia, and spread across the continent. Cut off from the larger world, the Aborigines, as Europeans later called them,* lived in small hunting and food-gathering bands, much as their Stone Age ancestors had. Aborigine groups spoke as many as 250 distinct languages. When white settlers arrived in Australia, the indigenous population suffered disastrously.

A Penal Colony Events halfway around the world in North America and Britain ended Australia's isolation and brought Europeans to the island continent. During the 1700s, Britain had sent convicts to its North American colonies, especially to Georgia. The American Revolution closed that outlet just when the Industrial Revolution was disrupting British society. Prisons in London and other cities were jammed with poor people arrested for crimes such as stealing food or goods to pawn, agitating against the government, or murder.

To fulfill the need for prisons, Britain made Australia into a penal colony. The first ships, carrying about 700 convicts, arrived in Botany Bay, Australia, in 1788. The men, women, and children who survived the gruel-ing eight-month voyage faced more hardships on shore. Many were city dwellers with no farming skills. Under the brutal discipline of soldiers, work gangs cleared land for the settlement.

Among these first arrivals was Matthew Everingham, who at the age of 14 had been sentenced to seven years in Australia for stealing two books.

---

*Aborigine was a word used by Europeans to denote the earliest people to live in a place. Today, many Australian Aborigines call themselves Kooris.

Primary Source

A Convict's Life
Convicts in the Australian penal colonies found that the attitudes of their masters determined the quality of their lives. Here, a son describes his father's life as a shepherd:

"He became a dreadful spectacle . . . weak and helpless as a child. . . . After my father had been out in the bush from sunrise to sunset, he had then to retire for repose to the watchbox, 6 feet by 18 inches, with a small bed and one blanket, where he could lie and gaze upon the starry heavens, and where the wind blew in at one end and out of the other, with nothing to ward off the pitiless storm. . . . Besides this he had to walk four miles [at night] for his rations."

—John Standfield, quoted in *The Fatal Shore* (Hughes)

Skills Assessment

Primary Source Why did a convict-shepherd have such a terrible life in Australia?

Background
Biography

William Bligh William Bligh served as a sailing master for Captain James Cook on his last voyage of exploration. Bligh later became captain of the *Bounty*. His mission was to sail to Tahiti, pick up a cargo of breadfruit trees, and bring them to British colonies in the West Indies, where, it was hoped, the plants could be used to feed the enslaved Africans working on plantations. In April 1789, mutineers set Bligh and 18 others adrift in an open boat. Bligh navigated the boat more than 3,600 miles (5,800 km) to Timor and on the way charted part of Australia's northeast coast.

After service under Admiral Horatio Nelson in the wars with France, Bligh was appointed in 1805 as governor of New South Wales in Australia. There, his vigorous attempts to combat an illegal rum trade and other forms of corruption resulted once again in mutiny. This time, the mutineers were army officers. They ruled New South Wales and kept Bligh under house arrest for about a year. In 1810, they finally sent Bligh back to England, where he eventually became a vice admiral.

Background
Global Connections

Threats to the Environment The European settlers who came to Australia brought rabbits with them, and in so doing unleashed an ecological nightmare. Without any natural predators in Australia, the rabbits lived up to their reputation and multiplied rapidly. Their numbers became so great that they soon competed with humans for available vegetation and crops. During the 1900s, the Australian government launched several wars of extermination against the massive rabbit population.

Skills Assessment

Geography Australia is both a continent and a country. Australia and its neighbor New Zealand feature a great variety of landforms.

1. **Location** On the map, locate **(a)** Great Barrier Reef, **(b)** Great Victoria Desert, **(c)** Central Lowlands, **(d)** Tasmania.
2. **Region** **(a)** In which region was gold found? **(b)** What geographic features did people encounter during the 1851 gold rush?
3. **Critical Thinking Drawing Conclusions** How does the map help you conclude that the population of Australia is not evenly distributed?

Despite illness and beatings during the course of his sentence, Everingham continued to have hope for the future:

> "I have now two years and seven months to remain a convict and then I am at liberty to act as a free-born Englishman ought to. . . . I am yet but young, only 19. If my health is spared I shall not be one jot the worse for being transported."
> —Matthew Everingham, quoted in "Children of the First Fleet," *National Geographic*

Everingham later married another convict, Elizabeth Rimes, and stayed in Australia. Their descendants, like those of other convicts and early settlers, carved out farms. Some prospered in their new homeland.

Into the Outback In the early 1800s, Britain encouraged free citizens to emigrate to Australia by offering them land and tools. As the newcomers occupied coastal lands, they thrust aside or killed the Aborigines. After settlers found that sheepherding was suited to the land and climate, a prosperous wool industry grew up in Australia.

In 1851, a gold rush in eastern Australia brought a population boom. Many gold hunters stayed on to become ranchers and farmers. They pushed into the rugged interior known as the Outback, displacing the Aborigines and carving out huge sheep ranches and wheat farms. By the late 1800s, Australia had won a place in a growing world economy.

Achieving Self-Government Like Canada, Australia was made up of separate colonies scattered around the continent. During the Age of Imperialism, Britain worried about interference from other powers. To counter this threat and to boost development, it responded to Australian

Skills Assessment

ANSWERS **1.** Review locations with students. **2. (a)** Western Plateau and the Great Victoria Desert **(b)** mountains **3.** Most of the cities are located along the coast.

Resource Directory

Teaching Resources
Viewpoint Activity *Australia's Convict Colonists,* Unit 6 booklet, p. 90
Section Quiz Unit 6 booklet, p. 83
Technology
Interactive Student Tutorial CD-ROM Ch. 26
Computer Test Bank Ch. 26

demands for self-rule. In 1901, Britain helped the colonies unite into the independent Commonwealth of Australia. The new country kept its ties to Britain by recognizing the British monarch as its head of state.

The Australian constitution drew on both British and American models. Like the United States Constitution, it set up a federal system that limited the power of the central government. As in Britain, Australia's executive is a prime minister chosen by the majority party in Parliament. Unlike Britain and the United States, Australia quickly granted women the right to vote. It also was the first nation to introduce the secret ballot.

New Zealand

Far to the southeast of Australia lies New Zealand. In 1769, Captain Cook claimed its islands for Britain. Missionaries landed there in 1814 to convert the local people, the Maoris, to Christianity.

Maori Struggles Unlike Australia, where the Aborigines were spread thinly across a large continent, the Maoris were concentrated in a smaller area. They were descended from seafaring people who had reached New Zealand from Polynesia in the 1200s. The Maoris were settled farmers. They were also determined to defend their land.

Missionaries were followed by white settlers, who were attracted by the mild climate and good soil. These settlers introduced sheep and cattle and were soon exporting wool, mutton, and beef. In 1840, Britain annexed New Zealand.

As colonists poured in, they took over more and more of the land, leading to fierce wars with the Maoris. Many Maoris died in the struggle. Still more perished from disease, alcoholism, and other misfortunes that followed European colonization.

By the 1870s, resistance crumbled. The Maori population had fallen drastically, from 250,000 to less than 50,000. Only in recent years has the Maori population started to grow once more.

Self-Government Like settlers in Australia and Canada, white New Zealanders sought self-rule. In 1907, they won independence, with their own parliament, prime minister, and elected legislature. They, too, preserved close ties to the British empire.

New Zealand pioneered in several areas of democratic government. In 1893, it became the first nation to give suffrage to women. Later, it was in the forefront of other social reforms, passing laws to guarantee old-age pensions and a minimum wage for all workers.

Did You Know?

The Mutiny on the *Bounty*

In 1808, an American ship sailing in the South Pacific unexpectedly came upon Pitcairn Island, about 3,000 miles east of New Zealand. To the American crew's amazement, many of the people on the island spoke English. They also had an unusual story to tell. They were the children of crew members of the *Bounty*, a British trading ship. The crew had mutinied against their harsh captain, William Bligh, more than 20 years before.

Today, the *Bounty* descendants continue to live on Pitcairn Island. The story of that mutiny and its aftermath has been the subject of several books and popular movies.

Theme: Geography and History Why do you think the mutineers stayed in the South Pacific instead of returning to England?

SECTION 3 Assessment

Recall
1. **Identify:** (a) Upper Canada, (b) Lower Canada, (c) British North America Act, (d) Aborigines, (e) Maoris.
2. **Define:** (a) indigenous, (b) confederation, (c) dominion.

Comprehension
3. What steps led to Canadian self-rule?
4. How did the British settle Australia?

5. Why did Maoris fight colonists in New Zealand?

Critical Thinking and Writing
6. **Analyzing Information** Why might young nations like Australia and New Zealand have been willing to grant women the right to vote before European nations did so?
7. **Synthesizing Information** What ethnic tensions did Australia, Canada, and New Zealand face?

Activity
Take It to the NET

Use the Internet to research the British Commonwealth. Then, write a report identifying the member countries and the purpose of the organization.

Chapter 26 **657**

Human Drama Note

Prestige and Power In the strictly hierarchical class system of traditional Maori society, woodcarvers held a position of power and respect. Their sculptures represented religious visions and helped the community to gain access to powerful gods and ancestors. The *rangatira,* the highest class of Maori society, claimed special woodcarving skills and a close relationship to the gods. All *rangatira* men were expected to develop an aptitude for carving. The younger men learned their craft by serving as apprentices to relatives who were master carvers. Thus, the *rangatira* class was able to preserve its political influence and prestige. As a sign of their upper-class status, Maori wood carvers were tattooed with complex spiral designs.

Did You Know?

ANSWER They might have faced prosecution if they had returned, or they may have been unable to return.

Reading Focus

- What political and economic problems faced new Latin American nations?

- How did Mexico struggle for stability?

- How did the United States influence Latin America?

Vocabulary

regionalism
caudillo
economic dependence
peonage

Taking Notes

Copy this concept web. As you read, fill in the major problems facing Latin American countries during the 1800s. To help you get started, parts of the diagram have been completed.

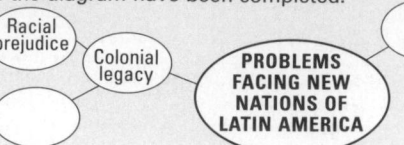

Racial prejudice — Colonial legacy — **PROBLEMS FACING NEW NATIONS OF LATIN AMERICA**

Main Idea The economy of Latin America became dependent on industrialized nations for investment, technology, and manufactured goods.

Setting the Scene The new technology of the Industrial Revolution allowed European nations to import goods from around the world. Meat, which spoiled easily and traditionally required drying before being transported, could now be shipped across the globe in refrigerated vessels. One observer noted: "Great Britain supplies Brazil with its steam and sailing ships, and paves and repairs its streets, lights its cities with gas, . . . carries its mail." These and other developments contributed to the intertwining of nations that might be thousands of miles apart.

During the Age of Imperialism, Latin American nations found their economies increasingly dependent on those of more developed countries. Britain, and later the United States, invested heavily in Latin America.

A City in Brazil
By 1900, the city of Rio de Janeiro, Brazil (below), was a bustling modern seaport. Yet much of the nation's wealth flowed out of the harbor and across the ocean to Europe.

Theme: Global Interaction Why might industrialized nations be eager to invest in Latin American countries?

Lingering Political Problems

Simón Bolívar had hoped to create strong ties among the nations of Latin America. After all, most people shared a common language, religion, and cultural heritage. But feuds among leaders, geographic barriers, and local nationalism shattered that dream of unity. In the end, 20 separate nations emerged.

These new nations wrote constitutions modeled on that of the United States. They set up republics with elected legislatures. During the 1800s, however, most Latin American nations were plagued by revolts, civil war, and dictatorships.

Colonial Legacy Many problems had their origins in colonial rule, as independence barely changed the existing social and political hierarchy. Creoles simply replaced peninsulares as the ruling class. The Roman Catholic Church kept its privileged position and still controlled huge amounts of land.

For most people—mestizos, mulattoes, blacks, and Indians—life did not improve after independence. The new constitutions guaranteed equality before the law, but deep-rooted inequalities remained. Voting rights were limited. Racial prejudice was widespread, and land remained in the hands of a few. Owners of haciendas ruled their great estates, and the peasants who worked them, like medieval European lords.

Instability With few roads and no tradition of unity, the new nations were weakened by regionalism, loyalty to a local area. Local strongmen, called *caudillos,* assembled private armies to resist the central government. At times, popular *caudillos* gained national power. They looted the treasury, ignored the constitution, and ruled as dictators. Power struggles led to frequent revolts that changed little except the name of the leader. In the long run, power remained in the hands of a privileged few who had no desire to share it.

As in Europe, the ruling elite in Latin America were divided between conservatives and liberals. Conservatives defended the old social order, favored press censorship, and strongly supported the Catholic Church. Liberals backed laissez-faire economics, religious toleration, greater access to education, and freedom of the press. Liberals saw themselves as enlightened supporters of progress but often showed little concern for the needs of the majority of the people.

The Economics of Dependence

Under colonial rule, mercantilist policies made Latin America economically dependent on Spain and Portugal. Colonies sent raw materials such as sugar, cotton, or precious metals to the parent country and had to buy manufactured goods from them. Strict laws kept colonists from trading with other countries or building local industries that might compete with the parent country.

After independence, this pattern changed very little. The new republics did adopt free trade, welcoming all comers. Britain and the United States rushed into the new markets, replacing Spain as the chief trading partners with Latin American nations. But the region remained as economically dependent as before.

Economic dependence occurs when less-developed nations export raw materials and commodities to industrial nations and import manufactured goods, capital, and technological know-how. The relationship is unequal because the more developed—and wealthier—nation can control prices and the terms of trade.

Foreign Influence In the 1800s, foreign goods flooded Latin America, creating large profits for foreigners and for a handful of local business people. Foreign investment, which could yield enormous profits, was often accompanied by interference. Investors from Britain, the United States, and other nations might pressure their own governments to take action if political events or reform movements in a Latin American country seemed to threaten their interests.

Economic Growth After 1850, some Latin American economies did grow. With foreign capital, they were able to develop mining and agriculture. Chile exported copper and nitrates, and Argentina expanded livestock and wheat production. Brazil exported coffee and rubber as well as sugar. By the early 1900s, both Venezuela and Mexico were developing important oil industries.

Throughout the region, foreigners invested in modern ports and railroads to carry goods from the interior to coastal cities. As in the United States, European immigrants poured into Latin America. The newcomers helped to promote economic activity, and a small middle class emerged.

Thanks to trade, investment, technology, and migration, Latin American nations moved into the world economy. Yet development was limited. The tiny elite at the top benefited from the economic upturn, but very little trickled down to the masses of people at the bottom. The poor earned too little to buy consumer goods. Without a strong demand, many industries failed to develop.

Primary Source

Imitating European Fashions
The wealthy in Brazil in the late 1800s regarded European goods and culture as superior to their own. Here, a Brazilian writer describes how the elite of his country copied British ways:

"At that time . . . Brazil did not manufacture a yard of silk, a shoe, a spool of thread; everything was imported. . . . Men's clothing for a tropical climate was made of English wool suitable for life in the unheated homes of an English winter. I asked myself: how did they stand the heat? The ladies when they took off their shoes at home used slippers of heavy wool, as if they were in Siberia. . . . Except for the poor, I never saw in the Pernambuco [his hometown] of my time anyone dressed in light clothing."

—Gilbert Amado,
História da Minha Infância

Skills Assessment

Primary Source Why did the elite in Pernambuco dress so impractically?

Background
Daily Life

The *Gauchos* On the *pampas,* or grasslands, of Argentina, *gauchos,* or cowboys, rode the range and herded cattle and horses. Their legendary pastimes, recorded in literature and song, included gambling, drinking, singing, playing the guitar, and fighting Native Americans. The tools of their trade were the lasso, knife, and *bola*—a device consisting of leather cords and three stones or iron balls. A *gaucho* would hurl the *bola* at an animal so that it would wrap around its legs and immobilize it. *Gauchos* lived in simple mud huts roofed with grass. They slept on beds made of hides and sat on stools made from the bones of steers. While the men took care of the horses and cattle, women sheared sheep, milked cows, wove cloth, grew corn, and cared for the children.

Block Scheduling Support

As a reinforcement activity, assign students to construct a time line documenting United States involvement in Latin America during the 1800s and early 1900s. Have students review the last two pages of this section and make a list of significant events and dates. They should then accurately place the events and dates from their list on a time line. Remind students to include benchmark dates at equal intervals along the time line. Finally, ask them to write a brief description for each event to accompany the completed time line. ✳

Primary Source

ANSWER They wanted to show their high class by imitating British people's clothes and customs.

Legend:
- United States possessions
- Under United States influence
- British possessions
- Dutch possessions
- French possessions
- Fishing
- Timber
- Bananas
- Coffee
- Sugar
- Cacao
- Tobacco

UNITED STATES

ATLANTIC OCEAN

Gulf of Mexico

MEXICO

BAHAMA ISLANDS (Br.)

Grand Cayman / CAYMAN IS. (Br.) / Little Cayman

CUBA

DOMINICAN REPUBLIC

HAITI

JAMAICA

PUERTO RICO

U.S. VIRGIN ISLANDS

ANTIGUA (Br.)

GUADELOUPE (Fr.)

DOMINICA

MARTINIQUE (Fr.)

ST. LUCIA

BARBADOS

ST. VINCENT

GRENADA

TOBAGO

TRINIDAD

BRITISH HONDURAS

Caribbean Sea

DUTCH ANTILLES

Aruba Curaçao Bonaire

GUATEMALA

HONDURAS

EL SALVADOR

NICARAGUA

PACIFIC OCEAN

COSTA RICA

CANAL ZONE

PANAMA

VENEZUELA

BRITISH GUIANA

DUTCH GUIANA

FRENCH GUIANA

COLOMBIA

Azimuthal Equal Area Projection

0   200   400 Miles

0   200   400 Kilometers

Skills Assessment

Geography In the early 1900s, foreign governments often intervened in the Caribbean to protect business interests there.

1. **Location** On the map, locate **(a)** Caribbean Sea, **(b)** Cuba, **(c)** Canal Zone, **(d)** Honduras.
2. **Place** **(a)** Which country controlled Martinique? **(b)** Name two United States possessions. **(c)** Which islands were controlled by the Dutch?
3. **Critical Thinking** **Applying Information** Why did the United States have a particularly strong interest in Caribbean affairs?

Mexico's Struggle for Stability

During the 1800s, each Latin American country followed its own course. In this section, we will explore the experiences of Mexico as an example of the challenges facing Latin American nations.

Large landowners, army leaders, and the Catholic Church dominated Mexican politics. However, bitter battles between conservatives and liberals led to revolts and the rise of dictators. Deep social divisions separated wealthy creoles from mestizos and Indians who lived in desperate poverty.

Santa Anna and War Between 1833 and 1855, an ambitious and cunning *caudillo*, Antonio López de Santa Anna, gained and lost power many times. At first, he posed as a liberal reformer. Soon, however, he reversed his stand and crushed efforts at reform.

In Mexico's northern territory of Texas, discontent grew. Settlers from the United States and other countries began an independence movement. In 1835, American settlers and some Mexicans in Texas revolted. The next year they set up an independent republic. In 1845, the United States annexed Texas. Mexicans saw this act as a declaration of war. In the fighting that followed, the United States invaded and defeated Mexico. In the treaty ending the war, Mexico lost almost half its territory. This defeat shook the creole ruling class and triggered new violence between conservatives and liberals.

La Reforma In 1855, Benito Juárez (WAHR ehz) and other liberals seized power and opened an era of reform known as La Reforma. Juárez, a Zapotec Indian, offered hope to the oppressed people of Mexico. He and his fellow reformers revised the Mexican constitution to strip the military of power and end the special privileges of the Church. They ordered the Church to sell unused lands to peasants.

660 *Chapter 26*

Skills Assessment

ANSWERS **1.** Review locations with students. **2. (a)** France **(b)** U.S. Virgin Islands, Puerto Rico **(c)** Dutch Antilles **3.** Many Caribbean islands were near Florida.

Resource Directory

Teaching Resources
Primary Source Activity *Jose Martí's "Our America,"* Unit 6 booklet, p. 89

Although conservatives resisted La Reforma and unleashed a civil war, Juárez was elected president in 1861. He used his new office to expand reforms. His opponents turned to Europe for help. In 1863, Napoleon III sent troops to Mexico and set up Austrian archduke Maximilian as emperor.

For four years, Juárez led Mexicans in battle against conservative and French forces. When France withdrew its troops, Maximilian was captured and shot. In 1867, Juárez was returned to power. Although he tried to renew reform, opponents resisted. Juárez, who died in office in 1872, never achieved all the reforms he envisioned. He did, however, help unite Mexico, bring mestizos into political life, and separate church and state.

Growth and Oppression After Juárez died, General Porfirio Díaz, a hero of the war against the French, gained power. From 1876 to 1880 and 1884 to 1911, he ruled as a dictator. In the name of "Order and Progress," he strengthened the army, local police, and central government. Any opposition was brutally crushed.

Under his harsh rule, Mexico made impressive economic advances. It built railroads, increased foreign trade, developed some industry, and expanded mining. Growth, however, had a high cost. Capital for development came from foreign investors, to whom Díaz granted special rights. He also let wealthy landowners buy up Indian lands.

The rich prospered, but most Mexicans remained poor. Many Indians and mestizos fell into peonage to their employers. In the peonage system, hacienda owners would give workers advances on their wages and require them to stay on the hacienda until they had paid back what they owed. Wages remained low, and workers were rarely able to repay the hacienda owner. Many children died in infancy. Others worked 12-hour days and never learned to read or write.

In the early 1900s, pressure mounted for real change. Middle-class Mexicans demanded democracy. Urban and rural workers joined protests and strikes. In 1910, Mexico plunged into revolution. It was the first true social revolution in Latin America.

The Influence of the United States

As nations like Mexico tried to build stable governments, a neighboring republic, the United States, was expanding across North America. At first, the young republics in the Western Hemisphere looked favorably on each other. Bolívar praised the United States as a "model of political virtues and moral enlightenment." In time, however, Latin American nations felt threatened by the "Colossus of the North," the giant power that cast its shadow over the entire hemisphere.

The Monroe Doctrine In the 1820s, Spain plotted to recover its American colonies. Britain opposed any move that might close the door to trade with Latin America. It asked the United States to join it in a statement opposing any new colonization of the Americas.

President James Monroe, however, wanted to avoid any "entangling alliance" with Britain. Acting alone, in 1823 he issued the Monroe Doctrine. "The American continents," it declared, "are henceforth not to be considered as subjects for future colonization by any European powers." The United States lacked the military power to enforce the doctrine. But knowledge that Britain was willing to use its strong navy to support the doctrine discouraged European interference. For more than a century, the Monroe Doctrine would be the key to United States policy in the Americas.

Expansion As a result of the war with Mexico, in 1848 the United States acquired the thinly populated regions of northern Mexico, including the Colorado River valley and California. The victory fed dreams of future

Global Connections

The Monroe Doctrine in Action

The statement of President Monroe has been interpreted many different ways since 1823. In 1845, President Polk used the doctrine to lay claim to all of the disputed Oregon territory and also to warn European powers not to interfere in the Mexican War of 1846–1848. In the early 1900s, President Theodore Roosevelt claimed that the Monroe Doctrine gave the United States the right to exercise an "international police power."

In 1939, the interpretation of the doctrine was narrowed. President Franklin Roosevelt declared that the doctrine only warranted opposition to European interference in the Western Hemisphere, not to United States interference in the affairs of other countries.

Theme: Global Interaction
Why would presidents interpret the Monroe Doctrine differently at different times?

Chapter 26 **661**

Background
Connections to Art

Artistic Opposition Although it was practically impossible to oppose the Díaz dictatorship on a political level, one artist managed to mount a continuous attack through his caricatures and drawings. José Guadalupe Posada, a graphic artist and printmaker, produced more than 20,000 illustrations depicting social conditions and satirizing the actions of the Díaz government. In his drawings, Posada used an expressionistic style that was characterized by violent images and distortion. Posada was a major influence on the generation of artists who followed him, including Diego Rivera and José Orozco.

Reading Strategy
Reinforcing Key Ideas

After they read the section, ask students to write a sentence summarizing the major problems faced by Latin American countries during the 1800s. If students completed the Taking Notes activity described at the beginning of this section, tell them to use their completed concept webs to help them write their sentences. If not, ask students to make a list of the problems that Latin American countries faced and use it to write their summarizing sentences. *(Less Advanced Readers)*

Human Drama Note

Hoy Decimos Basta! **(Today We Say Enough Is Enough!)** On January 1, 1994, a group of primarily indigenous men and women took advantage of government offices being closed for the holiday to seize towns in Chiapas, Mexico. Called *Zapatistas,* they invoked an article of Mexico's 1917 Constitution to declare a revolution against the Mexican government. The Zapatistas demanded better conditions for Mexico's indigenous peoples. Negotiations with the Mexican government have been on and off for several years, with no end to the impasse in sight.

Test Preparation

Have students read the section titled "Santa Anna and War" on the opposite page, and then answer the question below.

Which act by the United States did Mexico perceive as a declaration of war?

A Settlers in Texas began an independence movement.

B The United States invaded Mexico.

C American settlers and some Mexicans in Texas revolted.

D The United States annexed Texas.

Global Connections

ANSWERS Ways of thinking and of viewing the world change from one time period to another.

expansion. Before the century had ended, the United States controlled
much of North America and was becoming involved in overseas conflicts.

For decades, Cuban patriots had battled to free their island from
Spanish rule. As they began to make headway, the United States joined
their cause, declaring war on Spain in 1898. The brief Spanish-American
War ended in a crushing defeat for Spain.

In the peace treaty ending the war, the United States acquired Puerto
Rico in the Caribbean and the Philippines and Guam in the Pacific. Cuba
was granted independence, but in 1901 the United States forced Cubans to
add the Platt Amendment to their constitution. It gave the United States
naval bases in Cuba and the right to intervene in Cuban affairs.

Intervention American investments in Latin America soared in the early
1900s. Citing the need to protect those investments, in 1904 the United
States issued the Roosevelt Corollary to the Monroe Doctrine. Under this
policy, the United States claimed "international police power" in the
Western Hemisphere. When the Dominican Republic failed to pay its foreign debts, the United States sent in troops. It collected customs duties,
paid off the debts, and remained there for years.

In the next decades, the United States sent troops to Cuba, Haiti,
Mexico, Honduras, Nicaragua, and other countries in Central America and
the Caribbean. Like European powers in Africa and Asia, the United States
intervened in the Caribbean to protect American lives and investments.

Panama Canal From the late 1800s, the United States had wanted to
build a canal across Central America. A canal would let the American fleet
move swiftly between the Atlantic and Pacific oceans and protect its coastlines on either side of the continent. It would also greatly reduce the cost of
trade between the two oceans.

Panama, however, belonged to Colombia, which refused to sell the
United States land for the canal. In 1903, the United States backed a revolt
by Panamanians against Colombia. The Panamanians quickly won independence and gave the United States land to build the canal.

The Panama Canal opened in 1914. It was an engineering marvel that
boosted trade and shipping worldwide. To people in Latin America, however, the canal was another example of "Yankee imperialism." In those
years, nationalist feeling in the hemisphere was often expressed as anti-
Americanism. (In 1978, the United States agreed to a series of treaties that
would grant Panama control over the Canal Zone by the year 2000.)

Geography and History

French Failure in Panama

In 1879, even before the United
States envisioned a canal in
Panama, Frenchman Ferdinand de
Lesseps dreamed of completing the
engineering achievement for the
honor of his country. He had built
the Suez Canal in Egypt, but disease and disaster plagued him in
Panama. As fast as De Lesseps
could send engineers and construction workers to Panama, they
died of malaria, yellow fever, and
snakebite. Asked one magazine,
"Is De Lesseps a canal digger or
a grave digger?"

High costs drove his company
into bankruptcy within 10 years. It
would take another 25 years before
American engineers successfully
completed the canal.

 **Theme: Geography
and History** What
problems did De Lesseps
face in Panama that he had
not confronted in Egypt?

SECTION 4 Assessment

Recall
1. **Identify: (a)** Antonio López de
Santa Anna, **(b)** Benito Juárez,
(c) Porfirio Díaz, **(d)** Monroe
Doctrine, **(e)** Roosevelt Corollary.
2. **Define: (a)** regionalism,
(b) *caudillo,* **(c)** economic
dependence, **(d)** peonage.

Comprehension
3. What problems faced new nations
in Latin America?
4. How did imperialism encourage
economic dependence?
5. Describe two ways the United
States influenced Latin America.

Critical Thinking and Writing
6. **Identifying Main Ideas** Reformers
introduced many changes to Latin
America during the late 1800s and
early 1900s. Describe the reforms
and identify those that seem to
have been most successful. Explain.
7. **Defending a Position (a)** Why
might developing nations encourage foreign investment? **(b)** Do
you think foreign investors should
have the right to intervene in another nation's affairs to protect
their investments? Explain.

 ### Activity
Take It to the NET

Use the Internet to
research the building of
the Panama Canal. Write
a diary describing a week
in the life of a worker on
the canal.

Reading Focus

- How did imperialism lead to new economic patterns?

- What was the cultural impact of imperialism?

- How did new political tensions develop as the result of imperialism?

Taking Notes

Copy this concept web. As you read, fill in the information on the impact of imperialism on the different cultures. To help you get started, parts of the diagram have been completed.

Main Idea — Imperialism brought both benefits and challenges to every region of the world.

SECTION **5**

Bell Ringer Tell students that today civil wars disrupt nations in Africa and Asia and that Latin American nations struggle to build stable democracies. Based on what they have learned about imperialism and its effects, ask students to state opinions as to how imperialism may be one cause of civil wars and unstable governments in various parts of the world.

Setting the Scene

In 1900, Rudyard Kipling was among the most popular writers in the English-speaking world. Kipling was born in British-ruled India and, after being educated in England, returned to India as a journalist for a number of years. His stories and poems often glorified imperialism or presented it as a romantic adventure.

Like most British imperialists, Kipling emphasized the differences between what he saw as "exotic" India and his own English culture. In one famous poem, however, he recounted a dramatic clash between equals: a gallant Afghan chief and a heroic British officer. Though enemies, the two men respect each other and act with great nobility and courage. The poem begins and ends with these lines:

> "Oh, East is East, and West is West; and never the
> twain shall meet,
> Till Earth and Sky stand presently at God's great
> Judgment Seat;
> But there is neither East nor West, Border, nor Breed,
> nor Birth,
> When two strong men stand face to face, though
> they come from the ends of the Earth!"
> —Rudyard Kipling, "The Ballad of East and West"

The Age of Imperialism brought confrontations between differing cultures "from the ends of the Earth." By 1900, western nations had unfurled their flags over much of the globe. That expansion set off radical changes that reshaped the lives of subject people from Africa to Southeast Asia and the Pacific. For their western rulers, too, imperialism would bring about dramatic economic, political, and cultural changes.

New Economic Patterns

During the Age of Imperialism, a truly global economy emerged. It was dominated by the industrialized nations of the West, especially the United States, Britain, France, and Germany. From these nations, machine-made goods, investment capital, and technology flowed to the rest of the world. In return, the people of Africa, Asia, and Latin

One Link in a Global Economy

By the early 1900s, imperialism had created a global economy. The coffee grown at this plantation on the island of Java might have ended up in an American or Dutch dining room.

Theme: Economics and Technology Who might profit from this growing global economy?

Chapter 26 663

LESSON PLAN

1. Focus The Age of Imperialism produced a global economy in which industrialized nations provided machine-made goods, investment capital, and technology, and the rest of the world provided agricultural produce, natural resources, and cheap labor. The influence of western culture was both disruptive and beneficial to traditional cultures. Meanwhile, competition for colonies threatened to embroil the leading powers in a major war.

2. Instruct Divide the class into pairs. Have one student in each pair assume the role of an African or Asian who opposes westernization for its disruptive and corruptive influence. Have the other student assume the role of a western colonial official who praises westernization for its uplifting and modernizing influence. Assign each pair to write a dialogue in which they discuss and debate their opposing views on the value of westernization. Invite teams to present their dialogue to the class.

3. Assess Ask students to write three generalizations about the impact of imperialism.

4. Reteach If students' **Assess** activity does not reflect adequate understanding of the lesson, you might assign the *Guide to the Essentials* or the *Interactive Student Tutorial CD-ROM* for this section.

Block Scheduling Support

Remind students that as communications among countries continue to improve, different cultures increasingly influence one another. The United States is a blend of many cultures from many different countries. Conversely, the United States influences other countries, especially in entertainment and technology. Many countries want to curb the enormous influence the United States has globally. Divide the class into small groups to brainstorm the pros and cons of cultural interchanges. Then, have each group make a chart, giving specific examples of both the good and bad aspects of cultural exchanges. Have volunteers from each group share their ideas with the rest of the class.

Caption Answer

Most profits would go to the industrialized nations.

664 Chapter 26

America provided agricultural goods, natural resources, and cheap labor. Most profits from this global exchange went to the industrialized nations.

The demands of the new world economy disrupted traditional local economies in Africa and Asia. As in Europe before the Industrial Revolution, most people on these continents grew and produced goods by hand for local use. Under colonial rule, they were forced to supply products such as rubber, copper, and coffee needed by the industrial world.

Money Economy Western capitalists developed plantations and mines but relied on a steady supply of local labor to work them. At the same time, colonial rulers introduced a money economy that replaced the old barter system that existed in some countries. To cover the expense of governing their colonies, colonial authorities imposed heavy taxes on their subjects. The only way that people could earn money to pay the taxes was by working on plantations, in mines, or on projects such as railroad building.

Families were disrupted as men left their homes and villages to work in distant mines or cities. In southern and eastern Africa, especially, many men became migrant workers. Their departure shattered families and undermined village life as women were left alone to grow food and support their children. In other parts of the world, such as Japan and Latin America, sons were kept at home to farm while daughters were sent to cities to find work as domestics or in the growing textile industry.

Economic Dependency Mass-produced goods from the industrialized world further disrupted traditional economies. India, for example, was seen by Britain as a great market for its goods. It flooded the subcontinent with cheap, factory-made cloth. The British textile industry flourished. Indian weavers who produced cloth by hand, however, could not compete and were ruined. Elsewhere, too, artisan-run businesses and handicraft industries were destroyed.

Local economies that had once been self-sufficient became dependent on the industrial powers, which bought their raw materials and supplied them with manufactured goods. When the demand and prices for crops or minerals were high, colonies prospered. When demand and prices fell, people suffered. In addition, because many workers were producing export crops rather than food for local consumption, famines occurred in lands that had once fed themselves.

Modernization Colonial rule did bring some economic benefits. Westerners laid the groundwork for modern banking systems. They introduced new technology and built modern communication and transportation networks. Capitalists invested huge sums in railroad building to boost the export economy. Railroads linked plantations and mines to ports, which developers also modernized.

From China to Chile, some local leaders and business people benefited from the new economic system. Countries like Argentina, Brazil, and Chile, for example, used export profits to develop industry, buy modern farm equipment, and promote growth.

Cultural Impact

Like many other peoples in history, Europeans were convinced of their own superiority. During the Age of Imperialism, they also believed that they had a mission to "civilize" the world. Cecil Rhodes, a leading promoter of British imperialism, declared: "The more of the world we inhabit the better it is for the human race. . . . If there be a God, I think what he would like me to do is to paint as much of the map of Africa British red as possible."

Westernization As westerners conquered other lands, they pressed subject people to accept "modern" ways. By this, they meant western ideas,

---

Connections to Economics

Writing an Editorial Ask students to imagine that it is the late 1800s, and they are natives of an African or Asian land ruled by a western power. In this colony, they work as editors-in-chief of a local newspaper that opposes imperialism. Their assignment is to write editorials criticizing the economic policies of the western ruling power.

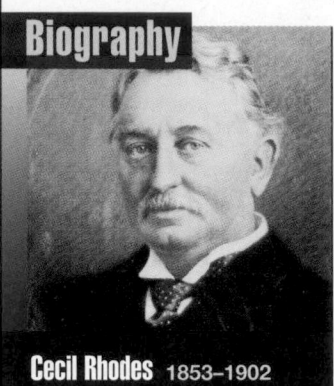

Biography

Cecil Rhodes 1853–1902

Cecil Rhodes arrived in South Africa at age 17, determined to make his fortune. He got off to a slow start. His first venture, a cotton-farming project, failed. Then Rhodes turned to diamond and gold mining. By the age of 40, he had become one of the richest men in the world.

However, money was not his real interest. "For its own sake I do not care for money," he once wrote. "I want the power." Rhodes strongly supported British imperialism in Africa. He helped Britain extend its African empire by 1,000,000 square miles and had an entire British colony named after himself—Rhodesia (now Zimbabwe). Rhodes also helped promote the policy of the separation of races in southern Africa.

Theme: Impact of the Individual How was Cecil Rhodes's desire for power illustrated by his actions?

Biography

ANSWER He pushed to acquire great wealth, to promote the status of the British in Africa, and even to name a country after himself.

government, technology, and culture. Thus, during the Age of Imperialism, modernization and westernization came to be seen as one and the same.*

Many nonwesterners, especially in conquered lands, came to accept a belief in western superiority. The overwhelming successes of the western imperialist nations sapped people's confidence in their own leaders and cultures. To share in the material advantages offered by western society, business and professional people and others who had contact with westerners learned western languages, wore western clothing, adopted western manners, and embraced many western ways.

Other nonwesterners, however, had great misgivings about abandoning their own age old traditions. They greatly resented—and often strongly resisted—western efforts to force new ways on them.

The new imperialism spread western culture around the world. Still, many regions were able to escape much of its influence. In remote areas of Africa, the Middle East, and Asia, many farming villagers and nomadic herders had virtually no contact with westerners. As a result, their lives continued with relatively few changes.

Schools and Hospitals Western culture was often spread by missionaries who built schools and hospitals. They taught children basic literacy and trained young men for jobs in colonial governments.

Western medicine brought many benefits. Missionaries introduced medical breakthroughs such as vaccines and modern methods of hygiene that saved lives. At the same time, however, modern medicine undermined traditional herbalists and local healers, who sometimes possessed useful knowledge of the medicinal value of plants.

Religion Imperialism enabled missionaries to spread their Christian faith across the globe. They had great success in some areas. In southern Africa, for example, Christianity became widespread, although Africans generally adapted its teachings and beliefs to their own traditions. In regions where other world religions or belief systems such as Islam, Hinduism, Buddhism, and Confucianism were deeply rooted, Christian missionaries won fewer converts.

Old and New Ways The pressure to westernize forced colonized people to reevaluate their traditions. In Asia, for example, people were proud of their ancient civilizations. On the other hand, they did work to discourage some customs, such as sati in India or footbinding in China, which they now saw as harmful. In the end, many nonwestern cultures created a complex blend of old and new ways.

As people moved into cities that had become westernized, many still felt the pull of the past. "People come to the city because they want to live

---

*The process of modernization along western lines has continued to the present. In today's world, however, modernization and westernization are often seen as separate and different courses.

Westernization and Tradition
In French colonies, local rulers kept their titles while real power was held by colonial officials. In this photo, a French colonial governor (left) meets with the king of Laos (right).

Theme: Continuity and Change What element of the king's clothing shows European influence?

Humanities Link

The Influence of African Art on Picasso

EXPLORING the HUMAN DRAMA
Humanities Link

Bell Ringer Have students study the two paintings and the African mask on this page. Ask them what similarities they notice among the three works of art.

Background Connections to Today

Ancient Influences on Modern Art Picasso's work is characteristic of the experimental trend in art during the first half of the twentieth century. African art influenced Picasso's move from realism to abstraction and showed a way of organizing elements that differed from the ways of western tradition. At almost the same time, Picasso realized the importance of Cézanne's art, which consisted of simplified forms painted with a shifting three-dimensional point of view. These influences helped lay the foundation for cubism, in which objects in paintings are presented from several angles.

Activity Cooperative Learning

Analyzing a Painting Divide the class into small groups to analyze any of Picasso's paintings that were influenced by African art. Group members should begin by taking notes about their own impressions of the painting. Then, groups should assign one member to research the painting, one to take notes, and one to write a brief analysis based on their research and their impressions.

Portfolio Assessment Rubrics

Share rubrics with students before they complete their displays.

Attempted Display does not identify similarities among the examples of the three cubist artists.

Minimal Display shows examples of cubism from all three artists and identifies some similarities among them.

Adequate Display shows good examples of cubism and identifies similarities that demostrate a good understanding of cubism.

Exemplary Identification of similarities among the attractively arranged display reveals the essence of cubism.

In 1907, Pablo Picasso was inspired while viewing an exhibition of African masks and sculpture in the Trocadéro museum in Paris. He rushed to his studio and repainted the heads of several figures in his painting *Les Demoiselles d' Avignon*. From then on, many of his portraits showed the influence of African art.

The distinctive abstract patterns of stripes and hatchmarks on this mother and child from 1907 show the influence of African art on Picasso's portraits.

Mother and child constituted a frequent theme in Picasso's work. He did this painting in 1903, before his introduction to African art.

Masks like this one inspired Picasso to move in a new direction. He wrote of his visit to the Trocadéro, "If you give spirits a shape, you break free from them. . . . I grasped why I was a painter. All alone in that museum, surrounded by masks. . . ."

Fast Facts

- Picasso's first word was "lápiz," the Spanish word for pencil, and he began drawing almost as soon as he began walking.

- Though many of his works are abstract, Picasso maintained a huge photography collection in his studio and often painted from photographs.

- Picasso lived to age 91 and continued to experiment with new styles until his death.

Portfolio Assessment

Use the Internet or library resources to find examples of cubist paintings by Picasso and his contemporaries, Juan Gris and Georges Braque. Assemble your examples into a class display. Then, use the display to identify similarities among the three artists' work.

Resource Directory

Teaching Resources
Humanities Link Chapter Extension Activities booklet, p. 64
Section Quiz Unit 6 booklet, p. 87
Geography Quiz Unit 6 booklet, p. 92
Chapter Test Forms A, B, and C Unit 6 booklet, pp. 93–97
Answer Key Unit 6 booklet, pp. 98–112
Technology
Interactive Student Tutorial CD-ROM Ch. 26
Computer Test Bank Ch. 26

like Europeans," admitted one Nigerian, "but we still feel close to our village and always go back to visit it."

Impact on Western Culture Western cultures changed, too, during the Age of Imperialism. The Columbian Exchange that had begun in 1492 picked up speed in the 1800s. Westerners drank coffee from Brazil and tea from Sri Lanka. They ate bananas from Honduras and pineapples from Hawaii. Their factories turned out products made from rubber harvested on plantations in Southeast Asia or South America.

Archaeologists and historians slowly unearthed evidence about ancient civilizations previously unknown to the West. Westerners who studied Hindu and Buddhist texts, Chinese histories, or Japanese poetry realized that they had much to learn from other civilizations. The arts of Japan, Persia, Africa, and Southeast Asia influenced western sculptors and painters. Western manufacturers also copied designs from other lands, launching fashions for Egyptian furniture, Japanese kimonos, and Chinese embroidery screens.

New Political Tensions

Imperialism had global political consequences, as you have seen. Europeans claimed and conquered large empires in Africa and Asia. They disrupted traditional political units such as tribes and small kingdoms. Often, they united rival peoples under a single government, imposing stability and order where local conflicts had raged for centuries.

By the early 1900s, however, resistance to imperialism was taking a new course. In Africa and Asia, western-educated elites were organizing nationalist movements to end colonial rule.

At the same time, the competition for imperial power was fueling tensions among western nations. In the Sudan in 1898, British forces expanding south from Egypt and French forces pushing east from West Africa met at Fashoda. An armed clash was barely avoided.

Elsewhere, the British and Russians played a cat-and-mouse game in Central Asia. The Great Powers—Germany, Britain, France, and Russia—tried to thwart one another's ambitions in Ottoman lands. More than once, Germany and France teetered on the brink of war over Morocco in North Africa. In 1914 and again in 1939, imperialist ambitions would contribute to the outbreak of two shattering world wars.

SECTION 5 Assessment

Recall

1. **Identify:** (a) Rudyard Kipling, (b) Cecil Rhodes.

Comprehension

2. Describe how each of the following affected industrialized nations and traditional cultures: (a) money economy, (b) dependency, (c) modernization.
3. How did imperialism affect cultures around the world?
4. Why did imperialism lead to increased tensions among the industrialized powers of Europe?

Critical Thinking and Writing

5. **Drawing Conclusions** List the benefits and disadvantages brought by colonial rule. Do you think subject people were better or worse off as a result of the Age of Imperialism? Explain.
6. **Recognizing Points of View** How might a subject person respond to the quotation by Cecil Rhodes in this section?

Activity

Creating a Chart
Create a chart showing the movement of goods and money in the global economy that emerged in the late 1800s. Be sure to include effects on traditional economies. Illustrate your chart with original drawings or pictures from magazines.

Human Drama Activity

Drawing a Self-Portrait Have students draw a self-portrait in the cubist style. Show students several examples of cubist paintings, or refer them to their displays if they completed the Portfolio Assessment activity on the opposite page. Remind students that cubism was a reflection of the historical period in which it was born. Influenced by Einstein's work in physics, cubism seeks to portray not only two-dimensional space but also the dimension of time since objects are shown from the views an observer would have at several different points of time.

SECTION 5 Assessment

Recall
1. (a) Rudyard Kipling, p. 663 (b) Cecil Rhodes, p. 664

Comprehension
2. (a) replaced barter system, led to high taxes, broke up families as people needed to work in distant locations (b) ruined traditional economies and industries, shifted agriculture from food crops to export crops (c) improved transportation systems, communication networks
3. Possible answers: Imperialism brought Christianity to many areas of Africa and Asia. Westernization caused people to reevaluate and, in some cases, change their traditional ways. 4. They competed for influence and control of colonies throughout the world. On several occasions, this competition led the imperialist powers of Europe to the brink of war.

Critical Thinking and Writing
5. Benefits included western technology, western government, economic modernization, improved education and health care, and the elimination of harmful customs. Disadvantages included the loss of traditions, disruption of family life, disruption of local economies, the undermining of village life, and economic dependence. Students' opinions on whether subject people were better or worse off should be well supported by evidence from the text.
6. Students' responses should recognize that some colonial people accepted western superiority, while others resented efforts at westernization.

Activity Rubrics

Share rubrics with students before they create their charts.

Attempted Chart does not meet the requirements nor does it reflect a basic understanding of the global economy of the late 1800s.

Minimal Chart reflects a basic understanding of the global economy. It shows movement of goods and money, includes some effects on traditional economies, and has illustrations.

Adequate Chart reflects a good understanding of the global economy. It shows movement of goods and money, includes effects on traditional economies, has good illustrations, and is neatly done.

Exemplary Chart reflects a comprehensive understanding of the global economy of the late 1800s. It is neatly done, and the illustrations are visually pleasing as well as informative.

CHAPTER **26** Review and Assessment

Creating a Chapter Summary

As a reteaching opportunity, pair a more able student with a less able student to complete this chapter summary.

Possible answers: **Southeast Asia** divided up among major powers, supplied Europe with natural resources **Canada** British and French sections are united, westward expansion destroys Native American way of life, gains self-rule and sets up government modeled after Britain **Australia** originally penal colony for Britain, westward expansion destroys Aboriginal way of life, gains self-rule and sets up government based on British model **Latin America** social divisions and political instability cause democratic constitutions to fail, becomes economically dependent on foreign nations, United States becomes "Colossus of the North" and intervenes to protect investments **Western Europe** fierce competition among countries competing for control of overseas land, African and Asian influences appear in European culture

Building Vocabulary

1–8. Students' sentences should reflect an understanding of each word.

Recalling Key Facts

9. As Japan modernized, it needed more resources and a greater market.
10. by modernizing and introducing reforms without western involvement and because its location led Britain and France to view it as a useful buffer state between their neighboring colonies
11. Unification encouraged expansion by providing a central government and simplifying the process of building a transcontinental railroad.
12. The United States backed a revolt in Panama and built the canal.
13. the industrialized nations of the West, especially the United States, Britain, France, and Germany
14. Competition from industrialized nations destroyed firms in nonindustrialized nations. Also, the need for trade with industrialized nations made non-industrialized nations dependent on high-priced foreign exports.

Critical Thinking and Writing

15. Possible answer: Colonies were sources of raw materials and markets

---

Creating a Chapter Summary

Copy this graphic organizer on a piece of paper. Include facts that describe the impact of the Age of Imperialism on different areas of the world.

For additional review and enrichment activities, see the interactive version of *World History* available on the Web and on CD-ROM.

REGION	IMPACT OF IMPERIALISM
JAPAN	• Meiji restoration and westernization • Becomes imperialist power
SOUTHEAST ASIA	• •
CANADA	
AUSTRALIA	
LATIN AMERICA	
WESTERN EUROPE	

Web Site Self-Test
For practice test questions for Chapter 26, see **www.phschool.com**.

Building Vocabulary

Review the meaning of the chapter vocabulary words listed below. Then, write a sentence for each word in which you define the word.

1. zaibatsu
2. homogeneous society
3. indigenous
4. confederation
5. regionalism
6. *caudillo*
7. economic dependence
8. peonage

Recalling Key Facts

9. How did modernization encourage Japan to seek its own colonies?
10. How did Siam avoid colonization by a European nation?
11. How did the creation of the Dominion of Canada encourage expansion?
12. What role did the United States play in the construction of the Panama Canal?
13. Which nations dominated the global economy that emerged in the late 1800s?
14. How did imperialism encourage economic dependence?

Critical Thinking and Writing

15. **Synthesizing Information** How did the Industrial Revolution contribute to imperialism?
16. **Comparing** Compare Japan's response to western imperialism with that of China. **(a)** How were the two responses similar? **(b)** How were they different?
17. **Connecting to Geography** Would you expect westernization to have a stronger impact in coastal cities or in rural areas? Explain.

18. **Applying Information (a)** What principle did the United States express in the Monroe Doctrine? **(b)** How did the Roosevelt Corollary alter the Monroe Doctrine?
19. **Defending a Position** Mexican President Porfirio Díaz defended his regime: "We were harsh. Sometimes we were harsh to the point of cruelty. But it was necessary then to the life and progress of the nation." Do you agree or disagree with Díaz's view that the end justifies the means? Explain.

---

for finished goods. With modern technology, industrialized nations could easily seize control of other lands.
16. **(a)** Both were forced to accept unequal treaties with the West. **(b)** The Chinese resisted the British but were defeated. The Japanese learned from the West and became an industrial and military power.
17. Possible answer: in coastal cities, because they would be centers of shipping and trade
18. **(a)** The Americas were no longer open to colonization by European powers. **(b)** The Roosevelt

Corollary claimed that the United States had police power in the Western Hemisphere.
19. Encourage students to explain the reasons for their opinions.

Skills Assessment
Analyzing Primary Sources

In the excerpt below, future Mexican president Benito Juárez describes growing up as a poor Zapotec Indian. Read the excerpt, then answer the questions that follow.

"As soon as I could think at all, I dedicated myself, insofar as my young age permitted, to work in the fields. In the few intervals in which we were not working, my uncle taught me to read; he showed me how useful and advantageous it would be for me to know the Spanish language, and since at that time it was extremely difficult for poor people, and especially for Indians, to follow any learned career except holy orders, he revealed that he wanted me to study for [the priesthood]. His desire, and the examples that I had before me of fellow countrymen who knew how to read, write, and speak the Spanish language, and of others in the priesthood, awakened in me a vehement desire to learn. . . . However, my uncle's work, and my own, in the fields, frustrated my ambition, and I advanced very little in my lessons. Furthermore, in a village as small as mine, which had hardly 20 families, at a time when hardly anyone was concerned with the education of youth, there was no school."

—Benito Juárez, *Notes for My Children*

20. What did Juárez's uncle encourage him to learn?
21. Why did his uncle want him to study for the priesthood?
22. What challenges did Juárez encounter?
23. Based on this excerpt, what reforms do you think Juárez might have introduced as president?

Skills Assessment
Take It to the NET

Use the Internet to research the history of one of the colonies in this chapter. Write a report summarizing its history since colonization. Include information on how it gained independence and major events that have occurred since independence.

Skills Assessment
Analyzing Charts

Cause *and* Effect

Causes

• Industrial Revolution strengthens the West
• Newly industrialized nations seek new markets
• Western nations compete for power
• Westerners feel duty to spread their culture

New Imperialism

Effects

• Europeans claim and conquer large empires in Africa and Asia
• Europeans gain control of global trading empires
• Western powers spread their ideas and adopt elements of nonwestern cultures
• Local people resist western domination
• Some nonwestern leaders attempt reforms in an effort to modernize

Connections to Today

• Nations in Africa, Asia, and Latin America struggle to build stable governments

Use the cause-and-effect chart to answer the following questions:

24. What did newly industrialized nations seek?
25. How did nonwestern peoples respond to colonization?
26. What is the central idea of this chart?
27. How do the events and developments identified in this chart continue to affect the world today?

Skills Tip

When reading a cause-and-effect chart, pay careful attention to the outcomes of events and developments,

Analyzing Primary Sources

20. the Spanish language
21. It was extremely difficult for poor Indians to pursue any learned career except for the priesthood.
22. He had to work in the fields, and there was no school in his village.
23. Possible answer: education for everyone and access to good jobs

Analyzing Charts

24. new markets
25. Some resisted foreign domination while others attempted to modernize.
26. Changes in the West led to western domination of much of the rest of the world.
27. Nations that were once colonized are still struggling with independence and stability.

Skills Tip

To understand the sequence of events in a cause-and-effect chart, read the chart by following the direction of the arrows, in this case from top to bottom. The Skills Handbook in the front of the book has a lesson that will help students with this feature.

Unit Theme Activity

Evaluate students' Unit Theme Activities by referring to the rubrics on the unit opener page in the Teacher's Edition.

Take It to the NET

Direct students to **www.phschool.com** for links to sites that will help them get started on this assignment. Share rubrics with students.
Attempted Report is incomplete.
Minimal Report has only a sketchy summary of the colony's history, fails to explain how the colony gained independence, or includes few main events that have happened since.
Adequate Report summarizes the colony's history, explains how the colony gained independence, and includes many major events that have happened since.
Exemplary Report is well written, organized, and comprehensive. It summarizes the colony's history, clearly explains how the colony gained independence, and includes a great number of the major events that have happened since.

Unit-in-Brief
6 Industrialism and a New Global Age

USING THESE PAGES

The Unit-in-Brief contains the main ideas of the unit chapters. You may use the Unit-in-Brief to preview, review, or condense the contents of each chapter.

The unit time line identifies key events in each world region that took place during the time span covered by the unit.

*A*ctivity
Unit Themes

Have students review the unit themes below. Then, ask them to find examples in the time line and summary to support each theme.

Diversity Rulers strengthened their nations by incorporating surrounding states and colonies. Conflicts arose as new subjects, often of different ethnic backgrounds, demanded independence. Women struggled to end restrictions on their lives and gain recognition of their rights.

Economics and Technology Developing factory systems, improved transportation and communication, and scientific advances contributed to overseas expansion by European powers. Industrialized nations grew wealthy, often at the expense of colonies.

Impact of the Individual Nationalist leaders in Italy and Germany used warfare and political alliances to forge new nations out of fragmented provinces.

Political and Social Systems In the 1800s, as the middle class grew, democratic rights were extended in Britain, France, and the United States. Urbanization and the impact of industrialization led to major changes in social values.

Chapter 22

Life in the Industrial Age (1800–1914)

From the mid-1800s, industrialism spread rapidly across Europe to North America and beyond. This second Industrial Revolution transformed the economies of the world and solidified patterns of life familiar to us today.

- By the mid-1800s, other western nations—particularly Germany and the United States—were challenging Britain's position as the world's industrial giant.
- Steel, electricity, and advances in communications and transportation marked the second Industrial Revolution.
- By the late 1800s, "big business" came increasingly to dominate industry.
- With the spread of industry, a more complex social structure, dominated by middle-class values, evolved. Although the poor endured harsh conditions, the overall standard of living for workers improved.
- Artistic movements such as romanticism, realism, and expressionism reflected various responses to social and technological changes.

Chapter 23

Nationalism Triumphs in Europe (1800–1914)

The 1800s saw an upsurge of nationalism in Europe. Nationalism unified some countries and sparked divisiveness and conflict in others.

- Between 1862 and 1890, Otto von Bismarck molded the German states into a powerful empire. To strengthen the German state, Bismarck promoted economic development, aggressive foreign policy goals, and domestic reforms.
- Although nationalist forces unified Italy in 1870, a long history of fragmentation created a host of problems for the new state.
- Nationalist feelings among diverse ethnic groups in Eastern Europe created widespread unrest and helped hasten the decline of the Ottoman and Hapsburg empires.
- Reluctant to surrender absolute power, Russian czars of the 1800s swung between reform and repression.

Chapter 24

Growth of Western Democracies (1815–1914)

In Britain, France, and the United States, reformers struggled for an extension of democratic rights and social change. Although many inequalities persisted, these efforts paved the way for great improvements in the quality of life.

- The British Parliament passed a series of reforms designed to help those whose labor supported the new industrial society. Suffrage was extended to all male citizens, prompting women to seek the vote as well.
- Following its defeat in the Franco-Prussian War and a fierce internal revolt, France established the Third Republic, which instituted a series of important reforms.
- By 1900, the United States had become the world's leading industrial giant, a global power, and a magnet for immigrants seeking freedom and opportunity.

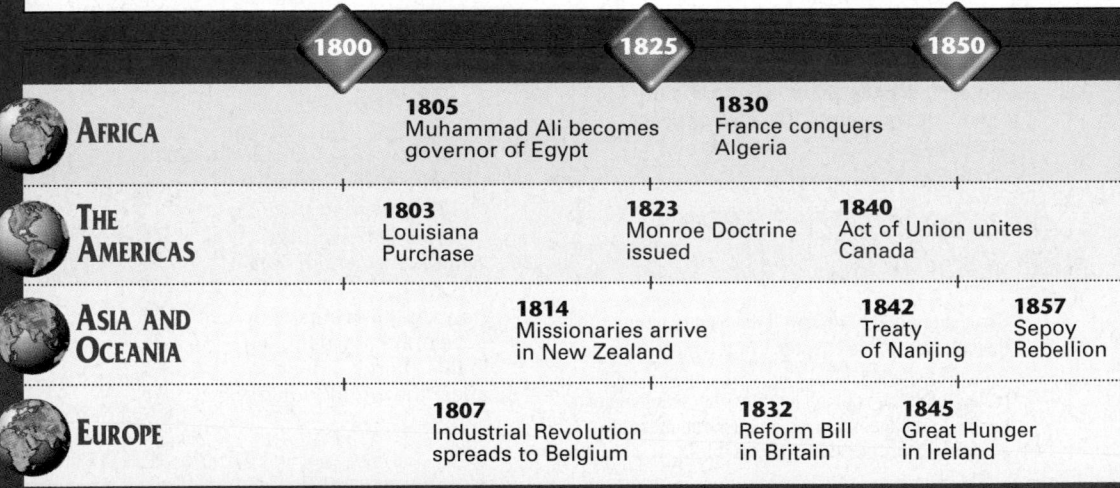

	1800	1825	1850
AFRICA	**1805** Muhammad Ali becomes governor of Egypt	**1830** France conquers Algeria	
THE AMERICAS	**1803** Louisiana Purchase	**1823** Monroe Doctrine issued	**1840** Act of Union unites Canada
ASIA AND OCEANIA	**1814** Missionaries arrive in New Zealand	**1842** Treaty of Nanjing	**1857** Sepoy Rebellion
EUROPE	**1807** Industrial Revolution spreads to Belgium	**1832** Reform Bill in Britain	**1845** Great Hunger in Ireland

Student Bibliography

Avakian, Monique. *The Meiji Restoration and the Rise of Modern Japan*. Silver Burdett Press, 1991. Detailed history of Japan from 1868 to 1912.

Bled, Jean-Paul. *Franz Joseph*. Blackwell, 1992. Biography of the monarch who presided over the decline and fall of the Austrian empire.

Hobsbawn, Eric. *Age of Empire*. McKay, 1989. Account of the Age of Imperialism from 1875 to 1914.

Hsu, Immanuel C. *The Rise of Modern China*. Oxford University Press, 1990. Covers historical events of China and how they contributed to the making of a modern nation.

Lipira, Benedict S. *Giuseppe Garibaldi: A Biography of the Father of Modern Italy*. Noble House, 1998. Biography of Garibaldi and history of the unification of Italy.

Tobias, Michael. *A Day in the Life of India*. Collins Publishers San Francisco, 1996. Beautiful photographs capture the essence of India.

Chapter 25

The New Imperialism
(1800–1914)

During the 1800s, European powers embarked on a period of aggressive expansion known as the Age of Imperialism. Despite fierce resistance, these powers brought much of the world under their control between 1870 and 1914.

- The Industrial Revolution gave western powers both the means and the motives to seek global domination.
- With little regard for traditional patterns of settlement, European powers partitioned almost the entire African continent.
- Taking advantage of the slowly crumbling Ottoman empire, Britain, France, and Russia competed to extend their influence over Algeria, Egypt, and other Ottoman lands.
- Britain set up a profitable system of colonial rule, controlling over 60 percent of India.
- Western powers carved out spheres of influence along the Chinese coast. China tried unsuccessfully to resist foreign influence with belated efforts at modernization and reform.
- By the early 1900s, leaders in many colonized regions were forging their own nationalist movements.

Chapter 26

New Global Patterns
(1800–1914)

Imperialism resulted in a global exchange that profited industrial nations but disrupted local economies in Africa, Asia, and Latin America. Radical changes reshaped the lives of both subject peoples and westerners.

- As a defense against western imperialism, Japan transformed itself into a modern industrial power and set out on its own imperialist path.
- By 1900, western powers had claimed most islands in the Pacific and divided up most of Southeast Asia.
- The British colonies of Canada, Australia, and New Zealand won independence relatively quickly.
- Although Latin American nations struggled to set up stable governments and economies, a pattern of military rule and economic dependency emerged.
- The United States created its own sphere of influence in the Western Hemisphere.
- Europeans forced subject peoples to accept western ideas about government, technology, and culture.

Activity

Summarizing the Main Idea

Have students use both the Unit-in-Brief and Chapters 22–26 to answer the following questions in order to summarize Unit 6: (1) What were some of the economic and social changes brought by the Industrial Revolution? (2) How did nationalism lead to both unity and division in Europe? (3) What changes made the British government more democratic in the 1800s? (4) Describe some of the results of the Age of Imperialism.

PRENTICE HALL
ASSESSMENT SYSTEM

Diagnose and Prescribe
- **Profile student skills with Diagnostic Tests A & B.**
- **Address student needs with program materials identified in the test.**

Review and Reteach
- **Provide cumulative content review with the Review Book.**

Practice and Assess
- **Build test-taking skills with Test-Taking Strategies With Transparencies.**

1875   **1900**   **1925**

1869 Suez Canal opens

1884 Berlin Conference carves up Africa

1896 Ethiopia defeats Italy at Battle of Adowa

1876 Diaz gains power in Mexico

1898 Spanish-American War

1914 Panama Canal opens

1868 Meiji restoration begins

1885 Indian National Congress formed

1900 Boxer Uprising in China

1908 Young Turks overthrow sultan

1870 Italy unified

1871 Germany unified

1894 Dreyfus affair begins

1905 Bloody Sunday in Russia

1918 Women win suffrage in Britain

Teacher Bibliography

Garrison, Webb B. *2,000 Questions and Answers About the Civil War: Unusual and Unique Facts About the War Between the States.* Grammercy, 1998. Valuable Civil War resource.

Lamar, Howard Roberts, ed. *The New Encyclopedia of the American West.* Yale University Press, 1998. Authoritative, comprehensive, and nicely illustrated resource about the American West.

Lincoln, W. Bruce. *The Great Reforms: Autocracy, Bureaucracy, and the Politics of Change in Imperial Russia.* Northern Illinois University Press, 1990. Synthesis of changes in Russia during this period.

Smith, Woodruff D. *European Imperialism in the Nineteenth and Twentieth Centuries.* Nelson-Hall, 1982. Brief overview of major issues and motives for the new imperialism.

Tsurumi, E. Patricia. *Factory Girls: Women in the Thread Mills of Meiji Japan.* Princeton University Press, 1992. Account of the contributions made by female textile workers in early industrialized Japan.

UNIT OVERVIEW

Unit 7 studies the first half of the twentieth century, a time of world wars, revolutions, economic crises, and emerging nationalism.

Chapter 27 studies World War I and the peace settlements that followed.

Chapter 28 studies the Russian Revolution and the establishment of totalitarian rule in the Soviet Union.

Chapter 29 focuses on the struggle for self-determination and democracy in Latin America, Africa, and Asia.

Chapter 30 examines the years after World War I, when political weakness, the Great Depression, and dictatorships threatened the West.

Chapter 31 describes World War II and the start of the Cold War.

Unit Theme Activity Rubrics

Share rubrics with students before they create their projects.

Attempted The project does not compare various solutions to worldwide economic challenges.

Minimal The project is poorly executed or only vaguely compares various solutions to worldwide economic challenges.

Adequate The project is well executed and clearly compares various solutions to worldwide economic challenges.

Exemplary The project is extremely well executed, ably compares various solutions to worldwide economic challenges, and is visually interesting or is extremely interesting and informative to read.

UNIT 7

World Wars and Revolutions

1910–1955

OUTLINE

Themes

As you read about global wars and revolutions, you will encounter the following themes.

Continuity and Change Nationalists in Asia, Latin America, and Africa challenged foreign domination and encouraged a revival of traditional culture. Tools of change ranged from civil disobedience in India to armed rebellion in Mexico.

Economics and Technology The Great Depression caused major economic problems around the world. Fascists and communists offered their own extreme solutions to the crisis.

Global Interaction Two world wars were fought in the first half of the twentieth century. Developed nations in the global North and developing countries in the global South became increasingly interdependent. Common concerns encouraged nations to support international organizations and agreements.

Political and Social Systems Democracy, communism, and fascism competed for influence and political power. Totalitarian dictatorships attempted to regulate all aspects of life and to place the needs of the state above individual rights.

Unit Theme Activity

For Your Portfolio The chapters in this unit examine economic challenges around the world. As you read the chapters, prepare a portfolio project comparing various solutions to the issues. Your project might take one of the following forms:
• **PowerPoint presentation**
• **Interview**
• **Photo essay**

Resource Directory

Teaching Resources

Teaching With Themes *How Did World Events Reflect Growing Interaction?*, p. 47

Technology

World History Visions, Voices, Views Scenes of an Age, *World Wars and Revolutions,* videodisc side 4 or videotape 7, running time 2:30 min.

Side 4: Fr. 228-3425

The official Japanese surrender was signed on September 2, 1945, on board the USS *Missouri* in Tokyo Bay. General Douglas MacArthur, commander in the Southwest Pacific and supreme commander for the Allied Powers, accepted the formal document, ending World War II.

Background
About the Picture

The Mighty Mo The USS *Missouri,* known as the Mighty Mo to its crew, was one of the largest warships of its time. Weighing in at 58,000 tons when fully loaded, the *Missouri* is an Iowa class battleship that measures over 887 feet in length, could reach speeds of 35 knots, and was equipped with nine 16-inch guns. This ship has been registered as a national historic landmark. It is now docked in the famous Battleship Row at Pearl Harbor, where it overlooks the fallen sailors of the USS *Arizona* and serves as a memorial museum.

Aboard the Mighty Mo is a plaque commemorating the Japanese surrender. It reads "USS Missouri. Over this spot on 2 September 1945 the instrument of surrender of Japan to the allied powers was signed thus bringing to a close the second world war. The ship at that time was at anchor in Tokyo Bay. Latitude 35° 21' 17" North. Longitude 139° 45' 36" East."

i TEXT

Don't miss the exclusive interactive version of *World History: Connections to Today* on the Internet and CD-ROM.

Block Scheduling Support

Using the Unit-in-Brief The Unit-in-Brief, found at the end of the unit, contains the main ideas of the unit chapters. You may use the Unit-in-Brief to preview, review, or condense the contents of each chapter.

Using the Unit Time Line The Unit Time Line, at the end of the unit, provides a chronology of world events during the period covered by this unit. By studying the time line in conjunction with the Unit-in-Brief, students may compare developments in various regions. You may use the time line to help condense the contents of the chapters.

Using the *Guide to the Essentials* The *Guide to the Essentials of World History* contains summaries and graphic organizers for each section of every chapter in this unit. You may use the *Guide to the Essentials* to help poor readers or students acquiring English access the main ideas of the chapters. You may also use it with all students to review or to condense topics in your world history course.

eTeach

Be sure to check out this month's online discussion with a World History Master Teacher.

Go to **www.phschool.com**.

Activity
Cooperative Learning

Painting a Picture Divide the class into five groups and assign each group a color: yellow, red, brown, black, and white. Instruct students in each group to use colored pencils, pens, markers, or paints of their assigned color to create pictures of things from everyday life that share their color. For example, students in the brown group could draw a cat; the black or white or yellow group could draw a cat as well. Groups should then combine all their pictures into one large mural to display on a wall. Then, ask students to find different-colored items among the pictures in the mural that are the same, like the cat. Point out that things—like the cats—can be alike, yet different. Ask students to name other things not shown on the mural that are also alike, yet different.

WHY STUDY HISTORY?

Because We Can Learn From the Mistakes of the Past

War. Economic depression. Genocide. Ethnic cleansing. Human history is filled with devastating tragedies. What causes these horrors? How do they begin? Most important, how can we use what we have learned about these tragedies of the past to ensure that they don't happen again?

War

Nations go to war for many different reasons. Looking back, sometimes we can see that the war was avoidable. In this cartoon, the artist shows how a disagreement can lead to violence. How might the combatants have avoided this conflict?

Genocide

During World War II, the leaders of Nazi Germany set out to exterminate all European Jews. In death camps, the Nazis built gas chambers to carry out their program of genocide. About six million Jews died in the Holocaust. Millions of others, considered "racially inferior" by the Nazis, were also killed. In this photo Nazi troops round up Polish Jews. Today, this tragedy serves as a reminder of the bitter legacy of hate.

674 Unit 7

Resource Directory

Teaching Resources

Why Study History? *Because We Can Learn From the Mistakes of the Past,* Why Study History? booklet, pp. 17–18

Spread of Nuclear Weapons

Toward the end of World War II, the United States deployed a deadly new weapon—the atomic bomb. Its fiery mushroom cloud gives a fearful hint of its vast destructive power. Though the two bombs dropped on Japan brought an end to the war, many people were appalled by the destruction such bombs could unleash. They feared that others might use the weapon.

Over time, other nations learned how to build nuclear weapons. With each new country that developed this capability, the risk of accident or use by terrorists grew. People began working to end the spread of nuclear weapons. In the picture at right, demonstrators oppose the testing of nuclear weapons by China, Russia, India, and other nations.

Overcoming the Past

Many times in the world's history, nations have fought wars and wreaked destruction on people and property. Yet, there have always been those who hoped to end such devastation and bring peace. In 1991, leaders of many nations (shown at right) met to discuss ways to improve the future for the world's children. They hoped that, by learning from the mistakes of the past, they could work together to bring about a better future for the next generation.

Portfolio Assessment

Connecting to Today The philosopher George Santayana wrote, "Those who do not remember the past are condemned to repeat it." Write a short paragraph explaining what he meant by this.

Background
Connections to Today

Hatred and Violence Ethnic and religious differences led to the deaths of millions of people in the twentieth century. They still plague the world today. In Northern Ireland, the Balkans, parts of Africa, South Asia, and the Middle East, ethnic or religious differences have caused wars or civil unrest. In the United States, too, minority groups still must struggle to enjoy full civil rights.

Background
About the Pictures

1. This Swiss cartoon *(opposite page, top)* by Pecub illustrates what might happen when two people have conflicting views.

2. Nazi soldiers rounding up Jews *(bottom)*. Historians trace the start of the Holocaust to the night of Nov. 9, 1938, when Nazis killed dozens of Jews and sent up to 30,000 to concentration camps. The Nazis also burned or demolished more than 200 synagogues and destroyed about 7,500 Jewish-owned businesses throughout Germany. This night has become known as *Kristallnacht,* or "Night of Broken Glass."

3. Nuclear explosion and protest *(above)*. The first atomic bomb was dropped on the city of Hiroshima, Japan, on Aug. 6, 1945, destroying about 4 square miles and killing an estimated 70,000 to 100,000 people.

4. International Conference on Children *(left)*. The Convention on the Rights of the Child, adopted by the United Nations in 1989, includes the rights to health care, proper nutrition, and education; freedom of expression; and protection from unfair treatment.

Portfolio Assessment Rubrics

Share rubrics with students before they write their paragraphs.

Attempted The paragraph is incomplete.

Minimal The paragraph is complete but is poorly written and has many mechanical errors.

Adequate The paragraph is complete and well written with few mechanical errors.

Exemplary The paragraph is complete and very well written. There are no mechanical errors.

Chapter 27 Planning Guide

Resource Manager

	CORE INSTRUCTION	READING/SKILLS
Chapter Level Resources	**Teaching Resources** ▪ Pacing Charts, Ch. 27 ▪ Teaching With Themes, p. 30 ▪ Color Transparencies, p. F–55 ▪ Resource Pro® Ch. 27 ▪ www.phschool.com • eTeach	▪ Book on CD, Ch. 27 ▪ Interactive Student Tutorial CD-ROM, Ch. 27 ▪ Social Studies Skills Tutor CD-ROM ▪ Skills Transparencies
1 The Stage Is Set 1. Summarize efforts toward peace in the early 1900s. 2. Describe how nationalism and international rivalries pushed Europe toward war. 3. Outline causes and effects of the European alliance system.	**Teaching Resources** ▪ Creative Teaching Activities, p. 121 ▪ Prentice Hall Presentation Pro, Ch. 27, Section 1 ▪ Section Reading Support Transparencies	**Teaching Resources** ▪ Unit 7 booklet • Guided Reading and Review, p. 2 ▪ Guide to the Essentials ▪ Guided Reading Audiotapes, Ch. 27, Section 1
2 The Guns of August 1. Describe how ethnic tensions in the Balkans sparked a political assassination. 2. Relate how the conflict between Austria-Hungary and Serbia widened. 3. Explain how historians view the outbreak of World War I.	**Teaching Resources** ▪ Creative Teaching Activities, p. 122 ▪ Prentice Hall Presentation Pro, Ch. 27, Section 2 ▪ Section Reading Support Transparencies	**Teaching Resources** ▪ Unit 7 booklet • Guided Reading and Review, p. 4 ▪ Guide to the Essentials ▪ Guided Reading Audiotapes, Ch. 27, Section 2

3 A New Kind of Conflict
1. Identify why a stalemate developed on the Western Front.
2. Assess how technology made World War I different from other wars.
3. Explain how the war became a global conflict.
	Teaching Resources
	▪ Unit 7 booklet
	   • Biography Activity, p. 12
	   • Viewpoint Activity, p. 14
	▪ Creative Teaching Activities, p. 123
	▪ Prentice Hall Presentation Pro, Ch. 27, Section 3
		Teaching Resources
		▪ Unit 7 booklet
		   • Guided Reading and Review, p. 6
		▪ Guide to the Essentials
		▪ Guided Reading Audiotapes, Ch. 27, Section 3

4 Winning the War
1. Explain how World War I became a total war.
2. Specify the effect that the continuing conflict had on morale.
3. Summarize causes and results of the American entry into the war.
	Teaching Resources
	▪ Unit 7 booklet
	   • Primary Source Activity, p. 13
	▪ Creative Teaching Activities, p. 124
	▪ Prentice Hall Presentation Pro, Ch. 27, Section 4
		Teaching Resources
		▪ Unit 7 booklet
		   • Guided Reading and Review, p. 8
		   • Skill Application Activity, p. 15
		▪ Guide to the Essentials

5 Making the Peace 1. Identify the costs of the war. 2. Enumerate the issues faced by the delegates to the Paris Peace Conference. 3. Explain the dissatisfaction with the Treaty of Versailles and other peace settlements.	**Teaching Resources** ▪ Creative Teaching Activities, p. 125 ▪ Prentice Hall Presentation Pro, Ch. 27, Section 5 ▪ Section Reading Support Transparencies	**Teaching Resources** ▪ Unit 7 booklet • Guided Reading and Review, p. 10 ▪ Guide to the Essentials ▪ Guided Reading Audiotapes, Ch. 27, Section 5

ENRICHMENT/PRE-AP

- **www.phschool.com**
  - Why Study History?

Teaching Resources
- **Chapter Extension Activities,** pp. 65–66
- **Geography and History,** pp. 14–15
- **www.phschool.com**
  - Internet Activities, Section 1

Teaching Resources
- **Chapter Extension Activities,** p. 67
- **History Through Literature,** pp. 57–58
- **Color Transparencies,** p. D–81
- **Visions, Voices, Views,** Global Issues Forum, tape 7

- **www.phschool.com**
  - Virtual Field Trip
  - Internet Activities, Section 4

Teaching Resources
- **Simulations,** pp. 12–15

ASSESSMENT

PRENTICE HALL ASSESSMENT *SYSTEM*

Core Assessment
- ExamView Test Bank booklet, Ch. 27
- ExamView Test Bank CD-ROM, Ch. 27

Standardized Test Preparation

Diagnose and Prescribe
- Diagnostic Tests for High School Social Studies Skills

Review and Reteach
- Review Book for World History

Practice and Assess
- Test-Taking Strategies With Transparencies for High School
- Alternative Assessment booklet
- Test Prep Book for World History

Teaching Resources
- **Unit 7 booklet**
  - Geography Quiz, p. 16
  - Section Quizzes, pp. 3, 5, 7, 9, 11
  - Chapter Tests A, B, and C, pp. 17–21
- **www.phschool.com**
  - Self-Test

CUSTOMIZE FOR INDIVIDUAL NEEDS

Gifted and Talented
- **Teacher's Edition,** Activities: Connections to Film, p. 688

Less Proficient Readers
- **Guide to the Essentials,** Ch. 27
- **Book on CD,** Ch. 27
- **Teacher's Edition,** Activities: Customize for Heterogeneous Groups, p. 680; Reading Strategy, p. 696

Less Proficient Writers
- **Teacher's Edition,** Activities: Cooperative Learning Activity, p. 686; Customize for Kinesthetic Learners, p. 688

Students Acquiring English/ESL
- **Guide to the Essentials, English/Spanish,** Ch. 27
- **Book on CD,** Ch. 27
- **Teacher's Edition,** Activities marked with an *

TEXT

Don't miss the exclusive interactive version of *World History: Connections to Today* on the Internet and CD-ROM.

INTRODUCTION

By 1914, Europeans had enjoyed almost a century without a major war. They had witnessed incredible changes. Rapid advances in science and industry had fed a belief in unlimited progress, peace, and prosperity. That confidence came crashing down in August 1914, buried in an avalanche of death and destruction. World War I marked the beginning of a disturbing new age.

Focusing on Themes

Suggest that students focus on these theme questions as they read:

Political and Social Systems
How did political and military rivalries push the European powers toward war in the early 1900s?

Global Interaction
Why did World War I become the first global war in history?

Economics and Technology
What impact did total war have on soldiers and civilians?

Continuity and Change
How did the peace treaties ending the war lead to both bitterness and hope?

◆ TIME LINE ACTIVITY

Share the About the Pictures note with students before asking questions about the time line such as these:

1. Which event happened first—the battle of the Somme or the assassination of Archduke Francis Ferdinand? *(assassination)*
2. How can you tell that World War I was extremely costly in terms of human lives? *(More than one million soldiers were killed in the battle of the Somme alone.)*
3. What event took place in the same year as the Treaty of Versailles? *(first Pan-African Congress)*

Don't Miss!

Comparing Viewpoints
Is War Ever Justified?
(Section 1)

You Are There . . .
Caring for the Wounded (Section 3)

World War I and Its Aftermath
1914–1919
Chapter Preview

1 The Stage Is Set
2 The Guns of August
3 A New Kind of Conflict
4 Winning the War
5 Making the Peace

1914
Archduke Francis Ferdinand of Austria-Hungary and his wife are killed in Sarajevo. The assassination sparks World War I.

1915
German submarines sink the ocean liner *Lusitania*.

1916
More than one million soldiers are killed in the battle of the Somme, shown above, but the war in Europe remains deadlocked.

CHAPTER EVENTS

1914   1915   1916

GLOBAL EVENTS

1914 The Panama Canal opens.

1916 Japan tries to establish a protectorate over China.

676 *Chapter 27*

▶ Resource Directory

Teaching Resources
Teaching With Themes Chapter Theme Activities, p. 30
Pacing Chart With Block Scheduling Guide Ch. 27

Technology
World History Color Transparencies Ch. 27 Graphic Organizer, p. F–55

The World at War, 1914–1918

World War I began in Europe. However, other world powers, as well as European colonies around the world, were drawn into the conflict.

Map labels: NORTH AMERICA, SOUTH AMERICA, EUROPE, ASIA, AFRICA, AUSTRALIA, ATLANTIC OCEAN, PACIFIC OCEAN, INDIAN OCEAN

Map Legend:
- Allies
- Central Powers
- Colonial possessions of Allies
- Colonial possessions of Central Powers

Robinson Projection
0   1500   3000 Miles
0   1500   3000 Kilometers

I WANT YOU FOR U.S. ARMY — NEAREST RECRUITING STATION

1917
The United States ends its policy of neutrality and enters the war. This famous poster is used to recruit American soldiers for the war effort.

1918
An armistice ends the war on November 11. This painting by George Luks shows an armistice celebration in New York.

1919
Delegates to the Paris Peace Conference draft the Treaty of Versailles, which blames Germany for the war.

1917 — 1917 The czar is overthrown in the Russian Revolution.

1918

1919 — 1919 The first Pan-African Congress meets in Paris.

Independent Assignments

Have students read one section as they prepare for class. After class, have them complete the assignment. Some students may benefit from using the Guided Reading and Review worksheets.

Section 1 Have students use the worksheet *Conflict in the Balkans: A Geographical Problem* in the Geography and History booklet, pp. 14–15, to learn about recent conflicts in the Balkans.

Section 2 Have students use the map *Europe in 1914* in the Historical Outline Map Book, p. 46, to locate and shade the countries of the Allied and Central Powers.

Section 3 Have students use the worksheet *Manfred, Baron von Richtofen* in the Unit 7 booklet, p. 12, to learn about the life of the "Red Baron."

Section 4 Have students use the worksheet *Recognizing Propaganda* in the Unit 7 booklet, p. 15, to learn more about government actions to encourage citizens to support the war effort.

Section 5 Have students use the map *Europe in 1918* in the Historical Outline Map Book, p. 47, to locate and label the countries of postwar Europe. Have them use shading to show territories lost by Austria-Hungary, Bulgaria, Germany, and Russia.

The World at War, 1914–1918

Activating Prior Knowledge
How might imperial rivalries explain why Germany opposed both France and Great Britain during World War I? *(Germany had not gained as much territory in Africa as had Britain and France. Germany might have hoped to gain territory by defeating France and Great Britain in a war.)*

Previewing
Have students look at the map. Ask which side might have a geographical advantage during the war. *(Possible answer: The Allies surrounded the Central Powers, which might give them an advantage during the war.)*

Background
About the Pictures

1. Archduke Francis Ferdinand hoped that his sympathy for Slavs would ease tensions between Austria-Hungary and the Balkans. His assassination, however, gave Austria-Hungary an excuse to crush Serbia, its long-time enemy in the Balkans.

2. At terrible cost (more than 600,000 Germans, more than 400,000 British, and nearly 200,000 French casualties), and after five months of fighting at the Battle of the Somme, the Allies gained only about seven miles. Still, the Western Front stood as solid as ever at the end of 1916.

3. After the United States entered the war, the government issued posters, such as this one, hoping to spark enthusiasm for the war and encourage enlistment in the armed forces.

4. In 1895 and 1896, during Cuba's fight for independence from Spain, George Benjamin Luks (1867–1933) was a war correspondent and artist for the *Philadelphia Bulletin*. Later, he was a member of the Ashcan school, young painters who broke with tradition and painted realistic and often gritty scenes of urban life.

eTeach

Be sure to check out this month's online discussion with a World History Master Teacher.

Go to **www.phschool.com**.

Bell Ringer

Have students scan this section and write down at least four general reasons why Europe was on the brink of war in the early 1900s. Ask students to comment on whether these same factors continue to cause international tension today.

LESSON PLAN

1. Focus After a century of relative peace in Europe, many felt optimistic about the future. However, aggressive nationalism, economic and imperial rivalries, militarism, and other forces pushed Europe toward war. By forming alliances to protect themselves, countries actually made war more likely.

2. Instruct Have students outline the various factors that helped lead to World War I. Advise students to first preview the section and to use the bold-faced heads to construct the skeleton of an outline. This skeleton outline should identify major causes of international tension in the early 1900s. Under each major cause, students should leave space for filling in supporting details. Next, have students read the section and complete their outlines by writing specific examples and supporting details under the appropriate head. Next, organize the class into small groups. Instruct the members of each group to compare and discuss their outlines. Students should use this time to make any necessary corrections or additions to their outlines.

3. Assess Ask students to review their outlines and to rank the causes of international tension from most significant to least significant. Invite students to share their rankings and to explain the reasons for their choices.

4. Reteach If students' Assess activity does not reflect adequate understanding of the lesson, you might assign the *Guide to the Essentials* or the *Interactive Student Tutorial CD-ROM* for this section.

Reading Focus

- What efforts in the early 1900s were made toward peace?
- How did nationalism and international rivalries push Europe toward war?
- What were the causes and effects of the European alliance system?

Vocabulary

pacifism
militarism
entente

Taking Notes

Copy this table. As you read, fill in the left-hand column with developments that promoted peace. In the right-hand column, list forces that were pushing Europe toward war.

EFFORTS AT PEACE	FORCES FOR WAR
• Modern Olympic games	• Aggressive nationalism
•	•
•	•

Main Idea In the late 1800s and early 1900s, a number of forces were pushing Europe to the brink of war.

Setting the Scene By 1914, Europe had enjoyed a century of relative peace. Many idealists hoped for a permanent end to the scourge of war. "The future belongs to peace," said French economist Frédéric Passy.

Others were less hopeful. "I shall not live to see the Great War," warned German chancellor Otto von Bismarck, "but you will see it, and it will start in the east." It was Bismarck's prediction, rather than Passy's, that came true.

The Pursuit of Peace

By the early 1900s, many efforts were underway to end war and foster understanding between nations. In 1896, the first modern Olympic games were held in Athens. Its founder hoped the games would promote "love of peace and respect for life." Alfred Nobel, the Swedish inventor of dynamite, regretted the military uses of his invention. In his will, he set up the annual Nobel Peace Prize to reward people who worked for peace.

The struggle for women's suffrage supported the peace movement. Dutch doctor Aletta Jacobs argued that if women won the vote, they could prevent war. "They don't feel as men do about war," Jacobs said. "They are the mothers of the race." Organizations such as the Women's International League for Peace and Freedom promoted pacifism, or opposition to all war.

Governments, too, backed peace efforts. In 1899, many world leaders attended the First Universal Peace Conference in the Netherlands. They set up the Hague Tribunal, a world court to settle disputes between nations. The Hague Tribunal could not force nations to submit their disputes, nor could it enforce its rulings. Still, it was a step toward keeping the peace.

Aggressive Nationalism

At the same time, other powerful forces were pushing Europe to the brink of war. Aggressive nationalism was one leading cause of international tension.

France and Germany Nationalist feelings were strong in both Germany and France. Germans were proud of their new empire's military power and industrial leadership. France longed to regain its position as Europe's leading power. The French were especially bitter about their 1871 defeat in the Franco-Prussian War and the German occupation of the border provinces of Alsace and Lorraine. Patriotic French citizens yearned for revenge against Germany and recovery of the "lost provinces."

678 Chapter 27

Resource Directory

Teaching Resources

Creative Teaching Activities Creative Teaching Activities booklet, p. 121
Guided Reading and Review Unit 7 booklet, p. 2
Comparing Viewpoints Chapter Extension Activities booklet, pp. 65–66

Is War Ever Justified?

In the years leading up to World War I, militarists glorified warfare, and pacifists strongly denounced war. Is war ever justified? Think about this enduring issue as you look at the following viewpoints.

China 300s B.C.

The warrior-philosopher Sun Tzu wrote *The Art of War,* an influential handbook of military strategy:

❝ A government should not mobilize an army out of anger, military leaders should not provoke a war out of wrath. Act when it is beneficial, desist when it is not. Anger can revert to joy, wrath can revert to delight, but a nation destroyed cannot be restored to existence, and the dead cannot be restored to life. **❞**

Germany 1913

Helmuth von Moltke, chief of the German General Staff, directed Germany's strategy at the beginning of World War I:

❝ The German people must be made to see that we have to attack because of our enemies' provocation. Things must be so built up that war will seem as a deliverance from the great armaments, the financial burdens, the political tensions. . . . Germany must regain what formerly she lost. **❞**

United States 1970s

The group Another Mother Against War created this poster.

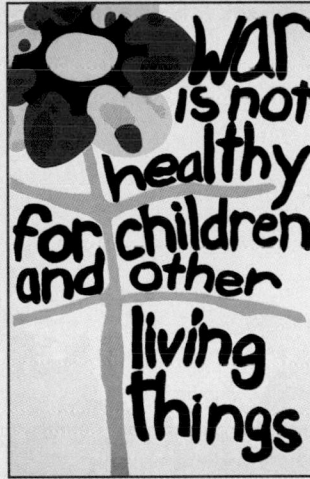

Zimbabwe 1978

Bishop Abel Muzorewa joined the struggle for majority rule in his nation and later served as prime minister:

❝ I question whether God himself would wish me to hide behind the principles of nonviolence while innocent persons were being slaughtered. **❞**

Skills Assessment

1. Which of the following would agree with the position that war should be avoided at all costs?
   A Sun Tzu
   B Helmuth von Moltke
   C Another Mother Against War
   D Abel Muzorewa

2. Sun Tzu and Bishop Muzorewa would probably agree that war
   E is justified in certain situations.
   F should be used by governments to gain revenge.
   G is a glorious and noble activity.
   H should be fought only to save innocent lives.

3. **Critical Thinking Making Decisions** You are running for the office of president of the United States. Write a brief position statement in which you explain under what circumstances you might send United States troops into action.

Skills Tip

Do not make hasty judgments about people's viewpoints. For example, you cannot automatically assume that every monarch will be against democracy or that every general will be in favor of war.

Background Other Viewpoints

Russia, 1700s Empress Catherine the Great, who greatly increased Russian territory, wrote of war: "The only way to save our empires from the encroaching of the people is to engage in war, and thus substitute national passions for social aspirations."

Cuba, Late 1800s Poet and revolutionary José Martí was a leader of his nation's fight against Spanish rule: "Anyone is a criminal who promotes an avoidable war. And so is he who does not promote an inevitable civil war."

India, 1948 Mohandas Gandhi, who led a nonviolent campaign to free India from British rule, denounced all forms of warfare and violence: "What difference does it make to the dead, the orphans and the homeless, whether the mad destruction is wrought under the name of totalitarianism or the holy name of democracy and liberty?"

Activity Interpreting Viewpoints

Critical Thinking: Comparing
Share the information in the Background note and then use these questions to generate class discussion.
1. How are the views of Martí, Gandhi, and Muzorewa alike? Different? *(All three are concerned about human rights, but only Gandhi flatly rejects violence.)*
2. How is the view of Sun Tzu similar to that of Martí? *(Both believe that there is an appropriate time and place for war, but it is better to wage war only when absolutely necessary.)*

Skills Tip

An individual's personal history and the sociopolitical history of the times affect that person's viewpoint. The Skills Handbook in the front of the book has a lesson that will help students with this feature.

Skills Assessment

ANSWERS 1. C **2.** E **3.** Students may cite defensive purposes or human rights violations as circumstances that might lead them to send troops into action.

▢ Block Scheduling Support

Share with students the information in the Human Drama Note in this section of the Teacher's Edition. Note that war toys, from action figures to tanks and machine guns, are available for children today. However, many parents refuse to buy toys of violence. Discuss with students whether they would buy such toys for their children. Why or why not? List students' reasons on the board. Then discuss whether attitudes about war have changed since World War I.

680 Chapter 27

Customize for...
Heterogeneous Groups

Relating Cause and Effect As a reinforcement activity, have students explain one effect of each of the following developments: (1) The French were defeated in the Franco-Prussian war and lost Alsace and Lorraine to Germany. (2) Russia felt kinship with other Slavic countries. (3) There was rising nationalism in Austria-Hungary and the Ottoman empire. (4) Germany gained territory as a result of the Moroccan crises. (5) Countries joined together in alliances. (Reteaching) ✳

Reading Strategy
Mapping Concepts

Have pairs of students construct a diagram or visual representation of key concepts and supporting details discussed in Section 1. To develop a conceptual map, students should (1) title their visual map "Forces Leading to War," (2) determine the main ideas surrounding this concept, and (3) determine supporting ideas for each main idea. *(Less Advanced Readers)*

European Alliances, 1914

Legend:
- Central Powers
- Allies
- Neutral Nations
- Neutral Nations that later joined the Central Powers
- Neutral Nations that later joined the Allies

Azimuthal Equal Area Projection
0   250   500 Miles
0   250   500 Kilometers

Standing Armies in Europe, 1914

Number of Soldiers (in millions)

ALLIES: Great Britain, France, Russia
CENTRAL POWERS: Austria-Hungary, Germany

Source: *The International Internet Encyclopedia*

Skills Assessment

Geography By 1914, most of Europe was divided into two armed camps. Millions of troops stood ready for war.

1. **Location** On the map, locate (a) Germany, (b) Austria-Hungary, (c) Serbia, (d) Russia, (e) France, (f) Great Britain.
2. **Region** Why would Germany worry about the alliance between France and Russia?
3. **Critical Thinking Synthesizing Information** Based on the map and the graph, which alliance do you think had the greater advantage in 1914?

Eastern Europe In Eastern Europe, Russia sponsored a powerful form of nationalism called Pan-Slavism. It held that all Slavic peoples shared a common nationality. As the largest Slavic country, Russia felt that it had a duty to lead and defend all Slavs. By 1914, it stood ready to support Serbia, a proud young nation that dreamed of creating a South Slav state.

Two old multinational empires particularly feared rising nationalism. Austria-Hungary worried that nationalism might foster rebellion among the many minority populations within its empire. Ottoman Turkey felt threatened by new nations on its borders, such as Serbia and Greece.

In 1912, several Balkan states attacked Turkey. The next year, the new Balkan states fought among themselves over the spoils of war. These brief but bloody Balkan wars raised tensions to a fever pitch. By 1914, the Balkans were the "powder keg of Europe"—a tiny spark might lead to an explosion.

Rivalries Among European Powers

Economic rivalries further poisoned the international atmosphere. Britain felt threatened by Germany's rapid economic growth. By 1900, Germany's new factories were outproducing Britain's older ones. Britain, therefore, had strong economic reasons to oppose Germany in any conflict. The Germans, in turn, thought the other great powers did not give them enough respect.

Imperialism Imperial rivalries also divided European nations. In 1905 and again in 1911, competition for colonies brought France and Germany to the brink of war. Germany wanted to prevent France from imposing a protectorate on Morocco. Although diplomats kept the peace, Germany did gain some territory in central Africa. As a result of the two Moroccan crises, Britain and France began to form closer ties against Germany.

680 Chapter 27

Skills Assessment

ANSWERS 1. Review locations with students. **2.** France and Russia bordered Germany on two sides and could attack from both directions at once. **3.** Possible answer: The Allies did. They had greater troop strength and they surrounded the major Central Powers.

Resource Directory

Teaching Resources

Geography and History Activity *Conflict in the Balkans: A Geographical Problem,* Geography and History booklet, pp. 14–15
Section Quiz Unit 7 booklet, p. 3

Technology

Interactive Student Tutorial CD-ROM Ch. 27
Computer Test Bank Ch. 27

Militarism and the Arms Race The 1800s saw a rise in militarism, the glorification of the military. It grew partly out of Social Darwinism. Echoing the idea of "survival of the fittest," one German militarist called war "a biological necessity of the first importance." Militarists painted war in romantic colors. Young men dreamed of blaring trumpets and dashing cavalry charges—not at all the sort of conflict they would soon face.

With international tensions on the rise, the great powers expanded their armies and navies. The result was an arms race that further increased suspicions and made war more likely. The fiercest competition was the naval rivalry between Britain and Germany. To protect its vast overseas empire, Britain had built the world's most respected navy. As Germany began acquiring overseas colonies, it began to build up its own navy. Suspicious of Germany's motives, Britain in turn increased naval spending.

As readiness for war came to dominate national policy, military leaders came to gain wider influence. On matters of peace and war, governments turned to military leaders for advice. German generals and British admirals enjoyed great respect and got more funds to build up their forces.

A Tangle of Alliances

Distrust led the great powers to sign treaties pledging to defend one another. These alliances were intended to create powerful combinations that no one would dare attack. Gradually, two huge alliances emerged.

The first of these alliances had its origins in Bismarck's day. He knew that France longed to avenge its defeat in the Franco-Prussian War. Sure that France would not attack Germany without help, Bismarck signed treaties with other powers. In 1882, he formed the Triple Alliance with Italy and Austria-Hungary. In 1914, when war did erupt, Germany and Austria-Hungary fought on the same side. They became known as the Central Powers.

A rival bloc took shape in 1894, when France and Russia formed an alliance. In 1904, France and Britain signed an entente (ahn TAHNT), a nonbinding agreement to follow common policies. Though not as formal as a treaty, the entente led to close military and diplomatic ties. Britain later signed a similar agreement with Russia. When war began, these powers became known as the Allies.

Other alliances also formed. Germany signed a treaty with the Ottoman empire, while Britain drew close to Japan. The growth of rival alliance systems increased international tensions. A local conflict could easily mushroom into a general war.

SECTION 1 Assessment

Recall
1. Identify: (a) Hague Tribunal,
(b) Pan-Slavism, **(c)** Central
Powers, **(d)** Allies.
2. Define: (a) pacifism,
(b) militarism, **(c)** entente.

Comprehension
3. Identify three peace efforts of the late 1800s and early 1900s.
4. Describe how each of the following served to inflame tensions in Europe: **(a)** nationalism,
(b) imperial rivalries,
(c) militarism.

5. (a) Why did European nations form alliances? **(b)** How did alliances increase fears of war?

Critical Thinking and Writing
6. Applying Information Reread Bismarck's statement at the start of this section. Why do you think he made this prediction?
7. Linking Past and Present Do you think the idea of going to war excites young people today in the same way that it did 100 years ago? Why or why not?

Activity
Take It to the NET
Use Internet sources to find out about peace efforts today. Then, choose someone whom you would nominate for the Nobel Peace Prize. Write a brief paragraph explaining why you think he or she deserves the honor.

SECTION 2 The Guns of August

Bell Ringer Have students consider an imaginary country whose head of state is murdered by a foreign assassin. Ask students whether they would blame the country from which the assassin came. Would they recommend punishing both the assassin and his homeland? Have students share their ideas in a class discussion.

Reading Focus

■ How did ethnic tensions in the Balkans spark a political assassination?

■ How did conflict between Austria-Hungary and Serbia widen?

■ How do historians view the outbreak of World War I?

Vocabulary

ultimatum
mobilize
neutrality

Taking Notes

Copy this flowchart. Include at least five empty boxes. As you read, fill in the chain of events in the summer of 1914 that led to an all-out war.

Francis Ferdinand is assassinated
↓
↓
↓
↓
Britain declares war on Germany

Main Idea The assassination of Archduke Francis Ferdinand ignited the Balkan "powder keg" and sparked World War I.

LESSON PLAN

1. Focus Long-simmering conflicts in the Balkans boiled over in 1914 when a Serb nationalist assassinated Archduke Francis Ferdinand. Self-interest, alliances, and a desire to punish past transgressions transformed the incident into a general European war. Today, most historians agree that the blame for World War I lies with all the nations involved.

2. Instruct On the board, work with the class to construct and fill in the flowchart described in Taking Notes at the top of this page. The flowchart should begin with the assassination of Archduke Francis Ferdinand and end with the British declaration of war on Germany. Discuss with students how each event led to the next.

3. Assess Ask students: (1) At what point do you think war became inevitable? (2) What actions might individual nations have taken to avoid war? (3) Could such a chain of events occur today? Why or why not?

4. Reteach If students' Assess activity does not reflect adequate understanding of the lesson, you might assign the *Guide to the Essentials* or the *Interactive Student Tutorial CD-ROM* for this section.

Connections to Today

A New Balkan Powder Keg?

"Crisis in the Balkans! Threat of War!" Some 80 years after the assassination of Francis Ferdinand, headlines like these flared in the world's newspapers. In 1991, rivalries among Eastern Orthodox Serbs, Muslim Bosnians, and Catholic Croats led to civil war in Bosnia. More than 250,000 people died, and millions fled their homes. In 1995, American and European troops helped restore peace.

Tensions flared again when Serbia moved to suppress an independence movement by Muslim Albanians in the province of Kosovo. In 1999, the United States and its allies took military action against the Serbian government.

Theme: Geography and History Identify two other places where religious or ethnic differences have led to conflict.

Setting the Scene

Bertha von Suttner devoted her life to peace. Though the daughter of a noble Austrian military family, she wrote a best-selling antiwar novel and organized a peace society. Her tireless work won her the nickname "Peace Bertha." Yet, in April 1913, Suttner wrote in her diary that "the great European disaster is well on its way. If so many seeds have been sown, surely the weeds will sprout up soon and surely so much stockpiled gunpowder will explode."

"Peace Bertha" died on June 20, 1914. Eight days later, an assassin's bullet set off the "gunpowder" and ignited a war that engulfed much of the world for four bloody years.

Assassination in Sarajevo

The crisis began when Archduke Francis Ferdinand of Austria-Hungary announced that he would visit Sarajevo (sar uh YAY voh), the capital of Bosnia. At the time, Bosnia was under the rule of Austria-Hungary. But it was also the home of many Serbs and other Slavs.

Serbian Outrage News of the royal visit angered many Serbian nationalists. They viewed the Austrians as foreign oppressors. Even worse, the date chosen for the archduke's visit, June 28, was a special date in Serbian history. It was on that date in 1389, Serbia had been conquered by the Ottoman empire. On the very same date in 1912, Serbia had at last freed itself from Turkish rule.

Some members of Unity or Death, a Serbian terrorist group commonly known as the Black Hand, vowed to take action. As one conspirator later recalled, "Our decision was taken almost immediately. Death to the tyrant!"

The Fatal Shots The archduke ignored warnings of anti-Austrian unrest in Sarajevo. On June 28, 1914, he and his wife, Sophie, rode through Sarajevo in an open car. Stationed along the route were several Black Hand conspirators. As the cars passed, one of the conspirators hurled a bomb. It missed the archduke but injured an officer in another car.

Later that day, the archduke asked to visit the wounded officer in the hospital. He did not know that one of the conspirators, Gavrilo Princip (GAHV ree loh PREEN tseep), was still waiting. As the car set out, Princip sprang forward and fired twice into the back seat. Moments later, the archduke and his wife were dead.

Connections to Today

ANSWER Answers may include the Middle East, Northern Ireland, India, and parts of Africa.

Resource Directory

Teaching Resources

Creative Teaching Activities Creative Teaching Activities booklet, p. 122

Guided Reading and Review Unit 7 booklet, p. 4

Technology

World History Color Transparencies political cartoon dealing with conditions that increase the possibility of war, p. E–45

Block Scheduling Support

Have students choose four countries that were involved in World War I and write a headline about the assassination that a newspaper of each country might have printed. Note that students must take into account the political viewpoint and bias that each newspaper might have had. Have students display their headlines—with the national origin of each clearly labeled—around the classroom. Invite other students to identify and explain any biases that they see in each headline. ※

The Conflict Widens

The news of his nephew's death shocked the aging Austrian emperor, Francis Joseph. Still, he was reluctant to go to war. His government in Vienna, however, saw the incident as an excuse to crush Serbia for good.

A Harsh Ultimatum Austria sent Serbia a sweeping ultimatum, or final set of demands. To avoid war, said the ultimatum, Serbia must end all anti-Austrian agitation and punish any Serbian official involved in the murder plot. It must even let Austria join in the investigation.

Serbia agreed to most, but not all, of the terms of Austria's ultimatum. This partial refusal gave Austria the opportunity it was seeking. On July 28, Austria declared war on Serbia.

From Capital to Capital A war between a major power and a small Balkan state might have been another "summer war," like most European wars of the past century. But as diplomats sent notes from capital to capital, larger forces drew the great powers deeper into conflict.

Austria-Hungary might not have pushed Serbia into war at all without the backing of its longtime ally, Germany. In Berlin, Kaiser William II was horrified at the assassination of a royal heir. He wrote to Francis Joseph, advising him to take a firm stand toward Serbia. The kaiser assured the emperor of Germany's full support. Thus, instead of urging restraint, William II gave Austria a "blank check."

Serbia meanwhile sought help from Russia, the champion of Slavic nations. From St. Petersburg, Nicholas II telegraphed William II. The czar asked the kaiser to urge Austria to soften its demands. When this plea failed, Russia began to mobilize, or prepare its military forces for war. Germany responded by declaring war on Russia.

Russia, in turn, appealed to its ally France. In Paris, nationalists saw a chance to avenge France's defeat in the Franco-Prussian War. Though French leaders had some doubts, they gave Russia the same kind of backing Germany offered Austria. When Germany demanded that France keep out of the conflict, France refused. Germany then declared war on France. By early August, the battle lines were hardening.

The Schlieffen Plan Italy and Britain remained uncommitted. Italy chose to remain neutral for the time being. Neutrality is a policy of supporting neither side in a war. Britain had to decide quickly whether or not to support its ally France. Then, Germany's war plans suddenly made the decision for Britain.

Years earlier, General Alfred von Schlieffen (SHLEE fuhn) had developed a plan of attack against France. The Schlieffen Plan was designed to avoid a two-front war—against France in the west and Russia to the east. Schlieffen reasoned that Russia's lumbering military would be slow to mobilize. Under the Schlieffen Plan, Germany first had to defeat France quickly. Then, it would fight Russia.

To ensure a swift victory in the west, the Schlieffen Plan required German armies to march through Belgium, then swing south behind French lines. On August 3, Germany invaded Belgium. However, Britain and other European powers had signed a treaty guaranteeing Belgian neutrality. Outraged by the invasion of Belgium, Britain declared war on Germany.

"Who Killed the Peace of Europe?"
One by one, the major powers of Europe were drawn into war. This cartoon appeared in an American newspaper in the summer of 1914.

Theme: Global Interaction What point is this cartoon making about the events leading up to the war?

Human Drama Note

How Harsh Was It? When British diplomat Edward Grey read Austria's ultimatum to Serbia, he declared it to be the most formidable demand ever imposed on one state by another. When the note reached Serbia, the minister of public information commented: "Well, there is nothing to do but die fighting." Meanwhile, Kaiser William II, who was vacationing aboard a cruise ship off the coast of Norway, dismissed the note as nothing more than "a spirited note."

Test Preparation

Have students read the third paragraph under "From Capital to Capital" on this page, and then answer the question below.

What does *champion* mean in this context?

(A) defender of others

B best of the group

C top winner

D prize winner

Caption Answer

The cartoon indicates that European nations blamed one another for the coming of the war. The large pointing finger, in the upper left, however, suggests that all were to blame.

Recall
1. **(a)** Francis Ferdinand, p. 682
(b) Gavrilo Princip, p. 682 **(c)** Schlieffen
Plan, p. 683 2. **(a)** ultimatum, p. 683
(b) mobilize, p. 683 **(c)** neutrality, p. 683

Comprehension
3. **(a)** Serbian nationalists planned the
assassination as a way to protest Austria-
Hungary's rule over Bosnia, where many
Serbs lived. **(b)** Austria-Hungary sent Serbia a harsh ultimatum. When Serbia did
not fully comply, Austria-Hungary declared
war. 4. **(a)** Germany gave Austria-Hungary
a "blank check," promising to support its
ally in taking a firm stand against Serbia.
(b) In response to Serbia's plea for help,
Russia mobilized its troops. **(c)** Germany
declared war on France because France
had an alliance with Russia. **(d)** Britain
declared war on Germany because Germany violated Belgian neutrality. 5. Most
historians believe that all the major European powers must share blame for the war.

Critical Thinking and Writing
6. Students' answer should demonstrate
understanding of the conditions that
existed in 1914 and the possible consequences of failing to support an ally.
7. Possible answer: Because of its location
between France and Russia, Germany
was in danger of fighting a war on two
fronts. The German invasion route
through Belgium helped bring Britain
into the war.

Activity Rubrics

Share rubrics with students before they
draw their cartoons.

Attempted Student does not complete
the cartoon, or the cartoon shows little
understanding of the subject.

Minimal The cartoon shows understanding of the subject but is poorly
rendered.

Adequate The cartoon shows a good
understanding of the subject and is
well rendered.

Exemplary The cartoon shows excellent understanding of the subject and is
exceptionally well rendered.

Caption Answer

To fulfill the Schlieffen Plan, these German
troops would first attempt to defeat France.
The picture shows that they were confident
of capturing Paris, the French capital.

Off to War
Like most European soldiers in 1914,
these young Germans optimistically
believed that they would be "home
by Christmas." They had no idea of
the horrors that lay ahead.

**Theme: Geography and
History** Why did these soldiers
write the word "Paris" on their
troop train?

The Historians' View

How could an assassination lead to all-out war in just
a few weeks? During the war, each side blamed the
other. Afterward, the victorious Allies placed all blame
on Germany, because it was the first country to invade
another. Today, most historians agree that all parties
must share blame for a catastrophe nobody wanted.

Each of the great powers believed that its cause
was just. Austria-Hungary wanted to punish Serbia for
encouraging terrorism. Germany felt that it must stand
by its one dependable ally, Austria-Hungary. Russia
saw the Austrian ultimatum to Serbia as an effort to
oppress Slavic peoples. France feared that if it did not
support Russia, it would have to face Germany alone
later. Britain felt committed to protect Belgium but also
feared the powerful German force on the other side of
the English Channel.

Once the machinery of war was set in motion, it
seemed impossible to stop. In *The Guns of August*, a
widely read study of the outbreak of the war, historian
Barbara Tuchman wrote:

> "[Military] staffs, goaded by their relent-
> less timetables, were pounding the table
> for the signal to move lest their oppo-
> nents gain an hour's head start. Appalled
> upon the brink, the chiefs of state who
> would be ultimately responsible for their
> country's fate attempted to back away but
> the pull of military schedules dragged
> them forward."
> —Barbara Tuchman, *The Guns of August*

Although leaders made the decisions, most people on both sides were
equally committed to military action. Young men rushed to enlist, cheered
on by women and their elders. Now that war had come at last, it seemed
an exciting adventure.

British diplomat Edward Grey was less optimistic. As armies began to
move, he predicted, "The lamps are going out all over Europe. We shall not
see them lit again in our lifetime."

SECTION 2 Assessment

Recall
1. **Identify:** **(a)** Francis Ferdinand,
(b) Gavrilo Princip, **(c)** Schlieffen
Plan.
2. **Define:** **(a)** ultimatum,
(b) mobilize, **(c)** neutrality.

Comprehension
3. **(a)** Why was Archduke Francis
Ferdinand assassinated? **(b)** How
did Austria-Hungary react?
4. Describe how each of the
following nations was drawn into
the conflict: **(a)** Germany,
(b) Russia, **(c)** France, **(d)** Britain.
5. Who do most modern historians
think was responsible for the war?

Critical Thinking and Writing
6. **Drawing Conclusions** Do you
think war could have been avoided in 1914? Why or why not?
7. **Connecting to Geography** What
role did geography play in the
outbreak of World War I?

Activity

**Drawing a Political
Cartoon**
Choose one of the
European powers involved
in the outbreak of World
War I. Then, from that
nation's point of view,
draw a cartoon assigning
blame for the war.

Resource Directory

Teaching Resources
Section Quiz Unit 7 booklet, p. 5
Creative Teaching Activities Creative Teaching
Activities booklet, p. 123
Guided Reading and Review Unit 7 booklet, p. 6
History Through Literature *All Quiet on the Western
Front*, History Through Literature booklet, pp. 57–58
Technology
Interactive Student Tutorial CD-ROM Ch. 27
Computer Test Bank Ch. 27

World History Color Transparencies *Troops
Resting*, p. D–81
World History Visions, Voices, Views Global Issues
Forum, *When Should the United States Use Force in
the Post-Cold War World?*, videodisc side 4 or video-
tape 7, running time 4:00 min.

Side 4: Fr. 15886-22920

SECTION **3** A New Kind of Conflict

Reading Focus

- Why did a stalemate develop on the Western Front?

- How did technology make World War I different from earlier wars?

- How did the war become a global conflict?

Vocabulary

stalemate

no man's land

zeppelin

U-boat

convoy

Taking Notes

Copy this concept web. As you read, fill in important facts about the various battle fronts of World War I. Add as many circles as you need.

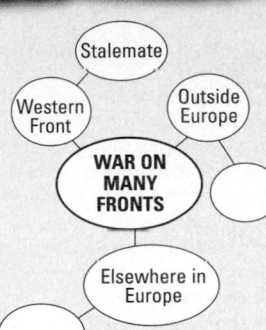

Main Idea Modern weapons resulted in huge numbers of casualties and helped prevent either side from gaining an advantage.

Setting the Scene The "Great War," as newspapers soon called it, was the largest conflict in history up to that time. The French mobilized almost 8.5 million men, the British 9 million, the Russians 12 million, and the Germans 11 million. But for those who fought, the statistics were more personal. "One out of every four men who went out to the World War did not come back again," recalled a survivor, "and of those who came back, many are maimed and blind and some are mad."

The early enthusiasm for the war soon faded. There were no stirring cavalry charges, no quick and glorious victories. This was a new kind of war, far deadlier than any ever fought before.

The Western Front

As the war began, German forces swept through Belgium toward Paris. German generals, however, soon violated the Schlieffen Plan. Russia mobilized more quickly than expected. After Russian forces won a few small victories in eastern Prussia, Germany hastily shifted some troops to the east. That move weakened German forces in the west. In September 1914, when British troops reached France, they joined the French along the Marne River. The battle of the Marne pushed back the German offensive and destroyed Germany's hopes for a quick victory on the Western Front.

Both sides then dug in for the winter. They did not know that the conflict would turn into a long, deadly **stalemate,** a deadlock in which neither side is able to defeat the other. Battle lines in France would remain almost unchanged for four years.

Trench Warfare On the Western Front, the warring armies burrowed into a vast system of trenches, stretching from the Swiss frontier to the English Channel. An American war correspondent described the scene:

"There were vast stretches of mud, of fields once cultivated, but now scarred with pits, trenches, rusty barbed wires. The roads were rivers of clay. They were lined with dugouts, cellars, and caves. These burrows in the earth were supported by beams, and suggested a shaft in a disused mine."
—Richard H. Davis, *With the French in France and Salonika*

An underground network linked bunkers, communications trenches, and gun emplacements. There, millions of soldiers roasted under the broiling

Did You Know?

The Christmas Truce

On December 24, 1914, British troops reported an amazing sight: Christmas trees and Chinese lanterns along the German front line. They were even more amazed to see some Germans walking toward the British trenches shouting, "Hello! I want to talk to you!" So began the unofficial Christmas Truce. Ignoring orders from headquarters, small groups of enemy soldiers drank a toast and exchanged gifts such as chocolate or jam. One German also recalled playing soccer against a Scottish regiment wearing kilts.

Theme: Global Interaction Why do you think commanders opposed the Christmas Truce?

CARING FOR THE WOUNDED

Bell Ringer Reruns of the TV show *M*A*S*H,* set in the Korean War, portray medical techniques that are often crude by today's standards. Point out that World War I took place about 35 years earlier than the Korean War. Modern medicine was still in its infancy, and no helicopters transported the critically wounded. Ask students to imagine being medical personnel at that time.

Background
About the Scene

Poison Gases Victims of poison gases (mustard, chlorine, phosgene) died horrible deaths, often taking days or weeks to die. Victims often had to be strapped to their beds because their agony made them thrash about. The first protective measures were crude—men breathed through their mouths while holding between their teeth a cloth pad soaked in hyposulphite and wrapped in thin fabric.

Activity
Cooperative Learning

Presenting Research Have pairs or small groups choose a subject related to the feature, research it, and present the results in a format of their choosing—skit, oral report, taped report, and so on. One interesting topic might be the story of Edith Cavell, a British nurse who died a martyr's death saving Allied soldiers.

Portfolio Assessment Rubrics

Share rubrics with students before they write their letters.

Attempted The letter is poorly written and organized, contains many mechanical errors, and shows little empathy with the medic.

Minimal The letter shows empathy with the medic, but is poorly written and organized, and contains many mechanical errors.

Adequate The letter shows empathy with the medic, is well written and organized, and contains few mechanical errors.

Exemplary The letter shows great empathy with the medic, is very well written and organized, and contains no mechanical errors.

The echoes of the last exploding shells have died away. The stench of poison gas still lingers, and cries of the wounded fill the air. You and the other medics pick your way through mud and corpses to retrieve the wounded, trying hard to ignore the horror of the scene. . . .

You find a soldier groaning in pain from a head wound. You and three other medics carry him on a stretcher through a long tunnel to a first-aid station in a dugout shelter. A doctor and a nurse evaluate his condition and treat him with the primitive supplies on hand. You hope this soldier survives until he is taken by ambulance or train for further treatment.

You have seen too many men felled by poison gas, which can cause blindness, skin rashes, and even death. To protect themselves, soldiers must wear masks that also allow them to talk and hear.

You pass by these French troops proudly displaying their catch of trench rats. The rats carry disease and feed on corpses.

Portfolio Assessment

After an exhausting day of caring for the wounded, you decide to write a letter to your family back home. In the letter, you describe your feelings of frustration at the hazards faced by soldiers and the limited supplies that you have to treat them.

Resource Directory

Teaching Resources
Viewpoint Activity *Soldier-Poets View World War I,* Unit 7 booklet, p. 14
You Are There Chapter Extension Activities booklet, p. 67

Europe at War, 1914–1918

Legend:
- Allies, 1918
- Central Powers, 1918
- Neutral Nations
- Farthest advance by Central Powers
- ★ Battle sites

Azimuthal Equal Area Projection
0   250   500 Miles
0   250   500 Kilometers

summer sun or froze through the long winters. They shared their food with rats and their beds with lice.

Between the opposing trench lines lay "no man's land." In this empty tract, pocked with shell holes, every house and tree had long since been destroyed. Through coils of barbed wire, soldiers peered over the edges of their trenches, watching for the next attack. They themselves would have to charge into this man-made desert when officers gave the order.

Sooner or later, soldiers would obey the order to go "over the top." With no protection but their rifles and helmets, they charged across no man's land toward the enemy lines. With luck, they might overrun a few trenches. In time, the enemy would launch a counterattack, with similar results. Each side then rushed in reinforcements to replace the dead and wounded. The struggle continued, back and forth, over a few hundred yards of territory.

Costly Battles In 1916, both the Allies and Central Powers launched massive offensives to break the stalemate. German forces tried to overwhelm the French at Verdun (vuhr DUHN). The French sent up the battle cry "They shall not pass." The French defenders held firm, but the 11-month struggle cost more than a half-million casualties on both sides.

An Allied offensive at the Somme (SAHM) River was even more costly. In a single grisly day, 60,000 British soldiers were killed or wounded. In the five-month battle, over one million soldiers were killed, without either side winning an advantage.

Technology of Modern Warfare

Modern weapons added greatly to the destructiveness of the war. Rapid-fire machine guns mowed down waves of soldiers, making it nearly impossible to advance across no man's land. Artillery allowed troops to shell enemy lines and cities from more than 10 miles away.

In 1915, Germany began using poison gas that blinded or choked its victims or caused agonizing burns and blisters. Later that year, the Allies also began to use gas. Though soldiers were eventually given gas masks, poison

Skills Assessment

Geography World War I was fought on many fronts, with massive losses of life and property.

1. **Location** On the map, locate (a) Tannenburg, (b) Verdun, (c) Paris, (d) Caporetto, (e) the Dardanelles.
2. **Movement** How far into France did the Central Powers advance?
3. **Critical Thinking Making Inferences** Based on this map, why were many Russians demoralized by the progress of the war?

Activity
Connections to Literature

Analyzing a Poem The massive destruction and brutality of World War I overwhelmed the sensibilities of writers who viewed the conflict firsthand. One such writer was Wilfred Owen, an English poet who shared his experiences in order to reveal the senseless nature of modern warfare. In his poem "Dulce et Decorum Est," found in many anthologies of English literature, Owen describes grueling marches, harsh conditions on the front, and the terror of a gas attack. His vivid, detailed account of violence and death nullifies patriotic sentiments about the glory of dying for one's country. He emphasizes the conflict between reality and idealism by repeating the Latin saying "Sweet and becoming it is to die for one's country."

Have students read the poem and answer the following questions:
(1) How does Owen describe life at the front? (2) Why does he describe the death of a soldier in such vivid detail? (3) What effect do you think he hoped to achieve by repeating the Latin quotation "Dulce et decorum est" at the end of the poem?

Human Drama Note

A Fine-Feathered Friend When American troops arrived in Europe, they brought with them some 15,000 specially trained carrier pigeons. Military officials later boasted that 95 percent of the messages carried by their pigeons arrived safely.

In 1918, a pigeon saved the American 77th Division from almost certain destruction. The Americans were caught behind enemy lines and under heavy bombardment from Allied artillery units. They released a pigeon with their location and this frantic message: "For heaven's sake, stop it." The pigeon reached the Allied lines missing an eye and a leg. But it delivered the message, and the shelling was stopped. The bird was later awarded a Distinguished Service Cross and was displayed in the Smithsonian Institution.

Skills Assessment

ANSWERS 1. Review locations with students. 2. within about 50 miles of Paris 3. The Central Powers had advanced far into Russia.

Activity
Connections to Film

Writing a Diary The 1981 Australian film *Gallipoli*, directed by Peter Weir and starring Mel Gibson, studies youthful idealism and the harsh realities of World War I. The film begins in Australia, where young men, driven by patriotism and adventure, eagerly volunteer to join the war. They happily march off to the sounds of cheering crowds and martial music. When they land on the beaches of Gallipoli, however, they must suddenly confront war's terrible destruction and the fact that many of them will never return home. The film's final scenes vividly reenact the carnage of trench warfare in World War I.

Have students imagine that they are among the Australian troops at Gallipoli. Assign them to write four diary entries that reflect their changing attitudes about World War I—one entry for each of the following events in the film: (1) their enlistment in the army, (2) their arrival and training in Egypt, (3) their first encounter with battle at Gallipoli, (4) their realization that they most likely will die in the next charge against the Turkish line. (*Gallipoli* is available on videocassette, laserdisc, and DVD.)

World War I Technology

Airplane

A one- or two-seat propeller plane was equipped with a machine gun. At first the planes were used mainly for observation. Later, "flying aces" engaged in individual combat, though such "dogfights" had little effect on the war.

Automatic machine gun

A mounted gun that fired a rapid, continuous stream of bullets made it possible for a few gunners to mow down waves of soldiers. This helped create a stalemate by making it difficult to advance across no man's land.

Submarine

These underwater ships, or U-boats, could launch torpedoes, or guided underwater bombs. Used by Germany to destroy Allied shipping, U-boat attacks helped bring the United States into the war.

Connections to Today

World War I was the first modern, fully industrialized war. Some weapons, such as submarines and machine guns, altered the nature of the fighting. Other new technology, such as airplanes, did not have its greatest impact until years later.

Skills Assessment **Chart** Which invention on this chart do you think has done the most to change how wars are fought? Explain.

gas remained one of the most dreaded hazards of the war. One British soldier recalled the effects of being gassed:

"I suppose I resembled a kind of fish with my mouth open gasping for air. It seemed as if my lungs were gradually shutting up and my heart pounded away in my ears like the beat of a drum. . . . To get air into my lungs was real agony."

—William Pressey, quoted in *People at War 1914–1918* (Moynihan)

Although poison gas could be fatal, it was an uncertain weapon. Shifting winds might blow the gas back on the side that launched it.

In 1916, Britain introduced a new weapon, the armored tank. Mounted with machine guns, the tanks were designed to move across broken ground and through barbed wire. Still, the first tanks moved slowly and broke down often. They did little to break the stalemate.

Both sides also used aircraft. At first, planes simply observed enemy troop movements. In 1915, Germany used **zeppelins,** large gas-filled balloons, to bomb the English coast. Later, both sides equipped airplanes with machine guns. Pilots known as "flying aces" battled in the skies. These "dogfights" were spectacular, but had little effect on the course of the war.

Submarines proved much more important. German submarines roamed the Atlantic. These **U-boats** did tremendous damage to the Allied side, sinking merchant ships that carried vital supplies to Britain. To counteract submarine warfare, the Allies organized **convoys,** or groups of merchant ships protected by warships. As you will read, Germany's policy of unrestricted submarine warfare would eventually help bring the United States into the war.

A Global Conflict

On Europe's Eastern Front, battle lines swayed back and forth, sometimes over large areas. Casualties rose even higher than on the Western Front, but the results were just as indecisive.

Eastern Europe In August 1914, Russian armies pushed into eastern Germany. Then, at the battle of Tannenburg, the Russians suffered one of the worst defeats of the war, causing them to retreat. After Tannenburg, armies in the east fought on Russian soil. As the least industrialized of the great powers, Russia was poorly equipped to fight a modern war. Troops sometimes lacked even rifles. Still, Russian commanders continued to throw masses of peasant soldiers into combat.

Southern Europe Southeastern Europe was another battleground. In 1915, Bulgaria joined the Central Powers and helped crush its old Balkan rival Serbia. That same year, Italy declared war on Austria-Hungary and, later on Germany. Italy had signed a secret treaty with the Allies to gain Austrian-ruled lands inhabited by Italians.

In October 1917, the Austrians and Germans launched a major offensive against the Italian position at Caporetto.

The Italians retreated in disarray. British and French forces later helped stop the Central Powers' advance into Italy. Still, Caporetto proved as disastrous for Italy as Tannenburg had been for Russia.

The War Outside Europe Though most of the fighting took place in Europe, World War I was a global conflict. Japan, allied with Britain, used the war as an excuse to seize German outposts in China and islands in the Pacific. It also tried to impose a protectorate on China.

The Ottoman empire joined the Central Powers in 1914. The Turks then closed off Allied ships from the Dardanelles, a vital strait connecting the Black Sea and the Mediterranean. In 1915, the Allies sent a massive force of British, Indian, Australian, and New Zealander troops to open up the strait. At the battle of Gallipoli (guh LIHP uh lee), Turkish troops tied down the trapped Allies on the beaches. In January 1916, after 10 months and more than 200,000 casualties, the Allies finally withdrew from the Dardanelles.

In turn, the Turks were hard hit in the Middle East. The Ottoman empire included vast areas of Arab land. In 1916, Arab nationalists led by Husayn ibn Ali declared a revolt against Ottoman rule. The British sent Colonel T. E. Lawrence—later known as Lawrence of Arabia—to support the Arab revolt. Lawrence led guerrilla raids against the Turks, dynamiting bridges and supply trains. Eventually, the Ottoman empire lost a great deal of territory to the Arabs, including the key city of Baghdad.

War and the Colonies European colonies were drawn into the struggle. The Allies overran scattered German colonies in Africa and Asia. They also turned to their own colonies and dominions for troops, laborers, and supplies. Canada, Australia, and New Zealand sent troops to Britain's aid. Colonial recruits from British India and French West Africa fought on European battlefields.

People in the colonies had mixed feelings about serving. Some were reluctant to serve the imperial powers. "When we speak of joining," remarked a South African man, "our women curse and spit at us, asking us whether the Government, for whom we propose to risk our lives, is not the one which sends the police to our houses at night . . . to trample upon us."

Other colonial troops volunteered eagerly. They expected that their service would be a step toward citizenship or independence. As you will read, such hopes would be dashed after the war.

SECTION 3 Assessment

Recall
1. **Identify:** (a) Western Front, (b) Verdun, (c) Somme, (d) Tannenburg, (e) Caporetto, (f) Gallipoli, (g) T. E. Lawrence.
2. **Define:** (a) stalemate, (b) no man's land, (c) zeppelin, (d) U-boat, (e) convoy.

Comprehension
3. Why did the war on the Western Front turn into a stalemate?
4. Describe three ways new technology affected the war.
5. What role did Europe's overseas colonies and dominions play in World War I?

Critical Thinking and Writing
6. **Linking Past and Present** Why do you think most nations today have agreed to ban the use of poison gas and other chemical and biological weapons?
7. **Predicting Consequences** Governments on both sides of World War I tried to keep full casualty figures and other bad news from reaching the public. What effect do you think news about disastrous defeats such as Tannenburg, Caporetto, or Gallipoli would have had on the attitude of people back home?

Activity

Conducting an Interview
With a partner, conduct an interview between a war correspondent and a soldier fighting on the Western Front during World War I. Include at least ten questions and answers. You may wish to tape your interview.

Chapter 27 **689**

Test Preparation

Have students read the quote in the second paragraph under the heading "War and the Colonies" on this page, and then answer the question below.

Which is the best summary of the passage?

A South African wives hated their husbands for fighting.

B The South African police forced men to fight in the war.

C South African wives encouraged their husbands to fight in World War I.

D South African wives did not want their husbands to fight to save a government that did not respect their rights.

SECTION 3 Assessment

Recall
1. (a) Western Front, p. 685 (b) Verdun, p. 687 (c) Somme, p. 687 (d) Tannenburg, p. 688 (e) Caporetto, p. 688 (f) Gallipoli, p. 689 (g) T.E. Lawrence, p. 689 2. (a) stalemate, p. 685 (b) no man's land, p. 687 (c) zeppelin, p. 688 (d) U-boat, p. 688 (e) convoy, p. 688

Comprehension
3. Due to deadly weapons, neither side was able to advance. They dug into trenches and fought, back and forth, over a few hundred yards of land. 4. Machine guns made it difficult for ground troops to advance. Airplanes supplied information on enemy troops. Germany used submarines to disrupt Allied shipping. 5. European powers turned to their colonies for troops, labor, and supplies. In some places, warring countries tried to seize one another's colonies.

Critical Thinking and Writing
6. Possible answer: Chemical and biological weapons can be particularly cruel and painful. They can cause terrible long-term health problems and may also poison the environment for years after the war is over. 7. Possible answer: During wartime, governments depend on the support of people back home. News of terrible defeats might have discouraged people from supporting the war effort.

Activity Rubrics

Share rubrics with students before they conduct their interviews.

Attempted The project is incomplete, or partners fail to cooperate in executing it.

Minimal Partners cooperate, but the interview shows limited understanding of the subject.

Adequate Partners work well together; the project reflects understanding of the human impact of the war.

Exemplary Partners work well together; the project is well presented, demonstrates excellent understanding of topic, and leads to an interesting and informative discussion.

Primary Source

ANSWER three

Bell Ringer Ask students to comment on the meaning of total war. How do they think total war affects the lives of civilians on the home front? Ask students to add to their definition of total war as they read this section.

LESSON PLAN

1. Focus In their efforts to win World War I, governments engaged in total war by committing all their nation's resources, controlling public opinion, and introducing economic restraints. Women contributed to the war effort in various ways. Russia withdrew from the war following its revolution. The United States, meanwhile, entered the war on the Allied side. In 1918, the Allies achieved victory.

2. Instruct Divide the class into groups of three. Have one student in each group assume the role of a talk show host while the other two students act as guests on the show. The two guests should choose one of the following roles: an antiwar poet, a government official waging total war, a woman supporting the war effort, a soldier who has mutinied and deserted, an American who believes the United States should enter the war against Germany. After choosing their roles, students should prepare for their shows by developing pertinent questions and answers. Each student should write notes on index cards that they can use during their interviews. Remind students that they should express not their own views but the views that their selected character would probably have had. Have the groups take turns presenting their shows.

3. Assess Ask students to write a brief review of the talk show presented by another group.

4. Reteach If students' **Assess** activity does not reflect adequate understanding of the lesson, you might assign the *Guide to the Essentials* or the *Interactive Student Tutorial CD-ROM* for this section.

Caption Answer

Possible answer: The German soldier is portrayed as an inhuman monster with blood on his hands and sword. He is looking over the edge of a trench as if he is ready to attack.

Reading Focus

- How did World War I become a total war?
- What effect did the continuing war have on morale?
- What were the causes and results of American entry into the war?

Vocabulary

total war
conscription
propaganda
atrocity
self-determination
armistice

Taking Notes

As you read, prepare an outline of this section. Use Roman numerals for major headings, capital letters for subheadings, and numbers for supporting details. The sample here will help you get started.

I. Total war
  A. Economic impact
    1.
    2.
  B. Propaganda war
    1.
    2.

Main Idea In their efforts to achieve victory, governments committed all their nations' resources to the war effort.

Setting the Scene By 1917, European societies were cracking under the strain of war. Instead of praising the glorious deeds of heroes, war poets began denouncing the leaders whose errors wasted so many lives. British poet and soldier Siegfried Sassoon captured the bitter mood:

> "You smug-faced crowds with kindling eye
> Who cheer when soldier lads march by,
> Sneak home and pray you'll never know
> The hell where youth and laughter go."
> —Siegfried Sassoon, "Suicide in the Trenches"

Three years into the war, a revolution in Russia and the entry of the United States into the war would upset the balance of forces and finally end the long stalemate.

Total War

As the struggle wore on, nations realized that a modern, mechanized war required the total commitment of their whole society. The result was what we today call total war, the channeling of a nation's entire resources into a war effort.

Economic Impact Early on, both sides set up systems to recruit, arm, transport, and supply armies that numbered in the millions. All of the warring nations except Britain imposed universal military conscription, or "the draft," which required all young men to be ready for military or other service. Germany set up a system of forced civilian labor as well.

Governments raised taxes and borrowed huge amounts of money to pay the costs of war. They rationed food and other products, from boots to gasoline. In addition, they introduced other economic controls, such as setting prices and forbidding strikes.

Propaganda War Total war meant controlling public opinion. Even in democratic countries, special boards censored the press. Their aim was to keep complete casualty figures and other discouraging news from reaching the people. Government censors also restricted popular literature, historical writings, motion pictures, and the arts.

Both sides waged a propaganda war. Propaganda is the spreading of ideas to promote a cause or to damage an opposing cause. Allied

Propaganda War
Name-calling is one of the most common techniques of propaganda. Allied propaganda often referred to Germans as Huns, the barbarian tribe who helped destroy Roman civilization.

Theme: Art and Literature How does the picture add to the emotional impact of this propaganda poster?

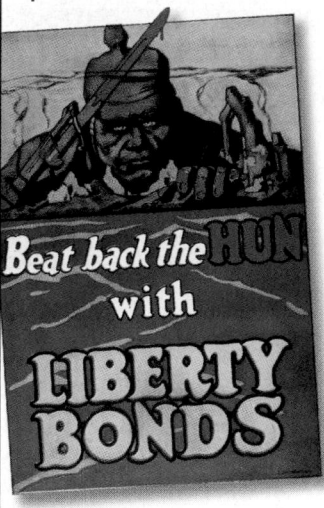

Resource Directory

Teaching Resources

Creative Teaching Activities Creative Teaching Activities booklet, p. 124
Guided Reading and Review Unit 7 booklet, p. 8
Primary Source Activity *Käthe Kollwitz's War Diary,* Unit 7 booklet, p. 13
Skill Application Activity *Recognizing Propaganda,* Unit 7 booklet, p. 15

propaganda often played up Germany's invasion of Belgium as a barbarous act. The British and French press circulated tales of atrocities, horrible acts against innocent people. Often, these stories were greatly exaggerated or completely made up. In Germany, propagandists encouraged people to sing a "Hymn of Hate" against the British:

"Hate by water and hate by land;
Hate of the head and hate of the hand;
We love as one, we hate as one;
We have one foe and one alone—
ENGLAND!"
     —Ernst Lissauer, "Hymn of Hate"

Impact on Women Women played a critical role in total war. As millions of men left to fight, women took over their jobs and kept national economies going. Many women worked in war industries, manufacturing weapons and supplies. Others joined women's branches of the armed forces. When food shortages threatened Britain, volunteers in the Women's Land Army went to the fields to grow their nation's food.

Nurses shared the dangers of the men whose wounds they tended. At aid stations close to the front lines, nurses often worked around the clock, especially after a big "push" brought a flood of casualties. In her diary, English nurse Vera Brittain describes sweating through 90-degree days in France, "stopping hemorrhages, replacing intestines, and draining and reinserting innumerable rubber tubes" with "gruesome human remains heaped on the floor."

War work gave women a new sense of pride and confidence. After the war, most women had to give up their jobs to men returning home. Still, they had challenged the idea that women were too "delicate" for demanding and dangerous jobs. In many countries, including Britain and the United States, women's support for the war effort helped them finally win the right to vote, after decades of struggle.

Collapsing Morale

By 1917, the morale of both troops and civilians had plunged. Germany was sending 15-year-old recruits to the front. Britain was on the brink of bankruptcy. Long casualty lists, food shortages, and the failure of generals to win promised victories led to calls for peace.

As morale collapsed, troops mutinied in some French units. In Italy, many soldiers deserted during the retreat at Caporetto. In Russia, soldiers left the front to join in a full-scale revolution back home.

Revolution in Russia Three years of war had hit Russia especially hard. Stories of incompetent generals and corruption destroyed public confidence. In March 1917, bread riots in St. Petersburg mushroomed into a revolution that brought down the Russian monarchy. (You will read more about the causes and effects of the Russian Revolution in the next chapter.)

At first, the Allies welcomed the overthrow of the czar. They hoped Russia would institute a democratic government and become a stronger ally. But later that year, when V. I. Lenin came to power, he promised to pull Russian troops out of the war. Early in 1918, Lenin signed the Treaty of Brest-Litovsk (brehst lih TAWFSK) with Germany. The treaty ended Russian participation in World War I.

Impact on the War Russia's withdrawal had an immediate impact on the war. With Russia out of the struggle, Germany could concentrate its forces on the Western Front. In the spring of 1918, the Central Powers stood ready to achieve the great breakthrough they had sought so long.

 Primary Sources and Literature

See "Erich Maria Remarque: All Quiet on the Western Front," in the Reference Section at the back of this book.

Virtual Field Trip

www.phschool.com

**The Imperial War Museum
London, United Kingdom**

To see other artworks, artifacts,
and documents relating to World
War I, use the Internet address
above to link to the Imperial War
Museum.

Allied Push Toward Victory
In September 1918, American
troops pushed German forces
back through the Argonne Forest
of France. This battle was the last
Allied offensive of the war.

**Theme: Geography and
History** What does this picture
suggest about the environmental
impact of the war?

The United States Declares War

Soon after the Russian Revolution began, however, another event altered
the balance of forces. The United States declared war on Germany. Why did
the United States exchange neutrality for war in 1917?

Unrestricted Submarine Warfare One major reason involved German
submarine attacks on merchant and passenger ships carrying American
citizens. Many of these ships were transporting supplies to the Allies. But
President Woodrow Wilson insisted that Americans, as citizens of a neutral
country, had a right to safe travel on the seas.

In May 1915, a German submarine torpedoed the British liner *Lusitania*.
Almost 1,200 passengers were killed, including 128 Americans. Germany
justified the attack, arguing that the *Lusitania* was carrying weapons. When
Wilson threatened to cut off relations with Germany, though, Germany agreed
to restrict its submarine campaign. Before attacking any ship, U-boats would
surface and give warning, allowing neutral passengers to escape to the lifeboats.
In December 1916, however, Germany announced that it would resume unrestricted submarine warfare. Wilson angrily denounced Germany.

Cultural Ties Many Americans supported the Allies. They felt ties of culture and language to Britain and sympathized with France as another
democracy. Still, some German Americans favored the Central Powers. So
did many Irish Americans, who resented British rule of Ireland, and Russian Jewish immigrants, who did not want to be allied with the czar.

Zimmermann Note In early 1917, the British intercepted a message from
the German foreign minister, Arthur Zimmermann, to his ambassador in
Mexico. Zimmermann promised that, in return for Mexican support,
Germany would help Mexico "to reconquer the lost territory in New Mexico,
Texas, and Arizona." Britain revealed the Zimmermann note to the American
government. When the note became public, anti-German feeling intensified
in the United States.

Declaring War In April 1917, Wilson asked Congress to declare war on Germany. "We have no selfish ends to serve," he stated. Instead, he painted the conflict idealistically as a war "to make the world safe for democracy" and as a "war to end war."

First, the United States needed months to recruit, train, supply, and transport a modern army across the Atlantic. By 1918, about two million fresh, confident American soldiers had joined the war-weary Allied troops fighting on the Western Front. Although relatively few American troops got into combat, they proved to be good fighters. Their arrival gave Allied troops a much-needed morale boost. Just as important to the debt-ridden Allies was the financial aid provided by the United States.

The Fourteen Points Though he had failed to maintain American neutrality, Wilson still hoped to be a peacemaker. In January 1918, he issued the Fourteen Points, a list of his terms for resolving this and future wars. He called for freedom of the seas, free trade, large-scale reductions of arms, and an end to secret treaties. For Eastern Europe, Wilson favored self-determination, the right of people to choose their own form of government. All those issues, he felt, had helped cause the war. Finally, he urged the creation of a "general association of nations" to keep the peace in the future.

Campaign to Victory

A final showdown got underway in early 1918. In March, the Germans launched a huge offensive that pushed the Allies back 40 miles by July. But the effort exhausted the Germans. The Allies then launched a counter-attack, slowly driving German forces back across France and Belgium. In September, German generals told the kaiser that the war could not be won.

The German people showed their monarch their frustration as uprisings exploded among hungry city dwellers. German commanders advised the kaiser to step down, as the czar had done. William II did so in early November, fleeing into exile in the Netherlands.

By autumn, Austria-Hungary was also reeling toward collapse. As the government in Vienna tottered, the subject nationalities revolted, splintering the empire of the Hapsburgs.

The new German government sought an armistice, or agreement to end fighting, with the Allies. At 11 A.M. on November 11, 1918, the Great War at last came to an end.

Geography and History

Getting "Over There"

By July 1918, the United States was sending some 10,000 troops every day to France. But transporting so many soldiers and supplies across the Atlantic Ocean was no easy task. Violent storms plagued the cold waters of the North Atlantic. Even more threatening were the German U-boats that patrolled Atlantic shipping lanes.

To protect the transport of men and supplies, naval destroyers escorted the convoys. Faster and more agile than the submarines, they outmaneuvered the enemy. The United States Navy was so effective that in just two years, 2.5 million American soldiers and 7.5 million tons of supplies reached France with few losses.

 Theme: Geography and History What geographic obstacle did the United States face when it entered World War I?

SECTION 4 Assessment

Recall
1. (a) Treaty of Brest-Litovsk, p. 691 (b) Woodrow Wilson, p. 692 (c) *Lusitania*, p. 692 (d) Fourteen Points, p. 693
2. (a) total war, p. 690 (b) conscription, p. 690 (c) propaganda, p. 690 (d) atrocity, p. 691 (e) self-determination, p.693, (f) armistice, p. 693

Comprehension
3. (a) Governments raised taxes, borrowed large amounts of money, rationed food and other supplies, and introduced price controls. (b) Both sides censored the press and used propaganda to win public support for the war effort. 4. Food shortages and collapsing morale led to a revolution that overthrew the czar. 5. (a) Americans were angered by German submarine warfare. The Zimmermann note further inflamed American feelings against Germany. (b) The arrival of American troops boosted Allied morale. American financial aid also helped the Allied war effort.

Critical Thinking and Writing
6. (a) civilian supporters of the war (b) Possible answer: Trench warfare was brutal and dehumanizing. 7. Possible answers: Yes, because women's support for the war effort might encourage the government to give women the vote. No, because many women's suffrage groups supported pacifism.

SECTION 4 Assessment

Recall
1. **Identify:** (a) Treaty of Brest-Litovsk, (b) Woodrow Wilson, (c) *Lusitania*, (d) Fourteen Points.
2. **Define:** (a) total war, (b) conscription, (c) propaganda, (d) atrocity, (e) self-determination, (f) armistice.

Comprehension
3. What measures did wartime governments take to control (a) national economies, (b) public opinion?
4. What impact did wartime failures have on Russia?

5. (a) Why did the United States declare war on Germany? (b) What impact did American entry have on the war?

Critical Thinking and Writing
6. **Analyzing Literature** Reread the poem at the beginning of this section. (a) To whom is the poem addressed? (b) What does it suggest about the effects of trench warfare?
7. **Defending a Position** If you had been a women's suffragist, would you have supported the war effort? Why or why not?

 Activity
Take It to the NET

Create a bibliography of five Web sites dealing with World War I. Rank the sites in order from 1 to 5, with 1 being the best. Consider content, images, and interactivity.

Chapter 27 **693**

Activity Rubrics

Share rubrics with students before they review the Web sites.

Attempted The bibliography is incomplete, or the Web sites chosen do not relate to the topic.

Minimal The bibliography is incomplete, and poor judgment is used in ranking the sites.

Adequate The bibliography is complete, and good judgment is used in ranking the sites.

Exemplary The bibliography is complete, and excellent judgment is used in ranking the sites.

Human Drama Activity

Recognizing Historical Significance The Americans arrived in France in June 1917. On July 4, General John Pershing led a battalion past cheering Parisians to Lafayette's tomb, where Pershing asked his friend Colonel (then Captain) Charles Stanton to speak. Stanton stepped up to the tomb, saluted, and then uttered those now famous words *"Lafayette, nous voilà!"* ("Lafayette, we are here!"). Ask students about the historical significance of his words. If needed, have students review Lafayette's role in the American Revolution.

Test Preparation

Have students read the section titled "Zimmermann Note," which begins on the opposite page, and then answer the question below.

Why would Americans have been angered by the Zimmermann note?

A It sought to involve a North American country in the war.

B It promised German help in Mexico's war with the U.S.

C It promised German help in taking U.S. territory.

D It promised to help Mexico take over the U.S.

Geography and History

ANSWER The Atlantic Ocean posed the greatest geographic obstacle for the United States, which had to send needed troops and supplies to the faraway European front across its dangerous waters.

Bell Ringer Note that one clause of the Treaty of Versailles put full blame on Germany for the war and the losses suffered by the Allies. Ask students whether they agree or disagree with that clause. Ask them to predict how that clause would affect the political climate in Germany and all of Europe after the war.

LESSON PLAN

1. Focus In 1918, Europeans struggled to recover from the devastation of World War I. Millions had been killed or wounded; famine and disease were prevalent; farms, factories, and homes were in ruins; several governments had collapsed. At the Paris Peace Conference, President Wilson urged "peace without victory," while France and Britain called for punishment and reparations. The Treaty of Versailles left many nations dissatisfied and resentful.

2. Instruct Divide the class into small groups. Ask group members to work together to list and describe the results of World War I and the Paris Peace Conference. Then, have them discuss responses to this question: How did the aftermath of World War I cause continued discontent and conflict? Allow students time to share and discuss their ideas.

3. Assess After students have discussed the question, assign students to write an essay in response to the discussion question. Remind students to outline their ideas, to write a first draft, and to edit their first draft before producing a final copy.

4. Reteach If students' *Assess* activity does not reflect adequate understanding of the lesson, you might assign the *Guide to the Essentials* or the *Interactive Student Tutorial CD-ROM* for this section.

Reading Focus

- What were the costs of the war?
- What issues faced the delegates to the Paris Peace Conference?
- Why were many people dissatisfied with the Treaty of Versailles and other peace settlements?

Vocabulary

pandemic

reparations

collective security

mandate

Taking Notes

Copy this chart. As you read, fill in the left-hand column with issues that faced the world after World War I. In the right-hand column, write how the Paris Peace Conference dealt with each of these issues.

ISSUE	SETTLEMENT
1. Debt	1. German reparations
2.	2. Reduced size of Germany
3. Nationalism	3.
4.	4. League of Nations
5.	5.

Main Idea As Europe struggled to recover from the devastation of war, world leaders met in Paris to craft a peace treaty.

Setting the Scene Just weeks after the war ended, President Wilson boarded a steamship bound for France. He had decided to go in person to Paris, where Allied leaders would make the peace. Wilson was certain that he could solve the problems of old Europe. "Tell me what is right," Wilson urged his advisers, "and I'll fight for it."

Sadly, it would not be that easy. Europe was a shattered continent. Its problems, and those of the world, would not be solved at the Paris Peace Conference, or for many years afterward.

The Costs of War

The human and material costs of the war were staggering. More than 8.5 million people were dead. Double that number had been wounded, many of them handicapped for life. Famine threatened many regions.

The devastation was made even worse in 1918 by a deadly pandemic of influenza. A pandemic is the spread of a disease across an entire country, continent, or—in this case—the whole world. In just a few months, the flu swept around the world, killing more than 20 million people—twice as many as the war itself.

Financial Burdens In battle zones from France to Russia, homes, farms, factories, roads, and churches had been shelled into rubble. The costs of rebuilding and paying off huge national war debts would burden an already battered world.

Shaken and disillusioned, people everywhere felt bitter about the war. The Allies blamed the conflict on their defeated foes and insisted that the losers make reparations, or payments for war damage. The stunned Central Powers, who had viewed the armistice as a cease-fire rather than a surrender, looked for scapegoats on whom they could blame their defeat.

Political Turmoil Under the stress of war, governments had collapsed in Russia, Germany, Austria-Hungary, and the Ottoman empire. Political radicals dreamed of building a new social order from the chaos, as revolutionaries

FACT FINDER

Casualties of World War I

	Deaths in Battle	Wounded in Battle
Allies		
France	1,357,800	4,266,000
British empire	908,371	2,090,212
Russia	1,700,000	4,950,000
Italy	462,391	953,886
United States	50,585	205,690
Others	502,421	342,585
Central Powers		
Germany	1,808,546	4,247,143
Austria-Hungary	922,500	3,620,000
Ottoman empire	325,000	400,000

Source: R. E. Dupuy and T. N. Dupuy, *The Encyclopedia of Military History*

Skills Assessment

Chart World War I resulted in more casualties than any previous war. **Which two nations suffered the most deaths? Why were American casualties relatively low?**

Skills Assessment

ANSWER Russia and Germany; American casualties were lower because the United States entered the war late.

Resource Directory

Teaching Resources

Creative Teaching Activities Creative Teaching Activities booklet, p. 125

Guided Reading and Review Unit 7 booklet, p. 10

Simulation *Rethinking the Treaty of Versailles,* Simulations booklet, pp. 12–15

in Russia seemed to be doing. Conservatives warned against the spread of bolshevism, or communism, as it soon came to be called.

Unrest also swept through Europe's colonial empires. African and Asian soldiers had discovered that the imperial powers were not as invincible as they seemed. Colonial troops returned home with a more cynical view of Europeans and renewed hopes for independence.

The Paris Peace Conference

To a weary world, Woodrow Wilson seemed a symbol of hope. His talk of self-determination and democracy raised expectations for a just and lasting peace, even in defeated Germany. Crowds cheered wildly as he rode along the Paris boulevards.

The Big Three Wilson was one of three strong personalities who dominated the Paris Peace Conference. A dedicated reformer, Wilson was so sure of his rightness that he could be hard to work with. Urging "peace without victory," he wanted the Fourteen Points to be the basis of the peace.

The other Allied leaders at the peace conference had different aims. The British prime minister, David Lloyd George, knew that his people demanded harsh treatment for Germany. He promised to build a postwar Britain "fit for heroes"—a goal that would cost money. The French leader, Georges Clemenceau (KLEHM uhn soh), bore the nickname "the Tiger" for his fierce anti-German war policy. His chief goal was to weaken Germany so that it could never again threaten France. "Mr. Wilson bores me with his Fourteen Points," complained Clemenceau. "Why, God Almighty has only ten!"

Difficult Issues Crowds of other representatives circled around the "Big Three" with their own demands and interests. The Italian prime minister, Vittorio Orlando, insisted that the Allies honor their secret agreement to give to Italy lands that were once ruled by Austria-Hungary. Such secret agreements violated Wilson's principle of self-determination.

Self-determination posed other problems. Many people who had been ruled by Russia, Austria-Hungary, or the Ottoman empire now demanded national states of their own. The territories claimed by these peoples often overlapped, so it was impossible to satisfy them all.

Faced with conflicting demands, Wilson had to compromise on his Fourteen Points. On one point, though, he stood firm. His dream was to create an international League of Nations. The League would be based on the idea of collective security, a system in which a group of nations acts as one to preserve the peace of all. With the League in place, Wilson felt sure that any mistakes made in Paris could be corrected in time.

The Treaty of Versailles

In June 1919, the peacemakers summoned representatives of the new German Republic to the palace of Versailles outside Paris. The Germans were ordered to sign the treaty drawn up by the Allies.

The German delegates read the document with growing horror. It forced Germany to assume full blame for causing the war. It also imposed huge reparations that would put an already damaged German economy under a staggering burden. The reparations covered not only the destruction caused by the war, but also pensions for millions of Allied soldiers or their widows and families. The total cost of German reparations would come to over $30 billion.

Other clauses were aimed at weakening Germany. The treaty severely limited the size of the once-feared German military. It returned Alsace and Lorraine to France, removed hundreds of square miles of territory from western and eastern Germany, and stripped Germany of its overseas colonies.

Primary Source

Signing the Peace Treaty
A British delegate describes how the German delegates were brought in to sign the Treaty of Versailles:

"Isolated and pitiable, come the two German delegates, Dr. Müller, Dr. Bell. The silence is terrifying. . . . They keep their eyes fixed away from those two thousand staring eyes, fixed up on the ceiling. They are deathly pale. . . . They are conducted to their chairs. Clemenceau at once breaks the silence. 'Messieurs,' he rasps, '[the meeting is open.]' He adds a few ill-chosen words. 'We are here to sign a Treaty of Peace.' The Germans leap up anxiously when he has finished, since they know that they are the first to sign. William Martin, as if a theater manager, motions them [crossly] to sit down again."

—Harold Nicolson, *Peacemaking, 1919*

Skills Assessment

Primary Source Do you think Nicolson approved of the way the German delegates were treated? Explain.

Background Historical Evidence

French War Losses France did not suffer the greatest number of dead and wounded during the war. Proportionately, however, France's losses were indeed greater. No other nation suffered a greater percentage of its population killed or wounded. Of Frenchmen who were between the ages of 20 and 32 at the start of the war, more than half were killed. Property damage in northern France, where much of the fighting took place, included 300,000 houses destroyed and 20,000 factories and workshops ruined or badly damaged. Some 1,360,000 head of livestock were killed or confiscated. Shell fire ravaged thousands of acres of forest and farmland. This was the country that Georges Clemenceau represented at the Paris Peace Conference.

Background Historical Evidence

German Defiance Rather than surrender its fleet to the Allied powers, the German navy sent it to the bottom of the sea. On June 21, 1919, the German fleet at Scapa Flow, under the command of Admiral Ludwig von Reuter, was scuttled. The ships that were sunk by their crews included more than 50 warships.

Background Historical Evidence

German Demilitarization The Treaty of Versailles limited the size of the German army to no more than 100,000 men. The treaty set the maximum size of the German navy at six warships. Germany could have no submarines and no military aircraft.

Primary Source

ANSWER Possible answer: Nicolson disapproved of the treatment of the Germans. He refers to them as "pitiable" and shows sympathy for their plight. Nicolson also presents Clemenceau as lofty and arrogant and calls his words "ill-chosen words."

Europe, 1914

Europe, 1920

Skills Assessment

Geography The peace treaties that ended World War I redrew the map of Europe.

1. **Location** *On the map, locate (a) Lithuania, (b) Latvia, (c) Estonia, (d) Poland, (e) Yugoslavia.*
2. **Region** *Which countries lost territory in Eastern Europe?*
3. **Critical Thinking Making Inferences** *Why do you think the war had no effect on national boundaries in southwestern Europe?*

The Germans signed because they had no choice. But German resentment of the Treaty of Versailles would poison the international climate for 20 years—and help spark an even deadlier world war.

Widespread Dissatisfaction

The Allies drew up separate treaties with the other Central Powers. Like the Treaty of Versailles, these treaties left widespread dissatisfaction.

Self-Determination in Eastern Europe Where the German, Austrian, and Russian empires had once ruled, a band of new nations emerged. They included the Baltic states of Latvia, Lithuania, and Estonia. Poland regained independence after more than 100 years of foreign rule.

Three new republics—Czechoslovakia, Austria, and Hungary—rose in the old Hapsburg heartland. In the Balkans, the peacemakers created a new South Slav state, Yugoslavia, dominated by Serbia. Eastern Europe, however, remained a center of conflict, as you will read.

Mandate System European colonies in Africa, Asia, and the Pacific had looked to the Paris Peace Conference with high hopes. Many people from these lands had fought alongside Europeans. Colonial leaders expected that the peace would bring new respect and an end to imperial rule. They took up Wilson's call for self-determination.

However, the leaders at Paris applied self-determination only to parts of Europe. Outside Europe, the victorious Allies added to their overseas empires. The treaties created a system of mandates, territories administered by western powers. Britain and France gained mandates over German colonies in Africa and Ottoman lands in the Middle East. In theory, mandates were to be held and modernized until they were able to "stand

ANSWERS **1.** Review locations with students. **2.** Germany, Russia, Austria-Hungary, and Bulgaria **3.** Spain had been neutral. As a result, it did not gain or lose territory to its Allied neighbors, France and Portugal.

Resource Directory

Teaching Resources
Section Quiz Unit 7 booklet, p. 11
Geography Quiz Unit 7 booklet, p. 16
Chapter Test Forms A, B, and C Unit 7 booklet, pp. 17–21
Answer Key Unit 7 booklet, pp. 96–109

Technology
Interactive Student Tutorial CD-ROM Ch. 27
Computer Test Bank Ch. 27

alone." In practice, they became European colonies. From Africa to the Middle East and across Asia, colonized peoples felt betrayed by the peacemakers.

Unfulfilled Goals Germany was not the only power dissatisfied by the peace. Italy was angry because it did not get all the lands promised in its secret treaty with the Allies. Japan protested the refusal of western nations to recognize its claims in China. At the same time, China was forced to accept former German holdings. Russia, excluded from the peace talks, resented the reestablishment of a Polish nation and three independent Baltic states on lands that had been part of the Russian empire. All of these discontented nations bided their time. They waited for a chance to revise the peace settlements in their favor.

Hopes for Global Peace The Paris Peace Conference did offer one beacon of hope in the League of Nations. In the aftermath of the war, millions of people looked to the League to ensure the peace. More than 40 nations joined the League. They agreed to negotiate disputes rather than resort to war. Members of the League promised to take common action—economic or even military—against any aggressor state.

Wilson's dream had become a reality. Yet his own Senate refused to ratify the treaty, and the United States never joined the League. Disillusioned with war, the United States chose to play a lone hand in world affairs. As time soon revealed, the League was powerless to prevent war. Still, it was a first step toward something genuinely new—an international organization dedicated to maintaining peace and advancing the interests of all peoples.

Cause *and* Effect

Long-Term Causes	Immediate Causes
• Imperialist and economic rivalries among European powers • European alliance system • Militarism and arms race • Nationalist tensions in Balkans	• Austria-Hungary's annexation of Bosnia and Herzegovina • Fighting in the Balkans • Assassination of Archduke Francis Ferdinand • German invasion of Belgium

World War I

Immediate Effects	Long-Term Effects
• Enormous cost in lives and money • Russian Revolution • Creation of new nations in Eastern Europe • Requirement that Germany pay reparations • German loss of its overseas colonies • Balfour Declaration • League of Nations	• Economic impact of war debts on Europe • Emergence of United States and Japan as important powers • Growth of nationalism in colonies • Rise of fascism • World War II

Connections to Today

• Ethnic tensions in Balkans
• International agreement banning poison gas
• Use of airplanes and submarines for military purposes
• Arab-Israeli conflict

Skills Assessment **Chart** Sparked by old rivalries in Europe, World War I helped shape our world today. **Which effect of the war do you think is most important today? Why?**

SECTION 5 Assessment

Recall
1. **Identify: (a)** David Lloyd George, **(b)** Georges Clemenceau, **(c)** League of Nations, **(d)** Treaty of Versailles.
2. **Define: (a)** pandemic, **(b)** reparations, **(c)** collective security, **(d)** mandate.

Comprehension
3. Describe conditions in Europe after World War I.
4. **(a)** Identify three issues to be settled at the Paris Peace Conference. **(b)** How did Woodrow Wilson's goals at the peace talks differ from those of other Allied leaders?

5. How did the peace treaties both follow and violate Wilson's principle of self-determination?

Critical Thinking and Writing
6. **Connecting to Geography** How might the creation of the mandate system affect the map of Africa after World War I?
7. **Making Inferences** Wilson's closest adviser wrote, "Looking at the conference in retrospect, there is much to approve and much to regret." What do you think he might have approved? What might he have regretted?

Activity

Writing an Editorial Choose *one* of the countries mentioned in this section. Write an editorial about the Paris Peace Conference that might have appeared in a newspaper in that country during or after the peace talks.

Chapter 27 **697**

SECTION 5 Assessment

Recall
1. **(a)** David Lloyd George, p. 695 **(b)** Georges Clemenceau, p. 695 **(c)** League of Nations, p. 695 **(d)** Treaty of Versailles, p. 695 2. **(a)** pandemic, p. 694 **(b)** reparations, p. 694 **(c)** collective security, p. 695 **(d)** mandate, p. 696

Comprehension
3. Millions of people had been killed or wounded. The destruction of homes, farms, and factories left nations in economic ruin. Governments had collapsed in Germany, Russia, Austria-Hungary, and the Ottoman empire. 4. **(a)** Possible answers: how to create a just and lasting peace, how to deal with secret agreements made by the Allies, how to handle demands for self-determination **(b)** Wilson wished to achieve "peace without victory" based on the Fourteen Points. Clemenceau and Lloyd George desired harsh punishment for Germany.
5. Self-determination was followed in Eastern Europe, leading to the creation of Poland and the Baltic states. However, by preserving colonies and creating mandates, the treaties violated colonial peoples' right to self-determination.

Critical Thinking and Writing
6. Possible answer: Most of Africa would still be shown as European colonies. However, former German colonies would be shown as being under English or French control. 7. He probably approved the creation of the League of Nations and several new nations in Eastern Europe. However, he probably disapproved of the harsh treatment of Germany.

Activity Rubrics

Share rubrics with students before they write their editorials.

Attempted The editorial is incomplete or is poorly written and organized and contains many mechanical errors. It shows little understanding of the topic.

Minimal The editorial is poorly written and organized and contains some mechanical errors. It shows limited understanding of the topic.

Adequate The editorial is well written and organized and contains few mechanical errors. It shows good understanding of the topic.

Exemplary The editorial is very well written and organized and contains no mechanical errors. It shows excellent understanding of the topic.

Skills Assessment

ANSWER Encourage students to explain fully the reasons for their opinions.

Human Drama Activity

Rewording a Speech Provide students the complete text of Wilson's "Fourteen Points" speech and have them choose one paragraph or point to explain in their own words. Then ask for volunteers to read each reworded paragraph. Discuss Wilson's ideas with the class. How might events have been changed if Wilson's ideas had been accepted?

Test Preparation

Have students look at the maps on the opposite page, and then answer the question below.

Which of the following is a country shown on the 1920 map that is in territory once held by Russia?

A Yugoslavia
(B) Finland
C Sweden
D Czechoslovakia

CHAPTER **27 Review and Assessment**

Creating a Chapter Summary

As a reteaching opportunity, pair a more able student with a less able student to complete this chapter summary.

Additional entries might include the following: Nations competed to build up their armies and navies. Industrial powers were economic rivals. Aggressive nationalism inflamed tensions. Governments tried to control wartime economies and public opinion. Women took an active role in the war effort. New nations were created in Eastern Europe. Germany resented having to pay reparations and take blame for the war. Colonies felt betrayed by the mandate system. The League of Nations was created.

Creating a Chapter Summary

Copy this concept web on a sheet of paper. For each statement in the light purple ovals, include two or more facts to support that statement, adding as many ovals as you need. Two examples have been filled in to help you get started.

For additional review and enrichment activities, see the interactive version of *World History* available on the Web and on CD-ROM.

Rivalry among European powers led to a global war.

European nations competed for overseas colonies.

WORLD WAR I AND ITS AFTERMATH

Modern weapons added to the destructiveness of the war.

Total war had a great impact on soldiers and civilians.

The peace treaties made many changes but left important issues unresolved.

Web Site Self-Test
For practice test questions for Chapter 27, see **www.phschool.com**.

Building Vocabulary

1–10. Puzzle clues should show a clear understanding of the meanings of the terms.

Building Vocabulary

Use the chapter vocabulary words listed below to create a crossword puzzle. Exchange puzzles with a classmate. Complete the puzzles and then check each other's answers.

1. **militarism**
2. **entente**
3. **ultimatum**
4. **mobilize**
5. **neutrality**
6. **propaganda**
7. **atrocity**
8. **armistice**
9. **reparations**
10. **mandate**

Recalling Key Facts

11. (a) the assassination of Archduke Francis Ferdinand of Austria-Hungary (b) Austria-Hungary
12. Central Powers—Germany and Austria-Hungary; Allies—France, Britain, Russia
13. Troops dug miles of trench networks. Occasionally, one side or another would charge into the no man's land between trenches. The other side would often counterattack.
14. European powers recruited troops from their colonies in Africa and Asia.
15. (a) the United States (b) Russia
16. It made Germany take blame for the war, ordered Germany to pay heavy reparations, limited the size of its military, stripped land from Germany's borders, and took away Germany's overseas colonies.

Recalling Key Facts

11. (a) What event sparked the outbreak of World War I? (b) Which nation was the first to declare war?
12. At the start of the war, which nations made up the Central Powers? Which nations made up the Allies?
13. Describe trench warfare.
14. How did troops from Europe's overseas colonies become involved in the war?
15. (a) What nation joined the war on the Allied side in 1917? (b) What Allied nation dropped out of the war in 1918?
16. How did the Treaty of Versailles punish Germany?

Critical Thinking and Writing

17. **Linking Past and Present** (a) What efforts were made to promote world peace before and after World War I? (b) How do individuals and governments work for peace today?
18. **Recognizing Points of View** (a) What arguments could Russia have used to blame Austria-Hungary for the start of World War I? (b) What arguments could Austria-Hungary have used to blame Russia?
19. **Recognizing Causes and Effects** How did the Industrial Revolution affect the course of World War I?
20. **Connecting to Geography** Review the map of the war in Europe in Section 3. (a) Locate the Dardanelles. How would control of the strait have been important to the Allies? (b) Why did submarine warfare play an important role in the war?

21. **Analyzing Ideas** (a) What do you think Woodrow Wilson meant by "peace without victory"? (b) Why do you think the European Allies were unwilling to accept this idea?

Critical Thinking and Writing

17. (a) Before: Nobel Peace Prize, Olympic games, peace societies, peace conferences; After: League of Nations (b) Possible answers: The United Nations mediates international disputes and intervenes in military conflicts. Individual leaders meet in private conferences.
18. (a) Russians might have argued that Austria-Hungary used the assassination of the archduke as an excuse to declare war on Serbia, even though Serbia had agreed to most of Austria's demands. (b) Austria-Hungary might

have argued that its conflict with Serbia could have been kept local. Russia's mobilization widened the war and activated the alliance system.
19. More deadly weapons were produced more rapidly. Transportation and communication improved.
20. (a) Possible answer: The strait links the Black Sea to the Mediterranean. Control of the strait would allow Allied ships to reach Russia as well as the Ottoman capital of Istanbul. (b) Most troops and supplies traveled by water. In addition, England was an island nation that depended heavily on its navy. Submarines could disrupt troop and supply transport and shipping.

21. Possible answers: (a) Wilson did not want the losers punished or the winners to gain any greater power as a result of the war. (b) Nations such as France and England had suffered more heavily than the United States had. They wanted to be compensated for their losses and remove the threat of further German attack.

Read this description of how the declaration of war was greeted in St. Petersburg, the capital of Russia. Then, answer the questions that follow.

"There was a crowd in front of a newspaper office. Every few minutes a momentous phrase scribbled in charcoal appeared in the window: 'ENGLAND GIVES UP PEACE NEGOTIATIONS. Germany invades Belgium. Mobilization progressing with Great Enthusiasm.' And at 7:50 p.m.:

'GERMANY DECLARES WAR ON RUSSIA.' Spontaneously the crowd started singing the national anthem. . . . The people were staring at the sprawling words, as if trying to understand what they actually meant as far as each personal little life was concerned.

Then the edges of the crowd started breaking off and drifting in one direction, up the Nevsky Prospect. I heard the phrase 'German Embassy' repeated several times."

—Sergyei N. Kurnakov, *Savage Squadrons*

22. Based on what you have read, during what month and year did this scene take place?
23. What is the first reaction of the crowd to news of the declaration of war?
24. "The people were staring at the sprawling words, as if trying to understand what they actually meant as far as each personal little life was concerned." Is this statement a fact, an opinion, or a mixture of both? Explain.
25. What do you think will happen when the crowd moves on up the Nevsky Prospect?
26. Based on what you have read, do you think similar scenes may have been taking place in France or Germany at this time? Explain.
27. How might the mood in St. Petersburg have been different three years later?

Take It to the NET

Use the Internet to research important battles, turning points, and changes in methods of warfare that took place during World War I. Begin by accessing the world history Web site at **www.phschool.com**. Then, create an illustrated map of Europe during World War I that highlights some of these events and explains their significance.

IN BELGIUM

HELP

THE NATIONAL COMMITTEE FOR RELIEF IN BELGIUM.
TRAFALGAR BUILDINGS, TRAFALGAR SQUARE, LONDON.

The poster above was created in 1916 by Louis Raemaekers, a Dutch artist who was then living in England. Study the poster and then answer the following questions:

28. Whom do the two figures on the poster represent?
29. (a) What organization distributed this poster? (b) Where was this organization located?
30. (a) Who was the intended audience for this poster? (b) What did the artist want the people who saw this poster to do?
31. Based on what you have read, why would people in England in 1916 have been sympathetic toward Belgium?
32. Describe how the poster appeals to the following emotions: (a) pity; (b) anger.
33. Would you consider this poster an effective piece of propaganda? Explain.

Skills Tip

As you analyze a work of propaganda, look for ways in which it tries to stir people to action by appealing to their emotions.

22. August 1914, the month Germany invaded Belgium
23. They sing the Russian national anthem.
24. Possible answer: a mixture of both. It may be a fact that people were staring, but Kurnakov can only give an opinion about what they were thinking.
25. Possible answer: They may attack the Germany embassy.
26. Possible answer: Yes. People in other nations were also excited and anxious. Many were eager for war.
27. By 1917, Russians were demoralized by the progress of the war. Food shortages led to bread riots in cities like St. Petersburg. Many Russians were calling for the overthrow of the czar.

28. women and children in war-torn Belgium
29. (a) The National Committee for Relief in Belgium (b) London
30. (a) English citizens (b) contribute money to aid Belgian victims of the war
31. England had entered the war in response to the German invasion of Belgium. Much English anti-German propaganda focused on atrocities Germans were supposed to have committed against Belgians.
32. (a) The poster would stir pity for the Belgians. It shows a suffering Belgian mother and child. They are in rags and the mother's hand is thin and bony. The child is crying, possibly from hunger. (b) The poster would stir anger against the Germans, who were blamed for causing such suffering.
33. Possible answer: Yes, it would probably make people want to help this mother and child.

Skills Tip

Physical features, facial expressions, and body language of the people in the poster help send the intended message. The Skills Handbook in the front of the book has a lesson that will help students with this feature.

Unit Theme Activity

Remind students about the Unit Theme Activity located on the unit opener page. Make sure students understand the assignment and have begun work.

Take It to the NET

Direct students to **www.phschool.com** for links to sites that will help them get started on this assignment. Share rubrics with students.
Attempted The map is missing most standard elements; labels are difficult to read, missing, or inaccurately placed. Few of the required elements are illustrated.
Minimal The map is missing some standard elements; most labels are included, but are somewhat difficult to read; several are inaccurately placed. Most of the required elements are illustrated.
Adequate The map includes most standard elements; all labels are included, and most are easy to read and accurately placed. All of the required elements are illustrated.
Exemplary The map includes all appropriate standard elements; all labels are included and are easy to read and accurately placed. All of the required elements are illustrated.

Chapter 28 Planning Guide

Resource Manager

	CORE INSTRUCTION	READING/SKILLS
Chapter Level Resources	**Teaching Resources** - **Pacing Charts**, Ch. 28 - **Teaching With Themes**, p. 31 - **Color Transparencies**, p. F–57 - **Resource Pro®** Ch. 28 - **www.phschool.com** • eTeach	- **Book on CD**, Ch. 28 - **Interactive Student Tutorial CD-ROM**, Ch. 28 - **Social Studies Skills Tutor CD-ROM** - **Skills Transparencies**

1 Two Revolutions in Russia
1. Explain why the revolution occurred in Russia in March 1917.
2. Outline why Lenin and the Bolsheviks launched the November revolution.
3. Analyze why the Communists defeated their opponents in the Russian civil war.
	Teaching Resources
	- **Unit 7 booklet**
	  • Viewpoint Activity, p. 30
	- **Creative Teaching Activities**, p. 126
	- **Prentice Hall Presentation Pro**, Ch. 28, Section 1
	- **Section Reading Support Transparencies**
		Teaching Resources
		- **Unit 7 booklet**
		  • Guided Reading and Review, p. 22
		  • Skill Application Activity, p. 31
		- **Guide to the Essentials**
		- **Guided Reading Audiotapes**, Ch. 28, Section 1

2 From Lenin to Stalin 1. Describe how the Communist state developed under Lenin. 2. Summarize the effects of Stalin's five-year plans. 3. Explain why Stalin launched the Great Purge. 4. Assess how Soviet foreign policy affected relationships with the western powers.	**Teaching Resources** - **Creative Teaching Activities**, p. 127 - **Prentice Hall Presentation Pro**, Ch. 28, Section 2 - **Section Reading Support Transparencies**	**Teaching Resources** - **Unit 7 booklet** • Guided Reading and Review, p. 24 - **Guide to the Essentials** - **Guided Reading Audiotapes**, Ch. 28, Section 2

3 Life in a Totalitarian State
1. Explain how Stalin created a totalitarian state.
2. Summarize how communism changed Soviet society.
3. Relate how state control affected the arts in the Soviet Union.
	Teaching Resources
	- **Unit 7 booklet**
	  • Primary Source Activity, p. 29
	- **Creative Teaching Activities**, p. 128
	- **Prentice Hall Presentation Pro**, Ch. 28, Section 3
	- **Section Reading Support Transparencies**
		Teaching Resources
		- **Unit 7 booklet**
		  • Guided Reading and Review, p. 26
		- **Guide to the Essentials**
		- **Guided Reading Audiotapes**, Ch. 28, Section 3

ENRICHMENT/PRE-AP

www.phschool.com
- Why Study History?

www.phschool.com
- Internet Activities, Section 1

Teaching Resources
- Chapter Extension Activities, p. 68
- History Through Literature, pp. 59–60

Teaching Resources
- Chapter Extension Activities, p. 69
- Listening to Literature World Masterpieces, poems by Anna Akhmatova and Boris Pasternak, side 8
- **www.phschool.com**
  - Virtual Field Trip
  - Internet Activities, *A Revolution in Filmmaking*

ASSESSMENT

PRENTICE HALL ASSESSMENT SYSTEM

Core Assessment
- ExamView Test Bank booklet, Ch. 28
- ExamView Test Bank CD-ROM, Ch. 28

Standardized Test Preparation

Diagnose and Prescribe
- Diagnostic Tests for High School Social Studies Skills

Review and Reteach
- Review Book for World History

Practice and Assess
- Test-Taking Strategies With Transparencies for High School
- Alternative Assessment booklet
- Test Prep Book for World History

Teaching Resources
- Unit 7 booklet
  - Geography Quiz, p. 32
  - Section Quizzes, pp. 23, 25, 27
  - Chapter Tests A, B, and C, pp. 33–37
- **www.phschool.com**
  - Self-Test

CUSTOMIZE FOR INDIVIDUAL NEEDS

Gifted and Talented
- Teacher's Edition, Activities: Connections to Literature, p. 715

Less Proficient Readers
- Guide to the Essentials, Ch. 28
- Book on CD, Ch. 28
- Teacher's Edition, Activities: Reading Strategy, p. 714

Less Proficient Writers
- Teacher's Edition, Activities: Customize for Auditory Learners, p. 705

Students Acquiring English/ESL
- Guide to the Essentials, English/Spanish, Ch. 28
- Book on CD, Ch. 28
- Teacher's Edition, Activities marked with an *

TEXT

Don't miss the exclusive interactive version of *World History: Connections to Today* on the Internet and CD-ROM.

INTRODUCTION

Discontent among the Russian people brought two revolutions and toppled the Romanov dynasty. Led by Lenin, the Bolsheviks won a civil war against the provisional government, setting up a new Communist government. After Lenin's death, Stalin became the leader of the Communist government. His goal was to make Russia a modern industrial power. His brutal dictatorship killed millions of people during the Great Purge and turned the Soviet Union into a totalitarian state.

Focusing on Themes

Suggest that students focus on these theme questions as they read:

Continuity and Change
How did political, social, and economic conditions in czarist Russia spark a revolution?

Impact of the Individual
What roles did Lenin and Stalin play in the emergence of the Soviet Union?

Economics and Technology
How did the Soviet economy develop?

Political and Social Systems
How did the Soviet Union become a totalitarian state?

◆ TIME LINE ACTIVITY

Share the About the Pictures note with students before asking these questions about the time line:

1. When did Bolsheviks storm the Winter Palace? *(in 1917)*
2. Why do you think the stock market crashing in New York triggered a global depression? *(Answers should reflect an understanding that what happens in one country affects the rest of the world.)*
3. When and why did World War II begin? *(1939; German forces invaded Poland)*

Don't Miss!

Synthesizing Information
Collectivization
(Section 2)

Humanities Link
A Revolution in Filmmaking
(Section 3)

CHAPTER
28

Revolution in Russia
1917–1939

Chapter Preview

1 Two Revolutions in Russia
2 From Lenin to Stalin
3 Life in a Totalitarian State

1917

Two revolutions lead to the creation of a communist government in Russia. In this painting, Bolsheviks storm the Winter Palace.

1921

Lenin, shown in the monument above, adopts the New Economic Policy.

CHAPTER EVENTS

1915 — 1920 — 1925

GLOBAL EVENTS

1919 After World War I, the Paris Peace Conference convenes.

1920s Mexico recovers from revolution and civil war.

Resource Directory

Teaching Resources
Teaching With Themes Chapter Theme Activities, p. 31
Pacing Chart With Block Scheduling Guide Ch. 28

Technology
World History Color Transparencies Ch. 28
Graphic Organizer, p. F–57

Russian Revolution and Civil War, 1917–1922

Between 1917 and 1922, revolution and civil war transformed Russia into the communist Soviet Union.

Map: Russian Revolution and Civil War, 1917–1922 showing Russia (Union of Soviet Socialist Republics, 1922), with labeled cities Murmansk, Archangel, Petrograd, Moscow, Kiev, Brest-Litovsk, and countries including ESTONIA, FINLAND, LATVIA, LITHUANIA, POLAND, ROMANIA, TURKEY, IRAN, AFGHANISTAN, INDIA, MONGOLIA, CHINA, JAPAN. Bodies of water: Barents Sea, Black Sea, Caspian Sea, Aral Sea, Mediterranean Sea, L. Balkhash, L. Baikal, Sea of Okhotsk, PACIFIC OCEAN. Robinson Projection, 0–1000 Miles / 0–1000 Kilometers.

Legend:
- Lands lost by Russia
- ★ Revolutionary outbreaks, 1917
- ✦ Major battle sites, 1918–1920
- → Foreign interventions

КОМСОМОЛ-УДАРНАЯ БРИГАДА ПЯТИЛЕТКИ.

1928
Stalin proposes a five-year plan for Soviet economic growth. This poster urges industrial workers to participate.

1934
Stalin launches the Great Purge. Millions will be executed or sent to forced-labor camps like the one shown here.

1930

1935

1940

1929 Stock market crash in New York triggers global depression of the 1930s.

1934 Chinese Communists make epic retreat known as the Long March.

1939 German forces invade Poland. World War II begins.

Russian Revolution and Civil War, 1917–1922

Activating Prior Knowledge
Which document was supposed to give people freedom of speech and assembly after the 1905 Revolution? *(October Manifesto)*

Previewing
Notice the arrows that show foreign intervention and the civil war battle sites on the map on this page. Why would foreign powers not want a radical Communist government in Russia? *(They did not want radical ideas and revolution to spread.)*

Background
About the Pictures

1. The Winter Palace was the residence of the czars from 1762 to 1904, when Nicholas II left St. Petersburg due to growing unrest. The provisional government was housed there in 1917. Today, it is home to the famous Hermitage Museum.

2. Vladimir Lenin held an exalted place in Soviet Russia. Statues, portraits, and banners celebrating him could be found throughout the country.

3. This propaganda poster, *The Young Communist League Is the Shock Battalion of the Five Year Plan* by Vladimir Lyushin, was painted in 1931 in the socialist realism style. Such paintings idealized workers and engineers for their heroism as builders of the Soviet state.

4. Have students contrast the idealized view of Soviet labor portrayed in Lyushin's propaganda poster with this photo of Russian slave laborers building a canal.

Independent Assignments

Have students read one section as they prepare for class. After class, have them complete the assignment. Some students may benefit from using the Guided Reading and Review worksheets.

Section 1 Have students use the worksheet *Women in the Russian Revolution* in the Unit 7 booklet, p. 30, to learn about women's contributions to the revolutionary cause.

Section 2 Have students use the worksheet *One Day in the Life of Ivan Denisovich* in the History Through Literature booklet, pp. 59–60, to learn about the harsh conditions in a Siberian forced-labor camp.

Section 3 Have students use the worksheet *Growing Up in Stalin's Russia* in the Unit 7 booklet, p. 29, to learn about an average boy living during Stalin's dictatorship.

eTeach

Be sure to check out this month's online discussion with a World History Master Teacher.

Go to **www.phschool.com**.

SECTION **1** Two Revolutions in Russia

🔔 **Bell Ringer** Ask students to recall what they have learned about World War I and conditions in Russia during the 1800s and early 1900s. Based on this knowledge, ask them to list possible causes for the revolutions that occurred in Russia in 1917.

Reading Focus

■ Why did revolution occur in Russia in March 1917?

■ Why did Lenin and the Bolsheviks launch the November revolution?

■ How did the Communists defeat their opponents in Russia's civil war?

Vocabulary

proletariat
soviet
commissar

Taking Notes

Copy this partially completed chart on the causes of revolution in Russia. As you read, finish the chart by writing in other causes.

National groups want self-rule

REVOLUTION IN RUSSIA

Main Idea After two revolutions and a civil war, Lenin and the Communist party were the new rulers of Russia.

LESSON PLAN

1. Focus Czarist rule and the extreme hardships of World War I set the stage for revolution in Russia. After their seizure of power, Lenin and the Bolsheviks attempted to establish socialism and a dictatorship of the proletariat. They also had to defeat rival forces and rebuild a nation ruined by war.

2. Instruct Divide the class into four groups—one for each of the subsections in this section. Assign each group one of the following topics: The March Revolution, Lenin and the Bolsheviks, The November Revolution, and Russian Civil War. Have students in each group work together to outline the major ideas of their topic. After students have finished this part of the lesson, regroup them so that each new group has at least one "expert" for each of the topics. Assign students to take turns teaching other group members about their area of expertise.

3. Assess Ask students to write on a sheet of paper three significant questions about the revolutions and civil war that took place in Russia. Collect the lists of questions. Shuffle the lists, redistribute them to the students, and assign the students to write answers to the three questions that they now have.

4. Reteach If students' Assess activity does not reflect adequate understanding of the lesson, you might assign the *Guide to the Essentials* or the *Interactive Student Tutorial CD-ROM* for this section.

Geography and History

A Land of Many Nations

Geography had long favored the growth of the Russian empire. The vast plain stretching from Moscow had few natural obstacles to halt the advance of Russian armies. For nearly four centuries, the empire grew steadily. This growth was a mixed blessing, however. In 1897, a census revealed that the Russians were a minority in their own empire. More than half the people under czarist rule were not Russians. The population included Poles, Finns, Ukrainians, Lithuanians, Latvians, Turkic peoples, and other groups.

Nationalism led to the rise of new political parties among these peoples. In addition to social and economic reform, the parties' leaders hoped for some degree of self-rule. Radicals even dreamed of independent nations—a revolutionary idea that contributed to unrest in the Russian empire.

Theme: Geography and History Refer to a modern map of Europe. Name two independent nations of today that were once part of the Russian empire.

Setting the Scene On Easter 1913, Czar Nicholas II gave his wife, Alexandra, a fabulous jeweled egg, made by the famous jewelry firm of Fabergé. The egg's enamel shell held tiny portraits of all the Romanovs who had reigned since Michael Romanov was elected to rule Russia in 1613. Balls, parades, and other festive events celebrated the 300th anniversary of the Romanov dynasty. Everywhere, Russians cheered wildly for the czar and his family.

Czarina Alexandra felt confident that the people loved Nicholas too much to ever threaten him. "They are constantly frightening the emperor with threats of revolution," she told a friend, "and here,—you see it yourself—we need merely to show ourselves and at once their hearts are ours."

Appearances were deceiving. After the Revolution of 1905, Nicholas had failed to solve Russia's basic political, economic, and social problems. Discontent sparked new eruptions. In March 1917, the first of two revolutions would topple the Romanov dynasty and pave the way for even more radical changes.

The March Revolution

In 1914, the huge Russian empire stretched from Eastern Europe to the Pacific Ocean. Unlike industrialized Western Europe, Russia was a backward land dominated by landowning nobles, priests, and an autocratic czar. Much of its majority peasant population endured stark poverty. A small middle class and an urban working class were emerging as Russia began to industrialize.

Long-Term Unrest Under pressure, czars had made some reforms, but too few to ease the nation's crisis. The elected Duma set up after the Revolution of 1905 had no real power. Moderates pressed for a constitution and social change. But Nicholas II, a weak and ineffectual man, blocked attempts to limit his authority. Like past czars, he relied on his secret police and other enforcers to impose his will. Adding to the problems of the government were a corrupt bureaucracy and an overburdened court system.

Revolutionaries hatched radical plots. Some hoped to lead discontented peasants to overthrow the czarist regime. Marxists tried to ignite revolution among the proletariat—the growing class of factory and railroad workers, miners, and urban wage earners. To outwit government spies and informers, revolutionaries worked in secrecy under rigid discipline. A revolution, they believed, would occur, when the time was ripe.

Geography and History

ANSWER Poland, Finland, Turkey, Ukraine, Lithuania, Latvia

Resource Directory

Teaching Resources
Creative Teaching Activities Creative Teaching Activities booklet, p. 126
Guided Reading and Review Unit 7 booklet, p. 22
Skill Application Activity *Documenting Your Sources,* Unit 7 booklet, p. 31

Impact of World War I The outbreak of war in 1914 fired national pride and united Russians. Armies dashed to battle with enthusiasm. But like the Crimean and Russo-Japanese wars, World War I quickly strained Russian resources. Factories could not turn out enough supplies. The transportation system broke down, delivering only a trickle of needed materials to the front. By 1915, many soldiers had no rifles and no ammunition. Badly equipped and poorly led, they died in staggering numbers. In 1915 alone, Russian casualties reached two million.

In a patriotic gesture, Nicholas II went to the front to take personal charge. The decision proved a disastrous blunder. The czar was no more competent than many of his generals. Worse, he left domestic affairs to the czarina, Alexandra. Many Russians already distrusted Alexandra because she was German born. She also knew little about government.

Rasputin Alexandra came to rely on the advice of Gregory Rasputin, an illiterate peasant and self-proclaimed "holy man." Rasputin's powerful personality had helped him gain a widespread reputation as a healer. The czarina, especially, came to believe in his "miraculous" powers after he helped ease the suffering of her son, who suffered from hemophilia, a disorder in which even the smallest injury can result in uncontrollable bleeding.

By 1916, Rasputin's influence over Alexandra had reached new heights and weakened confidence in the government. Officials were appointed or dismissed at his say-so. Those who flattered him won top jobs. Yet Alexandra ignored all warnings about Rasputin. Fearing for the monarchy, a group of Russian nobles killed Rasputin on December 29, 1916.

Collapse of the Monarchy By March 1917,* disasters on the battlefield, combined with food and fuel shortages on the home front, brought the monarchy to collapse. In St. Petersburg (renamed Petrograd during the war), workers were going on strike. Marchers, mostly women, surged through the streets, shouting, "Bread! Bread!" Troops refused to fire on the demonstrators, leaving the government helpless. Finally, on the advice of military and political leaders, the czar abdicated.

Duma politicians then set up a provisional, or temporary, government. Middle-class liberals in the government began preparing a constitution for a new Russian republic. At the same time, they continued the war against Germany. That decision proved fatal. Most Russians were fed up with the war. Troops at the front were deserting in droves. Peasants wanted land. City workers demanded food and an end to the desperate shortages.

Outside the provisional government, revolutionary socialists plotted their own course. In Petrograd and other cities, they set up soviets, or councils of workers and soldiers. At first, the soviets worked democratically within the government. Before long, though, the Bolsheviks, a radical socialist group, took charge. The leader of the Bolsheviks was a determined revolutionary, V. I. Lenin.

Lenin and the Bolsheviks

Vladimir Ilyich Ulyanov (ool YAHN awf) was born in 1870 to a middle-class family. Lenin was the name he adopted when he became a revolutionary. When he was 17, his older brother was arrested and hanged for plotting to kill the czar. The execution branded his family as a threat to the state and instilled in young Vladimir a hatred for the czarist government.

---

* The revolutions of March and November 1917 are known to Russians as the February and October revolutions. In 1917, Russia still used an old calendar, which was 13 days behind the one used in Western Europe. Not until 1918 did Russia adopt the western calendar.

Did You Know?

A Hard Man to Kill
The death of Gregory Rasputin was perhaps even more bizarre than his strange life.

To get rid of him, a group of nobles lured Rasputin to the palace of Prince Felix Yussoupov, where they served him cakes and wine laced with enough cyanide to kill several men. Incredibly, Rasputin was not affected. Next, Yussoupov shot him through the chest with a revolver. Rasputin fell. As the conspirators examined the body, Rasputin sprang to his feet and began to attack Yussoupov! The prince fled.

Then Rasputin attempted his own escape. He bolted outside and ran across the courtyard toward the gate. Another shot hit him, and he fell into the snow. The conspirators then clubbed him unconscious. Flinging Rasputin into the icy Neva River, they watched him sink.

Later, the body of Rasputin—poisoned, shot twice, and badly beaten—was recovered from the river and autopsied. The cause of death? Drowning.

Theme: Impact of the Individual Why did Yussoupov and others go to so much trouble to murder Rasputin?

Reading Strategy
Predicting Content

Before they read Section 1, have students skim the headings, subheadings, illustrations, and captions. Then ask them to predict what happens to the Russian czar and the Russian people and why it happens. *(More Advanced Readers)*

Customize for . . .
Kinesthetic Learners

Writing a Skit Invite volunteers to write and present a skit based on the political career and final days of Gregory Rasputin. Advise students to include the following roles in their skit: Rasputin, Nicholas II, Alexandra, Alexis (the son who had hemophilia), government officials who oppose the influence of Rasputin, and the assassins of Rasputin. In their skit, students should reveal the reason for Rasputin's influence over the royal family, the reasons for opposition to Rasputin, and the circumstances surrounding the assassination of Rasputin. ✳

Block Scheduling Support

Organize students into three groups. Assign one of the following to each group: American Revolution, Russian Revolution, and French Revolution. Have each group research its topic, looking at the ideology behind it, the political history that preceded it, the manner in which it was carried out, and the results and legacies of the revolution. Then, have each group make its presentation. In discussion, have the whole class compare and contrast the three revolutions.

Did You Know?

ANSWER The nobles were exasperated by Rasputin's influence over the royal family and his unseemly conduct.

Biography

ANSWER It is impossible to say, but the execution of Alexander was certainly a contributing factor, if not sufficient in its own right.

Activity
Connections to Film

Writing a News Article *Doctor Zhivago*, the 1965 epic film based on the novel by Boris Pasternak and directed by David Lean, presents its romantic drama against the backdrop of World War I and the Russian Revolution. The first hour of the film focuses on Russia's involvement in World War I. Initially, there are scenes of patriotic troops marching proudly off to war. But these quickly give way to scenes depicting the cruel hardships at the front, the collapse of Russian morale, mass desertion, and violent rebellion.

Ask students to assume the role of newspaper reporters accompanying the Russian troops. Assign them to write an article describing how and why Russian troops turned against their officers and czar to become the troops of the Russian Revolution. Advise them to address such factors as socioeconomic conditions, Bolshevik propaganda, conditions at the front, and the relations between the troops and their officers. (*Doctor Zhivago* is available on videocassette, laserdisc, and DVD.)

Biography

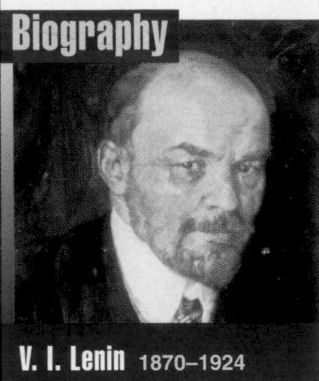

V. I. Lenin 1870–1924

Lenin was the son of a teacher and his wife who lived in a little town on the Volga River. Vladimir lived with his parents and five siblings in a rented wing of a large house. By all accounts it was a happy home. Vladimir excelled at school and looked up to his older brother Alexander. But, when Vladimir was 16, his father died. When he was 17, his beloved brother Alexander was hanged for plotting to kill the czar.

Still reeling from the death of his brother, Vladimir enrolled at Kazan University. There he met other discontented young people. They united to protest the lack of student freedom in the university. Vladimir was expelled within three months for his part in the demonstrations.

Theme: Impact of the Individual How do you think Lenin's early life affected his later political ideas?

Early Career As a young man, Lenin read the works of Karl Marx and participated in student demonstrations. He spread Marxist ideas among factory workers along with other socialists, including Nadezhda Krupskaya (nah DYEZH duh kroop SKĪ uh), the daughter of a poor noble family.

In 1895, Lenin and Krupskaya were arrested and sent to Siberia. During their imprisonment, they were married. After their release, they went into exile in Switzerland. There, they worked tirelessly to spread revolutionary ideas. A rival once described Lenin's total commitment to the cause: "There is no other man who is absorbed by the revolution 24 hours a day, who has no other thoughts but the thought of revolution, and who, even when he sleeps, dreams of nothing but the revolution."

A New View of Marx Lenin adapted Marxist ideas to fit Russian conditions. Marx had predicted that the industrial working class would rise spontaneously to overthrow capitalism. But Russia did not have a large urban proletariat. Instead, Lenin called for an elite group to lead the revolution and set up a "dictatorship of the proletariat." Though this elite revolutionary party represented a small percentage of socialists, Lenin gave them the name Bolsheviks, meaning "majority."

In Western Europe, many leading socialists had come to think that socialism could be achieved through gradual and moderate reforms such as higher wages, increased suffrage, and social welfare programs. The Bolsheviks rejected this approach. To Lenin, reforms of this nature were merely capitalist tricks to repress the masses. Only revolution, he said, could bring about needed changes.

Lenin Returns From Exile In March 1917, Lenin was still in exile. As Russia stumbled into revolution, Germany saw a chance to weaken its enemy by helping Lenin return home. In a special train, it rushed the Bolshevik leader across Germany to the Russian frontier.

On April 16, 1917, Lenin stepped off the train in Petrograd. A crowd of fellow exiles and activists recently released from the czar's prisons met him at the station. Lenin triumphantly addressed the crowd:

> "Dear Comrades, soldiers, sailors and workers! I am happy to greet in your persons the victorious Russian revolution, to greet you as the vanguard of the worldwide proletarian army. . . . Any day now the whole of European capitalism may crash. The Russian revolution accomplished by you has prepared the way and opened a new epoch. Long live the worldwide Socialist revolution!"
> —V. I. Lenin, quoted in *The Russian Revolution, 1917* (Sukhanov)

The November Revolution

Lenin threw himself into the work of furthering the revolution. He was assisted by another committed Marxist revolutionary, Leon Trotsky. To the hungry, war-weary Russian people, Lenin and the Bolsheviks promised "Peace, Land, and Bread."

The provisional government, meanwhile, continued the war effort and failed to deal with land reform. In the summer of 1917, the government launched a disastrous offensive against Germany. By November, according to one official report, the army was "a huge crowd of tired, poorly clad, poorly fed, embittered men." Growing numbers of troops mutinied. At the same time, peasants seized land and drove off fearful landlords.

The Bolshevik Takeover Conditions were ripe for the Bolsheviks to make their move. In November 1917, squads of Red Guards—armed factory workers—joined mutinous sailors from the Russian fleet in attacking

Resource Directory

Teaching Resource
Viewpoint Activity *Women in the Russian Revolution,* Unit 7 booklet, p. 30

the provisional government. In just a matter of days, Lenin's forces overthrew a government that no longer had any support.

In Petrograd, members of the government were meeting in a room at the Winter Palace. Suddenly, a young cadet entered the chamber to announce that Bolsheviks were storming the palace. "What are the provisional government's orders?" he asked.

"It's no use," one politician announced. "We give up. No bloodshed!" A moment later, armed rebels flooded into the room. The provisional government had fallen without a struggle.

The Bolsheviks in Charge The Bolsheviks quickly seized power in other cities. In Moscow, it took a week of fighting to blast the local government out of the walled Kremlin, the former czarist center of government. Moscow became the Bolsheviks' capital, and the Kremlin their headquarters.

"We shall now occupy ourselves in Russia in building up a proletarian socialist state," declared Lenin. The Bolsheviks ended private ownership of land and distributed land to peasants. Workers were given control of the factories and mines. A new red flag with an entwined hammer and sickle symbolized union between peasants and workers.

Throughout the land, millions thought they had at last gained control over their own lives. In fact, the Bolsheviks—renamed Communists—would soon become their new masters.

Russian Civil War

After the Bolshevik Revolution, Lenin quickly sought peace with Germany. Russia signed the Treaty of Brest-Litovsk in March 1918, giving up a huge chunk of its territory and its population. The cost for peace was extremely high, but the Communist leaders knew that they needed all their energy to defeat a battery of enemies at home.

Opposing Forces For three years, civil war raged between the "Reds," as the Communists were known, and the "Whites," counterrevolutionaries who remained loyal to the czar. National groups that the czars had conquered also took up arms against the Red Army. Poland, Estonia, Latvia, and Lithuania broke free, but nationalists in Ukraine, the Caucasus, and Central Asia were eventually subdued.

The Allied powers of World War I intervened in the civil war. They hoped that the Whites might overthrow the Communists and support the fight against Germany. Britain, France, and the United States sent forces to help the Whites. Japan seized land in East Asia that czarist Russia had once claimed. The Allied presence, however, did little to help the Whites. The Reds appealed to nationalism and urged Russians to drive out the foreigners. In the long run, the Allied invasion fed Communist distrust of the West.

Turning Points in Russia, 1914–1921

1914

August
World War I begins.

1917

March
Revolution forces the czar to abdicate. A provisional government is formed.

April
Lenin returns to Russia.

July
Russians suffer more than 50,000 casualties in battle against German and Austro-Hungarian forces.

November
A second revolution results in Bolshevik takeover of government.

December
Bolshevik government seeks peace with Germany.

1918

March
Russia signs treaty of Brest-Litovsk, losing a large amount of territory.

July
Civil war between the Reds and Whites begins. The czar and his family are executed.

August
British, American, Japanese, and other foreign forces intervene in Russia.

1921

March
Communist government is victorious. Only sporadic fighting continues.

Skills Assessment **Chart** Between 1914 and 1921, the Russian people struggled through World War I, two revolutions, and civil war. **How did the events of April and July 1917 contribute to revolution later that year?**

Customize for . . .
Auditory Learners

Analyzing a Primary Source The following excerpt from Lenin's *State and Revolution* compares democracy with the dictatorship of the proletariat. Read the excerpt to the class once or twice. Then ask the questions that follow.

"And so in the capitalist society we have a democracy that is curtailed, wretched, false, a democracy only for the rich, for the minority. The dictatorship of the proletariat, the period of transition to communism, will for the first time create democracy for the people, for the majority, along with the necessary suppression of the exploiters, the minority."

(1) Why does Lenin oppose the traditional type of democracy? (2) Why does he consider his dictatorship of the proletariat to be preferable? (3) Who will be suppressed under this dictatorship? (4) Do you agree or disagree with Lenin's analysis? Explain.

Human Drama Note

Trotsky's Red Army Leon Trotsky forged the Workers' and Peasants' Red Army from loyal Bolsheviks and from officers of the czar's army. The former imperial officers, threatened and bribed into accepting commissions, provided the discipline and experience that the new army needed. To ensure their loyalty to the Bolshevik cause, Trotsky appointed "military commissars" who carefully watched over them. In this way, Trotsky ensured political control over the Red Army.

Test Preparation

Have students read the excerpt on the opposite page by Lenin, and then complete the sentence: Lenin was trying to convince his audience that

A the Russian revolution was a failure.

B the Russian revolution was the beginning of a great change that would affect many countries.

C the International Socialist Revolution was complete.

D the governments of Europe were sending armies to put down the revolution.

Skills Assessment

ANSWER Lenin's arrival provided the leadership for the Bolshevik takeover. Heavy losses in battle furthered Russian dissatisfaction with the war.

Recall

1. (a) Nicholas and Alexandra, p. 702
(b) Gregory Rasputin, p. 703 (c) Bolsheviks, p. 704 (d) Leon Trotsky, p. 704
(e) Red Army, p. 705 (f) Whites, p. 705
(g) Cheka, p. 706 2. (a) proletariat, p. 702
(b) soviet, p. 703 (c) commissar, p. 706

Comprehension

3. Russia's massive defeats in World War I, food and fuel shortages, and low confidence in the government 4. (a) He called for an elite group to lead the revolution and set up a "dictatorship of the proletariat." (b) The provisional government had lost the support of the people by continuing the war against Germany.
5. The Bolsheviks, who became known as Reds, favored a socialist state. They appealed to nationalism and favored expelling foreigners from Russia. The Whites were counterrevolutionaries who were loyal to the czar.

Critical Thinking and Writing

6. (a) favor (b) He cited evidence that the revolution would otherwise fail.
(c) Answers are to be supported with facts. 7. Causes: Czarists battled Communists; nationalist groups tried to break away. Effects: foreign intervention, loss of territory, war, communism, country left in chaos

Activity Rubrics

Share rubrics with students before they begin the activity.

Attempted All three points of view are not included, or the summaries are incomplete.

Minimal Summaries are complete but show little understanding of the points of view.

Adequate Summaries show that all three points of view are well understood.

Exemplary Summaries show that all three points of view are well understood, and the information is presented in an interesting manner.

Primary Source

ANSWER The Red Army had developed a reputation for cruelty.

Primary Source

The Whites and the Reds

Like all modern wars, the Russian civil war involved civilians as well as soldiers. Here, an English eyewitness describes people fleeing from the advancing Red Army:

"Tens of thousands of peaceful people had fled . . . during that space of time, rushing away from the Red Terror with nothing but the clothes they stood in, as people rush in their nightdresses out of a house on fire. . . . Peasants had deserted their fields, students their books, doctors their hospitals, scientists their laboratories, workmen their workshops, authors their completed manuscripts. . . . We were being swept away in the wreckage of a demoralized army."

—quoted in *Russia Under the Bolshevik Regime* (Pipes)

Skills Assessment

Primary Source Why do you think people feared the Red Army?

Brutality was common in the civil war. Counterrevolutionary forces slaughtered captured Communists and tried to assassinate Lenin. The Communists, meanwhile, launched their own reign of terror. They organized the Cheka, a secret police force. They executed ordinary citizens, even if they were only suspected of taking action against the revolution. The former czar and czarina and their five children were shot to keep them from becoming a rallying symbol for counterrevolutionary forces.

War Communism The Communists adopted a policy known as "war communism." They took over banks, mines, factories, and railroads. Peasants were forced to deliver "surplus" food to hungry people in the cities. Peasant laborers were drafted into the military or into factory work.

Meanwhile, Trotsky turned the Red Army into an effective fighting force. He used former czarist officers under the close watch of commissars, Communist party officials assigned to the army to teach party principles and ensure party loyalty. Trotsky's passionate speeches roused soldiers to fight. So did the order to shoot every tenth man if a unit performed poorly—a tactic borrowed from the armies of ancient Rome.

The great Russian writer Maxim Gorky had supported revolution and was a friend of Lenin, but he opposed the severities of war communism. Gorky later recalled Lenin's response to his complaints:

"'Is it possible to act humanely in a struggle of such unprecedented ferocity? Where is there any place for softheartedness or generosity? We are being blockaded by Europe, we are deprived of the help of the European proletariat, counter-revolution is creeping like a bear on us from every side. What do you want? Are we not right?'"

—Maxim Gorky, "Days With Lenin"

A Costly Triumph By 1921, the Communists had defeated their scattered foes, but Russia was in chaos. Millions had died since the beginning of World War I. Millions more perished from the famine and disease that stalked the land. An American journalist, accompanying an international relief team in Russia, described the horrible desolation. In village after village, he noted, "no one stirred from the little wooden houses . . . where Russian families were hibernating and waiting for death." Although Lenin had triumphed, he faced an immense job of rebuilding a nation and an economy in ruins.

SECTION 1 Assessment

Recall

1. **Identify:** (a) Nicholas and Alexandra, (b) Gregory Rasputin, (c) Bolsheviks, (d) Leon Trotsky, (e) Red Army, (f) Whites, (g) Cheka.
2. **Define:** (a) proletariat, (b) soviet, (c) commissar.

Comprehension

3. What were the causes of the March Revolution?
4. (a) How did Lenin adapt Marxism to conditions in Russia? (b) Why were the Bolsheviks able to seize power in November 1917?
5. Describe the opposing forces in the Russian civil war.

Critical Thinking and Writing

6. **Analyzing Primary Sources** Review the excerpt from "Days With Lenin" by Maxim Gorky, quoted above. (a) Did Lenin favor or oppose war communism? (b) How did Lenin defend his position? (c) Do you agree or disagree with Lenin? Explain.
7. **Recognizing Causes and Effects** What were the causes and effects of the civil war in Russia?

Activity

Take It to the NET

Use the Internet to find three primary sources on the revolutions or civil war in Russia. Find one source for the Red point of view, one source for the White point of view, and a third for the viewpoint of the foreign powers that intervened in the civil war. Print the documents. Then, summarize the main ideas of each.

Resource Directory

Teaching Resources

Section Quiz Unit 7 booklet, p. 23
Creative Teaching Activities Creative Teaching Activities booklet, p. 127
Guided Reading and Review Unit 7 booklet, p. 24

Technology

Interactive Student Tutorial CD-ROM Ch. 28
Computer Test Bank Ch. 28

Reading Focus

- How did the Communist state develop under Lenin?
- What were the effects of Stalin's five-year plans?
- Why did Stalin launch the Great Purge?
- How did Soviet foreign policy affect relations with the western powers?

Vocabulary

command economy
collective
kulak

Taking Notes

Create a table like this one. As you read, list the policies and effects of Lenin's NEP and Stalin's five-year plans. Be sure to make your table large enough to allow a list of facts in each box.

	POLICIES	EFFECTS
THE NEP		Food production rose
THE FIVE-YEAR PLANS	Government made all economic decisions	

Main Idea After Lenin helped the country recover from civil war, Stalin established a brutal Communist dictatorship in the Soviet Union.

Setting the Scene

In January 1924, tens of thousands of people lined up in Moscow's Red Square. They had come to view the body of Lenin, who had died a few days earlier.

Meanwhile, Lenin's party colleagues debated what to do with his corpse. His widow, Krupskaya, wanted him buried simply, next to his mother's grave in Petrograd. Communist party officials—including Joseph Stalin—had other ideas. They wanted Lenin preserved and put on permanent display. In the end, the party had its way. Lenin's body would remain on display in Red Square for more than 65 years.

By having Lenin preserved, Stalin wanted to show that he would carry on the goals of the revolution. In the years that followed, he used ruthless measures to win dictatorial power and impose a new order on Russia.

Building the Communist Soviet Union

Lenin's first years as leader of Russia had been occupied in putting down civil war. Once the Communist victory and his personal power were secure, he turned to the enormous problem of rebuilding a state and an economy that had been shattered by World War I, two revolutions, and years of civil war.

Government In 1922, the Communists produced a constitution that seemed both democratic and socialist. It set up an elected legislature, later called the Supreme Soviet, and gave all citizens over 18 the right to vote. All political power, resources, and means of production would belong to workers and peasants. The new government united much of the old Russian empire in the Union of Soviet Socialist Republics (USSR), or Soviet Union. (See the map later in this section.) The Soviet Union was a multinational state made up of European and Asian peoples. In theory, all the member republics shared certain equal rights.

Reality, however, differed greatly from theory in the Soviet Union. The Communist party, not the people, reigned supreme. Like the Russian czars, the party used the army and secret police to enforce its will. Russia, which was the largest republic, dominated the other republics.

Lenin's NEP On the economic front, Lenin retreated from his policy of "war communism," which had brought the economy to near collapse. Under party control, factory and mine output had fallen. Peasants stopped producing grain, knowing it would only be seized by the government.

Symbols of the Soviet Union

The hammer and sickle were prominent symbols of the Soviet Union. The hammer represented industrial workers, and the sickle represented agricultural workers.

Theme: Political and Social Systems Why do you think Communist leaders placed the hammer and sickle over the world in the symbol below?

SECTION 2

Bell Ringer Inform students that before becoming a leader of the Soviet Union, Joseph Djugashvili changed his name to *Stalin*, which means "man of steel." Ask students to predict the types of policies that one might expect a man named Stalin to follow.

LESSON PLAN

1. Focus Lenin directed the establishment of the Soviet Union under the supreme authority of the Communist party. In economics, he mixed capitalism with socialism. After Lenin's death, Joseph Stalin gained power through ruthless measures. His economic goals were industrialization and collectivization. By launching the Great Purge and other acts of terror, Stalin gained absolute power.

2. Instruct Have students work individually or in groups to find evidence in the text to support the following generalizations: (1) In some ways, the Soviet Union remained similar to the old Russian empire. (2) Lenin retreated from pure communism. (3) Most Russians benefited little from the five-year plans. (4) Stalin was ruthless in both his economic and political policies. (5) In its foreign policy, the Soviet Union met with limited success. Encourage students to share the evidence they have gathered in a class discussion.

3. Assess Have students write one generalization of their own about the Soviet Union during this period.

4. Reteach If students' **Assess** activity does not reflect adequate understanding of the lesson, you might assign the *Guide to the Essentials* or the *Interactive Student Tutorial CD-ROM* for this section.

Block Scheduling Support

Have students work in pairs. Assign one member to become an expert on Lenin and the other to become an expert on Stalin. As students study Chapter 28, have them write a dialogue in which the two historic figures discuss the best way to seize and maintain power, achieve economic prosperity, pursue foreign policy, and the like. Ask for volunteers to read their dialogues to the class, and then have the class discuss whether they accurately reflect the two leaders' philosophies.

Caption Answer

The hammer symbolized workers and the sickle symbolized peasants. The globe was included because the revolution was to be worldwide.

Religious Policy Under the Communist government, the clergy of the Orthodox Church were declared "deprivees." As such, they were deprived of their voting rights, subjected to higher taxes, and provided with lower rations. Their children were denied access to higher education. Church buildings were destroyed or desecrated, while the priests themselves were beaten or killed. By 1921, 28 bishops and more than 1,000 priests had suffered either death or imprisonment.

Biography

Joseph Stalin 1879–1953

"The outstanding characteristic of Stalin's personality," one historian wrote, "was his total ruthlessness. No consideration of sentiment or pity seems to have influenced him in the slightest."

It is hard to disagree. Stalin left a wake of suffering and death that boggles the mind.

Stalin instituted "purges," sending millions of people to lives of misery in forced-labor camps. He sent millions more to their deaths. Many historians think that this one man was responsible for the deaths of some 20 million people. The only thing that stopped his killing was his own death. Just before he died, he was planning yet another wave of mass arrests and executions. Stalin is quoted as saying, "A single death is a tragedy, a million deaths is a statistic."

Theme: Impact of the Individual Why did Stalin's purges consolidate his power?

In 1921, Lenin adopted the New Economic Policy, or NEP. It allowed some capitalist ventures. Although the state kept control of banks, foreign trade, and large industries, small businesses were allowed to reopen for private profit. The government also stopped squeezing peasants for grain. Under the NEP, peasants held on to small plots of land and freely sold their surplus crops.

Lenin's compromise with capitalism helped the Soviet economy recover and ended armed resistance to the new government. By 1928, food and industrial production climbed back to prewar levels. The standard of living improved, too. But Lenin always saw the NEP as just a temporary retreat from communism. His successor would soon put the Soviet Union back on the road to "pure" communism.

Stalin Gains Power Lenin's sudden death in 1924 set off a power struggle among Communist leaders. The chief contenders were Trotsky and Joseph Stalin. Trotsky was a brilliant Marxist thinker, a skillful speaker, and an architect of the Bolshevik Revolution. Stalin, by contrast, was neither a scholar nor an orator. He was, however, a shrewd political operator and behind-the-scenes organizer.

Stalin was born Joseph Djugashvili (joo guhsh VEE lee) to a poor family in Georgia, a region in the Caucasus Mountains. As a boy, he studied for the priesthood. But his growing interest in revolution brought him under the seminary's harsh discipline. Once, he was confined to a punishment cell for reading a novel about the French Revolution.

By 1900, Djugashvili had joined the Bolshevik underground and had taken the name Stalin, meaning "man of steel." He organized robberies to get money for the party and spent time in prison and in Siberian exile. He played a far less important role in the revolution and the civil war than did Trotsky. But in the 1920s, he became general secretary of the party. He used that position to build a loyal group of Communist officials who owed their jobs to him.

As early as 1922, Lenin had expressed grave doubts about Stalin's ambitious nature: "Comrade Stalin . . . has concentrated an enormous power in his hands; and I am not sure that he always knows how to use that power with sufficient caution." To Lenin, Stalin was "too rude." Lenin urged the party to choose a successor "more tolerant, more loyal, more polite, and more considerate to comrades."

At Lenin's death, Trotsky and Stalin jockeyed for position. They differed on most issues, including the future of communism. Trotsky, a firm Marxist, urged support for a worldwide revolution against capitalism. Stalin took a more cautious view. Efforts to foster Marxist revolutions in Europe after World War I had failed. Instead, he wanted to concentrate on building socialism at home first.

With political cunning, Stalin put his own supporters into top jobs and isolated Trotsky within the party. Stripped of party membership, Trotsky fled the country in 1929. Still, he continued to criticize Stalin. In 1940, Trotsky was murdered in Mexico by a Stalinist agent.

Stalin's Five-Year Plans

Once in power, Stalin set out to make the Soviet Union into a modern industrial power. In the past, said Stalin, Russia had suffered defeats because of its economic backwardness. In 1928, therefore, he proposed the first of several "five-year plans" aimed at building heavy industry, improving transportation, and increasing farm output.

To achieve this growth, he brought all economic activity under government control. The Soviet Union developed a command economy, in which government officials made all basic economic decisions. Under Stalin, the government owned all businesses and allocated financial and other

Biography

ANSWER He eliminated all his enemies either by sending them to forced-labor camps or by sentencing them to death for trumped-up crimes such as treason.

Soviet Union, 1917–1938

Legend:
- Russian empire, 1914
- Area controlled by Bolsheviks, 1919
- Union of Soviet Socialist Republics, 1938

Azimuthal Equal Area Projection

0 500 1000 Miles
0 500 1000 Kilometers

Skills Assessment

Geography After the Bolshevik Revolution, the Soviet Union extended control over many areas of the former Russian empire.

1. **Location** On the map, locate (a) Turkmen S.S.R., (b) Poland, (c) China.
2. **Region** Name three countries that had been part of the Russian empire but were not part of the Soviet Union in 1938.
3. **Critical Thinking Applying Information** How does the map help explain why Russia was the most influential republic in the Soviet Union?

Activity
Cooperative Learning

Interpreting a Map Have students work together in small groups to answer the questions that follow. Instruct them to use the map of the Soviet Union on this page as well as other resources. (1) In what republics of the Soviet Union were there significant Muslim populations? (2) What countries were probably most fearful of an invasion by the Soviet Union? Why? (3) Why do you think the Soviet Union and Japan might have had an uneasy relationship? (4) How might nationalism have affected the Soviet Union? (5) Which of the Asian states bordering the Soviet Union was the first to become a communist state?

Background
Linking Past and Present

Food Shortages As the Soviet Union neared the end of its existence in the 1980s and 1990s, food shortages were still a critical problem. According to one newspaper article, 91 percent of all foodstuffs were sold with ration coupons or on special order through stores at workplaces. Soviet food stores typically carried from 5 to 40 separate items for sale, far different from supermarkets in the United States that carry between 25,000 and 35,000 different items.

resources. By contrast, in a capitalist economy, the free market controls most economic decisions. Businesses are privately owned and operated by individuals for profit.

Mixed Industrial Results Stalin's five-year plans set high production goals, especially for heavy industry and transportation. The government pushed workers and managers to meet these goals by giving bonuses to those who succeeded—and by punishing those who did not. Between 1928 and 1939, large factories, hydroelectric power stations, and huge industrial complexes rose across the Soviet Union. Oil, coal, and steel production grew. Mining expanded, and new railroads were built.

Despite the impressive progress in some areas, Soviet workers had little to show for their sacrifices. Some former peasants did improve their lives, becoming skilled factory workers or managers. Overall, though, standards of living remained poor. Wages were low, and consumer goods were scarce. Also, central planning was often inefficient, causing shortages in several areas and surpluses in others. Many managers, concerned only with meeting production quotas, turned out large quantities of low-quality goods.

During and after the Stalin era, the Soviet Union continued to do well in heavy industry, such as the production of farm machinery. However, its planned economy failed to match that of the capitalist world in making consumer goods such as clothing, cars, and refrigerators.

Revolution in Agriculture Stalin also brought agriculture under government control. Under the NEP, peasants had held on to small plots of land. But Stalin saw that system as being inefficient and a threat to state power. He forced peasants to give up their private plots and live on either state-owned farms or collectives, large farms owned and operated by peasants as a group. Peasants were permitted to keep their houses and personal

✓ Test Preparation

Have students read the first two paragraphs under the heading "Stalin's Five-Year Plans" on the opposite page, and then complete the sentence below.

Stalin set out to make Russia into

(A) a modern industrial power.

B a capitalist economy.

C a service-based economy.

D the world's leading agricultural nation.

Skills Assessment

ANSWERS 1. Review locations with students. **2.** Finland, Poland, Estonia, Latvia, Lithuania **3.** Russia was the largest of the republics.

A Powerless Constitution In 1936, the Soviet Union adopted a new constitution that contained a bill of rights. Among the rights guaranteed to Soviet citizens were freedom of speech, freedom of assembly, and freedom of religion. As the constitution was being adopted, the Great Purge and its accompanying show trials moved into full swing.

belongings, but all farm animals and implements were to be turned over to the collective. The state set all prices and controlled access to farm supplies.

On collectives, the government planned to provide tractors, fertilizers, and better seed, and to teach peasants modern farm methods. The government needed increased grain output to feed workers in the cities. Surplus grain would also be sold abroad to earn money to invest in industry.

A Ruthless Policy Peasants resisted collectivization by killing farm animals, destroying tools, and burning crops. The government responded with brutal force. An army officer described his horror at the orders he received:

> "I am an Old Bolshevik. . . . I worked in the underground against the czar and I fought in the civil war. Did I do all that in order that I should now surround villages with machine guns and order my men to fire indiscriminately into crowds of peasants? Oh, no, no!"
> —quoted in *Stalin: A Political Biography* (Deutscher)

Stalin sought to destroy the kulaks, or wealthy peasants. The government confiscated kulaks' land and sent them to labor camps. Thousands were killed or died from overwork.

Collectivization took a horrendous toll. Angry peasants often grew just enough to feed themselves. In response, the government seized all the grain, leaving the peasants to starve. This ruthless policy, combined with poor harvests, led to a terrible famine. Between five and eight million people died in Ukraine alone.

Although collectivization increased Stalin's control, it did not improve farm output. During the 1930s, grain production inched upward, but meat, vegetables, and fruits remained in short supply. Feeding the population would remain a major problem in the Soviet Union.

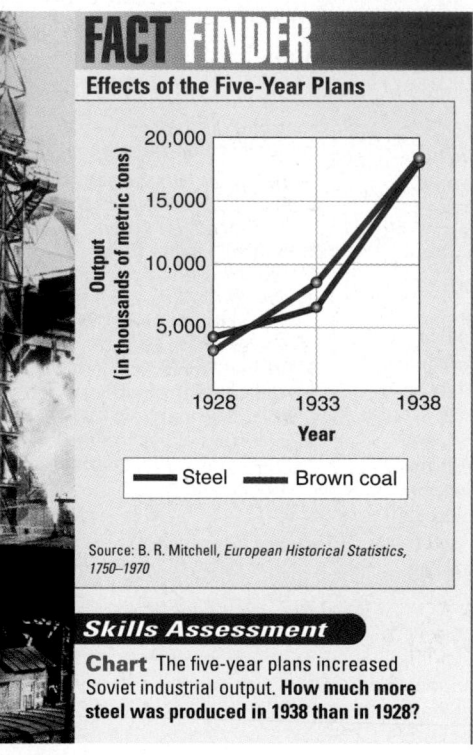

FACT FINDER

Effects of the Five-Year Plans

Output (in thousands of metric tons) vs. Year (1928, 1933, 1938)

— Steel — Brown coal

Source: B. R. Mitchell, *European Historical Statistics, 1750–1970*

Skills Assessment

Chart The five-year plans increased Soviet industrial output. **How much more steel was produced in 1938 than in 1928?**

The Great Purge

Even though Stalin's power was absolute, he harbored obsessive fears that rival party leaders were plotting against him. In 1934, he launched the Great Purge. In this reign of terror, Stalin and his secret police cracked down especially on Old Bolsheviks, or party activists from the early days. His net soon widened to target army heroes, industrial managers, writers, and ordinary citizens. They were charged with a wide range of crimes, from counterrevolutionary plots to failure to meet production quotas.

Between 1936 and 1938, Stalin staged a series of spectacular public "show trials" in Moscow. Former Communist leaders confessed to all kinds of crimes after officials tortured them or threatened their families or friends. Many purged party members were never tried but were sent to forced-labor camps in Siberia and elsewhere. Others were executed. Secret police files reveal that at least four million people were purged during the Stalin years. Some historians estimate the toll to be much greater.

The purges increased Stalin's power. Old revolutionaries were replaced by young party members who owed absolute loyalty to him. All Soviet citizens were now well aware of the consequences of disloyalty.

However, Stalin also paid a price. The victims of the purges included most of the nation's military officers. This loss of military leadership would weigh heavily on Stalin in 1941, when Germany invaded the Soviet Union.

Skills Assessment

ANSWER over three times more

Resource Directory

Teaching Resources

History Through Literature *One Day in the Life of Ivan Denisovich*, History Through Literature booklet, pp. 59–60
Synthesizing Information Chapter Extension Activities booklet, p. 68

Collectivization

Following their successful revolution, the Communists gave land to peasants. But after 1928, the five-year plans required peasants to give up their land and work on large, state-run farms called collectives. Collectivization was a disaster for farmers, leading to widespread famine and millions of deaths.

Stalin's Propaganda

This propaganda photograph shows farmers at the "Lenin's Way" collective in Vilshanka, Ukraine, as they remain in the field for a communal meal during harvest season.

Soviet Agricultural Output, 1928 and 1932

Bar graph showing Output (in millions of metric tons) for Oats, Wheat, and Potatoes in 1928 and 1932.

Legend: ▌ 1928   ▌ 1932

Source: B. R. Mitchell, *European Historical Statistics, 1750–1970*

Resistance to Collectivization

Many peasants resisted collectivization. In addition to slaughtering livestock and burning crops, they sold farm animals to keep them out of the hands of the government. The newspaper *Pravda* explained this practice:

"A mass sale of livestock is carried on by the middle and poor farmers before their entrance to the collective farms. . . . Buyers travel to different stations buying livestock at high prices, snatching them away from government markets, which are now at a standstill. . . . This practice is most evident in regions where there is all-out collectivization.

Before entering collective farming the middle, and even the poor farmers, try to get rid of their livestock, hoarding the money from the sale."

—*Pravda,* January 1930

Stalin hoped that collectivization would increase crop yields. Instead, collectivization contributed to a drop in output that continued until the 1950s.

Skills Assessment

1. What changes occurred in oat production between 1928 and 1932?
   A Production dropped by approximately five million metric tons.
   B Production increased by approximately five million metric tons.
   C It stayed the same.
   D Farmers were not producing oats at this time.

2. Which of the three pieces of evidence above suggests that peasants opposed collectivization?
   E the picture only
   F the primary source only
   G the graph and the picture
   H the picture and the primary source

3. **Critical Thinking Drawing Conclusions** (a) For each piece of evidence write a generalization about collective farming. (b) Use these generalizations to reach an overall conclusion about the social and economic impact of collectivization.

Skills Tip

Bar graphs show numerical information in graphic form for ease of comparison. Pay close attention to the labels that identify the quantities being compared.

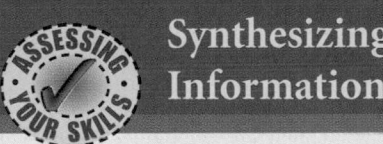

*B*ackground
About the Evidence

Women's Rebellion Women unwilling to give their land, livestock, and grain to the collective rebelled. Thousands of women broke into grain stores and stole the grain for their families. Several women were killed and many were arrested or deported. Still, women continued to rebel. In three villages, women regained their property after they replaced the local authorities. To avoid being attacked by armed forces, women would lead the attack, and then men would rally to the women's defense. In southern Ukraine, one collective farm collapsed as a result of the women's rebellion.

*A*ctivity
Interpreting the Evidence

Use this additional question to generate class discussion.
Critical Thinking: Drawing Conclusions What resulted from forcing people to relinquish private property? Why? (*Collectivization proved to be a disaster. The human spirit was broken. There was widespread famine, and millions of deaths.*)

Skills Tip

When creating a bar graph, use different colors to make comparisons easier to see. The Skills Handbook in the front of the book has a lesson that will help students with this feature.

Human Drama Note

Collectivization Soviet leaders were initially divided on the pace of the transition to collectivization. In December of 1927, the government decided to start collectivization slowly, on a voluntary basis. However, within a year, they were calling for 20 percent collectivization by 1933. By the winter of 1929–1930, Stalin increased the pace by calling for a "liquid[ation of] the kulaks as a class." The peasants violently opposed this policy, and Stalin was forced to back down somewhat, but the result of his action was a huge but temporary drop in enrollment. The party renewed the drive for collectivization, this time more slowly. The result: by 1936, almost all of the peasants were working on collective farms.

Skills Assessment

ANSWERS 1. A **2.** F **3.** (a) Collective farms stressed communal activities; collectivization led to a decrease in farm output; many peasants opposed collectivization. (b) In social terms, collectivization aimed to make peasants form communal units. The government had to force collectivization on many peasants. Economically, collectivization was a failure.

Recall

1. (a) USSR, p. 707 (b) NEP, p. 708
(c) Great Purge, p. 710 (d) Comintern,
p. 712 2. (a) command economy, p. 708
(b) collective, p. 709 (c) kulak, p. 710

Comprehension

3. (a) In 1921, Lenin replaced his policy of "war communism" with the New Economic Policy, which allowed for some capitalist ventures in an effort to boost output. (b) War communism had brought the economy to a near collapse. 4. Goals: building heavy industry, improving transportation, and increasing farm output. Results: impressive progress in heavy industry, the standard of living remained low, consumer goods were scarce and poor in quality, agricultural collectives proved to be a disaster. 5. Stalin launched the Great Purge to terminate anyone he considered a rival or threat. Because of the millions of people he purged, his power was absolute. Because Stalin had assassinated many of the military leaders, Russia was at a disadvantage when it was invaded in 1941 by Germany. 6. The Comintern's loud propaganda against capitalism made western powers highly suspicious of the Soviet Union. The fact that Lenin and Stalin kept secret that their ultimate goal was to bring about worldwide revolution did not sit well with world powers.

Critical Thinking and Writing

7. (a) different—increase in industry, decrease in agriculture (b) The emphasis on industry was successful, while anger against collectivization led to lower agricultural yields. 8. Under Stalin's economy, the government owned all businesses, allocated all resources, and made all economic decisions. In a capitalist economy, businesses are privately owned and operated, and the free market determines most economic decisions.

Activity Rubrics

Share rubrics with students before they design their political cartoons.

Attempted Student fails to finish the cartoon.

Minimal Student completes the cartoon, but its point about the policy is unclear, or it is messy.

Adequate The cartoon makes a clear comment on a policy and is well drawn.

Exemplary The cartoon is exceptionally well drawn and offers a strong comment on a policy.

Soviet Foreign Policy

Between 1917 and 1939, the Soviet Union pursued two very different goals in foreign policy. As Communists, both Lenin and Stalin wanted to bring about the worldwide revolution that Marx had predicted. But as Russians, they wanted to guarantee their nation's security by winning the support of other countries. The result of pursuing these two different goals was a contradictory and generally unsuccessful foreign policy.

Lenin formed the Communist International, or Comintern. It aided revolutionary groups around the world and urged colonial peoples to rise up against imperialist powers. Yet the Soviet Union also sought to join the League of Nations and to improve relations with western governments.

The Comintern's propaganda against capitalism made western powers highly suspicious of the Soviet Union. In the United States, fear of Bolshevik plots led to the "Red Scare" in the early 1920s. Britain broke off relations with the Soviet Union when evidence revealed Soviet schemes to turn a 1926 strike into a revolution. Even so, the Soviet Union slowly won recognition from western powers and increased trade with capitalist countries. It also joined the League of Nations. However, mistrust still poisoned relations, especially after the Great Purge.

Three Revolutions Compared

Historians often compare the Russian, French, and American revolutions. The American Revolution was in many ways the least radical of the three. American leaders did not order mass executions or seize property. French revolutionaries executed thousands and nationalized the lands of the Church and the aristocracy. In Russia, Stalin seized even the lands of the peasant masses. His policies caused millions of deaths.

All three revolutions had a worldwide impact. The Declaration of Independence and the United States Constitution served as models of democratic government. The French Revolution inspired revolts across Europe. As you will see, the Soviet Union supported revolts in many lands and became a model for other communist governments. Yet today, Russia and most of its allies have abandoned the goals of Lenin and Stalin. Democratic nations, meanwhile, continue to build on the principles preached during the American and French revolutions.

Recall

1. **Identify:** (a) USSR, (b) NEP, (c) Great Purge, (d) Comintern.
2. **Define:** (a) command economy, (b) collective, (c) kulak.

Comprehension

3. (a) How did Lenin make a compromise between the ideas of capitalism and communism? (b) Why did he think that the compromise was necessary?
4. What were the goals and results of Stalin's five-year plans?
5. What were the causes and effects of the Great Purge?

6. How did Soviet foreign policy lead to difficult relations with the West?

Critical Thinking and Writing

7. **Analyzing Information** Review the two charts in this section that show the effects of the five-year plans on industry and agriculture. (a) Were the effects on industry and agriculture similar or different? (b) Explain the reasons for the similar or different results.
8. **Comparing** How did the Soviet command economy under Stalin differ from a capitalist economy?

Activity

Drawing a Political Cartoon Draw a political cartoon that comments on one of Lenin's or Stalin's policies. Give your cartoon a title and a caption. Try to use symbolism, such as the hammer and sickle.

Resource Directory

Teaching Resources

Section Quiz Unit 7 booklet, p. 25
Creative Teaching Activities Creative Teaching Activities booklet, p. 128
Guided Reading and Review Unit 7 booklet, p. 26
Primary Source Activity *Growing Up in Stalin's Russia*, p. 29

Technology

Interactive Student Tutorial CD-ROM Ch. 28
Computer Test Bank Ch. 28

SECTION **3** Life in a Totalitarian State

Reading Focus

- How did Stalin create a totalitarian state?
- How did communism change Soviet society?
- How did state control affect the arts in the Soviet Union?

Vocabulary

totalitarian state
atheism
socialist realism

Taking Notes

Create a chart like this one. Fill in the chart as you read. In the left column, list ways in which people benefited from communist rule. In the right column, list ways in which people suffered.

COMMUNIST RULE	
Benefits	Drawbacks

> **Bell Ringer** Ask students to review the meaning of *propaganda*. Then have them study the art in this section. Ask students to describe how art served the needs of the Soviet state. Also have students describe what happened to artists who did not serve the needs of the state.

Main Idea Stalin turned the Soviet Union into a totalitarian state that regulated every aspect of the lives of its citizens.

Setting the Scene From the 1930s until his death in 1953, Stalin tried to boost morale and faith in the communist system by making himself a godlike figure. His propaganda mills described him as a devoted father of the Soviet people. Poets wrote hymns of praise to "Stalin the Wise" and the "Son of Lenin" who was "the unsinking sun of our times." This "cult of personality" was one more pillar to support Stalin's absolute power.

An Age of Totalitarian Control

Marx had predicted that under communism the state would wither away. The opposite occurred under Stalin. He turned the Soviet Union into a totalitarian state. In this form of government, a one-party dictatorship attempts to regulate every aspect of the lives of its citizens. You have already seen, for example, how Stalin imposed central government control over industry and agriculture.

Terror To ensure obedience, Stalin's Communist party used secret police, censorship, violent purges, and terror. Police spies did not hesitate to open private letters or plant listening devices. Nothing appeared in print without official approval. Grumblers or critics were rounded up and sent to brutal labor camps, where many died.

Propaganda Using modern technology, the party bombarded the public with relentless propaganda. Radios and loudspeakers blared into factories and villages. In movies, theaters, and schools, citizens heard about communist successes and the evils of capitalism. Newsreels and newspapers showed bumper harvests and new hydroelectric dams opening up, or proclaimed the misery of workers in the capitalist West. Billboards and posters urged workers to meet or exceed production quotas.

Stalinist propaganda also revived extreme nationalism. Headlines in the Communist party newspaper, *Pravda*, or "Truth," linked enemies at home to foreign agents seeking to restore power to the landowners and capitalists. Supporters of Stalin's aims were often glorified as national heroes. For example, the government put up statues honoring a 14-year-old boy who turned his own father over to the secret police for associating with kulaks.

Forced-Labor Camp
Accused of drawing an anti-Stalin caricature, Russian artist Nikolai Getman was convicted in a seven-minute trial. He spent the next seven years in forced-labor camps, where he painted haunting scenes such as this.

Theme: Art and Literature How does Getman convey the despair of camp life?

LESSON PLAN

1. Focus Under Stalin, the Soviet government used propaganda, censorship, and terror to establish a totalitarian state. Members of the Communist party and other leaders constituted a powerful new elite. The Soviet government forced artists and writers to praise the revolution, socialism, and Stalin.

2. Instruct Have students work in small groups to write a skit dramatizing life in the Soviet Union under Stalin. Assign each group one of the following as the central character of their skit: a member of the secret police, a producer of communist propaganda, a factory worker, a religious leader, a Communist party member, a teacher or student, a writer or artist. Advise students to include no more than three or four characters in their skits. They should first choose the characters that they will portray, and then gather information about the characters' lives. Finally they should write a simple plot and dialogue. Set aside time for each group to present its work.

3. Assess Ask students to comment on which of the skits had the greatest impact on them. Encourage students to explain the reasons for their choices.

4. Reteach If students' **Assess** activity does not reflect adequate understanding of the lesson, you might assign the *Guide to the Essentials* or the *Interactive Student Tutorial CD-ROM* for this section.

📋 Block Scheduling Support

Have students draw or paint a picture that depicts life in the Soviet Union under Stalin. Allow students to decide if they want to be a rebel artist or one who creates propaganda for the state. Pictures should therefore either support or criticize Stalin's regime. Then, have students display their drawings and explain why they chose as they did. Use their explanations as a basis for a discussion of life in a totalitarian state.

Caption Answer

The painting is dark. The men are emaciated from lack of adequate food. The facial expressions show despair.

Graphic Organizer

Ask students to draw a circle on a piece of paper. Have them write within the circle "the Soviet Union as a totalitarian state." Then ask students to read Section 3. As they read, have students add additional circles to form a web, linking main ideas and supporting details to the first circle. *(Less Advanced Readers)*

Activity
Connections to Math

Using Statistics In 1930, the membership of the Communist party in the Soviet Union was estimated to be about 1 million people. The total population of the Soviet Union at the time was about 150 million people. Have students compute the percentage of the Soviet population that made up the new elite of the Soviet Union.

Connections to Today

The Russian Orthodox Church

The Russian Orthodox Church survived more than half a century of Communist persecution. Millions of Russians continued to worship, in private and sometimes in public, in defiance of the government's prohibitions.

Today, the Communist government has fallen, and the Church is enjoying a revival. Its membership has swelled to perhaps as many as 50 million people.

Polls of the Russian people indicate that the Orthodox Church surpasses the government and the military as the most respected institution in the country. One Muscovite put it this way: "The Orthodox Church is perhaps the last, lone symbol of Russian national identity to have survived communism more or less intact. People . . . want and need such a symbol."

Theme: Religions and Value Systems Why is the Russian Orthodox Church experiencing a revival today?

War on Religion In accordance with the ideas of Marx, atheism, or the belief that there is no god, became an official state policy. Early on, the Communists targeted the Russian Orthodox Church, which had strongly supported the czars. The party seized religious property and converted churches into offices and museums. Many priests and other religious leaders were killed or died in prison camps.

Other religions were persecuted as well. At one show trial, 15 Roman Catholic priests were charged with "counterrevolutionary activities," such as teaching religion to the young. The state seized Jewish synagogues and banned the use of Hebrew. Islam was also officially discouraged. However, Muslims living in the Soviet Union generally faced fewer restrictions, partly because the Communists hoped to win support among colonized peoples in the Middle East.

The Communists replaced religion with their own ideology. Like a religion, communist ideology had its own "sacred" texts—the writings of Marx and Lenin—and its own shrines, such as the tomb of Lenin. Portraits of Stalin replaced religious icons in Russian homes.

Changes in Soviet Society

The Communists transformed Russian life. They destroyed the old social order of landowning nobles at the top and serfs at the bottom. But instead of creating a society of equals, as they promised, they created a society where a few elite groups emerged as a new ruling class.

The New Elite At the head of society were members of the Communist party. Only a small fraction of Soviet citizens were allowed to join the party. Many who did so were motivated by a desire to get ahead, rather than a belief in communist ideology.

The Soviet elite also included industrial managers, military leaders, scientists, and some artists and writers. The elite enjoyed benefits denied to most people. They had the best apartments in the cities and vacation homes in the country. They could shop at special stores for scarce consumer goods. Good shoes, noted one western visitor, distinguished the elite from the common citizen.

Social Benefits and Drawbacks Although excluded from party membership, most people did enjoy benefits unknown before the revolution. Free education was offered to all. The state also provided free medical care, day care for children, inexpensive housing, and public recreation.

While these benefits were real, the standard of living remained low. As elsewhere, industrial growth led millions of people to migrate to cities. Although the state built massive apartment complexes, housing was scarce. Entire families might be packed into a single room. Bread was plentiful, but meat, fresh fruit, and other foods were in short supply.

Education After the Russian Revolution, the Communists built schools everywhere and required all children to attend. The state supported technical schools and universities as well. Schools served many important goals. Educated workers were needed to build a modern industrial state. In addition to basic skills, schools taught communist values, such as atheism, the glory of collective farming, and love of Stalin.

The Communist party also set up programs for students outside school. These programs included sports, cultural activities, and political classes to train teenagers for party membership. Sometimes, young Communists would be sent to help harvest crops or to participate in huge parades.

Women Long before 1917, women such as Lenin's wife, Krupskaya, worked for the revolution, spreading radical ideas among peasants and workers. Some urged fellow Socialists to pay attention to women's needs.

Connections to Today

ANSWER Post-communist Russia is turbulent; many changes have come, so it might be comforting to people to have a symbol of stability that has lasted through all the changes.

Virtual Field Trip

www.phschool.com

Virtual Museum of Political Art
Vienna, Austria

To see other examples of socialist realism, use the Internet address above to link to the Virtual Museum of Political Art.

Socialist Realism
Bold, heroic images were the trademark of socialist realism. Here, workers and farmers hold aloft the Soviet hammer and sickle. Bright sunbeams suggest a glorious future just ahead.
Theme: Art and Literature
What values did socialist realism try to communicate?

In 1905, Alexandra Kollontai noted "how little our party concerned itself with the fate of women . . . [and] women's liberation." After the revolution, Kollontai became the only high-ranking woman to serve in Lenin's government. She vigorously campaigned for women's rights.

Under the Communists, women won equality under the law. They gained access to education and a wide range of jobs. By the 1930s, many Soviet women were working in medicine, engineering, or the sciences.

By their labor, women contributed to Soviet economic growth. They worked in factories, in construction, and on collectives. Within the family, their wages were needed because men earned low salaries. The government provided day nurseries for children.

The Arts and the State

The Bolshevik Revolution at first meant greater freedom for Russian artists and writers. "Art must serve politics," Lenin had insisted, but he generally did not interfere with artistic freedom. Artists welcomed the chance to experiment with ideas and forms.

Socialist Realism Under Stalin, however, the heavy hand of state control gripped the arts. Stalin forced artists and writers to conform to a style called socialist realism. Its goal was to boost socialism by showing Soviet life in a positive light. Artists and writers could criticize the bourgeois past or even, to a limited degree, point out mistakes under communism. Their overall message, though, had to promote hope in the communist future. Popular themes for socialist-realist artists were peasants, workers, heroes of the revolution, and—of course—Stalin.

Censorship Government controlled what books were published, what music was heard, and which works of art were displayed. Artists who ignored Communist guidelines could not get materials, work space, or jobs.

Under Stalin's totalitarian policies, writers, artists, and composers faced government persecution. The Jewish poet Osip Mandelstam, for example,

Bell Ringer Have students study the two still images from the film on this page. Ask them what feelings are evoked by these images and discuss how the images may have helped the Soviet cause.

Background
Connections to Today

Montage The movie industry, today dominated by American filmmakers, owes an artistic debt to Russia, where Sergei Eisenstein first developed the technique called *montage*. The first filmmaker to take a collage approach to editing, Eisenstein juxtaposed two separate images to convey a third idea. He likened this technique to Japanese writing, in which two separate characters combine to express a third notion. For example, the character for "dog" is combined with the one for "mouth" to create a character that means "bark."

Activity
Cooperative Learning

Creating a Storyboard Have students create a storyboard for a scene that would be part of a film on life under Stalin. Explain that a storyboard is a plan for a film showing the sequence of images that comprise a scene. Organize students into six groups. Tell them they should first outline their scene and then sketch out the images. Stick figures are okay to use. Display the completed storyboards in the classroom and use them to start a discussion of life under Stalin.

Portfolio Assessment Rubrics

Share rubrics with students before they prepare their class presentation.

Attempted Student does not complete presentation.

Minimal Student completes presentation but provides little information.

Adequate Presentation is well researched, designed, and presented.

Exemplary Presentation is well researched, designed, and presented and offers new insight into the director or film.

A Revolution in Filmmaking

In the Soviet Union, filmmakers used motion pictures to express revolutionary ideals. "Of all the arts, for us the cinema is the most important," said Lenin, who valued film as a propaganda tool. In 1925, director Sergei Eisenstein's *Battleship Potemkin* went far beyond propaganda. His techniques continue to influence filmmakers around the world.

In the film, sailors on the imperial ship *Potemkin* stage a successful mutiny. In the port city of Odessa, a crowd gathers in support of the mutineers and is fired upon by the czar's soldiers. Eisenstein fictitiously places this dramatic scene on a long flight of steps, where a woman stands among the shadows of the czar's soldiers who have killed her child.

In this dynamic sequence, a baby carriage bounces past murdered and wounded civilians. It evokes the helplessness of the unarmed civilians against armed soldiers. Many later directors from all over the world have copied this image.

Portfolio Assessment

 Use the Internet or library resources to find out more about the "golden era of Soviet film," which took place between 1925 and 1930. Then, prepare a class presentation on an important Soviet director or film from this era. Include photographs, drawings, diagrams, or videos that illustrate important aspects of the chosen director or film.

Eisenstein (right) won acclaim for his use of montage, a technique of cutting back and forth between clashing images. *Battleship Potemkin* was the last film over which Eisenstein had full control. After Stalin came to power, censorship was the rule. Eisenstein's last film was banned for criticizing the new leader. It was not shown in the Soviet Union until after Stalin's death.

Resource Directory

Teaching Resources

Section Quiz Unit 7 booklet, p. 27
Humanities Link Chapter Extension Activities booklet, p. 69
Geography Quiz Unit 7 booklet, p. 32
Chapter Test Forms A, B, and C Unit 7 booklet, pp. 33–37
Answer Key Unit 7 booklet, pp. 96–109

Technology

Listening to Literature World Masterpieces audiotapes two poems by Anna Akhmatova, side 8, running time 1:58 min.; two poems by Boris Pasternak, side 8, running time 1:56 min.
Interactive Student Tutorial CD-ROM Ch. 28
Computer Test Bank Ch. 28

was imprisoned, tortured, and exiled for composing a satirical verse that was critical of Stalin. Out of fear for his wife's safety, Mandelstam finally submitted to threats and wrote an "Ode to Stalin." Boris Pasternak, who would later win fame for his novel *Doctor Zhivago*, was afraid to publish anything at all during the Stalin years. Rather than write in the favored style of socialist realism, he became a translator of literary works.

Anna Akhmatova (ahk MAH taw vuh), one of Russia's greatest poets, could not publish her works because she had violated state guidelines. Still, she wrote secretly. In "Requiem," she described the ordeal of trying to visit her 20-year-old son, imprisoned during the Stalinist terrors:

> "For seventeen long months my pleas,
> My cries have called you home.
> I've begged the hangman on my knees,
> My son, my dread, my own.
> My mind's mixed up for good,
> And I'm no longer even clear
> Who's man, who's beast, nor how much time
> Before the end draws near."
> —Anna Akhmatova, "Requiem"

Despite restrictions, some Soviet writers produced magnificent works. *And Quiet Flows the Don,* by Mikhail Sholokhov, passed the censor. The novel tells the story of a man who spends years fighting in World War I, the Russian Revolution, and the civil war. Sholokhov later became one of the few Soviet writers to win the Nobel Prize for literature.

Looking Ahead

By the time Stalin died in 1953, the Soviet Union had become a military superpower and a world leader in heavy industry. Yet Stalin's efforts exacted a brutal toll. The Soviet people were dominated by a totalitarian system based on terror. Most people in the Soviet Union lived meager lives compared with people in the West.

The Soviet Union was not the only totalitarian state to emerge in the decades after World War I. As you will read, in the 1920s and 1930s, dictators arose in Italy and Germany. They, too, created one-party states and cults of personality to impose dictatorial rule on their people.

SECTION 3 Assessment

Recall
1. **Identify:** (a) *Pravda,*
   (b) Alexandra Kollontai,
   (c) Osip Mandelstam,
   (d) Anna Akhmatova,
   (e) Mikhail Sholokhov.
2. **Define:** (a) totalitarian state,
   (b) atheism, (c) socialist realism.

Comprehension
3. What methods did Stalin use to create a totalitarian state?
4. (a) Who made up the new elite in Soviet society? (b) What special privileges did they enjoy?
5. How did the Soviet government make sure that most writers and artists conformed to the style of socialist realism?

Critical Thinking and Writing
6. **Comparing** Compare life under Stalin's rule with life under the Russian czars. (a) Describe two similarities. (b) Describe two differences.
7. **Analyzing Information** One historian has said that socialist realism was "communism with a smiling face." What do you think he meant? (See the Virtual Field Trip in this section.)

Recall
1. (a) *Pravda,* p. 713 (b) Alexandra Kollontai, p. 715 (c) Osip Mandelstam, p. 715 (d) Anna Akhmatova, p. 717 (e) Mikhail Sholokhov, p. 717 2. (a) totalitarian state, p. 713 (b) atheism, p. 714 (c) socialist realism, p. 715

Comprehension
3. terror, propaganda, secret police, censorship, and violent purges
4. (a) the Communist party, industrial managers, military leaders, scientist, and some artists and writers (b) They enjoyed the best apartments in the city and vacation homes in the country. They could shop at special stores for scarce consumer goods, such as good shoes.
5. Artists who ignored Communist guidelines could not get materials, work space, or jobs. They also faced persecution, imprisonment, torture, and exile.

Critical Thinking and Writing
6. (a) Under both the standard of living remained low. Both used secret police. (b) Communists were atheists; under the czars, Russians worshiped in the Russian Orthodox Church. The Communist government provided people with free education, free medical care, inexpensive housing, and other social services; in czarist Russia, the land was owned by nobles and most of the people were peasants.
7. The Soviet arts policy dictated that artists could only show Soviet life in a positive light. Their message had to be a happy one, promoting hope in the socialist future.

Human Drama Note

Boris Pasternak For years, Boris Pasternak straddled the line between acceptance and censorship in Stalin's Russia. His early works, although described as avant-garde in comparison to his Russian contemporaries, were well received. His middle period pieces, 1933–1943, deviated too far from the government sanctioned art to be published. Yet he continued to write. Some believe that the only thing that saved Pasternak from Stalin's purges was his translations of works by poets who came from Stalin's native region. Finally, with the completion of *Doctor Zhivago* came his total censorship: Pasternak was ejected from the Union of Soviet Writers and forced to decline a Nobel Prize for Literature.

Creating a Chapter Summary

As a reteaching opportunity, pair a more able student with a less able student to complete this chapter summary.

Political one party; dictatorship with absolute power; cult of the dictator **Economic** collectivization of agriculture; no private ownership of property; central control of industry; state sets prices and provides needs of production **Social** attempt to regulate every aspect of life; propaganda as tool of social control, feeds extreme nationalism; atheism becomes official party policy; new central role for women; elite ruling class of party members **Cultural** art serves government goals; conformity of style (social realism); censorship **Military** secret police silences dissent with torture, exile, death; army used to enforce will of state

Building Vocabulary

1–8. Puzzles should contain a definition for each vocabulary word that demonstrates a clear understanding of each term.

Recalling Key Facts

9. Millions of Russian soldiers died; the czar, away at the front, neglected domestic affairs; popular discontent grew over battlefield defeats; and domestic shortages grew.
10. in November 1917, through an armed overthrow of the provisional government
11. By 1921, the Communists had triumphed.
12. Lenin's NEP allowed some capitalist ventures.
13. Stalin placed emphasis on high production of heavy industry and transportation. He brought agriculture under government control and set up collectives, large farms owned and operated by peasants as a group.
14. the arrest and execution of hundreds of thousands of people Stalin suspected of disloyalty
15. He used modern technology and education to bombard the public with messages that praised communism and the Soviet state while denouncing capitalism.
16. Communism became the religion.
17. to promote socialism by portraying Soviet life in a positive way

Critical Thinking and Writing

18. make social reforms and end Russian involvement in the war with Germany

---

Creating a Chapter Summary

Copy the chart below on a sheet of paper. Review what you have learned about communist dictatorship in the Soviet Union by completing the chart. A few entries have been made to help you get started.

COMMUNIST DICTATORSHIP IN THE SOVIET UNION

POLITICAL	ECONOMIC	SOCIAL	CULTURAL	MILITARY
• One party only	• Government makes all decisions			

For additional review and enrichment activities, see the interactive version of *World History* available on the Web and on CD-ROM.

Web Site Self-Test
For practice test questions for Chapter 28, see **www.phschool.com**.

Building Vocabulary

Use the chapter vocabulary words below to create a crossword puzzle. Exchange puzzles with a classmate. Complete the puzzles and then check each other's answers.

1. **proletariat**
2. **soviet**
3. **commissar**
4. **collective**
5. **kulak**
6. **totalitarian state**
7. **atheism**
8. **socialist realism**

Recalling Key Facts

9. How did World War I contribute to the collapse of the Russian monarchy?
10. How and when did the Bolsheviks take power in Russia?
11. What was the final outcome of the Russian civil war?
12. How was the NEP different from "pure communism"?
13. Describe Stalin's policies on agriculture and industry.
14. What was the Great Purge?
15. How did Stalin make use of propaganda?
16. What was the Soviet government's policy toward religion?
17. According to Stalin, what purpose should art serve?

Critical Thinking and Writing

18. **Identifying Alternatives** After the March Revolution, the provisional government of Russia chose a course that led to another revolution. What policies could the provisional government have followed that might have avoided a second revolution?
19. **Comparing** How were the Russian and French revolutions similar or different in terms of **(a)** long-term causes, **(b)** immediate causes, **(c)** effects, **(d)** world reaction?
20. **Synthesizing Information** **(a)** In what ways did Soviet communism conform to the teachings of Marx? **(b)** In what ways did Soviet communism differ from Marxist philosophy?
21. **Linking Past and Present** In the 1990s, the breakup of the Soviet Union led to a revival of religion. Why do you think the Soviets were unsuccessful in their attempt to destroy religion?
22. **Connecting to Geography** Review the map in Section 2. **(a)** How did the Soviet constitution try to satisfy the nationalist aspirations of non-Russians? **(b)** Do you think nationalist leaders in the Soviet Union were satisfied? Explain.

---

19. **(a)** Both countries had a long history of oppressive government. **(b)** Both revolutions were brought about by the costs of war, a failed economy, and food shortages. **(c)** Both revolutions experienced a moderate stage dominated by the bourgeoisie and a radical stage dominated by ideologues and the poorer classes. **(d)** In both cases, some foreign observers praised the revolution. But some foreign governments, fearing the spread of radicalism, sent military forces into the revolutionary country.

20. **(a)** Marx would have approved of the abolition of private property and businesses. **(b)** He would have disapproved of the rise of the Communist party as an elite group.
21. Religious faith, rooted in strong historical and cultural foundations, often survives repression.
22. **(a)** It was supposed to give each member of the republic equal rights, making no one republic more powerful than another. **(b)** No. Russia had to use the army to dominate the other republics.

Skills Assessment
Analyzing Primary Sources

The exerpt below, written by an American news reporter in Russia, is a dramatic eyewitness account of Stalin's brutal campaign against the kulaks. Read the excerpt and then answer the questions that follow.

"Obliteration of the . . . kulak elements was not only an end in itself, but a means for stampeding the rest of the population into submission to collectivization. . . . A population as large as all of Switzerland's or Denmark's was stripped clean of all their belongings—not alone their land and homes and cattle and tools, but often their last clothes and food and household utensils—and driven out of their villages. They were herded with bayonets at railroad stations, packed indiscriminately into cattle cars and freight cars, and dumped weeks later in the lumber regions of the frozen North, the deserts of Central Asia, wherever labor was needed, there to live or die. Some of this human wreckage was merely flung beyond the limits of their former villages, without shelter or food in those winter months, to start life anew if they could, on land too barren to have been cultivated in the past."

—Eugene Lyons, *Assignment in Utopia*

23. Who were the kulaks?
24. According to the reporter, what were the reasons for the policy toward the kulaks?
25. What do you think the government did with the confiscated property?
26. Do you think the kulaks prospered in the lands to which they were brought? Explain.
27. **(a)** What part of this account is most probably opinion? Explain. **(b)** What part is most probably fact? Explain.

Skills Assessment

Take It to the NET

Use the Internet to find examples of propaganda such as the Soviet poster on this page. You can look for posters, speeches, film clips, or other types. Print out two examples. For each example, identify the author and the intended audience, and explain the message that is being communicated.

Skills Assessment
Analyzing Propaganda

ЗНАНИЕ
РАЗОРВЕТ ЦЕПИ РАБСТВА.

Under the czars, few Russian peasants could read. The Soviet government launched a campaign to increase adult literacy. This Soviet propaganda poster proclaims, "Knowledge Will Break the Chains of Serfdom." Study the poster and answer the following questions:

28. **(a)** What symbol in the poster represents serfdom? **(b)** What symbols represent education?
29. Why do you think the Soviet government wanted people to learn to read?
30. Based on what you have read in this chapter, do you agree or disagree that education broke the "chains of serfdom" for the Russian people? Explain.

Skills Tip

To understand propaganda, try to recognize who the author is and who the intended audience is. Remember that propaganda uses lies, truths, or half-truths to sway opinion.

Analyzing Primary Sources

23. wealthy peasants
24. to cause the rest of the society to submit to collectivization
25. The property was turned into collectives.
26. No, most collectives were miserable failures.
27. **(a)** The first statement is probably an opinion. The reporter probably had no knowledge of the government's motives. **(b)** The statements about what happened to the kulaks are probably facts. He probably observed some of it and interviewed victims.

Analyzing Propaganda

28. **(a)** the chains **(b)** a stack of books, a quill pen, and a student's hand
29. The Soviet Union needed literate citizens to help build an economy based on modern technology.
30. Although free education enabled men and women to enter professions in science and industry, the people were still enslaved to the Soviet system. Peasants toiled in collectives as serfs of the Soviets or starved from lack of food.

Skills Tip

Propaganda may use exaggeration to make its point. Heroes are idealized, and enemies are demonized. The Skills Handbook in the front of the book has a lesson to help students with this feature.

Unit Theme Activity

Remind students to continue working on their Unit Theme Portfolio Activity. See rubrics for the activity on the unit opener page in the Teacher's Edition.

Take It to the NET

Direct students to **www.phschool.com** for links to sites that will help them get started on their assignments. Share rubrics with students.
Attempted Only one example is included or the explanations are missing.
Minimal The assignment is complete but does not adequately explain the message that is being communicated.
Adequate The assignment clearly explains the message that is being communicated.
Exemplary The assignment clearly and thoroughly explains the message that is being communicated; the assignment is creative and well written.

Chapter 29 Planning Guide

Resource Manager

Chapter Level Resources	CORE INSTRUCTION	READING/SKILLS
Chapter Level Resources	**Teaching Resources** 📖 Pacing Charts, Ch. 29 📖 Teaching With Themes, p. 32 📽 Color Transparencies, p. F–59 💿 Resource Pro® Ch. 29 **www.phschool.com** • eTeach	💿 Book on CD, Ch. 29 💿 Interactive Student Tutorial CD-ROM, Ch. 29 💿 Social Studies Skills Tutor CD-ROM 📽 Skills Transparencies
1 Struggle for Change in Latin America 1. Analyze causes of Mexican Revolution. 2. Cite reforms introduced in Mexico. 3. Explain how nationalism affected Mexico. 4. Describe the Good Neighbor Policy.	**Teaching Resources** 📖 Creative Teaching Activities, p. 129 💿 Prentice Hall Presentation Pro, Ch. 29, Section 1 📽 Section Reading Support Transparencies	**Teaching Resources** 📘 Unit 7 booklet • Guided Reading and Review, p. 38 📖 Guide to the Essentials 📼 Guided Reading Audiotapes, Ch. 29, Section 1

2 Nationalist Movements in Africa and the Middle East
1. Outline the ways Africans resisted colonial rule.
2. Describe signs of nationalism that developed in Africa.
3. Illustrate how Turkey and Iran modernized.
4. Explain how European mandates contributed to the growth of Arab nationalism.
	Teaching Resources
	📘 Unit 7 booklet
	  • Biography Activity, p. 48
	  • Viewpoint Activity, p. 50
	📖 Creative Teaching Activities, p. 130
	💿 Prentice Hall Presentation Pro, Ch. 29, Section 2
		Teaching Resources
		📘 Unit 7 booklet
		  • Guided Reading and Review, p. 40
		  • Skill Application Activity, p. 51
		📖 Guide to the Essentials
		📼 Guided Reading Audiotapes, Ch. 29, Section 2

3 India Seeks Self-Rule 1. Trace factors that sparked India's independence movement after World War I. 2. Assess how Mohandas Gandhi influenced the independence movement. 3. Interpret what the Salt March symbolized.	**Teaching Resources** 📖 Creative Teaching Activities, p. 131 💿 Prentice Hall Presentation Pro, Ch. 29, Section 3 📽 Section Reading Support Transparencies	**Teaching Resources** 📘 Unit 7 booklet • Guided Reading and Review, p. 42 📖 Guide to the Essentials 📼 Guided Reading Audiotapes, Ch. 29, Section 3

4 Upheavals in China
1. Point out key challenges to the Chinese Republic.
2. Identify leaders of the "new" China.
3. Determine how invasion by Japan affected China.
	Teaching Resources
	📘 Unit 7 booklet
	  • Primary Source Activity, p. 49
	📖 Creative Teaching Activities, p. 132
	💿 Prentice Hall Presentation Pro, Ch. 29, Section 4
		Teaching Resources
		📘 Unit 7 booklet
		  • Guided Reading and Review, p. 44
		📖 Guide to the Essentials
		📼 Guided Reading Audiotapes, Ch. 29, Section 4

5 Empire of the Rising Sun 1. Trace how liberal changes affected Japan in the 1920s. 2. Describe how nationalists reacted to Japan's problems during the Great Depression. 3. Summarize militarists' use of power.	**Teaching Resources** 📖 Creative Teaching Activities, p. 133 💿 Prentice Hall Presentation Pro, Ch. 29, Section 5 📽 Section Reading Support Transparencies	**Teaching Resources** 📘 Unit 7 booklet • Guided Reading and Review, p. 46 📖 Guide to the Essentials 📼 Guided Reading Audiotapes, Ch. 29, Section 5

ENRICHMENT/PRE-AP

www.phschool.com
- Why Study History?

Teaching Resources
- **Chapter Extension Activities,** p. 70
- **History Through Literature,** pp. 61–62

www.phschool.com
- Internet Activities, Section 1

- **Color Transparencies,** p. D–91
- **Listening to Literature World Masterpieces,** musical tribute to Africa as the cultural homeland of African Americans, side 9

www.phschool.com
- Virtual Field Trip
- Internet Activities, Section 3

- **Visions, Voices, Views,** Animated Map Story, tape 7

Teaching Resources
- **Chapter Extension Activities,** p. 71

www.phschool.com
- Internet Activities, The Tokyo Earthquake of 1922

ASSESSMENT

PRENTICE HALL
ASSESSMENT SYSTEM

Core Assessment
- ExamView Test Bank booklet, Ch. 29
- ExamView Test Bank CD-ROM, Ch. 29

Standardized Test Preparation

Diagnose and Prescribe
- Diagnostic Tests for High School Social Studies Skills

Review and Reteach
- Review Book for World History

Practice and Assess
- Test-Taking Strategies With Transparencies for High School
- Alternative Assessment booklet
- Test Prep Book for World History

Teaching Resources
- **Unit 7 booklet**
  - Geography Quiz, p. 52
  - Section Quizzes, pp. 39, 41, 43, 45, 47
  - Chapter Tests A, B, and C, pp. 53–57
- **www.phschool.com**
  - Self-Test

CUSTOMIZE FOR INDIVIDUAL NEEDS

Gifted and Talented
- **Teacher's Edition,** Activities: Connections to Literature, p. 727

Less Proficient Readers
- **Guide to the Essentials,** Ch. 29
- **Guided Reading Audiotapes, English,** Ch. 29
- **Book on CD,** Ch. 29
- **Teacher's Edition,** Activities: Customize for Visual Learners, p. 736

Less Proficient Writers
- **Teacher's Edition,** Activities: Customize for Visual Learners, p. 728; Customize for Heterogeneous Groups, p. 729; Connections to Math, p. 739

Students Acquiring English/ESL
- **Guide to the Essentials, English/Spanish,** Ch. 29
- **Guided Reading Audiotapes, English/Spanish,** Ch. 29
- **Book on CD,** Ch. 29
- **Teacher's Edition,** Activities marked with an *

iTEXT

Don't miss the exclusive interactive version of *World History: Connections to Today* on the Internet and CD-ROM.

INTRODUCTION

In the period between World War I and World War II, leaders around the world sought freedom from oppression and economic and political self-determination. Social and economic reforms were achieved in Mexico after years of civil war. Africans, Arabs, and Indians fought for an end to foreign domination of their lands. The Chinese endured civil war between communists and nationalists, while the Japanese set out on a path of militarism and expansion.

Focusing on Themes

Suggest that students focus on these theme questions as they read:

Political and Social Systems
How did nationalism and a desire for modernization affect countries around the world?

Impact of the Individual
How did nationalist leaders bring people together to change their countries?

Economics and Technology
How did the Great Depression affect world economies?

Global Interaction
What forces did anti-imperialism movements awaken?

◆ TIME LINE ACTIVITY

You may wish to share the About the Pictures note with your students before you ask these questions about the time line:

1. Which event probably brought a direct reaction by the United States? *(Villa invades New Mexico)*
2. Which events on the time line take place in the Western Hemisphere? *(Villa invades United States; New York Stock Exchange crashes)*
3. How many years after the Japanese captured Nanjing did the Germans invade Poland? *(two)*

Don't Miss!

Analyzing Primary Sources
Remembering the Revolution
(Section 1)

Disaster!
The Tokyo Earthquake of 1923
(Section 5)

Nationalism and Revolution Around the World

1910–1939

Chapter Preview

1 Struggle for Change in Latin America
2 Nationalist Movements in Africa and the Middle East
3 India Seeks Self-Rule
4 Upheavals in China
5 Empire of the Rising Sun

1914
New settlement increases the Jewish population of Palestine to 90,000. Leaders promote long-term development of the region's agriculture, as shown in this 1925 poster.

1916
Pancho Villa, shown here, invades the United States during the Mexican Revolution. He kills more than a dozen Americans in New Mexico.

1923
Atatürk begins modernizing Turkey.

CHAPTER EVENTS

1910   1916   1922

GLOBAL EVENTS

1914 World War I begins.

1917 Two revolutions lead to Bolshevik control of Russia.

Resource Directory

Teaching Resources
Chapter Theme Activities Teaching With Themes booklet, p. 32
Pacing Chart With Block Scheduling Guide Ch. 29
Technology
World History Color Transparencies Ch. 29 Graphic Organizer, p. F–59

Major Nationalist Movements, 1910–1939

The end of World War I motivated many people around the world to seek self-government.

ATLANTIC OCEAN

PACIFIC OCEAN

PACIFIC OCEAN

INDIAN OCEAN

MEXICO

TURKEY

IRAN

CHINA

JAPAN

EGYPT

INDIA

NIGERIA

KENYA

SOUTH AFRICA

Robinson Projection

0 1500 3000 Miles
0 1500 3000 Kilometers

1930
Thousands of Indians join Mohandas Gandhi in the Salt March to protest British rule.

1934
Mao Zedong leads the Long March.

1937
The Japanese army captures Nanjing. Here, Japanese soldiers enter the Chinese city, which has been under siege for weeks.

1928 — 1934 — 1940

1929 The New York Stock Exchange crashes.

1935 Italy invades Ethiopia.

1939 Germany invades Poland.

Independent Assignments

Have students read one section as they prepare for class. After class, have them complete the assignment. Some students may benefit from using the Guided Reading and Review worksheets.

Section 1 Have students use the worksheet *The Underdogs* in the History Through Literature booklet, pp. 61–62, to learn about the Mexican Revolution.
Section 2 Have students use the worksheet *T. E. Lawrence* in the Unit 7 booklet, p. 48, to learn about this famous soldier's efforts for Arab independence.
Section 3 Have students read *Mohandas Gandhi: Hind Swaraj* in the reference section at the back of the book to learn about the ideas behind nonviolent resistance.

Section 4 Have students use the worksheet *The Long March Across China* in the Unit 7 booklet, p. 49, to learn about this epic journey.
Section 5 Have students use the worksheet *Disaster!* in the Chapter Extension Activities booklet, p. 70, to learn more about earthquake damage.

Major Nationalist Movements, 1910–1939

Activating Prior Knowledge
The new imperialism of the 1800s produced European control of many lands on which two continents? *(Asia and Africa)*

Previewing
Mexico had already won independence from Spain. Why might Mexicans be involved in another revolution? Think about the revolutions in France and Russia before you answer. *(possible answers: to overthrow an autocratic ruler or government, to achieve economic and social reform)*

Background
About the Pictures

1 2 3

1. After the First Zionist Congress of 1897, thousands of Jews began returning to their historical homeland. The majority were Europeans fleeing discrimination or *pogroms*. Most of them joined collective farms called *kibbutzim* or *moshavim*.

2. Born in the late 1870s as Doroteo Arango, the young Villa led a checkered career that included cattle rustling and bank robbery. After he joined the revolution he became a sort of Mexican Robin Hood. His ability to escape government forces was legendary, but he had trouble dealing with his fellow revolutionaries, and broke relations with a succession of leaders. He was assassinated in 1923.

3. The atrocities that took place in Nanjing form a dark and shameful chapter in Japanese history that some have compared to the Holocaust.

eTeach

Be sure to check out this month's online discussion with a World History Master Teacher.

Go to **www.phschool.com**.

Bell Ringer Before assigning the section, display examples of the works of the Mexican muralists Diego Rivera, José Clemente Orozco, and David Alfaro Siqueiros. Invite students to comment on these murals and explain that they will learn more about them in this section.

LESSON PLAN

1. Focus Desires for land, better wages, and democratic reforms led to the Mexican Revolution. The revolution resulted in a new constitution that set goals for future social and political changes. In many areas of Latin America, economic and cultural nationalism encouraged people to oppose foreign influence and power.

2. Instruct Ask students to imagine that they are United States diplomats touring Mexico and other Latin American nations during the early 1900s. Their assignment is to file reports on political, economic, and cultural developments in the region. Their reports should describe the causes and effects of the Mexican Revolution, assess the impact of Mexican reforms during the 1920s, and analyze the rising tide of nationalism in Latin America. Finally, their reports should recommend policies that the United States can use to maintain friendly and profitable relations with Latin American countries. Encourage students to use library resources along with their texts. Invite volunteers to share their reports and encourage other students to offer critical comments.

3. Assess In a class discussion, ask students to comment on whether or not they think the Good Neighbor Policy was a wise response to the changes taking place in Latin America. Encourage students to explain the reasons for their opinions.

4. Reteach If students' Assess activity does not reflect adequate understanding of the lesson, you might assign the *Guide to the Essentials* or the *Interactive Student Tutorial CD-ROM* for this section.

Reading Focus

- What were the causes of the Mexican Revolution?
- What reforms were introduced in Mexico?
- How did nationalism affect Mexico?
- What was the Good Neighbor Policy?

Vocabulary

nationalization
economic
   nationalism
cultural
   nationalism

Taking Notes

Copy this diagram. As you read, fill in the major events in Mexican history. To help you get started, one part of the diagram has been completed.

STRUGGLE FOR CHANGE IN MEXICO			
1910s	1920s	1930s	1940s
• Dictator Porfirio Díaz rules • Prosperity for wealthy landowners	•	•	•

Main Idea The desire for lands, better wages, and democratic reforms led to the Mexican Revolution.

Setting the Scene The winds of revolution swept through Mexico between 1910 and 1920. "It is like a hurricane," says a peasant fighter in Mariano Azuela's novel *The Underdogs*. "If you're in it, . . . you're a leaf . . . blown by the wind."

The Mexican Revolution unleashed radical forces. As the revolution spread, Indian peasants battled to end centuries of oppression and to win land. A century after Miguel Hidalgo raised the "cry of Dolores," the Mexican Revolution finally opened the door to social and economic reform.

The Mexican Revolution

By 1910, the dictator Porfirio Díaz had ruled Mexico for almost 35 years, winning reelection as president again and again. On the surface, Mexico enjoyed peace and economic growth. Díaz welcomed foreign investors who developed mines, built railroads, and drilled for oil.

Sources of Discontent Prosperity benefited wealthy landowners, business people, and foreign investors. But most Mexicans were peasants who lived in desperate poverty. Without land or education, they had no hope of improving their situation.

Discontent rippled through Mexico in the early 1900s. Factory workers and miners earning meager wages were restless and angry. And middle-class liberals, who embraced democracy, opposed the Díaz dictatorship.

The Battle Begins The unrest boiled over when Francisco Madero, a liberal reformer, demanded free elections in 1910. After being imprisoned by Díaz, he began to encourage revolt. Faced with rebellion in several parts of the country, Díaz resigned in 1911. "Madero has unleashed a tiger, now let us see if he can control it," declared the dictator as he left Mexico. Díaz's taunt proved well founded. Madero became president of Mexico, but within two years he was murdered.

A Complex Upheaval During the power struggle that followed, several leaders emerged. Among them was Francisco "Pancho" Villa, a hard-riding rebel from the north. He fought mostly for personal power but won the loyalty of his followers. In southern Mexico, Emiliano Zapata led a peasant revolt. Zapata, himself an Indian tenant farmer, understood the misery of peasant villagers. His followers were called Zapatistas.

Fighting flared across Mexico for a decade, killing as many as a million people. Peasants, small farmers, ranchers, and urban workers were drawn

---

Resource Directory

Teaching Resources

Creative Teaching Activities Creative Teaching Activities booklet, p. 129
Guided Reading and Review Unit 7 booklet, p. 38
History Through Literature *The Underdogs,* History Through Literature booklet, pp. 61–62
Analyzing Primary Sources Chapter Extension Activities booklet, p. 70

Technology

Listening to Literature World Masterpieces audiotapes two poems by Gabriela Mistral, side 9, running time 4:56 min.

Remembering the Revolution

Zeferino Diego Ferreira was a peasant soldier in Pancho Villa's army. His experiences represent those of the Mexican masses who rallied to the revolutionary cause. Decades later, he shared his memories with an interviewer, who recorded the old man's tales of life as a revolutionary.

Poster of Emiliano Zapata
Zeferino Ferreira displayed a poster like this one on his living room wall. Asked years later what Zapata looked like, he snapped: "It's not important what he looked like. What is important was his politics."

"I was born in 1892. . . . We lived in a little room with no furniture . . . nothing. We slept on the floor. The only thing we had was a box with my mother's clothes in it. . . .

When I was about fourteen years old I got a job in some mines owned by an American company near Tlalpujahua. . . . At that time here in Mexico they didn't pay more than eighteen to twenty-five centavos. . . .

It was there in Tlalpujahua where I first saw firearms. . . . [A] friend of mine talked to me a lot about Villa and finally convinced me to go and join up. . . . My friend and I went north looking for Villa. And, yes, Villa was firing a shot here and there! . . .

In those days at the beginning of the revolution we didn't have many people and we weren't very well armed. You could say we were almost fighting without rifles. . . .

During the revolution I slept for only two hours at night, between two and four o'clock in the morning, and was always leaning against a wall or a rock or on my rifle. Sometimes we didn't have any hope of getting food, so we'd eat a mule, a skunk.

Yes! That was how we went through the revolution. . . .

[Villa] used to tell us: 'We are fighting for the people and we have to respect them.' . . . Villa wasn't like some people say. He was a well-liked person. Yes, he had people shot, but he'd also get his fill and stop the shootings. He was always in the battles. Sometimes he disguised himself but we would recognize him by his horse. Black. Villa never hid away all cozy and warm while his troops fought. He was right there in the middle. He said: 'Where my troops die, I'll die there, too.'

I am glad to have fought in the same cause with Zapata . . . and so many of my dear revolutionary friends who were left behind in the hills, their bones eaten by animals. I wasn't afraid. Just the opposite, I was glad. It's a beautiful thing to fight to realize an ideal."

—Zeferino Diego Ferreira, "The Life Story of a Villista"

Skills Assessment

1. Which term best describes Villa's peasant army?
   A well equipped
   B professional
   C poor
   D unmotivated

2. According to Ferreira, Villa was
   E a traitor to the peasant cause.
   F brave and decent.
   G seeking money and fame.
   H selfish and cruel.

3. **Critical Thinking Evaluating Information** (a) Ferreira spoke of events that had taken place more than 50 years earlier. How reliable do you think he is as a source of information about the Mexican Revolution? (b) How might a historian determine the truth of Ferreira's words?

Skills Tip
When reading oral history, try to imagine the person talking. This will make the reading "come to life" and help you get the most out of it.

Background
About the Primary Source

Zeferino Diego Ferreira Ferreira was 18 years old when he joined Villa's forces in 1910. He was badly wounded in 1916, and, unable to fight, went to the United States to look for work. He stayed there after the revolution ended, but, like many other Mexicans, he was deported during the Depression. Ferreira remained loyal to Villa into old age. In his words, "All the leaders of the revolution ended up being discredited except for Villa and Zapata. They remained spotless. Clean. Obregon, . . . Huerta, Madero, Orozco, Carranza . . . all of them betrayed the revolution. Madero's plan didn't have anything in it about agrarian reform. And Carranza. . . . was in the revolution out of pure self-interest. . . ."

Activity
Interpreting the Primary Source

Use this additional question to generate class discussion.
Critical Thinking: Asking Questions If you could talk to Ferreira, what would you ask him about the revolution? (*Students' questions will vary.*)

Skills Tip

In evaluating an oral history, look for statements that might be exaggerations, such as "I only slept for two hours a night" or "I wasn't afraid." The Skills Handbook in the front of the book has a lesson that will help students with this feature.

Skills Assessment

ANSWERS 1. C **2.** F **3.** Possible answers: **(a)** Students should be careful before accepting Ferreira's story at face value. Even though he was present at the events 50 years ago, over time he may have altered the facts without realizing it. **(b)** A historian would compare Ferreira's recollections with other oral histories and documents from the period.

Block Scheduling Support

Some of the conditions that led to the Mexican Revolution are still present in Mexico today, particularly the gap between rich and poor. In January 1994, peasant guerrillas again rose up against the government in the southern state of Chiapas. The revolt lasted only a couple of months, but it succeeded in gaining reforms benefiting the poor and the Indian population. Have students use library or Internet resources to find out about the goals and achievements of the guerrillas. How were they similar to the goals of the earlier revolutionaries?

Revolutionary Art Soon after the revolution, the new Mexican government commissioned artists such as José Orozco, David Siqueiros, and Diego Rivera to create public murals honoring Mexico's national heritage. These three artists had earlier issued a "manifesto" proclaiming that the future art of the Western Hemisphere would be true Indian art.

Diego Rivera's murals combined Mexican folk art with techniques used by fresco painters of the Renaissance. Following a 1927–1928 trip to Russia, Rivera began to place greater emphasis on Marxist themes. In his *History of Mexico,* which appears on this page, the struggle between social classes is portrayed on the lower part of the wall where Spanish conquistadors and native Indians clash. The underlying theme of the mural is the exploitation of the native people.

In the 1930s, Rivera's fame earned him invitations to work in the United States. He painted murals for the San Francisco Stock Exchange, the Detroit Institute of Arts, and Rockefeller Center in New York City. But at Rockefeller Center, Rivera's sponsors destroyed his mural because he had included in it a portrait of Lenin.

into the violent struggle. Women soldiers called *soldaderas* cooked, tended the wounded, and even fought alongside the men.

Reforms in Mexico

In 1917, voters elected Venustiano Carranza, a conservative, president of Mexico. That year, Carranza reluctantly approved a new constitution. With amendments, it is still in force today.

The Constitution of 1917 addressed three major issues: land, religion, and labor. It permitted the breakup of large estates, placed restrictions on foreigners owning land, and allowed nationalization, or government takeover, of natural resources. Church land was made "the property of the nation." The constitution set a minimum wage and protected workers' right to strike.

Although the constitution gave suffrage only to men, it did give women some protection. Women doing the same job as men were entitled to the same pay. In response to women activists, Carranza also passed laws allowing married women to draw up contracts, take part in legal suits, and have equal authority with men in spending family funds.

Social Change At first, the constitution was just a set of goals to be achieved sometime in the future. But in the 1920s, as the government finally restored order after years of civil war, it began to carry out reforms.

The government helped some Indian communities regain lands that had been taken from them. It supported labor unions and launched a massive effort to combat illiteracy. Schools and libraries were set up.

Dedicated teachers, often young women, worked for low pay. While they taught basic skills, they spread ideas of nationalism that began to bridge the gulf between the regions and the central government. As the revolutionary era ended, Mexico became the first Latin American nation to pursue real social and economic reforms for the majority of its people.

The PRI In 1929, government leaders organized what later became the Institutional Revolutionary Party (PRI). It has dominated Mexican politics ever since. The PRI managed to accommodate all groups in Mexican society, including business and military leaders, peasants, and workers. It backed reform but suppressed opposition. In 1938, the government nationalized foreign oil holdings, part of a program to reduce foreign influence.

Rising Tide of Nationalism

Mexico's move to reclaim its oil fields from foreign investors reflected a growing spirit of nationalism in Latin America. This spirit focused in part on ending economic dependence on the industrial powers, especially the United States.

Economic Nationalism During the 1920s and 1930s, world events affected Latin American economies. After World War I, trade fell off with Europe. The Great Depression that struck the United States in 1929 spread around the world in the 1930s. Prices for Latin American exports plunged as demand dried up. At the same time, the cost of imported consumer goods rose.

Murals
Diego Rivera painted murals with scenes of Mexico's history. The top portion of this mural section depicts people in the Mexican Revolution.
Theme: Art and Literature
How does Rivera show that people from all levels of society were involved in the revolution?

A tide of economic nationalism, or emphasis on domestic control of the economy, swept Latin American countries. They were determined to develop their own economies and end foreign economic control. Local entrepreneurs set up factories to produce goods. They urged their governments to raise tariffs to protect the new industries. Following Mexico's lead, some nations also nationalized resources or took over foreign-owned industries. The drive to create domestic industries had limited success. As in the past, the unequal distribution of wealth hampered economic development.

Cultural Nationalism By the 1920s, Latin American writers, artists, and thinkers began to reject European influences. Instead, they took pride in their own culture, with its blend of western and Indian traditions.

In Mexico, cultural nationalism, or pride in one's own culture, was reflected in the revival of mural painting, a major art form of the Aztecs. In the 1920s and 1930s, Diego Rivera, José Clemente Orozco (oh RAHS koh), David Alfaro Siqueiros (sih KAY rohs), and other muralists created magnificent works. On the walls of public buildings, they portrayed the struggles of the Mexican people for liberty, first from the Spanish and later during the Díaz era. The murals have been a great source of national pride ever since.

The "Good Neighbor" Policy

During and after World War I, investments by the United States in the nations of Latin America soared, especially as British influence declined. The United States continued to play the role of "international policeman," intervening to restore order when it felt its interests were threatened.

During the Mexican Revolution, the United States supported leaders who it thought would protect American interests. In 1914, it attacked the port of Vera Cruz to punish Mexico for imprisoning several American sailors. In 1916, it invaded Mexico after Pancho Villa killed more than a dozen Americans in New Mexico.

These actions stirred up anti-American feelings, which increased during the 1920s. In Nicaragua, Augusto César Sandino led a guerrilla movement against United States forces occupying his country. Many people in Latin America saw Sandino as a hero.

In the 1930s, President Franklin Roosevelt took a new approach to Latin America and pledged to follow "the policy of the good neighbor." Under the Good Neighbor Policy, the United States withdrew troops stationed in Haiti and Nicaragua. It also lifted the Platt Amendment, which had limited Cuban independence.

SECTION 1 Assessment

Recall

1. **Identify: (a)** Porfirio Díaz, **(b)** Francisco Madero, **(c)** Zapatistas, **(d)** Venustiano Carranza, **(e)** Diego Rivera, **(f)** Good Neighbor Policy.
2. **Define: (a)** nationalization, **(b)** economic nationalism, **(c)** cultural nationalism.

Comprehension

3. Describe three causes of the Mexican Revolution.
4. Explain how the Constitution of 1917 addressed each of these issues: **(a)** land, **(b)** religion, **(c)** labor.

5. Describe how nationalism affected Mexico.
6. How did Franklin Roosevelt change United States policy toward Latin America?

Critical Thinking and Writing

7. **Analyzing Information** How did world events affect the economies of Latin American nations during the 1920s and 1930s?
8. **Synthesizing Information** **(a)** How did opportunities for women change under the 1917 constitution? **(b)** How did women's lives stay the same?

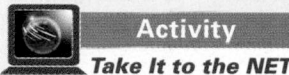
Activity
Take It to the NET

Use the Internet to research Emiliano Zapata and the Zapatista movement. Then, create a poster publicizing Zapatista goals.

SECTION 1 **Assessment**

Recall
1. **(a)** Porfirio Díaz, p. 722 **(b)** Francisco Madero, p. 722 **(c)** Zapatistas, p. 722 **(d)** Venustiano Carranza, p. 724 **(e)** Diego Rivera, p. 725 **(f)** Good Neighbor Policy, p. 725 2. **(a)** nationalization, p. 724 **(b)** economic nationalism, p. 725 **(c)** cultural nationalism, p. 725

Comprehension
3. Possible answers: Peasants desired land. Factory workers and miners wanted higher wages. Middle-class liberals favored democracy. 4. **(a)** The Constitution of 1917 permitted the breakup of large estates, placed restrictions on foreigners owning land, and allowed nationalization of natural resources. **(b)** The constitution made Church land "the property of the nation." **(c)** The constitution set a minimum wage for workers and protected their right to strike. 5. Possible answer: It led to the nationalizing of the oil fields and to a new pride in Mexican culture. 6. He introduced the Good Neighbor Policy, under which troops were withdrawn from Haiti and Nicaragua and the Platt Amendment, which limited Cuban independence, was lifted.

Critical Thinking and Writing
7. After World War I, trade with Europe fell off as new products competed with Latin American exports. The Great Depression hurt Latin American economies further. 8. **(a)** provided equal pay for equal work **(b)** did not allow women to vote

Activity Rubrics

Share rubrics with students before they begin their posters.

Attempted The poster is not complete or reveals little understanding of Zapatista goals.

Minimal The poster shows some awareness of Zapatista goals but is poorly executed.

Adequate The poster demonstrates a good grasp of Zapatista goals and is well presented.

Exemplary The poster shows a thorough understanding of Zapatista goals, is very well presented, and is original.

Human Drama Note

"Viva Roosevelt!" President Roosevelt's Good Neighbor Policy inspired Al Stillman and Xavier Cugat to write a song called "Viva Roosevelt!" Cugat, a Spanish American bandleader, wrote the music to a conga beat. The conga, a Cuban musical and dance form with African origins, was enormously popular in the 1930s.

Test Preparation

Have students read the third paragraph under "Reforms in Mexico" on the opposite page, and then answer the question below.

Which of the following is a right that women did *not* gain under the new constitution?

A equal pay for equal work

B the right to spend family money

C the right to sue someone

D the right to vote

Bell Ringer

Reading Focus

- How did Africans resist colonial rule?
- What signs of nationalism developed in Africa?
- How did Turkey and Iran modernize?
- How did European mandates contribute to the growth of Arab nationalism?

Vocabulary

apartheid
polygamy

Taking Notes

Copy this table. As you read, fill in the major nationalist developments in Africa and the Middle East. To help you get started, one row of the table has been completed.

NATION	LEADER	PROTESTS AGAINST	RESULTS
KENYA	Jomo Kenyatta	• Loss of land •	• Jailing of nationalist leaders •
SOUTH AFRICA			
EGYPT			
TURKEY			
IRAN			

Main Idea Following World War I, nationalist sentiment contributed to many changes in Africa and the Middle East.

LESSON PLAN

1. Focus Nationalist movements grew in Africa and the Middle East after World War I. In Africa, opposition to imperialism spread as the Pan-African and *négritude* movements developed. Mustafa Kemal in Turkey and Reza Khan in Iran tried to strengthen their countries through modernization. Elsewhere in the Middle East, the Pan-Arab movement sought Arab unity and freedom from foreign domination.

2. Instruct Ask students to imagine that they are living in Africa or the Middle East during the 1920s and 1930s. Have them assume one of the following roles: a Kikuyu, a Turk, an Iranian, an Arab, a Jew. Their assignment is to write a letter to a friend or family member in which they discuss their feelings about imperialism and nationalism. In their letters, they should also describe their hopes for the future and any actions that are being taken to achieve these goals. Invite volunteers to read their letters to the class. Encourage other students to make comments and ask questions.

3. Assess Ask students to write four generalizations about the nationalist movements that arose in Africa and the Middle East following World War I.

4. Reteach If students' *Assess* activity does not reflect adequate understanding of the lesson, you might assign the *Guide to the Essentials* or the *Interactive Student Tutorial CD-ROM* for this section.

Primary Source

An African Speaks Out Against Colonialism
Jomo Kenyatta was a leader in Kenya's struggle for independence from British rule. In the following quotation, he dramatizes his view of European colonialism:

"If you woke up one morning and found that somebody had come to your house, and had declared that house belonged to him, you would naturally be surprised, and you would like to know by what arrangement. Many Africans found that, on land that had been in the possession of their ancestors from time immemorial, they were now working as squatters or as laborers."

—Jomo Kenyatta, quoted in
A History of the African People
(July)

Skills Assessment

Primary Source Why was Kenyatta's house comparison an effective device for dramatizing the injustices of colonialism?

Setting the Scene

The Kikuyu people of Kenya were outraged. Not only had the British taken their land, but they also treated the Kikuyu like second-class citizens.

The Kikuyu were among many African people who resented colonial rule. During the 1920s and 1930s, a new generation of leaders, proud of their unique heritage, struggled to stem the tide of imperialism and restore Africa for Africans.

Resistance to Colonial Rule

During the early 1900s, Africans felt the impact of colonial rule. In Kenya and Rhodesia, for example, white settlers forced Africans off the best land. The few who kept their land were forbidden to grow the most profitable crops, such as coffee and sisal—only Europeans could grow these. In Kenya, too, the British made all Africans carry identification cards, imposed a tax, and restricted where they could live or travel.

Everywhere, Africans were forced to work on European-run plantations or in mines. The money they earned was needed to pay taxes to the colonial government. Farmers who had kept their land had to grow cash crops, such as cotton, instead of food. This led to famines in some regions. Increasingly, they lost their self-sufficiency and became dependent on European-made goods.

Resistance Opposition to imperialism grew among Africans. Resistance took many forms. Those who had lost their lands to Europeans sometimes squatted, or settled illegally, on European-owned plantations. In cities, workers began to form labor unions, even though such activity was illegal under the law codes imposed by imperialist nations.

Many western-educated Africans criticized the injustice of imperial rule. Although they had trained for professional careers, the best jobs went to Europeans. Inspired by President Woodrow Wilson's call for self-determination, they condemned the system that excluded Africans from political control of their own lands. Some eagerly read Lenin's writings that claimed imperialism was the final stage of a corrupt and dying capitalist society. In Africa, as in other regions around the world, socialism found a growing audience.

Protests Although large-scale revolts were rare, protests were common. In Kenya, the Kikuyu protested the loss of their land, forced labor, heavy

Primary Source

ANSWER It is a comparison to which almost anyone can relate.

taxes, and the hated identification cards. The British jailed the Kikuyu leaders, but protests continued.

In West Africa, women traditionally had controlled the marketplaces and the farmland. In the 1920s, Ibo women in Nigeria denounced British policies that threatened their rights and their economic role. They demanded a voice in decisions that affected them and their business activities. The "Women's War," as it was called, soon became a full-fledged revolt. Women armed with machetes and sticks mocked British troops and shouted down officials who ordered them to disperse.

Racial Segregation and Nationalism in South Africa Between 1910 and 1940, whites strengthened their grip on South Africa. They imposed a system of racial segregation. Their goal was to ensure white economic and political power and social supremacy. New laws, for example, restricted better-paying jobs in mines to whites only. Blacks were pushed into low-paid, less-skilled work. As in Kenya, South African blacks had to carry passes at all times. They were evicted from the best land, which was set aside for whites, and forced to live on crowded "reserves," which were located in dry, infertile areas.

Other laws chipped away at the rights of blacks. In one South African province, educated blacks who owned property had been allowed to vote in local elections. In 1936, the government abolished that right. The system of segregation set up at this time would become even more restrictive after 1948, when apartheid (uh PAHRT tīd) became law.

Yet South Africa was also home to a vital nationalist movement. African Christian churches and African-run newspapers demanded rights for black South Africans. In 1912, educated Africans organized a political party, later known as the African National Congress (ANC). Its members worked through legal means, protesting laws that restricted the freedom of black Africans. Their efforts, however, had no effect on South Africa's white government. Still, the ANC did build a framework for political action in later years.

Rise of Nationalism

During the 1920s, a movement known as Pan-Africanism began to nourish the nationalist spirit. Pan-Africanism emphasized the unity of Africans and people of African descent around the world. Among its most inspiring leaders was Jamaican-born Marcus Garvey. He preached a forceful and appealing message of "Africa for Africans" and demanded an end to colonial rule. Although Garvey never visited Africa, his ideas influenced a new generation of African leaders.

Pan-African Congress Led by African American scholar and activist W.E.B. DuBois (doo BOYS), Pan-Africanists tried to forge a united front. DuBois organized the first Pan-African Congress in 1919. It met in Paris, where the victorious Allies were holding their peace conference. Delegates from African colonies, the West Indies, and the United States called on the Paris peacemakers to approve a charter of rights for Africans. Although the western powers ignored their demands, the Pan-African Congress established cooperation among African and African American leaders.

Négritude French-speaking writers in West Africa and the Caribbean further awakened self-confidence among Africans. They expressed pride in their African roots through the *négritude* movement. Best known among them was the Senegalese poet Léopold Senghor, who celebrated Africa's rich cultural heritage. He fostered African pride by rejecting the negative views of Africa spread by colonial rulers. In his poem "Black Woman," he uses the image of an African woman to reflect on the beauty of Africa. Later, Senghor would take an active role in Senegal's drive to independence, and he would serve as its first president.

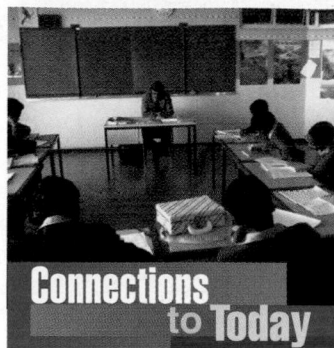

Connections to Today

Rekindling Hope in South Africa

Soweto, a poor suburb of Johannesburg, was a harsh symbol of apartheid. Created in the 1930s to house South Africa's black gold miners, it became a center of violent protest against apartheid in the 1970s. Forced into tiny hovels, Soweto's blacks lived lives marked by gunfire and tear gas and midnight visits from the police.

Today, Soweto has changed. In 1989, South Africa held its first all-race elections and began to dismantle apartheid. The new government brought electricity to most residents, built roads, and set up schools and libraries.

Life in post-apartheid Soweto is not perfect. Poverty is still widespread, and crime is a serious problem. Still, Soweto's residents have begun to feel hope for the future.

Theme: Continuity and Change How did the end of apartheid make it possible for Soweto to make social and economic gains?

<comment>Right sidebar</comment>

Background
Connections to Literature

Négritude This literary movement developed during the 1930s to the 1950s to protest mistreatment of Africa and its people by colonial powers. Négritude's early leaders included Léopold Sédas Senghor of French West Africa (now the Republic of Senegal) and Caribbean writers Aimé Césaire from Martinique and Léon Damas from French Guiana. The three developed an awareness of the injustices and indignities imposed upon their countrymen by colonial powers and resented the attitude of the West that Africans are inferior.

Senghor (b. 1906), the leading figure of négritude, also became a public figure greatly admired in his country and respected internationally. In the 1950s, he became involved in politics and worked to unify Africans politically. After he successfully appealed for Senegal's independence to French president Charles de Gaulle, Senegal became a republic, and soon after, in 1960, Senghor was elected its first president.

In 1948, Senghor edited an anthology of poetry by black, French-speaking Africans; the book became the seminal work of the négritude movement. Senghor's own poetry is found in the anthology *Poetical Work,* 1990. Among writers he inspired are poet Birago Diop and revolutionary protest poet David Diop from Senegal; Jacques Rabemananjara, poet from Madagascar; anticolonial novelists Mongo Beti and Ferdinand Oyono from the Cameroons; and poet Tchicaya U Tam'si from the Congo.

Activity
Connections to Literature

Writing a Poem Ask students to write a poem expressing some aspect of the African condition of the 1920s and 1930s from an African point of view. Students might write about exploitation, resistance, or the growing spirit of self-confidence. Display the poems for others to read.

Connections to Today

ANSWER The new government brought in electricity, built roads, and set up schools and libraries. These improvements will help residents live more comfortably and will provide the education they need to get better jobs.

Block Scheduling Support

In 1903, W.E.B. DuBois wrote, "One ever feels his twoness—an American, a Negro; two souls. . . . He simply wishes to make it possible . . . to be both a Negro and an American, without being cursed and spit upon by his fellow, without having the doors of opportunity closed roughly in his face."

Assign students to work together with a partner to analyze the above quotation. Distribute copies of the quotation or read it aloud several times. Ask students to rewrite the quotation in their own words. Then have them discuss how the experience of African Americans during the early 1900s compared to the experience of Africans during the same period.

Finding Evidence

Ask students to read Section 2. Have them list key events and ideas that led to nationalist movements in Africa and the Middle East. *(More Advanced Readers)*

Visual Learners

Creating a Poster Ask students to imagine that they are officials in a Middle Eastern country, such as Turkey or Iran, that is trying to modernize. Have students create a propaganda poster that urges people to break with a long-standing tradition and adopt a new, western custom, such as making Sunday a day of rest. What resistance would people make? What arguments would the poster use to be effective? Display finished posters around the classroom, and ask other students to interpret the posters' messages. ✳

Egyptian Independence African nationalism brought little political change, except to Egypt. During World War I, Egyptians had been forced to provide food and workers to help Britain. Simmering resistance to British rule flared as the war ended. Western-educated officials, peasants, landowners, Christians, and Muslims united behind the Wafd (WAHFT) party, which launched strikes and riots.

In 1922, the British finally agreed to declare Egypt independent. In fact, however, British troops stayed in Egypt to guard the Suez Canal, and Britain remained the real power behind Egypt's King Faud.

In the 1930s, many young Egyptians were attracted to an organization called the Muslim Brotherhood. This group fostered a broad Islamic nationalism that rejected western culture and denounced widespread corruption in the Egyptian government.

Modernization in Turkey and Iran

Nationalist movements brought immense changes to the Middle East in the aftermath of World War I. The defeated Ottoman empire collapsed in 1918. Its Arab lands, as you have read, were divided up between Britain and France. In Asia Minor, however, Turks resisted western control and fought to build a modern nation.

Atatürk Led by the determined and energetic Mustafa Kemal, Turkish nationalists overthrew the sultan, defeated western occupation forces, and declared Turkey a republic. Kemal later took the name Atatürk, meaning "father of the Turks." Between 1923 and his death in 1938, Atatürk forced through an ambitious program of radical reforms. His goals were to modernize Turkey along western lines and to separate religion from government.

Modernizing Turkey
Atatürk pushed radical reforms to make Turkey a modern nation. One of his changes was the replacement of Arabic with western script. Here, Atatürk reveals the new Turkish alphabet to a crowd in an Istanbul park.

Theme: Impact of the Individual Why do you think Atatürk introduced the new alphabet himself in a public ceremony?

Westernization Atatürk swept away centuries-old traditions when he replaced Islamic law with a new law code based on European models. He discarded the Muslim calendar in favor of the calendar based on western (Christian) traditions and moved the day of rest from Friday, traditional with Muslims, to Sunday, in line with Christian practice.

Like Peter the Great in Russia, Atatürk forced his people to wear western dress. He replaced Arabic script with the western (Latin) alphabet, stating it was easier to learn. He closed religious schools but opened thousands of state schools to prepare young Turks for the challenges of modern society.

Other reforms transformed the lives of women. They no longer had to veil their faces and were allowed to vote. Polygamy—the custom allowing men to have more than one wife—was banned. Given freedom to work outside the home, women became teachers, doctors, lawyers, and even politicians.

Under Atatürk, the government encouraged industrial expansion. The government built roads and railroads, set up factories, and hired westerners to advise on how to make Turkey economically independent.

To achieve his reforms, Atatürk ruled with an iron hand. To many Turks, he was a hero who was transforming Turkey into a strong,

728 Chapter 29

Possible answer: He wanted to show the importance of this reform by introducing it himself, rather than having a subordinate oversee the process.

Teaching Resources
Biography Activity *T. E. Lawrence,* Unit 7 booklet, p. 48
Skill Application Activity *Interpreting Graphs,* Unit 7 booklet, p. 51

modern power. Some Turkish Muslims, however, rejected his secular government. To them, the Quran and Islamic customs provided all needed guidance, from personal concerns such as prayer and behavior to national matters such as government, commerce, and education.

Nationalism and Reform in Iran The success of Atatürk's reforms inspired nationalists in neighboring Iran. They greatly resented the British and Russians, who had won spheres of influence in their land. In 1925, an ambitious army officer, Reza Khan, overthrew the shah. He set up his own Pahlavi dynasty, with himself as shah.

Like Atatürk, Reza Khan rushed to modernize Iran and make it fully independent. He built factories, roads, and railroads and strengthened the army. He, too, adopted the western alphabet, forced Iranians to wear western clothing, and set up modern, secular schools. In addition, he moved to replace Islamic law with secular law and encouraged women to take part in public life. Although many wealthy Iranians in cities supported Reza Khan, Muslim religious leaders fiercely condemned his efforts to introduce western ways to the nation.

As Iran modernized, it won better terms from the British company that controlled its oil industry. It persuaded the British to give it a larger share of the profits and insisted that Iranian workers be hired at all levels of the company. In the decades ahead, oil would become a major factor in Iranian economic and foreign affairs.

European Mandates and Arab Nationalism

Arab nationalism blossomed after World War I and gave rise to Pan-Arabism. This nationalist movement built on the shared heritage of Arabs who lived in lands from the Arabian Peninsula through North Africa.* It emphasized their common history and language and recalled the golden age of Arab civilization. Pan-Arabism sought to free Arabs from foreign domination and unite them in their own state. The national pact written at the First Arab Students' Conference spoke of this mission:

> "I am an Arab, and I believe that the Arabs constitute one nation. The sacred right of this nation is to be sovereign in her own affairs . . . to liberate the Arab homeland, to unite all its parts and to found [distinctively Arab] political, economic, and social institutions."
>
> —Arab pledge, quoted in *Arab Nationalism: An Anthology* (Haim)

Betrayal at the Peace Conference The mandates—territories administered by European nations—set up by the Paris Peace Conference outraged Arabs. During World War I, they had helped the Allies against the Central Powers, especially the Ottomans. In return, they had been promised independence. Instead, the Allies carved up the Ottoman lands, giving France

---

* The Arab lands included areas from the Arabian Peninsula through North Africa. Today, this area includes nations such as Syria, Jordan, Iraq, Egypt, Algeria, and Morocco.

The Middle East, 1920s

British mandates
French mandates
✡ Jewish settlements

Albers Equal Area Projection

Chapter 29 **729**

Skills Assessment

Geography After the end of World War I, Britain and France received mandates in the former Ottoman empire.

1. **Location** On the map, locate (a) Syria, (b) Palestine, (c) Trans Jordan, (d) Saudi Arabia, (e) Egypt, (f) Persian Gulf.
2. **Place** (a) Which areas became French mandates after World War I? (b) Which became British mandates?
3. **Critical Thinking Applying Information** Is this map a useful source of information about the origins of conflict in the Middle East? Explain.

Recall

1. (a) "Women's War," p. 727 (b) African National Congress, p. 727 (c) Pan-Africanism, p. 727 (d) négritude, p 727 (e) Pan-Arabism, p. 729 (f) Zionist, p. 730
2. (a) apartheid, p. 727 (b) polygamy, p. 728

Comprehension

3. People squatted on European plantations. City workers formed labor unions. They staged protests, and occasionally, as in the Women's War, revolted. 4. Pan-Africanism emphasized the unity of Africans and people of African descent. A Pan-African Congress called on Paris peacemakers to approve a charter of rights for Africans. Négritude writers awakened pride in African roots.
5. (a) adopted western calendar, opened secular schools, and allowed women to work outside the home (b) adopted western alphabet and secular law and built factories 6. (a) The mandate system kept their lands under European control. (b) The 1917 Balfour Declaration supported establishing in Palestine "a national home for the Jewish people." Conflict erupted between resident Arabs and Jews, who began moving there.

Critical Thinking and Writing

7. (a) Possible answers: Black South Africans formed the ANC to protest laws limiting their freedom. W.E.B. DuBois and others formed the Pan-African Congress. Egyptians staged strikes and riots. (b) They ignored African demands for independence. 8. Possible answer: It created conflict between Palestinians and Jews.

Activity Rubrics

Share rubrics with students before they write their speeches.

Attempted The speech shows little understanding of African culture and is poorly organized and delivered.

Minimal The speech makes some references to African culture but is poorly written and delivered.

Adequate The speech has several references to African culture and is well organized and delivered.

Exemplary The speech has many significant references to African culture, is perceptive, and is effectively delivered.

Geography and History

ANSWER They were collective farms whose members lived communally and shared belongings, labor, and proceeds.

Geography and History

Building New Settlements

During the early 1900s, many Jewish settlers in Palestine wanted to develop a new way of life. They organized collective farms, called *kibbutzim*. Members shared belongings, labor, and proceeds. The settlements were communal, with cooking done in a central dining hall. Children were raised in a home, separate from their parents, so that women could join the kibbutz work force.

Together, the settlers, called *kibbutzniks*, introduced new techniques of drainage and irrigation. Their efforts helped Israel become a world leader in agricultural production. The kibbutzniks grew grain, fruit trees, and vegetables. For meat, they raised chickens and cows. Cypress and palm trees were planted to provide shade from the desert sun.

Theme: Geography and History What were the main characteristics of the kibbutzim?

---

mandates in Syria and Lebanon and Britain mandates in Palestine and Iraq. Later, Trans-Jordan was added to the British mandate.

Arabs felt betrayed by the West—a feeling that has endured to this day. During the 1920s and 1930s, their anger erupted in frequent protests and revolts against western imperialism. A major center of turmoil was the British mandate of Palestine. There, Arab nationalists faced European Zionists, or Jewish nationalists, with dreams of a homeland of their own.

Promises in Palestine Since Roman times, Jews had dreamed of returning to Palestine. In 1897, Theodor Herzl (HER tsuhl) responded to growing antisemitism in Europe by founding the modern Zionist movement. His goal was to rebuild a Jewish state in Palestine, "our ever-memorable historical home." Soon, some Jews, mostly from Eastern Europe, migrated to Palestine. There they joined the small Jewish community that had survived since biblical times.

During World War I, the Allies made two vague sets of promises. First, they promised Arabs their own kingdoms in former Ottoman lands, including Palestine. Then, in 1917, the British issued the Balfour Declaration to win support of European Jews. In it, Britain supported the idea of setting up "a national home for the Jewish people" in Palestine. The declaration noted, however, that "nothing shall be done which may prejudice the civil and religious rights of existing non-Jewish communities in Palestine." Those communities were Arab. The stage was thus set for conflict between Arab and Jewish nationalists.

A Bitter Struggle In the 1930s, antisemitism, primarily in Germany and Eastern Europe, forced many Jews to seek safety in Palestine. Despite great hardships, they set up factories, built new towns, and turned arid desert into irrigated farmland.

At first, some Arabs welcomed the money and modern technical skills that the newcomers brought with them. But as Jews poured into the land of Palestine, tensions between the two groups developed. Sometimes, Jewish settlers bought land from absentee Arab landowners. In the cities, some Jewish factory owners refused to hire Arabs. These tensions were heightened by religious differences between Jews and Arabs. Although most Arabs were Muslim, some were Christian. Angry Arabs staged attacks on Jewish settlements, hoping to oust the Jews. For the rest of the century, Arab nationalists battled Zionists over the land that Arabs called Palestine and Jews called Israel.

SECTION 2 Assessment

Recall

1. **Identify:** (a) "Women's War," (b) African National Congress, (c) Pan-Africanism, (d) négritude, (e) Pan-Arabism, (f) Zionist.
2. **Define:** (a) apartheid, (b) polygamy.

Comprehension

3. How did Africans resist the impact of colonialism?
4. Describe three examples of the rise of nationalism in Africa.
5. What reforms were introduced in (a) Turkey, (b) Iran?

6. (a) Why were many Arabs angered by decisions made at the Paris Peace Conference after World War I? (b) Why did Palestine become a center of conflict?

Critical Thinking and Writing

7. **Synthesizing Information** (a) How did nationalist leaders in Africa oppose colonial rule? (b) How did colonial powers control African countries?
8. **Drawing Conclusions** How did the Balfour Declaration affect the Middle East?

Activity

Writing a Speech
Imagine that you are a member of the Pan-African movement in the 1920s. Use what you have learned about African culture in this and earlier chapters to write a speech extolling your unique heritage.

Resource Directory

Teaching Resources

Section Quiz Unit 7 booklet, p. 41
Creative Teaching Activities Creative Teaching Activities booklet, p. 131
Guided Reading and Review Unit 7 booklet, p. 42

Technology

World History Color Transparencies *Seascape From a Hill,* p. D–91
Interactive Student Tutorial CD-ROM Ch. 29
Computer Test Bank Ch. 29

Reading Focus

- What sparked the Indian independence movement after World War I?
- How did Mohandas Gandhi influence the independence movement?
- What did the Salt March symbolize?

Vocabulary

ahimsa

civil disobedience

Taking Notes

Copy this time line. As you read, fill in the key events in India's move to independence. To help you get started, one part of the time line has been completed.

```
        1900    1910    1920    1930    1940
   ─────┼───────┼───────┼───────┼───────┼─────
   ╱╱
   1858                1914
   Britain takes control
   of India
```

> **Main Idea** Mohandas Gandhi and the Congress party led the drive for independence in India.

Setting the Scene Tensions were running high in Amritsar, a city in northern India. Protests against British rule had sparked riots and attacks on British residents. On April 13, 1919, a large but peaceful crowd jammed into a walled field in the heart of the city. The British commander, General Reginald Dyer, had banned public meetings, but Indians either ignored or had not heard the order. As Indian leaders addressed the crowd, Dyer arrived with 50 soldiers. To clear the field, they opened fire on the unarmed men, women, and children. Within 10 minutes, they had killed 379 people and wounded more than 1,100. The Amritsar massacre was a turning point for many Indians. It convinced them of the evils of British rule.

Moves Toward Independence

The tragedy at Amritsar was linked to broader Indian frustrations after World War I. During the war, more than a million Indians had served overseas, suffering heavy casualties. As thousands died on distant battlefields, Indian nationalists grew angry that they had no freedom at home.

To quiet nationalist demands, the British promised India greater self-government after the war. But when the fighting ended, Britain proposed only a few minor reforms.

Since 1885, the Congress party had pressed for self-rule within the British empire. After Amritsar, it began to call for full independence. But party members were mostly a middle-class, western-educated elite who had little in common with the masses of Indian peasants. In the 1920s, a new leader emerged and united all Indians. Adoring Indians dubbed him Mahatma, or "Great Soul."

Mohandas Gandhi

The new leader was Mohandas Gandhi. Gandhi came from a middle-class Hindu family. At age 19, he went to England to study law. Like thousands of Indians before him, Gandhi went to South Africa. There he joined an Indian law firm. Although Gandhi was more successful financially than many Indians in South Africa, he too faced racial prejudice. For 20 years, Gandhi fought laws that discriminated against Indians in South Africa. In his struggle against injustice, he

Serving the Empire
Large numbers of Indians served in World War I. Here, Indian troops repel an air attack in Mesopotamia.

Theme: Political and Social Systems How did Indian nationalists respond to World War I?

Chapter 29 731

Cooperative Learning

Drawing a Political Cartoon Divide the class into small groups and have each group design a political cartoon about the Amritsar massacre. Remind students that political cartoons use images, symbols, but few, if any, words to convey a point of view. Ask each group to come to a consensus on what they want to emphasize. Group members should then discuss ways to express their viewpoint visually. Display the finished cartoons and call on students to interpret them.

Background
Historical Evidence

Witness to Civil Disobedience The American journalist Webb Miller was with Gandhi's followers when they marched on the government salt deposits in Dharsana. He described the determination and bravery of what he called "the Gandhi men" in this way:

"Suddenly, at a word of command, scores of native police rushed upon the advancing marchers and rained blows on their heads with their steel-shod *lathis*. . . . The waiting crowd of watchers groaned and sucked in their breaths in sympathetic pain at every blow. . . . Then another column formed. . . . They marched slowly toward the police. Although every one knew that within a few minutes he would be beaten down, perhaps killed, I could detect no signs of wavering or fear. They marched steadily with heads up, without the encouragement of music or cheering or any possibility that they might escape serious injury or death. The police rushed out and methodically and mechanically beat down the second column. There was no fight, no struggle."

You may wish to use the above excerpt as the basis for a class discussion on how news coverage of the Salt March may have affected public opinion.

Primary Source and Literature

See "Mohandas Gandhi: Hind Swaraj" in the Reference Section at the back of this book.

Biography

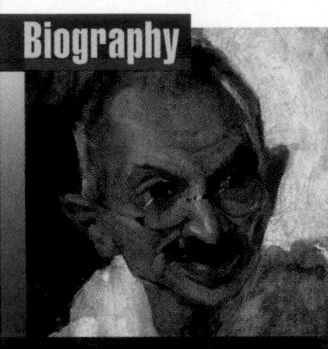

Mohandas K. Gandhi
1869–1948

A train trip in South Africa changed Gandhi's life. One day, the neatly dressed young lawyer bought a first-class ticket for a train. As he seated himself, a train official ordered him to move to a rear compartment.

At that time, South Africa had laws that required "coloured" travelers to sit separately from "whites." When Gandhi protested, the official forced him off the train.

This event inspired Gandhi to oppose injustice. Gradually, he developed his belief in nonviolent resistance. He pursued this battle—first in South Africa and later in India—for the rest of his life.

Theme: Impact of the Individual How did Gandhi's personal experience influence India's struggle for independence?

---

adopted the weapon of nonviolent (passive) resistance. He called it *satyagraha*, or "soul-force." In 1914, Gandhi returned to India, where his ideas inspired Indians of all religions and ethnic backgrounds.

Nonviolence While leaders like Atatürk adopted western solutions to national problems, Gandhi embraced Hindu traditions. Above all, he preached the ancient doctrine of *ahimsa* (uh HIM sah), or nonviolence and reverence for all life. By using the power of love, he believed, people could convert even the worst wrongdoer to the right course of action.

Gandhi's philosophy reflected western as well as Indian influences. He admired Christian teachings about love and had read the works of Henry David Thoreau, an American philosopher of the 1800s who believed in civil disobedience, the refusal to obey unjust laws. Gandhi also embraced western ideas of democracy and nationalism. He rejected the inequalities of the caste system and fought hard to end the harsh treatment of untouchables. He urged equal rights for all Indians, women as well as men.

Gandhi Sets an Example Abandoning western-style clothing, Gandhi dressed in the *dhoti*, the simple white garment traditionally worn by village Indians. During the 1920s and 1930s, he launched a series of nonviolent actions against British rule. He called for boycotts of British goods, especially textiles, and urged Indians to wear only cotton grown and woven in India. He worked to restore pride in India's traditional industries, making the spinning wheel a symbol of the nationalist movement. Many women joined the self-sufficiency movement, producing as much as they could in their homes.

Through his own example, Gandhi inspired Indians to "get rid of our helplessness." His campaigns of civil disobedience attracted wide support. But when protests led to violent riots, Gandhi was deeply upset. He would fast, pray, and call on patriots to practice self-control.

The Salt March

To mobilize mass support, Gandhi set out to end the British salt monopoly. Everyone needs salt to survive. But while natural salt was available in the sea, Indians were forbidden to touch it. They could buy only salt sold by the British government. To Gandhi, the government salt monopoly was a symbol of British oppression. Early in 1930, he wrote to the British viceroy in India, stating his intention to break the law.

Breaking the Law On March 12, Gandhi set out with 78 followers on a 240-mile march to the sea. As the tiny band passed through villages, crowds responded to Gandhi's message. By the time they reached the sea, the marchers numbered in the thousands. On April 6, Gandhi waded into the surf and picked up a lump of sea salt. Raising it over his head, he declared, "With this, I am shaking the foundations of the British empire."

Gandhi was arrested and jailed. Still, Indians followed his lead. Coastal villages started collecting salt. Congress party leaders sold salt on city streets, displayed it to enormous rallies—and were arrested. As Gandhi's campaign gained force, tens of thousands of Indians were imprisoned.

Toward Freedom All around the world, newspapers thundered against Britain. Stories revealed how police brutally clubbed peaceful marchers who tried to occupy a government saltworks. "Not one of the marchers even raised an arm to fend off the blows," wrote an outraged American reporter.

Gandhi's campaign of nonviolence and the self-sacrifice of his followers slowly forced Britain to agree to hand over some power to Indians. Britain also agreed to meet other demands of the Congress party. Complete independence, however, would not be achieved until 1947.

Biography

ANSWER His experience of discrimination led him to urge Indians to resist British rule.

Resource Directory

Teaching Resources
Section Quiz Unit 7 booklet, p. 43
Technology
Interactive Student Tutorial CD-ROM Ch. 29
Computer Test Bank Ch. 29

Virtual Field Trip

www.phschool.com

**ABC News
New York, NY**

To learn more about Gandhi and the Salt March, use the Internet address above to link to the ABC News Web site.

Defying British Law
The Salt March focused the attention of all India on Gandhi's challenge to the British. Supporters followed him from village to village until they reached the sea. Here, women boil ocean water to collect salt.

Theme: Global Interaction How did other countries react to the Salt March?

Looking Ahead

As India came closer to independence, Muslim fears of the Hindu majority increased. While millions of Muslims responded to Gandhi's campaigns, tensions between Hindus and Muslims often erupted into violence.

A Separate Muslim State During the 1930s, the Muslim League gained an able leader in Muhammad Ali Jinnah. Like Gandhi, Jinnah came from a middle-class background and had studied law in England. At first, he represented Muslim interests within the Congress party. Later, he threw his support behind the idea of a separate state for Muslims. It would be called Pakistan, meaning "land of the [ritually] pure."

World War II India was moving toward independence when a new world war exploded in 1939. Britain outraged Indian leaders by postponing further action on independence and then bringing India into the war without consulting them. Angry nationalists launched a campaign of noncooperation and were jailed by the British. Millions of Indians, however, did help Britain during the war. When the war ended in 1945, independence could no longer be delayed.

SECTION 3 Assessment

Recall
1. **Identify:** **(a)** Amritsar massacre, **(b)** Mohandas Gandhi, **(c)** Muhammad Ali Jinnah.
2. **Define:** **(a)** ahimsa, **(b)** civil disobedience.

Comprehension
3. How did the Amritsar massacre affect the movement for Indian independence?
4. How did Gandhi revive Indian pride?

5. Why did Gandhi organize the Salt March?

Critical Thinking and Writing
6. **Recognizing Causes and Effects** Why do you think Gandhi was able to unite Indians when earlier attempts had failed?
7. **Predicting Consequences** What conflicts would you expect to emerge in India after World War II?

Activity
Take It to the NET

Use the Internet to research the Amritsar massacre. Then, write two headlines about the event—one for an Indian newspaper and one for a British newspaper.

SECTION 3 Assessment

Recall
1. **(a)** Amritsar massacre, p. 731
(b) Mohandas Gandhi, p. 732
(c) Muhammad Ali Jinnah, p. 733
2. **(a)** ahimsa, p. 732 **(b)** civil disobedience, p. 732

Comprehension
3. After the Amritsar massacre, many Indians called for full independence rather than limited self-rule within the British empire. 4. Possible answers: Gandhi revived Indian pride by wearing traditional cotton clothing made in India, by urging others to do the same, and by urging them to boycott British textiles. 5. He wanted to end British control of Indian industries.

Critical Thinking and Writing
6. Possible answers: Gandhi gained support because of his personal character, the appeal of his beliefs, and his emphasis on equality. 7. Possible answer: India would experience a civil war.

Activity Rubrics

Share rubrics with students before they write their headlines.

Attempted The student does only one headline, or the headlines fail to reflect a viewpoint.

Minimal The student does both headlines, but they show little understanding of either viewpoint.

Adequate The student's headlines are interesting and reflect both viewpoints.

Exemplary The student's headlines are gripping and reflect both viewpoints.

Human Drama Activity

Creating a Presentation As a writer and educator Rabindranath Tagore worked to strengthen understanding between Indians and Westerners. His work includes poetry, novels, and songs (including the national anthems of India and of Bangladesh). Tagore received the Nobel Prize for literature in 1913 and was knighted by Britain's George V. After the Amritsar massacre, he gave up his knighthood. Have students find the anthems and other information about Tagore on the Internet and present their findings in a report to the class.

Test Preparation

Have students read the paragraph headed "Nonviolence" on the opposite page, and then complete the sentence below.

The doctrine of *ahimsa* is an example of

A a British tradition.

B civil disobedience.

C a Hindu tradition.

D the caste system.

Caption Answer

They bitterly criticized British repression of the Salt Marchers.

Bell Ringer

Bell Ringer Inform students that Sun Yixian called China "the poorest and weakest state in the world." Have them work in small groups to recall what they have previously learned about China in the late 1800s and early 1900s. Ask them to list ways in which China was weak and to recommend possible measures that could have made China strong.

LESSON PLAN

1. Focus The new republic of China was crippled by feuding warlords, a collapsed economy, famine, and increasing foreign influence. The May Fourth Movement hoped to solve China's problems by embracing western science and ideals. But in 1927, civil war erupted between the Guomindang led by Jiang Jieshi and the Communists led by Mao Zedong.

2. Instruct Inform students that China during the early 1900s was a battleground for competing ideas and forces. Rival warlords, the May Fourth Movement, the Guomindang, the Communists, and foreign powers all vied for greater influence in China. Have students complete the following three tasks: (1) Identify and define each of the groups that competed for power in China during the early and mid-1900s. (2) Outline the goals and methods of each group. (3) Decide which group was most likely to gain the support of the majority of China's people and explain why. Students may work on this lesson individually or in groups. Review students' findings in a class discussion.

3. Assess Ask students to write four newspaper headlines that summarize major developments in China during the early and mid-1900s.

4. Reteach If students' **Assess** activity does not reflect adequate understanding of the lesson, you might assign the *Guide to the Essentials* or the *Interactive Student Tutorial CD-ROM* for this section.

Reading Focus

- What were the key challenges to the Chinese republic?
- What leaders emerged in the "new" China?
- How did invasion by Japan affect China?

Taking Notes

As you read this section, prepare an outline of its contents. Use Roman numerals to indicate major headings. Use capital letters for subheadings, and use numbers for the supporting details. The example here will help you get started.

I. The Chinese republic
   A. Internal problems
      1. Yuan Shikai sets up dynasty with himself as emperor
      2.
   B. Foreign imperialism
      1.
      2.

Main Idea Civil war and foreign invasions plagued the new Chinese republic.

Setting the Scene Sun Yixian, "father" of the Chinese revolution, painted a grim picture of China after the overthrow of the Qing dynasty. "In comparison with other nations," he wrote, "we have the greatest population and the oldest culture, of 4,000 years' duration." In spite of this, he noted, China was "the poorest and weakest state in the world." Other countries were "the carving knife and the serving dish," and China was "the fish and the meat."

As the new Chinese republic took shape, nationalists like Sun Yixian set the goal of "catching up and surpassing the powers, east and west." But that goal would remain a distant dream as China suffered the turmoil of civil war and foreign invasion.

The Chinese Republic

In China, as you recall, the Qing dynasty collapsed in 1911. Sun Yixian hoped to rebuild China on the Three Principles of the People. But he made little progress. China quickly fell into chaos.

Internal Problems In 1912, Sun Yixian stepped down as president in favor of a powerful general, Yuan Shikai. Sun hoped that Yuan would restore order and create a strong central government. Instead, the ambitious general tried to set up a new dynasty, with himself as emperor. The military, however, did not support him, and opposition divided the nation. When Yuan died in 1916, China plunged into still greater disorder.

In the provinces, local warlords seized power. As rival armies battled for control, the economy collapsed and millions of peasants suffered terrible hardships. Warlords forced them to pay taxes to support their armies. The constant fighting ravaged the land. Famine and attacks by bandits added to their misery.

Foreign Imperialism During this period of upheaval, foreign powers increased their influence over Chinese affairs. Foreign merchants, missionaries, and soldiers dominated the ports China had opened to trade. They also exerted influence inland.

In 1915, Japan had begun to put new pressure on its once-powerful neighbor. While the attentions of the western powers were focused on World War I, Japan presented Yuan Shikai with the Twenty-One Demands, which sought to make China a Japanese protectorate. Too weak to resist, Yuan gave in to some of the demands.

Resource Directory

Teaching Resources
Creative Teaching Activities Creative Teaching Activities booklet, p. 132
Guided Reading and Review Unit 7 booklet, p. 44

Then, in 1919, at the Paris Peace Conference, the victorious Allies gave Japan control over former German possessions in China. That news infuriated Chinese nationalists, who blamed their leaders for "selling out" China in the Treaty of Versailles.

May Fourth Movement On May 4, 1919, student protests erupted in Beijing and later spread to cities across China—a startling event in those days. "China's territory may be conquered," they declared, "but it cannot be given away! The Chinese people may be massacred, but they will not surrender." Students organized boycotts of Japanese goods.

Student protests set off a cultural and intellectual ferment known as the May Fourth Movement. As with earlier reform movements, its goal was to strengthen China. Western-educated leaders blamed the imperialists' successes on China's own weakness. As in Meiji Japan, Chinese reformers wanted to learn from the West and use that knowledge to end foreign domination. Most reformers rejected Confucian traditions, and many turned to western science and ideas such as democracy and nationalism to solve China's problems.

Women played a key role in the May Fourth Movement, just as they had in earlier uprisings. They joined marches and campaigned to end a number of traditional practices, such as arranged marriages, footbinding, and the seclusion of women within the home. Their work helped open doors for women in education and the economy.

The Appeal of Marxism Some Chinese turned to the revolutionary ideas of Marx and Lenin. The Russian Revolution seemed to offer a model of how a strong, well-organized party could transform a nation. And Soviet Russia was more than willing to train Chinese students and military officers to become the vanguard, or elite leaders, of a communist revolution. By the 1920s, a small group of Chinese communists had formed their own political party.

Leaders for a New China

In 1921, Sun Yixian and his Guomindang (gwoh meen DAWNG), or Nationalist, party established a government in south China. Sun planned to raise an army, defeat the warlords, and spread his government's rule over all of China. When western powers ignored pleas for help in building a democratic China, Sun decided "that the one real and genuine friend of the

May Fourth Movement
In 1919, student protests spread across China. Reformers wanted to modernize the nation so that China would be able to expel foreign powers.

Theme: Political and Social Systems Why did some Chinese reformers adopt the ideas of Marx and Lenin?

Reading Strategy
Finding Evidence

Ask students to jot down facts as they read Section 4, supporting the idea stated on the opposite page that "... China suffered the turmoil of civil war and foreign invasion." (More Advanced Readers)

Background
Connections to Today

Tiananmen Square Almost 70 years to the day after the birth of the May Fourth Movement, student protests once again gripped the attention of China. In April 1989, student protesters organized rallies and demonstrations in many Chinese cities to demand democratic reforms. The Communist government issued a ban on public gatherings, but the protesters ignored it. On May 4, 1989, 100,000 students and workers descended on Tiananmen Square in Beijing. The protesters stayed week after week, and their numbers grew to about one million, as the news media of the world anxiously looked on. The government finally responded on June 3 and 4 by sending in tanks and soldiers to crush the protest. It is estimated that about 5,000 people died in the attack while some 10,000 more were injured.

Block Scheduling Support

Early in the Communist Long March, which started in 1934, one soldier described how he liked marching at night:

"Night marching is wonderful, if there is a moon and a gentle wind blowing. When no enemy troops were near, whole companies would sing and others would answer. We made torches from pine branches or trayed bamboo. When at the foot of a mountain we could look up and see a long column of lights coiling like a fiery dragon up the mountainside. From the summit we would look in both directions and see miles of torches."

Read the soldier's words to the class. Discuss how the soldier's description might have changed by the end of the march. What factors might have changed the attitudes of the marchers? What factors might help keep their spirits high? (This quote is from the chapter "The Long March" in *The Rise of the Chinese Republic*.)

Caption Answer

The Russian Revolution, which was inspired by the ideas of Marx and Lenin, seemed to offer a model of how a strong, well-organized party could transform a nation.

736 Chapter 29

Customize for...
Visual Learners

Illustrating a Story Have five or six students work together to illustrate a pamphlet that the Communists might have distributed to Chinese peasants in the 1930s. Students should first list the incidents and policies that they plan to illustrate. Each student should then take responsibility for creating one illustration and a caption to go along with it. Have students display their pamphlets around the classroom. ✳

Background
Perspectives

Lesser of Two Evils In the face of Japanese aggression, Jiang remained opposed to forming a united front with the Communists. Jiang expressed his feelings about his two enemies in this way, "The Japanese are a disease of the skin. The Communists are a disease of the heart." Finally, in December 1936, some of his generals convinced him to change his mind by taking him captive and holding him until he agreed to an alliance with the Communists.

Civil War in China, 1925–1935

→ Route of Jiang Jieshi, 1926–1928
→ Route of Long March, 1934–1935
▢ Controlled by Guomindang, 1927
▢ Communist bases

Azimuthal Equal Area Projection
0   150   300 Miles
0   150   300 Kilometers

Skills Assessment

Geography Beginning in 1925, the Guomindang and the Communists waged a long and bitter war for control of China.

1. **Location** On the map, locate **(a)** Beijing, **(b)** Nanjing, **(c)** Yenan, **(d)** Chongqing.
2. **Movement** Describe the route of the Long March.
3. **Critical Thinking Synthesizing Information** What types of natural features made the Long March difficult?

Chinese Revolution is Soviet Russia." Russian experts helped the Nationalists plan and carry out their campaign against the warlords.

Jiang Jieshi After Sun's death in 1925, an energetic young army officer, Jiang Jieshi* (jyawng jeh SHEE), took over the Guomindang. He had received military training in Japan. While he was determined to smash the power of the warlords and reunite China, Jiang had little interest in either democracy or communism.

In 1926, Jiang Jieshi began a march into northern China, crushing local warlords as he advanced and capturing Beijing. In midcampaign, he stopped to strike at the Chinese Communist party, which he saw as a threat to his power. While Jiang had the support of landlords and business leaders, the Communists were winning converts among the small proletariat in cities like Shanghai.

Early in 1927, on orders from Jiang, Guomindang troops slaughtered Communist party members and the workers who supported them. In Shanghai and elsewhere, thousands of people were killed. Anger over the massacre would fuel a bitter civil war that lasted for 22 years.

Mao Zedong Among the Communists who escaped Jiang's attack was a young revolutionary of peasant origins, Mao Zedong. Unlike earlier Chinese Communists, Mao believed that the Communists should seek support not among the small urban working class but among the large peasant masses.

Although the Communists were pursued at every turn by Guomindang forces, Mao was optimistic about eventual success. "A single spark can start a prairie fire," he once observed. For a time, Mao and the Communists organized the peasants in southeastern China. They redistributed land to peasants and offered them schooling and health care.

The Long March Jiang Jieshi, however, was determined to destroy the "Red bandits," as he called the Communists. He led the Guomindang in a series of "extermination campaigns" against them.

In 1934, in an epic retreat known as the Long March, Mao and about 100,000 of his followers fled the Guomindang. During the next year, they trekked more than 6,000 miles, facing daily attacks as they crossed rugged mountains, deep gorges, and mighty rivers. Only about 20,000 people survived the ordeal. For decades, the Long March stood as a symbol of Communist heroism to Chinese who opposed the Guomindang. The march also inspired new recruits to follow Mao.

During the Long March, the Communists enforced strict discipline. Soldiers had to follow three main rules: Obey orders, "do not take a single needle or a piece of thread from the people," and turn in everything you capture. Further, they were to treat peasants politely, pay for goods they wanted, and avoid damaging crops. Such behavior made Mao's forces welcome among peasants, many of whom had suffered greatly at the hands of the Guomindang.

At the end of the Long March, the Communists set up a new base in a remote region of northern China. There, Mao rebuilt his forces and plotted

---

* In earlier textbooks, this name is spelled Chiang Kai-shek.

ANSWERS 1. Review locations with students. **2.** west from bases in southeastern China and then north, curving east to Yenan **3.** rugged mountains, deep gorges, mighty rivers

Resource Directory

Teaching Resources
Primary Source Activity *The Long March Across China,* Unit 7 booklet, p. 49
Section Quiz Unit 7 booklet, p. 45

Technology
Interactive Student Tutorial CD-ROM Ch. 29
Computer Test Bank Ch. 29

World History Visions, Voices, Views Animated Map Story, *The Long March in China (1934–1935),* videodisc side 4 or videotape 7, running time 3:00 min.

Side 4: Fr. 10165-15882

new strategies for fighting the Guomindang. He claimed the great retreat as a victory. As he observed:

> "The Long March is also a seeding-machine. It has sown many seeds in eleven provinces, which will sprout, grow leaves, blossom into flowers, bear fruit, and yield a crop."
> —Mao Zedong, "On the Tactics of Fighting Japanese Imperialism"

Japanese Invasion

While Jiang was pursuing the Communists across China, the country faced another danger. In 1931, Japan invaded Manchuria in northeastern China, adding it to the growing Japanese empire. As Japanese aggression increased, some of Jiang's own generals began to doubt him. Why, they demanded, did he waste valuable resources fighting other Chinese instead of mobilizing against the foreign invaders? In the end, Jiang was forced to form a united front with the Communists against Japan.

In 1937, the Japanese struck again. As airplanes bombed Chinese cities, highly disciplined and well-equipped Japanese troops overran eastern China, including Beijing and Guangzhou. Jiang Jieshi retreated to the interior and set up his capital at Chongqing (chawng CHIHNG).

After a lengthy siege, Japanese troops marched into the city of Nanjing on December 13. Nanjing was an important cultural center, and had been the Nationalist capital before Chongqing. After the city's surrender, the Japanese killed hundreds of thousands of soldiers and civilians and brutalized still more. The cruelty and destruction became known around the world as the "rape of Nanjing."

Looking Ahead

From 1937 to 1945, the Guomindang, the Communists, and the Japanese were locked in a three-sided struggle. The bombing of Pearl Harbor in 1941 brought the United States not only into the war against Japan but into an alliance with the Chinese, as well. After Japan's defeat, the United States, which supported Jiang, tried to prevent renewed civil war in China, but with no success. Within a few years, the Communists would triumph, and Mao would move to impose revolutionary change on China.

SECTION 4 Assessment

Recall
1. **Identify:** (a) Sun Yixian, (b) May Fourth Movement, (c) Guomindang, (d) Jiang Jieshi, (e) Mao Zedong, (f) Long March.

Comprehension
2. Why did the new republic of China fall into chaos after 1912?
3. Describe the goals of each of the following: (a) Sun Yixian, (b) Jiang Jieshi, (c) Mao Zedong.
4. Why did Jiang side with the Communists after 1931?

Critical Thinking and Writing
5. **Recognizing Causes and Effects** (a) How did the actions of foreign imperialist powers help to strengthen nationalism in China? (b) How do you think the "rape of Nanjing" affected Japan's reputation around the world?
6. **Defending a Position** Do you think that Mao's order not to take a single needle or piece of thread from the people was a wise decision? Why or why not?

Activity

Drawing a Political Cartoon
Review Mao's statement about the Long March as a "seeding-machine." Draw a political cartoon illustrating this statement. Include a title and a caption for your political cartoon.

Chapter 29 **737**

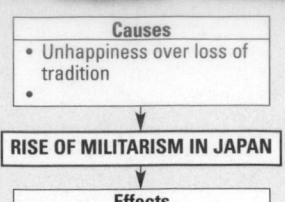

Reading Focus

■ How did liberal changes affect Japan during the 1920s?

■ How did nationalists react to Japan's problems during the Great Depression?

■ How did the militarists use their power?

Vocabulary

Diet
ultranationalist

Taking Notes

Copy this graphic organizer on a piece of paper. Include facts that describe the causes and effects of the rise of militarism in Japan. To help you get started, part of the graphic organizer has been completed.

Causes
• Unhappiness over loss of tradition
•

↓

RISE OF MILITARISM IN JAPAN

↓

Effects
• Withdrawal from League of Nations
•

Main Idea By the 1930s, the Japanese military dominated a government that emphasized service to the nation and a policy of imperialistic expansion.

Bell Ringer

Invite a student to read aloud the quotation from *The Way of Subjects* on the last page of this section. Ask students to explain the meaning of the quotation and to predict the consequences of this viewpoint.

LESSON PLAN

1. Focus In the 1920s, Japan's political parties and democratic parliament grew stronger. But the Great Depression fueled dissatisfaction among militarists and extreme nationalists. By the 1930s, the Japanese military dominated a government that emphasized obedience to the emperor, service to the state, and a policy of imperialist expansion.

2. Instruct Work with the class to construct on the chalkboard a graphic organizer outlining the factors that led to military domination of the Japanese government in the 1930s. Draw a circle on the board and label it Roots of Militarists' Power. Draw several branches leading away from the central circle. Write the following labels on the branches: Social Problems, Economic Problems, Foreign Influence, Western Imperialism, Nationalism. Invite students to come to the board and write specific facts and ideas at appropriate places on the graphic organizer. Encourage students to add other branches if necessary. Use the graphic organizer as the basis for a class discussion on the roots of Japanese militarism and imperialism in the 1930s.

3. Assess Ask students to imagine that they are working for the Japanese ministry of propaganda during this period. Have them create a propaganda poster supporting Japanese nationalism, militarism, or imperialism.

4. Reteach If students' **Assess** activity does not reflect adequate understanding of the lesson, you might assign the *Guide to the Essentials* or the *Interactive Student Tutorial CD-ROM* for this section.

Biography

Hirohito 1901–1989

Hirohito became emperor of Japan in 1926. As emperor, according to Japanese tradition, he was a living god and the nation's supreme authority—no one could look at his face or even mention his name. In practice, however, he merely approved the policies that his ministers formulated.

Hirohito was a private man who preferred marine biology to power politics. As a result, his role in Japan's move toward aggression is unclear. Some historians believe that Hirohito did not encourage Japanese military leaders. Others assert that he was actively involved in expansionist policies.

Theme: Impact of the Individual Why was Hirohito given great respect?

Setting the Scene

Solemn ceremonies marked the start of Emperor Hirohito's reign. A few honored participants gathered in the Secret Purple Hall. Other high-ranking guests sat in an outer chamber, able to hear but not to see the emperor.

In the hall, the new emperor sat on the ancient throne of Japan. Beside him was his wife, the empress Nagako. With great care, he performed purification rituals that were sacred going back thousands of years. Calling on the spirits of his ancestors, he pledged "to preserve world peace and benefit the welfare of the human race."

The prime minister then made his own brief speech, ending with a ringing cry: "May the Lord Emperor live 10,000 years!" This traditional wish for a long and successful reign echoed across Japan.

In fact, Hirohito reigned from 1926 to 1989—an astonishing 63 years. During those decades, Japan experienced remarkable successes and appalling tragedies. In this section, we will focus on the 1920s and 1930s, when the pressures of extreme nationalism and economic upheaval set Japan on a militaristic and expansionist path that would engulf all of Asia.

Liberal Changes of the 1920s

During the 1920s, Japan moved toward greater democracy. Political parties grew stronger, and elected members of the Diet—the Japanese parliament—exerted their power. By 1925, all adult men had won the right to vote. Western ideas about women's rights had brought a few changes. Overall, however, Japanese women remained subordinate to men, and they would not win suffrage until 1947.

Economic Growth During World War I, the Japanese economy enjoyed phenomenal growth. Its exports to Allied nations soared. Also, while western powers battled in Europe, Japan expanded its influence throughout East Asia. Additionally, it sought further rights in China with the Twenty-One Demands.

By the 1920s, the powerful business leaders known as the zaibatsu strongly influenced politics through donations to political parties. They pushed for policies to favor international trade and their own interests. At the same time, in the spirit of world peace, Japan signed an agreement with the United States and Britain to limit the size of its navy. The government also reduced military spending.

Biography

ANSWER According to tradition, he was a living god and the nation's supreme authority.

Resource Directory

Teaching Resources

Creative Teaching Activities Creative Teaching Activities booklet, p. 133
Guided Reading and Review Unit 7 booklet, p. 46

Serious Problems Behind this seeming well-being, Japan faced some grave problems. The economy grew more slowly in the 1920s than at any time since Japan had modernized. Rural peasants enjoyed none of the prosperity of city dwellers. In the cities, factory workers earning low wages were attracted to the socialist ideas of Marx and Lenin. As these workers won the right to vote, many of them elected socialists to the Diet.

In the cities, members of the younger generation were also in revolt against tradition. They adopted western fads and fashions and rejected family authority for the western notion of individual freedom.

During the 1920s, tensions between the government and the military simmered not far below the surface. Conservatives, especially military officers, blasted government corruption, including payoffs by powerful zaibatsu. They also condemned western influences for undermining basic Japanese values of obedience and respect for authority.

The Nationalist Reaction

In 1929, the Great Depression rippled across the Pacific, striking Japan with devastating force. Trade suffered as foreign buyers could no longer afford to purchase Japanese silks and other exports. Unemployment in the cities soared, while in the countryside peasants were only a mouthful from starvation.

A Worsening Crisis Economic disaster fed the discontent of the leading military officials and extreme nationalists, or **ultranationalists.** They condemned politicians for agreeing to western demands to stop overseas expansion. Western industrial powers, they pointed out, had long ago grabbed huge empires. By comparison, Japan's empire was tiny.

Japanese nationalists were further outraged by racial policies in the United States, Canada, and Australia that shut out Japanese immigrants. The Japanese took great pride in their industrial achievements and bitterly resented being treated as second-class citizens in other parts of the world.

As the crisis worsened, nationalists demanded renewed expansion. An empire in Asia, they argued, would provide much-needed raw materials as well as an outlet for Japan's rapidly growing population. They set their sights on the Chinese province of Manchuria. This region was rich in natural resources, and Japanese businesses had already invested heavily there.

The Manchurian Incident In 1931, a group of Japanese army officers provoked an incident that would provide an excuse to seize Manchuria. They set explosives and blew up tracks on a Japanese-owned railroad line. Then, they claimed that the Chinese had committed the act. In "self-defense," the army attacked Chinese forces. Without consulting their own government, the Japanese military forces conquered all of Manchuria and set up a puppet state there that they called Manzhouguo (mahn joh GWOH).

When the League of Nations condemned Japanese aggression against China, Japan simply

Japan's Expanding Empire to 1934

Map legend:
- Japan, 1890
- Territory added by 1918
- Territory added by 1934
- Main manufacturing areas
- Bauxite
- Coal
- Copper
- Gold
- Iron ore
- Petroleum

Azimuthal Equal Area Projection
0 — 400 — 800 Miles
0 — 400 — 800 Kilometers

Chapter 29 **739**

The Tokyo Earthquake of 1923

Bell Ringer For some people, the aftershocks of a major earthquake are more traumatizing than the actual quake. Ask students to speculate on why that may be true.

Background
Connections to Today

Kobe Earthquake, 1995 Although not as bad as the 1923 earthquake, the quake that struck Kobe, Japan, in January 1995 was horribly destructive. More than 5,000 people died and nearly 27,000 were injured. About 300,000 people were left homeless, and property damage was estimated at $400 billion. Rescue workers and firefighters were hampered by a city-wide traffic gridlock. The city and national governments came under sharp criticism because of their slow response to the emergency. The city's water lines, for example, were ruptured, and residents were without clean running water for weeks.

Activity
Cooperative Learning

Researching Earthquakes Have groups of students look into the scientific causes of earthquakes and make an illustrated report of their findings. Some groups may research the *tsunamis* that often accompany earthquakes. Alternately, one or more groups may do additional research on the 1923 earthquake. One book on the subject is *Two Minutes to Noon* by Noel F. Busch (New York: Simon & Schuster, 1962).

Portfolio Assessment Rubrics

Share rubrics with students.

Attempted The student does not complete the assignment.

Minimal The student lists three earthquakes but does not locate them on a map and does not accurately answer the questions.

Adequate The student accurately lists three earthquakes, locates them on a map, and completely answers the questions.

Exemplary The student accurately identifies and locates at least three earthquakes, provides illustrations, and gives thorough, well-researched answers to the questions.

On September 1, 1923, an earthquake of historic proportions struck the Tokyo-Yokohama area. One of the most destructive quakes in history, it was followed by widespread fires. The main quake, which lasted only four minutes, measured 8.3 on the Richter scale. It was followed by about 300 aftershocks.

Fleeing the flames and destruction, people poured into the streets. They used bicycles and wagons to salvage whatever belongings they could carry.

An office worker in Yokohama reported, "Without warning, came the first rumbling jar of an earthquake, a sickening sway, the vicious grinding of timbers and, in a few seconds, a crescendo of turmoil as the floor began to heave and the building to lurch drunkenly. . . . Walls bulged, spread and sagged, pictures danced on their wires, flew out and crashed to splinters."

—Otis Manchester Poole,
The Death of Old Yokohama

Most buildings were constructed in the traditional style with wood and paper, making them very vulnerable to fire.

Fast Facts

- An average of 1,500 earthquakes strike Japan each year.

- The 1923 earthquake caused the deaths of about 140,000 people and damaged as many as 700,000 buildings.

- Possibly 45 percent of surviving workers lost their jobs because so many businesses were destroyed.

Portfolio Assessment

INTERNET Use the Internet or other research sources to learn more about world earthquakes. List three of the most destructive earthquakes in modern history and pinpoint them on a map. Why are some regions of the world more vulnerable to earthquakes than others? How can buildings be designed to combat the effects of earthquakes?

Resource Directory

Teaching Resources

Disaster! Chapter Extension Activities booklet, p. 71
Section Quiz Unit 7 booklet, p. 47
Geography Quiz Unit 7 booklet, p. 52
Chapter Test Forms A, B, and C Unit 7 booklet, pp. 53–57
Answer Key Unit 7 booklet, pp. 96–109

Technology

Interactive Student Tutorial CD-ROM Ch. 29
Computer Test Bank Ch. 29

withdrew itself from the League. When politicians in Tokyo objected to the army's highhanded actions, public opinion sided with the military.

Militarists in Power

By the early 1930s, ultranationalists were winning popular support for foreign conquests and a tough stand against the western powers. Members of "patriotic" societies assassinated a number of politicians and business leaders who opposed expansion. Military leaders plotted to overthrow the government and, in 1936, briefly occupied the center of Tokyo.

Traditional Values Revived Civilian government survived, but by 1937 it had been forced to accept military domination. To please the ultranationalists, it cracked down on socialists and ended most democratic freedoms. It revived ancient warrior values and built a cult around the emperor, who was believed to be descended from the sun goddess.

To spread its nationalist message, the government focused on the schools. A government pamphlet, which became required reading in schools, criticized the Japanese adoption of western ideas:

> "With the influx of European and American culture into this country, . . . individualism, liberalism, utilitarianism, and materialism began to assert themselves, with the result that the traditional character of the country was much impaired and the virtuous habits and customs bequeathed by our ancestors were affected unfavorably."
> —from *The Way of Subjects,* quoted in *Human Record: Sources of Global History* (Andrea)

To practice "the way of subjects," students were taught absolute obedience to the emperor and service to the state.

Renewed Expansion During the 1930s, Japan took advantage of China's civil war to increase its influence there. Japan expected to complete its conquest of China within a few years. But in 1939, while the two nations were locked in deadly combat, World War II broke out in Europe. That conflict swiftly spread to Asia.

By 1939, Japan had joined with two aggressive European powers, Germany and Italy, in the alliance known as the Axis Powers. That alliance, combined with renewed Japanese conquests, would turn World War II into a brutal, wide-ranging conflict waged not only across the continent of Europe but across Asia and the islands of the Pacific as well.

SECTION 5 Assessment

Recall

1. **Identify:** (a) Hirohito, (b) Manzhouguo.
2. **Define:** (a) Diet, (b) ultranationalist.

Comprehension

3. What liberal changes occurred in Japan in the 1920s?
4. How did nationalists deal with the Great Depression?
5. (a) What goals did Japanese militarists pursue at home?
   (b) What goals did they pursue overseas?

Critical Thinking and Writing

6. **Comparing** Compare the policies pursued by Japanese liberals to those followed by Japanese conservatives during the 1920s and 1930s.
7. **Recognizing Cause and Effect** Why might a nation turn to military leaders and extreme nationalists during a time of crisis?

Activity

Creating a Time Line
Create a time line of the major events in Japan's shift from liberalism to militarism during the 1920s and 1930s. Briefly describe each event on the time line.

SECTION 5 Assessment

Recall
1. (a) Hirohito, p. 738 (b) Manzhouguo, p. 739 2. (a) Diet, p. 738 (b) ultranationalist, p. 739

Comprehension
3. In the 1920s, Japan experienced greater democracy as political parties grew stronger and elected members of the Diet exerted their power. By 1925, all adult men could vote. Women gained a few rights. The economy grew, and an international agreement with Britain and the United States limited naval power.
4. They demanded renewed expansion, and a group of Japanese army officers provoked an incident that provided the excuse to seize Manchuria. 5. (a) They wanted to revive ancient warrior values, build a cult centered on the emperor, crack down on socialists, and end most democratic freedoms. (b) They invaded China, hoping to build an Asian empire.

Critical Thinking and Writing
6. liberal policies: expanding democracy, encouraging international trade, signing treaties with Britain and the United States, decreasing military spending, and westernization; conservative policies: an end to democratic reforms, alliances with Germany and Italy, military expansion in Asia, and restoring traditional values 7. Possible answer: Military leaders and ultranationalists promised national security, military power, and cultural greatness.

Activity Rubrics

Share rubrics with students before they make their time lines.

Attempted The time line is not complete.

Minimal The time line has a rough scale and a few items; some are inaccurate, illegible, or misspelled.

Adequate The time line has several items and an accurate scale. Labels are legible and contain few mechanical errors.

Exemplary The time line has carefully chosen items and an accurate scale; labels are accurate and have no mechanical errors.

Human Drama Note

Lucky Escape When the Tokyo earthquake struck, the 88-year-old Prince Masayoshi Matsukata, a former samurai and politician who had by luck escaped more than one assassination attempt, was resting on the ground floor of his home in Kamakura. His son Saburo was on the second floor. After the quake struck, Saburo found himself inexplicably atop the roof of their collapsed villa. Fearing the worst, he and three servants began looking for the prince and his nurse. The prince's luck held: the two were found unhurt.

Test Preparation

Have students read the excerpt from *The Way of Subjects* on this page, and then answer the question below.

What does the word *bequeathed* mean in this passage?

A destroyed

B praised

C unaffected

(D) passed down

Creating a Chapter Summary

As a reteaching opportunity, pair a more able student with a less able student to complete this chapter summary.

Possible answers: **Sources of Discontent** *Mexico*—lack of land and education for peasants; lack of democracy; special privileges of wealthy landowners and foreign investors *Africa*—Europeans owned the best land and forced Africans to work on plantations or live in reserves; Africans were required to carry identification cards; and famine resulted from the emphasis on cash crops *Middle East*—resentment of Ottoman rule and European imperialism; feeling of betrayal by Europeans after World War I *India*—Amritsar massacre; forced reliance on British-made goods; inequalities of caste system *China*—Yuan's attempted dictatorship; foreign imperialism; the appeal of Marxism *Japan*—decline of traditions; economic depression; appeal of socialism; government corruption **Results** *Mexico*—civil war; new constitution; nationalization of industry; revival of native art forms *Africa*—British crushed protests; birth of Pan-Africanism; négritude movement stressed African roots in the arts *Middle East*—westernization of Egypt, Turkey, and Iran; rise of Arab nationalism; creation of mandates; conflict in Palestine between Arabs and Jews *India*—nonviolent protests led by Gandhi; restoration of Indian pride; increased tensions between Muslims and Hindus *China*—civil war; rise of communism under Mao Zedong; power struggle between Guomindang, Communists, and Japanese *Japan*—militarists and ultranationalists take power; restoration of traditional values; invasion of China; treaties with Germany and Italy

Building Vocabulary

1–6. Quiz definitions should show a clear understanding of the meanings of the terms.

Recalling Key Facts

7. It resulted in less interference in Latin American affairs. Troops were withdrawn from Haiti and Nicaragua, and the Platt Amendment limiting Cuban independence was lifted.

8. It brought together Africans and people of African descent who lived outside of Africa.

9. He replaced Islamic law and the Muslim calendar. He also replaced

---

Creating a Chapter Summary

Copy this chart on a piece of paper. Then, fill in the chart with facts about revolutions and national movements around the world. Some entries have been completed to serve as a sample.

For additional review and enrichment activities, see the interactive version of *World History* available on the Web and on CD-ROM.

NATIONALISM AND REVOLUTION AROUND THE WORLD (1910–1939)

SOURCES OF DISCONTENT		RESULTS
• Lack of land and education for peasants •	MEXICO	• Civil war •
•	AFRICA	•
•	MIDDLE EAST	•
•	INDIA	•
•	CHINA	•
•	JAPAN	•

Web Site Self-Test
For practice test questions for Chapter 29, see
www. phschool.com.

Building Vocabulary

Review the chapter vocabulary words listed below. Then, use the words and their definitions to create a matching quiz. Exchange quizzes with another student. Check each other's answers when you are finished.

1. **nationalization**
2. **apartheid**
3. **polygamy**
4. **ahimsa**
5. **civil disobedience**
6. **ultranationalist**

Recalling Key Facts

7. How did the Good Neighbor Policy change United States relations with Latin America?
8. How did Pan-Africanism affect people around the world?
9. How did Atatürk try to transform Turkey into a modern, secular state?
10. How did World War I affect relations between India and Britain?
11. What three-sided struggle took place in China from 1937 to 1945?
12. How did the Great Depression affect political activity in Japan?

Critical Thinking and Writing

13. **Making Inferences** **(a)** What were the three main issues addressed by the Mexican Constitution of 1917? **(b)** What groups do you think welcomed the constitution? **(c)** What groups might have opposed the constitution? Explain.
14. **Connecting to Geography** Why did some European Jews choose to move to Palestine in the early 1900s?
15. **Linking Past and Present** **(a)** Describe Gandhi's methods of nonviolence and civil disobedience. **(b)** How are methods used by other groups seeking social or political change similar to those used by Gandhi?
16. **Drawing Conclusions** Do you think the rise of militarism in Japan could have been avoided? Explain.
17. **Synthesizing Information** How is political independence related to economic independence? Explain your answer using examples from the nations in this chapter.

Muslim script with a western alphabet, forced people to wear western dress, closed religious schools, and changed rules regarding women.
10. India's sacrifices for Britain in World War I led to the growth of Indian demands for independence.
11. a struggle among the Guomindang, the Communists, and the Japanese
12. It raised ultranationalist influence by harming the economy.

Critical Thinking and Writing

13. **(a)** land, religion, and labor **(b)** peasants, factory workers, miners, women **(c)** large landowners,

foreign investors, the Church; they lost some control of resources
14. Possible answer: because of British promises to the Jews and the historical ties Jews had to Palestine
15. **(a)** He urged his followers to boycott British goods, demonstrate peacefully, and disregard unjust British laws. **(b)** They were also nonviolent means of protest.
16. Students who believe it was avoidable might argue that western imperialism provoked Japanese militarism. Those who think it was unavoidable might argue that there is a historical tradition of militarism in Japan.

Skills Assessment
Analyzing Primary Sources

Delegates to the Second Pan-African Congress wrote a manifesto to state their beliefs and goals. Use this excerpt from the *Manifesto* to answer the questions that follow.

> "The absolute equality of races— physical, political and social—is the founding stone of world peace and human advancement. . . .
>
> That in the vast range of time, one group should in its industrial technique, or social organization, or spiritual vision, lag a few hundred years behind another, or forge fitfully ahead, . . . is proof of the essential richness and variety of human nature. . . . The doctrine of racial equality does not interfere with individual liberty, rather, it fulfills it. . . .
>
> It is the duty of the world to assist in every way the advance of the backward and suppressed groups of mankind. . . .
>
> The habit of democracy must be made to encircle the earth. Despite the attempt to prove that its practice is the secret and divine gift of the few, no habit is more natural or more widely spread, . . . or more easily capable of development among masses. . . . "
>
> —*Manifesto of the Second Pan-African Congress*

18. What, according to the *Manifesto*, is proved by different levels of accomplishment among groups of people?

19. Why should wealthier nations aid poorer nations?

20. What does the *Manifesto* say about the spread of democracy?

21. How might the *Manifesto* encourage African pride and nationalism?

Skills Assessment

Take It to the NET

Use the Internet to research nationalist movements in Mexico, China, or an African nation during the early 1900s. Then, create a piece of artwork that reflects the ideals of the movement. You may want to create a sculpture or painting, or design a small mural.

Skills Assessment
Analyzing Maps

Civil War in China, 1925–1935

Legend:
→ Route of Jiang Jieshi, 1926–1928
→ Route of Long March, 1934–1935
▨ Controlled by Guomindang, 1927
▨ Communist bases

Use this map, as well as information from the chapter, to answer the following questions:

22. What areas were controlled by Japan?

23. When did Jiang Jieshi's march take place?

24. When did the Long March take place?

25. (a) In what region did the Long March begin? (b) In what city did it end?

26. Based on the map, which group would seem more likely to come into conflict with Japanese armies? Explain your answer.

Skills Tip

Many maps present information within a certain time period. Read the title, legend, and caption carefully to identify the time period shown in the map.

Analyzing Primary Sources

18. the essential richness and variety of human nature

19. It is their duty to do so.

20. Democracy is natural to all people and is attainable by all.

21. It would make Africans feel equal to people in developed nations.

Analyzing Maps

22. Formosa, Korea

23. 1926–1928

24. 1934–1935

25. (a) area around Hunan and Jiangxi; (b) Yenan

26. Jiang Jieshi, because the Japanese controlled Manchuria just north of Beijing.

Skills Tip

An equal area projection is one that shows areas in equal proportion to those on a globe of the same scale. The Skills Handbook in the front of the book has a lesson that will help students with this feature.

Unit Theme Activity

Remind students to continue working on their Unit Theme Activity. See rubrics for the activity on the unit opener page in the Teacher's Edition.

Take It to the NET

Direct students to **www.phschool.com** for links to sites that will help them get started on this assignment. Share rubrics with students.

Attempted The student does not complete the artwork, or the artwork reveals little understanding of the ideals of the particular nationalist movement.

Minimal The artwork shows some awareness of the ideals of the particular nationalist movement but is poorly executed.

Adequate The artwork is well conceived and clear, and it demonstrates a good grasp of the ideals of the particular nationalist movement.

Exemplary The artwork is original, creative, well researched, and well presented; and it shows a thorough understanding of the ideals of the particular nationalist movement.

Chapter 30 Planning Guide

Resource Manager

	CORE INSTRUCTION	READING/SKILLS
Chapter Level Resources	📁 **Teaching Resources** 📘 **Pacing Charts**, Ch. 30 📘 **Teaching With Themes**, p. 33 📺 **Color Transparencies**, p. F–61 💿 **Resource Pro®** Ch. 30 💻 **www.phschool.com** • eTeach	💿 **Book on CD**, Ch. 30 💿 **Interactive Student Tutorial CD-ROM**, Ch. 30 💿 **Social Studies Skills Tutor CD-ROM** 📺 **Skills Transparencies**

1 The Western Democracies
 	
1. Discuss issues that Europe faced after World War I.
2. Outline how the Great Depression began and spread.
3. Summarize the ways Britain, France, and the United States tried to meet the challenges of the 1920s and 1930s.
	📁 **Teaching Resources**
	📘 **Unit 7 booklet**
	   • Biography Activity, p. 66
	📙 **Creative Teaching Activities**, p. 134
	💿 **Prentice Hall Presentation Pro**, Ch. 30, Section 1
	📺 **Section Reading Support Transparencies**
		📁 **Teaching Resources**
		📘 **Unit 7 booklet**
		   • Guided Reading and Review, p. 58
		   • Skill Application Activity, p. 750
		📙 **Guide to the Essentials**
		📼 **Guided Reading Audiotapes**, Ch. 30, Section 1

2 A Culture in Conflict
 	
1. Analyze how new views revolutionized modern science and thought.
2. Identify the artistic and literary trends that emerged in the 1920s.
3. Summarize changes in western society after World War I.
	📁 **Teaching Resources**
	📘 **Unit 7 booklet**
	   • Primary Source Activity, p. 67
	📙 **Creative Teaching Activities**, p. 135
	💿 **Prentice Hall Presentation Pro**, Ch. 30, Section 2
	📺 **Section Reading Support Transparencies**
		📁 **Teaching Resources**
		📘 **Unit 7 booklet**
		   • Guided Reading and Review, p. 60
		📙 **Guide to the Essentials**
		📼 **Guided Reading Audiotapes**, Ch. 30, Section 2

3 Fascism in Italy 1. Explain how conditions in Italy favored the rise of Mussolini. 2. Describe how Mussolini reshaped Italy. 3. Restate the values and goals of fascist ideology.	📁 **Teaching Resources** 📙 **Creative Teaching Activities**, p. 136 💿 **Prentice Hall Presentation Pro**, Ch. 30, Section 3 📺 **Section Reading Support Transparencies**	📁 **Teaching Resources** 📘 **Unit 7 booklet** • Guided Reading and Review, p. 62 📙 **Guide to the Essentials** 📼 **Guided Reading Audiotapes**, Ch. 30, Section 3

4 Hitler and the Rise of Nazi Germany
 	
1. Identify the problems the Weimar Republic faced.
2. Trace how Hitler came to power.
3. Enumerate the political, social, economic, and cultural policies Hitler pursued.
4. Discuss how Hitler took action against German Jews.
	📁 **Teaching Resources**
	📘 **Unit 7 booklet**
	   • Viewpoint Activity, p. 68
	📙 **Creative Teaching Activities**, p. 137
	💿 **Prentice Hall Presentation Pro**, Ch. 30, Section 4
		📁 **Teaching Resources**
		📘 **Unit 7 booklet**
		   • Guided Reading and Review, p. 64
		📙 **Guide to the Essentials**
		📼 **Guided Reading Audiotapes**, Ch. 30, Section 4

ENRICHMENT/PRE-AP

www.phschool.com
- Why Study History?

Teaching Resources
- **Chapter Extension Activities**, p. 72

www.phschool.com
- Virtual Field Trip
- Internet Activities, Jazz!
- Internet Activities, Section 2

Teaching Resources
- **Chapter Extension Activities**, p. 73
- **History Through Literature**, pp. 63–64

Color Transparencies, p. D–83

www.phschool.com
- Internet Activities, Section 4

ASSESSMENT

PRENTICE HALL ASSESSMENT SYSTEM

Core Assessment
- ExamView Test Bank booklet, Ch. 30
- ExamView Test Bank CD-ROM, Ch. 30

Standardized Test Preparation

Diagnose and Prescribe
- Diagnostic Tests for High School Social Studies Skills

Review and Reteach
- Review Book for World History

Practice and Assess
- Test-Taking Strategies With Transparencies for High School
- Alternative Assessment booklet
- Test Prep Book for World History

Teaching Resources
- **Unit 7 booklet**
  - Geography Quiz, p. 70
  - Section Quizzes, pp. 59, 61, 63, 65
  - Chapter Tests A, B, and C, pp. 71–75

www.phschool.com
- Self-Test

CUSTOMIZE FOR INDIVIDUAL NEEDS

Gifted and Talented
- **Teacher's Edition**, Activities: Interpreting Viewpoints, p. 764

Less Proficient Readers
- **Guide to the Essentials**, Ch. 30
- **Guided Reading Audiotapes, English**, Ch. 30
- **Book on CD**, Ch. 30
- **Teacher's Edition**, Activities: Cooperative Learning Activity, p. 750; Reading Strategy, p. 763

Less Proficient Writers
- **Teacher's Edition**, Activities: Customize for Heterogeneous Groups, p. 747; Customize for Auditory Learners, p. 754

Students Acquiring English/ESL
- **Guide to the Essentials, English/Spanish**, Ch. 30
- **Guided Reading Audiotapes, English/Spanish**, Ch. 30
- **Book on CD**, Ch. 30
- **Teacher's Edition**, Activities marked with an *

iTEXT

Don't miss the exclusive interactive version of *World History: Connections to Today* on the Internet and CD-ROM.

INTRODUCTION

After World War I, political and economic turmoil in the 1920s and 1930s in Europe challenged democratic traditions and led to the rise of powerful dictators. The Great Depression of the 1930s created financial chaos and widespread suffering throughout the industrialized world. Scientific discoveries, new trends in the arts, and social changes contributed to a sense of uncertainty. In the 1920s, Mussolini created a Fascist state in Italy. In the 1930s, Hitler rose to power, turning Germany into a Nazi dictatorship.

Focusing on Themes

Suggest that students focus on these theme questions as they read:

Economics and Technology
What were the causes and effects of the Great Depression?

Art and Literature
How did writers and artists reflect the mood of postwar Europe and the United States?

Political and Social Systems
Why did some countries turn to authoritarian governments in the postwar era?

Religions and Value Systems
What values did fascism uphold?

TIME LINE ACTIVITY

You may wish to share the About the Pictures note with your students before asking these questions about the time line:

1. Who created Europe's first fascist dictatorship? *(Benito Mussolini)*
2. When did the Great Depression begin in the United States? *(1929)*
3. When did Japan conquer Manchuria? *(1931)*
4. What does *Kristallnacht* mean, and whom did it affect? *("Night of Broken Glass"; German Jewish communities)*

Don't Miss!

Humanities Link
Jazz! (Section 2)

Synthesizing Information
Totalitarianism (Section 3)

Crisis of Democracy in the West 1919–1939

Chapter Preview

1 The Western Democracies
2 A Culture in Conflict
3 Fascism in Italy
4 Hitler and the Rise of Nazi Germany

CHAPTER EVENTS

1920s
Modern art flourishes in Europe. Paintings like *Composition No. 4* by Fernand Leger challenge realistic traditions and disturb many viewers.

1922
Benito Mussolini comes to power in Italy. Mussolini will create Europe's first fascist dictatorship.

1925
Seven European nations sign the Locarno treaties, raising hopes for world peace.

| 1915 | 1920 | 1925 |

GLOBAL EVENTS

1919 Amritsar massacre takes place in India.

1922 Britain declares Egypt independent.

Resource Directory

Teaching Resources
Chapter Theme Activities Teaching With Themes booklet, p. 33
Pacing Chart With Block Scheduling Guide Ch. 30
Technology
World History Color Transparencies Ch. 30 Graphic Organizer, p. F–61

Rise of Dictatorships in Europe, 1917–1939

State controlled by communist regime

Areas controlled by fascist or right-wing regimes

Dates on map indicate year of rise of communist or fascist regime

After World War I, political and economic turmoil challenged democratic traditions. Dictatorships arose in many European countries.

Map labels:
FINLAND
NORWAY
SWEDEN
ESTONIA 1933
LATVIA 1934
DENMARK
LITHUANIA 1926
IRELAND
UNITED KINGDOM
NETH.
EAST PRUSSIA (Germany)
UNION OF SOVIET SOCIALIST REPUBLICS 1917
BELGIUM
GERMANY 1933
POLAND 1926
LUX.
CZECHOSLOVAKIA
To Germany 1938–1939
To Hungary 1938–1939
FRANCE
SWITZ.
AUSTRIA To Germany 1938
HUNGARY 1932
ROMANIA 1938
PORTUGAL 1926
SPAIN 1939
YUGOSLAVIA 1929
ITALY 1922
BULGARIA 1935
ALBANIA To Italy 1939
GREECE 1936
ATLANTIC OCEAN
Mediterranean Sea
Adriatic Sea
Baltic Sea
Black Sea

Lambert Azimuthal Equal Area Projection
0   250   500 Miles
0   250   500 Kilometers

"Mates! help me get a job."

1929
The Great Depression begins in the United States. Economic collapse also causes hardship for people in other countries, as this British poster shows.

1930

1931 Japan conquers Manchuria.

1933
Nazi leader Adolf Hitler comes to power in Germany and begins building a totalitarian state.

1935

1934 Stalin launches Great Purge in the Soviet Union.

1938
During *Kristallnacht*, or the "Night of Broken Glass," Nazi mobs attack Jewish communities in Germany.

1940

1938 Mexico nationalizes foreign oil holdings.

Independent Assignments

Have students read one section as they prepare for class. After class, have them complete the assignment. Some students may benefit from using the Guided Reading and Review worksheets.

Section 1 Have students complete the worksheet *Sean O'Casey* in the Unit 7 booklet, p. 66, to learn more about the life of this Irish playwright.
Section 2 Have students complete the worksheet *Studying at the Bauhaus* in the Unit 7 booklet, p. 67, to learn about an American architect's experience studying at this famous design school.
Section 3 Have students complete the worksheet

The Sound of the Cicadas in the History Through Literature booklet, pp. 63–64, to learn how Mussolini's dictatorship indoctrinated the youth of Italy in fascism.

Section 4 Have students complete the worksheet *Hitler's Propaganda Machine* in the Unit 7 booklet, p. 68, to read two viewpoints about the use of propaganda to support Hitler.

Rise of Dictatorships in Europe, 1917–1939

Activating Prior Knowledge
How does the map reflect political changes in Europe as a result of the treaties that ended World War I? *(Germany, Russia, Austria-Hungary lost territory; Latvia, Lithuania, Estonia, Poland, Czechoslovakia, Austria, Hungary, Yugoslavia became countries.)*

Previewing
Why do you suppose France retained its democratic form of government while much of Europe did not? *(Possible answer: The French economy recovered fairly quickly because France received territory and war reparations from Germany. The French were not as discontented as people in Germany.)*

Background About the Pictures

1   2   3   4

1. *Composition No. 4,* 1920, by Fernand Léger (1881–1955), reflects the influence of the cubists. Léger was among the first to use the machine as a reflection of modern life.

2. Benito Mussolini, Italian Fascist dictator, pictured here, was expelled from three schools for violent behavior before, ironically, becoming a schoolmaster. Unsuited for teaching, Mussolini later used a career in journalism and trade unionism as a springboard to politics.

3. This 1935 election poster from Great Britain's national elections reflects the high unemployment rates of the Great Depression.

4. These smashed shop windows in Berlin are the aftermath of *Kristallnacht,* a rampage by Nazis against Jews. More than 7,000 Jewish businesses were destroyed, and 91 Jews died in the violence.

eTeach

Be sure to check out this month's online discussion with a World History Master Teacher.

Go to **www.phschool.com**.

Bell Ringer Have small groups of students discuss the problems that may affect nations recovering from war. Assign each student to write about three problems that might have afflicted European countries following World War I.

LESSON PLAN

1. Focus Following World War I, diplomats tried to ensure a lasting peace. They drafted treaties that renounced war, and they encouraged international cooperation in the League of Nations. Britain, France, and the United States, the leading democratic powers, faced difficult political and economic challenges both at home and abroad. When the Great Depression struck, businesses closed, global trade declined, and unemployment and poverty grew.

2. Instruct Divide the class into five or more groups and assign each group one of the following topics: (1) Postwar Issues, (2) Recovery and Depression, (3) Britain in the Postwar Era, (4) France in the Postwar Era, (5) The United States in the Postwar Era. Ask the groups to outline the main ideas of their topic. Then, on a separate sheet of paper, have them write five key questions pertaining to the ideas in their outlines. Collect one list of questions from each of the groups. Next, distribute to each group a list of questions for one of the topics that they did not do. Allow them time to work together and answer the questions. Continue collecting and redistributing the questions until each group has worked on all five topics.

3. Assess Have students choose one of the topics and use the answers to the five questions as the basis for an essay.

4. Reteach If students' Assess activity does not reflect adequate understanding of the lesson, you might assign the *Guide to the Essentials* or the *Interactive Student Tutorial CD-ROM* for this section.

Caption Answer

The figures are not shown with individual features. Instead, they represent the emotions that are felt by all people who suffer the horrible pains of war.

Reading Focus

■ What issues faced Europe after World War I?

■ How did the Great Depression begin and spread?

■ How did Britain, France, and the United States try to meet the challenges of the 1920s and 1930s?

Vocabulary

disarmament
overproduction
margin buying
general strike

Taking Notes

On a sheet of paper, make a table like this one. As you read this section, add information about the three democracies in the years after World War I.

BRITAIN	FRANCE	UNITED STATES
Economic problems		
Political drift to right		

Main Idea Following World War I, the leading democratic powers moved to ensure peace but faced difficult political and economic challenges.

Disillusion in Postwar Europe
German artist Käthe Kollwitz lost a son in World War I. In her 1923 woodcut *The Parents* (below), Kollwitz mirrors the sense of despair that gripped postwar Europe.

Theme: Art and Literature How does this picture make a universal statement about war?

Setting the Scene In his 1929 novel, *All Quiet on the Western Front*, German writer Erich Maria Remarque captured the disillusionment of the World War I generation. The novel's hero, a young German soldier, endures three years of grueling trench warfare. His friends are dead—butchered by bullets, shrapnel, artillery, or poison gas. In the last chapter, he wonders how he can return to civilian life feeling dead inside:

"Had we returned home in 1916, out of the suffering and the strength of our experience we might have unleashed a storm. Now if we go back we will be weary, broken, burnt out, rootless, and without hope. We will not be able to find our way any more."
—Erich Maria Remarque, *All Quiet on the Western Front*

The catastrophe of World War I shattered the sense of optimism that had grown in the West since the Enlightenment. Despair gripped survivors on both sides as they added up the staggering costs of the war. Especially among the democracies, economic and political crises only added to the growing pessimism of the 1920s and 1930s.

Postwar Issues

In 1919, three western democracies—Great Britain, France, and the United States—appeared powerful. They had ruled the Paris Peace Conference and boosted hopes for democracy among the new nations of Eastern Europe.

Underlying Problems Beneath the surface, however, postwar Europe faced grave problems. At first, the most pressing issues were finding jobs for returning veterans and rebuilding war-ravaged lands. Many nations also owed huge debts because they had borrowed heavily to pay for the war. In the early postwar years, economic problems fed social unrest and made radical ideas more popular. The Russian Revolution unleashed fears of the spread of communism. Some people saw socialism as the answer to hardships. Others embraced nationalistic political movements.

Other troubles clouded the international scene. As you have read, the peace settlements dissatisfied many Europeans, especially in Germany and among various ethnic groups in Eastern Europe. Finally, Europe lacked strong leaders just when they were most needed. The war had killed many of those who might have helped solve critical problems.

746 Chapter 30

The Pursuit of Peace During the 1920s, diplomats worked hard for peace. Hopes soared in 1925 when representatives from seven European nations signed a series of treaties at Locarno, Switzerland. These treaties settled Germany's disputed borders with France, Belgium, Czechoslovakia, and Poland. The Locarno treaties became the symbol of a new era. "France and Germany Ban War Forever," trumpeted a *New York Times* headline.

The hopeful "spirit of Locarno" was echoed in the Kellogg-Briand Pact of 1928. Almost every independent nation signed this agreement, promising to "renounce war as an instrument of national policy." In this optimistic spirit, the great powers pursued disarmament, the reduction of armed forces and weapons. The United States, Britain, France, Japan, and other nations signed treaties to reduce the size of their navies. However, they failed to agree on limiting the size of their armies.

Despite grumblings about the Versailles treaty, people around the world put great hopes in the League of Nations. From its headquarters in Geneva, Switzerland, the League encouraged cooperation and tried to get members to make a commitment to stop aggression. In 1926, after signing the Locarno agreements, Germany joined the League. Later, the Soviet Union was also admitted.

Obstacles to Peace Although the Kellogg-Briand Pact outlawed war, there was no way of enforcing the ban. The League of Nations, too, was powerless to stop aggressors. It had also been damaged by the American refusal to join. In 1931, the League vigorously condemned Japan's invasion of Manchuria, but to no effect. Noting the League's weakness, ambitious dictators rearmed their military forces and pursued aggressive foreign policies, as you will read.

Recovery and Depression

During the 1920s, Europe made a shaky recovery. Economies returned to peacetime manufacturing and trade. Veterans gradually found jobs. Middle-class families generally enjoyed a rising standard of living, with money to buy new products such as cars, refrigerators, and radios.

The United States emerged from the war as the world's leading economic power. American banks and businesses controlled a global network of trade and finance. American loans and investments backed the recovery in Europe. As long as the American economy was healthy, the global economy remained relatively prosperous.

A Dangerous Imbalance Both the American and the world economy had weak spots, however. One major problem was overproduction, a condition in which production of goods exceeds the demand for them. The war had increased demand for raw materials from Latin America, Africa, and Asia. Improved technology and farming methods also contributed to higher output. After the war, the demand for raw materials dwindled and prices fell. Consumers benefited from the lower prices. But farmers, miners, and other suppliers of raw materials suffered severe hardships.

At the same time, industrial workers won higher wages, which raised the price of manufactured goods. An imbalance emerged. Because farmers' earnings had fallen, they could afford fewer manufactured goods. Despite the slowing demand, factories kept pouring out goods. This imbalance, combined with other problems, undermined industrial economies. By the late 1920s, conditions were ripe for disaster.

HAVING AN INSURANCE POLICY DOESN'T MEAN YOU CAN DO WITHOUT FIRE PREVENTION

An End to War?
The Kellogg-Briand Pact raised hopes for an end to war. But not everyone was so optimistic, as this 1929 American cartoon shows.

Theme: Global Interaction Summarize the main idea of this cartoon in your own words.

☐ Block Scheduling Support

Have students listen to Woody Guthrie's ballad *Tom Joad,* which was inspired by the film version of John Steinbeck's novel *The Grapes of Wrath.* Guthrie, a champion of the working class and the poor, wrote the song because he wanted all the American people to hear the story of the Joad family and their struggles during the Great Depression. After students have listened to the song, tell them to imagine they are teenagers living on a farm during the Great Depression. Have them write a letter to President Roosevelt telling about the hardships their families have faced and how a government-funded work program would help them. (The song can be found on the LP titled *Woody Guthrie: Dust Bowl Ballads,* RCA Victor Vintage Series, 1964.)

Caption Answer

Possible answer: Although the Kellogg-Briand pact promised to outlaw war, the cartoonist feels that nations should still prepare for war by building up their armed forces.

Background
Historical Evidence

Impact of the Crash The effects of the stock market crash of 1929 were swift and severe. In the following excerpt, industrialist Arthur Robertson describes the immediate impact of the crash on investors and corporate executives:

"A cigar stock at the time was selling for $115 a share. The market collapsed. I got a call from the company president. Could I loan him $200 million? I refused, because at the time I had to protect my own fences, including those of my closest friends. His $115 stock dropped to $2 and he jumped out of the window of his Wall Street office. . . . On Wall Street the people walked around like zombies. . . . You saw people who yesterday rode around in Cadillacs lucky now to have carfare. One of my friends said to me, 'If things keep on as they are, we'll all have to go begging.' I asked, 'Who from?'"

You may wish to use this excerpt as the basis for a class discussion on the devastating shock of the stock market crash of 1929.

Primary Source

The Great Depression in Europe
British author George Orwell describes the desperation of the unemployed poor:

"In the 'dirt' that is sent up from the [coal] pits there is a certain amount of broken coal. . . . In Wigan the competition among unemployed people for [this] waste coal has become so fierce that it has led to an extraordinary custom called 'scrambling for the coal.' . . . [The process] consists in getting on to the train while it is moving.

No one was hurt the afternoon I was there, but a man had had both his legs cut off a few weeks earlier, and another man lost several fingers a week later. Technically it is stealing but, as everybody knows, if the coal were not stolen, it would simply be wasted."

—George Orwell,
The Road to Wigan Pier

Skills Assessment

Primary Source **What dangers were involved in "scrambling for the coal"?**

Crash and Collapse Few people saw the danger. In the United States, prices on the New York Stock Exchange soared. Eager investors acquired stocks through margin buying, paying part of the cost and borrowing the rest from brokers. In the autumn of 1929, jitters about the economy caused brokers to call in these loans. Investors who were unable to repay were forced to sell their stocks. Financial panic set in. Stock prices crashed, wiping out the fortunes of many investors.

The stock market crash triggered the Great Depression of the 1930s, a painful time of global economic collapse. The crash created financial turmoil in the industrial world as American banks stopped making loans abroad and demanded repayment of foreign loans.

In the United States and elsewhere, banks failed and businesses closed, throwing millions out of work. The cycle spiraled steadily downward. The jobless could not afford to buy goods, so more factories had to close, which in turn increased the numbers of unemployed. In once-prosperous western cities, people slept on park benches and lined up to eat in charity soup kitchens. Former business leaders sold apples in the street.

Global Impact Desperate governments tried to protect their economies from foreign competition. The United States imposed the highest tariffs in its history. The policy backfired because other nations retaliated by raising their tariffs. In the end, all countries lost access to the larger global market. As you have read, the Great Depression spread misery from the industrial world to the suppliers of agricultural goods and raw materials.

As the depression dragged on, many people lost faith in the ability of democratic governments to solve the problems. Misery and hopelessness created fertile ground for extremists who promised radical solutions. Communists gloated that capitalism had collapsed. Right-wing extremists played on themes of intense nationalism, the failure of democracy, the virtues of authoritarian rule, and the need to rearm.

Britain in the Postwar Era

Even before the depression, Britain faced economic problems. Although it emerged victorious from the war, much of its overseas trade was lost. German U-boats had wreaked havoc on British shipping. The nation was deeply in debt, and its factories were out of date.

During the 1920s, unemployment was severe. Wages remained low, leading to worker unrest and frequent strikes. In 1926, a general strike, or strike by workers in many different industries at the same time, lasted nine days and involved some three million workers.

Economics and Politics During the 1920s, the Labour party surpassed the Liberal party in strength. Labour leaders gained support among workers by promoting a gradual move toward socialism. The middle class, however, firmly backed the Conservative party, which held power during much of this period. Widespread fear of communism contributed to a drift toward the right. After the general strike, Conservatives passed legislation limiting the power of workers to strike.

The Great Depression intensified the nation's economic woes. As the crisis worsened, Britain set up a coalition government made up of leaders from all three major political parties. The coalition government provided some unemployment benefits to ease the worst problems. Despite such efforts, millions of people suffered great hardships.

Primary Source

ANSWER Possible answer: People could get injured jumping onto moving trains.

Resource Directory

Teaching Resources
Biography Activity *Sean O'Casey,* Unit 7 booklet, p. 66

Irish Independence At the war's end, Britain still faced the "Irish question." In 1914, you will recall, Parliament passed a home-rule bill that was shelved when the war began. Militant Irish nationalists, however, were unwilling to wait. On Easter 1916, a small group launched a revolt against British rule. Although the Easter Rising was quickly suppressed, the execution of 15 rebel leaders stirred wider support for their cause.

When Parliament again failed to grant home rule in 1919, revolution erupted in Ireland. Members of the Irish Republican Army (IRA) carried on a guerrilla war against British forces and their supporters. Civilians were often caught in the middle of the violence.

In 1922, moderates in Ireland and England reached an agreement. Most of Ireland became the self-governing Irish Free State.* The largely Protestant northern counties (Ulster) remained under British rule. However, the IRA and other opponents of the treaty never accepted the division. Civil war broke out. Although peace was restored in 1923, the status of Northern Ireland would remain a thorny issue through the end of the century.

Commonwealth and Empire In 1931, four former colonies—Canada, Australia, New Zealand, and South Africa—became fully self-governing dominions within the newly formed British Commonwealth of Nations. Although linked by economic and cultural ties, each member of the Commonwealth pursued its own course.

Despite challenges from nationalists, Britain retained its colonies. To the British, their vast empire remained a source of wealth and pride. At the same time, Britain worked to improve agriculture and education in its colonies while planning for gradual independence at some uncertain date.

Foreign Policy Britain's postwar foreign policy created tensions with its ally France. Almost from the signing of the Treaty of Versailles, British leaders wanted to relax the treaty's harsh treatment of Germany. They feared that if Germany became too weak, the Soviet Union would be able to expand and France might gain too much control on the continent. Britain's leniency toward Germany helped push France in the opposite direction.

---

*Ireland later became a fully independent republic known as Eire.

Ireland's Easter Rising
Although the Easter Rising of 1916 failed, it was a turning point in the struggle for Irish independence. This photograph shows the ruins of a nationalist base of operations in Dublin.

Theme: Political and Social Systems How was the Easter Rising both a success and a failure?

Chapter 30 **749**

Geography and History

The Maginot Line

The Maginot Line was a masterpiece of engineering. Most of the line was built underground, with interconnecting tunnels that stretched for miles. Main forts, placed strategically to protect river crossings and crossroads, were located about every three to five miles. These were self-contained underground structures over 20 feet beneath the surface. Large enough to accommodate about 1,200 men, the forts contained barracks, kitchens, infirmaries, storage depots, telephone systems, electrical generating systems, and railways to move supplies. All that could be seen above ground were the barrels of the huge guns and gun placements.

In the end, the line failed to prevent a German invasion. In 1940, German troops simply bypassed the Maginot Line and marched into France.

Theme: Geography and History Look at a map of Europe. What routes could a German army take to bypass the German–French border and invade France?

France Pursues Security

Like Britain, France emerged from World War I both a victor and a loser. Fighting on the Western Front had devastated northern France. The French had suffered enormous casualties. Survivors felt battered and insecure.

The French economy recovered fairly rapidly, thanks in part to German reparations and to territories gained from Germany, including Alsace and Lorraine. Later, the Great Depression did not hurt France as much as it did some countries. French industry was not as centralized in the hands of big business. Small workshops served local regions and were less affected by global trends.

Coalition Governments Economic swings did occur, adding to an unstable political scene. Political divisions and financial scandals continued to plague the Third Republic. Many parties—from conservatives to communists—competed for power. During the postwar years, France was again ruled by a series of coalition governments.

In 1936, several leftist parties united behind the socialist leader Leon Blum. His Popular Front government tried to solve labor problems and passed some social legislation. But it could not satisfy more radical leftists. Strikes soon brought down Blum's government. Thus, France, like Britain, muddled through a series of crises. Democracy survived, but the country lacked strong leadership that could respond to the clamor for change.

The Maginot Line France's chief concern after the war was securing its borders against Germany. The French remembered with distrust the German invasions of 1870 and 1914. To prevent a third invasion, France built massive fortifications along the border. The Maginot (MA zhee noh) Line, as this defensive "wall" was called, offered a sense of security—a false one. The line would be of little use when Germany again invaded in 1940.

In its quest for security, France strengthened its military and sought alliances with other countries, including the Soviet Union. It insisted on strict enforcement of the Versailles treaty and complete payment of reparations, hoping to keep the German economy weak.

Prosperity and Depression in the United States

The United States emerged from World War I in excellent shape. A late entrant into the war, it had suffered relatively few casualties and little loss of property. It led the world in industrial and agricultural output. American money helped finance the European recovery.

Postwar Issues As you have read, the United States stayed out of the League of Nations. Arguing that membership might lead to involvement in future foreign wars, many Americans insisted that the nation maintain its free hand in foreign affairs. Still, during the 1920s, the United States took a leading role in international diplomacy. It sponsored the Kellogg-Briand Pact, pressed for disarmament, and worked to reduce German reparations.

Fear of bomb-throwing radicals and the Bolshevik Revolution in Russia set off a "Red Scare" in 1919 and 1920. Police rounded up suspected foreign-born radicals, and a number were expelled from the United States. The "Red Scare" fed growing demands to limit immigration. Millions of immigrants from southern and eastern Europe had poured into the United States between 1890 and 1914. Some native-born Americans sought to exclude these newcomers, whose cultures differed from those of earlier settlers from northern Europe. In response, Congress passed laws limiting immigration from Europe. Earlier laws had already excluded or limited Chinese and Japanese immigration.

Boom and Bust In the boom years of the 1920s, middle-class Americans were enjoying the benefits of capitalism. They stocked their homes with

Geography and History

ANSWER Possible answer: north of the line, through Belgium radios, refrigerators, and automobiles. Most Americans agreed with President Calvin Coolidge that "the business of America is business."

The 1929 stock market crash shattered this mood of prosperity. President Herbert Hoover firmly believed that the government should not intervene in private business matters. However, as hard times got worse, he did try a variety of limited measures to solve the crisis. Nothing seemed to work.

The New Deal In 1932, Americans elected a new President, Franklin D. Roosevelt. "FDR" projected a sense of energy and optimism. Arguing that the government had to take an active role in combating the Great Depression, he introduced the New Deal, a massive package of economic and social programs.

Under the New Deal, the federal government became more directly involved in people's everyday lives than ever before. New laws regulated the stock market and protected bank depositors' savings. Government programs created jobs for the unemployed and gave aid to farmers. A new Social Security system provided old-age pensions and other benefits that major European countries had introduced years earlier.

The New Deal failed to end the Great Depression, but it did ease the suffering for many. Still, some critics fiercely condemned FDR's expansion of the role of government. As a result of the New Deal, many Americans came to expect the government to intervene directly to promote their economic well-being. The debate about the size and role of the federal government continues to this day.

Cause and Effect

Long-Term Causes	Immediate Causes
• Worldwide interrelationship of governments and economies • Huge war debts • American loans to Europe • Widespread use of credit • Overproduction of goods • Industrial wages rise as farm earnings fall	• New York stock market crash • Farmers unable to repay loans • Banks demand repayment of loans • American loans to other countries dry up • Without capital, businesses and factories fail

Worldwide Economic Depression

Immediate Effects	Long-Term Effects
• Vast unemployment and misery • Protective tariffs imposed • Loss of faith in capitalism and democracy • Authoritarian leaders emerge	• Rise of fascism and Nazism • Governments experiment with social programs • People blame scapegoats • World War II begins

Connections to Today

• Government monitoring of or control of national economies, banks, credit, and stock markets
• Continuation of social programs
• Monitoring of worldwide economic developments by international agencies

Skills Assessment **Chart** Economists still debate the causes and effects of the Great Depression. **How do governments today deal with the kinds of conditions that caused the depression?**

SECTION 1 Assessment

Recall
1. **Identify:** (a) Locarno treaties, (b) Kellogg-Briand Pact, (c) IRA, (d) Commonwealth of Nations, (e) Leon Blum, (f) Maginot Line, (g) New Deal.
2. **Define:** (a) disarmament, (b) overproduction, (c) margin buying, (d) general strike.

Comprehension
3. (a) What steps did the major powers take to protect the peace? (b) Why did these moves have limited effects?
4. Explain how each of the following contributed to the outbreak or spread of the Great Depression: (a) overproduction, (b) margin buying, (c) high tariffs.
5. How did the Great Depression affect political developments in the United States?

Critical Thinking and Writing
6. **Understanding Causes and Effects** Why do you think the 1926 general strike in Britain strengthened the Conservative party?
7. **Applying Information** How did Britain and France emerge from World War I as both victors and losers?

Activity

Creating a Political Cartoon Draw a political cartoon that might have appeared in an American or British newspaper in 1932. The cartoon should show how the effects of the Great Depression often undermined confidence in democracy.

Chapter 30 **751**

SECTION 1 Assessment

Recall
1. (a) Locarno treaties, p. 747 (b) Kellogg-Briand Pact, p. 747 (c) IRA, p. 749 (d) Commonwealth of Nations, p. 749 (e) Leon Blum, p. 750 (f) Maginot Line, p. 750 (g) New Deal, p. 751 2. (a) disarmament, p. 747 (b) overproduction, p. 747 (c) margin buying, p. 748 (d) general strike, p. 748

Comprehension
3. (a) The major powers signed treaties to settle borders, to renounce the use of war, and to reduce the size of their navies. They also participated in the League of Nations. (b) The Kellogg-Briand Pact was unenforceable, and the League of Nations failed. 4. (a) Factories produced more goods than consumers could purchase, causing economic collapse. (b) Many investors bought stocks on margin. When brokers called in the loans, investors panicked, and stock prices crashed. (c) Governments tried to protect their economies from foreign competition by raising tariffs, which cut off all countries from global markets. 5. In response to the Depression, President Roosevelt introduced the New Deal, a massive package of economic and social programs, including social security.

Critical Thinking and Writing
6. Possible answer: The general strike disrupted businesses and services and raised fear of a communist revolt; many people turned to the Conservative party, which promised stability and limits on strikes. 7. They had won the war and gained territory, but the war had cost massive losses in life and property.

Activity Rubrics

Share rubrics with students before they begin their cartoons.

Attempted The cartoon is incomplete.

Minimal The cartoon shows limited understanding of the topic.

Adequate The cartoon is well researched and clearly drawn; it shows good understanding of the topic.

Exemplary The cartoon is original, well researched, perceptive, and well executed.

Skills Assessment

ANSWER Possible answer: Government measures include regulating stock markets, insuring savings accounts in banks, and providing unemployment and social security protection.

Human Drama Note

Works Progress Administration Responding to the nation's widespread unemployment, which by the spring of 1935 affected 20 percent of the labor force, Roosevelt created the Works Progress Administration (WPA). WPA workers improved roads, built bridges, repaired public buildings, created new parks, and engaged in archaeological digs. Non-construction projects included taking care of children, counting houses, painting murals, and canning peaches. Three years after its inception, the program came under attack in Congress by Republicans and conservative Democrats. Their concern was that there had been radical political activity in some states, particularly among WPA actors and writers. Congress eliminated theater and other projects, citing waste as well as unacceptable political activity. By the time the WPA was phased out in 1943, more than $10 billion had been pumped into the American economy and thousands of needy Americans had been employed.

SECTION 2   A Culture in Conflict

Bell Ringer

Bell Ringer To introduce this section, play recorded selections of early Duke Ellington, Louis Armstrong or other early jazz musicians' work. Point out that this music symbolized the era that students will read about in this section.

LESSON PLAN

1. Focus Western culture experienced much change in the years after World War I. Advances in chemistry, physics, and human psychology revolutionized science and thought. Writers expressed a loss of faith and purpose. Artists revolted against traditional styles and created new ways of viewing the world. Women continued to make gradual progress in politics, education, and other fields.

2. Instruct Organize students into groups. Tell them that they are to plan an exhibit that commemorates the changes western culture underwent during the early 1900s. Assign each group one of the following topics: Science; Art and Architecture; Literature; Film, Music, and Dance; Social Changes. The groups should use the text and outside resources to outline the major developments that occurred in their assigned areas. They should then make a list of the items that they will present as part of their exhibits. They might also present samples of these for the class to view or hear. Presentations could include works of art or literature, musical selections, dance performances, reenactments, dialogues, diagrams, excerpts from primary sources, or other exhibits.

3. Assess Ask students to explain the meaning of this section's title—"A Culture in Conflict."

4. Reteach If students' Assess activity does not reflect adequate understanding of the lesson, you might assign the *Guide to the Essentials* or the *Interactive Student Tutorial CD-ROM* for this section.

Biography

ANSWER Possible response: Most women of her time did not have both a family and a career, especially a career in science. She worked as a partner with her husband in research, and her achievements were considered as important as his.

SECTION 2 A Culture in Conflict

Reading Focus

■ How did new views revolutionize modern science and thought?

■ What artistic and literary trends emerged in the 1920s?

■ How did western society change after World War I?

Vocabulary

psychoanalysis
abstract
surrealism
stream of consciousness
flapper

Taking Notes

On a sheet of paper, draw a concept web like the one shown here. As you read this section, fill in important information about cultural changes. Add as many circles as you need.

Main Idea Western culture experienced great changes in the years following World War I.

Biography

Marie Curie 1867–1934

Marie Curie won two Nobel prizes, one in physics and one in chemistry. Still, like many other women, she had to balance her work with home duties. "I have a great deal of work," she said, "what with the housekeeping, the children, the teaching, and the laboratory, and I don't know how I shall manage it all."

Curie won worldwide fame for her groundbreaking research on radioactivity. But she paid a high price for knowledge. Her fingertips were often burned from handling radioactive material. Although she shrugged off the health dangers, she died from radiation poisoning.

Theme: Impact of the Individual Why do you think Marie Curie's achievements were unique for her time?

Setting the Scene In 1921, the Irish poet William Butler Yeats summed up the mood of many postwar writers and artists:

> "Things fall apart; the centre cannot hold;
> Mere anarchy is loosed upon the world,
> The blood-dimmed tide is loosed, and everywhere
> The ceremony of innocence is drowned."
> —William Butler Yeats, "The Second Coming"

It was not only the war that fostered this sense of uncertainty, of civilization falling apart. New ideas and scientific discoveries were challenging long-held ideas about the nature of the world.

New Views of the Universe

The ancient Greeks were the first to propose that all matter is composed of tiny, indivisible atoms. Over the centuries, most scientists came to accept this idea. But discoveries made in the late 1800s and early 1900s showed that the atom was more complex than anyone suspected.

Radioactivity By the early 1900s, the Polish-born French scientist Marie Curie and others were experimenting with radioactivity. They found that the atoms of certain elements, such as radium and uranium, spontaneously release charged particles. As scientists studied radioactivity further, they discovered that it could change atoms of one element into atoms of another. Such findings proved that atoms were not solid and indivisible.

Relativity By 1905, the German-born physicist Albert Einstein advanced his theories of relativity. Einstein argued that measurements of space and time are not absolute but are determined by many factors, some of them unknown. This idea raised questions about Newtonian science, which compared the universe to a machine operating according to absolute laws.

In the postwar years, many scientists came to accept the theories of relativity. To much of the general public, however, Einstein's ideas seemed to reinforce the unsettling sense of old certainties crumbling and a universe whirling beyond the understanding of human reason.

Probing the Mind The Austrian physician Sigmund Freud (FROID) also challenged faith in reason. He suggested that the subconscious mind drives much human behavior. Freud said that, in civilized society, learned values such as morality and reason help people repress, or check, powerful urges.

Resource Directory

Teaching Resources

Creative Teaching Activities Creative Teaching Activities booklet, p. 135

Guided Reading and Review Unit 7 booklet, p. 60

Virtual Field Trip

www.phschool.com

**The Salvador Dali Museum
St. Petersburg, Florida**

To see other works by this major artist, use the Internet address above to link to the Salvador Dali Museum.

A Masterpiece of Modern Art

The Persistence of Memory, by the Spanish artist Salvador Dali, is one of the most famous works of modern art. This 1931 painting seems to suggest a dream world where nothing is certain, not even time.

Theme: Art and Literature
How do you think people who admired traditional painting would have reacted to Dali's work?

Reading Strategy
Question Writing

Organize students into pairs. Have one student read aloud to the other student the main headings and subheadings of Section 2. Have the second student turn each heading into a question. Ask each pair to write down the questions and then work together to answer the questions as they read the section. *(More Advanced Readers)*

Background
Connections to Art

Painting the Subconscious Surrealist painters like Salvador Dali believed that rational thought thwarted true creativity and imagination. Dali portrayed this idea in his paintings, which he called "hand-colored photographs of the subconscious." The depiction of his subject matter in an altered state heightens the dreamlike and hallucinatory quality of his work. *The Persistence of Memory*, also known by its nickname "Soft Watches," destroys the notion of time as a concrete experience.

But an individual feels constant tension between repressed drives and social training. This tension, argued Freud, may cause psychological illness or physical symptoms, such as paralysis or blindness.

Freud pioneered psychoanalysis, a method of studying how the mind works and treating mental disorders. He analyzed dreams for clues to subconscious desires and developed ways to treat mental illnesses. His ideas had an impact far beyond medicine. Freud's work led artists and writers to explore the subconscious mind.

Modern Art and Architecture

In the early 1900s, many western artists rejected traditional styles. Instead of trying to reproduce the real world, they explored other dimensions of color, line, and shape. Painters, like Henri Matisse (mah TEES), outraged the public with their bold use of color and odd distortions. He and fellow artists were dubbed fauves (FOHVZ), or Wild Beasts.

New Directions in Painting Before the war, the Spanish artist Pablo Picasso and his friend Georges Braque (BRAHK) had created a revolutionary new style, called cubism. They broke three-dimensional objects into fragments and composed them into complex patterns of angles and planes. By redefining objects into separate shapes, they offered a new view of reality.

Later, the Russian Vasily Kandinsky and the German Paul Klee (KLAY) moved even further away from representing reality. Their artwork was abstract, composed of lines, colors, and shapes with no recognizable subject matter at all.

During and after the war, dada burst onto the Paris art world. Dada was a revolt against civilization. One dadaist proclaimed, "Dada is life without discipline or morality and we spit on humanity." Paintings by artists like Hans Arp and Max Ernst were intended to shock and disturb middle-class viewers.

Cubism and dada helped inspire surrealism, a movement that attempted to portray the workings of the unconscious mind. The Spanish surrealist Salvador Dali used images of melting clocks or burning giraffes to suggest the chaotic dream state described by Freud.

Background
Connections to Art

Fauvism The proliferation of photography was one of the reasons why Fauve painters rejected the idea of recreating the real world on canvas. If a photograph could show a sunset in all its detail, why should a painter try to reproduce the same image? This was the philosophy of Fauvists such as André Derain, who once noted:

"[Photography] counted in our reaction against anything that resembled a snapshot. No distance seemed great enough for us to take our stand in order to look at things. . . . Colours were supposed to become so many cartridges of dynamite, and they were supposed to let off light. We liked the idea, so new to us, that everything could be lifted above and beyond reality. And we took the idea seriously."

Block Scheduling Support

Have each student create flashcards for six individuals discussed in this section. On one side of each card, they should write the name of the person. On the other side, they should write a sentence describing that person's impact on postwar culture. When they have finished, have students form two lines facing each other. Instruct students in one line to show the sentence side of their cards one at a time to the person directly across from them. That person should read the cards and name the individuals, if they can. If they cannot, the holder of the cards should flip them over to reveal the answers. Students should then switch roles. When both students have seen each other's cards, they change partners by having one line move and the other remain stationary. Students in the moving line should take a few steps until they are facing the next person in the line opposite them. The person at the end of the moving line goes to the head of the line. Repeat the process until students in the moving line return to the position from which they started.

Caption Answer

Possible answer: They might have been confused and disturbed, because Dali's work did not depict reality in a familiar, comfortable way.

Connections to Literature

Making Inferences Ernest Hemingway served in World War I as an ambulance driver for the American Red Cross. His wartime experiences in Italy had a lasting influence on his writing. In his terse prose, Hemingway voiced the disillusionment and hopelessness of the postwar era's "lost generation."

Assign students to read "In Another Country," a work that can be found in various anthologies of Hemingway's short stories. In the story, which tells about the futility of trying to heal the wounds of war, doctors use modern technology to restore the damaged and lost limbs of wounded soldiers. However, no machine can replace the loss of meaning and purpose that cripples the hearts and wracks the minds of the war's survivors.

After students have read the story, have them answer the following questions: (1) In what ways are the veterans of World War I "crippled"? (2) Why do they have no faith in the restorative powers of modern technology? (3) How does this story reflect the "loss of faith" that is discussed in the text?

Customize for . . .
Auditory Learners

Linking Past and Present Read aloud the following observation made by the historian Frederick Lewis Allen. Then, ask students to discuss the questions that follow.

"All nations, in all eras of history, are swept from time to time by waves of contagious excitement over fads or fashions or dramatic public issues. . . . One of the striking characteristics of the . . . [1920s] was the unparalleled rapidity and unanimity with which millions of men and women turned their attention, their talk, and their emotional interest upon a series of tremendous trifles."

(1) What are some of the most popular fads and fashions of today? (2) Why do fads and fashions often spread rapidly and disappear rapidly? (3) Do you agree with the historian's observation that people are often captivated by "tremendous trifles"? Explain.

Connections to Today

ANSWER Possible answer: Movie stars are admired and imitated by many. They appeal to the imagination and fantacies of everyone.

Connections to Today

Going to the Movies
Movies have come a long way in 100 years. Yet today's traditions have roots in the early days of film.

- The first science fiction film was made in 1902. In *A Trip to the Moon,* French magician Georges Méliès pioneered stop motion photography and other special effects. Today, audiences flock to sci-fi spectaculars like the *Star Wars* series and *Men in Black.*

- In 1928, Walt Disney released the first animated cartoon with sound, *Steamboat Willie,* starring Mickey Mouse. Today, Mickey is loved around the world, and the Disney studios continue to make popular animated films such as *The Lion King* and *Tarzan.*

- In 1929, the first Academy Awards were given out at an 11-minute ceremony. Some 250 guests attended. Today, millions of people around the world watch the "Oscars"—and the ceremony takes more than three hours!

Theme: Continuity and Change Why do you think movies and movie stars continue to be popular around the world?

Architecture Architects, too, rejected classical traditions and developed new styles to match an industrial, urbanized world. The famous Bauhaus school in Germany influenced architecture by blending science and technology with design. Bauhaus designers used glass, steel, and concrete but little ornamentation.

The American architect Frank Lloyd Wright reflected the Bauhaus belief that the function of a building should determine its form. When designing a house, he used materials and forms that fit its environment.

The New Literature

In the 1920s, war novels, poetry, plays, and memoirs flowed off the presses. Works like Remarque's *All Quiet on the Western Front* exposed the grim horrors of modern warfare. Other writers heaped scorn on blundering military and political leaders. Their works reflected a powerful disgust with war that would color the European scene for decades.

A Loss of Faith To many postwar writers, the war symbolized the moral breakdown of western civilization. In 1922, the American-born English poet T. S. Eliot published *The Waste Land.* This long poem portrays the modern world as spiritually empty and barren. In *The Sun Also Rises,* the American novelist Ernest Hemingway shows the rootless wanderings of young people who lack deep convictions. "I did not care what it was all about," says the narrator. "All I wanted to know was how to live in it."

Literature of the Inner Mind As Freud's ideas became popular, some writers experimented with stream of consciousness. In this technique, a writer appears to probe a character's random thoughts and feelings without imposing any logic or order. In novels like *Mrs. Dalloway,* British novelist Virginia Woolf used stream of consciousness to explore the hidden thoughts of people as they go through the ordinary actions of their everyday lives.

The Irish novelist James Joyce went even further. In *Finnegans Wake,* he explores the inner mind of a hero who remains sound asleep throughout the novel. To convey the freedom and playfulness of the unconscious mind, Joyce invented many words—including some, like bababadalgharagtakamminarronnkonnbronntonnerronntuonnthunntrovarrhounawnskawntoohoohoordenenthurnuk, 100 letters long!

A Changing Society

In the aftermath of World War I, many people yearned to return to "normalcy"—to life as it had been before 1914. But rapid social changes would make it hard to turn back the clock.

A New Popular Culture New technologies helped create a mass culture shared by millions in the world's developed countries. Affordable cars gave middle-class people greater mobility. Movie stars such as Charlie Chaplin had fans on every continent. Radios brought news, music, and sports into homes throughout the western world.

Many radios were tuned to the new sounds of jazz. Jazz was pioneered by African American musicians who combined western harmonies with African rhythms. Jazz musicians, like trumpeter Louis Armstrong, took simple melodies and improvised endless subtle variations in rhythm and beat. They produced music that was both original and popular.

Europeans embraced American popular culture, with its greater freedom and willingness to experiment. The nightclub and the sound of jazz were symbols of that freedom. In fact, the 1920s are often called the Jazz Age.

The Younger Generation After the war, rebellious young people rejected the moral values and rules of the Victorian Age and chased after excitement.

Resource Directory

Teaching Resources
Primary Source Activity *Studying at the Bauhaus,* Unit 7 booklet, p. 67
Humanities Link Chapter Extension Activities booklet, p. 72

Technology
Listening to Literature World Masterpieces audiotapes poems by Paul Valéry and Federico García Lorca, side 8, running time 4:22 min.

Humanities Link

JAZZ!

Jazz is a lively improvisational musical style that first appeared in the bustling port of New Orleans in the early 1900s. It is actually a blend of many different musical traditions, including African rhythms and spirituals. Jazz caught on quickly, and by the 1920s there were jazz clubs in many cities across North America and Europe. Much of today's music, including rock and rap, has been influenced by jazz.

Louis Armstrong was one of the early jazz musicians from New Orleans. In 1922, he left New Orleans to play in Chicago. His improvised trumpeting and "scat" singing set a standard for later musicians.

Duke Ellington was a gifted piano player and composer. Born in Washington, D.C., he went to New York to pursue his career. His popular tunes include "Take the A Train."

In the 1920s, record companies began to record jazz music. The music was pressed onto vinyl discs, which were often marked with colorful labels.

Portfolio Assessment

INTERNET Use the Internet or library resources to find out more about jazz and listen to some recordings of jazz music. Then, write a song or a poem, either in the style of jazz lyrics or describing the sound of the music.

🔔 **Bell Ringer** Have students study the photograph of Duke Ellington on this page. Then, ask students to describe possible differences between his band and ones that are currently popular.

*B*ackground
Connections to Today

Modern Jazz Jazz continues to evolve as an art form. Its main characteristic, improvisation, has allowed it to borrow from and build upon other musical forms, often giving musical voice to changing times. Jazz mirrored the tumultuous years between World War I and the Great Depression. Large bands usually featured several trumpets, trombones, and saxophones in a brassy, exciting sound, combined with piano, bass, and drums. Closely associated with dance, jazz in the late 1920s and into the 1930s was often performed in large ballrooms. Innovations continued throughout the decades of the twentieth century, including avant-garde and "free jazz" in the 1960s and 1970s. Influenced by rock music, jazz adopted electronic instruments such as synthesizers and the electric piano.

*A*ctivity
Cooperative Learning

Interpreting Viewpoints Have small groups research a particular jazz musician, chosen from a short list of both early and contemporary musicians. Each group will prepare a five- to ten-minute presentation that should include information on the musician's contribution to the form, his or her impact on others, and a short selection of the artist's music.

Activity Rubrics

Share rubrics with students before they write their jazz song or poem.

Attempted The poem or song does not reflect jazz style or is incomplete.

Minimal The poem or song does not strongly present the jazz style.

Adequate The poem or song shows a good understanding of the jazz style.

Exemplary The poem or song is original, well executed, and representative of the jazz style.

Creating a Surreal Landscape Show students other examples of surreal art. Explain that the surrealist painter Salvador Dali created a surprise effect for viewers by juxtaposing objects with seemingly no relation to each other. His landscapes may seem normal in the context of dreams. Have students create their own surreal landscapes. Give them the option of drawing or painting their landscapes, or allow them to create a verbal landscape in a free verse poem.

 Test Preparation

Have students read the section titled "The New Literature" on the opposite page, and then answer the question below.

Which of following words would not be associated with the literature of the 1920s?

(A) optimism

B hopelessness

C pessimism

D emptiness

Recall

1. **(a)** Marie Curie, p. 752 **(b)** cubism, p. 753 **(c)** Bauhaus, p. 754 **(d)** T. S. Eliot, p. 754 **(e)** Virginia Woolf, p. 754 **(f)** James Joyce, p. 754 **(g)** Jazz Age, p. 754
2. **(a)** psychoanalysis, p. 753 **(b)** abstract, p. 753 **(c)** surrealism, p. 753 **(d)** stream of consciousness, p. 754 **(e)** flapper, p. 756

Comprehension

3. Einstein's ideas shattered the certainty of earlier theories; some felt that the universe was beyond human understanding. Freud's ideas challenged faith in reason by suggesting that the unconscious mind drives much of human behavior. 4. **(a)** Artists challenged traditional representational styles, using bold colors, distortions, abstract images, and dreamlike landscapes. **(b)** They stressed the horrors of modern warfare, military and political blunders, spiritual emptiness, the lack of conviction among the young, and people's hidden thoughts. 5. They were young and liberated; they rejected old ways and became enthusiastic over jazz and popular culture.

Critical Thinking and Writing

6. Possible answers: **(a)** Cars gave people greater mobility. Movies gained worldwide audiences. Radios brought news, music, and sports into homes. **(b)** More and more people use computers for work, play, and communication. Fiber-optic technology allows people to receive faxes, computer transmissions, and cable channels over telephone lines. 7. Possible answer: Eliot portrayed the modern world as spiritually empty and barren. Dali saw the world through the chaotic unconscious.

Activity Rubrics

Share rubrics with students before they begin their research.

Attempted The presentation is incomplete and shows little understanding of the artist.

Minimal The presentation shows some understanding of the artist but is disorganized and includes no visuals.

Adequate The presentation is well researched and thorough and includes several visuals.

Exemplary The presentation is well researched and well written, with interesting information and striking visuals.

Caption Answer

Possible answers: Short skirts and high heels were new and shocking. Answers about today's fashions should reflect current styles.

The Flapper
The flapper became a symbol of the rebellious "new woman" of the 1920s. Still, relatively few young women were flappers. Most continued to follow traditional lifestyles.

Theme: Continuity and Change What was new and shocking about this flapper's "look"? How are women's fashions today different from those of the 1920's?

Gertrude Stein, an American writer living in Paris, called them the "lost generation." Others saw them as immoral pleasure seekers.

The symbol of rebellious Jazz Age youth was the liberated young woman called the flapper. The first flappers were American, but their European sisters soon adopted the fashion. Flappers rejected old ways. Shocking their elders, they bobbed their hair and wore skirts far shorter than those of prewar fashions. They went out on dates unchaperoned, enjoyed wild new dance fads such as the Charleston, smoked cigarettes, and drank in nightclubs.

Women's Lives For most women, the postwar period brought limited progress. During the war, women had held a wide range of jobs. Although most women returned to the home when the war ended, their war work helped them win the vote in many western countries. A few women were elected to public office, such as Texas governor Miriam Ferguson or Lady Nancy Astor, the first woman to serve in the British Parliament.

By the 1920s, labor-saving devices had become common in middle-class homes. Washing machines, vacuum cleaners, and canned foods freed women from many time-consuming household chores. Some women found paid work outside the home. Others took volunteer jobs, providing social services or raising funds for charities.

In the new atmosphere of emancipation, women pursued careers in many arenas—from sports to the arts. Women golfers, tennis players, swimmers, and pilots set new records. Women worked as newspaper reporters, published bestselling novels, and won recognition for their artwork. Most professions, though, were still dominated by men. Women doing the same work as men earned much less.

Social Classes The war had changed social values and the class system itself. In Europe, noble families had lost sons in the fighting, while Russia's noble class was destroyed by the revolution. Peasants had suffered heavy losses. After the war, many filtered into the cities, adding their voices to protests against economic conditions. For many factory workers, wages improved in the postwar decades. Wealthy capitalists prospered in the boom times of the 1920s.

The lower middle class, however, often felt pinched. It resented the successes of big business and the rising wages of workers. As the Great Depression struck, many people from this class were attracted to radical right-wing groups.

SECTION 2 Assessment

Recall

1. **Identify:** **(a)** Marie Curie, **(b)** cubism, **(c)** Bauhaus, **(d)** T. S. Eliot, **(e)** Virginia Woolf, **(f)** James Joyce, **(g)** Jazz Age.
2. **Define:** **(a)** psychoanalysis, **(b)** abstract, **(c)** surrealism, **(d)** stream of consciousness, **(e)** flapper.

Comprehension

3. How did the ideas of Einstein and Freud contribute to a sense of uncertainty?
4. **(a)** How did postwar artists challenge older western traditions?

(b) What themes did postwar writers stress?
5. How did flappers symbolize changes in western society?

Critical Thinking and Writing

6. **Linking Past and Present** **(a)** How did technology shape popular culture in the 1920s? **(b)** What technologies are shaping popular culture today?
7. **Synthesizing Information** Choose one postwar writer and one postwar artist. Explain how the work of each reflected a new view of the world.

Activity
Take It to the NET

Use the Internet to find out more about Paul Klee and the ideas that affected his paintings. Choose one painting and prepare a description and explanation based on Klee's ideas, the period in which he worked, and your own reaction to the work.

Resource Directory

Teaching Resources

Section Quiz Unit 7 booklet, p. 61
Creative Teaching Activities Creative Teaching Activities booklet, p. 136
Guided Reading and Review Unit 7 booklet, p. 62

Technology

Interactive Student Tutorial CD-ROM Ch. 30
Computer Test Bank Ch. 30

Fascism in Italy

Reading Focus

- How did conditions in Italy favor the rise of Mussolini?
- How did Mussolini reshape Italy?
- What were the values and goals of fascist ideology?

Taking Notes

As you read this section, prepare an outline of its contents. Use Roman numerals to indicate major headings. Use capital letters for subheadings, and use numbers for the supporting details. The example here will help you get started.

I. Rise of Mussolini
  A. A leader emerges
    1.
    2.
  B. Seizing power
    1. Combat squads
    2.
    3.
  C.

Main Idea   Angered by political and economic problems, many Italians turned to fascism for solutions.

Setting the Scene

"I hated politics and politicians," said Italo Balbo. Like many Italian veterans of World War I, he had come home to a land of economic chaos and political corruption. Italy's constitutional government, he felt, "had betrayed the hopes of soldiers, reducing Italy to a shameful peace." Disgusted and angry, Balbo rallied behind a fierce nationalist, Benito Mussolini. Mussolini's rise to power in the 1920s served as a model for ambitious strongmen elsewhere in Europe.

Rise of Mussolini

In 1919, Italian nationalists were outraged by the Paris peace treaties. As one of the victorious Allies, Italy had expected to gain territory on the Adriatic. Instead, these lands became part of the new Yugoslavia.

At home, disorders multiplied. Inspired in part by the revolution in Russia, peasants seized land, and workers went on strike or seized factories. Amid the chaos, returning veterans faced unemployment. Trade declined and taxes rose. The government, split into feuding factions, seemed powerless to end the crisis.

A Leader Emerges   Into this turmoil stepped Benito Mussolini. The son of a socialist blacksmith and a teacher, Mussolini had been a socialist in his youth. During the war, however, he rejected socialism for intense nationalism. In 1919, he organized veterans and other discontented Italians into the Fascist party. They took the name from the Latin *fasces,* a bundle of sticks wrapped around an ax—a symbol of authority in ancient Rome.

With his jutting jaw and slashing phrases, Mussolini was a fiery speaker. He promised to end corruption and replace turmoil with order. He also spoke of reviving Roman greatness, pledging to turn the Mediterranean into a "Roman lake" once again.

Seizing Power   Mussolini organized his supporters into black-shirted "combat squads." Rejecting the democratic process in favor of violent action, "Black Shirts" broke up socialist rallies, smashed leftist presses, and attacked farmers' cooperatives. Through intimidation and terror, Fascist gangs ousted elected officials in northern Italy. Many Italians accepted these moves because they, too, had lost faith in constitutional government.

In 1922, the Fascists made a bid for power. At a rally in Naples, they announced a "march on Rome" to demand that the government make changes. Tens of thousands of Fascists swarmed into the capital. Fearing

Chapter 30 **757**

Bell Ringer Write the words *Il Duce* on the chalkboard and ask if students know who this is. What else do they know about Mussolini? Have students read the section to learn more.

LESSON PLAN

1. Focus Angered by unfulfilled foreign policy goals and facing political and economic turmoil at home, many Italians turned to Benito Mussolini and fascism. Mussolini's fascism was rooted in extreme nationalism, action, and discipline. As Il Duce, Mussolini established a totalitarian system in which the needs of the state took precedence over all else.

2. Instruct Have students work in small groups to construct a cause-and-effect chart titled "The Rise of Fascism in Italy." Among the causes on their charts they should note such issues as foreign policy, political conditions, economic conditions, and fascist methods. Among the effects on their charts they should note how fascism changed Italy's government, economy, society, educational system, and more. Students may model their charts after the one at the end of Section 1, or they may develop a design of their own. When they are finished, have them put their charts on display. Allow students time to view and compare the various charts. Then, use the charts as the basis for a class discussion on the causes and effects of the rise of Italian fascism.

3. Assess Remind the class that one of the slogans of Italian fascism was "Believe, Obey, Fight!" Ask students to write two or three other slogans that reflect ideals or goals of fascism. Invite volunteers to share their ideas with the class.

4. Reteach If students' Assess activity does not reflect adequate understanding of the lesson, you might assign the *Guide to the Essentials* or the *Interactive Student Tutorial CD-ROM* for this section.

Block Scheduling Support

Have students form small groups to create an educational poster about totalitarian governments. Their posters, which should be geared toward upper elementary students, could take the form of a two-column chart listing the six basic features of a totalitarian government in the left-hand column and examples from Mussolini's Fascist government in the right-hand column. To increase the appeal of their posters, encourage students to color and illustrate them. They might wish to include a map showing the location of countries ruled by totalitarian governments in the decades after World War I.

Social Goals In 1934, to help increase the Italian population, Mussolini decreed a special tax on bachelors. In 1938, he enacted a law that limited women to no more than 10 percent of higher-paying jobs in government and industry. He told women to stay at home and help the Italian population grow.

Background
Connections to Economics

Economic Success One of Mussolini's most successful projects was the drainage of several hundred thousand acres of marshland. The increase in farmland boosted wheat production by about 30 percent. Mussolini also directed the construction of a network of highways. With the help of private business, the first one was completed in 1924.

Background
Global Connections

Americans Respond Mussolini's program of intense nationalism and anti-communism had appeal in the United States as well as in Italy. During the 1920s, the *Saturday Evening Post* ran a series of articles praising fascism. In 1923, the American Legion invited Mussolini to speak at its annual convention.

Did You Know?

Mussolini's Plaster Rome

"The nation is in our hands now," declared Mussolini, "and we swear to lead her back to her ways of ancient greatness." In 1937, he inaugurated a celebration known as "The Augustan Exhibit of Roman Spirit" to commemorate the two-thousandth anniversary of the birth of Augustus Caesar. Many of the exhibits are still on display, including a scale plaster model of the city of Rome as it appeared in the 300s. Today the model, known as "Plastico," can be seen in the Museum of Roman Civilization, located in the heart of Rome. The Plastico is about 860 square feet, taking up an entire room in the museum.

Theme: Political and Social Systems Why do you think Mussolini wanted to glorify ancient Rome?

---

civil war, King Victor Emmanuel III asked Mussolini to form a government as prime minister. Without firing a shot, Mussolini thus obtained a "legal" appointment from the king, undermining constitutional democracy.

Mussolini's Italy

At first, Fascists held only a few cabinet posts. By 1925, though, Mussolini had assumed more power and taken the title Il Duce (eel DOO chay), "The Leader." He suppressed rival parties, muzzled the press, rigged elections, and replaced elected officials with Fascist supporters.

In theory, Italy remained a parliamentary monarchy. In fact, it was a dictatorship upheld by terror. Critics were thrown into prison, forced into exile, or murdered. Secret police and propaganda bolstered the regime.

Economic Policy To encourage economic growth and end conflicts between owners and workers, Mussolini brought the economy under state control. Unlike socialists, though, he preserved capitalism. Under Mussolini's "corporate state," representatives of business, labor, government, and the Fascist party controlled industry, agriculture, and trade. Although production increased, this success came at the expense of workers. They were forbidden to strike, and their wages lagged.

Social Policies To Fascists, the individual was unimportant except as a member of the state. Men, women, and children were bombarded with slogans glorifying the state and Mussolini. "Believe! Obey! Fight!" loudspeakers blared and posters proclaimed. Men were urged to be ruthless, selfless warriors for the glory of Italy. Women were pushed out of paying jobs. Instead, Mussolini called on women to "win the battle of motherhood." Those who bore more than 14 children were given a medal by Il Duce himself.

Shaping the young was a major Fascist goal. Fascist youth groups toughened children and taught them to obey strict military discipline. Boys and girls learned about the glories of ancient Rome. Young Fascists marched in torchlight parades, singing patriotic hymns and chanting, "Mussolini is always right." By the 1930s, a generation of young soldiers stood ready to back Il Duce's drive to expand Italian power.

What Is Fascism?

Historians still debate the real nature of fascist ideology. Mussolini coined the term, but fascists had no single unifying set of beliefs, as Marxists did. Today, we generally use the term to describe any authoritarian government that is not communist. In the 1920s and 1930s, though, fascism meant different things in different countries.

All forms of fascism, however, shared some basic features. It was rooted in extreme nationalism. Fascists glorified action, violence, discipline, and, above all, blind loyalty to the state. "Fascism conceives of the State as an absolute," declared Mussolini, "in comparison with which all individuals or groups are relative, only to be conceived of in their relation to the State."

Fascists were antidemocratic. They rejected the Enlightenment faith in reason and the concepts of equality and liberty spread by the French Revolution. To them, democracy led to corruption and weakness and put individual or class interests above national goals. Instead, fascists emphasized emotion and the need for the citizen to serve the state.

Fascists also pursued aggressive foreign expansion. Echoing the Social Darwinist idea of "survival of the fittest," Fascist leaders glorified warfare as a necessary and noble struggle for survival.

Compared to Communism Fascists were the sworn enemies of socialists and communists. While communists had hopes for international change, fascists pursued nationalist goals. Fascists found allies among business

---

Did You Know?

ANSWER Possible answers: He wanted to compare the glory of ancient Rome to Rome under his rule. He wanted to make people desire to restore Rome to what he thought was its glorious past under the caesars and hoped that people would identify his dictatorship with the dictatorship of the caesars.

Resource Directory

Teaching Resources

History Through Literature *The Sound of the Cicadas,* History Through Literature booklet, pp. 63–64
Synthesizing Information Chapter Extension Activities booklet, p. 73

Totalitarianism

In 1922, Benito Mussolini set up a fascist government, making Italy the first totalitarian state in Europe. Shortly afterward, Germany and the Soviet Union also came under totalitarian rule. Use the quotation, the poster, and the photograph to learn about the nature of totalitarianism.

Admiring the Leader

"[Only joy at finding such a leader] can explain the enthusiasm [Mussolini] evoked at gathering after gathering, where his mere presence drew the people from all sides to greet him with frenzied acclamations. Even the men who at first came out of mere curiosity and with indifferent or even hostile feelings gradually felt themselves fired by his personal magnetic influence. . . .

The women of the Abruzzi . . . strove to touch his hand as they would to touch a shrine or a relic. . . . The mayor of a little Sicilian village stopped his motor-car and said to him, 'I have nothing to ask of you, but this only. Perhaps you will never again pass over this ground of ours. Dismount that you may touch it with your feet!' "

—Margherita G. Sarfatti, *The Life of Benito Mussolini* (tr. Frederic Whyte)

Fascist Youth

A company of uniformed Italian boys, shouldering packs and rifles, proudly parades during a military drill.

Fascist Propaganda

FERROVIE DELLO STATO

LE PIU' RECENTI CARROZZE DI 3ª CLASSE

This propaganda poster celebrates the introduction of new passenger cars for the Italian state railroad. The words say, "State Railroad. The Newest Third-Class Carriages."

Skills Tip

When you analyze a work of propaganda, notice how images can convey an emotional impact, even when the words do not.

Skills Assessment

1. What value is reflected in both the photograph and the poster?
   - A personal freedom
   - B national pride
   - C prosperity
   - D individuality

2. According to Sarfatti, many Italians greeted Mussolini with
   - E petitions for jobs.
   - F complaints about his fascist government.
   - G calls for him to resign.
   - H deep respect.

3. **Critical Thinking Synthesizing Information** (a) How do the quotation, the poster, and the photograph illustrate some of the features of totalitarian states? (b) Based on your reading in the chapter and using the list (from the next page) of six basic features of a totalitarian state, name three additional traits of fascist Italy.

Background
About the Evidence

In the early days of fascism, millions of Italians enthusiastically supported Mussolini, as reflected in these anecdotes: A guide to some Etruscan tombs explained that the inscriptions, which are in a language not yet deciphered, had not been translated. A visitor replied, "Ah, that's because Mussolini has not yet been here. When he comes we shall see what he will find out." When Mt. Etna erupted, a newspaper proclaimed as fact a fanciful statement that the streaming lava of the volcano was stopped in its tracks by a glance from the dictator's eyes.

Activity
Interpreting the Evidence

Use these additional questions to generate class discussion.

1. Critical Thinking: Analyzing Primary Sources Why were people so happy to find a leader like Mussolini? *(His presence was reassuring and made people feel optimistic.)*

2. Critical Thinking: Recognizing Propaganda What might the image of the man lifting the train symbolize? *(Possible answer: the ability of powerful leaders to control and use technology)*

Skills Tip

Explain that the poster artist used exaggeration to emphasize praise of the new railroad cars. The Skills Handbook in the front of the book has a lesson that will help students with this feature.

Human Drama Note

Fascist Enterprises Mussolini started a large-scale public works program that included building, agricultural, and architectural restoration projects. Roads, schools, and train stations were built; swampland reclaimed; trees planted; and archaeological sites financed. Yet, end results did not match initial claims. Many projects were left unfinished, and huge sums of money lined the pockets of corrupt officials in charge of overseeing the programs. Although many Fascist enterprises fell far short of their promises, few people blamed Mussolini.

Test Preparation

Have students read the quotation by Mussolini in the section titled "What Is Fascism?" on the opposite page, and then complete the sentence.

According to the passage, Mussolini would probably agree that

A constitutional democracies are best.

B citizens should obey laws blindly.

C freedom of speech is an inalienable right.

D governments are subject to the will of the people.

Skills Assessment

ANSWERS 1. B **2.** H **3. (a)** The quote implies that Italians venerated Mussolini. The poster reflects a powerful state with control of the economy; the person holding up the train represents the state. The photograph shows the indoctrination of children. **(b)** Possible answers: Mussolini muzzled the press and controlled media. His dictatorship upheld terror; critics were thrown into prison, forced into exile, or murdered. Secret police and propaganda bolstered the regime.

Recall

1. (a) Black Shirts, p. 757 (b) Il Duce, p. 758

Comprehension

2. (a) unemployment, a decline in trade, rising taxes, and a weak and divided government (b) His promises to revive Rome's greatness and end corruption had great appeal. 3. Possible answer: Mussolini wanted economic growth and an end to workplace conflicts. He brought the economy under state control, allowed business, labor, and government to control various economic activities, and made strikes illegal. 4. Possible answers: (a) Fascism promoted action, violence, discipline, and blind loyalty. (b) Similar: During economic hard times, they promoted social change, imposed totalitarian governments, and claimed to rule in the national interest. Different: Communists sought world revolution; fascists pursued nationalism. Communist supporters were the urban working class; fascist supporters were business leaders, wealthy landowners, and the lower middle class.

Critical Thinking and Writing

5. Possible answer: Fascists said democracy put individuals above national goals, and promoted greed, selfishness, and corruption. 6. (a) Possible answers: Mussolini thought industrialization caused unemployment. He believed women, who had taken wartime jobs, were taking peacetime jobs away from men. (b) Fascists pushed women out of paying jobs and rewarded women for staying at home and having children.

Activity Rubrics

Share rubrics with students before they write their paragraphs.

Attempted The paragraph is incomplete and disorganized, with mechanical errors.

Minimal The paragraph is based on insufficient information, is disorganized, and has several mechanical errors.

Adequate The paragraph uses polling results from several people and is well organized, with few mechanical errors.

Exemplary The paragraph has information from a range of people, shows good analytical thinking and good organization, and has no mechanical errors.

Global Connections

ANSWER Possible answers: They could force groups to get along, and punish those who did not; they could forcibly separate ethnic groups.

Global Connections

Authoritarian Rule in Eastern Europe

Italy was not the only European nation to embrace authoritarian rule. The newly formed countries of Eastern Europe were in turmoil after World War I. They embraced democracy, but struggled with nationalist sentiments, ethnic tensions, wars, and economic problems. In 1926, General Joseph Pilsudski, a military hero who had helped liberate Poland, used the army to seize control of the country. Eventually every country in Eastern Europe, except Czechoslovakia, turned to some form of authoritarian government.

In the 1930s, President Franklin Roosevelt tried to explain why many nations had rejected democracy. "People . . . have grown tired of unemployment and insecurity," he said. "Finally, in desperation, they chose to sacrifice liberty in the hope of getting something to eat."

Theme: Political and Social Systems What methods might dictators use to reduce ethnic tensions?

---

leaders, wealthy landowners, and the lower middle class. Communists won support among urban and agricultural workers.

Despite such differences, these two ideologies had much in common. Both flourished during economic hard times by promoting extreme programs of social change. In Communist Russia as well as Fascist Italy, dictators imposed totalitarian governments in order to bring about social revolutions. In both, a party elite claimed to rule in the name of the national interest.

Totalitarian Rule Mussolini built the first totalitarian state, which became a model for others. Fascist rule in Italy was not as absolute as those of Stalin in the Soviet Union or Adolf Hitler in Germany. Still, all three governments shared these basic features: (1) a single-party dictatorship, (2) state control of the economy, (3) use of police spies and terror to enforce the will of the state, (4) strict censorship and government monopoly of the media, (5) use of schools and the media to indoctrinate and mobilize citizens, and (6) unquestioning obedience to a single leader.

Appeal Given its restrictions of individual freedom, why did fascism appeal to many Italians? First, it promised a strong, stable government and an end to the political feuding that had paralyzed democracy. Mussolini's intense nationalism also struck a chord among most ordinary Italians. He revived national pride, pledging to make the Mediterranean Sea a "Roman lake" once more. Finally, Mussolini projected a sense of power and confidence at a time of disorder and despair.

At first, Il Duce received good press outside Italy, too. Newspapers in Britain, France, and North America applauded the discipline and order of his government. "He got the trains running on time," admirers said. Only later, when Mussolini embarked on a course of foreign conquest, did western democracies protest his actions.

Looking Ahead

Three systems of government competed for influence in postwar Europe. Democracy endured in Britain and France but faced an uphill struggle in hard times. Communism emerged in Russia and won support elsewhere, but many people saw it as a dangerous threat.

In Italy, fascism offered a different formula. Its chest-thumping calls for action, national unity, and dedication to the state ignited patriotic feeling. As the Great Depression spread, other nations—most notably Germany—looked to leaders who preached fascist ideology.

SECTION 3 **Assessment**

Recall

1. **Identify:** (a) Black Shirts, (b) Il Duce.

Comprehension

2. (a) What problems did Italy face after World War I? (b) How did these problems help Mussolini win power?
3. Describe two economic or social goals of Mussolini, and explain the actions he took to achieve each goal.
4. (a) What values did fascism promote? (b) List two similarities and two differences between fascism and communism.

Critical Thinking and Writing

5. **Analyzing Information** Why do you think the Fascists blamed democracy for problems in Italy?
6. **Analyzing Primary Sources** Mussolini said, "Machines and women are the two main causes of unemployment." (a) What do you think he meant? (b) How did Mussolini's policies reflect his attitude toward women?

Activity

Taking a Poll
Many people today use the word *fascist* in discussing politics. Take a poll of several voters and ask what they think the word means. Then, write a paragraph comparing these definitions with what fascism meant under Mussolini.

Resource Directory

Teaching Resources

Section Quiz Unit 7 booklet, p. 63
Creative Teaching Activities Creative Teaching Activities booklet, p. 137
Guided Reading and Review Unit 7 booklet, p. 64

Technology

Interactive Student Tutorial CD-ROM Ch. 30
Computer Test Bank Ch. 30

SECTION 4 Hitler and the Rise of Nazi Germany

Reading Focus

- What problems did the Weimar Republic face?
- How did Hitler come to power?
- What political, social, economic, and cultural policies did Hitler pursue?
- How did Hitler take action against German Jews?

Vocabulary

chancellor
repudiate
concentration camp

Taking Notes

Make a cause-and-effect diagram about the rise of Hitler. This sample will help you get started.

| Versailles Treaty | Inflation | | |

RISE OF HITLER

Main Idea Under Adolf Hitler, the Nazi government used terror, repression, and one-party rule to establish a totalitarian state.

Setting the Scene In November 1923, a German army veteran and leader of an extremist party, Adolf Hitler, tried to follow Mussolini's example. His brown-shirted thugs burst into a beer hall in Munich, where a political meeting was set to start. Hitler climbed onto a table and fired his pistol. "The National Socialist revolution has begun!" he shouted.

The coup failed, and Hitler was soon behind bars. But Hitler was a force that could not be ignored forever. Within a decade, he made a new bid for power. This time, he succeeded by legal means.

Hitler's rise to power raises disturbing questions that we still debate today. Why did Germany, which had a democratic government in the 1920s, become a totalitarian state in the 1930s? How could a ruthless, hate-filled dictator gain the enthusiastic support of many Germans?

The Weimar Republic

As World War I drew to a close, Germany tottered on the brink of chaos. Under the threat of a socialist revolution, the kaiser abdicated. Moderate leaders signed the armistice and later, under protest, the Versailles treaty.

In 1919, German leaders drafted a constitution in the city of Weimar (vī mahr). It created a democratic government known as the Weimar Republic. The constitution set up a parliamentary system led by a chancellor, or prime minister. It gave women the vote and included a bill of rights.

Struggles of the Republic The republic faced severe problems from the start. Politically, it was weak because Germany, like France, had many small parties. The chancellor had to form coalitions that easily fell apart.

The government, led by moderate democratic socialists, came under constant fire from both the left and right. Communists demanded radical changes like those Lenin had brought to Russia. Conservatives—including the old Junker nobility, military officers, and wealthy bourgeoisie—attacked the government as too liberal and weak. They longed for another strong leader like Bismarck or the kaiser. Germans of all classes blamed the Weimar Republic for the hated Versailles treaty, with its war-guilt clause and heavy reparations. In their bitterness, they looked for scapegoats. Many blamed German Jews for economic and political problems.

Inflation Economic disaster fed unrest. In 1923, when Germany fell behind in reparations payments, France occupied the coal-rich Ruhr Valley. Ruhr Germans turned to passive resistance, refusing to work. To support them,

German Inflation
In 1923, runaway inflation caused prices in Germany to soar. Here, a housewife prepares to light her stove with several million marks.

Theme: Economics and Technology What does this picture suggest about the price of fuel at the time?

Heterogeneous Groups

Drawing Conclusions Ask students to review the provisions of the Versailles treaty and conditions in Weimar Germany. Then read aloud the following quotation from one of Hitler's early followers:

"Hitler responds to the vibrations of the human heart with the delicacy of a seismograph. . . . His words go like an arrow to their target; he touches each private wound on the raw, liberating the mass unconscious, expressing its innermost aspirations, telling it what it most wants to hear."

Ask students to interpret the meaning of the quotation. Then, based on what they know about the Versailles treaty and conditions in Weimar Germany, ask them to list the promises that they think Hitler would have made to the German people. *(Reteaching)*

Biography

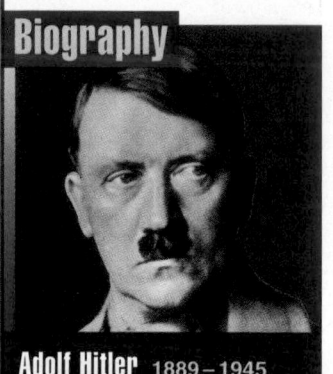

Adolf Hitler 1889–1945

As a boy, Adolf Hitler became obsessed with reading about Germany's 1871 victory in the Franco–Prussian War. "The great historic struggle would become my greatest spiritual experience," he later wrote. "I became more and more enthusiastic about everything . . . connected with war."

In school, young Hitler was known as a ring leader. One of his teachers recalled, "He demanded of his fellow pupils their unqualified obedience." He failed to finish high school and was later crushed when he was rejected by art school.

After Hitler came to power, he used his elite guard of storm troopers to terrorize his opponents. But when he felt his power threatened, Hitler had storm trooper leaders murdered during the "Night of the Long Knives," June 30, 1934.

Theme: Impact of the Individual Why do you think historians study the upbringing of Hitler?

the government printed huge quantities of paper money. This move set off inflation that spiraled out of control. The German mark became almost worthless. An item that cost 100 marks in July 1922 cost 944,000 marks by August 1923. A loaf of bread cost tens of thousands of marks.

Runaway inflation spread misery and despair. Salaries rose by billions of marks, but they still could not keep up with skyrocketing prices. Many middle-class families saw their savings wiped out.

Recovery and Collapse With help from the western powers, the government did bring inflation under control. In 1924, the United States gained British and French approval for a plan to reduce German reparations payments. Under the Dawes Plan, France withdrew its forces from the Ruhr, and American loans helped the German economy recover.

Germany began to prosper. Then, the Great Depression hit, reviving memories of the miseries of 1923. Germans turned to an energetic leader, Adolf Hitler, who promised to solve the economic crisis and restore Germany's former greatness.

Adolf Hitler

Hitler was born in Austria in 1889. When he was 18, he went to Vienna, hoping to enter art school, but he was turned down. Vienna was then the capital of the multinational Hapsburg empire. Austrian Germans made up just one of many ethnic groups. Yet they felt superior to Jews, Serbs, Poles, and other groups. While living in Vienna, Hitler developed the fanatical antisemitism that would later play a major role in his rise to power.

Hitler later moved to Germany and fought in the German army during World War I. Like many ex-soldiers, he despised the Weimar government which he perceived as weak and ineffectual. In 1919, he joined a small group of right-wing extremists. Within a year, he was the unquestioned leader of the National Socialist German Workers, or Nazi, party. Like Mussolini, Hitler organized his supporters into fighting squads. Nazi "Storm Troopers" battled in the streets against their political enemies.

Mein Kampf In 1923, as you have read, Hitler made a failed attempt to seize power in Munich. He was arrested, tried, and found guilty of treason. While in prison, Hitler wrote *Mein Kampf* ("My Struggle"). It would later become the basic book of Nazi goals and ideology.

Mein Kampf reflected Hitler's obsessions—extreme nationalism, racism, and antisemitism. Germans, he said, belonged to a superior "master race" of Aryans, or light-skinned Europeans, whose greatest enemies were the Jews. Hitler viewed Jews not as members of a religion but as a separate race. (He defined a Jew as anyone with one Jewish grandparent.) Echoing a familiar right-wing theme, he claimed that Germany had not lost the war but had been betrayed by a conspiracy of Marxists, Jews, corrupt politicians, and business leaders.

In his recipe for revival, Hitler urged Germans everywhere to unite into one great nation. Germany must expand, he said, to gain *Lebensraum,* or living space, for its people. Slavs and other inferior races must bow to Aryan needs. To achieve its greatness, Germany needed a strong leader, or *Führer* (FYOO ruhr). Hitler was determined to become that leader.

The Road to Power After serving less than a year, Hitler left prison. He soon renewed his table-thumping speeches. He found enthusiastic followers among veterans and lower-middle-class Germans who felt frustrated about their future. The Great Depression played into Hitler's hands. As unemployment rose, Nazi membership grew to almost a million. Hitler's program appealed to workers, the lower middle classes, small-town Germans, and business people alike. He promised to end reparations, create jobs, and defy the Versailles treaty by rearming Germany.

Biography

ANSWER Possible answer: They hope to understand the early experiences and attitudes that led to his later actions.

Resource Directory

Teaching Resources

Viewpoint Activity *Hitler's Propaganda Machine,* Unit 7 booklet, p. 68

Technology

World History Color Transparencies *Stadium Tribune, Nuremburg, Germany,* p. D–83

With the government paralyzed by divisions, both Nazis and Communists won more seats in the Reichstag, or lower house of the legislature. Fearing the growth of communist political power, conservative politicians turned to Hitler. Although they despised him, they believed they could control him. Thus, with conservative support, Hitler was elected chancellor in 1933 through legal, democratic means under the Weimar constitution.

Within a year, Hitler was master of Germany. He suspended civil rights, destroyed the socialists and Communists, and disbanded other political parties. Germany became a one-party state. Nazi flags, with their black swastikas, waved across the country. Like Stalin in Russia, Hitler purged his own party, brutally executing Nazis he felt were disloyal. Nazis learned that Hitler, the Führer, demanded unquestioning obedience.

Hitler's Third Reich

Once in power, Hitler moved to build a new Germany. Like Mussolini, Hitler appealed to nationalism by recalling past glories. Germany's First Reich, or empire, was the medieval Holy Roman Empire. The Second Reich was the empire forged by Bismarck in 1871. Under Hitler's new Third Reich, he boasted, the German master race would dominate Europe for 1,000 years.

Hitler soon **repudiated,** or rejected, the hated Treaty of Versailles. He began scheming to unite Germany and Austria. "Today Germany belongs to us," sang young Nazis. "Tomorrow, the world."

A Totalitarian State To achieve his goals, Hitler organized an efficient but brutal system of terror, repression, and totalitarian rule. Nazis controlled all areas of German life—from government to religion to education. Elite, black-uniformed SS troops enforced the Führer's will. His secret police, the Gestapo, rooted out opposition.

Few Germans saw or worried about this terror apparatus taking shape. Instead, they cheered Hitler's accomplishments in ending unemployment and reviving German power.

Economic Policy To combat the Great Depression, Hitler launched large public works programs (as did Britain and the United States). Tens of thousands of people were put to work building highways and housing or replanting forests. Hitler also began a crash program to rearm Germany, in violation of the Versailles treaty. Demand for military hardware stimulated business and helped eliminate unemployment.

Nazis March
Militarism was a key element of Nazi ideology. Here, German soldiers march at a Nazi party rally in Nuremberg. The swastika, which the Nazis adopted as a party symbol, actually dates back to ancient times.

Theme: Political and Social Systems Why would mass meetings and marches be important in a totalitarian state?

Chapter 30 **763**

Background
Historical Evidence

Hitler's Popularity Hitler promised Germany an economic recovery—and he delivered it. As most of the world was gripped by the Great Depression, Hitler launched a massive public works program. Millions of Germans were employed constructing superhighways, office buildings, sports arenas, public housing, and military materials. As a result, unemployment dropped from six million in 1932 to one million in 1936. By 1938, a shortage of workers developed and growing numbers of women began taking jobs outside the home. Between 1932 and 1938, the standard of living for employed Germans rose by more than 20 percent. For the masses of ordinary Germans, who were not Jews, Slavs, Gypsies, Communists, or other persecuted minorities, Hitler had produced an economic miracle.

Background
Global Connections

Global Connections The swastika, one of the oldest symbols in the world, has been found on Mesopotamian and Greek coins, as well as on Mayan monuments. In India, Hindus and Jains use it as a good-luck symbol on doorways and elsewhere. Swastikas may appear with arms rotating either clockwise, as in the Nazi swastika, or counterclockwise.

Reading Strategy
Reinforcing Key Ideas

Ask students to write two column headings on a piece of paper: the Weimar Republic and the Third Reich. Ask students to note distinguishing features, including key strengths and weaknesses that describe these very different twentieth-century German governments. *(Less Advanced Readers)*

Test Preparation

Have students read the subsection titled "Recovery and Collapse" on the opposite page, and then answer the question below.

Which of the following is true of the economic situation in Germany?

A The German economy never recovered until Hitler took power.

B The Great Depression ended Germany's economic recovery.

C French and British loans helped the German economy recover.

D The German economy recovered in 1924 and grew for the next 10 years.

Caption Answer

Possible answer: Totalitarian states encouraged conformity and absolute loyalty to the state. Parades and mass meetings emphasize such values.

Purging German Culture
The Nazis tried to "purify" German culture by destroying ideas they felt were dangerous. Here, enthusiastic youngsters participate in book burning.
Theme: Political and Social Systems What impression does this photograph give you of youth in Nazi Germany?

Like Mussolini, Hitler preserved capitalism but brought big business and labor under government control. Few objected to this loss of freedom because their standard of living rose. Propaganda highlighted the improvements. "Strength Through Joy" programs offered workers vigorous outdoor vacations that also made them physically fit for military service.

Social Policy Like the Fascists in Italy and the Communists in the Soviet Union, the Nazis indoctrinated young people with their ideology. In passionate speeches, the Führer spewed his message of racism. He urged young Germans to destroy their so-called enemies without mercy:

"Extremes must be fought by extremes. Against the infection of [Marxism], against the Jewish pestilence, we must hold aloft a flaming ideal. And if others speak of the World and Humanity, we must say the Fatherland—and only the Fatherland!"
—Adolf Hitler, *My New Order*

On hikes and in camps, the "Hitler Youth" pledged absolute loyalty to Germany and undertook physical fitness programs to prepare for war.

Like Fascists in Italy, Nazis sought to limit women's roles. Women were dismissed from upper-level jobs and turned away from universities. To raise the birthrate, Nazis offered "pure-blooded Aryan" women rewards for having more children. Still, Hitler's goal to keep women in the home and out of the work force applied mainly to the privileged. As German industry expanded, women factory workers were needed.

Purging German Culture

Nazis used education as a propaganda tool. School courses and textbooks were rewritten to reflect Nazi racial views. "We teach and learn history," said one Nazi educator, "not to say how things actually happened but to instruct the German people from the past."

The Arts The Nazis sought to purge, or purify, German culture. They denounced modern art, saying that it was corrupted by Jewish influences. They condemned jazz because of its African roots. Instead, the Nazis glorified old German myths such as those re-created in the operas of Richard Wagner.

At huge public bonfires, Nazis burned books of which they disapproved. *All Quiet on the Western Front* was one of many works that went up in flames. The Nazis viewed Remarque's novel as an insult to the German military.

Nazism and the Churches Hitler despised Christianity as "weak" and "flabby." He sought to replace religion with his racial creed. In an attempt to control the churches, the Nazis combined all Protestant sects into a single state church. They closed Catholic schools and muzzled the Catholic clergy.

Although some clergy supported the new regime or remained silent, others courageously denounced Hitler. Martin Niemoller, a Lutheran minister, preached against Nazi policies and was later jailed. He later commented:

"The Nazis came first for the Communists. But I wasn't a Communist, so I didn't speak up. Then they came for the Jews, but I wasn't a Jew so I didn't speak up. . . . Then they came for the Catholics, but I was a Protestant so I didn't speak up.

Then they came for me. By that time, there was no one left to speak up."

—Martin Niemoller, quoted in *Time* magazine

The Campaign Against the Jews Begins

In his fanatical antisemitism, Hitler set out to drive Jews from Germany. In 1935, the Nuremberg Laws placed severe restrictions on Jews. They were prohibited from marrying non-Jews, attending or teaching at German schools or universities, holding government jobs, practicing law or medicine, or publishing books. Nazis beat and robbed Jews and roused mobs to do the same. Many German Jews, including the brilliant scientist, Albert Einstein, fled the growing menace and sought refuge in other countries.

Night of Broken Glass On November 7, 1938, a young Jew, whose parents had been mistreated in Germany, shot and wounded a German diplomat in Paris. Hitler used the incident as an excuse to stage an attack on all Jews.

Kristallnacht (krihs TAHL nahkt), or the "Night of Broken Glass," took place on November 9 and 10. Nazi-led mobs attacked Jewish communities all over Germany, shouting "Revenge for Paris! Down with the Jews!" They smashed windows, looted shops, and burned synagogues. Many Jews were dragged from their homes and beaten in the streets.

Aftermath World reaction to *Kristallnacht* was swift and negative. Still, Hitler was unmoved. He even made the Jewish victims pay for the damage.

In the years that followed, Hitler's campaign against the Jews intensified. Tens of thousands of Jews were sent to concentration camps, detention centers for civilians considered enemies of the state. Before long, Hitler and his henchmen were making even more sinister plans for what they called the "final solution"—the extermination of all Jews.

Looking Ahead

In the 1930s, Germany became Europe's second fascist state. Germans of all classes responded to Hitler's hypnotic speeches and programs, which restored their national pride. Despite the warnings of some courageous Germans, most individuals ignored the ugly side of Nazi rule. Those who opposed Nazism were not united and were soon silenced.

While Hitler won absolute power at home, he moved boldly to expand Germany's power in Europe. In the next chapter, you will see how Nazi aggression set the stage for the largest war the world has yet seen.

Primary Source

Kristallnacht
A German Jewish woman recalls the "Night of Broken Glass":

"I was thirteen years old. We were all in bed sound asleep when we were suddenly woken by a loud knocking on the door—it was one or two o'clock in the morning. 'Open up! We're taking all of you to Palestine,' they shouted. . . . They broke our windowpanes, and the house became very cold. . . . We were standing there, outside in the cold, still in our nightclothes, with only a coat thrown over. They kept bringing more and more Jewish people from all over the neighborhood. . . . Then they made everyone lie face down on the ground. . . . 'Now, they will shoot us,' we thought. We were very afraid. Then abruptly, 'Get up!' They kept us there until the sky was light."
—Sophie Yaari, quoted in *To Save a Life: Stories of Holocaust Rescue* (Land-Weber)

Skills Assessment

Primary Source What did Sophie Yaari and the others fear most that night?

SECTION 4 Assessment

Recall

1. Identify: (a) Ruhr Valley,
(b) Dawes Plan, (c) *Mein Kampf,*
(d) Third Reich, (e) Gestapo,
(f) Nuremberg Laws,
(g) *Kristallnacht.*
2. Define: (a) chancellor,
(b) repudiate, (c) concentration camp.

Comprehension

3. List three problems faced by the Weimar Republic.
4. How did the depression pave the way for the rise of Hitler?
5. (a) How did Hitler create a one-party dictatorship? (b) What racial and nationalistic ideas did Nazis promote?

6. What were some of the restrictions that Hitler placed on German Jews?

Critical Thinking and Writing

7. **Defending a Position** Do you think that there are any circumstances under which a government would be justified in banning books or censoring ideas? Explain.
8. **Drawing Conclusions** Both Stalin in the Soviet Union and Hitler in Germany instituted ruthless campaigns against supposed enemies of the state. Why do you think dictators need to find scapegoats for their nation's ills?

Activity
Take It to the NET

Use the Internet to learn more about the rise of Hitler. Then, write a newspaper editorial for a western paper describing the day when Hitler became chancellor of Germany.

Human Drama Note

Hitler's Use of Propaganda Hitler explains in *Mein Kampf* that he recognized the importance of using propaganda to achieve political ends. He studied British and American propaganda techniques during World War I because they were superior to those of the Germans: "For what we failed to do, the enemy did, with amazing skill and really brilliant calculation. I, myself, learned enormously from this enemy war propaganda."

From the Allies, Hitler learned the value of establishing a central organization to coordinate and distribute propaganda. He also recognized the effectiveness of their use of emotional appeals such as the "atrocity story"—alleged reports of enemy cruelty—to fuel fear and hatred. Like the Allies, Hitler used political slogans to promote his agenda, such as his 25 theses, a historical allusion to Martin Luther's 95 theses.

SECTION 4 Assessment

Recall
1. (a) Ruhr Valley, p. 761 (b) Dawes Plan, p. 762 (c) *Mein Kampf*, p. 762 (d) Third Reich, p. 763 (e) Gestapo, p. 763 (f) Nuremberg Laws, p. 765 (g) *Kristallnacht*, p. 765 2. (a) chancellor, p. 761 (b) repudiate, p. 763 (c) concentration camp, p. 765

Comprehension
3. The Weimar government depended on coalitions that easily fell apart. People blamed the Weimar government for the hated Versailles treaty. In 1923, Germany was hit by severe inflation.
4. The Depression led to widespread unemployment and misery. Hitler's promises to end reparations, create jobs, and restore German greatness appealed to many Germans. 5. (a) He suspended civil rights, destroyed the Communists, and disbanded other political parties. (b) The Nazis promoted the idea of a German master race that would dominate Europe for 1,000 years. They promoted extreme antisemitism. 6. They were not allowed to marry non-Jews, attend or teach at German schools or universities, hold government jobs, practice law or medicine, or publish books.

Critical Thinking and Writing
7. Answers will vary. Encourage students to express their opinions clearly and to explain the reasons for their positions.
8. Possible answer: Dictators use scapegoats as an easy explanation for complex problems and to unite people against a common enemy.

Activity Rubrics

Share rubrics with students before they write their newspaper editorials.

Attempted The editorial is incomplete.

Minimal The editorial has limited information, reveals a weak grasp of the issue, is disorganized, and contains numerous mechanical errors.

Adequate The editorial reveals a good grasp of the issue and includes a few convincing details. It is clearly written and contains few mechanical errors.

Exemplary The editorial is very well researched and well written, includes interesting details, clearly and convincingly demonstrates the point of view of a western nation, and contains no mechanical errors.

Caption Answer

Possible answer: They were afraid of being killed.

Creating a Chapter Summary

As a reteaching opportunity, pair a more able student with a less able student to complete this chapter summary.

Possible information students might add to their diagrams includes: **Italy** women urged to "win battle of motherhood," revived Italian pride **Both** state control of economy, use of police spies and terror to enforce will of the state, strict censorship and government monopoly of media, use of school and media for propaganda, unquestioning obedience to single leader **Germany** brutal Nazi party, concept of *Lebensraum*, Third Reich appeals to nationalism, SS troops enforce totalitarian rule, program to rearm Germany, campaign against Jews

Building Vocabulary

1–10. Students' sentences should reflect an understanding of each word.

Recalling Key Facts

11. More goods were being produced than consumers could afford to buy.
12. fortifications that France built along several miles of its border with Germany
13. Writers expressed disgust and disillusionment with war, seeing it as a sign of moral breakdown.
14. It promised a strong and stable government and sought to revive national pride.
15. He started large public works projects, rebuilt the military, and brought big business and labor under government control.
16. He believed that Aryans were a master race and that others, including Slavs and Jews, were inferior.

Critical Thinking and Writing

17. **(a)** World War I had created a high demand for raw materials, but the need dwindled after the war. **(b)** Continued overproduction of goods caused prices to fall and contributed to the Great Depression.
18. Answers will vary, but many students will answer in the affirmative. They may cite generational differences that exist today in areas such as dress, musical taste, and interests.
19. Possible answers: **(a)** Textbooks were rewritten to reflect Nazi views. Old German myths, such as those in Wagner's operas, were espoused

---

CHAPTER **30 Review and Assessment**

Creating a Chapter Summary

On a sheet of paper, draw a Venn diagram to compare Italy and Germany in the postwar years. Place information relating to Italy in the circle marked Italy and information relating to Germany in the circle marked Germany. Place information that relates to both countries in the part of the circles that overlaps.

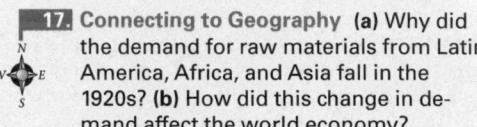

Italy
- Mussolini becomes *Il Duce*
- Black Shirts use intimidation and violence
-

Germany
- Hitler becomes *Führer*
-

- Single-party dictatorship
-

For additional review and enrichment activities, see the interactive version of *World History* available on the Web and on CD-ROM.

Web Site Self-Test
For practice test questions for Chapter 30, see **www. phschool.com**.

Building Vocabulary

Write sentences, using the chapter vocabulary words listed below, leaving blanks where the vocabulary words would go. Exchange your sentences with another student and fill in the blanks in each other's sentences.

1. **disarmament**
2. **overproduction**
3. **margin buying**
4. **psychoanalysis**
5. **surrealism**
6. **stream of consciousness**
7. **flapper**
8. **chancellor**
9. **repudiate**
10. **concentration camp**

Recalling Key Facts

11. What imbalances helped cause the Great Depression of the 1930s?
12. What was the Maginot Line?
13. How did the literature of the 1920s reflect the influence of World War I?
14. Why did the ideology of fascism appeal to many Italians?
15. Describe the economic policies that Hitler pursued as German leader.
16. How did racist theories shape Hitler's social policies?

Critical Thinking and Writing

17. **Connecting to Geography** **(a)** Why did the demand for raw materials from Latin America, Africa, and Asia fall in the 1920s? **(b)** How did this change in demand affect the world economy?
18. **Linking Past and Present** The manners and culture of the 1920s created a "generation gap" between young people and their elders. Do present-day manners and culture create a similar "generation gap"? Explain.
19. **Recognizing Propaganda** **(a)** Give three examples of Hitler's use of propaganda. **(b)** Why was propaganda an important Nazi tool?
20. **Identifying Main Ideas** Reread Martin Niemoller's words about Nazism. Then, restate Niemoller's main point in your own words.
21. **Recognizing Points of View** "England can only be saved by direct action. When it's saved, we can begin to think about Parliament again." Based on what you have read, which of the three competing postwar ideologies does this statement express—democracy, fascism, or communism? Explain.

---

because they glorified Germany, while Jewish works were deemed corrupt. Books considered unfavorable to Germany were burned. **(b)** It helped control and indoctrinate people.
20. Possible answer: It is important to take a stand against injustice, for inevitably it affects us all.
21. The statement reflects fascism's emphasis on nationalism, forceful action, and rejection of democratic institutions.

Gaetano Salvemini was an Italian college professor. In the 1920s, he was forced to resign his position and go into exile. Here, Salvemini describes events after an attempt was made on Mussolini's life in 1926. Read the passage, then answer the questions that follow.

"At Como, the Fascists got hold of many of the Opposition and painted their faces in three colors. Amongst the persons who suffered this vile treatment were the proprietor of a clock factory at Monte Olimpino, the proprietor of a cement factory at Pontchiano, and Commendatore Rosasco, one of the most important silk weavers of the district. The houses of Signor Noseda, a Member of Parliament, of the lawyer Beltramini-Frontini, and of the priest Primo Noiana, were sacked. . . .

At Brescia, the printing establishment of the paper Il Cittadino di Brescia, and the headquarters of the Christian-Democrat organizations were smashed and burnt."

—Gaetano Salvemini, *The Fascist Dictatorship in Italy*

22. How did the Fascists respond to the assassination attempt on Mussolini?
23. (a) Why do you think the Fascists painted the faces of some people? (b) Do you think this was an effective tactic?
24. (a) How would you describe the people persecuted by the Fascists? (b) Why do you think these people were chosen?
25. What message do you think the Fascists were trying to send?
26. Reread the description of *Kristallnacht* at the end of Section 4. (a) How were the tactics used by Italian Fascists and German Nazis similar? (b) Why do you think fascist dictatorships often used such tactics?

Use the Internet to research the economic systems of capitalism, socialism, and communism *or* the political systems of democracy and totalitarianism. Then, make a graphic organizer that compares and contrasts the systems you chose.

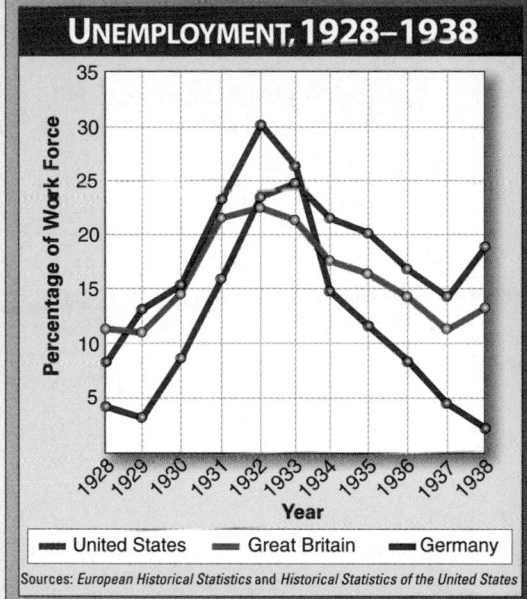

UNEMPLOYMENT, 1928–1938

Percentage of Work Force vs. Year (1928–1938)

Legend: United States | Great Britain | Germany

Sources: *European Historical Statistics* and *Historical Statistics of the United States*

Among the nations hardest hit by the Great Depression were the three titans of the Industrial Revolution—Britain, Germany, and the United States. Study the graph, then answer the following questions:

27. What was Britain's unemployment rate in 1928? In 1931?
28. Which nation shown here had the lowest unemployment rate in 1928? In 1933?
29. (a) During what year did unemployment in Germany reach its highest point? (b) In what year did Hitler become chancellor? (c) How are these events related?
30. (a) What trend do you see in the unemployment rate in the United States from 1933 to 1937? (b) Based on what you have read, how might you explain this trend?
31. (a) What trend do you see in Germany's unemployment rate from 1932 to 1938? (b) Based on what you have read, how might you explain this trend?

Skills Tip

When you look at a graph, be aware of what was going on during that time period. Knowing key events may indicate the causes of certain trends.

22. They painted people's faces, attacked people violently, looted and sacked homes and places of work, and imprisoned people.
23. Possible answers: (a) They wanted to humiliate some of their opponents. (b) Yes. Instead of making martyrs of their enemies, the fascists made them look ridiculous in public.
24. (a) They were business, religious, political, and community leaders. (b) They had important roles in society; they were Mussolini's opponents.
25. They wanted to show that they would not stand for any opposition; Mussolini would not be toppled or killed.
26. Possible answers: (a) Both groups used terror tactics against opponents. They raided communities, beat people, and destroyed property. (b) Fascists despised free speech and glorified strength. Terror tactics helped these governments silence opposition.

Analyzing Graphs

27. about 12%; about 22%
28. United States; Britain
29. (a) 1932 (b) 1933 (c) Possible answer: Hitler was able to use people's dissatisfaction with the high rate of unemployment to grab power by promising economic reforms.
30. (a) It goes steadily down. (b) In 1933, Franklin Roosevelt became President. Under his New Deal, government programs created jobs for the unemployed.
31. (a) It goes steadily down. (b) Hitler launched large public works programs and began to rearm Germany. These policies put many people to work.

Skills Tip

Point out that line graphs are good vehicles for showing change over time. Bar graphs are well suited to comparing many different values at the same time. The Skills Handbook in the front of the book has a lesson that will help students with this feature.

Direct students to **www.phschool.com** for links to sites that will help them get started on this assignment. Share rubrics with students before they make their organizers.
Attempted The graphic organizer is attempted but is not finished satisfactorily.
Minimal The graphic organizer is completed but shows limited comparison and contrast of the systems.
Adequate The graphic organizer reflects research and thought and is neatly done.
Exemplary The graphic organizer is comprehensive, reflects thorough research and thought, and is well executed.

Unit Theme Activity

Remind students to continue working on their Unit Theme Activity. See rubrics for the activity on the unit opener page in the Teacher's Edition.

Chapter 31 Planning Guide

Resource Manager

	CORE INSTRUCTION	READING/SKILLS
Chapter Level Resources	📁 Teaching Resources 📄 Pacing Charts, Ch. 31 📄 Teaching With Themes, p. 34 📺 Color Transparencies, p. F–63 💿 Resource Pro® Ch. 31 💻 www.phschool.com • eTeach	💿 Book on CD, Ch. 31 💿 Interactive Student Tutorial CD-ROM, Ch. 31 💿 Social Studies Skills Tutor CD-ROM 📺 Skills Transparencies
1 Aggression, Appeasement, and War 1. Articulate how dictators and the Spanish Civil War challenged peace. 2. Trace how continuing German aggression led toward war. 3. Outline the factors that encouraged the coming of war.	📁 Teaching Resources 📖 Creative Teaching Activities, p. 138 💿 Prentice Hall Presentation Pro, Ch. 31, Section 1 📺 Section Reading Support Transparencies	📁 Teaching Resources 📓 Unit 7 booklet • Guided Reading and Review, p. 76 📄 Guide to the Essentials 📼 Guided Reading Audiotapes, Ch. 31, Section 1
2 The Global Conflict: Axis Advances 1. Describe the early gains that allowed the Axis powers to control much of Europe. 2. Identify the Battle of Britain and Operation Barbarossa. 3. Summarize how Japan responded to growing American involvement.	📁 Teaching Resources 📖 Creative Teaching Activities, p. 139 💿 Prentice Hall Presentation Pro, Ch. 31, Section 2 📺 Section Reading Support Transparencies	📁 Teaching Resources 📓 Unit 7 booklet • Guided Reading and Review, p. 78 📄 Guide to the Essentials 📼 Guided Reading Audiotapes, Ch. 31, Section 2

3 The Global Conflict: Allied Successes
1. Describe how Germany and Japan treated people in occupied lands.
2. Outline how the Allies turned the tide of the war.
3. Explain how the Red Army and the Allied invasion of France undid German plans.
	📁 Teaching Resources
	📓 Unit 7 booklet
	    • Biography Activity, p. 86
	    • Viewpoint Activity, p. 88
	📖 Creative Teaching Activities, p. 140
	💿 Prentice Hall Presentation Pro, Ch. 31, Section 3
	📺 Section Reading Support Transparencies
		📁 Teaching Resources
		📓 Unit 7 booklet
		    • Guided Reading and Review, p. 80
		📄 Guide to the Essentials
		📼 Guided Reading Audiotapes, Ch. 31, Section 3

4 Toward Victory
1. Relate how the Pacific war was fought.
2. Reconstruct how the Allies defeated Nazi Germany.
3. Analyze the debates that surrounded the defeat of Japan.
	📁 Teaching Resources
	📓 Unit 7 booklet
	    • Primary Source Activity, p. 87
	📖 Creative Teaching Activities, p. 141
	💿 Prentice Hall Presentation Pro, Ch. 31, Section 4
	📺 Section Reading Support Transparencies
		📁 Teaching Resources
		📓 Unit 7 booklet
		    • Guided Reading and Review, p. 82
		    • Skill Application Activity, p. 89
		📄 Guide to the Essentials
		📼 Guided Reading Audiotapes, Ch. 31, Section 4

5 From World War to Cold War 1. Describe the issues that arose in the aftermath of war. 2. Explain why the Allies organized the United Nations. 3. Summarize how the breakup of the wartime alliance led to new conflicts.	📁 Teaching Resources 📖 Creative Teaching Activities, p. 142 💿 Prentice Hall Presentation Pro, Ch. 31, Section 5 📺 Section Reading Support Transparencies	📁 Teaching Resources 📓 Unit 7 booklet • Guided Reading and Review, p. 84 📄 Guide to the Essentials 📼 Guided Reading Audiotapes, Ch. 31, Section 5

ENRICHMENT/PRE-AP

Teaching Resources
Teaching With Themes
- Global View Activity, p. 47

www.phschool.com
- Global View Essay
- Why Study History?

Listening to Literature World Masterpieces, *A Song on the End of the World* by Czeslaw Milosz, side 10

www.phschool.com
- Internet Activities, Section 1

Teaching Resources
Chapter Extension Activities, p. 74

www.phschool.com
- Virtual Field Trip
- Internet Activities, Section 2

Teaching Resources
Chapter Extension Activities, p. 75
History Through Literature, pp. 65–66
Visions, Voices, Views, Daily Life CloseUp, tape 7

ASSESSMENT

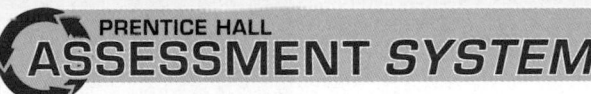
PRENTICE HALL ASSESSMENT SYSTEM

Core Assessment
- **ExamView Test Bank booklet,** Ch. 31
- **ExamView Test Bank CD-ROM,** Ch. 31

Standardized Test Preparation
Diagnose and Prescribe
- **Diagnostic Tests for High School Social Studies Skills**

Review and Reteach
- **Review Book for World History**

Practice and Assess
- **Document-Based Assessment,** pp. 33–37
- **Test-Taking Strategies With Transparencies**
- **Alternative Assessment booklet**
- **Test Prep Book for World History**

Teaching Resources
Unit 7 booklet
- Geography Quiz, p. 90
- Section Quizzes, pp. 77, 79, 81, 83, 85
- Chapter Tests A, B, and C, pp. 91–95

www.phschool.com
- Self-Test

CUSTOMIZE FOR INDIVIDUAL NEEDS

Gifted and Talented
- **Teacher's Edition,** Activities: Customize for Heterogeneous Groups, p. 779; Connections to Literature, p. 789; Customize for Heterogeneous Groups, p. 792

Less Proficient Readers
- **Guide to the Essentials,** Ch. 31
- **Guided Reading Audiotapes, English,** Ch. 31
- **Book on CD,** Ch. 31
- **Teacher's Edition,** Activities: Customize for Visual Learners, p. 773

Less Proficient Writers
- **Teacher's Edition,** Activities: Cooperative Learning Activities, p. 777; Customize for Kinesthetic Learners, p. 784

Students Acquiring English/ESL
- **Guide to the Essentials, English/Spanish,** Ch. 31
- **Guided Reading Audiotapes, English/Spanish,** Ch. 31
- **Book on CD,** Ch. 31
- **Teacher's Edition,** Activities marked with an *

iTEXT

Don't miss the exclusive interactive version of *World History: Connections to Today* on the Internet and CD-ROM.

World War II and Its Aftermath 1931–1955

INTRODUCTION

When Germany invaded Poland, France and Britain declared war on Germany. At first World War II's Axis powers won decisively. In the end, however, the Allies were victorious. During the war, German Nazis systematically destroyed Jews and others they considered "undesirable" in the Holocaust. Germany finally surrendered in May of 1945, and Japan surrendered the following September, after atomic bombs destroyed Hiroshima and Nagasaki. Later, the Soviet Union and the United States engaged in a Cold War of conflicting ideologies and mutual distrust.

Focusing on Themes

Suggest that students focus on these theme questions as they read:

Continuity and Change
Why was the world plunged into a second global conflict after World War I?

Economics and Technology
How did technology affect the fighting and destruction in World War II?

Political and Social Systems
How did totalitarian regimes carry out their goals during the war?

Global Interaction
How did World War II change the balance of world power?

Geography and History
How did geography influence the war in Eastern Europe and Russia?

◆ TIME LINE ACTIVITY

Share the About the Pictures note before you ask these questions:

1. What action did Italy take in 1935? *(invaded Ethiopia)*
2. How long after World War II began did the U.S. enter the war? *(two years)*
3. What took place in China after World War II ended? *(Mao founded the People's Republic.)*

Chapter Preview

1 Aggression, Appeasement, and War
2 The Global Conflict: Axis Advances
3 The Global Conflict: Allied Successes
4 Toward Victory
5 From World War to Cold War

1936

Spanish Civil War begins. This anti-fascist poster reads, "To Arms! No one is excused from duty."

1935

Italy invades Ethiopia.

1939

Germany invades Poland, sparking World War II. Here, a German tank and motorcycle corps speeds through the Polish countryside.

CHAPTER EVENTS

| 1930 | 1935 | 1940 |

GLOBAL EVENTS

1930 Mohandas K. Gandhi leads the Salt March in India.

1934 Chinese Communists flee the Guomindang in the Long March.

Don't Miss!

 You Are There . . .
Surviving the Blitz
(Section 2)

 Analyzing Primary Sources
The Holocaust
(Section 3)

Resource Directory

Teaching Resources
Chapter Theme Activities Teaching With Themes, p. 34
Pacing Chart With Block Scheduling Guide Ch. 31
Global View Activity *How Did World Events Reflect Growing Interaction?* Teaching With Themes booklet, p. 47

Technology
World History Color Transparencies Ch. 31 Graphic Organizer, p. F–63

Major Battles of World War II, 1939–1945

World War II was fought on land and sea. Battles took place on several continents.

Legend:
- Allied powers and areas under Allied control, 1939
- Axis powers and areas under Axis control, 1939
- ★ Battle sites

1939: German invasion of Poland

1945: Fall of Berlin

1942–1943: Battle of Stalingrad

1945: Atomic bombing of Hiroshima and Nagasaki

1944: Allied invasion of France (D-Day)

1942: Battle of Midway

1941: Japanese attack on Pearl Harbor

PACIFIC OCEAN

ATLANTIC OCEAN

PACIFIC OCEAN

INDIAN OCEAN

Robinson Projection

0   1500   3000 Miles
0   1500   3000 Kilometers

Honolulu Star-Bulletin 1st EXTRA

WAR!

OAHU BOMBED BY JAPANESE PLANES

SAN FRANCISCO, Dec. 7.—President Roosevelt announced this morning that Japanese planes had attacked Manila and Pearl Harbor.

1941
Japan bombs Pearl Harbor, on the the Hawaiian island of Oahu, and the United States enters the war.

1945
World War II ends. To honor the occasion, Allied troops in Paris march through the Arc de Triomphe.

1955
Postwar conflict between the Soviets and their former allies leads to the creation of the Warsaw Pact.

1945 ● **1950** **1955**

1947 Britain grants independence to India, and the separate nation of Pakistan is created.

1949 Mao Zedong founds the People's Republic of China.

Chapter 31 **769**

Independent Assignments

Have students read one section as they prepare for class. After class, have them complete the assignment. Some students may benefit from using the Guided Reading and Review worksheets.

Section 1 Have students use the map *World War II in Europe and North Africa* in the Historical Outline Map Book, p. 50, to show areas under German and Italian control in 1939.

Section 2 Have students use the Chapter Extension Activities sheet on p. 74 of the Chapter Extension Activities booklet to learn more about the London blitz.

Section 3 Have students use the worksheet *Raoul Wallenberg* in the Unit 7 booklet, p. 86, to learn how this man saved thousands of Jews from the Nazis.

Section 4 Have students use the worksheet *After the Battle at Kwajalein* in the Unit 7 booklet, p. 87, to learn about the aftermath of a battle in the Pacific.

Section 5 Have students use the worksheet *Night* in the History Through Literature booklet, pp. 65–66, to learn about Elie Wiesel's first night in a concentration camp.

Major Battles of World War II, 1939–1945

Activating Prior Knowledge
You have read about trends in each of the main Axis powers (Germany, Italy, Japan) that foreshadowed World War II. For each country, name one of those trends. *(Germany: rise of Nazism; Italy: rise of fascism; Japan: rise of militarism)*

Previewing
How does this map show you that the Axis powers were almost certainly doomed to fail? *(It shows that most of the world was under Allied control.)*

Background
About the Pictures

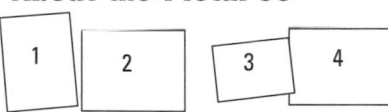

1. The Spanish Civil War ended on April 1, 1939. Despite Hitler's pressure on Franco, a fascist, Spain never entered World War II. Franco remained in power until his death on November 20, 1975.

2. Poland was ill-prepared for the German invasion. Many of its tanks and weapons were outdated. Also, the bulk of Polish forces were entrenched on the frontier and could be easily outflanked. The cavalry, though top-notch, could not withstand German motorized armor.

3. Pearl Harbor is an inlet on the south coast of Oahu, about 6 miles west of Honolulu. The Japanese attack was planned well in advance: their bombers were based on aircraft carriers, and their submarines were in position.

4. The Arc de Triomphe stands at the center of the Place Charles de Gaulle at the end of the Champs-Élysées. Although commissioned by Napoleon in 1806, construction of the Arc was not completed until 1835. The tomb of France's Unknown Soldier lies under the arch.

eTeach

Be sure to check out this month's online discussion with a World History Master Teacher.

Go to **www.phschool.com**.

Bell Ringer Ask students to use the text's glossary to define the words sanction, appeasement, and pacifism. Then have them read the Section Assessment questions. Ask them to predict what they will learn in this section.

Reading Focus

■ How did dictators and the Spanish Civil War challenge world peace?

■ How did continuing German aggression lead Europe toward war?

■ What factors encouraged the coming of war?

Vocabulary

sanction
appeasement
pacifism
Anschluss

Taking Notes

On a sheet of paper, make a table like the one shown here. As you read this section, complete the table by adding information about how dictators challenged world peace.

JAPAN	ITALY	GERMANY	SPAIN
• 1931 Manchuria seized	•	•	•
•			

Main Idea During the 1930s, dictators undermined world peace.

LESSON PLAN

1. Focus In the 1930s, dictators undermined the peace by committing acts of aggression and seizing foreign territories. They tested their military capabilities and technology by intervening in the Spanish Civil War. Fearing the horrors of another major war, the western democracies turned to appeasement, a policy that failed to stop the aggressions of the dictatorial powers.

2. Instruct Ask students to imagine themselves editors for an American, a British, or a French newspaper during the 1930s. Have each student choose an act of aggression committed by Germany, Italy, or Japan during this period. Their assignment is to write an editorial that describes the aggression and recommends how the western democracies should respond to it. Point out that students may choose to support the policy of appeasement or propose military or other action. Remind students to give reasons for the course of action that they suggest. Encourage them to use library resources in addition to the material in this section. Have volunteers read their editorials to the class. Then follow up with a discussion.

3. Assess Ask students to draw a political cartoon to illustrate the viewpoint contained in their editorial.

4. Reteach If students' Assess activity does not reflect adequate understanding of the lesson, you might assign the *Guide to the Essentials* or the *Interactive Student Tutorial CD-ROM* for this section.

Biography

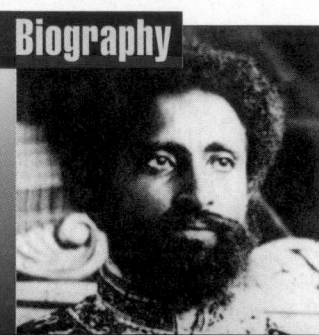

Haile Selassie 1892–1975

When Tafari Makonnen became emperor of Ethiopia in 1930, he took the name Haile Selassie, which means "Might of the Trinity," to show that his power was conferred by God. The Ethiopian people believed that their leader was descended from King Solomon.

Selassie was exiled during the Italian occupation, but returned after four years. He wanted to modernize his country. Selassie oversaw the writing of a constitution, established a parliament and cabinet, initiated land reforms, and encouraged all adults to vote. He remained in office until 1974, when a military group seized power.

Theme: Impact of the Individual How did Selassie share his power?

Setting the Scene During the 1920s, the western democracies tried to strengthen the framework for peace. In the 1930s, that structure crumbled. Dictators in Spain, Germany, and Italy, along with militarists in Japan, pursued ambitious goals for empire. They scorned peace and glorified war.

Unlike these dictators, leaders of the western democracies were haunted by memories of the Great War. Spurred by voters who demanded "no more war," the leaders of Britain, France, and the United States tried to avoid conflict through diplomacy. During the 1930s, the two sides tested each other's commitment and will.

Dictators Challenge World Peace

Challenges to peace followed a pattern throughout the 1930s. Dictators took aggressive action but met only verbal protests and pleas for peace from the democracies. Mussolini and Hitler viewed that desire for peace as weakness and responded with new acts of aggression. With hindsight, we can see the shortcomings of the democracies' policies. We must remember, however, that these policies were the product of long and careful deliberation. At the time, people strongly believed they would work.

Japan on the Move One of the earliest tests had been posed by Japan. Japanese military leaders and ultranationalists thought that Japan should have an empire equal to those of the western powers. In pursuit of this goal, Japan seized Manchuria in 1931. When the League of Nations condemned the aggression, Japan withdrew from the organization.

Japan's easy success strengthened the militarists. In 1937, Japanese armies overran much of eastern China. Once again, western protests had no effect on the conqueror.

Italy Invades Ethiopia In Italy, Mussolini used his new, modern military to pursue his own imperialist ambitions. He looked first to Ethiopia, in northeastern Africa. Italy's defeat by the Ethiopians at the battle of Adowa in 1896 still rankled.

In 1935, Italy invaded Ethiopia. Although the Ethiopians resisted bravely, their outdated weapons were no match for Mussolini's tanks, machine guns, poison gas, and airplanes. The Ethiopian king Haile Selassie (HĪ lee suh LAS ee) appealed to the League of Nations for help. The League voted sanctions, or penalties, against Italy for having violated international law. But the League had no power to enforce the sanctions, and by early 1936, Italy had conquered Ethiopia.

Biography

ANSWER He established a parliament and cabinet.

Resource Directory

Teaching Resources
Creative Teaching Activities Creative Teaching Activities booklet, p. 138
Guided Reading and Review Unit 7 booklet, p. 76

Hitler's Challenge By then, Hitler, too, had tested the will of the western democracies and found it weak. First, he built up the German military in defiance of the Versailles treaty. Then, in 1936, he sent troops into the "demilitarized" Rhineland bordering France—another treaty violation.

Germans hated the Versailles treaty, and Hitler's successful challenge won him greater popularity at home. Western democracies denounced his moves but took no real action. Instead, they adopted a policy of appeasement, giving in to the demands of an aggressor to keep the peace.

Appeasement and Neutrality The western policy of appeasement developed for a number of reasons. France was demoralized, suffering from political divisions at home. It could not move against Hitler without British support.

The British, however, had no desire to confront the German dictator. Some even thought that Hitler's actions constituted a justifiable response to the terms of the Versailles treaty, which they believed had been too harsh against Germany.

In both Britain and France, many saw Hitler and fascism as a defense against a worse evil—the spread of Soviet communism. Additionally, the Great Depression sapped the energies of the western democracies. Finally, widespread pacifism, or opposition to all war, and disgust with the destruction during the previous war pushed many governments to seek peace at any price.

As war clouds gathered in Europe in the mid-1930s, the United States Congress passed a series of Neutrality Acts. One law forbade the sale of arms to any nation at war. Others outlawed loans to warring nations and prohibited Americans from traveling on ships of warring powers. The fundamental goal of American policy, however, was to avoid involvement in a European war, not to prevent such a conflict.

Rome-Berlin-Tokyo Axis In the face of the democracies' apparent weakness, Germany, Italy, and Japan formed what became known as the Rome-Berlin-Tokyo Axis. The Axis powers agreed to fight Soviet communism. They also agreed not to interfere with one another's plans for expansion. The agreement cleared the way for these anti-democratic, aggressor powers to take even bolder steps.

The Spanish Civil War

In 1936, Spain plunged into civil war. Although the Spanish Civil War was a local struggle, it soon drew other European powers into the fighting.

From Monarchy to Republic In the 1920s, Spain was a monarchy dominated by a landowning upper class, the Catholic Church, and the military. Most Spaniards were poor peasants or urban workers. In 1931, popular unrest against the old order forced the king to leave Spain. A republic was set up with a new, more liberal constitution.

The republican government passed a series of controversial reforms. It took over some Church lands and ended Church control of education. It redistributed some land to peasants, gave women the vote, and ended some privileges of the old ruling class. Spanish public opinion was divided. Leftists demanded more radical reforms. Conservatives, who were backed by the military, rejected change. Although most Spaniards wanted a peaceful democracy, clashes between leftists and rightists created chaos.

Axis Leaders
Benito Mussolini (left) and Adolf Hitler (right) were two of the leaders in the Rome-Berlin-Tokyo Axis. Here, they view a parade staged in Mussolini's honor during his 1937 visit to Germany.

Theme: Political and Social Systems What did the Axis powers agree to do?

*A*ctivity
Connections to Film

Writing a News Article *Between the Wars* is an eight-part documentary series that uses original newsreels and eyewitness interviews to chronicle the critical years between the end of World War I and the start of World War II. Assign students to view *The Spanish Civil War*, a 30-minute program on tape six of the series. Ask them to imagine that they are war correspondents with the American Abraham Lincoln Brigade fighting in Spain. Their assignment is to write news articles explaining the complexities of the Spanish Civil War to the American public.

In their article, students should answer the following questions: (1) Who were the two opposing sides in the Spanish Civil War? (2) What role did other countries play in the civil war? (3) How did the conflict affect the lives of Spanish civilians? (4) Why was Francisco Franco victorious? (5) What were the lasting effects of the Spanish Civil War? (*Between the Wars*, released by Special Interest Videos in 1978, is available through Pacific Arts Publishing.) ✳

📖 Block Scheduling Support

The attack on Guernica in the Spanish Civil War (described on the following page) inspired Pablo Picasso's mural painting *Guernica*, perhaps one of the most famous antiwar paintings in the world. Share the background note on the next page with students and display a copy of the mural in the classroom. Then, have students create their own antiwar statement, using a different medium. Students might write a short poem, draw an editorial cartoon, or design a poster, for example. Have students share their work with the class and discuss how different forms of expression can convey similar messages.

Caption Answer

They agreed to fight Soviet communism and to refrain from interfering with one another's plans for expansion.

Picasso's Message The Spanish republican government in 1937 commissioned Pablo Picasso to paint a memorial to the destruction of Guernica. His painting, titled simply *Guernica,* is filled with fragmented structures and human bodies. Fear and anguish overwhelm a wailing mother holding her dead child; a distraught woman rushes from a building; and individuals appear with arms and heads extended in death's pain.

Picasso also made extensive use of symbolism in this work. A horse, a familiar figure in Spanish bullfighting, may represent Spain under attack. An electric light may symbolize the destructive power of modern technology, while an oil lamp may symbolize humanity's resistance to war's atrocities. A bull, often the adversary in Spanish folk tales, could represent human irrationality. In Picasso's *Guernica,* war's destructive power and irrational nature unleash terror and torment on mankind.

Global Connections

Fighting and Writing in Spain

Although the United States government remained neutral in the Spanish Civil War, nearly 3,000 American citizens, as members of the Abraham Lincoln Brigade, joined the Loyalists.

Some American journalists in Spain covered the war for newspapers or magazines. One was Ernest Hemingway, who described Madrid following a German air raid: ". . . with the air still full of heavy granite dust and high explosive smoke, the sidewalks scattered by new round jagged holes with blood trails leading into half the doorways you passed." Hemingway later turned his articles into a novel, *For Whom the Bell Tolls.*

Theme: Art and Literature
How might Hemingway's war experiences have contributed to the success of his novel?

Nationalists Versus Loyalists In 1936, a conservative general named Francisco Franco led a revolt that touched off a bloody civil war. Fascists and supporters of right-wing policies rallied to the banner of Franco's forces, called Nationalists. Supporters of the republic, known as Loyalists, included communists, socialists, and supporters of democracy.

Hitler and Mussolini sent arms and forces to help Franco. Close to 37,000 volunteers from Germany, Italy, the Soviet Union, and the western democracies joined the International Brigades and fought alongside the Loyalists against fascism. The governments of Britain, France, and the United States, however, remained neutral.

A Dress Rehearsal Both sides committed horrible atrocities. The ruinous struggle took almost one million lives. One of the worst horrors was a German air raid on Guernica, a small Spanish market town that lacked any military value. One April morning in 1937, German bombers streaked over the market square. They dropped their load of bombs and then swooped low to machine-gun anyone in the streets who had survived the first attack. An estimated 1,600 innocent people were killed.

To Nazi leaders, the attack on Guernica was an "experiment" to identify what their new planes could do. To the world, it was a grim warning of the destructive power of modern warfare.

By 1939, Franco had triumphed. Once in power, he created a fascist dictatorship like those of Hitler and Mussolini. He rolled back earlier reforms, killed or jailed enemies, and used terror to promote order.

German Aggression Continues

In the meantime, Hitler pursued his goal of bringing all German-speaking people into the Third Reich. He also took steps to gain "living space" for Germans in Eastern Europe. Hitler, who believed in the superiority of the German, or "Aryan race," thought that Germany had a right to conquer the inferior Slavs to the east. "Nature is cruel," he claimed, "so we may be cruel, too. . . . I have a right to remove millions of an inferior race that breeds like vermin."

Austria Annexed From the beginning, Nazi propaganda had found fertile ground in Austria. By 1938, Hitler was ready to engineer the Anschluss, or union of Austria and Germany. Early that year, he forced the Austrian chancellor to appoint Nazis to key cabinet posts. When the Austrian leader balked at other demands, Hitler sent in the German army "to preserve order." To indicate his new role as ruler of Austria, Hitler made a speech from the Hofburg Palace, the former residence of the Hapsburg emperors.

The Anschluss violated the Versailles treaty and created a brief war scare. But Hitler quickly silenced any Austrians who opposed him. And since the western democracies took no action, Hitler easily had his way.

The Czech Crisis Germany's next victim was Czechoslovakia. At first, Hitler insisted that the three million Germans in the Sudetenland—a region of western Czechoslovakia—be given autonomy. The demand set off new alarms among the democracies.

Czechoslovakia was one of only two remaining democracies in Eastern Europe. (Finland was the other.) Still, Britain and France were not willing to go to war to save it. As British and French leaders searched for a peaceful solution, Hitler increased his demands. The Sudetenland, he said, must be annexed to Germany.

At the Munich Conference in September 1938, British and French leaders again chose appeasement. They caved in to Hitler's demands and then persuaded the Czechs to surrender the Sudetenland without a fight. In exchange, Hitler assured Britain and France that he had no further plans to expand his territory.

Global Connections

ANSWER Since he had experienced the events, his novel would probably seem authentic.

Aggression in Europe to 1939

Legend:
- Under German control September 1, 1939
- Under Italian control September 1, 1939
- Maginot Line
- German concentration camps, 1939

Azimuthal Equal Area Projection

0 — 250 — 500 Miles

0 — 250 — 500 Kilometers

Map labels: NORWAY, SWEDEN, ESTONIA, LATVIA, LITHUANIA, DENMARK, IRELAND, GREAT BRITAIN, North Sea, Baltic Sea, Danzig, POLISH CORRIDOR, USSR, NETH., Sachsenhausen, GERMANY, BELG., Buchenwald, POLAND, LUX., RHINELAND March 1936, CZECHOSLOVAKIA March 1939, SUDETENLAND September 1938, Dachau, Mauthausen, FRANCE, SWITZ., AUSTRIA March 1938, HUNGARY, ROMANIA, ATLANTIC OCEAN, PORTUGAL, SPAIN, CORSICA, ITALY, YUGOSLAVIA, Black Sea, BULGARIA, ALBANIA April 1939, SARDINIA, GREECE, TURKEY, Mediterranean Sea, SICILY

"Peace for Our Time" Returning from Munich, British prime minister Neville Chamberlain told cheering crowds that he had achieved "peace for our time." To Parliament, he declared that the Munich Pact had "saved Czechoslovakia from destruction and Europe from Armageddon." French leader Edouard Daladier had a different reaction to the joyous crowds that greeted him in Paris. "The fools, why are they cheering?" he asked.

The Czech crisis revealed the Nazi menace. British politician Winston Churchill, who had long warned of the Nazi threat, judged the diplomats harshly: "They had to choose between war and dishonor. They chose dishonor; they will have war."

Europe Plunges Toward War

Just as Churchill predicted, Munich did not bring peace. Instead, Europe plunged rapidly toward war. In March 1939, Hitler gobbled up the rest of Czechoslovakia. The democracies finally accepted the fact that appeasement had failed. At last thoroughly alarmed, they promised to protect Poland, most likely the next target of Hitler's expansion.

Nazi-Soviet Pact In August 1939, Hitler stunned the world by announcing a nonaggression pact with his great enemy—Joseph Stalin, the Soviet dictator. Publicly, the Nazi-Soviet Pact bound Hitler and Stalin to peaceful relations. Secretly, the two agreed (1) not to fight if the other went to war and (2) to divide up Poland and other parts of Eastern Europe.

The pact was based not on friendship or respect but on mutual need. Hitler feared communism as Stalin feared fascism. But Hitler wanted a free hand in Poland. Also, he did not want to fight a war with the western democracies and the Soviet Union at the same time.

Recall

1. (a) Haile Selassie, p. 770 **(b)** Rome-Berlin-Tokyo Axis, p. 771 **(c)** Guernica, p. 772 **(d)** Munich Conference, p. 772 **(e)** Neville Chamberlain, p. 773 **(f)** Nazi-Soviet Pact, p. 773 **2. (a)** sanction, p. 770 **(b)** appeasement, p. 771 **(c)** pacifism, p. 771 **(d)** Anschluss, p. 772

Comprehension

3. Possible answer: **(a)** Each took aggressive action and seized other lands. **(b)** Germany and Italy sent forces to help Franco. The Soviet Union and a few volunteers from Western nations supported the Loyalists. **4.** It annexed Austria and the Sudetenland and invaded Poland. **5.** Hitler saw appeasement as a sign that other powers would not interfere with his plans for domination, and he continued to annex territory. Finally, France and Britain realized that appeasement had failed, and they agreed to protect Poland. When Poland was invaded, they declared war on Germany.

Critical Thinking and Writing

6. Possible answer: The Munich Conference showed that Britain and France favored appeasement and would not take a strong stand against Nazi aggression. This may have encouraged Hitler to further aggression, leading to the war. **7.** Possible answer: World War I left unresolved conflicts that led to World War II.

Activity Rubrics

Share rubrics with students before they write their letters.

Attempted The letter shows little research, is poorly written and organized, contains many mechanical errors, and fails to reflect a point of view.

Minimal The letter is poorly written and organized and contains some mechanical errors but shows some research and attempts to reflect a point of view.

Adequate The letter shows appropriate research, is well written and organized, contains few mechanical errors, and reflects a point of view.

Exemplary The letter shows extensive research, is very well written and organized, contains no mechanical errors, and strongly presents a point of view.

For his part, Stalin had sought allies among the western democracies against the Nazi menace. Mutual suspicions, however, kept them apart. By joining with Hitler, Stalin bought time to build up Soviet defenses. He also saw a chance for important territorial gains.

Invasion of Poland On September 1, 1939, a week after the Nazi-Soviet Pact, German forces invaded Poland. Two days later, Britain and France honored their commitment to Poland and declared war on Germany. World War II had begun. One British poet caught the overwhelming mood of gloom in these lines:

> "In the nightmare of the dark
> All the dogs of Europe bark,
> And the living nations wait,
> Each sequestered in its hate."
> —W. H. Auden, "In Memory of W. B. Yeats"

Why War Came

Many factors contributed to the outbreak of World War II. You have learned some of the reasons behind Axis aggression. You have also seen why western democracies adopted a policy of appeasement. Today, historians often see the war as an effort to revise the 1919 peace settlement. The Versailles treaty had divided much of the world into two camps—those who were satisfied with its terms and those who were not. Germany, Italy, Japan, and the Soviet Union all felt betrayed or excluded by the settlement.

Since 1939, people have debated issues such as why the western democracies failed to respond forcefully to the Nazi threat, and whether they could have stopped Hitler if they had responded. Dreading war, the democracies hoped that diplomacy and compromise would right old wrongs and prevent further aggression. They were distracted by their own political and economic problems and misread Hitler's intentions. Most disregarded even Hitler's declared goals in *Mein Kampf.*

Some historians assert that Britain and France could have stopped Hitler in 1936 by aiding Loyalist Spain before Germany was fully rearmed. But neither country was willing to risk war. The devastation of World War I, combined with awareness of the destructive power of modern technology, made the idea of more fighting unbearable. Unfortunately, when war came, it proved to be even more horrendous than anyone had imagined.

SECTION 1 Assessment

Recall

1. Identify: (a) Haile Selassie, **(b)** Rome-Berlin-Tokyo Axis, **(c)** Guernica, **(d)** Munich Conference, **(e)** Neville Chamberlain, **(f)** Nazi-Soviet Pact.
2. Define: (a) sanction, **(b)** appeasement, **(c)** pacifism, **(d)** Anschluss.

Comprehension

3. (a) How did Japan, Italy, and Germany test the resolve of western democracies before 1937? **(b)** Explain how other countries participated in the Spanish Civil War.

4. Identify major acts of German aggression in 1938 and 1939.
5. How did appeasement lead to the outbreak of war?

Critical Thinking and Writing

6. Recognizing Causes and Effects How was the Munich Conference a turning point in the road toward world war?

7. Analyzing Information Why do you think some historians call the period between 1919 and 1939 the 20-year armistice?

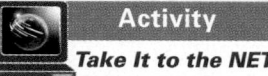

Activity
Take It to the NET

Use the Internet to find out more about the Munich Conference of 1938. Write a letter to the editor describing your opinion of Prime Minister Chamberlain's actions at the conference.

Resource Directory

Teaching Resources

Section Quiz Unit 7 booklet, p. 77
Creative Teaching Activities Creative Teaching Activities booklet, p. 139
Guided Reading and Review Unit 7 booklet, p. 78

Technology

Listening to Literature World Masterpieces audiotapes *A Song on the End of the World* by Czeslaw Milosz, side 10, running time 1:39 min.
Interactive Student Tutorial CD-ROM Ch. 31
Computer Test Bank Ch. 31

SECTION 2 The Global Conflict: Axis Advances

Reading Focus

- What early gains allowed the Axis powers to control much of Europe?
- What were the Battle of Britain and Operation Barbarossa?
- How did Japan respond to growing American involvement?

Vocabulary

blitzkrieg
radar
sonar

Taking Notes

As you read this section, make a time line on a separate sheet of paper. Record key events in the global conflict from 1939 to 1942. The sample on this page will help you get started.

1939	1940	1941	1942

Germany
invades Poland

Main Idea The early years of World War II were marked by Axis victories.

Setting the Scene

"Hitler will collapse the day we declare war on Germany," predicted a confident French general on the eve of World War II. He could not have been more wrong. World War II, the costliest war in history, lasted six years—from 1939 to 1945. It pitted the Axis powers, chiefly Germany, Italy, and Japan, against the Allied powers, which eventually included Britain, France, the Soviet Union, China, the United States, and 45 other nations.

Early Axis Gains

On September 1, 1939, Nazi forces stormed into Poland, revealing the enormous power of Hitler's blitzkrieg, or "lightning war." First, German planes bombed airfields, factories, towns, and cities, and screaming dive bombers fired on troops and civilians. Then, fast-moving tanks and troop transports roared into the country. The Polish army fought back unsuccessfully.

While Germany attacked from the west, Stalin's forces invaded from the east, grabbing lands promised to them under the Nazi-Soviet Pact. Within a month, Poland ceased to exist.

Hitler passed the winter without much further action. Stalin's armies, however, pushed on into the Baltic states of Estonia, Latvia, and Lithuania. Soviet forces also seized part of Finland, which put up stiff but unsuccessful resistance.

The "Phony War" During that first winter, the French hunkered down behind the Maginot Line. Britain sent troops to wait with them. Some reporters referred to this quiet time as the "phony war."

Then, in April 1940, the war exploded into action. Hitler launched a blitzkrieg against Norway and Denmark, both of which soon fell. Next, his forces slammed into the Netherlands and Belgium.

Miracle of Dunkirk By May, German forces were pouring into France. Retreating British forces were soon trapped between the advancing Nazis and the waters of the

Invasion of Poland
World War II was the first war to use airplanes in large-scale attacks. Here, German Stuka dive bombers fly over Poland.

Theme: Economics and Technology How would airplanes be used in wartime?

Chapter 31 **775**

Read aloud to students the following statement: "Unlike World War I, with its dug-in defensive trenches, the new global conflict was a war of aggressive movement." As students read Section 2, have them look for evidence that supports this statement. *(More Advanced Readers)*

Background
Daily Life

Phony Facts During the relatively peaceful days of the "phony war," wild rumors were rampant on the home front. In Britain, some widely circulated rumors included the following: Hitler had imported 30,000 gorillas from Brazil to be trained for immediate attack. The British government was adding cat fat to margarine and permitting restaurants to put cat meat in steak-and-kidney pie. Peace was being arranged so that Britain, France, and Germany could combine to attack the Soviet Union. The Russians had a device on their parachutes that could propel a paratrooper or downed flyer back into the air if he didn't like the spot where he was landing.

Background
Historical Evidence

A Fateful Decision Historians trying to explain the miracle of Dunkirk point to a fateful decision made by Hitler. He stopped his advancing German tanks just south of Dunkirk in order to reduce their losses and preserve them for later battles. He was assured by his closest advisers that the German Luftwaffe could easily prevent the escape of the reeling Allied army.

Hitler's advisers were wrong. The German planes were effective, but not nearly effective enough. Despite heavy attacks by the Luftwaffe, the British navy, along with hundreds of small boats captained by civilians, were able to get the job done. They ferried some 198,000 British and 140,000 French, Belgian, and other soldiers from the bombed and blazing beaches of Dunkirk to the shores of Britain.

Connections to Today

ANSWER Synthetic products replaced natural products that were in short supply.

Connections to Today

Rationing and New Products

What do nylon, margarine, and synthetic rubber have in common? All three were used during World War II to replace consumer goods needed for the war effort.

Before the war, women often wore silk stockings. The supply of silk dried up, however, as the army used it to make parachutes. In response, stocking manufacturers switched to nylon, a synthetic fabric developed just before the war.

During World War II, butterfat was needed to make cheese for soldiers. Stores replaced butter with margarine, a little-used vegetable oil substance that had been developed in the 1860s.

When the Japanese invaded Southeast Asia, they cut off the supply of rubber. The United States responded by developing synthetic rubber, modeled on a German invention from World War I.

Theme: Economics and Technology How did technology reduce the impact of shortages during World War II?

English Channel. In a desperate gamble, the British sent all available naval vessels, merchant ships, and even fishing and pleasure boats across the channel to pluck stranded troops off the beaches of Dunkirk and Ostend.

Despite German air attacks, the improvised armada ferried more than 300,000 troops to safety in Britain. This heroic rescue, dubbed the "miracle of Dunkirk," greatly raised British morale.

France Falls Meanwhile, German forces headed south toward Paris. Italy declared war on France and attacked from the south. Overrun and demoralized, France surrendered. On June 22, 1940, in a forest clearing in northeastern France, Hitler avenged the German defeat of 1918. He forced the French to sign the surrender documents in the same railroad car in which Germany had signed the armistice ending World War I. Following the surrender, Germany occupied northern France. In the south, the Germans set up a "puppet state," with its capital at Vichy (VIHSH ee).

Some French officers escaped to England and set up a government-in-exile. Led by Charles de Gaulle, these "free French" worked to liberate their homeland. Within France, resistance fighters used guerrilla tactics against German forces.

Africa and the Balkans Axis armies also pushed into North Africa and the Balkans. In September 1940, Mussolini ordered forces from Italy's North African colony of Libya into Egypt. When the British army repulsed these invaders, Hitler sent a brilliant commander, General Erwin Rommel, to North Africa. The "Desert Fox," as he was called, chalked up a string of successes in 1941 and 1942. He pushed the British back across the desert toward Cairo, in Egypt.

In October 1940, Italian forces invaded Greece. They encountered stiff resistance, and in 1941 German troops once again provided reinforcements. Both Greece and Yugoslavia were added to the growing Axis empire. Even after the Axis triumph, however, Greek and Yugoslav guerrillas plagued the occupying forces.

Meanwhile, both Bulgaria and Hungary had joined the Axis alliance. By 1941, the Axis powers or their allies controlled most of Western Europe.

The Technology of Modern Warfare The whirlwind Nazi advance revealed the awesome power of modern warfare. Air power took a prominent role. After its tryout in Spain, the Luftwaffe, or German air force, perfected methods of bombing civilian as well as military targets. Hitler also used fast-moving armored tanks and troop carriers along with parachute troops to storm through Europe.

Technology created a war machine with even greater destructive power. Scientists and engineers improved the design and effectiveness of airplanes and submarines. They produced ever more deadly bombs and invented hundreds of new devices, such as radar to detect airplanes and sonar to detect submarines. At the same time, research also led to medical advances to treat the wounded and new synthetic products to replace scarce strategic goods.

The Battle of Britain and the Blitz

With the fall of France in June 1940, Britain stood alone in Western Europe. Hitler was sure that the British would sue for peace. But Winston Churchill, who had replaced Neville Chamberlain as prime minister, had other plans. For many years, Churchill had been a lone voice against the Nazi threat. In 1940, he rallied the British to fight on:

> "We shall defend our island, whatever the cost may be. We shall fight on the beaches, we shall fight on the landing grounds, we shall fight in the fields and in the streets, we shall fight in the hills; we shall never surrender."
> —Winston Churchill, radio address, June 4, 1940

Resource Directory

Teaching Resources
You Are There Chapter Extension Activities booklet, p. 74

You Are There . . .

Surviving the Blitz

You are glad you heeded Churchill's warnings and prepared for a German assault on London. For the forty-fifth night in a row, the air-raid sirens wail. Soon, the unmistakable drone of German bomber engines will fill the air. This will be followed by the high-pitched shriek of falling bombs and the booming of antiaircraft guns.

You race with members of your family to the nearest shelter—an underground (subway) station. No trains run through it now. Instead, you and hundreds of others can sleep here for the night—safely, you hope. Someone begins an upbeat song. . . .

Bombs pound the city, turning buildings to rubble. At dawn, hours after the "all-clear" sirens sound, you climb up to the street and head home. Miraculously, the high dome of St. Paul's Cathedral stands proud above the damage. It is a symbol that "London can take it."

Portfolio Assessment

As a Londoner living through the wartime blitz, you are keeping a journal of your experiences. Write a journal entry describing your night in the underground during the raid and what you saw on your walk home in the morning.

Chapter 31 **777**

EXPLORING for **HUMAN DRAMA**

You Are There . . .

Bell Ringer Note that one very famous photograph of the London blitz shows a milkman making his rounds over the rubble left by bombs. What does that tell you about the spirit of the British? Why is it important to keep daily life as normal as possible in times of stress?

Background About the Scene

Underground Living The blitz drove thousands of Londoners to seek shelter in the subway stations of the London Underground system. Unlike the French Métro, the London Underground was far enough below the surface to offer adequate protection from bombings. By early 1941, the London Transport Board equipped subway stations with bunk beds so that people could sleep while the trains continued to function.

Activity Cooperative Learning

Presenting a Skit Have small groups write and present skits demonstrating life in England during the blitz. Suggest that students conduct research to find material for their skits. Students may discover, for example, that many London parents sent their young children to the country during the war. A resource for other ideas is the article "Remembering the Blitz," in the July 1991 issue of *National Geographic*.

Portfolio Assessment Rubrics

Share rubrics with students before they write their journal entries.

Attempted The journal entry is incomplete and shows little effort.

Minimal The journal entry reveals a little knowledge of the blitz and some feelings that a blitz survivor might have.

Adequate The journal entry reveals knowledge of the blitz, and the details show an understanding of the feelings that a blitz survivor might have.

Exemplary The journal entry reveals excellent knowledge of the blitz and conveys empathy for a blitz survivor's feelings, and it is well written.

Test Preparation

Have students read the information under the heading "The Battle of Britain and the Blitz" on the opposite page, and then complete the sentence below.

Based on the passage, you can tell that

A   Churchill wanted England to surrender to Germany.

B   Churchill had spoken up against Hitler for many years.

C   Churchill supported Hitler.

D   Churchill was a pacifist.

Early Warning Network Although the Royal Air Force was greatly outnumbered during the Battle of Britain, it managed to fend off German raids with remarkable success. One reason for its admirable record was radar. England had 21 long-range radar stations that could detect an enemy plane at a distance of 140 miles. Approaching Luftwaffe units were also tracked by trained civilian observers scattered throughout the countryside. Reports from the radar stations and civilian trackers were fed to an information clearing house near London. There, experts tracked the movements of enemy planes on giant maps and immediately telephoned new developments to RAF headquarters. In this way, the RAF was rarely taken by surprise and could rally its fighter pilots to face each new attack.

Faced with this defiance, Hitler ordered his generals to make plans for Operation Sea Lion—the invasion of Britain. In preparation for the invasion, he launched massive air strikes against the island nation.

The London Blitz Beginning on August 12, 1940, German bombers began a daily bombardment of England's southern coast. For a month, the British Royal Air Force valiantly battled the German Luftwaffe. Then, the Germans changed their tactics, turning their attention from military targets in the south to the blitz, or bombing, of London and other cities.

German bombers first appeared over London late on September 7. All through the night, relays of aircraft showered high explosives and firebombs on the sprawling capital. The bombing continued for 57 nights. Much of the city was destroyed, and some 15,000 people lost their lives.

London did not break under the blitz. Defiantly, Parliament continued to meet. Citizens carried on their daily lives, seeking protection in shelters and then emerging when the all-clear sounded to resume their routines. Even the British king and queen chose to support Londoners by joining them in bomb shelters rather than fleeing to the countryside.

Failure of the Blitz German planes continued to bomb London and other cities off and on until June 1941. But contrary to Hitler's hopes, British morale was not destroyed. In fact, the bombing only made the British more determined to turn back the enemy.

Operation Sea Lion was a failure. Hitler turned to a new target—the Soviet Union. The decision to invade Russia helped save Britain. It also proved to be one of Hitler's costliest mistakes.

Operation Barbarossa

In June 1941, Hitler embarked on Operation Barbarossa—the conquest of the Soviet Union.* Hitler made his motives clear. "If I had the Ural Mountains with their incalculable store of treasures in raw materials," he declared, "Siberia with its vast forests, and the Ukraine with its tremendous wheat fields, Germany under National Socialist leadership would swim in plenty." He also wanted to crush communism in Europe and defeat his powerful rival Joseph Stalin.

The German Advance In Operation Barbarossa, Hitler unleashed a new blitzkrieg. About three million Germans poured into the Soviet Union. They caught Stalin unprepared, his army still suffering from the purges that had wiped out many of its top officers.

The Russians lost two and a half million soldiers trying to fend off the invaders. As they were forced back, Russian troops destroyed factories and farm equipment and burned crops to keep them out of enemy hands. But they could not stop the German war machine. By autumn, the Nazis had smashed deep into Russia and were poised to take Moscow and Leningrad.

There, however, the German advance stalled. Like Napoleon's Grand Army in 1812, Hitler's forces were not prepared for the fury of Russia's "General Winter." By early December, temperatures plunged to –4 degrees. Thousands of German soldiers froze to death.

Siege of Leningrad The Russians, meanwhile, suffered appalling hardships. In September 1941, the two-and-a-half-year siege of Leningrad began. Food was soon rationed to two pieces of bread a day. Desperate Leningraders ate almost anything. They boiled wallpaper scraped off walls because its paste was said to contain potato flour. Owners of leather briefcases boiled and ate them—"jellied meat," they called it.

---

*The plan took its name from the Holy Roman emperor Frederick Barbarossa, a medieval Germanic leader who had won great victories in the East.

Although more than a million Leningraders died during the German siege, the survivors struggled to defend their city. Hoping to gain some relief for the exhausted Russians, Stalin urged Britain to open a second front in Western Europe. Although Churchill could not offer much real help, the two powers did agree to work together.

American Involvement Grows

When the war began in 1939, the United States declared its neutrality. Although isolationist feeling remained strong, many Americans sympathized with those who battled the Axis powers. Later, President Roosevelt found ways around the Neutrality Acts to provide aid, including warships, to Britain as it stood alone against Hitler.

The Arsenal of Democracy In early 1941, FDR persuaded Congress to pass the Lend-Lease Act. It allowed him to sell or lend war materials to "any country whose defense the President deems vital to the defense of the United States." The United States, said Roosevelt, would not be drawn into the war, but it would become "the arsenal of democracy," supplying arms to those who were fighting for freedom.

Atlantic Charter In August 1941, Roosevelt and Churchill met secretly on a warship in the Atlantic. The two leaders issued the Atlantic Charter, which set goals for the war—"the final destruction of the Nazi tyranny"—and for the postwar world. They pledged to support "the right of all peoples to choose the form of government under which they will live" and called for a "permanent system of general security."

Japan Attacks

In December 1941, the Allies gained a vital boost when a surprise action by Japan suddenly pitched the United States into the war. From the late 1930s, Japan had been trying to conquer China. Although Japan occupied much of eastern China, the Chinese would not surrender. When war broke out in Europe in 1939, the Japanese saw a chance to grab European possessions in Southeast Asia. The rich resources of the region, including oil, rubber, and tin, would be of immense value in fighting the Chinese war.

Growing Tensions In 1940, Japan advanced into French Indochina and the Dutch East Indies (present-day Indonesia). To stop Japanese aggression, the United States banned the sale to Japan of war materials, such as iron, steel, and oil for airplanes. This move angered the Japanese.

Japan and the United States held talks to ease the growing tension. But extreme militarists such as General Tojo Hideki were gaining power in Japan. They hoped to seize lands in Asia and the Pacific, and the United States was interfering with their plans.

Attack on Pearl Harbor With talks at a standstill, General Tojo ordered a surprise attack on the American fleet at Pearl Harbor, Hawaii. Early on December 7, 1941, Japanese airplanes damaged or destroyed 19 ships, smashed American planes on the ground, and killed more than 2,400 people.

The Eastern Front
In 1941, the German army attacked the Soviet Union. Here, Soviet soldiers crawl through the snow as they try to halt the German advance.

Theme: Geography and History Why was Russia's winter so devastating to the German army?

▶ **Primary Sources and Literature**

See "Franklin D. Roosevelt: The Four Freedoms" in the Reference Section at the back of this book.

Recall
1. (a) "phony war," p. 775 (b) Dunkirk, p. 776 (c) Winston Churchill, p. 776 (d) Battle of Britain, p. 776 (e) Operation Barbarossa, p. 778 (f) Lend-Lease Act, p. 779 (g) Pearl Harbor, p. 779 2. (a) blitz-krieg, p. 775 (b) radar, p. 776 (c) sonar, p. 776

Comprehension
3. by striking fast, using the awesome power of modern technology, never giving the enemy time to prepare or defend itself 4. It diverted much of Hitler's war machine away from Britain and aimed it at the Soviet Union. 5. (a) Japan wanted to conquer China and various Southeast Asian lands so that it could possess the oil, rubber, tin, and other valuable resources that these lands had. (b) Tojo ordered the attack because the United States had interfered in Japan's expansionary plans by imposing strict trade restrictions.

Critical Thinking and Writing
6. Answers should demonstrate a clear understanding of the conditions that existed at the time. 7. (a) Possible answer: Fast-moving planes made blitzkrieg possible. Sonar helped detect submarines. Radar could detect airplanes. (b) Warring states could inflict greater damage than ever before.

Activity Rubrics

Share rubrics with students before they prepare their radio broadcasts.

Attempted The student's broadcast is incomplete and reflects little research.

Minimal The student's broadcast is poorly written and organized and includes few facts.

Adequate The student's broadcast is well written, informative, and interesting.

Exemplary The student's broadcast is exceptionally well written, informative, and interesting. It is presented with flair.

Caption Answer

They attacked because the United States had banned the sale of war materials to Japan, which hampered Japanese expansion efforts in Southeast Asia. The United States responded by declaring war on Japan.

Virtual Field Trip

www.phschool.com

USS *Arizona* **Memorial Honolulu, Hawaii**

To learn more about the attack on Pearl Harbor, use the Internet address above to link to the USS *Arizona* Memorial Web site.

Pearl Harbor
On December 7, 1941, Japan attacked the United States naval base at Pearl Harbor, Hawaii. Here, the *Arizona* sinks after being destroyed by Japanese planes.

Theme: Global Interaction Why did the Japanese attack Pearl Harbor, and how did the United States respond?

The next day, a grim-faced President Roosevelt told the nation that December 7 was "a date which will live in infamy." He asked Congress to declare war on Japan. On December 11, Germany and Italy, as Japan's allies, declared war on the United States.

Japanese Victories In the long run, the Japanese attack on Pearl Harbor would be as serious a mistake as Hitler's invasion of Russia. But the months after Pearl Harbor gave no such hint. Instead, European and American possessions in the Pacific fell one by one to the Japanese. They captured the Philippines and seized other American islands across the Pacific. They overran the British colonies of Hong Kong, Burma, and Malaya, pushed deeper into the Dutch East Indies, and completed the takeover of French Indochina.

By the beginning of 1942, the Japanese empire stretched from Southeast Asia to the western Pacific Ocean. The Axis powers had reached the high point of their successes.

SECTION 2 Assessment

Recall
1. **Identify:** (a) "phony war," (b) Dunkirk, (c) Winston Churchill, (d) Battle of Britain, (e) Operation Barbarossa, (f) Lend-Lease Act, (g) Pearl Harbor.
2. **Define:** (a) blitzkrieg, (b) radar, (c) sonar.

Comprehension
3. How did the Axis powers achieve victories in 1939 and 1940?
4. How did Operation Barbarossa affect the Battle of Britain?

5. (a) What goals did Japan pursue in Asia? (b) Why did General Tojo order a surprise attack on the United States?

Critical Thinking and Writing
6. **Identifying Alternatives** Could the United States have stayed out of the war?
7. **Recognizing Causes and Effects** (a) Describe three technological advances during World War II. (b) How did this technology make war more destructive?

Activity

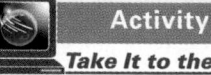

Take It to the NET

Use the Internet to learn more about the attack on Pearl Harbor in 1941. Prepare a radio broadcast giving a first-hand account of the attack and its toll on American ships.

Resource Directory

Teaching Resources
Section Quiz Unit 7 booklet, p. 79
Creative Teaching Activities Creative Teaching Activities booklet, p. 140
Guided Reading and Review Unit 7 booklet, p. 80
History Through Literature *Night,* History Through Literature booklet, pp. 65–66

Technology
World History Visions, Voices, Views Daily Life CloseUp, *A Resistance Fighter in the Warsaw Ghetto,* videodisc side 4 or videotape 7, running time 3:00 min.

Side 4: Fr. 3432-9245

The Global Conflict: Allied Successes

Reading Focus

- How did Germany and Japan treat people in occupied lands?
- How did the Allies turn the tide of war?
- How did the Red Army and the Allied invasion of France undo German plans?

Vocabulary

genocide
collaborator
reparations

Taking Notes

As you read this section, make an outline of its contents. Use Roman numerals for major headings. Use capital letters for subheadings, and use numbers for supporting details. The example at right will help you get started.

I. Occupied lands
  A. Nazi Europe
    1. Slavs considered inferior
    2. Plundered occupied lands
  B. Nazi genocide
  C.

Main Idea In 1942 and 1943, the tide of the war began to turn as Allied forces won key victories.

Setting the Scene

World War II was fought on a larger scale and in more places than any other conflict in history. It was also more costly in terms of human life than any previous war. Civilians, as well as soldiers, were targets. In 1941, a reporter visited a Russian town that had been home to 10,000 people before the German invasion. The reporter found a lone survivor: "[She was] a blind old woman who had gone insane. I saw her wandering barefooted around the village, carrying a few dirty rags, a rusty pail, and a tattered sheepskin."

From 1939 until mid-1942, the Axis ran up a string of successes. The conquerors blasted villages and towns and divided up the spoils. Then the Allies won some key victories. Slowly, the tide began to turn.

Occupied Lands

While the Germans rampaged across Europe, the Japanese conquered an empire in Asia and the Pacific. Each set out to build a "new order" in the occupied lands.

Nazi Europe Hitler's new order grew out of his racial obsessions. He set up puppet governments in Western European countries that were peopled by "Aryans" or related "races." The Slavs of Eastern Europe were considered to be an inferior "race." They were shoved aside to provide more "living space" for Germans, whom Hitler considered the ideal "race."

To the Nazis, occupied lands were an economic resource to be plundered and looted. The Nazis systematically stripped conquered nations of their works of art, factories, and other resources. They sent thousands of Slavs and others to work as slave laborers in German war industries. As resistance movements emerged to fight German tyranny, the Nazis took savage revenge, shooting hostages and torturing prisoners.

Nazi Genocide The most savage of Hitler's policies was his program to kill all people he judged "racially inferior," particularly Jews. Other targets included Slavs, Gypsies, and the mentally ill. At first, the Nazis forced Jews in Poland and other countries to live in ghettos and concentration camps. By 1941, however, German leaders had devised plans for the "final solution of the Jewish problem"—the genocide, or deliberate murder, of all European Jews.

To accomplish this goal, Hitler had special "death camps" built in Poland, at places like Auschwitz, Sobibor, and Treblinka. The Nazis

Bell Ringer Ask students to read the first paragraph on this page. Then have them name nearby towns that have a population of about 10,000. Ask them to imagine that town totally destroyed.

LESSON PLAN

1. Focus The Axis powers treated the people they conquered as inferiors. In many cases, this meant torture, forced labor, or death. Both the Axis and Allied nations committed all their resources to the war effort. Allied victories in North Africa, Italy, and Russia, along with the successful invasion of France in 1944, were major turning points in the war.

2. Instruct Assign each student one of the following roles: a Jewish resistance fighter; a member of the Big Three; a woman on the home front; a Russian soldier at Stalingrad; or a soldier with an Allied unit involved in the invasions of Italy, North Africa, and France. Have students write diary entries in which they describe the war from their particular point of view. In their entries, they should describe such things as their goals, their fears, and their actions against the Axis powers. Encourage students to supplement information in their text with material from outside resources. When students have finished, invite volunteers to read their diary entries to the class, without revealing the identity of their character.

3. Assess As students read their diaries, ask the remaining students to use clues in the diaries to identify each role. If there are problems identifying a particular student's role, have the class suggest details that would help in identification.

4. Reteach If students' **Assess** activity does not reflect adequate understanding of the lesson, you might assign the *Guide to the Essentials* or the *Interactive Student Tutorial CD-ROM* for this section.

Block Scheduling Support

Have students view *A Resistance Fighter in the Warsaw Ghetto* in World History Visions, Voices, Views, disc side 4 or tape 7. Then, read aloud excerpts from Helmuth von Moltke's *Letters to Freya* (available in libraries). Discuss with students the heroism and courage of the German resistance. Then ask students to speculate on why some who disagreed with Hitler became part of the resistance and others did not.

Geography and History

Working on a Deadly Railroad

In Southeast Asia, the Japanese captured tens of thousands of Allied prisoners of war (POWs) and turned them into a slave labor force. Nearly half of the POWs were forced to build a 250-mile rail line linking Siam (Thailand) and Burma (Myanmar). Engineers said the line would take from 2 to 5 years to build. Japanese generals ordered it completed in 18 months.

Geography made the task seem impossible. Not only were there mountains and ravines to cross but also winding rivers to be bridged again and again and a tropical jungle to be braved. Wild animals, deadly snakes, and tropical diseases threatened survival everywhere. Equipped only with pickaxes and shovels, the POWs completed the railway at the cost of thousands of lives.

 Theme: Geography and History How did geography contribute to the high death toll in building the Burma-Siam Railway?

shipped Jews from all over occupied Europe to the camps. There, Nazi engineers designed the most efficient means of killing millions of men, women, and children.

As Jews reached the camps, they were stripped of their clothes and valuables. Their heads were shaved. Guards separated men from women and children from their parents. The young, old, and sick were targeted for immediate killing. Within a few days, they were herded into "shower rooms" and gassed. The Nazis worked others to death or used them for perverse "medical" experiments. By 1945, the Nazis had massacred some six million Jews in what became known as the Holocaust. Almost as many other "undesirable" people were killed as well.

Jews resisted the Nazis even though they knew their efforts could not succeed. In October 1944, for example, a group of Jews in the Auschwitz death camp destroyed one of the gas chambers. The rebels were all killed. One woman, Rosa Robota, was tortured for days before she was hanged. "Be strong and have courage," she called out to the camp inmates who were forced by the Nazis to watch her execution.

In some cases, friends, neighbors, or strangers protected Jews. Sugihara Chiune, a Japanese diplomat in Lithuania, saved some 6,000 Jews by writing exit visas until he was ordered home by the Japanese government. Italian peasants hid Jews in their villages, and the nations of Denmark and Bulgaria saved almost all their Jewish populations. Most often, however, people pretended not to notice what was happening. Some were collaborators, helping the Nazis hunt down the Jews or, like the Vichy government in France, shipping tens of thousands of Jews to their death.

The scale and savagery of the Holocaust are unequaled in history. The Nazis deliberately set out to destroy the Jews for no reason other than their religious and ethnic heritage. Today, the record of that slaughter is a vivid reminder of the monstrous results of racism and intolerance.

The Co-Prosperity Sphere As Japan expanded across Asia and the Pacific, it donned the mantle of anti-imperialism. Under the slogan "Asia for Asians," it created the Greater East Asia Co-Prosperity Sphere. Japan's self-proclaimed mission was to help Asians escape western colonial rule. In fact, its real goal was a Japanese empire in Asia.

The Japanese treated the Chinese, Filipinos, Malaysians, and other conquered people with great brutality, killing and torturing civilians throughout East and Southeast Asia. People were shot simply for listening to Allied radio broadcasts. The Japanese seized food crops, destroyed cities and towns, and made local people into slave laborers. Whatever welcome the Japanese had at first met as "liberators" was soon turned to hatred. In the Philippines, Indochina, and elsewhere, nationalist groups waged guerrilla warfare against the Japanese invaders.

The Allied War Effort

After the United States entered the war, the Allied leaders met periodically to hammer out their strategy. In 1942, the Big Three—Roosevelt, Churchill, and Stalin—agreed to finish the war in Europe before turning their attention to Asia.

From the outset, the Allies distrusted one another. Churchill thought Stalin wanted to dominate Europe. Roosevelt felt that Churchill had ambitions to expand British imperial power. Stalin believed that the western powers wanted to destroy communism. At meetings and in writing, Stalin urged Roosevelt and Churchill to relieve the pressure on Russia by opening a second front in Western Europe. Not until 1944, however, did Britain and the United States make such a move. The British and Americans argued that they did not have the resources before then. Stalin saw the delay as a deliberate policy to weaken the Soviet Union.

Geography and History

ANSWER Rough terrain, dangerous animal life in tropical jungles, and tropical diseases all posed threats to life.

Analyzing Primary Sources

The Holocaust

As the Allied armies entered territories occupied by Germany, they came upon the concentration camps. The soldiers were horrified by what they saw. General Dwight Eisenhower of the United States insisted on having the camps photographed so others could see the conditions.

After camp inmates were killed, huge ovens like this one were used to cremate their bodies. Between 9 and 12 million people–including about 6 million Jews–died in concentration camps from 1939 to 1945.

These skeletal men were prisoners at Buchenwald camp in Germany. Inmates who escaped execution were used for forced labor. They suffered torture, starvation, and disease.

Children were among the millions of people shipped to the concentration camps. Most suffered the same ghastly fate as their parents.

Background
About the Primary Source

Concentration Camps Not all the Nazi concentration camps—and there were hundreds—were designed as death camps. Many were first used in the early 1930s for political prisoners. In the early 1940s, however, a number of new camps were built with gas chambers specifically created to exterminate large numbers of people at the same time. At all camps, conditions were so bad that thousands died of starvation, disease, or overwork. Near the end of the war, the Nazis tried to cover up the horror by removing prisoners and sending them to other camps as the Allies approached. Some prisoners were crowded on boxcars while others had to walk. Many more prisoners died on these forced marches.

Activity
Interpreting the Primary Source

Use this additional question to generate class discussion.
Critical Thinking: Making Inferences Why do you think the Nazis cremated the bodies of their victims? *(Possible answers: There were too many bodies even for mass burial. Cremation removed the evidence.)*

Skills Tip

Remember that photographs depict real scenes and were also taken for a particular purpose. Knowing this purpose can help you make sense of the photographs.

Skills Assessment

1. Based on the photographs, it can be assumed that
   A families were kept together.
   B conditions were the same in every camp.
   C conditions improved as the war continued.
   D the Nazis cared little about the well-being of their prisoners.

2. The photographs help historians to
   E explain Hitler's motives.
   F document conditions in concentration camps.
   G understand why the Nazis hated Jews.
   H identify the causes of World War II.

3. **Critical Thinking Making Inferences (a)** Based on the photographs, what do you think the Nazis thought about the camp inmates? **(b)** What does the ultimate purpose of the camps seem to have been?

Skills Tip

Looking at details helps one learn from photographs. The Skills Handbook in the front of the book has a lesson that will help students with this feature.

Test Preparation

Have students read the first paragraph under the heading "The Co-Prosperity Sphere" on the opposite page, and then answer the question below.

What does the word *mantle* mean in this context?

A ideals
B a framework
C a (symbolic) cloak
D pretense

Skills Assessment

ANSWERS 1. D **2.** F **3. (a)** The Nazis considered the inmates sub-human, not worth clothing properly, feeding, or even keeping alive. **(b)** The camps seem to have been designed to kill off the inmates, either by executing them or by starving them to death.

PAST

PRESENT

Women in Wartime
Women's military roles have changed dramatically. Although the British and American armies did not allow women to serve in combat positions during World War II, women did serve in auxiliaries such as the Women's Auxiliary Air Force, or WAAF (PAST). Today, women's roles are more active. During Operation Desert Storm in 1991 (PRESENT), women served as soldiers.

Theme: Continuity and Change What reasons might the military have for allowing women to serve as soldiers?

Total War Like the Axis powers, the Allies were committed to total war. Democratic governments in the United States and Britain increased their political power. They directed economic resources into the war effort, ordering factories to stop making cars or refrigerators and to turn out airplanes or tanks instead. Governments rationed consumer goods, from shoes to sugar, and regulated prices and wages. On the positive side, while the war brought shortages and hardships, it ended the unemployment of the depression era.

Under pressure of war, even democratic governments limited the rights of citizens, censored the press, and used propaganda to win public support for the war. In the United States and Canada, many citizens of Japanese descent lost their jobs, property, and civil rights. Japanese Americans and Japanese Canadians even lost their freedom and were forced into internment camps after governments decided that they were a security risk. The British took similar action against German refugees. Some 40 years later, both the United States and Canada apologized for the wartime policy and provided former internees with reparations, or payment for damages caused by the imprisonment.

Women Help Win the War As men joined the military and war industries expanded, millions of women around the world replaced them in essential jobs. Women built ships and planes, produced munitions, and staffed offices. A popular British song recognized women's contributions:

> "She's the girl that makes the thing that drills the hole
>   that holds the spring
> That drives the rod that turns the knob that works the
>   thingumebob. . . .
> And it's the girl that makes the thing that holds the
>   oil that oils the ring
> That works the thingumebob
>   THAT'S GOING TO WIN THE WAR!"
> —from *The People's War: Britain, 1939–1945* (Calder)

British and American women served in the armed forces in many auxiliary roles—driving trucks and ambulances, delivering airplanes, decoding messages, and assisting at antiaircraft sites. In occupied Europe, women fought in the resistance. Marie Fourcade, a French woman, directed 3,000 people in the underground and helped downed Allied pilots escape to safety. Many Soviet women played combat roles. Soviet pilot Lily Litvak, for example, shot down 12 German planes before she herself was killed.

Turning Points

During 1942 and 1943, the Allies won several victories that would turn the tide of battle and push back the Axis powers. The first of these turning points came in North Africa and Italy.

El Alamein In Egypt, the British under General Bernard Montgomery finally stopped Rommel's advance during the long, fierce Battle of El Alamein. They then turned the tables on the Desert Fox, driving the Axis forces back across Libya into Tunisia.

Later in 1942, American general Dwight Eisenhower took command of a joint Anglo-American force in Morocco and Algeria. Advancing on Tunisia from the west, he combined with the British forces to trap Rommel's army, which surrendered in May 1943.

World War II in Europe and North Africa

Legend:
- European Axis Powers, 1942
- Maximum extent of Axis control, 1942
- Neutral nations, 1942
- Allied territory, 1942
- → Allied advances
- ■ Concentration camps, 1939–1945

Azimuthal Equal Area Projection
0   300   600 Miles
0   300   600 Kilometers

Background Perspectives

News From the Front Ernie Pyle was a World War II war correspondent who wrote about the experiences of the American Infantry soldier, or "GI Joe." In his dispatches to the states, sent six times weekly, Pyle portrayed the fatigue, boredom, fear, and longing of the common American soldier. He carefully recorded their names, their daily routines, their combat experiences, and the places where they fought and often died. Pyle also observed and noted the character changes that came with the weeks, months, and years spent in combat. He lamented the lasting psychological impact that proximity to death and destruction had on the common man.

As an unarmed correspondent, Ernie Pyle accompanied American combat troops in Europe, North Africa, and the Pacific, where he was finally killed by Japanese gunfire. A compilation of his reports can be found in *Ernie's War: Best of Ernie Pyle's World War II Dispatches*, edited by David Nichols.

Invasion of Italy Victory in North Africa let the Allies leap across the Mediterranean into Italy. In July 1943, a combined British and American army landed first in Sicily and then in southern Italy. They defeated the Italian forces there in about a month.

Italians, fed up with Mussolini, overthrew Il Duce. The new Italian government signed an armistice, but the fighting did not end. Hitler sent German troops to rescue Mussolini and stiffen the will of Italians fighting in the north. For the next 18 months, the Allies pushed slowly up the Italian peninsula, suffering heavy losses against stiff German resistance. Still, the Italian invasion was a decisive event for the Allies because it weakened Hitler by forcing him to fight on another front.

The Red Army Resists

Another major turning point in the war occurred in the Soviet Union. After their triumphant advance in 1941, the Germans were stalled outside Moscow and Leningrad. In 1942, Hitler launched a new offensive. This

Skills Assessment

Geography Axis power reached its height in Europe in 1942. Then, the tide began to turn.

1. **Location** On the map, locate **(a)** Vichy France, **(b)** Soviet Union, **(c)** El Alamein, **(d)** Berlin, **(e)** Normandy, **(f)** Anzio.
2. **Movement** Describe the extent of the Axis advance to the east by 1942.
3. **Critical Thinking Analyzing Information** How did geography help or hinder Allied advances?

Human Drama Note

Invasion at Calais The Allied invasion of France in 1944 succeeded partly because of an elaborate diversion scheme. In the spring of that year, German intelligence units photographed "secret" Allied operations in southeastern England. Their photographs revealed large-scale movements of jeeps and tanks, busy army bases hidden under cover of forest, and a new oil refinery at Dover, across the English Channel from the French city of Calais. Based on this evidence and intercepted Allied radio transmissions, the German high command concluded that the Allies planned to invade Europe through Calais, probably in late July.

In truth, however, it was all a massive and very successful hoax. The oil refinery, made of old sewage pipes, had been built by movie set designers. The jeeps and tanks were replicas made of inflatable rubber. The military bases were equally fake. And the radio messages, which the Allies had intended to be intercepted, contained false and misleading information. The real invasion took place at Normandy on June 6, while German forces waited anxiously at Calais—for nothing.

Skills Assessment

ANSWERS 1. Review locations with students. **2.** The Axis controlled lands well within the borders of the Soviet Union, from Leningrad to Stalingrad and south to the Caucasus Mountains. **3.** They had to transport supplies and troops across the Atlantic, over the desert in Africa, and across large distances overland. The Mediterranean made advance from the south easier

Recall

1. (a) Holocaust, p. 782 (b) Greater East Asia Co-Prosperity Sphere, p. 782 (c) Battle of El Alamein, p. 784 (d) Battle of Stalingrad, p. 786 (e) D-Day, p. 786
2. (a) genocide, p. 781 (b) collaborator, p. 782 (c) reparations, p. 784

Comprehension

3. (a) Hitler's racial obsessions guided the "new order." Only "Aryans" were considered desirable. Slavs, Jews, the mentally ill, and others were designated for slave labor or extermination. All occupied lands were exploited for their economic wealth. (b) The Japanese treated conquered peoples with brutality. They killed and tortured civilians, seized food crops, and forced people into slave labor. 4. Democratic governments directed all economic resources into the war effort, replaced production of consumer goods with that of military goods, and regulated prices and wages. 5. (a) At El Alamein, the British stopped the German advance in Egypt, and pushed the Axis forces across Libya into Tunisia, ultimately forcing Rommel's army to surrender in 1943. (b) The German defeat at Stalingrad resulted in the loss of valuable equipment and some 300,000 German troops. Soviet troops were able to drive the Germans out of Russia and advance across Eastern Europe.

Critical Thinking and Writing

6. Students should weigh the temporary limit on freedom against the possible loss of democratic government. 7. Possible answer: Based on prejudices and stereotypes, they often lead to intolerance, discrimination, and violence.

Activity Rubrics

Share rubrics with students before they design their Holocaust memorials.

Attempted The memorial is incomplete or reveals little understanding of the Holocaust.

Minimal The memorial shows some understanding of the Holocaust but is poorly executed.

Adequate The memorial is well conceived and demonstrates a clear grasp of the Holocaust and its scope.

Exemplary The memorial is original and creative and movingly reflects a deep understanding of the Holocaust and its scope.

Primary Source

ANSWER because of its surprise appearance, size, and fire power

Primary Source

A Sea of Ships

As dawn broke on June 6, 1944, a German artillery officer in Normandy looked out across the English Channel and made an anxious phone call to Major Block at divisional headquarters:

"'There must be 10,000 ships out there,' I told him. 'It's unbelievable, fantastic. . . .' Block said, 'Look, Pluskat, are you really sure? The Americans and the British together don't have that many ships.' I just said, 'Come and look for yourself.'. . .

We watched absolutely petrified, as the armada steadily and relentlessly approached. . . . [T]hen the bombardment from the sea began. The shells screamed like a thousand express trains. . . . I was thrown to the ground . . . completely dazed and unable to speak."

—Werner Pluskat, quoted in *Nothing Less Than Victory* (Miller)

Skills Assessment

Primary Source Why were the German soldiers "absolutely petrified" as the armada approached?

---

time, he aimed for the rich oil fields of the south. His troops, however, got only as far as the city of Stalingrad.

Stalingrad The Battle of Stalingrad was one of the costliest of the war. Hitler was determined to capture Stalin's namesake city. Stalin was equally determined to defend it. The battle began when the Germans surrounded the city. The Russians then encircled their attackers. As winter closed in, a bitter street-by-street, house-by-house struggle raged. Soldiers fought for two weeks for a single building, wrote a German officer. Corpses "are strewn in the cellars, on the landings and the staircases," he said. Trapped, without food or ammunition and with no hope of rescue, the German commander finally surrendered in early 1943. The battle cost the Germans approximately 300,000 killed, wounded, or captured soldiers.

Counterattack After the Battle of Stalingrad, the Red Army took the offensive and drove the invaders out of the Soviet Union entirely. Hitler's forces suffered irreplaceable losses of both troops and equipment. By early 1944, Soviet troops were advancing into Eastern Europe.

Invasion of France

By 1944, the Allies were at last ready to open a second front in Europe—with the invasion of France. Eisenhower was made the supreme Allied commander. He and other Allied leaders faced the enormous task of planning the operation and assembling troops and supplies. To prepare the way for the invasion, Allied bombers flew constant missions over Germany. They targeted factories and destroyed aircraft that might be used against the invasion force. They also bombed a number of German cities.

The Allies chose June 6, 1944—D-Day, they called it—for the invasion of France. After midnight, Allied planes dropped paratroopers behind enemy lines. Then, at dawn, thousands of ships ferried 176,000 Allied troops across the English Channel. From landing craft, the troops fought their way to shore amid underwater mines and raking machine-gun fire. They clawed their way inland through the tangled hedges of Normandy. Finally, they broke through German defenses and advanced toward Paris. Meanwhile, other Allied forces sailed from Italy to land in southern France.

In Paris, French resistance forces rose up against the occupying Germans. Under pressure from all sides, the Germans retreated. On August 25, the Allies entered Paris. Within a month, all of France was free. Attention focused on conquering Germany itself—and defeating Japan.

Recall

1. **Identify:** (a) Holocaust, (b) Greater East Asia Co-Prosperity Sphere, (c) Battle of El Alamein, (d) Battle of Stalingrad, (e) D-Day.
2. **Define:** (a) genocide, (b) collaborator, (c) reparations.

Comprehension

3. (a) How did Hitler try to achieve a "new order" in Europe? (b) How did the Japanese treat conquered people?
4. How did democratic governments mobilize their economies for war?

5. Explain how each of the following battles was a turning point in the war: (a) El Alamein, (b) Stalingrad.

Critical Thinking and Writing

6. **Defending a Position** Do you think that democratic governments should be allowed to limit their citizens' freedoms during wartime? Defend your position.
7. **Applying Information** Hitler translated his hatred of Jews and others into a program of genocide. How do ethnic, racial, and religious hatreds weaken society?

Activity

Creating a Memorial Design a memorial commemorating the millions who died in the Holocaust. Include a brief description of any symbols you will use in your memorial.

Resource Directory

Teaching Resources

Section Quiz Unit 7 booklet, p. 81
Creative Teaching Activities Creative Teaching Activities booklet, p. 141
Guided Reading and Review Unit 7 booklet, p. 82
Primary Source Activity *After the Battle at Kwajalein,* Unit 7 booklet, p. 87
Skill Application Activity *Making Decisions,* Unit 7 booklet, p. 89

Technology

Interactive Student Tutorial CD-ROM Ch. 31
Computer Test Bank Ch. 31

SECTION 4 Toward Victory

Reading Focus

- How was the Pacific war fought?
- How did the Allies defeat Nazi Germany?
- What debates surrounded the defeat of Japan?

Vocabulary

island-hopping

kamikaze

Taking Notes

On a separate sheet of paper, copy the cause-and-effect chart shown here. As you read the section, complete the chart with information about how the Allies won in the Pacific and in Europe.

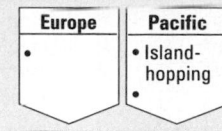

Europe	Pacific
•	• Island-hopping
	•

ALLIES WIN WORLD WAR II

Main Idea Continued Allied successes led to victory over Germany and Japan in 1945.

Setting the Scene

General Douglas MacArthur stood at the dock on Corregidor in March 1942. A boat waited to evacuate him from the fortified island in the Philippines. Although the United States Army and Filipino defense forces had battled to keep the Japanese out of the island chain, they had not been successful. Thousands of Allied civilians—men, women, and children—were being held in prison camps throughout the islands, and American and Filipino soldiers were under attack on the Bataan peninsula. After reaching Australia, MacArthur pledged his determination to free the Philippines with the words "I shall return."

Allied troops found that the war in Southeast Asia and the Pacific was very different from that in Europe. Most battles were fought at sea, on tiny islands, or in deep jungles.

War in the Pacific

At first, the Japanese won an uninterrupted series of victories. They controlled much of Southeast Asia and many Pacific islands. By May 1942, the Japanese had gained control of the Philippines, killing several hundred American soldiers and some 10,000 Filipino soldiers during the 68-mile Bataan Death March. One survivor described the ordeal as "a macabre litany of heat, dust, starvation, thirst, flies, filth, stench, murder, torture, corpses, and wholesale brutality that numbs the memory." Many Filipino

Storming the Beach
The Pacific war relied on the capture of individual islands. Here, United States Marines land on the island of Iwo Jima.

Theme: Geography and History How was the war in the Pacific different from the fighting in Europe?

Chapter 31 **787**

Bell Ringer Inform students that in certain ways the war against Japan was conducted differently than was the war against Germany. Ask students to list what the differences might have been and to offer possible explanations for those differences.

LESSON PLAN

1. Focus The Japanese advance in the Pacific was halted by American victories in the Coral Sea and at Midway Island. As Allied troops invaded Germany from both the west and the east, Germany finally surrendered. When Japan refused to surrender, the United States dropped atomic bombs on two Japanese cities to end the conflict.

2. Instruct Have students working in teams assume the role of radio news reporters during the final years of World War II. Ask each team to select a major battle, development, or event mentioned in this section. Teams should then research their selected topic and write the report that they will broadcast to the class. In their reports, students should answer the questions *who, what, where, when, why,* and *how.* Encourage students to also provide quotations from individuals who played a historic role. After each broadcast is presented, invite the radio audience to call in with questions for the announcers.

3. Assess Have students return to the Bell Ringer activity. Have them review and revise their responses in the light of what they have learned from the "radio broadcasts." Then lead the class in a discussion on how and why the war against Japan differed from the war against Germany.

4. Reteach If students' **Assess** activity does not reflect adequate understanding of the lesson, you might assign the *Guide to the Essentials* or the *Interactive Student Tutorial CD-ROM* for this section.

Caption Answer

Battles were generally fought at sea, on tiny islands, or in deep jungles.

🗐 Block Scheduling Support

One of the most famous images of the war in the Pacific is the photograph of Marines raising the flag at the tiny, but strategic, island of Iwo Jima. The photograph served as the basis for a sculpture that now stands in Arlington, Virginia. The sculpture has become a popular symbol. Provide students with a picture of the image and ask students to give their interpretation of what the image might symbolize for many Americans.

Biography

Erwin Rommel 1891–1944

When the war began, Erwin Rommel was personally responsible for guaranteeing Hitler's safety. Impressed with Rommel, in 1942, Hitler promoted him to field marshal. Rommel was the youngest person to hold that rank in the German army. The two men soon became disillusioned with each other. When Rommel tried to explain setbacks for his command in North Africa, Hitler branded him a defeatist. When Hitler refused to listen to military experts, Rommel came to believe that the Nazi leader was trying to destroy Germany. In 1944, Rommel was connected to a plot to assassinate Hitler, which led to his own destruction.

Theme: Impact of the Individual How did Rommel's attitude toward Hitler change?

civilians risked—and sometimes lost—their lives to give food and water to captives on the march.

Soon, however, the tide of the Pacific war began to turn. In May and June 1942, United States warships and airplanes severely damaged two Japanese fleets during the battles of the Coral Sea and Midway Island. These victories greatly weakened Japanese naval power and stopped the Japanese advance.

After the Battle of Midway, the United States took the offensive. That summer, under MacArthur's command, United States Marines landed at Guadalcanal in the Solomon Islands. Victory on Guadalcanal marked the beginning of an "island-hopping" campaign. The goal of the campaign was to recapture some Japanese-held islands while bypassing others. The captured islands served as steppingstones to the next objective. In this way, American forces gradually moved north toward Japan itself. By 1944, the United States Navy, commanded by Admiral Chester Nimitz, was blockading Japan, and American bombers pounded Japanese cities and industries.

In October 1944, MacArthur began the fight to retake the Philippines. The British, meanwhile, were pushing Japanese forces back in the jungles of Burma and Malaya. Despite such setbacks, the Japanese government rejected any suggestions of surrender.

The Nazis Defeated

Hitler, too, scorned talk of surrender. "If the war is to be lost," he declared, "the nation also will perish." To win the assault on "Fortress Europe," the Allies had to use devastating force.

The Allies Advance After freeing France, Allied forces battled toward Germany. As their armies advanced into Belgium in December 1944, Germany launched a massive counterattack. At the bloody Battle of the Bulge, which lasted more than a month, both sides took terrible losses. The Germans were unable to break through. The battle delayed the Allied advance, but it was Hitler's last success. His support within Germany was declining, and he had already survived one assassination attempt by senior officers in the German military.

By this time, Germany was reeling under round-the-clock bombing. For two years, Allied bombers had hammered military bases, factories, railroads, oil depots, and cities. In one 10-day period, bombing almost erased the huge industrial city of Hamburg. Allied raids on Dresden in February 1945 killed as many as 135,000 people.

By March, the Allies had crossed the Rhine into western Germany. From the east, Soviet troops closed in on Berlin. In late April, American and Russian soldiers met and shook hands at the Elbe River. Everywhere, Axis armies began to surrender.

The End in Europe In Italy, guerrillas captured and executed Mussolini. In Berlin, Hitler knew that the end was near. As Soviet troops fought their way into the city, Hitler committed suicide in his underground bunker. After just 12 years, Hitler's "thousand-year Reich" was bomb-ravaged. On May 7, Germany surrendered. Officially, the war in Europe ended the next day, May 8, 1945, which was proclaimed V-E Day (Victory in Europe).

Defeat of Japan

With war won in Europe, the Allies poured their resources into defeating Japan. By mid-1945, most of the Japanese navy and air force had been destroyed. Yet the Japanese still had an army of two million men. The road to victory, it appeared, would be long and costly.

World War II in the Pacific

Legend:
— Maximum extent of Japanese control, 1942
▨ Under Japanese control, 1942
→ Allied advances
★ Major battles
☁ Atomic bomb targets

Robinson Projection
0   750   1500 Miles
0   750   1500 Kilometers

Invasion Versus the Bomb Some American officials estimated that an invasion of Japan would cost a million or more casualties. In bloody battles on the islands of Iwo Jima and Okinawa, the Japanese had shown that they would fight to the death rather than surrender. Beginning in 1944, some young Japanese chose to become kamikaze (kah mih KAH zee) pilots who undertook suicide missions, crashing their explosive-laden airplanes into American warships. They hoped these efforts would stop the Allies and save their nation from defeat.

While Allied military leaders planned for invasion, scientists offered another way to end the war. Since the early 1900s, scientists had understood that matter, made up of atoms, could be converted into pure energy. In military terms, this meant that, by splitting the atom, scientists could create an explosion far more powerful than any yet known. During the war, Allied scientists, some of them German and Italian refugees, raced to harness the atom. In July 1945, they successfully tested the first atomic bomb at Alamogordo, New Mexico.

News of this test was brought to the new American president, Harry Truman. Truman had taken office after Franklin Roosevelt died unexpectedly on April 12. He realized that the atomic bomb was a terrible new force for destruction. Still, after consulting with his advisers, he decided to use the new weapon against Japan.

At the time, Truman was meeting with other Allied leaders in the city of Potsdam, Germany. They issued a warning to Japan to surrender or face "utter and complete destruction." When the Japanese ignored the deadline, the United States took action.

Hiroshima On August 6, 1945, an American plane dropped an atomic bomb on the mid-sized city of Hiroshima. The bomb flattened four square

---

Skills Assessment

Geography For six months, the Japanese won a series of uninterrupted victories. After the Battle of Midway, however, the Allies took the offensive in the Pacific.
1. **Location** On the map, locate (a) Japan, (b) Midway Island, (c) Pearl Harbor, (d) Iwo Jima, (e) Hiroshima, (f) Manila.
2. **Movement** (a) Did Japan ever gain control of New Guinea? Explain. (b) Which of the Allies advanced into Manchuria?
3. **Critical Thinking** Making Inferences How did geography make it difficult for Japan to maintain control of its empire?

Chapter 31 **789**

Recall

1. (a) Battle of the Coral Sea, p. 788
(b) Battle of the Bulge, p. 788 **(c)** V-E Day, p. 788 **(d)** Harry Truman, p. 789
2. (a) island-hopping, p. 788
(b) kamikaze, p. 789

Comprehension

3. Using an "island-hopping" campaign, American forces gradually moved closer to Japan. They captured Japanese-held islands in the Pacific so American ships could blockade Japan while American planes bombed Japan. **4.** As Allied ground troops neared Germany from the west and the east, Allied planes bombed Germany, targeting German military bases, factories, railroads, oil depots, and cities. **5.** The dropping of the atomic bombs convinced Emperor Hirohito to force the government to surrender.

Critical Thinking and Writing

6. Possible answer: the number of Japanese and American soldiers already killed in the war; estimates of the numbers who might be killed during an invasion; estimates of the number of deaths from dropping the atomic bomb; estimates of the likelihood of a Japanese surrender without it **7.** Possible answer: The Japanese ignored Truman's deadline and warning. Hitler committed suicide in the face of defeat. Both governments seemed willing to do anything to avoid surrender. Neither considered the death and destruction.

Activity Rubrics

Share rubrics with students before they write their headlines.

Attempted The student writes an incomplete headline.

Minimal The student writes a few headlines, but they are incorrect or inappropriate.

Adequate The student writes several headlines to cover the major events in the final months of war; they are well written. The student suggests visuals that are appropriate.

Exemplary The student writes many headlines to cover the major events in the final months of war. They are well written and appropriate in style. Suggestions for visuals are excellent.

Caption Answer

for: huge casualties expected if Japan were invaded; against: effects of bomb were brutal and enormously destructive

miles and instantly killed more than 70,000 people. In the months that followed, many more would die from radiation sickness, a deadly aftereffect from exposure to radioactive materials.

On August 8, the Soviet Union declared war on Japan and invaded Manchuria. Again, Japanese leaders did not respond. The next day, the United States dropped a second atomic bomb, this time on the city of Nagasaki. More than 40,000 people were killed in this second explosion.

Still, the Japanese cabinet argued. Should they surrender or continue to fight? Finally, on August 10, Emperor Hirohito intervened—an action unheard of for a Japanese emperor— and forced the government to surrender. On September 2, 1945, the formal peace treaty was signed on board the American battleship *Missouri,* which was anchored in Tokyo Bay.

The Atomic Bomb
President Harry Truman warned the Japanese that if they did not surrender, they would face "a rain of ruin from the air the like of which has never been seen on this Earth." This photo shows the destructive effects of the bomb on Hiroshima. The inset shows a watch stopped by the blast.

Theme: Religions and Value Systems What were some of the arguments for and against dropping the atomic bomb on Japan?

An Ongoing Controversy Dropping the atomic bomb brought a quick end to the war. It also unleashed terrifying destruction. Ever since, people have debated whether the United States should have used the bomb.

Why did Truman use the bomb? First, he was convinced that Japan would not surrender without an invasion that would result in an enormous loss of both American and Japanese lives. Truman also may have hoped that the bomb would impress the Soviet Union with American power. At any rate, the Japanese surrendered shortly after the bombs were dropped, and World War II was ended.

Looking Ahead

After the surrender, American forces occupied the smoldering ruins of Japan. In Germany, meanwhile, the Allies had divided Hitler's fallen empire into four zones of occupation. In both countries, the Allies faced difficult decisions about the future. How could they avoid the mistakes of 1919 and build the foundations for a stable world peace?

SECTION 4 Assessment

Recall

1. Identify: **(a)** Battle of the Coral Sea, **(b)** Battle of the Bulge, **(c)** V-E Day, **(d)** Harry Truman.
2. Define: **(a)** island-hopping, **(b)** kamikaze.

Comprehension

3. How did the United States fight the war in the Pacific?
4. How did the Allies weaken Germany?
5. How was Japan defeated?

Critical Thinking and Writing

6. Making Decisions Suppose that you are President Truman. What information would you want before deciding whether to drop an atomic bomb on Japan?
7. Making Generalizations How would you describe the attitudes of the Japanese government and of Hitler toward surrendering to the Allies?

Activity

Writing Headlines
Write a series of newspaper headlines reporting the final months of the war in Europe. Suggest photos or other visuals that might accompany a story for one of the headlines.

Resource Directory

Teaching Resources
Section Quiz Unit 7 booklet, p. 83
Creative Teaching Activities Creative Teaching Activities booklet, p. 142
Guided Reading and Review Unit 7 booklet, p. 84

Technology
Interactive Student Tutorial CD-ROM Ch. 31
Computer Test Bank Ch. 31

Reading Focus

- What issues arose in the aftermath of war?
- Why did the Allies organize the United Nations?
- How did the breakup of the wartime alliance lead to new conflicts?

Vocabulary

containment
satellite

Taking Notes

On a sheet of paper, make a concept web like the one shown here. As you read this section, add information about events that occurred after World War II. Add as many circles as you need.

Main Idea — As the war ended, new tensions developed between the United States and the Soviet Union.

Setting the Scene

"Give me ten years and you will not be able to recognize Germany," said Hitler in 1933. His prophecy proved correct—although not in the way he had intended. In 1945, Germany was an unrecognizable ruin. Poland, Russia, Japan, and many other countries also lay in ruins. Total war had gutted cities, factories, harbors, bridges, railroads, farms, homes—and lives. Millions of refugees, displaced by the fighting or liberated from prison camps, wandered the land. Amid the devastation, hunger and disease took large tolls for years after the fighting ended.

Aftermath of War

Even as the Allies celebrated victory, the appalling costs of the war began to emerge. It had killed as many as 75 million people around the world. In Europe, about 38 million people lost their lives, many of them civilians. The Soviet Union suffered the worst casualties, with more than 22 million dead.

Numbers alone did not tell the story of the Nazi nightmare in Europe or the Japanese brutality in Asia. In the aftermath of war, investigation brought new atrocities to light.

Horrors of the Holocaust During the war, the Allies were aware of the existence of Nazi concentration camps and death camps. But only at war's end did they learn the full extent of the inhumanity and misery of the Holocaust. United States general Dwight Eisenhower, who visited the camps, was stunned to come "face to face with indisputable evidence of Nazi brutality and ruthless disregard of every sense of decency."

Walking skeletons stumbled out of the death camps with tales of mass murder. Rudolf Hoess, Nazi commander at Auschwitz, would later admit that he had supervised the killing of some two and a half million people, not counting those who died of disease or starvation.

War Crimes Trials At wartime meetings, the Allies had agreed that Axis leaders should be tried for "crimes against humanity." In Germany, the Allies held war crimes trials in Nuremberg, where Hitler had staged mass rallies in the 1930s. A total of 177 Germans and Austrians were tried, and 142 were found guilty. A handful of top Nazis received death sentences. Others were imprisoned. Similar war crimes trials were held in Japan and Italy. The trials showed that political and military leaders could be held accountable for actions in wartime.

Chapter 31 **791**

SECTION 5

Bell Ringer Have students compare the words of Stalin, quoted in the second paragraph of the subsection "Origins of the Cold War," with those of President Truman, quoted in the first paragraph of the subsection "Truman Doctrine." Based on these viewpoints, ask students to predict the international climate that emerged in the years following World War II.

LESSON PLAN

1. Focus The cost of World War II in both human and material losses was immense. With the old European powers exhausted, the United States and the Soviet Union emerged as dominant new superpowers. Their different political systems and their differing goals in Europe helped bring about the Cold War.

2. Instruct Work with students to create on the chalkboard a time line of events related to the Cold War. Call on volunteers to come to the board and place significant events or developments at appropriate places on the time line. Students' responses should include such events as the installation of pro-Soviet governments in Eastern Europe, Churchill's warning about the "iron curtain," the conflicts in Greece and Turkey, the announcement of the Truman Doctrine, the Marshall Plan, the Berlin Airlift, the formation of NATO, the start of an arms race, and the start of a propaganda war. Encourage students to refer to various reference works to provide any dates that are missing. Use the completed time line as the focus for a discussion on the origins of the Cold War.

3. Assess Ask students to write three generalizations about the start of the Cold War.

4. Reteach If students' **Assess** activity does not reflect adequate understanding of the lesson, you might assign the *Guide to the Essentials* or the *Interactive Student Tutorial CD-ROM* for this section.

Block Scheduling Support

At the Nuremberg trials, defendants claimed they had violated no laws. In 1948, as a direct response, the United Nations (UN) passed the Genocide Convention, which made genocide a crime. In the same year, the UN also passed the Universal Declaration of Human Rights. Initiate a class discussion to address the following questions. How successful has the UN been in exposing and curbing human rights violations? What private organizations have similar goals?

Allied Occupation The war crimes trials served an additional purpose. By exposing the savagery of the Axis regimes, they further discredited the Nazi, fascist, and militarist ideologies that had led to the war.

Yet disturbing questions haunted people then, as now. What made the Nazi horrors possible? Why had ordinary people in Germany, Poland, France, and elsewhere accepted—and even collaborated in—Hitler's "final solution"? How could the world prevent the rise of future dictators?

The Allies tried to address those issues as their troops occupied Germany and Japan. The United States felt that strengthening democracy would ensure tolerance and peace. The western Allies built new governments with democratic constitutions to protect the rights of all citizens. In German schools, for example, Nazi textbooks and courses were replaced with a new curriculum that taught democratic principles.

The United Nations

As in 1919, the World War II Allies set up an international organization to ensure peace. In April 1945, delegates from 50 nations met in San Francisco to draft a charter for the United Nations. The UN would play a greater role in world affairs than did its predecessor, the League of Nations.

Under the UN Charter, each of the member nations had one vote in the General Assembly. A much smaller body called the Security Council was given greater power. Each of its five permanent members—the United States, the Soviet Union (today Russia), Britain, France, and China—had the right to veto any council decision. The goal was to give these great powers the authority to ensure the peace. Often, however, differences among these nations have kept the UN from taking action.

The UN's work would go far beyond peacekeeping. The organization would take on many world problems—from preventing the outbreak of disease and improving education to protecting refugees and aiding nations to develop economically. UN agencies like the World Health Organization and the Food and Agricultural Organization have provided help for millions of people around the world.

The Alliance Breaks Apart

Amid the rubble of war, a new power structure emerged. In Europe, Germany was defeated. France and Britain were drained and exhausted. Two other powers, the United States and the Soviet Union, had brought about the final victory. Before long, these two nations would become superpowers with the economic resources and military might to dominate the globe. They would also become tense rivals in an increasingly divided world.

Growing Differences During the war, the Soviet Union and the nations of the West had cooperated to defeat Nazi Germany. By 1945, however, the wartime alliance was crumbling. Conflicting ideologies and mutual distrust soon led to the conflict known as the Cold War. The Cold War was a state of tension and hostility among nations, without armed conflict between the major rivals. At first, the focus of the Cold War was Eastern Europe, where Stalin and the western powers had very different goals.*

---

*Stalin was deeply suspicious of other powers. Russia had been invaded by Napoleon's armies and by Germans in World Wars I and II. Also, the United States and Britain had both sent troops into Russia during World War I.

FACT FINDER

Casualties of World War II

	Military Dead*	Military Wounded*	Civilian Dead*
Allies			
Britain	389,000	475,000	65,000
France	211,000	400,000	108,000
Soviet Union	7,500,000	14,102,000	15,000,000
United States	292,000	671,000	**
Axis Powers			
Germany	2,850,000	7,250,000	5,000,000
Italy	77,500	120,000	100,000
Japan	1,576,000	500,000	300,000

* All figures are estimates.
** Very small number of civilian dead.
Source: Henri Michel, *The Second World War*

Skills Assessment

Chart World War II resulted in enormous casualties. Because planes carried destruction far beyond the battlefield, civilian deaths reached record numbers. **Which nation suffered the greatest number of both civilian and military casualties?**

Origins of the Cold War

Origins of the Cold War Stalin had two goals in Eastern Europe. First, he wanted to spread communism into the area. Second, he wanted to create a buffer zone of friendly governments as a defense against Germany, which had invaded Russia during World War I and again in 1941.

As the Red Army had pushed German forces out of Eastern Europe, it had left behind occupying forces. At wartime conferences, Stalin tried to persuade the West to accept Soviet influence in Eastern Europe. He bluntly stated, "Whoever occupies a territory also imposes his own social system. Everyone imposes his own system as far as his armies can reach. It cannot be otherwise."

The Soviet dictator pointed out that the United States was not consulting the Soviet Union about peace terms for Italy or Japan, defeated and occupied by American and British troops. In the same way, Russia would determine the fate of the Eastern European lands overrun by the Red Army on its way to Berlin.

Roosevelt and Churchill rejected Stalin's view, making him promise "free elections" in Eastern Europe. Stalin ignored that pledge. Backed by the Red Army, local communists in Poland, Czechoslovakia, and elsewhere destroyed rival political parties and even assassinated democratic leaders. By 1948, Stalin had installed pro-Soviet communist governments throughout Eastern Europe.

A Divided Europe Churchill had long distrusted Stalin. As early as 1946, during a visit to the United States, he described Soviet control of Eastern Europe as an "iron curtain" dividing the continent.

In the West, the "iron curtain" became a symbol of the Cold War. It expressed the growing fear of communism. More important, it described the division of Europe into "eastern" and "western" blocs. In the East were the Soviet-dominated, communist countries of Eastern Europe. In the West were the western democracies, led by the United States.

New Conflicts Develop

Like Churchill, President Truman saw communism as an evil force creeping across Europe and threatening countries around the world, including China. To deal with that threat, the United States abandoned its traditional isolationism. After World War I, it had withdrawn from global affairs, but after World War II, the nation took a leading role on the world stage.

Stalin soon showed his aggressive intentions. In Greece, Stalin backed communist rebels who were fighting to overturn a right-wing monarchy supported by Britain. By 1947, however, Britain could no longer afford to defend Greece. Stalin was also menacing Turkey in the Dardanelles, the strait linking the Russian Black Sea coasts and the Mediterranean.

Truman Doctrine Truman took action. On March 12, 1947, Truman outlined a new policy to Congress: "I believe that it must be the policy of the United States to support free people who are resisting attempted subjugation by armed minorities or by outside pressures."

This policy, known as the Truman Doctrine, would guide the United States for decades. It made clear that Americans would resist Soviet expansion in Europe or elsewhere in the world. Truman soon sent military and economic aid and advisers to Greece and Turkey so that they could withstand the communist threat.

The Truman Doctrine was rooted in the idea of containment, limiting communism to the areas already under Soviet control. George Kennan, the American statesman who first proposed this approach, believed that communism would eventually destroy itself. Stalin, however, saw containment as "encirclement" by the capitalist world that wanted to isolate the Soviet Union.

Curtaining Off Eastern Europe

In 1946, Winston Churchill traveled to Westminster College in Fulton, Missouri, and delivered an address analyzing the Soviet threat in Eastern Europe:

"A shadow has fallen upon the scenes so lately lighted by Allied victory. . . . From Stettin in the Baltic to Trieste in the Adriatic, an iron curtain has descended across the Continent. . . . Warsaw, Berlin, Prague, Vienna, Budapest, Bucharest, and Sofia, all these famous cities and the populations around them lie in what I must call the Soviet sphere, and all are subject . . . not only to Soviet influence but to a very high and, in many cases, increasing measure of control from Moscow. . . . I do not believe that Soviet Russia desires war. What they desire is the fruits of war and the indefinite expansion of their power and doctrines."

—Winston Churchill, speech delivered March 5, 1946

Skills Assessment

Primary Source What does Churchill believe are Soviet motives for isolating its territories?

Researching Ask students to review Winston Churchill's words quoted in the Primary Source on this page and to select one of the capital cities mentioned in the quotation. Assign them to research the political developments that took place in their selected cities between 1944 and 1946. Specifically, each student should determine the accuracy or inaccuracy of Churchill's charge that the Soviet Union dominated that capital and its nation. Ask students to present their findings in an oral or written report. *(Enrichment)*

Test Preparation

Have students read the passage by Churchill in the Primary Source on this page, and then complete the sentence below.

Based on the passage, you can tell that

A dark curtains blocked the sun in Stettin and Trieste.

B Churchill thought many Eastern European cities were better off than they had been before World War II.

C Churchill viewed the Soviet Union as a threat.

D Churchill felt that Western Europe was falling under the Soviet Union's control.

Primary Source

ANSWER to strengthen and expand its control and spread its political doctrines

The Truman Doctrine In his speech to Congress proclaiming the Truman Doctrine, the President described the polarization that was at the root of the Cold War:

"At the present moment in world history nearly every nation must choose between alternative ways of life. The choice is too often not a free one. One way of life is based upon the will of the majority and is distinguished by free institutions, representative government, free elections, guarantees of individual liberty, freedom of speech and religion, and freedom from political oppression.

The second way of life is based upon the will of a minority forcibly imposed upon the majority. It relies upon terror and oppression, a controlled press and radio, fixed elections, and the suppression of personal freedoms."

You may wish to use the above excerpt as the basis for a class discussion on the origins of the Cold War.

Customize for . . .
Heterogeneous Groups

Constructing a Model Assign students to make a locator map of Berlin and to construct the Berlin Wall dividing the city. Have them set the map into a map of Germany. Then, have them pose questions about political issues concerning the Berlin Wall and its location. Possible questions: Why did the Berlin Wall present a problem to residents of the city? How did the geographical distribution of residents affect the history of post–World War II Germany?

Cold War in Europe

Divided Germany, 1945

NATO nations, 1955 · Warsaw Pact nations, 1955 · Other communist countries · Territory added to Soviet Union

Skills Assessment

Geography By 1955, western nations had joined to form NATO, and the Soviet Union had formed the Warsaw Pact with its allies. Meanwhile, Germany was divided into communist and noncommunist zones of occupation.
1. **Location** On the main map, locate **(a)** West Germany, **(b)** East Germany, **(c)** Warsaw Pact nations.
2. **Region** Use the inset map to identify the occupation zone in which Berlin was located.
3. **Critical Thinking Synthesizing Information** Why would Turkey be a likely location for a Cold War conflict?

The Marshall Plan Postwar hunger and poverty made Western European lands fertile ground for communist ideas. To strengthen democratic governments, the United States offered a massive aid package, called the Marshall Plan. Under it, the United States funneled food and economic assistance to Europe to help countries rebuild. Billions in American aid helped war-shattered Europe recover rapidly.

President Truman also offered aid to the Soviet Union and its satellites, or dependent states, in Eastern Europe. Stalin, however, saw the plan as a trick to win Eastern Europe over to capitalism and democracy. He forbade Eastern European countries to accept American aid, promising help from the Soviet Union in its place.

Divisions in Germany Defeated Germany became another focus of the Cold War. Fearing the danger of a restored Germany, the Soviet Union dismantled factories and other resources in its occupation zone and used them to help rebuild Russia. France, Britain, and the United States, however, decided to unite their zones of occupation, encouraging Germans to rebuild businesses and industries.

Germany thus became a divided nation. In West Germany, the democratic nations allowed the people to write their own constitution and regain self-government. In East Germany, the Soviet Union installed a communist government tied to Moscow.

Berlin Airlift Stalin's resentment at western moves to rebuild Germany as a democracy triggered a crisis over Berlin. The former German capital was occupied by all four victorious Allies, even though it lay deep within the Soviet zone.

In 1948, Stalin tried to force the western Allies out of Berlin by sealing off every railroad and highway into the western sectors of the city. The

794 Chapter 31

Resource Directory

Teaching Resources
Section Quiz Unit 7 booklet, p. 85
Geography Quiz Unit 7 booklet, p. 90
Chapter Test Forms A, B, and C Unit 7 booklet, pp. 91–95
Answer Key Unit 7 booklet, pp. 96–109

Technology
Interactive Student Tutorial CD-ROM Ch. 31
Computer Test Bank Ch. 31

western powers responded to the blockade by mounting a round-the-clock airlift. For more than a year, cargo planes supplied West Berliners with food and fuel. Their success forced the Soviets to end the blockade. Although the West had won a victory, the crisis deepened hostilities.

Military Alliances Tensions continued to grow. In 1949, the United States, Canada, and nine Western European countries formed a new military alliance called the North Atlantic Treaty Organization (NATO). Members pledged to help one another if any one of them was attacked.

In 1955, the Soviet Union responded by forming its own military alliance, the Warsaw Pact. It included the USSR and seven satellites in Eastern Europe. Unlike NATO, however, the Warsaw Pact was a weapon used by the Soviets to keep its satellites in order.

The Arms Race Each side in the Cold War armed itself to withstand an attack by the other. At first, the United States held an advantage in its control of nuclear power. But Stalin's top scientists were under orders to develop an atomic bomb of their own. They succeeded in 1949, and the arms race was on. For four decades, the superpowers spent fantastic sums to develop new, more deadly nuclear and conventional weapons. They invested still more to improve "delivery systems"—bombers, missiles, and submarines to launch these weapons of mass destruction. Soon, the global balance of power became, in Churchill's phrase, a "balance of terror."

The Propaganda War Both sides participated in a propaganda war. The United States spoke of defending capitalism and democracy against communism and totalitarianism. The Soviet Union claimed the moral high ground in the struggle against western imperialism. Yet linked to those stands, both sides sought world power.

Looking Ahead

In 1945, the world hoped for an end to decades of economic crisis, bloody dictators, and savage war. Instead, it faced new tensions.

The Cold War would last for more than 40 years. Rivalry between the hostile camps would not only divide Europe but also fuel crises around the world. It would strain the resources of the United States and exhaust those of the Soviet Union. Though it would not erupt into large-scale fighting between the two superpowers, many small wars would break out, with the superpowers championing opposite sides. Meanwhile, the spread of ominous new weapons would raise the specter of global destruction.

SECTION 5 Assessment

Recall
1. **Identify:** (a) UN, (b) "iron curtain," (c) Truman Doctrine, (d) Berlin airlift, (e) NATO, (f) Warsaw Pact.
2. **Define:** (a) containment, (b) satellite.

Comprehension
3. How did the Allies try to hold the Axis leaders responsible for the suffering they caused during the war?
4. What was the main purpose of the UN?

5. List two causes of the Cold War.

Critical Thinking and Writing
6. **Recognizing Causes and Effects** Some historians argue that the Cold War began in 1918 when the World War I Allies, including the United States, sent forces to Russia to topple the Bolsheviks. How might they support this position?
7. **Linking Past and Present** Why do people feel it is so important to remember the inhumanity of the Holocaust?

Activity

Creating a Political Cartoon Use Churchill's "iron curtain" image to create a political cartoon about the Cold War. Write a caption for your cartoon.

Creating a Chapter Summary

As a reteaching opportunity, pair a more able student with a less able student to complete this chapter summary.

Students might add the following information to their flowcharts: Germany invades Poland—Britain/France declare war; German blitzkriegs overtake Europe—Britain stands alone; Hitler bombs London; Germany attacks Soviet Union; Japanese bomb Pearl Harbor—U.S. enters war; Japanese take Philippines; Battle of El Alamein—Germans driven out of Africa; Americans win battles of Coral Sea and Midway Island; Germans forced to surrender at Battle of Stalingrad; Allies invade Italy; D-Day; Allies free France; Battle of the Bulge; Hitler's suicide; V-E Day; Americans drop atomic bomb on Japan.

Building Vocabulary

1–10. (a) Possible answers: **Economics and technology**—sanction, radar, sonar **Global interaction**—appeasement, blitzkrieg, collaborator **Religions and value systems**—pacifism, genocide **Geography and history**—island-hopping, containment **(b)** Students' sentences should show an understanding of how each word relates to the theme.

Recalling Key Facts

11. British and French leaders appeased Hitler by agreeing to pressure the Czechs to surrender the Sudetenland to Germany.
12. German invasion of Poland; September 1, 1939
13. A large German army was destroyed in the battle, and after Stalingrad the Soviets went on the offensive.
14. It was established in 1945 to secure world peace and to deal with other world problems.
15. President Truman's declaration that the United States would support free peoples against domestic or foreign enemies

Critical Thinking and Writing

16. Possible answer: A powerful leader can exert enormous influence. Driven by hatred and fear, ordinary people are capable of unspeakable atrocities.
17. The war ended dictatorships in Germany, Italy, and Japan, but helped the totalitarian Soviet Union become a superpower.

Creating a Chapter Summary

Make a flowchart on a separate sheet of paper to show the main events of World War II and its aftermath, as well as related details. Use the chart below to help you get started.

For additional review and enrichment activities, see the interactive version of *World History* available on the Web and on CD-ROM.

> Dictators challenge world peace/Japan, Italy, Germany

> Spanish Civil War/Dress rehearsal

> Appeasement fails/Britain, France

Web Site Self-Test For practice test questions for Chapter 31, see **www.phschool.com.**

Building Vocabulary

(a) Classify each of the chapter vocabulary words listed below under one of the following themes: economics and technology, global interaction, religions and value systems, geography and history. **(b)** Choose one word in each category and write a sentence explaining how that word relates to the theme.

1. **sanction**
2. **appeasement**
3. **pacifism**
4. **blitzkrieg**
5. **radar**
6. **sonar**
7. **genocide**
8. **collaborator**
9. **island-hopping**
10. **containment**

Recalling Key Facts

11. What happened at the Munich Conference of 1938?
12. What event started World War II? When did it occur?
13. Why was the Battle of Stalingrad important?
14. When and why was the United Nations established?
15. What was the Truman Doctrine?

Critical Thinking and Writing

16. **Linking Past and Present** What lessons does the Holocaust have for us today?
17. **Analyzing Information** Explain the following statement: World War II brought down several dictatorships but increased the power of the world's largest totalitarian state.
18. **Defending a Position** Agree or disagree with the following statement: The western democracies could have prevented World War II. Explain.
19. **Synthesizing Information** **(a)** How did the United States help the Allies before entering World War II? **(b)** Was participation by the United States crucial to winning the war? Explain.
20. **Connecting to Geography** How were Hitler's plans to conquer Europe affected by the geography of **(a)** Britain, **(b)** Russia?
21. **Drawing Conclusions** **(a)** Which battle was most important in the war in Europe? **(b)** Which battle was most important in the war in the Pacific? Explain your answers.

---

18. Students should discuss the Treaty of Versailles and the policy of appeasement.
19. **(a)** The United States provided both military and economic aid. **(b)** Encourage students to provide clear and specific reasons for their opinions.
20. **(a)** Britain is an island nation, so it was nearly impossible to land ground troops, and the air war failed. **(b)** Russia's harsh winter climate inflicted heavy losses on the German army.
21. **(a)** Accept any well-supported response. **(b)** Accept any well-supported response.

The passage below is from a dispatch filed by Douglas Williams, a reporter for the London *Daily Telegraph*. The report describes Williams's first-hand observation of the evacuation of Dunkirk in May and June of 1940. Read the passage, then answer the questions that follow.

"All day long and during the night evacuation continued. Rescue vessels raced across the Channel loaded with men to the fullest capacity as fast as conditions would permit, steamed back at full speed across the narrow strip of water to return again with undiminished enthusiasm for fresh batches. . . .

Their position at Dunkirk becomes hourly more dangerous as German batteries begin to receive a full [supply] of ammunition from their supply columns. . . .

Parts of the town are in flames, and entire quarters in ruins. Outside, the main roads present scenes of confusion and destruction. Innumerable abandoned motorcars and [trucks] lie ditched in every field, while others set alight blaze fiercely.

Bodies of refugees killed by German machinegun bullets are seen at frequent intervals, and everywhere long lines of soldiers hurry down to the sea and safety.

Yet the work of evacuation continues uninterruptedly with calm efficiency, while a powerful rear-guard fights magnificently to delay the constantly increasing masses of German troops. . . ."

—Douglas Williams,
Dunkirk: May 28–June 4, 1940

22. **(a)** Describe the actions of people involved in the rescue operation. **(b)** According to Williams, what was the attitude of the rescuers?

23. **(a)** Why was the position of the Allied troops at Dunkirk becoming more dangerous? **(b)** How does Williams describe conditions at Dunkirk?

24. How would you describe Williams's point of view?

25. **(a)** How do you think the success of this operation affected British morale? **(b)** An American reporter wrote: "So long as the English tongue survives, the word Dunkirk will be spoken with reverence." What do you think the reporter meant by this?

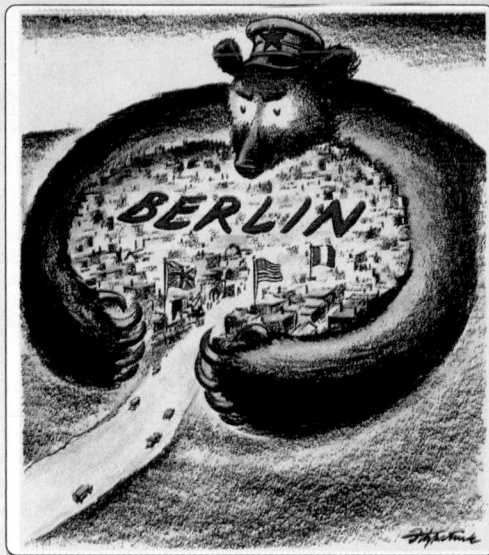

After World War II, relations between Russia and the western nations deteriorated. The cartoon is a comment on developments in Berlin. Study the cartoon, then answer the following questions:

26. What do the flags stand for?
27. **(a)** What does the bear represent? **(b)** What is the bear doing? Why?
28. Based on what you have learned, why did Russia want to close off Berlin?

Skills Tip

Pay careful attention to symbols in political cartoons. Determine how the cartoonist combines symbols to present a point of view.

Use the Internet to research important events of World War II. Then, create a time line that shows the progression of the war. Use a special color or other design to indicate important dates, such as major turning points.

Analyzing Primary Sources

22. **(a)** calm, efficient operation, and steady protection from the rear-guard **(b)** undiminished enthusiasm
23. **(a)** The Germans were getting new supplies of ammunition. **(b)** He describes a hectic scene full of destruction and chaos.
24. Possible answer: He is British and reflects admiration and respect for the rescuers and men being evacuated.
25. Possible answers: **(a)** It probably lifted morale considerably. **(b)** The Dunkirk rescue, accomplished under extremely difficult circumstances, will inspire pride in the British and their allies.

Analyzing Political Cartoons

26. They are the flags of Britain, France, and the United States.
27. **(a)** the Soviet Union **(b)** He is trying to encircle Berlin to cut it off from access by western nations.
28. to force the western Allies out of the city

Skills Tip

Note, for example, the red color on the bear's claws, which may stand for spilled blood or for the epithet *red*, which was used for the Russian communist government. Note, too, that a bear has been the symbol of Russia for many years. The Skills Handbook in the front of the book has a lesson that will help students with this feature.

Unit Theme Activity

Evaluate students' Unit Theme Activities by referring to the rubrics on the unit opener page in the Teacher's Edition.

Take It to the NET

Direct students to **www.phschool.com** for links to sites that will help them get started on this assignment. Share rubrics with students.

Attempted The time line has no apparent scale and few items, some of which are inaccurately placed. Labels are misspelled or illegible.

Minimal The time line has a rough scale and an adequate number of items, some of which are inaccurately placed. Labels are legible but contain some mechanical errors.

Adequate The time line has an appropriate number of items and an accurate scale. Labels are legible and contain few mechanical errors.

Exemplary The time line has an appropriate number of carefully chosen items and an accurate scale. Labels contain no mechanical errors. The time line is visually striking.

Using These Pages

The Unit-in-Brief contains the main ideas of the unit chapters. You may use the Unit-in-Brief to preview, review, or condense the contents of each chapter.

The unit time line identifies key events in each world region that took place during the time span covered by the unit.

Activity
Unit Themes

Have students review the unit themes below. Then, ask them to find examples in the time line and summary to support each theme.

Continuity and Change Nationalists in Asia, Latin America, and Africa challenged foreign domination and encouraged a revival of traditional culture. Tools of change ranged from civil disobedience in India to armed rebellion in Mexico.

Economics and Technology The Great Depression caused major economic problems around the world. Fascists and communists offered their own extreme solutions to the crisis.

Global Interaction Two world wars were fought in the first half of the twentieth century. Developed nations in the global North and developing countries in the global South became increasingly interdependent. Common concerns encouraged nations to support international organizations and agreements.

Political and Social Systems Democracy, communism, and fascism competed for influence and political power. Totalitarian dictatorships attempted to regulate all aspects of life and to place the needs of the state above individual rights.

Chapter 27

World War I and Its Aftermath (1914–1919)

Many forces—including nationalism, militarism, and imperialist rivalries—propelled Europe into World War I. This massive conflict engulfed much of the world for four years and ushered in a new age of modern warfare.

- Two huge alliances emerged in Europe: the Central Powers, dominated by Germany and Austria-Hungary, and the Allies, led by France, Britain, and Russia.
- Although the assassination of Archduke Francis Ferdinand in 1914 ignited World War I, historians agree that all the major powers share blame for the conflict.
- Trench warfare and new weapons contributed to a stalemate on the Western Front.
- In 1917, the United States entered the war, allowing the Allies to achieve victory.
- The Paris Peace Conference imposed heavy penalties on Germany and redrew the map of Eastern Europe.

Chapter 28

Revolution in Russia (1917–1939)

Lenin and his successors transformed czarist Russia into the communist Soviet Union. This experiment in single-party politics and a state-run economy would exert a powerful influence over the modern world for almost 75 years.

- In March 1917, political, social, and economic conditions in Russia sparked a revolution that overthrew the czar and paved the way for more radical changes.
- After leading the Bolsheviks to power in November 1917, Lenin hoped to build a communist state based on the ideas of Marx.
- Lenin's successor, Stalin, imposed "five-year plans" to build industry and increase farm output.
- Stalin created a totalitarian state, employing censorship, propaganda, and terror to ensure personal power and push the Soviet Union toward modernization.

Chapter 29

Nationalism and Revolution Around the World (1910–1939)

Between 1919 and 1939, the desire for democracy and self-determination contributed to explosive struggles in many regions. New leaders in Africa, Latin America, and Asia built liberation movements that would change the world.

- The Mexican revolution opened the door to social and economic reforms.
- African leaders opposed imperialism and reaffirmed traditional cultures.
- Arab Nationalism led to Pan-Arabism, uniting Arabs against foreign domination.
- In India, Gandhi led a campaign of nonviolent resistance to British rule.
- In China, foreigners extended their spheres of influence. Later, communists and nationalists engaged in civil war.
- In the 1920s and 1930s, extreme nationalism and economic upheaval set Japan on a militaristic and expansionist path.

	1910	1920	1930
AFRICA	**1912** African National Congress formed in South Africa	**1919** First Pan-African Congress held in Paris	
THE AMERICAS	**1910** Mexican Revolution begins	**1919** Red Scare in United States	**1929** Stock market crash
ASIA AND OCEANIA	**1911** Civil War in China	**1923** Atatürk begins modernization of Turkey	
EUROPE		**1914** World War I begins **1917** Russian Revolution	**1922** Mussolini rules Italy **1933** Hitler rules Germany

Student Bibliography

Beck, Earl R. *Under the Bombs: The German Home Front, 1942–1945.* University Press of Kentucky, 1999. A sensitive portrait of total war's impact on German civilians.

Gandhi, Mohandas Karamchand; Mahadev Desai, translator. *An Autobiography: The Story of My Experiments With Truth.* Beacon Press, 1993. Inspiring account of the inner world of Mohandas K. Gandhi.

Joll, James. *The Origins of the First World War.* Longman, 1992. Well-written synthesis examining the multiple causes of World War I.

Reed, John. *Ten Days That Shook the World.* Lightyear, 1992. Memoir of the October revolution by an American journalist.

Selden, Kyoko, and Mark Selden, eds. *The Atomic Bomb: Voices from Hiroshima and Nagasaki.* M.E. Sharpe, 1997. Account of the effects of the atomic bombs according to their victims.

Volkogonov, Dmitri. *Lenin: A New Biography.* Free Press, 1994. First biography of Lenin based on full access to the newly opened Russian archives.

Chapter 30

Crisis of Democracy in the West
(1919–1939)

After World War I, western nations worked to restore prosperity and ensure peace. At the same time, political and economic turmoil in the 1920s and 1930s challenged democratic traditions and led to the rise of dictators.

- The Great Depression of the 1930s created financial turmoil and widespread suffering throughout the industrialized world.
- Scientific discoveries, new trends in literature and the arts, and social changes all contributed to a sense of uncertainty.
- Unrest in Italy helped Mussolini lead his Fascist party to power in the 1920s.
- In Germany, Hitler rose to power by appealing to extreme nationalism, antisemitism, anti-communism, and resentment of the Treaty of Versailles. In the 1930s, he turned the German state into a totalitarian Nazi dictatorship.
- Three systems of government—democracy, communism, and fascism—competed for influence in postwar Europe.

Chapter 31

World War II and Its Aftermath
(1931–1955)

Between 1939 and 1945, nations all over the globe fought World War II, the largest and most costly conflict in history. The war shifted the balance of world power from Western Europe to the United States and the Soviet Union.

- The Axis powers—Germany, Italy, and Japan—embarked on a course of aggression in the late 1930s. France and Britain first adopted a policy of appeasement but declared war when Hitler invaded Poland.
- During the Holocaust, the Nazis systematically killed more than six million Jews, as well as millions of other people the Nazis considered undesirable.
- The United States, the Soviet Union, and the Allied Powers joined to defeat Germany.
- To force a Japanese surrender, the United States dropped two atomic bombs.
- The Cold War followed World War II, pitting the western democracies, led by the United States, against the communist bloc, dominated by the Soviet Union.

1940   **1950**   **1960**

1935
Italy invades
Ethiopia

1948 South Africa makes
apartheid the law of the land

1941
Bombing of
Pearl Harbor

1947
United States announces
Marshall Plan

1930s
Gandhi leads anti-British
protests in India

1945
Japan
surrenders and World War II ends

1949 People's Republic of China established

1939 World War II begins
1941 Holocaust begins

1949 NATO formed

1955 Warsaw Pact formed

Have students use both the Unit-in-Brief and Chapters 27–31 to answer the following questions in order to summarize Unit 7: (1) What were the major causes and effects of World War I? (2) Describe the political and economic conditions that existed in the Soviet Union under Stalin. (3) How did nationalism lead to the creation of many new nations? (4) What political and economic problems afflicted Europe after World War I? (5) How did World War II shift the balance of world power?

PRENTICE HALL
ASSESSMENT SYSTEM

Diagnose and Prescribe
- **Profile student skills with Diagnostic Tests A & B.**
- **Address student needs with program materials identified in the test.**

Review and Reteach
- **Provide cumulative content review with the Review Book.**

Practice and Assess
- **Build test-taking skills with Test-Taking Strategies With Transparencies.**

Teacher Bibliography

Burg, David F., and L. Edward Purcell. *Almanac of World War I.* University Press of Kentucky, 1998. Nicely illustrated chronological resource of the Great War.

Calvocoressi, P., G. Wint, and J. Pritchard. *Total War: Causes and Courses of the Second World War.* Pantheon, 1990. Detailed overview of World War II.

Figes, Orlando. *A People's Tragedy: The Russian Revolution 1891–1924.* Viking Books, 1997. Narrative, accessible account of the revolution.

Iriye, Akira. *After Imperialism: The Search for a New Order in the Far East, 1921–1931.* Imprint, 1990. Study of the growth of nationalism in Asia.

Langley, J.A. *Pan-Africanism and Nationalism in West Africa, 1900–1945.* Clarendon Press, 1973. Detailed study of pan-Africanism in West Africa.

Winn, Peter. *Americas: The Changing Face of Latin America and the Caribbean.* University of California Press, 1999. A general overview of the history of Latin America and the Caribbean.

UNIT 8

UNIT OVERVIEW

Unit 8 studies the world today by first providing an overview and then focusing on specific regions.

Chapter 32 provides an overview of major world trends and developments since World War II.

Chapter 33 focuses on Western Europe, the United States, Canada, the Soviet Union, and Eastern Europe.

Chapter 34 studies Japan, China, and other nations of East Asia and Southeast Asia.

Chapter 35 examines significant trends and developments in South Asia and the Middle East.

Chapter 36 provides in-depth coverage of the various forces that have brought change to Africa.

Chapter 37 surveys the forces that are shaping modern Latin America.

Unit Theme Activity Rubrics

Share rubrics with students before they create their projects.

Attempted The project does not examine how diversity poses a concern for a nation's development.

Minimal The project is poorly executed or only vaguely examines how diversity poses a concern for a nation's development.

Adequate The project is well executed and clearly examines how diversity poses a concern for a nation's development.

Exemplary The project is extremely well executed, ably examines how diversity poses a concern for a nation's development, and is visually interesting or is extremely interesting and informative to read.

UNIT 8

The World Today

1945–Present

OUTLINE

Themes

As you read about the developments and challenges over the last half of the twentieth century, you will encounter the following themes.

Diversity Conflicts flared between ethnic groups and between old and new ways of life. Urbanization, westernization, and the women's movement challenged the traditional culture.

Economics and Technology After a long struggle for control, communist state-run economies disappeared from Europe. Advances in science and technology dramatically changed human life and thought.

Global Interaction The Cold War between the United States and the Soviet Union dominated international relations in the second half of the century. Colonial empires collapsed as emerging nations in Africa, Asia, and elsewhere won their independence.

Geography and History Economic development often caused serious damage to the natural environment. Global warming, pollution, and diminishing resources were concerns of both rich and poor nations.

This satellite image of Earth shows the Arctic, Europe, Middle East, India, and Africa with a bit of South America. Nations around the world have become increasingly interdependent.

Unit Theme Activity

For Your Portfolio The chapters in this unit explore the challenge of ethnic groups to put aside differences and work together for a common good. As you read the chapters, prepare a portfolio project examining how diversity poses concern for a nation's development. Your project might take one of the following forms:
• **Poster**
• **Editorial**
• **Time line**

Resource Directory

Technology

World History Visions, Voices, Views Scenes of an Age, *The World Today,* videodisc side 4 or videotape 8, running time 2:30 min.

Side 4: Fr. 22926-28270

Radar Images Satellite technology has enabled scientists to gather a much more thorough picture of the Earth's surface. Starting in 1978 with the SEASAT spacecraft, NASA has used radar imaging to accurately plot the contours of the globe. This imaging technique works by projecting microwaves from a satellite in orbit to the Earth's surface. When these waves hit the surface, they are deflected. Some bounce back toward the satellite, while others are scattered in various directions. The satellite measures the strength of the waves, as well as the time it takes for the waves to return. It then converts this information into digital data which is used to compile a picture of the surface.

In February 2000, NASA embarked on what they hailed as the "most complete near-global high-resolution database of Earth's topography." After this mission, over 80 percent of the Earth's landmass will be mapped. Using equipment based on the Space Shuttle *Endeavour*, NASA was able to complete the imaging task in an amazing ten days.

iTEXT

Don't miss the exclusive interactive version of *World History: Connections to Today* on the Internet and CD-ROM.

Unit 8 **801**

eTeach

Be sure to check out this month's online discussion with a World History Master Teacher.

Go to **www.phschool.com**.

WHY STUDY HISTORY?
Because We Interact With People Around the World

Bell Ringer After students have read the text and looked at the pictures on these two pages, ask them to give examples of international cultural influences on their lives. Then, ask what they consider to be typical examples of American culture and whether they are found in other countries.

Activity
Cooperative Learning

An International Meal Organize the students into the following groups: Breakfast, Lunch, Snacks, Dinner, Beverages, Desserts. Then, using the local library, the Internet, or their own homes as resources, have students find recipes for their assigned meals from different countries around the world. For example, the lunch group can give lunch recipes for pizza from Italy, a lentil dish from Nicaragua, and stuffed grape leaves from the Middle East. Create a classroom menu of all of the meals, including drawings or photographs of the foods and ingredients.

Look around your classroom or home. Do you see running shoes made in Malaysia? A radio from Korea? Apples from New Zealand? Maybe you dance to Latin pop music or read Japanese comics. You might take part in online chats with teenagers from England. Or maybe you cheer for a U.S. sports team as it competes against teams from other nations. In all these ways, you are experiencing your link to people around the world.

These connections did not arise overnight, however. History helps explain how they developed.

Trading Around the World

Events in one country can affect prices in another. A bumper cotton crop in India can lead to cheaper clothing in Paris. An unexpected frost in South America can lead to expensive fruit juice in Chicago. The container ship shown here is carrying American products to overseas markets.

But how closely should one nation's economy be tied to others? Each nation must decide if it will promote trade with other countries or concentrate on helping its own industries. Throughout history, countries have grappled with this issue.

Meeting of Cultures

The world's people are on the move. In the 1990s, millions of people left their homes to live in a new country. Like immigrants in the past, these newcomers brought with them their recipes and music, their ideas and habits. These children proudly show off traditional clothing from their native lands. Over time, these traditions will become part of the culture of their adopted homeland.

Resource Directory

Teaching Resources

Why Study History? *Because We Interact With People Around the World,* Why Study History? booklet, pp. 19–20

Lending a Helping Hand

News of a disaster can bring help from people living thousands of miles away. After mudslides devastated Venezuela in 1999, American schoolchildren donated money and clothing. And when war in Kosovo left thousands of children in need, international organizations such as UNICEF helped out. Have people around the world always helped one another? History can help you learn the answer.

Sharing Moments

Events like the Olympics link athletes and spectators through competition and cooperation. Television, communications satellites, and the Internet allow people all over the world to experience an event at the moment when it happens. In 1998, millions of people watched the opening ceremonies of the Winter Olympic games in Nagano, Japan. Through the study of history, you can learn how nations came to compete in the Olympics and how technology has enabled us to share the events with people everywhere.

Chapter 32 Planning Guide

Resource Manager

	CORE INSTRUCTION	READING/SKILLS
Chapter Level Resources	📖 **Teaching Resources** 📄 **Pacing Charts**, Ch. 32 📄 **Teaching With Themes**, p. 35 ⚏ **Color Transparencies**, p. F–65 💿 **Resource Pro®** Ch. 32 🖥 **www.phschool.com** 　• eTeach	💿 **Book on CD**, Ch. 32 💿 **Interactive Student Tutorial CD-ROM**, Ch. 32 💿 **Social Studies Skills Tutor CD-ROM** ⚏ **Skills Transparencies**
1 The Changing Political Climate 1. Explain how the end of colonialism and the Cold War shaped the world. 2. Summarize the ways new nations tried to form stable governments. 3. Analyze the role world organizations played. 4. Discuss the enduring issues that the world faces today.	📖 **Teaching Resources** 📄 **Creative Teaching Activities**, p. 143 💿 **Prentice Hall Presentation Pro**, Ch. 32, Section 1 ⚏ **Section Reading Support Transparencies**	📖 **Teaching Resources** 📁 **Unit 8 booklet** 　• Guided Reading and Review, p. 2 📄 **Guide to the Essentials** 📼 **Guided Reading Audiotapes**, Ch. 32, Section 1
2 Global Economic Trends 1. Explain the ways that the global North and South are economically interdependent. 2. Outline the obstacles that developing nations face. 3. Relate how economic development and environmental issues are linked.	📖 Teaching Resources 📁 **Unit 8 booklet** 　• Biography Activity, p. 8 　• Viewpoint Activity, p. 10 📄 **Creative Teaching Activities**, p. 144 💿 **Prentice Hall Presentation Pro**, Ch. 32, Section 2 ⚏ **Section Reading Support Transparencies**	📖 Teaching Resources 📁 **Unit 8 booklet** 　• Guided Reading and Review, p. 4 📄 **Guide to the Essentials** 📼 **Guided Reading Audiotapes**, Ch. 32, Section 2
3 Changing Patterns of Life 1. Trace how new ways of life are replacing old ways. 2. Give examples of how modernization has affected the lives of women. 3. Compare and contrast the benefits and limits of modern science and technology. 4. Identify the forces that have shaped a new global culture.	📖 Teaching Resources 📁 **Unit 8 booklet** 　• Primary Source Activity, p. 9 📄 **Creative Teaching Activities**, p. 145 💿 **Prentice Hall Presentation Pro**, Ch. 32, Section 3 ⚏ **Section Reading Support Transparencies**	📖 Teaching Resources 📁 **Unit 8 booklet** 　• Guided Reading and Review, p. 6 　• Skill Application Activity, p. 11 📄 **Guide to the Essentials** 📼 **Guided Reading Audiotapes**, Ch. 32, Section 3

ENRICHMENT/PRE-AP

🖳 **www.phschool.com**
- Why Study History?

📕 Teaching Resources
📄 **History Through Literature**, p. 67

📕 Teaching Resources
📄 **Chapter Extension Activities**, pp. 76–77
📧 **Color Transparencies**, p. B–65
🖳 **www.phschool.com**
- Internet Activities, Section 2

📕 Teaching Resources
📄 **Chapter Extension Activities**, p. 78
📄 **Geography and History**, pp. 16–17
🖳 **www.phschool.com**
- Internet Activities, Computers and the Arts
- Virtual Field Trip
- Internet Activities, Section 3

ASSESSMENT

PRENTICE HALL
ASSESSMENT *SYSTEM*

Core Assessment
📘 ExamView Test Bank booklet, Ch. 32
💿 ExamView Test Bank CD-ROM, Ch. 32

Standardized Test Preparation

Diagnose and Prescribe
📘 Diagnostic Tests for High School Social Studies Skills

Review and Reteach
📘 Review Book for World History

Practice and Assess
📘 Test-Taking Strategies With Transparencies for High School
📘 Alternative Assessment booklet
📘 Test Prep Book for World History

📕 Teaching Resources
📂 **Unit 8 booklet**
- Geography Quiz, p. 12
- Section Quizzes, pp. 3, 5, 7
- Chapter Tests A, B, and C, pp. 13–17
🖳 **www.phschool.com**
- Self-Test

CUSTOMIZE FOR INDIVIDUAL NEEDS

Gifted and Talented
- **Teacher's Edition,** Activities: Customize for Heterogeneous Groups, p. 810

Less Proficient Readers
- **Guide to the Essentials,** Ch. 32
- **Guided Reading Audiotapes, English,** Ch. 32
- **Book on CD,** Ch. 32
- **Teacher's Edition,** Activities: Reading Strategy, p. 810; Cooperative Learning, p. 819

Less Proficient Writers
- **Teacher's Edition,** Activities: Customize for Kinesthetic Learners, p. 813; Cooperative Learning, p. 819

Students Acquiring English/ESL
- **Guide to the Essentials, English/Spanish,** Ch. 32
- **Guided Reading Audiotapes, English/Spanish,** Ch. 32
- **Book on CD,** Ch. 32
- **Teacher's Edition,** Activities marked with an *

TEXT

Don't miss the exclusive interactive version of *World History: Connections to Today* on the Internet and CD-ROM.

INTRODUCTION

After World War II, European colonial empires ended and dozens of new countries were born. The United States and the Soviet Union emerged as dominant powers. Locked in an ideological Cold War, these two superpowers realigned the world's economies into the capitalist West and the communist East. Industrialized nations of the global North and developing nations of the global South became increasingly interdependent. As urbanization and westernization became dominant forces, changes in women's roles, religions, and technology have helped shape a new global culture.

Focusing on Themes

Suggest that students focus on these theme questions as they read:

Political and Social Systems
What postwar developments have helped or hindered the spread of democracy?

Economics and Technology
How does the gap between rich and poor nations affect the world?

Global Interaction
How has global interdependence affected the world and its environment?

Continuity and Change
How has modernization and westernization brought about rapid social and cultural change?

TIME LINE ACTIVITY

Share the About the Pictures note with students before asking these questions:

1. When did the Green Revolution begin, and what were its results? *(It began in the 1960s; it helps feed people.)*
2. Why do you think the computer has become such an essential tool since 1980? *(Computers allow instant access to global information.)*
3. When did the Cold War end? *(1991)*

Don't Miss!

Comparing Viewpoints
What Is the Relationship Between People and the Environment? (Section 2)

Humanities Link
Computers and the Arts (Section 3)

The World Since 1945: An Overview 1945–Present

Chapter Preview

1 The Changing Political Climate
2 Global Economic Trends
3 Changing Patterns of Life

1969
On July 20, American astronauts become the first people to walk on the moon.

1945
The United Nations is formed. Today, the UN meets in this building in New York City.

1960s
The Green Revolution begins, increasing food production in many developing nations.

CHAPTER EVENTS

1940   1955   1970

Resource Directory

Teaching Resources
Chapter Theme Activities Teaching With Themes booklet, p. 35
Pacing Chart With Block Scheduling Guide Ch. 32
Technology
World History Color Transparencies Ch. 32 Graphic Organizer, p. F–65

The World Economy, 1990s

Per capita income
- Over $10,000
- $1,001–$10,000
- $100–$1,000
- Data unavailable

Source: *The World Almanac and Book of Facts, 1999*

The modern world is divided into the relatively rich nations of the global North and the relatively poor nations of the global South. Average income is one measure of a nation's wealth.

Robinson Projection
0   1500   3000 Miles
0   1500   3000 Kilometers

1980s
The computer becomes an essential tool in homes and offices. Here, a technician processes data in Senegal.

1991
The global Cold War ends.

2000
A new millennium, or thousand-year period, brings both hopes and fears. The Millennium Dome in Greenwich, England, was built to celebrate the start of this new era in history.

1985   2000   2015

Activating Prior Knowledge
How did World War II help shape the postwar world economy? *(Much of Europe and Japan lay in ruins. Many nations were unable to recover financially, so the balance of economic power shifted.)*

Previewing
Why do you think richer nations might be the ones to lead the campaign for the environment? *(They have the finances to do so; developing nations are more concerned with improving the standard of living.)*

Background
About the Pictures

 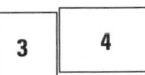

1. Outside the United Nations complex in New York City, flags of member nations from around the world are displayed prominently, symbolizing the UN's broad international scope.
2. Apollo 11 astronaut Edwin "Buzz" Aldrin, the second man to walk on the moon, was an air force pilot before becoming an astronaut. In 1969, Aldrin spent two hours on the moon.
3. The Colossus, built in England in 1943, and the ENIAC, built in the United States in 1945, were generally believed to be the first electronic digital computers. Actually, an American theoretical physicist, John V. Atanasoff, built the first electronic computer (1937–1942) at Iowa State College.
4. The largest dome in the world, the Millennium Dome in Greenwich, London, England, was built as a monument to the third millennium.

 eTeach

Be sure to check out this month's online discussion with a World History Master Teacher.

Go to **www.phschool.com**.

Independent Assignments

Have students read one section as they prepare for class. After class, have them complete the assignment. Some students may benefit from using the Guided Reading and Review worksheets.

Section 1 Have students read the selection *Kwame Nkrumah's Views on Independence* in Treasures of the World, pp.149–151, to explore the issues involved in the end of colonialism.
Section 2 Have students use the worksheet *Mother Teresa* in the Unit 8 booklet, p. 8, to learn about this unusual woman who devoted her life to helping the poor in developing countries.

Section 3 Have students use the worksheet *Media—"Hot" and "Cold"* in the Unit 8 booklet, p. 9, to learn more about how communications technology changed life in the later twentieth century.

Bell Ringer Before assigning the section, ask students to use the glossary at the back of the text to define the eight vocabulary words listed at the start of Section 1. As they read the section, ask students to list and define other key vocabulary words.

LESSON PLAN

1. Focus After World War II, European nations, lacking the strength and will to continue opposing nationalist movements, gradually lost their overseas colonies. As new nations emerged, the United States and the Soviet Union vied for influence. The new nations faced political instability due to ethnic and religious rivalries, the lack of democratic traditions, and the rise of dictatorships. Interdependence and global issues encouraged countries to enter into international agreements and organizations.

2. Instruct As they read this section, have students find evidence to support or dispute the five generalizations that follow. (1) World War II was a catalyst for ending imperialism. (2) New nations often failed in their attempts to establish democratic governments. (3) The Cold War brought both benefits and problems for new nations. (4) International organizations help shape global politics, economics, and social issues. (5) The arms trade, terrorism, and the violation of human rights are enduring issues of global concern.

3. Assess Conclude the lesson by discussing differing points of view within the class.

4. Reteach If students' **Assess** activity does not reflect adequate understanding of the lesson, you might assign the *Guide to the Essentials* or the *Interactive Student Tutorial CD-ROM* for this section.

Reading Focus
- How did the end of colonialism and the Cold War shape the world?
- How did new nations try to form stable governments?
- What role have world organizations played?
- What enduring issues face the world today?

Vocabulary
- modernization
- superpower
- ideology
- nonaligned
- interdependence
- summit
- human rights
- terrorism

Taking Notes
As you read this section, make an outline of its contents. Use Roman numerals for major headings. Use capital letters for subheadings, and use numbers for supporting details. This example will help you get started.

I. End to European colonial empires
  A. Nationalism and independence
    1. Nationalist leaders insist on independence
    2.
  B. Different roads to freedom
    1.
  C.

Main Idea After World War II, the Cold War and the decline of European influence shifted the balance of world power.

Connections to Today

The Last Shreds of an Empire

In the great tide of national liberation, Bermuda has gone its own way. It is one of a handful of remaining British colonies, all of them small island remnants of the once-mighty British empire.

A small group of islands that lures half a million visitors per year with soft ocean breezes, Bermuda did experience some political problems. The assassination of the British governor in 1973 and outbreaks of rioting in 1977 delayed independence negotiations. A vote for independence was finally held in August 1995. Prosperous and cautious, the Bermudans voted overwhelmingly to retain their ties to Great Britain.

Theme: Political and Social Systems Why might a colony choose to vote against independence?

Setting the Scene Two centuries ago, the American and French revolutions launched ideals such as the natural rights of all people. In 1972, President Julius Nyerere of Tanzania in East Africa put those ideas in modern terms when he spoke of the goals of new nations that had freed themselves from colonial rule:

> "There is a world-wide movement now—even within the imperialist countries it exists—to put an end to the exploitation [taking advantage] of man by man. This movement will succeed. Eventually, imperialism and racialism will become merely a chapter in the history of man—we shall hear about it in museums."
>
> —Julius K. Nyerere, *Freedom and Development*

The balance of world power changed dramatically after 1945. European influence declined while the United States and the Soviet Union emerged as the world's dominant powers, locked in a tense Cold War. Perhaps the greatest change, however, was the collapse of western overseas empires and the emergence of dozens of new countries.

An End to European Colonial Empires

The postwar decades brought a major turning point in world history. The colonial empires built by western powers during the Age of Imperialism crumbled. In Asia and Africa, people demanded and won freedom. Between 1950 and 1980, more than 50 new nations emerged in Africa alone.

Nationalism and Independence Resistance to colonial rule had begun long before. By the 1930s, nationalist movements had taken root in Africa, Asia, and the Middle East. After World War II, nationalist leaders such as Gandhi in India insisted on independence.

At first, Britain, France, and other powers tried to hold on to their empires. But the war had exhausted their military and financial resources. With subject peoples ready to fight for freedom, many war-weary Europeans had no desire for further conflict.

The Cold War, too, undermined imperialism. The United States backed the right of colonized people to self-determination. Its rival, the Soviet Union, also had long condemned western imperialism. Soon, both sides were seeking allies among emerging nations.

Connections to Today

ANSWER Their strong economy might make them reluctant to overturn an arrangement that has so far been more a benefit than a handicap to them.

Resource Directory

Teaching Resources
Creative Teaching Activities Creative Teaching Activities booklet, p. 143
Guided Reading and Review Unit 8 booklet, p. 2

Different Roads to Freedom In most areas, people achieved freedom largely through peaceful means. In a few regions, especially where many whites had settled, colonial rulers were reluctant to leave. Desperate wars of liberation often resulted. France, for example, fought to hold on to Algeria in North Africa and to French Indochina in Southeast Asia. By contrast, it gave up its vast colonial holdings in West Africa without a struggle.

Global Impact Altogether, around 90 new countries emerged during this "great liberation." Some, such as India and Nigeria, were large in area or population. Many others, such as Nepal, Kuwait, and Lesotho, were small.

The new nations of Africa and Asia, as well as the countries of Latin America, became known as the developing world.* Although these nations differed greatly from one another, they shared common goals. All were determined to pursue modernization, which meant building stable governments and developing their countries economically. They followed different paths toward modernization, but many experienced similar challenges.

The needs and goals of developing nations transformed the postwar world. Most joined the United Nations, where they have become an important voice by uniting their interests and often voting as a bloc. Individually and in regional groups, a number of them have played significant roles in global political and economic affairs.

The Cold War Goes Global

The new nations emerged into a world dominated and divided by the Cold War. The United States and Soviet Union emerged as superpowers, nations strong enough to influence the acts and policies of other nations. They competed for influence by offering economic and military aid to developing nations. Each superpower wanted new countries to adopt its ideology, or system of thought or belief—either capitalism or socialism. Many new nations favored socialism, in part because their old colonial rulers had been capitalist. Other nations were attracted by the greater prosperity of the capitalist West.

Nonaligned Nations To avoid superpower rivalry, many new nations chose to remain nonaligned, that is, not allied to either side in the Cold War. The goal of the nonaligned movement was to reduce world tensions and promote economic policies that would benefit developing nations. Giant India, which blended a democratic government with a socialist economy, was a leader in the nonaligned movement.

Hot Spots In Africa, Latin America, and Asia, local conflicts took on a Cold War dimension. Often, the West, led by the United States, supported one side, and the Soviet bloc supported the other. Through such struggles, the superpowers confronted each other indirectly rather than head to head.

Contributing to this tension was the Chinese Communist victory in 1949. When Mao Zedong's forces won control of mainland China, the United States feared that the "red tide" would sweep around the world. American policies, therefore, were designed to stop the communist threat.

On occasion, the Cold War did erupt into "shooting wars," especially in Asia. Both Korea and Vietnam were torn by brutal conflicts in which the United States and the Soviet Union played crucial roles, as you will read.

---

*During the Cold War, the term *Third World* was used to refer to these nations with less-advanced technology than that of the First World (the western industrial powers and Japan) or the Second World (the communist bloc nations).

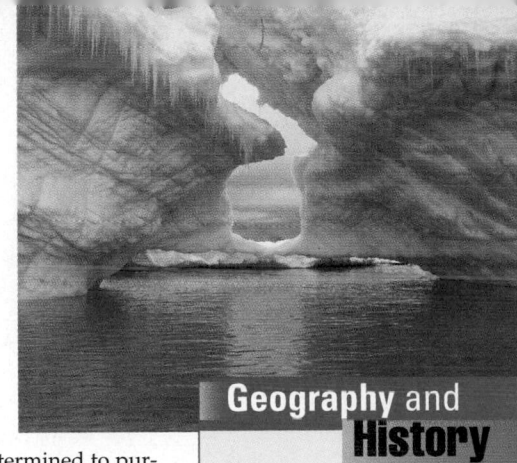

Geography and History

The Coldest Place on Earth

Oddly enough, the coldest place on Earth remained untouched by the Cold War. In 1959, twelve of the world's leading powers—including the United States and the Soviet Union—signed a treaty that made Antarctica a neutral zone of scientific research and cooperation. The continent was now off-limits to military bases, nuclear weapons testing, and radioactive-waste disposal. This treaty was followed in 1991 by a 50-year ban on oil and mineral exploration.

Antarctica is home to as many as 4,000 scientists who may stay for up to a year. Heavily wrapped in special cold-weather gear, they brave temperatures ranging from 32 degrees Fahrenheit to −100 degrees Fahrenheit. These men and women study topics such as global climate changes, ocean life, and geology.

Theme: Geography and History Why is Antarctica a symbol of international cooperation?

Connections to Math

Constructing a Graph Have students research population growth statistics for 10 different countries, five from the global South and five from the global North. They may gather statistics in terms of births per 100,000 people or in terms of an annual growth rate expressed as a percentage. Advise students that the data for the various countries should all represent the same year. Have them present their data in the form of a bar graph. Instruct them to use a key with one color representing the global South and the other color representing the global North. Display the finished graphs and call on students to use the statistics to draw conclusions about world population growth.

The Great Liberation and the Cold War, 1945–1990

Former European colonies that gained independence, 1945–1990 — Cold War hot spots

Robinson Projection

Geography As former European colonies won independence, they often became centers of Cold War rivalry.

1. **Location** On the map, locate (a) United States, (b) Soviet Union, (c) Cuba, (d) Congo, (e) Afghanistan, (f) Vietnam.
2. **Region** On which continent did the greatest number of nations win independence?
3. **Critical Thinking**
   Predicting Consequences What effect do you think the Cold War might have on new nations seeking to build stable governments?

The Cold War Ends The Cold War ended suddenly in 1991 when the Soviet Union collapsed. With the western victory in the Cold War, tensions eased and some long-standing conflicts were resolved. Many people hoped for a more peaceful world. But troubling local, regional, and global problems remained.

Ethnic and Religious Conflicts Within many nations, ethnic and religious groups have sometimes demanded greater independence to protect their cultural and political identity. Ethnic Kurds, for example, have long fought for autonomy in both Turkey and Iraq, while in Kashmir, the Muslim majority has struggled for decades for independence from predominantly Hindu India. In Nigeria, both ethnic and religious differences have repeatedly exploded into violent conflicts.

New Nations Seek Stability

After winning independence, new nations had high hopes for the future. Still, they faced immense problems. Especially in Africa, nations were created out of European colonies that had been carved up during the age of imperialism. People in new nations like Nigeria came from different cultural traditions and had few ties to unite them.

The new nations wrote constitutions modeled on those of western democracies. Only a few, however, like India, were able to sustain democratic rule. In general, colonial rulers had done little to prepare the people for self-government. Many new nations were shaken by revolution or civil war. Often, a wealthy, western-educated elite controlled the government and the economy. The great majority of people remained poor and cut off from advancement.

ANSWERS 1. Review locations with students. **2.** Africa **3.** The attempt to build stable governments might be disrupted as the superpowers compete for influence.

Teaching Resources
History Through Literature, *Half Measures,* History Through Literature booklet, p. 67

As problems multiplied, the military or authoritarian leaders often took control. Many times, these were the same people who had led the fight for liberation. They imposed order by building one-party dictatorships. They banned other political parties, claiming that a multiparty system threatened stability. Leaders waved the banner of nationalism, in hope of overcoming ethnic, religious, or regional divisions.

Despite setbacks, democracy did make some progress in the late 1980s and 1990s. In Africa, Asia, and Latin America, nations that had been ruled by dictators or by a single party held multiparty elections. Some of these new democracies have lasted. Others have not. Internal conflicts and lack of experience in representative government upset these fragile experiments in democracy.

Regional and Global Organizations

Since 1945, transportation and communications systems have made the world increasingly interdependent. Interdependence is the dependence of countries on goods, resources, and knowledge from other parts of the world. Political, economic, cultural, and other links have created both problems and opportunities. A number of international organizations deal with issues of global concern.

The United Nations The United Nations was set up at the end of World War II as a forum for settling disputes. Its responsibilities, along with its membership, have expanded greatly since 1945. The UN played a vital role in decolonization. Since then, it has tried to act as peacekeeper from Cambodia to the Middle East and from Africa to the Balkans. Some UN interventions have been successful. Others have failed, often because member nations could not agree on goals and methods.

UN agencies could provide services for millions of people worldwide. The World Health Organization (WHO), for example, helped wipe out smallpox through its program of vaccinations. Today, WHO works with other groups to seek a solution to the AIDS crisis. Other UN programs aim to reduce malnutrition or ensure access to safe drinking water. The UN has also sponsored global summits, conferences of leaders and experts from around the world. These summits have discussed issues such as the environment, women, and population.

Other Organizations Many nations formed regional groups to promote trade or meet other common needs. Powerful regional trading blocs have emerged. In later chapters, you will see how such groups as the European Union, the North American Free Trade Association, and the Association of Southeast Asian Nations have worked to lower trade barriers and promote the free exchange of goods and services.

The importance of global trade has been recognized by a series of international treaties. The General Agreement on Tariffs and Trade (GATT), signed in 1947, tried to establish fair trade policies for all nations. In 1995, more than 100 nations joined to form the World Trade Organization (WTO). Its goal was to establish global rules of trade "to ensure that trade flows as smoothly, predictably and freely as possible." Some people have opposed it.

At the highest levels, the Group of Seven, which represents the seven most productive economies—the United States, Canada, Japan, Germany, France, Britain, and Italy—has met annually to discuss common economic problems.*

The World Bank and the International Monetary Fund (IMF) play a large role in the world economy, as you will read, by making loans to

---

*Despite its weak economy, Russia has been invited to attend meetings of the Group of Seven because of its military strength, size, and potential for economic growth.

Chapter 32 **809**

Primary Source

Seeking World Peace
The Charter of the UN sets out the goals of the organization:

"WE THE PEOPLES OF THE UNITED NATIONS DETERMINED

to save succeeding generations from the scourge of war, which twice in our lifetime has brought untold sorrow to mankind . . .

to promote social progress and better standards of life in larger freedom . . .

to practice tolerance and live together in peace with one another as good neighbors . . .

to unite our strength to maintain international peace and security . . .

do hereby establish an international organization to be known as the United Nations."
—Charter of the United Nations

Skills Assessment

Primary Source Based on the goals listed above, why has the UN organized its own armed forces?

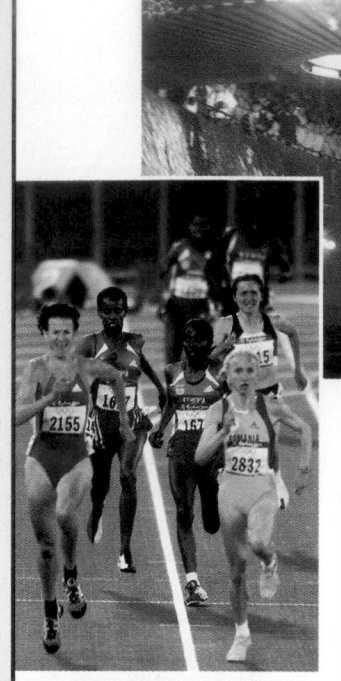

Games for an Interdependent World
Sprinter Cathy Freeman of Australia holds the Olympic flame during the opening ceremony of the 2000 Olympic games in Sydney, Australia. Through both the summer and the winter games, the International Olympic Committee works to promote international cooperation.
Theme: Global Interaction Why are the Olympic games a symbol of interdependence? Why might they also become a source of conflict?

 Primary Sources and Literature

See "The Universal Declaration of Human Rights" in the Reference Section at the back of this book.

developing nations. Many other types of nongovernmental organizations (NGOs) have forged valuable global networks, including the International Olympic Committee and the International Red Cross.

Global Issues

Many issues pose a challenge to world peace. Since the United States first exploded two atomic bombs in 1945, nations have poured resources into building nuclear weapons. The number of nuclear weapons grew from 3 in 1945 to over 50,000 in the 1980s.

Deadly Weapons During the Cold War, efforts to curb the arms race had only limited success. Yet in 1968, many nations signed the Nuclear Non-Proliferation Treaty (NPT), agreeing to halt the spread of nuclear weapons. In 1995, the treaty was renewed, but some nations still refused to sign. Why, they asked, could a few nations like the United States and Russia keep nuclear weapons if they could not? In 1998, for example, India and Pakistan stirred global concerns when they announced successful tests of nuclear weapons.

Even after the Cold War ended, many nations kept spending immense sums on the military. In nations split by ethnic or other conflicts, arms dealers sell weapons, including land mines. Many people have condemned the international arms trade. Others defend the economic right of arms makers to produce and sell their goods on the free market.

Human Rights In 1948, UN members approved the Universal Declaration of Human Rights. According to the document, all people are entitled to basic rights and freedoms "without distinction of any kind, such as race, color, sex, language, property, birth, or other status." Human rights include "the right to life, liberty, and security of person." In 1975, nations signing the Helsinki Accords guaranteed such basic rights as freedom of speech, religion, and the press as well as the rights to a fair trial, to earn a living, and to live in safety.

Despite these documents, human rights abuses, including torture and arbitrary arrest, occurred around the world. At times, the world community pressed countries to stop abuses. Economic pressure, for example, was used to push South Africa to end its system of apartheid.

In some countries, leaders have accused western nations of trying to impose their own ideas about individual freedom. They claim that their cultures value the community over the individual. Chinese leaders, for example,

810 *Chapter 32*

have argued that economic goals, such as improving the standard of living for their people, were more important than individual political freedom.

The Question of Intervention The human rights debate raised tough issues. Does the world community have a duty to step in to end abuses? How can it intervene when the UN Charter forbids any action that violates the independence of a member nation?

The UN and other organizations have a mixed record on intervention. In the 1990s, the UN sent peacekeepers to northern Iraq to protect the Kurds, an ethnic minority suffering brutal government persecution. For complex reasons, the UN was slow to move against Serbs who persecuted Muslims in Bosnia. The UN did not intervene when Hutus massacred an estimated one million Tutsis in Rwanda. In 1999, however, NATO forces bombed Serbia to stop its attacks on ethnic Albanians in Kosovo. Ethnic conflicts, especially, have fueled the debate over intervention to protect human rights.

Terrorism Since the 1960s, incidents of terrorism have increased around the world. Terrorism is the deliberate use of violence, especially against civilians, to achieve political goals. Through bombings, kidnappings, airplane hijackings, and shootings, terrorists focus attention on their causes and try to force governments to give in to their demands.

In Northern Ireland, extremists on both sides murdered civilians. Terrorists killed Israeli athletes at the 1972 Olympic games to push their demands for a Palestinian state. Terrorists murdered India's Rajiv Gandhi. Other groups bombed American embassies in Kenya and Tanzania.

In 2001, the deadliest terrorist outrage occurred in the United States. Suicide bombers opposed to American policies in the Middle East crashed several hijacked airplanes into the World Trade Center in New York and the Pentagon in Washington, D.C., killing thousands.

To combat terrorism, governments passed tough laws and increased watchfulness. They also tried to capture or kill terrorists, such as "Carlos," taken by the French in the 1990s, and Osama bin Laden, targeted by the United States after the 2001 World Trade Center and Pentagon attacks.

World Terrorism
This American cartoon appeared after the terrorist attack on the World Trade Center in New York. It expressed the feeling that the United States was now closer to dangers facing the rest of the world.

Theme: Global Interaction How do you think a terrorist attack like this could affect international relations?

SECTION 1 Assessment

Recall
1. **Identify:** (a) GATT, (b) International Monetary Fund, (c) NPT, (d) Universal Declaration of Human Rights.
2. **Define:** (a) modernization, (b) superpower, (c) ideology, (d) nonaligned, (e) interdependence, (f) human rights (g) summit, (h) terrorism.

Comprehension
3. (a) Why did European nations lose their colonial empires after World War II? (b) What was one effect of this "great liberation"?
4. Why did political instability plague many developing nations?
5. What two main roles has the UN played in world affairs?
6. Describe one effort nations have made to deal with each of the following issues: (a) the spread of nuclear arms, (b) human rights abuses, (c) terrorism.

Critical Thinking and Writing
7. **Predicting Consequences** Is interdependence likely to make the world more peaceful? Why or why not?
8. **Analyzing Information** (a) Why might lack of experience with representative government be a problem for developing nations? (b) Do you think democracy will help them solve their problems?

Activity

Designing an Invitation
Design an invitation to an international conference on nuclear arms, terrorism, or human rights. Your invitation should clearly state the goals of the meeting and who will participate. You may also design a logo relating to the theme of the meeting.

SECTION 1 Assessment

Recall
1. (a) GATT, p. 809 (b) International Monetary Fund, p. 809 (c) NPT, p. 810 (d) Universal Declaration of Human Rights, p. 810 2. (a) modernization, p. 807 (b) superpower, p. 807 (c) ideology, p. 807 (d) nonaligned, p. 807 (e) interdependence, p. 809 (f) human rights, p. 810 (g) summit, p. 809 (h) terrorism, p. 811

Comprehension
3. (a) Britain, France, and others were weakened by wars and reluctant to oppose national movements. The United States and Soviet Union pressured European powers to dissolve their empires. (b) Many newly independent states gained political influence in the United Nations. 4. In some new states, rival ethnic groups competed in violent civil wars. New nations often lacked experience in self-government. Frequently, authoritarian rulers established dictatorships. 5. It has served as peacekeeper and provider of services. 6. (a) Many nations signed the Nuclear Non-Proliferation Treaty. (b) Members of the United Nations approved the Universal Declaration of Human Rights and signed the Helsinki Accords. (c) Governments passed tough laws and tried to capture and kill terrorists.

Critical Thinking and Writing
7. Answers should demonstrate a clear understanding of interdependence. Encourage students to support their predictions. 8. Possible answers: (a) Without experience, people might be impatient with democracy and turn to dictators who promise quick solutions. (b) Students should support their answers with specific examples.

Activity Rubrics

Share rubrics with students before they begin their invitation.

Attempted The invitation is incomplete, missing either the goals or the participants, or is carelessly done.

Minimal The invitation includes required information but contains many errors.

Adequate The invitation is neat and clear and has few errors.

Exemplary The invitation is well executed and very attractive.

Caption Answer

Possible answer: A terrorist attack on one country could increase global cooperation to fight terrorism or could divide nations according to their self-interests.

LESSON PLAN

1. Focus The global North includes many prosperous industrial nations. The global South includes many developing nations. For developing nations, obstacles to economic development include factors related to geography, overpopulation, economic dependence, and political instability. For both rich and poor countries, economic development often causes serious damage to the natural environment.

2. Instruct Divide the class into groups and have each group create a poster that illustrates global economic trends. Students should focus on one of the following topics: (1) differences between the global North and global South, (2) obstacles that developing nations must overcome, (3) examples of economic interdependence, and (4) effects of economic development on the natural environment. Students' posters may consist of original illustrations as well as photocopies or clippings from newspapers and newsmagazines. Display the posters and have each group explain its work.

3. Assess Ask students to review the obstacles that often hinder economic development in the global South. Have them rank these obstacles in order of their importance and provide explanations for their choices.

4. Reteach If students' Assess activity does not reflect adequate understanding of the lesson, you might assign the *Guide to the Essentials* or the *Interactive Student Tutorial CD-ROM* for this section.

Reading Focus

- In what ways are the global North and South economically interdependent?
- Why have developing nations had trouble reaching their goals?
- How is economic development linked to the environment?

Vocabulary

multinational corporation
privatization
environmentalist
acid rain
global warming

Taking Notes

On a sheet of paper, draw a Venn diagram like the one shown here. As you read this section, add more information, including the area where the ovals overlap.

GLOBAL NORTH
- Industrial nations of Europe and North America
- Capitalism

GLOBAL SOUTH
- Nations of developing world

Main Idea The industrial nations of the global North and the developing nations of the global South have become increasingly interdependent.

Setting the Scene "Ours is a time of problems, of gigantic problems," noted Pope Paul VI in 1969. "And every day, if we want to live with open eyes, we have a problem to study, to resolve." Among these difficulties is the growing gulf between rich and poor nations. Yet in today's interdependent world, rich and poor nations are closely linked.

The Global North and South

The Cold War created an ideological split between the communist East and the capitalist West. Today, an economic gulf divides the world into two spheres—the relatively rich nations of the global North and the relatively poor nations of the global South.

Rich Nations The global North includes the industrial nations of Europe and North America, as well as Japan and Australia. Most are located in the temperate zone north of the Equator. They control most of the world's wealth. Although pockets of poverty exist, the standard of living in the North is generally high. Most people are literate, earn adequate wages, and have basic health services.

These rich nations have basically capitalist economies. Decisions about what to produce and for whom are generally regulated by the free market, not by the government. The governments of these nations do support economic growth through transportation and communication systems, public education, and social services. They also regulate their economies in various ways, from requiring pure food and drugs to preventing stock market fraud. Still, in the global North, economic success is driven by the free market.

Poor Nations The global South refers to the developing world. Most of these nations lie in Asia, Africa, and Latin America in the zone between the Tropics of Cancer and Capricorn. The South has 75 percent of the world's population and much of its natural resources. Some nations have enjoyed strong growth, especially the Asian "tigers," the oil-exporting nations of the Middle East, and several Latin American nations. Overall, though, the global South remains generally underdeveloped and poor. Unlike the nations that industrialized before 1900, newer nations have not had enough time to build up their capital, resources, or industries.

For most people in the developing world, life is a daily struggle for survival. About one billion people worldwide live in extreme poverty—many of them children.

Resource Directory

Teaching Resources
Creative Teaching Activities Creative Teaching Activities booklet, p. 144
Guided Reading and Review Unit 8 booklet, p. 4

Migration Despite some advances in the developing world, the gap between rich and poor nations is widening. The imbalance has sparked migration of people from poor regions to wealthier ones. Every year, refugees flee poverty or war to seek a better life in Western Europe, North America, and Australia. Millions of others, however, remain close to their homes.

Economic Interdependence

Rich and poor nations are linked by many economic ties. The nations of the global North control much of the world's capital, trade, and technology. But they depend increasingly on low-paid workers in developing states to produce manufactured goods as inexpensively as possible. This shift in labor has led to a loss of manufacturing jobs in many western nations.

Huge multinational corporations, with branches in many countries, have invested in the developing world. They bring new technology to mining, agriculture, transportation, and other industries. Rich nations also provide aid, technical advisers, and loans. At the same time, interdependence has often led to resentment. With its great buying power, the North controls the prices of goods and commodities produced by the South. In addition, multinational corporations remove many profits from developing countries and often limit workers' attempts to seek higher wages.

The Oil Crisis In an interdependent world, events in one country or region can affect people everywhere. A drastic example of this was the oil crisis of the 1970s. All nations use oil for transportation and for products ranging from plastics to fertilizers. This demand has allowed nations with oil resources to seek favorable prices on the world market.

Much of the world's oil comes from the Middle East. In 1973, a political crisis in the region led the Organization of Petroleum Exporting Countries (OPEC) to halt its oil exports and raise oil prices. Shortages and soaring fuel prices set off economic shock waves. Suddenly, industrialized nations realized how much they depended on imported oil. While some efforts were made to find other fuels or to conserve energy use, the energy crisis showed what impact a single vital product could have on the world economy.

The Debt Crisis Another complex economic problem involved the growing debt owed by poor nations to rich ones. Developing nations, needing capital to modernize,

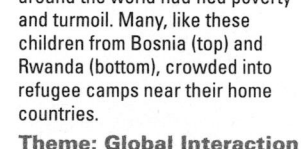

The World of Refugees
By 2000, nearly 20 million refugees around the world had fled poverty and turmoil. Many, like these children from Bosnia (top) and Rwanda (bottom), crowded into refugee camps near their home countries.

Theme: Global Interaction
Based on these pictures, how might you react to living in a refugee camp?

Chapter 32 **813**

Activity
Connections to Film

Comparing Assign students to view *Europe and the Third World,* Program 50 of the public television series *The Western Tradition.* The half-hour documentary compares conditions in the industrialized world with those that exist in developing countries. It suggests that developing nations, many of which are former colonies of the West, must somehow balance the traditions of their native cultures and the powerful influences of western culture. The documentary focuses especially on the increasing gap between the prosperity of the developed world and the poverty of the developing world. It examines such issues as overpopulation, single-export economies, runaway inflation, and political instability, among others.

Assign students to use the film as the basis for a chart comparing conditions in the developed and developing worlds. Have them also prepare an oral presentation that explains and supports the ideas contained in their charts. After each presentation, encourage other students to offer pertinent comments and questions. (*The Western Tradition,* released in 1989 as part of the Annenberg/CPB Collection, is distributed by Intellimation.) ✳

took loans offered by western banks. In the 1980s, however, bank interest rates rose, while the world economy slowed down. As demand for many of their goods fell, poor nations were unable to repay their debts or even the interest on their loans. Their economies stalled as they spent their income from exports on payments to their foreign creditors.

The debt crisis hurt rich nations, too, as banks were stuck with billions of dollars of bad debts. To ease the crisis, the International Monetary Fund, the World Bank, and private banks worked out agreements with debtor nations. Lenders lowered interest rates or gave some nations more time to repay the loans. In some cases, debts were even canceled altogether.

In return, debtor nations had to agree to adopt free-market policies. Many ended governmental supports for industry. They turned instead to privatization, selling off state-owned industries to private investors. Nations hoped that more efficient private enterprises would bring prosperity in the long run. Still, the immediate effects of privatization often hurt the poor.

The Asian Economic Crisis A third economic crisis highlighted the interdependence of the world's financial markets. The trouble began in the late 1990s with a recession in Japan, which had the world's second richest economy. Then, financial crises swept through other successful Asian economies, from South Korea to Singapore. All across the most developed nations of Asia, businesses closed down, workers lost jobs, and poverty spread.

Because all the economies of the world are linked, financial problems spread beyond Asia. Russia, trying to build a new capitalist economy after decades of communism, could not pay its debts. Brazil struggled to stabilize the value of its currency. The century ended with signs of an economic upturn, but the problems created by global financial links remained.

Economic Organizations A number of international economic organizations deal with the economic challenges that face rich and poor countries alike. The World Bank provides funding for major development programs and helps nations get through economic crises. The International Monetary Fund has become a lender of last resort in situations like the Asian financial crisis of the late 1990s.

Such organizations often help with global economic problems. But they have also caused serious social strains by requiring developing nations to abandon inefficient economic systems and end social programs they could not afford. In some cases, the poor in these countries have rioted, rebelled, or even overthrown their governments.

Obstacles to Development

Why have many developing nations been unable to make progress toward modernization? The answers vary from country to country, but many shared problems in five general areas: (1) geography, (2) population and poverty, (3) economic dependence, (4) economic policies, and (5) political instability.

Geography In parts of Africa, Asia, and Latin America, geography has posed an obstacle to development. For example, some of the African countries created since the 1950s are tiny and have few natural resources. Difficult climates, uncertain rainfall, lack of good farmland, and disease have added to the problems of some nations.

Population and Poverty The worldwide population boom that began in the 1700s has continued. Better medical care and increased food supplies have reduced death rates and led to explosive population growth. In the developing world, though, rapid growth is linked to poverty. Each year, the populations of countries like Nigeria and India increase by millions. All those people need food, housing, education, jobs, and medical care. Meeting these needs puts a staggering burden on developing nations.

Health Statistics of Selected Countries, 1999

Country	Population (thousands)	Life Expectancy at Birth (male/female)	Physicians (per 1,000 people)	Infant Mortality (deaths per 1,000)
Angola	10,865	45.6/50.2	*	132
Argentina	36,265	70.9/78.3	2.7	19
Guatemala	12,008	63.4/68.8	*	48
Japan	125,932	76.9/83.3	1.8	4
Jordan	4,435	71.0/74.8	1.6	33
Myanmar	47,305	53.0/56.1	0.3	78
Netherlands	15,731	75.1/81.0	2.4	5
Nigeria	110,532	52.7/54.5	0.2	71
Poland	38,607	68.6/77.2	2.3	13
United States	270,312	72.9/79.6	2.7	6

Source: *World Almanac and Book of Facts*   * Data unavailable

Across the developing world, people are caught in a cycle of poverty. Millions of people die each year from hunger-related illnesses. Children are the most vulnerable. The UN estimates that 35,000 children die each day from malnutrition, disease, and other effects of poverty.

Many developing nations have tried to slow population growth. Few countries, except China, want to force people to limit family size. In farming societies, children are a source of labor. They are seen as an insurance policy to support their parents in old age. Religious traditions often encourage large families. Also, despite education efforts, many people still lack information about or access to family planning.

Economic Dependence Often, economic patterns formed during the Age of Imperialism have survived. Most new nations remained dependent on their former colonial rulers. They sold agricultural products and raw materials to the industrial world. In turn, they relied on the West for manufactured goods, technology, and investment. Also, many new nations had only a single export crop or commodity, such as sugar, cocoa, or copper. Their economies depended on world demand for the product.

As you have read, developing nations borrowed heavily from foreign banks. These funds were intended for development. Once in debt, though, nations had to spend much of their resources to pay interest.

Economic Policies Many newly independent nations saw socialism, rather than capitalism, as a way to modernize quickly. They modeled their economies on those of China or the Soviet Union, rather than on those of their former colonial rulers. Under socialism, the government controls the economy. These nations had little private capital, so only the government could raise the money to finance large-scale development projects.

At first, emerging nations made some gains. But in the long run, socialism often blocked economic growth. Later, like their models China and Russia, many developing nations introduced free-market policies.

Political Instability Political unrest often hindered economic development. El Salvador, Lebanon, Cambodia, and Angola are among the many nations devastated by civil wars. Military dictators or other authoritarian leaders spent huge sums on weapons and warfare instead of on education, housing, or health care. In addition, war created millions of refugees. The loss of their labor further hurt war-torn countries.

Background
Connections to Science

Global Warming According to many scientists, global warming, also called the "greenhouse effect," is the result of emissions caused by the burning of fossil fuels and by other human activities. The increased level of carbon dioxide in the atmosphere traps heat that would otherwise radiate into space. The warming increases the amount of water vapor in the air, which in turn absorbs more of the Earth's heat. Eventually, rising temperatures melt snow and ice and cause ocean levels to rise. As the chain reaction progresses, low-lying coastal regions could be flooded, including parts of such cities as Charleston, South Carolina, and Galveston, Texas. The most damaging effect might be major climatic changes that could shift agriculture away from formerly fertile and productive lands.

What Is the Relationship Between People and the Environment?

Today, environmental issues are getting worldwide attention. Is it more important for a poor nation to protect its environment or to develop its resources? How much right do people have to alter the environment in the first place? To begin your investigation, examine the following viewpoints.

Background
Other Viewpoints

Brazil 1940s President Getúlio Vargas vowed to build Brazil's economy by subduing its mightiest resource—the Amazon River.

"Nothing will prevent us from accomplishing . . . the highest task of civilized man: the conquest and domination of great valleys of equatorial torrents, transforming their blind force and extraordinary fertility into disciplined energy."

Kenya 1960s Perez Olindo, a zoologist, explained why he resigned from the Kenya Game Department.

"I resigned in protest at having been assigned the duties . . . which, in effect, involved shooting elephants considered to be in conflict with economic activities. . . . I held, and still hold, the view that elephants and other animals have a right to live, and no human has any control over that right."

Greece 300s B.C.

The scientist and philosopher Aristotle used logic to explain relationships in the natural world:

" Plants exist for the sake of animals, and animals exist for the sake of man—the tame for use and food, and the wild, if not all, at least the greater part of them, for food and for the provision of clothing and various instruments. Now, if nature makes nothing in vain, [it follows] that she has made all animals for the sake of man. "

Russia 1890s

Concern that humankind is exploiting its environment drove famous Russian author Anton Chekhov to write:

" Man has been endowed with reason, with the power to create, so that he can add to what he's been given. But up to now he hasn't been a creator, only a destroyer. Forests keep disappearing, rivers dry up, wildlife's become extinct, the climate's ruined and the land grows poorer and uglier every day. "

Indonesia 1980s

Dr. Sumitro Djojohadikusumo, the former minister of trade and industry, gave his views on managing and protecting the environment:

" If we are to make further progress, we need the natural resources, we need the timber, we need the water, we need the fish. We can apply science to manage nature so that everyone benefits, even the animals. "

United States 1990s

American cartoonist Tom Toles commented on protecting biodiversity, the wide variety of plant and animal species on the planet.

Activity
Interpreting Viewpoints

Use these additional questions to generate class discussion.

1. Critical Thinking: Contrasting Do you think Olindo would agree or disagree with Vargas's way of building Brazil's economy? Explain. *(Olindo would disagree. Olindo believed that nature should be left alone; Vargas believed nature should be dominated.)*

2. Critical Thinking: Recognizing Points of View How would you explain these different points of view? *(Vargas was concerned with the economy; Olindo was concerned with animal rights.)*

Skills Assessment

1. Whose viewpoint emphasizes the complete dominance of people over nature?
   A Chekhov
   B Toles
   C Djojohadikusumo
   D Aristotle

2. Chekhov and Toles would agree that
   E the environment will continue to improve on its own.
   F humans have done much to alter the environment.
   G there are no environmental problems.
   H Aristotle was right.

3. **Critical Thinking Defending a Position** You are going to write a letter to Congress about an environmental issue. Include specific examples that support your point of view.

Skills Tip

When you express a point of view, you should cite specific examples to support your position.

Skills Tip

In an essay, adding quotations from original documents or experts can help support your position. The Skills Handbook in the front of the book has a lesson to help students with this feature.

Skills Assessment

ANSWERS 1. D **2.** F **3.** Letters should reflect an understanding of the issue and offer supporting facts.

Resource Directory

Teaching Resources

Viewpoint Activity *Approaches to the Environment,* Unit 8 booklet, p. 10
Comparing Viewpoints Chapter Extension Activities booklet, pp. 76–77
Section Quiz Unit 8 booklet, p. 5

Technology

Interactive Student Tutorial CD-ROM Ch. 32
Computer Test Bank Ch. 32

Development and the Environment

For both rich and poor nations, economic development has taken a heavy toll on the environment. Modern industry and agriculture have gobbled up natural resources and polluted much of the world's water, air, and soil.

Growing Threats Since earliest times, people everywhere have taken what they wanted from their environment. In the past, damage was limited because the world's population was relatively small and technology was simple. With the Industrial Revolution and the population explosion, the potential for widespread environmental damage grew.

By the 1970s, environmentalists raised the alarm about threats to the planet's fragile environment. Strip mining provided ores for industry but destroyed much land. Chemical pesticides and fertilizers produced more food crops but harmed the soil and water. Oil spills polluted vital waterways and killed marine life. Gases from power plants and factories produced acid rain, a form of pollution in which toxic chemicals in the air fall back to the Earth as rain, snow, or hail. Acid rain damaged forests, lakes, and farmland, especially in industrial Europe and North America.

Over the last century, world temperatures have increased. Scientists blame this global warming on the emission of gases into the upper atmosphere. Many warn that global warming will continue in the future.

Industrial accidents focused attention on threats to the environment. In Bhopal, India, a leak from a pesticide plant in 1984 killed 3,600 people. In 1986, an accident at the Chernobyl nuclear power plant in the Soviet Union exposed people, crops, and animals to deadly radiation over a wide area. Although industries and governments have developed safety measures, such measures are often expensive and not always successful.

Protecting the Environment Rich nations consume most of the world's resources and produce much of its pollution. At the same time, they have led the campaign to protect the environment. Most have laws to control pollution and ensure conservation.

At environmental summits, world leaders hotly debated how to preserve the planet. Should economic development take priority over protecting the environment? Are people, especially in rich nations, willing to do with less in order to conserve resources? Many agreed that permanent damage to the planet was too high a price for economic progress. Agreeing on solutions, however, is a challenge for the future.

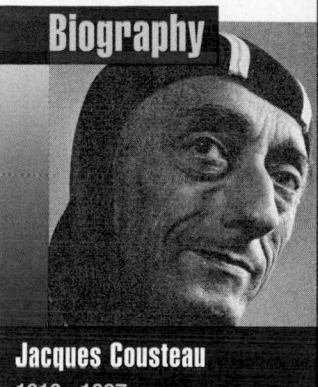

Biography

Jacques Cousteau
1910–1997

Jacques Cousteau introduced millions of people around the world to a wondrous and previously unexplored world within our world—the vast depths of the oceans.

Cousteau helped develop the aqualung, making it possible for divers to remain submerged for hours at a time. Aboard his research ship, the *Calypso*, he documented oceans, rivers, and the marine life they contained. His popular films, books, and television series educated the world about the beauty and fragility of the sea. Today, the Cousteau Society continues its founder's goal of preserving the undersea environment.

Theme: Impact of the Individual How did Cousteau help protect the world's oceans?

SECTION 2 Assessment

Recall
1. (a) OPEC, p. 813 (b) Chernobyl, p. 817
2. (a) multinational corporation, p. 813 (b) privatization, p. 814 (c) environmentalist, p. 817 (d) acid rain, p. 817 (e) global warming, p. 817

Comprehension
3. North—low-paid workers in developing nations of the South produce manufactured goods. South—multinational corporations from the North provide technology and money for development.
4. lack of resources, difficult climates, uncertain rainfall, and lack of good farmland; explosive population growth taxes services and resources; reliance on a single export and foreign loans; economic dependence on former colonial rulers; failed experiments with socialism; political problems 5. pollution and depletion of natural resources; examples—chemical fertilizers harm the soil and water; and air pollution produces acid rain, which damages forests, lakes, and farmland

Critical Thinking and Writing
6. (a) Industrialized nations that depended on imported oil experienced shortages and inflation. (b) Recession in Japan had an impact on other nations.
7. Answers should reflect the students' views and be well supported.

SECTION 2 Assessment

Recall
1. **Identify: (a)** OPEC, **(b)** Chernobyl.
2. **Define: (a)** multinational corporation, **(b)** privatization, **(c)** environmentalist, **(d)** acid rain, **(e)** global warming.

Comprehension
3. How do the nations of the global North and global South depend on one another?
4. What obstacles do developing nations face?
5. How has economic development increased the potential for widespread damage to the environment? Give two examples.

Critical Thinking and Writing
6. **Applying Information** Describe how each of the following showed interdependence: **(a)** the oil crisis, **(b)** the Asian financial crisis.
7. **Making Decisions** Would you be willing to pay much higher prices for manufactured goods such as clothing or your first car if it would help conserve the world's resources? Why or why not?

Activity
Take It to the NET

Use the Internet to do research on a current environmental issue such as acid rain, desertification, deforestation, waste disposal, or threats to endangered species. Then, write an editorial explaining the issue and taking a stand on it.

Activity Rubrics

Share rubrics with students before they write their editorials.

Attempted The editorial is poorly researched or incomplete.

Minimal The editorial shows limited research, is poorly organized, and reflects limited understanding of the issue.

Adequate The editorial is well researched and written, with few mechanical errors and sound reasoning.

Exemplary The editorial shows thorough research, is very well organized, contains forceful arguments, offers insight into the issue, and has no mechanical errors.

Human Drama Note

Amazing Amazon's Secret Cures Rainforests are one of the world's richest resources, containing millions of species of animals and plants, many of which scientists have never recorded. The Amazon rainforest is perhaps the most immense such ecosystem on the planet, covering about 40 percent of Brazil, or 2.3 million square miles. It is considered the world's richest resource for biodiversity. In addition to rubber, its forests are an important world source of fine woods such as rosewood and mahogany.

The Amazon's diverse plant life may hold the secrets of future cures for human diseases. About 70 percent of the world's medicinal drugs are derived from plants. However, the Amazon and other rainforests are disappearing at an alarming rate as a result of logging to clear the land for agriculture and cattle grazing. Natural disasters such as floods and fire also take their toll. Many conservation groups are working with the Brazilian government, the World Bank, and others, seeking effective ways to preserve the Amazon rainforest, which is estimated, at the current rate of depletion, to last only 50 more years!

Biography

ANSWERS Through his books, movies, and television specials, Cousteau educated people about the fragile undersea environment. He also founded the Cousteau Society to help preserve it.

Bell Ringer Ask students to read the Reading Focus questions at the start of Section 3. Have students use these points to write four generalizations about the contents of this section.

LESSON PLAN

1. Focus As people move to cities, they accept new ways and weaken their ties to traditional ideas and customs. Modernization has brought women additional opportunities and responsibilities. Scientific and technological advances have improved the quality of life for some, while creating new problems for others. Modern methods of communication have led to a dramatic increase in global exchanges.

2. Instruct Divide the class into groups and assign each group one of the following six topics: (1) traditional village life, (2) urbanization, (3) westernization, (4) religious influences, (5) the roles of women, or (6) science and technology. Have each group use the text and additional resources to become "experts" on their assigned topic. After students have completed this part of the lesson, regroup them so that each new group has at least one "expert" on each of the six topics. Have students take turns teaching the other group members about their particular area of expertise.

3. Assess Ask students to decide which changing pattern of life is most beneficial and which is most troublesome. Have them write a short essay in which they explain the reasons for their choices.

4. Reteach If students' Assess activity does not reflect adequate understanding of the lesson, you might assign the *Guide to the Essentials* or the *Interactive Student Tutorial CD-ROM* for this section.

Reading Focus

- How are new ways of life replacing old ways?
- How has modernization affected the lives of women?
- What are the benefits and limits of modern science and technology?
- What forces have shaped a new global culture?

Vocabulary

shantytown
fundamentalist
liberation theology
feminist movement
e-commerce
genetic engineering

Taking Notes

On a sheet of paper, draw a concept web to show the changing patterns of life in the past 50 years. Use this web to help you get started. As you read, add as many circles as you need.

Main Idea Forces such as urbanization, religion, and changing roles for women have shaped world societies.

Setting the Scene "My village is changing," observed Indian writer Prafulla Mohanti. A road was built there in the 1960s to carry iron ore from a nearby mine to a port city some 40 miles away. Since then, Mohanti said, "Nylon, stainless steel, plastic, [and] fizzy drinks have reached the village."

New products and technology are changing villages around the world. At the same time, millions of villagers have migrated to cities, and that has further transformed the lives of people in the developing world.

Old Ways and New

In the western world, industrialization and urbanization began more than 200 years ago during the Industrial Revolution. In the past 50 years, the rest of the world has experienced similar upheavals.

Urbanization Since 1945, people in the developing world have flocked to cities to find jobs and escape rural poverty. Cities offer not only economic opportunities but also attractions such as stores, concerts, and sports.

With no money and few jobs, some newcomers settled in shantytowns. These slums on the outskirts of cities are as crowded and dangerous as European cities were in the 1800s. They lack basic services such as paving, running water, or sewage. Drugs and crime are ever-present threats. Today, millions of people struggle to survive in these conditions.

In the cities, the extended family of rural villages is giving way to the nuclear family. As urban children go to school and learn how to read, they often reject their parents' ways. Without the support of the village and the extended family, older beliefs and values are undermined by such urban values as material wealth, education, and job status. Many villagers who move to cities suffer a sense of stress and isolation.

Westernization In cities, people frequently adopt western fashions and ideas. During the Age of Imperialism, westerners taught that their civilization was superior. Even after independence, many people in emerging nations felt that the way to modernize was to follow western models.

Some early nationalists, such as Mohandas Gandhi, rejected the rush to abandon traditional ways. Today, leaders in some Muslim lands have called for "modernization without westernization." Although they welcome modern technology, they want to preserve older traditions and religious beliefs. They reject western emphasis on material success and the individual, which they think undermines the community and family.

Global Connections

Endangered Languages
Of the 6,700 different languages spoken in the world today, many are spoken only in isolated rural areas or on remote islands among a handful of elderly residents. As families migrate to cities or other countries, their children often grow up speaking a dominant language, such as English, Hindi, or Spanish. In the next century, some linguists predict that 90 to 95 percent of all current languages will disappear. That is an average of more than one language every two weeks. Scholars are now working to preserve oral and written records of many of these disappearing languages.

Theme: Diversity How has migration affected the diversity of languages spoken?

Global Connections

ANSWER As families migrate to cities, the children often grow up speaking established national languages, rather than traditional languages of their ancestors.

Resource Directory

Teaching Resources
Creative Teaching Activities Creative Teaching Activities booklet, p. 145
Guided Reading and Review Unit 8 booklet, p. 6
Geography and History Activity *Globalization Means Movement,* Geography and History booklet, pp. 16–17
Skill Application Activity *Interpreting Statistical Tables,* Unit 8 booklet, p. 11

Village Life Despite urbanization, villages are still home to billions of people, mostly in the global South. Their lives vary widely, depending on climate, geographic isolation, and other factors. Still, village life follows similar patterns in much of the world. Many villagers are farmers. Their workday begins at sunrise. Women wash clothes in local streams. Young and old labor in fields or in workshops. Villagers exchange news at tiny shops in the village center and celebrate centuries-old religious festivals.

Westernization and technology are transforming villages. Changes such as roads, clinics, and television can enrich life. But they also weaken traditional cultures and lure young people to abandon villages for cities.

Religious Influences The major world religions and their offshoots still shape modern societies. In recent times, religious revivals have swept many regions. Christian, Muslim, Jewish, Buddhist, and Hindu reformers offer their own solutions to modern problems. Some of these reformers have been called **fundamentalists** because they stress what they see as the fundamental, or basic, values of their faiths. Many have sought political power in order to resist changes which they think undermine their beliefs.

In the West, evangelical Protestant groups emphasize salvation through faith and preaching, offering spiritual guidelines in a rapidly changing world. In the 1960s, the Second Vatican Council gave Roman Catholics more freedom to discuss issues and promoted cooperation with other Christian denominations. In Latin America, some Roman Catholic clergy backed a movement called **liberation theology**. They urged the Church to take a more active role in opposing the social conditions that contributed to poverty. Conservative Catholic forces often oppose such political activities.

In the Muslim world, too, religious reformers have called for change. They rejected what they saw as the West's emphasis on secular goals and the impact of western culture. Instead, they wanted to return to a strict version of Sharia, or Islamic law, to guide governments and people.

New Rights and Roles for Women

After 1945, women's movements brought changes to both the western and the developing nations. The UN Charter supported "equal rights for men and women." By 1950, women had won the right to vote in most European nations, as well as in Japan, China, Brazil, and other countries. In most African nations, both women and men won the vote at independence.

A small but growing number of women won elected office. Women headed democratic governments in Britain, Israel, India, Pakistan, the Philippines, and other countries. Still, a report to the UN noted that while women represent half of the world's people, "they perform nearly two thirds of all working hours, receive only one tenth of the world's income, and own less than one percent of world property."

The West In the industrialized world, more and more women worked outside the home. By the 1970s, the **feminist movement** sought greater access for women to jobs and promotions, equal pay for equal work, and an end to sexual harassment on the job. Women advanced into high-profile jobs as business owners and executives, astronauts, scientists, and technicians.

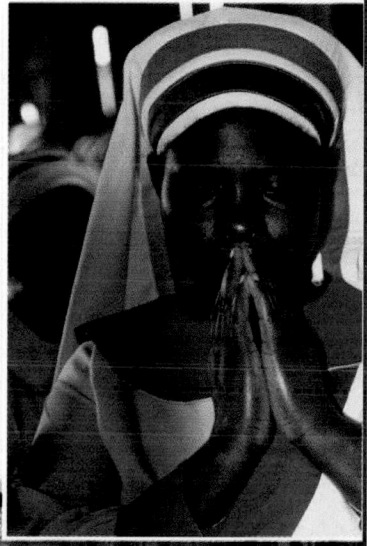

Religious Influences
Despite revolutionary changes, religious traditions remain a powerful force throughout the modern world. At top, a Christian woman prays in Kenya. At bottom, Buddhists gather at a temple in Vietnam.

Theme: Religions and Value Systems Besides those represented below, what other religions have millions of followers today?

Chapter 32 **819**

Activity
Cooperative Learning

Writing a Dialogue Have students work in pairs to write a dialogue commenting on the enduring traditions and changing patterns of life that may be found in developing countries. Have one student assume the role of an older person who is closely tied to the traditional ways of the past. Have the other student assume the role of a younger person who has moved to a city and is adopting many new ways of life. Students should develop two opposing viewpoints on the effects of change. Invite pairs to present their finished dialogues to the class. ✳

Background
Connections to Literature

African Literature Many African writers of the 1900s have sought to speak in an African voice. Like writers of other developing regions, they speak against western imperialism, against racial tensions, and against economic injustice. Some have written about Africa's struggle to create representative governments that are strongly committed to African traditions and to the protection of human rights.

Students may begin to explore modern African literature by reading the works of Wole Soyinka, a Nigerian playwright, poet, and Nobel Prize winner, whose tragedies combine western dramatic form with African music, dance, and mime. South African writer Alan Paton, in works of fiction and nonfiction, examines the tensions that exist between blacks and whites and between older and younger generations. Ama Ata Aidoo, a woman of Ghana, takes inspiration for her plays and poems from the rich and dynamic oral tradition of Ghana.

🗎 Block Scheduling Support

The conflict between traditional values and forces of westernization are brought out in the story "From Behind the Veil," by Dhu'l Nun Ayyoub, one of Iraq's most prominent fiction writers. When a teenage girl defies tradition and flirtatiously removes her facial veil before a young admirer in public, the reader is given insight into the cultural conflict confronting some young people in developing countries where traditional values are slipping away. Have students read the story, which is in the Prentice Hall Literature Library, *World Writers Today*, pp. 276–281. Have students write their responses to the story. Ask students to make a list of changing cultural values that they see in their own community. You may wish to use these lists as a basis for a class discussion on the merits and drawbacks of changing cultural values.

Caption Answer

Islam, Hinduism, Judaism

Primary Source

Women's Work
The following is an account of women's lives in the Kenyan countryside:

"One third of all rural households are headed by women, largely because men have migrated to the cities and towns in the hope of finding salaried work. Their wives continue to work the family plots of land and are always busy with some scheme to earn a bit of cash. Everywhere, one sees women walking to market with basketloads of vegetables on their heads, infants strapped to their backs, and older children following behind. Even while they are walking to the market, these women often are weaving baskets or fashioning other handiwork that they hope to exchange for cash needed for the family's support and for the children's education."

—P. Houston, *Third World Women Speak Out*

Skills Assessment

Primary Source **According to the passage, why are so many Kenyan women the heads of their households?**

New roles for women raised difficult social issues. Working women had to balance jobs with child rearing and household work. Some critics claimed that the growing number of women in the work force was partly responsible for rising divorce rates and a decline in family life. Others responded that many families required two incomes.

The Developing World In emerging nations, women worked actively in nationalist struggles. New constitutions spelled out equality for women, at least on paper. Although women still had less education than men, the gap narrowed. Women from the middle and elite classes entered the work force in growing numbers. Their skills contributed to their nations' wealth.

Still, women often shoulder a heavy burden of work in and out of the home. In rural areas, especially in Africa, women traditionally do much of the farmwork along with household tasks. In recent times, men have gone to cities to find work, leaving women with added responsibilities. In other regions, such as Southeast Asia, it is often young women who leave home to work, helping to support the family or pay for the education of their brothers. In many places, religious and cultural traditions confine women to the home or segregate men and women in the workplace.

Science and Technology

Since 1945, technology has transformed human life and thought. Instant communication via satellites has shrunk the globe. New forms of energy, especially nuclear power, have been added to the steam power, electricity, and gasoline energy of the first industrial age.

The Computer Revolution The computer has brought an information revolution. The first electronic computers, built in the 1940s, were huge, slow machines. Later, the computer was miniaturized, thanks to inventions like the silicon chip. By 2000, a huge computer network linked individuals, governments, and businesses around the world. Computerized robots operated in factories, and computers appeared in more and more homes and schools. E-commerce, or buying and selling on the Internet, contributed to economic growth and vitality. At the same time, however, access to computers widened the gap between the global North and South.

Medical and Biological Breakthroughs In the postwar era, the field of medicine achieved amazing successes. Vaccines helped prevent the spread of smallpox and other diseases. Toward the end of the century, however, the spread of deadly diseases such as AIDS created new challenges for researchers and public health officials.

In the 1970s, surgeons learned to transplant organs to save lives. Lasers made surgery safer. Scientists also had success in treating some cancers. Yet advances in medicine were costly and usually limited to people and nations that could afford them.

A controversial area of medical research is genetic engineering, which alters the chemical code carried by living things. Genetic research has produced new drug therapies. It has also created new strains of fruits and vegetables, which some see as unnatural and dangerous "Frankenfood." The possibility of cloning genetically identical mammals has also raised ethical questions about how far science should go to create and change life.

The Space Age In 1957, the space age started when the Soviet Union launched *Sputnik,* the first artificial satellite, into orbit. *Sputnik* set off a frantic "space race" between the superpowers. In 1969, the United States landed the first man on the moon. Both superpowers explored the military uses of space and sent spy satellites to orbit the Earth. Since the Cold War, the United States and Russia have cooperated in joint space ventures.

COMPUTERS and the Arts

Rapid advances in computer technology have revolutionized the arts. Computers have given artists, writers, musicians, photographers, and filmmakers new tools with which to release their imaginations. From computer-generated graphics to film animation to electronically synthesized music, digital technologies are transforming the practice and content of art.

Using a computer, a graphic artist manipulated reality to create this image of marbles in a maze.

Toy Story (1995) was the first full-length feature film in which all the images were computer-generated.

A composer uses a keyboard hooked up to a computer to create music.

Fast Facts

- It took animators 800,000 hours to generate the images for the movie *Toy Story*.

- The first electronic musical instrument, invented in 1919, was called the theremin. The performer waved his or her hands around two antennas to control the pitch and volume. No physical contact with the instrument was needed.

Portfolio Assessment

INTERNET Use the Internet to find samples of computer-generated graphics. Then, prepare a class presentation on the material you have found. Alternatively, you might research one of the instruments or techniques used to create electronic music, such as synthesizers, drum machines, sequencers, MIDI, or notation-based software. Download one or two selections to share with the class.

Chapter 32 **821**

Digital Filmmaking In the near future, people may be able to make films through use of the Internet. Amateur filmmakers will be able to record digital footage, edit their movies, and distribute them via the Internet. They may even be able to e-mail their films directly to theaters, where they will be screened using digital projectors. In the future, as digital filmmaking advances, watching a movie will be an experience in virtual reality. Hollywood filmmakers already are producing "filmless" films using digital equipment.

Bell Ringer Ask students what movies, television shows, and commercials they have seen that use computer graphics. Ask students how they could tell the graphics were computer generated.

*B*ackground
Connections to Today

Virtual reality uses computer graphics to create the illusion of a three-dimensional world. Users interact with different visual and sensory environments. The illusion of being in the environment is created through the wearing of goggles, headsets, gloves, or body suits. Users are so immersed in virtual environments that they seem to move and manipulate objects while experiencing the sensation of touch.

*A*ctivity
Cooperative Learning

Making a Visual Presentation Have the class brainstorm a list of ways or places virtual reality might be used now and in the future. To help students get started, suggest the following: museums, medical science, entertainment, education, music. Then, organize the class into groups, assigning each group one of the categories. Each group should research how virtual reality is currently being used in its category and make a presentation that includes visual information such as charts, graphs, and photos. Each student should be assigned a particular role, which may include researcher, interviewer, artist, speaker, or organizer.

Portfolio Assessment Rubrics

Share rubrics with students before they prepare their class presentations.

Attempted The presentation is sketchy and shows little research.

Minimal The presentation contains some information but is unclear, messily prepared, or has many errors.

Adequate The presentation is well researched and delivered and has few errors.

Exemplary The presentation is well researched, designed, and delivered and has outstanding examples.

Virtual Field Trip

www.phschool.com

Lyndon B. Johnson Space Center
Houston, Texas

To see other photographs of missions into outer space, use the Internet address above to link to the National Aeronautics and Space Administration.

The Space Age
At right, the International Space Station was built and is operated by the United States, Canada, Japan, Russia, Brazil, and 11 nations in Europe. An astronaut works on a robotic arm of the station in space.

Theme: Global Interaction
How does the International Space Station reflect changes in the world's political climate?

European nations, as well as Japan and China, launched their own satellites, mostly for peaceful purposes. Satellites mapped weather and tracked droughts, livestock diseases, and plagues. In the weightlessness of space, scientists experimented with promising new drugs and vaccines.

The Green Revolution Scientists applied new technology to increasing food production for the world's growing population. During the 1960s, they touched off the Green Revolution, developing new kinds of rice and other grains that yielded more food per acre than older strains. In India, Indonesia, and elsewhere, the Green Revolution doubled food output.

The Green Revolution had limits, however. It succeeded only in areas with regular moisture. Also, it required chemical fertilizers and pesticides as well as irrigation systems, which only wealthy farmers could afford. Unable to compete with larger, more efficient agricultural enterprises, many poor peasants were forced off their small farms.

Ongoing Issues Technology has improved life for people everywhere. Many people, especially in the industrial world, pin their hopes on technology to solve a variety of economic, medical, and environmental problems. Yet it has not solved such basic problems as hunger or poverty. Also, while technology has created many new kinds of jobs, it has threatened others. For example, a single computer can process thousands of telephone calls that were once handled by human operators.

A New Global Culture

"Radio has changed everything," noted Egyptian leader Gamal Abdel Nasser in the 1950s. "Today, people in the most remote villages hear of what is happening and form their opinions." Modern communications technology has indeed created a "new world." Radio, television, fax machines, satellites, and computer networks have put people everywhere in touch and helped create a new global culture.

Westernized Popular Culture The driving force behind this global culture has been the United States. American fashions, products, and entertainment have captured the world's imagination. American movies and television programs play in Beijing, Buenos Aires, and Cairo. English has become the leading language of international business.

Some critics have compared this westernization of culture to a foreign invasion. Yet the new global culture has sometimes balanced western and nonwestern traditions. From Latin America, popular music such as calypso and reggae gained international popularity. Movie makers like Japan's Akira Kurosawa and India's Satyajit Ray adapted western techniques to express their own distinct traditions.

The Arts Global exchanges have influenced literature and the visual arts for hundreds of years. By the 1700s, Europeans were copying Turkish carpets and Chinese pottery. A century later, European painters adapted the printmaking traditions of Japan. At the same time, Japanese artists were studying the styles of European painters. More recently, writers from Africa to India have adapted literary forms, such as the novel, from the West.

In the last 100 years, the western world has gained a new appreciation for the arts of other civilizations. Western artists studied Southeast Asian and African sculptures, dances, and music.

Global interest in the arts has led nations to value and protect ancient cultural treasures. The UN and other groups are helping countries preserve and restore temples, palaces, manuscripts, and other artifacts. Museums, too, preserve the heritage of the past. Traveling exhibits of Egyptian jewelry, Russian icons, Indian sculpture, or West African masks help modern audiences understand cultures from other times and places.

Looking Ahead

The recent past presents special problems for students of history. We can see the immediate results of recent events, but cannot know their long-term impact. Many recent trends and issues emerged long before 1945 and will continue for decades. At the same time, new issues and new conflicts will almost certainly take shape.

In the next five chapters, we will see how many of the trends and issues discussed in this chapter have affected different regions of the world. As you read, notice the impact of two contradictory trends. Nationalism, along with ethnic politics, is on the rise. Yet global interdependence has become an inescapable fact of life. Across the world, people must reconcile local and global interests.

SECTION 3 Assessment

Recall
1. **Identify: (a)** *Sputnik,* **(b)** Green Revolution.
2. **Define: (a)** shantytown, **(b)** fundamentalist, **(c)** liberation theology, **(d)** feminist movement, **(e)** e-commerce, **(f)** genetic engineering.

Comprehension
3. How has urbanization affected people in developing nations?
4. Describe two changes in the roles and rights of women.
5. How have three developments in science or technology affected the modern world?

6. How did American influences shape a new global culture?

Critical Thinking and Writing
7. **Predicting Consequences** What do you think might be some major global issues of the next century?
8. **Applying Information** "Educate a boy," says an African proverb, "and you educate a person. Educate a girl, and you educate a nation." **(a)** What does the proverb assume about the role of women in society? **(b)** What goal could this proverb be used to support?

Biography

Youssou N'Dour 1959—

In the 1980s, singer and musician Youssou N'Dour helped popularize "world beat" music. This new global rhythm mixes African, Latin, and western styles.

As a child, N'Dour absorbed the sounds of traditional Senegalese drum music. He was also inspired by reggae, funk, soul, jazz, and Cuban music. These influences created *mbalax*, music in which the "talking drum" is the main instrument.

Today, N'Dour considers himself "a modern griot." His music, he says, is "a representation of not only African music but of African life and the whole image of Africa."

Theme: Impact of the Individual How is N'Dour's music an example of international culture?

Activity
Take It to the NET

Use the Internet to learn about the history of computers and how they have affected contemporary society. Then, make a time line showing key events in the story of computers up to the present. You may illustrate your time line if you choose.

✓ Test Preparation

Have students read the section "The Arts" on this page, and then complete the sentence below.

For hundreds of years, literature and the visual arts have been influenced by

(A) global exchange.

B current political movements.

C Latin music.

D technology.

SECTION 3 Assessment

Recall
1. **(a)** *Sputnik,* p. 820 **(b)** Green Revolution, p. 822 **2. (a)** shantytown, p. 818 **(b)** fundamentalist, p. 819 **(c)** liberation theology, p. 819 **(d)** feminist movement, p. 819 **(e)** e-commerce, p. 820 **(f)** genetic engineering, p. 820

Comprehension
3. In cities, some people find greater economic and cultural opportunities. Others settle in shantytowns that lack basic services. People's traditional beliefs and values often are undermined, and the people may feel stress and isolation.
4. Women have the right to vote in most nations. More women now work outside the home, hold political office, and (in the developing world) have high-profile jobs.
5. Computers have led to an information revolution by storing and processing vast amounts of data. New medical treatments have helped prevent the spread of disease. Satellites have mapped weather and have helped fight disease. 6. Since World War II, American cultural items—clothing, products, and entertainment—have spread around the world. English has become the leading language of international business.

Critical Thinking and Writing
7. Students should base their answers on the contents of Section 3 and on their knowledge of current events. **8. (a)** It is women who pass on a society's knowledge and traditions. **(b)** The proverb supports the goal of educating young women.

Activity Rubrics

Share rubrics with students before they create their time lines.

Attempted The time line is poorly researched and incomplete.

Minimal The time line shows some research, but several items are inaccurately placed, and it has many errors.

Adequate The time line is well researched, contains several items that are accurately placed, and has few errors.

Exemplary The time line is well researched, comprehensive, and accurate; it contains interesting well-illustrated items and has no errors.

Biography

ANSWER Youssou N'Dour's *mbalax* style mixes native Senegalese drum music with western styles.

Creating a Chapter Summary

As a reteaching opportunity, pair a more able student with a less able student to complete this chapter summary.

Political Climate end to colonial empires; many new developing nations; political instability; UN as peace keeper; UN services; other organizations—WTO, Group of Seven, World Bank, IMF, NGOs; deadly weapons; human rights; terrorism

Patterns of Life urbanization; roles and rights for women; science and technology; new global culture

Economic Trends interdependence of global North and South; oil crisis; debt crisis; obstacles to development; environmental issues

Building Vocabulary

1–10. Students' sentences should show an understanding of each word.

Recalling Key Facts

11. Many former European colonies gained independence.
12. The global North includes the industrial nations of Western Europe and North America, as well as Japan and Australia. The global South includes the developing nations of Asia, Africa, and Latin America.
13. Poor nations borrowed from western banks to modernize, but interest rates rose and demand for exports slowed, and they did not have the money to repay these debts.
14. Large slums have emerged; the extended family is giving way to the nuclear family; many people are experiencing feelings of isolation.
15. new vaccines, organ transplantation, laser surgery, new cancer treatments

Critical Thinking and Writing

16. All three state that all people are entitled to basic rights and freedoms.
17. The IMF and World Bank have forced some governments in developing countries to abandon costly social programs. This move has led to hardship and resentment.
18. **(a)** Industrialization has caused severe damage to the natural environment. Many scientists predict that there will be future environmental crises of global impact. **(b)** Possible answer: Acid rain is caused by toxic chemicals being released into the air. When the chemicals come back to

---

Creating a Chapter Summary

On a sheet of paper, make a concept web like the one shown here. Add as many circles as you need to show the key ideas of this chapter.

 For additional review and enrichment activities, see the interactive version of *World History* available on the Web and on CD-ROM.

 Web Site Self-Test
For practice test questions for Chapter 32, see **www.phschool.com**.

Building Vocabulary

Review the meaning of the chapter vocabulary words listed below. Then, write a sentence for each word in which you define the word and describe its relation to the world in the second half of the twentieth century.

1. modernization
2. superpower
3. interdependence
4. multinational corporation
5. privatization
6. acid rain
7. global warming
8. fundamentalist
9. liberation theology
10. genetic engineering

Recalling Key Facts

11. Why did many new nations emerge in the years after World War II?
12. Explain what is meant by the terms "global North" and "global South."
13. What were the causes of the debt crisis of the 1980s?
14. How has urbanization affected life in the developing world?
15. List three medical breakthroughs in the postwar era.

Critical Thinking and Writing

16. **Linking Past and Present** How does the Universal Declaration of Human Rights echo the ideas of the American Bill of Rights and the French Declaration of the Rights of Man and the Citizen?
17. **Understanding Points of View** Why do some people resent the World Bank and IMF?
18. **Connecting to Geography (a)** Why has the environment become an area of growing concern in recent years? **(b)** Describe the causes and effects of one global environmental problem.

19. **Distinguishing Facts From Opinions** Harry Truman wrote, "The scientific and industrial revolution which began two centuries ago . . . caught up the peoples of the globe in a common destiny. Two world-shattering wars have proved that no corner of the Earth can be isolated from the affairs of mankind." **(a)** Which parts of Truman's statement are facts? **(b)** Which parts are opinions? **(c)** Do you think Truman's facts support his opinions? Explain.

Earth as rain or snow, they damage forests, lakes, and farmland.

19. **(a)** The scientific revolution, industrial revolution, and two world wars are factual events. **(b)** that all people share a common destiny and that no corner of the Earth can be isolated from the affairs of mankind **(c)** Answers should be well supported.

Nguyen Sa is one of the leading poets of modern Vietnam. Read these excerpts from Sa's poem "No Time," then answer the questions that follow.

"I must get far away from this city
with its soot-streaked curbs
and people who pass each other
without a smile or a word.
'No time! I have no time!' she answered me,
the girl dressed all in lavender.

Still, she did answer me, and yet
I didn't dare ask her,
'What important things have you time for?'
but whispered to myself instead
—the homeless whispering to the home-
    less—
there are those who love but have no time
    for loving.
If this is true, how can birds fly back to
    their nests?
How can poetry be written?
If this is true, birds and poems will die.

Yes, I must get away from the city
if there is no time, no time here
to speak one word,
to share one moment's laughter. . . ."

—Nguyen Sa, "No Time"

20. According to the first lines of the poem, what two qualities of cities does the speaker dislike?

21. How does the "girl dressed all in lavender" respond to the speaker?

22. Why does the speaker of the poem refer to himself as "homeless"?

23. Write a sentence summarizing the main point of this poem.

24. (a) How would you describe the mood of this poem? (b) How does it reflect what you have read about the psychological effects of urbanization?

Skills Tip

Modern poems often deal with the impact of modern life on the poet. When analyzing a poem, look for words that reveal the speaker's emotional or psychological state.

This political cartoon appeared in a Bombay newspaper in 1983. The woman in the cartoon is Indira Gandhi, India's prime minister at that time. Study the cartoon, then answer the following questions:

25. What familiar story does this cartoon recall?

26. (a) What does the boat represent? (b) What do the animals represent?

27. Cartoons often use familiar symbols for certain ideas. What idea does a dove symbolize?

28. (a) What dangers do the passengers on the boat face? (b) What is their goal?

29. (a) How does this cartoon reflect the position of India and many other developing nations during the Cold War? (b) Do you think the cartoonist supported or opposed this position? Explain.

Use the Internet to research one of the present-day issues mentioned in this chapter. You might choose a political issue such as human rights, an economic issue such as debt, an environmental issue such as global warming, or a social issue such as urbanization. Then, write a report on the status of that issue today. You may want to illustrate your report with photographs, diagrams, graphs, or charts.

Chapter 32 **825**

Analyzing Primary Sources

20. the dirt ("soot-streaked curbs") and unfriendly people who pass by "without a smile or a word"

21. She says she has no time to talk to him.

22. He is lonely and feels he does not belong in the city.

23. Answers should reflect the idea of urban life being too fast-paced and impersonal.

24. (a) depressed, hopeless, angry, lonely (b) People in the developing world who move from villages to cities frequently suffer a sense of stress and isolation.

Analyzing Political Cartoons

25. The Biblical story of Noah and the ark.

26. (a) the nonaligned movement during the Cold War (b) the nonaligned nations

27. peace

28. (a) the arms race and a world economic crisis (b) to survive; to build a peaceful world

29. (a) Many new nations did not ally themselves with either the Soviet Union or the United States. India was a leader of the nonaligned movement. (b) The cartoonist supported the nonaligned movement. The cartoon compares the nonaligned movement to Noah's quest for survival and associates India with peace.

Skills Tip

As you read a poem, try to understand why the poet chooses each word. Ask yourself, what emotional message does this word convey? The Skills Handbook at the front of the book has a lesson that will help students with this feature.

Unit Theme Activity

Remind students about the Unit Theme Activity located on the unit opener page. Make sure students understand the assignment and have begun work.

Take It to the NET

Direct students to **www.phschool.com** for links to sites that will help them get started on their assignments. Share rubrics with students.

Attempted The report is incomplete or extremely brief.

Minimal The report updates the issue but has little depth or many errors.

Adequate The report is well researched, updates the issue, and has many supporting illustrations.

Exemplary The report is well researched, updates the issue, is very well illustrated, and shows a deep understanding of the issue today.

Chapter 33 Planning Guide

Resource Manager

Chapter Level Resources	CORE INSTRUCTION	READING/SKILLS
Chapter Level Resources	**Teaching Resources** ▫ **Pacing Charts,** Ch. 33 ▫ **Teaching With Themes,** p. 36 ▥ **Color Transparencies,** p. F–67 ◉ **Resource Pro®** Ch. 33 ▥ **www.phschool.com** 　• eTeach	◉ **Book on CD,** Ch. 33 ◉ **Interactive Student Tutorial CD-ROM,** Ch. 33 ◉ **Social Studies Skills Tutor CD-ROM** ▥ **Skills Transparencies**
1 The Western World: An Overview 1. List issues that troubled Europe after the Cold War. 2. Describe how recent economic and political trends affected the West. 3. Explain how Europe has moved toward greater unity. 4. Summarize change in social trends.	**Teaching Resources** ▫ **Unit 8 booklet** 　• Viewpoint Activity, p. 30 ▫ **Creative Teaching Activities,** p. 146 ◉ **Prentice Hall Presentation Pro,** Ch. 33, Section 1	**Teaching Resources** ▫ **Unit 8 booklet** 　• Guided Reading and Review, p. 18 ▫ **Guide to the Essentials** ▰ **Guided Reading Audiotapes,** Ch. 33, Section 1
2 The Western European Democracies 1. Explain how Britain's policies changed after World War II. 2. Relate how French power was revived. 3. Describe how Germany reunified. 4. Enumerate problems of other democratic nations.	**Teaching Resources** ▫ **Creative Teaching Activities,** p. 147 ◉ **Prentice Hall Presentation Pro,** Ch. 33, Section 2 ▥ **Section Reading Support Transparencies**	**Teaching Resources** ▫ **Unit 8 booklet** 　• Guided Reading and Review, p. 20 ▫ **Guide to the Essentials** ▰ **Guided Reading Audiotapes,** Ch. 33, Section 2
3 North American Prosperity 1. Specify actions the United States took as a global superpower. 2. Outline developments that have shaped the United States. 3. Identify recent issues Canada has faced.	**Teaching Resources** ▫ **Creative Teaching Activities,** p. 148 ◉ **Prentice Hall Presentation Pro,** Ch. 33, Section 3 ▥ **Section Reading Support Transparencies**	**Teaching Resources** ▫ **Unit 8 booklet** 　• Guided Reading and Review, p. 22 　• Skill Application Activity, p. 31 ▫ **Guide to the Essentials**
4 The Soviet Union: Rise and Fall of a Superpower 1. Summarize the ideas that guided Soviet political, economic, and foreign policy. 2. Explain why the Soviet Union collapsed. 3. Describe Russia's current problems.	**Teaching Resources** ▫ **Creative Teaching Activities,** p. 149 ◉ **Prentice Hall Presentation Pro,** Ch. 33, Section 4 ▥ **Section Reading Support Transparencies**	**Teaching Resources** ▫ **Unit 8 booklet** 　• Guided Reading and Review, p. 24 ▫ **Guide to the Essentials** ▰ **Guided Reading Audiotapes,** Ch. 33, Section 4
5 A New Era in Eastern Europe 1. Describe how Eastern European nations opposed Soviet domination. 2. Identify effects of the fall of communism. 3. Enumerate causes and effects of the Yugoslavian civil war.	**Teaching Resources** ▫ **Unit 8 booklet** 　• Biography Activity, p. 28 　• Primary Source Activity, p. 29 ◉ **Prentice Hall Presentation Pro,** Ch. 33, Section 5	**Teaching Resources** ▫ **Unit 8 booklet** 　• Guided Reading and Review, p. 26 ▫ **Guide to the Essentials** ▰ **Guided Reading Audiotapes,** Ch. 33, Section 5

ENRICHMENT/PRE-AP

📖 **www.phschool.com**
- Why Study History?

📚 **Teaching Resources**
📗 **Chapter Extension Activities,** p. 79
📜 **Color Transparencies,** pp. B–59, B–61, B–63

📖 **www.phschool.com**
- Virtual Field Trip
- Internet Activities, Section 2

📚 **Teaching Resources**
📗 **History Through Literature,** pp. 68–69
📖 **www.phschool.com**
- Internet Activities, Section 3

📚 **Teaching Resources**
📗 **Chapter Extension Activities,** p. 80
📖 **www.phschool.com**
- Interne t Activities, Meltdown at Chernobyl

📜 **Color Transparencies,** pp. B–59, B–61, B–63, E–49
📺 **Visions, Voices, Views,** Daily Life CloseUp, tape 8

ASSESSMENT

PRENTICE HALL
ASSESSMENT SYSTEM

Core Assessment
📘 **ExamView Test Bank booklet,** Ch. 33
💿 **ExamView Test Bank CD-ROM,** Ch. 33

Standardized Test Preparation
Diagnose and Prescribe
📘 **Diagnostic Tests for High School Social Studies Skills**
Review and Reteach
📘 **Review Book for World History**
Practice and Assess
📘 **Test-Taking Strategies With Transparencies for High School**
📘 **Alternative Assessment booklet**
📘 **Test Prep Book for World History**

📚 **Teaching Resources**
📁 **Unit 8 booklet**
- Geography Quiz, p. 32
- Section Quizzes, pp. 19, 21, 23, 25, 27
- Chapter Tests A, B, and C, pp. 33–37
📖 **www.phschool.com**
- Self-Test

CUSTOMIZE FOR INDIVIDUAL NEEDS

Gifted and Talented
- **Teacher's Edition,** Activities: Customize for Heterogeneous Groups, p. 830

Less Proficient Readers
- **Guide to the Essentials,** Ch. 33
- **Guided Reading Audiotapes, English,** Ch. 33
- **Book on CD,** Ch. 33
- **Teacher's Edition,** Activities: Customize for Heterogeneous Groups, p. 846; Reading Strategy, p. 847

Less Proficient Writers
- **Teacher's Edition,** Activities: Customize for Kinesthetic Learners, p. 841; Cooperative Learning Activity, p. 845

Students Acquiring English/ESL
- **Guide to the Essentials, English/Spanish,** Ch. 33
- **Guided Reading Audiotapes, English/Spanish,** Ch. 33
- **Book on CD,** Ch. 33
- **Teacher's Edition,** Activities marked with an *

TEXT

Don't miss the exclusive interactive version of *World History: Connections to Today* on the Internet and CD-ROM.

CHAPTER
33

Europe and North America 1945–Present

INTRODUCTION

Western European nations, enjoying economic growth in the postwar years, expanded social welfare programs until the 1980s, when an economic slowdown forced cuts. Involved in the Cold War with the Soviet bloc, the United States led world opposition to communism, while expanding civil rights and pursuing prosperity at home. Reform efforts in the Soviet Union led to the nation's collapse. Eastern Europe faced economic challenges and ethnic conflicts after abandoning communist rule.

Focusing on Themes

Suggest that students focus on these theme questions as they read:

Economics and Technology
How are global economic changes affecting the industrial West?

Continuity and Change
Why is Western Europe struggling with the issue of unity?

Impact of the Individual
How did individual leaders in Europe and North America reshape their nations?

Political and Social Systems
Why did communism collapse in the Soviet Union and Eastern Europe?

Diversity
Why have ethnic tensions in Europe increased since the end of the Cold War?

Chapter Preview

1 The Western World: An Overview
2 The Western European Democracies
3 North American Prosperity
4 The Soviet Union: Rise and Fall of a Superpower
5 A New Era in Eastern Europe

◆ TIME LINE ACTIVITY

Share the About the Pictures note with students before asking these questions:

1. In what part of the world did the Korean War and the Vietnam War take place? *(eastern Asia)*
2. Why would Russians topple Lenin's statue to celebrate the end of a communist state? *(Lenin was a founder of the communist government.)*
3. In what year did Fidel Castro come to power in Cuba? *(1959)*

1960s
United States begins sending troops to battle communist forces in the Vietnam War. Here, American helicopters patrol a road in Vietnam.

1957
The Soviet Union launches *Sputnik,* the first artificial satellite, into orbit around the Earth.

CHAPTER EVENTS

| 1940 | 1955 | 1970 |

GLOBAL EVENTS

1950 The Korean War begins.

1959 Fidel Castro comes to power in Cuba.

1973 An oil crisis affects nations around the world.

826 Chapter 33

Don't Miss!

Synthesizing Information
The European Union (Section 1)

Disaster!
Meltdown at Chernobyl (Section 4)

Resource Directory

Teaching Resources
Teaching With Themes Chapter Theme Activities, p. 36
Pacing Chart With Block Scheduling Guide Ch. 33
Technology
World History Color Transparencies Ch. 33 Graphic Organizer, p. F–67

Political Map of Europe

Europe has undergone significant change since World War II. In the 1990s, many nations became independent.

1991
The Soviet Union collapses. In this scene, a man waves a Russian flag as others look upon a fallen statue of Lenin.

1999
The European Union introduces the euro, a common currency for member nations. Several examples are shown above.

1985

2000

2015

1980s A global economic slowdown causes many governments to reduce spending.

Take It to the NET
To learn about recent developments in Europe and North America, visit the World History section of www.phschool.com.

Independent Assignments

Have students read one section as they prepare for class. After class, have them complete the assignment. Some students may benefit from using the Guided Reading and Review worksheets.

Section 1 Have students use the worksheet *A Single Currency for Europe?* in the Unit 8 booklet, p. 30, to learn about both sides of the argument regarding the use of a common European currency.

Section 2 Have students use the reading *The Long March to Derry* in the Treasures of the World booklet, pp. 142–144, to learn about the strife in Northern Ireland.

Section 3 Have students use the worksheet *Cat's Eye* in the History Through Literature booklet,

pp. 68–69, to learn about an elementary school class in postwar Canada.

Section 4 Have students use the worksheet in the Chapter Extension Activities booklet, p. 80, to learn more about the meltdown at Chernobyl.

Section 5 Have students use the worksheet *Vaclav Havel* in the Unit 8 booklet, p. 28, to learn about this Czech playwright turned political leader.

Political Map of Europe

Activating Prior Knowledge
Which nations on this map were once part of the Soviet Union? *(Estonia, Latvia, Lithuania, Belarus, Ukraine, Moldova, Russia)*

Previewing
What movements do you suppose were involved in the breakup of nations such as Czechoslovakia (now the Czech Republic and Slovakia)? *(Possible answers: nationalism, anticommunism)*

Background
About the Pictures

1. The first *Sputnik* weighed only 184 pounds. The next one, which carried a dog named Laika, and the subsequent *Sputniks* were all much bigger. Laika died when her oxygen ran out, but most of the dogs who were sent into space on later *Sputnik* flights were safely recovered.

2. Antiwar sentiment grew after the 1971 leak of the Pentagon Papers to *The New York Times*. The documents, which were prepared by the Department of Defense, showed that the government had been deceiving the public about the war for many years.

3. When Mikhail Gorbachev resigned in December 1991, the Soviet Union had already ceased to exist. Earlier in the month, Russian president Boris Yeltsin and leaders from Ukraine and Belarus had signed a pact replacing that nation with a loose association of states.

4. There are 7 euro bills and 8 coins. On the face of the coins is a map of the European Union and the European flag. The design on the obverse is specific to the country minting the coin, although all coins may be used in any member country.

eTeach

Be sure to check out this month's online discussion with a World History Master Teacher.

Go to **www.phschool.com**.

LESSON PLAN

1. Focus The Cold War divided Europe into two hostile camps—the western democracies allied with the United States and the communist states allied with the Soviet Union. Western European economies rebounded after World War II but have sometimes been slowed by such factors as the oil crisis and the growth of Japanese industry. In the 1990s, the end of the Cold War and increased economic unity promised a new era of peaceful cooperation.

2. Instruct Work with the class to construct a concept chart. Begin by writing on the board the unifying theme "The Western World: An Overview." From this main title, draw three branches, labeled Political Trends, Economic Trends, and Social Trends. Now divide the class into several groups and assign each group one of the three topics. Have group members work together to list and briefly describe the major developments in their assigned area. When the groups have finished this task, call on volunteers from each group to take turns adding to the graphic organizer on the board.

3. Assess Ask students to answer the four Reading Focus questions that appear at the start of this section.

4. Reteach If students' **Assess** activity does not reflect adequate understanding of the lesson, you might assign the *Guide to the Essentials* or the *Interactive Student Tutorial CD-ROM* for this section.

Reading Focus

- What issues troubled Europe after the Cold War?
- How have recent economic and political trends affected the West?
- How has Europe moved toward greater unity?
- How have social trends changed the West?

Vocabulary

détente
welfare state
recession
service industry
euro

Taking Notes

As you read this section, make an outline of its contents. Use Roman numerals for major headings, capital letters for subheadings, and numbers for supporting details. The model at right will help you get started.

I. Europe: The Cold War and after
  A. The Berlin Wall
    1. Berlin divided into two zones
  B.
II. Economic and political trends
  A.
    1.
    2.
  B. The oil shock

Main Idea In the years since World War II, various economic, political, and social trends have shaped the western world.

Setting the Scene Western Europe rebounded out of the rubble of World War II. During the postwar years, standards of living rose dramatically. People earned higher wages, bought homes with central heating and running water, and enjoyed luxuries unheard of in earlier times. Amid these comforts, many other changes were shaping the western world.

Europe: The Cold War and After

For more than 40 years, the Cold War divided Europe into two hostile military alliances. The communist nations of Eastern Europe, dominated by the Soviet Union, formed the Warsaw Pact. The western democracies, led by the United States, formed NATO. The superpowers avoided direct confrontation in Europe, but some issues brought the continent to the brink of war.

The Berlin Wall Berlin was a focus of Cold War tensions. The city was split into democratic West Berlin and communist East Berlin. In the 1950s, West Berlin became a showcase for West German prosperity. Thousands of low-paid East Germans, discontented with communism, slipped into West Berlin. To stop the exodus, East Germany built a wall in 1961 that separated the two sectors of the city. When completed, the wall was a massive concrete barrier, topped with barbed wire and patrolled by guards.

The Berlin Wall was an ugly symbol of the Cold War and an embarrassment for the Soviets. It showed that workers, far from enjoying a communist paradise, had to be forcibly restrained from fleeing.

The Nuclear Threat The Cold War triggered an arms race, with both sides producing huge arsenals of nuclear weapons. Critics argued that a nuclear war would destroy both sides. Yet the superpowers claimed that they dared not stop. Each side wanted to have the power to deter the other from launching its nuclear weapons. The result was a "balance of terror."

During the arms race, both superpowers spent huge sums of money on weapons. Such spending meant cutbacks in other areas. In 1953, President Dwight Eisenhower warned Americans about the impact: "Every gun that is made, every warship launched . . . signifies . . . a theft from those who hunger and are not fed, those who are cold and are not clothed."

Disarmament and Détente To reduce the threat of nuclear destruction, both sides met at disarmament talks. Although mutual distrust often blocked progress, they did sign some agreements, such as the 1963 Nuclear

The Nuclear Threat
In Europe and other parts of the world, children were taught they could survive a nuclear attack. In 1954, the image above was used to advertise a bogus "radiation-resistant" blanket.

Theme: Economics and Technology How did nuclear weapons change the nature of war?

Caption Answer

Nuclear weapons are much more destructive than conventional weapons. In the Cold War, both sides had the capability of destroying each other.

Resource Directory

Teaching Resources
Creative Teaching Activities Creative Teaching Activities booklet, p. 146
Guided Reading and Review Unit 8 booklet, p. 18

Test Ban Treaty. It banned the testing of nuclear weapons in the atmosphere. Underground testing was still permitted, however.

By the 1970s, American and Soviet leaders promoted an era of détente (day TAHNT), or relaxation of tensions. The two superpowers made new agreements to reduce nuclear stockpiles. Détente ended, however, after the Soviet Union invaded Afghanistan in 1979.

End of the Cold War By the 1990s, as you will read, economic and foreign policy troubles threatened the Soviet Union. A new Soviet leader, Mikhail Gorbachev (mee kah EEL GOR bah chawf), eased the Soviet grip on Eastern Europe. One by one, communist governments collapsed. Communism even fell from power in the Soviet Union, which broke up into separate independent republics.

When the Cold War ended, nations in Western and Eastern Europe sought normal relations. Germany was reunited. The Warsaw Pact dissolved. NATO, originally formed to defend the West against communism, had to redefine its role in a post–Cold War world.

Troublesome Issues As the century neared its end, Europeans faced troublesome issues, new and old. Russia and the nations of Eastern Europe turned to the West for loans and investments to build capitalist economies. Ethnic clashes, especially in the Balkans, created conflicts that threatened the peace of Europe.

The nuclear peril was reduced, but it still remained. The United States, Russia, and other nations still had nuclear weapons. As disarmament talks continued, there were fears that some Russian nuclear materials might end up in the hands of other nations and groups.

NATO's New Role With the Cold War over, NATO allowed Eastern Europe's former communist nations to join the alliance. In 1999, Hungary, Poland, and the Czech Republic entered the organization. Despite Russian protests, several other Eastern European states also sought admission.

In the 1990s, conflict in the Balkans posed new challenges to NATO. When ethnic groups in Bosnia and Kosovo tried to break away from Yugoslavia, war erupted. Europeans witnessed the worst fighting since World War II and were shocked by horrible abuses of human rights. As you will read, NATO members finally sent military forces into both Bosnia and Kosovo. Those moves sparked debate over whether NATO should become Europe's peacekeeper and protector of human rights.

Economic and Political Trends

In the 1950s, Western Europeans recovered quickly from World War II. With Marshall Plan aid, their economies boomed. They rebuilt industries, farms, and transportation networks destroyed by the war.

Meanwhile, right-wing parties were discredited because they had supported fascism. Communists and socialists, who had resisted the Nazis during the war, enjoyed growing support. As a result, postwar governments in France, Italy, and Germany adopted many policies favored by the left.

The Welfare State A major goal of leftist parties was to extend the welfare state. Under this system, a government keeps most features of a capitalist economy but takes greater responsibility for the social and economic needs of its people. The welfare state had its roots in

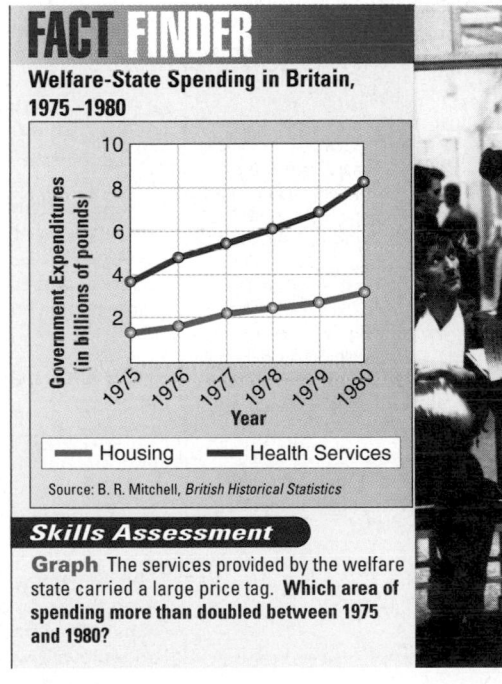

FACT FINDER

Welfare-State Spending in Britain, 1975–1980

Graph showing Government Expenditures (in billions of pounds) on the vertical axis from 2 to 10, and Year on the horizontal axis from 1975 to 1980. Two lines: Housing and Health Services.

— Housing   — Health Services

Source: B. R. Mitchell, *British Historical Statistics*

Skills Assessment

Graph The services provided by the welfare state carried a large price tag. **Which area of spending more than doubled between 1975 and 1980?**

Block Scheduling Support

Supply students with copies of the map *Europe Today* from p. B–59 of the World History Color Transparencies. Ask students to label the countries and their capitals. Then have them compare their maps to outdated maps from the 1980s and list the countries that have disappeared or emerged since then. After students have made their comparisons, you may wish to show them the map *Eastern Europe Updated* from p. B–63 in the World History Color Transparencies.

Customize for . . .
Auditory Learners

Recognizing a Viewpoint In 1964, American author and journalist Fred J. Cook expressed the following viewpoint on the nuclear arms buildup. Read the excerpt or distribute copies of it to the class. Have students use the excerpt to discuss the questions that follow.

"Now we have in our nuclear stock pile [weapons] equivalent in destruction to some 22 billion tons of TNT. Each of our 1,300 Strategic Air Force bombers, our intercontinental ballistic missiles, our Polaris submarines is equipped with hydrogen bombs 5,000 times more powerful than the primitive Hiroshima device that exterminated 100,000 lives in one blinding flash. To carry the analogy one inevitable step further, there are only 2,000 cities in the entire world with populations of 100,000. We have enough hydrogen bombs in our stock pile to deliver the equivalent of 2.5 million tons of TNT, 125 times the force of Hiroshima, upon each 100,000 population, not just upon each city — and we can deliver it not once, not twice, but 125 times."

(1) Did Cook believe that the United States had enough nuclear weapons? Explain. (2) What did he believe to be the primary targets of these weapons? (3) What recommendation about the arms race is implied in his analysis? Explain.

Skills Assessment

ANSWER health services

Geography and History

Offshore Oil Rigs

The oil crisis of 1973 spurred the West to search for new sources of oil. Exploration companies discovered rich deposits of petroleum and natural gas beneath the ocean floor. Today's offshore rigs are colossal steel structures that rise to heights taller than most skyscrapers. They are built to withstand 100-foot waves and 160-mph winds. The picture above shows a giant oil rig rising out of the North Sea, off the coast of Western Europe.

Living and working in this harsh environment is hard. Roughnecks, as the rig workers are called, must wrestle with heavy equipment, often in bitter winds or rain. Lodged in cramped quarters, the workers are subject to punishing conditions and long hours. They usually stay on the rigs for just a few weeks at a time. On a regular basis, helicopters or ships bring in a new crew and ferry exhausted workers ashore for rest.

Theme: Geography and History Why did exploration for oil increase after 1973?

the late 1800s, when governments passed reforms to ease the hardships of the industrial age. During that period, Germany, Britain, and other nations had set up unemployment insurance and old-age pensions.

After 1945, governments expanded these social programs. Both the middle class and the poor enjoyed increasing benefits from national health care, unemployment insurance, and old-age pensions. Other programs gave aid to the poor and created an economic cushion to help people get through difficult times. Still, the welfare state was costly, involving many burdensome taxes and greater government regulation of private enterprise.

Socialists supported the welfare state and a larger role for government in the economy. In Britain, France, and elsewhere, governments nationalized basic industries such as railroads, airlines, banks, steel, and energy. Conservatives condemned the drift from the free enterprise system toward socialism.

The Oil Shock In 1973, the West suffered an economic shock when OPEC cut oil production and raised prices. (See the previous chapter.) Because most Western European countries used imported oil to fuel industries, the higher oil prices caused inflation and slowed economic growth. In 1979, OPEC again raised prices, triggering a severe recession, in which business slowed and unemployment rates rose.

Economic Shifts At the same time, the West faced growing competition from other parts of the world. For 200 years, most manufactured goods came from factories in the West. By the 1980s, that pattern had changed. Japan's industrial economy boomed after World War II. Other countries, such as China and India, also expanded their industries. Western-based multinational corporations set up factories in the developing world, where labor was cheap. From there, they exported goods to the West.

In the West, economies changed. Many factories closed because they could not make goods as cheaply as competing industries did elsewhere. As manufacturing declined in the West, most new jobs were created in service industries. A service industry is one that provides a service rather than a product. Service industries include health care, finance, sales, education, and recreation. The shift from producing goods to services is a key feature of the post-industrial society that emerged in the West after World War II. In a post-industrial society, scientific and technical information dominate.

As economies slowed during the 1970s and 1980s, governments had to cut costs. Some moved away from the welfare state, reducing benefits. Conservative governments privatized state-owned industries. In the new political and economic climate, the gap between rich and poor grew, but most people still enjoyed a relatively high standard of living.

Toward European Unity

Economic cooperation helped Western Europe to recover from World War II. In 1952, six nations—France, West Germany, Belgium, Italy, the Netherlands, and Luxembourg—set up the European Coal and Steel Community. This independent agency set prices and regulated the coal and steel industries of member states. This small start spurred economic growth across Western Europe and led to further regional cooperation.

The Common Market In 1957, the same six nations signed a treaty to form the European Community (EC), or Common Market. Its goal was to expand free trade. The Common Market gradually ended tariffs on goods and allowed workers and capital to move freely across national borders. It

The European Union

In ancient times, the Roman empire united much of Europe politically. During the Middle Ages, many Europeans were joined by a common faith in Christianity. Today, some European nations are looking for a common economic bond through the European Union (EU). The map, the quotations, and the chart present evidence of the EU's efforts.

A Closely Tied European Union—For and Against

For

"[The European Union means that a] great power is being born, one at least as strong commercially, industrially and financially as the United States and Japan."

—French President François Mitterrand, 1991

Against

"We [do not want] a European super-state exercising a new dominance. . . . Europe will be stronger precisely because it has France as France, Spain as Spain, Britain as Britain, each with its own customs, traditions and identity. It would be folly to try to fit them into some sort of identical European personality."

—British Prime Minister Margaret Thatcher, 1988

European Union, 1957–2000

Azimuthal Equal Area Projection

Members by:
1957	1973	1986	2000

Votes in the European Union Council

Member State	Votes	Member State	Votes	Member State	Votes
France	10	Belgium	5	Sweden	4
Germany	10	Greece	5	Denmark	3
Italy	10	Netherlands	5	Finland	3
United Kingdom	10	Portugal	5	Ireland	3
Spain	8	Austria	4	Luxembourg	3

Source: European Union at www.eurunion.org

The Council of the European Union enacts European Union laws. This chart shows how many votes each member nation can cast in that Council.

Skills Assessment

1. Which of the following items pairs an oldest member with a youngest member of the European Union? (oldest/youngest)

   A Portugal/Italy
   B Germany/Sweden
   C France/Luxembourg
   D Greece/Ireland

2. Who are the most powerful members in the Council of the European Union?

   E France, Netherlands, Sweden, Denmark
   F United Kingdom, Belgium, Austria, Ireland
   G Germany, Spain, Portugal, Finland
   H France, Germany, Italy, United Kingdom

3. **Critical Thinking Making Inferences** (a) What do you think led Mitterrand to favor a united Europe? (b) What do you think led Thatcher to oppose the European Union?

Skills Tip

Maps that show change over time often use color coding. Check the map legend and match each color to its year.

Synthesizing Information

Background
About the Evidence

European Union In addition to the Parliament and the Council, the EU has a Council of Ministers, a Commission, a Court of Justice, and a Court of Auditors. Also included is the European Central Bank, which manages the euro and handles monetary affairs. In some ways, the EU is a federal system, in that it has power only in those areas that cannot be managed better at the local or national level. The European Parliament has 626 members who serve five-year terms and who are directly elected by voters in all EU nations. Although it cannot pass laws, it does have veto power over some laws passed by the European Union Council.

Activity
Interpreting the Evidence

Use these additional questions to generate class discussion.

1. **Critical Thinking: Defending a Position** With which position do you agree: Mitterrand's or Thatcher's? Why? (Accept reasonable answers.)

2. **Critical Thinking: Drawing Conclusions** Britain, Denmark, and Sweden have decided not to participate in the common currency (the euro). Why do you suppose they did so? (Possible answers: desire to control their own finances, skepticism about the euro's success, cost of producing new currency)

Skills Tip

Use recent history and the map to determine why EU members are all from Western Europe, not Eastern Europe. The Skills Handbook in the front of the book has a lesson that will help students with this feature.

Skills Assessment

ANSWERS 1. B **2.** H **3. (a)** Mitterrand uses the terms commercially, industrially, and financially; he concentrates on unity as a means to economic gains. **(b)** Since Thatcher fears a European "super-state" and favors European countries maintaining their identities, she favors nationalism.

Human Drama Activity

Saber Rattling or Serious Threat? For years, Soviet and then Russian military policy had been that nuclear weapons would be used only to defend national sovereignty. In mid-January 2000, however, Russia's acting president Vladimir V. Putin announced a change in policy that would allow Russia to make the first strike in a conflict. Some officials believed that this change was a result of frustration on the part of Russia's political and military leaders at their nation's declining clout in world affairs, their concerns that former Soviet satellites had become members of NATO, and worsening relationships between Russia and the West, particularly the United States. Another factor was the weakness and obsolescence of Russia's conventional weaponry. Have students look for a follow-up on this policy change. Is it still in effect? Are Russian military leaders gaining power? Have Russian relations with the United States improved? Have them report their findings to the class.

Background
Historical Evidence

Obstacle to Unity Nationalism is perhaps the main obstacle to European unity. In the 1960s, for example, the problem was resurgent French nationalism. French president Charles de Gaulle was dedicated to resurrecting the greatness and glory of France. Viewing the United States as the major threat to French independence, he removed French forces from the "American-controlled" NATO command. Because he felt that Britain was too closely allied with the United States, he vetoed British membership in the Common Market in 1963 and again in 1967. On several occasions, he forced French policies on the Common Market by refusing French cooperation under any other circumstances.

Migration to Western Europe

Major population movements

Countries attractive to immigrants, with foreign populations

NORWAY 150,000
SWEDEN 490,000
UNITED KINGDOM 1.9 million
DENMARK 160,000
NETH. 760,000
BELG. 920,000
GERMANY 6.7 million
FRANCE 3.6 million
SWITZ. 1.4 million
AUSTRIA 550,000
SPAIN 480,000
ITALY 1 million

North Sea
Baltic Sea
ATLANTIC OCEAN
Black Sea
Mediterranean Sea

Azimuthal Equal Area Projection
0 250 500 Miles
0 250 500 Kilometers

Skills Assessment

Geography In the 1990s, more than two million immigrants a year arrived in Western Europe.

1. **Location** On the map, locate (a) France, (b) Spain, (c) Germany, (d) United Kingdom.
2. **Place** Which three countries had the largest foreign populations?
3. **Critical Thinking** Drawing Conclusions Why did so many people move to Western Europe?

set up the European Parliament, a multinational body elected by citizens of the Common Market countries. Its powers were limited, however, as member states remained independent. Despite disputes between members, the Common Market prospered. In 1973, after much debate, Britain was admitted, along with Denmark and Ireland.

European Union In the 1980s and 1990s, the Common Market expanded further and took the name European Union (EU). By replacing destructive competition with greater cooperation, the EU promoted regional prosperity, peace, and security.

The EU pushed for complete economic unity and greater political unity. It replaced national passports with EU passports and ended most tariffs. In 1999, the EU began launching the euro, a single currency to be used by member nations. EU members welcomed the benefits of cooperation, but nationalist feelings remained strong in individual nations. Thus, a United States of Europe seemed unlikely to emerge any time soon.

Still, the EU was a powerful force, helping Europe compete with economic superpowers like the United States and Japan. With just over 6 percent of the world's population, the EU controlled about 20 percent of world trade. As the 1990s ended, growth of the EU seemed likely as Eastern European countries such as Hungary and the Czech Republic sought admission.

Social Trends

Social change speeded up after 1945 and class lines blurred as prosperity spread. For most of western history, a tiny wealthy class had dominated society. By the 1950s, though, more and more people belonged to the middle class. As wages rose, working-class people bought homes and cars, and

Skills Assessment

ANSWERS 1. Review locations with students. 2. Germany, France, United Kingdom 3. They wanted to enjoy the democracy and economic prosperity that most Western European nations had.

Resource Directory

Teaching Resources
Viewpoint Activity *A Single Currency for Europe?,* Unit 8 booklet, p. 30
Section Quiz Unit 8 booklet, p. 19

Technology
World History Color Transparencies *Europe Today* base map and overlay transparencies, set 7, pp. B–59, B–61, B–63
Interactive Student Tutorial CD-ROM Ch. 33
Computer Test Bank Ch. 33

their children attended universities. Although pockets of poverty remained, most people had opportunities unknown in earlier times.

Ethnic Diversity Since the 1950s, many immigrants from former colonies in Asia, Africa, and the Caribbean had settled in Europe. In Germany and other European countries, "guest workers" from Turkey and the Middle East provided low-wage labor for booming economies. Many Eastern Europeans fled economic hardships to find work in the West.

Some Europeans resented newcomers who competed with them for scarce jobs and brought new cultural influences. As a result, many newcomers faced discrimination and segregation. In a few countries, ultranationalists and racist thugs attacked and even killed foreign workers and immigrants. In 2000, in Austria, members of an anti-immigrant party assumed a leading role in a new coalition government.

Women In 1949, French writer Simone de Beauvoir (boh vwAHR) analyzed the status of women in western society:

> "The two sexes have never shared the world in equality. And even today woman is heavily handicapped, though her situation is beginning to change. Almost nowhere is her legal status the same as man's."
> —Simone de Beauvoir, *The Second Sex*

Since then, women in the West have made progress toward legal and economic equality. A growing number of women worked outside the home. Despite efforts to ensure equality, however, women's pay lagged behind that of men. Women often ran into a "glass ceiling," an invisible barrier that kept them from top jobs. However, women gradually chipped away at old attitudes and narrowed the gender gap in hiring, promotion, and pay. As a woman's income increased, so did her family's standard of living.

Family Life Devotion to family ideals remained strong in the West, but family life changed. Western families had fewer children than in the past. Children stayed in school longer to get needed skills. Family life seemed less stable as the divorce rate climbed. In cases in which a divorced parent failed to fulfill financial responsibilities, children suffered. At the same time, increasing numbers of children were being born to unwed mothers. Often dependent on one income, a growing number of single-parent families found themselves living in poverty.

SECTION 1 Assessment

Recall

1. **Identify:** (a) Berlin Wall, (b) Nuclear Test Ban Treaty, (c) NATO, (d) Common Market, (e) European Union.
2. **Define:** (a) détente, (b) welfare state, (c) recession, (d) service industry, (e) euro.

Comprehension

3. What were two effects of the end of the Cold War?
4. (a) How were western economies affected by growing international competition? (b) How did some governments respond?
5. How did the European Union benefit the economies of its member nations?
6. What social trends affected family life in the West?

Critical Thinking and Writing

7. **Predicting Consequences** Review the Fact Finder chart in this section. Based on the chart statistics, would you expect popular support for the welfare state to increase or decline? Explain.
8. **Connecting to Geography** How did the end of the Cold War change the map of Europe?

Activity

Drawing a Political Cartoon
Draw a political cartoon about one of the social or economic effects of the nuclear arms race. You may focus on the widespread fear that existed, the high costs of weapons production, or another idea.

Chapter 33 **833**

Bell Ringer

Bell Ringer Have students preview this section by studying its pictures and scanning its boldface headings. Ask students to identify and describe one challenge faced by each of the following nations since 1945: (1) Britain, (2) France, (3) Germany.

LESSON PLAN

1. Focus Under the Conservative leadership of Margaret Thatcher, Britain reversed many of its welfare state programs. After a period of ineffective government and colonial wars, Charles de Gaulle began the process of rebuilding French prosperity and power. West Germany experienced an economic miracle, while East Germany languished under communist rule. When Soviet support was removed, the communist rulers of East Germany fell from power and in 1990 Germany was reunited.

2. Instruct After they have read this section, have students write postcards from three different nations in Europe. Tell students to imagine that they are touring each country at a specific time in the 1980s or 1990s. Their postcard messages should describe a social, political, or economic situation of that time. Ask students to also indicate a pertinent picture that might appear on each postcard. For example, a student might create a card with a picture of Belfast and a message about the cease-fire in Northern Ireland.

3. Assess Have students take turns reading their postcards to the class, without identifying the nation from which it was sent. Ask the other students to identify the nation.

4. Reteach If students' Assess activity does not reflect adequate understanding of the lesson, you might assign the *Guide to the Essentials* or the *Interactive Student Tutorial CD-ROM* for this section.

Reading Focus

- How did Britain's policies change after World War II?
- How did French power and prosperity revive?
- How did Germany reunify?
- What problems have other democratic nations faced?

Vocabulary

chancellor
coalition

Taking Notes

Make a table like this partially completed model. As you read, identify main ideas about the Western European democracies and list them in the appropriate boxes.

COUNTRY	GOVERNMENT	ECONOMY
BRITAIN		• Industries nationalized •
FRANCE		
GERMANY		
ITALY		

Main Idea As a result of government policies and international cooperation, the people of Western European democracies have enjoyed freedom and prosperity.

Biography

Margaret Thatcher 1925—

Margaret Thatcher displayed qualities of leadership early in life. Inspired by her father, who was a politically active grocer, she ran errands for the local Conservative party at age 10. During her school years, she was a persistent academic leader and captain of sports teams. Thatcher always devoted much of her energy to her future: "I never went to a dance until I got to university," she later said. After earning an Oxford degree in the field of chemistry, she worked as a research chemist for several years before becoming a tax lawyer, a leading Conservative activist, and the "Iron Lady" prime minister of Great Britain.

Theme: Impact of the Individual How did Thatcher display leadership qualities early in life?

Setting the Scene

Setting the Scene In 1994, an army of bicycles sped through the English countryside, cheered by countless spectators. The event was the famous Tour de France race. The cyclists had crossed from France to England through the new English Channel tunnel, nicknamed Chunnel. For the first time since the ice age, a land route linked Britain and continental Europe.

The Chunnel reflected closer ties among Britain, France, and other European nations. After World War II, the Western European democracies worked within a framework of international cooperation, including NATO, the EU, and the UN. Each nation, however, faced its own problems and made its own contributions to freedom and prosperity.

Britain: Changing Policies

In 1945, British voters put the Labour party in power, hoping that it could help the nation recover from World War II. The war had helped change old attitudes toward the working class. A Labour official noted that if a working-class boy could save England in a fighter plane, "the same brain can be turned to produce a new world."

Rise and Fall of the Welfare State That "new world" gave rise to the welfare state, in which government expanded benefits such as unemployment insurance and old-age pensions. The British government nationalized major industries, built housing for the poor, and provided free or low-cost medical care. To pay for all this, taxes rose tremendously. By the late 1970s, Britain, like the rest of Europe, was reeling under economic hard times.

In 1979, British voters turned to the Conservative party, which denounced the welfare state as costly and inefficient. The Conservatives were led by Margaret Thatcher, who served 11 years as Britain's prime minister. Thatcher's tough determination to carry out her policies earned her the nickname Iron Lady. Stressing individual responsibility, Thatcher's government reduced social welfare programs and returned government-run industries to private control. The changes slowed government spending but did not revive the British economy as much as the Conservatives had hoped. Thatcher retired in 1990, but the Conservatives remained in power.

In 1997, however, the Labour party finally won a majority in Parliament. Tony Blair, the new prime minister, urged government to focus on the needs of all British citizens, not just one segment. He hoped to follow a "third way" between the traditional right and left.

Biography

ANSWER She ran errands for the local Conservative party at age 10, and she was an academic and athletic leader in high school.

Resource Directory

Teaching Resources
Creative Teaching Activities Creative Teaching Activities booklet, p. 147
Guided Reading and Review Unit 8 booklet, p. 20

A New World Role After the war, Britain adjusted to a new role in world affairs. The British empire shrank as colonies won independence. Still, some former colonies preserved their ties to Britain by joining the Commonwealth of Nations.

Weakened by World War II and the loss of empire, Britain gave up global leadership to its ally, the United States. Yet it remained a leader in the UN and NATO. Seeking closer ties with other Western European nations, it joined the Common Market in 1973. In the 1990s, however, British nationalism led some to reject greater European unity. As the European Union issued the euro currency, the British defended the pound. Many British people feared the growing international power of the EU.

Northern Ireland When Ireland won independence in 1922, Britain retained control of six northern counties where there was a Protestant majority. Faced with widespread discrimination, Catholics demanded civil rights and the reunification of Ireland. Protestants wanted to remain part of Britain.

Violence escalated in the 1960s and 1970s as extremists on both sides turned to terrorism. The Irish Republican Army (IRA) attacked Protestants, and Protestant militias targeted Catholics. Britain sent soldiers to keep order in Northern Ireland. But their presence inflamed tensions, especially as they jailed IRA members and violated their civil rights.

Peace talks were held on and off for years. Finally, in 1998, the main political parties signed a peace accord. Enacting the agreement proved difficult. Elections were held for a new government that would bring self-rule to Northern Ireland. But lasting peace and political stability were threatened by sporadic acts of violence and by the IRA's refusal to disarm.

France: Revival and Prosperity

Like Britain, France emerged from World War II greatly weakened. The Fourth Republic, set up in 1946, was ineffective and drew criticism from both communists and conservatives. Bloody colonial wars in Vietnam and Algeria further drained and demoralized France. In Algeria, longtime French settlers and the French military opposed Algerian nationalists who wanted independence for the North African country. France itself was so divided over the issue that civil war threatened.

De Gaulle As the crisis worsened, French voters turned to General Charles de Gaulle, a hero of World War II. In 1958, de Gaulle set up the Fifth Republic. Its constitution gave him, as president, great power. Although a staunch nationalist, de Gaulle realized that France must give up Algeria. In 1962, he made peace with the Algerians. Other French colonies in Africa soon won freedom without bloodshed.

De Gaulle worked hard to restore French prestige and power. He forged new ties with West Germany, ending the long hostility between the two nations. He developed a French nuclear force and challenged American dominance in Europe. He opposed the Cold War stance of the United States by opening talks with communist China and Cuba.

In 1968, youth revolts shook France. The next year, de Gaulle resigned. Although he was widely disliked by the left, he had successfully reasserted French leadership in Europe.

Economic Revival Like Britain, France nationalized some industries and expanded social welfare benefits after World War II. With government help, industry and business modernized, leading to new prosperity by the 1970s.

In the 1980s, French Socialists, led by François Mitterrand, won power just as a global recession hit. At first, Mitterrand tried to nationalize more industries and expand welfare benefits. But when those policies deepened the crisis, he encouraged the growth of private business.

In 1995, his successor, Jacques Chirac, took an even more conservative approach. Chirac cut government spending, despite protests by farmers, students, and others. Over the years, France overcame internal stresses and global economic swings to build the fourth largest economy in the world.

Germany: Division and Reunification

The early years after World War II were a desperate time for Germany. People were starving amid a landscape of destruction. German cities lay in ruins. "Nothing is left in Berlin," wrote an American reporter:

> "There are no homes, no shops, no transportation, no government buildings. Only a few walls. . . . Berlin can now be regarded only as a geographical location heaped with mountainous mounds of debris."
>
> —*New York Herald Tribune,* May 3, 1945

Germany Divided By 1949, the emerging Cold War had divided Germany. West Germany was a member of the western alliance, and East Germany lay in the Soviet orbit. For 40 years, differences between the two Germanys widened. The Soviet Union opposed a unified Germany that might threaten Soviet security.

West Germany's "Economic Miracle" Early in the Cold War, the United States rushed aid to its former enemy. It wanted to strengthen West Germany against communist Eastern Europe. From 1949 to 1963, Konrad Adenauer (AD ehn ow er) was West Germany's chancellor, or chief minister. He guided the rebuilding of cities, factories, and trade. Despite high taxes to pay for the recovery, West Germans created a booming industrial economy. This "economic miracle" raised European fears of a German revival. But West Germany worked closely with France and the United States, and played a key role in NATO and the European Community. This cooperation helped to reduce fear of German strength.

Later West German chancellors came from the Socialist party. West Germany remained a capitalist country, but the government expanded the social welfare benefits.

Virtual Field Trip

www.phschool.com

**The German Information Center
New York, New York**

To learn more about the fall of the Berlin Wall and Germany today, use the Internet address above to link to the German Information Center.

East Germany Under Communism Under communist rule, East Germany's economy stagnated. The Soviet Union exploited East German workers and industry for its own benefit. Still, unemployment was low, and workers had some basic benefits, such as health care, housing, and free education.

Lured by glittering views of life in the West, however, many East Germans fled. As you have read, this mass exodus led to the building of the Berlin Wall in 1961. Overnight, the migration ended. Occasionally, an East German made a dramatic escape. Many died in the attempt.

Reunification In 1969, West German chancellor Willy Brandt tried to ease tensions with communist neighbors to the east. He called his policy Ostpolitik, or "eastern policy." Brandt kept close ties to the West, but signed treaties with the Soviet Union and Poland. He established economic ties to Eastern Europe and signed a treaty of mutual recognition with East Germany. In the midst of the Cold War, however, Brandt's long-term goal of reunifying Germany seemed impossible.

In 1989, as Soviet communism declined, Germany was able to move toward reunification. Without Soviet backing, East German communist leaders were ousted. In Berlin, people from both Germanys clambered up the hated wall and began to tear it down. West German chancellor Helmut Kohl assured both the Soviet Union and the West that a united Germany would pose no threat to peace. In 1990, German voters approved reunification, and Kohl became chancellor of a united Germany.

New Challenges Germans welcomed unity even though it brought some serious problems. Prosperous West Germans had to pay higher taxes to finance the rebuilding of the east. At the same time, East Germans faced a difficult transition to a market economy. As old government-run factories closed, unemployment rose.

Political parties sought ways to deal with the economic troubles. A few right-wing extremists revived Nazi ideology. Seeing the answer to hard times in racism and hatred, these neo-Nazis viciously attacked foreign workers. Most Germans condemned such actions and worked instead to fulfill the hopes of unity. At the end of the 1990s, it seemed that an alliance

Fall of the Berlin Wall
In 1989, Germans celebrated as they tore down the wall that had divided communist East Berlin from democratic West Berlin. The entire nation was reunited soon after the collapse of communism in East Germany.

Theme: Political and Social Systems Who built the Berlin Wall? Why was it built?

**Activity
Connections to Film**

Writing a Diary Assign students to view *The Fall of the Berlin Wall,* an exciting and emotional 1990 documentary about the rise and fall of a famous symbol of the Cold War. Students will learn how the wall was constructed in 1961 to stop the flood of East Germans fleeing to the West. They will join in the celebration of the Wall's demise in 1989. They will see some of the dramatic escapes that occurred between those years—people jumping from buildings into rescue nets, using vehicles to crash through the Wall, tunneling underneath the Wall, and even flying over it in a balloon.

Have students who view the film assume the role of a German citizen of either East or West Berlin between 1949 and 1989. Ask them to write several diary entries for each decade during which Berlin was divided. In their diaries, they should describe the reasons for the Wall's construction, some attempts at escape, their personal feelings about the Wall, and the changing political climate of the 1980s. They should finally describe the joyous celebration that marked the fall of the Wall in 1989. Invite students to read their diaries to the class. (*The Fall of the Berlin Wall,* a 1990 coproduction of Studio Hamburg and WDR, is available through Warner Home Video.) ✳

Human Drama Note

Helmut Kohl As German chancellor from 1982 to 1998, Kohl was respected for his honesty and unpretentiousness. He was viewed as the chief figure in German reunification and was named one of the top 10 Germans ever in many "end-of-the-millennium" polls. Then, early in 2000, he became involved in a scandal over contributions to his party, but he refused to give up his seat in the German parliament.

Test Preparation

Have students read the first paragraph on this page, and then answer the question below.

Which of the following is true of the economic situation in East Germany?

A The economy was closely tied to West Germany's.

B Workers were unhappy over high unemployment.

C People enjoyed some basic welfare benefits.

D The economy produced more than West Germany's.

Caption Answer

The communist East German government had it built. Its purpose was to prevent East Germans from fleeing into West Germany.

SECTION 2 Assessment

Recall

1. **(a)** Margaret Thatcher, p. 834 **(b)** Tony Blair, p. 834 **(c)** IRA, p. 835 **(d)** Charles de Gaulle, p. 836 **(e)** François Mitterand, p. 836 **(f)** Konrad Adenauer, p. 836 **(g)** Helmut Kohl, p. 837 **(h)** neo-Nazis, p. 837 **2. (a)** chancellor, p. 836 **(b)** coalition, p. 838

Comprehension

3. They privatized industries, curbed the power of labor unions, and reduced social welfare programs. **4. (a)** He forged new ties to West Germany, developed a French nuclear force, and opened talks with communist nations such as China and Cuba. **(b)** He cut government spending. **5.** After the Soviet Union removed its support, the East German government collapsed. The German people then voted for reunification. **6.** Possible answers: regional economic differences divided the country; political divisions caused by lack of majority for any one party; corruption and financial scandals; inability to curb the Mafia

Critical Thinking and Writing

7. Students who agree could cite German aggression in World War I and World War II. Students who disagree could point to the record of West German democracy since World War II. **8.** Possible answer: Wars there had drained and demoralized France, and the French were so divided on the issue of Algerian independence that the nation was threatened with civil war.

Activity Rubrics

Share rubrics with students before they write their summaries.

Attempted The summary is incomplete because it does not include or adequately explain three points of view.

Minimal The summary shows limited understanding of the three points of view but is poorly written and organized.

Adequate The summary shows good understanding of the three points of view and is well written and organized.

Exemplary The summary shows thorough understanding of the three points of view and is very well written and organized.

---

of moderate political elements would lead Germany toward a prosperous period of social reform and economic growth.

Other Democratic Nations

Other parts of Western Europe slowly recovered from the war. The Scandinavian countries of Norway, Sweden, and Denmark created extensive socialist welfare programs. By the 1990s, rising costs revived debate about how much people were willing to pay for the welfare state. Yet many people saw these social programs as essential to a democratic society.

Italy In Italy, long-term regional differences continued to divide the country. In the urban north, industries rebuilt and prospered after World War II. In the rural south, the largely peasant population remained much poorer.

Political divisions also led to instability. Since no one political party could win a lasting majority, Italy experienced one coalition government after another. A coalition is a temporary alliance of political parties. Corruption and financial scandals added to the instability. Meanwhile, the Mafia, a violent criminal syndicate, defied government efforts to end its power, especially in the south. Despite these problems, Italy made impressive economic gains and ranked as a leading industrial nation.

Spain, Portugal, and Greece Change came slowly to other countries of southern Europe. In 1945, Spain, Portugal, and Greece were economically undeveloped with large peasant populations. In Spain and Portugal, dictators clung to power for decades.

Finally, in the 1970s, both Spain's Francisco Franco and Portugal's Antonio de Oliveira Salazar died. Their authoritarian governments soon collapsed. Both countries adopted democratic governments and eventually joined NATO and the EU. Their economies have grown rapidly.

Greece faced difficult obstacles on its path to democratic rule. After World War II, the Greek government needed American aid to defeat communist rebels. Then, in 1967, military rulers came to power. A crisis emerged in 1974, when the government supported an attempt to bring Cyprus under Greek rule. Cyprus is a Mediterranean island inhabited by Greeks and Turks. The incident brought Greece and Turkey to the brink of war and led to the downfall of the military regime. Cyprus was divided into two zones, one ruled by Greeks and the other ruled by Turks. In 1975, Greece returned to democratic rule.

SECTION 2 Assessment

Recall

1. **Identify:** **(a)** Margaret Thatcher, **(b)** Tony Blair, **(c)** IRA, **(d)** Charles de Gaulle, **(e)** François Mitterrand, **(f)** Konrad Adenauer, **(g)** Helmut Kohl, **(h)** neo-Nazis.
2. **Define:** **(a)** chancellor, **(b)** coalition.

Comprehension

3. What changes were introduced in Britain by Thatcher and the Conservative party?
4. **(a)** How did de Gaulle revive French power? **(b)** How did Chirac affect the French economy?

5. Why was Germany finally able to reunify?
6. Describe one problem that has troubled Italy in recent years.

Critical Thinking and Writing

7. **Defending a Position** Some people, especially in France, worried that a reunited Germany would pose a danger to Europe. Using historical evidence, explain why you agree or disagree.
8. **Making Inferences** Why did President de Gaulle decide that France had to give up Algeria?

Activity
Take It to the NET

Search online newspapers and magazines for recent articles on peace efforts in Northern Ireland. Print three articles—one from a United States source, one from an Irish source, and a third from a British source. Write a summary in which you point out how the three sources agree and disagree.

838 Chapter 33

Resource Directory

Teaching Resources

Section Quiz Unit 8 booklet, p. 21
Creative Teaching Activities Creative Teaching Activities booklet, p. 148
Guided Reading and Review Unit 8 booklet, p. 22

Technology

Interactive Student Tutorial CD-ROM Ch. 33
Computer Test Bank Ch. 33

SECTION 3 North American Prosperity

Reading Focus

- What actions has the United States taken as a global superpower?

- What developments have shaped the economy, government, and society of the United States?

- What issues has Canada faced in recent years?

Vocabulary

deficit
surplus
civil rights movement
segregation
separatism

Taking Notes

Copy this partially completed chart. As you read, list major ideas concerning the foreign policy, economy, and society of the United States since World War II.

UNITED STATES SINCE 1945		
Foreign Policy	**Economy**	**Society**
• Cold War with Soviet Union	•	• Minorities faced segregation
•	•	•

Main Idea Since the 1940s, the United States has asserted its role as a global superpower, promoted economic prosperity, and extended civil rights.

Setting the Scene In 1961, John F. Kennedy was sworn in as president of the United States. He proclaimed to the world:

> "Let every nation know that we shall pay any price, bear any burden, meet any hardship, support any friend, oppose any foe to assure the survival and the success of liberty."
> —John F. Kennedy, Inaugural Address

Kennedy's vow reflected a commitment to contain communism and promote democracy. During the postwar era, the United States also moved to extend civil rights and boost economic prosperity at home. To the north, meanwhile, Canada carved out its own world role.

The United States: A Global Superpower

During the Cold War, the United States used its vast economic and military resources to protect its interests and the security of the free, or noncommunist, world. In 1945, the United States was the world's greatest military power and the only country that possessed the atomic bomb. Yet it felt threatened by communist expansion, especially after the Soviet Union developed its own atomic bomb.

Global Commitments The United States built bases overseas and organized military alliances from Europe to Southeast Asia. Its fleets patrolled the world's oceans, and its air power provided protection for its allies.

As another way to contain communism, the United States provided economic aid to help Europe rebuild and to assist emerging nations. At times, American aid went to nations that were ruled by anti-communist dictators. Yet presidents such as Jimmy Carter pressed these countries to end human rights abuses.

Korea and Vietnam In 1950, the Korean War began in East Asia when communist North Korean forces invaded noncommunist South Korea. American troops made up the majority of a UN force sent to protect South Korea. During that war, anti-communist fears rose in the United States. Extremists such as Senator Joseph McCarthy charged that many Americans harbored communist sympathies.

By the early 1960s, the United States had become involved in Vietnam. Like Korea, this Southeast Asian nation was divided into a communist northern state and a noncommunist southern state. To prevent communist

Air and Sea Power
United States air and sea power has played a significant role in conflicts and peacekeeping missions around the world. The aircraft carrier *Philippine Sea*, shown above, saw action in the Korean War.

Theme: Global Interaction
Why did the United States become involved in the Korean War?

SECTION 3

🔔 **Bell Ringer** Invite a volunteer to read to the class the words of John F. Kennedy quoted on this page. Ask students whether they think these words characterize the policies of the United States government today. Encourage students to give reasons for their opinions. You may wish to return to this question after students have finished Section 3.

LESSON PLAN

1. Focus After World War II, the United States assumed the role of protecting the free world and stopping the spread of communism. As the economy prospered, the government pursued bold new programs to help the poor and disadvantaged. The civil rights movement brought progress for African Americans, Hispanics, Native Americans, women, and other groups. Canada, meanwhile, experienced economic growth, a rising tide of immigration, and increasing separatism among French-speaking Canadians.

2. Instruct Divide the class into five groups. Assign each group to work together to outline the main ideas of one of the subsections in Section 3. When they have finished this part of the lesson, ask a representative of each group to use the outline to give an oral presentation to the class. Encourage other students to ask questions about the topic. All group members should help answer these questions. Questions that the group cannot answer should be written down and saved. Continue in this way until all five subsections have been covered.

3. Assess Have each group use library resources to find information on the questions that they were unable to answer. Have them report their findings to the class.

4. Reteach If students' Assess activity does not reflect adequate understanding of the lesson, you might assign the *Guide to the Essentials* or the *Interactive Student Tutorial CD-ROM* for this section.

Caption Answer

to protect noncommunist South Korea from the invading communist North Korea

---

📖 **Block Scheduling Support**

British poet W. H. Auden satirizes western society's emphasis on materialism in his poem "The Unknown Citizen," written as an obituary to an unknown "hero." In the poem, a government official recounts the citizen's life by listing the statistics by which the man was known to society. While records of his life include the number of cars he owned, children he had, places he worked, and union dues he paid, questions of freedom and happiness are considered "absurd." Society is uninterested in his personal emotions; instead, his importance is measured in concrete terms of money and numbers.

Have students read "The Unknown Citizen," which may be found in various anthologies of British literature and poetry or on the Internet. Then, divide the class into groups to answer the following questions: (1) Why is the citizen considered a modern "hero"? (2) What values of modern western society does the poem satirize? (3) How is the title "The Unknown Citizen" ironic? When the groups have finished, bring them together to discuss their answers.

A National Investment In 1944, the United States Congress enacted the GI Bill of Rights to provide aid to returning veterans. The act provided billions of dollars to help veterans pay for a home, start a business, or get a higher education. For many, the GI Bill is an example of a government program that worked. It provided assistance to millions of veterans and ultimately made a net profit for the government. While the bill cost the government a total investment of $14.5 billion, it more than paid for itself in the income taxes that successful veterans paid to the government over their lifetimes.

Connections to Today

Social Security

The Social Security system of the United States began in the midst of the Great Depression during the presidency of Franklin D. Roosevelt. It provided for old-age assistance, unemployment insurance, and aid for dependent children.

Today, the Social Security system faces an uncertain future. Its funding is strained by the rising costs of benefits. One reason for increasing expenditures is that the population of older Americans who receive Social Security benefits is becoming a larger and larger percentage of the United States population.

Government leaders disagree on what to do. Some think that benefits need to be cut and taxes increased. Another idea is increasing the retirement age. Some recommend that, instead of paying Social Security taxes, people be allowed to save for retirement themselves by investing in stocks and bonds.

Theme: Continuity and Change Why are government leaders thinking about changing the Social Security system?

---

rebels from winning power in South Vietnam, Presidents Kennedy and Johnson sent economic and military aid plus a growing number of American troops. Soon, American forces there numbered half a million.

The Vietnam War led to bitter divisions among Americans. Many opposed supporting an unpopular government in South Vietnam. Antiwar protests spread from college campuses to city streets. In 1968, Richard Nixon was elected president with a promise to end American involvement in Vietnam. By 1974, Nixon finally negotiated an American withdrawal. Still, the divisions that had built up during the war took years to heal.

The Only Superpower After the Soviet Union collapsed, the United States was the world's only superpower. As conflicts erupted in various regions, it tried to resolve some of them. In 1991, it led a multinational force against Iraqi invaders of Kuwait. Along with its NATO allies, it provided peacekeeping forces to end bloody civil wars in Bosnia and Kosovo. In 2001, the nation faced a deadly new challenge after terrorists used hijacked airplanes to attack New York and Washington, D.C. President Bush vowed to wage war on terrorism, but rooting out diverse terrorist groups would be difficult.

Economy and Government

By the early 1950s, the American economy was booming. Unlike Europe, the United States emerged from World War II with its cities and industries undamaged. American factories quickly shifted from producing tanks and bombers to meeting the peacetime demand for cars and refrigerators.

The United States and the Global Economy In the postwar decades, American businesses expanded into markets around the globe. The United States profited greatly from the growing global economy. But interdependence also brought problems. In the 1970s, OPEC price hikes fed inflation and showed how much Americans relied on imported oil. Inflation also contributed to the Third World debt crisis, which involved American banks.

American industries faced stiff competition from Asian and other nations. Like Western Europe, the United States lost manufacturing jobs to the developing world. Some American corporations even moved operations to Mexico or Asia to take advantage of lower wages.

Wider Role for Government In the United States, as in Western Europe, the government's role in the economy grew. Under President Harry Truman, Congress created generous benefits that helped veterans attend college or buy homes. Other Truman programs expanded FDR's New Deal, providing greater Social Security benefits for the elderly and poor.

Truman's successor, Dwight Eisenhower, tried to reduce the government's role in the economy. At the same time, he approved government funding to build a vast interstate highway system. This program spurred the growth of auto, trucking, and related industries. Highways and home construction changed the face of the nation. As middle-class Americans moved out of cities to booming suburbs, urban neighborhoods declined.

During the 1960s, the government expanded social programs to help the poor and disadvantaged. Urged on by Presidents Kennedy and Johnson and other leaders of the Democratic party, Congress funded Medicare, providing health care for the elderly. Other programs offered job training and housing for the poor. Many Americans came to rely on these programs.

The Conservative Response In the 1980s, conservatives challenged costly social programs and the growth of government. Like Margaret Thatcher in Britain, President Ronald Reagan and the Republican party called for cutbacks in government spending on social programs. Congress ended some welfare programs, reduced government regulation of the economy, and cut taxes. At the same time, however, military spending increased.

Connections to Today

ANSWER The aging of the population has placed unprecedented financial stresses on the Social Security system.

Resource Directory

Teaching Resources
Skill Application Activity *Planning a Multimedia Presentation,* Unit 8 booklet, p. 31

The combination of government spending and tax cuts greatly increased the national budget deficit, the gap between what a government spends and what it takes in through taxes and other resources. To deal with the deficit, conservatives pushed for deeper cuts in social and economic programs, including education, welfare, and environmental protection.

Into the New Century In the 1990s, however, the American economy rebounded, producing record economic growth, full employment, a sky-rocketing stock market, and growing budget surpluses in Washington. A budget surplus is the amount of money left over after expenditures.

Americans entered the new century enjoying peace, prosperity, and unrivaled military power. Yet problems remained. The costs of medical care and social security were growing. So, too, until late in the decade was the gap between the nation's richest and poorest. To many, moral standards also seemed to be declining, a problem vividly illustrated by the impeachment of President Bill Clinton for personal misconduct while in office.

The turn of the century saw a decline in the stock market and growing fears of an impending recession. The terrorist attack on the World Trade Center and the Pentagon and its economic impact worried Americans. The nation rallied, however, to meet the challenge of terrorism.

Civil Rights and Society

During the 1950s and 1960s, many social changes took place. Some were linked to the civil rights movement that set out to end discrimination and ensure equal rights for all Americans.

Segregation and Discrimination Although slavery was abolished a century before, many states denied equality to various minority groups. They faced legal segregation, or separation, in education and housing. Minorities also suffered discrimination in jobs and voting. After World War II, President Truman desegregated the armed forces. Then, in 1954, the Supreme Court made a landmark ruling in *Brown* v. *Board of Education of Topeka*, declaring that segregated schools were unconstitutional.

Progress and Problems By 1956, a gifted preacher, Dr. Martin Luther King, Jr., emerged as a leader of the civil rights movement. Inspired by Gandhi's civil disobedience in India, King organized boycotts and led peaceful marches throughout the 1960s to end segregation in the United States. In 1963, at a huge civil rights rally in the nation's capital, King made a stirring speech. "I have a dream," he proclaimed, "that one day this nation will rise up and live out the true meaning of its creed: 'We hold these truths to be self-evident, that all men are created equal.'"

Americans of all races joined the civil rights movement, and their courage in the face of sometimes brutal attacks stirred the nation's conscience. Congress outlawed segregation in public accommodations, protected the rights of black voters, and required equal access to housing and jobs. Despite this, racial prejudice survived and poverty and unemployment still plagued many urban African Americans. Yet others won elected offices or gained top jobs in business and the military.

Other groups—such as Asians, Latinos, Native Americans, and women—also campaigned for equality. Civil rights laws banned discrimination based on gender as well as on race in hiring and promotion. More women were elected to political office, and many made progress toward higher salaries and positions in business.

Immigration In the years around 2000, the United States remained a magnet for immigrants, most of them from Latin America and Asia. The newcomers were met by tough laws that prohibited illegal entry into the country and restricted benefits to legal immigrants. Many new Americans, however, brought labor power and valuable skills to their new home.

Chapter 33 **841**

Biography

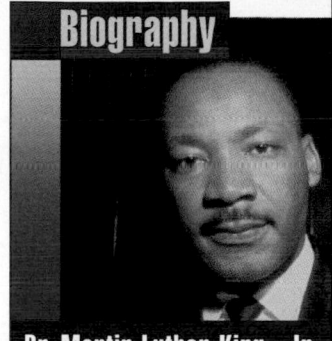

Dr. Martin Luther King, Jr.
1929–1968

In 1964, the year after his "I have a dream" speech, Martin Luther King, Jr., was awarded the Nobel Peace Prize for his civil rights work. He accepted the prize on behalf of the entire movement. After winning the prize, King continued his struggle to make his "dream" come true.

King led a massive drive to register African American voters in the South in 1965 and was thrown into a Selma, Alabama, jail for his efforts. He began a "Poor People's Campaign" to get help for the poor of all races—and received threats on his life. Even so, on the night of April 3, 1968, he could still say, "I'm not worried about anything. I'm not fearing any man." But he did have cause for fear. On the next day, in Memphis, Tennessee, Dr. King was killed by an assassin's bullet.

Theme: Impact of the Individual Why do you think King was such an effective leader in the civil rights movement?

Recall

1. (a) John F. Kennedy, p. 839 **(b)** Richard Nixon, p. 840 **(c)** Social Security, p. 840 **(d)** Medicare, p. 840 **(e)** Ronald Reagan, p. 840 **(f)** *Brown* v. *Board of Education of Topeka,* p. 841 **(g)** Martin Luther King, Jr., p. 841 **(h)** Quebec, p. 842 **2. (a)** deficit, p. 841 **(b)** surplus, p. 841 **(c)** civil rights movement, p. 841 **(d)** segregation, p. 841 **(e)** separatism, p. 842

Comprehension

3. The United States has used economic and military resources to protect its interests and the security of the noncommunist world and to help resolve international conflicts. **4. (a)** During the 1980s, the government cut spending on social programs, reduced government regulation of the economy, and cut taxes. However, increased military spending created a larger budget deficit. In the 1990s, military spending was cut back, and the economy grew and produced a budget surplus. **(b)** It created greater employment opportunities for minorities. **5.** Possible answer: defining a national identity, handling the impact of the United States

Critical Thinking and Writing

6. One similarity: they share a goal of preserving their cultural identities. One difference: minorities in the United States are not seeking to establish a separate, independent nation. **7.** Possible answer: Forced segregation has ended. African Americans and other groups enjoy wider opportunities, including equal access to housing and jobs.

Activity Rubrics

Share rubrics with students before they write their biographies.

Attempted The biography is very sketchy or has no illustrations.

Minimal The biography has only a brief account of Dr. King's life, is poorly written and organized, or has sparse illustrations.

Adequate The biography clearly outlines Dr. King's life, is well written, and has some illustrations.

Exemplary The biography is a detailed summary of Dr. King's life, is very well written, and is visually appealing.

Caption Answer

to protect their "distinct society" and culture

Quebec Separatism

Some French Canadians have urged that Quebec separate from the rest of Canada. Several times, they have come close to succeeding. Shown here are separatist buttons and French Canadians waving the blue-and-white flag of Quebec.

Theme: Diversity Why have some Quebeckers favored separatism?

Canada

After gaining independence, Canada charted its own course but still maintained links with Britain through the Commonwealth of Nations. Canada sided with the Allies in both world wars and became a member of NATO. Through diplomacy, Canada often worked to ease Cold War tensions. Its troops served in UN peacekeeping missions around the world.

Economic Growth Canada is a leading democratic and industrial power. It had a postwar economic boom, due in part to oil and gas deposits found in the western provinces. In 1959, Canada and the United States completed the St. Lawrence Seaway. It opened the Great Lakes to oceangoing ships and linked the interiors of both countries to the Atlantic Ocean.

With a population only a tenth that of the United States, Canada has encouraged immigration. Since the 1950s, Canada's population has grown increasingly diverse, with newcomers from Europe, Asia, Africa, Latin America, and the Caribbean.

Quebec Separatism Defining a national identity has remained a challenge for Canada. Quebec's French-speaking people saw themselves as a "distinct society." To protect their culture, Quebec demanded more autonomy within Canada.

Government leaders tried hard to meet those demands. But other provinces resisted any solutions that gave Quebec special treatment. Some Canadians favored separatism. They said that Quebec should separate from Canada and become an independent nation. In the 1990s, Quebec's future remained a subject of heated debate.

United States Influence Another challenge for Canada has been the immense impact of the United States. Although the two nations enjoyed close ties, many Canadians resented their neighbor's cultural domination. Economic competition led to disputes over trade and tariffs. To resolve issues of economic competition, the countries set up the North American Free Trade Association (NAFTA). It created a free trade zone between Canada, the United States, and Mexico.

Other issues between Canada and the United States concerned the environment. Chemical pollution from American smokestacks, for example, contributed to acid rain that fell on northeastern Canada. The two nations agreed to work together for a common solution.

Recall

1. Identify: (a) John F. Kennedy, **(b)** Richard Nixon, **(c)** social security, **(d)** Medicare, **(e)** Ronald Reagan, **(f)** *Brown* v. *Board of Education of Topeka,* **(g)** Martin Luther King, Jr., **(h)** Quebec.
2. Define: (a) deficit, **(b)** surplus, **(c)** civil rights movement, **(d)** segregation, **(e)** separatism.

Comprehension

3. What goals has the United States tried to achieve as a global superpower?
4. (a) How did government policies affect the American economy in the 1980s and 1990s? **(b)** How did the civil rights movement affect the economy?
5. What challenges have Canadians faced?

Critical Thinking and Writing

6. Comparing How is the situation of French-speaking Canadians similar to or different from that of minority groups within the United States?
7. Linking Past and Present Describe three ways the civil rights movement helped shape American life today.

Activity
Take It to the NET

On the Internet, find sites that specialize in biographies. From these and other sites, gather information and photographs about the life of Martin Luther King, Jr. Use the information and images to create a brief illustrated biography of King.

Resource Directory

Teaching Resources

History Through Literature *Cat's Eye,* History Through Literature booklet, pp. 68–69
Section Quiz Unit 8 booklet, p. 23
Creative Teaching Activities Creative Teaching Activities booklet, p. 149
Guided Reading and Review Unit 8 booklet, p. 24

Technology

Interactive Student Tutorial CD-ROM Ch. 33
Computer Test Bank Ch. 33
Listening to Literature World Masterpieces audiotapes *I Am Goya,* side 10, running time 2:04 min.; *Visit* and *Weddings,* side 10, running time 5:28 min.

The Soviet Union: Rise and Fall of a Superpower

Reading Focus

- What ideas guided Soviet political, economic, and foreign policy?
- Why did the Soviet Union collapse?
- What problems have Russia and the other republics faced since the fall of the Soviet Union?

Vocabulary

dissident
glasnost
perestroika
default

Taking Notes

Copy the before-and-after chart at right. As you read, write key facts about conditions before and after the collapse of the Soviet Union in the appropriate columns.

COLLAPSE OF THE SOVIET UNION

Before	After
• Cold War with the United States	• Attempts to cooperate with the United States
•	•
•	•

Main Idea After years of Communist rule, the Soviet Union collapsed and was replaced by Russia and other independent republics.

Setting the Scene

"We shall bury you," Soviet leader Nikita Khrushchev (KROOSH chawf) told the West during the Cold War. He later explained that his statement was not a military threat, as many westerners believed. Instead, he said, it was a reference to his belief that capitalism was doomed and that Soviet communism was the wave of the future.

Khrushchev's prediction did not come true. In fact, it was Soviet communism that was doomed. In the 1980s, the Soviet economy began to crumble. Efforts at reform led the Soviet empire to disintegration.

Soviet Government and Economy

After World War II, the Soviet Union emerged as a superpower. Under Stalin, it established a sphere of influence from the Baltic to the Balkans.

Victory, however, brought few rewards to the Soviet people. Stalin continued his ruthless policies. He filled slave labor camps with "enemies of the state" and seemed ready to launch new purges when he died in 1953.

Stalin's Successors Nikita Khrushchev emerged as the new Soviet leader. In 1956, he shocked top Communist party members when he publicly denounced Stalin's abuse of power. Khrushchev then pursued a policy of de-Stalinization. He did not change Soviet goals but did free many political prisoners and eased censorship. He sought a thaw in the Cold War, calling for a "peaceful coexistence" with the West.

The thaw had limits, though. When discontented Hungarians revolted against communist rule in 1956, Khrushchev sent tanks in to smash them. When critics at home grew too bold, he clamped down. It appeared that a return to Stalinism could happen at any time.

Khrushchev's successor, Leonid Brezhnev (BREHSH nehf) held power from the mid-1960s until he died in

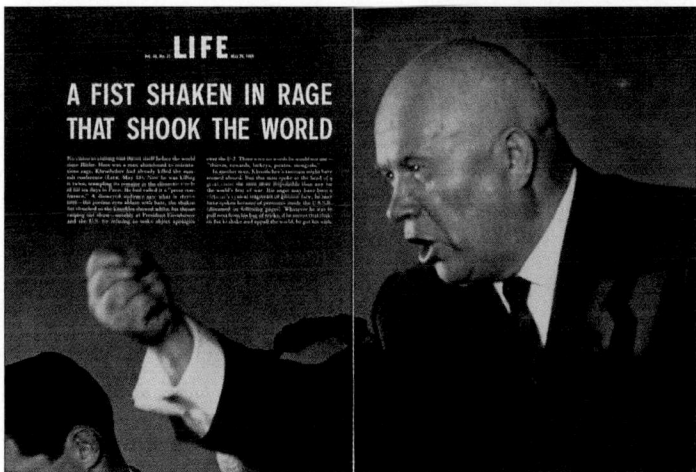

Khrushchev at the UN
Soviet leader Khrushchev was known for strong responses to the West. In 1960 at the UN, he emphasized a point by shaking his fist. *Life* magazine captured the moment and the feeling.

Theme: Global Interaction How did events in Europe cause the Cold War to heat up?

LIFE

A FIST SHAKEN IN RAGE THAT SHOOK THE WORLD

Chapter 33 **843**

Block Scheduling Support

Have students use text and atlas maps to create a map showing the 15 countries created out of the former Soviet Union. Then have them use almanacs to create a chart listing the name of each nation, its capital, population, and one interesting fact. Have students use these facts to sketch out a fictional travel brochure about one of these new countries. You may wish to display these brochures around the classroom.

SECTION 4

Bell Ringer Have students preview this section by studying the Section Assessment questions. Ask them to use the questions to write three generalizations about the historical content of Section 4. After they finish studying the section, assign them to review and revise their generalizations.

LESSON PLAN

1. Focus Stalin's successors eased some of his most repressive policies but continued to support communist dictatorship and military intervention in other nations. The Soviet economy enjoyed some success in industries connected to the military or to space exploration. However, severe problems existed in such areas as agriculture and the production of consumer goods. Gorbachev's revolutionary policies hastened the collapse of the Soviet Union and the birth of many new nations.

2. Instruct Ask students to imagine that they are Russians who were born sometime before World War II. They have witnessed and experienced all of the following: (1) the Cold War, (2) political oppression and dictatorship, (3) the failures of the Soviet economy, (4) the rise of Gorbachev and the collapse of the Soviet Union, and (5) the struggles of new nations to rise from the Soviet Union's ashes. Ask students to compose a diary in which they write at least one paragraph about each of the above topics. They should report historical events and how those events affected them. Invite students to read parts of their diaries to the class.

3. Assess Ask students to use what they have learned in this section to make up an interesting research assignment about the rise or fall of the Soviet Union. Encourage students to complete the assignment.

4. Reteach If students' **Assess** activity does not reflect adequate understanding of the lesson, you might assign the *Guide to the Essentials* or the *Interactive Student Tutorial CD-ROM* for this section.

Caption Answer

The Soviet crackdown on resistance in Eastern Europe, on dissidents at home, and the building of the Berlin Wall all brought strong responses from the West.

Economic Chaos A. G. Aganbegyan, an adviser to Mikhail Gorbachev, shared the following story as an example of the bureaucratic blundering that crippled the Soviet Union:

"I need wire. Some 9 months before I need the wire I submit a request at the respective office for material-technical supplies. That office sends my request to Moscow to the main Metal Administration. There someone looks at a list of the appropriate industrial enterprises and picks out the plant that can produce such wire. That enterprise gets an order which, however, is not final. I get the order sent to me. With Moscow's confirmation of it I go to the factory that produces that wire, a factory that may be located on the other side of the street from where I am."

You may wish to use the above excerpt as the basis for a class discussion on the economic problems of the Soviet Union.

Primary Source

Long Lines in the Soviet Command Economy
In the 1970s, Robert Kaiser lived and worked in Moscow as a reporter for the Washington Post. *He witnessed a noteworthy and frustrating result of the Soviet command economy—very long lines:*

"A good shopper will jump into a queue [line] wherever he or she finds it, taking a place and then asking what is being offered for sale at the other end. . . .

The queue is [everywhere] in Soviet life, and it comes in many forms. The queue to buy a private car may be five years long. . . . Mothers will spend an entire day at the Children's World department store hoping to buy an aluminum sled for winter. At the neighborhood bread store, three lines are not uncommon: one to make a selection, another to pay the cashier, a third to exchange the cashier's receipt for the chosen loaf."

—Robert G. Kaiser,
Russia From the Inside

Skills Assessment
Primary Source Why do you think waiting lines for goods were so long in the Soviet Union?

1982. Brezhnev rigorously suppressed dissidents, people who spoke out against the government. Critics faced arrest and imprisonment. Some were locked away in insane asylums, a policy once used by czarist Russia.

Some Successes After World War II, the Soviet Union had rebuilt its shattered industries, using factories and equipment stripped from Germany. As in the 1930s, priority was given to industries such as steel, coal, and heavy machinery. The government also poured resources into weapons, science, and technology. In 1957, the Soviets launched *Sputnik I,* the first artificial satellite to orbit the Earth. *Sputnik* was a propaganda victory for the Soviet Union because it suggested technological superiority over the United States.

The Soviets also claimed other successes. Citizens enjoyed benefits such as low rents, cheap bread, free health care, and day care for children. Although wages were low, unemployment was almost nonexistent.

Failure of the Command Economy In general, however, the Soviet economy was plagued by severe problems. Collectivized agriculture remained so unproductive that the Soviet Union frequently had to import grain to feed its people. Nor could the Soviet command economy match the free-market economies of the West in producing consumer goods. Soviet shoes, suits, and television sets were far inferior to those made in the West, and luxuries like clothes washers or automobiles remained rare. People spent many hours of their lives waiting in line to buy food and other goods.

Low output was the result of inefficiencies in central economic planning. A huge bureaucracy, rather than supply and demand, decided what to produce, how much, and for whom. Government planners in Moscow often had little knowledge of the local conditions. Sometimes, factories were forced to shut down because needed supplies never arrived. At the local level, workers set out to meet production quotas, regardless of quality. Because workers had lifetime job security, they had little incentive to produce better-quality goods.

Foreign Policy Issues
Stalin and his successors forcefully asserted Soviet control over Eastern Europe. In 1955, Khrushchev set up the Warsaw Pact, in theory to defend the communist bloc against NATO. In practice, it was used to suppress dissent within Eastern Europe.

The Developing World Both the Soviet Union and the United States sought allies among the developing nations. One way to win and keep allies was to offer military and economic aid. At times, this policy turned local conflicts into Cold War confrontations. In two bitter wars, Soviet-backed governments in North Korea and North Vietnam battled against American-backed governments in South Korea and South Vietnam.

Rivalry With the United States Soviet-American relations swung back and forth between confrontation and détente. In 1961, the building of the Berlin Wall increased Cold War tensions. A year later, Khrushchev tried to build nuclear missile bases in Cuba. That move triggered the dangerous Cuban missile crisis, which you will read about in a later chapter. The crisis brought the two superpowers to the brink of war.

Brezhnev invested in a huge military buildup. In the Brezhnev Doctrine, he asserted that the Soviet Union had a right to intervene militarily in any Warsaw Pact nation. At the same time, however, he also pursued détente and disarmament with the United States.

Détente came to an abrupt end in 1979, after the Soviets invaded Afghanistan to ensure Soviet influence in that neighboring nation. Like the Vietnam War for the United States, the Afghan War drained the Soviet economy and provoked a crisis in morale at home.

Primary Source
ANSWER because goods were scarce

Teaching Resources
Disaster! Chapter Extension Activities booklet, p. 80

MELTDOWN AT CHERNOBYL

In the early morning hours of April 26, 1986, disaster struck near the Ukrainian city of Prypyat. A full-scale nuclear meltdown had taken place in Reactor No. 4 of the Chernobyl nuclear power plant. The meltdown triggered a fire that released radiation-laden gas and dust particles. Countless civilians were contaminated by the radiation.

Radiation Warning Sign

These two children from Kiev, 65 miles southeast of Chernobyl, are being tested for radiation levels. Right now in the Ukraine, Belarus, and Russia, unusually high numbers of children suffer from thyroid cancer. Even children born after the accident are at risk.

The area surrounding the Chernobyl nuclear power plant was the worst hit by radiation, but much of the Northern Hemisphere was affected, as well.

The once thriving city of Prypyat is now a ghost town. People living within a 20-mile radius of the plant were evacuated immediately after the accident. The plant and surrounding area are now fenced, and it is still unsafe for humans to live there. Still, with nowhere else to go, hundreds of people have returned to their homes in Prypyat, despite the danger of contamination.

Radiation Levels

BELORUSSIAN S.S.R.

Dnieper R.
Savichi
Chernobyl Nuclear Power Plant — Prypyat
Cooling Pond — Chernobyl
Prypyat R.
Teterev R.
Ivankov
Dymer
Kiev Reservoir
Desna R.
UKRAINIAN S.S.R.

N W E S

0 10 Miles
0 10 Kilometers

Kiev

Initial evacuation zone
Severe radiation area
Most severe radiation area

Portfolio Assessment

INTERNET

Nuclear power is only one alternative form of energy. Using the Internet or library resources, learn more about other energy sources. Create a diagram or model that describes and illustrates how one new alternative energy source works.

Chapter 33 **845**

Bell Ringer Ask students to explain the dangers of radioactivity. If necessary, point out that effects range from immediate death to premature death from leukemia-like symptoms to mutations in offspring.

Background
Connections to Today

Recent Problems The United States has had its share of nuclear accidents, too. The best-known is probably the one at Three-Mile Island near Harrisburg, Pennsylvania, in 1979, but there have been many other accidents and near misses. In February 1993, for example, a New Jersey reactor had to be shut down manually when its automatic shutdown systems failed. Shutdown was achieved only 90 seconds before disaster.

In September 1999, a serious accident in Tokaimura, Japan, contaminated a large area. According to a Greenpeace energy specialist, the plant "had the safety standards of a bakery and not a nuclear facility. It was just a normal building."

Activity
Cooperative Learning

Conducting Research Organize the class into small groups to research and report on topics related to the feature. Possibilities include the arguments for and against the use of nuclear power, effects of radiation on animals and plants, and problems associated with storage and transport of nuclear materials or with disposal of nuclear wastes. Have groups present their reports to the class.

Portfolio Assessment Rubrics

Share rubrics with students before they create their diagrams or models.

Attempted The diagram or model is incomplete or unclear.

Minimal The diagram or model contains key elements but is poorly constructed.

Adequate The diagram or model clearly shows how the energy source works. A brief written explanation accompanies it.

Exemplary The diagram or model clearly shows how the energy source works and is accompanied by a well-written explanation.

Primary Sources and Literature

See "Mikhail Gorbachev: Perestroika" in the Reference Section at the back of this book.

Biography

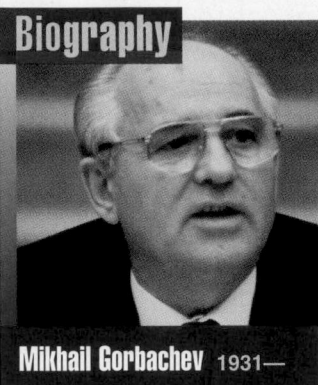

Mikhail Gorbachev 1931—

Before he led the Soviet Union, Mikhail Gorbachev knew hard times. He was born to a Russian family of peasant farmers. For a time, his mother kept him home from school because he had no shoes.

After falling from leadership, Gorbachev met hard times again. He lost some $80,000 in a Russian bank crisis. To earn money, he made a television commercial for a chain of pizza restaurants. In 1998, few Russians came to a press conference announcing his new book.

Many Russians blamed Gorbachev for their nation's troubles, charging that he had changed the Soviet Union without a plan or goal. In a 1999 interview, Gorbachev rejected the charge. "We had a concept," he said. "Give up the totalitarianism. Lead society to freedom: political, ideological, and religious pluralism. Economic freedom, too. . . . But when such developments get under way, no one can predict specifically what it will lead to."

Theme: Impact of the Individual Did Gorbachev achieve his goals? Explain.

Collapse of the Soviet Empire

In 1985, an energetic new leader, Mikhail Gorbachev, came to power in the Soviet Union. As the war in Afghanistan dragged on, Gorbachev was eager to bring about reforms. The changes he unloosed, however, soon spiraled out of control.

The Gorbachev Revolution In foreign policy, Gorbachev sought an end to costly Cold War tensions. He renounced the Brezhnev Doctrine, signed arms control treaties with the United States, and eventually pulled Soviet troops out of Afghanistan.

At home, Gorbachev launched a two-pronged effort at reform. First, he called for glasnost, or openness. He ended censorship and encouraged people to openly discuss the country's problems. Second, he urged perestroika (pehr uh STROI kuh), which meant the restructuring of the government and economy. He hoped that he could boost efficiency by reducing the size and complexity of the government bureaucracy. He backed some free-market ideas, including limited private enterprise, but he still wanted to keep the essence of communism.

Gorbachev wanted the Soviet economy to produce more and higher-quality consumer goods. To achieve this goal, factory managers, instead of central planners, were made responsible for decisions. To increase food supplies, farmers were allowed more land on which to grow food that they could sell on the free market.

Unexpected Results Gorbachev's reforms brought economic turmoil. Shortages grew worse and prices soared. Factories that could not survive without government help closed, leading to high unemployment. The reforms were denounced by old-line Communists and bureaucrats whose jobs were threatened. At the same time, other critics, like the popular Russian leader Boris Yeltsin, demanded even more radical changes.

Problems increased as glasnost fed unrest in the multinational Soviet empire. The Baltic republics of Estonia, Latvia, and Lithuania, which had been seized in 1940, regained full independence in 1991. In Eastern Europe, countries from Poland and East Germany to Romania and Bulgaria broke out of the Soviet orbit.

In response, hard-liners tried to overthrow Gorbachev and restore the old order. Their attempted coup failed, but it further weakened Gorbachev. In 1991, as more Soviet republics declared independence, Gorbachev resigned as president. After 74 years the Soviet Union ceased to exist.

The Russian Republic

Russia, the largest Soviet republic in size and population, had dominated the Soviet Union since its creation. After the breakup of the Soviet Union, Russia and its president, Boris Yeltsin, faced a difficult future.

Economic Problems To solve Russia's economic problems and gain western aid, Yeltsin privatized more state-run industries and collective farms. The changeover to a market economy was painful. Unemployment soared. Without government controls, prices skyrocketed. Older people on pensions were especially hard hit. Unlike East Germany, which got massive aid from West Germany, Russia got relatively little aid from the West.

Despite these difficulties, some Russians prospered in the new economy. Their success, however, fanned resentment among poorer Russians. Meanwhile, criminals flourished, and ruthless gangs preyed on the new business class.

In 1998, Russia barely avoided financial collapse when it defaulted, or failed to make payments, on much of its foreign debt. The value of Russia's currency, the ruble, collapsed. The economy survived, but many

Biography

ANSWER Students may note that despite all its problems, Russia has survived so far as a democratic nation.

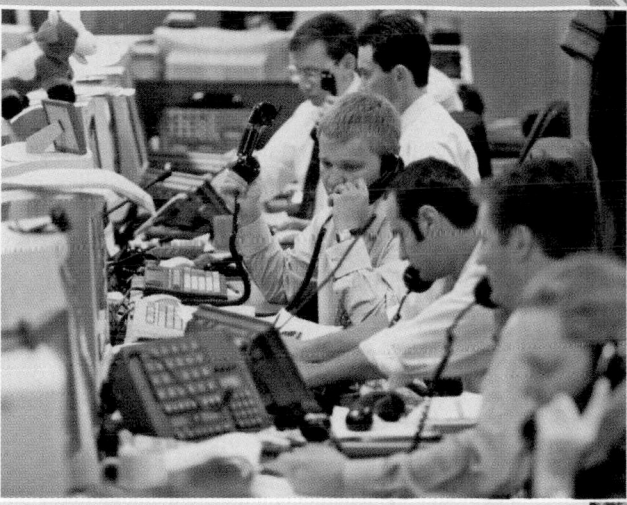

Reading Strategy
Check Comprehension

Write the following questions on the board: What was the main idea of this section? What did I already know about the postwar Soviet Union? What did I learn? What still puzzles me? What did I enjoy or dislike during my reading? Have students write for at least five minutes in response to these questions. Ask volunteers to share their written comments with the class. *(Less Advanced Readers)*

banks and businesses closed. People lost their savings and jobs. In time, a few industries began to recover, but experts predicted further problems. Yeltsin's failure to solve the crisis and frequent change of top officials fed uncertainty and unrest.

Further troubles arose when minorities within Russia sought greater autonomy or independence. In 1994, Yeltsin failed in his brutal attempt to crush a revolt in Chechnya, a region in the Caucasus Mountains. That region was home to a variety of ethnic and religious groups, including Muslims. In 1999, fighting between Russian troops and rebel forces again raged in Chechnya. At the same time, a wave of terrorist violence broke out in Moscow. By early 2000, Russian troops had gained the upper hand and the Muslim rebels were in retreat.

The future of democracy in Russia remained uncertain as politicians— from former communists to ultranationalists—jockeyed for position. In 1999, moderates made a strong showing in parliamentary elections. That same year, Boris Yeltsin resigned and Vladimir Putin, a veteran of the Soviet secret police, became acting president. In the presidential election of 2000, Putin was elected president through the first free elections in Russia's history.

Putin in Charge Many Russians thought Vladimir Putin would improve conditions. He brought Russia success in the humiliating war with the secessionist province of Chechnya, hope of a more orderly and less corrupt government, and some degree of economic improvement. He also projected a toughness and strength that Russians have traditionally admired in their leaders.

Some, however, felt that Putin, because of his former ties to the secret police, was not strongly committed to democracy. Critics worried about his muffling of critical journalists and his treatment of minority nationalities. Still, President Putin dealt as an equal with foreign leaders, a welcome relief to Russians after their steep international decline in the preceding decade. There was a sense of "someone in charge here" in Putin's Russia, as well as a feeling of economic and even political progress as the new century got underway.

Russia's Free-Market Economy
Since the collapse of communism, Russia has been struggling to make the difficult transition from a command economy to a free-market economy. Shown here are busy Russian stockbrokers and a Russian shopping mall.

Theme: Economics and Technology How is a free-market economy different from a command economy?

✓ Test Preparation

Have students read the section entitled "Putin in Charge" on this page and answer the question below.

Which of the following was a concern of some Russians about Vladimir Putin?

A He failed them in the war with Chechnya.

B He seemed weak as a leader.

C He was in an inferior position to foreign leaders.

(D) He wanted to silence journalists who criticized him.

Caption Answer

A free-market economy is directed by the decisions of individuals and factors such as supply and demand. A command economy is under state control and is directed by the decisions of leaders in government.

Recall

1. (a) Nikita Khrushchev, p. 843
(b) Afghan War, p. 844 **(c)** Mikhail Gorbachev, p. 846 **(d)** Boris Yeltsin, p. 846
(e) Chechnya, p. 847 **(f)** Vladmir Putin, p. 847
2. (a) dissident, p. 844 **(b)** glasnost, p. 846
(c) perestroika, p. 846 **(d)** default, p. 846

Comprehension

3. (a) The Soviet command economy was unable to match the free-market economies of the West in producing consumer goods, resulting in low output and inferior products. Factories lacking supplies sometimes had to shut down.
(b) huge and costly military buildup that drained resources from other areas of the economy **4.** Gorbachev's policies of perestroika and glasnost led to economic turmoil and multinational unrest. **5.** Possible answers: soaring unemployment and prices, rising crime rate, gang activity, bank and business failures, political division, ethnic conflict

Critical Thinking and Writing

6. Possible answer: The party would probably replace democracy and free-market reforms with a return to communism. **7.** Those in favor of investment may argue that, without it, these nations might again become dictatorships. Those who oppose the idea may argue that the investment might be lost.

Activity Rubrics

Share rubrics with students before they write their protest letters.

Attempted The letter is incomplete.

Minimal The letter shows little understanding of the issues involved, is poorly written and organized, and fails to convey a strong message.

Adequate The letter shows good understanding of the issues involved, is well written and organized, and conveys a strong message.

Exemplary The letter shows thorough understanding of the issues involved, is very well written and organized, and conveys a strong message.

Skills Assessment

ANSWER Possible answers: low output of crops and consumer goods, food and fuel shortages

---

Cause and Effect

Long-Term Causes	Immediate Causes
• Low output of crops and consumer goods • Cold War led to high military spending • Ethnic and nationalist movements • Denial of rights and freedoms	• War with Afghanistan • Food and fuel shortages • Demonstrations in the Baltic states • Gorbachev's rise to power

Collapse of the Soviet Union

Effects

• Soviet Union breaks up into 15 republics
• Russian republic approves a new constitution
• Changeover to market economy in Russia
• Cold War ends
• War in Chechnya

Connections to Today

• New republics struggle to achieve democratic reforms
• Difficulties adjusting to a free-market economy
• Increased danger of ethnic and religious conflict

Skills Assessment **Chart** It will be many years before the long-term effects of the fall of the Soviet Union are fully understood. **What was one economic cause of the fall of the Soviet Union?**

A World Power Even though Russia was no longer considered a superpower, it still exercised influence around the world. It retained a large military force and a nuclear arsenal. Western nations hoped that Russia might work to resolve global problems.

At times, relations between Russia and Eastern Europe were strained. Eastern European nations were alarmed when Russian nationalists urged Russia to reassert its power. Russia was unhappy when some of its former Warsaw Pact allies joined NATO. It saw such moves as a threat to its security.

The Other Republics

Like Russia, the other former Soviet republics wanted to build stable governments and improve their economies. They, too, faced unrest, corruption, and political divisions. In some countries, authoritarian rulers gained power. Ethnic conflict erupted in republics with a mix of national groups. Other conflicts arose over border disputes. Armenia, for example, seized a piece of neighboring Azerbaijan, where many Armenians lived. The republic of Georgia survived a bloody civil war.

These new nations endured hard times as they switched to market economies. With help from the UN, the World Bank, and the International Monetary Fund (IMF), the new nations worked to increase trade with the rest of the world. The republics of Ukraine, Kazakhstan, and Belarus gave up the nuclear weapons on their soil in return for trading privileges or investments from the West.

SECTION 4 Assessment

Recall

1. Identify: (a) Nikita Khrushchev, **(b)** Afghan War, **(c)** Mikhail Gorbachev, **(d)** Boris Yeltsin, **(e)** Chechnya, **(f)** Vladimir Putin.
2. Define: (a) dissident, **(b)** glasnost, **(c)** perestroika, **(d)** default.

Comprehension

3. What were the effects of each of the following Soviet policies: **(a)** command economy, **(b)** rivalry with the United States?
4. How did Gorbachev's reforms contribute to the collapse of the Soviet Union?

5. Describe two problems that have afflicted Russia and the other new republics since the breakup of the Soviet Union.

Critical Thinking and Writing

6. Predicting Consequences What do you think might happen in Russia if the Communist party won control of the government again?
7. Making Decisions Do you think the western democracies should invest large sums of money in Russia and other former Soviet republics? Why or why not?

Activity

Writing a Protest Letter
Write a letter to the leaders of the Russian republic in which you protest Russia's policy toward Chechnya. In your letter, demonstrate that you understand the issues involved, make your position clear, and offer reasons as to why Russian officials should change their policy.

848 Chapter 33

Resource Directory

Teaching Resources

Section Quiz Unit 8 booklet, p. 25
Creative Teaching Activities Creative Teaching Activities booklet, p. 150
Guided Reading and Review Unit 8 booklet, p. 26

Technology

Interactive Student Tutorial CD-ROM Ch. 33
Computer Test Bank Ch. 33

SECTION 5 A New Era in Eastern Europe

Reading Focus

- How did Eastern European nations oppose Soviet domination and strive for democracy?
- What were the effects of the fall of communism?
- What were the causes and effects of civil war in Yugoslavia?

Vocabulary

ethnic cleansing

war crime

Taking Notes

As you read, make a chart showing how the end of Soviet domination affected the countries of Eastern Europe. Use this partially completed chart as a model. Add as many countries as possible to the chart.

END OF SOVIET DOMINATION

Poland	East Germany	Romania	
•Solidarity legalized	•Berlin Wall toppled	• •	• •

Main Idea After years of Soviet domination, the countries of Eastern Europe were free of Russian control, facing new and sometimes difficult challenges.

Setting the Scene

For centuries, Eastern Europe lived in the shadow of larger powers. Before World War I, much of the region was divided among the German, Russian, Austrian, and Ottoman empires. Many small nations gained independence in 1919, only to be overrun by Germany in World War II. After the war, the region fell under Soviet domination.

Finally, in 1989, Eastern European nations again won their freedom. Vaclav Havel, a playwright and president of the Czech Republic, saw independence as a challenge. To him, it was not "just a state of being" but a "complex task." Independence, he noted, should benefit all citizens and be something worth fighting for and defending.

Under Soviet Domination

In 1945, as World War II ended, Soviet armies occupied much of Eastern Europe. By the end of the 1940s, most countries in the region were ruled by local Communist parties. Backed by Soviet power, they destroyed rival parties, silenced critics, and campaigned against religion. As in the Soviet Union, Communist leaders in Eastern Europe ended private ownership of businesses and turned to central economic planning. Because the countries of Eastern Europe were held in the orbit of the more powerful Soviet Union, they became known as satellites, or client states.

Unrest In the 1950s, the Soviet Union tightened its grip on its satellites. Stalin forced them to sell natural resources on terms favorable to the Soviet Union and to provide troops and money to support the Warsaw Pact. Soviet troops were stationed throughout Eastern Europe.

Yet in East Germany, Poland, Hungary, and elsewhere, unrest simmered. Despite some economic progress, many people despised the communist monopoly on power. Nationalists resented Russian domination.

Resistance and Repression In 1956, Imre Nagy (NOJ), a communist reformer and strong nationalist, gained power in Hungary. He ended one-party rule and withdrew Hungary from the Warsaw Pact. Khrushchev responded with force. Hungarian "freedom fighters" resisted Soviet

Primary Sources and Literature

See "Vaclav Havel: New Year's Address" in the Reference Section at the back of this book.

FACT FINDER

Soviet Domination of Eastern Europe

1945	After World War II, Soviet armies occupy much of Eastern Europe.
1949	Most Eastern European countries are under communist rule.
1956	Hungary withdraws from Warsaw Pact and ends one-party rule; Soviet troops crush Hungarian uprising.
1968	Czechoslovakia introduces reforms; Soviets use force to restore communist dictatorship.
1980	Polish government, under Soviet pressure, cracks down on trade union movement and arrests its leaders.

Skills Assessment

Graph The Soviet Union dominated Eastern Europe from 1945 through the 1980s. **How did World War II lead to the establishment of communism in most of Eastern Europe?**

Bell Ringer Before assigning this section, have students review the nations of Eastern Europe on a map. Discuss the location of each and its physical relationship to the Soviet Union and Western Europe.

LESSON PLAN

1. Focus After World War II, the Soviet military occupied much of Eastern Europe. Backed by the Russians, the local Communist parties took over, silencing critics and censoring the press. Economic hardships touched off rebellions in these nations and by late 1989 a "democracy movement" had taken place. Strong nationalism among groups in some countries resulted in civil wars after the downfall of communism.

2. Instruct Divide the class into cooperative groups. Assign each group one of the following rebellions to dramatize: the 1956 "Freedom Fighters" in Hungary; Alexander Dubček's reforms in Czechoslovakia; Lech Walesa and the Solidarity movement in Poland. Suggest that students use library or Internet resources to find additional information about their subjects. Have each group plan and prepare a script, assign roles, and rehearse their dramatizations before presenting them to the class.

3. Assess Ask students to speculate on the future of the nations in Eastern Europe. Which ones are stable? Which ones seem particularly troubled? Why?

4. Reteach If students' **Assess** activity does not reflect adequate understanding of the lesson, you might assign the *Guide to the Essentials* or the *Interactive Student Tutorial CD-ROM* for this section.

Block Scheduling Support

Assign students to draw two political cartoons about Eastern Europe in the late 1980s and 1990s, expressing two very different viewpoints. One cartoon should celebrate the end of communism, freedom from domination by the Soviet Union, or the birth of democratic rights and freedoms. The second cartoon should express discontent about unemployment, inflation, crime, ethnic violence, or other problems that have emerged since the end of communism. Have students display their pairs of cartoons around the classroom. ✳

Skills Assessment

ANSWER At the end of World War II, Soviet troops occupied most of the countries of Eastern Europe. Soviet forces influenced political developments in the region.

Tito After World War II, Tito gained control of Yugoslavia's government by having his chief rival, the anticommunist general Draza Mihajlovic, killed and by forcing the king to abdicate. Once in power, he organized a secret police force that eliminated any potential opposition. Tito then implemented his own brand of communism, which emphasized the idea that workers should manage their own factories. Although he was an authoritarian ruler, Tito did bring peace, security, and moderate prosperity to Yugoslavia, but it lasted only as long as Tito lived. He died in 1980.

Global Connections

The Enduring Impact of Pope John Paul II

This picture shows Lech Walesa holding a portrait of Pope John Paul II. Walesa knew how important the pope had been in helping to end communism in Poland. So did Soviet leader Mikhail Gorbachev, who said "Everything that happened in Eastern Europe in these last few years would have been impossible without the presence of this pope."

John Paul II was well known for his political activism. During World War II, before becoming a Catholic priest, Karol Wojtyla helped Polish Jews escape the Nazis. After he was elected pope in 1978, he visited well over 100 nations around the world. Wherever he went, he was outspoken. He was a vocal critic of communist dictatorship and other abuses of human rights. In a 1995 address to the UN, Pope John Paul II made a plea to leaders around the world. "The human person," he said, "must be the true focus of all social, political, and economic activity."

Theme: Global Interaction
What do you think was the meaning of the pope's speech at the UN?

▶ Primary Sources and Literature

See "Lech Walesa: Nobel Peace Prize Lecture" in the Reference Section at the back of this book.

tanks and troops, and called on the West for help. None came. Thousands died in the fighting, and Nagy was executed.

A dozen years later, Alexander Dubçek introduced liberal reforms in Czechoslovakia. He called for "socialism with a human face." Once again, the Soviets responded with force. Warsaw Pact troops ousted Dubçek and restored a communist dictatorship. As you have read, under the Brezhnev Doctrine, the Soviet Union claimed the right to intervene in the affairs of any Eastern European nation.

Yugoslavia's Independent Path Soviet power did not extend to Yugoslavia. During World War II, a fierce guerrilla leader, Josip Tito, had battled German occupying forces. Later, Tito set up a communist government in Yugoslavia, but he pursued a path independent of Moscow. He refused to join the Warsaw Pact and claimed to be neutral in the Cold War.

Poland's Road to Democracy

Poland was the Soviet Union's most troublesome satellite. Like Hungarians and Czechs, Poles wanted greater freedom within the Soviet bloc. Stalin had clamped down hard on Poland, but communist persecution of the Roman Catholic Church backfired. The Church became a rallying point for Poles opposed to the regime. In 1956, economic woes touched off riots and strikes. To end the turmoil, the Polish government made some reforms. Dissatisfaction with communism, however, would continue to surface.

Solidarity In 1980, economic hardships ignited strikes by shipyard workers. Led by Lech Walesa (vah LEHN sah), they organized Solidarity, an independent trade union. It won millions of members and demanded political change. Under pressure from the Soviet Union, the Polish government outlawed the union and arrested its leaders, including Walesa.

Still, unrest simmered. Walesa became a national hero. Pressure from the world community further strained the communist government. Pope John Paul II visited Poland in 1979, met with Solidarity leaders, and criticized communist policies. The pope was the former Karol Wojtyla, archbishop of the Polish city of Cracow.

Peaceful Transition In the late 1980s, Gorbachev declared he would not interfere in Eastern Europe. By then, Poland was introducing radical economic reforms similar to Gorbachev's changes in the Soviet Union. It also legalized Solidarity and, in 1989, held the first free elections in 50 years. Solidarity candidates triumphed. A year later, Lech Walesa was elected president of Poland. The new government began a difficult, but peaceful, transition from a planned to a market economy.

Fall of Communist Governments

By late 1989, a "democracy movement" was sweeping through Eastern Europe. Everywhere, people took to the streets, demanding reform. One by one, communist governments fell. A dissident writer and human rights activist, Vaclav Havel, was elected president of Czechoslovakia. The Berlin Wall was toppled and Germany was reunited. Most changes came peacefully. Only Romania's brutal longtime dictator, Nicolae Ceausescu (chah SHEHS koo), refused to step down. He was overthrown and executed.

For the first time since 1945, Eastern European countries were free to settle their own affairs. They withdrew from the Warsaw Pact and requested that Soviet troops leave. By then, Soviet power itself was crumbling.

Global Connections

ANSWER Possible answer: that governments and other institutions need to do what is best for the people, not what is best for the institution

Resource Directory

Teaching Resources
Biography Activity *Vaclav Havel,* Unit 8 booklet, p. 28
Technology
World History Color Transparencies *Europe Today,* base map and overlay transparencies, set 7, pp. B–59, B–61, B–63

New Challenges Like Russia and the former Soviet republics, Eastern European nations set out to build stable governments and free-market economies. Although the experiences of each nation differed, all faced similar challenges. Governments privatized industries and stopped keeping prices for basic goods and services artificially low. As in Russia, the many changes contributed to rising inflation, high unemployment, and crime waves. Consumer goods were certainly more plentiful, but many people could not afford to pay the high prices for them.

By the mid-1990s, some people were disillusioned with reform. As a result, former communists gained seats in some national parliaments. However, after initial hardships, the outlook began to brighten in Hungary, Poland, the Czech Republic, and other Eastern European countries.

In the 1990s, Eastern European nations looked to the West for aid, and many hoped to join the European Union and NATO. At first, Russia was opposed to NATO's expansion. Even so, Poland, Hungary, and the Czech Republic became members of the military alliance in 1999. Other Eastern European nations were expected to join NATO at a later date. As memory of the Cold War faded, Eastern and Western Europe moved closer together.

Ethnic Tensions Centuries of migration and conquest left most Eastern European countries with ethnically diverse populations. Most countries had a majority population, along with one or more ethnic minorities. Nationalism helped unite countries like Poland and Hungary, but it worked as a divisive force elsewhere. Hungarians in Romania demanded autonomy. Faced with ethnic tensions, Czechoslovakia peacefully split into two countries, the Czech Republic and Slovakia. In the 1990s, ethnic conflict tore Yugoslavia apart in a long civil war.

Civil War in Yugoslavia

Yugoslavia was created after World War I as a homeland for the South Slavs. It consisted of various republics—Serbia, Croatia, Bosnia and Herzegovina, Macedonia, Slovenia, and Montenegro. Yugoslavia's ethnic and religious groups included Serbs, who were Orthodox Christians; Croats, who were Roman Catholics; and Bosnians, who were Muslims. The groups had distinct customs and religions, but all spoke the same language, Serbo-Croatian. The Serbs dominated the multinational state.

Budapest, Hungary
In 1956, Soviet troops and tanks rolled through the streets of Budapest, crushing the freedom fighters of the Hungarian uprising (PAST). Today, the people of Budapest live in a nation with a democratic government and a free-market economy (PRESENT).

Theme: Continuity and Change Why was Hungary finally able to free itself from Soviet domination?

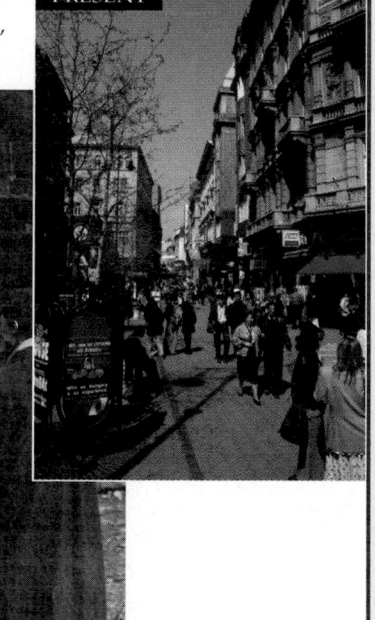

⊕ Human Drama Activity

Analyzing Literature Read the quotation below to the class.

"Today a shell fell on the park in front of my house, the park where I used to play and sit with my girl-friends. A lot of people were hurt. . . . AND NINA IS DEAD. A piece of shrapnel lodged in her brain and she died. She was such a nice, sweet girl."

Explain that these words came from the diary of an 11-year-old Yugoslavian on May 7, 1992. Then explain that one of the moving stories to come out of the breakup of Yugoslavia is that of Zlata Filipovic, who recorded her experiences as a young girl in war-torn Sarajevo in the book *Zlata's Diary* (Penguin Books, 1995). Have students read the book and choose one issue that she raises (such as the issue of why people are fighting one another because of their ethnic background) and respond to it as Zlata's mother or father might have responded.

Caption Answer

As a result of Gorbachev's leadership in the Soviet Union, Soviet forces were no longer used to prevent movements for independence and democracy.

Activity
Cooperative Learning

Solving a Problem In 1995, the United Nations proposed a peace plan that called for the partitioning of Bosnia. Fifty-one percent of Bosnia would be granted to the Bosnian government and its ally Croatia. The remaining 49 percent would be given to the Bosnian Serbs. The plan was accepted by Bosnia, Croatia, and Serbia. The Bosnian Serbs, who had gained control of about 70 percent of Bosnia during the war, at first refused to accept it. Not until December 1995 did all parties sign the treaty.

Divide the class into groups of four or five students and ask each group to come up with a proposal for bringing peace to this region. Encourage the groups to develop a list of arguments to support their plans. Then, have a classroom discussion in which each group presents its plan and the class tries to reach a consensus on the best plan to use.

New Nations in Eastern Europe

Former territory of
- Czechoslovakia
- Soviet Union
- East Germany
- Yugoslavia

Skills Assessment

Geography By the end of the 1990s, many nations in Eastern Europe had become newly independent.

1. **Location** On the map, locate (a) Latvia, (b) Ukraine, (c) Georgia, (d) Czech Republic, (e) Slovenia.
2. **Region** What three Baltic nations won independence from the Soviet Union?
3. **Critical Thinking** Comparing *Yugoslavia and the Soviet Union were multinational states. How does that help to explain what happened to both nations in the 1990s?*

Breakup For decades following World War II, Tito ruled Yugoslavia with an iron hand. He jailed critics and silenced nationalist and religious unrest. However, soon after his death and the fall of communism, nationalism tore Yugoslavia apart. The ruling Serbs tried in vain to keep the multinational state together and to hold onto power. In 1991, Slovenia declared independence. Croatia, Macedonia, and Bosnia-Herzegovina soon followed. Yugoslavia was left with only Serbia and Montenegro.

Fighting in Bosnia In Bosnia, civil war erupted among Muslims, Serbs, and Croats. Bosnian Serbs fought to set up their own autonomous regions. They received money and arms from Yugoslav president Slobodan Milosevic, an extreme Serb nationalist. The Muslims, who were the majority group in Bosnia, did not want the country divided into ethnic regions.

During the war, all sides committed atrocities. In a vicious campaign of ethnic cleansing, Serbs killed people of other ethnic groups or forcibly removed them from the areas they held. Tens of thousands of Bosnian Muslims were brutalized or killed, sometimes in mass executions. Muslim fighters committed acts of revenge. Innocent people were caught in the crossfire, and streams of refugees fled the war zones. To many, Serb efforts at ethnic cleansing recalled the horrors of Nazi Germany and the Holocaust.

The UN, NATO powers, and Russia all tried to bring about peace. Finally, in 1995, NATO launched air strikes against the Bosnian Serb military. Under that pressure, the warring parties began peace talks. Guided by the United States, Bosnia, Croatia, and Serbia signed the Dayton Accords, a series of peace agreements. International forces monitored the peace, but implementing the agreements was often difficult in the face of bitter feelings among the hostile groups.

852 Chapter 33

Skills Assessment

ANSWERS 1. Review locations with students. 2. Estonia, Latvia, Lithuania 3. Both the Soviet Union and Yugoslavia broke up as various nationalities established independent states.

Resource Directory

Teaching Resources
Primary Source Activity *A Family in Sarajevo*, Unit 8 booklet, p. 29
Section Quiz Unit 8 booklet, p. 27
Geography Quiz Unit 8 booklet, p. 32
Chapter Test Forms A, B, and C Unit 8 booklet, pp. 33–37
Answer Key Unit 8 booklet, pp. 110–125

Technology
World History Color Transparencies political cartoon about ways to encourage harmony, p. E–49

World History Visions, Voices, Views Daily Life CloseUp, *Children of War: Young People of Bosnia,* videodisc side 4 or videotape 8, running time 3:00 min.

Side 4: Fr. 28274-33825

Interactive Student Tutorial CD-ROM Ch. 33
Computer Test Bank Ch. 33

Fighting in Kosovo As Bosnia reached a tense peace, a new crisis rose in the Yugoslav province of Kosovo, a historic part of Serbia. Over the centuries, many ethnic Albanians, mostly Muslim, had settled in Kosovo. By the 1990s, they made up about 90 percent of the population. The rest of the population were mostly Serbs.

In 1989, President Milosevic ended the limited self-rule that Muslims in Kosovo had long enjoyed in Yugoslavia. Protests by Muslim Kosovars led to repression, and a small Kosovo Liberation Army waged guerrilla war against the Serbs.

Milosevic began ethnic cleansing in Kosovo as he had in Bosnia. When UN and NATO demands for a negotiated settlement failed, NATO launched air strikes against Serbia. As reports of Serbian massacres of Albanian Kosovars spread, hundreds of thousands fled.

Yugoslavia finally withdrew its forces from Kosovo, and NATO peace-keepers moved in, along with returning refugees. The international force had to help Kosovars organize a government and rebuild homes and factories while preventing ethnic Albanians from taking revenge on Serbs.

In Serbia, opposition to Milosevic's policies grew, which led to a military defeat, international condemnation, and the breakup of Yugoslavia. In 2000, mass political opposition toppled Milosevic and replaced him with the more democratic if still strongly nationalistic Vojislav Kostunica.

Although peace was restored, the Balkan region remained unstable. New nations needed massive aid to rebuild. Large numbers of refugees remained in temporary shelters for years after the fighting ended. And ethnic feuds, once unleashed, were hard to contain.

Looking Ahead

Bosnia and Kosovo were test cases for NATO in the post–Cold War world. In Bosnia, the United States and its European allies were hesitant to intervene militarily. In Kosovo, they took action more quickly.

During the Balkan conflicts, an international court charged Milosevic and others with war crimes for violating rules of war that forbid atrocities such as the mass killings of prisoners or civilians. When captured, they faced trial and possible punishment. To some, the interventions, the punishment of war crimes, and the widespread condemnation of human rights abuses suggested that a new era of international cooperation was emerging.

SECTION 5 Assessment

Recall
1. **Identify:** (a) satellites, (b) Imre Nagy, (c) Alexander Dubçek, (d) Josip Tito, (e) Lech Walesa, (f) Pope John Paul II, (g) Vaclav Havel, (h) Slobodan Milosevic.
2. **Define:** (a) ethnic cleansing, (b) war crime.

Comprehension
3. (a) How did Hungarians resist Soviet domination? (b) How did democracy emerge in Poland?
4. Why were some Eastern Europeans unhappy with the changes that came after the fall of communism?
5. Why did civil war break out in Yugoslavia?

Critical Thinking and Writing
6. **Analyzing Primary Sources** Mikhail Gorbachev said, "Everything that happened in Eastern Europe in these last few years would have been impossible without the presence of this pope." Explain the meaning of Gorbachev's words.
7. **Asking Questions** Suppose you are a journalist interviewing a Serb official. Make a list of questions about recent events in Yugoslavia.

Activity

Preparing a Dialogue
With a classmate, prepare a dialogue between two people in an Eastern European nation. Discuss the changes that have occurred in the country and the outlook for the future. Present your dialogue before the class.

Test Preparation

Have students look at the map "New Nations in Eastern Europe" on the opposite page, and then answer the question below.

Which of the following was once part of Yugoslavia?

(A) Croatia

B Slovakia

C Belarus

D Latvia

Recall
1. (a) satellites, p. 849 (b) Imre Nagy, p. 849 (c) Alexander Dubçek, p. 850 (d) Josip Tito, p. 850 (e) Lech Walesa, p. 850 (f) Pope John Paul II, p. 850 (g) Vaclav Havel, p. 850 (h) Slobodan Milosevic, p. 852 2. (a) ethnic cleansing, p. 852 (b) war crime, p. 853

Comprehension
3. (a) In 1956, Imre Nagy came to power and ended one-party rule and withdrew Hungary from the Warsaw Pact. When Moscow responded with force, Hungarian freedom fighters resisted but were overcome. (b) Poland had always been a rebellious satellite, but in 1980, economic hardships ignited strikes by shipyard workers, who formed an independent union called Solidarity. Although it was outlawed and its leaders arrested, unrest continued. Finally, with Gorbachev's policy of noninterference, Poland was able to make the transition to democracy and a market economy. 4. New freedoms have brought new problems, such as inflation, high unemployment, and crime waves. 5. Yugoslavia was a multinational state including Serbs, Croats, Muslims, and other ethnic groups. Each group had distinct customs and religions. When communist dictatorship was removed, nationalism swept the country, and it broke up into several smaller nations. The various nations and ethnic groups fought over disputed borders and religious or cultural practices.

Critical Thinking and Writing
6. He meant that Pope John Paul II had been an active and influential opponent of communist dictatorships and human rights abuses. 7. Students' questions should reflect a knowledge of recent events in Yugoslavia.

Activity Rubrics

Share rubrics with students before they present their dialogues.

Attempted The dialogue is poorly prepared and contains many factual errors.

Minimal The dialogue shows little understanding of conditions in Eastern Europe.

Adequate The dialogue is well prepared and informative about conditions in Eastern Europe.

Exemplary The dialogue is well prepared and presents strong, insightful information about life in Eastern Europe.

Creating a Chapter Summary

As a reteaching opportunity, pair a more able student with a less able student to complete this chapter summary.

Possible entries above the time line:
1954—*Brown* v. *Board of Education;* 1957—European Community (EC) founded; 1958—de Gaulle sets up Fifth Republic in France; 1959—St. Lawrence Seaway completed; 1961—Berlin Wall built; 1969—Brandt launches *Ostpolitik;* 1973—oil crisis; 1979—Thatcher becomes prime minister in United Kingdom; 1980s—Reagan follows conservative policies; 1990—Germany reunified; 1999—euro first issued
Possible entries below the time line:
1956—Hungarian rebellion suppressed; 1968—Soviet tanks crush revolt in Czechoslovakia; 1980—Solidarity forms in Poland; 1985—Gorbachev takes power in Soviet Union; 1989—communist governments fall in Eastern Europe; 1991—Soviet Union collapses, Yugoslavia breaks up; 1990s—fighting in former Yugoslavia

Building Vocabulary

1–8. Quiz sentences should show a clear understanding of the meanings of the terms.

Recalling Key Facts

9. increased fear of war, increased military spending and cutbacks in other economic areas
10. Possible answers: formation of the European Coal and Steel Community, formation of the Common Market, the EU's quest for greater economic and political unity through such measures as the introduction of a common currency, the euro
11. Brandt's *Ostpolitik* policy, the collapse of communism in East Germany, Gorbachev's decision not to send Soviet troops, and Kohl's assurances that a unified Germany would be peaceful
12. It created a free-trade zone.
13. Collectivized agriculture was unproductive; industries could not produce the consumer goods people wanted.
14. After World War II, Soviet armies occupied much of Eastern Europe. The Soviets backed local Communist parties and used force to quell unrest.
15. Possible answers: soaring unemployment and prices, rising crime rate, gang activity, bank and business failures, political division, ethnic conflict

---

Creating a Chapter Summary

To help you review the chapter, prepare a time line like the one below. Above the time line, list key events concerning Western Europe and North America. Below the time line, list key events concerning Eastern Europe and the Soviet Union.

		Youth riots in France		United States has budget surpluses
1945	1956		1968	1990s
Soviets occupy Eastern Europe	Soviets crush Hungarian revolt			

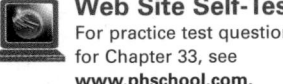

For additional review and enrichment activities, see the interactive version of *World History* available on the Web and on CD-ROM.

Web Site Self-Test
For practice test questions for Chapter 33, see **www.phschool.com.**

Building Vocabulary

Use the terms below to create a fill-in quiz. Write a sentence for each word, but leave a blank space where the word would appear.

1. **recession**
2. **euro**
3. **coalition**
4. **surplus**
5. **separatism**
6. **dissident**
7. **glasnost**
8. **ethnic cleansing**

Recalling Key Facts

9. What were the effects of the Cold War arms race?
10. Describe two steps Western European nations took toward unity.
11. What events led to German reunification?
12. How did NAFTA affect Canada and the United States?
13. Why was the Soviet command economy less successful than western capitalist economies?
14. How did the Soviet Union dominate Eastern Europe?
15. Describe three problems faced by former Soviet republics.

Critical Thinking and Writing

16. **Defending a Position** If you lived in a European country today, would you support a "United States of Europe"? Why or why not?
17. **Comparing** Compare the impact of Labour party leadership and Conservative party leadership on the citizens of Britain.
18. **Understanding Causes and Effects** What were the causes of the collapse of the Soviet Union?
19. **Drawing Conclusions (a)** Why do you think that many Russians considered Putin to be an improvement over Yeltsin? **(b)** Do you think Putin will benefit Russia in the long run? Explain.
20. **Connecting to Geography** What role might geography have played in Yeltsin's failure to crush revolts in Chechnya?
21. **Solving Problems** List possible solutions to the troubles in Yugoslavia. Describe the strengths and weaknesses of each possible solution.

Critical Thinking and Writing

16. Students who favor unity might cite the economic benefits. Students who oppose it might cite issues of nationalism.
17. Under the Labour party, Britain became a welfare state and eventually ran into severe economic problems. Conservatives reduced social welfare programs, curbed the power of labor unions, and returned nationalized industries to private control.
18. low output of crops and consumer goods, high military spending, ethnic and anti-nationalist movements, denial of rights and freedoms, war with Afghanistan, food and fuel shortages, demonstrations in the Baltic states, Gorbachev's rise to power
19. Possible answers: **(a)** Putin represents stability and strength; he may improve the economy; the government might be less corrupt. **(b)** Students who predict a positive result may argue that he will rebuild Russia's economy. Students may predict anything from Russia's rebuilding its economy to a continuation of Russia's troubles.

Read the excerpt below from a news article titled "Liberal Leaders Warn Yeltsin to Protect His People." Then, answer the questions that follow.

"MOSCOW, Oct 6, 1999—Liberal leaders urged Russian President Boris Yeltsin on Wednesday to defend his people by exercising caution in the advance of troops into the breakaway region of Chechnya. Liberal economist Grigory Yavlinsky said the troop movements and a two-week-old campaign of air raids ignored the 'tragic experience' of the 1994-96 Chechen war in which tens of thousands died on Russia's southern rim. . . .

[Yavlinsky] backed punitive measures against Chechen 'terrorists,' accused by Moscow of incursions in a neighboring region and of masterminding bomb blasts in Russian cities. But he urged the Kremlin to start talks with Chechen leaders. 'Russian forces should cooperate with those organizations which exist there . . . only contact with the people and with leaders can change the situation for the better,' he said. 'We insist on finding a balance between our security and your [Chechen] independence.'

. . . 'The development of events in Chechnya along the lines of 1994-96 will lead to Russia's colossal defeat,' Yavlinsky said. 'Russia will not be able to survive it.' "

—Reuters Information Service

22. Why were Russian troops advancing into Chechnya in 1999?

23. What policy does Yavlinsky recommend in Chechnya?

24. Why does Grigory Yavlinsky urge Yeltsin to exercise caution in Chechnya?

Do Internet research on a major current event or trend in Europe, the United States, or Canada. Use the information to produce a television news report on the topic. Remember to include maps, video, charts, or other visuals to go with the report.

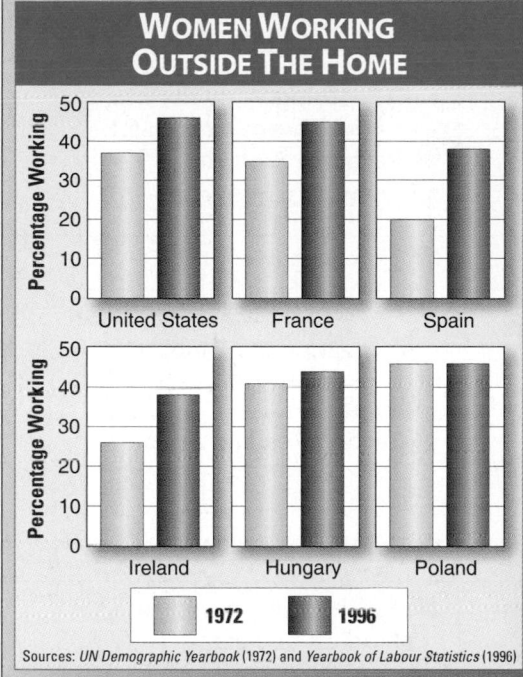

WOMEN WORKING OUTSIDE THE HOME

Sources: *UN Demographic Yearbook* (1972) and *Yearbook of Labour Statistics* (1996)

Study the series of bar graphs and answer the following questions:

25. What percentage of Spanish women worked outside the home in 1972? In 1996?

26. In 1996, which four countries had about the same percentage of women working outside the home?

27. In 1972, which country had the smallest percentage of women working outside the home?

28. **(a)** Which two countries experienced the smallest increase in women working outside the home between 1972 and 1996? **(b)** Based on what you have learned in this chapter, offer a possible explanation for the lack of change in these two countries.

Skills Tip

To understand a bar graph, use the title and key to identify what each bar represents. Read the numbers and labels on the vertical or horizontal axis to determine the measurements being compared.

20. Students should consult the political and physical maps of Russia in the Reference Section. Chechnya is about 1,000 miles southwest of Moscow, and between 7,000 and 14,000 feet above sea level. Distance and terrain could have hindered efforts to subdue revolts there.

21. Students should support their answers.

Analyzing Primary Sources

22. They are on a punitive mission in reaction to bomb blasts in Russian cities and incursions in regions neighboring Chechnya on the part of Chechen "terrorists."

23. contact with the Chechen leaders and organizations to work out the problems using mechanisms that are already in place

24. Yavlinsky warns that Russian people will again suffer numerous casualties as in the 1994-96 Chechen war, and that Russia will not be able to survive defeat.

Analyzing a Graph

25. 1972—20%; 1996—38%

26. United States, France, Hungary, Poland

27. Spain

28. **(a)** Hungary, Poland **(b)** Possible answer: To combat a consistent lower standard of living, women in Eastern European countries such as Hungary and Poland would have joined the workforce sooner than did women in the West.

Skills Tip

Unlike a table, a bar graph will not give you exact numbers, but it does give you a good idea of relative numbers or amounts. The Skills Handbook in the front of the book has a lesson that will help students with this feature.

Unit Theme Activity

Remind students to continue working on their Unit Theme Activity. See rubrics for the activity on the unit opener page in the Teacher's Edition.

Take It to the NET

Direct students to **www.phschool.com** for links to sites that will help them get started on this assignment. Share rubrics with students.

Attempted The news report is extremely brief and lacks any visuals.

Minimal The news report is poorly written and unorganized, contains many factual errors, and has poorly done graphics.

Adequate The news report is well written and organized, contains no factual errors, and has well-executed graphics.

Exemplary The news report is very well written and organized, provides insight into a current event, and has striking graphics.

Resource Manager

Chapter Level Resources	CORE INSTRUCTION	READING/SKILLS

	📁 Teaching Resources
	  📄 Pacing Charts, Ch. 34
	  📄 Teaching With Themes, p. 37
	  📖 Color Transparencies, p. F–69
	  💿 Resource Pro® Ch. 34
	  💻 www.phschool.com
	    • eTeach
		💿 Book on CD, Ch. 34
		💿 Interactive Student Tutorial CD-ROM, Ch. 34
		💿 Social Studies Skills Tutor CD-ROM
		📖 Skills Transparencies

1 Japan Becomes an Economic Superpower
1. Identify the factors that made Japan's recovery an economic miracle.
2. Summarize how Japan interacted economically and politically with other nations.
3. Analyze how patterns of life are changing in Japan.
	📁 Teaching Resources
	  📁 Unit 8 booklet
	    • Viewpoint Activity, p. 48
	  📄 Creative Teaching Activities, p. 151
	  💿 Prentice Hall Presentation Pro, Ch. 34, Section 1
	  📖 Section Reading Support Transparencies
		📁 Teaching Resources
		  📁 Unit 8 booklet
		    • Guided Reading and Review, p. 38
		    • Skill Application Activity, p. 49
		  📄 Guide to the Essentials
		  📼 Guided Reading Audiotapes, Ch. 34, Section 1

2 From Revolution to Reform in China
1. Describe effects of communist policies in China.
2. Enumerate challenges China faced during the Cold War.
3. Explain how calls for reform spurred renewed repression in China.
4. State the challenges that China faces today.
	📁 Teaching Resources
	  📁 Unit 8 booklet
	    • Primary Source Activity, p. 47
	  📄 Creative Teaching Activities, p. 152
	  💿 Prentice Hall Presentation Pro, Ch. 34, Section 2
	  📖 Section Reading Support Transparencies
		📁 Teaching Resources
		  📁 Unit 8 booklet
		    • Guided Reading and Review, p. 40
		  📄 Guide to the Essentials
		  📼 Guided Reading Audiotapes, Ch. 34, Section 2

3 The Asian Tigers
1. Relate how China has influenced Taiwan and Hong Kong.
2. Discuss how Singapore modernized.
3. Explain why Korea has remained divided for more than 50 years.
	📁 Teaching Resources
	  📄 Creative Teaching Activities, p. 153
	  💿 Prentice Hall Presentation Pro, Ch. 34, Section 3
	  📖 Section Reading Support Transparencies
		📁 Teaching Resources
		  📁 Unit 8 booklet
		    • Guided Reading and Review, p. 42
		  📄 Guide to the Essentials

4 Southeast Asia and the Pacific Rim
1. Analyze how war affected Vietnam and Cambodia.
2. Describe challenges faced by the Philippines and developing nations of Southeast Asia.
3. Summarize factors that make the Pacific Rim a vital region.
	📁 Teaching Resources
	  📁 Unit 8 booklet
	    • Biography Activity, p. 45
	  📄 Creative Teaching Activities, p. 154
	  💿 Prentice Hall Presentation Pro, Ch. 34, Section 4
		📁 Teaching Resources
		  📁 Unit 8 booklet
		    • Guided Reading and Review, p. 44
		  📄 Guide to the Essentials
		  📼 Guided Reading Audiotapes, Ch. 34, Section 4

ENRICHMENT/PRE-AP

- 🖥 **www.phschool.com**
  - Why Study History?

🗄 **Teaching Resources**
- 📕 **Chapter Extension Activities,** p. 81
- 📕 **History Through Literature,** pp. 70–71
- 🎞 **Color Transparencies,** p. C–59, D–85
- 🖥 **www.phschool.com**
  - Internet Activities, Section 2

🗄 **Teaching Resources**
- 📕 **Chapter Extension Activities,** p. 82
- 📼 **Listening to Literature World Masterpieces,** *High Mountain Plant, August River,* side 10

- 📼 **Listening to Literature World Masterpieces,** *Thoughts on Hanoi,* side 10
- 🖥 **www.phschool.com**
  - Internet Activities, Section 4

ASSESSMENT

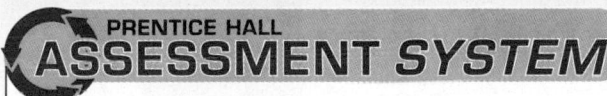

Core Assessment
- 📘 **ExamView Test Bank booklet,** Ch. 34
- 💿 **ExamView Test Bank CD-ROM,** Ch. 34

Standardized Test Preparation
Diagnose and Prescribe
- 📘 **Diagnostic Tests for High School Social Studies Skills**

Review and Reteach
- 📘 **Review Book for World History**

Practice and Assess
- 📘 **Test-Taking Strategies With Transparencies for High School**
- 📘 **Alternative Assessment booklet**
- 📘 **Test Prep Book for World History**

🗄 **Teaching Resources**
- 📁 **Unit 8 booklet**
  - Geography Quiz, p. 50
  - Section Quizzes, pp. 39, 41, 43, 45
  - Chapter Tests A, B, and C, pp. 51–55
- 🖥 **www.phschool.com**
  - Self-Test

CUSTOMIZE FOR INDIVIDUAL NEEDS

Gifted and Talented
- **Teacher's Edition,** Activities: Connections to Literature, p. 865

Less Proficient Readers
- **Guide to the Essentials,** Ch. 34
- **Book on CD,** Ch. 34
- **Teacher's Edition,** Activities: Customize for Visual Learners, p. 864

Less Proficient Writers
- **Teacher's Edition,** Activities: Customize for Auditory Learners, p. 863; Customize for Visual Learners, p. 864; Cooperative Learning Activity, p. 866

Students Acquiring English/ESL
- **Guide to the Essentials, English/Spanish,** Ch. 34
- **Book on CD,** Ch. 34
- **Teacher's Edition,** Activities marked with an *

Don't miss the exclusive interactive version of *World History: Connections to Today* on the Internet and CD-ROM.

INTRODUCTION

China, Japan, and other Asian nations achieved varying degrees of success in their efforts to modernize. After World War II, Japan introduced democratic reforms, emerging as an economic superpower in the 1960s. The People's Republic of China achieved modest economic gains under communist rule, while sacrificing individual freedoms. Taiwan, Hong Kong, Singapore, and South Korea became industrialized nations. Cold War tensions sparked long, devastating conflicts in Vietnam and Cambodia.

Focusing on Themes

Suggest that students focus on these theme questions as they read:

Continuity and Change
How did the Cold War affect the nations of East Asia and Southeast Asia?

Economics and Technology
How did technology and trade contribute to the success of Japan and the Asian "tigers"?

Political and Social Systems
How is the new China created by the communist revolution changing again today?

Global Interaction
Why did the Pacific Rim become a dynamic center of growth?

◆ TIME LINE ACTIVITY

You may wish to share the About the Pictures note with your students before asking these questions about the time line:

1. What happened in China in 1949? *(Mao Zedong announced the formation of the People's Republic of China.)*
2. What happened in 1962 to heighten Cold War tensions? *(Cuban missile crisis)*
3. What did the "people power" revolution in the Philippines force President Ferdinand Marcos to do in 1986? *(to hold elections)*

Don't Miss!

You Are There . . .
Helping Protesters in Tiananmen Square
(Section 2)

Analyzing Primary Sources
War Refugees in Korea
(Section 3)

CHAPTER
34

East Asia and Southeast Asia

1945–Present

Chapter Preview

1 Japan Becomes an Economic Superpower
2 From Revolution to Reform in China
3 The Asian Tigers
4 Southeast Asia and the Pacific Rim

1949

Mao Zedong announces the formation of the People's Republic of China. This idealized portrait of Mao was painted after he had ruled China for 20 years.

CHAPTER EVENTS

1950s

Japan's recovery from World War II begins, sparking an "economic miracle."

1968

During the Vietnam War, the Tet Offensive shows that guerrilla forces are determined to fight, no matter the cost. Here, American medical troops race to rescue a wounded Marine.

| 1940 | 1955 | 1970 |

GLOBAL EVENTS

1957 In Africa, the nation of Ghana gains independence from Britain.

1962 The Cuban missile crisis heightens Cold War tensions.

▶ Resource Directory

Teaching Resources
Teaching With Themes Chapter Theme Activities, p. 37
Pacing Chart With Block Scheduling Guide Ch. 34
Technology
World History Color Transparencies Ch. 34 Graphic Organizer, p. F–69

Nations of the Pacific Rim

[Map of the Pacific Rim region with countries labeled including CHINA, SOUTH KOREA, JAPAN, TAIWAN, Hong Kong, THAILAND, PHILIPPINES, BRUNEI, MALAYSIA, INDONESIA, SINGAPORE, PAPUA NEW GUINEA, AUSTRALIA, NEW ZEALAND, CANADA, UNITED STATES, MEXICO, CHILE, and oceans INDIAN OCEAN and PACIFIC OCEAN]

Resources and population enable nations of the Asia-Pacific Economic Cooperation group (APEC) to play a vital role in the global economy.

Robinson Projection
0   1000   2000 Miles
0   1000 2000 Kilometers

1986
In the Philippines, "people power" forces President Ferdinand Marcos to hold presidential elections after more than 20 years in power.

1987
South Korea holds direct elections, moving toward democracy.

1997
Britain returns Hong Kong to China. Ceremonies and fireworks commemorate the occasion.

1985 — 2000 — 2015

1989 The Berlin Wall falls.

1993 Israel and the PLO sign a peace accord.

1999 Control of the Panama Canal shifts from the United States to Panama.

Chapter 34 **857**

Independent Assignments

Have students read one section as they prepare for class. After class, have them complete the assignment. Some students may benefit from using the Guided Reading and Review worksheets.

Section 1 Have students use the worksheet *Looking at Teenagers in Japan* in the Unit 8 booklet, p. 48, to read two views on the experiences of Japanese students.

Section 2 Have students use the worksheet *The Trial* in the History Through Literature booklet, pp. 70–71, to read an excerpt from a novel that depicts the effects of Mao's victory in China.

Section 3 Have students use the map *The Korean War* in the Historical Outline Map Book, p. 57, to label geographical and historical features associated with the Korean War.

Section 4 Have students use the worksheet *Aung San Suu Kyi* in the Unit 8 booklet, p. 46, to learn about the Nobel Prize-winning leader of the opposition party in Myanmar.

Nations of the Pacific Rim

Activating Prior Knowledge
How did imperialism accelerate the advent of a global age? *(It forced western ideas about government, technology, and culture upon Asia.)*

Previewing
Why might the Pacific Ocean come to play an increasing role in global trade? *(It links the nations of the Pacific Rim.)*

Background
About the Pictures

1. This portrait of Mao Zedong was painted by Liu Chunhua, Dean of the Beijing Academy of Art. Mao's sympathy for the peasants of China had roots in his own history. Mao grew up in the rural village of Shaoshan, and his father had once been a poor peasant who became wealthy through farming.

2. The Tet Offensive, despite huge casualties for Communist forces, turned the tide for North Vietnam by convincing the American public that the war could not continue at current levels. Communist forces attacked some 100 cities and military bases in an effort that forced President Johnson to announce that he would not run for re-election and that bombing north of the 20th parallel would cease. This opened the way for negotiations with Hanoi.

3. The return of Hong Kong to China on June 30/July 1, 1997, which took 17 years to negotiate, ended 156 years of British rule. Britain gained Hong Kong from China after the Opium War of the mid-1800s. With the hand-over came fears that the Beijing government would end Hong Kong's relative freedom and prosperity.

eTeach

Be sure to check out this month's online discussion with a World History Master Teacher.

Go to **www.phschool.com**.

SECTION 1

Bell Ringer Ask students to imagine what Japan must have looked like at the end of World War II in 1945. If they had been citizens of Japan at the time, what predictions would they have made about their country's economic and political future?

LESSON PLAN

1. Focus At the end of World War II, American occupation forces took steps to destroy Japanese militarism and to ensure democracy for the Japanese people. Due to a number of favorable factors, Japan emerged as an economic superpower by the end of the 1980s. Today, Japan must face such challenging issues as its uncertain role in international politics, overcrowded living conditions, and the weakening of traditional values.

2. Instruct Ask students to make a chart showing the causes and effects of Japan's postwar economic recovery. Have students write Economic Recovery at the top of the chart. Under this have them make two columns labeled Reasons for Success and Effects of Success. In these columns, have students write all the relevant causes and effects that they can think of. Ask students to compare their charts with a partner's and to make any necessary additions or revisions. Use the completed charts to support a class discussion about Japan since World War II.

3. Assess Have students write down at least two ways that Japan's economic success has affected the people of Japan.

4. Reteach If students' Assess activity does not reflect adequate understanding of the lesson, you might assign the *Guide to the Essentials* or the *Interactive Student Tutorial CD-ROM* for this section.

Reading Focus

- What factors made Japan's recovery an economic miracle?
- How did Japan interact economically and politically with other nations?
- How are patterns of life changing in Japan?

Vocabulary

zaibatsu

gross domestic product

trade deficit

Taking Notes

Copy this concept web. Fill in each blank circle with key factors in Japan's emergence as an economic superpower. Add as many circles as you need.

[Concept web: JAPAN: ECONOMIC SUPERPOWER, with circles for Protectionist policies; Educated, skilled work force]

Main Idea After World War II, Japan rapidly rebuilt and became an economic superpower.

Setting the Scene Wartime destruction left cities crumbling throughout Japan. More than half of the homes in Tokyo had been destroyed. Agricultural production also suffered, as bad weather left rice harvests at only two thirds the prewar level.

With the end of the war came the need to rebuild. As in the past, the Japanese learned from outsiders. They selectively borrowed western ideas and technology and put them to their own use. In time, Japan emerged as an economic superpower.

Recovery and Economic Miracle

In 1945, Japan lay in ruins. It had suffered perhaps the most devastating property damage of any nation involved in World War II. Tens of thousands of Japanese were homeless and hungry.

The Occupation Under General Douglas MacArthur, the American military government set two main objectives for the occupation of Japan—to destroy militarism and to ensure democratic government. To achieve the first, Japan's armed forces were disbanded. As in Germany, trials were held to punish those responsible for wartime atrocities. Along with Japan's defeat, the trials further discredited the military. In 1946, a new constitution provided that "the Japanese people forever renounce war as a sovereign right of the nation." Japan, it said, would never maintain military forces except for its own defense.

The emperor lost all political power, and Japan became a constitutional monarchy. Power was held by the people, who elected representatives to the Diet, or parliament. The constitution also protected basic rights such as freedom of thought, press, and assembly. Occupation forces also brought social reforms. They opened the education system to all people and emphasized legal equality for women.

The Americans introduced economic reforms designed to promote democracy. The constitution protected the right of workers to organize unions.

Political and Economic Recovery
United States general Douglas MacArthur (left) led the occupation of Japan after World War II. This picture, showing him with Emperor Hirohito (right), was a great surprise to the Japanese people. MacArthur's casual appearance contrasted sharply with the emperor's formality.

Theme: Political and Social Systems How did political and social changes in Japan affect the nation's economic recovery?

Caption Answer

Through aid from the United States, by instituting a new constitution that put power in the hands of the people, and by enacting social reforms, the stage was set for greater economic growth.

Resource Directory

Teaching Resources
Creative Teaching Activities Creative Teaching Activities booklet, p. 151
Guided Reading and Review Unit 8 booklet, p. 38

A sweeping land-reform program divided up large estates among tenant farmers. The former owners received payment, and peasants owned land for the first time. This change erased lingering traces of feudalism in Japan. Although the Americans tried to disband the zaibatsu, or giant business organizations, the Japanese resisted. They felt that large firms were needed to compete internationally.

As Cold War tensions heightened, the United States grew eager to end the occupation. In 1952, it signed a peace treaty with Japan. Still, the two nations kept close ties. American military forces operated out of bases in Japan, which in turn was protected by the American "nuclear umbrella." They also were trading partners, eventually competing with each other in the global economy.

Japanese Success Between 1950 and 1975, Japan recovered and produced an economic miracle. Its gross domestic product (GDP) soared. GDP refers to the total value of all goods and services produced by a nation within a particular year.

Japan's success was built on producing goods for export. At first, the nation manufactured textiles. Later, it shifted to making steel for shipbuilding and machinery. How did Japan enjoy such success? After the war, Japan, like Germany, had to rebuild from scratch. Also like Germany, it had successfully industrialized in the past, so it quickly built efficient, modern factories that outproduced older industries in the West. It adapted the latest technology to create its own high-quality products.

Manufacturing By the 1970s, Japanese cars, cameras, and television sets found eager buyers on the world market. Its companies also moved into high technology. Soon, Japanese electronic goods—from computers in businesses to robots in factories—were competing with western, and especially American, products.

Japan benefited from an educated, highly skilled work force. Until recently, some Japanese companies guaranteed lifetime employment for their workers. In return, employees gave the company total loyalty.

Additionally, Japanese workers saved much of their pay. These savings gave banks the capital to invest in industrial growth. Further investment was possible because the government did not have to spend money on maintaining a large military force.

Trade and Investment As a small island nation with few resources, Japan depended on trade. It had to import oil and other raw materials like iron ore, but it exported the more profitable finished goods, such as steel. It marketed its products so successfully that it built a favorable balance of trade, exporting more goods than it imported.

As Japan's economy expanded, it invested in ventures around the world. In addition to investments in existing businesses and real estate, the Japanese financed and operated mines and plantations. They built airports and chemical plants. When a tire factory was to be built in East Africa or a dam in Central America, the engineers and managers were likely to be Japanese. Japan's presence everywhere showed that it not only had caught up with the West but was rapidly moving ahead of it.

Japan's protectionist policies angered its trading partners. The government protected domestic products by imposing tariffs and regulations that limited foreign imports. Partly because of this policy, and partly because of the quality of Japanese exports, other nations ran a trade deficit with Japan; they purchased more goods from Japan than Japan bought from them. So many Americans were buying Japanese-made cars, for example, that United States automakers felt that their own business was threatened.

The United States claimed that Japanese trade barriers deprived American corporations of a fair chance to sell their goods in Japan. To reduce its trade deficit with Japan, the United States threatened to raise tariffs on Japanese

Japanese Entrepreneurs Break With Tradition
Executives at the Toyota Corporation in Japan developed a new production system. The following excerpt describes the main features of this revolutionary new technique:

"The two executives [created] an entirely new system of production —dubbed . . . 'lean production.'. . . Its genius was to shift the focus of manufacturing . . . to 'economies of time.'

It did this in [several] ways. The first was by making every employee a quality checker. . . . Toyota gave workers the right to stop the production line as soon as they saw errors.

The second improvement came from introducing 'just-in-time' production. In the rest of the world, manufacturers made their components 'just in case' they were needed. They filled . . . warehouses with . . . costly parts, which gathered dust until they were finally needed. The Japanese started making components 'just in time,' with parts arriving just as they were needed on the production line."
—"The Art and Practice of Japanese Management" (Mickelthwaite)

Skills Assessment

Primary Source How would these techniques save time for Japanese companies?

Have students scan Section 1 and note the main headings. Then ask them to turn each heading into a question and to answer the questions as they read the section. *(More Advanced Readers)*

Activity
Connections to Film and Economics

Writing a Speech *A Proper Place in the World*, episode 4 of the four-part public television series *Japan*, analyzes the reasons for Japan's dramatic economic recovery following World War II. The program cites such contributing factors as American aid after the war, careful planning and direction by the Japanese government, and the production of high-quality goods by Japanese industry. Perhaps the most important reason for Japan's success, according to the documentary, is Japan's tradition of skillfully combining its own customs with ideas and technology imported from other cultures. The film also points out, however, that Japan's economy faces an uncertain future due to competition from other East Asian states, the high value of the yen, recurring trade conflicts with the United States, and other problems.

Ask students who view the film to assume the role of a Japanese economic minister. Their assignment is to write and present a speech profiling the status of the Japanese economy. In their speeches, they should review the reasons for Japan's economic successes. However, they should also warn their audience about the potential dangers that Japan may face in the future. (*Japan*, a 1987 coproduction of WTTW/Chicago and Central Independent Television, is distributed by MPI Home Video.) ✳

Chapter 34 **859**

Block Scheduling Support

Tell students to write a letter to the editor in which they take a position on whether people should support the policy of buying locally made goods. At issue is whether consumers should support their country's economy by purchasing items made in their country or look for the best buy in terms of price and quality, regardless of where a product is made. Remind students to state their opinion early in the letter and to support it with facts. You may wish to have students read the Skill Application worksheet *Synthesizing Information* in the Unit 8 booklet, p. 40. The worksheet provides evidence about Japan and the automobile industry that students may find useful.

ANSWER By eliminating waste and reducing defects, Japan could produce better-quality products at a lower cost. Also, by not having to store extra parts, the companies are able to save money.

Activity
Connections to Economics

Comparing Put the data below on the board and instruct students to express the data in graph form. After students have completed their graphs, ask them to compare what happened to the American and Japanese motor vehicle industries between 1950 and 1990. Then, have students discuss possible explanations for the differences. ✳

MOTOR VEHICLE PRODUCTION
(in thousands)

	JAPAN	U.S.
1950	32	8,006
1960	482	7,905
1970	5,289	8,284
1980	11,043	8,010
1990	13,487	9,783

Background
Connections to Economics

The *Keiretsu* System One of Japan's business practices that upsets its trading partners is called the *keiretsu* system. Many Japanese companies, such as automakers and auto parts suppliers, have become linked by cross-ownership. These businesses can make more money for themselves and their owners by doing business with one another. Foreign competitors complain that this practice unfairly locks them out of these markets in Japan.

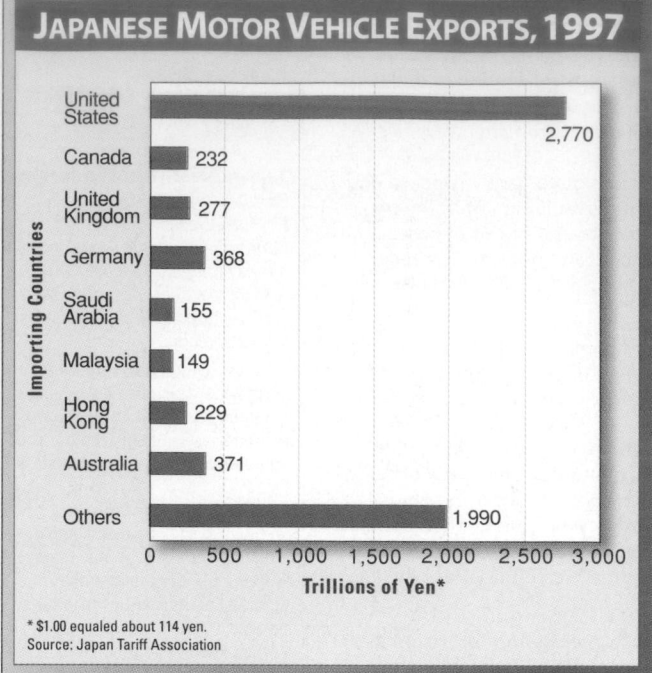

JAPANESE MOTOR VEHICLE EXPORTS, 1997

Importing Countries:
- United States — 2,770
- Canada — 232
- United Kingdom — 277
- Germany — 368
- Saudi Arabia — 155
- Malaysia — 149
- Hong Kong — 229
- Australia — 371
- Others — 1,990

x-axis: Trillions of Yen* (0, 500, 1,000, 1,500, 2,000, 2,500, 3,000)

* $1.00 equaled about 114 yen.
Source: Japan Tariff Association

Skills Assessment

Graph International sales of Japanese motor vehicles soared during the 1970s, and remained high through the 1980s and 1990s. The nation that imported the largest number of these vehicles was the United States. **Which individual nation was the second-largest importer of Japanese motor vehicles?**

imports, making them more expensive for American consumers. That threat was designed to force Japan to open its door to more American imports. Frequent trade talks between the two nations had only limited success.

Economic and Political Interaction

Economic success allowed Japan to benefit from the modern global economy. Yet Japan felt the negative effects of interdependence as well, especially because of its need for imported raw materials.

Dependence on Oil Nothing brought home Japan's dependence on world markets more than OPEC's price hikes in the 1970s. Japan's booming industries had fed on cheap imported oil. Higher energy costs sent shock waves through its economy.

In response to this economic challenge, Japan sought better relations with oil-producing nations of the Middle East. It also tried to reduce energy use by building more efficient power plants and expanding and improving public transportation. Still, Japan's modern economy required oil.

Japan and Its Neighbors As Japan sought economic openings in Asia, it had to deal with nations that still held bitter memories of World War II. China, Korea, and parts of Southeast Asia had suffered terribly under Japanese occupation. Japan was slow to apologize for its wartime actions, but it did work hard to regain the trust of neighboring peoples. By the 1980s, Japan was a major investor in China and the emerging nations of Southeast Asia. In the 1990s, Japanese leaders offered some public regrets for the death and destruction of the war years.

International Politics Although Japan was an economic superpower, it took a back seat in international politics for many years. During the Cold War, Japan supported the western alliance. More recently, it has edged toward a larger world role. For decades, Japan has given foreign aid to emerging nations. Today, it ranks as the world's largest donor nation.

In recent years, the United States has urged Japan to rearm and assume more of the costs for its own defense. Asian neighbors oppose Japan's rearmament, and the Japanese themselves are divided on the issue. Some think Japan's status as a world power requires rearmament. Most prefer to avoid the hazards and expense of becoming a military power.

Changing Patterns of Life

In the past 50 years, Japan has enjoyed many economic successes. In the 1990s, however, Japan faced its worst economic depression since the 1930s. Companies had to make cutbacks, and many workers lost the security of guaranteed lifetime employment. The Asian financial crisis, as you have read, further undermined confidence. The economy was recovering by the late 1990s, although unemployment remained high.

Skills Assessment

ANSWER Australia

Resource Directory

Teaching Resources
Skill Application Activity *Synthesizing Information,* Unit 8 booklet, p. 49
Viewpoint Activity *Looking at Teenagers in Japan,* Unit 8 booklet, p. 48
Section Quiz Unit 8 booklet, p. 39

Technology
Interactive Student Tutorial CD-ROM Ch. 34
Computer Test Bank Ch. 34

Political Stresses Japan's democracy has survived many crises. The Liberal Democratic Party (LDP) has dominated the government since the 1950s. But Japanese political parties differ from those in the United States. The LDP is, in fact, a coalition, or temporary alliance, of conservative factions that compete behind the scenes for top government positions. In the 1990s, charges of corruption greatly weakened the LDP. Some younger, reform-minded politicians broke with the LDP, threatening its monopoly on power.

Crowded Cities Today, most Japanese live in cities, which are hugely overcrowded. Housing is expensive, and space is scarce. Most people live in tiny, cramped apartments. Despite the crowded conditions, however, urban crime and violence are relatively rare. Many space-hungry Japanese move to the suburbs but then face long commutes between home and work.

Because Japan lies in a region often rocked by earthquakes, it built modern structures using "quake-proof" technology. Japanese highways and other structures were supposed to be designed to withstand strong quakes. In 1995, however, a severe earthquake badly damaged the city of Kobe (KOH BEE). The disaster raised questions about just how completely technology can protect against natural forces.

Women Japanese women have legal equality and often control the family finances. But traditional attitudes toward women continue to keep them in subordinate, or lower, positions in the workplace. About half the nation's adult women work outside the home, but most are in low-paying jobs or in family-run businesses. Fewer women than men get a university education, and only a handful have moved into higher-level jobs in business or government.

Work Ethic For decades, the Japanese sacrificed family life to work long hours. They also saved large portions of their earnings. Many younger Japanese, however, want more time to enjoy the benefits of economic success. Some older Japanese worry that the old work ethic is weakening. Also, as the tradition of lifetime employment fades, workers feel less loyalty to individual companies.

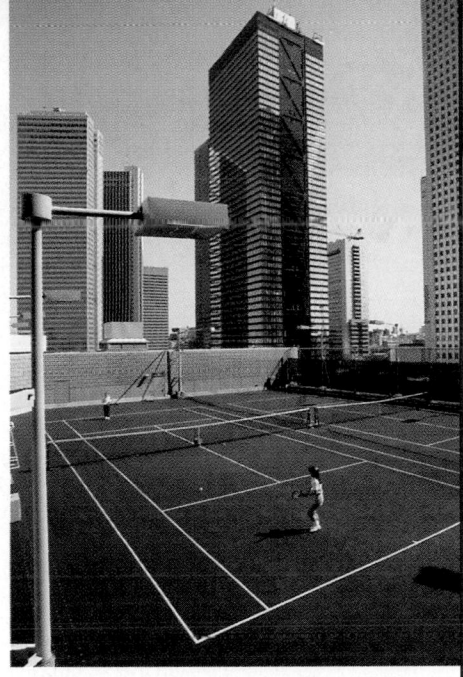

Crowded Cities
Japanese cities are so crowded that people must adapt their needs for parking and recreation. Here, people play tennis on a rooftop court.

Theme: Geography and History How have crowded Japanese cities adapted to limited space?

SECTION 1 Assessment

Recall
1. **Identify:** (a) Douglas MacArthur, (b) Diet, (c) Liberal Democratic Party.
2. **Define:** (a) zaibatsu, (b) gross domestic product, (c) trade deficit.

Comprehension
3. (a) How did Japan achieve political recovery? (b) What were three reasons for Japan's economic recovery?
4. What role has Japan played in world affairs in recent years?
5. What challenges face Japanese society today?

Critical Thinking and Writing
6. **Recognizing Points of View** Some nations complained that Japanese policies made it difficult for trading partners to sell goods to Japan, resulting in trade deficits. To the Japanese, however, these policies led to Japan's trade *surplus*. How might these differing perspectives affect trade talks?
7. **Synthesizing Information** How do you think occupation policies regarding Japan's armed forces and the zaibatsu affected the nation's economic success?

Activity
Writing a Letter Suppose that you are a Japanese teenager. Write a letter to the prime minister supporting or opposing the rearming of Japan. Prepare a bibliography of the sources you used to gather your information about this issue.

Chapter 34 **861**

🔔 **Bell Ringer** Ask students to recall what they have previously learned about communism and to list three common characteristics of a communist state. As they study this section, ask them to determine if those characteristics pertain to China today.

LESSON PLAN

1. Focus Backed by peasant support, Mao's communists emerged triumphant in their struggle against the nationalists. Once in power, the communists provided reforms in education, health care, and other areas while building a socialist, totalitarian state. Mao's more moderate successors introduced economic reforms but maintained a strict political dictatorship.

2. Instruct Work with students to construct on the board a time line of China from 1949 to the present. Divide the time line into segments of five years. Have students consult the text as well as other resources for pertinent information. Call on volunteers to come to the board to write significant events or trends in the appropriate place on the time line. Ask students to briefly describe the meaning and importance of the items they wrote. Use the completed time line to hold a class discussion on China under communist rule.

3. Assess Based on what they have learned, ask students to make predictions about future political, social, or economic developments in China.

4. Reteach If students' Assess activity does not reflect adequate understanding of the lesson, you might assign the *Guide to the Essentials* or the *Interactive Student Tutorial CD-ROM* for this section.

Reading Focus

- What were the effects of communist policies in China?
- What challenges did China face during the Cold War?
- How did calls for political reform lead to repression?
- What challenges face China today?

Vocabulary

collectivization
commune
joint venture
special enterprise zone

Taking Notes

Copy this table. As you read, list developments in the People's Republic of China under Mao Zedong and Deng Xiaoping.

MAO ZEDONG	DENG XIAOPING
• Great Leap Forward	• Joint ventures
•	•

Main Idea After a series of failed reforms in China, communist leaders introduced elements of capitalism.

Setting the Scene On October 1, 1999, China celebrated an important anniversary. Exactly 50 years earlier, in 1949, communist leader Mao Zedong had announced the birth of the People's Republic of China. He pledged "to build a new China, independent, . . . prosperous and strong." Under Mao, China experienced a revolution that ranks with Russia's as one of the major social transformations of the 1900s.

Communist Control of China

After World War II, civil war resumed between Mao Zedong's communist forces and Jiang Jieshi's nationalists. Battles raged until Mao's forces swept to victory and set up the People's Republic of China (PRC). Jiang Jieshi and his supporters fled to the island of Taiwan. After decades of struggle, China was finally united—with the communists in control.

Reasons for Victory The communists triumphed for a number of reasons. Mao won the support of China's huge peasant population. Peasants had long suffered from brutal landlords and crushing taxes. The communists pledged to redistribute land to poor peasants and end oppression by landlords.

Additionally, many women backed Mao's forces. The nationalists had made little effort to improve their harsh lives. Women were still seen as inferior to men and often were cruelly mistreated. The communists rejected the inequalities of the old Confucian order. To point out this break with tradition, Mao said: "Women hold up half the sky."

Mao's armies outfought Jiang's, and while support for the communists grew, the nationalists lost popularity. Many educated Chinese saw Jiang's government as morally and politically bankrupt. They hoped that the communists would build a new China and end foreign domination.

Reorganizing the Economy Once in power, the communists set out to turn China from a backward peasant society into a modern industrial nation. To build socialism and repair the economy, China nationalized all businesses. The government also drew up five-year plans to develop agriculture and heavy industry. With Soviet help, the Chinese built hydroelectric plants, railroads, and canals.

To boost agriculture, Mao distributed land to peasants. Then he called for collectivization, the pooling of peasant land and labor in an attempt to increase efficiency.

▶ **Primary Sources and Literature**

See "Mao Zedong: The People's Democratic Dictatorship" in the Reference Section at the back of this book.

Resource Directory

Teaching Resources

Creative Teaching Activities Creative Teaching Activities booklet, p. 152
Guided Reading and Review Unit 8 booklet, p. 40
History Through Literature *The Trial,* History Through Literature booklet, pp. 70–71

Technology

World History Color Transparencies *Goldfish From China,* p. C–59; *Wedding Group,* p. D–85

Remolding Society Like Lenin in the Soviet Union, Mao Zedong built a one-party totalitarian state, with the Communist party supreme. Communist ideology replaced Confucian beliefs and traditional religions. The government attacked crime and corruption. It did away with the old landlord and business classes. In their place, peasants and workers were honored as the builders of the new China. Many thousands of landlords and middle-class people were beaten and killed. One official justified the attacks, saying:

> "The freedom we uphold is not the same as that based on the type of democracy advocated by the bourgeoisie. . . . We, on the contrary, hold that there must be democratic liberties among the people, but that no freedom should be extended to counterrevolutionaries: for them we have only dictatorship."
> —Lu Ting-yi, speech delivered May 26, 1956

To increase literacy, the government simplified Chinese characters, making it easier to learn to read and write. Schools were opened for young and old. Reading and writing were mixed with political education. Students learned to praise the "Great Helmsman," Mao Zedong, who could do no wrong.

The Communists also sent health-care workers to remote rural areas. Although many of these "barefoot doctors" had limited training, they did help to reduce disease and teach better hygiene.

Changes for Women Under China's new constitution, women won equality under the law. They were expected to work alongside men in fields and factories. State-run nurseries were set up to care for the children. These changes weakened the old ideal of the extended family dominated by the oldest male. In China's cities, as elsewhere in the developing world, the nuclear family became increasingly common.

Although Chinese women made real progress, they did not enjoy full equality. Only a few won promotion to top jobs in government and industry. Women were often paid less than men for the same work. Also, after working at paid jobs, they still were responsible for cleaning, cooking, and child care.

Economic Disasters

Although some reforms did result in more access to education and greater equality, people in China paid a heavy cost for Mao's programs. During the 1950s and 1960s, two efforts in particular led to economic disaster and tremendous loss of life.

The Great Leap Forward In 1958, Mao launched a program known as the "Great Leap Forward." He urged people to make a superhuman effort to increase farm and industrial output. In an attempt to make agriculture more efficient, he created communes. A typical commune included several villages, thousands of acres of land, and up to 25,000 people. It had its own schools, factories, housing, and dining halls. Each commune had production quotas. Communes also mobilized labor brigades to build dams and irrigation systems. Rural communes set up "backyard" industries to produce steel and other products.

The Great Leap Forward was a dismal failure. Backyard industries turned out low-quality, useless goods. The commune system slowed food output. Bad weather and declining food production added to the problems and led to a terrible famine. Between 1959 and 1961, up to 30 million Chinese are thought to have starved to death. In response, China turned to more moderate policies.

The Cultural Revolution China slowly recovered from the Great Leap Forward. Then, in 1966, Mao launched the Great Proletarian Cultural Revolution. Its goal was to purge China of "bourgeois," or nonrevolutionary, tendencies. He urged young Chinese to experience revolution firsthand, as his generation had.

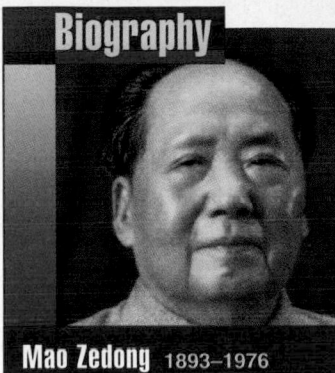

Biography

Mao Zedong 1893–1976

During the mid-1950s, divisions arose within the Communist party in China. In response, Mao launched a campaign under the slogan "Let a hundred flowers bloom, let a hundred thoughts contend." Mao hoped that by offering people the opportunity to openly express their views he would gain more support. When people began to criticize the Communist party, however, Mao ended the campaign. Of the nearly 550,000 Chinese who had spoken out, thousands were executed and hundreds of thousands were exiled to the countryside to "rectify their thinking through labor."

Theme: Impact of the Individual What methods did Mao use to keep power for himself?

Customize for . . .
Auditory Learners

Analyzing Quotations In 1957, Mao made this statement: "The policy of letting a hundred flowers blossom and a hundred schools of thought contend is designed to promote the flourishing of the arts and the progress of science." Only a few years later, however, Mao had this to say about intellectuals: "Swollen in head, weak in legs, sharp in tongue but empty in belly."

Read students the above two quotations and have them discuss the changes that they reflect in Mao's philosophy. Then, have students discuss possible reasons for the change. Finally, discuss what it might have felt like to be an artist or scientist in China during the two different times that surrounded these quotations.

Block Scheduling Support

Tell students to imagine that they are artists working for the Chinese government. Have them create posters supporting one of the programs introduced by the People's Republic. Students may wish to use an art style that was favored in China and other communist states. Called *socialist realism,* this style uses realistic and easily understood images to "educate" people about the principles, practices, and benefits of socialism. A central feature of socialist realism is the "positive hero," an individual who strives cheerfully and enthusiastically to achieve the goals of the people's state.

Biography

ANSWER He suppressed freedom of expression by exiling or executing those who criticized the Communist party.

Red Guards
During the Cultural Revolution, groups of teenagers known as Red Guards responded to Mao's call for renewed revolution. Here, young Red Guards read from Mao's "Little Red Book."

Theme: Impact of the Individual How does this photograph show Mao's importance in communist China?

In response, teenagers formed bands of Red Guards. Waving copies of the "Little Red Book" of Mao's sayings, Red Guards attacked those they claimed were counterrevolutionaries. They targeted people in authority, from party leaders and factory managers to teachers, writers, and artists. The accused were publicly humiliated or beaten, and sometimes even killed.

The Cultural Revolution convulsed China. Schools and factories closed. The economy slowed, and civil war threatened. Finally, Mao had the army restore order. Many Red Guards were sent to work on communes. They became a lost generation, undereducated and cut off from normal family life and careers. In the end, many became disillusioned with communism.

China and the Cold War

The Communist victory over the Nationalists dominated the Cold War in 1949. After Jiang Jieshi fled to Taiwan, the United States continued to support the Nationalist government. The United States refused to recognize the People's Republic of China, which it saw as an aggressive communist power and a threat to all of Asia.

Relations With the United States For years, the United States tried to isolate China. In 1971, however, China won admission to the United Nations. A year later, United States President Richard Nixon visited Mao in Beijing. Slowly, relations improved. Finally, in 1979, the United States set up formal diplomatic relations with China.

Split With the Soviet Union China and the Soviet Union were uneasy allies in the 1950s. Stalin sent economic aid and technical experts to help China modernize, but he and Mao disagreed on many issues.

Mao had adapted Marxism to Chinese conditions. Marx had predicted that the industrial working class—the proletariat—would lead the revolution. Because China had little industry, however, Mao's revolution relied on peasants rather than factory workers. Stalin rejected Mao's views. Mao, in turn, thought that the Soviets were too conservative and accused them of being too willing to "coexist" with the capitalist powers.

China and the Soviet Union also competed for influence in developing nations. In addition, border disputes triggered tensions between the two. By 1960, border clashes and disputes over ideology led the Soviets to withdraw all aid and advisers from China.

Reform and Repression

Mao Zedong died in 1976. Despite disastrous mistakes, many still saw him as the revolutionary hero who had restored order, ended foreign domination, and made China a world power once again.

After Mao, more moderate leaders controlled China. By 1981, Deng Xiaoping (duhng show PIHNG) had set China on a new path. Deng was a practical reformer, more interested in raising output than in political purity. "I don't care if a cat is black or white," he declared, "as long as it catches mice."

Economic Reforms Deng backed a program called the Four Modernizations, which emphasized agriculture, industry, science, and defense. As part of this plan, Deng introduced economic reforms, including some private ownership of property and free-market policies. In agriculture, the responsibility system replaced the communes. Peasant families were allotted plots of farmland. The government took a share of their crops, but the family could sell the rest on the free market.

Entrepreneurs were allowed to set up their own businesses. Managers of state-run factories were given more freedom but were expected to make their plants more efficient. Deng welcomed foreign capital and technology. Investors from Japan, Hong Kong, Taiwan, and the West organized joint ventures with China, in which foreign companies would organize a business with Chinese firms, with profits shared by both participants. The government also set up special enterprise zones, where foreigners could own and operate industries.

Deng's reforms brought a surge of growth and a better standard of living for some Chinese. They were soon buying motor scooters, televisions, and refrigerators. On the downside, crime and corruption grew. Inequalities increased as a new wealthy class emerged. An economic gap also grew between poor rural farmers in the interior and city dwellers on the coast who were exposed to western influences.

Tiananmen Square Massacre By the late 1980s, some Chinese were demanding greater political freedom as well as economic reform. In Beijing and other cities, students, workers, and others supported a democracy movement like those sweeping Eastern Europe. Deng, however, would not talk about political reform.

In May 1989, tens of thousands of demonstrators occupied Tiananmen Square. They raised banners calling for democracy and brought in a huge plaster statue called the Goddess of Democracy and Freedom. When the demonstrators refused to disperse, the government sent in troops and tanks. Thousands of demonstrators were killed or wounded. Many others were arrested and tortured. Some were put to death.

The crackdown showed that China's communist leaders were determined to maintain control. To them, order was more important than political freedom. During the 1990s, efforts to persuade China to end human rights violations had limited effects.

Challenges Today

By the mid-1990s, China had become a major industrial power. Its economy ranked among the fastest growing in the world, and it was building major trade ties with countries worldwide. Yet even as economic gains continued, the nation faced many unresolved issues.

Population Population growth posed a challenge for the future. Since 1949, China's population has more than doubled, to more than 1.2 billion. Such rapid growth strained the economy. In the 1980s, the government instituted

▶ **Primary Sources and Literature**

See "Harry Wu: The Outlook for China, Human Rights" in the Reference Section at the back of this book.

Population Density
Bicycles, trucks, and buses compete for space at a dangerous Beijing intersection.

Theme: Economics and Technology Why would the bicycle be a common form of transportation in Chinese cities?

You Are There . . .

Helping Protesters in Tiananmen Square

EXPLORING the HUMAN DRAMA

Bell Ringer Ask students what inference they can make about the convictions of the man standing in front of the tanks. How might his convictions reflect those of the student demonstrators in Tiananmen Square?

Background
About the Scene

Tiananmen Square A symbol of hope, Tiananmen Square has long been a historic space. Originally built in the 1420s, it played a significant role in government rituals, such as the issuing of edicts. Throughout the twentieth century, the space was used for assembly during moments of national crisis or victory—including Mao's victory in 1949. By 1989, Tiananmen Square had become the focal point for protesters who wanted further reforms and a chance to be listened to by government officials.

Activity
Cooperative Learning

Creating a Time Line Have students form groups of four to research the massacre at Tiananmen Square and make a time line of the major events. Divide the research into four periods of time—Part 1: April 1989, Part 2: May 1–15, Part 3: May 16–31, and Part 4: June. Each student is responsible for researching one of the four periods of time, taking notes, and sharing the information with the others. Group members should decide who will do the following: draw and label the time line, provide illustrations, proofread the time line for accuracy, and present the finished product to the class.

Activity Rubrics

Share rubrics with students.

Attempted The diary entry does not reflect an understanding of the events.

Minimal The diary entry reflects a basic understanding of the events, but descriptions are not detailed.

Adequate The diary entry reflects a basic understanding of the events, and descriptions have sufficient detail.

Exemplary The diary entry reflects a good understanding of the events, and the descriptions are interesting.

You are bringing food and supplies to the students in Tiananmen Square. They are protesting government corruption and the lack of democratic reform. As each day passes, the crowd of protesters grows—and tensions mount.

The government has declared military rule, and soldiers are moving into Beijing. In response, crowds of protesters build barricades. A wave of excitement ripples through the square as art students from Beijing University arrive. They have brought a statue that they call the "Goddess of Democracy and Freedom."

Finally, soldiers break through the barricades and march into the city. For 20 minutes, a lone man blocks a column of tanks. Eventually, however, the soldiers occupy Tiananmen Square and force the students out.

Portfolio Assessment

After you return home, you record all you have seen in your diary. In your entry, describe what you saw and how you felt about the demonstration.

866 Chapter 34

Resource Directory

Teaching Resources
You Are There Chapter Extension Activities booklet, p. 81
Section Quiz Unit 8 booklet, p. 41

Technology
Interactive Student Tutorial CD-ROM Ch. 34
Computer Test Bank Ch. 34

a one-child-per-family policy. Parents who had only one child were given rewards, such as better housing or improved medical benefits. Those who had more children faced fines and other penalties.

The campaign to slow the birthrate worked better in cities than in rural areas. Farm families, who wanted children to work the land, often paid fines rather than obey the policy. The one-child policy had a tragic effect in a country that still valued boys over girls. Female infanticide, or the killing of girl babies, increased despite efforts to prevent it.

Economic and Political Issues After Deng Xiaoping died in 1997, Jiang Zemin emerged as China's leader. He continued Deng's economic reforms and had to grapple with the same problems as Deng. Many state-run industries were inefficient, but they could not be closed without risking high unemployment and economic chaos. Cities overflowed with millions of peasants who poured in to seek new opportunities. Inequalities between rich and poor and between urban and rural Chinese continued to grow.

Across China, communist ideology was weakening. From party officials on down, people were more interested in profit than in socialism. Corruption was a growing problem. The government made some efforts to crack down on corruption and other criminal activity.

Human Rights Issues The Communist party maintained its monopoly on power and continued to jail critics. Its human rights abuses, however, brought strong pressure from trading partners such as the United States.

Advocates of western-style human rights did not focus only on the suppression of dissent in China. Some asserted that China used prison labor to produce cheap export goods. Others charged China with imperialistic tyranny in Tibet, where the indigenous culture had been swamped by Chinese immigrants and military suppression of the Tibetan form of Buddhism. At the end of the 1990s, the Chinese government had also cracked down on a new Chinese version of Buddhism, the Falun Gong sect, which claimed millions of members. Political dissidents, human rights advocates, and spokespeople for oppressed Tibet, such as Tibet's exiled religious leader the Dalai Lama, found widespread support in Europe and the United States.

China replied to the charges from the West by declaring that outsiders had no right to tell the Chinese leaders how to run their own domestic affairs. Chinese leaders also denied the right of the West to impose western standards of human rights on other cultures.

Geography and History

Three Gorges Dam

In the mid-1990s, China began construction on the world's largest dam. Located on the Yangzi River, Three Gorges Dam will be 607 feet high and 1.2 miles wide, creating a lake 370 miles long. The dam will cost between $14 billion and $75 billion and will take more than 15 years to complete.

The dam has sparked controversy. Officials say the dam will protect millions from floods and will generate electric power for one of the country's most underdeveloped regions. It will also improve navigation along the river.

Critics argue that the new lake will flood 13 cities and 140 towns, forcing some 1.5 million people to relocate. They point out that the lake will destroy important archaeological treasures in the region. Additionally, many fear that the dam will lead to greater pollution as industrial areas are flooded.

Theme: Economics and Technology
What are the benefits of the dam? What are the costs?

SECTION 2 Assessment

Recall
1. (a) People's Republic of China, p. 862 **(b)** five-year plan, p. 682 **(c)** Great Leap Forward, p. 863 **(d)** Cultural Revolution, p. 863 **(e)** "Little Red Book," p. 864 **(f)** Four Modernizations, p. 864 **(g)** Tiananmen Square, p. 865 **2. (a)** collectivization, p. 862 **(b)** commune, p. 863 **(c)** joint venture, p. 865 **(d)** special enterprise zone, p. 865

Comprehension
3. The Great Leap Forward resulted in famine. Attacks of the Red Guards brought China to the brink of civil war. **4.** At first, relations with the United States were tense. Relations improved after President Nixon visited China. China split with the Soviet Union, which Mao felt was linked too closely with capitalism. **5. (a)** some private ownership of property and free-market policies, responsibility system of agriculture, more freedom for managers of state-run factories, allowing foreign capital and technology **(b)** high population levels, outdated economic practices, urban crowding, weakening acceptance of communist ideology, opposition to treatment of political opponents

Critical Thinking and Writing
6. Encourage students to support their ideas. **7. (a)** Both introduced economic reforms, including private ownership and free-market policies. **(b)** Gorbachev: political and economic reform; Deng: economic reform only

Activity Rubrics

Share rubrics with students.

Attempted The database is incomplete, and the paragraph has inadequate information or is incomplete.

Minimal The database and paragraph have some information, but the paragraph is not well written and has many errors.

Adequate The database is good, and the paragraph has much information, is well written, and has few errors.

Exemplary The database is well constructed, and the paragraph has a great deal of information and is insightful, interesting, and well written, with no errors.

Geography and History

ANSWER benefits: provides protection from flooding, electricity for an underdeveloped area, and improved navigation; costs: destruction of towns and cities, displacement of people, loss of archaeological treasures, and possibly greater pollution

SECTION 2 Assessment

Recall
1. Identify: (a) People's Republic of China, **(b)** five-year plan, **(c)** Great Leap Forward, **(d)** Cultural Revolution, **(e)** "Little Red Book," **(f)** Four Modernizations, **(g)** Tiananmen Square.
2. Define: (a) collectivization, **(b)** commune, **(c)** joint venture, **(d)** special enterprise zone.

Comprehension
3. How did Mao's economic policies harm China?
4. What major issues did China face during the Cold War?

5. (a) What economic reforms did Deng Xiaoping introduce? **(b)** What challenges does China face today?

Critical Thinking and Writing
6. Predicting Consequences Do you think economic reforms can be successful without political reforms? Explain.
7. Comparing Compare Deng's reforms in China to those of Gorbachev in the Soviet Union. **(a)** How were the reforms similar? **(b)** How were they different?

Activity
Take It to the NET

Use the Internet to research the Tiananmen Square massacre. Create a database of the student protesters' criticisms of the government and the major actions the students took. Then, write a paragraph explaining the role of students in the 1989 demonstrations in Beijing.

Human Drama Note

Tiananmen Square Some likened the events at Tiananmen Square in the spring of 1989 to the final stages of decline that signal the end of every dynasty in China—in this case, the rule of the Chinese Communist party. Uncensored for the first time in 40 years, Chinese television broadcast the unfolding drama across the country. Although the protests ended in thousands of deaths and even more injuries at the hands of government troops, Tiananmen Square marked a turning point for many Chinese. Many people felt a sense of pride at what they had accomplished. Not only had they challenged their government, but the events in Tiananmen Square changed the way the younger generation perceived themselves. Although they did not achieve democracy, the seeds of change were planted.

Bell Ringer

Bell Ringer Have students read the section title and the Reading Focus questions at the start of the section. Then, have them scan the boldface heads throughout the section. Ask students to guess the meaning of the term *Asian tigers*. In addition, ask them to write three generalizations predicting what they will learn about in this section.

LESSON PLAN

1. Focus The nations known as the Asian tigers have combined industrialization, trade, finance, and excellent location to achieve remarkable economic growth. Taiwan, a former territory of China, cautiously pursues closer links with the mainland. The British colony of Hong Kong was returned to China in 1997. Singapore's prosperity is offset by troubling issues such as ethnic tensions and limits on individual freedoms. Korea is a divided nation—a communist totalitarian state in the north and a capitalist powerhouse in the south.

2. Instruct Divide the class into four groups. Assign each group one of the four Asian tigers—Hong Kong, Taiwan, Singapore, or South Korea. Have each group assemble information for a chart on the Asian tigers. Explain that students should include data for these six headings: (1) Traditions and Religion, (2) Relations With China, (3) Relations With Other Nations, (4) Government, (5) Economy, (6) Troubling Issues. While students are working, construct a skeleton of the chart on the board. When students have finished, have representatives from each group present their "tiger" to the class. Have them also fill out the chart on the board. Ask students to note how the four nations are similar and different.

3. Assess Ask students to update their knowledge by reading a recent newspaper or magazine article about any of the four Asian tigers. Have them submit the article and a summary. Display these around the classroom for others to read.

4. Reteach If students' **Assess** activity does not reflect adequate understanding of the lesson, you might assign the *Guide to the Essentials* or the *Interactive Student Tutorial CD-ROM* for this section.

Connections to Today

ANSWER The Taiwanese might lose some of the freedoms they recently achieved. Their economy might be hurt.

Reading Focus

- How has China influenced Taiwan and Hong Kong?
- How did Singapore modernize?
- Why has Korea remained divided for more than 50 years?

Taking Notes

Create an outline of this section. Use Roman numerals for major headings, capital letters for subheadings, and numbers for the supporting details. Use this sample as a starting point.

I. Taiwan and Hong Kong
  A. Taiwan
    1. Ruled by China until 1895
    2.
  B. Hong Kong
    1.

Main Idea Aggressive economic growth led to world prominence for several nations in East and Southeast Asia.

Connections to Today

Taiwan: Rebel Province or Independent State?

Since 1949, the People's Republic of China has considered Taiwan a "rebel province" that must be reunited with the parent country. In 1995, the Chinese drove home that point by conducting two months of missile tests and live-fire exercises in the island's waters.

In 1999, Taiwanese President Lee Teng-hui created a new uproar when he insisted that China deal with Taiwan as a separate state. The Chinese responded angrily, renewing their threats of force against Taiwan. In Beijing, the *People's Daily* compared Taiwan's efforts to influence China to "an ant trying to topple a tree."

Theme: Political and Social Systems How do you think reunion with mainland China would affect the lives of the Taiwanese?

Setting the Scene At a university in Taiwan, Professor Xu Wenxing proudly unveiled an invention he had worked on for 10 years. His invention was a computerized fingerprint-recognition device, which was soon put to use. To Xu, however, the most satisfying aspect of his success was that "the technology involved was developed in Taiwan."

Taiwan was one of four small Asian lands that vaulted into the class of "newly industrialized countries" by the 1980s. Besides Taiwan, Hong Kong, Singapore, and South Korea are also known for their aggressive economic growth. The four are often called the "Asian tigers." Although they differ in important ways, all followed similar roads to modernization after 1945. Additionally, all four nations were influenced to some degree by China and by Confucian traditions.

Taiwan and Hong Kong

Both Taiwan and Hong Kong have deep cultural and historical links to China. Both were once part of China. Neither, however, experienced Mao's communist revolution. The island of Taiwan was once ruled by the mainland. Today, the People's Republic still considers it part of China. Hong Kong was returned to China in 1997 after more than a century under British colonial rule.

Taiwan The island of Taiwan was ruled by China until 1895, when it fell to Japan. The Japanese built some industry, providing a foundation for later growth. In 1945, with Japan defeated, Taiwan reverted to China. But when Jiang Jieshi fled the mainland in 1949, he set up his Nationalist government on Taiwan. Despite Jiang's autocratic rule, Taiwan experienced rapid economic growth and enjoyed United States's support.

First, Taiwan set up light industries such as textiles. Later, it developed heavy industry. The Green Revolution of the 1960s, with its new seeds and fertilizers, helped Taiwan's agriculture become more productive. Trade boomed, industrial cities grew, and in time Taiwan's standard of living rose to one of the highest in Asia.

With economic success, the government slowly allowed people more political freedom. Hostility between Taiwan and the mainland eased somewhat as the Cold War ended in the 1990s. Taiwanese businesses took advantage of Deng Xiaoping's economic reforms to invest in companies on the mainland.

Resource Directory

Teaching Resources

Creative Teaching Activities Creative Teaching Activities booklet, p. 153

Guided Reading and Review Unit 8 booklet, p. 42

In recent years, Beijing reasserted its insistence that Taiwan must be reincorporated into China. Chinese military exercises in the area were perceived as threats, and when an advocate of Taiwanese independence was elected president, Beijing refused to negotiate with him until Taiwan accepted the "one country, two systems" principle on which Hong Kong had been incorporated into China.

Hong Kong Britain gained the tiny island of Hong Kong after the Opium War. Under British rule, Hong Kong and nearby territories grew into a center of trade. In 1949, millions of refugees from the Chinese Revolution flooded into Hong Kong, providing labor and capital to help the area.

Hong Kong's new prosperity was based largely on trade and light industry, such as textiles and electronics. It also became a world financial center with many foreign banks and a busy stock market. Wealth from these profitable industries helped Hong Kong modernize.

Hong Kong's amazing growth was also due in part to its location on China's doorstep. Hong Kong Chinese built commercial ties to the mainland at a time when the People's Republic was largely isolated from the world community. This gave Hong Kong the chance to buy and sell goods with a market that was unavailable to many other countries.

In 1997, Britain returned Hong Kong to China. Beijing agreed not to change Hong Kong's social or economic system for 50 years and to allow its people self-government. Still, many residents remained nervous about China's power and use of repressive measures against protests.

Singapore

The smallest Asian tiger is the city-state of Singapore. It sits on a tiny island at the tip of the Malay Peninsula in Southeast Asia. Its 200 square miles have a population of about two million.

In 1819, British empire builder Sir Stamford Raffles leased the island from a local ruler. Raffles recognized its ideal location on the Strait of Malacca, halfway between China and India. He and his successors turned the island's fishing villages into a seaport.

Under British rule, Singapore grew rapidly. The population came to include Malayans, British merchants and sailors, and Chinese and Indian immigrants. All hoped to prosper in the booming city. The British brought in Chinese workers to work in factories that processed tin and rubber from Malaya. In time, the Chinese, with their Confucian tradition, became the dominant ethnic group.

Order and Prosperity Singapore won independence first from Britain in 1959 and then from nearby Malaya in 1963. For 30 years, Lee Kwan Yew was Singapore's autocratic prime minister. Lee supported a free-market economy. By keeping labor costs low, Lee attracted foreign capital that helped the economy boom. He expanded Singapore's seaport into one of the world's busiest harbors.

The government welcomed skilled immigrants and insisted on education for all its people—in both English and Chinese. It encouraged high-tech industries, manufacturing, finance, and tourism. As Singapore's economy grew, its standard of living rose. The government set up a successful public housing program. Most married couples became homeowners with the help of government loans.

Ongoing Issues Lee's successors continued his strict policies, allowing little opposition. Critics condemned limits on freedom. In response, the government claimed that order was more important than individual freedoms. Still, it faced demands for more rights from many of its young, well-educated citizens.

Background
Historical Evidence

Boycott Blunder In response to North Korean aggression in 1950, the UN Security Council called on the North Korean government to cease hostilities. When that measure failed, the Security Council quickly passed a resolution that recommended that "members of the United Nations furnish such assistance to the Republic of Korea as may be necessary to repel the armed attack and to restore international peace and security in the area." The Soviet Union could not veto the resolution because at the time it was not represented in the Security Council. The Soviet Union was boycotting the Security Council in protest over the exclusion of Communist China from the United Nations.

Background
Daily Life

Thought Control The following excerpt is from an article titled "In the Land of the Single Tune," which appeared in the November 26, 1990, issue of *Time* magazine. It describes life in North Korea:

"Radios are fixed so they can receive only the one acceptable station, and a loudspeaker is installed in every home. The display case in a hotel bookstore features 114 different works, all by Kim Il Sung or his son and heir apparent, Kim Jong Il. Martial music is piped in throughout the country, even in the bus taking passengers from airplane to terminal; by daybreak, when workers march to their jobs, a fast furious female voice is already shouting exhortations from a hidden amplifier in the street."

Map legend:
- Line of farthest North Korean advance, September 1950
- UN invasion, September 1950
- Line of farthest UN advance, November 1950
- Line of farthest Chinese and North Korean advance, January 1951
- Armistice line, 1953

Skills Assessment

Geography After North Korean troops stormed across the 38th parallel, the UN sent an army to aid South Korea. Fighting continued for three years, until a cease-fire was signed in 1953.

1. **Location** On the map, locate (a) North Korea, (b) South Korea, (c) 38th parallel, (d) Yalu River, (e) Inchon.
2. **Movement** How far did UN forces advance into North Korea?
3. **Critical Thinking Making Inferences** Based on the map, why do you think the UN advance beyond the 38th parallel worried the Chinese?

Because Singapore depended heavily on trade, its economy was influenced by events elsewhere. Yet it weathered the Asian financial crisis. Over the years, it also faced ethnic tensions between the Chinese majority and Malay and Indian minorities.

Despite such issues, Singapore was often seen as a model of successful development. With few natural resources, it built a booming economy. How did it succeed? Lee Kwan Yew preached "Confucian values," such as hard work, loyalty toward family, and respectful obedience to authority. Lee and others also spoke of a "Confucian model of development." Singapore and the other Asian tigers, they noted, all had stable governments that invested in education. In each, the Confucian ethic shaped attitudes about work. People worked long hours for low wages. They also saved these wages, which enabled banks to invest in further development.

The Two Koreas

The fourth Asian tiger, South Korea, emerged during the Cold War. It occupies the southern half of the Korean peninsula. In 1910, Japan annexed the Korean peninsula, imposing harsh rule on it. After World War II, the Soviet Union and United States agreed to a temporary division of Korea along the 38th parallel of latitude. Before long, North Korea, ruled by Kim Il Sung, became a communist ally of the Soviet Union. In South Korea, the United States backed the authoritarian—but noncommunist—leader, Syngman Rhee.

The Korean War Both leaders wanted to end the division. In early 1950, Kim Il Sung called for a "heroic struggle" to reunite Korea. North Korean troops attacked and soon overran most of the south. The United States then organized a UN force to help South Korea.

UN forces were made up mostly of Americans and South Koreans. They were led by United States general Douglas MacArthur, who had commanded troops in World War I and World War II and headed the occupation of Japan. He landed troops behind enemy lines, drove the invaders back across the 38th parallel, and then pushed northward to the Yalu River, along the border of China. MacArthur's success alarmed China. Mao Zedong sent Chinese troops to help the North Koreans, who again advanced southward.

The Korean War turned into a stalemate. Finally, in 1953, both sides signed an armistice, or end to fighting. The armistice has held for nearly 50 years, but no peace treaty has ever been negotiated. More than a million North Korean and South Korean troops dug in on either side of the demilitarized zone (DMZ), an area with no military forces, near the 38th parallel. At the end of the 1990s, American forces were still in South Korea to help guarantee the peace.

After the war, the two Koreas slowly rebuilt economies destroyed by the fighting and by years of Japanese occupation. Both remained centers of Cold War tensions. The United States funneled aid to South Korea, while the Soviets helped the north.

Skills Assessment

ANSWERS 1. Review locations with students. 2. more than 100 miles into North Korea; almost to the border of China 3. The advance placed UN troops very close to China's border, which may have led Chinese leaders to fear an invasion.

Resource Directory

Teaching Resources
Analyzing Primary Sources Chapter Extension Activities booklet, p. 82
Technology
Listening to Literature World Masterpieces audiotapes
High Mountain Plant, side 10, running time 1:05 min.; *August River,* side 10, running time 1:19 min.

War Refugees in Korea

The power struggle over North and South Korea played a large part in the Cold War tensions of the late 1940s and 1950s. Those not involved in the politics were drawn in when the Cold War escalated into a hot war between Communist and UN-backed forces in 1950. Civilians, such as K. Connie Kang and her mother, were caught up in the fighting.

"On a cold January night in 1951, when North Korean troops were about to invade Seoul, I rode on the rooftop of the last train bound for Pusan with my mother to escape the oncoming Communists. Bone-chilling wind from Siberia whipped across the 'freedom train,' which was jam-packed with soldiers, the sick, and the injured. There was no room for able-bodied civilians—not even children.

'I don't want to go up there, Mommy,' I protested. 'It's too scary.'

'We will be all right,' Mother assured me, even though I could tell she was scared herself. 'See those fellows on the train? They will secure us.' she said, pointing to the men on top of the train with . . . straw rope in their hands. 'If we don't take this train, we will surely die in the hands of Communists. This is the last train to Pusan.'

Fleeing South
Thousands of Korean refugees struggle to board a train heading south out of Seoul to escape the advancing North Korean army.

Mother climbed very slowly up a small staircase at the back of the coach. When I got up on the top of the train, I was surprised to see how roomy it was. . . . My mother sat beside me and held me by the cord tied around my middle with one hand to make sure I didn't fall off the train. The 'freedom train' traveled all through the night. Not everyone was as fortunate as I on that fateful night. That night several youngsters fell accidentally to their death. Life was cheap. I could have been one of them, had my mother not secured me and grasped the rope tied to my waist through the long trip, her hand nearly frozen under her mittens from the exposure to the biting wind. Whenever my mother caught me dozing off, she pinched me. 'Don't fall asleep. . . . You'll fall off the train if you do,' she said, all the while not once letting go of the rope around my waist."

—K. Connie Kang, *Home Was the Land of Morning Calm*

Skills Assessment

1. Why was Kang forced to ride on top of the train with her mother?
   - **A** They had no money.
   - **B** Only soldiers, the sick, and the injured could ride inside.
   - **C** Passengers heading for Pusan had to ride on top.
   - **D** They had lost their tickets.

2. According to this excerpt, many South Koreans risked the train ride from Seoul because
   - **E** it would soon be winter in Seoul.
   - **F** their homes had been destroyed by bombs.
   - **G** they feared that invading Communists would kill them.
   - **H** there was no food left in Seoul.

3. **Critical Thinking Drawing Conclusions** List two conclusions you can draw from the information in the passage.

Skills Tip

When you analyze primary source material, be sure to think about the person or persons being quoted, how knowledgeable they might be about the subject, and what their biases might be.

Chapter 34 **871**

 Analyzing Primary Sources

Background
About the Primary Source

K. Connie Kang K. Connie Kang relocated to the U.S., where she eventually became an award-winning journalist for the *Los Angeles Times.* After Kang and her mother fled their ancestral home, they lived in Seoul and then fled to Pusan. After Pusan, Kang lived in Toyko until the 1960s, when she studied in the U.S. In the 1970s, she became a reporter in San Francisco, where she helped her family set up a grocery store.

Her father held an acute longing to return to his native soil and felt deeply disconnected. His daughter shares similar sentiments about her homeland. She spoke of the effect separation from North Korea has had on her: "I have longed to visit my native place in Tanchon . . . where my ancestors have lived for six centuries. . . . As long as the Korean Peninsula remains split, we [Koreans] are a crippled people longing to be made whole."

Activity
Interpreting the Primary Source

Use this additional question to generate class discussion.
Critical Thinking: Comparing Based on Kang's description, think of an experience you have had that involved danger or the unknown. How was your experience similar to and different from Kang's? *(Student responses should express an awareness of Kang's emotions, as well as physical pain and possibly their own similar feelings.)*

Human Drama Note

Human Costs of the Korean War More than 1.3 million South Koreans, many of them civilians, and half a million North Koreans lost their lives in the Korean War. American military casualties numbered 54,000. In addition, thousands of prisoners of war suffered at the hands of their captors. Millions of North Koreans fled their homeland, and today refugees are forbidden to return. These people are called *shilhangmin,* or people of lost homes. Each New Year, thousands of former North Koreans amass at the North/South border to pray and mourn.

Test Preparation

Have students read the paragraphs under the heading "The Korean War" on the opposite page, and then complete the sentence below.

Based on the passage, you can infer that
- **A** South Korea was opposed to the armistice.
- **B** a peace treaty will probably happen soon.
- **C** North Korea was willing to try economic reforms.
- **D** the stalemate could continue indefinitely.

Skills Tip

Point out that looking for exaggerated statements can help identify bias. The Skills Handbook in the front of the book has a lesson that will help students with this feature.

Skills Assessment

ANSWERS **1.** B **2.** G **3.** People were desperate to leave Seoul when the Communists came; the train ride was dangerous.

Recall

1. **(a)** Asian tigers, p. 868 **(b)** Lee Kwan Yew, p. 869 **(c)** Syngman Rhee, p. 870 **(d)** Kim Jong Il, p. 872

Comprehension

2. Taiwan and Hong Kong have deep cultural and historical links to China. Taiwan was once ruled by the mainland, which insists that Taiwan must be reincorporated into China. Hong Kong was returned to China in 1997 after more than a century under British rule. Many residents are nervous about China's power and its repressive government. 3. Leaders supported a free-market economy, encouraged immigration by skilled workers, and encouraged education in English and Chinese. Economic growth focused on high-tech industries, manufacturing, finance, and tourism.
4. **(a)** South Korea's capitalist economy has experienced tremendous growth while North Korea's communist economy has not. **(b)** Isolation and failed government policies contributed to a famine and widespread hunger. During the late 1990s, North Korea had to accept food aid from other nations.

Critical Thinking and Writing

5. Possible answer: Hard work and a willingness to save money instead of spending it have given these nations a large amount of cash to invest. 6. China, and therefore communism, continues to have a strong influence over the entire region, and this makes many of the countries ill at ease.

Activity Rubrics

Share rubrics with students before they write their position papers.

Attempted The paper does not reflect a basic understanding of the issue.

Minimal The paper reflects a basic understanding of the issue but is poorly written.

Adequate The paper reflects a basic understanding of the issue and is well written.

Exemplary The paper reflects a clear understanding of the issue and is well argued and well written.

Caption Answer

Possible answers: Political and economic differences divide the two countries. South Korea fears the threat of the North's nuclear weapons program.

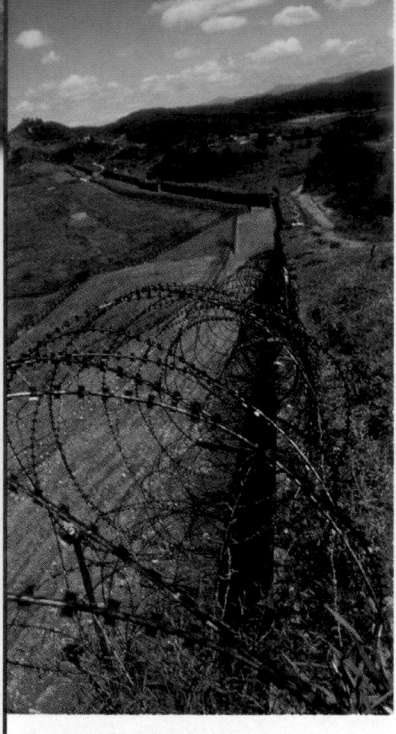

Demilitarized Zone
The border between South Korea and North Korea lies in the demilitarized zone, an area in which military forces are prohibited.

Theme: Political and Social Systems Why have tensions remained high between the two nations?

South Korea By the mid-1960s, South Korea's economy had leaped ahead. At first, it exported inexpensive textiles and manufactured goods. Later, it shifted to higher-priced exports such as automobiles and electronics. As in the other Asian tigers, its growth was partly due to low wages, long hours, and other worker sacrifices.

By the 1990s, South Korea was an economic powerhouse. With prosperity, workers won better pay, and the country's standard of living rose greatly. The 1997 Asian financial crisis brought hardships such as business failure and high unemployment. The government undertook difficult economic reforms, and by 2000, the nation's economy was recovering.

For decades after the Korean War, dictators backed by the military ruled in South Korea. By 1987, however, growing prosperity and fierce student protests pushed the government to hold direct elections. Since then, the nation has moved successfully toward democracy.

North Korea Under Kim Il Sung, state-owned industries and collective farms increased output in North Korea. That growth slowed, however, in the late 1960s. Kim's emphasis on self-reliance kept North Korea isolated. Even when its Soviet and Chinese allies undertook economic reforms, North Korea clung to hardline communism.

Propaganda constantly glorified Kim as the "Great Leader." After he died, his son Kim Jong Il, the "Dear Leader," took over. He faced huge problems. Failed government policies and terrible floods destroyed harvests, bringing widespread hunger. During the late 1990s, North Korea had to accept food aid from the United States, South Korea, and other nations to prevent mass starvation. Kim held onto power despite the misery and famine.

The Nuclear Issue Like several emerging nations, North Korea tried to develop nuclear power for electricity and for weapons. Under intense pressure from the United States, it agreed to end its nuclear weapons program in exchange for oil and other assistance. Yet North Korea continued to threaten South Korea and nearby Japan by testing missiles.

Outlook for Unity Despite differences between the two Koreas, most Koreans want to see their country reunited. After all, they share the same history, language, and culture. Restoring unity is of global interest because of Korea's strategic location in Asia.

SECTION 3 Assessment

Recall

1. **Identify:** **(a)** Asian tigers, **(b)** Lee Kwan Yew, **(c)** Syngman Rhee, **(d)** Kim Jong Il.

Comprehension

2. Describe how China's strength has affected the development of Taiwan and Hong Kong.
3. How did Singapore's leaders encourage economic growth?
4. **(a)** How do the economies of South Korea and North Korea differ? **(b)** How has the North

Korean government's policy on isolation affected the nation?

Critical Thinking and Writing

5. **Drawing Conclusions** What characteristic seems to have been most important to the economic success of the "Asian tigers"? Explain.
6. **Linking Past and Present** What conditions existing today in Taiwan, Hong Kong, Singapore, and Korea reflect lingering Cold War tensions?

Activity

Writing a Position Paper
In 1950, Kim Il Sung described North Korea's advances on the 38th parallel as the means to "achieve glorious, complete independence." Imagine that you are an official in the South Korean government. Write a position paper reacting to Kim's statement and identifying possible responses.

Resource Directory

Teaching Resources

Section Quiz Unit 8 booklet, p. 43
Creative Teaching Activities Creative Teaching Activities booklet, p. 154
Guided Reading and Review Unit 8 booklet, p. 44

Technology

Interactive Student Tutorial CD-ROM Ch. 34
Computer Test Bank Ch. 34

Reading Focus

■ How did war affect Vietnam and Cambodia?

■ What challenges faced the Philippines and the developing nations of Southeast Asia?

■ Why is the Pacific Rim a vital region?

Vocabulary

domino theory

cease-fire

embargo

Taking Notes

Create a time line that includes major events discussed in this section. The sample below will help you get started.

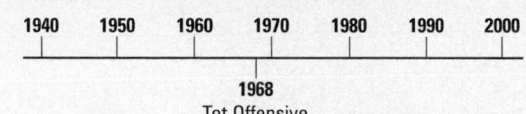

| 1940 | 1950 | 1960 | 1970 | 1980 | 1990 | 2000 |

1968
Tet Offensive

Main Idea Southeast Asian nations sought independence but also fell into divisive conflicts in the decades after World War II.

Setting the Scene Today, Southeast Asia is a key player in the global economy. For decades after the end of World War II, though, the region was shaped by the nationalist drive for independence. Some nations won freedom with little violence. Others faced long wars of liberation against European nations that wanted to reclaim their colonial empires after the war.

War in Vietnam and Cambodia

In mainland Southeast Asia, an agonizing liberation struggle tore apart the region once known as French Indochina. It affected the emerging nations of Vietnam, Cambodia, and Laos. The nearly 30-year conflict had two major phases. First was the battle against the French, dating from 1946 to 1954. Second were the civil war and Cold War conflicts that raged from 1959 to 1975.

In 1946, the French set out to regain Indochina, which Japan had seized during World War II. They faced fierce resistance from guerrilla forces led by Ho Chi Minh. Ho was a nationalist and communist who had fought the Japanese. He and his forces wore down the French and eventually forced them to leave Vietnam.

Vietnam Divided The struggle for Vietnam became part of the Cold War. At an international conference in 1954, western and communist powers agreed to a temporary division of Vietnam. Ho's communists ruled North Vietnam. Ngo Dinh Diem's noncommunist government, supported by the United States, ruled South Vietnam. Cambodia and Laos gained independence.

The agreement called for elections to reunite Vietnam. The elections were never held, however, largely because the Americans and Diem feared that the communists might win. American officials believed in the domino theory. It held that a communist victory in South Vietnam would cause noncommunist governments across Southeast Asia to fall to communism, like a row of dominoes.

American Involvement As the war continued, the United States became increasingly involved. Ho Chi Minh wanted to unite Vietnam under northern rule. He aided the National Liberation Front, communist rebels trying to overthrow Diem in South Vietnam. At first, the United States sent only military advisers and supplies to Diem. Later, it sent troops, turning a local struggle into a major Cold War conflict.

In 1964, the United States began bombing targets in North Vietnam. Eventually, more than 500,000 American troops were committed. At the

Primary Source

Vietnamese Declaration of Independence

Vietnamese nationalists led by Ho Chi Minh proclaimed the Democratic Republic of Vietnam on September 2, 1945. Following is an excerpt from their Declaration of Independence:

"The Declaration of the French Revolution . . . states: 'All men are born free with equal rights, and must always remain free and have equal rights.'. . .

Nevertheless, for more than eighty years, the French imperialists . . . have violated our Fatherland and oppressed our fellow-citizens. They have acted contrary to the ideals of humanity and justice. . . .

For these reasons, we . . . solemnly declare to the world that Vietnam has the right to be a free and independent country. . . . The entire Vietnamese people are determined to . . . sacrifice their lives and property in order to safeguard their independence and liberty."

—Vietnamese Declaration of Independence

Skills Assessment

Primary Source What document does this declaration cite? Why do you think the Vietnamese chose that document?

Chapter 34 **873**

SECTION **4**

Bell Ringer Inform students that from 1954 to 1975 Vietnam was divided into two separate states. Ask students to recall other nations that were divided during this same period. Have them write a paragraph explaining why these countries were divided after World War II.

LESSON PLAN

1. Focus Following World War II, Southeast Asian nations struggled to free themselves from colonial rule. They were also plagued by the Cold War, ethnic conflicts, dictatorial governments, and other problems. After freeing itself of French rule, Vietnam became a major battleground of the Cold War. The Pacific Rim countries, with their growing industry and huge market potential, are a vital part of the global economy.

2. Instruct Arrange students into five groups and assign each group one of the following countries: Vietnam, Cambodia, Myanmar, the Philippines, or Indonesia. Assign the students to work individually to list and describe obstacles that have limited development in their assigned nation. After students have finished, regroup them so that each new group has at least one "expert" on each country. Have students take turns teaching other group members about their area of expertise. Finally, each group should draw up a master list of the challenges facing Southeast Asia today.

3. Assess Ask students to predict the immediate and long-term effects of foreign trade and investment in Pacific Rim countries.

4. Reteach If students' **Assess** activity does not reflect adequate understanding of the lesson, you might assign the *Guide to the Essentials* or the *Interactive Student Tutorial CD-ROM* for this section.

Block Scheduling Support

Have students identify a list of major events in Vietnamese history during the 1900s. With a partner, students should then prepare a time line using their lists. Students should include a sentence that describes each event. Remind students to divide their time lines into equal intervals and to label each milestone marker with the year. Encourage students to make their time lines visually pleasing. You may wish to display the time lines around the classroom.

Primary Source

ANSWER It cites the Declaration of the Rights of Man, issued during the French Revolution. They probably chose the document for two reasons: first, it was written by the French, who controlled their land; second, it proclaimed the principle that all people must remain free with equal rights. They point to that statement to equate their position with that of the French during the Revolution and to justify their demands.

Chapter 34 **873**

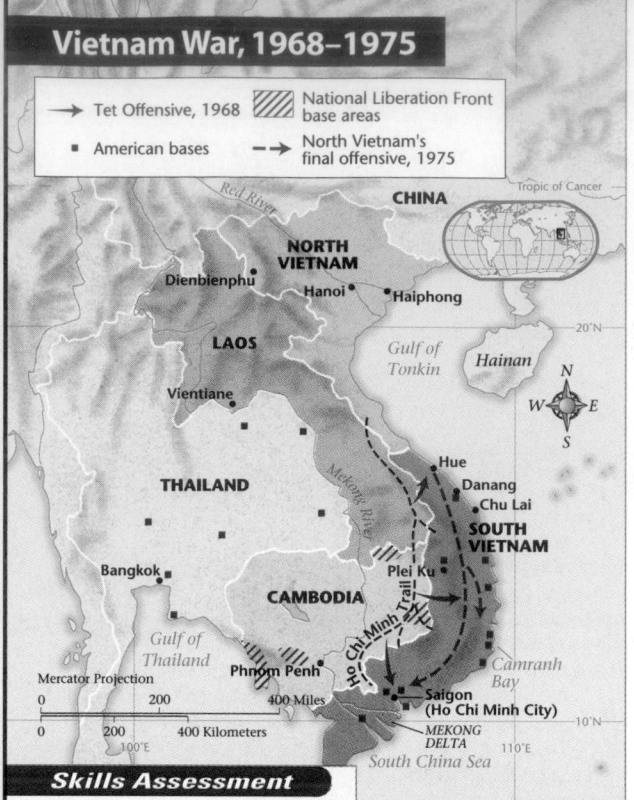

Vietnam War, 1968–1975

→ Tet Offensive, 1968
▨ National Liberation Front base areas
■ American bases
⇢ North Vietnam's final offensive, 1975

CHINA · Tropic of Cancer
NORTH VIETNAM
Dienbienphu · Hanoi · Haiphong
Red River
LAOS
Gulf of Tonkin · Hainan
20°N
Vientiane
THAILAND
Hue · Danang · Chu Lai
SOUTH VIETNAM
Bangkok · Plei Ku
CAMBODIA
Gulf of Thailand
Phnom Penh · Ho Chi Minh Trail
Mercator Projection
0 ... 200 ... 400 Miles
0 ... 200 ... 400 Kilometers
100°E
Camranh Bay
Saigon (Ho Chi Minh City)
MEKONG DELTA
South China Sea
10°N
110°E
Mekong River

Skills Assessment

Geography In the Vietnam War, the United States supported South Vietnam in its struggle against communist North Vietnam. Despite this help, the war ended with a North Vietnamese victory.

1. **Location** On the map, locate **(a)** North Vietnam, **(b)** South Vietnam, **(c)** Cambodia, **(d)** Laos, **(e)** Saigon, **(f)** Ho Chi Minh Trail.
2. **Movement** How did North Vietnam's use of the Ho Chi Minh Trail as a supply route help to spread the war beyond Vietnam?
3. **Critical Thinking Applying Information** Use the map to describe the "domino theory."

same time, both the Soviet Union and China sent aid—but no troops—to help North Vietnam.

Despite massive American aid, South Vietnam could not defeat the communist guerrillas and their North Vietnamese allies. In 1968, guerrilla forces launched a massive attack on American and South Vietnamese forces. The assault was unexpected because it took place at Tet, the Vietnamese New Year. Although the communists did not capture any cities, the Tet Offensive marked a turning point in public opinion in the United States. It also showed that the North Vietnamese would fight at any cost.

As the fighting continued, the bombing of North Vietnam and growing American casualties on the ground inflamed antiwar opinion in the United States. Under increasing pressure, President Nixon finally arranged a cease-fire, or halt in the fighting. He began withdrawing American forces in 1973. Two years later, the North Vietnamese captured Saigon, capital of the south, and reunited the country.

The Communist Victory Why did the communists win? In some ways, the Vietnam War mirrored the civil war in China that brought Mao to power in 1949. Diem and his successors in South Vietnam were unpopular leaders of a corrupt government. Ho Chi Minh was admired as a hero who had fought the Japanese and the French. Many Vietnamese saw the United States as another foreign power seeking to dominate their land. Also, despite American air power and advanced technology, guerrillas fought well in the jungle terrain.

Vietnam Today The communist victors imposed harsh rule on the south. Tens of thousands of Vietnamese fled in small boats. Many of these "boat people" drowned. Survivors landed in refugee camps. Eventually, some were accepted into the United States or other countries.

Vietnam had to rebuild a land destroyed by war. Recovery was slow due to government inefficiency and an American-led embargo, or blockage of trade. For years, the country remained mired in poverty and was unable to attract foreign capital.

In the early 1990s, Vietnam introduced some free-market reforms, opening the door to investors. The economy received a further boost after the United States lifted its embargo and restored diplomatic relations. Although Vietnam made some progress, it remained one of the poorest countries in Southeast Asia. The government's monopoly on political power and its complex laws made foreign investment difficult. Vietnam's best hope was the entrepreneurial spirit of its people.

Tragedy in Cambodia During the Vietnam War, fighting spilled over into neighboring Cambodia. North Vietnam sent supplies along the Ho Chi Minh Trail through Cambodia to guerrilla forces in South Vietnam. In 1970, the United States bombed that route and then invaded Cambodia. After the Americans left, Cambodian communist guerrillas called the Khmer Rouge overthrew the government.

Led by Pol Pot, the Khmer Rouge unleashed a reign of terror. To destroy all western influences, they drove people from the cities and forced them to work in the fields. They slaughtered or caused the death of more than a million Cambodians, perhaps a third of the population:

> "There were no more cities. No more markets, stores, restaurants, or cafes. . . . No schools. No books or magazines. No money. No clocks. No holidays and religious festivals. Just the sun that rose and set, the stars at night and the rain that fell from the sky. And work. Everything was work."
> —Haing Ngor, *A Cambodian Odyssey*

In 1979, Vietnam invaded and occupied Cambodia. Pol Pot and his forces retreated to remote areas. In the 1990s, the UN helped Cambodia hold elections. The new government, however, soon grew authoritarian. After Pol Pot died in 1998, a number of Khmer Rouge leaders gave up their guerrilla struggle. Cambodia debated whether to put Khmer Rouge leaders on trial.

Challenges for the Philippines

In 1946, the Philippines gained freedom peacefully after almost 50 years of American rule. The United States, however, continued to influence the country through military and economic aid. Although the Filipino constitution set up a democratic government, a wealthy elite controlled politics and the economy. The peasant majority was desperately poor. For a time, the government battled Huks, local communists with strong peasant support.

In 1965, Ferdinand Marcos was elected president. Marcos had promised reform but instead became dictator. He cracked down on free speech and forced opponents into exile. He even had Benigno Aquino (beh NEE nyoh ah KEE noh), a popular rival politician, murdered. Under heavy pressure, Marcos finally held elections in 1986. Voters elected Corazon Aquino, widow of the slain Benigno. Marcos tried to overturn the results, but the people of Manila forced him to leave in what was called the "people power" revolution.

Under Aquino and her successors, the fragile democracy survived. The country enjoyed economic growth during the 1990s, but many people remained poor. Government corruption and guerrilla wars waged by anti-government communists and separatist Muslims continued to raise questions about the nation's political future.

Like other developing nations, the Philippines experienced rapid urbanization. Newcomers crowded into the sprawling slums of Manila, the capital. Unrest surfaced in some areas. Natural disasters caused more setbacks. Many enterprising Filipinos left the country to build new lives in the United States and other parts of Asia.

Developing Nations of Southeast Asia

Southeast Asian nations faced many problems after independence. They lacked experience in self-government and were often hampered by complex ethnic and religious conflicts. Demands for political freedom and social justice were frequent. Some government leaders, however, claimed that order and economic development must take priority. All pursued the same goal, modernization, but their paths differed. Here, we will look at the experiences of two developing nations: Indonesia and Myanmar (formerly Burma).

Indonesia Geography posed an obstacle to unity in Indonesia, as in many developing nations. Indonesia includes more than 13,000 islands splashed across 3,200 miles of ocean—a distance equal to the width of the United States. Its large population is ethnically diverse. The Javanese dominate,

Corazon Aquino
The "people power" revolution of 1986 forced Ferdinand Marcos from power in the Philippines. Newly elected president Corazon Aquino, shown above, worked to preserve democracy.

Theme: Political and Social Systems What challenges faced the Philippines during the late 1980s and 1990s?

Connections to Art

A Demanding Art Batik originated over 1,000 years ago on the island of Java. It is a labor-intensive method of dyeing cloth in a creative and complex design. Before the fabric is dyed, it must be washed several times, dipped in a diluted starch solution for sizing, and then beaten to prepare the fibers for the dye. A design is drawn on the cloth and wax applied with a spouted applicator to those parts of the pattern that are not the first dye color. After the wax hardens, the fabric is dipped into the first dye. When the dye dries, the wax is removed from the fabric by scraping it or by dipping it in boiling water. The waxing and dyeing process is repeated for each color until the design is completed.

Biography

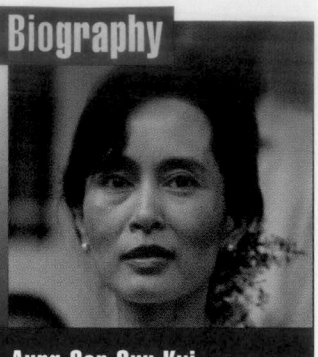

Aung San Suu Kyi 1945—

Aung San Suu Kyi was living in Britain with her husband and their sons when she decided to go home to Myanmar and oppose the military government. For safety, her family remained in Britain. After the 1990 election, the Myanmar government placed her under house arrest.

In 1991, the government announced that if Suu Kyi traveled to Norway to receive her Nobel Peace Prize, she would not be permitted to return to Myanmar. Her 18-year-old son Alexander accepted the award in her place.

Even after releasing Suu Kyi from house arrest in 1995, the government closely monitored her actions. Still, she resumed her post as general secretary of the opposition party. She gave weekly talks, held press conferences, and wrote speeches.

Theme: Impact of the Individual Why do many people in Myanmar consider Aung San Suu Kyi a hero?

 Primary Sources and Literature

See "Aung San Suu Kyi: Freedom From Fear" in the Reference Section at the back of this book.

but about 300 other groups, many with their own languages or dialects, also live in Indonesia. Despite this diversity, about 90 percent of Indonesians are Muslims.

Under authoritarian military rule, Indonesia made great economic progress. It benefited from exporting oil, tin, rubber, spices, and coffee. The rise and fall of world oil prices, however, meant that income was uncertain. Still, the government increased literacy and in the 1990s, introduced economic reforms that attracted more foreign capital.

The 1997 Asian financial crisis shook Indonesia to its roots. Riots erupted against a government accused of massive corruption. President Suharto, who had held power for more than 30 years, was forced to resign. Elections were held for a new government. It faced serious problems such as reforming and restarting the economy, meeting separatist demands, and restoring confidence in government. Meanwhile, many Indonesians sank back into poverty. The spread of religiously motivated violence pitted Muslims against Christians and other minorities.

For years after independence, the authoritarian government suppressed rebellions. In 1965, it crushed what looked like a communist uprising and massacred many suspected communists. Mobs also killed hundreds of thousands of Chinese whose ancestors had settled in Indonesia. Another struggle erupted in East Timor, which Indonesia seized from Portugal in 1975. The East Timorese, who were mostly Catholic, wanted independence. For years, Indonesia brutally suppressed the region. In 1999, under international pressure, it finally allowed a vote on the issue. When the East Timorese chose independence, pro-Indonesia forces unleashed a campaign of terror. Soon after, UN peacekeepers were sent in to restore order.

Myanmar Ethnic tensions have also plagued Burma. The majority, Burmans, long dominated the country. For years, repressive military rulers battled rebel ethnic minorities who wanted autonomy. In 1962, the military government isolated the country, thus limiting trade and foreign investment. It imposed state socialism modeled on Mao's system in China. These policies brought little improvement in the standard of living. In 1989, they renamed the country Myanmar, meaning "the People's Country," which recognized that other groups besides Burmans lived there.

Under mounting pressure, the government held elections in 1990. The opposition party won. It was led by Aung San Suu Kyi (AWNG SAHN SOO SHEE), whose father had helped Burma win independence. The military rejected the election results and jailed, killed, or exiled many opponents. Suu Kyi was held under house arrest. While still a prisoner, she won the Nobel Peace Prize for her "nonviolent struggle for democracy and human rights." Suu Kyi was finally released in 1995 and continued to push for democracy in Myanmar.

Regional Cooperation Demands for political freedom and social justice remained an issue in Southeast Asia. Some government leaders, however, argued that order and economic development must take priority over democracy. To achieve prosperity and improve regional self-reliance, six Southeast Asian countries formed the Association of Southeast Asian Nations (ASEAN) in 1967. Since then, ASEAN has expanded to include most Southeast Asian nations. They have worked to promote economic and cultural cooperation.

The Pacific Rim

In the modern global economy, Southeast Asia and East Asia are part of a vast region known as the Pacific Rim. It includes countries in Asia and the Americas that border the Pacific Ocean.

The Pacific first became an artery for world trade in the 1500s. By the mid-1900s, links across the Pacific had grown dramatically. By the 1990s,

Biography

ANSWER Possible responses: She risked her safety to oppose the military government.

Resource Directory

Teaching Resources

Biography Activity *Aung San Suu Kyi,* Unit 8 booklet, p. 46
Section Quiz Unit 8 booklet, p. 45
Geography Quiz Unit 8 booklet, p. 50
Chapter Test Forms A, B, and C Unit 8 booklet, pp. 51–55
Answer Key Unit 8 booklet, pp. 110–125

Technology

Interactive Student Tutorial CD-ROM Ch. 34
Computer Test Bank Ch. 34

Virtual Field Trip
www.phschool.com

**Batik of Indonesia
Jakarta, Indonesia**

To learn more about batik, use the Internet address above to link to Batik of Indonesia.

Indonesian Textiles
Batik is made by applying wax and then dye to fabric. The waxed portions of the fabric do not absorb the dye, creating intricate patterns and shapes.

Theme: Art and Literature
What kinds of skills would a batik artist need?

the volume of trade across the Pacific was greater than that across the Atlantic. Some analysts have predicted that the 2000s will be the "Pacific century" because of this region's potential for further growth.

Countries on the Asian Pacific Rim formed a huge market that lured investors, especially multinational corporations. American companies, too, sought a place on the Asian Pacific Rim. With more than 1.2 billion people, China has a fifth of the world's population. Indonesia, with 190 million people, and Japan, with 125 million, are also among the world's most populous nations. Since the 1960s, Japan has dominated the Asian Pacific Rim economically. By the 1990s, however, China was challenging Japan's economic empire.

Pacific Rim countries are enormously diverse. Indian, Hindu, Buddhist, and Confucian traditions, you will recall, helped shape Southeast Asian cultures. Later, Islam took root in some areas, while the Age of Imperialism brought western and Christian influences.

Today, cultural exchanges occur rapidly as radio and television programs are beamed by satellite across Asia. Businesses and tourists aid the exchange of technology and ideas. The development of the Pacific Rim promises to bring the Americas and Asia into closer contact.

SECTION 4 Assessment

Recall
1. **Identify:** (a) Ho Chi Minh, (b) Khmer Rouge, (c) Corazon Aquino, (d) Aung San Suu Kyi, (e) ASEAN.
2. **Define:** (a) domino theory, (b) cease-fire, (c) embargo.

Comprehension
3. Describe the effects of war on (a) Vietnam, (b) Cambodia.
4. What economic and ethnic issues have faced governments in the Philippines and Indonesia?
5. Why is the Pacific Rim seen as an important link in the global economy?

Critical Thinking and Writing
6. **Linking Past and Present** What effects of the Vietnam War can still be seen in the United States today?
7. **Connecting to Geography** How might Indonesia's geographic features affect its ability to create a national identity?

Activity
Take It to the NET

Use the Internet to research the ASEAN Promotion Centre on Trade, Investment, and Tourism. (a) List ASEAN's member countries. (b) Write a paragraph explaining Japan's economic relations with another member country.

SECTION 4 Assessment

Recall
1 (a) Ho Chi Minh, p. 873 (b) Khmer Rouge, p. 874 (c) Corazon Aquino, p. 875 (d) Aung San Suu Kyi, p. 876 (e) ASEAN, p. 876 2. (a) domino theory, p. 873 (b) cease-fire, p. 874 (c) embargo, p. 874

Comprehension
3. (a) Vietnam became united under a communist government. The destruction brought on by war and an American embargo meant that recovery was extremely slow. (b) The Khmer Rouge took over Cambodia, killing more than a million people. 4. Economic growth has been sporadic, leading to huge urban slums. Conflict has arisen among ethnic groups that feel underrepresented. 5. The Pacific Rim, with its very large population, represents a huge market for multinational corporations.

Critical Thinking and Writing
6. Possible answer: Signs of the war's effects today include war memorials, references to the war in debates over American involvement in overseas conflicts, and the large number of immigrants from Southeast Asia to the United States. 7. Indonesia's population is scattered among more than 13,000 islands across 3,200 miles of ocean. When distance and natural barriers divide people, it can be difficult to create a national identity.

Activity Rubrics

Share rubrics with students before they create their lists and paragraphs.

Attempted The list and paragraph are incomplete or inaccurate, reflecting insufficient research or effort.

Minimal The list is accurate, but the paragraph offers only a sketchy explanation of the two countries' economic relations.

Adequate The list is accurate, and the paragraph offers a strong explanation of the two countries' economic relations.

Exemplary The list is accurate, and the paragraph offers a comprehensive, clearly written explanation that reflects a strong understanding of the two countries' economic relations.

Caption Answer

Possible answers: knowledge of batiking process, draftsmanship, knowledge of materials

---

Human Drama Note

Global Culture The modern global economy is but one facet of the emerging global culture. Technology and communications have increased the speed at which old and new cultures intermingle and mutually transform themselves. On the Pacific Rim and in other parts of the world, an urban-based, technological culture is spreading. Disappearing fast are indigenous cultures, their traditions absorbed and diluted before scientists can fully study them. Loss of cultures means loss of different perspectives, knowledge, and languages. English is now spoken by one-fifth of the world's population, but perhaps the Penan people of Borneo could teach everyone about social cooperation. Their language has only one word for "he," "she," and "it" but six words for "we."

Creating a Chapter Summary

As a reteaching opportunity, pair a more able student with a less able student to complete this chapter summary.

Communist governments People's Republic of China, Vietnam, Cambodia, North Korea **Democratic or independent governments** Japan, Taiwan, Hong Kong, Singapore, South Korea, the Philippines, Indonesia, and Myanmar

Building Vocabulary

1–10. Students' sentences should reflect an understanding of each word.

Recalling Key Facts

11. It led to a famine that killed up to 30 million people.
12. When the communists won the civil war, the nationalists fled to Taiwan and established a separate government.
13. North Vietnam conquered South Vietnam and reunited the country.
14. through the "people power" revolution which pressured Marcos to hold elections in 1986 and forced him to leave
15. They have formed ASEAN to encourage regional and international trade.
16. The Pacific Rim includes countries that border the Pacific Ocean. Trade in the region has grown dramatically.

Critical Thinking and Writing

17. Possible answer: Prosperity and foreign influences may weaken the traditional work ethic and group loyalty.
18. Both introduced economic reforms, including private ownership and free-market policies. Gorbachev sought both political and economic reforms, while Deng allowed only economic reform.
19. North Korea and South Korea remain divided, with conflicting political and economic systems.
20. Possible answers: **(a)** Hong Kong may suffer loss of freedoms under communism. **(b)** Western ideas may enter China through Hong Kong and encourage Chinese people to push for democracy.

CHAPTER **34 Review and Assessment**

Creating a Chapter Summary

Copy this diagram on a sheet of paper. In the blank circles, write the names of nations that have communist governments and those that have independent or democratic governments. Add more circles as needed.

For additional review and enrichment activities, see the interactive version of *World History* available on the Web and on CD-ROM.

Web Site Self-Test
For practice test questions for Chapter 34, see **www.phschool.com**.

Building Vocabulary

Write a sentence for each of the following terms.

1. zaibatsu
2. gross domestic product
3. trade deficit
4. five-year plan
5. collectivization
6. commune
7. joint venture
8. special enterprise zone
9. domino theory
10. cease-fire

Recalling Key Facts

11. How did the Great Leap Forward affect China?
12. Why did Taiwan create a separate government from that of mainland China?
13. What was the outcome of the war in Vietnam?
14. How did supporters of democracy in the Philippines overturn Ferdinand Marcos's government?
15. How have Southeast Asian nations increased regional cooperation?
16. What is the Pacific Rim? What has happened to trade in this region?

Critical Thinking and Writing

17. **Recognizing Causes and Effects** How might Japan's emergence as an economic superpower threaten some of the values that contributed to that success?
18. **Comparing** How did Deng Xiaoping's reforms in China compare with Mikhail Gorbachev's reforms in the Soviet Union?
19. **Linking Past and Present** How are the effects of the Cold War still felt in Korea today?
20. **Predicting Consequences** What long-term effects might the takeover of Hong Kong by China have on **(a)** Hong Kong, **(b)** China? Explain your answers.
21. **Connecting to Geography** "Five hundred years ago," notes a modern economist, "the world's economic center moved from the Mediterranean to the Atlantic. Today, it has shifted again to the Pacific." Support this statement using details about Asia from this chapter.

21. During the 1500s, European exploration shifted commerce to the Atlantic. The Industrial Revolution increased Atlantic trade and commerce among industrialized western nations. Today, the industrialized Pacific Rim countries are assuming a dominant role in global commerce.

China's Cultural Revolution became an assault on intellectuals throughout Chinese society. In the excerpt below, a student describes some of the hardships he endured. Read the excerpt, then answer the questions that follow.

"When the Cultural Revolution began . . . my family was one of the first in the city to be ransacked. . . . At that time all the funds capitalists had in the banks were frozen. You couldn't withdraw anything. . . . My mother didn't know about that. She went to get some money out. The bank clerks immediately called the Red Guards. They showed up in no time at my home and started to search and ransack our apartment. . . .

The next day, I went to see the Red Guards responsible for ransacking my family. I figured I'd take anything from them: insults, criticism, and everything else. I was going to beg them to allow me to go home to have a look. . . .

I glanced over the rooms. . . . Lots of things were in shreds, smashed and torn. . . . The only thing left to me was the desire to survive. I forgot everything else, even hunger."

—quoted in *Voices From the Whirlwind* (Jicai)

22. Why was the student's home ransacked?
23. What type of damage did the student see?
24. What feelings did the student have after seeing his family's home?

A critical reader of Internet resources must be able to detect bias. Identify the source of information you are using, such as a university, news organization, or individual.

Use the Internet to research diverse opinions about the possibility of reunifying Taiwan and China. Then, write a paragraph explaining whether or not you support reunification.

Vietnam War, 1968–1975

→ Tet Offensive, 1968
■ American bases
▨ National Liberation Front base areas
⇢ North Vietnam's final offensive, 1975

CHINA
Red River
Tropic of Cancer
NORTH VIETNAM
Dienbienphu
Hanoi • Haiphong
LAOS
Gulf of Tonkin
Hainan
20°N
Vientiane
N
W E
S
THAILAND
Hue
Danang
Chu Lai
SOUTH VIETNAM
Bangkok
Plei Ku
CAMBODIA
Ho Chi Minh Trail
100°E
110°E
Gulf of Thailand
Camranh Bay
Phnom Penh
Saigon (Ho Chi Minh City)
Mercator Projection
0   200 Miles
0   200 Kilometers
MEKONG DELTA
South China Sea
10°N

Study this map of the Vietnam War. Then, answer the following questions:

25. In what nation did the National Liberation Front have its base areas?
26. What was the starting point for the Tet Offensive?
27. Describe the route of the Ho Chi Minh Trail.
28. What countries provided sites for American bases?
29. Examine the course of the Mekong River. How might different nations have been able to use the river to their advantage during the war?
30. Why do you think the name of the city of Saigon was changed?

22. His mother tried to withdraw funds from a frozen account. The Red Guard was called and ransacked their house for evidence.
23. Lots of things were in shreds, smashed, and torn.
24. He forgot everything except survival.

25. Cambodia
26. the Ho Chi Minh Trail
27. It started in North Vietnam, went through Laos and Cambodia, and there branched into South Vietnam.
28. South Vietnam, Thailand
29. North Vietnam could use it to get troops into South Vietnam. South Vietnamese and American troops could travel up river to reach near the Ho Chi Minh Trail.
30. The North Vietnamese changed it to display their victory and to crush the reminder of the former South Vietnam.

Explain to students the meaning of the following domains commonly found in Internet addresses: .edu, .org, .gov, and .com *(educational institution, organization, government, commercial)*. The Skills Handbook in the front of the book has a lesson that will help students with this feature.

Remind students to continue working on their Unit Theme Activity. See rubrics for the activity on the unit opener page in the Teacher's Edition.

Direct students to **www.phschool.com** for links to sites that will help them get started on this assignment. Share rubrics with students.
Attempted The paragraph is incomplete or does not reflect sufficient research.
Minimal The paragraph needs more support for its position or is poorly written.
Adequate The paragraph supports the writer's position with sufficient evidence and is well written.
Exemplary The paragraph clearly supports the writer's position with compelling evidence, is well written, and reflects a good understanding of the political situation.

Chapter 35 Planning Guide

Resource Manager

	CORE INSTRUCTION	READING/SKILLS
Chapter Level Resources	**Teaching Resources** 📘 Pacing Charts, Ch. 35 📘 Teaching With Themes, p. 38 📖 Color Transparencies, p. F–71 💿 Resource Pro® Ch. 35 📖 www.phschool.com • eTeach	💿 Book on CD, Ch. 35 💿 Interactive Student Tutorial CD-ROM, Ch. 35 💿 Social Studies Skills Tutor CD-ROM 📖 Skills Transparencies

1 Nations of South Asia
1. Explain why India was partitioned.
2. Discuss how India has dealt with political, economic, and social change.
3. Identify problems Pakistan and Bangladesh faced.
4. Show how South Asia is linked to world affairs.
	Teaching Resources
	📘 Unit 8 booklet
	  • Biography Activity, p. 64
	📘 Creative Teaching Activities, p. 155
	💿 Prentice Hall Presentation Pro, Ch. 35, Section 1
		Teaching Resources
		📘 Unit 8 booklet
		  • Guided Reading and Review, p. 56
		📘 Guide to the Essentials
		📼 Guided Reading Audiotapes, Ch. 35, Section 1

2 Forces Shaping the Modern Middle East
1. Point out how diversity and nationalism shaped the Middle East.
2. Identify political and economic patterns that emerged.
3. Explain why an Islamic revival grew.
4. Describe how women's lives vary in the Middle East.
	Teaching Resources
	📘 Creative Teaching Activities, p. 156
	💿 Prentice Hall Presentation Pro, Ch. 35, Section 2
	📖 Section Reading Support Transparencies
		Teaching Resources
		📘 Unit 8 booklet
		  • Guided Reading and Review, p. 58
		  • Skill Application Activity, p. 67
		📘 Guide to the Essentials
		📼 Guided Reading Audiotapes, Ch. 35, Section 2

3 Nation Building in the Middle East: Three Case Studies 1. Outline issues that Turkey faced. 2. Analyze why Egypt was a leader in the Arab world. 3. Summarize causes and results of the revolution in Iran.	**Teaching Resources** 📘 Creative Teaching Activities, p. 157 💿 Prentice Hall Presentation Pro, Ch. 35, Section 3 📖 Section Reading Support Transparencies	**Teaching Resources** 📘 Unit 8 booklet • Guided Reading and Review, p. 60 📘 Guide to the Essentials 📼 Guided Reading Audiotapes, Ch. 35, Section 3

4 The Middle East and the World
1. Describe how the Cold War increased tensions in the Middle East.
2. Analyze why Arab–Israeli conflict was difficult to resolve.
3. Restate why conflicts arose in Lebanon and the Persian Gulf.
	Teaching Resources
	📘 Unit 8 booklet
	  • Primary Source Activity, p. 65
	  • Viewpoint Activity, p. 66
	📘 Creative Teaching Activities, p. 158
	💿 Prentice Hall Presentation Pro, Ch. 35, Section 4
		Teaching Resources
		📘 Unit 8 booklet
		  • Guided Reading and Review, p. 62
		📘 Guide to the Essentials
		📼 Guided Reading Audiotapes, Ch. 35, Section 4

ENRICHMENT/PRE-AP

www.phschool.com
- Why Study History?

Teaching Resources
- History Through Literature, pp. 72–74
- Color Transparencies, pp. B–53, B–55, B–57
- www.phschool.com
  - Internet Activities, Section 1

Teaching Resources
- Chapter Extension Activities, p. 83
- Color Transparencies, p. D–89
- www.phschool.com
  - Virtual Field Trip

Teaching Resources
- Chapter Extension Activities, p. 84
- www.phschool.com
  - Internet Activities, Naguib Mahfouz: Views of Egypt
  - Internet Activities, Section 3

Listening to Literature World Masterpieces, *The Diameter of a Bomb,* side 10

ASSESSMENT

PRENTICE HALL
ASSESSMENT *SYSTEM*

Core Assessment
- ExamView Test Bank booklet, Ch. 35
- ExamView Test Bank CD-ROM, Ch. 35

Standardized Test Preparation

Diagnose and Prescribe
- Diagnostic Tests for High School Social Studies Skills

Review and Reteach
- Review Book for World History

Practice and Assess
- Test-Taking Strategies With Transparencies for High School
- Alternative Assessment booklet
- Test Prep Book for World History

Teaching Resources
- Unit 8 booklet
  - Geography Quiz, p. 68
  - Section Quizzes, pp. 57, 59, 61, 63
  - Chapter Tests A, B, and C, pp. 69–73
- www.phschool.com
  - Self-Test

CUSTOMIZE FOR INDIVIDUAL NEEDS

Gifted and Talented
- Teacher's Edition, Activities: Customize for Heterogeneous Groups, p. 883

Less Proficient Readers
- Guide to the Essentials, Ch. 35
- Book on CD, Ch. 35
- Teacher's Edition, Activities: Reading Strategy, p. 895; Customize for Heterogeneous Groups, p. 896

Less Proficient Writers
- Teacher's Edition, Activities: Cooperative Learning Activity, p. 897; Customize for Auditory Learners, p. 900

Students Acquiring English/ESL
- Guide to the Essentials, English/Spanish, Ch. 35
- Guided Reading Audiotapes, English/Spanish, Ch. 35
- Book on CD, Ch. 35
- Teacher's Edition, Activities marked with an *

TEXT

Don't miss the exclusive interactive version of *World History: Connections to Today* on the Internet and CD-ROM.

INTRODUCTION

In South Asia and the Middle East, nations cast off western rule and begin to modernize. They have similar challenges—religious and ethnic strife, border conflicts, urbanization, and population growth. In India, leaders create the world's largest democracy. In Iran, leaders rejected western models and created a theocracy. In Israel, after long conflict, Palestinians and Jews seek peace.

Focusing on Themes

Suggest that students focus on these theme questions as they read:

Diversity
What impact did diversity have on challenges to nations in South Asia and the Middle East?

Economics and Technology
How did emerging nations use technology to develop economically?

Geography and History
Why was geography a significant force in shaping the modern Middle East?

Continuity and Change
How did modernization pose a challenge to older cultural values and traditions?

Religions and Value Systems
Why did the Islamic revival have a strong appeal to many Muslims?

◆ TIME LINE ACTIVITY

Share the About the Pictures note with students before asking these questions:

1. What common themes do events on the time line share? *(possible answers: religious and ethnic conflict, independence)*
2. What two events before 1984 seem to have religion as a motive? *(India is divided, 1947; revolution in Iran, 1979)*
3. What problem would be caused by burning oil wells in Kuwait in 1991? *(air pollution)*

Don't Miss!

Synthesizing Information
Water Scarcity in the Middle East (Section 2)

Humanities Link
Naguib Mahfouz: Views of Egypt (Section 3)

South Asia and the Middle East 1945–Present

Chapter Preview

1 **Nations of South Asia**
2 **Forces Shaping the Modern Middle East**
3 **Nation Building in the Middle East: Three Case Studies**
4 **The Middle East and the World**

1947
India wins independence from Britain. The subcontinent is divided into Hindu India (top) and Muslim Pakistan (bottom).

1956
Egyptian president Gamal Abdel Nasser (above) nationalizes the Suez Canal, ending British and French control of the vital waterway.

1979
Revolutionaries in Iran oust the shah and declare an Islamic republic.

CHAPTER EVENTS

1940

1955

1970

GLOBAL EVENTS

1941 Nazis begin to implement "Final Solution"

1957 Ghana wins independence.

1966 Cultural Revolution begins in China.

◆ Resource Directory

Teaching Resources
Chapter Theme Activities Teaching With Themes booklet, p. 38
Pacing Chart With Block Scheduling Guide Ch. 35
Technology
World History Color Transparencies Ch. 35 Graphic Organizer, p. F–71

Independence in South Asia and the Middle East

In South Asia and the Middle East, large nations like India and tiny ones like Jordan won independence. Since then, each has charted its own path toward modernization.

TURKEY 1923
LEBANON 1941 · Beirut
SYRIA 1946 · Damascus
ISRAEL 1948
JORDAN 1946 · Amman · Jerusalem
IRAQ 1932 · Baghdad
Cairo
EGYPT 1922
KUWAIT 1961 · Kuwait
BAHRAIN 1971 · Manama
QATAR 1971 · Riyadh · Doha
UNITED ARAB EMIRATES 1971 · Abu Dhabi · Muscat
OMAN 1951
SAUDI ARABIA 1932
YEMEN 1990 · Sanaa
AFGHANISTAN
PAKISTAN 1947 · Islamabad
NEPAL
INDIA 1947 · New Delhi
BHUTAN
BANGLADESH 1971 · Dhaka
SRI LANKA 1948 · Colombo

Ankara

Black Sea · Caspian Sea · Mediterranean Sea · Red Sea · Persian Gulf · Gulf of Aden · Arabian Sea · Bay of Bengal · INDIAN OCEAN

Tropic of Cancer · Ganges R.

AFRICA · ASIA

Dates on map indicate date of creation or independence

Mercator Projection
0   400   800 Miles
0   400   800 Kilometers

1984
Sikh separatists clash with Indian troops at the Golden Temple in Amritsar.

1991
The Persian Gulf War ends an Iraqi invasion of Kuwait. Retreating Iraqi troops set fire to hundreds of Kuwaiti oil wells.

1999
General Pervez Musharraf of Pakistan (shown in portrait above) deposes the civilian government in the name of fighting corruption and restoring a stable government.

1985 · 2000 · 2015

1991 The Soviet Union collapses.

Take It to the NET
To learn about recent developments in South Asia and the Middle East, visit the World History section of **www.phschool.com**.

Independence in South Asia and the Middle East

Activating Prior Knowledge
In which nation was the modernization movement led by Mustafa Kemal? *(Turkey)*

Previewing
Which nations became independent within two years of the end of World War II? *(Syria, Jordan, Pakistan, India)*

Background
About the Pictures

   4

1. Adopted in 1947, the flag of India bears the wheel of dharma as the national emblem. The image is taken from one of the stelae that Asoka erected in the 200s B.C. The star and crescent that adorn the Pakistani flag are traditional symbols of Islam.

2. After the canal was nationalized, Israel, Britain, and France attacked Egypt in 1956. Egypt then blocked the canal by sinking 40 ships in it. A truce brokered by the UN led to the removal of the foreign forces and the reopening of the canal in 1957.

3. It took firefighters, many of whom were from the United States, 10 months to put out the fires and cap the wells.

4. During a crisis in 1999 between India and Pakistan over Kashmir, a part of India with a majority Muslim population, General Musharraf was the military chief of Pakistan. After the increasingly unpopular prime minister fired Musharraf, the general deposed him and established military rule, pledging to cleanse the government of corruption.

 eTeach

Be sure to check out this month's online discussion with a World History Master Teacher.

Go to **www.phschool.com**.

Independent Assignments

Have students read one section as they prepare for class. After class, have them complete the assignment. Some students may benefit from using the Guided Reading and Review worksheets.

Section 1 Have students use the worksheet *Satyajit Ray* in the Unit 8 booklet, p. 64, to learn about this Indian filmmaker.

Section 2 Have students use the worksheet *Revising Your Writing* in the Unit 8 booklet, p. 67, to learn how to improve their writing.

Section 3 Consult lesson ideas at the front of the Historical Outline Map Book and have students use the map *Southwest Asia*, p. 69, to learn the locations of various nations in the Middle East.

Section 4 Have students use the worksheet *An Encounter With the Israeli Army* in the Unit 8 booklet, p. 65, to learn about a confrontation between a female Arab professor and Israeli soldiers.

Bell Ringer Ask students to scan the section and to study the map on the next page. Then, have them list the countries that make up the region of South Asia. Ask them to recall what they have previously learned about the region and to write three facts that they think have a significant impact on the region today.

LESSON PLAN

1. Focus The partition of India in 1947 created two states—India, with its Hindu majority, and Pakistan, with its Muslim majority. The new nations of South Asia sought industrial growth, increased agricultural production, solutions for complex social issues, and other goals. Significant problems for the region have included population growth and regional, religious, and ethnic conflicts. Both India and Pakistan have played important roles in world affairs.

2. Instruct Work with the class to construct a chart about India on the chalkboard. Construct the chart with two columns and six or more rows. Use the following labels for the two columns: Problems, Progress. Use the following labels for the rows: Government, Economy, Religious Tensions, Education, Social Inequality, International Relations. Allow students time to complete the chart by working individually or in groups. When they have finished, invite students to come to the board and fill in details for each section of the chart. You may wish to use the completed chart as the focus for a discussion on India.

3. Assess Ask students to find current news and magazine articles about India. Have students bring in their articles to share with the class. Have students evaluate the information according to the chart categories: Does it represent a problem or progress or both?

4. Reteach If students' Assess activity does not reflect adequate understanding of the lesson, you might assign the *Guide to the Essentials* or the *Interactive Student Tutorial CD-ROM* for this section.

Primary Source

ANSWER Possible answers: very substantially, awake to life and freedom, soul of a nation . . . finds utterance

Reading Focus

- Why was India partitioned?
- How has India dealt with political, economic, and social change?
- What problems did Pakistan and Bangladesh face?
- How is South Asia linked to world affairs?

Vocabulary

partition
federal system
harijan
deforestation
debt service
cyclone

Taking Notes

On a sheet of paper, make a Venn diagram like this one. As you read, add information about developments in India and Pakistan after winning independence.

INDIA • World's largest democracy • Ethnic rivalries • Military leaders seize power **PAKISTAN**

Main Idea After winning independence, Hindu India and Muslim Pakistan pursued separate roads to modernization.

Primary Source

Nehru's Vision of Independence

As the Indian Assembly met to celebrate independence, Prime Minister Jawaharlal Nehru spoke:

"Long years ago we made an [appointment] with destiny, and now the time comes when we shall redeem our pledge, not wholly or in full measure, but very substantially. At the stroke of the midnight hour, when the world sleeps, India will awake to life and freedom. A moment comes, which comes but rarely in history, when we step out from the old to the new, when an age ends and when the soul of a nation long suppressed finds utterance. It is fitting that at this solemn moment we take the pledge of dedication to the service of India and her people and to the still larger cause of humanity."

—Jawaharlal Nehru, "Tryst With Destiny" speech

Skills Assessment

Primary Source What words or phrases did Nehru use to express his optimism about India's future?

Setting the Scene August 15, 1947, was a joyful day in India. Everywhere, crowds gathered to watch parades and fireworks. At the stroke of midnight, power had passed from British colonial rulers into the hands of Indians themselves. This was India's Independence Day.

Three years later, India adopted a new democratic constitution. It set lofty goals for the nation:

". . . to secure to all its citizens: JUSTICE, social, economic, and political; LIBERTY of thought, expression, belief, faith and worship; EQUALITY of status and opportunity; and to promote among them all FRATERNITY assuring the dignity of the individual and the unity of the Nation."

—Indian National Constitution

Achieving those goals would be difficult. Most Indians were poor, uneducated, and divided by caste, region, language, and religious and ethnic background. Other nations on the subcontinent faced similar challenges.

Independence and Partition

As you have read, Indian nationalists had demanded independence since the late 1800s. After World War II, Britain finally agreed to these demands. As independence neared, a long-simmering issue surfaced. What would happen to the Muslim minority in a Hindu-dominated India?

Two Nations Muhammad Ali Jinnah, leader of the Muslim League, insisted that Muslims have their own state, Pakistan. Riots between Hindus and Muslims helped persuade Britain to partition, or divide, the subcontinent. Drawing fair borders was impossible because Hindus and Muslims lived side by side. Still, in 1947, British officials hastily created Hindu India and Muslim Pakistan. Pakistan was made up of two widely separated areas in the northern part of the subcontinent that had large Muslim populations.

Tragedy Unfolds In 1947, millions of Hindus and Muslims crossed the borders of India and Pakistan in both directions. During the mass migration, centuries of mistrust—which the British had exploited to keep the population divided—plunged northern India into savage violence. Sikh and Hindu mobs slaughtered Muslims fleeing into Pakistan. Muslims massacred Hindu and Sikh neighbors. An estimated 10 million refugees fled their homes. One million or more, mostly Muslims, may have died.

Resource Directory

Teaching Resources

Creative Teaching Activities Creative Teaching Activities booklet, p. 155
Guided Reading and Review Unit 8 booklet, p. 56
History Through Literature *The Day Gandhi Was Shot*, History Through Literature booklet, pp. 72–74

Technology

World History Color Transparencies *South Asia, 1945–Present*, base map and overlay transparencies, set 6, pp. B–53, B–55, B–57

Horrified at the partition and the violence, Mohandas Gandhi, the "father of the nation," turned once more to satyagraha to restore peace. But on January 30, 1948, he was shot and killed by a Hindu extremist. Jawaharlal Nehru, India's first prime minister, told a stricken nation, "The light has gone out of our lives and there is darkness everywhere." Gandhi's death discredited the extremists and helped to end the worst violence. Still, Hindu-Muslim tensions persisted.

India: World's Largest Democracy

India built on the legacy of British government, including its system of law and government. Today, with a population of about one billion, it is the world's largest democratic nation.

Unity and Diversity To achieve independence, Indians had united behind the Congress party. Still, the new nation was deeply divided. It included hundreds of princely states that had survived British rule. Indians spoke a wide variety of languages and dialects. The majority of Indians were Hindu, but millions of others were Muslim, Sikh, Christian, or Buddhist.

India's constitution set up a federal system, like that of the United States. Under this system, powers are divided between a strong central government and smaller local governments. In time, the government reorganized the princely states into a smaller number of states. It recognized 15 official languages and 35 major regional languages.

The "Nehru Dynasty" For 40 years after independence, members of the Nehru family led India. From 1947 to 1964, Jawaharlal Nehru worked to build a modern, secular state dedicated to promoting social justice. After he died, his daughter Indira Gandhi and, later, his grandson Rajiv Gandhi, served as prime minister. Both were popular, energetic leaders, but at times their highhanded policies eroded goodwill. In the end, both fell victim to violence, as you will read. Today, Sonia Gandhi, the Italian-born widow of Rajiv, has entered the political arena.

Under the "Nehru dynasty," the Congress party dominated Indian politics. In the early 1990s, though, support deepened for the fundamentalist Bharatiya Janata party (BJP). Unlike the Congress party, which wanted to separate religion and government, the BJP called for a government built on Hindu principles. For a few years, the BJP held power. In 1999, the Congress party was returned to power, but it was a shadow of its former self. As the millennium turned, India's political future remained uncertain.

Ongoing Divisions India's size and diversity have contributed to religious and regional divisions. In 1992, the BJP backed calls for the destruction of a mosque in Ayodhya (uh YOHD yuh). Hindu fundamentalists claimed that it stood on a sacred Hindu site seized by Muslim invaders centuries earlier. The BJP wanted a Hindu temple built there. The conflict touched off rioting at Ayodhya and the mosque was destroyed.

Other divisions affected the prosperous Punjab region of northwestern India. There, some Sikhs wanted an independent state. In 1984, these Sikh separatists occupied the Golden Temple in Amritsar. When talks failed to

Partition of India, 1947

India, 1947
Pakistan, 1947
Disputed areas

Mercator Projection
0   300   600 Miles
0   300   600 Kilometers

Skills Assessment

Geography The partition of India created two populous new nations but also led to widespread violence.

1. **Location** On the map, locate (a) India, (b) East Pakistan, (c) West Pakistan, (d) Kashmir, (e) Afghanistan.
2. **Movement** Based on this map, describe the migration of Hindus and Muslims across the India–West Pakistan border in 1947.
3. **Critical Thinking Linking Past and Present** Compare this map with the map of Asia in the Reference Section. Identify two changes that have taken place since 1947.

Customize for . . .
Heterogeneous Groups

Writing an Editorial Ask students to imagine that they are newspaper editors in India in 1947. Tell them to write an editorial in which they favor or oppose partition. Students should include an explanation of why they believe partition is either a good or a bad plan for the subcontinent. When students are finished, have several volunteers read their editorials to the class. List on the chalkboard the arguments that are presented both for and against partition. When the lists are completed, ask students to decide which position is backed by the most convincing arguments. (Enrichment)

Background
Historical Evidence

Ayodhya's Aftermath The 1992 destruction of the mosque in Ayodhya initiated a wave of violence and turmoil in India. Hundreds died and thousands more were wounded or arrested. Strikes and protests immobilized many cities. Mob attacks on Muslim mosques and Hindu temples were accompanied by police shootings, arson, and other acts of violence. The majority of those killed were Muslims. While many of the police shootings were provoked by mob actions, journalists on the scene reported that incidents of police violence were often unprovoked or were overreactions.

Block Scheduling Support

Have students read the selection titled "Mohandas Gandhi: *Hind Swaraj*" in the Reference Section at the back of their textbooks. The selection explains the leader's ideas that motivated his nonviolent method of passive resistance. Have students complete the questions at the end of the selection, and then ask them to respond to the following questions: (1) Since Gandhi was shot and killed by an extremist, does this prove that his ideas were wrong? Explain. (2) How does Gandhi reply to the objection that in justifying his use of passive resistance he can disobey any law he does not like? (3) Would Gandhi's methods have been as successful in a totalitarian state like Hitler's Germany or Stalin's Soviet Union?

Skills Assessment

ANSWERS 1. Review locations with students. 2. Hindus moved eastward from West Pakistan into India. Muslims moved westward from India into West Pakistan. 3. Possible answer: East Pakistan is now Bangladesh. Ceylon won independence and is now Sri Lanka. Kashmir has been divided between Pakistan and India.

Protest at the Golden Temple
Although the Sikh religion has roots in Hinduism, conflict has often erupted between India's Sikh minority and Hindu majority. Here, Sikh separatists occupy the Golden Temple in Amritsar in 1984.

Theme: Diversity **What were these protesters demanding?**

oust them, Indira Gandhi sent troops. Thousands of Sikhs died in the fighting. A few months later, Gandhi was killed by two of her Sikh bodyguards. The assassination ignited battles between Hindus and Sikhs.

Economic Growth and Challenges

Like other developing nations, India wanted to apply modern technology to expand agriculture and industry. The government adopted a largely socialist model, drawing up five-year plans to set economic goals and manage resources.

Industry and Agriculture British-built railroads gave India its basic transportation network. Under Nehru, India built dams to produce hydroelectric power and poured resources into heavy industries such as steel. By the 1960s, India was on its way to becoming an industrial power. Development, however, remained uneven. India lacked oil and natural gas—two resources essential to economic growth. It had to rely on costly imported oil.

To turn out the educated work force essential to a developing industrial economy, the Indian government built schools and universities. The nation's literacy rate climbed, but unevenly. Boys were more likely to attend school than were girls. Also, children from poor families often received little schooling because they were needed to work.

Seeking to make India self-sufficient in food production, Nehru took advantage of the Green Revolution. New seeds, chemical fertilizers, and irrigation methods boosted crop output. Still, only farmers with enough land and money could afford to grow the new crops. Most farmers continued to use the same methods as in the past. They depended on the monsoons and produced enough to survive but had little surplus.

The Population Issue Rapid population growth hurt efforts to improve living conditions. India's population has tripled since independence. While food output rose, so did demand. More than a third of Indians live below the poverty level, eating only one meal a day.

As the population boomed and the Green Revolution eliminated many agricultural jobs, millions of people streamed into cities like Calcutta and Bombay to find work. But these overcrowded cities did not have enough jobs. Often, they could not provide basic services such as water or sewage. To help the urban poor, Mother Teresa, a Roman Catholic nun, founded an order in Calcutta called the Missionaries of Charity. Its branches in India and elsewhere have provided food and medical care to thousands.

The government encouraged family planning but did not impose harsh population control measures, as China did. Efforts to slow down population growth met with limited success. Many Indians, especially in rural areas, saw children as an economic resource. Children were expected to work the land and to care for parents in old age.

Economic Reform An economic slowdown and pressure from international lenders forced India to make reforms. Turning from the socialist model, it looked to the successes of the Asian tigers. It privatized some industries and made foreign investment easier. By the 1990s, India had a significant role in textiles, technology, and other industries. Computer experts at India's software center at Madras gained a worldwide reputation.

Social Change

In India, as elsewhere, urbanization undermined some traditions. Yet most Indians continued to live in villages, where centuries-old attitudes and values remained strong.

Reforming the Caste System Discrimination based on caste continued. In the 1930s, Gandhi had campaigned to end the inhumane treatment of untouchables, whom he called harijans—children of God. India's 1950 constitution banned discrimination against untouchables. The government set aside jobs and places in universities for these long-mistreated groups.

Despite such programs, deep prejudice persisted. Higher-caste Hindus still received better schooling and jobs. In the 1990s, the government tried to open more jobs to untouchables. Violent protests by higher-caste Hindus who feared losing their jobs forced the government to back off from its plan.

Women At independence, women gained the vote along with other legal rights. A few educated women, like Indira Gandhi, won elected office or entered professions. In the cities, upper- and middle-class families sought to educate their daughters as a sign of modernization and accomplishment.

Yet, because of class and caste differences, many girls from poor families receive little or no education. Women on the lower rungs of society cluster in menial, low-paying jobs. In rural areas, women make up a majority of the work force, but few receive wages for their labor.

Indian women have formed organizations and movements to meet their needs. The Self-Employed Women's Association (SEWA) formed production and marketing cooperatives, opened banks, and provided classes and legal advice for poor women. Women's groups have also fought violence against women, protested dowry laws, and called for environmental protection.

Pakistan and Bangladesh

At independence, Pakistan faced severe problems. Early on, military leaders seized power and ruled as dictators. The country lacked many essential natural resources for industry. Ethnic rivalries also fueled conflicts.

A Divided Nation West Pakistan and East Pakistan were separated by a wide swath of Indian territory. The people of both regions were Muslim, but their languages and cultures differed. Bengalis in the east outnumbered Punjabis in the west, yet Punjabis dominated the government and economy.

As tensions mounted, Bengalis broke away. In 1971, they declared independence for Bangladesh, or "Bengal Nation." The Pakistani military ruler ordered the army to crush the rebels. To escape the bloodbath, millions of Bengalis fled west into India. India responded by attacking and defeating the Pakistani army in Bangladesh.

Government Defeat discredited Pakistan's ruling general. A new civilian president, Zulfikar Ali Bhutto, promised to make a "prosperous and progressive Pakistan." Bhutto was in turn overthrown, tried, and executed by the military. Later, civilian government was restored. Twice between 1988 and 1996, Bhutto's daughter Benazir served as prime minister, but was also ousted from power twice.

By 1999, Pakistan's elected government faced severe challenges. Muslim militants demanded that Pakistan aggressively assert its right to rule India's largely Muslim province of Kashmir. (See next page.) Severe economic woes and widespread corruption plagued the government.

Once again, the military stepped in. Led by General Pervez Musharraf, the military "dismissed" the elected government and suspended the constitution. Musharraf claimed that "the choice before us was of saving the body, the nation, at the cost of losing a limb, the constitution." The military promised to revive the economy, fight corruption, and restore stable government.

Biography

Indira Gandhi 1917–1984

"On her fragile shoulders rests the huge destiny of India—and they don't shrink from the burden," noted French leader Charles de Gaulle of Prime Minister Indira Gandhi. Early in life, Gandhi's strength was forged by her family's participation in the independence struggle. "I was part of the processions and meetings and everything that took place," she said. As a young woman, she was imprisoned by British authorities for her part in the independence campaign.

Gandhi continued her central role in Indian politics after her father, Jawaharlal Nehru, became prime minister. With him she traveled throughout India and went on official trips abroad. Her experience and connections to Nehru helped her become prime minister after his death.

Theme: Impact of the Individual How did Gandhi's experiences as Nehru's daughter influence her political career?

Cycle of Destruction In 1991, a cyclone and accompanying storm surge ravaged Bangladesh, killing an estimated 140,000 people and leaving perhaps 10 million people homeless. As the president of Bangladesh toured his devastated country, he sighed, "I don't know why God should punish us like this."

Bangladesh is punished not only by nature but also by human activity. The Ganges and other rivers that flow through Bangladesh all have their watersheds in the southern slopes of the Himalayas. As a result of deforestation, these slopes are no longer able to absorb heavy monsoon rains. Year after year, therefore, the volume of runoff water pouring into Bangladesh increases and, with it, so does the devastation caused by floods. Poverty-stricken Bangladesh is ill-equipped to deal with the onslaught caused by both people and nature.

Sirimavo Bandaranaike In 1960, Sri Lanka became the world's first nation to elect a woman prime minister. Sirimavo Bandaranaike became interested in politics when she married political leader Solomon W.R.D. Bandaranaike in 1940. Her husband later became Sri Lanka's prime minister but was assassinated in 1959. It was then that Sirimavo decided to enter politics herself. She led the Sri Lanka Freedom party to victory in 1960 and served as prime minister until 1965. Bandaranaike again led her country as prime minister from 1970 to 1977. Her daughter, Chandrika Kumaratunga, followed in her mother's footsteps when she became prime minister of Sri Lanka in 1994. Later that year she was elected president and appointed her mother as prime minister.

Geography and History

Scaling Mt. Everest

Its summit soars above 29,000 feet, making Mt. Everest in the Himalayas the highest mountain in the world. On May 29, 1953, Tenzing Norgay of Nepal and Edmund Hillary of New Zealand were the first climbers to reach the top. Since then, some 700 others have risked avalanches, altitude sickness, and blinding snowstorms to reach the "top of the world." More than 150 mountaineers have died in the attempt.

The grueling climb requires sturdy equipment—oxygen tanks, snow tents, thick down suits, and aluminum ladders to cross crevasses—and extreme physical endurance. Explains one veteran climber, "Climbing above 26,000 feet, even with bottled oxygen, is like running on a treadmill and breathing through a straw."

 Theme: Economics and Technology What technology has made it possible for climbers to reach the top of Mt. Everest?

At the same time, many nations, including the United States, denounced the military takeover and called for a return to democratic rule.

Economy After independence, Pakistan moved to improve agriculture. It distributed unused lands to landless farmers, experimented with new high-yield crops, and financed irrigation projects. Building dams and clearing land helped boost food production, but at a high cost to the environment. Deforestation, or destruction of forest land, caused terrible floods when monsoon rains were heavy.

To modernize, Pakistan nationalized major industries. More recently, the government has encouraged private or mixed government and private ownership of businesses. Like other developing nations, Pakistan faces an ongoing financial crisis. It has borrowed heavily from lenders such as the World Bank and IMF. Yet debt service, paying interest on loans, takes 40 percent of the nation's budget, leaving little for development.

Some international authorities have urged outright cancellation of the debts of Pakistan and other developing nations. Yet such a move might discourage further foreign investment in nations that desperately need it.

Trials of Bangladesh Since 1971, Bangladesh has struggled to rise out of poverty, but geography often stands in the way. Its large population is crowded on a low-lying coastal plain. The region is subject to devastating floods when monsoon rains are too heavy or to droughts if the rains are too light. Cyclones, fierce circular windstorms, are another frequent threat.

Explosive population growth has strained resources still further. More than 50 million people, many of them women and children, live below the poverty level. Large amounts of foreign aid have brought little relief, in part because various military governments have misused the assistance.

Since the early 1990s, civilian governments have worked to encourage foreign investment. Foreign businesses took advantage of cheap labor costs to make clothes in Bangladesh for export to Japan and the West. However, human rights groups revealed that textile workers, often young children, were treated like slaves. Development in Bangladesh seemed to mirror the miseries of the early Industrial Revolution in the West.

South Asia and the World

India and Pakistan achieved their independence as the Cold War began, and each followed its own path. Nehru welcomed economic aid from both superpowers, but otherwise embraced the nonaligned movement. Pakistan, feeling threatened not only by India but by the Soviet Union to the north, accepted United States military aid. Partly to counter this alliance, Indira Gandhi signed a treaty of friendship with the Soviet Union in the 1970s. With the end of the Cold War in the early 1990s, both India and Pakistan sought aid from the western powers, especially the United States.

Conflict Over Kashmir Fear and mistrust marred relations between India and Pakistan. At independence, border conflicts ignited a war over Kashmir, a princely state in the Himalayas. Its Hindu monarch decided to join India, but its Muslim majority wanted to be part of Pakistan. Since then, Pakistan and India have fought several wars over Kashmir.

In 1999, the border conflict erupted anew. India accused Pakistan of funding groups inside Kashmir who opposed Indian rule and sending troops to fight there. Even after the fighting ended, tensions remained high, especially because India and Pakistan were flexing their muscles on another front, nuclear weapons.

The Nuclear Issue India tested its first nuclear bomb in 1974. India was proud of its new status as a nuclear power. But Pakistan felt threatened. It tried to acquire its own nuclear technology.

Geography and History

ANSWER bottled oxygen, aluminum ladders, and cold-weather tents and suits

Resource Directory

Teaching Resources
Section Quiz Unit 8 booklet, p. 57
Technology
Interactive Student Tutorial CD-ROM Ch. 35
Computer Test Bank Ch. 35

In 1998, Pakistan and India both tested nuclear weapons. As the nuclear rivalry raised new fears, leaders of the two nations met. They agreed to "confidence-building measures" to ease tensions and improve relations. Still, both countries faced strong nationalist and religious pressure to use at least the threat of nuclear conflict in future confrontations.

Afghanistan This Central Asian country has suffered years of civil war. From 1979 to 1989, Soviet troops supported a harsh communist government. With American aid, Afghan guerrillas forced the Soviets to withdraw.

The Soviet exit did not end the fighting. Civil war between rival factions went on for years. In the late 1990s, the Taliban, a fundamentalist Muslim group, gained power. They restored order but imposed an extreme form of Islam on Afghanistan.

The Taliban also supported al-Qaida, an international terrorist group led by a Saudi named Osama bin Laden. Bin Laden and al-Qaida terrorists planned and carried out the attacks on New York and Washington, D.C., on September 11, 2001. As you will read in the next section, this led to serious consequences.

Sri Lanka Ethnic tensions have fed guerrilla warfare in the island nation of Sri Lanka. Most Sri Lankans are Buddhists who speak Singhalese. The Tamil-speaking Hindu minority faced discrimination. For years, Tamil rebels have fought to set up a separate nation.

In the 1980s, India's Rajiv Gandhi sent troops to smash the rebels. Although the attempt failed, outraged Tamil extremists assassinated Gandhi in 1991. The violence has continued despite efforts to ease tensions.

Cause *and* Effect

Long-Term Causes	Short-Term Causes
• Muslim conquest of northern India in 1100s • British imperialism in India • Nationalists organize the Indian National Congress in 1885 • Muslim nationalists form separate Muslim League in 1906	• World War II weakens European colonial empires • Pressure from Indian nationalists increases • Insistence by Muhammad Ali Jinnah and the Muslim League that Muslims have their own state • Rioting between Hindus and Muslims throughout northern India

Partition of India

Effects

• Violence erupts as millions of Hindus and Muslims cross the border between India and Pakistan
• Gandhi is assassinated by Hindu extremists
• India and Pakistan become centers of Cold War rivalry
• Establishment of the state of Bangladesh

Connections to Today

• Continuing clash between India and Pakistan over Kashmir
• Nuclear arms race as both India and Pakistan refuse to sign Non-Proliferation Treaty

Skills Assessment **Chart** The conflicts that led to the partition of India continue to affect the subcontinent. **How have the long-term effects of the partition spread beyond India and Pakistan?**

SECTION 1 Assessment

Recall
1. **Identify:** (a) Jawaharlal Nehru, (b) Indira Gandhi, (c) Rajiv Gandhi, (d) BJP, (e) Mother Teresa, (f) Zulfikar Ali Bhutto, (g) Osama bin Laden.
2. **Define:** (a) partition, (b) federal system, (c) harijan, (d) deforestation, (e) debt service, (f) cyclone.

Comprehension
3. Why was the Indian subcontinent divided into two nations?
4. (a) What economic goals did India pursue? (b) Why has progress been limited?

5. Describe one problem facing (a) Pakistan, (b) Bangladesh.
6. How did Cold War rivalries affect South Asia? Give two examples.

Critical Thinking and Writing
7. **Applying Information** "The past still clings to us," said Jawaharlal Nehru. Give two examples that support his statement.
8. **Defending a Position** (a) Why would nationalists in India and Pakistan favor development of nuclear weapons? (b) Why did world leaders worry about the arms race in South Asia?

Activity
Take It to the NET

Use the Internet to find out more about a recent flood in Bangladesh. Then, with a partner, prepare an action report outlining local and international efforts to relieve flood victims. You may wish to include an illustrated map of the flood plain.

Chapter 35 **887**

EXPLORING HUMAN DRAMA — Human Drama Note

Muhammad Ali Jinnah The architect of Pakistani independence was born on December 25, 1876, to a wealthy merchant family. At age 16, he went to London to study law. Admitted to the bar in 1895, Jinnah quickly earned a reputation for brilliance. Strikingly thin (about 6 feet 2 inches tall and weighing less than 120 pounds), he had a powerful voice and presence. According to one of his peers, "When he stood up in court, slowly looking toward the judge, placing his monocle in his eye—with the sense of timing you would expect from an actor—he became omnipotent. Yes, that is the word—omnipotent."

Jinnah at first favored Muslim-Hindu unity, speaking eloquently for the idea at the 1916 meeting of the Indian National Congress and the Muslim League in Lucknow. He later changed his views, and, as the force behind the Muslim League, worked for partition. Terminally ill with tuberculosis, Jinnah lived long enough to see the bloody birth of Pakistan. At the time of his death, he voiced regret for his choice, saying that Pakistan was "the biggest blunder" of his life.

SECTION 1 Assessment

Recall
1. **(a)** Jawaharlal Nehru, p. 883 **(b)** Indira Gandhi, p. 883 **(c)** Rajiv Gandhi, p. 883 **(d)** BJP, p. 883 **(e)** Mother Teresa, p. 884 **(f)** Zulfikar Ali Bhutto, p. 885 **(g)** Osama bin Laden, p. 887 **2. (a)** partition, p. 882 **(b)** federal system, p. 883 **(c)** harijan, p. 885 **(d)** deforestation, p. 886 **(e)** debt service, p. 886 **(f)** cyclone, p. 886

Comprehension
3. Muslim demands for a separate state and riots between Hindus and Muslims convinced the British to partition.
4. **(a)** India wanted to use modern technology to expand its agriculture and industry. **(b)** India lacks the oil and natural gas needed for economic growth. Most farmers are too poor to take advantage of the Green Revolution. Population growth has reduced the benefits of increased production. **5.** Possible answers: **(a)** Pakistan has had periods of military rule. Efforts to improve agriculture have caused environmental problems. **(b)** Bangladesh is subject to floods and cyclones. Population growth has strained its resources.
6. India led the nonaligned movement; Pakistan accepted American military aid. The Soviet Union invaded and set up a puppet government in Afghanistan.

Critical Thinking and Writing
7. Possible answers: Despite government protection, untouchables still face discrimination; equality remains a distant goal for women. **8.** Possible answer: **(a)** as an expression of national power **(b)** The effects of a nuclear war, such as contamination of air, land, and water, can spread.

Activity Rubrics

Share rubrics with students before they do their reports.

Attempted The report is poorly written and organized and has many mechanical errors. The map is missing or incomplete.

Minimal The report is poorly written and organized and has mechanical errors. The map is messy.

Adequate The report is complete, well written, and well organized and has few mechanical errors. The map is well executed.

Exemplary The report is very well written and organized and has no mechanical errors. The map is striking.

Skills Assessment

ANSWER Possible answer: Nuclear war between India and Pakistan could have global effects.

Bell Ringer

Bell Ringer Have students skim through Section 2. Ask them to identify two natural resources that are of vital importance to the Middle East today.

LESSON PLAN

1. Focus Diversity and nationalism blocked the Pan-Arab dream of a united Arab state. Control of water and oil resources has a major impact on the countries of the Middle East. Ethnic and religious diversity, the influence of western culture, and the Islamic revival are some of the forces shaping the Middle East today.

2. Instruct Help students identify the various forces that are shaping the Middle East today. List these on the chalkboard. For example, students might name ethnic diversity, nationalism, western influence, religious differences, vital resources, Islamic reforms, or other factors. Define and discuss each item on the list. Then, ask students to rank these forces in the order of their importance to the Middle East. Invite volunteers to share their rankings with the class. Encourage students to explain the reasoning behind their choices.

3. Assess Ask students to create a political cartoon based on one of the issues the class has discussed.

4. Reteach If students' Assess activity does not reflect adequate understanding of the lesson, you might assign the *Guide to the Essentials* or the *Interactive Student Tutorial CD-ROM* for this section.

Reading Focus

- How have diversity and nationalism shaped the Middle East?
- What political and economic patterns have emerged?
- Why has an Islamic revival spread across the region?
- How do women's lives vary in the Middle East?

Vocabulary

recognize
kibbutz
desalinization
hejab

Taking Notes

As you read this section, prepare an outline of its contents. Use Roman numerals to indicate major headings. Use capital letters for subheadings, and use numbers for the supporting details. The example here will help you get started.

I. Diversity and nationalism
  A. Religious and cultural diversity
    1. Judaism, Christianity, Islam
    2. Different languages
    3.
  B. Winning independence

Main Idea Three forces shaping the modern Middle East are nationalism, religious and cultural diversity, and access to resources such as oil and water.

Setting the Scene In the Arab world, as in South Asia, nationalists sought to free themselves from the legacy of imperialism. "We are [erasing] the traces of the past," declared Egyptian president Gamal Abdel Nasser in the 1950s. "We are building our country on strong and sound bases."

Leaders of Nasser's generation embarked on ambitious reforms. Their policies, however, often failed to bring promised improvements. By the 1970s, Islamic reformers began to offer another route to modernization.

Diversity and Nationalism

What does the term *Middle East* mean? Western powers first used the term to refer to the region between Europe and what they called the "Far East"— China, Japan, and Southeast Asia. To avoid this western bias, some people now call the region Southwest Asia. Yet the UN and many scholars and journalists continue to use the term *Middle East*.

Experts differ on what areas lie in the Middle East. In this chapter, we use the term to refer to the region from Egypt in the west to Iran in the east and from Turkey in the north to the Arabian Peninsula in the south.

Religious and Cultural Diversity Judaism, Christianity, and Islam all emerged in the Middle East. Today, most people in the region are Muslims, but many Jews and Christians also live there. Different sects within these religions add to the diversity.

Middle Eastern peoples speak more than 30 different languages, including Arabic, Turkish, Persian, Hebrew, Kurdish, and Armenian. Every country is home to minority groups—some, as many as a dozen. The Kurds, for example, are an ethnic group divided by modern borders among Turkey, Iraq, and Iran. Their efforts to win autonomy have led to repression.

Like Christians in Europe, Muslims in the Middle East share the same basic faith but belong to different national groups. Arabs, Iranians, and Turks have their own cultures, languages, and histories. Often, such differences have created divisions.

Winning Independence In the Middle East, as elsewhere, imperialism and nationalism were powerful forces. In the decades after World War I, Arab nationalists opposed the mandate system that placed Arab territories under European rule. Iraq won freedom from Britain in 1932. After World War II, British and French mandates won complete independence as the nations of Lebanon, Syria, and Jordan.

Connections to Today

A People Without a Nation

Numbering some 25 million, the Kurds today are the world's largest ethnic group without a homeland. After World War I, world leaders had promised the Kurds a nation. But these promises were broken. Since then, the Kurds have fought for autonomy and independence.

However, politics has often driven a wedge among Kurds and weakened these efforts. In 1994, a civil war divided the two main Kurdish political parties in northeastern Iraq. In 1994, radical Kurds in Turkey led by rebel leader Abdullah Ocalan began a guerrilla war for independence. In 2000, rebel leaders called a halt to the fighting. They pledged to work for Kurdish rights "within a framework of peace and democratization."

Theme: Geography and History Why might Kurd rebels in Turkey have decided to halt the guerrilla war?

Connections to Today

ANSWER Possible answer: to win support from other nations

Resource Directory

Teaching Resources

Creative Teaching Activities Creative Teaching Activities booklet, p. 156

Guided Reading and Review Unit 8 booklet, p. 58

Skill Application Activity *Revising Your Writing,* Unit 8 booklet, p. 67

🖥 Virtual Field Trip

www.phschool.com

Jerusalem, Israel

To take a virtual tour of this important city—including sites sacred to Jews, Christians, and Muslims—use the Internet address above to link to the city of Jerusalem.

A Diverse City
The streets of Jerusalem are filled with a wide mix of people, including Jews and Palestinian Arabs. The street sign—written in Hebrew, Arabic, and English—reflects the city's diversity.
Theme: Diversity Why might Jerusalem become a center of conflict?

The Pan-Arab dream of a united Arab state foundered as nations pursued individual goals. Still, their common heritage linked Arabs across borders. Pan-Arabism survived in the Arab League, which promoted Arab solidarity in times of crisis and worked for common economic goals.

Colonial Legacy Despite winning independence, Arab nations remained economically dependent on the West. Westerners owned industries and banks. They provided the capital and technology needed for development, as well as the principal market for exports. Ending western economic domination became a key goal of many governments.

Imperialism left another legacy. Britain and France had drawn borders to serve their own interests. At independence, Arab nations inherited these borders, which often led to disputes. For example, Iraq included diverse and sometimes hostile groups. Colonial borders also limited Iraq's access to the Persian Gulf. Religious and ethnic tensions, plus a desire for outlets on the gulf, continue to fuel conflicts in Iraq.

Conflict Over Palestine As you read, in 1917, Britain issued the Balfour Declaration, which pledged support for a Jewish national home in Palestine. The declaration deepened tensions in that region. Both Jews and Palestinian Arabs claimed a historical right to the land. Jewish migration to Palestine, which began in the late 1800s, increased after World War II. In the United States, especially, the horrors of the Holocaust created strong support for a Jewish homeland. But growing migration and conflicting British policies led to violent clashes.

As turmoil increased, Britain turned over its mandate to the United Nations. In 1947, the UN drew up a plan to partition Palestine into an Arab and a Jewish state. Jews accepted the plan, but Arabs rejected it. They saw it as a plan to relocate European Jews on Arab territory.

The Birth of Israel After Britain withdrew in 1948, Jews proclaimed the independent state of Israel. The United States and Soviet Union both recognized Israel, that is, they formally agreed to treat it as a legitimate government. Arab states, however, launched a military attack on the new nation. Israeli forces fought well against the poorly equipped and badly led Arab forces. In the end, Israel increased its territory. Other Arab-Israeli wars would follow, as you will read.

Chapter 35 **889**

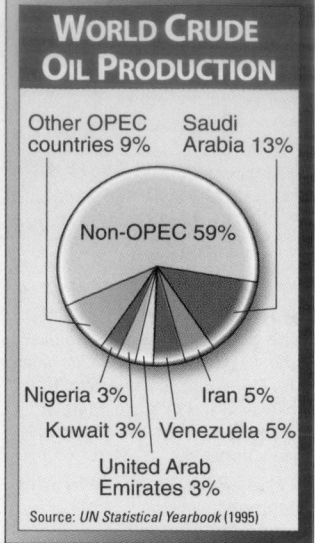

WORLD CRUDE OIL PRODUCTION

Other OPEC countries 9%
Saudi Arabia 13%
Non-OPEC 59%
Nigeria 3%
Iran 5%
Kuwait 3%
Venezuela 5%
United Arab Emirates 3%

Source: *UN Statistical Yearbook* (1995)

Skills Assessment

Graph In the 1970s, OPEC nations produced more than half of the world's oil. Today, that figure is much lower, but many nations still depend on OPEC fuel. **Which OPEC member produces the largest share of the world's oil? Identify two OPEC nations located outside the Middle East.**

Israel developed rapidly after 1948. The government built towns for settlers and provided many services. American aid and high taxes gave Israel the capital to invest in industry and agriculture. In spite of scarce natural resources, a skilled and educated work force made rapid progress. Israelis built factories and developed methods to farm their arid land. Kibbutzim, or collective farms, produced crops for export.

The Refugee Issue The Arab-Israeli War of 1948 uprooted 700,000 Arabs from Palestine. The UN set up temporary shelters for Palestinian refugees. These poverty-stricken camps have since become permanent homes. Recent generations of Palestinian refugees have grown up bitterly determined to win a homeland of their own. Resolving the refugee issue would remain a thorny problem in the peace process for decades.

Political and Economic Patterns

After winning independence, Middle Eastern nations worked to modernize their governments and economies. Parts of the region sit atop the world's largest oil reserves, which brought regional and global consequences.

Governments Most Middle Eastern nations developed authoritarian governments. In Egypt and Iraq, revolutionary military leaders toppled monarchs who were closely tied to western powers. In other countries, such as Jordan and Saudi Arabia, hereditary monarchs remained in power but took steps to adapt to the modern world. In Iraq and Syria, a single party won power. Dictators like Iraq's Saddam Hussein brutally suppressed opponents but enjoyed some popular backing because their social and economic policies improved life for many.

Only Israel and Turkey formed multiparty democratic systems. In both of these countries, however, minority groups—Kurds in Turkey and Arabs in Israel—faced restrictions or serious discrimination.

Impact of Oil Because the Middle East commanded vital oil resources, the United States and other powers increased their political and military presence in the region. At the same time, the 1973 OPEC oil embargo showed that oil could be a powerful diplomatic and economic weapon.

Oil is unevenly distributed. Only a few countries, mostly on the Persian Gulf, have large oil reserves. Oil-rich Saudi Arabia and Kuwait have small populations. Turkey and Egypt, with much larger populations, have little oil. As a result, differences between "haves" and "have-nots" fueled resentments within the region. Oil-rich nations built roads, hospitals, and schools. Poorer countries lacked the capital needed for development.

Water Resources Many experts have predicted that water, not oil, may soon become the most valuable resource in the Middle East. Most of the region has limited rainfall. Growing populations and rising standards of living have increased demands for water. Farmers can produce good crops—if they can get water. Farming accounts for 80 percent of water use in the Middle East. To meet this urgent demand, oil-rich countries have built desalinization plants that convert salty sea water into fresh water.

Individual nations have built dams to supply water both for crops and for hydroelectric power. Turkey, for example, erected 22 dams in the late 1980s, including the giant Atatürk Dam. Its goal was to irrigate southeastern Turkey with water from the Tigris and Euphrates rivers, turning the region into a breadbasket.

Yet dam building has sparked explosive debates over water resources. Many rivers run through several countries. The Euphrates rises in Turkey but flows through Syria and Iraq. Israel, Jordan, and Syria all have claims on the waters of the Jordan River. As water needs grow, nations that share river systems must seek ways to use that scarce resource cooperatively.

Synthesizing Information

Water Scarcity in the Middle East

Arid lands stretch across vast areas of the Middle East, where fresh water and rainfall are scarce. With new technology and massive investment, however, the nations in this dry region are trying to meet the water needs of growing populations.

Piping Water In

Once connected, this long line of pipes will snake across the desert in Saudi Arabia. Rather than carrying oil, these pipes will transport water. Pipelines bring treated water from desalinization plants on the coast to Riyadh and other inland cities.

Expensive projects such as dams and desalinization plants help Middle Eastern nations harness rivers and seas to make the desert bloom.

The Most Important Resource

Water conservation is critical in the Middle East. In many cases, peace hangs in the balance where water is concerned. Anis Muasher, founder of Jordan's Royal Society for the Protection of Nature, had this to say about water rights along the Jordan River:

"It becomes of no use to anybody if we continue behaving with nature the way we are behaving. . . . The whole world knows that water in the Middle East could be the cause of future wars, and we are fed up with wars. So the reasonable thing to do is to sit together, look at what we have, try to analyze it scientifically, take the consequences bravely, and do our job. Anything short of that will get nobody anywhere."

—Anis Muasher, *Audubon* magazine, September–October 1994

Water Resources in the Middle East

- Major dams
- Desalinization plants

Skills Assessment

1. Which Middle Eastern nation has the most desalinization plants?
   A Turkey
   B Syria
   C Saudi Arabia
   D Kuwait

2. Based on the picture, what can you conclude about Saudi Arabia?
   E It lacks natural resources.
   F Its terrain is flat.
   G It has a tropical climate.
   H It has an arid climate.

3. Critical Thinking Connecting to Geography Analyze each of the pieces of evidence above to describe how nations have used technology to change their environment. How might these changes affect international relations?

Skills Tip

Map symbols convey important geographic information while summarizing the main idea of the map.

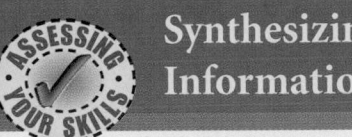
Background
About the Evidence

Desalinization Desalinization plants use a variety of processes, the most simple of which is distillation. In this process, salt water is boiled, and the resulting steam is collected and condensed into desalinized water. In other methods, such as electrodialysis and reverse osmosis, salt water is passed through special membranes that separate the salts and the water.

Activity
Interpreting the Evidence

Use these additional questions to generate class discussion.
1. **Critical Thinking: Recognizing Points of View** Building dams on the Tigris and Euphrates will create lakes that cover unexplored archaeological sites. Which is more important: present water needs or preservation of the sites? Why?
2. **Critical Thinking: Solving Problems** Syria and Iraq both use water from the Tigris and Euphrates. They are concerned that their share of the water will be reduced. How could the two nations resolve that issue?

Skills Tip

Since you know that rivers generally originate in high ground, the mountain symbols on the map can help determine the direction of their flow. The Skills Handbook in the front of the book has a lesson that will help students with this feature.

Skills Assessment

ANSWERS 1. C **2.** H **3.** Middle Eastern nations have built dams and desalinization plants to provide fresh water. Countries may become angry if dams built upriver reduce the water available to them.

Test Preparation

Have students read the passage by Anis Muasher on this page, and then answer the question below.

Which of the following gives the main idea of the passage?

A Nations of the Middle East have fought wars over water.

B Jordan has all the water it needs.

C Water is not a problem in the Middle East.

D The nations of the Middle East need to negotiate to settle water issues.

Economic Policies In the 1950s, some Arab nations turned to socialism as a way to end foreign economic control and modernize rapidly. They nationalized banks, oil companies, and factories. Despite such moves, they still depended on the industrial world for much of their technology.

To get capital, governments took foreign loans. They then built large projects in industry and agriculture, especially dams and other irrigation systems. In some countries, they redistributed land to peasants. But small farmers did not produce efficiently, and food output did not keep pace with rapid population growth. By the 1990s, under pressure from the IMF and other international lenders, many governments eased restrictions on foreign ownership. They privatized some state-run enterprises.

The Middle East, like other developing regions, faced grave economic challenges. Heavy borrowing left them deeply in debt and owing massive sums just in debt service. Also, while nations had built some industry and cities had boomed, large segments of the people still lived in poverty.

Islamic Revival

Islam has been a shaping force in the Middle East for more than 1,300 years. As in the past, the Quran and Sharia provide guidance on all aspects of life—from religious faith, law, and government to family and business relationships.

Western Influences During the Age of Imperialism, westerners urged Muslim nations to modernize. To the West, modernization meant adopting western forms of secular government and law. It also meant keeping religion and government separate.

After nearly a century of western influence, some Middle Eastern leaders adopted western models of development, promising economic progress and social justice. In the 1950s and 1960s, western cultural influences increased. In the growing cities, people wore western-style clothing, watched American television programs, and bought foreign products. Yet despite government promises, life improved very little for many people. When their leaders were unable to solve mounting problems, many people became disillusioned.

Call for Reform By the 1970s, in the face of failed development and repressive regimes, many Muslim leaders and writers called for a return to the Sharia. They blamed social and economic ills on blind imitation of western models and applied Islamic principles to the search for solutions.

Islamic reformers, often called fundamentalists by westerners, did not reject modernization, but they did reject westernization. They argued that a renewed commitment to Islam was the only way out of their current problems. Offering Islam as an inspiration, the movement appealed to poor and educated Muslims alike.

Impact By the 1990s, the Islamic revival had spread across the Muslim world, from Morocco to Indonesia. Its impact varied from country to country. In Iran, as you will read, revolutionaries overthrew an unpopular shah as early as 1979. In Algeria, voters supported members of a party that had pledged to restore the Sharia. In Egypt and elsewhere, some extremists justified terrorist acts as a weapon against authoritarian, secular governments. Other Muslim groups worked within the system for political reforms and social programs.

Across the Muslim world, the Islamic revival sparked heated debates between reformers and secularists. Issues ranged from science to crime. Like Christian fundamentalists in the West, many devout Muslims opposed any scientific view of the world that excluded belief in God as creator and ruler of the universe. They also urged political restructuring to put power in the hands of religious leaders.

A Profession of Islamic Faith
The Arabic lettering on this ceramic by Iraqi artist Wasma'a K. Chorbachi proclaims, "There is no God but God and Muhammad is his prophet." Chorbachi said that she turned away from western artistic styles to express her "inner identity" as an Arab and Muslim.

Theme: Religions and Value Systems Why do you think Chorbachi chose to inscribe this phrase on a work of art?

Resource Directory

Teaching Resources
Section Quiz Unit 8 booklet, p. 59
Technology
World History Color Transparencies *Village of Chtouka,* p. D–89
Interactive Student Tutorial CD-ROM Ch. 35
Computer Test Bank Ch. 35

Women in the Muslim World

Conditions for women vary greatly from country to country in the modern Middle East. Since the 1950s, women in most countries have won voting rights and equality before the law. They attend schools and universities in growing numbers. Middle- and upper-class women have entered professions such as law, engineering, and medicine.

The changes have taken place at different rates in different places. In Turkey, Syria, and Egypt, many urban women gave up long-held practices such as wearing hejab, or cover.[*] On the other hand, conservative countries like Saudi Arabia and Iran have opposed the spread of many western secular influences among women.

Return to Hejab In recent decades, many educated Muslim women have returned to wearing hejab. For some women, the movement symbolized resistance to unpopular governments or a refusal to imitate western culture. "I think of Muslim dress as a kind of uniform," one Egyptian student said. "I can sit in class with men and there is no question of attraction and so on—we are all involved in the same business of learning." Most important, women who elected to return to hejab saw it as an expression of sincere loyalty to Muslim values and practices.

Continuing Issues Still, some women in Muslim countries were dismayed. They argued against social and political forces that put severe limits on their lives.

Under Sharia, women traditionally held powerful positions in the family and played important economic roles. In some countries, though, laws and traditions emerged that limited women's right to vote, work, or even drive cars. Many Muslim and non-Muslim women spoke out on the need for women to realize their full potential and contribute to national life.

[*] The Arabic word *hejab* means "following Islamic guidelines for women's dress in public." The practice includes a variety of head coverings as well as a long, loose-fitting garment. In English, the word is often translated as "veiling," though only a small fraction of Muslim women cover their faces.

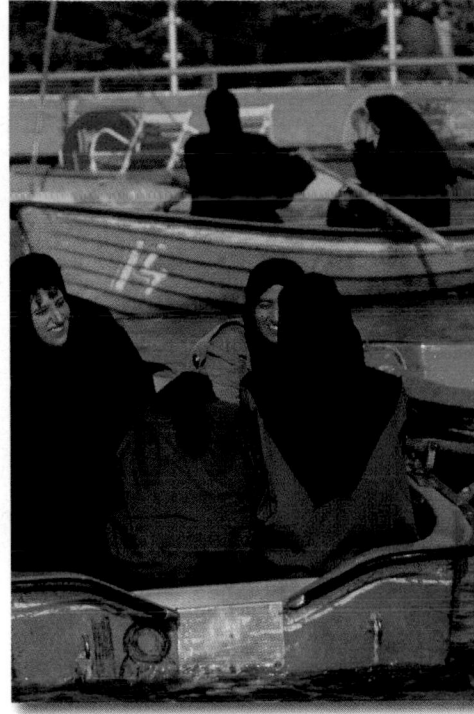

Return to Hejab
Today, many Muslim women have adopted the traditional form of dress known as hejab. Here, these Iranian women enjoy an afternoon of boating.

Theme: Continuity and Change How does the return to hejab reflect continuity in the Muslim world?

SECTION 2 Assessment

Recall
1. **Identify:** (a) Kurds, (b) Arab League.
2. **Define:** (a) recognize, (b) kibbutz, (c) desalinization, (d) hejab.

Comprehension
3. (a) What forces have linked Arab nations? (b) Give one example of how diversity has caused tension in a Middle Eastern nation.
4. How has oil shaped Middle Eastern economies?
5. How was the Islamic revival linked to social and political development?

6. (a) What rights have women gained in the Middle East? (b) Why did some Muslim women favor a return to hejab?

Critical Thinking and Writing
7. **Understanding Causes and Effects** (a) How did events of the early 1940s increase European and American support for the creation of Israel? (b) Why was such support needed?
8. **Defending a Position** Would you agree that water is a more valuable resource than oil? Why or why not?

Activity

Holding a Debate
With a group of classmates, stage a debate about paths to development in the Middle East. Have one team present arguments in favor of modernization and westernization. Have the other team present the opposing viewpoint. Have one student act as moderator.

Recall
1. (a) Kurds, p. 888 (b) Arab League, p. 889 2. (a) recognize, p. 889 (b) kibbutz, p. 890 (c) desalinization, p. 890 (d) hejab, p. 893

Comprehension
3. (a) the Muslim religion and a shared heritage (b) Answers include the Kurdish struggle for autonomy and the conflict between Israel and its Arab neighbors.
4. Oil-rich nations have used profits from petroleum exports to develop their economies and improve their standards of living. 5. Islamic reformers said that imitation of western culture had brought few political or economic benefits. They urged people to reject westernization and renew their commitment to Islam. Extremists have threatened some governments.
6. (a) Women in most countries have won suffrage and equality before the law. More of them attend universities and have entered professions. (b) To some women, it symbolized a resistance to westernization and an expression of loyalty to Islam.

Critical Thinking and Writing
7. (a) The horrors of the Holocaust helped convince many people of the need for a safe Jewish homeland. (b) Israel needed the support of Britain, which controlled Palestine. Israel also needed aid to build its economy and defend itself against attack. 8. Students should weigh the value of the two resources and consider the possible results of a shortage or lack of each.

Activity Rubrics

Share rubrics with students before they present their debates.

Attempted The debate team is poorly prepared, offers unsound arguments with factual errors, and is disorganized.

Minimal The debate team offers a few sound arguments, but most are weak and poorly organized.

Adequate The debate team is well prepared and offers strong, well-organized arguments and convincing support.

Exemplary The debate team's arguments are thoroughly researched, carefully prepared, insightful, and well reasoned.

Caption Answer

Possible answer: It is a return to traditional dress that connects Muslim women to the past.

Bell Ringer

Bell Ringer Ask students to skim through the section and identify the three Middle Eastern countries that the section uses as case studies. Have them write one general statement about each country.

LESSON PLAN

1. Focus In the late 1900s, Turkey struggled to build a stable government, cope with modernization and social upheaval, and settle conflicts with Kurds and Greek Cypriots. Egypt changed policies several times in its drive for modernization. In Iran, a revolution toppled the government of the shah and replaced it with an Islamic republic.

2. Instruct Divide the class into three groups. Assign each group one of the following nations: Turkey, Egypt, or Iran. Have students gather and outline information about their nation in each of the following areas: government, economy, religion, social issues, world affairs. Ask representatives from each group to report to the class. You may wish to compile the information into a large chart on the chalkboard that you may then use as the basis for a class discussion.

3. Assess Ask students to write predictions about the future of Turkey, Egypt, and Iran. Ask them to select the nation that they think is in the best position for the twenty-first century. Have them explain the reasons for their choices.

4. Reteach If students' *Assess* activity does not reflect adequate understanding of the lesson, you might assign the *Guide to the Essentials* or the *Interactive Student Tutorial CD-ROM* for this section.

Reading Focus

- What issues has Turkey faced?
- Why was Egypt a leader in the Arab world?
- What were the causes and results of the revolution in Iran?

Vocabulary

delta
ayatollah
theocracy

Taking Notes

Prepare a table comparing the three nations discussed in this section. The table here has been partly filled in to help you get started.

	TURKEY	EGYPT	IRAN
GOVERNMENT	• Multiparty democracy		
ECONOMY	• Expanding agriculture		
CONFLICTS	• Kurds		
OTHER ISSUES			

Main Idea Since World War II, Turkey, Egypt, and Iran have followed different routes to modernization.

Setting the Scene An Iranian religious leader, Ruhollah Khomeini (roo HOH luh koh MAY nee), angrily denounced the government. While the shah lived off the riches of the land, claimed Khomeini, most people lived in misery, especially in the capital city of Tehran:

> "Look at those pits, those holes in the ground where people live, dwellings you reach by going down a hundred steps into the ground, homes people have built out of rush matting or clay so their poor children can have somewhere to live."
> —*Declarations of the Ayatollah Khomeini*

Khomeini's fiery speeches helped spur an Iranian revolution in 1979.

In this section, we will see how three nations pursued modernization. Turkey, Egypt, and Iran are the three most populous nations in the Middle East. While they have faced similar issues, each followed its own course.

Turkey Moves Toward Democracy

In the 1920s, Kemal Atatürk began his campaign to transform Turkey into a modern secular state. At the beginning of the Cold War, the Soviets tried to expand southward into Turkey to gain control of the Bosporus. With American aid, Turkey held off the Soviet threat. Later, Turkey joined NATO and remained an important western ally in the Mediterranean.

Government and Economy Turkey struggled to build a stable government. At first, the military seized power in times of unrest. In time, a multiparty democracy emerged. In recent decades, however, Muslim reformers won support and played a larger role in Turkish politics.

Turkey transformed its economy by expanding agriculture through increased irrigation and by promoting industry. It exported crops and manufactured goods to Europe and hoped to join the European Union. While the EU agreed to build closer ties, it denied Turkey full membership.

As elsewhere, modernization and urbanization brought social turmoil. Istanbul could not provide jobs for millions of newcomers. The jobless and the poor lived in shantytowns, where desperate conditions fed unrest.

Tragic Earthquakes Turkey lies in a region of frequent earthquakes. The nation has the technology to erect buildings that can withstand most tremors. Yet, because of rapid urbanization and poorly enforced building codes, many structures were hastily put up without adequate safeguards.

894 *Chapter 35*

Resource Directory

Teaching Resources

Creative Teaching Activities Creative Teaching Activities booklet, p. 157
Guided Reading and Review Unit 8 booklet, p. 60

In 1999, a series of powerful earthquakes shook western Turkey, including major industrial areas. Poorly constructed buildings collapsed, killing or injuring tens of thousands of people. Many more were left homeless. The government's response to the disaster was widely criticized as slow and inadequate. The earthquakes were a catastrophe that an already embattled nation did not need.

Conflicts For decades, Turkey tried to force its Kurdish citizens to abandon their identity. Kurds were forbidden to speak, publish, or broadcast in their own language. Kurdish revolts were fiercely suppressed. Although the Turkish government slowly agreed to abolish laws against Kurdish culture, Kurdish nationalists continued to press for autonomy.

Turkey also waged a long struggle over Cyprus, an island in the eastern Mediterranean. The roots of conflict dated back to Ottoman times. In the 1970s, clashes between the Greek majority and Turkish minority led Turkey to invade. The island was then partitioned. Today, UN peacekeepers monitor the tense dividing line between Turkish and Greek communities.

Finally, Turkey itself was divided politically. On one side stood secular politicians, who were backed up by the military. On the other side stood Islamic reformers who demanded a larger role for religion in society. Although the military seemed to retain the upper hand, Islamists kept up their pressure for change.

Egypt, A Leader in the Arab World

Egypt has roots both in Africa, where it is located, and in the Arab world. Geography has always played a key role in Egypt's destiny. Its location between the Mediterranean and Red seas is strategically important. It shares a long border with Israel and controls the Suez Canal. It is a rich agricultural region. But, since most of Egypt is desert, 99 percent of its people live on four percent of the land, in the fertile Nile Valley.

Nasser In the 1950s, Gamal Abdel Nasser emerged as a towering Arab leader. Like Atatürk, Nasser was a military officer who rose to power after the overthrow of a weak ruler who had allowed foreigners to dominate his country. Nasser set out to modernize Egypt and end western domination. In 1956, he nationalized the Suez Canal, ending British and French control. "The Canal is the property of Egypt," he declared. It "was dug by Egypt's sons and 120,000 of them died while working" on it. Nasser's defiance of the West boosted his prestige in the Arab world.

An outspoken enemy of Israel, Nasser led two wars against the Zionist state. Although defeated each time, he nevertheless remained a symbol of Arab independence and pride.

Economic Development Like leaders of other developing nations, Nasser turned to socialism. He nationalized banks and businesses. He launched land reforms that broke up large estates and distributed the land to peasant farmers. Nasser's economic policies had only limited success.

In the 1960s, with Soviet help, Nasser built the giant Aswan High Dam on the upper Nile. The dam created a huge reservoir, Lake Nasser, as well

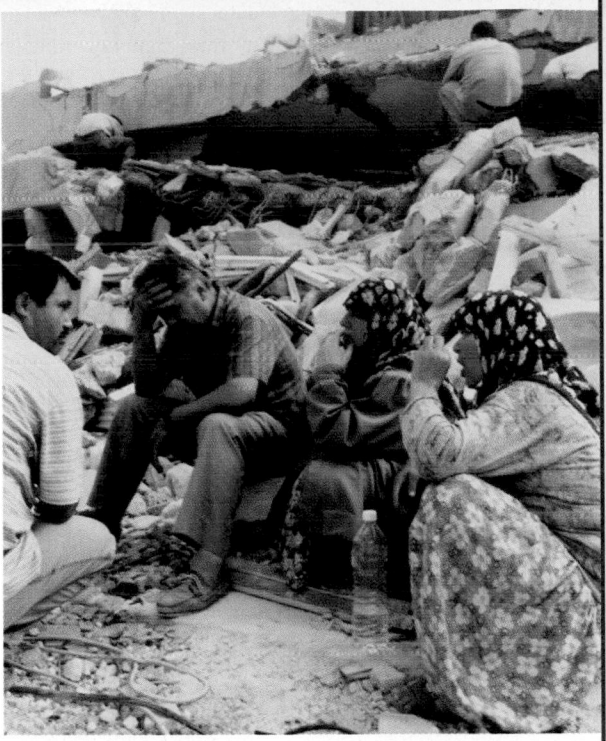

Earthquake in Turkey
Residents of Istanbul survey the ruins of their apartment building after the August 17, 1999, earthquake. The disaster sparked a massive international relief and rescue effort.
Theme: Geography and History Why might an earthquake be especially harmful for a developing nation?

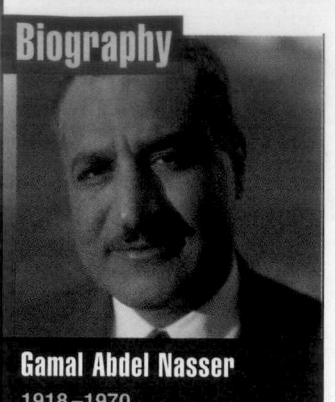
as more than two million acres of new farmland. It controlled Nile floodwaters and made year-round irrigation possible. But such benefits had a price. The dam increased the salt content of the Nile, destroyed fish hatcheries in the eastern Mediterranean, and caused erosion of the delta, the triangular area of marshland at the mouth of the river. As Lake Nasser rose, many ancient temples had to be relocated to higher ground.

Sadat After Nasser's death in 1970, the new president, Anwar Sadat, took steps to open Egypt to foreign investment and private business. In foreign affairs, Sadat moved away from the Soviet camp and closer to the United States. In 1979, he became the first Arab leader to make peace with Israel. Although that move angered other Arab states, Sadat promised Egyptians that peace would have economic benefits. It did bring American aid but did not improve life for most Egyptians.

Continuing Issues In 1981, Sadat was assassinated by Muslim extremists. His successor, Hosni Mubarak, reaffirmed the peace with Israel. At the same time, he mended fences with his Arab neighbors. Under Mubarak, Egypt continued to push for peace in the region.

At home, Mubarak faced serious problems. Although industry and farm output expanded, the economy could not keep pace with population growth. Most rural families who streamed into cities like Cairo barely managed to survive in teeming slums. The thousands of families living in the City of the Dead, a Cairo cemetery, symbolized the miseries of urbanization.

Islamic reformers denounced the government's failure to solve economic and social ills. Their model for change, based on Islamic solutions, seemed to offer a vision for a better future. Muslim groups set up schools and offered the poor many other social services, which tight government budgets did not provide. Extremists turned to terrorist attacks, and harsh government crackdowns tended to increase support for the dissenters.

Iran's Ongoing Revolution

Iran is the most ethnically diverse country in the Middle East. About half the people are Persian-speaking Iranians. The rest come from many groups. Unlike their neighbors, most Iranians are Shiite, not Sunni, Muslims.

Nationalism and Oil Because of its vast oil fields, Iran became a focus of British, Soviet, and American interests. In 1945, Shah Muhammad Reza Pahlavi had western backing but faced many opponents at home. Iranian nationalists wanted to end British control of Iran's oil wealth and limit the shah's dictatorial powers.

Led by Muhammad Mosaddiq (мон sah dehk), nationalists in Iran's parliament voted to nationalize the oil industry. That action set off a long, complex crisis involving the shah, Mosaddiq, Britain, and the United States. In 1953, the United States helped the shah oust Mosaddiq, a move that outraged many Iranians. The United States wanted the anti-communist shah as an ally against the Soviets. For the next 25 years, American weapons and experts helped the shah stay in power.

Reform From Above To strengthen Iran and to quiet unrest, the shah pushed for modernization. He used oil wealth to build roads and industries, redistributed some land to peasants, and extended new rights to women. To separate religion and government, he reduced the power of Islamic scholars, teachers, and legal experts.

The shah's "reform from above" was supported by the army, the westernized elite, and others who prospered under the shah. Opposition came from landowners, merchants, students, and religious leaders. As protests grew, the shah became more repressive. His secret police arrested critics. Some were tortured, executed, or forced into exile.

Naguib Mahfouz

Naguib Mahfouz: Views of Egypt

Since the 1930s, writer Naguib Mahfouz has woven stories that capture the rich tapestry of twentieth-century Egyptian life. He has long been considered one of the greatest Arabic writers and in 1988 won the Nobel Prize for literature. The following excerpts evoke the sights and sounds of Mahfouz's Egypt.

In his 1957 novel *Palace of Desire,* Mahfouz shows how ancient and modern exist side by side:
"The automobile stopped near the foot of the great pyramid. . . . The expanse of land seemed vast and limitless, but the pyramid shot up in the center like a legendary giant. On the far side, beyond the downward-sloping plateau, the city of Cairo was visible with the tops of its trees, a thread of water, and the roofs of its large buildings."

The 1961 novel *The Thief and the Dogs* reflects the continuing traditions of the Egyptian people:
"[He] . . . saw the Sheikh sitting cross-legged on the prayer carpet, absorbed in quiet recitation. The old room had hardly changed. The rush mats had been replaced by new ones, thanks to his disciples, but the Sheikh's sleeping mattress still lay close to the western wall. . . . The other walls of the room were half-covered with rows of books on shelves. The odor of incense lingered."

In *Miramar,* written in 1967, two characters discuss the changing lives of Egyptian women:
"'What about this decision to study? What made you think of it?'
'All girls go to school now. The streets are full of them.'
'But you never thought of it before.'
'It's your fault,' she smiled. 'You said . . . there was no reason why they should read and write while I stayed illiterate.' . . .
'When I learn to read and write,' she said thoughtfully, 'I'll try and learn some profession. Like dressmaking, perhaps.'"

Portfolio Assessment

 Use the Internet or library resources to find out more about twentieth-century Arabic literature. Then, prepare a class presentation on the significance of an important Arabic writer. Summarize a book or story that illustrates the writer's style and themes.

Researching a Topic Despite promises of a homeland during World War I, Kurds have never had their own nation. They have continually been subject to repression both in Turkey and in Iraq, which has a sizable Kurdish population. The plight of Iraq's Kurds was highlighted during the 1991 Persian Gulf War, when thousands of Kurds fled to the mountains of northern Iraq and remained there for months under extremely difficult conditions. Have students use Internet or library resources to research and report on Kurdish struggles.

 Test Preparation

Have students read the excerpt from *The Thief and the Dogs* on this page, and then answer the question below.

Which of the following would the sheikh most likely be reciting?

A a passage from a novel

B a prayer or passage from the Quran

C a poem

D instructions to his disciples

🔔 ***Bell Ringer*** Ask students to name examples of the contrast between old and new that is shown in these pictures. *(pyramids with modern city in the background, man in western dress kneeling on a prayer rug, women in traditional clothing wearing sneakers)*

*B*ackground
Connections to Today

Nobel Prizes The Nobel Prize consists of a large cash award, a gold medal, and a diploma-like certificate citing the winner's name and field. Funding comes from the interest on investments made by the executors of Alfred Nobel's estate. Nobel, a chemist and philanthropist, was the inventor of dynamite. His will set up equal prizes in five areas—physics, chemistry, physiology or medicine, literature, and peace. A sixth prize—in economics—was set up in 1968 by the Swedish national bank to honor its 300th anniversary. Most winners of the prize for literature have been from Europe or the United States, but a few have been from Latin America, Asia, and elsewhere. Mahfouz was the first Arab to win it.

*A*ctivity
Cooperative Learning

Plotting a Story Have pairs of students choose a place or an event in their community that could be a focal point for a children's story that juxtaposes the old and the new. Have them outline the plot and list illustrations. If time permits, have them write, illustrate, and edit the story.

Portfolio Assessment Rubrics

Share rubrics with students.

Attempted The presentation is incomplete.

Minimal The presentation shows little understanding of the topic and is poorly executed.

Adequate The student identifies a theme of an important Arabic writer, shows some understanding of the topic, and makes a clear presentation.

Exemplary The student shows a very good understanding of the significance of an important Arabic writer. The presention is clear, very well executed, and interesting.

Leader of the Iranian Revolution
In 1979, the Ayatollah Khomeini
returned to Iran after a 15-year
exile to direct an Islamic revolution. He was almost 80 years old
at the time.

**Theme: Impact of the
Individual** Why was Khomeini
exiled from Iran?

Islamic Revolution In the 1970s, the shah's foes rallied behind the exiled
Ayatollah Ruhollah Khomeini. Ayatollah is a title given to learned Shiite
legal experts. He condemned western influences and accused the shah of
violating Islamic law. In 1979, massive unrest forced the shah to flee. As
Khomeini returned to Iran, his supporters proclaimed an Islamic republic
based on the Quran and Sharia. They set up a theocracy, or government
ruled by religious leaders.

Revolutionaries attacked corruption. They replaced secular courts with
religious ones, abolished the shah's laws favoring women's rights, and
banned western books, music, and movies. At first, the new government
allowed some open discussion. Before long, though, the revolutionaries
suppressed opponents, just as the shah had.

Foreign Policy The new leaders bitterly denounced the West. When the
shah was allowed into the United States for medical treatment, angry revolutionaries seized the American embassy in Tehran and held 52 hostages for
over a year. Iran also tried to export its revolution. It urged Muslims
in countries like Egypt and Turkey to overthrow secular governments.
Although the revolution seemed to strengthen the Islamic revival, it was
not reproduced in other Muslim lands.

In 1980, as you will read, Iraq took advantage of the turmoil to invade
Iran. In Iran, the war helped rally support for the new government, but the
eight-year ordeal took a huge economic and human toll.

Moderate Voices The end of the Iran-Iraq War and Khomeini's death in
1989 helped more moderate voices gain power. They worked to rebuild the
economy. Industries began producing much-needed consumer goods. Low
oil prices in the 1990s hurt Iran's income, and the country faced the pressing needs of a large population of young people for education and jobs.

In the later 1990s, moderate politicians began to win elections and to
ease some restrictions. Conservative clerics responded by encouraging
attacks on students, journalists, and other liberals. Street demonstrations
emphasized divisions between moderates and conservatives. Iran did,
however, take concrete steps toward improving its relations with western
nations, including the United States.

Impact The revolution changed Iran's foreign policy and some forms of
public behavior. Although some reforms helped rural people, the revolution did not improve life greatly for most Iranians. Corruption resurfaced.
Poverty, unemployment, and other problems remained. As Iran marked the
twentieth year of its revolution, moderates and radicals still debated how to
achieve its goal of modernization within an Islamic republic.

SECTION 3 Assessment

Recall
1. **Identify: (a)** Gamal Abdel Nasser,
(b) Aswan High Dam, **(c)** Anwar
Sadat, **(d)** Muhammad Mosaddiq,
(e) Ruhollah Khomeini.
2. **Define: (a)** delta, **(b)** ayatollah,
(c) theocracy.

Comprehension
3. **(a)** What kind of government did
Turkey build? **(b)** Describe one
challenge Turkey faced.
4. What steps did Egypt take toward
modernization?

5. **(a)** Why did discontent spread in
Iran under the shah? **(b)** Describe
two effects of the Iranian revolution.

Critical Thinking and Writing
6. **Making Inferences** Why do you
think Turkey would want to force
its Kurdish citizens to abandon
their language and culture?
7. **Recognizing Points of View**
(a) Who might consider the Iranian revolution a success? Why?
(b) Who might criticize the revolution? Why?

Activity
Take It to the NET

Use the Internet to find
more information about
Turkey, Egypt, or Iran.
Then, create a statistical
profile of that nation. You
could include information
about population, ethnic
and religious groups,
literacy rate, health, or the
economy.

The Middle East and the World

Reading Focus

■ How did the Cold War increase tensions in the Middle East?

■ Why has the Arab-Israeli conflict been difficult to resolve?

■ Why did conflicts arise in Lebanon and the Persian Gulf?

Vocabulary

client state
intifada
militia
no-fly zone

Taking Notes

Copy this time line. As you read, fill in the time line with important events from the section. Some entries have been included to help you get started.

```
1960        1967        1980        2000
 |           |           |           |
          Third       Iraq invades
          Arab-Israeli Iran
          war
```

Main Idea The Middle East has been the focus of conflicts that have had an impact far beyond the region.

Setting the Scene To David Ben-Gurion, Israel's first prime minister, the birth of modern Israel in 1948 was the fulfillment of God's promise to the ancient Israelites. He quoted Scripture:

> "The land whereto we have returned to inherit it, it is the inheritance of our fathers and within it no stranger has part or parcel. . . . We have taken unto us our fathers' inheritance."
> —First Book of Maccabees

But to the Arabs then living on the land called Palestine, the creation of Israel was an illegal "invasion." The land, they felt, was rightfully theirs:

> "Palestine is the homeland of the Arab Palestinian people. It is an indivisible part of the Arab homeland, and the Palestinian people are an integral part of the Arab nation."
> —The Palestinian National Charter, Article 1

These conflicting claims to the same land touched off repeated violence. The Arab-Israeli struggle was one of many issues that focused worldwide attention on the Middle East.

The Cold War and After

Today, as in the past, the Middle East is a strategic region. It commands vital oil resources as well as key waterways such as the Bosporus, the Suez Canal, and the Persian Gulf. During the Cold War, both the United States and the Soviet Union were anxious to have access to the oil and the waterways. Superpower rivalries had a far-reaching impact on the region.

Superpower Rivalries In their global rivalry, each of the superpowers tried to line up allies in the Middle East. The United States sent aid to stop a communist threat to Turkey in 1947. For years, it supported the strongly anti-communist shah of Iran despite his repressive actions.

In Egypt, Nasser saw himself as a leader of the nonaligned movement. Still, the Soviets showered aid on Egypt during the Nasser years. Iraq, Syria, and Libya also became Soviet client states, dependent on the support of a stronger power. All of these Arab nations mistrusted their former colonial rulers in the West and condemned western support for Israel.

Weapons Pile Up Each superpower sold arms to its allies in the region. In the Arab-Israeli conflict, the United States helped Israel, while the Soviet

Did You Know?

Israel's Citizen Army

At the age of 18, most young men and women in Israel are drafted for military service. The men spend three grueling years training as infantry soldiers, elite paratroopers, or tank soldiers. They must then serve one month a year in the reserves for some 30 years.

After independence, women did not serve in combat. Now, they serve in both support and combat support roles. Since 1995, women can also serve as paramilitary border police in combat positions, and a few have become pilots.

Theme: Political and Social Systems Why do you think Israel introduced such an extensive military draft?

Primary Source

A Palestinian Refugee Camp
A few months before the intifada began, a young Israeli writer visited a refugee camp on the West Bank:

"Twelve thousand Palestinians live here in one of the highest population densities in the world; the houses are piled together, and the house of every extended family branches out in ugly cement growths, rooms and niches, rusty iron beams spread throughout as sinews, jutting like disconnected fingers.

In Deheisha, drinking water comes from wells. The only running water is the rainwater and the sewage flowing down the paths between the houses. . . .

Beside each house—a yard. They are small, fenced in with corrugated aluminum, and very clean. A large [jar] filled with springwater and covered with cloth stands in each yard. But every person here will tell you without hesitation that the water from the spring of his home village was sweeter."
—David Grossman,
The Yellow Wind

Skills Assessment
Primary Source Do you think the author feels sympathetic toward the Palestinian refugees? Explain.

Union gave aid to the Arabs. After each Arab-Israeli war, the superpowers rearmed their allies with expensive new weapons. Other nations also benefited from lavish arms sales, including such valued American allies as oil-rich Saudi Arabia.

During and after the Cold War, the development of weapons of mass destruction in the Middle East became a global concern. International military experts believed that Israel was developing nuclear weapons to defend itself against hostile Arab neighbors. Iraq under Saddam Hussein was also thought to be building a nuclear capability, as well as stockpiling chemical and biological weapons. Iraq used some of its poison gas supplies to suppress a Kurdish liberation movement within its own borders.

The Arab-Israeli Conflict

After the 1948 war, Israel and its Arab neighbors fought again in 1956, 1967, and 1973. In these conflicts, Israel defeated Arab attacks and gained territory. In between the wars, Israel faced guerrilla warfare and terrorist activity. Despite the long conflict, the UN, the United States, and others kept pushing for peace negotiations.

The Occupied Territories In the 1967 war, Israeli forces won the Golan Heights from Syria, East Jerusalem and the West Bank from Jordan, and the Gaza Strip and Sinai Peninsula from Egypt. In 1973, Arabs attacked Israel but failed to regain these occupied territories.

Israel refused to give up the territories until Arab nations recognized Israel's right to exist. Later, Israel annexed East Jerusalem and the Golan Heights. The government helped Jewish settlers build homes in the occupied territories, displacing more Palestinian Arabs.

Palestinian Resistance The number of Palestinians in refugee camps had grown since 1948. Many supported the Palestine Liberation Organization (PLO), headed by Yasir Arafat. Its stated goal was the destruction of Israel, which the PLO claimed had no right to exist on the land they called Palestine.

For years, the PLO waged guerrilla warfare against Israelis at home and abroad. Bombings, airplane hijackings, and the massacre of Israeli athletes at the 1972 Olympic games brought PLO demands to the attention of the world. At the same time, though, such attacks stiffened Israel's resolve not to negotiate with the PLO.

In the late 1980s and again starting in 2000, large numbers of young Palestinians mounted intifadas, or uprisings, against Israeli occupation. Demanding a Palestinian homeland of their own, they disobeyed curfew laws and stoned Israeli troops. Palestinian gunmen fired on Israeli soldiers and civilians. Israeli soldiers responded to the intifadas with force. Hundreds of Palestinians were injured or killed in bloody street fights. Israeli troops repeatedly sealed off Palestinian towns and villages, crippling the already fragile Palestinian economy and intensifying Palestinian bitterness.

Peace Efforts Despite these conflicts, some progress toward peace was made. As you have read, Israel returned the Sinai Peninsula to Egypt. After the collapse of the Soviet Union in 1991 put an end to Soviet aid, some other Arab governments accepted the need to negotiate with Israel. Talks between Israel and Syria stalled on the issue of the Golan Heights, but in the early 1990s, Jordan and Israel signed a peace agreement.

A further breakthrough seemed possible in 1993 when Israel and the PLO held direct talks for the first time. Arafat and Israeli prime minister Yitzhak Rabin signed the Oslo accord, based on secret discussions held earlier in Oslo, Norway. These accords gave Palestinians in Gaza and the West Bank limited self-rule under an independent Palestinian Authority headed by Arafat. Later agreements, negotiated at the urging of United States

---

Primary Source

ANSWER Possible answer: Yes, because although he talks about the squalor and ugliness, he also describes the cleanliness of the yards and the cloth-covered jar of springwater. He also has talked to the residents and adds the poignant observation about the water in the home villages.

Resource Directory

Teaching Resources
Primary Source Activity *An Encounter with the Israeli Army,* Unit 8 booklet, p. 65

Technology
Listening to Literature World Masterpieces audiotapes *The Diameter of the Bomb,* side 10, running time 1:03 min.

president Bill Clinton, further extended Palestinian self-rule and arranged timetables for Israeli withdrawal from disputed lands. In return, the Authority recognized Israel's right to exist and promised to end terrorist activity against the Israeli state.

Still, discontent with these agreements continued to run high on both sides. Many Palestinians remained dissatisfied because the accords did not promise them an independent homeland and because the region remained heavily dependent on Israel economically. Radical groups like Hamas and Hizbullah continued their terrorist attacks after the PLO had renounced terrorism.

Some Israeli citizens were willing to give up occupied territory in exchange for peace. Others, however, remained determined to keep and settle lands they had won or simply continued to distrust and fear their Arab neighbors. A Jewish student who opposed Rabin's peace policy assassinated the prime minister who had signed the Oslo accords. Early in the new century, prime minister Ariel Sharon, a conservative Israeli, announced that there would be no further talks until all anti-Israeli terrorism ceased.

Continuing Issues A number of specific issues continued to divide the two sides. Many Palestinians whose families had fled their farms and villages during the Arab-Israeli wars demanded recognition of their right to return to the land where their families had lived. Israelis opposed the return of large numbers of Palestinians.

Many Israelis, on the other hand, insisted that any peace settlement guarantee the survival of Israeli settlements in the occupied territories. Palestinians, however, rejected the idea of Israeli settlements scattered across a future Palestinian state.

Finally, the city of Jerusalem was sacred to both sides, as well as to Christians. It had been captured by Israeli troops during their wars with the Arabs. Palestinians demanded that Muslims control Islamic holy places in the city and that part of Jerusalem become the capital of a future Palestinian nation. Israeli conservatives insisted that the city remain undivided as the capital of Israel. Peace in the Middle East has remained an elusive goal.

Civil War in Lebanon

In the 1970s, the Arab-Israeli conflict fueled tensions in nearby Lebanon. After winning independence, Lebanon became a thriving center of international commerce. People of diverse ethnic and religious groups lived mostly in harmony. But the surface prosperity masked deep problems.

Growing Tensions The government depended on a delicate balance among Maronites (a Christian sect), Sunni and Shiite Muslims, Druze (a sect derived from Islam), and others. Maronites held the most power, but local bosses controlled their own districts backed by private armies.

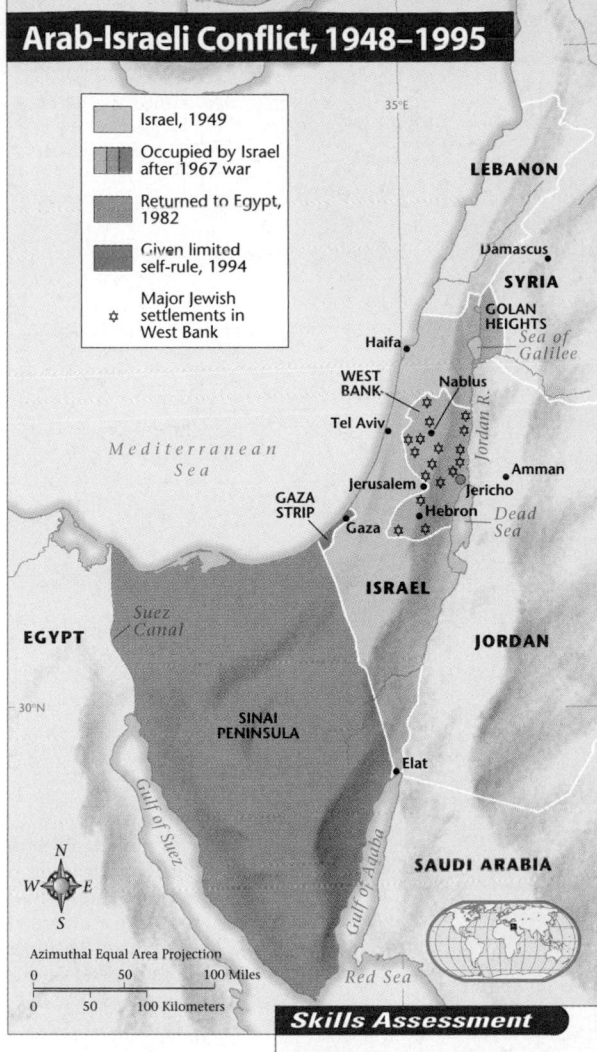

Arab-Israeli Conflict, 1948–1995

- Israel, 1949
- Occupied by Israel after 1967 war
- Returned to Egypt, 1982
- Given limited self-rule, 1994
- ☆ Major Jewish settlements in West Bank

LEBANON
SYRIA
Damascus
GOLAN HEIGHTS
Sea of Galilee
Haifa
WEST BANK
Nablus
Tel Aviv
Mediterranean Sea
Jerusalem
Jericho
Amman
Hebron
Dead Sea
GAZA STRIP
Gaza
ISRAEL
JORDAN
EGYPT
Suez Canal
30°N
SINAI PENINSULA
Elat
Gulf of Suez
Gulf of Aqaba
SAUDI ARABIA
Red Sea

Azimuthal Equal Area Projection
0   50   100 Miles
0   50   100 Kilometers

Skills Assessment

Geography Israel and its Arab neighbors have fought four wars since 1948.

1. **Location** On the map, locate (a) Israel, (b) Egypt, (c) West Bank, (d) Gaza Strip, (e) Sinai Peninsula, (f) Jerusalem.
2. **Region** What areas did Israel gain as a result of the 1967 war?
3. **Critical Thinking Making Inferences** Why would cities like Hebron and Jericho be likely points of conflict?

Chapter 35 **901**

Chapter 35 **901**

Activity
Connections to Literature

Analyzing a Poem The Israeli writer Yehuda Amichai explores the "range" of a terrorist bomb in his poem "The Diameter of a Bomb." Each detonation kills only a certain number of people, but reaches out to have a devastating impact on the families and homeland of the victims. By the end of his poem, Amichai shows how violence has created ever-widening circles of despair and mourning that have "no end" and can be motivated by "no God."

Play the selection "The Diameter of a Bomb," in the *Listening to Literature World Masterpieces* audiotapes, side 10, for the class. Then, ask students to respond to the following questions: (1) How does the poet extend the effect of the bomb from the initial body count to the whole world? (2) Why does the poet say there is "no God" behind the bomb? (3) Do you think the poet is against all terrorism or only Palestinian terrorism? Explain.

EXPLORING THE HUMAN DRAMA
Human Drama Activity

Summarizing an Event In 1999, PBS aired a documentary series (produced jointly by PBS and the BBC) on the Arab-Israeli conflict: *The Fifty Years' War: Israel and the Arabs.* The series is available as a video package containing two videotapes (running time: 5 hours). It begins with the 1947 UN decision to partition Palestine and ends with events of the late 1990s. Told through the words of statesmen, generals, terrorists, and others, it provides, according to one reviewer, "in the main, [a] carefully rendered, factual and balanced" picture. The story is also available as a book: *The Fifty Years' War: Israel and the Arabs,* by Ahron Bregman and Jihan El-Tahri, (New York: TV Books, 1998). Have students view parts of the video or skim the book and choose one event or interview to summarize in their own words. (The book and the video are available from PBS as a package or separately.)

Skills Assessment

ANSWERS 1. Review locations with students. **2.** the Sinai Peninsula, the Golan Heights, the Gaza Strip, and the West Bank **3.** These cities are located on the West Bank. The growth of Jewish settlements in these cities would lead to conflict with the Palestinians who lived there.

Costs of the Iran-Iraq War The eight-year war between Iraq and Iran (1980–1988) was costly, with an estimated 1.5 million people killed, two-thirds of whom were Iranians, and 1.7 million wounded. On both sides more than 90,000 of the soldiers killed were under 15 years of age. In addition, Iranians sent pre-teenage youths before their tanks to blow up mines. Iran and Iraq made prisoner-of-war (POW) exchanges over the years, and in 1998 they completed repatriation of more than 5,500 prisoners, some of whom had been captive for more than 15 years. When the war was at its highest point, each country spent an estimated $10 billion per year on weapons alone. Iraq sustained $100 billion in economic losses from the war, with crippling damage inflicted on its oil export facilities. The battle front along the Shatt al Arab waterway created a wasteland. The sheer volume of artillery fire left whole forests of trees cut off at the trunk, leaving only burnt stumps that resembled a bed of nails.

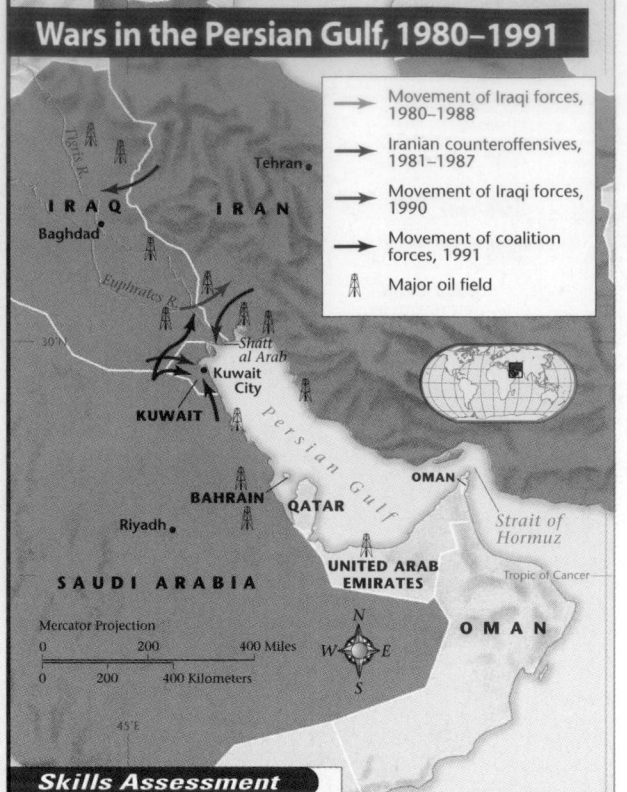

Wars in the Persian Gulf, 1980–1991

→ Movement of Iraqi forces, 1980–1988

→ Iranian counteroffensives, 1981–1987

→ Movement of Iraqi forces, 1990

→ Movement of coalition forces, 1991

⚒ Major oil field

Mercator Projection

0   200   400 Miles

0   200   400 Kilometers

Skills Assessment

Geography Since 1980, the area around the Persian Gulf has been the site of two wars.

1. **Location** On the map, locate (a) Persian Gulf, (b) Strait of Hormuz, (c) Iraq, (d) Iran, (e) Kuwait, (f) Saudi Arabia.

2. **Movement** Why would the Strait of Hormuz be vital to the world oil trade?

3. **Critical Thinking Drawing Conclusions** Describe two advantages Iraq would gain by taking control of Kuwait.

A growing number of Palestinian refugees crossed the border from the occupied territories into Lebanon. Their needs strained resources. Also, the Muslim population began to outnumber Maronites, creating unrest. Adding to the tensions, the PLO developed into an important force in the Palestinian refugee camps. From Lebanon, PLO guerrillas crossed into Israel to attack civilian and military targets. To end the threat to its security, Israel tried to influence events in southern Lebanon.

Years of Violence In 1975, Lebanon was plunged into a seemingly endless civil war. Christian and Muslim militias, bands of citizen soldiers, battled for control of villages and of Beirut, the capital city. Israel invaded the south to clear out PLO bases and advanced almost as far as Beirut. Syria occupied eastern Lebanon.

Lawlessness led to massacres on all sides. As Palestinian refugee camps came under fire, thousands were killed. A UN peacekeeping force tried to restore order, but it withdrew after hundreds of French and American peacekeepers were killed in a series of suicide bombings.

Rebuilding By 1990, Lebanese leaders finally restored some measure of order. The PLO was forced out of southern Lebanon, private armies began to disarm, and the ruined capital slowly rebuilt. Over the following decade, the economic outlook improved, and many Lebanese who had fled their homeland returned. By 2000, Beirut was poised to return to its former status as a leading economic center of the Middle East.

Despite the hopeful outlook, divisions remained. Syria was still a dominant presence and Israeli forces continued to take military action against suspected terrorists in southern Lebanon. The future of this small nation seemed to depend on the prospects for peace among its neighbors.

Two Wars in the Persian Gulf

Border disputes, oil wealth, foreign intervention, and ambitious rulers fed tensions along the Persian Gulf. In 1980, Iraqi dictator Saddam Hussein seized a disputed border region from Iran. Iraqi forces then pushed deeper into Iran, which was embroiled in its recent Islamic revolution. Before long, the Iranians launched a counterattack. They urged young soldiers to spread their revolution to Iraq.

Iraq used its superior weapons, tanks, airplanes, and even poison gas to stop waves of Iranian soldiers. Fighting threatened to spread as both sides attacked international tankers and offshore oil fields in the Persian Gulf. The United States sent naval forces to protect shipping lanes in the Gulf and the Strait of Hormuz. The war dragged on for eight years, ending in a stalemate. For both nations, the human and economic toll was enormous.

A Second Gulf War In 1990, Iraqi troops invaded the oil-rich nation of Kuwait. Saddam Hussein argued that historically the region was part of Iraq. Control of Kuwait would give Iraq not only one of the world's largest oil-producing areas but also access to the Persian Gulf.

The United States saw the invasion as a threat to its ally Saudi Arabia, as well as to oil flow from the Persian Gulf. President George Bush therefore

Skills Assessment

ANSWERS 1. Review locations with students. 2. Whoever controls the Strait of Hormuz controls oil shipments from Iran, Iraq, Kuwait, Saudi Arabia, and the United Arab Emirates. 3. Iraq would win control of more oil fields and gain greater access to the Persian Gulf.

Resource Directory

Teaching Resources

Section Quiz Unit 8 booklet, p. 63
Geography Quiz Unit 8 booklet, p. 68
Chapter Test Forms A, B, and C Unit 8 booklet, pp. 69–73
Answer Key Unit 8 booklet, pp. 112–127

Technology

Interactive Student Tutorial CD-ROM Ch. 35
Computer Test Bank Ch. 35

organized a coalition of American, European, and Arab powers to drive Iraqi forces out of Kuwait. In the 1991 Gulf War, American missiles and bombers destroyed targets in Iraq. Then, under the UN banner, coalition forces pushed across the desert to liberate Kuwait. As they retreated, Iraqi troops blew up hundreds of Kuwaiti oil wells.

Saddam Remains Despite defeat, Saddam Hussein remained in power. He brutally suppressed all critics and persecuted Kurds and Shiites. To protect these minorities, the UN enforced no-fly zones, areas over which Iraqi aircraft were not permitted to fly.

For years, UN economic sanctions kept Iraq from selling oil on the world market and from importing most goods. The goal was to stop Saddam Hussein from building chemical and nuclear weapons, but the sanctions hurt the Iraqi people.

In the late 1990s, the UN set up an oil-for-food program. It allowed Iraq to sell some oil on the world market and use the profits to buy food and medicines. Still, the standard of living in Iraq fell. Some people called for an end to sanctions, which they said were not effective. Others responded that ending sanctions would reward Saddam Hussein, who was still trying to build weapons of mass destruction.

Uncertainties Continue

The Middle East remained the focus of many conflicting forces. Nationalist conflicts, clashes between religious and secular goals, and competition for water resources were among many forces that carried the potential for future violence. The area's vast supplies of oil guaranteed that outside powers would continue to intervene in the region.

The region became the center of another crisis after al-Qaida terrorists attacked New York and Washington, D.C., on September 11, 2001. Thousands of people died in these attacks.

Al-Qaida had bases in Afghanistan and in about 60 other countries. After the attacks, the United States vowed to declare war on terrorism. It launched an attack on Afghanistan that drove the Taliban from power. Even after a fragile peace was restored in Afghanistan, the country faced frequent outbreaks of violence. In 2002, a new Afghan government set out on the difficult task of restoring peace to a divided nation. The United States began sending advisers to other countries that were threatened by terrorist groups.

Take It to the NET

Go to **United We Stand** for updated articles and lessons to guide your classroom discussion of September 11 and beyond. **www.phschool.com/ social_studies/special_ report/index.html**

SECTION 4 Assessment

Recall
1. **Identify:** (a) PLO, (b) Yasir Arafat, (c) Yitzhak Rabin, (d) Palestinian Authority, (e) Ariel Sharon, (f) Saddam Hussein.
2. **Define:** (a) client state, (b) intifada, (c) militia, (d) no-fly zone.

Comprehension
3. How did the Cold War affect the Middle East?
4. (a) Why were the occupied territories a source of conflict? (b) What steps were taken toward peace?

5. Describe one cause of each of the following: (a) the civil war in Lebanon, (b) the Iran-Iraq war, (c) the Persian Gulf War.

Critical Thinking and Writing
6. **Making Decisions** If you had been an Israeli leader in the late 1980s, what response to the intifada would you have favored? Explain your reasons.
7. **Solving Problems** If you were organizing a Middle East peace conference, whom would you invite and what issues would you put on the table?

Activity

Drawing a Political Cartoon Draw a cartoon about the role of oil in fueling tensions in the Persian Gulf. Take the viewpoint of an Iraqi, a Kuwaiti, a Saudi, or an outside observer. Identify the time period of your cartoon.

Chapter 35 **903**

SECTION 4 Assessment

Recall
1. (a) PLO, p. 900 (b) Yasir Arafat, p. 900 (c) Yitzhak Rabin, p. 900 (d) Palestinian Authority, p. 900 (e) Ariel Sharon, p. 901 (f) Saddam Hussein, p. 902 2. (a) client state, p. 899 (b) intifada, p. 900 (c) militia, p. 902 (d) no-fly zone, p. 903

Comprehension
3. The United States and the Soviet Union backed opposite sides in the Arab-Israeli conflict. Each superpower sold arms to its allies, creating an arms race in the region. 4. (a) Israel refused to give up the territories unless Arab nations recognized Israel's right to exist. Tension increased as Jewish settlers built homes, displacing more Palestinian Arabs. (b) Israel and the PLO reached an agreement to give Palestinians in Gaza and Jericho limited self-rule. Israel also signed accords with Egypt and Jordan. 5. (a) Tensions increased among Christian and Muslim groups, especially after large numbers of Palestinian refugees entered Lebanon. (b) Iraq took advantage of turmoil in Iran to occupy a disputed border area. (c) Iraq invaded oil-rich Kuwait to gain greater access to the Persian Gulf.

Critical Thinking and Writing
6. Students should demonstrate an understanding of the dangers of suppressing the revolt and of the dangers of allowing it to continue. 7. Students' responses should demonstrate a knowledge of the major players and sources of conflict in the Middle East today.

Activity Rubrics

Share rubrics with students before they draw their cartoons.

Attempted The cartoon is incomplete or has little relation to the assignment.

Minimal The cartoon is complete but does not indicate a clear viewpoint and is poorly executed.

Adequate The cartoon clearly expresses a viewpoint on the issue and is well executed.

Exemplary The cartoon expresses a viewpoint in a clever and creative manner and is well executed.

CHAPTER **35 Review and Assessment**

Creating a Chapter Summary

As a reteaching opportunity, pair a more able student with a less able student to complete this chapter summary.

Possible answers: **Modernization** Green Revolution, Shah's reforms in Iran, oil-rich nations improve standards of living **Ethnic and Religious Conflicts** Hindus and Muslims in India, Sikh separatism, civil war in Lebanon. **Other Issues** Islamic revival, Iraqi invasion of Kuwait

Creating a Chapter Summary

On a sheet of paper, draw a concept web like this one. Fill in the outer circles with supporting details relating to the themes shown. Add extra circles as needed.

For additional review and enrichment activities, see the interactive version of *World History* available on the Web and on CD-ROM.

Web Site Self-Test
For practice test questions for Chapter 35, see **www.phschool.com**.

Building Vocabulary

1–10. (a) Possible answers: **Political and Social Systems** federal system, harijan, theocracy, intifada **Economics and Technology** debt service, kibbutz, desalinization, deforestation **Religions and Value Systems** hejab, ayatollah **(b)** Students' sentences should show an understanding of how each word relates to the theme.

Building Vocabulary

(a) Classify each of the chapter vocabulary words listed below under *one* of the following themes: Political and Social Systems; Economics and Technology; Religions and Value Systems. **(b)** Choose *one* word in each category and write a sentence explaining how that word relates to the theme.

1. **federal system**
2. **harijan**
3. **deforestation**
4. **debt service**
5. **kibbutz**
6. **desalinization**
7. **hejab**
8. **ayatollah**
9. **theocracy**
10. **intifada**

Recalling Key Facts

11. He built dams for hydroelectric power, poured resources into heavy industries, and took advantage of the Green Revolution in an effort to make India self-sufficient in food production.
12. Tensions grew between Bengalis in East Pakistan and Punjabis in West Pakistan. In 1971, Bengalis in East Pakistan declared independence.
13. Arabs saw the creation of Israel as a plan to relocate European Jews on Arab territory. Palestinian Arabs believed the land belonged to them.
14. Many Middle Eastern leaders had adopted western models of development but were unable to solve social and economic problems. Also, Islamic reformers opposed the western idea of separation of religion and state.
15. He wanted to end western domination of the region.
16. The first war ended in a stalemate. The economic and human costs were enormous. The second ended with the defeat of Iraqi forces and the liberation of Kuwait. Environmental damage was great, Iraqi dictator Saddam Hussein remained in power, and the UN maintained sanctions on Iraq for years after the war.

Recalling Key Facts

11. What economic policies did Nehru pursue in India?
12. How was Bangladesh created?
13. Why did Arab nations oppose the creation of Israel?
14. Why did Islamic reformers oppose westernization?
15. Why did Nasser nationalize the Suez Canal?
16. What were the results of the two wars in the Persian Gulf?

Critical Thinking and Writing

17. **Linking Past and Present** Give three examples of how the legacy of imperialism has influenced recent developments in South Asia and the Middle East.
18. **Comparing (a)** How is India's attempt to reform the caste system similar to the civil rights movement in the United States? **(b)** How is it different?
19. **Connecting to Geography (a)** What region do historians mean when they refer to the Middle East? **(b)** Why do some people prefer to use the term *Southwest Asia*? **(c)** Describe three ways that geographic features have influenced recent events in the region.
20. **Identifying Alternatives** Developing nations have often alternated between periods of military and civilian rule. **(a)** Identify two nations of South Asia or the Middle East that have followed this pattern. **(b)** What are the benefits and dangers of each alternative?
21. **Asking Questions** Imagine that you are going to interview the current leaders of Israel and the PLO. Write a list of five questions to ask them about their plans for achieving a lasting and just peace.

Critical Thinking and Writing

17. Possible answers: British-built railroads supported India's economic development. Arab nations remained economically dependent upon the West. The British role in the creation of Israel, Iraq, and Kuwait contributed to conflicts in the region.
18. Possible answers: **(a)** Both countries sought to end discrimination against a group of people by passing laws and trying to increase economic and educational opportunities. Some people in each country responded to reform efforts with violence. **(b)** In the United States, the civil rights movement dealt largely with discrimination on account of race, rather than social position. Violent protests in India forced the government to back off from its plan to open more jobs to untouchables.
19. **(a)** The region from Egypt in the west to Iran in the east and from Turkey in the north to the Arabian Peninsula in the south. **(b)** The term *Middle East* reflects a European bias. *Southwestern Asia* is a neutral term for a geographical location. **(c)** Possible answers: Nations with large oil deposits have been able to build their economies. Water resources have become an important issue in dry desert regions. Iraq invaded Kuwait in order to gain wider access to the Persian Gulf.
20. **(a)** Pakistan and Turkey **(b)** Possible answers: The military often steps in to bring stability in times of disorder. However, military rule is usually authoritarian and leads to a reduction of basic rights. Civilian rule has brought widespread government corruption and political instability.

Skills Assessment
Analyzing Primary Sources

Zade Teherani was a Shiite preacher and scholar in Iran. In 1986, he was interviewed by a British journalist. Here, Teherani describes how he and other Muslim clergy were arrested by the shah's secret police. Read the passage, then answer the questions that follow.

"I was arrested in August 1978 with several other members of the clergy. We were told to take off our clerical robes, but we refused. We said to them that only those who had given us our clothes, at the theological [religious] school, could take them away from us. They tried to make us sign a paper saying that we would never preach again. And they asked us questions continually, just as you are doing. But they let us go in the end. It was nothing more than intimidation. They wouldn't have dared to do anything serious to us. Things were so tense in Iran then that it would have caused a real upheaval."

—Zade Teherani, quoted in
Inside Iran (Simpson)

22. **(a)** Who ruled Iran at the time that Teherani was arrested? **(b)** Who ruled Iran at the time that he gave this interview? **(c)** What significant event occurred between these two dates?
23. **(a)** What did the secret police order Teherani and the other clergy to do? **(b)** How did the clergy respond?
24. How would you describe the attitude shown by the clergy toward the secret police?
25. According to Teherani, why were the prisoners released?
26. Based on what you have read, why would the shah's secret police want to arrest these prisoners?
27. Do you think Teherani was probably a supporter of the Ayatollah Khomeini? Explain.
28. **(a)** What seems to be Teherani's mood as he looks back at past events? **(b)** How might his mood be different if this interview had taken place in 1978?

Skills Tip

Interviews are part of oral history, or a spoken record of events. When you read an interview, make sure that you understand the relationship of the speaker to the events he or she is describing.

Skills Assessment
Analyzing Photographs

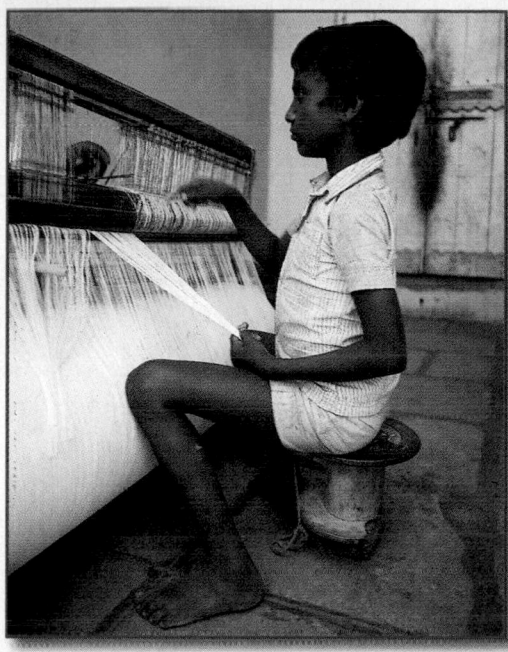

This photograph shows a young worker in an Indian textile factory. Look at the photograph and answer the following questions:

29. How would you describe **(a)** the child, **(b)** his surroundings? Identify at least two specific details relating to each.
30. **(a)** How could a human rights activist make use of this photograph? **(b)** How might the factory owner respond?
31. Compare this picture with what you have seen and read about the early Industrial Revolution in Britain. What similarities can you recognize?

Skills Assessment
Take It to the NET

Use the Internet to research modern-day life in one of the countries of South Asia or the Middle East. Then, choose one country as the site of a "virtual vacation." Write a brochure describing sites to visit, as well as the climate and natural features.

21. Questions should reflect students' understanding of issues causing Israeli-Palestinian conflicts and recent efforts to resolve them.

Analyzing Primary Sources

22. **(a)** the shah Muhammad Reza Pahlavi **(b)** the Ayatollah Khomeini **(c)** the Iranian revolution
23. **(a)** to remove their clerical robes and to sign a paper agreeing not to preach **(b)** They refused.
24. Possible answer: defiant and proud
25. He says that any attempt to punish the clergy harshly would have sparked an upheaval.
26. Shiite Muslim leaders were the shah's chief critics, opposing his efforts to separate religion and government and limit the power of Islamic leaders.
27. Yes. Like Khomeini, Teherani was a Shiite scholar and a critic of the shah.
28. Possible answers: **(a)** He seems calm and serene, recalling a past conflict that his side had won. **(b)** Possible answers: He might have been angrier immediately after his arrest and more anxious because the struggle against the shah was ongoing.

Analyzing Photographs

29. Possible answers: **(a)** He is thin and barefoot, indicating that he is poor. His expression seems grim and hopeless. **(b)** The factory is bleak, with bare floors and walls. He is sitting on a broken spool.
30. **(a)** A human rights activist might use this picture to stir up opposition to child labor. **(b)** A factory owner might answer that cheap child labor is contributing to economic growth.
31. Child labor was common in the early Industrial Revolution in Europe and the United States.

Skills Tip

In evaluating information from an interview, consider whether the interviewee was an eyewitness to the events being described. The Skills Handbook in the front of the book has a lesson that will help students with this feature.

Unit Theme Activity

Remind students to continue working on their Unit Theme Activity. See rubrics for the activity on the unit opener page in the Teacher's Edition.

Take It to the NET

Direct students to **www.phschool.com** for links to sites that will help them get started on this assignment. Share rubrics with students.

Attempted The brochure shows little research, is poorly written and organized, and contains many mechanical errors. It contains no illustrations.

Minimal The brochure shows some research but is poorly written and organized and contains some mechanical errors. A few illustrations are included.

Adequate The brochure shows appropriate research, is well written and organized, and contains few mechanical errors. Several illustrations are included.

Exemplary The brochure shows extensive research, is very well written and organized, and contains no mechanical errors. Many illustrations are included.

Chapter 36 Planning Guide

Resource Manager

	CORE INSTRUCTION	READING/SKILLS
Chapter Level Resources	📗 Teaching Resources 📘 **Pacing Charts**, Ch. 36 📘 **Teaching With Themes**, p. 39 📖 **Color Transparencies**, p. F–73 💿 **Resource Pro®** Ch. 36 💻 **www.phschool.com** • eTeach	💿 **Book on CD**, Ch. 36 💿 **Interactive Student Tutorial CD-ROM**, Ch. 36 💿 **Social Studies Skills Tutor CD-ROM** 📖 **Skills Transparencies**

1 Achieving Independence
1. Explain how the colonial legacy contributed to a growing spirit of nationalism.
2. Trace routes to freedom that Ghana, Kenya, and Algeria followed.
3. Summarize how the Cold War affected Africa.
	📗 Teaching Resources
	📁 **Unit 8 booklet**
	   • Biography Activity, p. 82
	📘 **Creative Teaching Activities**, p. 159
	💿 **Prentice Hall Presentation Pro**, Ch. 36, Section 1
	📖 **Section Reading Support Transparencies**
		📗 Teaching Resources
		📁 **Unit 8 booklet**
		   • Guided Reading and Review, p. 74
		   • Skill Application Activity, p. 85
		📘 **Guide to the Essentials**
		📼 **Guided Reading Audiotapes**, Ch. 36, Section 1

2 Programs for Development
1. Discuss barriers to unity and stability in Africa.
2. Outline economic choices that African nations faced.
3. Identify critical issues that affect Africa today.
4. Give examples of how modernization affected patterns of life in Africa.
	📗 Teaching Resources
	📁 **Unit 8 booklet**
	   • Viewpoint Activity, p. 84
	📘 **Creative Teaching Activities**, p. 160
	💿 **Prentice Hall Presentation Pro**, Ch. 36, Section 2
	📖 **Section Reading Support Transparencies**
		📗 Teaching Resources
		📁 **Unit 8 booklet**
		   • Guided Reading and Review, p. 76
		📘 **Guide to the Essentials**
		📼 **Guided Reading Audiotapes**, Ch. 36, Section 2

3 Three Nations: A Closer Look
1. Enumerate the pressures for change in Nigeria.
2. Describe the effects dictatorship had on Congo.
3. Discuss the outcome of Tanzania's socialism experiment.
	📗 Teaching Resources
	📁 **Unit 8 booklet**
	   • Primary Source Activity, p. 83
	📘 **Creative Teaching Activities**, p. 161
	💿 **Prentice Hall Presentation Pro**, Ch. 36, Section 3
		📗 Teaching Resources
		📁 **Unit 8 booklet**
		   • Guided Reading and Review, p. 78
		📘 **Guide to the Essentials**
		📼 **Guided Reading Audiotapes**, Ch. 36, Section 3

4 Struggles in South Africa 1. Identify challenges that Zimbabwe faced. 2. Explain how the long struggle to end apartheid led to a new South Africa. 3. Discuss how the Cold War affected southern African nations.	📗 Teaching Resources 📘 **Creative Teaching Activities**, p. 162 💿 **Prentice Hall Presentation Pro**, Ch. 36, Section 4 📖 **Section Reading Support Transparencies**	📗 Teaching Resources 📁 **Unit 8 booklet** • Guided Reading and Review, p. 80 📘 **Guide to the Essentials** 📼 **Guided Reading Audiotapes**, Ch. 36, Section 4

ENRICHMENT/PRE-AP

🖥 **www.phschool.com**
  • Why Study History?

📗 Teaching Resources
  📘 **Chapter Extension Activities,** p. 85

📖 **Color Transparencies,** p. D–87

🖥 **www.phschool.com**
  • Internet Activities, Section 3

📗 Teaching Resources
  📘 **Chapter Extension Activities,** p. 86
  📘 **History Through Literature,** p. 75
  📘 **Simulations,** p. 16
  📖 **Color Transparencies,** p. C–61
  🖥 **www.phschool.com**
    • Virtual Field Trip
    • Internet Activities, Section 4

ASSESSMENT

PRENTICE HALL
ASSESSMENT SYSTEM

Core Assessment
  📘 **ExamView Test Bank booklet,** Ch. 36
  💿 **ExamView Test Bank CD-ROM,** Ch. 36

Standardized Test Preparation
Diagnose and Prescribe
  📘 **Diagnostic Tests for High School Social Studies Skills**
Review and Reteach
  📘 **Review Book for World History**
Practice and Assess
  📘 **Test-Taking Strategies With Transparencies for High School**
  📘 **Alternative Assessment booklet**
  📘 **Test Prep Book for World History**

📗 Teaching Resources
  📘 **Unit 8 booklet**
    • Geography Quiz, p. 86
    • Section Quizzes, pp. 75, 77, 79, 81
    • Chapter Tests A, B, and C, pp. 87–91
  🖥 **www.phschool.com**
    • Self-Test

CUSTOMIZE FOR INDIVIDUAL NEEDS

Gifted and Talented
  • **Teacher's Edition,** Activities: Customize for Heterogeneous Groups, p. 918; Customize for Heterogeneous Groups, p. 925

Less Proficient Readers
  • **Guide to the Essentials,** Ch. 36
  • **Guided Reading Audiotapes, English,** Ch. 36
  • **Book on CD,** Ch. 36
  • **Teacher's Edition,** Activities: Customize for Auditory Learners, p. 909

Less Proficient Writers
  • **Teacher's Edition,** Activities: Customize for Auditory Learners, p. 909; Cooperative Learning Activity, p. 917

Students Acquiring English/ESL
  • **Guide to the Essentials, English/Spanish,** Ch. 36
  • **Guided Reading Audiotapes, English/Spanish,** Ch. 36
  • **Book on CD,** Ch. 36
  • **Teacher's Edition,** Activities marked with an *

𝒊 TEXT

Don't miss the exclusive interactive version of *World History: Connections to Today* on the Internet and CD-ROM.

INTRODUCTION

After World War II, the colonial legacy in Africa created a growing spirit of nationalism. Many African nations declared independence. As new nations established their governments, they faced challenges in unity and stability. Civil war broke out in many new nations, and most faced economic hardships. Nations in southern Africa faced challenges and turmoil as the people struggled for equal rights.

Focusing on Themes

Suggest that students focus on these theme questions as they read:

Political and Social Systems
What kinds of governments did the new nations of Africa develop?

Economics and Technology
Why did developing nations of Africa remain economically dependent on the industrialized world?

Diversity
How did diversity pose problems for emerging African nations?

Continuity and Change
Why have many Africans called for their nations to seek African solutions to African problems?

◆ TIME LINE ACTIVITY

You may wish to share the About the Pictures note with your students before you ask questions about the time line such as the following:

1. When did the Sudan gain independence from Britain? *(in 1956)*
2. How many years passed between India's independence and Ghana's independence *(10 years)*
3. What year did South Africa hold its first all-race elections? Who was elected president? *(1994; Nelson Mandela)*

Don't Miss!

Analyzing Primary Sources
Ghana Wins Independence (Section 1)

You Are There . . .
Reporting on the Election in South Africa (Section 4)

Africa
1945–Present

Chapter Preview

1 Achieving Independence
2 Programs for Development
3 Three Nations: A Closer Look
4 Struggles in Southern Africa

1956
The Sudan gains independence from Britain. Here, the changing of the flags symbolizes the transfer of power.

1957
Ghana becomes the first African nation south of the Sahara to free itself from colonial rule. This arch commemorates Ghanaian independence.

1961
Tanzania gains independence.

CHAPTER EVENTS

1940 ● ● 1955 ● ● ● 1970

GLOBAL EVENTS

1947 India wins independence.

1957 The European Community is formed.

1966 Mao Zedong announces the Cultural Revolution in China.

Resource Directory

Teaching Resources
Teaching With Themes Chapter Theme Activities, p. 39
Pacing Chart With Block Scheduling Guide Ch. 36
Technology
World History Color Transparencies Ch. 36 Graphic Organizer, p. F–73

African Independence

In the decades after World War II, African nationalist movements gained strength. More than 50 new nations emerged.

Legend:
- Independent nations by 1945
- Gained independence, 1945–1959
- Gained independence since 1959
- Status in dispute
- ★ Sites of civil wars and ethnic clashes, 1990s

Map labels:

TUNISIA 1956
MOROCCO 1956
WESTERN SAHARA
ALGERIA 1962
LIBYA 1951
EGYPT 1922
MAURITANIA 1960
MALI 1960
NIGER 1960
CHAD 1960
SUDAN 1956
ERITREA 1993
SENEGAL 1960
BURKINA FASO 1960
THE GAMBIA 1965
GUINEA 1958
GUINEA BISSAU 1974
BENIN 1960
GHANA 1957
NIGERIA 1960
DJIBOUTI 1977
CÔTE D'IVOIRE 1960
SIERRA LEONE 1961
LIBERIA
TOGO 1960
CENTRAL AFRICAN REPUBLIC 1960
ETHIOPIA
EQUATORIAL GUINEA 1968
CAMEROON 1960
SÃO TOMÉ AND PRÍNCIPE 1975
GABON 1960
DEMOCRATIC REPUBLIC OF CONGO 1960
UGANDA 1962
KENYA 1963
SOMALIA 1960
CABINDA (TO ANGOLA)
CONGO 1960
RWANDA 1962
BURUNDI 1962
TANZANIA 1961
ANGOLA 1975
MALAWI 1964
ZAMBIA 1964
MOZAMBIQUE 1975
MADAGASCAR 1960
NAMIBIA 1990
ZIMBABWE 1980
BOTSWANA 1966
SWAZILAND 1968
SOUTH AFRICA 1910
LESOTHO 1966

ATLANTIC OCEAN
INDIAN OCEAN
Mediterranean Sea
Red Sea
Tropic of Cancer
Tropic of Capricorn
Equator

Mercator Projection
0   400   800 Miles
0   400   800 Kilometers

Timeline

1980s Zimbabwe begins land and economic reforms.

1994 South Africa holds its first all-race elections and elects Nelson Mandela (right) as president. With Mandela is F. W. de Klerk, the previous president of South Africa.

2000 Religious violence strikes Nigeria after several states adopt Sharia, or Islamic law.

1985   2000   2015

1989 The Berlin Wall falls.

Take It to the NET
To learn about recent developments in Africa, visit the World History section of www.phschool.com.

Chapter 36 **907**

Independent Assignments

Have students read one section as they prepare for class. After class, have them complete the assignment. Some students may benefit from using the Guided Reading and Review worksheets.

Section 1 Have students use the worksheet *Youssou N'Dour* in the Unit 8 booklet, p. 82, to learn about how one African performer's work covers both his personal memories and social and political issues.

Section 2 Have students use the worksheet *Saving Africa's Environment?* in the Unit 8 booklet, p. 84, to learn about economic development and the environment in Africa.

Section 3 Have students use the worksheet *Growing Up in Nigeria* in the Unit 8 booklet, p. 83, to learn what it was like for one writer as he was growing up in Nigeria.

Section 4 Have students use the worksheet *Poems About Prison* in the History Through Literature booklet, p. 75, to read a poem by Dennis Brutus about his experience in a South African jail.

African Independence

Activating Prior Knowledge
Name four African countries that were independent prior to World War II. *(Egypt, Liberia, South Africa, and Ethiopia)*

Previewing
Why do you think so many countries came into existence after World War II? *(Following World War II, western imperialism stopped. Europe, exhausted from the war, gave up its colonial governments. Nationalism rose in Africa.)*

Background
About the Pictures

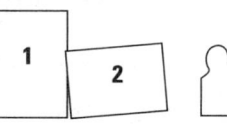

1   2   3

1. The Sudan, the largest African country, has a land area that represents over eight percent of the continent's area and almost two percent of the world's land area. The Sudan has been involved in conflict for many of the years since its independence. From 1956 until 1972, the country was involved in a costly civil war. In 1983, civil war broke out again.

2. The Independence Arch stands in Black Star Square in Ghana's capital, Accra. The square serves as the location for many national celebrations. One such celebration was the visit of Queen Elizabeth II in 1961, four years after Ghana gained its independence. Her arrival prompted what one observer described as "the biggest and most colourful military parade in Accra."

3. Following the Sharpeville massacre of 1960 and the subsequent ban on the African National Congress, Nelson Mandela, once a proponent of nonviolence, began to advocate attacks against the South African government. Mandela was sentenced to life in prison when the headquarters of the military wing of the ANC, which Mandela helped found, were raided.

eTeach

Be sure to check out this month's online discussion with a World History Master Teacher.

Go to www.phschool.com.

Bell Ringer Ask students to preview this section by scanning the illustrations and boldface heads. Have them write three generalizations about the African experience since 1945.

LESSON PLAN

1. Focus After World War II, a tide of nationalism swept through Africa, resulting in independence for many nations. The pattern of dependence fostered by colonialism made it difficult for most nations to build strong economies and stable political systems. In the years after independence, African leaders struggled to encourage national unity and to modernize their nations.

2. Instruct Have students work in pairs to prepare and present an imaginary interview with either Kwame Nkrumah or Jomo Kenyatta. Have each pair write five questions for their interview. Then, have them create answers that are consistent with the philosophy and experience of their chosen leader. Advise students that they may use classroom or library resources to formulate their questions and answers. Ask volunteers to perform their interviews for the class.

3. Assess Before closing, draw students' attention to the words of Ngugi wa Thiong'o on this page. Have students paraphrase the quotation in their own words. Then lead a discussion about how they might feel if they had been present as a citizen of Kenya.

4. Reteach If students' Assess activity does not reflect adequate understanding of the lesson, you might assign the *Guide to the Essentials* or the *Interactive Student Tutorial CD-ROM* for this section.

Reading Focus

- How did colonialism contribute to a growing spirit of nationalism?
- What routes to freedom did Ghana, Kenya, and Algeria follow?
- How did the Cold War affect Africa?

Taking Notes

On a sheet of paper, create a time line to show important events in the struggle for African independence. Use the time line shown here to help you get started.

```
1945    1950    1955    1960    1965
                        1957
                        Ghana declares
                        independence
```

Main Idea As many African nations won independence in the 1950s and 1960s, they held great hopes and faced great challenges.

Primary Sources and Literature

See "Chinua Achebe: Things Fall Apart" in the Reference Section at the back of this book.

Setting the Scene "Kenya regained her *Uhuru* [freedom] from the British on 12 December 1963," writes Ngugi wa Thiong'o in a novel about Kenya's struggle for independence. One scene describes the moment of independence in Nairobi, Kenya's capital:

"A minute before midnight, lights were put out at the Nairobi stadium. . . . In the dark, the Union Jack [British flag] was quickly lowered. When next the lights came on the new Kenya flag was flying and fluttering, and waving in the air."
—Ngugi wa Thiong'o, *A Grain of Wheat*

In Nairobi and in villages throughout Kenya, bands played the new national anthem and crowds cheered the good news. During the 1950s and 1960s, dozens of new nations emerged in Africa. As people across the continent celebrated their newfound freedom, they also faced many challenges.

The Colonial Legacy

Scholars trace many of Africa's recent problems to the colonial experience. Western imperialism had a complex and contradictory impact on Africa. Some changes brought real gains. Others had a destructive effect on African life that is felt down to the present.

Economics In their colonies, Europeans introduced new crops, technologies, and cash economies. They built roads, railroads, harbors, and cities. The new forms of transportation were meant to make the colonies profitable by linking plantations and mines to ports. Exporting raw materials and cash crops helped pay for European rule. Most Africans, who were subsistence farmers, gained little or nothing from these facilities.

After liberation, the pattern of economic dependence continued. To pay for expensive development projects, African nations exported minerals and agricultural goods to the industrial world. But most profits flowed out of Africa because the new nations had to buy expensive manufactured goods and technology from the West. Also, many large farms and mines were still owned by westerners.

Politics During the colonial period, Europeans undermined Africa's traditional political systems. Even when they left African rulers in place, they told Africans how to govern. In other cases, Europeans denied educated Africans top jobs in colonial governments.

908 *Chapter 36*

Resource Directory

Teaching Resources

Creative Teaching Activities Creative Teaching Activities booklet, p. 159
Guided Reading and Review Unit 8 booklet, p. 74
Biography Activity *Youssou N'Dour*, Unit 8 booklet, p. 82
Skill Application Activity *Analyzing Cartograms*, Unit 8 booklet, p. 85

At independence, colonial powers expected that African leaders would almost immediately transform authoritarian colonies into democratic nations. These powers seemed to forget that many western nations themselves had achieved democracy only after centuries of turmoil—and with the help of strong industrial economies.

Health Care and Education Colonial governments had an impact on health care and education in Africa. Western doctors developed vaccines for yellow fever and smallpox, and helped reduce deaths from malaria. These governments usually did not emphasize general health care, however. Medical attention was more likely to be provided by missionary groups.

By the 1950s, in response to nationalist demands, colonial rulers built more hospitals and schools. They emphasized elementary education, but established relatively few secondary schools and only a handful of universities. With limited access to education, people in liberated colonies faced additional challenges in the modern world.

National Borders At independence, African nations inherited borders drawn by colonial powers. These borders often caused immense problems. Europeans had staked out colonies according to their own political and economic interests, regardless of who lived in a particular region. Colonies therefore included people from diverse ethnic groups and with different—even conflicting—interests. As a result, many new nations were made up of hostile groups forced to live together in the same country. Some borders also split people of the same ethnic group into two separate nations. Rather than draw new borders, leaders of the new nations worked to build a sense of unity where none existed.

A Growing Spirit of Nationalism

In 1945, four European powers—Britain, France, Belgium, and Portugal—controlled almost all of the African continent. Only Egypt, Ethiopia, Liberia, and white-ruled South Africa were independent nations. The rising tide of nationalism, however, was sweeping over European colonial empires. Around the world, liberation would follow this tide.

Impact of World War II World War II sharpened the edges of nationalist movements in Africa. Early Japanese victories in Asia shattered the West's reputation as an unbeatable force. Also, African troops provided support for Allied armies in Africa, the Middle East, and other parts of the world. When they returned to find discrimination and second-class citizenship at home, these ex-soldiers became easy recruits for growing nationalist movements. Nationalists also found support among workers in wartime defense industries. Often, strikes by workers over issues such as pay escalated into demands for freedom.

The Global Setting After the war, most people in Europe had had their fill of fighting. Many were reluctant to return to combat over their overseas colonies. Britain and France, the largest imperialist powers, were faced with growing nationalist demands. In response, they adopted new policies toward their African colonies. Both countries introduced political reforms that would lead to gradual independence. Colonial powers soon learned, however, that they could dictate neither the terms nor the pace of change.

African Soldiers
During World War II, African troops helped Allied armies around the world. Here, members of the Nyasaland Battalion of the King's African Rifles prepare for action.

Theme: Political and Social Systems How did wartime experiences contribute to the growth of nationalist movements?

Analyzing Primary Sources

Background
About the Primary Source

Ghana and American Foreign Policy As a reporter for an American newspaper, Thomas Brady may have produced an account of these events colored by American views regarding Ghana's independence. First, at this time, an American foreign policy goal was halting the spread of communism. Friendly relations with Ghana might influence emerging nations in Africa.

Second, during the 1950s, many African Americans involved in the civil rights movement saw Ghana's independence as a hopeful sign that might aid their struggle for equality in the United States.

Activity
Interpreting the Primary Source

Use this additional question to generate class discussion.
Critical Thinking: Recognizing Points of View Many African leaders spent time in prison during the colonial period for crimes against the government. Why do you think this is so? *(Imprisonment is one way governments have tried to silence dissenters.)*

Skills Tip

Point out to students that they should be particularly sensitive to the possibility of bias in reports about other countries. The Skills Handbook in the front of the book has a lesson that will help students with this feature.

Skills Assessment

ANSWERS **1.** C **2.** F **3. (a)** They were happy. **(b)** economic development

Ghana Wins Independence

On March 6, 1957, Ghana became the first African nation south of the Sahara to win independence. The following is an eyewitness account of the events celebrating the birth of the new nation.

"**Nation of Ghana Is Born In Africa**
Accra, Ghana, Wednesday, March 6, 1957—A new . . . nation was born at midnight.

As the British flag was lowered from the staff of the Legislative Assembly here and the new red, green and gold flag bearing a star rose in its place, the British colony known as the Gold Coast ceased to exist and the sovereign state of Ghana became the ninth member of the Commonwealth [of Nations].

Prime Minister Kwame Nkrumah had told the final session of the colony's Legislative Assembly a few minutes earlier that the 'chains of imperialism and colonialism which have hitherto bound us to Britain' were left behind as Ghana redeemed 'her lost freedom.'

Ghana is the name of the ancient West African empire that flourished about a thousand years ago. After it disintegrated, it remained a legend of . . . power and magnificence.

Attending the celebration of the rebirth of Ghana are representatives of more than fifty nations, including the Soviet Union and Communist China. Vice President Richard M. Nixon heads the United States delegation. . . .

Thousands of Ghanaians marched in the streets of Accra this morning singing, thumping drums and shooting firecrackers. At least 30,000 of them came from the polo grounds where the Prime Minister had told them in English and in the Fanti language that they were free people—no longer 'slaves'—and that they must throw out their chests when they walk.

Mr. Nkrumah addressed them after his long and serious speech in Parliament House. He was still inside when the flag of Ghana rose on the mast and the crowd in the streets began to cheer and yell. . . .

Mr. Nkrumah told the final session of the Assembly that the Government would seek to help 'all African peoples in their pursuit of freedom and social progress.' He also emphasized that foreign investment would be encouraged."
—Thomas F. Brady, special to *The New York Times*

Kwame Nkrumah (center), prime minister and later president of Ghana, addresses the public during Ghana's independence celebration.

Skills Tip

Keep in mind that a newspaper article reports only on facts that are available at the moment. Often, additional information emerges through the years that helps historians gain a deeper understanding of events.

Skills Assessment

1. According to this report, the name *Ghana* calls up images of
   A colonial oppression.
   B bloody civil war.
   C past greatness.
   D successful diplomacy.

2. The article conveys the international importance of Ghana's independence mainly in its description of
   E Ghana's new flag.
   F the foreign officials in attendance.
   G the cheering crowds in Accra.
   H Nkrumah's speech.

3. **Critical Thinking Making Inferences (a)** Based on this account, how did the people of Ghana react to their independence? **(b)** What issues faced the new nation?

Resource Directory

Teaching Resources
Analyzing Primary Sources Chapter Extension Activities booklet, p. 85

Pressures for independence built up both within and outside Africa. After India won independence from Britain in 1947, African leaders grew impatient. Furthermore, both the United States and the Soviet Union rejected colonialism. Everywhere, the cry rose: "Freedom Now."

Nationalist Leaders Most nationalist leaders were western educated. Many were powerful speakers whose words inspired their supporters. Kwame Nkrumah in Gold Coast (later Ghana), Jomo Kenyatta in Kenya, and Léopold Senghor in Senegal, to name just a few, also were skilled political organizers.

In colonies throughout Africa, leaders organized political parties. In the cities, these political parties published newspapers, held mass rallies, and mobilized support for independence. Demonstrations, strikes, and boycotts were designed to pressure European governments into negotiating timetables for freedom.

Routes to Freedom

During the great liberation, each African nation had its own leaders and its own story. Here, we will look at three examples: Ghana in West Africa, Kenya in East Africa, and Algeria in North Africa.

Ghana The first African nation south of the Sahara to win freedom was the British colony of Gold Coast. During the late 1940s, Kwame Nkrumah (kwah MEE ehn KROO muh) was impatient with Britain's policy of gradual movement toward independence. Nkrumah had spent time in the United States, where he was inspired by the Pan-Africanist Marcus Garvey and other civil rights leaders. He also studied the nonviolent methods of India's Mohandas Gandhi.

Back in Gold Coast, Nkrumah organized a radical political party. Through strikes and boycotts, he tried to win concessions from Britain. When mass actions led to riots, Nkrumah was imprisoned. His supporters continued the struggle.

In 1957, Gold Coast finally won independence. Nkrumah, who had emerged from prison to become prime minister of the new nation, named it Ghana, after the ancient West African empire.* The symbolism was clear. *Gold Coast* reflected European interests in Africa. *Ghana* linked the new nation with the region's African past. "Before the arrival of the Europeans," Nkrumah said, "our ancestors had attained a great empire. . . . Thus we may take pride in the name of Ghana, not out of romanticism, but as an inspiration for the future."

Kenya In Kenya, freedom came only with armed struggle. White settlers had carved out farms in the fertile highlands, where they displaced African farmers, mostly Kikuyu (kih KOO yoo). Settlers saw Kenya as their homeland and had passed laws to ensure their domination.

Even before World War II, Jomo Kenyatta had been a leading spokesman for the Kikuyu. "The land is ours," he said. "When Europeans came, they kept us back and took our land." Kenyatta supported nonviolent methods to end oppressive laws.

More radical leaders turned to guerrilla warfare. They burned farms and destroyed livestock, hoping to scare whites into leaving. In 1952, they began to attack settlers and Africans who worked with the colonial rulers. The British called the guerrillas Mau Mau and pictured them as savages. To stop the violence, the British arrested Kenyatta and forced thousands of Kikuyu into concentration camps. Kikuyu casualties rose when British bombers pounded Mau Mau armed mostly with swords. All told, casualties totaled about 75 dead among the whites, and about 13,000 Kenyans.

*Ancient Ghana was located to the north and west of modern Ghana.

▶ **Primary Sources and Literature**

See "*Kwame Nkrumah: Autobiography*" in the Reference Section at the back of this book.

Biography

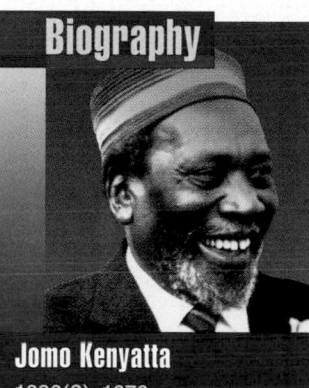

Jomo Kenyatta
1890(?)–1978

Jomo Kenyatta was born in a small Kikuyu village and educated at a Christian mission. Moving to Nairobi, he was quickly drawn to the first stirrings of the nationalist cause. He became a prominent anticolonial organizer and was eventually elected president of the Kenya Africa Union.

Kenyatta was arrested in 1952 and convicted in 1953 on charges of inciting the Mau Mau uprising against the British. Released in 1961, he resumed leadership of the movement for independence, which was finally granted in December 1963. When Kenya became a republic in 1964, Kenyatta was elected its first president. Under his 15-year rule, Kenya enjoyed political stability and economic advances. Each year, October 20, the date of his arrest, is celebrated as Kenyatta Day.

Theme: Impact of the Individual What role do you think national heroes play in helping to form a nation's identity?

The Roots of War In the 1950s, many Algerians became increasingly active in movements for independence. Under French rule, Muslims faced a great deal of discrimination. European settlers, most of whom were French, owned and operated large farms, businesses, and industries. Meanwhile, most Algerian Muslims labored on tiny plots of land. They were hired by Europeans to fill only the most menial jobs. Although Muslims had been granted equality under the law, they were prevented from taking an active role in government.

Under these conditions, it was inevitable that resentment would build. With France unwilling to grant Algeria independence, Muslims and other Algerians rose in revolution.

Reading Strategy
Relating to Topic

Have students answer the following questions as they read: What political similarities did the liberated nations of Ghana, Kenya, and Algeria share in their routes to freedom? How did Africa's colonial heritage affect the more than 50 new nations that were born on that continent after World War II? *(More Advanced Readers)*

The rebels were crushed, but the movement lived on. Eventually, the British released Kenyatta, whose imprisonment had made him a national hero. In 1963, he became the first prime minister of an independent Kenya. The next year, Kenya became a republic, with Kenyatta as president.

Algeria From 1954 to 1962, a longer and even costlier war of liberation raged in Algeria. In the 1800s, France had conquered Algeria after a brutal struggle. Over the years, the French had come to see Algeria, located across the Mediterranean from France, as part of their country. Along with the million Europeans who had settled there, they were determined to keep the Arab-Berber people of Algeria from winning independence.

Muslim Algerian nationalists set up the National Liberation Front (FLN). In 1954, the group turned to guerrilla warfare to win freedom. France, which had just lost its Asian colony of Vietnam, was unwilling to retreat from Algeria. As the fighting escalated, a half-million French troops went to Algeria. Thousands of these troops were killed. Additionally, hundreds of thousands of Algerians died during the long war.

Eventually, public opinion in France turned against the war. After Charles de Gaulle, a World War II hero, became president of France in 1958, he began talks to end the war. In 1962, Algeria celebrated its freedom.

Modernization and Challenges More than 50 new nations were born in Africa during the great liberation. Throughout the continent, Africans had great hopes for the future. People looked forward to rapid political and economic development. African leaders knew they had much to do to build modern nations, but they welcomed the chance to deal on an equal footing with the other nations of the world. After 70 years of colonial rule, Africans were again in control of their destinies.

During the early decades after independence, the new nations took different paths to modernization. Some made progress despite huge obstacles. Others were plunged into crisis by civil war, natural disasters, military rule, or corrupt dictators. In some parts of Africa, standards of living actually fell after liberation. In many countries, a small elite enjoyed wealth and privileges, while the majority lived in poverty.

The Cold War and Africa

African nations emerged into a world dominated by rival blocs led by the United States and the Soviet Union. Although many African nations supported the nonaligned movement, they generally could not avoid the pressures of the Cold War. Those who embraced socialism, such as Tanzania's Julius Nyerere, were viewed with suspicion by the West. In turn, the Soviet Union frowned on nations that decided to pursue capitalist goals. Each superpower supplied arms to governments it favored. That policy boosted the power of the military in many countries, contributing to instability.

Cold War rivalries affected local conflicts within Africa. The Soviet Union and the United States supported rival groups in the liberation struggles in southern Africa. Along the Red Sea, the two superpowers became involved in a long, bloody war between the nations of Ethiopia and Somalia.

Like the colonial experience, the Cold War left a painful legacy. Weapons supplied by the superpowers came into the hands of traditional tribes and clans or of modern militias and guerrilla forces. Thus, armed

The Cold War
Cold War rivalries had devastating effects in Africa. One of the bloodiest struggles took place in Somalia and Ethiopia. In this cartoon, American and Soviet advisers rush to help their allies, but head for their own collision.

Theme: Global Interaction Why did the two superpowers care about which political system African nations adopted?

912 *Chapter 36*

Caption Answer

Each wanted to be the dominant power in the world and hoped to increase control by persuading developing nations to adopt a particular economic system.

Resource Directory

Teaching Resources
Section Quiz Unit 8 booklet, p. 75

Technology
Interactive Student Tutorial CD-ROM Ch. 36
Computer Test Bank Ch. 36

with modern weapons, these groups spread violence across many lands.

Organization of African Unity The new nations of Africa were determined to carve out their own position in the world. To do so, they joined both regional and global organizations. In 1963, they set up the Organization of African Unity (OAU). It promoted cooperation among members, supported independence, and sought peaceful settlement of disputes.

Since then, the OAU has provided African nations with a forum to discuss and settle common problems. The OAU set up the African Development Bank to channel much-needed investment capital from foreign sources into development programs. The impact of the OAU was limited, however, because it had no power to enforce decisions. It also strongly opposed interfering in the internal affairs of member states.

The UN After independence, African nations joined the United Nations. They contributed to and benefited from the UN and its many agencies. Africans served in UN peacekeeping missions around the world.

African countries and other developing nations focused world attention on issues including health care, literacy, and economic development. They called for an end to racism and imperialism. They also pressed nations of the global North to deal with the unequal distribution of wealth.

Disaster Relief The UN—along with individual nations and private agencies like the International Red Cross, Oxfam, and Doctors Without Borders—responded to famine and other crises that struck African nations. In the early 1960s, UN peacekeepers helped stop the fighting in Zaire. Later, UN efforts helped save millions from starvation in Biafra during Nigeria's civil war.

Some international efforts had limited success. In the early 1990s, UN forces, with massive American help, brought food to Somalians caught up in a civil war. Outsiders tried, but failed, to restore peace to Somalia. In the end, the UN and most foreigners withdrew, concluding that only Somalians could solve their own problems. In Burundi and Rwanda, the UN and private aid groups again fed refugees of civil wars.

Turmoil and Survival
Although civil wars caused great hardship, people throughout Africa were determined to create better lives. Here, women build new homes after war in Rwanda forced them to abandon their villages.

Theme: Economics and Technology What economic and political changes did reformers support during the 1980s?

SECTION 1 Assessment

Recall

1. **Identify: (a)** Kwame Nkrumah, **(b)** Jomo Kenyatta, **(c)** National Liberation Front, **(d)** Charles de Gaulle, **(e)** Organization of African Unity.

Comprehension

2. **(a)** What challenges faced African nations as a result of colonialism? **(b)** How did nationalist leaders respond to these challenges?

3. Describe the conflicts that arose during independence in the following countries: **(a)** Ghana, **(b)** Kenya, **(c)** Algeria.

4. What role did international organizations play in Africa during the Cold War?

Critical Thinking and Writing

5. **Connecting to Geography** How might Africa's size and diversity have affected early reform efforts?

6. **Making Inferences** Review the subsection A Growing Spirit of Nationalism. Why might European enthusiasm for colonization have declined after World War II? Provide details from the text to support your answer.

Chapter 36 **913**

Chapter 36 **913**

Bell Ringer
Read aloud the quotation that begins the section. Tell students to imagine that this is the first line in a speech that they are giving to the government of a newly independent African nation. Give students two or three minutes to list the ideas they might include in such a speech.

Reading Focus
- What were barriers to unity and stability in Africa?
- What economic choices did African nations make?
- What critical issues affect African nations today?
- How has modernization affected patterns of life?

Vocabulary
one-party system
mixed economy
desertification

Taking Notes
As you read this section, prepare an outline of its contents. Use Roman numerals to indicate major headings. Use capital letters for sub-headings, and use numbers for the supporting details. The example here will help you get started.

I. Seeking unity and stability
  A. Divisions
    1. Diversity
    2.
  B. Civil war
  C.
II. Economic choices
  A. Socialism or capitalism
  B.

Main Idea New African nations faced many choices and challenges as they established new governments.

LESSON PLAN

1. Focus New African nations sought unity and stability as they set up political and economic systems. But civil wars, population explosions, drought, famine, and other problems made these goals difficult to achieve. In many cases, one-party rule or military rule was established. Often, socialism or mixed economies replaced capitalism.

2. Instruct Ask students to work with a partner to create a two-column chart describing the African experience since 1945. Instruct them to label one column "Goals" and the other "Obstacles." Have them work together using information in the section to fill in the chart. When they have finished this part of the lesson, ask each pair to choose one African nation as the subject of a case-study. Their assignment is to research the goals and obstacles that their chosen nation has encountered since 1945. Invite volunteers to present their findings to the class.

3. Assess Ask students to create a bulletin board display of news about the governments, economies, and social conditions that exist in African nations today.

4. Reteach If students' *Assess* activity does not reflect adequate understanding of the lesson, you might assign the *Guide to the Essentials* or the *Interactive Student Tutorial CD-ROM* for this section.

Setting the Scene
"Independence is the beginning of a real struggle," declared one liberation leader in Africa. The new nations faced two critical issues. First, they needed to create unified states with stable governments. Second, they had to achieve economic growth that would improve the standard of living of their people. Meeting those challenges would be a long, complex process—one that is still incomplete.

After independence, African governments experimented with various programs. They made some progress but also took some wrong turns. In this section, we will look at the political and economic challenges faced by nations across Africa.

Seeking Unity and Stability
At independence, African nations set up governments modeled on those of departing colonial rulers. But parliamentary systems did not work in the new African countries as they did in European nations, where they had evolved over centuries.

New Governments
Many African nations adapted colonial structures for new uses. The Presidential Palace in Senegal, shown here, originally served as the home of the governor-general for French West Africa.

Theme: Political and Social Systems Why might a nation choose to use an existing structure rather than construct new government buildings?

914 Chapter 36

Resource Directory

Teaching Resources
Creative Teaching Activities Creative Teaching Activities booklet, p. 160
Guided Reading and Review Unit 8 booklet, p. 76

Divisions Colonial borders had left most African nations a patchwork of people with diverse cultures, languages, and histories. Nationalism had helped unify Africans within each colony to end foreign rule. But once freedom was won, many Africans felt their first loyalty was to their own ethnic group, not to a faceless national government.

Like Eastern European nations, African nations were plagued by ethnic and regional conflict. In Sudan, for example, the Arabic-speaking Muslim majority in the north dominated and persecuted the minority, mostly African Christian groups, in the south. These southerners tried to break away, resulting in a civil war that has continued to the present.

Civil War Westerners often blamed African civil wars on old "tribal" rivalries.* But most conflicts were more complex. Some were rooted in colonial history. Britain, for example, often chose to rule a colony through what it called "tribal" leaders. It assigned Africans within a colony to tribes, and then chose one tribe to rule the others. This system fostered ill will that continued long after independence.

Civil wars also erupted when liberation leaders monopolized political and economic power for their own group. In Nigeria and Zaire, civil war erupted when economically successful groups tried to set up their own nations. In Africa, as elsewhere, civil wars unleashed terrible violence.

One-Party Rule Faced with divisions that threatened national unity, many early leaders turned to a one-party system. Under this political structure, a country has a single political party, or only one party that has any real likelihood of winning elections. Multiparty systems, these leaders declared, encouraged disunity. In Tanzania, Julius Nyerere (nyuh RAIR ay) claimed that a one-party system could be democratic and offered voters a choice of candidates within the party.

In fact, most one-party nations became authoritarian states. After the struggle for independence, some nationalist leaders became dictators. Some used their position to enrich themselves and a privileged elite. Others used force to hold onto power.

Military Rule When bad government led to unrest, the military often seized power. More than half of all African nations suffered military coups. Military leaders claimed that they—unlike politicians, who they said sought power and wealth—were motivated by a sense of duty to their country. Some military rulers, like Idi Amin, who murdered thousands of citizens in Uganda, were brutal tyrants. Others sought to end abuses and improve conditions.

Military leaders usually promised to restore civilian rule once they had cleaned up the government. In many cases, however, they gave up power only when they were toppled by other military coups.

Reforms By the mid-1980s, political and economic woes brought Africa to the brink of crisis. Demands for change came from inside and outside the continent. African thinkers looked for African solutions to their problems. They studied precolonial African societies that had limited a ruler's power and allowed people a share in decision making. They did not propose returning to the past, but hoped instead to build on traditions that had worked before.

While some Africans demanded this sort of "people participation," external sources called for democratic reforms. Western governments and the World Bank, for example, required such reforms before making more loans. Under that pressure, some governments eased autocratic policies.

---

*The word *tribe* was used by westerners to describe people living in small-scale societies and implied backwardness. The term is misleading, however. Like societies elsewhere, Africans in precolonial times belonged to ethnic or social groups that shared a common culture or loyalty. But these groups changed over time and continue to change today.

Primary Source

Building New Nations
Kenneth Kaunda delivered this speech in 1966, when he was president of Zambia. In this excerpt, Kaunda emphasizes the need for elected leaders to serve their nation:

"We must think and think and think again about how best we shall serve and not how important we are as leaders of our people or how we can safeguard our own positions as leaders. . . . We must remember we are *not* elected kings. . . .

Selfishness in leaders and followers inevitably leads to corruption. I cannot see, however, that uniformed men replacing elected leaders, by either killing them, imprisoning them, or, indeed, sending them into exile is the answer to this problem. . . .

To my fellow leaders on the continent of Africa I would . . . send this message—that our task and challenge is to try and help establish governments of the people, by the people, and for the people."

—Kenneth Kaunda, speech delivered March 18, 1966

Skills Assessment

Primary Source What is Kaunda's opinion of military rule?

Activity
Connections to Literature

Analyzing a Short Story During the bloody civil war in Mozambique, millions of people endured violence, famine, and disease. In her short story "The Ultimate Safari," South African Nadine Gordimer, winner of the 1991 Nobel Prize for literature, traces the upheavals in one girl's family as they try to escape the brutality of Mozambique's civil war.

After the disappearance of the parents, the remaining members of the family face death unless they can escape to the refugee camps. The hardships experienced while keeping themselves hidden from soldiers and game hunters, who would return them to Mozambique, leave the grandfather dead, the infant boy retarded, and the others near starvation. Once in the refugee camp, the grandmother fights to provide the children with food, clothing, and shelter.

Have students read the story. Then, organize them into groups to answer the following questions: (1) Identify three reasons the family must flee Mozambique. (2) Why must the refugees stay hidden from the game hunters? (3) Why does the grandmother leave the grandfather behind in the game park? (4) Why does the girl's attitude differ from her grandmother's at the end of the story? (5) Why do you think the author titled her story "The Ultimate Safari"?

Block Scheduling Support

Have students create a classroom government. Appoint students to research types of government they could create. Appoint another group to act as the council that will decide the form of government. Once the council has decided on the form of government to be created, have other groups brainstorm about problems this new government faces, such as how to discipline students who break rules. Some students may even set up a class economy—money to be used for a future event. Once this exercise is complete, you may wish to assign a brief essay in which students compare what they have experienced with what they know about newly independent African nations.

Primary Source

ANSWER Kaunda believes that military rule is not for the good of the people.

Background
Connections to Economics

Economic Success One of Africa's more economically successful nations is Mauritius. When this island nation became independent from Britain in 1968, Mauritius basically had a one-crop economy. Sugar was grown on most of its farmland and accounted for most of its exports. To reduce the nation's dependence on sugar, the new government encouraged farmers to grow other crops and helped light industry to expand. Today, Mauritius's major industries include tourism, food processing, and knitwear. By the 1990s, the nation had a per capita gross national product of $2,980, one of the highest in Africa. Meanwhile, its literacy rate reached more than 90 percent.

Geography and History

Preserving Africa's Wildlife

Logging, farming, and urban development have devoured nearly 70 percent of Africa's animal habitats. The black rhinoceros, wildebeest, and hartebeest have been pushed to the edge of extinction. Populations of elephant, zebra, and antelope are in decline.

Some governments have responded with strong conservation measures. In fact, national parks and game reserves encompass 185,000 square miles of Africa, a higher proportion than on any other continent. Still, Africa's wildlife faces threats from many sources, among them real estate developers, farmers who view wild beasts as a threat to their crops and livestock, and poachers who traffic in ivory elephant tusks and black rhino horns. Wildlife officials face an uphill battle in persuading Africans that the benefits they will gain from protecting their natural heritage will outweigh the costs.

Theme: Political and Social Systems Why are some African governments having a hard time protecting endangered wildlife?

Economic Choices

A key to modernization was building productive economies and raising standards of living. Developing modern economies meant improving agriculture and developing industry. To achieve those goals, African nations had to build transportation systems, develop resources, increase literacy, and solve problems of rural poverty. Many had little capital to invest in such projects. As a result, they had to make difficult choices.

Socialism or Capitalism Many newly independent nations chose socialism, which meant that the government made economic decisions about using resources and producing goods. Socialist governments wanted to control scarce resources, using them where government planners thought they were most needed. They hoped to end foreign economic influence and prevent inequalities between rich and poor. But to regulate the economy, socialism created large bureaucracies, which generally were inefficient. Often, policies imposed by the national government were ill suited to local farming communities.

Some African nations set up mixed economies, with both private and state-run enterprises. These, too, had problems. These nations relied heavily on foreign aid from the UN, the World Bank, and industrial nations. Foreign capital was used to build airports, hydroelectric plants, and factories, and to improve farming. Some programs succeeded. Others were costly failures, due partly to mistakes by government planners or foreign advisers.

Although African nations did build some industries, they remained heavily dependent on imports. Most people were subsistence farmers. As a result, there was too little demand for manufactured goods to make local industries prosper.

Cash Crops or Food In the early years, governments pushed programs to increase earnings by growing more cash crops for export. But land used for crops such as cotton, tea, coffee, or sisal could not also be used to produce food. As a result, African countries that once had fed their people from their own land had to import food.

Urban or Rural Needs The food dilemma had another aspect. Many city dwellers earned low wages and needed cheap food to survive. Farmers, however, would grow food crops only if they received good prices for them. Many governments kept food prices artificially low to satisfy poor city people. As a result, farmers either used their land for export crops or produced only for themselves.

Many early government programs neglected rural development in favor of industrial projects. By the 1980s, though, governments realized they must pay more attention to farmers' needs. In Zimbabwe, the government helped small farmers buy tools, fertilizer, and seed. Additionally, it made sure farmers received higher prices for their crops. The policy paid off in higher food output.

The Debt Crisis Soaring oil prices in the 1970s also hurt developing economies. Most African nations were oil importers and had to pay out large amounts of currency for much-needed fuel. Prices for African exports fell, plunging the young nations deep into debt. Governments had to pay so much interest on loans that they had little money for development.

The debt crisis led the World Bank and other lenders to require developing nations to make tough economic reforms before extending new loans. African governments had to privatize businesses, cut spending on

Geography and History

ANSWER Farmers want to protect their crops and livestock from wildlife, poachers can make a great deal of money from elephant tusks and rhino horns, and real estate developers want to develop the land.

Resource Directory

Teaching Resources
Viewpoint Activity *Saving Africa's Environment?,* Unit 8 booklet, p. 84

development projects, and stop subsidizing prices of basic foods for the urban poor. In the long term, the reforms were designed to help economies grow. In the short term, however, they increased unemployment and led to higher prices that the poor could not pay.

Critical Issues

The population explosion put a staggering burden on Africa's developing economies. In 1965, Africa's population was about 280 million. By 1990, that figure had increased to over 650 million. The continent's population was expected to double before 2020. As in other developing nations around the world, rising population meant that the least-developed countries had to find ways to feed, educate, and generate jobs for the fastest-growing number of people.

Drought and Famine In the early 1970s and again in the 1980s, prolonged drought contributed to famine in parts of Africa. Livestock died. As farmland turned to dust and blew away, millions of people became refugees. The Sahel was especially hard hit. This semidesert region stretches across Africa just south of the Sahara. There, overgrazing and farming removed topsoil and speeded up desertification, or the spread of desert areas.

In countries like Ethiopia and Sudan, civil war intensified the effects of drought and famine. Each side in the conflict tried to keep relief supplies from reaching the other. On several occasions, huge international efforts helped save millions of people facing starvation.

Deforestation Rain forests, too, came under attack. To boost badly needed export earnings, African governments allowed hardwood trees to be cut and shipped to the global North. Once forests were cleared, heavy tropical rains washed nutrients from the soil and destroyed its fertility. In Kenya, an environmental activist named Wangari Maathi challenged government policy by starting the Greenbelt movement. She hoped to restore the environment and create job opportunities for women in areas such as planting trees, marketing, and forestry.

AIDS The AIDS epidemic spread rapidly across parts of Africa. Nations such as Uganda and Tanzania were particularly hard hit. In 1998, the Joint United Nations Programme on HIV/AIDS estimated that more than 21 million Africans might be infected with the virus believed to cause the disease, with about 4 million new infections each year. Many victims were young people in their twenties and thirties, as well as children born to infected mothers.

New treatments for the disease were emerging as the century ended. Many of these, however, were too expensive for people in the poorer African nations to afford. And for Africa as for the rest of the world, there was as yet no cure for AIDS.

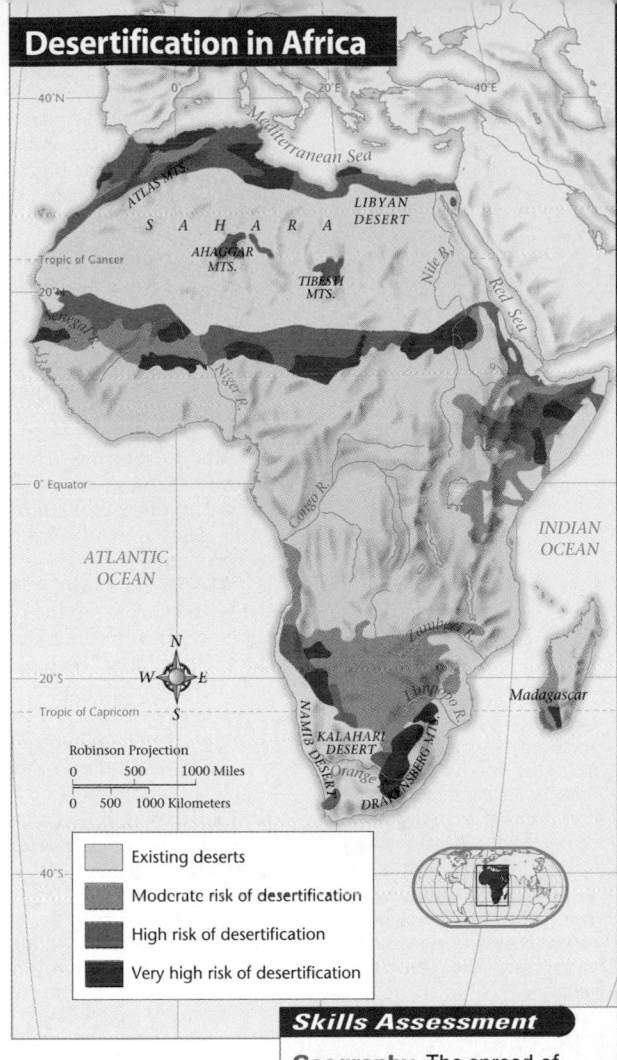

Desertification in Africa

Existing deserts

Moderate risk of desertification

High risk of desertification

Very high risk of desertification

Skills Assessment

Geography The spread of deserts in Africa results in the loss of farmlands and grazing lands.

1. **Location** On the map, locate **(a)** Sahara, **(b)** Kalahari Desert, **(c)** Namib Desert, **(d)** Libyan Desert.
2. **Region** Which regions of Africa are least likely to experience desertification?
3. **Critical Thinking Drawing Conclusions (a)** Based on this map, in which direction would you expect the Sahara to expand? **(b)** the Kalahari Desert?

Activity
Cooperative Learning

Solving a Problem After students have read the section titled "Critical Issues," divide the class into small groups. Instruct each group to choose one of Africa's population or environmental problems and to brainstorm possible solutions. Advise the groups that they should be able to explain how and why their solutions might work. When the groups are finished, have them present and defend their ideas. Then, encourage discussion of which solutions seem most practical and likely to succeed. ✳

✓ Test Preparation

Have students read the paragraph with the heading "Deforestation" on this page, and then answer the question below.

Which of the following is a result of rain forests being cleared?

A There was an economic boom.

(B) The soil's fertility was destroyed.

C There was an AIDS epidemic.

D There was greater food production for export.

Skills Assessment

ANSWERS 1. Review locations with students. **2.** the southern part of West Africa, Central Africa, the area along the southernmost coast, and the northern three quarters of Madagascar **3. (a)** south **(b)** north and east

Urban Growth
Throughout Africa, people continue to seek jobs in cities such as Pretoria, South Africa, shown here. Although such migration can disrupt traditional cultures, it has also promoted national unity.

Theme: Economics and Technology Why might new nations choose to spend money on the construction of modern buildings?

Old and New Patterns

In Africa, as elsewhere, modernization disrupted old ways. Colonial rule also undermined African traditions by promoting western cultural influences. Today, people across Africa face a similar dilemma. On the one hand, they want the high standard of living, advanced technology, and other benefits associated with modern societies. On the other, they value and want to preserve their own culture and traditions.

Impact of Urbanization By 2000, almost half of all Africans lived in towns and cities, and rural people were still migrating to cities at a rapid rate. Although urbanization contributed to the development of a larger national identity, it weakened traditional cultures and undermined ethnic and kinship ties that unified rural communities. Young urban dwellers who returned to their villages often scorned traditional ways. Yet many educated Africans took pride in those traditions.

Effects on Women The great migration to the cities had some effect on women. A few educated women joined the urban elite, working in civil service or other professional positions. Most urban women, however, struggled to feed and keep their families together in poverty-stricken urban slums.

Despite urbanization, most African women still live in rural areas, where they make up the bulk of the population. As men moved to the cities, rural women took on the sole responsibility of caring and providing for their children. They planted and harvested food crops, collected wood and water, and prepared food. In some areas, they found paid work on large farms. In West Africa, their historical role as market traders allowed some women to gain considerable economic power.

The constitutions of most African nations promised women generous rights. But often those rights were not enforced, and women's lives were still ruled by traditional laws. A small but powerful group of well-educated African women has worked to make national governments more responsive to women's issues.

Christianity in Africa Today, as in the past, Africa is home to many religious traditions. Colonialism and modernization disrupted traditional practices, but in rural areas, people remained faithful to their own beliefs. Both Christianity and Islam spread to Africa centuries ago, and both have grown since their introduction. Almost three fourths of African Christians are Roman Catholic. Others belong to Orthodox Christian or Protestant sects. These churches sometimes combine Christian and traditional African beliefs.

At times, African clergy risked their lives to stand up to dictators in Zaire, Uganda, and elsewhere. Sometimes, though, they were unable to stop violence. In Rwanda, for example, most people are Christian. But ethnic conflict in that nation led to mass killings, even in churches where people had taken refuge.

Islamic Revival Islam has long influenced the northern half of Africa and linked it to the Middle East. Islam, you will recall, spread along trade routes into both East and West Africa. Today, Nigeria has the largest Muslim population south of the Sahara.

Muslim African nations felt the effects of the Islamic revival that began in the Middle East. Its message of reform based on Islamic traditions and its call for social justice were welcomed by people in Africa and around the world. So, too, was its rejection of western influences. In the early 1990s, Algeria's Islamic party did so well in elections that the government feared an Islamic revolution like Iran's. The military canceled further elections. That action outraged Islamic extremists, who attacked politicians, scholars, and others, sometimes massacring whole villages. The government responded with force. More than 70,000 people were killed in the fighting.

In other African lands, as in parts of Asia, the Islamic revival stimulated deeper religious commitment. Many Muslims, like some Christians in the West, believed that the world had become too secularized and returned to the faith of their ancestors.

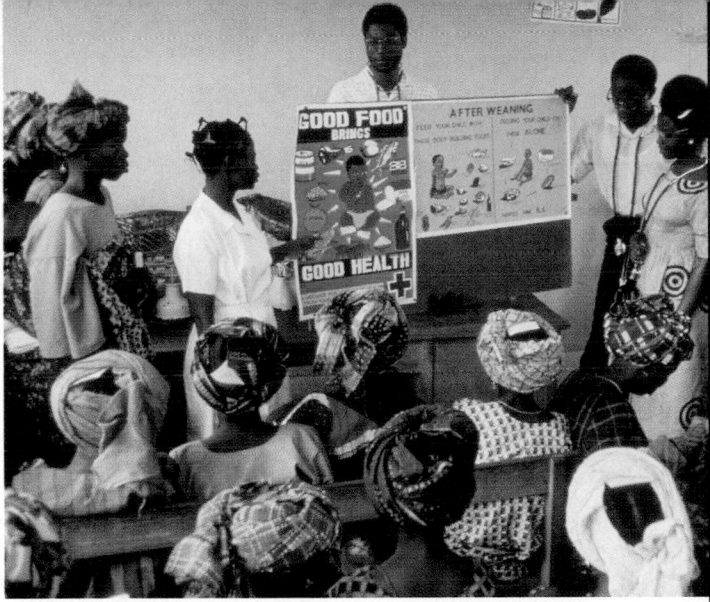

Improving Health Care
Providing medical care has been a goal of many African nations. Because there are few hospitals in many areas, health projects often focus on prevention. Here, doctors at a rural Nigerian clinic teach women about the importance of good nutrition in raising healthy children.

Theme: Political and Social Systems Why is preventive medicine especially important in areas with few doctors or hospitals?

SECTION 2 Assessment

Recall
1. **Identify:** (a) Julius Nyerere, (b) Wangari Maathi, (c) AIDS epidemic.
2. **Define:** (a) one-party system, (b) mixed economy, (c) desertification.

Comprehension
3. Why were unity and stability difficult to achieve?
4. Describe the choices faced by African nations after independence.
5. What environmental challenges does Africa face?
6. How did modernization and the growth of cities change daily life for many Africans?

Critical Thinking and Writing
7. **Analyzing Information** How did governments of new African nations respond to political and economic challenges?
8. **Identifying Alternatives** How might development in Africa have been different if nationalist leaders had chosen to draw new national boundaries based on ethnicity?

Activity

Creating a Development Program
Suppose that you have been elected president of a newly independent nation. Outline a development program that identifies the nation's needs and suggests ways to address them.

SECTION 2 Assessment

Recall
1. (a) Julius Nyerere, p. 915 (b) Wangari Maathi, p. 917 (c) AIDS epidemic, p. 917
2. (a) one-party system, p. 915 (b) mixed economy, p. 916 (c) desertification, p. 917

Comprehension
3. They were hindered by divisions among people within nations, civil wars, authoritarian leaders, and military rule.
4. socialism or capitalism, cash crops or food, urban or rural needs, solutions for debt crisis 5. African nations need to feed and support a growing population in the face of droughts and famines. They also need to find ways to create a healthy economy without deforestation, which causes more problems. 6. Cities grew dramatically, often weakening traditional cultures even as national unity increased. Women took on the bulk of farm labor as men migrated to cities.

Critical Thinking and Writing
7. Some governments tried to foster national unity through one-party systems, but these often produced authoritarian states. Others fell to military rule. In many cases, governments tried to develop reforms that would build on local traditions.
8. National boundaries would have been redrawn, leading to a need for brand new governments. While people might have felt more immediate loyalty to their nations, leaders might have had difficulty organizing international movements.

Activity Rubrics

Share rubrics with students before they outline their programs.

Attempted Student does not complete the development program.

Minimal Student completes the development program, but it is brief and shows little effort or has many errors.

Adequate Student's development program identifies the nation's needs, offers good suggestions to address these needs, and is well written.

Exemplary Student's development program identifies the nation's needs, offers insightful suggestions to address these needs, is well written, and is presented in a creative manner.

Caption Answer

It is harder for people in these areas to get care when they are sick, making it more important to limit the chances of becoming ill or injured.

Human Drama Activity

Designing a Magazine Cover Organize the class into small groups and then explain to students that they are going to design a magazine cover highlighting one of the problems facing young African nations. The problems addressed may include establishing a new government, moving toward an independent economy, solving environmental issues, improving national health and education levels, and resolving ethnic and religious conflicts. Then have students write a short "Message from the Publisher" describing the problem and presenting possible solutions.

🔔 **Bell Ringer** Begin by reading aloud the lines from John Pepper Clark's poem, "The Casualties." Encourage students to share their interpretations of the poem.

LESSON PLAN

1. Focus Upon attaining independence, each African nation faced a unique set of challenges. Nigeria faced ethnic strife and an oil-based economy. Congo was plagued by civil war and a harsh dictator. In Tanzania, Julius Nyerere introduced socialism.

2. Instruct Ask students to choose one of the following African leaders: General Ibrahim Babangida, Mobutu Sese Seko, Julius Nyerere, or Ali Hassan Mwinyi. Have students write a letter of advice to the leader they selected. In their letters, they should review the problems faced by the leader's nation. They should then express agreement or disagreement with the leader's policies. Finally, they should offer other possible solutions to the problems that plague the nation. Encourage students to use both their textbooks and other resources. Invite volunteers to read their letters to the class.

3. Assess Ask students to reread the letters that they wrote. Have them underline the most important ideas.

4. Reteach If students' **Assess** activity does not reflect adequate understanding of the lesson, you might assign the *Guide to the Essentials* or the *Interactive Student Tutorial CD-ROM* for this section.

Reading Focus

- What were some pressures for change in Nigeria?
- What effects did dictatorship have on the Congo?
- What was the outcome of Tanzania's experiment in socialism?

Taking Notes

Create a concept web that shows key issues discussed in this section. Use this sample as a starting point, and add more circles as needed.

Main Idea Nigeria, the Congo, and Tanzania provide examples of paths followed by African nations.

Setting the Scene Nigerian poet John Pepper Clark saw his nation torn by civil war. In one poem, he chronicled both the obvious effects and the unseen costs of the war:

> "The casualties are not only those who are dead;
> They are well out of it.
> The casualties are not only those who are wounded,
> Though they await burial by installment. . . .
> The casualties are not only those led away by night;
> The cell is a cruel place. . . .
> The casualties are many, and a good number well
> Outside the scenes of ravage and wreck; . . .
>
> We fall,
> All casualties of the war,
> Because we cannot hear each other speak
> Because eyes have ceased to see the face from the crowd."
> —John Pepper Clark, "The Casualties"

Nigeria was only one of many African nations that suffered a disastrous civil war after independence. In this section, we will take a closer look at Nigeria, the Democratic Republic of Congo (formerly called Zaire), and Tanzania. Their experiences, resources, populations, and leaders differed.

Oil Drilling
Oil produced from wells such as the one shown here provides income for a number of West African countries. Several nations have used their oil wealth to industrialize their economies.

Theme: Economics and Technology In what ways might the people and the government disagree about how income from oil should be spent?

Caption Answer

People might feel their immediate needs should be met, while the government might feel that money should be spent on long-term goals.

Resource Directory

Teaching Resources
Creative Teaching Activities Creative Teaching Activities booklet, p. 161
Guided Reading and Review Unit 8 booklet, p. 78
Primary Source Activity *Growing Up in Nigeria*, Unit 8 booklet, p. 83

But through their efforts to modernize, they illustrate the patterns that were common during the post-independence years.

Pressures for Change in Nigeria

When Nigeria won independence in 1960, it hoped to develop rapidly. This large West African nation had rich resources, especially oil. Its population was the largest in Africa south of the Sahara, giving it a potentially strong internal market. Its fertile farming areas produced exports of cocoa and palm oil as well as food crops. The Niger and Benue rivers provided a good transportation network.

Diversity and Civil Strife Nigeria's borders, drawn in colonial times, lumped together 250 ethnic groups. Several regional groups competed for power. In the north were the Muslim Hausa and Fulani, heirs to a strong empire since the early 1800s. Christian Ibo dominated the oil-rich south. Some of the Yoruba of the southwest were Christian and others were Muslim. Many others still practiced traditional religions.

At independence, Nigeria drew up a federal constitution to protect various national interests. The system did not work well, however. At first, the Hausa dominated the government, and ethnic rivalries increased. In the 1960s, massacres of tens of thousands of Ibo triggered a bloody civil war. Ibo leaders in the southeast declared their region the independent state of Biafra. The two-and-a-half-year struggle that followed cost hundreds of thousands of lives, including vast numbers who starved to death in the long blockade of Biafra.

Economic Recovery The 1970s oil boom helped Nigeria recover from the war. With its massive oil wealth, the government spent lavishly on development projects. It set up industries, including a steel mill, auto assembly plant, and petrochemical works. To pay for prestige projects like a new capital, it also borrowed heavily from the West.

Rural people flooded into the cities, hoping to share in the economic boom. During the last four decades of the century, for instance, the population of Lagos grew from about 500,000 to 11 million people. But while cities grew, the government paid little heed to farmers. Nigeria, once a food exporter, bought expensive imported grain. Local food production fell, and rural poverty increased.

Later, when oil prices fell, the economy almost collapsed. A huge debt burden combined with waste, mismanagement, and corruption strangled the young nation. Though a small elite continued to profit enormously, the majority of the people suffered.

Military and Civilian Rule Since independence, Nigeria has often lived under military rule. The military usually took over in the name of reform, arguing that something needed to be done to end the lavish lifestyle and corrupt practices of civilian politicians. Though many citizens welcomed the military as a force for order and honest government, military dictators imposed rigid political controls, often without providing either greater efficiency or economic progress.

During Nigeria's debt crisis in the 1980s, General Ibrahim Babangida imposed harsh economic reforms to restore economic stability. He attacked corruption, prohibited imports, and raised the prices paid farmers for agricultural produce. But he also cracked down on his critics, outraging the international community by executing Ken Saro-Wiwa, a renowned writer and critic of the regime.

The people democratically elected Babangida's successor, Olusegun Obasanjo, a former dictator. Accepting tight IMF reform requirements, he moved to privatize state industries. Supported by a big rise in world oil prices, he promised more roads, schools, and clinics for Nigeria's people.

Primary Source

A Nigerian Speaks Out
Convicted by a military tribunal in 1995 of inciting violence, Nigerian author Ken Saro-Wiwa tried in vain to read a statement to the court:

"I am a man of peace, of ideas.

Appalled by the deplorable poverty of my people . . . angered by the devastation of their land, anxious to preserve their right to life and to a decent living, and determined to usher to this country as a whole a fair and just democratic system, I have devoted all my intellectual and material resources—my very life—to a cause in which I have total belief and from which I cannot be blackmailed or intimidated. . . .

In my innocence of the false charges I face here, in my utter conviction, I call upon the Ogoni people, the peoples of the Niger delta, and the oppressed ethnic minorities of Nigeria to stand up and fight fearlessly and peacefully for their rights. History is on their side, God is on their side. . . ."

—Ken Saro-Wiwa,
unpublished remarks

Skills Assessment

Primary Source What grievances against the government does Ken Saro-Wiwa cite in his speech?

Block Scheduling Support

Read the following quotation aloud to students:
"It is the elites who have chosen their own narrow interests over everything else. Now the whole place is twisted because you cannot expect justice, you cannot expect your fair share. They have robbed the country and ruined it."

Explain to students that this statement was written by a Nigerian editor in response to the debt crisis. Then organize the class into two groups. Have one group take the side of the Nigerian poor and the other take the side of the wealthy elite. Have the poor present their grievances to the wealthy and challenge the wealthy to justify their actions.

Primary Source

ANSWER The people live in terrible poverty and have no political rights, and he was falsely accused and condemned.

Dictatorship in Congo

After World War II, Belgium, determined to keep the Congo, did nothing to prepare the huge central African colony for freedom. Then, in 1960, fearing a struggle like the French war in Algeria, Belgium suddenly rushed the Congo to independence. Unprepared for self-government and with few trained leaders, the new nation was soon plunged into civil war.

Physically, the new country had many advantages. It had many rich resources, including vast tropical forests, plantations, and great mineral wealth. In addition, the immense Congo River and its tributaries flowed from the interior to the coast, providing water resources as well as an extensive transportation network.

Yet the new nation included some 200 ethnic groups and had no sense of unity. At independence, more than 100 political parties sprang up. They represented diverse regional and ethnic groups. Within months after independence, the nation split apart.

Mobutu in Power Civil war raged for almost three years before the UN peace-keeping troops ended the worst fighting. Two years later, in 1965, an army general, Mobutu Sese Seko, seized power and imposed some kind of order. He renamed the nation Zaire, meaning "big river."

For the next 34 years, Mobutu built an increasingly brutal dictatorship. He slaughtered rivals and ran the economy into the ground. He also bilked the treasury of millions stolen from the nation and stored in foreign bank accounts. Mobutu survived for more than three decades because he represented order in a land formerly torn by civil war and because his strong anti-communist stance won favor with the West during the Cold War.

Further Struggles In the late 1990s, ethnic violence in the neighboring countries of Rwanda and Burundi spilled over into eastern Zaire. In the escalating tumult that followed, rebels overthrew Mobutu at last, renaming the country Congo and promising reforms. But continuing power struggles within the country and interventions by other central African states led to continuing violence. By the time the rebel leader who had overthrown Mobutu was himself murdered, in 2001, ten countries—Congo and its nine neighbors—were involved in the violence, which resulted in hordes of refugees and may have cost more than a million lives.

Tanzania's Experiment in Socialism

In sharp contrast to Zaire's greedy and corrupt dictator, Tanzania's first president, Julius Nyerere, set out on a high-minded crusade. Tanganyika had been a German colony until World War I, when it was transferred to British control. After independence in 1961, nationalist leaders hoped for great changes for their country, which became known as Tanzania. Nyerere's goals included improving rural life, building a classless society, and creating a self-reliant economy.

To carry out his program, Nyerere embraced what he called "African socialism." This system was not a western import, he declared, but was based on African village traditions of cooperation and shared responsibility. Nyerere was a strong supporter of women's rights, claiming that their subservient position was "inconsistent with our socialist conception of the equality of all human beings."

In the 1960s, Nyerere introduced a command economy, nationalizing all banks and foreign-owned businesses. Drawing on traditional images of community, he emphasized the idea that Tanzania was "a rural society where improvement will depend largely upon the efforts of the people in agriculture and village development." Nyerere also tried to prevent the rise of a wealthy elite.

One-Party Rule At independence, Tanzania was a large country with plenty of land and labor but very little capital or technology. Its main exports were coffee, cotton, tea, and tobacco. Most people worked as farmers or herders.

Tanzania included about 120 ethnic groups. Most groups were small, however, and the country escaped the type of conflicts that ravaged Nigeria and Zaire. To promote unity, Nyerere set up a one-party system. Under this system, several candidates could run for each office. They were permitted to debate any topic except those related to ethnic or regional issues.

Mutual Cooperation Nyerere promoted the idea of *ujamaa*, a Swahili word that means "familyhood" or "mutual cooperation." Rural farmers were encouraged to live in large villages and to farm the land collectively. The government pledged to build roads and provide tools, clean water, health care, and schools. Under this arrangement, Nyerere believed, output would increase. The government would then sell the surplus crops to towns or export them for sale in other nations.

Nyerere's bold experiment did not work as planned. Many families refused to leave land they had farmed for generations, so the government forced them to move to *ujamaa* villages. Those farmers who did relocate resented experts who tried to teach them to farm. In the end, farm output did not rise.

Reforms High oil prices, inflation, and a bloated bureaucracy plunged Tanzania into debt. In 1985, Nyerere resigned. His successor, Ali Hassan Mwinyi, introduced reforms. He cut government spending by reducing bureaucracy and privatized some businesses. These moves toward a market economy brought some improvement.

Although it faced serious problems, Tanzania did have some successes. Unlike that of many African nations, its food output did not decline. With foreign aid, the government provided basic services such as clean water, schools, and health care to many rural villages.

Farming in Tanzania
New farming methods and seeds are helping some Tanzanian farmers to grow more than they could in the past. Changes like these are designed to improve Tanzania's economy.

Theme: Economics and Technology Under Tanzania's socialist government, who was likely to make decisions about the use of new agricultural techniques?

SECTION 3 Assessment

Recall
1. **Identify:** (a) Biafra, (b) General Ibrahim Babangida, (c) Ken Saro-Wiwa, (d) Olusegun Obasanjo, (e) Mobutu Sese Seko.

Comprehension
2. How has Nigeria responded to economic pressures?
3. (a) What challenges faced the Congo at independence? (b) How did Mobutu Sese Seko's policies affect the nation?
4. What programs did Julius Nyerere introduce in Tanzania after independence?

Critical Thinking and Writing
5. **Analyzing Information** What effects did the rise of military dictatorships have on Nigeria and the Congo?
6. **Drawing Conclusions** Why did socialist policies fail in Tanzania?

Take It to the NET
Research current events in one of the nations discussed in this chapter. Write a paragraph summarizing an important issue or event in that nation.

SECTION 3 Assessment

Recall
1. (a) Biafra, p. 921 (b) General Ibrahim Babangida, p. 921 (c) Ken Saro-Wiwa, p. 921 (d) Olusegun Obasanjo, p. 921 (e) Mobutu Sese Seko, p. 922

Comprehension
2. Oil wealth encouraged urbanization, but the government paid little attention to farmers. Food production declined, and the country had to import grain. When oil prices dropped, many people were thrown out of work. 3. (a) civil war caused by different ethnic groups with no sense of unity (b) Mobutu stole millions, killed many people, and destroyed the nation's economy. 4. African socialism, command economy, one-party rule, collective farming, and forced relocation

Critical Thinking and Writing
5. great loss of life, political corruption, economic instability 6. People did not want to leave lands that their families had worked on for generations, and they resented interference from experts.

Activity Rubrics

Share rubrics with students before they write their paragraphs.

Attempted The paragraph is very sketchy.

Minimal Student's paragraph is unclear, focuses on minor events or issues, or has many mechanical errors.

Adequate Student's paragraph is well researched and well written, and it summarizes an important issue or event.

Exemplary Student's paragraph is well written and shows astute insight into an important issue or event.

 Human Drama Note

Tanzania Tanzania has coastal lowlands, volcanic highlands, and the Great Rift Valley. Africa's highest mountain, Mount Kilimanjaro, is in Tanzania. One third of the country is part of a national park or game reserve, with herds of buffalo, rhinoceroses, elephants, and giraffes. Both the Ngorongoro Crater and the Serengeti Plain are in Tanzania. Because of these attractions, tourism has seen a sharp increase since 1990.

Test Preparation

Have students read the paragraphs under the heading "Mutual Cooperation" on this page, and then answer the question below.

What does *ujamaa* mean?

A a one-party political system

B the state provides for people's needs

C families live in government housing

D familyhood or mutual cooperation

Caption Answer

the government

Bell Ringer Write the word *apartheid* on the board. Ask students to describe in their notebooks what this word means to the people of South Africa. Ask them to describe what they know about the role of Nelson Mandela in dismantling the system of apartheid.

LESSON PLAN

1. Focus Under apartheid all South Africans were classified by race. Whites were in control, and the lives of all non-whites were restricted. Pressure to end apartheid came from within South Africa as well as from other nations. In 1994, Nelson Mandela and F. W. de Klerk worked to move the nation from white rule to majority rule. In Angola and Mozambique, power struggles, complicated by Cold War interests, resulted in years of war.

2. Instruct Divide the class into groups. Ask each group to plan a one-minute skit about the life of Nelson Mandela. Tell groups to choose one event or period of Mandela's life to portray. Have each group research and prepare a script. The groups can take turns presenting their skits to the class.

3. Assess Have students write critical reviews of the various skits that are presented. They should comment on historical accuracy and the quality of presentation.

4. Reteach If students' *Assess* activity does not reflect adequate understanding of the lesson, you might assign the *Guide to the Essentials* or the *Interactive Student Tutorial CD-ROM* for this section.

Reading Focus

- What challenges faced Zimbabwe?
- How did the long struggle to end apartheid lead to a new South Africa?
- How did the Cold War affect nations of southern Africa?

Taking Notes

Create a table that shows important information about southern Africa. Use this sample as a starting point.

	ZIMBABWE	SOUTH AFRICA	NAMIBIA	ANGOLA	MOZAMBIQUE
NATIONAL LEADERS	Robert Mugabe, Joshua Nkomo				
SOCIAL AND POLITICAL CONFLICTS					
REFORMS					

Main Idea Nations in southern Africa experienced turmoil as people sought majority rule and equal rights.

> **Primary Sources and Literature**
>
> See *"Nelson Mandela: Glory and Hope"* in the Reference Section at the back of this book.

Setting the Scene On May 10, 1994, Nelson Mandela stood before a wildly cheering crowd. He had just been inaugurated as South Africa's first president elected by voters of all races. "The time for the healing of wounds has come," he told black and white South Africans.

For almost 350 years, whites had dominated South Africa and had denied blacks the most basic civil rights. Mandela's election marked a new beginning for South Africa. In his inauguration speech, he spoke of the need for a new unity, not of revenge for the losses suffered by black South Africans. The crowd sang "Nkosi Sikelel' iAfrika" (God Bless Africa)—the anthem that had come to symbolize South Africa's struggle for freedom.

Zimbabwe's Road to Majority Rule

During the Age of Imperialism, European nations had carved up southern Africa. In the 1890s, British businessman Cecil Rhodes took control of the region known as Southern Rhodesia. Later, white settlers turned the region into a self-governing British colony. Whites made up only five percent of the population but owned half the land and controlled the government. As the tide of nationalism swept through Africa in the 1960s, white Southern Rhodesians flatly rejected any move to give up power to the black majority. When Britain supported demands for majority rule, conservative whites led by Ian Smith declared independence in 1965.

Armed Struggle In response, nationalist groups waged guerrilla war to achieve majority rule. Among their leaders were Robert Mugabe (moo GAH beh) and Joshua Nkomo (uhn KOH moh). The long struggle caused much suffering. As guerrilla forces won more successes, many whites fled. UN sanctions hurt the economy. Smith finally had to accept a negotiated settlement. In 1980, Southern Rhodesia became the nation of Zimbabwe. It took its name from the ancient kingdom of Great Zimbabwe and the stone structures built there by earlier African peoples.

Rebuilding The new nation faced severe challenges after years of war. International sanctions had further damaged the economy, and droughts caused additional problems. Recovery was also slowed by a power struggle between Mugabe and Nkomo. In the end, Mugabe won and became the elected president of Zimbabwe. He called for a one-party system to promote national unity and tolerated little opposition. In 2000, tensions over land ownership led to renewed violence.

South Africa's Long Struggle

In 1910, South Africa won self-rule from Britain. Freedom, however, was limited to white settlers. Whites, who made up less than 20 percent of the population, controlled vast mineral resources and the most fertile land. Over the next decades, the white-minority government passed racial laws to keep the black majority in a subordinate position.

Afrikaner Nationalism After World War II, thousands of blacks moved to towns and cities. There, as elsewhere in Africa, black nationalism stirred demands for equality. In response, Afrikaners, who were descended from Dutch settlers, demanded severe new limits on blacks.

In 1948, the Afrikaner National party won a majority in a "whites-only" parliament. They then extended the existing system of racial segregation, creating what was known as apartheid, or the separation of the races. Under apartheid, all South Africans were registered by race: Black, White, Colored (people of mixed descent), and Asian. Afrikaners claimed that apartheid would allow each race to develop its own culture. In fact, it was designed to give whites control over South Africa.

Apartheid in Action For nonwhites, apartheid meant a life of restrictions. Blacks were treated like foreigners in their own land. They had to get permission to travel and had to carry passbooks or face arrest. The pass laws were an especially heavy burden for women, who had to get permission from their parents, guardian, or husband, as well as from the authorities, in order to move from one district to another.

Blacks were assigned to "homelands" based on their ethnic group. Homelands were located in arid, unproductive parts of the country. More than 80 percent of South Africa, including cities, mines, and the richest farmland, was reserved for whites. Apartheid laws banned marriages between the races and set up segregated restaurants, beaches, schools, and other facilities. Blacks who worked in factories, mines, and other jobs were paid less than whites for the same work. Low wages and inferior schooling condemned blacks to poverty.

Black Resistance From the beginning, black South Africans protested apartheid. In 1912, an organization, later called the African National Congress (ANC), was set up to oppose white domination. In the 1950s, as Afrikaner nationalists imposed harsh new laws, the ANC organized marches, boycotts, and strikes. As protests continued, government violence increased. In 1960, police gunned down 69 men, women, and children taking part in a peaceful demonstration in Sharpeville, a black township outside Johannesburg. In the wake of the incident, the government outlawed the ANC and cracked down on groups that opposed apartheid.

The massacre at Sharpeville stunned the world. At home, it pushed some ANC activists to shift from nonviolent protest to armed struggle. Some leaders left South Africa to wage the battle for freedom from abroad. Others went underground, including Nelson Mandela.

Mandela's Struggle As a young lawyer, Mandela had helped organize the ANC Youth League. With other league leaders, he mobilized young South Africans to take part in acts of civil disobedience against apartheid laws. As government suppression grew, Mandela joined ANC militants who called for armed struggle against the white-minority government.

In the early 1960s, Mandela was arrested, tried, and condemned to life in prison for conspiracy. "I have cherished the ideal of a democratic and free society," he declared at his trial. It was an ideal Mandela hoped "to live for and to achieve." It was also "an ideal for which I am prepared to die." Mandela spent 27 years in prison, often in isolation. Yet he remained a popular leader and powerful symbol of the struggle against apartheid.

Apartheid and Business
The diamond industry provides great wealth for South Africa. Mined in a rough state (right), diamonds later are cut and polished (left). For decades, white-run companies in South Africa have controlled the world's diamond market.

Theme: Economics and Technology How did white-controlled companies benefit from apartheid?

Background
Connections to Art

Tribal Art Redirected The connection between art and society is a fundamental principle of traditional tribal art. Traditional stories taught values, songs aided communal work, and masks articulated spiritual beliefs. However, in the 1980s, the anti-apartheid movement needed art not to preserve traditions, but to act as an agent of change. Music, posters, songs, and paintings began to expose the harsh reality of life under apartheid and to direct the people to resist political oppression. The immediacy and strength of artistic messages rallied people of all races to unite against the tyranny of apartheid.

Activity
Connections to Film

Writing a Speech Assign students to view *Mandela: The Man and His Country*, a 1990 documentary film produced by ABC News. The 50-minute program presents a rich visual chronicle of the career of Nelson Mandela and the rise and fall of apartheid in South Africa.

Ask students to imagine that they are at an African National Congress rally celebrating Mandela's release from prison. Their assignment is to write a speech reviewing the injustices of apartheid and Nelson Mandela's long and ultimately successful struggle. Invite volunteers to deliver their speeches to the class. As an enrichment activity, ask students to use other resources to outline Mandela's achievements in the years following his release from prison. (*Mandela: The Man and His Country* is distributed by MPI Home Video.) ✳

Biography

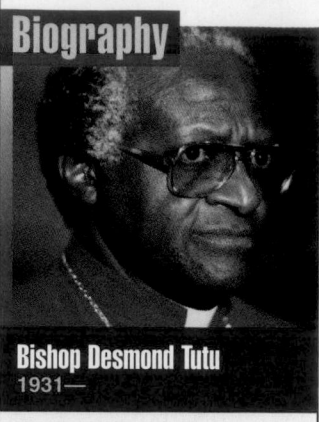

Bishop Desmond Tutu
1931—

Desmond Tutu grew up in the Transvaal region of South Africa, where he attended mission schools as a child. Lacking the money to pursue his dream of attending medical school, he first became a schoolteacher. Later, he took up the study of theology. He was ordained as an Anglican priest in 1961 and was made bishop in 1976.

Tutu used his growing influence to crusade against the brutal laws of apartheid. Although there was the constant threat of violent rebellion, he never wavered from his message of peace and reconciliation. In 1980, Tutu said, "I will never tell anyone to pick up a gun. But I will pray for the man who picks up a gun, pray that he will be less cruel than he might otherwise have been. . . ."

Theme: Impact of the Individual How did people like Desmond Tutu influence South Africa's battle against apartheid?

By the 1980s, demands for an end to apartheid and for Mandela's release intensified. Many countries, including the United States, imposed strict economic sanctions on South Africa. South African athletes were banned from world sports events such as the Olympic games. In 1984, the black Anglican bishop Desmond Tutu won the Nobel Peace Prize for his nonviolent opposition to apartheid.

Toward Reform Foreign boycotts hurt South Africa's economy. Even worse, in 1985, protests and growing violence at home forced the government to impose a state of emergency. Many South African whites questioned the oppressive measures used by the government.

By 1989, a new South African president, F. W. de Klerk, boldly accepted the need for reform. He abandoned apartheid, repealed the hated pass laws, and lifted the ban on the ANC. A year later, he freed Mandela. Over the next four years, Mandela and de Klerk negotiated the terms by which South Africa would move to majority rule. White voters overwhelmingly approved the reforms that would allow "one person, one vote."

Majority Rule In 1994, South Africa held its first multiracial elections. Black, mixed race, and Asian South Africans, young and old, lined up with white voters to cast their ballots. They elected Nelson Mandela as the first president of a new, democratic South Africa. In a speech to supporters, Mandela echoed the African American civil rights leader Martin Luther King, Jr.: "We can loudly proclaim from the rooftops: Free at last!"

The New South Africa

As president, Mandela offered a striking example to other African nations when he welcomed longtime political foes into his government. If he could work with Afrikaners who had once tyrannized the black majority, perhaps other leaders could learn to accept democratic, multiparty systems. "Let us build together," *masakhane*, was Mandela's slogan and guiding policy.

Mandela's government faced the huge challenge of meeting people's high expectations for change. Mandela had promised a better life to the black majority. Delivering on those promises would be difficult. South Africa was a rich country with a strong industrial base. But it could afford only a limited amount of spending for housing, education, and other programs. The gap between blacks and whites remained large.

Even in Mandela's South Africa, whites owned three fourths of the land, black unemployment remained high, and the crime rate made both cities and the shantytowns around them unsafe. But South Africa's first black president did bring both a peaceful transition to democratic rule and soaring international prestige to his country. He also introduced new programs, from public housing to school lunches, making such necessities as pure water and electrical power available to the masses.

In 1999, a second all-race election brought Thabo Mbeki to the presidency. The democratic process seemed to be successful, and people were hopeful for the future. Given the nation's accumulated problems, major changes might take decades rather than years. But a start had been made.

Other Nations of Southern Africa

The colonies of southern Africa were among the last to win independence. From the 1960s to the 1980s, South Africa's white-minority government intervened to prevent neighboring peoples from achieving freedom.

Namibia In 1920, South Africa received German Southwest Africa as a mandate from the League of Nations. After World War II, the UN asked South Africa to prepare the territory for independence. Instead, South Africa backed the oppressive regime run by the white minority.

Biography

ANSWER In an atmosphere of intense racial oppression and violence, Tutu encouraged South Africans to rise above the culture of hatred and achieve their goals through nonviolent opposition.

Resource Directory

Teaching Resources
History Through Literature *Poems About Prison,* History Through Literature booklet, p. 75
You Are There Chapter Extension Activities booklet, p. 86
Simulation *Looking Beyond Apartheid,* Simulations booklet, p. 16

Reporting on the Election in
South Africa

As an American journalist covering South Africa's second all-race elections, you are excited to find that people here feel strongly about exercising their right to vote. Nelson Mandela, the national hero who became president in 1994, has turned down a second term. Which party's candidate will succeed him? All of South Africa holds its breath to see what happens. . . .

When you arrive at the polling station at 8 A.M., you find a line of voters stretching for more than two miles. Because of the enormous turnout, some people will have to wait more than four hours to vote.

Inside the polling station, voters show signs of weariness. The elderly and sick are ushered to the front of the line. Despite the long wait, most people remain patient, knowing their turn will come.

After the station closes, you learn that someone may have tampered with three of the ballot boxes. If this proves to be true, election officials will have to discard hundreds of votes. Despite the problems, you reflect that South Africans have once again demonstrated their commitment to democracy.

Portfolio Assessment

After you return to the United States, your editor asks you to write an article comparing the attitudes toward democracy and elections in South Africa and in the United States.

Chapter 36 **927**

Bell Ringer Ask students to look at the pictures on this page and then speculate why all these people are standing in line. What kinds of events would draw this kind of a line in the United States?

Background
About the Scene

Election Glitches Only minor problems occurred on election day in South Africa. A few polling stations opened late. Ballot papers arrived late in some places, and people claimed that the ANC was in possession of the registration papers that were needed to vote. Final results of the vote were delayed, and violence or disruption did occur in a few polling stations. However, the voter turnout was high, and South Africans showed determination and courage in their commitment to the democratic process.

Activity
Cooperative Learning

Inviting Speakers to Class Organize students into small groups. One group should research community organizations in order to locate someone to speak about the local and global importance of all-race voting in South Africa. Another group should invite this person to speak to the class. A third group will write a series of questions for the speaker. A fourth group will write a thank-you note to the speaker.

Portfolio Assessment Rubrics

Share rubrics with students before they write their articles.

Attempted The article is incomplete.

Minimal The article addresses the differences in attitudes toward democracy and elections but is not well written.

Adequate The article identifies differences in attitudes toward democracy and elections and is well written.

Exemplary The article shows insight in identifying the differences in attitudes toward democracy and elections and is very well written.

Human Drama Note

South Africa South Africa is one of the richest countries in the world in natural resources. At one time, it supplied nearly 50 percent of the world's gold. It is also rich in diamonds and had dominated the world's diamond market. In spite of this, only about one-half of South African black adults are employed. Black South Africans are the poorest people of the nation even though they are the majority. Whites, who are the minority, are still the wealthiest, enjoying one of the world's highest standards of living. There are only a small number of middle-class non-white communities.

Economic Cooperation During the days of apartheid, the other nations of southern Africa tried to reduce their economic dependence on South Africa. Many of these nations were landlocked and needed access to South Africa's ports. In 1979, they organized a group called the Southern Africa Development Coordination Council (SADCC), which focused most of its energies on rebuilding rail routes from the interior to ports in Angola and Mozambique. After South Africa abolished apartheid in 1992, the organization renamed itself the Southern African Development Community. Members hoped that South Africa would join and help the organization operate as a regional common market.

Virtual Field Trip

www.phschool.com

Republic of Namibia
Namibia

For more information about Namibia since independence, use the Internet address above to link to the official Web site of the Republic of Namibia.

Freedom for Namibia
Like many African peoples, Namibians waged a long, armed struggle to win independence. Here, a group of Namibian women celebrate the birth of their nation in 1990.

Theme: Global Interaction
How did the Cold War affect Namibia's struggle for independence?

By the 1960s, the Southwest African People's Organization (SWAPO) had turned to armed struggle to win independence. For years, SWAPO guerrillas battled South African troops. The struggle became part of the Cold War, with the Soviet Union and Cuba lending their support to SWAPO. As the Cold War ground to a halt, an agreement was finally reached to hold free elections. In 1990, Namibia—as the new country was called—celebrated independence.

Portuguese Colonies As Britain and France took steps to meet nationalist demands in their African possessions, Portugal clung fiercely to its colonies in Angola and Mozambique. During the 1960s, the Portuguese dictator António Salazar rejected African demands for freedom. In response, nationalists turned to guerrilla warfare. Portugal responded by sending almost its entire army to defend its last outposts of empire.

After 15 years of fighting, many Portuguese army officers realized that they could not succeed in the struggle. In 1974, an army coup in Portugal toppled the dictatorship of Salazar's successor. The new Portuguese government quickly agreed to withdraw from southern Africa. In 1975, Angola and Mozambique celebrated independence.

Wars Continue Independence did not end the fighting in Angola and Mozambique. Bitter civil wars, fueled by Cold War rivalries, raged for years in both countries. Both South Africa and the United States had seen the struggles for freedom in southern Africa as a threat because some liberation leaders were socialists. To undermine the new governments, South Africa aided rebel groups in both countries that wanted power for themselves.

From 1975 to 1992, rebels in Mozambique starved and killed tens of thousands of civilians. They destroyed schools and health clinics in an effort to overturn the government. The end of the Cold War and South Africa's move to majority rule helped stop the conflict. Although the task of rebuilding was staggering, by the late 1990s, many had confidence that democratic reforms would succeed.

In Angola, a complicated power struggle dragged on for years. The Soviet Union helped one side in the struggle by financing more than 50,000 Cuban troops that went to fight in Angola. South Africa supported a rival

Caption Answer

Their struggle became part of the Cold War, with the Soviet Union and Cuba lending support to SWAPO.

Resource Directory

Teaching Resources

Section Quiz Unit 8 booklet, p. 81
Geography Quiz Unit 8 booklet, p. 86
Chapter Test Forms A, B, and C Unit 8 booklet, pp. 87–91
Answer Key Unit 8 booklet, pp. 110–125

Technology

World History Color Transparencies *African Textiles*, p. C–61
Interactive Student Tutorial CD-ROM Ch. 36
Computer Test Bank Ch. 36

group, supplying weapons and troops. The United States, too, tried to undermine the Soviet-backed government. Even after the Cold War ended, the fighting continued between the rival factions in Angola.

Outlook and Gains

Making accurate generalizations about Africa is difficult. Every nation is different. Some nations have rich resources to help finance progress. Others lack resources. Each country has its own set of circumstances and its own history. Despite many setbacks, African nations have made progress. As independent nations, they carved out a place on the world scene and won the power to shape their own future. Within each nation, the process of building a national identity went slowly. But education and urbanization did begin to break the localism of the past.

Education and Health Care As governments set up more schools, literacy rates rose. Every year, more students entered high school. Universities trained a new generation of leaders.

A few countries promoted higher education for women, and great strides were made in providing girls with elementary school education. Relatively few girls, however, went on to high school because they were needed to help their mothers with farm work and household chores. As a result, illiteracy among African women remained high, especially in rural areas.

Most African nations sought to improve health care and created family planning programs. Governments saw that population growth had profound effects on the standards of living.

Economic Opportunity Despite often-depressing economic news, Africa has enormous potential for growth. By the 1990s, many nations had learned from failed policies of the past. With free-market reforms, countries such as Ghana enjoyed economic growth. Other nations expanded mining and manufacturing. Some built factories and expanded communication and transportation networks.

Cultural Influence In literature, film, and the arts, Africans made major contributions to global culture. Writing in African languages produced many writers with large local audiences. Other African writers used western languages to reach a world audience. In music and dance, Africans and members of the "African diaspora"—African-descended citizens of other lands—helped shape the culture of the century. Influential diaspora musical forms included jazz, blues, reggae, and samba.

Global Connections

The Scars of War

After Angola gained independence in 1975, a bitter civil war broke out. Angolans found themselves in the middle of a Cold War battlefield. The Soviet Union offered the Popular Liberation Movement of Angola (MPLA), millions of dollars in arms. It also arranged for thousands of Cuban soldiers to travel to Angola to bolster support. The United States, on the other hand, provided aid to the National Union for the Total Independence of Angola (UNITA), which opposed the MPLA's Marxist policies.

Fighting finally ended in 1991, but the unrest continues. Today, UNITA controls about 70 percent of Angola, including most of the diamond trade, while the MPLA retains the oil-rich regions. Caught between the two are thousands of refugees who still wait for life to return to normal.

Theme: Political and Social Systems How did Angola become a victim of the Cold War?

SECTION 4 Assessment

Recall

1. (a) Robert Mugabe, p. 924 **(b)** Joshua Nkomo, p. 924 **(c)** African National Congress, p. 925 **(d)** Nelson Mandela, p. 925 **(e)** F. W. de Klerk, p. 926 **(f)** Southwest African People's Organization, p. 928

Comprehension

2. The white-run government declared independence but kept most of the power for itself. Nationalists waged a guerrilla war and forced out many whites. The prime minister finally agreed to turn over power. **3. (a)** formation of ANC, police crack down at Sharpeville, end to nonviolent protest, imprisonment of Mandela, international sanctions imposed, nation banned from Olympics, imposition of state of emergency, growing opposition from whites as well as blacks **(b)** held all-race elections; instituted new programs to improve people's lives **4.** Cold War powers became directly involved in independence movements and civil wars. **5.** made strides in education, carved out a place on the world scene, improved health care, created family planning programs, and improved standard of living

Critical Thinking and Writing

6. Challenges would be greater if independence came through fighting, because armed factions would continue to exist after independence and might continue to cause problems. **7.** Africans had been ruled for so long by a white minority that ruling themselves—the majority—was vital to their sense of independence.

SECTION 4 Assessment

Recall

1. Identify: (a) Robert Mugabe, **(b)** Joshua Nkomo, **(c)** African National Congress, **(d)** Nelson Mandela, **(e)** F. W. de Klerk, **(f)** Southwest African People's Organization.

Comprehension

2. How did Zimbabwe achieve independence?

3. (a) Identify major events leading to the elimination of apartheid. **(b)** Describe how South Africa has changed since 1989.

4. How did the Cold War affect independence movements in southern Africa?

5. How have African nations worked to improve conditions?

Critical Thinking and Writing

6. Drawing Conclusions Would a country be likely to face greater challenges after independence if it won freedom through fighting or through negotiation? Explain.

7. Identifying Main Ideas Why was the idea of majority rule so important to people in African nations?

Activity
Take It to the NET

Research the history of one of the nations discussed in this section. Create an illustrated time line that shows important dates and events in that nation's history.

Activity Rubrics

Share rubrics with students.

Attempted The time line is poorly researched and incomplete.

Minimal The time line shows some research, but several items are inaccurately placed, and it has many errors.

Adequate The time line is well researched; contains several items, accurately placed; and has few errors.

Exemplary The time line is well researched, comprehensive, and accurate; contains interesting, well-illustrated items; and has no errors.

Global Connections

ANSWER To promote their own interests, the Soviet Union and the United States involved themselves in the internal affairs of foreign nations. When the Cold War was over, the superpowers disengaged themselves but left Angola with the war that they had helped keep alive.

✓ Test Preparation

Have students read the section titled "Outlook and Gains" on this page, and then complete the sentence below.

Illiteracy among African women remained high because instead of finishing high school they

A got married and started their families.

B were needed to fight in the civil wars.

C moved to the cities where they found jobs in factories.

D were needed to help their mothers with farm work and household chores.

Creating a Chapter Summary

As a reteaching opportunity, pair a more able student with a less able student to complete this chapter summary.

Possible answers: Economic choices rural or urban, cash crops or food **People and the environment** expanded farmlands, deforestation and desertification, drought and famine, AIDS **Colonial legacy** changes for women, growing slums **Types of government** democratic—South Africa; military rule—Nigeria; dictatorship—Congo; socialist—Tanzania

Building Vocabulary

1–3. Students' sentences should reflect a clear understanding of the terms.

Recalling Key Facts

4. Many of Africa's problems can be traced to the colonial legacy. There was a pattern of economic dependence, and African nations inherited borders drawn by colonial powers. New countries were made up of peoples from diverse cultures.
5. Ghana: strikes and boycotts, nonviolent protest; Kenya: guerrilla warfare; Algeria: extended war
6. International organizations provided opportunities for cooperation among African nations and gave them a voice in world debates.
7. choices about using resources and producing goods, ending foreign economic influences, preventing inequalities between rich and poor, land use, urbanization, and debt
8. caused massive movement to cities, overgrazing, desertification, and deforestation
9. **(a)** rapid urbanization and growth of slums **(b)** increased burdens as many men moved to cities for work **(c)** often disrupted local beliefs and sometimes led to persecution
10. Oil brought great wealth, which was often mismanaged. A worldwide drop in oil prices led to widespread unemployment and poverty.
11. improve rural life, build classless society, create self-reliant economy
12. ANC relied on nonviolent protest until the Sharpeville massacre; continued pressure from domestic reformers and the international community persuaded leaders to end apartheid.

CHAPTER **36** Review and Assessment

Creating a Chapter Summary

Complete the concept web by filling in circles with appropriate information from the chapter. Add more circles as needed.

For additional review and enrichment activities, see the interactive version of *World History* available on the Web and on CD-ROM.

Web Site Self-Test
For practice test questions for Chapter 36, see **www.phschool.com**.

Building Vocabulary

For each of the terms below, write a sentence using the term.
1. **one-party system**
2. **mixed economy**
3. **desertification**

Recalling Key Facts

4. How did the colonial legacy affect independence movements in Africa?
5. Compare independence movements in Ghana, Kenya, and Algeria.
6. What role did international organizations play in Africa during the Cold War?
7. What choices did new nations face as they tried to build productive economies?
8. Describe the effects of the population explosion on the African environment.
9. Explain how modernization affected **(a)** cities, **(b)** women, **(c)** religious groups.
10. How has oil affected Nigeria's development?

11. What were Julius Nyerere's goals for Tanzania?
12. How did South Africa overcome apartheid?
13. How did the Cold War affect southern Africa?
14. Describe how education and urbanization have encouraged development in Africa.

Critical Thinking and Writing

15. **Synthesizing Information** How were African nations affected by military dictatorships? Support your answer with examples.
16. **Connecting to Geography** How have subsistence farming and population growth affected desertification in Africa?
17. **Making Inferences** Based on information in this chapter, what types of economic development seem to have been most successful? Explain.
18. **Drawing Conclusions** How has majority rule affected political stability in southern African nations?

---

13. Cold War powers became directly involved in a number of independent movements and civil wars.
14. Both have encouraged people to move beyond localism and see themselves as participants in global affairs.

Critical Thinking and Writing

15. Military dictatorships led to greater instability and corruption. For example, in Zaire, Mobutu Sese Seko ruled with great brutality and stole large quantities of money from the nation.

16. Subsistence farming has often led to overgrazing and depletion of the soil, encouraging desertification of exhausted lands. Similarly, population growth has required even greater agricultural expansion, further taxing the environment.
17. Capitalism seems to be the most successful basis for economic development in Africa, as free-market reforms and infrastructure development have had success.

Skills Assessment
Analyzing Primary Sources

In 1998, Catherine Bertini, executive director of the World Food Programme, gave a speech about hunger issues in Africa. Read this excerpt and answer the questions that follow.

"In Africa, women provide roughly 80 percent of the labor to grow, process, and store food. They account for 60 percent of the labor needed to harvest and market food. They must be involved and benefit from agricultural innovations and reforms, and from food aid and other forms of assistance. . . .

Emphasizing women is done because it is the most efficient way to improve the nutrition of families. . . . Robert Fogel, a Nobel laureate in economics, . . . estimates . . . that almost a third of the growth in per capita income in Britain in the last two centuries can actually be attributed to better nutrition in the workforce. Study after study . . . has shown a clear connection between nutritional status and the productivity and wage earnings of workers. . . ."

—Catherine Bertini, speech delivered February 19, 1998

19. What role do women play in African agriculture?
20. What assistance does Bertini recommend?
21. Why, according to Bertini, must women be at the center of efforts to improve nutrition?
22. **(a)** What economic information does she use to support her point? **(b)** Does this theory seem reasonable? Explain your answer.

Skills Tip

When you read a primary source, pay careful attention to the information used to support the writer's or speaker's opinion.

Skills Assessment
Take It to the NET

Use the Internet to research current development projects in one African nation. Create a poster that shows how these projects are supposed to affect your chosen nation.

Skills Assessment
Analyzing Graphs

POPULATION PYRAMIDS

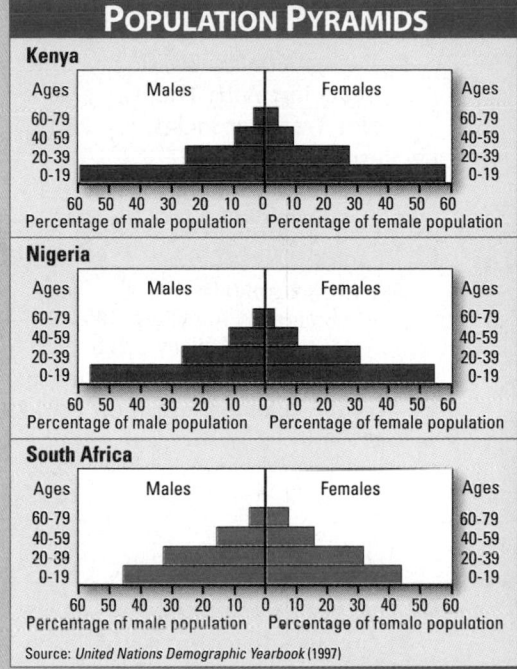

Source: *United Nations Demographic Yearbook* (1997)

A population pyramid is a bar graph that shows the percentages of males and females by age group in a particular country. The shape can also tell you whether a population is growing or declining. A wide base indicates growth, and a narrow base indicates decline. Study the graphs and answer the following questions:

23. Which country has the highest percentage of females ages 60–79?
24. Which country has the lowest percentage of males ages 0–19?
25. Which is the largest age group in each of the three countries?
26. How would you explain the great difference in size between age ranges 0–19 and 20–39?
27. According to the population pyramids, which nation seems to be experiencing the fastest rate of growth?

Analyzing Primary Sources

19. They provide 80 percent of the labor to grow, process, and store food, and 60 percent of the labor to harvest and market it.
20. Involve women in agricultural reform plans.
21. That is the most efficient way to improve nutrition.
22. **(a)** studies that link good nutrition to economic growth **(b)** Students' responses should be supported by good arguments.

Analyzing Graphs

23. South Africa
24. South Africa
25. 0–19
26. People in the 20–39 age group are having many children.
27. Kenya

Skills Tip

Point out that writers often use statistics to support their statements. The Skills Handbook in the front of the book has a lesson that will help students with this feature.

Unit Theme Activity

Remind students to continue working on their Unit Theme Activity. See rubrics for the activity on the unit opener page in the Teacher's Edition.

 Take It to the NET

Direct students to **www.phschool.com** for links to sites that will help them get started on their assignments. Share rubrics with students.
Attempted The poster is incomplete or does not show how development projects help.
Minimal The poster is complete but does not show how development projects help.
Adequate The poster is well researched, shows how development projects affect the nation, and is well illustrated.
Exemplary The poster is well researched, shows deep understanding of the effects of development projects, and is very well illustrated.

Resource Manager

Chapter Level Resources	CORE INSTRUCTION	READING/SKILLS
Chapter Level Resources	📖 Teaching Resources 📘 **Pacing Charts**, Ch. 37 📘 **Teaching With Themes**, p. 40 📽 **Color Transparencies**, p. F–75 💿 **Resource Pro®** Ch. 37 🖥 **www.phschool.com** • eTeach	💿 **Book on CD**, Ch. 37 💿 **Interactive Student Tutorial CD-ROM**, Ch. 37 💿 **Social Studies Skills Tutor CD-ROM** 📽 **Skills Transparencies**
1 Forces Shaping Modern Latin America 1. Explain why Latin America is culturally diverse. 2. Summarize conditions that contributed to unrest in Latin American countries. 3. Analyze forces that shaped political, economic, and social patterns in Latin America.	📖 Teaching Resources 📗 **Unit 8 booklet** • Biography Activity, p. 100 • Viewpoint Activity, p.102 📘 **Creative Teaching Activities**, p. 163 💿 **Prentice Hall Presentation Pro**, Ch. 37, Section 1	📖 Teaching Resources 📗 **Unit 8 booklet** • Guided Reading and Review, p. 92 📘 **Guide to the Essentials** 📼 **Guided Reading Audiotapes**, Ch. 37, Section 1
2 Latin America, the United States, and the World 1. Describe how communist rule affected Cuba. 2. Identify policies the United States followed in Latin America. 3. Point out global issues that link Latin America to other regions of the world.	📖 Teaching Resources 📘 **Creative Teaching Activities**, p. 164 💿 **Prentice Hall Presentation Pro**, Ch. 37, Section 2 📽 **Section Reading Support Transparencies**	📖 Teaching Resources 📗 **Unit 8 booklet** • Guided Reading and Review, p. 94 📘 **Guide to the Essentials** 📼 **Guided Reading Audiotapes**, Ch. 37, Section 2
3 Mexico, Central America, and the Caribbean 1. Compare conditions that have changed and those that have remained the same in Mexico. 2. Determine why Central American countries suffer civil wars. 3. Restate causes of Haiti's political and economic struggles.	📖 Teaching Resources 📗 **Unit 8 booklet** • Primary Source Activity, p. 101 📘 **Creative Teaching Activities**, p. 165 💿 **Prentice Hall Presentation Pro**, Ch. 37, Section 3 📽 **Section Reading Support Transparencies**	📖 Teaching Resources 📗 **Unit 8 booklet** • Guided Reading and Review, p. 96 📘 **Guide to the Essentials** 📼 **Guided Reading Audiotapes**, Ch. 37, Section 3
4 Focus on Argentina and Brazil 1. Identify challenges Argentina has faced on the road to democracy. 2. Describe how Brazil's government changed in the late 1900s. 3. Determine what has limited Brazil's "economic miracle."	📖 Teaching Resources 📘 **Creative Teaching Activities**, p. 166 💿 **Prentice Hall Presentation Pro**, Ch. 37, Section 4 📽 **Section Reading Support Transparencies**	📖 Teaching Resources 📗 **Unit 8 booklet** • Guided Reading and Review, p. 98 • Skill Application Activity, p. 103 📘 **Guide to the Essentials**

ENRICHMENT/PRE-AP

- www.phschool.com
  - Why Study History?

- Listening to Literature World Masterpieces, poems by Octavio Paz, Derek Walcott, and Gabriela Mistral, sides 9 and 10.
- www.phschool.com
  - Internet Activities, Section 1

- www.phschool.com
  - Internet Activities, Section 2

Teaching Resources
- Chapter Extension Activities p. 87
- History Through Literature, pp. 76–77
- Visions, Voices, Views, Animated Map Story, tape 8
- www.phschool.com
  - Internet Activities, Hurricane Strikes!
  - Virtual Field Trip

Teaching Resources
- Chapter Extension Activities p. 88

ASSESSMENT

PRENTICE HALL ASSESSMENT SYSTEM

Core Assessment
- ExamView Test Bank booklet, Ch. 37
- ExamView Test Bank CD-ROM, Ch. 37

Standardized Test Preparation

Diagnose and Prescribe
- Diagnostic Tests for High School Social Studies Skills

Review and Reteach
- Review Book for World History

Practice and Assess
- Test-Taking Strategies With Transparencies for High School
- Alternative Assessment booklet
- Test Prep Book for World History

Teaching Resources
Unit 8 booklet
- Geography Quiz, p. 104
- Section Quizzes, pp. 93, 95, 97, 99
- Chapter Tests A, B, and C, pp. 105–109
- www.phschool.com
  - Self-Test

CUSTOMIZE FOR INDIVIDUAL NEEDS

Gifted and Talented
- Teacher's Edition, Activities: Interpreting Viewpoints, p. 938

Less Proficient Readers
- Guide to the Essentials, Ch. 37
- Guided Reading Audiotapes, English, Ch. 37
- Book on CD, Ch. 37
- Teacher's Edition, Activities: Reading Strategy, p. 951

Less Proficient Writers
- Teacher's Edition, Activities: Customize for Kinesthetic Learners, p. 935; Cooperative Learning Activity, p. 942

Students Acquiring English/ESL
- Guide to the Essentials, English/Spanish, Ch. 37
- Guided Reading Audiotapes, English/Spanish, Ch. 37
- Book on CD, Ch. 37
- Teacher's Edition, Activities marked with an *

i TEXT

Don't miss the exclusive interactive version of *World History: Connections to Today* on the Internet and CD-ROM.

INTRODUCTION

Most Latin American nations have had a long history of poverty and social inequality. Those problems continue today, despite postwar efforts to develop their economies. Many nations have suffered political unrest, and a number have been ruled by dictators or the military.

Focusing on Themes

Suggest that students focus on these theme questions as they read:

Economics and Technology
How did Latin American nations evolve economic policies to meet changing needs?

Political and Social Systems
Why did Latin American nations have trouble preserving democratic governments?

Continuity and Change
How did colonialism and independence influence present-day Latin America?

Global Interaction
How did the Cold War affect Latin America?

Impact of the Individual
How did leaders like Juan Perón and Fidel Castro reshape their nations?

TIME LINE ACTIVITY

Share the About the Pictures note with your students before asking these questions about the time line:

1. Castro established a communist regime in Cuba. Why might that have had more significance at the time than if he had done so after 1991? *(The Cold War was at its height in 1959 but had ended by 1991.)*
2. Which nations named on the time line are in South America? *(Argentina)*

Don't Miss!

Disaster!
Hurricane Strikes!
(Section 3)

Analyzing Primary Sources
Helping the Street Children of Brazil
(Section 4)

Latin America
1945–Present

Chapter Preview

1 Forces Shaping Modern Latin America
2 Latin America, the United States, and the World
3 Mexico, Central America, and the Caribbean
4 Focus on Argentina and Brazil

1948
The Organization of American States is formed. Its colorful symbol, above, consists of the furled flags of its member nations.

1959
In Cuba, Fidel Castro and his guerrilla army overthrow a corrupt dictator. Later, Castro establishes a communist dictatorship.

CHAPTER EVENTS

1940 • • 1955 • • 1970

GLOBAL EVENTS

1949 The People's Republic of China is founded.

1960s Many African nations gain independence from European rule.

Resource Directory

Teaching Resources

Chapter Theme Activities Teaching With Themes booklet, p. 40
Pacing Chart With Block Scheduling Guide Ch. 37
Global View Activity *What Trends Are Influencing the Direction of World History Today?* Teaching With Themes booklet, p. 48

Technology

World History Color Transparencies Ch. 37 Graphic Organizer, p. F–75

Population Density of Latin America

Latin America is a diverse region that stretches across Mexico, Central America, the Caribbean, and South America. The region's population is very unevenly distributed.

Robinson Projection

Persons per sq. mi.	Persons per sq. km.
250 +	100 +
100–249	40–99
25–99	10–39
5–24	3–9
0–4	0–2
Data unavailable	Data unavailable

1983
In Argentina, people celebrate the end of military rule and the restoration of democracy.

2000
After more than 70 years of rule by the Institutional Revolutionary Party (PRI), Mexico elects the opposition candidate Vicente Fox as president (above, at left).

1985   2000   2015

1980s A global economic slowdown causes many governments to reduce spending.

Take It to the NET
To learn about recent developments in Latin America, visit the World History section of **www.phschool.com**.

Chapter 37 **933**

Independent Assignments

Have students read one section as they prepare for class. After class, have them complete the assignment. Some students may benefit from using the Guided Reading and Review worksheets.

Section 1 Have students use the Viewpoint Activity worksheet *Democracy in Latin America* in the Unit 8 booklet, p. 102, to learn about Latin American hopes for democracy.

Section 2 Have students use the maps *South America* and *Central America and the Caribbean* in the Historical Outline Map Book, pp. 65 and 66, to locate and label the political boundaries and major geographic features of Latin America.

Section 3 Have students use the Primary Source worksheet *Witness to War* in the Unit 8 booklet, p. 101, to learn about Chilin Hultaxh's experiences with the military in Guatemala.

Section 4 Have students use the Skill Application Activity *Predicting Consequences* in the Unit 8 booklet, p. 103, to learn about the problems of saving the Amazon rain forests.

Population Density of Latin America

Activating Prior Knowledge
From your knowledge of history and geography, explain why the highest population densities are found along the coasts. *(People settle on the coasts because overland travel is difficult.)*

Previewing
Why do you suppose data is unavailable for the large area in central Brazil? *(It is in the middle of the rain forest, and it is difficult to count people there.)*

Background
About the Pictures

1   2   3   4

1. Among other functions, OAS is responsible for the administration of the Rio Treaty of 1947, in which member nations pledged mutual help in case of attack. The OAS in the 1990s played a role in protecting democratic governments in Haiti, Peru, and Guatemala.

2. Ironically, Castro became just as much of a dictator as the man he replaced. He killed or jailed thousands of dissidents and imposed severe restrictions on private enterprise, a policy that Cuba's Communist party reaffirmed in 1996.

3. These celebrators have climbed onto a statue to demonstrate approval of the new president, Raúl Alfonsín. Argentina's huge debts and an inflation rate of more than 900 percent are two challenges Alfonsín faced.

4. Swept to power on a mandate of change and the end of government corruption, Vicente Fox took office as president of Mexico in December 2000. The PRI had ruled Mexico since its formation in 1929 and had in later decades been accused of fixing elections and assassinating rival politicians.

eTeach

Be sure to check out this month's online discussion with a World History Master Teacher.

Go to **www.phschool.com**.

Have students preview this section by studying the Reading Focus questions on this page and the Section 1 Assessment questions. Ask them to use the questions to write three generalizations predicting the contents of the section.

LESSON PLAN

1. Focus Social inequality, population growth, poverty, and rapid urbanization all contributed to unrest in Latin America. Many ideologies competed for power. To promote economic growth, governments encouraged economic nationalism and expanding agriculture. Urbanization, competing political groups, religious movements, and the struggles of individuals have all led to social change.

2. Instruct As students read the section, have them find evidence to support or challenge the following generalizations: (1) Most people in Latin America share a common heritage and the same culture. (2) Class structure is a significant influence on the lives of most Latin Americans. (3) Democracy has had a troubled history in Latin America. (4) Economic development has had mixed success. (5) Religious leaders play a significant role in Latin American politics. (6) The role of women has remained unchanged in this century.

3. Assess Have students write generalizations of their own about Latin American population growth and urbanization.

4. Reteach If students' Assess activity does not reflect adequate understanding of the lesson, you might assign the *Guide to the Essentials* or the *Interactive Student Tutorial CD-ROM* for this section.

Skills Assessment

ANSWER (a) African (b) European (c) Native American

Reading Focus

- Why is Latin America a culturally diverse region?
- What conditions contributed to unrest in Latin American countries?
- What forces shaped political, economic, and social patterns in Latin America?

Vocabulary

import substitution
agribusiness
liberation theology

Taking Notes

As you read this section, make an outline of its contents. Use Roman numerals for major headings, capital letters for subheadings, and numbers for supporting details. The model at right will help you get started.

I. A diverse region
  A. Geographic diversity
    1.
    2.
  B. Cultural diversity
II. Sources of unrest
  A. Social structure
    1.
    2.
  B. Population and poverty

Main Idea Latin America's development is influenced by geography, culture, social patterns, and political and economic conditions.

Setting the Scene For Carolina Maria de Jesus, life in the slums of São Paulo, Brazil, was filled with hardship. Like millions of other poor people, she had moved from the country to the city. To earn money to feed her family, she combed garbage for paper, cans, and other scraps to sell. In her diary, De Jesus described her daily struggle against poverty:

> "July 16. I went to Senhor Manuel, carrying some cans to sell. . . . He gave me 13 [coins]. I kept thinking that I had to buy bread, soap, and milk. . . . The 13 [coins] wouldn't make it. I returned . . . to my shack, nervous and exhausted. I thought of the worrisome life that I led, carrying paper, washing clothes for the children, staying in the street all day long."
> —Carolina Maria de Jesus, *Child of the Dark*

After 1945, Latin American nations faced problems similar to those of other emerging nations—rapid population growth, poverty, illiteracy, political instability, and authoritarian governments. In Latin America, as elsewhere, each country pursued its own course toward modernization.

A Diverse Region

Latin America stretches across an immense region from Mexico, Central America, and the Caribbean through South America. It includes 33 independent countries that range from tiny island nations like Grenada and Haiti to giant Brazil, which is almost as large as the United States.

Skills Assessment

Graph Latin America is a region of ethnic and cultural diversity. **What ethnic group is the largest in each of the following countries?** (a) Haiti, (b) Argentina, (c) Peru.

ETHNIC DIVERSITY IN LATIN AMERICA

Argentina 3 / 97	Brazil 1 6 / 55 38	Haiti 5 / 95	Mexico 1 9 / 60 30	Peru 3 / 15 45 37

Percentage of Population

African   European   Mestizo   Mulatto   Native American   Other

Source: *CIA World Factbook 2000*

Resource Directory

Teaching Resources

Creative Teaching Activities Creative Teaching Activities booklet, p. 163
Guided Reading and Review Unit 8 booklet, p. 92
Biography Activity *Pablo Neruda*, Unit 8 booklet, p. 100
Viewpoint Activity *Democracy in Latin America*, Unit 8 booklet, p. 102
Prentice Hall Literature Library "The Rebellion of the Magical Rabbits," *World Writers Today*, pp. 462–474

Technology

Listening to Literature World Masterpieces audiotapes poems by Octavio Paz and Derek Walcott, sides 9 and 10, running time 6:56 min.

Conquest, immigration, and intermarriage made Latin America culturally diverse. After 1492, Europeans imposed their civilization on Native Americans. They later brought millions of Africans to the region. As these populations mingled, they created vital new cultures. Since the late 1800s, immigrants from Europe and Asia have further contributed to the diversity. Today, people of Indian descent are still the majority population in Mexico, Guatemala, Peru, and Bolivia. Brazil has more people of African descent than any other Latin American nation. Although Spanish is the chief language of the region, Portuguese, French, English, Creole, and hundreds of Native American languages and African dialects are also spoken.

Sources of Unrest

For decades after World War II, uprisings and revolutions shook much of Latin America. Although they grew in part out of changes brought by modernization, they also reflected the failure to reform deep-rooted inequalities.

Social Structure Since colonial days, a key feature of Latin America has been the uneven distribution of wealth. In most countries, a tiny elite controlled the land, mines, businesses, and factories. The wealthy few opposed reforms that threatened their economic power. A growing gulf between rich and poor fueled discontent in the postwar era.

Poverty was linked to the social structure that had survived since colonial times. The upper classes were mostly descended from Europeans. The great majority of the population—the urban and rural poor—were mestizos, Native Americans, or people of African descent.

By the mid-1900s, two social classes were emerging as important forces. As cities grew, the middle class and urban working class expanded. They were less tied to particular ethnic groups than the old aristocracy and peasantry. Both had their own hopes for progress and prosperity.

Population and Poverty In Latin America, as elsewhere, the population explosion contributed to poverty. Between 1930 and 1985, for example, the populations of both Brazil and Mexico increased by more than four times. Growth rates in some countries slowed during the 1990s, but economies were still hard pressed to keep pace with population. Overall populations kept rising because a large proportion of the people were young and just starting their own families. Latin America's population reached 400 million in 1990 and exceeded 600 million in 2000.

In rural areas, where most of the people were peasant farmers, population growth put stress on the land. A family might own a small plot for growing food. But most farmers worked for low wages on the estates of wealthy landlords who held the best land. Many had to borrow money from their landlords just to get by from harvest to harvest. Burdened by this so-called debt slavery, they were tied to the land unless they ran away to the cities.

Urbanization Pressure on the land contributed to the great migration that sent millions of peasants to the cities. Today, about 70 percent of all Latin Americans live in cities. Some newcomers found jobs in factories,

Source of Unrest
The gulf between rich and poor contributes to unrest in Latin America. This family lives in a shack near Lima, Peru.

Theme: Political and Social Systems Why do you think poor health is often a problem for people who live in communities such as this?

Military Regimes
Military officers ruled many Latin American countries in the 1960s and 1970s. In other nations, elected officials stayed in power only with the army's support. In this painting, *The Parrots,* Colombian artist Beatriz González uses the repeating image of a civilian president flanked by generals.

Theme: Art and Literature Why do you think the artist did not stress the leaders' facial features?

offices, or stores. Many more survived by working odd jobs such as doing laundry or mending shoes. Others scavenged at the city garbage dump.

In the shantytowns that ringed Latin American cities, people lived in shacks without electricity, sewage, or other services. Yet because they were near urban centers, they were more likely to attend school or have access to health care than were the rural poor. As a result, poor city children were sometimes in a better position to move ahead than rural children.

Politics: Reform, Repression, or Revolution

Most Latin American states had constitutions modeled on those of France or the United States. On paper, they protected the rights of individuals. Yet real democracy seemed difficult to achieve in nations plagued by poverty and inequality.

Competing Ideologies After World War II, various groups pressed for reforms. They included liberals, socialists, students, labor leaders, peasant organizers, and Catholic priests and nuns. Although they differed over how to achieve their goals, all wanted to improve conditions for the poor. Most called for schools, housing, health care, and land reform.

Conservative forces, however, resisted reforms that might undermine their power. These elite groups included the military, the traditional landed aristocracy, and the growing business middle class. They often had strong ties to foreign investors and corporations. Conflict between conservatives and reformers contributed to political instability in many nations.

Military Regimes Military leaders, like *caudillos* of the 1800s, held power in many Latin American nations. They often served conservative interests. However, some supported modest social and economic reforms, in part because a growing number of officers came from the working classes.

In the 1960s and 1970s, as social unrest increased, military governments seized power in Argentina, Brazil, Chile, and elsewhere. Claiming the need to restore order, they imposed harsh regimes. They outlawed political parties, censored the press, and closed universities. In Argentina and Chile, the military imprisoned and executed thousands of dissidents. Others were murdered by illegal "death squads" allied to the government.

Some military rulers tried to solve economic problems by sponsoring capitalism. In Chile, General Augusto Pinochet (pee noh SHAY), who ruled from 1973 to 1990, promoted foreign investment and privatized industry. The Chilean economy did expand. In general, however, most military regimes were unable to solve basic problems.

Caption Answer

Possible answer: By repeating the same images and not stressing individual facial features, the artist conveys the idea that military rulers and the civilian officials under their control are all very much the same. The nature of military dictatorship stays the same regardless of who the individual rulers may be.

The Threat of Revolution

During the 1960s and 1970s, guerrillas and urban terrorists battled repressive governments in many Latin American countries. Rebel groups used bombings, kidnappings, and assassinations. The leaders of many of these groups supported Marxist goals. Only a socialist revolution, they said, could end inequalities. Marxism won support among peasants, urban workers, and some intellectuals. Other revolutionaries were motivated by nationalism. They condemned economic and cultural domination by the United States.

During the Cold War, the spread of Marxism complicated moderate reform efforts. Conservatives tended to view any effort at reform as a communist threat and often won support from the United States.

Revival of Democracy By the mid-1980s, inflation, debt, and growing protests led repressive leaders to step aside. Argentina, Brazil, Chile, and other countries held multiparty elections to replace military governments with civilian governments. As the twenty-first century began, the only major nonelected ruler in Latin America was Cuba's Fidel Castro.

Still, elections alone could not ensure a truly democratic government. In Peru, for example, President Alberto Fujimori suspended the nation's constitution to crush antigovernment guerrillas and engineered his own reelection before fleeing the country. President Hugo Chavez of Venezuela centralized power in his own hands to advance his populist and nationalist "Bolivarian revolution." Heavy debt burdens and economic slowdowns have threatened the success of Latin America's elected rulers, putting the stability of democratic governments in the region in doubt.

Economic Development

Except during the Great Depression of the 1930s, most Latin American nations experienced economic growth between 1900 and the 1960s. Their economies, though, were influenced by global economic trends and dependence on industrial nations. Many relied on the export of a single crop or commodity, so they were hard hit if harvests failed or demand declined. By the 1960s, Latin America faced growing competition from African and Asian nations seeking to export their crops and commodities.

Industry To reduce dependence on imported goods, many Latin American governments encouraged the development of local industries. This policy, called import substitution, had mixed success. The middle class prospered, but life did not improve for most people. Many of the new industries were inefficient and needed government help or foreign capital

Background
Daily Life

Tale of Two Cities In 1994, a reporter for *The New York Times* interviewed Bernardo Ruz, a 22-year-old Chilean electrician, about the effects of economic reform on his life. At the time, Ruz, his wife, and infant son were living on the outskirts of Santiago in a drafty wooden shack with no heat and no running water. Said Ruz, "There are a lot of fancy buildings that have been built, making the big businessman richer. The humble people like us got jobs for a while, but that is over. I haven't had work in months and everything is now more expensive. We've forgotten what meat tastes like."

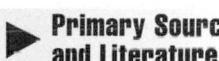

▶ **Primary Sources and Literature**

See "Mario Vargas Llosa: Latin America, the Democratic Option" in the Reference Section at the back of this book.

Human Drama Activity

Drawing a Political Cartoon A highly respected poet and political activist, Pablo Neruda worked to help Gabriel González Videla win the presidency of Chile in 1946. Videla had pledged to promote economic and social justice. Once in office, though, he cracked down on workers, censored the press, and even persecuted former supporters. Neruda used his pen for revenge in the epic *Canto general*. He writes of González Videla:

"He has *betrayed* everything.
He climbed like a rat to my people's shoulders
and there, gnawing on my country's sacred
flag, he twitches his rodent's tail
telling landowners and foreigners, the owners
of Chile's subsoil: 'Drink all this nation's blood.'"

Have students paraphrase Neruda's poem and then draw a political cartoon protesting political corruption in Latin America.

Analyzing Poetry Mexican poet Octavio Paz, winner of the 1990 Nobel Prize for Literature, often portrays a magical sense of life in his works. Asking his readers to suspend their understanding of reality, he invites them into a world where fantastic images, dreams, and the irrational reign. In his poem "Fable," Paz accounts for the loss of an idyllic period of history when the world "shattered" into the "broken mirrors" of language that keep all men apart.

Have students listen to the poem on the Listening to Literature World Masterpieces audiotapes, side 9, or read it, if an anthology of Paz's works or of Latin American poetry is available. Ask students to identify and explain the fantastic images used at the start of the poem to portray an idyllic world. Ask them to interpret the meaning of the lines "Everything was for everyone/Everyone was everything." Next, have them describe the change that occurs in the last four lines of the poem. Finally, ask students to identify the aspects of contemporary society that are addressed by Paz's "Fable."

Women in Government
Today, a growing number of women are becoming leaders in government. Mireya Moscoso was elected the first woman president of Panama. She follows in the footsteps of her husband, Arnulfo Arias, a former president.

Theme: Continuity and Change How does Mireya Moscoso represent both continuity and change?

to survive. Also, industry did not expand rapidly enough to produce new jobs for a rapidly growing population. Eventually, governments returned to promoting agricultural exports.

Expanding Agriculture Over the past 60 years, large areas of land were opened up for farming through irrigation and the clearing of forests. Much of the best farmland belonged to **agribusinesses,** or giant commercial farms owned by multinational corporations. They used modern technology to develop the land and operate processing plants. In Central America and Brazil, developers cleared tropical forests to provide new farmlands.

Commercial agriculture increased the need to import food. Production of some food crops declined as land was turned over to growing crops for export. As a result, more food had to be imported, at a high cost.

Crisis and Reform In the 1980s, Latin American nations were buffeted by economic storms, including high oil costs, rising interest rates, and a worldwide recession. As interest rates rose, nations that had borrowed to develop industry were crushed by a debt crisis.

To combat the crisis, nations like Mexico and Brazil resorted to strong measures. They cut spending on social programs, raised prices on goods, stopped financing local businesses, and opened their markets to foreign companies. Most governments brought their debt payments under control.

In the 1990s, free-trade organizations modeled loosely on the European Common Market promised some economic improvement. The Southern Common Market (Mercosur) linked some of Latin America's most productive economies, including those of Argentina and Brazil and, in an associate capacity, Chile. The North American Free Trade Association (NAFTA) linked Mexico to the prosperous markets of the United States and Canada. The mutual support and expanded markets of such organizations did bring some economic growth in the years around 2000.

Changing Social Patterns

In Latin America, as elsewhere, urbanization brought social upheaval. City life weakened the extended family of rural villages and often replaced it with the smaller nuclear family. Instead of raising food, family members had to earn cash. The struggle to make a living caused some families to fall apart. In large cities, thousands of abandoned or runaway children roamed the streets. Many were caught up in crime and violence. To support their families, many women took jobs outside the home.

Women Throughout the 1900s, Latin American women worked hard to increase their role in public life and to win equality, including the right to vote. By 1961, women had won the vote throughout the Americas. By the

1990s, women moved into the political arena in small but growing numbers. Argentina, Nicaragua, and Panama had women presidents, and Benedita da Silva became the first black woman elected to the Brazilian congress.

Women's status varied according to class and race. Generally, women were responsible for the home and for child care. Upper-class women had access to education and professional careers and could hire servants to care for their homes and children. Rural women of Indian or African descent faced prejudice and poverty. They lacked schooling and basic health care, and they often labored for low pay.

A peasant woman from El Salvador, who began harvesting coffee and cotton at age 16, described the injustices she endured. One problem was the quota system: "They'd give you two and a half sacks as a quota for every day and if you didn't manage it, they didn't pay you anything." Another complaint was unequal treatment: "Men have always been paid 5 colones more than women or children and we all do exactly the same work."

Women struggled to win change. To help their families and communities, some peasant women pushed for schools and health care. In Argentina and elsewhere, women protested human rights abuses by brutal military governments. During the harsh Pinochet years in Chile, women in Santiago organized food kitchens to serve meals to the poor. Others protested violence against women or challenged the subordinate position of women within the family.

Religion The Catholic Church has remained a powerful force throughout Latin America. Traditionally, it was often tied to the conservative ruling class. However, some Church leaders had always spoken up for the poor. During the 1960s and 1970s, many priests, nuns, and church workers crusaded for social justice and an end to poverty. Their movement became known as liberation theology. These activists saw Jesus as a "liberator of the poor." They urged the Church to become a force for reform. Many joined the struggle against oppressive governments. Some became objects of violence themselves. In El Salvador, for example, Archbishop Oscar Romero was assassinated by a right-wing death squad.

Some evangelical Protestant groups won a growing following among the poor. Their message, which emphasized the power of faith, had an especially strong appeal among women, who then brought other family members into the faith.

Catholics Take Action
Dom Hélder Câmara, a Catholic bishop, outlined his vision for the Catholic Church in Brazil:

"We will [help] to keep poverty from sinking into misery. . . . But I have not come here to help anyone [trick] himself into thinking that a little charity and social work will [be enough]. . . . If we really want to get to the root of our social ills, we will have to help our country break out of the vicious circle of underdevelopment and misery. . . . It would be an unpardonable scandal if the Church were to abandon the masses in their hour of greatest need, as if [it] took no interest in helping them reach a level of human, Christian dignity compatible with real citizenship."

—Dom Hélder Câmara, *Revolution Through Peace*

Skills Assessment
Primary Source On what problem does Bishop Câmara suggest that the Catholic Church focus in Brazil?

SECTION 1 Assessment

Recall
1. **(a)** debt slavery, p. 935 **(b)** Alberto Fujimori, p. 937 **(c)** Hugo Chavez, p. 937 **(d)** Benedita da Silva, p. 939
2. **(a)** import substitution, p. 937 **(b)** agribusiness, p. 938 **(c)** liberation theology, p. 939

Comprehension
3. Conquests, immigration, and intermarriage have led to diversity. 4. the gulf between rich and poor, inequalities among the social classes, a population explosion, rapid urbanization 5. **(a)** Most imposed harsh regimes, outlawing political parties, censoring the press, and closing universities. In some countries, the military imprisoned and executed thousands of dissidents. **(b)** Results were mixed. The middle class prospered, but life did not improve for most. Many new industries were inefficient. Commercial agriculture produced more crops, but many of these were for export, so food had to be imported at a high cost. **(c)** Some Roman Catholic Church leaders spoke up for the poor, but the Church was tied to mostly the ruling class. In the 1960s and 1970s, Church activists crusaded for social justice and an end to poverty.

Critical Thinking and Writing
6. Students' editorials should reflect an understanding of life for the poor.
7. Causes included high oil costs, rising interest rates, and worldwide recession. Effects included reduced spending on social programs, increasing prices on goods, elimination of financing for local businesses, and opening of markets to foreign companies.

SECTION 1 Assessment

Recall
1. **Identify: (a)** debt slavery, **(b)** Alberto Fujimori, **(c)** Hugo Chavez, **(d)** Benedita da Silva.
2. **Define: (a)** import substitution, **(b)** agribusiness, **(c)** liberation theology.

Comprehension
3. How does the history of Latin America explain its cultural diversity today?
4. Describe four conditions that fed unrest in Latin America.
5. Describe how each of the following has affected Latin America: **(a)** military regimes, **(b)** economic nationalism, **(c)** religion.

Critical Thinking and Writing
6. **Synthesizing Information** Review the Setting the Scene and the picture of Lima, Peru, on the first pages of the section. Use the primary source and the picture to write an editorial commenting on the condition of poor families in Latin America.
7. **Recognizing Causes and Effects** Explain the causes and effects of the debt crisis that afflicted Latin America and other parts of the world in the 1980s.

Activity
Take It to the NET

Use the Internet to find information about urban populations in Latin America. Identify the largest cities in Latin America in order of population, and plot these cities on a map. Create a database to accompany your map that indicates each city's population and the year the data were gathered.

Chapter 37 **939**

Activity Rubrics

Share rubrics with students.

Attempted The map is incomplete, and the database is missing.

Minimal The map includes the largest cities, but the database is not complete.

Adequate The map includes the largest cities; labels are easy to read and accurate; and the database is complete.

Exemplary The map includes all the largest cities and is clear and attractive; labels are accurate; and the database is complete.

Primary Source

ANSWER Câmara urges the Church to focus on the problem of economic development in Brazil to ease social problems.

Have students read the first paragraph of "Changing Social Patterns" on the opposite page and then answer the question below.

What is an extended family?

A one in which members live far apart

B one that is made up of the parent(s) and children

C one that includes parent(s), children, aunts, uncles, and grandparents

D one that has moved to a city

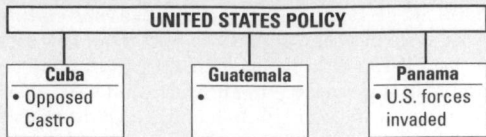

Reading Focus

- How did communist rule affect Cuba?

- What policies has the United States followed in Latin America?

- What global issues have linked Latin America to other regions of the world?

Vocabulary

literacy rate

embargo

Taking Notes

Make an organizer like the one shown here to outline relations between the United States and nations of Latin America. Complete the chart as you read. Add as many boxes as you need.

UNITED STATES POLICY		
Cuba • Opposed Castro	**Guatemala** •	**Panama** • U.S. forces invaded

Main Idea   Latin American nations have developed policies in response to United States influence, regional issues, and global issues.

LESSON PLAN

1. Focus By establishing a communist state in the Western Hemisphere, the Cuban Revolution had great impact on relations between Latin American nations and the United States. The United States pursued Cold War goals in Latin America. It backed anti-communist governments, promoted capitalism, and exerted its influence and power in the region. Issues concerning trade, illegal drug trafficking, immigration, and the environment have linked Latin America more closely with the rest of the world.

2. Instruct Organize the class into two or more teams to play a quiz game. Provide each team with index cards or slips of paper. Ask each team to write on individual cards the name of a person, organization, event, or significant development presented in Section 2. A sample list might include: Fidel Castro, Good Neighbor Policy, Jacobo Arbenz, Bay of Pigs, environmental protection, drug wars. Instruct each team to check their cards and eliminate any duplicates.

3. Assess Have teams take turns sending one member to pick a card from another team. To win a point, the team member must identify the name or term on the card by providing two significant facts about it. After the game is finished, follow up with a discussion of the issues represented by the names and terms used in the game.

4. Reteach If students' Assess activity does not reflect adequate understanding of the lesson, you might assign the *Guide to the Essentials* or the *Interactive Student Tutorial CD-ROM* for this section.

Biography

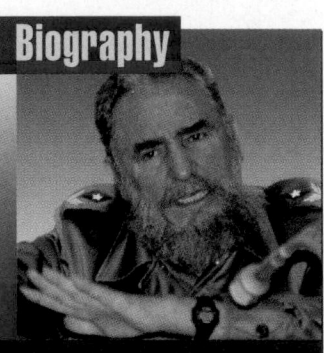

Fidel Castro 1926(?) —

Castro was the son of a wealthy farmer who employed several hundred workers. While studying law at the University of Havana, he and other students took part in a failed attempt to invade the Dominican Republic and overthrow its dictator, Rafael Trujillo. Castro earned his law degree and became a vocal opponent of dictator Fulgencio Batista. In 1953, Castro led an attack on an army barracks. The assault failed and resulted in his imprisonment. After his release, he went into exile in Mexico. In 1956, he returned to Cuba and launched the guerrilla war that eventually led to his victory.

Theme: Impact of the Individual How did Castro demonstrate an ability to overcome failure?

Biography

ANSWER Castro maintained his goal of overthrowing Batista after his failed attacks and kept implementing new strategies.

Setting the Scene "The duty of every revolutionary is to make revolution," declared Cuban dictator Fidel Castro in 1962. After bringing about sweeping changes in his island nation, Castro vowed to export communism to other countries in the region. During the Cold War, the threat of communist revolution had a strong influence on United States policy toward Latin America. Meanwhile, Latin American nations tried to limit United States influence in the region. Today, Latin American nations are building new political and economic relations in the global arena.

Communism in Cuba

After the Spanish-American War, Cuba won independence from Spain. However, Cuba was controlled by the United States under the Platt Amendment to the Cuban Constitution until 1935. During this time, American investors bought up Cuban plantations and mills, and the United States became the chief buyer of Cuba's sugar. It continued to support military dictators.

Castro In the 1950s, a young lawyer, Fidel Castro, rallied forces opposed to the corrupt Batista regime. By 1959, Castro had led his tiny guerrilla army to victory. Cubans cheered the rebel as a hero. For many, the joy soon wore off as Castro turned Cuba into a communist state. Castro nationalized foreign-owned sugar plantations and other businesses. He put most land under government control and distributed the rest to peasant farmers.

While Castro imposed harsh authoritarian rule, he did improve conditions for the poor. During the 1960s, Cuba provided basic health care for all, promoted equality for women, and increased the nation's literacy rate, the percentage of a population that can read and write. But communist dictatorship angered middle-class Cubans. Critics were jailed or silenced, and hundreds of thousands fled to the United States.

Cold War Tensions The Cuban Revolution alarmed the United States, especially as Castro turned to the Soviet Union for aid. In 1961, the United States backed a plot by anti-Castro exiles to invade Cuba and overthrow Castro. An invasion force landed at the Bay of Pigs in Cuba but was quickly crushed. The next year, the United States imposed an embargo on Cuba. An embargo is a ban on trade. Castro sought closer ties to the Soviet Union. He let the Soviets build nuclear missile bases in Cuba, just 90 miles from Florida. The threat of nearby Soviet nuclear bases outraged the United States and touched off a dangerous crisis.

In October 1962, President John Kennedy declared a naval blockade of Cuba and demanded that the Soviets remove the weapons. For several days during the Cuban missile crisis, the superpowers stood on the brink of nuclear war. In the end, Soviet leader Nikita Khrushchev backed down. He agreed to remove the missiles from Cuba.

Over the next decades, Castro tried to encourage revolution in other Latin American nations. Cuba also sent troops to Africa to help the socialist government of Angola. In response, the United States continued its efforts to isolate Cuba and undermine Castro. The Soviets, meanwhile, provided massive economic and military aid to Cuba.

Recent Trends When the Soviet Union collapsed in the early 1990s, Cuba lost its chief ally and trading partner. Without Soviet financial aid, Cuba's economy fell into a shambles. In response, Castro encouraged tourism, allowed some features of a market economy, and welcomed foreign investment. At the same time, however, he vowed to preserve communism.

The United States refused to negotiate with Castro, despite the urgings of the United Nations and Latin American leaders, who argued that Cuba no longer posed a threat. Still, as American business people visited the country and baseball teams from the two nations competed, it seemed less and less likely that either Cuban communism or the American embargo would endure for long.

The United States and Latin America

Like powerful nations in many times and places, the United States developed a sphere of influence that included smaller neighboring states. The United States was the leading investor and trading partner for most nations in Latin America. Profits from United States-owned companies flowed from Latin America to the north. At the same time, cultural influences drifted both north and south.

Despite their links, the United States and its neighbors had very different views of one another. The United States saw itself as the defender of democracy and capitalism and the source of humanitarian aid. Many Latin Americans, however, resented that they lived under the shadow of the "colossus of the north."

Intervention During the Cold War, the United States intervened repeatedly in Latin America. It did so to protect its interests and to prevent the spread of communism. The United States backed anti-communist dictators and helped equip and train their soldiers to fight rebel uprisings. It even helped topple leftist leaders.

In 1954, for example, the United States helped Guatemalan soldiers overthrow a popularly elected president, Jacobo Arbenz. This action came after he had enacted land reforms that threatened United States-owned businesses. In the 1970s, after socialist Salvador Allende (ah YEHN day) was elected president of Chile, President Richard Nixon told officials to "make the [Chilean] economy scream." In 1973, the United States quietly lent its support to a military coup that overthrew Allende.

Other United States interventions in Latin America were unrelated to the threat of communism. In 1989, United States forces invaded Panama and overthrew the government of General Manuel Noriega. Noriega was removed from Panama and then tried, convicted, and imprisoned for drug trafficking. In the 1990s, the United States used economic pressure and the threat of military action to force military rulers from power in Haiti.

Many Latin Americans opposed United States economic and military intervention. Although they perhaps admired the wealth and technology of the United States, they often resented its political, economic, and cultural influence in Latin America.

Escape From Cuba

To flee poverty and political repression, many Cuban *balseros* (rafters) braved 90 miles of open sea to reach the United States. Men, women, and children crossed the Straits of Florida on rickety rafts, small boats, and smugglers' speedboats. Not all survived the trip.

Sun, waves, winds, and even hurricanes imperiled those trying to escape from Cuba. "The weather was so bad that we were lost for the next two days," said one balsero. "We were pushed into the middle of the Atlantic . . . [and] were followed by sharks." The sole survivor of another voyage recalled: "When the raft fell apart, all of us grabbed whatever tire and wood we could."

Theme: Political and Social Systems Why were people willing to risk the voyage from Cuba to Florida?

Analyzing a Quotation Inform students that the leftist Arbenz government fell in June 1954 when Guatemalan exiles invaded Guatemala from bases in Honduras and Nicaragua. The Arbenz government appealed to the UN for help, but United States pressure helped convince the UN to take no action. In July 1954, the British politician Clement Atlee openly criticized the UN with these words:

"The fact is that this was a plain act of aggression, and one cannot take one line on aggression in Asia and another line in Central America. . . . [W]e cannot pass this off as just a Central American squabble. . . . There was a principle involved and that principle was the responsibility of the United Nations."

Ask students to respond to the following questions: (1) What Asian aggression of the period was Atlee probably referring to? (2) What was the UN's response in that case? (3) How does Atlee find the UN to be inconsistent? (4) What do you think Atlee wanted the UN to do in the future?

Fidel Castro's overthrow of the corrupt Batista regime in 1959 was followed by an improved standard of living. The beneficiaries of the communist dictator's policies were the peasants, but the middle class suffered a diminished standard of living and curtailment of personal liberties. Thousands of people subsequently escaped to the United States to seek a better life. Have students read *The Program of the Cuban Revolution* in Treasures of the World, pp. 157–158, an excerpt of Castro's speech before the UN in 1960. It describes his idealistic goals. Then have students complete the questions at the end of the reading. Students will be asked to compare the conditions in Cuba that Castro condemns with conditions today as described in Section 2 of the textbook.

Cooperative Learning

Solving a Problem In 1995, Colombian police made major headway in the drug wars by arresting most of the leaders of the Cali drug cartel. This cartel, which a U.S. official described as "the biggest organized-crime syndicate there has ever been," was allegedly responsible for handling 80 percent of the world's cocaine traffic. In 1994, it is estimated that the Cali cartel made $7 billion in the U.S. alone. However, as a noted Colombian university professor commented, "The Scorpions [members of the cartel] will fall. But there are always going to be others to replace them until you tackle [drug] consumption."

Organize the class into small groups and assign them to come up with solutions to the drug consumption problem. Suggest to students that they brainstorm and list ways to sharply reduce the demand for illegal drugs. They should then discuss and evaluate their ideas, and narrow their lists to include only those ideas that seem to offer the greatest chance for success. When groups are done, have them share their solutions with the class. Ask them to explain the reasoning that led to their conclusions.

Global Connections

Cutting Down Lives?

As loggers cut down trees in the Amazon rain forest, medical experts worry. They worry because they know that vital medicines—both discovered and undiscovered—are derived from plants and animals found only in the Amazon and other rain forests. For example, the bark of the cinchona tree produces quinine, which is used for treating malaria. Curare, used by Indians of the Amazon as a dart poison, serves as a muscle relaxant during surgery. A wild Amazonian yam provides a drug that can be used in the treatment of autoimmune diseases and some forms of cancer. One day, the medical experts fear, the loss of plant and animal life in the rain forests and other ecosystems might result in the loss of human life.

Theme: Global Interaction
How might destruction of rain forests lead to loss of human life?

Regional Organizations Despite disagreements, Latin American nations and the United States did work together. The Organization of American States (OAS) was formed in 1948 to promote democracy, economic cooperation, and human rights. Members pledged not to interfere "directly or indirectly, for any reason whatever, in the internal or external affairs of any other State." Although the United States often dominated the OAS, Latin American members did at times pursue an independent line.

The Castro revolution and other Cold War tensions led President Kennedy to launch the Alliance for Progress in 1961. Under this ambitious program, the United States offered billions in loans and investments. In exchange, Latin American governments were to enact genuine reforms. The goals were to promote education and land reform, reduce inequality and poverty, weaken dictatorships, and help countries avoid revolutions.

The alliance produced little progress. Landowners and the business elite in many countries opposed basic reforms. The United States provided aid to Latin America, but never on the scale proposed by Kennedy.

Regional and Global Issues

By the end of the Cold War, many Latin American nations had reduced their dependence on the United States, although it remained their chief trading partner. Increasingly, they were tied to the global economy. Oil-rich Venezuela joined Arab nations in OPEC, while Brazil worked with coffee-exporting nations of Africa to support coffee prices.

Many Latin American nations increased trade and cultural links to European countries. Some exported food or minerals to Asian nations. Japanese investments in Latin America, especially in Brazil, rose rapidly.

Regional Ties In Latin America, as elsewhere around the world, regional trading blocs gained importance in the 1990s. Such groups created larger markets by lowering trade barriers among neighboring countries. In 1993, Mexico linked its economy to those of the United States and Canada through NAFTA. Two years later, a new South American trading bloc, Mercosur, paved the way for increased trade among Argentina, Brazil, Paraguay, and Uruguay. The new groups operated alongside older blocs that linked Andean, Caribbean, or Central American nations. Talks were also underway to create a hemisphere-wide free-trade zone that would be even larger than the expanding European Union.

The Drug Wars Regional cooperation was essential to efforts to control the illegal drug trade. Indians in Colombia, Peru, and Bolivia had for centuries grown coca for their own uses. However, as drug use increased in various parts of the world, criminal gangs, also known as drug cartels, began producing and exporting ever-larger quantities of cocaine and other drugs. By the 1970s, drug lords were reaping huge profits, which they used to bribe government officials. They also hired assassins to kill judges, journalists, and others who spoke out against them.

In the 1980s, the United States declared a "war on drugs." To halt the flow of drugs, the United States pressed governments in Colombia, Peru, and other countries to destroy coca crops and move against the cartels. Governments cooperated, but many Latin Americans argued that the root of the problem was not the supply of drugs but the growing demand for illegal drugs in the United States.

Development Versus the Environment Concerns about the environment also raised some troubling issues for Latin America and the world.

Global Connections

ANSWER Possible answer: Plants from which medicines might have been derived will become extinct before scientists discover their usefulness.

Resource Directory

Teaching Resources
Section Quiz Unit 8 booklet, p. 95
Technology
Interactive Student Tutorial CD-ROM Ch. 37
Computer Test Bank Ch. 37

Developing nations insisted that they needed to exploit their land and other resources if they wanted economic growth. "You cannot talk ecology to people who are struggling to survive," said a Brazilian delegate at an international conference on the environment. Developing nations pointed out that western powers had long since cleared many of their forests and mined their lands. What right, they asked, did industrial nations have to tell them to stop developing their resources?

The most widely publicized issue was the rapid destruction of the Amazon rain forest, which occupies more than a million square miles in the heart of Brazil. It is rich in mineral resources needed for economic growth. It also could provide land to millions of landless peasants. Since the 1930s, Brazil has opened more and more of this area to development. By the 1970s and 1980s, vast tracts of forest were being bulldozed and burned for farms, cattle ranches, highways, and even newly planned cities.

Environmentalists argued that deforestation had enormous costs. They called the Amazon rain forest "the lungs of the world" because it plays a key role in absorbing poisonous carbon dioxide from the air and releasing essential oxygen. It has been home to 15 million species of plants and animals, which have been threatened by development. Some forms of plant life might even hold undiscovered cures for diseases.

Another environmental concern was rapid development, which meant disaster for many native peoples. Isolation had protected bands of Native American forest dwellers for centuries. Land-hungry farmers, speculators, or foreign mining companies converged on the forest, threatening these ancient ways of life. Many Indians died of strange diseases introduced by the newcomers. Others were killed in conflicts provoked by impatient developers moving into the forest.

Migration Latin American immigration to the United States increased rapidly after the 1970s. Poverty, civil war, and repressive governments led many people to flee their homelands. Like earlier immigrants, they sought freedom and economic opportunity.

By the end of the 1990s, the United States had more than 11 million Latin American immigrants. Many immigrants entered the United States legally and eventually became citizens. A large number, however, were illegal immigrants. As a result, pressure increased in the United States to halt illegal immigration, deny services to illegal aliens, and return them to their countries of origin.

SECTION 2 Assessment

Recall
1. **Identify:** (a) Fidel Castro, (b) Bay of Pigs, (c) Cuban missile crisis, (d) Salvador Allende, (e) Manuel Noriega, (f) OAS, (g) Alliance for Progress, (h) NAFTA, (i) Mercosur, (j) drug cartel.
2. **Define:** (a) literacy rate, (b) embargo.

Comprehension
3. What changes did communism bring to life in Cuba?
4. Describe how United States political and economic policies have affected relations with countries of Latin America.
5. How have Latin American nations addressed regional and global issues?

Critical Thinking and Writing
6. **Connecting to Geography**
   (a) What environmental issues face Latin American nations?
   (b) Which of the five themes of geography seems most closely linked to these issues? Explain.
7. **Recognizing Causes and Effects**
   (a) How did the anti-communist stance of the United States affect Cuba? (b) How did the collapse of the Soviet Union affect Cuba?

Activity
Take It to the NET

Use the Internet to find recent news articles concerning one Latin American nation's involvement with one of the regional or global issues discussed in this section. Using the news articles, prepare a radio broadcast to deliver to the class.

SECTION 2 Assessment

Recall
1. (a) Fidel Castro, 940 (b) Bay of Pigs, p. 940 (c) Cuban missile crisis, pp. 940–941 (d) Salvador Allende, p. 941 (e) Manuel Noriega, p. 941 (f) OAS, p. 942 (g) Alliance for Progress, p. 942 (h) NAFTA, p. 942 (i) Mercosur, p. 942 (j) drug cartel, p. 942
2. (a) literacy rate, p. 940 (b) embargo, p. 940

Comprehension
3. Possible answer: improved conditions for the poor, harsh authoritarian rule, and an exodus of middle-class Cubans to the United States 4. Possible answers: The United States intervened in Latin American affairs by training and equipping the military of many nations and by sending American troops into Latin American trouble spots. It also engaged in undercover operations to preserve its power in the hemisphere. These interventions created deep resentment towards the United States. 5. They created larger markets by forming regional trading groups and lowering trade barriers among group members. They cooperated with one another and the U.S. in fighting drug trafficking. They are looking for ways to reconcile global environmental issues with local economic concerns.

Critical Thinking and Writing
6. (a) destruction of rain forest and subsequent loss of air purification and plant and animal species, rapid development that has disastrous effect on native peoples (b) human-environment interaction; Students' answers should be well supported. 7. (a) It led Cuba to seek closer ties with the Soviet Union, especially after the U.S. imposed a trade embargo on Cuba. It meant that Cuba was isolated to some degree. (b) The Cuban economy fell apart without Soviet aid, which led Castro to encourage tourism, allow some features of a market economy, and welcome foreign investment.

Activity Rubrics

Share rubrics with students before they deliver their radio broadcasts.

Attempted The broadcast is poorly researched, written, and organized, and delivery is poor.

Minimal The broadcast is adequately researched but poorly written and organized, and the delivery is fair.

Adequate The broadcast is well researched, written, and organized, and the delivery is good.

Exemplary The broadcast is very well researched, written, and organized, and the delivery is excellent.

Human Drama Activity

Researching the Penan Development has threatened indigenous peoples in other parts of the world. The Penan, a nomadic group of hunter-gatherers, live in the rain forest of Borneo. Commercial logging is destroying their ancient way of life. Many Penan have barricaded logging roads and used other forms of nonviolent protest. Have students find out more about the situation on the Internet.

Test Preparation

Have students read "The Drug Wars" on the opposite page, and then complete the sentence below.

The war on drugs is an attempt to

A keep illegal drugs in the country where they were produced and out of the U.S.

B teach people about the dangers of drug use.

C protect judges and journalists.

D stop cartels from producing and selling illegal drugs.

Reading Focus

- What conditions have changed and what conditions have remained the same in Mexico?

- Why did Central American countries suffer civil wars?

- What were the causes of Haiti's political and economic struggles?

Vocabulary

ejido
maquiladora
contra

Taking Notes

Make a table like the one below. Add key information about Mexico, Nicaragua, and two other countries.

	MEXICO	NICARAGUA		
POLITICS				
ECONOMICS	Land redistribution			

Main Idea Although Mexico underwent change with relatively little turmoil, several Central American countries were torn by civil war.

Primary Source

Heading Toward Democracy
Octavio Paz, a Mexican poet, philosopher, and winner of a Nobel Prize for Literature, comments on democracy in Latin America:

"Latin American democracy was a late arrival on the scene, and it has been disfigured and betrayed time and time again. It has been weak, hesitant, rebellious, its own worst enemy, all too eager to worship the demagogue, corrupted by money, riddled with favoritism and nepotism. And yet almost everything good that has been achieved in Latin America in the last century and a half has been accomplished under democratic rule, or, as in Mexico, a rule heading toward democracy. A great deal still remains to be done."

—Octavio Paz, *One Earth, Four or Five Worlds: Reflections on Contemporary History*

Skills Assessment

Primary Source Does Paz favor or oppose democracy? Explain.

Setting the Scene Oscar Romero was a conservative member of El Salvador's elite until he became archbishop. Then, he began to condemn government death squads that were killing peasants and students opposed to the government. From his pulpit, he announced, "The church would betray . . . its fidelity to the gospel if it stopped being . . . a defender of . . . every legitimate struggle to achieve a more just society."

Romero's outspoken stance cost him his life. On March 24, 1980, as he said mass, shots rang out. Moments later, Romero lay dead, a victim of the death squads he had denounced. But others took his place, and the protest against injustice continued. As one Salvadoran activist commented, "If you silence a prophet, he will speak out through his people."

In the latter half of the 1900s, El Salvador and other Central American countries were battered by civil wars. To the north, their larger and richer neighbor, Mexico, weathered those decades with relatively less turmoil.

Continuity and Change in Mexico

As you have read, Mexico endured a long, violent revolution in the early 1900s. After the revolution, government officials became committed—at least in theory—to improving conditions for the poor.

The Rural Poor In the 1930s, Mexico's president, Lázaro Cárdenas, had taken steps to fulfill the promises of the Mexican Revolution—especially land reform. He distributed millions of acres of land to peasants. Most was given to *ejidos* (eh HEE dohs), or peasant cooperatives. Some families also received small plots to farm themselves.

Over the years, however, the land reform program proved unsuccessful. Much of the land given to peasants was arid. It needed to be irrigated and fertilized to be productive. As rural populations grew, the land was subdivided and exhausted from overfarming. Presidents after Cárdenas paid less attention to Mexico's rural poor. Instead, they favored agribusinesses that produced cash-earning export crops.

As conditions worsened, many peasants migrated to towns and cities, especially to the capital. The population of Mexico City mushroomed from 1.5 million in 1940 to about 20 million in 1995.

The PRI in Control Since the Mexican Revolution, a single party—the Institutional Revolutionary Party (PRI)—dominated Mexican politics. It claimed to represent all groups—from workers and peasants to business-

944 *Chapter 37*

Primary Source

ANSWER He favors it because, although it is not strong in Latin America, he feels that almost everything good that has happened there has happened under democratic rule or under rule heading toward democracy.

industrial interests and the military. There were some other small political parties, but PRI bosses moved forcefully against any serious opposition.

In part, the PRI held on to power by responding to social ills with reform programs for education, welfare, and health. As a result, the party generally kept discontent from exploding into violence. Yet, in 1968, student protests shook Mexico as they did other western countries. Riot police and the army brutally suppressed the turmoil. The riots and the government's response received worldwide attention because the summer Olympic games were held in Mexico City that year. Despite widespread criticism, the PRI remained in power.

From time to time, the government faced rebel uprisings. One outbreak occurred in Chiapas, a state in southern Mexico which had a large Native American population. Discontent was high there because most Indians had benefited little from the nation's economic growth. In 1994, rebels took up arms and challenged the government. They demanded land reforms and rights for Native Americans. By skillfully using the media, the Chiapas rebels became international heroes. Yet they failed to achieve their goals.

Political Reforms Under pressure from all sides, the PRI made some election reforms in the 1990s. The PRI's hold on power was further undermined by reports of political corruption, repeated drug scandals, and splits within the party's own ranks. As a result, the PRI lost its majority in the national legislature. And in 2000, opposition candidate Vicente Fox won election as Mexico's president, breaking the PRI's long tenure of power. Fox, a rancher with entrepreneurial instincts, promised change, including more rapid economic growth, the reduction of poverty by one third, and a sweeping assault on corrupt police, judges, and politicians.

Economic Ups and Downs After World War II, Mexico pushed ahead with efforts to foster import substitution, reduce foreign influence, and expand agriculture. To promote industry, the government worked closely with private businesses. It invested in building roads, dams, and ports. It also encouraged tourism.

From the 1940s to the early 1980s, both manufacturing and agriculture made huge gains. Mexico's economy became the second largest in Latin America after that of Brazil. This growth turned Mexico from an agricultural society into a mostly urban, industrial society. In the late 1970s, new oil discoveries and rising oil prices spurred an economic boom.

In the 1980s, however, global economic trends worked against Mexico. A worldwide recession, falling oil prices, and rising interest rates plunged the country deeply into debt. Like other debtor nations, Mexico cut spending on social and other programs so that it could make its debt payments. To spur economic recovery, the government reduced barriers to foreign businesses and privatized some industries.

Poverty and Prosperity As the 1900s came to an end, Mexico remained a disturbing mix of prosperity and poverty. *Maquiladoras* (mah kee luh DOHR uhs), or assembly plants owned by multinational corporations, flourished along Mexico's northern border. These plants used cheap Mexican labor to assemble imported parts for cars and electronic goods. Finished products were then exported to the United States, Japan, and elsewhere. The *maquiladoras* provided jobs for many Mexicans—most of them women.

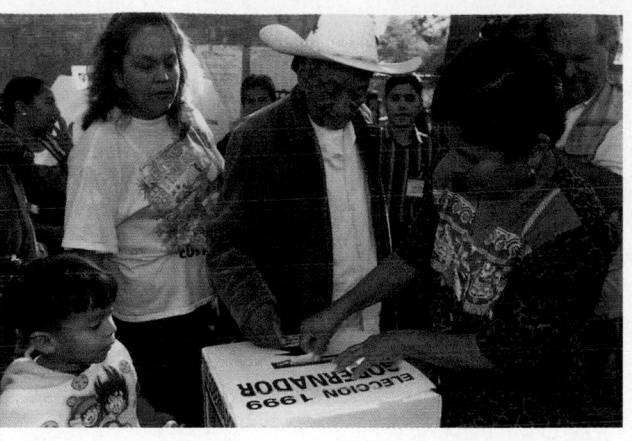

Mexican Democracy
As the 1990s came to an end, it seemed possible that Mexico's government would no longer be dominated by a single party. Above, a husband and wife drop their votes into the ballot box.

Theme: Political and Social Systems Why is it important for a democracy to have at least two major political parties?

Block Scheduling Support

Have students view *Unfinished Business,* Program 5 in the video documentary series entitled *The Buried Mirror: Reflections on Spain and the New World.* In the hour-long program, host Carlos Fuentes identifies Latin America's problems today as the "4Ds"—debt, drugs, development, and democracy. He suggests that to solve these problems, Latin Americans must find their own solutions rooted in their culture, which combines Spanish, Indian, and African influences. Change will come not from the governments that tie themselves to foreign models or influence but from the society itself.

Ask students who view the film to outline the many difficult challenges facing Latin America today. Then, ask them to summarize the solutions that the film offers. Finally, use their outlines and summaries as the basis for a class discussion. (*The Buried Mirror: Reflections on Spain and the New World,* produced by Sogetel in association with the Smithsonian Institution, is a Films Incorporated Video.)

Caption Answer

If there is only one party, then people do not have a real choice. If there are two or more political parties, then the voters have two or more candidates to choose from.

Activity

Connections to Economics

Evaluating Data Write the data in the table below on the chalkboard. You may wish to have students organize the data in graphic form to help them see trends. Inform students that NAFTA went into effect on January 1, 1994. Then, have students use the data to answer the questions that follow.

Year	Mexican Exports To U.S.*	U.S. Exports To Mexico*
1989	27.6	25.0
1990	30.8	28.4
1991	31.9	33.3
1992	35.9	40.6
1993	40.7	41.6
1994	48.0	49.1
1995	61.7	46.3
1996	74.3	56.8
1997	85.9	71.4
1998	94.6	78.7

*(estimated, in billions of dollars)

(1) In what years did Mexico have a trade deficit with the United States? *(1991, 1992, 1993, 1994)* (2) In what year did Mexico import the most from the United States? *(1998)* (3) In what year did Mexican exports to the United States increase the most? *(1995)* (4) How would you describe the effect of NAFTA on trade between Mexico and the United States? *(Since NAFTA went into effect, Mexico has begun to export far more to the U.S. than the U.S. exports to Mexico.)* ✳

Customize for . . .
Heterogeneous Groups

Relating Cause and Effect In 1990, there were an estimated 74,000 refugees from Nicaragua, El Salvador, and Guatemala living in the United States. Assign students to select one of these three Central American countries and to describe the political, social, and economic conditions that would have caused thousands of people to leave their countries and move to the United States. *(Reteaching)* ✳

Connections to Today

ANSWER Some feared that U.S. naval ships would be threatened by Chinese pilots. Others were more worried about the stability of the Panamanian government.

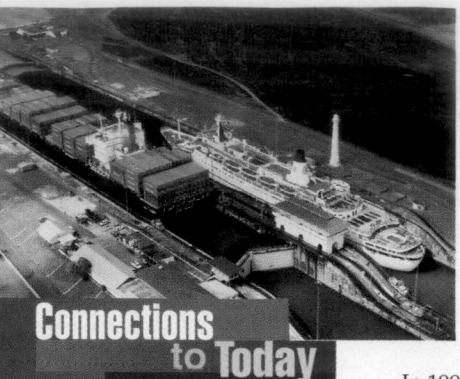

Connections to Today

The China-Panama Connection

In the 1970s, the United States hoped for the best when it agreed to give up control of the Panama Canal at the end of the century. But in 1999, some United States leaders were not so optimistic. Senator Trent Lott sounded the alarm that "U.S. naval ships will be at the mercy of Chinese-controlled pilots."

The root of his fear was that the Panamanian government had made a deal with a company based in Hong Kong to run two ports near the canal entrances. Most observers felt that Senator Lott's fears were groundless. After all, the Hong Kong company had an impressive record in managing 19 other ports around the world.

Of more concern, thought some observers, was the fragile Panamanian government. In 1999, Mireya Moscoso took office as president. Her late husband had been elected president three times. He was also deposed by the Panamanian army three times.

Theme: Continuity and Change Why did the change in canal ownership cause some to worry?

Still, environmental problems in the plants, plus the government's refusal to let workers organize, led to labor protests.

Despite economic growth, most Mexicans remained poor. The economy could not produce enough jobs to keep up with rapid population growth. Wealth continued to be unequally distributed. The top 10 percent of the people controlled over 40 percent of the wealth, while the poorest 20 percent earned less than 2 percent of national income.

Links to the United States Mexico has felt the powerful influence of its northern neighbor. In the 1930s, Mexico set out to reduce economic influence through import substitution. Yet the nation continued to rely on investment capital from the United States. In 1995, a $20 billion loan from the United States bailed Mexico out of an economic crisis.

In 1993, Mexico, the United States, and Canada signed NAFTA. Supporters claimed that the free-trade association would boost prosperity by lowering trade barriers, thus opening up a huge regional market. NAFTA did bring some new business and investments to Mexico. At the same time, however, it hurt Mexican manufacturers, who could not compete with a flood of goods from the United States.

Issues such as illegal immigration and drug smuggling created tension between Mexico and the United States. Some employers in the United States, especially commercial farmers, relied on Mexican migrant workers to harvest crops for low wages. But as growing numbers of Mexicans crossed the border illegally, many people in the United States came to resent the newcomers. Despite their differences, both nations cooperated on solving issues of international concern such as environmental problems.

War and Peace in Central America

In Central America, unrest threatened the ruling elite of military, business, and landowning interests. Discontent grew in the cities and among rural Indian communities that had long suffered from poverty and oppression. Fearing the spread of communism, the United States intervened repeatedly in the region.

Nicaragua Along with Mexico and Cuba, Nicaragua was one of three Latin American countries to have a genuine revolution in the twentieth century. From 1936 to 1979, the Somoza family ruled—and looted—Nicaragua. Due to their strong anti-communist stand, they enjoyed United States backing. In the 1970s, various groups opposed to Anastasio Somoza joined forces. They called themselves Sandinistas after Augusto Sandino, a revolutionary of the 1930s. Like Sandino, they were reform-minded nationalists. The Sandinistas included a large number of women and leftist students.

In 1979, the revolutionaries ousted Somoza and set out to reshape Nicaragua. Under Sandinista president Daniel Ortega, they introduced land reform and other socialist policies. Fearing that Nicaragua would become "another Cuba," President Ronald Reagan secretly backed the contras—guerrillas who fought against the Sandinistas.

A long civil war weakened the economy but did not unseat the Sandinistas. Other Central American countries finally helped both sides to reach a compromise and stop the fighting. In 1990, Violeta Chamorro, a moderate, won election as president. The Sandinistas peacefully handed over power but kept control of the army.

Over the next decade, rival political parties, including the Sandinistas, competed for power in Nicaragua. Although the economy has grown as exports have dramatically risen, many people remained poor, unemployment was still high, and the country had a heavy debt burden. In 1998,

Hurricane Strikes!

In October 1998, Hurricane Mitch hovered just off the coast of Honduras for two days, dumping a torrent of rain. Then, Mitch swept across much of Central America. Widespread flooding and mud-slides killed thousands, making this hurricane the deadliest Atlantic storm in 200 years.

Fast Facts

- Some regions received up to two feet of rain a day during Hurricane Mitch.

- It has been estimated that it will take more than 15 years for the economies of Central America to recover.

- Earlier deforestation contributed to the devastating mudslides.

The Impact of Hurricane Mitch

Nation	Deaths	Property Loss (estimated)
Honduras	5,657	$3,705 million
Nicaragua	3,045	$969 million
Guatemala	268	$698 million
El Salvador	240	$334 million

Source: Inter-American Development Bank

Hurricane Mitch dealt a devastating social and economic blow to Central America, whose nations were just recovering from decades of civil war.

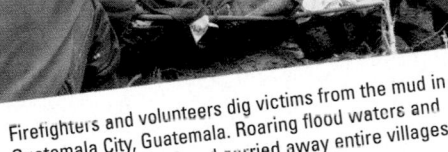

Firefighters and volunteers dig victims from the mud in Guatemala City, Guatemala. Roaring flood waters and fast-flowing rivers of mud carried away entire villages.

A resident of Mango Bay, Honduras, sal-vages what he can from his home. Almost 130,000 homes across Central America were destroyed or damaged, leaving an estimated 460,000 people homeless.

Portfolio Assessment

Use the Internet or library resources to find out more about a recent hurricane. Then, prepare a class presentation on its impact. If possible, include first-person accounts or photographs of the hurricane you have selected.

Test Preparation

Have students read the second paragraph under "Nicaragua" on the opposite page, and then complete the sentence below.

When President Reagan expressed the fear that Nicaragua would become "another Cuba," he meant that he was afraid that Nicaragua would

(A) become a communist country.

B become a dictatorship.

C be ruled by Fidel Castro.

D be ruled by Somoza.

Bell Ringer Have students look at a relief map of Honduras to find out why defor-ested areas of the country would have been so hard-hit by mud-slides. *(Much of the country is mountainous.)*

Background Connections to Today

Slow Progress More than a year after the storm, much remained to be done to repair the damage in Honduras. Many roads still awaited repairs, and bridges, schools, homes, and businesses still needed to be rebuilt. Progress was particularly slow in the region called Mosquitia, where many of the Miskito people live. Part of the problem was that the area's infrastructure was poor even before the storm. Also, it is a low-lying coastal area, and so it was especially hard hit. Unfortunately, greed and cor-ruption seemed to be affecting recon-struction as well. Local people claimed that town and village officials had pock-eted relief funds and kept supplies for their own use. They also complained about shoddy work.

Activity Cooperative Learning

Following Up Have students work in small groups to find out what progress has been made on reconstruction in the various Central American nations that were hit by Hurricane Mitch. Have the groups present their findings to the class.

Portfolio Assessment Rubrics

Share rubrics with students.

Attempted The presentation is incomplete.

Minimal The presentation demonstrates adequate research and identifies the impact of a recent hurricane, but without specific details.

Adequate The presentation demon-strates extensive research, identifies the impact of a recent hurricane, and uses specific details.

Exemplary The presentation demon-strates extensive research and pre-paration, fully outlines the social and economic impact of a recent hurricane, and communicates the human dimen-sions of the tragedy.

Virtual Field Trip
www.phschool.com

Honduras This Week
Tegucigalpa, Honduras

To learn more about culture and current events in Central America, use the Internet address above to link to the online newspaper *Honduras This Week*.

Central American Street Scene
In this colorful folk art painting by Jorge Ferman, one can learn much about the culture of the Central American country of Honduras. Note especially the architecture, clothing, landscape, and plant life in the painting.

Theme: Geography and History What does the painting suggest about the climate and landscape of Central America?

Hurricane Mitch, one of the most destructive storms of the century, added to the nation's woes by devastating much of the country. As the new century began, both developed democracy and real prosperity still lay in the future.

Guatemala Fearing growing communist influence and threats to American interests, the United States helped oust Guatemala's reformist government in 1954. Although the military and landowners regained power, they faced constant challenges from leftist guerrilla movements. During decades of civil war, the government routinely tortured and murdered critics, including student and labor leaders.

The chief victims were the Native American majority, some of whom had taken part in antigovernment actions. An estimated 30,000 died during the 1980s alone. Some were killed fighting for the land they tilled but did not own. Others were shot as military forces exterminated whole villages.

Although a civilian government took power in the mid-1980s, the military remained a powerful force behind the scenes. The United States pressured the government to halt the fighting. In 1996, the 30-year civil war finally ended when the government and guerrillas signed a peace agreement that recognized the rights of the Guatemalan people.

El Salvador The ruling class of military officials and wealthy landowners was also challenged in El Salvador. Here, as elsewhere in Latin America, reformers and revolutionaries found new support in the Catholic Church. In the 1970s, some Church leaders in Latin America abandoned traditional ties to the elite and instead pressed for reform. Inspired by the ideas of liberation theology, Salvadoran priests preached that God was "a God of justice and love who acts on the side of the poor and oppressed." Archbishop Oscar Romero even proclaimed: "When all peaceful means have been exhausted, the church considers insurrection moral and justified."

During a vicious 12-year civil war, right-wing death squads slaughtered church workers, student and labor leaders, and anyone else thought to sympathize with leftists. In 1980, Archbishop Romero fell victim to the fighting, gunned down as he celebrated mass in a chapel. Meanwhile, the United States pressed the government to make some reforms. However, it also provided weapons and other aid to help the military battle rebel guerrillas.

Finally, in 1991, both sides agreed to a UN-brokered peace. After elections were held, former enemies met in the congress, not in battle. However, problems remained. The civil war had ravaged the economy, which still depended on a single export—coffee. Despite large-scale aid from the International Monetary Fund, El Salvador remained a developing nation with a fragile democracy.

Struggle in Haiti

Like other Latin American countries, the Caribbean nation of Haiti has endured a history of dictatorial rule and rebellion. Since independence in 1804, a small upper class controlled the economy and ruled the rural poor majority.

From Dictatorship to Democracy From 1957 to 1971, Dr. François Duvalier (doo vahl YAY) ruled Haiti. "Papa Doc," as he was called, used his brutal secret police, the *Tontons Macoutes,* to crush opposition and terrorize the people. His son, "Baby Doc," was driven into exile in 1986, but a succession of military leaders then ruled the island nation.

In 1990, in its freest election in recent times, Haiti chose Jean-Bertrand Aristide as president. A former Catholic priest, supporter of liberation theology, and hero to the poor, Aristide hoped to advance his country at least "from misery to dignified poverty." Overthrown by a military coup and restored when the United States threatened military action, the Haitian leader proclaimed that "This is a day on which democracy rises, never to set."

An Uncertain Future Despite Aristide's pledge, however, he had little success in imposing meaningful reforms. He and his successors faced many problems. The poorest state in the Western Hemisphere, Haiti lacked adequate roads, electricity, and other services. The weakness of the government discouraged foreign investment, while intense party rivalries, street demonstrations, and soaring crime all pointed toward difficult times ahead.

Haiti was only one of many Central American and Caribbean countries that faced a devastating combination of natural and social problems. Almost all were affected by rapidly growing populations. On average, their economies produced roughly a tenth as much per person as the United States economy did. And in most of them, a skewed distribution of wealth put most of the productive land in the hands of one or two percent of the citizens. Poverty and social conflict were widespread consequences.

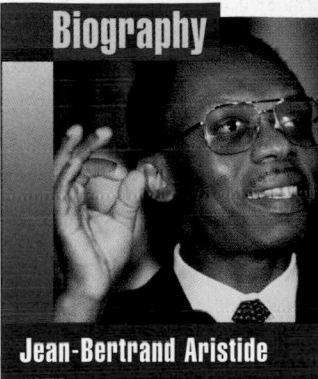

Biography

Jean-Bertrand Aristide
1953—

"Can we continue to find this situation of violence that is imposed on the poor normal?" asked Jean-Bertrand Aristide in a 1982 sermon. "No. We must end this regime," the young priest concluded.

In September 1988, an armed group of Haitian security forces, known as the *Tontons Macoutes,* attacked Aristide and his followers in church. They set fire to the church and killed a number of Aristide's supporters. Aristide escaped, but he was soon forced to resign as a priest. Two years later, Aristide became a presidential candidate—in part, to bring the killers to justice.

Theme: Impact of the Individual Why did Aristide become involved in politics?

SECTION 3 Assessment

Recall
1. **(a)** Lázaro Cárdenas, p. 944 **(b)** PRI, p. 944 **(c)** Chiapas, p. 945 **(d)** Vicente Fox, p. 945 **(e)** Sandinistas, p. 946 **(f)** Violeta Chamorro, p. 946 **(g)** Oscar Romero, p. 948 **(h)** Jean-Bertrand Aristide, p. 949 **2. (a)** *ejido,* p. 944 **(b)** *maquiladora,* p. 945 **(c)** contra, p. 946

Comprehension
3. **(a)** PRI made election reforms in the 1990s; opposition candidate was elected as Mexico City's mayor; opposition candidate Vicente Fox was elected president of Mexico. **(b)** NAFTA linked Mexico to the prosperous markets of the United States and Canada, bringing some economic growth. **4. (a)** reformers and revolutionaries against wealthy landowners and the military government **(b)** Both sides agreed to a UN-brokered peace. **5.** Possible answer: a history of dictatorial rule and rebellion; poorest nation in Western Hemisphere; soaring crime; intense party rivalries

Critical Thinking and Writing
6. There will be a better prospect for peace in Central America because the United States will probably not consider rebellions or shifts toward socialism to be as threatening. 7. Haiti has often been ruled by dictators representing a small upper class. From 1957 to 1986, the Duvaliers used brutal force to crush opposition. In 1990, Aristide was voted in, but a military coup removed him from power soon after. Aristide was returned to power but unable to achieve meaningful reform. Haiti faced devastating natural and social problems, creating poverty and social conflict.

SECTION 3 Assessment

Recall
1. **Identify: (a)** Lázaro Cárdenas, **(b)** PRI, **(c)** Chiapas, **(d)** Vicente Fox, **(e)** Sandinistas, **(f)** Violeta Chamorro, **(g)** Oscar Romero, **(h)** Jean-Bertrand Aristide.
2. **Define: (a)** *ejido,* **(b)** *maquiladora,* **(c)** contra.

Comprehension
3. **(a)** How has Mexican politics changed in recent years? **(b)** Identify recent developments in the Mexican economy.
4. **(a)** Who were the opposing sides in El Salvador's civil war? **(b)** How did the civil war end?
5. What problems have hindered the development of democracy in Haiti?

Critical Thinking and Writing
6. **Predicting Consequences** How might the collapse of the Soviet Union and the end of the Cold War affect relations between the United States and the nations of Central America?
7. **Identifying Main Ideas** Reread the subsection Struggle in Haiti. Then, write the main idea of each paragraph in the subsection.

Activity

Analyzing a Newspaper Article Find a newspaper article on a recent election in Central America. Read it to find out the "Five W's": *who, what, where, when,* and *why.* Write down questions about the article and answers to those questions using information you learn from the article.

Chapter 37 **949**

Activity Rubrics

Share rubrics with students.

Attempted Questions and answers are incomplete.

Minimal Questions are asked, but answers do not reflect information in the article.

Adequate Questions and answers are complete and reflect information in the article.

Exemplary Questions and answers are insightful, very well written, and provide extensive information.

EXPLORING THE HUMAN DRAMA — Human Drama Note

Rigoberta Menchú Menchú grew up in a poor farming village in the Guatemalan highlands. The land was so poor that villagers could not support themselves by farming alone, so children and adults alike worked part of the year on coffee or cotton plantations. Wages were tiny and living conditions abominable. While Menchú was a child, one brother died of malnutrition and another of poisoning from the pesticide used on the crops. That was not the end of tragedy in her life, however. Members of Menchú's family later became activists for human rights for indigenous people, which made them targets of the Guatemalan government. Soldiers tortured her brother and other villagers and then burned them alive. Soldiers also caused a fire at the Spanish embassy where her father and others were protesting, killing everyone inside. Her mother was tortured, raped, mutilated, and left to die slowly. Menchú continued working for the cause, and in 1992, received the Nobel Peace Prize. Her story is told in the book *I, Rigoberta Menchú; an Indian Woman in Guatemala* and in the film *When the Mountains Tremble.*

Biography

ANSWER to end violence aimed at the poor and to bring murderers to justice

LESSON PLAN

1. Focus Juan Perón became a popular dictator by appealing to Argentine nationalism and providing benefits to the working class. For both Argentina and Brazil, erratic economic swings have contributed to political and social unrest. In both nations, periods of dictatorship and military rule have limited the growth of democracy.

2. Instruct Assign half the class to study Argentina and the other half to study Brazil. Have students work on their own to outline the major developments in their assigned country. Students' outlines should address the following issues: cultural background, social divisions, economic strengths and weaknesses, causes and effects of dictatorship, and efforts at democracy. After students have finished their outlines, organize the class into small groups. Make sure that each group consists of students who have studied both countries. Assign the groups to compare the two South American nations and to make notes on similarities and differences. Conclude the lesson by conducting a class discussion on this topic.

3. Assess Ask students to use what they have learned about Argentina and Brazil to speculate on what they think will occur in those nations in the years ahead.

4. Reteach If students' **Assess** activity does not reflect adequate understanding of the lesson, you might assign the *Guide to the Essentials* or the *Interactive Student Tutorial CD-ROM* for this section.

Caption Answer

The Peróns appealed to Argentine nationalism. They also raised wages, strengthened labor unions, and enacted social reform.

Reading Focus

- What challenges has democracy faced in Argentina?
- How did Brazil's government change in recent times?
- Why did Brazil's "economic miracle" have limited success?

Vocabulary

favela
plebiscite
squatter

Taking Notes

Make a Venn diagram like the one below. Use it to record important facts about recent developments in Argentina and Brazil. In the middle section, list things that are true of both nations.

ARGENTINA • Facts revealed about the "dirty war" — • Democratic elections restored in 1980s — **BRAZIL** • People voted against a monarchy

Main Idea Both Argentina and Brazil have overcome serious political and economic challenges as they became modernized.

Setting the Scene One year at Rio de Janeiro's annual carnival parade, a float was based on the story of *Alice's Adventures in Wonderland.* After Alice shrank to tiny size and then grew very tall, a caterpillar on the float asked her, "Who are you?"

Alice replied: "I no longer know who I am. First, I was small like Brazil, underdeveloped, with many problems. Suddenly I grew, became a giant, a great power, but with many problems."

The caterpillar reassured Alice: "I am a caterpillar, but I turn myself into a butterfly. This could happen to you." The float expressed optimism for Brazil, a nation that has experienced many changes over recent decades.

Brazil is one of a dozen independent nations of South America. Here we will look at the two largest South American republics—Argentina and Brazil. History, geography, and other forces have shaped each country's efforts to develop a stable government and a strong, modern economy.

Dictatorship and Democracy in Argentina

In the early 1900s, Argentina was the largest Spanish-speaking nation in the world and the richest nation in Latin America. It had a fairly stable government dominated by the wealthy elite. Its economy was fed by exports of beef and wheat, mostly to Britain. Argentina attracted millions of immigrants, many of whom worked in the factories of Buenos Aires. Then the Great Depression struck. For the next 50 years, Argentina was plagued by economic crises, social unrest, and military rule.

Juan and Eva Perón
Despite their authoritarian rule, the charismatic Peróns captured the imagination of working-class Argentinians. Years later, audiences around the world were captivated by *Evita,* a musical play based on the life of Mrs. Perón.

Theme: Impact of the Individual How did the Peróns win popular support?

Perón in Power In 1946, Juan Perón was elected president. He appealed to Argentine nationalism by limiting foreign-owned businesses and promoting import substitution. By boosting wages, strengthening labor unions, and enacting social reforms, Perón won the loyalty of the working classes.

Perón was helped by his glamorous wife Eva Duarte Perón, who had risen from poverty to fame as an actress. As Perón's chief aide, she had clinics built and gave money to the sick and

950 *Chapter 37*

Resource Directory

Teaching Resources
Creative Teaching Activities Creative Teaching Activities booklet, p. 166
Guided Reading and Review Unit 8 booklet, p. 98

unemployed. To secure more votes for her husband, she helped women gain the right to vote. Meanwhile, she used public funds to enjoy an extravagant lifestyle. "You, too, will have clothes as rich as mine," she promised the poor women of Argentina.

While Juan Perón wooed the urban poor, his authoritarian government stifled opposition. Many educated people fled Argentina. Perón's policies led to a huge debt and soaring inflation. In 1955, Perón was ousted by a military coup and forced into exile.

Military Rule For two decades, the military was in and out of power, and supporters of Perón urged a return to his policies. In 1973, an aging Perón did return, and he was again elected president. His new wife, Isabel, was chosen vice president. When he died the next year, Isabel Perón became president—the first woman head of state in the Western Hemisphere. As she faced economic and political crises, terrorists on the left and on the right disrupted the country. In 1976, the military took power.

To combat leftist guerrillas, the army waged a "dirty war," terrorizing people that they claimed were enemies of the state. They tortured and murdered thousands of citizens. As many as 20,000 people disappeared after being taken from their homes. Week after week, in the Plaza de Mayo in Buenos Aires, mothers marched silently, holding pictures of their children who had disappeared. The "Mothers of the Plaza de Mayo" gained worldwide attention.

In 1982, the military hoped to mask economic troubles by seizing the British-ruled Falkland Islands. Argentina had long claimed these islands, which it called the Malvinas. The military mistakenly believed that Britain would not fight to keep the islands. In a brief but decisive war fought on land, on sea, and in the air, the British recaptured the Falklands. Defeat undermined the power and prestige of Argentina's military, and it was forced to hold free elections.

Democracy Restored In 1983, an elected government restored democracy to Argentina. Despite economic setbacks and scandals of corruption, democratic rule survived. Gradually, more and more facts emerged about the military's "dirty war" against the people. Nearly all who disappeared were murdered—often by being thrown into the ocean from aircraft.

In the 1990s, Argentina's democracy took hold and the economy grew, aided by plentiful natural resources and the highest literacy rate in Latin America. President Carlos Menem was able to cut inflation and enact government financial reforms urged by the International Monetary Fund.

Critics, however, objected to the privatization of government-run industries and noted that unemployment remained high. In some years, one in five adults was jobless. Another persistent problem was that wealth remained concentrated in the hands of a few. In 1999, Argentines elected Fernando de la Rua to the presidency. De la Rua pledged to work for better living conditions for all Argentines.

Economic Activity in Argentina

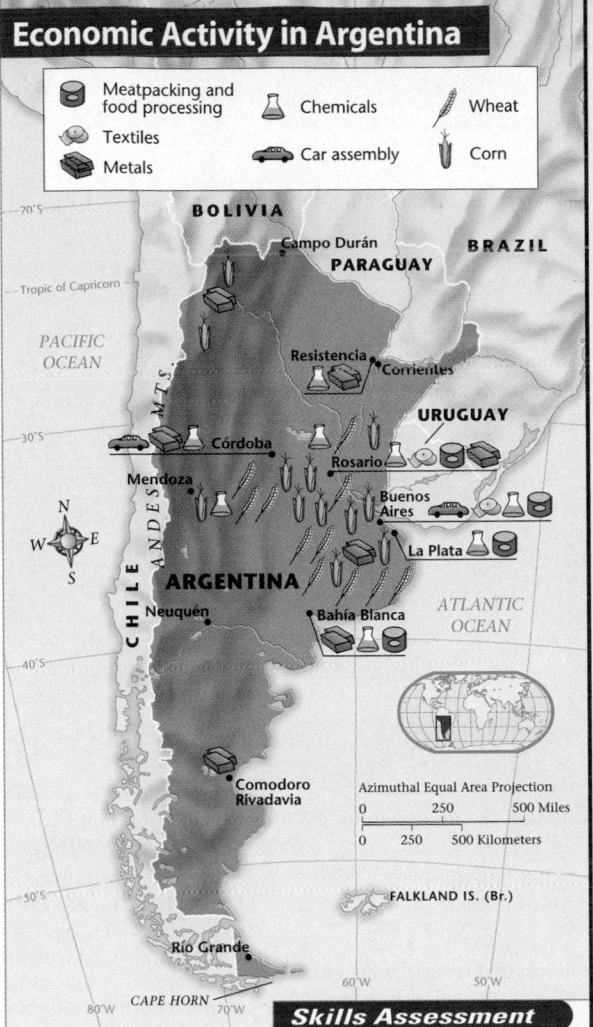

Legend:
- Meatpacking and food processing
- Textiles
- Metals
- Chemicals
- Car assembly
- Wheat
- Corn

Drawing a Map Provide students with an outline map of Brazil or have students draw their own maps of the country. Assign them to indicate the various climate zones of Brazil by doing research, devising a key, and marking the map appropriately. Have them also use various symbols to indicate Brazil's major economic resources and activities. Display finished maps around the class for all to see. Now have students compare these maps of Brazil with the population density map on the chapter opener. Ask them to compare the two maps and to offer possible explanations for the distribution of population in Brazil. ✳

Urbanization in Brazil

1994
22.4% rural
77.6% urban

2025 (estimate)
11.1% rural
88.9% urban

Source: UN Population Division

Skills Assessment

Graph The cityscape above is of São Paulo. Unlike other Latin American countries that have only one major city, Brazil has more than a dozen. **Over the years, have more Brazilians migrated *to* cities or *from* cities? How do you think this pattern affects the Brazilian economy? Explain.**

Brazil's People and Government

Brazil occupies almost half of South America. Its varied landscapes include the mighty Amazon River and the world's largest tropical forest. Northeastern Brazil, however, is an arid plain. Brazil's rich resources include minerals, timber, and rich farmlands that yield cash crops such as coffee and sugar. Geographic conditions have contributed to uneven settlement patterns. About 90 percent of Brazilians live within 200 miles of the Atlantic coast. To draw settlers inland, the government has encouraged development of the interior.

Population Unlike its South American neighbors, Brazil was settled by people from Portugal, not Spain. With a population over 173 million, the nation has more people than any of its Spanish-speaking neighbors. Brazil has a diverse society. Afonso Celso, a noted Brazilian patriot, considered this diversity to be a source of national strength. In his words, "Three elements contributed to the formation of the Brazilian people: the American Indian, the African, and the Portuguese." In the 1900s, many Japanese and Germans settled in Brazil, adding to its cultural mix.

Most Brazilians are Roman Catholic, but a growing number of people embrace evangelical Protestant faiths. Others practice Candomblè, a form of worship that blends African and Christian beliefs.

Rapid population growth and class divisions have contributed to poverty in Brazil. In the cities, where more than 75 percent of Brazilians live, the sharp contrast between rich and poor is seen everywhere. Teeming, garbage-strewn *favelas,* or slums, ring the major cities, which boast luxurious high-rise apartment buildings and wealthy shopping areas. In the *favelas* around São Paulo and Rio de Janeiro, thousands of homeless children survive on the streets without families or education.

Skills Assessment

ANSWER More have migrated to cities. The economy is probably becoming less dependent on agriculture and more dependent on industry. People in the cities are more likely to work in industry than in agriculture.

Political Instability Like its neighbors, Brazil has had its share of dictators and military rulers. They pursued modernization under the motto "order and progress."

Between 1930 and 1945, dictator Getúlio Vargas allied himself with the working poor. Like Perón in Argentina, he improved wages and workers' benefits, favored labor unions, and gave women the right to vote. The military eventually toppled Vargas, but they allowed elected presidents to rule Brazil for 20 years thereafter.

By 1964, economic problems and fear of communism led the military to take over again. The seizure of power was quietly supported by the United States, which was even willing to provide some aid to the military. The assistance was not needed. Backed by the middle and upper classes, the generals wielded enormous power. They tortured and jailed critics, censored the press, and ignored calls for social reform.

In the mid-1980s, though, the military gradually eased their grip on power. In 1989, Brazilians were finally able to vote directly for a president for the first time in 29 years. To determine if Brazil should remain a republic or return to being a monarchy, a plebiscite was held in 1993. A plebiscite is a vote in which people approve or reject a proposal. The people of Brazil voted to keep their republic.

Brazil's "Economic Miracle"

"Brazil is a country of the future, and always will be." This Brazilian saying suggests both the nation's potential and its many setbacks. For more than a century, Brazil has weathered many boom-and-bust cycles.

Early Development In the early 1900s, the huge demand for Brazilian rubber suddenly fell off, causing economic hardships. Coffee then replaced rubber as the major export. But again and again, declining prices for coffee or natural disasters wreaked havoc on the economy.

In the 1930s, Brazil moved away from dependence on a single export by diversifying its economy. Vargas encouraged industry. He built highways, hydroelectric plants, and schools. During and after World War II, industry continued to expand. In the 1950s, President Juscelino Kubitschek (zhooh suh LEE nuh KOO bih chehk) promised "fifty years of progress in five." He opened up the Amazon forest region to settlers by carving out a new capital, Brasília, hundreds of miles from the Atlantic coast.

Brazil's Economic Miracle Diversification, modernization, and foreign investments have helped Brazil's economy grow. In the picture, robots assemble cars in a Ford automotive plant in Brazil.

Theme: Economics and Technology Why did Brazil's economy suffer when it relied too much on a single export?

Background
Connections to Art

International Style President Kubitschek's decision to build a new national capital at Brasília was accompanied by a national competition to choose a design. The winner was Lucio de Costa, considered by many to be the father of modern architecture in Brazil. Costa laid out the city in the shape of an airplane and gave it a modernistic design. He worked closely with architect Oscar Niemeyer, who designed all of the city's major buildings, including the President's Palace, the Congress Building, and the cathedral.

Niemeyer and Costa were both "International Style" architects. International Style architecture made use of new structural materials such as steel, glass, and concrete. Before working on Brasília, Niemeyer had made a name for himself designing the Ministry of Education and Health in Rio de Janeiro and working on the team that designed the United Nations building in New York City.

Human Drama Note

Books About South America One of the most interesting of recent books on South America is a success story out of Colombia—*Gaviotas: A Village To Reinvent the World,* by Alan Weisman (White River Junction, Vermont: Chelsea Green Publishing, 1998). It is the story of how a group of Colombians built a viable community in the harsh environment of the country's savannas. Some of their inventions are so environmentally friendly and cost-effective that a Bogotá hospital and a housing complex have adopted them. Another book is *Makuna: Portrait of a People,* by Kaj Arhem (Washington, D.C.: Smithsonian Institution, 1998). It discusses the lifestyle of an indigenous rain forest people threatened by modern development. The book *The Elder Brothers,* by Alan Ereira (New York: Alfred A. Knopf, 1992), describes the author's encounter with Kogi civilization. The Kogi decide to break with their habit of isolation because they feel that the rest of the world needs to be warned that they are destroying themselves. The film *From the Heart of the World* is based on this book.

Caption Answer

Economic hardships resulted when demand fell.

Analyzing Primary Sources

Background
About the Primary Source

Axé is supported by donations from Brazilian businesses and by foreign donors. Its 98 employees work with more than 2,500 children. It spends about $45 a month per child, which contrasts very well with the estimated $2,000 a month that state reformatories spend on each child in their custody.

One of Axé's success stories is a youngster named Sinval, who joined the program at age 15. He had been earning small sums washing windows of cars stopped for a traffic light. His home was a shanty he shared with his mother, stepfather, and six brothers and sisters. If he returned home at night without cigarette money for his stepfather, he was beaten. Sometimes he was beaten anyway. With skills he learned through Axé, Sinval was able to get a job at a popsicle factory, and he hoped to soon have enough money to live on his own, away from the abuse.

Activity
Interpreting the Primary Source

Use this additional question to generate class discussion.
Critical Thinking: Defending a Position Which do you think is more important for the street children: building self-esteem or learning reading, writing, and job skills? Why?

Skills Tip

In a photograph, as in a painting, the central image is usually the most important. The Skills Handbook in the front of the book has a lesson that will help students with this feature.

Skills Assessment

ANSWERS **1.** A **2.** F **3. (a)** By juxtaposing poor street children next to symbols of wealth the photographer draws attention to the inequalities in São Paulo. **(b)** Society views them as problems who face "death or jail," but who can be helped to lead productive lives.

Analyzing Primary Sources

Helping the Street Children of Brazil

Poverty is a widespread problem in Brazil. Of the poor who wander the streets in search of work, food, or shelter, thousands are children. Journalist James Brooke describes Projecto Axé (Project Force), which helps Brazilian street children.

"Salvador, Brazil 1993

'Street children face two choices: death or jail,' said Cesare de Florio La Rocca, director of the program and an immigrant from Italy. 'These youths are beings in development. If we don't act here and now, it will be too late.' . . .

To compete with the lure of street life, which can be fascinating as well as deadly, Mr. La Rocca's social workers offer their own lure, Afro-Brazilian culture. . . .

When Salvador's children show interest, Axé workers offer drumming lessons in the youth corps of the city's internationally known Afro dance and drum groups . . . and culture classes at one of the city's most important Afro-Brazilian religious centers. . . .

Using activities that appeal to children, Axé builds bridges for them to leave a short-term world of the street to a world of plans for the future. 'They are assimilating life habits of discipline and punctuality,' Mr. La Rocca said. 'If a youth goes straight from the street to a job, he will fail.'

Moving beyond cultural activities, Axé offers literacy classes and apprenticeships in a recycled paper workshop and in a silk-screen T-shirt design studio. Each child taking part in activities gets three meals every weekday, bus fare, new clothes, and a spending allowance of $8 a week. In existence for three years, Axé says that last year it helped 768 Axé children reestablish family links and return home. In a measure of growing business interest in the program . . . a local construction company has started taking older Axé boys as apprentice laborers."

—James Brooke, *The New York Times*

Street children wash their clothes in a public fountain in São Paulo, Brazil.

Skills Tip

Photographers sometimes combine two contrasting images in a single frame to convey a message. This technique is called juxtaposition.

Skills Assessment

1. La Rocca believes that street youths who learn discipline are more likely to
   A hold down a job.
   B survive on the streets.
   C get along with others.
   D commit crimes.

2. Projecto Axé tries to help street children by offering
   E shelter.
   F apprenticeships.
   G family counseling.
   H medical care.

3. **Critical Thinking Analyzing Primary Sources** **(a)** What point is the photographer trying to make? **(b)** Based on both the primary source and the photograph, what assumptions can you make about the street children and how society views them?

Resource Directory

Teaching Resources
Skill Application Activity *Predicting Consequences,* Unit 8 booklet, p. 103
Analyzing Primary Sources Chapter Extension Activities booklet, p. 88
Section Quiz Unit 8 booklet, p. 99
Geography Quiz Unit 8 booklet, p. 104
Chapter Test Forms A, B, and C Unit 8 booklet, pp. 105–109
Answer Key Unit 8 booklet, pp. 110–125

Technology
Interactive Student Tutorial CD-ROM Ch. 37
Computer Test Bank Ch. 37

Impressive Growth "Power in the world," said one Brazilian leader, "is a great nation that has territory, population, wealth, financial resources, technology, material goods, minerals." Brazil had almost all of these. Under the military, experts ran the economy, which for a time chalked up impressive growth. Brazil began producing everything from steel and cars to shoes. People talked of Brazil's "economic miracle," like those in postwar Germany or Japan. The miracle enriched a few. To most Brazilians, however, it brought little or no benefit.

Economic Challenges In the 1980s, Brazil, like other developing nations, faced a host of economic problems—from inflation fed by higher oil prices to a staggering debt. Population growth and migration strained the government's ability to provide services as millions of people flooded Brazil's major cities. Conditions for the poor worsened when the government cut spending in response to the debt crisis. Despite environmental concerns, economic development of the Amazon region continued.

One of the most persistent economic problems in Brazil was the unequal distribution of land. Less than 3 percent of the population owned more than 50 percent of the land, much of which remained unused. In protest, some Brazilians formed an organization called the Landless Movement. This group urged peasants to become squatters, or people who settle on land that they do not own. Violent clashes erupted between the squatters and the landowners.

In the 1990s, President Fernando Henrique Cardoso, a respected economist, provided strong leadership for Brazil. His policies promoted rapid economic growth and helped to limit inflation. In response to the Landless Movement, he promised to distribute land to nearly 300,000 families. While landowners opposed the president's policy, others accused Cardoso of not doing enough for the poor. Critics of the president also objected to the privatization of state-run industries, and many were very concerned about high unemployment rates.

Looking Ahead

In recent years, Brazil produced two fifths of Latin America's output and numbered among the top ten economies in the world. With ample human and natural resources, Brazil was determined to become an economic superpower—and to become the country of the future today.

SECTION 4 Assessment

Recall

1. **Identify:** (a) Juan Perón, (b) Eva Perón, (c) Isabel Perón, (d) "dirty war," (e) Falklands, (f) Carlos Menem, (g) Getúlio Vargas, (h) Brasília.
2. **Define:** (a) *favela*, (b) plebiscite, (c) squatter.

Comprehension

3. (a) How have dictatorships affected Argentina? (b) What steps did the nation take toward democracy during the 1980s and 1990s?
4. Why did military rulers seize power in Brazil?

5. (a) Describe the Brazilian economic miracle. (b) What problems have threatened Brazil's economy since the 1980s?

Critical Thinking and Writing

6. **Analyzing Information** What benefits and drawbacks might result from building a "cult of personality" around figures like Juan and Eva Perón?
7. **Comparing** Review the political developments that occurred in Brazil and Argentina between 1945 and the 1980s. Were the political conditions generally similar or different? Explain.

SECTION 4 Assessment

Recall

1. (a) Juan Perón, p. 950 (b) Eva Perón, p. 950 (c) Isabel Peron, p. 951 (d) "dirty war," p. 951 (e) Falklands, p. 951 (f) Carlos Menem, p. 951 (g) Getúlio Vargas, p. 953 (h) Brasília, p. 953 2. (a) *favela*, p. 952 (b) plebiscite, p. 953 (c) squatter, p. 955

Comprehension

3. (a) Perón's policies created huge debt and soaring inflation. Under the military's "dirty war" in the 1970s, thousands of people disappeared, were tortured, or murdered on suspicion of being enemies of the state. "Mothers of the Plaza de Mayo" gained worldwide recognition for the situation. (b) It elected a government and restored democracy. 4. because of economic problems and the fear of communism 5. (a) After World War II, Brazil experienced impressive economic growth under military rule. Brazil produced everything from steel and cars to shoes. It enriched some but brought no benefits to most. (b) inflation, foreign debt, and rapid population growth

Critical Thinking and Writing

6. Possible answer: Charismatic leaders can inspire people to work hard for the common good. But people may become too devoted to such leaders and overlook their shortcomings, misdeeds, or even criminal acts. 7. Students will probably think that conditions were similar, since both countries experienced dictatorships, military rule, and democratically elected governments.

CHAPTER **37** **Review and Assessment**

Creating a Chapter Summary

As a reteaching opportunity, pair a more able student with a less able student to complete this chapter summary.

Possible answers: **Religion:** Catholicism —liberation theology; Protestant groups **Economy:** local industry; end of single import dependency **Social:** extreme poverty; human rights violations; urbanization; women—voting, in politics **Political:** left vs. right; military dictatorships; revolutions; democracy

Building Vocabulary

1–5. Sentences should show a clear understanding of the meanings of the terms.

Recalling Key Facts

6. In most countries, a small group of people held almost all the wealth, while most people lived in abject poverty. This situation caused social discontent.

7. They outlawed political parties, censored the press, closed universities, and imprisoned and executed opponents.

8. After Fidel Castro took power in a revolution, he nationalized foreign-owned businesses and turned to the Soviet Union for support.

9. The *maquiladoras* are assembly plants—located in Mexico and owned by multinational corporations—in which Mexicans assemble imported parts to make finished goods. They provided jobs for many poor Mexicans, but caused environmental problems and had few protections for workers.

10. **(a)** a military coup **(b)** The threat of American military action returned him to power.

11. Free elections were held, and a civilian government took power.

12. No. Most Brazilians are poor and landless.

Critical Thinking and Writing

13. Possible answer: The rich often have greater political power than the poor and can block democratic reform.

14. **(a)** Rain forests play an important role in removing carbon dioxide from the atmosphere and replenishing oxygen. They provide a habitat for thousands of species of animals, contain plants that may be medicinally valuable, and are home to native peoples

---

Creating a Chapter Summary

Make a concept web like the partially completed model below. Fill in the blank circles. Add branches and circles as needed.

For additional review and enrichment activities, see the interactive version of *World History* available on the Web and on CD-ROM.

Web Site Self-Test
For practice test questions for Chapter 37, see **www.phschool.com**.

Building Vocabulary

Review the meanings of the terms below. For each term, write a sentence that includes the term.

1. import substitution
2. liberation theology
3. literacy rate
4. embargo
5. squatter

Recalling Key Facts

6. How did the distribution of wealth in Latin America cause problems after World War II?

7. How did military regimes affect nations such as Argentina and Chile?

8. Why did relations between the United States and Cuba worsen after 1959?

9. Describe the *maquiladoras* and their effect on Mexico.

10. **(a)** Who forced Jean-Bertrand Aristide from power in Haiti? **(b)** Who returned him to power?

11. What steps did Argentina take toward democratic rule in the 1980s?

12. Has economic growth benefited all Brazilians? Explain.

Critical Thinking and Writing

13. **Drawing Conclusions** How can a wide gap between rich and poor make it difficult for democracy to flourish?

14. **Recognizing Points of View** Environmentalists have called on Brazil to halt destruction of the Amazon rain forest. **(a)** Why do environmentalists take this view? **(b)** Why do some people think that it is unfair for developed nations to urge developing nations to protect the environment?

15. **Linking Past and Present** How does Latin America's colonial past help to explain the uneven distribution of land that is common in much of the region today?

16. **Connecting to Geography (a)** How do geography and climate benefit economic growth in Latin America? **(b)** How do they hinder economic growth?

17. **Making Generalizations** Do you think the general trend in Latin America in the 1980s and 1990s was toward democracy or toward dictatorship? Explain.

---

whose way of life would be threatened by development. **(b)** Many of the developed nations have long since cleared their forests, and the developing nations have an immediate need to develop the land because of economic pressure.

15. In colonial times, most of the land was in the hands of a very small number of people of European descent.

16. Possible answer: **(a)** South America, for example, has huge amounts of land suitable for ranching and farming. It has vast mineral and timber resources. In many places, the climate is mild. The continent's mountains offer the potential for development of ski resorts and other tourist attractions,

while many coastal areas also attract tourists. The warm sunny islands of the Caribbean make them ideal for tourism, as well. **(b)** South America's dense rain forests are difficult to develop, and the climate is oppressive. Southern South America has a harsh climate, as do the highest parts of the Andes. Parts of Latin America are subject to frequent hurricanes and earthquakes. Many islands of the Caribbean have few natural resources needed for economic development.

17. Students will probably answer democracy. They should back up their choices with examples.

Read the news article below about the 1996 visit of Pope John Paul II to Nicaragua. Then, answer the questions that follow.

"MANAGUA, Nicaragua (Feb. 7, 1996)— Pope John Paul on Wednesday hailed Central America's transformation from superpower battleground to peaceful democracy, saying the change showed the hand of God in human history. In impromptu remarks at the end of a joyful open-air Mass celebrated before more than 150,000 cheering supporters in a lakeside plaza, John Paul . . . said, 'Today we can see that you are the master of your own human, Christian, Nicaraguan destiny.' The crowd gathered beneath the tropical blue sky roared 'Pope, Pope, Pope' in approval and thundered its applause. . . . During his 1983 visit, the Pope was forced to shout for silence as Sandinista protesters heckled him during Mass. . . . The Pope said on arriving on Wednesday that his message remained the same as in 1983—one of peace and reconciliation. . . . Analysts say the Sandinistas, now in opposition, have no option but to play the Catholic card if they want to have a chance of winning the presidential election this year in a country where enthusiasm for the Pope has reached fever pitch."

—Reuters Information Service

18. Why do you think the pope called Nicaragua a superpower battleground?
19. **(a)** How did the response to the pope in 1996 differ from the response to him in 1983? **(b)** How can you explain the change?
20. Based on the article, what type of government did Nicaragua have in 1996? Explain.
21. What information in the article is opinion rather than fact?

Skills Tip

Note that a news article can contain both factual reporting and author commentary.

This photograph shows Cuban refugees. Use the photograph and information from the chapter to answer the following questions:

22. What land are the people probably trying to reach?
23. What means of propulsion does the raft rely on?
24. How seaworthy does the raft appear to be? Explain.
25. Why were these people willing to make this voyage?
26. What risks might they face during the voyage from Cuba?

Search the Internet to learn more about the Organization of American States. Design a brochure that includes a brief description of the group's history, a list of its current goals, and a diagram of its organizational structure.

18. Nicaragua is part of Central America, where the United States repeatedly intervened to prevent the spread of communism there.
19. **(a)** In 1983, he was heckled. In 1996, he received thunderous ovations. **(b)** Analysts said that the Sandinistas needed the support of the Catholics in order to win election.
20. democracy, because there is a reference to a presidential election
21. the pope's remark that "the change showed the hand of God in human history"; also the analyst's assessment of the need for "playing the Catholic card"

22. Florida in the United States
23. oars
24. Possible answer: not very; because it is overcrowded, rides quite low in the water, and generally looks as if it was put together with found objects
25. Possible answer: to seek freedom from an oppressive regime, to escape poverty and unemployment
26. They might face being caught leaving Cuba, dangers at sea, and the possibility of being intercepted and sent back to Cuba.

Skills Tip

When an article mentions something that may occur in the future (such as the prediction of the analysts in this article), that is a clue that it is probably an opinion, since one cannot be sure of what will happen in the future. The Skills Handbook in the front of the book has a lesson that will help students with this feature.

Unit Theme Activity

Evaluate students' Unit Theme Activities by referring to the rubrics on the unit opener page in the Teacher's Edition.

Take It to the NET

Direct students to **www.phschool.com** for links to sites that will help them get started on this assignment. Share rubrics with students.
Attempted The brochure shows little research, is poorly written and organized, and contains many mechanical errors. The diagram, if included, is poorly done.
Minimal The brochure shows some research, but is poorly written and organized, and contains some mechanical errors. The diagram is included but is messy.
Adequate The brochure shows appropriate research, is well written and organized, and contains few mechanical errors. The diagram is well executed.
Exemplary The brochure shows extensive research, is very well written and organized, and contains no mechanical errors. The diagram is very well executed.

USING THESE PAGES

The Unit-in-Brief contains the main ideas of the unit chapters. You may use the Unit-in-Brief to preview, review, or condense the contents of each chapter.

The unit time line identifies key events in each world region that took place during the time span covered by the unit.

Activity
Unit Themes

Have students review the unit themes below. Then, ask them to find examples in the time line and summary to support each theme.

Diversity Conflicts flared between ethnic groups and between old and new ways of life. Urbanization, westernization, and the women's movement challenged the traditional culture.

Economics and Technology After a long struggle for control, communist state-run economies disappeared from Europe. Advances in science and technology dramatically changed human life and thought.

Global Interaction The Cold War between the United States and the Soviet Union dominated international relations in the second half of the century. Colonial empires collapsed as emerging nations in Africa, Asia, and elsewhere won their independence.

Geography and History Economic development often caused serious damage to the natural environment. Global warming, pollution, and diminishing resources were concerns of both rich and poor nations.

Chapter 32

The World Since 1945: An Overview (1945–Present)

Since the end of World War II, the world has changed rapidly. Although we cannot yet determine the long-term impact of events of the recent past, we can identify political, social, and economic trends that have shaped the postwar years.

- The collapse of western colonial empires led to the emergence of nearly 100 new countries, mostly in Africa and Asia.
- Nuclear weapons, terrorism, and human rights are enduring issues in an increasingly interdependent world.
- Complex economic ties link the rich nations of the global North and the poor nations of the global South.
- Urbanization, modernization, women's movements, and technology have brought dramatic social changes.
- Technology has revolutionized medicine and agriculture and helped create a global, westernized popular culture.

Chapter 33

Europe and North America (1945–Present)

Within a framework of growing regional cooperation, Western Europe enjoyed tremendous economic growth after World War II. At the same time, the Cold War pitted the West, led by the United States, against the Soviet Union and its allies.

- In the postwar era, Western European nations expanded social programs and introduced the welfare state. By the 1980s, an economic slowdown forced cuts in social programs.
- The United States led world opposition to communism, pursued economic prosperity, and extended civil rights.
- Efforts to reform inefficiencies in government and the economy led to the collapse of the Soviet Union.
- After shaking off Soviet domination, nations of Eastern Europe faced economic challenges and ethnic conflicts.

Chapter 34

East Asia and Southeast Asia (1945–Present)

China, Japan, and other Asian nations have achieved varying degrees of success in their efforts to modernize. Several of these nations enjoy growing trade and other ties, linking the nations of the Pacific Rim from Asia to the Americas.

- After World War II, Japan introduced democratic reforms and by the 1960s had emerged as an economic superpower.
- Under communist rule, the People's Republic of China achieved modest economic gains while sacrificing individual political freedoms.
- The "Asian tigers"—Taiwan, Hong Kong, Singapore, and South Korea—vaulted into the class of newly industrialized nations.
- Cold War tensions sparked long, devastating conflicts in Korea, Vietnam, and Cambodia.

	1940		1955		1970
AFRICA		**1948** Apartheid is law in South Africa		**1957** Ghana gains independence	**1966** Civil war begins in Nigeria
THE AMERICAS		**1946** Perón becomes president of Argentina	**1954** *Brown* v. *Board of Education of Topeka*	**1962** Cuban missile crisis	
ASIA AND OCEANIA		**1947** India wins independence / **1954** French leave Vietnam		**1966** Cultural Revolution in China	
EUROPE		**1945** Labour party gains power in Britain	**1956** Hungarian uprising / **1957** European Community formed		

Student Bibliography

Abel, Elie. *The Shattered Bloc: Behind the Upheaval in Eastern Europe*. Houghton Mifflin, 1990. Discussion of the political and economic transformation in Eastern Europe in 1989.

Burns, E. Bradford. *Latin America: A Concise Interpretive History*. Prentice Hall, 1986. Looks at Latin America and its transition toward a more modern society.

Fairbank, John King, and Merle Goldman. *China: A New History*. Harvard University Press, 1998. Well-researched, authoritative account of China.

Friedman, Thomas L. *From Beirut to Jerusalem*. Doubleday, 1990. An account of war between Lebanon and Israel in the 1980s, by a reporter for *The New York Times*.

Gates, Jr., Henry Louis, and Lynn Davis. *Wonders of the African World*. Knopf, 1999. Beautifully photographed, unique narrative of Africa.

Tutu, Desmond Mpilo. *No Future Without Forgiveness*. Doubleday, 1999. Personal memoir of Archbishop Tutu's work as chairman of the Truth and Reconciliation Commission in South Africa after apartheid.

Chapter 35

South Asia and the Middle East (1945–Present)

In South Asia and the Middle East, nations cast off western rule and set out to modernize. They have often confronted similar challenges—from religious strife and border conflicts to urbanization and population growth.

- Upon achieving independence, India built on the legacy of British rule to create the world's largest democracy.
- Ethnic and religious rivalries have fueled ongoing conflict among people of South Asia.
- When secular governments in the Middle East did not yield promised improvements, some reformers rejected western models and called for a reaffirmation of Islamic values.
- The long Arab-Israeli struggle and other conflicts have focused world attention on the Middle East.

Chapter 36

Africa (1945–Present)

Leaders of new African nations set out to build strong central governments, achieve economic growth, and raise standards of living. They have faced a variety of obstacles, including economic dependency and political instability.

- After independence, a number of new nations experienced military or one-party rule. Many have since introduced multi-party democracy.
- African nations experimented with different economic systems, including socialism and mixed economies.
- After decades of conflict, South Africa abandoned its system of apartheid in the 1990s and made a transition to democratic rule.
- In Africa, as elsewhere, modernization and urbanization have disrupted traditional cultures and ways of life.

Chapter 37

Latin America (1945–Present)

Despite setbacks, Latin American nations have tried to sustain economic growth and overcome a legacy of poverty and social inequality. Marxism, military rule, and the Roman Catholic Church have been continuing influences in the region.

- In the postwar period, poverty and uneven distribution of wealth fed social unrest in many nations.
- Latin America was a focus of Cold War politics, especially after a communist revolution in Cuba in 1959.
- Through trade, investment, and military intervention, the United States was a dominant force in Latin America.
- Although Mexico enjoyed economic gains in agriculture and manufacturing, most people remained in poverty.
- Argentina and Brazil experienced economic growth and long periods of military rule.

1985   **2000**   **2015**

1980s Drought causes famine in parts of Africa
1994 Mandela wins first multiracial election in South Africa

1993 Canada, United States, and Mexico sign NAFTA
2000 Control of Panama Canal shifts to Panama

1979 Revolution in Iran   **1993** Israel and PLO sign peace accord
1997 Hong Kong returned to China
1989 Tiananmen Square massacre in China

1970s Greece restores civilian rule   **1989** Berlin Wall falls
1991 Breakup of Soviet Union
1999 European Union introduces common currency

Activity
Summarizing the Main Idea

Have students use both the Unit-in-Brief and Chapters 32–37 to answer the following questions in order to summarize Unit 8: (1) Why did many new countries emerge in Africa and Asia? (2) What caused the collapse of the Soviet Union? (3) How did Japan fare after its defeat in World War II? (4) How has religion been a source of conflict in both South Asia and the Middle East? (5) What are some obstacles that have hindered economic progress in both Africa and Latin America?

PRENTICE HALL
ASSESSMENT *SYSTEM*

Diagnose and Prescribe
- Profile student skills with Diagnostic Tests A & B.
- Address student needs with program materials identified in the test.

Review and Reteach
- Provide cumulative content review with the Review Book.

Practice and Assess
- Build test-taking skills with Test-Taking Strategies With Transparencies.

Teacher Bibliography

Corbin, Jane. *The Norway Channel: The Secret Talks That Led to the Middle East Peace Accord.* Atlantic Monthly Press, 1994. Account of the Palestinian-Israeli peace talks.

Echikson, William. *Lighting the Night.* William Morrow, 1990. Account of the collapse of communism by a reporter for *The Christian Science Monitor.*

El-Agraa, Ali M. *The Economics of the European Community.* St. Martin's, 1990. Study of the EC's economic policy and its worldwide impact.

Kothari, Rajni. *Politics and People: In Search of a Humane India.* New Horizons, 1989. Account of post-independence India.

Osborne, Milton. *Southeast Asia: An Introductory History.* Allen & Unwin, 1985. Comprehensive general survey presenting the region as a coherent whole.

Salisbury, Harrison. *The New Emperors: China in the Era of Mao and Deng.* Little, Brown, 1992. Discussion of two powerful leaders of the Chinese Communist party.

Reference Section

CONTENTS

PRIMARY SOURCES AND LITERATURE

Background
About the Document

Worldly Success Unlike later Egyptian writings, this document from the Old Kingdom focuses on a quest for success during one's lifetime rather than concerns about the afterlife. Ptah-hotep advocates seeking truth and what is right over greed and what is evil. Wealth comes from following the right course. Later, more chaotic periods of Egyptian history witnessed a preoccupation with righteousness or good deeds as a means of securing happiness in the afterlife.

Activity
Interpreting the Document

Use this additional question to generate class discussion.

Critical Thinking: Making Generalizations Ask students to read the description of a vizier's duties in the text on page 23, then ask them to describe how Ptah-hotep's advice relates to his job and life experience. *(Answers will vary. Much of his advice relates to obedience. Obedience would be viewed as an admirable trait in a highly structured government.)*

Analyzing Primary Sources

ANSWERS **1.** A **2.** G **3.** The author may be implying that a person who is greedy loses the companionship of friends and relatives, and therefore is not respected after his or her death.

Vocabulary Answers

arrogant—full of self-importance; **counsel**—advice; **venture**—a business enterprise in which there is danger of loss as well as chance for profit; **council**—group of advisers

Instruction of Ptah-hotep

Ptah-hotep, who lived around 2450 B.C. in Egypt, was a vizier, or chief minister, to a pharaoh during the Old Kingdom. In the excerpt below, Ptah-hotep describes some practical rules for behavior that he believes will help his son live a successful life.

Vocabulary Before you read the selection, look up the following words in a dictionary: **arrogant, counsel, venture, council.**

> **Main Idea** In this letter, Ptah-hotep describes rules of behavior that he believes will help his son live a successful life.

Be not arrogant because of your knowledge, and be not puffed up because you are a learned man. Take counsel with the ignorant as with the learned, for the limits of art cannot be reached, and no artist is perfect in his skills. . . .

If you are a leader, commanding the conduct of many, seek out every good aim, so that your policy may be without error. A great thing is truth, enduring and surviving; it has not been upset since the time of Osiris. He who departs from its laws is punished. It is the right path for him who knows nothing. Wrongdoing has never brought its venture safe to port. Evil may win riches, but it is the strength of truth that it endures long. . . .

If you want your conduct to be good, free from every evil, then beware of greed. It is an evil and incurable sickness. No man can live with it; it causes divisions between fathers and mothers, and between brothers of the same mother; it parts wife and husband; it is a gathering of every evil, a bag of everything hateful. A man thrives if his conduct is right. He who follows the right course wins wealth thereby. But the greedy man has no tomb. . . .

If you are a worthy man sitting in the council of his lord, confine your attention to excellence. Silence is more valuable than chatter. Speak only when you know you can resolve difficulties. He who gives good counsel is an artist, for speech is more difficult than any craft. . . .

If you listen to my sayings, then all your affairs will go forward. . . . If the son of a man accepts what his father says, no plan of his will fail. . . . Failure follows him who does not listen. . . .

Egyptian tomb painting

Analyzing Primary Sources

1. Which of the following statements best summarizes the main idea of the fourth paragraph?

   A Speak only when you have something helpful to say.

   B Achieve excellence so that you may council the lord.

   C Remain silent while in the council of the lord.

   D Give good counsel in order to gain wealth.

2. The author wishes his son to listen to his advice so that his son will be

   E greedy.

   F sick.

   G successful.

   H arrogant.

3. **Critical Thinking Making Inferences** What do you think Ptah-hotep means by the phrase "the greedy man has no tomb" (third paragraph)?

> ## Resource Directory

Teaching Resources

History Through Literature *Poems of Ancient Egypt,* History Through Literature booklet, pp. 5–6

Other Resources

Griffith, F. L., trans. *A Library of the World's Best Literature,* Volume XIII, pp. 5329–5340.

The Epic of Gilgamesh

The Sumerian *Epic of Gilgamesh* dates from about 2000 B.C. It is a collection of tales about a hero named Gilgamesh. The main themes of the poem are the unpredictability of the gods and the inevitability of death. These themes may be a reflection of life in Sumer, where the flooding of the Tigris and Euphrates rivers was both unpredictable and devastating.

Vocabulary Before you read the selection, look up the following words in a dictionary: **attain, slough, boon.**

Main Idea In this epic poem, Gilgamesh comes to realize that death is the common lot of all people, even fearless heroes.

Utnapishtim says to him, to Gilgamesh. . . .
"About a plant I will tell thee. . . .
Its thorns will prick thy hands just as does the rose.
If thy hands obtain the plant, thou wilt attain [eternal] life."
No sooner had Gilgamesh heard this, . . .
He tied heavy stones to his feet.
They pulled him down into the deep and he saw the plant.
He took the plant, though it pricked his hands.
He cut the heavy stones from his feet.
The sea cast him up upon its shore.
Gilgamesh says to him, to Urshanabi, the boatman:
"Urshanabi, this plant is a plant apart,
Whereby a man may regain his life's breath. . . .
Its name shall be 'Man Becomes Young in Old Age.'
I myself shall eat it
And thus return to the state of my youth."
Gilgamesh saw a well whose water was cool.
He went down into it to bathe in the water.
A serpent snuffed the fragrance of the plant;
It came up from the water and carried off the plant,
Going back to shed its slough.
Thereupon Gilgamesh sits down and weeps.
His tears running down over his face.
He took the hand of Urshanabi, the boatman:
"For whom, Urshanabi, have my hands toiled?
For whom is being spent the blood of my heart?
I have not obtained a boon for myself.
For the serpent have I effected a boon!"

Sumerian sculpture

Analyzing Literature

1. What does Gilgamesh decide to do after hearing Utnapishtim?
   A seek help from a boatman named Urshanabi
   B search for a plant that brings eternal life
   C bathe in a well with cool water
   D battle a serpent who carries away youth

2. At the end of this selection, Gilgamesh weeps because
   E the serpent has shed its skin.
   F he has toiled with his hands for too long.
   G he has failed to find everlasting life and must accept death.
   H he has eaten all of the plant.

3. **Critical Thinking** Synthesizing Information Which physical characteristic of a snake leads the author to choose it as the creature who benefits from the plant?

Reference Section **963**

Background About the Document

The Uncertainty of Life This epic poem is one of the world's oldest pieces of literature. It tells the story of Gilgamesh, a semi-legendary Sumerian king of Uruk around 2700 B.C. The main theme of the poem is death and the realization that death is inevitable. In this excerpt, Utnapishtim—who, along with his family and the animals on his ship, is the only survivor of a great flood—tells Gilgamesh about a Plant of Life that can give immortality. Gilgamesh finds the plant but his hopes are dashed when it is eaten by a snake.

Activity Interpreting the Document

Use these additional questions to generate class discussion.
1. Describe how Gilgamesh obtained the plant. *(He tied stones to his feet in order to reach the bottom of the water. When he reached the plant, he cut the stones from his feet and rose to the surface.)*
2. Critical Thinking: Making Comparisons Think of one or more examples of stories, movies, or legends in which a person is seeking immortality. Why is this a common theme in literature? *(Examples include* Cocoon, Ponce de Leon and the Fountain of Youth, *and* The Portrait of Dorian Gray. *Humans have always been intrigued by the mystery of death.)*

Analyzing Literature

ANSWERS 1. B **2.** G **3.** A snake is a symbol of immortality because it can constantly shed its skin and rejuvenate itself.

Vocabulary Answers

attain—gain; **slough**—the outer layer of a snake's skin that is periodically cast off; **boon**—welcome benefit, blessing

Resource Directory

Teaching Resources
History Through Literature *The Odyssey,* History Through Literature booklet, pp. 11–12

Other Resources
Leonard, William Ellery, trans. *Gilgamesh.* Penguin, 1962.

Pritchard, James B., ed. *Ancient Near Eastern Texts Relating to the Old Testament.* Princeton: Princeton University Press, 1969.

Sanders, N. K., trans. *The Epic of Gilgamesh.* New York: Penguin, 1972.

Background
About the Document

Role of the Psalms The psalms were meant to be sung to the accompaniment of a stringed instrument. The English word *psalm* comes from the Greek word *psalmos*. Written originally in Hebrew, the psalms were translated into Greek, from which they were translated into other languages, including English.

Psalm 23 is taken from the Book of Psalms, a section of the Old Testament that is sacred to both Jews and Christians and that plays an important role in both their liturgies.

Activity
Interpreting the Document

Use these additional questions to generate class discussion.

1. Critical Thinking: Identifying Main Ideas What does the psalm say the Lord provides to the Israelites? What phrases are clues? *(comfort, peace— "still waters," "green pastures"; food— "preparest a table before me/in the presence of my enemies"; protection— "fear no evil . . . thou art with me," "dwell in the house of the Lord")*

2. Critical Thinking: Drawing Conclusions Based on what you already know, why might the Israelites choose certain things to be thankful for that are mentioned in the answer to the question above? *(Possible answer: The Israelites lived in the desert, so water and green pastures would be symbols of refreshment. The image of eating in the presence of enemies might suggest that the Israelites were persecuted. Under the Lord's protection, they would be able to eat at their leisure and not on the run, despite the presence of enemies.)*

Analyzing Literature

ANSWERS 1. A **2.** F **3. (a)** God provides for the Israelites, leads them, comforts and protects them. **(b)** It asserts the goodness of God, who delivers the speaker from evil and protects him from enemies.

Vocabulary Answers

righteousness—acting without sin; **anoint**—to apply oil, indicating divine election

Psalm 23

The Psalms are a collection of 150 religious hymns. These songs reflect the Israelites' belief in their God as the powerful savior of Israel. Many of the psalms praise the faithfulness of God to each of his people. In this psalm, the speaker describes his faith in God's protection.

Vocabulary Before you read the selection, look up the following words in a dictionary: **righteousness, anoint.**

Main Idea The Twenty-Third Psalm celebrates the Israelites' sense of a special relationship with a loving God.

The LORD is my shepherd, I shall not want;

he makes me lie down in green pastures.
He leads me beside still waters;

he restores my soul.
He leads me in paths of righteousness
for his name's sake.

Even though I walk through the valley of the shadow of death,
I fear no evil;
for thou art with me;
thy rod and thy staff,
they comfort me.

Thou preparest a table before me
in the presence of my enemies;
thou anointest my head with oil,
my cup overflows.

Surely goodness and mercy shall follow me
all the days of my life;
and I shall dwell in the house of the LORD
for ever.

Prayer book in Hebrew

Analyzing Literature

1. The speaker of the Twenty-Third Psalm says that he

A feels protected by God.

B feels abandoned by God.

C fears the anger of God.

D fears Israel's enemies.

2. According to the speaker, God's strength

E helps the sheep find water.

F overcomes the power of death.

G provides housing and food for the Israelites.

H builds an army to defeat the enemies of the Israelites.

3. Critical Thinking Making Generalizations
(a) Identify the qualities of God and the Israelites that lead the speaker to compare God to a shepherd. **(b)** How does the Twenty-Third Psalm reflect some of the basic beliefs of Jewish monotheism?

Resource Directory

Technology
Listening to Literature World Masterpieces audiotapes *Psalm 23,* side 1, running time 1:34 min.

Other Resources
Boadt, Lawrence. *Reading the Old Testament: An Introduction.* New York: The Paulist Press, 1984.

Holy Bible: Updated New American Standard Bible: Containing the Old Testament and the New Testament. Grand Rapids, Mich.: Zondervan, 1999.

Pritchard, James B., ed. *Ancient Near Eastern Texts Relating to the Old Testament.* Princeton: Princeton University Press, 1969.

Confucius: *Analects*

The *Analects* are a collection of 497 verses recorded by Confucius' followers long after his death (perhaps in the fourth century B.C.). Confucius' teachings emphasize duty and responsibility as a means of ensuring social order and good government.

Vocabulary Before you read the selection, look up the following words in a dictionary: **homage, bias, induce, piety, incompetent.**

> **Main Idea** In these sayings, Confucius emphasizes that education and self-sacrifice are the keys to becoming a superior person.

The Master said, He who rules by moral force is like the pole-star, which remains in its place while all the lesser stars do homage to it.

The Master said, If out of the three hundred Songs I had to take one phrase to cover all my teaching, I would say 'Let there be no evil in your thoughts.'

Mêng Wu Po asked about the treatment of parents. The Master said, Behave in such a way that your father and mother have no anxiety about you, except concerning your health.

Tzu-kung asked about the true gentleman. The Master said, He does not preach what he practices till he has practiced what he preaches.

The Master said, A gentleman can see a question from all sides without bias. The small man is biased and can see a question only from one side.

The Master said, Yu, shall I teach you what knowledge is? When you know a thing, to recognize that you know it, and when you do not know a thing, to recognize that you do not know it. That is knowledge.

Chi K'ang-tzu asked whether there were any form of encouragement by which he could induce the common people to be respectful and loyal. The Master said, Approach them with dignity, and they will respect you. Show piety towards your parents and kindness towards your children, and they will be loyal to you. Promote those who are worthy, train those who are incompetent; that is the best form of encouragement.

Confucius

Analyzing Primary Sources

1. According to the excerpts, which one saying did Confucius pick to best summarize his teachings?

   A Show piety towards your parents and kindness towards your children.

   B Let there be no evil in your thoughts.

   C He does not preach what he practices till he has practiced what he preaches.

   D A gentleman can see a question from all sides without bias.

2. Confucius says that a gentleman

   E is knowledgeable.

   F is respectful and loyal.

   G can understand more than one point of view on a question or issue.

   H can recognize those who are worthy.

3. **Critical Thinking Identifying Main Ideas** Use your own words to describe Confucius' definition of knowledge.

Reference Section **965**

*B*ackground
About the Document

Inner Virtues The Chinese philosopher Confucius (551–479 B.C.) believed in the perfectibility of all people. A morally superior person—a *chün-tzu*—possessed the five inner virtues of (1) integrity, (2) righteousness, (3) loyalty and conscientiousness toward others, (4) altruism and reciprocity, and (5) virtue, love, and human-heartedness. Confucius' teachings were not accepted during his lifetime, but for more than 2000 years his philosophy had an enormous influence on East Asian culture.

*A*ctivity
Interpreting the Document

Use this additional question to generate class discussion.

Critical Thinking: Defending a Position Do you agree with the last saying that the best way to win respect is to treat others with respect? Why or why not? *(Answers will vary. Students may differentiate between respect and fear.)*

Analyzing Primary Sources

ANSWERS 1. B **2.** G **3.** Knowledge is described as an awareness of what you know as well as what you don't know.

Vocabulary Answers

homage—anything given or done to show honor or respect; **bias**—prejudice; **induce**—cause, influence; **piety**—loyalty and devotion; **incompetent**—unqualified

Resource Directory

Teaching Resources

Creative Teaching Activities *Philosophy and Religion in China,* Creative Teaching Activities booklet, p. 22

Other Resources

Waley, Arthur, trans. *The Analects of Confucius.* HarperCollins Publishers Limited.

Background
About the Document

Thucydides Thucydides was an Athenian general who failed in battle and was relieved of his duties by the people. Thucydides wrote a precise history of the Peloponnesian War, recording information about troop numbers, equipment, and battles. Although Thucydides was not present for many of the speeches he recorded in his history, he claims to give an accurate account of their content. In this speech, Pericles appeals to the patriotic feelings of the citizens to defend at any price the superior system of democracy that they inherited from their ancestors.

Activity
Interpreting the Document

Use this additional question to generate class discussion.
How would Pericles describe a good citizen? *(one who takes care of his own private duties and participates fully in government)*

Analyzing Primary Sources

ANSWERS **1.** B **2.** E **3.** He means that Athens and its system of democracy should be a model or example for the rest of the Greek city-states.

Vocabulary Answers

extravagance—going beyond proper limits; **vainglory**—extreme self-pride and boastfulness; **degradation**—to be lowered in status; **absorption**—the state of being much interested; **aloof**—apart; **notwithstanding**—nevertheless, in spite of the fact that; **attainment**—accomplishment

Primary Sources and Literature

Thucydides: *History of the Peloponnesian War*

This excerpt from Thucydides' *History of the Peloponnesian War* records a speech made by the Athenian leader Pericles in honor of those who died fighting Sparta in the first year of the war (431 B.C.). In the speech, Pericles describes the superior qualities of Athenian democracy as compared with life in Sparta.

Vocabulary Before you read the selection, look up the following words in a dictionary: **extravagance, vainglory, degradation, absorption, aloof, notwithstanding, attainment.**

Main Idea This speech by the Athenian leader Pericles is one of the most famous defenses of democracy of all time.

For our government is not copied from those of our neighbors: we are an example to them rather than they to us. Our constitution is named a democracy, because it is in the hands not of the few but of the many. But our laws secure equal justice for all in their private disputes, and our public opinion welcomes and honors talent in every branch of achievement, not for any sectional reason but on grounds of excellence alone. And as we give free play to all in our public life, so we carry the same spirit into our daily relations with one another. . . .

We are lovers of beauty without extravagance, and lovers of wisdom without unmanliness. Wealth to us is not mere material for vainglory but an opportunity for achievement; and poverty we think it no disgrace to acknowledge but a real degradation to make no effort to overcome. Our citizens attend both to public and private duties, and do not allow absorption in their own various affairs to interfere with their knowledge of the city's. We differ from other states in regarding the man who holds aloof from public life not as 'quiet' but as useless; we decide or debate, carefully and in person, all matters of policy, holding, not that words and deeds go ill together, but that acts are foredoomed to failure when undertaken undiscussed. For we are noted for being at once adventurous in action and most reflective beforehand. Other men are bold in ignorance, while reflection will stop their onset. But the bravest are surely those who have the clearest vision of what is before them, glory and danger alike, and yet notwithstanding go out to meet it. . . . In a word I claim that our city as a whole is an education to Greece, and that her members yield to none, man by man, for independence of spirit, many-sidedness of attainment, and complete self-reliance in limbs and brain.

The Parthenon in Athens

Analyzing Primary Sources

1. Pericles defines democracy as a system based on
   A equal justice for all in their private disputes.
   B the say of many citizens, not just a few.
   C beauty without extravagance and wisdom without unmanliness.
   D free play in public life.

2. According to Pericles, a good citizen
   E participates fully in public debate.
   F is quiet during public debate.
   G acts boldly without discussion.
   H attends exclusively to his own business.

3. **Critical Thinking Synthesizing Information** What does Pericles mean when he states that Athens is "an education to Greece"?

Resource Directory

Teaching Resources
Creative Teaching Activities *Victory and Defeat in the Greek World,* Creative Teaching Activities booklet, p. 26
Viewpoint Activity *The Values of Sparta and Athens,* Unit 2 booklet, p. 34

Other Resources
Ravitch, Diane, and Abigail Thernstrom, eds. *The Democracy Reader.* New York: HarperCollins, 1992.

Thucydides, *History of the Peloponnesian War,* in *The Greek Commonwealth: Politics and Economics in Fifth-Century Athens.* Oxford, 1924.

Safire, William, ed. "Pericles Extols the Glory That Is Greece," in *Lend Me Your Ear.* New York: Norton, 1997.

Aristotle: *The Politics*

The Greek philosopher Aristotle (384 B.C.–322 B.C.) was suspicious of democracy, which he thought could lead to mob rule. Instead, Aristotle favored rule by a single strong and virtuous leader. In this excerpt from *The Politics*, Aristotle outlines the forms of government and discusses the strengths and weaknesses of each form.

Vocabulary Before you read the selection, look up the following words in a dictionary: **treatise, constituted, despotic, generic.**

> **Main Idea** In this selection, Aristotle describes the characteristics of an ideal state as well as practical matters relating to the preservation and improvement of government.

First let us consider what is the purpose of a state and how many forms of government there are by which human society is regulated. We have already said, earlier in this treatise . . . that man is by nature a political animal. And therefore men, even when they do not require one another's help, desire to live together all the same, and are in fact brought together by their common interests. . . . Well-being is certainly the chief end of individuals and of states. . . .

The conclusion is evident: governments which have a regard to the common interest are constituted in accordance with strict principles of justice, and are therefore true forms; but those which regard only the interest of the rulers are all defective and perverted forms. For they are despotic, whereas a state is a community of free men. . . .

We call that form of government in which one rules, and which regards the common interest, kingship or royalty; that in which more than one, but not many, rule, aristocracy. It is so called, either because the rulers are the best men, or because they have at heart the best interest of the state and of the citizens. But when the citizens at large administer the state for the common interest, the government is called by the generic name—constitutional government. . . .

Of the above-mentioned forms, the perversions are as follows: of royalty, tyranny; of aristocracy, oligarchy; of constitutional government, democracy. For tyranny is a kind of monarchy which has in view the interest of the monarch only; oligarchy has in view the interest of the wealthy; democracy, of the needy; none of them the common good of all.

Students at an Athenian school

Analyzing Primary Sources

1. According to Aristotle, the form of government known as constitutional government is one in which
   A one rules, and which regards the common interest.
   B the citizens at large administer the state for the common interest.
   C more than one, but not many, rule.
   D the interests of the needy are placed above all.

2. Which of the following does Aristotle describe as the corrupt form of aristocracy?
   E tyranny
   F oligarchy
   G monarchy
   H democracy

3. **Critical Thinking Identifying Main Ideas** What do you think Aristotle means when he states that "man is by nature a political animal"?

Reference Section **967**

Resource Directory

Other Resources

Aristotle. *Politics*. Penguin Classics, 1981.

Ravitch, Diane, and Abigail Thernstrom, eds. *The Democracy Reader*. New York: HarperCollins, 1992.

Background
About the Document

Aristotle Aristotle was the tutor of Alexander the Great in Macedonia. When Alexander died, Aristotle became unpopular in Athens because of his association with the conqueror. He fled the city, remembering what had happened to Socrates, and not wishing, as he said, "to give the Athenians a second chance of sinning against philosophy."

Aristotle was a very productive thinker. His works include major studies in astronomy, botany, and physics, as well as ethics, poetry, and politics. Aristotle's two most influential works, *Ethics* and *Politics*, investigate human character and conduct in order to discover and build a society that provides the greatest amount of happiness for the greatest number of people.

Activity
Interpreting the Document

Use this additional question to generate class discussion.
How does Aristotle distinguish between good governments and bad governments? *(Good governments operate with regard for the good of everyone. Bad governments operate only in the interest of the rulers.)*

Analyzing Primary Sources

ANSWERS **1.** B **2.** F **3.** He means that it is human nature for people to seek association with other people.

Vocabulary Answers

treatise—a systematic article on a subject; **constituted**—set up, established; **despotic**—autocratic, tyrannical; **generic**—general kind

The Mahabharata

An epic of the ancient Aryans, the *Mahabharata* became a major source of Hindu social and religious doctrine. Indian storytellers still recite segments of the 100,000 stanzas to entertain and instruct village audiences. This excerpt tells of the rewards the god Indra bestows upon a dutiful king, Vasu.

Vocabulary Before you read the selection, look up the following words in a dictionary: **accustomed, celestial, crystalline, garland, lotuses, sustain, renowned.**

Main Idea In this epic, an Indian king is given earthly rule and supernatural gifts as reward for upholding the law of the gods.

Two Hindu gods

Indra said:

May never on earth, O lord of this earth, the Law be confused! Protect it, for the upheld Law holds up all the world. Guard thee this worldly Law, forever on guard and attentive; if yoked to the Law, you shall win the blessed worlds of eternity. You standing on earth have become the dear friend of me standing in heaven—now possess . . . a country beyond all others, with riches and jewels and all good things—Mother Earth, mother of plenty: live on her in the land of the Cedis, king of the Cedis!

The country people are accustomed to the Law, quite content and upright. No lies are spoken there even in jest, let alone in earnest. Sons are devoted to their elders there; they do not divide off from their fathers. Cows are never yoked to the cart, and even lean cows yield plenty. All the classes abide by their own Law, in this land of the Cedis. . . .

This large celestial crystalline chariot in the sky, which it is the God's privilege to enjoy, this airborne chariot will come to you as my gift. Among all mortals you alone shall stand upon a grand and sky-going chariot, and indeed, you will ride there above, like a God come to flesh! And I give you this garland Vaijayanti, woven of lotuses that never fade, which shall sustain you in battle, never hurt by swords. That shall be your mark of distinction here, sovereign of men—grand, rich, unmatched, and renowned as "India's Garland"!

Background
About the Document

Long Digression The great Sanskrit epic of western India, the *Mahabharata,* is probably based on fact—a war for control of the Ganges Valley around 1000 B.C. Twice the length of the western epics the *Iliad* and the *Odyssey* combined, the *Mahabharata* is the longest poem ever created. In addition to the main story line—the struggle of five brothers to regain their kingdom—the *Mahabharata* gathers many myths, episodes, prayers, narratives, and delightful and tender stories. These elements are presented as subplots and digressions to the main narrative, which makes up a relatively small portion of the whole. One of the elements that has become very popular in the West is the *Bhagavad Gita,* a classic Hindu text of devotion that is analogous to Christ's Sermon on the Mount in that each work contains essential teachings of Hinduism and Christianity, respectively. The principal teaching of the *Mahabharata's* stories is *dharma,* or devotion to one's duty.

Activity
Interpreting the Document

Use this additional question to generate class discussion.
Critical Thinking: Analyzing Information What seems to be the king's most important function, and why do you think it is so important? *(upholding the law, because it creates an orderly, just society where people are peaceful and happy)*

Analyzing Literature

ANSWERS 1. C **2.** E **3.** Answers will vary. Answers should include that Vasu is obedient to the laws of the gods and fulfills his duty as an earthly king.

Vocabulary Answers

accustomed—being in the habit of; used to; **celestial**—relating to the sky; **crystalline**—sparkling; made of crystal; **garland**—wreath; **lotuses**—water lilies; **sustain**—nourish; **renowned**—famous

Analyzing Literature

1. What does Indra say will be Vasu's reward for pleasing the gods?
   A Vasu will be given a place among the gods.
   B Vasu will receive jewels and a herd of cattle.
   C Vasu will ride through the skies on a crystal chariot.
   D Vasu will not be required to obey the Law.

2. According to Indra, Vasu will rule
   E Mother Earth.
   F the heavens.
   G his sons.
   H the afterlife.

3. **Critical Thinking Making Inferences** The heroes of epics frequently embody the values of the cultures that produced them. Describe some of the values that King Vasu represents.

Resource Directory

Teaching Resources
Creative Teaching Activities *Kingdoms of the Ganges,* Creative Teaching Activities booklet, p. 17
Other Resources
Mahesh Yogi, Maharishi. *Bhagavad-Gita: A New Translation and Commentary with Sanskrit Text.* Los Angeles: SRM International Publications, 1967.

Narayan, R.K., trans. *The Mahabharata.* New York: Viking Press, 1978.

Prabhavananda, Swami, and Christopher Isherwood, trans. *The Song of God: Bhagavad Gita.* New York: New American Library, 1944.

The Bhagavad-Gita (audiotapes). Berkeley: Audio Literature, 1987.

Asoka: *Edicts*

During his rule of Maurya India beginning in 268 B.C., Asoka converted to Buddhism, rejected violence, and resolved to rule by moral example. Asoka had stone pillars set up across India announcing laws, or edicts, and describing the just actions of his government. The following are excerpts from several of the pillars.

Vocabulary Before you read the selection, look up the following words in a dictionary: **righteousness, circumspection, disparages, concord, conformity, exhortation, abstention.**

> ### Main Idea
> The stone pillars set up across India by Asoka announced laws and promised fair and just government.

This world and the other are hard to gain without great love of Righteousness, great self-examination, great obedience, great circumspection, great effort. Through my instruction respect and love of Righteousness daily increase and will increase. . . . For this is my rule—to govern by Righteousness, to administer by Righteousness, to please my subjects by Righteousness, and to protect them by Righteousness.

Whoever honors his own [religion] and disparages another man's, whether from blind loyalty or with the intention of showing his own [religion] in a favorable light, does his own [religion] the greatest possible harm. Concord is best, with each hearing and respecting the other's teachings. It is the wish of the [king] that members of all [religions] should be learned and should teach virtue.

All the good deeds that I have done have been accepted and followed by the people. And so obedience to mother and father, obedience to teachers, respect for the aged, kindliness . . . to the poor and weak, and to slaves and servants, have increased and will continue to increase. . . . And this progress of Righteousness . . . has taken place in two manners, by enforcing conformity to Righteousness, and by exhortation. I have enforced the law against killing certain animals and many others, but the greatest progress of Righteousness . . . comes from exhortation in favor of noninjury to life and abstention from killing living beings.

I have done this that it may endure . . . as long as the moon and sun, and that my sons and my great-grandsons may support it; for by supporting it they will gain both this world and the next.

Sculpture from one of Asoka's pillars

Analyzing Primary Sources

1. This excerpt from the Edicts provides evidence that Asoka

   A was in favor of performing animal sacrifices.

   B wanted to place Buddhism above all other religions.

   C believed in the power of daily religious rituals.

   D sought to promote tolerance of diverse religions.

2. Based on the passage you can tell that Asoka was probably a

   E vegetarian.

   F monk.

   G dictator.

   H judge.

3. **Critical Thinking Drawing Conclusions** Which of his actions does Asoka view as the best promotion of Righteousness? Why do you think this is so?

Reference Section **969**

Resource Directory

Teaching Resources

Creative Teaching Activities *Hinduism and Buddhism,* Creative Teaching Activities booklet, p. 19

Other Resources

de Bary, William Theodore, ed. *Sources in Indian Tradition,* Vol. I. New York: Columbia University Press, 1958.

Background
About the Document

Authorship The edicts of Asoka were written on pillars and rocks throughout Asoka's empire. They were written in such clear, heartfelt language that historians believe they were written by Asoka himself.

Activity
Interpreting the Document

Use these additional questions to generate class discussion.

1. According to Asoka, what is the result of religious intolerance? *(If one is intolerant of another's religion, it reflects badly on one's own religion.)*

2. Critical Thinking: Identifying Main Ideas What are the major themes in these excerpts by Asoka? *(respect for all living things and righteousness)*

Analyzing Primary Sources

ANSWERS 1. D **2.** E **3.** Asoka states that the greatest progress of righteousness comes from urging people not to injure life and not to kill living beings. Asoka probably sees noninjury of life as the most important component of building a peaceful life.

Vocabulary Answers

righteousness—the act of behaving in a just, upright manner; doing what is right or virtuous; **circumspection**—careful consideration before acting; **disparages**—belittles, puts down, speaks badly of; **concord**—harmony, peace; **conformity**—obedience, act in accordance with a rule or custom; **exhortation**—urging or pleading; **abstention**—refraining, voluntarily doing without

Primary Sources and Literature

Background
About the Document

Addressing Problems Now part of the New Testament Bible, St. Paul's *First Letter to the Corinthians* was written about A.D. 53–54 from the city of Ephesus in Asia Minor. Paul had set up a Christian community in Corinth in A.D. 50–51. He later learned that disagreements about principles of the faith among the new converts were threatening the stability of the community. Paul's letter was a response to those problems. He addressed issues such as marriage, celibacy, conduct of women, and jealousy about how spiritual gifts are given. The most significant part of the letter is Paul's discourse on the place of love in the Christian faith. The idea of love that he expounds has become the core Christian belief.

Activity
Interpreting the Document

Use this additional question to generate class discussion.
Critical Thinking: Synthesizing Information According to St. Paul, how should Christians conduct themselves? *(possible answer: without jealousy, boasting, arrogance, or insisting on one's way, without rejoicing in wrong)*

Analyzing Primary Sources

ANSWERS 1. B 2. G 3. Love overcomes knowledge, martyrdom, the barrier of language, and death.

Vocabulary Answer

prophetic—foretelling events

St. Paul:
First Letter to the Corinthians

Around A.D. 51, Paul founded a Christian community in the thriving commercial city of Corinth. After his departure, he wrote two letters to the newly converted Christians to encourage and guide them in their faith. This excerpt from Paul's First Letter to the Corinthians focuses on the importance of love in a Christian life.

Vocabulary Before you read the selection, look up the following word in a dictionary: **prophetic**.

> **Main Idea** In this letter, Paul declares that, for a Christian, love is more important than any other quality.

If I speak in the tongues of men and of angels, but have not love, I am a noisy gong or a clanging cymbal. And if I have prophetic powers and understand all mysteries and all knowledge, and if I have all faith, so as to remove mountains, but have no love, I am nothing. If I give away all I have, and if I deliver my body to be burned, but have not love, I gain nothing.

Love is patient and kind; love is not jealous or boastful; it is not arrogant or rude. Love does not insist on its own way; it is not irritable or resentful; it does not rejoice at wrong, but rejoices in the right. Love bears all things, believes all things, hopes all things, endures all things.

Love never ends; as for prophecies, they will pass away; as for tongues, they will cease; as for knowledge, it will pass away. For our knowledge is imperfect and our prophecy is imperfect; but when the perfect comes, the imperfect will pass away. When I was a child, I spoke like a child, I thought like a child, I reasoned like a child; when I became a man, I gave up childish ways. For now we see in a mirror dimly, but then face to face. Now I know in part; then I shall understand fully, even as I have been fully understood. So faith, hope, love abide, these three; but the greatest of these is love.

Early Christian symbols

Analyzing Primary Sources

1. In his letter to the Corinthians, Paul states that love
   A can be fully understood by people in this life.
   B is a greater virtue than knowledge or faith.
   C has the power to remove mountains.
   D will pass away with an individual's death.

2. According to Paul, people will be able to achieve perfect knowledge when they
   E reach adulthood.
   F love their neighbors.
   G come face to face with God.
   H have prophetic powers.

3. **Critical Thinking Synthesizing Information** What does Paul mean when he says love "endures all things"?

> ### Resource Directory

Other Resources

Barrett, C. K. *A Commentary on the First Epistle to the Corinthians.* New York: Harper & Row, 1968.

Holy Bible: Updated New American Standard Bible: Containing the Old Testament and the New Testament. Grand Rapids: Zondervan Publishing House, 1999.

Perkins, Pheme. *Reading the New Testament: An Introduction.* New York: The Paulist Press, 1984.

The Quran

The Quran, the holy scriptures of Islam, contains 114 suras, or verses. Muslims believe that the Quran is the actual word of God as revealed to the prophet Muhammad. This excerpt from the Quran tells the faithful what they should do to be righteous and faithful Muslims.

Vocabulary Before you read the selection, look up the following words in a dictionary: **wayfarers, redemption, alms, perchance.**

Main Idea This excerpt from the Quran encourages believers to fast and observe the holy month of Ramadan.

Righteousness does not consist in whether you face towards the east or the west. The righteous man is he who believes in God and the Last Day, in the angels and the Scriptures and the prophets; who for the love of God gives his wealth to his kinsfolk, to the orphans, to the needy, to the wayfarers and to the beggars, and for the redemption of captives; who attends to his prayers and pays the alms-tax; who is true to his promises and steadfast in trial and adversity and in times of war. Such are the true believers; such are the god fearing. . . .

Believers, fasting is decreed for you as it was decreed for those before you; perchance you will guard yourselves against evil. Fast a certain number of days, but if any one of you is ill or on a journey let him fast a similar number of days later on; and for those that can afford it there is a ransom: the feeding of a poor man. He that does good of his own account shall be rewarded; but to fast is better for you, if you but knew it.

In the month of Ramadan the Quran was revealed, a book of guidance with proofs of guidance distinguishing right from wrong. Therefore whoever of you is present in that month let him fast. But he who is ill or on a journey shall fast a similar number of days later on.

God desires your well-being, not your discomfort. He desires you to fast the whole month so that you may magnify Him and render thanks to Him for giving you his guidance.

Pages from the Quran

Analyzing Primary Sources

1. According to the excerpt above, what is one goal of the Quran?

   A It helps the faithful distinguish right from wrong.

   B It helps the faithful guard against evil.

   C It helps the faithful question the will of God.

   D It helps the faithful increase their worldly wealth.

2. The "righteous man" does not have to fast during Ramadan if he

   E gives money to the poor.

   F is ill.

   G believes in God.

   H has not committed evil acts.

3. **Critical Thinking Applying Information** How does this passage from the Quran support the five pillars of Islam?

PRIMARY SOURCES AND LITERATURE

Background
About the Document

Development of the Quran For Muslims, the Quran is the revealed word of God, and it is the ultimate authority on legal and religious questions. It is believed that the angel Gabriel revealed the content of the Quran to Muhammad piecemeal over a span of twenty years. Muhammad recited the words he received, and followers wrote them down on various media that were available—paper, stone, palm leaves, animal shoulder blades, and pieces of leather. The words were memorized and eventually collected.

Composed of 114 chapters, or *surahs*, of rhythmic prose and rhymed verse, the Quran is written in Arabic. It is composed of history and moral, religious, and political dictates, as well as promises. It charges the faithful to be honest and ethical and to spread their beliefs.

Activity
Interpreting the Document

Use these additional questions to generate class discussion.

1. Critical Thinking: Synthesizing Information What are the faithful to be thankful for, and how does the Quran instruct the faithful to give thanks to God? *(The faithful should be thankful for God's guidance in distinguishing right from wrong. The faithful should show their thankfulness for this guidance by fasting.)*

2. Critical Thinking: Comparing What similarities and differences can you detect between the teachings of the Quran and the teachings of Jews and Christians? *(Answers will vary and may include the following: similarities— monotheism, revealed religion, heaven, just and benevolent God; differences— prayer and fasting, almsgiving.)*

Resource Directory

Teaching Resources

Creative Teaching Activities *Rise of Islam,* Creative Teaching Activities booklet, p. 49
Treasures of the World *In the Name of Allah,* pp. 53–55

Other Resources

Ali, Ahmed, trans. *al-Qur'an: A Contemporary Translation.* Princeton, N.J.: Princeton University Press, 1994.

Bell, Richard. *Introduction to the Qur'an.* Edinburgh: Edinburgh University Press, 1970.

Cragg, Kenneth. *The Event of the Qur'an.* Oxford: Oneworld, 1994.

Gätje, Helmut. *The Qur'an and Its Exegesis: Selected Texts with Classical and Modern Muslim Interpretations.* Berkeley: University of California Press, 1976.

Analyzing Primary Sources

ANSWERS 1. A **2.** F **3.** It encourages giving alms, making a pilgrimage, fasting, prayer, and belief in God.

Vocabulary Answers

wayfarers—foot travelers; **redemption**—freeing; **alms**—something given to the poor; **perchance**—possibly, perhaps

Background
About the Document

Culture of Aesthetics The author was born in Kyoto around 978. She served empress Joto mon' and had first-hand knowledge of court life. Her true name is unknown, and she was assigned the name Murasaki Shikibu, after the novel's heroine.

The Tale of Genji is a very long and complex novel written between A.D. 1001 and 1005. There are no great action scenes, but it captures the flavor of the esthetics cultivated by the aristocracy. It inspired the development of Nō plays, and the establishment of a very refined esthetic sense in Japanese culture, culminating in the tea ceremony.

Activity
Interpreting the Document

Use these additional questions to generate class discussion.

1. Critical Thinking: Identifying Main Ideas What facts does the passage reveal about pastimes in court life? *(Royal stables and royal hawks and the gift of the falcon reveal that equestrian activity and falconry were common.)*

2. Critical Thinking: Making Inferences How do you know that people liked Genji's dance? What do you think they liked about his dance, and what does this tell you about the audience? *(They wept because the prince was so graceful. This reveals that the audience held grace and beauty in great regard.)*

Analyzing Literature

ANSWERS 1. B **2.** G **3.** Answers will vary. Students might mention bar mitzvahs, bat mitzvahs, sweet-sixteen parties, confirmations, high school and college graduations.

Vocabulary Answers

initiation—rites and rituals marking entry into a phase of life or a group; **zeal**—enthusiasm; **prescribed**—designated; **loath**—greatly dislike; **homage**—expression of respect; **chamberlain**—chief household officer; **obeisance**—bow indicating respect

Murasaki Shikibu:
The Tale of Genji

Murasaki Shikibu's *Tale of Genji* is considered one of the finest works of Japanese literature. The novel provides insight into the court life and mores of tenth-century Japan. In this excerpt, the elaborate rituals associated with Prince Genji's transition from childhood to manhood are described. The passage also reflects the Japanese aristocracy's emphasis on official titles and social ranks.

Vocabulary Before you read the selection, look up the following words in a dictionary: **initiation, zeal, prescribed, loath, homage, chamberlain, obeisance.**

> **Main Idea** This excerpt from the novel describes the royal coming of age ceremony in Heian Japan.

Though it seemed a shame to put so lovely a child into man's dress, he was now twelve years old and the time for his Initiation was come. The Emperor directed the preparations with tireless zeal and insisted upon a magnificence beyond what was prescribed. . . .

Genji arrived at the hour of the Monkey [3 P.M.]. He looked very handsome with his long childish locks, and the Sponsor, whose duty it had just been to bind them with the purple filet, was sorry to think that all this would soon be changed and even the Clerk of the Treasury seemed loath to sever those lovely tresses with the ritual knife. . . .

Duly crowned, Genji went to his chamber and changing into man's dress went down into the courtyard and performed the Dance of Homage, which he did with such grace that tears stood in every eye. . . .

When the courtiers assembled to drink the Love Cup, Genji came and took his place among the other princes. The Minister of the Left came up and whispered something in his ear; but the boy blushed and could think of no reply. A chamberlain now came over to the Minister and brought him a summons to wait upon His Majesty immediately. . . . Then, when he had made him drink out of the Royal Cup, the Emperor recited a poem in which he prayed that the binding of the purple filet might symbolize the union of their two houses; and the Minister answered him that nothing should sever this union save the fading of the purple band. Then he descended the long stairs and from the courtyard performed the Grand Obeisance. Here too were shown the horses from the Royal Stables and the hawks from the Royal Falconry, that had been decreed as presents for the Genji. At the foot of the stairs, the Princes and the Courtiers were lined up to receive their bounties, and gifts of every kind were showered upon them.

Lady Murasaki Shikibu

Analyzing Literature

1. Genji's initiation into manhood is symbolized by

   A his honored position at the Emperor's banquet.

   B the cutting of his hair and changing of his garments.

   C the lining up of the Princes for their gifts.

   D the Emperor's show of affection for the Prince.

2. The importance of the ceremony is reflected in the

   E social rank of the Minister of the Left.

   F performance of the Dance of Homage.

   G elaborate preparations and emphasis on social rank.

   H binding of the hair.

3. **Critical Thinking Linking Past and Present** What kinds of ceremonies do we have today that recognize the transition from childhood to adulthood?

> ## Resource Directory

Teaching Resources
Creative Teaching Activities *The Emergence of Japan,* Creative Teaching Activities booklet, p. 61
History Through Literature *The Pillow Book,* History Through Literature booklet, pp. 30–31

Other Resources
Puette, William J. *The Tale of Genji by Murasaki Shikibu: A Reader's Guide.* Rutland, Vermont: Tuttle, 1993.

Shikibu, Murasaki. *The Tale of Genji.* Tokyo: Tuttle, 1978.

The Illustrated Handscroll Tale of Genji (video-recording). Princeton, N.J.: Video Champ, co-production, CR-NEXUS, Films for the Humanities & Sciences, 1993.

Geoffrey Chaucer:
The Canterbury Tales

In *The Canterbury Tales,* Geoffrey Chaucer presents a portrait of English society in the 1300s. The story involves 29 men and women who tell stories to one another while on pilgrimage to the tomb of Thomas Becket in Canterbury. The detailed descriptions of each character provide a sharp look at three classes of medieval society: clergy, nobles, and common people. In these passages, Chaucer describes a noble knight, a wealthy merchant, and a humble plowman.

Vocabulary Before you read the selection, look up the following words in a dictionary: **sovereign, heathen, motley, estimable, negotiation.**

Main Idea In this poem, Chaucer describes three characters who represent different classes and occupations of medieval society.

There was a *Knight,* a most distinguished man,
Who from the day on which he first began
To ride abroad had followed chivalry,
Truth, honor, generousness, and courtesy.
He had done nobly in his sovereign's war
And ridden into battle, no man more,
As well in Christian as heathen places,
And ever honored for his noble graces....

There was a Merchant with a forking beard
And motley dress; high on his horse he sat,
Upon his head a Flemish beaver hat
And on his feet daintily buckled boots....
He was expert at currency exchange.
This estimable Merchant so had set
His wits to work, none knew he was in debt,
He was so stately in negotiation,
Loan, bargain, and commercial obligation....

[The Plowman] was an honest worker, good and true,
Living in peace and perfect charity....
For steadily about his work he went
To thrash his corn, to dig or to manure
Or make a ditch; and he would help the poor
For love of Christ and never take a penny
If he could help it, and, as prompt as any,
He paid his tithes in full when they were due....

A medieval town

Analyzing Literature

1. What quality do the Knight and the Plowman have in common?
   A wealth
   B bravery
   C honesty
   D sharp wits

2. What conclusion can you draw from these passages?
   E The Knight fought in the Crusades.
   F The Merchant is successful at business.

   G The Plowman is overworked and desperately poor.
   H The Knight and the Merchant look down on the Plowman.

3. **Critical Thinking** Applying Information
   (a) Which of the three characters described in these excerpts represents a class of people who were powerful in early feudal society? (b) Which of these characters represents a class that grew more powerful in the High Middle Ages?

Reference Section **973**

Resource Directory

Other Resources

Chaucer, Geoffrey. *The Canterbury Tales: A Verse Translation.* Oxford: Oxford University Press, 1985.

Coulton, George G. *Chaucer and His England.* Williamstown, Mass.: Corner House Publishers, 1976.

Donaldson, Ethelbert T. *Chaucer's Poetry: An Anthology for the Modern Reader.* New York: Ronald Press Co., 1983.

The Canterbury Tales (sound recording). New York: Caedmon, 1962.

PRIMARY SOURCES AND LITERATURE

Background
About the Document

Poet of the World The selections from the General Prologue presented here introduce characters from Chaucer's long masterpiece. During the pilgrimage, the characters agree that each will tell a story.

Chaucer, who lived from c. 1340 to 1400 in London, was the first English poet to write realistically about his own times. He came from a middle class family; his father was a successful vintner who had connections at court. Chaucer himself held important positions as a civil servant under three kings—Edward III, Richard II, and Henry IV. He worked his way up the ranks in the court and became very successful. He served as a diplomat, handling the king's business in France and Italy. Chaucer was knowledgeable in French, Italian, Latin, astronomy, philosophy, rhetoric, and bookkeeping.

Chaucer was a poet by avocation. *The Canterbury Tales,* the longest of many works, was written over a period of years toward the end of the 1300s.

Activity
Interpreting the Document

Use this additional question to generate class discussion.
Critical Thinking: Making Inferences
What clues reveal (a) how the Merchant makes his living, (b) the sort of character he is? *(a) makes his living—"currency exchange," "loan, bargain, and commercial obligation" (b) character—proud: "high on his horse"; ostentatious: "daintily buckled boots," "Flemish beaver hat," "motley dress"; and crafty—"forking beard," "stately in negotiation"; "set/His wits to work, none knew he was in debt"*

Analyzing Literature

ANSWERS 1. C **2.** E **3. (a)** the Knight **(b)** the Merchant

Vocabulary Answers

sovereign—lord; **heathen**—uncivilized, unreligious person; **motley**—variegated color garment of wool; **estimable**—valuable; **negotiation**—making deals

Primary Sources and Literature

Background
About the Document

Machiavelli In his most notorious work, *The Prince*, Machiavelli seems to endorse the idea that in politics the ends always justify the means. Like many people during the later Renaissance, Machiavelli looked to the Roman Republic for answers regarding the problems of the day. In his *Discourses on the First Ten Books of Titus Livy*, Machiavelli describes the means for founding and preserving republics based on the Roman method described by Livy.

Activity
Interpreting the Document

Use this additional question to generate class discussion.

Critical Thinking: Synthesizing Information Do you agree with Machiavelli that tyrants or dictators can take over during times of chaos or confusion? Why? *(Answers will vary. Students may suggest that when life becomes too confusing, violent, or uncertain, people look to a strong leader to solve their problems. They may be willing to give up their rights to the leader in exchange for security.)*

Analyzing Primary Sources

ANSWERS 1. B **2.** E **3. (a)** They have lasted long and must be regulated by laws to function properly. **(b)** Machiavelli states that it is easy to criticize the populace in general without fear of punishment whereas criticizing a prince can be dangerous.

Vocabulary Answers

populace—population, masses; **subservient**—inferior; **licentious**—disregarding rules; **trepidation**—fearful uncertainty

Niccolò Machiavelli: *Discourses*

The Florentine writer Niccolò Machiavelli (1469–1527) is best known for his book *The Prince*, in which he describes how a ruler can get and keep power. However, in his book *Discourses on the First Ten Books of Titus Livy*, Machiavelli concludes that the best-governed state is ruled by the people rather than by a ruthless prince.

Vocabulary Before you read the selection, look up the following words in a dictionary: **populace, subservient, licentious, trepidation.**

> **Main Idea** In his *Discourses,* Machiavelli describes methods for establishing and preserving republics.

In short, to bring this topic to conclusion, I say that, just as princely forms of government have endured for a very long time, so, too, have republican forms of government; and that in both cases it has been essential for them to be regulated by laws. For a prince who does what he likes is a lunatic; and a populace which does what it likes is unwise. If, therefore, it be a question of a prince subservient to the laws and of a populace chained up by laws, more virtue will be found in the populace than in the prince; and if it be a question of either of them loosed from control by the law, there will be found fewer errors in the populace than in the prince, and these of less moment and much easier to put right. For a licentious and turbulent populace, when a good man can obtain a hearing, can easily be brought to behave itself; but there is no one to talk to a bad prince, nor is there any remedy except the sword. . . .

When the populace has thrown off all restraint, it is not the mad things it does that are terrifying, nor is it of present evils that one is afraid, but of what may come of them, for amidst such confusion there may come to be a tyrant. In the case of bad princes it is just the opposite: it is present evils that are terrifying, but for the future there is hope, since men are convinced that the evil ways of a bad prince may make for freedom in the end. . . . The reason why people are prejudiced against the populace is because of the populace anyone may speak ill without fear and openly, even when the populace is ruling. But of princes people speak with the utmost trepidation and the utmost reserve.

Analyzing Primary Sources

1. Machiavelli states that the only way to bring an unruly prince under the law is to
   - **A** obtain a hearing.
   - **B** use physical combat.
   - **C** discuss the people's legal rights.
   - **D** choose a tyrant.
2. Machiavelli concludes that the greatest threat posed by an unlawful populace is the
   - **E** rise of a dictator.
   - **F** violence of the mob.
   - **G** loss of a prince.
   - **H** destruction of property.
3. **Critical Thinking Making Inferences (a)** According to Machiavelli, what do princely and republican forms of government have in common? **(b)** Why do you think Machiavelli believes that the populace loosed from control is more subject to criticism than a prince loosed from control?

Resource Directory

Teaching Resources
History Through Literature *The Prince,* History Through Literature booklet, pp. 32–33
Creative Teaching Activites *The Renaissance in Italy,* Creative Teaching Activities booklet, p. 63

Other Resources
Machiavelli, Niccolò. *The Discourses,* in *The Prince and The Discourses.* New York: Modern Library, 1950.

Ravitch, Diane, and Abigail Thernstrom, eds. *The Democracy Reader.* New York: HarperCollins, 1992.

Bernal Díaz: *The True History of the Conquest of New Spain*

Bernal Díaz del Castillo (c. 1492–1581) accompanied Hernan Cortés on his conquest of the Aztecs in present-day Mexico. Díaz wrote his history many years later to refute what he viewed as inaccurate accounts of the conquest. The following excerpt describes a meeting between Cortés and Moctezuma, the Aztec king, in the Aztec city of Tenochtitlán.

Vocabulary Before you read the selection, look up the following words in a dictionary: **oratory, league.**

> **Main Idea** This memoir provides an account of the Aztec capital of Tenochtitlán at the time of the Spanish conquest.

When we climbed to the top of the great [temple] there was a kind of platform, with huge stones where they put the poor Indians to be sacrificed, and an image like a dragon and other evil figures, with a great deal of blood that had been shed that day. Moctezuma, accompanied by two priests, came out from an oratory dedicated to the worship of his cursed idols. . . .

Then Moctezuma took him [Cortés] by the hand and bade him look at his great city and at all the other cities rising from the water, and the many towns around the lake. . . .

There we stood looking, for that large and evil temple was so high that it towered over everything. From there we could see all three of the causeways that led into Mexico. . . .

We saw the fresh water that came from Chapultepec, which supplied the city, and the bridges on the three causeways, built at certain intervals so the water could go from one part of the lake to another, and a multitude of canoes, some arriving with provisions and others leaving with merchandise. We saw that every house in this great city and in the others built on the water could be reached only by wooden drawbridges or by canoe. We saw temples built like towers and fortresses in these cities, all white-washed; it was a sight to see. . . .

After taking a good look and considering all that we had seen, we looked again at the great square and the throngs of people, some buying and others selling. The buzzing of their voices could be heard more than a league away. There were soldiers among us who had been in many parts of the world, in Constantinople and Rome and all over Italy, who said that they had never before seen a market place so large and so well laid out, and so filled with people.

Aztec gold ornament

Analyzing Primary Sources

1. What scene is Bernal Díaz describing in this excerpt?

   A a view of Tenochtitlán's market and surroundings from the top of a tall temple

   B an indoor temple with many religious statues

   C a view of Tenochtitlán's temple from the market place

   D a view of the markets in Constantinople and Rome

2. Which of the following best describes the author's view of the Aztecs?

   E generous and busy

   F evil and prosperous

   G loving and kind

   H athletic and loud

3. **Critical Thinking Recognizing Points of View** Which words and phrases in the excerpt above reveal the author's opinion of the Aztec's religion?

Background
About the Document

Bernal Díaz del Castillo Bernal Díaz set out from Spain to travel to the New World when he was 18. Before joining Cortés in Mexico, he explored Cuba and the Yucatán. Díaz remained in Central America for most of his life and settled in what is today Guatemala. His papers, including the original copy of this document, are still in Guatemala today. Díaz was an eyewitness to the events in Mexico, but his version of the events was written many years later, and it was written to refute other accounts and is probably, therefore, somewhat distorted.

Activity
Interpreting the Document

Use this additional question to generate class discussion.
What do Cortés and his soldiers view from the top of the temple? *(the surrounding lake, towns on the lake, causeways, houses, canoes, market place, temples, people)*

Analyzing Primary Sources

ANSWERS 1. A **2.** F **3.** The phrases "poor Indians," "evil figures," "cursed idols," and "evil temple" reveal that the author views the Aztecs' religion as evil.

Vocabulary Answers

oratory—a small chapel, especially for private prayer; **league**—about three miles

Resource Directory

Teaching Resources

Simulations *Encounter in Tenochtitlán,* Simulations booklet, p. 8
Primary Source Activity *The Massacre in the Temple of Tenochtitlán,* Unit 4 booklet, p. 51
History Through Literature *The Broken Spears,* History Through Literature booklet, pp. 35–36

Other Resources

Idell, Albert, trans. *The Bernal Díaz Chronicles.* Albert Idell, 1956.

Background
About the Document

An Unanswered Appeal In this letter, Affonso appeals to the king of Portugal to end the slave trade in Kongo. His appeal failed, however, and the slave trade increased and relations between Kongo and Portugal worsened. To ensure that Kongo continued to supply them with slaves, the Portuguese invaded in the mid-1600s and killed the kingdom's ruler, Antonio I. The kingdom of Kongo never recovered from this invasion, and what was once a prosperous empire disappeared.

Activity
Interpreting the Document

Use this additional question to generate class discussion.
Critical Thinking: Making Inferences Which lines in the document reveal Affonso's beliefs about the causes of the slave trade? *(Affonso says that "the thieves and men of bad conscience grab them [the people to be enslaved] wishing to have the things and wares of this Kingdom which they are ambitious of.")*

Analyzing Primary Sources

ANSWERS 1. B **2.** E **3.** The Portuguese have undermined his rule of the kingdom because the people now have more goods (or wealth) than he does. Also, they are depopulating the kingdom by taking people away as slaves.

Vocabulary Answers

comply—obey; **jurisdiction**—authority or power; **depopulated**—loss of people

---

Primary Sources and Literature

King Affonso I:
Letter to King John of Portugal

In 1490, the Portuguese converted the son of a Kongo king to Christianity and then helped him to assume his father's throne. The king, born Nzinga Mbemba, was renamed Affonso. King Affonso soon realized that his relationship with Portugal had extremely negative consequences, as can be seen from his letter in 1526 to King John of Portugal.

Vocabulary Before you read the selection, look up the following words in a dictionary: **comply, jurisdiction, depopulated.**

Main Idea In this letter, the king of Kongo asks the king of Portugal to end the slave trade.

African carving of Portuguese soldiers

Sir, Your Highness of Portugal should know how our Kingdom is being lost in so many ways. This is caused by the excessive freedom given by your officials to the men and merchants who are allowed to come to this Kingdom to set up shops with goods and many things which have been prohibited by us. Many of our vassals, whom we had in obedience, do not comply because they have the things in greater abundance than we ourselves. It was with these things that we had them content and subjected under our jurisdiction, so it is doing a great harm not only to the service of God, but to the security and peace of our Kingdoms and State as well.

And we cannot reckon how great the damage is, since the mentioned merchants are taking every day our natives, sons of the land and the sons of our noblemen and vassals and our relatives. The thieves and men of bad conscience grab them wishing to have the things and wares of this Kingdom which they are ambitious of; they grab them and get them to be sold. And so great, Sir, is the corruption and licentiousness that our country is being completely depopulated, and your Highness should not agree with this nor accept it as in your service. And to avoid it we need from those your Kingdoms no more than some priests and a few people to teach in schools, and no other goods except wine and flour for the holy sacrament.

That is why we beg of Your Highness to help and assist us in this matter, commanding your factors that they should not send here either merchants or wares, because *it is our will that in these kingdoms there should not be any trade of slaves nor outlet for them.* Concerning what is referred to above, again we beg of Your Highness to agree with it. . . .

Analyzing Primary Sources

1. Which of the following best describes the author's purpose in writing this letter?

   A to ask the king for money to help in ending the slave trade

   B to inform the king of the abuses taking place and to ask for his help in ending them

   C to inform the king about the extent of trade taking place in the kingdom

   D to ask the king for an explanation for why people are being enslaved

2. What does Affonso request of King John in the last paragraph?

   E that he not send any merchants or wares

   F that he send teachers

   G that he send priests

   H that he pray for Affonso

3. **Critical Thinking Recognizing Causes and Effects** According to King Affonso, how have the Portuguese affected his kingdom and state?

Resource Directory

Teaching Resources
Creative Teaching Activities *Turbulent Centuries in Africa,* Creative Teaching Activities booklet, p. 75
Biography Activity *Olaudah Equiano,* Unit 4 booklet, p. 50

Other Resources
Clark, Leon E., ed. *The African Past and the Coming of the European.* New York: Praeger Publishers, 1970.

Miguel de Cervantes: *Don Quixote*

In his novel *Don Quixote*, Spanish writer Miguel de Cervantes tells the story of a madman who thinks he is a medieval knight. While Don Quixote's exploits often seem ridiculous, his devotion to the virtues underlying chivalry give his actions dignity. In this famous excerpt, Don Quixote does battle with a group of windmills against the advice of his down-to-earth companion, Sancho Panza.

Vocabulary Before you read the selection, look up the following words in a dictionary: **nigh, leagues, millstone, caitiffs**.

> **Main Idea** In this excerpt, Don Quixote's devotion to knighthood leads him to attack a windmill, which he sees as a menacing giant.

Just then they came in sight of thirty or forty windmills that rise from that plain, and no sooner did Don Quixote see them than he said to his squire: "Fortune is guiding our affairs better than we ourselves could have wished. Do you see over yonder, friend Sancho, thirty or forty hulking giants? I intend to do battle with them and slay them. With the spoils we shall begin to be rich, for this is a righteous war. . . ."

"What giants?" asked Sancho Panza.

"Those you see over there," replied his master, "with the long arms; some of them have them well-nigh two leagues in length."

"Take care, sir," cried Sancho. "Those over there are not giants but windmills, and those things that seem to be armed are their sails, which when they are whirled around by the wind turn the millstone."

"It is clear," replied Don Quixote, "that you are not experienced in adventures. Those are giants, and if you are afraid, turn aside and pray whilst I enter into fierce and unequal battle with them."

Uttering these words, he clapped spurs to Rozinante, his steed, without heeding the cries of his squire, Sancho, who warned him that he was not going to attack giants, but windmills. But so convinced was he that they were giants that he neither heard his squire's shouts nor did he notice what they were, though he was very near them. Instead, he rushed on, shouting in a loud voice: "Fly not, cowards and vile caitiffs; one knight alone attacks you!" At that moment a slight breeze arose and the great sails began to move. . . .

He ran his lance into the sail, but the wind twisted it with such violence that it shivered the lance in pieces and dragged both rider and horse after it, rolling them over and over on the ground, sorely damaged.

Analyzing Literature

1. When Don Quixote attacks the giants, he expects

    A to gain great wealth.

    B to fail because he fights alone.

    C Sancho to join him.

    D to be tossed in the air.

2. Don Quixote believes a knight should

    E attack only after being attacked.

    F act boldly when he finds an enemy.

    G seek help before fighting an unequal battle.

    H enter a battle only to gain material wealth.

3. **Critical Thinking Drawing Conclusions** (a) What values of chivalry motivate Don Quixote's attack on the windmills? (b) How do you think Cervantes feels about Don Quixote and his ideals? Explain.

> ## Resource Directory

Other Resources

Cervantes, Miguel Saavedra de. *The Adventures of Don Quixote.* Baltimore: Penguin, 1962.

Nelson, Lowry, Jr., ed. *Cervantes: A Collection of Critical Essays.* Englewood Cliffs, N.J.: Prentice-Hall, 1969.

PRIMARY SOURCES AND LITERATURE

Background About the Document

Dreaming of Reality Written in two parts (Part 1, 1605, and Part 2, 1615), *Don Quixote* began as a parody satirizing the chivalric romances that dominated writing in Cervantes's Spain. By the time Cervantes wrote his novel, the romance was a tired genre on its way out. The first part of *Don Quixote* follows the knight's misadventures and is written in the style of mock heroic. But the second part takes on a more serious tone as the protagonist's search for the real behind the appearances becomes more philosophical. Instead of laughing at him, the reader begins to admire him and his efforts to find the ideal. The themes of morality, government, and society all are confronted as Don Quixote emerges as the man who only wants to do the right thing. The second part also contains vivid descriptions of Spanish life of the period.

Activity Interpreting the Document

Use this additional question to generate class discussion.

Critical Thinking: Analyzing Information What are some examples of how Don Quixote presents the *opposite* values of a true knight? *(selfish—attacks giants to become rich; overconfident—boastful that he can defeat larger enemy; blindness—can't see reality before him; foolish—won't consider the squire's warning)*

Analyzing Literature

***ANSWERS* 1.** A **2.** H **3. (a)** Answers will vary. Answers might include: battle fiercely against odds; bravery and boldness; sense of adventure. **(b)** Cervantes feels Don Quixote's ideals are silly because he makes the knight mistake windmills for fantastic giants and has Don Quixote speak with overconfidence and righteousness about himself and his exaggerated pursuit.

Vocabulary Answers

nigh—nearly, almost; **league**—unit of measure, about three miles; **millstone**—circular stone used to grind grain; **caitiffs**—cowardly, despicable characters

977

Primary Sources and Literature

The English Bill of Rights

When the Catholic king, James II, was forced from the English throne in 1688, Parliament offered the crown to his Protestant daughter Mary and her husband William of Orange. But Parliament insisted that William and Mary submit to a Bill of Rights. This document, a continuation of the struggle between the crown and Parliament, sums up the powers that Parliament had been seeking since the Petition of Right in 1628.

Vocabulary Before you read the selection, look up the following words in a dictionary: **subvert, extirpate, abdicated, prerogative, redress.**

Main Idea This document ensured the superiority of Parliament over the monarchy and spelled out basic rights.

Whereas, the late King James II . . . did endeavor to subvert and extirpate the Protestant religion and the laws and liberties of this kingdom . . . and whereas the said late King James II having abdicated the government, and the throne being vacant. . . .

The said lords [Parliament] . . . being now assembled in a full and free representative [body] of this nation . . . do in the first place . . . declare:

1. That the pretended power of suspending of laws or the execution of laws by regal authority without consent of Parliament is illegal. . . .
4. That levying money for or to the use of the crown by pretense of prerogative without grant of Parliament . . . is illegal;
5. That it is the right of the subjects to petition the king, and all commitments and prosecutions for such petitioning are illegal.
6. That . . . raising or keeping a standing army within the kingdom in time of peace, unless it be with consent of Parliament, is against law. . . .
8. That election of members of Parliament ought to be free. . . .
9. That the freedom of speech and debates or proceedings in Parliament ought not to be challenged or questioned in any court or place out of Parliament. . . .
10. That excessive bail ought not to be required, nor excessive fines imposed, nor cruel and unusual punishments inflicted. . . .
13. And that, for redress of all grievances and for the amending, strengthening, and preserving of the laws, Parliaments ought to be held frequently. . . .

English Houses of Parliament (1800s)

Analyzing Primary Sources

1. Which of the following statements best summarizes these excerpts from the Bill of Rights?

   A The king's powers are limited by the Parliament.

   B The Parliament's powers are limited by the monarch.

   C The Parliament's duty is to amend and preserve laws.

   D The king's powers to raise an army are unlimited.

2. This Bill of Rights required the monarch to

   E raise money for paying the members of Parliament.

   F summon Parliament regularly.

   G cancel laws he or she considered unjust.

   H keep a standing army to defend the country.

3. **Critical Thinking Making Inferences** Why do you think the members of Parliament included item 9? Why do you think this item was important?

John Locke: *Two Treatises on Government*

English philosopher John Locke (1632–1704) published *Two Treatises on Government* in 1690. In the writings, Locke holds that all people possess natural rights, including property and personal freedom. Locke also states that governments hold their power only with the consent of the people. Locke's ideas heavily influenced revolutions in America and France.

Vocabulary Before you read the selection, look up the following words in a dictionary: **promulgated, extemporary, inroads, transgress, endeavor, forfeit, devolves.**

Main Idea In this essay, Locke states that the primary purpose of government is to protect the natural rights of the people.

But though men, when they enter into society give up the equality, liberty, and executive power they had in the state of Nature into the hands of society . . . the power of the society or legislative constituted by them can never be supposed to extend farther than the common good. . . . Whoever has the legislative or supreme power of any commonwealth, is bound to govern by established standing laws, promulgated and known to the people, and not by extemporary decrees, by [unbiased] and upright judges, who are to decide controversies by those laws; and to employ the force of the community at home only in the execution of such laws, or abroad to prevent or redress foreign injuries and secure the community from inroads and invasion. And all this to be directed to no other end but the peace, safety, and public good of the people. . . .

The reason why men enter into society is the preservation of their property; and the end while they choose and authorize a legislative is that there may be laws made, and rules set, as guards and fences to the properties of all the society, . . .

Whensoever, therefore, the legislative [power] shall transgress this fundamental rule of society, and either by ambition, fear, folly, or corruption, endeavor to grasp themselves, or put into the hands of any other, an absolute power over the lives, liberties, and estates of the people, by this breach of trust they forfeit the power the people had put into their hands for quite contrary ends, and it devolves to the people; who have a right to resume their original liberty, and by the establishment of a new legislative (such as they shall think fit), provide for their own safety and security. . . .

Analyzing Primary Sources

1. Which of the following statements best summarizes the excerpt above?

   A People should give up their fundamental rights in order to establish absolute monarchies.

   B People establish governments in order to set and enforce laws. If a government does not do this, the people may abolish it.

   C Most legislative powers are corrupt.

   D Judges may need to act outside the law.

2. Which of the following groups has the final authority of government in Locke's opinion?

   E the legislature

   F the prince

   G the people

   H the judges

3. **Critical Thinking Making Inferences** According to Locke, what do people give up when they enter into a society? Why do you think people do this?

Background
About the Document

John Locke Locke wrote *Two Treatises on Government* in 1690 in part to "establish the throne of our great restorer, the present King William, to make good his title in the consent of the people." In other words, he wanted to make sure that this king was viewed as legitimate. Locke wrote that a ruler who fails to protect the rights of the people can be overthrown and replaced by the people.

Activity
Interpreting the Document

Use this additional question to generate class discussion.
Critical Thinking: Comparing How is the text of this excerpt similar to the text of the American Declaration of Independence? *(Students should be able to identify many similarities.)*

Analyzing Primary Sources

ANSWERS **1.** B **2.** G **3.** Locke says they give up the equality, liberty, and executive power that they had in the state of Nature in order to secure peace and safety through just government, rules, and laws.

Vocabulary Answers

promulgated—published or made known; **extemporary**—without any preparation; **inroads**—advances at the expense of someone; **transgress**—go beyond, break; **endeavor**—try; **forfeit**—lose something; **devolves**—passes

Resource Directory

Other Resources

Goldie, Mark, ed. *Locke: Political Essays.* New York: Cambridge University Press, 1997.

Kimmel, Michael S. and Charles Stephen, eds. *Social and Political Theory: Classical Readings.* Boston: Allyn and Bacon, 1998.

Ravitch, Diane, and Abigail Thernstrom, eds. *The Democracy Reader.* New York: HarperCollins, 1992.

Primary Sources and Literature

Jean-Jacques Rousseau:
The Social Contract

In *The Social Contract*, Rousseau (1712–1778) proposes an ideal society formed through a "social contract," and based on the natural will of the people. Rousseau believed that people in their natural state were basically good but were corrupted by the evils of society. The first lines of *The Social Contract*, "Man is born free, but is everywhere in chains," reflect this idea.

Vocabulary Before you read the selection, look up the following words in a dictionary: **indivisible, sovereign**.

> **Main Idea** — In consenting to form a government, Rousseau says, individuals choose to give up their self-interest in favor of the common good.

Find a form of association that defends and protects the person and goods of each associate with all the common force, and by means of which each one, uniting with all, nevertheless obeys only himself and remains as free as before. This is the fundamental problem which is solved by the social contract. . . .

[F]irst of all, since each one gives his entire self, the condition is equal for everyone, and since the condition is equal for everyone, no one has an interest in making it burdensome for the others. . . .

If, then, everything that is not the essence of the social compact is set aside, one will find that it can be reduced to the following terms: Each of us puts his person and all his power in common under the supreme direction of the general will; and in a body we receive each member as an indivisible part of the whole.

Instantly, in place of the private person of each contracting party, this act of association produces a moral and collective body, composed of as many members as there are voices in the assembly, which receives from this same act its unity, its common self, its life, and its will. This public person, formed thus by the union of all the others, formerly took the name City, and now takes that of Republic or body politic, which its members call State when it is passive, Sovereign when active, Power when comparing it to similar bodies. As for the associates, they collectively take the name People; and individually are called Citizens as participants in the sovereign authority, and Subjects as subjects to the laws of the State. . . .

*B*ackground
About the Document

Jean-Jacques Rousseau Rousseau believed that people were essentially good. He believed that educated people could improve modern civilization by taking control of their political, social, and educational environments. According to Rousseau, all people should be directly involved in political decision-making. He sometimes neglected to protect individual rights because he believed that a well-informed "general will" would always act in the public interest. In Rousseau's view, if a person was forced against his or her own will to obey the general will, that person was merely being led to do what the person would want to do if he or she fully understood the matter. Rousseau's ideas were influential in shaping the French Revolution.

*A*ctivity
Interpreting
the Document

Use this additional question to generate class discussion.
Critical Thinking: Recognizing Points of View What assumptions does Rousseau make about human nature? *(Rousseau assumes that people are basically good and that the "general will" will be moral.)*

Analyzing Primary Sources

ANSWERS **1.** B **2.** G **3.** The condition is equal for everyone, and no one has an interest in making it burdensome for others.

Vocabulary Answers

indivisible—not capable of being divided; **sovereign**—independent, superior to all others

Analyzing Primary Sources

1. According to Rousseau, "social contract" provides a solution to the fundamental problem of finding a form of government in which
   A people's differences can be solved peacefully.
   B people remain as free as they were without government.
   C people are not subject to unjust or immoral laws.
   D minorities are protected.

2. The Republic or body politic is defined by Rousseau as the
   E assembly.
   F collective body formed when the social contract is dissolved.
   G collective body formed when private persons enter into the social contract.
   H collective body appointed by the king.

3. **Critical Thinking Drawing Conclusions** Why does Rousseau believe that people are safe putting themselves under the direction of the "general will"?

980 *Reference Section*

Resource Directory

Teaching Resources
Viewpoint Activity *Enlightenment Views on Education,* Unit 5 booklet, p. 12

Other Resources
Cole, G. D. H., trans. *The Social Contract and Discourses.* New York: Everyman Paperback, 1973.

Gourevitch, Victor, trans. *The Social Contract and Other Later Political Writings.* New York: Cambridge University Press, 1997.

Declaration of the Rights of Man and the Citizen

The French National Assembly issued this document in 1789 after having overthrown the established government in the early stages of the French Revolution. The document was modeled in part on the English Bill of Rights and on the American Declaration of Independence.

Vocabulary Before you read the selection, look up the following words in a dictionary: **auspices, imprescriptible, indispensable.**

> **Main Idea** This declaration states the natural rights of French citizens and establishes the equality of all citizens before the law.

Therefore the National Assembly recognizes and proclaims, in the presence and under the auspices of the Supreme Being, the following rights of man and of the citizen:

1. Men are born and remain free and equal in rights. Social distinctions may be founded only upon the general good.
2. The aim of all political association is the preservation of the natural and imprescriptible rights of man. These rights are liberty, property, security, and resistance to oppression. . . .
4. Liberty consists in the freedom to do everything which injures no one else. . . .
5. Law can only prohibit such actions as are hurtful to society. . . .
6. Law is the expression of the general will. Every citizen has a right to participate personally, or through his representative, in its formation. It must be the same for all, whether it protects or punishes. All citizens, being equal in the eyes of the law, are equally eligible to all dignities and to all public positions and occupations, according to their abilities, and without distinction except that of their virtues and talents.
7. No person shall be accused, arrested, or imprisoned except in the cases and according to the forms prescribed by law. . . .
9. As all persons are held innocent until they shall have been declared guilty, if arrest shall be deemed indispensable, all harshness not essential to the securing of the prisoner's person shall be severely repressed by law. . . .
11. The free communication of ideas and opinions is one of the most precious of the rights of man. Every citizen may, accordingly, speak, write, and print with freedom. . . .
13. A common contribution is essential for the maintenance of the public [military] forces and for the cost of administration. This should be equitably distributed among all the citizens in proportion to their means.

Paris protesters during the French Revolution

Analyzing Primary Sources

1. Which of the following describes the tax policy set forth in this document?

   A All citizens must pay the same amount of tax.

   B Only citizens in the military must pay taxes.

   C All citizens pay taxes in proportion to their wealth.

   D There should be no taxes imposed on citizens.

2. Which article above specifically protects citizens from police brutality and torture?

   E 5

   F 6

   G 9

   H 11

3. **Critical Thinking Applying Information** Give one real-life example of each of the four natural rights listed under article 2.

Resource Directory

Teaching Resources

Creative Teaching Activities *On the Eve of Revolution* and *Revolutions of 1830 and 1848,* Creative Teaching Activities booklet, pp. 86 and 96

History Through Literature *A Tale of Two Cities* and *Les Misérables,* History Through Literature booklet, pp. 41–42 and pp. 45–46

Biography Activity *Maximilien Robespierre,* Unit 5 booklet, p. 30

Primary Source Activity *The Royal Family in Prison,* Unit 5 booklet, p. 31

Other Resources

Ravitch, Diane, and Abigail Thernstrom, eds. *The Democracy Reader.* New York: HarperCollins, 1992.

Background
About the Document

Citizenship This document was written in the early stages of the French Revolution when tensions were high due to high prices and shortages of food and work. It was issued on August 26 following the storming of the Bastille on July 14, an insurrection by peasants in the countryside in late July, and the abolishment of feudalism on August 4. It is significant that the Declaration speaks of both the man and of the citizen. Man possesses rights, but a citizen, as a member of the state, also possesses power.

Activity
Interpreting the Document

Use this additional question to generate class discussion.

Critical Thinking: Recognizing Points of View Which lines in this document show evidence of Jean-Jacques Rousseau's influence? *(Answers include, "men are born and remain free," "general good," "the aim of all political association is the preservation of the natural . . . rights of man," and "general will.")*

Analyzing Primary Sources

ANSWERS 1. C **2.** G **3.** Answers will vary. Sample answers include: liberty—the right to do everything that injures no one else; property—the right to own property; security—the right to be free from danger; resistance to oppression—the right to bear arms.

Vocabulary Answers

auspices—support, guiding sponsorship; **imprescriptible**—not able to command as a rule; **indispensable**—absolutely necessary

Background
About the Document

The Grito de Dolores Prior to issuing the Decree of Hidalgo, Miguel Hidalgo made a speech known as the *Grito de Dolores,* or Cry of Dolores. This speech said in part: "My children: a new dispensation comes to us today. Will you receive it? Will you free yourselves? Will you recover the lands stolen three hundred years ago from your forefathers by the hated Spaniards? We must act at once. . . . Will you not defend your religion and your rights as true patriots?"

Activity
Interpreting the Document

Use these additional questions to generate class discussion.

1. The introduction to this document says that the Mexicans must throw off those duties that do not contribute to the country's well-being. What are those two "duties"? *(slavery and taxation—the seal being a form of taxation)*

2. Critical Thinking: Predicting Consequences What is the inherent weakness of item number 1? *(Hidalgo needed the support of many people to enforce it. He also needed a strong and well-equipped army or court system.)*

Analyzing Primary Sources

ANSWERS 1. C **2.** E **3.** rights of liberty (slavery), equality (taxes based on race), and free speech (seal).

Vocabulary Answers

yoke—wooden bar with loops at either end, fitted around the necks of oxen; **exactions**—taxes

Miguel Hidalgo:
Decree of Hidalgo

Father Miguel Hidalgo of Mexico called for freedom from Spanish rule in 1810. The following decree, also issued in 1810 from Guadalajara, Jalisco, was an attempt to gain additional support for the uprising from Native Americans, blacks, and mestizos. In the end, Hidalgo's rebellion failed because creoles feared that more rights for Native Americans and an end to slavery would cost them power. Less than one year after the start of the uprising, Hidalgo was captured and executed, and his followers scattered.

Vocabulary Before you read the selection, look up the following words in a dictionary: **yoke, exactions**.

Main Idea In this decree, Hidalgo calls for an end to slavery and to the heavy taxes imposed on the poor in Mexico.

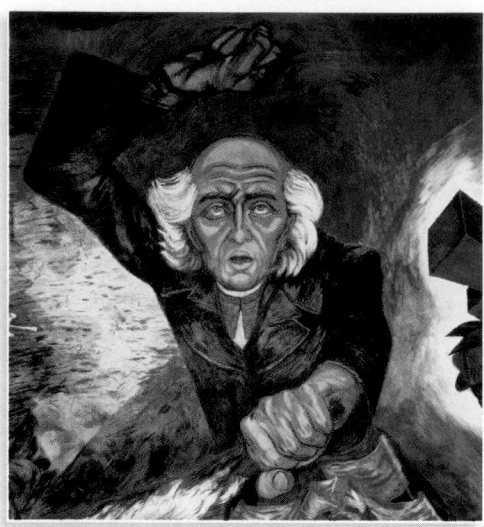
Miguel Hidalgo

From the happy moment that the valiant American nation took up arms to shake off the heavy yoke that has oppressed it for three centuries, one of the principal objectives has been to extinguish such duties that cannot advance its fortune, especially those which in these critical circumstances do not well serve that end or provide for the real need of the kingdom in meeting the costs of the struggle, so therefore there is now put forward here the most urgent remedy in the following declarations:

1. That all owners of slaves shall give them their freedom before the end of ten days, under penalty of death, which shall be applied to those who violate this article.
2. That from now on the collection of tributes according to [race] shall cease, as shall exactions that are demanded of the Indians.
3. That all legal business, documents, letters and actions can be on common paper, with the requirement of the seal totally abolished.

Analyzing Primary Sources

1. Item 2 of the Decree of Hidalgo calls for an end to
   A slavery.
   B collection of any taxes.
   C collection of taxes based on race.
   D all business transactions with mestizos and Indians.

2. What does "the seal" probably symbolize in item 3 above?
   E approval from Spanish authorities
   F a postage stamp
   G a special type of paper used for legal documents
   H respect for Native American traditions

3. **Critical Thinking Defending a Position** Latin American liberation movements were often based on Enlightenment ideas about natural rights. Describe some of the natural rights Hidalgo could have listed in his decree as explanations for why he wished to abolish slavery, taxes based on race, and the requirement of the seal.

982 *Reference Section*

Resource Directory

Teaching Resources
Biography Activity *Miguel Hidalgo y Costilla,* Unit 5 booklet, p. 64

Other Resources
Meyer, Michael C., and William L. Sherman, eds. *The Course of Mexican History.* New York: Oxford University Press, 1979.

Simón Bolívar: *Address to the Congress of Venezuela*

Encouraged by the revolutions in British North America and France, colonists in Spanish South America soon began to create a force for independence. Simón Bolívar was one of the leaders of this movement. The excerpt below, from Bolívar's Address to the Second National Congress of Venezuela, was given in 1819.

Vocabulary Before you read the selection, look up the following words in a dictionary: **pernicious, inflexible, arduous, erroneous, incentives, succulent.**

Main Idea   **In this speech, Bolívar offers advice on what type of government to set up in Venezuela.**

Subject to the threefold yoke of ignorance, tyranny, and vice, the American people have been unable to acquire knowledge, power, or [civic] virtue. The lessons we received and the models we studied, as pupils of such pernicious teachers, were most destructive. . . .

If a people, perverted by their training, succeed in achieving their liberty, they will soon lose it, for it would be of no avail to endeavor to explain to them that happiness consists in the practice of virtue; that the rule of law is more powerful than the rule of tyrants, because, as the laws are more inflexible, everyone should submit to their beneficent austerity; that proper morals, and not force, are the bases of law; and that to practice justice is to practice liberty. Therefore, Legislators, your work is so much the more arduous, inasmuch as you have to reeducate men who have been corrupted by erroneous illusions and false incentives. Liberty, says Rousseau, is a succulent morsel, but one difficult to digest. . . .

Legislators, meditate well before you choose. Forget not that you are to lay the political foundation for a newly born nation which can rise to the heights of greatness that Nature has marked out for it if you but proportion this foundation in keeping with the high plane that it aspires to attain. Unless your choice is based upon the peculiar . . . experience of Venezuelan people—a factor that should guide you in determining the nature and form of government you are about to adopt for the well-being of the people . . . the result of our reforms will again be slavery.

Simón Bolívar

Analyzing Primary Sources

1. Which statement best summarizes Bolívar's view of the people of Latin America?

   A They have not been well prepared for self-government by their former Spanish rulers.

   B They have been well prepared for self-government by the Spanish.

   C They had been ruled fairly by the Spanish.

   D They have very little desire for self-government.

2. Bolívar states that a government will be most effective if it

   E adheres closely to theories of good government.

   F imitates other successful governments.

   G is molded to fit the character of the nation for which it is built.

   H is based on the rule of law.

3. **Critical Thinking Defending a Position** Would you describe Bolívar as practical or idealistic? Use examples from the excerpt to defend your opinion.

Reference Section **983**

PRIMARY SOURCES AND LITERATURE

Background
About the Document

Simón Bolívar In addition to his military successes, Bolívar was an accomplished political thinker. As a pragmatist he wrote, "We must never forget that the excellence of a government lies not in its theories, not in its form or mechanisms, but in its being suited to the nature and character of the nation for which it is instituted."

Activity
Interpreting the Document

Use this additional question to generate class discussion.
Why does Bolívar think that the legislator's task of establishing a government is a difficult one? *(The people have been corrupted by the Spanish rulers; they are accustomed to bribery as a way of getting things, and they are not prepared to practice liberty.)*

Analyzing Primary Sources

ANSWERS 1. A **2.** G **3.** Answers will vary. Most students may see Bolívar as practical because he sees that governments cannot be based on theories alone, but must be adapted to suit the experience of the people for whom they are built.

Vocabulary Answers

pernicious—wicked; **inflexible**—unyielding, unable to change; **arduous**—difficult; **erroneous**—mistaken, wrong; **incentives**—rewards; **succulent**—juicy, not dry or dull

---

Resource Directory

Teaching Resources
Viewpoint Activity *Why Latin Americans Wanted Independence,* Unit 5 booklet, p. 66
Skill Application Activity *Identifying Ideologies,* Unit 5 booklet, p. 67

Other Resources
Bolívar, Simón. *Selected Writings.* New York: The Colonial Press, 1951.

Background
About the Document

Voice of Conscience Dickens wrote this novel in 1854 after visiting the city of Preston, England, which in the mid-1800s was a growing industrial center. Preston had about 40 factories, mostly spinning mills, and was also a port for coal.

Hard Times, as many of his novels, criticized social and political shortcomings, helping gain Dickens the reputation of being a voice of conscience for his age. In the character of Thomas Gradgrind, the extremely practical factory owner, Dickens criticized the attitude that suppressed imagination and individuality.

Activity
Interpreting the Document

Use this additional question to generate class discussion.
Critical Thinking: Analyzing Information
Why do you think Dickens mentions good, evil, patriotism, virtue, and vice in the third paragraph? *(These qualities are essential differences that exist between machine and man. These qualities are suppressed and lie dormant when people are put in the role of machines, or "Hands" working machines.)*

Analyzing Primary Sources

ANSWERS 1. C 2. H 3. (a) The work they do involves only their hands and requires no thinking. **(b)** He seems to pity them. **(c)** The general attitude is negative. It creates a dirty environment and turns people into machines.

Vocabulary Answers

clogs—wooden-soled shoes; **melancholy**—depressed or pensive mood; **monotony**—tedious sameness; **consign**—turn over control; **decomposition**—corruption; **unfathomable**—unable to be understood; **shrouded**—veiled or obscured

Charles Dickens: *Hard Times*

In *Hard Times*, Charles Dickens protests the dehumanizing conditions of factory life in nineteenth-century England. In this excerpt from the novel, Dickens describes early morning in a fictional factory town named Coketown. (Coke is a form of coal.)

Vocabulary Before you read the selection, look up the following words in a dictionary: **clogs, melancholy, monotony, consign, decomposition, unfathomable, shrouded.**

Main Idea In this excerpt from the novel, Dickens depicts the labor conditions of the early Industrial Revolution.

The Fairy palaces burst into illumination, before pale morning showed the monstrous serpents of smoke trailing themselves over Coketown. A clattering of clogs upon the pavement; a rapid ringing of bells; and all the melancholy mad elephants, polished and oiled up for the day's monotony, were at their heavy exercise again.

Stephen bent over his loom, quiet, watchful, and steady. A special contrast, as every man was in the forest of looms where Stephen worked, to the crashing, smashing, tearing piece of mechanism at which he laboured. Never fear, good people of an anxious turn of mind, that Art will consign Nature to Oblivion. Set anywhere, side by side, the work of God and the work of man; and the former, even though it be a troop of Hands of very small account, will gain in dignity from the comparison.

So many hundred Hands in this Mill; so many hundred horse Steam Power. It is known, to the force of a single pound weight, what the engine will do; but, not all the calculators of the National Debt can tell me the capacity for good or evil, for love or hatred, for patriotism or discontent, for the decomposition of virtue into vice, or the reverse, at any single moment in the soul of one of these its quiet servants, with the composed faces and the regulated actions. There is no mystery in it; there is an unfathomable mystery in the meanest of them, for ever. . . .

The day grew strong, and showed itself outside, even against the flaming lights within. The lights were turned out, and the work went on. The rain fell, and the Smoke-serpents, submissive to the curse of all that tribe, trailed themselves upon the earth. In the waste-yard outside, the steam from the escape pipe, the litter of barrels and old iron, the shining heaps of coals, the ashes everywhere, were shrouded in a veil of mist and rain.

The work went on, until the noon-bell rang. More clattering upon the pavements. The looms, and wheels, and Hands all out of gear for an hour.

A spinning mule

Analyzing Primary Sources

1. What are the "melancholy mad elephants" to which Dickens refers in the excerpt above?
   A factory workers
   B factory owners
   C power looms
   D steam locomotives

2. According to this passage, facts cannot predict
   E the national debt.
   F the potential output of a factory.
   G the amount of work an individual can complete in a day.
   H the capacity of any individual for good or evil.

3. **Critical Thinking Making Inferences**
   (a) Why does Dickens refer to the factory workers as "Hands"? **(b)** What seems to be his attitude toward the workers? **(c)** What seems to be his general attitude toward the Industrial Revolution?

Resource Directory

Other Resources

Doorway to Dickens (videorecording). BBC Education in association with the Dickens Project, University of California, 1997.

Ford, George, and Sylvère Monod. *Hard Times: An Authoritative Text, Backgrounds, Sources, and Contemporary Reactions, Criticism.* New York: Norton, 1990.

Leavis, R., and Q.D. *Dickens, the Novelist.* Chatto & London: Windus, 1979.

Rooke, Patrick J. *The Age of Dickens.* New York: Putnam, 1970.

Wilson, Angus. *The World of Charles Dickens.* New York: Viking Press, 1970.

Fukuzawa Yukichi: *Autobiography*

In 1860, Fukuzawa Yukichi joined the first Japanese mission to the United States. When he returned home, he wrote articles and books explaining western customs and practices to the Japanese. This selection from his *Autobiography* recalls his impressions of his first days in San Francisco.

Vocabulary Before you read the selection, look up the following words in a dictionary: **inexplicable, revered**.

> **Main Idea** In this autobiography, Fukuzawa Yukichi shows some of the differences between American and Japanese cultures and attitudes.

All of us wore the usual pair of swords at our sides and the [rope] sandals. So attired, we were taken to the modern hotel. There we noticed, covering the interior, the valuable carpets which in Japan only the more wealthy could buy from importers' shops at so much a square inch to make purses and tobacco pouches with. Here the carpet was laid over an entire room—something quite astounding—upon this costly fabric walked our hosts wearing the shoes with which they had come in from the streets!

One evening our hosts said that some ladies and gentlemen were having a dancing party and that they would be glad to have us attend it. We went. To our dismay we could not make out what they were doing. The ladies and gentlemen seemed to be hopping about the room together. As funny as it was, we knew it would be rude to laugh, and we controlled our expressions with difficulty as the dancing went on. These were but a few of the instances of our bewilderment at the strange customs of American society.

When we were taking leave, our host and hostess kindly offered us horses to ride home on. This pleased us, for a chance to ride horseback again was a relief. . . . We touched whip to the horses and rode back to our quarters at a trot. The Americans watched us and exclaimed at the Japanese ability in riding. So neither of us really knew much about the other after all. . . .

Things social, political, and economic proved most inexplicable. One day, on a sudden thought, I asked a gentleman where the descendants of George Washington might be. He replied, "I think there is a woman who is directly descended from Washington. I don't know where she is now, but I think I have heard she is married." His answer was so very casual that it shocked me.

Of course, I knew that America was a republic with a new president every four years, but I could not help feeling that the family of Washington would be revered above all other families. My reasoning was based on the reverence in Japan for the founders of the great line of rulers. . . .

Japanese textile workers

Analyzing Primary Sources

1. Fukuzawa views the dance with
   A fear.
   B horror.
   C reverence.
   D amusement.

2. What conclusion does Fukuzawa come to after the incident with the horses?
   E Americans do not understand the Japanese.
   F Americans do not respect the Japanese.
   G Americans are not as skilled riders as the Japanese.
   H Americans are more skillful riders than the Japanese.

3. **Critical Thinking Recognizing Points of View** (a) Why did Fukuzawa Yukichi expect Americans to treat the descendants of George Washington with respect? (b) What does this incident suggest about the differing cultural values of Japan and the United States?

Background
About the Document

Opening Japan Fukuzawa Yukichi was an educator who became a leader in opening Japan to western ways after a period of isolation. After traveling to the West in 1862, he wrote *Conditions in the West,* an account of western ways that became an overnight success in Japan. Conservative opponents, however, made several attempts on his life. In 1868, he founded a school in Tokyo that later became Keio University, Japan's first large university that was independent of government control. Many business leaders were educated there.

Fukuzawa worked to develop his simple, clear writing style to describe western political, economic, and cultural traditions and institutions. He wrote more than 100 books on how to introduce change in Japan. He founded "Current Events," which became the most influential newspaper in Japan and cultivated many liberal politicians and journalists. Just before he died in 1901, he completed his *Autobiography,* in which he expressed his gratification to see the fulfillment of his goals for Japan.

Activity
Interpreting the Document

Use this additional question to generate class discussion.
Critical Thinking: Making Inferences How might Fukuzawa's description of the way the carpet was treated in the hotel have created a myth about America? *(It gives the impression that Americans are so wealthy they can walk on expensive carpets, which, in Japan, would be used for making luxury items.)*

Analyzing Primary Sources

ANSWERS **1.** D **2.** E **3. (a)** He was the founder of the Republic. **(b)** Answers might include that the Japanese have great reverence for their leaders and the families of their leaders.

Vocabulary Answers

inexplicable—unexplainable; **revered**—highly respected

Background
About the Document

Disillusionment with War *All Quiet on the Western Front,* a title that reflects the terse style of military communiqués, expresses the disillusionment with the war among participants who were shocked by the disjuncture between the rhetoric of patriotism and the reality of trench warfare. The book became an immediate success, and in 1930 an American film was made based on it. *The Road Back,* Remarque's sequel to *All Quiet on the Western Front,* deals with the collapse of Germany in 1918. Nazis banned his books in 1933. Remarque, a German, left his homeland and became an American citizen. He later moved to Switzerland, where he lived until his death in 1970.

Activity
Interpreting the Document

Use this additional question to generate class discussion.
Critical Thinking: Making Inferences What effect does this experience have on the narrator, and how does he believe it will affect his life after the war? Explain. *(It transforms him. He suddenly realizes that he has killed at least one soldier who might have been his best friend or brother, someone like himself. He seems to have lost hope, and he is unsure that he will ever be able to lead a normal life.)*

Analyzing Literature

ANSWERS **1.** D **2.** E **3. (a)** that enemy soldiers are fellow humans alike **(b)** It expresses disillusionment about the war. Soldiers join the fighting without realizing what it means to kill another human.

Vocabulary Answer

abstraction—a theoretical notion, detached from the actual thing

Erich Maria Remarque:
All Quiet on the Western Front

Erich Maria Remarque was wounded five times while serving in the German army during World War I. In 1928, he published *All Quiet on the Western Front,* which is often considered the greatest novel about the war. It follows the narrator, Paul Baumer, from eager recruit to disillusioned veteran. In this passage, Paul is trapped for hours in a foxhole with a French soldier he has just killed.

Vocabulary Before you read the selection, look up the following word in a dictionary: **abstraction.**

Main Idea | In this excerpt from a novel, a young German soldier expresses his horror at killing a man hand-to-hand.

In the afternoon, about three, he is dead.

I breathe freely again. But only for a short time. Soon the silence is more unbearable than the groans. I wish the gurgling were there again, gasping hoarse, now whistling softly and again hoarse and loud.

It is mad, what I do. But I must do something. I prop the dead man up again so that he lies comfortably, although he feels nothing any more. I close his eyes. They are brown, his hair is black and a bit curly at the sides. . . .

German soldiers on their way to the front

The silence spreads. I talk and must talk. So I speak to him and say to him: "Comrade, I did not want to kill you. If you jumped in here again, I would not do it, if you would be sensible too. But you were only an idea to me before, an abstraction that lived in my mind and called forth its appropriate response. It was that abstraction I stabbed. But now, for the first time, I see you are a man like me. I thought of your hand-grenades, of your bayonet, of your rifle; now I see your wife and your face and our fellowship. Forgive me, comrade. We always see it too late. Why do they never tell us that you are poor devils like us, that your mothers are just as anxious as ours, and that we have the same fear of death, and the same dying and the same agony—Forgive me, comrade; how could you be my enemy? If we threw away these rifles and this uniform you could be my brother just like Kat and Albert. Take twenty years of my life, comrade, and stand up—take more, for I do not know what I can even attempt to do with it now."

Analyzing Literature

1. Why does Paul finally speak to the French soldier?

   A He does not know that the French soldier is dead.

   B He hopes to nurse the French soldier back to life.

   C He wants to brag about his victory over his enemy.

   D He can no longer stand the silence in the foxhole.

2. According to Paul, he can no longer see the French soldier as

   E an abstraction.

   F a human being.

   G a "poor devil."

   H a dead body.

3. **Critical Thinking Recognizing Points of View (a)** What does Paul mean by "We always see it too late"? **(b)** How does this passage reflect what you know about the morale of soldiers late in the war?

986 *Reference Section*

Resource Directory

Teaching Resources
Creative Teaching Activities *A New Kind of Conflict,* Creative Teaching Activities booklet, p. 123
History Through Literature *All Quiet on the Western Front,* History Through Literature booklet, pp. 57–58

Other Resources
Milestone, Lewis (director). *All Quiet on the Western Front* (videorecording). Universal City, Cal.: Universal-International, MCA Videocassette, 1981.

Remarque, Erich Maria. *All Quiet on the Western Front.* Greenwich, Conn.: Fawcett Publications, 1965.

Remarque, Erich Maria. *The Road Back.* Toronto: McClelland & Steward, 1931.

Mohandas Gandhi: *Hind Swaraj*

Mohandas Gandhi led a successful, peaceful revolution in India against British rule. In the following excerpt from his book *Hind Swaraj* (*Indian Home Rule*), published in 1938, Gandhi explains the ideas behind his nonviolent method of passive resistance in the form of an imaginary conversation between an editor and a reader.

Vocabulary Before you read the selection, look up the following words in a dictionary: **repugnant, breach.**

> **Main Idea** In this imaginary interview, Gandhi explains the ideas behind his nonviolent method of passive resistance.

Editor: Passive resistance is a method of securing rights by personal suffering; it is the reverse of resistance by arms. When I refuse to do a thing that is repugnant to my conscience, I use soul-force. For instance, the Government of the day has passed a law which is applicable to me. I do not like it. If by using violence I force the Government to repeal the law, I am employing what may be termed body-force. If I do not obey the law and accept the penalty for its breach, I use soul-force. It involves sacrifice of self.

Everybody admits that sacrifice of self is infinitely superior to sacrifice of others. Moreover, if this kind of force is used in a cause that is unjust, only the person using it suffers. He does not make others suffer for his mistakes. . . . No man can claim that he is absolutely in the right or that a particular thing is wrong because he thinks so, but it is wrong for him so long as that is his deliberate judgment. It is therefore meet [proper] that he should not do that which he knows to be wrong, and suffer the consequence whatever it may be. This is the key to the use of soul-force.

Reader: You would then disregard laws—this is rank disloyalty. We have always been considered a law-abiding nation. You seem to be going even beyond the extremists. They say that we must obey the laws that have been passed, but that if the laws be bad, we must drive out the lawgivers even by force.

Editor: Whether I go beyond them or whether I do not is a matter of no consequence to either of us. We simply want to find out what is right and to act accordingly. The real meaning of the statement that we are a law-abiding nation is that we are passive resisters. When we do not like certain laws, we do not break the heads of law-givers but we suffer and do not submit to the laws.

Mohandas Gandhi

Analyzing Primary Sources

1. What is the goal of passive resistance?

   A to bring about peaceful change

   B to gain support for violence

   C to discover truth

   D to injure wrongdoers

2. The author defines soul-force as

   E weapons used for peaceful purposes.

   F refusal to obey a law that is unjust and accepting the penalty.

   G trying to determine what is right.

   H obeying all laws while working to overthrow the lawmakers.

3. **Critical Thinking Understanding Sequence** (a) According to Gandhi, could soul-force ever be used to support an unjust cause? (b) What does Gandhi mean when he says that a person using soul-force "does not make others suffer for his mistakes"?

Reference Section **987**

PRIMARY SOURCES AND LITERATURE

*B*ackground
About the Document

Mohandas Gandhi Mohandas Gandhi was trained as a lawyer in England and practiced in South Africa where he was politically active in opposing race policies. In India following World War I he became the head of the Indian National Congress and worked for independence from British rule. Gandhi consistently opposed armed opposition to the British. The moral pressure he applied gradually wore down the British resolve to rule the country, and in 1947 he negotiated with the British for Indian independence. He was assassinated in 1948.

*A*ctivity
Interpreting the Document

Use these additional questions to generate class discussion.

1. Why does soul-force involve sacrifice of self? *(The person practicing soul-force must accept the consequences of breaking a law.)*

2. Critical Thinking: Making Inferences What character traits would a person who practices passive resistance need? *(courage, honesty, bravery, patience, thoughtfulness, self-discipline)*

Analyzing Primary Sources

ANSWERS 1. A **2.** F **3. (a)** Yes. The one using it for unjust causes is not making others suffer for his mistakes because he is sacrificing himself for what he believes in. **(b)** He is not acting violently toward others to accomplish his goal. If he is mistaken—if what he believes in is not the truth—he has hurt only himself.

Vocabulary Answers

repugnant—opposed, offensive; **breach**—being broken

Resource Directory

Teaching Resources

History Through Literature *The Day Gandhi Was Shot,* History Through Literature booklet, pp. 72–74

Creative Teaching Activities *India Seeks Self-Rule,* Creative Teaching Activities booklet, p. 131

Other Resources

Parel, Anthony J. *Hind Swaraj and Other Writings of M.K. Gandhi.* New York: Cambridge University Press, 1997.

Primary Sources and Literature

Background
About the Document

Preparations for War Roosevelt delivered this address to Congress in January 1941. Roosevelt knew in 1940 that the United States would have to help Great Britain if Britain was not to fall to Hitler. But could he convince the country in time? Roosevelt's plan to build 50,000 planes in 1941 and his development of the Lend-Lease program were practical preparations for involvement in the war. This Four Freedoms speech was in some ways a spiritual or moral preparation, outlining for the nation the underlying purpose for fighting the war.

Activity
Interpreting
the Document

Use this additional question to generate class discussion.
Critical Thinking: Drawing Conclusions What does Roosevelt mean when he says that "this nation has placed its destiny in the hands and heads and hearts of its millions of free men and women"? *(He means that because we are a democracy, the people decide what the future will be like through their political participation, acts of charity, work, and ability to use their ideas to solve problems and build a better country.)*

Analyzing Primary Sources

ANSWERS **1.** C **2.** G **3. (a)** Answers will vary. Students may suggest the following: disarmament, mediation of potential conflicts, an end to torture and political imprisonment. **(b)** America's neutrality and Roosevelt's Lend-Lease program reflected Roosevelt's belief that free countries should work together to preserve freedom.

Vocabulary Answers

perpetual—continuing indefinitely without interruption; **quick-lime**—calcium oxide; substance that is used to decompose corpses

Franklin D. Roosevelt:
The Four Freedoms

Franklin D. Roosevelt delivered the following address to Congress in January 1941, after having been elected to a third term as president of the United States. In the speech, he described the "four freedoms" that he hoped would be secured throughout the world. As he spoke, most of Europe had already fallen to Hitler's tyranny and Great Britain was struggling against the threat of German invasion.

Vocabulary Before you read the selection, look up the following words in a dictionary: **perpetual, quick-lime.**

Main Idea In this speech, Roosevelt vows to protect what he describes as the four "essential human freedoms."

In the future days, which we seek to make secure, we look forward to a world founded upon four essential human freedoms.

The first is freedom of speech and expression—everywhere in the world.

The second is freedom of every person to worship God in his own way—everywhere in the world.

The third is freedom from want—which translated into world terms, means economic understandings which will secure to every nation a healthy peace time life for its inhabitants—everywhere in the world.

The fourth is freedom from fear—which translated into world terms, means a worldwide reduction of armaments to such a point and in such a thorough fashion that no nation will be in a position to commit an act of physical aggression against any neighbor—anywhere in the world. . . .

Since the beginning of our American history we have been engaged in change—in a perpetual peaceful revolution—a revolution which goes on steadily, quietly adjusting itself to changing conditions—without the concentration camp or the quick-lime in the ditch. The world order which we seek is the cooperation of free countries, working together in a friendly civilized society.

This nation has placed its destiny in the hands and heads and hearts of its millions of free men and women; and its faith in freedom under the guidance of God. Freedom means the supremacy of human rights everywhere. Our support goes to those who struggle to gain those rights or keep them. Our strength is in our unity of purpose.

To that high concept there can be no end save victory.

Honolulu Star-Bulletin 1st EXTRA

WAR!

(Associated Press by Transpacific Telephone)
SAN FRANCISCO, Dec. 7.—President Roosevelt announced this morning that Japanese planes had attacked Manila and Pearl Harbor.

OAHU BOMBED BY JAPANESE PLANES

Newspaper headline, December 7, 1941

Analyzing Primary Sources

1. Being able to make a living and support one's family is an example of
   A freedom of speech.
   B freedom of worship.
   C freedom from want.
   D freedom from fear.
2. Roosevelt thinks the nation's strength comes from
   E citizens worshipping together.
   F its support for other nations.
   G citizens working together for a common purpose.
   H carrying out change in a peaceful manner.
3. **Critical Thinking Applying Information**
   (a) Describe some of the specific actions that might be necessary to secure "freedom from fear," as Roosevelt describes it.
   (b) How does American foreign policy in the years before the United States entered World War II reflect Roosevelt's views?

988 *Reference Section*

Resource Directory

Teaching Resources
Creative Teaching Activities *The Global Conflict: Allied Successes,* Creative Teaching Activity booklet, p. 140
Other Resources
Ravitch, Diane, and Abigail Thernstrom, eds. *The Democracy Reader.* New York: HarperCollins, 1992.

The Universal Declaration of Human Rights

The General Assembly of the United Nations adopted this declaration on December 10, 1948. They hoped that it would become a standard by which liberty and freedom could be judged throughout the world.

Vocabulary Before you read the selection, look up the following words in a dictionary: **servitude, arbitrary**.

Main Idea This UN declaration sets forth the basic liberties and freedoms to which all people are entitled.

Article 1 All human beings are born free and equal in dignity and rights. They are endowed with reason and conscience and should act towards one another in a spirit of brotherhood.

Article 2 Everyone is entitled to all the rights and freedoms set forth in this Declaration, without distinction of any kind, such as race, color, sex, language, religion, political or other opinion, national or social origin, property, birth or other status. . . .

Article 3 Everyone has the right to life, liberty and security of person.

Article 4 No one shall be held in slavery or servitude. . . .

Article 5 No one shall be subjected to torture or to cruel, inhuman or degrading treatment or punishment. . . .

Article 9 No one shall be subjected to arbitrary arrest, detention or exile. . . .

Article 13 Everyone has the right to freedom of movement. . . .

Article 18 Everyone has the right to freedom of thought, conscience and religion. . . .

Article 19 Everyone has the right to freedom of opinion and expression. . . .

Article 20 Everyone has the right to freedom of peaceful assembly and association. . . .

Article 23 Everyone has the right to work, to free choice of employment, to just and favorable conditions of work and to protection against unemployment. . . .

Article 25 Everyone has the right to a standard of living adequate for the health and well-being of himself and of his family, including food, clothing, housing and medical care and necessary social services, and the right to security in the event of unemployment, sickness, disability, widowhood, old age or other lack of livelihood. . . .

Article 26 Everyone has the right to education. Education shall be free, at least in the elementary and fundamental stages.

United Nations building in New York City

Analyzing Primary Sources

1. Which of the following statements would best be supported by Article 5?

   A The United Nations will take action to punish a nation that uses torture.

   B Trial by jury should be considered a basic human right.

   C Punishments that inflict pain on prisoners are a violation of basic human rights.

   D Long prison sentences are a form of cruel and inhuman punishment.

2. Which of the following articles states that a person has the right to live free from hunger?

   E Article 1

   F Article 9

   G Article 23

   H Article 25

3. **Critical Thinking Drawing Conclusions** In what ways might the existence of this declaration benefit people living under an oppressive government?

Reference Section **989**

Background
About the Document

Eleanor Roosevelt Eleanor Roosevelt served as chairperson of the United Nations committee appointed to draft this declaration. The document enumerates political and civil rights (that were insisted upon by the western democracies) as well as social and economic rights (insisted upon by the socialist countries). Although many United Nations members regularly ignore provisions of the document, it still serves as a reminder of the freedoms and liberties to which humans aspire.

Activity
Interpreting the Document

Use this additional question to generate class discussion.

Critical Thinking: Comparing This document can be viewed as a summary of the rights of citizens and restraints on the power of the state that had evolved over centuries. Compare this document to the Magna Carta, the English Bill of Rights, the Declaration of the Rights of Man, and the Decree of Hidalgo. What does this document have in common with those? *(Sample answers include statements of rights and liberties, freedom of religion, abolishing slavery, freedom from arbitrary arrest, and freedom of speech or expression.)*

Analyzing Primary Sources

ANSWERS 1. C 2. H 3. People living under an oppressive government can use the legal and moral authority of this document to press for change and to draw international attention to their cause.

Vocabulary Answers

servitude—forced labor; **arbitrary**—not fixed by rules, based on whim, dictatorial

Primary Sources and Literature

Background
About the Document

Mao Zedong The 1949 victory of the Communists in the Chinese civil war made way for the leadership of Mao Zedong. Mao's argument, excerpted here, that there is only room in a country for one voice or for those who agree with the Communist Party's views reached its height during the anarchy of the Red Guards in 1967.

Activity
Interpreting the Document

Use this additional question to generate class discussion.
Critical Thinking: Recognizing Propaganda How does Mao use the word democracy? *(Students may point out that democracy means rule by the people, not rule by some of the people. Also, it is clear from the document that people who do not agree with the communist leadership are not considered "people" and are not allowed to vote. People cannot disagree or make choices as in a real democracy.)*

Analyzing Primary Sources

ANSWERS **1.** C **2.** H **3. (a)** They are denied a voice because their voice would be in opposition to "the people," and their opposition would interfere with the revolution. **(b)** Mao does not view the members of the landlord and capitalist classes as "the people." Most Americans believe all classes in society are "the people."

Vocabulary Answers

henchmen—the followers of a criminal gang leader; **reactionaries**—people who favor moving back to a less advanced condition; extreme conservatives; **apparatus**—the system by which something is kept in action; instruments, tools

Mao Zedong: *The People's Democratic Dictatorship*

In this speech, given in 1949 on the anniversary of the founding of the Communist Party, Mao Zedong explains the philosophy that guides China under his leadership. Mao's ideas were heavily influenced by the communist philosopher Karl Marx.

Vocabulary Before you read the selection, look up the following words in a dictionary: **henchmen, reactionaries, apparatus.**

Main Idea In this speech, Mao explains what groups of people will be denied basic rights in his government and why.

Who are the "people"? At the present stage in China, they are the working class, the peasantry, the petit bourgeoisie and the national bourgeoisie.

Under the leadership of the working class and the Communist Party, these classes unite to create their own state and elect their own government so as to enforce their dictatorship over the henchmen of imperialism—the landlord class and bureaucratic capitalist class. . . . The people's government will suppress such persons. It will only permit them to behave themselves properly. It will not allow them to speak or act wildly. Should they do so, they will be instantly curbed and punished. The democratic system is to be carried out within the ranks of the people, giving them freedom of speech, assembly and association. The right to vote is given only to the people, not to the reactionaries.

These two things, democracy for the people and dictatorship for the reactionaries, when combined, constitute the people's democratic dictatorship.

Why must things be done in this way? Everyone is very clear on this point. If things were not done like this, the revolution would fail, the people would suffer and the state would perish. . . .

Our present task is to strengthen the people's state apparatus—meaning principally the people's army, the people's police and the people's courts—thereby safeguarding national defense and protecting the people's interests. Given these conditions, China, under the leadership of the working class and the Communist Party, can develop steadily from an agricultural into an industrial country and from a New Democratic into a Socialist and, eventually, Communist society, eliminating classes and realizing universal harmony.

Mao Zedong

Analyzing Primary Sources

1. According to Mao, what class of people are the "reactionaries"?
   A the peasants
   B the bourgeoisie
   C the landlords and capitalists
   D the working class
2. Mao claims that the Communist Party in China represents the interests of
   E landlords.
   F capitalists.
   G imperialists.
   H working class.
3. **Critical Thinking Recognizing Points of View (a)** Why does Mao Zedong claim that the "people's government" is justified in denying some groups of people the right to freedom of speech? **(b)** How does Mao's view of democracy differ from that generally accepted by most Americans?

Resource Directory

Teaching Resources
Primary Source Activity *The Long March Across China,* Unit 7 booklet, p. 49
Other Resources
Tse-tung, Mao. *On People's Democratic Dictatorship.* Peking: Foreign Language Press, 1950.

Chinua Achebe: *Things Fall Apart*

In his famous 1959 novel *Things Fall Apart*, Nigerian writer Chinua Achebe described the effects imperialism had on traditional Ibo society. In this excerpt, Okonkwo returns to his village to discover that the traditional laws have been supplanted by European religion and government.

Main Idea In this excerpt from a novel, two characters discuss the ways in which Europeans were able to gain power in an African village.

"Perhaps I have been away too long," Okonkwo said almost to himself. "But I cannot understand these things you tell me. What is it that has happened to our people? Why have they lost the power to fight?"

"Have you not heard how the white man wiped out Abame?" asked Obierika.

"I have heard," said Okonkwo. "But I have also heard that Abame people were weak and foolish. Why did they not fight back? . . . We would be cowards to compare ourselves with the men of Abame. Their fathers had never dared to stand before our ancestors. We must fight these men and drive them from the land."

"It is already too late," said Obierika sadly. "Our own men and our sons have joined the ranks of the stranger. They have joined his religion and they help to uphold his government. If we should try to drive out the white men in Umuofia we should find it easy. There are only two of them. But what of our own people who are following their way and have been given power? They would go to Umuru and bring the soldiers, and we would be like Abame." He paused for a long time and then said: "I told you on my last visit to Mbanta how they hanged Aneto."

"What has happened to that piece of land in dispute?" asked Okonkwo.

"The white man's court has decided that it should belong to Nnama's family, who had given much money to the white man's messengers and interpreter."

"Does the white man understand our custom about land?"

"How can he when he does not even speak our tongue? But he says that our customs are bad; and our own brothers who have taken up his religion also say that our customs are bad. How do you think we can fight when our own brothers have turned against us? The white man is very clever. He came quietly and peaceably with his religion. We were amused at his foolishness and allowed him to stay. Now he has won our brothers, and our clan can no longer act like one. He has put a knife on the things that held us together and we have fallen apart."

Analyzing Primary Sources

1. In this passage, Okonkwo says that he wants to
   A drive the Europeans away.
   B learn European customs.
   C teach African customs to the Europeans.
   D go to war against Abame.

2. In this passage, Obierika feels helpless because
   E Okonkwo stayed away too long.
   F he fears the Abame tribe.

   G the tribe has divided into opposing factions.
   H he has lost his family's land in a court dispute.

3. **Critical Thinking Recognizing Points of View** (a) According to Obierika, how have Europeans "put a knife on the things that held us together"? (b) Why do you think a contemporary Nigerian author would choose to write a novel about the early days of imperialism?

Reference Section **991**

*B*ackground
About the Document

Conflicting Values The main themes that concern the novels of prominent Ibo writer Chinua Achebe are the changes brought on his people by the introduction of western society and its values. In his first novel, *Things Fall Apart,* published in 1959, he explores the effects of the first contact with missionaries on traditional values. In later novels he explores the moral dilemmas and conflicts of values faced by individuals who live under the new order of postcolonial Africa. Achebe's other novels include *No Longer at Ease, Arrow of God, A Man of the People,* and *Anthills of the Savannah.*

*A*ctivity
Interpreting the Document

Use this additional question to generate class discussion.

Critical Thinking: Synthesizing Information How did the white man gain power, and what criticisms does Obierika make of the white man? *(Gain power—At first the people did not take the missionaries seriously but tolerated their unusual ways. Gradually, however, the people were converted and turned against their traditional values and each other. Criticisms—The white man did not speak the local language or understand the people's laws, as the incident of the disputed land shows. Also, white officials took bribes and were not interested in justice.)*

Analyzing Primary Sources

ANSWERS **1.** A **2.** G **3. (a)** The white man has divided the people so that they no longer support the same religious, political, and social systems. **(b)** Answers will vary. Students' answers should show an understanding that the author felt it is important for people to be aware that imperialism inflicted an injustice on his people. In the process, aspects of Nigerian culture and identity were lost.

Resource Directory

Teaching Resources
Viewpoint Activity *Two Views of Imperialism in Africa,* Unit 6 booklet, p. 70
Prentice Hall Literature Library *World Writers Today,* pp. 192–200

Other Resources
Achebe, Chinua. *Things Fall Apart.* New York: Anchor Books, 1994.

Lindfors, Bernth, ed. *Approaches to Teaching Achebe's Things Fall Apart.* New York: Modern Language Association of America, 1991.

Petersen, Kirsten Holst, and Anna Rutherford, eds. *Chinua Achebe: A Celebration.* Portsmouth, N. H.: Heinemann, 1991.

Podis, Leonard A., and Yakubu Saaka, eds. *Challenging Hierarchies: Issues and Themes in Colonial and Postcolonial African Literature.* New York: P. Lang, 1998.

Wren, Robert M. *Achebe's World: The Historical and Cultural Context of the Novels of Chinua Achebe.* Washington, D.C.: Three Continents Press, 1980.

Background
About the Document

Kwame Nkrumah In his *Autobiography*, written in the 1950s, Nkrumah looked beyond the immediate goal of independence for Gold Coast to the economic challenges that the nation would face following independence. Nkrumah began addressing these challenges as leader of Ghana in its early years, but in 1966 he was overthrown by an army coup and forced into exile.

Activity
Interpreting the Document

Use these additional questions to generate class discussion.

1. Ask students why Nkrumah believed that disturbances and political tension were a logical result of colonialism. *(The system is not designed to benefit the colonized people, and such people will try to rid themselves of colonial rule.)*

2. Critical Thinking: Making Inferences Ask students how they think Nkrumah would have responded to the following statement: Colonists should ask their colonial rulers to maintain political control over them while helping them develop economically; only after economic development has been achieved should colonies receive political independence. *(Nkrumah would probably have responded that economic development cannot proceed as long as colonies remain under foreign domination.)*

Analyzing Primary Sources

ANSWERS 1. D 2. E 3. Without economic independence, a country will not be able to maintain political independence.

Kwame Nkrumah: *Autobiography*

Kwame Nkrumah led the people of Gold Coast in their quest for independence from Britain. After succeeding in 1957, Nkrumah became the first prime minister and renamed the country Ghana. In this excerpt from his *Autobiography*, Nkrumah speaks of the need to establish economic independence as a means of maintaining political independence.

> **Main Idea** In this excerpt, Nkrumah describes his goals of political freedom and the difficult work of building an independent economy.

Independence for the Gold Coast was my aim. It was a colony, and I have always regarded colonialism as the policy by which a foreign power binds territories to herself by political ties, with the primary object of promoting her own economic advantage. No one need be surprised if this system has led to disturbances and political tension in many territories. There are few people who would not rid themselves of such domination if they could. . . .

I saw that the whole solution to [our] problem lay in political freedom for our people, for it is only when a people are politically free that other races can give them the respect that is due them. It is impossible to talk of equality of races in any other terms. No people without a government of their own can expect to be treated on the same level as people of independent sovereign states. It is far better to be free to govern or misgovern yourself than to be governed by anybody else. . . .

Once freedom is gained, a greater task comes into view. All dependent territories are backward in education, in science, in agriculture, and in industry. The economic independence that should follow and maintain political independence demands every effort from the people, a total mobilization of brain and manpower resources. What other countries have taken three hundred years or more to achieve, a once dependent territory must try to accomplish in a generation if it is to survive.

Kwame Nkrumah (second from right) at an independence celebration

Analyzing Primary Sources

1. In this passage, how does the author define colonialism?

A a balanced political alliance between a foreign power and a territory

B a balanced economic alliance between a foreign power and a territory

C a system in which a ruling country helps residents of a colony develop their economy

D a system in which a ruling country administers a colony in order to promote its own economic gain

2. Nkrumah viewed political independence as a means of gaining

E respect from other sovereign states.

F great personal wealth.

G a better system of education.

H better resources.

3. Critical Thinking Defending a Position Nkrumah states that newly independent countries must establish economic independence quickly in order to survive. Give reasons to support this statement.

Resource Directory

Teaching Resources
History Through Literature *The Gentlemen of the Jungle,* History Through Literature booklet, pp. 53–54
Treasures of the World *Kwame Nkrumah's Views on Independence,* pp. 149–151

Other Resources
Nkrumah, Kwame. *The Autobiography of Kwame Nkrumah.* London: Panaf Books, 1973.

Lech Walesa:
Nobel Peace Prize Lecture

Lech Walesa organized an independent trade union in Poland known as Solidarity. After a successful strike by Solidarity members in 1980, the Polish Communist government granted the workers many new rights and higher wages. A year later, however, the gains were withdrawn and Solidarity was outlawed. Lech Walesa was awarded the Nobel Peace Prize in 1983 for his work promoting freedom in Poland. This lecture was delivered at a time when Solidarity was still illegal.

Main Idea In this speech, Walesa declares his solidarity with all people in the world who work to secure peace, justice, and human rights.

May I repeat that the fundamental necessity in Poland is now understanding and dialogue. I think that the same applies to the whole world: we should go on talking, we must not close any doors or do anything that would block the road to an understanding. And we must remember that only peace built on the foundations of justice and moral order can be a lasting one.

In many parts of the world the people are searching for a solution which would link the two basic values: peace and justice. The two are like bread and salt for mankind. Every nation and every community have the inalienable right to these values. No conflicts can be resolved without doing everything possible to follow that road. Our times require that these aspirations which exist the world over must be recognized.

Our efforts and harsh experiences have revealed to the world the value of human solidarity. Accepting this honorable distinction I am thinking of those with whom I am linked by the spirit of solidarity.

—first of all, of those who in the struggle for the workers' and civic rights in my country paid the highest price—the price of life;
—of my friends who paid for the defense of "Solidarity" with the loss of freedom, who were sentenced to prison terms or are awaiting trial;
—of my countrymen who saw in the "Solidarity" movement the fulfillment of their aspirations as workers and citizens, who are subjected to humiliations and ready for sacrifices, who have learn[ed] to link courage with wisdom and who persist in loyalty to the cause we have embarked upon;
—of all those who are struggling throughout the world for workers' and union rights, for the dignity of a working man, for human rights.

Lech Walesa holding up a picture of Pope John Paul II

Background
About the Document

Lech Walesa This is an excerpt of a Nobel Peace Prize lecture, which was delivered by the wife of the award recipient—Danuta Walesa—because the recipient himself had been denied permission to leave his country. In his speech Walesa warned that "the Polish aspirations to freedom will never be stifled." Indeed, six years after this 1983 speech, Poland held free elections, and Walesa himself later became president of a free Poland.

Activity
Interpreting the Document

Use these additional questions to generate class discussion.

1. Ask students what they think Walesa means by the terms "peace" and "justice." *(Answers will vary, but "peace" suggests an absence of conflict or violence, and "justice" suggests respect for human rights.)*

2. Critical Thinking: Analyzing Information Ask students why it is often difficult for large numbers of people to unify in pursuit of a common goal. *(Answers will vary. Students should recognize that people will disagree over leadership, tactics, priorities, and even goals of the movement.)*

Analyzing Primary Sources

ANSWERS **1.** C **2.** G **3.** Answers will vary. Students should support their opinions.

Analyzing Primary Sources

1. What does Walesa claim has been the result of the struggles of the Polish workers?

   A They have succeeded in bringing peace and justice to Poland.

   B They have failed to encourage the growth of understanding and dialogue.

   C They have taught the world the value of human solidarity.

   D They have taught the world the value of freedom.

2. What were the members of Solidarity struggling for?

   E government loyalty

   F shorter prison terms

   G workers' and civic rights

   H bread and salt

3. **Critical Thinking Defending a Position** Do you agree with Walesa's idea that the only way to build a lasting peace is to establish justice?

Reference Section **993**

Resource Directory

Other Resources
Ravitch, Diane, and Abigail Thernstrom, eds. *The Democracy Reader.* New York: HarperCollins, 1992.

Primary Sources and Literature

About the Document

Accepting Change When Mikhail Gorbachev became General Secretary of the Communist Party in 1985, he saw that the country's economy was in ruins. He hoped his program of *perestroika* would be a remedy. He realized that the central planning system that had brought the Soviet Union into the modern industrial age was not working and that a change to a market economy was necessary. Many people in the Soviet Union were wary of the changes brought on by perestroika. Many political leaders, including Boris Yeltsin, opposed Gorbachev. The speech excerpted here is an example of Gorbachev's efforts to hold the people together despite difficulties.

*A*ctivity
Interpreting the Document

Use this additional question to generate class discussion.
Point out to students that Gorbachev was repeatedly criticized both by opponents of reform and by supporters of radical reforms. Ask them how this speech reflects Gorbachev's position between those two extremes. *(Gorbachev attacks both those who want to abandon perestroika and those who want to speed it up.)*

Analyzing Primary Sources

ANSWERS **1.** C **2.** G **3. (a)** He accuses them of being prompted by ambition rather than concern for real progress, and he argues that their ambition will produce rash decisions and hasty projects. **(b)** As a program that he initiated, he would not want it to fail.

Mikhail Gorbachev: *Perestroika*

Mikhail Gorbachev's economic and political reforms paved the way for the independence of Eastern Europe, the breakup of the Soviet Union, and the end of the Cold War. In the following speech delivered in 1989, Gorbachev asks the people of the Soviet Union to maintain confidence in the changes brought about by perestroika despite the difficulties and criticisms of the program.

Main Idea | In this speech, Gorbachev restates the benefits of his program of political and economic reform.

Good evening, comrades, I am here to talk to you about our current affairs. The situation in the country is not simple. We all know and feel this. Everything has become entangled in a tight knot: Scarcity on the consumer goods market, conflicts in ethnic relations, and difficult and sometimes painful processes in the public consciousness, resulting from the overcoming of distortions and from the renewal of socialism. People are trying to understand where we have found ourselves at the moment, evaluating the pluses and minuses of the path we have covered during the last four-plus years, the development of democracy and the pace of the economic and political reforms. . . .

Some are ready to give up perestroika and return to the past. Others, who consider themselves "active reformers," want to head perestroika onto the path of rash decisions and hasty projects, prompted by ambition rather than concern for real progress. . . .

True, perestroika is meeting with many difficulties. But it is radical change, a revolution in the economy and in policy, in the ways of thinking and in people's consciousness, in the entire pattern of our life. Besides, we have not been able to avoid mistakes in our practical actions in the course of perestroika. But perestroika has opened up realistic opportunities for society's renewal, for giving society a new quality and for creating truly humane and democratic socialism. It has returned to the great nation a sense of dignity and given the Soviet people a sense of freedom. It is a powerful source of social, spiritual, and, I should say, patriotic energy for decades to come.

That is why we must do everything to continue perestroika on the basis of the ideas and principles proclaimed by the party. And we must not allow those who are using the difficulties we have met to impose on society doubts about the correctness of the path we have chosen.

Mikhail Gorbachev

Analyzing Primary Sources

1. Which of the following statements best summarizes this excerpt?

   A Perestroika imposes too many reforms on society.

   B Perestroika is a great source of human dignity.

   C Perestroika must continue despite mistakes and criticism.

   D Perestroika does not allow for enough freedom.

2. Gorbachev states that the "active reformers" want to

   E return to the past.

   F end the policy of perestroika.

   G speed up the pace of reforms under perestroika.

   H further debate the policy of perestroika.

3. **Critical Thinking Recognizing Bias (a)** How does Gorbachev discredit the ideas of "active reformers" in this excerpt? **(b)** Why would Gorbachev be anxious to defend perestroika?

994 *Reference Section*

Vaclav Havel: *New Year's Address*

Vaclav Havel was a leading dissident and human rights activist in communist Czechoslovakia. When the "democracy movement" swept through Eastern Europe in 1989, Havel was elected president. In the following speech delivered on January 1, 1990, Havel asks the citizens of Czechoslovakia to accept responsibility for their past and to move forward in building a democracy.

Vocabulary Before you read the selection, look up the following words in a dictionary: **immutable, perpetuate.**

Main Idea In this speech, Havel calls upon Czech citizens to be active participants in their new democracy.

Our country is not flourishing. The enormous creative and spiritual potential of our nations is being wasted. Entire branches of industry produce goods that are of no interest to anyone, while we lack the things we need. . . . We now have the most contaminated environment in all of Europe. . . .

But all this is not even the main problem. The worst thing is that we live in a contaminated moral environment. We have fallen morally ill because we became used to saying one thing and thinking another. We have learned not to believe in anything, to ignore each other, to care only about ourselves. Notions such as love, friendship, compassion, humility, or forgiveness have lost their depth and dimensions. . . . Only a few of us managed to cry out loud that the powers-that-be should not be all-powerful. . . .

We have all become used to the totalitarian system and accepted it as an immutable fact, thus helping to perpetuate it. In other words, we are all . . . responsible for the creation of the totalitarian machinery. . . .

Why do I say this? It would be very unwise to think of the sad legacy of the last forty years as something alien or something inherited from a distant relative. On the contrary, we have to accept this legacy as something we have inflicted on ourselves. If we accept it as such, we will understand that it is up to all of us, and only us, to do something about it. We cannot blame the previous rulers for everything—not only because it would be untrue, but also because it could weaken our sense of duty, our obligation to act independently, freely, sensibly, and quickly. Let us not be mistaken: even the best government in the world, the best parliament, and the best president cannot do much on their own. And in any case, it would be wrong to expect a cure-all from them alone. Freedom and democracy, after all, require everyone to participate and thus to share responsibility.

PRIMARY SOURCES AND LITERATURE

Background
About the Document

The Velvet Revolution Czechoslovakia's Communist Party leader announced in November 1989 that the party would not relax its hold on the country. When large demonstrations occurred a few weeks later, however, the leader resigned. Pressures on the party increased when millions of Czechs and Slovaks went out on a general strike. The Communist government collapsed peacefully and opposition leader Vaclav Havel—who had been arrested just two months earlier—was elected interim-president by the (still-Communist) parliament.

Activity
Interpreting the Document

Use this additional question to generate class discussion.
Critical Thinking: Drawing Conclusions Ask students what parts of Havel's message are relevant to people living in nations with long democratic traditions. *(Answers will vary. Students should focus on Havel's message that people should participate in public life.)*

Analyzing Primary Sources

ANSWERS **1.** A **2.** E **3.** Answers will vary. Students' answers should reflect Havel's argument that if people do not accept responsibility for the past, they will not work to rebuild the nation.

Vocabulary Answers

immutable—unchangeable;
perpetuate—prolong

Analyzing Primary Sources

1. What does Havel mean when he says that the people of Czechoslovakia "have the most contaminated environment in all of Europe"?

   A The people have become dishonest and uninterested.

   B The people have been disrespectful of the environment.

   C The people are by nature unwise and unruly.

   D The people have lost their respect for the law.

2. According to Havel, why must everyone participate in the new democracy?

   E to correct the wrongs of the past

   F to share responsibility

   G to prevent totalitarianism

   H to prevent environmental pollution

3. **Critical Thinking Recognizing Causes and Effects** Why does Havel ask that the people of Czechoslovakia accept their responsibility for the totalitarian machinery of the past?

Reference Section **995**

Resource Directory

Teaching Resources
Biography Activity *Vaclav Havel,* Unit 8 booklet, p. 28
Other Resources

Havel, Vaclav. "New Year's Day Address," in *Uncaptive Minds* (quarterly). New York: Institute for Democracy in Eastern Europe.

Ravitch, Diane, and Abigail Thernstrom, eds. *The Democracy Reader.* New York: HarperCollins, 1992.

Safire, William, comp. "Playwright-Dissident Vaclav Havel Assumes the Presidency," in *Lend Me Your Ear.* New York: Norton, 1997.

Primary Sources and Literature

Background
About the Document

Economic Growth and Tolerance In the 1990 speech from which this excerpt was taken, Vargas Llosa asked how Latin Americans could strengthen and sustain the trend toward democracy in the region. Vargas Llosa outlined two tasks: continued economic development, on which a strong democracy depends, and a shift in popular attitudes away from absolutism and toward tolerance.

Activity
Interpreting the Document

Use this additional question to generate class discussion.

Ask students to explain how, according to Vargas Llosa, Latin America's economic problems are threatening its democratic institutions. *(Democratic governments need to improve the lives of the people in order to maintain support, yet economic problems, including foreign debt, are forcing these governments to demand even more sacrifices from people.)*

Analyzing Primary Sources

***ANSWERS* 1.** A **2.** F **3.** Answers will vary. Students should explain that Latin America's long history of non-democratic government has shaped the attitudes of its people.

Vocabulary Answers

unprecedented—having no previous example; **superficial**—not deeply rooted; **oligarchies**—governments dominated by a small group

Mario Vargas Llosa: *Latin America, The Democratic Option*

In this speech delivered in 1990, Peruvian writer Mario Vargas Llosa describes the changes that are needed to maintain and extend democracy in Latin America.

Vocabulary Before you read the selection, look up the following words in a dictionary: **unprecedented, superficial, oligarchies**.

Main Idea In this speech, Vargas Llosa describes what is needed to sustain democracy in Latin America.

The democratization of Latin America, even though it has today an unprecedented popular base, is very fragile. To maintain and extend this popular base, governments will have to prove to their citizens that democracy means not only the end of political brutality but progress—concrete benefits in areas such as labor, health, and education, where so much remains to be done. But, given Latin America's current economic crisis, when the prices of its exports are hitting record lows and the weight of its foreign debt is crushing, those governments have virtually no alternative but to demand that their citizens—especially the poor—make even greater sacrifices than they've already made. . . . A realistic and ethically sound approach that our creditors could take would be to demand that each debtor nation pay what it can without placing its stability in jeopardy. . . .

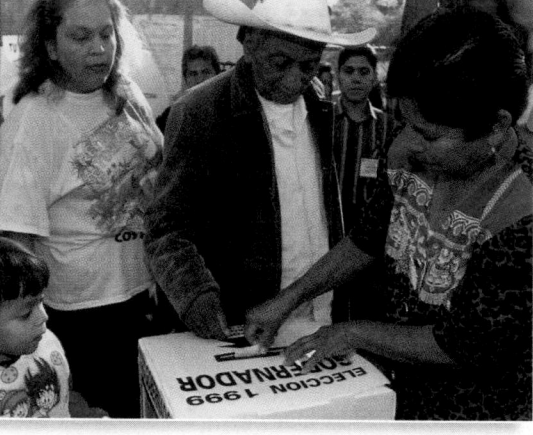
Mexicans voting

If we want democracy to take hold in our countries, our most urgent task is to broaden it, give it substance and truth. Democracy is fragile in so many countries because it is superficial, a mere framework within which institutions and political parties go about their business in their traditionally arbitrary, bullying way. . . .

Perhaps the hardest struggle we Latin Americans will have will be against ourselves. Centuries of intolerance, of absolute truths, of despotic governments, weigh us down—and it won't be easy to shake that burden off. The tradition of absolute power that began with our pre-Columbian empires, and the tradition that might makes right that the Spanish and Portuguese explorers practiced, were perpetuated in the nineteenth century, after our independence, by our caudillos and our oligarchies, often with the blessing or direct intervention of foreign powers.

Analyzing Primary Sources

1. The author states that democratic governments in Latin American countries have to provide
   A real improvements in labor, health, and education.
   B higher incomes.
   C a stronger, more authoritative government.
   D greater understanding of their history.

2. The author states that many democratic governments are fragile because they
   E lack authority.
   F do not always act democratically.
   G lack international support.
   H lack strong political parties.

3. **Critical Thinking Identifying Main Ideas** In the last paragraph, the author describes obstacles to democracy in Latin America. Restate the main idea in your own words.

Resource Directory

Other Resources

Llosa, Mario Vargas. "To Nurture Latin Democracy," *Harper's Magazine*, June 1987.

Ravitch, Diane, and Abigail Thernstrom, eds. *The Democracy Reader*. New York: HarperCollins, 1992.

Aung San Suu Kyi:
Freedom From Fear

Aung San Suu Kyi, leader of Myanmar's National League for Democracy and winner of the Nobel Peace Prize, has worked courageously for human rights and democracy in her country. Because of her opposition to Myanmar's ruling military junta, she was held under house arrest from 1989 to 1995 and severely restricted thereafter.

Vocabulary Before you read the selection, look up the following words in a dictionary: **unremitting, insidious, inherent, enervating, miasma, wellspring, trite, bulwarks.**

Main Idea | **In this essay, Aung San Suu Kyi describes the need for courage when living under an oppressive government.**

Fearlessness may be a gift but perhaps more precious is the courage acquired through endeavor, courage that comes from cultivating the habit of refusing to let fear dictate one's actions, courage that could be described as 'grace under pressure'—grace which is renewed repeatedly in the face of harsh, unremitting pressure.

Within a system which denies the existence of basic human rights, fear tends to be the order of the day. Fear of imprisonment, fear of torture, fear of death, fear of losing friends, family, property or means of livelihood, fear of poverty, fear of isolation, fear of failure. A most insidious form of fear is that which masquerades as common sense or even wisdom, condemning as foolish, reckless, insignificant or futile the small, daily acts of courage which help to preserve man's self-respect and inherent human dignity. It is not easy for a people conditioned by fear under the iron rule of the principle that might is right to free themselves from the enervating miasma of fear. Yet even under the most crushing state machinery courage rises up again and again, for fear is not the natural state of civilized man.

The wellspring of courage and endurance in the face of unbridled power is generally a firm belief in the sanctity of ethical principles combined with a historical sense that despite all setbacks the condition of man is set on an ultimate course for both spiritual and material advancement. . . . It is man's vision of a world fit for rational, civilized humanity which leads him to dare and to suffer to build societies free from want and fear. Concepts such as truth, justice and compassion cannot be dismissed as trite when these are often the only bulwarks which stand against ruthless power.

Aung San Suu Kyi

Background
About the Document

The Struggle for Democracy A military junta known as the State Law and Order Restoration Council seized power in Burma in 1988 and used the military to put down democracy protests throughout the country. In 1989 Aung San Suu Kyi began working to unite the opposition party for upcoming elections. She was placed under house arrest for this activity until July 1995 when she was released. When student protests broke out again in the fall of 1996, Aung San Suu Kyi's movements were severely restricted.

Activity
Interpreting the Document

Use this additional question to generate class discussion.
Have students list the fears that, according to the author, afflict people who live in countries where human rights are denied. *(fear of imprisonment, torture, death, losing friends, family, property or means of livelihood, poverty, isolation, and failure)*

Analyzing Primary Sources

ANSWERS 1. A **2.** F **3.** Answers will vary.

Vocabulary Answers

unremitting—constant; **insidious**—more dangerous than seems evident; **inherent**—part of the general nature of something; **enervating**—weakening; **miasma**—pollution; **wellspring**—source; **trite**—worn out; **bulwarks**—defenses

Analyzing Primary Sources

1. According to the author, why do people work against all odds to build societies free from want and fear?
   A because they have a dream of a just world
   B because they dismiss truth and justice as trite
   C because they are powerless against injustice
   D because they want to learn how to gain courage

2. What are the sources of courage according to the author?
   E power and history
   F belief in ethical principles and a sense that progress is inevitable
   G belief in truth and compassion
   H power and endurance

3. **Critical Thinking Applying Information** Give one example of a person refusing to let fear dictate his or her actions.

Resource Directory

Teaching Resources
Biography Activity *Aung San Suu Kyi,* Unit 8 booklet, p. 46
Other Resources
Kyi, Aung San Suu. *Freedom from Fear and other Writings.* New York: Penguin Books, 1995.

Background
About the Document

Rebuilding South Africa After 1984, violence was increasing in white-ruled South Africa, and the world was isolating the country through economic sanctions. Under this pressure, the South African government began to abandon its policy of apartheid. In 1990, Nelson Mandela, who had been sentenced to life in prison in 1964, was freed. Despite opposition from many whites and bloody fighting between black factions, apartheid was abolished, and in 1994 Mandela was elected president in the country's first multiracial elections. This speech addresses the difficult task of rebuilding South Africa.

Activity
Interpreting the Document

Use this additional question to generate class discussion.

Critical Thinking: Synthesizing Information Ask students to find and list the phrases in Mandela's speech that call for unity among all South Africans. *(Phrases include: "our hopes for a glorious life for all"; "liberate all our people"; "all South Africans, both black and white"; and "act together as a united people, for national reconciliation.")*

Analyzing Primary Sources

ANSWERS **1.** A **2.** G **3. (a)** Mandela calls for freedom from poverty, deprivation, suffering, and gender discrimination and other forms of discrimination. **(b)** He means that blacks and whites should try to forget past injustices and work together for the good of the nation.

Vocabulary Answers

emancipation—liberation; **covenant**—agreement; **reconciliation**—the settling of differences

Nelson Mandela: *Glory and Hope*

Nelson Mandela delivered this speech after having been elected president in South Africa's first multiracial elections in 1994. Knowing that the injustices of apartheid would not be easily erased, Mandela asked the people to work together for peace and justice.

Vocabulary Before you read the selection, look up the following words in a dictionary: **emancipation, covenant, reconciliation.**

Main Idea In this speech, Mandela calls upon black and white South Africans to work together to build a new nation based on justice.

Today, all of us do, by our presence here, and by our celebrations . . . confer glory and hope to newborn liberty.

Out of the experience of an extraordinary human disaster that lasted too long must be born a society of which all humanity will be proud.

Our daily deeds as ordinary South Africans must produce an actual South African reality that will reinforce humanity's belief in justice, strengthen its confidence in the nobility of the human soul and sustain all our hopes for a glorious life for all. . . .

Nelson Mandela (right) with F. W. de Klerk

The time for the healing of the wounds has come. . . .

The time to build is upon us.

We have, at last, achieved our political emancipation. We pledge ourselves to liberate all our people from the continuing bondage of poverty, deprivation, suffering, gender and other discrimination.

We have triumphed in the effort to implant hope in the breasts of the millions of our people. We enter into a covenant that we shall build the society in which all South Africans, both black and white, will be able to walk tall, without any fear in their hearts, assured of the inalienable right to human dignity—a rainbow nation at peace with itself and the world. . . .

We understand it still that there is no easy road to freedom.

We know it well that none of us acting alone can achieve success.

We must therefore act together as a united people, for national reconciliation, for nation building, for the birth of a new world.

Let there be justice for all. Let there be peace for all. Let there be work, bread, water, and salt for all. . . . The sun shall never set on so glorious a human achievement!

Analyzing Primary Sources

1. In this speech, Mandela is celebrating

A the birth of a new, free nation.

B decades of peace and justice.

C the easy road to freedom.

D the end of violence.

2. Which of the following best summarizes the excerpt?

E We must find work for all.

F We must not take the path of violence.

G We must now finish the work of freedom that we have started.

H We must correct the injustices of South Africa's past through severe punishments.

3. Critical Thinking Making Inferences (a) In addition to political freedom, what further "freedoms" does Mandela call for in his speech? **(b)** What does Mandela mean by "reconciliation"?

998 *Reference Section*

Resource Directory

Teaching Resources

History Through Literature *Poems About Prison,* History Through Literature booklet, p. 75
Simulations *Looking Beyond Apartheid,* Simulations booklet, p. 16

Other Resources

Mandela, Nelson. "Glory and Hope," *in Vital Speeches of the Day,* May 10, 1994.

Harry Wu: *The Outlook for China, Human Rights*

Author and human rights activist Harry Wu was imprisoned in China for 19 years because of his criticisms of the communist regime. The excerpt below is from a speech Wu delivered in 1996.

Vocabulary Before you read the selection, look up the following words in a dictionary: **specter, superstructure, vulcanizing.**

Main Idea In this speech, Wu describes the system of forced labor camps run by China's communist government.

Sometimes people ask me, "What are you fighting for?" And my answer is quite simple. I want to see the word *laogai* in every dictionary in every language in the world; I want to see the laogai ended. . . .

The economic boom made possible by capitalism makes profits for both the West and China. But despite the huge profits earned by China's external trade, ordinary people enjoy only a tiny part. The communist government puts most of the profits into upgrading its weapons systems, into internal and external political activities, and into maintaining the nation's political stability. . . .

Today, a specter is hovering over Mainland China—capitalism. Communism is dead; it is no longer believed in by the Chinese in general nor even by the majority of Communist Party members. The "capitalistic" economic boom has made the superstructure of the communist regime appear pretty on the outside, but its pillars are heavily damaged. Looming in front of China are some huge crises.

At the core of the human rights question in China today is China's fundamental machinery for crushing human beings physically, psychologically and spiritually: the laogai camp system, of which we have identified 1,100 camps. It is also an integral part of the national economy. Its importance is illustrated by some basic facts: one third of China's tea is produced in laogai camps; 60 percent of China's rubber vulcanizing chemicals are produced in a single laogai camp in Shanghai; the first and second chain hoist works in the country to receive direct export authority are laogai camps in Zhejiang Province; one of the largest and earliest exporters of hand tools is a camp in Shanghai; an unknown but significant amount of China's cotton crop is grown by prisoners. I could go on and on and on. . . . The laogai is not simply a prison system, it is a political tool for maintaining the Communist Party's totalitarian rule.

Chinese human rights protester

Analyzing Primary Sources

1. What is a laogai?
   - **A** a labor camp for prisoners
   - **B** a warehouse for exports
   - **C** a chemical plant
   - **D** a tea or cotton plantation

2. The damaged "pillars" described by Wu in the third paragraph of this excerpt are a symbol of the
   - **E** non-communist leadership.
   - **F** economy of the country.
   - **G** communist regime's lack of true support by the people.
   - **H** Chinese prison system under the Communist government.

3. **Critical Thinking Synthesizing Information** **(a)** Why do you think the author describes the laogai as "a political tool for maintaining the Communist Party's totalitarian rule"? **(b)** What is the economic role of the labor camps?

Reference Section **999**

Primary Sources and Literature

The World: Political

North America

CANADA
NORTH
AMERICA
★ Ottawa
UNITED STATES
★ Washington, D.C.
Bermuda (Br.)
ALASKA (U.S.)
Greenland (Denmark)
Azores (Port.)
ATLANTIC OCEAN

ARCTIC OCEAN
Arctic Circle

Tropic of Cancer
HAWAII (U.S.)
MEXICO
★ Mexico City
See inset below
Caribbean Sea
Caracas GUYANA ★
VENEZUELA
Bogotá ★ Georgetown
★ Paramaribo
COLOMBIA Cayenne ★
Quito ★ FR. GUIANA (Fr.)
Galápagos Is. (Ecuador) ECUADOR SOUTH SURINAME
AMERICA
CAPE VERDE

PACIFIC OCEAN

Equator

KIRIBATI
SAMOA
American Samoa (U.S.)
FIJI IS.
Cook Islands (N.Z.)
French Polynesia (Fr.)
TONGA
BRAZIL
Lima ★ ★ Brasília
PERU
La Paz ★
★ BOLIVIA
Sucre
PARAGUAY

Tropic of Capricorn
Pitcairn I. (Br.)
Easter I. (Chile)
CHILE
Santiago ★
★ Asunción
Buenos Aires ★ ★ URUGUAY
★ Montevideo
ARGENTINA

International Date Line

Robinson Projection
0   1000   2000 Miles
0   1000   2000 Kilometers

Falkland Is. (Br.)

Antarctic Circle
SOUTHERN OCEAN

Central America and the Caribbean

UNITED STATES
B A H A M A S
Nassau ★
Tropic of Cancer
Gulf of Mexico
Havana ★
CUBA
ATLANTIC OCEAN

Puerto Rico (U.S.)
Virgin Is. (Br.)
Virgin Islands (U.S.)
DOMINICAN REPUBLIC
HAITI
Port-au-Prince ★ Santo Domingo ★
JAMAICA
Kingston
ANTIGUA AND BARBUDA
ST. KITTS AND NEVIS
Guadeloupe (Fr.)
DOMINICA

MEXICO
Belmopan ★
BELIZE
GUATEMALA
Guatemala ★ HONDURAS
★ Tegucigalpa
San Salvador ★
EL SALVADOR NICARAGUA
Managua ★

Caribbean Sea
Martinique (Fr.)
ST. LUCIA
ST. VINCENT AND THE GRENADINES
BARBADOS
Aruba (Neth.)
Netherlands Antilles (Neth.)
GRENADA

COSTA RICA ★ San José
PANAMA
Panama ★
Azimuthal Equal Area Projection
0   200   400 Miles
0   200   400 Kilometers

Port of Spain ★ TRINIDAD AND TOBAGO
Caracas ★
VENEZUELA
SOUTH AMERICA
COLOMBIA
GUYANA
★ Georgetown
SURINAME
Paramaribo ★

World Atlas

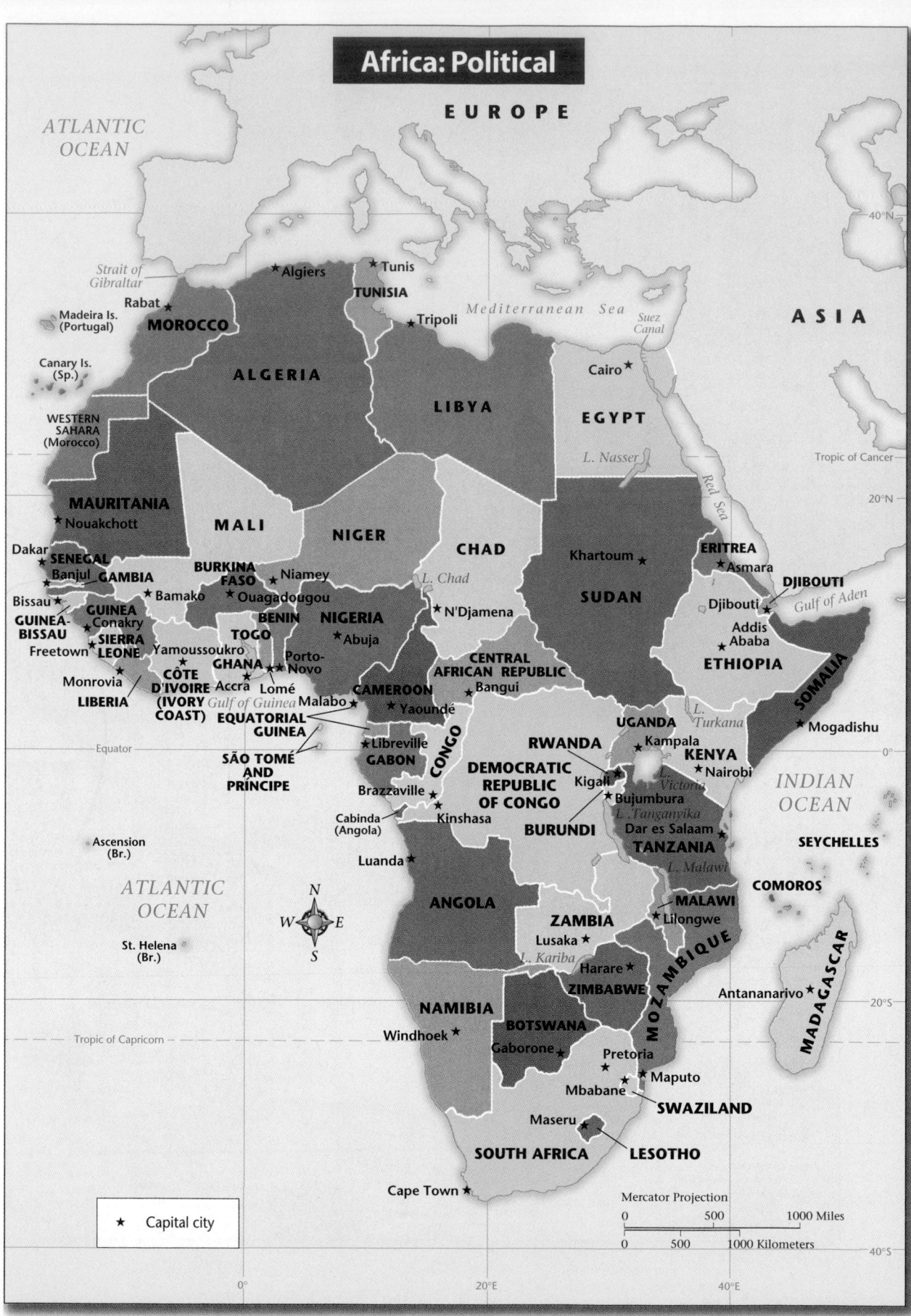

Africa: Political

EUROPE

ATLANTIC OCEAN

Strait of Gibraltar

★Algiers ★Tunis
TUNISIA
Rabat ★
Madeira Is. (Portugal)
MOROCCO ★Tripoli
Mediterranean Sea Suez Canal

ASIA

Canary Is. (Sp.)

ALGERIA **LIBYA** **EGYPT** Cairo ★

WESTERN SAHARA (Morocco)

L. Nasser Tropic of Cancer

20°N

MAURITANIA
★Nouakchott **MALI** **NIGER** **CHAD** Khartoum ★ **ERITREA** ★Asmara **DJIBOUTI**

Dakar
★**SENEGAL** **BURKINA FASO** ★Niamey *L. Chad* **SUDAN** Djibouti ★ *Gulf of Aden*
Banjul ★ **GAMBIA** ★Bamako ★Ouagadougou ★N'Djamena Addis Ababa ★
Bissau ★ **BENIN** **NIGERIA** **ETHIOPIA** **SOMALIA**
GUINEA-BISSAU **GUINEA** ★Conakry **TOGO** ★Abuja **CENTRAL AFRICAN REPUBLIC**
★★**SIERRA LEONE** Yamoussoukro **GHANA** Porto-Novo ★Bangui
Freetown ★ ★ Accra Lomé **CAMEROON**
Monrovia ★ **CÔTE D'IVOIRE (IVORY COAST)** *Gulf of Guinea* Malabo ★ ★Yaoundé **UGANDA** ★Kampala *L. Turkana* Mogadishu ★
LIBERIA **EQUATORIAL GUINEA** ★Libreville **RWANDA** **KENYA** ★Nairobi
Equator **SÃO TOMÉ AND PRÍNCIPE** **GABON** **CONGO** **DEMOCRATIC REPUBLIC OF CONGO** Kigali ★ *L. Victoria* 0° **INDIAN OCEAN**
Brazzaville ★ ★Bujumbura ★
Cabinda (Angola) ★Kinshasa **BURUNDI** Dar es Salaam ★ **SEYCHELLES**
Ascension (Br.) Luanda ★ **TANZANIA** *L. Tanganyika*
L. Malawi **COMOROS**
ANGOLA **ZAMBIA** **MALAWI** ★Lilongwe
St. Helena (Br.) Lusaka ★ *L. Kariba* **MOZAMBIQUE**
Harare ★ Antananarivo ★ **MADAGASCAR** 20°S
NAMIBIA **ZIMBABWE**
Tropic of Capricorn **BOTSWANA**
Windhoek ★ Gaborone ★ Pretoria ★
★Maputo
Mbabane ★ **SWAZILAND**
Maseru ★
SOUTH AFRICA **LESOTHO**
Cape Town ★

Mercator Projection
0   500   1000 Miles
0   500   1000 Kilometers

40°N
20°N
Equator
20°S
40°S

0°   20°E   40°E

★ Capital city

World Atlas

Africa: Physical

ATLANTIC OCEAN

EUROPE

Strait of Gibraltar

Madeira Is.

Canary Is.

ATLAS MOUNTAINS

Mediterranean Sea

Suez Canal

ASIA

Nile R.

S A H A R A

LIBYAN DESERT

L. Nasser

Tropic of Cancer

TIBESTI MTS.

NUBIAN DESERT

Red Sea

20°N

Senegal R.

Niger R.

L. Chad

White Nile R.

Blue Nile R.

Gulf of Aden

ETHIOPIAN HIGHLANDS

HORN OF AFRICA

Gulf of Guinea

Congo R.

GREAT RIFT VALLEY

Turkana

Equator

CONGO BASIN

L. Victoria

0°

INDIAN OCEAN

L. Tanganyika

KATANGA PLATEAU

L. Malawi

ATLANTIC OCEAN

N
W   E
S

Zambezi R.

L. Kariba

Madagascar

20°S

NAMIB DESERT

KALAHARI DESERT

Tropic of Capricorn

DRAKENSBERG RANGE

Orange R.

Land Elevation

Feet	Meters
14,000	4,000
7,000	2,000
1,500	500
700	200
0	0
Below sea level	Below sea level

Mercator Projection

0   500   1000 Miles

0   500   1000 Kilometers

40°S

0°   20°E   40°E

Asia: Political

World Atlas

★ Capital city

EUROPE

ARCTIC OCEAN

RUSSIA

Moscow ★

Barents Sea

East Siberian Sea

Bering Sea

Sea of Okhotsk

Sakhalin (Russia)

Kuril Islands (Russia)

PACIFIC OCEAN

Aleutian Islands (U.S.)

Sea of Japan (East Sea)

JAPAN
Tokyo ★

Lake Baikal

MONGOLIA
Ulan Bator ★

NORTH KOREA
P'yongyang ★

Beijing ★

SOUTH KOREA
Seoul ★

East China Sea

Ryukyu Islands (Japan)

Taipei ★
TAIWAN

CHINA

GEORGIA
Tbilisi ★
Yerevan ★
ARMENIA
AZERBAIJAN
Baku ★

TURKEY
Ankara ★

CYPRUS
Nicosia ★
Beirut ★
LEBANON
ISRAEL
Jerusalem ★
JORDAN
Amman ★
Damascus ★
SYRIA

Caspian Sea

KAZAKHSTAN
Astana ★

Aral Sea

L. Balkhash

Bishkek ★
Tashkent ★
UZBEKISTAN
KYRGYZSTAN
Dushanbe ★
TAJIKISTAN

TURKMENISTAN
Ashgabat ★

Tehran ★
IRAN

Baghdad ★
IRAQ
Kuwait ★
KUWAIT
BAHRAIN
Riyadh ★
QATAR
Doha ★
Abu Dhabi ★
UNITED ARAB EMIRATES
OMAN
Muscat ★

SAUDI ARABIA

YEMEN
Sanaa ★

Red Sea

Gulf of Aden

Socotra (Yemen)

Arabian Sea

AFGHANISTAN
Kabul ★

PAKISTAN
Islamabad ★

New Delhi ★

Kathmandu ★
NEPAL
BHUTAN
Thimphu ★

BANGLADESH
Dhaka ★

INDIA

Bay of Bengal

SRI LANKA
Colombo ★

Male ★ MALDIVES

INDIAN OCEAN

MYANMAR (BURMA)
Yangon (Rangoon) ★

Hanoi ★
LAOS
Vientiane ★
THAILAND
Bangkok ★
CAMBODIA
Phnom Penh ★
VIETNAM

South China Sea

Hong Kong
Macao

Manila ★
PHILIPPINES

Bandar Seri Begawan ★
BRUNEI

MALAYSIA
Kuala Lumpur ★
SINGAPORE ★

Borneo

Celebes

INDONESIA

Sumatra
Jakarta ★
Java

Timor

PAPUA NEW GUINEA
Port Moresby ★

AUSTRALIA

AFRICA

Mediterranean Sea

Black Sea

Persian Gulf

Azimuthal Equal Area Projection

0   500   1000 Miles

0   500   1000 Kilometers

Tropic of Cancer

Equator

N
W   E
S

40°N

60°N

80°N

Arctic Circle

20°N

40°E

60°E

80°E

100°E

120°E

140°E

160°E

180°

160°W

Asia: Physical

Land Elevation

Feet	Meters
14,000	4,000
7,000	2,000
1,500	500
700	200
0	0
Below sea level	Below sea level

Azimuthal Equal Area Projection

1000 Miles

1000 Kilometers

EUROPE

ARCTIC OCEAN

Arctic Circle

Barents Sea

Kara Sea

URAL MTS.

WEST SIBERIAN PLAIN

Ob R.

Irtysh R.

SIBERIA

Lena R.

L. Baikal

East Siberian Sea

Bering Sea

KOLYMA RANGE

KAMCHATKA PENINSULA

Sea of Okhotsk

Sakhalin

Kuril Islands

Hokkaido

Honshu

Sea of Japan (East Sea)

Shikoku

Kyushu

KOREAN PENINSULA

Amur R.

MONGOLIAN PLATEAU

GOBI DESERT

ALTAI MTS.

TIEN SHAN

KUNLUN MTS.

TIBETAN PLATEAU

HIMALAYAS

Huang He

Chang Jiang

Yangtze R.

Ryukyu Is.

East China Sea

Taiwan

PACIFIC OCEAN

Tropic of Cancer

Equator

Luzon

Mindanao

Philippine Islands

East Indies

Celebes

Borneo

New Guinea

AUSTRALIA

Timor

Java

Sumatra

MALAY PENINSULA

INDOCHINA PENINSULA

Mekong R.

South China Sea

Irrawaddy R.

Bay of Bengal

Sri Lanka

EASTERN GHATS

DECCAN PLATEAU

WESTERN GHATS

INDIAN PENINSULA

Ganges R.

Indus R.

Brahmaputra

Aral Sea

L. Balkhash

Caspian Sea

CAUCASUS MTS.

Black Sea

ZAGROS MTS.

Tigris R.

Euphrates R.

Persian Gulf

ANATOLIAN PLATEAU

Mediterranean Sea

Red Sea

Gulf of Aden

ARABIAN PENINSULA

Arabian Sea

INDIAN OCEAN

AFRICA

Yenisei R.

Don R.

Volga R.

World Atlas

Europe: Political

30°W · 20°W · 10°W · 0° · 10°E · 20°E · 30°E · 40°E · 50°E · 70°N

Barents Sea

ICELAND
★Reykjavik

Arctic Circle

60°N

Norwegian Sea

Faroe Is.
(Den.)

Shetland Is.
(Br.)

**ATLANTIC
OCEAN**

Scotland

North Sea

FINLAND

Gulf of Bothnia

Helsinki
★

NORWAY
Oslo ★ **SWEDEN**
★Stockholm

St. Petersburg ●

Tallinn
★

ESTONIA

RUSSIA

Baltic Sea

Riga
★ **LATVIA**

Moscow ★

N.
Ireland
Dublin
**UNITED
KINGDOM**

DENMARK
Copenhagen ★

LITHUANIA
Vilnius
★

★Minsk

50°N

★

IRELAND

Wales

England

The
Hague

★Amsterdam

RUSSIA

BELARUS

London ★

NETHERLANDS

Berlin
★

POLAND
Warsaw ★

★Kiev

English Channel

Brussels
★
BELGIUM

GERMANY

LUXEMBOURG

Prague
★
CZECH REP.

SLOVAKIA

★Bratislava

UKRAINE

★Paris

*Bay of
Biscay*

FRANCE

LIECHTENSTEIN

Bern
★
SWITZ.

Vienna
★

AUSTRIA
Ljubljana
★
SLOVENIA

★Budapest

HUNGARY

MOLDOVA

★Chisinau

ROMANIA

CROATIA
★Zagreb

PORTUGAL

ANDORRA

**SAN
MARINO**

Adriatic Sea

Belgrade
★

★Bucharest

Black Sea

40°N

MONACO

ITALY

**BOSNIA–
HERZEGOVINA**

Sarajevo
★ **YUGOSLAVIA**

BULGARIA
Sofia
★

Bosporus

★Lisbon

Corsica
(Fr.)

★Madrid

SPAIN

**VATICAN
CITY**

★Rome

ALBANIA

Tirana
★

★Skopje
MACEDONIA

Istanbul ●

TURKEY

★Ankara

Sardinia
(It.)

Balearic Is.
(Sp.)

*Strait of
Gibraltar*

Gibraltar
(Br.)
●

GREECE

*Aegean
Sea*

Mediterranean

Sicily

Athens ★

AFRICA

MALTA

Sea

Crete

30°N

N
W ✦ E
S

★ Capital city

● Major city

Azimuthal Equal Area Projection

0 · 250 · 500 Miles

0 · 250 · 500 Kilometers

Europe: Physical

30°W 20°W 10°W 0° 10°E 20°E 30°E 40°E 50°E

70°N

60°N

50°N

40°N

30°N

Barents Sea

Iceland

Arctic Circle

Norwegian Sea

Faroe Is.

Shetland Is.

ATLANTIC
OCEAN

KJØLEN MTS.

SCANDINAVIAN PENINSULA

Gulf of Bothnia

Volga R.

North Sea

Baltic Sea

British Isles

JUTLAND
PENINSULA

Thames R.

Elbe R.

Ruhr
Valley

NORTHERN EUROPEAN PLAIN

Oder R.

Vistula R.

Dnieper R.

English Channel

Seine R.

Rhine R.

Dniester R.

CARPATHIAN MTS.

Don

Bay of
Biscay

Loire R.

Garonne R.

Rhône R.

A L P S

Po R.

Danube R.

DINARIC ALPS

BALKAN MTS.

Black Sea

Bosporus

PYRENEES

Ebro R.

IBERIAN
PENINSULA

Tagus R.

APENNINES

ITALIAN PENINSULA

Adriatic Sea

BALKAN
PENINSULA

Corsica

Guadiana R.

Sardinia

Balearic
Islands

PINDUS MTS.

*Aegean
Sea*

Dardanelles

Strait of
Gibraltar

Sicily

Crete

Mediterranean Sea

AFRICA

Land Elevation

Feet	Meters
14,000	4,000
7,000	2,000
1,500	500
700	200
0	0
Below sea level	Below sea level

Icecaps

N
W E
S

Azimuthal Equal Area Projection

0 250 500 Miles

0 250 500 Kilometers

North and South America: Political

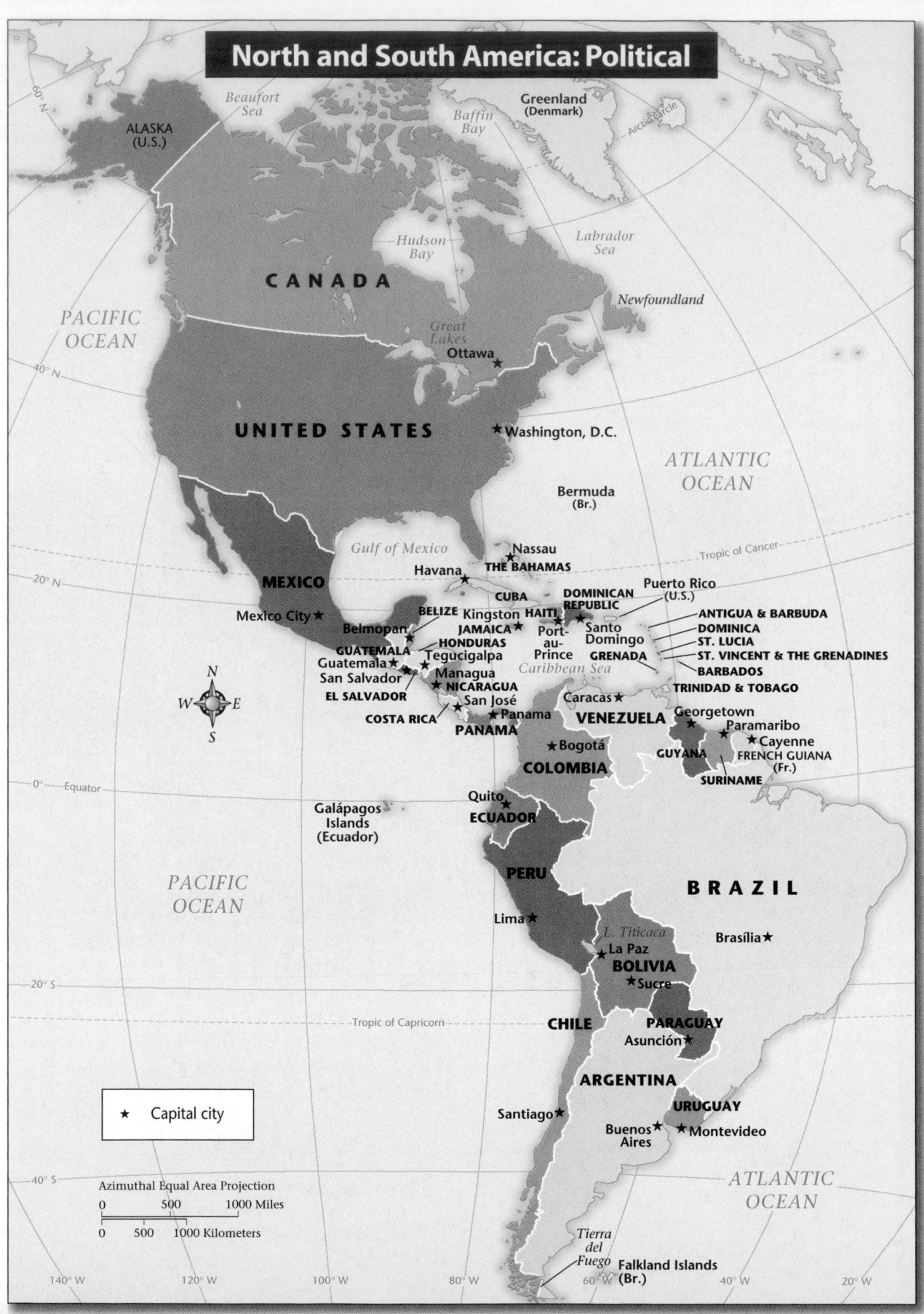

Beaufort Sea

ALASKA (U.S.)

Baffin Bay

Greenland (Denmark)

Arctic Circle

PACIFIC OCEAN

Hudson Bay

Labrador Sea

CANADA

Newfoundland

Great Lakes

Ottawa ★

40° N

UNITED STATES

★ Washington, D.C.

ATLANTIC OCEAN

Bermuda (Br.)

Gulf of Mexico

Nassau

Tropic of Cancer

20° N

Havana

THE BAHAMAS

Puerto Rico (U.S.)

MEXICO

CUBA

DOMINICAN REPUBLIC

Mexico City ★

BELIZE

Kingston HAITI

ANTIGUA & BARBUDA

Belmopan

JAMAICA ★

Port-au-Prince

Santo Domingo

DOMINICA

ST. LUCIA

GUATEMALA

HONDURAS

GRENADA

ST. VINCENT & THE GRENADINES

Guatemala ★

Tegucigalpa

Caribbean Sea

BARBADOS

San Salvador

Managua

NICARAGUA

TRINIDAD & TOBAGO

EL SALVADOR

San José

Caracas ★

COSTA RICA

Panama

VENEZUELA

Georgetown

Paramaribo

PANAMA

★ Bogotá

GUYANA

Cayenne

FRENCH GUIANA (Fr.)

N W E S

COLOMBIA

SURINAME

0° Equator

Quito

Galápagos Islands (Ecuador)

ECUADOR

PERU

B R A Z I L

PACIFIC OCEAN

Lima ★

L. Titicaca

Brasília ★

★ La Paz

20° S

BOLIVIA

★ Sucre

Tropic of Capricorn

CHILE

PARAGUAY

Asunción ★

ARGENTINA

URUGUAY

Santiago ★

Buenos Aires ★

★ Montevideo

40° S

Azimuthal Equal Area Projection

0   500   1000 Miles

0   500   1000 Kilometers

ATLANTIC OCEAN

Tierra del Fuego

Falkland Islands (Br.)

140° W   120° W   100° W   80° W   60° W   40° W   20° W

★ Capital city

World Atlas

North and South America: Physical

Land Elevation

Feet		Meters
14,000		4,000
7,000		2,000
1,500		500
700		200
0		0
Below sea level		Below sea level

Icecaps

Azimuthal Equal Area Projection

0   500   1000 Miles

0   500   1000 Kilometers

Australia, New Zealand, and Oceania: Political–Physical

World Atlas

A S I A

Philippine Sea

Northern
Mariana
Islands
(U.S.)

Guam
(U.S.)

PALAU ✪ Koror

Wake Island
(U.S.)

Timor Sea

Arafura Sea

Darwin ★

KIMBERLEY
PLATEAU

ARNHEM
LAND

BARKLY
TABLELAND

**Northern
Territory**

SIMPSON
DESERT

GREAT SANDY
DESERT

GIBSON DESERT

GREAT VICTORIA
DESERT

**Western
Australia**

*Great
Australian
Bight*

NULLARBOR PLAIN

Perth ★

DARLING RANGE

*INDIAN
OCEAN*

M I C R O N E S I A

Palikir ✪

Caroline Islands

FEDERATED STATES OF MICRONESIA

**MARSHALL
ISLANDS** ● Majuro

Tarawa
✪ Gilbert
Islands

Yaren ✪
NAURU

**SOLOMON
ISLANDS**
Honiara ✪

M E L A N E S I A

*New
Hebrides*

VANUATU
✪ Port-Vila

New Caledonia
(Fr.)

*Coral
Sea*

GREAT BARRIER REEF

CAPE
YORK
PENINSULA

Queensland

GREAT
ARTESIAN
BASIN

GREAT DIVIDING RANGE

Brisbane ★

Sydney ●

Canberra ✪

**New
South
Wales**

Murray River

Darling River

Lake
Eyre

**South
Australia**

Adelaide ★

Victoria ★

Melbourne ●

*Bass
Strait*

Tasmania

Hobart ★

*Tasman
Sea*

A U S T R A L I A

GREAT DIVIDING RANGE

PACIFIC OCEAN

P O L Y N E S I A

Line
Islands

Hawaiian
Islands
(U.S.)

Midway Islands
(U.S.)

Tropic of Cancer

Equator

KIRIBATI

Funafuti ✪
TUVALU

SAMOA
✪ Apia
American
Samoa
(U.S.)

**FIJI
ISLANDS**
● Suva

Nukualofa ✪ **TONGA**

International Date Line

Marquesas
Islands

French Polynesia (Fr.)

Society
Islands
● Tahiti

Cook
Islands
(N.Z.)

Tropic of Capricorn

Pitcairn
Island
(Br.)

**NEW
ZEALAND**

Auckland ●
*North
Island*

Wellington ✪

Christchurch ●

Dunedin ●

Cook Strait

SOUTHERN ALPS

*South
Island*

*Stewart
Island*

Aukland
Islands
(N.Z.)

15°N

0°

15°S

30°S

45°S

135°W

150°W

165°W

180°

165°E

150°E

135°E

120°E

N
W E
S

Land Elevation

Feet	Meters
14,000	4,000
7,000	2,000
1,500	500
700	200
0	0
Below
sea level	Below
sea level

✪ National
capital

★ State or
territorial
capital

● Other city

Mercator Projection

0   500   1000 Miles

0   500   1000 Kilometers

Understanding Map Projections

Geographers and historians use globes and maps to represent the Earth. A globe is like a small model of the Earth. It shows major geographic features, representing the land-masses and bodies of water accurately. How-ever, a globe is not always convenient to use. A map, on the other hand, which can be printed on a piece of paper or in a book, is a more con-venient way to show the Earth. Unfortunately, no map can be an exact picture of the Earth be-cause all maps are flat and the Earth's surface is curved.

Mapmakers have developed many ways of showing the curved Earth on a flat surface. Each of these ways is called a map projection. The three maps on this page show different types of map projections—each with its advan-tages and disadvantages.

Robinson Projection The Robinson pro-jection shows correct shapes and sizes of land-masses for most parts of the world. They are commonly used today by geographers. You will find numerous Robinson projections in this book. The locator maps that appear with most of the maps in the book are Robinson projections.

Mercator Projection The Mercator projec-tion, one of the earliest projections developed, accurately shows the directions north, south, east, and west. As you can see, the parallels and meridians are straight lines intersecting each other at right angles. This makes it easy to plot distances on the map. As a result, Mercator pro-jections are useful for showing sailors' routes and ocean currents. Sizes become distorted, however, as you move farther away from the equator.

Interrupted Projection The Interrupted projection shows the sizes and shapes of land-masses accurately. However, the interruptions in the oceans make it difficult to measure dis-tances and judge directions across water.

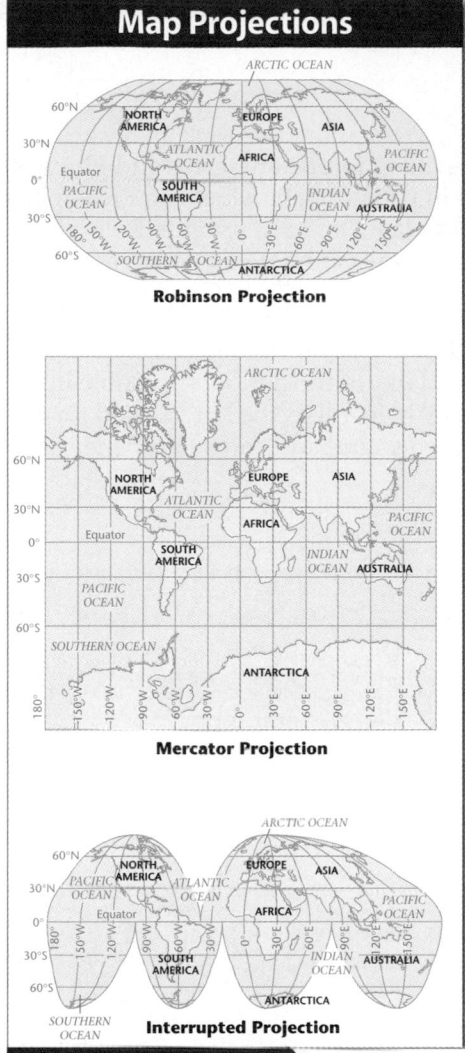

Map Projections

Robinson Projection

Mercator Projection

Interrupted Projection

Skills Assessment

Geography Map projections enable mapmakers to show the curved Earth on a flat page. Each of the projections shown here has its advantages and disadvantages.

1. **Location** On the maps, locate **(a)** North America, **(b)** Africa, **(c)** Australia.
2. **Region** **(a)** On an Interrupted projection, which continent is divided into sections? Why is it divid-ed? **(b)** List three pages in this textbook on which you can find a Robinson projection.
3. **Critical Thinking Comparing** Locate Antarctica on the Robinson and Mercator projections. On which map is its size shown more accurately? Explain why this is so.

Reference Section **1011**

Glossary

This Glossary defines many important terms and phrases. Some terms are phonetically respelled to aid in pronunciation. See the Pronunciation Key below for an explanation of the respellings. The page number following each definition is the page on which the term or phrase is first discussed in a chapter. All terms that appear in blue type in the text are included in this Glossary.

PRONUNCIATION KEY When difficult terms or names first appear in the text, they are respelled to aid in pronunciation. A syllable in small capital letters receives the most stress. The key below lists the letters used for respelling. It includes examples of words using each sound and shows how they are respelled.

SYMBOL	EXAMPLE	RESPELLING
a	hat	(hat)
ay	pay, late	(pay), (layt)
ah	star, hot	(stahr), (haht)
ai	air, dare	(air), (dair)
aw	law, all	(law), (awl)
eh	met	(meht)
ee	bee, eat	(bee), (eet)
er	learn, sir, fur	(lern), (ser), (fer)
ih	fit	(fiht)
ī	mile	(mīle)
ir	ear	(ir)
oh	no	(noh)
oi	soil, boy	(soil), (boi)
oo	root, rule	(root), (rool)
or	born, door	(born), (dor)
ow	plow, out	(plow), (owt)
u	put, book	(put), (buk)
uh	fun	(fuhn)
yoo	few, use	(fyoo), (yooz)
ch	chill, reach	(chihl), (reech)
g	go, dig	(goh), (dihg)
j	jet, gently, bridge	(jeht), (JEHNT lee), (brihj)
k	kite, cup	(kīt), (kuhp)
ks	mix	(mihks)
kw	quick	(kwihk)
ng	bring	(brihng)
s	say, cent	(say), (sehnt)
sh	she, crash	(shee), (krash)
th	three	(three)
y	yet, onion	(yeht), (UHN yuhn)
z	zip, always	(zihp), (AWL wayz)
zh	treasure	(TREH zher)

A

abdicate give up a high office (p. 490)

abolitionist one who fought for the end of slavery in the United States (p. 609)

absentee landlord one who owns a large estate but does not live there (p. 600)

absolute monarch ruler with complete authority over the government and lives of the people he or she governs (p. 413)

abstract style of art composed of lines, colors, and shapes, usually having no recognizable subject matter (p. 753)

acid rain form of pollution in which toxic chemicals in the air come back to the Earth as rain, snow, or hail (p. 817)

acropolis (uh KRAHP uh lihs) highest and most fortified point within a Greek city-state (p. 106)

acupuncture medical treatment in which needles are inserted under the skin at specific points to relieve pain or treat various illnesses (p. 96)

agribusiness large commercial farm owned by a multinational corporation (p. 938)

ahimsa (uh HIM sah) Hindu belief in nonviolence and a reverence for all life (pp. 78, 732)

alliance formal agreement between two or more nations or powers to cooperate and come to one another's defense (pp. 111, 387)

alloy mix or blend one metal with another (p. 167)

alphabet letters that represent spoken sounds (p. 44)

anarchist someone who wants to abolish all government (p. 580)

anesthetic drug that prevents pain during surgery (p. 498)

animism belief that spirits and forces may live in animals, objects, or dreams (p. 12)

annex add a territory onto an existing state or country (pp. 486, 573)

annul cancel or invalidate (pp. 214, 352)

Anschluss union of Austria and Germany (p. 772)

anthropology study of the origins and development of people and their societies (p. 8)

antisemitism prejudice against Jews (p. 196)

apartheid policy of strict racial separation in South Africa; abolished in 1989 (p. 727)

apostle leader or teacher of a new faith or movement (p. 142)

appeasement policy of giving in to an aggressor's demands in order to keep the peace (p. 771)

apprentice young person learning a trade from a master (p. 200)

aqueduct in ancient Rome, bridgelike stone structure that carried water from the hills into the cities (p. 138)

arabesque intricate design made up of curved lines that suggest floral shapes, used to decorate rugs, textiles, and glassware (p. 263)

archaeology study of past people and cultures (p. 8)

archipelago (ahr kuh PEHL uh goh) chain of islands (p. 316)

aristocracy government headed by a privileged minority or upper class (p. 106)

armada fleet of ships (p. 414)

armistice agreement to end fighting in a war (p. 693)

artifact object made by human beings (p. 8)

artisan skilled craftworker (p. 16)

assassination murder of a public figure, usually for political reasons (p. 120)

assembly line production method that breaks down a complex job into a series of smaller tasks (p. 546)

assimilate absorb or adopt another culture (p. 122)

astrolabe instrument used to determine latitude by measuring the position of the stars (p. 365)

atheism belief that there is no god (p. 714)

atman (AHT muhn) in Hindu belief, a person's essential self (p. 77)

atrocity brutal act committed against innocent people (p. 691)

autocrat ruler who has complete authority (p. 236)

autonomy self-rule (p. 520)

ayatollah title given to a learned Shiite Muslim legal expert (p. 898)

B

balance of power distribution of military and economic power that prevents any one nation from becoming too strong (p. 420)

baroque ornate style of art and architecture popular in the 1600s and 1700s (p. 453)

barter economy system in which one set of goods or services is exchanged for another (p. 43)

bill of exchange issued by a banker in one city to a merchant who could exchange it for cash in a distant city, thus freeing him from traveling with gold, which was easily stolen (p. 199)

bishop high-ranking Church official with authority over a local area, or diocese (p. 145)

blitzkrieg lightning war (p. 775)

blockade shutting off of a port to keep people or supplies from moving in or out (p. 487)

bourgeoisie (boor zhwah ZEE) the middle class (p. 469)

boyar landowning noble in Russia under the czars (pp. 242, 432)

brahman according to Aryan belief, the single spiritual power that resides in all things (p. 57)

bunraku Japanese puppet plays (p. 325)

bushido (BOO shee doh) code of conduct for samurai during the feudal period in Japan (p. 320)

C

cabinet parliamentary advisors to the king who originally met in a small room, or "cabinet" (p. 458)

caliph successor to Muhammad as political and religious leader of the Muslims (p. 256)

calligraphy fancy or stylized handwriting (pp. 63, 263)

canon law body of laws of a church (p. 195)

canonize recognize one as a saint (p. 352)

capital money or wealth (pp. 199, 501)

capital offense crime punishable by death (p. 598)

capitalism economic system in which the means of production are privately owned and operated for profit (p. 404)

caravel improved type of sailing ship in the 1400s (p. 365)

Glossary

Glossary

cartel association of large corporations formed to fix prices, set production quotas, or divide up markets (p. 550)

cartographer mapmaker (p. 365)

caste in traditional Indian society, unchangeable social group into which a person is born (pp. 57, 267)

cataract waterfall (p. 25)

caudillo military dictator in Latin America (p. 659)

cease-fire halt in fighting (p. 874)

celadon porcelain with an unusual blue-green glaze (p. 314)

censorship restriction on access to ideas and information (p. 451)

census population count (p. 135)

chancellor prime minister (pp. 571, 761, 836)

charter in the Middle Ages, a written document that set out the rights and privileges of a town (p. 199)

chinampas artificial islands made of earth piled on reed mats anchored to a shallow lake bed (p. 159)

chivalry code of conduct for knights during the Middle Ages (p. 189)

circumnavigate travel all the way around the Earth (p. 368)

city-state political unit made up of a city and the surrounding lands (p. 18)

civil disobedience refusal to obey unjust laws (p. 732)

civil law body of law dealing with private rights of individuals (p. 40)

civilization complex, highly organized social order (p. 15)

civil rights movement effort in the 1950s and 1960s to end discrimination and ensure equal rights for all Americans (p. 841)

civil war war fought between two groups of people in the same nation (p. 387)

clan group of families with a common ancestor (p. 62)

client state nation dependent on the support of a stronger power (p. 899)

coalition temporary alliance of various political parties (pp. 605, 838)

codify arrange and set down in writing (p. 40)

collaborator person who cooperates with an enemy (p. 782)

collective large farm owned and operated by peasants as a group (p. 709)

collective security system in which a group of nations acts as one to preserve the peace of all (p. 695)

collectivization pooling of land and labor in an attempt to increase efficiency (p. 862)

colony territory settled and ruled by people from another land (p. 44)

colossus giant (p. 584)

comedy in ancient Greece, play that mocked people or social customs (p. 119)

command economy system in which government officials make all basic economic decisions (p. 708)

commissar communist party official assigned to the army to teach party principles and ensure party loyalty (p. 706)

commodity valuable product (p. 284)

common law system of law that is the same for all people, based on court decisions that have become accepted legal principles (p. 207)

commune community in which property is held in common, living quarters are shared, and physical needs are provided in exchange for work at assigned jobs (p. 863)

communism form of socialism advocated by Karl Marx; according to Marx, class struggle was inevitable and would lead to the creation of a classless society in which all wealth and property would be owned by the community as a whole (p. 512)

compact agreement (p. 395)

compromise acceptable middle ground (p. 352)

concentration camp detention center for civilians who are considered enemies of a state (p. 765)

concession special economic rights given to a foreign power (p. 630)

confederation unification (p. 654)

conquistador (kahn KEES tuh dor) name for the Spanish explorers who claimed lands in the Americas for Spain in the 1500s and 1600s (p. 386)

conscription "the draft," which required all young men to be ready for military or other service (p. 690)

constitutional government government whose power is defined and limited by law (p. 457)

consul in ancient Rome, official from the patrician class who supervised the government and commanded the armies (p. 129)

containment Cold War policy of limiting communism to areas already under Soviet control (p. 793)

contra guerrilla who fought against the Sandinistas in Nicaragua (p. 946)

convoy group of merchant ships protected by warships (p. 688)

corporation business owned by many investors who buy shares of stock and risk only the amount of their investment (p. 549)

covenant binding agreement (p. 46)

creole person in Spain's colonies in the Americas who was an American-born descendant of Spanish settlers (pp. 390, 527)

criminal law branch of law that deals with offenses against others, such as robbery, assault, or murder (p. 40)

crusade holy war (p. 214)

cult of domesticity idealization of women and the home (p. 556)

cultural diffusion spread of ideas, customs, and technologies from one people to another (p. 19)

culture way of life of a society that is handed down from one generation to the next by learning and experience (p. 8)

cuneiform (kyoo NEE uh form) wedge-shaped writing of the ancient Sumerians (p. 36)

curriculum formal course of study (p. 185)

cyclone fierce circular windstorm (p. 886)

czar title of the ruler of the Russian empire (p. 243)

D

daimyo (DĪ myoh) warrior lord directly below the shogun in feudal Japan (p. 320)

debt service paying interest on loans (p. 886)

decimal system system of numbers based on 10 (p. 83)

decipher decode (p. 32)

default fail to make payments (p. 846)

deficit gap between what a government spends and what it takes in through taxes and other sources (p. 841)

deficit spending situation in which a government spends more money than it takes in (p. 470)

deforestation the destruction of forest land (pp. 633, 886)

delta triangular area of marshland formed by deposits of silt at the mouth of some rivers (pp. 25, 896)

democracy government in which the people hold ruling power (p. 107)

demotic system of ancient Egyptian writing, simpler than hieroglyphics, that was developed for everyday use (p. 32)

depopulation reduction in population (p. 428)

desalinization process of converting salty sea water into fresh water (p. 890)

desertification process by which fertile or semidesert land becomes desert (pp. 281, 916)

détente easing of tensions between the United States and the Soviet Union in the 1970s (p. 829)

dharma (DAHR muh) in Hindu belief, an individual's religious and moral duties (p. 77)

diaspora (di AS puhr uh) the scattering of people (p. 47)

dictator ruler who has complete control over a government; in ancient Rome, a leader appointed to rule for six months in times of emergency (p. 129)

diet assembly or legislature (pp. 247, 647)

diocese district or region under the care of a bishop (p. 145)

direct democracy system of government in which citizens participate directly in the day-to-day affairs of government rather than through elected representatives (p. 112)

disarmament reduction of armed forces and weapons (p. 747)

dissent different or opposing ideas (p. 81)

dissenter Protestant whose views and opinions differed with those of the Church of England (p. 422)

dissident someone who speaks out against the government (p. 844)

divine right belief that a ruler's authority comes directly from God (p. 413)

domesticate tame animals and adapt crops for the purpose of cultivation (p. 12)

dominion self-governing nation (p. 654)

domino theory belief that if one nation fell to communism, neighboring nations would also fall, like a row of falling dominoes (p. 873)

dowry payment to the bridegroom or his family in an arranged marriage (p. 87)

Duma elected national legislature in Russia (p. 589)

dynamo machine used to generate electricity (p. 546)

dynastic cycle rise and fall of Chinese dynasties according to the Mandate of Heaven (p. 64)

dynasty ruling family (p. 25)

E

e-commerce business and trade conducted over the Internet (p. 820)

economic dependence economic relationship, con-trolled by a developed nation, in which a less-developed nation exports raw materials to the developed nation and imports manufactured goods, capital, and technological know-how (p. 659)

ejido (eh HEE doh) Mexican peasant cooperative (p. 944)

elector one of seven German princes who would choose the Holy Roman emperor (p. 427)

electorate body of people allowed to vote (p. 595)

elite upper class (p. 626)

emancipation granting of freedom to serfs or slaves (p. 586)

embargo ban on trade (pp. 874, 940)

emigration movement away from one's homeland (p. 580)

émigré (EHM ih gray) person who flees his or her country for political reasons (p. 476)

empire group of states or territories controlled by one ruler (p. 18)

enclosure in England in the 1700s, the process of taking over and fencing off public lands (p. 499)

encomienda right the Spanish government granted to its American colonists to demand labor or tribute from Native Americans (p. 390)

engineering application of science and mathematics to develop useful structures and machines (p. 138)

engraving art form in which an artist etches a design on a metal plate with acid and then uses the plate to make multiple prints (p. 342)

enlightened despot absolute ruler who uses his or her power to bring about political and social change (p. 452)

entente nonbinding agreement to follow common policies (p. 681)

entrepreneur person who assumes financial risks in the hope of making a profit (p. 404)

environmentalist one who raises an alarm about threats to the planet's fragile environment (p. 817)

epic long, narrative poem (p. 222)

epidemic outbreak of a rapidly spreading disease (p. 225)

ethics moral standards of behavior (p. 47)

ethnic cleansing policy of killing or forcibly removing people of certain ethnic groups (p. 852)

ethnic group large group of people who share the same language and cultural heritage (p. 245)

euro common currency used by member nations of the European Union (p. 832)

exchequer treasury (p. 207)

excommunication exclusion from the Roman Catholic Church as a penalty for refusing to obey Church laws (p. 195)

expansionism policy of increasing the amount of territory a government holds (pp. 95, 608)

extraterritoriality right of foreigners to be protected by the laws of their own nation (p. 636)

F

faction small group (p. 473)

factory place in which workers and machines are brought together to produce large quantities of goods (p. 502)

favela Brazilian slum (p. 952)

Glossary

federal republic government in which power is divided between the national, or federal, government and the states (p. 463)

federal system system in which powers are divided between a strong central government and local governments (p. 883)

feminist movement sought equal access for women to jobs and promotions, equal pay for equal work, and an end to sexual harassment on the job (p. 819)

feudal contract exchange of pledges between lords and vassals (p. 186)

feudalism (FYOO duhl ihz uhm) loosely organized system of government in which local lords governed their own lands but owed military service and other support to a greater lord (pp. 64, 186)

fief (FEEF) in the Middle Ages, an estate granted by a lord to a vassal in exchange for service and loyalty (p. 186)

filial piety respect for parents (p. 90)

flapper in the United States and Europe in the 1920s, a rebellious young woman (p. 756)

flying buttress stone support on the outside of a building that allowed builders to construct higher walls and leave space for large stained-glass windows (p. 223)

free trade trade between countries without quotas, tariffs, or other restrictions (p. 597)

fresco colorful painting completed on wet plaster (p. 102)

friar monk who traveled throughout Europe's growing towns to preach to the poor (p. 195)

frontier sparsely populated, undeveloped area on the outskirts of civilization (p. 182)

fundamentalist one who stresses the fundamental, or basic, values of his or her faith (p. 819)

G

general strike strike by workers in many different industries at the same time (p. 748)

genetic engineering altering of the chemical code carried by all living things (p. 820)

genocide deliberate attempt to destroy an entire religious or ethnic group (pp. 629, 781)

gentry wealthy, landowning class (p. 304)

geography study of people, their environments, and their resources (p. 6)

germ theory idea that certain microbes might cause specific infectious diseases (p. 551)

ghetto separate section of a city where members of a minority group are forced to live (p. 355)

glacier thick sheet of ice that covered parts of the Earth during the ice age (p. 12)

glasnost policy of openness instituted by Soviet leader Mikhail Gorbachev in the 1980s (p. 846)

global warming worldwide temperature increase (pp. 157, 817)

glyph pictograph or other symbol carved into a surface (p. 164)

golden age period of great cultural achievement (p. 83)

gravity force that tends to pull one mass or object to another (p. 358)

griot (GREE oh) professional storyteller in early West Africa (p. 297)

gross domestic product total value of all goods and services produced by a nation (p. 859)

guerrilla warfare fighting carried on through hit-and-run raids (p. 489)

guild in the Middle Ages, association of merchants or artisans who cooperated to protect their economic interests (p. 200)

H

habeas corpus principle that a person cannot be held in prison without first being charged with a specific crime (p. 426)

haiku form of Japanese poetry that expresses a feeling, thought, or idea in three lines, or 17 syllables (p. 325)

hajj one of the Five Pillars of Islam, the pilgrimage to Mecca that all Muslims are expected to make at least once in their lifetime (p. 254)

hangul alphabet that uses symbols to represent the sounds of spoken Korean (p. 315)

harijan "child of God," Gandhi's term for an untouchable in the caste system (p. 885)

hejab traditional form of dress worn by Muslim women (p. 893)

heliocentric based on the belief that the sun is the center of the universe (pp. 123, 356)

helot member of a class of state-owned slaves in ancient Sparta (p. 106)

heresy religious belief that is contrary to the official teachings of a church (p. 146)

hierarchy (HĪ uhr ahr kee) system of ranking people within a society (p. 35)

hieroglyphics (hi er oh GLIHF ihks) form of picture writing developed by the ancient Egyptians (p. 32)

hijra Muhammad's flight from Mecca to Medina in 622 (p. 253)

historian person who studies how people lived in the past (p. 10)

home rule local self-government (p. 602)

homogeneous society society that has a common culture and language (p. 648)

humanism intellectual movement at the heart of the Italian Renaissance that focused on worldly subjects rather than on religious issues (p. 337)

humanities study of subjects taught in ancient Greece and Rome, such as grammar, rhetoric, poetry, and history (p. 338)

human rights basic rights and freedoms (p. 810)

hypothesis possible explanation (p. 357)

I

icon holy image of Christ, the Virgin Mary, or a saint venerated in the Eastern Orthodox Church (p. 237)

ideogram picture that symbolizes an idea or action (p. 32)

ideology system of thought and belief (pp. 518, 807)

illumination artistic decoration in books (p. 224)

immunity natural protection (p. 386)

imperialism domination by one country of the political, economic, or cultural life of another country or region (pp. 133, 618)

Glossary

import substitution government policy of encouraging local manufacturers to produce goods that would replace imports (p. 937)

impressionism school of painting of the late 1800s and early 1900s that tried to capture fleeting visual impressions (p. 565)

indemnity payment for losses in war (p. 636)

indigenous original or native to a country or region (p. 653)

indulgence in the Roman Catholic Church, pardon for sins committed during a person's lifetime (p. 346)

inflation economic cycle that involves a rapid rise in prices linked to a sharp increase in the amount of money available (pp. 148, 226, 404)

intendant official appointed by French king Louis XIV to govern the provinces, collect taxes, and recruit soldiers (p. 418)

interchangeable parts identical components that can be used in place of one another in manufacturing (p. 546)

interdependence mutual dependence of countries on goods, resources, and knowledge from other parts of the world (p. 809)

interdict in the Roman Catholic Church, excommunication of an entire region, town, or kingdom (p. 195)

intifada mass uprising mounted by Palestinians in territory held by Israel (p. 900)

island-hopping method used by Allied forces to recapture some Japanese-held islands in the Pacific while bypassing others (p. 788)

isolationism policy of limited involvement in world affairs (p. 613)

J

janizary elite force of the Ottoman army (p. 273)

jihad in Islam, an effort in God's service (pp. 254, 621)

joint family family organization in which several generations share a common dwelling (p. 87)

joint stock company private trading company in which shares are sold to investors to finance business ventures (p. 404)

joint venture business organized by two parties, with profits shared by both participants (p. 865)

journeyman salaried worker who was employed by a guild master (p. 200)

jury group of people sworn to make a decision in a legal case (pp. 112, 207)

K

kabuki (kuh BOO kee) form of Japanese drama developed in the 1600s (p. 323)

kaiser (KĪ zer) emperor of Germany (p. 573)

kamikaze (kah mih KAH zee) Japanese pilot who undertook a suicide mission (p. 789)

kana in the Japanese writing system, phonetic symbols representing syllables (p. 318)

karma in Hindu belief, all the actions that affect a person's fate in the next life (p. 77)

kibbutz collective farm in Israel (p. 890)

kiva large underground chamber used by the Anasazi for religious ceremonies (p. 169)

knight noble in Europe who served as a mounted warrior for a lord in the Middle Ages (p. 187)

kulak wealthy peasant in the Soviet Union in the 1930s (p. 710)

Kulturkampf Bismarck's "battle for civilization," in which his goal was to make Catholics put loyalty to the state above their allegiance to the Church (p. 575)

L

labor union workers' organization (p. 509)

laissez faire policy allowing business to operate with little or no government interference (p. 450)

land reform breakup of large agricultural holdings for redistribution among peasants (p. 303)

latifundia huge estates bought up by newly wealthy Roman citizens (p. 133)

latitude distance north or south of the Equator (p. 6)

lay investiture creation of bishops by anyone who is not a member of the clergy (p. 213)

legion basic unit of the ancient Roman army, made up of about 5,000 soldiers (p. 131)

legislature lawmaking body (p. 108)

legitimacy principle by which monarchies that had been unseated by the French Revolution or Napoleon were restored (p. 493)

levée morning ritual during which nobles would wait upon King Louis XIV (p. 418)

levy collect (p. 218)

libel knowing publication of false and damaging statements (p. 606)

liberation theology movement in the 1960s and 1970s urging the Roman Catholic Church to take a more active role in changing the social conditions that contributed to poverty and oppression in Latin America (pp. 819, 939)

limited monarchy government in which a constitution or legislative body limits the monarch's powers (p. 426)

lineage group claiming a common ancestor (p. 295)

literacy rate percentage of people who can read and write (pp. 315, 940)

loess fine windblown yellow soil (p. 60)

logic rational thinking (p. 115)

longbow six-foot-long bow that could rapidly fire arrows with enough force to pierce most armor (p. 228)

longitude distance east or west of the Prime Meridian (p. 6)

Loyalist colonist who supported Britain during the American Revolution (p. 462)

M

mandate after World War I, a territory that was administered by a western power (p. 696)

manor during the Middle Ages in Europe, a lord's estate, which included one or more villages and the surrounding lands (p. 189)

mansa title for the king of Mali (p. 285)

maquiladora (mah kee luh DOHR uh) foreign-owned industrial plant in Mexico in which local workers assemble imported parts into finished goods (p. 945)

margin buying paying part of the cost of stocks while borrowing the rest from brokers (p. 748)

martyr person who suffers or dies for his or her beliefs (p. 144)

matrilineal term for a family organization in which kinship ties are traced through the mother (pp. 295, 370)

means of production farms, factories, railways, and other large businesses that produce and distribute goods (p. 511)

medieval referring to the Middle Ages in Europe or the period of history in between ancient and modern times (p. 182)

mercantilism policy by which a nation sought to export more than it imported in order to build its supply of gold and silver (p. 406)

mercenary soldier serving in a foreign army for pay (pp. 149, 428)

messiah savior sent by God (p. 142)

mestizo person in Spain's colonies in the Americas who was of Native American and European descent (pp. 391, 527)

middle class new class of people, including merchants, traders, and artisans—who stood between peasants and nobles (p. 200)

militarism glorification of the military (p. 681)

militia band of citizen soldiers (p. 902)

millet in the Ottoman empire, a religious community of non-Muslims (p. 273)

minaret slender tower of a mosque, from which Muslims are called to prayer (p. 259)

missi dominici agents of Emperor Charlemagne who traveled throughout the empire to check the condition of the roads, listen to grievances, and see that justice was done (p. 184)

missionary someone sent on a religious mission (pp. 82, 622)

mixed economy economic system with both private and state-run enterprises (p. 916)

mobilize prepare military forces for war (p. 683)

modernization building a stable government while developing a country economically (p. 807)

moksha (MAHK shuh) in Hindu belief, the ultimate goal of existence, achieving union with brahman (p. 77)

monarchy government in which a king or queen exercises central power (p. 106)

money economy system by which goods and services are paid for through the exchange of a token of agreed value (p. 43)

monopoly complete control of a product or business by one person or group (pp. 95, 401)

monotheistic believing in one God (pp. 46, 253)

monsoon seasonal wind; in India, the winter monsoon brings hot, dry weather and the summer monsoon brings rain (p. 53)

mosaic picture made from chips of colored stone or glass (p. 138)

mosque Muslim house of worship (p. 254)

muezzin mosque official who climbs to the top of a minaret to call the faithful to prayer (p. 259)

mulatto in Spain's colonies in the Americas, person who was of African and European descent (pp. 391, 527)

multinational corporation enterprise with branches in many countries (p. 813)

mummification (muhm mih fih KAY shuhn) practice of preserving the bodies of the dead (p. 29)

mural large wall painting (p. 85)

mutual-aid society self-help group set up to aid sick or injured workers (p. 553)

mystic person who devotes his or her life to seeking spiritual truths (p. 57)

N

nationalism a strong feeling of pride in and devotion to one's country (p. 483)

nationalization takeover of property or resources by the government (p.724)

natural law rule or law that governs human nature (p. 446)

natural right right that belongs to all humans from birth (p. 447)

neutrality policy of supporting neither side in a war (p. 683)

nirvana in Buddhism, union with the universe and release from the cycle of rebirth (p. 79)

no-fly zone area over which Iraqi aircraft were not permitted to fly after the Persian Gulf War (p. 903)

nomad person who moves from place to place in search of food (p. 11)

no man's land empty tract of land where everything has been destroyed by war (p. 687)

nonaligned not allied with either side in a conflict (p. 807)

nuclear family family unit consisting of parents and children (p. 295)

O

oasis fertile area in a desert, watered by a natural well or spring (p. 252)

oba title for the king of Benin (p. 288)

oligarchy government in which ruling power belongs to a few people (pp. 106, 458)

one-party system country that has a single political party (p. 915)

oracle bone bone used by priests in Shang China to predict the future (p. 63)

ostracism used in ancient Greece to banish or send away a public figure who threatened democracy (p. 112)

outpost distant military station (pp. 283, 373)

overproduction condition in which production of goods exceeds the demand for them (p. 747)

P

pacifism opposition to all war (pp. 678, 771)

padi field (p. 372)

pagoda multistoried Buddhist temple with eaves that curve up at the corners (p. 307)

pandemic spread of a disease across a large area, country, continent, or the entire world (p. 694)

papal supremacy authority of medieval popes over all secular rulers (p. 193)

Glossary

papyrus (puh PĪ ruhs) plant that grows along the banks of the Nile; used by the ancient Egyptians to make a paperlike material (p. 32)

partition divide (pp. 435, 882)

partnership group of merchants who joined together to finance a large-scale venture that would have been too costly for any individual trader (p. 199)

pasha provincial ruler in the Ottoman empire (p. 628)

patriarch in the Byzantine empire, highest church official in a major city (pp. 145, 237)

patriarchal describing a family headed by the father, husband, or oldest male (p. 47)

patrician member of the landholding upper class in ancient Rome (p. 129)

patrilineal term for a family organization in which kinship ties are traced through the father (p. 295)

patron person who provides financial support for the arts (p. 337)

penal colony place where people convicted of crimes are sent (p. 598)

peninsular member of the highest class in Spain's colonies in the Americas (pp. 390, 527)

peon worker forced to labor for a landlord in order to pay off a debt (p. 390)

peonage system by which workers owe labor to pay their debts (p. 661)

perestroika restructuring of the Soviet government and economy in the 1980s (p. 846)

perspective artistic technique used to give drawings and paintings a three-dimensional effect (p. 339)

phalanx in ancient Greece, a massive formation of heavily armed foot soldiers (p. 106)

pharaoh (FAIR oh) title of the rulers of ancient Egypt (p. 25)

philosophe member of a group of Enlightenment thinkers who tried to apply the methods of science to the improvement of society (p. 447)

philosophy system of ideas (p. 89)

physiocrat Enlightenment thinker who searched for natural laws to explain economics (p. 450)

pictogram drawing used to represent a word (p. 17)

plains fertile flatlands (p. 157)

plantation large estate run by an owner or overseer and worked by laborers who live there (p. 390)

plateau raised area of level land (p. 52)

plebeian (plih BEE uhn) member of the lower class in ancient Rome, including farmers, merchants, artisans, and traders (p. 129)

plebiscite ballot in which voters have a direct say on an issue (pp. 485, 953)

pogrom violent mob attack on a Jewish community (p. 588)

polis city-state in ancient Greece (p. 106)

polygamy custom that allows men to have more than one wife (p. 728)

polytheistic believing in many gods (p. 16)

pope head of the Roman Catholic Church (p. 146)

potlatch ceremonial giftgiving by wealthy Native Americans of the Northwest Coast (p. 171)

predestination idea that God long ago determined who will gain salvation (p. 350)

prehistory period of time before writing systems were invented (p. 8)

premier prime minister (p. 605)

prime minister head of the cabinet in a parliamentary government; usually the leader of the largest party in the legislature (p. 458)

privateer pirate (p. 393)

privatization selling off of state-owned industries to private investors (p. 814)

proletariat working class (pp. 512, 702)

propaganda spreading of ideas to promote a certain cause or to damage an opposing cause (p. 690)

prophet spiritual leader believed to be interpreting God's will (p. 47)

protectorate country with its own government but under the control of an outside power (p. 620)

province land outside the city of Rome that was controlled by the Roman government (p. 133)

provisional temporary (p. 605)

psychoanalysis method of studying how the mind works and treating mental disorders (p. 753)

pueblo Southwestern Native American village (p. 168)

purdah isolation of women in separate quarters (p. 633)

Q

quipu knotted strings used by Incan officials for record keeping (p. 164)

R

racism belief that one racial group is superior to another (p. 561)

radar device used to detect the flight of airplanes (p. 776)

rajah elected warrior chief of an Aryan tribe in ancient India; local Hindu ruler in India (pp. 57, 268)

realism artistic movement whose aim was to represent the world as it is (p. 563)

Realpolitik realistic politics based on the needs of the state (p. 571)

recant give up one's views or beliefs (p. 347)

recession period of reduced economic activity (pp. 522, 830)

recognize formally agree to treat a country as a legitimate state with a legitimate government (p. 889)

regionalism loyalty to a local area (p. 659)

Reich German empire (p. 573)

reincarnation in Hinduism, belief in the rebirth of the soul in another bodily form (p. 77)

religious toleration policy of allowing people to worship as they choose (p. 219)

reparation payment for war damages or damages caused by imprisonment (pp. 694, 784)

repeal cancel (pp. 400, 598)

republic system of government in which officials are chosen by the people (pp. 129, 477)

repudiate reject (p. 763)

revenue money taken in through taxes (p. 394)

rhetoric art of skillful speaking (p. 115)

rococo personal, elegant style of art and architecture made popular during the mid-1700s and featuring fancy design in the shape of leaves, shells, and scrolls (p. 453)

Glossary

romanticism nineteenth-century artistic movement that appealed to emotion rather than reason (p. 562)

rotten borough rural town in England that sent members to Parliament despite having few or no voters (p. 595)

S

sabbath holy day for rest and worship (p. 47)

sacrament sacred ritual of the Roman Catholic Church (p. 191)

salon informal social gathering at which writers, artists, and philosophers exchanged ideas; originated in France in the 1600s (p. 451)

samurai member of the warrior class in Japanese feudal society (p. 320)

sanction penalty (p. 770)

satellite dependent state (p. 794)

sati Hindu custom that called for a wife to join her husband in death by throwing herself on his funeral pyre (p. 631)

satirize make fun of (p. 137)

satrap governor of a province in the Persian empire (p. 42)

savanna grassy plain with irregular patterns of rainfall (p. 280)

scapegoat person, group, or thing forced to take the blame for the crimes or mistakes of others (p. 354)

schism permanent division in a church (p. 216)

scholasticism in medieval Europe, school of thought that used logic and reason to support Christian belief (p. 221)

scientific method painstaking method used to confirm findings and to prove or disprove a hypothesis (p. 357)

scribe in ancient civilizations, specially trained person who knew how to read, write and keep records (p. 18)

scurvy disease caused by the lack of vitamin C in someone's diet (p. 365)

secede withdraw (p. 611)

secret ballot votes cast without announcing them publicly (p. 595)

sect small religious group (p. 80)

secular having to do with worldly, rather than religious, matters (pp. 193, 483)

segregation separation of the races (pp. 611, 841)

selective borrowing adopting or adapting some cultural traits but discarding others (p. 318)

self-determination right of people to choose their own form of government (p. 693)

separatism movement advocating that Quebec separate from Canada and become an independent nation (p. 842)

sepoy Indian soldier who served in an army set up by the French or English East India company (pp. 376, 631)

serf in medieval Europe, peasant bound to the lord's land (p. 189)

service industry industry that provides a service rather than a product (p. 830)

shah king (p. 274)

shantytown slum on the outskirts of a city that lacks basic services, such as running water (p. 818)

shogun in Japanese feudal society, supreme military commander who held more power than the emperor (p. 320)

shrine altar, chapel, or other place that is sacred (p. 102)

silt rich soil carried by flooding rivers (p. 24)

simony selling of Church offices (p. 195)

slash-and-burn agriculture farming method in which forest and brush are cut down and burned to create planting fields (p. 294)

smelt melt in order to get the pure metal away from its waste matter (p. 500)

social contract agreement by which people give up their freedom to a powerful government in order to avoid chaos (p. 447)

social gospel movement of the 1800s that urged Christians to do social service (p. 561)

socialism system in which the people as a whole rather than private individuals own all property and operate all businesses (p. 511)

socialist realism artistic style whose goal was to promote socialism by showing Soviet life in a positive light (p. 715)

social mobility ability to move up in social class (p. 261)

social welfare programs to help people in need (p. 576)

sonar device used to detect the path of submarines (p. 776)

soviet council of workers and soldiers set up by Russian revolutionaries in 1917 (p. 703)

special enterprise zone area in China where foreigners can own and operate industries (p. 865)

sphere of influence area in which an outside power claims exclusive investment or trading privileges (p. 620)

squatter person who settles on land he or she does not own (p. 955)

stalemate deadlock in which neither side is able to defeat the other (p. 685)

standard of living measures the quality and availability of necessities and comforts in a society (p. 554)

steppe sparse, dry grassland (pp. 18, 240)

stipend a fixed salary given to public office holders (p. 112)

stock shares in a company (p. 549)

strait narrow water passage (p. 103)

stream of consciousness literary technique that probes a character's random thoughts and feelings (p. 754)

stupa large domelike Buddhist shrine (pp. 83, 371)

subcontinent large landmass that juts out from a continent (p. 52)

suffrage right to vote (p. 478)

sultan Muslim ruler (p. 259)

sultanate land ruled by a sultan (p. 267)

summit conference of leaders and experts from around the world (p. 809)

superpower nation strong enough to influence the acts and policies of other nations (p. 807)

surplus extra or excess (pp. 15, 284, 841)

surrealism artistic movement that attempts to portray the workings of the unconscious mind (p. 753)

T

tariff tax on imported goods (p. 406)

technology tools and skills people use to meet their basic needs (p. 8)

temperance movement campaign to limit or ban the use of alcoholic beverages (p. 558)

tenant farmer someone who would pay rent to a lord in order to farm the land (p. 199)

tenement building multistory building divided into crowded apartments (p. 505)

terrorism deliberate use of random violence, especially against civilians, to achieve political goals (p. 811)

theocracy government run by religious leaders (pp. 350, 898)

tithe payment to a church equal to one tenth of a person's income (p. 192)

tolerance acceptance (p. 42)

total war channeling of a nation's entire resources into a war effort (p. 690)

totalitarian state government in which a one-party dictatorship regulates every aspect of citizens' lives (p. 713)

tournament mock battle in which knights would compete against one another to show off their fighting skills (p. 187)

trade deficit situation in which a country imports more than it exports (pp. 635, 859)

trade surplus situation in which a country exports more than it imports (p. 635)

tragedy in ancient Greece, a play that focused on human suffering and very often ended in disaster (p. 117)

triangular trade colonial trade route among Europe and its colonies, the West Indies, and Africa in which goods were exchanged for slaves (p. 399)

tribune official in ancient Rome who was elected by the plebeians to protect their interests (p. 129)

tributary state independent state that has to acknowledge the supremacy of another state and pay tribute to its ruler (p. 303)

tribute payment that conquered peoples were forced to make to their conquerors (p. 160)

troubadour wandering poet in Europe in the Middle Ages (p. 189)

truce temporary peace (p. 528)

tsunami very large, damaging wave caused by an earthquake or very strong wind (p. 317)

turnpike privately built road that charges a fee to travelers who use it (p. 504)

tyrant in ancient Greece, ruler who gained power by force (p. 108)

U

U-boat submarine (p. 688)

ultimatum final set of demands (p. 683)

ultranationalist extreme nationalist (p. 739)

ultraroyalist émigré noble or member of the clergy in France who opposed constitutional government and favored the restoration of the old regime (p. 521)

universal manhood suffrage right of all adult men to vote (p. 519)

urbanization movement of people from rural areas to cities (p. 505)

urban renewal rebuilding of the poor areas of a city (p. 552)

usurp illegally take over a throne (p. 302)

usury (YOO zhuh ree) practice of lending money with interest (p. 200)

utilitarianism idea that the goal of society should be to bring about the greatest happiness for the greatest number of people (p. 511)

utopia ideal society (p. 343)

V

vassal in medieval Europe, a lord who was granted land in exchange for service and loyalty to a greater lord (p. 186)

veneration special regard (p. 54)

vernacular everyday language of ordinary people (pp. 222, 343)

veto power to block a government action (p. 129)

viceroy representative who ruled one of Spain's provinces in the Americas in the king's name; one who governed in India in the name of the British monarch (pp. 389, 632)

vizier chief minister who supervised the business of government in ancient Egypt (p. 25)

W

war crime act that violates international rules of war (p. 853)

warlord local military ruler (p. 96)

warm-water port port that is free of ice all year (p. 433)

welfare state system in which the government takes responsibility for its citizens' social and economic needs (p. 829)

westernization adoption of western ideas, technology, and culture (p. 431)

women's suffrage right of women to vote (p. 558)

Z

zaibatsu (ZĪ BAHT soo) since the late 1800s, powerful banking and industrial families in Japan (pp. 647, 859)

zemstvo local elected assembly set up in Russia under Alexander II (p. 586)

zeppelin large, gas-filled balloon (p. 688)

ziggurat (ZIHG oo rat) pyramid-temple dedicated to the chief god or goddess of an ancient Sumerian city-state (p. 36)

A

abdicate/abdicar renunciar a un alto puesto oficial (pág. 490)

abolitionist/abolicionista persona que luchó para poner fin a la esclavitud en Estados Unidos (pág. 609)

absentee landlord/dueño ausente dueño de una gran propiedad que no vive en ella (pág. 600)

absolute monarch/monarca absoluto gobernante que tiene autoridad absoluta sobre la administración y la vida de los que están bajo su mando (pág. 413)

abstract/abstracto estilo artístico caracterizado por líneas, colores y formas que generalmente no tienen un tema reconocible (pág. 753)

acid rain/lluvia ácida forma de polución en la que los productos químicos tóxicos que se encuentran en el aire vuelven a la tierra en la lluvia, nieve o granizo (pág. 817)

acropolis/acrópolis el punto más alto y fortificado de una ciudad estado griega (pág. 106)

acupuncture/acupuntura tratamiento médico por el que se introducen agujas en la piel en puntos específicos, para aliviar el dolor o como tratamiento de diversas enfermedades (pág. 96)

agribusiness/agroindustria gran granja comercial que pertenece a una corporación multinacional (pág. 938)

ahimsa/*ahimsa* creencia hindú en la no violencia y en el respeto a todas las formas de vida (págs. 78, 732)

alliance/alianza acuerdo formal de cooperación y defensa mutua entre dos o más naciones o poderes (págs. 111, 387)

alloy/aleación mezcla o fusión de dos metales (pág. 167)

alphabet/alfabeto letras que representan los sonidos del lenguaje hablado (pág. 44)

anarchist/anarquista persona que quiere abolir toda forma de gobierno (pág. 580)

anesthetic/anestesia droga que suprime el dolor durante la cirugía (pág. 498)

animism/animismo creencia de que los espíritus y fuerzas pueden vivir en animales, objetos o sueños (pág. 12)

annex/anexar agregar un territorio a un estado o país existente (págs. 486, 573)

annul/anular cancelar o invalidar (págs. 214, 352)

Anschluss/Anschluss unión de Austria y Alemania (pág. 772)

anthropology/antropología estudio del origen y desarrollo de los pueblos y sus sociedades (pág. 8)

antisemitism/antisemitismo prejuicio contra los judíos (pág. 196)

apartheid/*apartheid* política de estricta separación racial en Sudáfrica que fue abolida en 1989 (pág. 727)

apostle/apóstol líder o maestro de una nueva fe o movimiento (pág. 142)

appeasement/contemporización política de aceptación de las exigencias de un agresor para mantener la paz (pág. 771)

apprentice/aprendiz joven que aprende un oficio de su maestro (pág. 200)

aqueduct/acueducto en la antigua Roma, estructura parecida a un puente que llevaba agua desde las colinas hasta las ciudades (pág. 138)

arabesque/arabesco diseño intrincado formado por líneas curvas que sugieren formas florales y que se usa para decorar alfombras, tejidos y objetos de vidrio (pág. 263)

archaeology/arqueología estudio de pueblos y culturas antiguas (pág. 8)

archipelago/archipiélago cadena de islas (pág. 316)

aristocracy/aristocracia gobierno encabezado por una minoría privilegiada o de clase alta (pág. 106)

armada/armada flota de barcos (pág. 414)

armistice/armisticio acuerdo para dejar de luchar en una guerra (pág. 693)

artifact/artefacto objeto hecho por seres humanos (pág. 8)

artisan/artesano trabajador cualificado que hace objetos a mano (pág. 16)

assassination/asesinato acto de dar muerte a una figura pública, generalmente por razones políticas (pág. 120)

assembly line/cadena de montaje método de producción que divide un trabajo complejo en una serie de tareas menores (pág. 546)

assimilate/asimilar absorber o adoptar otra cultura (pág. 122)

astrolabe/astrolabio instrumento que mide la posición de las estrellas para determinar la latitud (pág. 365)

atheism/ateísmo creencia de que Dios no existe (pág. 714)

atman/*atman* según la creencia hindú, el ser esencial de una persona (pág. 77)

atrocity/atrocidad acto brutal cometido en contra de inocentes (pág. 691)

autocrat/autócrata gobernante que tiene autoridad total (pág. 236)

autonomy/autonomía autogobierno (pág. 520)

ayatollah/ayatolá título que le se da al líder religioso musulmán chiíta que interpreta las leyes del corán (pág. 898)

B

balance of power/equilibrio de poder distribución del poder militar y económico que evita que una nación se vuelva demasiado fuerte (pág. 420)

baroque/barroco estilo artístico y arquitectónico elaborado que se dio en los siglos XVII y XVIII (pág. 453)

barter economy/economía de trueque sistema en el que se utiliza el intercambio de mercancías o servicios (pág. 43)

bill of exchange/letra de cambio documento emitido por un banco a un comerciante que podía cambiar por dinero en una ciudad distante, para evitar que viajara con oro, que se podía robarse fácilmente (pág. 199)

bishop/obispo funcionario eclesiástico de alto nivel con autoridad sobre un área local o diócesis (pág. 145)

blitzkrieg/guerra relámpago guerra intensa y muy breve (pág. 775)

blockade/bloqueo cierre de un puerto para evitar que las personas o provisiones puedan entrar o salir (pág. 487)

bourgeoisie/burguesía clase media (pág. 469)

boyar/*boyar* noble ruso que poseía tierras en la época de los zares (págs. 242, 432)

brahman/brahmán de acuerdo con la creencia aria, el poder espiritual que reside en todas las cosas (pág. 57)

bunraku/*bunraku* en Japón, funciones teatrales de títeres (pág. 325)

bushido/*bushido* código de conducta de los samuráis durante el período feudal japonés (pág. 320)

C

cabinet/gabinete miembros del parlamento consejeros del rey que originalmente se reunían en un pequeño cuarto o "gabinete" (pág. 458)

caliph/califa sucesor de Mahoma como líder religioso y político de los musulmanes (pág. 256)

calligraphy/caligrafía escritura refinada o estilizada que se realiza a mano (pág. 263)

canon law/derecho canónico conjunto de leyes de una iglesia (pág. 195)

canonize/canonizar reconocer a alguien como santo (pág. 352)

capital/capital dinero o riqueza (págs. 199, 501)

capital offense/ofensa capital crimen que puede castigarse con la muerte (pág. 598)

capitalism/capitalismo sistema económico por el que los medios de producción son propiedad privada y se administran para obtener beneficios (pág. 404)

caravel/carabela embarcación rápida y ligera a vela del siglo XV (pág. 365)

cartel/cartel asociación de grandes corporaciones formada para fijar precios, establecer cuotas de producción o repartirse los mercados (pág. 550)

cartographer/cartógrafo persona que hace mapas (pág. 365)

caste/casta grupo social en la sociedad tradicional de India, en el que una persona nace y del que no se puede cambiar (págs. 57, 267)

cataract/catarata cascada, caída de agua (pág. 25)

***caudillo*/caudillo** térmiono que se refiere a un dictador militar en América Latina (pág. 659)

cease-fire/tregua alto en la lucha (pág. 874)

celadon/celadón esmalte poco común de color verde azulado (pág. 314)

censorship/censura restricción en el acceso a ideas o información (pág. 451)

census/censo recuento de la población (pág. 135)

chancelor/canciller primer ministro (págs. 571, 761, 836)

charter/fueros en la Edad Media, documento escrito que establecía los derechos y privilegios de una ciudad (pág. 199)

chinampas/chinampas islas artificiales hechas de tierra apilada sobre bases de juncos en lagos de poca profundidad (pág. 159)

chivalry/caballerosidad código de conducta de los caballeros durante la Edad Media (pág. 189)

circumnavigate/circunnavegar navegar alrededor de la Tierra (pág. 368)

city-state/ciudad estado unidad política compuesta por una ciudad y las tierras que la rodean (pág. 18)

civil disobedience/desobediencia civil negarse a obedecer leyes injustas (pág. 732)

civil law/ley civil cuerpo legal que trata de los derechos privados de los individuos (pág. 40)

civilization/civilización orden social complejo y altamente organizado (pág. 15)

civil rights movement/movimiento por los derechos civiles esfuerzo en las décadas de los años 50 y 60 para acabar con la discriminación y asegurar los mismos derechos para todos los estadounidenses (pág. 841)

civil war/guerra civil guerra en la que luchan dos grupos de personas de una misma nación (pág. 387)

clan/clan grupo de familias con un antepasados comunes (pág. 62)

client state/estado dependiente nación que depende del apoyo de una potencia mayor (pág. 899)

coalition/coalición alianza temporal de varios partidos políticos (págs. 605, 838)

codify/codificar organizar y dejar por escrito (pág. 40)

collaborator/colaborador persona que coopera con el enemigo (pág. 782)

collective/granja colectiva granja grande que pertenece a campesinos que la administran en grupo (pág. 709)

collective security/seguridad colectiva sistema por el que un grupo de naciones actúa como una para preservar la paz común (pág. 695)

collectivization/colectivización unión de tierras y del trabajo de varias personas o entidades para lograr una mayor eficacia (pág. 862)

colony/colonia territorio poblado y gobernado por personas de otro lugar (pág. 44)

colossus/coloso gigante (pág. 584)

comedy/comedia en la antigua Grecia, obra de teatro donde se hacía burla de personas o costumbres (pág. 119)

command economy/economía de control sistema en el que los funcionarios del gobierno toman todas las decisiones económicas básicas (pág. 708)

commissar/comisario funcionario del partido comunista asignado al ejército para enseñar los principios del partido y asegurar la lealtad al mismo (pág. 706)

commodity/mercancía producto valioso (pág. 284)

common law/ley común sistema legal igual para todos, basado en las decisiones de las cortes que se han vuelto principios legales aceptados (pág. 207)

commune/comuna comunidad en la que la propiedad es común, se comparte la vivienda y se cubren las necesidades físicas a cambio de trabajar en ocupaciones asignadas (pág. 863)

Spanish Glossary

communism/comunismo forma de socialismo defendida por Karl Marx; según él la lucha de clases era inevitable, y llevaría a la creación de una sociedad sin clases en la que todas las propiedades pasarían a ser propiedad de la comunidad (pág. 512)

compact/pacto acuerdo (pág. 395)

compromise/acuerdo aceptación de una posición intermedia (pág. 352)

concentration camp/campo de concentración centro de detención para civiles a los que se considera enemigos del estado (pág. 765)

concession/concesión derechos económicos especiales que se dan a un poder extranjero (pág. 630)

confederation/confederación unificación (pág. 654)

conquistador/conquistador término que se refiere a los exploradores españoles que apropiaron tierras en América para España en los siglos XVI y XVII (pág. 386)

conscription/conscripción llamado a filas que exigía que todos los hombres jóvenes estuvieran listos para el servicio militar u otro servicio (pág. 690)

constitutional government/gobierno constitucional gobierno cuyo poder está definido y limitado por la ley (pág. 457)

consul/cónsul funcionario de la clase patricia que en la Roma antigua supervisaba el gobierno y dirigía los ejércitos (pág. 219)

containment/contención política de la Guerra Fría para limitar el comunismo a las áreas bajo control soviético (pág. 793)

contra/contra guerrilla que luchaba contra los sandinistas en Nicaragua (pág. 946)

convoy/convoy grupo de barcos mercantes protegidos por barcos de guerra (pág. 688)

corporation/corporación negocio propiedad de muchos inversores que compran acciones, y sólo arriesgan el monto de su inversión (pág. 549)

covenant/convenio acuerdo que obliga a las partes (pág. 46)

creole/criollo descendiente de colonos españoles nacido en las colonias españolas de América (págs. 390, 527)

criminal law/ley criminal rama de la ley que se ocupa de las ofensas contra otros, tales como robo, agresión u homicidio (pág. 40)

crusade/cruzada guerra santa (pág. 214)

cult of domesticity/culto a lo doméstico idealización de las mujeres y del hogar (pág. 556)

cultural diffusion/difusión cultural divulgación de ideas, costumbres y tecnología a distintos pueblos o culturas (pág. 19)

culture/cultura forma de vida de una sociedad que se pasa de una generación a la siguiente mediante el aprendizaje y la experiencia (pág. 8)

cuneiform/cuneiforme tipo de escritura de los antiguos sumerios cuyos caracteres tenían forma de cuña (pág. 36)

curriculum/currículo curso formal de estudios (pág. 185)

cyclone/ciclón fuerte tormenta de viento de forma circular (pág. 886)

czar/zar título del regente del imperio ruso (pág. 243)

D

daimyo/daimio señor de la guerra que en el Japón feudal estaba directamente abajo del shogún (pág. 320)

debt service/obligación de deuda pago de interés sobre préstamos (pág. 886)

decimal system/sistema decimal sistema numérico basado en el número 10 (pág. 83)

decipher/descifrar decodificar (pág. 32)

default/cese de pagos imposibilidad de realizar pagos (pág. 846)

deficit/déficit lapso entre los gastos de un gobierno y las recaudaciones por impuestos y otras fuentes de ingresos (pág. 841)

deficit spending/gasto deficitario situación en la que un gobierno gasta más de lo que recauda (pág. 470)

deforestation/deforestación destrucción de tierras forestales (págs. 633, 886)

delta/delta área triangular de tierra pantanosa que se forma en la boca de algunos ríos con los depósitos de limo (págs. 25, 896)

democracy/democracia gobierno en el que es el pueblo quien tiene el poder de gobernar (pág. 107)

demotic/demótico sistema de escritura del antiguo Egipto, más simple que los jeroglíficos, que se desarrolló para el uso diario (pág. 32)

depopulation/despoblación reducción del número de la población (pág. 428)

desalinization/desalinización proceso para convertir el agua salada del mar en agua dulce (pág. 890)

desertification/desertización proceso por el que la tierra fértil o semifértil se convierte en desierto (págs. 281, 916)

détente/distensión relajamiento de las tensiones entre Estados Unidos y la Unión Soviética en los años 70 (pág. 829)

dharma/dharma entre los hindúes, las obligaciones morales y religiosas de un individuo (pág. 77)

diaspora/diáspora diseminación de un pueblo (pág. 47)

dictator/dictador dirigente con control absoluto sobre el gobierno; en la antigua Roma, líder designado para gobernar durante seis meses en casos de emergencia (pág. 129)

diet/asamblea legislatura o asamblea legislativa (págs. 247, 647)

diocese/diócesis distrito o región a cargo de un obispo (pág. 145)

direct democracy/democracia directa sistema de gobierno en el que los ciudadanos participan directamente en lugar de a través de representantes electos en los asuntos del día a día del gobierno (pág. 112)

disarmament/desarme reducción de las fuerzas armadas y del armamento (pág. 747)

dissent/desacuerdo ideas diferentes u opuestas (pág. 81)

dissenter/disidente protestante cuyos puntos de vista y opiniones diferían de los de la Iglesia de Inglaterra (pág. 422)

dissident/disidente alguien que habla en contra del gobierno (pág. 844)

divine right/derecho divino creencia de que la autoridad de un gobernante proviene directamente de Dios (pág. 413)

domesticate/domesticar entrenar o adaptar animales y plantas con el propósito de cultivarlos (pág. 12)

dominion/dominio nación que se gobierna a sí misma (pág. 654)

domino theory/teoría del dominó creencia de que si una nación caía ante el comunismo, las naciones vecinas también caerían, como una hilera de piezas de dominó (pág. 873)

dowry/dote en un matrimonio de conveniencia, pago al futuro esposo o a su familia (pág. 87)

Duma/Duma en Rusia, asamblea legislativa nacional electa (pág. 589)

dynamo/dinamo máquina que se usa para generar electricidad (pág. 546)

dynastic cycle/ciclo dinástico florecimiento y caída de las dinastías chinas de acuerdo con el Mandato del Cielo (pág. 64)

dynasty/dinastía familia gobernante (pág. 25)

E

e-commerce/comercio electrónico comercio y negocios que se realizan en Internet (pág. 820)

economic dependence/dependencia económica relación económica controlada por una nación desarrollada, en la que una nación menos desarrollada exporta materias primas e importa objetos manufacturados, capital y conocimiento tecnológico (pág. 659)

ejido/ejido cooperativa de campesinos mexicanos (pág. 944)

elector/elector uno de los siete príncipes germanos que elegían al emperador sagrado de Roma (pág. 427)

electorate/electorado conjunto de personas a quienes se permite votar (pág. 595)

elite/élite clase alta (pág. 626)

emancipation/emancipación concesión de libertad a esclavos o siervos (pág. 586)

embargo/embargo prohibición de comerciar (págs. 874, 940)

emigration/emigración trasladarse de su propio país a otro (pág. 580)

émigré/exiliado persona que deja su país por razones políticas (pág. 476)

empire/imperio grupo de estados o territorios controlados por un gobernante (pág. 18)

enclosure/cercamiento en Inglaterra en el siglo XVIII, el proceso de apropiación y cercado de tierras públicas (pág. 499)

encomienda/encomienda derecho a exigir tributo o trabajo a los nativos americanos, que el gobierno español otorgó a sus colonos en América (pág. 390)

engineering/ingeniería aplicación de las ciencias y matemáticas al desarrollo de máquinas y estructuras útiles (pág. 138)

engraving/grabado forma de arte en la que un artista graba un diseño con ácido en una placa de metal y después la usa para producir múltiples impresiones (pág. 342)

enlightened despot/déspota ilustrado gobernante absoluto que usa su poder para precipitar cambios políticos y sociales (pág. 452)

entente/pacto acuerdo no obligatorio de seguir una política en común (pág. 681)

entrepreneur/empresario persona que asume riesgos financieros con la esperanza de obtener beneficios (pág. 404)

environmentalist/ecologista quien saca a la luz las amenazas contra el frágil medio ambiente del planeta (pág. 817)

epic/poema épico largo poema narrativo (pág. 222)

epidemic/epidemia brote de una enfermedad que se extiende rápidamente (pág. 225)

ethics/ética estándar moral de conducta (pág. 47)

ethnic cleansing/limpieza étnica política de matar o expulsar a las personas de ciertos grupos étnicos (pág. 852)

ethnic group/grupo étnico grupo grande de personas que comparten el idioma y la herencia cultural (pág. 245)

euro/euro moneda usada por las naciones que pertenecen a la Unión Europea (pág. 832)

exchequer/erario público tesoro de la nación (pág. 207)

excommunication/excomunión exclusión de la Iglesia Católica Romana como castigo por negarse a obedecer las leyes de la iglesia (pág. 195)

expansionism/expansionismo política de aumentar el territorio que posee un gobierno (págs. 95, 608)

extraterritoriality/extraterritorialidad derecho de los extranjeros a recibir protección de las leyes de su propio país (pág. 636)

F

faction/facción grupo pequeño (pág. 473)

factory/fábrica lugar donde los trabajadores y las máquinas producen grandes cantidades de mercaderías (pág. 502)

favela/favela en Brasil, barriada de casas muy pobres (pág. 952)

federal republic/república federal gobierno en el que el poder se divide entre el gobierno nacional o federal y los estados (pág. 463)

federal system/sistema federal sistema en el que el poder se divide entre un gobierno central fuerte y los gobiernos locales (pág. 883)

feminist movement/movimiento feminista movimiento que procura el acceso igualitario de las mujeres al trabajo y las promociones, igualdad de salario por un igual trabajo y el fin del acoso sexual (pág. 819)

feudal contract/contrato feudal intercambio de promesas entre señores y vasallos (pág. 186)

feudalism/feudalismo vago sistema de gobierno en el que los señores gobernaban sus propias tierras pero debían servicio militar y otras formas de apoyo a un superior (págs. 64, 186)

fief/feudo en la Edad Media, propiedad que el señor daba a un vasallo a cambio de servicios y lealtad (pág. 186)

filial piety/piedad filial respeto hacia los padres (pág. 90)

flapper/*flapper* mujer joven y rebelde en los años 20 en Estados Unidos y Europa (pág. 756)

flying buttress/contrafuerte soporte de piedra en el exterior de un edificio que permitía la construcción de paredes más altas que dejaban espacio para grandes vidrieras (pág. 223)

free trade/libre comercio comercio entre países, sin cuotas, tasas u otras restricciones (pág. 597)

fresco/fresco pintura colorida realizada sobre una pared de yeso húmedo (pág. 102)

friar/fraile monje que viajaba por las ciudades europeas en desarrollo para predicar a los pobres (pág. 195)

frontier/frontera área poco poblada y subdesarrollada, situada en las afueras de la civilización (pág. 182)

fundamentalist/fundamentalista persona que pone énfasis en los valores fundamentales o básicos de su fe (pág. 819)

G

general strike/huelga general huelga de trabajadores de muchas industrias diferentes al mismo tiempo (pág. 748)

genetic engineering/ingeniería genética alteración del código genético que portan todas las formas de vida (pág. 820)

genocide/genocidio intento deliberado de destruir la totalidad de un grupo religioso o étnico (págs. 629, 781)

gentry/alta burguesía la aristocracia rural (pág. 304)

geography/geografía estudio de las personas, el entorno y los recursos (pág. 6)

germ theory/teoría de los gérmenes idea de que ciertos microbios podrían causar enfermedades infecciosas específicas (pág. 551)

ghetto/ghetto área separada de una ciudad donde se fuerza a vivir a los miembros de una minoría (pág. 355)

glacier/glaciar gruesa capa de hielo que cubría parte de la Tierra durante la era glacial (pág. 12)

glasnost/*glasnost* política de apertura instituida por el líder soviético Mikhail Gorbachev en los años 80 (pág. 846)

global warming/calentamiento global aumento de la temperatura del planeta (págs. 157, 817)

glyph/glifo pictografía u otro símbolo tallado en una superficie (pág. 164)

golden age/edad de oro período de grandes logros culturales (pág. 83)

gravity/gravedad fuerza que atrae una masa u objeto hacia otro (pág. 358)

griot/*griot* antiguo narrador de historias profesional en África Occidental (pág. 297)

gross domestic product/producto interior bruto valor de todos los productos y servicios producidos por una nación (pág. 859)

guerrilla warfare/guerra de guerrillas lucha que se caracteriza por rápidos ataques y retiradas (pág. 489)

guild/gremio en la Edad Media, asociación de comerciantes o artesanos que cooperaban para proteger sus intereses económicos (pág. 200)

H

habeas corpus/habeas corpus principio por el que no puede encarcelarse a una persona sin haber sido antes condenada formalmente por un crimen específico (pág. 426)

haiku/haiku poema japonés que expresa un sentimiento, pensamiento o idea en tres líneas o 17 sílabas (pág. 325)

hajj/hayyi uno de los Cinco Pilares del Islam, la peregrinación a la Meca que se espera hagan todos los musulmanes por lo menos una vez en la vida (pág. 254)

hangul/*hangul* alfabeto que usa símbolos para representar gráficamente los sonidos del idioma coreano (pág. 315)

harijan/*harijan* "niño de Dios," término usado por Gandhi para designar al intocable de la sistema de castas (pág. 885)

hejab/*hejab* vestido tradicional usado por las mujeres musulmanas (pág. 893)

heliocentric/heliocéntrico sistema basado en la creencia de que el sol es el centro del universo (págs. 123, 356)

helot/ilota en la antigua Esparta, miembro de una clase de esclavos que pertenecían al estado (pág. 106)

heresy/herejía creencia religiosa contraria a las enseñanzas oficiales de la iglesia (pág. 146)

hierarchy/jerarquía sistema que clasifica a las personas de una sociedad (pág. 35)

hieroglyphics/jeroglíficos escritura pictográfica desarrollada en el antiguo Egipto (pág. 32)

hijra/héjira trayecto de Mahoma de la Meca a Medina en el año 622 (pág. 253)

historian/historiador persona que estudia el modo de vida de la gente en el pasado (pág. 10)

home rule/autogobierno autogobierno local (pág. 602)

homogeneous society/sociedad homogénea sociedad que tiene un lenguaje y una cultura común (pág. 648)

humanism/humanismo movimiento intelectual en el apogeo del Renacimiento italiano centrado en temas de este mundo en lugar de en temas religiosos (pág. 337)

humanities/humanidades estudio de materias que se enseñaban en la antigua Grecia y Roma, tales como gramática, retórica, poesía e historia (pág. 338)

human rights/derechos humanos básico derechos y libertades (pág. 810)

hypothesis/hipótesis explicación posible (pág. 357)

I

icon/ícono imagen sagrada de Cristo, la Vírgen María o de un santo venerado por la iglesia ortodoxa oriental (pág. 237)

ideogram/ideograma imagen que simboliza una idea o acción (pág. 32)

ideology/ideología sistema de pensamiento y creencias (págs. 518, 807)

illumination/iluminación decoración artística en libros (pág. 224)

immunity/inmunidad protección natural (pág. 386)

imperialism/imperialismo dominio por parte de un país de la vida política, económica o cultural de otro país o región (págs. 133, 618)

import substitution/substitución de importaciones política del gobierno de alentar a los fabricantes locales para que produzcan mercaderías que reemplacen importaciones (pág. 937)

impressionism/impresionismo escuela de pintura de finales del siglo XIX y principios del siglo XX que trataba de captar impresiones visuales fugaces (pág. 565)

indemnity/indemnización compensación como pago por pérdidas de guerra (pág. 636)

indigenous/indígena original o nativo de un país o región (pág. 653)

indulgence/indulgencia perdón por los pecados cometidos en vida concedido por la Iglesia Católica Romana (pág. 346)

inflation/inflación ciclo económico caracterizado por un rápida subida de los precios ligada a un aumento rápido del dinero disponible (págs. 148, 226, 404)

intendant/intendente oficial nombrado por el rey francés Luis XIV para gobernar las provincias, recaudar impuestos y reclutar soldados (pág. 418)

interchangeable parts/repuestos intercambiables componentes idénticos que pueden usarse unos en lugar de los otros en el proceso de producción (pág. 546)

interdependence/interdependencia dependencia mutua de los países con los de otras partes del mundo en cuanto a productos, recursos y conocimiento (pág. 809)

interdict/interdicto en la Iglesia Católica Romana, excomunión de una región, ciudad o reino (pág. 195)

intifada/intifada rebelión masiva de los palestinos en territorios ocupados por Israel (pág. 900)

island-hopping/salteo de islas método usado por las fuerzas aliadas para recapturar ciertas islas del Pacífico en poder de los japoneses, mientras salteaban otras (pág. 788)

isolationism/aislamiento política de intervención limitada en asuntos de orden mundial (pág. 613)

J

janizary/jenízaro fuerza de élite del ejército otomano (pág. 273)

jihad/yihad en el Islam, un esfuerzo al servicio de Dios (págs. 254, 621)

joint family/familia extendida organización familiar en la que varias generaciones comparten una vivienda (pág. 87)

joint stock company/compañía de capital social compañía comercial privada cuyas acciones se venden a inversores para financiar aventuras empresariales (pág. 404)

joint venture/empresa en común negocio organizado por dos partes, que comparten las ganancias (pág. 865)

journeyman/jornalero trabajador asalariado empleado por un jefe de gremio (pág. 200)

jury/jurado grupo de personas que bajo juramento deben tomar una decisión en un caso legal (págs. 112, 207)

K

kabuki/kabuki género teatral japonés desarrollado en el siglo XVII (pág. 323)

kaiser/kaiser emperador de Alemania (pág. 573)

kamikaze/kamikaze piloto japonés que emprendía una misión suicida (pág. 789)

kana/kana en el sistema japonés de escritura, símbolos fonéticos que representan sílabas (pág. 318)

karma/karma según la creencia hindú, todas las acciones que afectan el destino de una persona en su próxima vida (pág. 77)

kibbutz/kibbutz granja colectiva en Israel (pág. 890)

kiva/kiva gran cámara subterránea usada por los anazasi para realizar ceremonias religiosas (pág. 169)

knight/caballero en Europa medieval, noble que servía como guerrero a caballo para un señor (pág. 187)

kulak/kulak campesino adinerado de la Unión Soviética en los años 30 (pág. 710)

Kulturkampf/Kulturkampf "batalla por la civilización" de Bismarck, cuyo objetivo era que los católicos pusieran la lealtad al estado por encima de la lealtad a la Iglesia (pág. 575)

L

labor union/sindicato organización de trabajadores (pág. 509)

laissez faire/laissez faire política que permite que los negocios operen con poca o ninguna intervención del estado (pág. 450)

land reform/reforma agraria división de grandes propiedades dedicadas a la agricultura para distribuirlas entre los campesinos (pág. 303)

latifundia/latifundios grandes propiedades adquiridas por los ciudadanos romanos que se habían vuelto ricos recientemente (pág. 133)

Spanish Glossary

latitude/latitud distancia hacia el norte o sur del ecuador (pág. 6)

lay investiture/investidura laica creación de obispos por parte de alguien que no es clérigo (pág. 213)

legion/legión unidad básica del ejército de la antigua Roma, que consistía de unos 5,000 soldados (pág. 131)

legislature/asamblea legislativa cuerpo encargado de hacer las leyes (pág. 108)

legitimacy/legitimidad principio por el que las monarquías que habían sido derrocadas por la Revolución Francesa o por Napoleón debían restituirse (pág. 493)

levée/recepción matutina ritual de la mañana en el que los nobles atendían al rey Luis XIV (pág. 418)

levy/recaudar cobrar impuestos (pág. 218)

libel/libelo publicación intencional de declaraciones falsas que perjudican a alguien (pág. 606)

liberation theology/teología de la liberación movimiento de los años 60 y 70 que urgía a la Iglesia Católica Romana a adoptar un rol más activo para cambiar las condiciones sociales que contribuían a la pobreza y la opresión en Latinoamérica (págs. 819, 939)

limited monarchy/monarquía limitada gobierno en el que la constitución o el cuerpo legislativo limitan los poderes de la monarquía (pág. 426)

lineage/linaje grupo de antepasados comunes (pág. 295)

literacy rate/tasa de alfabetización porcentaje de personas que pueden leer y escribir (págs. 315, 940)

loess/loes tierra fina y amarilla que se lleva el viento (pág. 60)

logic/lógica pensamiento racional (pág. 115)

longbow/arco largo arco de seis pies de largo que podía lanzar con rapidez flechas con suficiente fuerza como para atravesar casi todos los tipos de armaduras (pág. 228)

longitude/longitud distancia hacia el este o el oeste del Primer Meridiano (pág. 6)

Loyalist/*Loyalist* colono leal a Gran Bretaña durante la Revolución Americana (pág. 462)

M

mandate/mandato territorio administrado por un poder occidental después de la Primera Guerra Mundial (pág. 696)

manor/feudo propiedad de un Señor que incluía uno o más pueblos y las tierras que los rodeaban en la Edad Media en Europa (pág. 189)

mansa/mansa título del rey de Mali (pág. 285)

***maquiladora*/maquiladora** planta industrial mexicana de dueños extranjeros en la que los trabajadores locales ensamblan partes importadas para obtener productos acabados (pág. 945)

margin buying/transacción a crédito operación en la que se paga parte del costo total de unas acciones, y se pide prestado el resto a los corredores de bolsa (pág. 748)

martyr/mártir persona que sufre o muere por sus creencias (pág. 144)

matrilineal/matrilineal organización familiar en la que los lazos de parentesco se siguen a través de la madre (págs. 295, 370)

means of production/medios de producción granjas, fábricas, ferrocarriles y otros grandes negocios que producen y distribuyen mercancías (pág. 511)

medieval/medieval que se refiere a la Edad Media en Europa o al período histórico situado entre la época antigua y la moderna (pág. 182)

mercantilism/mercantilismo política por la que una nación trataba de exportar más de lo que importaba para aumentar sus reservas de oro y plata (pág. 406)

mercenary/mercenario soldado que sirve en un ejército extranjero a cambio de dinero (págs. 149, 428)

messiah/mesías salvador enviado por Dios (pág. 142)

mestizo/mestizo persona de las colonias españolas de América descendiente de nativos y europeos (págs. 391, 527)

middle class/clase media nueva clase social, situada entre los campesinos y los nobles, que incluye mercaderes, comerciantes y artesanos (pág. 200)

militarism/militarismo glorificación de los militares (pág. 681)

militia/milicia tropas de soldados civiles (pág. 902)

millet/millet comunidad religiosa no musulmana en el impero otomano (pág. 273)

minaret/minarete torre esbelta de una mezquita desde la que se convoca a los musulmanes a la oración (pág. 259)

missi dominici*/*missi dominici agentes del emperador Carlomagno que viajaban por el imperio para comprobar el estado de los caminos, oir quejas, y asegurarse de que se hiciera justicia (pág. 184)

missionary/misionero persona a quien se envía en una misión religiosa (págs. 82, 622)

mixed economy/economía mixta sistema económico que combina empresas estatales y privadas (pág. 916)

mobilize/mobilizar preparar las fuerzas militares para la guerra (pág. 683)

modernization/modernización construir un gobierno estable mientras se desarrolla económicamente un país (pág. 807)

moksha/moksha según la creencia hindú, el objetivo final de la existencia, llegar a la unión con el brahman (pág. 77)

monarchy/monarquía gobierno en el que el poder reside en el rey o la reina (pág. 106)

money economy/economía de dinero sistema por el que las mercancías y servicios se pagan mediante el intercambio de una moneda con un valor establecido (pág. 43)

monopoly/monopolio control total de un producto o negocio por una persona o grupo (págs. 95, 401)

monotheistic/monoteísta creencia en un solo Dios (págs. 46, 253)

monsoon/monzón viento de temporada; en India, el monzón de invierno trae tiempo seco y caliente, y el de verano trae lluvias (pág. 53)

mosaic/mosaico imagen hecha con pedazos de piedras o vidrio de colores (pág. 138)

mosque/mezquita templo musulmán (pág. 254)

muezzin/muecín musulmán que desde lo alto de un minarete llama a los religiosos a la oración (pág. 259)

mulatto/mulato en las colonias españolas de América, descendiente de africanos y europeos (págs. 391, 527)

multinational corporation/corporación multinacional empresa con sucursales en muchos países (pág. 813)

mummification/momificación práctica de preservar los cuerpos de los muertos (pág. 29)

mural/mural pintura de gran tamaño sobre una pared (pág. 85)

mutual-aid society/sociedad de socorro mutuo grupo de auto apoyo establecido para ayudar a los trabajadores enfermos o heridos en accidente laboral (pág. 553)

mystic/místico persona que dedica su vida a buscar verdades espirituales (pág. 57)

N

nationalism/nacionalismo fuerte sentimiento de orgullo y devoción hacia el propio país (pág. 483)

nationalization/nacionalización apropiación de propiedades o recursos por parte del gobierno (pág. 724)

natural law/ley natural reglas o leyes que gobiernan la naturaleza humana (pág. 446)

natural right/derecho natural derechos que todas las personas tienen desde el momento en que nacen (pág. 447)

neutrality/neutralidad política de no apoyar en una guerra a ninguno de los bandos (pág. 683)

nirvana/nirvana en el budismo, unión con el universo y liberación del ciclo de la reencarnación (pág. 79)

no-fly zone/zona de vuelo prohibido área sobre la que no se permitía volar a los aviones iraquíes después de la Guerra del Golfo Persa (pág. 903)

nomad/nómada persona que se traslada de un lugar a otro en busca de alimentos (pág. 11)

no man's land/tierra de nadie área de tierra vacía donde la guerra lo ha destruido todo (pág. 687)

nonaligned/no alineado que no se alía con ninguno de los bandos en un conflicto (pág. 807)

nuclear family/familia nuclear unidad familiar que consiste en los padres y sus hijos (pág. 295)

O

oasis/oasis área fértil de un desierto, regada por aguas subterráneas o por un manantial (pág. 252)

oba/oba título del rey de Benin (pág. 288)

oligarchy/oligarquía gobierno en el que el poder de gobernar está en manos de unas pocas personas (págs. 106, 458)

one-party system/sistema de partido único país que tiene un solo partido político (pág. 915)

oracle bone/huesos oraculares huesos usados por los sacerdotes de la China Shang para predecir el futuro (pág. 63)

ostracism/ostracismo en la Grecia antigua, el acto de desterrar o enviar lejos una figura pública que amenazaba la democracia (pág. 112)

outpost/puesto de avanzada estacionamiento militar distante (págs. 283, 373)

overproduction/superproducción condición en la que la producción de mercancías excede la demanda (pág. 747)

P

pacifism/pacifismo oposición a las guerras (págs. 678, 771)

padi/arrozal campo de arroz (pág. 372)

pagoda/pagoda templo budista de varios pisos con aleros que se curvan en las esquinas (pág. 307)

pandemic/pandemia propagación de una enfermedad a una gran área, país, continente o al mundo entero (pág. 694)

papal supremacy/supremacía papal en la Edad Media, autoridad de los papas sobre los demás gobernantes (pág. 193)

papyrus/papiro planta que crece a lo largo de los bancos del Nilo; usado por los antiguos egipcios para hacer un material parecido al papel (pág. 32)

partition/partición parte, división (págs. 435, 882)

partnership/sociedad grupo de comerciantes que se unen para financiar un negocio a gran escala que hubiera sido demasiado costoso para un comerciante individual (pág. 199)

pasha/bajá gobernante provincial del imperio otomano (pág. 628)

patriarch/patriarca en el imperio bizantino, el funcionario de rango más alto en la Iglesia de una ciudad importante (págs. 145, 237)

patriarchal/patriarcal familia regida por el padre, esposo o varón de mayor edad (pág. 47)

patrician/patricio miembro de la clase alta terrateniente en la antigua Roma (pág. 129)

patrilineal/patrilineal organización familiar en la que los lazos de parentesco se siguen a través del padre (pág. 295)

patron/mecenas persona que proporciona apoyo financiero a la cultura y las artes (pág. 337)

penal colony/colonia penal lugar al que se manda a los condenados por crímenes (pág. 598)

peninsular/peninsular miembro de la clase más alta en las colonias españolas de América (págs. 390, 527)

peon/peón trabajador forzado a trabajar para un terrateniente para pagar una deuda (pág. 390)

peonage/peonaje sistema en el que los trabajadores deben trabajo como pago por sus deudas (pág. 661)

perestroika/perestroika reestructuración del gobierno y la economía soviética en los años 80 (pág. 846)

perspective/perspectiva técnica artística usada para lograr el efecto de tercera dimensión en dibujos y pinturas (pág. 339)

phalanx/falange en la antigua Grecia, formación masiva de soldados de infantería fuertemente armados (pág. 106)

Spanish Glossary

pharaoh/faraón título de los gobernantes del antiguo Egipto (pág. 25)

philosophe/philosophe miembro de un grupo de pensadores de la Ilustración que trataron de aplicar métodos científicos para mejorar la sociedad (pág. 447)

philosophy/filosofía sistema de ideas (pág. 89)

physiocrat/fisiócrata pensador de la Ilustración que buscaba leyes naturales para explicar la economía (pág. 450)

pictogram/pictograma dibujo utilizado para representar una palabra (pág. 17)

plains/planicies tierras planas y fértiles (pág. 157)

plantation/plantación gran propiedad administrada por un dueño o capataz y cultivada por trabajadores que viven en ella (pág. 390)

plateau/meseta área elevada de tierra plana (pág. 52)

plebeian/plebeyo en la antigua Roma, miembro de clase baja, que incluía granjeros, mercaderes, artesanos y comerciantes (pág. 129)

plebiscite/plebiscito votación en la que los votantes expresan su opinión sobre un tema en particular (págs. 485, 953)

pogrom/pogrom ataque violento de una multitud hacia una comunidad judía (pág. 588)

polis/ciudad estado ciudad de la antigua Grecia que tenía su propio gobierno (pág. 106)

polygamy/poligamia costumbre que permite a los hombres tener más de una esposa (pág. 728)

polytheistic/politeísta creencia en muchos dioses (pág. 16)

pope/papa cabeza de la Iglesia Católica Romana (pág. 146)

potlatch/*potlatch* entre los americanos nativos de la costa noroeste, entrega ceremonial de presentes (pág. 171)

predestination/predestinación idea de que Dios determinó hace mucho tiempo quién alcanzaría la salvación (pág. 350)

prehistory/prehistoria período de tiempo anterior a la invención de los sistemas de escritura (pág. 8)

premier/*premier* primer ministro (pág. 605)

prime minister/primer ministro jefe del gabinete en un gobierno parlamentario; generalmente el líder del partido mayoritario de la legislatura (pág. 458)

privateer/bucanero pirata (pág. 393)

privatization/privatización venta de industrias del estado a inversores privados (pág. 814)

proletariat/proletariado clase trabajadora (págs. 512, 702)

propaganda/propaganda divulgación de ideas para promover cierta causa o para perjudicar una causa opuesta (pág. 690)

prophet/profeta líder espiritual a quien se le atribuye la interpretación de la voluntad de Dios (pág. 47)

protectorate/protectorado país con su propio gobierno pero que está bajo el control de una potencia exterior (pág. 620)

province/provincia territorio situado fuera de Roma que estaba controlado por el gobierno romano (pág. 133)

provisional/provisional temporal (pág. 605)

psychoanalysis/psicoanálisis método que estudia el funcionamiento de la mente y trata los desórdenes mentales (pág. 753)

pueblo/pueblo poblado de los nativos americanos del Sudoeste (pág. 168)

purdah/*purdah* aislamiento de las mujeres en residencias separadas (pág. 633)

Q

quipu/quipo cuerdas con nudos que usaban los aztecas como sistema de registro (pág. 164)

R

racism/racismo creencia de que un grupo racial es superior a otro (pág. 561)

radar/radar mecanismo usado para detectar el vuelo de aviones (pág. 776)

rajah/rajá jefe guerrero electo de una tribu aria en la antigua India; gobernante local hindú en India (págs. 57, 268)

realism/realismo movimiento artístico cuyo objetivo era representar el mundo tal como es (pág. 563)

Realpolitik/Realpolitik política realista basada en las necesidades del estado (pág. 571)

recant/retractarse abandonar las propias creencias o puntos de vista (pág. 347)

recession/recesión período de reducción de la actividad económica (págs. 522, 830)

recognize/reconocer aceptar formalmente tratar a un país como un estado legítimo con un gobierno legítimo (pág. 889)

regionalism/regionalismo lealtad a un área local (pág. 659)

Reich/Reich imperio alemán (pág. 573)

reincarnation/reencarnación en el hinduismo, creencia del renacimiento del alma en otra forma corporal (pág. 77)

religious toleration/tolerancia religiosa política que permite a las personas practicar su religión como quieran (pág. 219)

reparation/indemnización pago por daños de guerra o daños causados por encarcelamiento (págs. 694, 784)

repeal/revocar cancelar (págs. 400, 598)

republic/república sistema de gobierno en el que los gobernantes son elegidos por el pueblo (págs. 129, 477)

repudiate/repudiar rechazar (pág. 763)

revenue/rentas públicas dinero que se recauda por impuestos (pág. 394)

rhetoric/retórica arte de hablar con habilidad (pág. 115)

rococo/rococó estilo artístico y arquitectónico elegante y personal que se dio a mediados del siglo XVIII y que presentaba sofisticados diseños en forma de hojas, conchas marinas y volutas (pág. 453)

romanticism/romanticismo movimiento artístico del siglo XIX que apelaba a la emoción más que a la razón (pág. 562)

rotten borough/"distrito podrido" en Inglaterra, ciudad rural que enviaba miembros al parlamento a pesar de no tener o tener pocos votantes (pág. 595)

S

sabbath/sabbat día sagrado para descansar y rendir culto (pág. 47)

sacrament/sacramento ritual sagrado de la Iglesia Católica Romana (pág. 191)

salon/salón reunión social informal en la que escritores, artistas y filósofos intercambian ideas; comenzó en Francia en el siglo XVII (pág. 451)

samurai/samurai miembro de la clase guerrera en la sociedad japonesa feudal (pág. 320)

sanction/sanción pena (pág. 770)

satellite/satélite término que se refiere a un estado dependiente (pág. 794)

sati/sati costumbre hindú que requería que la esposa se uniera a su marido en la muerte arrojándose a su pira funeraria (pág. 631)

satirize/satirizar burlarse de algo (pág. 137)

satrap/sátrapa gobernador de una provincia del imperio persa (pág. 42)

savanna/sabana planicie con pastizales cuyo régimen de lluvias es irregular (pág. 280)

scapegoat/chivo expiatorio persona, grupo o cosa a quien se culpa por los crímenes o faltas de otros (pág. 354)

schism/cisma división permanente de una iglesia (pág. 216)

scholasticism/escolasticismo en la Europa medieval, escuela de pensamiento que usaba la lógica y la razón para apoyar las creencias cristianas (pág. 221)

scientific method/método científico método concienzudo que se usa para confirmar hallazgos y poner a prueba hipótesis (pág. 357)

scribe/escriba en las civilizaciones antiguas, persona especialmente entrenada que sabía leer, escribir y mantener registros (pág. 18)

scurvy/escorbuto enfermedad causada por la falta de vitamina C en la dieta (pág. 365)

secede/separar retirarse (pág. 611)

secret ballot/voto secreto votos que se dan sin hacerlos públicos (pág. 595)

sect/secta pequeño grupo religioso (pág. 80)

secular/secular que tiene que ver más con asuntos mundanos que religiosos (págs. 193, 483)

segregation/segregación separación de las razas (págs. 611, 841)

selective borrowing/préstamo selectivo adoptar o adaptar algunos rasgos culturales y descartar otros (pág. 318)

self-determination/autodeterminación derecho de los pueblos a elegir su propia forma de gobierno (pág. 693)

separatism/separatismo movimiento que apoyaba la separación de Quebec de Canadá y buscaba el hacer de Quebec una nación independiente (pág. 842)

sepoy/cipayo soldado de India que servía en un ejército inglés o francés de la East India Company (págs. 376, 631)

serf/siervo en la Europa medieval, campesino ligado a la tierra del Señor (pág. 189)

service industry/industria de servicios industria que ofrece servicios en vez de productos (pág. 830)

shah/sha rey (pág. 274)

shantytown/ciudad perdida viviendas precarias en las afueras de una ciudad que carecen de servicios básicos como agua corriente (pág. 818)

shogun/shogún en la sociedad feudal japonesa, jefe militar supremo con más poder que el emperador (pág. 320)

shrine/altar capilla u otro lugar sagrado (pág. 102)

silt/limo tierra fértil que arrastran las crecidas de los ríos (pág. 24)

simony/simonía venta de objetos religiosos (pág. 195)

slash and burn agriculture/agricultura de cortar y quemar método de cultivo que consiste en cortar selva o matorrales y quemarlos para crear campos de cultivo (pág. 294)

smelt/fundir fundir mineral para separar el mineral puro del desperdicio (pág. 500)

social contract/contrato social acuerdo por el que las personas entregan su libertad a un gobierno poderoso para evitar el caos (pág. 447)

social gospel/evangelio social movimiento del siglo XIX que urgía a los cristianos a que hicieran el servicio social (pág. 561)

socialism/socialismo sistema en el que el pueblo como un todo, más que los individuos, son dueños de todas la propiedades y manejan todos los negocios (pág. 511)

socialist realism/realismo socialista estilo artístico cuyo objetivo era promover el socialismo mostrando la vida en la Unión Soviética desde una perspectiva positiva (pág. 715)

social mobility/mobilidad social capacidad para ascender de clase social (pág. 261)

social welfare/bienestar social programas de ayuda a las personas necesitadas (pág. 576)

sonar/sonar aparato que se usa para detectar la ruta de los submarinos (pág. 776)

soviet/soviet consejo de trabajadores y soldados establecido por los revolucionarios rusos en 1917 (pág. 703)

special enterprise zone/zona especial de empresas área en China donde los extranjeros pueden dirigir y ser dueños de industrias (pág. 865)

sphere of influence/esfera de influencia área en la que un poder exterior se reserva privilegios comerciales o la exclusividad de realizar inversiones exclusivas (pág. 620)

squatter/ocupante ilegal persona que se establece en tierras que no le pertenecen (pág. 955)

stalemate/punto muerto estancamiento en una confrontación, en el que ninguna de las partes puede vencer a la otra (pág. 685)

standard of living/estándar de vida medida de la calidad y disponibilidad de las necesidades básicas y de los lujos en una sociedad (pág. 554)

steppe/estepa tierra de pastos escasos y secos (págs. 18, 240)

stipend/estipendio salario fijo de los funcionarios públicos (pág. 112)

stock/acciones títulos o valores de una compañía (pág. 549)

strait/estrecho paso angosto de agua (pág. 103)

stream of consciousness/flujo de conciencia técnica literaria que investiga pensamientos y sentimientos de un personaje, al azar (pág. 754)

stupa/*stupa* gran altar budista en forma de cúpula (págs. 83, 371)

subcontinent/subcontinente gran masa de tierra que sobresale de un continente (pág. 52)

suffrage/sufragio derecho al voto (pág. 478)

sultan/sultán gobernante musulmán (pág. 259)

sultanate/sultanía territorio regido por un sultán (pág. 267)

summit/cumbre reunión de líderes y expertos de distintas partes del mundo (pág. 809)

superpower/superpotencia nación lo suficientemente poderosa como para influir en los actos y políticas de otras naciones (pág. 807)

surplus/excedente exceso, extra (págs. 15, 284, 841)

surrealism/surrealismo movimiento artístico que trata de mostrar el funcionamiento del inconciente (pág. 753)

T

tariff/tasa impuesto a mercancías importadas (pág. 406)

technology/tecnología herramientas y conocimiento que usan las personas para satisfacer sus necesidades básicas (pág. 8)

temperance movement/campaña de moderación campaña para limitar o prohibir el uso de bebidas alcohólicas (pág. 558)

tenant farmer/campesino arrendatario persona que paga una renta a un Señor por trabajar en sus tierras (pág. 199)

tenement building/inquilinato edificio de varios pisos dividido en apartamentos llenos de gente (pág. 505)

terrorism/terrorismo uso deliberado de la violencia al azar, especialmente en contra de civiles, para lograr fines políticos (pág. 811)

theocracy/teocracia gobierno administrado por líderes religiosos (págs. 350, 898)

tithe/diezmo pago a la iglesia, igual a un décimo de los ingresos de una persona (pág. 192)

tolerance/tolerancia aceptación (pág. 42)

total war/estado de guerra canalización de todos los recursos de una nación hacia la guerra (pág. 690)

totalitarian state/estado totalitario gobierno en el que una dictadura de partido único regula todos los aspectos de la vida de los ciudadanos (pág. 713)

tournament/torneo batalla fingida en la que los caballeros competían entre sí para mostrar sus habilidades en la lucha (pág. 187)

trade deficit/déficit comercial situación en la que un país importa más de lo que exporta (págs. 635, 859)

trade surplus/excedente comercial situación en la que un país exporta más de lo que importa (pág. 635)

tragedy/tragedia en la antigua Grecia, obra teatral que trataba del sufrimiento humano y que acababa en un desastre (pág. 117)

triangular trade/comercio triangular ruta colonial de comercio entre Europa y sus colonias en las Indias Occidentales y África, en donde las mercancías se cambiaban por esclavos (pág. 399)

tribune/tribuno funcionario de la antigua Roma elegido por los plebeyos para proteger sus intereses (pág. 129)

tributary state/estado tributario estado independiente que debe reconocer la supremacía de otro estado y pagar tributo a su gobernante (pág. 303)

tribute/tributo pago obligatorio de los pueblos conquistados a los conquistadores (pág. 160)

troubadour/trobador en la Edad Media, poeta europeo ambulante (pág. 189)

truce/tregua paz temporaria (pág. 528)

tsunami/tsunami ola enorme y destructiva causada por un terremoto o vientos muy fuertes (pág. 317)

turnpike/carretera de peaje camino construido por intereses privados que cobran un peaje a los viajeros que lo usan (pág. 504)

tyrant/tirano en la antigua Grecia, gobernante que llegó al poder por medio de la fuerza (pág. 108)

U

U-boat/submarino nave que puede viajar bajo el agua (pág. 688)

ultimatum/ultimatum conjunto final de exigencias (pág. 683)

ultranationalist/ultranacionalista nacionalista extremo (pág. 739)

ultraroyalist/ultrarealista en Francia, noble exiliado o miembro de la iglesia que se oponía al régimen constitucional y apoyaba la reinstauración del antiguo régimen (pág. 521)

universal manhood suffrage/sufragio universal masculino derecho de todos los hombres adultos a votar (pág. 519)

urbanization/urbanización movimiento de personas de las áreas rurales a las ciudades (pág. 505)

urban renewal/renovación urbana reconstrucción de las áreas pobres de una ciudad (pág. 552)

usurp/usurpar apoderarse ilegalmente de un trono (pág. 302)

usury/usura práctica de prestar dinero con interés (pág. 200)

utilitarianism/utilitarismo idea de que el objetivo de la sociedad debería ser lograr la mayor felicidad posible para el mayor número posible de personas (pág. 511)

utopia/utopía sociedad ideal (pág. 343)

V

vassal/vasallo en la Europa Medieval, señor a quien se le otorgaron tierras a cambio de servicios y lealtad a un señor más poderoso (pág. 186)

veneration/veneración estima especial (pág. 54)

vernacular/vernacular lenguaje diario de las personas comunes (págs. 222, 343)

veto/veto poder de bloquear una acción del gobierno (pág. 129)

viceroy/virrey representante que regía una de las provincias de España en las Américas en nombre del rey; quien gobernaba en India en nombre del monarca británico (págs. 389, 632)

vizier/visir ministro principal que supervisaba los asuntos de gobierno en el antiguo Egipto (pág. 25)

W

war crime/crimen de guerra acto que viola las leyes internacionales de guerra (pág. 853)

warlord/jefe militar cabeza de un ejército local (pág. 96)

warm-water port/puerto de aguas templadas puerto que carece de hielo en todo el año (pág. 433)

welfare state/estado de bienestar social sistema en el que el gobierno acepta la responsabilidad de las necesidades sociales y económicas de sus ciudadanos (pág. 829)

westernization/occidentalización adopción de las ideas, tecnología y cultura occidentales (pág. 431)

women's suffrage/sufragio femenino derecho de las mujeres a votar (pág. 558)

Z

zaibatsu/*zaibatsu* familias japonesas de banqueros e industriales poderosos desde finales del siglo XIX (págs. 647, 859)

zemstvo/*zemstvo* asamblea local electa que se estableció en Rusia en la época de Alejandro II (pág. 586)

zeppelin/zepelín dirigible, gran globo lleno de gas (pág. 688)

ziggurat/zigurat templo piramidal dedicado al dios o diosa principal de una antigua ciudad estado sumeria (pág. 36)

Spanish Glossary

Index

Index

Index

Index

Index

Index

Index

Index

Index

Index

Index

Index

Index

Index

Index

Index

Credits

Illustration Credits

Maps: Mapping Specialists Limited
Features 61, 286 José Morales, S.I. International; **139** Malcolm McGregor; **227, 507** Ben Stahl, Klimt Represents; **375, 740** Richard Courtney, S.I. International; **375, 740** Richard Courtney, S.I. International; **557** Penny Haufe, Klimt Represents; **637** Paul Bachem, Artworks;
Cover: Eiffel Tower, Strasbourg Statue and Obelisk of Luxor, (Paris, France) 1991, Stephen Simpson/FPG International Corp. **Cover and title page border:** clockwise from top left: Ife Figure. South-Western Nigeria, c.12-15th centuries A.D., Bronze (Nigeria National Museum, Lagos, Nigeria). Photo: John Picton; Heiroglyphs. Bas-Relief, near White Chapel of Karnak dedicated to Amon-Min, ithyphallic god of fertility, limestone (Egypt). Erich Lessing/Art Resource, NY; Zapotec Urn from Monte Alban (Mexico), Charles & Josette Lenars/CORBIS; Detail of Greek translation of discourse by Emperor Nero on the freedom of Greeks, stone. Museo della Civilta Romana, Rome, Italy/Roger-Viollet, Paris/Bridgeman Art Library, London/NY; Queen Elizabeth I (England) Bedfordshire, Woburn Abbey/A.K.G., Berlin/Superstock; Copy of the Aztec Sun Stone Calender c. 16th, Malachite (Mexico) Ian Mursell/Mexicolore/Bridgeman Art Library, London/NY; Terra-cotta warriors from tomb of Qin Shinuang (China), Christopher Arnesen/Tony Stone

Images; Mohandas Gandhi, CORBIS/Hulton-Deutsch Collection; Enconium of Darius I, Acheamenid Period, Archaelogical Museum, Teheran, Iran, SEF/Art Resource, NY
Interior: iv top: Ministere de la Culture et de la Communication. Direction Regionale des affaires Culturelles de Rhone-Alpes. Service Regional de l'Archeologie; bottom: Scala/Art Resource, NY. **v** top: O. Louis Mazzatenta/NGS Image Collection; middle: C. M. Dixon; bottom: Lee Boltin Picture Library. **vi** top: © University Museum of Cultural Heritage, University of Oslo bottom: Christel Gerstenberg/CORBIS **vii** top: *A Qadi Hears a Case* (detail), Bibliothéque Nationale de France, Paris; middle: © British Museum; bottom: © Copyright 1998 PhotoDisc, Inc. **viii** top: Library of Congress; middle: The Science Museum/Science & Society Picture Library; bottom: Hermitage, St. Petersburg, Russia/The Bridgeman Art Library, London/NY **ix** top: SuperStock; middle: The Granger Collection, NY; bottom: Dannielle Hayes/Omni-Photo Communications, Inc. **x** top: The Granger Collection, NY; bottom: Carpenter Center for the Visual Arts, Harvard University, Cambridge, MA **xi** top: Staatliche Museen zu Berlin - PreuBischer Kulturbesitz Museum für Volkerkunde; bottom: Museum of Fine Arts, Boston/Laurie Platt Winfrey, Inc. **xii** top: Culver Pictures, Inc.; bottom: (detail) Photograph © The Detroit Institute of Arts, 1995. Palacio Nacional stairway, Mexico City. © Dirk Bakker, photographer. **xiii** CORBIS **xiv** top: NASA/Science Photo Library /Photo Researchers, Inc.; middle: ©Regis Bossu/CORBIS Sygma **xv** top: ©T. Hegenbart/Black Star; bottom: Mireille Vautier/Woodfin Camp & Associates **xvi** SuperStock **xvii** *Paso de los Andes*, Vilas y Prades, Museo Historico y Militar de Chile **xviii** EddieAdams/Liaison Agency **xxi** (detail) Topkapi Sarayi Museum, Istanbul/Ergun Cagatay/ Tetragon. **xxvi** top: Library of Congress; left: Palace of Versailles, France/SuperStock **xxvii:** Bibliothéque Nationale de France top: Library of Congress **xxx** middle, right: © Dan Groshong/CORBIS Sygma; top: NASA/Science Photo Library /Photo Researchers, Inc.; bottom, SEF/Art Resource, NY **xxxi** middle, right: © Dan Groshong/CORBIS Sygma; top: Ray Ellis/Photo Researchers; middle, left: Collection-Academia Sinica, Taipei; photo: Wan-go Weng; bottom: Picasso Museum, Paris, France/Giraudon, Paris / SuperStock ©2001 Estate of Pablo Picasso/Artists Rights Society (ARS), NY; **xxxviii** ©Hulton Getty/Liaison Agency **xxxix** Mireille Vautier/Woodfin Camp & Associates **xl** Arcadio Cartoonists & Writers Syndicate,cartoonweb.com **xliii** The Granger Collection, NY **xliv** The ScienceMuseum/Science & Society Picture Library **xlv** *A Spaniard, his Mexican Wife, and their daughter from a series on mixed marriages,* Miguel Cabrera, Museo de America, Madrid/The Bridgeman Art Library,

London/NY **xlviii** Walker Art Gallery, Liverpool/The Bridgeman Art Library, London/NY **liv–1** Richard Passmore/Tony Stone Images **2** top: Garrett/National Geographic Society; middle: Collection-Academia Sinica, Taipei, photo: Wan-go Weng; bottom: Arvind Garg/Liaison International **3** top, left: Corel Professional Photos CD-ROM™; top, right: Photofest; bottom: John Elk/Tony Stone Images, Inc. **4** left: Lascaux Caves, France/SuperStock; middle: The Granger Collection, NY; right: Ministere de la Culture et de la Communication. Direction Regionale des affaires Culturelles de Rhone-Alpes. Service Regional de l'Archeologie **5** left: SuperStock; middle: Dorling Kindersley Ltd. courtesy of the Museum of London; right–2: © G. Dagli Orti, Paris, France **7** top: © Geoffrey Clifford/Woodfin Camp & Associates; bottom: Novosti Press/The Image Bank **9** top, right: CORBIS; bottom, left: Brett Houk; bottom, right–4: Corel Professional Photos CD-ROM™; background: Arvind Garg/Liaison Agency **11** CORBIS/Bettmann—UPI **12** Lascaux Caves, France/SuperStock **13** left: Illustration by Peter McCarty from FROZEN MAN by David Getz, 1994, by Peter McCarty. Reprinted by permission of Henry Holt and Company, LLC; middle, left: Bernhard Grobruck/Contrast/Liaison Agency; middle, right: and top, right: CORBIS Sygma **14** bottom: Erich Lessing/Art Resource, NY; top: © George Holton/Photo Researchers, Inc. **17** top: © J. M. Kenoyer/Dept. of Archaeology and Museums, Government of Pakistan; middle: © Jehangir Gazdar/Woodfin Camp & Associates, Inc; bottom: © J. M. Kenoyer/Dept. of Archaeology and Museums, Government of Pakistan **18** The Kon-Tiki Museum, Oslo **21** © Punch-Bill Tidy/Rothco Cartoons **22** top, left: Musée du Louvre, Paris/Giraudon, Paris/SuperStock; left: Courtesy of The Oriental Institute of the University of Chicago; right: Tony Stone Images **23** left: Scala/Art Resource, NY; right: Museum of Israel, Jerusalem—Lauros-Giraudon, Paris/SuperStock **25** Kenneth Garrett/National Geographic Society **27** The Granger Collection, NY **28** Musée du Louvre, Paris/Giraudon, Paris/SuperStock **29** *Mummified Cat,* The Louvre © Photo Réunion des Musées Nationaux **30** left–2: Scala/Art Resource, NY; top, right: Erich Lessing/Art Resource, NY; bottom, right: © Fred J. Maroon/Photo Researchers, Inc. **32** Gary Cralle/The Image Bank **36** The Granger Collection, NY **39** The Granger Collection, NY **41** top and middle: © Michael Holford; bottom: The Metropolitan Museum of Art, Purchase, H. Dunscombe Colt Gift, 1961 (61.62) **42** top: The Granger Collection, NY; bottom: © Kevin Schafer/Peter Arnold, Inc. **45** Scala/Art Resource, NY **46** top: Rafael Macia/Photo Researchers, Inc.; bottom, left: The Jewish Museum, NY/Art Resource, NY **50** top, left: The Victoria and Albert Museum; left: Paolo Koch/Photo Researchers, Inc.; right: The

Granger Collection, NY **51** left: *Dragon Head,* late Zhou dynasty. Courtesy of the Freer Gallery of Art, Smithsonian Institution, Washington, D.C. (32.14); right: CORBIS **54** Hulton Getty/Liaison Agency **57** National Museum of India, New Delhi, India/The Bridgeman Art Library, London/NY **59** SuperStock **62** left: *"Fu" Kuang-Ting, Shang Dynasty,* c. 1700 B.C.–1100 B.C. The Lowe Art Museum, The University of Miami/SuperStock; right: National Museum, Beijing, China/Erich Lessing/Art Resource, NY **63** © Dan Groshong/CORBIS Sygma **67** *The Earliest Cities* by Jean-Michel Coblence/CASTERMAN S.S. **68** left: Ministere de la Culture et de la Communication. Direction Regionale des affaires Culturelles de Rhone-Alpes. Service Regional de l'Archeologie; right: Kenneth Garrett/National Geographic Society **69** *Dragon Head,* late Zhou dynasty. Courtesy of the Freer Gallery of Art, Smithsonian Institution, Washington, D.C. (32.14) **70–71** SuperStock **72** top, left: E T Archive; top, right: © British Museum; bottom, left: Ralph Rainer Steffens/Bildarchiv Steffens, Mainz; bottom, right: Laurie Platt Winfrey, Inc. **73** top, right: © The Stock Market; bottom: SuperStock **72–73** National Museum of Scotland **74** left: The Ashmolean Museum/© Copyright Dorling Kindersley; middle: Archaeological Museum, Sarnath/Robert Harding Picture Library; right: Keren Su/Tony Stone Images **75** left: Christie's Images/The Bridgeman Art Library, London/NY; right: CORBIS/Richard A. Cooke **76** Lauros-Giraudon/Art Resource, NY **77** *Krishna's Combat with Indra,* c. 1585–90, Gouache, (detail) Courtesy of the Trustees of the Victorian & Albert Museum **78** W. Hille/Leo de Wys, Inc. **81** © Viren Desai/Dinodia Picture Agency **84** left: Abdullah Khandwani; right: Dorling Kindersley Ltd. **86** SEF/Art Resource, NY **87** Los Angeles County Museum of Art, From the Nasli and Alice Heeramaneck Collection, Museum Associates Purchase **88** © 1983 Steve McCurry/Magnum Photos **90** Bibliothèque Nationale, Paris, France/The Bridgeman Art Library/London/NY **91** The Ashmolean Museum/© Dorling Kindersley **92** Chengde, Hubei Province, China/Kurt Scholz/SuperStock **93** O. Louis Mazzatenta/NGS Image Collection **95** Werner Forman/Art Resource, NY **96** Garry Gay/The Image Bank **100** top, left: © Copyright 1998 PhotoDisc, Inc.; left: SuperStock; right: © Peter Connolly, Spalding, Lincolnshire—Trustees of the National Museum of Scotland, Edinburgh **101** left: Lee Boltin Picture Library; right: Giraudon/Art Resource, NY **103** Knossos, Crete/Kurt Scholz/SuperStock **104** C. M. Dixon **107** Vanni/Art Resource, NY **108** Bildarchiv Preussischer Kulturbesitz **109** Stephen Dunn/Allsport **113** Benito/Liaison Agency **115** Alinari/Art Resource, NY **117** © Copyright 1998 PhotoDisc, Inc. **118** top: Martha Swope © Time Inc.; bottom: (detail), The Art Museum, Princeton University. Museum purchase, Caroline G. Mather Fund. Photographer: Bruce White **120** Erich Lessing/Art Resource, NY **122** Private Collection/The Bridgeman Art Library, London/NY **125** © Michael Holford **126** top, left: Paola Koch/Photo Researchers, Inc.; left: CORBIS/Gianni Dagli Orti; right: CORBIS **127** left: McRae Books Srl; right: E T Archive **128** CORBIS/Gianni Dagli Orti **130** *Lady Playing the Cithara* (detail), The Metropolitan Museum of Art, Rogers Fund, 1903 (03.14.5) Photograph © 1986 The Metropolitan Museum of Art **132** Scala/Art Resource, NY **133** © Stephane Compoint/CORBIS Sygma **135** Direzione Generale Musei Vaticani **136** H. M. Herget/NGS Image Collection **138** Paola Koch/Photo Researchers, Inc. **139** bottom, left: CORBIS **140** © Leonard Von Matt/Photo Researchers, Inc. **142** © André Held **143** Masolino da Panicale/E T Archive **145** top: Byzantine Collection, Dumbarton Oaks, Washington, D.C.; bottom: The Metropolitan Museum of Art, The Cloisters Collection, 1950. (50.4) Photograph © 1978 The Metropolitan Museum of Art, NY **147** McRae Books Srl **149** Walters Art Gallery, Baltimore **150** Illustration by Matthew Frey-Wood Ronsaville Harlin, Inc. **154–155** Michael Holford **154** top, left: M. L. Corvetto/The Image Works; left: Lee Boltin Picture Library **155** right: Trans. no. 3519(2) (Photo by P. Hollembeak/J. Beckett) Courtesy Department of Library Services, American Museum of Natural History **158** top: Otis Imboden © National Geographic Society; bottom: Chris Trotman/Duomo Photography, Inc. **159** top: Lee Boltin Picture Library; bottom: © Justin Kerry **161** top: Museum für Völkerivnde Wien, Foto-Archiv, Foto Nr. 61.240; middle: *La Gran Tenochtitlán,* 1940, (detail) Reproduccion Autorizada Por El Instituto Nacional De Bellas Artes Y Literatura/Banco de Mexico. Photo: Bob Schalkwijk; bottom: National Museum of Anthropology, Mexico City/Werner Forman, Art Resource, NY **163** Museo Nacional de Antropologia y Arqueologia Lima, Peru/Loren McIntyre **164** North Wind Picture Archives **166** M. L. Corvetto/The Image Works **169** top and middle: CORBIS/Richard A. Cooke; bottom: Ohio State Museum/Werner Forman Archive/Art Resource, NY **170** © British Museum **173** The Bodleian Library, Oxford, UK **174** left: Christie's Images/The Bridgeman Art Library, London/NY; right: Bildarchiv Preussischer Kulturbesit **175** left: CORBIS; right: Lee Boltin Picture Library **176–177** SuperStock **178** left: The Granger Collection, NY; bottom, left: Photo: Kim Yong-chui/Korean Cultural Service; right: Korean Cultural Service **179** top, left: AP/Wide World Photos; top, right: Hulton Getty/Liaison Agency; middle: NASA; bottom: Lisa Quinones/Black Star **180** left: Pierre Belzeaux/Rapho Agence/Photo Researchers, Inc.; right: Giraudon/Art Resource, NY **181** left: SuperStock; right: Bibliothèque Nationale/Archiv für Kunst und Geschichte, Berlin **185** © University

Museum of Cultural Heritage—University of Oslo **187** image © Copyright 1998 PhotoDisc, Inc. **188** left: © British Museum **189** Private Collection/The Bridgeman Art Library, London/NY **190** *February* from the Tres Riches Heures du duc de Berry (book of hours) painted by the Flemish [Limbourg, Limburg] Brothers from 1415, Giraudon/Art Resource, NY **193** *Virgin and Child,* miniature from the Book of Kells, Hiberno-Saxon ms., c. A.D. 800, Folio 7V. The Granger Collection, NY **194** top, right: Archiv Gerstenberg; bottom, right: The Pierpont Morgan Library/Art Resource, NY; bottom, left: The Granger Collection, NY; background: © G. Dagli Orti, Paris; **195** The Granger Collection, NY **196** © Israel Museum, Jerusalem **200** C. M. Dixon **204** top, left: image © Copyright 1998 PhotoDisc, Inc.; left: *The Siege of Antioch (First Crusade) 1098,* William of Tyre, Bibliothèque Nationale, Paris, France/The Bridgeman Art Library, London, NY; right: Christopher Guy/reproduced by the kind permission of the Dean and Chapter of Worcester **205** *The Entrance of Joan of Arc into Orleans,* Jean-Jacques Sherrer, Musée des Beaux-Arts, Orleans, France/Roger Viollet, Paris/The Bridgeman Art Library, London/NY **206** Philip Mould, Historical Portraits Ltd, London, UK/The Bridgeman Art Library, London, NY **207** image © Copyright 1998 PhotoDisc, Inc. **208** The Royal Collection © 2000 Her Majesty Queen Elizabeth II **209** The Granger Collection, NY **212** © Meyer/Kunsthistorisches Museum, Vienna **214** Scala/Art Resource, NY **218** The Granger Collection, NY **220** Giraudon/Art Resource, NY **221** By permission of The British Library (Harley ms 4431) **223** top: © Agence Top, Paris; bottom: SuperStock **224** Sonia Halliday Photography **227** top, left: *La Ferte Loupiere,* © G. Dagli Orti, Paris **228** top: Froissart's Chronicle, Battle of Janera, 1367 (detail), Bibliothèque Nationale, Paris/The Bridgeman Art Library, London/NY; middle: CORBIS; bottom: Courtesy of the Trustees of British Library, Roy.14.E.IV. **232** top, left: Robert Frerck/Odyssey Productions, Chicago; left: Christel Gerstenberg/CORBIS; right: Bernard Cox/John Bethell PhotoLibrary, St. Albans **233** left, middle: Zamek Krolewski W. Warszawie/Collection of the Royal Castle in Warsaw; right: Hermitage, St. Petersburg, Russia/Bridgeman Art Library, London/NY **235** top, right: Marvin Trachtenberg; bottom: CORBIS/Gianni Dagli Orti; background: Robert Frerck/Odyssey Productions, Chicago **236** Scala/Art Resource, NY **237** Icon of Christ and St. Maenas, Photo Jacqueline Hyde © Réunion des Musées Nationaux **241** © G. Dagli Orti, Paris **243** Archiv für Kunst und Geschichte, Berlin **245** © Artephot/R. Percheron, Paris **250** top, left: Robert Freck/Odyssey Productions/Chicago; left: Giraudon/Art Resource, NY; right: Private Collection/The Bridgeman Art Library, London/NY **251** left: © D. Banerjeb/Dinodia Picture Agency **251**

right: Topkapi Sarayi Museum, Istanbul/Ergun Cagatay/Tetragon **252** Mohamed Lounes/Liaison Agency **253** Courtesy of the Trustees of British Library **254** © M. Reichenthal/The Stock Market **255** *A Qadi Hears a Case,* (detail), Bibliothèque Nationale de France, Paris **257** Robert Freck/Odyssey Productions/Chicago **259** Historical Pictures/Stock Montage, Inc. **261** British Library/The Bridgeman Art Library, London/NY **262** top: (detail), Topkapi Sarayi Museum, Istanbul/Ergun Cagatay/Tetragon, bottom: Joseph Nettis/Photo Researchers, Inc. **263** The Granger Collection, NY **264** top: The Metropolitan Museum of Art, Harris Brisbane Dick Fund, 1939. (39.20) Photograph © 1982 The Metropolitan Museum of Art, NY; middle: British Museum, London/The Bridgeman Art Library, London/NY; bottom: Scala/Art Resource NY **266** By permission of The British Library [1.0. 1379 (Ethé 2296) Folio 34] **269** (detail) Victoria & Albert Museum/The Bridgeman Art Library, London, NY **270** Donato-Toronto Sun, Canada/Rothco Cartoons **273** © Sonia Halliday Photographs **278** top, left: © British Museum; middle: © British Museum; right: Werner Forman/Art Resource, NY **279** Kal Muller/Woodtin Camp & Associates **280** Martin Dohrn-Science Photo Library/Photo Researchers, Inc. **282** (detail), Museum Expedition. Courtesy, Museum of Fine Arts, Boston, MA **285** Lee Boltin Picture Library **288** © British Museum **292** Georg Gerster/Photo Researchers, Inc. **294** left: Lee Boltin Picture Library; right: Robert Harding Picture Library **298** M. & E. Bernheim/ Woodfin Camp & Associates **297** A. Ramsey/Stock, Boston **299** Jason Laure **300** top, left: E T Archive; left: Michael Holford; right: © Copyright 1998 PhotoDisc, Inc. **301** left: Collection of the National Palace Museum. Taiwan, Republic of China; right: Victoria & Albert Museum, London/Art Resource, NY **303** top: Science Museum/ Michael Holford; middle: © Uniphoto, Inc.; bottom: © Jonathan Wallen/Harry N. Abrams, Inc. **305** Werner Forman Archive—Idemitsu Museum of Arts, Tokyo/Art Resource, NY **306** *Travelers Among Mountains and Streams* (detail), Fan K'uan, National Palace Museum, Taiwan, Republic of China **308** James Stanfield/National Geographic Society **310** The Metropolitan Museum of Art, Gift of Robert E. Tod, 1937. (37.191.1) **313** Carmen Redondo/CORBIS **315** Flags of North and South Korea © Copyright 1998 PhotoDisc, Inc. **316** Janette Ostier Gallery, Paris, France/Giraudon, Paris/SuperStock **318** Laurie Platt Winfrey, Inc. **319** E T Archive **320** © 1998 PhotoDisc, Inc. **321** left: Werner Forman/Art Resource, NY; right: The Metropolitan Museum of Art, Rogers Fund, 1904. (04.4.2) Photograph by Schecter Lee. Photograph © 1986 The Metropolitan Museum of Art **322** © John Bryson/The Image Bank **324** left: Charles & Josette Lenars/CORBIS; right: Torii Kiyonaga © British Mu-

seum; bottom: Stapleton Collection, UK/The Bridgeman Art Library, London/NY **328** left and middle: Giraudon/Art Resource, NY; right: Bernard Cox/John Bethell PhotoLibrary, St. Albans **329** left: Giraudon/Art Resource, NY; middle, left: Robert Harding Picture Library; middle, right: Lee Boltin Picture Library; right: Werner Forman Archive—Idemitsu Museum of Arts, Tokyo/Art Resource, NY **330–331** Werner Forman/Art Resource, NY **332** top and middle: The Granger Collection, NY; bottom: North Wind Picture Archives **333** top, left: The Granger Collection, NY; left: National Maritime Museum/© Dorling Kindersly Ltd.; top, right: © 1994 Larry Kunkel/FPG International Corp.; middle: The Granger Collection, NY; bottom: Mary Kate Denny/PhotoEdit; top, left: Science Museum, London/The Bridgeman Art Library, London/NY; left: Scala/Art Resource, NY; top, right: Dorling Kindersley Ltd. Courtesy of St. Bride Printing; bottom, right: Courtesy of the Trustees of British Library **335** left: *Mona Lisa,* Leonardo da Vinci, Scala/Art Resource NY; right: Private Collection, Great Britain **336** Richard Elliott/Tony Stone Images **338** *St. Jerome in His Study,* Antonello da Messina, The National Gallery, London **339** Library of Congress **340** *The Creation of Adam,* Michelangelo, Scala/Art Resource, NY **343** left: Library of Congress; right: *Self Portrait,* Albrecht Dürer, SuperStock **344** top: Scala/Art Resource, NY; left: Tom Skudra/Stratford Festival Archives; bottom, right: Clive Barda/Performing Arts Library **347** Mansell Collection/Time Inc. **348** The Granger Collection, NY **349** Cambridge Education Corp. **351** Portrait of Henry VIII, Hans Holbein, the Younger, Belvoir Castle, Leicestershire/The Bridgeman Art Library, London/NY **352** Walker Art Gallery, Liverpool/The Bridgeman Art Library, London/NY **356** Science Museum, London/The Bridgeman Art Library, London/NY **358** left: Windsor Castle, Royal Library/Archiv für Kunst und Geschichte, Berlin; right: CNRI—Science Photo Library/Photo Researchers, Inc. **361** Scala/Art Resource, NY **362** left: The Granger Collection, NY; middle: Index/The Bridgeman Art Library, London/NY; right: The Granger Collection, NY **363** *The Emperor Ch'ien-lung as a Young Man:* The Metropolitan Museum of Art, Rogers Fund, 1942. (42.141.8) Photograph © 1980 The Metropolitan Museum of Art **364** top, left: Barry Runk/Grant Heilman Photography; top, right: Barry L. Runk/Grant Heilman Photography; bottom, left: Felicia Martinez/PhotoEdit; bottom, right: Runk/Schoenberger/Grant Heilman Photography **365** Robert Frerck/Odyssey Productions/Chicago **367** top: Bibliothèque Nationale de Cartes et Plans, Paris/The Bridgeman Art Library, London/NY; bottom: The Science Museum/Science & Society Picture Library **369** Van Bucher/Photo Researchers, Inc. **370** SuperStock **374** George Bernard/Photo Researchers,

ates; right: Marco Ugarte/AP/Wide World Photos; **935** Vera Lentz/Black Star **936-937** Courtesy of the artist. **938** ©Reuters/Eliana Aponte/ Archive Photos **940** ©P.Robert/ CORBIS Sygma **941** CORBIS **942** Mireille Vautier/Woodfin Camp & Associates **945** AP/Wide World Photos **946** Don Goode/Photo Researchers, Inc. **947** background: ©Ilkka Ulimonen/ CORBIS Sygma; middle: AP/Wide World Photos **948** Mireille Vautier/Woodfin Camp & Associates **949** and **950** AP/Wide World Photos **952** Ary Diesendruck/Tony Stone Images **953** ©Les Stone/CORBIS Sygma **954** Ben Gibson/Katz/Woodfin Camp & Associates **957** AP/Wide World Photos **958** left: NASA/SCIENCE Photo Library/Photo Researchers, Inc.; middle: ©Regis Bossu/Corbis Sygma; right: SuperStock **959** left: Marlene Nelson/ Copyright Wasma'a K. Chorbachi; middle: Nik Wheeler/Corbis; right: Mireille Vautier/Woodfin Camp & Associates **960-961** CORBIS/Pablo Corral V **962** Musee du Louvre, Paris/Giraudon, Paris/SuperStock **963** The Oriental Institute Museum **964** The Jewish Museum, NY/Art Resource, NY **965** Bibliotheque Nationale, Paris, France/The Bridgeman Art Library/London/NY **966** ©Copyright 1998 PhotoDisc, Inc. **967** Bildarchiv Preussischer | Kulturbesitz **968** CORBIS **969** Archaeological Museum, Sarnath/Robert Harding Picture Library **970** McRae Books Srl **971** Giraudon/Art Resource, NY **972** E T Archive **973** Bibliotheque Nationale/Archiv für Kunst und Geschichte, Berlin **975** Lee **973** Archaelogical Museum, Sarnath/Robert Harding Picture Library **975** LeeBoltin Picture Library **976** Nationalmuseet, Copenhagen/The Bridgeman Art Library, London **978** British Information Service **981** Private Collection/The Bridgeman Art Library, London/New York **982** Schalkwijk/Art Resource, NY **983** Dannielle Hayes/Omni-Photo Communications, Inc. **984** The Election II-Canvassing for Votes by William Hogarth, Sir John Soane Museum, London/The Bridgeman Art Library, LondonNY **984** The Science Museum/Science & Society Picture Library **985** Museum of Fine Arts, Boston/Laurie Platt Winfrey, Inc. **986** Bildarchiv Preussischer Kulturhesitz, Berlin **987** By permission of The British Library (F839) **988** The Granger Collection, NY **989** Rudi Von Briel/PhotoEdit **990** SuperStock **992** CORBIS/Bettmann-UPI **993** © Chuck Fishman/Contact Press Images **994** Shone/Liaison Agency **996** AP/Wide World Photos **997** ©Stuart Isett/CORBIS Sygma **998** Reuters/CORBIS/Bettmann **999** © Fallender/Sipa Press

Acknowledgments

6 Excerpt from *The Overview Effect* by Frank White. Copyright © 1987, Houghton Mifflin. **55** "The Rig Veda/Hymn to Indra" from *Reading About the World, Volume 1.* Used by permission of Michael Myers, Translator, Washington State University. **65** "The Spirits Are Good" from *The Book of Songs* by Arthur Waley, Translator. Copyright © 1937 by Arthur Waley, Translator. Used by permission of Grove/Atlantic Inc. **67** Excerpt from *The Ramayana*, translated by Kenneth Anderson, aka Krishna Dharma. Copyright © 1998 by Kenneth Anderson, aka Krishna Dharma. Published by Torchlight Publishing, Inc. **80** Excerpt from *The Dhammapada*, edited by Anne Bancroft. Copyright © 1997 Element Books Limited. Used by permission of Element Books Limited and Anne Bancroft, editor. **104** Excerpt from *The Illiad* by Homer; translated by Robert Fitzgerald. Copyright © 1974 by Robert Fitzgerald. Published by Anchor Books/Doubleday. **137** Excerpt from *The Aeneid of Virgil*, translated by C. Day Lewis, reprinted by permission of Oxford University Press, Inc. **191** Excerpt from *The Canterbury Tales* by Geoffrey Chaucer, translated into modern English by Nevill Coghill. Copyright © 1951, 1958, 1960 by Neville Coghill. Reproduced by permission of Penguin Books Ltd. **222** From *The Song of Roland Done into English in the Original Measure*, translated by C. Scott Moncrieff. Copyright © 1919 Chapman & Hall Ltd. Used by permission of the publishers and the executors of the Estate of C. Scott Moncrieff. **287** Excerpt from *Leo Africanus: Description of Timbuktu*, translated by Paul Brians. Copyright © 1998 by Paul Brians, Department of English, Washington State University. **296** Excerpt from *Through African Eyes Volume 1: The Past; the Road to Independence* by Leon E. Clark. Copyright © 1988, 1991 by Leon E. Clark. Published by CITE Books and Distributed by Apex Press. **307** "Letter to His Small Children" from *Li Po and Tu Fu Poems*, translated by Arthur Cooper. Copyright © 1973 by Arthur Cooper. **529** Excerpt from *The Black Jacobins: Toussaint L'Ouverture and the San Domingo Revolution* by C. L. R. James. Copyright © 1963 by Random House, Inc. **579** From "A Foreign Volunteer at the Battle of the Volturno, April 2, 1860" from *Garibaldi: Great Lives Observed*, edited by Denis Mack Smith. Copyright © 1969 by Prentice Hall, Inc. Reprinted by permission of the author. **717** Excerpt from "Requiem," translated by Robin Kemball, Copyright © 1974 by Robin Kemball, from *Selected Poems* by Anna Akhmatova, edited and translated by Walter Arndt. Reprinted by permission of Ardis. **719** From *Assignment in Utopia* by Eugene Lyons. Copyright © 1937, by Harcourt, Brace & World, Inc., and reproduced with their permission. Published in Great Britain by George G. Harrap & Co. Ltd. Reprinted by permission. **723** Excerpt from "Zeferino Diego Ferreira: The Life Story of a Villista," by Laura Cummings. Copyright © 1999 by University of Arizona *Journal of the Southwest.* **737** Excerpt from *Japanese Imperialism and the Massacre in Nanjing*, translated by Robert P. Gray. Copyright © 1996. **765** "Sophie Yaari Tells Her Story" from *To Save A Life: Stories of Jewish Rescue* by Ellen Land-Weber. Copyright © 1984, 1999 to Ellen Land-Weber. **774** Four lines of "In Memory of W. B. Yeats," from *W. H. Auden: Collected Poems* by W. H. Auden. Copyright © 1940 and renewed 1968 by W. H. Auden. Reprinted by permission of Random House, Inc. and Faber and Faber Limited. **786** From "Major Werner Pluskat, aged 32, 352 Artillery Regiment, 352nd Division" from *Nothing Less Than Victory: An Oral History of D-Day* by Russell Miller. Copyright © 1993 by Russell Miller. Reprinted by permission of Peters Fraser & Dunlop Group, Ltd. **825** "No Time" by Nguyen Sa from *A Thousand Years of Vietnamese Poetry* (ed. Nguyen Ngoc Bich). Copyright © 1962, 1967, 1968, 1969, 1970, 1971, 1972, 1974, by Asia Society, Inc. **833** "A Man's Place" from *The New York Times Magazine*, May 16, 1999 by Claudia Goldin in a conversation moderated by Michael Weinstein. Copyright © 1999, The New York Times Company. **855** "Liberal Leaders Warn Yeltsin to Protect His People," Reuters Limited, October 6, 1999. Copyright © 1999 Reuters Limited. **859** "The Art and Practice of Japanese Management" by John Micklethwait and Adrian Wooldridge. This article is adapted from *The Witch Doctors.* (c) 1996 by Times Books. **871** "War Refugees in Korea" from *Home Was the Land of the Morning Calm* by Koynshill Kang. Copyright © 1995 by K. Connie Kang. Reprinted by permission of Perseus Books Publishers, a member of Perseus Books, L.L.C. **879** From "A Modern Rouge et Noir," translated by Deborah Cao and Lawrence Tedesco from *Voices from the Whirlwind: An Oral History of the Chinese Cultural Revolution*, edited by Feng Jicai. Copyright © 1990 by Foreign Language Press, Beijing, China. Reprinted by permission of the publisher. **901** Excerpt adapted from "A Man is Like a Stalk of Wheat" from *The Yellow Wind* by David Grossman. Copyright © 1988 by David Grossman and Koteret Rashit. English translation copyright © 1988 by Haim Watzman. Reprinted by permission of Farrar, Straus & Giroux, Inc. **910** Excerpt from "Negro Nation of Ghana is Born in Africa" by Thomas F. Brady. Copyright © 1957, The New York Times Company. **939** Excerpt from *Revolution Through Peace* by Dom Helder Camara, translated by Amparo McLean. English translation copyright © 1971 by Harper & Row Publishers, Inc. **954** Excerpt from "For Brazil's Street Children, a Happy Path to Take" by James Brooke. Copyright © 1993, The New York Times Company. **968** Excerpt from *The Mahabharata*, translated by J. A. B. van Buitenen. Copyright © 1973 by University of Chicago Press. **971** From *The Koran*, translated by N. J. Dawood. Copyright © 1956, 1959, 1966, 1968, 1974 by N. J. Dawood. Published by Penguin Books, Ltd. **973** "The Prologue" from *The Canterbury Tales* by Geoffrey Chaucer, translated into modern English by Nevill Coghill. Copyright © 1951, 1958, 1960 by Neville Coghill. Reproduced by permission of Penguin Books Ltd. **975** "The True History of the Conquest of New Spain" from *The Bernal Diaz Chronicles*, translated by Albert Idell. Translation copyright © 1956 by Albert Idell. Used by permission of Doubleday, a division of Bantam Doubleday Dell Publishing Group, Inc. **977** Excerpt from *Don Quixote of La Mancha* by Miguel de Cervantes; translated by Walter Starkie. Copyright © 1957 by Macmillan & Co., Ltd., London. Translation copyright © 1964 by Walter Starkie and published by The New American Library. **985** Excerpt from *The Autobiography of Fukuzawa Yukichi*, by Fukuzawa Yukichi, translated by Eiichi Kiyooka. Translation copyright © 1960 by Eiichi Kiyooka. Copyright © 1966 by Columbia University Press. **986** Excerpt from *All Quiet on the Western Front* by Erich Maria Remarque. Copyright © 1929, 1930 by Little, Brown and Company; copyright © renewed 1957, 1958 by Erich Maria Remarque. **991** Excerpt from *Things Fall Apart* by Chinua Achebe. Copyright © 1959 by Chinua Achebe. Published by Doubleday Dell Publishing Group, Inc. Originally published by Heinemann Educational Books, Ltd. **994, 998, 999** "Perestroika" by Mikhail Gorbachev, "Glory and Hope" by Nelson Mandela, and "The Outlook for China: Human Rights" by Harry Wu from *Vital Speeches Of the Day.* Used by permission of The City News. **995** "New Years Address" from *Uncaptive Minds* by Vaclav Havel. Reprinted by permission of Uncaptive Minds, a publication of the Institute for Democracy in Eastern Europe. **996** "Latin America: the Democracy Option" by Mario Vargas Llosa from *Harper's Magazine.* Copyright © 1987 by Harper's Magazine. Reproduced from the June issue by special permission. **997** From *Freedom From Fear and Other Writings* by Aung San Suu Kyi, forwarded by Vaclav Havel, translated by Michael Aris. Translation copyright © 1991 by Aung San Suu Kyi and Michael Aris. Used by permission of Penguin, a division of Penguin Books USA, Inc.

Note: Every effort has been made to locate the copyright owner of material reprinted in this book. Omissions brought to our attention will be corrected in subsequent printings.

INDEX

Italicized page numbers refer to either Background or Human Drama notes. The *b* preceding the number indicates a Background note and the *hd* preceding the number indicates a Human Drama note.

Abu Simbel *b1*

Activities analyzing a graph, 387; analyzing a musical, 951; analyzing a painting, 666; analyzing a poem, 149, 687, 865, 901, 938; analyzing a primary source, 112, 195, 417, 469, 691, 705; analyzing a quotation, 310, 449, 492, 645, 851, 863, 909, 941; analyzing a short story, 915; analyzing a song, 187, 523; analyzing a speech, 117; analyzing fiction, 792; analyzing literature, 457, 522; analyzing propaganda, 764; applying information, 340; assessing impact of ancient Middle East, 41; charting skills, 9; comparing, 814; comparing ancient, modern practices, 32; comparing arts and crafts, 264; comparing leaders, 896; comparing maps, 245; comparing state homes, 419; comparing statistics, 860; comparing viewpoints, 270, 547, 651, 764; conducting a survey, 820; conducting research, 845; constructing a chart, 332, 413, 454, 531, 633, 660; constructing a diagram, 208, 257; constructing a graph, 792, 935; constructing a model, 688; constructing an outline, 121; constructing a poster, 159, 528, 728; constructing a propaganda poster, 474; constructing charts and graphs, 469, 599, 601, 612, 808, 814; cooperative learning, 2, 72; creating a booklet, 286; creating a display, 392; creating a meal, 802; creating a memorial, 311; creating a mosaic, 235; creating an advertisement, 216; creating an illustration, 166, 482; creating a storyboard, 716; creating a time line, 866; critical thinking, 270; debating, 116; debating an issue, 512, 545; defending a point of view, 948, 954; discussing a topic, 461, 918; discussing viewpoints, 113; drawing a cartoon, 18, 414, 575, 595, 628, 715, 732, 807, 864, 909; drawing a map, 952; drawing conclusions, 396, 480, 485, 606, 762, 925; evaluating data, 946; expressing an opinion, 747, 810; giving an oral report, 660; giving a presentation, 442; illustrating a manuscript, 194; illustrating a story, 736; interpreting a map, 709; interpreting a primary source, 13, 91, 209, 296, 305; interpreting history, 184; interpreting the document, 962, 963, 964, 965, 966, 967, 968, 969, 970, 971, 972, 973, 974, 975, 976, 977, 978, 979, 980, 981, 982, 983, 984, 985, 986, 987, 988, 989, 990, 991, 992, 993, 994, 995, 996, 997, 998, 999; interpreting the evidence, 56, 165, 188, 405, 425, 503, 610, 646, 711, 759, 831, 891; interpreting the primary source, 379, 479, 529, 625, 723, 783, 871, 910; interpreting viewpoints, 349, 448, 679, 759,

816; interviewing, 17, 449, 638, 813, 841; investigating dialects, 63; inviting speakers, 927; letter writing, 26; linking past and present, 199, 754, 836; making a map, 122, 258, 303, 375, 582; making a presentation, 587, 821; making a report, 210; making comparisons, 39; making generalizations, 572; making inferences, 63, 625, 645, 739, 754, 900; outlining, 453; painting a picture, 674; performing a play, 324; performing a tragedy, 118; performing Shakespeare, 344; planning a presentation, 507; planning tribute to famous persons, 30; plotting a story, 897; predicting outcomes, 795; preparing a speech, 390; preparing an exhibit, 161; presenting a dramatization, 606; presenting an informational poster, 227; presenting a skit, 78, 107, 777, 784; presenting research, 540, 686; reading a map, 773; reading historical fiction, 236; recognizing bias, 142; recognizing viewpoints, 282, 476, 829; relating cause and effect, 237, 588, 680, 750, 890, 946; report writing, 36; researching, 268, 291, 810, 830; researching disasters, 61; researching earthquakes, 740; researching historical photographs, 611; researching jazz musicians, 755; researching leaders, 889; researching monsoons, 87; researching political changes, 793; researching storm recovery, 947; researching the Forbidden City, 637; researching the Moscow retreat, 491; researching trade, 135; solving a problem, 852, 917, 942; summarizing the main idea, 69, 175, 329, 439, 537, 671, 799, 959; supporting a generalization, 138; time line, 4, 22, 26, 50, 74, 100, 126, 154, 180, 204, 232, 250, 278, 300, 334, 362, 384, 410, 444, 466, 496, 516, 542, 568, 592, 616, 642, 676, 700, 720, 744, 768, 804, 826, 856, 880, 906, 932; unit themes, 68, 174, 328, 438, 536, 670, 798, 958; using biographical information, 135, 352, 432; using fiction as historical evidence, 380, 556; using hand gestures, 84; using photography as a source, 564; using statistics, 714, 739; using visual evidence, 322, 339; viewing a film, 77; writing a dialogue, 258, 519, 560, 609, 629, 819; writing a diary, 612, 688, 779, 837; writing a headline, 226; writing a letter, 486, 512, 729; writing a news article, 321, 422, 623, 704, 771, 846; writing an editorial, 532, 664, 883; writing an essay, 139, 552, 557; writing a poem, 16, 727, 789; writing a report, 199, 309; writing a response, 789; writing a skit, 178, 228, 703; writing a speech, 609, 859, 926

Address to the Congress of Venezuela (Bolívar) 983, *b983*

Africa art, *b926*; early civilizations, 282; exploring in, *b622*; development issues, 917, 919; independence leaders, 910; literature of, *b819*; myths about,

hd365; self-government, 909; student poem about, 727

"Africa" poem by David Diop, *hd729*

African words *hd297*

agriculture *hd499*

Agrippina *hd131*

Akbar regulations of, *b269*

Alexander the Great, empire of extent of, 121; division of, 122

Algeria *b912*

al-Idrisi *b265*

All Quiet on the Western Front (Remarque), 986, *b986*

al-Rashid, Harun *b259*

Amazon biodiversity in, *hd817*

Amichai, Yehuda 901

Amritsar massacre 732

Analects (Confucius), 965, *b965*

Angkor Wat *hd371*

Animal Farm (Orwell), 792

Anthony, Susan B. *b610*

appeasement and war *b739*

Arabian Nights, The *b265*

Arabic words *hd259*

archaeology destruction of evidence, *b35*; Enlightenment and, *b447*; finds *b148*

architectural structures *hd291*

Aroostook "War" *b654*

art and architecture Muslim, 263, *b264*

Art of the Western World 339

Aryan invasion *b57*

as-Sahili, Abu Ishaq *hd287*

Athenian oath 112

Attila the Hun *hd151*

Australia rabbits in, *b656*

Austria's ultimatum *hd683*

Autobiography (Nkrumah), 992, *b992*; (Yukichi), 985, *b985*

Axé *b954*

Axis Powers aggression in Europe of, 773

Ayodhya aftermath of, *b883*

Aztecs farming by, *b160*; life, 161; music, *b159*; sacred crop of, *b159*; tacos and, *b160*

Babur's death *hd269*

Background notes listed under individual topics

bad students *b221*

Balkan culture *hd583*

Bandaranaike, Sirimavo *b886*

Bangladesh cyclones in, *b886*

banking *b198*

Bastille life at, *b471*; storming of, *hd471*

batik *b876*

bazaars rules for, *b262*

Bazaine, Marshal *b604*

Becket *b207*

Beethoven, Ludwig van *b563*

being informed *b443*

Benedictine order *b194*

Berlin Wall 837

Biafra *b921*

Bill of Rights, The American, 442; English, *b425*, 978, *b978*

Bismarck, Otto Von and German unification, *b572*; personal life of, *hd575*

Black Death *b226*

Bligh, William *b656*

Block Scheduling Support 7, 11, 15, 25, 29, 35, 39, 45, 52, 55, 59, 77, 81, 86, 89, 93, 102, 105, 111, 115, 121, 129, 133, 137, 141, 147, 157, 163, 169, 183, 187, 191, 197, 207, 212, 215, 221, 225, 235, 241, 245, 253, 257, 261, 267, 273, 281, 285, 289, 293, 303, 309, 313, 317, 321, 337, 343, 347, 351, 357, 365, 369, 373, 377, 386, 389, 395, 399, 403, 413, 417, 421, 427, 431, 447, 451, 457, 461, 469, 473, 479, 485, 489, 498, 501, 505, 511, 518, 521, 527, 545, 551, 555, 563, 571, 574, 577, 581, 585, 594, 597, 603, 609, 618, 621, 627, 631, 635, 645, 650, 653, 659, 663, 679, 682, 685, 691, 695, 703, 707, 713, 723, 727, 731, 735, 739, 747, 753, 757, 761, 771, 775, 781, 787, 791, 807, 813, 819, 829, 835, 839, 843, 849, 859, 863, 869, 873, 883, 889, 895, 899, 909, 915, 921, 925, 935, 941, 945, 951

Bolívar, Simón 532, 533

Bonampak the murals of, *hd9*

Bosnia 852

bow *b169*

Brady, Mathew *b611*

brain drain *b782*

Brazil 952

Britain Asantes and, *b401*; attitudes, *hd633*; middle class in, *b595*; overseas markets, *b502*; Redcoats, *b423*; reforms in, 595, 599

British Isles music from the, *hd457*

British rule effects of, 633

Brontë sisters *hd565*

bubonic plague *b95*, 227

Buddha life of, 78

Buddhism and Japan, *b318*; today, 79

butter war *b546*

Byzantine word origin of, *b238*

Byzantine empire emperors, 237; intrigue in, 236

Calais invasion at, *hd785*

calligraphy *hd893*

camel caravans *b262*

Canaan and China punishment in, *b39*

Canadian separatism *b655*

Canterbury Tales, The (Chaucer), 973, *b973*

carbon dating *b8*

carrier pigeons *hd573*, *hd687*

cartels *b549*

casualties 792

cave paintings *b12*

Central America early civilizations of, 9

Chadwick, Edwin *b599*

Art/Photo Credits